The Macmillan Dictionary
of
Canadian Biography

The Macmillan Dictionary
of
Canadian Biography

EDITED BY
W. STEWART WALLACE

FOURTH EDITION REVISED, ENLARGED, AND UPDATED
by W. A. McKay

MACMILLAN OF CANADA
TORONTO

Canadian Cataloguing in Publication Data

Main entry under title:
The Macmillan dictionary of Canadian biography

Canadians who died before 1976.
Includes bibliographical references.
ISBN 0-7705-1462-6

1. Canada — Biography — Dictionaries.
I. Wallace, William Stewart, 1884-1970.
II. McKay, William Angus, 1914-

FC25.M33 1977   920'.071   C77-001038-5
F1005.M33 1977

Printed in Canada for
The Macmillan Company of Canada Limited
70 Bond Street, Toronto, Ontario
M5B 1X3

Preface to the Fourth Edition

This, the fourth revision of the *Macmillan Dictionary of Canadian Biography*, has been designed to bring up to date the biographies of those who have made a contribution to Canadian life.

In general I have followed the trail blazed by W. Stewart Wallace, who wrote in the first edition (1926):

> It has, of course, been difficult to decide what Canadian biographies should be included and what omitted. Since this is purely a Canadian biographical dictionary, it has not been thought advisable to include, as a rule, the names of soldiers who fought or served in Canada for a brief time, without holding civil office, or of navigators and explorers who came and touched the coast and sailed away. An attempt has been made, however, to include all those who have held important offices of state, such as governors, lieutenant-governors, administrators, ministers of the Crown, speakers of the House of Commons, and other politicians, such as senators and provincial cabinet ministers, when especially notable. An attempt has been made also to include outstanding Canadian jurists, scholars, scientists, artists, explorers, soldiers, and capitalists; and especial efforts have been made to make the book useful as an author dictionary. People who leave behind them something tangible, like books, are much more likely to have inquiries made about them than people who do not leave anything tangible behind them; and this will explain why, in the present volume, comparatively obscure authors are included, while men of much greater consequence in their own day and generation are deliberately omitted. The rule which the author has tried to follow has been to include only those names which seemed most likely to be the object of inquiry.

In revising the dictionary I have attempted to include a somewhat wider spectrum of people than he did, particularly in the world of business and in science. All the biographies included in previous editions have been re-examined in the light of new research and information which is available. New bibliographical references have been added and some dates and narratives changed in the interests of accuracy.

A few names have been deleted from this volume in an effort to keep it within manageable limits, as some four hundred additional biographies had to be included.

Undertaking a work such as this has given me a better understanding of the great amount of work which went into the first edition, and has demonstrated again the richness of the Canadian heritage and the remarkable achievements of some outstanding Canadians.

I would like to thank the staff of the library of Scarborough College, University of Toronto, for the patient help I received. I would also thank Phil Baker, Marjorie Westheuser, and Joyce Lawlor for their valuable assistance and Professor John Moir for his advice.

W. A. McKay

Key to Bibliographical Abbreviations

Allaire, *Dict. biog.*	J. B. A. Allaire, *Dictionnaire biographique du clergé canadien-français* (6 vols., St. Hyacinthe, Que., 1908-34).
Bibaud, *Panth. can.* (1891)	Maximilien Bibaud, *Le Panthéon canadien* (nouvelle édition, par A. et V. Bibaud, Montreal, 1891).
Bull. rech. hist.	*Bulletin des recherches historiques* (Lévis, P.Q., 1895 —).
Can. ann. review	J. Castell Hopkins, *The Canadian annual review* (Toronto, 1902-38).
Can. Arch. reports	Canada, *Archives reports* (Ottawa, 1881 —).
Can. biog. dict., Ontario vol.	*The Canadian biographical dictionary and portrait gallery of eminent and self-made men,* Ontario volume (Toronto, Chicago, and New York, 1880).
Can. biog. dict., Quebec and Maritime provinces vol.	*The Canadian biographical dictionary and portrait gallery of eminent and self-made men,* Quebec and Maritime provinces volume (Toronto, Chicago, and New York, 1880).
Can. hist. rev.	*The Canadian historical review* (Toronto, 1920 —).
Can. law times	*The Canadian law times* (1881-1922), continued as *The Canadian bar review* (1922 —).
Can. mag.	*The Canadian magazine* (Toronto, 1893 —).
Can. parl. comp.	*The Canadian parliamentary companion,* later *The Canadian parliamentary guide* (Ottawa, 1862 —).
Can. parl. guide	*The Canadian parliamentary guide* (Ottawa, 1898 —) continuing *The Canadian parliamentary companion* (q.v.)
Can. who's who (1910)	*The Canadian who's who* (London, *The Times,* 1910).
Can. who's who (1936-7 and 1938-9)	Sir C. G. D. Roberts and A. L. Tunnell (eds.), *The Canadian who's who,* vols. II and III (Toronto, 1937-9).
Can. who's who (1948, 1949-51, 1952-54, 1955-57, 1958-60, 1961-3, 1964-6, 1967-9, 1970-2)	A. L. Tunnell (ed.), *The Canadian who's who* (Toronto, 1948-72).
Can. who was who	Sir C. G. D. Roberts and A. L. Tunnell (eds.), *A standard dictionary of Canadian biography. Canadian who was who* (2 vols., Toronto, 1934-8).
Coll. Nova Scotia Hist. Soc.	*Collections of the Nova Scotia Historical Society* (Halifax, 1880 —).

Cyc. Am. biog.	J. G. Wilson and John Fiske (eds.), *Appleton's cyclopaedia of American biography* (7 vols., New York, 1887-1900).
Dent, *Can. port.*	J. C. Dent, *The Canadian portrait gallery* (4 vols., Toronto, 1880-1).
Dict. Am. biog.	A. Johnson and D. Malone (eds.), *Dictionary of American biography* (21 vols., New York, 1928-36).
Dict. Can. biog.	Marc La Terreur (ed.), *Dictionary of Canadian Biography* (10 vols., Toronto, 1966 —).
Dict. nat. biog.	Leslie Stephen and Sidney Lee (eds.) *Dictionary of national biography* (63 vols. and supplements, London, 1885-1912).
Dom. ann. reg.	H. J. Morgan (ed.), *The Dominion annual register* (8 vols., 1878-86).
Encyc. Can.	John E. Robbins (ed.), *Encyclopedia Canadiana* (10 vols., Ottawa, 1960).
Le Jeune, *Dict. gén.*	L. Le Jeune, *Dictionnaire général du Canada* (2 vols., Ottawa, 1931).
Morgan, *Bib. can.*	H. J. Morgan, *Bibliotheca canadensis, or A manual of Canadian literature* (Ottawa, 1867).
Morgan, *Can. men* (1898)	H. J. Morgan (ed.), *The Canadian men and women of the time* (Toronto, 1898).
Morgan, *Can. men* (1912)	H. J. Morgan (ed.), *The Canadian men and women of the time* (Toronto, 1912).
Morgan, *Cel. Can.*	H. J. Morgan, *Sketches of celebrated Canadians* (Quebec, 1862).
Newfoundland Supp.	R. H. Blackburn, *Newfoundland* (Toronto, 1949); supplementary volume to W. S. Wallace (ed.), *The Encyclopedia of Canada* (6 vols., Toronto, 1948).
Ont. Hist. Soc., papers and records	*Ontario Historical Society, papers and records* (Toronto, 1899 —).
Proc. Roy. Soc. Can.	*Proceedings of the Royal Society of Canada* (Ottawa, 1883 —).
Rose, *Cyc. Can. biog.* (1886)	G. M. Rose (ed.), *A cyclopaedia of Canadian biography* (Toronto, 1886).
Rose, *Cyc. Can. biog.* (1888)	G. M. Rose (ed.), *A cyclopaedia of Canadian biography* (Toronto, 1888).
Taché, *Men of the day*	L. H. Taché, *Men of the day, a Canadian portrait gallery* (Ottawa, 1890).
Taylor, *Brit. Am.*	W. Notman and Fennings Taylor, *Portraits of British Americans, with biographical sketches* (3 vols., Montreal, 1865-8).
Trans. Roy. Soc. Can.	*Transactions of the Royal Society of Canada* (Ottawa, 1883 —).
Who was who in Am.	*Who was who in America* (Chicago, 1942).

The Macmillan Dictionary
of
Canadian Biography

Abbott, Sir John Joseph Caldwell (1821-1893), prime minister of Canada (1891-92), was born on March 12, 1821, at St. Andrews, Lower Canada, the eldest son of the Rev. Joseph Abbott (q.v.). He was educated at the University of McGill College and was called to the bar in 1847 (Q.C., 1862). He became one of the leading authorities on commercial law in Lower Canada, dean of the faculty of law in McGill University (1855-80), and standing counsel to the Canadian Pacific Railway Company (1880-87). His political career began in 1849, when his name appeared among the signatories of the famous annexation manifesto of that year. In 1857 he was elected a member of the Legislative Assembly of Canada for Argenteuil; and, with the exception of the years 1874-80, when he was out of parliament, he continued to represent this constituency, first in the Legislative Assembly of Canada, and then in the Canadian House of Commons, until his appointment to the Senate in 1887. In 1862 he was for a short time solicitor-general in the Macdonald-Sicotte administration. As legal adviser to Sir Hugh Allan (q.v.), he was implicated in the "Pacific Scandal" of 1873; and it was a confidential clerk of his who revealed the evidence that brought about the fall of the Macdonald government in that year. This fact was no doubt in part responsible for his defeat in the elections of 1874. When he was appointed to the Senate in 1887, he was made government leader in the upper house; and, on the death of Sir John Macdonald (q.v.) in 1891, he was chosen, as a compromise nominee, to succeed Macdonald as prime minister. His conduct of the government was marked by great astuteness, though he had little in him of the politician. "I hate politics," he once wrote, "and what are considered their appropriate methods. I hate notoriety, public meetings, public speeches, caucuses, and everything that I know of that is apparently the necessary incident of politics — except doing public work to the best of my ability." On December 5, 1892, he was compelled by ill-health to resign the prime-ministership; and he died on October 30, 1893. He was created a K.C.M.G. in 1892.

[*Dict. nat. biog.*, supp. I; Dent, *Can. port.*, vol. 3; Rose, *Cyc. Can. biog.*; Taché, *Men of the day*; Sir J. Pope, *The correspondence of Sir John Macdonald* (Toronto, 1920); Sir R. Cartwright, *Reminiscences* (Toronto, 1913).]

Abbott, Johnston (pseud.). See **Ashworth, Edward Montague.**

Abbott, Joseph (1789-1863), author and clergyman, was born in Cumberland, England, in 1789, and was educated at Marischal College, Aberdeen. In 1818 he was sent out to Canada as a missionary by the Society for the Propagation of the Gospel, and first at St. Andrews, and then at Grenville, in Lower Canada, he served in this capacity until his retirement on pension, in 1847. He wrote *The emigrant to North America, from memoranda of a settler in Canada* (Montreal, 1842), and *Philip Musgrave, or the adventures of a missionary in Canada* (London, 1846). He died in Montreal in January, 1863. He married Harriet Bradford; and he was the father of Sir J. J. C. Abbott (q.v.).

[Morgan, *Bib. can.*; L. J. Burpee and L. E. Horning, *A bibliography of Canadian fiction* (Toronto, 1904).]

Abbott, Maude Elizabeth Seymour (1869-1940), physician and educationist, was born at St. Andrews, Quebec, in 1869. She was educated at Bishop's College, Lennoxville (M.D., C.M., 1894) and at McGill University (B.A., 1910; hon. M.D., 1910), was a fellow in pathology at McGill University from 1912 to 1923, and was appointed in 1923 a research professor in the medical faculty of McGill. She died at Montreal, Quebec, on September 2, 1940. She was the author of *History of medicine in the province of Quebec* (Montreal, 1931) and *Atlas of congenital cardiac disease* (Montreal, 1936).

[H. E. McDermott, *Maude Abbott* (Toronto, 1941); J. B. Scriver, in Mary Quayle Innis (ed.), *Clear spirit* (Toronto, 1966); *Can. who's who*, 1936-37.]

Abercrombie, James (d. 1775), soldier, was a captain in the 42nd Regiment of Royal

Highlanders in 1756. In 1759 he was appointed aide-de-camp to General Amherst (q.v.); and he took part in the campaigns in Canada in that and the following year. In 1760 he was gazetted major in the 78th Regiment (Fraser's Highlanders); and in September of that year he was the emissary who conducted the negotiations with the Marquis de Vaudreuil (q.v.) which resulted in the surrender of Montreal. In 1763 he retired on half-pay; but in 1770 he resumed active service as lieutenant-colonel commanding the 22nd Regiment, which was then serving in America. He was killed at the battle of Bunker Hill on June 17, 1775.

[*Cyc. Am. biog.*]

Abercromby, James (1706-1781), soldier, was born in Scotland, in 1706. He entered the British army as an infantry officer; in 1756 he was promoted to the rank of major-general, and appointed second-in-command of the British forces in North America. In 1758 he became commander-in-chief in North America; and was in command of the British force which marched on Ticonderoga in June of that year. Here his incapacity for supreme command showed itself clearly; and he was compelled, after repeated assaults on the French position, to fall back. In the autumn of 1758 he was recalled to England. In 1772 he was appointed deputy-governor of Stirling Castle; and he died on April 23, 1781.

[*Dict. Am. biog.*]

Aberdeen and Temair, John Campbell Hamilton Gordon, first Marquess of (1847-1934), governor-general of Canada (1893-98), was born in Edinburgh, Scotland, on August 3, 1847, the son of the fifth Earl of Aberdeen. He was educated at St. Andrews University and at University College, Oxford (B.A., 1871; M.A., 1877; D.C.L., 1907). While still an undergraduate, he succeeded to the earldom of Aberdeen on the death of his elder brother, the sixth earl, in 1870. From 1893 to 1898 he was governor-general of Canada; and it fell to him to deal with the difficult situations created by the death of Sir John Thompson (q.v.) in 1894, the revolt of the "seven bolters" in the cabinet of Sir Mackenzie Bowell (q.v.) in January, 1896, and the defeat of Sir Charles Tupper (q.v.) in June, 1896. From January to June, 1886, and again from 1905 to 1915, he was lord lieutenant of Ireland. He died at the House of Cromar, Tarland, Aberdeenshire, on March 7, 1934. In 1877 he married the Hon. Ishbel Maria Marjoribanks, daughter of the first Baron Tweedmouth; and by her he had two sons and one daughter. Throughout life both he and his wife took an active interest in many aspects of social welfare; and Lady Aberdeen was instrumental, during her stay in Canada, in founding the National Council

of Women and the Victorian Order of Nurses. In 1915 Lord Aberdeen was created first Marquess of Aberdeen and Temair; and he was an honorary LL.D. of Aberdeen, St. Andrews, Queen's, McGill, Ottawa, Toronto, Harvard, Princeton, and Laval universities. In 1913 he was elected lord rector of St. Andrews University. With Lady Aberdeen, he published his reminiscences under the title *We twa* (2 vols., London, 1925). After his death, Lady Aberdeen published *The musings of a Scottish granny* (London, 1936). She was the author also of *Through Canada with a Kodak* (Edinburgh, 1893) and her *Canadian journal* has been edited for the Champlain Society by John T. Saywell (Toronto, 1960).

[Marjorie Pentland, Baroness, *A bonnie Fechter* (London, 1953); *Dict. nat. biog.*; *Who was who*, 1928-40.]

Aberhart, William (1878-1943), prime minister of Alberta (1935-43), was born in Hibbard township, Ontario, on December 30, 1878, the son of William Aberhart and Louisa Pepper. He was educated at Queen's University, Kingston (B.A., 1906), and became a school-teacher. From 1915 to 1935 he was principal of the Crescent Heights High School in Calgary, Alberta; and in 1918 he founded the Calgary Prophetic Bible Institute. He became an advocate of the principle of Social Credit, and was elected as a Social Credit candidate to represent the Okotoks–High River constituency in the Alberta legislature in 1935. On the triumph of the Social Credit party in the general elections later in that year, he became prime minister of the province and minister of education. Though he encountered insuperable obstacles to the consummation of his plans for bringing Social Credit into effect in Alberta, he continued prime minister until his death at Vancouver, British Columbia, on May 23, 1943.

[L. P. V. Johnson and Ola J. MacNutt, *Aberhart of Alberta* (Edmonton, 1970); *Can. who's who*, 1936-37.]

Abraham, Robert (d. 1854), author and journalist, was a native of Cumberlandshire, England, who was educated at Edinburgh University, and who emigrated to Canada about 1843. He became the editor of the Montreal *Gazette*, and later of the Montreal *Transcript* and of the *Lower Canada Agricultural Journal*. He died at Montreal on November 10, 1854. He was the author of a pamphlet entitled *Some remarks upon the French tenure of "Franc-alleu roturier" and its relation to the feudal and other tenures* (Montreal, 1849) and a paper on *Tracks of a Chelonian reptile in the Lower Silurian formation at Beauharnois* (British American journal, 1851).

[Morgan, *Bib. can.*]

Acheson, Sir Archibald. See **Gosford, Sir Archibald Acheson, second Earl of.**

Achintre, Auguste (1834-1886), author and journalist, was born in Besançon, France, in 1834. He was educated at Aix-en-Provence and in Paris, and, after spending five years in Haiti, he came to Canada shortly before Confederation. He was successively editor of *Le Pays* and *L'Opinion Publique*, Montreal; and he was the author of *Portraits et dossiers parlementaires du premier parlement de Québec* (Montreal, 1871) and *L'Ile Ste. Hélène* (Montreal, 1876). He died at Montreal on June 25, 1886.

[*Bull. rech. hist.*, 1914; *Dom. ann. reg.*, 1886.]

Adair, Edward Robert (1888-1965), historian, was born in 1888 in London, England, the son of Col. Edward A. Adair, former colonel in the army of the Confederate States of America. He was educated at Peterhouse School, Cambridge University, and the University of London. He became senior lecturer at University College, London, in 1919 and in 1925 accepted a position in the department of history of McGill University which he held until retirement. He had a great depth of knowledge of British and European history of the sixteenth and seventeenth centuries. He died in Austin, Texas, on April 12, 1965. He was the author of *Sources for the history of the council in the sixteenth and seventeenth centuries* (London, S.P.C.K., 1924), *A short biography of William Thomas, clerk of the council* (in Tudor studies, London, 1924). *The extraterritoriality of ambassadors in the sixteenth and seventeenth centuries* (London, 1929), and numerous articles on the French régime in Canada.

[*Can. hist. rev.*, vol. XLVI, 1965; *Can. who's who*, 1961-63.]

Adam, Graeme Mercer (1839-1912), publisher, journalist, and author, was born at Loanhead, Midlothian, Scotland, the son of James Adam and Margaret Wishart. He was educated at Edinburgh, and emigrated to Canada in 1858. He entered the book trade in Toronto, and in 1860 became a partner in the publishing firm of Rollo and Adam. In the *British American Magazine*, which was published by this firm, appeared his first literary efforts. In 1866 the firm was reorganized as Adam, Stevenson and Co. As its senior partner, he founded the *Canada Bookseller* (1869) and the *Canadian Monthly and National Review* (1872-82), the latter a periodical of first-rate quality, in which Goldwin Smith (q.v.) was interested. In 1876, however, the firm failed; and Adam gradually drifted into journalism and literary work. In 1879 he established and for five years edited the *Canada Educational Monthly*; from 1880 to 1883 he was the editor of the *Canadian Monthly*; and during these years he was also literary assistant to Goldwin Smith and business manager of *The Bystander* (1880-81, 1883). He was the author or editor of a considerable number of school-books and illustrated guide-books; he brought out, at the time of the second Riel Rebellion, a book on *The Canadian North-West, its history and its troubles* (Toronto, 1885); in collaboration with Ethelwyn Wetherald (q.v.) he tried his hand at novel-writing in *An Algonquin maiden* (Toronto, 1886); and he wrote *An outline history of Canadian literature* (Toronto, 1887). In 1892 he removed to New York, to become reader and literary adviser to the United States Book Co. In the United States he engaged in literary work of a miscellaneous character: from 1896 to 1905, for instance, he was the editor of a periodical entitled *Self-Culture* at Chicago. Much of his later work, in fact, was mere hack-work; but during his earlier years, from 1862 to 1892, he played a conspicuous part in the development of Canadian letters. He died in New York on October 30, 1912.

[Rose, *Cyc. Can. biog.* (1886); Morgan, *Can. men* (1912); *Can. who was who*, vol. 1.]

Adami, John George (1862-1926), pathologist, was born at Ashton-on-Mersey, Lancashire, England, on January 12, 1862. He was educated at Christ's College, Cambridge (M.A., 1887; M.D., 1891), and in 1891 won a fellowship in Jesus College, Cambridge. From 1892 to 1919 he was professor of pathology in McGill University, Montreal; but he spent the years 1914-19 on military service in England, and in 1919 he was elected vice-chancellor of the University of Liverpool. He died in hospital at Ruthin Castle, near Liverpool, on August 29, 1926. In 1905 he was elected a fellow of the Royal Society.

[M. Adami, *J. George Adami: A memoir* (London, 1930); *Who was who*, 1916-28; Morgan, *Can. men* (1912).]

Adams, Frank Dawson (1859-1942), geologist, was born in Montreal, Canada East, on September 17, 1859. He was educated at McGill University (B.A.Sc., 1878; M.A.Sc., 1884; D.Sc., 1902) and at Heidelberg University (Ph.D., 1892), and, after serving on the staff of the Canadian Geological Survey, he was appointed in 1889 lecturer in geology at McGill University, and in 1893 professor of geology. In 1908 he was appointed dean of the faculty of applied science in McGill University, and later he became vice-principal and, for a short time, acting principal. He was elected a fellow of the Royal Society of Canada in 1896, and its president in 1913; and he was elected a fellow of the Royal Society of London in 1907. He was president of the International

Geological Society in 1913, and of the Geological Society of America in 1918; and he received honorary degrees from a number of Canadian and American universities. He died at Montreal, Quebec, on December 29, 1942. He was the author of many papers dealing with the igneous rocks of North America and the flow of these rocks under changing conditions of temperature and pressure, and of *A history of Christ Church Cathedral, Montreal* (Montreal, 1941).

[*Can. who's who,* 1936-37; *Proc. Roy. Soc. Can.,* 1943.]

Adams, John (*fl.* 1673-1745), administrator of Nova Scotia, was born in Boston, Massachusetts, about 1673; and was appointed a member of the council of Nova Scotia in 1720. After the death of Lawrence Armstrong (q.v.) he administered the government of the colony from 1739 to 1740. He was smitten with blindness, and, being unable to attend to his duties, resigned and retired to Boston, where he died after 1745.

[B. Murdoch, *History of Nova Scotia* (3 vols., Halifax, N.S., 1865-67); *Dict. Can. biog.,* vol. 3.]

Adams, Levi (d. 1832), author, was a native of the Eastern Townships, Lower Canada, and lived for many years at Henryville, Lower Canada. In 1827 he was called to the bar of Lower Canada as an advocate; and he died at Montreal, of cholera, on July 21, 1832. He was the author of *Jean Baptiste: A poetic olio* (Canadian review, 1826), and *The young lieutenant* and *The wedding* (Canadian magazine and literary repository, 1826).

[Morgan, *Bib. can.*]

Adamson, William Agar (1800-1868), clergyman and author, was born in Dublin, Ireland, on November 21, 1800, the son of James Adamson. He was educated at Trinity College, Dublin (B.A., 1821), and was ordained to the priesthood of the Church of England in 1824. In 1840 he came to Canada as chaplain to Lord Sydenham (q.v.), and in 1841 he was appointed chaplain and librarian of the Legislative Council of Canada. He was a frequent contributor to English and Canadian periodicals; but, apart from a number of sermons, his only publication in separate form was *Salmon fishing in Canada,* edited by Colonel Sir J. E. Alexander (London, 1860). He died at Ottawa on August 7, 1868. In 1824 he married Sarah, second daughter of John Walsh, of Walsh Park, Tipperary, Ireland.

[Taylor, *Brit. Am.,* vol. 3; Morgan, *Bib. can.;* N.O. Côté, *Political appointments* (Ottawa, 1896).]

Adaskin, John (1908-1964), musician, was born in Toronto, Ontario, June 4, 1908, and educated at the Hamburg Conservatory, and the Toronto Conservatory of Music. He was a cellist with the Toronto Symphony Orchestra from 1925 to 1936 and during the Second World War he directed three seasons of Victory Loan concerts. He became first program director of the Canadian Radio Commission (now the CBC) in 1934 and was responsible for commissioning many Canadian works, including the opera *Transit through fire* by Healey Willan and John Coulter in 1942. He left the CBC in 1943 to direct his own radio productions. He became executive secretary of the Canadian Music Centre, a non-profit organization founded in 1959 by the Canadian Music Council to promote music in Canada and abroad. In July 1961 he was elected a fellow of the Royal Society of Arts, London, and in August of that year became secretary of the International Association of Music Information Centres. He died at Toronto, Ontario, March 4, 1964.

[*Can. who's who,* 1961-63; Metropolitan Toronto Library Board, *Biographical scrapbooks,* vol. 22; Information from Canadian Music Centre.]

Addison, Robert (1754?-1829), clergyman, was born in Westmoreland, England, about 1754, and was educated at Trinity College, Cambridge. He came to Canada in 1791 as a missionary of the Society for the Propagation of the Gospel, and in the summer of 1792 he settled at Niagara, Upper Canada, where he became the first rector of St. Mark's Church (1792-1829). He died in Niagara on October 6, 1829. He was married, and his widow and daughter survived him.

[A. H. Young, *The Rev. Robert Addison and St. Mark's Church* (Ont. Hist. Soc., Papers and records, 1922); Janet Carnochan, *History of Niagara* (Niagara, 1914).]

Adhémar de Saint-Martin, Jean Baptiste Amable (1736-1800), notary public, was born at Montreal on January 29, 1736, the son of Jean Baptiste Adhémar de Saint-Martin and Catherine Moreau. In 1783 he was chosen, with William Dummer Powell (q.v.) and Jean-Guillaume Delisle (q.v.), to go to England to urge on the British government the desire of the inhabitants of Canada for a house of assembly and the retention of the French civil law. He returned to Canada in 1786; and he died in 1800.

[B. Sulte, *Mélanges historiques,* vol. 1 (Montreal, 1918); *Bull. rech. hist.,* vol. 12 and vol. 26.]

Ahern, George (1887-1927), physician, was born at Quebec, Que., on February 3, 1887, the son of Dr. Michael Joseph Ahern (q.v.). He became a physician in Quebec; and he completed and edited the volume prepared by his father, entitled *Notes pour servir à l'histoire de la médecine dans le Bas-Canada*

(Quebec, 1923). He died at Quebec on August 27, 1927.

[*Bull. rech. hist.*, 1942, p. 101.]

Ahern, John (1851-1933), educationist, was born at Quebec, Canada East, on January 23, 1851. He was a school-teacher successively at St. Romuald, at Lévis, at Montreal, and at Quebec; and he died at Quebec, Que., on September 13, 1933. He was the author of *Leçons d'anglais* (Quebec, 1895) and *Principles of book-keeping* (Quebec, 1897); and he was joint author, with C. J. Magnan (q.v.), of *Mon premier livre* (Quebec, 1900).

[*Bull. rech. hist.*, 1942, p. 101.]

Ahern, Michael Joseph (1844-1914), physician, was born at Quebec, Canada East, on March 19, 1844, the son of Patrick Ahern and Catherine Noonan. He became a doctor of medicine in 1868; and during the later years of his life he was a professor in the faculty of medicine of Laval University. He died at Quebec on April 18, 1914. In the *Bulletin médical de Québec* he published a large number of biographical sketches of medical men in the province of Quebec, which were after his death published in book form by his son, Dr. George Ahern (q.v.), under the title *Notes pour servir à l'histoire de la médecine dans le Bas-Canada* (Quebec, 1923).

[Morgan, *Can. men* (1912).]

Ahrens, Carl (1863-1936), painter, was born at Wingfield, Canada West, in 1863, the son of Herman Ahrens. He studied art in Toronto under George A. Reid (q.v.) and J. W. L. Forster (q.v.), and in New York; and he had a studio in or near Toronto for many years. After 1923 he lived near Galt, Ontario. He died in Toronto, Ontario, on February 27, 1936. In 1916 he married Madonna Niles, a singer; and by her he had one son and two daughters. He was outstanding as a painter of trees; and examples of his work are to be found in the National Gallery at Ottawa.

[Toronto *Mail and Empire*, Feb. 28, 1936.]

Aikins, Sir James Albert Manning (1851-1929), lieutenant-governor of Manitoba (1916-26), was born in Peel county, Ontario, on December 10, 1851, the son of the Hon. James Cox Aikins (q.v.). He was educated at Upper Canada College and at the University of Toronto (B.A., 1875; M.A., 1876), and was called to the bar in Ontario in 1878, and in Manitoba in 1879 (Q.C., 1884). He practised law in Winnipeg, and from 1881 to 1911 he was western solicitor for the Canadian Pacific Railway Company. From 1911 to 1915 he represented Brandon in the Canadian House of Commons. In 1915 he resigned to accept the leadership of the Conservative party in Manitoba; but the Conservatives were defeated in the provincial elections of that year, and in 1916 he was appointed lieutenant-governor of Manitoba. His period of office ended in 1926; and he died at Winnipeg, Manitoba, on March 1, 1929. In 1919 he was made an hon. LL.D. of Manitoba University; and from 1914 to his death he was president of the Canadian Bar Association. He was twice married, (1) in 1884 to Mary, daughter of the Hon. A. W. McLelan (q.v.), whom he divorced in 1892, and (2) in 1899 to Mary, daughter of the Hon. C. C. Colby (q.v.).

[*Can. who was who*, vol. 1; *Who was who*, 1928-40; Morgan, *Can. men* (1912); *Can. parl. comp.*]

Aikins, James Cox (1823-1904), secretary of state for Canada (1867-73 and 1878-80) and lieutenant-governor of Manitoba (1882-88), was born on March 30, 1823, in the township of Toronto, and was the eldest son of James Aikins from the county of Monaghan, Ireland. He was educated at the public schools and at Upper Canada Academy in Cobourg. He settled on a farm in the county of Peel, and in the general elections of 1854, he was elected to the Legislative Assembly as the representative of the county. He associated himself with the "Clear Grits" in the House, and was opposed to the Hincks-Morin administration. In the elections of 1861, he was defeated by John Hillyard Cameron (q.v.); but in 1862 he was elected a member of the Legislative Council for the Home division, which comprised the counties of Peel and Halton. At Confederation, he was called to the Senate of the Dominion; and on December 9, 1867, he accepted the office of secretary of state under Sir John Macdonald. This office he retained until the fall of the government at the time of the "Pacific Scandal" in 1873. Upon Sir John Macdonald's return to power in 1878, Aikins again took office as secretary of state. In November, 1880, there was a readjustment of portfolios, and he became minister of inland revenue. This office he held until his resignation from the cabinet in March, 1882. On September 22, 1882, he was appointed lieutenant-governor of Manitoba and Keewatin; and his term of office expired in 1888. In 1896 he was again called to the Senate; and he died on August 6, 1904.

[Rose, *Cyc. Can. biog.* (1888); Dent, *Can. port.*, vol. 3; N. F. Davin, *The Irishman in Canada* (Toronto, 1877).]

Ailleboust de Coulonge, Louis d' (1612-1660), governor of New France, was born in 1612 in Champagne, at Ancy-le-Franc, the son of Antoine d'Ailleboust and Suzanne Hotman. He was sent to New France to engage in missionary work among the Indians, and he arrived at Quebec on August 15, 1643. In October, 1645, he became governor of Montreal in the absence of Maisonneuve; and in 1648, he was appointed governor-general of New France for the term of three years. On September 12, 1657, he was again appointed temporarily governor of New France, and this interim appointment he held until July 11, 1658. He died at Montreal on May 31, 1660. He married on September 6, 1638, in Paris, Marie-Barbe de Boullonge, by whom he had no children.

[A. Fauteux, *La famille d'Ailleboust* (Montreal, 1916); E. Gagnon, *Feuilles volantes et pages d'histoire* (Quebec, 1911); E. Gagnon, *Louis d'Ailleboust: Louis d'Ailleboust de Coulonge et d'Aigentenay, troisième gouverneur de la Nouvelle-France*, 2 ed. rev. (Montreal, 1931); Bibaud, *Panth. can.*; Morgan, *Cel. Can.*; *Dict. Can. biog.*, vol. 1.]

Aird, Sir John (1855-1938), banker, was born at Longueuil, Canada East, on November 15, 1855. He was educated at the Model School, Toronto, and entered the service of the Canadian Bank of Commerce in 1878. He became general manager of the bank in 1915, and president in 1924. He died in Toronto, Ontario, on Nov. 30, 1938. He was created a knight bachelor in 1917.

[F. Griffin, *Sir John Aird* (Canadian banker, 1936); *Can. who's who*, 1936-37.]

Aitken, William Maxwell (1879-1964), first Baron Beaverbrook, publisher, was born at Maple, Ontario, May 25, 1879. He was educated at Newcastle, New Brunswick, where his father was minister of St. James Presbyterian Church. He studied law at the University of New Brunswick for a year. He was largely responsible for the reorganization of the Canada Car and Foundry Company, the Steel Company of Canada, the Dominion Steel and Coal Company, the Canada Cement Company, and the Royal Securities Corporation, by amalgamating companies which were in similar businesses into large corporate holdings. In England he was a member of parliament from 1910 to 1916. He was raised to the peerage in 1917. In the Second World War he re-entered the government as minister of aircraft production (1940-41); minister of supply (1941-42); and Lord Privy Seal (1943-45). He bought his first daily paper, the London *Daily Express*, in 1917 and added the *Sunday Express*, the *Evening Standard*, and the Glasgow *Evening Citizen*, having a total circulation of eight million copies. He was an honorary chancellor of the University of New Brunswick and was generous with his gifts to the university and to Fredericton, to which he gave a theatre and library. He was author of *Canada in Flanders* (2 vols., London, 1916, 1917); *Success* (London, 1921); *Politicians and the press* (London, 1925); *Politicians and the war* (London, 1928); *Resources of the Brit-*

ish Empire (London, 1934); *Men and power* (London, 1956); *Don't trust to luck* (London, 1954); *Three keys to success* (London, 1954); *Friends* — a biography of R. B. Bennett (London, 1959); *Courage* — a biography of Sir Jas. Dunn (London, 1960); *The divine propagandist* (London, 1962); *The decline and fall of Lloyd George* (London, 1963); *My early life* (London, 1965). He died at Cherkley, near London, England, June 9, 1964.

[*Can. who's who*, 1955-57; *Encyc. Can.* (1971); R. A. Tweedie, *The arts in New Brunswick*; E. Middleton, *Beaverbrook, the statesman and the man* (London, 1934); P. Howard, *Beaverbrook* (Fredericton, 1964); A. Wood, *The true story of Lord Beaverbrook* (London, 1965).]

Akins, Thomas Beamish (1809-1891), barrister and author, was born at Liverpool, Nova Scotia, on February 1, 1809, the only son of Thomas Akins, merchant. He studied law in the office of Beamish Murdoch (q.v.), and was admitted to the bar of Nova Scotia in 1831. He assisted both Haliburton (q.v.) and Murdoch in the preparation of their histories of Nova Scotia. In 1857 he was appointed commissioner of Public Records by the House of Assembly of Nova Scotia. He published a prize essay entitled *History of Halifax, Nova Scotia* (Halifax, 1847); this he revised and expanded from time to time until the year of his death, and it was published in the *Collections of the Nova Scotia Historical Society, 1892-94* (Halifax, 1895). He published also *A sketch of the rise and progress of the Church of England in the British North-American provinces* (Halifax, 1849); *A brief sketch of the origin, endowment and progress of the University of King's College, Windsor, Nova Scotia* (Halifax, 1865); and he edited *Selections from the public documents of the province of Nova Scotia* (Halifax, 1869), published under a resolution of the House of Assembly passed March 15, 1865. In 1865 he received the honorary degree of LL.D. from King's College, Windsor. He died on May 6, 1891, at Halifax.

[Rose, *Cyc. Can. biog.* (1886); Nova Scotia Hist. Soc., *Collections*, 1889-91; Sheila I. Stewart, *A catalogue of the Akins collection of books and pamphlets* (Halifax, 1933).]

Albanel, Charles (1616-1696), priest and explorer, was born in Auvergne, France, in 1616. He entered the Jesuit novitiate in 1633, and in 1649 he joined the Jesuit mission in Canada. He was employed for many years at Tadoussac, whence he made many expeditions into the surrounding wilderness. His most notable journey was his overland expedition to Hudson Bay in 1671-72; he was probably the first white man to reach Hudson Bay by land. His journal of this expedition is contained in the Jesuit *Relation* of

1672. In 1674 he returned to Hudson Bay, was captured by the English, and was sent back to Europe. He returned to Canada, however, in 1676, and from that time until his death, which occurred on January 11, 1696, he laboured in the Canadian missions, first on the Ottawa, then at Green Bay on Lake Michigan, and lastly at Sault Ste. Marie. "There was in him more of the explorer than of the missionary" (Rochemonteix).

[R. G. Thwaites (ed.), *The Jesuit relations* (Cleveland, 1898); Le Jeune, *Dict. gén.; Dict. Can. biog.*, vol. 1.]

Albert, Thomas (1879-1924), priest and historian, was born at St. Hilaire-de-Madawaska, New Brunswick, on June 17, 1879. He was ordained a priest of the Roman Catholic Church in 1905; and he served in several parishes in New Brunswick. He died at Grand Sault, New Brunswick, on November 16, 1924. He was the author of *Histoire de Madawaska* (Quebec, 1920).

[*Bull. rech. hist.*, 1930.]

Alderdice, Frederick Charles (1872-1936), prime minister of Newfoundland (1928 and 1932-34), was born in Belfast, Ireland, on November 10, 1872. He was educated at Belfast, but in 1886 emigrated to Newfoundland, where he became a successful business man. He was appointed to the Legislative Council of Newfoundland in 1924, and in 1928 became government leader in the Council. The same year he succeeded the Hon. W. S. Monroe (q.v.) as prime minister of Newfoundland, but his party was defeated in the subsequent election. In 1932, however, his party swept the country, and he was prime minister again until 1934, when government by commission was introduced. He died at St. John's, Newfoundland, on February 26, 1936.

[*Encyc. Can.*; *Newfoundland Quarterly*, 1936; St. John's *Daily News*, Feb. 28, 1936.]

Alexander, Sir James Edward (1803-1885), author, was born at Stirling, Scotland, on October 16, 1803. In 1841 he was appointed to the staff of the commander-in-chief of the forces in Canada; and he lived in Canada for several years. He died in 1885. He was the author of *Transatlantic sketches* (2 vols., London, 1833), and *L'Acadie, or Seven years' exploration in British America* (2 vols., London, 1849); and he edited *Salmon fishing in Canada* (London, 1860).

[*Dict. nat. biog.*, supp. I; Morgan, *Bib. can.*; Le Jeune, *Dict. gén.*]

Alexander, James Lynne (1800-1879), clergyman and poet, was born at Glenhead, Antrim, Ireland, in 1800. He emigrated to Canada, with his parents, about 1816; and

for over ten years he was a school-teacher. He took holy orders in the Church of England, becoming a deacon in 1829, and a priest in 1832. From 1831 to 1845 he was a missionary at Leeds in the Eastern Townships, and from 1845 to 1873 he was incumbent of Saltfleet and Binbrook in Ontario. He died at Grimsby, Ontario, on August 22, 1879. As a young man he published, under the nom-de-plume of "A Canadian", one of the first volumes of poetry printed in Upper Canada, entitled *Wonders of the West; or, A day at the Falls of Niagara* (York, 1825).

[C. C. James, *A bibliography of Canadian poetry* (Toronto, 1899); *Dict. Can. biog.*, vol. 10.]

Alexander, Sir William. See **Stirling, Sir William Alexander, Earl of.**

Alexander, William John (1855-1944), educationist, was born at Hamilton, Canada West, in 1855. He was educated at the University of Toronto and at London University, England (B.A., 1877), and at Johns Hopkins University (Ph.D., 1883). From 1884 to 1889 he was professor of English language and literature at Dalhousie University, Halifax; and from 1889 to 1926 he was professor of English literature in University College, Toronto. He died at Halifax, Nova Scotia, on June 28, 1944. He was the author of *An introduction to the poetry of Robert Browning* (Boston, 1888), joint author, with M. F. Libby, of *Composition from models* (Toronto, 1894), and editor of *The University of Toronto and its colleges* (Toronto, 1907) and several anthologies for academic use.

[Morgan, *Can. men* (1912); *Univ. of Toronto monthly*, 1944.]

Alexis de Barbezieux (1854-1941), priest, was born near Barbezieux, France, on November 3, 1854. His baptismal name was Georges Derouzier; but after he had been ordained a priest of the Roman Catholic Church in 1882, he joined the Capuchin order in 1887, and took the name in religion of Alexis. He came to Canada in 1890, and here he founded the Canadian branch of the Capuchin order. He died at Pointe-aux-Trembles, Quebec, on April 9, 1941. He was the author of *Histoire de la province ecclésiastique d'Ottawa et de la colonisation dans la vallée de l'Ottawa* (2 vols., Ottawa, 1897), as well as of some volumes of religious edification.

[R. P. Justin de Montagnac, *Le P. Alexis de Barbezieux* (Montreal, 1943); Allaire, *Dict. biog.*]

Alfonse, Jean Fonteneau dit (1484?-1544), pilot and author, was born around 1484 at the village of Saintonge, France, and at an early age went to sea. He visited India and both North and South America; and in

1542 he served as pilot in the expedition of Roberval (q.v.) to the St. Lawrence. His account of this expedition is to be found in a manuscript written by him and preserved in the Bibliothèque Nationale in Paris, which has been edited by G. Musset under the title *La cosmographie avec l'espère et régime du soleil et du nord par Jean Fonteneau dit Alfonse de Saintonge* (Paris, 1904), and extracts from it have been reproduced in Hakluyt, *Principall navigations*, vol. 3, and in H. P. Biggar, *The voyages of Jacques Cartier* (Ottawa, 1924). The manuscript was also the basis of Jean de Marnef de Poitiers, *Les voyages avantureux du Capitaine Jan Alfonce Sainctongeois* (Poitiers, 1559). Alfonse was killed in 1544, just after the completion of his *Cosmographie*, when on a buccaneering expedition against the Spaniards. He married a Portuguese, Valentine Alfonse, whose name he seems to have adopted.

[H. P. Biggar, *The voyages of Jacques Cartier* (Ottawa, 1924); *Dict. Can. biog.*, vol. 1.]

Alfred, Brother. See **Dooner, Alfred James.**

Algie, James (1857-1928), physician and novelist, was born at Ayr, Ontario, in 1857. He was educated at Trinity University, Toronto (M.B., 1878), and for many years practised medicine at Alton, Ontario. In 1908 he joined the staff of the Queen Street Insane Asylum, Toronto; and later he was physician in charge of the Mercer Reformatory, Toronto. He died suddenly, at St. Petersburg, Florida, on January 16, 1928. He wrote under the pseudonym of "Wallace Lloyd"; and he was the author of three novels, *Houses of glass* (Toronto, 1899), *Bergen Worth* (Toronto, 1900), and *The sword of Glenvohr* (Toronto, n.d.).

[Morgan, *Can. men* (1912); L. E. Horning and L. J. Burpee, *A bibliography of Canadian fiction* (Toronto, 1904).]

Allan, Andrew (1822-1901), capitalist, was born in 1822 at Saltcoats, Ayrshire, Scotland, the son of Captain Alexander Allan, and the younger brother of Sir Hugh Allan (q.v.). In 1846 he joined his brother in business in Canada, and on his brother's death in 1882 he succeeded him as president of the Montreal Ocean Steamship Company. He was also president of the Merchant's Bank, and chairman of the Board of Harbour Commissioners for Montreal. He died at Montreal on June 27, 1901. In 1846 he married Isabella (d. 1881), daughter of John Smith, Montreal; and by her he had eight children.

[Morgan, *Can. men* (1898).]

Allan, Andrew Edward Fairbairn (1907-1974), was born in Arbroath, Scotland,

August 11, 1907. He was educated in Australia and the United States and attended Peterborough Collegiate and the University of Toronto (B.A., 1930) in Canada. He began his radio career at CFRB, Toronto, in 1931 but left in 1937 to return to England to work in radio advertising. He was returning to Canada on the *Athenia* in 1939 when the ship was torpedoed. He joined the CBC in Vancouver as regional drama supervisor and went to Toronto in 1944 to work with CBC Stage. In 1945 he became national supervisor of drama and continued until 1958 during the period of rapid development of radio drama. With the rise of interest in television, the broadcasting format changed and Allan became, from 1967 to 1974, a radio essayist and commentator. He was artistic director of the Shaw Festival, Niagara-on-the-Lake (1963-65). In 1969 he received the John Drainie Award for his contribution to broadcasting. He wrote *Narrow passage*, a play; *The adventure of Falstaff* (1964), a radio play. He died at Toronto, Ontario, January 15, 1974.

[*Creative Canada*, vol. I (Victoria University, 1971); *Globe and Mail* (January 16, 1974); *Can. who's who*, 1970-72; Andrew Allan, *A self-portrait* (Toronto, 1974).]

Allan, George William (1822-1901), lawyer and politician, was born at York, Upper Canada, on January 9, 1822, the son of William Allan (q.v.) and Leah Tyrer Gamble. He was educated at Upper Canada College, and was called to the bar in 1846. He early took a part in municipal politics, became an alderman of Toronto in 1849, and in 1855 was elected mayor. In the autumn of 1858 he was appointed to the Legislative Council of Canada for the York division; and for a few years was chairman of the private bills committee of the Council. In 1867 he was called to the Senate of Canada, and from 1888 to 1891 he was its speaker. In May, 1891, he was sworn of the Queen's Privy Council of Canada. His death occurred at Toronto on July 24, 1901. He married, first, in 1846, Louisa Maud, third daughter of Sir John Beverley Robinson (q.v.), and, second, in 1851, Adelaide Harriet Schreiber, by whom he had six children. In 1872, he received the degree of D.C.L. from Trinity University; and from 1877 until his death he was chancellor of this university. He was a fellow of the Royal Geographical Society of England, president of the Ontario Society of Artists, president of the Horticultural Society of Toronto, president of the Upper Canada Bible Society, president of the Toronto Conservatory of Music, and president of the Historical Society of Ontario.

[Rose, *Cyc. Can. biog.* (1886); Dent, *Can. port.*, vol. 4; Morgan, *Can. men* (1898).]

Allan, George William (1860-1940), lawyer, was born at Toronto, Canada West, on August 13, 1860, the son of the Hon. George William Allan (q.v.). He was educated at Upper Canada College, at Trinity College School, and at Trinity University, Toronto (B.A., 1880; M.A., 1886). He read law with the Hon. Edward Blake (q.v.), and was called to the bar in Manitoba in 1882 (K.C., 1914). From 1917 to 1925 he represented Winnipeg in the Canadian House of Commons. He was a director of many financial and commercial organizations, and for many years he was the chairman of the Canadian Committee of the Hudson's Bay Company. He died at Victoria, British Columbia, on December 6, 1940.

[*Can. who's who*, 1936-37.]

Allan, Sir Hugh (1810-1882), capitalist and founder of "the Allan Line", was born on September 29, 1810, at Saltcoats, Ayrshire, Scotland, the second son of Captain Alexander Allan, shipmaster. After three years in a counting-house in Greenock, he came to Canada in 1826, and obtained employment with the firm of William Kerr and Company, dry-goods merchants of Montreal. In 1831 he entered the ship-building firm of John Millar and Company, and in 1835 was taken into partnership. Upon the death of the head of the firm in 1839, Allan formed a new partnership with Edmonstone, the third partner; and together they founded the great shipping firm of which Allan subsequently became the head. In 1852 they were granted a contract by the government to establish a line of screw steamers on the St. Lawrence. In 1856, with four steamers, they instituted a fortnightly service; and this was succeeded by a weekly service, with eight vessels, in the following year. During the Crimean War two of the company's ships were employed as transports by the governments of Great Britain and France; and again in 1874 two ships were employed to carry troops to South Africa. Allan was also one of the original projectors of the Canadian Pacific Railway, and in 1872 he was given a contract by the Macdonald government for its construction; but the fact that he had made large contributions to the campaign funds of Sir John Macdonald was made public, and the consequent fall of the government in 1873 brought the contract to nought. In 1871 Allan was knighted for his services to Canadian commerce. He died in Edinburgh, Scotland, on December 9, 1882. He married, in 1844, Matilda, second daughter of John Smith of Montreal; and by her he had nine daughters and four sons.

[Morgan, *Cel. Can.*; Dent, *Can. port.*, vol. 4; *Dom. ann. reg.*, 1882; Taylor, *Brit. Am.*]

Allan, Sir Hugh Montagu (1860-1951), financier, was born at Montreal, Quebec, on October 13, 1860, the second son of Sir Hugh Allan (q.v.). In 1878, to distinguish himself from a cousin of the same name, he changed his name from Hugh Andrew (his baptismal name) to Hugh Montagu. He was educated at Bishop's College School and in France, and in 1881 he entered his father's business. He became a highly successful financier, and from 1901 to 1922 he was president of the Merchants' Bank. Because of his benefactions he was created a knight bachelor in 1904. In 1910 he gave the Allan Cup for competition among amateur hockey teams. He died at Montreal, Quebec, on September 26, 1951. In 1893 he married Marguerite Ethel Mackenzie, and by her he had one daughter, Marguerite Martha (q.v.).

[*Can. who's who*, 1949-51; *Encyc. Can.*]

Allan, Isaac (1741-1806), executive councillor of New Brunswick, was born in England in 1741. He emigrated to America and settling at Trenton, New Jersey, became a judge of the Supreme Court of the province. During the American Revolution he commanded a regiment of New Jersey Volunteers. At the close of hostilities he went to Nova Scotia and thence to New Brunswick. In 1784 he was appointed a judge of the Supreme Court and a member of the New Brunswick Executive Council. He died in 1806.

[J. W. Lawrence, *The judges of New Brunswick* (Saint John, N.B., 1907).]

Allan, Marguerite Martha (1895-1942), amateur dramatist, was born in Montreal in 1895, the daughter of Sir Hugh Montagu Allan (q.v.), and died at Victoria, British Columbia, on March 31, 1942. She organized in Montreal an amateur dramatic group which came to be known as the Montreal Repertory Theatre; this became one of the most successful amateur dramatic groups in Canada. In 1935 she received the Canadian Drama Award "for outstanding service in the development of the Canadian theatre". At the annual Dominion Drama Festival the Martha Allan Trophy is awarded in her memory for the best visual performance. She was the author of three plays: *What fools we mortals be*; *All of a summer's day*; and *Summer solstice*.

[Montreal *Gazette*, April 2, 1942; *Can. who's who*, 1938-39; *Encyc. Can.*]

Allan, Marvin Francis (1905-1964), architect, was born in Delhi, Ontario, in 1905 and educated at the University of Toronto, where he graduated in architecture in 1929, and in Paris and Berlin. He established a private practice in Hamilton but left it to join the firm of Marani and Morris in 1946 and was involved in the design of York University, the Confederation Life building, the Metropolitan Toronto Courthouse, and the Bell Telephone building. He was chief architect for Housing Enterprises of Canada in 1945 and 1946. He was a fellow of the

Royal Institute of Architects of Canada. He died at Saint John, New Brunswick, June 22, 1964. During the Second World War he was an officer with the Royal Canadian Engineers and commanded field companies in England and North-West Europe. He served on the headquarters staff of the 21st Army Group in 1944-45, was awarded an O.B E. for his service in airfield planning and retired with the rank of colonel.

[Metropolitan Toronto Library Board *Biographical scrapbooks*, vol. 22.]

Allan, Peter John (1825-1848), poet, was born in York, England, on June 6, 1825, the son of Colin Allan, a surgeon in the British army. He came as an infant to Halifax, Nova Scotia, where his father was until 1836 senior medical officer; and later he lived in Fredericton, New Brunswick. He was educated at the University of New Brunswick, and had begun the practice of law when he died suddenly in 1848. He was engaged, at the time of his death, in the preparation of a volume of verse, and this was published posthumously, under the editorship of the Rev. Henry Christmas, in London in 1853.

[Rev. H. Christmas (ed.), *The poetical remains of Peter John Allan* (London, 1853); W. G. MacFarlane, *New Brunswick bibliography* (Saint John, N.B., 1895).]

Allan, William (1770-1853), capitalist, was born in 1770 near Huntly, Aberdeenshire, Scotland, the son of Alexander Allan and Margaret Mowatt. He came to Upper Canada between 1792 and 1798, and settled first at Niagara, and then at York, where he became about 1800 the postmaster and collector of customs. He served as a major in the militia during the War of 1812; and fought at Queenston Heights and at the capture of York. In 1821 he became first president of the Bank of Upper Canada, and in 1833 first president of the British America Assurance Company. In 1825 he was appointed a member of the Legislative Council of the province; and he was regarded as one of the pillars of the "Family Compact". In 1836, Sir F. Bond Head (q.v.), on the resignation of the members of the Executive Council, appointed Allan to one of the vacancies, and he continued to be an executive councillor until 1840. He died in Toronto on July 11, 1853. He married Leah Tyrer, and by her he had, besides others who died in infancy, one son, George William (q.v.).

[A. Shortt, *The Hon. William Allan* (Journal of the Can. Bankers' Association, 1923); E. M. Chadwick, *Ontarian families*, vol. 1 (Toronto, 1894); J. E. Middleton and others, *The municipality of Toronto* (3 vols., Toronto, 1923).]

Allardyce, Sir William Lamond (1861-1930), governor of Newfoundland (1922-28), was born on November 14, 1861, and died in London, England, on June 9, 1930. He entered the colonial service in 1879, and became the governor successively of the Falkland Islands (1904-14), the Bahamas (1915-20), Tasmania (1920-22), and Newfoundland, where his period of office coincided with a period of economic crisis. He was created a K.C.M.G. in 1916 and a G.C.M.G. in 1927.

[*Who was who*, 1929-40.]

Allcock, Henry (d. 1808), chief justice, was an English barrister who studied law at Lincoln's Inn, and was called to the English bar in 1791. In November, 1798, he was appointed a judge of the Court of King's Bench in Upper Canada, and in October, 1802, he became chief justice of Upper Canada. In January, 1803, he was made also speaker of the Legislative Council. On July 1, 1805, he became chief justice of Lower Canada, and in January, 1807, he was appointed speaker of the Legislative Council of that province. Some constitutional importance attaches to his election, while a judge, in 1800, to represent the electors of Durham, Simcoe, and East York in the Legislative Assembly of Upper Canada; he took his seat, but in June, 1801, was unseated by the Assembly on a petition from certain of his constituents, on the ground that he was ineligible for election. He died at Quebec on February 22, 1808.

[D. B. Read, *Lives of the judges* (Toronto, 1888); P. G. Roy, *Les juges de la province de Québec* (Quebec, 1933); Morgan, *Cel. Can.*]

Allen, Andrew (Ralph) (1913-1966), writer and editor, was born in Winnipeg, Manitoba, August 25, 1913, and educated in Saskatchewan schools. He began his career as a newsman with the Winnipeg *Tribune* (1930-38). He joined the Toronto *Globe and Mail* in 1938 and became war correspondent for the paper in 1943, covering campaigns in Sicily, Italy, and North-West Europe. From 1941 to 1943 he served with the Royal Canadian Artillery and was discharged with the rank of sergeant in 1943. He received the O.B.E. for his war service, and on his return to Canada joined *Maclean's* magazine as assistant editor in 1945. He worked as sports writer for the *Toronto Telegram* from 1948 to 1950 and was editor of *Maclean's* magazine from 1950 to 1960. After four years of freelance writing he joined the *Toronto Star* as managing editor in 1964, a position which he held until his death on December 3, 1966. In addition to his newspaper writing, Allen did a number of wartime radio broadcasts and later appeared as a television personality. His writings also include the novels *Homemade banners* (1946); *Peace River country* (1958); *The chartered libertine*, a satire on the entertainment industry (1954); *Ordeal by fire, Canada 1910-1945*, being Volume V of the Canadian History Series (1961); *Ask the name of the lion* (1962), about the Congo.

[C. M. Newman (ed.), *The man from Oxbow: The best of Ralph Allen* (Toronto, 1967); *Can. who's who*, 1964-66; Metropolitan Toronto Library Board, *Biographical scrapbooks*, vols. 26, 51.]

Allen, Ethan (1737-1789), soldier, was born at Litchfield, Connecticut, on January 10, 1737 (old-style), the son of Joseph Allen and Mary, daughter of Remember Baker. He saw service in the Seven Years' War, and in 1770 organized the "Green Mountain Boys" in Vermont. With Benedict Arnold (q.v.) he captured Ticonderoga from the British on May 10, 1775; but later in that year he was captured by the British when attempting to surprise Montreal, and he spent two years as a prisoner of war. In 1780 he became deeply implicated in an attempt to bring Vermont under the British flag, but the attempt miscarried. He died at Burlington, Vermont, on February 12, 1789. He was the author of *A narrative of Col. Ethan Allen's captivity* (Philadelphia, 1779), which went into many editions, as well as a number of controversial books and pamphlets, including what was perhaps the first anti-Christian book published in America, *Reason the only oracle of man* (Bennington, Vermont, 1784).

[S. H. Holbrook, *Ethan Allen* (New York, 1940); J. Pell, *Ethan Allen* (Boston, 1929); Henry Walter DePuy, *Ethan Allen and the green-mountain heroes of '76* (Freeport, L.I., 1975); Charles A. Jellison, *Ethan Allen: Frontier rebel* (Syracuse, N.Y., 1969); *Dict. Am. biog.*; *Cyc. Am. biog.*]

Allen, Frank (1874-1965), first professor of physics at the University of Manitoba, was born in Meductic, New Brunswick, on February 6, 1874. He graduated (M.A.) from the University of New Brunswick in 1897 and became principal of a county grammar school. He received his Ph.D. from Cornell University in 1902, where he taught until appointed professor of physics at the University of Manitoba in 1904. Besides teaching, he carried on his research into colour vision and by applying the concepts of measurement of the physics discipline established a link between a biological system and its environment. His papers, which probably would not be classified as pure physics, are considered to be major contributions to physiological optics and the theory of perception. He published some sixty interrelated papers in this field as well as a popular book, *The Universe from crystal spheres to relativity* (New York, 1931). He was a fellow of the Royal Society of Canada and winner of the Society's Tory medal in 1944. He died at Winnipeg, Manitoba, November 19, 1965.

[*Proc. Roy. Soc. Can.* (1967); *Can. who's who*, 1955-57.]

Allen, Sir John Campbell (1817-1898), politician and judge, was born at Kingsclear, New Brunswick, on October 1, 1817, the son of John Allen, quartermaster-general of the militia. He was educated at the Fredericton Grammar School, and in 1840 was called to the bar of New Brunswick. From 1852 to 1855 he was mayor of Fredericton; in February, 1856, he was elected a member of the House of Assembly in New Brunswick for York county; and in May, 1856, he became solicitor-general. He was also speaker of the Assembly from 1862 until the dissolution of 1865. To Confederation he was strongly opposed, and in June, 1865, he was sent with the Hon. Albert J. Smith (q.v.) as a delegate to Great Britain to urge on the British government the objections of New Brunswick to Confederation. In September of the same year he was appointed puisne judge of the Supreme Court of New Brunswick; and on October 8, 1875, he became chief justice of the province. He retired from the bench in 1896; and he died on September 27, 1898. In 1845, he married Margaret, daughter of Captain Charles Drury. He published in 1847 *Rules of the Supreme Court of New Brunswick*, with notes; and from 1849 to 1865 he was reporter of the decisions in the Supreme Court. In 1882 he was made an LL.D. of the University of New Brunswick; and in 1889 he was created a knight bachelor.

[Rose, *Cyc. Can. biog.* (1888); Dent, *Can. port.*, vol. 1; W. G. MacFarlane, *New Brunswick bibliography* (Saint John, N.B., 1895); J. W. Lawrence, *The judges of New Brunswick* (Saint John, N.B., 1907).]

Allen, Joseph Antisell (1814-1900), clergyman and author, was the son of Jonathan Allen, a member of the Irish bar, and Eliza Josephine Antisell, and was born at Arbor Hill, Tipperary, Ireland, on February 27, 1814. He was educated at private schools and at Trinity College, Dublin, but went to London before taking his degree, and there engaged in literary work. In 1840 he was ordained as a priest of the Church of England, and came to Canada. His first charge was at Christieville, Canada East. In 1848 he removed to Canada West, and resided at Ardath, Wolfe Island, where he took charge of Trinity Church, which had been built by his wife, the Baroness de Longueuil. In 1861 he gave up the charge of a parish and went to live in New Haven, Connecticut. Subsequently, however, he returned to Canada, and he died on October 6, 1900, at Alwington, in Kingston, Ontario. Among his published works were the following: *Day dreams by a butterfly*, a philosophical poem (Kingston, 1854); *The Lambda-nu-tercentary poem on Shakespeare* (Stratford-upon-Avon, 1864); *Orangeism, Catholicism, and Sir Francis Hincks* (Toronto, 1877); *The true and* *romantic love story of Col. and Mrs. Hutchinson*, a drama in verse (London, 1884); *The church of the Pope and primitive Christianity* (Kingston, 1891). He married in September, 1843, Charlotte, only daughter of Charles William Grant, fifth Baron de Longueuil (d. April, 1894); and he was the father of Grant Allen, the novelist (d. 1899).

[Morgan, *Cel. Can.* and *Can. men* (1898); *Can. who was who*, vol. 1; Edward Clodd, *Grant Allen, a memoir* (London, 1900).]

Alleyn, Charles (1817-1890), lawyer and politician, eldest son of Commander R. I. Alleyn, R.N., and Margaret O'Donovan, was born at Myrus Wood, County Cork, Ireland, on September 11, 1817. He was educated at Fermoy School and Clongowes College. In 1834 he came to Canada with his parents, and settled at Quebec. He was called to the bar of Lower Canada in 1840 (Q.C., 1857). In 1854 he was elected mayor of Quebec. In the same year he was elected to the Legislative Assembly for Quebec City, and he continued to represent that constituency until Confederation. From November, 1857, to July, 1858, he was the chief commissioner of public works in the Macdonald-Cartier government. In August, 1858, after the defeat of the short-lived administration, he was made provincial secretary in the Cartier-Macdonald government, and he held this office until the fall of that government in May, 1862. From 1866 to 1889 he was sheriff of Quebec, and he died at Quebec on April 4, 1890. He married, in 1849, Zoé, daughter of P. J. Aubert de Gaspé (q.v.), and by her he had several children.

[Morgan, *Cel. Can.*; J. C. Dent, *The last forty years* (Toronto, 1881); J. O. Côté, *Political appointments* (Ottawa, 1866).]

Allin, Cephas Daniel (1874-1927), educationist and author, was born at Clinton, Ontario, on August 18, 1874, the son of the Rev. Roger Allin and Jane Williams. He was educated at the University of Toronto (B.A., 1897; LL.B., 1899) and at Harvard University (M.A., 1900); and he later studied at Berlin and Oxford. In 1907 he became an instructor in political science in the University of Minnesota; and in 1920 he became chairman of the department. He died at Minneapolis, Minnesota, on October 23, 1927. He was the author of *The early federation movement of Australia* (Kingston, 1907), *A history of the tariff relations of the Australian colonies* (Minneapolis, 1917), and *Australasian preferential tariffs and imperial free trade* (Minneapolis, 1929); and he collaborated with G. M. Jones (q.v.) in *Annexation, preferential trade, and reciprocity* (Toronto, 1911).

[*Who was who in Am.*; "In memoriam: Cephas Daniel Allin", in C. D. Allin, *Aus-*

tralasian preferential tariffs and imperial free trade (Minneapolis, 1929).]

Alline, Henry (1748-1784), clergyman, was born in Rhode Island in 1748, and in 1760 went with his parents to Nova Scotia. He became an itinerant preacher, and founded a sect known as the "New Lights" or "Allinites", some of whom later became "Free Christian Baptists". He returned to New England in 1783, and he died at North Hampton, New Hampshire, in 1784. He was the author of *Two mites on some of the most important and much disputed points of divinity* (Halifax, 1781) and some sermons printed in Halifax; and his *Life and journals* were published posthumously (Boston, 1806).

[J. Bumsted, *Henry Alline, 1748-1784* (Toronto, 1971); Gordon Stewart and George Rawlyk, *A people highly favoured of God* (Toronto, 1972); M. W. Armstrong, *The great awakening in Nova Scotia* (Hartford, 1947); Marie Tremaine, *Bibliography of Canadian imprints, 1751-1800* (Toronto, 1952); R. J. Long, *Nova Scotia authors* (East Orange, N.J., 1918); Morgan, *Bib. can.*]

Allison, David (1836-1924), educationist, was born at Newport, Nova Scotia, on July 3, 1836, the son of James Allison, a member of the Legislative Assembly of Nova Scotia, and Margaret Elder. He was educated at Halifax Academy (afterwards Dalhousie University); at the Wesleyan Academy, Sackville, New Brunswick, and at the Wesleyan College, Middletown, Connecticut (B.A., 1859; M.A., 1862). From 1859 to 1862 he was instructor in classics at Sackville Academy, and from 1862 to 1869 in Mount Allison College. From 1869 to 1877 he was president of Mount Allison College, and again from 1891 to 1910, of Mount Allison University. In the interim, he was superintendent of education in Nova Scotia. In 1873 he was made an LL.D. by Victoria University, Cobourg, Ontario, and in 1903 by the Wesleyan University, Middletown, Connecticut. After 1910 he lived in retirement; and he died at Halifax on February 13, 1924. He married, first, in 1862, Elizabeth Powell of Richibucto, New Brunswick (d. 1898), and second, in 1902, H. E. Cummings of Souris, Prince Edward Island. He was the author of *History of Nova Scotia* (3 vols., Halifax, N.S., 1916).

[Morgan, *Can. men* (1912); Rose, *Cyc. Can. biog.* (1888); *Can. who was who*, vol. 1.]

Allison, Joseph (1755?-1839), merchant and banker, was born at Newton Limavady, near Londonderry, Ireland, about 1755, the son of Joseph Allison and Alice Pollock, who settled in Horton, Kings county, Nova Scotia, in 1769. He became an associate of Enos Collins (q.v.), and was one of the original partners of the Halifax Banking Company in 1825. He represented the town of Horton in the Nova Scotia Assembly from 1799 to 1806; and he was appointed a member of the "Council of Twelve" in Nova Scotia in 1832. He died in Halifax in 1839. He married, probably in 1788, Alice, daughter of Israel Harding; by her he had six sons and three daughters.

[V. Ross, *History of the Canadian Bank of Commerce* (2 vols., Toronto, 1920); A. W. H. Eaton, *The history of Kings County, Nova Scotia* (Salem, Mass., 1910).]

Allison, William Talbot (1874-1941), poet and educationist, was born at Unionville, Ontario, on December 20, 1874. He was educated at Victoria College, University of Toronto (B.A., 1899; M.A., 1900) and at Yale University (B.D., 1901; Ph.D., 1910), and was ordained a minister of the Presbyterian church in 1902. He held charges at Stayner, Ontario, and at Middletown, Connecticut, from 1902 to 1910; from 1910 to 1920 he was professor of English at Wesley College, Winnipeg; and he was professor of English in the University of Manitoba from 1920 until his death at Winnipeg, Manitoba, on February 4, 1941. He was the author of *The amber army, and other poems* (Toronto, 1909); and he edited John Milton's *The tenure of kings and magistrates* (New York, 1911).

[*Can. who's who*, 1936-37.]

Allouez, Claude Jean (1622-1689), Jesuit missionary, was born at St. Didier, France, on June 6, 1622. He entered the Jesuit novitiate at Toulouse, and pursued his studies there and at Billom and Rodez. In 1658 he came to Canada, and he served at Three Rivers and other St. Lawrence settlements for seven years. In August, 1665, he went to labour among the Ottawas on Lake Superior, and in 1668 he laid the foundations of the mission of St. Francis Xavier. In 1671 he went to Green Bay, and in 1676 he was appointed to the Illinois missions. He spent twenty-five years among the Indians of what are now the states of Wisconsin, Michigan, and Minnesota; and he died on August 27, 1689. He wrote *Récit d'un 3e voyage fait aux Illinois* (c. 1679).

[J. G. Shea, *Discovery and exploration of the Mississippi valley* (Albany, 1903); R. G. Thwaites (ed.), *The Jesuit relations* (Cleveland, 1898),*Dict. Can. biog.*, vol. 1.]

Alloway, Mrs. Mary, *née* **Wilson** (1848-1919), author, was born at Montreal, Canada East, on December 3, 1848; and died while on a visit to California on January 11, 1919. She was the author of *Famous firesides of French Canada* (Montreal, 1899) and a novel, *Crossed swords* (Toronto, 1912).

[Morgan,*Can. men* (1912).]

Allsopp, George (*fl.* 1761-1806), merchant and legislative councillor, was an Englishman who came to Canada and settled in Quebec in 1761. He became a champion of the rights of the English mercantile element in the colony, and early incurred the hostility of General Murray (q.v.). When he obtained in 1766 the appointment of deputy secretary, registrar, and clerk of the Council from the patentee, Henry Ellis (q.v.), Murray refused to admit him to office, and he was not admitted until 1768. From 1771 to 1776 he was also deputy commissary-general. In 1775 he was appointed a member of the Legislative Council of Quebec; and in the Council he was active in opposition first to Carleton (q.v.) and then to Haldimand (q.v.). In 1783 he was dismissed from the Council by Haldimand, and he then retired from political life. He died at Cap Santé, Quebec, in April, 1806. He was the proprietor of the Jacartier Paper Mills at Cap Santé, Quebec.

[W. S. Wallace (ed.), *The Maseres letters* (Toronto, 1919); J. M. LeMoine, *Picturesque Quebec* (Montreal, 1882); A. Shortt and A. G. Doughty (eds.), *Constitutional documents* (2 vols., Ottawa, 1918); *Bull. rech. hist.*, 1939.]

Allward, Walter Seymour (1876-1955), sculptor, was born in Toronto, Ontario, on November 18, 1876, and died in Toronto on April 24, 1955. He was educated at the Central Technical School in Toronto, and entered an architect's office. Although he was mainly self-taught, he became Canada's most successful sculptor. He designed public statues and monuments in Toronto and Ottawa, as well as in other places, and his crowning achievement was his design for the Vimy Memorial in 1921. This was unveiled by King Edward VIII at Vimy Ridge in France in 1936, before an assemblage of several thousand Canadians who had made a pilgrimage to witness the event. In 1898 he married Margot Kennedy, of Galt, Ontario, and by her he had two children.

[*Encyc. Can.*; *Can. who's who*, 1952-54; Augustus Bridle, *Sons of Canada* (Toronto, 1916); O. J. Stevenson, *A people's best* (Toronto, 1927).]

Almon, William Johnson (1816-1901), senator of Canada, was born at Halifax, Nova Scotia, on January 27, 1816, the son of the Hon. William Almon, a member of the Legislative Council of Nova Scotia. He was educated at King's College, Nova Scotia (B.A., 1834; D.C.L., 1893), and at the universities of Edinburgh and Glasgow (M.D., 1838). For many years he was president of the Liberal-Conservative Association of Halifax; from 1872 to 1874 he represented Halifax in the Canadian House of Commons; and in 1879 he was called to the Senate of Canada. He died at Halifax, on February 18, 1901. In 1840 he married Elizabeth, daughter of Thomas Ritchie (q.v.), of Annapolis, N.S.

[Morgan, *Can. men* (1898); *Can. parl. comp.*]

Almond, John Macpherson (1872-1939), clergyman, was born at Shigawake, Quebec, on July 27, 1872. Educated at Bishop's College, Lennoxville (B.A., 1894; M.A., 1901), he was ordained a priest of the Church of England in 1897. He served as a chaplain in the South African war; and he was senior chaplain of the Canadian forces in the European War of 1914-18. In 1932 he became archdeacon of Montreal. He died at Montreal, Quebec, on September 17, 1939.

[*Can. who's who*, 1936-37.]

Althouse, John George (1889-1956), educationist, was born at Ailsa Craig, Ontario, in 1889, and died at his summer place in Temagami on August 2, 1956. He graduated from the University of Toronto (M.A., 1914; D.Paed., 1929), and became a school-teacher. In 1923 he became headmaster of the University of Toronto Schools, in 1934 dean of the Ontario College of Education, and in 1944 chief director of education for Ontario. In 1948 he was elected president of the Canadian Educational Association. He was the author, among other papers, of *The Ontario teacher: An historical sketch of progress, 1800-1910* (Toronto, 1929).

[*Can. who's who*, 1955-57.]

Altschul, Rudolf (1901-1963), anatomist, was born in Prague, February 24, 1901, and educated there, graduating in dentistry and medicine in 1925. He did post-graduate work in neurology and neuropathology in Paris and Rome. He practised medicine in Prague from 1929 to 1939 when he and his wife fled to Canada. They were on the S.S. *Athenia*, the first ship torpedoed in the Second World War. Dr. Altschul became an instructor in the anatomy department of the University of Saskatchewan and was head of the department from 1955 until his death. He undertook many studies of the nervous system and of cholesterol metabolism and his extensive work in this field led to the introduction of niacin therapy for lowering blood serum cholesterol. In addition to some one hundred scientific papers he published *Selected studies on arteriosclerosis* (Springfield, 1950); *Endothelium — its development morphology, function and pathology* (New York, 1954); *Niacin in vascular disorders and hyperlipemia* (Springfield, 1964). He was a fellow of the Royal Society of Canada and of the Gerontological Society, past president of the Canadian Association of Anatomists, and a director of the American Association for the study of arteriosclerosis. He died at Saskatoon, Saskatchewan, November 4, 1963.

[*Proc. Roy. Soc. Can.* (1964).]

Alverstone, Richard Everard Webster, first Viscount (1842-1915), an eminent British jurist, was born in England on December 22, 1842. He was the British attorney-general (1885-86, 1886-92, and 1895-1900); and in 1900 he became lord chief justice, and was raised to the peerage. He represented Great Britain in the arbitration with the United States regarding the Bering Sea (1893) and in the Venezuelan and Guiana boundary question (1898-99), and was one of the three British commissioners on the Alaska boundary dispute, 1903. He was president of the commission, and in this capacity voted against the Canadian claims. In 1913 he was created a viscount. He was the author of *Recollections of bar and bench* (London, 1914), and he died on December 12, 1915.

[*Dict. nat. biog.*; *Who was who*, 1897-1918.]

Alward, Silas (1842-1919), lawyer, was born at New Canaan, Queens county, New Brunswick, on April 14, 1842. He was educated at Acadia University (B.A., 1860; M.A., 1863; D.C.L., 1882) and at Brown University (M.A., 1871), and was called to the bar in 1865 (Q.C., 1891). He became one of the leaders of the bar in New Brunswick, and dean of the law faculty of King's College, Windsor, Nova Scotia. He died at Saint John, New Brunswick, on June 13, 1919. He was the author of *The unity of the empire* (Windsor, N.S.) and other public addresses.

[W. G. MacFarlane, *New Brunswick bibliography* (Saint John, N.B., 1895); Morgan, *Can. men* (1912).]

Amaron, Calvin Elijah (1852-1917), clergyman, was born at De Ramsay, Canada East, on September 4, 1852, of Swiss parentage. He was educated at McGill University (B.A., 1877; M.A., 1880) and at the Presbyterian Theological College, Montreal (B.D., 1884), and he was ordained a minister of the Presbyterian Church in 1879. He founded in Springfield, Massachusetts, the French Protestant College; and he became a leader in the movement toward conversion of the French Canadians in Canada and the United States to Protestantism. He returned to Canada in 1896, and became pastor of French Protestant churches successively at Montreal, Longueuil, Joliette, and Quebec. He also published a newspaper, *L'Aurore*, as the organ of the French Protestants of America. He died in Montreal, Quebec, on March 15, 1917. He was the author of *Your heritage; or, New England threatened* (Springfield, Mass., 1891).

[Morgan, *Can. men* (1912).]

Ames, Sir Herbert Brown (1863-1954), publicist, was born in Montreal, Quebec, on June 27, 1863, of American parents. He was educated at the Montreal High School and at Amherst College (B.A., 1885; LL.D., 1915). He went into business in Montreal, and from 1898 to 1906 was an alderman of the city. From 1904 to 1920 he represented Montreal–St. Antoine in the Canadian House of Commons. He then became financial director of the secretariat of the League of Nations, and in 1926 he was appointed Canadian delegate to the assembly of the League of Nations. He was created a K.B. in 1915, and was awarded several foreign honours. He was the author of *"The city below the hill": a sociological study of a portion of the city of Montreal* (Montreal, 1887) and other pamphlets. He died in Montreal on March 30, 1954. In 1890 he married Louise Marion, daughter of Sir John Kennedy (q.v.).

[*Can. who's who*, 1952-54; *Encyc. Can.*]

Amherst, Jeffery, first Baron (1717-1797), field-marshal, was the second son of Jeffery Amherst of Riverhead, Kent, and was born on January 29, 1717. In 1731 he became an ensign in the Guards, and later acted as aide-de-camp to General Ligonier and to the Duke of Cumberland. In 1756 he was made a lieutenant-colonel, and in 1758 Pitt gave him command of the expedition to North America, with the rank of major-general. After the capture of Louisbourg on July 26, 1758, Amherst was appointed commander-in-chief of the forces in North America; and on the surrender of Montreal in 1760, he became governor-general of British North America. In 1761 he was made a knight of the Bath. On his failure to cope with Pontiac's rebellion, he returned to England in 1763, and was made governor of Virginia. In 1770 he became governor of Guernsey; in 1772 he was made a privy councillor, and commander-in-chief of the forces; and in 1776 he was created a baron of the United Kingdom. He served as adviser to the government during the American revolutionary war, and in the suppression of the Gordon riots in 1780. In 1796 he was made a field-marshal; but he did not long survive this last honour, and died at Montreal, his seat in Kent, England, on August 3, 1797. Amherst's *Journal . . . from 1758 to 1763* has been edited, with introduction and notes, by J. C. Webster (Toronto, 1931).

[L. S. Mayo, *Jeffery Amherst* (New York, 1916); J. C. Long, *Lord Jeffery Amherst* (New York, 1933); Louis Des Cognets, *Amherst and Canada* (Princeton, 1962); *Dict. nat. biog.*; Morgan, *Cel. Can.*]

Ami, Henri Marc (1858-1931), geologist and palaeontologist, was born at Belle Rivière, near Montreal, Quebec, on November 23, 1858, the son of the Rev. Marc Ami, of Geneva, Switzerland. He was educated at McGill University (B.A., 1882; M.A., 1885; D.Sc., 1907); and from 1882 to 1912 was on the staff of the Geological Survey of Canada. From 1895 to 1900 he was editor of the Ottawa *Naturalist*; and he contributed many papers on the geology and palaeontology of Canada to scientific journals and the transactions of learned societies. In 1900 he was elected a fellow of the Royal Society of Canada; and after his retirement from the Geological Survey, he founded the Canadian School of Prehistory in France. He died at Mentone, France, on January 4, 1931. In 1892 he married Clarissa, daughter of George B. Burland, of Montreal. He was the author of *North America*, vol. 1 in Stanford's *Compendium of geography* (10 vols., London, 1893-1915).

[Morgan, *Can. men* (1912); *Proc. Roy. Soc. Can.*, 1931; *Can. who was who*, vol. 2.]

Amundsen, Roald (1872-1928), navigator, was born at Borge, Norway, on July 16, 1872, the son of Jens Amundsen, a ship-owner. He was educated at Christiania (Oslo), but, after studying medicine for two years, he went to sea. From 1903 to 1906 he commanded the *Gjoa* on the first voyage made from the Atlantic to the Pacific by way of the North West passage. In 1910-12 he commanded, in the *Fram*, the Norwegian Antarctic Expedition which reached the South Pole; and in 1926 he made an airplane flight from Spitzbergen to Teller, Alaska, over the North Pole. He was lost in the Arctic in 1928, while on a rescue expedition by airplane. He was the author of *The north west passage* (2 vols., London, 1908), *The South Pole* (London, 1913), *Our polar flight* (New York, 1925), and *My life as an explorer* (Garden City, N.Y., 1927).

[C. Turley, *Roald Amundsen* (London, 1935); *Americana annual*, 1929.]

Anderson, Alexander Caulfield (1814-1884), fur-trader and author, was born at Calcutta, India, on March 10, 1814. In 1831 he entered the service of the Hudson's Bay Company; and from 1832 to 1858 he was engaged in the fur-trade on the Pacific slope. In 1858 he was appointed the first collector of customs for British Columbia, and the first postmaster at Victoria. He was subsequently commissioner of fisheries for British Columbia. He died at Victoria, B.C., on May 9, 1884. He was the author of *The Dominion of the West* (Victoria, B.C., 1872), *Notes on north-western America* (Montreal, 1876), and of an unpublished "History of the Northwest coast", of which H. H. Bancroft made use in his *History of British Columbia* (San Francisco, 1887).

[E. E. Rich (ed.), *The letters of John McLoughlin*, 2d series (Toronto and London, 1943); *Dom. ann. reg.*, 1884.]

Anderson, David (1814-1885), bishop of Rupert's Land, was born in London, England, in 1814. He was educated at Edinburgh Academy and at Exeter College, Oxford (B.A., 1836). He was ordained a priest of the Church of England; and in 1849 he was consecrated at Canterbury Cathedral bishop of Rupert's Land. He arrived at York Factory (Hudson Bay) on August 16, 1849, and reached the Red River Settlement on October 3. In 1864 he returned to England, and resigned his see; and subsequently he became vicar of Clifton and chancellor of St. Paul's Cathedral, London. In 1878 he was attacked by a lingering illness, and he died in 1885. He married, in 1841, the eldest daughter of James Marsden, of Liverpool, and he had three sons. He was the author of *Notes of the flood at the Red River, 1852* (London, 1853) and *The net in the bay, a journal by the bishop of Rupert's Land* (London, 1854).

[B. Heeney, *Leaders of the Canadian church: Third series* (Toronto, 1943); C. H. Mockridge, *The bishops of the Church of England in Canada* (Toronto, 1896); Morgan, *Bib. can.*]

Anderson, Sir David Murray (1874-1936), governor of Newfoundland (1933-35), was born on April 11, 1874, the son of General David Anderson, colonel of the Cheshire Regiment. He entered the Royal Navy in 1889, and became admiral in 1931. He went on the retired list in 1932; in 1933 he was appointed governor and commander-in-chief of Newfoundland. It was during his period of office that the constitution of Newfoundland was suspended. In 1936 he was appointed governor of New South Wales, but he died shortly after assuming office, on October 30, 1936, at Sydney, Australia. He was created a K.C.B. in 1930.

[*Who was who*, 1928-40; *Encyc. Can.*]

Anderson, Duncan (1828-1903), clergyman and poet, was born in Rayne, Aberdeenshire, Scotland, in 1828, and was educated at King's College, Aberdeen (M.A., 1848). He taught school for several years; but in 1854 he was ordained a minister of the Presbyterian Church. The same year he came to Canada as minister of St. Andrews Church, Lévis, Lower Canada, and he remained in this charge until his retirement from the ministry in 1886. His later years were devoted to ornithological and literary work; and he was the author of *Lays of Canada, and other poems* (Montreal, 1890), and *Scottish folklore* (London, 1895). He died on April 3, 1903.

[Morgan, *Can. men* (1898); C. C. James, *A bibliography of Canadian poetry* (Toronto, 1899).]

Anderson, Fulton Henry (1895-1968), philosopher, was born at Morell, Prince Edward Island, May 23, 1895. He graduated from Dalhousie University in 1917 and from the University of Toronto (M.A., 1918; Ph.D., 1920), after which he studied at Princeton and at Munich. He taught at the University of Colorado for three years and was appointed to the University of Toronto's department of philosophy in 1924. By 1945 he had become head of the department of philosophy and head of the department of ethics of University College and retained these posts until his retirement in 1963. Three years later, in 1966, he accepted the position of visiting professor and acting chairman of the department of philosophy at Huntington College, Laurentian University, Sudbury. He was a scholar of distinction, a teacher of great influence, and a unique and colourful personality. His studies in philosophy were centred on Plato, Bacon, and Locke. He edited, with introductions, three of Plato's dialogues (*Symposium, Meno,* and *Phaedo*) and Bacon's *Novum Organum*. He published *The influence of contemporary science on Locke's methods and results* (Toronto, 1923); *The arguments of Plato* (London, 1935); *The philosophy of Francis Bacon* (Chicago, 1948); *Francis Bacon: His career and his thought* (Los Angeles, 1962). He died at Charlottetown, Prince Edward Island, January 11, 1968.

[*Proc. Roy. Soc. Can.*, vol. VI (1968); *Can. who's who*, 1955-57.]

Anderson, James Thomas Milton (1878-1946), prime minister of Saskatchewan (1929-34), was born at Fairbanks, Ontario, on July 23, 1878. He was educated at the West Toronto High School, the University of Manitoba (B.A., 1911; LL.B., 1913; M.A., 1914), and at the faculty of education in the University of Toronto (D.Paed., 1918). He taught school at several places in Ontario, Manitoba, and Saskatchewan, and in 1918 became director of education among new Canadians in Saskatchewan. In 1924 he was chosen as leader of the Conservative party in Saskatchewan, and in 1925 was elected a member of the Legislative Assembly. In 1929 the Conservatives obtained a majority in the legislature, and Anderson became prime minister of the province. But in the years that followed, Saskatchewan suffered from a series of calamities, such as drought, duststorms, and low prices for agricultural products; and in the election of 1934 the Anderson government was defeated by the Liberals under J. G. Gardiner. Two years later Anderson retired from politics. In his later years he was superintendent of the School for the Deaf in Saskatoon. He died at Saskatoon on December 29, 1946. He was the author of *The education of the new Canadian* (New York, 1918).

[*Who was who*, 1941-58; *Can. who's who*, 1938-39; *Encyc. Can.*; J. F. C. Wright, *Saskatchewan: The history of a province* (Toronto, 1955).]

Anderson, Rudolph Martin (1876-1961), zoologist, was born in Winneshiek county, Iowa, June 30, 1876. He attended high school in Forest City, Iowa and published his first paper *The marsh hawk* at the age of seventeen. He graduated from the University of Iowa (Ph.B., 1903; Ph.D., 1906), where he was assistant in the Zoological Museum of Natural History. He served in the Spanish-American War, 1898. He did exploratory work in the Yukon and North-West Territories from 1908 to 1912 as field agent and assistant in mammalogy of the American Museum of Natural History of New York. From 1913 to 1920 he was zoologist with the Canadian Geological Survey and was second in command, under Vilhjalmur Stefansson (q.v.), and chief of the southern party of the Canadian Arctic Expedition of 1913-18. In 1920 he became chief of the division of biology of the National Museum of Canada, a position which he held until his retirement in 1946. He went to Greenland with the Canadian expedition of 1928 and did exploratory work in every province of Canada. He was a world authority on zoology and was author of *Birds of Iowa* (Iowa City, 1907), *Report on the natural history collections of the 1908-1912 Arctic expedition* (New York, 1913), *Recent explorations on the Canadian Arctic coast* (Geographical Review, 1917), *Present status and future prospects of the larger mammals of Canada* (Scottish Geog. mag., 1924), *Summary of the large wolves of Canada* (Journal of mammalogy, 1943) and numerous articles on birds and animals of Canada. A complete bibliography appears in the *Canadian field naturalist*, vol. 76 for 1962. He died at Ottawa, June 21, 1961.

[*Can. who's who*, 1955-57; N. Story, *The Oxford companion to Canadian history and literature* (Toronto, 1967); *Canadian field naturalist*, vol. 76 (1962).]

Anderson, Thomas Gummersall (1779-1875), superintendent of Indian affairs for Canada West, was born at Sorel, Quebec, on November 12, 1779, the son of Captain Samuel Anderson, of the Royal Regiment of New York. After serving an apprenticeship with a merchant at Kingston, Upper Canada, he went into the fur-trade at Michilimackinac; and in 1814 was in command of a party of volunteers that re-took Prairie-du-Chien from the Americans. After the war he was appointed an officer of the Indian department, with the rank of captain; and he was stationed in turn at Drummond Island, Penetanguishene, Coldwater, and Manitoulin Island. In 1845 he succeeded Colonel S. P. Jarvis (q.v.) as superintendent of Indian affairs for Canada West; and he held this post until his retirement in 1858. He died at Port Hope on February 10, 1875.

[Mrs. S. Rowe, *Anderson record, from 1699 to 1896* (Ont. Hist. Soc., papers and records, 1905); *Dict. Can. biog.*, vol. 10.]

Anderson, William James (1812-1873), physician and journalist, was born at sea of Scottish parents, and was educated at Edinburgh University (M.D., L.R.C.S.). He came to Canada in the 1830s, and worked as a doctor and a journalist, first in Nova Scotia, and then in Quebec. He died at Quebec, Que., on May 15, 1873. He was the author of *The gold fields of the world* (Quebec, 1864), *Canadian history and biography, and passages in the lives of a British prince and a Canadian seigneur* (Quebec, 1867), *The life of F.M. H.R.H. Edward, Duke of Kent* (Montreal, 1870), *The valley of the Chaudière* (Quebec, 1872), *The lower St. Lawrence* (Quebec, 1872), and several papers in the *Transactions* of the Literary and Historical Society of Quebec, of which he was president in 1872.

[Morgan, *Bib. Can.*; *Bull. rech. hist.*, 1929; *Dict. Can. biog.*, vol. 10.]

André, Brother (1845-1937), religious mystic, was born at St. Grégoire d'Iberville, Lower Canada, on August 9, 1845. His baptismal name was Alfred Bissette; and he was the son of a poor working man, who left him an orphan at the age of five. He had no education, and reached middle age before he could read or write. After working in various kinds of manual labour, he became the door-keeper of a commercial school in Montreal; and here he worked for forty years. Then, having been admitted a lay brother of the Congregation of the Holy Cross, and having acquired a great reputation for piety and for the performance of miracles, he was given permission to erect on the north slope of Mount Royal, in Montreal, a shrine to Saint Joseph, his patron saint. This shrine became the Mecca for the sick, the halt, and the blind from all over the North American continent; and it is said that during the twenty-nine years that elapsed between the building of the original shrine and Brother André's death, which took place at Montreal, Quebec, on January 6, 1937, over three million persons had visited it, and that large numbers of these went away cured of their ailments. Brother André disclaimed any healing power in himself, and averred that the cures were wrought "by the good St. Joseph". After his death, his body lay in state at the shrine for five days; and it is said that during this time half a million persons climbed the thirty-three steps that led to St. Joseph's Oratory.

[George H. Ham, *The miracle man of Montreal* (Toronto, 1922); T. F. Cashen, *Brother André, as he was* (Montreal, 1937); J. Drouin, *Le Frère André* (Montreal, 1937); H. P. Bergeron, *Le Frère André* (Montreal, 1938); Étienne Catta, *Le Frère André, 1845-1937, et l'Oratoire Saint Joseph du Mont-Royal* (Montreal, 1965);

Alden Hatch, *The miracle of the mountain: The story of Brother André and the shrine on Mount Royal* (Toronto, 1959); *Can. who's who*, 1936-37; *Americana annual*, 1938.]

Anger, Joseph Humfrey (1862-1913), musician, was born in Berkshire, England, on June 3, 1862, and was educated at Oxford University (Mus. Bac., 1889). He came to Canada, and was for many years professor of harmony in the Toronto Conservatory of Music. In 1902 he received from Trinity University, Toronto, the honorary degree of Mus. Doc. He died at Toronto, Ontario, on June 11, 1913. He was the author of *Forum in music* (London, 1900) and *A treatise on harmony* (3 vols., Boston, 1906-12).

[Morgan, *Can. men* (1912).]

Angers, Sir Auguste Réal (1838-1919), lieutenant-governor of Quebec (1887-92) and minister of agriculture for Canada (1892-95), was born in the city of Quebec, Lower Canada, on October 4, 1838, the son of François R. Angers (q.v.). He was educated at Nicolet College, and was called to the bar in 1860. He entered into partnership with Sir N. Casault (q.v.) and Jean Langlois, and was made a Q.C. in 1874. In 1874 he was elected to the Quebec legislature, and in the same year was given the portfolio of solicitor-general under Boucherville (q.v.). In 1875 he became government leader in the Assembly; and attorney-general on January 26, 1876. On the dismissal of Boucherville, he took the leadership of the Conservative opposition; but in the general election of May, 1878, was defeated in his constituency. In 1880 he was elected a member of the House of Commons for the county of Montmorency, and, after sitting for one session, was elevated to the bench as a puisne judge of the Superior Court of Quebec. After the election of 1886, the premiership of Quebec was offered to him, but was refused. On October 20, 1887, he was appointed lieutenant-governor of Quebec; and it was he who dismissed Mercier (q.v.) from office as prime minister of Quebec in 1891. On December 5, 1892, he entered the administration of Sir John Thompson (q.v.) as minister of agriculture, and he continued in office under Sir Mackenzie Bowell (q.v.). Owing to differences with his colleagues on the Manitoba School Question, he retired from the cabinet on July 8, 1895, and resumed his practice at the bar. In September, 1895, he declined re-appointment to the Superior Court, but in May, 1896, he entered the government of Sir Charles Tupper (q.v.) as president of the Council, being also leader in the province of Quebec. At the general election in June, 1896, he was defeated as a candidate in Quebec Centre, and retired from public life. He died in Montreal on April 15, 1919. He married first, in 1869, Julia Marguerite (d. 1879), daughter of Senator Chinic, and second, in April, 1890, Madeleine Alphonse Hamel, daughter of Alexander Lemoine of Quebec. He was created a knight bachelor in 1913; and in 1888 he was made a LL.D. of Laval University.

[Morgan, *Can. men* (1898); Rose, *Cyc. Can. biog.* (1888); Taché, *Men of the day*; *Can. parl. comp.*; *Can. who was who*, vol. 1.]

Angers, Charles (1854-1929), author, was born at Murray Bay, Quebec, the son of Elie Angers and Marie Perron, and the brother of Félicité Angers (q.v.). He was first a schoolteacher, and then a lawyer; and from 1896 to 1900 he represented Charlevoix in the Canadian House of Commons. Under the pseudonym of "Jean du Sol", he published *Le docteur Hubert Larue et l'idée canadienne-française* (Quebec, 1912), and he contributed to *La Nouvelle-France* in 1913 a series of chapters on *La traite des pelleteries et la colonisation en la Nouvelle-France*. He died at Quebec on March 9, 1929.

[P. G. Roy, *Les avocats de la région de Québec* (Lévis, Que., 1936).]

Angers, Félicité (1845-1924), author, was born at Murray Bay, Lower Canada, in 1845, the daughter of Elie Angers and Marie Perron. She was educated at the Ursuline Convent in Quebec, and she spent most of her life in Murray Bay. She died at Quebec, Que., on June 7, 1924. She was the pioneer among women writers in the province of Quebec; and under the pen-name of "Laure Conan" she published the following novels: *Un amour vrai* (Quebec, 1879), republished under the title *Larmes d'amour* (Montreal, 1897), *Angéline de Montbrun* (Quebec, 1884), *L'oublié* (Montreal, 1902), and *L'obscure souffrance* (Revue canadienne, 1919). She was also the author of *A l'oeuvre et à l'épreuve* (Quebec, 1891), *Elizabeth Seton* (Montreal, 1903), and *Silhouettes canadiennes* (Montreal, 1915).

[C. ab der Halden, *Nouvelles études* (Paris, 1907); Morgan, *Can. men and women* (1912); *Can. who was who*, vol. 1; Le Jeune, *Dict. gén.*]

Angers, François-Réal (1812-1860), lawyer, was born at Pointe aux Trembles, Lower Canada, on November 20, 1812; and was called to the bar of Lower Canada in 1837. He died at Quebec, Canada East, on March 23, 1860. He was the author of *Les révélations du crime de Cambray et ses complices* (Quebec, 1837).

[Morgan, *Bib. can.*; P. G. Roy, *Les avocats de la région de Québec* (Lévis, Que., 1936).]

Angers, Philippe (1858-1935), notary public, was born at Quebec, Canada East, on April 28, 1858; and died at Beauceville,

Quebec, on March 21, 1935. He was the author of *Les seigneurs et premiers censitaires de Saint-Georges (Beauce) et la famille Pozer* (Beauceville, Que., 1927).

[*Bull. rech. hist.*, 1942, p. 118.]

Anglin, Francis Alexander (1865-1933), chief justice of Canada (1924-33), was born at Saint John, New Brunswick, on April 2, 1865, the son of the Hon. Timothy Warren Anglin (q.v.). He was educated at St. Mary's College, Montreal, and at Ottawa University (B.A., 1885), and was called to the bar of Ontario in 1888 (K.C., 1902). He was appointed a judge of the High Court of Ontario in 1904, and of the Supreme Court of Canada in 1909. He became chief justice of Canada in 1924; and he died at Ottawa on March 2, 1933. In 1892 he married Harriet Isabel, daughter of Archibald Fraser, of Fraserfield, Glengarry, Ontario; and by her he had one son and three daughters. In 1924 he was made an imperial privy councillor, and a knight commander of the order of St. Gregory the Great.

[Morgan, *Can. men* (1912); *Can. parl. comp.*; *Can. who was who*, vol. 1.]

Anglin, Margaret Mary (1876-1958), actress, was born at Ottawa, Ontario, on April 3, 1876, the daughter of the Hon. T. W. Anglin (q.v.). She was educated at Loretto Abbey, Toronto, and at the Convent of the Sacred Heart, Montreal; and she studied at the Empire Dramatic School in New York. She became one of the most distinguished actresses on the American stage, and for a time toured with her own company. She died at Toronto, Ontario, on January 7, 1958.

[*Can. who's who*; *Encyc. Can.*; O. J. Stevenson, *A people's best* (Toronto, 1927).]

Anglin, Timothy Warren (1822-1896), journalist and politician, was born on August 31, 1822, at Clonakilty, county Cork, Ireland, the son of Francis Anglin, an officer in the service of the East India Company, and Joanna Warren. He was educated in the village grammar school. In 1849 he emigrated to Saint John, New Brunswick, where he became a journalist. In August, 1849, he established the *Weekly Freeman*, which he published until the autumn of 1850, when it was suspended. In February, 1851, he founded the *Morning Freeman*, a Liberal paper, and the recognized mouthpiece of the Roman Catholics of New Brunswick. In 1860 he was elected representative of the city and county of Saint John in the New Brunswick House of Assembly. He was opposed to Confederation, and became a member without portfolio of the administration of Albert J. Smith (q.v.). He resigned his seat, however, when his colleagues leased to a company of speculators the building of the road to connect New Brunswick and the United States, and he was defeated in the general election

which followed the Fenian agitation. In 1867 he was elected to the House of Commons for the county of Gloucester, and was re-elected in 1872 and 1874. On March 26 of the latter year he was elected speaker of the House of Commons. In 1877 he was obliged to resign this position, as it was held that his printing contract with the government was an infringement of the Independence of Parliament Act; but he was re-elected by his constituents, and in 1878 he was again chosen speaker. In 1879, however, he was not re-elected to this post. From 1879 to 1882 he was a prominent member of the Liberal opposition in parliament; but in the general elections of 1882 he was defeated. In 1883 he removed to Toronto, and became the editor of the Toronto *Tribune*. He died in Toronto on May 4, 1896. He was twice married, first in 1853, to his cousin, Margaret O'Ryan, and second, in September, 1862, to the daughter of Alexander McTavish of Saint John. He had several children, among them the Hon. F. A. Anglin (q.v.) and Margaret Anglin (q.v.), the actress.

[*Can. parl. comp.*; Dent, *Can. port.*, vol. 4.]

Angus, Richard Bladworth (1831-1922), banker and capitalist, was born in Bathgate, Scotland, on May 28, 1831. He received his first training in banking with the Manchester and Liverpool Bank. In 1857 he came to Canada, and entered the service of the Bank of Montreal. From 1869 to 1879 he was its general manager, and from 1910 to 1913 its president. In 1879 he became general manager of the St. Paul, Minneapolis, and Manitoba Railway, which had been bought in 1878 by Donald Smith (q.v.), George Stephen (q.v.), and two other financiers; and it was to the success of this enterprise that he, in conjunction with his associates, owed the foundation of his fortune. In 1880 he was one of the syndicate formed for the construction of the Canadian Pacific Railway, and he was one of the directors of the Canadian Pacific Railway Company from its formation until his death. He died at Senneville, Quebec, on September 17, 1922. In 1857 he married Mary Daniels, and by her he had three sons and five daughters.

[*Can. who was who*, vol. 1; Rose, *Cyc. Can. biog.* (1888); Morgan, *Can. men* (1912); *Can. who's who* (1910); H. A. Innis, *History of the Canadian Pacific Railway* (London, 1923).]

Annand, William (1808-1877), politician, was born in Halifax, Nova Scotia, on April 10, 1808, the son of a well-to-do merchant from Banffshire, Scotland. He was educated in Halifax and in Scotland, and early in 1836 he was chosen to represent Halifax county in the Nova Scotia House of Assembly, with Joseph Howe (q.v.) as his colleague. Thus began an intimate friendship between these two men which lasted until Howe's desertion of the anti-Confederation party. Annand became editor of the *Nova Scotian* in 1843, and shortly afterwards he founded the *Morning Chronicle*, a paper with which Howe was for some time associated. From 1860 to 1863 he was the financial secretary of the province in Howe's ministry; and he went in the autumn of 1866 with Howe and Hugh McDonald to London, to oppose the inclusion of Nova Scotia in Confederation. In 1867 he became the head of the anti-Confederation government of Nova Scotia, and in 1868 he went again to England, to urge the repeal of the British North America Act. When Howe went over to the Confederationists, Annand filled the columns of the *Morning Chronicle* with an unceasing stream of abuse of his old-time leader and friend. His last years were spent in England, where for a time he was agent-general of the Dominion government, and afterwards agent for Nova Scotia. He died in London, England, on October 12, 1887.

[M. O. Hammond, *Confederation and its leaders* (Toronto, 1917); E. M. Saunders, *Three premiers of Nova Scotia* (Toronto, 1909); *Can. who was who*, vol. 2.]

Anson, Sir Archibald Edward Harbord (1826-1925), lieutenant-governor of Prince Edward Island (1867-70), was born in London, England, in 1826, the son of General Sir William Anson, bart. He entered the army in 1844, and served in the Crimea. From 1867 to 1870 he was lieutenant-governor of Prince Edward Island; and later he was governor of the Straits Settlements. He died on February 26, 1925. He published his reminiscences under the title *About others and myself* (London, 1920).

[*Who was who*, 1916-28.]

Anspach, Lewis Amadeus (*fl.* 1799-1822), clergyman and historian, came to Newfoundland about 1799, when he opened the first grammar school at St. John's. From 1800 to 1812 he was the Church of England rector at Harbour Grace. The dates of his birth and death have not been ascertained. He was the author of *Summary of the laws of commerce and navigation, adapted to the present state, government, and trade of the island of Newfoundland* (London, 1809), *History of Newfoundland* (London, 1819), and a German translation of the latter volume (Weimar, 1822).

[*Newfoundland supp.*]

Arbuthnot, Marriott (1711?-1794), lieutenant-governor of Nova Scotia (1776-78), was born at Weymouth, England, about 1711, and entered the Royal Navy. In 1775 he was appointed naval commissary at Halifax; and he was lieutenant-governor of Nova Scotia from 1776 to 1778 in succession

to Michael Francklin (q.v.). From 1779 to 1781 he was in command of the British fleet in North American waters, but he was recalled to England in 1781, and was never again employed at sea, though he became by reason of seniority in 1793 an admiral of the blue. He died at London, on January 31, 1794.

[W. B. Willcox, "Arbuthnot, Gambler and Graves, 'old women' of the navy", in George Ethan Billias (ed.), *George Washington's opponents* (Toronto, 1969); *Dict. nat. biog.*; Le Jeune, *Dict. gén.*]

Arcand, Adrien (1900-1967), Canadian Fascist leader and career journalist, first came to national attention as the leader of the Quebec-based anti-Semitic Parti de l'Unité Nationale which claimed to have 100,000 members across Canada in 1938. He promised a blue-shirt march on Ottawa in 1940 to take over the country but instead spent the years 1940 to 1945 in an internment camp. On his release he returned to journalism and retired to Lanoraie, Quebec, where he continued to correspond with groups in other parts of the world and to write anti-Semitic articles. He ran unsuccessfully for the federal riding of Richelieu-Verchères in 1949 and then dropped out of politics. He published *A bas la haine* in 1965 in an attempt to discredit the reports of Jewish persecution and death in the Second World War. He died at Montreal, Quebec, August 1, 1967.

[Metropolitan Toronto Library Board, *Biographical scrapbooks*, vol. 33.]

Archambault, Sir Horace (1857-1918), chief justice of Quebec (1911-18), was born at L'Assomption, Lower Canada, on March 6, 1857, the son of the Hon. Louis Archambault and Elizabeth Dugal. He was educated at Laval University (LL.L., 1878; LL.D., 1886), and was called to the Quebec bar in 1878 (Q.C., 1889). In 1888 he was called to the Legislative Council of Quebec; and from 1897 to 1908 he was speaker of the Council. From 1897 to 1905 he was also attorney-general in the Marchand and Parent administrations. In 1905 he was appointed a puisne judge of the Court of King's Bench in Quebec; and in 1911 chief justice of this court. He died at Trois Pistoles, Quebec, on August 25, 1918. In 1882 he married Elizabeth, daughter of Roger Lelièvre, Quebec. He was created a knight bachelor in 1914.

[F. J. Audet, *Les juges en chef de la province du Québec* (Quebec, 1933); Morgan, *Can. men* (1912); *Can. parl. comp.*; Le Jeune, *Dict. gén.*]

Archambault, Joseph Louis (1849-1925), lawyer and author, was born at Varennes, Canada East, on June 19, 1849, the son of J. N. A. Archambault and Aurélie

Mongeau. He was called to the Quebec bar in 1871, and he was for several years corporation counsel for Montreal. In 1913 he was elected *bâtonnier* of the Montreal bar. He died at Montreal on May 27, 1925. He was the author of *Jacques Cartier, ou le Canada vengé* (Montreal, 1879), an historical drama; *Le barreau canadien au Conseil Privé* (Montreal, 1880; 2nd ed., 1889), and *Conservateurs et libéraux: Etude politique* (Montreal, 1887).

[Morgan, *Can. men* (1912).]

Archambault, Louis Misaël (1812-1894), priest, was born at Chambly, Lower Canada, on July 14, 1812; and died at St. Hugues, Quebec, July 10, 1894. He was the author of *Généalogie de la famille Archambault* (Montreal, 1891).

[Allaire, *Dict. biog.*]

Archibald, Sir Adams George (1814-1892), lieutenant-governor of Manitoba (1870-72) and of Nova Scotia (1873-83), was born at Truro, Nova Scotia, on May 18, 1814, the son of Samuel Archibald and Elizabeth, daughter of Matthew Archibald. He was educated at Pictou Academy, studied law, and was called to the bar of Prince Edward Island in 1838, and of Nova Scotia in 1839. From 1851 to 1867 he represented the county of Colchester in the Nova Scotia Assembly. In 1856 he was appointed solicitor-general, and in 1860 attorney-general. He was a strong advocate of Confederation, and was a delegate to the Charlottetown Conference of September, 1864, to the Quebec Conference of October, 1864, and finally to the conference held in London during the winter of 1866-67 to complete the terms of Confederation. On July 1, 1867, he became secretary of state for Canada; but he resigned in May, 1870, and he was appointed lieutenant-governor of Manitoba and the North West Territories. During his administration, which lasted until 1872, he laid the foundation of the civil institutions of Manitoba and the Territories. On his return from Manitoba he was appointed, on June 24, 1873, judge in equity of Nova Scotia; but this office he held only until July 4 of the same year, when, upon the death of Joseph Howe (q.v.), he was appointed lieutenant-governor of Nova Scotia and this office he held until July 4, 1883. In 1888 he was elected to the Canadian House of Commons for Colchester, but he resigned in 1891. He died at Truro on December 14, 1892. For his services in Manitoba he was in 1872 created a C.M.G., and in 1886 he was created a K.C.M.G. In 1884 he was chosen chairman of the board of governors of Dalhousie College; and in 1885 he was elected president of the Nova Scotia Historical Society. He married on June 1, 1843, Elizabeth, daughter of the Rev. John Burnyeat, by whom he had four children.

[E. Parker, *Manitoba's first lieutenant-*

governor (Dalhousie review, 1931); R. Craggs, *Sir Adams G. Archibald: Colchester's Father of Confederation* (Truro, 1967); *In memoriam* (Coll. Nova Scotia Hist. Soc., 1895); C. Bruce Fergusson, *Adams George Archibald* (Coll. Nova Scotia Hist. Soc., 1968); *Dict. nat. biog.*, supp. I; Rose, *Cyc. Can. biog.* (1886); Dent, *Can. port.*, vol. 1.]

Archibald, Mrs. Edith Jessie, *née* **Archibald** (1854-1934), author, was born in Newfoundland in 1854, the daughter of Sir Edward Mortimer Archibald. She was the author of her father's *Life and letters* (Toronto, 1924) and of a novel, *The token* (London, 1930). She married Charles Archibald, a distant cousin; and she died in Halifax, Nova Scotia in 1934.

[Clara Thomas, *Canadian novelists* (Toronto, 1946).]

Archibald, Edward Spinney (1885-1968), agriculturalist and director of Experimental Farms Service, 1919-51, was born in Yarmouth, Nova Scotia, on May 12, 1885. He was educated at Acadia University (B.A., 1905) and at the University of Toronto (B.S.A., 1908). He was awarded a D.Sc. by Acadia University in 1930. He lectured at the Agricultural College in Truro, Nova Scotia, from 1908 until appointment to the Canadian Public Service in 1912 where he became director of the Experimental Farms in 1919. The most serious problem confronting Canadian agriculture during Dr. Archibald's term as director of Experimental Farms was the protracted prairie drought of 1930-35. He was responsible for much of the experimental work in connection with the Prairie Farm Rehabilitation program established by Act of the Canadian parliament of 1935. The experimental farms undertook demonstrations of accepted methods of combating drought conditions through new tillage practices, changes in cropping practices and the encouragement of cooperative programs for land reclamation through grass and tree planting. In addition, pressure was maintained to complete the prairie soil surveys begun in the previous decade as a means of assessing the future of Canadian agriculture in the prairie region. Dr. Archibald combined empirical methods for finding solutions for immediate farm problems with the development of basic research techniques which would help deal with problems of genetics, plant diseases, soil fertility, and animal improvement. He was liaison officer with the agricultural division of the Food and Agricultural Organization of the United Nations at Addis Ababa from 1950 to 1952. He was a fellow of the Royal Society of Canada and a Companion of the Order of Canada. A continuing view of his work in agricultural rehabilitation is to be found in the *Canadian Geographical Journal: Prairie farm rehabilitation* (October, 1940), and *Research* *in prairie farm rehabilitation*, with Wm. Dickson (February, 1944), also *Financial Post* (April 16, 1949).

[*Proc. and Trans. Roy. Soc. Can.*, 1968; *Can. who's who*, 1955-57.]

Archibald, Samuel George William (1777-1846), politician and judge, was born at Truro, Nova Scotia, on February 5, 1777, the son of Samuel Archibald. He was educated at Andover and for a time at Harvard University, and was called to the bar of Nova Scotia on April 6, 1805. In 1806 he was returned to the Nova Scotia House of Assembly for Halifax, and he continued to represent this county until 1835, when it was divided. He was then returned for Colchester county, and remained its representative until 1844. From 1824 to 1828 he was at the same time chief justice of Prince Edward Island. In 1830 he was elected speaker of the Nova Scotia House of Assembly, and became solicitor-general of the province; and on April 29, 1844, he was appointed master of the rolls, and judge of the Court of Vice-Admiralty. This office he held until his death in Halifax, on January 28, 1846.

[I. Longworth, *Life of S. G. W. Archibald* (Truro, N.S., 1881); D. Campbell, *History of Nova Scotia* (Montreal, 1873); A. B. Warburton, *A history of Prince Edward Island* (Saint John, N.B., 1923); Edith Jessie Archibald, *Life and letters of Sir Edward Mortimer Archibald* (Toronto, 1924).]

Archibald, Thomas Dickson (1813-1890), senator of Canada, was born at Onslow, Nova Scotia, on April 8, 1813, the son of David Archibald. He was educated at Pictou Academy, and became a member of the firm of Archibald and Co., merchants. From 1856 to 1867 he was a member of the Legislative Council of Nova Scotia, and from 1860 to 1863 he was a member of the Executive Council. In 1867 he was called by royal proclamation to the Senate of Canada. He died at Sydney Mines, Nova Scotia, on October 18, 1890.

[*Cyc. Am. biog.; Can. parl. comp.*]

Archibald, Sir Thomas Dickson (1817-1875), judge, was born at Truro, Nova Scotia, on August 23, 1817, the sixth son of the Hon. Samuel George William Archibald (q.v.). He was educated at Pictou Academy, studied law with his father, and was called to the bar of Nova Scotia in 1837. He went to England, and became a member of the Middle Temple in 1840. In 1872 he was made a judge of the Court of Queen's Bench in England; and he died in England on October 18, 1875. He was created a knight bachelor in 1873.

[Mrs. C. Archibald, *The Hon. Thomas Dickson Archibald* (Coll. Nova Scotia Hist. Soc., 1927).]

Argall, Sir Samuel (1572?-1626?), adventurer, was probably born in Bristol, England. He was one of the early adventurers to Jamestown, Virginia; and in 1613-14 he commanded the English expedition which captured Port Royal in Acadia, the French settlements in Acadia being regarded by the authorities in Virginia as an infringement of their charter. He received the honour of knighthood from James I in 1622; and he might have died early in 1626 shortly after an unsuccessful attempt on the part of the expedition headed by Lord Wimbledon and himself to capture Cadiz.

[*Dict. Can. biog.*, vol. 1; *Dict. nat. biog.*; Le Jeune, *Dict. gén.*]

Argenson, Pierre de Voyer, Vicomte d' (1625-1709?), governor of New France (1658-61), was born in 1625, the son of René de Voyer, Comte d'Argenson. He became a soldier, and distinguished himself at the battle of Lens in 1648, and at the siege of Bordeaux in 1649. For a time he was bailiff of Touraine. On January 27, 1657, he was appointed governor-general of New France, and he arrived at Quebec in July of the following year. He speedily came into conflict with Laval over the question of precedence and, worn out by the ceaseless intrigues, asked for his recall. He left Canada on September 19, 1661, and he died about the year 1709.

[Bibaud, *Panth. Can.*; Le Jeune, *Dict. gén.*; F. Parkman, *The old régime in Canada* (Boston, 1874); *Lettres inédites du gouverneur d'Argenson* (Bull. rech. hist., 1921); *Dict. Can. biog.*, vol. 2.]

Argyll, Duke of. See **Lorne, Marquis of.**

Arles, Henri d' (pseud.). See **Beaudé, Henri.**

Armitage, William James (1860-1929), clergyman and author, was born at Bryanston, near London, Canada West, on February 6, 1860. He was educated at Wycliffe College, Toronto, at Dalhousie University, and at the University of New Brunswick (Ph.D., 1905); and he was ordained a priest of the Church of England in 1885. He was successively rector of churches in St. Catharines, Ontario, and Halifax, Nova Scotia; and in 1906 he became archdeacon of Halifax. In 1911 he was elected president of the Nova Scotia Historical Society. He died at Halifax, N.S., on September 10, 1929. He was the author of *The story of the Canadian revision of the prayer book* (Toronto, 1922).

[Morgan, *Can. men* (1912).]

Armour, Edward Douglas (1851-1922), lawyer and author, was born at Port Hope, Ontario, in 1851, the son of Robert Armour.

He was educated at Trinity University, Toronto (D.C.L., 1902), and was called to the bar in Ontario in 1876 (Q.C., 1890). He practised law in Toronto; and he was the founder, and for nineteen years the editor, of the *Canadian Law Times*. He died at Toronto on October 3, 1922. In addition to a number of legal text-books, he was the author of *Law lyrics* (Toronto, 1918) and *Odes from Horace* (Toronto, 1922).

[Morgan, *Can. men* (1912).]

Armour, Eric Norman (1877-1934), jurist, was born at Cobourg, Ontario, on February 15, 1877, the youngest son of Chief Justice J. D. Armour (q.v.). He was educated at the University of Toronto (B.A., 1899) and at Osgoode Hall, Toronto, and was called to the bar of Ontario in 1902 (K.C., 1924). He saw service in the Canadian Army, with the rank of major, from 1915 to 1919; and in 1925 he was appointed Crown attorney of Toronto. He was made a judge of the Supreme Court of Ontario in 1933; and in 1932 he was elected president of the Champlain Society. For many years he was a governor of the University of Toronto. He died at Toronto, Ontario, on March 11, 1934.

[Morgan, *Can. men* (1912).]

Armour, John Douglas (1830-1903), chief justice of Ontario, was born in Otonabee, Peterborough county, Upper Canada, on May 4, 1830, the youngest son of the Rev. Samuel Armour, rector of Cavan. He was educated at Upper Canada College and the University of Toronto (B.A., 1850). He was called to the bar in 1853, and in 1867 he was appointed a Q.C. On November 30, 1877, he became puisne judge of the Court of Queen's Bench, and in 1890 chief justice of Ontario and president of the Court of Appeal. He was one of the two commissioners for Canada appointed to act with Lord Alverstone on the Alaska Boundary Commission of 1903; but he died in London while the argument was being heard, on July 11, 1903. On April 28, 1855, he married Eliza, daughter of Freeman S. Clench, of Cobourg; and by her he had eleven children. He was an honorary LL.D. of the University of Toronto (1902).

[*Dict. nat. biog.*, supp. II; Dent, *Can. port.*, vol. 4; Morgan, *Can. men* (1898); *Cyc. Can. biog.* (1888).]

Armour, Robert (1781?-1857), publisher and bookseller, was born in Kilmarnock, Scotland, about 1781. He emigrated to Canada about 1800, and became a publisher and bookseller in Montreal. In 1829 he founded the Montreal *Almanack*; and for many years he was one of the proprietors of the Montreal *Gazette*. He died in Montreal on April 16, 1857. His son, Robert Armour, Jr., who was for a time editor of the Montreal *Gazette*, and who was born in 1809, died in Montreal on October 4, 1845.

[Morgan, *Bib. can.*]

Armstrong, Ernest Howard (1864-1946), prime minister of Nova Scotia (1923-25), was born at North Kingston, Kings county, Nova Scotia, on July 27, 1864, and died at Bridgewater, Nova Scotia, on February 15, 1946. He was educated at Acadia and Dalhousie universities, and was called to the bar in Nova Scotia in 1888. He practised law first at Weymouth and then at Yarmouth, Nova Scotia. He represented Yarmouth county as a Liberal in the legislature of Nova Scotia from 1906 to 1920, and Shelburne county from 1920 to 1925. He was prime minister of the province from 1923 to 1925. In 1926 he was appointed a county court judge, but retired from the bench because of ill-health in 1932.

[*Encyc. Can.*; *Who's who in Canada*, 1925-26.]

Armstrong, George Henry (1858-1938), educationist, was born at Yonge, Leeds county, Canada West, on January 2, 1858. He was educated at the University of Toronto (B.A., 1896; B.Paed., 1897; M.A., 1898), and became a school-teacher and, later, a school-inspector. He died at Kingston, Ontario, on April 14, 1938. He was the author of *The origin and meaning of place-names in Canada* (Toronto, 1930).

[Morgan, *Can. men* (1912).]

Armstrong, Lawrence (1664-1739), lieutenant-governor of Nova Scotia (1724-1739), was born in 1664, and came to Annapolis Royal, Nova Scotia, as lieutenant-colonel in General Philipps's regiment, when the latter (q.v.) was "Captain-General and Governor-in-Chief" of Nova Scotia. He was appointed to the first council in Annapolis Royal in 1720, and in 1724 became lieutenant-governor of Nova Scotia. He was a man of unfortunate temper and sensitive disposition, and his difficulties preyed so upon his mind that on December 6, 1739, he committed suicide.

[Le Jeune, *Dict. gén.*; *Dict. Can. biog.*, vol. 2.]

Armstrong, Philip Christian (1883-1952), economist, was born in 1883. In 1930 he joined the staff of the Canadian Pacific Railway in Montreal as a special representative in the office of the vice-president in charge of traffic; and in 1944 he became economic consultant for the C.P.R. He died at Montreal on March 25, 1952. He was the author of *A report of the economic situation and outlook at the close of 1940* (Montreal, 1941) and *Two and two: A study of economic superstitions* (Toronto, 1948), and joint author, with F. E. M. Robinson, of *City and county: A* *study in fundamental economics* (Toronto, 1939).

[*New York Times*, March 26, 1953.]

Arnold, Benedict (1741-1801), soldier, was born at Norwich, Connecticut, on January 14, 1741, the son of Benedict Arnold and Hannah King Waterman. He saw service as a boy in the Seven Years' War, and he was one of the first militia officers to enlist in the Revolutionary Army in 1775. With Ethan Allen (q.v.), he was in command of the revolutionary force which captured Ticonderoga on May 10, 1775; and in the autumn of 1775 he commanded the force which made its way to the valley of the St. Lawrence by way of the Kennebec River, and joined the force under Richard Montgomery (q.v.) before Quebec. After Montgomery's death, Arnold succeeded to the command of the American forces invading Canada, and conducted their retreat by way of Montreal in the spring of 1776. In 1779 he became a traitor to the revolutionary cause; and in September, 1780, he was forced to take refuge within the British lines. He spent most of the rest of his life in England, in comparative poverty and disgrace; and he died in London on June 14, 1801. In 1797 he was granted 13,400 acres of land in Upper Canada; and two of his sons settled in Upper Canada.

[M. Decker, *Benedict Arnold* (Tarrytown, N.Y., 1932); E. D. Sullivan, *Benedict Arnold* (New York, 1932); O. Sherwin, *Benedict Arnold* (New York, 1931); Lauran Paine, *Benedict Arnold, hero and traitor* (New York, 1965); Brian Richard Boylan, *Benedict Arnold: The dark eagle* (New York, 1973); Willard Mosher Wallace, *Traitorous hero: The life and fortunes of Benedict Arnold* (Freeport, L.I., 1970); *Dict. Am. biog.*; *Cyc. Am. biog.*]

Arnoldi, Daniel (1774-1849), physician, was born at Montreal, Quebec, on March 4, 1774, the son of Johann Peter Arnoldi, who had settled in Canada in the early days of British rule. He became one of the pioneer physicians of Montreal, and was the first president of the College of Physicians and Surgeons of Lower Canada. He died at Montreal on July 19, 1849. He married Elisabeth Franchère; and by her he had three sons and seven daughters.

[J. Gauvreau, *Daniel Arnoldi* (Journal of the Canadian Medical Association, July, 1932); E. Fabre-Surveyer, *Une famille d'orfèvres* (Bull. rech. hist., 1940).]

Arthur, Sir George, Bart. (1784-1854), lieutenant-governor of Upper Canada (1838-41), was the youngest son of John Arthur of Norley House, Plymouth, and was born on June 21, 1784. On August 25, 1804, he entered the army. In 1806 he served in Sir James Craig's expedition to Italy, in 1807 in

General Fraser's expedition to Egypt, in 1808 under Sir James Kempt in Sicily, and in 1809 in the expedition to Walcheren. He was twice wounded, once in the attack on Rosetta in 1807, and again in the attack on Flushing in 1809. In 1814 he was appointed lieutenant-governor of Honduras, and in 1823 lieutenant-governor of Van Diemen's Land. On March 23, 1838, he became lieutenant-governor of Upper Canada. This position he held until 1841, when Upper and Lower Canada were united. His tenure of office thus coincided with the troubled period following the Rebellion of 1837, and was marked by great firmness and some severity. His refusal to grant a reprieve to the rebels Lount and Mathews before their execution in Toronto — although, as it turned out, instructions were already on their way to him from the Colonial Office to temper justice with mercy — greatly embittered the Reform element in the province. His services in keeping Upper Canada quiet and intact from invaders were, however, rewarded with a baronetcy; and he was given the governorship of Bombay, which he retained until 1846. On returning finally to England, he was made a privy councillor, and was given the honorary degree of D.C.L. at Oxford. He died on September 19, 1854. In 1814 he married Eliza Orde Usher, second daughter of Lieutenant-General Sir John Frederick Sigismund Smith, and by her he had twelve children. *The Arthur papers* have been edited by C. R. Sanderson (Toronto, 1943).

[W. Sage, *Sir George Arthur* (Queen's quarterly, vol. 26); D. B. Read, *The lieutenant-governors of Upper Canada and Ontario* (Toronto, 1900); W. D. Forsyth, *Governor Arthur's convict system: Van Diemen's Land, 1824-36* (Sydney, 1970); *Dict. nat. biog.*; Morgan, *Cel. Can.*]

Arthur, Julia (1869-1950), actress, was born in Hamilton, Ontario, on May 3, 1869. Her baptismal name was Ida Lewis, but she assumed the stage name of Julia Arthur when she went on the stage, Arthur being her mother's family name. She made her debut as an actress at the age of fourteen in United States. In 1895 she went to London, and played at the Lyceum Theatre with Sir Henry Irving and Ellen Terry. In 1898 she retired temporarily from the stage on her marriage to Benjamin Pearce Cheney of Boston, but in 1914 she returned to the stage, and in 1924 she scored a triumphant success when she toured Canada in Bernard Shaw's *Saint Joan*. She died at Boston, Massachusetts, on March 28, 1950.

[*Can. who's who*, 1948; *Ency. Can.*; O. J. Stevenson, *A people's best* (Toronto, 1927).]

Ascher, Isidore Gordon (1835-1914), lawyer and poet, was born at Glasgow, Scotland, in 1835. He came with his parents to

Canada in 1843, and was educated at McGill College (B.C.L., 1847). He was called to the bar in Lower Canada, but in 1864 he removed to England, where he lived until his death at London, England, in 1914. While in Canada he published *Voices from the hearth* (Montreal, 1863); and after he left Canada he was the author of *An odd man's story* (London, 1889), *The doom of destiny* (London, 1895), *A social upheaval* (London, 1898), *One hundred and five sonnets* (Oxford, 1912), and *Collected poems* (London, 1929).

[Morgan, *Bib. can.*]

Ashburton, Alexander Baring, Baron (1774-1848), statesman, was born in London, England, on October 27, 1774. In 1806 he was elected a member of the British House of Commons. In 1842 he was appointed a commissioner to adjust the rival claims of England and the United States on account of a dispute in regard to the north-eastern boundary. He has been attacked, especially by Canadian writers, for sacrificing Canada's interests, but the United States was actually awarded less territory than had previously been granted it by the King of the Netherlands, an award the United States Senate refused to accept. Lord Ashburton died on May 13, 1848.

[*Dict. nat. biog.*]

Ashworth, Edward Montague (1880-1954), engineer and novelist, was born at Newmarket, Ontario, in 1880, and was educated at Harbord Collegiate Institute, Toronto, and at the University of Toronto (B.A., 1907). He joined the staff of the Toronto Hydro-Electric Commission, and in 1924 became its general manager. He retired from this position in 1952, and died at Toronto on March 26, 1954. His *Toronto Hydro recollections* was published after his death (Toronto, 1955). Earlier he had published, under the pseudonym of Johnston Abbott, two novels: *La roux* (Toronto, 1924) and *The seigneurs of La Saulaye* (Toronto, 1928).

[*Can. who's who*, 1949-51.]

Askin, John (1739?-1815), merchant, was born at Strabane, county Tyrone, Ireland, about 1739, the son of John Askin (or Erskine) and Alice Rea. He migrated to America in 1758, and served in the army during the later stages of the Seven Years' War. About 1761 he established himself in business as a merchant at Albany, New York; and in 1765 he went to Michilimackinac, where he became commissary in the military department. In 1780 he settled in Detroit; and he lived there until Detroit was handed over to the United States in 1802. He thereupon moved to Amherstburg, in Upper Canada; and there he died in April, 1815. He married, first, an Indian woman, by whom he had three children; and, secondly, in 1772,

Archange Barthe, of Detroit, by whom he had nine children. *The John Askin papers* have been edited by Milo M. Quaife, and published by the Detroit Library Commission (2 vols., Detroit, 1928-31).

[W. S. Wallace (ed.), *Documents relating to the North West Company* (Toronto: The Champlain Society, 1934).]

Askin, John (1765?-1820), superintendent of Indian affairs at Amherstburg, was born at L'Arbre Croche, a town of the Ottawas, about 1765, the son of John Askin (q.v.) and an Indian woman. He spent his life in the fur-trade and in the service of the Indian Department. He led the Indians in the attack on Michilimackinac in July, 1812; and he remained at this post during the whole of the War of 1812. He then became superintendent of Indian affairs at Amherstburg, and major commanding the second regiment of Essex militia. He died at Amherstburg on January 1, 1820. In 1791 he married, at Detroit, Mary Madelaine Peltier.

[M. M. Quaife (ed.), *The John Askin papers* (2 vols., Detroit, 1928-31).]

Asselin, Joseph François Olivar (1874-1937), journalist, was born at St. Hilarion, Quebec, on November 9, 1874. He was educated at Rimouski College, and became a journalist. He became an outstanding French-Canadian nationalist, and was one of the founders of the Nationalist League; but, on the outbreak of the First World War, he enlisted in the Canadian Army, and served overseas as a major from 1915 to 1917. In 1917 he was appointed secretary of the Canadian Military Mission in Paris, and he was attached to the Canadian delegation at the Peace Conference in Paris in 1919. From 1919 to 1930 he engaged in the investment business; but he then returned to journalism. Though a leader of French-Canadian nationalism, he was never elected to parliament; he was an unsuccessful candidate for election to the Quebec lower chamber in 1904, and to the Canadian House of Commons in 1911. In 1919 he was awarded by the French government the Légion d'Honneur. He died at Montreal, Quebec, on April 18, 1938. He was the author of *A Quebec view of Canadian nationalism* (Montreal, 1909), *L'oeuvre de l'Abbé Groulx* (Montreal, 1923), and *Pensée française* (Montreal, 1938). In 1903 he married Alice Le Bouthillier; but he had no children.

[J. Gauvreau, *Olivar Asselin* Montreal, 1937); H. Bastien, *Oliver Asselin* (Montreal, 1938); M. Hébert, *Deux protagonistes de notre pensée française* (Canada français, 1938); Marcel A. Gagnon, *La vie orageuse d'Olivar Asselin* (2 vols., Montreal, 1962); *Can. who's who*, 1936-37.]

Astor, John Jacob (1763-1848), fur-trader and capitalist, was born in the village of Waldorf, Baden, Germany, on July 17, 1763, the son of Jacob Astor. He emigrated to America in 1784, and became interested in the fur-trade. In 1808 he formed the American Fur Company, of which he was sole proprietor, and in 1810 the Pacific Fur Company, the story of which has been told in Washington Irving's *Astoria* (Philadelphia, 1836). The fort which his partners built in 1811 at the mouth of the Columbia River was in 1813 handed over to the North West Company of Canada, but by 1817 he had driven the North West Company from the Mississippi valley, and by 1827 he acquired a virtual monopoly of the fur-trade in the middle west of the United States. He retired from the fur-trade in 1834, and he died at New York on March 29, 1848. At his death he was estimated to be worth $20,000,000.

[K.W. Porter, *John Jacob Astor* (2 vols., Cambridge, Mass., 1931); *Dict. Am. biog.*; *Cyc. Am. biog.*]

Atherton, William Henry (1867-1950), historian, was born at Salford, England, on November 15, 1867. He was educated at Stonyhurst College, England, and taught classics at Stonyhurst College and at Beaumont College, Old Windsor. He came to Canada in 1907, and after teaching in Alberta and in Montreal, he was appointed a professor of history and literature in the University of Montreal in 1920. He was the author of *Montreal, 1535-1914* (3 vols., Montreal, 1914), and he was joint editor, with William Wood (q.v.) and others, of *The storied province of Quebec* (4 vols., Montreal, 1931). He died at Montreal, Quebec, on July 6, 1950. He was not married.

[*Can. who's who*, 1948.]

Athlone, Alexander Augustus Frederick William Alfred George Cambridge, Earl of (1874-1957), governor-general of Canada (1940-46), was born at Kensington Palace, London, on April 14, 1874, the son of the Duke of Teck and Princess Mary, daughter of the first Duke of Cambridge. He was thus a brother of Her Majesty Queen Mary. He was educated at Eton and Sandhurst, and was commissioned in the Life Guards. He served in the Matabeleland campaign and in the South African War, and was awarded the D.S.O. and the Queen's medal. From 1923 to 1930 he was governor-general of South Africa; and from 1940 to 1946 he served as governor-general of Canada, his period of office practically coinciding with the years of the Second World War. In 1904 he married the Princess Alice of Albany, grand-daughter of Queen Victoria; they had one son (d. 1928) and one daughter. The Earl of Athlone died in London, England, on January 16, 1957. He was created a K.G., a

G.C.B., and a G.C.M.G.

[M. E. Sara, *The Rt. Hon. the Earl of Athlone* (London, 1941); J. Cowan, *Canada's governors-general* (Toronto, 1952); *Encyc. Can.*; *Can. parl. guide*, 1940-46; *Who's who*, 1956.]

Atholstan, Sir Hugh Graham, first Baron (1848-1938), newspaper publisher and philanthropist, was born at Atholstan, Huntingdon county, Canada East, on July 18, 1848, of Scottish parentage. In 1863 he entered the employ of the Montreal *Daily Telegraph*, under his uncle, E. H. Parsons; and in 1869 he founded his own paper, the *Evening Star*. This paper, which became the *Montreal Daily Star* and the *Family Herald and Weekly Star*, he conducted with amazing success for nearly seventy years. His editorial policy was Conservative and Imperialist; but he himself never took an active part in politics. Having become wealthy, he devoted himself mainly to private philanthropy; and his gifts to cancer research and to various charities were on a munificent scale. It was largely because of his benefactions that he was created a knight bachelor in 1908, and in 1917 first Baron Atholstan of Huntingdon in the province of Quebec and of Edinburgh in Scotland, the first Canadian journalist to receive such honours. In 1892 he married Annie Beekman Hamilton of Montreal; and by her he had one daughter. His title lapsed with his death.

[*Who was who*, 1929-40; *Can. who's who*, 1936-37; Morgan, *Can. men* (1912).]

Atkinson, William Edwin (1862-1926), landscape painter, was born in Toronto, Ontario, on March 22, 1862, the son of W. T. Atkinson, a chemist. He studied painting at the Toronto Art School, the Pennsylvania Academy of Fine Arts, and the Atelier Julien, Paris. He specialized in landscape painting; and in 1902 he was elected an associate of the Royal Canadian Academy. He exhibited in the Paris Salon in 1890; and some of his landscapes are in the National Gallery at Ottawa. He died at Toronto on August 1, 1926. In 1899 he married Laura Davidge, who was also an artist; and by her he had two sons.

[Morgan, *Can. men* (1912); N. MacTavish, *The fine arts in Canada* (Toronto, 1925).]

Aubert de Gaspé, Philippe (1786-1871), seignior and author, was born at Quebec on October 30, 1786, the son of the Hon. Pierre Ignace Aubert de Gaspé, a member of the Legislative Council of Lower Canada, and Catherine Tarieu de Lanaudière. He was the descendant of Charles Aubert de la Chesnaye (q.v.), who came to Canada in 1655, and in 1693 was granted a patent of nobility by Louis XIV. Educated at the Quebec Seminary, he studied law under Jonathan Sewell (q.v.), was called to the bar, and for a number of years was high sheriff of the district of Quebec. Business troubles compelled his resignation of this office, and he retired to his manor at St. Jean Port-Joli. Here the later years of his life were passed in seclusion, and here he wrote, at the age of seventy-six years, his first book, *Les anciens canadiens* (Quebec, 1863), an historical romance which ranks as one of the classics of French-Canadian literature. Two English translations of the book have been published, under the title *The Canadians of old*, the first by Georgiana M. Pennée (Quebec, 1864) and the second by Charles G. D. Roberts (London, 1890). In 1866 Gaspé published his *Mémoires* (Ottawa), a volume of reminiscences of great value to the historian; and in 1893 his son, Alfred Aubert de Gaspé, brought out a posthumous volume of sketches by him entitled *Divers* (Montreal). He died in Quebec on January 29, 1871.

[H. R. Casgrain, *Philippe Aubert de Gaspé* (Quebec, 1871) and *Biographies canadiennes* (Montreal, 1885); C. Roy, *Etude sur "Les anciens canadiens"* (Trans. Roy. Soc. Can., 1906); Morgan, *Cel. Can.* and *Bib. can.*; L. M. Darveau, *Nos hommes de lettres* (Montreal, 1873); *Dict. Can. biog.*, vol. 10.]

Aubert de Gaspé, Philippe, Jr. (d. 1841), novelist, was the son of Philippe Aubert de Gaspé (q.v.), the author of *Les anciens canadiens*. He wrote one of the first Canadian novels, *L'influence d'un livre, roman historique* (Quebec, 1837). He died on March 7, 1841, at Halifax, Nova Scotia, where he was reporter to the Legislative Assembly.

[Morgan, *Bib. can.*; *Bull. rech. hist.*, vol. 12.]

Aubert de la Chesnaye, Charles (1632-1702), merchant and fur-trader, was born at Amiens, France, on February 12, 1632. He came to Canada in 1655, and in 1666 became agent of the Compagnie des Indes Occidentales in Canada. In 1696 he prepared an important memoir on the commerce of Canada. He died at Quebec on September 20, 1702. In 1693 he was granted by Louis XIV a patent of nobility.

[P. G. Roy, *La famille Juchereau Duchesnay* (Lévis, 1903); *Dict. Can. biog.*, vol. 2.]

Aubin, Napoléon (1812-1890), journalist and author, was born at Chaynes, near Geneva, in French Switzerland, in 1812. He came to America about 1833, and in 1834 settled in Quebec. He became a journalist, and founded the famous *Fantasque* (1837-45), a humorous and satirical journal; and he was imprisoned as a rebel in 1838. He then edited successively *Le Castor, Le Canadien, Le*

Canadien Indépendant, the *Tribune*, and *Le Pays*. In 1847 he was secretary of the "Association de la réforme et du progrès", and in 1869 he was elected president of the Institut Canadien at Montreal. For many years he was the Swiss consul at Montreal. Apart from some scientific treatises, such as *La chimie agricole mise à la portée de tout le monde* (Quebec, 1847), and a volume entitled *Les veillées du Père Bonsens* (Montreal, 1873), most of his writings are to be found in newspapers or in such collections as *Le répertoire national* (4 vols., Montreal, 1848-50). He died at Montreal on June 12, 1890.

[Jean Paul Tremblay, *A la recherche de Napoléon Aubin* (Quebec, 1969); Bibaud, *Panth. can.*; L. M. Darveau, *Nos hommes de lettres* (Montreal, 1873); E. Lareau, *Histoire de la littérature canadienne* (Montreal, 1874).]

Auclair, Elie Joseph Arthur (1866-1946), priest and historian, was born at St. Vincent de Paul, Quebec, in 1866. He studied in Rome and Paris, and for five years he taught in the Sherbrooke Seminary. For twenty-five years he was editor of *La semaine religieuse de Montréal*, and for fifteen years secretary of the *Revue canadienne*. But he devoted himself chiefly to the local history of the province of Quebec; and he wrote the parish histories of St. Jérôme, the Cedars, Terrebonne, and Châteauguay. He also wrote *Histoire des Soeurs de Sainte-Anne* (Montreal, 1922), *Vie de Mgr. John Forbes* (Quebec, 1929), *Les de Jordy de Cabanac* (Montreal, 1930), and *Figures canadiennes* (2 vols., Montreal, 1933). He was elected a fellow of the Royal Society of Canada in 1919. He died at Montreal in 1946.

[*Proc. Roy. Soc. Can.*, 1947; *Can. who's who*, 1936-37.]

Auclair, Joseph (1813-1887), priest, was born at Jeune Lorette, Lower Canada, on June 16, 1813; and died at Quebec, Que., November 29, 1887. He was the author of *Le congrès de la Baie Saint-Paul* (Quebec, 1875) and *Les danses et las bals* (Quebec, 1879).

[Allaire, *Dict. biog.*]

Auden, Henry William (1867-1940), educationist, was born at Wellinborough, England, in 1867. He was educated at Shrewsbury School, at Christ's College, Cambridge (B.A., 1890), and at Marburg University, Germany. From 1891 to 1903 he was a master at Fettes College, Edinburgh; and in 1903 he was appointed headmaster of Upper Canada College, Toronto. He remained in this position until his resignation in 1918; and shortly afterwards he was appointed to the chair of Latin in the University of Western Ontario, London, Ontario, a position he retained until his death at London, Ontario, on June 26, 1940. He was joint author, with A. E. Taylor, of *A minimum of Greek* (Toronto, 1906); and he was the editor of several classical school-texts.

[*Can. who's who*, 1936-37.]

Audet, François Joseph (1867-1943), archivist and author, was born at Detroit, Michigan, on July 29, 1867, the son of François Audet and Delphine Goulet. He was educated at the Christian Brothers School, Ottawa, and the Christian Brothers Academy, Montreal; and in 1889 he entered the Archives Branch at Ottawa as a clerk. He became chief clerk and head of the Information Branch of the Public Archives of Canada in 1906; and he continued in this position until shortly before his death. In 1923 he was elected a fellow of the Royal Society of Canada; and in 1927 he was president of Section I. He died at Ottawa, Ontario, on September 13, 1943. He was the author of *Historique des journaux d'Ottawa* (Ottawa, 1896), *Canadian historical dates and events* (Ottawa, 1917), *Jean-Daniel Dumas* (Montreal, 1920), *Les juges en chef de la province de Québec* (Quebec, 1927), *Le comté de Maskinongé* (Three Rivers, 1934), *Contrecoeur: famille, seigneurie, paroisse, village* (Montreal, 1940), and *Les deputés de Montréal* (Montreal, 1943); and he was joint author, with Mr. Justice Fabre-Surveyer, of a series of pamphlets on the members of parliament of the Three Rivers region (Three Rivers, 1934) and, with G. Malchelosse, of *Pseudonymes canadiens* (Montreal, 1936).

[*Can. who's who*, 1936-37; *Proc. Roy. Soc. Can.*, 1943.]

Audette, Louis Arthur (1856-1942), jurist, was born at Quebec, Canada East, on December 14, 1856. He was educated at the Quebec Seminary, and was called to the Quebec bar in 1880. From 1887 to 1912 he was registrar of the Exchequer Court of Canada; and from 1912 to his death he was a judge in this court. He died at Ottawa, Ontario, on January 19, 1942. He was the author of *The practice of the Exchequer Court of Canada* (Ottawa, 1895; 2nd ed., 1909).

[P. G. Roy, *Les juges de la province de Québec* (Quebec, 1933); *Can. parl. comp.*]

Auger, Joseph Cyrille (1836-1901), notary public, was born at Terrebonne, Lower Canada, on March 25, 1836; and died at Montreal, Quebec, on January 18, 1901. He was the author of *Compilation et recueil des lois statutaires* (Montreal, 1899).

[*Bull. rech. hist.*, 1899.]

Auld, Frederick Clyde (1893-1959), lawyer and educationist, was born at Charlottetown, Prince Edward Island, on May 10, 1893, and died at Toronto, Ontario, on September 29, 1959. He was educated at Prince of Wales College, Charlottetown, at McGill University (B.A., 1917), and at Oxford University (B.A., 1921; M.A. and B.C.L., 1922). He was a member of the teaching staff of the School of Law in the University of Toronto from 1929 to 1952, and he was the editor of *The Canadian abridgement* (35 vols., Toronto, 1935-46) and the *Canadian encyclopaedic digest* (2nd ed., 14 vols., Toronto, 1949-56).

[*Can. who's who*, 1948.]

Aulnay, Charles de Menou Charnisay, Seigneur d'. See **Charnisay, Charles de Menou.**

Aulneau, Jean Pierre (1705-1736), Jesuit missionary, was born at Moutiers-sur-le-Lay, in La Vendée, France, on April 21, 1705, and entered the novitiate of the Jesuit order in 1720. He came to Canada in 1734, and the following year he went west with La Vérendrye (q.v.) as a missionary to the Indians. With twenty other Frenchmen, he was massacred by the Sioux on an island in the Lake of the Woods on June 8, 1736.

[L. J. Burpee (ed.), *Journals and letters of Pierre Gaultier de Varennes de la Vérendrye and his sons* (Toronto: The Champlain Society, 1927); Le Jeune, *Dict. gén.*; *Dict. Can. biog.*, vol. 2.]

Austin, Benjamin Fish (1850-1932), author, was born near Brighton, Ontario, on September 21, 1850, and was educated at Albert College, Belleville (B.A., 1877; B.D., 1881). He was ordained a minister of the Methodist Episcopal Church in 1877; and from 1881 to 1897 he was principal of Alma College, St. Thomas. He became a spiritualist and in 1899 was expelled from the Methodist Church. In his later years he was pastor of spiritualist churches in Rochester, New York, and Los Angeles, California. He died in Los Angeles in 1932. He edited *The Methodist Episcopal church pulpit* (Toronto, 1879), and he was the author of *Popular sins* (Toronto, 1880), *The gospel to the poor versus pew rents* (Toronto, 1884), *The Jesuits* (St. Thomas, Ont., 1889; 2nd ed., London, Ont., 1890), *Woman* (Brantford, 1890; 2nd. ed., Toronto, 1898), *The prohibition leaders of America* (Toronto, 1895), *Success* (Rochester, N.Y., 1904), *Rational memory training* (Rochester, N.Y., 1905), and *How to make money* (Los Angeles, California, 1913). He was also the author of two novels, *The mystery of Ashton Hall* (Rochester, N.Y., 1910) and *Christ or Barabbas: A psychic novel* (Los Angeles, California, 1921).

[Morgan, *Can. men* (1912).]

Austin, James (1813-1897), president of the Dominion Bank (1871-97), was born in county Armagh, Ireland, and came to Canada with his parents about 1829. He was first apprenticed to the printing trade, but later entered the wholesale and retail grocery business. In 1871 he founded the Dominion Bank, and he became its first president. He died in Toronto in February, 1897.

[O. D. Skelton and others, *The Dominion Bank* (Toronto, 1922).]

Avaugour, Pierre du Bois, Baron d' (d. 1664), governor of New France (1661-63), was descended from a cadet branch of the family of the Counts of Brittany. In 1658 he was French minister in Sweden, and in 1661 he was appointed governor of New France in succession to Argenson (q.v.). He arrived at Quebec on the last day of August, 1661. He soon quarrelled with Bishop Laval (q.v.) over the question of the liquor traffic with the Indians, and that powerful prelate had him recalled in 1663. On his return to France, he took service in Hungary, and was killed at the taking of Fort Serin, in July, 1664.

[R. Roy, *M. Pierre du Bois, baron d'Avaugour* (Bull. rech. hist., vol. 22); Le Jeune, *Dict. gén.*; *Dict. Can. biog.*, vol. 1.]

Aylesworth, Sir Allen Bristol (1854-1952), lawyer and statesman, was born of United Empire Loyalist stock, in Camden township, Ontario, on November 27, 1854. He was educated at the University of Toronto (B.A., 1874; M.A., 1875) and at Osgoode Hall, and was called to the bar of Ontario in 1878 (Q.C., 1889). He practised law in Toronto until he retired from active practice in 1923, and was a bencher of the Law Society of Upper Canada from 1891 until his death. In 1903 he was appointed a member of the Imperial Alaska Boundary Tribunal, and with Sir L. A. Jetté (q.v.) declined to sign the award. He was elected a member of the Canadian House of Commons for North York in 1905, and was appointed a member of the Laurier cabinet, first as postmaster general and minister of labour, and then as minister of justice from 1905 to 1911. He retired from the House of Commons in 1911, and was appointed a member of the Senate by the Mackenzie King government in 1923. He remained a member of the Senate until his death at Toronto, Ontario, on February 13, 1952. In 1911 he was created a K.C.M.G. for his services as an agent representing Great Britain and Canada in the fisheries dispute before the Hague Tribunal. His portrait, painted by Sir Wyly Grier (q.v.) hangs in Osgoode Hall, Toronto.

[D. Cole, *Allen Aylesworth on the Alaska boundary award* (Can. hist. rev., 1971); *Can. who's who*, 1949-51; *Can. parl. guide*, 1950; *Encyc. Can.*; *Americana annual*, 1952.]

Aylmer, Matthew Aylmer, eighth Baron (1842-1923), inspector-general of the Canadian militia (1904-07), was born at Melbourne, Lower Canada, on March 28, 1842, the son of Udolphus, seventh Baron Aylmer, and Mary Eliza, daughter of Edward Journeaux. He was educated at the Montreal High School and at Trinity College, Dublin, and in 1864 he obtained a commission in the 7th Royal Fusiliers. He saw service with his regiment during the Fenian Raids in Canada; in 1870 he entered the permanent militia of Canada. He rose to the position of inspector-general in the militia, and he held this post from 1904 to 1907, when he retired with the rank of major-general. During his later years he lived at Kootenay, British Columbia; and he was president of the Kootenay Gold Mines, Limited. He died at Queen's Bay, Kootenay Lake, British Columbia, on June 12, 1923. In 1875 he married Amy Gertrude, daughter of the Hon. John Young (q.v.), of Montreal, and by her he had three sons and two daughters.

[*Debrett's Peerage*, 1923; Morgan, *Can. men* (1912); *Who's who in Canada*, 1922.]

Aylmer, Matthew Whitworth-Aylmer, fifth Baron (1775-1850), governor-in-chief of Canada (1831-35), was born in England on May 24, 1775, the eldest son of Henry, fourth Baron Aylmer, and Catherine, second daughter of Sir Charles Whitworth, and sister of Charles, Earl of Whitworth, at whose death in 1825 Aylmer assumed the surname of Whitworth. He succeeded to the barony on October 22, 1785, on his father's death; and in 1787 he entered the army as an ensign in the 49th Foot. He served throughout the wars with France; and in 1825 he attained the full rank of general. On February 4, 1831, he assumed office as governor of Canada, and his administration of the province lasted until August 24, 1835. From the beginning he encountered the hostility of Louis Joseph Papineau (q.v.) and the extreme *patriotes*, and in the famous Ninety-two Resolutions of 1834 the Assembly of Lower Canada actually demanded his impeachment. His recall in 1835, however, carried with it no censure, and perhaps no governor could at this period have established friendly relations with the majority in the Assembly. Aylmer died in London, England, on February 23, 1850. In 1801 he married Louisa Anne, second daughter of Sir John Call, Bart.; and by her he had no issue. In 1815 he was gazetted a K.C.B., and in 1836 a G.C.B.

[Morgan, *Cel. Can.*; R. Christie, *History of Lower Canada* (6 vols., Quebec and Montreal, 1848-56); W. Kingsford, *History of Canada* (10 vols., Toronto, 1887-95); A. D. DeCelles, *Louis-Joseph Papineau* (Toronto, 1904).]

Aylwin, Thomas Cushing (1806-1871), judge and politician, was born in the city of Quebec, Lower Canada, on January 5, 1806.

His father was a merchant, the son of Thomas Aylwin, who settled in Quebec about 1763, and his mother was Louisa Catherine, the daughter of John Connolly. He was educated privately, and for a short time at Harvard University. In 1827 he was called to the bar of Lower Canada. He early showed strong political leanings towards Reform, and during Lord Gosford's administration distinguished himself by his championship of the French Canadians. In 1841 he was returned to the first parliament of united Canada for Portneuf; and in 1842 he was included in the first Baldwin-Lafontaine administration as solicitor-general for Lower Canada. He resigned with his colleagues on December 11, 1843. In opposition he had the reputation of being the most brilliant debater in the House. On March 4, 1848, on the formation of the second Baldwin-Lafontaine administration, he was again appointed solicitor-general for Lower Canada, but little more than six weeks later he was appointed a puisne judge in the Court of Queen's Bench. Failing health caused his resignation from this post in 1868, and he died in Montreal on October 14, 1871.

[C. Langelier, *L'Hon. T. C. Aylwin* (Quebec, 1904); A. W. P. Buchanan, *The bench and bar of Lower Canada* (Montreal, 1925); P. G. Roy, *Fils de Québec*, vol. 3 (Lévis, Que., 1933); Morgan, *Cel. Can.*; Dent, *Can. port.*, vol. 4; *Dict. Can. biog.*, vol. 10.]

B

Babkin, Boris Petrovich (1877-1950), physiologist, was born in Koursk, Russia, on January 4, 1877. He was educated at the Military Academy in St. Petersburg, Russia (M.O., 1904), and in 1915 became professor of physiology at the University of Odessa. In 1924, after spending two years in England, he came to Canada as professor of physiology at Dalhousie University. In 1928 he was appointed research professor of physiology at McGill University; and he continued in this post until shortly before his death. He died on a train between Atlantic City and Montreal, on May 3, 1950. He was elected a fellow of the Royal Society of Canada in 1930, and in 1943 was awarded the Flavelle Medal. He was the author of *Secretory mechanism of the digestive glands* (New York, 1944; 2nd ed., 1950) and *Pavlov: A biography* (Chicago, 1949).

[*Can. who's who*, 1948; *Proc. Roy. Soc. Can.*, 1950.]

Baby, Charles François Xavier (1794-1864), legislative councillor of Canada, was born on June 19, 1794, the son of François Baby (q.v.) and Marie-Anne Tarieu de Lanaudière. At an early age he failed in business, and fled to the United States; but he later returned to Canada, paid off his creditors, and amassed a fortune as a government contractor. In 1861, he was elected to represent the Stadacona division in the Legislative Council of United Canada, and he remained a legislative councillor until his death on August 6, 1864. He married a sister of Mgr Pinsonnault, bishop of London; by her he had one son and one daughter.

[P. B. Casgrain, *Mémorial des familles Casgrain, Baby, et Perreault* (Quebec, 1899), and *L'honorable C.-F.-X. Baby* (Bull. rech. hist., vol. 13).]

Baby, Francis or **François** (1763-1856), landowner, was the son of Jacques Duperron Baby (q.v.) and Suzanne de la Croix Rhéaume and was born at Detroit on December 7, 1763. From 1792 to 1796 he represented the constituency of Kent in the first Legislative Assembly of Upper Canada; and he died at Windsor, Canada West, on November 24, 1856. He married on September 9, 1795, Frances, daughter of James Abbott, a British officer, and had by her twelve children.

[P. B. Casgrain, *Mémorial des familles Casgrain, Baby, et Perreault* (Quebec, 1899); M. M. Quaife (ed.), *The John Askin papers*, vol. I (Detroit, 1928).]

Baby, François (1733-1820), executive councillor of Lower Canada, was the son of Raymond Baby and Thérèse Le Compte Dupré, and the grandson of Jacques Baby de Ranville, an officer of the Carignan-Salières regiment, who came to Canada in 1662. He was born at Montreal on October 4, 1733, and was educated at the Jesuit College at Quebec. Throughout the Seven Years' War he fought on the French side, but on the conclusion of peace, after two years spent in France, he took the oath of allegiance to the British crown, and became a staunch upholder of British rule. In 1774 he was appointed a member of the Council of the province of Quebec; and from 1774 to 1783 he took a prominent part in the defence of the province against the Americans. From 1789 to 1811 he was adjutant-general of the provincial militia. In 1791 he was sworn of both the Executive and Legislative councils of Lower Canada, and became a leading member of the so-called "Château clique". He died on October 9, 1820, at Montreal. In 1786 he married Marie-Anne (d. 1844), daughter of the Hon. Charles François Tarieu de Lanaudière; by her he had several children.

[P. B. Casgrain, *Mémorial des familles Casgrain, Baby, et Perreault* (Quebec, 1899), and *L'honorable François Baby* (Bull. rech. hist., vol. 12).]

Baby, Jacques Duperron (1731-1789), fur-trader, was born at Montreal in 1731, the youngest son of Raymond Baby and Thérèse Le Compte Dupré, and the brother of François Baby (q.v.). After the Seven Years' War, throughout which he fought in the French colonial forces, he settled at Detroit, where his family had fur-trading interests. During Pontiac's conspiracy, he was of service to the British; and he was staunchly loyal to the

British Crown during the American Revolution. In consequence, he lost his properties on the Detroit side of the St. Clair River, and was compelled to move to Sandwich, on the Canadian side. Here he died about August 2, 1789. He married at Detroit, in 1760, Suzanne de la Croix Rhéaume (d. 1813).

[J. Tassé, *Les canadiens de l'ouest* (2 vols., Montreal, 1878); P. B. Casgrain, *Mémorial des familles Casgrain, Baby, et Perreault* (Quebec, 1899); M. M. Quaife (ed.), *The John Askin papers* (2 vols., Detroit, 1928-31); W. L. Baby, *Souvenirs of the past* (Windsor, Ont., 1898).]

Baby, Jacques Duperron or **James** (1762-1833), inspector-general of Upper Canada, was born at Detroit, the son of Jacques Duperron Baby (q.v.) and Suzanne de la Croix Rhéaume. He was educated at the Quebec Seminary, and after a prolonged visit to England engaged in the fur-trade at Detroit. In 1792 he was appointed a member of the Executive and Legislative councils of Upper Canada, and he continued to sit in these councils until his death at York (Toronto) on February 19, 1833. He was long regarded as one of the inner circle of the "Family Compact". From 1815 to 1833 he was inspector-general of Upper Canada; and in 1824 two of his sons were implicated in the attack on W. L. Mackenzie's printing-press at York. He married Elizabeth (d. *circa* 1812), the daughter of James Abbott of Detroit.

[P. B. Casgrain, *Mémorial des familles Casgrain, Baby, et Perreault* (Quebec, 1899); Brother Alfred, *The Honourable James Baby* (Canadian Catholic Hist. Ass., annual report, 1933-34); Abbé Daniel, *Nos gloires nationales* (Montreal, 1867); W. L. Baby, *Souvenirs of the past* (Windsor, Ont., 1898); Morgan, *Cel. Can.*]

Baby, Louis François Georges (1834-1906), politician and judge, was the son of Joseph Baby and Caroline Guy, and the grandson of François Baby of Montreal (q.v.). He was born in Montreal on August 26, 1834, and was educated at the College of St. Sulpice and at Joliette College. He was called to the bar in 1857, and practised law, first in Montreal, and then in Joliette. From 1872 to 1880 he represented Joliette in the Canadian House of Commons, and was thus one of Sir John Macdonald's "Old Guard". In 1878 he was appointed minister of inland revenue in the Macdonald government; but in 1880 he went on the bench, becoming a judge first of the Superior Court of Quebec, and then, in 1881, of the Queen's Bench. He was one of the founders of the Historical Society of Montreal, president of the Antiquarian and Numismatic Society of Montreal, and an honorary LL.D. of Laval University (1888). In 1893 he was also one of

the founders of the Canadian National League. He retired from the bench in 1896; and he died at Montreal on May 13, 1906. In July, 1873, he married Marie-Hélène-Adelaide, daughter of Dr. Berthelet of Montreal; by her he had no children.

[P. B. Casgrain, *Mémorial des familles Casgrain, Baby, et Perreault* (Quebec, 1898); P. G. Roy, *Les juges de la province de Québec* (Quebec, 1933); Dent, *Can. port.*, vol. 2; Morgan, *Can. men* (1898); Rose, *Cyc. Can. biog.* (1886); Bibaud, *Panth. can.*; *Can. who was who*, vol. 1.]

Baby, William Lewis (1812-1897), author, was born at Sandwich, Upper Canada, on April 3, 1812, the son of the Hon. James Baby (q.v.). He had a varied and adventurous career, and when an old man he published his reminiscences under the title *Souvenirs of the past* (Windsor, Ont., 1896). He died at Windsor, Ontario, on November 9, 1897.

[P. B. Casgrain, *Mémorial des familles Casgrain, Baby, et Perreault* (Quebec, 1898).]

Back, Sir George (1796-1878), explorer, was born in Stockport, England, on November 6, 1796. He entered the British navy as a first-class volunteer in 1808, and was promoted lieutenant in 1821, commander in 1825, vice-admiral in 1863, and admiral in 1876. In 1818, in 1819-22, and in 1824-27, he accompanied Sir John Franklin (q.v.) on his Arctic expeditions; and in 1833-35 he led an expedition, through what is now northern Canada, to the shores of the Arctic Ocean, to ascertain the fate of Sir John Ross (q.v.). The expedition resulted in the exploration of the Great Fish River, which was renamed Backs River in honour of its explorer. In 1836 he explored the Arctic coast of North America, between Regent Inlet and Cape Turnagain; and he was knighted, in acknowledgment of his services, in 1839. He died in London, England, on June 23, 1878. He was the author of a *Narrative of the Arctic land expedition* (London, 1836) and of a *Narrative of the expedition of H. M. Ship Terror* (London, 1838).

[*Dict. nat. biog.*; *Dict. Can. biog.*, vol. 10.]

Badeau, Jean Baptiste (1741-1796), diarist, was born at Quebec, New France, on April 29, 1741, the son of Charles Badeau and Catherine Loisy. In 1767 he was appointed notary for the city and district of Three Rivers; and during the American invasion he kept a diary of what passed before his eyes, which was first printed in the *Revue Canadienne* for 1870, and has been reprinted by the Literary and Historical Society of Quebec (Montreal, 1871) and by the Abbé Verreau (q.v.) in his *Invasion du Canada*, vol. 2 (Montreal, 1873).

[Le Jeune, *Dict. gén.*; P. G. Roy, *Fils de Québec*, vol. 2 (Lévis, Que., 1933).]

Badgley, William (1801-1888), attorney-general for Lower Canada (1847-48), was born in Montreal on May 2, 1801, the son of Francis Badgley, a member of the Legislative Assembly of Lower Canada (1801-05). He was called to the bar of Lower Canada in 1823. In 1836 he was a moving spirit in the proceedings of the Constitutional Association of Montreal, and in 1837 went to England to press on the Colonial Office the views of the British inhabitants of Lower Canada. In 1844 he was appointed a circuit-judge; and in April, 1847, he became attorney-general for Lower Canada in the Draper administration. He was elected to the Legislative Assembly for Missisquoi county, and he continued to sit in the legislature until 1855. From 1848 to 1854 he was a conspicuous member of the Conservative opposition; but he was not included in the MacNab-Morin government of 1854, and in January, 1855, he accepted an appointment as judge of the Superior Court of Lower Canada. On September 12, 1862, he was transferred to the Court of Queen's Bench, as assistant judge; and on July 17, 1866, he was appointed a puisne judge of that court. In 1874 he retired from the bench; and he died in Montreal on December 24, 1888. In 1843 he was made a D.C.L. of McGill University. He married on April 22, 1834, Elizabeth Wallace, eldest daughter of Col. J. W. Taylor, of the East India Company; and by her he had four sons and two daughters.

[P. G. Roy, *Les juges de la province de Québec* (Quebec, 1933); J. P. Noyes, *Hon. Judge Badgley* (Missisquoi County Hist. Soc., 4th annual report, 1908-09.]

Baffin, William (1584?-1622), navigator, was born, probably in London, about 1584. The earliest mention of him is as pilot on an expedition of discovery to Greenland in 1612. In 1615 he took service with the company formed for the discovery of the north-west passage, and was appointed pilot of the *Discovery*, under Captain Robert Bylot. He explored Hudson Strait, but came to the conclusion that there was no passage to the west; in 1616 he made another northern voyage; and in 1617 he took service with the East India Company. He was killed at the siege of Ormuz on January 23, 1622. His *Voyages* have been edited, with notes and introduction, by Sir Clements Markham, for the Hakluyt Society (London, 1881).

[*Dict. nat. biog.*; *Dict. Can. biog.*, vol. 1.]

Bagnall, John Stanley (1888-1962), dentist, was born in Charlottetown, Prince Edward Island, December 21, 1888. He was educated at Prince of Wales College, Charlottetown, and at Dalhousie University (O.D.S., 1921). He became chief of the dental department at Victoria General Hospital, Halifax, in 1922. He was a member of the dental section of the National Research Council and secretary (1922-42) of the International Dental Research Society. He was dean of the faculty of dentistry at Dalhousie University from 1947-54. He served in the First World War (1914-19) as captain with the 8th Canadian Siege Battery. He died at Halifax, January 11, 1962. He wrote *Bibliography of dental caries* (Ottawa, 1950); *Caries research* (Ottawa, 1951); *Trends in caries research: A brief review and bibliography* (Ottawa, 1950).

[*Can. who's who*, 1955-57.]

Bagot, Sir Charles, Bart. (1781-1843), governor-general of British North America (1841-43), was born at Blithfield House, Rugeley, in Staffordshire, England, on September 23, 1781, the second son of William, first Baron Bagot, and Lady Louisa St. John. He was educated at Rugby and at Christ Church, Oxford. In 1807 he entered parliament, and became under-secretary of state for foreign affairs in the Conservative administration of the Duke of Portland. In 1818 he was instrumental, while British minister at Washington, in concluding the Rush-Bagot Treaty. In 1841, on the death of Lord Sydenham (q.v.), he was appointed by the Conservative administration of Sir Robert Peel governor-general of British North America. He arrived in Kingston, then the temporary capital of Canada, on January 10, 1842; and he administered the government under the strain of rapidly failing health, until the arrival of his successor, Sir Charles Metcalfe (q.v.), on March 30, 1843. Six weeks later, on May 18, he died at Alwington House, in Kingston. He was married to Lady Mary, daughter of the third Earl of Mornington, and niece of the Duke of Wellington; and by her he had three sons and five daughters. He was created a privy councillor in 1815, and a G.C.B. in 1820.

His period of office in Canada was marked by constitutional changes of great importance. Lord Sydenham, his predecessor, had declined to accept the principle of responsible government in Canada, but had set up the machinery of responsible government — that is, a cabinet of ministers sitting in the legislature — except that he acted as his own prime minister, and himself presided at the meetings of council. Bagot, partly through ill-health, frequently absented himself from the meetings of council, and so made possible the development in Canada of the office of prime minister; and when the Conservative administration formed by Sydenham lost control of the Assembly, Bagot sent for the opposition leaders, Robert Baldwin (q.v.) and Louis Lafontaine (q.v.), and invited them to form a ministry. His action caused consternation in England, and incurred the displeasure of both Queen Victoria and the Duke of Wellington; his policy was virtually repudiated by his successor, Sir Charles Metcalfe; and it was not until the arrival of the Earl of Elgin (q.v.) in 1848 that his policy triumphed. Yet to him belongs the credit for giving to the principle of responsible government in Canada its first practical application.

[G. P. de T. Glazebrook, *Sir Charles Bagot in Canada* (London, 1929); J. L. Morison, *Sir Charles Bagot* (Queen's quarterly, 1912) and *British supremacy and Canadian self-government* (Toronto, 1919); Dent, *Can. port.*, vol. 3, and *The last forty years* (2 vols., Toronto, 1881); *Dict. nat. biog.*; Morgan, *Cel. Can.*]

Bailey, Jacob (1731-1808), clergyman, was born in Massachusetts in 1731. He took orders in the Church of England, and was employed by the Society for the Propagation of the Gospel as a missionary in Maine. During the war of the Revolution he adhered to the Loyalist side, and took refuge in Nova Scotia. His diaries give a valuable account of the Loyalist migration of 1782-83. He died at Annapolis, Nova Scotia, in 1808.

[Rev. W. S. Bartlett, *The frontier missionary: A memoir of the life of the Rev. Jacob Bailey* (Boston, 1853); *Dict. Am. biog.*]

Bailey, Loring Woart (1839-1925), scientist, was born at West Point, New York, on September 28, 1839, the son of Professor Jacob Whitman Bailey, of the United States Military Academy. He was educated at Harvard College (B.A., 1859), and was for a time assistant to the professor of chemistry at Harvard. In 1861 he was appointed professor of chemistry and natural science at the University of New Brunswick; and he retained this post until his retirement on pension in 1907. He died at Fredericton, New Brunswick, on January 10, 1925. In addition to many scientific papers, he was the author of an *Elementary natural history* (Saint John, N.B., 1887). His reminiscences have been edited by his son, Joseph Whitman Bailey, in a volume entitled *Loring Woart Bailey: The story of a man of science* (Saint John, N.B., 1925).

[Morgan, *Can. men* (1912); W. G. MacFarlane, *New Brunswick bibliography* (Saint John, N.B., 1895).]

Baillargé, Charles (1825-1906), architect and author, was born at Quebec, Lower Canada, on September 27, 1825, the son of P. F. Baillargé and Charlotte Horsley. He was educated at the Quebec Seminary, and became a provincial land surveyor in 1847. He was architect of Laval University and many other buildings in Quebec; and he was

one of the architects of the Parliament Buildings in Ottawa. For many years he was city engineer of Quebec. He died at Quebec on May 10, 1906. In 1880 he was appointed a charter member of the Royal Canadian Academy of Arts, and in 1882 a charter fellow of the Royal Society of Canada. In addition to numerous papers of a scientific character, he was the author of a *Nouveau traité de géométrie et de trigonométrie* (Quebec, 1866), *Clef du tableau stéréométrique* (Quebec, 1876; Eng. translation, Quebec, 1876), *Nouveau dictionnaire français du système éducationnel* (Quebec, 1888), *Vocabulaire des homonymes simples* (Joliette, 1891), *Vocabulary of English homonyms* (Quebec, 1891), and *Divers, ou Les enseignements de la vie* (Quebec, 1898).

[Le Jeune, *Dict. gén.*; Morgan, *Can. men* (1898).]

Baillargé, François (1759-1830), sculptor and architect, was born at Quebec on January 21, 1759, the fourth son of Jean Baillargé. He studied art in Paris, France, from 1778 to 1781. He then returned to Quebec, and for thirty years was an architect and sculptor. In 1812 he became treasurer of the city of Quebec; and this post he held until his death in 1830. He married Josephte Boutin de Piémont; and his son Thomas (d. 1859) was also a sculptor.

[G. F. Baillargé, *François Baillargé* (Bull. rech. hist., 1914) and *Thomas Baillargé* (Bull. rech. hist., 1914).]

Baillargé, Frédéric Alexandre (1854-1928), priest and educationist, was born at Morrisburg, Canada West, on January 5, 1854; and died at Verchères, Quebec, on March 12, 1928. He was the author of *Coups de crayon* (Joliette, Que., 1889), *La nature, la race, et la santé dans leur rapports avec la productivité du travail* (Joliette, Que., 1890), *La littérature au Canada en 1890* (Joliette, Que., 1891), *Traité classique d'économie politique* (Joliette, Que., 1892), *Traité de la Sainte Trinité* (Joliette, Que., 1893), *La terre à vol d'oiseau* (Joliette, Que., 1898), *La gratuité des livres* (Montreal, 1901), *Histoire sainte* (Montreal, 1923), *Histoire du temps primitifs* (Montreal, 1923), and *Danserons-nous* (Montreal, 1926).

[Allaire, *Dict. biog.*]

Baillargeon, Charles François (1798-1870), Roman Catholic archbishop of Quebec (1867-70), was born at Ile-aux-Grues, Lower Canada, on April 26, 1798, the son of François Baillargeon. He was educated at the seminary of Nicolet, and in 1822 was ordained a priest of the Roman Catholic Church. He was consecrated coadjutor to the archbishop of Quebec in 1850, and in 1867 succeeded to the archiepiscopal see. He died on October 13, 1870. He was the author of

Recueil des ordonnances synodales et épiscopales du diocèse de Québec (Quebec, 1859). [Allaire, *Dict. biog.*]

Baillie, Sir Frank Wilton (1875-1921), financier, was born in Toronto on August 19, 1875, son of John Baillie and Marian Wilton. He was educated in the public schools; and had a meteoric career in business, becoming in 1902 the first general manager of the Metropolitan Bank. In 1903 he resigned this post, and became a member of the Toronto Stock Exchange. He organized several successful companies; and, at the outbreak of the European war, he formed the Canadian Cartridge Company of Hamilton, for the manufacture of war munitions. In December, 1916, he was appointed director of aviation for Canada, and became president of Canadian Aeroplanes Ltd. For his war services he was created, on January 9, 1918, a K.B.E. He died on January 8, 1921, at Toronto. On June 8, 1900, he married Edith Julia, daughter of Aubrey White, Toronto; by her he had three sons and two daughters.

[H. Charlesworth (ed.), *A cyclopaedia of Canadian biography* (Toronto, 1919); Morgan, *Can. men* (1912).]

Bain, Francis (1842-1894), naturalist, was born at North River, Prince Edward Island, in 1842; and died at the same place on November 20, 1894. He was the author of *The natural history of Prince Edward Island* (Charlottetown, P.E.I., 1890) and *Birds of Prince Edward Island* (Charlottetown, P.E.I., 1891).

[Private information.]

Bain, James (1842-1908), librarian, was born in London, England, on August 2, 1842, the son of James Bain and Joanna Watson, both natives of Edinburgh, Scotland. He was educated at the Toronto Academy and the Toronto Grammar School. After a commercial career, first as a bookseller, and then as a publisher, he was appointed in 1883 chief librarian of the Toronto Public Library; this position he held until his death, on May 22, 1908. He acquired a wide and deserved reputation as a bibliographer and scholar; and he built up in the Toronto Public Library one of the finest collections of *Canadiana* in existence. His most important publication was an edition of Alexander Henry, *Travels and adventures* (Toronto, 1901). He was the first president of the Ontario Library Association, serving from 1900 to 1902. He was one of the founders of the Champlain Society; and in 1902 he received the honorary degree of D.C.L. from Trinity University, Toronto. He married, in 1875, Jessie N. Paterson, of Edinburgh, Scotland.

[Morgan, *Can. men* (1898); *Can. who was who*, vol. 2.]

Bain, James Watson (1875-1964), chemist, was born in London, England, November 14, 1875, son of James Bain (q.v.). He was educated at the University of Toronto (B.A. Sc., 1897). He remained at the university, rising from fellow (1897-99) to professor of chemical engineering (1916) and head of the department (1920). He established the first department of chemical engineering in Canada at the University of Toronto. He was a founder of the Canadian Institute of Chemistry, which became the Chemical Institute of Canada, and was president of the Royal Canadian Institute in 1948. During the First World War he was liaison officer for the explosives program of the Canadian War Mission at Washington. He was a fellow of the Royal Society of Canada, of the Institute of Chemistry of Great Britain, and a member of the American Institute of Chemical Engineers. He died at Toronto, Ontario, January 23, 1964.

[*Can. who's who*, 1961-63; Metropolitan Toronto Library Board, *Biographical scrapbooks*, vols. 10 & 22.]

Baird, William Thomas (1819?-1897), soldier and author, was born in Fredericton, New Brunswick, about 1819, the son of John Baird and Anne Diggin. He was paymaster of military district No. 8 in Canada from 1867 to 1887, and he rose in the militia to the rank of lieutenant-colonel. He died at Woodstock, New Brunswick, on February 23, 1897. He was the author of a volume of autobiographical sketches entitled *Seventy years of New Brunswick life* (Saint John, N.B., 1890).

[W. G. MacFarlane, *New Brunswick bibliography* (Saint John, N.B., 1895).]

Baker, Edwin Albert (1893-1968), director of the Canadian National Institute for the Blind, was born at Collins Bay, Ontario, January 9, 1893, and educated at Queen's University (B.Sc., 1914). He lost his sight in the First World War where he was a lieutenant in the Royal Canadian Engineers and was awarded the Military Cross and the Croix de Guerre. He was trained at St. Dunstan's Hostel for Blinded Soldiers in England and held positions with the Ontario Hydro Electric Power Commission and the Department of Soldiers' Civil Re-establishment on his return to Canada. He became vice-president of the Canadian National Institute for the Blind in 1918 and from 1920 to 1962 was managing director and general secretary of the Institute. He was first president of the World Council for the Welfare of the Blind. His work for the blind in Canada was recognized when he was awarded the O.B.E. in 1935 and created Companion of the Order of Canada in 1967. He died at Collins Bay, Ontario, April 7, 1968.

[Can. who's who, 1955-57; Encyc. Can. (1972).]

Baldwin, Augustus Warren (1776-1866), admiral, was born in Ireland, on October 1, 1776, the son of Robert Baldwin of Summerhill and Barbara Spread. He entered the Royal Navy in 1794, and retired from service in 1846, with the rank of admiral. Before this, however, in 1817, he had settled near York (Toronto), Upper Canada, and in 1836 he was appointed by Sir Francis Bond Head (q.v.) a member of the Executive Council of Upper Canada. In 1831 he had been made a member of the Legislative Council of the province, and he retained this seat until the union of 1841. He died at Toronto on January 5, 1866. In 1827 he married Augusta Melissa, the daughter of John Mills Jackson (q.v.); and by her he had one son and two daughters, all of whom died without issue.

[E. M. Chadwick, Ontarian families (2 vols., Toronto, 1894-98); Morgan, Cel. Can.; N. F. Davin, The Irishman in Canada (Toronto, 1877).]

Baldwin, Frederick Walker, commonly known as "Casey" (1882-1948), aeronaut and engineer, was born in Toronto on January 2, 1882, the son of Robert Baldwin, and the grandson of the Hon. Robert Baldwin (q.v.). He was educated at Ridley College and at the University of Toronto (B.Sc., 1905); and he joined the Aerial Experiment Association at Baddeck, Nova Scotia, under Alexander Graham Bell (q.v.). In 1908 he became the first British subject to fly an airplane; but he discontinued flying in 1911. From 1909 to 1932 he was manager of the Graham Bell Laboratories in Baddeck. In 1933 he was elected a member of the House of Assembly in Nova Scotia, and in 1937 he became president of the Nova Scotia Conservative Association. He died at Neareagh, Nova Scotia, on August 7, 1948.

[Can. who's who, 1948; Encyc. Can.; F. H. Ellis, Canada's flying heritage (Toronto, 1954); John H. Parkin, Bell and Baldwin: Their development of aerodomes and hydrodomes at Baddeck, Nova Scotia (Toronto, 1964).]

Baldwin, Lawrence Counsell Martin (1891-1968), art gallery director, was born at Toronto, August 31, 1891, and educated at Trinity College School, Port Hope, and at the University of Toronto (B.A.; Sc. Arch., 1913). He joined Sproatt and Rolph, architects, in 1911 and was a partner in Baldwin and Green, architects, from 1926 to 1933; he was in private practice from 1921 to 1926. During the First World War he served in the South Lancashire regiment. He was made curator of the Toronto (now the Ontario) Art Gallery in 1932 and retained his position until retirement thirty years later. He was instrumental in arousing great public interest in the gallery by bringing many outstanding exhibits from outside Canada and encouraging public participation in adding new pictures to the Gallery collection. He died at Toronto, May 11, 1968.

[Can. who's who, 1955-57; Metropolitan Toronto Library Board, Biographical scrapbooks, vol. 68.]

Baldwin, Maurice Scollard (1836-1904), Anglican bishop of Huron, was born in Toronto, Upper Canada, on June 21, 1836, the fourth son of John Spread Baldwin and Anne, daughter of Major-General Aeneas Shaw. He was educated at Upper Canada College and at the University of Trinity College, Toronto (M.A., 1859), and was ordained a priest of the Church of England in 1861. In 1872 he became rector of Christ Church Cathedral, Montreal; and in 1879 dean of Montreal. In 1883 he was elected bishop of Huron; and this diocese he administered until his death on October 19, 1904. In 1861 he married Maria (d. 1863), daughter of Edward Ermatinger; and in 1870 Sarah Jessie, daughter of J. J. Day, of Montreal. In 1882 he received the degree of D.D. from Trinity University. He was the author of Life in a look (Montreal, 1883).

[Dyson Hague, Bishop Baldwin (Toronto, 1927); Morgan, Can. men (1898); Can. who was who, vol. 1; E. M. Chadwick, Ontarian families (2 vols., Toronto, 1894-98).]

Baldwin, Robert (1804-1858), statesman, was born at York (Toronto), Upper Canada, on May 12, 1804, the eldest son of William Warren Baldwin (q.v.) and Phoebe Willcocks. He was educated at the Home District Grammar School, studied law under his father, and was called to the bar of Upper Canada in 1825. In 1829 he was elected to the Legislative Assembly of Upper Canada, but at the general elections of 1830 he was defeated, and he did not again sit in the legislature until after the Union of 1841. His ability and his high character, however, early won for him a general esteem; and in 1836 he was appointed by Sir Francis Bond Head (q.v.) to the Executive Council of Upper Canada. His tenure of office lasted less than four weeks (February 20-March 12), as the result of a disagreement with the lieutenant-governor which brought about the resignation of the whole council. Later in the year, when in England, he submitted to the Colonial Office a memorandum in which, for the first time, the project of responsible government in Canada was fully and clearly elaborated. With the wing of the Reform party led by W. L. Mackenzie (q.v.) he had never, however, much sympathy; and it was significant that during the rebellion of 1837, Head confided to him the task of parleying with the rebels.

In February, 1840, Baldwin was persuaded by Poulett Thomson to accept the post of solicitor-general of Upper Canada, and in February, 1841, he became solicitor-general of Canada West, with a seat in the Executive Council. At the same time he was elected as a Reformer to represent Hastings in the Assembly; and when the governor-general declined to reconstruct the administration to accord with the views of the Reformers, Baldwin resigned from the Council, and went into opposition. In September, 1841, he introduced into the Assembly a series of resolutions in favour of responsible government; and when the government was defeated in the House in September, 1842, it was to Baldwin that the new governor, Sir Charles Bagot (q.v.), turned to form an administration. Together with Louis Lafontaine (q.v.), Baldwin formed a ministry — known as the first Baldwin-Lafontaine administration — which held office until the crisis of November 26, 1843, when nine of the ten ministers resigned in consequence of a disagreement with Sir Charles Metcalfe (q.v.). From 1843 to 1848 Baldwin was in opposition; but the defeat of the Draper government in the general elections of 1847 led to the formation in 1848 of the second Baldwin-Lafontaine administration, sometimes called "The Great Ministry". It was under this administration that the principle of responsible government in Canada was finally and indisputably established. Always a moderate Reformer, Baldwin found, however, as time went on, that he was out of sympathy with many of his more radical supporters; and when, in the session of 1851, a resolution favouring the abolition of his own creation, the Court of Chancery, was carried by a majority of Upper Canadian votes, he resigned from office. At the subsequent election, in 1851, he was defeated in North York by a considerable majority; and he thereupon retired to private life. In 1854 he gave his approval to the formation of the union of the Conservatives and the "Baldwin Liberals" in what came to be known as the Liberal-Conservative party. The same year he was created a C.B. — a somewhat paltry recognition of his public services.

He died in Toronto on December 9, 1858. In 1827 he married his cousin, Augusta Elizabeth (d. 1836), daughter of Daniel Sullivan; and by her he had two sons and two daughters.

[George E. Wilson, *The life of Robert Baldwin* (Toronto, 1933); S. Leacock, *Baldwin, Lafontaine, Hincks* (Toronto, 1910); R. M. Baldwin and J. Baldwin, *The Baldwins and the great experiment* (Toronto, 1969); Dent, *Can. port.*, vol. 1; Morgan, *Cel. Can.*; Taylor, *Brit. Am.*, vol. 3; *Dict. nat. biog.*, supp. I. The Baldwin papers are in the Toronto Public Library.]

Baldwin, William Warren (1775-1844), physician, lawyer, and politician, was born in Ireland on April 25, 1775, the eldest son of Robert Baldwin, of Knockmore, near Carrigoline, county Cork, who came to Upper Canada in 1798. He had studied medicine at the University of Edinburgh (M.D., 1796), and came to Canada with his father. In 1802 he settled in York (Toronto), and in 1803 he was granted a licence to practise here as an advocate and attorney. For many years he practised successfully in York both law and medicine; and in 1822 he became wealthy through the inheritance of the estate of Peter Russell (q.v.). He became a member of the Legislative Assembly of Upper Canada (1824-30), and was regarded as one of the leaders of the Reform party in the province. In 1830 he was defeated at the polls, and in 1835 he declined to submit himself for election; but in 1836 he became president of the Constitutional Reform Society, formed by the more moderate Reformers. He was elected, after the Union of 1841, to represent Norfolk in the Legislative Assembly of Canada; and in 1843 he was appointed to the Legislative Council. He died, only a few months later, on January 8, 1844, at Toronto. He married in 1803 Margaret Phoebe, the daughter of William Willcocks; and by her he had five sons.

[E. M. Chadwick, *Ontarian families* (2 vols., Toronto, 1894-98); Rose, *Cyc. Can. biog.* (1886); J. C. Dent, *The Upper Canadian rebellion* (2 vols., Toronto, 1881); N.F. Davin, *The Irishman in Canada* (Toronto, 1877).]

Baldwyn, Augusta (1821?-1884), poet, was born about 1821, the daughter of the first Anglican rector of St. Johns, Lower Canada; and died at St. Johns, Quebec, on May 9, 1884. She was the author of a volume of *Poems* (Montreal, 1859).

[*Dom. ann. reg.*, 1884.]

Balfour, Grant (pseud.). See **Grant, James Miller.**

Balfour, William (1759-1811), president and commander-in-chief of New Brunswick (1811), was born in 1759, the fourth son of John Balfour, of Edinburgh, Scotland. He entered the British army in 1775 as an engineer, and rose to the rank of lieutenant-general. In 1784 he was in command at Fort Howe, in New Brunswick; and in 1811 he became president and commander-in-chief of the province. He died at Fredericton, after holding office for only two months, on December 2, 1811.

[J. W. Lawrence, *The judges of New Brunswick* (Saint John, N.B., 1907).]

Ballantyne, Charles Colquhoun (1867-1950), minister of marine and fisheries for

Canada (1917-21), was born at Colquhoun, Ontario, on August 9, 1867. He became a prominent business executive in Montreal; and in the Canadian general election of 1917 he was returned as member for the St. Lawrence-St. George division of Montreal in the House of Commons. He was sworn in as minister of marine and fisheries in the coalition government formed by Sir Robert Borden (q.v.) in 1917; and he continued to hold this portfolio until the defeat of the Meighen government in 1920. He was defeated in the general election of 1921; but in 1932 he was appointed to the Senate. He died at Montreal on October 19, 1950.

[*Can. who's who*, 1949-51; *Can. parl. comp.*]

Ballantyne, Robert Michael (1825-1894), author, was born in Edinburgh, Scotland, in 1825. As a youth he entered the service of the Hudson's Bay Company, and his experience in Rupert's Land supplied him with abundant material for books of adventure, books that are still popular. His stories number over sixty: among the best known are *Hudson's Bay, or Life in the wilds of North America* (1848); *The young fur traders*; *Ungava, a tale of Eskimo land*; *The world of ice*; and *The coral island*. He died in Rome, Italy, on February 8, 1894.

[Eric Quayle, *Ballantyne the brave: A Victorian and his family* (London, 1967); *Dict. nat. biog.*]

Ballard, Bristow Guy (1902-1975), engineer, was born at Fort Stewart, Ontario, June 19, 1902, and educated at Queens University (B.Sc., 1924; D.Sc., 1956). He worked for the Westinghouse Electrical and Manufacturing Company in the design department before joining the National Research Council in Ottawa, where he was in charge of electrical-engineering research from 1930 to 1945. He was director of the Radio and Electrical Engineering Division (1948-63), vice-president (Scientific) (1954-63), and president (1963-67). He was a member of the Engineering Institute of Canada, and president of the Canadian Standards Association (1961-63). During the Second World War he worked on the development of anti-magnetic-mine equipment. He was awarded the O.B.E. in 1946. He was a fellow of the Royal Society of Canada. He died at Ottawa, Ontario, on September 22,1975.

[*Can. who's who*, 1967-69.]

Baltimore, George Calvert, first Baron (1580-1632), colonizer, was born in Yorkshire, England, about 1580, and was educated at Trinity College, Oxford (B.A., 1597). He was knighted in 1617, and in 1625 was created Baron Baltimore. Between 1621 and 1627 he made an unsuccessful attempt to found a colony in Newfoundland. He bought the northern half of the grant of land made to William

Vaughan in 1616, and in 1621 and 1622 he sent out colonists to settle at Ferryland. In 1623 he received a royal charter for what was to be called the province of Avalon; but his colony did not prosper, and he himself found the climate of Newfoundland too severe. He therefore turned his efforts at colonization to a more southerly region; and he had virtually succeeded in obtaining a charter for Maryland when he died in London, England, on April 15, 1632.

[D. W. Prowse, *A history of Newfoundland* (London, 1895); *Encyc. Can.*; *Dict. Can. biog.*, vol. 1.]

Bancroft, Hubert Howe (1832-1918), historian, was born in Granville, Ohio, May 5, 1832. He went to California in 1852 and devoted his life to studying the history of the Pacific coast. He published five volumes on *The Native Races of the Pacific States* and forty on the *History of the Pacific States of North America*. He devoted one volume to the history of British Columbia. He died on March 2, 1918.

[*Dict. Am. biog.*; *Cyc. Am biog.*]

Banks, Charles Arthur (1885-1961), mining engineer, was born in Auckland, New Zealand, on May 18, 1885. He was educated at Thames College and Thames School of Mines, Auckland, and at the Colorado State School of Mines. He was managing director of Placer Development Limited; Bulolo Gold Dredging Limited; and Consolidated Dredging Limited. He served during the First World War with the Royal Engineers as captain. During the Second World War he served in London as representative of the Canadian department of munitions and supply (1940-45). He became lieutenant-governor of British Columbia (1946-50). He was awarded the gold medal of the Mining and Metallurgical Society of America for his work in developing remote mines by air transport (1937). He died at Vancouver, September 28, 1961.

[*Can. who's who*, 1955-57.]

Banks, William (d. 1920), author, was for many years a journalist on the staff of the Toronto *Globe*. He died in Toronto, Ontario, on March 15, 1920. He was the author of a novel, *William Adolphus Turnpike* (Toronto, 1913). He is to be distinguished from his son, William Banks, Jr. (1875-1931), who was also for many years a journalist on the staff of the Toronto *Globe*, and who died at Toronto, Ontario, on July 14, 1931.

[Private information.]

Bannatyne, Andrew Graham Ballenden (1829-1889), councillor of Assiniboia and the North West Territories, was born in South Ronaldshay, Orkney Islands, on October 31, 1829. He entered the service of the Hudson's Bay Company in 1846, and for several years was at Norway House. In 1851 he went into business in the Red River colony; in 1861 he was appointed a magistrate; and in 1868 a member of the Council of Assiniboia. In 1869 he was a member of the provisional government established by Louis Riel (q.v.), with the portfolio of postmaster-general. In 1872 he was appointed a member of the North-West Council; and in 1875 he was elected to represent Provencher in the Canadian House of Commons on the expulsion of Riel. He withdrew from politics in 1878; and he died on May 18, 1889. He was the first postmaster of Fort Garry, and the first police magistrate of Winnipeg. About 1850 he married Annie, daughter of Andrew McDermott, of Norway House; and he was a brother-in-law of William Mactavish (q.v.).

[J. P. Robertson, *Political manual of Manitoba* (Winnipeg, 1887); *Can. parl. comp.*; Rev. W. Cochrane, *Men of Canada* (Brantford, Ont., 1895).]

Bannerman, Sir Alexander (1783-1864), lieutenant-governor of Prince Edward Island (1851-54), was born in 1783, and became a banker in Aberdeen, Scotland. From 1832 to 1847 he sat in the House of Commons at Westminster; and in 1851 he was appointed lieutenant-governor of Prince Edward Island, being created at the same time a knight bachelor. He retired from office in 1854. From 1857 to 1863 he was governor of Newfoundland. He died in 1864.

[Le Jeune, *Dict. gén.*; D. Campbell, *History of Prince Edward Island* (Charlottetown, 1865).]

Banting, Sir Frederick Grant (1891-1941), physician, was born at Alliston, Ontario, on November 14, 1891, the youngest child of William Thompson Banting and Margaret Grant. He was educated at the University of Toronto (M.B., 1916; M.D., 1922; D.Sc., 1923); and he served as a medical officer in the First World War. He was wounded in the battle for Cambrai in 1918, and was awarded the Military Cross for gallantry in the field. On his return to Canada he commenced practice as a surgeon in London, Ontario; but he had hardly entered on this practice when he conceived the idea that was to be the starting-point of his discovery of insulin as a remedy for diabetes. He brought his idea to Professor J. J. R. Macleod, the head of the department of physiology in the University of Toronto; and working under Professor Macleod's direction, and with the assistance of several fellow-workers, he succeeded in isolating insulin and demonstrating its beneficial effect on diabetes — one of the great medical discoveries of the twentieth century. In recognition of his discovery he was awarded the Nobel Prize, which he characteristically shared with his colleagues in the research; and in 1923 he was appointed the first professor of medical

research in the University of Toronto. For the rest of his life, honours were showered upon him. He was elected a Fellow of the Royal Society of Canada in 1926, of the Royal College of Surgeons of Canada in 1931, and of the Royal Society of London in 1935. He received the award of numerous gold medals and prizes, and of honorary degrees from several universities. Finally, in 1934, he was created a knight commander of the civil division of the Order of the British Empire. As professor of medical research, he never succeeded in repeating the resounding success of his discovery of insulin; but, especially after he obtained suitable quarters for his department, with the building of the Banting Institute in 1930, he and his staff made many notable contributions to medical knowledge in several widely different fields. He was interested also in the fine arts; and he became a serious amateur of painting.

His first marriage, by which he had one son, ended unhappily in divorce in 1932; and in 1939 he married, secondly, Henrietta Ball, of Newcastle, New Brunswick. Shortly after this marriage, on the outbreak of war, he enlisted for the second time in the Royal Canadian Army Medical Corps, and placed his unrivalled knowledge of medical problems at the disposal of the government. It was while he was flying to Great Britain on "a mission of high national and scientific importance", that the plane on which he was a passenger crashed in attempting a forced landing in a remote region of eastern Newfoundland; he received severe injuries, from which he died, probably on February 21, 1941.

[*Proc. Roy. Soc. Can.*, 1941; C. H. Best, *Sir Frederick Banting* (University of Toronto quarterly, 1941); A. Y. Jackson, *Banting as an artist* (Toronto, 1934); L. G. Stevenson, *Sir Frederick Banting* (Toronto, 1946); Israel E. Levine, *The discoverer of insulin: Dr. Frederick G. Banting* (Toronto, 1959); Viola W. Pratt, *Famous doctors: Osler, Banting, Penfield* (Toronto, 1967).]

Baranov, Aleksandr (1745-1819), Russian governor of Alaska (1804-18), was born in Kargopol, Russia, in 1745. He became in 1799 chief manager of the Russian American Company, which traded in Alaska and the Aleutian Islands; and in 1804 he was given by the Czar official status. He laid the foundations in 1804 of the present town of Sitka. His tenure of authority came to an end in 1818; and he died at sea on his return voyage to Russia on April 13, 1819.

[H. Chevigny, *Lord of Alaska* (New York, 1942); A. Laut, *Vikings of the Pacific* (Toronto, 1904); Le Jeune, *Dict. gén.*]

Barbeau, Charles Marius (1883-1969), ethnologist, was born at Ste. Marie de Beauce, Quebec, March 5, 1883. He was educated at Laval University (B.A., LL.L.,

1907); Oxford University (1907-10); and at the Sorbonne in Paris. He began his work as an ethnologist and folklorist with the National Museum of Canada in 1911 and remained with the museum until his retirement in 1949; thereafter, for another fifteen years, he was an active consultant to the museum. He began collecting songs and tales in the spring of 1911, shortly after his appointment, and eventually assembled 195 Eskimo, more than 3,000 Indian, close to 7,000 French-Canadian, and 1,500 English-Canadian songs — many of them on old Edison tube records.

In an age of increasing specialization, his interests ranged over the whole field of folklore, folk arts, and cultures in Canada and, as he himself said, "I would need two lives to process all my research." He published 50 major books, 700 articles, produced a number of recordings, and delivered many lecture series. He was completely bilingual and did more than anyone of his day to preserve and promote folk culture in Canada. In 1956 he organized the Canadian Folk Music Society and was its president until 1963. He was awarded the Gold Medal of the Royal Society of Canada of which he was a fellow; honorary degrees from Montreal, Laval, and Oxford universities; and in 1967 was named Companion of the Order of Canada.

He died at Ottawa, February 27, 1969. His writings include *Indian days in the Canadian Rockies* (1923); *Totem poles of the Gitksan, Upper Skeena River, British Columbia* (1929); *Alaska beckons* (1947); *Totem poles* (2 volumes, 1949-52); *Mountain cloud* (1944-1948); *Huron and Wyandot mythology* (1915). A bibliography of Barbeau's writing until 1947 is to be found in *Les Archives de Folklore*, Laval University, Quebec, No. 2 (1947), and a bibliography of his writings is in the library of the University of Ottawa.

[N. Story, *The Oxford companion to Canadian history and literature* (1967).]

Barclay, James (1844-1920), clergyman, was born at Edinburgh, Scotland, on June 19, 1844, and was educated at Glasgow University (D.D., 1892). He was ordained a minister of the Church of Scotland in 1871; and in 1883 he came to Canada as minister of St. Paul's Presbyterian Church, Montreal. He retired from this charge in 1910; and he died at Keswick, England, on May 18, 1920. In 1902 he was offered the principalship of Queen's University, Kingston; but declined it. He received the honorary degree of LL.D. from McGill University.

[*Who was who*, 1916-28; Morgan, *Can. men* (1912).]

Barclay, Robert Heriot (1785-1837), naval officer, was born in Scotland in 1785, and became an officer in the British navy. He lost an arm at the battle of Trafalgar; and

in 1813 he was placed in command of the British naval force on Lake Erie. He was defeated on September 10, 1813, by a superior American naval force under Commodore Perry. He died at Edinburgh, Scotland, on May 8, 1837.

[L. H. Irving, *Officers of the British forces in Canada during the war of 1812-15* (Welland, Ont., 1908).]

Barclay, Thomas (1753-1830), loyalist, was born in New York on October 12, 1753, the son of the Rev. Henry Barclay, rector of Trinity Church, New York. He was educated at King's College (Columbia University), and studied law under John Jay. During the American Revolution he was an officer in the Loyal American Regiment; and at the end of the war he went with his family to Nova Scotia. In 1785 he was elected to represent Annapolis in the House of Assembly of Nova Scotia, and in 1793 he was elected speaker of the House. In 1799 he was appointed British consul general at New York; and in 1816 he was one of the commissioners appointed under the Treaty of Ghent. He died at New York in 1830.

[*Dict. Am. biog.*; *Cyc. Am. biog.*]

Barker, Edward John (1799-1884), physician and journalist, was born in Islington, London, England, on December 31, 1799. He graduated from the London College of Medicine, and for ten years practised medicine in East Smithfield. In 1832, however, he emigrated to Canada, and settled in Kingston, Upper Canada. Here he embarked on journalism as a means of supplementing the meagre returns from his medical practice; and in 1834 he founded in Kingston the *British Whig*. In 1849 he founded also *Barker's Canadian Magazine*, a literary periodical which had only a short existence. In 1871 he was appointed registrar of the city of Kingston; and he died at Pittsburgh, Ontario, on April 27, 1884.

[*Dom. ann. reg.*, 1884.]

Barker, Sir Frederick Eustache (1838-1915), chief justice of New Brunswick (1908-13), was born at Sheffield, New Brunswick, on December 27, 1838, and was educated at the University of New Brunswick (B.A., 1856; M.A., 1858; B.C.L., 1861; D.C.L., 1866). He was called to the bar in 1861 (Q.C., 1873), and practised law in Saint John. From 1885 to 1887 he represented Saint John in the Canadian House of Commons as a Conservative, and in 1893 he was appointed a puisne judge of the Supreme Court of New Brunswick. In 1908 he became chief justice of New Brunswick; he retired from the bench in 1913; and he died at Saint John on December 15, 1915.

[Morgan, *Can. men* (1912); *Can. parl. comp.*; *Can. who was who*, vol. 1.]

Barker, William George (1894-1930), aviator, was born in Manitoba, Canada, on November 3, 1894. He was educated in Winnipeg, and in 1914 enlisted in the Canadian Expeditionary Force. In England, he transferred to the Royal Flying Corps, with which he served until 1918, first on the French front, and later on the Italian. He brought down fifty-two enemy aeroplanes, was twice wounded, rose to the rank of lieutenant-colonel, and was awarded the Victoria Cross, the Distinguished Service Order, with bar, the Military Cross, with two bars, the Croix de Guerre, and two Italian decorations. After the war, he became president of the Middleton Tobacco Company and the Norfolk Tobacco Plantations in Canada. He died at Ottawa, Ontario, on March 12, 1930.

[*Who's who in Can.*, 1929.]

Barkley, Charles William (1759-1832), navigator, was born in 1759, and in 1786 set out from Ostend in command of the trading-ship *Imperial Eagle* for the coast of what is now British Columbia. He discovered in 1787 Barkley Sound, and re-discovered the Strait of Juan de Fuca. He made a second expedition to the north-west coast of America in 1792. He died at North Crescent, Hartford, in 1832.

[J. T. Walbran, *British Columbia coast names* (Ottawa, 1909); W. K. Lamb, *The mystery of Mrs. Barkley's diary* (British Columbia historical quarterly, 1942).]

Barlow, Alfred Ernest (1861-1914), geologist, was born in Montreal on June 17, 1861, the younger son of Robert Barlow, cartographer to the Geological Survey of Canada. He was educated at McGill University (B.A., 1883; M.A., 1889; D.Sc., 1900), and on graduation joined the Geological Survey of Canada. He remained on the staff of the Survey until 1907, when he resigned to become a consulting geologist in Montreal. Between 1890 and 1915 there were published over sixty reports, memoirs, papers, and pamphlets from his pen, some of which contributed greatly to the knowledge of the geology of Canada. In 1903 he was elected a member of the Royal Society of Canada. He was drowned in the *Empress of Ireland* disaster in the St. Lawrence River on May 29, 1914. He married, in 1887, Frances, daughter of William Toms of Ottawa.

[*Proc. Roy. Soc. Can.*, 1915; *Can. who was who*, vol. 1; Morgan, *Can. men* (1912).]

Barnard, Edouard André (1835-1898), agriculturist and author, was born at Three Rivers, Lower Canada, on September 20, 1835, and died at L'Ange Gardien, near Quebec, on August 19, 1898. He became interested in scientific agriculture, and in 1876 he was appointed director of the Quebec department of agriculture. In 1877 he founded *Le journal d'agriculture*; and of this he remained editor until his death. He was the author of *Causeries agricoles* (Montreal, 1875), *Manuel d'agriculture* (Montreal, 1895), *L'agriculture dans la province de Québec* (St. Hyacinthe, 1896), and *La colonisation par les travailleurs et les ouvriers* (Quebec, 1897).

[M. A. Perron, *Un grand éducateur agricole, Edouard-A. Barnard* (Montreal, 1955); *Bull. rech. hist.*, vol. 19.]

Barnard, Sir Frank Stillman (1856-1936), lieutenant-governor of British Columbia (1914-21), was born in Toronto, Canada West, on May 16, 1856. He was educated at Hellmuth College, London, Ontario, and entered business in British Columbia. From 1886 to 1896 he represented Cariboo in the Canadian House of Commons as a Conservative; and in 1914 he was appointed lieutenant-governor of British Columbia. He retired from office in 1921; and he died in Victoria, British Columbia, on April 11, 1936. He was created a K.C.M.G. in 1918.

[Morgan, *Can. men* (1912); *Can. parl. comp.*]

Barnard, Leslie Gordon (1890-1961), author, was born at Montreal on January 16, 1890. He was educated at King's School, Westmount, Que., and the Westmount Academy. He served in the military Young Men's Christian Association during the First World War in France. After the war he began writing short stories and radio scripts, and in 1940 his novel *Jancis* won the Quebec Government Award for fiction. He married Margaret Elizabeth Elliot of Toronto in 1923. He died at Montreal, October 28, 1961. He was author of *One generation away* (short stories, Montreal, 1931), *Jancis* (Toronto, 1935), *The immortal child* (essay, Montreal, 1941), and *So near is grandeur* (short stories, Toronto, 1945).

[*Can. who's who*, 1955-57; R. E. Watters, *A checklist of Canadian literature, 1678-1960.*]

Barnes, Wilfred Molson (1892-1955), painter, was born in Montreal, Quebec, and studied in the Art Association of Montreal under William Brymner (q.v.) and Maurice Cullen (q.v.) and at the Art Students' League in New York. He became noted for his landscapes, two of which are in the National Gallery of Canada. He was elected an A.R.C.A. in 1920, and an R.C.A. in 1946. He died at Montreal on February 14, 1955.

[National Gallery of Canada, *Catalogue of paintings* (Ottawa, 1948).]

Barnsley, James Macdonald (1861-1929), landscape painter, was born in Toronto, Ontario, in 1861. He was educated at Washington University, and he studied art at the School of Fine Arts, St. Louis, Missouri, and later in Paris, France. He exhibited in the Paris Salon when only 21 years of age. He returned to Canada about 1890, and he achieved an international reputation as a landscape painter. He died at Montreal, Quebec, on February 25, 1929. Several of his landscapes are in the National Gallery, Ottawa, and the Art Gallery, Montreal.

[Morgan, *Can. men* (1912).]

Barnston, George (1800-1883), fur-trader and naturalist, was born in Edinburgh, Scotland, in 1800, and in 1820 entered the service of the Hudson's Bay Company. In 1825 he crossed the Rockies, and he spent many years in the Fraser River valley. He retired from the service of the Hudson's Bay Company, with the rank of chief factor, in 1867; he settled later at Montreal; and there he died on March 14, 1883. During his years in the North-West, he was a diligent collector of botanical and zoological specimens; and he contributed a number of papers, describing these, to the *Canadian Naturalist*, between 1857 and 1863.

[G. A. Dunlop and C. P. Wilson, *George Barnston* (Beaver, 1941); *Dom. ann. reg.*, 1883.]

Barr, Allan (1890-1959), painter, was born in London, England, on January 10, 1890. He studied at the London School of Art, and came to Canada after serving in the First World War. He achieved some distinction as a portrait painter; his portrait of Sir Charles G. D. Roberts (q.v.) is in the National Art Gallery at Ottawa. He was elected an associate of the Royal Canadian Academy in 1928. He died at Toronto, Ontario, on August 14, 1959.

[*Can. who's who*, 1955-57; *Who's who in American Art* (New York, 1959).]

Barr, Robert (1850-1912), author, was born in Glasgow, Scotland, on September 16, 1850. He came to Canada at an early age and was educated in Toronto. For a time he taught school, but having an aptitude for writing, joined the editorial staff of the Detroit *Free Press*, to which he contributed under the name "Luke Sharpe". He went to London, England, in 1881, and with Jerome K. Jerome, founded a monthly magazine, the *Idler*. Among his most popular books are: *In the midst of alarms,* a story based on the Fenian invasion of Canada; *A woman intervened*; *The Countess Tekla*; *The face and the mask*; and *The unchanging East*. He died on October 22, 1912.

[*Who was who*, 1897-1916; Morgan, *Can. men* (1912).]

Barrass, Edward (1821-1898), clergyman and author, was born at Rainton Colliery, Durham, England, on July 22, 1821, the son of Henry Barrass, a colliery agent. He was educated at the grammar school in Houghton-le-Spring, and in 1840 entered the Methodist ministry. He came to Canada in 1853, and was stationed at Toronto, Gananoque, Sherbrooke, and other places. He published several books: *A gallery of deceased ministers* (London, 1853), *Class meetings, their origin and advantages* (Sherbrooke, 1865), *A gallery of distinguished men* (Napanee, 1870), and *Smiles and tears, or sketches from real life* (Toronto, 1879). He died in Toronto, Ontario, in 1898.

[Morgan, *Can. men* (1898).]

Barrington, E. (pseud.). See **Beck, Mrs. Lily Adams.**

Barrison, Mabel (d. 1912), actress, was born in Toronto, Ontario, the daughter of E. J. Farrance. She went on the stage in 1902, and became a "star" in 1905. She made a great success in *The blue mouse* in New York in 1908; but in 1911 she was compelled to retire from the stage because of illness, and she died in Toronto on November 1, 1912. In 1907 she married Joseph T. Howard.

[Morgan, *Can. men and women* (1912).]

Barron, John Augustus (1850-1936), jurist, was born at Toronto, Canada West, on July 11, 1850, the son of Frederick William Barron, sometime principal of Upper Canada College. He was educated at Upper Canada College, and was called to the bar of Ontario in 1872 (Q.C., 1890). He represented North Victoria in the Canadian House of Commons from 1887 to 1891; and in 1897 he was appointed a county court judge for Perth county. He retired from this position in 1925; and he died at Stratford, Ontario, on January 21, 1936. He was the author of *The bills of sale and chattel mortgage acts of the several provinces of the Dominion* (Toronto, 1880), *A handbook on the conditional sales act* (Toronto, 1890), and *The law of automobiles and motor vehicles in Canada* (Toronto, 1926).

[*Who's who in Can.*; Morgan, *Can. men* (1912).]

Barry, Robertine (1863-1910), author and journalist, was born at L'Ile Verte, Lower Canada, in 1863, the daughter of John Edmund Barry. She was educated at the Ursuline Convent, Quebec, and became a journalist. For many years she was on the staff of *La Patrie*, to which she contributed under the pen-name of "Françoise". In 1901 she left *La Patrie*, and founded *Le Journal de Françoise*, a bi-monthly review, and this she edited until her death in 1910. She published a collection of stories and sketches entitled *Fleurs champêtres* (Montreal, 1895).

[Renée Des Ormes, *Robertine Barry; en littérature, Françoise: Pionnière du journalisme féminin au Canada, 1863-1910*

(Quebec, 1949); *Can. who was who*, vol. 2; Morgan,*Can. men and women* (1898).]

Barthe, Georges Isidore (1834-1900), journalist, was born at Restigouche, New Brunswick, on November 16, 1834, the younger brother of J. G. Barthe (q.v.). He was educated at Nicolet College, and was admitted to the bar in 1855; but most of his life was devoted to journalism. From 1857 to 1882 he was the editor of the Sorel *Gazette*; later he was the editor at Three Rivers of the *Ere nouvelle* and *Indépendance canadienne*. He represented Richelieu in the Canadian House of Commons from 1870 to 1872, and from 1874 to 1878. In 1897 he was appointed official translator to the House of Commons; and he died in Ottawa on August 11, 1900. He married Charlotte, daughter of J. B. Meilleur (q.v.), and by her he had nine children. He was the author of a novel entitled *Drame de la vie réelle* (Sorel, 1896).
[Le Jeune, *Dict. gén.*; Morgan, *Can. men* (1898); *Can. parl. comp.*; P. G. Roy, *La famille Barthe* (Bull. rech. hist., 1935).]

Barthe, Joseph Guillaume (1818-1893), journalist, was born in 1818 on board his father's trading ship, on a voyage between the Bay of Chaleur and the Antilles. He was educated at Nicolet College, and studied first medicine and then law. During the troubles of 1837-38 he was arrested. In 1841 he was elected to the Legislative Assembly of United Canada as member for Yamaska. He took a prominent part in the Assembly; but in 1845 he was defeated at the polls, and never again sat in parliament. In 1855 he published a book dealing with French emigration to Canada, *Le Canada reconquis par la France* (Paris); and in 1885, after a long journalistic career, he published *Souvenirs d'un demi-siècle* (Montreal). He died at Montreal on August 4, 1893.
[Le Jeune, *Dict. gén.*; Morgan, *Cel. Can.* and *Bib. can.*; P. G. Roy, *La famille Barthe* (Bull. rech. hist., 1935).]

Barthe, Ulric (1853-1921), journalist, was born at Quebec, Canada East, on September 13, 1853, the nephew of Georges Isidore Barthe (q.v.) and Joseph Guillaume Barthe (q.v.). He became a journalist, first in Sorel and then in Quebec; and he died at Quebec, Que., on August 3, 1921. He compiled a collection of the speeches of Sir Wilfrid Laurier (q.v.) under the title *Sir Wilfrid Laurier on the platform* (Quebec, 1890); and he was the author of *Similia similibus* (Quebec, 1916).
[Morgan, *Can. men* (1912); P. G. Roy, *La famille Barthe* (Bull. rech. hist., 1935).]

Bartlett, Robert Abram (1875-1946), explorer, was born at Brigus, Newfoundland, on August 15, 1875, and died in New York on April 28, 1946. Both his father, Captain

William Bartlett, and his grandfather, Captain Abram Bartlett, had been Arctic explorers, and he followed in their wake. His first trip to the Arctic was made in 1897 as first officer in Peary's *Windward*; and he commanded one of Peary's ships in his Arctic voyages in 1908-09. Later, in 1914, he commanded the *Karluk* in Stefansson's expedition through Bering Strait; and in his later years he made almost annual voyages into Arctic waters in his own schooner. He was the author of *The last voyage of the Karluk* (Toronto, n.d.) and *Sails over ice* (New York, 1934).
[G. P. Putnam, *Mariner of the north* (New York, 1947); Paul Sarnoff, *Ice pilot Bob Bartlett* (New York, 1966); *Who was who in Am.*, 1943-50; *Encyc. Can.*; *Newfoundland supp.*]

Bartlett, William Henry (1809-1854), illustrator, was born in Kentish Town, London, England, on March 26, 1809. He entered an architect's office, and became a skilled draughtsman. He was employed to make sketches illustrating books dealing with many countries in Europe and Asia, and between 1836 and 1852 he made four trips to the United States and Canada. The drawings made on these trips appeared in N. P. Willis, *American scenery* (2 vols., London, 1840) and *Canadian scenery* (2 vols., London, 1842). His pictures of Canadian scenery are an important contribution to Canadian pictorial history. He died at sea, between Malta and Marseilles, on his return from a voyage to the East, on September 14, 1854, and was buried at sea.
[A. M. Ross, *William Henry Bartlett 1809-1854: Artist, author, and traveller* (Toronto, 1973); *Dict. nat. biog.*; *Cyc. Am. biog.*]

Barton, George Samuel Horace (1883-1961), agriculturalist, was born at Vankleek Hill, Ontario, June 29, 1883. He graduated from the University of Toronto in 1907 (B.S.A.). Upon graduation from the University of Toronto he joined the animal husbandry department at Macdonald College, Ste. Anne de Bellevue, Quebec, becoming head of the department and dean (1925-32). He joined the department of agriculture of the government of Canada in 1932 as deputy minister and remained in the government service until 1953. When he assumed his position as deputy minister, Canadian agriculture was suffering from depressed prices and severe drought conditions which had hardly been alleviated when the Second World War brought great strains on the food-producing capacity of Canada. Responsibility for food supply was given to the combined food board on which Dr. Barton worked in co-operation with members from the United States. He was a strong influence in the formation of the food and agriculture organization of the United Nations in 1945, being a member of its council and chairman of the finance committee. He was interested in promoting high standards of agricultural education in Canada. He received an honorary degree (D.Sc.A.) from Laval University in 1928 and in 1929 was created Commander Agricole Mérite by the government of Quebec. In 1935 he became a Companion of the Order of St. Michael and St. George. He died at Ottawa in 1961.

[*Can. who's who*, 1955-57; *Proc. Roy. Soc. Can.*, (1962).]

Bate, Sir Henry Newell (1829-1917), capitalist, was born at Truro, Cornwall, England, on April 9, 1829. He came to America as a young man, and settled in Bytown (Ottawa) in 1853. He entered the wholesale grocery business, and built up the firm of H. N. Bate and Sons. He was created a knight bachelor in 1910; and he died in Ottawa on April 6, 1917.

[Morgan, *Can. men* (1912).]

Bates, Stewart (1907-1964), economist, was born in Greenock, Scotland, November 8, 1907, and educated at Glasgow University (M.A., 1929), and Harvard University. Before coming to Canada he was employed by the Empire Marketing Board in London, England, and as a lecturer in economics at Edinburgh University (1931-34). He was secretary of the Nova Scotia Economic Council in 1936 and became economist with the Rowell-Sirois Commission in 1937 and 1938. He was professor of commerce at Dalhousie University from 1938 to 1942, when he became special assistant to the deputy minister of fisheries at Ottawa. He was deputy director general of economic research of the department of reconstruction and supply in 1945 and director general in 1946. He became deputy minister of fisheries in 1947 and president of Central Mortgage and Housing in 1954, a position which he held until his death, May 24, 1964. He wrote *Financial history of Canadian governments* (1939); and *Canadian Atlantic sea fishery* (1944).

[Metropolitan Toronto Library Board, *Biographical scrapbooks*, vol. 22.]

Bates, Walter (1760-1842), author, was born in Connecticut in 1760, and settled in New Brunswick at the close of the American Revolution. For many years he was sheriff of Kings county, New Brunswick; and he died in 1842. He was the author of *Companion for Cariboo: A narrative of the conduct and adventures of Henry Frederick Moon, alias Henry Fred. More Smith, alias William Newman* (London, 1817). This edition was reprinted at Charlottetown, Prince Edward Island, in 1855, and another edition was published under the title *The mysterious stranger: or,*

Memoirs of the noted Henry More Smith (Saint John, N.B., 1837; 3rd ed., 1854; 4th ed., 1875; 5th ed., 1877).

[W. G. MacFarlane, *New Brunswick bibliography* (Saint John, N.B., 1895).]

Baxter, Arthur Beverley (1891-1964), writer and politician, was born in Toronto, Ontario, January 8, 1891. At fifteen he left Harbord Collegiate and took a job with Nordheimer Piano Company and became a piano salesman. He served in the Canadian army from 1915 to 1918; after the war he stayed in London and in 1920 got a job as editorial writer with Lord Beaverbrook's *Express*. He was soon put in charge of the feature page. In 1924 he became managing editor and in 1930 became editor. He left the paper in 1933 to become public-relations man in the motion-picture industry, and in 1935 he ran for parliament and was elected. He remained in parliament from then until he died on April 26, 1964. He was knighted in 1954. He was known in Canada, India, and Australia through his *London Letters* which appeared in national publications for twenty-five years. He also wrote four novels, a play, and two autobiographies.

[*Can. who's who*, 1961-63; Metropolitan Toronto Library Board, *Biographical scrapbooks*, vol. 23; *Encyc. Can.* (1972).]

Baxter, John Babington Macaulay (1868-1946), prime minister of New Brunswick (1925-31), was born at Saint John, New Brunswick, on February 16, 1868. He was educated at the King's College Law School, Windsor, N.S. (B.C.L., 1890), and was called to the bar in New Brunswick (K.C., 1909). He practised law in Saint John, and from 1892 to 1910 was a member of the Saint John Common Council. From 1911 to 1921 he represented Saint John county as a Conservative in the New Brunswick legislature, and in 1920 became leader of the Conservative opposition. In 1921 he became minister of customs in the short-lived Meighen administration at Ottawa, representing Saint John-Albert in the Canadian House of Commons; but in 1925 he resigned his seat, and returned to provincial politics. He led the Conservative party to victory in the general election of 1925 in New Brunswick, and he became prime minister and attorney-general from 1925 to 1931. He then retired from politics to accept appointment to the Supreme Court of New Brunswick, and in 1935 he became chief justice of the province. He died at Saint John on December 27, 1946. He was the author of *Historical records of the New Brunswick Regiment, Royal Artillery* (Saint John, 1896), a unit whose commanding officer he was from 1907 to 1912.

[*Can. who's who*, 1936-37; *Can. parl. comp.*; *Encyc. Can.*]

Bayfield, Henry Wolsey (1795-1885), naval officer and surveyor, was born at Hull,

Yorkshire, England, on January 21, 1795. He entered the Royal Navy in 1806, when only eleven years of age, and was in the service for more than fifty years. In June, 1817, he was appointed Admiralty surveyor in British North America; and during the forty years that followed he surveyed lakes Erie, Huron, and Superior, the Gulf of St. Lawrence, the Straits of Belle Isle, the coast of Labrador, the Island of Anticosti, Prince Edward Island, the Magdalen Islands, Cape Breton, Sable Island, and the coast of Nova Scotia from Halifax to the gut of Canso. He attained the rank of commander in 1826, flag rank in 1856, the rank of vice-admiral in 1863, and that of admiral in 1867. From 1827 to 1841 he lived in Quebec, and from 1841 to his death, in Charlottetown, Prince Edward Island. Here he died on February 10, 1885. In 1838 he married Fanny, only daughter of General Charles Wright.

[*Dict. nat. biog.*; Capt. J. G. Boulton, *Admiral Bayfield* (Trans. Lit. and Hist. Soc., Quebec, no. 28).]

Baylis, Samuel Mathewson (1854-1941), merchant and author, was born at Montreal, Canada East, on September 3, 1854, and was educated at the Montreal High School. He became associated with his father in the firm of Baylis and Son, carpet manufacturers; and he was one of the founders of the Montreal Amateur Athletic Association. But he had also strong literary and historical tastes; and he was the author of several books and pamphlets: *Camp and lamp* (Montreal, 1897), *At the sign of the beaver* (Montreal, 1907), *Shakespeare: An inquiry* (Toronto, 1910), *Echoes of the Great War* (Montreal, 1919), and *Enchanting Métis* (Montreal, 1928). He died at Montreal, Quebec, on July 12, 1941.

[Montreal *Gazette*, July 14, 1941.]

Bayne, John (1806-1859), clergyman, was born in Greenock, Scotland, on November 16, 1806. He was educated at Glasgow University and Edinburgh University, and became a minister of the Church of Scotland. He removed to Canada in 1835, and became minister of the Presbyterian Church at Galt, Upper Canada—a charge in which he served until his death. In 1843 he was a leader in the disruption of the Church of Scotland, and in the formation of the Free Church in Canada. He died at Galt, Canada West, on November 3, 1859.

[Rev. G. Smellie, *Memoir of the Rev. John Bayne* (Toronto, 1871); *Cyc. Am. biog.*]

Beadle, Delos White (1823-1905), lawyer and horticulturist, was born at St. Catharines, Upper Canada, on October 17, 1823. He was educated at Yale University (B.A., 1844), became a lawyer, and published, when a young man, *The American lawyer and business man's form book* (New York, 1851). Later he became interested in gardening, and was the author of *The Cana-*

dian fruit, flower, and kitchen gardener (Toronto, 1872). He died at Toronto, Ontario, on August 30, 1905.

[*Obituary record of graduates of Yale University, deceased during the academical year ending in 1906* (New Haven, Conn., 1906).]

Beatty, Sir Edward Wentworth (1877-1943), president of the Canadian Pacific Railway Company (1918-43) and chairman of the board of directors (1924-43), was born in Thorold, Ontario, on October 16, 1877. He was educated at the University of Toronto (B.A., 1898; LL.D., 1925) and at the Osgoode Hall Law School, Toronto. He was called to the bar of Ontario in 1901 (K.C., 1915), and entered the legal department of the Canadian Pacific Railway. He was appointed general counsel for the railway in 1913; and in 1918 he became president of the railway. In 1924 he became also chairman of the board of directors. His period of office coincided with a period of great difficulty for railways everywhere; and he had to cope with problems that seemed to defy solution. He took also during this period a foremost part in the affairs of McGill University, of which he was elected the chancellor in 1921. He received honorary degrees from McGill University, McMaster University, the University of Western Ontario, and Bishop's University, Lennoxville; and in 1935 he was made a G.B.E. He died, unmarried, at Montreal, Quebec, on March 23, 1943.

[*Who's who*, 1942; *Can. who's who*, 1938-39; D. H. Miller-Barstow, *Beatty of the C.P.R.* (Toronto, 1951).]

Beatty, John William (1869-1941), painter, was born in Toronto, Ontario, on May 30, 1869. He studied art in Toronto and at the Julien Academy in Paris, France; and for many years he had a studio in Toronto. He was elected an associate of the Royal Canadian Academy of Arts in 1903, and an academician in 1913. In 1917 he served as an official artist in England and France for the Canadian War Memorials. He was especially noted for his landscapes, several of which are in the National Gallery at Ottawa. He died at Toronto, Ontario, on October 4, 1941.

[*Can. who's who*, 1936-37; N. MacTavish, *The fine arts in Canada* (Toronto, 1925); D. Hoover, *J. W. Beatty* (Toronto, 1948).]

Beaubien, Charles Philippe (1843-1914), priest and historian, was born at Montreal, Canada East, on October 17, 1843; and died at Sault-au-Récollet, Quebec, on July 2, 1914. He was the author of *Le Sault au Récollet* (Montreal, 1898) and *Ecrin d'amour familial* (Montreal, 1914).

[Allaire, *Dict. biog.*]

45

Beaubien, Louis (1837-1915), politician, was born at Montreal, Quebec, on July 27, 1837, and was educated at the Sulpician College in Montreal. He represented Hochelaga in the Legislative Assembly of Quebec from 1867 to 1886, and Nicolet from 1892 to 1897, as well as Hochelaga in the Canadian House of Commons from 1872 to 1874. He was speaker of the Legislative Assembly of Quebec from 1876 to 1878, and commissioner of agriculture in the Boucherville and Flynn administrations from 1892 to 1897. A famous breeder of cattle and horses, he did much to improve stock-breeding in Quebec. He died at Outremont, near Montreal, on July 19, 1915. In 1864 he married Susanna Lauretta, daughter of Sir Andrew Stuart (q.v.).
[Morgan, *Can. men* (1912); *Can. parl. comp.*; *Can. who was who*, vol. 1.]

Beauchemin, Nérée (1850-1931), poet, was born at Yamachiche, Lower Canada, in 1850, and died at Three Rivers, Quebec, on June 29, 1931. He was the author of *Les floraisons matutinales* (Three Rivers, 1897) and *Patrie intime* (Montreal, 1928).
[É. Chartier, *Un poète patriote et mystique: Nérée Beauchemin* (Trans. Roy. Soc. Can., 1929).]

Beauchêne, Robert Chevalier, dit. See **Chevalier**, dit **Beauchêne, Robert**.

Beauchesne, Arthur (1876-1959), civil servant, was born at Carleton, Quebec, on June 15, 1876, and died at Ottawa, Ontario, on April 7, 1959. After a varied career in journalism, he studied law at Laval University, and was called to the bar in Quebec in 1904 (K.C., 1914). After practising law in Montreal, he became, in 1913, legal adviser to the department of justice at Ottawa, in 1916, assistant clerk of the House of Commons, and, in 1925, clerk of the House — a post he filled with great distinction until his retirement in 1949. His *Rules and forms of the House of Commons of Canada* (Toronto, 1922), which went into four editions, made him the outstanding authority in Canada on parliamentary procedure. He was the author also of *Procedure at meetings in Canada* (Toronto, 1954). In 1924 he was elected a fellow of the Royal Society of Canada; and in 1934 he was awarded the C.M.G.
[*Proc. Roy. Soc. Can.*, 1960; *Can. who's who*, 1952-54; *Encyc. Can.*]

Beaudé, Henri (1870-1930), priest and author, was born at Arthabaskaville, Quebec, on September 9, 1870. He was educated at Quebec, entered in 1890 the Dominican order, and was ordained a priest in 1895. He served in various parishes in Canada and in the United States; and he died in Rome, Italy, on July 11, 1930. Under the pseudonym of "Henri d'Arles", he was the author of *Propos d'art* (New York, 1903), *Pastels* (New York, 1905), *Le collège sur la colline* (Paris, 1908), *Essais et conférences* (Quebec, 1909), *Lacordaire* (Quebec, 1911), *Eaux-fortes et taille-douces* (Quebec, 1913), *Acadie* (3 vols., Quebec, 1916-21), *Les grands jours* (Quebec, 1920), *Nos historiens* (Montreal, 1921), *Arabesques* (Paris, 1923), *Louis Fréchette* (Toronto, 1924), *Laudes* (Paris, 1925), *Estampes* (Montreal, 1926), *Miscellanées* (Montreal, 1927), and *Horizons* (Montreal, 1929).
[F. Walter, *Henri d'Arles* (Canadian forum, Jan., 1933); Allaire, *Dict. biog.*]

Beaudoin, Jean (1662-1698), missionary, was born at Nantes, France, about 1662. He began life as a soldier, and was a musketeer in the Royal Guard. In 1682, however, he entered the Nantes seminary and later the Sulpician college at Paris, and in 1685 was ordained a priest. In 1688 he went to Acadia as a missionary to the Indians, and he distinguished himself by the part he took in the struggle between the English and the French for control of Acadia. In 1696-97 he accompanied Iberville (q.v.) on his expedition to Pemaquid and Newfoundland; and he left a journal of the expedition, which has been published by the Abbé A. Gosselin, under the title *Les Normands au Canada: Journal de M. Beaudoin* (Evreux, France, 1900). He died at Beaubassin, in Acadia, in 1698.
[Allaire, *Dict. biog.*; *Dict. Can. biog.*, vol. 1.]

Beaudoin, Joseph Damase (1856-1917), priest and historian, was born at St. Isidore, Canada East, on October 29, 1856; and died at Quebec, Que., on March 5, 1917. He was the author of *Jean Cabot* (Lévis, Que., 1898).
[Allaire, *Dict. biog.*]

Beaudry, Cyrille (1835-1904), priest and educationist, was born in 1835, and died at Joliette, Quebec, on May 3, 1904. He was for many years superior of the College of Joliette.
[A. C. Dugas, *Un éducateur apôtre: Le R. Père C. Beaudry* (Montreal, 1910).]

Beaudry, David Hercule (1822-1876), priest, was born at Quebec, Lower Canada, on July 11, 1822, and died at Napierville, Quebec, on January 2, 1876. He was the author of *Le conseiller du peuple* (Montreal, 1861), and *Nouveau mois de Marie* (Montreal, 1865); and he translated from English *Les jeunes converties* (Montreal, 1866).
[Allaire, *Dict. biog.*; Morgan, *Bib. can.*]

Beaudry, Jean Louis (1809-1886), legislative councillor, was born in Lower Canada in 1809. He was descended from a French family which came to Canada in 1666. He was a successful merchant and financier in Montreal, and was three times mayor of the city, in 1862-66, in 1877-79, and in 1881-84. He was called to the Legislative Council of Quebec in 1867. He died at Montreal, Quebec, on June 25, 1886.

[*Dom. ann. reg.; Can. parl. comp.*]

Beaudry, Joseph Ubald (1816-1876), jurist, was born at Montreal, Lower Canada, on May 15, 1816. He was called to the bar of Lower Canada in 1838, and practised law in Montreal. He was appointed a judge of the Superior Court of Quebec for the district of Montreal in 1869; and he died at Montreal on January 12, 1876. He was the author of *Code des curés, marguilliers, et paroissiens* (Montreal, 1870).

[P. G. Roy, *Les juges de la province de Québec* (Quebec, 1933); *Dict. Can. biog.*, vol. 10.]

Beaugrand, Honoré (1849-1906), journalist and author, was born at Lanoraie, Lower Canada, on March 24, 1849, the son of Louis Beaugrand and Josephine Marion. He was educated at the College of Joliette and at the Montreal Military School; and in 1865 he enlisted with the French army in Mexico. The next fourteen years he spent in journalism either in Europe or in the United States; but he returned to Canada in 1879, and founded at Montreal *La Patrie*. This paper he conducted until 1897, when he sold it to the Hon. Israel Tarte (q.v.) and his associates. He died at Westmount, Quebec, on October 7, 1906. In 1873 he married Eliza, daughter of S. Walker, of Fall River, Massachusetts. He was an officer of the French Academy and a commander of the Legion of Honour (1889). A copious contributor to periodical literature, both French and English, he published among other things *Mélanges: Trois conférences* (Montreal, 1888), *Lettres de voyage* (Montreal, 1889), *Six mois dans les Montagnes Rocheuses* (Montreal, 1890), and a novel, *Jeanne la fileuse* (Fall River, 1878; Montreal, 1888).

[Le Jeune, *Dict. gén.*; Bibaud, *Panth. can.*; Morgan, *Can. men* (1898).]

Beauharnois, Charles, Marquis de (1670-1749), governor of New France (1726-46), was born in 1670, and was the son of François de Beauharnois and Marguerite-Françoise Pyvart de Chastullé. In 1692 he became an ensign, in 1696 a lieutenant, in 1699 captain of a company of marines, and in 1708 "capitaine de vaisseau". In 1718 he was made a knight of the order of Saint-Louis and in 1726 he was appointed governor-general of New France. This position he occupied until 1746, when because of his advanced age he was recalled. In October, 1747, he returned to France, where he became lieutenant-general of the naval forces. He

died in Paris on July 12, 1749.

[R. Roy, *Intendants de la Nouvelle-France* (Trans. Roy. Soc. Can., 1903), with portrait; B. Sulte, *Les Beauharnois au Canada* (Bull. rech. hist., vol. 3); A. Gosselin, *Charles de Beauharnois* (Bull. rech. hist., vol. 7); *Dict. Can. biog.*, vol. 3.]

Beauharnois, François de (1665-1746), intendant of New France, was born in 1665, and was the son of François de Beauharnois and Marguerite Françoise Pyvart de Chastullé, and brother of the Marquis de Beauharnois (q.v.), governor-general of New France. From a naval commissary, he became intendant of New France on April 1, 1702, a position which he held until 1705, when he was named intendant of the naval forces. On returning to France in the autumn of that year, he was given a grant of land in Acadia, and created Baron de Beauville. He occupied various posts as intendant until his death on September 9, 1746. He married Anne des Grés (d. Sept. 24, 1731), and died without issue.

[R. Roy, *Intendants de la Nouvelle-France* (Trans. Roy. Soc. Can., 1903); R. Roy, *François de Beauharnois* (Bull. rech. hist., vol. 7); B. Sulte, *Les Beauharnois au Canada* (Bull. rech. hist., vol. 3); *Dict. Can. biog.*, vol. 3.]

Beaujeu, Daniel Hyacinthe Liénard de (1711-1755), soldier, was born at Montreal on August 19, 1711, the son of Louis Liénard, Sieur de Beaujeu. He became an officer in the French army, and in 1749 was appointed commandant at Niagara. He was in command at the battle of the Monongahéla on July 9, 1755, and was killed early in the action. For many years he was regarded as "the hero of the Monongahéla"; but it has now been shown that the battle was really won by the officer who succeeded him in command, Jean-Daniel Dumas. In 1737 he married at Quebec Michelle-Elisabeth Foucault; and he had by her nine children. Some of his letters, written while in command at Niagara in 1749, have been published in the *Bulletin des recherches historiques*, 1931.

[F. J. Audet, *Jean-Daniel Dumas* (Montreal, 1920); Le Jeune, *Dict. gén.*; *Dict. Can. biog.*, vol. 3.]

Beaujeu, Louis Liénard de (1716-1802), soldier, was born at Montreal on September 16, 1716, and entered the French army. He was promoted lieutenant in 1744, and captain in 1751; and in 1754 he was created a chevalier de St. Louis. In 1760 he was in command at the post of Michilimackinac; and on receipt of the news of the fall of Montreal he took refuge in the Illinois country. In 1775 he distinguished himself at the defence of St. John against the Americans, and was taken prisoner. After the American

war, he retired to the manor of Ile-aux-Grues, and he died here on June 5, 1802.
[Le Jeune, *Dict. gén.*]

Beaujeu, Monongahéla de (1870-1928), historian, was born at Côteau-du-Lac, Quebec, on December 16, 1870, the son of Georges-Raoul de Beaujeu and Henriette-Marie Lamothe. He was all his life a collector of *Canadiana*. For many years he lived at Côteau-du-Lac and at Montreal; but his later years were spent in New York. He died on board the *Empress of France*, off Buenos Aires, in the Argentine, on March 19, 1928, in the course of a cruise. He published *Documents inédits sur le colonel de Longueuil* (Montreal, 1890) and *Le héros de la Monongahéla, esquisse historique* (Montreal, 1892).
[*Bull. rech. hist.*, 1928.]

Beaulieu, Jean Joseph (1895-1965), teacher, poet, and composer, was born at Mattawa, Ontario, May 21, 1895. He was educated at the University of Ottawa and began teaching at Glen Robertson. He taught at the University of Ottawa High School from 1924 to 1942, when he became assistant director of music for Ontario and moved to North Bay. He was conductor of "Les Petits Chanteurs Céciliens" in North Bay and established an opera society. He composed the music for 200 songs and wrote a number of lyrics. His songs, used in schools under the title *Chansons à l'école*, are part of the program of bilingual musical education for which Mr. Beaulieu was largely responsible. He retired as assistant director of music in May, 1965, and died October 1 at North Bay, Ontario.
[Montreal *Gazette* (Oct. 2, 1965); Ontario Department of Education, *Report of the minutes for 1965.*]

Beaumont, Charles (1820-1889), priest and genealogist, was born at Charlesbourg, Lower Canada, on November 3, 1820. He was ordained a priest in 1844 and served in various parishes in Quebec until his retirement from active parochial work in 1873. He died on September 2, 1889. His genealogical researches have been published by the Public Archives of Canada under the titles of *Généalogies des familles de la Beauce* (Ottawa, 1905) and *Généalogies des familles de la Côte de Beaupré* (Ottawa, 1912).
[Allaire, *Dict. biog.*; *Bull. rech. hist.*, 1926.]

Beaumouchel, Robert Anne d'Estimauville, Chevalier de. See **Estimauville, Robert Anne d'**.

Beaurégard, Alphonse (1885-1924), poet, was born at St. Hyacinthe, Quebec, in 1885; and died at Montreal, on January 15, 1924. He was the author of two volumes of poetry:

Les forces (Montreal, 1912) and *Les alternances* (Montreal, 1921).
[*Bull. rech. hist.*, 1924.]

Beausoleil, Joseph Maxime (1852-1928), physician, was born at St. Félix de Valois, Canada East, on April 7, 1852, practised medicine in Montreal, and died at St. Félix de Valois, Quebec, on September 11, 1928. He was the author of a pamphlet entitled *Le dernier chant des serins de Laval* (Montreal, 1890).
[*Bull. rech. hist.*, 1943.]

Beaven, Mrs. Elizabeth Speed (d. 1871), author, was born in England, the eldest daughter of John Speed Frowd, of Croscombe House, Somersetshire, married the Rev. James Beaven (q.v.), and died in Toronto, Canada, on September 14, 1871. She published a little volume of *Devotions for school girls* (Toronto, n.d.).
[Morgan, *Bib. can.*]

Beaven, James (1801-1875), clergyman and scholar, was born in England in 1801, and was educated at Oxford University (B.A., 1824; D.D., 1842). In 1843 he came to Canada as professor of divinity in King's College, Toronto; and when the chair of divinity was abolished in 1849, he became professor of metaphysics and ethics in the University of Toronto. He retired from academic work in 1871, and became rector of the Church of England in Whitby, Ontario. He died at Niagara, Ontario, on November 8, 1875. In addition to a number of devotional books, he was the author of an *Account of the life and writings of St. Irenaeus* (London, 1841), *Recreations of a long vacation; or, A visit to Indian missions in Upper Canada* (Toronto, 1846; London, 1847), and *Elements of natural theology* (London, 1850).
[J. Campbell, *The Reverend Professor James Beaven* (Univ. of Toronto monthly, 1902); J. King, *McCaul, Croft, Forneri* (Toronto, 1914); Morgan, *Bib. can.*; *Dict. Can. biog.*, vol. 10.]

Beaven, Robert (1836-1920), prime minister of British Columbia (1882-83), was born at Leigh, Staffordshire, England, on January 28, 1836, the son of the Rev. James Beaven (q.v.). He was educated at Upper Canada College, Toronto; and in 1858 he joined in the "gold rush" to British Columbia. He spent several years mining in the Cariboo district, and eventually he settled in Victoria as a merchant. He was one of the leaders in the movement which ended in the inclusion of British Columbia in the Dominion of Canada in 1871, and was the first secretary of the Confederate League. From 1871 to 1894 he represented Victoria in the Legislative Assembly of British Columbia. He was chief commissioner of lands and works in the

De Cosmos administration from 1872 to 1876, and minister of finance and agriculture in the Walkem government from 1878 to 1882; and from 1882 to 1883 he was prime minister of the province. His government was defeated in 1883; and from that date to 1894 he was leader of the Conservative opposition. In 1892, in 1893, and in 1897 he was mayor of Victoria. His last active participation in public affairs was his attempt to form a government on the fall of the Turner administration in 1898. He died at Victoria on September 19, 1920. In 1866 he married Susan, daughter of the Rev. Canon Ritchie, of Georgina, Ont.

[J. B. Kerr, *Biographical dictionary of British Columbians* (Vancouver, 1890); Morgan, *Can. men* (1912); F. W. Howay, *British Columbia* (Vancouver, 1914).]

Béchard, Auguste (1828-1893), biographer and historian, was born at Longueuil, Lower Canada, on February 18, 1828, the son of Rémi Béchard and Sophie Pinet. He was in turn a school-teacher, a civil servant, and a journalist; and he died at Danville, Quebec, on August 30, 1893. He was the author of *Histoire de la Banque Nationale* (Quebec, 1878); *Biographie de François Vézina* (Quebec, 1878); *L'honorable Pierre Garneau* (Quebec, 1883); *L'honorable Joseph G. Blanchet* (Quebec, 1884); *Histoire de la paroisse de St. Augustin* (Quebec, 1885); *L'honorable A. N. Morin* (Quebec, 1885); *Monographies: Gouverneurs, intendants, et évêques de Québec* (Ottawa, 1888); *L'ancien Québec* (Quebec, 1890); and *Histoire de l'Ile-aux-Grues* (Arthabaskaville, 1902).

[*Bull. rech. hist.*, 1923.]

Becher, Henry Corry Rowley (1817-1885), author, was born in London, England, on June 5, 1817, the youngest son of Alexander Becher, an officer in the Royal Navy. He came to Canada in 1835, and settled in London, Upper Canada. He studied law under John Wilson (q.v.), and for many years was a lawyer of outstanding eminence in western Ontario. He died at Sidcup, near Falmouth, England, on July 6, 1885, and was buried in the Isle of Wight. He was the author of *A trip to Mexico, being notes of a journey from lake Erie to lake Tezcuco and back* (Toronto, 1880); and his diary for 1835 has been printed in the *Papers and records* of the Ontario Historical Society for 1939.

[*Dom. ann. reg.*, 1885.]

Beck, Sir Adam (1857-1925), chairman of the Ontario Hydro-Electric Power Commission (1906-25), was born at Baden, Ontario, on June 20, 1857, the son of Jacob Beck and Charlotte Hespeler. He was educated at the Galt Grammar School under Dr. Tassie (q.v.), and went into business in London, Ontario, as a manufacturer. From 1902 to 1919,

and from 1923 to his death, he represented London in the Legislative Assembly of Ontario; and from 1905 to 1914, and again from 1923 until his death, he was minister without portfolio. In 1903 he was appointed a commissioner to investigate the development and distribution of power from Niagara Falls; he introduced into the Ontario legislature in 1906 the bill creating the Hydro-Electric Power Commission of Ontario; and from 1906 to his death he was the chairman and presiding genius of this commission. He died at London, Ontario, on August 15, 1925. In 1898 he married Lillian, daughter of C. J. Ottaway, barrister, of the Inner Temple, London, England; and he had one daughter. He was created a knight bachelor in 1914.

[A. C. Carty, *Sir Adam Beck* (Waterloo Hist. Soc., annual report, 1925); *Who was who*, 1916-28; H. Charlesworth (ed.), *Cyclopaedia of Canadian biography* (Toronto, 1919); *Can. parl. comp.*; Morgan, *Can. men* (1912); J. Mavor, *Niagara in politics* (New York, 1925); W. R. Plewman, *Adam Beck and the Ontario Hydro* (Toronto, 1947); Merrill Denison, *The people's power: The history of Ontario Hydro* (Toronto, 1960).]

Beck, Mrs. Lily Adams, *née* **Moresby** (d. 1931), novelist, was the daughter of Admiral John Moresby, R.N., and until going to live in British Columbia, spent many years in the Orient. She did not begin to write until 1919, and her first book did not appear until 1922; but in the remaining years of her life she wrote nearly thirty books, and she performed the remarkable feat of achieving a contemporaneous success both under her own name and under a *nom-de-plume*. In the last years of her life she lived in Japan. She died at Kyoto, Japan, on January 3, 1931. She was the author of *The ninth vibration* (New York, 1922); *Dreams and delights* (New York, 1922); *The key of dreams* (Toronto, 1922); *The perfume of the rainbow* (Toronto, 1923); *The treasure of Ho* (Toronto, 1925); *The way of stars* (Toronto, 1925); *The splendour of Asia* (Toronto, 1926); *The way of power* (New York, 1928); *The story of Oriental philosophy* (New York, 1928); *The garden of vision* (New York, 1929); and *The joyous story of Astrid* (New York, 1921). Under the pen-name of E. Barrington she wrote *The ladies* (Boston, 1922); *The chaste Diana* (New York, 1923); *The gallants* (Boston, 1924); *The divine lady* (Toronto, 1924); *Glorious Apollo* (Toronto, 1925); *The exquisite Perdita* (New York, 1926); *The house of fulfilment* (London, 1927); *The thunderer* (London, 1927); *The empress of hearts* (New York, 1928); *The laughing queen* (New York, 1929); *The duel of the queens* (New York, 1930); *The Irish beauties* (Garden City, N.Y., 1931); *Anne Boleyn* (Garden City, N.Y., 1932); and *The great romantic* (Garden City, N.Y., 1933); and under the pen-name of L. Moresby she wrote

The glory of Egypt (New York, 1926); *Rubies* (New York, 1927); and *Captain Java* (Garden City, N.Y., 1928).
[*Publishers' weekly*, 1931.]

Becker, Mrs. Abigail, *née* **Jackson,** afterwards **Mrs. Rohrer** (1830-1905), heroine, was born in the township of Portland, Frontenac county, Upper Canada, on March 14, 1830. At eighteen she married a widower named Becker, who was a trapper on Long Point Island, Lake Erie, and in November, 1854, she was instrumental in saving the lives of the master and six men of the crew of the schooner *Conductor*, wrecked off Long Point Island. After the death of her husband, she married a second time, in 1869, a widower named Rohrer, and moved to Walsingham Centre, Ontario. Here she died on March 21, 1905.
[John G. Whittier, *The heroine of lake Erie* (Atlantic monthly, 1869), Rev. R. Calvert (ed.), *The story of Abigail Becker* (Toronto, 1899).]

Beckwith, Julia Catharine. See **Hart, Julia Catharine.**

Bédard, Elzéar (1799-1849), politician and judge, was born at Quebec on July 24, 1799, the second son of Pierre Stanislas Bédard (q.v.). He was educated at the College of Nicolet and the Quebec Seminary, and studied law under Andrew Stuart (q.v.). He was called to the bar of Lower Canada; and in 1832 he was elected to the Legislative Assembly of Lower Canada for Montmorency. In the Assembly he allied himself with the followers of Louis-Joseph Papineau (q.v.), and in 1834 he moved the Ninety-two Resolutions, which embodied the platform of the *patriote* party. Soon after this, however, he parted company with Papineau and the extremists of the party; and in 1836 he accepted appointment as a judge of the Court of King's Bench. In 1838 he was suspended from the bench on account of a judgment given by him in regard to the right of *habeas corpus*; but he was reinstated in 1841. He died at Montreal, of cholera, on August 11, 1849. In 1827 he married at Quebec Julie Henriette, daughter of James Lemprière Marett, merchant; and by her he had one daughter, who died an infant. In 1833 he was elected first mayor of Quebec.
[N. E. Dionne, *Pierre Bédard et ses fils* (Quebec, 1909); Morgan, *Cel. Can.*; Bibaud, *Panth. can.*]

Bédard, Joseph Edouard (1845-1927), lawyer, was born at Beauport, Canada East, on August 22, 1845, the son of Joseph Bédard. He was educated at Laval University (B.A., 1864; LL.B., 1867; LL.D., 1902), and was called to the bar of Quebec in 1868 (K.C., 1893). He was the *bâtonnier* of the

Quebec bar in 1900; and in 1907 he was created by the Pope a chevalier of St. Gregory the Great. He died at Beauport, Quebec, on January 30, 1927. He was the author of *Code-manuel des huissiers et des shérifs* (Quebec, 1892) and *Code municipal de la province de Québec annoté* (Quebec, 1898).
[Morgan, *Can. men* (1912); *Bull. rech. hist.*, 1927; P. G. Roy, *Les avocats de la région de Québec* (Lévis, Que., 1936).]

Bédard, Joseph Isidore (1806-1833), poet, was born at Quebec on January 9, 1806, the third son of Pierre Stanislas Bédard (q.v.). He was educated at the College of Nicolet, and was called to the bar of Lower Canada in 1829. In 1830 he was elected the representative of the county of Saguenay in the Legislative Assembly of Lower Canada. He actually sat, however, in the House for only one session, as he left for Europe in the early summer of 1831, and died in Paris, France, on April 14, 1833. He was the author of a famous Canadian song, *Sol canadien, terre chérie!*
[N. E. Dionne, *Pierre Bédard et ses fils* (Quebec, 1909); Morgan, *Bib. can.*]

Bédard, Pierre Joseph, physician, was born at Montreal, Quebec, on August 26, 1869; and died on July 5, 1905. He was the author of *Etudes et récits* (Montreal, 1890).
[*Bull. rech. hist.*, 1923.]

Bédard, Pierre Stanislas (1762-1829), politician and judge, was born at Charlesbourg, near Quebec, on November 13, 1762, the son of Pierre Stanislas Bédard and Marie-Josephte Thibault. He was educated at the Quebec Seminary, and was called to the bar of Lower Canada in 1790. In 1792 he was elected to the Legislative Assembly of Lower Canada for Northumberland, and he sat in the Assembly continuously until his appointment to the bench in 1812. He became the leader of the French-Canadian party in the House, and in 1806 he was mainly instrumental in founding *Le Canadien*, a French-Canadian journal. As one of the editors of this journal he was in 1810 imprisoned by Sir James Craig (q.v.), but was later released without being brought to trial. In 1812 Sir George Prevost (q.v.) made amends for this illegal imprisonment by appointing him a judge. He sat on the bench, with some interruptions caused by ill-health, until his death at Three Rivers, Lower Canada, on April 26, 1829. In 1796 he married Jeanne Louise Luce Françoise Frémiot de Chantal, daughter of François Lajus, a physician of Quebec; and by her he had four sons.
[F. J. Audet, *L'hon. Pierre-Stanislas Bédard* (Trans. Roy. Soc. Can., 1926); N. E. Dionne, *Pierre Bédard et ses fils* (Quebec,

1909) and *Pierre Bédard et son temps* (Trans. Roy. Soc. Can., 1898).]

Bédard, Théophile Pierre (1837-1900), historian, was born in Quebec, Lower Canada, in 1837, and was educated at the Quebec Seminary. He was called to the bar of Lower Canada and practised law at Quebec. At the early age of twenty-five years he published a volume entitled *Histoire de cinquante ans, 1791-1841* (Quebec, 1869). In his later years he contributed to the early volumes of the *Bulletin des Recherches Historiques*; and a list of his publications is in the *Bulletin* for 1926. He died at Lynn, Massachusetts, on January 16, 1900.

[E. Lareau, *Histoire de la littérature canadienne-française* (Montreal, 1873); C. Roy, *French-Canadian literature*, in A. Shortt and A. G. Doughty (eds.), *Canada and its provinces*, vol. 12 (Toronto, 1914); Le Jeune, *Dict. gén.*]

Beers, William George (1843-1900), sportsman and author, was born at Montreal, Lower Canada, on May 5, 1843, the son of J. C. Beers and Isabella Hope. He was educated at Lower Canada College. He became a dentist, and was the founder of the *Canada Journal of Dental Science*, the first dental journal in Canada. He was regarded as the father of the modern game of lacrosse, since it was he who first reduced the game to a set of rules; and he organized in 1876 the first Canadian lacrosse team that visited the British Isles. He died at Montreal on December 26, 1900. Besides numerous articles contributed to periodicals, he was the author of *Lacrosse: The national game of Canada* (Montreal, 1869), *Over the snow; or, The Montreal carnival* (Montreal, 1883), and *Young Canada's reply to annexation* (Montreal, 1888).

[Morgan, *Can. men* (1898).]

Begbie, Sir Matthew Baillie (1819-1894), frontier judge, was born in Edinburgh, Scotland, in 1819, the eldest son of Colonel T. S. Begbie, of the 44th Foot. He was educated at St. Peter's College, Cambridge (B.A., 1841; M.A., 1844), and was called to the English bar from Lincoln's Inn in 1844. For fourteen years he practised law in England; but in 1858 he was appointed a judge in the crown colony of British Columbia. In this capacity he played a signal part in preserving law and order on the mainland of British Columbia during the days of the "gold rush". In 1866, on the union of British Columbia and Vancouver Island, he became chief justice of the mainland of British Columbia, and in 1870 chief justice of the province of British Columbia. This position he retained until his death at Victoria on June 11, 1894. In 1875 he was created a knight bachelor.

[W. Kaye Lamb (ed.), *Memoirs and doc-*uments relating to Judge Begbie (British Columbia historical quarterly, 1941); R. G. MacBeth, *A famous frontier judge* (Can. mag., 1918); E. Nicolls, *Sir Matthew Baillie Begbie* (Can. mag., 1898); J. B. Kerr, *Biographical dictionary of well-known British Columbians* (Vancouver, B.C., 1890); S. Banwell, *A frontier judge* (Toronto, 1938).]

Begg, Alexander (1825-1905), journalist and author, was born in Watten, Caithness, Scotland, on May 7, 1825, the son of Andrew Begg and Jane Taylor. He came to Canada in 1846. After various experiences as a schoolteacher, a journalist, and a customs officer, he went to the North-West in 1869; and for most of the rest of his life he was connected with the North-West in one way or another. He published a *History of British Columbia* (Toronto, 1894). He died in New York in March, 1905.

[Rose, *Cyc. Can. biog.* (1888); Morgan, *Can. men* (1898); *Can. who was who*, vol. 1; M. Wolfenden, *Alexander Begg versus Alexander Begg* (British Columbia historical quarterly, 1937).]

Begg, Alexander (1839-1897), author, was born in Quebec, Lower Canada, on July 19, 1839. At an early age he engaged in business, and in 1867 he took the first shipment of goods of Canadian manufacture to Winnipeg. He settled in Manitoba, and from November, 1878, to September, 1884, he was deputy treasurer of the province. Later, he was for a number of years general immigration agent of the Canadian Pacific Railway in England. Besides a story entitled *Dot it down, a story of life in the north-west* (Toronto, 1871), he published several historical works, *The creation of Manitoba* (Toronto, 1871), *Ten years in Winnipeg* (Winnipeg, 1879), *The great Canadian north-west* (Montreal, 1881), and *The history of the north-west* (3 vols., Toronto, 1894-95). He died in Victoria, British Columbia, on September 6, 1897.

[Morgan, *Can. men* (1898); P. G. Roy, *Fils de Québec*, vol. 4 (Lévis, Que., 1933); M. Wolfenden, *Alexander Begg versus Alexander Begg* (British Columbia historical quarterly, 1937).]

Bégin, Louis Nazaire (1840-1925), cardinal of the Roman Catholic Church, was born at Lévis, Lower Canada, on January 10, 1840, the son of Charles Bégin and Luce Paradis. He was educated at the Quebec Seminary, at the Gregorian University in Rome, and at the University of Innsbrück; and he was ordained a priest of the Roman Catholic Church in 1865. From 1868 to 1884 he was on the staff of Laval University; from 1884 to 1888 he was principal of the Normal School in the University; and in 1888 he was elected bishop of Chicoutimi. In 1891, he became co-adjutor of Cardinal Taschereau (q.v.); and in 1898 archbishop of Quebec. In 1914 he was appointed a member of the College of Cardinals; and he died at Quebec on July 20, 1925. In 1882 he was elected a fellow of the Royal Society of Canada.

[A. Robert, *S. É. le Cardinal Bégin* (Canada français, 1925); Allaire, *Dict. biog.*; *Cyc. Am. biog.*; *Can. who was who*, vol. 1.]

Bégon, Michel, Sieur de la Picardière (1667-1747), intendant of New France (1712-26), was born at Blois, France, on March 21, 1667. In 1707 he became inspector-general of the navy, and on March 31, 1710, he was appointed intendant of Canada. He arrived at Quebec in September, 1712, and held the position of intendant until 1724, when he was made intendant of Havre. He left Canada on October 14, 1726. About 1736 he became intendant of Normandy. He died in 1747. In 1711 he married Jeanne-Elisabeth de Beauharnois, sister of the Marquis de Beauharnois (q.v.), governor-general of New France, and by her he had eight children.

[R. Roy, *Intendants de la Nouvelle-France* (Trans. Roy. Soc. Can., 1903), with portrait; R. Roy, *Michel Bégon* (Bull. rech. hist., vol. 8); *Dict. Can. biog.*, vol. 3.]

Beioley, Joseph (1785?-1859), fur-trader, was born about 1785, and entered the service of the Hudson's Bay Company in 1800. In 1819 he acted as governor of the Southern Department in the absence of Thomas Vincent (q.v.); and in 1821 he was made a chief factor. He retired from the service of the Company in 1843, and he died in 1859.

[E. E. Rich (ed.), *Colin Robertson's correspondence book* (Toronto, 1939).]

Béique, Frédéric Ligori (1845-1933), senator of Canada, was born at St. Mathias, Canada East, on May 20, 1845. He was educated at the College of Marieville, and was called to the bar of Quebec in 1868 (Q.C., 1885). He practised law in Montreal, and became in 1891 and 1893 *bâtonnier* of the Montreal bar. In 1902 he was called to the Senate of Canada; and he continued to sit in the Senate until his death at Montreal, Quebec, on September 12, 1933. In his later years he was president of the Banque Canadienne Nationale. In 1875 he married Caroline, daughter of the Hon. L. A. Dessaulles; and by her he had several children.

[Mme Caroline Béique, *Quatre-vingts ans de souvenirs* (Montreal, 1939); *Can. parl. comp.*; Morgan, *Can. men* (1912); *Can. who's who* (1910).]

Béland, Henri Sévérin (1869-1935), physician and politician, was born at Louiseville, Quebec, on October 11, 1869. He was educated at Laval University (M.D., 1893), and practised medicine at St. Joseph de Beauce, Quebec. In 1897 he was elected to represent Beauce in the Quebec Legislative Assembly; and from 1902 to 1925 he was a member of the Canadian House of Commons. From August 19 to October 6, 1911, he was postmaster-general in the Laurier administration; and from 1921 to 1925 he was minister of soldiers' civil re-establishment and public health in the King administration. He was then called to the Senate of Canada; and he sat in the Senate until his death at Eastview, near Kingston, Ontario, on April 22, 1935. During the War of 1914-18 he was interned for three years in a German prison in Berlin; and he published an account of his experiences in *My three years in a German prison* (Toronto, 1919).

[*Can. parl. comp.*; *Who's who in Can.*, 1934.]

Belaney, Archibald Stansfeld, alias **Grey Owl** (1888-1938), author, was born at Hastings, England, in 1888, the son of George Belaney and a mother about whom some mystery exists. Grey Owl always maintained that his mother was an Indian woman of the Apache tribe named Katherine Cochise; but no proof of this statement has been found, and the available evidence suggests that he had no Indian blood in his veins. He emigrated to Canada in 1903, and became a trapper, guide, and forest ranger in New Ontario. Gradually he assumed the Indian mode of life, and posed as a half-breed. He served for three years in the Canadian Expeditionary Force in the First World War, and was wounded in France. On his return to Canada he lived the life of an Indian, first in New Ontario, then in Témiscouata county, Quebec, and finally in the Prince Albert National Park in Saskatchewan. In 1931 he published his first book, *The men of the last frontier*; and this was followed by *Pilgrims of the wild* (London, 1934), *The adventures of Sajo and her beaver people* (London, 1935), *Tales of an empty cabin* (London, 1936), and *The tree* (Toronto, 1937). Especially in England, where Grey Owl made two lecture tours, his books achieved a great success. He died at Prince Albert, Saskatchewan, on April 13, 1938.

[Anahareo, *Devil in deerskins: Grey Owl* (Toronto, 1972); Lovat Dickson, *Wilderness man: The strange story of Grey Owl* (Toronto, 1973).]

Bélanger, Jean Amable, poet, was born at Rivière-Ouelle, Lower Canada, on September 22, 1832, and died at Ottawa, Ontario, on March 16, 1913. He published a collection of poems under the title *Mes vers* (Ottawa, 1882).

[*Bull. rech. hist.*, 1925.]

Belcher, Alexander Emerson (1844-1926), civil servant and author, was born near Toronto, Canada West, on January 30, 1844, and died at Toronto on November 26, 1926. He was educated at Rockwood Academy, and became a commercial traveller. In 1911 he entered the Ontario civil service. He was the author of *What I know about commercial travelling* (Toronto, 1883).

[Morgan, *Can. men* (1912).]

Belcher, Sir Edward (1799-1877), sailor and author, was born in Nova Scotia in 1799, the son of Andrew Belcher, and grandson of the Hon. Jonathan Belcher (q.v.), chief justice of Nova Scotia. At the age of thirteen he entered the navy; five years later he received his lieutenancy; and at the age of thirty he was made commander. He showed great skill as a surveyor; and was knighted in 1843 for his services in surveying the west coast of America. From 1852 to 1854 he commanded an expedition in search of Sir John Franklin, but this Arctic expedition was his last. He died on March 18, 1877. In 1867 he was created a K.C.B., and in 1872 he attained the rank of admiral. He published *On nautical surveying* (London, 1835); *Narrative of a voyage round the world in H.M.S. Sulphur, from 1836 to 1843* (2 vols., London, 1843); *Narrative of the voyage of H.M.S. Samarang in surveying the islands of the Eastern Archipelago* (2 vols., London, 1855); and *Horatio Howard Brenton*, a novel (3 vols., London, 1856).

[*Dict. nat. biog.*; *Cyc. Am. biog.*; *Nova Scotia Hist. Soc. Coll.*, vol. xviii; Morgan, *Bib. can.*; *Dict. Can. biog.*, vol. 10.]

Belcher, Jonathan (1710-1776), chief justice of Nova Scotia, was born on July 23, 1710, the son of Jonathan Belcher, governor of Massachusetts and New Jersey, and Mary Partridge. He graduated from Harvard University in 1728, and studied law. In 1754 he was appointed chief justice of Nova Scotia and a member of the Executive Council. It was owing to his contention that laws made by the Council were not legal that the first Assembly of the province was called together on October 7, 1758. On the death of Governor Lawrence (q.v.) in October, 1760, he administered the government of the province for nearly four years; and in 1761 he was made lieutenant-governor. He died on March 29, 1776. In 1756 he married Abigail (d. 1771), daughter of Jeremiah Allen; and by her he had five sons and two daughters. In 1767 he published a volume on the laws of Nova Scotia.

[C. Townshend, *Jonathan Belcher* (Coll. Nova Scotia Hist. Soc., vol. xviii); *Cyc. Am. biog.*]

Belcourt, Georges Antoine (1803-1874), missionary, was born at Baie-du-Fèbvre, Lower Canada, on April 22, 1803. He was educated at the College of Nicolet, was ordained a priest in 1827, and in 1831 went to the West as a missionary. From 1832 to 1858 he devoted himself to the evangelization of the Indians in the valleys of the Red and Assiniboine rivers, and to the study of their language. In 1859 he returned to the east, and he passed his later years in charge of parishes in Prince Edward Island and New Brunswick. He died at Shediac, New Brunswick, on May 31, 1874, and was buried at Memramcook. He was the author of *Principes de la langue des sauvages appelés Sauteux* (Quebec, 1839); he left behind him a *Dictionnaire Sauteux*, which was published by Father Lacombe (q.v.); and his *Itinéraire de Lac des Deux-Montagnes à la Rivière-Rouge* has been printed in the *Bulletin de la Société Historique de Saint-Boniface*, vol. iv, 1913.

[L. A. Prud'homme, *Monsieur Georges-Antoine Belcourt* (Trans. Roy. Soc. Can., 1921); J. M. Reardon, *George Anthony Belcourt, pioneer Catholic missionary to the north-west, 1803-1874, his life and times* (St. Paul, Minn., 1955); Le Jeune, *Dict. gén.*; *Dict. Can. biog.*, vol. 10.]

Belcourt, Napoléon Antoine (1860-1932), senator of Canada, was born at Toronto, Ontario, on September 15, 1860. He was educated at Laval University (LL.L., 1882; LL.D., 1909), and was called to the bar in 1882 (Q.C., 1898). He represented Ottawa in the Canadian House of Commons from 1896 to 1907; and from 1904 to 1906 he was speaker of the House. In 1907 he was called to the Senate of Canada, and he remained a senator until his death at Blue Sea Lake, Quebec, on August 7, 1932. In 1924 he was minister plenipotentiary at the Inter-allied Conference and at the International Conference of London. He was the author of a number of pamphlets and articles dealing with the question of the French language in Ontario.

[*Can. parl. comp.*; Morgan, *Can. men* (1912).]

Belford, Charles (1837-1880), journalist, was born in Cork, Ireland, on April 25, 1837. He emigrated to Canada in 1857, and entered the office of the Toronto *Leader*. In 1867 he became chief editor of the *Leader*; and in 1872 he was appointed chief editor of the Toronto *Mail*. In 1878 his health gave way; and in 1879 he was appointed secretary to the Dominion Board of Appraisers at Ottawa. He died in Ottawa on December 19, 1880.

[*Dom. ann. reg.*, 1880-81; *Dict. Can. biog.*, vol. 10.]

Bell, Alexander Graham (1847-1922), inventor, was born in Edinburgh, Scotland, on March 3, 1847, the son of Alexander Melville Bell, afterwards professor of elocution in Queen's University, Kingston. He was educated at Edinburgh and at University College, London; but did not proceed to a degree. In 1870 he came, with his father, to Canada, and settled in Brantford, Ontario. It was here, in 1874, that he first conceived the idea of transmitting speech over a telephone wire. He patented his invention, and was the founder of the Bell Telephone Company. Later, he invented also the graphophone. For many years before his death he lived in Washington, D.C., or at his summer home in Baddeck, Nova Scotia, where he conducted many experiments with flying machines, with only partial success. He died at Baddeck on August 2, 1922. He received many honorary degrees from American and European universities: Ph.D. (Würzburg, 1882), M.D. (Heidelberg, 1886), LL.D. (Harvard, 1896; Illinois, 1896; Amherst, 1901; St. Andrew's, 1902; Queen's, 1909), D.Sc. (Oxford, 1907). In 1877 he married Mabel Gardiner, daughter of G. G. Hubbard; by her he had two daughters. He published his autobiography under the title of *Prehistoric telephone days* in the *National Geographic Magazine*, 1922.

[C. Mackenzie, *Alexander Graham Bell* (Boston, 1928); G. Keenan, *A few recollections of Alexander Graham Bell* (Outlook, 1922); Robert V. Bruce, *Bell: Alexander Graham Bell and the conquest of solitude* (Boston, 1973); Morgan, *Can. men* (1912); *Can. who was who,* vol. 1; *Who was who in Am.*]

Bell, Andrew James (1856-1932), educationist, was born at Ottawa, Canada West, on May 12, 1856; and was educated at the University of Toronto (B.A., 1878), and at Breslau University (Ph.D., 1889). In 1889 he was appointed professor of the Latin language and literature in Victoria University, Toronto; and he held this position until his retirement in 1926. He died at Toronto, Ontario, on December 24, 1932. A great scholar of the old-fashioned type, he was the author of *The Latin dual and poetic diction* (London, 1923).

[*In memoriam, Andrew James Bell* (Toronto, 1934); Morgan, *Can. men* (1912); *Univ. of Toronto monthly,* 1933.]

Bell, Charles Napier (1854-1936), historian, was born at Perth, Canada West, in 1854, the son of James Bell. He went to Manitoba with the first Red River expedition in 1870, and remained there for the rest of his life. He was successively employed in the civil service, in the railway service, and as secretary-treasurer of the Winnipeg Grain Exchange. Throughout life he interested himself in the history of Manitoba and the North-West, and he became president, and later honorary president, of the Historical and Scientific Society of Manitoba. He died

at Winnipeg, Manitoba, on August 29, 1936. Among his publications were *Our northern waters* (Winnipeg, 1884), *The Selkirk settlement and the settlers* (Winnipeg, 1887), *The old forts of Winnipeg* (Winnipeg, 1927), and *The journal of Henry Kelsey* (Winnipeg, 1928).

[*Can. who's who,* 1936-37.]

Bell, Charles William (1876-1938), lawyer and playwright, was born at Hamilton, Ontario, on April 25, 1876, the son of William Bell and Emily Rogers. He was educated at Trinity University, Toronto (B.A., 1896), and at Osgoode Hall, and was called to the Ontario bar in 1889 (K.C., 1912). He practised law in Toronto and Hamilton, and became an outstanding criminal lawyer. He represented Hamilton West in the Canadian House of Commons from 1925 to 1935, but did not seek re-election in the general elections of 1935. He wrote several successful plays: "A Prince of Zanzibar", performed at the Bijou Theatre in London, England, in 1904; "Her First Divorce", played at the Comedy Theatre, New York, in 1913; "Parlor, Bedroom, and Bath", produced at the Republic Theatre, New York, in 1917; and three others, "Elsie", "Thy neighbor's wife", and "Paradise Alley". He was the author also of a volume of legal reminiscences entitled, *Who said murder?* (Toronto, 1935). He died at Hamilton, Ontario, on February 8, 1938. In 1904 he married Beatrice Emmeline Gates, of Hamilton, and by her he had two sons and two daughters.

[*Can. who's who,* 1936-37.]

Bell, Frederick McKelvey (1878-1931), physician and author, was born at Kingston, Ontario, on April 10, 1878. He was educated at Queen's University, Kingston (M.D., 1903), and began the practice of medicine in Ottawa in 1904. In 1907 he became medical officer of the Princess Louise Dragoon Guards in Ottawa, and he went overseas with the first Canadian contingent in 1914. Later, he was appointed deputy director of medical services for Canada, and medical director of the department of Soldiers' Civil Re-establishment. He died at New York on January 6, 1931. He was the author of *The first Canadians in France* (Toronto, 1917) and *A romance of the Halifax disaster* (Halifax, N.S., 1918).

[Morgan, *Can. men* (1912).]

Bell, James Mackintosh (1877-1934), geologist and author, was born at St. Andrew's, Quebec, on September 23, 1877, the son of Andrew Bell and Marian Rosamund, and the nephew of Dr. Robert Bell (q.v.). He was educated at Queen's University, Kingston (M.A., 1899), and at Harvard University (Ph.D., 1904). Between 1899 and 1901 he carried out explorations for the Geological

Survey of Canada in the Mackenzie Valley and Great Bear Lake region; from 1905 to 1911 he was director of the Geological Survey of New Zealand; and he then returned to Canada, and became a consulting engineer and geologist. He went overseas in the Canadian Expeditionary Force in 1915; and from 1917 to 1919 he was on the staff of the British military mission to Russia, with the rank of temporary colonel. In 1920 he became managing director of the Atlas Exploration Company. He died at Almonte, Ontario, on March 31, 1934. In 1909 he married Vera, daughter of Sir Harold Beauchamp, and sister of the writer Katherine Mansfield; and by her he had two sons. In 1919, for his services in the war, he was created an O.B.E. He was the author of *The wilds of Maoriland* (London, 1914), *Sidelights on the Siberian campaign* (Toronto, 1920), and *Far places* (Toronto, 1931), and with Abbie F. Brown was co-author of *Tales of the red children* (New York, 1909).

[*Proc. Roy. Soc. Can.*, 1934; *Can. who was who*, vol. 2.]

Bell, John (1799-1868), fur-trader, was born in the Isle of Mull, Scotland, in 1799, and entered the service of the North West Company in 1818. He was taken over by the Hudson's Bay Company in 1821; and from 1821 to 1824 he was in the Winnipeg district. From 1824 to 1850, with the exception of the years 1847-48, when he was told off to assist in Arctic exploration, he was stationed in the Mackenzie River department. In 1851 he was at Oxford House; in 1852, at Cumberland House; from 1853 to 1856, at Fort Chipewyan; and from 1858 to 1860, in the Montreal department, at St. Maurice. He was promoted to be a chief trader in 1840; and he retired from the fur-trade in 1860, and died in 1868. He married a daughter of Peter Warren Dease (q.v.); and by her he had at least one daughter.

[R. Harvey Fleming (ed.), *Minutes of Council, Northern Department of Rupert's Land, 1821-31* (Toronto, 1940).]

Bell, John Howatt (1845-1929), prime minister of Prince Edward Island (1919-23), was born at Cape Traverse, Prince Edward Island, on December 9, 1845. He was educated at the Prince of Wales College, Charlottetown, and at Albert College, Belleville, Ontario (B.A., 1868; M.A., 1869), and was called to the bar in 1874 (K.C., 1910). For many years he was a member of the Legislative Assembly of Prince Edward Island; and from 1898 to 1900 he represented East Prince in the Canadian House of Commons. From 1915 to 1923 he represented the fourth district of Prince in the Legislative Assembly of Prince Edward Island; and from 1919 to 1923 he was prime minister of that province. He died

at Los Angeles, California, on January 29, 1929.

[*Can. parl. comp.*]

Bell, Leslie Richard (1906-1962), musician and conductor, was born in Toronto, Ontario, in 1906. He was educated at the University of Toronto (M.A., 1932; Ph.D., 1940), and at the University of Montreal (Mus.D.). After teaching English and history at Parkdale Collegiate (1934-39) he became professor of music at the College of Education and the faculty of music of the University of Toronto in 1939, where he was supervisor and director of choral technique. He was founder and conductor of the Leslie Bell singers, making concert tours and recordings from 1939 to 1962. He was music columnist with the *Toronto Star* and assistant editor of the *Canadian Music Journal* (1956-62). He contributed "popular music" to *Music in Canada* (ed. Sir Ernest MacMillan; Toronto, 1955) and articles to popular magazines and to *Canadian Music Journal*. He was the composer of *In winter cold* (choral, 1950), *Glorious is the land* (band, 1954), *Awakening* (unison, 1957). He died at Toronto, January 19, 1962.

[*Can. who's who*, 1955-57; *Creative Canada* (Toronto, 1971).]

Bell, Robert (1841-1917), scientist and explorer, was born in Toronto, Canada West, on June 3, 1841, the son of the Rev. Andrew Bell, a clergyman of the Church of Scotland, and Elizabeth Notman. He was educated at the grammar school of the county of Prescott and at McGill University (B.Sc., 1861; M.D., 1878; D.Sc., 1901). From 1863 to 1867 he was professor of chemistry and natural science at Queen's University, Kingston; but as early as 1857 he had connected himself with the Geological Survey of Canada, and with this branch of the public service he continued to be identified for over fifty years. In 1877 he was appointed assistant director of the Geological Survey; in 1890 he became its chief geologist; and from 1901 to 1906 he was its director. His surveys covered a large part of northern Quebec and Ontario, the country about Hudson Bay, northern Manitoba, Alberta, and the North West Territories, and some parts of these regions were surveyed by him for the first time. In 1884, in 1885, and in 1897, he took part also in expeditions to Hudson Bay; and in 1897 he explored Baffinland. The bibliography of his writings includes over two hundred pamphlets, most of which are to be found in the publications of the Geological Survey; and these cover geology, geography, forestry, biology, and folklore. He was a charter member of the Royal Society of Canada; in 1893 he was given the degree of LL.D. by Queen's University, and in 1903 that of D.Sc. by Cambridge University; and in 1903 he was created a companion of the Imperial Service Order. In 1908 he was superannuated; and he died on his farm at Rathwell, Manitoba, on June 17, 1917. In 1873, he married Agnes, daughter of Alexander Smith, of Westbourne, Glasgow, and Auchentroig, Stirlingshire, Scotland.

[Rev. R. Campbell, *The jubilee of a scientist* (Can. mag., 1908); C. Hallock, *One of Canada's explorers* (Washington, 1901); *Proc. Roy. Soc. Can.*, 1918; Morgan, *Can. men* (1912).]

Bell, Walter Andrew (1889-1969), earth scientist, was born in St. Thomas, Ontario, January 4, 1889. He was educated in local schools and at Queen's University (B.Sc., 1911). He then enrolled at Yale University and had completed most of the requirements for the Ph.D. degree when he joined the Canadian Field Artillery, serving in Europe until 1919. At the close of the war he was able to study at Cambridge University and the School of Mines in Paris and received a Ph.D. from Yale in 1920. He joined the Geological Survey of Canada as assistant palaeobotanist and spent his working life with the Survey, rising to chief palaeontologist in 1938, senior geologist in 1946, and director of the Geological Survey in 1949. He retired in 1956 but continued to work for the Geological Survey and as consultant with the department of mines of Nova Scotia. He published many major works on the stratigraphy, floral zonation, and structure of maritime coalfields including *Carboniferous rocks and fossil floras of northern Nova Scotia*; *The Pictou coal field, Nova Scotia*; *Fossil flora of Sydney coalfield, Nova Scotia* as memoirs or bulletins of the Geological Survey. In 1965 his previous work in cataloguing and classification was brought together in three handbooks in the *Illustrations of Canadian Fossils* series. He was a fellow of the Royal Society of Canada and an honorary member of the Geological Association of Canada, and received numerous medals and awards. He died at Ottawa on January 28, 1969.

[*Proc. and Trans. Roy. Soc. Can.*, fourth series, vol. VII.]

Bell, William (1780-1857), clergyman and author, was born in Scotland on May 20, 1780, and died at Perth, Canada West, on August 16, 1857. He was ordained a minister of the Secession Church of Scotland in 1817, and was sent to Canada to minister to the settlers at Perth in Upper Canada. Here he remained for the rest of his life. His diary depicting his experience of pioneer life over forty years has been preserved, and is in the Queen's University Library. He was the author of *Hints to emigrants, in a series of letters from Upper Canada* (Edinburgh, 1824).

[Isabel Skelton, *A man austere: William Bell, parson and pioneer* (Toronto, 1947).]

Bell, Winthrop Picard (1884-1965), scholar and author, was born in Halifax, Nova Scotia, May 12, 1884. He was educated at Mount Allison University (B.A., 1904) and Göttingen, Germany, where he was interned for the duration of the First World War. He was awarded his Ph.D. in philosophy in 1919. He taught for a short time at the University of Toronto and at Harvard. Returning to Nova Scotia he went into business but gave much of his time to history and philosophy. He died at Chester, Nova Scotia, on April 4, 1965. He was author of *The foreign Protestants and the settlement of Nova Scotia* (Toronto, 1961).

[*Can. hist. rev.*, vol. XLVI, 1965.]

Belleau, Sir Narcisse Fortunat (1808-1894), prime minister of Canada and lieutenant-governor of Quebec, was born near Quebec on October 20, 1808, the son of Gabriel Belleau and Marie de Kostka Hamel. He was called to the bar in Lower Canada in 1832, and was made a Q.C. in 1854. In 1852 he was appointed to the Legislative Council of Canada, and in 1857 he was made speaker of the Council, with a seat in the Macdonald-Cartier administration of that year. As speaker of the Upper House, he was knighted by the Prince of Wales in 1860; and when, in 1865, Sir Etienne Taché (q.v.) was compelled to retire as the head of the coalition government formed to bring in Confederation, Belleau became prime minister of Canada in his place. The real head of the government, however, was John A. Macdonald (q.v.); and when Confederation was achieved, Macdonald became prime minister of the new Dominion and Belleau was appointed the first lieutenant-governor of the province of Quebec (1867-73). In 1879 he was made a K.C.M.G. He died at Quebec, on September 14, 1894. In 1835 he married Marie Reine Josephte, daughter of Louis Gauvreau and Marie Josephte Vanfelson; she died at Quebec, on December 11, 1884, and there was no issue by the marriage.

[S. Drapeau, *Biographie de Sir N. F. Belleau* (Quebec, 1883); H. Fry, *Biographical sketch of Sir N. F. Belleau* (Quebec, 1894); Rose, *Cyc. Can. biog.* (1888); Taylor, *Brit. Am.*]

Bellefeuille, Joseph Edouard Lefebvre de (1840-1926), lawyer, was born at St. Eustache, Lower Canada, on June 13, 1840, the eldest son of Joseph Lefebvre de Bellefeuille and Caroline Leprohon. He was educated at St. Mary's College, Montreal, and was called to the bar of Lower Canada in 1861 (Q.C., 1889). He carried on the practice of law in Montreal. He was one of the founders of *La Revue Canadienne*, and was a frequent contributor to it. He died at Montreal, Quebec, on January 12, 1926. He was the author of *Thèse sur les mariages clandestins*

(Montreal, 1860), *Code civil du Bas-Canada* (Montreal, 1866), *Le Canada et les zouaves pontificaux* (Montreal, 1868), and *Code municipale de la province de Québec* (Montreal, 1879).

[Morgan, *Can. men* (1912); *Bull. rech. hist.*, 1926.]

Bellemare, Joseph Elzéar (1849-1924), priest and historian, was born at Yamachiche, Canada East, was the son of Joseph Bellemare and Hermine Gélinas. He was ordained a priest of the Roman Catholic Church in 1872, and he served successively as a professor at the Nicolet Seminary, vicar at Baie-du-Fèbvre, assistant at Yamaska, curé of Ste. Hélène de Chester, curé of Saint Cyrille de Wendover, and lastly curé of Baie-du-Fèbvre. He died at Nicolet on February 29, 1924. He was the author of two local histories: *Histoire de la Baie-Saint-Antoine, dite Baie-du-Fèbvre* (Montreal, 1911) and *Histoire de Nicolet* (Montreal, 1924).

[Allaire, *Dict. biog.*]

Bellemare, Raphaël (1821-1906), civil servant and historian, was born at Yamachiche, Lower Canada, on February 22, 1821. He was appointed an inspector of inland revenue in 1855, and he continued a member of the civil service of Canada until his retirement in 1893. He was one of the founders of La Société Historique de Montréal; and after his retirement from the civil service he was the author of *Les bases de l'histoire d'Yamachiche* (Montreal, 1901). He died at Montreal, Quebec, in 1906.

[Morgan, *Can. men* (1898).]

Bellerive, Georges (1859-1935), lawyer and author, was born in 1859, was called to the bar, and practised law in Quebec, Que. He died at Quebec on May 23, 1935. He took an interest in art and literature, and was the author of *Orateurs canadiens-français aux Etats-Unis* (Quebec, 1908), *Orateurs canadiens-français en Angleterre, en Ecosse, et en Irelande* (Quebec, 1912), *Brèves apologies de nos auteurs féminins* (Quebec, 1924), *Artistes, peintres canadiens-français* (2 vols., Quebec, 1925-26), and *Nos auteurs dramatiques* (Quebec, 1933).

[G. Tougas, *A check-list of printed materials relating to French-Canadian literature* (Vancouver, 1958).]

Belley, Louis de Gonzague (1863-1930), postmaster-general of Canada (1921), was born at Ha Ha Bay, Chicoutimi county, Quebec, on February 3, 1863. He was educated at Laval University, and was called to the bar of Quebec. From 1892 to 1896 he represented Chicoutimi in the Canadian House of Commons; and in 1921 he was appointed postmaster-general in the short-lived Meighen administration of that year. He died at Quebec on July 9, 1930. In 1889 he married Lydia Guay, of Chicoutimi; and by her he had five sons and five daughters.

[*Can. parl. comp.*]

Bell-Smith, Frederick Marlett (1846-1923), painter, was born in London, England, on September 26, 1846, the eldest son of John Bell-Smith (q.v.). He came to Canada with his father in 1866, and for a number of years (1882-89) taught drawing in the public schools of London, Ontario. In 1888 he was elected a member of the Royal Canadian Academy of Arts, whereupon he removed to Toronto, and devoted himself to painting. In 1891 he went to Paris, and studied under Courtois, Blanc, and Dupain. He was best known for his landscapes; but he was successful also with pictures of city streets, and he did some acceptable portraits. He was for many years an enthusiastic member of the Toronto Dickens fellowship and was for a time its president. He had a flair for Dickens and French-Canadian characters and was noted for his impersonations of them. He died in Toronto on June 23, 1923. In 1871 he married Annie Myra, daughter of Samuel Dyde. From 1904 to 1908 he was president of the Ontario Society of Artists.

[Morgan, *Can. men* (1912); *Who was who*, 1916-28; *Can. who was who*, vol. 2.]

Bell-Smith, John (1810-1883), painter, was born in London, England, in 1810. Before coming to Canada in 1866, he was secretary-treasurer and trustee of the Institute of Fine Arts, London, and he exhibited his pictures frequently at the Royal Academy. In 1867 he founded in Montreal, and was the first president of, the Society of Canadian Artists; but failing health compelled him to decline the invitation to join the Royal Canadian Academy of Arts in 1880. He died in Toronto, Ontario, on December 30, 1883.

[*Dom. ann. reg.*, 1883; *Can. who was who*, vol. 2.]

Belmont, François Vachon de (1645-1732), superior of the Sulpician Seminary in Montreal (1701-27), was born on April 2, 1645, at Grenoble, France. He came to Canada as a Sulpician missionary in 1680; and after devoting himself for twenty years to the Indians on the island of Montreal, he was appointed superior of the Sulpician Seminary in Montreal. He died on May 22, 1732. He left behind him a history of Canada from 1608 to 1700, which was published in 1840 by the Literary and Historical Society of Quebec in its first series of *Historical Documents*.

[Allaire, *Dict. biog.*; Le Jeune, *Dict. gén.*; *Dict. Can. biog.*, vol. 2.]

Bender, Louis Prosper (1844-1917), physician and author, was born at Quebec, Canada East, on July 30, 1844. He was educated at the Quebec Seminary and at McGill University (M.D., 1865), and served as a medical officer in the American Civil War. In 1884 he removed from Quebec to Boston; but toward the end of his life he returned to Quebec, and he died there on January 24, 1917. He was the author of *Literary sheaves* (Montreal, 1881), *Old and new Canada* (Montreal, 1882), and *Canada's actual condition* (New York, 1886).

[Morgan, *Can. men* (1912).]

Bengough, John Wilson (1851-1923), cartoonist and poet, was born in Toronto, Canada West, on April 7, 1851, the son of John Bengough and Margaret Wilson. He was educated in the Whitby district and grammar schools, and became a printer. In 1873 he founded *Grip*, a humorous weekly published in Toronto, and his cartoons in this journal attained a wide celebrity. Selections from them were twice published between boards, first under the title of *Grip's cartoons* (Toronto, 1875), and second under the title *Caricature history of Canadian politics* (2 vols., Toronto, 1886). In 1892 he severed his connection with *Grip*, and thereafter he was successively cartoonist with the Montreal *Star* and the Toronto *Globe*. An ardent advocate of single tax, prohibition, and free trade, he published several political brochures, *The up-to-date primer, a first book of lessons for little political economists* (Toronto, 1896), *The gin mill primer* (Toronto, 1898), and *The whole hog book* (Toronto, 1911). He published also two volumes of verse, *Motley: Verses grave and gay* (Toronto, 1895), and *In many keys* (Toronto, 1902). He was a popular entertainer by humorous lecturing and cartooning local celebrities. He died in Toronto on October 2, 1923.

[Morgan, *Can. men* (1912); *Can. who was who*, vol. 1.]

Benjamin, George (1799-1864), politician, was born in England in 1799. He came to Canada in 1830, and settled in Belleville, Upper Canada. In 1848 he was elected grand master of the Orangemen of British North America; and from 1856 to 1861 he represented North Hastings in the Legislative Assembly of Canada. He died at Belleville, Upper Canada, on July 6, 1864.

[*Cyc. Am. biog.*]

Bennett, Charles Fox (1793-1883), prime minister of Newfoundland (1870-74), was born at Shaftesbury, Dorset, England, on June 11, 1793, and died at St. John's, Newfoundland, on December 5, 1883. He came to Newfoundland at an early age, and became a successful merchant in St. John's. He was the leader of the party opposing the proposed union with Canada in 1869, and he was elected to the House of Assembly for Placentia–St. Mary's. In 1870 he was invited to form a government, and he remained prime minister of Newfoundland until the defeat of his party at the polls in 1874. It was due to his efforts that the entrance of Newfoundland into the Canadian Confederation was postponed for eighty years.

[D. W. Prowse, *A history of Newfoundland* (London, 1895); *Encyc. Can.*]

Bennett, Richard Bedford, first Viscount (1870-1947), prime minister of Canada (1930-35), was born on July 3, 1870, at Hopewell Hill, Albert county, New Brunswick, the son of Henry John Bennett and Henrietta Stiles, descendants of pre-Loyalist settlers from Connecticut. He was educated at the Provincial Normal School, and was for a short time a school-teacher. In 1893, however, he graduated from the law school at Dalhousie University, and was called to the bar of New Brunswick. He practised law for four years in Chatham, New Brunswick, with L. J. Tweedie (q.v.). He then went to Calgary, North West Territories, and became a partner of Senator (later Sir) James Lougheed (q.v.).

His first entry into politics was in 1898, when he was elected Conservative member for Olds in the legislature of the North West Territories. He was defeated in 1905 in the first general election of the newly created province of Alberta, but was re-elected in 1909. In 1911 he resigned from the Alberta legislature, and was elected to represent Calgary East in the Canadian House of Commons. In the election of 1917 he declined nomination, but he accepted office briefly as minister of justice in the short-lived Meighen administration in 1921, and again as minister of finance in the second Meighen administration in 1926. In 1925 he was elected to represent Calgary West, and he represented this constituency until his retirement from Canadian politics in 1938.

In 1927, at a convention held in Winnipeg, Bennett was chosen leader of the Conservative party; and in the general election of 1930 he led his party to victory. He became prime minister, taking over at the same time the portfolios of finance and external affairs. His period of office coincided with the most severe years of the Great Depression; and his efforts to counteract the effects of the depression did not prove very successful. The truth is that, although a very able lawyer, he was not an economist. He had, moreover, a domineering manner which tended to alienate even his supporters; and the fact that he had acquired a controlling interest in the E. B. Eddy Company of Ottawa, and was a very rich man, did not tend to commend him to the electorate. The result was that, when the general election became due in 1935, the

Bennett government suffered a more disastrous defeat than any other government since Confederation. Bennett himself retained his seat, and became leader of the opposition until, in 1938, he retired from political life. In 1939 he went to live in England, where he purchased an estate in Surrey; and here he lived, a lonely and embittered old man, until his death at Dorking, on June 27, 1947. In 1941 he was created Viscount Bennett of Mickleham, Calgary, and Hopewell. He was a bachelor, and the title died with him. His papers are in the Bonar Law – Bennett Library at the University of New Brunswick.

[Lord Beaverbrook, *Friends: Sixty years of intimate personal relations with Richard Bedford Bennett* (London, 1959); A. D. MacLean, *R. B. Bennett* (Toronto, 1934); Ernest Watkins, *R. B. Bennett* (Toronto, 1963); *Who was who*, 1941-50; *Can. who's who*, 1938-39; *Encyc. Can.*]

Benoît, Joseph Paul Augustin (1850-1915), priest and author, was born and educated in France, and died at St. Boniface, Manitoba, in 1915. He came to Canada in 1891, as the first superior of Notre Dame de Lourdes in Manitoba. He was the author of *Vie de Mgr. Taché* (2 vols., Montreal, 1904).

[Morgan, *Can. men* (1912).]

Bensley, Benjamin Arthur (1875-1934), biologist, was born at Barton, Ontario, on November 5, 1875; and was educated at the University of Toronto (B.A., 1896) and Columbia University (Ph.D., 1902). He was appointed associate professor of biology in the University of Toronto in 1906, and professor in 1912. He died at Toronto, Ontario, on January 20, 1934. He was the author of *Practical anatomy of the rabbit* (Toronto, 1910).

[*University of Toronto monthly*, 1934.]

Benson, James Rea (1807-1885), senator, was for many years engaged in milling and shipping. He had large financial interests, and was president of the Niagara District Bank and later director of the Imperial Bank of Canada. He was elected a member of the Legislative Council of Canada in 1867, and when Confederation was consummated in that year he was elected a member of the House of Commons. He was appointed to the Senate in 1868. He died in 1885.

[*Dom. ann. reg.*, 1885; *Can. parl. comp.*]

Benson, Nathaniel Anketell Michael (1903-1966), poet, was born in Toronto, Ontario, October 11, 1903, and educated at the University of Toronto (B.A., 1927; M.A., 1928) and at the Ontario College of Education. He worked on newspapers in Toronto and Winnipeg and as an advertising writer in Toronto and New York before returning to Canada in 1949. He taught English in To-

ronto collegiate institutes and wrote drama criticism for the Toronto *Saturday Night*. From 1937 to 1943 he was editor of *Canadian Poetry Magazine*. He published six volumes of poetry: *Poems* (1927); *Twenty and after* (1927); *The wanderer* (1930); *Dollard* (1933); *The glowing years* (1937); *One man's pilgrimage* (1962). He also wrote *None of it came easy* (1956), a biography of the Rt. Honourable J. G. Gardiner, and three one-act plays, *Three plays for patriots* (1930). He died at Toronto, Ontario, July 19, 1966.

[*Can. who's who*, 1964-66; Metropolitan Toronto Library Board, *Biographical scrapbooks*, vol. 27.]

Berczy, Charles Albert (1794-1858), post-master of Toronto, was born at Newark (Niagara), Upper Canada, on August 22, 1794, the son of William von Moll Berczy (q.v.). During the War of 1812 he served in the commissariat. In 1837 he acted as a confidential agent of Sir Francis Bond Head (q.v.), and was appointed postmaster of Toronto, in place of James Scott Howard, dismissed. He died in Toronto in June, 1858. By his wife, who was Anne Eliza, daughter of Joseph Stace Finch, of Greenwich, England, he had a large family.

[Morgan, *Cel. Can.*]

Berczy, William von Moll (1748-1813), colonizer and artist, was born in Saxony in 1748. He was educated at the universities of Leipzig and Jena. In 1790 he went to England, and there undertook to act as the agent of an English association owning land in the Genesee Valley, New York, in bringing out German settlers. In 1792 he brought out sixty families; but in 1793 he had a disagreement with his employers; and in 1794 he brought his settlers to Upper Canada, and placed them on the land in the township of Markham, north of York (Toronto). The colony, for various reasons, proved a failure; and in 1805, Berczy went to live in Montreal. Here he supported himself and his family by painting, and his name is one of the earliest in the history of Canadian art. He died in February, 1813, in New York, whither he had gone on business. He married on December 15, 1785, in Switzerland, Charlotte Allemand.

[Morgan, *Cel. Can.*; P. Gagnon, *Bibliographie canadienne* (Quebec, 1895), no. 3796.]

Bering, Vitus (1680-1741), navigator, was born at Horsen, Denmark, in 1680. He took service in the Russian navy established by Peter the Great; and in 1725 was chosen to command an expedition of discovery in the sea of Kamchatka. In 1728 he explored the north-eastern coasts of Asia, discovered the strait which now bears his name, and proved that Asia and America are not united by land. Later, he undertook a second expedition with the object of discovering whether the land opposite Kamchatka was the coast of America, or merely intervening islands. In 1741 he sailed from Okhotsk and reached the coast of Alaska; but storms and sickness interrupted his plans, and he died on December 19, 1741, on a desolate island which now bears his name, off the coast of Kamchatka.

[F. A. Golder, *Bering's voyages* (2 vols., New York, 1922).]

Berkeley, Thomas Charles (1892-1957), philatelist, was born in England in 1892, and died at Toronto, Ontario, on December 15, 1957. He came to Canada in 1923, and was employed as an engineer by the Toronto Transportation Commission. An ardent philatelist, he was the author of *The history of Canada in stamps* (Toronto, 1957).

[Toronto *Globe and Mail*, Dec. 16, 1957.]

Bernard, Alexis Xyste (1847-1923), Roman Catholic bishop of St. Hyacinthe (1905-23), was born at Beloeil, Quebec, on December 29, 1847, and was ordained a priest in 1871. He was elected bishop of St. Hyacinthe in 1905, and died at St. Hyacinthe on June 18, 1923. He edited *Les lettres pastorales et circulaires des évêques de Saint-Hyacinthe* (9 vols., St. Hyacinthe, 1888-99).

[Allaire, *Dict. biog.*]

Bernard, Hewitt (1825-1893), soldier and civil servant, was born in Jamaica in 1825, the son of Thomas James Bernard, sometime attorney-general of Jamaica, and Theodora Folks Hewitt. He came to Canada with his mother, after the death of his father, and settled at Barrie, Upper Canada. In 1855 he entered the volunteer militia, and in 1860 he was appointed deputy judge advocate general. From 1858 to 1866 he was private secretary to John A. Macdonald (q.v.), whose brother-in-law he became. In 1864 he was secretary to the Quebec Conference, and in 1866 he accompanied Macdonald to London, and acted as secretary to the London Conference. From 1867 to 1876 he was deputy minister of justice. In 1872 he was created a C.M.G.; and he died on February 24, 1893. He was not married.

[E. M. Chadwick, *Ontarian families* (2 vols., Toronto, 1894-98); J. Pope, *Memoirs of Sir J. A. Macdonald* (2 vols., Ottawa, 1895).]

Bernier, Joseph Elzéar (1852-1934), navigator and explorer, was born at L'Islet, Quebec, on January 1, 1852, the son of Capt. Thomas Bernier and Célina Paradis. He went to sea when 12 years of age, and became master of a brigantine at 17 years. In 1887 he was appointed dockmaster at Lévis, and from 1893 to 1897 he was governor of the Quebec jail. He then turned, however, to Arctic exploration; and he made, in the service of the Canadian government, no fewer than twelve voyages of exploration to the Arctic archipelago. He was in no small measure responsible for asserting Canada's claim to the Arctic islands, and in awaking the Canadian government and public to their importance. He died at Lévis, Quebec, on December 26, 1934. His *Report on the Dominion government expedition to the Arctic islands and Hudson strait on board the D.G.S. "Arctic"*, with maps and charts, was published by the Canadian government (Ottawa, 1910). His autobiography was published posthumously under the title, *Master mariner and arctic explorer: A narrative of sixty years at sea* (Ottawa, 1939).

[*Americana annual*, 1935; W. Q. Ketchum, *Last of the great master mariners* (Can. geog. journal, 1937); H. Steele, *Captain goes ashore* (Can. mag., 1935); Morgan, *Can. men* (1912); Gilberte Tremblay, *Bernier, capitaine à 17 ans* (Montreal, 1972).]

Bernier, Michael Esdras (1841-1921), minister of inland revenue (1900-1904), was born at St. Hyacinthe, Quebec, on September 28, 1841, the son of Étienne Bernier and Julie Lussier. He was educated at St. Hyacinthe College, and in 1867 became a notary public. He sat in the Canadian House of Commons as a Liberal for the constituency of St. Hyacinthe from 1882 to 1904; and from June, 1900, to January, 1904, he was minister of inland revenue in the Laurier administration. On January 18, 1904, he was appointed a member of the Board of Railway Commissioners for Canada, and he continued to be a member of this board until his death, at St. Hyacinthe, on July 29, 1921. In 1865 he married Alida, daughter of S. Marchesseault, of St. Hyacinthe.

[*Can. parl. comp.*; Morgan, *Can. men* (1912).]

Bernières, Henri de (1635-1700), priest, was born at Caën, Normandy, France, in 1635, the son of Pierre de Bernières, Baron d'Acqueville. He studied for the priesthood at Caën, and in 1660 was ordained a priest of the Roman Catholic Church by Bishop Laval (q.v.). From 1660 to 1687 he was curé of the cathedral at Quebec, and from 1684 to 1700 a canon of the cathedral and dean of the chapter. He died at Quebec on December 4, 1700.

[A. Gosselin, *Henri de Bernières* (Quebec, 1902); Allaire, *Dict. biog.*; *Dict. Can. biog.*, vol. 1.]

Berthelot, Amable (1777-1847), author, was born in Quebec in 1777, the son of Michel-Amable Berthelot d'Artigny. He was educated at the Quebec Seminary, and was called to the bar of Lower Canada, but practised law for only a few years. He devoted the latter part of his life to the study of a variety of sciences; and he collected one of the earliest libraries of books relating to Canada. He represented Three Rivers in the Assembly of Lower Canada from 1824 to 1827 and the upper town of Quebec from 1834 to 1838; and from 1841 to his death he represented the county of Kamouraska in the Assembly of united Canada. He died at Quebec on November 24, 1847. He was the author of an *Essai de grammaire française* (Quebec, 1840) and an *Essai d'analyses grammaticales* (Quebec, 1843; new and rev. ed., 1847); and, in addition to some speeches, he published two pamphlets of historical interest, *Dissertation sur le canon de bronze que l'on voit dans le musée de M. Casseur à Québec* (Quebec, 1830), and *Discours fait devant la Société de Discussion de Québec, le 15 juillet, 1844, sur le vaisseau trouvé à l'embouchure du ruisseau St. Michel, et que l'on prétend être la Petite Hermine de Jacques Cartier* (Quebec, 1844).

[*Bull. rech. hist.*, 1903 and 1935; Bibaud, *Panth. can.*; E. Lareau, *La littérature canadienne* (Montreal, 1874).]

Berthelot, Hector (1842-1895), humorist, was born at Three Rivers, Canada East, on March 4, 1842. He was called to the bar in 1865, but practised law for only a short time. He was successively a teacher of French, a photographer, a politician, and a journalist. He died at Montreal, Quebec, on September 15, 1895.

[Mme Henriette L. Tassé, *La vie humoristique d'Hector Berthelot* (Montreal, 1934); P. G. Roy, *Les avocats de la région de Québec* (Lévis, Que., 1936).]

Berthon, George Théodore (1806-1892), portrait-painter, was born in Vienna in the year 1806, the son of René Théodore Berthon (1777-1859), a painter at the court of Napoleon, and a pupil of the painter David. The younger Berthon early showed an aptitude for portrait-painting, and studied in various capitals in Europe. After spending fourteen years in England, he came to Canada in 1841, and settled in Toronto. There, despite the limited field for art at that time, he came into great demand as a portrait-painter; and a large number of portraits in Osgoode Hall and Government House, Toronto, and in the Senate Chamber, Ottawa, are by him. Of these he himself regarded his portrait of Sir John Beverley Robinson (q.v.) as his masterpiece. He died in Toronto on January 18, 1892; and at the time of his death was the oldest member of the Ontario Society of Artists. He was twice married, (1) to Zélie Boisseau (d. 1847), daughter of a surgeon in Napoleon's army, and (2) in 1850 to Claire, daughter of J. P. de la Haye, the first French master at Upper Canada College, Toronto. By his first wife he had one daughter, and by his second, six sons and five daughters.

[W. Colgate, *George Theodore Berthon* (Ont. Hist. Soc., papers and records, vol. XXXIV, 1942); *Can. who was who*, vol. 2; E. Morris, *Art in Canada: The early painters* (Toronto, 1911); N. MacTavish, *The fine arts in Canada* (Toronto, 1925).]

Bertram, Sir Alexander (1853-1926), manufacturer and soldier, was born at Dundas, Ontario, on February 18, 1853, the second son of John Bertram and Elizabeth Bennett. He became a partner in his father's Canadian Tool Works in Dundas in 1886; and later he became president of the firm of John Bertram and Sons. He entered the 77th Wentworth Militia Regiment as a bugler, and rose to be the officer commanding the regiment. In 1905 he was appointed to the command of the 3rd Infantry Brigade, western Ontario; and in 1909 he commanded the Canadian rifle team that went to Bisley. He was promoted colonel in 1910, brigadier-general in 1915, and major-general in 1916. In 1915 he was appointed deputy chairman of the Canadian Imperial Munitions Board, and in 1916 he was created for his services a knight bachelor. He died at Montreal on April 24, 1926.

[*Who was who*, 1916-28; Morgan, *Can. men* (1912).]

Bertrand, Jean-Jacques (1916-1973), lawyer and premier, was born at Ste-Agathe-des-Monts, Quebec, June 20, 1916, and educated at Bishop's University, the University of Ottawa, and the University of Montreal. He practised law in Cowansville, Quebec, and was elected to the Quebec Assembly as the member for Missisquoi in 1948, serving as minister of lands and forests from 1958 until he became minister for youth for six months in 1960. He was re-elected at each election until his death in Quebec City on February 22, 1973. He was minister of justice and minister of education on the election of the Union Nationale to power in 1966, and was chosen as leader of the party on the death of Daniel Johnson in 1968, becoming premier and minister of intergovernmental affairs as well as minister of justice from October, 1968, until the defeat of his government in the election of 1970. He relinquished the leadership of the Union Nationale party to Gabriel Loubier at the leadership convention in June, 1971. He continued his law practice with Bertrand, Turmel and Mennier.

[*Can. who's who*, 1970-72; *Canadian News Facts*, 1971-73.]

Bessborough, Sir Vere Brabazan Ponsonby, ninth Earl of (1880-1956), governor-general of Canada (1931-35), was born on October 27, 1880, the eldest son of the eighth Earl of Bessborough. He was educated at Harrow and Trinity College, Cambridge (B.A., 1901), and was called to the bar in 1903. After serving as a Conservative member in the House of Commons for several years, he succeeded to the earldom in 1920. He was appointed governor-general of Canada in 1931, and his period of office, which came to an end in 1935, virtually coincided with the Bennett régime. In 1912 he married Roberte, daughter of Baron de Neuflize, of Paris, France; and both he and his wife took an active interest in amateur theatricals in Canada. They initiated the Dominion Drama Festival, and presented the Bessborough trophy for competition. He edited *Lady Charlotte Elizabeth Guest; Extracts from her journal, 1833-1852* (London, 1950), *Lady Charlotte Schreiber; Extracts from her journal, 1853-1891* (London, 1952), and, with A. Aspinall, *Lady Bessborough and her family circle* (London, 1940). He died at Rowlands Castle, Hampshire, England, on March 10, 1956.

[John Cowan, *Canada's governors-general* (Toronto, 1952); *Burke's Peerage*; *Who's who*, 1955; *Encyc. Can.*]

Bethune, Alexander Neil (1800-1879), Anglican bishop of Toronto, was born at Williamstown, Glengarry, Upper Canada, on August 28, 1800, the fifth son of the Rev. John Bethune (q.v.), the first Presbyterian minister in Canada. He was educated at Cornwall, Upper Canada, under the Rev. John Strachan (q.v.), whose *protégé* he became. In 1824 he was admitted to the priesthood of the Church of England, and in 1827 he was presented with the living of Cobourg, Upper Canada. In 1849, Strachan, on his consecration as bishop of Toronto, appointed him archdeacon of York; in 1867 he became bishop of Niagara and coadjutor to the bishop of Toronto; and, on Strachan's death later in the same year, he succeeded him as the second bishop of Toronto. He died in Toronto, on February 3, 1879. In addition to a number of his sermons which were printed — one collection of which, entitled *Six sermons on the liturgy of the Church of England* (York, U.C., 1829), is an early Upper Canadian imprint — he published *Thoughts upon the clergy reserve question* (Toronto, 1856), *Thirteen lectures on historical portions of the Old Testament* (New York, n.d.), *Thirteen lectures, expository and practical, on the liturgy of the Church of England* (Toronto, 1862), and *Memoir of the Right Reverend John Strachan* (Toronto, 1870).

[C. H. Mockridge, *The bishops of the Church of England in Canada* (Toronto, 1896); A. H. Young, *The Bethunes* (Ont. Hist. Soc., papers and records, 1931); Rose, *Cyc. Can. biog.* (1886); *Dict. Can. biog.*, vol. 10.]

Bethune, Angus (1783-1858), fur-trader, was born at Carleton Island, in Lake Ontario, on September 9, 1783, the eldest son of the Rev. John Bethune (q.v.) and Veronica, daughter of Jean Etienne Wadden (q.v.). He entered the service of the North West Company, and in 1806 was a clerk at Lake Winnipeg. In 1813 he was transferred to the Columbia; and in 1814 he was made a partner of the North West Company. He was at Fort William in the summer of 1817, and again in the summer of 1820; and on the latter occasion he was appointed by the wintering partners as a delegate, with John McLoughlin (q.v.), to go to London to open separate negotiations with the Hudson's Bay Company. He spent the winter of 1820-21 in London; and on the union of the North West and Hudson's Bay companies in 1821, he was made a chief factor. He seems to have retired from the fur-trade before 1825; and he died in Toronto on November 13, 1858. He married Louisa, daughter of the Hon. Roderick McKenzie (q.v.), of Terrebonne; and by her he had five sons and one daughter.

[E.E. Rich (ed.), *Colin Robertson's correspondence book* (Toronto, 1939); A. H. Young, *The Bethunes* (Ont. Hist. Soc., papers and records, 1931).]

Bethune, Charles James Stewart (1838-1932), clergyman and entomologist, was born at West Flamborough, Upper Canada, on August 11, 1838, the third son of the Right Rev. A. N. Bethune (q.v.). He was educated at Upper Canada College and Trinity University (B.A., 1859; M.A., 1861; D.C.L., 1883), and was ordained a priest of the Church of England in 1862. From 1870 to 1899 he was headmaster of Trinity College School, Port Hope; and from 1906 to 1920 he was professor of entomology and zoölogy at the Ontario Agricultural College, Guelph. For many years he was editor of the *Canadian Entomologist*. In 1913 he was president of the Entomological Society of America. He died at Toronto on April 17, 1932. In 1863 he married Harriet Alice Mary, daughter of Lieut.-Col. James Forlong, K.H., and by her he had two sons and two daughters.

[A. H. Young, *The Bethunes* (Ont. Hist. Soc., papers and records, 1931); Morgan, *Can. men* (1912); *Can. who was who*, vol. 1.]

Bethune, James Gray (1793-1841), banker, was born in Charlottenburg, Upper Canada, on April 1, 1793, the third son of the Rev. John Bethune (q.v.). He became a banker in Cobourg, Upper Canada, but suffered bankruptcy in 1834. In his later years he lived in Rochester, New York; and he died there in October, 1841. He was the author of a pamphlet entitled *A schedule of real estate in the Newcastle district* (Cobourg, 1833).

[A. H. Young, *The Bethunes* (Ont. Hist. Soc., papers and records, 1931).]

Bethune, John (1751-1815), clergyman, was born in the Isle of Skye in 1751, and was educated at King's College, Aberdeen. He emigrated to South Carolina before the outbreak of the American Revolution; and, during the revolutionary war, he was the chaplain of the 84th Regiment (Royal Highland Emigrants). In 1786 he organized at Montreal the first Presbyterian congregation in Canada; and from May, 1787, to his death on September 13, 1815, he was pastor of the Presbyterian church at Williamstown, Glengarry, Upper Canada.
[A. H. Young, *The Bethunes* (Ont. Hist. Soc., papers and records, 1931); W. Gregg, *History of the Presbyterian church in the Dominion of Canada* (Toronto, 1880); W. Canniff, *A history of the early settlement of Upper Canada* (Toronto, 1809).]

Bethune, Norman (1890-1939), surgeon, was born at Gravenhurst, Ontario, in 1899, the son of the Rev. Malcolm N. Bethune; and was educated at the University of Toronto (M.B., 1916). He interrupted his course to enlist in the first contingent of the Canadian Expeditionary Force in 1914, but was invalided back to Canada in 1915, and completed his course. In the latter half of the First World War, he was a surgeon-lieutenant in the Navy. In 1936-37 he served as a surgeon with the Spanish government forces in Madrid; and he then went to China, where he served as a surgeon with the Eighth Route Army, in the war with Japan. He died at Wupaishan, Shansi province, China, in November, 1939.
[G. Nadeau, *A T.B.'s progress, the story of Norman Bethune* (Bulletin of the history of medicine, 1940); *New York Times*, Nov. 26, 1939; *Saturday night*, Dec. 9, 1939; T. Allen and S. Gordon, *The scalpel, the sword: The story of Dr. Norman Bethune* (Boston, 1952); Roderick Stewart, *Bethune* (Toronto, 1973).]

Bettridge, William (1791-1879), soldier and clergyman, was born in Warwickshire, England, on August 30, 1791. At an early age he became an ensign in the 81st Foot, and served throughout the later stages of the Napoleonic wars. At the time of the battle of Waterloo, he was town adjutant of Brussels. In 1816 he retired on half-pay, and entered on a course of studies first at the University of Jena and then at St. John's College, Cambridge. In 1824 he took holy orders in the Church of England, and in 1834 he came to Upper Canada, where he was appointed rector of Woodstock. He continued in this charge until his retirement in 1874; and he died in Strathroy, Ontario, on November 21, 1879. He wrote *A brief history of the Church in Upper Canada* (London, 1838).
[*Dom. ann. reg.*, 1879; Morgan, *Bib. can.*; *Dict. Can. biog.*, vol. 10.]

Biard, Pierre (1567?-1622), Jesuit missionary, was born at Grenoble, France, about 1567. He entered the Society of Jesus in 1583, and for many years was a professor of theology at Lyons. In 1611 he was sent as a missionary to Acadia. In 1613 he helped to found a settlement at St. Sauveur (now Bar Harbor), but was taken prisoner by the English, was carried to Virginia, and only succeeded in getting back to France after many thrilling adventures. He was accused of being in league with the English captors of the French settlements; and he embodied his defence in his *Relation de la Nouvelle France*, 1616. He died at Avignon, France, on November 17, 1622.
[Louis Pelletier, *Pierre Biard* (Montréal, 1962); Le Jeune, *Dict. gén.*; *Dict. Am. biog.*; *Cyc. Am. biog.*; *Dict. Can. biog.*, vol. 1.]

Bibaud, François Marie Uncas Maximilien (1824-1887), author, was born at Montreal, Lower Canada, in November, 1824, the son of Michel Bibaud (q.v.). He was educated in Montreal, was called to the bar, and was one of the founders of the school of law at the Jesuit College in Montreal. In this school he was for a time a professor. He died, unmarried, at Montreal on July 9, 1887. He was the author of a number of works of unequal value: *Biographie des sagamos illustres de l'Amérique septentrionale* (Montreal, 1848), *Essai logique judiciaire* (Montreal, 1853), *Catéchisme de l'histoire du Canada* (Montreal, 1853), *Les institutions de l'histoire du Canada, ou Annales canadiennes* (Montreal, 1855), *Le charlatanisme dans l'histoire* (Montreal, 1855), *Deux pages de l'histoire d'Amérique* (Montreal, 1857), *Dictionnaire historique des hommes illustres du Canada et de l'Amérique* (Montreal, 1857), *Opuscules* (Montreal, 1857), *Le Panthéon canadien* (Montreal, 1858; new and rev. ed., 1891), *Tableau historique des progrès matériels et intellectuels du Canada* (Montreal, 1858), *Bibliothèque canadienne, ou Annales bibliographiques* (Montreal, 1858), *Commentaires sur les lois du Bas-Canada* (Montreal, 1859), *Tablettes historiques canadiennes* (Montreal, 1859; 2nd ed., 1861), *Les Machabées canadiens* (Montreal, 1859), *Notice historique sur l'enseignement du droit en Canada* (Montreal, 1862), *L'honorable L. A. Dessaulles et le système judiciaire des Etats Pontificaux* (Montreal, 1862), *La confédération du Sud* (Montreal, 1864), *Le mémorial des vicissitudes et des progrès de la langue française en Canada* (Montreal, 1879), and *Mémorial des honneurs étrangers conférés à des canadiens* (Montreal, 1885).
[Le Jeune, *Dict. gén.*; Morgan, *Bib. can.*]

Bibaud, Michel (1782-1857), journalist and historian, was born at Côte des Neiges, near Montreal, on January 20, 1782, of *habitant* stock. He was educated at the college of St. Raphael (1800-06), and for many years supported himself by teaching. Meanwhile, he drifted into journalism. He was one of the editors of *Le Spectateur* (1813-29), and in succession he founded and edited a number of periodicals, *L'Aurore* (1816-19), *Le Courrier du Bas-Canada* (1819), *La Bibliothèque canadienne* (1825-30)', *L'Observateur* (1831-32), *Le Magasin du Bas-Canada* (1832), and *L'Encyclopédie canadienne* (1842-43). In 1830 he published *Epîtres, satires, chansons, épigrammes et autres pièces de vers* (Montreal), the first volume of verse printed by a French Canadian. He published also a text-book on arithmetic (Montreal, 1816). But it is as one of the pioneers in Canadian historiography that he is best remembered. In 1820 he published the *Relation d'un voyage à la côte du nord-ouest de l'Amérique septentrionale, dans les années 1810-14, par G. Franchère* (Montreal). This volume, which is now very rare, was published also in an English translation; and in 1854 a second edition of the translation was brought out in New York by Franchère himself, though without acknowledgment of Bibaud's authorship. In 1837 there appeared in Montreal the first volume of his *Histoire du Canada* (2nd ed., revised and enlarged, 1843); in 1844 he published the second volume; and in 1878 his son, Dr. J. G. Bibaud, published the third volume. The work, which was the first account of Canadian history by a French Canadian, had many defects, and it has never been popular in French Canada, because of its Tory leanings; but it contains materials which might otherwise have been lost. Bibaud died in Montreal on August 3, 1857. He had four sons and one daughter. His portrait is in the Château de Ramezay, Montreal.

[L. W. Sicotte, *Michel Bibaud* (Can. Antiq. and Num. Jl. of Montreal, 3rd series, vol. v), reprinted in both English and French in pamphlet form (Montreal, 1908); Morgan, *Cel. Can.* and *Bib. can.*; Bibaud, *Panth. can.*; *Bull. rech. hist.*, 1906 and 1913 (bibliography).]

Bidwell, Barnabas (1763-1833), author, was born at Monterey, Mass., on August 23, 1763, and was educated at Yale College (B.A., 1785). He became attorney-general of Massachusetts; but in 1810 he was compelled to flee from the United States because of charges of malversation made against him as treasurer of Berkshire county, Massachusetts. He settled first in Bath, Upper Canada, where he became a school-teacher, and then in Kingston. In 1821 he was elected to represent Lennox and Addington in the Legislative Assembly of Upper Canada; but he was immediately expelled from the As-

sembly, and an Act was passed making him ineligible for election. He died in Kingston in 1833. Besides contributing to Gourlay's *Statistical account of Upper Canada* the historical and topographical sketches comprising the first half of the first volume, he was the author of *The prompter* (Kingston, 1821). While an undergraduate at Yale, he published a tragedy entitled *The mercenary match* (New Haven, Conn., 1784?).

[*Dict. Am. biog.*]

Bidwell, Marshall Spring (1799-1872), politician and lawyer, was born at Stockbridge, Massachusetts, in February, 1799, the only son of Barnabas Bidwell (q.v.). In 1810, Barnabas Bidwell came to Canada with his family to escape prosecution on a charge of misappropriation of public funds, and settled first at the village of Bath, Upper Canada, and then at Kingston. In 1821, he was elected to the Assembly of Upper Canada for Lennox and Addington, but his election was voided on the ground that he was an alien. Marshall Spring Bidwell, who had in 1821 been called to the bar of Upper Canada, was then elected in his father's stead; but he, too, was declared ineligible to sit. In 1824, however, the election law was changed; and in 1825 Marshall Spring Bidwell was re-elected for Lennox and Addington, and took his seat in the Assembly. He was a member of the Assembly from 1825 to 1836, and on two occasions (1829 and 1835) was elected its speaker. He was during these years regarded as the leader of the moderate wing of the Reform party in Upper Canada. He had no connection with the Rebellion of 1837; and indeed never identified himself with the proceedings of William Lyon Mackenzie (q.v.). He was, however, accused of complicity in the rebellion, and was advised by Sir Francis Bond Head (q.v.) to leave the province. Head had just been dismissed from office for declining to appoint Bidwell to the bench; and he was anxious to be able to advise the Colonial Office that Bidwell had fled the country. Bidwell, however, thinking that Head's advice proceeded from kindness, accepted it, and went to live in Albany, New York. Here he rose to a high place at the bar, and here he died on October 24, 1872. After his departure from Canada, his innocence of complicity in the Rebellion of 1837 was vindicated in two powerful letters to the *Upper Canada Herald*, May 8 and May 29, 1838, written by Egerton Ryerson (q.v.), the first signed "A United Empire Loyalist", the second signed with Ryerson's own name. It is said on fairly good authority that, at a later date, Sir John Macdonald (q.v.) endeavoured to persuade Bidwell to re-enter Canadian politics, but without success.

[*Dict. Am. biog.*; R. G. Riddell (ed.), *Canadian portraits* (Toronto, 1940); *In memoriam, M. S. Bidwell* (New York,

1872); E. F. DeLancey, *A memoir, historical and biographical* (New York, 1890; reprinted from the *Genealogical Record,* January, 1890);*Dict. Can. biog.*, vol. 10.]

Biencourt de Poutrincourt, Charles de (1591?-1623?), was the son of Jean de Biencourt de Poutrincourt (q.v.) and came with his father in May, 1606, on de Poutrincourt's second voyage to Acadia. On his father's return to France in 1611, he was left in command of Port Royal. In 1613 Port Royal was attacked and burnt by Argall, but Biencourt partially rebuilt it and remained in Acadia until 1621. He died about 1623.

[G. Patterson, *Last Years of Charles de Biencourt* (Trans. Roy. Soc. Can., 1895); F. Parkman, *Pioneers of France in the New World* (Boston, 1865); Le Jeune, *Dict. gén.*; *Dict. Can. biog.*, vol. 1.]

Biencourt de Poutrincourt, Jean de, Baron de St. Just (1557-1615), soldier and colonizer, was a native of Picardy. He fought in the ranks of the Catholics during the wars of the League, and later was attached to the service of Henry IV. In 1603 he was living in his barony of Saint-Just, in Champagne, when his former companion in arms, the Sieur de Monts (q.v.), asked him to join his expedition to colonize Acadia. They sailed from France in 1604, and Poutrincourt was given a grant of the lands about the Annapolis basin. In 1606 he accompanied Champlain in his exploration of the bay of Fundy. After the abandonment of the colony in 1607, he went to France, but he returned to Acadia in 1610. In 1613 Port Royal was destroyed, and Poutrincourt once again returned to France. Here the Jesuits had him thrown into prison, but he regained his liberty and visited Port Royal for the last time in 1614. He returned to France the same year, and he was fatally wounded in the attack on Méry in 1615.

[H. P. Biggar, *The death of Poutrincourt* (Can. hist. review, 1920); F. Parkman, *Pioneers of France in the New World* (Boston, 1865); M. Lescarbot, *Histoire de la Nouvelle France* (Paris, 1609); Le Jeune, *Dict. gén.*;*Dict. Can. biog.*, vol. 1.]

Bienville, Jean Baptiste Le Moyne, Sieur de (1680-1767), governor of Louisiana (1732-40), was born in February, 1680, the twelfth son of Charles Le Moyne, Sieur de Longueuil, and Catherine Thierry. He entered the navy and in 1697 accompanied his brother, Iberville (q.v.), in his expedition to Hudson Bay, and took part in the capture of Fort Nelson. He also accompanied Iberville to the Mississippi in 1698-99, and acted as lieutenant for the latter in his absence from the colony. In 1701 he became commandant and served in a variety of military positions until he became governor of Louisiana in 1732. In 1740 he asked to be relieved of his position, and in 1743 when the new governor, Vaudreuil, arrived, he returned to France, where he died in 1767.

[Grace King, *Jean Baptiste Le Moyne, Sieur de Bienville* (New York, 1892); *Dict. Am. biog.*; *Cyc. Am. biog.*; Le Jeune, *Dict. gén.*;*Dict. Can. biog.*, vol. 3.]

Big Bear (d. 1888), a chief of the Plains Cree, who took part in the North West Rebellion of 1885. His band were responsible for the massacre at Frog Lake and the capture of Fort Pitt. After the rebellion, he was captured near Fort Carlton, was tried, found guilty, and sentenced to two years in prison. Not long after his release, he died, in the beginning of 1888, near Battleford.

[W. B. Cameron, *The war trail of Big Bear* (Toronto, 1926).]

Biggar, Charles Robert Webster (1847-1909), lawyer and author, was born at Murray, Ontario, in 1847, the son of James Lyons Biggar. He was educated at the University of Toronto (B.A., 1869; M.A., 1873), and was called to the bar in 1873 (Q.C., 1890). He died at Toronto, Ontario, on October 16, 1909. In 1875, he married Jane Helen, eldest daughter of Sir Oliver Mowat (q.v.); and he wrote his father-in-law's biography, *Sir Oliver Mowat: A biographical sketch* (2 vols., Toronto, 1905).

[Morgan,*Can. men* (1898).]

Biggar, Emerson Bristol (1853-1921), journalist and author, was born at Winona, Ontario, on March 6, 1853. He became a journalist in 1873; and with the exception of the years 1875-80, when he was in South Africa, he was connected with journalism in Canada, in one way or another, until his death at Toronto on May 31, 1921. He was the author of an *Anecdotal life of Sir John Macdonald* (Montreal, 1891), *Reciprocity: The trade treaty of 1854-66* (Toronto, 1911), *The Canadian railway problem* (Toronto, 1917), and *Hydro-electric development in Ontario* (Toronto, 1920).

[Morgan, *Can. men* (1912); *Who's who among North American authors,* 1921; *Can. who was who,* vol. 1.]

Biggar, Henry Percival (1872-1938), historian and archivist, was born at the Carrying Place, Ontario, on August 9, 1872, the son of James Lyons Biggar and Isabel Hodgins. He was educated at the University of Toronto (B.A., 1894) and at Oxford University (B.Litt., 1899; D.Litt., 1927). He entered the service of the Public Archives of Canada, and from 1905 to his death he was the chief archivist for Canada in Europe. He died at Worplesdon, Surrey, England, on July 25, 1938. He was the author of a treatise on *The early trading companies of New France* (Toronto, 1901), of which only 300 copies survived destruction by fire; and he edited *The precursors of Jacques Cartier* (Ottawa, 1911), *The works of Samuel de Champlain* (6 vols., Toronto, The Champlain Society, 1922-36), *The voyages of Jacques Cartier* (Ottawa, 1924), and *A collection of documents relating to Jacques Cartier and the Sieur de Roberval* (Ottawa, 1930). In 1924 he was made an LL.D. of Queen's University, Kingston.

[*Can. who's who*, 1936-37.]

Bigot, François (*fl.* 1703-1777?), intendant of New France (1748-59), was the son of Louis-Amable Bigot, and was born on January 30, 1703, at Bordeaux, France. He became a lawyer and entered the civil service. On September 9, 1739, he arrived at Louisbourg, where he had been appointed commissary; and it is probable that his malversation of the funds intended for its fortification caused the downfall of Louisbourg in 1744. He returned to France in 1745, and his influence at court obtained for him the appointment of intendant of New France. He arrived in Quebec on August 26, 1748. His official position made him here almost superior to the governor in power, and he was able to carry on the most astounding frauds. Under the name of Claverie, he established huge stores at Quebec and Montreal, where he sold goods at retail to the public at enormous profits. Rich furs belonging to the Crown were disposed of at low prices to his friends; and, in league with Cadet, the commissary general, he sold provisions to the government at profits exceeding one hundred per cent. At the same time supplies intended for the various military posts were retained, and false receipts given; and a great part of the supplies granted for the use of the Indians never reached them, being stolen on the way. In 1755 Bigot made a journey to France, and having assured himself that he would remain unmolested in that quarter, proceeded to plunder the people by buying up large quantities of flour, which he sold back at an immense advance. He issued an ordinance to compel farmers to sell their grain at a low price, and not only took it by force, but threatened them with imprisonment if they complained. This corrupt administration brought the colony to financial ruin, and paved the way for the conquest. In 1759 Bigot returned to France, where he was arrested and thrown into the Bastille for eleven months. On his release, he was compelled to make restitution, and was banished from the kingdom. The date of his death is not known; but probably took place in 1777.

[R. Roy, *Intendants de la Nouvelle-France* (Trans. Roy. Soc. Can., 1903); R. Bellemare, *Les malversations de l'intendant Bigot* (Bull. rech. hist., vol. iv); E. Z Massicotte, *L'intendant Bigot* (Bull. rech. hist., vol. ii); Le Jeune, *Dict. gén.*; H. M.

Thomas, *The mechanics of Bigot's system* (Trans. Roy. Soc. Can., 1938); *Mémoire pour Messire François Bigot* (Paris, 1763); G. Frégault, *François Bigot* (Montreal, 1948). Some documents relating to Bigot are printed in the *Can. Arch. report*, 1904, and in A. Shortt (ed.), *Documents relating to Canadian currency, exchange, and finance during the French period* (2 vols., Ottawa, 1925).]

Bilkey, Paul Ernest (1878-1962), journalist, was born in St. George, Bermuda, on January 26, 1878, and he was educated in schools in Toronto and Bowmanville. He joined the *Evening Star* in Toronto in 1896, became parliamentary correspondent for the Toronto *Telegram* in 1900, and for the Toronto *Mail and Empire* from 1912 to 1917 when he joined the Montreal *Gazette* as vice-president and editor-in-chief; he remained in these positions until his retirement. He was author of *Persons, papers and things* (Toronto, 1940). He died at Montreal on April 20, 1962.

[*Can. who's who*, 1955-57; R. E. Watters, *A check list of Can. literature*.]

Bill, Ingraham E. (1805-1891), clergyman and author, was born at Billtown, Kings county, Nova Scotia, in 1805, and was ordained a Baptist minister in 1829. He held pastorates at Nictaux, Nova Scotia, and Fredericton and Saint John, New Brunswick; and he died at St. Martins, New Brunswick, in 1891. In 1881 he was made a D.D. of Acadia University. He was the author of *Fifty years with the Baptists of the maritime provinces* (Saint John, N.B., 1880), and of several published sermons.

[W. G. MacFarlane, *New Brunswick bibliography* (Saint John, N.B., 1895).]

Billings, Elkanah (1820-1876), palaeontologist, was born in the township of Gloucester, Upper Canada, on May 5, 1820. He was educated at the St. Lawrence Academy, Potsdam, New York, and in 1843 he was called to the bar of Upper Canada. He practised law in Bytown (Ottawa) and in Renfrew; but his chief interest was in biology and natural history, and in 1856 he was appointed palaeontologist to the Geological Survey of Canada. Early in the same year he issued the first number of the *Canadian Naturalist*; and for the rest of his life he was a voluminous contributor to Canadian scientific literature. He died in 1876.

[H. M. Ami, *Brief biographical sketch of Elkanah Billings* (American geologist, 1901), with portrait and bibliography; B. E. Walker, *List of the published writings of Elkanah Billings* (Canadian record of science, July, 1901); Morgan, *Cel. Can. and Bib. can.*; *Dict. Can. biog.*, vol. 10.]

Binney, Hibbert (1819-1887), Anglican bishop of Nova Scotia (1851-87), was born at Sydney, Cape Breton, on August 12, 1819, the son of the Rev. Hibbert Binney, rector of Sydney. Educated at King's College, London, and Worcester College, Oxford (B.A., 1842; M.A., 1844; D.D., 1851), he became a fellow and tutor of Worcester College. In 1843 he was ordained a priest of the Church of England, and in 1851 he was appointed by the Crown bishop of Nova Scotia, at the age of 31 years. For more than 36 years he had oversight of the diocese of Nova Scotia, and he died in New York on April 30, 1887. In 1854 he married Mary, the daughter of the Hon. William Blowers Bliss (q.v.), Halifax; by her he had two sons and three daughters.

[Rose, *Cyc. Can. biog.* (1888); Dent, *Can. port.*, vol. 3; C. H. Mockridge, *The bishops of the Church of England in Canada* (Toronto, 1896).]

Birch, Sir Arthur (1837-1914), administrator, was born in England in 1837, the son of the Rev. W. H. R. Birch, rector of Reydon and Bedfield. He entered the Colonial Office in 1855, and he was successively private secretary to Sir E. B. Lytton, the Duke of Newcastle, and Chichester Fortescue. In 1864 he was appointed colonial secretary of British Columbia, and in 1866 he was sent out to this colony as acting governor. His term of office lasted from August, 1865, to November, 1866. He then returned to the Colonial Office, and became successively lieutenant-governor of Penang (1871-72), colonial secretary of Ceylon (1873-76), and lieutenant-governor of Ceylon (1876-78). In 1886 he was created a K.C.M.G., and he died in London on October 31, 1914.

[*Who was who*, 1897-1916.]

Birchall, Reginald (d. 1890), murderer, was born in England, the son of the Rev. Joseph Birchall, rector of Church Kirk, Lancashire. In 1885 he became a gentleman commoner of Lincoln College, Oxford; but he left Oxford without taking a degree. In 1888 he eloped with the daughter of David Stevenson, the general traffic superintendent of the London and North Western Railway. With his wife, he emigrated to Canada, and he spent part of 1889 in Woodstock, Ontario, posing as "Lord Somerset". Toward the end of 1889 he returned with his wife to England, and lured two young Englishmen, F. C. Benwell and Douglas Pelly, into a scheme whereby they were to pay for the privilege of entering into a partnership with him for farming in Canada. He and his wife sailed for Canada early in 1890, with Benwell and Pelly; and on February 17, 1890, Birchall murdered Benwell in a swamp near Woodstock, Ontario. He was arrested a few days later, was tried and found guilty, and was hanged at Woodstock on November 14, 1890. The case created a sensation, not only in Canada, but also in England.

[J. W. Murray, *Memoirs of a great detective* (London, 1905); W. S. Wallace, *Murders and mysteries* (Toronto, 1931).]

Bird, James (1773?-1856), fur-trader, was born at Acton, Middlesex, England, about 1773; and entered the service of the Hudson's Bay Company in 1788. He became "a master and trader inland", and was appointed a chief factor on the union of the Hudson's Bay and North West Companies in 1821. He retired to the Red River Settlement in 1824; and he died there on October 18, 1856.

[E. E. Rich (ed.), *Journal of occurrences in the Athabasca department by George Simpson* (Toronto: The Champlain Society, 1938).]

Bishop, William Avery (1894-1956), airman and author, was born at Owen Sound, Ontario, on February 8, 1894, and died at Palm Beach, Florida, on September 11, 1956. He was educated at the Royal Military College, Kingston, and went overseas in the First World War with the Canadian cavalry. In 1915 he transferred to the Royal Flying Corps, and after a period of training went to France in 1917. He proved to be one of the most successful "fighting airmen" in the Allied forces; and was awarded, in rapid succession, the V.C., the D.S.O. and bar, and the D.F.C. He shot down a total of seventy-two enemy aircraft. In August, 1918, he was appointed to the staff of the British Air Ministry, and he had a hand in forming the Royal Canadian Air Force as a separate brigade. In 1936 he was promoted to be honorary air vice-marshal of the R.C.A.F., and during the Second World War he became honorary air-marshal. In 1919 he was one of the first to enter the field of commercial aviation. He was the author of *Winged warfare* (New York, 1918) and *Winged peace* (Toronto, 1944), and, joint author, with Major R. Stuart-Wortley, of *The flying squad* (London, 1928). In 1917 he married Margaret Burden, a grand-daughter of Timothy Eaton (q.v.), and by her he had one son and one daughter.

[William Arthur Bishop, *The courage of the early morning: The story of Billy Bishop* (Toronto, 1965); G. A. Drew, *Canada's fighting airmen* (Toronto, 1930); *Can. who's who*, 1952-54; *Encyc. Can.*]

Bisshopp, Cecil (1783-1813), soldier, was born in Spring Gardens, London, England, on June 23, 1783, the son of Sir Cecil Bisshopp, Bart., afterwards Baron de la Zouche. He obtained a commission in the First Foot Guards in 1799, and after serving in Flanders, Portugal, and Spain during the Napoleonic wars, was sent to Canada in 1812, with the rank of lieutenant-colonel. He took part in the campaigns in the Niagara

Peninsula in 1812 and 1813; he was mortally wounded at Black Rock on July 11, 1813, died on July 16, and was buried in the village of Stamford, Upper Canada.

[L. H. Irving, *Officers of the British forces in Canada during the war of 1812-15* (Welland, Ont., 1908).]

Bissot, François (1613?-1673), merchant, was born about 1613 at Pont-Audemer, Normandy, the son of Jean Bissot and Marie Assour, and came to Canada about 1639. He established himself at Pointe Lévy, on the St. Lawrence River, and there he founded the first tannery in Canada. He engaged also in the culture of the soil and in the Labrador fisheries; and he amassed a considerable fortune. On October 25, 1648, he married Marie, fifth daughter of Guillaume Couillard and Guillemette Hébert; by her he had five sons and seven daughters, most of whom intermarried with the upper classes of the colony. Bissot died at Quebec, on July 26, 1673.

[J. E. Roy, *François Bissot* (Trans. Roy. Soc. Can., 1892); P. G. Roy, *Fils de Québec*, vol. 1 (Lévis, Que., 1933); *Dict. Can. biog.*, vol. 1.]

Black, Davidson (1884-1934), anthropologist, was born in Toronto, Canada, on July 25, 1884, the son of Davidson Black, Q.C. He was educated at the University of Toronto (M.D., 1906; hon. D.Sc., 1932); and from 1909 to 1916 he was on the staff of the Western Reserve University, Cleveland, Ohio. In 1918 he was appointed professor of neurology, and in 1921 professor of anatomy, on the staff of the Peking Medical Union College; and he achieved there international fame as the discoverer of the "Peking man", a primitive type of man resembling the anthropoid ape. In 1931 he was made an honorary fellow of the Royal Anthropological Institute; and in 1932 a fellow of the Royal Society. He died at Peiping, China, on March 15, 1934. His only publications were papers on physical anthropology and human palaeontology in scientific journals and the transactions of learned societies.

[Dora Hood, *Davidson Black: A biography* (Toronto, 1964); *Univ. of Toronto monthly*, 1934.]

Black, Mrs. George. See **Black, Mrs. Martha Louise,** *née* **Munger**.

Black, John (*fl.* 1784-1819), member of the Legislative Assembly of Lower Canada (1796-1800), was born in Scotland, came to Canada about 1784, and set up at Quebec as a ship-builder. In 1796 he was elected to represent Quebec in the Lower Canadian legislature; and in 1797 he was instrumental in bringing about the arrest of David McLane, a revolutionary agent. In 1800 he retired from the legislature, and in 1802 he failed in business. He then devoted himself to trying to obtain from the British government a recompense for his services, but without success; and some time after 1819 he died in Scotland. In 1806 he presented to the Duke of Kent a memoir on the government of Canada which has been printed in A. G. Doughty and D. McArthur, *Documents relating to the constitutional history of Canada, 1791-1818* (Ottawa, 1918), pp. 327-8.

[Abbé I. Caron, *John Black* (Bull. rech. hist., 1921).]

Black, John (1817-1879), recorder of Rupert's Land (1862-70), was born in Scotland in 1817. He went to the Red River Settlement with Adam Thom (q.v.) in 1839, and eventually entered the service of the Hudson's Bay Company. He rose to the position of a chief trader; but in 1852 he resigned, and the following ten years he spent in Scotland and Australia. In 1862, however, on his return from Australia to Scotland, he was appointed recorder of Rupert's Land, and this position he occupied until the creation of Manitoba as a province in 1870. In 1870 he was a member of the delegation sent by the Red River settlers to Ottawa. He did not return to the west, and he died at St. Andrew's, Scotland, on February 3, 1879.

[*Don. ann. reg.*, 1799; E. H. Oliver, *The Canadian north-west*, vol. 1 (Ottawa, 1914); *Dict. Can. biog.*, vol. 10.]

Black, John (1818-1882), Presbyterian clergyman, was born at Dumfries, Scotland, on January 8, 1818. He was educated at Delaware Academy, Delhi, New York, and at Knox College, Toronto; and was ordained a minister of the Presbyterian Church in 1851. The same year he went as a missionary to the Red River Settlement, and he was the only Presbyterian clergyman there until 1862. He died at Kildonan, Manitoba, on February 11, 1882. The degree of D.D. was conferred on him by Queen's University, Kingston.

[G. Bryce, *John Black, the apostle of the Red River* (Toronto, 1898); Olive Elsie Knox, *John Black of old Kildonan* (Toronto, 1958); *Dom. ann. reg.*, 1882.]

Black, Mrs. Martha Louise, *née* **Munger** (1866-1957), author of a notable autobiography, was born in Chicago, Illinois, on February 24, 1866, and died at Whitehorse, Yukon Territory, on October 31, 1957. She was educated at St. Mary's College, Notre Dame, Indiana, and in 1887 married William Purdy, by whom she had three children. She and her husband separated in 1898, and she went with her children to the Yukon. Here she obtained a divorce from her husband, and later married George Black, who became commissioner of the Yukon in 1912, represented the Yukon in the Canadian House of

Commons from 1921 to 1935 and from 1940 to 1949, and was speaker of the House from 1930 to 1935. When ill-health compelled him to interrupt his political career in 1935, his wife was elected to represent the Yukon in the House of Commons, and was then the second woman to sit in the House, the first having been Agnes Macphail (q.v.). Her autobiography, "as told to Elizabeth Bailey Price", was published under the title *My seventy years* (London, 1938); she was the author also of *Yukon flowers* (Toronto, 1936).

[*Can. who's who*, 1956-58;*Encyc. Can.*]

Black, Samuel (d. 1841), fur-trader, was a native of Aberdeen, Scotland, and must have been born about 1785. He came to Canada in 1802 as a clerk in the XY Company, at the instance of Edward Ellice (q.v.); and in 1804 he was absorbed by the North West Company. In the struggle between the North West Company and the Hudson's Bay Company under Lord Selkirk (q.v.), he took such an active part that, at the time of the union of 1821, he was deliberately excluded from employment by the Hudson's Bay Company. In 1823, however, Governor Simpson (q.v.) relented, and he was given a commission as chief trader. In 1824 he was employed in exploring the Finlay River. He was then transferred to the Columbia, where he was in charge, first, of Fort Walla Walla, and second, of Kamloops. He was promoted to be chief factor in 1837; and his career was cut short when he was murdered by an Indian on January 8, 1841, at a place near the mouth of the Columbia.

[J. N. Wallace, *The explorer of Finlay River* (Can. hist. rev., 1928); E. E. Rich (ed.), *Journal of occurrences in the Athabasca department by George Simpson* (Toronto, 1938).]

Black, William (1760-1834), "the father of Methodism in Nova Scotia", was born in Huddersfield, West Yorkshire, England, in 1760. He came to Nova Scotia with his parents in 1775, and at the age of twenty years became a Methodist preacher. He was the founder of the Wesleyan Methodist Church in Nova Scotia, and ultimately became general superintendent of the British American Wesleyan missions. He died at Halifax, Nova Scotia, on September 8, 1834.

[M. Richey, *Memoir of the late Rev. William Black* (Halifax, N.S., 1839); R. J. Long, *Nova Scotia authors* (East Orange, N.J., 1918).]

Black, William (1770-1866), president and administrator of the government of New Brunswick (1829-31), was born at Aberdeen, Scotland, in 1770; and was a member of the Legislative Council of New Brunswick from 1819 to his death at Fredericton in 1866. From 1844 to 1866 he was president of the

Legislative Council, and from 1829 to 1831 he administered the government of New Brunswick, with the title of president and commander-in-chief. He was thrice mayor of Saint John, N.B., in 1828, in 1832, and in 1840. He married one of the daughters of Lieut.-Col. the Hon. Christopher Billop, a member of the executive council of New Brunswick.

[J. W. Lawrence, *The judges of New Brunswick* (Saint John, N.B., 1907).]

Black, William Anderson (1847-1934), minister of railways for Canada (1926), was born in Windsor, Nova Scotia, in 1847, the son of Samuel G. Black, and the grandson of the Rev. William Black (q.v.), the founder of Methodism in the Maritime provinces. He was educated at Mount Allison Academy and at King's College, Windsor; and he entered business as a ship chandler. He became the head of a shipping firm which did an extensive business with the West Indies, and did much to develop the West Indian trade. He represented Halifax in the Canadian House of Commons from 1923 to his death at Halifax, Nova Scotia, on September 2, 1934; and he was minister of railways and canals in the short-lived Meighen administration of 1926. In 1875 he married Annie, daughter of Joseph Bell, Halifax; and by her he had one son and two daughters.

[*Can. parl. comp.*]

Blackadder, Edward (1869-1922), physician and poet, was born at Wolfville, Nova Scotia, on April 18, 1869; and died at Bedford, Nova Scotia, on October 22, 1922. He was the author of *Fancies of boyhood: Poems original and translated* (Halifax, N.S., 1890) and *Poems: Sonnets, lyrics, and miscellaneous* (Halifax, N.S., 1895).

[R. J. Long, *Nova Scotia authors* (East Orange, N.J., 1918).]

Blackburn, Victoria Grace (d. 1928), journalist, was born in Quebec, Que., the fifth daughter of Josiah Blackburn, who was for forty years editor and proprietor of the London *Free Press*. Throughout life she was a constant contributor to the *Free Press*, and became widely known under her pseudonym of "Fanfan". She died in London, Ontario, on March 4, 1928. She left behind her in manuscript a novel which was published under the title, *The man child* (Ottawa, 1930).

[*Can. who was who*, vol. 2.]

Blackmore, John Horne (1890-1971), politician, was born in Sublett, Idaho, on March 27, 1890, of Mormon parents who moved to Alberta in 1892. He was educated at the University of Alberta (B.A., 1913), and the Calgary Normal School. He taught at Raymond, Alberta, for many years and in 1916-17 was a member of the Raymond

School Board. He was elected a member of parliament for Lethbridge in 1935 and became leader of the seventeen-member Social Credit group in the House of Commons. He was re-elected in 1940, 1945, 1949, 1953, and 1957, but was defeated in the 1958 general election and retired. He died at Cardston, Alberta, May 2, 1971.

[*Can. who's who*, 1955-57, and 1967-69.]

Blackstock, George Tate (1857-1921), lawyer, was born at Newcastle, Ontario, in 1857, the son of the Rev. W. S. Blackstock. He was educated at Upper Canada College, and was called to the bar in 1879 (Q.C., 1889). He defended Reginald Birchall (q.v.) in 1890; and he was frequently employed as a Crown prosecutor, notably in the Kinrade case of 1909. He died at Toronto on December 27, 1921. In 1880 he married Emeline Moulton, daughter of James Fraser, Inverness, Scotland; but she divorced him in 1896.

[Morgan, *Can. men* (1912).]

Blackstone, Henry (1763-1825), sheriff of the district of Three Rivers, was born in England in 1763, the son of Sir William Blackstone, the famous commentator on the laws of England. He was educated at Queen's College, Oxford (B.A., 1783); but was apparently a source of trouble to his family, for in 1799 he was shipped out to Canada. Here he was, first, comptroller of customs at St. Johns, Lower Canada, then sheriff of Three Rivers, and finally coroner at Quebec. He died at Quebec on February 2, 1825.

[G. Malchelosse, *Les Blackstone* (Cahiers des dix, 1936).]

Blackwood, Frederick Temple. See **Dufferin and Ava, Marquess of.**

Blair, Adam Johnston Fergusson (1815-1867), lawyer and statesman, was born in Perthshire, Scotland, on November 4, 1815, the son of Adam Fergusson (q.v.) and Jemima Johnston Blair. He was educated at Edinburgh, came to Canada with his parents in 1833, and settled near Hamilton, Upper Canada. He was called to the bar of Upper Canada in 1839 (Q.C., 1867). From 1849 to 1854 he was a member of the Legislative Assembly of Canada for Waterloo, and from 1854 to 1857 for Wellington South. From 1860 to 1867 he was an elected member of the Legislative Council of Canada for the "Brock" division; and in 1867 he was called to the Senate of Canada. In 1863 he was appointed receiver-general in the Macdonald-Sicotte administration; and on the reconstruction of the government, later in the same year, he became provincial secretary. On the defeat of the Macdonald-Dorion government in 1864, he was invited to form a moderate or coalition administration, but failed. In 1866 he replaced George Brown

(q.v.) as president of the Council in the coalition government of Sir Narcisse Belleau (q.v.); and he was president of the Privy Council in the first Dominion government of Sir John Macdonald (q.v.), until his death on December 30, 1867. In 1862, on his coming into the possession of a Scottish estate, he assumed the name of Blair. He was not married.

[Taylor, *Brit. Am.*, vol. 2; *Cyc. Am. biog.*; *Can. parl. comp.*, 1864; F. Driscoll, *Sketch of the Canadian ministry* (Montreal, 1866).]

Blair, Andrew George (1844-1907), prime minister of New Brunswick (1883-96) and minister of railways and canals for Canada (1896-1903), was born in Fredericton, New Brunswick, on March 7, 1844. He was educated at the Collegiate School, Fredericton, and was called to the bar of New Brunswick in 1866 (Q.C., 1891). In 1878 he was elected to the Legislative Assembly of New Brunswick for York county, and he represented this constituency continuously until 1896. In 1879 he was elected leader of the Liberal opposition in the Assembly, and in 1883, on the defeat of the Hanington ministry, he became prime minister of New Brunswick. His government was sustained in the elections of 1886, 1890, and 1894; but in 1896 he resigned as prime minister of New Brunswick in order to accept the portfolio of railways and canals in the Laurier administration at Ottawa, and was elected to the Canadian House of Commons for Queen's-Sunbury. In 1903 he resigned from the cabinet as a result of a disagreement with the policy of Sir Wilfrid Laurier (q.v.) in regard to the building of the Grand Trunk Pacific Railway; and in 1904 he accepted appointment as chairman of the board of railway commissioners for Canada. He died at Fredericton on January 25, 1907. In 1866 he married Annie, eldest daughter of George Thompson, of Fredericton; and by her he had ten children.

[T. G. Marquis, *Hon. Andrew G. Blair* (Can. mag., 1904); *Can. who was who*, vol. 1; Morgan, *Can. men* (1898); Rose, *Cyc. Can. biog.* (1888); Taché, *Men of the day*; J. Hannay, *The premiers of New Brunswick since Confederation* (Can. mag., 1907); O. D. Skelton, *The life and letters of Sir Wilfrid Laurier* (2 vols., Toronto, 1921).]

Blake, Edward (1833-1912), lawyer and statesman, was born in the township of Adelaide, county of Middlesex, Upper Canada, on October 13, 1833, the eldest son of William Hume Blake (q.v.). He was educated at Upper Canada College and at the University of Toronto (B.A., 1854; M.A., 1858; LL.D., 1889), and was called to the bar of Upper Canada in 1856 (Q.C., 1864). He became one of the leading equity lawyers of

Upper Canada, and after Confederation was regarded as one of the foremost authorities on the Canadian constitution, his services being in great demand as counsel before the Judicial Committee of the Privy Council. In 1879 he was elected treasurer of the Law Society of Upper Canada; and he repeatedly declined appointment to high positions on the bench.

His political career began in 1867, when he was elected as a Liberal to the Canadian House of Commons for West Durham, and to the Legislative Assembly of Ontario for South Bruce. In 1869 he became leader of the Liberal opposition in Ontario; and in 1871, on the defeat of the government of Sandfield Macdonald (q.v.), he became prime minister of Ontario. In 1872, however, on the abolition of dual representation, he elected to sit in the House of Commons, and resigned as prime minister of Ontario. He became a minister without portfolio in the administration of Alexander Mackenzie (q.v.) in 1873; but gave the ministry at first a wavering support. After holding office for three months, he resigned, and in his famous "Aurora speech" of 1874 he aligned himself with the new "Canada First" or nationalist party. In 1875, however, he returned to the fold, and became minister of justice in the Mackenzie government. This office he retained for two years; and in this time he effected a number of important constitutional changes, notably a change in the royal instructions to the governor-general in regard to the reservation of bills. In 1877 he resigned as minister of justice and became president of the council; but he took no part in the general elections of 1878, and virtually withdrew from the government.

From 1879 to 1887 he was the successor of Alexander Mackenzie as leader of the Liberal party in the Dominion; but he did not prove an unqualified success as a politician in opposition, and led his party to defeat in the elections in 1882. In 1890 he declined nomination to parliament; and thereafter he withdrew completely from Canadian politics. In 1892 he was returned as an Irish nationalist to the British House of Commons for South Longford; but he scarcely achieved the position at Westminster which had been expected of him. He died at Toronto, Canada, on March 1, 1912.

In 1858 he married Margaret, daughter of the Rt. Rev. Benjamin Cronyn, bishop of Huron, and by her he had several children. From 1873 to 1900 he was chancellor of the University of Toronto. A number of his speeches have been published in pamphlet form. His papers are in the University of Toronto library.

[*Dict. nat. biog.*, supp. III; *Who was who*, 1897-1916; Morgan, *Can. men* (1912); Dent, *Can. port.*, vol. I; Rose, *Cyc. Can. biog.* (1886); W. S. Wallace, *The mystery of*

Edward Blake (Can. mag., 1912); J. Loudon, *Edward Blake* (Univ. of Toronto monthly, 1912); Margaret A. Banks, *Edward Blake, Irish nationalist* (Toronto, 1957); Joseph Schull, *Edward Blake: The man of the other way (1833-1881)* (Toronto, 1975); Joseph Schull, *Edward Blake: Leader and exile (1881-1912)* (Toronto, 1976).]

Blake, Samuel Hume (1835-1914), judge and lawyer, was born in Toronto, Upper Canada, on August 31, 1835, the second son of William Hume Blake (q.v.). He was educated at Upper Canada College and at the University of Toronto (B.A., 1858), and was called to the bar of Upper Canada in 1860 (Q.C., 1872). He was appointed vice-chancellor of Ontario in 1872, but resigned from the bench in 1881 to resume his legal practice. He was long one of the leaders of the Ontario bar; but he was equally notable as a religious controversialist. He was one of the champions of evangelical doctrines in the Church of England in Canada; he wrote many pamphlets on religious questions; and he was one of the founders of Wycliffe College, Toronto. He died in Toronto on June 23, 1914. He was twice married, (1) in 1859 to Rebecca, third daughter of the Rt. Rev. Benjamin Cronyn, bishop of Huron, by whom he had one son; and (2) in 1909 to Miss Baird, of Toronto.

[H. J. Cody, *Samuel Hume Blake* (Univ. of Toronto monthly, 1914); *Can. who was who*, vol. 1; Dent, *Can. port.*, vol. 3; Morgan, *Can. men* (1912).]

Blake, William Hume (1809-1870), chancellor of Upper Canada (1849-62), was born at Kiltegan, county Wicklow, Ireland, on March 10, 1809, the second son of the Rev. Dominick Edward Blake, and Anne Margaret Hume. He was educated at Trinity College, Dublin (B.A., 1830), and came to Canada in 1832. He settled first in the township of Adelaide, Middlesex county, Upper Canada, and took out a grant of land. But he found farming distasteful, and removed to York about 1835, to engage in the study of law. He was called to the bar of Upper Canada in 1838, and soon became one of the foremost counsel in the province. In 1847 he was elected as a Liberal to the Legislative Assembly of Canada for East York, and in 1848 he became solicitor-general for Upper Canada in the second Baldwin-Lafontaine administration. On the reorganization of the court of Chancery in 1849, however, he was appointed chancellor of Upper Canada; and this post he retained until failing health compelled his resignation in 1862. In 1864 he accepted a judgeship in the Court of Appeals; and he died at Toronto on November 17, 1870. In 1832 he married his first cousin, Catharine Hume; and by her he had two sons. From 1853 to 1856 he was chancellor of the University of Toronto.

[D. B. Read, *Lives of the judges* (Toronto, 1880); N. F. Davin, *The Irishman in Canada* (Toronto, 1877); Dent, *Can. port.*, vol. 3.]

Blake, William Hume (1861-1924), lawyer and author, was born in Toronto on November 2, 1861, the son of Samuel Hume Blake (q.v.) and Rebecca Cronyn. He was educated at the University of Toronto (B.A., 1882), and was called to the Ontario bar in 1885 (K.C., 1902). He was the author of *Brown waters* (Toronto, 1915) and *A fisherman's creed* (Toronto, 1923), as well as of a highly successful translation of Louis Hémon's *Maria Chapdelaine* (Toronto, 1921). He died at Victoria, British Columbia, on February 5, 1924. In 1889 he married Alice Jean, second daughter of David Law, of Montreal.

[F. C. Wade, *William Hume Blake* (Univ. of Toronto monthly, 1924); *Can. who was who*, vol. 2; Morgan, *Can. men* (1912).]

Blanchard, Hiram (1820-1874), prime minister of Nova Scotia (1867), was born in West River, Nova Scotia, in 1820, the brother of Jotham Blanchard (q.v.). He was educated at the Pictou Academy, and was called to the bar of Nova Scotia in 1843. In 1857 he was elected to represent Inverness in the House of Assembly as a Liberal; and in 1864 he supported Confederation. In 1867 he was chosen to form the first administration of Nova Scotia under Confederation; but, although elected for Inverness in the general elections of 1867, he was later unseated, and in November, 1867, he resigned from office. He was again elected to represent Inverness in 1871; and he was leader of the opposition in the Assembly of Nova Scotia until his death at Halifax, Nova Scotia, on December 17, 1874.

[J. W. Longley, *Premiers of Nova Scotia since 1867* (Can. mag., 1897); *Can. parl. comp.*; *Bull. rech. hist.*, 1934; *Dict. Can. biog.*, vol. 10.]

Blanchard, Jotham (1800-1840), journalist, was born at Peterboro', New Hampshire, on March 15, 1800, the eldest son of Jonathan Blanchard. His parents moved to Truro, Nova Scotia, in 1801; and he was educated at the Pictou Academy. He was admitted to the bar of Nova Scotia in 1821; and in 1827 he helped to establish, and edited anonymously, the *Colonial Patriot*, the first paper published in Nova Scotia outside Halifax. The radical views expressed in this paper had a wide influence, and in particular they helped to mould the politics of Joseph Howe (q.v.). In 1830 Blanchard was elected to represent the county of Halifax in the House of Assembly; but in 1836 his health began to fail, and in 1838 his mind gave way. He died in Nova Scotia in 1840.

[Morgan, *Bib. can.*]

Blanchet, François Norbert (1795-1883), Roman Catholic archbishop of Oregon, was born at St. Pierre, Rivière-du-Sud, Lower Canada, on September 3, 1795. He was ordained a priest in 1819, and in 1838 he went to British Columbia as a missionary. In 1845 he was consecrated bishop of Oregon, and in 1850 archbishop. He died on June 18, 1883. He was the author of an anonymous pamphlet entitled *Historical studies of the Catholic Church in Oregon* (Portland, Ore., 1878), reprinted from the *Catholic Sentinel* of Oregon.

[*Dict. Am. biog.*; Allaire, *Dict. biog.*; Sister Letitia Mary Lyons, *Francis Norbert Blanchet and the founding of the Oregon missions* (Washington, D.C., 1940).]

Blanchet, François Xavier (1776-1830), physician and politician, was born at St. Pierre, Rivière-du-Sud, Lower Canada, on April 3, 1776, the son of a farmer. He was educated at the Quebec Seminary, and he studied medicine in New York. He practised medicine in Quebec; and from 1809 to 1816 he represented Hertford in the Legislative Assembly of Lower Canada. In 1806 he was one of the founders of *Le Canadien*; and in 1810 he was arrested and imprisoned by Sir J. Craig (q.v.), but was released on promise of good behaviour. In 1820 he revived *Le Canadien*. He died at Quebec on June 24, 1830. In 1802 he married Catherine-Henriette Juchereau Duchesnay; and by her he had three daughters and one son. He published *Recherches sur la médecine* (New York, 1800) and *Appel au gouvernement impérial* (pamphlet, Quebec, 1824).

[P. G. Roy, *La famille Juchereau Duchesnay* (Lévis, 1903); *François Blanchet* (Bull. rech. hist., 1904).]

Blanchet, Joseph Goderic (1829-1890), speaker of the Canadian House of Commons (1879-82), was born at St. Pierre, Rivière-du-Sud, Lower Canada, on June 7, 1829, the son of Louis Blanchet and Marguerite Fontaine. He was educated at the Quebec Seminary and at the College of Ste. Anne, and was admitted to practise as a physician in 1850. In 1852 he began to practise medicine at Lévis, Lower Canada; and from 1855 to 1861 he was mayor of Lévis. He represented Lévis in the Legislative Assembly of Canada from 1861 to 1867, in the Legislative Assembly of Quebec from 1867 to 1875, and in the Canadian House of Commons from 1867 to 1874. From 1875 to 1878 he represented Bellechasse in the House of Commons; and from 1878 to 1883 he again represented Lévis. From 1867 to 1875 he was speaker of the Quebec Assembly; and from 1879 to 1882 he was speaker of the House of Commons. He retired from political life in 1883, on his appointment as collector of customs at the port of Quebec; and he died at Quebec on January 2, 1890. In 1850 he married Emilie, daughter of G. D. Balzaretti, of Milan, Italy; and by her he had six children.

[A. Béchard, *L'Hon. J. G. Blanchet* (Quebec, 1884); Rose, *Cyc. Can. biog.* (1888); Dent, *Can. port.*, vol. 4; *Can. biog. dict.*, Quebec vol. (Chicago, 1881); *Cyc. Am. biog.*; *Can. parl. comp.*]

Bland, Salem Goldworth (1859-1950), clergyman and author, was born in Lachute, Quebec, on August 25, 1859, and died at Toronto, Ontario, on February 7, 1950. He was educated at McGill University (B.A., 1877), and was ordained a minister of the Methodist Church in 1884. He was stationed at various places in Ontario and Quebec, and became a minister of the United Church of Canada in 1925. In 1927 he became a special writer on the Toronto *Daily Star*; and he was the author of *The new Christianity* (Toronto, 1920) and *James Henderson* (Toronto, 1927). His portrait, painted by Lawren Harris, hangs in the Toronto Art Gallery.

[*Can. who's who*, 1948.]

Blanshard, Richard (1817?-1894), governor of Vancouver Island (1849-51), was born in England about 1817, the eldest son of T. Henry Blanshard, of Kirby, Essex. He was educated at Queen's College, Cambridge (B.A., 1840), and was called to the bar at Lincoln's Inn in 1845. In 1849 he was appointed governor of Vancouver Island, and he arrived in the colony in 1850; but he resigned in 1851, and returned to England. He died in London, England, on June 5, 1894.

[W. N. Sage, *Early days of representative government in British Columbia* (Can. hist. rev., 1922); F. W. Howay and E. O. S. Scholefield, *British Columbia* (4 vols., Vancouver, B.C., 1914); A. Begg, *History of British Columbia* (Toronto, 1894).]

Blatchly, William Daniel (1838-1903), painter, was born in Bristol, England, in 1838. He came to Canada in 1881, and joined the staff of a lithographing firm in Toronto. In 1893 he opened his own studio, and painted in water-colours and oils. He was the first president of the Toronto Art Students' League; and he made a noteworthy series of drawings illustrating the North-West Rebellion of 1885. He died at Toronto on December 31, 1903.

[Private information.]

Blatz, William Emet (1895-1964), psychologist and professor, was born in Hamilton, Ontario, June 30, 1895, and educated at the University of Toronto (B.A., 1916; M.B., 1921); and the University of Chicago (Ph.D., 1923). He began teaching at the University of Toronto, where he opened the St. George School for Child Studies, a forerunner of the Institute of Child Study and one of the earliest research centres for the systematic study of child development in North America. During the Second World War he lectured on morale to army and air force officers in England. He set up a school at Birmingham to train day-care nursery staff for wartime service. He challenged many accepted ideas on child-rearing and insisted on a minimum of spanking and scolding. He sought to remove the competitive factor from formal education and would have abolished report cards and prizes. He was author of *Parents and the pre-school child* (1927); *Management of young children* (1931); *The five sisters* (1938) — on the Dionne quintuplets; *Hostages to peace* (1940); *Understanding the young child* (1944); and numerous other articles and addresses. He retired as director of the Institute of Child Study in 1960 but continued to lecture in psychology. He was past president of the Canadian Psychological Society. He died at Toronto, Ontario, November 1, 1964.

[*Can. who's who*, 1961-63; Metropolitan Toronto Library Board, *Biographical scrapbooks*, vols. 22 and 25.]

Blewett, George John (1873-1912), clergyman and scholar, was born near St. Thomas, Ontario, on December 9, 1873, the son of William Blewett and Mary Baker. He was educated at the University of Toronto (B.A., 1897) and at Harvard University (Ph.D., 1900), and was ordained a minister of the Methodist Church in 1898. From 1901 to 1906 he was lecturer in philosophy at Wesley College, Winnipeg; and from 1906 to his death he was professor of moral philosophy at Victoria College, Toronto. He died at Go-Home Bay, Ontario, on August 15, 1912. He was the author of *The study of nature and the vision of God* (Toronto, 1907).

[Morgan, *Can. men* (1912).]

Blewett, Mrs. Jean, *née* **McKishnie** (1862-1934), author, was born at Scotia, Harwich township, Kent county, Ontario, on November 4, 1862, the daughter of John McKishnie and Janet McIntyre. She was educated at the St. Thomas Collegiate Institute; and in 1879 married Bassett Blewett (d. 1919), a native of Cornwall. For many years she was a contributor to the Toronto *Globe*, and later she joined the staff of this paper, and became editor of the "Homemaker's Department". She retired from active journalism in 1925, and she died at Chatham, Ontario, on August 19, 1934. She was the author of a novel entitled *Out of the depths* (1890), and she published several volumes of poetry: *Heart songs* (Toronto, 1897), *The cornflower and other poems* (Toronto, 1906), and *Poems* (Toronto, 1922).

[A. MacMurchy, *Canadian literature* (Toronto, 1906); Morgan, *Can. men and women* (1912).]

Bligh, Harris Harding (1842-1918), lawyer and author, was born at Cornwallis, Nova Scotia, on April 14, 1842, the son of James Bligh. He was educated at Acadia University (B.A., 1864; M.A., 1867; D.C.L., 1897), and was called to the bar of Nova Scotia in 1868 (Q.C., 1884). In 1892 he was appointed librarian of the Supreme Court of Canada; and he died at Ottawa on August 21, 1918. He was the author of the *Index to the revised statutes of Canada* (Ottawa, 1884); he edited the *Consolidated orders-in-council of Canada* (Ottawa, 1889) and the *Statutory annotations to the revised statutes of Canada, 1906, and other Canadian statutes* (Ottawa, 1910); and he was one of the compilers of the *Dominion law index* (Ottawa, 1890, 1898, and 1915), the *Ontario law index* (Toronto, 1895 and 1900), and the *Quebec law index* (Montreal, 1898).

[Morgan, *Can. men* (1912).]

Bliss, Daniel (1740?-1806), loyalist, was born at Concord, Massachusetts, about 1740. He was educated at Harvard College (B.A., 1760), and was called to the bar in Massachusetts. During the Revolutionary War he served as a commissary with the British forces; and in 1784 he was appointed a member of the first council of New Brunswick. He settled at "Belmont" on the St. John River; and here he died in 1806. In 1770 he married Isabella, daughter of Colonel John Murray, of Rutland, Massachusetts.

[*Cyc. Am. biog.*; J. W. Lawrence, *The judges of New Brunswick* (Saint John, N.B., 1907); J. Hannay, *History of New Brunswick* (Saint John, N.B., 1909).]

Bliss, Henry (1797-1873), lawyer and author, was born at Saint John, New Brunswick, in 1797, the youngest son of the Hon. Jonathan Bliss (q.v.). He was educated at King's College, Windsor, Nova Scotia; and was called to the English bar from Lincoln's Inn. For many years he was agent for New Brunswick in London; and he published the following pamphlets on colonial questions: *Consideration of the claims and conduct of the United States respecting their northeastern boundary, and the value of the British colonies in North America* (London, 1826); *On colonial intercourse* (London, 1830); *Letter to Sir Henry Parnell, bart., on the new colonial trade bill* (London, 1831); and *Statistics of the trade, industry and resources of Canada, and the other plantations in British America* (London, 1833). He died in London, England, on July 31, 1873.

[W. G. MacFarlane, *New Brunswick bibliography* (Saint John, N.B., 1895); *Dict. Can. biog.*, vol. 10.]

Bliss, John Murray (1771-1834), judge, was born in Massachusetts in 1771, the son of Daniel Bliss (q.v.). He settled in New Brunswick with his father in 1786, studied law, and was called to the bar of New Brunswick. In 1809 he was appointed solicitor-general of the province; in 1813 he was elected to represent York in the House of Assembly; and in 1816 he was made a judge of the Supreme Court of New Brunswick. For a few months in 1824 he was president and commander-in-chief of the province. He died, while on a visit to Saint John, N.B., on August 29, 1834. By his wife, who was a daughter of the Hon. Joshua Upham (q.v.), he had one son and two daughters.

[J. W. Lawrence, *The judges of New Brunswick* (Saint John, N.B., 1907); *Cyc. Am. biog.*]

Bliss, Jonathan (1742-1822), chief justice of New Brunswick (1809-22), was born at Springfield, Massachusetts, in 1742. He was educated at Harvard College (B.A., 1763), and studied law in the office of Lieutenant-governor Hutchinson. In 1778 he was proscribed as a loyalist, and went to England. In 1785 he was appointed attorney-general of New Brunswick, and settled at Saint John. The same year he was elected to represent Saint John in the House of Assembly of New Brunswick. In 1809 he was appointed chief justice of the province; and this office he held until his death, at Fredericton, New Brunswick, on October 1, 1822. In 1789 he married a daughter of the Hon. John Worthington, formerly of Springfield, Massachusetts; she died in 1799, and by her he had four sons.

[*Dict. Am. biog.*; *Cyc. biog.*; J. W. Lawrence, *The judges of New Brunswick* (Saint John, N.B., 1907).]

Bliss, William Blowers (1795-1874), judge, was born in Saint John, New Brunswick, on August 24, 1795, the third son of the Hon. Jonathan Bliss (q.v.). He was educated at King's College, Windsor (B.A., 1813), and he studied law at the Inner Temple in London, England. After being called to the English bar, he returned to Nova Scotia, and practised law in Halifax. In 1830 he was elected to represent Hants in the House of Assembly of Nova Scotia; and in 1834 he was appointed a judge of the Supreme Court of Nova Scotia. He retired from the bench in 1869; and he died at Halifax on March 16, 1874. He married an adopted daughter of the Hon. Sampson Salter Blowers (q.v.); and by her he had three sons and four daughters. He was the author of *Translations from Catullus, Horace, etc.* (Halifax, N.S., 1872).

[Sir C. J. Townshend, *Memoir of the life of the Hon. William Blowers Bliss* (Nova

Scotia Hist. Soc., collections, 1913); J. W. Lawrence, *The judges of New Brunswick* (Saint John, N.B., 1907); *Dict. Can. biog.*, vol. 10.]

Blondeau, Barthélemi (*fl.* 1743-1790), fur-trader, was born at Michilimackinac on August 24, 1743, the son of Thomas Blondeau and Marie-Josephte Celles-Duclos, and a first cousin of Maurice Régis Blondeau (q.v.). He was one of the first traders to reach the North-West after the British conquest. He was on the Red Deer River in 1772; and it is possible that he reached the Assiniboine as early as 1767 or 1769. In 1773 he was "up the Saskatchewan"; in 1774 he went "southwest, when a little above the Great lake"; and in 1777-78 he was at Sturgeon River Fort, near what is now Prince Albert. He was not included in the original North West Company in 1779; and he seems thereafter to have turned his energies toward the Illinois country. He was at Michilimackinac in 1790; but after that he disappears from view.

[W. S. Wallace, *Documents relating to the North West Company* (Toronto: The Champlain Society, 1934).]

Blondeau, Maurice Régis (1734-1809), merchant, was born in Montreal on June 20, 1734, the second son of Jean Baptiste Blondeau and Geneviève Lefèbvre. Like others of his family, which had in it an early strain of Indian blood, he engaged in the fur-trade; and in 1772 he was one of the group of merchants that sent Thomas Corry (q.v.) to the West. On April 2, 1773, he was granted a seigniory on the west bank of the St. Lawrence, adjoining the Seigniory des Cèdres; and during his later years he appears to have taken little part in the fur-trade. He died at Montreal on July 20, 1809.

[B. Sulte, *La chute à Blondeau* (Bull. rech. hist., vol. 19); W. S. Wallace, *Documents relating to the North West Company* (Toronto: The Champlain Society, 1934).]

Blondin, Pierre Edouard (1874-1943), speaker of the Senate of Canada (1930-35), was born at St. François du Lac, Quebec, on December 14, 1874. He became a notary public; and he represented Champlain in the Canadian House of Commons from 1908 to 1917. He was minister of inland revenue in the Borden administration from 1914 to 1915, and secretary of state from 1915 to 1917; and in 1917 he became postmaster-general. He was defeated in the general elections of 1917; but in 1918 was appointed to the Senate of Canada. He was again postmaster-general in the Meighen administration from 1920 to 1921; and from 1930 to 1935 he was speaker of the Senate. In 1917 he raised the 258th Overseas Battalion in the Canadian Expeditionary Force; and he served overseas from 1917 to 1918. He was the chief French-Canadian supporter of Sir Robert Borden (q.v.) in the formation of the Union government of 1917. He died at St. François du Lac, Quebec, on October 29, 1943.

[*Can. who's who*, 1936-37; *Can. parl. comp.*; C. Hébert, *L'Honorable P. E. Blondin* (n.p., n.d.).]

Blowers, Sampson Salter (1743-1842), chief justice of Nova Scotia (1797-1833), was born in Boston, Massachusetts, in March, 1743, the son of John Blowers, a lieutenant who died at the siege of Louisbourg. He was educated at the grammar school in Boston, and at Harvard College (B.A., 1763); and was admitted an attorney and barrister of the Supreme Court at Boston in 1767. In 1779 he was appointed judge of the Vice-Admiralty Court of Rhode Island; but the following year he went to England, and after a few months was appointed solicitor-general for New York. He returned to New York; but on the evacuation of that city he moved to Halifax. In 1785 he was appointed attorney-general of Nova Scotia, and was elected speaker of the House of Assembly; in 1788 he became a member of the Legislative Council of the province; and in 1797 he was appointed chief justice and president of the Legislative Council. He retired from public life in 1833, and died at Halifax, Nova Scotia, on October 25, 1842.

[*Dict. Am. biog.*]

Blue, Archibald (1840-1914), journalist and civil servant, was born at Oxford, Kent county, Upper Canada, on February 3, 1840, the son of John Blue and Mary McTavish. He was educated at the public school in Oxford, and for a time was a school-teacher. In 1867 he embarked in journalism, and was successively on the staff of the St. Thomas *Journal*, the Toronto *Globe*, and the Toronto *World*. In 1884 he was appointed deputy minister of agriculture in Ontario, and in 1891 he became head of the Ontario Bureau of Mines. In 1900 he was appointed chief census commissioner for Canada; and it was under his direction that the *Canada Year Book* was founded. He died at Ottawa on July 27, 1914. He was twice married, (1) to Mary, daughter of John Black, Yarmouth township, Ontario; and (2) to Amelia, daughter of Ledley Brabant, of Toronto; and he had three sons. In 1908 he was made an LL.D. of McMaster University, Toronto.

[Morgan, *Can. men* (1912); *Can. who's who* (1910).]

Blue, John (1875-1945), librarian and author, was born at Tara, Ontario, in 1875, and died at Edmonton, Alberta, on September 15, 1945. He was educated at the University of Toronto (B.A., 1906); and during the latter part of his life he was librarian of the Alberta Provincial Library at Edmonton. He was the author of *Alberta, past and present, historical and biographical* (3 vols., Chicago, 1924).

[Private information.]

Boak, Sir Robert (1822-1904), president of the Legislative Council of Nova Scotia (1878-1904), was born in Leith, Scotland, the son of Robert Boak, an officer in the British army. He came to Halifax, Nova Scotia, with his parents in 1831; and in 1839 his father, on retirement from the army, became an officer of Her Majesty's Customs at Halifax. The son entered business, and eventually became the head of Robert Boak and Son, engaged in the West Indian trade. In 1867-68 he was president of the Nova Scotia Repeal League; and in 1872 he was appointed a member of the Legislative Council of the province. From 1877 to 1878 he was provincial treasurer; and in 1878 he was appointed president of the Legislative Council. This office he held for twenty-five years. He died at Halifax on December 5, 1904. In 1902 he was created a knight bachelor.

[*Can. parl. comp.*]

Bochart de Champigny, Jean. See **Champigny, Jean Bochart de.**

Bohn, Eric (pseud.). See **Price-Brown, John.**

Bois, Louis Edouard (1813-1889), priest and historian, was born at Quebec, Lower Canada, on September 11, 1813, the son of Firmin Bois and Marie Anne Boissonneau. He was ordained a priest of the Roman Catholic Church in 1837; and he became curé of Maskinongé, Lower Canada, in 1848. He published an edition of the *Relations des Jésuites* (3 vols., Quebec, 1858); and he issued anonymously a large number of historical and biographical studies. Among these were *Esquisse de la vie de Mgr. François-Xavier de Laval-Montmorency* (Quebec, 1845), *Études et recherches biographiques sur le chevalier Noël Brulard de Sillery* (Quebec, 1855), *Notice sur Michel Sarrazin* (Quebec, 1857), *La découverte du Mississippi* (Quebec, 1873), *Esquisse du service postal* (Quebec, 1875), *Le colonel Dambourgès* (Quebec, 1877), *Le juge Mabane* (Quebec, 1881), and *Notes sur l'Isle d'Orléans* (Quebec, 1895). He died at Maskinongé, Quebec, in September, 1889. His papers were bequeathed to the College of Nicolet, Que.

[T. M. Charland, *L'oeuvre historique de l'abbé Louis-Édouard Bois* (Société Canadienne d'histoire de l'Eglise catholique, rapport, 1935-36); P. G. Roy, *Les oeuvres de M. l'abbé L. E. Bois* (Bull. rech. hist., 1900); Allaire, *Dict. biog.*; Le Jeune, *Dict. gén.*]

Boishébert, Charles des Champs de (1727-1797), soldier, was born at Quebec on February 7, 1727, the son of Henri Louis des Champs de Boishébert and Louise-Geneviève, daughter of Claude de Ramezay (q.v.). He entered the army in 1742, and in 1746-47 he saw service in Acadia. During the Seven Years' War, he played an important part in the course of events in Acadia; and he was present also at the battle of the Plains of Abraham in 1759 and that of St. Foy in 1760. After the British conquest he returned to France; and he died on January 9, 1797.

[J. C. Webster, *Charles des Champs de Boishébert* (Shediac, N.B., 1931); Le Jeune, *Dict. gén.*]

Boisseau, Nicolas Gaspard (1765-1842), notary public, was born at St. Pierre, on the Island of Orleans, on October 15, 1765. He became a notary public; and from 1792 to 1796 he represented the Island of Orleans in the Legislative Assembly of Lower Canada. He died at Montmagny, Canada East, on March 9, 1842. He left behind him in manuscript some autobiographical notes which were published by Dr. P. G. Roy under the title *Mémoires de Nicolas-Gaspard Boisseau* (Lévis, Que., 1907).

[Le Jeune, *Dict. gén.*; *Bull. rech. hist.*, 1926.]

Boivin, George Henry (1882-1926), minister of customs and excise for Canada (1925-26), was born at Granby, Quebec, on December 26, 1882, the son of Henri Boivin and Sarah Bray. He was educated at Laval University, Montreal (B.A., 1902), and was called to the Quebec bar in 1907 (K.C., 1918). From 1911 to his death he represented Shefford in the Canadian House of Commons; and from 1918 to 1921 he was deputy speaker of the Commons. From September, 1925, until the resignation of the King government in 1926, he was Canadian minister of customs and excise. He died at Philadelphia, Pennsylvania, on August 7, 1926, while attending a convention of the Knights of Columbus, of the Canadian branch of which he was "Supreme Director".

[*Can. parl. comp.*]

Boland, Frank John (1916-1969), theologian and historian, was born in Toronto, Ontario, June 30, 1916. He was educated at St. Michael's College, Toronto, and at St. Basil's Seminary, being ordained to the priesthood in 1942. He was awarded a B.A. (Toronto, 1938); M.A. (Detroit University, 1948); and Ph.D. (University of Ottawa, 1955). He taught at St. Michael's High School in Toronto and joined the faculty of Assumption University, Windsor, in 1955. He was founder and director of the Seminar on Canadian-American Relations. He died on April 6, 1969, at Amersfoort, Holland. He contributed articles on early French administrators in Canada to the *New Catholic Encyclopedia* (New York, 1967).

[*Can. hist rev.*, vol. L (1969).]

Bolduc, Evelyn (1888-1939), civil servant and author, was born at St. Victor de Beauce, Quebec, on July 8, 1888, the daughter of the Hon. Joseph Bolduc (q.v.). She was for many years a translator on the staff of the Canadian Senate; and she died at St. Georges de Beauce, Quebec, on December 22, 1939. She was the author of a *Manuel de l'étiquette* (Ottawa, 1937).

[Private information.]

Bolduc, Jean Baptiste Zacharie (1818-1889), missionary, was born at St. Joachim, Lower Canada, on November 30, 1818, and was educated at the Quebec seminary. He was ordained a priest of the Roman Catholic Church in 1841, and was immediately sent as a missionary to the Oregon country. He was with Sir James Douglas (q.v.) at the founding of Fort Victoria in 1843; and later he was a missionary in the Willamette Valley. On his return to Canada he became the parish priest of St. Roch, Quebec. He died near Quebec on May 8, 1889. He was the author of two valuable pamphlets now much sought after by collectors: *Mission de la Colombie: Lettre et journal* (Quebec, 1843) and *Mission de la Colombie: Deuxième lettre et journal* (Quebec, 1845).

[Rev. A. G. Morice, *Dictionnaire historique des canadiens et des métis français de l'ouest* (Kamloops, B.C., 1908); Le Jeune, *Dict. gén.*]

Bolduc, Joseph (1847-1924), speaker of the Senate of Canada (1916-22), was born at St. Victor de Tring, Lower Canada, on June 22, 1847, the son of Capt. A. Bolduc. He was educated at Laval University, and became a notary public, as well as a farmer and lumber merchant. From 1876 to 1884 he represented Beauce as a Conservative in the Canadian House of Commons; and in 1884 he was summoned to the Senate. He was appointed speaker of the Senate in 1916, and he served in this position until 1922. He died at St. Victor de Tring, Quebec, on August 13, 1924. In 1921 he was sworn of the Privy Council of Canada.

[*Can. parl. comp.*; Morgan, *Can. men* (1912).]

Bolvin, Gilles (1710-1766), sculptor, was born in France in 1710, and came to Canada about 1729. He was employed as a sculptor of religious statues for churches; and his sculpture has been much admired. He died in January, 1766.

[E. Z. Massicotte, *Le sculpteur Bolvin* (Bull. rech. hist., 1935); *Dict. Can. biog.*, vol. 3.]

Bombardier, Armand (1908-1964), inventor, was born in Valcourt, Quebec, in 1908. A garage operator, he began attempting to construct an all-terrain vehicle in 1926. He produced his first commercial snowmobile in 1937 and by 1947 was producing twelve-passenger snowmobiles. In 1959 he introduced the smaller skidoo, a 230-pound snow-vehicle on tracks. Within a few years this machine had almost displaced the dog-team in northern regions and had been used in arctic and antarctic exploration. Armand Bombardier and his brothers revolutionized winter travel in out-lying parts of the world and invented a new winter sport, snowmobiling. Mr. Bombardier died at Sherbrooke, Quebec, February 18, 1964.

[Metropolitan Toronto Library Board, *Biographical scrapbooks*, vol. 22.]

Bompas, William Carpenter (1834-1906), missionary bishop of the Church of England in Canada, was born in London, England, on January 20, 1834. He was ordained a priest of the Church of England in 1865, and became a missionary in the Mackenzie River district. In 1874 he was consecrated first bishop of Athabaska, in 1884 first bishop of Mackenzie River, and in 1891 first bishop of Selkirk. He died at Cariboo Crossing, in the Yukon, on June 9, 1906. He was the author of a *History of the diocese of Mackenzie River* (London, 1888). His wife's letters have been edited by S. A. Archer (New York, 1929).

[H. A. Cody, *An apostle of the north* (Toronto, 1908); *Dict. nat. biog.*, supp. II; *Who was who*, 1897-1916; Rev. W. B. Heeney (ed.), *Leaders of the Canadian church*, vol. 2 (Toronto, 1920); C. H. Mockridge, *The bishops of the Church of England in Canada* (Toronto, 1896).]

Bond, William Bennett (1815-1906), archbishop of the Church of England and primate of all Canada (1903-6), was born in Truro, Cornwall, England, on September 15, 1815. He came to Newfoundland about 1832, and thence to Canada in 1840; and in 1841 he was ordained at Montreal a priest of the Church of England. He began his ministry as a travelling missionary in the Eastern Townships, but in 1862 he was appointed rector of St. George's church, Montreal. In 1878 he was elected bishop of Montreal; in 1901 he became metropolitan of the Province of Canada, and in 1903, primate of all Canada. He died at Montreal on October 9, 1906. In 1870 he was made an LL.D. of McGill University.

[*Can. who was who*, vol. 1; Morgan, *Can. men* (1898); Dent, *Can. port.*, vol. 3; W. B. Heeney (ed.), *Leaders of the Canadian church* (Toronto, 1918); C. H. Mockridge, *Bishops of the Church of England in Canada* (Toronto, 1896).]

Bonin, Joseph (1845-1917), priest, was born at Lanoraie, Canada East, on January 6, 1845; and died at Berthier-en-haut, Quebec, on December 26, 1917. He was the author of *Biographies de l'honorable Barthélemy Joliette et de M. le grand vicaire Antoine Manseau* (Montreal, 1874).

[Allaire, *Dict. biog.*; *Bull. rech. hist.*, 1930.]

Bonnar, Robert Andrew (1860-1932), lawyer, was born at King, North York, Canada West, on May 16, 1860. He went to the west as a young man, and was called to the bar of Manitoba in 1889 (K.C., 1915). He practised law in Winnipeg, and became one of the most successful criminal lawyers in Canada, losing only one of forty-six murder trials in which he represented the defendant. He died at Headingly, Manitoba, on August 13, 1932.

[*Can. who was who*, vol. 1; R. St. G. Stubbs, *Lawyers and laymen of western Canada* (Toronto, 1939).]

Bonne, Pierre Amable de. See **De Bonne, Pierre Amable.**

Bonnycastle, Sir Richard Henry (1791-1847), soldier and author, was born in England in 1791, the son of John Bonnycastle, professor of mathematics in the Royal Military Academy, Woolwich. He obtained a commission in the Royal Engineers, and served in Canada during the War of 1812. From 1837 to 1839 he commanded the Royal Engineers in Upper Canada, and he was knighted in 1838 for his services in the rebellion of 1837-38. He was subsequently commandant of the Royal Engineers in Newfoundland; and he died at Kingston, Canada, on November 3, 1847, soon after having retired with the rank of lieutenant-colonel. He published *Spanish America* (London, 1818; Philadelphia, 1819); *The Canadas in 1841* (London, 1841); *Newfoundland in 1842* (London, 1842); *Canada and the Canadians in 1846* (London, 1846); and *Canada as it was, is, and may be* (London, 1852).

[*Dict. nat. biog.*; *Cyc. Am. biog.*; Morgan, *Cel. Can.* and *Bib. can.*]

Booth, John Rudolphus (1826-1925), capitalist, was born in Shefford county, Quebec, in 1826. In 1837 he built a small lumber-mill at Ottawa; and he developed this into an enormous industry. In 1905 the Grand Trunk Railway acquired 500 miles of railway which he had built as an adjunct of his business. He died at Ottawa on December 8, 1925.

[Morgan, *Can. men* (1912); *Can. who was who*, vol. 1.]

Borden, Byron Crane (1850-1929), president of Mount Allison University (1911-23), was born at Avonport, Nova Scotia, on November 27, 1850, the son of George Newton Borden. He was educated at Mount Allison University (B.A., 1878; M.A., 1886; D.D., 1893), and in 1885 was appointed principal of Mount Allison Ladies' College. He became also professor of political science at Mount Allison University; and from 1911 to 1923 he was president of this university. He died at Annapolis Royal, Nova Scotia, on July 17, 1929. He was an honorary D.C.L. of King's College, Windsor, and an honorary LL.D. of Acadia and Dalhousie universities.

[Morgan, *Can. men* (1912).]

Borden, Sir Frederick William (1847-1917), Canadian minister of militia and defence (1896-1911), was born at Cornwallis, Nova Scotia, on May 14, 1847, the son of Dr. Jonathan Borden and Maria Frances Brown. He was educated at King's College University, Windsor, Nova Scotia (B.A., 1866), and at Harvard Medical School, Boston, Massachusetts (M.A., 1868), and he practised medicine for many years at Canning, Nova Scotia. In 1874 he was elected as a Liberal to the Canadian House of Commons for King's county, Nova Scotia; and, except for the years 1882-87, when he was out of parliament, he continued to represent this constituency until his defeat in the general elections of 1911. From 1896 to 1911 he was minister of militia and defence in the Laurier administration; and his period of office was marked by striking changes. It was under his régime that the last British troops were withdrawn from Canada in 1901, and that the practice ceased of appointing a British general officer to command the Canadian militia. Though not open to the suggestions of military experts for the improvement of the Canadian militia, he raised on the whole the standard of the militia during his time. He died at Canning, Nova Scotia, on January 6, 1917. He was twice married, (1) to Julia Maud (d. 1880), daughter of John H. Clark, Canning, Nova Scotia; and (2) to Bessie Blanche, another daughter of John H. Clark; and he had two daughters and one son. In 1911 he was made LL.D. of the University of New Brunswick; and in 1902 he was created a K.C.M.G.

[*Who was who*, 1916-28; Morgan, *Can. men* (1912); *Can. who's who* (1910); Rose, *Cyc. Can. biog.* (1888); *Can. parl. comp.*; O. D. Skelton, *The life and times of Sir Wilfrid Laurier* (2 vols., Toronto, 1921).]

Borden, Sir Robert Laird (1854-1937), prime minister of Canada (1911-20), was born at Grand Pré, Nova Scotia, on June 26, 1854, the son of Andrew Borden. He was educated at Acacia Villa Seminary, Horton, Nova Scotia, studied law, and was called to the bar in Nova Scotia in 1878 (Q.C., 1891). He practised law in Halifax, and from 1893 to 1904 was president of the Barristers' Society of Nova Scotia. From 1896 to 1904 he represented Halifax in the Canadian House of Commons; and in 1901 he was chosen leader of the Conservative opposition in parliament, in succession to Sir Charles Tupper, Bart. (q.v.). He was defeated in Halifax in 1904, but was elected for Carleton in 1905; he represented Halifax again from 1908 to 1917; and from 1917 to 1921 he sat for King's county. In 1911 he became prime minister of Canada; and he remained at the head of affairs in Canada throughout the whole period of the Great War. In 1918 he formed a Unionist government of Conservatives and Liberals on a platform of compulsory military service. He represented Canada at the meetings of the Imperial War Cabinet and the Imperial War Conference in 1917 and 1918; and he was the chief plenipotentiary delegate of Canada at the Peace Conference in Paris, in 1919. Through ill-health, he was compelled to resign as prime minister in July, 1920; and he then retired from active politics. In 1921-22 he was the Canadian delegate at the Washington Conference; and in 1922 he represented Great Britain in an arbitration between Great Britain and Peru, in Paris. From 1918 to 1920 he was chancellor of McGill University, and from 1924 to 1930 of Queen's University, Kingston. After his retirement from politics, he published two volumes of lectures, *Canadian constitutional studies* (Toronto, 1922) and *Canada in the Commonwealth* (Oxford, 1929); and in 1928 he was elected a fellow of the Royal Society of Canada. He was created a member of the King's Privy Council in 1912, and a G.C.M.G. in 1914. He was a D.C.L. of Queen's University (1903), and an LL.D. of St. Francis Xavier University (1905), McGill University (1913), McMaster University (1916), Edinburgh University (1917), Cambridge University (1917), and Dalhousie University (1918). He died in Ottawa, Ontario, on June 10, 1937. His *Memoirs* were edited and published posthumously by his nephew, Henry Borden (2 vols., Toronto, 1938).

[*Who was who*, 1928-40; *Americana annual*, 1938; *Can. who's who*, 1936-37; H. Charlesworth, *A cyclopaedia of Canadian biography* (Toronto, 1919); Morgan, *Can. men* (1912); Le Jeune, *Dict. gén.*; H. Borden, (ed.), *Robert Laird Borden: His memoirs* (2 vols., Toronto, 1938); Robert Craig Brown, *Robert Laird Borden* (Toronto, 1975).]

Borduas, Paul Emile (1905-1960), painter, was born at St. Hilaire, Quebec, in 1905, and died at Paris, France, on February 22, 1960. He studied painting in Montreal and Paris, and became a teacher at Ecole du Meuble, Montreal. In 1948, however, he was dismissed from this post because of "an im-passioned manifesto explaining his school of objectivity", and he became the mentor of a group of sixteen young painters who called themselves "Les Automatistes Surrationnels". He was the author, with others, of *Refus global* (Montreal, 1948).

[R. Elie, *Borduas* (Montreal, 1943); Guy Robert, *Borduas* (Montreal, 1972); D. W. Buchanan, *The growth of Canadian painting* (London, 1950); *Can. who's who*, 1958-60.]

Borenstein, Samuel (1908-1969), painter, was born in Suwalkie, Poland, in 1908; he came to Canada at the age of thirteen. He had no formal education and was a self-taught artist. He began painting as a career in the early 1930s and held seven exhibitions at the Montreal Museum of Fine Arts where several of his paintings are on permanent display. His works are characterized by multi-varied colours. He is represented in the National Gallery of Canada, at Concordia University, and in the Joseph Hirshorn Collection. He died at Montreal, December 15, 1969.

[E. Gottesman, *Who's who in Canadian Jewry* (1967); *Montreal Star* (16 December, 1969).]

Borgia, Joseph LeVasseur (1773-1839), politician, was born at Quebec, on January 13, 1773, the son of Louis LeVasseur dit Borgia and Marie Anne Trudel. He was not, as has been stated, of Italian origin. Educated at the Quebec Seminary, he was called to the bar in 1800. In 1806 he was one of the founders of *Le Canadien*; in 1808 he was deprived of his commission in the militia by Sir James Craig (q.v.), because of his connection with this newspaper, and in 1810 he was imprisoned. From 1808 to 1820, and again from 1824 to 1830, he represented Cornwallis in the Legislative Assembly of Lower Canada; and he was regarded as one of the more moderate reformers in the House. In his later years poverty compelled him to withdraw from politics, and he died at Quebec on June 28, 1839.

[F. J. Audet, *Joseph LeVasseur Borgia* (Trans. Roy. Soc. Can., 1925); Bibaud, *Panth. can.*]

Borthwick, John Douglas (1832-1912), clergyman and author, was born at Glencourse, near Edinburgh, Scotland, in 1832, and came to Canada about 1850. He taught school, first in Upper Canada, and then in Montreal; and in 1866 he was ordained a clergyman of the Church of England. For twenty-five years he was incumbent of St. Mary's, Hochelaga, and in his later years he was Protestant chaplain of the Montreal prison. He died at Montreal on January 14, 1912. In his earlier days he published a number of general or reference books, such as *Examples of historical and geographical autonomiasis* (Montreal, 1858), *A cyclopedia of history and geography* (Montreal, 1859), *The harp of Canaan, or selections from the poets on Bible historical incidents* (Montreal, 1866), *The battles of the world* (Montreal, 1866), *Everyman's mine of useful knowledge* (Montreal, 1869), and *The Dominion geography* (Montreal, 1871). He published also *The history of Scottish song* (Montreal, 1874), *Borthwick castle, or scenes from Scottish history* (Montreal, 1880), and *Poems and songs on the South African War* (Montreal, 1901). But he is remembered chiefly as the historian of Montreal, and was the author of *Montreal, its history* (Montreal, 1875), *History of Montreal and commercial registrar for 1885* (Montreal, 1885), *History and biographical gazetteer of Montreal* (Montreal, 1892), *History of Montreal, including the streets of Montreal* (Montreal, 1897), *Authentic history of the eight prisons of Montreal* (Montreal, 1907), and *History of the diocese of Montreal, 1850-1910* (Montreal, 1911).

[Morgan, *Can. men* (1912).]

Bossin, Hye (1906-1964), editor, was born in Toronto, Ontario, in 1906. He was a journeyman printer with Ruddy Brothers when he decided to go to Hollywood, where he became a script-writer. Returning to Toronto, he published *A tattler's tale of Toronto*, originally written as a series of newspaper articles. In 1941 he formed a company which began publishing *Canadian Film Weekly* and wrote a regular column for it. He was official historian of Canadian Picture Pioneers and a consultant with the National Film Board in making a documentary on sixty years of film in Canada. He received an award in 1955 for his promotion of a Canadian film archive. He died at Toronto, Ontario, September 12, 1964.

[Metropolitan Toronto Library Board, *Biographical scrapbooks*, vol. 22.]

Bostock, Hewitt (1864-1930), speaker of the Senate of Canada (1922-30), was born at Walton Heath, Surrey, England, on May 31, 1864, the son of Samuel Bostock, of The Hermitage, Walton Heath, and Marion Iliff. He was educated at Trinity College, Cambridge (B.A., 1885; M.A., 1888); and he was called to the bar at Lincoln's Inn in 1888, but never practised law. In 1893 he went to British Columbia, became a rancher and fruit-farmer at Monte Creek, and the proprietor of the Victoria *Province*. In 1896 he was elected to represent Yale and Cariboo in the Dominion House of Commons; and in 1904 he was called to the Senate. In 1914 he became leader of the Liberal party in the Senate; from 1921 to 1922 he was minister of public works in the King government; and in 1922 he was appointed speaker of the Senate. He died at Monte Creek, British Columbia, on

April 28, 1930. In 1880 he married Lizzie Jean McCombie, daughter of Hugh Cowie, Q.C., chancellor of the county palatine of Durham; and by her he had three sons and four daughters.

[*Can. parl. comp.*; *Can. who was who*, vol. 2.]

Bosworth, Newton (d. 1848), author, was a Baptist minister who was stationed, first in Montreal, and later in Paris, Upper Canada. He died in Paris, Upper Canada, on July 14, 1848. He was the author of *Hochelaga depicta* (Montreal, 1839).

[Morgan, *Bib. can.*]

Botsford, Amos (1744-1812), first speaker of the House of Assembly of New Brunswick, was born at Newtown, Connecticut, on January 31, 1744, the son of Gideon Botsford. He was educated at Yale College (B.A., 1763), and was called to the bar in Connecticut. During the American Revolution he adhered to the Loyalist side, and in 1782 he was appointed an agent of the British government in connection with the settlement of the Loyalists in Nova Scotia. He settled in the county of Westmoreland, New Brunswick; and he represented Westmoreland in the House of Assembly of the province from 1785 to his death. During this period he was elected by each successive House its speaker. He died at Saint John, New Brunswick, on September 14, 1812. He married Sarah, second daughter of Joshua Chandler; and by her he had one son and two daughters.

[F. D. Dexter, *Biographical sketches of the graduates of Yale College*, vol. 3 (New York, 1903).]

Botsford, Amos Edwin (1804-1894), senator of Canada, was born at Saint John, New Brunswick, September 5, 1804, the second son of the Hon. William Botsford (q.v.). He was educated at Sackville Academy, and devoted himself to agriculture. From 1833 to 1867 he was a member of the Legislative Council of New Brunswick; and from 1838 to 1840 a member of the Executive Council. In 1867 he was called by royal proclamation to the Senate of Canada; and he was speaker of the Senate in 1872, and again in 1880. He died on March 22, 1894. In 1864 he married Mary, widow of T. F. Allison, of Sackville, New Brunswick.

[*Can. parl. comp.*]

Botsford, William (1773-1864), judge, was born in New Haven, Connecticut, on April 29, 1773, the son of Amos Botsford (q.v.). He was educated at Yale College (B.A., 1792; M.A., 1796), and was called to the bar of New Brunswick in 1795. In 1812 he succeeded his father as representative of Westmoreland in the House of Assembly, and from 1817 to

1823 he was its speaker. In 1817 he became also solicitor-general of the province; and in 1823 he was appointed a judge of the Supreme Court, with a seat in the Legislative and Executive councils. He retired from the bench in 1845; and the rest of his life he spent on his estate at West Cock, Westmoreland county. He died there on May 8, 1864. In 1802 he married Sarah Lowell, daughter of the Hon. William Hazen, of Saint John; and they had eight sons and two daughters.

[F. D. Dexter, *Biographical sketches of the graduates of Yale College*, vol. 5 (New York, 1911); J. W. Lawrence, *The judges of New Brunswick* (Saint John, N.B., 1907).]

Boucher, Adélard (1835-1912), musician, was born at Maskinongé, Lower Canada, on June 28, 1835, the son of François-Xavier-Olivier Boucher and Emily Munro. He became the proprietor of a music shop in Montreal, and took a prominent part in the encouragement of good music in the Province of Quebec. He died at Outremont, Quebec, in November, 1912. Before going into business as a vendor of music and musical instruments, he published a *Tableau synoptique de l'histoire du Canada* (Montreal, 1888).

[Mgr O. Maurault, *Adélard Boucher* (Trans. Roy. Soc. Can., 1938).]

Boucher, Pierre (1622-1717), governor of Three Rivers, was born in France in 1622, and came to Canada with his father in 1635. He spent four years in the country of the Hurons learning several Indian languages, and on his return to Quebec became interpreter in the garrison, and took part in various expeditions against the Iroquois. In 1645 he settled at Three Rivers, where he became chief interpreter, and for nearly a quarter of a century he served there in various capacities, civil and military. In 1652 he became governor of Three Rivers, and he filled this office, with short intervals, until 1667. In 1661 he was sent to France to obtain reinforcements, was received by Louis XIV, and given a patent of nobility, and returned to Quebec with a number of colonists. Although he was not an educated man, he wrote at this period a work entitled *Histoire véritable et naturelle des moeurs et des productions de la Nouvelle-France*, which has remained an authority, and which has been four times reprinted since its first publication in Paris, in 1664. In 1667, as a reward for saving Three Rivers from an attack of the Iroquois, he was granted the seigniory of Boucherville, whither he retired to spend the rest of his life. He died there on April 19, 1717. He married first, in 1649, Marie Chrestienne, a Huron girl, and second, on July 9, 1652, Jeanne Crevier, by whom he had fifteen children.

[S. Marion, *Un pionnier canadien* (Quebec, 1927); Laure Conan, *Pierre Boucher* (Revue canadienne, 1913); B. Sulte, *Pierre Boucher et son livre* (Trans. Roy. Soc. Can., 1896-97); M. Boucher de la Bruère, *Pierre Boucher* (Les Cahiers des dix, vol. 2, 1937); Estelle Mitchell, *Messire Pierre Boucher (écuyer) seigneur de Boucherville, 1622-1717* (Montreal, 1967); Le Jeune, *Dict. gén.*; Bibaud, *Panth. can.*; *Bull. rech. hist.*, vols. 2, 22, and 32.]

Boucher-Belleville, Jean Baptiste (1763-1839), priest, was born at Quebec, Canada, on July 23, 1763, and was ordained a priest in 1787. In 1792 he was appointed parish priest at Laprairie, Lower Canada; and he died at Laprairie on September 6, 1839. He was the author of *Les principes de la langue latine* (Montreal, 1832) and *Les principes de la langue française* (Montreal, 1855); and he translated from the English J. Mannock, *Manuel abrégé de controverse* (Quebec, 1806).

[Allaire, *Dict. biog.*; P. G. Roy, *Fils de Québec*, vol. 2 (Lévis, Que., 1933).]

Boucher de Boucherville, Sir Charles Eugène. See Boucherville.

Boucher de la Bruère, Pierre (1837-1917), politician and author, was born at St. Hyacinthe, Lower Canada, on July 5, 1837, the son of Pierre Boucher de la Bruère, M.D. He was educated at Laval University, and was called to the bar in 1860. From 1877 to 1895 he was a member of the Legislative Council of the Province of Quebec, and he was speaker of the Assembly, with a seat in the provincial cabinet, from 1882 to 1889 and from 1892 to 1895. In 1895 he was appointed superintendent of education in the Province of Quebec; and he died at Quebec on March 17, 1917. In addition to a number of pamphlets, he was the author of *Le Canada sous la domination anglaise* (St. Hyacinthe, 1863), *Histoire de la séminaire de St. Hyacinthe* (St. Hyacinthe, 1879), *Les conservateurs et la politique nationale* (St. Hyacinthe, 1882), *Les principes de l'honorable M. Mercier* (St. Hyacinthe, 1890), *Education et constitution* (Montreal, 1904), and *Le Conseil de l'Instruction Publique et le Comité Catholique* (Montreal, 1918).

[Morgan, *Can. men* (1912).]

Boucher de Niverville, Joseph Claude (1715-1804), soldier and explorer, was born on September 22, 1715, the second son of Jean-Baptiste Boucher de Niverville and Marguerite-Thérèse, daughter of François Hertel de la Frenière. He became an ensign in 1742, and in 1746 and 1747 took part in the war with the English colonies. In 1749 he accompanied Céloron (q.v.) to the Ohio, and in 1750 he accompanied Legardeur de St. Pierre's expedition to Upper Saskatchewan, where he built Fort La Jonquière in 1751, but was forced by illness to return in 1753. In 1756 he became a lieutenant, and in 1757 was in command of the Abenaki at the taking of Fort William Henry. During the American invasion of 1775, he again took up arms; and from 1775 to 1795 he was superintendent of the Indians in the district of Three Rivers. On March 4, 1790, he was made a colonel of militia. He died on August 31, 1804. He married on October 5, 1757, Josephte, daughter of François Chatelain; and he had by her one son and three daughters.

[B. Sulte, *Le Chevalier de Niverville* (Trans. Roy. Soc. Can., 1909); A. G. Morice, *Dictionnaire historique* (Kamloops, B.C., 1908); Le Jeune, *Dict. gén.*]

Boucherville, Sir Charles Eugène Boucher de (1822-1915), prime minister of Quebec (1874-78 and 1891-92), was born at Boucherville, Lower Canada, on May 4, 1822, the son of the Hon. Pierre Boucher de Boucherville and Marguerite Amélie Sabrevois de Bleury. He was educated at the College of St. Sulpice, Montreal, and studied medicine at Paris, France (M.D., 1843). In 1861 he was elected as a Conservative to the Legislative Assembly of Canada for the county of Chambly; and in 1867 he was appointed to the Legislative Council of the Province of Quebec. From 1867 to 1873 he was speaker of the Council, and as such a member of the Chauveau ministry; and in 1874 he became prime minister of Quebec. In 1878 he was dismissed from office by the lieutenant-governor, the Hon. Luc Letellier de St. Just (q.v.); and in 1879 he was called to the Senate of Canada. In 1891 he became for the second time prime minister of Quebec; but he resigned a year later, in 1892, and thereafter retired to private life. He died at Montreal on September 11, 1915. He was twice married, (1) to Susanne, daughter of R. L. Morrogh, of Montreal; and (2) to C. Lussier, daughter of the seignior of Varennes. He was created a C.M.G. in 1894, and a K.C.M.G. in 1914.

[*Who was who*, 1897-1916; Morgan, *Can. men* (1898); Dent, *Can. port.*, vol. 3; R. P. Lalande, *Boucherville* (Montreal, 1890); P. B. Casgrain, *Letellier de St. Just et son temps* (Quebec, 1885).]

Boucherville, Pierre Georges Boucher de (1814-1894), lawyer and author, was born at Quebec, Lower Canada, on October 21, 1814. He was admitted to the bar of Lower Canada on January 26, 1837; but later in the year left Canada for Louisiana because of the part he had taken in the organization of the revolutionary Fils de la Liberté. Later, when an amnesty was granted, he returned to Canada; and in 1867 he was appointed clerk of the Legislative Council of Quebec. He retired from this post in 1889, and he died at

St. Laurent, on the Island of Orleans, Quebec, on September 6, 1894. He was the author of a novel, *Une de perdue, deux de trouvées* (2 vols., Montreal, 1874) and three other books, *Le crédit foncier* (Quebec, 1863), *Le code du whist* (Montreal, 1877), and *Dictionnaire du langage des nombres* (Quebec, 1889).

[P. G. Roy, *Fils de Québec* (Lévis, Que., 1933).]

Bouchette, Jean Baptiste (1736-1804), naval captain, was born at Quebec on July 5, 1736, the son of Marc Bouchet and Marie-Thérèse Grenet. He served in the Canadian militia during the Seven Years' War; and after the war he engaged in the fisheries of the Gulf of St. Lawrence. In 1775 he was instrumental in securing the escape of Guy Carleton (q.v.) from Montreal when the Americans captured it. During the latter part of his life he was commandant of the British naval forces on the Great Lakes, with headquarters at Fort Frederick, near Kingston, on Lake Ontario. Here he died in 1804.

[B. Sulte, *Jean Baptiste Bouchette* (Trans. Roy. Soc. Can., 1908); E. Fabre Surveyer, *The Bouchette family* (Trans. Roy. Soc. Can., 1941).]

Bouchette, Joseph (1774-1841), surveyor-general of Lower Canada (1804-41), was born at Quebec, Lower Canada, on May 14, 1774, the son of Jean Baptiste Bouchette (q.v.). About 1790 he entered the office of his uncle, Samuel Holland (q.v.), surveyor-general of Quebec; and in 1804 he succeeded to the office of surveyor-general of Lower Canada. He was the author of a number of important topographical maps of Upper and Lower Canada, and of four books, *Description topographique de la province du Bas-Canada* (London, 1815), *General report of an official tour through the new settlements of the province of Lower Canada* (Quebec, 1825), *The British dominions in North America* (2 vols., London, 1831), and *A topographical dictionary of the province of Lower Canada* (London, 1831). He died in Montreal on April 9, 1841.

[*Sketch of the chief features of the services of Joseph Bouchette* (pamphlet, about 1835); N. E. Dionne, *Joseph Bouchette* (Bull. rech. hist., 1914); Morgan, *Cel. Can. and Bib. can.*; Taylor, *Brit. Am.*, vol. 2; Bibaud, *Panth. can.*; Le Jeune, *Dict. gén.*; E. Fabre Surveyer, *The Bouchette family* (Trans. Roy. Soc. Can., 1941); Gérard Parizeau, *Joseph Bouchette: L'homme et le haut fonctionnaire* (Trans. Roy. Soc. Can., 1971).]

Bouchette, Robert Errol (1863-1912), author and civil servant, was born in Quebec on June 2, 1863, the son of Robert Shore Milnes Bouchette (q.v.) and Clara Lindsay.

He was educated at the Quebec Seminary and Laval University (LL.B., 1885), and was called to the bar of the province of Quebec in 1885. He practised as an advocate, first in Quebec and then in Montreal. From 1898 to 1900 he was private secretary to Sir Henri Joly de Lotbinière (q.v.) when minister of inland revenue; and in 1900 he was appointed chief clerk in the Library of Parliament, Ottawa. He died in Ottawa on August 13, 1912. In 1891 he married Alice, daughter of the Hon. E. L. Pacaud, a member of the Legislative Council of Quebec; and by her he had three sons and two daughters. In 1905 he was elected a member of the Royal Society of Canada. He published several books on economic subjects: *Emparons-nous de l'industrie* (Ottawa, 1901), *L'indépendance économique du Canada français* (Arthabaska, 1906; new and revised ed., Montreal, 1913), and *Etudes sociales et économiques sur le Canada* (Montreal, 1905), as well as a novel, *Robert Lozé* (Montreal, 1903). He edited also the *Mémoires* of his father, R. S. M. Bouchette (Montreal, 1904).

[*Proc. Roy. Soc. Can.*, 1913; *Can. who was who*, vol. 1; Morgan, *Can. men* (1912); Le Jeune, *Dict. gén*; E. Fabre Surveyer, *The Bouchette family* (Trans. Roy. Soc. Can., 1941).]

Bouchette, Robert Shore Milnes (1805-1879), rebel and civil servant, was born in Quebec on March 12, 1805, the fourth and youngest son of Joseph Bouchette (q.v.). He was called to the bar of Lower Canada in 1826, and he joined the ranks of the *patriotes*. He was implicated in the rebellion of 1837, was arrested, and was banished by Lord Durham (q.v.) to Bermuda. On his return to Canada under the amnesty, he received the appointment of law clerk in the attorney-general's office; and in 1851 he became commissioner of customs for Canada. He retired from the civil service in 1875; and he died at Quebec on June 4, 1879. With Wolfred Nelson (q.v.) he was the joint author of a *Brief sketch of Canadian affairs* (Can. Antiquarian and Numismatic Journal, 1916), dealing with the events of 1837; and his *Mémoires* were published by his son, Errol Bouchette (Montreal, 1904).

[*Dom. ann. reg.*, 1879; Le Jeune, *Dict. gén.*; *Dict. Can. biog.*, vol. 10.]

Bougainville, Louis Antoine, Comte de (1729-1811), soldier and sailor, was born at Paris on November 11, 1729, the son of a notary. He was educated to become an advocate before the *Parlement de Paris*; but he early abandoned law, and turned to mathematics. At the age of twenty-two he published a *Traité de calcul intégral* (Paris, 1751), which brought him in 1756 election to the Royal Society of London. In 1756 he was sent to Canada as aide-de-camp to Montcalm (q.v.),

and he served in Canada during the campaigns of 1756-58. He was wounded at Ticonderoga, and was sent while convalescent to France to secure reinforcements. He returned to Quebec shortly before the arrival of the British fleet in April, 1759; and he played an important part in the defence of Quebec. Though blamed for the failure to reinforce the post at Wolfe's Cove before the battle of the plains of Abraham, he was undoubtedly one of the most brilliant of Montcalm's officers. He returned to France in 1761, and later entered the naval service of France. Between 1766 and 1769 he made a voyage around the world; during the American Revolution he served in the French navy, and he commanded the advance guard of the French fleet in the action of Chesapeake Bay in 1780. He retired from active service in 1790; and, though a royalist, survived the French Revolution, and won the favour of Napoleon. Napoleon granted him a pension, and appointed him a senator, a count of the Empire, and a grand officer of the Legion of Honour. He died in Paris on August 31, 1811. He was the author of *Un voyage autour du monde* (Paris, 1771), *Journal de l'expédition d'Amérique*, published in the *Rapport de l'Archiviste de Québec*, 1923-24, and some papers in the early volumes of the *Académie des sciences morales et politiques*.

[R. de Kerallain, *La jeunesse de Bougainville* (Paris, 1896); M. Thiéry, *Bougainville, soldier and sailor* (London, 1932); Le Jeune, *Dict. gén.*]

Boulton, Charles Arkoll (1841-1899), senator of Canada, was born in Cobourg, Upper Canada, on September 17, 1841, the eldest son of Lieut.-Col. D'Arcy Edward Boulton and Emily, daughter of Brig.-Gen. Charles Heath. He obtained a commission in the Royal Canadian Regiment, on its organization in 1857, and served in the army for ten years. During the Red River Rebellion of 1869-70 he fought against the rebels, and was captured, condemned to death, and reprieved; during the second North-West Rebellion in 1885 he commanded as major in the militia a corps organized by himself, and known as "Boulton's Scouts". In 1889 he was appointed to the Canadian Senate; and he died at Shellmouth, Manitoba, on May 18, 1899. He published *Reminiscences of the North-West Rebellion* (Toronto, 1886).

[Morgan, *Can. men* (1898); *Can. parl. comp.*; *Cyc. Am. biog.*, vol. VII.]

Boulton, D'Arcy (1759-1834), judge, was born in England on May 20, 1759, the son of Henry Boulton, a barrister. He came to Upper Canada about 1797, and in 1803 was created a barrister by Act of the legislature. In 1805 he was appointed solicitor-general of Upper Canada; in 1814, attorney-general; and in 1818, a judge of assize and *nisi prius*.

He died in York (Toronto) on May 23, 1834. In 1782 he married in Westminster, England, Elizabeth, daughter of James Forster, sergeant-at-law; and by her he had four sons. He was the author of a *Sketch of his Majesty's province of Upper Canada* (London, 1805).

[D. B. Read, *Lives of the judges* (Toronto, 1888); Morgan, *Bib. can.*]

Boulton, George Strange (1797-1869), legislative councillor, was born in 1797 in the State of New York, the third son of D'Arcy Boulton (q.v.). He was educated at Cornwall by the Rev. John Strachan (q.v.), and was called to the bar of Upper Canada in 1818. He represented Durham in the Legislative Assembly of Upper Canada from 1830 to 1841; and he was appointed a member of the Legislative Council of Canada in 1847. He was not, like most of the legislative councillors, appointed to the Senate of Canada in 1867; and he died at Cobourg on February 13, 1869. He was twice married, (1) in 1824 to Elizabeth (d. 1836), daughter of Henry Boulton, of Geddington House, Northamptonshire, England; and (2) in 1840 to Anna Maria, daughter of J. Walton, of Schenectady, and widow of N. F. Berk, of Albany, New York. He was a colonel in the Canadian militia, having commanded in military district No. 4.

[*Can. parl. comp.*, 1864; Toronto *Globe*, Feb. 20, 1869.]

Boulton, Henry John (1790-1870), attorney-general of Upper Canada (1829-33), was born in Kensington, London, England, in 1790, the second son of D'Arcy Boulton (q.v.). He came to Canada with his parents about 1797, but was educated in England and in 1815 was called to the English bar from the Middle Temple. He began the practice of law in York (Toronto), Upper Canada; and in 1818 was appointed solicitor-general, and in 1829 attorney-general of the province. In 1830 he was elected to represent Niagara in the Legislative Assembly of Upper Canada; and in 1833 he was dismissed from office as attorney-general by the colonial secretary, because of an attack on the Colonial Office made by him in the legislature in connection with the reception accorded William Lyon Mackenzie (q.v.) in Westminster in 1832. He went to England, and though he did not succeed in having himself reinstated, he was appointed chief justice of Newfoundland. This office he held until his dismissal for political reasons in 1838; and he then returned to Toronto. From 1841 to 1844 he represented Niagara in the Legislative Assembly of Canada, and from 1848 to 1851 he represented Norfolk. In his later years he retired to private life, and he died at Toronto on June 18, 1870. He was the author of *A short sketch of the province of Upper Canada* (London, 1826).

[Morgan, *Cel. Can.* and *Bib. can.*; J. C. Dent, *The Upper Canadian rebellion* (2 vols., Toronto, 1885) and *The last forty years* (2 vols., Toronto, 1881).]

Boulton, Henry John (1824-1876), author, was born in Toronto on April 21, 1824, the eldest son of the Hon. Henry John Boulton (q.v.). He was educated at Upper Canada College, where he was head boy in 1840; and he died in Toronto on June 11, 1876. He was the author of two pamphlets, *The drainage of land, and its necessity in the present state of the agricultural interests of Canada* (Toronto, 1859), and *On thorough land drainage, and the results of actual operations in Canada* (Toronto, 1860).

[A. H. Young (ed.), *The roll of pupils of Upper Canada College* (Kingston, Ont., 1917); Morgan, *Bib. can.*]

Boulton, William Henry (1812-1874), politician, was born in 1812, the grandson of D'Arcy Boulton (q.v.), and the son of D'Arcy Boulton, jr. From 1844 to 1853 he represented Toronto in the Legislative Assembly of Canada; and from 1845 to 1847 he was mayor of Toronto. He died in February, 1874. He married Harriette Elizabeth, daughter of Thomas Dixon, of Boston; and in 1875 she married Goldwin Smith (q.v.).

[Goldwin Smith, *Reminiscences* (New York, 1910); *Dict. Can. biog.*, vol. 10.]

Bouquet, Henry (1719-1765), soldier, was born in 1719 in the canton of Berne, Switzerland, and was a childhood friend of Sir Frederick Haldimand (q.v.). He served in the Sardinian and Dutch armies, and in 1754 took service in the British army. He was employed in America during the Seven Years' War, and from 1759 to 1762 he was commandant of the western posts, with the rank of colonel. In 1763 he put an end to the Conspiracy of Pontiac at Bushy Run. He died at Pensacola, Florida, of fever, in September, 1765. His papers, which are an important source of information for the history of the Seven Years' War and the Conspiracy of Pontiac, are in the British Museum; and copies of them are in the Canadian Archives, Ottawa.

[*Dict. nat. biog.*; Le Jeune, *Dict. gén.*]

Bourassa, Gustave (1860-1904), priest and author, was born at Montebello, Quebec, on June 15, 1860, the son of Napoléon Bourassa (q.v.) and Azélie Papineau. He was ordained a priest of the Roman Catholic Church in 1884; and after studying for three years in Rome, became secretary of Laval University at Montreal. He died at Montreal on November 20, 1904. In 1902 he was elected a member of the Royal Society of Canada.

He was the author of *Mme. Gamelin et les origines de la providence* (Montreal, 1892), *L'hotel de Rambouillet* (Montreal, 1897), and *Conférences et discours* (Montreal, 1899).

[Allaire, *Dict. biog.*; Le Jeune, *Dict. gén.*]

Bourassa, Henri (1868-1952), journalist and politician, was born at Montreal, Quebec, on September 1, 1868, the son of Napoléon Bourassa (q.v.) and Azélie Papineau, and the grandson of Louis Joseph Papineau (q.v.). He was educated by tutors, and became a journalist. He was a contributor to *Le Nationaliste*, a journal published in Montreal; and in 1896 he was elected to represent Labelle as an independent Liberal in the Canadian House of Commons. He became a pronounced "Nationalist"; and in 1910 he founded *Le Devoir,* a Nationalist newspaper in Montreal, of which he became the editor-in-chief; and he continued as editor until he broke with many of the Nationalists, and resigned from the paper in 1932. A man of erratic impulses, he resigned from the Commons in 1907, sat in the Quebec Legislative Assembly from 1908 to 1912, and again in the Commons from 1925 to 1935, when he was defeated in his old constituency, Labelle. Though an outstanding political figure and a first-rate orator, he never attained cabinet rank. He was an inveterate pamphleteer, and published scores of pamphlets on political questions, both in French and English. One of the most contentious of his publications was *Que devons-nous à l'Angleterre?* (Montreal, 1915). A partial list of his publications will be found in *Hier, aujourd'hui, demain; Problèmes nationaux* (Montreal, 1916). He died at Outremont, Quebec, on August 30, 1952.

[Patrick Allen, *et al., La pensée de Henri Bourassa* (Montreal, 1954); Robert Rumilly, *Henri Bourassa: La vie publique d'un grand Canadien* (Montreal, 1953); *Can. who's who,* 1948; *Encyc. Can.*]

Bourassa, Napoléon (1827-1916), author, architect, and painter, was born at L'Acadie, Lower Canada, on October 21, 1827, the son of François Bourassa of Montebello. He was educated at the seminary of St. Sulpice, Montreal, and studied painting under Théophile Hamel (q.v.). He spent three years in Rome and Florence, and on his return to Canada he became an architect and painter. An example of his work as an architect is the church of Notre Dame de Lourdes, Montreal. In 1880 he was appointed a charter member of the Royal Canadian Academy of Arts, and he was for a number of years its vice-president. In 1864 he was one of the founders of the *Revue Canadienne,* and many papers by him are scattered through the early volumes of that periodical. He published an historical novel, *Jacques et Marie* (Montreal, 1866; new ed., 1886), a descriptive sketch entitled *Nos grand'-mères* (Montreal, 1887), and two or three volumes of lectures. His letters have been published by Mlle. A. Bourassa (Bruges, 1929). He died at Lachenaie, Quebec, on August 27, 1916. In 1857 he married Azélie, youngest daughter of Louis Joseph Papineau (q.v.); and his son was Henri Bourassa (q.v.).

[Anne Bourassa, *Napoléon Bourassa* (Montreal, 1968); *Napoléon Bourassa* (Revue canadienne, 1916); *Bull. rech. hist.,* 1916; Morgan, *Can. men* (1912); Le Jeune, *Dict. gén.*; *Can. who was who,* vol. 1.]

Bourdages, Louis (1764-1835), member of the Legislative Assembly of Lower Canada (1804-35), was born at Lorette, near Quebec, on July 6, 1764, the son of Raymond Bourdages, an Acadian refugee who settled in Quebec, and Esther Leblanc. He was educated at the seminary of Quebec; and first served in the merchant marine. He then, after 1787, settled on a farm on the Chambly River; and ultimately he became a notary public. In 1804 he was elected to the Legislative Assembly of Lower Canada for the county of Richelieu, and he became a vehement opponent of the administration of Sir James Craig (q.v.). He commanded a militia battalion during the War of 1812, and his strict discipline later cost him his seat in the Assembly. He was, however, immediately returned for the county of Buckingham, and this constituency he represented until his death. He became the leader of the French-Canadian party in the House, and a close colleague of Louis Joseph Papineau (q.v.). He died at St. Denis de Richelieu, Lower Canada, on January 20, 1835. In 1787 he married Louise Catherine Soupiran, of Quebec, and by her he had several children.

[A. Bernard, *Louis Bourdages* (Canada français, 1926); Morgan, *Cel. Can.*; *Bull. rech. hist.,* 1905.]

Bourdon, Jean (1602?-1668), surveyor and explorer, was born at Rouen, Normandy about 1602, and came to Canada in 1634. He settled near Quebec, and in 1661 his holdings of land were erected into a seigniory. He was one of the first surveyors and civil engineers in the colony; he was employed on several diplomatic missions to the Iroquois; and in 1657 he made an abortive attempt to reach Hudson Bay by water. In 1663 he was appointed *procureur-général* of the Sovereign Council; and he died at Quebec on January 12, 1668. About 1635 he married Jacqueline Potel, and by her he had four sons and four daughters.

[Abbé A. Gosselin, *Jean Bourdon et son ami, l'abbé de Saint-Sauveur* (Quebec, 1904); J. E. Roy, *Jean Bourdon et la Baie d'Hudson* (Quebec, 1896); Abbé I. Caron, *Les censitaires du coteau Sainte-Geneviève*

(Bull. rech. hist., 1921); *Dict. Can. biog.*, vol. 1.]

Bourgault, Médard (1897-1967), woodcarver, was born at St. Jean Port Joli, Quebec, June 8, 1897. His father was a shipbuilder. Médard became a navigator and spent several years at sea. Encouraged by Marius Barbeau (q.v.), he left the sea and became a full-time carver. His themes are mainly religious rather than secular and his style is that of the Quevillon school, light and deeply incised. Neighbours and friends appear in Biblical scenes which are done in a simple and direct manner. A series of his bas-reliefs, "Via Crucis", hangs in the church of St. Nicolas in Lévis county. He and his brother Jean-Julien carved the pulpit of the church in St. Jean Port Joli and together trained a new generation of Canadian carvers. Other examples of his work are to be found in the garden of the Scholasticat Immaculée-Conception, Montreal and in the Provincial Museum of Quebec. He died at Port Joli, September 21, 1967.

[*Canadian Geographical Journal* (December, 1952).]

Bourgeau, Eugène (1813-1877), botanist, was born at Brizon, a village of eastern France, near the Swiss border, in 1813, the son of a sheep-farmer. He was self-educated, but his aptitude for natural history led to his employment in the Botanic Garden at Lyons. Thence he went to Paris, and there he became a collector of botanic specimens on behalf of a French botanical society. In 1857 he was appointed by the British government botanist to the Palliser expedition to the Canadian North West; and he proved one of the most valuable officers of the expedition. He was the first botanist to examine the Rocky mountains south of Athabaska pass, and the prairie south of North Saskatchewan River. After his return to Europe in 1859, he made collecting expeditions to Asia Minor and to Mexico; and he died in Paris, France, in February, 1877.

[J. N. Wallace, *Eugène Bourgeau* (Canadian Alpine journal, 1928); *Dict. Can. biog.*, vol. 10.]

Bourgeois, Philéas Frédéric (1855-1913), priest and author, was born at Memramcook, New Brunswick, of Acadian parentage, on November 17, 1855. He was educated at St. Joseph's College, and was ordained a priest of the Roman Catholic Church in 1879. For most of his life he was a professor at St. Joseph's College. He died at Moncton, New Brunswick, on April 3, 1913. He was the author of *L'École des apparitions mystérieuses* (Montreal, 1896), *L'Histoire du Canada en 200 leçons* (Montreal, 1903), and a series of *Livres de lecture* (Edinburgh, 1907).

[Allaire, *Dict. biog.*]

Bourgeoys, Marguerite (1620-1700), nun, was born in Troyes, Champagne, France, in 1620. She emigrated to Canada with Maisonneuve (q.v.) in 1653, and founded in Montreal a religious order, known as the congregation of Notre Dame, of which she became the first superior. She resigned the post of superior in 1693, and henceforth performed the humblest tasks in the institution she had founded. She died at Montreal on January 12, 1700.

[M. Ransonnet, *La vie de la vénérable Soeur Marguerite Bourgeoys* (Ville-Marie, 1818); Abbé Faillon, *Vie de la Soeur Bourgeoys* (Paris, 2 vols., 1853); *Abbé* Sausseret, *Eloge historique de la Soeur Marguerite Bourgeoys* (Troyes, 1864); C. W. Colby, *Canadian types of the old régime* (New York, 1908); R. Rumilly, *Marguerite Bourgeoys* (Paris, 1936); *Dict. Can. biog.*, vol. 1; *Cyc. Am. biog.*; Le Jeune, *Dict. gén.*; Bibaud, *Panth. can.*]

Bourget, Ignace (1799-1885), Roman Catholic bishop of Montreal (1840-76), was born at Point Lévis, Lower Canada, on October 30, 1799. He was educated at the Quebec Seminary and at Nicolet College, and was ordained a priest of the Roman Catholic Church in 1822. He was appointed vicar-general of Montreal in 1836, coadjutor bishop of Montreal in 1837, and bishop of Montreal in 1840. During his oversight of this see, which lasted until his appointment as archbishop of Martianopolis *in partibus* in 1876, he displayed great energy. He was instrumental in founding many religious communities, charitable institutions, and colleges; and he became a champion of ultramontane doctrines in Canada. In 1842 it was through his invitation that the Jesuits returned to Canada; and from 1858 to 1876 he waged a bitter warfare against the liberally minded Institut Canadien at Montreal. He died at Sault-aux-Récollets, near Montreal, on June 8, 1885. He is said to have published nearly one thousand *mandements* and pastorals during his episcopate, extracts from which were published under the title *Fioretti vescovili* (Montreal, 1872); and he was the author of *Le cérémonial des évêques* (Montreal, 1855).

[A. Leblond de Brumath, *Mgr. Ignace Bourget* (Montreal, 1885); Abbé Bourassa, *Mgr. Bourget* (pamphlet, Montreal, 1903); Gérard Parizeau, *Monseigneur Ignace Bourget, deuxième évêque de Montréal* (Trans. Roy. Soc. Can., 1970); *Can. who who*, vol. 1; *Dom. ann. reg.*, 1885; *Catholic encyclopaedia*; Bibaud, *Panth. can.*; Le Jeune, *Dict. gén.*; Allaire, *Dict. biog.*; Morgan, *Bib. can.*]

Bourinot, Arthur Stanley (1893-1969), poet and author, was born in Ottawa, October 3, 1893. He was educated at the University of Toronto (B.A., 1915) and Osgoode Hall, Toronto. He was called to the bar in 1920. He served in the First World War and his poems entitled *Canada's fallen* won the National Poetry Competition prize in 1919. He published *Laurentian lyrics* (1915); *Selected poems* (1935); *Under the sun* (1939); *More lines from Deepwood* (1949) — winner of the Governor General's award; *Treasures of the snow* (1950); *The green earth* (1953); *Tom Thomson and other poems* (1954); *Ten narrative poems* (1955); *Everything in earth must die* (1955); *A gathering of poems* (1959); and *To and fro in the earth: poems* (1963). His book *Five Canadian poets* (1954) deals with Scott, Lampman, Sangster, Cameron, and Marshall. He also compiled and edited *Edward William Thomson (1849-1924): A bibliography with notes and some letters* (1955); *Letters of Archibald Lampman to Edward William Thomson (1890-1898)* (1956); *The letters of Edward William Thomson to Archibald Lampman 1891-1897* (1957); *At the mermaid inn* (1958), a selection of Lampman newspaper writing. He published *Some letters of Duncan Campbell Scott, Archibald Lampman and others* (1959); and *More letters of Duncan Campbell Scott (second series) with some personal recollections by the author* (1960). He was editor of the *Canadian Poetry magazine* (1948-54) and editor of the *Canadian Author and Bookman* (1953-54). He was a fellow of the Royal Society of Literature (1950). He died at Ottawa, January 17, 1969.

[N. Story, *Oxford companion to Canadian history and literature* (Toronto, 1967); *Can. who's who,* 1958-60; Rhodenizer, *Canadian Literature in English* (Montreal, 1965).]

Bourinot, Sir John George (1837-1902), historian, was born at Sydney, Cape Breton, on October 24, 1837, the eldest son of the Hon. John Bourinot, a senator of Canada, and Mary Jane Marshall. He was educated at Trinity University, Toronto (B.A., 1857), and then became a journalist. In 1860 he founded the Halifax *Herald,* and was for several years its editor. In 1861 he was appointed chief reporter of the Legislative Assembly of Nova Scotia; and in 1868 he joined the Hansard staff at Ottawa. In 1873 he was appointed an assistant clerk of the Canadian House of Commons, and in 1880 chief clerk, a position he retained until his death. He devoted himself to the study of the constitutional law and history of Canada, and became a foremost authority in this field. He published *The intellectual development of the Canadian people* (Toronto, 1881), *Parliamentary procedure and practice in Canada* (Montreal, 1884; new ed., Toronto, 1903), *Local government in Canada* (Baltimore, 1887), *Manual of the constitutional history of Canada* (Montreal, 1888; new and revised ed., Toronto, 1901), *Federal government in Canada* (Baltimore, 1889), *Historical descriptive account of the Island of Cape Breton* (Montreal, 1892), *How Canada is governed* (Toronto, 1895), *The story of Canada* (London, 1897), *Canada under British rule* (Cambridge, 1900), and *Lord Elgin* (Toronto, 1903). He contributed also many papers to the Transactions of the Royal Society of Canada, of which he was the first secretary in 1882, and the president in 1892. He died at Ottawa on October 13, 1902. He was married three times, (1) in 1858 to Delia, daughter of John Hawke; (2) in 1865 to Emily Alden, daughter of John Pilsbury, the American consul at Halifax; and (3) in 1889 to Isabelle, daughter of John Cameron, of Toronto. He had four sons and one daughter. He was an LL.D. of Queen's University, Kingston (1887), and of Trinity University, Toronto (1889); a D.C.L. of the University of New Brunswick (1890), and of Bishop's College, Lennoxville (1895); and a D. ès L. of Laval University (1893). In 1890 he was created a C.M.G., and in 1898 a K.C.M.G.

[*Dict. nat. biog.,* supp. II; *Proc. Roy. Soc. Can.,* 1903; *Can. who was who,* vol. 1; Morgan, *Can. men* (1898); Rose, *Cyc. Can. biog.* (1886); Le Jeune, *Dict. gén.*]

Bourlamaque, François Charles de (1716-1764), soldier, was born in Paris, France, of Italian descent, in 1716. He entered the French army, and in 1756 was promoted to the rank of colonel in the Dauphin regiment. He was sent to Canada in 1756 as third-in-command, after Montcalm (q.v.) and Lévis (q.v.), of the regular troops; and he served with distinction throughout the subsequent campaign in Canada. He commanded at Ticonderoga in 1757; and at the battle of Carillon in 1758 he commanded the French left, and was severely wounded. He was made a brigadier-general in 1759; and in 1762, after his return to France, he became a major-general. He was appointed in 1763 governor of Guadeloupe; and he died on this island in 1764. His Canadian correspondence has been preserved, and has been calendared in the Report of the Public Archives of Canada for 1923.

[Le Jeune, *Dict. gén.; Dict. Can. biog.;* vol. 3.]

Bouteroue, Claude de (1620-1680), intendant of New France (1668-70), was born in 1620, the son of Claude de Bouteroue, a councillor in the "Cour des Monnaies". On April 8, 1668, he was appointed intendant of New France during the absence of Talon (q.v.) in France, and he arrived in Quebec in the following September. Courcelle (q.v.), the governor, complained that he was under the influence of Bishop Laval (q.v.), and he was recalled in October, 1670. On his return he lived in Paris, and he died in 1680.

[R. Roy, *Claude de Bouteroue* (Bull. rech. hist., vol. viii); *Dict. Can. biog.*, vol. 1.]

Bovell, James (1817-1880), author, was born in the Barbados, West Indies, in 1817, and was educated at London, Edinburgh, and Dublin. He took holy orders in the Church of England, and also acquired the degree of M.D. He came to Canada about 1848, and settled in Toronto. Here he took part in 1850 in founding the medical faculty of Trinity University, and he became its first dean. On the disruption of this faculty in 1856, he joined the Toronto School of Medicine, and became the lecturer on physiology and pathology. He left Canada in 1870; and he died in Nevis, West Indies, on January 6, 1880. In 1851 he was one of the founders of the *Upper Canada Medical Journal*; and he was the author of a *Plea for inebriate asylums* (Toronto, 1862). He published also a number of religious works: *Constitution and canons of the synod of the diocese of Toronto* (Toronto, 1858), *Outlines of natural theology* (Toronto, 1859), *Preparation for holy communion* (Toronto, 1859), *Outlines of the history of the British church* (Toronto, 1860), *Passing thoughts on man's relation to God and God's relation to man* (Toronto, 1862), *Letters addressed to the Rev. Mr. Fletcher and others, framers of a series of resolutions on "ritual"* (Toronto, 1867), and *The world at the advent of the Lord Jesus* (Toronto, 1868).

[*Dom. ann. reg.*, 1880-81; *Can. who was who*, vol. 2; *Dict. Can. biog.*, vol. 10.]

Bovey, Henry Taylor (1852-1912), dean of the faculty of applied science, McGill University (1888-1908), was born in Devonshire, England, on May 7, 1852. He was educated at Cambridge University, and became a fellow of Queen's College, Cambridge. In 1887 he was appointed professor of civil engineering at McGill University, Montreal; and in 1888 he became a dean of the new faculty of applied science in the university. He resigned this post in 1908, to accept appointment as rector of the Imperial College of Science and Technology, London, England; but he was forced to resign this appointment in 1909 because of ill-health, and he died at Eastbourne, England, on February 2, 1912. In 1880, he married Emily Jane Bonar, daughter of John Redpath, Montreal; and by her he had several children. He was a D.C.L. of Bishop's College, Lennoxville (1892), and an LL.D. of Queen's and McGill universities (1893); and he was elected a fellow of the Royal Society of Canada in 1888, and of the Royal Society in 1902. He was the author of *Applied mechanics* (Montreal, 1882), *The theory of structures and strength of materials* (New York, 1893; 6th ed., 1905), *A treatise on hydraulics* (New York, 1895; 6th ed., 1904),

and *The strength of Canadian Douglas fir, red pine, white pine, and spruce* (n.p., 1895), as well as many contributions to scientific periodicals.

[Morgan, *Can. men* (1912); *Proc. Roy. Soc. Can.*, 1912.]

Bovey, Wilfrid (1882-1956), educationist and author, was born at Montreal, Quebec, on December 13, 1882, the son of Professor Henry Taylor Bovey (q.v.), and died at Montreal on October 11, 1956. He was educated at McGill University (B.A., 1903) and at Cambridge University (LL.B., 1906). He was called to the Quebec bar in 1907, and for some years practised law in Montreal. He served overseas with the Canadian Corps, latterly at Corps headquarters, during the First World War, and rose to the rank of lieutenant-colonel. In 1923, he was appointed director of extramural relations and extension at McGill University, and he continued in this position until his retirement in 1948; he was also chairman of the Canadian Legion Educational Services from 1939 to 1946. In 1942 he was appointed a member of the Legislative Council of Quebec. He was the author of *Canadien* (Montreal, 1935) and *The French-Canadians today* (Toronto, 1938), both of which were translated into French. He received the honorary degree of D.Litt. from Laval University (1934) and the University of Montreal (1935), and that of LL.D. from the University of Ottawa (1941).

[*Can. who's who*, 1952-54; *Encyc. Can.*]

Bowell, Sir Mackenzie (1823-1917), prime minister of Canada (1894-96), was born at Rickinghall, Suffolk, England, on December 27, 1823, the son of John Bowell. He came to Canada with his parents in 1833, and became a printer's apprentice in the office of the *Intelligencer* of Belleville, Upper Canada — a journal of which he ultimately became the editor and proprietor. At an early age he joined the Orange order, and for many years he was grand master of the Orange Association of British America. In 1867 he was elected as a Conservative for North Hastings in the Canadian House of Commons, and this constituency he represented continuously until 1892. He was then appointed a member of the Senate of Canada, and he continued a senator until 1906, when he retired to private life. In 1878 he became minister of customs in the Macdonald government; and it fell to him to put into operation the "National Policy". In the government of Sir John Abbott (q.v.), he was minister of militia; and in the government of Sir John Thompson (q.v.), minister of trade and commerce.

On the death of Sir John Thompson in 1894 Bowell became prime minister and president of the council. It was not long, however, before serious dissatisfaction with his leadership arose in the cabinet; and in January, 1896, half the ministers — the "nest of traitors", as Bowell called them—resigned in a body. These resignations were followed on April 27, 1896, by that of Bowell himself; and Sir Charles Tupper (q.v.) succeeded him. After the defeat of the Conservatives in the general elections of 1896, Bowell was chosen leader of the opposition in the Senate; but he played henceforth a minor part in politics, and in 1906 he retired to private life. He died at Belleville, Ontario, on December 10, 1917. In 1847 he married Harriet Louise (d. 1884), daughter of Jacob G. Moore, of Belleville. He was created a K.C.M.G. in 1895.

[*Who was who*, 1897-1916; Morgan, *Can. men* (1912); *Can. who's who* (1910); Dent, *Can. port.*, vol. 2; Rose, *Cyc. Can. biog.* (1886); *Can. parl. comp.*; J. S. Willison, *Sir Wilfrid Laurier and the Liberal party* (2 vols., Toronto, 1903); Sir R. Cartwright, *Reminiscences* (Toronto, 1912); J. Young, *Public men and public life in Canada* (2 vols., Toronto, 1912).]

Bowen, Edward (1780-1866), legislator and judge, was born at Kinsdale, Ireland, on December 1, 1780, and was educated at the Drogheda Academy. He came to Canada in 1797, entered the law office of Jonathan Sewell (q.v.), and was called to the bar of Lower Canada in 1803. From 1808 to 1812 he represented Sorel in the Legislative Assembly of Lower Canada; and during these years he was attorney-general of Lower Canada. In 1812 he was appointed a judge of the Court of King's Bench in the province; and in 1849 he became chief justice of the Superior Court of Lower Canada. In 1821 he was appointed a member of the Legislative Council of Lower Canada, and from 1835 to 1838 he was its speaker. He died on April 11, 1866, after sitting on the bench continuously for fifty-four years. In 1807 he married Eliza, daughter of James Davidson, surgeon to the Royal Canadian Volunteers; and by her he had eight sons and eight daughters.

[F. J. Audet, *Edward Bowen* (Les Annales, 1924); P. G. Roy, *Les jeunes de la province de Québec* (Quebec, 1933).]

Bowman, Mrs. Louise, *née* **Morey** (1882-1944), poet, was born at Sherbrooke, Quebec, in 1882, and died at Montreal, Quebec, on September 28, 1944. She married Archibald Abercromby Bowman in 1909, and lived in Toronto until 1925. Thereafter she lived in Montreal. She was the author of three volumes of poetry: *Moonlight and common day* (Toronto, 1922), *Dress tapestries* (Toronto, 1924), and *Characters in cadence* (Toronto, 1938).

[*Encyc. Can.*; *Can. who's who*, 1938-39; J. D. Logan and D. G. French, *Highways of Canadian literature* (Toronto, 1924).]

Bowring, Benjamin (1778-1846), merchant and shipowner, was born in Exeter, En-

gland, in 1778, and died in Liverpool, England, on June 1, 1846. He emigrated to Newfoundland in 1811 as a clock-maker, and became a general merchant in St. John's. By 1823 he had acquired the schooner *Charlotte*, which was destined to be the first ship in the fleet that the Bowring family built up during the next century. He returned to England in 1834; but the Newfoundland business remained in the hands of his sons.

[A. C. Wardle, *Benjamin Bowring and his descendants* (London, 1938); *Encyc. Can.*]

Bowring, Sir Edgar Rennie (1858-1943), high commissioner of Newfoundland in London (1918-22 and 1933-34), was born at St. John's, Newfoundland, on August 17, 1858. He became chairman of the shipping company of Bowring Brothers, Ltd.; in 1897 he was appointed a member of the Legislative Council of Newfoundland; and in 1918 he became the first high commissioner of Newfoundland in London. He was created a K.C.M.G. in 1934. He died in London on June 23, 1943.

[*Who was who*, 1941-50; *Encyc. Can.*; *Newfoundland supp.*]

Bowser, William John (1867-1933), prime minister of British Columbia (1915-16), was born at Rexton, New Brunswick, on December 2, 1867. He was educated at Dalhousie University, Halifax, and was called to the bar in 1890 (Q.C., 1900). He went to British Columbia in 1891, and from 1903 to his death he represented Vancouver in the legislature of British Columbia. From 1907 to 1916 he was attorney-general in the provincial cabinet, and from 1915 to 1916 prime minister. He was then leader of the opposition in the legislature; and he died at Vancouver, in the midst of the general elections, on October 26, 1933.

[*Can. parl. comp.*]

Boyd, John (1826-1893), lieutenant-governor of New Brunswick (1893), was born at Magherafelt, county Derry, Ireland, on September 28, 1826. He came to New Brunswick about 1833, and became a prominent wholesale merchant of Saint John. He was a supporter of Sir Leonard Tilley (q.v.), and a strong advocate of Confederation. In 1879 he was called to the Senate of Canada; and on September 22, 1893, he was appointed lieutenant-governor of New Brunswick. He died only a few weeks later on December 4, 1893.

[*Can. parl. comp.*; Le Jeune, *Dict. gén.*; W. G. MacFarlane, *New Brunswick bibliography* (Saint John, N.B., 1895).]

Boyd, John (1864-1933), journalist and author, was born at Montreal, Canada East, on May 2, 1864, the son of John Boyd, a merchant. He was educated at the Montreal High School, and became a journalist. He was at various times on the staff of the

Montreal *Herald,* the Montreal *Witness,* and the Montreal *Gazette.* He retired from active journalism in 1913; and he died at Lake Ouimet, near St. Jovite, Quebec, on January 31, 1933. He was the author of *Sir George Etienne Cartier, bart., his life and times* (Toronto, 1914), some political pamphlets, and some occasional poetry.

[Morgan, *Can. men* (1912).]

Boyd, Sir John Alexander (1837-1916), chancellor of Ontario (1881-1916), was born at Toronto, Upper Canada, on April 23, 1837, the son of John Boyd, principal of the Bay Street Academy, Toronto. He was educated at Upper Canada College and at the University of Toronto (B.A., 1860; M.A., 1861); and he was called to the bar of Upper Canada in 1863 (Q.C., 1880). In 1881 he was appointed chancellor of Ontario, and in 1887 president of the High Court of Justice. These positions he retained until his death at Toronto, on November 23, 1916. In 1863 he married Elizabeth, daughter of David Buchan, bursar of the University of Toronto; and by her he had several children. In 1889 he was made an LL.D. of the University of Toronto; in 1899 he was created a knight bachelor; and in 1901 a K.C.M.G. He was the author of a *Summary of Canadian history* (Toronto, 1862).

[*The last chancellor of Ontario* (Can. law times, December, 1916); *Who was who,* 1897-1916; Morgan, *Can. men* (1912).]

Boyer, Charles (*fl.* 1767-1795), fur-trader, seems to have been a French Canadian, possibly a native of Michilimackinac. A Charles Boyer was trading in furs at Rainy Lake as early as 1744; and this may have been the same person. He was in partnership with Forrest Oakes (q.v.) as early as 1767; and he was one of the earliest traders to reach the North-West. A letter of John Askin (q.v.) dated May 18, 1778, seems to indicate that he was then a clerk of Alexander Henry the elder (q.v.). In 1780 he was with William Bruce (q.v.) at Fort des Trembles on the Assiniboine River; and in the spring of 1781 he and Bruce were attacked by the Indians, but saved the fort after an heroic defence. Later, Boyer went as a clerk of the North West Company to the Peace River, and he is said to have founded Fort Vermillion in 1787, near what is still known as Boyer River. In 1788 he was back at Lake Athabaska; but in 1789 he retired from the western fur-trade, and in 1793-95 he was living at Rainy Lake.

[A. S. Morton, *Forrest Oakes, Charles Boyer, Joseph Fulton, and Peter Pangman in the north-west* (Trans. Roy. Soc. Can., 1937).]

Boyle, Sir Cavendish (1849-1916), governor of Newfoundland (1901-04), was born on May 29, 1849, the son of Capt. Cavendish Spencer Boyle of the 72nd Highlanders. He was educated at Charterhouse, and entered the British colonial service. He was governor of Newfoundland from 1901 to 1904; retired from the colonial service on pension in 1911; and died on September 17, 1916. He was created a C.M.G. in 1888, and a K.C.M.G. in 1897. He was the author of what is described as the national ode of Newfoundland, which is reproduced in J. R. Smallwood, ed., *The book of Newfoundland* (2 vols., St. John's, 1937).

[*Who was who,* 1916-28.]

Boyle, David (1842-1911), ethnologist and archaeologist, was born at Greenock, Scotland, on May 1, 1842, and came to Canada with his parents in 1856. He became a school-teacher, and was for ten years principal of the public school at Elora, Ontario. He made himself an authority on the archaeology of Ontario, and was appointed successively curator of the museum of the Canadian Institute, Toronto, and of the museum of the Ontario Department of Education. His *Archaeological reports,* issued for many years as supplements to the reports of the minister of education of Ontario, contained much material of great value; and he published also *Notes on the life of Dr. Joseph Workman* (Toronto, 1894), *Notes on primitive man in Ontario* (Toronto, 1895), *The township of Scarboro* (Toronto, 1896), and *Uncle Jim's Canadian nursery rhymes* (Toronto, 1908). He died at Toronto on February 14, 1911. In 1909 he was made an LL.D. of the University of Toronto.

[A. F. Chamberlain, *David Boyle* (American anthropologist, 1911); *Can. who was who,* vol. 2; Morgan, *Can. men* (1912).]

Boyle, George (1902-1956), author and journalist, was born in 1902, and died at Antigonish, Nova Scotia, on October 18, 1956. At the time of his death he was editor of the Antigonish *Casket,* and professor of journalism in St. Francis Xavier University at Antigonish. He was the author of *Democracy's second chance* (New York, 1941), *The poor man's prayer* (New York, 1951), *Pioneer in Purple* (Montreal, 1951), and *Father Tompkins of Nova Scotia* (New York, 1953).

[*New York Times,* Oct. 21, 1956.]

Boylen, James (1907-1970), mining executive, was born at Weston, Ontario, August 10, 1907. He was educated in Western Canada and returned to Northern Ontario at age fourteen where he was engaged in fur-trading and trapping around Larder Lake. In 1923 he began prospecting and by 1927 had become a full-time prospector in many parts of Canada. He established an office in Toronto in 1934. His main achievement was the discovery of the Bathurst mining area of New Brunswick. He was chairman and director of Advocate Mines Limited; president and director of Key Anacon Mines Limited; president, Atlantic Coast Copper Corporation Limited; chairman and president of Brunswick Mining and Smelting Corporation Limited and numerous other mining and financial companies. He died at Toronto July 7, 1970.

[*Can. who's who,* 1967-69; *Who's who in Can.,* 1966-68.]

Brabant, Augustus Joseph (d. 1912), missionary, was born at Courtray, West Flanders, Belgium. He was educated at the University of Louvain, and was ordained a priest of the Roman Catholic Church in 1868. Shortly afterwards he came to British Columbia, and in 1874 he established an Indian mission at Hesquiat, on the west coast of Vancouver Island. Here he spent all but the last four years of his life. In 1908 he was appointed apostolic administrator of the diocese of Victoria; and he died at Victoria, British Columbia, on July 4, 1912.

[Allaire,*Dict. biog.*]

Bracken, John (1883-1969), agronomist and politician, was born in Ellisville, Ontario, June 22, 1883, and educated at Brockville High School, the Ontario Agricultural College, and the University of Illinois (B.S.A., 1906). He represented Manitoba on the Dominion Seed Board (1906); became superintendent of fairs and farmers' institutes for Saskatchewan (1907); and became professor of field husbandry, University of Saskatchewan (1910-20). In 1920 he was made principal of the Manitoba Agricultural College and he entered politics in 1922 as a farmer's candidate and was elected to the Manitoba legislature. He became president of the executive council and was re-elected in 1927, 1932, and 1936. He was premier of Manitoba from 1922 to 1943. His party, which changed its name as it continued in office, was in large measure a reflection of the economical, honest, conservative views of its rural supporters. Mr. Bracken was chosen leader of the National Progressive Conservative party in 1942 and resigned from the Manitoba legislature to enter federal politics. He was elected to the House of Commons for Neepawa in the general election of 1945, but was defeated in the 1949 election. He resigned the leadership of his party and retired to his farm at Manotick, Ontario. John Bracken symbolized the pre-Second World War agricultural outlook of rural Canada which was changing rapidly by the time he emerged on the national scene. His style was not attractive to the growing urban electorate. He was the author of *Crop production in Western Canada* (1920); *Dry farming in Western Canada* (1921). He died at Ottawa, March 18, 1969.

[*Can. who's who,* 1964-66; *Encyc. Can.* (1972).]

Braddock, Edward (1695-1755), soldier, was born in 1695, the son of Major-General Edward Braddock. He entered the British army in 1710 as an ensign in the Coldstream Guards; and he became lieut.-colonel in command of this regiment in 1745. In 1754 he was appointed commander-in-chief of the British forces in North America, with the rank of major-general. He was in command of the force sent to reduce Fort Duquesne in 1755; and he was mortally wounded in the battle of the Monongahéla on July 9, 1755. He died four days later.

[*Dict. nat. biog.; Dict. Am. biog.;* Le Jeune,*Dict. gén.*]

Bradshaw, Thomas (1868-1939), actuary, was born in Manchester, England, on April 22, 1868, and came to Canada as a child. He entered the service of the North American Life Assurance Company in Toronto in 1881, and he rose to the presidency of this company. From 1915 to 1920 he was finance commissioner of the city of Toronto; and he came to be regarded as an outstanding authority on finance. He was one of only three Canadians who have been admitted as fellows of the Institute of Actuaries of Great Britain. He died at Toronto, Ontario, on November 10, 1939. He was the author of *Essential features of life assurance organization* (Toronto, 1902); joint author, with F. Sanderson, of *British office life tables* (Toronto, 1905); and joint compiler, with others, of *Tables of net premiums* (Toronto, n.d.).

[*Can. who's who,* 1936-7.]

Bradstreet, John (1714-1774), soldier, was born on December 21, 1714, at Annapolis Royal. He entered the British army in 1735, and was present at the capture of Louisbourg in 1745. In 1746 he was appointed lieutenant-governor of St. John's, Newfoundland, and during the Seven Years' War he was deputy quartermaster-general of the British forces in America. In 1758 he commanded the force which captured Fort Frontenac; and in 1764 he commanded the expedition to Detroit, which resulted in the submission of the Indians who had taken part in Pontiac's rebellion. He died at New York on September 25, 1774, two years after his promotion to the rank of major-general.

[*An impartial account of Lt.-Col. Bradstreet's expedition to Fort Frontenac* (London, 1759); *Dict. nat. biog.; Dict. Am. biog.;* Le Jeune,*Dict. gén.*]

Bradwin, Edmund William (1877-1954), educationist and author, was born at Lynden, Ontario, in 1877, and died at Toronto, Ontario, on February 19, 1954. He became a school-teacher, and in 1903 joined the staff of the Frontier College, which had been founded in 1900 by Alfred Fitzpatrick (q.v.) for the education of workers in mining, logging, and other camps. On Fitzpatrick's death in 1936, Bradwin succeeded him as principal. He received his M.A. from Queen's University and his Ph.D. from Columbia University, and in 1952 he was made an honorary LL.D. of the University of Toronto. He was the author of *The bunkhouse man: A study of work and pay in the camps of Canada* (New York, 1928).

[Toronto *Globe and Mail,* Feb. 20, 1954.]

Braithwaite, Edward Ernest (1865-1928), president of the University of Western Ontario (1914-19), was born at Unionville, Ontario, on March 14, 1865. He was educated at McGill University (B.A., 1886), at the Congregational College, Oberlin University (B.D., 1890), and at Harvard University (M.A., 1901; Ph.D., 1904). After acting for one year as professor of Old Testament language and literature at Oberlin College and Theological Seminary, he engaged in pastoral work in Massachusetts and in Ontario; but in 1912 he was appointed dean of a projected University or College at Calgary, Alberta. In 1914 he was appointed president of the Western University, London, Ontario; and he presided over the affairs of this institution during the difficult period of the Great War, but resigned in 1919. He died at Unionville, Ontario, on December 29, 1928.

[*Who's who and why,* 1921; Morgan, *Can. men* (1912).]

Brandtner, Fritz (1896-1969), painter, was born in Danzig, Germany, July 28, 1896. He served in the German army during the First World War, first as a cavalryman on the Russian front, and later in France, where he became a prisoner of war. He was in a French labour corps, as a prisoner, after the armistice, returning to Germany in 1920. In Danzig, he worked as a commercial designer, studied contemporary art movements and taught at the University of Danzig (1924-26). In 1928 he came to Winnipeg, Canada, where he worked as a house-painter, a window-display artist, and commercial artist. Here he met Lionel Lemoine Fitzgerald (q.v.), principal of the Winnipeg School of Art and a gifted landscape painter with whom he formed a close friendship. Brandtner held his first Canadian exhibition in the Winnipeg School of Art in 1928. His work was not well received by local critics. In 1934 he moved to Montreal where he felt his experimental art would be more acceptable. Again he worked in display art and design and held an exhibition of his paintings in 1936. He worked with Marian Scott and Norman Bethune (q.v.) in setting up a children's art centre, which he and Mrs. Scott operated from 1936 to 1950 with ever-growing success. From 1944 to 1966 he

taught at Miss Edgar's and Miss Cramp's school and for a number of years (1947-56) he lectured at McGill University School of Social Work. He was awarded the Jessie Dow Prize for water-colour painting in 1946; first prize in the Canadian Olympic Contest (1948); and the Visual Arts Award of the Canada Council in 1968. He was vice-president of the Canadian Group of Painters (1944-48 and 1953); and of the Canadian Society of Water-Colour Painters (1945). He died at Montreal, November 7, 1969. Brandtner's was a continuously experimental and creative approach to painting. He searched out new and original ideas and brought them into his work. He introduced German Expressionism to Canada but was not himself bound by it. Instead he pushed on into a world of brilliant colours, very much his own world.

His paintings may be found in the National Gallery of Canada, the Confederation Gallery in Charlottetown, in the Winnipeg Art Gallery, the Art Gallery of Ontario, the New Brunswick Museum, as well as in private collections.

[J. R. Harper, *Fritz Brandtner, 1896-1969* (a retrospective) (Montreal, 1969); D. W. Buchanan, *The growth of Canadian painting* (Toronto, 1955); P. Duval, *Canadian water-colour painting* (Toronto, 1954); G. McInnes, *Canadian art* (Toronto, 1950).]

Brant, Joseph (1742-1807), principal chief of the Six Nations Indians, was born on the banks of the Ohio River in 1742. He fought on the British side in the war of the American Revolution, and after the war led the Mohawk tribe to the valley of the Grand River, in the present province of Ontario. He died on November 24, 1807, at his house in Wellington Square (now Burlington), Upper Canada. He translated into Mohawk part of the Church of England prayer book and part of the Gospels.

[W. L. Stone, *Life of Joseph Brant* (Cooperstown, 1845); L. A. Wood, *The war chief of the Six Nations* (Toronto, 1915); M. L. Bonham, *The religious side of Joseph Brant* (Journal of religion, 1929); John W. Jakes, *Mohawk: The life of Joseph Brant* (New York, 1969); Ethel Brant Monture, *Famous Indians: Brant, Crowfoot, Oronhyatekha* (Toronto, 1960); Dent, *Can. port.,* vol. 1; Morgan, *Cel. Can.* and *Bib. can.*]

Braun, Antoine Nicolas (1815-1885), priest, was born at St. Avold, France, on February 5, 1815, and entered the Society of Jesus in 1839. He came to Canada in 1851, and served successively at Laprairie, Montreal, Quebec, and Montreal. He died at Sault-au-Récollet, Quebec, on February 1, 1885. He was the author of *Instructions dogmatiques sur le mariage chrétien* (Quebec,

1866) and *Une fleur de Carmel* (Quebec, 1881).

[Allaire, *Dict. biog.*]

Breakenridge, John (1820-1854), lawyer and poet, was born at Niagara in 1820, the son of John Breakenridge (d. 1828). He became a ward of Dr. William Warren Baldwin (q.v.), and was educated at Upper Canada College. He was called to the bar of Upper Canada, practised law in Kingston and Belleville, and died in 1854. He wrote under the pseudonym of "Claude Halcro"; and he was the author of *The Crusades, and other poems* (Kingston, 1846).

[A. H. Young (ed.), *The roll of pupils of Upper Canada College* (Kingston, Ont., 1917).]

Brébeuf, Jean de (1593-1649), Jesuit martyr, was born at Condé-sur-Vire, France, on March 25, 1593. Having entered the Society of Jesus, he came to Canada, with Samuel Champlain (q.v.), in 1625. He spent the years 1626-29 among the Hurons, and subsequently the years 1633-49. On March 16, 1649, he was tortured and put to death by the Iroquois at the village of St. Ignace in the Huron country. He wrote two of the Jesuit *Relations*. He was canonized on June 29, 1930.

[T. Besterman (ed. and tr.), *Travels and sufferings of Father Jean de Brébeuf* (London, 1938); C. W. Colby, *Canadian types of the old régime* (New York, 1908); C. de Rochemonteix, *Le Père Jean de Brébeuf* (Bull. rech. hist., 1898); F. Parkman, *The Jesuits in North America* (2 vols., Boston, 1867); R. G. Thwaites (ed.), *The Jesuit relations* (73 vols., Cleveland, 1897-1901); *Dict. Can. biog.*, vol. 1.]

Brebner, John Bartlet (1895-1957), historian, was born at Toronto, Ontario, on May 12, 1895, the son of James Brebner, the registrar of the University of Toronto. He was educated at the University of Toronto, but his course was interrupted in 1915 by his enlistment in the Canadian overseas forces, in which he served until the end of the war. He then resumed his studies as an exhibitioner in St. John's College, Oxford (B.A., 1920; B.Litt., 1925), and in 1921 he was appointed a lecturer in the department of modern history at the University of Toronto. He left Toronto in 1925 to accept an appointment in the department of history at Columbia University, New York. Here he obtained the degree of Ph.D. in 1927; and in 1942 he was appointed full professor. He was the author of *New England's outpost* (New York, 1927), *The explorers of North America* (London, 1933; new ed., 1955), *The neutral Yankees of Nova Scotia* (New York, 1937), *The making of modern Britain* (New York, 1943), *North Atlantic triangle* (New Haven, Conn., 1945),

Scholarships for Canada (Ottawa, 1945), and *Canada, a modern history* (Ann Arbor, Mich., 1960); and he was joint author, with M. L. Hansen, of *The mingling of the Canadian and American peoples* (New Haven, Conn., 1940). In 1957 he was offered the honorary degree of LL.D. by the University of Toronto, but he did not live to receive it. He died at New York on November 9, 1957.

[D. G. Creighton, *John Bartlet Brebner* (Can. hist. rev., 1958); *Can. who's who*, 1955-59; *Who's who in America*, 1956-57; *Encyc. Can.*]

Breckenridge, James (d. 1879), clergyman and poet, was born in Scotland, and on coming to Canada became a school-teacher. In 1865 he entered Knox College, Toronto; and in 1871 he was ordained a minister of the Presbyterian Church. He died at Streetsville, Ontario, on December 10, 1879. While still a school-teacher, he published a volume of *Poems* (Toronto, 1860).

[*Dom. ann. reg.*, 1879.]

Breithaupt, Louis Orville (1890-1960), lieutenant-governor of Ontario (1952-57), was born in Kitchener (then Berlin), Ontario, on October 28, 1890. He was educated at Northwestern College, Naperville, Illinois, and at the University of Toronto. He entered his family's leather business in Kitchener, and became its president in 1930. He represented North Waterloo in the Canadian House of Commons as a Liberal from 1940 to 1952; and in 1952 he was appointed lieutenant-governor of Ontario. He retired in 1957; and he died at Toronto on December 6, 1960. He received the honorary degree of LL.D. from McMaster University, the University of Toronto, the University of Western Ontario, and Queen's University; and in 1959 he was sworn in as chancellor of Victoria University.

[Toronto *Globe and Mail*, Dec. 7, 1960; *Can. who's who*, 1958-60; *Encyc. Can.*]

Bremner, Archibald (1849-1901), journalist, was born in Newfoundland in 1849, was educated there, and became a journalist successively in Montreal, Toronto, and London, Ontario. He died in London, Ontario, in 1901; and he was the author of a history of the city of London (London, Ont., 1897).

[Morgan, *Can. men* (1898).]

Bremner, Benjamin (1851-1938), local historian, was born in 1851 and died at Charlottetown, Prince Edward Island, on December 29, 1938. He was the author of *Memories of long ago* (Charlottetown, P.E.I., 1930), *An island scrap-book* (Charlottetown, P.E.I., 1932), and *Tales of Abegweit* (Charlottetown, P.E.I., 1936).

[Private information.]

Bressani, Francesco Giuseppe (1612-1672), Jesuit missionary, was born at Rome, Italy, on May 6, 1612, and in 1626 became a novice in the Society of Jesus. In 1642 he was sent as a missionary to Canada and in 1645 he was captured by the Iroquois and cruelly tortured. He was ransomed by the Dutch and returned to France; but in 1646 he returned to Canada, and joined again the Huron mission. He witnessed the destruction of the mission, and in 1650 he went back to Europe. He died in Florence, Italy, on September 9, 1672. Soon after his return to Italy he published his *Breve relatione d'alcune missioni ... nella Nuova Francia* (Macerata, 1653); this has been translated by the Rev. F. Martin (Montreal, 1852), and by R. G. Thwaites in the *Jesuit relations* (Cleveland, 1898).

[Le Jeune, *Dict. gén.*; Bibaud, *Panth. can.*; Allaire, *Dict. biog.*; F. Parkman, *The Jesuits in North America* (Boston, 1867); T. J. Campbell, *Pioneer priests,* vol. I (New York, 1908); *Dict. Can. biog.*, vol. 1.]

Brett, George Sidney (1879-1944), philosopher, was born at Briton Ferry, South Wales, on August 5, 1879. He was educated at Christ Church, Oxford (B.A., 1899; M.A., 1902); and after teaching in England for two or three years, he was appointed, in 1904, professor of philosophy in the Government College at Lahore, India. In 1908 he came to Canada as lecturer in classics in Trinity College, Toronto; in 1921 he was appointed professor of philosophy in the University of Toronto; and in 1932 he became dean of the faculty of graduate studies in the University. He was elected a fellow of the Royal Society of Canada in 1919; and he was the first editor of the *University of Toronto Quarterly.* He died at Toronto on October 27, 1944. He was the author of *The philosophy of Gassendi* (London, 1908), *The history of psychology* (3 vols., London, 1912-21), *The government of man* (London, 1913; 2nd ed., 1930), *Psychology, ancient and modern* (New York, 1928), and *Introduction to psychology* (Toronto, 1929).

[John A. Irving, *The achievement of George Sidney Brett* (University of Toronto Quarterly, July, 1945); C. Martin, *George Sidney Brett* (Proc. Roy. Soc. Can., 1945); *Can. who's who,* 1936-37; *Encyc. Can.*]

Brett, Robert George (1851-1929), lieutenant-governor of Alberta (1915-25), was born at Strathroy, Ontario, on November 15, 1851, the son of James Brett and Catherine Mallon. He was educated at the University of Toronto (M.D., 1874), and practised medicine successively at Arkona, Ont., and Winnipeg, Man., and at Banff, N.W.T. From 1888 to 1901 he was a member of the Legislative Assembly of the North West Territories; and from 1889 to 1891 he was president of the executive council. He was lieutenant-governor of Alberta from 1915 to 1925; and he died at Calgary, Alberta, on September 16, 1929. In 1878 he married Louise, daughter of Samuel Hungerford, Watford, Ont., and by her he had one son.

[*Can. parl. comp.*]

Brewster, Harlan Carey (1870-1918), prime minister of British Columbia (1916-18), was born at Harvey, Albert county, New Brunswick, on November 10, 1870, the son of Gilbert Brewster and Amelia Wells. He was educated in New Brunswick and at Boston, Mass. He went to British Columbia, and became manager and director of the Clayoquot Sound Canning Co. From 1907 to 1912 he represented Alberni in the Legislative Assembly of British Columbia. In 1912 he ran as leader of the Liberal opposition against Sir Richard McBride (q.v.), in Victoria city, and was defeated; but he was elected for Victoria at a by-election in March, 1916. In November, 1916, on the resignation of the Bowser government, he became prime minister, with the portfolio of president of the council. His term of office was, however, cut short by his death at Calgary, Alberta, on March 1, 1918. In 1892 he married Annie Lucinda Downie; and by her he had a son and two daughters.

[*Can. parl. guide,* 1916-18.]

Briand, Jean Olivier (1715-1794), Roman Catholic bishop of Quebec (1766-84), was born in France in 1715. He was ordained a priest of the Roman Catholic Church in 1739, and came to Canada in 1741. For many years he was a canon of the cathedral at Quebec; and in 1766 the British government gave an informal consent to his consecration as bishop of Quebec, with the official title of superintendent of the Roman Catholic Church in Canada. He played an important part in keeping the French Canadians at least passively loyal to the British crown during the period of the American Revolution. In 1784 he retired on a pension; and he died at Quebec on June 25, 1794.

[A. Gosselin, *L'église du Canada après la conquête* (2 vols., Quebec, 1916-17); W. S. Wallace (ed.), *The Massères letters* (Toronto, 1919); Allaire, *Dict. biog.*; Le Jeune, *Dict. gén.*]

Bridle, Augustus (1869-1952), journalist and author, was born in Dorset, England, in 1869; and died in Toronto, Ontario, on December 21, 1952. He came to Canada during boyhood, and became a journalist. He was associate editor of the *Canadian Courier* from 1908 to 1916, and editor from 1916 to 1930; and for many years he was the art, drama, and music editor of the Toronto *Daily Star.* He was the author of a novel entitled *Hansen* (Toronto, 1925) and of two collections of biographical sketches, *Sons of Canada*

(Toronto, 1917), and *Masques of Ottawa* (Toronto, 1921), the latter under the pseudonym "Domino".

[*Can. who's who*, 1949-51; *Encyc. Can.*]

Brierley, James Samuel (1858-1935), journalist, was born at London, Canada West, on March 4, 1858. He learned the printing business in the office of the London *Free Press,* and became a journalist. In 1881 he became editor and part proprietor of the St. Thomas *Home Journal;* and in 1896 he was appointed managing director of the Montreal *Daily Herald.* In his later years he retired from journalism, and devoted himself to his business interests. He died at Montreal, Quebec, on December 1, 1935. He was the author of *1881 and onward: Reminiscences of St. Thomas and Elgin county half a century ago* (St. Thomas, Ont., 1931).

[Morgan, *Can. men* (1912).]

Brigden, Frederick Henry (1871-1956), painter, was born in London, England, on April 9, 1871, and came to Canada in 1878. He was the son of the founder of an engraving business in Toronto, Ontario, known as Brigden's Ltd.; and he himself ultimately became the manager of the business. He studied painting under William Cruikshank and George A. Reid (qq.v.), and in 1943 retired from business to devote his whole time to painting. He was president of the Ontario Society of Artists from 1927 to 1931; and he was elected an A.R.C.A. in 1934, and an R.C.A. in 1937. Twenty-four of his paintings were reproduced in full colour in *Canadian landscapes, as pictured by F. H. Brigden,* with notes by J. E. Middleton (Toronto, 1944); and three of his paintings are in the National Gallery of Canada at Ottawa. He died while on a sketching trip at Bolton, Ontario, on March 24, 1956.

[W. Colgate, *Canadian art* (Toronto, 1943); H. A. Robson, *Canadian landscape painters* (Toronto, 1932); N. MacTavish, *The fine arts in Canada* (Toronto, 1925); *Can. who's who,* 1952-54; *Encyc. Can.*]

Briggs, William (1836-1922), clergyman and publisher, was born at Banbridge, county Down, Ireland, on September 9, 1836, the son of Thomas Briggs. He was educated at the Mount Street school and the Collegiate Institute, Liverpool, England, and came to Canada about 1859. He was ordained a minister of the Methodist Church in 1863, and was stationed at various places in Ontario during the next fifteen years. In 1879 he was elected book steward of the Methodist Book and Publishing House (later the Ryerson Press); and under him this became one of the largest publishing houses in Canada. He retired from charge of the business in 1919, and he died at Port Credit, near Toronto, on November 5, 1922. In 1865 he

married Rosalie Marian Clark, of Melbourne, Australia; and by her he had one son. In 1886 he was made a doctor of divinity of Victoria University, Cobourg.

[*Can. who was who,* vol. 2; H. Charlesworth (ed.), *A cyclopaedia of Canadian biography* (Toronto, 1919); Morgan, *Can. men* (1912); *Can. who's who* (1910); J. E. Middleton and others, *The municipality of Toronto* (3 vols., Toronto, 1923).]

Bristol, Edmund (1861-1927), politician, was born at Napanee, Ontario, on September 4, 1861, the son of A. S. Bristol, M.D. (McGill), and Sarah Everitt. He was educated at the University of Toronto (B.A., 1883), and at Osgoode Hall, Toronto; and was called to the bar in 1886 (K.C., 1908). From 1905 to his death he represented Toronto Centre in the Canadian House of Commons; and from September 21 to December 29, 1921, he was minister without portfolio in the Meighen administration. He died at Toronto on July 14, 1927. In 1889 he married Mary Dorothy, daughter of the Hon. J. D. Armour (q.v.).

[*Can. parl. comp.*; Morgan, *Can. men* (1912).]

Britnell, George Edwin (1903-1961), economist, was born in London, England, on June 9, 1903. The Britnells came to Canada in 1910 as homesteaders in Saskatchewan. George Britnell was educated at the University of Saskatchewan (B.A., 1929), at the London School of Economics and Political Science (1929-30), and at the University of Toronto (M.A., 1934; Ph.D., 1938). He was appointed lecturer in political economy at the University of Saskatchewan in 1930. In 1934 and 1935 he lectured at the University of Toronto, returning to Saskatchewan as assistant professor in 1936. He remained at the University of Saskatchewan until 1941 when he went to Ottawa to serve on the Wartime Prices and Trade Board, returning to the University of Saskatchewan in 1945 as professor and head of the department of economics and political science; he remained there until his retirement in 1961. Professor Britnell was chairman of the Economic Advisory Committee of the first Saskatchewan C.C.F. government, member of the research staff of the Rowell-Sirois Commission on Dominion-Provincial relations (1937-38), and chief economist of the mission to Guatemala for the International Bank for Reconstruction and Development (1950-51). He died at Saskatoon on October 14, 1961. He wrote *The wheat economy* (Toronto, 1939); *The economic development of Guatemala* (Washington, 1951) — with R. F. Behrendt, George de Fleurieu, and others; *Economia de Guatemala* (Guatemala, 1958) — with D. L. Grove, C. L. Jones, and others: *Canadian agriculture in war and peace* (Stanford, 1962) — with V. C. Fowke; and many research papers and briefs dealing mainly with Western Canadian economic problems.

[*Canadian journal of economics and political science*, vol. XXVII; *Can. who's who*, 1958-60.]

Brittain, Horace Leslie (1874-1957), political scientist, was born at Apohaqui, New Brunswick, on January 14, 1874, and died at Toronto, Ontario, on November 1, 1957. He was educated at the University of New Brunswick (B.A., 1895; M.A., 1898) and at Clark University (Ph.D., 1907). From 1914 to 1947 he was managing director of the Bureau of Municipal Research in Toronto; and he was the author of *Local Government in Canada* (Toronto, 1951).

[*Can. who's who*, 1954-56.]

Brittain, Miller Gore (1912-1968), artist and painter, was born in Saint John, New Brunswick, in 1912. He studied at the Art Students League in New York with Harry Wickey (1930-32) and during the thirties did works which were social comments on the period. During the Second World War he served as a bombardier on thirty-seven bombing sorties and received the Distinguished Flying Cross (D.F.C.). In April, 1945, he was appointed an official war artist and returned to Canada the same year. He found religious studies, particularly the Book of Job and the writings of William Blake, provided some relief from the emotional trauma of war and began to paint religious subjects. In 1957 his wife died of cancer; Brittain suffered increasing despair which was only partially lifted by the passage of time. His early painting, influenced by the Art Students League, was for publication and was a comment on the society of the thirties; his wartime painting was realistic and sometimes caustic. It was in the postwar years that he moved through a period of visionary religious and biblical themes to the more abstract and personal surrealism of his later years. A number of his early works appeared in *Saturday Night* and his paintings were shown in exhibits in Canada and the United States. One of his most interesting works, the cartoons which he did for murals at the Saint John Tuberculosis Hospital, was never completed and only the massive drawings on paper remain. Many of his paintings are in private collections in New Brunswick although he is represented in the National Gallery at Ottawa and the Beaverbrook Gallery in Moncton, New Brunswick. He died in Saint John, New Brunswick, January 21, 1968.

[B. Lord, *The History of painting in Canada* (1974); C. S. MacDonald, *A dictionary of Canadian artists*, vol. 1 (1967); *Atlantic Advocate* (March, 1965, and March, 1968).]

Broadus, Edmund Kemper (1876-1936), educationist and author, was born at Alexandria, Virginia, on August 27, 1876. He was educated at the George Washington University (B.A., 1898), the University of Chicago (M.A., 1900), and Harvard University (Ph.D., 1908); and after holding positions in the John B. Stetson University, the University of South Dakota, and Harvard University, he was appointed in 1908 professor of English in the University of Alberta — a position which he held until his death at Edmonton, Alberta, on December 17, 1936. He was the author of *The laureateship: A study of the office of poet-laureate in England* (Oxford, 1921), *The story of English literature* (New York, 1931), and *Saturday and Sunday* (Toronto, 1935); and he was joint editor, with R. K. Gordon, of *English prose from Bacon to Hardy* (London, 1918), and, with Eleanor H. Broadus, of *A book of Canadian prose and verse* (Toronto, 1923). In 1934 he was elected a fellow of the Royal Society of Canada: and in 1935 he was made an honorary LL.D. of the University of Alberta.

[*Can. who's who*, 1936-37.]

Brock, Sir Isaac (1769-1812), soldier, was born in the island of Guernsey, on October 6, 1769, the eighth son of John Brock and Elizabeth de Lisle. In 1785 he obtained a commission, by purchase, in the 8th Regiment; and by 1797, at the early age of twenty-eight years, he was lieut.-colonel of the 49th Regiment. In 1799-1801 he saw service in Holland and at Copenhagen; and in 1802 he was sent with his regiment to Canada. Here he was stationed, either at Quebec, at Niagara, or at York, until the outbreak of the War of 1812. He was promoted colonel in 1805, and major-general in 1811; and, just before the outbreak of hostilities, in 1812, he was appointed president and administrator of Upper Canada. In the early months of the war, he was the heart and soul of the defence of Upper Canada. With brilliant audacity, he captured Detroit on August 15; and on October 13 his troops defeated the American invaders at Queenston Heights on the Niagara frontier. During the engagement, however, Brock fell, mortally wounded, and died the same day. For his services in connection with the capture of Detroit, he had been gazetted, three days before his death, a K.C.B. He was not married.

[F. B. Tupper, *Life and correspondence of Sir Isaac Brock* (London, 1845); Lady Edgar, *General Brock* (Toronto, 1904); D. B. Read, *Life and times of Brock* (Toronto, 1894); W. R. Nursey, *The story of Isaac Brock* (Toronto, 1908); T. G. Marquis, *Brock, the hero of Upper Canada* (Toronto, 1912); H. Eayrs, *Isaac Brock* (Toronto, 1924); and E. A. Cruikshank, *Some unpublished letters from General Brock* (Ont. Hist. Soc., papers and records, 1915), *Doc-*

uments relating to the invasion of Canada and the surrender of Detroit 1812 (Ottawa, 1913), and *The documentary history of the campaigns on the Niagara frontier in 1812-14* (9 vols., Lundy's Lane Historical Society, 1896-1905).]

Brock, Isaac (1829-1911), clergyman and author, was born near Winchester, Hampshire, England, in 1829. His paternal grandfather was a first cousin of Sir Isaac Brock (q.v.). He was educated at Queen's College, Oxford (M.A., 1851), and was ordained a priest of the Church of England in 1853. He came to Canada in 1868, and from 1868 to 1872 he was principal of Huron College, London. Subsequently he was rector at Galt, Ontario, at Sherbrooke, Quebec, and at Londonderry and Kentville, Nova Scotia. From 1885 to 1888 he was president of King's College, Windsor. He died on January 1, 1911. He was the author of *Sermons on the Apostles' Creed* (London, 1864), and some pamphlets.

[*Crockford's Clerical directory;* Morgan, *Can. men* (1898); R. J. Long, *Nova Scotia authors* (East Orange, N.J., 1918).]

Brockington, Leonard Walter (1888-1966), lawyer and orator, was born in Cardiff, Wales, April 6, 1888. He was educated at the University of Wales and was classics master at Cowley Grammar School, St. Helen's, before coming to Canada in 1912. He worked as a newspaper reporter and as a civil servant in Edmonton while enrolled as an extramural law student. In 1913 he left Edmonton for Calgary and studied law with Lougheed and Bennett (q.v.). On completion of his studies in 1921 he became solicitor for the city of Calgary. Brockington's gifts as a speaker were well known in Western Canada and he was invited to become counsel for the North West Grain Dealers' Association at Winnipeg in 1935. The following year he became first chairman of the Canadian Broadcasting Corporation and was responsible, in large measure, for the policy of granting free air time rather than selling time for the discussion of controversial issues. During the Second World War he was special advisor to Mackenzie King (q.v.) and his powers as a speaker were in demand in Canada, the United Kingdom, and Australia as an interpreter of the Commonwealth war effort. He was an adviser on commonwealth affairs to the British Ministry of Information during the last years of the war and spent much of his time, despite his crippling arthritis, in the war zone. Brockington and radio developed together and his voice became one of the best known in the English-speaking world of the forties. He was in great demand at universities and association gatherings and was in receipt of innumerable honours and degrees. He was rector of Queen's University from 1947 to 1966, and an arbitrator in labour disputes, including a dispute between the United States government and its employees at the United Nations. He was a director of the Odeon Theatre chain, the *Globe and Mail*, Boeing of Canada, the Lord Simcoe Hotel, the Windsor Hotel; and a member of the law firm of Gowling, McTavish, Osborne and Henderson. He died at Toronto, Ontario, September 15, 1966.

[*Can. who's who,* (1964-66); *Maclean's* magazine, vol. 66 (April 15, 1953); Metropolitan Toronto Library Board, *Biographical scrapbooks,* vols. 27, 51, 67, 89.]

Broder, Andrew (1845-1918), politician, was born in Franklin, Canada East, on April 16, 1845, the seventh son of William Broder and Mary McKee. He was educated at the Huntingdon Academy and at Malone Academy, New York; and in 1866 he went into business in the county of Dundas, Ontario. From 1875 to 1886 he represented Dundas in the Legislative Assembly of Ontario and from 1896 to 1917 in the Canadian House of Commons. In 1916 he was appointed a member of the Privy Council for Canada. He died at Morrisburg, Ontario, on January 4, 1918.

[*Can. parl. comp.*; Morgan, *Can. men* (1912).]

Brodeur, Louis Philippe (1862-1924), minister of marine and fisheries for Canada (1906-11), was born at Beloeil, Quebec, on August 21, 1862, the son of Toussaint Brodeur, a rebel of 1837, and Justine Lambert. He was educated at the college of St. Hyacinthe and at Laval University (LL.B., 1884; LL.D., 1904), and was called to the bar of Quebec in 1884 (Q.C., 1889). From 1891 to 1911 he represented Rouville in the Canadian House of Commons; and in 1901 he was elected speaker of the House. In 1904 he became minister of inland revenue in the Laurier government, and in 1906 minister of marine and fisheries. He was one of the representatives of Canada at the Imperial Conferences of 1907 and 1911, and in 1910 he introduced the bill which created the Canadian navy. In 1911 he was appointed a judge of the Supreme Court of Canada. In 1923 he resigned from the bench to accept appointment as lieutenant-governor of Quebec; but he had hardly entered on the duties of this office when he died, at Quebec, on January 1, 1924. In 1887 he married Emma, daughter of J. R. Brillon, N.P., of Beloeil, Quebec.

[*Can. parl. comp.*; Morgan, *Can. men* (1912).]

Bronfman, Abraham (1882-1968), industrialist, was born in Winnipeg, Manitoba, March 15, 1882. He was associated with the family's hotel and liquor business and became vice-president of Distillers Corporation-Seagrams Limited. He was director of Bronfman Interests and secretary-treasurer and director of Brintcan Holdings (Canada) Limited. He was honorary president of the Federation of Jewish Community Services and was associated with many charitable medical and social causes both within and outside the Jewish community in Canada. He died in Safety Harbor, Florida, on March 16, 1968.

[*Canadian News Facts*, March 16-31, 1968; *Who's who in Canadian Jewry* (Montreal, 1967).]

Bronfman, Samuel (1891-1971), industrialist, was born in Brandon, Manitoba, March 4, 1891, and educated in public and high schools in Brandon and Winnipeg. He entered the hotel business in 1909, and with his father and brothers operated hotels in Manitoba and Saskatchewan along with a mail-order ·liquor business during the prohibition era. He organized Distiller's Corporation in 1924, acquired Joseph E. Seagram and Sons in 1928, and established Distiller's Corporation–Seagram's Limited of which he remained president from 1928 until 1971. He was associated with charitable and philanthropic organizations in Canada and Israel. He died at Montreal, Que., July 10, 1971.

[*Can. who's who*, 1967-69; J. H. Gray, *Booze* (Toronto, 1972).]

Bronson, Franklin Henry (1817-1889), lumberman, was born in Moreau, Saratoga county, New York State, on February 24, 1817. He was a pioneer of the lumber industry in the Ottawa Valley. He came to Canada in 1852, and in 1853 erected the first saw-mill in the Ottawa district for the manufacturing of lumber for the United States market. He died in 1889.

[Rose, *Cyc. Can. biog.* (1886); H. Charlesworth (ed.), *A cyclopaedia of Canadian biography* (Toronto, 1919).]

Brooke, Frances, *née* **Moore** (1745-1789), novelist, was born in England in 1745. She was the wife of the Rev. John Brooke, rector of Colney in Norfolk and afterwards (*circa* 1760-68) garrison chaplain at Quebec. She joined her husband in Quebec about 1764, and while in Canada wrote what may be described as the first Canadian novel, *The history of Emily Montague* (4 vols., London, 1769; new ed., Ottawa, 1931). She returned to England in 1768, and died in 1789.

[Frances Brooke, *The history of Lady Julia Mandeville* (London, 1792), to which are prefixed biographical anecdotes of the author; Morgan, *Bib. can.*; A. Blue, *Canada's first novelist* (Can. mag., 1921).]

Brooker, Bertram (1888-1955), advertising executive and author, was born at Croydon, England, in March, 1888; and died at Toronto, Ontario, on March 20, 1955. He came

to Canada in 1905, and became a journalist and later an advertising executive. He became interested in art; and he was the editor of the *Yearbook of the Arts in Canada* (2 vols., Toronto, 1929 and 1936). In 1936 he was elected a member of the Ontario Society of Artists. He was also the author of three novels: *Think of the earth* (London, 1936), *The tangled miracle* (Toronto, 1936), under the pseudonym of Huxley Herne, and *The robber* (New York, 1949).

[*Can. who's who*, 1952-54; *Encyc. Can.*]

Brooks, Allan (1869-1946), ornithologist, was born in 1869, and died at Courtenay, British Columbia, on January 4, 1946. With Harry S. Swarth, he was joint author of *A distributional list of the birds of British Columbia* (Berkeley, Calif., 1925).

[Private information.]

Brophy, Reginald McLaren (1902-1971), industrialist, was born in Montreal, Que., June 6, 1902, and educated at Westmount High School. He joined Canadian Marconi Company in Montreal in 1919, and worked in various factory positions until 1924, when he was appointed assistant general sales manager, becoming sales manager from 1926 to 1933 and assistant general manager from 1933 to 1934. From 1934 to 1937 he was director of station relations for the National Broadcasting Company of New York. He returned to Canadian Marconi in 1937 as general manager. He became president and managing director of Rogers Majestic, DeForest Radio, and Rogers Electronic Tubes Limited. He became president of Canadian Radio Manufacturing Corporation in 1950 and chairman of Canadian Motorola Products in 1957. During 1950 he represented Canada on a NATO committee which studied defence production facilities throughout Western Europe and the United Kingdom. He was co-ordinator of defence production for Canada (1952) and deputy minister (1952-54). He died at his home at Claremont, Ontario, September 1, 1971.

[*Can. who's who*, 1967-69.]

Brown, Adam (1826-1926), merchant and politician, was born at Edinburgh, Scotland, on April 3, 1826, and came to Canada in 1833. He entered mercantile life, first in Montreal, then in Hamilton; and he became in Hamilton the head of one of the largest wholesale grocery houses in Canada. He was one of the "fathers" of the National Policy of protection; and he represented Hamilton in the Canadian House of Commons from 1887 to 1891. In 1891 he was appointed postmaster of Hamilton; and he died at Hamilton on January 16, 1926.

[Morgan, *Can. men* (1912).]

Brown, Alan (1887-1960), paediatrician, was born at Toronto, Ontario, on September 27, 1887, and died at Toronto on September

7, 1960. He was educated at the University of Toronto (M.D., 1909), and after spending five years as resident physician at the Babies' Hospital, New York, he studied abroad in Germany, France, and England. He returned to Toronto to practise paediatrics, and in 1919 he was appointed physician-in-chief at the Hospital for Sick Children — a position he retained until his retirement in 1951. He was also for many years head of the department of paediatrics in the University of Toronto: and he was the author of *Common procedures in the practice of paediatrics* (Toronto, 1926) and *The normal child, its care and feeding* (Toronto, 1929) — both of which books ran to four editions.

[D. Sangster, *Alan Brown of Sick Kids* (Maclean's magazine, Aug. 1, 1952); *Can. who's who*, 1958-60.]

Brown, Edward Killoran (1905-1951), educationist and author, was born at Toronto, Ontario, on August 15, 1905. He was educated at the University of Toronto (B.A., 1926), and did post-graduate work at the University of Paris (D.-ès-L., 1935). He joined the teaching staff of the department of English in University College, Toronto, in 1929; and he was successively professor and head of the department of English in the University of Manitoba (1935-37), associate professor, and then professor, in University College, Toronto (1937-41), professor and head of the department of English at Cornell University (1941-44), and, lastly, professor of English at the University of Chicago (1944-51). His career was cut short by his sudden death at Chicago, Illinois, on April 24, 1951. He was the author of *Edith Wharton* (Paris, 1935), *Studies in the text of Matthew Arnold's prose works* (Paris, 1935), *On Canadian poetry* (Toronto, 1943; 2nd ed., 1944), *Matthew Arnold: A study in conflict* (Chicago, 1948), *Rhythm in the novel* (Toronto, 1950), and *Willa Cather: A critical biography* (Toronto, 1953), the latter completed by his friend, Leon Edel; and he was the editor of *Matthew Arnold: Representative essays* (New York, 1936), *Victorian poetry* (New York, 1940), and *Duncan Campbell Scott: Representative poems* (Toronto, 1951). From 1936 to 1950 he contributed an annual survey of Canadian poetry to the *University of Toronto Quarterly*'s "Letters in Canada".

[*Can. who's who; Encyc. Can.*]

Brown, Eric (1877-1939), director of the National Gallery, Ottawa (1913-1939), was born in Nottingham, England, and studied art in England. He came to Canada in 1909, and in 1910 he was appointed curator, and in 1913 director, of the National Gallery at Ottawa. He died at Ottawa, Ontario, on April 6, 1939.

[F. Maud Brown, *Breaking barriers: Eric Brown and the National Gallery* (Ottawa, 1964); *Can. who's who*, 1936-37.]

Brown, George (1818-1880), journalist and statesman, was born at Alloa, near Edinburgh, Scotland, on November 29, 1818, the son of Peter Brown (q.v.) and Isabella Mackenzie. He was educated at the High School and at the Southern Academy, Edinburgh; and in 1838 he migrated, with his father, to the United States. In 1842 the father and son founded in New York the *British Chronicle* (1842-43); but in 1843, finding New York uncongenial, they removed to Toronto, and founded there the *Banner* (1843-48), a weekly paper for Presbyterian readers. This was followed in 1844 by the *Globe,* a political journal, of which George Brown became the editor and guiding spirit. First as a weekly, then as a bi-weekly, then as a tri-weekly, and lastly as a daily, the *Globe,* under Brown's management, set a new pace in Canadian journalism; and before long it had earned for itself a political influence in Upper Canada such as no other journal has ever possessed.

In 1851 Brown was elected to the Legislative Assembly of Canada as a Reform member from the county of Kent. In the assembly he played at first a lone hand: he opposed the Hincks-Morin administration, and he refused to coalesce with the "Clear Grits". But his advocacy of representation by population, and his campaign against French-Canadian and Roman Catholic domination in Canada, eventually made him the most outstanding Reform leader in Upper Canada; and when the Macdonald-Cartier government resigned in 1858, he was called upon to form an administration. With A. A. Dorion (q.v.) he formed the short-lived Brown-Dorion government (August 2-4, 1858). He stood aloof from the S. Macdonald-Sicotte and S. Macdonald-Dorion governments of 1862-64; but when the second Taché-Macdonald government fell in June, 1864, and the "Great Coalition" was formed to bring about Confederation, he was included in it as the chief representative of the Reformers.

In October, 1864, Brown played a prominent part in the Quebec Conference; but in December, 1865, he resigned from the government, before Confederation was completed, through inability to work in harmony with his colleagues, and particularly with John A. Macdonald (q.v.), between whom and himself there had been for years a bitter personal enmity. Thereafter he played little or no part in parliament. In the first elections to the Canadian House of Commons, in 1867, he was defeated in South Ontario; and though he was appointed to the Senate in 1874, he spoke seldom in that house. In the country, however, he remained a force to be reckoned with. He was regarded as the power

99

behind the Mackenzie administration of 1873-78; and he was certainly the extra-parliamentary leader of the Liberals, who, in 1871, drove Sandfield Macdonald (q.v.) from office in Ontario.

Brown was a great journalist and a dominating personality. As a politician, his actions did not always square with his pretensions; and his editorship of the *Globe* was, as Goldwin Smith said, "a long reign of literary terror". But sometimes, as in 1864, he was capable of taking really statesmanlike views.

He died in Toronto on May 9, 1880, from a bullet wound inflicted by a discharged employee. In 1862 he married in Edinburgh Anne (d. 1906), daughter of Thomas Nelson, the publisher; and by her he had one son and two daughters.

[A. Mackenzie, *Life and speeches of the Hon. George Brown* (Toronto, 1882); J. Lewis, *George Brown* (Toronto, 1906); *Dict. nat. biog.*; Dent, *Can. port.*, vol. 2.; J. Young, *Public men and public life in Canada* (2 vols., Toronto, 1912); C. Clarke, *Sixty years in Upper Canada* (Toronto, 1908); Sir J. Willison, *Reminiscences* (Toronto, 1919); J. M. S. Careless, *Brown of The Globe* (2 vols., Toronto, 1959 and 1963); *Dict. Can. biog.*, vol. 10.]

Brown, Sir George McLaren (1865-1939), railwayman, was born in Hamilton, Ontario, on January 29, 1865, the son of Adam Brown (q.v.). He was educated at Upper Canada College, and entered the service of the Northern and Northwestern Railway in Hamilton. In 1887 he entered the service of the Canadian Pacific Railway; and in this service he rose until he became in 1910 European general manager of the railway. During the War of 1914-18 he was assistant director-general of movements and railways in the British War Office; and in 1919 he was created, in recognition of his services, a K.B.E. He retired from the European general managership of the Canadian Pacific Railway in 1937; and he died at Toronto, Ontario, on June 28, 1939.

[*Who was who*, 1928-40; *Can. who's who*, 1936-37; Morgan, *Can. men* (1912).]

Brown, George William (1860-1919), lieutenant-governor of Saskatchewan (1910-15), was born at Holstein, Ontario, on May 30, 1860, the son of Thomas Brown and Hannah Acheson. He was educated at Brantford Collegiate Institute and the University of Toronto (B.A., 1881); and in 1882 he went to the North West Territories. In 1892 he was called to the bar, and for many years he practised law at Regina, as well as ranching in the Qu'Appelle Valley. From 1894 to 1906 he sat for Regina in the Legislative Assembly of the North West Territories; and in 1910 he was appointed the second lieutenant-governor of the province of Saskatchewan. His term of office ended in 1915, and he died at Regina on February 17, 1919. In 1895 he married Anna Gardiner, youngest daughter of James Barr, Norwich, Ontario.

[*Can. parl. comp.*; Morgan, *Can. men* (1912); N. F. Black, *A history of Saskatchewan and the old North West* (Regina, 1913).]

Brown, George Williams (1894-1963), historian and editor, was born in Glencoe, Ontario, on April 3, 1894. He was educated at the University of Toronto (B.A., 1915) and at the University of Chicago (Ph.D., 1924). He married Vera Beatrice Kenny in 1920, and had four children by her. He served in the Canadian army (1914-18). He was a teacher in Saskatoon Collegiate Institute (1919-20); lecturer at the University of Michigan (1924-25); and a member of the department of history, University of Toronto, from 1925 until his death. He was editor of University of Toronto Press and was appointed editor of the *Dictionary of Canadian biography* in 1959. He was editor of *Readings in Canadian history* (Toronto, 1940); *Building the Canadian nation* (Toronto, 1942); *Canadian democracy in action* (Toronto, 1945), and *Canada in the making* (Toronto, 1953).

[*Can. hist. rev.*, vol. XLV (1964); *Can. who's who*, 1961-63.]

Brown, J. Archibald (1862-1948), painter, was born in Liverpool, England, on February 28, 1862, of Scottish parentage. He came to Canada in 1885, and, after trying business life, turned to painting for a livelihood, though he was mainly self-taught. He was elected an A.R.C.A. in 1898, and an R.C.A. in 1919. Three of his landscapes are in the National Gallery in Ottawa. In his later years he had a studio at Lancaster, Ontario. He died at Cornwall, Ontario, on November 7, 1948.

[N. MacTavish, *The fine arts in Canada* (Toronto, 1925); *Can. who's who*, 1948; Toronto *Globe and Mail*, Nov. 9, 1948.]

Brown, James (1790-1870), poet and surveyor-general of New Brunswick, was born in Forfarshire, Scotland, in 1790, and came to New Brunswick in 1808. He settled on a farm near St. Andrews, Charlotte county, and here he lived for the remainder of his life. For over thirty years he represented Charlotte in the Legislative Assembly of New Brunswick; and in 1854 he became surveyor-general in the Fisher administration. The government was defeated in 1856, and Brown lost his seat in the House; but he was re-elected in 1857, and resumed office as surveyor-general. Soon afterwards, however, he retired from political life, and was appointed a special commissioner to visit

Great Britain and advertise New Brunswick as a home for immigrants. He published, in this connection, a pamphlet entitled *New Brunswick as a home for immigrants* (Saint John, 1860). He is remembered, however, chiefly for his famous verses entitled *The de'il's reply to Robert Burns* (first published anonymously in the *Scottish American Journal*, 1859). Brown died at Tower Hill, near St. Andrews, New Brunswick, in 1870.

[D. F. Maxwell, *Hon. James Brown* (Acadiensis, 1903); W. G. MacFarlane, *New Brunswick bibliography* (Saint John, N.B., 1895).]

Brown, John Gordon (1827-1896), journalist, was born in Alloa, Scotland, on November 16, 1827, the son of Peter Brown (q.v.), and the brother of George Brown (q.v.). He was educated partly in Edinburgh, and partly in New York, and came with his parents and brother to Canada in 1843. He eventually joined the staff of the Toronto *Globe*, under his brother's management; and on George Brown's death in 1880, he succeeded him as managing editor. He retired from the *Globe* in 1882, and in 1883 he was appointed registrar of the surrogate court, Toronto. He died in Toronto on June 13, 1896.

[Rose, *Cyc. Can. biog.* (1886); Sir J. Willison, *Reminiscences* (Toronto, 1919).]

Brown, John Henry (1859-1946), poet and civil servant, was born at Ottawa, Ontario, on April 29, 1859, and died at Ottawa on November 30, 1946. He entered the Dominion civil service in 1882; and he published *Poems, lyrical and dramatic* (Ottawa, 1892).

[C. C. James, *Bibliography of Canadian poetry (English)* (Toronto, 1899); Morgan, *Can. men* (1912).]

Brown, John Price. See **Price-Brown, John.**

Brown, Lewis (1858-1930), local historian, was born on August 12, 1858, and died at Simcoe, Ontario, on November 26, 1930. He was the author of *A history of Simcoe* (Simcoe, Ont., 1929).

[Private information.]

Brown, Peter (1784?-1863), author and journalist, was born in Scotland about 1784. In his earlier years he was a merchant in Edinburgh; but in 1838 he emigrated with his family to New York. There he became a contributor to the *Albion*, and afterwards editor and proprietor of the *British Chronicle*. In 1843 he removed to Toronto, Canada, and founded here the *Banner*, a semi-religious newspaper; and in 1844 he joined with his son George Brown (q.v.) in founding the *Globe*. He died at Toronto in 1863. Under

the pen-name of "Libertas", he published *The fame and glory of England vindicated* (New York and London, 1842), in reply to C. E. Lester, *The shame and glory of England* (New York, 1841).

[*Cyc. Am. biog.*]

Brown, Robert Anthony (1914-1972), oil company president, was born at Calgary, Alberta, March 20, 1914. He was educated at the University School, Victoria, British Columbia, and at the University of Alberta. He was associated with the early days of oil exploration in Alberta and became president and managing director of Home Oil Company Limited, president of Cygnus Corporation, president of Natural Resources Growth Fund Limited, and director of several other companies associated with the power and petroleum industries. He was a member of the American Petroleum Institute and an associate member of the Canadian Institute of Mining and Metallurgy. He died at Calgary, Alberta, January 4, 1972.

[*Can. who's who,* vol. XI, (1967-69).]

Brown, Thomas Storrow (1803-1888), journalist and rebel, was born at St. Andrews, New Brunswick, in 1803, the son of Henry B. Brown, registrar of wills, and the grandson of a Loyalist. He went to Montreal at an early age, and in 1832 was one of the founders of the Montreal *Vindicator*. He allied himself with the French-Canadian *patriotes*, and took a leading part in the rebellion of 1837. At the battle of St. Charles he was the "general" in command of the rebel forces. After the battle he escaped to the United States, and from 1839 to 1842 he was a journalist at St. Augustine, Florida. In 1844 he returned to Canada under the amnesty, and for the remainder of his life he lived in Montreal. He lost his sight in 1876, and he died at Montreal in December, 1888. He published a *History of the Grand Trunk Railway* (Quebec, 1864), and a temperance pamphlet entitled *Strong drink, what it is, and what it does* (Montreal, 1884); and after his death there was published in *Le Courrier du Livre* (Quebec) a series of papers by him entitled *1837, and my connection with it*.

[J. Boyd, *Thomas Storrow Brown* (Revue canadienne, 1916); Morgan, *Bib. can.*; W.G. MacFarlane, *New Brunswick bibliography* (Saint John, N.B., 1895.)]

Brown, William (1738-1789), printer, was born in Scotland about 1738, the son of John Brown and Mary Clark, of Nunton, Kirkcudbrightshire. At the age of fifteen years he was sent to America, and he became an apprentice with William Dunlop, a printer of Philadelphia, and brother-in-law of Benjamin Franklin. In 1760 Dunlop sent him to establish a printing shop at Bridgetown, in the Barbados; but in 1763 his health compelled him to abandon this enterprise, and he obtained Dunlop's assistance in establishing a printing shop in Canada. He brought a press out from England, and set up at Quebec the first printing establishment in the colony. He published in 1764 the first number of the *Quebec Gazette;* and he continued to print the *Gazette* until his death, when it was taken over by his relatives, the Neilsons (q.v.). He died, unmarried, on March 22, 1789, having amassed what was, for those days, a large fortune.

[F. J. Audet, *William Brown* (Trans. Roy. Soc. Can., 1932); Ae. Fauteux, *The introduction of printing into Canada* (Montreal, 1930).]

Browne, Patrick William (1864-1937), priest and author, was born at Carbonear, Newfoundland, in 1864. He became a priest of the Roman Catholic Church, and in his later years was on the staff of the Catholic University of America. He died at Washington, D.C., in 1937. Among his publications was *Where the fishers go: The story of Labrador* (New York, 1909).

[*Guide to Catholic literature, 1888-1940* (Detroit, 1940).]

Brownell, Peleg Franklin (1856-1946), artist, was born at New Bedford, Massachusetts, in 1856. He studied under well-known artists in Boston and in Paris, France; and he came to Canada in 1886 as the headmaster of the Ottawa Art School. He was elected to the R.C.A. in 1895; and many of his paintings are in the National Gallery at Ottawa. He died at Ottawa on March 13, 1946.

[N. MacTavish, *The fine arts in Canada* (Toronto, 1925); *Can. who's who*, 1936-37; Toronto *Globe and Mail*, March 14, 1946.]

Brownlee, John Edward (1884-1961), politician, was born at Port Ryerse, Ontario, August 27, 1884. He was educated at Sarnia High School and the University of Toronto (B.A., 1908). He was called to the bar in Alberta in 1912 (K.C., 1921). He was attorney-general of Alberta from 1921 to 1924 and premier of the province from 1924 to 1934. He was head of the United Farmers of Alberta. He died at Port Ryerse, July 15, 1961.

[*Can. who's who*, 1955-57.]

Brownlow, Edward Burrough (1857-1895), journalist and poet, was born in London, England, on November 27, 1857, became a journalist in Montreal, Canada, and died in Montreal on September 8, 1895. After his death, William McLennan (q.v.) edited his collected poems under the title *Orpheus and other poems* (Montreal, 1896).

[C. C. James, *A bibliography of Canadian poetry* (Toronto, 1899).]

Brownridge, Earl Kitchener (1916-1973), business executive, was born in Toronto, Ontario, July 28, 1916. He was educated at Oakwood Collegiate Institute, and at the University of Waterloo. He joined the Victory Aircraft, Malton, Ontario, in 1944 and transferred to A. V. Roe when that company bought Victory Aircraft in 1945. He rose from works manager to president of Orenda Engines, a Roe subsidiary. He resigned in 1959 to become manager of American Motors, becoming president in 1961. He resigned to enter politics in 1968 and was unsuccessful Conservative candidate for Peel South. He became president of Brewers' Warehousing in 1969, of Formosa Spring Brewery (1970-71), and at his death was executive vice-president of the Security Capital Corporation Limited. During the Second World War he served with the Royal Canadian Artillery. In 1956 he received the McCurdy Trophy for outstanding contribution to Canadian aviation. He died at Mississauga, Ontario, November 15, 1973.

[*Can. who's who*, 1970-72.]

Bruce, Charles Tory (1906-1971), novelist and newspaperman, was born in Port Shoreham, Nova Scotia, May 11, 1906, and educated at Mount Allison University (B.A., 1927). He began his career as a reporter for the *Morning Chronicle*, Halifax, in 1927, and in 1928 went to New York as editor for Canadian Press. From 1929 to 1933 he was night editor in Halifax and from 1933 to 1939 was editor in Toronto. He became superintendent in New York (1939-40) and acting general superintendent in Toronto (1940-42), and general news editor (1942-45). He spent part of 1944 and 1945 in London, England, co-ordinating reports of Canadian Press war correspondents. He was general superintendent of the Canadian Press from 1945 to 1963.

Charles Bruce published a number of books of poetry, novels, and historical works — *Wild apples* (1927); *Tomorrow's tide* (1932); *Personal note* (1941); *Grey ship moving* (1945); *The flowing summer* (1947); *The channel shore* (1954); *The township of time* (1959); *News and the Southams* (1968). *The Mulgrave road* (1951) won the Governor General's Award for poetry. He died at Toronto, Ontario, December 19, 1971.

[*Can. who's who*, 1967-69.]

Bruce, Herbert Alexander (1868-1963), surgeon and politician, was born at Blackstock, Ontario, September 28, 1868. He attended Port Perry High School and the University of Toronto (M.D., 1892), winning the University gold medal and Starr silver medal; L.R.C.P. (London), and F.R.C.S. (1896). He also studied in Paris, Berlin, and Vienna. He served in the First World War with the Canadian Army Medical Corps, becoming Inspector General of Canadian Medical Services in July, 1916. His controversial report, highly critical of some aspects of the medical services, resulted in his being relieved of his position. He was a founder of the Wellesley Hospital in Toronto and continued a close association with it throughout his life. He was appointed lieutenant-governor of Ontario in 1932 and became involved in Mitchell Hepburn's (q.v.) campaign to close government house. Although government house remained open during Bruce's term as lieutenant-governor it was closed in 1937. He was elected to the House of Commons in 1940 and 1945, resigning in 1946. He was a professor of surgery at the University of Toronto for many years, a director of many Canadian companies, and a member of the Board of Governors of the University of Toronto. He was twice mentioned in despatches and was made a chevalier of the Order of Leopold of Belgium for service in the First World War. He was made a Knight of Grace of the Order of St. John of Jerusalem in 1934. He wrote *Politics and the C.M.A.C.* (1919), explaining his work as inspector general; *Our heritage* (1934); and *Varied operations,* his memoirs, in 1958. He died at Toronto, Ontario, June 23, 1963.

[*Can. who's who,* 1961-63; Bruce, *Politics and the C.M.A.C.* (1919); Metropolitan Toronto Library Board, *Biographical scrapbooks,* vols. 21 and 45.]

Bruce, James, eighth Earl of Elgin. See **Elgin, James Bruce, eighth Earl of.**

Bruce, Robert (1802-1885), philanthropist, was born in Aberdeen, Scotland, in 1802. He came to Canada in 1835, and became a market gardener in Quebec. He died in 1885, and his estate of $50,000 was left to his heirs in trust. In 1922 the last of his heirs died; and his estate is now devoted "by means of scholarships and bursaries to aid young men or young women to obtain the benefits of a university education." As a result of this bequest, scholarships have been established in Dalhousie University, Bishop's University, McGill University, Queen's University, the University of Toronto, and the University of Manitoba. It is directed that "the scholarships shall be given for the first twenty-five years of their existence to students of Scottish extraction, if such should offer for examination."

[Private information.]

Bruce, Robert Randolph (1863-1942), lieutenant-governor of British Columbia (1926-31), was born at St. Andrews, Elgin, Scotland, on July 16, 1863; and was educated at Glasgow University (B.Sc., 1886). He came to Canada in 1887, and for ten years was on the engineering staff of the Canadian Pacific Railway. He then devoted himself to the development of silver and lead mines in British Columbia. From 1926 to 1931 he was lieutenant-governor of British Columbia; and from 1936 to 1938 he was Canadian envoy extraordinary and minister plenipotentiary to Japan. He died at Montreal, Quebec, on February 21, 1942. In 1915 he married Lady Elizabeth Northcote (d. 1916), daughter of the second Earl of Iddesleigh; and in 1932 he married Edith, daughter of W. A. Molson, M.D., of Montreal.

[*Can. who's who,* 1938-39.]

Bruce, William (d. 1781), fur-trader, was engaged in the fur-trade at La Baye, on Lake Michigan, as early as 1763. He first appears in the North West in 1772, when Matthew Cocking (q.v.) met him at Basquia on the Saskatchewan. He told Cocking that "he had been a trader among the Indians at Mississippi, where a difference happening between his men and the natives he had killed one of the latter, and was obliged to leave that part and entered into this trade, being the first time of his being up." In 1773 he was near the Red Deer River; and in 1774, near Fort Dauphin. In 1778 he was described in a list of North West traders as "bad and rebel"; and he does not appear to have been included in the North West Company formed in 1779. In 1781 he made, with Charles Boyer (q.v.), a gallant defence of Fort des Trembles on the Saskatchewan, when it was attacked by the Indians; but shortly afterward he was carried off by the small-pox epidemic of 1781-82.

[W. S. Wallace, *The pedlars from Quebec* (Can. hist. rev., 1932).]

Bruce, William (1833-1927), astronomer, was born in the Shetland Islands, Scotland, on November 7, 1833, and came to Canada with his parents in 1838. He was educated in Hamilton, Ontario, and at Oberlin College, Ohio. He became a patent attorney in Hamilton; but devoted much time to the study of astronomy. He was for many years president of the Hamilton centre of the Royal Astronomical Society of Canada, and he founded the Elmwood Astronomical Observatory. He died in Hamilton on March 7, 1927.

[Private information.]

Bruce, William Blair (1859-1906), painter, was born at Hamilton, Upper Canada, on October 8, 1859, the son of William Bruce (q.v.) and Jennette Blair. At an early age, he entered the office of an architect, and studied art in the Hamilton Art School. In 1881 he went to France and studied in the Académie Julien at Paris under Fleury and Bourguereau. Henceforth, except for occasional visits to Canada, he lived in France and Sweden. He exhibited at the Paris Salon; and he acquired a notable reputation. One of his most famous pictures, "The Forgers", is in the National Gallery at Ottawa. He died at Stockholm, Sweden, on November 17, 1906; and in 1907 his widow, a wealthy Swedish sculptress, Mme Karoline Benedicks-Bruce, organized a retrospective exhibition of no fewer than one hundred and twenty-two of his paintings at the George Petit Galleries, Paris. A collection of his paintings is housed in Hamilton, Ont., as a public loan.

[E. Morris, *Art in Canada* (Toronto, 1912); N. MacTavish, *The fine arts in Canada* (Toronto, 1925); Morgan, *Can. men* (1898); *Can. who was who*, vol. 2.]

Bruchési, Louis Joseph Paul Napoléon (1855-1939), Roman Catholic archbishop of Montreal, was born at Montreal, Canada East, on October 29, 1855. He was educated at the Montreal Seminary, at Issy, France, and at Rome, Italy (D.D., 1878), and was ordained a priest of the Roman Catholic Church in 1878. In 1887 he was appointed professor in the Montreal branch of Laval University; and in 1897 he became archbishop of Montreal. He continued to administer the affairs of this archdiocese until his death at Montreal, Quebec, on September 20, 1939. In 1905 he was elected a fellow of the Royal Society of Canada. He was the author of *Conférence de la charité* (Quebec, 1882) and *Les catacombes de Rome* (Lévis, Que., 1886).

[J. Bruchési, *La vocation sulpicienne de Monseigneur Bruchési* (Trans. Roy. Soc. Can., 1941), *Un Inlassable Épistolier: Paul-Napoléon Bruchési (1855-1939)* (Trans. Roy. Soc. Can., 1972); *Can. who's who*, 1936-37; Allaire, *Dict. biog.*; Le Jeune, *Dict. gén.*]

Brûlé, Etienne (1592-1633), interpreter and explorer, was born in Champigny, south-east of Paris, France, toward the end of the sixteenth century. He came to Canada as a boy in 1608, became an Indian interpreter, and accompanied Champlain (q.v.) to the Huron country in 1615. In 1618 he pushed south through Pennsylvania to Chesapeake Bay; and in 1622 he penetrated, first of white men, to Lake Superior. He was murdered by the Hurons, near the site of the present town of Penetanguishene, Ontario, in June, 1633.

[B. Sulte, *Etienne Brûlé* (Trans. Roy. Soc. Can., 1907); C. W. Butterfield, *History of Brûlé's discoveries and explorations* (Cleveland, 1898); J. Tremblay, *La Sépulture d'Etienne Brûlé* (Trans. Roy. Soc. Can., 1915); J. H. Cranston, *Etienne Brûlé, immortal scoundrel* (Toronto, 1949); *Dict. Can. biog.*, vol. 1.]

Brumath, Adrien Leblond de. See **Leblond de Brumath, Adrien.**

Bruneau, Arthur Aimé (1864-1940), jurist, was born at St. Athanase d'Iberville,

Canada East, on March 4, 1864. He was educated at Sorel and at Montreal, and was called to the bar of Quebec in 1887. He represented Richelieu county in the Canadian House of Commons from 1892 to 1907; and in 1907 he was appointed a judge of the Superior Court of Quebec. He retired from the bench in 1928; and he died at Montreal, Quebec, on December 1, 1940. He was the author of *Questions de droit sur le mariage* (Montreal, 1921).

[P. G. Roy, *Les juges de la province de Québec* (Quebec, 1933).]

Brunet, Louis Ovide (1826-1877), priest and botanist, was born at Quebec, Lower Canada, on March 10, 1826. He was ordained a priest of the Roman Catholic Church in 1848; and in 1854 he was appointed professor of botany in the Quebec Seminary. Later, in 1863, he became professor of botany in Laval University at Quebec. He retired to private life in 1871; and he died at Quebec on October 2, 1877. He was the author of *Enumération des genres des plantes de la flore du Canada* (Quebec, 1864), *Catalogue des plantes canadiennes* (Quebec, 1865); *Catalogue des végétaux ligneux du Canada* (Quebec, 1867), and *Éléments de botanique et de physiologie végétale* (Quebec, 1870).

[Allaire, *Dict. biog.*; Morgan, *Bib. can.*; P. G. Roy, *Fils de Québec*, vol. 4 (Lévis, Que., 1933); *Dict. Can. biog.*, vol. 10.]

Bryce, George (1844-1931), historian, was born at Mount Pleasant, Upper Canada, on April 22, 1844, the son of George Bryce and Catherine Henderson, natives of Perthshire, Scotland. He was educated at the University of Toronto (B.A., 1867; M.A., 1868; LL.B., 1878; LL.D., 1884), and he studied theology at Knox College, Toronto (D.D., 1903). He was ordained a minister of the Presbyterian Church in 1871, and was immediately sent to Winnipeg, Manitoba, to organize the work of the Presbyterian Church there. He founded Manitoba College, and had a part in founding the University of Manitoba, in 1871. From 1871 to 1909 he occupied various positions in Manitoba College and the University of Manitoba; and in 1902 he was moderator of the Presbyterian Church in Canada. He died at his brother's house in Ottawa on August 5, 1931. In 1901 he was elected a member of the Royal Society of Canada, and in 1909 its president. Besides many pamphlets and articles of a miscellaneous character, he was author of *Manitoba: Its infancy, progress, and present condition* (London, 1882), *A short history of the Canadian people* (London, 1887; new ed., Toronto, 1914), *John Black, the apostle of the Red river* (Toronto, 1898), *The remarkable history of the Hudson's Bay Company* (London, 1900; 2nd ed., 1903; 3rd. ed., 1910), *Mackenzie, Selkirk, Simpson* (Toronto, 1905; new ed., 1926),

The romantic settlement of Lord Selkirk's colonists (Toronto, 1909), and *The life of Lord Selkirk* (Toronto, 1912); and he collaborated with W. W. Campbell (q.v.) in *The Scot in Canada* (2 vols., Toronto, 1911). A collection of the pamphlets published by him is in the Library of Congress, Washington.

[*Proc. Roy. Soc. Can.*, 1932; *Can. who was who*, vol. 2; Morgan, *Can. men* (1912); Rose, *Cyc. Can. biog.* (1886).]

Bryden, Walter Williamson (1883-1952), theologian, was born in Galt, Ontario, in 1883, and died at Toronto, Ontario, on March 23, 1952. He was educated at the University of Toronto (B.A., 1907) and Knox College; and was ordained a minister of the Presbyterian Church in 1909. He joined the staff of Knox College, and in 1945 became its principal. He was the author of *The spirit of Jesus in St. Paul* (New York, 1925), *Why I am a Presbyterian* (Toronto, 1934), and *The Christian's knowledge of God* (Toronto, 1941).

[Toronto *Globe and Mail*, March 24, 1952; *Can. who's who*, 1948.]

Brydges, Charles John (1827-1889), railway manager, was born in London, England, in 1827. He gained his apprenticeship in railway management with the South Western Railway in England; and in 1852 he came to Canada as general manager of the Great Western Railway of Canada. In 1861 he was appointed general manager of the Grand Trunk Railway, and he retained this position until 1874. He then became one of the commissioners of the Intercolonial Railway; and in his later years he was land commissioner of the Hudson's Bay Company at Winnipeg. He died in Winnipeg on February 16, 1889.

[*Cyc. Am. biog.*]

Brydone-Jack, William. See **Jack, William Brydone.**

Brymner, Douglas (1823-1902), archivist, was born on July 3, 1823, at Greenock, Scotland, the fourth son of Alexander Brymner and Elizabeth Fairlie. He was educated in the grammar school at Greenock, and went into business; but his health failed him, and in 1857 he came to Canada to engage in farming. He settled in the Eastern Townships, and gradually drifted into journalism. He became editor of the *Presbyterian*, the official organ of the Presbyterian Church in Canada, and associate editor of the Montreal *Daily Herald*. In 1872 he was appointed to the newly created post of Dominion archivist; and the Archives Branch, over which he presided for thirty years, was mainly his creation. Apart from a seven-page essay in verse entitled *The two mongrels: A modern eclogue,* "by Tumas Treddles, Esq., Thrums Cottage" (Toronto, 1876), he published noth-

ing; and the record of his life-work is to be found in the *Reports* of the Canadian Archives from 1872 to 1902. In 1892 he was given the degree of LL.D. by Queen's University, Kingston; and in 1895 he was elected a fellow of the Royal Society of Canada. He died at Victoria, British Columbia, on June 18, 1902. In 1853 he married Jean (d. 1884), daughter of William Thomson, of Hill End.

[D. C. Harvey, *Douglas Brymner* (Can. hist. rev., 1943); *Proc. Roy. Soc. Can.*, 1903; Morgan, *Can. men* (1898); Rose, *Cyc. Can. biog.* (1886).]

Brymner, William (1855-1925), painter, was born at Greenock, Scotland, on December 14, 1855, the son of Douglas Brymner (q.v.). He was educated at St. Francis College, Richmond, and the College of Ste. Thérèse de Blainville, Quebec; and he studied painting in Paris, France, under Bouguereau and Fleury. He was elected a member of the Royal Canadian Academy in 1886, and in 1909 he was elected its president. He was distinguished as a painter both of landscape and of the human figure. For many years he taught art in Montreal; and he died at Wallasey, England, on June 18, 1925. In 1910 he was made a C.M.G.

[N. MacTavish, *The fine arts in Canada* (Toronto, 1925); H. G. Jones and E. Dyonnet, *History of the Royal Canadian Academy of Arts* (n.p., 1934); Morgan, *Can. men* (1912); *Can. who was who*, vol. 2.]

Buchan, John. See **Tweedsmuir, John Buchan, first Baron.**

Buchanan, Alexander Carlisle (1808-1868), immigration agent, was born near Omagh, county Tyrone, Ireland, on December 25, 1808, the son of James Buchanan. He came with his parents in 1816 to New York, where his father had been appointed British consul; and in 1825 he came from the United States to Canada. In 1838 he was appointed chief immigration agent at Quebec; and during the important period that followed he established a reputation for kindliness and efficiency in dealing with immigrants into Canada. He died on February 3, 1868. In 1840 he married Charlotte, daughter of the Hon. Edward Bowen (q.v.); and by her he had several children. He was the author of *Emigration practically considered, with detailed directions to emigrants proceeding to British North America* (London, 1828).

[A. W. P. Buchanan, *The Buchanan book* (Montreal, 1911); Taylor, *Brit. Am.*, vol. 3.; Morgan, *Bib. can.*]

Buchanan, Arthur William Patrick (1870-1939), lawyer and author, was born in Montreal, Quebec, in 1870; and was educated at McGill University and at Laval University (LL.B., 1893). He was called to the bar in

1894 (K.C., 1908), and practised law in Montreal. He died at Montreal on October 31, 1939. He was the author of *The Buchanan book* (Montreal, 1911) and *The bench and bar of Lower Canada* (Montreal, 1925).

[*Can. who's who*, 1936-37.]

Buchanan, Donald William (1908-1966), author, collector, was born in Lethbridge, Alberta, April 9, 1908. He was educated at the University of Toronto, and at Oxford University. He founded the National Film Society of Canada in 1935. From 1937 to 1940 he was supervisor of the Talks and Public Affairs Division of the Canadian Broadcasting Corporation and later was with the National Film Board as supervisor of rural circuits and displays. He published three books on Canadian painters, *James Wilson Morrice* (1937); *Canadian painters* (1946); and *The growth of Canadian painting* (1950); and a number on films and design, *Documentary and educational films in Canada* (1952); *Design for use in Canadian products* (1947), as well as *This is Canada* (1945). He joined the staff of the National Gallery of Canada in 1947 and retired as associate director in 1960. His first photographic exhibition, *A not always reverent journey* (1959), received wide acclaim. Buchanan's interest in photography led him to publish *To have seen the sky* (1962); *A nostalgic view of Canada* (1963); and *Sausages and roses* (1963). He was an editor of *Canadian Art*. He died at Ottawa, Ontario, February 28, 1966.

[*Can. who's who*, 1961-63.]

Buchanan, Isaac (1810-1883), merchant and politician, was born in Glasgow, Scotland, on July 21, 1810, the fourth son of Peter Buchanan. He was educated at the Glasgow Grammar School; and in 1825 became an employee of William Guild and Co., West Indian merchants. He came to Canada in 1830 as the representative of this firm, and in 1831 established a branch of the firm in Toronto. In 1833 he became a partner, and was placed in charge of the firm's Canadian business. He established branches of the business at Hamilton and London, Upper Canada; and he became one of the leading wholesale merchants in Canada. From 1841 to 1844 he represented Toronto in the Legislative Assembly of Canada; and from 1857 to 1867 he represented Hamilton. A moderate Liberal, he supported the Macdonald-Sicotte government of 1862-63, but opposed the Macdonald-Dorion government of 1863-64; and in 1864 he accepted office as president of the council in the short-lived Taché-Macdonald administration. He retired to make way for George Brown (q.v.), in the coalition government of June, 1864; and in 1865 he withdrew from parliament. He died in Hamilton, Ontario, on October 1, 1883. In 1843 he married Agnes, second daughter of Robert Jarvis, a Glasgow merchant; and by her he had eleven children.

He is chiefly remembered as a controversial writer on trade and currency. At one time he advocated the adoption of an irredeemable paper currency, basing his arguments on the steadily declining gold supply preceding the gold discoveries in Australia and California; and he was one of the earliest advocates of tariff protection in Canada. He has sometimes been described as the real father of the "National Policy". In his later days, however, he came out in favour of commercial union with the United States, and a customs union for all North America. A collection of his speeches and papers was edited by H. J. Morgan (q.v.), under the title *The relations of the industry of Canada with the mother country and the United States* (Montreal, 1864); and some of his later publications were *The British American federation* (Hamilton, 1865) and *A government specie-paying bank of issue* (Hamilton, 1866). Perhaps his best-known pamphlet was *Britain the country versus Britain the Empire* (Hamilton, 1860).

[Morgan, *Cel. Can.* and *Bib. can.*; Taylor, *Brit. Am.*, vol. 1; *Dom. ann. reg.*, 1883; *Cyc. Am. biog.*; *Can. parl. comp.*, 1867; J. C. Dent, *The last forty years* (2 vols., Toronto, 1881); W. J. Rattray, *The Scot in British North America* (4 vols., Toronto, 1880).]

Buchanan, Milton Alexander (1878-1952), educationist, was born at Zurich, Ontario, on July 17, 1878. He was educated at the University of Toronto (B.A., 1901) and at the University of Chicago (Ph.D., 1906); and during the years 1902-04 he studied at Paris and Madrid. In 1906 he was appointed a lecturer in the department of Italian and Spanish in the University of Toronto, and he rose rapidly until he became head of the department in 1917. He became an Hispanic scholar with an international reputation; and in 1932 he was elected president of the Modern Language Association, the only Canadian ever elected to this position. In 1935 he was elected a fellow of the Royal Society of Canada. He retired from teaching in 1946, and he died at Toronto on May 2, 1952. He left his magnificent library of Spanish literature to the University of Toronto Library. He compiled a *Graded Spanish wordbook* (Toronto, 1927); he was chairman of the committee that prepared *Modern language instruction in Canada* (2 vols., Toronto, 1928); and he edited *Spanish poetry of the golden age* (Toronto, 1942).

[J. H. Parker, *Milton Alexander Buchanan* (Hispanic Review, vol. xx, 1952); A. F. B. Clark, *Milton Alexander Buchanan* (Proc. Roy. Soc. Can., 1955); *Can. who's who,* 1948.]

Buchanan, William Asbury (1876-1954), journalist and senator, was born at Fraserville, Ontario, on July 2, 1876, and died at Lethbridge, Alberta, on July 11, 1954. He became a journalist in Ontario, but in 1905 moved to Alberta, and acquired an interest in the Lethbridge *Herald*. He soon became its sole owner, turned it from a weekly into a daily, and eventually made it one of the most influential newspapers in the West. He was elected to the Canadian House of Commons in 1911 and again in 1917, as a Liberal; and in 1925 he was appointed a senator of Canada.

[C. F. Steele, *Prairie editor: The life and times of Buchanan of Lethbridge* (Toronto, 1961); *Can. who's who*, 1952-54; *Can. parl. comp.*, 1953; *Encyc. Can.*]

Bucke, Richard Maurice (1837-1902), physician and author, was born at Methwold, Norfolk, England, on March 18, 1837, the son of the Rev. Horatio Walpole Bucke and Clarissa Andrews. He was brought to Canada by his parents in 1838, and was educated at the London Grammar School. He studied medicine at McGill University (M.D., 1862), and at London and Paris; and he eventually began the practice of medicine at Sarnia, Ontario. In 1876 he was appointed superintendent of the Asylum for the Insane at Hamilton, Ontario; and in 1877 he became superintendent of the Asylum for the Insane at London, Ontario. This position he filled until his death at London on February 19, 1902. He was the author of *Man's moral nature* (New York and Toronto, 1879), *Walt Whitman* (Philadelphia, 1883), and *Cosmic consciousness* (Philadelphia, 1901). He was one of the literary executors of Walt Whitman, and edited a number of his literary remains.

[J. H. Coyne, *Richard Maurice Bucke* (Trans. Roy. Soc. Can., 1906; new and revised ed., Toronto, 1923); G. H. Stevenson, *The life and work of Richard Maurice Bucke* (Am. journal of psychiatry, 1937); *Can. who was who*, vol. 1; Morgan, *Can. men* (1898); Rose, *Cyc. Can. biog.* (1886).]

Buckingham, William (1832-1915), journalist, was born in Devonshire, England, on December 3, 1832. He came to Canada in 1857, and entered journalism. He was successively the editor and proprietor of the *Nor'wester*, the first newspaper in Winnipeg, of the Norfolk *Reformer*, and of the Stratford *Beacon*. From 1873 to 1878 he was private secretary to the Hon. Alexander Mackenzie (q.v.); and he was, with Sir George Ross (q.v.), joint author of *The Hon. Alexander Mackenzie, his life and times* (Toronto, 1892). He died at Stratford, Ontario, on June 11, 1915.

[*Can. who was who*, vol. 1; Morgan, *Can. men* (1912).]

Buffalo Child Long Lance (d. 1932), Blackfoot chief and author, was born in Montana, and was educated at Carlisle University and the Manlius Military Academy. He served for three years with the Canadian forces in the First World War, was twice wounded, and was decorated with the Croix de Guerre. After the war, he was attached to the American Museum of Natural History, and in 1928-29 was a member of the Burden expedition sent by the Museum to the far north. He was a licensed air pilot. He died, presumably by his own hand, on March 20, 1932. He was the author of an autobiography, *Long Lance* (New York, 1928).

[*New York Times,* March 21, 1932.]

Buies, Arthur (1840-1901), author, was born near Montreal on January 24, 1840, the son of William Buies, a banker, and Marie Antoinette Leocadie d'Estimauville. His parents went, while he was an infant, to live in British Guiana; and he was brought up by two aunts at Quebec. He led a strange and eventful life. After an education at the colleges of Nicolet and Ste. Anne de la Pocatière, he went in 1846 to British Guiana, and from there to Dublin and Paris. In 1859 he took service with Garibaldi in Italy; but the same year he returned to Canada to study law, and he was called to the bar of Lower Canada in 1866. He launched himself into journalism, and published in 1868-69 a periodical entitled *La Lanterne* (Montreal; new ed., 1884), and in 1876 one entitled *Le Réveil* (Quebec); and these were so strongly anti-clerical that they roused the condemnation of Cardinal Taschereau (q.v.). To other periodicals he contributed also short *chroniques* which were later collected under the titles *Chroniques: humeurs et caprices* (Quebec, 1873; new ed., Montreal, 1884), *Chroniques, voyages* (Quebec, 1875), and *Petites chroniques pour 1877* (Quebec, 1878). Among his other publications were *Lettres sur le Canada* (1862-63), *Le Saguenay et la vallée du lac Saint-Jean* (Quebec, 1880; 2nd ed., 1896), *Anglicismes et Canadianismes* (Quebec, 1888), *L'Outaouais supérieur* (Quebec, 1889), *Récits de voyages* (Quebec, 1890), *Au portique des Laurentides* (Quebec, 1891), *Reminiscences* (Quebec, 1892), *La vallée de la Matapédia* (Quebec, 1895), *La province de Québec* (anonymous, Quebec, 1900), and *Les poissons et les animaux à fourrure du Canada* (Ottawa, 1900). In his later years his radicalism abated, and he descended to writing immigration literature for the Quebec government. He died at Quebec on January 26, 1901.

[C. ab der Halden, *Nouvelles études de littérature canadienne-française* (Paris, 1907); P. G. Roy, *Les ouvrages d' Arthur Buies* (Bull. rech. hist., 1901); Léopold Lamontagne, *Arthur Buies, homme de lettres* (Quebec, 1957); Marcel A. Gagnon,

Le ciel et l'enfer d'Arthur Buies (Quebec, 1965); Le Jeune, *Dict. gén.*]

Bulger, Andrew (1789-1858), governor of Assiniboia, was born in Newfoundland in 1789, and served on the British side throughout the War of 1812. He was appointed governor of Assiniboia in 1822, and remained in office for a little more than a year. He died in Montreal, on March 28, 1858. His correspondence is preserved in the Canadian Archives.

[E. H. Oliver, *The Canadian North-West* (2 vols., Ottawa, 1914).]

Bulkeley, Richard (1717-1800), secretary of the province of Nova Scotia (1757-92), was born in Dublin on December 26, 1717, the son of Sir Lawrence Bulkeley and Elizabeth Freke. He was educated by a tutor, and spent three years at Trinity College, Dublin. In 1727 he entered the Dragoon Guards (captain, 1741), and from 1742 to 1747 he held the post of king's messenger at Whitehall. In 1749 he arrived in Nova Scotia with Governor Cornwallis, and in 1757 he was made secretary of the province. This post he held under thirteen governors until 1792, when his son was appointed in his place. In 1758 he undertook the editorship of the *Royal Gazette*. He was made clerk of the Council in 1763, and from 1775 to his death he was a judge of the Court of Admiralty. On November 26, 1791, on the death of Governor Parr (q.v.), he assumed, as senior councillor, the administration of the government until the arrival of Governor Wentworth (q.v.), on May 14, 1792. After a career of fifty-two years as a social and political leader in Nova Scotia, he died on December 7, 1800, "the father of the province". He married (1) in 1757, Amy (d. 1775), daughter of Captain John Rous, R.N.; and (2) in 1782, a daughter of Captain Mostyn, R.N.; and he had three sons.

[J. A. Macdonald, *Richard Bulkeley* (Coll. Nova Scotia Hist. Soc., vol. xii); D. Campbell, *Nova Scotia* (Montreal, 1873).]

Bull, William Perkins (1870-1948), lawyer and author, was born at Downsview, Ontario, on July 25, 1870. He was educated at Victoria College, University of Toronto (B.A., 1893; LL.B., 1895), and at Osgoode Hall. He was called to the bar in 1897 (K.C., 1908), and for a time practised law in Toronto. He then went to England, and conducted a convalescent hospital for Canadian officers in London during the First World War. He returned to Toronto about 1929, and devoted the later years of his life to compiling a series of volumes on the history of Peel county, Ontario. These bore the titles *From medicine man to medical man* (1934), *From rattlesnake hunt to hockey* (1934), *From Brock to Currie* (1935), *Spadunk* (1935),

From humming bird to eagle (1935), *From Boyne to Brampton* (1936), *From spring to autumn* (1937), *From Strachan to Owen* (1938), *From amphibians to reptiles* (1939), and *From Macdonell to McGuigan* (1940). He died at Niagara-on-the-Lake, Ontario, on June 30, 1948. In 1938 he was made an honorary LL.D. of Ottawa University.

[*Can. who's who*, 1936-37; *Who was who*, 1941-50.]

Buller, Arthur Henry Reginald (1874-1944), botanist, was born at Moseley, Birmingham, England, on August 19, 1874. He was educated at Queen's College, Taunton, and at the universities of Leipzig and Munich; and after serving on the staff of Birmingham University for a short time, was appointed professor of botany in the University of Manitoba in 1904. This position he held until his retirement in 1936. He was elected a fellow of the Royal Society of Canada in 1909, and its president in 1927; and he became a fellow of the Royal Society of London in 1937. He was an LL.D. of the University of Manitoba (1924) and a D.Sc., of the University of Pennsylvania (1933). He died at Winnipeg, Manitoba, on July 3, 1944. He was the author of *Researches on fungi* (6 vols., London, 1909-34), *Essays on wheat* (New York, 1919), and *Practical botany* (London, 1929).

[*Can. who's who*, 1936-37; *Trans. Roy. Soc. Can.*, 1945.]

Bullock, William (1797-1874), clergyman and author, was born in Prittlewell, Essex, England, on January 12, 1797. He was educated at the Blue Coat School, London; and became an officer in the Royal Navy. In 1821, however, he resigned his commission, and was ordained a priest of the Church of England. Until 1841 he was a missionary in Newfoundland. The rest of his life was spent in parochial work in Nova Scotia; and he was the first dean of the diocese of Nova Scotia. He died at Halifax, Nova Scotia, on March 7, 1874. He was the author of *Song of David* (London, 1822), *Practical lectures upon the story of Joseph and his brethren* (London, 1826), *The Baptist answered* (Boston, 1843), *The ruler's daughter raised* (Halifax, N.S., 1851), and *Songs of the church* (Halifax, N.S., 1854; 2nd ed., London, 1855).

[R. H. Bullock, *A memoir of the Very Rev. William Bullock* (Halifax, N.S., 1899); C. E. Thomas, *Dean William Bullock, D.D.* (Coll. Nova Scotia Hist. Soc., vol. xxxvii); *Dict. Can. biog.*, vol. 10.]

Bulyea, George Hedley Vicars (1859-1928), lieutenant-governor of Alberta (1905-15), was born at Gagetown, New Brunswick, on February 17, 1859. He was educated at the University of New Brunswick (B.A., 1878; LL.D., 1908), and from

1878 to 1882 he was principal of the Sunbury Grammar School. In 1882 he went to the North West, and he held various offices in the government of the North West Territories. In 1905 he was appointed first lieutenant-governor of Alberta, and in 1910 he was appointed for a second term. He died at Peachland, British Columbia, on July 28, 1928. He was the author of an official handbook of the North West Territories, published in 1902.

[*Can. parl. comp.*; Morgan, *Can. men* (1912).]

Bunn, John (1800?-1861), pioneer physician, was born at a Hudson's Bay Company post on Hudson Bay about 1800, the son of Thomas Bunn (q.v.). He studied medicine at Edinburgh University in 1817-19 and 1831-32, and became a licentiate of the Royal College of Surgeons of Edinburgh. On his return to the Hudson's Bay Territories, he became the sole physician for many years at the Red River Settlement. In 1835 he was appointed a member of the Council of Assiniboia, and he held several public offices. He died at Upper Fort Garry on May 31, 1861.

[R. Mitchell, *Doctor John Bunn* (Beaver, 1938).]

Bunn, Thomas (1764-1853), fur-trader, was born at Hendon, Middlesex, England, in 1764. He entered the service of the Hudson's Bay Company in 1797, when he became a writer at Albany Factory. In 1803 he was transferred to York Factory, and here he spent most of his service. He retired to the Red River Settlement in 1822; and he died there on January 15, 1853.

[E. E. Rich (ed.), *Journal of occurrences in the Athabasca department, by George Simpson* (Toronto: The Champlain Society, 1938).]

Burd, Frank J. (1870-1962), journalist, was born at Muskegon, Michigan, on January 7, 1870. He went west with his family in 1883 and was employed by the *Manitoba Free Press* in the circulation department. He joined the Klondike gold rush of 1898 with his brother and established a newspaper at White Horse in the Yukon Territories. After the gold rush he returned to Vancouver and worked for the *News Advertiser* and later the Vancouver *Province*, becoming managing director and president. He died at Vancouver on January 6, 1962.

[*Can. who's who*, 1955-57.]

Bureau, Jacques (1860-1933), minister of customs (1921-25), was born at Three Rivers, Quebec, on July 9, 1860, the son of Joseph Napoléon Bureau, Q.C., and Sophie Gingras. He was educated at Nicolet College and Laval University, and was called to the bar in 1882 (K.C., 1903). From 1882 to 1898 he

practised law in Manitoba and in Wisconsin; but in 1898 he returned to Three Rivers, and from 1900 to 1925 he represented Three Rivers and St. Maurice in the Canadian House of Commons. He was solicitor-general in the Laurier government from 1907 to 1911, and minister of customs in the King government from 1921 to 1925. In 1925 he was appointed a member of the Canadian Senate; and he died at Montreal on January 23, 1933. In 1884 he married Ida Beliveau; and by her he had one son.

[*Can. parl. comp.*; *Can. who was who*, vol. 1; Morgan, *Can. men* (1912).]

Bureau, Jacques Olivier (1820-1883), provincial secretary for Canada (1863), was born in Three Rivers, Lower Canada, in February, 1820. He became a notary public; and in 1854 he was elected as a *Rouge* to the Legislative Assembly of Canada for Napierville. This constituency he represented until 1862; he was then elected to the Legislative Council for the De Lorimier division; and in 1867 he was called to the Senate of Canada. For a few months in 1863 he held office as provincial secretary in the Sandfield Macdonald government. He died at St. Rémi, Quebec, on February 7, 1883.

[*Dom. ann. reg.*, 1883; *Can. parl. comp.*]

Burke, Edmund (1753-1820), first vicar apostolic of Nova Scotia, was born in Kildare, Ireland, in 1753. He was ordained a priest of the Roman Catholic Church, and came to Canada in 1786. He was appointed first vicar apostolic of Nova Scotia, with the title of bishop of Zion *in partibus infidelium*, in 1817; and he died at Halifax on November 29, 1820. He was the author of some early Nova Scotian imprints, such as *Remarks on the Rev. Mr. Stanser's Examination of the Rev. Mr. Burke's Letter of instruction* (Halifax, 1805), *A treatise on the first principles of Christianity* (Halifax, 1808), *Remarks on a pamphlet entitled Popery condemned* (Halifax, 1808), *Continuation of the first principles of Christianity* (Halifax, 1810), and *A treatise on the ministry of the church* (Dublin, 1817).

[C. O'Brien, *Memoirs of the Rt. Rev. Edmund Burke* (Ottawa, 1894); Rev. Brother Alfred, *The Right Rev. Edmund Burke* (Can. Catholic Hist. Ass., report, 1940-41); R. J. Long, *Nova Scotia authors* (East Orange, N.J., 1918).]

Burn, Sir George (1847-1932), banker, was born in Thurso, Scotland, on April 10, 1847, the son of the Rev. David Burn. He came to Canada in 1866, and entered the service of the Royal Canadian Bank in Toronto. In 1880 he became general manager of the Bank of Ottawa, and he retired from this position only in 1917. In 1915 he was elected president of the Canadian Bankers' Association, and in 1916 its honorary president. He died at Ottawa on December 5, 1932. In 1872 he married Kate Fraser, daughter of Matthew Drummond, Toronto; and by her he had four daughters. He was created a knight bachelor in 1917.

[*Who's who in Canada,* 1932; *Who was who,* 1929-40.]

Burn, William Scott (d.1851), author, was for a number of years secretary of the County of York Building Society, and was the author of *Principles of book-keeping by single and double entry* (Toronto, 1844). He published also *Connection between literature and commerce: Two essays read before the Literary and Historical Society of Toronto* (pamphlet, Toronto, 1845). He died in Toronto on September 30, 1851.

[Private information.]

Burnham, John Hampden (1860-1940), lawyer, author, and politician, was born at Peterborough, Canada West, on October 14, 1860, of United Empire Loyalist descent. He was educated at the University of Toronto (B.A., 1883; M.A., 1886), and was called to the bar of Ontario in 1886. He practised law in Peterborough; and from 1911 to 1925 he represented West Peterborough in the Canadian House of Commons as a Conservative. He died at Peterborough, Ontario, on April 25, 1940. He was the author of *Canadians in the imperial naval and military service abroad* (Toronto, 1891) and two novels, *Jack Ralston* (Edinburgh, 1900) and *Marcelle* (Toronto, 1905).

[Morgan, *Can. men* (1912); *Can. who's who,* 1936-37.]

Burns, Patrick (1856-1937), cattle king, was born at Oshawa, Canada West, on July 6, 1856. He went to the west in 1878, and became a dealer in cattle. He established a slaughter-house in Calgary in 1890, and he built up a business that became one of the largest meat-packing businesses in the world, with branches at London, Liverpool, and Yokohama. In 1931 he was summoned to the Senate of Canada; but he relinquished his seat in the Senate in 1936. He died at Calgary, Alberta, on February 24, 1937.

[*Can. who's who,* 1936-37; *Can. parl. comp.*]

Burns, Robert (1789-1869), clergyman and author, was born at Barrowstowness, Linlithgowshire, Scotland, on February 13, 1789. He graduated in arts at Edinburgh University in 1805, and in divinity in 1810. From 1811 to the disruption of 1843 he was minister of St. George's Church, Paisley; in 1843 he came out with the Free Church; and in 1845 he came to Canada. He was minister of Knox Church, Toronto, Canada West, from 1845 to 1856; and from 1856 to his death he

was professor of church history and apologetics in Knox College, Toronto. Before coming to Canada he published many books and pamphlets, notably an edition of Wodrow's *History of the sufferings of the Church of Scotland* (4 vols., Glasgow, 1830); but in Canada he published only two or three pamphlets. He died at Toronto on August 19, 1869. In 1828 he was made a D.D. of the University of Glasgow.

[R. F. Burns, *Life and times of the Rev. Robert Burns* (Toronto, 1872); Taylor, *Brit. Am.*, vol. 2; Morgan, *Bib. can.*]

Burns, Robert Easton (1805-1863), judge, was born at Niagara, Upper Canada, on December 26, 1805, the son of the Rev. John Burns, a Presbyterian minister who had come to Canada in 1803. He was educated at the Niagara Grammar School, and was called to the bar of Upper Canada in 1827. In 1836 he was appointed judge of the Niagara district, but he resigned in 1838, and took up practice in Toronto. His partners were Oliver Mowat (q.v.) and Philip M. Vankoughnet (q.v.). From 1844 to 1848 he was judge of the Home district; and in 1850 he was appointed puisne judge of the Court of Queen's Bench. This office he retained until his death at Toronto on January 12, 1863. He was twice married: (1) to Anne Taylor, by whom he had four sons, and (2) to Agnes Nanton. He was the author of a *Letter to the Hon. Robert Baldwin on the subject of division courts* (pamphlet, Toronto, 1847).

[D. B. Read, *Lives of the judges* (Toronto, 1888); *Cyc. Am. biog.*; Morgan, *Bib. can.*]

Burns, Robert Ferrier (1826-1896), clergyman and author, was born in Paisley, Scotland, on December 23, 1826, the son of the Rev. Robert Burns (q.v.). He was educated at the University of Glasgow, at New College, Edinburgh, and at Knox College, Toronto; and in 1847 he was ordained a minister of the Presbyterian Church in Canada. He was successively stationed at Kingston and at St. Catharines, Upper Canada, at Chicago, Illinois, at Montreal, Quebec, and at Halifax, Nova Scotia. In 1887 he was elected moderator of the General Assembly of the Presbyterian Church in Canada. He died at Broughty Ferry, near Dundee, Scotland, on April 5, 1896. Besides the life of his father, he published *Maple leaves for the grave of Abraham Lincoln* (St. Catharines, 1865), *A plea for the Lord's day* (Montreal, 1874), *Maine law* (Halifax, 1875), *Modern Babylon* (Halifax, 1876), and *Confession and absolution* (Halifax, 1883).

[*Cyc. Am. biog.*; Dent, *Can. port.*, vol. 3; Rose, *Cyc. Can. biog.* (1888).]

Burns, William (1757?-1829), legislative councillor of Lower Canada, was born in England about 1757, the son of a British army officer. At the age of fifteen, he emigrated to Canada with his father; but his father died on the voyage, and the boy arrived in Quebec a penniless orphan. He was adopted, however, by a merchant of Quebec, John Melvin, and eventually succeeded to the direction of his benefactor's business. In 1818 he was appointed a member of the Legislative Council of Lower Canada. He died, unmarried, at Quebec on September 25, 1829.

[P. G. Roy, *L'honorable William Burns* (Bull. rech. hist., 1935, pp. 740-43).]

Buroyne, St. George (1882-1964), painter, was born in England in 1882 and came to Canada in 1897. He was mainly self-taught and worked in Montreal. His water colour *Late Afternoon* is in the collection of the National Gallery of Canada. He died in 1964.

[C. S. MacDonald, *A dictionary of Canadian artists*, vol. 1 (Ottawa, 1967).]

Burpee, Isaac (1825-1885), merchant and minister of customs, was born at Sheffield, New Brunswick, on November 28, 1825, the eldest son of Isaac Burpee and Phoebe, daughter of Moses Coban. He was educated at the county grammar school, and in 1848 he moved to Saint John, where with his younger brother he founded the firm of I. & F. Burpee, hardware merchants. His first appearance in politics was in 1872, when he was returned to the Canadian House of Commons for the city and county of Saint John. Though a Liberal, he gave an independent support to the government of Sir John A. Macdonald until the fall of that government in 1873. He then became a vigorous opponent of the Conservative party, and on December 7, 1873, he accepted the portfolio of minister of customs in the Mackenzie administration. He remained a member of the government until its defeat and resignation in October, 1878, and he remained a member of the House of Commons until his death on March 1, 1885. He married, on March 8, 1855, Henrietta, youngest daughter of Thomas Robertson of Sheffield, England.

[*Dom. ann. reg.*, 1885; Dent, *Can. port.*, vol. 4; *Can. parl. comp.*]

Burpee, Lawrence Johnston (1873-1946), civil servant and author, was born in Halifax, Nova Scotia, on March 5, 1873. He entered the civil service at Ottawa in 1890, and was private secretary to three successive ministers of justice. After serving as librarian of the Ottawa Public Library from 1905 to 1912, he was appointed first Canadian secretary of the International Joint Commission, and this post he occupied for the rest of his life. He was honorary secretary of the Royal Society of Canada from 1926 to 1935, and he was its president in 1936-37. In 1927 the University of Toronto conferred on him the honorary degree of LL.D. His contributions to Canadian history, geography, and bibliography were extensive. He was the author of *The search for the western sea* (London, 1908; new and enlarged ed., 2 vols., Toronto, 1935), *Sandford Fleming, empire builder* (London, 1915), *Pathfinders of the great plains* (Toronto, 1915), *On the old Athabaska trail* (Toronto, 1927), *The discovery of Canada* (Ottawa, 1929; new and rev. ed., Toronto, 1944), and *Jungling in Jasper* (Ottawa, 1929); he was joint author, with H. J. Morgan, of *Canadian life in town and country* (Toronto, 1905); he edited *An historical atlas of Canada* (Toronto, 1927) and *The journals and letters of La Vérendrye and his sons* (Toronto, The Champlain Society, 1937); and he was joint editor, with L. E. Horning, of *A bibliography of Canadian fiction* (English) (Toronto, 1904), and, with A. G. Doughty, of *An index and dictionary of Canadian history* (Toronto, 1911; new ed., Toronto, 1926). He edited also a series of small volumes, entitled *By Canadian streams* (Toronto, 1909), *Flowers from Canadian streams* (Toronto, 1909), *A little book of Canadian essays* (Toronto, 1909), *Songs of French Canada* (Toronto, 1909), *Canadian eloquence* (Toronto, 1910), *A century of Canadian sonnets* (Toronto, 1910), and *Humour of the north* (Toronto, 1912). He died in the deanery of Christ Church, Oxford, England, on October 13, 1946, while visiting his son-in-law, the Very Rev. John Lowe (q.v.).

[Pelham Edgar, *Lawrence J. Burpee* (Proc. Roy. Soc. Can., 1947); *Who was who, 1941-50*; *Can. who's who, 1938-39*.]

Burque, François Xavier (1851-1923), priest and author, was born at St. Hyacinthe, Quebec, on April 20, 1851, the son of François Xavier Burque and Justine Jacques. He was ordained a priest of the Roman Catholic Church in 1874, was for a time a professor at the St. Hyacinthe Seminary, and was latterly curé of Fort Kent, Maine. He died at Quebec on October 22, 1923. He was the author of *La pluralité des mondes habités considérés au point de vue negatif* (Montreal, 1898), *Le docteur Pierre-Martial Bardy* (Quebec, 1907), *Elévations poétiques* (2 vols., Quebec, 1906-7; new ed., 1921), and *Le nouveau chansonnier canadien-français: Recueil de chansons populaires* (Quebec, 1923).

[Allaire, *Dict. biog.*]

Burr, Reuben (1766-1842), loyalist, was born in Bucks county, Pennsylvania, on March 14, 1766. He emigrated to Canada in 1787, and settled in the Niagara peninsula; but in 1790 he returned to Pennsylvania. In 1805 he again came to Upper Canada, and this time he settled near the present town of Aurora. He died near Woodbridge, Canada West, on September 21, 1842. A valuable series of his letters has been preserved.

[J. B. Tyrrell, *Reuben Burr, loyalist* (Ont. Hist. Soc., papers and records, 1942).]

Burrell, Martin (1858-1938), politician, librarian, and author, was born at Faringdon, Berkshire, England, on October 15, 1858. He came to Canada in 1886, and for nearly twenty years was engaged in fruit-farming, first in the Niagara peninsula and then in British Columbia. In 1908 he was elected to represent Yale-Cariboo in the Canadian House of Commons as a Conservative; and in 1911 he was sworn of the Privy Council for Canada, and became minister of agriculture in the Borden government. On the formation of a Union government in 1917, he became secretary of state and minister of mines; and he held these portfolios until after the close of the World War. Then, in 1920, he retired from political life, and was appointed parliamentary librarian in the Library of Parliament at Ottawa — a position he occupied until his death at Ottawa on March 20, 1938. In 1928 he was made an LL.D. of Queen's University, Kingston. From 1924 to his death he conducted a literary column in the *Ottawa Journal*; and he was the author of *Betwixt Heaven and Charing Cross* (Toronto, 1928) and *Crumbs are also bread* (Toronto, 1934).

[Morgan, *Can. men* (1912); *Can. who's who*, 1936-37; *Can. parl. comp.*]

Burrows, Acton (1853-1948), journalist and author, was born at Bosbury, Hertfordshire, England, on September 18, 1853, and died at Toronto, Ontario, on November 15, 1948. He came to Canada in 1873, and engaged in journalism successively in Elora, Guelph, Winnipeg, and Toronto. In 1898 in Toronto, he founded the *Railway and shipping world*, which was later renamed *Canadian transportation*. He was the author of *Annals of the town of Guelph* (Guelph, Ont., 1877) and *North Western Canada* (Winnipeg, 1880).

[Toronto *Globe and Mail,* Nov. 16, 1948; *Can. who's who*, 1938-39.]

Burrows, Theodore Arthur (1857-1929), lieutenant-governor of Manitoba (1927-29), was born at Ottawa, Ontario, on August 15, 1857, the son of Henry J. Burrows. He was educated at Manitoba College, Winnipeg; and became a lumber manufacturer, with mills at Dauphin and Edson, Manitoba. He represented Dauphin in the Manitoba legislature from 1892 to 1903, and in the Canadian House of Commons from 1904 to 1908. In 1927 he was appointed lieutenant-governor of Manitoba; and he died in office, at Winnipeg, on January 18, 1929.

[*Can. parl. comp.*; *Can. who was who,* vol. 2.]

Burt, Alfred Leroy (1888-1970), historian, was born at Listowel, Ontario, November 28, 1888. He was educated at Victoria College, University of Toronto (B.A., 1910), Rhodes Scholar for Ontario (1910), Oxford University (B.A., 1912; M.A., 1916). He was appointed to the staff of the University of Alberta in 1913, becoming head of the history department in 1921 after a period of military service during the First World War. He became professor of history at the University of Minnesota, 1930, where he remained during the balance of his teaching career. He died June 21, 1970.

Dr. Burt was one of the first to undertake a study of Canada's dual nationality. He made exhaustive use of material in the Canadian archives and produced a study of Quebec under the French régime entitled, *The old province of Quebec* (Toronto, Minneapolis, 1933). Other works were *The United States, Great Britain and British North America* (New Haven, 1940), *The evolution of the British Empire and Commonwealth from the American revolution* (Boston, 1956), and *Imperial architects* (Oxford, 1913).

[*Can. hist. rev.*, vol. LII (1971).]

Burton, Charles Luther (1876-1961), company president, was born at Malvern, Ontario, on September 9, 1876. His father was a small shopkeeper, first at Green River and later in Toronto. Burton was educated at Jarvis Collegiate Institute in Toronto and after graduation he joined Thompson, Henderson and Bell. From 1891 to 1899 he was associated with H. H. Fudger in the wholesale fancy goods trade. He was a traveller for various wholesale companies until 1912 when he became associated with the Robert Simpson Company, becoming president and chairman of the board of directors. He retired from active participation in the company in 1956. He published his autobiography, *A sense of urgency* (Toronto, 1952).

[*Can. who's who*, 1955-57.]

Burton, Edgar Gordon (1903-1968), merchant, was born in Toronto, Ontario, October 26, 1903, and educated at the University of Toronto. He joined the law firm of Star, Spencer and Fraser in 1922 and in 1923 became buyer for Carson, Pirie, Scott and Company of Chicago. He joined the Robert Simpson Company in 1925, becoming general manager in 1937, and managing director in 1945, president in 1948, and chairman in 1956. During the Second World War he was an administrator of the Wartime Prices and Trade Board. He was president of the Toronto Board of Trade (1949-50), and a member of the Board of Governors of York University. He was awarded the C.B.E. for his work in the Second World War. He died at Toronto, Ontario, May 8, 1968.

[*Can. who's who*, 1964-66.]

Burton, Eli Franklin (1879-1948), physicist, was born at Green River, Ontario, on February 14, 1879. He was educated at the University of Toronto (B.A., 1901; Ph.D., 1910) and at Emmanuel College, Cambridge (B.A., 1906); and he joined the staff of the department of physics in the University of Toronto in 1916. He became the head of the department in 1932, and continued in this position until shortly before his death at Toronto on July 6, 1948. He became a physicist of world-wide reputation, and was especially noted for his researches in liquid helium, colloids, cosmic rays, and radar. He was elected a fellow of the Royal Society of Canada in 1913, and was awarded the O.B.E. in 1943. His publications included *The physical properties of colloidal solutions* (London, 1916; 3rd. ed., 1938), *Lectures on general physics* (Toronto, 1933; 3rd ed., 1935), *The phenomena of superconductivity* (Toronto, 1934), *Phenomena at the temperature of liquid helium* (New York, 1940), *The electron microscope* (New York, 1942; 2nd. ed., 1946), and, with others, *College physics* (Toronto, 1947; 3rd ed., 1957).

[J. Satterly, *Eli Franklin Burton* (Proc. Roy. Soc. Can., 1949); *Who was who*, 1941-50; Toronto *Globe and Mail*, July 7, 1948.]

Burton, Sir Francis Nathaniel (1766-1832), lieutenant-governor of Lower Canada (1808-32), was born in London, England, on December 26, 1766, the younger twin son of Francis Pierpoint Burton (afterwards Conyngham), Baron Conyngham of Mount Charles, and Elizabeth, daughter of the Rt. Hon. Nathaniel Clements. In 1808 he was appointed lieutenant-governor of Lower Canada, a sinecure office, and he held this office until his death at Bath, England, on January 27, 1832. In 1822 he was created a K.C.H., and in 1825 he was administrator of the government of Canada during the absence of Lord Dalhousie (q.v.).

[*Dict. nat. biog.*]

Burton, Sir George William (1818-1901), judge, was born at Sandwich, Kent, England, on July 21, 1818, the second son of Admiral George Guy Burton, R.N. He came to Canada in 1836, studied law at Ingersoll, Upper Canada, and was called to the bar of Upper Canada in 1842 (Q.C., 1863). He practised law for many years in Hamilton, Upper Canada; and in 1874 he was raised to the bench as a judge of the Court of Error and Appeal. From 1897 to 1900 he was chief justice of the Supreme Court of Ontario; and he died in Toronto, on August 22, 1901. In 1850 he married Elizabeth, daughter of Dr. F. Perkins, of Kingston, Jamaica; and by her he had several children. He was created a knight bachelor in 1898.

[Morgan, *Can. men* (1898); Dent, *Can. port.*, vol. 3.]

Burton, John (1834-1897), clergyman and author, was born at Gailsham, Sussex, England, in 1834. He came to Canada as a young man, and was educated at Knox College, Toronto, and Albert College, Belleville (B.A., 1879; M.A., 1880). He was ordained a minister of the Presbyterian Church in 1864, and occupied charges at Prescott, Toronto, and Gravenhurst, Ontario. From 1890 to 1892 he was president of the Upper Canada Tract Society. He died at Gravenhurst on July 6, 1897. He was the author of *Congregational polity and work* (Bowmanville, 1885), *The French-Canadian: Imperium in imperio* (Toronto, 1887), *How to read the Bible* (Toronto, 1891), and *Social reform* (Toronto, 1892).

[Morgan, *Can. men* (1898).]

Burton, Ralph (d. 1768?), military governor of Three Rivers (1760-62), was a British army officer who came to America at the beginning of the Seven Years' War. As lieutenant-colonel of the 48th Foot, he fought with Braddock at the Monongahéla, and was wounded. He served at Louisbourg in 1758 and at Quebec in 1759, and was again wounded at the battle of Montmorency. After the capture of Quebec in 1759, he was appointed lieutenant-governor of the town under James Murray (q.v.); and after the capture of Montreal in 1760, he was appointed governor of the district of Three Rivers. With the exception of the year 1763, spent with his regiment in Cuba, he remained governor of Three Rivers throughout most of the period of military rule in Canada. In 1760 he was promoted to be colonel of the 95th Regiment; and in 1762 he was gazetted a major-general. After the institution of civil government in Canada in 1764, he was given command of the troops in the Northern Department; and trouble occurred between him and Murray, who had become civil governor at Quebec. He seems to have died in 1768, since his name disappears from the Army list in 1769.

[E. B. O'Callaghan, *Le major-général Ralph Burton* (Bull. rech. hist., 1901); Le Jeune, *Dict. gén.*; *Dict. Can. biog.*, vol. 3]

Burwash, Lachlan Taylor (1874-1940), mining engineer, was born at Cobourg, Ontario, on September 5, 1874, the son of the Rev. Nathanael Burwash (q.v.). He was educated at Albert College, Belleville, Ontario, at Victoria College, Cobourg, and at the University of Toronto (M.E., 1912). He went to the Klondike in 1892, and remained there until 1912, latterly as an engineer in the government service. He served in the first Great War as a major in the 1st Battalion, Canadian Pioneers; and after the war he was employed by the Canadian government to conduct explorations in the Canadian Arctic. His report, entitled *Canada's Western Arctic*, was published by the government at Ottawa in 1931. After 1932 he was interested in mining development in the Mackenzie River and Great Bear Lake regions, and became president of the Burwash Yellowknife Gold Mines, Limited. He died at Cobourg, Ontario, on December 21, 1940.

[*Can. who's who*, 1936-37.]

Burwash, Nathanael (1839-1918), chancellor of Victoria University (1887-1913), was born near St. Andrews, Lower Canada, on July 25, 1839, the son of John Burwash and Anne Taylor. He was educated at Victoria University, Cobourg (B.A., 1859; M.A., 1867; LL.D., 1892), and at the Garrett Biblical Institute, Evanston, Ill. (B.D., 1871; S.T.D., 1876). He was ordained a Methodist minister in 1864, and in 1866 was appointed to the staff of Victoria University. From 1866 to 1872 he was professor of natural science in this University; from 1874 to 1887 he was professor of biblical and systematic theology; and from 1887 to 1913 he was president and chancellor. In 1887-89 he played a foremost part in bringing about university federation in Ontario. Besides a number of theological works, he published *Memorials of Edward and Lydia Jackson* (Toronto, 1874), *Egerton Ryerson* (Toronto, 1903), and some chapters in *The University of Toronto and its colleges* (Toronto, 1906). A *History of Victoria College* written by him was published posthumously (Toronto, 1927). In 1913 he retired from the chancellorship of Victoria University; and he died at Toronto on March 30, 1918. In 1868 he married Margaret Proctor, of Sarnia, Ontario; and by her he had four sons. In 1902 he was elected a fellow of the Royal Society of Canada.

[*Proc. Roy. Soc. Can.*, 1918; Morgan, *Can. men* (1912); *Can. who's who* (1910); Rose, *Cyc. Can. biog.* (1888); W. S. Wallace, *A history of the University of Toronto* (Toronto, 1927).]

Burwell, Adam Hood (1790?-1849), clergyman, was born in England about 1790, and was a brother of Mahlon Burwell (q.v.). He came to Canada in 1831 as an assistant missionary of the Society for the Propagation of the Gospel; and was stationed first at Nicolet, in Lower Canada, and then at Bytown (now Ottawa). He died at Kingston, Canada West, on November 2, 1849. He was the author of two early Upper Canada imprints: *Doctrine of the Holy Spirit* (Toronto, 1835) and *A voice of warning* (Kingston, 1835).

[Frances M. Staton and Marie Tremaine (eds.), *A bibliography of Canadiana* (Toronto, 1934).]

Burwell, Mahlon (1783-1846), surveyor, was born in New Jersey on February 18, 1783, the eldest son of Adam Burwell. He came to Canada with his parents after the American Revolutionary War and studied surveying. He was employed as a surveyor by the government of Upper Canada from 1809 to 1840; and a large part of the western part of the province was surveyed by him. In 1811 he was appointed registrar of land titles for the district of Middlesex; and from 1812 to 1824 and from 1830 to 1834 he represented Middlesex in the Legislative Assembly of Upper Canada. In 1836 he was elected the first representative of London in the legislature. He died at his farm near Port Talbot, Ontario, on January 25, 1846.

[A. Blue, *Colonel Mahlon Burwell, land surveyor* (Proceedings of the Canadian Institute, 1899).]

Bury, Sir George (1866-1958), railway executive, was born in Montreal, Quebec, in 1866, and died at Vancouver, British Columbia on July 20, 1958. He entered the service of the Canadian Pacific Railway as a junior clerk in 1883, and rose to be vice-president. He retired from office in 1918, and lived in Vancouver for the last forty years of his life. He was created a knight bachelor in 1917 for his services in helping to reorganize the railway lines behind the western front during the First World War.

[*Can. who's who*, 1956-58; Toronto *Globe and Mail*, July 21, 1958.]

Bury, William Coutts Keppell, Viscount, and later **Earl of Albemarle** (1832-1894), civil servant, was born in 1832. He was educated at Eton. From 1850 to 1851, he was private secretary to Lord John Russell. He was a member of the British House of Commons from 1857 to 1865 and from 1868 to 1874. He held office as treasurer of the household (1859-66), and under-secretary of war (1878-80). He was created Baron Ashford in 1876, and succeeded to the earldom of Albemarle in 1891. In 1854 he was appointed civil secretary and superintendent of Indian affairs in Canada, and although his term of office was short he did much useful work. His *Report on the condition of Indians of North America* was a result of this work. He is best remembered by his *Exodus of the western nations* (2 vols., London, 1855). He was one of the founders, and for several years president of the Royal Colonial Institute. He died in 1894.

[*Dict. nat. biog.*]

Butler, John (d. 1794), soldier, was born in Connecticut, and became an important figure in the Mohawk Valley, in northern New York, before the American Revolution. In 1759 he commanded the Indians under Sir William Johnson in the campaign against Niagara, and in 1760 in the campaign against Montreal. He espoused the loyalist cause at the beginning of the Revolution, and in 1776 he organized Butler's Rangers, an irregular corps that fought at Oriskany in 1777, in Wyoming in 1778, in central New York in 1779, and in Schoharie and Mohawk settlements in 1780. He was charged with the commission of great atrocities; but these have been much exaggerated. After the war he came to Canada, disbanded the Rangers, and took up land in the Niagara peninsula. He was appointed superintendent of Indian affairs in Canada, and he continued in this office until his death at Niagara, Upper Canada, in 1794.

[E. Cruickshank, *The story of Butler's Rangers* (Lundy's Lane Historical Society, Welland, 1893); J. M. Dixon, *The real Wyoming Butler* (American illustrated Methodist magazine, 1900); H. Swiggett, *A portrait of Colonel John Butler* (New York history, 1937).]

Butler, Walter (d. 1781), soldier, was a son of Colonel John Butler (q.v.), of Butler's Rangers. He served throughout the American Revolutionary War as an officer in Butler's Rangers, and he commanded the Rangers at Cherry Valley in 1778. He was killed in a skirmish which took place on the banks of Canada Creek, which flows into the Mohawk River, in New York, on October 30, 1781. His "Journal of an expedition along the north shore of Lake Ontario, 1779" has been published, with notes and introduction by J. F. Kenney, in the *Canadian Historical Review*, 1920.

[H. Swiggett, *War out of Niagara: Walter Butler and the Tory Rangers* (New York, 1933).]

Butler, Sir William Francis (1838-1910), soldier and author, was born at Suirville, county Tipperary, Ireland, on October 31, 1838, the son of Richard Butler. In 1858 he obtained a commission in the 69th Foot; and in 1867 his regiment was sent to Canada at the time of the Fenian Raids. In 1870 he was sent as an *avant-courrier* of the Red River expeditions, and had an interview with Louis Riel (q.v.). He was then sent on a further mission, to report on conditions in the Saskatchewan country; and he made a journey to the Rocky Mountains, and back. The story of this is told in *The great lone land* (London, 1872). In 1872 he made a trip to Lake Athabaska, and he told the story of this in *The wild north land* (London, 1873). He left Canada in 1873, and the rest of his life was spent in other parts of the British Empire, notably in Egypt and South Africa. He attained the rank of lieutenant-general in 1900, and he retired from service in 1905. He died at Bansha Castle, county Tipperary, Ireland, on June 7, 1910. In 1874 he received the C.B.; in 1885 he was made a K.C.B.; and

in 1906, a G.C.B. Beside the works mentioned and others, he wrote *Far out: Rovings retold* (London, 1880) and *Red Cloud, the solitary Sioux* (London, 1882). After his death his daughter edited and published his *Autobiography* (London, 1911).

[Edward McCourt, *Remember Butler: The story of Sir William Butler* (Toronto, 1967); *Dict. nat. biog.*, supp. II; *Who was who*, 1897-1916.]

Button, Sir Thomas (d. 1634), sailor, was a native of Glamorganshire, Wales, and the son of Miles Button, of Worlton. He entered the Royal Navy about 1589; and in 1612 he was placed in charge of an expedition, consisting of two vessels, the *Resolution* and the *Discovery*, which had as their object the discovery of the north west passage. At the entrance to Hudson Strait, he discovered a group of islands which still bear his name; and he penetrated Hudson Strait across Hudson Bay to the mouth of the Albany River. He wintered here, and in the spring he took possession of the country in the name of the king of England, calling it New Wales. Having proved to his own satisfaction that there was no outlet from Hudson Bay to the west, he returned to England in 1613; and, as a reward for his discoveries, he was promoted to the rank of admiral. In 1620 he took part in the expedition sent against the Algerian pirates; and in his later years he became embroiled in several disputes with the Admiralty. He died in 1634, leaving children of both his wives.

[*Dict. nat. biog.*; *Dict. Can. biog.*, vol. 1.]

By, John (1781-1836), military engineer, was born in 1781. He was educated at the Royal Military Academy, Woolwich, and in 1799 was commissioned a second lieutenant in the Royal Engineers. He was stationed in Canada during the years 1802-11, and in 1826 he was sent out, as a lieutenant-colonel of the Royal Engineers, to design and construct the Rideau Canal. He chose for his headquarters a spot near the junction of the Ottawa and Rideau rivers; and about this place there grew up the village of Bytown (now Ottawa), which was named after him. He completed the canal and returned to England in 1832; and he died at Shernfold Park, Sussex, on February 1, 1836. He married in 1818 Esther, daughter of John March; and by her he had two daughters.

[A. Blue, *Colonel John By* (Canadian magazine, 1912); H. P. Hill, *Lieut.-Colonel John By* (Engineering journal, 1931).]

Byerly, Alpheus Edward (1894-1960), local historian, was born in 1894, and died at Guelph, Ontario, on June 10, 1960. He was the author of *The beginning of things in Wellington and Waterloo counties* (Guelph, 1935) and *Fergus, or the Fergusson-Webster settlement* (Elora, 1932-34).

[Private information.]

Byng of Vimy, Julian Hedworth George Byng, Viscount (1862-1935), governor-general of Canada (1921-26), was born on September 11, 1862, the seventh son of the second Earl of Strafford. He entered the British army in 1883 as a junior officer in the 10th Royal Hussars, and served in the Sudan expedition of 1884 and in the South African War from 1899 to 1902. In the First World War he commanded in 1914-15 the 3rd Cavalry Division, with the rank of major-general, and then the Cavalry Corps. After commanding the 9th and 17th Army Corps with the rank of lieutenant-general, he was appointed in 1916 to the command of the Canadian Corps, and he was in command of this corps during the battle of Vimy Ridge. In 1917 he was given command of the 3rd Army, with the rank of general, and this position he occupied until the end of the war, when he was thanked by parliament, and granted a large gratuity. In 1921 he became governor-general

of Canada; and he discharged the duties of this position with general acceptability until shortly before the expiration of his term of office, when he became involved in controversy as a result of his refusal of dissolution to the Right Hon. W. L. Mackenzie King (q.v.) and his subsequent granting of a dissolution to the Right Hon. Arthur Meighen (q.v.). The point on which he had to make a decision is one on which constitutional experts are still divided in opinion. On his return to Great Britain, he was appointed in 1928 commissioner of police in the metropolitan area in London, England; and this position he retained until 1934. He died at Thorpe-le-Soken, Essex, England, on June 6, 1935. He was created a K.C.M.G. in 1915, a K.C.B. in 1916, a G.C.B. in 1919, a G.C.M.G. in 1921, Baron Byng of Vimy in 1926. In 1902 he married Marie Evelyn, daughter of the Hon. Sir Richard Moreton; and she published two novels, *Barriers* (London, 1912) and *Anne of the marshland* (London, 1913), and an autobiography, *Up the stream of time* (Toronto, 1945).

[*Who was who*, 1928-40; *Americana annual*, 1936; J. Cowan, *Canada's governors-general* (Toronto, 1952).]

Cabot, John (*fl.* 1461-1498), explorer, was a native of Italy. Neither the date nor place of birth of Giovanni (or Zuan) Caboto, of which John Cabot was an anglicized version, is known. The earliest documents suggest that he went to Venice in 1461, where he resided continuously for the next fifteen years. For the next eleven years, a period during which he probably conceived the idea of a westward voyage to the Indies, information about Cabot is limited. By 1495, however, he had arrived in England, with a view to prosecuting this project, and he enlisted the aid of the merchants of Bristol. In 1497 Cabot set sail westward on a voyage of discovery from Bristol and made landfall on some part of the coast of northeastern America, possibly southern Nova Scotia. The following year he made a second expedition, with five ships, and possibly explored some part of the coast of northeastern America, though his course is a matter of conjecture. Cabot failed to find on the bleak coasts he visited the wealth of which he was in search and his expedition was a commercial failure. But if he failed to find the wealth of Asia, he led the way to a source of wealth hardly less great — the American fisheries. After his expedition of 1497, Cabot was granted a pension by Henry VII, and, although the pension was paid in 1498 and 1499, it is probable that he never returned to England, for after September, 1498, nothing more was heard about Cabot's voyage and he disappeared from view.

[J. A. Williamson, *The voyages of the Cabots* (London, 1929); H. P. Biggar, *The precursors of Jacques Cartier* (Ottawa, 1923), and *The voyages of the Cabots and of the Cortereals* (Revue hispanique, x, 485-593); R. Beazley, *John and Sebastian Cabot* (London, 1898); H. Harrisse, *John Cabot, the discoverer of North America, and Sebastian his son* (London, 1896); *Dict. Can. biog.,* vol. 1.]

Cadet, Joseph Michel (1719-1781), purveyor-general to the French forces in Canada, was born in or near Quebec on December 24, 1719, the son of a butcher. He began life as a cattle-dealer; and in 1748 he was appointed purveyor-general for the French forces in Canada. He played a dominant part in the economic life of New France in its last years, and after 1756 practically discharged the function of commissary-general of the colony. He has been regarded as one of those who bled New France to death; and after its fall he was condemned at Paris to make restitution and was banished. Recent investigations, however, have tended to clear his name of the charges made against him; and it is significant that he was pardoned in 1764, and was allowed to return to Canada to settle his affairs. He embarked in France on a career of land speculation which ended in disaster, and he died in France in 1781.

[A. Shortt, *Documents relating to Canadian currency, exchange, and finance during the French period* (2 vols., Ottawa, 1926); Le Jeune, *Dict. gén.*]

Cadieux, Louis Marie (1783-1838), priest, was born at Montreal, Canada, in 1783; was ordained a priest of the Roman Catholic Church in 1810; and died at Rivière-Ouelle, Lower Canada, on June 13, 1838. He was the author of *Observations sur un écrit intitulé: Questions sur le gouvernement ecclésiastique du district de Montréal* (Three Rivers, L.C., 1823).

[Allaire, *Dict. biog.*; Morgan, *Bib. can.*]

Cadillac, Antoine de Lamothe. See **Laumet, Antoine,** dit **de Lamothe Cadillac.**

Cadot, Jean Baptiste (*fl.* 1723-1803), trader, was born at Batiscan, Canada, on December 5, 1723, the son of Jean Cadot and Marie-Joseph Proteau. He settled at Sault Ste. Marie before 1751 and was left in charge of the French fort there when the French troops were withdrawn in 1758. Alexander Henry (q.v.) says that he was "the last governor of the French fort". After the British conquest, he entered partnership with Alexander Henry (q.v.); and during the Conspiracy of Pontiac saved Henry's life from the Indians. He continued to take part in the fur-trade at Sault Ste. Marie until 1796, when he handed over his business to his sons. He is said to have died about 1803; but there is some doubt about this, as there is evidence he was still alive at Sault Ste. Marie in 1812. In 1756 he had his marriage with Anastasia, a Nipissing woman, legitimized by the Church; and by her he had two daughters and two sons.

[J. Tassé, *Les Canadiens de l'ouest* (2 vols., Montreal, 1878).]

Cadot, Jean Baptiste (1761-1818), fur-trader, was born at Sault Ste. Marie on October 25, 1761, the elder son of Jean Baptiste Cadot (q.v.) and his wife Anastasia, a Nipissing woman. He was educated in Lower Canada, and David Thompson (q.v.), who met him in 1798 says that he "spoke fluently his native language, with Latin, French, and English". He entered the service of the North West Company, and in 1798-99 was a senior clerk in the Fond du Lac department. He was admitted a partner of the North West Company in 1801, but was expelled in 1803 for intemperance. From 1801 to 1813 he received an annual pension of £100 from the Company, but in the latter year this pension was discontinued, because about that time he had received an appointment as an interpreter in the Indian department of Upper Canada. He died in 1818.

[W. S. Wallace (ed.), *Documents relating to the North West Company* (Toronto: The Champlain Society, 1934).]

Cadot, Michel (1764-1836), fur-trader, was born at Sault Ste. Marie on July 22, 1764, the younger son of the elder Jean Baptiste Cadot (q.v.) and his wife Anastasia. He entered the employ of the North West Company, and in 1798 was in charge of a post on the river Tortue in the Fond du Lac department. He spent most of his life at La Pointe, Madelaine Island, in what is now Wisconsin; and there he died in 1836. He married the daughter of White Crane, a hereditary chief of the Chippewa tribe; and by her he had several daughters, two of whom married in 1821 two New England traders named Warren. Another daughter married Léon St. Germain.

[W. S. Wallace (ed.), *Documents relating to the North West Company* (Toronto: The Champlain Society, 1934).]

Cahan, Charles Hazlitt (1861-1944), secretary of state for Canada (1930-35), was born at Yarmouth, Nova Scotia, on October 31, 1861. He was educated at Dalhousie University (B.A., 1886; L.L.B., 1890), and was called to the bar of Nova Scotia in 1893 (K.C., 1907). He practised law in Halifax, Nova Scotia, in Mexico and in Montreal, Que. From 1890 to 1894 he represented Shelburne in the Legislative Assembly of Nova Scotia, and was during these years leader of the Conservative opposition. In 1925 he was elected to represent St. Lawrence-St. George in the Canadian House of Commons; and in 1927 he was a candidate for the leadership of the Conservative party at the Winnipeg convention of the party. From 1930 to 1935 he was secretary of state in the Bennett government. He was defeated in the general elections of 1940, and then retired to private life. He died at Montreal, Que., on August 15, 1944. He was an honorary LL.D. of Dalhousie University and of the University of Montreal.

[*Can. parl. comp.*; *Can. who's who, 1936-37.*]

Calder, Robert Louis (1878-1944), lawyer, was born at Sherbrooke, Quebec, on March 26, 1878, the son of John Calder and Delphine Primeau. He was educated at Laval University (B.A., 1897) and McGill University (B.C.L., 1906), and was called to the bar in Quebec in 1906 (K.C., 1922). He practised law in Montreal; and from 1923 to 1924 was crown prosecutor in Montreal. He served in the European war of 1914-18, with the rank of major, was wounded, and was awarded the M.C.; and from 1923 to 1930 he was officer commanding the Châteauguay regiment, with the rank of lieut.-colonel. He died at Westmount, Quebec, on May 12, 1944. He was author of *Comment s'éteint la liberté* (Lachute, Que., 1935).

[*Can. who's who, 1938-39; Who's who in Canada.*]

Caldwell, Henry (1738-1810), legislative councillor, was born in Ireland in 1738. In 1757 he was commissioned a lieutenant in the 69th Regiment, and in 1758 he was at Louisbourg, where he attracted the attention of Wolfe (q.v.), who remembered him in his will. At the capture of Quebec he served as deputy quartermaster-general under Guy Carleton (q.v.); and after the conquest he remained in Canada. In 1774 he was named agent and lessee for the seigniory of Lauzon. During the American invasion of Canada in 1775-76 he commanded the British militia at Quebec, and his account of the invasion was published nearly a century later (*Trans. Lit. and Hist. Soc., Quebec,* 1865). In 1776 he was made a legislative councillor of Quebec; and in 1784 he was appointed temporary receiver-general of the province, an appointment made permanent in 1794. His administration of the finances resulted in heavy losses to the Crown; but these did not become apparent until after his death. This occurred, on May 28, 1810, at Belmont Manor, Quebec, where during his later years he had lived in almost feudal splendour. He married Anne, the sister of Alexander Hamilton of Knoch and Hampton, county Dublin; by her he had one son.

[Sir J. M. LeMoine, *Maple leaves,* 7th series (Quebec, 1906), pp. 74-90; J. E. Roy, *Histoire de la seigneurie de Lauzon* (6 vols., Lévis, 1897); A. G. Doughty (ed.), *The journal of Captain John Knox* (3 vols., Toronto: The Champlain Society, 1914-16); Le Jeune, *Dict. gén.*]

Caldwell, Sir John, Bart. (1775-1842), receiver-general of Lower Canada, was born at Quebec in 1775, the only son of Henry

Caldwell (q.v.). He was privately educated, and in 1798 was called to the Quebec bar. In 1804 and in 1809 he was elected a member of the Legislative Assembly of Lower Canada for the county of Dorchester; and in 1810 he succeeded his father as receiver-general of the province. Defalcations amounting to £96,000 led to his dismissal in 1823. In 1830 he succeeded to the baronetcy of his cousin, Sir John Caldwell, of Castle Caldwell, County Fermanagh, Ireland; and he died at Boston, Mass., on October 26, 1842. He married, in 1800, Jane, daughter of James Davidson, surgeon to the 2nd battalion of the Royal Canadian Volunteers: she died at Quebec in 1805, leaving one son, Henry John, who in 1842 succeeded to the baronetcy.

[Sir J. M. LeMoine, *Maple leaves,* 7th series (Quebec, 1906); G. E. C., *Complete baronetage,* vol. 4 (Exeter, 1904); Le Jeune, *Dict. gén.*]

Caldwell, William (1863-1942), educationist, was born in Edinburgh, Scotland, on November 10, 1863, and was educated at Edinburgh University (M.A., 1884). After serving on the staff of Edinburgh University and several universities in the United States, he was appointed in 1903 Macdonald professor of moral philosophy at McGill University, Montreal. He retired in 1933; and he died at Montreal, Quebec, on December 14, 1942. He was the author of *Schopenhauer's system in its philosophical significance* (Edinburgh, 1896) and *Pragmatism and idealism* (London, 1913).

[*Can. who's who,* 1936-37.]

Caldwell, William Bletterman (*fl.* 1814-1857), governor of Assiniboia, was a British officer who obtained a commission as ensign in the 60th Regiment of Royal Americans in 1814. He was promoted to the rank of lieutenant in 1824, of captain in 1831, and of major in 1846. On the withdrawal of the British troops from Assiniboia in 1840, he took out to the Red River a corps of enrolled pensioners who were intended to combine agriculture and police duties. He was governor of Assiniboia from June, 1848, to June, 1855. He then returned to England, was promoted to the rank of lieutenant-colonel, and retired from the army. The history of his connection with the Red River settlement is given in the minutes of evidence taken before the select committee on the Hudson's Bay Company, 1857.

[E. H. Oliver (ed.), *The Canadian northwest* (2 vols., Ottawa, 1914); Le Jeune, *Dict. gén.*]

Calkin, John Burgess (1829-1918), teacher and author, was born at Cornwallis, Nova Scotia, in 1829, the son of Elias Calkin. He was educated at the Free Church College, Halifax, and at the Normal School, Truro, and became a school-teacher. From 1869 to 1900 he

was headmaster of the Truro Normal School; and he died at Truro on September 14, 1918. In 1909 he was made an honorary LL.D. of Dalhousie University. He was the author of *A geography and history of Nova Scotia* (Halifax, 1859; 2nd ed., 1864), *History and geography of the world* (Halifax, 1868; 2nd ed., 1872), *The world: An introductory geography* (Halifax, 1874), *History of British America* (Halifax, 1882), *Notes on education* (Truro, 1888), *History of the Dominion of Canada* (Halifax, 1898), and *Historical geography of Bible lands* (Halifax, 1905).

[R. J. Long, *Nova Scotia authors* (East Orange, N.J., 1918); Morgan, *Can. men* (1912).]

Callard, Keith Brendon (1924-1961), teacher, scholar, and CBC commentator, was born in 1924. He was educated at the London School of Economics and at Harvard University (1950-52). He taught in the department of economics and political science at McGill University from 1948 to 1950, returning again in 1952. In 1954 he spent a year's leave of absence in Pakistan and in 1957 published *Pakistan, a political study* (London, 1957) and *Pakistan's foreign policy* (New York, 1957). He applied his own discipline to many areas of inquiry and made a contribution to the study of local government in Canada and developing governments in Asia and Africa. He wrote a number of articles on local government and public administration. He died suddenly at Accra, Ghana, on September 26, 1961.

[*Can. journ. ec. pol. sc.,* vol. XXVIII.]

Callière, Louis Hector de (1648-1703), governor of New France (1699-1703), was the son of Jacques de Callières, governor of Cherbourg, and Madeleine Potier, and was born at Thorigny-Sur-Vive in 1648. He entered the army, and became a regimental captain. In the autumn of 1684 he came to Canada as governor of Montreal, and commanded the troops against the Iroquois. In 1694 he was made a chevalier of St. Louis. In 1699 he succeeded Frontenac as governor-general of New France, and he displayed great sagacity in his dealings with the Iroquois, concluding the memorable peace of 1701. He died in Quebec on May 26, 1703.

[B. Sulte, *La famille de Callières* (Trans. Roy. Soc. Can., 1890); Bibaud, *Panth. can.*; Le Jeune, *Dict. gén.*; *Dict. Can. biog.*, vol. 2.]

Calnek, William Arthur (1822-1892), author, was born at Granville, Nova Scotia, in 1822, and was educated at the Collegiate School, Windsor. He was successively a school-teacher, a journalist, and a land surveyor; but he was also for many years interested in historical research. He died suddenly at Bridgewater, Nova Scotia, on June 11, 1892. He was the author of *A brief memoir of the late Hon. James William Johnstone*

(Halifax, 1884), and a *History of the county of Annapolis,* completed by Judge Savary, and published posthumously (Halifax, 1897).

[R. J. Long, *Nova Scotia authors* (East Orange, N.J., 1918).]

Calvert, George. See **Baltimore, George Calvert, first Baron.**

Calvin, Delano Dexter (1881-1948), author and architect, was born at Garden Island, near Kingston, Ontario, in 1881, and died at Toronto, Ontario, on November 3, 1948. He was educated at Woodstock College and at Queen's University, Kingston (B.A., 1902), later studied architecture in Paris, France, and became an architect, practising in Toronto. The last years of his life he devoted to writing. He was the author of a centennial history of *Queen's University at Kingston* (Kingston, 1941) and of *A saga of the St. Lawrence* (Toronto, 1945); he was joint author, with T. B. Glover, of *A corner of Empire* (Toronto, 1937); and he edited John Macnaughton's *Essays and addresses* (Kingston, 1946).

[Toronto *Globe and Mail,* Nov. 4, 1948.]

Cameron, Aeneas (1757?-1822), fur-trader, was born in the parish of Kirkmichael, Banffshire, Scotland, about 1757. He emigrated to America, and first spent some time in Jamaica with an uncle, John Grant, who was chief factor of the island from 1783 to 1790. He then came to Canada, and in 1794 he was employed in the fur-trade at Fort Timiskaming, under James Grant, who was perhaps another uncle. He succeeded James Grant in charge of Fort Timiskaming in 1798, and became a partner in the North West Company. He returned to Montreal about 1807, when he was elected a member of the Beaver Club; and he was employed in a financial capacity at the headquarters of the North West Company until 1815, though he never became a partner in McTavish, McGillivrays, and Co. In 1812 he was appointed paymaster to the Corps of Canadian Voltigeurs raised by the North West Company in that year. He died at Montreal on August 18, 1822.

[W. S. Wallace, *An unwritten chapter of the fur-trade* (Trans. Roy. Soc. Can., 1939).]

Cameron, Agnes Deans (1863-1912), educationist and writer, was the daughter of Duncan Cameron and Jessie Anderson, and was born in Victoria, British Columbia, on December 20, 1863. She was educated in the public schools there, and was for eighteen years a teacher in the public and high schools of British Columbia. In 1906 she was elected school trustee of Victoria. In 1908 she made a 10,000-mile journey from Chicago to the Arctic Ocean by way of Athabaska, Great Slave Lake, and the Mackenzie River, returning by the Peace River and Lesser Slave Lake. In the following year she published an account

of her journey, *The new north* (New York, 1909). She contributed articles to numerous magazines, and lectured in Canada, the United States, and England. She died in Victoria, British Columbia, on May 14, 1912.

[Morgan, *Can. men and women* (1912); *Can. who was who,* vol. 2.]

Cameron, Angus (1782?-1876), fur-trader, was born in Scotland about 1782, a nephew of Aeneas Cameron (q.v.), and when a young man entered the service of the North West Company. Most of his life was spent in the Timiskaming district. At the time of the union of the North West and Hudson's Bay companies, in 1821, he was appointed a chief trader; and in 1838 he was promoted to be chief factor. In 1843 he returned to Scotland; and he died at his residence of Firhall, near Nairn, on August 11, 1876, aged 94 years. He should be distinguished from Angus Cameron, jr., who joined the North West Company as a clerk in 1819, was employed in the Timiskaming district until 1823, and retired from the fur-trade in 1825.

[W. S. Wallace, *An unwritten chapter of the fur-trade* (Trans. Roy. Soc. Can., 1939); R. Harvey Fleming (ed.), *Minutes of Council, Northern Department of Rupert's Land* (Toronto: The Champlain Society, 1940); *Dict. Can. biog.,* vol. 10.]

Cameron, Charles Innes (1837-1879), clergyman and poet, was born in Scotland in 1837, became a Presbyterian minister in Canada, and died at New Edinburgh, Ontario, on March 3, 1879. He was the author of *Poems and hymns* (Toronto, 1879).

[*Dom. ann. reg.,* 1879.]

Cameron, David (1804-1872), chief justice of Vancouver Island, was born in Perth, Scotland, in 1804, and began life as a cloth merchant. In 1830, after difficulties with his creditors, he emigrated to Demerara, and became overseer of a sugar plantation. In 1838 he bought a small property on the Essequibo River; but this business failed in 1851, and two years later Colville, governor of the Hudson's Bay Company, offered him a position as superintendent of the coal mines at Nanaimo. He arrived on Vancouver Island with his family in July, 1853. In September, 1853, he became one of the justices of the peace, and in December, he was made a judge of the Supreme Court. It was alleged that the fact that he was a brother-in-law of Governor Douglas (q.v.) accounted for his appointment, and a strict inquiry was asked. But, after two years of petitions and counter-petitions, Douglas was authorized to appoint him chief justice of Vancouver Island. He retired from the bench in 1864; and he died at Belmont, Vancouver Island, in 1872.

[E. O. S. Scholefield and F. W. Howay, *British Columbia* (Vancouver, B.C., 1914);

H. H. Bancroft, *History of British Columbia* (San Francisco, Cal., 1887); *Dict. Can. biog.*, vol. 10.]

Cameron, Sir Douglas Colin (1854-1921), lieutenant-governor of Manitoba (1911-16), was born at Hawkesbury, Upper Canada, on June 8, 1854, the son of Colin Cameron and Annie McLaurin. He was educated at the High School, Vankleek Hill, Ontario; and in 1880 he went to Manitoba. Here he entered the lumber business, and organized the Rat Portage Lumber Co., of which he was after 1894 its president. In 1902 he was elected as a Liberal to represent Fort William and the Lake of the Woods in the Ontario legislature, but he was defeated in the general elections of 1905 and 1908. In 1908 he was defeated also in the Dominion elections in Winnipeg. In 1911 he was appointed lieutenant-governor of Manitoba; in 1913 he was created a K.C.M.G.; and he retired from office in 1916. He died in Toronto on November 26, 1921. In 1880 he married Margaret, daughter of William Ferguson of Vankleek Hill, Ontario; by her he had two sons and one daughter.
[H. Charlesworth, *A cyclopaedia of Canadian biography* (Toronto, 1919); Morgan, *Can. men* (1912); *Can. parl. comp.*]

Cameron, Duncan (d. 1838), provincial secretary of Upper Canada (1817-38), was born in Scotland, and appears as a merchant in York, Upper Canada, in 1801. He was in command of the company of York Volunteers at the battle of Queenston Heights in 1812. In 1817 he was appointed to succeed William Jarvis (q.v.) as secretary of the province, and in 1820 he became a member of the Legislative Assembly of Upper Canada. He died in Toronto on September 9, 1838. He appears to have been unmarried; and his heir was his sister, Janet Cameron, who lived in his house at Gore Vale, near Toronto, until her death in 1853.
[J. Ross Robertson, *Landmarks of Toronto*, sixth series (Toronto, 1914).]

Cameron, Duncan (d. 1842), soldier, was an officer of the 79th Foot, or Cameron Highlanders, and was second-in-command of the regiment at the battle of Waterloo, and subsequently succeeded to the command of the regiment, with the rank of lieut.-colonel. He retired from the army in 1820; and in 1836, with his wife and nine children, he came to Canada and settled at York Mills, near Toronto. In 1838, after the rebellion of 1837, he was appointed colonel commanding the First Regiment of the North York militia. He died at York Mills in 1842, and was buried in the churchyard of St. John's Church, York Mills, which he was instrumental in building.
[T. W. L. MacDermot, *Some opinions of a Tory in the 1830's* (Can. hist. rev., 1930).]

Cameron, Duncan (1764?-1848), furtrader, was born at Glenmorriston, Inverness-shire, Scotland, about 1764, the son of Alexander Cameron and Margaret McDonell. His parents emigrated to America when he was a child, and settled at Schenectady, New York. During the American Revolution the family came north to Canada and settled at Williamstown, Glengarry. In 1784 Duncan entered the service of the North West Company, and for many years was employed in the Nipigon department. He was elected a partner of the North West Company about 1800; and until 1807 he was proprietor in charge at Nipigon. From 1807 to 1811 he was stationed at Lake Winnipeg; and from 1811 to 1814, at Rainy Lake. In 1814, he was placed in charge of the Red River department; and it fell to him to deal with the situation created by the establishment of the Selkirk colony. He was taken prisoner by the officers of the Hudson's Bay Company in the attack on Fort Gibraltar in April, 1816, and was sent to England, by way of Hudson Bay, for trial. In England he was released, and obtained damages from the Hudson's Bay Company for false imprisonment. About 1820 he returned to Canada, and settled at Williamstown, Glengarry; and in 1824 he was elected to represent Glengarry in the Legislative Assembly of Upper Canada, but was unseated. He died at Williamstown on May 15, 1848, age 84 years. In 1820 he married Margaret, daughter of Capt. McLeod of Hamer, and by her had several children, one of whom later became Sir Roderick W. Cameron, of New York. Duncan Cameron's *Nipigon journal* and his *Sketch of the customs of the natives of the Nipigon country* have been printed in L. R. Masson, *Les bourgeois de la Cie. du Nord-Ouest* (2nd series, Quebec, 1890).
[G. Bryce, *The remarkable history of the Hudson's Bay Company* (London, 1900); E. Coues, *New light on the early history of the great north west* (New York, 1897); J. A. Macdonell, *Sketches illustrating the early settlement and history of Glengarry* (Montreal, 1893).]

Cameron, Edward Robert (1857-1931), lawyer and author, was born at London, Ontario, on March 18, 1857, the son of Daniel Cameron and Louisa, daughter of Major John Parke. He was educated at the University of Toronto (B.A., 1879; M.A., 1882), and was called to the bar of Ontario in 1882 (K.C., 1902). After practising law in Strathroy and London, Ontario, he was appointed in 1898 registrar of the Supreme Court of Canada. He died at Ottawa on February 1, 1931. He was the author of *The Memoirs of Ralph Vansittart* (Toronto, 1902; 2nd ed., 1924), *The practice and jurisprudence of the Supreme Court of Canada* (Toronto, 1906), *The Canadian constitution as interpreted by the Judicial Committee of the Privy Council* (2 vols., Winnipeg and Toronto, 1915-30), *Canadian com-*

panies and the Judicial Committee (Toronto, 1922), and other legal works.

[Morgan, *Can. men* (1912).]

Cameron, George Frederick (1854-1885), poet and journalist, was born in New Glasgow, Nova Scotia, on September 24, 1854. At the age of fifteen years he went with his parents to live in Boston, Massachusetts, and most of his life was spent in the United States. In 1882, however, he returned to Canada, and became editor of the *News* in Kingston, Ontario. He died at Kingston on September 17, 1885. In 1887 his brother, Charles J. Cameron, published a collection of his verse under the title, *Lyrics on freedom, love and death* (Kingston and Boston, 1887).

[J. D. Logan and D. French, *Highways of Canadian literature* (Toronto, 1924); A. MacMurchy, *Handbook of Canadian literature* (Toronto, 1906); C. C. James, *A bibliography of Canadian poetry* (Toronto, 1899).]

Cameron, James (1817?-1851), fur-trader, was born in Scotland, about 1817, a nephew of Angus Cameron (q.v.), and came to Canada in 1836. He was employed as a clerk of the Hudson's Bay Company in the Timiskaming district, under his uncle; and in 1847 he succeeded his uncle in charge of Fort Timiskaming. He was promoted to the rank of chief trader in 1849; but he was accidentally shot by one of his clerks in 1850, and returned to Scotland a dying man. He died at Ballinish, the home of his family, in Kirkmichael parish, Banffshire, Scotland, on January 28, 1851.

[W. S. Wallace, *An unwritten chapter of the fur-trade* (Trans. Roy. Soc. Can., 1939).]

Cameron, John (1843-1908), journalist, was born at Markham, Upper Canada, on January 21, 1843. He was early apprenticed as a printer; and in 1863 he founded the London *Advertiser*. In 1875 he founded also the Toronto *Liberal* (1875-76), as the the organ of the Blake wing of the Liberal party. From 1882 to 1890 he was editor and general manager of the Toronto *Globe*. He died in London, Ontario, on December 1, 1908. He married, in 1869, Elizabeth, daughter of Capt. D. Miller, Royal Canadian Rifles.

[Morgan, *Can. men* (1898).]

Cameron, John Dugald (1777?-1857), fur-trader, was a younger brother of the Hon. Duncan Cameron (q.v.), for many years secretary and registrar of Upper Canada, and was born about 1777. He entered the service of the North West Company about 1795; and for many years was a clerk in the Nipigon district. In 1811 he was placed in charge of the Lake Winnipeg district, and in 1813 was made a partner of the North West Company. He took little part in the struggle between the North West Company and the Hudson's Bay Company; and on the union of the companies in 1821 he was appointed a chief factor. He became a great favourite with Sir George Simpson (q.v.), who described him as "a happy fellow, nothing seems to concern him, and an excellent well-meaning man he is". Some glimpses of him may be obtained from the *Letters of Rev. James Evans,* edited by F. Landon (Ont. Hist. Soc., papers and records, xxviii, 1932). He retired from the fur-trade in 1844, and settled at Grafton, near Cobourg, Upper Canada. Here he died on March 21, 1857, at the age of 80 years. By his Indian wife he had several children.

[E. E. Rich (ed.), *Colin Robertson's correspondence book* (Toronto: The Champlain Society, 1939).]

Cameron, John Hillyard (1817-1876), lawyer, businessman, and politician, was born at Blendecques, France, on April 14, 1817, the son of Angus Cameron of the 79th Highlanders. In 1825 Angus Cameron emigrated to Canada, where he became paymaster of the Royal Canadian Rifles. John Hillyard Cameron was educated at Upper Canada College, and was called to the bar of Upper Canada in 1838. From 1843 to 1846 he was reporter to the court of Queen's Bench, Upper Canada; and he began the publication of the *Upper Canada law reports.* In July, 1846, he was appointed solicitor-general for Upper Canada in the Draper administration, was elected to the Legislative Assembly in August, and in 1847 was included in the executive council; but in 1848 the administration was defeated, and Cameron never again occupied cabinet office. He continued for many years, however, to be a prominent figure in politics. He was out of parliament from 1851 to 1854, and from 1857 to 1861. In 1859 he became grand master of the Orange Association of British North America; and in 1860 he was elected treasurer of the Law Society of Upper Canada. After Confederation he sat in the House of Commons, first for Peel (1867-72), and then for Cardwell (1872-76), and in 1873 he was chairman of the parliamentary committee appointed to inquire into the "Pacific scandal". He died at Toronto on November 14, 1876. In 1843 he married (1) Elizabeth (d. 1844), third daughter of Henry John Boulton (q.v.); and in 1849 he married (2) Ellen, second daughter of General Mallett. His second wife died in Toronto on June 24, 1915. He was a prominent member of the Church of England, and was one of the founders of the University of Trinity College, from which he received in 1855 the degree of D.C.L., and of which he became in 1864 chancellor. He published *A digest of cases determined in the Upper Canada Court of Queen's Bench* (Toronto, 1840), and *The rules of court and statutes relative to practice and pleading in the Court of Queen's Bench, U.C.* (Toronto, 1844).

[*Can. parl. comp.,* 1876; Morgan, *Cel. Can.* and *Bib. can.*; Taylor, *Brit. Am.*; W. J. Rattray, *The Scot in British North America* (4 vols., Toronto, 1880); J. C. Dent, *The last forty years* (2 vols., Toronto, 1881); J. Pope, *Memoirs of the Right Hon. Sir John A. Macdonald* (2 vols., Ottawa, 1895); Sir R. Cartwright, *Reminiscences* (Toronto, 1912); *Dict. Can. biog.*, vol. 10.]

Cameron, Malcolm (1808-1876), politician and businessman, was born at Three Rivers, Lower Canada, on April 25, 1808, the son of Angus Cameron, hospital sergeant in a Highland regiment, and Euphemia McGregor. He was almost wholly self-educated, his early years having been spent as a farm-labourer, a shop assistant, a stable-boy, and a clerk in a distillery. In 1832 he and two partners established a successful business as general merchants and he branched out into real estate around Perth, Upper Canada. In 1834 he founded the *Bathurst Courier* at Perth; and in 1836 he was returned to the Legislative Assembly of Upper Canada for the county of Lanark. He was a moderate Reformer who generally sided with Baldwin and Bidwell. In 1842 he accepted office under Sir Charles Bagot in the Baldwin-Lafontaine ministry as inspector of revenue but resigned in 1843 over the move of the capital from Kingston to Montreal. In 1848 he became a member of the second Baldwin-Lafontaine ministry, as assistant commissioner of public works. This office he resigned late in 1850 after several disputes with his cabinet colleagues; but in 1852 he was included in the Hincks-Morin ministry, and was successively president of the council, minister of agriculture, and postmaster-general. At this time he was regarded as one of the leaders of the "Clear Grit" party, and he assisted William McDougall (q.v.) in founding the *North American*, the organ of that party; but when returned to parliament in 1857, after an absence of three years, he was found supporting the Macdonald-Cartier administration. In 1860 he resigned from the Assembly, and was elected to represent the St. Clair division in the Legislative Council. In 1863 he resigned his seat once more, and for six years (1863-69) he was Queen's printer. After several unsuccessful attempts to recover a seat in parliament, he was finally in 1874 elected for South Ontario to the House of Commons as a Liberal; but his day was past, and he played only an inconspicuous part in the house. He died at Ottawa on June 1, 1876. About 1833 he married, on a visit to Scotland, his cousin, Christina, daughter of Robert McGregor, of Glasgow; and by her he had one daughter. He was a prominent and life-long advocate of the prohibition of the sale of spiritous liquors, when the "prohibition" movement was in its infancy; but as a politician his course was erratic, and he was popularly nick-named "the Coon".
[A. Haydon, *Pioneer sketches of the district of Bathurst* (Toronto, 1925); Dent, *Can.*

port., vol. 4; Morgan, *Cel. Can.* and *Bib. can.*; Rose, *Cyc. Can. biog.* (1886); *Can. parl. comp.*; E. Barrass, *A gallery of distinguished men* (Napanee, Ont., 1870); J. M. S. Careless, *Brown of The Globe*, vol. 1 (Toronto, 1959); *Dict. Can. biog.*, vol. 10.]

Cameron, Malcolm Colin (1832-1898), politician, was born at Perth, Upper Canada, on April 12, 1832, the adopted son of Malcolm Cameron (q.v.). He was educated in Toronto and was called to the bar of Upper Canada in 1860. He practised law in Goderich, Ontario; and he represented South Huron in the House of Commons from 1867 to 1882, and West Huron from 1882 to 1887. He was re-elected for West Huron at a by-election in January, 1896, and at the general elections of the same year. On June 7, 1898, he was sworn in as lieutenant-governor of the North West Territories; but he died shortly afterwards at Regina on September 26, 1898. In 1855 he married Jessie, daughter of Dr. John McLean, R.N.; by her he had several children.
[Morgan, *Can. men* (1898); *Can. parl. comp.*]

Cameron, Malcolm Graeme (1857-1925), jurist, was born at Goderich, Canada West, on February 24, 1857, the eldest son of the Hon. Malcolm Colin Cameron (q.v.). He was called to the bar of Ontario in 1879 (K.C., 1902), and practised law in Goderich. In 1920 he was appointed county court judge of Northumberland and Durham counties, Ontario; and he died at Cobourg, Ontario, on August 10, 1925. He was the author of *A treatise on the law of dower* (Toronto, 1882).
[Morgan, *Can. men* (1912).]

Cameron, Sir Matthew Crooks (1822-1888), politician and judge, was born at Dundas, Upper Canada, on October 2, 1822, the son of John McAlpine Cameron, who came to Canada from Scotland in 1819, and was subsequently an officer of the Canada Company, and Nancy Foy. He was educated at the Home District Grammar School and Upper Canada College, and in 1849 was admitted to the bar of Upper Canada. As an attorney he attained a position of great eminence in the province; and in 1861 he entered political life. From 1861 to 1863 and from 1864 to 1867, he sat in the Legislative Assembly of Canada as Conservative member for North Ontario. He opposed Confederation; but in 1867 he became provincial secretary in the first Ontario government, formed by John Sandfield Macdonald (q.v.), and was returned to the Ontario legislature for East Toronto. In July, 1871, he exchanged the provincial secretaryship for the commissionership of crown lands; but in December, 1871, he went out of office with his colleagues, on the defeat of the government. From 1871 to 1878 he was the leader of the Conservative opposition in the Ontario legislature; but his High Tory views and his erratic course in the House did not make him an ideal leader. In 1878 he was appointed a judge of the Court of Queen's Bench of Ontario, and in 1884 chief justice of the Court of Common Pleas. He was created a knight bachelor in 1886; and he died at Toronto on June 25, 1888. He married, in 1851, Charlotte Ross (d. 1868), daughter of William Wedd; by her he had three sons and three daughters.

[Rose, *Cyc. Can. biog.* (1888); Dent, *Can. port.,* vol. 3; D. B. Read, *Lives of the judges* (Toronto, 1888); C. Clarke, *Sixty years in Upper Canada* (Toronto, 1908).]

Cameron, Ranald (*fl.* 1793-1817), fur-trader, first appears in the literature of the fur-trade as a clerk in the service of David and Peter Grant (q.v.) in their opposition to the North West Company in 1793-95. Later, he appears as a clerk of the North West Company at Nipigon in 1797, together with John Dugald Cameron (q.v.). In 1806 he was a clerk on the Montreal River; and in 1808 he was admitted a partner at the North West Company. From 1807 to 1815 he was proprietor at Lac des Isles; and in August, 1817, Ross Cox (q.v.) met him at Fort William. He died some time between 1817 and 1821.

[W. S. Wallace (ed.), *Documents relating to the North West Company* (Toronto: The Champlain Society, 1934).]

Cameron, William A. (1882-1956), clergy-man, was born near Palmyra, Ontario, in 1882, and died at Toronto, Ontario, on July 15, 1956. He was educated at Woodstock College and at McMaster University (B.A., 1904), and was ordained a minister of the Baptist Church in 1908. He became the pastor of the Bloor St. Baptist Church in Toronto until 1928, when the church was demolished, rebuilt on Yonge St., and renamed Yorkminster Church. He continued as pastor of this church until his retirement in 1948. A very popular preacher, he was the author of *The gift of God and other sermons* (New York, 1925), *The potter's wheel* (Toronto, 1937), *The clinic of a cleric* (Toronto, 1931), *Jesus and the rising generation* (Toronto, 1932), *Songs of the ages* (Toronto, 1934), and *Not by eastern windows only* (Toronto, n.d.).

[Toronto *Globe and Mail,* July 17, 1956.]

Cameron, William Bleasdell (1862-1951), journalist and author, was born at Trenton, Canada West, on July 26, 1862; and was educated at the Trenton High School. He went to the North West in 1881, and when the North West Rebellion broke out in 1885 he was in charge of the Hudson's Bay Company's post at Frog Lake. He was the sole survivor of the Frog Lake massacre, and was held as a prisoner for two months by Big Bear's band of Crees. He afterwards described his experiences in *The war trail of Big Bear* (Toronto,

1926), republished under the title, *Blood red the sun* (Toronto, 1950); and he was joint author, with H. J. Moberly, of *When fur was king* (London, 1929). He was the founder and editor of the Vermilion *Signal.* He died at Meadow Lake, Saskatchewan, on March 3, 1951.

[*Encyc. Can.*]

Campbell, Sir Alexander (1822-1892), lawyer and statesman, was born at the village of Hedon, near Kingston-upon-Hull, York-shire, England, on March 9, 1822, the son of James Campbell, M.D. His father came to Canada in 1823, practised medicine at Mont-real until 1832, then at Lachine until 1836, and finally at Kingston. Campbell was educated at St. Hyacinthe College and at the Kings-ton Grammar School, and in 1843 was called to the bar of Upper Canada. He entered into partnership with John A. Macdonald (q.v.), and between Macdonald and himself there was a close and life-long association. In 1858 he was elected as a Liberal-Conservative to the Legislative Council of Canada for the Cataraqui division, and in 1863 he became for a few months (February-May) its speaker. In 1864 he was appointed commissioner of crown lands in the "Great Coalition"; and he was a member of the Quebec Conference. At Confed-eration he was appointed to the Canadian Sen-ate, and became postmaster-general in the first Dominion cabinet. In July, 1873, he was placed in charge of the newly-created department of the interior; but he left office with the rest of his colleagues at the end of the year. From 1873 to 1878 he was leader of the opposition in the Senate; and on the return of Sir John Macdonald to power he occupied suc-cessively the offices of receiver-general (Octo-ber, 1878–May, 1879), postmaster-general (May, 1879–January, 1880), minister of militia (January, 1880–October, 1880), postmaster-general (October 1880–May, 1881), minister of justice (May, 1881–Sep-tember, 1885), and postmaster-general (Sep-tember, 1885–February, 1887). In June, 1887, he was appointed lieutenant-governor of Ontario; but before assuming office he repre-sented Canada at the Imperial Conference of 1887. He died at Toronto on May 24, 1892, just before the conclusion of his term of five years as lieutenant-governor. In 1855 he married Georgina Frederica Locke, daughter of Thomas Sandwith, of Beverley, Yorkshire. In 1856 he was created a Q.C., and in 1879 a K.C.M.G. A collection of his speeches was printed for private circulation under the title, *Speeches on divers occasions* (Ottawa, 1885).

[M. O. Hammond, *Confederation and its leaders* (Toronto, 1917); *In memoriam Sir Alexander Campbell* (pamphlet, Toronto, 1892); *Dict. nat. biog.,* supp. I; Dent, *Can. port.,* vol. 3; Rose, *Cyc. Can. biog.* (1888); Sir J. Pope, *Memoirs of the Right Hon. Sir John A. Macdonald* (2 vols., Ottawa, 1895).]

Campbell, Alexander Colin (1857-1943), journalist and civil servant, was born at Shannonville, Canada West, in 1857. He became a journalist; and in 1894 he was appointed one of the reporters of debates in the Canadian House of Commons. He became associate editor of debates in 1917, and editor in 1919. He retired on pension in 1926, and he died at Ottawa, Ontario, in 1943. He was the author of *Insurance and crime* (New York, 1902); and he was the editor of *Rose's Handbook of Dominion politics* (Toronto, 1886).

[*Canadian author and bookman,* 1944; Morgan, *Can. men* (1912).]

Campbell, Sir Archibald, Bart. (1769-1843), lieutenant-governor of New Brunswick (1831-37), was born on March 12, 1769, the son of Captain Archibald Campbell. At the age of eighteen he entered the British army as an ensign, and he served with distinction first in India, then in Portugal, and then again in India. From 1831 to 1837 he was lieutenant-governor of New Brunswick, where he was very unpopular, by reason of his arbitrary rule and his stubborn resistance to the desire of the House of Assembly to transfer the control of the crown lands to the government of the province. He returned to England in 1838, and he died there on October 6, 1843. He married Helen, daughter of Sir John Macdonald of Garth, and by her he had one son. In 1814 he was knighted, given the gold cross with one clasp, and made an aide-de-camp to the prince regent; in 1815 he was made a K.C.B.; in 1826 a G.C.B.; and in 1831 he was created a baronet, with special arms by royal licence.

[*Dict. nat. biog.*; J. Hannay, *History of New Brunswick* (Saint John, N.B., 1909).]

Campbell, Archibald (1790-1862), notary, was born at Quebec, Lower Canada, on June 29, 1790; and was admitted to practice as a notary public in 1812. In 1821 he was appointed royal notary at Quebec; and in 1822 he bought the seigniory of Bic. He died at Bic, Lower Canada, on July 16, 1862.

[P. G. Roy, *Le notaire du roi Archibald Campbell* (Bull. rech. hist., 1926).]

Campbell, Sir Colin (1776-1847), lieutenant-governor of Nova Scotia (1834-40), was born in 1776, the fifth son of John Campbell of Melfort, and Colina, daughter of John Campbell of Auchalader. He was educated at the Perth Academy. In 1793 he became a midshipman on an East Indiaman; but two years later he entered the army, and he served with credit in India and in the Peninsular War. In 1833 he was appointed lieutenant-governor of Nova Scotia; but in spite of his personal popularity his resignation was asked for by the House of Assembly, on account of his resistance to their demand for responsible government. He was recalled in 1840, and he died in England on June 13, 1847. In 1814 he was decorated with the gold cross and six clasps, and was created a K.C.B.

[*Dict. nat. biog.*; D. Campbell, *Nova Scotia* (Montreal, 1873); E. M. Saunders, *Three premiers of Nova Scotia* (Toronto, 1909).]

Campbell, Colin (1787-1853), fur-trader, was born at River Beaudette, Lake St. Francis, in Glengarry county, Canada, on November 25, 1787, the son of Alexander Campbell, a United Empire Loyalist, who represented Cornwall in the first legislature of Upper Canada, and his wife Magdalena Van Sice. He entered the service of the North West Company as a clerk in 1804, doubtless through the influence of his elder brother, John Duncan Campbell (q.v.). He spent most of his life in the Athabaska district. He was taken over by the Hudson's Bay Company in 1821, and he remained in the Athabaska district until 1846. In 1828 he was promoted to be chief trader; but he did not attain the rank of chief factor. After several years spent in charge of the Kenogamissee district, he retired from the fur-trade in 1853; and a few months later he died, on November 9, 1853, at the Red River Settlement. He married Elizabeth, daughter of the Hon. John McGillivray (q.v.).

[E. E. Rich (ed.), *Journal of occurrences in the Athabasca department, by George Simpson* (Toronto: The Champlain Society, 1938).]

Campbell, Colin H. (1859-1914), politician, was born in Burlington, Upper Canada, on December 25, 1859, the son of John H. Campbell and Jane Kennedy. He was christened merely "Colin Campbell", but assumed the middle initial "H" early in life, in order to distinguish himself from others of the same name. He was called to the Ontario bar in 1881, and to the Manitoba bar in 1882 (Q.C., 1893). In 1899 he was elected to represent Morris as a Conservative in the Legislative Assembly of Manitoba; in 1900 he was appointed attorney-general in the Manitoba government, and he remained a member of the government, first as attorney-general, and then as minister of public works, until ill-health compelled his resignation in 1913. He died in Winnipeg on October 24, 1914. In 1884 he married Minnie Julia Beatrice, daughter of Anson Buck, M.D., of Palermo, Ontario.

[Morgan, *Can. men* (1912); *Can. who's who* (1910); *Can. parl. comp.*; Can. who was who, vol. 1.]

Campbell, Sir Donald, Bart. (1800-1850), lieutenant-governor of Prince Edward Island, was born on August 3, 1800, the son of Sir Colin Campbell (q.v.). He was created a baronet of the United Kingdom in 1836; and in 1847 he was appointed lieutenant-governor of Prince Edward Island. He died in office at Charlottetown on October 18, 1850. In 1823 he married Carolina Elisa, daughter of Sir William Plomer; and by her he had four sons and one daughter.

[*Annual register,* 1850; Le Jeune, *Dict. gén.*; D. Campbell, *A history of Prince Edward Island* (Charlottetown, P.E.I., 1865).]

Campbell, Duncan (1819?-1886), historian, was born in Scotland about 1819, came to Nova Scotia in 1860, and died at Halifax, Nova Scotia, on August 26, 1886. He was the author of *A history of Prince Edward Island* (Charlottetown, 1865) and *Nova Scotia in its historical, mercantile, and industrial relations* (Montreal, 1873).

[*Dom. ann. reg.,* 1886.]

Campbell, Grace MacLennan Grant (1895-1963), novelist, was born at Williamstown, Glengarry county, Ontario, on March 18, 1895, of Highland and United Empire Loyalist stock. She was educated at Williamstown High School, Queen's University (gold medal in English, B.A. 1915), and at the faculty of education. She taught for three years and in 1919 married the Reverend Harvey Campbell. As a clergyman's wife she lived in Saskatchewan and in Quebec in both small towns and cities. She was a popular and gifted speaker. She wrote articles and short stories and the following novels: *Thorn-apple tree* (Toronto, 1942), set on the farm of her childhood; *The higher wall* (Toronto, 1944); *Fresh wind blowing* (Toronto, 1947); *The tower and the town* (Toronto, 1950); *Torberg* (Toronto, 1953). She died at Niagara-on-the-Lake, Ontario, May 31, 1963.

[*Can. who's who* (1955-57); C. Thomas, *Canadian novelists 1920-1945* (Toronto, 1946); V.B. Rhodenizer, *Canadian literature in English* (Montreal, 1965).]

Campbell, John (1840-1904), clergyman and scholar, was born in Edinburgh, Scotland, in 1840, the son of James Campbell. He came to Canada in 1861, and graduated from the University of Toronto in 1865 (M.A., 1866). He then studied theology at Knox College, Toronto, and New College, Edinburgh, and was ordained a minister of the Presbyterian Church in 1868. After a pastorate of five years in Toronto, he was appointed, in 1873, professor of church history and apologetics in the Presbyterian College, Montreal. This position he held until his death in Muskoka on July 30, 1904. In 1875 he married Mary Helen, daughter of John Stuart Playfair, of Toronto. He was elected a fellow of the Royal Society of Canada in 1893; and in 1889 he was made an LL.D. of the University of Toronto. His chief work was *The Hittites* (2 vols., Toronto, 1890); but he wrote on a variety of other subjects, and under the pen-name of "J. Cawdor Bell" he published a novel entitled *Two knapsacks* (Toronto, 1892).

[*Proc. Roy. Soc. Can.,* 1905; Morgan, *Can. men* (1898).]

Campbell, Sir John Douglas Sutherland. See Lorne, Marquis of.

Campbell, John Duncan (1773-1835), fur-trader, was born at Scoharie, New York, on February 21, 1773, the son of Alexander Campbell and Magdalena Van Sice. His parents emigrated to Canada, as United Empire Loyalists, during the American Revolution, and settled ultimately at Cornwall, which Alexander Campbell represented in the first legislature of Upper Canada. John Duncan Campbell entered the employ of the North West Company as clerk some time before 1799, when he appears as a clerk at Upper Fort des Prairies. For most of his service he was stationed, however, in the English River department. He was admitted a partner of the North West Company in 1803, and from that date to 1819 he was in charge of this department. In 1809 he was elected a member of the Beaver Club. After the Selkirk troubles, he was arrested by officers of the Hudson's Bay Company at the Grand Rapid on June 18, 1819, and was taken, with Benjamin Frobisher (q.v.), to Hudson Bay. He was kept a prisoner for several months and then brought down to Canada, under guard, and released. (See S. H. Wilcocke, *The death of B. Frobisher,* in L. R. Masson, *Les bourgeois de la Cie. du Nord-Ouest,* 2nd series, Quebec, 1890.) On the union of the North West and Hudson's Bay companies in 1821, he retired from the fur-trade, and settled in Cornwall, Upper Canada. Here he died on May 6, 1835. He married Elizabeth, daughter of John McDonald of Garth (q.v.) and his Indian wife Nancy, daughter of Patrick Small (q.v.); and by her he had several children.

[E. E. Rich (ed.), *Journal of occurrences in the Athabasca department, by George Simpson* (Toronto: The Champlain Society, 1938).]

Campbell, Robert (1808-1894), fur-trader and explorer, was born in Glenlyon, Perthshire, Scotland, on February 21, 1808, the son of a sheep-farmer. In 1832 he came to the Red River in the service of the Hudson's Bay Company; and he rose in this service to the rank of chief factor. He carried out many explorations in the Mackenzie River basin and in the Yukon; and in particular he discovered the Upper Yukon River in 1848. He retired from the service of the Hudson's Bay Company in 1871; and in 1880 he took up ranching in Manitoba. Here he died on May 9, 1894. About 1860 he married Eleanora Sterling, who came from Scotland to Athabaska to marry him, and by her he had two sons and one daughter.

[G. Bryce, *Sketch of the life and discoveries of Robert Campbell,* with portrait (Hist. and Sci. Soc. of Manitoba, Trans. No. 52, Winnipeg, 1898); G. W. Bartlett, *The diary of Robert Campbell* (Can. mag., 1915); J. P.

Kirk and C. Parnell, *Campbell of the Yukon* (Beaver, 1942); Clifford Wilson, *Campbell of the Yukon* (Toronto, 1970).]

Campbell Robert (1835-1921), clergyman and author, was born in the township of Drummond, Lanark county, Upper Canada, on June 21, 1835, the son of Peter Campbell. He was educated at Queen's University, Kingston (B.A., 1856; M.A., 1858; D.D., 1887). In 1861 he was ordained a minister of the Presbyterian Church; and from 1866 to 1909 he was pastor of the St. Gabriel Street Presbyterian Church, Montreal. His *History of the Scotch Presbyterian Church, St. Gabriel St., Montreal* (Montreal, 1887) is a valuable contribution to Canadian history. For many years he was senior clerk of the General Assembly of the Presbyterian Church in Canada; and in 1907 he was elected its moderator. He died at Montreal on March 13, 1921. In 1863 he married Margaret, daughter of the Rev. George Macdonnell; and by her he had three sons and two daughters.
[*Can. who was who*, vol. 1; Morgan, *Can. men* (1912); J. T. McNeill, *History of the Presbyterian Church in Canada* (Toronto, 1925).]

Campbell, Rollo (1803-1871), publisher, was born at Dunning, Perthshire, Scotland, on December 18, 1803. He emigrated to Canada in 1822, and entered the printing office of the Montreal *Courant*. In 1834 he became business manager of the *Morning Courier*; and in 1849 he purchased from Francis Hincks (q.v.) the *Pilot*. Of this paper he was the proprietor from 1849 to its discontinuance in 1862; and during these years he carried on perhaps the most extensive printing business in Canada. He died at Montreal on January 2, 1871. He was the author of *Two lectures on Canada* (Greenock and Toronto, 1857).
[Morgan, *Bib. can.*; W. H. Kesterton, *A history of journalism in Canada* (Toronto, 1967); *Dict. Can. biog.*, vol. 10.]

Campbell, Lord William (d. 1778), governor of Nova Scotia (1766-73), was the fifth and youngest son of John Campbell, fourth Duke of Argyle. He entered the Royal Navy, and in 1762 was gazetted a post captain. From 1764 to 1766 he represented Argyleshire in the British House of Commons; and in 1766 he was appointed governor of Nova Scotia. He administered the affairs of his colony until 1773, when he was appointed royal governor of South Carolina. During the American Revolution he served as a volunteer in the British navy, and he was severely wounded in the attack on Fort Sullivan on June 28, 1776. He died, from the effects of his wounds, on September 5, 1778. In 1763 he married Sarah, daughter of Ralph Izard, of Charleston, South Carolina; and by her he had one son and two daughters.
[*Dict. Am. biog.*; *Cyc. Am. biog.*; Sir J. B. Paul (ed.), *The Scots peerage,* vol. 1 (Edinburgh, 1904), *sub* "Argyle".]

Campbell, Sir William (1758-1834), chief justice of Upper Canada, was born in Caithness, Scotland, in 1758, the son of Capt. Alexander Campbell, R.N. He served in the Royal Navy until 1784, and then settled at Guysborough, Nova Scotia. There he studied law, and in 1804 he was appointed attorney-general of Cape Breton. He was removed from office in 1807; but in 1811 he became a judge of the King's Bench in Upper Canada, and in 1825 he was appointed chief justice of the King's Bench in Upper Canada. At the same time he became speaker of the Legislative Council. In 1829 he was compelled by ill-health to retire from the bench, and was gazetted a knight bachelor. He died in Toronto on January 18, 1834.
[D. B. Read, *The lives of the judges* (Toronto, 1888); Morgan, *Cel. Can.*; J. Ross Robertson, *The history of freemasonry in Canada* (2 vols., Toronto, 1900).]

Campbell, William Wilfred (1861-1918), poet, was born in Berlin (Kitchener), Ontario, on June 1, 1861, the son of the Rev. Thomas Swaniston Campbell and Matilda Frances, daughter of Major Francis Wright, Royal Horse Guards. He was educated at Upper Canada College and the University of Trinity College, and in 1885 took orders in the Church of England. In 1888 he became rector of St. Stephen, New Brunswick; but in 1891 he resigned his charge, and entered the Canadian civil service at Ottawa. He published the following volumes of poetry: *Lake lyrics* (Saint John, N.B., 1889), *The dread voyage* (Toronto, 1893), *Beyond the hills of dream* (Boston, 1899), *Collected poems* (Toronto, 1906), *Sagas of vaster Britain* (Toronto, 1914), and *War lyrics* (Toronto, 1915). In 1895 he published two versified tragedies, *Mordred* and *Hildebrand* (Ottawa), and these were included, with two others, *Daulac* and *Morning*, in a volume entitled *Poetical tragedies* (Toronto, 1908). He wrote also two novels, *Ian of the Orcades* (New York, 1906) and *A beautiful rebel* (Toronto, 1909), and a descriptive work on *The Canadian lake region* (Toronto, 1910). He collaborated with T. M. Martin in a book entitled *Canada* (London, 1907), and with the Rev. George Bryce in a work entitled *Scotsmen in Canada* (Toronto, 1911); and he was the editor of the *Oxford book of Canadian verse* (Toronto, n.d.). His reputation rests mainly, however, on his poetry. He died near Ottawa on January 1, 1918. He was elected to the Royal Society of Canada in 1893, and in 1906 was given the degree of LL.D. by Aberdeen University.
[C. F. Klinck, *Wilfred Campbell* (Toronto, 1942); *Proc. Roy. Soc. Can.*, 1918; Morgan,

Can. men (1912); *Can. who was who,* vol. 1; L. Pierce, *An outline of Canadian literature* (Toronto, 1927).]

Campion, Etienne (1737-1795), fur-trader, was born in Montreal on January 15, 1737, the son of Etienne Campion. He became an Indian trader, and first wintered in the Indian country in 1753. With his younger brother Alexis, he engaged in the Illinois trade after the British conquest of Canada. He signed the agreement for a general store at Michilimackinac in 1779; and his name constantly appears in the Michilimackinac register between the years 1765 and 1794. He was a charter member of the Beaver Club in Montreal, in 1787; and in his later years he was a member of the firm of Grant, Campion and Co. He died in Montreal in December, 1795.

[W. S. Wallace (ed.), *Documents relating to the North West Company* (Toronto: The Champlain Society, 1934).]

Camsell, Charles (1876-1958), geologist, was born at Fort Liard, North West Territories, on February 8, 1876, the son of Julian Stewart Camsell, a chief factor of the Hudson's Bay Company. He was educated at St. John's College, Winnipeg, and at the University of Manitoba (B.A., 1894), and he pursued postgraduate studies at Queen's University, Kingston, at Harvard University, and at the Massachusetts Institute of Technology. In 1904 he was appointed a geologist in the Canadian Geological Survey, with the title after 1914 of "Geologist in charge of exploration", and from 1920 to 1948 he was deputy minister of mines. From 1935 to 1946 he was also commissioner of the North West Territories. He was elected a fellow of the Royal Society of Canada in 1918, and became its president in 1930. He was created a C.M.G. in 1935, and received a number of medals and awards. He died at Ottawa, Ontario, on December 19, 1958. A few years before his death he published his autobiography, under the title *Son of the North* (Toronto, 1954).

[*Proc. Roy. Soc. Can.,* 1959; *Encyc. Can.*; *Can. who's who,* 1956-58.]

Canniff, William (1830-1910), physician and author, was born on June 20, 1830, at Thurlow, near Hastings, Upper Canada, the son of Jonas Canniff and Letta Flagler, both of United Empire Loyalist descent. He was educated at the University of Victoria College, Cobourg, at the Toronto School of Medicine, and at the University of New York (M.D., 1854). In 1855 he was admitted a member of the Royal College of Surgeons in England, and he served as a medical officer in the Crimean War. On his return to Canada, he practised medicine first in Belleville, and later in Toronto. He was professor of general pathology and of surgery in the University of Victoria College, and later sub-dean of the

Toronto Medical School. He was also the first medical health officer in Toronto (1883-91). His chief medical publication was *A manual of the principles of surgery* (Philadelphia, 1866). He was a member of the "Canada First" party, was president of the North West Emigration Aid Society (1870), and published a pamphlet on *Canadian nationality, its growth and development* (Toronto, 1875). His fame rests mainly, however, on his historical works, *A history of the early settlement of Upper Canada* (Toronto, 1869), and *The medical profession in Upper Canada, an historical narrative* (Toronto, 1894). He died in Belleville, Ontario, on October 18, 1910. His papers, which were left to the Lennox and Addington Historical Society, are calendared in the *Papers and records* of the Society (Napanee, Ontario), vol. ix.

[*Can. who was who,* vol. 1; Morgan, *Can. men* (1898); *Can. who's who* (1910).]

Cannon, Edward (1739-1814), architect, was born in Wexford county, Ireland, in 1739. He emigrated from Ireland to Newfoundland in 1774, and from Newfoundland to Canada in 1795; and during the remainder of his life he was an architect and contractor in Quebec. Among the buildings of which he was architect is the English church cathedral in Quebec. He died in Quebec, Lower Canada, on July 28, 1814.

[R. Cannon, *Edward Cannon* (Can. Cath. Hist. Assn., report, 1935-36).]

Cannon, Lawrence Arthur Dumoulin (1877-1939), jurist, was born at Arthabaskaville, Quebec, on April 28, 1877, the son of the Hon. Lawrence John Cannon, a judge of the Superior Court of the province of Quebec. He was educated at Laval University (B.A., 1896; LL.L., 1899; LL.D., 1927), and was called to the bar of Quebec in 1899 (K.C., 1910). He practised law in the city of Quebec, and was *bâtonnier* of the Quebec bar in 1924. He was twice elected to represent Quebec Centre in the Quebec legislature, in 1916 and in 1919; and in 1924 he was appointed a judge of the Court of King's Bench in Quebec. In 1930 he was appointed a judge of the Supreme Court of Canada; and this position he occupied until his death at Ottawa, Ontario, on December 5, 1939. In 1904 he married Corinne, daughter of Sir Charles Fitzpatrick (q.v.); and by her he had four sons and one daughter.

[*Can. who's who,* 1936-37; P. G. Roy, *Les juges de la province de Québec* (Quebec, 1933).]

Caouette, Jean Baptiste (1854-1922), author, was born at Quebec on July 29, 1854, the son of Germain Caouette and Caroline Sauviat. He was successively postmaster at St. Roch, near Quebec, and archivist of the judicial district of Quebec. He died at Beauport, Quebec, on August 2, 1922. He was the author of a volume of poetry, *Les voix intimes* (Quebec,

1892), and two novels, *Le vieux muet; ou, Un héros de Châteauguay* (Quebec, 1901) and *Une intrigante sous le régime de Frontenac* (Quebec, 1921).

[*Bull. rech. hist.*, 1926.]

Cappon, James (1855-1939), educationist, was born at Dundee, Scotland, on March 8, 1855; and was educated at Glasgow University (M.A., 1881). He came to Canada in 1888, as professor of the English language and literature in Queen's University, Kingston; and he continued in this position until his retirement in 1919. He died in Kingston, Ontario, on September 19, 1939. For many years he was one of the editors of *Queen's Quarterly*; and he was the author of *Britain's title in South Africa* (London, 1901), *Roberts and the influences of his time* (Toronto, 1905), *Charles G. D. Roberts* (Toronto, n.d.), and *Bliss Carman and the literary currents and influences of his time* (Toronto, 1930).

[R. C. Wallace (ed.), *Some great men of Queen's* (Toronto, 1941); *Proc. Roy. Soc. Can.*, 1940; *Can. who's who*, 1936-37.]

Capreol, Frederick Chase (1803-1886), commission merchant and financier, was born at Bishop Stortford, Hertfordshire, England, on June 10, 1803. He came to Canada in 1829, and in 1833 he settled in York (Toronto). Here he died on October 12, 1886. In the fifties he promoted the building of the Northern Railway, one of the first in Ontario. He also secured a charter for the building of a ship canal between Lake Huron and Lake Ontario.

[*Dom. ann. reg.*, 1886; W. H. Pearson, *Recollections and records of Toronto of old* (Toronto, 1908).]

Cardin, Pierre Joseph Arthur (1879-1946), politician, was born at Sorel, Quebec, on June 18, 1879. He was educated at the University of Montreal, and for many years practised law in Sorel. He was elected to represent Richelieu in the Canadian House of Commons in 1911; and he continued to represent this constituency until his death at Sorel on October 18, 1946. From 1924 to 1926, and again from 1926 to 1930, he was minister of marine and fisheries in the King administration; and from 1935 to 1942 he was minister of transport and public works. In 1942 he resigned his portfolio because of a disagreement with his colleagues over the conscription issue, much to the regret of the prime minister, who described him as "my oldest colleague in the cabinet".

[*Can. parl. guide*, 1942; *Can. who's who*, 1938-39; Toronto *Globe and Mail*, Oct. 19, 1946.]

Cardinal, Joseph Narcisse (1808-1838), rebel, was born at St. Constant, Lower Canada, on February 8, 1808. He was educated at the College of Montreal, and was commissioned a notary public in 1829. In 1834 he was elected to represent Laprairie in the Legislative Assembly of Lower Canada. He did not take part in the insurrection of 1837; but he was forced to flee to the United States, and in 1838 he took part in the disturbances on the Canadian border. He was captured and convicted of high treason; and he was executed at Montreal on December 21, 1838.

[*Cyc. Am. biog.*; L. O. David, *Les patriotes de 1837-1838* (Montreal, 1884); Le Jeune, *Dict. gén.*]

Carheil, Etienne de (1633-1726), Jesuit missionary, was born at Carentoir, France, in November, 1633. He entered the Society of Jesus in 1653, was ordained a priest in 1666, and was then sent to Canada. After spending two years at Quebec, he was sent to the Iroquois mission at Cayuga; and he remained there, with one interval, until he was driven out in 1683. In 1686 he was sent to the mission of Saint-Ignace near the Straits of Mackinac; and he remained there until 1703. During the remainder of his life he worked among the French in Montreal and other towns; and he died at Quebec on July 27, 1726. He left behind him two manuscript volumes entitled *Racines huronnes*, a work of value to the student not only of the Huron language, but of all those languages allied with it.

[*Catholic encyclopedia*; R. G. Thwaites (ed.), *The Jesuit relations* (73 vols., Cleveland, 1896-1901); P. de Rochemonteix, *Les Jésuites et la Nouvelle France au XVIIe siècle* (3 vols., Paris, 1895-96); *Dict. Can. biog.*, vol. 2.]

Carleton, Sir Guy, first Baron Dorchester (1724-1808), governor-in-chief of British North America, was born at Strabane, county Tyrone, Ireland, on September 3, 1724, the son of Christopher Carleton of Newry, county Down, and Catherine Ball. On May 21, 1742, he was commissioned an ensign in Lord Rothes's regiment (the 25th Foot); and by 1757 was a lieutenant-colonel commanding the 72nd Foot. He was a friend of James Wolfe (q.v.), and in 1759 Wolfe took him with him as quartermaster-general on the expedition against Quebec. During the siege of Quebec he was one of Wolfe's right-hand men; and he was wounded at the battle of the Plains of Abraham.

In 1766 he was appointed lieutenant-governor of the province of Quebec, and in 1768 its governor. His period of office lasted on this occasion until 1778, and was of cardinal importance in several ways. It was largely through Carleton's influence that the policy of the conciliation of the French-Canadian seigniors and clergy triumphed in the Quebec Act of 1774, and that the advent of representative government was postponed. It was also through his efforts that the American invasion of Canada in 1775-76 was defeated. In 1778 he retired as the result of differences between himself and Lord George Germain, the secretary of state for the colonies; but in 1782 he was brought forth from his retirement, and appointed commander-in-chief of the British forces in North America. In this capacity, he had oversight of the evacuation of New York by the British troops and the loyalists in 1783.

In 1786 he was once again appointed to the Government of Canada, this time as Baron Dorchester with a commission as governor-in-chief of British North America. His second term of office lasted until 1796, and was chiefly notable for the passage of the so-called Constitutional Act of 1791. In the framing of this Act his influence was not so marked as in the framing of the Quebec Act; but his firm administration of the government was in part responsible for the successful inauguration of representative institutions in Canada at the moment when the French Revolution was threatening the foundations of government elsewhere. A man of decidedly arbitrary and autocratic methods, he was yet perhaps the sort of pro-consul who was required to guide the destinies of Canada during the difficult and dangerous periods with which his two administrations coincided.

In 1796 he retired to private life, first at his estate of Kempshot, near Basingstoke, and later at Stubbings, near Maidenhead. It was at the latter place he died suddenly on November 10, 1808. In 1772 he married Lady Maria Howard, third daughter of the Earl of Effingham; she bore him nine sons and two daughters, and survived him for twenty-eight years.

[A. G. Bradley, *Lord Dorchester* (Toronto, 1907); W. Wood, *The father of British Canada* (Toronto, 1916); W. Smith, *The struggle over the laws of Canada, 1763-1783* (Can. hist. rev., 1920); A. L. Burt, *Sir Guy Carleton and his first council* (Can. hist. rev., 1923), and *The old province of Canada* (Minneapolis, 1933); *Dict. nat. biog.*; *Cyc. Am. biog.*]

Carleton, Thomas (1735-1817), governor of New Brunswick, was born in Ireland in 1735, the youngest son of Christopher Carleton of Newry, county Down, and Catherine Ball, and the brother of Sir Guy Carleton (q.v.). He joined the 20th Foot as a volunteer in 1753, was commissioned ensign in 1755, and promoted lieutenant and adjutant the same year. He served on the continent during the Seven Years' War, was four years in garrison at Gibraltar from 1765 to 1769, and in 1774 obtained leave of absence to serve with the Russians against the Turks. In 1776 he came to Canada, and became quartermaster-general of the forces commanded by Sir Guy Carleton. On August 16, 1784, he was appointed first governor of the newly created province of New Brunswick; on May 20, 1786, his title was changed to lieutenant-governor, and he continued to occupy this position until his death in 1817. In 1803, however, he returned to England, and for the rest of his life

New Brunswick was governed by administrators. He died on February 2, 1817, at Ramsgate, England. In 1782 he married Hannah Van Horne, the widow of Captain Edward Foy, Royal Artillery; by her he had one son and two daughters.

[W. O. Raymond, *A sketch of the life and administration of General Thomas Carleton* (Coll. New Brunswick Hist. Soc., No. 6, 1905), *The first governor of New Brunswick* (Trans. Roy. Soc. Can., 1914), and *The Winslow papers* (Saint John, N.B., 1901).]

Carling, Sir John (1828-1911), brewer and politician, was born in the township of London, Middlesex county, Upper Canada, on January 23, 1828, the son of Thomas Carling, a brewer. He was educated at the common schools in London, entered his father's business, and ultimately succeeded him as president of the Carling Brewing and Malting Co. From 1857 to 1867 he was the representative of London in the Legislative Assembly of Canada; and from 1867 to 1873 he represented London in the Legislative Assembly of Ontario, and from 1867 to 1874, from 1878 to 1891, and from 1892 to 1895 in the Canadian House of Commons. From 1891 to 1892 he sat in the Senate of Canada; and in 1896 he was re-appointed to the Senate. He several times held cabinet office. In 1862 he was for a short time receiver-general in the Cartier-Macdonald government; from 1867 to 1871 he was commissioner of agriculture and public works in the first administration of Ontario; from 1882 to 1885 he was postmaster-general in the Dominion government and from 1885 to 1892 minister of agriculture; and from 1892 to 1894 he was a minister without portfolio in the Thompson administration. He died at London, Ont., on November 6, 1911. In 1849 he married Hannah (d. 1909), daughter of Henry Dalton, of London; and by her he had several children. He was created a K.C.M.G. in 1893.

[Morgan, *Can. men* (1912); Rose, *Cyc. Can. biog.* (1886); Dent, *Can. port.*, vol. 4; *Can. parl. comp.*; Sir J. Pope, *Memoirs of the Right Hon. Sir John A. Macdonald* (2 vols., Ottawa, 1894) and *Correspondence of Sir John Macdonald* (Toronto, 1921).]

Carlyle, Florence (d. 1923), painter, was born in Galt, Ontario, the daughter of William Carlyle and Ella Youmans, and a grand-niece of Thomas Carlyle, the essayist and historian. She was educated in Woodstock, Ontario, and studied art in Paris, France, from 1893 to 1898, under Lefèbvre, Fleury, and Rolshoven. In 1897 she was elected an associate member of the Royal Canadian Academy; and she won a reputation for figure painting. She died at Crowborough, England, on May 7, 1923. Some of her paintings are in the National Gallery at Ottawa, and in one or two public buildings in the province of Ontario.

[Morgan, *Can. men and women* (1912); *Can. who was who*, vol. 1.]

Carman, Albert (1833-1917), clergyman and educationist, was born at Iroquois, Upper Canada, on June 27, 1833, the son of Philip Carman and Emmeline, daughter of Peter Shaver, sometime member of the Legislative Assembly of Upper Canada. He was educated at the Dundas Grammar School and at Victoria University, Cobourg (B.A., 1855; M.A., 1860; D.D., 1891). He was headmaster of the Dundas Grammar School (1855-57), the first principal of Albert College (1858-68), and the first chancellor of Albert University (1868-74). He was ordained a deacon of the Methodist Episcopal Church in Canada in 1859, an elder in 1863, and from 1874 to 1883 he was a bishop. In 1883 he was elected general superintendent of the Methodist Church in Canada. He was repeatedly re-elected to this post until 1915, when he was made general superintendent emeritus, and he died at Toronto on November 3, 1917. In 1860 he married Mary, eldest daughter of James Sisk; by her he had three sons and one daughter.

[Morgan, *Can. men* (1912); Dent, *Can. port.*, vol. 2; J. E. Sanderson, *The first century of Methodism in Canada* (Toronto, 1910).]

Carman, Albert Richardson (1865-1939), journalist and novelist, was born at Belleville, Canada West, on February 8, 1865, the son of the Rev. Albert Carman (q.v.). He was educated at Albert College, Belleville (B.A., 1883), and became a journalist. He served successively on the staffs of the Toronto *Globe*, the *Montreal Star*, and the Philadelphia *Ledger*; and in 1921 he was appointed editor-in-chief of the *Montreal Star*. He died at Montreal, Quebec, on October 16, 1939. He was the author of two novels, *The preparation of Ryerson Embury* (Toronto, 1900) and *The pensionnaires* (Toronto, 1903).

[*Can. who's who*, 1936-37.]

Carman, Bliss (1861-1929), poet, was born in Fredericton, New Brunswick, on April 15, 1861, the son of William Carman and Sophia Mary Bliss, both of United Empire Loyalist descent. He was educated at the Collegiate School in Fredericton and at the University of New Brunswick (B.A., 1881; M.A., 1883; LL.D., 1906); and later he studied at Edinburgh and Harvard universities. In 1890 he went to New York, and became literary editor of the *Independent*; in 1894 he established the *Chap Book*; and from 1895 to 1900 he wrote a weekly column for the *Boston Transcript*. Gradually, however, he deserted journalism, and turned to work of a purely literary character. In his later days he was acclaimed as "Canada's poet laureate". His health was threatened, and in 1908 he went to live at New Canaan, Connecticut. There he died unmar-

ried on June 8, 1929. The bibliography of his poetry is very long and intricate, since many of his poems were first issued in broad-sheets and on Christmas cards; but the volumes of poetry he published were *Low tide on Grand Pré* (Toronto, 1893; 2nd ed. New York, 1893; 3rd ed., Cambridge and Chicago, 1894), *Behind the arras* (Boston and New York, 1895; 2nd ed., Boston, 1899), *Ballads of lost haven* (Boston, 1897), *By the Aurelian wall* (New York, 1898), *Ballads and lyrics* (London, 1902), *Ode on the coronation of King Edward VII* (Boston, 1902), *Pipes of Pan* (5 vols., Boston, 1902-5; definitive ed., 1906), *Sappho* (Boston, 1904; London, 1906), *Poems* (2 vols., New York, 1904; new ed., 1905), *The rough rider, and other poems* (New York, 1909), *Echoes from Vagabondia* (Boston, 1913), *April airs* (Boston, 1916), *Later poems* (Toronto, 1921), *Ballads and lyrics* (Toronto, 1923), *Far horizons* (Toronto, 1925), *Wild garden* (Toronto, 1929), *Sanctuary* (Toronto, 1929), and *Poems* (Toronto, 1931). With Richard Hovey he wrote *Songs from Vagabondia* (Boston, 1894), *More songs from Vagabondia* (Boston, 1896), and *Last songs from Vagabondia* (Boston, 1901); and he collaborated with Mary Perry King in *Daughters of dawn: A lyrical pageant* (New York, 1913), and *Earth deities, and other rhythmic masques* (New York, 1914). He edited *The world's best poetry* (10 vols., Philadelphia, 1904), and *The Oxford book of American verse* (New York, 1927). In prose, he was the author of several volumes of essays, *The kinship of nature* (Boston, 1904), *The friendship of art* (Boston, 1904), *The poetry of life* (Boston, 1905), *The making of personality* (Boston, 1908), and *Talks on poetry and life* (Toronto, 1926).

[J. Cappon, *Bliss Carman and the literary currents and influences of his time* (Toronto, 1930); O. Shepard, *Bliss Carman* (Toronto, 1923); L. Pierce (ed.), *Bliss Carman's scrapbook* (Toronto, 1931); M. Miller, *Bliss Carman* (Toronto, 1935); *Can. who was who*, vol. 1; Morgan, *Can. men* (1912).]

Carmichael, Franklin (1890-1945), painter, was born in Orillia, Ontario, in 1890. He studied painting at the Ontario College of Art in Toronto under G. A. Reid and William Cruikshank (qq.v.) and at the Académie Royale in Antwerp. He became an original member of the Group of Seven in 1919, and was elected an A.R.C.A. in 1935 and an R.C.A. in 1938. In 1932 he was appointed an instructor in the Ontario College of Art, and he retained this post until his death on October 24, 1945. He died in his car shortly after leaving the Ontario College of Art for his home in Lansing. He was chiefly a painter of landscapes, and three of his landscapes are in the National Gallery at Ottawa.

[F. B. Housser, *A Canadian art movement* (Toronto, 1926); *Encyc. Can.*; Toronto *Globe and Mail*, Oct. 25, 1945.]

Carnarvon, Henry Howard Molyneux Herbert, fourth Earl of (1831-1890), statesman, was born in London, England, in 1831. He was educated at Christ Church, Oxford (B.A., 1852; D.C.L., 1859), and on coming of age took his seat in the House of Lords. He was secretary of state for the colonies in the British government from 1858 to 1859, from 1866 to 1867, and from 1874 to 1878. He presided over the Westminster conference in 1866, introduced the British North America Act into the House of Commons in 1867, and laid down the so-called "Carnarvon terms" with British Columbia in 1874. He died in London, England, on June 28, 1890. His *Speeches on Canadian affairs* were published posthumously (London, 1902).

[Sir A. H. Hardinge, *The life of Henry Howard Molyneux Herbert, fourth Earl of Carnarvon* (3 vols., Oxford, 1925); *Dict. nat. biog.*]

Carnochan, Janet (1839-1926), author, was born at Stamford, Ontario, on November 14, 1839. For many years she was a high school teacher in Niagara-on-the-Lake, Ontario; and on retiring from teaching she devoted herself to the work of the Niagara Historical Society. To her efforts were largely due the erection of the Niagara Memorial Hall, opened in 1907, which contains an historical museum of great value and interest; and for many years she edited the publications of the Niagara Historical Society. She died at Niagara-on-the-Lake on March 31, 1926. She was the author of *The history of St. Mark's Church* (Toronto, 1892), *The history of St. Andrew's Church* (Toronto, 1895), and *The history of Niagara* (Toronto, 1914).

[Morgan, *Can. men and women* (1912).]

Caron, Ivanhöe (1875-1941), priest and historian, was born at L'Islet, Quebec, on October 12, 1875. He was educated at the Quebec Seminary, and studied afterwards at Rome; and he was ordained a priest of the Roman Catholic Church in 1900. He served for a time as a parish priest, but eventually found his life-work in the employ of the Quebec Archives. He became an authority on certain phases of the history of French Canada, and in 1921 he was elected a fellow of the Royal Society of Canada. He died at Quebec, Que., on October 1, 1941. He was the author of *La colonisation de la province de Québec* (2 vols., Quebec, 1923-27).

[*Proc. Roy. Soc. Can.*, 1942; Allaire, *Dict. biog.*]

Caron, Sir Joseph Philippe René Adolphe (1843-1908), politician, was born in Quebec on December 24, 1843, the son of René Edouard Caron (q.v.) and Josephine, daughter of Germain de Blois, of Quebec. He was educated at the Quebec Seminary and at McGill University (B.C.L., 1865). He was called to the

bar in 1865, and in 1879 was created a Q.C. In March, 1873, he was elected to the Canadian House of Commons as a Conservative for Quebec county. This constituency he represented continuously until 1887; he was then elected for Rimouski, and in 1896 for Three Rivers and St. Maurice. In 1880 he became minister of militia under Sir John Macdonald (q.v.), and he was at the head of the militia department during the North West rebellion of 1885. For his services on this occasion he was created a K.C.M.G. In 1892 he became postmaster-general, and he held this portfolio in the ministries of Sir John Abbott, Sir John Thompson, and Sir Mackenzie Bowell. In the formation of Sir Charles Tupper's short-lived ministry of 1896, he was omitted; and in 1900 he retired from parliament. He died at Montreal on April 20, 1908. In 1867 he married Alice, daughter of Charles François Xavier Baby (q.v.).

[Morgan, *Can. men* (1898); Dent, *Can. port.*, vol. 4; *Can. parl. comp.*; Sir R. Cartwright, *Reminiscences* (Toronto, 1912).]

Caron, René Edouard (1800-1876), politician, judge, and lieutenant-governor of Quebec, was born in the parish of Ste. Anne, Côte de Beaupré, on October 21, 1800, the son of Augustin Caron, sometime member of the Legislative Assembly of Lower Canada. He was educated at the College of St. Pierre, Rivière du Sud, and at the Quebec Seminary and was called to the bar of Lower Canada in 1826. From 1834 to 1836, and again from 1840 to 1846, he was mayor of Quebec. In 1834 he was elected to the Legislative Assembly of Lower Canada for the upper town of Quebec, but in 1836 he resigned in consequence of a heated disagreement with Louis Joseph Papineau (q.v.), the speaker of the Assembly. In 1841 he was appointed to the Legislative Council of Canada, and he was speaker of the Council from 1843 to 1847, and from 1848 to 1853. As such he was a member of both the Baldwin-Lafontaine and the Hincks-Morin administrations. In 1853 he was created a judge of the Superior Court of Lower Canada, and later he became a judge of the Court of Queen's Bench. In 1873 he succeeded Sir N. F. Belleau (q.v.), as lieutenant-governor of Quebec, and he filled this position until his death at Spencer Wood, Quebec, on December 13, 1876.

[L. P. Turcotte, *L'Honorable R. E. Caron* (Quebec, 1873); P. G. Roy, *Les juges de la province de Québec* (Quebec, 1933); Taylor, *Brit. Am.*, vol. 1; Morgan, *Cel. Can.*; Dent *Can. port.*, vol. 1; *Dict. Can. biog.*, vol. 10.]

Carpenter, George Hiram (1889-1971), newspaper editor, was born in Richmond, Vermont, July 26, 1889. He was educated at the Feller Institute, Grande Ligne, Quebec, and in Vermont and Massachusetts. He became a reporter with the Montreal *Gazette* in 1910. He served with the Canadian Artillery (1915-16), joined the United States Regular Army in 1917, and became a lieutenant in France (1918). He returned to the *Gazette* and served in many editorial and administrative positions but was best known for his contribution to the encouragement of conservation when he was Outdoor Editor from 1959 until his retirement. He wrote many newspaper and magazine articles under the pen names "Izaak Hunter" and "Isaac Le Chasseur". He died at Montreal, Quebec, February 12, 1971.

[*Can. who's who,* 1967-69.]

Carr, Emily (1871-1945), painter and author, was born in Victoria, British Columbia, on December 13, 1871, and died there on March 2, 1945. She studied art at the Mark Hopkins School of Art in San Francisco and at the Westminster School of Art in London, England, and later at the Académie Colarossi in Paris, France. On her return to British Columbia, she found that recognition of her painting was discouragingly slow, and for many years she gave up painting altogether. Eventually, however, her genius came to be recognized, and in 1933 she became a member of the Canadian Group of Painters. Her painting had a strongly individual style. In her last years failing health compelled her to turn from painting and sketching to writing, and her first book, *Klee Wyck* (London, 1941), won the Governor-General's award for non-fiction. It was followed by *The book of Small* (Toronto, 1942) and *The house of all sorts* (Toronto, 1944). Her autobiography, *Growing pains* (Toronto, 1946), was edited after her death by her literary executor, Ira Dilworth, as was *The heart of a peacock* (Toronto, 1953). Some of her sketches were also published posthumously, under the title *Pause: A sketch book* (Toronto, 1953).

[Ira Dilworth and others, *Emily Carr, her paintings and sketches* (Toronto, 1945); C. Pearson, *Emily Carr as I knew her* (Toronto, 1953); D. Buchanan, *The growth of Canadian painting* (London, 1950); B. H. Sanders, *Canadian portraits — Famous women* (Toronto, 1958); *Encyc. Can.*]

Carr, William James Guy (1895-1959), naval officer and author, was born at Formby, Lancashire, England, on June 2, 1895. He was educated in Scotland, and went to sea at the age of fourteen. He served as a naval officer in the British navy in the First World War and with the Canadian navy during the Second World War. He died at Toronto, Ontario, on October 2, 1959. He was the author of several successful books about war at sea: *By guess and by God* (New York, 1930), *Hell's angels of the deep* (London, 1932), *High and dry* (London, 1935), *Brass hats and bell-bottomed trousers* (London, 1939), *Out of the mists* (London, 1942), *Checkmate in the north*

(Toronto, 1944), and *The red fog over America* (Toronto, 1955).

[*Can. who's who,* 1955-57; Toronto *Globe and Mail,* Oct. 3, 1959.]

Carrel, Frank (1870-1940), journalist and author, was born at Quebec, Que., on September 7, 1870, the son of James Carrel, proprietor of the Quebec *Daily Telegraph.* He was educated at Stanstead Wesleyan College, Stanstead, Quebec; and was from an early age employed on the staff of the Quebec *Daily Telegraph,* of which he became, on the death of his father in 1891, proprietor and editor-in-chief. Later he became president of the Chronicle-Telegraph Publishing Company, when the Quebec *Chronicle* was merged with the *Telegraph.* In 1918 he was appointed a member of the Legislative Council of Quebec; and in 1926 he was elected president of the Canadian Daily Newspapers Association. He died at Quebec on July 30, 1940. He was the author of *Canada's west and farther west* (Quebec, 1911), *Around the world cruise* (Quebec, 1917), *Impressions of war* (Quebec, 1919), and *Touring South Africa* (Quebec, 1937), and compiler of *Guide to the city of Quebec* (Quebec, 1902).

[*Can. who's who,* 1936-37.]

Carr-Harris, Mrs. Bertha, *née* **Wright** (1863-1949), author, was born in 1863, and died at Ottawa, Ontario, on November 22, 1949. She married Robert Carr-Harris, professor of engineering at the Royal Military College at Kingston, and lived at Kingston for many years. After her husband's death, she lived in Toronto. She was the author of *The white chief of the Ottawa* (Toronto, 1903), *The hieroglyphics of the heavens* (Toronto, 1933), and *Love's immensity* (Pickering, Ont., 1935).

[Toronto *Globe and Mail,* Nov. 24, 1949.]

Carrier, Louis Napoléon (1837-1912), author, was born at St. Henri de Lévis, Lower Canada, on August 19, 1837, the son of Jean-Baptiste Carrier and Marie-Ursule Patry. He was admitted a notary public in 1863, and from 1879 to 1908 was registrar of the county of Lévis. He died at Lévis on July 19, 1912. He was the author of *Les évènements de 1837-1838* (Quebec, 1880; 2nd ed., Beauceville, 1914) and *Les institutions de crédit foncier* (Quebec, 1880).

[P. G. Roy, *Dates Lévisiennes,* vol. 6 (Lévis, Que., 1933); *Bull. rech. hist.,* 1928.]

Carroll, Henry George (1865-1939), lieutenant-governor of Quebec (1929-34), was born at Kamouraska, Canada East, on January 31, 1865. He was educated at Laval University (LL.B., 1889; LL.D., 1902), and was called to the bar of Quebec in 1889 (K.C., 1899). He represented Kamouraska in the Canadian House of Commons from 1891 to 1904, and was solicitor-general in the Laurier government from 1902 to 1904. In 1904 he was appointed a judge in the Superior Court of Quebec, and in 1908 a judge in the court of King's Bench. In 1929 he was appointed lieutenant-governor of the province of Quebec; and he occupied this position until 1934. He died at Quebec on August 20, 1939.

[*Can. who's who,* 1936-37; Morgan, *Can. men* (1912); *Can. parl. comp.*]

Carroll, John (1809-1884), clergyman and author, was born on an island in the Bay of Fundy in 1809. He removed, with his parents, to York (Toronto), Upper Canada, in 1818; and he became a Methodist preacher in 1829. He was superannuated in 1870; and he died at Toronto, Ontario, on December 13, 1884. He was the author of *The stripling preacher* (Toronto, 1852), *Past and present; or, A description of persons and events connected with Canadian Methodism* (Toronto, 1860), *Case and his contemporaries* (5 vols., Toronto, 1867-77), *The school of the prophets* (Toronto, 1876), *"Father Corson"* (Toronto, 1879), *The "Exposition" expounded, defended, and supplemented* (Toronto, 1881), and *My boy life* (Toronto, 1882).

[*Dom. ann. reg.,* 1884; L. E. Horning and L. J. Burpee, *A bibliography of Canadian fiction* (Toronto, 1904).]

Carruthers, John (d. 1866), missionary, was a school-teacher who was appointed in 1832 a catechist and exhorter of the Church of Scotland in Canada, and made many missionary journeys through Upper Canada in subsequent years. He died in 1866. He published his autobiography under the title, *Retrospect of thirty-six years' residence in Canada West, being a Christian journal and narrative* (Hamilton, C.W., 1861).

[Frances M. Staton and M. Tremaine (eds.), *A bibliography of Canadiana* (Toronto, 1934).]

Carry, John (1824-1891), clergyman, was born in Ireland in 1824, and came to Canada when a young man. He was ordained a clergyman of the Church of England in 1850; and he served in various country parishes in Quebec and Ontario. The University of Bishop's College conferred on him the degree of D.D. in 1883. He died in 1891. He was the author of *Sermons, doctrinal, devotional, and practical* (Quebec, 1860) and *An exposure of the mischievous perversions of Holy Scripture in the National Temperance Society's publications* (Toronto, 1885).

[Toronto *Globe,* Jan. 15, 1891.]

Carson, Sir Frederick (1886-1960), engineer, was born at Kingston, Ontario, in 1886; and died at Montreal, Quebec, on May 3, 1960. He was educated at Queen's University and at the Royal Military College, and was commissioned in the Royal Engineers in 1908. He served with the Royal Engineers throughout the First World War, and was awarded the M.C. and bar. From 1919 to 1940 he served with the State Railways in India, and from 1936 to 1940 he was general manager of the Northwest Railway. During the Second World War he was chief engineer of a special force in London from 1940 to 1941, with the rank of brigadier, and from 1941 to 1943 he was the director of transportation in Iraq. He was created a knight bachelor in 1941.

[*Can. who's who,* 1955-57; Toronto *Globe and Mail,* May 4, 1960.]

Carson, Sir John Wallace (1864-1922), mining capitalist and soldier, was born in Montreal on October 13, 1864, the son of William Carson and Mary Johnston. He was lieutenant-colonel of the 5th Royal Highlanders of Montreal (retired, 1909), and in 1916 was appointed special representative of the Canadian minister of militia in England, with the rank of major-general. In 1917, on the appointment of Sir G. Perley (q.v.) as overseas minister of militia, his appointment terminated. In 1916 he was created a C.B., and in 1918 a knight bachelor. He died in Montreal on October 13, 1922. In 1885 he married Minnie, daughter of Henry Corran of St. Johns, Quebec.

[*Who was who,* 1916-28.]

Carson, William (1770-1843), physician and reformer, was born in Scotland in 1770, studied medicine at the University of Edinburgh, and became a physician in Birmingham. He moved to Newfoundland in 1808, and there took a leading part in the agitation for reform of the system of government. He was partly responsible for the introduction of representative government in Newfoundland in 1832; and though at first he failed of election to the House of Assembly, he was later elected, and was mainly responsible for the dismissal of H. J. Boulton (q.v.) as chief justice in 1838. He died at St. John's, Newfoundland, on February 26, 1843.

[J. R. Smallwood (ed.), *The book of Newfoundland* (2 vols., St. John's, 1937); *Encyc. Can.*; *Newfoundland supp.*]

Carter, Sir Frederic Bowker Terrington (1819-1900), prime minister of Newfoundland (1865-70 and 1874-78), was born at St. John's, Newfoundland, on February 12, 1819. He was called to the bar in Newfoundland in 1842, and was appointed a Q.C. in 1859. He was a member of the Newfoundland House of Assembly from 1855 to 1878, was speaker of the House from 1861 to 1865, and was prime minister and attorney-general from 1865 to 1870, and again from 1874 to 1878. He attended the Quebec Conference on Confederation in 1864; but his advocacy of Newfoundland's entry into Confederation with Canada brought about his defeat in the election of 1865. He was appointed a judge of the Supreme Court of

Newfoundland in 1878, and chief justice of the island in 1880; and he died at St. John's on February 28, 1900. He was created a K.C.M.G. in 1878.

[*Who was who,* 1897-1916; Morgan, *Can. men* (1898); *Encyc. Can.*; *Newfoundland supp.*]

Carter, Sir James (1805-1878), chief justice of New Brunswick (1851-65) was born in 1805, the son of James Carter, of Portsmouth, England. He was educated at Trinity College, Cambridge, and was called to the bar at the Inner Temple in 1832. In 1834 he was appointed a puisne judge of the Supreme Court of New Brunswick, and in 1851 he became chief justice of this court. He retired on a pension in 1865; and he died in England, where he had been living for some years, on March 9, 1878. He was knighted in 1859.

[J. W. Lawrence, *The judges of New Brunswick and their times* (Saint John, N.B., 1907); *Dom. ann. reg.,* 1878; J. Hannay, *History of New Brunswick* (2 vols., Saint John, N.B., 1909); *Dict. Can. biog.,* vol. 10.]

Cartier, Sir George Etienne, Bart. (1814-1873), statesman, was born at St. Antoine, county of Verchères, Lower Canada, on September 6, 1814, the son of Lt.-Col. Jacques Cartier and Marguerite Paradis. He was educated at the college of St. Sulpice, in Montreal; and in 1835 he was called to the bar of Lower Canada. In 1837 he shouldered a musket, fought at St. Denis on the rebel side, and was forced to take refuge in the United States. He returned to Canada in 1838; and in 1848 he was elected to the Legislative Assembly of Canada for the county of Verchères. He continued to represent Verchères until 1861, when he was elected for Montreal East; and for this constituency he sat in the Legislative Assembly and the House of Commons until his death. He first entered office in 1856, when he was appointed first provincial secretary and then attorney-general for Lower Canada, in the MacNab-Taché ministry. In 1857 he became leader of the Lower Canadian section of the government in the Macdonald-Cartier administration. He remained in power until the defeat of this government in 1862; and in the short-lived Taché-Macdonald ministry of 1864 he was again attorney-general for Lower Canada.

In the movement toward Confederation he played a conspicuous part. He was the leading French-Canadian member of the "Great Coalition"; he was a delegate to the Quebec Conference of 1864; and it was largely through his efforts that French Canada accepted the federation proposals. He was minister of militia in the first government of the Dominion of Canada; and was regarded as Sir John Macdonald's chief lieutenant. In 1872-73 he became implicated in the so-called "Pacific Scandal"; but before parliament had pronounced its verdict on that episode, he died in London, England, on May 20, 1873.

He was a politician of indomitable energy and good executive ability; and his hold over the people of French Canada was, from 1858 to 1873, almost unchallenged. His political methods were perhaps not always above reproach; but his services in connection with Confederation outweigh any shortcomings he may have had.

He married, in 1846, Hortense, daughter of Edouard Raymond Fabre, of Montreal; and by her he had three daughters. In 1868 he was created a baronet of the United Kingdom. He was the author of a song which at one time seemed likely to become the national anthem of Canada, *O Canada! mon pays, mes amours!*

[J. Boyd, *Sir George Etienne Cartier* (Toronto, 1914); A. Dansereau *et al., Georges-Etienne Cartier* (Montreal, 1914); C. E. Lavergne, *Georges-Etienne Cartier* (Montreal, 1914); B. Sulte, *Georges Cartier* (Montreal, 1919); A. D. DeCelles, *Cartier et son temps* (Montreal, 1907); L. O. David, *Esquisse biographique* (Montreal, 1873) and *Canada sous l'union* (2 vols., Quebec, 1871-72); J. C. Dent, *The last forty years* (2 vols., Toronto, 1881); J. Pope, *Memoirs of the Right Hon. Sir John A. Macdonald* (2 vols., Ottawa, 1894) and *Correspondence of Sir John Macdonald* (Toronto, 1921); M. O. Hammond, *Confederation and its leaders* (Toronto, 1917); *Dict. nat. biog.*; Morgan, *Cel. Can.*; Taylor, *Brit. Am.,* vol. 1; Dent, *Can. port.,* vol. 1; *Bull. rech. hist.,* 1916; *Dict. Can. biog.,* vol. 10.]

Cartier, Jacques (1491-1557), navigator, was born at St. Malo, France, in 1491. Of his early life little is known; but in 1534 he was commissioned by the French king to make a voyage of exploration to the Gulf of St. Lawrence. He passed through the Strait of Belle Isle, crossed to the coast of Gaspé, where he first came into contact with the Indians, and penetrated the Gulf of St. Lawrence as far as Anticosti. In the spring of 1535 he made a second voyage, and on this he ascended the St. Lawrence River as far as the island of Montreal. He wintered in the neighbourhood of the present city of Quebec, and in 1536 returned to France. His third voyage did not take place until 1541; and on this occasion he was subordinate to the Sieur de Roberval, to whom the king of France had issued a commission as lieutenant-general. Cartier re-visited the island of Montreal, and again spent a winter in Canada, waiting for Roberval; but in the spring of 1542 he returned to France, passing Roberval at St. John's, Newfoundland, on the way. It is probable that the voyage of 1541-42 was his last visit to the St. Lawrence valley, of which he had been the discoverer. He died at St. Malo on September 1, 1557. In 1519 he married Marie Catherine, daughter of the high constable of St. Malo; but he had no children.

Cartier left narratives of his first and second voyages. The account of the second voyage was published under the title *Brief récit et succinte narration* (Paris, 1545), and has been reprinted with the manuscript variants (Paris, 1863). The account of the first voyage first appeared, in an Italian translation, in Ramusio, *Navigationi e viaggi,* vol. iii (Venice, 1565); secondly, in an English translation from Ramusio by John Florio (London, 1580); thirdly, in a French translation of a translation, under the title *Discours du voyage* (Rouen, 1598). For the third voyage the authority is Hakluyt.

[H. P. Biggar, *The voyages of Jacques Cartier* (Ottawa, 1924) and *Collection of documents* (Ottawa, 1930); G. Vathier, *Jacques Cartier et la découverte du Canada* (Paris, 1937); J. P. Baxter, *A memoir of Jacques Cartier* (New York, 1906); J. Pope, *Jacques Cartier* (Ottawa, 1890); N. E. Dionne, *Jacques Cartier* (Quebec, 1889; new ed., 1934); H. B. Stephens, *Jacques Cartier and his four voyages to Canada* (Montreal, 1890); F. J. des Longrais, *Jacques Cartier* (Paris, 1888); S. Leacock, *The mariner of St. Malo* (Toronto, 1914); S. E. Dawson, *The St. Lawrence basin* (New York, 1905); C. de La Roncière, *Histoire de la marine française,* vol. iii (Paris, 1906); W. F. Ganong, *Cartier's first voyage* (Trans. Roy. Soc. Can., 1887) and *Cartography of the Gulf of St. Lawrence* (Trans. Roy. Soc. Can., 1889); Abbé H. A. Verreau, *Jacques Cartier* (Trans. Roy. Soc. Can., 1890, 1891, and 1897); P. de Cazes, *Les points obscurs des voyages de Jacques Cartier* (Trans. Roy. Soc. Can., 1890). For bibliographical information about Cartier's narratives, see H. Harrisse, *Notes pour servir à l'histoire de la Nouvelle France* (Paris, 1872); *Dict. Can. biog.*, vol. 1.]

Cartwright, Conway Edward (1837-1920), clergyman and author, was born at Kingston, Upper Canada, on May 15, 1837, the son of the Rev. R. D. Cartwright. He was educated at Trinity College, Dublin (B.A., 1869), took holy orders in the Church of England, and in 1875 was appointed Protestant chaplain to the Portsmouth Penitentiary, near Kingston. He died at Vancouver, British Columbia, on January 26, 1920. When a young man he published a small volume of poetry, *Lena, a legend of Niagara, and other poems* (Dublin, 1860); and he was the author of *The life and letters of the late Hon. Richard Cartwright* (Toronto, 1876).

[C. C. James, *A bibliography of Canadian poetry* (Toronto, 1899).]

Cartwright, George (1739-1819), author, was born at Marnham, Nottinghamshire, England, on February 12 (old style), 1739, the second son of William Cartwright. He entered the British army, and became a captain in the 37th Foot; but in 1770 he went to live on the coast of Labrador, and he spent sixteen years there. On his return to England, he became barrack-master at Nottingham; and he died at Mansfield, Nottinghamshire, on February 19, 1819. He published a *Journal of transactions and events during a residence of nearly sixteen years on the coast of Labrador* (3 vols., Newark, 1792); and extracts of this journal, with a brief biography of its author, have been printed in C. W. Townsend (ed.), *Captain Cartwright and his Labrador journal* (London, 1911).

[W. G. Gosling, *Labrador* (London, 1910).]

Cartwright, John Solomon (1804-1845), banker, was born on September 17, 1804, the son of the Hon. Richard Cartwright (q.v.). He studied law in York (Toronto) and at Lincoln's Inn, London; and he returned to Canada in 1830. In 1831 he became the first president of the Commercial Bank of Kingston. In 1836 he was elected to the Legislative Assembly of Upper Canada, and in 1841 to the Legislative Assembly of United Canada, for Lennox and Addington. A supporter of the "Family Compact", he opposed the Union of 1840, and in 1842 he declined the offer of the solicitor-generalship from Sir Charles Bagot (q.v.). He died at Kingston on December 15, 1845. In 1831 he married Sarah Hayter, daughter of Dr. James Macaulay; and by her he had two sons and two daughters.

[A. Shortt, *Founders of Canadian banking: John Solomon Cartwright* (Journal of the Canadian Bankers Association, 1923); E. M. Chadwick, *Ontarian families* (2 vols., Toronto, 1894-98).]

Cartwright, Richard (1759-1815), pioneer merchant, was born at Albany, New York, on February 2, 1759, the son of Richard Cartwright, who came to America about 1742. During the American Revolutionary War he was secretary to Colonel Butler (q.v.), of the Queen's Rangers; and about 1780 he settled in Upper Canada, first at Niagara, and then at Kingston. He entered into partnership with Robert Hamilton (q.v.), and became one of the foremost merchants of the province. In 1788 he was appointed judge of the court of Common Pleas for the district of Mecklenburgh; and in 1792 he became a member of the Legislative Council of Upper Canada. During the War of 1812 he was commandant of the Midland District. He died at Montreal on July 27, 1815.

[C. E. Cartwright, *Life and letters of the late Hon. Richard Cartwright* (Toronto, 1876); E. M. Chadwick, *Ontarian families* (2 vols., Toronto, 1894-98); W. Canniff, *History of the settlement of Upper Canada* (Toronto, 1869); J. Ross Robertson (ed.), *The diary of Mrs. Simcoe* (Toronto, 1911); D. C. Macdonald, *Three history theses* (Toronto, 1962).]

Cartwright, Sir Richard John (1835-1912), statesman, was born in Kingston, Upper Canada, on December 4, 1835, the son of the Rev. Robert David Cartwright and Harriet Dobbs, and grandson of the Hon. Richard Cartwright (q.v.). He was educated at Trinity College, Dublin. On returning to Canada, he went into business, and became president of the Commercial Bank of the Midland District. In 1863 he was elected as a Conservative to the Legislative Assembly of Canada for Lennox and Addington, and in 1867 he was elected for the same constituency to the Canadian House of Commons. In 1870 he was an unsuccessful rival of Sir Francis Hincks (q.v.) for the office of finance minister, and thereafter he drifted into the ranks of the Liberal party. From 1873 to 1878 he was minister of finance in the Mackenzie administration. In 1878 he was defeated in Lennox and Addington, but was elected for Centre Huron, and he continued to sit in the House of Commons continuously until 1904, first for Centre Huron (1878-82), then for South Huron (1882-87), and lastly for South Oxford (1887-1904). In 1896 he became minister of trade and commerce in the Laurier administration; in 1904 he was appointed to the Senate; and in 1909 he became government leader in the Senate. On four occasions, in 1897, in 1902, in 1907, and in 1911, he was acting prime minister, during Sir Wilfrid Laurier's absence; he was for nearly forty years the chief spokesman of the Liberal party in regard to fiscal matters; and the vigour and trenchancy of his speeches won for him the *sobriquet* of "the Rupert of debate".

He died at Kingston, on September 24, 1912. He married, in 1859, Frances, eldest daughter of Col. Alexander Lawe, of Cork, Ireland; and by her he had six sons and three daughters. He was created a K.C.M.G. in 1879, and a G.C.M.G. in 1907; and in 1902 he was appointed a member of the privy council. He was the author of *Memories of Confederation* (Ottawa, 1906) and *Reminiscences* (Toronto, 1912).

[W. L. Grant, *Sir Richard Cartwright* (Can. mag., 1913); *Who was who*, 1897-1916; *Can. who was who*, vol. 1; Morgan, *Can. men* (1912); Dent, *Can. port.*, vol. 3; Taché, *Men of the day*; Rose, *Cyc. Can. biog.* (1886); *Can. parl. comp.*]

Carvell, Frank Broadstreet (1862-1924), minister of public works for Canada (1917-19), was born at Bloomfield, Carleton county, New Brunswick, on August 14, 1862, the son of A. Bishop Carvell and Margaret Lindsay. He was educated at Boston University (LL.B., 1890), and was called to the bar in New Brunswick (K.C., 1907). From 1899 to 1900 he represented Carleton in the Legislative Assembly of New Brunswick; and from 1904 to 1919 he represented the same constituency in the Canadian House of Commons. In 1917 he became minister of public works in the Union

government under Sir Robert Borden; but he resigned this post in 1919 to become chairman of the board of railway commissioners for Canada. He died at Woodstock, New Brunswick, on August 9, 1924. In 1887 he married Carrie B. Parks. He was popularly known as "fighting Frank Carvell".

[*Can. who was who*, vol. 1; Morgan, *Can. men* (1912); *Can. parl. comp.*]

Carvell, Jedediah Slason (1832-1894), lieutenant-governor of Prince Edward Island, was born at Newcastle, New Brunswick, on March 16, 1832. In his early years he was a merchant and became mayor of Charlottetown, Prince Edward Island, in 1877. He was appointed to the Senate of Canada in 1879, and was a senator until September, 1889, when he became lieutenant-governor of Prince Edward Island. He died at Charlottetown on February 14, 1894.

[*Can. parl. comp.*; Le Jeune, *Dict. gén.*]

Carver, Jonathan (1710-1780), author, was born on April 13, 1710, at Weymouth, Massachusetts, the son of David Carver and Hannah Dyer. He fought in the Seven Years' War, and in 1760 became a captain in a Massachusetts regiment. In 1766 he was persuaded by Major Robert Rogers (q.v.) to undertake an exploration of the country west of Michilimackinac; and he made a journey to the Mississippi and St. Peter's rivers, going by way of Lake Michigan, and returning by way of Lake Superior. His account of this journey was published by him in his *Travels in the interior parts of America* (London, 1878). This ran through many editions and translations, for which see John Thomas Lee, *A bibliography of Carver's travels* (Proceedings of the Wisconsin Historical Society, 1909), and *Additional data* (1912). He died in poverty in London, England, on January 31, 1780. Over his motives and reliability a considerable controversy has been waged.

[L. P. Kellogg, *The mission of Jonathan Carver* (Wisconsin magazine of history, 1928); E. G. Bourne, *The travels of Jonathan Carver* (American historical review, 1904); William Browning, *Early history of Jonathan Carver* (Wisconsin magazine of history, 1919); T. C. Elliott, *The strange case of Jonathan Carver and the name Oregon* (Quarterly of the Oregon Historical Society, 1920); M. M. Quaife, *Carver and the Carver grant* (Mississippi Valley historical review, 1921); *Dict. Am. biog.*]

Cary, Thomas (1751-1823), journalist, was born near Bristol, England, in 1751. After a period of service with the East India Company, he came to Canada, and in 1797 became secretary of Robert Prescott (q.v.), the governor of Canada. In 1805 he founded the Quebec *Mercury* (1805-1903), as the organ of the official or Tory party in Lower Canada; and this paper remained in the possession of his family for three generations. In 1789 his name appeared on an early Canadian imprint, *Abram's Plains, a poem* (Quebec). He died at Quebec on January 29, 1823.

[Morgan, *Bib. can.*; P. G. Roy, *Les avocats de la région de Québec* (Lévis, Que., 1936).]

Casault, Sir Louis Napoléon (1823-1908), chief justice of the Supreme Court of Quebec (1894-1904), was born at St. Thomas, Lower Canada, on July 10, 1823, the son of Louis Casault. He was educated at the Quebec Seminary, and was called to the bar of Lower Canada in 1847 (Q.C., 1867). He sat as a Conservative in the Legislative Assembly of Canada for Montmagny from 1854 to 1857, and in the Canadian House of Commons for Bellechasse from 1867 to 1870. In 1870 he was appointed a puisne judge of the Superior Court of Quebec, and in 1894 he became chief justice of this court. He retired from the bench in 1904, and he died at Quebec on May 18, 1908. In 1870 he married Jane Elmire, daughter of John Pangman, seignior of Lachenaye, near Montreal. From 1858 to 1891 he was professor of commercial law in Laval University; and he was an LL.D. of Laval (1865) and a D.C.L. of Bishop's College, Lennoxville (1895). In 1894 he was created a knight bachelor.

[P. G. Roy, *Les juges de la province de Québec* (Quebec, 1933); *Can. parl. comp.*; Morgan, *Can. men* (1898); Le Jeune, *Dict. gén.*]

Casavant, Joseph (1807-1874), organ-builder, was born in 1807, and became an organ-builder at St. Hyacinthe, Lower Canada. He built, among many others, the organs in the Roman Catholic cathedrals at Kingston and Ottawa. He died at St. Hyacinthe on March 9, 1874, but his work was carried on by his sons, Claver and Samuel, under the firm name of Casavant Frères.

[Brother Élie, *La famille Casavant* (Montreal, 1914); *Dict. Can. biog.*, vol. 10.]

Case, William (1780-1855), Methodist missionary, was born in Swansea, Massachusetts, in 1780. He entered the ministry of the Methodist Episcopal Church, and was first stationed in the district of the Bay of Quinte, Upper Canada. In 1809 he was stationed at Detroit; and from 1810 to 1827 he was presiding elder of the Methodist Church in Canada and north-western New York. In 1828 on the separation of the Canadian Methodists from their brethren in the United States, he became superintendent of Indian missions and schools in Upper Canada; and from 1830 to 1833 he was general superintendent of the Wesleyan Methodists in Canada. From 1837 to 1851 he was in charge of the Wesleyan industrial school for Indians at Alnwick, Upper Canada; and he obtained over the Indians a great influence for good. He died at the Alnwick mission

house, Upper Canada, on October 19, 1855. Shortly before his death he delivered before the Methodist Conference in London, Upper Canada, a *Jubilee sermon* (Toronto, 1855), which embodied his reminiscences.

[J. Carroll, *Case and his contemporaries* (5 vols., Toronto, 1867-77); J. E. Sanderson, *The first century of Methodism in Canada* (2 vols., Toronto, 1908-10); Morgan, *Bib. can.*]

Casey, George Elliott (1850-1903), politician, was born in Southwold, Elgin county, Canada West, in March, 1850. He was educated at the University of Toronto (B.A., 1871); and in 1872 he was elected to represent West Elgin in the Canadian House of Commons as a Liberal. He continued to represent this constituency until 1900; and he became the leading advocate in the Canadian parliament of the abolition of patronage in the Canadian civil service and of the introduction of the merit system. He died on November 30, 1903.

[*Can. parl. comp.*; Morgan, *Can. men* (1898).]

Casey, Timothy (1862-1931), Roman Catholic archbishop, was born at Flume Ridge, Charlotte county, New Brunswick, on February 20, 1862. He was educated at St. Joseph's College, Memramcook, and at Laval University, and was ordained a priest in 1886. In 1901 he was appointed bishop of Saint John; and in 1912 he became archbishop of Vancouver and metropolitan of British Columbia. He died at Vancouver, British Columbia, on October 5, 1931.

[*Can. who was who*, vol. 2; E. O. S. Scholefield and F. W. Howay, *British Columbia*, vol. 3 (Vancouver, B.C., 1914).]

Casgrain, Henri Raymond (1831-1904), priest and historian, was born at Rivière Ouelle, Lower Canada, on December 16, 1831, the son of the Hon. Charles Eusèbe Casgrain and Anne Elizabeth, daughter of the Hon. Jacques Baby (q.v.). He was educated at the College of Ste. Anne and the Quebec Seminary, and was ordained a priest of the Roman Catholic Church in 1856. In 1874 he was compelled to give up active parochial duties; but long before this he had turned his energies toward literary and historical work. His first important publication was a volume of *Légendes canadiennes* (Quebec, 1861), and this was followed by his *Histoire de la Mère Marie de l'Incarnation* (Quebec, 1864; new and revised ed., Montreal, 1886), *Vie des Saints* (Ottawa, 1867), *Les pionniers canadiens* (Quebec, 1876), *Opuscules* (Quebec, 1876), *Histoire de l'Hôtel Dieu de Québec* (Quebec, 1878), and *Une paroisse canadienne au xviie siècle* (Quebec, 1880). Together with a number of short biographies, most of these were collected in his *Oeuvres complètes* (4 vols., Montreal, 1884). His *Pèlerinage au pays d'Evangeline* (Quebec, 1888) was crowned by the French Academy. But his chief work was his *Montcalm et Lévis* (2 vols., Quebec, 1891; Tours, 1898) and this was followed by *Une seconde Acadie* (Quebec, 1894), *Les sulpiciens et les prêtres des missions étrangères en Acadie* (Quebec, 1897), *Les origines du Canada* (Quebec, 1898), and *Montcalm and Wolfe* (Toronto, 1905). He published also two small volumes of verse, *A ma soeur Rosalie* (privately printed, 1860) and *Les miettes* (Quebec, 1869); and he edited, with a memoir of his mother, his mother's *Mémoires de famille* (Rivières Ouelle, 1891). He died in Quebec, on February 12, 1904. In 1877 he was made a LL.D. of Laval University; and in 1889 he was elected president of the Royal Society of Canada, of which he was a charter member, and in the proceedings of which a number of papers by him appeared.

[A. B. Routhier, *Eloge historique de M. l'Abbé H. R. Casgrain* (Trans. Roy. Soc. Can., 1904); C. Roy, *L'Abbé Casgrain* (La Nouvelle-France, 1904); Morgan, *Can. men* (1898); Le Jeune, *Dict. gén.*; Allaire, *Dict. biog.*; L. M. Darveau, *Nos hommes de lettres* (Montreal, 1873).]

Casgrain, Joseph Philippe Baby (1856-1939), senator of Canada, was born at Quebec, Canada East, on March 1, 1856, the son of Philippe Baby Casgrain (q.v.). He was educated at the Quebec Seminary, and became a civil engineer and land surveyor. He was summoned to the Senate of Canada in 1900; and he continued a senator of Canada until his death at Montreal, Quebec, on January 6, 1939.

[*Can. who's who,* 1936-37; *Can. parl. comp.*]

Casgrain, Philippe Baby (1826-1917), historian, was born in Quebec, on December 30, 1826, the son of the Hon. Charles Eusèbe Casgrain and Anne Elizabeth, daughter of the Hon. Jacques Baby (q.v.). He was educated at the College of Ste. Anne, and was called to the bar of Lower Canada in 1850 (Q.C. 1879). From 1872 to 1891 he sat in the Canadian House of Commons for L'Islet. He then became clerk of the Circuit and Revision Court of the province of Quebec. He was the author of *Letellier de St. Just et son temps* (Quebec, 1885), *Mémorial des familles Casgrain, Baby, et Perrault* (Quebec, 1898), *La vie de Joseph François Perrault* (Quebec, 1898), and a number of publications dealing with the history and archaeology of the city of Quebec and its environs. He died at Quebec on May 23, 1917. In 1854 he married Mathilde, daughter of Col. F. X. Perrault, and by her he had three sons. In 1898, 1899, and 1906, he was president of the Literary and Historical Society of Quebec.

[H. Charlesworth (ed.), *A cyclopaedia of Canadian biography* (Toronto, 1919); *Can. who was who,* vol. 1; Morgan, *Can. men* (1912); Le Jeune, *Dict. gén.*; *Bull. rech. hist.*, 1917.]

Casgrain, Pierre François (1886-1950), secretary of state for Canada (1940-41), was born at Montreal, Quebec, on August 4, 1886; and died at Westmount, Quebec, on August 26, 1950. He was educated at Laval University (B.A., 1907; LL.M., 1910), and was called to the bar. He represented Charlevoix-Saguenay as a Liberal in the Canadian House of Commons from 1917 to 1941, was elected speaker of the House in 1936, and was appointed secretary of state in the Mackenzie King government in 1940. In 1941 he was appointed a justice of the Superior Court of Quebec.

[*Can. who's who,* 1948; *Can. parl. guide,* 1940.]

Casgrain, René Édouard (1839-1917), priest, was born at Rivière Ouelle, Lower Canada, on February 4, 1839, the son of the Hon. Charles Eusèbe Casgrain. He was ordained a priest of the Roman Catholic Church in 1873; and he held various charges in the province of Quebec. He died at Quebec City, on April 25, 1917. He was the author of *Histoire de la paroisse de l'Ange-Gardien de Québec* (Quebec, 1902).

[Allaire, *Dict. biog.*; *Bull. rech. hist.*, 1929.]

Casgrain, Thomas Chase (1852-1916), postmaster-general of Canada (1914-16), was born in Detroit, Michigan, on July 28, 1852, the son of the Hon. Charles Eusèbe Casgrain, and a nephew of the Abbé H. R. Casgrain (q.v.) and P. B. Casgrain (q.v.). He was educated at the Quebec Seminary and at Laval University, and was called to the bar of Quebec in 1877 (Q.C., 1887). In 1894 he was *bâtonnier-général* of the Quebec bar. From 1886 to 1890 and from 1892 to 1896, he was a member of the Legislative Assembly of Quebec, first for Quebec county, and secondly for Montmorency; and he was attorney-general in the Boucherville and Taillon administrations. From 1896 to 1904 he was a member of the Canadian House of Commons for Montmorency; and from 1911 to 1914 he was chairman of the International Joint Commission. Shortly after the outbreak of the First World War, he accepted the office of postmaster-general in the Borden administration; and he died, in office, on December 29, 1916.

[*Can. parl. comp.*; Morgan, *Can. men* (1912); *Encyclopedia Americana.*]

Cashin, Sir Michael Patrick (1864-1926), prime minister of Newfoundland (1919), was born at Cape Broyle, Newfoundland, on September 9, 1864. He was educated at St. John's, and became a fish merchant. He was a member of the House of Assembly in Newfoundland from 1898 to 1923, and was minister of finance in the Morris administration from 1909 to 1919. He became prime minister in 1919, but was defeated at the polls after holding office for only a few months. He was leader of the opposition from 1919 to 1923; then he surrendered the position to Sir John Bennett (q.v.), and in 1924 he retired from public life. He died at St. John's on August 30, 1926. In 1918 he was created a K.B.E.

[J. R. Smallwood, ed., *The book of Newfoundland* (2 vols., St. John's, 1937); *Who was who*, 1916-28; *Encyc. Can.*; *Newfoundland supp.*]

Cassegrain, Arthur (1835-1868), poet, was born at L'Islet, Lower Canada, on October 4, 1835, the son of Eugène Casgrain and Hortense Dionne; and he died on February 9, 1868. He was the author of a humorous poem entitled *La grande tronciade; ou, Itineraire de Québec à la Rivière-du-Loup* (Ottawa, 1866).

[*Bull. rech. hist.*, 1927; Morgan, *Bib. can.*]

Cassels, Hamilton (1854-1925), lawyer, was born in Quebec on April 2, 1854, the seventh son of Robert Cassels. He was educated at Morrin College and at McGill University (B.A., 1873), and was called to the bar in 1877 (K.C., 1902). He was keenly interested in welfare work, was president of the Penny Bank in 1905, was chairman of the Ontario Parole Board for several years, and for many years was interested in the Prisoners' Aid Association. He died in Toronto, Ontario, on November 2, 1925.

[Morgan, *Can. men* (1912).]

Cassels, Robert (1843-1898), lawyer and author, was born in Quebec on April 27, 1843, the third son of Robert Cassels. He was educated at Morrin College (B.A., 1866), and he was called to the bar of Lower Canada in 1864, and that of Upper Canada in 1866. In 1875 he was appointed first registrar of the Supreme Court of Canada, and he retained this position until his death on June 17, 1898. He was the author of *A manual of procedure in the Supreme and Exchequer Courts of Canada* (Toronto, 1877), *A digest of all cases reported and unreported by the Supreme Court of Canada* (Toronto, 1886; 2nd ed., 1893), and *The practice of the Supreme Court of Canada* (Toronto, 1888; 2nd ed., 1899).

[Morgan, *Can. men* (1898).]

Cassels, Sir Walter (1845-1923), judge, was born at Quebec on August 14, 1845, the son of Robert Cassels. He was educated at the University of Toronto (B.A., 1865), and was called to the bar in 1872 (Q.C., 1883). He was judge of the Exchequer Court of Canada from 1908 to his death at Ottawa on March 1, 1923. He was created a knight bachelor in 1917.

[*Who was who*, 1916-28; Morgan, *Can. men* (1912).]

Cassidy, Harry Morris (1900-1951), social worker and educationist, was born at Vancouver, British Columbia, on January 18, 1900, and died at Toronto, Ontario, on November 2,

1951. He was educated at the University of British Columbia (B.A., 1923), the University of California, and the Robert Brookings Graduate School of Economics and Government (Ph.D., 1926). Between 1926 and 1934, he served successively on the teaching staff of the University of North Carolina, Rutgers University, and the University of Toronto. He then served for five years as director of social welfare for the province of British Columbia, and for another five years as dean of the School of Social Welfare at the University of California. Finally, in 1945, he was appointed professor of social welfare and director of the School of Social Work in the University of Toronto, a position he held until his early death. He was the author of *Unemployment and relief in Ontario* (Toronto, 1932), *Social security and reconstruction in Canada* (Toronto, 1943), and *Public health and welfare reorganization* (Toronto, 1943); and he was joint author, with F. R. Scott, of *Labour conditions in the men's clothing industry* (Toronto, 1935).

[Toronto *Globe and Mail*, Nov. 3, 1951; *Encyc. Can.*; *Can. who's who*, 1948.]

Caswell, Edward Samuel (1861-1938), librarian, was born at Goderich, Canada West, in 1861. From 1881 to 1909 he was employed in the publishing house of William Briggs; and from 1909 to his death he was assistant librarian and secretary-treasurer of the Toronto Public Library. He died at Toronto, Ontario, on January 25, 1938. He was the author of *Canadian singers and their songs* (Toronto, 1925).

[*Can. who's who*, 1936-37.]

Catalogne, Gédéon de (1662-1729), soldier and engineer, was born at Arthez in the province of Béarn, France, in 1662, and was the son of Gédéon de Catalogne and Marie de Capdeviolle. He came to Canada in 1683, took part in La Barre's expedition against the Iroquois in 1684, and was in the French expedition to Hudson Bay in 1686. In 1687 he accompanied Denonville in his expedition against the Senecas, and he was present at the siege of Quebec in 1690, having had charge of constructing the fortifications. In 1702 he built the fortifications at Bécancour and Three Rivers, and from 1708 to 1709 he prepared maps of the districts of Quebec, Montreal, and Three Rivers. He was the author of an interesting memoir on the plans of the seigniories of Quebec, Three Rivers, and Montreal, written in 1712. He died at Louisbourg on January 5, 1729. He married, in 1690, at Montreal, Marie Anne Lemire; by her he had ten children.

[P. G. Roy, *Gédéon de Catalogne* (Bull. rech. hist., 1907); G. Catalogne, *Mémoire sur les seigneuries* (Bull. rech. hist., 1915); C. Tanguay, *Etude sur une famille canadienne* (Trans. Roy. Soc. Can., 1884); Le Jeune, *Dict. gén.*; *Dict. Can. biog.*, vol. 2.]

Cates, Harry Arthur (1890-1953), anatomist, was born in England in 1890, and came to Canada in 1908. He was educated at the University of Toronto (M.B., 1915), and served with the Royal Medical Corps during the First World War. He joined the staff of the department of anatomy in the University of Toronto at the end of the war, became a full professor in the department, and in 1949 was appointed director of the School of Physical and Health Education. He died at Toronto on July 2, 1953. He was the author of *Primary anatomy* (Baltimore, 1948), and joint author, with J. C. B. Grant, of *A handbook for dissectors* (Baltimore, 1940).

[Toronto *Globe and Mail,* July 4, 1953.]

Cathcart, Charles Murray Cathcart, second Earl (1783-1859), governor-general of Canada (1846-47), was born at Walton, Essex, England, on December 21, 1783, the son of William Schaw Cathcart, first Earl Cathcart, and Elizabeth Elliott. He entered the army in 1799, and fought throughout the Napoleonic wars. He was promoted colonel in 1819 and general in 1854. From 1845 to 1847 he was commander-in-chief of the forces in Canada; from November 26, 1845, to April 23, 1846, he was administrator of the government of Canada; and from April 24, 1846, to January 29, 1847, he was governor-general. He was created a C.B. in 1815, a K.C.B. in 1838, and a G.C.B. in 1859. He died at St. Leonards-on-Sea, England, on July 16, 1859. In 1818 he married Henrietta, second daughter of Thomas Mather, and by her he had three sons and three daughters. He was the author of several papers on geology and other scientific subjects; and he discovered a new mineral, a sulphate of cadmium.

[*Dict. nat. biog.*; Sir J. B. Paul (ed.), *The Scots peerage,* vol. 2 (Edinburgh, 1905); J. C. Dent, *The last forty years* (2 vols., Toronto, 1881) and *Can. port.,* vol. 4.]

Cauchon, Joseph Edouard (1816-1885), journalist, politician, and lieutenant-governor of Manitoba (1877-82), was born at St. Roch, Quebec, on December 31, 1816, the son of Joseph Ange Cauchon and Marguerite Vallée. He was educated at the Quebec Seminary, and was called to the bar of Lower Canada in 1843, but never practised. In 1841, he succeeded Etienne Parent (q.v.) as editor of *Le Canadien,* and during the following year he founded the *Journal de Québec.* In 1844 he was elected to the Legislative Assembly of Canada for Montmorency, and he continued to sit in this House and in the Canadian House of Commons without interruption until 1872. On the reorganization of the MacNab-Morin government in 1855, he became commissioner of crown lands, but he resigned in 1857. In the Cartier-Macdonald government he held the post of commissioner of public works from 1861 to 1862. He supported Confederation, and in 1867 became speaker of the Senate; but in 1872 he resigned his seat in the Senate, and was elected once more to the House of Commons, as an independent member for Quebec Centre. Meanwhile, he had been also member for Montmorency in the Legislative Assembly of Quebec, and in 1872 charges of political corruption were made against him which brought about his resignation from this House. He was re-elected by his constituents; but the charges were not disproved, and there was some surprise when Alexander Mackenzie, whom he had been supporting in the federal house, included him in the Dominion cabinet in 1875 as president of the council. In June, 1877, he was transferred to the department of inland revenue; but Mackenzie found that his usefulness had gone, and in October, 1877, he was appointed lieutenant-governor of Manitoba. He administered the government until 1882, and then retired from public life. He died at Whitewood, near Qu'Appelle, N.W.T., on February 23, 1885. He was thrice married: first, to Julie (d. 1864), eldest daughter of Charles Lemieux, of Quebec; secondly, to Maria (d. 1877), daughter of Martin Nolan, of Quebec; and thirdly, to Emma, daughter of Robert LeMoine, clerk of the Senate. His chief publication was *L'union des provinces de l'Amérique Britannique du Nord* (Quebec, 1865), a book which had an influence in disposing the French Canadians favourably toward Confederation.

[*Dom. ann. reg.,* 1885; Taylor, *Brit. Am.,* vol. 1; Dent, *Can. port.,* Vol. 4; *Revue Canadienne,* 1884; J. C. Dent, *The last forty years* (2 vols., Toronto, 1881); J. Pope, *Memoirs of the Right Hon. Sir John A. Macdonald* (2 vols., Ottawa, 1894).]

Caulfield, Thomas (1685-1717), lieutenant-governor of Nova Scotia (1711-1717), was born in England in 1685. He entered the army, and fought in Spain under Lord Peterborough. In 1710 he was at the capture of Port Royal in Acadia by the English; and in 1711 he was temporarily appointed lieutenant-governor, a position in which he was confirmed in 1712. He died at Annapolis Royal on March 2, 1717.

[Le Jeune, *Dict. gén.*; *Dict. Can. biog.,* vol. 2.]

Cavell, Reginald George (Nik) (1894-1967), diplomat, was born in Hampshire, England, February 27, 1894, and educated for the army, which he joined (Indian cavalry) in 1913. He was wounded in Mesopotamia in the First World War and after the war returned to Burma and the Indian North West frontier areas. He operated a sheep ranch in South Africa, was employed by International Telephone Company, London, in 1924, becoming president of the Automatic Telephone Company in China and Japan in 1932. He came to Canada in 1934 as vice-president of Automatic Electric (Canada) Limited, and Phillips

Electrical Works of Toronto. In 1951 he was appointed administrator of the International Economic and Technical co-operation division of the Department of Trade and Commerce of Canada to supervise Canada's commitments under the Colombo plan. He was appointed high commissioner to Ceylon in 1957, retiring in 1961, to become a director of Balfour, Beatty and Company (Canada) Limited. In his work with the Colombo plan he was more concerned with the need for aid than the political complexion of the recipient and generated some conflict with Canadian politicians. He died at Ottawa, Ontario, January 19, 1967.

[*Can. who's who,* 1964-66; Metropolitan Toronto Library Board, *Biographical scrapbooks,* vol. 33.]

Caven, William (1830-1904), principal of Knox College, Toronto (1873-1904), was born in the parish of Kirkcolm, Wigtonshire, Scotland, on December 26, 1830, the son of John Caven, a school-teacher. He came to Canada with his parents in 1847, and was privately educated for the Presbyterian ministry. He was licensed to preach in 1852, and from 1852 to 1866 was pastor of the United Presbyterian Church of St. Mary's, Canada West. He was then appointed professor of exegetics at Knox College, Toronto; and in 1873 he became principal of the College. In 1875 he was moderator of the General Assembly of the Canada Presbyterian Church, and played a foremost part in bringing about in that year the union with the Church of Scotland which resulted in the formation of the Presbyterian Church in Canada. He was one of the leaders in the agitation in Ontario against the Jesuits' Estates Act of 1888, and against separate schools in Manitoba in 1896. He died at Toronto on December 1, 1904. In 1856 he married Margaret, daughter of John Goldie (q.v.), of Ayr, Ontario; and by her he had six children. He was a D.D. of Queen's University (1875) and of Princeton University (1896), and an LL.D. of the University of Toronto (1896). From 1900 to 1904 he was president of the Pan-Presbyterian Alliance. After his death a number of his papers were collected under the title, *Christ's teaching concerning the last things* (London and Toronto, 1908), with a biographical sketch by J. A. Macdonald (q.v.).

[Morgan, *Can. men* (1898); Rose, *Cyc. Can. biog.* (1886); Dent, *Can. port.,* vol. 2.]

Cawdell, James Martin (d. 1842), journalist, was an officer in the 100th Regiment in Canada prior to the War of 1812, but resigned his commission a few months before war broke out. He was successively a commissary of stores, a school-teacher, and librarian and secretary to the Law Society of Upper Canada. He was one of the earliest writers of verse in Upper Canada, and he edited in 1823 at York (Toronto) a periodical named the *Rose Harp,* which was chiefly filled with contributions by himself. He died at Toronto on July 13, 1842.

[A. Shortt (ed.), *The memorial of J. M. Cawdell* (Can. hist. rev., 1920).]

Cawthra, William (1801-1880), capitalist, was born at Yeadon, Yorkshire, England, on October 29, 1801, the son of Joseph Cawthra. He came to Canada with his parents in 1803, and settled in York (Toronto), Upper Canada. He became one of the early merchants of York and ultimately one of the wealthiest capitalists in Canada. At his death, which took place at Toronto, Ontario, on October 26, 1880, he was reputed to be "worth three or four million dollars".

[A. Maude Brock (comp.), *Past and present: Notes by Henry Cawthra and others* (Toronto, 1924); *Dict. Can. biog.,* vol. 10.]

Cayley, William (1807-1890), inspector-general of Canada (1845-48 and 1854-58), was born in St. Petersburg, Russia, on May 26, 1807, the son of John Cayley and Harriet Raikes. He was educated at Christ Church, Oxford; and in 1834 he was called to the English bar from Lincoln's Inn. He came to Canada about 1836; and in 1838 he was called to the bar of Upper Canada. In 1846 he was elected to the Legislative Assembly of Canada as member for Huron; and, except for the years 1851-54, he continued to be a member of the legislature until 1861, first for Huron and Bruce (1854-57), and lastly for Renfrew (1858-61). From 1845 to 1848 he was inspector-general of accounts in the Draper administration, and from 1854 to 1858 in the MacNab-Morin, the MacNab-Taché, the Taché-Macdonald, and the Macdonald-Cartier administrations. In the formation of the Cartier-Macdonald government of 1858 he was omitted; and in 1861 he retired from political life. He represented the "Family Compact" wing of the Liberal-Conservative party; and his disappearance from political life marked the end of the influence of this group. His period of office was mainly notable for the introduction of the Tariff Act of 1858, in which the principle of "protection for home industries" was first applied. In 1869 he was appointed provincial auditor for Ontario; and he died in Toronto on February 23, 1890. In 1836 he married Emma Robinson, daughter of D'Arcy Boulton, of The Grange, Toronto; and he had by her eight sons and three daughters. He published a pamphlet entitled *Finances and trade of Canada at the beginning of 1855* (London, 1855).

[E. M. Chadwick, *Ontarian families* (2 vols., Toronto, 1894-98); Burke, *Colonial gentry* (2 vols., London, 1891-95); Toronto *Mail,* Feb. 24, 1890; J. C. Dent, *The last forty years* (2 vols., Toronto, 1881); J. Pope, *Memoirs of the Right Hon. John A. Macdonald* (2 vols., Ottawa, 1894).]

Cazeau, François (1734-1815), merchant, was born at Angoulême, France, in 1734, and came to Canada before the British conquest. He became a merchant in Montreal, and during the American invasion of 1775 he supplied the Continental troops with provisions. He was arrested by Haldimand, on the charge of having assisted the enemy, and imprisoned. About 1785 he went to Paris to try to collect some of his debts; and he died in Paris, after a long illness, shortly after April, 1815. He appears to have been twice married, (1) in 1759 to Marguerite, daughter of Pierre Vallée, and (2) later to a daughter of John Reeves, of Montreal.

[B. Sulte, *François Cazeau,* and Ae. Fauteux, *François Cazeau* (Bull. rech. hist., 1916).]

Cazes, Paul de (1841-1913), author, was born in France on June 17, 1841, the son of Charles de Cazes, who came to Canada about 1850, settled in the Eastern Townships, and represented Richmond in the Canadian legislature from 1861 to 1863. Called to the bar in 1869, he practised law at St. Hyacinthe, Quebec, until 1880. He then entered the civil service at Quebec, and in 1885 he was appointed secretary of the department of public instruction. On his retirement from office, he returned to France; and he died at Neuilly-sur-Seine on May 28, 1913. He was the author of *Notes sur le Canada* (Quebec, 1878), *L'instruction publique dans la province de Québec* (Quebec, 1884), *Code de l'instruction publique* (Quebec, 1890), *Code scolaire de la province de Québec* (Quebec, 1905), as well as a number of historical papers contributed to the *Transactions* of the Royal Society of Canada.

[Morgan, *Can. men* (1912); *Bull. rech. hist.,* 1927.]

Céloron de Blainville, Pierre Joseph (1693-1759), soldier, was born at Montreal on December 29, 1693, the eldest son of Jean Baptiste Céloron de Blainville and Hélène Picoté de Belestre. He was commandant successively at Michilimackinac, at Detroit, at Niagara, and again at Detroit. In 1749 he took possession of the valley of the Ohio, in the name of the king of France. He died at Montreal on April 12, 1759. In 1741 he was made a chevalier de St. Louis. His *Journal* of the expedition to the Ohio Valley has been published in P. Margry, *Mémoires et documents* (6 vols., Paris, 1879-88).

[P. G. Roy, *La famille Céloron de Blainville* (Bull. rech. hist., 1909); C. G. Galbraith, *The expedition of Céloron* (Ohio archaeological and historical quarterly, 1920); A. A. Lambing, *Céloron's Journal* (Ohio archaeological and historical quarterly, 1920); G. A. Wood, *Céloron de Blainville and French expansion in the Ohio valley* (Mississippi Valley historical review, 1923);

Dict. Am. biog.; Le Jeune, *Dict. gén.*; *Dict. Can. biog.,* vol. 3.]

Chabanel, Noël (1613-1649), Jesuit missionary, was born in France on February 2, 1613, and entered the Jesuit novitiate at Toulouse in 1630. In 1643 he came to Canada as a missionary, and in 1644 was sent to the Jesuit mission in Huronia. He was murdered by an apostate Huron on December 8, 1649, and was canonized in 1930.

[R. G. Thwaites (ed.), *The Jesuit relations* (73 vols., Cleveland, 1898-1900); Le Jeune, *Dict. gén.*; *Bull. rech. hist.,* 1925; *Dict. Can. biog.,* vol. 1.]

Chaboillez, Charles (1772-1812), fur-trader, was born in Montreal in 1772, the son of Charles Jean Baptiste Chaboillez (q.v.), and was educated at the College of Montreal. He entered the service of the North West Company about 1793, when his sister married Simon McTavish (q.v.); and he became a partner of the Company before 1799. For many years he was in the Red River and Assiniboine district; but from 1807 to 1809 he was at the Pic, on Lake Superior. He retired from the fur-trade in 1809, and was elected a member of the Beaver Club of Montreal. He died at St. Henri de Mascouche, Lower Canada, and was buried at Terrebonne, on December 29, 1812. He brought back with him from the West four half-breed children, who were baptized at Terrebonne in 1811; and the same year he married Jessy Dunbar Selby Bruyères, daughter of Capt. John Bruce, adjutant of the 10th Veteran Battalion, but he had by her no children.

[E. Z. Massicotte, *Les Chaboillez* (Bull. rech. hist., 1922); A. G. Morice, *Dictionnaire historique des canadiens et des métis français de l'ouest* (Kamloops, B.C., 1908).]

Chaboillez, Charles Jean Baptiste (1736-1808), fur-trader, was born at or near Michilimackinac in 1736, the eldest son of Charles Chaboillez, a fur-trader, and Marie Anne, daughter of Jean Baptiste Chevalier. He engaged in the fur-trade, and his name occurs repeatedly in the fur-trade licences from 1769 to 1787. The statement has been repeatedly made that he became a partner in the North West Company; but there is no evidence of this. It is clear that he has been hopelessly confused with his son Charles (q.v.). He died in Montreal on September 25, 1800. In 1769 he married Marguerite (d. 1798), daughter of Jacques Larchevêque *dit* La Promenade; and by her he had two sons and seven daughters. One of his daughters, Marie Marguerite, married in 1793 Simon McTavish (q.v.); another, Adelaide, married Joseph Bouchette; and a third, Marie Louise Rachel, married in 1803 the Hon. Roderick Mackenzie (q.v.).

[E. Z. Massicotte, *Les Chaboillez* (Bull. rech. hist., 1922); A. G. Morice, *Dictionnaire historique des canadiens et des métis français de l'ouest* (Kamloops, B.C., 1908).]

Chabot, Jean (1807-1860), commissioner of public works for Canada (1849-54), was born at St. Charles de Bellechasse, Lower Canada, on October 15, 1807, the son of Basile Chabot and Josephte Prévost. He was educated at the Quebec Seminary, and was called to the bar of Lower Canada in 1834. From 1843 to 1856 he was, almost without intermission, the representative of Quebec in the Legislative Assembly of Canada; and in 1849 he became commissioner of public works in the Baldwin-Lafontaine administration. He resigned this portfolio, for private reasons, in 1850. In 1852, however, he resumed the portfolio of public works in the Hincks-Morin government, and he continued to hold it in the MacNab-Morin government. In 1855 he was not included in the MacNab-Taché administration; and in 1856 he was appointed a judge of the Superior Court of Lower Canada. He died on May 31, 1860. He married Hortense Hamel, but had no children.

[*L'honorable Jean Chabot* (Bull. rech. hist., 1905).]

Chadwick, Edward Marion (1840-1921), genealogist, was born at Cravendale, Ancaster, Upper Canada, on September 22, 1840, the third son of John Craven Chadwick and Louisa Bell. He was called to the bar of Upper Canada in 1863 (K.C., 1910), and for many years practised law in Toronto. He was an authority on Ontario genealogies, and from 1898 to 1901 edited *The Ontarian genealogist and family historian.* He was the author of *Ontarian families* (2 vols., Toronto, 1894-98) and *The people of the long house* (Toronto, 1898). In 1908 he presented the Ontario government with a manuscript volume embodying the results of his investigations into coats-of-arms borne in Ontario. He died at Toronto on December 15, 1921.

[E. M. Chadwick, *The Chadwicks of Guelph and Toronto* (Toronto, 1914); H. Charlesworth (ed.), *A cyclopaedia of Canadian biography* (Toronto, 1919); Morgan, *Can. men* (1912).]

Chagnon, François-Xavier (1842-1911), priest, was born at Verchères, Canada East, on February 18, 1842, and was ordained a priest of the Roman Catholic Church in 1870. He served in parishes both in Canada and in the United States; and he died at Champlain, Quebec, on October 9, 1911. He was the author of *Annales, religieux et historiques, de la paroisse de Saint-Jacques-le-Majeur, vulgo de L'Achigan* (Montreal, 1872).

[*Bull. rech. hist.,* 1928.]

Challener, Frederick Sproston (1869-1959), painter, was born at Whetstone, Middlesex, England, on July 7, 1869; and died at Toronto, Ontario, on September 30, 1959. He came to Canada in 1883, and studied art at the Central Ontario School of Art in Toronto and under G. A. Reid (q.v.). He became one of Canada's most successful painters, and was elected a member of the Ontario Society of Artists in 1889, an A.R.C.A. in 1891, and an R.C.A. in 1899, probably the youngest artist ever to attain that honour. He is represented by mural decorations in many Canadian cities, and five of his oil paintings are in the National Gallery in Ottawa.

[Toronto *Globe and Mail,* Oct. 1, 1959; *Can. who's who,* 1955-57; Morgan, *Can. men* (1912); N. MacTavish, *The fine arts in Canada* (Toronto, 1925).]

Chamberlain, Alexander Francis (1865-1914), anthropologist, was born at Kenninghall, Norfolk, England, on January 12, 1865. He came to Canada as a child, and was educated at the University of Toronto (B.A., 1886; M.A., 1889). From 1887 to 1890 he was a fellow in modern languages in University College, Toronto; and from 1890 to his death he was successively fellow, lecturer, and professor of anthropology in Clark University, Worcester, Mass. From 1901 to 1908 he was editor of the *Journal of American Folk-lore.* He died at Worcester, Mass., on April 8, 1914. In addition to numerous papers on the North American Indian contributed to learned periodicals, he was the author of *The child and childhood in folk-thought* (New York, 1896), *The child: A study in the evolution of man* (London, 1900; 2nd ed., 1906), and a volume of *Poems* (Boston, 1904).

[*Alexander Francis Chamberlain, In Memoriam* (Publications of the Clark University Library, vol. iv, no. 2); *Dict. Am. biog.*]

Chamberlin, Brown (1827-1897), civil servant and author, was born at Frelighsburg, Lower Canada, on March 26, 1827, the son of Brown Chamberlin, M.D. He was educated at McGill University (B.C.L., 1850; D.C.L., 1867), and was called to the bar of Lower Canada in 1850. He became one of the proprietors of the Montreal *Gazette*; and in 1867 he was elected to represent Missisquoi in the first parliament of the Dominion of Canada. In 1870 he was appointed Queen's printer at Ottawa; and he held this position until 1891. He died at Lakefield, Ontario, on July 13, 1897. In 1870 he married Agnes, daughter of Sheriff Moodie of Belleville, widow of Charles FitzGibbon, and illustrator of *Canadian wild flowers* (Montreal, 1868). He was the author of a *Lecture delivered before the Mercantile Library Association of Montreal on the British North American colonies* (Montreal, 1853), and a *Report upon institutions in London, Dublin, Edinburgh, and Paris, for the promotion of industrial education* (Montreal, 1859).

[Morgan, *Can. men* (1898); Rose, *Cyc. Can. biog.* (1886); *Can. parl. comp.*]

Chamberlin, Edson Joseph (1852-1924), president of the Grand Trunk Railway (1912-17), was born in Lancaster, New Hampshire, on August 25, 1852. He was educated at the Montpelier Methodist Seminary, and in 1871 entered the service of a New England railway. In 1886 he became general manager of the Canada Atlantic Railway, and in 1909 general manager and vice-president of the Grand Trunk Railway. In 1912 he became president of this railway, but he resigned in 1917. He died at Pasadena, California, on August 27, 1924.

[Morgan, *Can. men* (1912); *Who's who in America;* H. A. Lovett, *Canada and the Grand Trunk* (Montreal, 1924).]

Chambers, Edward Thomas Davies (1852-1931), journalist and author, was born at Saffron Walden, Essex, England, on June 26, 1852, the son of Edward Thomas Chambers and Louisa Davies. He came to Canada in 1870, and was at first a school-teacher. He then turned to journalism, and in 1897 he became editor-in-chief of the Quebec *Daily Chronicle*. In his later years he was an official of the department of colonization and fisheries at Quebec. He died at Quebec on October 5, 1931. He was the author of *The past of Quebec* (Quebec, 1890), *Quebec, ancient and modern* (Montreal, 1892), *Guide to Quebec* (Quebec, 1895), *The ouananiche and its Canadian environment* (New York, 1896), *The angler's guide to eastern Canada* (Quebec, 1898), *The sportsman's companion* (Quebec, 1899), and *The Quebec centenary commemorative history* (Quebec, 1909).

[Morgan, *Can. men* (1912).]

Chambers, Ernest John (1862-1925), author, was born at Penkridge, Staffordshire, England, on April 16, 1862, the son of Edward Thomas Chambers, and the younger brother of E. T. D. Chambers (q.v.). He came to Canada as a child, and was educated at the Montreal High School. He became a journalist, and was chief correspondent of the Montreal *Star* during the North West Rebellion of 1885. In 1904 he was appointed gentleman usher of the black rod at Ottawa; and he held this post for the rest of his life. From his youth he was an officer in the militia, and in 1915 was promoted to the rank of lieutenant-colonel in the Corps of Guides. At the outbreak of the First World War he was appointed censor at Military Headquarters, Ottawa, and in 1915 chief press censor for Canada. He died at Ottawa on May 11, 1925. For many years he edited the *Canadian parliamentary guide*; and he was the author of *The book of Montreal* (Montreal, 1903), *The book of Canada* (Montreal, 1905), *The Canadian marine* (Toronto, 1905), *The Canadian militia* (Montreal, 1907), *The*

unexploited west (Ottawa, 1914), *The Athabaska country* (Ottawa, 1916), and *The Peace River country*, as well as the following regimental histories: *The origin and services of the 32nd (Montreal) Field Battery of Artillery* (Montreal, 1898), *The Montreal Highland Cadets* (Montreal, 1901), *The Queen's Own Rifles of Canada* (Toronto, 1901), *The Governor-General's Body Guard* (Toronto, 1902), *The Duke of Cornwall's Own Rifles* (Toronto, 1903), *The Third Regiment, Active Militia of Canada* (Ottawa, 1903), *The Royal Grenadiers* (Toronto, 1904), *The Fifth Regiment, Royal Scots of Canada Highlanders* (Montreal, 1904), *Histoire de 65ème Régiment* (Montreal, 1906), and *The Royal North West Mounted Police* (Montreal, 1906).

[Morgan, *Can. men* (1912).]

Chambly, Jacques de (d. 1687), governor of Acadia (1673-77), came to Canada as an officer of the Carignan Regiment in 1665. He built Fort St. Louis (now Fort Chambly) on the Richelieu, and was its commandant. In 1672 he was granted the seigniory of Chambly; but he did not live long on his seigniory. From 1673 to 1677 he was governor of Acadia; from 1677 to 1679 he was commandant of the troops in the Isles; in 1679 he was appointed provisionally governor of Grenada, and in 1680 governor of Martinique. He died at Martinique on August 15, 1687.

[P. Gaudet, *Le capitaine Jacques de Chambly* (Bull. rech. hist., 1917); B. Sulte, *Le régiment de Carignan* (Montreal, 1922) and *Le fort de Chambly* (Montreal, 1922); Le Jeune, *Dict. gen.*; *Dict. Can. biog.*; vol. 1.]

Champigny, Jean Bochart de (*fl.* 1645-1720), intendant of New France (1686-1702), belonged to a distinguished family in the civil service in France. In 1686 he was appointed intendant of New France and he arrived at Quebec in September of that year. In 1687 he took part in Denonville's expedition against the Senecas; he was present at the siege of Quebec in 1690; and he accompanied Frontenac in his expedition against the Iroquois in 1696. In 1701 he was appointed intendant at Le Havre and he returned to France in August, 1702. He died on September 27, 1720.

[R. Roy, *Bochart de Champigny* (Bull. rech. hist., 1914); B. Sulte, *Un intendant de la Nouvelle France* (in *Mélanges historiques* vols. 1-2); J. Shea, *Charlevoix's History of New France* (New York, 1900); Le Jeune, *Dict. gén.*; *Dict. Can. biog.*, vol. 2.]

Champion, Thomas E. (1843?-1910), journalist, was born in Toronto, Canada West, about 1843, and became a journalist. During his later years he was on the staff of the Toronto *Evening Telegram*; and he assisted John Ross Robertson (q.v.) in the preparation of *Landmarks of Toronto* (6 vols., Toronto, 1894-1914). He was also the editor of *The Methodist Church of Toronto* (Toronto, 1899).

He died at Toronto, Ontario, on April 20, 1910.
[Private information.]

Champlain, Samuel de (1567?-1635), explorer and colonizer, was born at Brouage, in Saintonge, France, about 1567. During the religious wars, he fought under Henry of Navarre; and, on demobilization in 1598, he took service with the king of Spain, and visited America. In 1601, on his return to France, he was appointed royal geographer; and in 1603 he made his first visit to the St. Lawrence. In 1604 he accompanied Monts's expedition to Acadia, and he spent the next three years exploring and mapping the coasts of Acadia and northern New England. In 1608 he commanded the expedition which founded the post of Quebec; and the rest of his life was mainly devoted to making this settlement a success. In 1612 he was appointed commandant in New France; and in 1627 he became governor of New France under the Company of One Hundred Associates. In 1628 Quebec was captured by the English; but Champlain's efforts resulted in its return to France in 1632, and in his last years he had the satisfaction of seeing the colony firmly established.

His work as an explorer and geographer, was, however, no less noteworthy than his work as a colonizer. In 1613 he visited the upper Ottawa, and in 1615-16 he reached Georgian Bay, by way of the Ottawa and Lake Nipissing, spent a winter among the Huron Indians, followed the Trent Valley south to Lake Ontario, and penetrated into the Iroquois country in northern New York. He had here an encounter with the Iroquois which proved later disastrous for the French; but this result he could hardly have foreseen.

He wrote and published a number of books describing his explorations. These were *Des sauvages* (Paris, 1604), *Les voyages du Sieur de Champlain* (Paris, 1613), *Voyages et découvertes faites en la Nouvelle-France* (Paris, 1619), *Les voyages du Sr. de Champlain* (Paris, 1620), and *Les voyages de la Nouvelle France occidentale* (Paris, 1632). A *Brief récit* of his voyage to central America has been preserved in manuscript, and was first printed in the original by the Abbé Laverdière in 1870, and in translation by the Hakluyt Society in 1859. Champlain died at Quebec on December 25, 1635. He married, in 1610, Hélène, daughter of Nicholas Boullé, secretary of the king's chamber; but had no children.

[N. E. Dionne, *Samuel Champlain, fondateur de Québec* (2 vols., Quebec, 1891-1906) and *Champlain* (Toronto, 1905); G. Gravier, *Vie de Samuel Champlain* (Paris, 1900); H. D. Sedgwick, *Samuel de Champlain* (Boston, 1902); C. W. Colby, *The founder of New France* (Toronto, 1915); H. A. Verreau, *Samuel de Champlain* (Trans. Roy. Soc. Can., 1899); F. Parkman, *The pioneers of France in the new world* (Boston, 1865); M. Bishop, *Champlain, the life of fortitude* (New York, 1948); S. E. Morison, *Samuel de Champlain, Father of New France* (Boston, 1972). The works of Champlain have been edited by the Abbé C. H. Laverdière (6 vols., Quebec, 1870), and have been re-edited by H. P. Biggar (6 vols., Toronto, The Champlain Society, 1922-36); and parts of his works have been translated into English by S. Purchas (London, 1625), by A. Wilmere (London, Hakluyt Society, 1859), by C. P. Otis (3 vols., Boston, The Prince Society, 1878-82), by E. G. and A. N. Bourne (New York, 1906), and by W. L. Grant (New York, 1907). The Champlain Society's edition by H. P. Biggar contains the first English translation of all Champlain's works. For full bibliographical information, see H. Harrisse, *Notes pour servir à l'histoire de la Nouvelle France* (Paris, 1872) and P. Gagnon, *Notes bibliographiques sur les écrits de Champlain* (Bulletin de la Société de Géographie de Québec, 1908); *Dict. Can. biog.*, vol. 1.]

Chandler, Edward Barron (1800-1880), one of the Fathers of Confederation, was born at Amherst, Nova Scotia, on August 22, 1800, the son of C. H. Chandler, of Cumberland, Nova Scotia, and the grandson of Joshua Chandler, of New Haven, Connecticut, a well-known loyalist. He studied law, and was called to the bar of New Brunswick in 1823. From 1827 to 1836 he represented Westmoreland in the House of Assembly of New Brunswick; and from 1836 to 1878 he was a member of the Legislative Council of the province. From 1843 to 1858 he was almost continuously a member of the Executive Council. He took a prominent part in the negotiations leading up to Confederation and the construction of the Intercolonial Railway; and was a delegate from New Brunswick at the Charlottetown, Quebec, and London Conferences in 1864-66. In 1867 he was called, by royal proclamation, to the Senate of Canada, but declined the appointment. In 1868 he was appointed a commissioner for the construction of the Intercolonial Railway; and in 1878 he succeeded Sir Leonard Tilley (q.v.) as lieutenant-governor of New Brunswick. He died, before the completion of his term of office, at Fredericton, New Brunswick, on February 6, 1880.

[*Dom. ann. reg.*, 1880-81; *Can. parl. comp.*; *Cyc. Am. biog.*; Dent, *Can. port.*, vol. 1; J. W. Lawrence, *The judges of New Brunswick and their times* (Saint John, N.B., 1907); *Dict. Can. biog.*, vol. 10.]

Chant, Clarence Augustus (1865-1956), astronomer, was born in York county, Ontario, on May 31, 1865. He was educated at the University of Toronto (B.A., 1890; M.A., 1900) and at Harvard University (Ph.D., 1901); and he spent his entire academic career at the University of Toronto, first in the department of physics, and later as head of the department of astronomy. In 1927 he was instrumental in persuading Mrs. D. A. Dunlap to build a large research observatory, near Yonge St., to be known as the David Dunlap Observatory, in memory of her husband; and this observatory, which contained at that time the second largest reflecting telescope in the world, was formally dedicated in 1935, the year of Professor Chant's retirement. He was the founder of the Royal Astronomical Society of Canada, and was the editor of its *Journal* from 1907 until his death at Richmond Hill, Ontario, on November 18, 1956. He was elected a fellow of the Royal Society of Canada in 1923, and was president of Section III of the Society in 1932. He was the author of *Our wonderful universe* (London, 1928; new ed., 1940), which was translated into five European languages, and of *Astronomy at the University of Toronto* (Toronto, 1954), which was partly autobiographical; and he was joint author, with others, of several text-books on physics and mechanics.

[*Varsity graduate,* Jan. 1957; *Proc. Roy. Soc. Can.*, 1957; *Can. who's who*, 1955-57.]

Chapais, Jean Charles (1811-1885), one of the Fathers of Confederation, was born at Rivière Ouelle, Lower Canada, on December 2, 1811, the son of J. C. Chapais, a merchant. He was educated at Nicolet College and at the Quebec Seminary, and became, like his father, a merchant. From 1851 to 1867 he represented Kamouraska in the Legislative Assembly of Canada; and in 1864 he became commissioner of public works in the short-lived Taché-Macdonald administration. He continued to hold this portfolio in the coalition government of 1864-67; and he was one of the delegates to the Quebec Conference. From 1867 to 1871 he represented Champlain in the Legislative Assembly of Quebec; and in 1867 he contested Kamouraska as a candidate for the Canadian House of Commons, but no election was declared, and in 1868 he was appointed a member of the Senate of Canada. From 1867 to 1869 he was minister of agriculture in the first Dominion government under Sir John Macdonald (q.v.), and from 1869 to 1873 he was receiver-general. He died at Ottawa, Ontario, on July 17, 1885. He married Henriette Georgina, daughter of the Hon. Amable Dionne, a member of the Legislative Council of Canada; and by her he had several children.

[C. E. Rouleau, *L'honorable Jean-Charles Chapais* (Bull. rech. hist., 1899); *Dom. ann. reg.*, 1885; *Can. parl. comp.*; Garland, *Parliamentary directory*, 1885; J. C. Dent, *The last forty years* (2 vols., Toronto, 1881).]

Chapais, Jean Charles Louis Thomas (1850-1926), civil servant, was born at St. Denis de Kamouraska, Canada East, on March 6, 1850, the son of the Hon. Jean Charles Chapais (q.v.). He was called to the bar of Quebec in 1875; but in 1890 he entered the Canadian civil service as a dairy commis-

sioner, and he became a well-known writer on agriculture. He was the author of *Guide illustré du sylviculteur canadien* (Montreal, 1883) and several pamphlets on agriculture. He died at St. Denis de Kamouraska, Quebec, on July 23, 1926.

[Morgan, *Can. men* (1912).]

Chapais, Sir Thomas (1858-1946), historian and legislator, was born at St. Denis de Kamouraska, Canada East, on March 23, 1858, the son of the Hon. Jean Charles Chapais (q.v.). He was educated at Ste. Anne's College at Ste. Anne de la Pocatière and at Laval University (LL.B., 1875). He was called to the Quebec bar, but turned to journalism, and from 1884 to 1901 was editor of *Le Courrier du Canada* at Quebec. He was called to the Legislative Council of Quebec in 1892, became its president in 1895, and held portfolios in the Taillon, Flynn, and Duplessis cabinets. In 1919 he was called to the Senate of Canada, and set a precedent by becoming a member of both upper houses. It was, however, for his historical work that he was best known. He was the author of *Discours et conférences* (4 series, Quebec, 1897, 1913, 1935, and 1943), *Jean Talon* (Quebec, 1904), *Mélanges* (Quebec, 1905), *Le Marquis de Montcalm* (Quebec, 1911), *The great intendant* (Toronto, 1914), and *Cours d'histoire du Canada, 1760-1841* (8 vols., Quebec, 1919-1934). He was elected a member of the Royal Society of Canada in 1902, and became its president in 1923; he received the honorary degree of LL.D. from several universities; and he was created a knight bachelor in 1935. He died at St. Denis de Kamouraska, Quebec, on July 15, 1946. In 1884 he married Hectorine (d. 1934), daughter of Sir Hector Langevin (q.v.); they had no children.

[P. E. Gosselin, *L'oeuvre historique de Thomas Chapais* (Revue de l'Université Laval, Oct., 1946); J. C. Bonenfant, *Sir Thomas Chapais* (Culture, Sept., 1945); *Proc. Roy. Soc. Can.*, 1947; *Can. who's who*, 1938-39; *Can. parl. guide*, 1944; *Encyc. Can.*]

Chapleau, Sir Joseph Adolphe (1840-1898), prime minister of Quebec (1879-82), secretary of state for Canada (1882-92), and lieutenant-governor of Quebec (1892-98), was born at Ste. Thérèse de Blainville, Lower Canada, on November 9, 1840, the son of Pierre Chapleau. He was educated at Masson College, and at the seminary of St. Hyacinthe; and in 1861 he was called to the bar of Lower Canada (Q.C., 1873). From 1867 to 1882 he represented Terrebonne in the Legislative Assembly of Quebec. He was solicitor-general in the Ouimet administration (1873-74) and provincial secretary in the Boucherville administration (1876-78); and from 1879 to 1882 he was prime minister of Quebec, holding the portfolio of public works, railways, and agriculture. In 1882 he became secretary of state for Canada in the government of Sir John Macdonald (q.v.), and he held this office, with the exception of ten days in June, 1891, until 1892. He then became, from January to December, 1892, minister of customs in the Abbott government. On December 7, 1892, he was appointed lieutenant-governor of Quebec; and he retired from this post only six months before his death at Montreal, on June 13, 1898. In 1874 he married Marie Louise, daughter of Lieut.-Col. Charles King. In 1896 he was created a K.C.M.G.; and he was an LL.D. of Laval University, Montreal. He was the author of *Léon XIII, homme d'état* (pamphlet, Montreal, 1888), as well as of a number of political pamphlets.

[*L'honorable J. A. Chapleau, sa biographie, ses discours* (Montreal, 1887), with biography by A. de Bonneterre; *Dict. nat. biog.*, supp. I; Morgan, *Can. men* (1898); Rose, *Cyc. Can. biog.* (1886); Dent, *Can. port.*, vol. 4; Taché, *Men of the day*; Le Jeune, *Dict. gén.*; *Can. parl. comp.*]

Chaplin, James D. (1863-1937), minister of trade and commerce for Canada (1926), was born on March 20, 1863, and was educated at St. Catharines, Ontario. He became president of the Welland Vale Manufacturing Company of St. Catharines; and he was a member of the Canadian House of Commons continuously from 1917 to 1935. In 1926 he was sworn in as minister of trade and commerce in the short-lived Meighen administration of that year. He died at St. Catharines, Ontario, on August 23, 1937.

[*Can. who's who*, 1936-37.]

Chapman, Edward, (1821-1904), geologist, was born in Kent, England, in 1821, and was educated in France and Germany. He became a civil engineer, and from 1850 to 1853 was professor of mineralogy in University College, London. In 1853 he came to Canada as professor of mineralogy and geology in University College, Toronto; and he resigned this post only in 1890. He then returned to England; and he died at Hampton Wick, near London, on January 28, 1904. He was a Ph.D. of Göttingen University (1862) and an LL.D. of Queen's University, Kingston (1867); and in 1883 he became a charter member of the Royal Society of Canada. Besides many books and papers on geology and mineralogy, he was the author of a volume of poetry, *A song of charity* (Toronto, 1857; 2nd ed., London, 1858). A bibliography of his scientific publications is to be found in the *Proceedings* of the Royal Society of Canada, 1894.

[*Dict. nat. biog.*, supp. II; *Univ. of Toronto monthly*, 1904; J. King, *McCaul: Croft: Forneri* (Toronto, 1914).]

Chapman, William (1850-1917), poet, was born at St. François de la Beauce, Lower Canada, on December 14, 1850, the son of an English father and a French-Canadian mother. He was educated at Lévis College, studied law for a time, then went into business, and finally took refuge in the civil service. In 1902 he became a French translator for the Senate of Canada; and he died at Ottawa on February 23, 1917. In poetry, he published *Les Québecoises* (Quebec, 1876), *Les feuilles d'érable* (Montreal, 1890), *Les aspirations* (Paris, 1904), *Les rayons du nord* (Paris, 1910), and *Les fleurs de givre* (Paris, 1912), the last three of which were crowned by the French Academy. In prose he published *Le lauréat* (Quebec, 1894), a critique of the work of Louis Fréchette (q.v.), and *Deux copains* (Quebec, 1894).

[C. ab der Halden, *Nouvelles études de littérature canadienne française* (Paris, 1907); Morgan, *Can. men* (1912); *Bull. rech. hist.*, 1917; Le Jeune, *Dict. gén.*]

Charbonneau, Robert (1911-1966), writer, was born in Montreal, Que., February 3, 1911. He was educated at College Sainte-Marie and the University of Montreal (journalism, 1934). He was script supervisor for the Canadian Broadcasting Corporation and later (1950-55) was with the Press and Information department of the corporation. From 1940 to 1948 he was literary director of Editions de l'Arbre. He wrote *Ils posséderont la terre* (1941); *Petits poems retrouvés* (1944); *Fontile* (1945); *Connaissance du personnage* (1945); *La France et nous* (1947); *Les désirs et les jours* (1948). He died at St. Jovite, Quebec, June 26, 1966.

[*Can. who's who*, 1955-57.]

Charbonnel, Armand François Marie de (1802-1891), Roman Catholic bishop of Toronto, was born at the Château of Flachats, near Monistrol-sur-Loire, France, on December 1, 1802. He joined the Sulpician order in 1825, and was ordained a priest in 1826. In 1839 he came to America, and was in Montreal from 1840 to 1847. In 1850 he was consecrated bishop of Toronto. He founded St. Michael's College in Toronto, and he brought about the division of his diocese into the dioceses of Toronto and Hamilton, in 1855. In 1860 he retired from his see, and was made archbishop of Sozopolis. He returned to France, and there he died in retirement at Crest, near Valence, on March 25, 1891.

[Allaire, *Dict. biog.*; Le Jeune, *Dict. gén.*]

Charland, Louis (1772-1813), surveyor and cartographer, was born at Quebec, Lower Canada, the son of Alexis Charland and Marie Poulin, on April 7, 1772; and died at Montreal about September 1, 1813. He was with William Vondenvelden (q.v.) joint author of the first exact map of Lower Canada, published in London in 1813, and he prepared valuable plans of Quebec and Montreal.

[P. Scribe, *Louis Charland* (Bull. rech. hist., 1928); P. G. Roy, *Fils de Québec,* vol. 2 (Lévis, Que., 1933).]

Charland, Paul Victor (1858-1939), priest and historian, was born at St. Roch, Canada East, on May 23, 1858. He was educated at the Quebec Seminary and Laval University (Litt.D., 1902), and was ordained a priest of the Roman Catholic Church in 1881. From 1881 to 1886 he was professor of rhetoric at Notre Dame College, Lévis, Quebec; he then joined the Dominican order, and was stationed successively at St. Hyacinthe, Quebec, at Ottawa, Ontario, at Lewiston, Maine, and at Fall River, Massachusetts. He died at Quebec City, on December 24, 1939. In 1900 he was elected a fellow of the Royal Society of Canada; and he was the author of *Questions d'histoire littéraire* (Lévis, Que., 1884), *Les trois légendes de Madame Saincte Anne* (Montreal, 1898), *La culte de Sainte Anne en Amérique* (Lévis, Que., 1898), *La bonne sainte* (Quebec, 1904), *Madame Saincte Anne et son culte au moyen age* (2 vols., Paris, 1911-13), *La famille Canac-Marquis et familles alliées* (Quebec, 1918), *La culte de Sainte Anne en occident* (Quebec, 1921), and *La grande artiste; ou, Le zèle artistique de l'Eglise* (Quebec, 1923).

[*Can. who's who,* 1936-37; *Proc. Roy. Soc. Can.,* 1940.]

Charlebois, Ovide (1862-1933), Roman Catholic missionary, was born at Oka, Quebec, on February 12, 1862, was educated at the College of L'Assomption, entered the Oblate order, and was ordained a priest in 1887. From 1887 to 1903 he was a missionary in Saskatchewan; and from 1903 to 1920 he was director of the industrial school at Lac aux Canards. He became in 1910 apostolic vicar of Keewatin, with the title of bishop of Berenice *in partibus;* and in 1925 he organized the first missions of the Roman Catholic Church on Hudson Bay. He died on November 20, 1933.

[J. M. Pénard, *Mgr Charlebois* (Montreal, 1937); Gaston Carrière, *Le Pere du Keewatin: Mgr Ovide Charlebois* (Montreal, 1962); Allaire, *Dict. gén.*]

Charlesworth, Hector (1872-1945), journalist and author, was born in Hamilton, Ontario, on September 28, 1872, and was educated in Toronto. Though he qualified as a chartered accountant, he turned to journalism. He was city editor of the Toronto *Mail and Empire* from 1904 to 1910; and was associate editor of *Saturday Night* from 1910 to 1925, and editor-in-chief from 1925 to 1932. In 1932 he was appointed first chairman of the Canadian Radio Broadcasting Commission, which preceded the Canadian Broadcasting Corporation. This position he held for four years, during which his relations with the politicians became increasingly difficult. He then returned to journalism as a music and dramatic critic in Toronto. He died at Toronto on December 30, 1945. He was the author of three books of reminiscences, *Candid chronicles* (Toronto, 1925), *More candid chronicles* (Toronto, 1928), and *I'm telling you* (Toronto, 1937), in the last of which he told the story of his four years in Ottawa with the Canadian Radio Broadcasting Commission. He was the author also of a volume of essays, *The Canadian scene* (Toronto, 1927).

[Toronto *Globe and Mail,* Dec. 31, 1945; *Can. who's who,* 1938-39; *Encyc. Can.*]

Charlevoix, Pierre François Xavier de (1682-1761), historian, was born at St. Quentin, France, on October 24, 1682. In 1698 he became a novice of the Society of Jesus in Paris, and in 1705 he was sent to Canada. He reached Quebec in September, and taught grammar in the college at Quebec until 1709, when he returned to France and became a professor in the college of Louis-le-Grand at Paris. In 1720 he again came to Canada, commissioned by the French government to seek a route to the western sea. He journeyed to Lake Superior and descended the Mississippi, visiting the posts of what was then the extreme western frontier of New France. He returned to France in 1723. His report of this journey is printed in P. Margry (ed.), *Mémoires et documents,* vol. vi (Paris, 1888). In 1733 he became one of the editors of *Mémoires de Trévoux,* a monthly journal published by the Jesuits from 1701 to 1762. The later years of his life were occupied with various literary works, and he died at La Flèche on February 1, 1761. His published works include *Histoire de l'établissement, des progrès et de la décadence du christianisme dans l'empire du Japon* (Paris, 1715), *La vie de la Mère Marie de l'Incarnation* (Paris, 1724), *Histoire de l'Isle Espagnole ou de Saint-Domingue* (Paris, 1730), *Histoire et description générale du Japon* (Paris, 1736), *Histoire et description général de la Nouvelle-France* (3 vols., Paris, 1744), and *Histoire du Paraguay* (Paris, 1756). His history of New France, which was the first general history of Canada to be published, was translated into English by J. G. Shea (6 vols., New York, 1866-72; new ed., New York, 1900); and his *Journal* has been translated by Louise P. Kellogg (Chicago, Caxton Club, 1923).

[J. E. Roy, *Essai sur Charlevoix* (Trans. Roy. Soc. Can., 1907); Louise P. Kellogg, introduction to *Journal* (Chicago, 1923); N. F. Morrison, memoir and bibliography in J. G. Shea, *History* (New York, 1900); R. G. Thwaites (ed.), *The Jesuit relations,* vol. 69 (Cleveland, 1900); Le Jeune, *Dict. gén.; Dict. Can. biog.,* vol. 3.]

Charlton, John (1829-1910), merchant and politician, was born near Caledonia, New York, on February 3, 1829, the son of Adam Charlton and Ann Gray. He was educated at the Springville Academy, New York, and came to Canada with his parents in 1849. In 1853 he opened a general store at Lynedoch, Norfolk county, Upper Canada; and in 1859 he became Canadian manager of a firm of lumber merchants at Tonawanda, New York. In 1861 he bought the Canadian business of this firm; and under varying names carried on the business for more than forty years. He represented North Norfolk in the Canadian House of Commons from 1872 to 1904; and during this period took an active part in the debates on the tariff. Though a moderate protectionist, he was a Liberal in politics, and was in favour of commercial union with the United States. He died at Lynedoch, Ontario, on February 11, 1910. In 1854 he married Ella, daughter of George Gray of Charlotteville, Upper Canada. A few years before his death he published a volume of *Speeches and addresses* (Toronto, 1905).

[*Can. parl. comp.*; Morgan, *Can. men* (1898); Rose, *Cyc. Can. biog.* (1886); *Canadian biographical dictionary,* Ontario vol. (Toronto, 1880).]

Charnisay, Charles de Menou, Seigneur d'Aulnay (1604?-1650), governor of Acadia (1635-50), came of an old family of Touraine, and was born near Loches about 1604. He came to Acadia with his cousin Rasilly (q.v.), in August, 1632, as his lieutenant, and Rasilly appointed him his successor in 1635. There followed years of strife with Charles de La Tour (q.v.), who also claimed to represent the king. Charnisay, however, with superior influence at court, had La Tour's commission revoked, and in 1645 he attacked and captured La Tour's headquarters, Fort St. John. La Tour fled from the country, and Charnisay remained with almost unlimited power in Acadia. In May, 1650, he was drowned in the Annapolis River by the upsetting of his canoe. He married Jeanne Molin, daughter of the Seigneur de Courcelles, by whom he had eight children.

[A. Couillard-Després, *Charles de Saint-Etienne de la Tour* (Arthabaska, Que., 1930); G. O. Bent, *Fortunes of La Tour* (University magazine, vol. xi); R. G. Thwaites (ed.), *The Jesuit relations,* vol. 30 (Cleveland, 1898); Le Jeune, *Dict. gén.*; *Dict. Can. biog.*, vol. 1.]

Chartier, Étienne (1798-1853), priest, was born at St. Pierre-de-la-Rivière-du-Sud, Lower Canada, on December 23, 1798. He was educated at the Quebec Seminary, and was ordained a priest of the Roman Catholic Church in 1828. He was the only priest who joined in the Rebellion of 1837; and he was compelled to flee to the United States. He returned to Canada in 1845; and he died at Quebec on July 6, 1853.

[F. J. Audet, *L'Abbé Etienne Chartier* (Les cahiers des dix, 1941).]

Chartier, Joseph-Etienne Emile (1876-1963), educator and educationalist, was born in Sherbrooke, Que., on June 18, 1876, and died there on February 27, 1963. He was educated at the Séminaire de Saint-Hyacinthe, and ordained a priest of the Roman Catholic Church in 1899. He began teaching Greek and Latin in his *alma mater* at the age of eighteen and continued from 1894 to 1903 when he began studies abroad of modern Greek in Athens, at Paris, and at Rome where he received a doctorate in Thomistic philosophy from the Gregorian University. He returned to Saint-Hyacinthe and taught there until appointed secretary-general of the Université de Montréal (1914-19). He taught Greek in the University until his retirement in 1944 and was for many years bursar. From 1919 to 1944 he was also vice-rector and dean of the Faculté des Lettres. He received numerous honours — M. A. (Laval); docteur ès lettres (Montreal); LL.D. (Queen's, McGill); docteur de l'Université (Montreal, Sherbrooke); member of the Royal Society of Canada (1916). He belonged to several language and historical societies and contributed articles to such publications as *La revue canadienne*, *Dictionnaire des lettres françaises,* and *Mémoires de la Société royale*. In addition to extensive writings on Greek grammar and literature, he was the author of seven books, including *Littérature canadienne* (1923); *La vie de l'esprit au Canada français* (1941); and *Lectures littéraires en deux volumes* (1948, 1961).

[*Proc. and Trans. Roy. Soc. Can.*, 1963.]

Chartrand, Joseph Demers (1852-1905), soldier, was born at St. Vincent de Paul, Canada East, on November 23, 1852. In 1877 he left Canada, and enlisted in the French Foreign Legion. He obtained a commission, first in the 3rd Zouaves, and later in the Chasseurs Alpins, and saw service in the Tonquin War. He retired from the French army in 1894, with the rank of captain, and returned to Canada. He died at Kingston, Ontario, in April, 1905. He was the author of *Expéditions autour de ma tente* (Paris, 1887), *Saint-Maxent: Souvenirs d'école militaire* (Paris, 1889), and *Au pays d'étapes: Notes d'un légionnaire* (Paris, 1892).

[Morgan, *Bib. can.* (1898); *Bull. rech. hist.*, 1925.]

Chaste, Aymar de. See **Chatte, Aymar de.**

Chatte, Aymar de (d. 1603), lieutenant-general of New France (1602-3), was a younger son of François de Clermont, baron de Chatte, and Paule de Joyeuse. He entered the order of St. John of Jerusalem in 1566, and rose in this order to the rank of marshal. In 1589 he was appointed governor of Dieppe; and in 1602 he was commissioned as lieutenant-general of New France, having organized a company for trade in Canada. He died in May, 1603.

[R. La Roque de Roquebrune, *Aymar de Clermont-Chatte* (Nova Francia, 1927); Le Jeune, *Dict. gén.*]

Chaumonot, Pierre Joseph Marie (1611-1693), Jesuit missionary, was born on March 9, 1611, in a village in Burgundy, France. He entered the Company of Jesus in 1632, and was ordained a priest in 1637. He was sent to Canada in 1639, and spent nearly ten years in the Huron missions. He escaped martyrdom, and accompanied the Hurons, first to the Christian Islands, and then to Quebec. Under him, the refugees settled on the island of Orleans; and he had oversight of this mission for thirty-five years, except for short absences. In 1692 his advanced age compelled him to retire to Quebec; and there he died on February 21, 1693. In 1688 he wrote his autobiography, which has been preserved; and his Huron grammar has been translated into English, and published in the *Transactions* of the Literary and Historical Society of Quebec for 1831.

[Le Jeune, *Dict. gén.*; Allaire, *Dict. biog.*; R. G. Thwaites (ed.), *The Jesuit relations* (73 vols., Cleveland, 1898-1900); *Dict. Can. biog.*, vol. 1.]

Chauveau, Charles Auguste (1877-1940), lawyer, was born at Quebec City, on October 28, 1877, the grandson of the Hon. P. J. O. Chauveau (q.v.). He was educated at Georgetown University, Washington, D.C., and at Laval University (B.A., 1896; LL.L., 1899; LL.D., 1903); and was called to the bar of Quebec in 1899 (K.C., 1917). He practised law in Quebec, and died there on December 17, 1940. In 1902 he married Amélie, daughter of the Hon. E. J. Flynn (q.v.); and by her he had three children. He was the author of *De l'autorité de la chose jugée en matière civile* (Quebec, 1903).

[Morgan, *Can. men* (1912); *Can. who's who*, 1936-37.]

Chauveau, Pierre Joseph Olivier (1820-1890), prime minister of Quebec (1867-73), was born at Quebec, Lower Canada, on May 30, 1820, the son of Charles Chauveau and Marie Louise Roy. He was educated at the Quebec Seminary, and was called to the bar of Lower Canada in 1841 (Q.C., 1853). He represented Quebec county in the Legislative Assembly of Canada from 1844 to 1855, and in the Canadian House of Commons and the Legislative Assembly of Quebec from 1867 to 1873. From 1851 to 1853 he was solicitor-general for Lower Canada in the Hincks-Morin administration, and provincial secretary from 1853 to 1854. He continued as provincial secretary in the MacNab-Morin administration of 1854; but in 1855 he resigned from parliament in order to accept the appointment of superintendent of public instruction in Lower Canada. His tenure of this office was marked by the founding in 1857 of the *Journal of public instruction* (published, both in English and French, until 1879), by the establishment of normal schools in Lower Canada, and by the creation of separate schools in Lower Canada in 1863. In 1867 he became first prime minister of the province of Quebec, holding the portfolios of minister of education and provincial secretary. In 1873 he resigned, and was called to the Senate of Canada, of which he was speaker from 1873 to 1874. In 1878 he was appointed professor of Roman law at Laval University, Montreal, and later became dean of the law faculty. He died at Quebec on April 4, 1890. In 1840 he married Marie Louise Flore, daughter of Pierre Massé; and by her he had two sons and six daughters.

He was no less notable as a *littérateur* than as a politician. He was an LL.D. of McGill University and a D.C.L. of Laval; and at different times he was president of the Quebec Literary and Historical Society, the Royal Society of Canada, the Institut Canadien of Quebec, and the Institut Canadien Français of Montreal. His writings include poems, novels, and political and educational essays. His poetry, most of which appeared in *Le Canadien* and other journals between 1838 and 1850, was collected in *Le répertoire national* (Montreal, 1848-50). His best-known novel was *Charles Guérin, roman de moeurs canadiennes* (Montreal, 1852). Among his other publications, the most notable were *Relation du voyage de S. A. R. le Prince de Galles en Amérique* (Montreal, 1861), *L'instruction publique au Canada* (Quebec, 1876), *Souvenirs et légendes* (Quebec, 1877), *François-Xavier Garneau* (Montreal, 1883), and *Bertrand de la Tour* (Lévis, 1898). A history of the universities of Laval, McGill, and Toronto, written by him, appeared serially in his *Journal of Public Instruction*.

[L. O. David, *Biographies et portraits* (Montreal, 1876), *Feu P. J. O. Chauveau* (Trans. Roy. Soc. Can., 1891), and *Mes contemporains* (Montreal, 1894); Bibaud, *Panth. can.*; Le Jeune, *Dict. gén.*; Rose, *Cyc. Can. biog.* (1886); Dent, *Can. port.*, vol. 4; Morgan, *Cel. Can.* and *Bib. can.*; Taylor, *Brit. Am.*, vol. 3; *Can. biog. dict.*, Quebec vol., Chauveau, Pierre (Chicago, 1880); J.D. Borthwick, *Montreal, its history* (Montreal, 1875); L. P. Audet, *P. J. O. Chauveau* (Trans. Roy. Soc. Can., 1967, 1971).]

Chauvin, Jean (1895-1958), journalist and art critic, was born at Ste. Rose, Quebec, on July 20, 1895, and died at Montreal on September 15, 1958. He was educated at the University of Montreal, and was called to the Quebec bar. But the First World War cut short his legal career; for, though rejected by the Canadian army because of poor eyesight, he enlisted with the French Foreign Legion, was twice gravely wounded, and was awarded the Croix de Guerre with two stars. On his return to Canada he became a journalist, and ultimately became editor-in-chief of the *Revue Populaire*. He was the author of an important book on Canadian artists, entitled *Ateliers* (Montreal, 1928). He was elected a fellow of the Royal Society of Canada in 1946.

[*Proc. Roy. Soc. Can.*, 1959.]

Cheadle, Walter Butler (1835-1910), physician and explorer, was born at Colne, Lancashire, on October 15, 1835, the son of the Rev. James Cheadle. He was educated at Caius College, Cambridge (B.A., 1859; M.B., 1861); and in 1862 he started with Lord Milton on an expedition of exploration in the North-West Territories. The account of the expedition, published by Milton and Cheadle jointly under the title, *The north west passage by land* (London, 1865; new ed., Ottawa, 1931), was really written by Cheadle. Cheadle's *Journal across the mountains* has been published by James White in the *Canadian Alpine Journal*, 1924, and his *Journal of a trip across Canada* was edited for publication by A. G. Doughty and Gustave Lanctot (Ottawa, 1931). In 1865 he was elected a member of the Royal College of Surgeons, and he became in his later years a distinguished London physician. In 1884 he visited Canada with the British Association, and contracted dysentery, which permanently injured his health. He died in London, England, on March 25, 1910.

[*Dict. nat. biog.*, supp. II; *Who was who, 1897-1916; Can. who was who*, vol. 1.]

Chénier, Jean Olivier (1806-1837), physician and rebel, was born at Longueuil, Lower Canada, in 1806. He was educated at Montreal, studied medicine under Dr. Kimber of Montreal, and was admitted to practice as a physician in 1828. He first practised at St. Benoit in the county of Two Mountains, and later at St. Eustache. He became a leader of the local *patriotes*, and in 1837 he headed the insurgents in the Two Mountains district. He was killed at the battle of St. Eustache on December 14, 1837. In 1831 he married the daughter of Dr. Jacques Labrie (q.v.).

[L. O. David, *Les patriotes de 1837-38* (Montreal, 1884); Bibaud, *Panth. can.*; Le Jeune, *Dict. gén.*; *Cyc. Am. biog.*]

Cherrier, Côme Séraphin (1798-1885), lawyer, was born at Repentigny, Lower Canada, on July 22, 1798, and was for many years the dean of the Quebec bar. He was called to the bar of Lower Canada in 1822 (Q.C., 1842) and practised law in Montreal for over half a century. He twice declined appointment to the bench, and in 1864 he declined the chief justiceship of Lower Canada. From 1834 to 1837 he represented Montreal in the Legislative Assembly of Lower Canada; and he was arrested on suspicion of being implicated in the rebellion of 1837, but was released. In later life he became wealthy, and was for many years president of the Banque du Peuple. He died at Montreal on April 10, 1885. In 1834 he married the widow of Jean Coursol, of the Hudson's Bay Company, and mother of the Hon. C. J. Coursol (q.v.); and by her he had two daughters.

[H. Mercier, *Conférence sur C. S. Cherrier* (Montreal, 1885); L. O. David, *Biographies et portraits* (Montreal, 1876); *Dom. ann. reg.*, 1885; Le Jeune, *Dict. gén.*]

Chevalier, Henri Émile (1828-1879), journalist and novelist, was born at Chatillon, France, on September 13, 1828. He fled from France on the accession of Napoleon III in 1851, and in 1852 settled in Canada. He was employed on the staff of several newspapers in Montreal, and was for a time librarian of the Institut Canadien. In 1860 he returned to France; and he died in Paris on August 25, 1879. While in Canada he published several novels, *L'héroine de Châteauguay* (Montreal, 1858), *L'Iroquoise de Caughnawaga* (Montreal, 1858), and *Le pirate du St. Laurent* (Montreal, 1859); and he translated Ebenezer Clemo's *Canadian homes* under the title, *Le foyer canadien ou le mystère dévoilé* (Montreal, 1859). In 1853 he became editor of *La Ruche Littéraire* (Montreal, 1853-59).

[B. Corrigan, *Henri-Emile Chevalier and his novels of North America* (Romanic review, 1944); E. Z. Massicotte, *Emile Chevalier* (Bull. rech. hist., 1914); Le Jeune, *Dict. gén.*; Morgan, *Bib. can.*; *Dict. Can. biog.*, vol. 10.]

Chevalier, dit Beauchêne, Robert (1686-1731), buccaneer, was born at Pointe-aux-Trembles, New France, on April 23, 1686, the son of Jacques Chevalier and Jeanne Villain. At an early age he embarked on a life of adventure, and became a pirate captain. He retired on his gains to France; and he was killed in a brawl at Tours on December 11, 1731. His memoirs were published after his death by Alain René Le Sage, under the title *Aventures de M. Robert Chevalier dit le Beauchesne, capitaine, filibustier dans la Nouvelle-France* (2 vols., Paris, 1732). Until recently it was thought these memoirs were apocryphal; but it has now been established that they are genuine, but considerably amplified by Le Sage.

[A. Fauteux, *Les aventures de Chevalier de Beauchêne* (Les cahiers des dix, vol. 2, 1937); Le Jeune, *Dict. gén.*; *Dict. Can. biog.*, vol. 2.]

Chewett, William (1753-1849), surveyor, was born in London, England, on December 21, 1753, and was educated as a hydrographical engineer in the service of the East India Company. He came to Canada in 1771, and served as an engineer in the defence of Quebec in 1775-76. In 1791 he was appointed deputy surveyor-general of Upper Canada, and afterwards he became, with Thomas Ridout, joint surveyor-general. A considerable part of the province of Ontario was first surveyed by him, and his maps were among the earliest sources of exact information regarding the topography of the province. He retired from the public service in 1832, and he died at Toronto on September 24, 1849. In 1791 he married Isabella, daughter of Major Archibald McDonell, of the Long Sault; and by her he had three sons and one daughter.

[*Biographical sketch of the late Colonel Chewett* (Proceedings of the Association of Provincial Land Surveyors of Ontario, 1890); W. Canniff, *The medical profession in Upper Canada* (Toronto, 1894); E. M. Chadwick, *Ontarian families*, vol. 2 (Toronto, 1898); Morgan, *Cel. Can.*]

Chiniquy, Charles Paschal Télesphore (1809-1899), clergyman and author, was born at Kamouraska, Lower Canada, on July 30, 1809, the son of Charles Chiniquy and Marie Reine Perrault. He was educated at the Quebec Seminary, and was ordained a priest in the Roman Catholic Church in 1833. After serving as vicar, or curé, in several parishes, he deserted in 1858 the Roman Catholic Church and became a minister of the Presbyterian Church. He died in Montreal on January 16, 1899. In 1864 he married Euphémie Allard, of St. Anne, Kankakee. He was the author of a *Manuel ou règlement de la Société de Temperance* (Quebec, 1844), *Lettre à Mgr. Pinsonnault, évêque de London* (Montreal, 1857), *Letter to Mr. Brassard, curate of St. Roch l'Achigan* (Montreal, 1857), *L'Eglise de Rome* (Montreal, 1870), *Le prêtre, la femme, et le confessionel* (Montreal, 1875), *Fifty years in the Church of Rome* (Chicago, 1885), *The murder of Abraham Lincoln planned and executed by Jesuit priests* (Indianapolis, 1893), *The perversion of Dr. Newman to the Church of Rome* (Montreal, 1896), and *Forty years in the church of Christ* (Chicago, 1899). Some of these publications have been translated into several languages and have reached many editions.

[Morgan, *Can. men* (1898); Le Jeune, *Dict. gén.*]

Chipman, Clarence Campbell (1856-1924), chief commissioner of the Hudson's Bay Company (1891-1911), was born in Amherst, Nova Scotia, in 1856. In 1882 he became private secretary to Sir Charles Tupper (q.v.), and in 1891 he was appointed chief commissioner in Canada for the Hudson's Bay Company. He retired from this position in 1911, and he died at Leamington, England, on February 13, 1924. He was the author of *A treatise on the fisheries of Canada* (1891).

[Morgan, *Can. men* (1912); *Beaver* (1924).]

Chipman, Ward (1754-1824), solicitor-general of New Brunswick (1784-1808), was born in Marblehead, Massachusetts, on July 30, 1754, the son of John Chipman. He was educated at Harvard College (B.A., 1770), was called to the bar in Massachusetts, and practised law in Boston from 1774 to 1777. From 1777 to 1783 he was deputy muster-master-general of the British forces in North America; and on the evacuation of New York he accompanied Sir Guy Carleton (q.v.) to England. In 1784 he was appointed solicitor-general of New Brunswick, and he held this position until 1808. In 1785 he was elected to represent Saint John in the House of Assembly of New Brunswick, and in 1789 Northumberland. In 1806 he was appointed a member of the Executive Council of the province, and in 1808 he was made a judge of the Supreme Court. In 1823, on the death of the lieutenant-governor, he was sworn as president and commander-in-chief of the province; but he presided at only one session of the legislature, and he died on February 9, 1824. In 1786 he married Elizabeth (d. 1852), daughter of the Hon. William Hazen.

[J. W. Lawrence, *Judges of New Brunswick* (Saint John, N.B., 1907); W. O. Raymond (ed.), *The Winslow papers* (Saint John, N.B., 1901); *Dict. Am. biog.*; *Cyc. Am. biog.*]

Chipman, Ward (1787-1851), chief justice of New Brunswick (1834-51), was born in Saint John, New Brunswick, on July 10, 1787, the son of Ward Chipman (q.v.), solicitor-general of the province. He was educated at Harvard College (B.A., 1805), and in 1808 he was called to the bar of New Brunswick. He then spent several years at the Inner Temple in London, completing his legal studies; and in 1815 he was appointed recorder of Saint John, N.B. In 1820 he was elected to represent Saint John in the House of Assembly; and in 1823 he was chosen speaker of the House. In 1824, on his father's death, he was appointed a judge of the Supreme Court of the province, with a seat in the Legislative Council; and in 1834 he reached the summit of his ambition, when he became chief justice of the province. He resigned his seat in the Legislative Council in 1842; and he retired from the bench in 1850. He died at Saint John on November 26, 1851. In 1817 he married Elizabeth (d. 1876), daughter of Henry Wright. He was the author of a *Report of the commissioners for ascertaining the losses occasioned by the late fires in New Brunswick* (Fredericton, 1826), and *Remarks upon the disputed points of boundary under the fifth article of the Treaty of Ghent* (Saint John, 1839).

[J. W. Lawrence, *The judges of New Brunswick* (Saint John, N.B., 1907); W. G. MacFarlane, *New Brunswick bibliography* (Saint John, N.B., 1895).]

Chisholm, Arthur Murray (1872-1960), novelist, was born in Toronto in 1872, was educated at the University of Toronto (B.A., 1895; LL.B., 1896), and died at Windermere, British

Columbia, on January 24, 1960. He was the stepson of Sir George Foster (q.v.). Though his work was little known in Canada, he published no fewer than twelve novels: *The boss of Wind River* (Garden City, N.Y., 1911), *Precious waters* (Garden City, N.Y., 1913), *The land of strong men* (New York, 1919), *The land of big rivers* (New York, 1924), *When Stuart came to Sitkum* (New York, 1924), *The red-headed kids* (New York, 1925), *Black Powder Dan* (London, 1925), *The red heads* (London, 1926), *Yellow Horse* (London, 1926), *Red* (London, 1927), *Prospectin' fools* (London, 1927), and *Red Bill* (New York, 1929).

[R. E. Watters, *A check list of Canadian literature* (Toronto, 1959).]

Chisholm, George Brock (1896-1971), psychiatrist, was born at Oakville, Ontario, May 18, 1896. He was educated at the Galt Collegiate, the Oakville High School, and at the University of Toronto (M.D., 1924). He undertook postgraduate studies in London, England, and at Yale University. He had a psychiatric practice in Toronto (1934-40), was deputy minister of National Health (1944-46), Interior commissioner of the World Health Organization (1946-48), and director-general of the World Health Organization (1948-53). During the First World War he served with the 15th Canadian Battalion, Canadian Militia. Between 1919 and 1939 he maintained his military connection and commanded the Lorne Scots, 25th Infantry brigade from 1935 to 1940, the 5th Infantry brigade from 1940 to 1941, was general staff-officer at National Defence Headquarters (1941) and director of personnel selection (1941) and was deputy adjutant general and director-general of medical services (1942-44). He received the Military Cross and bar in the First World War. A controversial figure, Chisholm questioned many of the accepted moral codes and standards of behaviour which have been handed on from one generation to another. His questioning of Santa Claus almost cost him his position with the Canadian government in 1945. He received many awards for his forthright approach to world health problems and was a member of many international organizations. He was a member of the Executive of the World Federation for Mental Health, was vice-president of the World Federalists Association, and was created Commander of the Order of the British Empire. He died at Victoria, British Columbia, February 2, 1971. He published: *Prescription for survival* (New York, 1958); *Can people learn to learn?* (New York, 1958).

[*Can. who's who* 1967-69; *Encyc. Can.* (1966); *Maclean's* magazine, vol. 63 (May 1, 1950).]

Chisholm, Sir Joseph Andrew (1863-1950), chief justice of the Supreme Court of Nova Scotia (1931-50), was born at St.

Andrews, Nova Scotia, on January 9, 1863; and died at Halifax, Nova Scotia, on January 22, 1950. He was educated at St. Francis Xavier College and Dalhousie University, and was called to the bar in Nova Scotia in 1886 (K.C., 1907). In 1889 he joined the law firm in Halifax headed by R. L. (later Sir Robert) Borden (q.v.); from 1909 to 1911 he was mayor of Halifax; and in 1916 he was appointed a justice of the Supreme Court of Nova Scotia. He became chief justice of this court in 1931, and continued as such until his death. In 1935 he was created a K.B. He edited a new and enlarged edition of *The speeches and public letters of Joseph Howe* (2 vols., Halifax, 1909), originally published by William Annand (2 vols., Halifax, 1858).

[*Who was who,* 1941-50; *Can. who's who,* 1948; *Encyc. Can.*]

Chisholme, David (1796?-1842), journalist and author, was born in Ross-shire, Scotland, about 1796. He came to Canada in 1822, and became the editor, first, of the *Canadian Magazine and Literary Repository* (Montreal, 1823-25), and then of the *Canadian Review and Literary and Historical Journal* (Montreal, 1824-26). Through the patronage of Lord Dalhousie (q.v.), he was appointed clerk of the peace for the district of Three Rivers; but in 1836 he was dismissed from office on account of his high Tory views, and for the remainder of his life he edited the Montreal *Gazette*. He published *The annals of Canada* (Three Rivers, 1831), and *Observations on the rights of the British colonies to representation in the imperial parliament* (Three Rivers, 1832); and an early Upper Canadian imprint, *The Lower Canada watchman* (Kingston, 1829), is attributed to him. He died on September 24, 1842, at Montreal. At the time of his death, he was engaged on a history of Lower Canada, and the papers which he had collected are in the Library of Parliament, Ottawa.

[Morgan, *Bib. can.*; W. Kingsford, *Early bibliography of Ontario* (Toronto, 1892); P. Gagnon, *Essai de bibliographie canadienne* (Quebec, 1895).]

Choquette, Ernest (1862-1941), physician and author, was born at Beloeil, Canada East, on November 18, 1862. He was educated at Laval University (M.B., M.D.), and practised medicine for many years at St. Hilaire, Quebec. He was repeatedly elected mayor of St. Hilaire; and in 1910 he was appointed a member of the Legislative Council of Quebec for the Rougemont division. He died at Montreal, Quebec, on March 29, 1941. He was the author of *Les Ribaud* (Montreal, 1898), *Claude Paysan* (Montreal, 1899), *Carabinades* (Montreal, 1900), and *La terre* (Montreal, n.d.).

[*Can. who's who,* 1936-37.]

Chouart des Groseilliers, Médard (b. 1618), explorer and fur-trader, was born in

July, 1618, at Charly-sur-Marne, France. He came to Canada, probably in 1642; and for several years served as a *donné* in the Jesuit missions among the Hurons. He became a fur-trader, and in 1654-56 he made a momentous trip to the West which opened up the western fur-trade again. In 1659-60 he made, in company with his brother-in-law, Pierre Esprit Radisson (q.v.), another journey to the North West. Whether, as has been maintained, he reached the Mississippi River, on the first of these journeys, and Hudson Bay, on the second, is extremely doubtful; but there is no doubt that he was one of the first white men, with Radisson, to visit the Old North-West. In 1665, he went with Radisson to England, and in 1668-69 he accompanied an English expedition to Hudson Bay. The outcome of this expedition was the formation in 1670 of the Hudson's Bay Company; and in the service of this company Chouart remained until 1675. He returned to Canada, and in 1682 he accompanied Radisson on his expedition against the English on Hudson Bay. In 1684 he was in Paris, and presented a memorial of his grievances to the king's minister. Thereafter he disappears from view; and he seems to have died, probably in Hudson Bay, before 1690. He married (1) Hélène, the daughter of Abraham Martin, of Quebec, and (2) about 1652 Marguerite, daughter of Sebastien Hayet, of St. Malo, and half-sister of Pierre Esprit Radisson.

[Grace L. Nute, *Caesars of the wilderness* (New York, 1943); N. E. Dionne, *Chouart and Radisson* (Quebec, 1910); W. Upham, *Groseilliers and Radisson* (Minnesota historical collections, 1905); G. Bryce, *The remarkable history of the Hudson's Bay Company* (London, 1900); A. Laut, *Pathfinders of the west* (New York, 1904) and *The conquest of the great north west* (Toronto, 1908); L. J. Burpee, *The Search for the western sea* (London, 1908); *Dict. Can. biog.*, vol. 1.]

Chouinard, Ernest (1856-1924), journalist and author, was born at Lévis, Canada East, in 1856. He was educated at Laval University (LL.M., 1883), and became a journalist in Quebec. He died at Quebec City, on November 3, 1924. He was the author of *Sur mer et sur terre* (Quebec, 1919), *Croquis et marines* (Quebec, 1920), and *L'oeil de phare* (Quebec, 1923).

[Morgan, *Can. men* (1912); *Bull. rech. hist.*, 1925.]

Chouinard, Honoré Julien Jean Baptiste (1850-1928), historian, was born at Quebec on June 18, 1850, the son of Honoré Julien Chouinard and Marie Pelletier. He was educated at Laval University, Quebec (LL.B., 1873), and was called to the bar of Quebec in 1873. He represented Dorchester in the Canadian House of Commons from 1888 to 1890;

and in 1908 he was largely responsible for organizing the celebration of the tercentenary of the founding of Quebec. He was appointed the secretary of the Quebec Battlefields Commission; and for his work in this connection he received, in 1908, the C.M.G. He died at Quebec on November 27, 1928. In 1884 he married Marie Louise Isabelle, the youngest daughter of the Hon. Juchereau Duchesnay and niece of Cardinal Taschereau (q.v.). He was the author of *La Pologne* (Quebec, 1875), *Fête nationale des canadiens-français* (Quebec, 1881), *Paul de Chomedey, Sieur de Maisonneuve* (Quebec, 1882), *Inauguration du monument Champlain à Québec* (Quebec, 1902), *Annales de la Société Saint-Jean-Baptiste de Québec* (Quebec, 1902-03), and *Monographie d'une famille canadienne-française* (Quebec, 1903).

[Morgan, *Can. men* (1912).]

Chown, Alice Amelia (1866-1949), suffragist and author, was born at Kingston, Ontario, in 1866, was educated at Queen's University (B.A., 1887), and died at Toronto, Ontario, on March 2, 1949. She devoted her energies to forwarding female suffrage, women's trade unions, and women's support of the League of Nations; and she was the author of an autobiographical work, *The stairway* (Boston, 1921).

[Toronto *Globe and Mail*, March 3, 1949.]

Chown, Samuel Dwight (1853-1933), clergyman and author, was born in Kingston, Ontario, on April 11, 1853. He was educated at Victoria University (D.D., 1898), and was ordained a Methodist minister in 1879. From 1914 until the union of the Methodist with the Presbyterian and the Congregational churches in 1925, he was general superintendent of the Methodist Church; and his influence was no small factor in bringing this union about. He died in Toronto, Ontario, on January 30, 1933. He was the author of *Church union in Canada* (Toronto, 1930).

[*Who's who in Canada*; Morgan, *Can. men* (1912).]

Christie, Alexander (1792-1872), governor of Assiniboia (1833-39 and 1844-48), was a native of Scotland. He entered the service of the Hudson's Bay Company in 1809; and in the deed poll of 1821 he appears as a chief factor. In 1822 he was appointed councillor for the governor of the Company's territories, and in 1833 governor of Assiniboia. In 1839 he was appointed also a councillor of Rupert's Land. He retired in 1849, and died in Scotland in 1872.

[E. H. Oliver (ed.), *The Canadian northwest* (2 vols., Ottawa, 1914); Rose, *Cyc. Can. biog.* (1886), *sub nomine* Hon. J. W. Christie; *Dict. Can. biog.*, vol. 10.]

Christie, Alexander James (d. 1843), journalist, was born in Scotland, the son of the dean of the diocese of Aberdeen, was educated at the University of Aberdeen, and studied medicine at Edinburgh University. He emigrated to Canada in 1817, and for the rest of his life combined journalism with agriculture and the practice of medicine. From 1819 to 1822 he was editor of the Montreal *Herald*; from 1823 to 1824 he edited the Montreal *Gazette*; and in 1836 he founded the *Bytown Gazette*. He died at Bytown (Ottawa) in November, 1843. He was the author of *The emigrant's assistant; or, Remarks on the agricultural interest of the Canadas* (2 vols., Montreal, 1821).

[H. P. Hill, *The Bytown gazette* (Ont. Hist. Soc., papers and records, 1931); C. C. J. Bond, *A. J. Christie, Bytown pioneer* (Ont. Hist., 1964).]

Christie, Mrs. Annie Rothwell, *née* **Fowler** (1837-1927), author, was born in London, England, on March 31, 1837, the eldest daughter of Daniel Fowler (q.v.). She came to Canada in 1843, and lived with her parents on Amherst Island, near Kingston. She married, first, one Rothwell, but was early widowed; and in 1895 she married, secondly, the Rev. I. J. Christie (d. 1905), rector of North Gower, Ontario. Her later years were spent in Ottawa; and she died in New Liskeard, Ontario, on July 2, 1927. She wrote three novels which were published in serial form: *Alice Gray* (1873), *Edged tools* (Appleton's journal, 1880), and *Requital* (1886); and one novel published in book form, *Loved I not honour more* (Toronto, 1887). She contributed short stories to American, English, and Canadian periodicals; and she contributed poetry to the *Magazine of poetry*. "The best war-songs of the Half-breed Rebellion," wrote Sir Edwin Arnold, "were written by Annie Rothwell."

[*Can. who was who*, vol. 2; Morgan, *Can. men and women* (1912); L. E. Horning and L. J. Burpee, *A bibliography of Canadian fiction* (Toronto, 1904).]

Christie, David (1818-1880), secretary of state for Canada, was born in Edinburgh, Scotland, in 1818. He was educated at the Edinburgh High School, and came to Canada in 1833. He became a farmer and stockbreeder, and later was elected president of the Agricultural Association of Upper Canada. He was one of the founders of the "Clear Grit" party, and sat in the Legislative Assembly of United Canada as member for Wentworth (1851-54) and for East Brant (1855-58). In 1858 he was elected to the Legislative Council for the Erie division; and in 1867 he was appointed to the Canadian Senate. On November 7, 1873, he became secretary of state in the Mackenzie administration; but on January 9, 1874, he was appointed speaker of the Senate, and he continued to preside over the Senate until the

fall of the administration in 1878. He died at Paris, Ontario, on December 15, 1880. He married, first, in 1850, Isabella, eldest daughter of Robert Turnbull, and second, in 1860, Margaret, daughter of William Telfer.

[*Dom. ann. reg.*, 1880-81; *Can. parl. comp.*; W. J. Rattray, *The Scot in British North America*, vol. 2 (Toronto, 1880); *Dict. Can. biog.*, vol. 10.]

Christie, Gabriel (1722-1799), soldier, was born in England in 1722. He entered the British army, and was present at the capture of Quebec in 1759. After 1763, he settled in Canada, and became the proprietor of the seigniories of Bleury, Sabrevois, Noyan, and Lacolle on the Upper Richelieu. In the army he rose to the rank of major-general. He died at Montreal on January 26, 1799. By his wife, Sara Stevenson, he had one son and two daughters; and by a mistress, Rachel Plenderleath, he had three other sons, who bore the patronymic of Plenderleath, but whom he recognized in his will.

[J. B. A. Allaire, *Gabriel Christie* (Bull. rech. hist., 1923).]

Christie, Loring (1885-1941), diplomat, was born at Amherst, Nova Scotia, on January 21, 1885. He was educated at Acadia University (B.A., 1905) and at the Harvard Law School (LL.B., 1909); and, after spending several years in the United States, he was in 1913 appointed legal adviser to the department of External Affairs at Ottawa. He resigned this position in 1923, to take up a financial career in London, England; but in 1935 he returned to the department of External Affairs as legal adviser, and in 1939 he was appointed Canadian minister to the United States. His tenure of this post was interrupted by illness; and he died at New York, N.Y., on April 8, 1941.

[*Can. parl. comp.*; *Records of the graduates of Acadia University* (Wolfville, N.S., 1926); *Encyc. Can.*]

Christie, Robert (1788-1856), politician and historian, was born in Windsor, Nova Scotia, in 1788. He was educated in Nova Scotia, but before the War of 1812 came to Canada, settled in Quebec, and was called to the bar of Lower Canada. He was elected in 1827 a member of the Legislative Assembly of Lower Canada for Gaspé, but was in 1829 expelled for having, as chairman of the quarter sessions of the district of Quebec, advised the omission of the names of certain Reformers from the commission of the peace. Between 1829 and 1834 he was five times re-elected by his constituents and five times expelled by the Assembly. He then retired from the contest; but in 1841 he was again elected to represent Gaspé in the first parliament of United Canada. He continued to represent this constituency in parliament until the general election of 1854; but he did not play an important part in the House. His reputation rests, not on his parliamentary career, but on the historical researches to which he devoted himself for many years. As early as 1818, he had published *Memoirs of the administration of the colonial government of Lower Canada by Sir James Henry Craig and Sir George Prevost* (Quebec). This was followed by *Memoirs of the administration of the government of Lower Canada by Sir Gordon Drummond, Sir John Coape Sherbrooke, the late Duke of Richmond, James Monk, Esquire* (Quebec, 1820), *Memoirs of the administration of Lower Canada by the Right Honourable the Earl of Dalhousie* (Quebec, 1829), and *Administration of the Honourable Sir Francis Burton* (Quebec, n.d.). All these were later incorporated in his *History of the late province of Lower Canada* (vols. i-v, Quebec, 1848-54; vol. vi, Montreal, 1855), a work without literary pretensions but scrupulously impartial, and containing a great many documents of cardinal importance. The work was hardly completed when its author died in Quebec, on October 13, 1856. He married Olivette Doucet; she died at Quebec on January 18, 1865.

[Morgan, *Cel. Can.* and *Bib. can.*; J. C. Dent, *The last forty years* (2 vols., Toronto, 1881); Sir J. M. LeMoine, *Monographies et esquisses* (Quebec, 1885); *Bull. rech. hist.*, 1914.]

Churchill, Charles (*fl.* 1837-1879), clergyman and author, was ordained a clergyman of the Wesleyan Methodist Church in 1841, after having been received on trial in 1837, and served in the Maritime provinces and Canada East. From 1856 to 1861 he was book steward of the Wesleyan Methodist Church at Halifax, Nova Scotia. In 1862 he removed to England; and in 1879 he was living at Clapton, near London. He was the author of *Memorials of missionary life in Nova Scotia* (London, 1845).

[G. H. Cornish, *Cyclopaedia of Methodism in Canada*, vol. 1 (Toronto, 1881).]

Clapin, Sylva (1853-1928), author, was born at St. Hyacinthe, Quebec, on July 15, 1853, the son of Joseph Clapin and Léocadie Lupien. He was educated at the college of St. Hyacinthe, and became a bookseller, successively at St. Hyacinthe, Paris, and Boston. He was also for a time engaged in journalism, first at St. Hyacinthe, and then at Worcester, Massachusetts. From 1902 to 1921 he was translator of the Canadian House of Commons at Ottawa. He died at Ottawa on February 17, 1928. He was the author of *Souvenirs et impressions de voyage* (St. Hyacinthe, 1880), *La France transatlantique* (Paris, 1885), *Dictionnaire canadien-français* (Montreal, 1894; new ed., 1902), *A new dictionary of Americanisms* (New York, 1900), *Histoire des États-Unis depuis les premiers établissements* (Montreal, 1903), *Inventaire de nos fautes les*

plus usuelles (Worcester, Mass., 1913; new ed., Montreal, 1918); and a translation of John Boyd's *Sir George Etienne Cartier* (Montreal, 1918).

[Le Jeune, *Dict. gén.*; *Bull. rech. hist.*, 1930; Morgan, *Can. men* (1912).]

Clark, Arthur Lewis (1873-1956), educationist, was born at Worcester, Massachusetts, on February 19, 1873, and was educated at the Worcester Polytechnic and at Clark University (Ph.D., 1905). He came to Canada in 1906 as professor of physics in Queen's University, Kingston; and in 1919 he became dean of the faculty of applied science at Queen's. He retired from this position in 1943; and he died at Kingston on September 1, 1956. He was elected a fellow of the Royal Society of Canada in 1915; and he was the author of a history of the science faculty at Queen's University, under the title *The first fifty years* (Kingston, Ont., 1944).

[*Proc. Roy. Soc. Can.*, 1958; *Can. who's who*, 1955-57.]

Clark, Daniel (1835-1912), physician and author, was born at Grantown, Inverness-shire, Scotland, on August 29, 1835, the son of Alexander Clark and Anne McIntosh. He came to Canada with his parents in 1847, and was educated at the Simcoe Grammar School, at Victoria University (M.D., 1858), and at Edinburgh University, Scotland. From 1875 to 1905 he was superintendent of the Provincial Lunatic Asylum, Toronto, Ontario. In addition to many publications on medical and psychological subjects, he was the author of *Pen photographs of celebrated men and noted places* (Toronto, 1873), and of a novel dealing with the rebellion of 1837, entitled *Josiah Garth* (Toronto, n.d.). He died in Toronto on June 4, 1912. In 1859 he married Jennie F. Gissing, of Princeton, Upper Canada.

[Morgan, *Can. men* (1912); Rose, *Cyc. Can. biog.* (1886); L. E. Horning and L. J. Burpee, *A bibliography of Canadian fiction* (Toronto, 1904).]

Clark, John Murray (1860-1929), lawyer and author, was born at St. Mary's, Ontario, on July 6, 1860, and was educated at the University of Toronto (B.A., 1882; M.A., 1884; LL.B., 1891). He was called to the bar of Ontario (Q.C., 1889), and practised law in Toronto. He died in Toronto on December 3, 1929. He was the author of a number of papers on legal and historical subjects; and he collaborated with D. W. McPherson in *The law of mines in Canada* (Toronto, 1898).

[Morgan, *Can. men* (1912); H. Charlesworth (ed.), *A cylopaedia of Canadian biography* (Toronto, 1919); *Can. who was who*, vol. 1.]

157

Clark, Michael (1861-1926), politician, was born at Belford, Northumberland, England, in 1861. He was educated at Edinburgh University (M.B., C.M.), and practised medicine and surgery at Newcastle-on-Tyne. He came to Canada, and about 1902 began farming and ranching near Red Deer, Alberta. From 1908 to 1921 he was Liberal member for the Canadian House of Commons for Red Deer; and he played a prominent part as a Liberal-Unionist in the elections of 1917. In 1921 he was defeated, and retired to private life. He died at Olds, Alberta, on July 29, 1926. In 1882 he married Elizabeth, daughter of George Smith, of Cherrybank Farm, Hamilton, Ontario, and by her he had four sons.

[*Can. parl. comp.*; R. G. Riddell (ed.), *Canadian portraits* (Toronto, 1940).]

Clark, Robert Harvey (1880-1961), professor and chemist, was born at Blyth, Ontario, June 4, 1880. He attended the University of Toronto (B.A., 1905; M.A., 1906), and Leipzig University (Ph.D., 1909). After teaching for several years at Clark University and Whitman College in the United States he was appointed to the chemistry department of the University of British Columbia in 1916. He was head of the department from 1927 until his retirement in 1948. He was made a fellow of the Royal Society of Canada in 1928. He served as a member of the council of the National Research Council of Canada from 1937 to 1943 and maintained an interest in research throughout his career. In collaboration with his students he published over one hundred papers and reports. He was particularly interested in the development of the natural resources of British Columbia. He died at Vancouver, July 25, 1961.

[*Can. who's who*, 1955-57; *Trans. Roy. Soc. Can.*, 1962.]

Clark, William Clifford (1889-1952), educationist and civil servant, was born in Glengarry county, Ontario, in 1889; and was educated at Queen's University, Kingston (M.A., 1910), and at Harvard University (A.M. 1915). In 1915 he joined the staff of the department of political and economic science at Queen's. In 1923 he accepted a position with an investment firm in Chicago and New York, but in 1931 he returned to Queen's. In 1932 he was appointed deputy minister of finance at Ottawa; and he continued to hold this very responsible office until his death at Chicago, on December 27, 1952. In 1935 he received from Queen's the honorary degree of LL.D.; the same year he was awarded the C.M.G.; and in 1939 he was elected a fellow of the Royal Society of Canada. He was the author of *The skyscraper: A study of the economic height of modern office buildings* (New York, 1930).

[*Proc. Roy. Soc. Can.*, 1953; *Can. who's who*, 1949-51.]

Clark, William George (1865-1948), lieutenant-governor of New Brunswick (1940-45), was born in Queensbury, York county, New Brunswick, on October 1, 1865; and died at Fredericton, New Brunswick, on January 18, 1948. He became a manufacturer of farm implements, was mayor of Fredericton from 1926 to 1936, and represented York-Sunbury as a Liberal in the Canadian House of Commons from 1935 to 1940. From 1940 to 1945 he was lieutenant-governor of New Brunswick. He was the first president of the York-Sunbury Historical Society; and he endowed the building that houses the museum of the society and the Fredericton Public Library.

[*Encyc. Can.*; *Can. parl. guide*, 1945; Fredericton *Daily Gleaner*, Jan. 19, 1948.]

Clark, Sir William Mortimer (1836-1917), lieutenant-governor of Ontario (1903-08), was born in Aberdeen, Scotland, on May 24, 1836, the son of John Clark. He was educated at Marischall College, Aberdeen, and at Edinburgh University, and became a writer to the signet in 1859. In 1859 he came to Canada, and in 1861 he was admitted to the bar of Ontario (Q.C., 1887). In 1888 he was vice-president of the Equal Rights Association; and he was a political ally of D'Alton McCarthy (q.v.). From 1903 to 1908 he was lieutenant-governor of Ontario; and he was created a knight bachelor in 1907. He died at Prout's Neck, Maine, on August 11, 1917. In 1866 he married Helen, daughter of Gilbert Gordon; and by her he had one son and two daughters. He was an LL.D., of the University of Toronto (1902) and of Queen's University, Kingston (1903). From 1880 to his death he was chairman of the board of management of Knox College, Toronto.

[Morgan, *Can. men* (1912); *Can. who's who* (1910); *Can. who was who*, vol. 2.]

Clark, William Robinson (1829-1912), clergyman and scholar, was born at Inverurie, Aberdeenshire, Scotland, on March 26, 1829, the son of the Rev. James Clark and Catherine Lyon. He was educated at King's College, Aberdeen (B.A., 1848) and at Hertford College, Oxford (B.A., 1853; M.A., 1856). He was ordained a priest of the Church of England in 1858; and in 1882 he came to Canada as professor of mental and moral philosophy in Trinity University, Toronto. This chair he held until 1908, when he retired; and he died in Toronto on November 12, 1912. He was an LL.D. of Hobart College, New York (1888), a D.C.L., of Trinity University, Toronto (1891), and a D.D. of Queen's University, Kingston (1902). In 1891 he was elected a fellow of the Royal Society of Canada, and in 1910 he was its president. In addition to a number of theological works and literary lectures, he was the author of *Savonarola, his life and times* (Chicago, 1892), *The Anglican Reformation*

(Edinburgh, 1899), and *Pascal and the Port Royalists* (Edinburgh, 1902).

[*Proc. Roy. Soc. Can.*, 1913; Morgan, *Can. men* (1912); *Can. who's who* (1910).]

Clarke, Sir Alured (1745?-1832), lieutenant-governor of Lower Canada (1791-96), was born about 1745, and was probably the son of Charles Clarke, baron of the Exchequer, London, England. He became an ensign in the 50th Foot in 1759; and he served in America during the revolutionary war. From 1782 to 1790 he was lieutenant-governor of Jamaica; and in 1791 he was appointed lieutenant-governor of Lower Canada. During the absence of Lord Dorchester (q.v.), it fell to him to put into operation the Constitutional Act, and he opened the first legislature of Lower Canada. He left Canada, however, in 1793, though his commission as lieutenant-governor did not terminate until 1796. From 1798 to 1801 he was commander-in-chief in India; and in 1830 he was promoted a field-marshal. He died at Llangollen, Wales, on September 16, 1832. In 1797 he was created a K.B.

[*Dict. nat. biog.*; A. G. Doughty and D. McArthur (eds.), *Documents relating to the constitutional history of Canada, 1791-1818* (Ottawa, 1914).]

Clarke, Andrew D. (1882-1948), broadcaster, was born at Grimsby, Ontario, in 1882, and was educated there. He became a journalist; then in 1940 the Canadian Broadcasting Corporation put him on the air with a broadcast entitled "Neighbourly News", which became very popular from one end of Canada to the other. Clarke died at York Mills, Ontario, on May 19, 1948; after his death some of his broadcasts were published under the title *Andy Clarke and his neighbourly news* (Toronto, 1949).

[Toronto *Globe and Mail*, May 20, 1948.]

Clarke, Charles (1826-1909), politician and author, was born in Lincoln, England, on November 28, 1826. He came to Canada in 1843, and settled near Elora, Upper Canada. In 1871 he was elected a member of the second Legislative Assembly of Ontario for Wellington Centre, and he sat for this constituency continuously until 1894. From 1880 to 1885 he was speaker of the Assembly; and from 1901 to 1907 he was clerk of the Assembly. He died at Elora, Ontario, on April 6, 1909. Just before his death he published a volume of reminiscences entitled *Sixty years in Upper Canada* (Toronto, 1908).

[Morgan; *Can. men* (1898); *Can. parl. comp.*; Dent, *Can. port.*]

Clarke, Charles Kirk (1857-1924), psychiatrist, was born at Elora, Ontario, in 1857, the son of the Hon. Charles Clarke (q.v.). He was educated at the University of Toronto (M.B., 1878; M.D., 1879), and specialized in the study of mental diseases. From 1885 to 1905 he was superintendent of the Rockwood Asylum for the Insane. From 1911 to 1918 he was superintendent of the Toronto General Hospital; and from 1908 to 1920 dean of the faculty of medicine in the University of Toronto. He died at Toronto on January 20, 1924. In 1906 Queen's University, Kingston, conferred on him the honorary degree of LL.D. He was the author of *A history of the Toronto General Hospital* (Toronto, 1913).

[Morgan, *Can. men* (1912); *Univ. of Toronto monthly*, 1924; C. Greenland, *C. K. Clarke: A pioneer of Canadian psychiatry* (Toronto, 1966).]

Clarke, Douglas (1893-1962), musician and composer, was born in England, April 4, 1893. He was educated at the Reading University School of Composition under Sir Hugh Allen (1909-12) and at Christ's College, Cambridge, where he took the degrees of M.A. and Mus. B. He also studied composition with Gustav Holst, Vaughan Williams, and Charles Wood. He was a conductor of the Cambridge Musical Society and had compositions performed by the London Symphony Orchestra. He came to Canada in 1927 as conductor of the Winnipeg Male Voice Choir and Winnipeg Philharmonic Society. In 1928 he organized the first performance of Bach's St. Matthew Passion in western Canada. He was appointed principal of the conservatory of music of McGill University at Montreal in 1929 and became conductor of the Montreal Symphony. Shortly thereafter he became dean of the faculty of music at McGill. He died at Montreal on November 13, 1962.

[*Grove's dictionary of music and musicians*, vol. II; *Can. who's who*, 1955-57.]

Clarke, Edward Frederick (1850-1905), journalist and politician, was born at Bailieboro', county Cavan, Ireland, on April 24, 1850, the son of Richard Clarke and Ellen Reynolds. He came to Canada in 1864, was apprenticed as a printer, and became a journalist. In 1877 he was selected as editor of the Toronto *Sentinel*, the organ of the Orange Association; and in 1887 he became deputy grand master of the Orange Association in British America. From 1888 to 1891 he was mayor of Toronto. He sat in the Legislative Assembly of Ontario from 1886 to 1894; and in 1896 he was elected to the Canadian House of Commons for West Toronto as an independent Conservative, pledged to support D'Alton McCarthy (q.v.), and to oppose separate schools in Manitoba. This constituency he represented in parliament until his death in Toronto on March 3, 1905. In 1884 he married Charlotte Elizabeth Scott, of Toronto; and by her he had two daughters.

[Morgan, *Can. men* (1898); Rose, *Cyc. Can. biog.* (1888); *Can. parl. comp.*]

Clarke, George Herbert (1873-1953), educationist and poet, was born at Gravesend, England, on August 27, 1873, and came to Canada at an early age. He was educated at McMaster University (B.A., 1895; M.A., 1896), and became a professor of English literature in several American universities, notably the University of Tennessee and the University of the South. He returned to Canada in 1925 as head of the department of English in Queen's University, Kingston, a post that he held until his retirement in 1943. He was chairman of the editorial board of *Queen's Quarterly* for many years until his death at Kingston on March 27, 1953. He received honorary doctorates from three Canadian universities, McMaster, Bishop's, and Queen's; and he was elected a fellow of the Royal Society of Canada in 1930. He published four volumes of poetry: *Wayfaring* (Chicago, 1901), *At the shrine and other poems* (Cincinnati, 1914), *The hasting day* (London, 1930), and *Halt and parley, and other poems* (Toronto, 1934); his *Selected poems* appeared after his death (Toronto, 1954); and he edited three anthologies of war poetry (Boston, 1917, 1919, and 1943).

[*Proc. Roy. Soc. Can.*, 1953; *Encyc. Can.*; *Can. who's who*, 1949-51.]

Clarke, George Johnson (1857-1917), prime minister of New Brunswick (1914-17), was born at St. Andrews, New Brunswick, the son of Nelson and Mary Clarke. He was educated at St. Andrews, New Brunswick, and Fredericton, was called to the bar, and became a K.C. in 1907. He entered the Legislative Assembly of New Brunswick in 1903, and was elected speaker of Assembly in 1909. In 1914 he became attorney-general in the Fleming administration, and at the end of the year he became prime minister. He resigned on February 1, 1917, and died on February 26 of that year.

[*Can. who's who* (1910); *Can. parl. comp.*]

Clarke, James Paton (1807?-1877), musician, was born about 1807, and graduated in music at King's College, Toronto (Mus. Bac., 1846; Mus. Doc., 1856). He died at Yorkville, near Toronto, on August 27, 1877. He published a *Canadian church psalmody* (Toronto, 1845).

[H. Kallmann, *A history of music in Canada* (Toronto, 1960); Morgan, *Bib. Can.*; *Dict. Can. Biog.*, vol. 10.]

Clarke, John (1781-1852), fur-trader, was born in Montreal, Canada, in 1781, the son of Simon Clarke and Ann Waldorf. He entered the service of the North West Company as a clerk in 1800 and served successively on the Mackenzie River and on the Peace River. In 1810 he left the North West Company, and joined the Pacific Fur Company of John Jacob Astor, who appears to have been a relative of his mother. In 1811 he commanded the second expedition to Fort Astoria, and he was present in 1812 when the fort was surrendered to the Nor'-Westers. On his return to Canada in 1814 he took service with Lord Selkirk; and during the years 1815 to 1819 he was the leader in the opposition which the Hudson's Bay Company offered the Nor'-Westers along the Peace River. At the time of the union of the two companies, in 1821, he was made a chief factor. He retired from the fur-trade in 1830; and he spent the rest of his days in Montreal. There he died in 1852. He was twice married, first, to a half-breed named Sapphira Spence, who died shortly afterwards; and second in 1821, to Marian Tranclar, of Neuchâtel, Switzerland, by whom he had four sons and four daughters.

[Adèle Clarke, *Old Montreal: John Clarke, his adventures, friends, and family* (Montreal, 1906); E. E. Rich (ed.), *Simpson's Athabasca journal* (Toronto: The Champlain Society, 1938).]

Clarke, Lionel Herbert (1859-1921), lieutenant-governor of Ontario (1919-21), was born in Guelph, Ontario, in 1859, the son of William Clarke, M.D. (T.C.D.), and Clara Pigott Strange, widow of William Dummer Powell. He was educated at Trinity College School, Port Hope, Ontario, and in Edinburgh, Scotland; and early in life he entered business in Palmerston, Wellington county, Ontario. Later he moved to Toronto. He devoted his energies chiefly to the grain trade; and he became president of the Canadian Malting Company, as well as a director of numerous other companies, and he was appointed later a member of the Board of Grain Supervisors. In 1908 he was elected president of the Toronto Board of Trade; and he became chairman of the Toronto Harbour Commission, as well as a member of the Niagara Falls Park Commission. In 1919 he was appointed lieutenant-governor of Ontario; but he died, after only a year and a half of office, at Toronto, on August 29, 1921. In 1891 he married Anne Clara Gertrude, daughter of Sydenham Small, of Toronto; and by her he had three sons and one daughter.

[Le Jeune, *Dict. gén.*; *Can. parl. comp.*]

Claus, Daniel (1727-1787), deputy superintendent of Indian affairs, was born in Germany in 1727, and emigrated to America in 1748. He became attached as an interpreter to the Indian Department under Sir William Johnson (q.v.), and in 1760 was appointed deputy superintendent of the Canadian Indians. He held this position throughout the American Revolution, and his property in New York was confiscated. On the declaration of peace he went to England to attempt to obtain compensation; and he died at Cardiff, Wales, in the latter part of 1787. In 1762 he married Ann (Nancy), daughter of Sir William Johnson,

Bart. (q.v.). She died at Niagara, Upper Canada, in 1801.

[L. Sabine, *The American loyalists* (Boston, 1847); W. L. Stone, *Life and times of Sir William Johnson* (2 vols., Albany, 1865); J. Carnochan, *History of Niagara* (Toronto, 1914).]

Claus, William (1763-1826), executive councillor of Upper Canada, was born in 1763, the son of Daniel Claus (q.v.). After the American Revolution, he settled in Upper Canada, and in 1799 he was appointed deputy superintendent of Indian affairs. From 1812 to 1825 he was a member of the Legislative Council of Upper Canada; and from 1818 to 1824 he was also a member of the Executive Council. He died on November 12, 1826.

[E. Cruikshank, *Reminiscences of Colonel Claus* (Canadiana, 1889).]

Claxton, Brooke (1898-1960), minister of national defence for Canada (1946-54), was born at Montreal, Que., on August 23, 1898; and died at Ottawa, Ontario, on June 13, 1960. He was educated at Lower Canada College and McGill University (B.C.L., 1921). During the First World War he served with the 10th Canadian Siege Battery, and won the D.C.M. He was called to the Quebec bar (K.C., 1939), practised law in Montreal, and from 1930 to 1944 was associate professor of commercial law at McGill. He was elected to represent St. Lawrence—St. George as a Liberal in the Canadian House of Commons in 1940, and held this seat until his resignation in 1954. In 1944 he was appointed minister of national health and welfare in the Mackenzie King government, and in 1946, minister of national defence. He retired from political life in 1954, to accept a position as vice-president of the Metropolitan Life Insurance Co.; and in 1957 he was appointed the first chairman of the Canada Council. He was the author of *Notes on military law and discipline for Canadian soldiers* (Montreal, 1939).

[*Can. who's who*, 1958-60; *Encyc. Can.*; *Can. parl. guide*, 1954.]

Claxton, Mrs. Lionel, *née* **Holland**. See **Holland, Norah Mary.**

Cleary, James Vincent (1828-1898), Roman Catholic archbishop of Kingston, was born in Dungarvan, Waterford, Ireland, on September 18, 1828. He studied theology at Rome, at the Royal College, Maynooth, Ireland, and at the University of Salamanca, and was ordained to the priesthood in 1851. In 1854 he became a professor of theology in St. John's College, Waterford (D.D., 1862); and from 1873 to 1876 he was its president. In 1880 he was appointed bishop of Kingston, in Canada; and he came to Canada in 1881. In 1889, Kingston having been made the metropolitan see of a new ecclesiastical province, he was

raised to the dignity of archbishop. In 1896 he was instrumental in re-opening Regiopolis College; and his episcopate was notable in other ways. He died on February 24, 1898.

[Morgan, *Can. men* (1898); Le Jeune, *Dict. gén.*]

Clemens, Wilbert Amie (1887-1964), biologist, was born at Millbank, Ontario, December 22, 1887. He was educated at the University of Toronto (B.A.,1912; M.A.,1913), and at Cornell University (Ph.D.,1915). He began his career at the University of Maine in 1915 as an instructor, moving to the University of Toronto in 1916, where he remained until 1924. He was director of the Pacific Biological Station at Nanaimo, British Columbia, from 1924 to 1940 when he became head of the department of zoology at the University of British Columbia. In 1920 he set up the Ontario Fisheries Research Laboratory on Lake Nipigon, where he undertook the first limnobiological studies in Canada. From 1924 to 1940 he built up a full-time staff at the British Columbia Marine Biology Station and was able to direct thorough studies of salmon, herring, pilchard, shellfish, as well as general oceanography. With G. V. Wilby he published the illustrated *Fishes of the Pacific Coast of Canada* in 1946. During his time as head of zoology in the University of British Columbia an Institute of Oceanography was established in 1949 and a beginning made on an Institute of Fisheries. He retired in 1953. He was president of the Pacific Division of the American Association for the Advancement of Science in 1961, and was a fellow of the Royal Society of Canada. He died at Vancouver on June 21, 1964.

[*Proc. Roy. Soc. Can.* (1965).]

Clement, William Henry Pope (1858-1922), judge and author, was born at Vienna, Upper Canada, on May 13, 1858, the son of Rev. Edwin Clement and Mary C. Pope. He was educated at the University of Toronto (B.A., 1878), and was called to the Ontario bar in 1880. From 1898 to 1900 he was legal adviser to, and a member of, the Yukon Council; and in 1905 he was appointed judge of Yale county, British Columbia. In 1906 he was appointed a judge of the Supreme Court of British Columbia; and this office he held until his death at Vancouver, British Columbia, on May 3, 1922. In 1899 he married Elsie L. Main, and by her he had one son and two daughters. He was the author of *The law of Canadian constitution* (Toronto, 1892; 3rd edition, 1916) and of a *History of Canada* (Toronto, 1897).

[*Who's who in Can.*]

Clemo, Ebenezer (1831?-1860), novelist, was born in London, England, about 1831. He came to Canada in 1858, and employed himself in writing, for a Canadian publisher, two novels, *The life and adventures of Simon Seek,* by "Maple Knot" (Montreal, 1858), and *Canadian homes; or, The mystery solved* (Montreal, 1858). He is said to have been the inventor also of making paper pulp from straw. He died at Morristown, New Jersey, in 1860.

[Morgan, *Bib. can.*; Rose, *Cyc. Can. biog.* (1888).]

Clouston, Sir Edward Seaborne, Bart. (1849-1912), banker, was the son of James Stewart Clouston, a chief factor of the Hudson's Bay Company, and Margaret, eldest daughter of Robert S. Miles, of the Hudson's Bay Company, and was born at Moose Factory, Hudson Bay, on May 9, 1849. He was educated at the Montreal High School, and after one year in the service of the Hudson's Bay Company, joined the staff of the Bank of Montreal as a clerk in 1865. In 1887 he was appointed assistant general manager of the bank, in 1890 general manager, and in 1906 first vice-president. In 1908 he was created a baronet. He died at Montreal on November 23, 1912. In 1878 he married Annie, youngest daughter of George Easton of Brockville, Ontario; by her he had one daughter.

[*Who was who*, 1897-1916; Morgan, *Can. men* (1912); *Can. who's who* (1910); *Can. mag.*, vol. 12.]

Cloutier, Albert (1902-1965), painter and art director, was born at Leominster, Massachusetts, June 12, 1902. He was educated in Montreal and began art classes at the Monument National at age eleven. He painted with A.Y. Jackson and Edwin Holgate although he was mainly self-taught. He worked as art director for Batten Limited of Montreal (1926-29); as a freelance artist (1930-40); as director of posters and publications of the Department of National War Services (1940-43); as an official Royal Canadian Air Force war artist (1944-46); and as consulting art director for Rapid Grip and Batten. He also taught at the École des Beaux Arts, Montreal. He was a member of the Canadian Society of Painters in Water Colour, the Canadian Society of Graphic Art, and the Royal Canadian Academy. His murals may be seen in the Queen Elizabeth Hotel and the Place Ville Marie, Montreal. He designed *Pathway to greatness* (Montreal, 1959), a book on the St. Lawrence Seaway. His paintings may be seen at the National Gallery of Canada. His early work was influenced by French Impressionism and the work of the Group of Seven; in later years he inclined to intensified realism. He died at St. Hilaire, June 9, 1965.

[C. S. MacDonald, *A dictionary of Canadian artists*, vol. 1 (Ottawa, 1967); *Can. who's who*, 1955-57.]

Coady, Moses Michael (1882-1959), priest and educationist, was born at North East Margaree, Nova Scotia, on January 3, 1882, and died at Antigonish, Nova Scotia, on July 28, 1959. He was educated at St. Francis Xavier University (B.A.,1905) and at Urban College in Rome (Ph.D., 1907; D.D.,1910). In 1910 he returned to Canada as an instructor in St. Francis Xavier University, and in 1928 he became the first director of the University's extension department. He launched a most successful programme of adult education among the fishermen of the Maritime Provinces, and helped to organize co-operatives and credit unions that greatly improved economic conditions among the fishermen. His own account of the Antigonish movement was published under the title *Masters of their own destiny* (New York, 1939), which ran into three editions, and was translated into French (Gardenvale, Que., 1948).

[M. Hoehn (ed.), *Catholic authors* (Newark, 1940); *Encyc. Can.*]

Coaker, Sir William Ford (1871-1938), union organizer, was born at St. John's, Newfoundland, in 1871, and died at Boston, Massachusetts, on October 29, 1938. He was educated at Bishop Field College. He became interested in the lot of the Newfoundland fishermen, and in 1908 he organized the first local of a co-operative that he named the Fishermen's Protective Union. The union grew rapidly, and he founded the community of Port Union as its headquarters in 1914. In 1912 he formed the Fishermen's Union Party, and he represented this party in the Assembly from 1913 to 1924. From 1919 to 1924 he was minister of marine and fisheries; in 1923 he was created a K.B.E. He was the author of *Twenty years of the Fishermen's Protective Union of Newfoundland from 1909-1929* (St. John's, 1930).

[J. R. Smallwood, *Coaker of Newfoundland* (London, 1927); *Who was who*, 1929-40; *Encyc. Can.*; *Newfoundland supp.*]

Coats, Robert Hamilton (1874-1960), statistician, was born at Clinton, Ontario, on July 25, 1874, and died at Ottawa, Ontario, on February 7, 1960. He was educated at the University of Toronto (B.A., 1896), and for some years was a journalist in Toronto. In 1902 he went to Ottawa as assistant editor of the *Labour Gazette*, published by the Department of Labour. He remained with this department until 1916, when he was transferred to the Department of Trade and Commerce, with the title of "Dominion Statistician". He organized the Dominion Bureau of Statistics in 1918, and continued as its head until his retirement in 1942. He was elected a fellow of the Royal Society of Canada in 1923; and he received the honorary degree of LL.D. from McGill University in 1934, from the University of Toronto in 1937, and from Dalhousie University in 1938. He was joint author, with R. E. Gosnell (q.v.) of *Sir James Douglas* (Toronto, 1908), and with R. M. McLean, of *The American born in Canada* (Toronto, 1943).

[*Proc. Roy. Soc. Can.,* 1960; *Can. who's who,* 1958-60; *Encyc. Can.*]

Coburn, Frederick Simpson (1871-1960), painter, was born in Upper Melbourne, Quebec, in 1871, and died there on May 26, 1960. He studied art in Montreal, New York, Munich, Paris, London, and Antwerp, returning to Canada about 1898 to illustrate books by Louis Fréchette and W. H. Drummond (qq.v.). He became noted especially for his oil paintings of Quebec landscapes. He is represented by three paintings in the National Gallery at Ottawa; he was elected an A.R.C.A. in 1920, and an R.C.A. in 1927.

[*Montreal Star,* May 27, 1960; *Can. who's who,* 1937-38; N. MacTavish, *The fine arts in Canada* (Toronto, 1926).]

Coburn, John (1874-1954), clergyman and author, was born at Neenah, Wisconsin, on April 19, 1874, and died at Toronto, Ontario, on May 21, 1954. He was educated at Victoria College, Toronto, and was ordained a minister of the Methodist Church in 1897. He served in many charges in Ontario; then in 1920 he became secretary of the Board of Evangelism and Social Services of the Methodist Church, and later, after Church union, of the United Church of Canada. He retired in 1945; and after retirement he published two books of reminiscences: *I kept my powder dry* (Toronto, 1950) and *Grace, grit, and gumption* (Toronto, 1952).

[Toronto *Globe and Mail,* May 22, 1954; *Can. who's who,* 1952-54.]

Cochran, Andrew William (1792-1849), civil secretary to the governor of Lower Canada, was born at Windsor, Nova Scotia, in 1792, the son of the Rev. William Cochran (q.v.). He was educated at King's College, Windsor, and studied law. In 1812, however, he became assistant civil secretary to the governor of Lower Canada, under the administration of Sir G. Prevost (q.v.); and under Sir John Sherbrooke (q.v.) and Lord Dalhousie (q.v.) he was civil secretary. From 1827 to 1841 he was a member of the Executive Council of Lower Canada; and he held various other offices under the Crown; but after 1841 he resumed the practice of law. He died at Quebec, of Asiatic cholera, on July 11, 1849. He was a D.C.L. of King's College, Windsor; and in 1837 he was president of the Quebec Literary and Historical Society. To the transactions of this society he contributed several papers.

[Morgan, *Cel. Can.* and *Bib. can.*]

Cochran, William (1745?-1833), vice-president of King's College, Windsor, Nova Scotia, was born in Ireland about 1745. He was educated at Trinity College, Dublin; and in 1784 he was appointed professor of Greek and Latin in Columbia College, New York. He came to Nova Scotia in 1789, and was appointed the first vice-president of King's College, Windsor. He died at Windsor, Nova Scotia, on August 4, 1833.

[Morgan, *Bib. can.*]

Cochrane, Charles Norris (1889-1945), classical scholar, was born at Omemee, Ontario, on August 21, 1889, and died at Toronto, Ontario, on November 23, 1945. He was educated at the University of Toronto (B.A., 1911) and at Corpus Christi College, Oxford. On his return from Oxford he joined the staff of the classical department in University College; in 1919 he was appointed assistant professor of Ancient History, and in 1929 professor. In his chosen field, he was the author of *Thucydides and the science of history* (London, 1929) and *Christianity and classical culture* (London, 1940; rev. ed., 1944). He was elected a fellow of the Royal Society of Canada in 1937.

[M. D. C. Tait, *Charles Norris Cochrane* (Phoenix, 1946); *Proc. Roy. Soc. Can.,* 1946; *Encyc. Can.*]

Cochrane, Francis (1852-1919), minister of railways and canals for Canada (1911-17), was born at Clarenceville, Lower Canada, on November 18, 1852, the son of Robert Cochrane and Mary Anne Hunter. He was educated at the Clarenceville Academy, and ultimately became a merchant at Sudbury, Ontario. In 1905 he was elected as a Conservative to the Legislative Assembly of Ontario for East Nipissing, and became minister of lands and mines in the Whitney administration. In 1911 he left provincial politics to become minister of railways and canals in the Dominion government of Sir Robert Borden. He resigned this portfolio in 1917, on the reconstruction of the government, but continued as a minister without portfolio in the Union government. He died at Ottawa on September 22, 1919. In 1882 he married Alice Levina Dunlap; and by her he had two sons and one daughter.

[*Can. parl. comp.;* Morgan, *Can. men* (1912); *Can. who's who* (1910); A. and S. Young, *Silent Frank Cochrane* (Toronto, 1973).]

Cochrane, Thomas (1777-1804), judge, was born in Halifax, Nova Scotia, in 1777, the son of the Hon. Thomas Cochrane, a member of the Council of that province. He was educated at King's College, Windsor, Nova Scotia, studied law in England, and in 1801 was called to the bar from Lincoln's Inn. The same year he was appointed chief justice of the Supreme Court of Prince Edward Island; and in 1803 he became a puisne judge of the Court of King's Bench in Upper Canada. He was drowned in the loss of the government schooner *Speedy* on Lake Ontario on October 7, 1804.

[D. B. Read, *Lives of the judges* (Toronto, 1888); A.B. Warburton, *A history of Prince Edward Island* (Saint John, N.B., 1923); Morgan, *Cel. Can.*]

Cochrane, Sir Thomas John (1789-1872), governor of Newfoundland (1825-34), was born on February 5, 1789, the eldest son of Admiral Sir Alexander Forrester Inglis Cochrane. He entered the British Navy at an early age, and rose rapidly, attaining the rank of captain in 1806. In 1825 he was appointed the first resident governor of Newfoundland, shortly after Newfoundland was granted colonial status. His period of office was marked by an agitation in the island for the granting of representative institutions, which he opposed; but when representative institutions were granted by the British government, he strove to make the new constitution work harmoniously, although not with complete success. He was recalled in 1834. He was created a K.C.B. in 1847 and a G.C.B. in 1860; and he was promoted to the rank of admiral in 1865. He died in 1872.

[*Dict. nat. biog.*; *Encyc. Can.*; *Newfoundland supp.*; *Dict. Can. biog.*, vol. 10.]

Cochrane, William (1831-1898), clergyman and author, was born at Paisley, Scotland, in 1831, and was educated at Glasgow University, at Hanover College, Indiana (M.A., 1857; D.D., 1875), and at the Princeton Theological Seminary. He came to Canada in 1862; and he was pastor of the Zion Presbyterian Church, Brantford, Ontario, until his death in 1898. He was the author of *The heavenly vision* (Toronto, 1874), *Christ and the Christian life* (Toronto, 1875), *The Church and the commonwealth* (Brantford, 1887), *Memoirs and remains of the Rev. Walter Inglis* (Toronto, 1887), *Future punishment* (Brantford, 1888), and he was the editor of *The Canadian album: Men of Canada* (5 vols., Brantford, 1891-96).

[R. W. Grant, *The life of the Rev. William Cochrane* (Toronto, 1899); Morgan, *Can. men* (1898).]

Cockburn, Alexander Peter (1837-1905), politician and author, was born in the township of Finch, Stormont, Upper Canada, on April 7, 1837, the son of Peter Cockburn and Mary McMillan. He was educated at the local schools, and went into business for himself in Victoria county. In 1865 he became interested in the settlement and development of the Muskoka district; and he organized the Muskoka Lakes Navigation and Hotel Company. From 1867 to 1872 he represented North Victoria in the Ontario legislature; and from 1872 to 1882 he represented Muskoka, and from 1882 to 1887 North Ontario, in the Canadian House of Commons, as a Liberal. He died in 1905. In addition to some immigration literature, he published an historical work entitled *Political annals of Canada* (Toronto, 1905).

[Morgan, *Can. men* (1898); *Can. parl. comp.*]

Cockburn, George Ralph Richardson (1834-1912), educationist and financier, was born at Edinburgh, Scotland, on February 15, 1834; and was educated at Edinburgh University (M.A., 1857). He came to Canada in 1857 as rector of the Model Grammar School at Toronto; and in 1861 he became principal of Upper Canada College. He held this position until 1881, when he resigned to enter politics and business. From 1887 to 1896 he represented Centre Toronto as a Conservative in the Canadian House of Commons; and from 1894 to 1906 he was president of the Ontario Bank. He died in London, England, on January 18, 1912. His son, Major Hampden Zane Churchill Cockburn (1867-1913), was awarded the Victoria Cross in the South African War.

[Morgan, *Can. men* (1912).]

Cockburn, James (1819-1883), one of the Fathers of Confederation, was born at Berwick-on-Tweed, England, on February 13, 1819, the son of James Cockburn and Sarah Turnbull. He came to Canada about 1832, and was educated at Upper Canada College, Toronto. In 1846 he was called to the bar of Upper Canada (Q.C., 1863), and practised law at Cobourg, Upper Canada. He represented the west riding of Northumberland in the Legislative Assembly of Canada from 1861 to 1867, and in the Canadian House of Commons from 1867 to 1874, and from 1878 to 1881. In 1864 he was appointed solicitor-general for Upper Canada in the second Taché-Macdonald administration; he held the same portfolio in the "Great Coalition"; and he was one of the delegates from Upper Canada at the Quebec Conference. In 1867 he was chosen first speaker of the Canadian House of Commons, and he continued to preside over the deliberations of the House, with only a short intermission, until 1874. His tact and courtesy did much to establish a high tradition in the speaker's office. He died at Ottawa on August 14, 1883.

[*Dom. ann. reg.*, 1883; Taylor, *Brit. Am.*, vol. 3; *Can. parl. comp.*; W. J. Rattray, *The Scot in British North America* (4 vols., Toronto, 1881); J. C. Dent, *The last forty years* (2 vols., Toronto, 1881).]

Cockin, Hereward Kirby (1854-1917), poet and journalist, was born at Frizinghall, Yorkshire, England, the younger son of the Rev. Joseph Cockin. He was educated at Oxford University, and came to Canada about 1877. He was for a time associate editor of the *Week* in Toronto; and later he joined the staff of the Guelph *Mercury*, to which he contributed a weekly column, under the pen-name of "The Blacksmith". He died at Guelph, Ontario, on June 22, 1917. He was the author of *The happy family; or, Deacon Brown's dream and the lord mayor of York and his brother Ned* (Toronto, n.d.) and *Gentleman Dick o' the Greys, and other poems* (Toronto, 1889).

[Morgan, *Can. men* (1912); C. C. James, *A bibliography of Canadian poetry* (Toronto, 1899).]

Cocking, Matthew (d. 1799), fur-trader, was engaged by the Hudson's Bay Company in 1765 as a "writer" at York Factory, and in 1770 was appointed second-in-command at York Factory. He was sent inland in 1772 and was one of the first of the Hudson's Bay Company's servants to come into touch with the "Canada pedlars". From 1774 to 1781 he was master at Severn House; and later he became master at York Factory. He died in 1799. An incomplete version of the journal of his expedition into the interior in 1772-73 has been published by L. J. Burpee, under the title *An adventurer from Hudson Bay* (Trans. Roy. Soc. Can., 1908).

[J. B. Tyrrell (ed.), *Journals of Samuel Hearne and Philip Turnor* (Toronto: The Champlain Society, 1934).]

Cockrel, Richard (1773?-1829), schoolteacher and journalist, was born in England about 1773, and came to Upper Canada by way of the United States. As early as 1796 he conducted a school at Newark (Niagara); and this school obtained a reputation second only to that of the Rev. John Strachan (q.v.) at Cornwall. In 1816 he founded the St. David's *Spectator,* the first newspaper published in the Niagara peninsula after the War of 1812; and in 1818 he founded in Dundas, Upper Canada, the *Upper Canada Phoenix,* the first newspaper published in the province west of York (Toronto). He died at Ancaster, Upper Canada, on July 7, 1829.

[W. S. Wallace, *The periodical literature of Upper Canada* (Can. hist. rev., 1931).]

Coderre, Louis (1865-1935), secretary of state for Canada (1912-15), was born at St. Ours, Quebec, on November 1, 1865. He was educated at Laval University (LL.B., 1892), and was called to the bar in 1892. In 1911 he was elected to represent Hochelaga in the Canadian House of Commons; and in 1912 he became secretary of state in the Borden government. He retired from office in 1915 to accept appointment as a judge of the Superior Court of Quebec. He died at Montreal on January 29, 1935.

[P. G. Roy, *Les juges de la province de Québec* (Quebec, 1933); *Can. parl. comp.*]

Cody, Henry John (1868-1951), clergyman and educationist, was born at Embro, Ontario, on December 6, 1868. He was educated at the Galt Collegiate Institute and the University of Toronto (B.A., 1889; M.A., 1890), and was ordained a priest of the Church of England in 1894. For nearly forty years he served in St. Paul's Church, Toronto, the last twenty-five as rector. He was appointed a canon of St. Alban's Cathedral in 1903, and was archdeacon of York, from 1909 to 1918; but he repeatedly declined episcopal or archiepiscopal preferment. He was elected a member of the Ontario legislature in 1918, and for one year was minister of education in the Hearst government. In 1917 he was appointed a member of the Board of Governors of the University of Toronto, and from 1925 to 1932 he was its chairman. He became president of the University in 1932, and continued as such until his election as chancellor in 1944. His period of office as chancellor was terminated in 1947, and he died at Toronto on April 27, 1951. He was elected an unattached fellow of the Royal Society of Canada in 1935; he was created a C.M.G. in 1943; and received honorary degrees from many universities.

[W.C. White, *Henry John Cody* (Toronto, 1953); *Proc. Roy. Soc. Can.,* 1951; *Can. who's who,* 1949-51; Toronto *Globe and Mail,* April 28, 1951.]

Cody, Hiram Alfred (1872-1948), clergyman and author, was born at Cody's, New Brunswick, on July 3, 1872; and he died at Saint John, New Brunswick, on February 9, 1948. He was educated at King's College, Windsor (B.A., 1897; M.A., 1908). He was ordained a priest of the Church of England and from 1905 to 1910 served as a missionary in the Yukon and Northwest Territories. While there he published a life of Bishop Bompas (q.v.), entitled *An apostle of the North* (London, 1908). He returned to New Brunswick in 1910, as rector of St. James Church in Saint John; and here he began the publication of a long series of novels, first dealing with life in the North, and later with life in the Loyalist settlements in New Brunswick. He was the author of the following novels (all published in Toronto): *The frontiersman* (1910), *The fourth watch* (1911), *The chief of the ranges* (1913), *If any man sin* (1915), *Rod of the long patrol* (1916), *Under sealed orders* (1917), *The unknown wrestler* (1918), *The touch of Abner* (1919), *Glen of the high north* (1920), *Jess of the rebel trail* (1921), *The king's arrow* (1921), *The trail of the Golden Horn* (1923), *The master revenge* (1924), *The fighting slogan* (1926), *Fighting stars* (1927), *The stumbling shepherd* (1929), *The river fury* (1930), *The red ranger* (1931), *The girl at Bullet Lake* (1933), *The crimson sign* (1935), and *Storm king banner* (1937). He also wrote a volume of verse, *Songs of a bluenose* (1925).

[Clara Thomas, *Canadian novelists* (Toronto, 1946); *Can. who's who,* 1948; *Encyc. Can.*]

Coffin, John (1756-1838), loyalist, was born in Boston, Massachusetts, in 1756. He fought on the loyalist side throughout the American Revolution; and at the close of the war he settled in New Brunswick, at "Alwyngton Manor" on the Nerepis River. For many years he represented King's county in the Legislative Assembly of New Brunswick, and he became a member of the Executive Council of the province. In 1819 he attained the rank of general in the British army. He died at Alwyngton Manor on May 12, 1838.

[Capt. H. Coffin, *A memoir of General Coffin* (Reading, Eng. 1874); L. Sabine, *The American loyalists* (Boston, 1847); *Dict. Am. biog.*; *Cyc. Am. biog.*; W. O. Raymond (ed.), *The Winslow papers* (Saint John, N.B., 1901); P. G. Roy, *La famille Coffin* (Bull. rech. hist., 1934).]

Coffin, Thomas (1817-1890), receiver-general of Canada (1873-78) was born at Barrington, Nova Scotia, in 1817, the son of Thomas Coffin and Margaret Horner. He was educated at Barrington, Nova Scotia, and became a merchant and shipbuilder. He represented Shelburne in the Legislative Assembly of Nova Scotia from 1851 to 1855, and again from 1859 to 1867. From 1867 to 1878 he represented Shelburne in the Canadian House of Commons; and from 1873 to 1878 he was receiver-general in the Mackenzie administration. On his defeat in the general election of 1878, he retired from public life; and he died at Barrington on July 12, 1890. He was twice married (1) in 1841 to Sarah Doane (d.1860), and (2) in 1871 to Adeline Coffin. By his first wife he had five sons and three daughters; and by his second wife four sons and three daughters.

[Burke's *Colonial gentry* (2 vols., London, 1891); *Can. parl. comp.*]

Coffin, Thomas Aston (1754-1810), loyalist, was born in Boston, Massachusetts, on March 31, 1754, and was educated at Harvard University (B.A., 1772). At the end of the American Revolution he was private secretary to Sir Guy Carleton (q.v.); and during the latter's second governorship of Canada, from 1786 to 1794, he was civil secretary and comptroller of accounts in Lower Canada. He died in London on May 31, 1810.

[*Cyc. Am. biog.*; W. O. Raymond (ed.), *The Winslow papers* (Saint John, N.B., 1901).]

Coffin, William Foster (1808-1878), civil servant and author, was born at Bath, England, on November 5, 1808, the son of a British army officer. He was educated at Eton, and came to Canada in 1830. In 1835 he was called to the bar of Lower Canada, and in 1838 he became assistant civil secretary of Lower Canada. From 1842 to 1851 he was joint sheriff of the district of Montreal; and in 1856 he was appointed commissioner of ordnance lands in Canada. This post he held until shortly before his death at Ottawa on January 28, 1878. In 1855 he raised the Montreal Field Battery, and became its commanding officer, with the rank of lieutenant-colonel in the militia. He was the author of *Three chapters on a triple project* (Montreal, 1848), *1812: The war and its moral* (Montreal, 1864), *Thoughts on defence from a Canadian point of view* (Ottawa, 1870), and *Quirks of diplomacy* (Ottawa, 1874). Some of his papers are included in the *Transactions*

of the Literary and Historical Society of Quebec.

[*Dom. ann. reg.*, 1878; Le Jeune, *Dict. gén.*; A MacMurchy, *Handbook of Canadian literature* (Toronto, 1906); *Dict. Can. biog.*, vol. 10.]

Cohen, Nathan (1923-1971), critic, was born in Sydney, Nova Scotia, April 16, 1923. He was educated at Mount Allison University (B.A.), and at Osgoode Hall Law School in Toronto. For a time he was the one-man staff of *The Gazette*, Glace Bay, Nova Scotia. In 1945 he came to Toronto and began contributing articles and reviews to newspapers there. From 1948 to 1958 he was drama critic for the Canadian Broadcasting Corporation and broadcast on radio and television. He had a weekly theatre column for the Toronto *Telegram* (1957-58) and was story editor for C.B.C. television (1956-58). He joined the Toronto *Star* in 1959 as entertainment editor and was well known as chairman of the television program "Fighting Words". He was a demanding critic, kind to newcomers but merciless in his assessment of mature professionals. He wrote a number of articles in *The Tamarack Review*, *Queen's Quarterly*, *The Dancing Times*, and *Ballet*, and was editor of *The Critic* from 1950 to 1953. He died March 26, 1971, at Toronto.

[*Can. who's who*, 1967-69.]

Colborne, Sir John, first Baron Seaton (1778-1863), lieutenant-governor of Upper Canada (1829-1836), was born at Lyndhurst, Hants, England, on February 16, 1778, the only son of Samuel Colborne. He entered the British army as an ensign in the 20th Regiment in 1794; and fought throughout the Revolutionary and Napoleonic wars. At the battle of Waterloo, where he commanded the 52nd Regiment, he was chiefly responsible for the defeat and rout of Napoleon's Old Guard. In 1825 he was appointed lieutenant-governor of Guernsey, and in 1829 lieutenant-governor of Upper Canada. He administered the affairs of Upper Canada with much prudence under several colonial secretaries until 1836, when he was allowed to retire. In 1835, however, he had been appointed commander-in-chief of the forces in Canada; and it fell to him, therefore, to deal with the rebellions of 1837 and 1838. Both before and after Lord Durham's period of office, he was administrator of the government; and in 1839 he was appointed governor-in-chief of British North America. At the end of the year, however, he gave place to Poulett Thomson (q.v.), and was raised to the peerage as Baron Seaton of Seaton. From 1843 to 1849 he was lord high commissioner of the Ionian Islands; and from 1855 to 1860 he was commander-in-chief of the forces in Ireland, with the rank of general. In 1860, on his retirement, he was promoted to be a field-marshal; and he died at Torquay, England, on April 17, 1863. In 1813 he married Elizabeth, daughter of the Rev. J. Yonge, rector of Newton Ferrers, Devonshire; and by. her he had several children, including two sons who rose to the rank of general. In 1814 he was created a K.C.B., in 1838 a G.C.B., and in 1843 a G.C.M.G.

[Rev. Wm. Leeke, *The history of Lord Seaton's regiment* (2 vols., London, 1866; suppl., London, 1871); *Dict. nat. biog.*; *Cyc. Am. biog.*; Morgan, *Cel. Can.*; D. B. Read, *The lieutenant-governors of Upper Canada* (Toronto, 1900); J. C. Dent, *The Upper Canadian rebellion* (2 vols., Toronto, 1885); W. S. Wallace, *The Family Compact* (Toronto, 1915).]

Colby, Charles Carroll (1827-1907), president of the Privy Council for Canada (1889-91), was born at Derby, Vermont, on December 10, 1827, the son of Moses French Colby, M.D., and came with his parents to Stanstead, Lower Canada, in 1832. He was educated at Dartmouth College, New Hampshire (B.A., 1847), and was called to the bar of Lower Canada in 1855. He began the practice of law at Stanstead; and in 1867 he was elected by Stanstead as a Liberal-Conservative in the Canadian House of Commons. This constituency he represented continuously until 1891. From 1887 to 1889 he was deputy speaker of the House, and from 1889 to 1891 he was president of the Privy Council. He then retired from public life; and he died at Stanstead, Quebec, on January 10, 1907. In 1858 he married Harriet Child, of Waybridge, Vermont; and by her he had two sons and two daughters. He was the author of a small book entitled *Parliamentary government in Canada* (Montreal, 1886).

[*Can. parl. comp.*; Morgan, *Can. men* (1898); Rose, *Cyc. Can. biog.* (1886); Garland, *Parliamentary directory* (1885).]

Colby, Charles William (1867-1955), historian, was born at Stanstead, Quebec, on March 28, 1867, the son of the Hon. C. C. Colby (q.v.); and he died at Montreal, Quebec, on December 10, 1955. He was educated at McGill University (B.A., 1887) and at Harvard (M.A., 1889; Ph.D., 1890); and he joined the staff of McGill University in 1893 as a lecturer in English language and history. In 1895 he was appointed Kingsford professor of history, and he held this chair until 1910 when he resigned to pursue a business career. He was elected a fellow of the Royal Society of Canada in 1909. He was the author of *Canadian types of the old régime* (New York, 1908) and *The founder of New France* (Toronto, 1915); and he edited *Selections from the sources of English history* (London, 1899).

[*Proc. Roy. Soc. Can.*, 1956; *Can. who's who*, 1952-54.]

Coldwell, Albert Edward (1841-1916), educationist, was born at Gaspereau, Nova Scotia, on September 18, 1841, and was educated at Horton Academy and Acadia University (B.A., 1869; M.A., 1872). He was instructor in mathematics at Horton Academy from 1871 to 1882, and professor of natural science at Acadia University from 1882 to 1898. He died at Wolfville, Nova Scotia, on November 30, 1916. He was the author of *Memorials of Acadia College and Horton Academy* (Montreal, 1881).

[Morgan, *Can. men* (1912).]

Coldwell, Major James William (1888-1974), political leader, was born in Seaton, Devon, England, December 2, 1888. He was educated at Exeter University College and emigrated to Canada in 1910 where he taught in the Dowling school district of Alberta. He later became principal of various Regina schools (1914-34). He was an alderman of the city of Regina and unsuccessfully contested the Regina seat for the Progressive party in the 1925 general elections. As provincial leader of the Farmer-labour party of Saskatchewan (1932-35) he helped launch the Co-operative Commonwealth Federation at Calgary in 1932 and attended the National C.C.F. Convention in Regina in 1934. He contested a seat in the provincial legislature unsuccessfully in 1934 but was successful in the 1935 federal election when he became the member for Rosetown-Biggar, a seat which he held until his retirement in 1958. He was parliamentary leader of the party from 1940 to 1958 and national president from 1942 to 1960. Coldwell gained valuable experience as president of the Saskatchewan Teachers' Alliance (1924-25) and as president and then secretary-treasurer of the Canadian Teachers' Federation (1926-34). He was a believer in co-operative socialism and was the author of *Left turn, Canada* (1945), which is in part autobiographical. He also wrote a number of pamphlets and magazine articles. He represented Canada at many international meetings such as the San Francisco Conference of 1945, the General Assembly of the United Nations in 1946, 1950, 1952, and 1953. He was chairman of the United Nations Commission to evaluate community development in India (1958-59). He was created a Companion of the Order of Canada (1967). He died at Ottawa, Ontario, August 25, 1974.

[*Can. who's who*, 1970-72; *Encyc. Can.* (1972).]

Coldwell, William (1834-1907), journalist, was born in London, England, in 1834, and was educated in Dublin, Ireland. He came to Toronto, Canada, in 1854, and joined the staff of the Toronto *Leader*. In 1859 he went to Winnipeg, and with William Buckingham (q.v.) established the *Nor'Wester*, the first newspaper in the Canadian Northwest. Most of the rest of his life was spent as a journalist in the

Northwest; and he died at Victoria, British Columbia, on February 18, 1907.

[J. P. Robertson, *A political manual of the province of Manitoba* (Winnipeg, 1887).]

Colebrooke, Sir William MacBean George (1787-1870), lieutenant-governor of New Brunswick (1841-48), was born in 1787, the son of Colonel Paulet Colebrooke, R.A. He was educated at Woolwich, and obtained a commission in the Royal Artillery in 1803. He saw service successively in the East Indies, in India, in Java, in Sumatra, and in Bengal, and he accompanied the expedition to the Persian Gulf in 1818. In 1834 he was appointed lieutenant-governor of the Bahamas, and in 1837 governor of the Leeward Islands and Antigua. In 1841, he became lieutenant-governor of New Brunswick, and his tenure of office, which was uneventful, lasted for seven years. From 1848 to 1856 he was governor of Barbados. He died at Salt Hill, Buckinghamshire, on February 6, 1870. He was created a K.H. in 1834, a K.B. in 1837, and he received the C.B. (civil) in 1848. In 1820 he married Emma Sophia (d. 1851), daughter of Lieutenant-Colonel Robert Colebrooke, surveyor-general of Bengal.

[*Dict. nat. biog.*, supp. II; James Hannay, *History of New Brunswick* (Saint John, N.B., 1909).]

Coleman, Arthur Philemon (1852-1939), geologist, was born at Lachute, Canada East, on April 4, 1852, the son of the Rev. Francis Coleman and Emmeline Adams. He was educated at Victoria University, Cobourg, Ont. (B.A., 1876; M.A., 1880), and at Breslau University, Germany (Ph.D., 1881). From 1882 to 1891, he was professor of geology and natural history at Victoria University; from 1891 to 1901, professor of geology at the School of Practical Science, Toronto; from 1901 to 1922, professor of geology in the University of Toronto; and, from 1919 to 1922, dean of the faculty of arts in the University of Toronto. He was elected a fellow of the Royal Society of Canada in 1900, was elected its president in 1921, and was awarded its Flavelle medal in 1928. He was elected a fellow of the Royal Society of London in 1910; and in 1915 he was honoured with the presidency of the Geological Society of America. He received the degree of LL.D from Queen's University in 1913, and from the University of Western Ontario in 1922, as well as the degree of D.Sc. from the University of Toronto in 1922. He died, unmarried, at Toronto on February 26, 1939. He was the author of *The Canadian Rockies* (London, 1911) and *Ice ages, recent and modern* (Toronto, 1926); and he was joint author, with W. A. Parks (q.v.), of *Elementary geology* (1922).

[*Proc. Roy. Soc. Can.*, 1939; *Can. who's who*, 1936-37.]

Coleman, Ephraim Herbert (1890-1961), diplomat, was born in Renfrew county, Ontario, July 21, 1890. He was educated at the University of Manitoba (LL.B., 1922) and called to the bar of Manitoba the same year. He practised law in Winnipeg and was secretary-treasurer of the Canadian Bar Association (1919-33) and dean of the Manitoba Law School from 1929 to 1933. From 1933 to 1949 he was under-secretary of state and registrar-general of Canada. He was appointed minister to Cuba in 1949, and became ambassador in 1950. From 1951 to 1953 he was ambassador to Brazil. He retired to private practice in Ottawa in 1954. During the First World War he was an N.C.O. in the Canadian Expeditionary Force to Siberia. During the Second World War he was chief of the Voluntary Service Registration Bureau and was responsible for dealing with the internment of enemy aliens, with the custody of enemy property, and with press censorship. He died at Ottawa, Ontario, December 4, 1961.

[*Can. who's who*, 1949-51; Metropolitan Toronto Library Board, *Biographical scrapbooks*, vol. 18.]

Coleman, Mrs. Kathleen Blake, *née* **Watkins** (1864-1915), journalist, was born at Castle Blakeney, Ireland, in 1864. She came to Canada in 1884, and from 1890 to 1911 she conducted a woman's page, under the pseudonym of "Kit", in the Toronto *Mail and Empire*. In 1898 she married Dr. Theodore Coleman. She died at Hamilton, Ontario, on May 16, 1915. Besides occasional contributions to the magazines, she was the author of *To London for the Jubilee* (Toronto, 1897).

[Morgan, *Can. men and women* (1912).]

Coles, George (1810-1875), one of the Fathers of Confederation, was born in Prince Edward Island on September 20, 1810, the eldest son of James Coles. He established a brewery and distillery; and in 1842 he was elected to represent the first district of Queen's in the House of Assembly. He was an outstanding advocate of responsible government; and in 1864 he was a delegate of Prince Edward Island at both the Charlottetown and Quebec Conferences in regard to Confederation. In 1867 his health broke down, and he retired from public life in 1868. He died at Charlottetown, Prince Edward Island, on August 21, 1875. In 1833 he married, in England, Mercy Haine, of East Penard, Somersetshire.

[D. Campbell, *History of Prince Edward Island* (Charlottetown, P.E.I., 1875); *Dict. Can. biog.*, vol. 10.]

Collette, Jacques Philippe Emile (1898-1963), manufacturer, was born in Montreal, December 5, 1898. He worked with J. O. Bourcier Limited, of Montreal before joining Associated Textiles of Canada as sales manager in 1929. He became president of the company in

1945. He was president of Canadian Javelin Limited. He worked with Boys' Town in Montreal. He was a member of the Unemployment Insurance Commission, of the National Selective Service during the Second World War, and of the R.C.A.F. benevolent fund committee, and was an executive member of the Canadian Manufacturers' Association. He died at Montreal, September 15, 1963.

[*Can. who's who*, 1955-57.]

Collier, Eric (1903-1966), writer, frontiersman, was born in Northampton, England, in 1903 and was educated at Dauntsey Agricultural College in Wiltshire. He spent a year as a law student and at the age of seventeen went to Canada to a cousin's ranch at Clinton, British Columbia. He then went on to Riske Creek, and while working there at the trading post he met and married Lillian, whose grandmother was an Indian. In 1931 he and his wife and son went to Meldrum Creek, where they built a cabin and began a wilderness life of hunting and trapping. His book *Three against the wilderness* (Toronto, 1959), which was translated into French as *La rivière des castors* (Montreal, 1961), describes how they restored the parched area by repairing old beaver dams and how the beaver, when reintroduced after being extinct in the area, multiplied, and the other animals and the forest came back to life. Collier also wrote a number of articles all dealing with conservation and natural phenomena for *Outdoor Life*. He died at Williams Lake, British Columbia, in March, 1966.

[N. Story, *The Oxford companion to Canadian history and literature* (Toronto, 1967); V. B. Rhodenizer, *Canadian Literature in English* (Montreal, 1965); *The Beaver* (Spring, 1960).]

Collins, Enos (1774-1871), merchant and banker, was born at Liverpool, Nova Scotia, on September 5, 1774, the eldest son of Hallet Collins and Rhoda Peek. He began his business career as the first lieutenant of a Nova Scotian privateer during the Napoleonic War; and partly from the booty of privateering during this war and the War of 1812 he amassed a large fortune. In 1822 he was appointed to the "Council of Twelve" in Nova Scotia; and in 1825 he was the chief promoter of the Halifax Banking Company, which was for many years regarded as a synonym for the executive government of the province. In 1840 he was retired from the Council by Lord Falkland, and in 1859 he withdrew from active business. He married in 1825 Margaret, the daughter of Sir Brenton Halliburton (q.v.); and he died in Halifax on November 18, 1871. At the time of his death, he was reputed to be the wealthiest man in British North America, his fortune being estimated at between six and nine million dollars.

[V. Ross, *The history of the Canadian Bank of Commerce*, vol. 1 (Toronto, 1920); P. Lynch, *Early reminiscences of Halifax* (Coll. Nova Scotia Hist. Soc., vol. xvi); *Dict. Can. biog.*, vol. 10.]

Collins, Francis (1801-1834), journalist, was born in Ireland in 1801, and came to Canada about 1820. He obtained employment as a printer on the staff of the *Upper Canada Gazette* in York (Toronto), and for a time reported the debates of the Legislative Assembly of Upper Canada. In 1825 he established the *Canadian Freeman*, a paper violently opposed to the "Family Compact"; and in 1826 he published a very early Upper Canadian political pamphlet, *An abridged view of the alien question unmasked* (York, U.C.). He ran foul of the government, and in 1828 he was found guilty of libel and subjected to fine and imprisonment. He died of cholera in Toronto in 1834. One of his daughters, Mother St. Maurice, of the Congregation of Notre Dame, died in Montreal in 1911.

[Brother Alfred, *Francis Collins* (Can. Cath. Hist. Ass., report, 1938-39); Morgan, *Bib. can.*; W. S. Wallace, *The periodical literature of Upper Canada* (Can. hist. rev., 1931).]

Collins, John (d. 1795), surveyor, came to Canada with the British army under Wolfe (q.v.) in 1759, and in 1760 was a merchant at Quebec. In 1764 he was appointed deputy surveyor-general under Samuel Holland (q.v.), and he was for many years engaged in surveying various parts of the old province of Quebec. In 1783 he was employed also in laying out the townships on the north shore of the St. Lawrence and about the Bay of Quinte in anticipation of the settlement of the Loyalists. In 1775 he was appointed a member of the Legislative Council of Quebec, and in 1792 of the Legislative Council of Lower Canada. He died at Quebec on April 15, 1795.

[J. Desjardins, *Guide parlementaire historique de la province de Québec* (Quebec, 1902).]

Collins, Joseph Edmund (1855-1892), journalist and author, was born at Placentia, Newfoundland, on October 22, 1855. He came to Canada in 1875, and engaged in journalism as the editor of newspapers in Fredericton and Chatham, New Brunswick, and later as city editor of the *Globe* in Toronto. He published several works of fiction, *The story of a Greenland girl* (Toronto, 1884), *Annette, the Métis spy* (Toronto, 1886), and *The four Canadian highwaymen* (Toronto, 1886). Better known are his historical effusions, *The life and times of the Rt. Hon. Sir John A. Macdonald* (Toronto, 1883), *Canada under the administration of Lord Lorne* (Toronto, 1884), and *The story of Louis Riel* (Toronto, 1885). He died in New York in 1892.

[W. G. MacFarlane, *New Brunswick bibliography* (Saint John, N.B., 1895); *Dom. ann. reg.*, 1885; Rose, *Cyc. Can. biog.* (1886); L. E. Horning and L. J. Burpee, *A bibliography of Canadian fiction* (Toronto, 1904).]

Collip, James Bertram (1892-1965), endocrinologist, professor of medicine, was born in Belleville, Ontario, November 20, 1892. He entered Trinity College, University of Toronto, at the age of fifteen, receiving his B.A. in 1912, M.A., in 1913, and Ph.D. in biochemistry in 1916. On graduation he became lecturer in biochemistry at the University of Alberta. He returned to Toronto on a travelling fellowship in 1921 and worked with Banting, Best, and Professor J. J. R. Macleod on the purification of insulin. He remained in Toronto for a year and then returned to Edmonton as professor of biochemistry. His interest in endocrinology led him to enrol as a part-time medical student and he graduated in 1926. Two years later he accepted the chair of biochemistry at McGill, where he worked with David Thompson and Hans Selye in intensive research in his chosen field including preliminary clinical studies on ACTH. In 1941, as director of the new Institute of Endocrinology at McGill University, Collip became involved in extensive war-related research projects and gradually became concerned in the organization and fund-raising necessary to carry on advanced medical research. One of his satisfactions was to see the division of medical research of the National Research Council become an independent Medical Research Council. He joined the University of Western Ontario in 1947 as director of research and dean of medicine, a position he held until retirement in 1961. He was a member of the Royal Society of Canada and winner of the Flavelle Gold Medal for natural science in recognition of his work in insulin, the parathyroid hormones, and placental hormones, as well as awards and degrees from a number of universities. He died at London, Ontario, June 19, 1965.

[*Can. who's who*, 1961-63; *Proc. Roy. Soc. Can.* (1968).]

Collison, William Henry (1847-1922), clergyman and author, was born in Ireland in 1847, and was educated at the Church Missionary College, Islington, England. He was ordained a priest of the Church of England in 1878, and became a missionary among the Indians of northern British Columbia. Here he spent the rest of his life, and he published a valuable account of his work under the title *In the wake of the war canoe* (Toronto, 1916). He died in 1922.

[Morgan, *Can. men* (1912).]

Colquhoun, Arthur Hugh Urquhart (1861-1936), journalist, civil servant, and author, was born at Montreal, Canada East, in 1861, and died at Toronto, Ontario, on February 9, 1936. He was educated at McGill University (B.A., 1885), and for twenty years was a journalist in Montreal, Ottawa, and Toronto. In 1906 Sir James Whitney (q.v.) appointed him deputy minister of education for Ontario, and he held this post under various changes of government until his retirement in 1934. He was the author of *The Hon. James R. Gowan: A memoir* (Toronto, 1894), *The fathers of Confederation* (Toronto, 1915), and *Press, politics and people: The life and letters of Sir John Willison* (Toronto, 1935); and he was the editor of *A history of Canadian journalism* (Toronto, 1908). In 1906 the University of Toronto conferred on him the degree of LL.D.

[W. S. Wallace, *Arthur Hugh Urquhart Colquhoun* (Can. hist. rev., 1936); H. Charlesworth (ed.), *A cyclopaedia of Canadian biography* (Toronto, 1919); Morgan, *Can. men* (1912); Toronto *Globe and Mail*, Feb. 10, 1936.]

Coltman, William Bacheler (d. 1826), executive councillor, was a merchant of Quebec who was appointed in 1812 a member of the Executive Council of Lower Canada. In 1816 he was made by Sir John Coape Sherbrooke (q.v.) a commissioner to investigate the disturbances in the Indian countries; and in 1817 he visited the Red River Settlement. His report was printed in a blue-book entitled *Papers relating to the Red River Settlement* (London, 1819), and has been reprinted in the *Collections of the State Historical Society of North Dakota*, vol. iv (Fargo, N.D., 1913). He died on January 2, 1826.

[E. E. Rich (ed.), *Journal of occurrences in the Athabasca department, by George Simpson* (Toronto: The Champlain Society, 1938).]

Colvile, Eden (1819-1893), governor of Rupert's Land (1850-51), was born in 1819, the son of Andrew Colvile, founder of the Royal Mail Steamship line. He was educated at Eton and at Trinity College, Cambridge; and in 1844 he was sent to Canada by the London Land Company to take charge of the seigniory of Beauharnois. He represented Beauharnois in the Legislative Assembly from 1844 to 1847. In 1850 he was appointed governor of Rupert's Land by the Hudson's Bay Company; but he returned to England in 1851. In 1872 he became deputy governor of the Hudson's Bay Company, and from 1880 to 1889 its governor. He died in Devonshire, England, on April 2, 1893. In 1845 he married, at Montreal, Anna, daughter of Lieut.-Colonel John Maxwell.

[*Annual register,* 1893.]

Conant, Gordon Daniel (1885-1953), prime minister of Ontario (1942-43), was born in Oshawa, Ontario, on January 11, 1885. He was educated at the University of Toronto (B.A., 1908; LL.B., 1912), and was called to the bar in 1912 (K.C., 1933). He practised law in Oshawa, and in 1916 was elected mayor of Oshawa. He was elected to represent the Ontario riding as a Liberal in the Ontario legislature in 1937, and was appointed attorney-general in the Hepburn administration. On Hepburn's resignation in October, 1942, Conant succeeded him for a few months as prime minister; but in May, 1943, he retired from politics, and accepted appointment as master of the Supreme Court of Ontario. He died at Oshawa on January 2, 1953.

[*Can. who's who*, 1949-51; *Can. parl. guide*, 1943; *Encyc. Can.*; Toronto *Globe and Mail*, Jan. 6, 1953.]

Conant, Thomas (1842-1905), author, was born at Oshawa, Canada West, on April 15, 1842, the son of Daniel Conant and Mary Shipman. He was educated at the Eddytown Seminary, near Geneva, New York; and then returned to Oshawa to administer his father's property. He contributed frequently to the Toronto *Globe*; and he published *Upper Canada sketches* (Toronto, 1898), and *Life in Canada* (Toronto, 1903). He died at Oshawa, Ontario, on March 14, 1905.

[Morgan, *Can. men* (1898); *Can. who was who*, vol. 1.]

Congdon, Frederick Tennyson (1858-1932), commissioner of the Yukon Territory (1903-04), was born at Annapolis Royal, Nova Scotia, on November 16, 1858. He was educated at Yarmouth High School and at the University of Toronto (B.A., 1879; LL.B., 1883), and was called to the bar in 1883 (K.C., 1903). He practised law in Halifax for many years; but in 1901 he was appointed legal adviser to the government of the Yukon Territory, and from 1903 to 1904 he was commissioner of the Yukon. From 1909 to 1911 he represented the Yukon in the Canadian House of Commons. He died at Ottawa on March 13, 1932. He was the author of *Congdon's digest of Nova Scotia reports* (Halifax, 1891).

[*Can. parl. comp.*; Morgan, *Can. men* (1912).]

Connaught and Strathearn, H.R.H. Arthur William Patrick Albert, first Duke of (1850-1942), governor-general of Canada (1911-16), was born at Buckingham Palace, London, England, on May 1, 1850, the third son of H.M. Queen Victoria and H.R.H. Albert, Prince Consort. He was educated at the Royal Military Academy, Woolwich, England; and entered the British army as a subaltern in 1868. He saw service in Canada during the Red River Rebellion and Fenian raid of 1870; and he had a distinguished career as a soldier, rising to the rank of field-marshal in 1902. In 1911 he was appointed governor-general of Canada; and in this position his military knowledge and experience was of inestimable value during the early stages of the First World War. He retired from office as governor-general of Canada in 1916; and during his later years he took little more part in public life than was demanded of a distinguished member of the Royal Family. He died at Bagshott Park, Surrey, England, on January 16, 1942. In 1879 he married Princess Louise Margaret Alexandra Victoria Agnes (d. 1917), daughter of Prince Frederick Charles of Prussia; and by her he had one son, Prince Arthur of Connaught, and two daughters, the Crown Princess of Sweden, and Princess Patricia, who, on her marriage with Captain the Hon. A. R. M. Ramsay in 1919, assumed the style of Lady Patricia Ramsay. After Princess Patricia was named a famous Canadian regiment, the Princess Patricia's Canadian Light Infantry. The Duke of Connaught was a K.G., a K.P., a G.M.B., a G.C.S.J., a G.C.M.G., a G.C.I.E., and a G.C.V.O.; and he received honorary degrees from Oxford University, Cambridge University, the University of Cape Town, McGill University, and the University of Toronto.

[*Who's who*, 1940; *Can. who's who*, 1936-37; *Americana Annual*, 1943; Le Jeune, *Dict. gén.*; Sir George Aston, *His Royal Highness The Duke of Connaught and Strathearn* (London, 1929).]

Connolly, Thomas Louis (1814-1876), Roman Catholic archbishop of Halifax (1859-76) was born in county Cork, Ireland, in 1814. He was educated at Rome, joined the Capuchin order, and was ordained a priest at Lyons, France. After serving for several years in Ireland, he came to Nova Scotia in 1842, as secretary to Archbishop Walsh (q.v.), and in 1845 he became vicar-general of the diocese of Halifax. In 1852 he became bishop of Saint John, New Brunswick; and in 1858 he succeeded to the archbishopric of Halifax. His chief work was in charitable and educational lines; but his influence was thrown also against the Fenian movement. He died at Halifax, Nova Scotia, on July 27, 1876.

[*Can. who was who*, vol. 2; Dent, *Can. port.*, vol. 2; Le Jeune, *Dict. gén.*; N. F. Davin, *The Irishman in Canada* (Toronto, 1877); *Dict. Can. biog.*, vol. 10.]

Connor, George Skeffington (1810-1863), jurist, was born in Dublin, Ireland, in 1810, the son of a Dublin lawyer. He was educated at Trinity College, Dublin, and was called to the Irish bar. In 1832, however, he emigrated to Canada, and settled in the township of Oro in Upper Canada. In 1842 he was called to the bar of Upper Canada, and engaged in the practice of law in Toronto. In 1858 he was elected to the Legislative Assembly of Canada, and he became solicitor-general west in the short-lived Brown-Dorion administration of that year. He retired from parliament in 1862, and early in 1863 he was appointed a judge of the Court of Queen's Bench in Upper Canada.

After only a few months on the bench, he died in Toronto on April 29, 1863.

[D. B. Read, *The lives of the judges of Upper Canada* (Toronto, 1888).]

Connor, Ralph (pseud.). **See Gordon, Charles William.**

Conolly, William (1787?-1849), fur-trader, was born at Lachine, near Montreal, about 1787, and entered the service of the North West Company as a clerk about 1801. He was made a partner of the North West Company about 1818; and in 1819 he was in charge of Cumberland House, where he received Franklin (q.v.) on his first expedition to the Arctic. At the union of the North West and Hudson's Bay companies in 1821, he was made a chief trader; and in 1825 he was promoted to the rank of chief factor. From 1824 to 1831 he was in charge of the district of New Caledonia, and in 1831 he retired from the fur-trade. He died at Montreal on June 3, 1849. In 1805 he married, "according to the custom of the country", a Cree woman named Susanne; and by her he had six children, one of whom became in 1828 the wife of James (afterwards Sir James) Douglas (q.v.). In 1832, however, Conolly repudiated his Indian wife, having been advised by the Church that an Indian marriage was not valid, and married in Montreal his cousin, Julia Woolrich, the daughter of a wealthy Montreal merchant, by whom he had several children. His Indian wife was sent to a convent on the Red River, where she was supported, first by Conolly himself, and after his death by his white wife. On the death of the Indian wife, the eldest of Conolly's half-breed sons, then a middle-aged man, brought suit in the courts to obtain his share of Conolly's estate. The Canadian courts ruled that the Indian marriage was valid; but the case was carried to the Judicial Committee of the Privy Council, and before judgment was given the case was settled out of court. Some account of the litigation over Conolly's estate will be found in the *Lower Canada Jurist*, vol. xi, pp. 197 ff.

[E. E. Rich (ed.), *Colin Robertson's correspondence book* (Toronto: The Champlain Society, 1939).]

Contrecoeur, Claude Pierre Pécaudy, Sieur de (1706-1775), soldier, was born in New France in 1706, the son of François-Antoine Pécaudy, sieur de Contrecoeur. He became a captain in the marine troops, and in 1754 was placed in command at Fort Duquesne, in the Ohio valley. Owing to illness, he was not actually present at the action of the Monongahéla, in which Braddock fell; but he commanded the French troops after the action, and was partly responsible for the excesses of the Indians. In 1756 he was created a chevalier of the order of St. Louis. He died at Montreal on December 13, 1775.

[*Cyc. Am. biog.*; Bibaud, *Panth. can.*; Le Jeune, *Dict. gén.*; *Bull. rech. hist.*, 1905.]

Conybeare, Charles Frederick Pringle (1860-1927), lawyer and poet, was born at Little Sutton, Middlesex, England, on May 19, 1860, the son of Henry Conybeare, an eminent engineer. He was educated at Westminster School, and in 1875 entered the merchant service as a midshipman; but in 1880 he came to Canada, and studied law. He was called to the bar in the North West Territories in 1885 (Q.C., 1894), and practised law in Lethbridge, Alberta. He became president of the Alberta Law Society; and he died at Lethbridge on July 31, 1927. He was the author of *Vahn Fried* (Toronto, 1903) and *Lyrics from the West* (Toronto, 1907).

[Morgan, *Can. men* (1912).]

Cook, James (1728-1779), navigator, was born at Marton, Yorkshire, England, on October 27, 1728, the son of an agricultural labourer. He entered the Royal Navy, and rose to the rank of master. The charts and observations which he made as marine surveyor of Newfoundland and Labrador, after the conquest of Canada, brought him to the attention of the Royal Society; and in 1768 he was offered command of an expedition to the Pacific Ocean, for the purpose of observing the transit of Venus over the face of the sun. This expedition, on which he explored the coasts of New Zealand and Australia, was the first of three which he made to the South Seas. He returned to England in 1771; and in 1772 he set out on a second expedition, during which he made further explorations in the Pacific. He set out on his third and final expedition in 1776; and in the course of this voyage he explored the coast of North America as far north as Bering Strait. He was killed by the natives on the Island of Hawaii on February 24, 1779. After his death his widow and children were granted pensions by the British government; and the Royal Society struck a medal in memory of his work. He was the author of *An account of a voyage round the world in the years 1768-71* (vols. ii and iii of Hawkeworth's *Voyages*, 1773), *A voyage toward the South Pole and round the world ... in the years 1772-75* (2 vols., London, 1777), and a *Voyage to the Pacific ocean ... in the years 1770-80* (3 vols. and atlas, London, 1784), the last volume of which was written by James King.

[There is a voluminous literature relating to Cook's voyages: Sir Maurice Holmes, *Captain James Cook: A bibliographical excursion* (London, 1952); *Bibliography of Capt. James Cook*, published by the Public Library, Sydney, New South Wales (Sydney, 1928). Biographies of Cook include J. R. Muir, *The life and achievements of Captain James Cook* (London, 1939), H. Carrington, *Life of Captain Cook* (London, 1939).]

Cook, John (1805-1892), clergyman, was born in Sanquhar, Dumfriesshire, Scotland, on April 13, 1805, and was educated at Glasgow and Edinburgh universities. He was ordained a clergyman of the Church of Scotland in 1835, and came to Canada in 1836. For many years the minister of St. Andrew's Church, Quebec, he played a prominent part in bringing about the union of Presbyterians in Canada in 1875, and was the first moderator of the Presbyterian Church in Canada. He was also one of the founders of Queen's University, Kingston, and was its principal in 1857-58. In 1861 he was appointed principal of Morrin College, Quebec, and this position he retained until his death at Quebec on April 1, 1892. In 1880 the degree of LL.D. was conferred on him by Queen's University, Kingston.

[Rose, *Cyc. Can. biog.* (1888); Morgan, *Cel. Can.*]

Coombs, Albert Ernest (1871-1957), educationist and local historian, was born in 1871, and died at St. Catharines, Ontario, on January 9, 1957. He was educated at the University of Toronto (B.A., 1892; M.A., 1895; B. Paed., 1897), and became a school-teacher. In his later years he was head of the classical department at the St. Catharines Collegiate Institute. He was the author of *History of the Niagara Peninsula and the new Welland canal* (Toronto, 1930) and *City of St. Catharines: Historical facts* (St. Catharines, 1948).

[Private information.]

Cooney, Robert (1800-1870), clergyman and historian, was born in Dublin, Ireland, on June 24, 1800, and came to New Brunswick in 1824. In 1831, he became a convert from Roman Catholicism to Protestantism, and a clergyman of the Wesleyan Methodist Church. He was stationed at various places in the Maritime provinces and in Lower Canada, and about 1858 he removed to Upper Canada. He died at Toronto, Ontario, on March 17, 1870. Besides some sermons, he published a *Compendious history of the northern part of the province of New Brunswick and of the district of Gaspé in Lower Canada* (Halifax, 1832; reprinted by D. G. Smith, at Chatham, Miramichi, N.B., in 1896), and *The autobiography of a Wesleyan Methodist missionary* (Montreal, 1856).

[W. O. Raymond, *Robert Cooney* (Collections of the New Brunswick Historical Society, No. 10); W. G. MacFarlane, *New Brunswick bibliography* (Saint John, N.B.,1895).]

Cooper, Charles W. (1819?-1893), lawyer, was born in England about 1819, and came to Canada in youth. He was called to the bar of Upper Canada, and practised law in Toronto. In 1849 he was secretary of the central committee of the British-American League; and for many years he was legal editor and repor-

ter to the Toronto *Globe*. He died in Toronto, Ontario, on January 15, 1893. He was the author of *A prize essay on the features and resources of the united counties of Frontenac, Lennox, and Addington* (Kingston, C.W., 1856).

[Morgan, *Bib. can.*]

Cooper, John Alexander (1868-1956), editor, was born at Clinton, Ontario, on February 5, 1868, and died at Toronto, Ontario, on January 18, 1956. He was educated at the University of Toronto (B.A., 1892; LL.B., 1893). From 1895 to 1906 he was the editor of the *Canadian Magazine*, and from 1906 to 1920, editor of the *Canadian Courier*. He then entered the motion picture industry, and was one of its pioneers in Canada. He was the author of *Canada under Victoria* (Toronto, 1901); he edited *Men of Canada* (Montreal, 1901-2); and he was joint editor, with others, of *The bench and bar of Ontario* (Toronto, 1905).

[Toronto *Globe and Mail*, Jan. 19, 1956; *Can. who's who*, 1948.]

Cooper, Robert (1822?-1866), jurist, was born in England about 1822, a younger brother of Charles W. Cooper (q.v.). He came to Canada at an early age, was called to the bar of Upper Canada, and practised law in Toronto. In 1856 he was appointed county judge of the united counties of Huron and Bruce; and he died at Goderich, Canada West, on June 19, 1866. He was the author of *Rules and practice of the court of chancery of Upper Canada* (Toronto, 1851), as well as of a prize essay on agriculture published in the *Anglo-American Magazine* for 1852.

[Morgan, *Bib. can.*]

Copway, George (1818-1863), author, was born near the mouth of the Trent River, in Ontario, in the autumn of 1818, the son of Chippewa parents. His Indian name was Kagigegabo ("He who stands forever"). He was educated in Illinois, and became a Wesleyan missionary to his people. For many years he was connected with the press of New York City, and he lectured extensively in Europe and the United States. He is said to have died near Pontiac, Michigan, in 1863. He was a prolific writer, and he published *The life, history, and travels of Kah-ge-ga-gah-bowh (George Copway)* (Albany and Philadelphia, 1847), *The life, letters, and speeches of Kah-ge-ga-gah-bowh* (New York, 1850), *The traditional history and characteristic sketches of the Ojibway nation* (London, 1850; Boston, 1851), *Recollections of forest life* (London, 1851; new ed., 1855), *Indian life and Indian history* (Boston, 1858), *The Ojibway conquest* (New York, 1860), and *Running sketches* (New York, 1861). He also wrote a hymn in the Chippewa language (London, 1851), and collaborated with the Rev. Sherman Hall in the translation of the *Gospel of St. Luke* (Boston, 1837) and the *Acts of the Apostles* (Boston, 1838).

[*Dict. Am. biog.*]

Coquart, Claude Godefroy (1706-1765), Jesuit missionary, was born at Melun, France, on February 2, 1706, and entered the Jesuit novitiate in Paris in 1726. He was sent to Canada in 1740, and from 1741 to 1744 he was with La Vérendrye (q.v.) in the West. In 1746 he was assigned to the Saguenay mission where he remained for eleven years. From 1757 to 1762 he spent most of his time at Quebec. He then returned to the Saguenay mission; and he died at Chicoutimi on July 4, 1765. He compiled an Abnaki grammar and dictionary, and a valuable memoir by him on the King's Posts has been printed in R. G. Thwaites (ed.), *The Jesuit relations* (73 vols., Cleveland, 1897-1901).

[*Catholic encyclopedia*; *Dict. Can. biog.*, vol. 3.]

Corbett, Edward Annand (1887-1964), educator, was born in Truro, Nova Scotia, April 12, 1887, and educated at Huntingdon Academy, Quebec, McGill University, and the Presbyterian Theological College in Montreal. He served in the First World War with the rank of captain and taught at Khaki College. After the war he was treated for tuberculosis and on release from the sanitorium joined the extension department of the University of Alberta. He became director of extension and was founder of the Banff School of Fine Arts. He became first director of the Canadian Association for Adult Education in 1937, a position he retained until retirement in 1951. He wrote *Blackfoot trails* (1934); *McQueen of Edmonton* (1934); *Father, God bless him* (1953); *Henry Marshall Tory, beloved Canadian* (1954); *Sidney Earle Smith* (1961); and his memoirs, *We have with us tonight* (1957). He died at Toronto, Ontario, November 28, 1964.

[*Encyc. Can.*, vol. 3; *Can. who's who*, 1961-63; Metropolitan Toronto Library Board, *Biographical scrapbooks*, vol. 22.]

Corey, Albert Bickmore (1898-1963), historian, was born in India, December 17, 1898. Dr. Corey was educated at Acadia University (B.A., 1922), Harvard (M.A., 1923), and Clark University (Ph.D., 1934). He taught at Waynesburg College, Pennsylvania, and St. Lawrence University. In 1944 he was appointed State historian of New York. As a young man he had served in the Canadian army and the Royal Air Force in the First World War. He was a leading scholar in the field of Canadian-American relations. He was author of *The crisis of 1830-1842 in Canadian-American relations* (New Haven and Toronto, 1941), and numerous articles and papers.

[*Who was who in Am.*, vol. IV; *Can. hist. rev.*, 1964.]

Cormack, William Epps (1796-1868), explorer, was born in St. John's, Newfoundland, on May 5, 1796. In 1822 he crossed Newfoundland from east to west, with a Micmac guide, the first white man to do so. His account of his journey has been reprinted several times. Part of it was published in the Edinburgh *Philosophical Journal* in 1824; it was fully printed, under the title *Narrative of a journey across the island of Newfoundland* (St. John's, Newfoundland, 1856 and 1873); and a new edition was published in London in 1928. In his later years Cormack lived in Australia, in New Zealand, and in California; he died in New Westminster, British Columbia, in 1868.

[J. P. Howley, *The Beothuks* (Cambridge, 1915); *Encyc. Can.*; *Newfoundland supp.*]

Cornell, Beaumont Sandfield (1892-1958), physician and author, was born at Athens, Ontario, on March 26, 1892, and died at Huntington, Indiana, on September 16, 1958. He was educated at the University of Toronto (M.B., 1916), and practised medicine, first in Canada, and later in the United States. He was the author of *Pernicious anemia* (Durham, N.C., 1927), and he published two novels, *Renaissance* (Toronto, 1922) and *Lantern Marsh* (Toronto, 1923).

[Clara Thomas, *Canadian novelists* (Toronto, 1946).]

Cornell, John A. (1841-d.?), local historian, was born in 1841. He was the author of *The pioneers of Beverly* (Dundas, Ontario, 1889) and *The first church of Beverly* (Toronto, 1921). The date of his death has not been ascertained.

[Private information.]

Cornish, George Augustus (1872-1960), educationist, was born at Courtright, Ontario, in 1872, and died at Toronto, Ontario, on April 29, 1960. He was educated at the University of Toronto (B.A., 1900), and became a schoolteacher. In 1921 he was appointed a professor in the Ontario College of Education in Toronto; and he taught geography there until his retirement in 1944. He was the author of several text-books on geography for use in secondary schools.

[Toronto *Globe and Mail*, April 30, 1960.]

Cornish, George Henry (1834-1912), clergyman and author, was born in Exeter, England, on June 26, 1834. He came to Canada when a child, and was educated at the Toronto Academy and at Victoria University, Cobourg. In 1862 he was ordained a minister of the Methodist Church, and for nearly forty years he served in various pastorates in Ontario. He was superannuated in 1901, and he died at Toronto on August 25, 1912. In 1862 he married Elizabeth Frances, daughter of Captain Reynell, Ballinalach, Westmeath, Ireland. He was the author of *A handbook of Canadian*

COSTAIN

Methodism (Toronto, 1867), and *The cyclopedia of Methodism in Canada* (2 vols., Toronto, 1880-1903).

[Morgan, *Can. men* (1912).]

Cornwall, Clement Francis (1836-1910), lieutenant-governor of British Columbia (1881-86), was born at Ashcroft, Gloucestershire, England, in 1836, the son of the Rev. Alan Gardner Cornwall and Caroline, daughter of Thomas Kingscote. He was educated at Magdalene College, Cambridge (B.A., 1858), and was called to the bar at the Inner Temple. He emigrated to British Columbia in 1862, and in 1865 became a member of the Legislative Council of British Columbia. In 1871, when British Columbia entered the Dominion, he was appointed a member of the Senate of Canada; and he sat in this house until his appointment as lieutenant-governor of British Columbia in 1881. This position he held until 1886. In 1889 he was appointed to the bench as the county court judge of Cariboo, and he retired from this post only at the end of 1906. He died at Victoria, British Columbia, on February 15, 1910. In 1871 he married Charlotte, daughter of the Rev. A. G. Pemberton, vicar of Kensal Green, London, England.

[J. B. Kerr, *Biographical dictionary of well-known British Columbians* (Vancouver, 1890); Morgan, *Can. men* (1898); *Can. parl. comp.*; F. W. Howay and E. O. S. Scholefield, *British Columbia* (4 vols., Vancouver, 1914).]

Cornwallis, Edward (1713-1776), governor of Nova Scotia (1749-52), was born in London, England, on February 22, 1713, the son of Charles, fourth Baron Cornwallis, and Lady Charlotte Butler, daughter of the Earl of Arran. He and his twin brother, who became archbishop of Canterbury, were appointed royal pages, when they were twelve years old, and both of them were aided by the influence of the court all their lives. In 1731 he joined the army, and he served until 1748, when he retired with the rank of lieutenant-colonel. In May, 1749, he was appointed governor and captain-general of Nova Scotia, and was sent out to Nova Scotia with a company of 2,500 settlers. He remained governor of Nova Scotia for three years; and on his return to England in 1753, he left a flourishing little town, with three courts for the administration of the law, a body of militia, and several fortifications. His later military life was unfortunate, for he shared in the disgrace of Admiral John Byng at Minorca in 1756, and of General Sir John Mordaunt in Africa in 1760, and only the influence of his friends saved him from dismissal. In 1762, he was appointed governor of Gibraltar; and he held this office until his death there on January 23, 1776. He married in 1753 Mary (d. 1775), daughter of Viscount Townshend, and he had no children.

[J. Macdonald, *The Hon. Edward Cornwallis* (Coll. Nova Scotia Hist. Soc., vol. xii); D. Campbell, *Nova Scotia* (Montreal, 1873); B. Murdoch, *History of Nova Scotia* (3 vols., Halifax, N.S., 1867).]

Corry, Thomas (d. 1792), fur-trader, was one of the earliest fur-traders to penetrate to the valley of the Saskatchewan in the early days of British rule. He engaged in the fur-trade as early as 1767, when he obtained a licence to take two canoes to Kaministiquia, on Lake Superior. He reached the Saskatchewan in 1771; and he spent the winters of 1771-72 and 1772-73 on the Saskatchewan. He did so well that he was able to retire with a competency. He settled first in Montreal, and then in L'Assomption, where he kept a shop from 1779 to 1785 or later. He died in Montreal on July 20, 1792.

[W. S. Wallace, *The pedlars from Quebec* (Can. hist. rev., 1932).]

Cortereal, Gaspar (1450?-1501?), navigator, was a native of the Island of Terceira, in the Azores. In 1500 he was commissioned by the king of Portugal to make a voyage of exploration to the New World, and was appointed governor of whatever countries he might discover, within the limits assigned to Portugal under the Treaty of Tordesillas. In the summer of 1500 he explored part of the east coast of Greenland, but was turned back by the ice; and in 1501 he made a second expedition, with three ships, during which he visited the shores of Labrador and Newfoundland. At Hamilton Bay, he seized about 60 natives, and sent them back to Lisbon as slaves. He himself proceeded south of Newfoundland; but his ship was never heard of again, and it is probable that it was lost with all on board some time in the autumn of 1501. In 1502 Michel Cortereal, his brother, set out in search of him, but he too disappeared.

[H. P. Biggar, *The precursors of Jacques Cartier* (Ottawa, 1913); *Dict. Can. biog.*, vol. 1.]

Costain, Thomas Bertram (1885-1965), novelist, was born in Brantford, Ontario, May 3, 1885. He was educated in Brantford and began his writing career with the Brantford *Expositor* as a reporter; he then became editor of the Guelph *Courier* and *Mercury* in 1908. He became editor of the Maclean-Hunter publication *Hardware and Metal* in 1911, and later was editor of *Maclean's* magazine. He left to become general editor of the *Saturday Evening Post* in 1920. He began publishing his fiction in 1942 after he had spent two years with 20th Century Fox motion pictures as story editor and then returned as advisory editor to Doubleday and Company. His first novel, *For my great folly* (1942), sold more than 132,000 copies and was followed by thirteen novels, two biographies, five histories, and five

175

anthologies of short stories. His most famous novel, *The black rose* (1945), sold nearly one million copies. He died in New York, October 8, 1965.

[*Maclean's* magazine (Jan. 15, 1946); Norah Story, *Oxford companion to Canadian history and literature* (Toronto, 1967); *Can. who's who*, 1949-51.]

Costebelle, Philippe Pastour, Sieur de (1661-1717), governor of Louisbourg, was born in the south of France in 1661, and entered the French army in 1683. In 1692 he was sent to Newfoundland, where he served in several positions for a number of years; and in 1706 he was appointed governor of Placentia. In 1714 he became the first governor of Louisbourg; and he died at Louisbourg on November 16, 1717.

[J. S. McLennan, *Louisbourg* (London, 1918); Le Jeune, *Dict. gén.*; *Dict. Can. biog.*, vol. 2.]

Costigan, John (1835-1916), politician, was born at St. Nicholas, Lower Canada, on February 1, 1835, the son of Irish Roman Catholic parents. He was educated at Ste. Anne's College, Lower Canada, but early moved to New Brunswick. In 1861 he was elected a member of the New Brunswick Assembly for Victoria; defeated over the issue of Confederation in 1866, he was elected to the Canadian House of Commons in 1867; and he was continuously a member of this House until 1905. He was in parliament the chief spokesman of the Irish Roman Catholics of Canada, and was the author of the "Costigan resolutions" in favour of home rule for Ireland passed by the Canadian House of Commons in 1882. The same year he became a member of the Macdonald government, and he continued to hold office, first as minister of inland revenue (1882-92), then as secretary of state (1892-94), and lastly as minister of marine and fisheries (1894-96), until the defeat of the Conservative administration of Sir Charles Tupper in 1896. During the Laurier régime, Costigan deserted the Conservative party, and supported the government. His reward came in January, 1907, when he was appointed to the Senate. He died at Ottawa on September 29, 1916. In 1885 he married Harriet, daughter of J. R. Ryan of Grand Falls, New Brunswick; by her he had two sons and three daughters.

[Mrs. W. Armstrong, *Some Confederation reminiscences of the Hon. Senator Costigan* (Transactions of the Women's Historical Society of Ottawa, vol. vi); Rose, *Cyc. Can. biog.* (1888); Morgan, *Can. men* (1912); *Can. parl. comp.*]

Côté, Cyrille Hector Octave (1809-1850), physican, politician, and clergyman, was born at Quebec in 1809. He was educated at the College of Montreal and at the University of Vermont (M.D., 1831). In 1834 he was elected

to the Legislative Assembly of Lower Canada for L'Acadie as a reformer, and in 1837 he was one of the leaders of the Lower Canadian Rebellion. He fled to the United States, and became there a convert to Protestantism and a Baptist minister. On his return to Canada, he published *Un mot en passant à ceux qui ont abandonné l'église romaine et ses traditions* (Montreal, 1848). He died at Burlington, Vermont, on October 4, 1950. He married Marguerite Jobson.

[Rev. N. Cyr, *Memoirs of the Rev. C.H.O. Côté, M.D.* (Philadelphia, 1854); E. Z. Massicotte, *Le docteur Côté* (Bull. rech. hist., 1923); P.G. Roy, *Fils de Québec*, vol. 3 (Lévis, Que., 1933).]

Côté, Jean Baptiste (1834-1907), woodcarver, was born near Quebec in 1834, and was educated at the Quebec Seminary. He became a wood-carver, and devoted himself at first to the carving of figure-heads for ships and of Red Indians for tobacco-shops. Then he turned to the carving of wooden effigies for churches. His work, which carried on an artistic tradition in French Canada, is now recognized as having high artistic merit; and his woodcarving of the Last Supper is in the Royal Ontario Museum. He died, however, poor and unknown, in 1907.

[M. Barbeau, *Côté the wood-carver* (Toronto, 1943) and *Côté, sculpteur sur bois* (Trans. Roy. Soc. Can., 1942).]

Côté, Joseph Olivier (1820-1882), civil servant, was born in Quebec on April 7, 1820, and in 1845 entered the Canadian civil service as a clerk in the Executive Council office. He ultimately became clerk of the Queen's Privy Council for Canada (1880-82). He published a useful book of reference, *Political appointments and elections in the province of Canada* (Quebec, 1860; new ed., Ottawa, 1866); and he compiled a valuable index to the state papers of Canada, 1841-67. He died in Ottawa, on April 24, 1882. A sequel to his *Political appointments* was published by his son, N. Omer Côté.

[*Dom. ann. reg.*, 1882; P. G. Roy, *Fils de Québec*, vol. 4 (Lévis, Que., 1933).]

Côté, Narcisse Omer (1859-1944), civil servant and author, was born at Quebec, Canada East, on September 14, 1859, the son of Joseph Olivier Côté (q.v.), and was educated at Ottawa University. He entered the civil service in 1879, and became in 1906 controller of the lands patent branch of the department of the interior. He retired from the civil service in 1931, and he died at Ottawa, Ontario, on January 11, 1944. He was the author of *Political appointments, parliaments, and the judicial bench in the Dominion of Canada, 1867-1895* (Ottawa, 1896) and *Political appointments, parliaments, and the judicial bench in* the Dominion of Canada, 1896-1917 (Ottawa, 1918).

[Morgan, Can. men (1912).]

Côté, Thomas (1869-1918), journalist and author, was born at Trois Pistoles, Quebec, on September 22, 1869, the son of Théophile Côté and Flavie Larivée. He was educated at Laval University (B.A., 1889), became a journalist, and was from 1904 to 1909 managing-editor of La Presse, Montreal. He then accepted a position in the Dominion civil service; and he died at Montreal on January 16, 1918. He was the author of Trois études (Lévis, 1891).

[Morgan, Can. men (1912).]

Cotes, Mrs. Everard. See **Duncan, Sara Jeannette.**

Cotton, William Lawson (1848-1928), journalist, was born in New London, Prince Edward Island, on July 23, 1848. He became a journalist, and after serving on newspapers in Charlottetown and Halifax, he became in 1873 editor of the Charlottetown Examiner. Even after the Examiner was absorbed by the Charlottetown Guardian in 1922, he continued his connection with the paper. He died at Charlottetown on March 31, 1928. He was the author of Chapters in our island story (Charlottetown, P.E.I., 1927).

[Private information.]

Couët, Thomas Cyrille (1861-1931), priest, was born at Quebec, Canada East, on April 11, 1861. He was educated at the Quebec Seminary, and joined the Dominican order in 1881. He was ordained a priest in 1886; and he served in various places in Ontario and Quebec. He was accidentally drowned in the Chicoutimi River, near Portage des Roches, Quebec, on September 17, 1931. He was the author of La franc-maçonnerie et la conscience catholique (Quebec, 1910), Bas les masques (Quebec, 1911), and La Mère-Marie de la Charité et les soeurs dominicaines de Québec (Quebec, 1925).

[Bull. rech. hist., 1931.]

Couillard-Després, Azarie (1876-1939), priest and historian, was born at St. Albans, Vermont, on March 4, 1876, a descendant of Louis Hébert (q.v.), the first Canadian colonist. He was educated at the St. Hyacinthe seminary and at the Sulpician seminary at Montreal; and was ordained a priest of the Roman Catholic Church in 1905. He served as parish priest in various places in the province of Quebec; and from 1932 to his death on December 8, 1939, he was curé of the parish of Notre Dame de Sorel. An indefatigable student of history, he was elected a fellow of the Royal Society of Canada in 1918; and he was the author of La première famille française au Canada (Montreal, 1907), Histoire des seigneurs de la Rivière du sud (St. Hyacinthe,

Que., 1912), L'histoire de la seigneurie et de la paroisse de Saint-Ours (2 vols., Montreal, 1915-16), La noblesse de France et du Canada (Montreal, 1916), Histoire de Sorel (Montreal, 1926), Charles de Saint-Etienne de la Tour ... et son temps (Arthabaska, Que., 1930), and Charles de Saint-Etienne de la Tour, au tribunal de l'histoire (St. Hyacinthe, Que., 1932).

[Proc. Roy. Soc. Can., 1940; Can. who's who, 1936-37.]

Courcelle, Rémy, Sieur de (1626-1698) governor of New France (1665-72), was a soldier who had been governor of Thionville. On March 23, 1665, he received the appointment of governor of New France. In 1666 he led an expedition against the Mohawks, and though he was forced to retreat, the courage showed by this sally had a salutary effect on the Iroquois tribes. Later in the year, he aided Tracy in subduing the Mohawks, and in 1668 he concluded peace with the Iroquois. In 1669 his firmness and impartiality in executing three French soldiers who had murdered an Indian chief, saved the colony from another war. Failing health compelled him to request his recall, and he left Canada in 1672. On his return to Paris, he was appointed commander of the citadel at Arras and is reported to have been governor of Toulon at his death on October 14, 1698.

[R. Roy, Rémy de Courcelles (Bull. rech. hist., vol. xx); Le Jeune, Dict. gén.; F. Parkman, The old régime in Canada (Boston, 1892); Dict. Can. biog., vol. 1.]

Coursol, Charles Joseph (1819-1888), jurist and politican, was born near Amherstburg, Upper Canada, on October 3, 1819, the son of Michel Coursol, a servant of the Hudson's Bay Company, and Marie Mélaine, daughter of Joseph Quesnel (q.v.). He was educated at Montreal College, and was called to the bar of Lower Canada in 1841 (Q.C., 1873). In 1870 he was appointed a judge of the sessions of the peace in Montreal; but in 1878 he retired from this post to contest Montreal East for the House of Commons. He was elected, and he continued to represent this constituency until his death in Montreal on August 4, 1888. He married the daughter of Sir Etienne Taché (q.v.).

[J. Tassé, Le 38me fauteuil (Montreal, 1891); Cyc. Am. biog.; Can. parl. comp.; Rose, Cyc. Can. biog. (1886).]

Courtice, Mrs. Ada Mary, née **Brown** (1860-1923), educationist, was born at Pickering, Ontario, of Quaker descent. She was educated at the Ontario Ladies College, Whitby; and in 1888 she married the Rev. Andrew Cory Courtice, for many years the editor of the Christian Guardian. After his death she opened a private school in Toronto; and she became a member of the Board of Education in Toronto, and an authority on child psychology.

In 1914 she founded the Home and School Movement in Toronto, and she lived to see the movement spread across Canada. She died in Toronto in 1923.

[L. M. Montgomery and others, *Courageous women* (Toronto, 1935); *Can. who was who*, vol. 2.]

Courtney, John Mortimer (1838-1920), civil servant, was born at Penzance, England, on July 22, 1838, the second son of John Sampson Courtney. He was privately educated, and was for some years in the service of the Bank of Agra, India. In 1869 he came to Canada, at the invitation of Sir John Rose (q.v.), and became chief clerk and assistant secretary of the Treasury Board of Canada. In 1878 he was promoted to the position of deputy minister of finance; and this post he occupied until his retirement in 1906. In 1907 he was the chairman of the commission appointed to investigate the working of the Civil Service Act; and the report which he submitted in 1908 was the basis for legislation establishing the Civil Service Commission, and making competitive examinations obligatory. He died at Ottawa on October 8, 1920. In 1870 he married Mary Elizabeth Sophia, second daughter of John Fennings Taylor (q.v.); and by her had one son. In 1897 he was created a C.M.G., and in 1903 a companion of the Imperial Service Order.

[*Can. parl. comp.*; *Can. who's who* (1910); Morgan, *Can. men* (1898); Rose, *Cyc. Can. biog.* (1886); J. M. Courtney and A. Shortt, "Dominion finance, 1867-1912", in A. Shortt and A. G. Doughty (eds.), *Canada and its provinces*, vol. 7 (Toronto, 1914).]

Coverdale, William Hugh (1871-1949), engineer and capitalist, was born at Kingston, Ontario, on January 27, 1871, and died at New York, on August 10, 1949. He was educated at Geneva College, Beaver Falls, Pennsylvania (B.A., 1891), and became a highly successful consulting engineer, with a wide variety of interests, including the Canada Steamships Company. He was a collector of historical Canadiana; he presented his collection to the Manoir Richelieu at Murray Bay, and a catalogue of part of the collection was published in 1942, under the title *Catalogue of Canadiana: being a selection of prints, water colour drawings, oil paintings and maps drawn from the William H. Coverdale Collection. — Exhibited under the auspices of the Maple Leaf Fund* (New York: Grand Central Art Galleries). He was the author of *Tadoussac then and now* (n.p., 1942). Geneva College conferred on him the honorary degree of D.Sc. in 1914, and Queen's University that of LL.D. in 1922.

[*New York Times*, Aug. 11, 1949; *Can. who's who*, 1948; *Encyc. Can.*]

Covert, Walter Harold (1865-1949), lieutenant-governor of Nova Scotia (1931-37), was born at Musquash, New Brunswick, on December 23, 1865, and died at Dartmouth, Nova Scotia, on August 20, 1949. He was called to the bar in 1887, and practised law, first in Saint John, New Brunswick, and then in Halifax, Nova Scotia. He was appointed lieutenant-governor of Nova Scotia in 1931, and held office until 1937. He was created a K.C. in 1909.

[*Can. who's who*, 1948; *Can. parl. guide*, 1936; *Encyc. Can.*]

Cowan, Hugh (1870-1943), clergyman and author, was born on Manitoulin Island, Ontario, in 1870, and died at Owen Sound in April, 1943. He was educated at the University of Manitoba, Queen's University, and Knox College, and was ordained a minister of the Presbyterian Church. He was the author of *La Cloche* (Toronto, 1928), *The Detroit River district* (Toronto, 1929), and *The great drama of human life* (Toronto, 1937).

[Toronto *Globe and Mail*, April 20, 1943; R. E. Watters, *A check list of Canadian literature* (Toronto, 1959).]

Cowie, Isaac (1848-1917), author, was born at Lerwick, in the Shetland Islands, Scotland, in 1848. He was educated at Edinburgh University, and in 1867 entered the service of the Hudson's Bay Company. He was employed at various posts in the North West Territories, and exerted an influence in restraining the Métis during the North West Rebellion of 1885. He left the service of the Hudson's Bay Company in 1891, and went into business for himself, first in Edmonton, and later in Winnipeg. He died at Winnipeg on May 18, 1917. He was the author of *The company of adventurers* (Toronto, 1913).

[Private information.]

Cowie, Robert (1795?-1859), fur-trader, was born about 1795 and entered the service of the North West Company about 1811. He was employed as a clerk and accountant, and was present at Fort William when it was captured by Lord Selkirk. He was clerk and accountant at Lachine from 1825 to 1829, and he was in charge of the affairs of McTavish, McGillivrays and Company from 1825 to 1826, between the departure of Thomas Thain (q.v.) and the arrival of Sir George Simpson (q.v.). He was appointed a chief trader in 1829, and was employed consecutively at Portneuf, Fort Vancouver, and Moose Factory. He retired in 1846, and died on June 6, 1859.

[W. S. Wallace (ed.), *Documents relating to the North West Company* (Toronto: The Champlain Society, 1934).]

Cox, Arthur (1840-1917), painter, was born in England in 1840, and came to Canada as a young man. Failing to make a living as an artist, he entered the employ of the Great Western Telegraph Company, and eventually became its secretary. He continued to paint, however, and was elected an associate of the Royal Canadian Academy. On retirement from business, he returned to England, where he died, at Nottingham, in August, 1917.

[Private information.]

Cox, George Albertus (1840-1914), senator of Canada and capitalist, was born at Colborne, Upper Canada, on May 7, 1840, the son of Edward W. Cox and Jane Tanner. He was educated at the grammar school in Colborne, and began life as an operator in the service of the Montreal Telegraph Company. In 1858 he was moved to Peterborough, Upper Canada; and he lived there until 1888. From 1878 to 1884 he was president of the Midland Railway, which was absorbed in the Grand Trunk Railway; and in 1881 he was one of the Howland syndicate which offered to build the Canadian Pacific Railway. In 1888 he removed to Toronto, and he became actively interested in a great number of financial and mercantile organizations. He unsuccessfully contested West Peterborough as a Liberal in the provincial elections of 1872, and in the Dominion elections of 1887; and in 1896 he was called to the Senate of Canada. He was regarded as one of the powerful interests behind the Laurier government of 1896-1911; and he was one of the outstanding capitalists of Eastern Canada. He died at Toronto on January 16, 1914. He was twice married, (1) in 1862 to Margaret Young (d. 1905), second daughter of Daniel Hopkins of Peterborough; and (2) in 1909 to Amy Gertrude, eldest daughter of Walter Sterling, Toronto.

[Morgan, *Can. men* (1912); *Can. who's who* (1910); *Can. parl. comp.*]

Cox, Ross (1793-1853), author, was born in Dublin, Ireland, in 1793, the son of Samuel Cox, of the Ordnance Office, and his wife Margaret Thorpe. He emigrated to America about 1811, and took service as a clerk in J. J. Astor's American Fur Company. He reached Astoria in the spring of 1812 and was present at the surrender of Astoria to the North West Company, in 1813. He then took service as a clerk with the North West Company; but he retired from the fur-trade in 1817, returning to Ireland by the overland route from the Columbia to Montreal. His *Adventures on the Columbia River* (London, 1831; 2nd ed., 1832; New York, 1832) is one of the most important documents relating to the later history of the North West Company. On his return to Dublin, he became the Irish correspondent of the London *Morning Herald* and a clerk in the Dublin police office. He died in Dublin in 1853. In 1819 he married Hannah Cumming, and by her had a large family.

[W. S. Wallace, *A note on Ross Cox* (Can. hist. rev., 1933).]

Coyne, James Henry (1849-1942), lawyer and historian, was born in St. Thomas, Canada West, on October 3, 1849. He was educated at the University of Toronto (B.A., 1870; M.A., 1905; LL.D., 1930), and was called to the bar of Ontario in 1874. He practised law in St. Thomas until 1888, when he was appointed registrar of deeds in the county of Elgin. This position he held until his death at St. Thomas, Ontario, on January 5, 1942. He was a life-long student of Canadian history; and in 1906 he was elected a fellow of the Royal Society of Canada, and in 1926 its president. Queen's University in 1909 and the University of Western Ontario in 1927 conferred on him the degree of LL.D. He edited *The Talbot papers* (St. Thomas, Ont., 1909); and he contributed many papers to the *Transactions* of the Royal Society of Canada and the *Papers and records* of the Ontario Historical Society.

[*Proc. Roy. Soc. Can.,* 1942; *Can. who's who,* 1936-37.]

Craig, Sir James Henry (1748-1812), governor-in-chief of Canada (1807-11), was born in 1748 at Gibraltar, where his father was civil and military judge. He entered the British army in 1763 as an ensign in the 30th Regiment, and he served in America throughout the American Revolutionary War. He was wounded at the battle of Bunker Hill, and was with Burgoyne at Saratoga. In 1795, with Major-General Alured Clarke (q.v.), he effected the capture of the Dutch colony at the Cape of Good Hope, and he administered the government of the colony until 1797. From 1797 to 1802 he commanded a division in India; and in 1801 he was promoted to be lieutenant-general. From 1802 to 1805 he was in command of the Eastern district in England; and from 1805 to 1806 he commanded an army in the Mediterranean theatre of operations. Ill-health having compelled his return to England, he was appointed in 1807 governor-in-chief of Canada, and he arrived in Quebec on October 18, 1807.

His period of office in Canada has been described by French-Canadian writers as "a reign of terror". Influenced by the official oligarchy at Quebec, he came into conflict with the Assembly; and he imprisoned Pierre Bédard (q.v.) and others connected with the newly-founded French-Canadian journal *Le Canadien*. These arrests were, no doubt, illegal and arbitrary; but to describe them as part of a "reign of terror" is an abuse of language. A man of transparent simplicity and honesty, Craig was at the worst a governor who was misled by unwise counsellors; and he himself realized this before he left the country. During the whole of his term of office, moreover, he was a dying man; and his death occurred soon after his return to England in 1811, at London, on January 12, 1812. In 1797 he was created a

K.C.B. Just before his death, he was promoted to be general.

[E. A. Cruickshank, *The administration of Sir James Craig* (Trans. Roy. Soc. Can., 1908); *Dict. nat. biog.*; R. Christie, *History of Lower Canada,* vol. 1 (Quebec, 1848); A.G. Doughty and D. A. McArthur (eds.), *Documents relating to the constitutional history of Canada, 1791-1818* (Ottawa, 1914).]

Craig, John (1852-1923), missionary, was born near Toronto, Canada West, in 1852; was educated at the University of Toronto (B.A., 1873) and at the Rochester Theological Seminary; and became a missionary in India. He died at Cocanada, India, on July 20, 1923. He was the author of *Forty years among the Telugus* (Toronto, 1909).

[Morgan, *Can. men* (1912).]

Craig, John Roderick (1837-d.?), rancher and author, was born at Toronto, Upper Canada, in 1837. He is said to have been educated at Victoria University, but does not appear to have graduated from it. He became interested in the importation and breeding of livestock, and in 1881 he organized the Oxley Ranch Company in the West, the story of which he told in *Ranching with lords and commons* (Toronto, 1903). The date and place of his death have not been ascertained.

[Morgan, *Can. men* (1912).]

Cramahé, Hector Theophilus (1720-1788), lieutenant-governor of Quebec (1771-82), was born in England of French parentage in 1720. He served as a captain in the 15th Regiment in the expedition against Louisbourg in 1758, and he was deputy judge-advocate in the expedition against Quebec in 1759. From 1759 to 1764 he was secretary to General Murray (q.v.); and he was appointed in 1764 a member of the first Council of the province of Quebec. When Carleton (q.v.) returned to England temporarily in 1771, Cramahé was appointed lieutenant-governor of Quebec, and he administered the affairs of the province until 1774. He retained his position as lieutenant-governor until 1782. In 1785 he was appointed lieutenant-governor of Detroit, but he does not appear to have entered on his duties at that place. He died in England, on June 8, 1788.

[A. Shortt and A. G. Doughty (eds.), *Documents relating to the constitutional history of Canada, 1759-1791* (new and rev. ed., 2 vols., Ottawa, 1918).]

Cramp, John Mockett (1796-1881), president of Acadia College (1851-69), was born at St. Peter's, Isle of Thanet, England, on July 25, 1796. He was educated at Stepney College, and became a Baptist minister. He came to Canada in 1844, and became president of the Montreal Baptist College. In 1851 he was appointed president of Acadia College,

Wolfville, Nova Scotia; and he held this post until his retirement in 1869. He died at Wolfville on December 6, 1881. He was the author of a large number of books and pamphlets, many of which were published before he came to Canada. Among those published after his arrival in Canada were *A portraiture from life* (Halifax, 1862), *A catechism of Christian baptism* (London, 1865), *Baptist history* (London, 1868), *The lamb of God* (London, 1871), *Paul and Christ* (London, 1873), and *A memoir of Madame Feller, with an account of the origin of the Grande Ligne mission* (London, 1876).

[Rev. T. A. Higgins, *The life of John Mockett Cramp* (Montreal, 1887); *Dom. ann. reg.,* 1880-81.]

Crankshaw, James (1844-1921), lawyer, was born at Manchester, England, on July 20, 1844, and came to Canada in 1876. He studied law at McGill University (B.C.L., 1882), and was called to the bar of Quebec in 1883 (K.C., 1906). He practised law in Montreal, and was the author of *The criminal code of Canada* (Montreal, 1894) and *A practical guide to police magistrates and justices of the peace* (Montreal, 1895), both of which reached several editions. He died at Montreal, Quebec, on December 16, 1921.

[Morgan, *Can. men* (1912).]

Cranston, James Herbert (1880-1952), journalist and author, was born at Galt, Ontario, on July 26, 1880, and died at Midland, Ontario, on December 18, 1952. He was educated at Woodstock College and McMaster University (B.A., 1905), and became a journalist. For many years he was on the staff of the Toronto *Daily Star,* latterly as editor of the *Star Weekly.* In 1935 he became editor and publisher of the *Midland Free Press,* retiring from this position in 1947. He was the author of *Etienne Brûlé, immortal scoundrel* (Toronto, 1949); and his autobiography was published posthumously, under the title *Ink on my fingers* (Toronto, 1953). In 1949 McMaster University conferred on him the honorary degree of LL.D.

[Toronto *Globe and Mail,* Dec. 19, 1952; *Can. who's who,* 1949-51.]

Crawford, Alexander Wellington (1866-1933), educationist, was born at Branchton, Ontario, on January 15, 1866. He was educated at Victoria College, University of Toronto (B.A., 1895; M.A., 1898) and at Cornell University (Ph.D., 1902). He was ordained a minister of the Methodist Church in 1896; but devoted his life to educational work. After holding several academic appointments in the United States, he was appointed in 1909 professor of English in the University of Manitoba. He retired from this post in 1930; and he died at Hamilton, Ontario, on May 3, 1933. He was the author of *The philosophy of F. H.*

Jacobi (New York, 1905), *Hamlet, an ideal prince, and other essays in Shakesperean interpretation* (Boston, 1916), *Germany's moral downfall* (New York, 1919), *Poems of yesterday* (Toronto, 1924), and *The genius of Keats* (London, 1932); and he was editor, with others, of *Greater English poets* (Toronto, 1929).

[*Canadian bookman,* August, 1933; *Who's who among North American authors,* vol. 6; Morgan, *Can. men* (1912).]

Crawford, Isabella Valancy (1850-1887), poet, was born in Dublin, Ireland, on December 25, 1850, the daughter of Dr. Stephen Dennis Crawford and Sydney Scott. She came to Canada with her parents in 1858, and her father practised medicine successively in the village of Paisley, at Lakefield, and at Peterborough, Ontario. After her father's death, she moved with her mother to Toronto, and here she died, in poverty, on February 12, 1887. During her life, apart from verses and stories published in the newspapers, she issued only one volume, *Old Spookses' Pass, Malcolm's Katie, and other poems* (Toronto, 1884). After her death her *Collected poems* were edited (Toronto, 1905) by J. W. Garvin, with an introduction by Ethelwyn Wetherald.

[Katherine Hales (Mrs. J. W. Garvin), *Isabella Valancy Crawford* (Toronto, 1923), with bibliography; Thomas O'Hagan, *Canadian essays* (Toronto, 1901); A. MacMurchy, *Handbook of Canadian literature* (Toronto, 1906); L. J. Burpee, *A little book of Canadian essays* (Toronto, 1909); *Can. who was who,* vol. 2.]

Crawford, John Willoughby (1817-1875), lieutenant-governor of Ontario (1873-75), was born at Manor Hamilton, Ireland, the son of George Crawford, afterwards a senator of Canada. He came to Canada in 1824 with his parents, was educated in Toronto, and was called to the bar of Upper Canada (Q.C., 1867). He represented East Toronto in the Legislative Assembly of United Canada from 1861 to 1863; and in the Canadian House of Commons, after Confederation, he represented South Leeds from 1867 to 1872, and West Toronto from 1872 to 1873. In 1873 he was appointed lieutenant-governor of Ontario; and he died in office, on May 13, 1875, at Government House, Toronto. He married Helen, daughter of Mr. Justice Sherwood (q.v.), and by her he had one son and five daughters.

[D. B. Reed, *The lieutenant-governors of Upper Canada and Ontario* (Toronto, 1900); *Can. parl. comp.*; D. Swainson, *Business and politics: The career of John Willoughby Crawford* (Ont. Hist., 1969); *Dict. Can. biog.,* vol. 10.]

Crawford, Julia (1896-1968), painter, was born in Kingston, New Brunswick, in 1896. She attended the provincial Normal School and was, for a time, a rural school-teacher. In 1925 she entered the Pratt Institute in Boston, where she won honours in design. She later studied at the Cape School of Art, Provincetown, and travelled in Europe. From 1928 to 1944 she was on the staff of the Saint John Vocational School. Her work reveals freedom and spontaneity within the limitations of a strongly developed sense of design. She painted in many styles and media. She was a member of the New York Water Color Club and the Canadian Society of Painters in Water Colour. She died at Saint John, New Brunswick, in 1968.

[R. A. Tweedie, *Arts in New Brunswick* (Fredericton, 1967); C. S. MacDonald, *A dictionary of Canadian artists,* vol. 1 (Ottawa, 1967).]

Crawley, Edmund Albern (1799-1888), president of Acadia University, was born at Ipswich, Suffolk, England, in 1799. He was educated at King's College, Nova Scotia (B.A., 1820; M.A., 1823; D.C.L., 1888), and was called to the bar in Nova Scotia. In 1828 he decided to enter the Baptist ministry; and he studied at the Andover Theological Seminary, Massachusetts, and at Brown University, Providence, Rhode Island. He was alternately engaged in pastoral work in Halifax and in academic work at Acadia University. From 1851 to 1853 he was president of this university. He died in 1888. He was the author of *A treatise on baptism* (Halifax, 1835).

[R. J. Long, *Nova Scotia authors* (East Orange, N.J., 1918).]

Crease, Sir Henry Pering Pellew (1825-1905), judge, was born in England in 1825, the eldest son of Captain Henry Crease, R.N. He was educated at Clare College, Cambridge (B.A., 1847), and was called to the bar from the Middle Temple in 1849. In 1858 he went to British Columbia, and became the first practising barrister in Vancouver Island. In 1860 he was elected to represent Victoria in the Legislative Assembly of Vancouver Island; and in 1864 he was appointed the first attorney-general of British Columbia. He occupied this position until 1870; and he was then appointed a judge of the Supreme Court of British Columbia. He retired from the bench in 1896, and he died on February 27, 1905. In 1853 he married Sarah, daughter of John Lindley, F.R.S. In 1896, on retiring from the bench, he was created a knight bachelor.

[*Who was who,* 1897-1916; J. B. Kerr, *A biographical dictionary of well-known British Columbians* (Vancouver, B.C., 1890); Morgan, *Can. men* (1898); G. R. Elliott, *Henry P. Pellew Crease* (B.C. Studies, 1971-72).]

Creighton, Letitia. See **Youmans, Mrs. Letitia,** *née* **Creighton.**

Creighton, William Black (1864-1946), clergyman and author, was born at Dorchester, Ontario, on July 20, 1864, and died at Toronto, Ontario, on October 30, 1946. He was educated at Victoria University, Cobourg (B.A., 1890), and was ordained a minister of the Methodist Church. In 1900 he was appointed assistant editor, and in 1906 editor, of the *Christian Guardian*; and when Church union took place in 1925, he continued as editor of the *New Outlook* (which combined the papers of the Methodist, Presbyterian, and Congregational churches), until his retirement in 1937. The honorary degree of D.D. was conferred on him by Victoria University in 1909. Shortly before his death he published two books, *Life is like that* (Toronto, 1945) and *Round 'bout sun-up* (Toronto, 1946).

[Toronto *Globe and Mail,* Oct. 31, 1946; *Can. who's who,* 1936-37.]

Crémazie, Joseph Jacques (1810-1872), lawyer and author, was born at Quebec, Lower Canada, on October 10, 1810. He became dean of the faculty of law in Laval University; and he died at Quebec City, on July 11, 1872. He was the author of *Les lois criminelles anglaises* (Quebec, 1842), *Manuel des notions utiles sur les droits politiques* (Quebec, 1852), and *Notions élémentaires de cosmographie and de météorologie* (Quebec, 1857).

[P.G. Roy, *Fils de Québec,* vol. 3 (Lévis, Que., 1933); Morgan, *Bib. can.; Dict. Can. biog.,* vol. 10.]

Crémazie, Octave (1827-1879), poet, was born at Quebec, Lower Canada, on April 16, 1827. He was educated at the Quebec Seminary, and when he finished his studies in 1844 he joined his brother Joseph in a bookselling business in Quebec. He began to contribute verses to the *Journal de Québec,* and it was for the readers of this journal that his verses were first issued in separate form. In 1862 business reverses compelled his departure from Quebec, and he took refuge in France. There he spent the remainder of his days, under a false name, in the employ of a mercantile firm. During these years he wrote nothing but a *Journal du siège de Paris,* in which he described day by day the siege of 1870. He died at Havre, France, on January 16, 1879. After his death his friends published his *Oeuvres complètes* (Montreal, 1883). "Crémazie may justly be called the father of French-Canadian poetry" (Abbé C. Roy).

[Abbé H. R. Casgrain, *Octave Crémazie* (Montreal, 1912) and *Biographies canadiennes* (Montreal, 1885); T. Chapais, *Octave Crémazie* (Nouvelles soirées canadiennes, vol. ii, 1883); F. Rinfret, *Octave Crémazie* (Montreal, 1906); C. ab der Halden, *Etudes de littérature canadienne-française* (Paris, 1904); C. Darveau, *Nos hommes de lettres* (Montreal, 1873); *Dict. Can. biog.,* vol. 10.]

Crerar, Henry Duncan Graham (1888-1965), soldier, was born in Hamilton, Ontario, April 28, 1888. He was educated at Upper Canada College, in Switzerland, and at the Royal Military College, Kingston, Ontario. He became a lieutenant with the 4th Field Battery, Canadian Artillery, in 1910. He served in the First World War as captain, 11th Battery, 1914; major, 1916; lieutenant-colonel, 1918. He was counter battery officer with the Canadian Corps, 1918. He became general staff officer (2) at the War Office, London (1925), returning to Canada as officer commanding B Battery, R.C.H.A. (1927), and professor of Tactics at Royal Military College (1928-29). He planned the reorganization of the Canadian Militia and was director of military operations and intelligence at the Department of National Defence (1935-38). He was commandant at the Royal Military College, Kingston, (1938-39). At the outbreak of the Second World War he organized Canadian Military Headquarters in London, England, returning to Canada in 1940 as chief of the general staff. He went back to England in 1941 as acting general officer commanding the First Canadian Corps. As Corps commander he served in Britain and Italy (1942-44). When the First Canadian Army was formed in 1944 he became commander-in-chief and directed operations in France, the Low Countries, and Germany. He returned to Canada in 1945 and retired in 1946. He headed the Canadian mission on the Japanese peace settlement in 1947; was appointed first Canadian A.D.C. (General) to the King in 1948, an appointment that was renewed on the accession of Queen Elizabeth II. He has been called Canada's most distinguished soldier and received many military and civil honours. He died at Ottawa, April 1, 1965.

[*Can. who's who,* 1955-57; Metropolitan Toronto Library Board, *Biographical scrapbooks,* vol. 23.]

Crerar, Thomas Alexander (1876-1975), senator, was born June 17, 1876, at Molesworth, Ontario. His family moved to Western Canada in 1881, and Crerar was educated at the Portage la Prairie Collegiate. After teaching in rural schools he became manager of the Grain Grower's Grain Company in 1907. This later became the United Grain Grower's Limited, and he was president until 1929. He was also president of the associated companies: Grain Grower's Export Company; Public Press Limited; and Country Guide Publishing Company. He was elected to the House of Commons for Marquette in 1917 and joined the Union government of Sir Robert Borden (q.v.) where he became minister of agriculture. He resigned his portfolio in 1919 in a dispute over tariff proposals. He was re-elected for Marquette in the general elections of 1921 and became leader of the sixty-six-member Progressive group in the House of Commons. In

November, 1922, he resigned and returned to private life. However, he was elected again in a 1930 by-election after having been appointed minister of railways and canals in the Mackenzie King government. He was defeated, along with the government, in the general election of 1930, but was returned in the general election of 1935 when he became minister of mines and resources following reorganization. He resigned from the government in 1945 and was summoned to the senate from which he retired in 1966. He played a key role in the Western farmers' revolt against the old grain-marketing system during the first quarter of the twentieth century and continued to fight for low tariffs and freight rates. He supported Borden (1917) and King (1944) in their conscription legislation. He died in Victoria, British Columbia, April 11, 1975.

[*Can. who's who,* 1970-72; *Encyc. Can.* (1972); W. L. Morton, *The Progressive Party in Canada* (Toronto, 1950); A. Wood, *Farmers' movements in Canada* (Toronto, 1926).]

Crespel, Emmanuel (1703?-1775), missionary and author, was born at Douai, Flanders, about 1703. He became a Récollet, and was sent to Canada in 1724. He was ordained a priest in 1726, and he served at Sorel, at Niagara, at Cataraqui, and with a mission to the Wisconsin country. He returned to France in 1738, after having been shipwrecked in 1736 on Anticosti; but he came back to Canada in 1752, and he died at Quebec on April 28, 1775. He was the author of a volume entitled *Voyages* (Frankfort-on-Main, 1742; 2nd ed., Amsterdam, 1757; 3rd ed., with biography, Quebec, 1884); and this was translated into English, under the title *Crespel's Travels in North America* (London, 1797; new ed., New York, 1908).

[*Cyc. Am. biog.*; Allaire, *Dict. biog.*]

Cresswell, William Nichol (1822-1888), painter, was born in Devonshire, England, in 1822, and studied art under W.E. Cook, R.A. He emigrated to Canada, and settled near Seaforth, Huron county, Ontario. There he continued painting; and he was elected a charter member of the Ontario Society of Artists in 1872 and of the Royal Canadian Academy of Arts in 1880. He died near Seaforth, Ontario, in 1888.

[H. G. Jones and E. Dyonnet, *History of the Royal Canadian Academy of Arts* (Montreal, 1934); N. MacTavish, *The fine arts in Canada* (Toronto, 1925).]

Cridge, Edward (1871-1913), bishop of the Reformed Episcopal Church, was born at Bratton-Heming, Devonshire, England, on December 17, 1817, the son of John Cridge. He was educated at St. Peter's College, Cambridge (B.A., 1848), and was ordained a priest of the Church of England in 1849. In 1854 he was appointed chaplain of the

Hudson's Bay Company in Vancouver Island, and was rector of the church at Victoria until 1874. He then rejoined the Reformed Episcopal Church, and became rector of the Church of Our Lord at Victoria. In 1875 he was elected bishop of the Reformed Episcopal Church, his diocese including all of Canada and the United States west of the Rocky Mountains. This diocese he administered until his death at Victoria on May 6, 1913. In 1854 he married Mary, daughter of George Winnelle, of Boniford, Essex, England. He was the author of *As it was in the beginning* (Chicago, 1890).

[*Can. who was who,* vol. 2; Morgan, *Can. men* (1912).]

Croft, Henry Holmes (1820-1883), chemist, was born in London, England, on March 6, 1820, the youngest son of William Croft. He was educated at University College, London, and at the University of Berlin; and in 1842 was appointed professor of chemistry and experimental philosophy in King's College (later the University of Toronto), Toronto. He held this chair until ill-health compelled his resignation in 1880; and he died near San Diego, Texas, on March 1, 1883. In 1844 he married Mary, daughter of Capt. Alexander Shaw, and grand-daughter of Major-General Aeneas Shaw (q.v.). By her he had three sons and four daughters. In 1850 he was made a D.C.L. of the University of Toronto.

[J. King, *McCaul: Croft: Forneri* (Toronto, 1914).]

Crofton, Francis Blake (1841-1912), author, was born at Crossboyne, Mayo county, Ireland, in 1841, the youngest son of the Rev. William Crofton. He was educated at Trinity College, Dublin (B.A., 1863); and from 1864 to 1865 was professor of classics at the University of Bishop's College, Lennoxville, Canada. For a number of years he was engaged in journalism in New York; but in 1882 he was appointed librarian to the Legislature of Nova Scotia, at Halifax, and he retired from this post only in 1906. He died in 1912. In addition to numerous contributions to English, American, and Canadian magazines, he was the author of *The bewildered querists and other nonsense* (New York, 1875), *The major's big talk stories* (London, 1882), *The hairbreadth escapes of Major Mendax* (Philadelphia, 1889), *Haliburton, the man and the writer* (Windsor, N.S., 1889), *For closer union* (Halifax, 1897), *Is it too late?* (London, 1902), and a volume of verse, *In sombre tones* (Halifax, 1904).

[Morgan, *Can. men* (1912).]

Crofton, John Folliott (1801-1885), acting governor of Assiniboia, was born in 1801, the son of the Rev. Henry Crofton. He entered the British army as an ensign in the 6th Regiment in 1824, and rose to the rank of general in 1877. In 1846 he was sent to the Red River, in the Canadian West, in charge of a military detachment; and from June to August, 1847, he was acting governor of Assiniboia. He died on July 17, 1885.

[*Annual register,* 1885; E. H. Oliver (ed.), *The Canadian north-west* (2 vols., Ottawa, 1914-15).]

Crofton, Walter Cavendish (1806?-1870), author, was born about 1806, and was successively employed as a clerk in the Canadian civil service and in the court of chancery in Upper Canada. He died in Toronto on July 26, 1870. Under the *nom de plume* of "Uncle Ben", he published a *Brief sketch of the life of Charles Baron Metcalfe* (Kingston, 1846), and under the *nom de plume* of "Erinensis", *Sketches of the thirteenth parliament of Upper Canada* (Toronto, 1840).

[Morgan, *Bib. can.*]

Croil, James (1821-1916), historian and journalist, was born in Glasgow, Scotland, on September 4, 1821, the third son of James Croil, a West India merchant. He was educated at Glasgow University, and came to Canada in 1841. For twenty-three years he was a farmer at Crysler's Farm, Williamsburg, Upper Canada; and he was then appointed general agent of the Church of Scotland in Canada. Later he was the editor of the *Presbyterian*, the official organ of the Presbyterian Church in Canada; and he remained an official of the Church until 1891. He died at Montreal on November 28, 1916. He was the author of *Dundas, a sketch of Canadian history* (Montreal, 1861), *Historical and statistical report of the church of Scotland in Canada* (Montreal, 1867), *The life of Rev. Alexander Mathieson* (Montreal, 1870), *The story of the kirk in the maritime provinces* (published in the *Presbyterian,* Montreal, 1875), *The missionary problem* (Toronto, 1883), *Steam navigation* (Toronto, 1898), and *The genesis of the churches in the United States of America, in Newfoundland, and in the Dominion of Canada* (Montreal, 1907).

[*Can. who was who,* vol. 2; Morgan, *Can. men* (1912).]

Croke, Sir Alexander (1758-1842), jurist, was born at Aylesbury, England, on July 22, 1758, and was educated at Oriel College, Oxford. He was called to the bar at the Inner Temple in 1786; and in 1801 he was appointed a judge in the vice-admiralty court at Halifax, Nova Scotia. He held this position until 1815. He then returned to England, and was created in 1816 a K.C.M.G. He died at Studley, England, on December 27, 1842.

[*Dict. nat. biog.*]

Crooks, Adam (1827-1885), lawyer and politician, was born at West Flamboro', Upper Canada, on December 11, 1827, the fourth son of James Crooks (q.v.) and of the daughter of James Cummings, a United Empire Loyalist.

He was educated at Upper Canada College and at the University of Toronto (B.A., 1850). He was called to the bar in 1852, and was created a Q.C. in 1863. In 1871 he was elected as a Liberal to the legislature of Ontario for West Toronto; and from December, 1871, to October, 1872, he was attorney-general during the premiership of Edward Blake. Under Oliver Mowat, he became first provincial treasurer (1872-77) and then minister of education (1877-83). In 1883 he was obliged by mental ill-health to retire from public life; and he died, at Hartford, Connecticut, on December 11, 1885. His name is chiefly remembered through his connection with the Ontario Liquor Licence Act of 1876, popularly known as the "Crooks Act"; but he played also an important part in the history of education in Ontario.

[*Dom. ann. reg.,* 1885; *Can. parl. comp.*; Dent, *Can. port.,* vol. 2; Rose, *Cyc. Can. biog.* (1888); C. R. W. Biggar, *Sir Oliver Mowat* (2 vols., Toronto, 1905).]

Crooks, James (1778-1860), legislative councillor of Upper Canada, was born in Kilmarnock, Scotland, in 1778, and came to Canada in 1794. He went into business at Niagara, and became one of the leading merchants of Upper Canada. He is said to have made the first shipment of wheat and flour from the Niagara Peninsula to Montreal; and he established at West Flamboro' the first paper mill in Upper Canada. In 1821 he was elected a member of the Legislative Assembly of Upper Canada, and in 1831 he was appointed to the Legislative Council. In 1841 he was made a legislative councillor of united Canada; and he died at Flamboro' West on March 2, 1860.

[Morgan, *Cel. Can.*; *Cyc. Am. biog.*; W. J. Rattray, *The Scot in British North America* (4 vols., Toronto, 1880).]

Crosbie, Chesley Arthur (1905-1962), merchant, was born in St. John's, Newfoundland, on November 4, 1905. He was elected to the Newfoundland National Convention in 1946 as president of a party advocating economic union with the United States. In 1948 he was a member of the delegation which concluded the terms under which Newfoundland entered the Canadian Confederation. He was president of Crosbie and Company Limited (fish merchants), of Gadens Limited, Olsen Whaling and Sealing Limited, and numerous other companies. He died in Honolulu on December 26, 1962.

[*Can. who's who,* 1955-57.]

Crosby, Thomas (1840-1914), missionary, was born in Pickering, Yorkshire, England, on June 21, 1841, and came to Canada with his parents in 1856. He became a minister of the Methodist Church in 1868, and for the rest of his life, until superannuated, was a missionary in British Columbia. He died at Vancouver, British Columbia, on January 13, 1914. He was the author of *Among the An-ko-me-nums or Flathead tribes of Indians of the Pacific coast* (Toronto, 1907) and *Up and down the north Pacific coast by canoe and mission ship* (Toronto, 1914).

[Morgan, *Can. men* (1912).]

Croskill, John H. (1810-1855), journalist, was born in Halifax, Nova Scotia, in 1810. In 1840 he established the Halifax *Morning Post*, and in 1845 he made this the first daily newspaper in the Maritime provinces. From 1845 to 1848 he was king's printer in Nova Scotia; but in 1851 he returned to journalism, and founded the *British North American*. He died in 1855. He was the author of *A comprehensive outline of the geography and history of Nova Scotia from the discovery of America to the reign of Queen Victoria* (Halifax, 1838).

[R. J. Long, *Nova Scotia authors* (East Orange, N.J., 1918).]

Cross, Austin Fletcher (1898-1961), journalist, was born at Oshawa, Ontario, July 3, 1898. He was educated at Ottawa Collegiate and at Queen's University (B.A., 1923). He began his career with the Ottawa *Citizen* in 1923 and also worked for the Hamilton *Spectator*, the *Hamilton Herald*, the Toronto *Globe* and the *Montreal Star*. He joined the staff of the Ottawa *Citizen* in 1943 as parliamentary and political writer. He died at Ottawa, on December 24, 1961. He wrote *Cross roads* (Montreal, 1936), *Snobs and spies* (Toronto, 1937), *The people's mouths* (Toronto, 1943), *Plow to parliament* (Ottawa, 1946).

[*Can. who's who*, 1955-57.]

Crothers, Thomas Wilson (1850-1921), minister of labour for Canada (1911-18), was born at Northport, Canada West, on January 1, 1850, the son of William Crothers and Nancy Gray. He was educated at Albert College and at Victoria University (B.A., 1873), and from 1874 to 1876 he was headmaster of the High School at Wardsville, Ontario. In 1880 he was called to the bar of Upper Canada (K.C., 1908), and for many years he practised law at St. Thomas, Ontario. In 1908 he was elected as a Conservative for West Elgin in the Canadian House of Commons; and in 1911 he became minister of labour in the Borden administration. On him fell the duty of suppressing strikes and lockouts during the War of 1914-18, and he incurred during this period some unpopularity. In 1918 he retired from the cabinet on account of ill-health; and he was thereupon appointed a senator of Canada. He died at Ottawa, on December 10, 1921. In 1883 he married Mary, daughter of Dr. J.A. Burns, of St. Thomas, Ontario.

[*Can. parl. comp.*; Morgan, *Can. men* (1912).]

Crowfoot (d. 1890), chief of the Blackfoot Indians, was born on the western prairies about 1830. He became the most influential chief among the Blackfoot Indians and was largely instrumental in preserving the peace between them and the whites, both at the time of the coming of the North-West Mounted Police and during the North West Rebellion of 1885. He died on April 25, 1890, near Gleichen, Alberta, aged about sixty.

[F. W. Howay, *Crowfoot, the great chief of the Blackfoot* (Canadian Historical Association Report, 1930); H.A. Dempsey, *Crowfoot, chief of the Blackfeet* (Edmonton, 1972).]

Crozier, Leif Newry Fitzroy (1847-1901), superintendent of the North-West Mounted Police (1875-85), was born at Newry, Ireland, in 1847, and died at Oklahoma, United States, on February 25, 1901.

[*Canadian annual review*, 1901; T. M. Longstreth, *The silent force* (Toronto, 1928).]

Cruikshank, Ernest Alexander (1853-1939), soldier and historian, was born in Bertie township, Welland county, Canada West, on June 29, 1853. He was educated at Upper Canada College; and during his earlier years he farmed near Fort Erie, Ontario. He took an active interest in municipal affairs, and in 1886 was elected warden of Welland county. In 1877 he was commissioned as an ensign in the militia, and he rose in rank until he became in 1899 commanding officer of the Lincoln and Welland Regiment, and in 1904 officer commanding the 5th Infantry Brigade. In 1909 he was appointed district officer commanding Military District No. 3, with head-quarters at Calgary; and he remained in this post until 1917, having been promoted brigadier-general in 1915. In 1918 he was appointed director of the Historical Section of the General Staff at Ottawa; from this position he retired on pension in 1921. For the remainder of his life he was chairman of the Historic Sites and Monuments Board of Canada. He died at Ottawa, Ontario, on June 23, 1939. In 1906 he was elected a fellow of the Royal Society of Canada; and in 1935 he was awarded the Society's Tyrrell medal for distinguished work in Canadian history. Over a period of fifty years he contributed a long series of papers to the *Transactions* of the Royal Society of Canada, the *Papers and Records* of the Ontario Historical Society, and the publications of various local historical societies; he was the author of *The life of Sir Henry Morgan* (Morgan, 1935) and *The political adventures of John Henry* (Toronto, 1936); and he edited *The documentary history of the campaign on the Niagara frontier in 1812-14* (9 vols., Welland, Ont., 1896-1908), *The Simcoe papers* (5 vols., Toronto, 1923-31), and *The Russell papers* (3 vols., Toronto 1932-36).

[*Can. who's who*, 1936-37; *Proc. Roy. Soc. Can.*, 1940.]

Cruikshank, William (1848-1922), painter, was born at Broughty Ferry, Scotland, on December 25, 1848, and was the grandnephew of George Cruikshank, the illustrator of Charles Dickens's works. He studied art at the Royal Scottish Academy, Edinburgh, at the Royal Academy, London, and in Paris. His studies in Paris were interrupted by the Franco-Prussian War, and in 1871 he settled in Canada. He opened a studio in Toronto; and for twenty-five years he was an instructor in the Central Ontario School of Art, later the Ontario College of Art. In 1894 he was elected a member of the Royal Canadian Academy of Arts; and he acquired a considerable reputation as a portrait and figure painter, and a painter of Canadian scenes. He died at Kansas City, Missouri, on May 19, 1922. Some of his paintings are in the National Gallery at Ottawa.

[J. Mavor, *William Cruikshank, R.C.A* (Can. mag., 1926); *Can. who was who*, vol. 2; N. MacTavish, *The fine arts in Canada* (Toronto, 1925).]

Cudmore, Sedley Anthony (1878-1945), statistician, was born in Ireland in 1878, and died suddenly at Quebec City, on October 17, 1945. He came to Canada as a child, and was educated at the University of Toronto (B.A., 1905) and at Wadham College, Oxford (M.A., 1908). He was appointed an instructor on the staff of the department of economics in the University of Toronto in 1908, and later an assistant professor. In 1919 he joined the staff of the Dominion Bureau of Statistics in Ottawa; in 1921 he became editor of the *Canada Year Book*; in 1930 he was appointed Assistant Dominion Statistician; and in 1942 he succeeded R. H. Coats (q.v.) as Dominion Statistician. He was the author of *A history of the world's commerce, with especial reference to Canada* (Toronto, 1929; rev. ed., 1932). He was elected a fellow of the Royal Society of Canada in 1941; and the University of Toronto conferred on him the degree of LL.D. a few months before his death.

[*Proc. Roy. Soc. Can.*, 1946; *Can. who's who*, 1936-37).]

Cugnet, François Joseph (1720-1789), lawyer, was born at Quebec on June 26, 1720, the eldest son of François-Étienne Cugnet and Louise-Madeleine DuSautoy. Before the conquest he was counsellor to the Superior Council of New France; and in 1760 he was attached by General Murray (q.v.) to the military court at Quebec. In 1766 Carleton (q.v.) appointed him French secretary to the governor and council, and employed him in drawing up an abstract of the laws during the French régime. The result was published in four volumes, *Traité abrégé des anciennes loix* (Quebec, 1775), *Extraits des édits, declarations, ordonnances, et règlements* (Quebec, 1775), *Traité de la loi des fiefs* (Quebec, 1775), and *Traité de la*

police (Quebec, 1775). He took part in the controversy over the framing of the Quebec Act, and was the object of attack by Francis Maseres (q.v) in his *Mémoire à la défence d'un plan d'acte de parlement ... contre les objections de M. François Joseph Cugnet* (London, 1773). He died at Quebec on September 16, 1789. In 1757 he married Marie-Josephte de la Fontaine de Belcour, one of the heirs of the Bissot estate, and by her he had five sons.

[P. G. Roy, *La famille du légiste François-Joseph Cugnet* (Bull, rech. hist., 1915); and *Fils de Québec*, vol. 1 (Lévis, Que., 1933); Morgan, *Bib. can.*; Le Jeune, *Dict. gén.*]

Cullen, Maurice Galbraith (1866-1934), landscape-painter, was born at St. John's, Newfoundland, in 1866, and came to Montreal with his parents as a child. He studied sculpture in Montreal, under Hébert, and painting in Paris, France, under Delauny and Roll. He exhibited for the first time in the Paris salon in 1894. He was elected an associate of the Royal Canadian Academy of Arts in 1895, and a member in 1907. He lived in Canada after 1906, specializing in winter landscapes. He was also a member of the Canadian War Memorial staff, and painted a number of pictures relating to the Great War. He died in Chambly Canton, Quebec, on March 28, 1934.

[Morgan, *Can. men* (1912); N. MacTavish, *The fine arts in Canada* (Toronto, 1925); *Can. who was who*, vol. 2.]

Culliton, John Thomas (1905-1963), economist, was born at Englevale, North Dakota, on April 23, 1905, the son of Joseph Culliton, a railway telegrapher. He was educated at Elbow, Saskatchewan, and entered the University of Saskatchewan in 1921, graduating in 1926 (B.A.). He then went to McGill University (M.A., 1927), and was appointed lecturer in economics under Stephen Leacock (q.v.). In 1931 he received a Royal Society Fellowship and after touring the British universities he spent a year at the London School of Economics. He returned to McGill University in 1932 as assistant professor of economics, becoming associate professor in 1952. During the Second World War he was an administrative officer with the Royal Canadian Air Force. His early life on the farm and the railroad gave him a great interest in the themes of transportation, land settlement, and wheat. He died at Montreal in 1963. He wrote *Leacock's Montreal*, with S. Leacock (Toronto, 1963).

[*Can. journ. ec. pol. sc.*, vol. XXX.]

Cumberland, Frederic Barlow (1846-1913), author, was born in Portsmouth, England, in 1846, the son of Lieut.-Col. Frederic William Cumberland (q.v.). He came to Canada with his parents in 1847, and was educated at the Toronto Grammar School, at Cheltenham College, England, and at Trinity University, Toronto (M.A., 1867). For a number of years he was in the service of the Great Western and the Northern Railways; from 1885 to 1892 he was traffic manager of the Lake Superior line of steamships; and he was one of the organizers, and later the president, of the Niagara Navigation Company. He wrote *A century of sail and steam on the Niagara river* (Toronto, 1913), and a *History of the Union Jack* (3rd and rev. ed., Toronto, 1909), as well as a number of historical papers such as *The Fenian raid of 1866* (Trans. Roy. Soc. Can., 1912) and *The battle of York* (pamphlet, Toronto, 1913). He died at Port Hope, Ontario, on September 1, 1913. In 1871 he married Seraphina, daughter of William Fraser, of Port Hope; and by her had one daughter.

[Morgan, *Can. men* (1912); *Can. who was who*, vol. 1.]

Cumberland, Frederic William (1821-1881), engineer and architect, was born in London, England, on April 10, 1821. He was educated at King's College, London, studied architecture and engineering, and obtained employment, first as a railway engineer, and then in the engineering department of the Admiralty. In 1847 he came to Canada. He settled in Toronto, entered into partnership with W. G. Storm, and became the architect of St. James Cathedral, of Osgoode Hall, and of University College, Toronto. At the same time, he interested himself in railway construction and operation and became in 1860 managing director of the Northern Railway — a position he occupied until his death. In 1861 he organized the 10th Royal Grenadiers of Toronto, and he was the commanding officer of this regiment until 1865. He represented Algoma in the Legislative Assembly of Ontario from 1867 to 1875, and in the Canadian House of Commons from 1871 to 1872. His death took place at Toronto on August 5, 1881. He married Wilmot Bramley, whose sister was the wife of Thomas Gibbs Ridout (q.v.).

[*Dom. ann. reg.*, 1880-81; *Cyc. Am. biog.*; Rose, *Cyc. Can. biog.* (1886); C. Clarke, *Sixty years in Upper Canada* (Toronto, 1908).]

Cumming, Cuthbert (1787-1870), furtrader, was born in Banffshire, Scotland, in 1787, and entered the service of the North West Company as a clerk at Fort Dauphin in 1804. He was taken over as a clerk by the Hudson's Bay Company in 1821; and in 1827 he was promoted to be a chief trader. From 1821 to 1828 he was employed mainly in the Swan River department; in 1828 he was moved to the Montreal department; and from 1831 to 1837 he was at the Mingan Islands. From 1841 to 1843 he was at the Pic; and in 1843-44 he was at Fort Pelly, in the Swan River district. In 1844 he resigned, and settled at Colborne, Ontario. There he died in April, 1870, aged 83 years. In 1842 he married at the Pic, Lake Superior, Jane, daughter of Thomas McMurray (q.v.), and he was survived by his widow and three sons.

[G. de T. Glazebrook (ed.), *The Hargrave correspondence* (Toronto: The Champlain Society, 1938).]

Cummings, Mrs. Emily Ann McCausland, *née* **Shortt** (1851-1930), journalist, was born in Port Hope, Ontario, on May 11, 1851, the daughter of the Rev. Jonathan Shortt. In 1871 she married Willoughby Cummings (d. 1892), a journalist; and from 1893 to 1903 she was on the editorial staff of the Toronto *Globe*. She then entered the civil service at Ottawa, as field secretary of the women's department of the annuities branch of the department of the interior. From 1894 to 1910 she was corresponding secretary of the National Council of Women. She died at Toronto on November 1, 1930. In 1910 she received the honorary degree of D.C.L. from King's College, Windsor, being the first woman to receive an honorary degree from a Canadian university.

[Morgan, *Can. men and women* (1912); *Can. who was who*, vol. 1.]

Cunard, Sir Samuel, Bart. (1787-1865), shipowner, was born at Halifax, Nova Scotia, on November 21, the son of Abraham Cunard. He became a successful merchant of Halifax, was one of the founders of the Halifax Banking Company in 1825, and in 1831 was appointed a member of the Council of Twelve in Nova Scotia. In 1838 he founded the British and North American Royal Mail Steam Packet Company, from which originated the Cunard line of steamships; and he was thus the pioneer of regular trans-Atlantic steam navigation. During the latter part of his life he lived in England; and there he died on April 28, 1865. In 1859 he was created a baronet of the United Kingdom for the services rendered by the Cunard line during the Crimean War.

[A. M. Payne, *Life of Sir Samuel Cunard* (Coll. Nova Scotia Hist. Soc., 1918); L. Cox, *A pioneer of ocean navigation* (Can. geographical journal, 1935); *Dict. nat. biog.*; *Cyc. Am. biog.*; H.K. Grant, *Samuel Cunard, pioneer of the Atlantic steamship* (London, 1967).]

Cuoq, Jean André (1821-1898), priest and philologist, was born at Puy-en-Vélay, Haute Loire, France, on June 6, 1821, the son of Jean Pierre Cuoq and Rosalie Delholme. Ordained a priest of the Roman Catholic Church in 1845, he came to Canada in 1846, and was appointed a missionary to the Indians at the Lake of Two Mountains, Lower Canada. Here he remained for many years, and he became an authority on the Indian languages. In his later years he retired to the Seminary of St. Sulpice, Montreal, and he died at Oka, Quebec, on July 21, 1898. In 1882 he was chosen a charter member of the Royal Society of Canada. His chief publications were *Etudes philologiques sur quelque langues sauvages de l'Amérique* (Montreal, 1866), *Lexique de la langue Iroquoise* (Montreal, 1882, with "additamenta", 1883), *Lexique de la langue Algonquine* (Montreal, 1886), *Grammaire de la langue Algonquine* (Trans. Roy. Soc. Can., 1891-92). He published also an anonymous pamphlet entitled *Jugement erroné de M. Ernest Renan sur les langues sauvages* (Montreal, 1864; 2nd ed., 1869).

[O. Maurault, *Un Sulpicien indianisant: M. André Cuoq* (Trans. Roy. Soc. Can., 1932); *Can. who was who*, vol. 2; *Proc. Roy. Soc. Can.*, 1901; Morgan, *Can. men* (1898); Allaire, *Dict. biog.*; Le Jeune, *Dict. gén.*]

Curran, James Watson (1865-1952), journalist and author, was born in Armagh, Ireland, on April 24, 1865, and died at Sault Ste. Marie, Ontario, on February 20, 1952. He came to Canada with his parents when a child, and was educated in the public schools of Orillia, Ontario. He became a journalist, first in Toronto, and then in Montreal; but in 1901 he bought the Sault Ste. Marie *Star*, a weekly journal which he turned into a daily in 1914. He was the author of two books, *Here was Vinland* (Sault Ste. Marie, Ont., 1939) and *Wolves don't bite* (Sault Ste. Marie, Ont., 1940).

[Toronto *Globe and Mail*, Feb. 21, 1952; *Can. who's who*, 1949-51).]

Curran, John Joseph (1842-1909), politician and judge, was born in Montreal on February 22, 1842, the son of Charles Curran and Sarah Kennedy. He was educated at St. Mary's College, Montreal, at the University of Ottawa (LL.D., 1891), and at McGill University (B.C.L., 1862). He was called to the bar in 1863 (Q.C., 1876), and practised law in Montreal. He was elected to represent Montreal Centre in the Canadian House of Commons, in 1882, and he continued to sit for this constituency until his elevation to the bench as a puisne judge of the Superior Court of Quebec in 1895. From 1892 to 1895 he was solicitor-general in the governments of Sir John Thompson (q.v.) and Sir Mackenzie Bowell (q.v.). He died in Montreal on October 1, 1909. In 1865 he married Mary Elizabeth, daughter of Patrick Brennan, Montreal, and by her he had several children.

[P. G. Roy, *Les juges de la province de Québec* (Quebec, 1933); *Can. parl. comp.*; Morgan, *Can. men* (1898).]

Currelly, Charles Trick (1876-1957), archaeologist, was born at Exeter, Ontario, on January 11, 1876, and died at Baltimore, Maryland, on April 17, 1957. He was educated at Victoria College, University of Toronto (B.A., 1898; M.A., 1902); and during the years following graduation he devoted himself to archaeological work, first in Egypt, and later in Crete and Asia Minor. When the Royal Ontario Museum of Archaeology was projected in 1907, he was appointed its curator, and in 1914 its director. This position he held until his retirement in 1946; and during these years he built up one of the most outstanding archaeological museums in North America. He was elected a fellow of the Royal Society of Canada in 1917; and honorary degrees were conferred on him by the University of Toronto and Queen's University. Shortly before his death he published his autobiography, entitled *I brought the ages home* (Toronto, 1956).

[*Proc. Roy. Soc. Can.*, 1957; *Can. who's who*, 1956-58; *Encyc. Can.*; Toronto *Globe and Mail*, April 18, 1957.]

Currie, Sir Arthur William (1875-1933), soldier and educationist, was born in the village of Napperton, Middlesex county, Ontario, on December 5, 1875, the son of William Garner Currie and Jane Patterson. He was educated at the Strathroy Collegiate Institute. In 1893 he went to British Columbia, and became a school-teacher. Eventually, he went into business in Victoria, British Columbia; and there became the senior partner in one of the leading real estate firms on Vancouver Island. When the First World War broke out, in 1914, he was also a lieut.-colonel in the militia, having risen from the ranks to command the 5th Canadian Garrison Artillery; and he was given command of the Vancouver Highland Battalion in the First Canadian contingent. After the battle of St. Julien, in 1915, he was given command of a brigade, with the rank of brigadier-general. In 1916 he was placed in command of the First Canadian Division, with the rank of major-general; and in 1917 he succeeded Sir Julian Byng (q.v.) as the commander of the Canadian Corps, with the rank of lieutenant-general. This last position he retained, with great credit to himself and to the Corps, throughout the remainder of the war. He rode into Mons at the head of his troops as the Armistice came into effect on November 11, 1918. After the Armistice he commanded the Canadian forces on the Rhine; and on his return to Canada in 1919 he was appointed inspector-general of the Canadian militia. In 1920 he was offered and accepted the position of principal and vice-chancellor of McGill University, Montreal; and he retained this post until his death in Montreal, on November 30, 1933. In 1901 he married Lucy Sophia, youngest daughter of William Chaworth Chaworth-Musters, of Nottingham, England; and by her he had one son and one daughter. He received many honours. He was created a C.B. in 1915, a K.C.M.G. in 1917, a K.C.B. in 1918, and a G.C.M.G. in 1919; and the honorary degree of LL.D. was conferred on him by the following universities: Cambridge, McGill, Toronto, New York, Acadia, Edinburgh, Pennsylvania, Princeton, McMaster, Dartmouth, Vermont, Western, British Columbia, Middlebury,

Harvard, Queen's, and Union. At the time of his death, he was grand president of the Canadian Legion of the British Empire Service League.

[Sir A. Macphail, *Sir Arthur Currie* (Queen's quarterly, 1934); W. Bovey, *General Sir Arthur Currie* (Canadian defence quarterly, 1934); *Who was who*, 1929-1940; *Who's who in Canada*; H.M. Urquhart, *Arthur Currie* (Toronto, 1950); J. A. Swettenham, *To seize the victory* (Toronto, 1965).]

Currie, John Allister (1868-1931), politician and soldier, was born at the village of Nottawa, Simcoe county, Ontario, on February 25, 1868. He was educated at the Collingwood Collegiate Institute, and began life as a journalist in Toronto; but later went into business and became managing-director of the Imperial Steel Corporation. From 1908 to 1921 he represented North Simcoe in the Canadian House of Commons; and in 1914 he went overseas as officer commanding the 15th Battalion (48th Highlanders), but was invalided to Canada in 1915. From 1922 to 1925 he represented south-east Toronto in the Legislative Assembly of Ontario. He died at Miami, Florida, on June 28, 1931. He was the author of *The Red Watch: With the First Canadian Division in Flanders* (Toronto, 1916), the sale of which exhausted three editions.

[*Can. who was who*, vol. 1; *Can. parl. comp.*; Morgan, *Can. men* (1912); *Can. who's who* (1910).]

Curzon, Mrs. Sarah Anne (1833-1898), author, was born at Birmingham, England, in 1833. In 1858 she married Robert Curzon, of Norfolk, England, and with him she came to Canada in 1862. She became a champion in Canada of woman's rights; and she was a frequent contributor to Canadian periodical literature. She died at Toronto, Ontario, on November 8, 1898. Her chief publication was *Laura Secord, the heroine of 1812: A drama, and other poems* (Toronto, 1887).

[Morgan, *Can. men and women* (1898); C. C. James, *A bibliography of Canadian poetry* (Toronto, 1899).]

Cuthbert, James (*fl.* 1741-1798), legislative councillor, was the son of Alexander Cuthbert, of Inverness, Scotland, and Beatrix, daughter of David Cuthbert, of Ardresier, and belonged to a cadet branch of the barons of Castlehill. He served first in the British navy, and was present at the bombardment of Cartagena, Colombia, in 1741. Later he obtained a commission in the British army. He was attached first to the Black Watch, and then to the 15th Regiment, and attained the rank of captain. He was present at Louisbourg in 1758 and the Plains of Abraham in 1759; and he was sent by General Murray (q.v.), whose aide-de-camp he was, to England to carry the news of the capture of Quebec. In 1765 he acquired the seigniory of Berthier, and he lived at Berthier for the rest of his life. In 1766 he was appointed by Murray to the Executive Council; and in 1775 he became a member of the Legislative Council. He encountered the hostility of both Carleton (q.v.) and Haldimand (q.v.); and in 1786 he was dropped from the Council. He died in 1798. He was thrice married. By his wife Catherine Cairns (d. 1785), he had three sons and seven daughters.

[S. A. Moreau, *L'honorable James Cuthbert, père* (Bull. rech. hist., 1901); R. Roy, *Cuthbert* (Bull. rech. hist., 1934).]

Cuthbert, James (1769-1849), president of the Special Council of Lower Canada (1838), was the second son of James Cuthbert (q.v.), the first English seignior of Berthier. He inherited the seigniory of Berthier, and lived there all his life. From 1796 to 1811 he was a member of the Legislative Assembly of Lower Canada for Warwick; and from 1811 to 1838 he was a member of the Legislative Council. In 1838 he was appointed president of the Special Council appointed to administer the affairs of Lower Canada after the suspension of the constitution; and he was one of three members of the Council that opposed union with Upper Canada. In his later years he became involved in financial difficulties, and obtained the post of *grand-voyer* of the province. He died at the manor house of Berthier on March 4, 1849. He was twice married, first to Marie-Claire Fraser (d. 1811), and then in 1814 to Marie-Louise-Amable Cairns (d. 1878).

[S. A. Moreau, *L'honorable Jacques Cuthbert, fils* (Bull. rech. hist., 1902); R. Roy, *Cuthbert*, (Bull. rech. hist., 1934).]

Cuthbert, Ross (1776-1861), executive councillor of Lower Canada (1812-41), was born on February 17, 1776, the third son of James Cuthbert, the elder (q.v.). He was educated at the College of Douai, in France; and he inherited from his father the seigniory of Lanoraie and Dautray. He was called to the bar of Lower Canada in 1803, and practised law in Quebec. In 1812 he was sworn of the Executive Council, and he held his seat in the Council until 1841. From 1800 to 1810, from 1812 to 1816, and again in 1820, he also represented Warwick in the Legislative Assembly of Lower Canada, and during the years 1812-16 he was the spokesman of the government on the floor of the House. He was the author of three early items in Canadian literature, *L'Aréopage* (Quebec, 1803), *An apology for Great Britain* (Quebec, 1809), and *New theory of the tides* (Quebec, 1810). He died on August 28, 1861.

[Morgan, *Bib. can.*; Le Jeune, *Dict. gén.*; R. Roy, *Cuthbert* (Bull. rech. hist., 1934).]

Cutts, William Malcolm (1857-1943), painter, was born at Allahabad, India, in 1857, and came to Canada in early youth. He began his career as a painter at Stratford, Ontario, in 1870, and opened a studio in Toronto in 1880. He was elected an associate of the Royal Academy of Arts in 1908; and he became well known as a portrait painter and a painter of marine subjects. He died at Port Perry, Ontario, on January 29, 1943.

[*Can. who's who*, 1936-37.]

Cuvillier, Augustin or **Austin** (1779-1849), merchant and banker, was born in Quebec on August 21, 1779, the eldest son of Augustin Cuvillier. He was educated at the College of Montreal, and went into business in Montreal. He was one of the pioneers of Canadian banking, and was closely associated in 1817 with the founding of the Bank of Montreal. In 1814 he was elected a member of the Legislative Assembly of Lower Canada for Huntingdon; and he represented this constit-uency continuously until 1830. He then sat for four years for Laprairie. During this time he supported Papineau and the *patriote* party; but he broke with Papineau over the Ninety-Two Resolutions of 1834, and in the elections of that year was defeated. He thereupon retired from political life, and devoted himself for a time to business. After the union of 1841 he was, however, again elected to the Assembly for Huntingdon; and he was chosen the first speaker of the Legislative Assembly of United Canada. In 1844 his support of Sir Charles Metcalfe (q.v.) once again cost him his seat; and on this occasion he retired finally to private life. He died in Montreal on July 11, 1849. In 1802 he married a daughter of Joseph Marie Perrault, of Montreal.

[A. Shortt, *Founders of Canadian banking* (Journal of the Canadian Bankers' Association, 1923); F. J. Audet, *Augustin Cuvillier* (Bull. rech. hist., 1922 and 1927); Morgan, *Cel. Can.*; Le Jeune, *Dict. gén.*]

D

Dablon, Claude (1619-1697), missionary, was born at Dieppe, France, June 21, 1619. He became a member of the Society of Jesus, and was sent to Canada in 1655. In 1671 he was appointed superior of the Jesuit missions in Canada, and he edited the *Relation* of 1671-72. He died in Quebec in 1697. A description by him of the journey of Marquette (q.v.) to the Mississippi has been published in J. G. Shea, *Discovery and exploration of the Mississippi valley* (New York, 1853).

[*Cyc. Am. biog.*; R. G. Thwaites (ed.), *The Jesuit relations* (73 vols., Cleveland, 1897); *Dict. Can. biog.*, vol. 1.]

Dadson, Ebenezer W. (1845-1900), clergyman, was born in England on July 10, 1845, and came to Canada with his parents in 1849. He was educated at the Toronto Model School and Woodstock College; and became an outstanding preacher of the Baptist Church. From 1881 to 1888 he was editor of the *Canadian Baptist*. He died on March 12, 1900.

[J. H. Farmer (ed.), *E. W. Dadson, B.A., D.D.: The man and his message* (Toronto, 1902).]

Dafoe, Allan Roy (1883-1943), physician, was born at Madoc, Ontario, on May 29, 1883. He was educated at the University of Toronto (M.B., 1907); and became a general practitioner at Callander, Ontario. Here, on May 28, 1934, he attended the birth of the Dionne quintuplets; and he was shortly afterwards placed in charge of their welfare by an Act of the Ontario legislature. He died at North Bay, Ontario, on June 2, 1943. He was the author of *Dr. Dafoe's guide-book for mothers* (New York, 1936).

[F. Hunt, *The little doc: The story of Allan Roy Dafoe* (New York, 1939); *Can. who's who*, 1938-39.]

Dafoe, Elizabeth (1900-1960), librarian, was born in Montreal, Quebec, on October 22, 1900, the daughter of John W. Dafoe (q.v.). She was educated at the University of Manitoba (B.A., 1923), and took library training at Columbia University and the University of Chicago. She joined the staff of the University of Manitoba Library, and in 1937 became chief

librarian. She died at Winnipeg, Manitoba, on April 25, 1960. In 1948 she was president of the Canadian Library Association.

[*Can. who's who*, 1958-60.]

Dafoe, John Wesley (1866-1944), journalist, was born at Combermere, Ontario, on March 8, 1866. He was educated at the public and high schools in Arnprior, Ontario; and became for a time a school-teacher. In 1883, however, he entered journalism as the parliamentary correspondent at Ottawa of the *Montreal Star*; from 1885 to 1886 he was editor of the *Ottawa Evening Journal*; from 1886 to 1892 he was on the staff of the *Manitoba Free Press*; and in 1901, after serving in various capacities on Montreal newspapers, he returned to the *Manitoba Free Press* (later known as the *Winnipeg Free Press*), as editor-in-chief. This position he retained during the rest of his life; and during this period he became a figure of national importance in Canadian affairs, and perhaps the last of the great journalists of an earlier day. He was a member of the Canadian delegation at the Peace Conference of 1919; and he was a Canadian representative at repeated Imperial Press Conferences. He was elected a fellow of the Royal Society of Canada in 1926; he was elected chancellor of the University of Manitoba in 1934; and he was an honorary LL.D. of the University of Manitoba and of Queen's University. He died at Winnipeg, Manitoba, on January 9, 1944. He was the author of *Over the Canadian battlefields* (Toronto, 1919), *Laurier, a study in Canadian politics* (Toronto, 1922), *Clifford Sifton in relation to his times* (Toronto, 1931), and *Canada, an American nation* (New York, 1935); and he was the editor of *Canada fights* (New York, 1941). More recently W. L. Morton has published some of his editorials under the title *The voice of Dafoe* (Toronto, 1945).

[R. A. McKay, *John W. Dafoe* (Canadian journal of economics and political science, 1944); *Can, who's who*, 1938-39; *Can. hist. rev.*, 1944; *Proc. Roy. Soc. Can.*, 1944; G. V. Ferguson, *John W. Dafoe* (Toronto, 1948); R. Cook, *The Politics of John Dafoe and the Free Press* (Toronto, 1963); M. Donnelly, *Dafoe of the Free Press* (Toronto, 1968).]

Dale, Arch (1882-1962), cartoonist, was born in Dundee, Scotland, in 1882. He began his professional career as a cartoonist for the Dundee *Courier* and then the *Manchester Despatch*. He was a member of the Harmsworth Group in London. He came to Canada as a homesteader in Saskatchewan and, while there, sent his first cartoon to the *Winnipeg Free Press*. He abandoned homesteading for a freelance cartooning career with his syndicated "doo-dads". He joined the *Winnipeg Free Press* in 1927, where he remained until retirement. Among his publications are *Five years of R.B. Bennett with Arch Dale and the Winnipeg Free Press* (Winnipeg, 1935), and *The left and the right* (Winnipeg, 1945). He died at Winnipeg June 18, 1962.
[*Can. who's who*, 1955-59.]

Dale, James Alfred (1874-1951), educationist, was born at Birmingham, England, on June 11, 1874, and died at Hamilton, Ontario, on November 27, 1951. He was educated at Merton College, Oxford (B.A., 1901; M.A., 1903), and came to Canada in 1908 as first professor of education at McGill University. In 1920 he was appointed professor of social science at the University of Toronto, but was compelled to resign this chair in 1930 because of ill-health. He edited *Education and life* (Toronto, 1923).
[*Can. who's who*, 1949-51.]

Dalgleish, Oakley (1910-1963), newspaperman, was born at New Liskeard, Ontario, in 1910. He was educated in Moose Jaw, Saskatchewan, and at the University of Toronto. He began his newspaper career in Vancouver with the *Star* and then moved to the Regina *Star*. He worked in London, England, for the Sifton newspapers and for the *Daily Express* and the *Morning Post*. Upon the establishment of the Dominion News Bureau he became a member of its European staff and worked out of a number of European capitals. He joined the Toronto *Globe* in 1935 and in 1939 became a member of the staff of the Dominion Bureau of Information. In 1940 he became the Ottawa correspondent for the *Globe and Mail* and editorial writer, becoming editor in 1948 and assistant publisher in 1952. He died at Toronto, August 16, 1963.
[*Can. who's who*, 1955-57.]

Dalhousie, George Ramsay, ninth Earl of (1770-1838), governor-in-chief of Canada (1819-28), was born on October 23, 1770, the eldest son of George Ramsay, eighth Earl of Dalhousie, and Elizabeth Glen. He entered the 3rd Dragoon Guards in 1788; in 1794 he became lieutenant-colonel of the 2nd Foot; in 1809 he attained the rank of major-general, and in 1830 that of general. He fought throughout the Revolutionary and Peninsular wars, and was present at the battle of Waterloo. In 1816 he was appointed lieutenant-governor of Nova Scotia; and from 1819 to 1828 he was governor-in-chief of Canada. During his period of office he came into conflict with Louis Joseph Papineau (q.v.) and the French-Canadian majority in the Assembly; and he was instrumental in founding in 1824 the Quebec Literary and Historical Society, the first learned society in Canada. In 1829 he was appointed commander-in-chief in India; and in 1830 he was elected captain-general of the Royal Company of Archers, the king's bodyguard for Scotland. He died at Dalhousie Castle on March 21, 1838. In 1805 he married Christian, daughter of Charles Broun of Coalstoun; and by her he had three sons. He succeeded his father in the earldom in 1788: and from 1796 to 1815 he was a representative peer of Scotland; and in 1815 he was created Baron Dalhousie of Dalhousie Castle in the peerage of the United Kingdom. In 1813 he was created a K.B., and in 1815 a G.C.B.
[*Dict. nat. biog.*; Morgan, *Cel. Can.*; Sir J. B. Paul (ed.), *The Scots peerage*, vol. 3 (Edinburgh, 1906); R. Christie, *History of Lower Canada* (6 vols., Montreal and Quebec, 1848-56).]

Dallaire, Jean (1916-1965), painter, was born in Hull, Quebec, in 1916. He had little formal art training until he went to Central Technical School in Toronto where he studied with Charles Goldhamer, Peter Haworth, and Elizabeth Wyn Wood. On his return to Quebec he did two murals, one in Ottawa, and one in Fall River, Massachusetts, for the Dominican Fathers. He won an overseas scholarship from the Beaux-Arts in Montreal and went to Paris in 1938 to the Atelier d'Art Sacré to study with Maurice Denis. When the Germans invaded Paris, Dallaire and his wife were interned. Madame Dallaire was released after six months but Jean remained interned in Stalag 220 at St. Denis for four years. On his release he studied tapestry design and on his return to Canada began to teach tapestry design at the Ecole des Beaux-Arts in Quebec. In 1952 he joined the National Film Board, where he worked as a film-strip artist. He illustrated three film-strip productions of the folk song "Cadet Rouselle II" for use in schools. At the same time he maintained a studio where he created large canvasses. It has been said that his work was affected by the years of internment, by cubist analysis of form, by the decorative limitations and possibilities of tapestry design in which he had specialized, and by his sensitivities to the myths of French Canada against the realities of Canadian life. He died in 1965. He is represented in the National Gallery of Canada, the Art Gallery of Ontario, and the Museum of the Province of Quebec.
[C. S. MacDonald, *A dictionary of Canadian artists,* vol. 1 (Ottawa, 1967); Donald Buchanan, *The art of Jean Dallaire* (Canadian art, vol. 12, no. 4, 1955).]

Dallas, Alexander Grant (1818?-1882), governor of Rupert's Land, was born in Scotland about 1818. He engaged in trade in China, retired from business, and about 1850 was appointed chief factor of the Hudson's Bay Company at Fort Victoria, Vancouver Island. In 1862 he was appointed governor of Rupert's Land, in succession to Sir George Simpson (q.v.); but he resigned this position in 1864. He then returned to Scotland, and he died there on January 2, 1882. He married a daughter of Sir James Douglas (q.v.).

[G. Bryce, *The remarkable history of the Hudson's Bay Company* (London, 1900); J. J. Hargrave, *Red River* (Montreal, 1871); Sir E. W. Watkin, *Canada and the States* (London, 1887); Le Jeune, *Dict. gén.*; B. E. McKelvie, *Successor to Simpson* (Beaver, 1951).]

Dalton, Mrs. Annie Charlotte, *née* **Armitage** (1865-1938), poet and story-writer, was born at Birkby, Huddersfield, England, on December 9, 1865. She married Willie Dalton, of Huddersfield, in 1891; and came to Vancouver, British Columbia, in 1904. She died in Vancouver on January 12, 1938. She was the author of *The marriage of music* (Vancouver, B.C., 1910), *Flame and adventure* (New York, 1924), *Songs and carols* (Vancouver, B.C., 1925), *The ear trumpet* (Toronto, 1926), *The silent zones* (Vancouver, B.C., 1927), *The call of the carillon* (Vancouver, B.C., 1928), *The amber riders* (Toronto, 1929), *The neighing north* (Toronto, 1931), and *Lilies and leopards* (Toronto, 1935).

[*Can. who's who*, 1936-37.]

Dalton, Thomas (1792-1840), journalist, was born in Birmingham, England, on April 29, 1792. He emigrated to Canada about 1812, and settled in Kingston. There he began in 1828 the publication of a weekly newspaper, the *Patriot*. In 1832 he transferred the *Patriot* to York (Toronto); and became one of the apologists for the "Family Compact". He died in Toronto on October 26, 1840. He was the author of a pamphlet on banking, *Money is power* (Toronto, 1835).

[R. Card, *The Daltons and the Patriot* (Can. hist. rev., 1935).]

Daly, Sir Dominick (1798-1868), administrator, was born in Galway, Ireland, on August 11, 1798, the third son of Dominick Daly, an Irish landowner. He came to Canada as the private secretary of Sir Francis Burton (q.v.) in 1822; and in 1827 he was appointed provincial secretary for Lower Canada. He was continued in this office under the Act of Union in 1841, having been elected to the Legislative Assembly for Megantic. During the years 1841-48 he clung to office in successive administrations, and from November, 1843, to August, 1844, he was the governor's sole constitutional adviser; but in 1848 he was not in-cluded in the second Baldwin-Lafontaine administration. He was the last survivor of the old Canadian bureaucracy, and was commonly known as "the perpetual secretary". In 1851 he returned to England, and was appointed successively governor of Tobago (1851-54), lieutenant-governor of Prince Edward Island (1854-57), and governor of South Australia (1860-68). He was knighted in 1857; and he died in South Australia on February 19, 1868. In 1826 he married Caroline Maria, daughter of Col. Ralph Gore of Kilkenny, Ireland.

[Morgan, *Cel. Can.*; Dent, *Can. port.*, vol. 3; Taylor, *Brit. Am.*; N. F. Davin, *The Irishman in Canada* (Toronto, 1877); J. C. Dent, *The last forty years* (2 vols., Toronto, 1881).]

Daly, John Corry Wilson (1796-1878), pioneer, was born in Liverpool, England, on March 24, 1796, of Irish parentage. He served as a surgeon's assistant in the Royal Navy; then he emigrated to the United States, where he settled in Cooperstown, New York. In 1826 he came to Upper Canada, and in 1827 he entered the service of the Canada Company. He was a pioneer of settlement in the Huron tract, and founder of Stratford, Ontario. In 1831, he became the agent of the Canada Company, and later became the agent for the Bank of Upper Canada. He was the first banker, the first post-master, the first coroner, and the first militia officer in the Huron tract. He died at Stratford, Ontario, on April 1, 1878. He was thrice married, and had, by his first wife, one son and one daughter.

[*Dom. ann. reg.*, 1878; *Dict. Can. biog.*, vol. 10.]

Daly, Sir Malachy Bowes (1836-1920), lieutenant-governor of Nova Scotia, was born in Quebec on February 6, 1836, the son of Sir Dominick Daly (q.v.). He was educated in England, was called to the bar in Halifax in 1864, and was successively private secretary to his father, to Sir R.G. MacDonnell (q.v.), to Sir Hastings Doyle (q.v.), and to Sir W. F. Williams of Kars (q.v.). He represented Halifax in the House of Commons from 1878 to 1887, and from 1882 to 1886 he was deputy speaker of the House. In 1890 he was appointed lieutenant-governor of Nova Scotia and in 1895 his appointment was continued for a second term. On retiring from office in 1900, he was made a K.C.M.G. He died in Halifax on April 26, 1920. In July, 1859, he married Joanna, daughter of Sir Edward Kenny (q.v.); she died in May, 1908.

[*Can. who was who*, vol. 1; *Can. parl. comp.*; Morgan, *Can. men* (1912); *Bull. rech. hist.*, 1926.]

Daly, Thomas Mayne (1828-1885), politician, was born in Hamilton, Upper Canada, on February 7, 1828, the son of John Corry Wilson Daly (q.v.) and was educated at Upper

Canada College, Toronto. From 1854 to 1863 he represented Perth in the Canadian Assembly; and from 1872 to 1874 he represented North Perth in the Canadian House of Commons. During the crisis of the "Pacific Scandal", he was chief government whip. In 1874 he was elected for North Perth to the Ontario legislature; but in 1875 he retired from public life. He died at Stratford, Ontario, on March 4, 1885.

[*Dom. ann. reg.*, 1885; *Can. parl. comp.*; Rose, *Cyc. Can. biog.* (1888).]

Daly, Thomas Mayne (1852-1911), lawyer and politician, was born at Stratford, Ontario, on August 16, 1852, the second son of Thomas Mayne Daly (q.v.) and Helen McLaren. He was educated at Upper Canada College, Toronto, and was called to the Ontario bar in 1876. In 1881 he went to Manitoba, and in 1882 he became the first mayor of Brandon. From 1887 to 1896 he represented Selkirk in the Dominion House of Commons; and from 1892 to 1896 he was minister of the interior in the administrations of Sir John Thompson (q.v.) and Sir Mackenzie Bowell (q.v.). He was not included in the cabinet formed in 1896 by Sir Charles Tupper (q.v.), and declined to stand for re-election at the polls. From 1901 to 1908 he was police magistrate of Winnipeg, and from 1909 to his death judge of the juvenile court in Winnipeg. He died in Winnipeg on June 24, 1911. In 1879 he married Margaret Annabella, daughter of P. R. Jarvis, Stratford; she bore him two sons.

[*Can. who's who* (1910); *Can. parl. comp.*; Morgan, *Can. men* (1912); Rose, *Cyc. Can. biog.* (1888).]

Dambourgès, François (1742-1798), soldier, was born in 1742, at Salies, Béarn, France, the son of Jean Baptiste Dambourgès and Anne de Lambeye. He emigrated to Canada in the summer of 1763, and went into business at Saint Thomas. In 1775 he played an important part in the defence of Quebec against the Americans; and for his services on this occasion he was given a commission in the 84th Regiment. In 1785 he received a commission as captain in the Royal Canadian Volunteers, and later he became a colonel in the militia. From 1792 to 1796 he represented Devon in the Legislative Assembly of Lower Canada; and he died at Montreal on December 13, 1798. In 1786 he married Marie-Josephte, daughter of François Boucher, of Quebec.

[Abbé L. E. Bois, *Le colonel Dambourgès* (Quebec, 1877); *Bull. rech. hist.*, 1895; Le Jeune, *Dict. gén.*]

Dandurand, Raoul (1861-1942), senator of Canada, was born at Montreal, Canada East, on November 4, 1861. He was educated at Laval University (LL.B., 1882; LL.D., 1909), and was called to the Quebec bar in 1883 (Q.C., 1898). He was called to the Senate of Canada

in 1898; and from 1905 to 1909 he was speaker of the Senate. He was appointed a minister without portfolio, and the representative of the government in the Senate, in the King governments of 1921, 1926, and 1935. From 1930 to 1935 he was leader of the Liberal party in the Senate. In 1925, and again from 1927 to 1930 he was a representative of Canada in the Assembly of the League of Nations; and in 1925 he was elected president of the Assembly. He received honorary degrees from McGill University (1910), from the University of Toronto (1925), and from Queen's University (1927). He died at Ottawa, Ontario, on March 18, 1942. In 1886 he married Josephine, second daughter of the Hon. Félix Gabriel Marchand (q.v.). He was joint author, with C. Lanctôt, of *Manuel de juge de paix* (Montreal, 1891).

[*Can. who's who*, 1936-37; *Can. parl. comp.*; Morgan, *Can. men* (1912); M. Hamelin (ed.), *Les Mémoires du senateur Raoul Dandurand* (Quebec, 1967).]

Daniel, François (1820-1908), priest and author, was born in Normandy, France, on September 6, 1820. He entered the Sulpician Seminary in Paris in 1844, and in 1847 he was ordained a priest and sent to the Sulpician Seminary in Montreal. Here he remained until his death at Montreal on February 20, 1908. He was the anonymous author of *Le vrai canadien, ou Notice sur M. J.-B. Bruyère de Montréal* (Montreal, 1859), *Une page de notre histoire* (Montreal, 1865), *Notice sur la famille Guy* (Montreal, 1867), *Le Vicomte C. de Léry* (Montreal, 1867), and *Histoire des grandes familles françaises du Canada* (Montreal, 1867), the last of which was republished in 1867 under the titles *Les français de l'Amérique du Nord* and *Nos gloires nationales*.

[Allaire, *Dict. biog.*; Le Jeune, *Dict. gén.*]

Dansereau, Clément Arthur (1844-1918), journalist, was born at Contrecoeur, Lower Canada, on July 5, 1844, the son of Clément Dansereau and Louise Fiset. He was educated at L'Assomption Collège and at McGill University (B.C.L., 1865). From 1863 to 1876 he was one of the editors of *La Minerve*, a Conservative newspaper of Montreal; and he then became editor of *La Presse*. From 1891 to 1899 he was postmaster of Montreal; and in 1899 he again became editor of *La Presse*, in support of the Laurier government. He died at Montreal on March 27, 1918.

[*Can. who was who*, vol. 1; Morgan, *Can. men* (1912); *Can. who's who* (1910); Bibaud, *Panth. can.*; "Vieux-Rouge", *Les contemporains*, vol. 1 (Montreal, 1898); *Bull. rech. hist.*, 1928.]

Daoust, Charles Roger (1865-1924), journalist, was born at Montreal, Canada East, on March 30, 1865; and died at Manchester,

Quebec, on November 17, 1924. He was the author of *Cent-vingt jours de service actif* (Montreal, 1886).

[*Bull. rech. hist.*, 1935.]

Darling, Sir Charles Henry (1809-1870), governor of Newfoundland (1855-57), was born at Annapolis Royal, Nova Scotia, in 1809, and died at Cheltenham, England, on January 25, 1870. After serving as lieutenant-governor of the island of St. Lucia and of Cape Colony, he was successively governor of Newfoundland, of Jamaica, and of Victoria. As governor of Newfoundland he assisted in the introduction of responsible government. He was created a K.C.B. in 1862.

[*Dict. nat. biog.*; *Encyc. Can.*; *Newfoundland supp.*]

Darling, Frank (1850-1923), architect, was born in Toronto, Canada West, in 1850, the eldest son of the Rev. W. Stewart Darling (q.v.). He was educated at Upper Canada College, and studied architecture in England. He became senior member in the firm of Darling and Pearson, architects, Toronto; and a large number of public buildings in Toronto and Montreal were designed by him. He was elected a fellow of the Royal Canadian Academy in 1886. In 1915 he was awarded the King's gold medal for architecture, and received the degree of LL.D. from the University of Toronto. He died in Toronto on May 19, 1923.

[*Can. who was who*, vol. 2; Morgan, *Can. men* (1912).]

Darling, William Stewart (1818-1886), clergyman and author, was born in Scotland in 1818, and came to Canada with his parents as a youth. He was brought up on a bush farm near Orillia, Upper Canada; and in 1842 he was ordained by Bishop Strachan (q.v.) a minister of the Church of England. For many years he was rector of the Church of Holy Trinity, Toronto. He died at Alassio, Italy, on January 19, 1886. Under the pen-name of "A presbyter of the diocese of Toronto", he published *Sketches of Canadian life, lay and ecclesiastical* (London, 1849); and he was the author of *Papers on the unpopularity of religious truth* (Toronto, 1857), and *The emigrants (A tale in verse)* (Toronto, 1863).

[*Dom. ann. reg.*, 1886; Morgan, *Bib. can.*]

Darnell, Henry Faulkner (1831-1915), author and clergyman, was born in London, England, in 1831, the son of Rev. J. Darnell, of Tunbridge Wells. He was privately educated and took holy orders. In 1861 he came to Canada as rector of St. John's, Canada East; and he remained in this charge until 1883, when he became rector of Zion Episcopal Church, Avon, New York. He died at Easton, Pennsylvania, in 1915. While in Canada he contributed both prose and verse to the *British American Magazine* (1863-64); and he was the author of

Songs by the way (Montreal, 1862), *Verses in memory of the Right Rev. G. I. Mountain, Lord Bishop of Quebec* (St. John's, L.C., 1863), and three novels, *Philip Hazelbrook, or The junior curate* (Buffalo, 1887), *Flossy, or A child of the people* (Buffalo, 1889), and *The craze of Christian Englehart* (New York and London, 1890).

[Morgan, *Can. men* (1912).]

Dart, John (1837-1910), bishop, was born in Devonshire, England, in 1837. He was ordained a priest of the Church of England in 1861, and later graduated at St. Mary's Hall, Oxford (B.A., 1867; M.A., 1871). He came to Canada in 1876, as president of King's College, Windsor; and in 1895 he was consecrated bishop of New Westminster, British Columbia. He received the degree of D.C.L. from King's College, Windsor, in 1877, and that of D.D. from Oxford University in 1895. He died at New Westminster, British Columbia, on April 15, 1910.

[Morgan, *Can. men* (1898).]

Darveau, Jean Édouard (1816-1844), priest and missionary, was born at Quebec, Lower Canada, on March 17, 1816, and was ordained a priest of the Roman Catholic Church in 1841. He was sent to the Hudson's Bay territories as a missionary; and in the summer of 1844 he was murdered by his Indian guides, when travelling from St. Boniface to The Pas.

[A. G. Morice, *M. Darveau, martyr de Manitoba* (Winnipeg, 1934); P. G. Roy, *Fils de Québec* (Lévis, Que., 1933); Le Jeune, *Dict. gén.*]

Dashwood, Richard Lewes (d. 1905), soldier and author, was the second son of S. V. Dashwood, of Stanford Park, Nottinghamshire, England. He entered the British army as a subaltern in the 15th Foot, and he served in Canada and in Afghanistan. At the time of his death, which occurred on July 11, 1905, he had attained the rank of major-general. He was the author of *Chiploquorgan; or, Life by the camp-fire* (Dublin, 1871).

[*Who was who*, 1897-1916; W. G. MacFarlane, *New Brunswick bibliography* (Saint John, N.B., 1895).]

Daulac, Adam. See **Dollard des Ormeaux, Adam.**

David, Ivor (1912-1961), economist and professor, was born at Strathroy, Ontario, in 1912. He was educated at the University of Western Ontario (B.A., 1933; M.A., 1936). He was awarded a British Council Scholarship in 1939 and enrolled in the London School of Economics. From 1940 until the end of the Second World War he served at Canadian Army Headquarters in London. In 1946 he received a Ph.D. in economics from the University of London. He was appointed assistant professor of economics and political science at the University of Western Ontario in 1946 and became head of the department at Middlesex College of the University of Western Ontario in 1960. He died in London, England, on September 22, 1961, while engaged in research for a book on public finance.

[*Can. journ. ec. pol. sc.*, vol. XVIII.]

David, Laurent Olivier (1840-1926), author, was born at Sault-au-Récollet, Quebec, on March 24, 1840, the son of Major Stanislaus David and Elisabeth Tremblay. He was educated at the Collège de Ste. Thérèse, and was called to the bar of Lower Canada in 1864. He became a journalist, and was the founder and editor of several periodicals, notably *L'Opinion publique* (1870) and *Le Bien public* (1874). Later he practised law in Montreal in partnership with J. A. Mousseau (q.v.). From 1886 to 1890 he represented Montreal East in the Legislative Assembly of Quebec; and in 1903 he was appointed a member of the Canadian Senate. He was elected a fellow of the Royal Society of Canada in 1890. He died in Montreal on August 24, 1926. He was the author of *Biographies et portraits* (Montreal, 1876), *Le héros de Châteauguay* (Montreal, 1883), *Les patriotes de 1837-38* (Montreal, 1884), *Mes contemporains* (Montreal, 1894), *Les deux Papineau* (Montreal, 1896), *Le clergé canadien* (Montreal, 1896), *L'union des deux Canadas, 1841-67* (Montreal, 1898), *Le drapeau de Carillon: Drame en 5 actes* (Montreal, 1900), *Laurier et son temps* (Montreal, 1905), *Histoire du Canada depuis la Confédération* (Montreal, 1909), *Souvenirs et biographies* (Montreal, 1911), *Mélanges historiques et littéraires* (Montreal, 1917), *Laurier, sa vie, ses oeuvres* (Beauceville, 1919), and *Les gerbes canadiennes* (Montreal, 1921).

[*Proc. Roy. Soc. Can.*, 1927; Morgan, *Can. men* (1912); *Can. parl. comp.*; Rose, *Cyc. Can. biog.* (1888); Le Jeune, *Dict. gén.*]

Davidson, Sir Charles Peers (1841-1929), jurist, was born at Huntingdon, Lower Canada, in January, 1841, the son of Capt. Alexander Davidson and Marion Peers. He was educated at McGill University (B.A., 1863; M.A., 1867; B.C.L., 1873; D.C.L., 1875; LL.D., 1912), and was called to the bar of Quebec in 1864 (Q.C., 1876). In 1887 he was appointed a puisne judge of the Superior Court of the province of Quebec; and from 1912 to 1915 he was chief justice of this court. In 1913 he was created a knight bachelor. He died at New York on January 29, 1929. He was the author of *Statutes relating to banks and banking* (Montreal, 1876).

[F. J. Audet, *Les juges en chef de la province de Québec* (Quebec, 1927); Morgan, *Can. men* (1912).]

Davidson, Gordon Charles (1884-1922), historian, was born in 1884, and obtained his professional training as a historian at the University of California (Ph.D., 1916). He served as an officer in the 1st Canadian Mounted Rifles in France during the First World War; and he died at Vancouver, British Columbia, in May, 1922. He was the author of *The North West Company* (Berkeley, Cal., 1918).

[Private information.]

Davidson, John (1869-1905), political economist, was born in Edinburgh, Scotland, in 1869, the son of William Davidson, a produce broker. He was educated at Edinburgh University (B.A., 1890), and he studied at the University of Berlin (Ph.D., 1897). In 1891 he was appointed professor of philosophy and political economy at the University of New Brunswick, and he held this post until his death at Edinburgh, on July 31, 1905. In 1895 he married Helen, daughter of T. Watt, Edinburgh. He was the author of *The growth of the French Canadian race in America* (Annals of the Am. Academy of Social and Political Science, 1896), *The bargain theory of wages* (New York, 1898), and *Commercial federation and colonial trade policy* (London, 1900).

[*Can. who was who*, vol. 1; Morgan, *Can. men* (1898).]

Davidson, Sir Walter Edward (1859-1923), governor of Newfoundland (1913-17), was born in Ulster on April 20, 1859, and died in Australia on September 14, 1923. He entered the British civil service in 1880, and served successively in Ceylon, the Transvaal, the Seychelles, Newfoundland, and New South Wales. He was created a K.C.M.G. in 1914, while he was governor of Newfoundland.

[*Who was who*, 1916-28; *Encyc. Can.*; *Newfoundland supp.*]

Davie, Alexander Edmund Batson (1848-1889), prime minister of British Columbia (1887-89), was born in Somersetshire, England, in November, 1848, the son of John Chapman Davie, M.R.C.S. He was educated at Silcoates College, near Wakefield, Yorkshire. In 1862 he emigrated to British Columbia with his family, and he studied law in Victoria. He was admitted an attorney of British Columbia in 1868, and was called to the bar in 1873 (Q.C., 1883). From 1862 to 1874 he was law clerk of the Assembly of British Columbia; and he represented Cariboo in the Assembly from 1875 to 1877, and Lillooet from 1882 to 1889, as a Conservative. In 1877 he was appointed provincial secretary in the Elliott administration, but resigned on failing to secure his re-election. In 1883 he became attorney-general in the Smithe administration; and on the death of William Smithe (q.v.) he became prime minister of the province. He died in office on July 31, 1889. In 1874 he married Constance Langford, third daughter of T.O. Skinner, of Farleigh, near Maple Bay.

[J. B. Kerr, *Biographical dictionary of well-known British Columbians* (Vancouver, B.C., 1890); *Can. parl. comp.*]

Davie, Theodore (1852-1898), prime minister of British Columbia (1892-95), was born in Brixton, Surrey, England, on March 22, 1852, the son of John Chapman Davie, M.R.C.S. He was brought by his parents to British Columbia in 1862, and was educated at Victoria. In 1873 he was admitted an attorney of British Columbia, and in 1877 was called to the bar (Q.C., 1888). He represented Victoria in the Legislative Assembly of British Columbia from 1882 to 1895. In 1889, on the death of his brother, A. E. B. Davie (q.v.), he was appointed attorney-general in the Robson administration; and in 1892 he became prime minister. In 1895 he resigned office to become chief justice of British Columbia; and he died at Victoria, British Columbia, on March 7, 1898. In 1884 he married Alice Mary, daughter of Gregory Yorke, of Galway, Ireland. He was made an LL.D. of Ottawa University in 1895.

[J. B. Kerr, *Biographical dictionary of well-known British Columbians* (Vancouver, B.C., 1890); Morgan, *Can. men* (1898); *Can. parl. comp.*]

Davies, Blodwen (1897-1966), author, was born in Montreal, Quebec, in 1897 and educated in public and private schools in Ontario and Quebec. She worked for a time as a reporter in Fort William and then came to Toronto in 1921 to meet the Group of Seven Canadian painters. She learned of Tom Thomson through the Group and wrote *A study of Tom Thomson* (1935). She was a long-time member of the Canadian Authors' Association. During the early forties Miss Davies became influenced by scientific humanism and collaborated with Oliver Reiser in writing *Planetary democracy* (1944). She lived for some years in the United States but returned to live in Markham, Ontario, in 1946. Among her other writings are *Storied streets of Quebec* (1927); *Ottawa: Portrait of a capital* (1954); *Quebec: Portrait of a province* (1951-52); *Romantic Quebec* (1932); *Storied York* (1931); *Old Father Forest* (1930) (for children); *Saguenay and Gaspé* (1932); *The charm of Ottawa* (1932); *Gaspé: Land of history and romance* (1949); *Youth, marriage and the family* (1948); *Youth speaks out on citizenship* (1948); *Youth speaks its mind* (1948); *Daniel Du Lhut* (1930); *Ruffles and rapiers* (1930). She died September 10, 1966.

[Metropolitan Toronto Library Board, *Biographical scrapbooks*, vol. 26; C. Thomas, *Canadian novelists, 1920-1945* (Toronto, 1946); V.B. Rhodenizer, *Canadian literature in English* (Montreal, 1965); N.

Story, *The Oxford companion to Canadian history and literature* (Toronto, 1967).]

Davies, Henry William (1834-1895), clergyman and grammarian, was born in Cleveland, Ohio, on June 24, 1834, and was educated at Trinity University, Toronto (B.A., 1855; D.D., 1860). In 1866 he was appointed English master at the Toronto Normal School; and in 1871 he became its principal. He retired in 1885; and he died at Toronto on March 19, 1895. He was the author of *An analytical and practical grammar of the English language* (Toronto, 1868), and *An English grammar for the use of junior pupils* (Toronto, 1869).

[Rose, *Cyc. Can. biog.* (1886).]

Davies, Sir Louis Henry (1845-1924), chief justice of the Supreme Court of Canada (1918-24), was born in Prince Edward Island on May 4, 1845, the son of the Hon. Benjamin Davies and Kezia Attwood Watts. He was educated at Prince of Wales College, Charlottetown, and studied law at the Inner Temple, London, England. He was called to the English bar in 1866, and to the bar of Prince Edward Island in 1867 (Q.C., 1880). From 1872 to 1879 he was a member of the Legislative Assembly of Prince Edward Island, and from 1876 to 1879 he was prime minister of the province. In 1882 he was elected as a Liberal to the Canadian House of Commons for Queen's; and he represented this constituency continuously until 1901. He was one of the leaders of the Liberal opposition from 1882 to 1896; and from 1896 to 1901 he was minister of marine and fisheries in the Laurier administration. In 1901 he was appointed a judge of the Supreme Court of Canada; and in 1918 he became its chief justice. He died at Ottawa on May 1, 1924. In 1872 he married Susan, fourth daughter of the Rev. Dr. Wiggins. He was created a K.C.M.G. in 1897, and an imperial privy councillor in 1919.

[*Who was who*, 1916-28; *Can. who was who*, vol. 1; *Can. parl. comp.*; Morgan, *Can. men* (1912); O. D. Skelton, *The life and letters of Sir Wilfrid Laurier* (2 vols., Toronto, 1921).]

Davies, Rupert William (1879-1967), senator and publisher, was born in Welshpool, Wales, in 1879. He came to Canada in 1894 and became an apprentice printer in Brantford. He published weekly newspapers in Thamesville and Renfrew from 1908 to 1925 before buying the *British Whig*, Kingston. He merged this with the Kingston *Daily Standard* in 1926. In 1936 he bought the Peterborough *Examiner*. He also owned radio and television stations in Kingston and Peterborough. He became president of the Canadian Press in 1939, 1940, and 1941 and was a director of the Canadian Daily Newspaper Publishers' Association. He was appointed to the Senate in 1942.

He died at Toronto, Ontario, March 11, 1967.

[Metropolitan Toronto Library Board, *Biographical scrapbooks*, vol. 33; *Can. who's who*, 1961-63.]

Davies, Thomas (1737?-1812), soldier and artist, was born in England about 1737, and died at Blackheath, near Woolwich, England, on March 16, 1812. He entered the British army as a cadet in 1755, and rose to the rank of lieutenant-general in 1803. He was stationed in Canada twice, first after 1757 in Halifax, and secondly from 1786 to 1790 in Quebec. He was an artist, and his water-colours of Canadian scenes, of which the National Gallery acquired about twenty in 1955, are among the most important that we owe to the soldier-artists stationed in Canada during the early days of British rule.

[Kathleen M. Fenwick and C. P. Stacey, *Thomas Davies, soldier and painter of eighteenth-century Canada* (Canadian Art, Spring, 1956); R. H. Hubbard, *Thomas Davies, gunner and artist* (Trans. Roy. Soc. Can., 1971).]

Davies, William H. A. (d. 1867), fur-trader, was a servant of the Hudson's Bay Company who was in 1841 in charge of the district of Esquimaux Bay, on the Labrador coast. On retiring from the fur-trade he lived in Montreal; and he died in 1867. He was the author of two papers, *Notes on Esquimaux Bay* and *Notes on Ungava Bay*, published in the *Transactions* of the Literary and Historical Society of Quebec for 1855.

[Morgan, *Bib. can.*]

Davin, Nicholas Flood (1843-1901), lawyer, journalist, and politican, was born at Kilfinane, county Limerick, Ireland, on January 13, 1843, the son of Nicholas Flood Davin, M.D., and Eliza Lane. He was educated at Queen's College, Cork, and at London University, and was called to the English bar at the Middle Temple in 1868. He became a journalist, and was a war correspondent during the Franco-Prussian War. In 1872 he came to Canada, and joined the staff of the Toronto *Globe*, and later the staff of the Toronto *Mail*. In 1874 he was called to the Ontario bar; and in the general elections of 1878 he was the unsuccessful Conservative candidate for the House of Commons in Haldimand. In 1883 he went to the North West, and established the Regina *Leader*, the first newspaper issued in Assiniboia; and in 1887 he was elected member for West Assiniboia in the House of Commons. He continued to represent this constituency in parliament until 1900; and in 1897 he was elected president of the Liberal-Conservative Association for the North West Territories. On October 18, 1901, he committed suicide in Winnipeg.

Brilliant, but erratic and uneven, he published a number of books which do not fairly represent the best work of which he was capable, or fully explain the wide reputation he acquired. These were *British versus American civilization* (Toronto, 1873), *The fair Grit; or the advantages of coalition, a farce* (Toronto, 1876), *The Irishman in Canada* (Toronto, 1877), *Album verses and other poems* (Ottawa, 1882), *Eos, a prairie dream* (Ottawa, 1884), *Eos, an epic of the dawn* (Regina, 1889), and *Culture and practical power, an address* (Regina, 1889).

[Morgan, *Can. men* (1898); *Who was who*, 1897-1916; C. M. Whyte-Edgar, *A wreath of Canadian song* (Toronto, 1910); A. MacMurchy, *A handbook of Canadian literature* (Toronto, 1906); R. St. G. Stubbs, *Lawyers and laymen of western Canada* (Toronto, 1939).]

Davis, John (1550?-1605), explorer, was born at Sandridge, near Dartmouth, Devonshire, about 1550. He went to sea as a boy, and became one of the most famous of Elizabethan sea-captains. In 1585, 1586, and 1587 he made voyages to the north-east coast of America, and explored the shores of Davis Strait, Cumberland Gulf, and Baffin Bay. He narrowly escaped discovering Hudson Strait and Hudson Bay. In 1588 he took his share in repelling the Spanish Armada; and in his later years he made several expeditions to the South Seas. He was killed by Japanese pirates at Bintang, near Singapore, on December 27, 1605. He was the author of a treatise on navigation entitled *The seaman's secrets* (London, 1594); and his own accounts of his voyages have been published by A. H. Markham for the Hakluyt Society (London, 1880).

[Clements R. Markham, *Life of John Davis, the navigator* (London, 1889); *Dict. nat. biog.*; *Dict. Can. biog.*, vol. 1.]

Davis, John (1802-1875), clergyman, was born in Liverpool, England, in 1802. He was educated at Stepney College, and was ordained a minister of the Baptist Church in 1829. After serving as pastor of several churches in England, he was sent to the Maritime provinces of British North America as an agent of the American and Foreign Bible Society. He settled in 1858 in Charlottetown, Prince Edward Island; and he died in Charlottetown in 1875. He was the author of *The patriarch of western Nova Scotia: Life and times of the late Rev. Harris Harding* (Charlottetown, P.E.I., 1866).

[R. J. Long, *Nova Scotia authors* (East Orange, N.J., 1918); *Dict. Can. biog.*, vol. 10.]

Davis, Sir Mortimer Barnett (1864-1928), manufacturer and philanthropist, was born in Montreal, Quebec, in 1864, the son of Samuel Davis, a manufacturer and importer of cigars. He was educated at the Montreal High School, and entered his father's business. In 1895 he became the president of the American Tobacco

Company of Canada, and later he formed the Imperial Tobacco Company of Canada. The establishment of a market for Canadian leaf tobacco was largely due to his foresight and energy. He was known as "the Tobacco King of Canada". He made large benefactions to many objects; and in 1917 he was created a knight bachelor. He died at Cannes, France, on March 22, 1928.

[*Who was who*, 1916-28.]

Davis, Robert (1800?-1838), author and rebel, was born in Killeshandra, county Cavan, Ireland, about 1800, and came to Canada with his parents in 1819. He settled in Missouri township, Oxford county, Upper Canada; and was one of the leaders of the rebels in the western part of the province in 1837-38. He was in command of the rebels on the schooner *Anne*, which attacked Amherstburg on January 9, 1838. He was mortally wounded in this engagement, and died of his wounds shortly afterward. He was the author of *The Canadian farmer's travels in the United States of America* (Buffalo, N.Y., 1938).

[J. J. Talman, *The value of Crown lands papers in historical research* (Trans. Roy. Soc. Can., 1936).]

Dawson, Aeneas McDonell (1810-1894), priest and poet, was born at Redhaven, Banffshire, Scotland, on July 30, 1810. He was ordained a priest of the Roman Catholic Church in 1835, and in 1854 he came to Canada. He published several volumes of verse: *The massacre of Oszmania* (Glasgow, 1844), *Lament for the Rt. Rev. James Gillis, D.D., bishop of Edinburgh, and other poems* (London and Ottawa, 1864), *Our strength and their strength* (Ottawa, 1870), *Zenobia, queen of Palmyra* (Ottawa, 1883), and *Dominion day, Caractacus, Malcolm and Margaret* (Ottawa, 1886). He was the author also of a number of translations from the French, of a descriptive volume entitled *The North West Territory and British Columbia* (Ottawa, 1881), and of a history of *The Catholics of Scotland* (Ottawa, 1890). He died at Ottawa on December 29, 1894.

[H. J. Morgan, *In memoriam: Recollections of Father Dawson* (Ottawa, 1895); *Proceedings at the presentation of a public testimonial to the Very Rev. A. McD. Dawson* (Ottawa, 1891); C. C. James, *A bibliography of Canadian poetry* (Toronto, 1899); *Can. who was who*, vol. 2.]

Dawson, Carl Addington (1887-1964), sociologist, was born in Tryon, Prince Edward Island, in 1887. He was educated in Prince Edward Island, at Acadia University, Wolfville, Nova Scotia, and at the University of Chicago (M.A., Ph.D.). During the First World War he served overseas with the Y.M.C.A., completing his education on his return. He joined the staff of McGill University in 1922 to establish the first department of

sociology and social work. In 1948 it became the department of sociology and anthropology. He retired in 1952. Carl Dawson introduced the idea to Canada that the task of sociologists was to study society at close hand and his early studies of immigrant settlements became models for sociology students. He wrote *The settlement of the Peace River country: A study of a pioneer area* (with R. W. Murchie; Toronto, 1934); *Group settlement: Ethnic communities in Western Canada* (Toronto, 1936); *The new north-west* (Toronto, 1947); and *Pioneering in the prairie provinces* (with E. R. Younge; Toronto, 1940). The text *An introduction to sociology*, which he wrote with W.E. Gettys, went through several editions (1929, 1935, 1948) and was widely used in North America. He died at Whitby, Ontario, January 16, 1964.

[*Proc. Roy. Soc. Can.* (1964).]

Dawson, George Mercer (1849-1901), geologist, was born in Pictou, Nova Scotia, on August 1, 1849, the son of Sir John William Dawson (q.v.) and Margaret Mercer. He was educated at McGill University and at the Royal School of Mines, London. In 1873 he was appointed geologist and botanist to the North American Boundary Commission; and in this capacity he published a *Report on the geology and resources of the region in the vicinity of the forty-ninth parallel* (Montreal, 1875). In 1875 he joined the staff of the Canadian Geological Survey; in 1883 he became assistant director of the Survey, and in 1895 director. His work on the Survey lay chiefly in the North West Territories and British Columbia; and its results are mainly embodied in the reports of the Geological Survey. He was one of the British commissioners appointed to inquire into the resources of the Bering Sea in 1892, and he was, with Sir G. Baden Powell, joint author of the *Report of the British Behring Sea commissioners* (London, 1892). With A. R. C. Selwyn (q.v.), he published a *Descriptive sketch of the physical geography and geology of the Dominion of Canada* (Montreal, 1884); with W. F. Tolmie, *Comparative vocabularies of the Indian tribes of British Columbia* (Montreal, 1884); and with Alexander Sutherland, a *Geography of the British colonies* (London, 1892). He died at Ottawa on March 2, 1901. In 1892 he was created a C.M.G.; in 1890 he was given the degree of LL.D. by Queen's University, and in 1891 by McGill University; and in 1891 he was elected a fellow of the Royal Society, and in 1893 president of the Royal Society of Canada. He was not married.

[Morgan, *Can. men* (1898); *American geologist*, August, 1901; *Trans. Roy. Soc. Can.*, 1894; A. H. Lang, *G. M. Dawson and the economic development of western Canada* (Cdn. Publ. Admin., 1971).]

Dawson, Sir John William (1820-1899), educationist and naturalist, was born at Pictou, Nova Scotia, on October 13, 1820, the son

199

of James Dawson. He was educated at Pictou Academy and the University of Edinburgh. In 1846 and in 1852 he was associated with Sir Charles Lyell in investigating the geology and mineralogy of the maritime provinces. In 1850 he was appointed superintendent of education for Nova Scotia; and in 1855 he became principal of McGill University. This post he occupied until his retirement in 1893. He was a voluminous writer; and, apart from a large number of papers contributed to scientific periodicals and learned societies, he published a *Handbook of the geography and natural history of Nova Scotia* (Pictou and Edinburgh, 1848), *Scientific agriculture in Nova Scotia* (Halifax, 1852), *Acadian geology* (Edinburgh, 1855), *Archaia* (Montreal, 1857), *Agriculture for schools* (Montreal, 1864), *Handbook of Canadian zoology* (Montreal, 1871), *The story of the earth and man* (London, 1872), *Nature and the Bible* (New York, 1875), *Life's dawn on earth* (London, 1875), *The origin of the world* (London and New York, 1878), *Fossil men* (London, 1880), *The chain of life in geological time* (London, 1881), *The geological history of plants* (London and New York, 1888), *Modern science in Bible lands* (London and New York, 1888), *Handbook of Canadian geology* (Montreal, 1889), *Modern ideas of evolution* (London, 1890), *Some salient points in the history of the earth* (London and New York, 1893), *The ice age in Canada* (Montreal, 1894), *The meeting-place of geology and history* (Montreal, 1894), *Peter Redpath* (Montreal, 1894), *Eden lost and won* (London, 1895), *Science the ally of religion* (Montreal, 1896), *Relics of primeval life* (London, 1897), and *Testimony of the Holy Scriptures respecting wine and drink* (Montreal, 1898). He died at Montreal on November 19, 1899.

In 1847 he married Margaret, daughter of G. Mercer, Edinburgh, Scotland; and had by her three sons and two daughters. In 1881 he was created a C.M.G., and in 1884 a knight bachelor. In 1882 he was the first president of the Royal Society of Canada; and he was an LL.D. (Edin.), a D.C.L. (Lennoxville), and a D.L. (Columbia). In 1892 he was president of the American Association for the Advancement of Science, and in 1886 of the British Association.

[R. Dawson (ed.), *Fifty years of work in Canada*, autobiography (London, 1901); H. M. Ami, *Sir John William Dawson* (American geologist, July, 1900), with bibliography; and F. D. Adams, *Sir William Dawson* (Journal of geology, November, 1899); B. G. Trigger, *Sir John William Dawson: A faithful anthropologist* (Anthropological, 1966); *Dict. nat. biog.*; Dent, *Can. port.*, vol. 2; Rose, *Cyc. Can. biog.* (1888); Taylor, *Brit. Am.*; Morgan, *Bib. can.* and *Can. men* (1898).]

Dawson, Robert MacGregor (1895-1958), political scientist, was born at Bridgewater,

Nova Scotia, on March 1, 1895. He was educated at Dalhousie University (B.A., 1915; M.A., 1916), at Harvard University (A.M., 1917), and at the London School of Economics (M.Sc. Econ., 1921; D.Sc. Econ., 1922). He was appointed a lecturer at Dalhousie University in 1921, moved to the Carnegie Institute of Technology in 1923, and then to Rutgers University in 1926. He returned to Canada in 1929 as professor of political science in the University of Saskatchewan; and in 1937 he was appointed to the staff of the University of Toronto as associate professor, and later professor, of political science. In 1935 he was elected a fellow of the Royal Society of Canada. He died at Bridgewater, Nova Scotia, on July 16, 1958. He was the author of *The principle of official independence* (London, 1922), *The civil service of Canada* (London, 1929), *Constitutional issues in Canada, 1900-1931* (London, 1933), *The development of Dominion status* (Toronto, 1937), *Canada in world affairs: Two years of war, 1939-1941* (Toronto, 1942), *The government of Canada* (Toronto, 1947), and *Democratic government in Canada* (Toronto, 1949). The first volume of the official life of William Lyon Mackenzie King (q.v.), which he had been commissioned to write, appeared posthumously (Toronto, 1959), as did *The conscription crisis of 1944* (Toronto, 1961). He was the editor of *Problems of modern government* (Toronto, 1941).

[*Proc. Roy. Soc. Can.*, 1960; *Can. who's who*, 1956-58; *Encyc. Can.*]

Dawson, Samuel Edward (1833-1916), critic and historian, was born in Halifax, Nova Scotia, on June 1, 1833, the son of the Rev. Benjamin Dawson, a native of Prince Edward Island. He was educated at McCulloch's School, Halifax, and came with his father to Montreal in 1847. He became a partner, and subsequently head, of the firm of B. Dawson and Son (afterwards Dawson Bros.), publishers and booksellers, Montreal. In 1891 he was appointed King's printer at Ottawa. He was superannuated in 1909, and he died at Westmount, Montreal, on February 9, 1916. For many years he contributed fugitive papers on a wide variety of subjects to newspapers and other periodicals; but his most important publications were *A study, with critical and explanatory notes, of Lord Tennyson's poem, The Princess* (Montreal, 1882), *Handbook of the Dominion of Canada* (Montreal, 1884), and *The St. Lawrence basin* (New York, 1905), a work of capital importance for the history of early exploration in Canada. He married, in 1858, Annie, daughter of Gilbert Bent, of Saint John, New Brunswick. He was created a C.M.G. in 1906; and he was a Litt.D. of Laval University (1890) and an LL.D. of McGill University (1911). In 1907 he was elected president of the Royal Society of Canada.

[*Proc. Roy. Soc. Can.*, 1916; Morgan, *Can. men* (1912).]

Dawson, Simon James (1820-1902), civil engineer and member of parliament, was born in 1820 at Redhaven, Banffshire, Scotland. He came to Canada as a young man, and became a civil engineer. In 1857 he was appointed by the Canadian government to explore the country from Lake Superior westward to the Saskatchewan; and his report (Toronto, 1859) was among the first to attract attention to the possibilities of the North West as a home for settlers. In 1868 he was employed to open communications with the Red River country, by what was later known as "the Dawson Route"; and in 1870 he superintended the transportation over this route of the troops comprising the Red River expedition. His *Report on the line of route between lake Superior and the Red River settlement* was published as a government document (Ottawa, 1868). From 1875 to 1878 he was Conservative member of the Ontario legislature for Algoma; and from 1878 to 1891 he sat in the Canadian House of Commons for the same constituency. He died at Ottawa, Ontario, on November 20, 1902.

[Rose, *Cyc. Can. biog.* (1886); *Cyc. Am. biog.*; *Can. parl. comp.*]

Day, Mrs. Catherine Matilda, *née* **Townsend** (1815-1899), historian, was born at East Farnham, Eastern Townships, Quebec, on January 1, 1815, the daughter of Samuel Wells Townsend and Pamelia Lawrence. In 1840 she married, at Chambly, Henry M. Day (d. 1854); and she died at South Stukeley, Eastern Townships, on August 24, 1899. She was the author of *Pioneers of the Eastern Townships* (Montreal, 1863), and a *History of the Eastern Townships* (Montreal, 1869).

[Private information.]

Day, Charles Dewey (1806-1884), chancellor of McGill University (1857-84), was born at Bennington, Vermont, in 1806, the son of Ithamar H. Day. He came to Montreal, Lower Canada, in 1812, and was there educated. He was called to the bar of Lower Canada in 1827 (Q.C., 1838), and in 1838 he was appointed deputy judge-advocate-general at the courts-martial held in Montreal for the trial of the political prisoners arrested during the rebellion of 1837-38. In 1840 he was appointed solicitor-general of Lower Canada, with a seat in the Special Council; and in 1841 he was elected to the Legislative Assembly of Canada, and became solicitor-general for Lower Canada in the first administration under the Union. His presence in the Executive Council was, however, obnoxious to the Reformers; and in 1842 he accepted an appointment as a judge of the Court of Queen's Bench. He was transferred to the Superior Court in 1849, but in 1862 he retired from the bench. In 1857 he was elected chancellor of McGill University; and

this position he occupied until his death in England, on January 31, 1884.

[*Dom. ann. reg.*, 1884; Taylor, *Brit. Am.*, vol. 3; C. Macmillan, *McGill and its story* (Toronto, 1921); Morgan, *Bib. can.*]

Day, Forshaw (1837-1903), painter, was born in London, England, on November 4, 1837. He studied architecture and design in Dublin, and art in London; and in 1862 he emigrated to Canada. For some years he taught art in Halifax, Nova Scotia, while employed as a draughtsman in the government navy yard; and from 1879 to 1897 he was professor of drawing at the Royal Military College, Kingston, Ontario. He became especially noted as a marine painter; and in 1880 he was chosen a member of the Royal Canadian Academy of Arts. He died on July 22, 1903.

[Morgan, *Can. men* (1898); N. MacTavish, *The fine arts in Canada* (Toronto, 1925).]

Day, Frank Parker (1881-1950), educationist and novelist, was born at Shubenacadie, Nova Scotia, on May 9, 1881, and died near Yarmouth, Nova Scotia, on July 30, 1950. He was educated at Mount Allison University (B.A., 1903) and at Oxford University (B.A., 1907; M.A., 1912). From 1909 to 1912 he was a professor of English at the University of New Brunswick; and from 1912 to 1927 he was on the staff of the Carnegie Institute of Technology, except for the years 1914 to 1919, when he was on active service with the Canadian Expeditionary Force, latterly commanding the 25th Overseas Battalion. From 1927 to 1929 he was professor of English at Swarthmore College, and from 1929 until his retirement in 1936 he was president of Union College, Schenectady. He was the author of four novels: *River of strangers* (New York, 1926), *Autobiography of a fisherman* (New York, 1927), *Rock-bound* (New York, 1928), and *John Paul's rock* (New York, 1932). Mount Allison University conferred on him the degree of LL.D. in 1927, and New York University that of Litt.D. in 1929.

[*New York Times*, Aug. 1, 1950.]

Deane, Richard Burton (1848-1930), superintendent of the Royal North West Mounted Police, was born in India, on April 30, 1848. He was gazetted a lieutenant in the Royal Marine Light Infantry in 1866, served during the Ashanti War, and retired with the rank of captain in 1882. He came to Canada, was appointed an inspector of the Royal North-West Mounted Police in 1883, served throughout the Northwest Rebellion of 1885, and rose to the rank of senior superintendent in the R.N.W.M.P. He died at Diano, Mariana, Italy, on December 13, 1930. He published his reminiscences in *Mounted police life in Canada* (New York, 1916).

[Morgan, *Can. men* (1912).]

Dease,[1] **Charles Johnson Watts** (*fl.* 1797-1826), fur-trader, was the youngest son of Dr. John Dease, of the Indian Department, a nephew of Sir William Johnson, Bart., and was born at Côte des Neiges, near Montreal, on December 13, 1797. He entered the service of the North West Company as a clerk in 1814, and was, after 1821, for several years a clerk in the Hudson's Bay Company. In 1822-23 he was stationed in the Athabaska district; and from 1824 to 1826 he was in the Mackenzie River district. In 1826 he retired from the fur-trade, and returned to Canada.

[R. Harvey Fleming (ed.), *Minutes of Council, Northern Department of Rupert's Land* (Toronto: The Champlain Society, 1939).]

Dease, Francis Michael (1786-1864), soldier, was born at Niagara on August 10, 1786, the third son of Dr. John Dease, of the Indian Department, a nephew of Sir William Johnson, Bart. During the War of 1812, he commanded the Chippewa at the capture of Michilimackinac in July, 1812; and in July, 1814, he took part in the engagement at Prairie-du-Chien as captain commanding Dease's Mississippi Volunteers. On September 2, 1814, he was appointed a captain in the Indian department; but in 1827 he entered the service of the Hudson's Bay Company. He died at St. Boniface, on the Red River, on July 29, 1864. He was not married.

[R. Harvey Fleming (ed.), *Minutes of Council, Northern Department of Rupert's Land* (Toronto: The Champlain Society, 1939).]

Dease, John Warren (1783-1829), fur-trader, was born at Niagara on June 9, 1783, the second son of Dr. John Dease, of the Indian department, a nephew of Sir William Johnson, Bart. He entered the service of the North West Company, and in 1816 he was in charge of the important post of Rainy Lake. After the union of 1821 he was transferred to the Pacific slope, and was promoted to be a chief trader. He died at Fort Colville, in what is now the state of Washington, in December, 1829; and his will is on record at Hudson's Bay House, in London. He was elected a member of the Beaver Club in Montreal in 1815. He was twice married: first, to Mary Cadot, by whom he had two children, and secondly, to Jenny Benoist, by whom he had five children.

[R. Harvey Fleming (ed.), *Minutes of Council, Northern Department of Rupert's Land* (Toronto: The Champlain Society, 1939).]

Dease, Mary Teresa (1820-1889), superior-general of the Institute of the Blessed Virgin Mary in America, was born in Dublin, Ireland, on May 7, 1820, the daughter of Oliver

[1]Pronounced as though *Dace*.

and Ann Dease. Her baptismal name was Ellen; but this was changed to Mary Teresa when she entered Loretto Abbey, near Dublin, as a novice. She was sent to Canada in 1847, and was one of the nuns who founded in Toronto the first home of the Institute of the Blessed Virgin Mary in America. In 1851 she became mother superior of this house; and during the remainder of her life she saw the establishment of daughter houses in all parts of Ontario and even in the United States. She died at Loretto Abbey, Toronto, on July 1, 1889.

[*Life and letters of Rev. Mother Teresa Dease*, ed. by a member of the community (Toronto, 1916).]

Dease, Peter Warren (1788-1863), fur-trader and explorer, was born at Michilimackinac on January 1, 1788, the fourth son of Dr. John Dease, who was a nephew of Sir William Johnson (q.v.), and first cousin of Sir John Johnson (q.v.). He was named after Admiral Sir Peter Warren, an uncle of Sir William Johnson. He entered the service of the North West Company; and for some years prior to the union of the North West and Hudson's Bay companies in 1821 he was in the Mackenzie River district. At the time of the union he became a chief trader in the Hudson's Bay Company; and in 1825 he was placed in charge of the commissariat in Sir John Franklin's second expedition to the Arctic. In 1826 he was made a chief factor; and in 1831 he succeeded William Conolly (q.v.) in charge of the New Caledonia district. In 1836-39 he was, with Thomas Simpson (q.v.), in command of the expedition which explored the Arctic coast of North America from the mouth of the Mackenzie to Point Barrow; and for his services in connection with this expedition he is said to have been offered the honour of knighthood, but to have refused it. He retired from the Hudson's Bay Company in 1842, and settled in the immediate vicinity of Montreal. There he died on January 17, 1863. He married, in the North West, Elizabeth Chouinard, a half-breed; and by her he had eight children.

[R. Harvey Fleming (ed.), *Minutes of Council, Northern Department of Rupert's Land* (Toronto: The Champlain Society, 1939).]

Debartzch, Pierre Dominique (1784?-1846), legislative and executive councillor of Lower Canada, was seignior of St. Charles, in the Richelieu Valley. From 1809 to 1814 he was a member of the Legislative Assembly of the province, and in 1814 he was appointed to the Legislative Council. He opposed the Union bill of 1822, and supported the Ninety-Two Resolutions in 1834, but in 1837 he was appointed by Gosford (q.v.) to the Executive Council, and henceforth he opposed the *patriote* party. His manor house at St. Charles (otherwise known as Debartzch village) was the centre of the first engagement of the rebellion of 1837. He died on September 6, 1846.

[J. J. Lefebvre, *Pierre-Dominique Debartzch* (Revue trimestrielle canadienne, 1941); Bibaud, *Panth. can.*; R. Christie, *History of Lower Canada*, vol. 4 (Montreal, 1866).]

De Blaquière, Peter Boyle (1784-1860), legislative councillor of Canada, was born in Ireland on April 27, 1784, the fourth and youngest son of John, first Baron De Blaquière. He came to Canada in 1837, and in 1839 he was appointed a member of the Legislative Council of Upper Canada. He was reappointed to the Legislative Council of United Canada in 1841. From 1850 to 1852 he was chancellor of the University of Toronto. He died at Yorkville, near Toronto, on October 23, 1860.

[G.E.C. (ed.), *Complete peerage*, vol. 3 (London, 1890); *Cyc. Am. biog.*]

DeBonne, Pierre Amable (1758-1816), executive councillor of Lower Canada, was born at Montreal on November 25, 1758, the son of the Chevalier Louis de Bonne de Misèle, captain in the regiment of Condé, and Marie-Louise Prudhomme. He was educated at the Quebec Seminary, and in 1780 was licensed to practise law. He sat in the Legislative Assembly of Lower Canada from 1792 to 1796 as the member for York, from 1796 to 1804 as the nember for Three Rivers, and from 1804 to 1810 as the member for Quebec county. In the house he was the chief protagonist of the "Château party"; and in 1794 he was appointed a judge, first of the Court of Common Pleas, and then of the Court of King's Bench. In 1794 he was appointed also a member of the Executive Council. He retired from the bench in 1812; and he died at Beauport, Lower Canada, on September 6, 1816.

[*Bull. rech. hist.*, 1904; *Cyc. Am. biog.*; Bibaud, *Panth. can.*; P. Gagnon, *Essai de bibliographie canadienne* (Quebec, 1895), no. 3926.]

De Brisay, Jacques-René, Marquis de Denonville. See **Denonville, Jacques-René de Brisay, Marquis de.**

De Cazes, Paul. See **Cazes, Paul de.**

DeCelles, Alfred Duclos (1843-1925), librarian and author, was born at St. Laurent, Lower Canada, the son of A. D. DeCelles and Sarah Holmes, on August 15, 1843. He was educated at the Quebec Seminary and at Laval University (B.A., 1867; Litt.D., 1890); and in 1873 he was called to the Quebec bar, but never practised law. He began life as a journalist, and was successively editor of the *Journal de Québec, La Minerve,* and *L'Opinion publique.* From 1880 to 1885 he was an assistant librarian in the Library of Parliament, Ottawa; and from 1885 to 1920 he was general librarian in this library. He died at Ottawa on October 5, 1925. In 1876 he married Eugénie Dorion, of Ottawa. He was elected a member of the Royal Society of Canada in 1885; in 1903 he was made a chevalier of the Legion of Honour, France, and in 1907 a C.M.G. A voluminous writer, he was the author of *Les États Unis* (Montreal, 1898), *A la conquête de la liberté religieuse en France et en Canada* (Lévis, 1898), *Papineau* (Montreal, 1905), *Papineau, Cartier* (Toronto, 1906), *Lafontaine et son temps* (Montreal, 1907), *The patriotes of '37* (Toronto, 1916), *Les constitutions du Canada* (Montreal, 1918), and *Laurier et son temps* (Montreal, 1920).

[T. Chapais, *Alfred Duclos DeCelles* (Canada français, 1925); Morgan, *Can. men* (1912).]

De Cosmos, Amor (1825-1897), prime minister of British Columbia (1872-74), was born at Windsor, Nova Scotia, in 1825. His baptismal name was William Alexander Smith. In 1852, he went to California, and there he had his name changed by Act of the legislature to Amor de Cosmos, which he seems to have thought meant "lover of the world". It is said that an amendment, whereby his name would have been "Amor de Bacchus", narrowly escaped adoption. In 1858 he went to British Columbia and founded at Victoria the *British Colonist* newspaper. From 1863 to 1866 he represented Victoria in the Legislative Assembly of Vancouver Island; and from 1867 to 1871 in the Legislative Council of British Columbia. During this period he was a leader in the battle for responsible government in the colony, and in the agitation for confederation with the Dominion of Canada. In 1871 he was elected to represent Victoria as a Liberal in the Canadian House of Commons and in the Legislative Assembly of British Columbia; and from 1872 to 1874 he was prime minister of British Columbia. In 1874 he retired from the provincial legislature, owing to the operation of the law against dual representation; but he continued to represent Victoria in the House of Commons until 1882, when he was defeated at the polls. He then retired to private life; and he died at Victoria, British Columbia, on July 4, 1897. He was not married.

[*Can. who was who*, vol. 2; J. B. Kerr, *Biographical dictionary of well-known British Columbians* (Vancouver, B.C., 1890); *Can. parl. comp.*; A. Begg, *A history of British Columbia* (Toronto, 1894); R. Wild, *Amor de Cosmos* (Toronto, 1952).]

De Grassi, Philip (1793-1877), soldier, was born in Rome, Italy, in 1793. He became an officer in Napoleon's army, and saw service in the Peninsular War. He was taken prisoner by the British; and in England he obtained a commission in the British army. He was in the British West Indies with his regiment from

1812 to 1815; and he was then placed on half-pay. After eking out a living in England by teaching languages, he emigrated, with his family, to Canada in 1831, and settled near York (Toronto), Upper Canada. In the rebellion of 1837, two of his daughters, Cornelia (d.1885) and Charlotte (d.1872), played a romantic and adventurous part; and he himself served with the loyalist forces. He died at Lindsay, Ontario, in 1877.

[W. S. Wallace, *The story of Charlotte and Cornelia De Grassi* (Trans. Roy. Soc. Can., 1941).]

De Koninck, Charles (1906-1965), philosopher and theologian, and for over twenty years dean of the faculty of philosophy, Laval University. Born at Thourhout, Belgium, July 29, 1906, he emigrated with his family as a child to Detroit but returned to Ostende in 1917 for his secondary education. After completing his docteur en philosophie at the Université de Louvain he joined the faculty of Laval University in 1934 as professor of philosophy. Drawing on his anglophone background he introduced French-speaking students to contemporary English philosophy. The breadth of his academic interests was reflected in his published works on the incarnation, *La philosophie politique et la Confédération,* and *Doctrine sur la sobriété.* His reputation was international — he received six honorary degrees and was an invited speaker in Europe, Asia, and the two Americas. He acted in Rome as theological advisor to Maurice, Cardinal Roy, Archbishop of Quebec, at the Second Vatican Council, and received the Aquinas Spellman Medal of the American Catholic Philosophical Association in 1964. A member of several learned societies, including the Roman Pontifical Academy of St. Thomas Aquinas, he was also a founder of the Canadian Society for the History and Philosophy of Science and president of the Canadian Philosophical Association. He died suddenly in Rome on February 13, 1965, survived by his wife Zoé Decruydt.

[*Trans. and Proc. Roy. Soc. Can.* (1965), vol. 3.]

Delafosse, Frederick Montague (1860-1950), librarian, was born in Bengal, India, in 1860, the son of an English army officer. He was educated at Wellington College, and came to Canada in 1878. His first experience of life in Canada was helping to clear a bush farm in Muskoka, an experience on which he drew in writing his *English Bloods* (Ottawa, 1930), under the *nom de plume* of "Roger Vardon". After various experiences, he was appointed librarian of the Peterborough Public Library in 1900; and this position he held with distinction until 1946. He died at Peterborough, Ontario, on September 29, 1950. Under his own name he published a *Centenary history of St.*

John's Church (Peterborough, 1927) and *Verses grave and gay* (Peterborough, 1937).

[*Ontario Library Review*, Nov., 1950.]

Delâge, Cyrille Fraser (1869-1957), educationist, was born in Quebec City in 1869, and died there on November 27, 1957. He was educated at Laval University (LL.B., 1892). He represented Quebec in the provincial Legislative Assembly from 1901 to 1916; and from 1912 to 1916 he was speaker of the House. He then accepted appointment as superintendent of public instruction for the province, and he held this post until his retirement in 1939. He was elected a fellow of the Royal Society of Canada in 1916; and he was the author of two volumes of *Conférences, discours, lettres* (Quebec, 1919 and 1937).

[*Proc. Roy. Soc. Can.*, 1958; *Can. who's who,* 1955-57.]

De la Roche, Mazo (1879-1961), novelist, was born in Toronto in 1879, a descendant on her mother's side of United Empire Loyalists, a circumstance which influenced her work as a novelist. She was educated at Parkdale Collegiate Institute in Toronto and at the University of Toronto. Her first short story appeared in the *Atlantic Monthly* in 1915, and her first novel of the Jalna series won the *Atlantic Monthly* $10,000 prize and brought its author immediate fame. Miss de la Roche built her novels around a large family in a large house on a large estate dominated by the matriarch, Adeline Whiteoak, mistress of Jalna. The atmosphere is horsy, loyalist, and at times threadbare. The novels, twenty-four in the series, have found world-wide readership in half a dozen languages. *Whiteoaks,* a play, ran two years on the London stage and was produced also in New York and Montreal. Miss de la Roche was awarded the Medal of the Royal Society of Canada, in 1938, for distinguished literary contribution. She died at Toronto, July 12, 1961. She was the author of four plays, *Come true* (Toronto, 1927), *The return of the immigrant* (Boston, 1929), *Low life and other plays* (Boston, 1929), and *Whiteoaks* (Boston, 1936). She also wrote *Explorers of the dawn* (New York, 1922), *Possession* (New York, 1923), *Delight* (New York, 1926), *Jalna* (Boston, 1927), *Whiteoaks of Jalna* (Boston, 1929), *Portrait of a dog, essays* (Boston, 1930), *Finch's fortune* (London, 1931), *Lark ascending* (Boston, 1932), *The master of Jalna* (Toronto, 1933), *Beside a Norman tower* (Toronto, 1934), *Young Renny* (Toronto, 1935), *Whiteoak harvest* (Boston, 1936), *The very house* (London, 1937), *Growth of a man* (Boston, 1938), *The sacred bullock and other stories of animals* (London, 1939), *Whiteoak heritage* (Boston, 1940), *The Whiteoak chronicles* (London, 1940), *Wakefield's course* (Boston, 1941), *The two saplings* (London, 1942), *The building of Jalna* (Boston, 1944), *Mary Wakefield* (Boston, 1949), *Renny's daughter* (Boston, 1951), *Boy in* the house and other stories (Boston, 1952), Bill and Coo (Toronto, 1958), Centenary at Jalna (Toronto, 1958), Morning at Jalna (London, 1960), The Whiteoak brothers: Jalna 1923 (Toronto, 1953), Return to Jalna (Boston, 1946), The song of Lambert (Toronto, 1955), The thunder of new wings (Boston, 1932), Variable winds at Jalna (Toronto, 1954), Ringing the changes: autobiography (Toronto, 1957), Quebec, historic seaport (Toronto, 1944).

[Can. who's who, 1958-60; R. E. Watters, A check list of Canadian literature, 1628-1950 (Toronto, 1959); N. Story, The Oxford companion to Canadian history and literature (Toronto, 1967).]

Delfosse, Georges (1869-1939), painter, was born at Les Rapides, St. Henri de Mascouche, Quebec, on December 8, 1869, of mixed French and United Empire Loyalist stock. He studied painting in Canada and Europe, and became a portrait painter and a painter of religious and historical tableaux. He died, after several years of illness, on December 24, 1939.

[Mgr. O. Maurault, Georges Delfosse (Trans. Roy. Soc. Can., 1940); Morgan, Can. men (1912).]

Delisle, David Chabrand (1730?-1794), clergyman, was born at Auduxe, France, about 1730. He is said to have been a Jesuit, and to have been converted to Protestantism. In 1769 he came to Montreal from England as the authorized Protestant clergyman; and he continued as rector of the parish of Montreal until 1794. He died at Montreal on June 28, 1794. In 1769 he married Margaret Henry; and by her he had three sons and four daughters. At the time of his death he was chaplain to the garrison at Montreal.

[R. Campbell, A history of the Scotch Presbyterian Church, St. Gabriel St., Montreal (Montreal, 1887); Bull. rech. hist., 1912.]

DeLisle, Jean (d. 1814?), notary public, was a native of Nantes, France, and came to Canada by way of New York. In 1768 he became a notary public in Montreal. In 1783-84 he went, with Adhémar (q.v.), to England as agent of the French Canadians in their request for an assembly. He seems to have died about 1814. He was twice married, (1) about 1753 in New York to an Englishwoman named Danton, by whom he had one son, named Jean-Guillaume (d. 1819); and (2) in Montreal to Suzanne de Mézières de l'Epervanche, by whom he had two sons, Ambroise and Auguste. In 1777 Jean-Guillaume DeLisle published a work on the administration of the fabriques; but this is not to be found in any of the usual bibliographies or library catalogues.

[B. Sulte, La délégation envoyée en Angleterre en 1783 (Bull. rech. hist., 1901); E. Z. Massicotte, La famille de Jean de Lisle (Bull. rech. hist., 1919); MM. Adhémar et Delisle (Bull. rech. hist., 1906); Abbé Daniel, Notice sur la famille Guy (Montreal, 1867).]

De Lury, Alfred Tennyson (1864-1951), mathematician, was born at Manilla, Ontario, on May 13, 1864, and died at Lindsay, Ontario, on November 12, 1951. He was educated at the University of Toronto (B.A., 1890; M.A., 1902), and in 1892 was appointed a lecturer in mathematics in this university. He became head of the department in 1919, and dean of the faculty of arts in 1922; and he retired on pension in 1934. He was elected a fellow of the Royal Society of Canada in 1918; and he was the author of several textbooks in algebra and arithmetic. He left his extensive collection of Irish literature to the University of Toronto Library.

[Proc. Roy. Soc. Can., 1952; Can. who's who, 1936-37.]

Demers, Benjamin (1848-1919), priest, was born at St. Romuald d'Etchemin, Canada East, on October 9, 1848; became a parish priest in the Roman Catholic Church; and died at Quebec, Que., on July 31, 1919. He was the author of Notes sur la paroisse de Saint-François de la Beauce (Quebec, 1891), La famille Demers d'Etchemin (Lévis, Que., 1905), and La paroisse de Saint-Romuald d'Etchemin (Quebec, 1906).

[Allaire, Dict. biog.; Bull. rech. hist., 1930.]

Demers, Hector (1878-1917), poet, was the author of Les voix champêtres (Montreal, 1912). He was in 1912 president of the École Littéraire de Montréal.

[Bull. rech. hist., 1912.]

Demers, Jérôme (1774-1853), priest and educationist, was born at St. Nicholas, Quebec, on August 1, 1774, was ordained a priest of the Roman Catholic Church in 1798, and became superior of the Quebec Seminary. He died at Quebec, Canada East, on May 17, 1853. He was the author of Institutiones philosophicae (Quebec, 1935) and other textbooks for the use of pupils in the Seminary.

[Allaire, Dict. biog.]

Demers, Modeste (1809-1871), first Roman Catholic bishop of Victoria (1847-71), was born at St. Nicolas, Lower Canada, on October 11, 1809. He was educated at the Quebec Seminary, and was ordained a priest in 1836. In 1837 he was sent as a missionary to the west; and in 1847 he was consecrated the first bishop of Victoria. In 1856 he imported a printing-press, and established a journal at Victoria, entitled Le Courier de la Nouvelle Caledonia. He died at Victoria, British Columbia, on July 28, 1871.

[Allaire, Dict. biog.; Le Jeune, Dict. gén.; Ae. Fauteux, The introduction of printing into Canada (Montreal, 1930); Dict. Can. biog., vol. 10.]

De Mille, James (1833-1880), novelist, was born in Saint John, New Brunswick, on August 23, 1833. He was educated at Acadia College, Wolfville, Nova Scotia, and at Brown University, Providence, Rhode Island (M.A., 1854). From 1860 until 1864 he was professor of classics at Acadia College; and from 1865 to his death he was professor of history and rhetoric at Dalhousie College, Halifax. He was a voluminous writer of novels. He published *Martyrs of the catacombs* (New York, 1865), *Helena's household* (London and New York, 1868), *The Dodge Club* (New York, 1869), *Cord and crease* (New York, 1869), *The lady of the ice* (New York, 1870), *An open question* (New York, 1870), *The cryptogram* (New York, 1871), *The American baron* (New York, 1872), *A comedy of terrors* (Boston, 1872), *An open question* (New York, 1873), *Old Garth* (New York, 1873), *The lily and the cross* (Boston, 1874), *The living link* (New York, 1874), *The babes in the wood* (Boston, 1875), and *A castle in Spain* (New York, 1878). He published also a number of books of adventure for boys; and a book on *The elements of rhetoric* (New York, 1878). He died at Halifax, Nova Scotia, on January 28, 1880. After his death there was published perhaps the best-known of all his novels, *A strange manuscript found in a copper cylinder* (New York, 1888); and in 1893 there appeared, edited by A. MacMechan, a poem by him entitled *Behind the veil* (Halifax).

[A. MacMechan, *DeMille, the man and the writer* (Canadian magazine, 1906); R. W. Douglas, *James DeMille* (Canadian bookman, 1922); W. G. MacFarlane, *New Brunswick bibliography* (Saint John, N.B., 1895); L. E. Horning and L. J. Burpee, *A bibliography of Canadian fiction* (Toronto, 1904); A. MacMurchy, *Handbook of Canadian literature* (Toronto, 1906); *Dict. Can. biog.*, vol. 10.]

Denis, Joseph (1657-1736), priest, was born at Three Rivers, Canada, on November 7, 1657, the son of Pierre Denis and Cathérine Le Neuf. His baptismal name was Jacques, but later in life he took the religious name of Joseph. He was the first native-born Canadian to enter the Récollet order, and he was ordained a priest at Paris, France, in 1682. He served at Gaspé, in Newfoundland, at Montreal, Quebec, and Three Rivers, at Louisbourg, and finally at Quebec. He died at Quebec on January 25, 1736.

[R. P. Hugolin, *Le Père Joseph Denis* (2 vols., Quebec, 1926); Allaire, *Dict. biog.*; Le Jeune, *Dict. gén.*; *Dict. Can. biog.*, vol. 2.]

Denison, Mrs. Flora Macdonald, *née* **Merrill** (1867-1921), journalist and suffragist, was born near Bridgewater, Ontario, in 1867, and died at Toronto, Ontario, on May 23, 1921. In 1892 she married Howard Denison, by whom she had one son, Merrill, later a well-known Canadian author. She became a suc-cessful business woman in Toronto, and a leader in the campaign for woman suffrage. From 1911 to 1914 she was president of the Canadian Suffrage Association, and for several years she conducted a labour column in the *Sunday World,* which was not without influence in bringing about woman suffrage in most of the provinces of Canada a few years later

[C. L. Cleverdon, *The woman suffrage movement in Canada* (Toronto, 1950); *Encyc. Can.*]

Denison, Frederick Charles (1846-1896), soldier, was born in Toronto on November 22, 1846, the second son of Colonel George Taylor Denison (q.v.). He entered "Denison's Horse" as a cornet in 1865, and he rose to the rank of lieutenant-colonel, in 1884. In 1870 he was orderly officer to General Wolseley in the Red River Expedition; and in 1884-85 he commanded the Canadian *Voyageurs* in the Soudan. From 1887 to 1896 he represented West Toronto, as a Conservative, in the Canadian House of Commons; and he died at Toronto on April 15, 1896. In 1874 he married Julia Abigail, daughter of Oliver Tiffany Macklem; and by her he had six sons and two daughters. He was created a C.M.G. in 1885. He was the author of *The historical record of the Governor-General's Body Guard* (Toronto, 1876).

[*Can. parl. comp.*; E. M. Chadwick, *Ontarian families* (2 vols., Toronto, 1894-98).]

Denison, George Taylor (1783-1853), soldier, was born at Hedon, Yorkshire, England, on December 29, 1783, the son of John Denison and Sophia Taylor. He came to Canada with his parents in 1792, and settled in York (Toronto) in 1796. He served as a militia officer in the War of 1812; and during the Rebellion of 1837 he commanded a troop of dragoons — a unit which was disbanded in 1839, but was immediately organized as a volunteer corps, known as "Denison's Horse", and played an important part in the formation of the volunteer militia of Canada. He died at his place "Bellevue", Toronto, on December 18, 1853. He was married four times, and had of the first marriage three sons and three daughters, and of the third marriage two sons and one daughter.

[E. M. Chadwick, *Ontarian families* (2 vols., Toronto, 1894-98).]

Denison, George Taylor (1816-1873), soldier, was born at York (Toronto), Upper Canada, on July 17, 1816, the second son of Lieut.-Col. George Taylor Denison (q.v.) and Esther Borden Lippincott. He succeeded his father in 1853 as lieutenant-colonel commanding "Denison's Horse"; and he took part in the organization of the Toronto Field Battery and of the Queen's Own Rifles. In 1860 he was gazetted a colonel, and was appointed commandant of the 5th and 10th military districts. He died at Toronto on May 30, 1873. He married Mary Anne Dewson; and by her he had seven sons and two daughters.

[*Cyc. Am. biog.*; E. N. Chadwick, *Ontarian families* (2 vols., Toronto, 1894-98); *Dict. Can. biog.*, vol. 10.]

Denison, George Taylor (1839-1925), soldier and author, was born in Toronto on August 31, 1839, the eldest son of Col. George Taylor Denison (q.v.) and Mary Anne Dewson. He was educated at Upper Canada College and at the University of Toronto (LL.B., 1861), and was called to the bar of Upper Canada in 1861. He joined "Denison's Horse" in 1855 as a cornet, and in 1866 he became lieutenant-colonel commanding the Governor-General's Body Guard, as the unit was henceforth to be known. He saw active service in 1866 during the Fenian Raids, and in 1885 during the North West Rebellion. In 1868 he was one of the group of young men who founded the "Canada First" movement; and twenty-five years later he was the chief figure in Canada in the Imperial Federation movement. From 1877 to 1923 he was senior police magistrate of Toronto, and he died at Toronto on June 6, 1925. He was twice married, (1) to Caroline Macklem (d. 1885), by whom he had three sons and three daughters, and (2) to Helen Amanda Mair, by whom he had two daughters. In 1882 he was appointed a charter member of the Royal Society of Canada, and in 1903 he was elected its president. He was the author of *The Fenian raid at Fort Erie* (Toronto, 1866), *Modern cavalry* (London, 1868), *A history of cavalry* (London, 1877), *Soldiering in Canada* (Toronto, 1900), *The struggle for imperial unity* (Toronto, 1909), and *Recollections of a police magistrate* (Toronto, 1920).

[Morgan, *Can. men* (1912); *Cyc. Am. biog.*; E. M. Chadwick, *Ontarian families* (2 vols., Toronto, 1894-98); D. Gagan, *The Denison family of Toronto, 1792-1925* (Toronto, 1973).]

Denison, Mrs. Grace Elizabeth, *née* **Sandys** (d. 1914), journalist and author, was born in Chatham, Ontario, the daughter of the Ven. Archdeacon Sandys. She was educated in New York and in London; and she married Albert Ernest, son of Lieut.-Col. R. L. Denison (q.v.). She became a journalist, and wrote under the *nom de plume* of "Lady Gay". She died at Toronto, Canada, on February 1, 1914. Among her publications were *A happy holiday* (Toronto, 1890), and *The new cook book* (Toronto, 1903).

[Morgan, *Can. men and women* (1912).]

Denison, John (1853-1939), naval officer, was born in Toronto, Canada West, on May 25, 1853, the fifth son of Colonel George Taylor Denison (q.v.). He was educated at Upper Canada College, Toronto, and entered the

Royal Navy as a midshipman in 1867. He rose to the rank of admiral, and commanded the Devonport division of the Home Fleet in 1908-09. He then retired, but served as temporary captain and commodore during the First World War. He died at Alverstoke, England, on March 8, 1939. He was awarded the D.S.O. in 1917.

[*Who was who*, 1928-40.]

Denison, Richard Lippincott (1814-1878), soldier, was born near York (Toronto) on June 13, 1814, the eldest son of Colonel George Taylor Denison (q.v.) and Esther Borden, daughter of Lieut.-Col. Richard Lippincott. He served in the militia during the rebellion of 1837, and from 1838 to 1846 he was officer commanding the Queen's Light Dragoons, later the Governor-General's Body Guard. During his later years he commanded the West Toronto Reserve Militia. He died at Toronto on March 10, 1878. He married Susan Maria Hepburn, of Chippawa, and by her he had eight sons and one daughter.

[*Dom. ann. reg.*, 1878; E. M. Chadwick, *Ontarian families* (2 vols., Toronto, 1894-98).]

Denison, Septimus Julius Augustus (1859-1937), soldier, was born at Toronto, Canada West, on September 3, 1859, the seventh son of Colonel George Taylor Denison (q.v.). He was educated at Upper Canada College, Toronto, and at the Royal Military College, Kingston. He rose to the rank of major-general in the Canadian Permanent Force, and was awarded the C.M.G. in 1901. He served as A.D.C. to Lord Aberdeen (q.v.) when governor-general of Canada, to Field Marshal Lord Roberts during the South African War, and to H.R.H. the Prince of Wales (later King George V) during his visit to Canada in 1901. He died at Toronto, Ontario, on November 8, 1937. He was the author of a volume of *Memoirs* (Toronto, 1927).

[*Who was who*, 1928-40.]

Denison, Walter Wallbridge (1879-1944), soldier and lawyer, was born at Toronto, Ontario, on August 27, 1879, the son of Lieut.-Col. Clarence A. Denison. He was educated at Upper Canada College and at the Royal Military College; and was called to the bar of Ontario in 1905 (K.C., 1928). He served during the First World War with the 4th Canadian Mounted Rifles, and was awarded the D.S.O. in 1916. After the war, he occupied various positions in the civil service in Ontario; and he died at Toronto on October 1, 1944. He was the author of *The A B C of company incorporation in Ontario* (Toronto, 1925), which was republished as *Denison's manual of companies* (Toronto, 1928).

[*Can. who's who*, 1936-37.]

Dennis, John Stoughton (1820-1885), surveyor and civil servant, was born on October 19, 1820, near York, Upper Canada, the son of Joseph Dennis, of "Buttonwood". He was commissioned as a surveyor of public lands in 1842. In 1869 he was sent by the Canadian government to organize a system of surveys in the North West; and his handling of the difficulties confronting him was partly responsible for the first Riel Rebellion. In March, 1871, he was appointed surveyor-general of Dominion lands, and from 1878 to 1881 he was deputy minister of the interior. In 1882 he was created, for his services, a C.M.G.; and he died at "Kingsmere", near Ottawa, on July 7, 1885.

[*Dom. ann. reg.*, 1885; J. P. Robertson, *Political manual of Manitoba* (Winnipeg, 1887).]

Dennis, William (1856-1920), journalist, was born in Cornwall, England, on March 4, 1856. He came to Canada in 1873, and joined the staff of the Halifax *Herald*. In 1890 he became editor-in-chief of this paper, and later its proprietor. In 1912 he was appointed to the Senate of Canada. He died at Boston, Massachusetts, on July 12, 1920.

[Morgan, *Can. men* (1912); *Can. parl. comp.*]

Denny, Sir Cecil Edward, Bart. (1850-1928), author, was born on December 14, 1850, the second son of the Rev. Robert Day Denny, and grandson of the third baronet of Tralee Castle, county Kerry, Ireland. He was educated at Cheltenham College, England; and in 1874 became a sub-inspector in the Royal North West Mounted Police in Canada, and later an inspector. He resigned in 1881, and became an officer of the Indian department. In his later years he was archivist of the province of Alberta; and he died at Edmonton, Alberta, unmarried, on July 24, 1928. In 1921 he succeeded his half-brother in the baronetcy of Tralee Castle, and became the sixth baronet. He was the author of *The riders of the plains* (Calgary, Alta., 1905).

[*Who was who*, 1916-28.]

Denonville, Jacques-René de Brisay, Marquis de (1637-1710), governor of New France (1685-89), was a colonel of dragoons and had spent thirty years in military service when he was appointed governor of New France in 1685. On his arrival he at once saw the necessity of open war with the Iroquois and sent to France for reinforcements, in the meantime strengthening Fort Frontenac, and constructing a fort at Niagara. Although Denonville never received significant reinforcements from France, he initiated several engagements against the Iroquois, partially restoring the military balance that had been upset before his arrival. In 1688 he entered peace negotiations with the Iroquois, but in 1689, when the treaty was to be ratified by the Five Nations, war broke out between England and France and the Iroquois ceased talking of peace. Denonville, however, was recalled to France in that year. On his return he was named deputy governor of the Dauphin's children. He died on September 22, 1710.

[R. Roy, *Denonville* (Bull. rech. hist., 1919); T. Prince-Falmagne, *Un marquis de grand siècle: Jacques-René de Brisay de Denonville* (Montréal, 1965); W. J. Eccles, *Canada under Louis XIV* (Toronto, 1964); Le Jeune, *Dict. gén.*; *Dict. Can. biog.*, vol. 2.)]

Dent, John Charles (1841-1888), journalist and historian, was born at Kendal, England, on November 8, 1841. He came to Canada with his parents when an infant, and was educated in Canada. He was called to the bar of Upper Canada in 1865, but practised law for only a short time. He returned to England, and was on the staff of the London *Daily Telegraph*. In 1876 he came back to Canada, and for a year was editor of the Toronto *Evening Telegram*. He then joined the editorial staff of the Toronto *Globe*; but later drifted from journalism to the writing of books. In 1880 he published *The Canadian portrait gallery* (4 vols., Toronto); in 1881 *The last forty years; Canada since the union of 1841* (2 vols., Toronto); and in 1884 *The story of the Upper Canadian rebellion* (2 vols., Toronto). In 1884 he collaborated with the Rev. Henry Scadding (q.v.) in a volume celebrating the semi-centennial of the city of Toronto; and in 1884 he published a volume of short stories entitled *The Gerrard Street mystery, and other weird tales* (Toronto). He died at Toronto on September 27, 1888.

[*Can. who was who*, vol.2; A. MacMurchy, *Handbook of Canadian literature* (Toronto, 1906); L. E. Horning and L. J. Burpee, *A bibliography of Canadian fiction* (Toronto, 1904).]

Denys, Nicolas (1598-1688), trader and author, was born in Tours, France, in 1598. In 1633 he became interested in Acadia; and from that date until about 1671 he was almost continuously engaged in its exploitation. In 1654 he was appointed governor of the coasts and islands of the Gulf of St. Lawrence from Canso to Gaspé, as well as of Newfoundland. He returned to France in 1671, and there published his *Description géographique et historique des costes de l'Amérique septentrionale* (2 vols., Paris, 1672). In 1685 he came back to Acadia; and he died, probably at his post of Nepisiguit, in 1688.

[W. F. Ganong (ed.), *The description and natural history of the coasts of North America (Acadia)*, by Nicolas Denys (Toronto: The Champlain Society, 1908); F. Pacifique, *Nicolas Denys* (Bulletin de la Société de Géographie de Québec, 1929); *Dict. Can. biog.*, vol. 1.]

De Peyster, Arent Schuyler (1736-1832), soldier, was born in New York on June 27, 1736, the grandson of Abraham De Peyster, chief justice of New York. In 1755 he obtained a commission in the 8th Regiment of Foot, and he served in various parts of North America during the Seven Years' and American Revolutionary wars. For a time he was in command at Michilimackinac; and in 1779 he took command at Detroit. At the close of the American Revolution he settled at Dumfries, Scotland; and here he lived until his death in November, 1832. At Dumfries he was a friend of Robert Burns, and to him Burns addressed one of his poems. He was the author of a volume of verse, entitled *Miscellanies* (Dumfries, Scotland, 1813).

[J. Watts De Peyster (ed.), *Miscellanies*, by an officer (New York, 1888); *Cyc. Am. biog.*; *Michigan Pioneer and Hist. Soc. Coll.*, vol. 20 (Lansing, Mich., 1892).]

Derbishire, Stewart (1797?-1863), Queen's printer, was born in London, England, about 1797, the son of Philip Derbishire, M.D., and Ann Masterton. He was called to the English bar, and in 1838 came to Canada as an attaché to Lord Durham (q.v.). After the union of Upper and Lower Canada, in 1841, he was appointed Queen's printer; and he also sat in the Legislative Assembly of United Canada for Bytown (later Ottawa), from 1841 to 1844. He died at Quebec, Canada East, on March 27, 1863.

[J. C. Dent, *The last forty years* (2 vols., Toronto, 1881).]

Desaulniers, François Sévère Lesieur (1850-1913), politican and author, was born at Yamachiche, Canada East, on September 19, 1850. He was educated at Nicolet College, and was called to the bar of Quebec in 1879. He sat in the Legislative Assembly of Quebec from 1875 to 1881, and in the Canadian House of Commons from 1887 to 1892. He died at Montreal, Quebec, on January 28, 1913. He was the author of *Réunions des paroissiens d'Yamachiche* (Quebec, 1876), *Les vieilles familles d'Yamachiche* (4 vols., Montreal, 1898-1908), *Charles Lesieur et la fondation d'Yamachiche* (Montreal, 1902), *Recherches généalogiques* (Montreal, 1902), *Notes historiques sur la paroisse de Saint-Guillaume d'Upton* (Montreal, 1905), *La généalogie des familles Gouin et Allard* (Montreal, 1909), and *La généalogie des familles Richer de la Flèche et Hamelin* (Montreal, 1909).

[*Can. parl. comp.*; *Bull. rech. hist.*, index.]

Desautels, Joseph (1814-1881), priest, was born at Chambly, Lower Canada, on October 26, 1814, and was ordained a priest of the Roman Catholic Church in 1838. After serving as a missionary in the lumbercamps on the Ottawa River, he was successively parish priest at Rigaud and at Varennes, Quebec. He died at Salem, Massachusetts, on August 4, 1881. He was the author of *Manuel des curés pour le bon gouvernement temporel des paroisses et des fabriques* (Montreal, 1864).

[Allaire, *Dict. biog.*]

Desbarats, Georges Edouard (1838-1893), printer and publisher, was born at Quebec, Lower Canada, on April 5, 1838, the son of Georges Paschal Desbarats (q.v.) and Henriette Dionne. He succeeded his father (q.v.) as Queen's printer in 1865; but resigned soon afterwards. In 1869 he began the publication of the *Canadian Illustrated News*, and in 1870 that of *L'Opinion Publique*. In 1888 he founded the *Dominion Illustrated*. He died on February 18, 1893. He was the author of a pamphlet entitled *L'esclavage dans l'antiquité* (Montreal, 1858).

[Le Jeune, *Dict. gén.*; *Bull. rech. hist.*, 1928.]

Desbarats, Georges Paschal (1808-1864), printer and publisher, was born in Quebec, Lower Canada, on August 11, 1808, the son of Pierre-Édouard Desbarats and Marie-Josephte Voyer. He became one of the editors of the Quebec *Mercury*; and in 1844 he was appointed Queen's printer. This post he held until his death, in Montreal, on November 12, 1864.

[Le Jeune, *Dict. gén.*; *Bull. rech. hist.*, 1928.]

DesBarres, Joseph Frederic Wallet (1722-1824), lieutenant-governor of Cape Breton (1784-87), and of Prince Edward Island (1804-12), was born in 1722, of Huguenot descent. He was educated at Basel, Switzerland, and at the Royal Military College, Woolwich, England. He then entered the British army, and came to America at the beginning of the Seven Years' War. He was present at Ticonderoga in 1757, at the second capture of Louisbourg in 1758, and at Quebec in 1759. From 1763 to 1773 he was engaged in surveying the coast of Nova Scotia and Cape Breton; and he published the result of his surveys in a magnificent collection of charts, plans, and views, entitled *The Atlantic Neptune* (4 vols., London, 1777). When Cape Breton was erected into a separate government in 1784, he was appointed its first lieutenant-governor; but he was relieved of his post in 1787. In 1804 he was appointed lieutenant-governor of Prince Edward Island, and his term of office there lasted until 1812. He then returned to Halifax, Nova Scotia, and he died there on October 24, 1824, aged one hundred and three.

[J. C. Webster, *The life of Joseph Frederick Wallet DesBarres* (Shediac, N.B., 1933); G. N. D. Evans, *Uncommon obdurate: The several public careers of J. F. W. DesBarres* (Toronto, 1969); *Dict. nat. biog.*; *Cyc. Am. biog.*; W. G. MacFarlane, *New Brunswick bibliography* (Saint John, N.B., 1895); *Can. arch. report*, 1896.]

DesBarres, William Frederick (1800-1885), jurist, was born at the Elysian Fields, Cumberland, Nova Scotia, on February 14, 1800, the grandson of J. F. W. DesBarres (q.v.). He was educated at the Halifax grammar school, and was called to the bar of Nova Scotia in 1821. From 1836 to 1848 he represented Guysboro' in the House of Assembly of Nova Scotia; and he was solicitor-general in the administration formed by Joseph Howe (q.v.) in 1848. Later in the same year he was appointed a judge of the Supreme Court of Nova Scotia. He retired from the bench in 1881; and he died at Halifax, Nova Scotia, on June 16, 1885.

[*Dom. ann. reg.*, 1885; *Cyc. Am. biog.*]

Des Brisay, Alexander Campbell (1888-1963), judge, was born in Winnipeg, Manitoba, June 27, 1888. He was educated at Western Canada College, Calgary, Alberta, at the University of Manitoba and at Queen's University (B.A., 1910). He entered the law office of Bowser, Reid and Wallbridge in Vancouver, and was called to the British Columbia bar in 1913. He was a partner in Bourne, Des Brisay and Bourne, a director of O'Brien Advertising Limited, Georgia Hotel Company Limited, Pacific Western Hotels Limited, Torbit Silver Mines Limited, M. Des Brisay and Company Limited. He was commissioner for British Columbia at the conference of commissions on uniformity of legislation in Canada, and was president of the Vancouver Conservative Association, 1926-28. He became chief justice of British Columbia in 1958. He died at Vancouver, on November 30, 1963.

[*Can. who's who*, 1955-57; 1961-63.]

D'Eschambault, Antoine (1896-1960), priest and historian, was born at Letellier, Manitoba, on October 15, 1896, and died at St. Boniface, Manitoba, on May 18, 1960. He was educated at the College of St. Boniface, at Laval University (D.Th., 1921), and at Apollinaris College, Rome (D.C.L., 1923). He returned to Manitoba in 1924, and became secretary to the bishop, and later, chancellor and archivist of the diocese. He became an authority on the history of the West; and at the time of his death was president of the Historic Sites and Monuments Board of Canada. He was elected a fellow of the Royal Society of Canada in 1955.

[*Proc. Roy. Soc. Can.*, 1960; *Can. who's who*, 1958-60.]

Deschamps, Isaac (1722?-1801), jurist, was born, apparently in Switzerland, about 1722. He came to America as a young man, and was in Halifax, Nova Scotia, as early as 1752. In 1768 he was appointed a judge of the Court of Common Pleas in Prince Edward Island; and in 1770 he was transferred to the Supreme Court of Nova Scotia. He became chief justice of this court in 1785; and he died on August 13,

1801. He was the author of a description of Nova Scotia.

[F. J. Audet, *Isaac Deschamps* (Bull. rech. hist., 1935).]

Des Ecorres, Charles (pseud.). See **Chartrand, Joseph Demers.**

Des Groseilliers, Médard Chouart. See **Chouart des Groseilliers, Médard.**

Desjardins, Alphonse (1841-1912), minister of militia for Canada (1896), was born at Terrebonne, Lower Canada, on May 6, 1841. He was educated at Masson College and at the Seminary of Nicolet, and was called to the bar of Lower Canada in 1862. He practised law in Montreal until 1868, when he entered journalism, and became one of the editors of *L'Ordre.* Later he became chief editor of *Le Nouveau Monde.* From 1874 to 1896 he represented Hochelaga in the Canadian House of Commons; and in 1896 he was first minister of militia in the reconstructed Bowell administration, and then minister of public works in the Tupper administration. At the general election of 1896 he was defeated in Richelieu, and he then retired from political life. He died at Montreal on June 4, 1912. He was twice married, (1) in 1864 to Virginie (d. 1879), eldest daughter of Hubert Paré, and (2) in 1880 to Hortense, daughter of Joseph Barsalou. In 1872 he was created a knight of the order of Pius IX.

[Morgan, *Can. men* (1912); *Cyc. Am. biog.*; *Can. parl. comp.*]

Desjardins, Alphonse (1854-1920), journalist and reporter, was born at Lévis, Lower Canada, on November 5, 1854, and became a journalist. From 1879 to 1890 he published, at his own risk, the debates of the legislature of Quebec; and from 1892 to 1917 he was an official reporter of the debates in the House of Commons at Ottawa. In his later days he interested himself in the foundation of popular banks (*caisses populaires*); and he died at Lévis, Quebec, on October 31, 1920. He was created by the Pope a commander of the order of St. Gregory.

[Y. Roby, *Alphonse Desjardins et les caisses populaires, 1854-1920* (Montreal, 1964); Le Jeune, *Dict. gén.*]

Desjardins, Louis Georges (1849-1928), civil servant and author, was born at St. Jean Port Joli, Quebec, on May 12, 1849, and was educated at Lévis College. From 1881 to 1890 he represented Montmorency in the Legislative Assembly of Quebec; and from 1890 to 1892 he represented L'Islet in the House of Commons. He was then appointed clerk of the Legislative Assembly of Quebec; and he died at Montreal on June 8, 1928. He was the author of *Précis historique de 17e Bataillon d'Infanterie de Lévis* (Lévis, 1872),

M. Laurier devant l'histoire (Quebec, 1877), *Considérations sur l'annexion* (Quebec, 1891), *Decisions of the speakers of the House of Commons of Canada* (Quebec, 1901), *Decisions of the speakers of the Legislative Assembly of Quebec* (Quebec, 1902), and *England, Canada and the Great War* (Quebec, 1918), the last three being published also in French.

[Morgan, *Can. men* (1912); *Can. parl. comp.*; Rose, *Cyc. Can. biog.* (1888); *Bull. rech. hist.*, 1930.]

Desmazures, Adam Charles Gustave (1818-1891), priest, was born at Nogent-sur-Seine, France, on January 15, 1818. He became first a lawyer, and then entered the Sulpician order, and was ordained a priest of the Roman Catholic Church in Paris in 1848. He came to Canada in 1851, and for forty years he was vicar of a parish in Montreal. He died in Montreal on September 30, 1891. He was the author of *Colbert et le Canada* (Paris, 1879), *M. Faillon, prêtre de St. Sulpice* (Montreal, 1879), and *Histoire du Chevalier d'Iberville* (Montreal, 1890).

[Allaire, *Dict. biog.*; Le Jeune, *Dict. gén.*]

De Smet, Pierre Jean. See **Smet, Pierre Jean de.**

Desprairies, Jean (pseud.). See **Lacasse, Pierre Zacharie.**

Desroches, J. Israel (1850-1922), physician, was born at St. Esprit, Canada East, on November 18, 1850; and died at Montreal, Quebec, on November 25, 1922. He was the author of *Traité élémentaire d'hygiène privée* (Montreal, 1889), *Catéchisme d'hygiène privée et publique* (Montreal, 1897), *Morte apparente et morte réelle* (Montreal, 1911), and *Les doctrines évolutionistes* (Montreal, 1913).

[*Bull. rech. hist.*, 1928.]

Desrosiers, Léo Paul (1896-1967), writer and librarian, was born at Berthier, Quebec, April 11, 1896, and educated at Berthier and the University of Montreal. He became chief librarian, Civic Library of Montreal. He was a member of the Montreal Historical Society and of the Académie canadienne-française. He wrote *L'accalmie, Lord Durham au Canada* (1937); *Ames et paysages* (1922); *Commencements* (1939); *Les engagés du Grand Portage* (1938); *Nord-sud* (1943); *Sources* (1942); *Iroquoise* (1947). He died at Montreal, Quebec, April 20, 1967.

[*Can. who's who*, 1949-51.]

Dessaulles, Louis Antoine (1819-1895), politician and author, was born at St. Hyacinthe, Lower Canada, on January 31, 1819, the son of the Hon. Jean Dessaulles, seignior of St. Hyacinthe, and Rosalie, sister of the Hon. L. J. Papineau (q.v.). He was educated at the College of Montreal, and was admitted to practice as a physician in Lower Canada. From 1856 to 1863 he represented the Rougemont division in the Legislative Council of Canada; and during this period he was one of the leaders of the *parti rouge*. For a time he was editor-in-chief of *Le Pays*, the *rouge* newspaper; and he was for several years president of the Institut Canadien of Montreal. In 1863 he retired from politics, and was appointed clerk of the crown and peace for Montreal. He retired from this office in 1875; and he died in Paris, France, on August 5, 1895. In 1848 he published anonymously a pamphlet written in defence of his uncle, the Hon. L. J. Papineau (q.v.), entitled *Papineau et Nelson: Blanc et noir* (Montreal, 1848), and this was followed by a number of books and pamphlets under his own name: *Six lectures sur l'annexion du Canada aux Etats Unis* (Montreal, 1851); *Galilée, ses travaux scientifiques et sa condamnation* (Montreal, 1856); *A messieurs les électeurs de la division de Rougemont* (Montreal, 1858); *La guerre américaine* (Montreal, 1865); *Dernière correspondance entre S. E. le Cardinal Barnabo et l'hon. M. Dessaulles* (Montreal, 1871); *La grande guerre ecclésiastique* (Montreal, 1873); *Réponse honnête à une circulaire assez peu chrétienne* (Montreal, 1873); and *L'index* (Montreal, 1873).

[Morgan, *Bib. can.*; *Can. parl. comp.*; Le Jeune, *Dict. gén.*; J. D. Borthwick, *Montreal, its history* (Montreal, 1875); C. Piette-Samson, *Louis-Antoine Dessaulles, journaliste libéral* (Recherches sociographiques, 1969).]

Des Voeux, Sir George William (1834-1909), governor of Newfoundland (1886), was born in Baden, Germany, on September 22, 1834, and died in London, England, on December 15, 1909. He was educated at Charterhouse, at Balliol College, Oxford, and at the University of Toronto (B.A., 1858). In 1861 he was called to the bar in Upper Canada; but in 1863 he entered the British colonial service as a magistrate in British Guiana. He became governor successively of Fiji, Newfoundland (for part of the year 1886), and Hong Kong. In 1893 he was created a G.C.M.G.; and he was the author of an autobiography, entitled *My colonial service* (2 vols., London, 1903).

[*Dict. nat. biog.*; *Who was who*, 1897-1916; *Encyc. Can.*; *Newfoundland supp.*]

Desy, Jean (1893-1960), diplomat, was born in Montreal, January 8, 1893. He was educated at Collège Ste. Marie; at Laval University (LL.D.); at Ecole Libre des Sciences Politiques; at the Sorbonne; and at Collège de France, Paris. He was called to the bar in Quebec in 1915 and in 1919 became professor of law specializing in international law, political history, and constitutional law, at the University of Montreal. In 1924 he went to the Sorbonne as professor of Canadian history. He was counsellor in the Department of External

Affairs of the Canadian government and advisor to the Canadian delegation to the League of Nations (1925-27); in 1927 he became Canadian representative to the Council of the League. In 1939 he was appointed Canadian minister to Belgium and the Netherlands, and in 1941 he went to Brazil as minister and ambassador remaining until 1947 when he became minister and ambassador to Italy. He was director of the International Service of the Canadian Broadcasting Corporation in 1952 and in 1954 became Canadian ambassador to France. By his humanity and understanding of both the European and American worlds he helped his fellows to understand one another. He died at Paris, France, on December 19, 1960.

[*Can. who's who*, 1955-57; *Proc. Roy. Soc. Can.* (1961).]

Deville, Edouard Gaston (1849-1924), surveyor, was born at La Charité sur Noire, Nièvre, France, on February 21, 1849. He was educated at the naval school at Brest, and for several years he served in the French navy. He had charge of hydrographic surveys in the South Sea islands, Peru, and other countries. In 1875, on his retirement from the French navy, he was appointed inspector of surveys in the province of Quebec; and in 1881 he became an inspector of Dominion land surveys. In 1885 he was appointed surveyor-general of Dominion lands, and he continued to serve in this post until his death at Ottawa on September 21, 1924. In 1881 he married Josephine, daughter of the Hon. Gédéon Ouimet (q.v.). He was the author of *Photographic surveying* (Ottawa, 1889; 2nd ed., 1895).

[Morgan, *Can. men* (1912); Rose, *Cyc. Can. biog.* (1886).]

Devine, Edward James (1860-1927), priest and author, was born at Bonnechère Point, near Ottawa, Ontario, on March 3, 1860, the son of John Devine and Marion McDonnell. He was educated at the St. Francis Xavier College, New York, and joined the Society of Jesus in 1879. He was ordained a priest of the Roman Catholic Church in 1889, and he spent several years as a missionary in the Canadian North West and in Alaska. In his later years he was editor of the *Canadian Messenger*, a religious monthly, published in Montreal by the Roman Catholic Church. He died at Toronto, on November 5, 1927. Besides a novel, entitled *The training of Silas* (New York, 1906; French translation, Abbeville, 1908), he wrote *Across widest America: Newfoundland to Alaska* (Montreal, 1905), *Fireside messages* (Montreal, 1911), *Historic Caughnawaga* (Montreal, 1922), and *The Jesuit martyrs of Canada* (Montreal, 1923; French translation, Paris, 1925).

[*Can. who was who*, vol. 1; Morgan, *Can. men* (1912); Le Jeune, *Dict. gén.*]

Devlin, Charles Ramsay (1858-1914), politician, was born at Aylmer, Lower Canada, on October 29, 1858, the son of Charles Devlin. He was educated at Montreal College and Laval University (LL.D., 1908). From 1891 to 1896 he sat in the Canadian House of Commons for Ottawa county, and from 1896 to 1897 for Wright. From 1897 to 1903 he was Canadian trade commissioner in Ireland; and from 1903 to 1906 he sat for Galway city in the British House of Commons. In 1907 he became minister of colonization, mines, and fisheries in the Gouin administration in the province of Quebec, being elected to the Quebec Assembly for Nicolet, and this portfolio he held until his death at Aylmer, Quebec, on March 1, 1914. In 1893 he married Blanche, daughter of Testard de Montigny, Ste. Scholastique, Quebec. In 1910 he was made an LL.D. of Ottawa University.

[Morgan, *Can. men* (1912); *Can. parl. comp.*]

Devonshire, Victor Christian William Cavendish, ninth Duke of (1868-1938), governor-general of Canada (1916-21), was born on May 31, 1868, the eldest son of Lord Edward Cavendish, and nephew of the eighth Duke of Devonshire. He was educated at Eton and at Trinity College, Cambridge; and from 1891 to 1908, when he succeeded his uncle as Duke of Devonshire, he sat in the House of Commons for West Derbyshire as a Liberal Unionist. From 1903 to 1905 he was financial secretary to the Treasury; and in 1915-16 he was a civil Lord of the Admiralty. In 1916 he was appointed to succeed H.R.H. the Duke of Connaught (q.v.) as governor-general of Canada; and his term of office lasted until 1921. It was under him as representative of the Crown that the Union government of Sir Robert Borden (q.v.) was formed in 1917. After his return to Great Britain he took little part in public affairs; and he died at Chatsworth House, Devonshire, England, on May 6, 1938. In 1892 he married Lady Evelyn Emily Mary Fitzmaurice, daughter of the fifth Marquis of Lansdowne (q.v.); and by her he had two sons and five daughters. He was created a G.C.V.O. in 1912, a G.C.M.G. in 1916, and a K.G. in 1916.

[*Who was who*, 1929-40; Le Jeune, *Dict. gén.*]

Dewart, Edward Hartley (1828-1903), clergyman and author, was born at Stradone, County Cavan, Ireland, in 1828, the son of James Dewart and Margaret Hartley. He came to Canada with his parents at the age of six years, and settled in the township of Dummer, county of Peterborough, Upper Canada. He was educated at the Normal School, Toronto, and for a time taught school; but in 1851 he became a probationer in the Methodist Church, and in 1855 was ordained a minister. He was stationed at various places in Upper and Lower Canada; but in 1869 he was elected editor of the *Christian Guardian*, and thereafter he lived in Toronto. He published a number of books on religious and theological subjects; and he was the author of a volume of verse, *Songs of life* (Toronto, 1869), and a volume of essays and verse, *Essays for the times* (Toronto, 1898). He is remembered chiefly, however, as the editor of an excellent anthology of Canadian verse, *Selections from the Canadian poets* (Toronto, 1864). He died in Toronto on June 17, 1903. In 1856 he married Dorothy Matilda, daughter of Daniel Hunt, of Hamilton, and by her he had three sons. In 1879 he was made a D.D. of Victoria University.

[Morgan, *Can. men* (1898); Rose, *Cyc. Can. biog.* (1886).]

Dewdney, Edgar (1835-1916), civil engineer and administrator, was born in Devonshire, England, in 1835. He went to British Columbia in 1859, and for several years was engaged in surveying in that province. In 1869 he was elected to the British Columbia legislature; and in 1872, on the inclusion of British Columbia in the Dominion, he was elected to the Canadian House of Commons. He was a supporter of Sir John Macdonald during the period of the "Pacific Scandal" and during the Mackenzie régime. In 1879 he was appointed Indian commissioner, and in 1881 lieutenant-governor of the North West Territories. It was while he occupied these posts that the Riel Rebellion of 1885 took place, and his careful handling of the situation was partly responsible for the pacific behaviour of the Indians. In August, 1888, he became minister of the interior in the Macdonald government, and he continued to hold office until October, 1892. From 1892 to 1897 he was lieutenant-governor of British Columbia. He died at Victoria, British Columbia, on August 8, 1916. He was twice married, first, in 1864, to Jane Shaw, eldest daughter of Stratton Moir, of Colombo, Ceylon, and second, in 1909, to Blanche, youngest daughter of Col. Charles John Kemeys-Tynte, of Halswell, Somersetshire, England.

[Morgan, *Can. men* (1912); Le Jeune, *Dict. gén.*; *Can. parl. comp.*; Sir J. Pope, *Correspondence of Sir John Macdonald* (Toronto, 1921); S. Baptie, *Edgar Dewdney* (Alberta Historical Review, 1968); J. Larmour, *Edgar Dewdney and the aftermath of the rebellion* (Saskatchewan History, 1970).]

De Witt, Norman Wentworth (1876-1958), educationist, was born at Tweedside, Ontario, on September 18, 1876, and died at Lincoln, Illinois, on September 20, 1958. He was educated at the University of Toronto (B.A., 1889) and at the University of Chicago (Ph.D., 1901), and he studied later at Jena University and at the American School of Classical Studies in Rome. After holding brief appointments in

several universities in the United States, he became, in 1908, professor of Latin in Victoria College, in the University of Toronto; and he continued to hold this chair until his retirement in 1945. He was elected a fellow of the Royal Society of Canada in 1925; and he was the author of *Virgil's biographia litteraria* (Toronto, 1923), *Ancient history* (Toronto, 1927), *A brief world history* (Toronto, 1934), *Epicurus and his philosophy* (Minneapolis, 1954), and *St. Paul and Epicurus* (Minneapolis, 1954).

[*Can. who's who*, 1955-57.]

Dexter, Alexander Grant (1896-1961), journalist, was born at St. Andrew's, Manitoba, on February 3, 1896. He was educated at Hamilton Collegiate Institute (Hamilton, Ontario), and Brandon College (Manitoba). He joined the staff of the *Winnipeg Free Press* in 1912, becoming Ottawa correspondent in 1923 and London correspondent from 1936 to 1938. He became associate editor in 1944, executive editor in 1946, and editor from 1948 to 1954. During the First World War he served in France with Lord Strathcona's Horse; he was wounded and invalided out in 1917. He was awarded the Columbia University Cabot medal for journalism in 1946. He died at Winnipeg on December 12, 1961. He wrote, *The roots of the Nazi tree* (Toronto, 1939), *Canada and the building of peace* (C.I.I.A., Toronto, 1946), *The conscription debates of 1917 and 1944* (Winnipeg, 1944), *Family Allowances* (Winnipeg, 1945), *Canada and the building of the post-war world* (Toronto, 1946).

[*Can. who's who*, 1955-57; *Short title catalogue of Canadiana*, vol. 2.]

Dick, David B. (1846-1925), architect, was born in Scotland in 1846. He studied at the Edinburgh School of Design, and came to Canada in 1873. He was the architect of the University of Toronto Library, and other public buildings in Toronto. In 1893 he was elected a member of the Royal Canadian Academy of Arts. He returned to England before 1914; and he died in England in 1925.

[H. G. Jones and E. Dyonnet, *History of the Royal Canadian Academy of Arts* (Montreal, 1934).]

Dickens, Francis Jeffrey (1844-1886), inspector of the North-West Mounted Police, was born at London, England, on January 15, 1844, the third son of Charles Dickens, the novelist. He went first to India and became district superintendent of the Bengal Police; and after his father's death, he came in 1876 to Canada, and became an inspector in the North-West Mounted Police. He played an important part in the troubles connected with the North West Rebellion of 1885; and his diary for part of this year has been published in *Queen's Quarterly*, 1930. He died at Moline, Illinois, on June 11, 1886.

[*Dom. ann. reg.*, 1886.]

Dickey, Arthur Rupert (1854-1900), politician, was born at Amherst, Nova Scotia, on August 18, 1854, the second son of Robert Barry Dickey (q.v.). He was educated at the Collegiate School, Windsor, Nova Scotia, and at the University of Toronto (B.A., 1875), and was called to the bar of Nova Scotia in 1878 (Q.C., 1890). From 1888 to 1896 he was Conservative member for Cumberland in the Canadian House of Commons; and in 1894 he became secretary of state in the administration of Sir Mackenzie Bowell (q.v.). In 1895 he became minister of militia and defence, and in 1896 minister of justice. He was one of the "nest of traitors" in the Bowell cabinet; and he continued as minister of justice in the short-lived Tupper administration of 1896. In the elections of 1896 he was defeated, and he then retired to private life. He was drowned, while bathing, at Amherst, Nova Scotia, on July 4, 1900.

[Morgan, *Can. men* (1898); *Can. parl. comp.*; *Annual register*, 1900.]

Dickey, Robert Barry (1811-1903), one of the Fathers of Confederation, was born at Amherst, Nova Scotia, on November 10, 1811, the son of Robert McGowan Dickey and Eleanor Chapman. He was educated at Truro grammar school and at Windsor Academy, Nova Scotia; and was called to the bar of Nova Scotia in 1834 and of New Brunswick in 1835 (Q.C., 1863). From 1858 to 1867 he sat in the Legislative Council of Nova Scotia; and he was a delegate to the Quebec Conference in 1864. He declined to subscribe to the resolutions of the Quebec Conference; but in 1866 he supported Confederation, and in 1867 he was appointed to the Senate of Canada. In the Senate he gave a general support to the Conservative party, but played a comparatively minor part in politics. He died on July 14, 1903. In 1844 he married Mary Blair, daughter of the Hon. Alexander Stewart, C.B., Halifax; and by her he had three sons and two daughters.

[Morgan, *Can. men* (1912); Rose, *Cyc. Can. biog.* (1886); *Can. parl. comp.*]

Dickson, Robert (1767?-1823), fur-trader, was born in Scotland about 1767, and came to Canada in 1781. In 1786 he embarked in the fur-trade at Michilimackinac, and for many years he was an important trader in the valley of the upper Mississippi. During the War of 1812 he was largely instrumental in ensuring the allegiance to the British flag of the Indians in this region. After the war he was associated with Lord Selkirk (q.v.) in the establishment of his colony on the Red River. He died at Drummond Island, on his way to the Mississippi, on June 20, 1823. He married To-to-win, a Sioux woman; and a number of his descendants are living in South Dakota.

[L. A. Tohill, *Robert Dickson, British fur-trader on the upper Mississippi* (Ann Arbor, Michigan, 1927).]

Dickson, Robert (1796-1846), legislative councillor of Canada, was born at Niagara, Upper Canada, in 1796, the eldest son of the Hon. William Dickson (q.v.). He was appointed a member of the Legislative Council of United Canada in 1842; and he died at Leghorn, Italy, on November 27, 1846.

[J. Young, *Reminiscences of the early history of Galt* (Toronto, 1890).]

Dickson, Walter Hamilton (1806-1885), senator of Canada, was born at Niagara on January 4, 1806, the youngest son of the Hon. William Dickson (q.v.). He was called to the bar of Upper Canada in 1830; and from 1844 to 1851 he represented Niagara in the Legislative Assembly of Canada. In 1855 he was appointed a member of the Legislative Council; and in 1867 he was called by royal proclamation to the Senate of Canada. He died at Niagara on July 30, 1885.

[*Dom. ann. reg.*, 1885; *Can. parl. comp.*]

Dickson, William (1769-1846) legislative councillor of Upper Canada, was born in Dumfries, Scotland, in 1769. He emigrated to Canada in 1792, settled in Newark (Niagara), and began the practice of law. In 1806 he engaged in a duel with an Irish barrister, William Weekes, in which Weekes was killed. He served as an officer in the Canadian militia during the War of 1812, and was taken prisoner by the Americans. In 1815 he was commissioned a member of the Legislative Council of Upper Canada; and in the same year he purchased the township of Dumfries, Upper Canada, and was chiefly instrumental in bringing about its settlement. From 1827 to 1836 he lived in Galt, Upper Canada, supervising the work of settlement. He died at Niagara, to which he had returned in 1836, on February 19, 1846.

[J. Young, *Reminiscences of the early history of Galt* (Toronto, 1890).]

Dièreville, Monsieur de (*fl.* 1699-1711), was a French surgeon who made in 1699-1700 a trading expedition to Acadia. He is thought to have been born at Pont l'Evêque, Calvados, France, but the dates of his birth and death are not known. On his return to France from Acadia, he was appointed surgeon to the Hospice of Pont l'Evêque, and he held this position until 1711, when he disappears from view. He published an account of his visit to Acadia under the title *Relation du voyage du Port Royal de l'Acadie ou de la Nouvelle France* (Rouen, 1708); and this has been reprinted three times, first (in a pirated edition) at Amsterdam in 1710, secondly, at Quebec in 1885, and thirdly, with introduction, notes, and translation by Dr. and Mrs. J. C. Webster, at Toronto, in 1933.

[J. C. Webster (ed.), *Relation of the voyage to Port Royal in Acadia or New France* (Toronto: The Champlain Society, 1933); L. U.

Fontaine, *Voyage du sieur de Dièreville* (Quebec, 1885); Le Jeune, *Dict. gén.*; *Dict. Can. biog.*; vol. 2.]

Dieskau, Jean Armand, Baron (1701-1767), soldier, was born in Saxony in 1701. He entered the French army, became aide-de-camp of Marshal Saxe, and in 1747 became a major-general and military governor of Brest. In 1755 he was sent to Canada as commander-in-chief of the French troops in the colony; and in September, 1755, he was defeated at Lake George, and taken prisoner by the English. He remained a prisoner until 1763, when he was exchanged and returned to France; and he died at Suresnes, near Paris, on September 8, 1767. [*Cyc. Am. biog.*; Le Jeune, *Dict. gén.*; *Dict. Can. biog.*, vol. 3.]

Dilworth, Ira (1894-1962), radio executive, was born at High Bluff, Manitoba, on March 25, 1894. His father became a pioneer cattle-rancher in British Columbia, and Ira was educated in Victoria, British Columbia, at McGill University (B.A., 1915), and at Harvard (M.A., 1920). He began teaching in Victoria High School (1915-26), becoming principal (1926-34). He was a member of the English department at the University of British Columbia (1934-38), becoming manager of radio station CBR Vancouver (1938-47). In 1947 he moved to Montreal with the CBC International Service, and to Toronto as national director of program planning and production in 1950. He was editor and literary executor of the estate of Emily Carr (q.v.) and edited *The heart of a peacock* by Emily Carr (Toronto, 1953); he also wrote *Scenes from Shakespeare* (Toronto, 1930); *Nineteenth-century verse*, an anthology (Oxford, 1945). He died at Vancouver on November 23, 1962. [*Can. who's who*, 1955-57.]

Dionne, Charles Eusèbe (1846-1925), naturalist, was born at St. Denis de la Bouteillerie, Quebec, on July 11, 1846, the son of Eusèbe Dionne and Emélie Lavoie. In 1882 he was appointed director of the zoological museum of Laval University, Quebec; and he died at Quebec on January 25, 1925. He contributed many papers to the *Auk* and to the *Naturaliste canadien*, and he was the author of *Les oiseaux du Canada* (Quebec, 1883), *Catalogue des oiseaux de la province de Québec* (Quebec, 1889), *Les mammifères de la province de Québec* (Quebec, 1902), *Les oiseaux de la province de Québec* (Quebec, 1906), and *Nos araignées* (Quebec, 1910). [Morgan, *Can. men* (1912); *Bull. rech. hist.*, 1930.]

Dionne, Narcisse Eutrope (1848-1917), historian and bibliographer, was born at St. Denis de la Bouteillerie, Lower Canada, on May 18, 1848, the son of Narcisse Dionne and Elizabeth Bouchard. He was educated at Laval University (M.B., 1872; M.D., 1874; Lit.D., 1900), and he practised medicine from 1873 to 1880. In 1880 he became editor of the *Courrier du Canada*, and in 1892 he was appointed librarian of the Quebec Legislative Library. He died at Quebec on March 30, 1917. For thirty-five years he was a voluminous contributor to Canadian historical literature. He published, among other works, *Le tombeau de Champlain* (Quebec, 1880), *Jacques Cartier* (Quebec, 1889), *La Nouvelle France de Cartier à Champlain* (Quebec, 1891), *Samuel Champlain* (2 vols., Quebec, 1891-1906), *Vie de C. F. Painchaud* (Quebec, 1894), *Mgr. de Forbin-Janson* (Quebec, 1895), *Les ecclésiastiques et les royalistes français refugiés au Canada* (Quebec, 1905), *Champlain* (Toronto, 1906), *Le parler populaire des Canadiens-français* (Quebec, 1909), *Pierre Bédard et ses fils* (Quebec, 1909), *Chouart et Radisson* (Quebec, 1910), *Gabriel Richard* (Quebec, 1911), *Une dispute grammaticale en 1842* (Quebec, 1912), *La "Petite Hermine" de Jacques Cartier et diverses monographies historiques* (Quebec, 1913), *Les Canadiens-français: Origine des familles* (Quebec, 1914), and in collaboration with A. G. Doughty, *Quebec under two flags* (Quebec, 1903). But his most important work was his *Inventaire chronologique* (4 vols., Quebec, 1905-09) of books, pamphlets, maps, and periodicals published in and about the province of Quebec, a bibliography such as no other province in Canada possesses.

[N. E. Dionne, *Travaux historiques publiés depuis trente ans* (Quebec, 1909); *Bull. rech. hist.*, 1917; Morgan, *Can. men* (1912); *Can. who's who* (1910); Le Jeune, *Dict. gén.*]

Dixon, Frederick Augustus (1843-1919), playwright, was born in England on May 7, 1843. He came to Canada shortly after 1870, and was first a journalist on the staff of the Toronto *Mail*. He entered the civil service of Canada in 1878, and was employed in the department of railways and canals. He died at Ottawa in 1919. He was the author of several plays, which were presented at Rideau Hall, Ottawa: *The maire of St. Brieux* (Ottawa, 1875), *Little nobody* (Ottawa, 1875), *Fifine, the fisher maid* (Ottawa, 1877), and *A masque entitled "Canada's welcome"* (Ottawa, 1879). [Morgan, *Can. men* (1912).]

Dixon, George (d. 1800?), mariner, was captain of the *Queen Charlotte*, one of the two vessels under Capt. Nathaniel Portlock, which explored the coast of British Columbia in 1787. He died about 1800; and he was the author of *A voyage round the world* (London, 1789). [F. W. Howay (ed.), *The Dixon-Meares controversy* (Toronto, 1929).]

Dobell, Richard Reid (1837-1902), merchant and politician, was born in Liverpool, England, in 1837, the son of George Dobell, a merchant of Liverpool. He came to Canada in

1857, and built up in Quebec a very prosperous lumber business. His political leanings were at first Conservative, but in 1896 he stood as the Liberal candidate for Quebec West in the House of Commons. On his election he was included in the Laurier government as a minister without portfolio, and he continued to be a member of the administration until his death on January 11, 1902. He married Elizabeth Francis, eldest daughter of Sir D. L. Macpherson (q.v.), of Toronto, and by her had three sons and two daughters.

[Morgan, *Can. men* (1898); Rose, *Cyc. Can. biog.* (1888).]

Doherty, Charles Joseph (1855-1931), minister of justice for Canada (1911-21), was born at Montreal, Quebec, on May 11, 1855, the son of the Hon. Marcus Doherty and Elizabeth O'Halloran. He was educated at St. Mary's Jesuit College and at McGill University (B.C.L., 1876; D.C.L., 1893), and was called to the Quebec bar in 1877 (Q.C., 1887). He practised law in Montreal, and in 1891 he was appointed a puisne judge of the Superior Court of the province of Quebec. He retired from the bench with a pension, in 1906, and entered political life. From 1908 to 1921 he represented the St. Anne's division of Montreal in the Canadian House of Commons; and from 1911 to 1921 he was minister of justice in the Borden and Meighen administrations. In 1918 he was one of the Canadian representatives at the Peace Conference at Paris, and he signed the Treaty of Versailles on behalf of Canada. He also represented Canada at the Assembly of the League of Nations in Geneva in 1920-21. On his defeat in the general elections of 1921 he retired to private life, and he died at Montreal on July 28, 1931. He was an LL.D. of Ottawa University (1895) and of McGill University (1913); and in 1920 he was made an imperial privy councillor. In 1888 he married Catherine Lacy, daughter of Edmund Barnard, K.C., Montreal, and by her he had one son and four daughters.

[*Can. who was who*, vol. 1; *Can. parl. comp.*; Morgan, *Can. men* (1912).]

Doherty, Patrick (1838-1872), priest, was born at Quebec, Lower Canada, on June 2, 1838; was ordained a priest of the Roman Catholic Church in 1865; and died at Quebec, Que., May 21, 1872. After his death, a volume entitled *Ses principaux écrits en français* (Quebec, 1872) was published by an anonymous friend.

[*Cyc. Am. biog.*; Allaire, *Dict. biog.*; *Dict. Can. biog.*, vol. 10.]

Dollar, A. Melville (d. 1932), business man, was the son of Captain Robert Dollar (q.v.). He was a prominent business man of Vancouver, British Columbia, and a past-president of the Canadian Chamber of Commerce. He died suddenly at Vancouver, British Columbia, on March 31, 1932, in his 53rd year.

[*Americana annual*, 1933.]

Dollar, Robert (1844-1932), ship-owner, was born in Falkirk, Scotland, on March 20, 1844. While a boy of thirteen, he found his way to Canada, and engaged in Muskoka in the lumber business; later he went to California with the same business in view. This led him to shipping in a small way; in course of time he entered overseas trade, and finally organized the great "Dollar Steamship Line", whose policies he is said to have dictated to the very end. He died at San Rafael, California, on May 16, 1932. He was the author of *Memories of Robert Dollar* (San Francisco, 1917; 3rd ed., 1925), and *One hundred and thirty years of steam navigation* (San Francisco, 1931). Throughout most of his life he carried with him the courtesy title of "Captain".

[*Who was who in America*.]

Dollard, James Barnard (1872-1946), priest and poet, was born at Mooncoin, Kilkenny, Ireland, in 1872, and died at Toronto, Ontario, on April 28, 1946. He came to Canada in 1890, was educated at Laval University, Montreal, and was ordained a priest of the Roman Catholic Church. He was the pastor of several churches in Ontario, and during the last twenty-five years of his life he was the pastor of Our Lady of Lourdes at Toronto. He was the author of three volumes of poetry: *Irish mist and sunshine* (Boston, 1901), *Poems* (Toronto, 1910), and *Irish lyrics and ballads* (Toronto, 1917), as well as a volume of short stories entitled *The Gaels of Moondharig* (Dublin, 1907).

[Toronto *Globe and Mail*, April 29, 1946; *Can. who's who*, 1938-39.]

Dollard des Ormeaux, Adam (1635-1660), soldier, was a native of France. He came to Canada in 1657, and was appointed commandant of the garrison at Ville-Marie (Montreal). In the spring of 1660 he led a party of sixteen Frenchmen up the Ottawa River to wage war on the Iroquois; and at the Long Sault he and his companions died, May, 1660, after defending for a week an improvised fort against many times their number of Iroquois.

[E. Z. Massicotte, *Dollard des Ormeaux et ses compagnons* (Montreal, 1920); E. R. Adair, *Dollard des Ormeaux and the fight at the Long Sault* (Can. hist. rev., 1932); L. Groulx, *Dollard: Est-il un mythe?* (Montreal, 1960); *Dict. Can. biog.*, vol. 1.]

Dollier de Casson, François (1636-1701), priest and explorer, was born in the Château de Casson, near Nantes, in 1636. He became a soldier, and before the age of twenty was a cavalry captain under Turenne. In 1657 he entered the seminary of Saint-Sulpice at Paris; and he came to Canada to engage in missionary work in 1666. In 1669 he was sent with Galinée (q.v.) to try to reach the Mississippi, in order to pave the way for Sulpician missions among the western tribes. The two priests spent the winter of 1669-70 on the northern shore of Lake Erie, where they took possession of the country in the name of Louis XIV. In the spring of 1670 they proceeded to Sault Ste. Marie, and thence they returned to the St. Lawrence. In the autumn of 1670, Dollier de Casson became superior of the seminary of Montreal, and later he was vicar-general of the diocese of Quebec. He died on September 25, 1701, leaving an *Histoire du Montréal* covering the years 1640-72, and this was published by the Société Historique de Montreal in 1868, and also by the Literary and Historical Society of Quebec in its third series of *Historical Documents* (Quebec, 1871), and has been translated and annotated by R. Flenley (Toronto, 1928).

[O. Maurault, *Dollier de Casson* (Revue trimestrielle canadienne, 1919); R. G. Thwaites (ed.), *The Jesuit relations*, vol. 50 (Cleveland, 1899); J. H. Coyne, *Exploration of the great lakes* (Ont. Hist. Soc., papers and records, 1903); Le Jeune, *Dict. gén.*; *Dict. Can. biog.*, vol. 2.]

Domville, James (1842-1921), senator of Canada, was born at Belize, British Honduras, on November 29, 1842, the son of Lieut.-Gen. D. Domville, R.A., and Frances, daughter of the Hon. William Usher. He was educated at Woolwich, England, and came to Canada in 1866. He settled in New Brunswick, and was the father of many railway and mercantile enterprises. In 1897 he built and navigated the first British vessel that established contact with the Yukon. From 1872 to 1882 he represented Kings county, as a Conservative, in the Canadian House of Commons; and from 1896 to 1900, as a Liberal. In 1903 he was called to the Senate of Canada, and he retained his seat until his death at Rothesay, New Brunswick, on July 30, 1921. In 1867 he married Isabella, daughter of W. H. Scovill, of Saint John, New Brunswick. He organized the 8th Princess Louise Hussars of New Brunswick, commanded this regiment for twenty years, and in 1904 was appointed its honorary lieutenant-colonel.

[*Can. who was who*, vol. 1; *Can. parl. comp.*; Morgan, *Can. men* (1912).]

Donlevy, Charles (1813-1858), journalist, was born in county Sligo, Ireland, in 1813, and came to Canada in 1831. In 1837 he founded the Toronto *Mirror* as a Roman Catholic newspaper; and he edited this paper until his death at Toronto, Canada West, on July 22, 1858.

[J. E. Middleton, *The municipality of Toronto* (3 vols., Toronto, 1923).]

Doolittle, Perry E. (1861-1933), physician and automobilist, was born in 1861, and was educated at Trinity University, Toronto, in medicine (M.D., C.M., 1885). In 1884 he was one of the promoters of the Wheelmen's Association; and when the motor-car was introduced, he became one of its most enthusiastic devotees. From 1920 to his death, at Toronto, on December 31, 1933, he was president of the Canadian Automobile Association.

[*Who's who in Canada*, 1933.]

Dooner, Alfred James (1875-1949), historian, was born at Osceola, Ontario, on July 24, 1875, and died at Toronto, Ontario, on April 20, 1949. He was educated at St. Joseph's College, New York, at De La Salle College, Toronto, and at Mount St. Louis College, Montreal; and in 1891 he joined the Christian Brothers. He was instrumental in establishing Roman Catholic schools for boys in several centres, and for ten years he conducted a summer camp for boys. He became an authority on some phases of Canadian history; he was partly responsible for organizing the Canadian Catholic Historical Association in 1933; and under his religious name, Brother Alfred, he was the author of *Catholic pioneers in Upper Canada* (Toronto, 1947).

[*Can. who's who*, 1948.]

Dorchester, Sir Guy Carleton, first Baron. See **Carleton, Sir Guy.**

Dorey, George (1884-1963), churchman, was born in Jersey, in the Channel Islands, in 1884 and came to Canada in 1905. He graduated from Wesley College, Winnipeg, and was ordained in 1914 in the Methodist Church. He served in Saskatchewan both before and after ordination and during the 1930s was superintendent of missions for Southern Saskatchewan and organized relief work in the province. He became secretary of the Board of Home Missions in 1945 and moderator of the United Church in 1954. He was president of the Canadian Council of Churches in 1958 and at his death, May 12, 1963, was a member of the Department of Pensions. Dr. Dorey was the first bilingual moderator of the United Church and a strong advocate of union with the Anglican Church and of the ecumenical mission of the church. He died at Toronto, Ontario, October 4, 1963.

[Metropolitan Toronto Library Board, *Biographical scrapbooks*, vol. 21.]

Dorion, Sir Antoine Aimé (1818-1891), politician and jurist, was born in the parish of Ste. Anne de la Pérade, Champlain county, Lower Canada, on January 17, 1818, the son of Pierre Antoine Dorion and Geneviève Bureau. He was educated at Nicolet College, was called to the bar of Lower Canada in 1842 (Q.C., 1863), and entered on the practice of law in Montreal. He became a member of the Institut Canadien and of the *parti rouge*, and in 1854 was elected to represent Montreal in the

Legislative Assembly of Canada. He sat for this constituency until 1861, when he was defeated by George Etienne Cartier (q.v.); in 1862 he was elected for Hochelaga, and he held this seat, first in the Assembly, and then in the Canadian House of Commons, until 1872; finally, he represented Napierville in the House of Commons from 1872 to 1874. In 1858 he joined with George Brown (q.v.) in forming the short-lived Brown-Dorion administration, in which he held the portfolio of Crown lands; in 1862 he became provincial secretary in the S. Macdonald-Sicotte government; and in 1863 he became Lower Canadian leader in the reorganized S. Macdonald-Dorion government, with the office of attorney-general. He opposed Confederation, but accepted it when completed; and in 1873 he became minister of justice in the Mackenzie administration. This portfolio, however, he held for only a few months. In 1874 he was appointed chief justice of the Court of Queen's Bench, Quebec, and he presided over this court until his death at Montreal on May 31, 1891. In 1848 he married a daughter of Dr. Trestler, of Montreal. He was created a knight bachelor in 1877.

[*Dict. nat. biog.*, Supp. I; Rose, *Cyc. Can. biog.* (1888); *Cyc. Am. biog.*; Dent, *Can. port.*, vol. 4; Taylor, *Brit. Am.*, vol. 1; Bibaud, *Panth. can.*; Le Jeune, *Dict. gén.*; J. C. Dent, *The last forty years* (2 vols., Toronto, 1881); F. J. Audet, *Les juges en chef de la province de Québec* (Quebec, 1927).]

Dorion, Jean Baptiste Eric (1826-1866), journalist and politician, was born at Ste. Anne de la Pérade, Champlain county, Lower Canada, on September 16, 1826, the son of Pierre Antoine Dorion and Geneviève Bureau. He was educated at his birthplace, and became a journalist. In 1848 he was one of the founders of *L'Avenir* (1848-52), the mouthpiece of the *parti rouge*; and later he founded at L'Avenir, Lower Canada, *Le Défricheur*, a local newspaper to which Wilfrid Laurier (q.v.) succeeded as editor. He sat in the Legislative Assembly of Canada for Drummond and Arthabaska from 1854 to 1857 and from 1861 to his death on November 1, 1866. An advanced radical, he was known to his contemporaries by the nickname of "l'enfant terrible". For several years he was president of the Institut Canadien in Montreal.

[Morgan, *Bib. can.*; J. C. St. Amant, "*L'enfant terrible*" (Bull. rech. hist., 1898); J. C. Dent, *The last forty years* (2 vols., Toronto, 1881).]

Doty, John (d. 1842), clergyman, was born in England, and was one of the first Anglican clergymen sent out to Canada. He reached Canada in 1784; and from 1784 to 1803 he was Anglican rector at Sorel. He then moved to Three Rivers, and devoted himself to teaching. He died in 1842.

[*Bull. rech. hist.*, 1932.]

Dougall, John (1808-1886), journalist, was born at Paisley, Scotland, on July 8, 1808, the eldest son of John Dougall, manufacturer. He came to Canada at the age of eighteen, as a commercial traveller. In 1835 his interest in temperance reform led him to accept the editorship of the *Canada Temperance Advocate*; and in 1846 he founded the *Montreal Witness*, first as a weekly, then in 1860 as a daily newspaper. The success of this paper, which appealed to strict religious and temperance sentiment, was unprecedented. In 1871 Dougall founded a similar paper in New York, the *Daily Witness*, but this disappeared in 1878, leaving behind it, however, the *Weekly Witness*, which long enjoyed a large circulation. On August 19, 1886, he died suddenly at Flushing, Long Island, New York. He married Elizabeth, eldest daughter of John Redpath, Montreal.

[*Dom. ann. reg.*, 1886.]

Dougall, Lily (1858-1923), novelist, was born in Montreal on April 16, 1858, the daughter of John Dougall (q.v.). She was educated in Brooklyn, New York, and at Edinburgh and St. Andrew's universities, Scotland. From 1891 to her death she lived in England, with the exception of the years 1897-1903, which were spent in Montreal. She wrote *Beggars all* (London, 1891), *What necessity knows* (London, 1893), *The mermaid* (London, 1895), *Zeitgeist* (London, 1895), *A question of faith* (London, 1895), *The madonna of a day* (London, 1896), *A dozen ways of love* (London, 1897), *The Mormon prophet* (Toronto, 1899), *The earthly purgatory* (London, 1904), *The Spanish dowry* (London, 1906), and *Paths of the righteous* (London, 1908). She died in October, 1923.

[Morgan, *Can. men and women* (1912); *Can. who was who*, vol. 1; L. E. Horning and L. J. Burpee, *A bibliography of Canadian fiction* (Toronto, 1904).]

Doughty, Sir Arthur George (1860-1936), archivist and historian, was born at Maidenhead, England, on March 22, 1860; and came to Canada in 1886. He was for several years a clerk in a mercantile firm in Montreal; but he devoted his leisure to musical, dramatic, and literary criticism, and became a figure in literary and artistic circles in Montreal. In 1897 he entered the civil service of the province of Quebec, and in 1901 he was appointed joint librarian of the Legislative Library at Quebec. In 1904 he succeeded Douglas Brymner (q.v.) as Dominion archivist; and he discharged the duties of this office with great distinction until his retirement in 1935. As a collector and a showman, he revealed a touch of genius; and the Public Archives of Canada are today very largely his creation. A mere administrator could hardly have obtained the results he achieved. He was honoured with the degrees of D. ès L. from

Laval University (1901) and LL.D. from Queen's University (1912); he was created a C.M.G. in 1905, and a K.C.M.G. in 1935. He died at Ottawa, Ontario, on December 1, 1936. Though twice married, he had no children. His publications were numerous. He was the author of two volumes of verse, *Rose leaves* (London, 1894) and *Nugae canorae* (Portland, Me., 1897), and of several historical works, *The fortress of Quebec* (Quebec, 1904), *The cradle of New France* (Montreal, 1908), *The Acadian exiles* (Toronto, 1915), *A daughter of New France* (Edinburgh, 1915), *Under the lily and the rose* (2 vols., Ottawa, 1929), and *The wee story of Canada* Ottawa, 1930). He was joint author, with G. W. Parmalee, of *The siege of Quebec and the battle of the Plains* (6 vols., Quebec, 1901-02), with N. E. Dionne, of *Quebec under two flags* (Quebec, 1903), with L. J. Burpee, of *The index and dictionary of Canadian history* (Toronto, 1911), and with William Wood, of *The King's book of Quebec* (Quebec, 1911); he was the editor of Knox *An historical journal of the campaigns in North America* (3 vols., Toronto, 1914-16); and he was joint editor, with Adam Shortt, of *Documents relating to the constitutional history of Canada, 1759-1791* (Ottawa, 1907) and *Canada and its provinces* (22 vols., Toronto, 1914), with D. A. McArthur, of *Documents relating to the constitutional history of Canada, 1791-1818* (Ottawa, 1914), and with Chester Martin, of *The Kelsey papers* (Ottawa, 1929).

[*Can. who's who*, 1936-37; *Trans. Roy. Soc. Can.*, 1937.]

Douglas, David (1798-1834), botanist, was born at Scone, Perthshire, Scotland, in 1798. He obtained employment in the botanic garden of the University of Glasgow, and was appointed botanical collector in the United States for the Horticultural Society of London. In 1824 he visited Oregon and California; and in 1827 he made an expedition from Fort Vancouver to Hudson Bay. Here he met Sir John Franklin, and with him he returned to England, having acquired many valuable botanic specimens. He visited the Oregon country for a second time in 1829; and thence he went to the Hawaiian Islands. There he was gored to death by an enraged bull on July 12, 1834. A species of pine which he discovered on the Pacific slope of North America has been named after him *Pinus Douglassii*. The *Journal* of his travels in North America, 1823-27, has been published posthumously (London, 1914).

[G. Barnston, *Abridged sketch of the life of Mr. David Douglas* (Canadian naturalist, 1859); A. G. Harvey, *David Douglas in British Columbia* (British Columbia historical quarterly, 1940); A. G. Harvey, *Douglas of the fir; A biography of David Douglas, botanist* (Cambridge, Mass., 1947); W. Morwood, *Traveller in a vanished landscape*

(London, 1973); *Dict. nat. biog.*; *Cyc. Am. biog.*]

Douglas, George (1825-1894), clergyman, was born in Ashkirk, Roxburghshire, Scotland, in October, 1825. He was brought to Canada by his parents in 1832, and lived in Montreal. In 1849 he went to England to study for the Methodist ministry; and in 1850 he was ordained. From 1850 to 1852 he served in the Bermudas; but in 1853 he returned to Canada. He occupied charges successively at Montreal, Kingston, Toronto, and Hamilton; and in 1864 he was appointed principal of the Wesleyan Theological College, Montreal. He died at Montreal on February 11, 1894. In 1869 he was made an LL.D. of McGill University.

[*Cyc. Am. biog.*; Dent, *Can. port.*, vol. 2.]

Douglas, Sir Howard, Bart. (1776-1861), soldier, author, and lieutenant-governor of New Brunswick (1823-31), was born at Gosport, England, in 1776, the son of Vice-Admiral Sir Charles Douglas, by his second wife, Sarah, daughter of James Wood. He was educated at the grammar school of Musselburgh and at the Royal Military Academy, Woolwich. In 1795 he was sent on an expedition to Quebec, but the transport was wrecked and the castaways were carried by a trader to Labrador, where they passed the winter. Douglas spent some time at Halifax, at Quebec, and at Kingston, and returned to England in 1799. After a period of active service in Spain, and as commandant of the Royal Military Academy (1804-08 and 1812-22), he was appointed lieutenant-governor of New Brunswick in 1823. He was a popular and successful governor; and it was during his term of office that savings banks were established, and a charter was granted to the University of Fredericton. It was due also to his firmness and tact that the attempted American invasion of the frontier of Maine was checked in 1828; and when the question of the boundary was referred to the King of the Netherlands, Douglas was recalled to England to assist in preparing the British case. He was later for a time lord high commissioner of the Ionian Islands. But he spent most of the rest of his life in politics in England, where he died at Tunbridge Wells, on November 9, 1861. In July, 1799, he married Anne (d. 1854), daughter of James Dundas of Edinburgh, and by her he had three daughters and six sons. He was a fellow of the Royal Society, and of the Royal Geographical Society; an associate of the Institute of Naval Architects; a D.C.L. of Oxford, and first chancellor of the University of New Brunswick. He was made C.B. in 1814, K.C.B. in 1821, G.C.M.G. in 1835, and G.C.B. in 1841. He published a large number of essays on military and political subjects, and amongst these *Considerations on the value and importance of the British North American* *provinces, and the circumstances on which depend their prosperity and connection with Great Britain* (London, 1831).

[S. W. Fullom, *Life of Sir Howard Douglas* (London, 1863); *Dict. nat. biog.*; W. G. MacFarlane, *New Brunswick bibliography* (Saint John, N.B., 1895).]

Douglas, James (1800-1886), physician, was born in Brechin, Scotland, on May 20, 1800. He studied medicine in Edinburgh, and in 1821 was admitted a member of the Royal College of Surgeons. After serving as a medical officer in India and on the Mosquito coast, he migrated to North America, and in 1826 he settled in Quebec, Lower Canada. He was one of the founders of the Beauport Lunatic Asylum, near Quebec, and became in 1846 its first superintendent. He died in New York, on April 14, 1886.

[J. Douglas (ed.), *Journals and reminiscences of James Douglas, M.D.* (privately printed, New York, 1910); *Cyc. Am. biog.*]

Douglas, Sir James (1803-1877), governor of Vancouver Island (1851-63) and of British Columbia (1858-64), was born at Demerara, British Guiana, on August 15, 1803. He was educated at Lanark, Scotland, and in 1819 came to Canada to take service with the North West Company. In 1821 he entered the employ of the Hudson's Bay Company, when the North West Company was amalgamated with it; and he remained with it until his retirement as chief factor in 1858. In 1843 he founded, on the site of the present Victoria, the first Hudson's Bay Company post in Vancouver Island. In 1851 he was appointed governor of Vancouver Island; and in 1858 there were added to his duties those of governor of the new colony of British Columbia. His administration of the mainland colony during and after the "gold rush" of 1858 was remarkable for its firmness and vigour; he enjoyed almost despotic power, but seldom has despotic power been more wisely and conscientiously used. In 1863 his commission as governor of Vancouver Island expired; and the following year he retired from the government of British Columbia. He then withdrew to private life; and he died at Victoria, the city which he had founded, on August 2, 1877. In 1829 he married Amelia, daughter of William Conolly (q.v.), chief factor of New Caledonia; and by her he had several children. In 1863 he was created, for his services, a K.C.B.

[Walter N. Sage, *Sir James Douglas and British Columbia* (Toronto, 1930); R. H. Coats and R. E. Gosnell, *Sir James Douglas* (Toronto, 1908); B. A. McKelvie, *Sir James Douglas: A new portrait* (British Columbia historical quarterly, 1943); D. B. Smith, *James Douglas: Father of British Columbia* (Toronto, 1971); *Can. who was who*, vol. 2; *Cyc. Am. biog.*; *Dict. Can. biog.*, vol. 10.]

Douglas, James (1837-1918), chancellor of Queen's University, Kingston (1915-18), was born at Quebec, Lower Canada, in 1837, the son of James Douglas, M.D. (q.v.). He was educated at Edinburgh University and at Queen's University, Kingston, Canada (B.A., 1858), and was ordained a minister of the Presbyterian Church. He retired from the ministry, after a brief experience, and became professor of chemistry in Morrin College, Quebec; and in 1869 he was elected president of the Quebec Literary and Historical Society. In 1875 he went to the United States as manager of a copper works at Phoenixville, Pennsylvania; and he became an outstanding authority in mining and metallurgy. He was twice president of the Institute of Mining Engineers, and in 1900 he represented the United States at the Mining Congress in Paris, France. He was a benefactor of Queen's University, Kingston; and in 1915 he was elected its chancellor. He died at New York on June 25, 1918. In 1860 he married Naomi, third daughter of Walter Douglas, of Glasgow, Scotland. He was the author of a number of papers contributed, before 1875, to the *Canadian Monthly*, and, among other works, of a *Memoir of T. Sterry Hunt* (Philadelphia, 1898), *Untechnical addresses on technical subjects* (New York, 1905), *Old France in the New World* (Cleveland, 1905), and *New England and New France* (New York, 1913). He also edited his father's *Journals and reminiscences* (New York, 1910).

[H. H. Langton, *James Douglas, a memoir* (Toronto, 1940); Morgan, *Can. men* (1912); *Queen's quarterly*, 1918; *Can. who was who*, vol. 1.]

Douglas, James Robson (1876-1934), lieutenant-governor of Nova Scotia (1925), was born at Amherst, Nova Scotia, on March 27, 1876. He became a successful broker, and on January 23, 1925, was appointed lieutenant-governor of Nova Scotia. He resigned office eight months later; and he died at Montreal on December 17, 1934.

[*Can. parl. comp.*]

Douglas, Thomas, fifth Earl of Selkirk. See **Selkirk, Thomas Douglas, fifth Earl of.**

Doutre, Gonzalve (1842-1880), law reformer and author, was born at Montreal, Lower Canada, on July 12, 1842. He was educated at McGill University (B.C.L., 1861; D.C.L., 1873), and was called to the bar of Lower Canada in 1863 (Q.C., 1879). He devoted himself to the reform of law in Lower Canada, and drafted the Act of 1866 which raised the standards of admission to the bar in that part of the province. He was professor of civil procedure at McGill University; and he published *Lois de la procédure civile* (2 vols., Montreal, 1867-69). With Edmund Lareau, he was joint author of *Le droit civil canadien*, vol. i (Montreal, 1872). He was also president of the

Institut Canadien of Montreal. He died at Montreal on February 28, 1880.

[*Dom. ann. reg.*, 1880-81; Morgan, *Bib. can.*; *Revue canadienne*, 1869; E. Lareau, *Histoire de la littérature canadienne* (Montreal, 1874); *Dict. Can. biog.*, vol. 10.]

Doutre, Joseph (1825-1886), lawyer and author, was born at Beauharnois, Lower Canada, on March 11, 1825. He was educated at Montreal College, and was called to the bar of Lower Canada in 1847 (Q.C., 1863). Though he never sat in parliament, he was one of the leading members of the *parti rouge*; and it was under his presidency that the Institut Canadien was incorporated in 1852. He was an advocate of the abolition of seigniorial tenure in Lower Canada; he fought a duel with George Etienne Cartier (q.v.); and he opposed, vehemently and successfully, the attempt of Bishop Bourget (q.v.) and other ecclesiastics to crush Liberalism in the province of Quebec. Especially noteworthy was his battle with Bishop Bourget (q.v.) over the Guibord case in 1869. In his earlier years he was a constant contributor to such journals as *Les Mélanges Religieux*, *L'Aurore des Canadas*, *Le Courrier des Etats-Unis* (New York), and the *Lower Canada Jurist*. He was one of the founders of *Le Pays*, and he contributed a series of contemporary biographies to Papineau's *L'Avenir*. He published also, in his earlier years, two novels, *Les fiancés de 1812* (Montreal, 1844) and *Le frère et la soeur*, in J. Huston (ed.), *Le répertoire national* (4 vols., Montreal, 1848-50). He died at Montreal on February 3, 1886.

[*Dom. ann. reg.*, 1866; Bibaud, *Panth. can.*; Le Jeune, *Dict. gén.*; Morgan, *Bib. can.*; J. D. Borthwick, *Montreal, its history* (Montreal, 1875); E. Lareau, *Histoire de la littérature canadienne* (Montreal, 1874); J. S. Willison, *Sir Wilfrid Laurier and the Liberal party* (2 vols. Toronto, 1903).]

Dowling, Donaldson Bogart (1858-1925), geologist, was born in Camden township, Addington county, Ontario, on November 5, 1858. He was educated at McGill University (B.A.Sc., 1883; D.Sc., 1921), and entered in 1884 the service of the Geological Survey of Canada. He spent his life on the staff of the Geological Survey; and he had charge of a number of important explorations in the Canadian West. He died at Ottawa on May 26, 1925.

[Morgan, *Can. men* (1912); *Proc. Roy. Soc. Can.*, 1926.]

Doyle, Sir Charles Hastings (1804-1883), lieutenant-governor of Nova Scotia (1867-73), was born on April 10, 1804, the son of Sir Charles William Doyle, and Sophia, daughter of Sir John Coghill. He was educated at Sandhurst; saw active service in the East and West Indies; and was inspector-general of militia in Ireland. In 1861 he was appointed to command

the troops in Nova Scotia, where he showed great skill in dealing with the questions which arose in connection with the civil war in the United States. In 1867 he was appointed lieutenant-governor of Nova Scotia, and he resigned from this post in May, 1873. He died in London, England, on March 19, 1883. He was created a K.C.M.G. in 1869.

[*Dict. nat. biog.*; *Dom. ann. reg.*, 1883.]

Doyle, Lawrence O'Connor (*fl.* 1804-1855), politician, was born in Halifax on February 27, 1804, the son of Lawrence Doyle, a native of Ireland, and his wife Bridget O'Connor. He was educated abroad, probably at Stoneyhurst College, since being a Roman Catholic he could not obtain admittance into any of the schools of Nova Scotia. He studied law, and was admitted to the bar in 1829. He was elected to represent the Isle Madame in the House of Assembly in the early thirties; and he was one of the most energetic of the younger reformers, famous for his wit. In 1849 he represented Halifax in the House of Assembly; he retired from public life in 1855, and died in New York. He married Sarah, daughter of Lieutenant Driscoll, and she died in 1842.

[G. Mullane, *A sketch of Lawrence O'Connor Doyle* (Coll. Nova Scotia Hist. Soc., 1913); Sir J. G. Bourinot, *Builders of Nova Scotia* (Trans. Roy. Soc. Can., 1899).]

Drapeau, Stanislaus (1821-1893), journalist and author, was born at St. Roch, near Quebec, Lower Canada, on July 28, 1821. He was educated at the Quebec Seminary, and in 1837 was apprenticed to a printer. From printing he graduated into journalism, and in 1859 he entered the civil service of Canada. He died at Point Gatineau, on the Ottawa River, on February 21, 1893. He was the author of *Etudes sur les développements de la colonisation du Bas-Canada depuis dix ans* (Quebec, 1863), *Histoire des institutions de charité, de bienfaisance, et d'éducation du Canada* (Ottawa, 1878), *Biographie de Sir N. F. Belleau* (Quebec, 1883), *Canada: Le guide de colon* (Ottawa, 1888), and a number of pamphlets. Three of these dealt with the question of the burial place of Champlain (q.v.): *Observations sur la brochure de MM. les abbés Laverdière et Casgrain, relativement à la découverte du tombeau de Champlain* (Quebec, 1866), *Le Journal de Québec et le tombeau de Champlain* (Quebec, 1867), and *Notes et éclaircissements: La question du tombeau de Champlain* (Ottawa, 1880).

[C. Thibault, *Biographie de Stanislaus Drapeau* (Ottawa, 1891); P. G. Roy, *Fils de Québec*, vol. 4 (Lévis, Que., 1933); Morgan, *Bib. can.*; Le Jeune, *Dict. gén.*]

Draper, William George (d. 1868), lawyer and author, was the eldest son of the Hon. William Henry Draper (q.v.). He was educated at

King's College, Toronto (M.A., 1850), and was called to the bar of Upper Canada. In 1864 he was appointed county judge of Frontenac; and he died at Kingston on December 17, 1868. Besides some law books he published a *Short sketch of the history of Kingston* (Kingston, 1862).

[Morgan, *Bib. can.*]

Draper, William Henry (1801-1877), politician and jurist, was born near London, England, on March 11, 1801, the son of the Rev. Henry Draper, a clergyman of the Church of England. He came to Canada in 1820, and studied law at Port Hope and Cobourg, Upper Canada. He was called to the bar in 1828 (Q.C., 1842), and in 1829 he entered the law office of John Beverley Robinson (q.v.) in York (Toronto). From 1836 to 1840 he represented Toronto in the Legislative Assembly of Upper Canada; and in 1836 he was appointed a member of the Executive Council of the province. During the rebellion of 1837 he served as aide-de-camp to Sir Francis Bond Head (q.v.). In 1837 he was appointed solicitor-general for the province, and in 1840 attorney-general. On the completion of the Union of 1841 he became attorney-general for Upper Canada in the administration formed by Lord Sydenham (q.v.), and he retained this office until the defeat of the government and the formation of the Baldwin-Lafontaine administration in 1842. In 1843 he was appointed a member of the Legislative Council; and on the resignation of Baldwin and Lafontaine later in the year, he was again sworn of the Executive Council, and became the chief adviser of Sir Charles Metcalfe (q.v.). With Dominick Daly (q.v.) and Denis Benjamin Viger (q.v.), he carried on the government for several months; and then he formed an administration, in which he took again the portfolio of attorney-general for Upper Canada. He resigned from the Legislative Council, and was in 1845 returned for London in the Legislative Assembly. His government having been sustained in the general elections of 1844, he was for three years the virtual head of the government, though without the recognized title of prime minister; but the difficulty of carrying on the administration with the small majority at his disposal was too much for him, and in 1847 he resigned office. A few weeks later he was appointed to the bench, and as a judge he spent the rest of his life. He was successively a puisne judge of the Court of Queen's Bench in Upper Canada (1847-56), chief justice of the Common Pleas (1856-63), chief justice of Upper Canada (1863-69), and president of the Court of Error and Appeal (1869-77). He died at Yorkville, near Toronto, on November 3, 1877.

In 1827 he married the daughter of Captain George White, R.N., and by her he had several children. In 1854 he was made a C.B. Though not commonly regarded as a member of the

"Family Compact", and though theoretically in favour of responsible government, he was an old-fashioned Conservative. He was a speaker of very persuasive powers; and hence came his parliamentary sobriquet of "Sweet William".

[Rose, *Cyc. Can. biog.* (1886); J. C. Dent, *Can. port.*, vol. 2, and *The last forty years* (Toronto, 1881); D. B. Read, *Lives of the judges* (Toronto, 1888); J. Pope, *Memoirs of the Right Hon. Sir John A. Macdonald* (2 vols., Ottawa, 1894); J. L. Morison, *British supremacy and Canadian self-government* (Edinburgh, 1919); *Cyc. Am. biog.*; *Dict. Can. biog.*, vol. 10.]

Drayton, Sir Henry Lumley (1869-1950), minister of finance for Canada (1919-1921), was born at Kingston, Ontario, on April 27, 1869, and died at Muskoka, Ontario, on August 29, 1950. He was called to the Ontario bar in 1891 (K.C., 1908); and he held successive legal appointments in Toronto and its vicinity. From 1912 to 1919 he was chairman of the Canadian Board of Railway Commissioners; and for his services in this capacity during the First World War, he was created a knight bachelor in 1915. From 1919 to 1928 he represented first Kingston, and then West York, in the Canadian House of Commons as a Conservative; and from 1919 to 1921 he was minister of finance in the Borden and Meighen administrations. He was also minister of immigration and colonization in the short-lived Meighen administration of 1926.

[*Who was who*, 1941-50; *Can. who's who*, 1948; *Can. parl. comp.*, 1928; *Encyc. Can.*]

Dressler, Marie (1873-1934), the stage-name of Leila von Koerber, actress, who was born in Cobourg, Ontario, on November 9, 1873. She was educated in Toronto, and began her career as an actress on the local stage. She became a famous comedienne, and enjoyed various successes, notably as "Flo Honeydew" in *The lady slavey*, and in *Tillie's nightmare*. In later life she became famous as a motion-picture actress, and was in receipt of a fabulous salary. She was married twice; and she died in 1934. She was the author of an autobiography, *My own story* (Boston, 1934), published posthumously.

[*Who was who in America.*]

Drew, Andrew (1792-1878), naval officer, was born in 1792, and entered the British Navy in 1806. He served throughout the later stages of the Napoleonic Wars. In 1824 he distinguished himself in the defence of Cape Coast Castle against the Ashantees, and for this service he was promoted to the rank of commander. In 1832 he settled in Upper Canada, having bought an estate in Oxford county; and at the time of the rebellion of 1837 he was the senior naval officer in the colony. He was appointed commander of the provincial marine, and was in command of the party which "cut out" the *Caroline* at Port Schlosser in December, 1837. He left Canada in 1842, because of several attempts made against his life; in 1843 he retired on half-pay; and from 1850 to 1862 he was naval store-keeper at the Cape of Good Hope. He died in England on December 19, 1878. He was promoted to be an admiral in 1875. His reminiscences of the rebellion of 1837 were published in the *Hamilton Spectator*, and were republished by Judge Woods under the title *The burning of the Caroline* (Chatham, Ontario, 1896).

[J. Ireland, *Andrew Drew and the founding of Woodstock* (Ont. Hist. Soc., papers and records, 1968); J. Ireland, *Andrew Drew: The man who burned the Caroline* (Ont. Hist. Soc., papers and records, 1967); *Dom. ann. reg.*, 1878; *Dict. Can. biog.*, vol. 10.]

Drew, George Alexander (1894-1973), lawyer, soldier, political leader, was born in Guelph, Ontario, May 7, 1894. He was a son and grandson of distinguished lawyers. George Drew was educated at Upper Canada College and the University of Toronto. He was called to the bar of Ontario in 1920 and practised law in Guelph until he was appointed assistant master of the Supreme Court of Ontario in 1926, becoming master in 1929. He was chairman of the Ontario Securities Commission from 1931 to 1934 and became active in the Liberal-Conservative campaign committee for Ontario. He was elected to the Ontario Legislature for Simcoe East in 1939 and re-elected for High Park in 1943 and 1945. was premier of Ontario and minister of education from 1943 to 1948. In the Conservative leadership convention of October, 1948, he was elected national leader on the first ballot and became leader of the opposition in the House of Commons from 1949 until 1956. He resigned his seat in the Commons to become Canadian High Commissioner to the United Kingdom (1957-65).

During the First World War Drew served with the 16th Battery, Canadian Expeditionary Force. He was wounded in 1916 and returned to service as commanding officer of the 64th Battery, C.F.A. During the inter-war years he maintained his close association with the militia. He wrote a number of books on military affairs including: *The truth about the war* (Toronto, 1928); *The truth about the war-makers* (Toronto, 1932); *Salesman of death* (Toronto, 1933); *Canada's fighting airmen* (Toronto, 1930). He died at Toronto, Ontario, January 4, 1973.

[*Can. who's who*, 1970-72.]

Driscoll, Frederick (*fl.* 1830-1866), journalist, was born in Montreal, Lower Canada, in 1830, and became a journalist in Montreal. He went to New York, and was on the staff of the New York *Tribune* during the American civil war. After 1866 he passed from view. He

was the author of *The twelve days campaign* (Montreal, 1866) and *Sketch of the Canadian ministry* (Montreal, 1866).

[Morgan, *Bib. can.*]

Drolet, Gustave Adolphe (1844-1904), lawyer and author, was born at St. Pie, Quebec, on February 16, 1844, and was educated at the College of St. Hyacinthe and at Masson College, Terrebonne. He was called to the bar in 1866, and practised law in Montreal. In 1896 he undertook, at the instance of Sir Wilfrid Laurier (q.v.), a political mission to Rome in connection with the Manitoba school question. He died at Montreal on October 17, 1904. Besides numerous contributions to periodicals, he was the author of *Zouaviana* (Montreal, 1893).

[Morgan, *Can. men* (1898).]

Drucourt, Augustin de (1703?-1762), the last French governor of Louisbourg, was born about 1703, probably in Normandy, and entered the French naval service. He rose to the rank of captain in 1751; and in 1754 he was appointed governor of Ile Royale (Cape Breton Island). It fell to him, after a brave defence of Louisbourg, to surrender the fortress to the British in 1758. He died on August 28, 1762. In 1749 he was created a chevalier de St. Louis.

[R. Roy, *Drucourt* (Bull. rech. hist., 1938); Le Jeune, *Dict. gén.*; *Dict. Can. biog.*, vol. 3.]

Drummond, Sir George Alexander (1829-1910), president of the Bank of Montreal (1905-10), was born in Edinburgh, Scotland, on October 11, 1829, the son of George Drummond and Margaret Pringle. He was educated at Edinburgh High School and University; and emigrated to Canada in 1854. He became manager of John Redpath and Son, sugar refiners, Montreal; and in 1879 he founded the Canada Sugar Refining Company. In 1882 he was elected a director of the Bank of Montreal; in 1887, a vice-president; and in 1905, its president. In 1885 he was called to the Senate of Canada, and he sat in the Senate until his death at Montreal on February 2, 1910. He was twice married, (1) in 1857 to Helen, daughter of John Redpath, of Montreal, by whom he had five sons and two daughters; and (2) in 1884 to Grace Julia, daughter of A. D. Parker, of Montreal, by whom he had two sons. He was created a K.C.M.G. in 1904 and a C.V.O. in 1908. He was the possessor of a notable collection of paintings, and was chairman of the National Gallery of Canada and president of the Art Association of Montreal.

[*Dict. nat. biog.*, supp. II; *Can. who was who*, vol. 1; Morgan, *Can. men* (1898); *Can. parl. comp.*]

Drummond, Sir Gordon (1771-1854), administrator of Upper Canada (1813-15) and of Canada (1815-16), was born in Quebec in 1771, the youngest son of Colin Drummond, paymaster-general of the forces in Lower Canada. He entered the British army in 1789 as an ensign in the First Regiment of Foot, and rose rapidly in rank, becoming in 1794 lieutenant-colonel commanding the Eighth Regiment. He served throughout the Revolutionary and Napoleonic wars; and in 1813 he was appointed second-in-command to Sir George Prevost (q.v.) in Canada, having attained in 1811 the rank of lieutenant-general. He commanded on the Niagara frontier during the winter of 1813-14 and the summer of 1814, and was wounded at Lundy's Lane. In the autumn of 1814 he was ordered to Quebec, to succeed Prevost as commander-in-chief, and to assume the administration of the Canadas. He returned to England in 1816, and in 1826 he was promoted to be full general. His later years were spent in retirement, and he died in London, England, on October 10, 1854. In 1809 he married Margaret, daughter of William Russell, of Brancipath Castle, Durham; and by her he had two sons and one daughter. He was created a K.C.B. in 1815 and a G.C.B. in 1817.

[D. B. Read, *The lieutenant-governors of Upper Canada* (Toronto, 1900); Morgan, *Cel. Can.*; *Cyc. Am. biog.*; E. A. Cruikshank, *Documentary history of the campaign on the Niagara frontier* (9 vols., Welland, Ont., 1900-08).]

Drummond, Lewis Henry (1848-1929), priest and author, was born in Montreal on October 29, 1848, the son of the Hon. Lewis Thomas Drummond (q.v.). He was educated at St. Mary's College, Montreal; entered the Society of Jesus in 1868; and was ordained a priest of the Roman Catholic Church in 1883. He served in various capacities in different parts of Canada, Great Britain, and the United States; and he died at Guelph, Ontario, on July 29, 1929. He was a voluminous contributor to both poetry and prose to various periodicals; and he translated Edouard Richard's *Acadia* (2 vols., New York, 1895).

[Morgan, *Can. men* (1912).]

Drummond, Lewis Thomas (1813-1882), politician and jurist, was born in Londonderry, Ireland, on May 28, 1813. He emigrated to Canada with his widowed mother in 1825, and was educated at Nicolet College. He was called to the bar of Lower Canada in 1836, and in 1838 he distinguished himself as one of the counsel in defence of the political prisoners arrested in connection with the rebellion of 1837. He sat in the Legislative Assembly of Canada almost continuously from 1844 to 1863, representing successively Portneuf, Shefford, Lotbinière, and Rouville. From 1848 to 1851, he was solicitor-general for Lower Canada in the Baldwin-Lafontaine administration; from 1851 to 1856 he was attorney-general for Lower Canada in the Hincks-Morin, MacNab-Morin, and MacNab-Taché adminis-

trations; in 1858 he held the same office in the short-lived Brown-Dorion government; and in 1863 he was for a few months commissioner of public works in the Sandfield Macdonald government. His most notable achievement was the abolition of the seigniorial tenure in Lower Canada in 1856. In 1864 he was appointed a judge of the Court of Appeal of Lower Canada, and he sat on the bench until his retirement in 1873. He died at Montreal on November 24, 1882. In 1842 he married Josephte Eléonore, daughter of the Hon. P. D. Debartzch (q.v.).

[*Dom. ann. reg.*, 1882; J. C. Dent, *The last forty years* (2 vols., Toronto, 1881); J. D. Borthwick, *History and biographical gazetteer of Montreal* (Montreal, 1892).]

Drummond, William (d. 1814), soldier, was born at Keltire, Perthshire, Scotland. He entered the British army at an early age, and he served in Canada during the War of 1812. He was wounded in the attack on Sackett's Harbour in 1813, and he served under Sir Gordon Drummond (q.v.) as quartermaster-general on the Niagara frontier in 1814, with the rank of lieutenant-colonel. He was killed at the siege of Fort Erie on August 5, 1814.

[E. A. Cruikshank, *The documentary history of the campaign on the Niagara frontier* (9 vols., Welland, Ont., 1908).]

Drummond, William Henry (1854-1907), dialect poet, was born at Currawn House, county Leitrim, Ireland, on April 13, 1854, the son of George Drummond, Royal Irish Constabulary, and Elizabeth Morris Loden. He came to Canada with his parents in 1864, and was educated at the Montreal High School. He studied medicine at Bishop's College, Lennoxville (M.D., 1884), and for many years was a physician in general practice, first in the country, and then in Montreal. He died at Cobalt, Ontario, on April 6, 1907. His first volume of verse was entitled *The habitant* (New York and London, 1897), and was couched in an approximation to the dialect of the French-Canadian *habitant* speaking English. This was followed in the same strain by *Phil-o-Rum's canoe* (New York and London, 1898), *Johnnie Courteau* (New York and London, 1901), and *The voyageur* (New York, 1905); and there was published a posthumous volume entitled *The great fight* (New York and London, 1908), prefaced by a biographical memoir. He married, in 1894, May Isabel, only daughter of Dr. O. C. Harvey of Savanna la Mar, Jamaica. He was elected a fellow of the Royal Society of Canada in 1899; and he was made an LL.D. of the University of Toronto in 1902.

[W. H. Drummond, *The great fight* (New York and London, 1908), with biographical sketch; *Dict. nat. biog.*, supp. II; *Can. who was who*, vol. 1; Morgan, *Can. men* (1898);

Proc. Roy. Soc. Can., 1907; A. MacMurchy, *Handbook of Canadian literature* (Toronto, 1906); L. Pierce, *An outline of Canadian literature* (Toronto, 1927).]

Drummond, William Malcolm (1897-1965), economist, was born in Bristol, Quebec, in 1897. He was educated at Queen's University (B.A., 1923), the University of Toronto (M.A., 1924), the Ecoles Libres des Sciences Politiques in Paris, and Harvard University, (Ph.D., 1955). He lectured at the University of Alberta from 1924 to 1926 and at the University of Toronto from 1929 to 1937 when he left to become professor and head of the department of agricultural economics at the Ontario Agricultural College at Guelph. Dr. Drummond remained at O.A.C. for fifteen years, developing a strong department. In 1952 he resigned from O.A.C. to serve with the United Nations' economic mission in Korea. He was a member of the Royal Commission on Newfoundland Agriculture, and the Canadian Commission on price spreads, and on Canada's economic prospects. At the time of his death he was a member of the Agricultural Economics Research Council. He was a fellow of the Agricultural Institute of Canada. His special interests lay in the fields of agricultural policy, agricultural marketing, and foreign agriculture. He wrote *A review of agricultural policy in Canada* with W. J. Anderson and T. C. Kerr (Ottawa, 1966), and *Wheat surpluses and their impact on Canada-United States relations* with W. E. Hamilton (Montreal, 1959). He died at Ottawa, April 7, 1965.

[*Can. journal of economic and political science*, vol. XXXII; *Journal of farm economics*, vol. XLIII, no. 4, part 11 (November, 1961).]

Drury, Ernest Charles (1878-1968), premier, and former head of the United Farmers of Ontario, was born at Crown Hill, Ontario, January 22, 1878, the son of the Honourable Charles Drury, the first minister of agriculture for Ontario. He was educated at Ontario Agricultural College (B.S.A., 1900). Active in farm associations he was first secretary of the Canadian Council of Agriculture in 1909. He was elected president of the United Farmers of Ontario in 1913. He was defeated as Liberal candidate for the House of Commons in the 1917 election. When the United Farmers of Ontario won their unexpected victory in the general provincial election of 1919, although he had not been a candidate for election, he was invited to head the Farmer government, which remained in power until defeated in 1923. The success of the United Farmers of Ontario in 1919 was a class victory; its defeat in 1923 sprang from its failure to grow from a movement into a political party. Drury's broadening policy designed to appeal to a wider section of the population was rejected by his own followers. He was an ardent free-trader and wrote *Forts of folly* in 1932. He became registrar, Supreme Court of Ontario, and county court clerk in 1934 as well as sheriff of Simcoe county, retiring in 1957. He has left an account of his life in *Farmer Premier* (Toronto, 1966). He died at Barrie, Ontario, February 17, 1968.

[*Can. who's who*, 1961-63; E. C. Drury, *Farmer Premier* (Toronto, 1966).]

Drury, Victor Montague (1884-1962), industrialist, was born at Quebec City on February 20, 1884. He was educated at Queen's University. Mr. Drury joined the Bank of Montreal, Kingston, in 1902, leaving in 1908 to join Montreal Trust Company. In 1909 he became an employee of Royal Securities Corporation, rising to vice-president (1919). He resigned in 1924 to form Drury and Company. He was president and chairman of the executive committee and director of Canadian Car and Foundry Company until 1953; chairman of the Board of Provincial Transport Company and a number of other Canadian firms in the construction and financial sectors. He died at Montreal July 29, 1962.

[*Can. who's who*, 1955-57.]

Du Bois, Pierre, Baron d'Avaugour. See **Avaugour, Pierre du Bois, Baron d'**.

Dubuc, Sir Joseph (1840-1914), chief justice of Manitoba (1903-09), was born at Ste. Martine, Lower Canada, on December 26, 1840, the son of Joseph Dubuc and Phebée Euphémie Garand. He was educated at Montreal College and McGill University (LL.B., 1869), and was called to the bar of Quebec in 1869, and of Manitoba in 1871. He settled in Winnipeg in June, 1870, became a member of Louis Riel's provisional council, and in December, 1870, was elected to represent St. Norbert in the first Legislative Assembly of Manitoba. He sat in the Assembly until 1878; in 1874 he was for a short time attorney-general in the Girard administration, and from 1875 to 1878 he was speaker of the Assembly. In 1872 he was also appointed a member of the Council of the North West Territories. In 1878 he was elected to represent Provencher in the Canadian House of Commons, as a Conservative; and he sat for this constituency until his appointment in 1879 as a judge of the Court of Queen's Bench in Manitoba. In 1903 he became chief justice of Manitoba, and he retired from the bench in 1910. He died at Los Angeles, California, on January 7, 1914. In 1872 he married Maria Anne Hénault of St. Cuthbert, Quebec. He was an LL.D. of the University of Toronto (1907), and he was created a knight bachelor in 1912.

[E. LeCompte, *Sir Joseph Dubuc* (Montreal, 1923); L. A. Prud'homme, *Sir Joseph Dubuc* (Revue canadienne, 1914); Morgan, *Can. men* (1912); J. P. Robertson, *Political manual of Manitoba* (Winnipeg, 1887); *Can. parl. comp.*; Le Jeune, *Dict. gén.*]

DuCalvet, Pierre (d. 1786), merchant, was a native of France who came to Canada by way of Acadia. In 1760 he was engaged in the fur-trade at Quebec. He espoused the cause of the Americans in 1775-78, and was in 1781 imprisoned for the remainder of the war by Haldimand (q.v.). In 1783 he went to London, England, and published, with the aid of Roubaud (q.v.) and Maseres (q.v.), his *Appel à la justice* (London, 1784). This was published also in English under the title *The case of Peter DuCalvet* (London, 1784). He was lost at sea when returning to America in 1786.

[B. Sulte, *Pierre DuCalvet* (Trans. Roy. Soc. Can., 1919) and *Mélanges historiques*, vol. vii (Montreal, 1921); *Can. arch. report*, 1885; *Cyc. Am. biog.*; Le Jeune, *Dict. gén.*]

Ducharme, Dominique (1765-1853), soldier, was born at Lachine, Quebec, on May 15, 1765, the son of Jean Marie Ducharme (q.v.) and Marie Roy-Portelance. He was educated at the College of Montreal; and his early days were spent in the fur-trade. About the year 1800 he was appointed captain of the Indian militia in the Lake of Two Mountains district; and in the War of 1812 he greatly distinguished himself at the head of his Indians. He and his Caughnawagas deserve the credit for the defeat and capture of the American force at Beaver Dam in 1813; and later in the same year he was mentioned in despatches after the battle of Châteauguay. At the end of the war, he was appointed Indian agent and interpreter at the Lake of Two Mountains, and he occupied this position until his death at the Lake of Two Mountains on August 3, 1853. He married on June 26, 1810, Agathe Chamilly de Lorimier; and by her he had several children, of whom five daughters survived him.

[P. Hudon, *Le capitaine Dominique Ducharme* (Revue canadienne, 1878).]

Ducharme, Jean Marie (1723-1807), fur-trader, was born at Lachine, Canada, on July 20, 1723, and engaged in the western fur-trade. In 1780 he led a party of Indians in an abortive attack on the post of St. Louis on the Mississippi. After his retirement from the fur-trade, he represented the county of Montreal in the Legislative Assembly of Lower Canada from 1796 to 1800. He died at Lachine, Lower Canada, on July 20, 1807.

[F. J. Audet, *Jean-Marie Ducharme* (Trans. Roy. Soc. Can., 1939); J. Tassé, *Les canadiens de l'ouest* (2 vols., Montreal, 1878).]

Ducharme, Louis Léandre (*fl.* 1815-1845), *patriote*, was born at Lachine, Lower Canada, on January 15, 1815, the son of Louis Ducharme, and the grandson of Jean Marie

Ducharme (q.v.). He took part in the rebellion of 1837 in Lower Canada, and on December 1, 1838, was condemned to death. Later, this sentence was commuted; and he was deported to Australia. On his return to Montreal, he published his *Journal d'un exilé politique aux terres Australes* (Montreal, 1845). The date and the place of his death have not been ascertained.

[F. J. Audet, *Jean-Marie Ducharme* (Trans. Roy. Soc. Can., 1939).]

Duchaussois, Pierre Jean Baptiste (1878-1940), missionary and author, was born at Wallincourt, France, on August 4, 1878, and died in 1940. He was educated at Liège, Belgium, was ordained a priest in the Oblate order in 1903, and came to Canada shortly afterwards. After serving in various capacities in Ottawa and Edmonton, he spent the years 1915 to 1921 exploring the Canadian North, with a view to writing the history of the Catholic missionaries in the Far North. He published three volumes: *Femmes héroïques* (Paris, 1917), republished in English under the title *The Grey Nuns in the far north* (Toronto, 1919); *Aux glaces polaires* (Lyons, 1921), translated later under the title *Mid snow and ice* (London, 1922); and *Apôtres inconnues* (Paris, 1924), translated later under the title *Hidden apostles* (Buffalo, N.Y., 1937). He returned to France in 1921, and spent five years in Ceylon; in 1929 he came back to Canada, to write the life of Mère Marie-Rose Durocher, under the title *Rose du Canada* (Montreal, 1932), translated into English under the title *Rose of Canada* (Montreal, 1934).

[J. B. A. Allaire, *Dictionnaire biographique du clergé canadien-français*, vol. 6 (St. Hyacinthe, Que., 1934).]

Duchesnay, Antoine Juchereau (1740-1806), executive councillor of Lower Canada, was born at Beauport, near Quebec, on February 7, 1740, the son of Antoine Juchereau Duchesnay, seignior of Beauport, and Marie-Françoise Chartier de Lotbinière. He fought in the Seven Years' War as an ensign in the *troupes de la marine*; but remained in Canada after the conquest. In 1775 he served against the Americans, was captured, and remained a prisoner of war for eighteen months. From 1792 to 1796 he represented Buckingham in the Legislative Assembly of Lower Canada. In 1794 he was appointed a member of the Executive Council of Lower Canada. He died at Beauport on December 15, 1806. He was twice married, (1) in 1765 to Julie-Louise Liénard de Beaujeu (d. 1773), by whom he had five children, and (2) in 1778 to Catherine LeCompte Dupré (d. 1836), by whom he had four children.

[P. G. Roy, *La famille Juchereau Duchesnay* (Lévis, 1903).]

Duchesnay, Antoine Louis Juchereau (1767-1825), legislative and executive councillor of Lower Canada, was born at Quebec on February 18, 1767, the eldest son of Antoine Juchereau Duchesnay (q.v.). In 1804 he was elected to represent the county of Hampshire (Portneuf) in the Legislative Assembly of Lower Canada; and in 1810 he was appointed a member of the Legislative Council. He died suddenly at his manor-house of Beauport on February 17, 1825. In 1793 he married Marie-Louise Fleury de la Gorgendière; and by her he had seven children.

[P. G. Roy, *La famille Juchereau Duchesnay* (Lévis, 1903).]

Duchesnay, Henri Elzéar Juchereau (1809-1871), senator of Canada, was born at Beauport, Lower Canada, on July 19, 1809, the third son of the Hon. Antoine Louis Juchereau Duchesnay (q.v.). He was called to the bar of Lower Canada in 1832, and from 1839 to 1843 he was police magistrate of Montreal. In 1856 he was elected to the Legislative Council of Canada for the division of Lauzon; and in 1867 he was called by royal proclamation to the Senate of Canada. He died at Ste. Marie de la Beauce, Quebec, on May 12, 1871. He was twice married, (1) in 1834 to Julie Perrault (d. 1838) by whom he had three children, and (2) in 1844 to Elisabeth-Suzanne Taschereau, by whom he had seven children.

[P. G. Roy, *La famille Juchereau Duchesnay* (Lévis, 1903); *Dict. Can. biog.*, vol. 10.]

Duchesnay, Henri Jules Juchereau (1845-1887), agriculturist, was born at Ste. Marie de la Beauce, Lower Canada, on July 6, 1845, the third son of the Hon. Henri Elzéar Juchereau Duchesnay (q.v.). He was educated at the Quebec Seminary, studied law at Laval and McGill universities, and was called to the bar of Quebec in 1866. He settled at Ste. Marie de la Beauce, became in 1871 lieutenant-colonel of the 23rd Battalion of Beauce, and in 1874 stipendiary magistrate of the county of Beauce. In February, 1887, he was elected to represent Dorchester in the Canadian House of Commons. He died shortly afterwards, however, at Ste. Marie de la Beauce, on July 6, 1887. In 1869 he married Marie Caroline Têtu; and by her he had ten children. He is chiefly remembered as the first dairy farmer to introduce the cream separator into America.

[P. G. Roy, *La famille Juchereau Duchesnay* (Lévis, 1903); Errol Bouchette, *Les débuts d'une industrie et notre classe bourgeoise* (Trans. Roy. Soc. Can., 1912).]

Duchesnay, Jean Baptiste Juchereau (1779-1833), legislative councillor of Lower Canada, was born at Beauport, near Quebec, on February 16, 1779, the son of Antoine Juchereau Duchesnay (q.v.) and Catherine LeCompte Dupré. For several years he held a commission in the 60th Regiment; and he commanded a company in the Canadian Vol-

tigeurs at the battle of Châteauguay in 1813. In 1832 he was appointed a member of the Legislative Council of Lower Canada; but he died of cholera at Quebec on January 12, 1833. He married Eliza Jones; and by her he had four children.

[P. G. Roy, *La famille Juchereau Duchesnay* (Lévis, 1903).]

Duchesneau, Jacques (*fl.* 1664-1696), intendant of New France (1675-82) was the son of Guillaume Duchesneau and Anne de La Lande. About 1664 he became commissary of Tours, and later a king's councillor, "trésorier de France et général des finances de la Touraine". On May 30, 1675, he was named intendant of New France. His commission invested him with the title of president of the Sovereign Council, an office which had hitherto been filled by the governor. This incurred the wrath of Frontenac (q.v.), who was then governor, and endless disputes occurred between governor and intendant on questions of precedence. On May 9, 1682, Duchesneau was recalled, and he died in France in 1696.

[R. Roy, *Les intendants de la Nouvelle-France* (Trans. Roy. Soc. Can., 1903); R. Roy, *Jacques Duchesneau* (Bull. rech. hist., vol. ix); Le Jeune, *Dict. gén.*; *Dict. Can. biog.*, vol. 1.]

Duckworth, Henry Thomas Forbes (d. 1927), scholar and author, was born at Liverpool, England; and was educated at Merton College, Oxford (B.A., 1889). He was ordained a priest of the Church of England in 1894, and was appointed in 1896 to special duty in Cyprus in connection with an inquiry into the liturgy and doctrines of the Eastern Church. In 1900 he became English chaplain at Cairo; but in 1901 he was appointed professor of Greek in Trinity College, Toronto. He died in hospital at Rouen, France, on September 7, 1927. He was the author, among other books and pamphlets, of *The church of Cyprus* (London, 1900), *Greek manuals of church doctrine* (London, 1901), *The Church of the Holy Sepulchre* (London, 1922), and *Pages of Levantine history* (London, n.d.).

[Morgan, *Can. men* (1912).]

Du Creux, François (1596-1666), priest and historian, was born in 1596 at Saintes, a town midway between Rochelle and Bordeaux in France. He was admitted to the Society of Jesus in 1614, taught *belles-lettres* for twelve years, and then devoted the rest of his life to "apostolic labour". He died at Bordeaux in 1666. Besides new editions of Greek and Latin grammars, and translations into Latin of the lives of St. Francis Regis and St. Francis de Sales, he was the author of a history of Canada in Latin, *Historia canadensis* (Paris, 1664), which was largely a compilation of the Jesuit *Relations* and which was translated by Percy

J. Robinson (q.v.) and edited by J. B. Conacher for the Champlain Society (2 vols., Toronto, 1951).

[R. G. Thwaites (ed.), *The Jesuit relations* (73 vols., Cleveland, 1900).]

Duff, Emma Lorne (d. 1935), schoolteacher and author, was a daughter of the Rev. Charles Duff, and a sister of Chief Justice Sir Lyman P. Duff. She became a kindergarten teacher in Toronto, Ontario, in 1888, and she taught in Toronto for over 25 years. She died in Toronto on March 31, 1935. She was the author of *A cargo of stories for children* (Toronto, 1931).

[*The Globe*, Toronto, April 1, 1935.]

Duff, Louis Blake (1878-1959), journalist and author, was born at Bluevale, Huron county, Ontario, in 1878, and died at Welland, Ontario, on August 29, 1959. After four years of school-teaching, he became a journalist in western Ontario; and in 1907 he became part owner of the Welland *Telegraph*, and later, owner and editor. He sold the paper in 1926; and from 1926 to 1945 he was the head of the Niagara Finance Company. He was the author of *Burnaby* (Welland, Ont., 1926), *Crowland* (Welland, Ont., 1928), and *The county kerchief* (Toronto, 1949), as well as numerous articles on historical, literary, and bibliographical subjects. In 1953 the University of Western Ontario conferred on him the honorary degree of LL.D.

[Toronto *Globe and Mail*, Aug. 30, 1959; *Can. who's who*, 1955-57.]

Duff, Sir Lyman Poore (1865-1955), chief justice of Canada (1933-44), was born at Meaford, Ontario, on January 7, 1865, and died at Ottawa, Ontario, on April 26, 1955. He was educated at the University of Toronto (B.A., 1887; LL.B., 1889), and was called to the bar of Ontario in 1893, and later to that of British Columbia. He practised law in Victoria, British Columbia, and was appointed a puisne judge of the Supreme Court of British Columbia in 1904. He became a justice of the Supreme Court of Canada in 1906, and chief justice of Canada in 1933. He retired from the bench in 1944. In 1934 he was created a G.C.M.G.; and the honorary degree of LL.D. was conferred on him by the University of Toronto, McGill University, the University of Montreal, Queen's University, Dalhousie University, the University of British Columbia, Laval University, the University of Pennsylvania, and Columbia University. He was to a large extent the author of the Report of the Royal Commission on Transportation (popularly known as the Duff Commission), of which he was chairman.

[*Can. who's who*, 1952-54; *Encyc. Can.*]

Dufferin and Ava, Frederick Temple Blackwood, Marquess of (1826-1902),

governor-general of Canada (1872-78), was born in Florence, Italy, on June 21, 1826, the son of Price, fourth Baron Dufferin and Clandeboye, and Helen Selina Sheridan, a granddaughter of Richard Brinsley Sheridan. He was educated at Eton and at Christ Church, Oxford, but did not graduate. He succeeded to his father's peerage in 1841; and from 1848 to 1852, and from 1854 to 1858, he was lord-in-waiting to Queen Victoria. He entered politics, and from 1864 to 1866 he occupied successively the offices of undersecretary of state for India and undersecretary for war. In 1868 he became chancellor of the Duchy of Lancaster in the Gladstone government; and in 1872 he was appointed governor-general of Canada. It fell to him, during his term of office, to deal with the difficult questions connected with the "Pacific scandal" charges; and he handled these questions with much tact and judgment. In 1876 he visited British Columbia, and by his able diplomacy succeeded in allaying in that province the growing discontent with Confederation. A facile and eloquent speaker, he achieved great popularity in Canada; though his speeches gave rise to some criticism, and were characterized by Goldwin Smith (q.v.) as "elegant flummery".

In 1879 he was appointed British ambassador at St. Petersburg, and in 1881 he was transferred to Constantinople. From 1884 to 1888 he was viceroy of India; from 1888 to 1891 he was ambassador extraordinary at Rome; and from 1891 to 1896 he was ambassador at Paris. He died at Clandeboye, Ireland, on February 12, 1902. In 1862 he married Harriet Georgiana, eldest daughter of Archibald Rowan Hamilton, of Killyleagh Castle, County Down, Ireland; and by her he had several children. In 1871 he was created Viscount Clandeboye and Earl of Dufferin, in the peerage of the United Kingdom; and in 1888 Marquess of Dufferin and Ava. He was the author of *Letters from high latitudes* (London, 1860) and of a number of essays on Irish affairs; and collections of his speeches were published in Toronto (1878) and in London (1882). C. W. de Kiewiet and F. H. Underhill edited for the Champlain Society *The Dufferin-Carnarvon Correspondence, 1874-78* (Toronto, 1955).

[Sir A. C. Lyall, *The life of the Marquess of Dufferin* (2 vols., London, 1905); C. E. D. Black, *The Marquess of Dufferin and Ava* (Toronto, 1903); G. Stewart, *Canada under the administration of the Earl of Dufferin* (Toronto, 1878); W. Leggo, *The history of the administration of the Right Hon. Frederick Temple, Earl of Dufferin* (Montreal, 1878); H. Nicolson, *Helen's tower* (London, 1937); *Who was who*, 1897-1910.]

Duffy, Augustine Michael (1905-1966), merchant, was born at St. John's, Newfoundland, February 18, 1905, and educated at St.

Bonaventure's College at St. John's. He was a commission merchant for church supplies and furnishings and managing director of A. M. Duffy Limited and Colonial Stationery Limited of St. John's. He was elected a member of the provincial legislature in 1951 and on a recount in 1956 as one of the four members of the opposition Conservative party. He broke with the party in 1959 over Prime Minister John Diefenbaker's handling of the financial terms of the Confederation agreement and founded the United Newfoundland party. He was defeated in the election of 1963 and retired from politics. He died at St. John's, Newfoundland, July 26, 1966.

[*Can. parl. comp.*, 1958; Montreal *Gazette* (July 27, 1966).]

Dugas, Alphonse Charles (1858-1924), priest, was born at St. Liguori, Canada East, on August 8, 1858; and died at St. Polycarpe, Quebec, on October 21, 1924. He was the author of *Histoire de la paroisse de Saint-Liguori* (n.p., 1902), *Gerbes de souvenirs* (2 vols., Montreal, 1914), and *Soeur Marie de Sainte-Amélie* (Montreal, 1922).

[Allaire, *Dict. biog.*]

Dugas, Georges (1833-1928), priest and author, was born at St. Jacques de l'Achigan, Lower Canada, on November 5, 1833, the son of Edouard Dugas and Hedwige Lagarde. He was educated at L'Assomption College, and was ordained a priest of the Roman Catholic Church in 1862. He went to the West as a missionary, and served in various capacities in Manitoba from 1866 to 1888. He then became curé of the parish of Ste. Anne des Plaines, Quebec; and he died there on December 14, 1928. He was the author of *La première canadienne du Nord-Ouest* (Montreal, 1883), *Mgr. Provencher et les missions de la Rivière-Rouge* (Montreal, 1889), *Légendes du Nord-Ouest* (Montreal, 1890), *Un voyageur des pays d'en haut* (Montreal, 1890), *L'Ouest canadien* (Montreal, 1896; English trans., Montreal, 1905), *Histoire de la paroisse de Sainte-Anne-des-Plaines* (Montreal, 1900), *Histoire véridique des faits qui ont préparé le mouvement des Métis à la Rivière Rouge en 1869* (Montreal, 1905), and *Histoire de l'Ouest canadien de 1822 à 1869* (Montreal, 1906).

[Morgan, *Can. men* (1912); Allaire, *Dict. biog.*; Le Jeune, *Dict. gén.*]

Dugas, Marcel Henri (1883-1947), author, was born at St. Jacques de l'Achigan, Quebec, in 1883. He was educated at the Collège de l'Assomption and later, after studying law and reporting for journals in Montreal, he went to France to study at the Sorbonne. He returned to Canada in 1914, and joined the staff of the Bibliothèque Cinque in Montreal. In 1920 he returned to France as assistant archivist at the Public Archives of Canada in Paris; and he

remained in this post until 1940. He then returned to Montreal, where he died on January 7, 1947. His interests were literary rather than historical, and he was the author of over a dozen books: *Le théâtre à Montréal* (Paris, 1911), under the pseudonym "Marcel Henry"; *Feux de Bengale à Verlaine glorieux* (Montreal, 1915); *Psyché au cinéma* (Montreal, 1916); *Confins* (Montreal, 1918); *Apologies* (Montreal, 1919); *Flacons à la mer* (Paris, 1923); *Littérature canadienne* (Paris, 1929); *Cordes anciennes* (Paris, 1933); *Un romantique Canadien, Louis Fréchette* (Paris, 1934); *Nocturnes* (Paris, 1937), under the pseudonym of "Sixte le Débonnaire"; *Salve alma parens* (Quebec, 1941); *Pots de fer* (Quebec, 1941); *Approches* (Quebec, 1942); and *Paroles en liberté* (Montreal, 1944).

[C. Rocheleau-Rouleau, *Marcel Dugas, l'homme et son oeuvre* (Bull. rech. hist., 1948).]

Duley, Margaret Iris (1895-1968), novelist, was born at St. John's, Newfoundland, in 1895. She lived most of her life in Newfoundland although she spent some time in Britain, the United States, and the Canadian mainland. In 1936 she earned international acclaim for her novel *Eyes of the gull* (London, 1936) and went on to publish *Cold pastoral* (London, 1939); *Highway to valour* (London, 1941); *Novelty on earth* (London, 1942); *Green afternoon* (1944); and *The Caribou hut*. All her novels have Newfoundland settings and she was the first Newfoundland woman writer to be recognized as a novelist outside her own province. She depicts the harshness as well as the beauty of the land and seems to have lived in a kind of love-hate relationship with the society of the island. She died at St. John's, Newfoundland, March 22, 1968.

[St. John's *Evening Telegram*, March 25, 1968; *Saturday Night*, September, 1941; May, 1942.]

DuLhut, or DuLuth, Daniel Greysolon (1639?-1710), *coureur-de-bois*, was born about 1639 at St. Germain-en-Laye, France, and came to Canada about 1674. In 1678 he left Montreal, with seven Frenchmen, to explore the Sioux country; he took possession of this country in the name of the king of France; and he returned to Quebec in 1681. During the greater part of the following ten years he was in the Northwest, exploring and trading with the Indians, and for a time acting as commandant for the government of New France. In 1686 he built a small fort on the Detroit Strait, near the outlet of Lake Huron; and in 1696 he appears as commandant at Fort Frontenac on Lake Ontario. He died at Montreal on February 25, 1710. The city of Duluth, Minnesota, is named in honour of him. DuLhut wrote accounts of his earlier journeys, but these have been lost. A memorandum by him on the western country has, however, been published in Margry, *Découvertes et établissements*, vol. v, 3-72.

[C. W. Colby, *Canadian types of the old régime* (New York, 1908); W. McLennan, *The death of Duluth* (Trans. Roy. Soc. Can., 1903); B. Sulte, *DuLhut* (Revue canadienne, 1893); Le Jeune, *Dict. gén.*; *Cyc. Am. biog.*; *Dict. Can. biog.*, vol. 2.]

Dulongpré, Louis (1759?-1843), painter, was born in Paris, France, about 1759, the son of Louis Dulongpré and Marie-Jeanne Duguay. He fought under Rochambeau in the War of American Independence; but after the war he came to Canada, and settled in Montreal. He achieved success as a painter of portraits and religious pictures; and he died at St. Hyacinthe, Lower Canada, on April 26, 1843. In 1787 he married in Montreal Marguerite Campeau.

[*Bull. rech. hist.*, 1902, 1917, and 1920.]

Dumas, Jean Daniel (*fl.* 1750-1780), soldier, was born in the province of Agenais, France, and was "brought up by the banks of the Garonne". He became a captain in the Agenais regiment; in 1750 he came to Canada as a captain in the Marine troops; and he served in Canada throughout the Seven Years' War. At the battle of the Monongahéla in 1755, he succeeded to the command of the French troops on the death of Beaujeu (q.v.); and the defeat of Braddock (q.v.) was largely due to him. In 1759 he became inspector-general of the Marine troops in Canada, with the rank of colonel; and he commanded the right wing of the French army at the battle of the Plains of Abraham. In 1760 he returned to France; in 1768 he was promoted to be a brigadier-general; and in 1780 he became a field-marshal. The date of his death does not appear to be known.

[F. J. Audet, *Jean-Daniel Dumas, le héros de la Monongahéla* (Montreal, 1920); *Cyc. Am. biog.*]

Dumont, Gabriel (1838-1906), rebel, was born in Assiniboia in 1838, the son of Isidore Dumont and Louise Laframboise, both half-breeds. He took no part in the North West Rebellion of 1870; but he was adjutant-general of the rebel forces in the rebellion of 1885. After the battle of Batoche, he escaped to the United States, and lived there for a number of years. He died at Batoche, Saskatchewan, on May 19, 1906. He married Magdeleine Welkey, a Scottish half-breed, but he had no children.

[A. Ouimet, *La vérité sur la question métisse: Biographie et récit de Gabriel Dumont* (Montreal, 1889); A. G. Morice, *Dictionnaire historique des canadiens de l'ouest* (Quebec, 1908); *Can. who was who*, vol. 2; G. Woodcock, *Gabriel Dumont: The Métis chief and his lost world* (Edmonton, 1975).]

DuMoulin, John Philip (1834-1911), Anglican bishop of Niagara, was born in Dublin, Ireland, on January 9, 1834, and was educated at Trinity College, Dublin, and Bishop's College, Lennoxville, Quebec (M.A., 1878). He came to Canada in 1862, and was ordained a priest of the Church of England in 1863. He was elected third bishop of Niagara in 1896; and he continued the oversight of this see until his death at Hamilton, Ontario, on March 29, 1911. He was the author of *The eternal law* (Toronto, 1906).

[*Can. who was who*, vol. 1; Morgan, *Can. men* (1912); C. H. Mockridge, *The bishops of the Church of England in Canada* (Toronto, 1896).]

Duncan, Dorothy (1903-1957), author, was born in East Orange, New Jersey, in 1903, and died at Montreal, Quebec, on April 22, 1957. In 1936 she married Hugh MacLennan, the novelist; but as an author she used her maiden name. She wrote *You can live in an apartment* (New York, 1939), *Here's to Canada* (New York, 1941), *Bluenose: A portrait of Nova Scotia* (New York, 1942), and *Partner in three worlds* (New York, 1944).

[*Can. who's who*, 1952-54; *Encyc. Can.*]

Duncan, James (1805-1881), illustrator, was born at Coleraine, Ireland, in 1805, and emigrated to Canada in 1830. He became a teacher of art in Montreal; and he illustrated *Hochelaga depicta*, by Newton Bosworth (q.v.). He died at Montreal, Quebec, on September 28, 1881.

[E.-Z. Massicotte, *L'illustrateur du vieux Montréal* (Bull. rech. hist., 1940).]

Duncan, John Morison (1795?-1825), author, was born in Scotland about 1795, the son of Andrew Duncan, printer to the University of Glasgow. He was educated at the University of Glasgow (B.A., 1816); and in 1818-19 he made a trip to the United States and Canada. He died at Glasgow on October 3, 1825. He was the author of *A Sabbath among the Tuscarora Indians* (Glasgow, 1819), and *Travels through part of the United States and Canada* (2 vols., Glasgow, 1823; Amer. ed., New York, 1823).

[W. Innes Addison (ed.), *The matriculation albums of the University of Glasgow* (Glasgow, 1913).]

Duncan, Norman (1871-1916), novelist, was born at Brantford, Ontario, on July 2, 1871, the son of Robert Augustus Duncan and Susan Hawley. He was educated at the University of Toronto, but did not graduate. In 1896 he joined the staff of the New York *Evening Post*, and his first book, *The soul of a street* (New York, 1900), dealt with life in New York. His reputation was won, however, by his stories of Labrador: *The way of the sea* (New York, 1903), *Dr. Luke of the Labrador* (New

York, 1904), *Dr. Grenfell's parish* (New York, 1905), *The adventures of Billy Topsail* (New York, 1906), *The cruise of the Shining Light* (New York, 1907), *Billy Topsail and Company* (New York, 1910), *Billy Topsail, M.D.* (Toronto, 1916), and *Harbour tales* (Toronto, 1918). He published also *The mother* (New York, 1905), *Every man for himself* (New York, 1908), *The suitable child* (New York, 1909), *Going down from Jerusalem* (New York, 1909), *The best of a bad job* (Toronto, 1912), *The bird-store man* (Toronto, 1914), and *Battles royal* (Toronto, 1918). During the last twenty years of his life he lived almost continuously in the United States; and he died at Buffalo, New York, on October 18, 1916.

[Morgan, *Can. men* (1912); *Who was who in America*; L. Pierce, *An outline of Canadian literature* (Toronto, 1927).]

Duncan, Sara Jeannette, afterwards **Mrs. Everard Cotes** (1862-1922), novelist, was born in Brantford, Ontario, in 1862, the eldest daughter of Charles Duncan. She began her literary career as a journalist, first with the Washington *Post*, and then with the Toronto *Globe*, writing under the pseudonym "Garth Grafton". Her first, and perhaps best known, book was *A social departure* (London, 1890), an entertaining account of "how Orthodocia and I went round the world by ourselves." This was followed by *An American girl in London* (Toronto, 1891), *The simple adventures of a memsahib* (New York, 1893), *A daughter of to-day* (New York, 1894), *Vernon's aunt* (London, 1894), *The story of Sonny Sahib* (London, 1894), *His honour and a lady* (New York, 1896), *Hilda, a story of Calcutta* (New York, 1898), *A voyage of consolation* (New York, 1898), *The path of a star* (Toronto, 1899), *On the other side of the latch* (London, 1901), *Those delightful Americans* (New York, 1902), *The pool in the desert* (New York, 1903), *The imperialist* (New York, 1904), *Set in authority* (London, 1906), *Cousin Cinderella* (London, 1908), *The burnt offering* (London, 1909), *The consort* (London, 1912), and *His royal happiness* (Toronto, 1914). In 1891 she married Everard Charles Cotes, of the Indian Museum, Calcutta; and most of her later life was spent in India. She died at Ashmead, England, on July 22, 1922.

[*Can. who was who*, vol. 1; Morgan, *Can. men and women* (1912); L. E. Horning and L. J. Burpee, *Bibliography of Canadian fiction* (Toronto, 1904).]

Duncan, William (1832-1918), missionary, was born at Bishop's Burton, near Beverley, Yorkshire, England, on April 3, 1832. He was educated at Highbury College, and in 1856 he was sent as a lay missionary to British Columbia. In 1862 he founded a mission for the Tsimshian Indians at Metlakahtla, near Fort Simpson. In 1887, as a result of a dispute with

the Anglican bishop of Caledonia and the government of British Columbia, he removed his mission to New Metlakahtla, on Annette Island, in Alaska; and here he built up a remarkable industrial community. He never took holy orders, but was always merely a lay missionary. He died at Metlakahtla, Alaska, on August 30, 1918.

[J. W. Arctander, *The apostle of Alaska* (New York, 1909); H. S. Wellcome, *The story of Metlakahtla* (New York, 1887); *Can. who was who*, vol. 2.]

Duncombe, Charles (1794-1875), physician and politician, was born in Connecticut, United States, in 1794. He came to Canada in 1820, and settled in Burford, Upper Canada. In 1819 he was licensed as a physician, and for many years he practised medicine in the western part of Upper Canada. In 1834 he was returned to the legislature of Upper Canada as a member for Oxford; and in 1836 he was chairman of a parliamentary committee which published an important report on education in the province. In 1836 he went to England as an emissary of the Reform party; and in 1837 he was the leader of the rebels in western Upper Canada. He fled to the United States; and, though granted a pardon in 1843, he continued to live in the United States for the rest of his life. He died in Hicksville, California, on October 1, 1875.

[W. Canniff, *The medical profession in Upper Canada* (Toronto, 1894); J. Ross Robertson, *The history of freemasonry in Canada* (2 vols., Toronto, 1899).]

Dundas, George (1819-1880), lieutenant-governor of Prince Edward Island (1859-68), was born in England in 1819, and entered the British army in 1839. After serving in the Bermudas and in Nova Scotia, he resigned his commission in 1844; and from 1847 to 1858 he represented Linlithgow in the British House of Commons. From 1859 to 1868 he was lieutenant-governor of Prince Edward Island; and in 1875 he was appointed governor of the island of St. Vincent in the Antilles. He died there on March 18, 1880. In 1879 he was created a C.M.G.

[*Dom. ann. reg.*, 1880-81; Sir B. Burke, *A history of the landed gentry in Great Britain* (London, 1914); *Dict. Can. biog.*, vol. 10.]

Dundonald, Douglas Mackinnon Baillie Hamilton, 12th Earl of (1852-1935), soldier, was born on October 29, 1852, the son of the 11th Earl of Dundonald. He was educated at Eton, and entered the 2nd Life Guards in 1870. He served in the Nile expedition of 1884-85 and in the South African War, and rose in 1900 to the rank of major-general. In 1902 he was appointed general officer commanding the Canadian militia; but in 1904 he fell foul of the Laurier government over its exercise of political patronage in militia appointments, and was dismissed from office. In 1907 he was promoted to be lieutenant-general; and he served overseas in the First World War. He died on April 11, 1935. He published his autobiography under the title, *My army life* (London, 1926).

[*Who was who*, 1928-40; Morgan, *Can. men* (1912); O. D. Skelton, *The life and letters of Sir Wilfrid Laurier* (2 vols., Toronto, 1921).]

Dunham, Bertha Mabel (1881-1957), librarian and author, was born at Harriston, Ontario, in 1881, and died at Kitchener, Ontario, on June 21, 1957. She was educated at the University of Toronto (B.A., 1908) and at McGill Library School; and from 1908 to 1944 she was the librarian of the Kitchener Public Library. She was the author of three novels, *The trail of the Conestoga* (Toronto, 1924), *Toward Sodom* (Toronto, 1927), and *The trail of the King's men* (Toronto, 1931); of a local history, *Grand River* (Toronto, 1945); and of a book for children, *Kristli's trees* (Toronto, 1948). In 1947 the University of Western Ontario conferred on her the honorary degree of D.Litt.

[*Can. who's who*, 1952-54; *Encyc. Can.*]

Dunkin, Christopher (1812-1881), politician and jurist, was born in London, England, on September 25, 1812. He was educated at the University of London, at Glasgow University, and at Harvard University. At Harvard he was, for a short time, a tutor in Greek. He came to Canada in 1837, and from May, 1837, to June, 1838, he edited the Montreal *Morning Courier*. He then became secretary to the commission appointed by Lord Durham to inquire into education, and as such had a share in the preparation of Lord Durham's *Report* (London, 1839). From 1839 to 1847 he occupied an official position in the Post Office; but in 1847, having been called to the bar in 1846, he resigned to devote himself to the practice of law. From 1858 to 1861 he represented Drummond and Arthabaska in the Canadian Assembly, and from 1862 to 1871 he was the member for Brome, first in the Assembly of Old Canada, and then in both the Canadian House of Commons and the Quebec legislature. Though nominally a Conservative, he opposed Confederation, and he was its ablest and most cogent critic in the debates in the Canadian Assembly. He accepted Confederation, however, when completed, and played a part in setting the machinery of the new Dominion to work, first as provincial treasurer of Quebec (1867-69), and then as minister of agriculture in the Dominion government (1869-71). On October 25, 1871, he was appointed a puisne judge of the Superior Court of Quebec, and this position he occupied until his death, at Knowlton, Quebec, on January 6,

1881. He married Mary, daughter of Dr. Jonathan Barber of Montreal. He was the author of the Canada Temperance Act of 1864, commonly known as the "Dunkin Act".

[*Dom. ann. reg.*, 1880-81; Dent, *Can. port.*, vol. 4; Morgan, *Bib. can.*; M. O. Hammond, *Confederation and its leaders* (Toronto, 1917).]

Dunlap, David Alexander (1863-1924), financier and philanthropist, was born in Pembroke, Ontario, on October 13, 1863. He was educated at Pembroke, and at Osgoode Hall, Toronto; and was called to the bar in 1885. For a number of years he practised law in Mattawa, Ontario; but, on the discovery of silver in the Cobalt area, he became actively interested in mining. With some of his friends, he acquired a controlling interest in La Rose mine in Cobalt; and later he entered the field of gold-mining in the Porcupine area, and became vice-president and treasurer of the Hollinger Consolidated Gold Mines, Ltd. He died, after a lingering illness, at Donalda Farm, near Toronto, on October 29, 1924; and he left in his will large bequests to the University of Toronto and Victoria University, as well as to other institutions. He married Jessie Donalda Bell, of Pembroke; and he had by her one son. In his memory, his widow and son presented to the University of Toronto in 1931 an astronomical observatory, to be known as the David Dunlap Observatory.

[*University of Toronto monthly*, 1924.]

Dunlop, James (1755?-1815), merchant, was probably a native of Scotland. He came to Canada in 1777, and became a general merchant in Montreal. He amassed a fortune "supposed to be greater than ever was acquired by an individual of this country." In the War of 1812 he served as a major in the Montreal Volunteers, and was in January, 1814, court-martialled and dismissed from the service. He died on August 28, 1815.

[R. Campbell, *A history of the Scotch Presbyterian church*, *St. Gabriel St.*, *Montreal* (Montreal, 1887).]

Dunlop, William (1792-1848), author, was born at Greenock, Scotland, in 1792. He became an assistant surgeon in the 89th Regiment, and served in Canada during the War of 1812. He then is said to have accompanied his regiment to India, where his prowess in hunting tigers won for him the sobriquet of "Tiger" Dunlop. An attact of fever compelled his return to England on half-pay, and he there employed himself in literary journalism. He came to Canada in 1826 with John Galt (q.v.), and settled in the Huron district, in the service of the Canada Company. In 1841 he was elected a member of the Legislative Assembly of Canada for Huron as an independent; and he continued to sit in the

Assembly until 1846. He died at Lachine, near Montreal, on June 28, 1848. He was not married; and his will, which has been several times reprinted, is one of the curiosities of early Canadian literature. Both before and after coming to Canada, he was a contributor to *Blackwood's Magazine*; and his *Autobiography of a rat* (vol. xxiv) is typical of the character of his work. In Canada, he was the founder of the Toronto Literary Club in 1836; and he contributed to the *Canadian Literary Magazine* (Toronto) and the *Literary Garland* (Montreal). Under the *nom de plume* of "A Backwoodsman" he published *Statistical sketches of Upper Canada* (London, 1833).

[A. H. U. Colquhoun (ed.), *Recollections of the War of 1812*, by Dr. Wm. Dunlop (Toronto, 1908), with biographical sketch; F. S. L. Ford, *William Dunlop* (pamphlet, Toronto, 1931); W. J. Rattray, *The Scot in British North America* (4 vols., Toronto, 1881); R. and K. M. Lizars, *In the days of the Canada Company* (Toronto, 1896) and *Humours of '37* (Toronto, 1897); Morgan, *Bib. can.*; W. H. Graham, *The tiger of Canada West* (Toronto, 1952).]

Dunn, Alexander Roberts (1833-1868), soldier, was born in York (Toronto), Upper Canada, in 1833. He obtained a commission in the 11th Hussars, and greatly distinguished himself in the charge of the Light Brigade at Balaclava in the Crimea in 1856, winning the coveted Victoria Cross. In 1858 he was gazetted a major in the Royal Canadian Regiment, and he became its commanding officer; but he was later transferred to a regiment in India. In 1867 he accompanied his regiment on an expedition into Abyssinia; and he was killed by the accidental discharge of his rifle while hunting near Serafe, Abyssinia, on January 25, 1868.

[Morgan, *Cel. Can.*]

Dunn, Andrew Hunter (1839-1914), Anglican bishop of Quebec (1892-1914), was born at Saffron Walden, Essex, England, on October 16, 1839. He was educated at Corpus Christi College, Cambridge (B.A., 1863; M.A., 1866; D.D., 1893), was ordained a priest of the Church of England in 1865, and was vicar of All Saints', South Acton, Middlesex, from 1872 to 1892. In 1892 he was elected fifth bishop of Quebec, and he continued in charge of this diocese until 1914. He died at sea on November 14, 1914. In 1866 he married Alice, daughter of William Hunter, of Croydon, Surrey, England; and by her he had five sons and two daughters. He was a D.C.L. of Bishop's College, Lennoxville (1907).

[P. Jolliffe, *Andrew Hunter Dunn* (London, 1919); Morgan, *Can. men* (1912); *Can. who's who* (1910).]

Dunn, Sir James Hamet, Bart. (1875-1956), financier, was born at Bathurst, New Brunswick, on October 29, 1875. He was educated at Dalhousie University (LL.B., 1898), and was called to the bar. Soon, however, he gravitated from law to finance. In 1902 he became a member of the Montreal stock exchange, and from that point his rise was meteoric. He planned the merger that brought about the Brazilian Traction, Light, and Power Company and the Barcelona Traction, Light, and Power Company; and in 1935 he became president of the Algoma Steel Corporation. Even before his death, he was described as "the last of the multimillionaires". He died at St. Andrews, New Brunswick, on January 1, 1956. He was created a baronet in 1921.

[Lord Beaverbrook, *Courage: The story of Sir James Dunn* (Fredericton, N.B., 1961); *Can. who's who*, 1950-54; *Encyc. Can.*]

Dunn, Oscar (1844-1885), journalist, was born at Côteau du Lac, Lower Canada, in 1844, the son of a Scottish father and a French-Canadian mother. He was educated at the College of St. Hyacinthe, and soon after graduation became editor of the *Courrier de Saint-Hyacinthe*. He then went to Paris, France, to study journalism, and was there on the staff of the *Journal de Paris*. On his return to Canada, he joined the staff of the *Minerve* of Montreal. He edited *L'Opinion Publique*, a weekly journal; and he was one of the editors of the *Revue Canadienne*. In 1872, and again in 1875, he stood for parliament, but was defeated on both occasions; and, after his second defeat, he became librarian of the department of Public Instruction at Quebec. Later, he became secretary of the department; and he held this post at the time of his early death, in Quebec, on April 15, 1885. His chief publication was a *Glossaire franco-canadien* (Quebec, 1880); but he published also two volumes of papers and essays, *Dix ans de journalisme* (Montreal, 1876), and *Lectures pour tous* (Quebec, 1878), as well as a number of pamphlets, such as *Pourquoi nous sommes français* (Montreal, 1870), *L'union des catholiques* (Montreal, 1871), and *L'Amérique avant Christophe Colomb*. Strongly nationalist and clerical, he anticipated tendencies in French Canada which have become more pronounced since his day. In 1882 he was selected a charter member of the Royal Society of Canada.

[F. J. Audet, *Oscar Dunn* (Bull. rech. hist., 1928); J. Bruchési, *A propos Oscar Dunn* (Bull. rech. hist., 1928), and *Oscar Dunn et son temps* (Bull. rech. hist., 1928); A. D. DeCelles, *Oscar Dunn* (Trans. Roy. Soc. Can., 1886); Le Jeune, *Dict. gén.*; *Dom. ann. reg.*, 1885; *Cyc. Am. biog.*]

Dunn, Thomas (1729-1818), president and administrator of Lower Canada (1805-07 and 1811), was an English merchant who came to Quebec during the period of military rule. From 1764 to 1774 he was a member of the Executive Council of the province of Quebec; and from 1775 to 1791 he was a member of the Legislative Council. After 1791 he became a member of both the Executive and Legislative Councils of Lower Canada; and during five different periods he was president of the Legislative Council. As the senior councillor, he was president and administrator of the province on two occasions, first during the interval between the departure of Sir Robert Milnes (q.v.) in 1805 and the arrival of Sir James Craig (q.v.) in 1807, and secondly in 1811 between the departure of Craig and the arrival of Sir George Prevost (q.v.). In 1775 he was appointed a puisne judge of the Court of King's Bench in Quebec; and he died at Quebec on April 5, 1818. He married a French Canadian, Mme. Henriette Fargues, *née* Guichaud; and his son William became a major-general in the British army.

[*Cyc. Am. biog.*; Morgan, *Cel. Can.*; Le Jeune, *Dict. gén.*; R. Christie, *History of Lower Canada* (6 vols., Quebec and Montreal, 1848-56); F. J. Audet, *Gouverneurs, lieutenant-gouverneurs, et administrateurs de la province de Québec* (Trans. Roy. Soc. Can., 1908).]

Dunning, Charles Avery (1885-1958), politician and financier, was born in Leicestershire, England, on July 31, 1885, and came to Canada as an immigrant at the age of seventeen. He began as a farm-hand in Saskatchewan, became a homesteader, and took part in the Grain Growers' Movement in Saskatchewan. He was elected a member of the legislature in 1912, became minister of agriculture in 1919, and prime minister of the province in 1922. In 1926 he resigned as prime minister of Saskatchewan to accept the post of minister of railways and canals in the Mackenzie King government at Ottawa. He became minister of finance in 1929, and was defeated at the polls in 1930, but resumed his post of minister of finance after the Liberal victory of 1935. His health brought about his retirement from politics, however, in 1939; and his last years were devoted to looking after his business at Montreal. He died at Montreal on October 1, 1958. In 1940 he was chosen as chancellor of Queen's University, Kingston; and the honorary degree of LL.D. was conferred on him by several Canadian universities.

[*Can. who's who*, 1955-57; *Encyc. Can.*]

Dunsmuir, James (1851-1920), prime minister of British Columbia (1900-02) and lieutenant-governor (1906-09), was born at Fort Vancouver, Washington, on July 8, 1851, the son of Robert Dunsmuir (q.v.) and Joanna White. He was educated at the Collegiate, Hamilton, Ontario, and at the Military School, Blackburg, Virginia. He entered his father's business, and in 1889 inherited his father's great wealth. From 1898 to 1902 he rep-

resented East Yale in the Legislative Assembly of British Columbia as a Conservative; and from 1900 to 1902 he was prime minister of the province, and president of the council. In 1906 he was appointed lieutenant-governor of British Columbia; but he resigned in 1909. He died at Cowichan, British Columbia, on June 6, 1920. In 1908 he was elected a director of the Canadian Pacific Railway. He married in 1876 Laura, daughter of W. B. Surles, of Fayetteville, North Carolina.

[*Can. who was who*, vol. 2; Morgan, *Can. men* (1912); *Can. parl. comp.*; Le Jeune, *Dict. gén.*; J. B. Kerr, *A biographical dictionary of well-known British Columbians* (Vancouver, B.C., 1890).]

Dunsmuir, Robert (1825-1889), president of the council of British Columbia (1887-89), was born in Hurlford, Ayrshire, Scotland, in 1825, the son of an Ayrshire "coal master". He emigrated to British Columbia about 1850, as a coal-mining expert, and was employed for a number of years by the Vancouver Coal Company. He discovered a rich vein of coal at Wellington, British Columbia, and this coal mine was the basis of a large fortune. He became president of the Esquimalt and Nanaimo Railway; and there was hardly an enterprise of any magnitude in British Columbia in which he was not financially interested. In 1882 he was elected to represent Nanaimo in the Legislative Assembly of British Columbia; and in 1886 he became president of the council in the A. E. B. Davie administration. He died at Victoria, British Columbia, on April 12, 1889. In 1847 he married Joanna, daughter of Alexander White, of Kilmarnock, Scotland.

[*Can. who was who*, vol. 2; J. B. Kerr, *Biographical dictionary of well-known British Columbians* (Vancouver, B.C., 1890); *Can. parl. comp.*; J. Audain, *From coal mine to castle* (New York, 1955).]

Duplessis, Maurice (1890-1959), prime minister of Quebec (1936-39 and 1944-59), was born at Three Rivers, Quebec, on April 20, 1890. He was educated at Laval University (B.A., 1911; LL.B., 1913), and was called to the Quebec bar in 1913 (K.C., 1931). He practised law in Three Rivers, and in 1937 was elected *bâtonnier* of the Quebec bar. In 1927 he was elected to represent Three Rivers in the Quebec legislature as a Conservative, and in 1933 he became leader of the Conservative party in Quebec. He reorganized his supporters as the Union Nationale party; and in the election this party was returned with a large majority, and Duplessis became prime minister and attorney-general. He and the Union Nationale party were defeated in the elections of 1939; but they came back to power in 1944, and from this date until his sudden death at Schefferville, Quebec, on September 7, 1959, he had no rival near the throne. He carried the province like a dictator in the elections of

1948, 1952, and 1956. After his death, the Union Nationale fell on evil days, and was defeated in the elections of 1960. Over Duplessis's record as an administrator and politician there will probably always be a good deal of controversy.

[P. Laporte, *Le vrai visage de Duplessis* (Montreal, 1960); L. Roberts, *The chief: A political biography of Maurice Duplessis* (Toronto, 1963); R. Rumilly, *Maurice Duplessis et son temps* (Montreal, 1973); C. Black, *Duplessis* (Toronto, 1977); *Can. who's who*, 1958-60; *Can. parl. comp.*, 1959; *Encyc. Can.*]

Du Pont, François Gravé, Sieur (*fl.* 1554-1629), sailor and trader, was born at St. Malo, France, in 1554. He became interested in the Canadian fur-trade, and was connected with almost all the early attempts at colonization in Canada. He was an associate of Chauvin in 1599, of Monts (q.v.) in 1604-07, of Champlain (q.v.) in 1608-23. He was in Quebec in 1629, but thereafter he disappears from view.

[H. P. Biggar, *The early trading companies of New France* (Toronto, 1900); *Cyc. Am. biog.*; Le Jeune, *Dict. gén.*; *Dict. Can. biog.*, vol. 1.]

Dupré, Maurice (1888-1941), solicitor-general of Canada (1930-35), was born at Lévis, Quebec, on March 20, 1888, the son of H. Edmond Dupré and Marie Emilie, daughter of the Hon. J. G. Blanchet (q.v.). He was educated at Laval University (LL.L., 1911), was called to the bar of Quebec in 1911 (K.C., 1922), and practised law in Quebec. He represented Quebec West in the Canadian House of Commons from 1930 to 1935, and during this period he was solicitor-general in the Bennett administration. He was a Canadian delegate to the Imperial Conference in 1930 and to the Assembly of the League of Nations at Geneva in 1932. His death occurred at Three Rivers, Quebec, on October 3, 1941.

[*Can. who's who*, 1935-37; *Can. parl. comp.*; P. G. Roy, *La famille Le Compte Dupré* (Lévis, Que., 1941).]

Dupuis, Nathan Fellowes (1836-1917), scientist, was born in Portland township, Frontenac county, Upper Canada, on April 13, 1836, the son of Joseph Dupuis. He was educated at Queen's University, Kingston (B.A., 1866; M.A., 1868; LL.D., 1911), and became professor of mathematics, and later dean of the faculty of applied science, at Queen's University. He retired from this position in 1911, and he died at Long Beach, California, on July 20, 1917. He was a charter member of the Royal Society of Canada; and was the author of *Elements of geometrical optics* (Kingston, 1868), *Junior algebra* (Kingston, 1882), *Geometry of the point, line, and circle in the plane* (London,

1889), *Principles of elementary algebra* (London, 1893), *Elements of trigonometry* (Kingston, 1902), *Elements of astronomy* (Kingston, 1910), and *Measurement of time* (Kingston, 1917).

[*Can. who was who*, vol. 1; Morgan, *Can. men* (1912); *Queen's quarterly*, 1917.]

Dupuy, Claude Thomas (1687-1738), intendant of New France (1726-28), was born on December 10, 1687, in France. He became an advocate in the Châtelet of Paris, King's councillor, advocate-general in the grand council, and "maître des requêtes". He was named intendant of New France in October, 1725, and took possession of his office on September 2, 1726. During his period of office he was involved in constant quarrels with the governor and the bishop; and he was recalled in 1728, and sailed for France on October 1. He died in France on September 15, 1738.

[H. M. Thomas, *A Canadian pooh-bah* (Dalhousie review, 1927); R. Roy, *Les intendants de la Nouvelle-France* (Trans. Roy. Soc. Can., 1903); J. C. Dubé, *Claude-Thomas Dupuy, intendant de la Nouvelle-France, 1678-1738* (Montreal, 1968); Le Jeune, *Dict. gén.*; *Dict. Can. biog.*, vol. 2.]

Duquesne, Michel Ange Duquesne-Menneville, Marquis de (1701-1778), governor of New France (1752-55), was the son of Alexandre Duquesne-Monnier and Ursule Possel. He entered the navy at an early age, and became successively ensign (1727), lieutenant (1735), and major (1746). On March 1, 1752, he was appointed governor of New France, and was given the title of Marquis. His policy as governor was to intercept communication between New England and the western Indians, and in 1753 he sent a force to the Ohio district to build forts and institute war if necessary. Owing to disease, the troops were forced to return; nevertheless, the Indians were brought into submission to the French. Duquesne resigned his governorship in 1755, and returned to France. In January, 1763, he was made a commander of St. Louis. He retired from service on April 8, 1776, and died at Anthony (Seine) on September 17, 1778.

[R. Roy, *Le gouverneur Du Quesne* (Bull. rech. hist., vol. xii); Le Jeune, *Dict. gén.*]

Duquet, Joseph Norbert (1828-1891), journalist and author, was born at St. Charles de Bellechasse, Lower Canada, on October 7, 1828, became a journalist in Quebec, and died at Quebec on August 10, 1891. He was the author of *Le petit véritable Albert, ou Secret pour acquérir un trésor* (Quebec, 1861).

[Morgan, *Bib. can.*; *Bull. rech. hist.*, 1928.]

Durand, Charles (1811-1905), author, was born near the site of the present city of Hamilton, Ontario, on April 9, 1811, the son of James

Durand; and he died at Toronto, Ontario, on August 16, 1905. He published his *Reminiscences* (Toronto, 1897).

[Toronto *Globe*, Aug. 17, 1905.]

Durand, Evelyn (1870-1900), poetess, was born in Toronto, Ontario, in 1870, the daughter of Charles Durand (q.v.), and died at Boulder, Colorado, on December 5, 1900. She was educated at the University of Toronto (B.A., 1896); and some of her literary remains were published posthumously by her sister, Laura Durand (q.v.), under the title, *Elise Le Beau, a dramatic idyll, and lyrics and sonnets* (Toronto, 1921).

[*University of Toronto monthly*, 1901.]

Durand, Laura Bradshaw (1865-1925), journalist, was born in Toronto in 1865, the daughter of Charles Durand (q.v.). She joined the staff of the Toronto *Globe* in 1894, and became its literary editor. She wrote under the *nom de plume* of "Pharos", and conducted under that name a page for children. She died on July 10, 1925.

[Morgan, *Can. men and women* (1912).]

Durell, Philip (1707-1766), naval officer, was a native of England who entered the British navy, and rose to the rank of captain in 1742. In 1758 he was appointed commander-in-chief of the fleet centred at Halifax, and his soundings of the St. Lawrence in 1759 made possible the success of Admiral Saunders (q.v.) in passing his ships up the river to Quebec. He was promoted to be vice-admiral of the blue in 1762, and was appointed to command the American station. His death occurred at Halifax, Nova Scotia, in August, 1766.

[E. Arma Smillie, *The achievement of Durell in 1759* (Trans. Roy. Soc. Can., 1925); Le Jeune, *Dict. gén.*; *Dict. Can biog.*, vol. 3.]

Durham, John George Lambton, first Earl of (1792-1840), governor-in-chief of British North America and lord high commissioner (1838), was born in London, England, on April 12, 1792, the eldest son of William Henry Lambton, M.P., and Lady Anne Barbara Frances Villiers, second daughter of George, fourth Earl of Jersey. He was educated at Eton, and in 1809 entered the army as a cornet in the 10th Hussars. In 1813 he was elected to the House of Commons for the county of Durham; and he continued to represent this constituency in parliament until his elevation to the peerage as Baron Durham in 1828. He was a pronounced radical, his popular sobriquet being "Radical Jack'; and the Reform Bill of 1832 was first drafted in his house. In 1830 he became lord privy seal in the Grey administration; but in 1833 ill-health compelled his resignation of office. In 1835-37 he was British ambassador at St. Petersburg; and

he had hardly returned from Russia when he was invited by the Melbourne ministry to assume the government of Canada. He at first declined the offer; but, after the outbreak of the rebellions of 1837 in Upper and Lower Canada, he yielded to the personal solicitations of Queen Victoria, and was appointed governor-in-chief of British North America, with extraordinary powers as lord high commissioner.

He arrived in Canada on May 28, 1838, and he resigned his office on September 28, just four months later, because of the disallowance by the Melbourne government of his ordinance dealing with the political prisoners in Canada. His actual departure from the country took place on November 1, 1838. Yet in these few months he and his staff instituted inquiries which resulted in his famous *Report on the affairs of British North America* (2 vols., London, 1839; new ed., by Sir C. P. Lucas, 3 vols., Oxford, 1912), a classic of English political literature. The recommendations made in this report led to the union of Upper and Lower Canada in 1841, the introduction of "responsible government" and municipal government in Canada, and the growth of Canadian national feeling. The report did less than justice to the French Canadians, but in view of the circumstances of the time that was perhaps not surprising.

Durham's Canadian experience undermined his health, never robust, and he had hardly completed his report when his health broke down. He died at Cowes, in the Isle of Wight, on July 28, 1840. He married, first, in 1812, Henriette Cholmondeley (d. 1815), natural daughter of Lord Cholmondeley, by whom he had three daughters; and, secondly, in 1816, Lady Louisa Elizabeth Grey, eldest daughter of Charles, second Earl Grey, by whom he had two sons. He was created first Earl of Durham on his resignation of the office of lord privy seal in 1833.

[C. W. New, *Lord Durham* (Oxford, 1929); W. Smith, *Lord Durham's administration* (Can. hist. rev., 1927); S. J. Reid, *Life and letters of the first Earl of Durham*, London, 1906); L. Cooper, *Radical Jack: The life of the First Earl of Durham* (London, 1959); R. Garnett, *The authorship of Lord Durham's Canada report* (Eng. hist. rev., 1902); *Dict. nat. biog.*; F. Bradshaw, *Self-government in Canada* (London, 1903); Sir C. P. Lucas (ed.), *Lord Durham's Report* (3 vols., Oxford, 1912); J. L. Morison, *British supremacy and colonial self-government* (Glasgow, 1919).]

Duvernay, Ludger (1799-1852), journalist, was born at Verchères, Lower Canada, in 1799. From 1817 to 1827 he was a journalist at Three Rivers. In 1827 he acquired *La Minerve*, a Montreal newspaper, and it became the mouthpiece of the *patriote* party. In 1837 he was elected to represent Lachenaye in the

Legislative Assembly of Lower Canada; at the time of the rebellion he took refuge at Burlington, Vermont; and there he published the *Patriote*. He died at Montreal on November 28, 1852. In 1834 he founded the Société St. Jean Baptiste; and he is said to have been the first to suggest the maple leaf as the national emblem of Canada. His papers have been published in the *Canadian Antiquarian and Numismatic Journal*, 1908-09.

[*Cyc. Am. biog.*; Abbé Daniel, *Histoire des grandes familles françaises du Canada* (Montreal, 1867); Bibaud, *Panth. can.*; Le Jeune, *Dict. gén.*]

DuVernet, Frederick Herbert (1860-1924), Anglican archbishop of Caledonia, and metropolitan of British Columbia, was born at Hemmingford, Quebec, on January 20, 1860, the son of the Rev. Canon DuVernet and Francis Eliza Ellegood. He was educated at King's College, Windsor, Nova Scotia, and at the University of Toronto; and was ordained a priest of the Church of England in 1883. From 1885 to 1895 he was a professor in Wycliffe College, Toronto; and from 1895 to 1904 rector of St. John's Church, Toronto Junction. In 1904 he was consecrated bishop of Caledonia (British Columbia); and in 1915 he became archbishop of Caledonia and metropolitan of British Columbia. He died at Prince Rupert, British Columbia, on October 22, 1924. In 1885 he married Stella, daughter of Horatio Yates, M.D., of Kingston, Ontario. He was a D.D. of Trinity University (1904), of King's College, Windsor (1905), and of Wycliffe College, Toronto (1921). After his death there was published a book by him entitled *Out of a scribe's treasure* (Toronto, 1927).

[*Can. who was who*, vol. 1; Morgan, *Can. men* (1912).]

Dyde, Samuel Walters (1862-1947), educationist, was born at Ottawa, Ontario, on March 11, 1862, and died at Edmonton, Alberta, on January 22, 1947. He was educated at Queen's University (B.A., 1883; M.A., 1884; D.Sc., 1887) and in Germany. From 1886 to 1889 he was professor of mental and moral philosophy at the University of New Brunswick; and from 1889 to 1911, professor of mental philosophy at Queen's University. He then became principal of Robertson College at Edmonton, but in 1918 he returned to Queen's as principal of the Queen's Theological College. In 1900 the University of New Brunswick conferred on him the LL.D. degree. He published several small volumes of verse: *War verses* (Kingston, 1924), *From my gallery* (Kingston, 1925), *A year* (Kingston, 1927), and *The highway* (Kingston, 1928).

[*Can. who's who*, 1936-37; Morgan, *Can. men* (1912).]

Dymond, Alfred Hutchinson (1827-1903), journalist, politician, and educationist, was born at Croydon, Surrey, England, on August 2, 1827. He became a journalist in London; but in 1869 he emigrated to Canada, and obtained employment on the editorial staff of the Toronto *Globe*. From 1874 to 1878 he represented North York as a Liberal in the Canadian House of Commons. In 1881 he was appointed principal of the Ontario Institute for the Education of the Blind, at Brantford, Ontario; and he remained in this post until his death at Brantford, on May 11, 1903.

[Morgan, *Can. men* (1898); Rose, *Cyc. Can. biog.* (1888); *Can. parl. comp.*]

Dyonnet, Edmond (1859-1954), painter, was born in France in 1859, and died in Montreal, Quebec, on July 8, 1954. He came to Canada in 1874, settled in Montreal, and lived there for the rest of his life. He became a successful portrait painter and art teacher; was elected an A.R.C.A. in 1892 and an R.C.A. in 1901; and was secretary of the Royal Canadian Academy from 1910 to 1948. He was the author, with H. C. Jones, of a *History of the Royal Canadian Academy of Arts* (Montreal, 1934), published in mimeographed form; and he was also the author of an autobiography, entitled *Memories of a Canadian artist* (Montreal, 1951), a copy of the French text of which was deposited in the Bibliothèque Cinque in Montreal, and an English translation in the Westmount Public Library.

[*Can. who's who*, 1952-54; *Encyc. Can.*; N. MacTavish, *The fine arts in Canada* (Toronto, 1926).]

Eakins, William George (1854-1913), librarian, was born at Vienna, Ontario, on November 16, 1854, and was educated at the University of Toronto (B.A., 1876; M.A., 1877). He was called to the bar in 1880, but after practising law in Woodstock, Ontario, for several years, he became a leader-writer on the staff of the Toronto *Mail*. In 1891 he was appointed librarian at the Law Society of Upper Canada, at Osgoode Hall, Toronto, and he retained this position until his death at Toronto on December 31, 1913. He was the author of a valuable *Bibliography of Canadian statute law* (Index to Legal Periodicals and Law Library Journal, Chicago, 1908, pp. 61-71).

[Morgan, *Can. men* (1912).]

Eaton, Arthur Wentworth Hamilton (1849-1937), clergyman and author, was born at Kentville, Nova Scotia, on December 10, 1849. He was educated at Harvard University (B.A., 1880), and was ordained in 1885 a priest of the Protestant Episcopal Church. For many years he was head of the department of English literature at the Cutler School in New York; and he lived in the United States, first in New York, and then after 1907 in Boston, until his death at Boston on July 11, 1937. He returned to Nova Scotia, however, annually; and most of his writings have reference to Nova Scotia. He was the author of *Genealogical sketch of the Nova Scotia Eatons* (Halifax, N.S., 1885), *The heart of the creeds* (New York, 1888), *Acadian legends and lyrics* (New York, 1889), *The Church of England in Nova Scotia and the Tory clergy of the revolution* (New York, 1891), *Acadian ballads and De Soto's last dream* (New York, 1905), *Poems of the Christian year* (New York, 1905), *The lotus of the Nile, and other poems* (New York, 1907), *The history of King's county, Nova Scotia* (Salem, Mass., 1910), *The famous Mather Byles* (Boston, 1914), *The Eaton family of Nova Scotia* (Cambridge, Mass., 1929), and *Acadian ballads and lyrics in many moods* (Toronto, 1930); and he was joint editor, with C. L. Betts, of *Tales of a garrison town* (New York, 1892).

[*Coll. Nova Scotia Hist. Soc.*, vol. 24 (1938); *Who was who in America*; Morgan, *Can. men* (1912); R. J. Long, *Nova Scotia authors* (East Orange, N.J., 1918).]

Eaton, Edith (1867-1914), author, was born in 1867, and died at Montreal, Quebec, on April 7, 1914. She was the author of *Mrs. Spring Fragrance* (Chicago, 1912).

[Private information.]

Eaton, Flora McCrae (1881-1970), philanthropist, wife of Sir John Craig Eaton (q.v.), was born at Omemee, Ontario, in 1881 and on completing high school there went to Toronto for nursing training. She married John Eaton in 1901 and devoted her life to her family and her various charities, including the Toronto Symphony Orchestra, the Institute for the Blind, Children's Welfare, and numerous other worthy projects. She was a director of the T. Eaton Company and vice-president and director of the Eaton Knitting Company Limited. In 1956, she wrote *Memory's wall*, her autobiography, for her grandchildren. She died at Toronto, July 9, 1970.

[*Can. who's who*, 1967-69.]

Eaton, Sir John Craig (1876-1922), merchant and philanthropist, was born in Toronto, Ontario, on April 28, 1876, the third son of Timothy Eaton (q.v.) and Margaret Beattie. He received his education at the Model School and Upper Canada College, Toronto, and as a young man he entered business in the departmental store which his father had founded. In 1898 he became a director of the T. Eaton Company; and in 1900, on the death of his elder brother, Edward Young Eaton, he became vice-president. In 1907, on his father's death, he succeeded his father as president; and he continued at the head of the business for the rest of his life. A man of great wealth, he was famous for his benefactions; and during the First World War he contributed in many different ways to the Allied cause. For his war services, he was created in 1915 a knight bachelor. He died at Toronto on March 30, 1922. In 1901 he married Flora, (q.v.), daughter of John McCrae, of Omemee, Ontario; they had four sons and one daughter.

[H. Charlesworth (ed.), *A cyclopaedia of Canadian biography* (Toronto, 1919); Morgan, *Can. men* (1912); J. E. Middleton and others, *The municipality of Toronto* (3 vols., Toronto, 1923).]

Eaton, John David (1909-1973), merchant, was born in Toronto, Ontario, October 4, 1909, son of John Craig (q.v.) and Flora (McCrae) Eaton (q.v.). He was educated at Stowe School in England and at Cambridge University. He joined the T. Eaton Company in 1930, became a director in 1934, vice-president in 1937, and president in 1942. Under his direction plans were laid for the Eaton Centre, replacing many of the old Eaton buildings in downtown Toronto. He was associated with the Royal Winter Fair and with many philanthropic causes including the Crippled Children's Centre, the Toronto General Hospital, and the Salvation Army. He died at Toronto, Ontario, August 4, 1973.

[*Can. who's who*, 1967-69.]

Eaton, Timothy (1834-1907), merchant, was born in 1834 near Ballymena, county Antrim, Ireland, the posthumous son of John Eaton, a farmer. He came to Canada about 1854, and eventually went into partnership with two of his elder brothers, Robert and James Eaton, who had established a general shop at St. Mary's, Ontario. In 1868 he removed to Toronto and here went first into the dry-goods business, until in 1869 he established the firm of T. Eaton and Company. By selling at a fixed price and for cash, he revolutionized commercial methods at that time, and built up one of the largest departmental stores on the North American continent. He died in Toronto on January 31, 1907. In 1862 he married Margaret Beattie of Woodstock, Ontario; and by her he had three sons and three daughters.

[G. G. Nasmith, *Timothy Eaton* (Toronto, 1923); M. E. Macpherson, *Shopkeepers to a nation: The Eatons* (Toronto, 1963); Morgan, *Can. men* (1898).]

Eaton, Wyatt (1849-1896), painter, was born at Phillipsburg, Lake Champlain, Lower Canada, on May 6, 1849. He studied at the National Academy of Design, New York, and in the *atelier* of Gérôme at the Beaux Arts, Paris. He became a friend of the painter Millet (see his "Recollections of J. F. Millet" in the *Century Magazine*, vol. xvi); and exhibited in the Paris Salon. In 1873 he returned to New York, and there for many years he taught and painted. In 1892 he returned to Canada, and painted a number of Canadian portraits. His health gave out, however, and on June 7, 1896, he died at Newport, Rhode Island.

[*Can. who was who*, vol. 2; *Dict. Am. biog.*; *Cyc. Am. biog.*; E. Morris, *Art in Canada: The early painters* (Toronto, 1911); N. MacTavish, *The fine arts in Canada* (Toronto, 1925).]

Eayrs, Hugh Smithurst (1894-1940), publisher, was born at Leeds, England, on March 11, 1894. He came to Canada in 1912, and entered the service of the Macmillan Company of Canada. Of this company he became president in 1921; and in this capacity he did a great deal to encourage the production of Canadian literature. He died in Toronto, Ontario, on April 19, 1940. He was the author of *Sir Isaac Brock* (Toronto, 1917), and he was joint author of *The amateur diplomat* (Toronto, 1916).

[*Can. who's who*, 1936-37.]

Eccles, Henry (1817-1863), lawyer, was born at Bath, England, in 1817, the son of Capt. Hugh Eccles, of the 61st Regiment. He came to Canada with his parents as a child, and was educated in York (Toronto), Upper Canada. He was called to the bar of Upper Canada in 1842, and became perhaps the best-known special pleader among the Canadian counsel of his day. He was elected a bencher of the Law Society of Upper Canada in 1853, and was created a Q.C. in 1856. He died at Toronto on November 2, 1863.

[*Solicitor's journal and reporter*, vol. 8 (1863), p.71.]

Eddy, Ezra Butler (1827-1906), manufacturer, was born near Bristol, Vermont, on August 22, 1827, the son of Samuel Eddy and Clarissa Eastman. In 1851 he embarked on the manufacture of friction matches at Burlington, Vermont; and in 1854 he removed to Hull, Canada East, where he built up one of the largest match factories in the world. In 1886 he reorganized the business as the E. B. Eddy Co., and became its president. From 1871 to 1875 he represented Ottawa county in the Legislative Assembly of Quebec. He died at Hull, Quebec, on February 12, 1906.

[Morgan, *Can. men* (1898).]

Edgar, Sir James David (1841-1899), speaker of the Canadian House of Commons (1896-99), was born at Hatley, Lower Canada, on August 10, 1841, the son of James Edgar and Grace Fleming. He was educated at Lennoxville, Lower Canada, and at Quebec; and in 1864, having moved to Toronto, he was called to the bar of Upper Canada (Q.C., 1890). He was elected to the House of Commons in 1872 as Liberal member for Monck; and he was chief Liberal whip during the parliamentary crisis of 1873, which culminated in the downfall of Sir John Macdonald (q.v.). In 1874 he was defeated at the polls; and he did not return to the House of Commons until 1884. He was then elected by acclamation in West Ontario; and this constituency he represented continuously for the rest of his life. He was from 1884 to 1896 one of the leaders of the Liberal party in parliament; and in 1896 he was chosen speaker of the House of Commons. He died at Toronto on July 31, 1899. In 1865, he married Matilda, daughter of Thomas Gibbs Ridout (q.v.); and by her he had six sons and three daughters. In 1897 he was elected a member of the Royal Society of Canada; and he was the author of a volume of verse, *This Canada of ours* (Toronto,

1893), and a descriptive work, *Canada and its capital* (Toronto, 1898). In 1898 he was created a K.C.M.G.

[*Who was who*, 1897-1916; *Can. parl. comp.*; *Proc. Roy. Soc. Can.*, 1900; Morgan, *Can. men* (1898); Rose, *Cyc. Can. biog.* (1888).]

Edgar, Matilda, Lady (1844-1910), historian, was born in Toronto on September 29, 1844, the second daughter of Thomas Gibbs Ridout (q.v.). In 1865 she married James David (afterwards Sir James) Edgar (q.v.); and she died in London, England, on September 29, 1910. She was the author of *Ten years of Upper Canada in peace and war* (Toronto, 1895), *General Brock* (Toronto, 1904), and *A colonial governor in Maryland* (London, 1912).

[H. J. Morgan (ed.), *Types of Canadian women* (Toronto, 1903).]

Edgar, Oscar Pelham (1871-1948), educationist and author, was born in Toronto, Ontario, on March 17, 1871, the son of Sir James David Edgar and Lady Edgar (qq.v.), and died at Canton, Ontario, on October 7, 1948. He was educated at Upper Canada College, at the University of Toronto (B.A., 1892), and at Johns Hopkins University (Ph.D., 1897). In 1897 he was appointed professor of French in Victoria College, Toronto; and in 1902, professor of English. This chair he occupied until his retirement in 1938. He was elected a fellow of the Royal Society of Canada in 1915; and he was the author of *Henry James, man and author* (Boston, 1927) and *The art of the novel* (New York, 1933). Some autobiographical materials by him were published after his death, under the title, *Across my path* (Toronto, 1952), edited by Northrop Frye. A striking portrait of him was painted by Alan Barr (q.v.).

[*Proc. Roy. Soc. Can.*, 1949; *Can. who's who*, 1948; *Encyc. Can.*]

Edmunds, Frederic Harrison (1898-1965), geologist, was born in Hawarden, Flintshire, North Wales, on January 27, 1898. He served in the Special Brigade, Royal Engineers, during the First World War and later attended the University of Liverpool (B.Sc., 1922; M.Sc., 1923). In 1925 he left England and joined the soils department of the University of Saskatchewan, transferring in 1929 to the department of geology. Professor Edmunds undertook a comprehensive study of the glacial geology of Saskatchewan and was involved in the early development of the Lloydminster Oil Field. In 1952 he was appointed to the Saskatchewan Oil and Gas Conservation Board and in 1961 he became chairman of the department of geological sciences at the University of Saskatchewan. He was a fellow of the Royal Society of Canada, a fellow of the Geological Society (London), a fellow of the Geological Society of America, and a member of the council of the Canadian Institute of Mining and Metallurgy of the Geological Association of Canada. At the University of Saskatchewan he was very interested in theatre and was largely responsible for the creation there of the first department of drama in Canada. He died on February 28, 1965.

[*Proc. Roy. Soc. Can.*, 1965.]

Edson, Allan (1846-1888), landscape painter, was born at Stanbridge, Missiquoi county, Lower Canada, in 1848. He studied painting in Paris, France, under Pelouse; and on his return to Canada he became a charter member of the Royal Canadian Academy and of the Ontario Society of Artists. He died in 1888.

[N. MacTavish, *The fine arts in Canada* (Toronto, 1925); H. G. Jones and E. Dyonnet, *History of the Royal Canadian Academy of Arts* (Montreal, 1934); Le Jeune, *Dict. gén.*]

Edwards, John Wesley (1865-1929), minister of immigration and colonization for Canada (1921), was born in Storrington township, Frontenac county, Ontario, on May 25, 1865, the son of George Edwards and Elizabeth Jane Lyon. He was educated at the Ottawa Normal School, and was for ten years a school-teacher; but he subsequently graduated from Queen's University, Kingston (B.A., 1900; M.D., 1900). From 1908 to 1921, and from 1926 to 1929, he represented Frontenac in the Canadian House of Commons; and from September 21 to December 6, 1921, he was minister of immigration and colonization and minister of health in the Meighen administration. From 1921 to 1923 he was grand master of the Grand Orange Lodge of eastern Ontario. He died at Ottawa on April 18, 1929.

[*Can. parl. comp.*; Morgan *Can. men* (1912); H. Charlesworth (ed.), *A cyclopaedia of Canadian biography* (Toronto, 1919).]

Edwards, Joseph Plimsoll (1857-1930), historian, was born in 1857, and lived first in Montreal, and later in Londonderry and Halifax, Nova Scotia. He died at Halifax, on February 3, 1930. He was the author of a number of historical papers and pamphlets, notably, *Louisbourg: An historical sketch* (Halifax, N.S., 1895), and *The public records of Nova Scotia* (Halifax, N.S., 1920).

[Morgan, *Can. men* (1912); *Can. who was who*, vol. 2.]

Edwards, Robert Chambers (1864-1922), journalist, was born on September 12, 1864, at Edinburgh, Scotland, the son of Alexander Mackenzie Edwards and Mary Chambers. He was educated at St. Andrew's, Fife, and at Glasgow University; and he came to Canada in 1895. He settled in Calgary, Alberta; and he issued at irregular intervals, for many years, the *Calgary Eye-opener*, a paper which, by reason of its unconventional character, became famous all over Canada. He also published a humorous annual, known as *Bob Edwards' Annual*. In 1921 he was elected as an independent to represent Calgary in the Legislative Assembly of Alberta; but he died at Calgary on November 14, 1922. He was married in 1918, but died without issue.

[R. G. Riddell (ed.), *Canadian portraits* (Toronto, 1940); *Can. parl. comp.*; J. W. G. MacEwan, *Eye-opener Bob: The story of Bob Edwards* (Edmonton, 1957).]

Edwards, William Cameron (1844-1921), senator of Canada, was born in the township of Clarence, Russell county, Upper Canada, on May 7, 1844, the son of William Edwards, a native of Portsmouth, England. He was educated at the Ottawa grammar school; and in 1868 he founded the firm of W. C. Edwards and Co., lumber merchants. From 1887 to 1903 he represented Russell as a Liberal in the Canadian House of Commons; and in 1903 he was summoned to the Senate. He died at Ottawa on September 17, 1921. In 1885 he married Catherine, daughter of William Wilson, of Cumberland, Ontario.

[*Can. parl. comp.*; Morgan, *Can. men* (1912); H. Charlesworth (ed.), *A cyclopaedia of Canadian biography* (Toronto, 1919).]

Egan, Sir Henry Kelly (1848-1925), capitalist, was born at Aylmer, Canada East, on January 15, 1848, the son of John Egan and Anne Gibson. He was educated at the Montreal High School, and went into the lumbering business. He was one of the founders, and became managing director, of the Hawkesbury Lumber Company; and he became interested in a variety of projects in the Ottawa Valley. He died at Ottawa on October 19, 1925. In 1878 he married Harriet Augusta, daughter of W. A. Himsworth, clerk of the Queen's Privy Council in Canada. He was created a knight bachelor in 1914.

[*Who was who*, 1916-28.]

Egbert, William (1857-1936), lieutenant-governor of Alberta (1926-31), was born in Welland county, Canada West, on February 25, 1857. He was educated at the University of Toronto (M.B., 1889), and practised medicine in Calgary, Alberta. From 1917 to 1925 he was president of the Alberta Liberal Association; and in 1926 he was appointed lieutenant-governor of Alberta. He retired from office in 1931; and he died at Calgary, Alberta, on October 15, 1936.

[*Can. parl. comp.*]

Elder, Samuel (1817-1853), clergyman and poet, was born at Halifax, Nova Scotia, on February 6, 1817. He was educated at Acadia College (B.A., 1844), and was ordained a minister of the Baptist Church in 1845. While an undergraduate, he read at college gatherings some poems that gave great promise, notably one on "The expulsion of the Acadians". He died at Philadephia, Pa., on May 23, 1853.

[*Records of the graduates of Acadia University* (Wolfville, N.S., 1926); R. J. Long, *Nova Scotia authors* (East Orange, N.J., 1918); Morgan, *Bib. can.*]

Elder, William (1784-1848), clergyman and author, was born in Hants county, Nova Scotia, in 1784. He became a Baptist minister, but in 1834 took orders in the Church of England. In 1848 he died in Cape Breton. He was the author of *Infant baptism weighed in the balance and found wanting* (Halifax, N.S., 1823), and *A series of letters on infant baptism* (Halifax, N.S., 1834).

[Morgan, *Bib. can.*]

Elgin, James Bruce, eighth Earl of (1811-1863), governor-general of British North America (1847-54), was born in London, England, on July 20, 1811, the eldest son of Thomas, seventh Earl of Elgin, and his second wife, Elizabeth, daughter of J. T. Oswald, of Dunnikier, Fifeshire, Scotland. He was educated at Eton and at Christ Church, Oxford (B.A., 1833; M.A., 1835); and in 1833 was elected a fellow of Merton College, Oxford. In 1840, on the death of his elder brother, he became heir to the earldom of Elgin in the Scottish peerage, and in 1841, on the death of his father, he succeeded to the peerage. In 1841 he had been elected to the House of Commons for the borough of Southampton in the Tory interest; but his succession to the peerage cut short his parliamentary career, and in 1842 he accepted appointment as governor of Jamaica. His successful administration of this post led in 1846 to the offer by Lord John Russell's Whig government of the governor-generality of British North America. The Colonial Office, under Earl Grey, had decided on giving the principle of "responsible government", as advocated by Lord Durham (q.v.), a fair trial in Canada; and the task of putting the new policy into effect was confided to Elgin. He accepted the appointment, and arrived in Canada on January 30, 1847. He found in office the Draper-Viger government formed by Lord Metcalfe (q.v.), and for over a year he worked in harmony with it, though he made it clear that he was prepared, if necessary, to work in harmony with any other advisers who had the confidence of the Assembly. In the general elections of 1848 the government was defeated; and Elgin thereupon entrusted office to the second Baldwin-Lafontaine administration. To these advisers he gave "all constitutional support", in the face, at the time of the passage of the Rebellion Losses Act of 1849, of violent Tory opposition, culminating in personal attacks on himself and in the burning of the parliament buildings at Montreal. Through his firmness and patience on this oc-

241

casion, the triumph of "responsible government" was assured.

During Elgin's régime four ministries in Canada held power, the Draper-Viger, the Baldwin-Lafontaine, the Hincks-Morin, and the MacNab-Morin administrations; and with all his relations were harmonious. He played a more active part than later governors in some respects; and in 1854 it was largely through his personal diplomacy at Washington that the Reciprocity Treaty of that year was ratified by the United States Senate. But in general he laid down the lines of conduct which all governors-general of Canada have followed since his time.

After leaving Canada, he was twice a special commissioner to China, in 1857-59 and in 1860-61. In 1858 he made an official visit to Japan. In 1859-60 he was postmaster-general in the Palmerston cabinet, and in 1862 he became the viceroy of India. While administering this office, he died at Dhurmsala, in the Himalayas, on November 20, 1863.

In 1841, he married (1) Elizabeth Mary (d. 1843), daughter of C. L. Cumming Bruce, by whom he had two daughters; and in 1846 (2) Lady Mary Louisa Lambton, daughter of the first Earl of Durham (q.v.), by whom he had four sons and one daughter. In 1840 he was created a peer of the United Kingdom with the title of Baron Elgin, was sworn of the privy council, and invested with the Order of the Thistle. In 1856 Oxford University recognized his services in Canada by conferring upon him the degree of D.C.L.

[T. Walrond (ed.), *Letters and journals of James, eighth Earl of Elgin* (London, 1873); *Extracts from the letters of James, Earl of Elgin, to Mary Louisa, Countess of Elgin, 1847-1862* (privately printed, 1864); Sir J. G. Bourinot, *Lord Elgin* (Toronto, 1903); G. M. Wrong, *The Earl of Elgin* (London, 1905); Sir J. M. Lemoine, *Le Comte d'Elgin* (Trans. Roy. Soc. Can., 1894); J. L. Morison, *The eighth Earl of Elgin* (London, 1928); W. P. M. Kennedy, *Lord Elgin* (Toronto, 1926).]

Ellice, Alexander (1743-1805), merchant, was born in 1743, and about 1765 emigrated to New York, where he purchased a partnership in a firm at Schenectady, later known as Phyn, Ellice and Co., which was interested in the fur-trade. In 1774 the headquarters of the firm were transferred to London; and from 1774 to 1779 Alexander Ellice was the partner who looked after the affairs of the firm in Montreal. In 1779 he returned to London, leaving the Montreal office in charge of his younger brother Robert (q.v.); and he died in London on September 29, 1805, possessed of considerable wealth. His will is on file at Somerset House in London. He married a daughter of George Phyn, laird of the Corse of Monelly in Scotland, and thus became the brother-in-law of James Phyn (q.v.), and the uncle by marriage of the Hon. John Forsyth (q.v.) and the Hon. John Richardson (q.v.).

[R. H. Fleming, *Phyn, Ellice and Company of Schenectady* (Contributions to Canadian economics, 1932).]

Ellice, Edward (1781-1863), merchant, was born in 1781, the third son of Alexander Ellice (q.v.). He was educated at Marischall College, Aberdeen (B.A., 1797; M.A., 1800); and he became a partner in the firm of Phyn, Ellices and Inglis, which had become interested in the XY Company in Canada. He was sent to Canada about 1803, and in 1804 became a party to the union of the XY and North West companies. He became a partner in the North West Company, and during the struggle with Lord Selkirk (q.v.) he played a not unimportant part. He was the anonymous author of *The communications of Mercator* (Montreal, 1817), in which the claims of the North West Company were upheld. In 1820-21, he was, with William and Simon McGillivray (q.v.), active in bringing about the union of the North West and the Hudson's Bay companies; and it was actually with him and the McGillivrays that the union was negotiated. On the death of William McGillivray (q.v.) and the failure of the firm of McTavish, McGillivrays, and Co., in 1825, he became the only member of the trio who stood between the Hudson's Bay Company and the claims of the discontented members of the North West Company; and he became involved in a series of litigations which lasted for a quarter of a century. He was made a member of the Committee of the Hudson's Bay Company, however, and a fund, known as the North West Partners' Trust Fund, was set aside to satisfy the claims of those who had just claims on the North West Company. It has frequently been said that he became a deputy-governor of the Hudson's Bay Company, but this is a mistake. It was his son Edward who occupied this position; and it was the son who became in 1857 a member of the committee of the British House of Commons appointed to inquire into the affairs of the Hudson's Bay Company. But the father came to play a conspicuous part in English politics. From 1818 to 1826, and from 1830 to 1863, he represented Coventry in the House of Commons; and from 1830 to 1832 he was secretary to the treasury in Earl Grey's government, and from 1832 to 1834 secretary of war. He died at Ardochy, on his estate in Glengarry, Scotland, on September 17, 1863. He was known as "Bear" Ellice, probably from his connection with the Canadian fur-trade. In 1809 he married Lady Hannah Altheah Bettesworth (d. 1832), widow of Captain Bettesworth, R.N., and youngest sister of the second Earl Grey, and by her he had one son, Edward. In 1843, he married, secondly, Lady Leicester, widow of the first Earl of Leicester; and she died in 1844.

[D. E. T. Long, *The elusive Mr. Ellice* (Can. hist. rev., 1942); *Dict. nat. biog.*]

Ellice, James (d. 1787), merchant, was a younger brother of Alexander Ellice (q.v.), who was left in Schenectady in charge of the affairs of Phyn, Ellice and Company in 1775, after the headquarters of the firm were transferred to London. After suffering "heavy suspicion" and "close confinement", he was allowed to take the oath of allegiance to the State of New York in 1779. He remained for several years in charge of the declining affairs of the Schenectady office of the firm, until his death in Montreal, on October 15, 1787.

[R. H. Fleming, *Phyn, Ellice and Company of Schenectady* (Contributions to Canadian economics, 1932).]

Ellice, Robert (d. 1790), merchant, was a younger brother of Alexander Ellice (q.v.), who was taken into the firm of Phyn, Ellice and Co. in Schenectady in 1768. From 1779 to 1790 he was in charge of the Montreal office of the firm, which was known as Robert Ellice and Co., and in 1787 he became a partner in the London firm of Phyn, Ellices, and Inglis. He died in 1790.

[R. H. Fleming, *Phyn, Ellice and Company of Schenectady* (Contributions to Canadian economics, 1932).]

Elliot, Gilbert John, fourth Earl of Minto. See **Minto, Gilbert John Elliot, fourth Earl of.**

Elliot, Joseph (1810-1885), clergyman, was born in Roxburghshire, Scotland, in 1810, and died at Guelph, Ontario, on September 3, 1885. He was ordained a minister of the Congregational Church in 1836, and was for some years stationed at Bury St. Edmunds, England. He came to Canada about 1855, and in 1875 became a minister of the Presbyterian Church in Canada. He was the author of *Walks about Zion* (Toronto, 1881).

[*Dom. ann. reg.*, 1885.]

Elliott, Andrew Charles (d. 1889), prime minister of British Columbia (1876-78), was born and educated in Ireland, and was called to the English bar in 1854 from Lincoln's Inn. He emigrated to British Columbia in 1859, and in 1860 he was appointed a county court judge. After 1867 he became police magistrate of Victoria; and in 1875 he was elected to represent Victoria in the Legislative Assembly of British Columbia. From 1876 to 1878 he was prime minister of the province, with the portfolios of attorney-general and provincial secretary; but he was defeated in the elections of 1878, and he thereupon retired from political life. He died at San Francisco, California, on April 9, 1889.

[*Can. parl, comp.*, 1878.]

Elliott, John Campbell (1872-1941), postmaster-general of Canada (1935-39), was born in Ekfrid township, Middlesex county, Ontario, on July 25, 1872. He was educated at Trinity University, Toronto (B.C.L., 1898; D.C.L., 1905), and at Osgoode Hall, Toronto; and was called to the bar in Ontario (K.C., 1908). He practised law in London, Ontario; and from 1908 to 1918 he represented Middlesex in the Ontario legislature. From 1925 to 1939 he represented West Middlesex in the Canadian House of Commons; and he held office in the first, second, and third administrations formed by the Right Hon. W. L. Mackenzie King. He was first minister of labour, and then minister of health, in 1926; he was minister of public works from 1926 to 1930; and he was postmaster-general from 1935 until his resignation in 1939. He died at London, Ontario, on December 20, 1941. He was not married.

[*Can. who's who*, 1936-37.]

Ellis, Henry (1721-1806), governor of Nova Scotia (1761-63), was born in England in 1721. In 1746-47 he made a voyage of exploration to Hudson Bay, an account of which was published in his *A voyage to Hudson's bay* (London, 1748); and in 1749 he was elected a fellow of the Royal Society. From 1758 to 1760 he was governor of Georgia; and from 1761 to 1763 he held the commission of governor of Nova Scotia, though he did not enter on the duties of his office. He had much to do with the framing of the Royal Proclamation of 1763, whereby civil government was established in Quebec; and from 1763 to 1769 he held the offices of secretary, clerk of the council, commissary-general, and clerk of the enrolments in the province of Quebec, with power to appoint deputies. He died in Naples, Italy, on January 21, 1806.

[*Dict. nat. biog.*; *Cyc. Am. biog.*]

Ellis, John Valentine (1835-1913), journalist and politician, was born at Halifax, Nova Scotia, on February 14, 1835. He went to Saint John, New Brunswick, in 1857, and founded there the *Saint John Globe*, of which he remained throughout life the proprietor and editor. He represented Saint John in the Legislative Assembly of New Brunswick from 1882 to 1887, and in the Canadian House of Commons from 1887 to 1891 and 1896 to 1900. In 1900 he was called to the Senate of Canada, and he remained a member of the Senate until his death, at Saint John, New Brunswick, on June 10, 1913. He was the author of *New Brunswick as a home for emigrants* (Saint John, N.B., 1860).

[Morgan, *Can. men* (1912); *Can. parl comp.*; W. G. MacFarlane, *New Brunswick bibliography* (Saint John, N.B., 1895).]

Ells, Robert Wheelock (1845-1911), geologist, was born at Sheffield Mills, Nova

Scotia, on July 26, 1845. He was educated at Horton Academy and McGill University (B.A., 1872; M.A., 1875; LL.D., 1887), and in 1872 he joined the staff of the Geological Survey of Canada. He rose in the service of the Survey until he became senior geologist; and in 1893 he was elected a fellow of the Royal Society of Canada. He died at Ottawa, Ontario, on May 23, 1911. In addition to numerous papers printed in the reports of the Geological Survey and in the transactions of the Royal Society of Canada and other learned bodies, he was the author of *A history of New Brunswick geology* (Montreal, 1887) and *The geology and mineral resources of New Brunswick* (Ottawa, 1907).

[*Proc. Roy. Soc. Can.*, 1912; Morgan, *Can. men* (1898).]

Elmsley, John (1762-1805), chief justice of Upper Canada (1796-1802) and of Lower Canada (1802-05), was born in 1762, the son of Alexander Elmsley, of the parish of Marylebone, Middlesex, England. He was called to the English bar at the Middle Temple in 1790; and in 1796 he was appointed chief justice of Upper Canada. The same year he was sworn of the Legislative Council of the province; and in 1799 he became its speaker. In 1802, the position of chief justice of Lower Canada having fallen vacant, he was transferred to this post; and he held it until his death at Montreal on April 29, 1805.

[D. B. Read, *Lives of the judges* (Toronto, 1888); F. J. Audet, *Les juges en chef de la province de Québec* (Montreal, 1927); Le Jeune, *Dict. gén.*]

Elmsley, John (1801-1863), executive councillor of Upper Canada, was born in York (afterwards Toronto), Upper Canada, on May 19, 1801, the son of John Elmsley (q.v.). He was a member of the Executive Council of Upper Canada from 1831 to 1833, and from 1836 to 1838. He died at Toronto on May 8, 1863.

[Brother Alfred, *Honourable John Elmsley* (Report of the Canadian Catholic Historical Association, 1936-37).]

Elson, John Melbourne (1880-1966), author and newspaper proprietor, was born at Byron, near London, Ontario, December 25, 1880, and educated at London Collegiate Institute and the University of Western Ontario. He was associated with the London (Ontario) *News* and the Montreal *Gazette* and became editor of the Toronto *Sunday World* (1907). For some years he was owner-editor of the St. Catharines *Journal*. He wrote *Reciprocity: The outcome of evolution* (1911). He died at Toronto, Ontario, August 30, 1966.

[*Can. who's who*, 1949-51.]

Emard, Joseph Médard (1853-1927), bishop, was born at Laprairie, Canada East, on April 1, 1853; and was educated at the Sulpician College and the Grand Seminary in Montreal. He was ordained a priest of the Roman Catholic Church; and in 1892 he became the first bishop of Valleyfield. He died at Ottawa, Ontario, on March 28, 1929. He was the author of *Souvenirs d'un voyage en Terre-Sainte* (Montreal, 1884) and *Oeuvres complètes* (5 vols., Montreal, 1921-24).

[Allaire, *Dict. biog.*; Morgan, *Can. men* (1912); Le Jeune, *Dict. gén.*; *Bull. rech. hist.*, 1930.]

Emerson, Sir Lewis Edward (1890-1949), chief justice of the Supreme Court of Newfoundland (1944-49), was born at St. John's, Newfoundland, on May 12, 1890, and died there on May 19, 1949. He was called to the Newfoundland bar in 1912 (K.C., 1928); and he was elected a member of the legislature as a Conservative from 1928 to 1934. From 1932 to 1934 he was minister of justice and attorney-general. After the suspension of representative government, he served as commissioner for justice in 1937 and commissioner for defence from 1940 to 1944. In 1944 he was appointed chief justice of the Supreme Court of Newfoundland. He was created a knight bachelor in 1944.

[*Who was who*, 1941-50; *Encyc. Can.*]

Emerson, Robert Alton (1911-1966), railway executive, was born at Plum Coulee, Manitoba, April 12, 1911, and attended schools there. He graduated from the University of Manitoba (B.Sc. engineering, 1930) and attended Yale University as Strathcona Memorial Fellow in Transportation (1933-34). He joined the Canadian Pacific Railway as a summer employee in 1928. From 1931 to 1933 he was a locating engineer with the Ontario Department of Northern Development and worked on C.P.R. track-engineering from 1935 to 1939 when he became roadmaster of the Manitoba district and then division engineer at Brandon, Manitoba, and Moose Jaw, Saskatchewan. He rose to be chief engineer in 1951 and became vice-president of operations and maintenance in 1955. He was elected vice-president of the C.P.R. in 1958, and president in 1964, a position which he held until his death. He presided over the $2.9-billion company during a period of declining passenger traffic and changes in transportation patterns. He came under heavy criticism for the company's policy of phasing out unprofitable passenger trains and railway lines. He died at Montreal, Quebec, March 14, 1966.

[*Can. who's who*, 1961-63; Metropolitan Toronto Library Board, *Biographical scrapbooks*, vol. 26.]

Emmerson, Henry Robert (1853-1914), prime minister of New Brunswick (1897-1900) and minister of railways and canals for Canada (1904-07), was born at Maugerville, Sunbury county, New Brunswick, on September 25, 1853, the son of the Rev. R. H. Emmerson and Augusta Read. He was educated at Acadia College (M.A., 1897; D.C.L., 1904) and at Boston University (LL.B., 1877). He was called to the bar of New Brunswick in 1878 (Q.C., 1899), and practised law at Dorchester, New Brunswick. He sat in the Legislative Assembly of New Brunswick from 1888 to 1890, in the Legislative Council from 1891 to 1892, and in the Assembly again from 1892 to 1900. From 1892 to 1900 he was minister of public works in New Brunswick, and from 1897 to 1900 attorney-general and prime minister. In 1900 he was elected to represent Westmoreland in the Canadian House of Commons, and he sat in the House until his death on July 9, 1914. In 1904 he became minister of railways and canals in the Laurier government; but in 1907 he was compelled to resign his portfolio as the result of charges brought against his private character. In 1878 he married Emily (d. 1901), daughter of C. B. Record, of Moncton, New Brunswick; and by her he had one son and four daughters. He was an LL.D. of the University of New Brunswick (1900); and he was president of the Baptist convention of the Maritime provinces in 1899, and of the Baptist Congress of Canada in 1900.

[*Can. who was who*, vol. 2; Morgan, *Can. men* (1912); *Can. parl. guide*; O. D. Skelton, *Life and letters of Sir Wilfrid Laurier* (2 vols., Toronto, 1920).]

England, Richard (1750-1812), the last British commandant at Detroit, was born in Ireland about 1750, and entered the British army as an ensign in 1766. He rose to the rank of lieutenant-colonel in 1781, of major-general in 1796, and lieutenant-general in 1801. From 1775 to 1781 he served with distinction in the American Revolutionary War. In 1791, and again from 1793 to 1796, he was commandant at Detroit; and it was he who handed Detroit over to the Americans in 1796. He was also a member of the land board of the district of Hesse, Upper Canada, and was instrumental in encouraging immigration into the district in its earliest days. He died in England in 1812. His son, Sir Richard England (1793-1883), was born in Detroit in 1793, entered the British army, achieved distinction in the Afghan and Crimean wars, and also rose to the rank of lieutenant-general.

[M. M. Quaife (ed.), *The John Askin papers* (2 vols., Detroit, Mich., 1928-31).]

Englehart, Jacob Lewis (1847-1921), chairman of the Temiskaming and Northern Ontario Railway Board (1905-21), was born at Cleveland, Ohio, on November 2, 1847, the son of John Joel Englehart. In 1866 he became head of the firm of J. L. Englehart and Co., engaged in the production of Canadian petroleum, with headquarters at London, Ontario, and later at Petrolia, Ontario; and in 1881 he was elected a vice-president of the Imperial Oil Company. In 1905 he was appointed chairman of the board of the Temiskaming and Northern Railway; and he administered the affairs of this government railway with unusual success until shortly before his death at Toronto, on April 6, 1921. In 1891 he married Charlotte Eleanor, daughter of Thomas Thompson, of Adelaide, Ontario; but he had no children.

[Morgan, *Can. men* (1912); *Can. ann. rev.*, supp., 1916.]

Erichsen-Brown, Frank (1878-1967), lawyer and painter, was born in Galt, Ontario, August 29, 1878, and was educated at the University of Toronto, graduating from Osgoode Hall in 1903. He began painting as a hobby as a young man and held several exhibitions of his mainly northern scenes. He was also a close friend of members of the Group of Seven and of the Canadian Group. He was a legal insurance expert on fire insurance law and laws related to legal negligence, and a director of Crown Life. He died at Toronto, Ontario, March 27, 1967.

[*Can. who's who*, 1955-57; The Metro Toronto Library Board, *Biographical Index*, vols. 33 and 53.]

Ermatinger, Charles Oakes (1780?-1853), fur-trader, was born about 1780, a son of Lawrence Ermatinger (q.v.) and Jemima Oakes (d. 1809), a sister of Forrest Oakes (q.v.). He became an Indian trader, and lived for many years at Sault Ste. Marie. In 1805 he was admitted a partner of the North West Company, to begin with the outfit of 1808; and he acted as an agent of the North West Company at Sault Ste. Marie for several years. His later days were spent on the island of Montreal, where he bought a property at Elmwood, Long Point; and there he died on September 4, 1853. He married an Indian woman, named Charlotte Kallawabide, who died at Philipsburgh on July 9, 1850, aged 65 years; and by her he had three sons, Charles Oakes, William and James, and four daughters, Frances, Jemima, Jane, and Ann. His eldest son, Capt. Charles Oakes Ermatinger, died at Montreal on January 14, 1857, aged 55 years.

[W. S. Wallace (ed.), *Documents relating to the North West Company* (Toronto, 1934).]

Ermatinger, Edward (1797-1876), fur-trader and author, was born on the Island of Elba, in the Mediterranean Sea, in February, 1797, the son of Lawrence Edward Ermatinger, who was the eldest son of Lawrence Ermatinger (q.v.). His father was employed in the commissariat of the British Army, under the patronage of his relative, Sir Hildebrand Oakes (see *Dict. Nat. Biog.*). Edward Ermatinger was educated in England, and in 1818 he was, with his brother Francis (q.v.), apprenticed to the Hudson's Bay Company. He remained in the service of the Company for ten years; but in 1830 he retired from the fur-trade, and settled at St. Thomas, Upper Canada. There he died in 1876. He was the author of a *Life of Colonel Talbot* (St. Thomas, C.W., 1859); and his *York Factory express journal* has been edited by his son, Judge C. O. Ermatinger (Trans. Roy. Soc. Can., 1912).

[E. E. Rich (ed.), *Colin Robertson's correspondence book* (Toronto: The Champlain Society, 1939); *Dict. Can. biog.*, vol. 10.]

Ermatinger, Francis (1798-1858), fur-trader, was born in Lisbon, Portugal, in 1798, the son of Lawrence Edward Ermatinger. He was educated in England, and, with his brother Edward (q.v.), was apprenticed to the Hudson's Bay Company in 1818. He spent between thirty and forty years in the service of the Company, mostly on the Pacific coast; and was promoted to the rank of chief trader in 1841. He was described by Sir George Simpson (q.v.) in 1830 as "a bustling, active, boisterous fellow". He retired from the Company in 1853; and he died at St. Thomas, Canada West, on August 12, 1858. He married a daughter of William Sinclair, a chief factor of the Hudson's Bay Company, and a relative by marriage of John McLoughlin (q.v.).

[E. E. Rich (ed.), *Colin Robertson's correspondence book* (Toronto: The Champlain Society, 1939).]

Ermatinger, Lawrence (d. 1789), fur-trader, was a Swiss merchant who appears to have made his way from London to Canada in the early days of British rule. An Ermatinger child (Ann Mary) was born in Montreal in 1766. In 1770 Lawrence Ermatinger was declared a bankrupt in London; but he evidently succeeded in re-establishing himself in Canada, for his name appears in the fur-trade licences as trading to Grand Portage between 1779 and 1783. He died in Montreal on October 6, 1789. He married Jemima Oakes (d. 1809), the sister of Forrest Oakes (q.v.); and by her he had several children.

[W. S. Wallace (ed.), *Documents relating to the North West Company* (Toronto, 1934).]

Ernst, William Gordon (1897-1939), minister of fisheries for Canada (1935), was born at Mahone Bay, Nova Scotia, on October 18, 1897, of German descent. He was educated at King's College, Windsor (B.A., 1917), and at Oxford University (B.A., 1921), where he was a Rhodes scholar. He served in the War of 1914-18 as an officer in the Canadian infantry, and was awarded the Military Cross and bar. He was called to the bar of Nova Scotia in 1922 (K.C., 1932); and he represented Queens-Lunenburg in the Canadian House of Commons from 1926 to 1935 as a Conservative. In August, 1935, he was sworn of the Privy Council of Canada and appointed minister of fisheries in the Bennett government; but was defeated in the general elections of 1935. He died at Bridgewater, Nova Scotia, on July 12, 1939.

[*Can. parl. comp.*; *Can. who's who*, 1936-37.]

Esglis, Louis Philippe Mariauchau d' (1710-1788), eighth bishop of Quebec, was born in Quebec in 1710, the second son of François Mariauchau D'Esglis, an officer of the Dauphiné regiment who came to Canada in 1689. He was ordained a priest in 1734, and became curé of St. Pierre, on the Island of Orleans. In 1770 he became coadjutor of Bishop Briand (q.v.), and in 1772 he was appointed bishop of Dorylaeum *in partibus*. On the retirement of Briand in 1784, he became bishop of Quebec, being the first native-born Canadian to wear the mitre. He died at St. Pierre, on the Island of Orleans, on June 4, 1788.

[P. G. Roy, *La famille Mariauchau d'Esgly* (Lévis, 1908); Le Jeune, *Dict. gén.*; Allaire, *Dict. biog.*; A. Gosselin, *L'église du Canada après la conquête* (Quebec, 1916).]

Esten, James Christie Palmer (1805-1864), judge, was born in St. George, Bermuda, the son of the Hon. John C. Esten, chief justice of Bermuda. He was educated at the Charterhouse school, London, and was called to the English bar from Lincoln's Inn. After spending some time in Virginia, he came to Upper Canada in 1836; and on the establishment of a court of chancery in 1837, became a barrister in this court. In 1849 he was appointed a judge in the court of chancery; and he occupied this post until his death at Toronto on October 25, 1864.

[D. B. Read, *The lives of the judges of Upper Canada* (Toronto, 1888); *Cyc. Am. biog.*]

Estimauville, Robert Anne d', Chevalier de Beaumochel (1754-1831), author, was born at Louisbourg, Cape Breton, on December 3, 1754. He entered the French army, and served in the Napoleonic wars; but he returned to Canada after the Peace of Amiens in 1802, and he held various posts under the government of Lower Canada. In 1823 he was appointed gentleman usher of the black rod. He died on July 31, 1831. In 1821 he published at Quebec a short-lived monthly periodical, the *Inquirer*; and he was the author of *A cursory view of the local, social, moral, and political state of the colony of Lower Canada* (Quebec, 1829).

[P. G. Roy, *La famille d'Estimauville* (Lévis, 1909).]

Éthier, Joseph Arthur Calixte (1868-1936), politician and jurist, was born at St. Benoît, Quebec, on May 26, 1868. He was educated at the Collège de Montréal, and was admitted to the bar of Quebec in 1895. He practised law at Ste. Scholastique, Quebec; and from 1896 to 1925 he represented the constituency of Two Mountains in the Canadian House of

Commons. In 1925 he was appointed chief justice of the circuit court of the district of Montreal; and he held this position until his death on August 14, 1936.

[*Can. who's who*, 1936-37; P. G. Roy, *Les juges de la province de Québec* (Quebec, 1933).]

Evans, James (1801-1846), missionary, was born at Kingston-upon-Hull, England, in 1801. He came to Canada in 1823, and in 1828 he became teacher of an Indian school at Rice Lake, Upper Canada. In 1833 he was ordained a minister of the Methodist Church, and in 1834 he was sent as a missionary to the Ojibway Indians on the St. Clair River. From 1838 to 1840 he served among the Indians of Lake Superior; and in 1840 he was appointed general superintendent of the Northwest Indian Missions, and was stationed at Norway House. Here he invented the system of syllabic characters still in use among the Cree Indians; and the books of hymns and texts which he printed for the Indians were the first examples of printing in the North West. He died at Keilby, Lincolnshire, England, on November 23, 1846.

[Rev. E. R. Young, *The apostle of the north* (New York, 1899); Rev. J. Maclean, *Brief sketch of the life and work of Rev. James Evans* (Toronto, n.d.); N. Burwash, *The gift to a nation of written language* (Trans. Roy. Soc. Can., 1911).]

Evans, William (1786-1857), author, was born at Carana, Ireland, on November 22, 1786. He emigrated to Canada in 1819, and settled in Montreal. In 1843 he founded at Montreal the *Canadian Agricultural Journal*; and he edited this journal until his death at Montreal in 1857. He published *A treatise on the theory and practice of agriculture* (Montreal, 1835; supplement, Montreal, 1836), *Agricultural improvements* (Montreal, 1837), and *Suggestions sur la subdivision et l'économie d'une ferme, dans les seigneuries du Bas-Canada* (Montreal, 1854).

[Morgan, *Bib. can.*]

Evans, William Sanford (1869-1949), publicist and author, was born at Spencerville, Ontario, on December 18, 1869, and died at Winnipeg, Manitoba, in 1949. He became a journalist, first in Toronto, and then in Winnipeg; and from 1901 to 1905 he was editor-in-chief of the Winnipeg *Telegram*. From 1905 to 1911 he was mayor of Winnipeg. He abandoned journalism, and became a successful broker and investment dealer; then in 1921 he established the Sanford Evans Statistical Services. He represented Winnipeg as a Conservative in the Manitoba legislature from 1922 to 1935, and from 1933 to 1936 was leader of the opposition. He was the author of *The Canadian contingents and Canadian imperialism* (London, 1901). In 1936 the University of Manitoba conferred on him the honorary degree of LL.D.

[Morgan, *Can. men* (1912); *Can. who's who*, 1948.]

Evanturel, François (1821-1891), politician and author, was born at Quebec, Lower Canada, on October 22, 1821. He was called to the bar of Lower Canada in 1845; and he sat in the Legislative Assembly of United Canada from 1855 to 1857 and from 1861 to 1867. From 1862 to 1863 he was minister of agriculture in the Macdonald-Sicotte administration. He died at Quebec City on March 12, 1841. He was the author of *Les deux cochers de Québec; Souvenirs historiques* (Quebec, 1886).

[P. G. Roy, *Fils de Québec*, vol. 4 (Lévis, Que., 1933).]

Evanturel, François Eugène Alfred (1849-1908), lawyer and politician, was born at Quebec, Canada East, on August 31, 1849, the eldest son of the Hon. François Evanturel (q.v.). He was educated at Laval University (LL.B., 1869), and was called to the bar of Lower Canada in 1871. Later he removed to the county of Prescott, Ontario; and in 1886 he was elected to represent this constituency in the Legislative Assembly of Ontario. He continued to represent Prescott in the Ontario legislature until 1905; and he was speaker of the Assembly from 1897 to 1902, and a member of the Ross government from 1904 to 1905. He died at Alfred, Ontario, on November 14, 1908.

[Morgan, *Can. men* (1898); *Can. parl. comp.*]

Evanturel, Joseph Eudore Alphonse (1852-1919), poet, was born at Quebec, Canada East, on September 22, 1852, and was educated at the Quebec Seminary. He spent most of his life in the civil service of the province of Quebec; and he died at Boston, Massachusetts, on May 16, 1919. He was the author of *Premières poésies* (Quebec, 1878).

[*Bull. rech. hist.*, 1926.]

Ewan, John Alexander (1854-1910), journalist, was born in Aberdeen, Scotland, in 1854, and came to Canada in early youth. He entered the office of the Toronto *Globe*; and except for some years when he was on the staff of the Toronto *Mail* and later of the Toronto *World*, his life was spent on the *Globe* staff. He rose to the position of associate editor, and came to be regarded as one of the outstanding journalists of Canada. He died at Toronto on July 28, 1910.

[*A tribute to John A. Ewan* (pamphlet, Toronto, 1910); *Can. who was who*, vol. 2; *Can. who's who* (1910); Morgan, *Can. men* (1898).]

Ewart, John Skirving (1849-1933), lawyer and author, was born at Toronto, Ontario, on

August 11, 1849, the son of Thomas Ewart and Catherine Seaton Skirving. He was educated at Upper Canada College and at Osgoode Hall, Toronto, and was called to the bar in 1871 (Q.C., 1884). He practised law in Winnipeg from 1882 to 1904; and he took a prominent part in the controversy over separate schools in Manitoba. In 1904 he removed to Ottawa, and he became an outstanding counsel before the Supreme Court of Canada and the Judicial Committee of the Privy Council. In his later years, he became famous as an advocate of the independence of Canada. He died at Ottawa on February 21, 1933. In addition to a number of legal works, he was the author of *The Kingdom of Canada, Imperial federation, The Colonial Conference, The Alaska boundary, and other essays* (Toronto, 1908), *John A. Macdonald and the Canadian flag* (Toronto, 1908), *Canadian independence* (Toronto, 1911), *The roots and causes of the wars (1914-1918)* (2 vols., New York, 1925), and two series of brochures, *The Kingdom papers*, nos. 1-19 (Ottawa, 1911-14), and *The independence papers* (Ottawa, 2 vols., 1925-30).

[D. M. L. Farr, *John S. Ewart* (Our Living Tradition, Third Series, 1959); *Can. who was who*, vol. 1; Morgan, *Can. men* (1912).]

Ewing, Juliana Horatia (1841-1885), author, was born at Ecclesfield, Yorkshire, England, on August 3, 1841, the second daughter of the Rev. Alfred Gatty, D.D. In 1867 she married Major Alexander Ewing, A.P.D., and the first two years of her married life were spent at Fredericton, New Brunswick, where her husband was stationed. Both before and after her marriage she wrote stories and verses for children, which attained a wide-spread popularity. Notable among her verses were some lines entitled *Canada Home*, published in 1879. She died at Bath, England, on May 13, 1885.

[H. K. F. Gatty, *Juliana Horatia Ewing and her books* (London, 1885); Elizabeth T. Tucker, *Leaves from Juliana Horatia Ewing's "Canada Home"* (Boston, 1897); W. G. MacFarlane, *New Brunswick bibliography* (Saint John, N.B., 1895); *Dict. nat. biog.*]

Eyre, Sir William (1805-1859), administrator of Canada (1857), was born at Hatfield, England, in 1805, the second son of Vice-admiral Sir George Eyre. He entered the British army in 1823, served with distinction in the Crimean War, was created a K.C.B. in 1855, and was appointed in 1856 commander-in-chief of the forces in Canada. In 1857, during the absence of Sir Edmund Head (q.v.), he was administrator of the government of Canada. He returned to England in 1858, and he died there in 1859.

[*Dict. nat. biog.*; Le Jeune, *Dict. gén.*]

Fabre, Edouard Charles (1827-1896), first Roman Catholic archbishop of Montreal, was born in Montreal, Lower Canada, on February 28, 1827, the son of Edouard Raymond Fabre and Luce Perrault. He was educated at the college of St. Hyacinthe, and at Issy, near Paris, France. He was ordained a priest in 1850. In 1873 he became coadjutor of Bishop Bourget (q.v.), with the title of bishop of Gratianopolis, and in 1876 he succeeded him as bishop of Montreal. In 1886 the see of Montreal was made an archbishopric, and Bishop Fabre received the pallium. He died at Montreal on December 30, 1896.

[Allaire, *Dict. biog.*; Le Jeune, *Dict. gén.*; Rose, *Can. biog.* (1888).]

Fabre, Hector (1834-1910), journalist and Canadian commissioner in Paris, was born in Montreal on August 9, 1834, the son of E. R. Fabre and Luce Perrault, and the brother of Archbishop Fabre (q.v.). He was educated at L'Assomption and St. Hyacinthe colleges, and at the College of St. Sulpice, Montreal, and studied law with his brother-in-law, George Etienne Cartier (q.v.). He was called to the bar in 1856, but drifted into journalism, becoming successively the editor of *L'Ordre* (Montreal), *Le Canadien* (Quebec), and *L'Evénement* (Quebec). In 1873 he unsuccessfully contested as a Liberal the representation of Quebec county in the House of Commons; and in 1875 he was appointed to the Senate by the Mackenzie government. In 1882 he resigned his seat in the Senate to become agent for the Canadian government in Paris, and he continued to represent Canada in Paris during the remainder of his life. In 1886 he was created a C.M.G.; and in 1882 he was appointed one of the charter members of the Royal Society of Canada. He published *Esquisse biographique sur Chevalier de Lorimier* (Montreal, 1856), *Sur la littérature canadienne* (Quebec, 1866), *Confédération, indépendance, annexion* (Quebec, 1871), and *Chroniques* (Quebec, 1877). He died in Paris on September 2, 1910.

[Morgan, *Can. men* (1898) and *Bib. can.*; *Can. who's who* (1910); L. M. Darveau, *Nos hommes de lettres* (Montreal, 1873).]

Faillon, Etienne Michel (1799-1870), priest and historian, was born at Tarascon in France on May 1, 1799. He studied at Tarascon, at Avignon, and at Paris, and was ordained a priest in 1824. He entered the Sulpician order, and between 1826 and 1849 held various positions in the order in France. He visited Canada in 1849-50 and in 1854, and from 1858 to 1862 he lived in Montreal. In 1862 he returned to Europe, and his remaining years were spent in Rome and Paris. He died in Paris on October 25, 1870. A voluminous writer, he published several books dealing with Canadian history, *Vie de la Soeur Bourgeois* (2 vols., Paris, 1853), *Vie de Mademoiselle Mance* (2 vols., Paris, 1854), *Vie de Madame d'Youville* (Paris, 1852), and *Histoire de la colonie française en Canada* (3 vols., Paris, 1865-66).

[*M. Faillon, sa vie, ses oeuvres* (Montreal, 1879); *Bull. rech. hist.*, 1900; Allaire, *Dict. biog.*; Le Jeune, *Dict. gén.*]

Fairchild, George Moore (1854-1912), author, was born at Quebec, Canada East, in 1854, the son of G. M. Fairchild. He was educated at the University of New York, and went into business in New York. He retired from business with a competency in 1880, and settled in Quebec. He married in 1880 the granddaughter of the Hon. John Neilson (q.v.), and he devoted himself to literary and historical pursuits, and to the collection of a library of "Canadiana". He died at Quebec on September 18, 1912. He was the author of *Oritani snow shoe club souvenir* (New York, 1888), *A short account of ye Quebec winter carnival* (Quebec, 1894), *Rod and canoe, rifle and snowshoe in Quebec's Adirondacks* (Quebec, 1896), *Quebec, the sportsman's land of plenty* (Quebec, 1899), *A ridiculous courting, and other stories of French Canada* (Chicago, 1900), and *From my Quebec scrap-book* (Quebec, 1907); and he edited *Canadian leaves* (New York, 1887) and *The journal of an American prisoner at Ford Malden and Quebec in the War of 1812* (Quebec, privately printed, 1909).

[Morgan, *Can. men* (1912).]

Fairford, Alan (pseud.). See **Kent, John.**

Falardeau, Antoine Sébastien (1823-1889), painter, was born near Quebec, Lower Canada, in 1823. He went to Italy about 1844, and became a copyist in Florence. His work was in great demand, and he was created a chevalier by the Grand Duke of Tuscany. Very little of his work, however, was original. He died in Florence, Italy, on August 14, 1889.

[H. R. Casgrain, *Biographies canadiennes* (Montreal, 1885); E. de Rives, *Le chevalier Falardeau* (Quebec, 1862); Morgan, *Cel. Can.*; Bibaud, *Panth. can.*; Le Jeune, *Dict. gén.*]

Falcon, Pierre (1793-1876), composer of *chansons*, was born at Elbow Fort, Swan River, in the *pays d'en haut*, the son of Pierre Falcon, a clerk of the North West Company, and an Indian mother. He entered the service of the North West Company, and was one of the half-breeds who accompanied Cuthbert Grant (q.v.) at the massacre of Seven Oaks in 1816. He became famous on the prairies as a composer and singer of *chansons*; and one of these, the "Chanson de la Grenouillère", is a narrative of the episode at Seven Oaks. Falcon died at St. François Xavier, Manitoba, on October 26, 1876. In 1812 he married Marie, a daughter of Cuthbert Grant the Nor'Wester (q.v.), and a sister of Cuthbert Grant (q.v.), the Warden of the Plains.

[M. Complin, *Pierre Falcon's "Chanson de la Grenouillère"* (Trans. Roy. Soc. Can., 1939); *Dict. Can. biog.*; vol. 10.]

Falconbridge, Sir William Glenholme (1846-1920), chief justice of the King's Bench in Ontario (1900-20), was born at Drummondville, Upper Canada, on May 12, 1846, the son of John Kennedy Falconbridge, J.P., and Sarah Fralick. He was educated at the University of Toronto (B.A., 1866; M.A., 1871) and was called to the bar of Ontario in 1871 (Q.C., 1885). From 1872 to 1881 he was registrar of the University of Toronto. He devoted himself later, however, to law; and in 1887 he was appointed a judge of the Queen's Bench division of the Supreme Court of Ontario. In 1900 he became chief justice of this court, and he continued in this office until his death at Toronto on February 8, 1920. In 1908 he was created a knight bachelor. He married in 1873 Mary Phoebe, youngest daughter of the Hon. Robert Baldwin Sullivan (q.v.); and by her he had one son and five daughters.

[W. S. Herrington, *Sir Glenholme Falconbridge* (Canadian bar review, 1925); Morgan, *Can. men* (1912); *Can. who's who* (1910).]

Falconer, Sir Robert Alexander (1867-1943), president of the University of Toronto (1907-32), was born at Charlottetown, Prince Edward Island, on February 10, 1867, the son of the Reverend Alexander Falconer, D.D., and Susan Douglas. He was educated at the Queen's Royal College, Trinidad, British West Indies, at London University (B.A., 1888), at Edinburgh University (M.A., 1889; B.D., 1892), and at Marburg University. He was ordained a minister of the Presbyterian Church in Canada in 1892, and was appointed lecturer in New Testament Greek in Pine Hill College, Halifax, Nova Scotia. In 1895 he was made professor; and in 1904 he became principal of the College. In 1907 he was appointed president of the University of Toronto; and during his presidency this university became the largest in point of attendance in the British Empire. He retired because of ill-health in 1932; and he died in Toronto, Ontario, on November 4, 1943. In 1897 he married Sophie, daughter of the Reverend J. Gandier; and by her he had two sons. In 1911 he was created a C.M.G., and in 1917 a K.C.M.G. He received honorary degrees from a score of universities in America and Europe; and he was president of the Royal Society of Canada in 1932, of the Royal Canadian Institute from 1932 to 1935, and of the Champlain Society from 1935 to 1941. He was the author of *The German tragedy and its meaning for Canada* (Toronto, 1915), *Idealism in national character* (Toronto, 1920), *The United States as a neighbour* (Cambridge, Mass., 1925), *Citizenship in an enlarging world* (Sackville, N.B., 1928), *The idea of immortality and western civilization* (Cambridge, Mass., 1930), and *The pastoral epistles* (Oxford, 1937).

[*Proc. Roy. Soc. Can.*, 1944; *Who's who*, 1943; *Can. who's who*, 1936-37; A. Bridle, *Sons of Canada* (Toronto, 1917); *Univ. of Toronto monthly*, 1943; *Univ. of Toronto quarterly*, 1944.]

Falkland, Lucius Bentinck Cary, tenth Viscount of (1803-1884), governor of Nova Scotia (1840-46), was born on November 5, 1803, the son of Charles John, ninth Viscount of Falkland, in the peerage of Scotland, and Christiana Anton. He succeeded to the viscountcy on the death of his father in 1809; and in 1830 he was appointed a lord of the bedchamber to William IV. In 1831 he was elected a representative peer from Scotland; but in 1832 he took his seat in the House of Lords in his own right, having been created Baron Hunsdon in the peerage of the United Kingdom. In 1840 he was appointed governor of Nova Scotia, and it fell to him to resist the demand for the full introduction of responsible government in the province. He came into violent collision with Joseph Howe (q.v.), who lampooned him mercilessly, and even threatened to "horse-whip" him; and he left the province in 1846 under something of a cloud. From 1846 to 1848 he was captain of the Yeomen of the Guard; and from 1848 to 1853 he was governor of Bombay. He died at Montpelier, France, on March 12, 1884. He married (1) in 1830 Amelia Fitz-Clarence (d. 1858), illegitimate daughter of King William

IV, and (2) in 1859 Elizabeth Catherine, dowager Duchess of St. Albans. By his first wife he had one son (d. 1871). In 1831 he was made a G.C.H., and in 1837 a privy councillor.

[*Burke's peerage; Ann. reg.*, 1884; E. M. Saunders, *Three premiers of Nova Scotia* (Toronto, 1909); J. Howe, *Letters and speeches*, ed. by J. A. Chisholm (2 vols., Halifax, N.S., 1909).]

Fallon, Michael Francis (1867-1931), Roman Catholic bishop of London, was born at Kingston, Ontario, in 1867, the son of Dominick Fallon. He was educated at Ottawa College and at the Gregorian University in Rome, and was ordained a priest in 1894. He was first professor of English on the staff of the University of Ottawa then a parish priest in Buffalo, New York, and in 1910 he was created bishop of London. As bishop he took an active part in the discussion of public questions, as the champion of the Irish element in the Roman Catholic Church. He died at London, Ontario, on February 22, 1931.

[*Can. who was who*, vol. 1; Morgan, *Can. men* (1912).]

Falloon, Daniel (d. 1862), clergyman, was born in Ireland, and became a clergyman of the Church of England in Canada. He died in Montreal, Canada West, in September, 1862. He was the author of *An historical view of the Church of England* (2 vols., Dublin, 1830), *Dialogues on the apostolic church* (London, 1837), and *History of Ireland, civil and ecclesiastical* (Montreal, 1863).

[Morgan, *Bib. can.*]

Fanning, Edmund (1737-1818), lieutenant-governor of Nova Scotia (1783-86) and of Prince Edward Island (1787-1804), was born in New York on April 24, 1737, the son of James Fanning, a captain in the British army. He was educated at Yale College, New Haven (B.A., 1757; M.A., 1758), and was admitted to the bar of North Carolina in 1762. In 1765 he was appointed a judge of the Supreme Court of North Carolina. On two occasions, before the actual outbreak of the American Revolution, he raised a corps of loyalists to suppress insurgent outbreaks; and during the Revolution he commanded the King's American Regiment, which he had raised. In 1783 he was appointed lieutenant-governor of Nova Scotia, and in 1787 he succeeded Walter Patterson (q.v.) as lieutenant-governor of Prince Edward Island. His term of office lasted until 1804, when he was retired on full salary. He died in London, England, on February 28, 1818. In 1774 he was made a D.C.L. of Oxford University. He retired from the army with the rank of general (gazetted 1808).

[A. P. Stokes, *Memorials of eminent Yale men* (2 vols., New Haven, Conn., 1914); L. Sabine, *Biographical sketches of loyalists of the American revolution* (2 vols., Boston,

1864); *Cyc. Am. biog.*; A. B. Warburton, *A history of Prince Edward Island* (Saint John, N.B., 1923).]

Fargues, Thomas (1780-1847), physician, was born at Quebec in 1780. He was educated at Harvard College (B.A., 1797), and at the University of Edinburgh (M.D., 1811). After spending some years in London, he returned to practise medicine in Quebec about 1811; and he occupied an outstanding position in his profession in Canada for the next generation. He died in Quebec on December 11, 1847. In 1831 he was made an honorary M.D. of Harvard University.

[Morgan, *Cel. Can.*; M. J. and G. Ahern, *Notes pour servir à l'histoire de la médecine dans le Bas Canada* (Quebec, 1923).]

Faribault, George Barthélmi (1789-1866), bibliographer, was born at Quebec on December 3, 1789. He was called to the bar of Lower Canada in 1810, but in 1822 entered the civil service of the province. In 1840 he was appointed assistant clerk of the Legislative Assembly, and this post he occupied until his retirement on pension in 1855. He twice made for the Assembly a collection of books and papers relating to Canadian history; but the first collection was wholly destroyed in the burning of the Parliament Buildings at Montreal in 1849, and the second partially destroyed in the burning of the government offices at Quebec in 1854. He died at Quebec on December 21, 1866. His *Catalogue d'ouvrages sur l'histoire de l'Amérique, et en particulier sur celle du Canada* (Quebec, 1837) is the first essay in Canadian bibliography.

[H. R. Casgrain, *Faribault* (Quebec, 1867); *La famille Faribault* (Bull. rech. hist., 1912); Bibaud, *Panth. can.*; Le Jeune, *Dict. gén.*]

Faries, Hugh (1779-1852), fur-trader, was born in Montreal in 1779, the son of Hugh Faries and Mary Warfinger. He entered the service of the North West Company as a clerk, and in 1804-06 was at Rainy Lake. He was one of the first officers of the Company to cross the Rocky Mountains, and in 1807 was the first master of Fort George in New Caledonia. Later, from 1812 to 1817, he was at Cumberland House on the Saskatchewan. At the union of the North West and Hudson's Bay companies in 1821, he was made a chief trader; and from 1821 to 1826 he was employed in the Peace River district. In 1827 he was proposed as a member of the Beaver Club in Montreal. From 1827 to 1837 he was stationed in the Kenogamissie district; and he was promoted to the rank of chief factor in 1838. He retired from the fur-trade in 1840; and he died at Berthier, Canada East, on March 23, 1852.

[C. M. Gates (ed.), *Five fur-traders of the Northwest* (Minneapolis, Minn., 1933).]

Farquharson, Ray Fletcher (1897-1965), professor of medicine, was born in Claude, Ontario, August 4, 1897. After early education in Durham he entered the University of Toronto Medical School in 1917, graduating M.B. (Toronto) in 1922. He spent the next six years in medical research in Toronto and in Boston before being appointed to the staff of the University of Toronto School of Medicine in 1928. By 1947 he had become head of the department of medicine and physician-in-chief at Toronto General Hospital.

Among his major contributions to medical knowledge was the discovery of the "Farquharson phenomenon", with Dr. A. H. Squires, in which the principle was developed which showed that the secretory activity of a hormone-producing organ of an individual is markedly suppressed, and the organ itself temporarily atrophied, by continuous exogenous administration of relatively large doses of the hormone which the organ normally produces. In 1957 Dr. Farquharson was appointed vice-president (medical) of the National Research Council. The following year he became chairman of a Privy Council Committee on medical research and out of this investigation came the "Farquharson Committee Report" of 1959 which showed the need for greatly increased government assistance to medical research if present projects were to be sustained and future plans carried out. As a result of the report the Medical Research Council of Canada was established in 1960 with Dr. Farquharson, who had retired from his teaching post at the University of Toronto, as chairman. In this position he succeeded in putting medical research in Canada on a much better financial basis.

He died at Ottawa on June 1, 1965. He was a fellow of the Royal Society and an M.B.E., and he received honours and awards from governments and universities in Canada and abroad as an outstanding physician, a first-rate investigator, an enthusiastic teacher, and an able administrator.

[*Can. who's who*, 1955-57; *Proc. Roy. Soc. Can.* (vol. IV, 1965).]

Farthing, John Colborne (1897-1954), educationist, was born at Woodstock, Ontario, on March 18, 1897, the son of the Right Rev. John Cragg Farthing (q.v.). He was educated at McGill University (B.A., 1921), his course having been interrupted by service overseas during the First World War; and then he took Modern Greats at New College, Oxford. He returned to Canada in 1924, and became a lecturer in economics and political science under Stephen Leacock (q.v.) at McGill, but resigned his lectureship in 1929. He resumed teaching from 1940 to 1949, when he was master at Bishop's College School, Lennoxville, Quebec. He died at Montreal on March 9, 1954. After his death his book *Freedom wears a crown* (Toronto, 1957), was edited for publication by Judith Robinson, with an introduction by E. D. Fulton.

[Montreal *Gazette*, March 10, 1954.]

Farthing, John Cragg (1861-1947), bishop, was born in Cincinnati, Ohio, on December 13, 1861. He was educated in England, and after several years with a mercantile firm in Liverpool, decided to study for holy orders. He graduated from Caius College, Cambridge (B.A., 1885; M.A., 1888) and went to Canada, where he was ordained a priest of the Church of England in 1886. After serving as curate and rector in several charges in Ontario, he was elected bishop of Montreal in 1909; and he continued in this position for thirty years. His last years he spent with his elder son in Calgary, Alberta; and shortly before his death at Calgary, on May 6, 1947, he published his *Recollections* (n.p., 1945).

[*Can. who's who*, 1938-39; Morgan, *Can. men* (1912).]

Faucher de Saint-Maurice, Narcisse Henri Edouard (1844-1897), author, was born at Quebec, Lower Canada, on April 18, 1844, the son of Narcisse Constantin Faucher de Saint-Maurice, seigneur of Beaumont and Vincennes, and Catherine Henriette Mercier. He was educated at the Quebec Seminary and in 1864 he took service, as a captain of sharpshooters, in the army of the Emperor Maximilian in Mexico. He served throughout the Mexican War, was twice wounded, and returned to Canada in 1866. From 1867 to 1881 he was clerk of the Legislative Council of Quebec; and in 1883 he became the editor-in-chief of the *Journal de Québec*, and in 1885 of *Le Canadien*. From 1881 to 1890 he represented Bellechasse in the Legislative Assembly of Quebec. He published a large number of books. His first publications were military: *L'ennemi! L'ennemi! Étude sur l'organisation militaire du Canada* (Quebec, 1862), and *Course de tactique* (Quebec, 1863). After his return from Mexico he published successively *De Québec à Mexico: Souvenirs de voyage* (2 vols., Montreal, 1874), *A la brunante: Contes et récits* (Montreal, 1874), *Choses et autres* (Montreal, 1874), *De tribord à babord* (Montreal, 1877), *A la veillée* (Quebec, 1878), *Deux ans au Mexique* (Montreal, 1878), *Procédure parlementaire* (Montreal, 1885), *En route* (Quebec, 1888), *Joies et tristesses de la mer* (Montreal, 1888), *Loin du pays* (2 vols., Quebec, 1889), *Notes pour servir à l'histoire de l'Empéreur Maximilian* (Quebec, 1889), *La question du jour: Resterons-nous français?* (Quebec, 1890), *Honi soit qui mal y pense* (Montreal, 1892), *Notes pour servir à l'histoire du Général Richard Montgomery* (Montreal, 1893), *Les états de Jersey et la langue française* (Montreal, 1893), *Notes pour servir à l'histoire des officiers de la marine et de l'armée française, qui ont fait la guerre de l'indépendance américaine* (Quebec, 1896), and *Promenades* *dans le golfe St-Laurent* (2 vols., Montreal, n.d.). He was a charter member of the Royal Society of Canada, and to its transactions he contributed a number of papers, mostly on historical subjects. He died in April, 1897. In 1868 he married Josephine Berthelot d'Artigny, niece of Sir Louis H. Lafontaine (q.v.). In 1881 he was created by the French government a chevalier of the Legion of Honour.

[L. H. Taché, *Faucher de Saint-Maurice* (Montreal, 1886); *Proc. Roy. Soc. Can.*, 1897; G. Parizeau, *Faucher de Saint-Maurice: Écrivain, journaliste, député président de la section française de la société royal du Canada* (Trans. Roy. Soc. Can., 1969); *Bull rech. hist.*, 1923; Bibaud, *Panth. can.*; *Can. parl. comp.*; Rose, *Cyc. Can. biog.* (1886); Le Jeune, *Dict. gén.*]

Faull, Joseph Horace (1870-1961), botanist, was born at L'Anse, Michigan, on May 3, 1870. His father, who awakened his interest in plants, was a minister. Joseph was educated at Napanee, Ontario, and at the University of Toronto (B.A., 1898). He entered graduate school at Harvard University and in 1902 began teaching at Toronto. He was awarded his Ph.D. from Harvard in 1904. He taught at Toronto until 1928, when he accepted a position at Harvard, retiring in 1940. He has been called the founder of forest pathology in Canada, initiating the study of tree diseases and wood decay and establishing research stations for the Ontario government and the government of Canada. By his study of tree rusts and tree fungi during the first decade of this century he made valuable contributions to the later study of wheat diseases on the Canadian prairies. He was a fellow of the Royal Society, an honorary life member of the Royal Canadian Institute, and a fellow of the American Academy of Arts and Sciences. He died June 30, 1961.

[*Trans. Roy. Soc. Can.* (1963).]

Fauteux, Aegidius (1876-1941), librarian and historian, was born at Montreal, Quebec, on September 27, 1876; and was educated at Laval University, Montreal. He studied first for the priesthood, but turned later to the study of law, and was called to the Quebec bar in 1903. He never practised law, however, having already drifted into journalism. He served on the staff of both *La Patrie* and *La Presse* of Montreal; and from 1909 to 1912 he was editor-in-chief of *La Presse*. In 1912 he was appointed librarian of the newly founded Sulpician Library in Montreal, and he continued in this position until the Sulpician Library was closed for lack of funds in 1931. He then became librarian of the Bibliothèque Civique in Montreal; and he discharged the duties of this office until his death at Montreal on April 22, 1941. A scholar of rare qualities, he became one of the most outstanding authorities on the history and bibliography of Canada; in 1918 he

was elected a fellow of the Royal Society of Canada, and in 1937 he was awarded the Society's Tyrrell medal. In 1936 he was honoured by the University of Montreal with the degree of D. ès L. He was the author of *La famille d'Ailleboust* (Montreal, 1917), *Monsieur Lecoq* (Montreal, 1927), *The introduction of printing into Canada* (1930), *Le duel au Canada* (Montreal, 1934), and *Les chevaliers de Saint-Louis en Canada* (Montreal, 1940); and he was a regular contributor to the annual volume of historical essays published in Montreal under the title *Les cahiers des dix*. In 1911 he married Antonia Chevrier; but he had no children.

[*Can. who's who*, 1936-37; *Proc. Roy. Soc. Can.*, 1941.]

Fauteux, Guillaume André (1874-1940), solicitor-general of Canada (1926), was born at St. Benoit, Quebec, on October 20, 1874. He was called to the bar of Quebec in 1900 (K.C., 1926); and he was Conservative candidate for the Canadian House of Commons for Terrebonne in 1921 and for Bagot in 1925, 1926, and 1930; but was defeated in each of these elections. In the short-lived Meighen administration of 1926 he was sworn in as solicitor-general; but held office for only a few months, from August 23 to December 25. He was called to the Senate in 1933; and in 1934-35 he was *bâtonnier* of the Montreal bar. He died at Montreal, Quebec, on September 10, 1940.

[*Can. who's who*, 1938-39; *Can. parl. comp.*]

Fay, Charles Lyle (1884-1961), economist and professor, was born in England on January 13, 1884. He was educated at Cambridge University (fellow, 1908) and lectured there until joining the British army in 1914. He served until 1918, when he returned to the University. He was professor of economic history at the University of Toronto (1921-30); he then returned to Cambridge as reader in economic history, remaining there until his death on November 9, 1961. He was a frequent visitor to Canada and lectured at Toronto, British Columbia and Memorial universities. He was author of *Cooperation at home and abroad* (vol. I, Cambridge, 1908; vol. II, 1939), *Copartnership in industry* (Cambridge, 1913), *Life and labour in the 19th century* (Cambridge, 1920), *Great Britain from Adam Smith to the present day* (London, 1928), *Youth and power* (London, 1931), *The corn laws and social England* (Cambridge, 1932), *English economic history, mainly since 1700* (Cambridge, 1940), *Huskisson and his age* (London, 1951), *Palace of industry, 1851* (Cambridge, 1951), *Life and labour in Newfoundland* (Toronto, 1956), *Imperial economy and its place in the formation of economic doctrine 1600-1932* (Oxford, 1934).

[*Can. journ. ec. pol. sc.*, vol. XXVII; *Who was who*, vol. VI.]

Feild, Edward (1801-1876), Anglican bishop of Newfoundland (1844-76), was born in Worcester, England, on June 7, 1801. He was educated at Rugby and Queen's College, Oxford (B.A., 1823; M.A., 1826); and from 1825 to 1833 he was a fellow of Queen's College, Oxford. He was ordained a priest in the Church of England in 1827, and in 1844 he was appointed bishop of Newfoundland. He held this office for the rest of his life, and played an important part in the ecclesiastical history of the island. In 1875 he moved to Bermuda, which was part of his diocese; and he died there on June 8, 1876.

[H. W. Tucker, *Memoir of the life and episcopate of Edward Feild* (London, 1877); C. H. Mockridge, *The bishops of the Church of England in Canada and Newfoundland* (Toronto, 1896); *Dict. nat. biog.*; *Encyc. Can.*; *Dict. Can. biog.*, vol. 10.]

Feller, Mme Henrietta, *née* **Odin** (1800-1868), missionary and educationist, was born in Montagny, Switzerland, on April 22, 1800. In 1822 she married Louis Feller, of Lausanne; but he died in 1826, and after his death his widow took refuge in religious activity. In 1835 she offered herself as a Protestant missionary among the Roman Catholics of Quebec; and she arrived in Canada the same year. In 1838 she established a Baptist mission-house and school at Grande Ligne, Lower Canada; and she continued in charge of this mission and school until her death at Grande Ligne, on March 29, 1868.

[W. N. Wyeth, *Henrietta Feller and the Grande Ligne mission* (Philadelphia, 1898); J. M. Cramp (comp.), *A memoir of Madam Feller* (London, 1876); *Cyc. Am. biog.*]

Fénelon, François de Salignac de (1641-1679), missionary, was born in 1641, and was the half-brother of the Archbishop Fénelon. At the age of twenty-four he entered the Seminary of Saint-Sulpice in Paris, France; and in the spring of 1667 he sailed for New France. He arrived at Quebec on June 21. On October 2, 1668, he set out from Lachine with the Abbé Trouve on a mission to Lake Ontario, and established himself among the Cayuga at Kenté Bay. This was the first Sulpician mission among the Iroquois, and was maintained until 1673, when Fénelon founded a school for Indian children at Gentilly. In 1674 he incurred Frontenac's displeasure by his opposition to the arrest of Perrot, and was summoned to Quebec to appear before the Council. Here he was severely censured, and sent back to France, where he went into retirement and died in 1679.

[H.-A. Verreau, *Les deux Abbés de Fénelon* (Lévis, 1898); *Dict. Can. biog.*, vol. 1.]

Fenety, George Edward (1812-1899), journalist, was born in Halifax, Nova Scotia, in 1812. In 1829 he entered the office of the *Nova Scotian*, the newspaper of Joseph Howe (q.v.). He went to the United States in 1835, and he became the editor and proprietor of the *Planter's Advocate*, at Donaldsville on the Mississippi. In 1839, however, he returned to the Maritime provinces, and founded at Saint John, New Brunswick, the *Commercial News*. This journal, which was the first penny newspaper in the Maritime provinces, he conducted until 1863. He then became Queen's printer for New Brunswick, and continued in this office until 1895, when it was abolished. He died at Fredericton, New Brunswick, on September 30, 1899. In 1847 he married Eliza, daughter of Robert Arthur of New York. He was the author of *The lady and the dress-maker; or, A peep at fashionable folly* (Saint John, N.B., 1842), *Political notes and observations* (Fredericton, N.B., 1867), and *The life and times of the Hon. Joseph Howe* (Saint John, N.B., 1896).

[Morgan, *Can. men* (1898) and *Bib. can.*; W. G. MacFarlane, *New Brunswick bibliography* (Saint John, N.B., 1895).]

Ferguson, Bartimus (1792?-1832), journalist, was born about 1792. He became the editor in 1818 of the Niagara *Spectator*; and he printed in this journal some of the "libels" against the government of Upper Canada, for which Robert Gourlay (q.v.) was convicted and banished from the province in 1819. Ferguson himself was fined and imprisoned for printing these libels. In 1829 he founded the *Gore Balance*, the first newspaper published in Hamilton, Upper Canada; but this paper ceased publication in 1831, and in 1832 Ferguson died in the hospital in York (Toronto).

[W. S. Wallace, *The periodical literature of Upper Canada* (Can. hist. rev., 1931).]

Ferguson, Donald (1839-1909), minister without portfolio in the Canadian government (1894-96), was born at Marshfield, Prince Edward Island, on March 7, 1839, the son of John Ferguson. He was a member of the Legislative Assembly of Prince Edward Island from 1878 to 1891; and he held in turn, in the government of the island, the portfolio of public works (1879-80) and the provincial secretaryship and the commissionership of Crown lands (1880-91). He unsuccessfully contested Queen's county, Prince Edward Island, for the Canadian House of Commons in 1891; and in 1893 he was summoned to the Senate of Canada. He was a member of the Bowell and Tupper administrations (1894-96), without portfolio; and for a short time in 1896 was acting minister of agriculture. He died at Marshfield, Prince Edward Island, on September 3, 1909. In 1873 he married Elizabeth, daughter of John Scott, Charlottetown; and by her he had three sons and two daughters.

[Morgan, *Can. men* (1898); Rose, *Cyc. Can. biog.* (1888); *Can. parl. comp.*]

Ferguson, George Dalrymple (1829-1926), historian, was born in Montreal, Lower Canada, on Christmas Day, 1829, the son of Archibald Ferguson, proprietor of the Montreal *Herald*. He was educated at Queen's University, Kingston (B.A., 1851), at Edinburgh University, and at the University of Halle. In 1854 he was ordained a minister of the Church of Scotland in Canada, and for fifteen years he was in charge of St. Andrew's Church, Hawkesbury, Ontario. From 1869 to 1908 he was professor of history at Queen's University, Kingston; and for several years he was also on the staff of the Royal Military College, Kingston. He died at Kingston on August 21, 1926. He was the author of *Lectures on the history of the Middle Ages* (Kingston, 1904).

[*Queen's quarterly*, 1926; K. Ferguson, *George Dalrymple Ferguson, first professor of history at Queen's University* (Historic Kingston, 1965); Morgan, *Can. men* (1898).]

Ferguson, George Howard (1870-1946), prime minister of Ontario (1923-30), was born at Kemptville, Ontario, on June 18, 1870. He was educated at the University of Toronto (B.A., 1891) and Osgoode Hall, and was called to the bar in 1894 (K.C., 1908). In 1905 he was elected member of the Legislative Assembly as a Conservative for Grenville, and he continued to represent this constituency for twenty-five years. He was minister of lands and mines in the Hearst government from 1914 to 1919, and in 1920 he was elected Conservative leader in the legislature, and in 1923 he led his party to victory at the polls, and became prime minister of Ontario. He combined the offices of prime minister and minister of education until 1930, when he resigned to accept appointment as Canadian high commissioner in London. He resigned from this post in 1935, and then retired from political life. He died at Toronto, Ontario, on February 21, 1946.

[J. Henderson, *Howard Ferguson: The romance of a personality* (Toronto, 1930); *Who was who, 1941-50*; *Can. who's who, 1938-39*; *Can. parl. guide*, 1930; *Encyc. Can.*]

Ferguson, John Bright (1889-1963), chemist and professor, was born at Londesborough, Ontario, November 2, 1889. He graduated from Victoria College in the University of Toronto in chemistry and mineralogy (B.A., 1912). From Toronto he went to the Geophysical Laboratory in the Carnegie Institute in Washington. During service at the Geophysical Laboratory he solved wartime problems related to the manufacture of optical glass and the composition and stability of certain silicate materials. After a short period with the Western Electric Company of New York he returned, in 1920, as associate professor of research at the University of Toronto, remaining at the University until retirement in 1948. In 1928 he was chosen as a co-

operating expert and editor of "systems containing refractory substances" for *International critical tables*. He was a fellow of the Royal Society of Canada, and of the Canadian Institute of Chemistry. He was author of more than one hundred scientific papers. He died at Toronto, Ontario, on January 7, 1963.

[*Trans. Roy. Soc. Can.* (1963).]

Fergusson, Adam (1782-1862), legislative councillor of Canada, was born at Woodhill, Perthshire, Scotland, in 1782. He first visited Canada in 1831, and shortly afterwards settled at Woodhill, Upper Canada. A prominent Reformer and agriculturist in Scotland, he was appointed in 1839 a member of the Legislative Council of Upper Canada, and in 1841 of the Legislative Council of united Canada. He was also president of the Agricultural Association of Upper Canada. He died at Woodhill, Upper Canada, in 1862. He was the author of *Practical notes made during a tour in Canada and a portion of the United States* (Edinburgh, 1834).

[J. C. Boylen, *The Hon. Adam Fergusson* (Can. mag., 1913); Taylor, *Brit. Am.*, vol. 2; Morgan, *Bib. can.*; W. Kingsford, *The early bibliography of Upper Canada* (Montreal, 1891).]

Fergusson, Adam Johnston. See **Blair, Adam Johnston Fergusson.**

Fergusson, W. Neil (1869?-1954), missionary and author, was born at Bond Head, Ontario, about 1869, and died at Glen Orchard, Muskoka, Ontario, on July 18, 1954. He graduated from Knox College, Toronto, in 1894; and for twenty-five years he was a Presbyterian missionary in China, under the British and Foreign Bible Society. He returned to Canada in 1924, and occupied several charges in Ontario. He was the author of *Adventure, sport, and travel on Tibet steppes* (London, 1911).

[Toronto *Globe and Mail*, July 19, 1954.]

Ferland, Albert (1872-1943), poet and artist, was born at Montreal, Quebec, on August 23, 1872. He was privately educated, and in later years was employed as a draughtsman in the General Post Office in Montreal. He was one of the founders of the "École Littéraire de Montréal" in 1895, and became its president in 1904. He was the author of *Mélodies poétiques* (Montreal, 1893), *Femmes rêvées* (Montreal, 1899), *Le Canada chanté* (4 vols., Montreal, 1908), and *Opuscules* (Montreal, 1912); and he illustrated his own books. He was elected a fellow of the Royal Society of Canada in 1928; and he died at Montreal, Quebec, on November 9, 1943.

[*Proc. Roy. Soc. Can.*, 1944; *Can. who's who*, 1936-37; J. Léger, *Le Canada français et son expression littéraire* (Paris, 1938).]

Ferland, Jean Baptiste Antoine (1805-1865), priest and historian, was born at Montreal, Lower Canada, on December 26, 1805, the son of Antoine Ferland and Elizabeth LeBrun de Duplessis. He was educated at Nicolet College; and in 1828 was ordained a priest of the Roman Catholic Church, and was appointed vicar at Quebec. Subsequently he served in several parishes in Lower Canada. In 1841 he became professor of philosophy in Nicolet College; and in 1848 he was appointed superior of the college. In 1855 he was appointed professor of Canadian history in Laval University, Quebec, and in 1864 dean of the Faculty of Arts. He entered the field of historical writing with his *Observations sur un ouvrage intitulé "Histoire du Canada", par M. L'abbé Brasseur de Bourbourg* (Quebec, 1853). This was followed by *Notes sur les régistres de Notre Dame de Québec* (Quebec, 1854; 2nd ed., Quebec, 1863). His best-known work, however, is his *Cours d'histoire du Canada* (2 vols., Quebec, 1861-65). He died at Quebec on January 11, 1865; and some of his work, which had appeared in the *Foyer canadien* and *Soirées canadiennes* and elsewhere, was republished posthumously in separate form — notably *Opuscules* (Quebec, 1876), *La Gaspésie* (Quebec, 1877), *Louis Olivier Gamache* (Quebec, 1877), and *Mgr. J. O. Plessis* (Quebec, 1878).

[H. d'Arles, *Nos historiens* (Montreal, 1921); Bibaud, *Panth. can.*; Morgan, *Cel. Can.* and *Bib. can.*; *Cyc. Am. biog.*; Allaire, *Dict. biog.*; Le Jeune, *Dict. gén.*]

Fernie, William (1837-1921), miner and capitalist, was born at Kimbolton, Huntingdonshire, England, in 1837. After leading an adventurous life in Australia and South America, he settled in British Columbia in 1860; and from 1873 to 1882 he was gold commissioner of the province. In 1887 he located coal deposits at Crow's Nest, and was one of the promoters of the Crow's Nest Pass Coal Company and the British Columbia Southern Railway. He was the founder of the city of Fernie, British Columbia, which derived its name from him. He died at Victoria, British Columbia, on May 15, 1921.

[Morgan, *Can. men* (1912); J. B. Kerr, *Biographical dictionary of well-known British Columbians* (Vancouver, 1890).]

Fernow, Bernhard Edouard (1851-1923), forester, was born on January 7, 1851, in Posen, Prussia. He was educated at the University of Königsberg, and served in the Prussian army during the Franco-Prussian War. He emigrated to the United States in 1876; and from 1886 to 1898 he was chief of the division of forestry in the United States department of agriculture. From 1898 to 1903 he was director of the New York State College of Forestry at Cornell University. In 1907 he became dean of the Faculty of Forestry in the University of Toronto, and this position he retained until his retirement in 1919. He died at Toronto on February 6, 1923. In addition to many technical contributions to scientific periodicals, he was the author of *Economics of forestry* (New York, 1902), *A brief history of forestry* (New Haven, Conn., 1907), and *The care of trees in lawn, park, and street* (New York, 1910). He was an LL.D. of the University of Wisconsin and of Queen's University, Kingston.

[Morgan, *Can. men* (1912); *Who's who in Canada*, 1922; *Univ. of Toronto monthly*, 1923.]

Ferrie, Adam (1777-1863), merchant, was born at Irvine, Scotland, on March 15, 1777. He became a merchant in Glasgow, interested in the Canadian trade; and in 1829 he himself came out to Canada. He founded a general importing business in Montreal, and his sons established a branch of the business in Hamilton, Upper Canada. He retired from active business in 1855; and he died at Hamilton on December 24, 1863. He was appointed a member of the Legislative Council of Upper Canada in 1841.

[Adam Shortt, *The Hon. Adam Ferrie* (Journal of the Canadian Bankers' Association, 1924).]

Ferrie, William (1815-1903), clergyman, was born at St. Andrew's, Scotland, in 1815, and became for some years minister of a Presbyterian church in Saint John, New Brunswick. Later he removed to the United States; and he died at Monticello, Ohio, on December 29, 1903. He was the author, while in British North America, of *The cream of Scottish history* (Saint John, N.B., 1857), and *The papacy* (Halifax, N.S., 1858).

[Morgan, *Bib. can.*; W. G. MacFarlane, *New Brunswick bibliography* (Saint John, N.B., 1895).]

Ferrier, Alan (1894-1971), aviation pioneer, was born at Ootacamund, India, May 26, 1894. He was educated at Berkhamsted School in England, at McGill University (B.Sc., 1920) and at the Imperial College of Science, London (D.I.C., 1927). He served in the First World War with the Royal Engineers. Subsequently he worked with T. Pringle and Sons of Montreal on water power and textile machinery engineering. He joined the Canadian Air Board in 1921 as an engineering clerk and was commissioned in the R.C.A.F. in 1922. He was loaned to the Department of Transport in 1937 as chief aeronautical engineer. On the outbreak of war he returned to the R.C.A.F. as director of aeronautical engineering, in charge of design, development, and inspection. He became a member of the Canadian Air Transport Board on its formation in 1944 and in 1949 left the board to join the International Civil Aviation Organization as assistant secretary general for air navigation. He retired in 1957. He is recognized as a pioneer in Canadian military and civil aviation. He died at Montreal, Quebec, June 26, 1971.

[*Can. who's who*, 1967-69.]

Ferrier, James (1800-1888), capitalist and politician, was born in Fifeshire, Scotland, on October 22, 1800. He came to Canada in 1821, and became a successful merchant in Montreal. He was one of the promoters of the Montreal and Lachine Railway, and in 1857 he became a director of the Grand Trunk Railway. In 1845 he was elected mayor of Montreal; and in 1847 he was appointed to the Legislative Council of Canada. In 1867 he was called to the Senate of Canada, and at the same time was appointed a member of the Legislative Council of Quebec. He died in Montreal, Quebec, on May 30, 1888.

[Dent, *Can. port.*, vol. 4; Taylor, *Brit. Am.*, vol. 1; *Can. parl. comp.*; *Can. biog. dict.*, Quebec vol. (Chicago, 1881); W. J. Rattray, *The Scot in British North America* (4 vols., Toronto, 1881).]

Fessenden, Mrs. Clementina, *née* **Trenholme** (d. 1918), imperialist, was born in the province of Quebec, the daughter of Edward Trenholme, of Trenholme, Quebec, and Marian Kidley. She was educated in Montreal, and in 1867 married the Rev. E. G. Fessenden, who died and left her a widow. She became organizing secretary of the Imperial Order of the Daughters of the Empire; and it was largely owing to her efforts that Empire Day (May 24, the birthday of Queen Victoria) was established in Canada. She died at Hamilton, Ontario, on September 14, 1918. She was the author of *Our Union Jack, The genesis of empire day,* and other pamphlets.

[Morgan, *Can. men and women* (1912).]

Fetherstonhaugh, Robert Collier (1892-1949), military historian, was born in Montreal, Quebec, in 1892, and died there on January 13, 1949. He was educated at the Montreal High School, and went into business; but his health gave way, and limited his activities for the rest of his life. He was not able to enlist in the Canadian forces during the First World War, but he took an intense interest in following the course of the war, and was the author of the following regimental or unit histories: *The 13th Battalion, Royal Highlanders of Canada* (Toronto, 1925); *The Royal Montreal Regiment* (Montreal, 1927); *No. 3 Canadian General Hospital* (Montreal, 1928); *The 24th Battalion, C.E.F., Victoria Rifles of Canada* (Montreal, 1930); *The Royal Canadian Regiment* (Montreal, 1936); *The Royal Canadian Mounted Police* (New York, 1938); and *McGill University at war* (Montreal, 1947). He was the author also of a biography, *Charles Fleetwood Sise* (Montreal, 1944); and he translated into English A. J.

Lapointe, *Soldier of Quebec* (Montreal, 1931). In 1946 McGill University conferred on him the LL.D. degree.

[Montreal *Gazette*, Jan. 14, 1949.]

Fewster, Ernest Philip (1868-1947), physician and poet, was born in Berkshire, England, in August, 1868, and died at Vancouver, British Columbia, in 1947. He was educated in England and at a medical college in Chicago (M.D., 1901). For many years he practised as a physician and surgeon in Vancouver. He was the author of the following volumes of poetry: *White desire* (Ottawa, 1930), *The immortal dwellers* (Vancouver, 1938), *Litany before the dawn of fire* (Toronto, 1942), *The wind and the sea* (Vancouver, 1946), and *Rejoice O my heart* (Vancouver, 1949), the last published by his widow, Dr. Grace Fewster. He was the author also of a book of essays, *My garden dreams* (Ottawa, 1926).

[*Can. who's who*, 1936-37.]

Fidler, Peter (1769-1822), fur-trader and surveyor, was born at Bolsover, Derbyshire, England, on August 16, 1769. He was apprenticed to the Hudson's Bay Company in 1788, and he spent the rest of his life in the service of the Company in the Canadian North West. He learnt surveying from Philip Turnor (q.v.), and his surveys were later incorporated in a map of the North West Territories made for J. G. MacTavish (q.v.). He died at Manitoba Post, in the Swan River district of the Hudson's Bay territories, on December 17, 1822. He married an Indian woman; and by her he had at least four sons.

[J. B. Tyrrell, *Peter Fidler, trader and surveyor* (Trans. Roy. Soc. Can., 1913); W. S. Wallace, *Peter Fidler looks ahead 200 years* (Beaver, 1943).]

Fielding, William Stevens (1848-1929), finance minister of Canada (1896-1911 and 1921-25), was born in Halifax, Nova Scotia, on November 24, 1848, the son of Charles Fielding. He was educated at Halifax, and in 1864 he entered the office of the Halifax *Morning Chronicle*. He was on the staff of this paper for twenty years, and became its managing editor. From 1882 to 1896 he represented Halifax in the Legislative Assembly of Nova Scotia, and from 1884 to 1896 he was Liberal prime minister of the province. In 1896 he deserted the provincial arena to become minister of finance in the Dominion government formed by Sir Wilfrid Laurier (q.v.); and from 1896 to 1911 he held the portfolio of finance in this government, representing Shelburne and Queens in the House of Commons. In 1910-11 he played a leading part in the negotiations for reciprocity in trade with the United States; and in the general elections of 1911 he was defeated. In 1917 he broke with Sir Wilfrid Laurier over the question of compulsory military service, and in the elections of that year he was returned to the Canadian House of Commons as a Liberal Unionist. He did not enter the Unionist cabinet formed by Sir Robert Borden; but he gave it a general support. At the end of the war, he reverted to the Liberal party; and after the death of Sir Wilfrid Laurier in 1919, he was a candidate for the leadership of the Liberal party, but his age and his desertion of the party in 1917 told against him, and he failed to gain a majority of votes in the Liberal convention of 1920. In 1921, however, he again took office as finance minister in the Mackenzie King government, and he retained this portfolio until 1925, when he retired on an annuity voted him by parliament. He died at Ottawa on June 23, 1929. In 1876 he married Hester, daughter of Thomas A. Rankine of Saint John, New Brunswick; and by her he had one son and four daughters. He was created an imperial privy councillor in 1923; and he was a D.C.L. of Acadia University and an LL.D. of Queen's, McGill, Dalhousie, and McMaster universities.

[B. Russell, *Recollections of W. S. Fielding* (Dalhousie review, 1929); *Can. parl. comp.*; Morgan, *Can. men* (1912); O. D. Skelton, *The life and letters of Sir Wilfrid Laurier* (2 vols., Toronto, 1921); C. B. Fergusson, *Hon. W. S. Fielding* (Windsor, N.S., 1970).]

Fields, John Charles (1863-1932), educationist, was born at Hamilton, Canada West, on May 14, 1863. He was educated at the University of Toronto (B.A., 1884), at Johns Hopkins University (Ph.D., 1887), and at Paris, Göttingen, and Berlin; and after three years as professor of mathematics in Allegheny College, Pennsylvania, he was appointed in 1902 lecturer in mathematics in the University of Toronto. Here he remained for the rest of his life, rising to the rank of professor. In 1909 he was elected a fellow of the Royal Society of Canada, and in 1913 of the Royal Society of London; and he was president of the Royal Canadian Institute from 1919 to 1925. He died in Toronto, Ontario, in August, 1932. He was the author of *Theory of the algebraic functions of a complex variable* (Berlin, 1906).

[*Proc. Roy. Soc. Can.*, 1933; *University of Toronto monthly*, 1932; Morgan, *Can. men* (1912).]

Fingold, Samuel (1911-1970), industrialist, was born at Lemonville, Ontario, April 17, 1911, and educated at Claremont, Ontario, public and continuation schools. He was chairman of Slater Steel Industries, Burlington Steel Company, and N. Slater Company; and chairman of the Board and director of Canadian Foundation Company and associated companies throughout Eastern Canada. He was honorary governor of the Canadian Association for Retarded Children. He died at Toronto, August 2, 1970.

[*Can. Who's Who*, 1967-69.]

Finlay, Hugh (1732-1801), deputy postmaster-general of British North America (1774-99), was born in Scotland in 1732, and came to Canada about 1760. In 1765 he was appointed a member of the governors' council; and later he became postmaster at Quebec. In 1774 he was appointed deputy postmaster-general of British North America; and he occupied this post, which was an imperial appointment, until 1799. During this period he played an important part in the government of Canada; and in particular he laid the foundation of the Canadian postal services. He died on December 26, 1801. A journal kept by him when surveyor of post roads in 1773-74 has been edited and published by F. H. Norton (Brooklyn, 1867); a journal in which he described the siege of Quebec in 1775-76 has been printed in the *Manuscripts* published by the Literary and Historical Society of Quebec, 4th series (1875); and a number of his letters dealing with political affairs in Canada have been printed in A. Shortt and A. G. Doughty, *Documents relating to the constitutional history of Canada* (2 vols., Ottawa, 1918).

[J. G. Hendy, *Hugh Finlay, pioneer of Canadian posts* (Empire review, 1902); W. Smith, *The history of the post office in British North America* (Cambridge, 1920).]

Finlay, James (d. 1797), fur-trader, was a native of Scotland who came to Canada in the early days of British rule. Here he engaged in the fur-trade, and the date on the medal given him by the Beaver Club of Montreal, of which he became a charter member in 1785, shows him to have wintered in the Indian country as early as 1766. He was the first of the "Old Subjects" to reach the valley of the Saskatchewan, and in 1768 he built what was known as Finlay's House near Neepawin. Later, he entered into partnership with a young Englishman named John Gregory (q.v.); and from 1773 to 1783 the firm of Finlay and Gregory appears in the fur-trade licences as sending canoes to the West. In 1783, James Finlay retired from the fur-trade; and in his later years he was inspector of chimneys in Montreal. He died in Montreal in 1797. He married in Montreal, apparently, about 1765, Christiana Youel; and by her he had two sons, James (q.v.) and John (q.v.), and two daughters, Anne and Christy, the latter of whom became the wife of Capt. Edward Townsend Jones of the 34th Foot.

[W. S. Wallace, *The pedlars from Quebec* (Can. hist. rev., 1932).]

Finlay, James (1766-1830), fur-trader, was born in Montreal in 1766, the son of James Finlay (q.v.) and Christiana Youel. He entered the service of the "Little Company", in opposition to the North West Company, as an apprentice clerk, in 1784, at the same time as the Hon. Roderick Mackenzie (q.v.). He became a clerk of the North West Company in 1787, and in 1792 he was made a wintering partner of the

Company, in charge of Fort de l'Isle, on the Saskatchewan. He relinquished his two shares in the Company in 1805, and in 1814 he was a merchant at Beloeil on the river Chambly, in Lower Canada. From 1814 to 1817 he was store-keeper of the Indian department at Lachine, and in 1817 he petitioned for the position held by his father as inspector of chimneys at Montreal. He died at Montreal on January 3, 1830. In 1798 he married Elizabeth Grant, daughter of John Grant (q.v.), and granddaughter of Richard Dobie (q.v.); and by her he had "a large family". His daughter Elizabeth married on March 26, 1835, Frederick, son of Sir John Chetwode, Bart., of Oakley Park, Cheshire.

[W. S. Wallace (ed.), *Documents relating to the North West Company* (Toronto: The Champlain Society, 1934).]

Finlay, John (1774-1833), fur-trader, was born in Montreal in 1774, the son of James Finlay (q.v.) and Christiana Youel. He became a clerk of the North West Company in 1789, and in 1792 was with Alexander Mackenzie (q.v.) on the Peace River. By 1799 he had been admitted to partnership in the Company, and was proprietor in charge at Lake Athabaska. He signed the agreement of 1802; but he retired from the fur-trade in 1804, and in 1805 he relinquished one of his two shares in the Company. In 1807 he was elected a member of the Beaver Club in Montreal; and in 1827 he presided over the last meeting of the Club. He obtained an appointment as deputy assistant commissary-general at Montreal; and he died at Montreal on December 19, 1833.

[W. S. Wallace (ed.), *Documents relating to the North West Company* (Toronto: The Champlain Society, 1934).]

Finlayson, Duncan (1796?-1862), fur-trader, was born at Dingwall, Scotland, about 1796, the son of John Finlayson, later of Montreal, and younger brother of Nicol Finlayson (q.v.). He entered the service of the Hudson's Bay Company in 1815. He was promoted to the rank of chief factor in 1831, and was in that year in charge at Red River. From 1833 to 1837 he was on the Columbia; from 1839 to 1844 he was governor of Assiniboia; and in 1844 he succeeded James Keith (q.v.) in charge at Lachine. He retired from the Company in 1855, but was re-appointed, and retired finally only in 1859. He died in London, England, on July 25, 1862. He was a brother-in-law of Lady Simpson, the wife of Sir George Simpson (q.v.).

[E. E. Rich (ed.), *Journal of occurrences in the Athabasca department, by George Simpson* (Toronto: The Champlain Society, 1938).]

Finlayson, Nicol (1795-1877), fur-trader, was born in Scotland, in 1795, the son of John Finlayson, later of Montreal, and elder brother

of Duncan Finlayson (q.v.). He entered the service of the Hudson's Bay Company in 1815. He was promoted to the rank of chief trader in 1833, and to that of chief factor in 1846. He retired from the Company in 1855, and he died in 1877.

[G. P. de T. Glazebrook, *The Hargrave correspondence* (Toronto: The Champlain Society, 1938); *Dict. Can. biog.*, vol. 10.]

Finlayson, Roderick (1818-1892), fur-trader, was born in the parish of Lochalsh, Ross-shire, Scotland, on March 16, 1818, and was probably a relative of Duncan Finlayson (q.v.). He came to America in 1837, and entered the service of the Hudson's Bay Company as a clerk. In 1839 he was sent across the Rocky Mountains to the Pacific slope; and here he spent most of the rest of his life. He was at Fort Simpson, on the Mackenzie River, in 1842; but in 1843 he returned to the Pacific coast, and he took part in the founding of Fort Victoria. For many years he was in charge of this post, and may be described as "the founder of Victoria". He was promoted to the rank of chief trader in 1850, and to that of chief factor in 1859. From 1851 to 1863 he was a member of the Legislative Council of Vancouver Island. He retired from the Company's service in 1872; and he died at Victoria, British Columbia, on January 30, 1892. His unpublished autobiography, covering the years from 1837 to 1851, is in the Provincial Archives of British Columbia.

[J. B. Kerr, *Biographical dictionary of well-known British Columbians* (Vancouver, B.C., 1890).]

Finley, Frederick James (1894-1968), painter and teacher, was born in Newcastle, New South Wales, June 4, 1894. He attended Sydney Art School (1919-20), the Académie Julien, Paris (1920-23), the Bavarian Academy in Munich (1930-31), and the Ontario College of Art (1932-34). He served with the Australian army (1914-19) in New Guinea, Egypt, Sinai, and France. He came to Canada in 1925 and worked as a commercial artist until he joined the Ontario College of Art in 1946 as director of advertising and design. He held this position until retirement in 1960. He is represented in the National Gallery of Canada, the National Gallery of New South Wales, Sarnia Public Library, and the Royal Canadian Academy Deposit collection. He was a member of the R.C.A. (A.R.C.A., 1949), (R.C.A., 1954), of the Ontario Society of Artists, and of the Society of Canadian Painters, Etchers and Engravers. His early work was influenced by the work of Vatican Renaissance painters. His work is representational rather than abstract. Primarily a figure painter he did many paintings of rural and contemporary Indian life as well as landscapes and portraits. He died at Toronto in 1968.

[(*Can. who's who*, 1955-57; C. S. Mac-

Donald, *A dictionary of Canadian artists,* vol. 1 (Ottawa, 1967).]

Finucane, Bryan (d. 1785), chief justice of Nova Scotia (1778-85), was born in county Clare, Ireland, and was called to the bar in Dublin. In 1778 he was appointed chief justice of Nova Scotia, and a member of the Council. He died at Halifax on August 3, 1785, and was buried in a private vault in St. Paul's Church, Halifax.

[R. V. Harris, *Catalogue of portraits of the judges of the Supreme Court of Nova Scotia* (Halifax, n.d.).]

Fiset, Sir Eugène Marie Joseph (1874-1951), lieutenant-governor of Quebec (1939-50), was born at Rimouski, Quebec, on March 15, 1874. He was educated at Laval University (B.A., 1894; M.B., 1896; M.D.C.M., 1898), and took post-graduate work in medicine in London and Paris. He served with the Royal Canadian Regiment in the South African War, and was awarded the D.S.O. In 1906 he was appointed deputy minister of militia and defence (after 1915, deputy minister of national defence), and continued as such until 1923, when he retired with the rank of major-general. From 1924 to 1939 he represented Rimouski in the Canadian House of Commons, as a Liberal; and from 1939 to 1950 he was lieutenant-governor of Quebec. He died at Rivière-du-Loup, Quebec, on June 7, 1951. He was created a K.B. in 1917.

[*Can. who's who,* 1949-51; *Can. parl. guide,* 1950; *Encyc. Can.*]

Fiset, Louis Joseph Cyprien (1825-1898), poet, was born at Quebec, Lower Canada, on October 3, 1825; and died in 1898. He was the author of *Jude et Grazia; ou, Les malheurs de l'émigration canadienne* (Quebec, 1861).

[*Cyc. Am. biog.,* vol. 7; Morgan, *Bib. can.*]

Fisher, Alexander (1783?-1847), fur-trader, was born about 1783, and was possibly the son of Alexander Fisher, the first judge of the Midland district of Upper Canada. In any case, he appears from his will, which is preserved in Hudson's Bay House in London, to have come from the neighbourhood of Kingston, Upper Canada. He entered the service of the North West Company as a clerk some years before the union of 1821, and he was taken over as a clerk by the Hudson's Bay Company in that year. In 1823 he was promoted to the rank of chief trader; and he retired from the Company's service in 1845. He died on April 2, 1847. He is not to be confused with another Alexander Fisher, who entered the service of the North West Company in 1815, and was taken over by the Hudson's Bay Company in 1821, but retired from the fur-trade in 1824.

[W. S. Wallace (ed.), *John McLean's Notes of a twenty-five years' service in the Hudson's*

Bay Company (Toronto: The Champlain Society, 1932).]

Fisher, Charles (1808-1880), judge and politician, was born in Fredericton, New Brunswick, on September 16, 1808, the son of Peter Fisher (q.v.), and Susanna Williams. He was educated at King's College, Fredericton (B.A., 1830), studied law, and was called to the bar of New Brunswick in 1833 (Q.C., 1855). In 1837 he was elected to represent York in the Legislative Assembly of New Brunswick, in the Liberal interest, and he continued to hold this seat with but slight interruption until 1868, when he retired from political life. He was a member of the Executive Council from 1848 to 1851; and in 1854 he became prime minister and attorney-general. His government resigned on the prohibitory liquor law question in 1856, but was returned to power the following year, and he remained in office until 1861, when he resigned owing to questions arising out of a Crown Lands investigation, though he kept his seat as a private member. In 1864 he attended the Quebec Conference as a delegate from New Brunswick, and his advocacy of Confederation cost him his seat in the election of 1865. In 1866, however, he was re-elected for his old constituency; and he was one of the delegates sent to England for the final conferences in 1866-67. Upon his return, he was elected to the Canadian House of Commons for the county of York; and he also resumed his old position of attorney-general of New Brunswick. In 1868, however, he retired from political life, and was appointed a puisne judge of the Supreme Court of New Brunswick. He died in Fredericton on December 8, 1880. In September, 1836, he married Amelia, seventh daughter of David Hatfield, a United Empire Loyalist. He was given the degree of D.C.L. by the University of New Brunswick in 1866. He declined at one time the chief justiceship. In 1852 he was appointed one of a commission to codify the provincial statutes; and the results of the work of this important commission were embodied in several volumes, issued in 1854.

[J. W. Lawrence, *Lives of the judges of New Brunswick and their times* (Saint John, N.B., 1907); Dent, *Can. port.,* vol. 4; *Dom. ann. reg.,* 1880-81; *Dict. Can. biog.,* vol. 10.]

Fisher, Edward (1848-1913), musician, was born at Jamaica, Vermont, on January 11, 1848. He obtained his training in music at the New England Conservatory, in Boston, and in Berlin, Germany; and in 1875 he came to Canada as music director of the Ottawa Ladies' College. In 1879 he became organist and choirmaster of St. Andrew's Church, Toronto; and in 1887 he founded the Toronto Conservatory of Music. Of this institution he remained the director until his death at Toronto, on May 31, 1913.

[O. Thompson (ed.), *The international cyc-*

lopedia of music and musicians (New York, 1939).]

Fisher, James (1840-1927), lawyer and politician, was born at Glenquaich, Perthshire, Scotland, on November 6, 1840. He came to Canada when a child, and was educated at the University of Toronto (B.A., 1862; M.A., 1872). He was called to the bar in 1867; and after practising law in Stratford, Ontario, removed to Winnipeg, and was called to the bar of Manitoba in 1883 (Q.C., 1893). He represented Russell in the Manitoba legislature from 1888 to 1899; and was a leading advocate of the building of the Hudson's Bay Railway. He died at Whitby, Ontario, on May 10, 1927. He was the author of several pamphlets.

[Morgan, *Can. men* (1912); *Can. parl. comp.*]

Fisher, John Charlton (1794-1849), journalist, was born at Carlisle, England, on October 23, 1794. He edited the *Albion* newspaper in New York for some years; and in 1823 he accepted the editorship of the *Quebec Gazette*, and with it the office of Queen's printer. In 1831 he incurred censure on account of his political articles, which were not in accord with the policy of the government, and he was forced to resign. He then became the editor of the Quebec *Mercury*; and in 1841 he founded a journal of his own, the *Conservative*. He died at sea on August 10, 1849, when returning to Canada from England. He was for a time president of the Literary and Historical Society of Quebec. He contributed frequently to the *Canadian Magazine* (Montreal, 1823-25); and wrote also a *Note on the ancient English or Anglo-Saxon language* (Trans. Lit. and Hist. Soc., Quebec, vol. iii).

[Morgan, *Bib. can.* and *Cel. Can.*]

Fisher, Peter (1782-1848), the first historian of New Brunswick, was born in Staten Island, New York, on June 9, 1782, the youngest son of Lodewick Fisher, a New Jersey Loyalist. In September, 1783, he was brought by his parents to Saint John, and the family settled at St. Ann's Point, now Fredericton. He carried on an extensive lumber business; and he published anonymously two books, *Sketches of New Brunswick, containing an account of the first settlement of the province* (Saint John, N.B., 1825), and *Notitiae of New Brunswick* (Saint John, N.B., 1838). These entitle him to be described as the first historian of New Brunswick. He died in New Brunswick on August 15, 1848. He married on August 15, 1807, Susanna Williams, by whom he had seven sons and four daughters.

[W. O. Raymond, *Peter Fisher* (Collections of the New Brunswick Historical Society, No. 10, 1919); J. W. Lawrence, *Lives of the judges of New Brunswick* (Saint John, N.B., 1907); W. G. MacFarlane, *New Brunswick bibliography* (Saint John, N.B., 1895).]

Fisher, Sydney Arthur (1850-1921), minister of agriculture for Canada (1896-1911), was born in Montreal, Lower Canada, on June 12, 1850, the son of Arthur Fisher, M.D., and Susanna Corse. He was educated at McGill University and at Trinity College, Cambridge (B.A., 1871), and devoted himself to scientific farming in the Eastern Townships of Quebec. He represented Brome as a Liberal in the Canadian House of Commons from 1882 to 1891, and from 1896 to 1911; and from 1896 to 1911 he was minister of agriculture in the Laurier government. He was defeated in the general elections of 1911, and in a by-election in Châteauguay in 1913, and he thereupon retired to private life. He died at Ottawa on April 9, 1921. He was unmarried.

[*Can. who was who,* vol. 1; *Can. parl. comp.*; Morgan, *Can. men* (1912); O. D. Skelton, *The life and letters of Sir Wilfrid Laurier* (2 vols., Toronto 1922).]

Fitch, Ernest Robert (1878-1935), clergyman, was born at Kingsville, Ontario, in 1878. He was educated at McMaster University, Toronto (B.A., 1905; B.D., 1910; M.A., 1918), and became a Baptist minister. After holding several pastorates in Canada, he removed in 1918 to the United States; and he died at Granville, Ohio, in February, 1935. He was the author of *The Baptists of Canada* (Toronto, 1911).

[*McMaster University monthly*, 1935.]

Fitzgerald, John Gerald (1882-1940), physician and educationist, was born at Drayton, Ontario, in 1882. He was educated at the University of Toronto (M.B., 1903; M.D., 1920) and at Harvard University; and in 1909 he was appointed lecturer in bacteriology in the University of Toronto. Apart from a year spent at the Pasteur Institutes at Paris and Brussels, and two years as associate professor of bacteriology at the University of California, he spent the rest of his life on the staff of the University of Toronto. In 1913 he was appointed associate professor of hygiene in this University, and in 1920 professor of hygiene and preventive medicine. At the same time he became director of the Connaught Laboratories, which he had been instrumental in founding; and in 1924 he was appointed director of the School of Hygiene. From 1932 to 1936 he was also dean of the faculty of medicine in the University of Toronto. He was elected a fellow of the Royal Society of Canada in 1920; and in 1925 he received the degree of LL.D. from Queen's University. He died, after a prolonged illness, at Toronto, Ontario, on June 20, 1940. He was joint author, with others, of *An introduction to the practice of preventive medicine* (St. Louis, Mo., 1922).

[*Proc. Roy. Soc. Can.*, 1941; *Can. who's who*, 1936-37).]

Fitzgerald, Lionel LeMoine (1890-1956), painter, was born at Winnipeg, Manitoba, in

1890, and died there on August 5, 1956. He studied painting in Winnipeg, at the Carnegie Institute in Pittsburgh, and at the Art Students' League in New York. From 1929 to 1947 he was principal of the Winnipeg School of Art; he became a member of the Group of Seven in 1932, on the death of J. E. H. MacDonald (q.v.); and in 1933 he was one of the founders of the Canadian Group of Painters. Three of his Manitoba landscapes hang in the National Gallery at Ottawa. In 1947 the University of Manitoba conferred on him the honorary degree of LL.D.

[R. Ayre, *Lionel LeMoine Fitzgerald* (Canadian Art, Autumn, 1956); *Encyc. Can.*]

FitzGibbon, James (1780-1863), soldier, was born in Ireland on November 16, 1780, the son of Gerald FitzGibbon and Mary Wyndham. He served in the British army as a non-commissioned officer during the Napoleonic Wars, and received his commission in 1806. He came to Canada in 1802, and in the War of 1812 he received the surrender of the American forces at Beaver Dams. In 1822 he was appointed assistant adjutant-general; and during the rebellion of 1837 he was acting adjutant-general. In 1846 he returned to England, and in 1850 was appointed a military knight of Windsor. He died in England on December 10, 1863. In 1814 he married Mary Haley; and by her he had four sons and one daughter.

[M. A. FitzGibbon, *A veteran of 1812* (Toronto, 1895); E. M. Chadwick, *Ontarian families* (2 vols., Toronto, 1894-98); Morgan, *Cel. Can.*]

FitzGibbon, Mary Agnes (1851-1915), author, was born at Belleville, Upper Canada, on June 18, 1851, the eldest daughter of Charles FitzGibbon and Agnes Dunbar Moodie. She was educated in Belleville and at Pinehurst, Toronto; and she lived most of her life in Toronto. In 1894 she founded the Canadian Women's Historical Society of Toronto; and she was actively engaged in philanthropic work. She died at Toronto on May 17, 1915. She wrote *A trip to Manitoba* (London, 1880), *A veteran of 1812* (Toronto, 1895), and *Historic days* (Toronto, 1898).

[Morgan, *Can. men and women* (1912).]

FitzGibbon, Mrs. Mary Agnes, *née* **Bernard** (1862-1933), journalist, was born at Barrie, Canada West, in 1862, the daughter of R. B. Bernard and Agnes Elizabeth Lally, and a niece of the Baroness Macdonald of Earnscliffe. In 1882 she married Clare Valentine FitzGibbon, son of the Hon. Gerald and Lady Louise FitzGibbon; and for fourteen years she lived abroad. In 1896, however, she returned to Canada, and went to live with her step-father, D'Alton McCarthy (q.v.). She became a journalist, and wrote under the nom-de-plume of "Lally Bernard". In her later years she lived in Victoria, British Columbia; and

she died there on July 17, 1933. She was the author of *The Canadian Doukhobor settlements* (Toronto, 1899).

[Morgan, *Can. men and women* (1912).]

Fitzpatrick, Alfred (1862-1936), clergyman and educationist, was born at Millsville, Nova Scotia, April 22, 1862. He was educated at Queen's University, Kingston (B.A., 1890) and at McMaster University, Hamilton (M.A., 1922), and he was ordained a minister of the Presbyterian Church. After serving in several charges and mission fields, he felt the need for an educational programme in the lumber and mining camps, and founded in 1900 what became the Frontier College, an organization which received a Dominion charter in 1922. He was the author of *Handbook for new Canadians* (Toronto, 1919) and *The university in overalls* (Toronto, 1920). He died at Toronto, Ontario, on June 16, 1936. In 1935 he received the honour of O.B.E. He was not married.

[Morgan, *Can. men* (1912).]

Fitzpatrick, Sir Charles (1853-1942), minister of justice for Canada (1902-06), chief justice of Canada (1906-18), and lieutenant-governor of Quebec (1918-23), was born at Quebec, Canada East, December 19, 1853. He was educated at Laval University (B.A., 1873; LL.B., 1876; LL.D., 1902); and was called to the bar in 1876 (Q.C., 1893). He practised law in Quebec, and distinguished himself as a criminal lawyer. He was the chief counsel for Louis Riel (q.v.) in 1885; and he defended the Hon. Honoré Mercier (q.v.) against charges made following the fall of the Mercier administration in Quebec in 1892. He sat as a Liberal for Quebec county in the Legislative Assembly of Quebec from 1890 to 1896, and in the Canadian House of Commons from 1896 to 1906. He became solicitor-general in the Laurier government in 1896, and minister of justice in 1902; but in 1906 he resigned this portfolio to accept the appointment of chief justice of the Supreme Court of Canada. He retired from the bench in 1918; and for the years 1918-23 he served as lieutenant-governor of the province of Quebec. His later years were spent in retirement; and he died at Quebec, Que., on June 17, 1942. In 1879 he married Corinne, daughter of the Hon. R. E. Caron (q.v.), and sister of Sir Adolphe Caron; and by her he had one son and four daughters. He was created a K.C.M.G. in 1907 and a G.C.M.G. in 1911; and he received the honorary degree of LL.D. from University of Ottawa, McGill University, the University of Notre Dame, and the University of Toronto.

[*Americana annual*, 1943; *Who's who*, 1942; *Can. who's who*, 1938-39; *Can. parl. comp.*; Le Jeune, *Dict. gén.*]

FitzRoy, Sir Charles Augustus (1796-1858), lieutenant-governor of Prince Edward Island (1837-41), was born on May 10, 1796, the eldest son of Lord Charles FitzRoy by his first wife, Frances Mundy. He obtained a commission in the Horse Guards, and was at the battle of Waterloo. He retired from active service, and was elected member for Bury St. Edmunds in the British House of Commons; and in 1837 he was appointed lieutenant-governor of Prince Edward Island, and was knighted before his departure. He returned to England in 1841, and was subsequently appointed governor of the Leeward Islands (1841-45), governor of New South Wales (1846-50), and governor-general of Australia (1850-55). He died in London on February 16, 1858. He married (1) on March 11, 1820, Lady Mary Lennox (d. 1847), daughter of the Duke of Richmond; and (2) on December 11, 1855, Margaret Gordon.

[*Dict. nat. biog.*]

Flanders, Charles Ruston (1852-1920), clergyman and educationist, was born at Shefford, Canada East, on August 2, 1852. He was educated at Waterloo Academy, and at Victoria University (B.A., 1881), and entered the ministry of the Methodist Church in 1873. From 1893 to 1907 he was principal of Stanstead College. He died in Winnipeg, Manitoba, on November 9, 1920.

[Morgan, *Can. men* (1912).]

Flavelle, Sir Joseph Wesley, Bart. (1858-1939), financier, was born at Peterborough, Canada West, on February 15, 1858. He was educated in Peterborough, and afterwards engaged there in the produce business. In 1887 he moved to Toronto; and here he became one of the leading industrialists and financiers. He became president of the William Davies Company, pork packers, Toronto, and vice-president of the Robert Simpson Company. In 1905 he was appointed chairman of the royal commission which reorganized the University of Toronto; and he became a prominent member of the board of governors of the University, as well as trustee of the Royal Ontario Museum and chairman of the board of trustees of the Toronto General Hospital. From 1914 to 1920 he was chairman of the Imperial Munitions Board; and for his notable work in this capacity he was created in 1917 a baronet of the United Kingdom. In 1920-21 he was chairman of the board of the Grand Trunk Railway Company; and later he was chairman of the board of the Canadian Bank of Commerce and of the National Trust Company. He died at Palm Beach, Florida, March 7, 1939. In 1882 he married Clara Ellsworth (d. 1932); and by her he had one son and two daughters. He received honorary degrees from the University of Toronto and Mount Allison University. He was the author of *The Canadian National Railway system* (Toronto, 1921), and other pamphlets.

[*Who was who*, 1928-40; *Can. who's who*, 1938-39; *University of Toronto monthly*,

1939; D. Carnegie, *The history of munitions supply in Canada, 1914-1918* (London, 1925).

Fleming, Mrs. Ann Cuthbert (d. 1860), author and school-teacher, was a native of Scotland who came to Canada about 1815. She published at this time two small volumes of poetry, *Home, a poem* (Edinburgh, 1815), and *A year in Canada, and other poems* (Edinburgh, 1816). She founded later a ladies' school in Montreal, and published three early Canadian school-books, *First book for Canadian children* (Montreal, 1844), *The prompter* (Montreal, 1844), and *Progressive exercises on the English language, to correspond with the prompter* (Montreal, 1845). She married James, a younger brother of John Fleming (q.v.), of Montreal; and she died in 1860.

[Morgan, *Bib. can.*]

Fleming, Archibald Lang (1883-1953), Anglican bishop of the Arctic, was born at Greenock, Scotland, on September 8, 1883, and died at Toronto, Ontario, on May 17, 1953. He came to Canada as a young man, and entered Wycliffe College as a theological student in 1908. He was ordained a priest of the Church of England in 1913; and for several years served as a missionary to the Eskimos of Baffin Land. He then served as rector in several churches in Canada, notably at St. John's Church, Saint John, New Brunswick; and for three years he was chaplain of Wycliffe College. He then returned to the North in 1927 as archdeacon of the Arctic, and in 1933 he became the first Anglican bishop of the Arctic. He returned to Toronto in 1948. He was the author of *A book of remembrance; or, The history of St. John's Church, Saint John, New Brunswick* (Saint John, N.B., 1925), *Dwellers in Arctic night* (Westminster, 1929), and *Perils of the polar pack* (Toronto, 1932). His autobiography was published posthumously, under the title *Archibald the Arctic* (New York, 1956).

[*Can. who's who*, 1949-51; *Encyc. Can.*]

Fleming, John (1786?-1832), merchant and author, was born in Aberdeenshire, Scotland, about 1786, and emigrated to Canada about 1803. He became head of the firm of Hart, Logan and Co., and president of the Bank of Montreal. A man of literary interests, he gathered what was for that time a very large library, which was sold by auction in 1843; and he published *The political annals of Lower Canada* (Montreal, 1828). He died at Montreal of cholera on July 30, 1832.

[Morgan, *Bib. can.*; P. Gagnon, *Bibliographie canadienne* (Quebec, 1895), no. 2732.]

Fleming, Michael Anthony (1792-1850), Roman Catholic bishop of Newfoundland (1829-50), was born in Tipperary, Ireland, in

1792, and died at Belvedere, Newfoundland, on July 14, 1850. He became a member of the Franciscan Order in 1808; and he was brought to Newfoundland as a missionary in 1823 by Bishop Scallan. He succeeded to the bishopric of Newfoundland in 1829, and in 1841 he laid the corner-stone of the Roman Catholic cathedral in St. John's. He was instrumental in persuading several religious orders to open schools in Newfoundland.

[M. F. Howley, *The Ecclesiastical history of Newfoundland* (Boston, 1888); *Encyc. Can.*; *Newfoundland supp.*]

Fleming, Sir Sandford (1827-1915), civil engineer, was born at Kirkcaldy, Fifeshire, Scotland, on January 7, 1827, the son of Andrew Greig Fleming and Elizabeth Arnot. He studied surveying and engineering in Scotland, came to Canada in 1845, and entered the service of the Northern Railway. Of this railway he became chief engineer in 1857. He was chief engineer of the Intercolonial Railway during its construction; and in 1871 he was appointed engineer-in-chief to superintend the surveys for the Canadian Pacific Railway. He surveyed the route through the Yellowhead Pass which is now followed by the Canadian National Railway; and he was the first to demonstrate the practicability of the route through the Kicking Horse, Eagle, and Rogers passes. In 1880 he retired from the service of the government; and thereafter he devoted himself to literary and scientific work.) He was the pioneer of the twenty-four-hour-day system of time reckoning; and he was the father of the idea of an intra-imperial system of cable communication; Though never a member of parliament, he played a prominent part in public life. He was an ardent imperialist; and it is worthy of record that it was he in 1849 who rescued from the burning Parliament Buildings at Montreal the portrait of Queen Victoria. He became a vice-president of the United Empire League; and he was one of the Canadian representatives at the Colonial Conferences of 1887 and 1894. He was created a C.M.G. in 1877, and a K.C.M.G. in 1897. In 1855 he married Ann Jean, daughter of Sheriff Hall of Peterborough, Upper Canada, and he had six children. In 1882 he was chosen a charter member of the Royal Society of Canada, and in 1888 he became its president. He was an LL.D. of St. Andrews University (1884), of Columbia University (1887), of the University of Toronto (1907), and of Queen's University, Kingston (1908). Of Queen's University he was for thirty-five years (1880-1915) the chancellor. He was also for many years a director of the Hudson's Bay Company and of the Canadian Pacific Railway. He died at Halifax, Nova Scotia, on July 22, 1915.

His chief publications were *Railway inventions* (Toronto, 1847), *A railway to the Pacific through British territory* (Port Hope, 1858), *The Intercolonial* (Montreal, 1876), and *Can-*

ada and British imperial cables (Ottawa, 1900), besides numerous reports on railway surveys and construction work, and papers contributed to scientific periodicals.

[L. J. Burpee, *Sandford Fleming, empire builder* (Oxford, 1915), with portrait and bibliography; Sir A. Macphail, *Sir Sandford Fleming* (Queen's quarterly, 1929); H. Mac-Lean, *Man of Steel: The story of Sir Sandford Fleming* (Toronto, 1969); Morgan, *Can. men* (1912); Rose, *Cyc. Can. biog.* (1886).]

Flemming, James Kidd (1868-1927), prime minister of New Brunswick (1911-14), was born at Woodstock, New Brunswick, on April 27, 1868, of Irish parentage. He became a merchant and lumber-manufacturer in Woodstock, and in 1900 he was elected to represent Carleton county in the Legislative Assembly of New Brunswick. From 1908 to 1911 he was provincial secretary in the Hazen government; and from 1911 to 1914 he was prime minister of New Brunswick. He resigned as the result of charges made against him in regard to contributions made to the Conservative campaign funds, and for some years retired to private life. In 1925, however, he was elected to represent Victoria-Carleton in the Canadian House of Commons, and he sat for this constituency until his death at Woodstock, New Brunswick, on February 10, 1927.

[*Can. parl. comp.*; Morgan, *Can. men* (1912); *Can. who was who*, vol. 2.]

Flenley, Ralph (1886-1969), historian, was born in Liverpool, England, on January 2, 1886. He was educated at Liverpool University (M.A., 1908) and New College, Oxford (B. Litt., 1910). He began teaching at the University of Manitoba in 1911. He served with the Royal Field Artillery during the First World War, becoming captain and battery adjutant. He was twice mentioned in despatches. He returned to the University of Manitoba in 1919 and joined the staff of the University of Toronto in 1920 where he remained a member and then chairman of the history department (1952-55) until his retirement in 1955. He was, in many respects, the complete historian. He wrote textbooks for schools as well as specialist studies for scholars. He died at Parkgate, Cheshire, on March 21, 1969. He was author of *Six town chronicles* (Oxford, 1911), *A calendar of the register of the Queen's Majesty's council in the principality of Wales and the marches of the same (1569-1591)* (Cardiff, 1916), *A life of Samuel Champlain* (Toronto, 1924), translated *Dollier de Casson's Histoire de Montréal (1640-1672)* (Toronto, 1928), *Makers of the nineteenth century* (London, 1927), *World history* (London, 1936), *Modern German history* (London, 1953).

[*Can. hist. rev.*, vol. L, 1969.]

Fletcher, Charles G. (1881-1961), actor, was born in Toronto, Ontario, in 1881. He was a member of the original New York Company of the *Red Mill* and of the *Merry Widow* in its first North American production. He played with the Vaughan Glaser Players in Toronto's Uptown and Victoria theatres from 1923 to 1935 when he retired from the stage. He continued to live in Toronto until his death in December, 1961.

[Metropolitan Toronto Library Board, *Biographical scrapbooks*, vol. 18.]

Fletcher, Edward Taylor (1816?-1897), civil servant and author, was born in Canterbury, England, about 1816, the son of Capt. Fletcher, of the Royal York Regiment of Rangers. He was educated in Quebec, and became in 1842 a land surveyor. He was for many years an officer of the surveyor-general's department in the old province of Canada, and afterwards in the province of Quebec. In 1878 he was appointed surveyor-general of Quebec; but he retired on pension in 1882, and his later years were spent living with one of his sons, first in Victoria, and then in New Westminster, British Columbia. He died in New Westminster, British Columbia, on January 30, 1897. In 1846 he married Henrietta Amelia, fourth daughter of William Burns Lindsay, and by her he had three sons and one daughter. In his early days he was a contributor to the *Literary Garland* (Montreal, 1838-51), and to the *Transactions* of the Quebec Literary and Historical Society. He was the author of an *Essay on language* (Toronto, 1857), of a poem entitled *The lost island* (Ottawa, 1889; 2nd ed., 1895), and of a paper entitled *Reminiscences of old Quebec* (Canadian antiquarian and numismatic journal, July, 1913).

[Morgan, *Bib. can.*]

Fletcher, James (1852-1908), naturalist, was born at Ashe, near Wrotham, Kent, England, on March 28, 1852, the second son of Joseph Flitcroft Fletcher and Mary Ann Hayward. He was educated at King's School, Rochester; and in 1871 he entered the service of the Bank of British North America in London. In 1874 he was transferred to Canada; but in 1876 he left the bank to accept an appointment in the Library of Parliament at Ottawa. He was employed here until 1884; and he then became Dominion entomologist in the department of agriculture. He was one of the founders of the Ottawa Field Naturalists' Club, and in 1885 he was elected a member of the Royal Society of Canada. Seventeen species of butterflies bear his name. He was a voluminous contributor to scientific periodicals; and he published, in collaboration with George H. Clark, *The farm weeds of Canada* (Ottawa, 1906). He died at Montreal on November 8, 1908. In 1879 he married Eleanor Gertrude, eldest daughter of Sir Collingwood

Schreiber (q.v.); and by her he had two daughters. He was an LL.D. of Queen's University, Kingston (1896).

[*Dict. nat. biog.*, supp. II; *Can. who was who*, vol. 1; Morgan, *Can. men* (1898); *Ottawa naturalist*, 1909; *Proc. Roy. Soc. Can.*, 1909; *Can. who was who*, vol.1.]

Fletcher, John (1787-1844), jurist, was born in England in 1787, and was called to the English bar. He came to Canada in 1810, and began the practice of law in Quebec. In 1816 he was appointed a commissioner, with the Hon. W. B. Coltman (q.v.), for the purpose of investigating the disturbances in the Indian country; but he did not go farther west than Fort William. In 1823 he was appointed provincial judge of the district of St. Francis; and he died at Sherbrooke, in the Eastern Townships, on November 11, 1844.

[P. G. Roy, *Les juges de la province de Québec* (Quebec, 1933).]

Fletcher, John (1850-1917), educationist, was born in London, England, in 1850. He was educated at Upper Canada College, Toronto, at the University of Toronto (B.A., 1872), and at Balliol College, Oxford (M.A., 1880). From 1881 to 1895 he was professor of classics at Queen's University, Kingston; and from 1895 to his death he was professor of Latin in University College, Toronto. He died at Toronto, Ontario, on July 15, 1917. He was the author of *A short handbook of Latin* (Toronto, 1912); and, with J. Henderson, he was joint author of *Latin prose composition* (Toronto, 1894) and *First Latin book* (Toronto, 1900).

[Morgan, *Can. men* (1912); *University of Toronto monthly*, 1917.]

Flint, Billa (1805-1894), senator of Canada, was born in Elizabethtown, Leeds county, Upper Canada, on February 9, 1805. He became a successful merchant in Belleville. He sat for Hastings in the Legislative Assembly of Canada from 1847 to 1851, and for South Hastings from 1854 to 1857; and he was elected to the Legislative Council for the Trent division in 1863. In 1867 he was called to the Senate by royal proclamation; and he died at Belleville on June 14, 1894.

[*Can. parl. comp.*]

Flynn, Edmund James (1847-1927), prime minister of Quebec (1896-97), was born at Percé, Gaspé county, Canada East, on November 16, 1847, the son of James Flynn and Elizabeth Tostevin. He was educated at the Quebec Seminary and at Laval University (LL.L., 1873; LL.D., 1878), and was called to the Quebec bar in 1873 (Q.C., 1887). In 1874 he was appointed professor of Roman law in Laval University. He represented Gaspé in the Legislative Assembly of Quebec almost continuously from 1878 to 1900, and Nicolet from 1900 to 1904; and he was commissioner of crown lands in the Chapleau government from 1879 to 1882, solicitor-general in the Ross government from 1884 to 1887, and commissioner of crown lands in the Boucherville and Taillon governments from 1891 to 1896. From May 11, 1896, to May 22, 1897, he was prime minister and minister of public works. From 1897 to 1904 he was leader of the opposition, and he then retired to private life. He died at Quebec on June 7, 1927. In 1875 he married Mathilde Augustine, daughter of Augustin Coté, proprietor of *Le Journal de Québec*; and by her he had three sons and two daughters.

[*Can. parl. comp.*; Morgan, *Can. men* (1912).]

Foley, Michael Hamilton (1820-1870), postmaster-general of Canada (1858, 1862-63, and 1864), was born in Sligo, Ireland, in 1820. His parents emigrated to Canada in 1822, and he was educated at Port Colborne, Upper Canada. He became a journalist, and between 1845 and 1853 he was successively editor of the *Simcoe Advocate*, the *Norfolk Messenger*, and the *Brantford Herald*. From 1854 to 1864 he represented North Waterloo in the Legislative Assembly of Canada. He was postmaster-general in the short-lived Brown-Dorion administration of 1858, and again in the Macdonald-Sicotte administration of 1862-63. In 1863 he went with D'Arcy McGee (q.v.) and L. V. Sicotte (q.v.) into opposition; and in 1864 he became postmaster-general in the second Taché-Macdonald government. He failed, however, to secure his re-election; and, in the formation of the Great Coalition, he made way for a supporter of George Brown (q.v.). In 1864 he was admitted, by special Act of parliament, to practise as a barrister in Upper Canada. He died at Simcoe, Ontario, on April 8, 1870.

[N. F. Davin, *The Irishman in Canada* (Toronto, 1877); J. C. Dent, *The last forty years* (2 vols., Toronto, 1881); Morgan, *Bib. can.*; *Can. parl. comp.*, 1864.]

Foley, Pearl Beatrix (d. 1953), novelist, was born at Toronto, Ontario, and died there on October 12, 1953. She attended the University of Toronto, but apparently did not graduate. She was the author of four novels: *The gift of the gods* (Toronto, 1921), *The octagon crystal* (New York, 1929), *The Gnome Mine mystery* (London, 1933) (published under the pseudonym "Paul de Mar"), and *The yellow circle* (Toronto, 1937).

[Clara Thomas, *Canadian novelists* (Toronto, 1946); Toronto *Globe and Mail*, Oct. 14, 1953.]

Fontaine, Raphaël Ernest (1840-1902), jurist, was born at St. Hugues-de-Bagot, Lower Canada, on October 27, 1840. He was educated at the St. Hyacinthe Seminary, and was called to the bar of Lower Canada in 1862. He practised law at St. Hyacinthe, and was for many years mayor of St. Hyacinthe. He was appointed a judge of the Superior Court of the province of Quebec for the district of Richelieu in 1901; but died in office, at Sorel, Quebec, only eighteen months later, on September 20, 1902. He was the author of *Un duel à poudre: Comédie en trois actes* (St. Hyacinthe, Que., 1868).

[P. G. Roy, *Les juges de la province de Québec* (Quebec, 1933).]

Foran, Joseph Kearney (1857-1931), author, was born at Aylmer, Quebec, on September 5, 1857, the son of John Foran and Catharine F. Kearney. He was educated at the University of Ottawa (Litt.D., 1894) and at Laval University (LL.B., 1880), and was called to the bar in 1881. He was successively a lawyer, a journalist, and a civil servant; and eventually he became law clerk of the Canadian House of Commons. He died at Mount Royal, Quebec, in 1931. He was the author of *The spirit of the age, on faith and infidelity* (Montreal, 1885), *An essay on obligations* (Toronto, 1886), *Irish-Canadian representatives* (Ottawa, 1886), *Poems and lyrics* (Montreal, 1895), *A garland: Lectures and poems* (Montreal, 1931), *Jeanne Mance* (Montreal, 1931), and *Blossoms of the past* (Montreal, 1935).

[Morgan, *Can. men* (1912); *Guide to Catholic literature* (Detroit, Mich., 1940).]

Forbes, Sir Francis (1784-1841), chief justice of the Supreme Court of Newfoundland (1816-22), was born in Bermuda in 1784, and died near Sydney, Australia, on November 9, 1841. He was called to the bar in England from Lincoln's Inn in 1812. In 1816 he was appointed chief justice of the Supreme Court of Newfoundland. His decisions were influential in helping to secure for Newfoundland colonial status and in paving the way for the advent of constitutional government. He was chief justice of New South Wales from 1823 to 1837, and he was knighted in 1839.

[*Dict. nat. biog.*; *Encyc. Can.*]

Forbes, John Colin (1846-1925), painter, was born in Toronto, Canada, on January 23, 1846, the son of Duncan Forbes and Jane Turner. He was educated at Upper Canada College, and studied art in London and Paris. In 1882 he was elected a member of the Royal Canadian Academy. His chief work was as a portrait-painter; and he executed portraits of King Edward VII and Queen Alexandra, in addition to portraits of many of the outstanding figures in Canadian public life since Confederation. He died in Toronto on October 28, 1925.

[Morgan, *Can. men* (1912); *Can. who was who*, vol. 2; N. MacTavish, *The fine arts in Canada* (Toronto, 1925).]

Forbin-Janson, Charles Auguste Marie Joseph (1785-1844), French Roman Catholic prelate, was born in Paris, France, on November 3, 1785, and died at Marseilles, France, on July 11, 1844. He was ordained a priest in 1811, was created bishop of Nancy in 1824, and from 1839 to 1842 carried on evangelistic work in the United States and Canada. He interested himself in the fate of the French Canadians exiled to New South Wales after the rebellion of 1837-38.

[N. E. Dionne, *Mgr de Forbin-Janson* (Quebec, 1895; new ed., 1910); Allaire, *Dict. biog.*; Le Jeune, *Dict. gén.*]

Forget, Amédée Emmanuel (1847-1923), lieutenant-governor of the North West Territories (1898-1905) and of Saskatchewan (1905-10), was born at Marieville, Lower Canada, on November 12, 1847, the son of Jérémie Forget and Marie Guenette. He was educated at the College of Marieville, and was called to the bar of Quebec in 1871. In 1875 he was appointed one of the commissioners for the settlement of half-breed claims in the North West Territories; and in 1876 he was appointed secretary to the lieutenant-governor of the Territories, and clerk of the council. In 1888 he became assistant commissioner of Indian affairs for Manitoba and the North West Territories, and in 1895 commissioner. In 1898 he was gazetted lieutenant-governor of the North West Territories, and in 1905 he became first lieutenant-governor of Saskatchewan. His term of office ended in 1910, and in 1911 he was summoned to the Senate of Canada. He sat in the Senate until his death, at Ottawa, on June 8, 1923. In 1876 he married Henriette Drolet.

[*Can. parl. comp.*; Morgan, *Can. men* (1912); Le Jeune, *Dict. gén.*]

Forget, Sir Joseph David Rodolphe (1861-1919), financier, was born at Terrebonne, Canada East, on December 10, 1861, the son of David Forget and Angèle Limoges. He was educated at Masson College, Terrebonne. In 1890 he became a member of the Montreal Stock Exchange, and in 1908 he was elected its president. He had widespread financial interests, and was president of the Richelieu and Ontario Navigation Company, of the Quebec and Saguenay Railway, of the Eastern Canada Steel and Iron Works, of the Canada Car Foundry Company, and other corporations. In 1911 he founded also the Banque Internationale du Canada. From 1904 to 1917 he represented Charlevoix in the Canadian House of Commons, as an independent Conservative. He died at Montreal on February 19, 1919. He was twice married, (1) in 1885 to Alexandra Tourville, and (2) in 1895 to Blanche, daughter of A. R. McDonald, of Quebec. He was appointed honorary lieutenant-colonel of the 65th Carabiniers of Montreal in 1907; and in 1912 he was created a knight bachelor.

[*Who was who*, 1916-28; Morgan, *Can. men* (1912); *Can. parl. comp.*; *Can. who was who*, vol. 1.]

Forgues, Michel (1811-1882), priest, was born at St. Michel de Bellechasse, Lower Canada, on February 13, 1811. He was ordained a priest of the Roman Catholic Church; and he served in several parishes in the province of Quebec. He died at St. Laurent, in the Island of Orleans, Quebec, on November 28, 1882. He was the author of a *Dictionnaire généalogique des familles de l'Ile d'Orléans*, which was published by the Public Archives of Canada (Ottawa, 1905).

[*Bull. rech. hist.*, 1926.]

Forke, Robert (1860-1934), minister of immigration and colonization for Canada (1926-29), was born at Gordon, Berwickshire, Scotland, on June 2, 1860. He emigrated to Canada in 1882, and became a farmer at Pipestone, Manitoba. In 1921 he was elected to the Canadian House of Commons as a Progressive; and in 1922 he was appointed leader of the Progressive members in the House. From 1926 to 1929 he was minister of immigration and colonization in the Mackenzie King administration; and in 1929 he was called to the Senate of Canada. He died at Winnipeg, Manitoba, on February 2, 1934.

[*Can. parl. comp.*]

Forneri, James (1789-1869), professor of modern languages in University College, Toronto (1853-66), was born near Turin, Piedmont, Italy, about the end of June, 1789, the son of David Emmanuel de Forneri and Margharitta Gorresio. He was educated at the University of Turin, and in 1809 was called to the bar of that city. In 1812 he obtained a commission in the 4th Regiment of the *Gardes d'Honneur* of the Emperor Napoleon, and in 1814 he was captured by the Russians. He returned to Italy in 1815, and in 1820 he joined the Carbonari revolutionists. Forced to flee from Italy in 1821, he went to Spain, and took service in the Spanish army. In 1824 he went to England; and there he made a living as a teacher of modern languages. In 1836 he went to Belfast, Ireland, and there he became professor of modern languages in the Belfast Royal Academical Institution. In 1851 he received the appointment as modern language master in the collegiate school at Windsor, Nova Scotia; and in 1853 he was appointed professor of modern languages in University College, Toronto. This position he retained until his retirement in 1866. He died at Toronto on September 5, 1869. In 1836 he married Elizabeth, daughter of William Wells; and he was survived by four sons and four daughters.

[J. King, *McCaul: Croft: Forneri* (Toronto, 1914).]

Forrest, Edmund William (d. 1880), soldier and author, was born in London, England, and entered at an early age the service of the East India Company. He served throughout the Persian war and the Indian mutiny; but a sunstroke, ending in blindness, brought about his retirement from the company's service, with the rank of captain. He settled in Canada; and he died at Hull, Quebec, on July 4, 1880. After coming to Canada, he wrote *Ned Fortescue; or, Roughing it through life* (Ottawa, 1869).

[*Dom. ann. reg.*, 1880-81.]

Forrest, John (1842-1920), clergyman and educationist, was born at New Glasgow, Nova Scotia, on November 25, 1842. He was educated at the Presbyterian College at Halifax, Nova Scotia, and was ordained a minister of the Presbyterian Church in 1866. From 1866 to 1881 he was pastor of St. John's church, Halifax; and from 1881 to 1885 he was professor of history in Dalhousie University. In 1885 he was appointed president of Dalhousie University; and he remained president until his retirement in 1911. He died at Halifax, Nova Scotia, on June 27, 1920. He received the honorary degree of D.D. from Queen's University, Kingston, in 1863; that of D.C.L. from King's College, Windsor, in 1890; and that of LL.D. from St. Francis Xavier University in 1905.

[Morgan, *Can. men* (1912).]

Forrester, Alexander (1805-1869), clergyman and educationist, was born in Scotland in 1805, and was educated at the University of Edinburgh. He was ordained a minister of the Church of Scotland in 1835; but in 1843 he became a minister of the Free Church. He emigrated to Nova Scotia in 1848, and in 1855 he was appointed superintendent of education in Nova Scotia. He retired from this office in 1864, and he died in New York on April 20, 1869. He was the author of several pamphlets.

[Morgan, *Bib. can.*; R. J. Long, *Nova Scotia authors* (East Orange, N.J., 1918).]

Forster, John Wycliffe Lowes (1850-1938), portrait-painter, was born at Norval, Canada West, on December 31, 1850. He studied portrait-painting in Paris, and some of his portraits were exhibited at the first exhibition of the Ontario Society of Artists in 1872. He was later elected an associate of the Royal Canadian Academy of Arts. He died at Toronto, Ontario, on April 24, 1938. He was the author of *Under the studio light: Leaves from a portrait-painter's sketch book* (Toronto, 1928) and *Sight and insight* (Toronto, 1941).

[*Can. who's who*, 1936-37; Morgan, *Can. men* (1912); N. MacTavish, *The fine arts in Canada* (Toronto, 1925).]

Forsyth, George (1755-1806), merchant, was the eldest son of William Forsyth, of Huntly, Scotland, and Jean, daughter of George Phyn, laird of the Corse of Monelly, Aberdeenshire, and was born in Scotland on April 2, 1755. He came to Canada; and was a merchant at Niagara. He died at Niagara on September 15, 1806. He married a woman named Tenbroeck, who died at Niagara in 1817; and by her he had a daughter, Mary Ann, who lived afterwards at Brechin, Scotland, and who died, unmarried, about 1862.

[W. S. Wallace, *Forsyth, Richardson and Company in the fur-trade* (Trans. Roy. Soc. Can., 1940).]

Forsyth, James Bell (1803-1869), merchant and author, was born in Kingston, Upper Canada, in 1803, the son of Joseph Forsyth (q.v.) and Alicia Robins; and died at Quebec, Canada, in 1869. In 1828 he married Frances, daughter of the Hon. Matthew Bell of Three Rivers; and by her he had two sons and two daughters. He was the author of *A few months in the east; or, A glimpse of the Red, the Dead, and the Black Seas* (Quebec, 1861).

[W. S. Wallace, *Forsyth, Richardson and Company in the fur-trade* (Trans. Roy. Soc. Can., 1940).]

Forsyth, John (1762-1837), merchant, was born in Scotland on December 8, 1762, the sixth son of William Forsyth, of Huntly, and Jean, daughter of George Phyn, laird of the Corse of Monelly. His mother's sister married Alexander Ellice (q.v.); her brother George married the sister of Edward Ellice (q.v.); another brother, James (q.v.), became the head of the firm of Phyn, Inglis, and Ellice, in London; and another sister was the mother of the Hon. John Richardson (q.v.). John Forsyth emigrated to Canada in 1779, and about 1790 he became the head of the firm of Forsyth, Richardson and Co., which was one of the firms behind the so-called XY Company, and which acquired an interest in the North West Company in 1804. In 1827 he was appointed a member of the Legislative Council of Lower Canada, and he continued a legislative councillor of the province until his death in London on December 29, 1837. He died at Morley's Hotel, which used to stand at the south-west corner of Trafalgar Square; and he was buried in Kensal Green. He married Margaret, the daughter of Charles Grant (q.v.); and by her he had two sons and one daughter. The elder son, William, married his cousin, Eweretta Jane, daughter of Joseph Forsyth (q.v.), and later assumed the name of Forsyth Grant. The younger, John Blackwood, married Mary, daughter of Samuel Gerrard (q.v.); and the daughter, Jane Prescott, married George Gregory, the son of John Gregory (q.v.).

[W. S. Wallace, *Forsyth, Richardson and Company in the fur-trade* (Trans. Roy. Soc. Can., 1940); R. Campbell, *A history of the Scotch Presbyterian Church, St. Gabriel St., Montreal* (Montreal, 1887); *Centenary of the Bank of Montreal* (Montreal, 1917).]

Forsyth, Joseph (1764-1813), merchant, was the seventh son of William Forsyth, of Huntly, and Jean Phyn, and was born on January 24, 1764. He came to Canada about 1784, and became a merchant in Kingston, Upper Canada. He died in Kingston in September, 1813. He married, first, the daughter of one Bell, by whom he had a son, William, who died unmarried; and second, he married in Kingston, Alicia, daughter of James Robins, by whom he had three sons and three daughters, descendants of some of whom are still living.

[W. S. Wallace, *Forsyth, Richardson and Company in the fur-trade* (Trans. Roy. Soc. Can., 1940).]

Forsyth Grant, Mrs. Minnie Caroline, *née* **Robinson** (d. 1923), author, was born in Toronto, Canada, the daughter of the Hon. John Beverley Robinson (q.v.) and Mary Jane Hagerman. In 1881 she married Captain William Forsyth Grant, the son of William Forsyth, of Ecclesgreig, Kincardineshire, Scotland, who took in 1842 the name of Grant, and was the descendant of two families closely connected with the early history of the fur-trade in Canada. After the death of her husband, she returned to Toronto; and she died there on November 2, 1923. She was the author of *Scenes in Hawaii; or, Life in the Sandwich Islands* (Toronto, 1888), and she contributed to the *Canadian Magazine*, in 1914, a valuable series of papers on "Bygone days in Toronto".

[Morgan, *Can. men and women* (1912).]

Fortin, Marc-Aurèle (1888-1970), painter, was born at Ste. Rose, Quebec, March 14, 1888. He studied at the Monument National in Montreal (1904-08) and at Chicago, New York, and Boston under Tarbell, Timmons, Vanderpoel, and Alexander. He returned to Canada in 1914. His style is direct, simple, and massive, much of his work being done in water-colour. In 1938 he won the Jessie Dow Award in Montreal and in 1939 was awarded a bronze medal at the New York World's Fair. In 1955 he became ill and had both his legs amputated. He stopped painting for several years but began again in the early sixties. Writing of his retrospective 1963 exhibition, Raymond Heard wrote, "A gentle and nostalgic world is reflected in Mr. Fortin's canvasses." His work hangs in the Musée du Québec, the Art Gallery of Ontario, and the Montreal Museum of Fine Arts, as well as in private collections. He was elected A.R.C.A. in 1942. He died at Ste. Rose, Quebec, March 2, 1970.

[*Can. who's who*, 1955-57; C. M. Barbeau, *Painters of Quebec* (Toronto, 1941); G. McInnes, *Canadian art* (Toronto, 1950); P. Duval, *Canadian water colour painting* (Toronto, 1952); C. S. MacDonald, *A dictionary of Canadian artists*, vol. 1 (Ottawa, 1967).]

Fortin, Pierre (1823-1888), senator of Canada, was born at Verchères, Lower Canada, in 1823; and was educated at McGill College (M.D., 1845). He served as a surgeon at Grosse Isle during the cholera epidemic of 1847-48; but did not thereafter practise medicine. From 1852 to 1867 he was a stipendiary magistrate for the protection of the fisheries in the Gulf of St. Lawrence. He represented Gaspé in the Canadian House of Commons from 1867 to 1874, and in the Quebec Legislative Assembly from 1867 to 1878; and he was commissioner of crown lands in the Ouimet administration in Quebec from 1873 to 1874. In 1887 he was called to the Senate of Canada; but he died the following year, on June 15.

[*Can. parl. comp.*]

Fosbery, Ernest George (1874-1960), painter, was born at Ottawa, Ontario, on December 29, 1874, and died at Cowansville, Quebec, on February 7, 1960. He studied at the Ottawa Art School under Franklin Brownell (q.v.), and in Paris. In 1907 he became headmaster of the Art Students' League in Buffalo. He returned to Canada in 1911 and opened a studio in Ottawa, where he worked chiefly as a portrait-painter. He served overseas with the Canadian Army during the First World War, and was employed by the Canadian War Memorials in 1918 as an official artist for the Canadian Army. He was elected an A.R.C.A. in 1912, and an R.C.A. in 1929; and in 1943-44 he was president of the Royal Academy. Several of his paintings are in the National Art Gallery at Ottawa.

[*Can. who's who*, 1958-60; *Encyc. Can.*; Montreal *Gazette*, Feb. 8, 1960.]

Foster, Sir George Eulas (1847-1931), statesman, was born in Carleton county, New Brunswick, on September 3, 1847, the son of John Foster and Margaret Heine. He was educated at the University of New Brunswick (B.A., 1868; LL.D., 1894); and he was professor of classics in this university from 1873 to 1879. He represented Kings county, New Brunswick, in the Canadian House of Commons from 1882 to 1896. In 1885 he became minister of marine and fisheries in the Macdonald government, and in 1888 minister of finance. This portfolio he retained in the Abbott, Thompson, Bowell, and Tupper administrations from 1891 to 1896, with the exception of a few days in January, 1896, when he was one of the so-called "nest of traitors" who retired from the Bowell cabinet. From 1896 to 1900 he represented York county, New Brunswick, in the Commons, and was the first lieutenant of Sir Charles Tupper (q.v.) in opposition. From 1900 to 1904 he was out of parliament; but in 1904 he was elected to the Commons to represent North Toronto, and this constituency he retained, with ever increasing majorities, until 1921, when he was summoned to the Senate of Canada. Between 1906 and 1910 he was the subject of an attempt on the part of the Liberal party to drive him from public life, by means of charges made against his administration of the affairs of the Union Trust Company, of which he was appointed general manager in 1901; but this attempt failed, and in 1911 he was appointed minister of trade and commerce in the Borden government. He played a conspicuous part in the government of Canada during the Great War; and in 1917 his was the first of four names submitted by the western Liberals as head of a Union government. In 1918-19 he accompanied Sir Robert Borden (q.v.) to Paris as one of the Canadian delegates to the Peace Conference; and he would have been one of the signatories of the Treaty of Versailles had he not been called home to Canada by the mortal illness of his wife. In 1920 he was acting prime minister of Canada during the absence of Sir Robert Borden through ill health; and in 1920-21 he was chairman of the Canadian delegation to the first Assembly of the League of Nations at Geneva, and was elected a vice-president of the Assembly. He continued as minister of trade and commerce in the Meighen administration, declining to allow his name to be put forward as a candidate for the prime ministry; but at the end of 1921 he accepted appointment to the Senate, and for the rest of his days played only an intermittent part in Canadian politics. He died at Ottawa, on December 30, 1931. He was created a K.C.M.G. in 1912, and a G.C.M.G. in 1918; and in 1916 he was appointed an imperial privy councillor. In 1889 he married Addie (d. 1918), daughter of Milton Davies, and former wife of D. B. Chisholm; and in 1920 he married Jessie, daughter of Sir William Allan, M.P. He was the author of *Canadian addresses* (Toronto, 1914) and *Citizenship: The Josiah Wood lectures* (Sackville, N.B., 1927).

[W. S. Wallace, *The memoirs of the Rt. Hon. Sir George Foster* (Toronto, 1933); *Who was who*, 1929-40; *Can. parl. comp.*; Morgan, *Can. men* (1912); Rose, *Cyc. Can. biog.* (1888).]

Foster, George Greene (1860-1931), senator of Canada, was born at Knowlton, Quebec, on January 21, 1860, the son of Samuel E. Foster and Ellen Greene. He was educated at Knowlton Academy and McGill University, and was called to the Quebec bar in 1881 (Q.C., 1896). He was called to the Senate of Canada in 1917; and he died at Montreal on May 1, 1931. In 1896, he married Mary Maud, daughter of the Hon. G. C. V. Buchanan.

[*Can. parl. comp.*]

Foster, John Stuart (1890-1964), physicist, was born in Clarence, Nova Scotia, in 1890 and graduated from Acadia and Yale universities (Ph.D., 1924). He came to McGill in 1924 and was head of the department of physics from 1952 to 1955 and Rutherford professor of physics from 1955 to 1960, when he became Professor Emeritus and Macdonald travelling Fellow of McGill (1960-64).

In 1927 he published the definitive paper on the quantum mechanical theory of the Stark effect in helium. During the Second World War he invented the Foster microwave rapid scanner. By 1949 he had persuaded McGill to build a Radiation Laboratory and cyclotron and began training students in nuclear physics at the John Stuart Foster Radiation Laboratory which is named in his honour. He was a fellow of the Royal Society of Canada, fellow of the Royal Society (London), member of the Council of the American Physical Society, and Tory medallist (R.S.C., 1946), and he received the Medal of Freedom and Bronze Palm (U.S.A., 1947). He died in Berkeley, California, September 9, 1964.

[*Proc. Roy. Soc. Can.* (1965).]

Foster, Walter Edward (1874-1947), prime minister of New Brunswick (1917-23), was born at St. Martin's, New Brunswick, on April 9, 1874. He was educated at the Saint John Grammar School, and became at first a bank clerk. He then entered the employ of a dry-goods firm, of which he eventually became president. In 1916 he was chosen as leader of the New Brunswick Liberals, and in 1917 he led his party to victory in the provincial elections. He became prime minister, and remained in office until 1923. In 1925 he was made secretary of state for Canada in the Mackenzie King administration, but he was defeated later in the year in the general election. In 1928 he was appointed to the Senate, and from 1936 to 1940 he was speaker of the Senate. He died at Saint John, New Brunswick, on November 14, 1947.

[*Can. who's who*, 1938-39; *Can. parl. guide*, 1940; *Encyc. Can.*]

Foster, William Alexander (1840-1888), lawyer and nationalist, was born in Toronto on July 16, 1840, the son of James Foster and Mary Morrison. He was educated at the University of Toronto (LL.B., 1860), and was called to the Ontario bar in 1861. He was one of the chief founders of the "Canada First" movement in 1868-75; and his pamphlet, *Canada first* (Toronto, 1871), provided the Canadian nationalists of that time with a rallying-point. He was one of the founders of the *Nation* (1874-76), and of the National Club in Toronto. He died in Toronto on November 1, 1888. In 1877 he married Margaret, daughter of John George Bowes, of Toronto; and by her he had three children, of whom two survived him.

[*Canada first: A memorial of the late William A. Foster, Q.C.*, with introduction by Goldwin Smith (Toronto, 1890); G.T. Denison, *The struggle for imperial unity* (Toronto, 1909), and W. S. Wallace, *The growth of Canadian national feeling* (Can. hist. rev., 1920).]

Fothergill, Charles (1782-1840), journalist and author, was born in Yorkshire, England, on May 23, 1782. He emigrated to Canada in 1816, and from 1822 to 1827 he was King's Printer in Upper Canada, and editor of the *Upper Canada Gazette.* From 1827 to 1830 he represented Durham in the Legislative Assembly of Upper Canada. In 1837 he founded in Toronto the *Palladium of British America,* a semi-weekly newspaper; and he was editor of this until his death in Toronto on May 22, 1840. In 1825 he married at Port Hope, Upper Canada, Eliza Richardson, of Pickering; and by her he had several children. He was one of the first students of natural history in the province; and he was the author of *A sketch of the state of Upper Canada* (York, U.C., 1822).

[J. L. Baillie, Jr., *Charles Fothergill* (Can. hist. rev., 1944); Morgan, *Bib. can.*]

Foucher, Louis Charles (1760-1829), jurist, was born at Rivière-des-Prairies, Lower Canada, on September 13, 1760. He was called to the bar of Quebec in 1787; and from 1795 to 1804 he was solicitor-general of Lower Canada. He represented Montreal West in the Legislative Assembly of Lower Canada from 1796 to 1800, York from 1800 to 1804, and Three Rivers from 1804 to 1808. In 1804 he was appointed provincial judge at Three Rivers; and in 1812 he became a judge of the Court of King's Bench for the district of Montreal. He died at Montreal, Lower Canada, on December 26, 1829. He was throughout life a supporter of government, and has been severely condemned by French-Canadian historians.

[P. G. Roy, *Les juges de la province de Québec* (Quebec, 1933).]

Foulkes, Charles (1903-1969), soldier, was born at Stockton-on-Tees, England, January 13, 1903. He was educated in London, Ontario, and joined the Canadian Army in 1926. He attended the Staff College in Camberley, England, in 1938, and a year later went overseas with the First Canadian Division as brigade major in the 3rd Canadian Infantry Brigade. In 1941 he returned to Canada and became senior general-staff officer of the 3rd Canadian Division. He took command of the 2nd Canadian Infantry Division in 1944 and led this formation during the Normandy and Dutch campaigns. General Eisenhower considered him to be largely responsible for Canada's great contribution to the Allied victory. During the battle for Antwerp he was commander of the 2nd Canadian Corps. In November, 1944, he became commander of the First Canadian Corps in Italy and in 1945 was transferred again to North-West Europe. He became chief of the Canadian General Staff in August, 1945, and in 1951 became the first

chairman of the Canadian chiefs-of-staff, a position which he held to retirement in 1960. He received many military honours including the Croix de Guerre, Order of Orange-Nassau, Ordre de Couronne, C.B., C.B.E., D.S.O. (1944), C.D. (1951). He died at Ottawa, September 12, 1969.

[*Can. who's who,* 1955-57; *Canadian Forces Sentinel* (January, 1970); C.P. Stacey, *The Canadian Army 1939-1945* (Ottawa, 1948).]

Fournier, Télesphore (1824-1896), politician and jurist, was born at St. François, Montmagny county, Lower Canada, on August 5, 1824, the son of Guillaume Fournier of Bécancour. He was educated at Nicolet College, and was called to the bar of Lower Canada in 1846. He became one of the leaders of the *parti rouge*; and from 1856 to 1858 he was one of the editors of *Le National*, the French-Canadian Liberal newspaper. After several unsuccessful attempts to enter parliament, he was elected in 1870 to represent Bellechasse in the Canadian House of Commons, and in 1871 to represent Montmagny in the Legislative Assembly of Quebec. His seat in the Quebec Assembly he resigned in 1873, when he was appointed minister of inland revenue in the Dominion government of Alexander Mackenzie (q.v.). In 1874 he exchanged this portfolio for that of minister of justice, and later for that of postmaster-general; and in 1875 he was appointed a judge of the newly created Supreme Court of Canada. He resigned from the bench in 1895, and he died on May 10, 1896. In 1857 he married Hermine, daughter of Wilbrod Demers; and by her he had nine children.

[T. Rinfret, *Le juge Télesphore Fournier* (Revue trimestrielle canadienne, 1926); Bibaud, *Panth. can.*; Rose, *Cyc. Can. biog.* (1888); *Can. parl. comp.*; Le Jeune, *Dict. gén.*]

Fowler, Daniel (1810-1894), painter, was born at Down, Kent, England, in 1810. He studied law, but on the death of his father he entered the studio of the English water-colour painter, J. D. Harding. He spent a year on the continent, and then set up his own studio in London. His health broke down, however, and he was forced to come to Canada. Here he lived for fifty-one years on Amherst Island, near Kingston, Ontario. Though for the first fourteen years in Canada he led an out-door life and ceased to paint, a visit to London revived his old desire, and in 1857 he began to send his pictures to the exhibitions. His subjects ranged from landscape to still life, and his work was vigorous and strong in colour. In 1879 he became a charter member of the Royal Canadian Academy of Arts. He died in Toronto in 1894.

[H. Charlesworth, *Autobiography of a Canadian painter* (Queen's quarterly, 1938); E. Morris, *Art in Canada: The early painters*

FOX

(Toronto, 1911); N. MacTavish, *The fine arts in Canada* (Toronto, 1925); A. Graves, *Dictionary of artists* (London, 1885); *Can. who was who*, vol. 2.]

Fox, William Sherwood (1878-1967), president of the University of Western Ontario for twenty years (1927-47), was born in Throopsville, New York, June 17, 1878. His father, the Reverend E. T. Fox, had received his training in the Baptist seminary at Rochester and was pastor of the Throopsville Church. In 1889 the family returned to Canada and William attended schools in Toronto and McMaster University (B.A., 1900). He was instructor in classics at Brandon College, Manitoba, from 1900 to 1909 when he left to continue his graduate studies at Johns Hopkins University (Ph.D., 1911). He then taught at Princeton until he became professor of classics at the University of Western Ontario, London. In 1917, Western had no buildings on its 150-acre campus and it was not until after the First World War that funds became available for building. Dr. Fox, who had been dean of arts since 1919, became president in 1927 and continued to hold this position through a period of slow and then rapidly accelerating growth until 1947. The story of Western is in his own book, *Sherwood Fox of Western: Reminiscences* (Toronto, 1964). Among his other works are *Greek and Roman mythology* (Princeton, 1917); *Letters of William Davies* (ed., Toronto, 1945); *T'aint runnin' no more: The story of Grand Bend, the Pinery, and the old river bed* (London, Ontario, 1946); *St. Ignace: Canadian altar of martyrdom* with W. Jerry (Toronto, 1949); his best-known work, *The Bruce beckons: The story of Huron's great peninsula* (Toronto, 1952), has been credited with the establishment of the Bruce hiking trail. He was a fellow of the Royal Society of Canada and a member of archaeological and philological societies in Canada and the United States. He died on August 14, 1967, at the age of eighty-nine.
[*Proc. and Trans. Roy. Soc. of Can.* (1968).]

Foxe, Luke (1586-1635), explorer, was born in Hull, Yorkshire, England, on October 20, 1586, the son of a master mariner; and he became himself a master mariner. In 1631, he made an important voyage to Hudson Bay, and explored the west coast of the bay so thoroughly that it became clear the northwest passage did not lie in that direction. He published an account of his voyage under the title *Northwest Fox* (London, 1635); and shortly afterwards he died at Whitby, Yorkshire, on or about July 15, 1635.
[M. Christy, *The voyages of Captain Luke Foxe of Hull and Captain Thomas James of Bristol in search of a north-west passage* (2 vols., London, Hakluyt Society, 1894); *Dict. Can. biog.*, vol. 1.]

Foy, James Joseph (1847-1916), attorney-general of Ontario (1905-16), was born in Toronto, Canada West, on February 22, 1847. He was educated at St. Michael's College, Toronto, and at Ushaw College, England; and was called to the bar in Ontario in 1871 (Q.C., 1883). In 1882 he was elected a bencher of the Law Society of Upper Canada. From 1898 to his death he represented South Toronto in the Ontario legislature; and from 1905 to his death he was attorney-general of the province, in the Whitney and Hearst administrations. He died at Toronto, Ontario, on June 13, 1916. In 1902 he was made an LL.D. of the University of Toronto.
[*Can. parl. comp.*; Morgan, *Can. men* (1912).]

Frame, Elizabeth (1820-1913), schoolteacher and author, was born in Shubenacadie, Nova Scotia, in 1820. She was educated at Truro Academy and Normal School, and was for many years a school-teacher in Nova Scotia. She died in Shubenacadie, Nova Scotia, in 1913. She was the author of *Descriptive sketches of Nova Scotia* (Halifax, N.S., 1864) and *The twilight of faith* (Boston, 1891).
[R. J. Long, *Nova Scotia authors* (East Orange, N.J., 1918); Morgan, *Can. men and women* (1912) and *Bib. can.*]

Franchère, Gabriel (1786-1863), furtrader, was born at Montreal, Canada, on November 3, 1786, the son of Gabriel Franchère, a merchant. In 1810 he took service with the Pacific Fur Company of John Jacob Astor, and in 1811 he took part in the founding of Astoria, at the mouth of the Columbia River. After the surrender of Astoria to the North West Company in 1812, he returned to Montreal; and in 1820 he published at Montreal his *Relation d'un voyage à la côte du nord-ouest de l'Amérique septentrionale dans les années 1810, 11, 12, 13, et 14*, a book now rare and much sought after by collectors. In 1854 an English translation of this work, edited by J. V. Huntington, was published at New York, and in 1969 the Champlain Society published another English translation of this work, edited by W. Kaye Lamb. After his return to Montreal, Franchère lived successively in Sault Ste. Marie, in St. Louis, and in New York. He died on April 12, 1863, at St. Paul, Minnesota, at the home of his stepson. In 1815 he married Sophie (d. 1837), daughter of J. B. Routhier; and by her he had several children.
[J. Tassé, *Les canadiens de l'ouest* (2 vols., Montreal, 1878); A. G. Morice, *Dictionnaire historique des canadiens et des Métis français de l'ouest* (Kamloops, B.C., 1908); Morgan, *Bib. can.*; *Cyc. Am. biog.*]

Franchère, Joseph Charles (1866-1921), painter, was born in Montreal, Quebec, on March 4, 1866. He studied at the École des Beaux-Arts in Paris, France; and while in

272

France won several honourable mentions. In 1902, after his return to Canada, he was elected an associate of the Royal Canadian Academy. He died at Montreal on May 12, 1921.

[N. MacTavish, *The fine arts in Canada* (Toronto, 1925).]

Francis, Walter Joseph (1872-1924), civil engineer, was born in York township, near Toronto, Ontario, on January 28, 1872. He was educated at the University of Toronto (C.E., 1901); and after serving on the engineering staffs of the Canadian Pacific Railway, the Grand Trunk Railway, and the Department of Railways and Canals, he became a consulting engineer in Montreal. He died suddenly at Montreal, on March 7, 1924. At the time of his death he was president of the Engineering Institute of Canada.

[Morgan, *Can. men* (1912).]

Francklin, Michael (1720-1782), lieutenant-governor of Nova Scotia (1766-76), was born in Devonshire, England, in 1720, and emigrated to Nova Scotia in 1752. He was a man of education and ability, and though his career in Halifax began with only a small rum shop, his enterprise and integrity brought him such success that he soon had an enormous business in supplying stores to the military and naval forces stationed in and passing through Halifax. He was elected to the House of Assembly for Halifax in 1759; and in 1762 he was made a justice of the peace, and a member of the old "Council of Twelve". On March 28, 1766, he was appointed lieutenant-governor of the province, and his administration was both wise and popular, being remarkable chiefly for his great influence over the Indians and Acadians. In 1768 he was appointed lieutenant-governor of the Island of St. John (Prince Edward Island). In 1773 Major Francis Legge (q.v.) was appointed governor of Nova Scotia, and through his influence Francklin was removed from office in 1776. He went to England in 1781 to plead his case, but was given only the satisfaction of being made superintendent of Indian affairs. He died very suddenly in Halifax on November 8, 1782. In 1762 he married Susannah, daughter of Joseph Boutineau; and by her he had five sons and five daughters.

[J. S. Macdonald, *Memoirs of Lieut.-Governor Michael Francklin* (Coll. Nova Scotia Hist. Soc., 1912); B. Murdoch, *History of Nova Scotia* (3 vols., Halifax, 1867).]

Francoeur, Louis (1895-1941), journalist and radio commentator, was born at Montreal, Quebec, on April 3, 1895. He became a journalist, and in the later years of his life a very popular radio announcer. He died, as the result of a motor accident near Montreal, on June 1, 1941. He was joint author, with Philippe Panneton, of *Littératures ... à la*

manière de... (Montreal, 1924); and he published a series of radio broadcasts under the title *La situation ce soir* (11 nos., Montreal, 1941).

[O. Blaise, *Louis Francoeur, journaliste* (Ottawa, 1941).]

Franklin, Sir John (1786-1847), explorer, was born on April 16, 1786, the twelfth and youngest son of Willingham Franklin, of Spilsby, Lincolnshire, England. He entered the Royal Navy in 1800, and he fought under Nelson at Trafalgar. In 1819 he was appointed to command an expedition to explore the Arctic coast of North America eastward from the mouth of the Coppermine; and he returned from this expedition in 1822, after a narrow escape from death by starvation. In 1825-27 he made a second expedition; and on this occasion he succeeded in exploring the Arctic coast of North America both east and west of the mouth of the Mackenzie River. In 1836 he was appointed lieutenant-governor of Van Diemen's Land; and he occupied this position until 1843. In 1845 he was appointed to command a third expedition to the Arctic regions, this time with the object of penetrating by water from the Atlantic to the Pacific. On this expedition, his two ships, the *Erebus* and the *Terror*, were held up in the ice; and he and all his companions perished. Franklin himself died on June 11, 1847. In the search for Franklin nearly fifty expeditions were sent out during the years 1847-57; but it was only in 1857 that the fate of himself and his men was fully discovered, by Captain McClintock, in a yacht fitted out by Lady Franklin. Franklin was twice married, (1) to Eleanor Anne Porde (d. 1825), by whom he had one daughter, and (2) in 1828 to Jane Griffin (d. 1875). In 1829 he was created a knight bachelor, and Oxford University conferred on him the degree of D.C.L. He was the author of a *Narrative of a journey to the shores of the Polar Sea in the years 1819-22* (London, 1823), and a *Narrative of a second expedition to the shores of the Polar Sea in the years 1825-7* (London, 1828).

[H. D. Traill, *Life of Sir John Franklin* (London, 1896); S. Osborn, *Career, last voyage, and fate of Sir John Franklin* (London, 1865); F. L. McClintock, *Narrative of the discovery of the fate of Sir John Franklin and his companions* (Boston, 1860); S. Leacock, *Adventurers of the far north* (Toronto, 1914); P. Nanton, *Arctic breakthrough: Franklin's expeditions* (Toronto, 1970); L. H. Neatby, *The search for Franklin* (Edmonton, 1970); *Dict. nat. biog.*; Le Jeune, *Dict. gén.*; G. F. Lamb, *Franklin, happy voyager* (London, 1956).]

Franquelin, Jean Baptiste Louis (*fl.* 1653-1712), geographer, was born in France between 1651 and 1653. He came to Canada about 1672, and was appointed royal hydrographer in 1686 or 1687. Many of the early maps and plans of New France were prepared by him. He returned to France about 1692 and he died there some time after 1712.

[P. G. Roy, *Un hydrographe du roi à Québec* (Trans. Roy. Soc. Can., 1919); Le Jeune, *Dict. gén.*; *Dict. Can. biog.*, vol. 2.]

Fraser, Alexander (1729-1799), soldier, was a subaltern of Fraser's Highlanders who was born about 1729, who served in Canada from 1758 to 1763, and who retired on half-pay in 1763, and settled in Canada. He acquired the seigniory of Beauchamp in 1773, that of Vitré in 1775, and that of St. Gilles or Beaurivage in 1782. He served as a captain in the Royal Highland Emigrants during the American revolutionary war; and he died at St. Charles, Lower Canada, on April 19, 1799.

[W. S. Wallace, *Alexander Fraser of Beauchamp* (Bull. rech. hist., 1937).]

Fraser, Alexander (1761?-1837), furtrader, was born at Murray Bay, Canada, about 1761, the eldest son of Malcolm Fraser (q.v.). He entered the service of the North West Company as a clerk prior to 1789, possibly through the influence of Simon Fraser, Sr., a merchant of Quebec, known as "the Bonhomme", who was his father's financial agent, and was a cousin of Simon McTavish (q.v.). He seems to have been employed mainly in the English River district. In 1789-90 he wintered at the Côte des Serpents; in 1797 he was in charge of the post to which David Thompson (q.v.) came, when he transferred from the service of the Hudson's Bay Company to that of the North West Company; and in 1799 he is described as "proprietor, Lower English River". He must, therefore, have become a partner of the North West Company before 1799. In 1801 he went to Montreal on leave; and in 1802-03 he was "employed as a partner assisting the Company's concerns in the King's Posts and Hudson's Bay". In 1804 he returned to the North West; but he retired from the fur-trade about 1806, and settled at Rivière-du-Loup. He had bought the seigniory of Rivière-du-Loup-en-Bas in 1802; and he lived here until his death on June 14, 1837. He married in the Indian country an Indian wife, known as Angélique Meadows (d. 1833); and by her he had one son and three daughters. After settling down at Rivière-du-Loup, and while his Indian wife was living, in Indian fashion, at the Point at Rivière-du-Loup, he married, secondly, Pauline Michaud, and by her he had seven children. On his death a prolonged litigation over his estate took place between the children of his white and his Indian wife; and this was terminated only when in 1884 the court adjudged his marriage to his Indian wife valid.

[W. S. Wallace, *Notes on the family of Malcolm Fraser of Murray Bay* (Bull. rech. hist., 1933).]

Fraser, Alexander (1785?-1853), soldier and politician, was born near Fort Augustus, Inverness-shire, Scotland, about 1785; and came to Canada early in the nineteenth century. During the War of 1812 he was quartermaster of the Canadian Fencible Infantry Regiment; and at the close of the war he settled at Fraserfield, in the township of Charlottenburgh, Glengarry county, Upper Canada. He represented Glengarry county in the House of Assembly of Upper Canada from 1828 to 1834; in 1839 he was appointed a member of the Legislative Council of the province, and in 1841 he was appointed a member of the Legislative Council of United Canada. In 1822 he became commanding officer of the 1st Regiment of Glengarry militia; and he commanded this regiment on active service during the rebellion of 1837-38. He died in 1853. He married Anne Macdonell; and by her he had two sons and four daughters.

[J. F. Pringle, *The genealogy of Jacob Farrand Pringle and his wife, Isabella Fraser Pringle* (Cornwall, Ont., 1892); W. L. Scott, *Glengarry's representatives in the Legislative Assembly of Upper Canada* (Canadian Catholic Historical Association report, 1939-40).]

Fraser, Alexander (1860-1936), journalist, archivist, and historian, was born near Inverness, Scotland, on November 2, 1860. He came to Canada in 1886, and became city editor of the Toronto *Mail and Empire*. In 1903 he was appointed provincial archivist of Ontario; and he continued in this position until his retirement from the civil service in 1935. He took a great interest in Scottish organizations in Canada, and was grand chief of the Sons of Scotland, president of the Gaelic Society of Canada, and president of the Scottish-Canadian Association. For twenty years he was also aide-de-camp to the lieutenant-governor of Ontario. He died at Toronto, Ontario, on February 9, 1936. He was the author of *The last laird of MacNab* (Toronto, 1899), *The 48th Highlanders of Toronto* (Toronto, 1900), and *The history of Ontario* (2 vols., Toronto, 1907); and he was editor of *The clan Fraser in Canada* (Toronto, 1895).

[*Can. hist. rev.*, 1936; Morgan, *Can. men* (1912).]

Fraser, Sir Charles Frederick (1850-1925), educationist, was born at Windsor, Nova Scotia, on January 4, 1850, the son of B. D. Fraser, M.D., and Elizabeth Allison. He was educated at King's College, Windsor (M.A., 1884); and he studied at the Perkins Institute for the Blind, Boston, Massachusetts. From 1873 to shortly before his death he was superintendent of the Halifax School for the Blind; and he was regarded as a foremost authority on the education of the blind. He was created a knight bachelor in 1915. He died at Halifax, Nova Scotia, on July 5, 1925.

[*Who was who*, 1916-28; Morgan, *Can. men* (1912).]

Fraser, Christopher Findlay (1839-1894), minister of public works in Ontario (1874-94), was born at Brockville, Upper Canada, in October, 1839, the son of John Fraser and Sarah Burke. He was largely self-educated, and began life as a printer's devil in the office of the Brockville *Recorder*. In 1865 he was called to the bar of Upper Canada. In 1872 he was elected to represent South Grenville in the Legislative Assembly of Ontario; and he continued to represent this constituency until shortly before his death. In 1873 he became provincial secretary in the Mowat administration, and in 1874 minister of public works. He was one of the founders of the Roman Catholic League, and was regarded as the political leader of the Roman Catholics of Ontario. In 1894 he resigned from the government, and was appointed inspector of registry offices; but he had hardly entered on his new duties when he died suddenly, at Toronto, on August 24, 1894.

[*Can. parl. comp.*; *Canada year book*, 1894; Dent, *Can. port.*, vol. 3; Rose, *Cyc. Can. biog.* (1886); C. Clarke, *Sixty years in Upper Canada* (Toronto, 1908).]

Fraser, Donald (1826-1892), clergyman and author, was born in Inverness, Scotland, on January 15, 1826, the son of John Fraser, afterwards commissioner in Canada of the British North American Land Company. He was educated at the University of Aberdeen (M.A., D.D., 1872), and studied divinity at Knox College, Toronto, and New College, Edinburgh. He was ordained in 1851 a minister of the Presbyterian Church in Canada; and from 1851 to 1859 he was minister of the Coté St. Presbyterian Church in Montreal. He then accepted a charge in Inverness, Scotland, and in 1870 he became minister of the Marylebone Presbyterian Church in London, England. He died in London on February 13, 1892. While in Canada he published *Leaves from a minister's portfolio* (Montreal, 1858).

[*Dict. nat. biog.*, supp. II.]

Fraser, Duncan Cameron (1845-1910), lieutenant-governor of Nova Scotia (1906-10), was born at New Glasgow, Nova Scotia, on October 1, 1845, the son of Alexander Fraser and Annie Chisholm. He was educated at Dalhousie University (B.A., 1872), and was called to the bar of Nova Scotia in 1873. In 1878 he was appointed a member of the Legislative Council of Nova Scotia, and was for a short time a member without portfolio of the Hill administration. He then retired to private life, but in 1888 he was again appointed to the Legislative Council, and became government leader, with a seat in the Executive Council. From 1891 to 1904 he represented Guysborough in the Canadian House of Commons, as a Liberal. In 1904 he was appointed a judge of the Supreme Court of Nova Scotia; and in 1906 he became lieutenant-governor of Nova Scotia. He died, while in office, at Halifax, on September 27, 1910. In 1878 he married Bessie, daughter of William Graham, of New Glasgow. He was a D.C.L. of St. François-Xavier College and of King's College, and an LL.D. of Dalhousie University. In 1892 and 1893 he was grand master of the Free Masons of Nova Scotia.

[*Can. parl. comp.*; Morgan, *Can. men* (1898); Rose, *Cyc. Can. biog.* (1888).]

Fraser, Horace John (1905-1969), mining executive, was born at Girvin, Saskatchewan, on November 27, 1905. He graduated from the University of Manitoba in 1925 with a gold medal in science and was awarded a travelling fellowship. He received an M.A. and Ph.D. (1930) from Harvard University in economic geology. After serving with International Nickel Company, he became assistant professor of geology at the California Institute of Technology in 1935, where he remained until 1942, when he went to Washington to become assistant divisional chief in charge of ferro alloys in the wartime Foreign Economics administration.

He returned to Canada in 1945 to become manager of Falconbridge Nickel Mines Limited. Fraser's Washington experience enabled him to negotiate a large contract with the American government and the anticipated revenue allowed Falconbridge to carry out its expansion program. He became president and general manager of Falconbridge in 1957 and a year later manager of Ventures Limited. As a result of this, he was able to merge the two companies. Dr. Fraser spent many years working on methods of ore refining for the lateritic nickel deposits of Cuba and the Dominican Republic and succeeded in perfecting a method of recovering high-grade nickel from lateritic nickel. He had a strong belief in education and in the equalization of educational opportunity. This led him to undertake a leading role in the establishment of Laurentian University in Sudbury. He was chairman of the building committee and in 1965 became chairman of the Board of Governors. He also acted as an adviser on courses and fund raising for Queen's University, which granted him an LL.D. in 1958. He was president of the Ontario Mining Association (1953-56) and of the Canadian Institute of Mining and Metallurgy (1957, 1958). The association awarded him the Selwyn Blaylock medal in 1964. He was a fellow of the Royal Society of Canada, of the Geological Society of America, and the Geological Association of Canada. He died at his farm at Palgrave, Ontario, February 2, 1969.

[*Proc. and Trans. Roy. Soc. Can.*, fourth series, vol. VII (1969); *Can. who's who*, 1961-63.]

Fraser, Hugh (1818-1870), founder of the Fraser Institute, Montreal, was born near Lachine, Lower Canada, in 1818, the son of John Fraser and Catherine, sister of Hon. Alexander Fraser (q.v.), of Fraserfield, Upper Canada. He was educated at Lachine, and became a wine merchant in Montreal. He died in Montreal on May 15, 1870, unmarried; and by his will he left his estate to be applied to founding a free public library in Montreal to be called the Fraser Institute. The will was disputed by his brother John (q.v.) and other heirs; but the bequest was finally validated by the Judicial Committee of the Privy Council.
[Private information.]

Fraser, James (1802-1884), chief of the clan Fraser in British North America, was born at Boleskine, Inverness-shire, Scotland, on April 7, 1802, and was brought by his parents to Nova Scotia in 1804. In 1825 he founded a prosperous business at New Glasgow, Nova Scotia; and in 1867 he was appointed a member of the Legislative Council of New Brunswick. In 1868 he was elected head of the clan Fraser in British North America. He died at New Glasgow, Nova Scotia, on May 8, 1884.
[A. Fraser, *The clan Fraser in Canada* (Toronto, 1895); *Dom. ann. reg.*, 1884.]

Fraser, John (d. 1795), judge, was a half-pay captain of the 78th Regiment (Fraser's Highlanders) who became, after 1760, paymaster of the British troops in Montreal. He had been educated at the Jesuit College in Douai, Flanders. In 1764 he was made a judge of the Court of Common Pleas at Montreal; in 1775 he was made a member of the Legislative Council of Quebec; and in 1792 a member of the Legislative Council of Lower Canada. He died in December, 1795; and a memorial of his widow, stating her husband's services, is in the Canadian Archives (Q., 75-1, p. 54).
[W. S. Wallace, *Some notes on Fraser's Highlanders* (Can. hist. rev., 1937).]

Fraser, John (1820-1899), author, was born at Lachine, Lower Canada, on May 20, 1820, the younger brother of Hugh Fraser (q.v.). He was for a time in partnership with his brother Hugh in the wine business; but retired from the partnership, and later lost his money. He was chiefly instrumental in trying to upset his brother's will establishing the Fraser Institute, Montreal; and his failure to do so somewhat embittered his later years. He died on the family farm at Lachine on October 12, 1899. In 1857 he married Eliza Malcolm, the headmistress of a girls' school in Montreal; and by her he had one daughter. He was the author of *Canadian pen and ink sketches* (Montreal, 1890).
[Private information.]

Fraser, John Arthur (1838-1898), painter, was born in London, England, in 1838, and came to Canada about 1860. He entered the employ of William Notman, the photographer, in Montreal; and in 1868 he moved to Toronto as a resident partner in the firm of Notman and Fraser. In 1873 he was one of the founders of the Ontario Society of Artists; and in 1880 he was appointed a charter member of the Royal Canadian Academy. In 1883 he removed to the United States, and lived there until his death in New York on January 1, 1898. Most of his work was done in water-colours.
[Morgan, *Can. men* (1898); E. Morris, *Art in Canada: The early painters* (Toronto, 1906); N. MacTavish, *The fine arts in Canada* (Toronto, 1925).]

Fraser, John James (1829-1896), prime minister of New Brunswick (1878-82) and lieutenant-governor (1893-96), was born at Miramichi, New Brunswick, on August 1, 1829, the son of John Fraser. He was educated at the Newcastle Grammar School, and in 1852 was called to the bar of New Brunswick (Q.C., 1873). He was elected a member of York county in the Legislative Assembly of New Brunswick in 1865, as an opponent of Confederation; but was defeated in the elections of 1866. From 1871 to 1872 he was president of the Executive Council in the King administration, with a seat in the Legislative Council; and from 1872 to 1878 he was provincial secretary, with a seat in the Legislative Assembly. From 1878 to 1882 he was attorney-general and prime minister. In 1882 he was appointed a judge of the Supreme Court; and in 1893 he became lieutenant-governor. He died on November 24, 1896, in Italy, whither he had gone in search of health. He was twice married, (1) in 1867 to Martha (d. 1871), daughter of Alexander Cumming, of Fredericton; and (2) in 1884 to Jane, daughter of Mr. Justice Fisher, of Fredericton.
[J. Hannay, *Premiers of New Brunswick* (Can. mag., 1897); Rose, *Cyc. Can. biog.* (1888); *Can. parl. comp.*]

Fraser, John Zimmerman (1855-1932), farmer and political organizer, was born at St. George, Canada West, on October 14, 1855. He became a farmer, and was in his early days interested in the Grange movement. In 1914 he was one of the founders of the United Farmers of Ontario; from 1919 to 1931 he was president of the United Farmers' Publishing Company, which took over the *Farmers' Sun*, founded in 1891 by Goldwin Smith (q.v.); and in 1922 he was elected president of the U.F.O. Co-operative Company. He opposed direct political action by the farmers, however; and was opposed to the policies of the Drury administration, which was in power in Ontario from 1919 to 1923. He died at Brantford, Ontario, on November 23, 1932.
[*Can. who was who*, vol. 2; *Can. ann. rev.*, 1933.]

Fraser, Joshua (*fl.* 1858-1883), clergyman and author, was a native of Lanark, Upper Canada. He was educated at Queen's University, Kingston, (B.A., 1858), and became a minister of the Church of Scotland, and later of the Presbyterian Church in Canada. He was pastor of several churches in Ontario and Quebec; but shortly after 1880 he seems to have retired from the ministry. The date of his death has not been ascertained, but it would seem to have been about 1888. He was the author of *Three months among the moose* (Montreal, 1881) and *Shanty, forest and river life in the backwoods of Canada* (Montreal, 1883).
[Private information.]

Fraser, Malcolm (1733?-1815), soldier and seignior, was born in Scotland about 1733, and in 1757 he obtained a commission in the 78th Highlanders. He served under Wolfe (q.v.) at Louisbourg and Quebec in 1758-59; and he was wounded at Ste. Foy in 1760. In 1761 he acquired the seigniory of Mount Murray at Malbaie; and here he spent, with intervals of absence, the rest of his life. In 1775 he took part in the defence of Quebec against the Americans; and he served as a captain in the Royal Highland Emigrants during the later stages of the revolutionary war. He died at Malbaie, Lower Canada, on June 17, 1815. His journal of the siege of Quebec in 1759 is published in the *Transactions* of the Literary and Historical Society of Quebec for 1868.
[G. M. Wrong, *A Canadian manor and its seigneurs* (Toronto, 1908); W. S. Wallace, *Notes on the family of Malcolm Fraser of Murray Bay* (Bull. rech. hist., 1933).]

Fraser, Paul (d. 1855), fur-trader, was a brother of the Hon. Alexander Fraser (q.v.) of Fraserfield, Glengarry, Upper Canada, and entered the service of the North West Company in 1819. He was taken over as a clerk by the Hudson's Bay Company in 1821; and from 1822 to 1824 he was stationed on Lesser Slave Lake. From 1825 to 1832 he was in the Athabaska department, latterly in charge of Fort Vermilion; and in 1832 he was transferred to New Caledonia, and he spent the rest of his life there. He was promoted to the rank of chief trader in 1843; and he died on July 29, 1855. His will is preserved in Hudson's Bay House in London.
[Information from Hudson's Bay House.]

Fraser, Richard Duncan (1783?-1857), fur-trader, was born about 1783, the son of Capt. Thomas Fraser, a United Empire Loyalist. He entered the service of the North West Company when a young man, and in 1805 was a clerk at Lake Nipigon. He seems to have left the service of the Company, however, before 1812; and he died at Frasersfield, Edwardsburgh, Canada West, on April 1, 1857, aged 75 years. He married Mary Macdonell, who died at Brockville, Ontario, on October 27, 1871; and by her he had several children.
[T. H. W. Leavitt, *History of Leeds and Grenville* (Brockville, Ont., 1879).]

Fraser, Robert Blair (1909-1968), journalist, was born in Sydney, Nova Scotia, April 17, 1909. He was educated at Sydney Academy and Acadia University (B.A., 1928). He taught for a year at Stanstead College, near Montreal, before joining the Montreal *Herald* in 1927. A year later he got a job on the *Montreal Star* and then moved to the *Gazette,* where he became an editorial writer and by 1940 had established a regular book-review page. He resigned in 1943 to become Ottawa editor of *Maclean's* magazine. In Ottawa he soon became known as a perceptive reporter of political events and a first-rate radio commentator for the Canadian Broadcasting Corporation. His association with *Maclean's* magazine continued until his death on May 12, 1968. From radio he moved into television and was a respected reporter on the Canadian and international scene. Fraser expressed in his writing and his lifestyle the Canada which emerged from the Second World War — a country at once strong and plagued by self-doubts. At forty-three years of age he began his discovery of the historic north of Canada, voyaging with a small group of friends along the old fur-trade routes which criss-cross the Canadian north. His writings, particularly *The search for identity* (1967), emphasized the "love of the land itself" as the strongest bond of unity among Canadians. His reports on the British and American elections as well as reports from the Far East and the Middle East broadened the horizons of Canadians, while his Ottawa reports helped them to understand themselves. Fraser drowned while on a canoe trip on the Petawawa River. After his death a collection of his writings was assembled by his two sons as *Blair Fraser reports* (Toronto, 1969).
[*Can. who's who*, 1955-57; *Maclean's* Magazine (August, 1968); *The Beaver* (Autumn, 1968).]

Fraser, Simon (1760?-1839), fur-trader, was born about 1760, probably in the parish of Boleskine, Stratherrick, Inverness-shire, Scotland, the son of Capt. Alexander Fraser. He came to Canada, and entered the fur-trade prior to the year 1789, when he and Toussaint Lesieur (q.v.) took the posts of Rivière des Trembles and Portage de l'Isle on a sort of lease from the North West Company. He appears to have become a partner of the North West Company about 1795; and in 1797 he was in charge at Grand Portage. He retired from the fur-trade about 1800; and in 1805 he relinquished his two shares in the North West Company. He was elected a member of the Beaver Club in Montreal in 1803, and he continued an active member until 1816. In 1807 he purchased from John Gregory (q.v.) the fief

Bellevue, on the Lake of Two Mountains; and he lived here until the house in which he lived was burned in 1820, when he bought a property at Ste. Anne's on the Island of Montreal, where he lived until his death at Ste. Anne's, on May 6, 1839. In 1804 he married Catherine (d. 1846), daughter of Donald McKay, and sister of William Alexander, and Donald McKay (q.v.); and by her he had five sons and three daughters. In his obituary notice in the *Quebec Gazette*, he is described as "formerly a partner of the North West Company, and subsequently one of the firm of Fraser, Caldwell, and Co., of Albany."

[W. S. Wallace, *Simon Fraser of Ste. Anne's* (Trans. Roy. Soc. Can., 1934).]

Fraser, Simon (1769-1844), physician, was born at Murray Bay, Quebec, on January 1, 1769, the son of Malcolm Fraser (q.v.). He was educated as a physician and surgeon, and he practised medicine for many years at Terrebonne, Lower Canada. He was a frequent correspondent with his nephew, John McLoughlin (q.v.). He died at Terrebonne on February 20, 1844. He directed that he should be buried without any religious ceremony and without "either priest or minister".

[W. S. Wallace, *Notes on the family of Malcolm Fraser of Murray Bay* (Bull. rech. hist., 1933); E. E. Rich (ed.), *The letters of John McLoughlin* (Toronto: The Champlain Society, 1941).]

Fraser, Simon (1776-1862), fur-trader and explorer, was born at Bennington, New York, in 1776, the youngest son of Capt. Simon Fraser of Guisachan and Isabella Grant, daughter of the laird of Daldreggan. His father, who joined the Loyalist forces during the American Revolution, was captured by the revolutionists, and died in prison at Albany. His mother came to Canada, and ultimately settled near Cornwall. Simon Fraser, the son, was educated at Montreal, where his uncle, John Fraser (q.v.), was a judge of the Court of Common Pleas; and in 1792 he was apprenticed to the North West Company. He was employed in the Athabaska department as early as 1799; and he continued to be attached to this department until 1805. In 1801 he was elected a partner of the North West Company; and in 1805 he was placed in charge of the Company's operations beyond the Rocky Mountains. In 1808 he explored to its mouth the river that bears his name; and the journal of his exploration has been published in L. R. Masson, *Les bourgeois de la Cie. du Nord-Ouest*, vol. i (Quebec, 1889). In 1811 he took charge of the Red River department; and in 1817 he was one of those arrested by Lord Selkirk (q.v.) as an accessory to the massacre at Seven Oaks. He retired from the North West Company before 1820, and settled at St. Andrew's, Upper Canada. Here he died on April 19, 1862, aged 86 years. After he returned from the West, he

married a daughter of Allan Macdonell, at Matilda, Upper Canada.

[W. N. Sage, *Simon Fraser, explorer and fur-trader* (Proceedings of the Pacific Coast Branch of the Amer. Hist. Assoc., 1929); A. Fraser, *The clan Fraser in Canada* (Toronto, 1895); L. J. Burpee, *The search for the western sea* (London, 1908); *Cyc. Am. biog.*]

Fraser, William (1779-1851), first Roman Catholic bishop of Halifax, was born in the vale of Strathglass, Scotland, in 1779. He was educated at the Scots College of Valladolid, Spain; and was ordained a priest in 1804. He came out as a missionary to Nova Scotia in 1822. In 1826 he was created second vicar apostolic of Nova Scotia and titular bishop of Tanen, and in 1842 first Roman Catholic bishop of Halifax. He died at Antigonish, Nova Scotia, on October 4, 1851.

[Rev. A. A. Johnston, *The Right Reverend William Fraser* (Canadian Catholic Historical Association report, 1935-36).]

Fraser, William Alexander (1859-1933), author, was born at River John, Pictou county, Nova Scotia, in 1859. He was educated in New York and Boston; and as a young man he spent seven years prospecting for oil in India. He returned to Canada, and spent six years prospecting in the Canadian North West. Illness, which incapacitated him for field work, caused him to turn to writing; and he began his literary career as a special writer for the *Detroit Free Press* and other periodicals. As a writer of short stories and novels dealing with life in India, the Canadian North West, and horse-racing, he achieved a distinct success; and he was sometimes described as "the Canadian Kipling". In his later years he lived in Georgetown, Ontario, and in Toronto; and he died at Toronto on November 9, 1933. In 1889 he married Jessie Maud Barber, of Georgetown, Ontario; and by her he had several children. He was the author of *Sorrow* (Philadelphia, 1896), *The eye of a god* (New York, 1890), *Mooswa and others of the boundaries* (New York, 1900; new ed., 1923), *The outcasts* (New York, 1901), *Thoroughbreds* (New York, 1902), *The blood lilies* (New York, 1903), *Brave hearts* (New York, 1904), *Thirteen men* (New York, 1906), *Sa'Zada tales* (New York, 1906), *The lone furrow* (New York, 1907), *The three sapphires* (Toronto, 1918), *Bull-dog Carney* (Toronto, 1919), *Red Meekins* (Toronto, 1921), *Caste* (Toronto, 1922), and *Delilah plays the ponies* (Toronto, 1927).

[D. G. French, *W. A. Fraser* (Canadian bookman, Feb., 1930); Morgan, *Can. men* (1912); L. Pierce, *Outline of Canadian literature* (Toronto, 1927).]

Fraser, William Henry (1853-1916), grammarian, was born at Bond Head, Ontario, in 1853, the son of the Rev. William Fraser, D.D., and Nancy McCurdy. He was educated at the University of Toronto (B.A., 1880), and from 1880 to 1887 he was a master at Upper Canada College, Toronto. In 1887 he became lecturer in Italian and Spanish at the University of Toronto; in 1892, associate professor; and in 1901, professor. He died at York Mills, near Toronto, on December 28, 1916. With John Squair (q.v.) he was author of *The high school French grammar* (Toronto, 1891), and with W. H. Vander Smissen (q.v.) of *The high school German grammar* (Toronto, n.d.).

[Morgan, *Can. men* (1912); *Univ. of Toronto monthly*, 1916.]

Fraser, William Kaspar (1884-1949), lawyer, was born in Toronto, Ontario, in 1884, the son of Professor William Henry Fraser (q.v.), and died in Toronto on February 22, 1949. He was educated at the University of Toronto (B.A., 1908) and at Balliol College, Oxford, where he was a Rhodes scholar. He studied law at Osgoode Hall, Toronto, and was called to the bar in 1913. He became the leading authority on Canadian company law, and was joint author, with C. A. Masten, of *The company law of Canada* (Toronto, 1920), together with *Canadian company forms* (Toronto, 1920) and *Handbook on company law* (Toronto, 1925) — all of which ran into several editions.

[Private information.]

Fréchette, Louis Honoré (1839-1908), poet, was born at Lévis, Lower Canada, on November 16, 1839, the son of Louis Fréchette and Marguerite Martineau de Lormière. He was educated at Laval University (Quebec), at McGill University, and at Queen's University. In 1862 he was called to the bar of Lower Canada, but he did not practise law seriously. From 1865 to 1871 he was engaged in journalism in Chicago, and in 1871 he went for a short time to New Orleans. The same year he returned to Quebec, and entered politics. Defeated in Lévis in the elections of 1871, he was returned for this seat as a member of the Canadian House of Commons in 1874, and he sat until 1878. Defeated again in 1878 and in 1882, he turned once more to journalism; and in 1884-85 was editor of *La Patrie*, of Montreal. In 1889 he was appointed by the Mercier government clerk of the Legislative Council of Quebec; and this post he held until his death at Montreal on May 31, 1908. In 1876 he married Emma, daughter of Jean-Baptiste Beaudry, of Montreal; and by her he had three daughters.

His first volume of poetry was *Mes loisirs* (Quebec, 1863); and this was followed by *La voix d'un exilé* (Chicago, 1866-68), *Pêlemêle* (Montreal, 1877), *Les oiseaux de neige* (Quebec, 1880), *Les fleurs boréales* (Dijon, 1881), *La légende d'un peuple* (Paris, 1887), and *Les feuilles volantes* (Montreal, 1891). He published also some prose works, *Lettres à Basile* (Quebec, 1872), *Histoire critique des rois de France* (Montreal, 1881), *Originaux et*

détraqués (Montreal, 1892), and a collection of tales, *La Noël au Canada* (Toronto, 1900), the latter translated into English under the title, *Christmas in French Canada* (Toronto, 1899). He attempted drama in *Félix Poutré* (Montreal, 1871), *Papineau* (Montreal, 1880), and *Véronica* (Montreal, 1908); but these dramas were not conspicuously successful. At his death he had in preparation a collected edition of his poems, and this appeared posthumously in three volumes (Montreal, 1908). Several of his works were crowned by the French Academy; the honorary degree of LL.D. was conferred upon him by McGill University (1881), by Queen's University (1881), and by the University of Toronto (1900), and the degree of D.Litt. by Laval University (1888); and he was created a C.M.G. in 1897. He was a charter member of the Royal Society of Canada, and in 1900 was elected its president. His *Mémoires intimes* have recently been edited by George A. Klinck (Montreal, 1961).

[Henri d'Arles, *Louis Fréchette* (Toronto, 1925); M. Dugas, *Un romantique canadien: Louis Fréchette* (Paris, 1934); *Dict. nat. biog.*, Supp. II; *Proc. Roy. Soc. Can.*, 1909; Taché, *Men of the day*; Dent, *Can. port.*, vol. 4; L. M. Darveau, *Nos hommes de lettres* (Montreal, 1873); L. O. David, *Souvenirs et biographies* (Montreal, 1911); C. ab der Halden, *Etudes de littérature canadienne-française* (Paris, 1904); C. Roy, *Essais sur la littérature canadienne-française* (Quebec, 1914).]

French, Donald Graham (1873-1945), literary editor, was born at Beaverton, Ontario, in 1873, and died at Toronto, Ontario, on August 5, 1945. He was first a schoolteacher, and then a journalist; and for the last twenty-five years of his life he was literary editor and adviser for McClelland and Stewart, Toronto publishers. He was joint author, with J. D. Logan (q.v.), of *Highways of Canadian literature* (Toronto, 1924; 2nd ed., 1928).

[Toronto *Globe and Mail*, Aug. 6, 1945; *Can. who's who*, 1938-39.]

Frédéric de Ghyvelde (1838-1916), Franciscan priest, was born at Ghyvelde, France, on November 19, 1838, the son of Pierre Antoine Tanssoone. He entered the Franciscan order at Amiens in 1864, took the name of Frédéric de Ghyvelde, and was admitted to the priesthood in 1870. He was sent to Canada in 1878; and he died at Montreal, Quebec, on August 4, 1916. He was the author of *Vie de la bienheureuse Jeanne-Marie de Maillé* (Bordeaux, 1871), *Notice historique sur l'oeuvre de Terre-Sainte* (Quebec, 1882), *Le tiers-ordre* (Three Rivers, Que., 1889), *Vie du frère Didace, récollet* (Montreal, 1894), *Vie de Saint François d'Assise* (Montreal, 1894), *Vie de N. S. Jésus-Christ* (Quebec, 1894), *La bonne Ste. Anne* (Quebec, 1896), *Saint Antoine de Padoue*

(Quebec, 1896), *Saint Joseph* (1902), and *La Vierge immaculée* (Quebec, 1904).
[*Bull. rech. hist.*, 1926.]

Frémont, Donatien (1881-1967), writer, was born in Erbray, France, January 7, 1881, and was educated at Nantes. He came to Canada in 1904 and began farming in Saskatchewan. In 1910 he turned to journalism as founder of *Patriote de l'Ouest* in Prince Albert, Saskatchewan, and from 1923 to 1941 he was editor of *La Liberté*, Winnipeg. He then worked with the Wartime Information Board in Ottawa (1941-47) and was associate editor of *Le Canada* (1947-52). He was a witness and faithful reporter of the development of the Canadian west in the early decades of the twentieth century. He was a fellow of the Royal Society of Canada. Among his published works are: *Mgr. Taché et la naissance du Manitoba* (Winnipeg, 1930); *Sur le ranch de Constantin-Weyer* (Winnipeg, 1932); *Pierre Radisson, roi des coureurs de bois* (Montreal, 1933); *Mgr. Provencher et son temps* (Winnipeg, 1935); *Les secrétaires de Riel* (Montreal, (1953); *Les Français dans l'ouest canadien* (Winnipeg, 1959). He died at Verdun, Quebec, June 19, 1967.
[*Proc. and Trans. Roy. Soc. Can.* (1968); *Can. who's who*, 1967-69.]

Frémont, Thaïs (1886-1963), lecturer and women's spokesman, was born in Montreal, Quebec, October 18, 1886. She was a welfare worker and one of the founders of the Ste. Justine Children's Hospital in Montreal in 1907. She was active in politics and founded the Conservative Women's Association for Quebec City in 1926. In 1927 she became the Quebec women's representative to the National Council for the Conservative party. She was Canadian delegate to the League of Nations Assembly in 1932. From 1933 to 1936 she was vice-president of the League of Nations Society in Canada. In 1943 she was appointed to the Women's National Advisory Committee on problems of post-war rehabilitation and in 1947 to the joint committee on the legal status of married women in the province of Quebec. She died at Montreal, April 6, 1963.
[*Encyc. Can.*, vol. IV (1972).]

French, Sir George Arthur (1841-1921), first commissioner of the North-West Mounted Police, was born at Roscommon, Ireland, on June 19, 1841, the eldest son of John French, of Mornington Park, county Dublin. He was educated at Sandhurst and Woolwich, and in 1860 obtained a commission in the Royal Artillery. In 1870 he was appointed inspector of artillery by the Canadian government, with the rank of lieutenant-colonel in the Canadian militia. In 1873 he organized the North-West Mounted Police, became its first commissioner, and commanded it on its famous march to the foothills of the Rockies in 1874. He resigned his post in Canada in 1876; and in subsequent years he occupied various military positions in Queensland, in Bombay, and in New South Wales, attaining finally the rank of major-general. He died on July 28, 1921. In 1862 he married Janet Clark, daughter of Robert Long Innes, of Kingston, Ontario. He was created a C.M.G. in 1877, and a K.C.M.G. in 1902.
[*Who was who*, 1916-28; R. G. MacBeth, *Policing the plains* (Toronto, 1922); A. L. Hayden, *The riders of the plains* (London, 1910).]

Freshman, Charles (1819-1875), rabbi and clergyman, was born at Micklosh, Hungary, in 1819. He came to Canada, and was rabbi of the Jewish Synagogue at Quebec. Later he became a minister of the Wesleyan Methodist Church. He died at Ingersoll, Ontario, on January 4, 1875. He was the author of *The pentateuch* (Toronto, 1864), and *Autobiography* (Toronto, 1868).
[Morgan, *Bib. can.*]

Fricker, Herbert Austin (1868-1943), musician, was born at Canterbury, England, on February 12, 1868. He was educated at Leeds University (M.A.) and Durham University (Mus.B.); and for many years was an organist and choirmaster in England. In 1917 he came to Canada as organist and choirmaster of the Metropolitan Church, Toronto, and as conductor of the famous Mendelssohn Choir of Toronto. These positions he held until his death at Toronto, Ontario, on November 11, 1943. In 1923 he was made an honorary doctor of music of the University of Toronto.
[*Can. who's who*, 1936-37.]

Friedlander, Ernst Peter (1906-1966), musician, was born October 6, 1906, in Vienna. He came to Canada in 1958 and settled in British Columbia. He studied cello in Vienna with Dr. Anton Walter and conducting under Dr. Hans Pless. He made his formal debut as a performer in 1935 and played with orchestras in Vienna and in the United States. He lectured in music at the University of Oklahoma and came to the University of British Columbia music department in 1958. He also became a member of the Vancouver Symphony, the Vancouver chamber orchestra, and the Vancouver string quartet. He gave the first performance of Kodaly's *Sonata for cello* in 1936 and made a number of recordings. He composed music for voice and string quartet as well as cello and brass instruments. He died October 28, 1966, at Vancouver, British Columbia.
[*Creative Canada*, vol. 1 (1971).]

Frobisher, Benjamin (1742?-1787), fur-trader, was born in Yorkshire, England, about 1742. He emigrated to Canada, and embarked in the fur-trade as early as 1765, in partnership with John Welles; and he was later associated in turn with James McGill (q.v.),

Richard Dobie (q.v.), and his brothers Joseph (q.v.) and Thomas (q.v.). So far as can be discovered, he never went west of Grand Portage; but he looked after the Montreal end of the business of Frobisher and Co., in which his brothers were partners with him. He died at Montreal on April 14, 1787.

[Rev. R. Campbell, *A history of the Scotch Presbyterian Church, St. Gabriel St., Montreal* (Montreal, 1887); G. C. Davidson, *The North West Company* (Berkeley, Cal., 1919); *Can. Arch. report,* 1890, note C.]

Frobisher, Benjamin Joseph (1782-1819), fur-trader, was born in Montreal in 1782, the son of Joseph Frobisher (q.v.). He entered the service of the North West Company in 1799, and in that year was a clerk at Lake Winnipeg. From 1804 to 1808 he represented the county of Montreal in the Legislative Assembly of Lower Canada. In 1819, during the Selkirk troubles, he was captured by the Hudson's Bay men, was carried to York Factory, and perished from exhaustion at Cedar Lake in an attempt to escape to a North West Company post.

[S. H. Wilcocke, "Death of B. Frobisher", in L. R. Masson, *Les bourgeois de la Compagnie du Nord-Ouest* (2 vols., Quebec, 1890); F. J. Audet, *Les députés de Montréal* (Montreal, 1943).]

Frobisher, Joseph (1740-1810), fur-trader, was born in Halifax, Yorkshire, England, on April 15, 1740. He appears to have followed his brother Benjamin (q.v.) to Canada, and to have first gone to the West in 1768. It is known that he made an attempt to pass beyond Grand Portage in 1769, but was turned back by the Indians. The statement is made in the McDonell diary, under date of September 4, 1793, that he wintered on the Red River in 1770-71; but this statement is open to doubt. Certainly he reached the Saskatchewan in 1773, with his brother Thomas (q.v.); and spent the winter near the site of what afterwards became Fort Cumberland. In 1774-75 he wintered on the Athabaska River, in the hope of cutting off the fur-trade from Fort Churchill, and nearly perished of starvation. He was an original member of the North West Company in 1779; and he became one of its great figures. On the death of his brother Benjamin in 1787, he joined forces with Simon McTavish (q.v.), to form McTavish, Frobisher and Co., which was for many years the virtual directorate of the North West Company. He retired from business in 1798, and lived at his place, Beaver Hall, in Montreal. He represented the East Ward of Montreal in the Legislative Assembly of Lower Canada from 1792 to 1796; and he died in Montreal on September 12, 1810. In 1779 he married Charlotte Joubert, of Montreal. His letter-book and his "Diary of my dinners" are preserved in the Library of McGill University.

[F. J. Audet, *Les députés de Montréal* (Montreal, 1943); G. C. Davidson, *The North West Company* (Berkeley, Cal., 1919); W. S. Wallace, *The pedlars from Quebec* (Can. hist. rev., 1932); *Can. Arch. report,* 1890, note C.]

Frobisher, Sir Martin (d. 1594), explorer, was a native of Doncaster, England. He was a pioneer in England in advocating a search for the north-west passage to China; and he made three successive expeditions to the north-eastern coast of North America in 1576, 1577, and 1578. In 1576 he discovered the strait that now bears his name; but he does not appear to have penetrated the Arctic archipelago much further than this. In 1588 he distinguished himself in the fight with the Spanish Armada, and was knighted. He died on November 22, 1594, from the effects of a wound received while leading an attack by sea against Brest. An account of his voyages was printed by Richard Hakluyt in his *Principall navigations*, and was reprinted by the Hakluyt Society under the title, *The three voyages of Martin Frobisher* (London, 1867).

[William McFee, *Sir Martin Frobisher* (London, 1928); *Dict. nat. biog.*; *Dict. Can. biog.*, vol. 1.]

Frobisher, Thomas (1744-1788), fur-trader, was born in Yorkshire, England, in 1744, the brother of Benjamin and Joseph Frobisher (q.v.). He came to Canada about 1769, and engaged in the fur-trade with his brothers. He was on the Saskatchewan in 1773 and on the Athabaska River in 1774; and in 1776 he founded the first post at Isle à la Crosse. Though a good man in the bush, he apparently lacked the business capacity of his brothers. He died at Montreal on September 12, 1788.

[G. C. Davidson, *The North West Company* (Berkeley, Cal., 1919); W. S. Wallace (ed.), *Documents relating to the North West Company* (Toronto, 1934); R. H. Fleming, *McTavish, Frobisher and Company* (Can. hist. rev., 1929).]

Frontenac, Louis de Buade, Comte de Palluau et de (1622-1698), governor of New France (1672-82 and 1689-98), was born in 1622, the son of Henri de Buade, colonel of the regiment of Navarre. In 1635 he entered the army, and saw service in the Low Countries and in Italy. In 1646 he attained the rank of *maréchal de camp*. He was appointed governor of New France in 1672; and, except for an interval of seven years, from 1682 to 1689, he continued to administer the government of the colony until his death at Quebec on November 28, 1698. A man of proud and overbearing temper, he quarrelled with successive bishops and intendants; and it was because of these quarrels that he was recalled in 1682. As a civil administrator he was not without decided defects. But as a military governor he was without a rival among all the governors of New France. His handling of the Indians, among whom he was known as the "Great Onontio", was marked by qualities approaching genius; and his defence of Quebec against the English in 1690 afforded a good example of his talent for war. It was under him that the military organization of New France took shape, an organization that enabled New France, with a comparatively small population, to hold its own against the populous English colonies to the south.

In 1648 he married Anne de la Grange-Trianon, daughter of the Sieur de Neuville; and by her he had one son, who died apparently in youth. But he early separated from his wife, and she did not accompany him to Canada.

[W. D. LeSueur, *Count Frontenac* (Toronto, 1906); H. Lorin, *Le comte de Frontenac* (Paris, 1895); E. Myrand, *Frontenac et ses amis* (Quebec, 1902); F. Parkman, *Frontenac and New France under Louis XIV* (Boston, 1877); T. P. Bédard, *La comtesse de Frontenac* (Lévis, 1904); W. J. Eccles, *Frontenac, the courtier governor* (Toronto, 1959); *Dict. Can. biog.*, vol. 1.]

Frost, Leslie Miscampbell (1895-1975), lawyer and premier, was born in Orillia, Ontario, September 20, 1895. He was educated at the University of Toronto and Osgoode Hall. He served in France and Belgium with the 20th Canadian Battalion and was severely wounded (1918). He was discharged with the rank of captain. Leslie Frost was called to the bar of Ontario in 1921. He was first elected to the legislature of Ontario in 1937 and re-elected at each election until his retirement in 1959. He was treasurer of Ontario and minister of mines in the George Drew (q.v.) administration and the T. L. Kennedy (q.v.) administration. He was chosen leader of the provincial Progressive Conservative party in 1949 and was sworn in as premier and provincial treasurer on May 4, 1949. He remained premier until 1961 and was treasurer until 1955. He was a member of the legal firm of Frost, Inrig, and Gorwill, an honorary bencher of the Law Society of Upper Canada, a member of the Board of Governors of the University of Toronto, and chancellor of Trent University. He was the last of the old-style, rural, conservative premiers of Ontario and in himself embodied the transition to the post-war urban industrialization that characterizes the province. He wrote *Fighting men* (Toronto, 1967). He died at Lindsay, Ontario May 4, 1973.

[*Can. who's who*, 1967-69; *Encyc. Can.* (1972).]

Fulford, Francis (1803-1868), Anglican bishop of Montreal, was born at Sidmouth, England, on June 30, 1803, the second son of Baldwin Fulford. He was educated at Exeter College, Oxford (B.A., 1824), and in 1825 was elected a fellow of his college. He was ordained a priest of the Church of England in 1828. From 1832 to 1842 he was rector of Trowbridge, in Wiltshire; from 1842 to 1845 rector of Croydon, in Cambridgeshire; and from 1845 to 1850 minister of Curzon Chapel, Mayfair. In 1850 he was consecrated first bishop of Montreal; and in 1860 he became metropolitan of Canada. He died at Montreal on September 9, 1868. He was the author of a number of sermons and lectures.

[F. Taylor, *The last three bishops appointed by the Crown for the Anglican Church in Canada* (Montreal, 1869); *Brit. Am.*, vol. 2; C. H. Mockridge, *The bishops of the Church of England in Canada* (Toronto, 1896); *Cyc. Am. biog.*; Morgan, *Bib. can.*]

Fuller, Thomas Brock (1810-1884), first Anglican bishop of Niagara, was born at Kingston, Upper Canada, on July 16, 1810, the son of Major Thomas Fuller, 41st Regiment. He took holy orders in the Church of England in 1833, and served successively at Montreal, Chatham, Thorold, and Toronto. In 1869 he was appointed archdeacon of Niagara; and in 1875 he became the first bishop of the new diocese of Niagara. He died at Hamilton, Ontario, on December 17, 1884. In 1835 he married Cynthia, daughter of Samuel Street, of Clarkhill. He was the author of an anonymous pamphlet entitled *The state and prospects of the church in Canada* (Toronto, 1836), and of a number of religious tracts.

[Rev. C. H. Mockridge, *The bishops of the Church of England in Canada* (Toronto, 1896); E. M. Chadwick, *Ontarian families* (2 vols., Toronto, 1894-98); Morgan, *Bib. can.*; *Dom. ann. reg.*, 1884.]

Fuller, William Henry (*fl.* 1870-1898), playwright and satirist, was born at Ramsgate, England, at a date not ascertained, and was educated there. After spending several years in a bank in India, he came to Canada about 1870, and took service in the Ontario Bank. He then became interested in mining. At the same time he blossomed forth as a playwright and a writer of political skits. None of his plays or pamphlets bore his name, and a bibliography of his publications is difficult to compile, but at least two of his plays were printed in Ottawa. These were: *The unspecific scandal* (Ottawa, 1874) and *H.M.S. "Parliament"; or, The lady who loved a government clerk* (Ottawa, 1880). He was also the author of *Flapdoodle: A political encyclopaedia and manual for public men* (Toronto, 1881). In 1898 he was apparently living at the Rideau Club in Ottawa, but he seems to have died before 1912.

[Morgan, *Can. men* (1898).]

Fullerton, Charles Percy (1870-1938), jurist, was born at Amherst, Nova Scotia, on

July 18, 1870. He was educated at Dalhousie University, and was called to the bar of Nova Scotia in 1896, and to that of Manitoba in 1906 (K.C., 1908). From 1917 to 1931 he was a justice of the court of appeal in the Supreme Court of Manitoba; from 1931 to 1933 he was chief commissioner of the Board of Railway Commissioners for Canada; and from 1934 to 1936 he was chairman of the board of trustees of the Canadian National Railways. He died at Winnipeg, Manitoba, on October 5, 1938.

[*Can. who's who*, 1936-37.]

Fyfe, Robert Alexander (1816-1878), principal of the Canadian Literary Institute, Woodstock, Ontario (1860-78), was born at St. André, near Montreal, Lower Canada, in 1816, of Scottish parentage. He was educated at Madison University, New York, and at the Newton Theological Seminary, near Boston, where he graduated in 1842. He was ordained a minister of the Baptist Church, and was the pastor of several churches in Canada and in the United States. In 1860 he became principal of the newly organized Baptist college at Woodstock, Ontario, and he retained this position until his death at Woodstock on September 4, 1878. He was the author of *The teaching of the New Testament in regard to the soul* (Toronto, 1859), and several pamphlets.

[J. E. Wells, *Life and labors of Robert Alex. Fyfe* (Toronto, n.d.); *Dom. ann. reg.*, 1878; Dent, *Can. port.*, vol. 2; Morgan, *Bib. can.*; *Dict. Can. biog.*, vol. 10.]

Fyfe, William Hamilton (1878-1965), school and university principal, was born in London, England, July 9, 1878. He attended school in Scotland and graduated in honours classics from Merton College, Oxford. After two years as a classics master at Radley College he returned to Oxford in 1904 and remained as fellow, tutor, and principal of the Postmasters for fifteen years. In 1919 he was made headmaster of Christ's Hospital, the Bluecoat School, where he introduced many needed reforms to the three-hundred-and-fifty-year-old school. He believed, as he said, that the finest form of teaching and the aim of all education is "the ability to encourage young people to do something for themselves, not to sit passively listening, not merely to accumulate from dictation a number of facts and then in due course at the end of the term to regurgitate them whole, but really do something because they are interested in it and be-

cause they want to do it better and better". In 1930 Fyfe was offered the principalship of Queen's University in Kingston and began a six-year association with the University at a time of severe financial pressure. However, he succeeded in modernizing some of the University buildings, he introduced the new academic posts of resident artist and resident musician, and he established a series of scholarships, one for each Canadian province, which allowed many able students to attend Queen's University.

He left Queen's in 1936 to become principal and vice-chancellor of the University of Aberdeen, a post which he retained until 1948. At Aberdeen he continued his policies of updating and improving the academic program of the university, creating five new chairs, doubling the number of readers and lecturers, and improving the facilities for post-graduate research.

On retirement he moved to Blackheath, continuing his interest in education and serving on numerous committees, including the executive of the Association of Universities of the British Commonwealth. He was a fellow of the Royal Society of Canada, the holder of a number of honorary degrees from universities in Canada and Britain and was an Officier de l'Académie Française. His publications were mainly in the classical field and include: *Aristotle — the poetics; Longinus on the sublime* with an English translation by W. H. Fyfe (London, 1927); *Aristotle's art of poetry — a Greek view of poetry and drama* (translated by I. Bywater) with introduction and explanation by W. H. Fyfe (Oxford, 1940); *Tacitus dialogues, Agricola and Germania* translated with introduction and notes (Oxford, 1908); *Tacitus, the histories*, translated with introduction and notes (2 vols., Oxford, 1912). He died at Blackheath, June 13, 1965.

[*Proc. Roy. Soc. Can.*, vol. V (1967).]

Fyshe, Thomas (1845-1911), banker, was born in East Lothian, Scotland, on October 3, 1845. He came to Canada as a young man, and entered the Bank of British North America. He became cashier of the Bank of Nova Scotia; and in 1897 he was appointed joint general manager of the Merchants Bank of Canada, but resigned in 1905. He died at Montreal on November 26, 1911. He was the author of a pamphlet entitled *Letters on municipal taxation* (Halifax, 1880).

[Morgan, *Can. men* (1912).]

Gage, Thomas (1721-1787), military governor of Montreal (1760-63), was born in 1721, the second son of Thomas, first Viscount Gage, in the peerage of Ireland, and Benedicta Hall. He entered the British army, as a lieutenant in the 48th Foot, in 1741, and he rose to the rank of general in 1782. He was with Braddock (q.v.) at the Monongahéla in 1755, with Abercrombie (q.v.) at Ticonderoga in 1758, and with Amherst (q.v.) at Montreal in 1760. From 1760 to 1763 he was military governor of Montreal; and his rule was marked by great leniency toward the French Canadians. In 1763 he became commander-in-chief of the British forces in North America, with headquarters at New York, and he retained this post until 1772. In 1774 he was appointed governor of Massachusetts, and he was in command at Boston during the outbreak of the American Revolution. In 1775 he was a second time appointed commander-in-chief in North America, but within a few weeks he resigned and returned to England. He died on April 2, 1787. In 1758 he married Margaret, daughter of Peter Kemball, president of the Council of New Jersey; and by her he had six sons and five daughters. His *Correspondence with the secretaries of state, 1763-1775*, has been edited by C. E. Carter (2 vols., New Haven, Conn., 1931-33).

[*Dict. Am. biog.*; *Dict. nat. biog.*; *Cyc. Am. biog.*; Morgan, *Cel. Can.*; B. Sulte, *Le régime militaire* (Trans. Roy. Soc. Can., 1907); J. R. Alden, *General Gage in America* (Baton Rouge, La., 1948).]

Gage, Sir William James (1849-1921), publisher, was born near Brampton, Canada West, on September 16, 1849. He was educated at the Toronto Normal School, and was for a time a school-teacher. In 1874 he entered the employ of the publishing house of Adam Miller and Company, in Toronto; and, after the death of the head of the firm, he reorganized it in 1880 as W. J. Gage and Company. This firm specialized in the publication of educational books, and became one of the most successful publishing houses in Canada. As he acquired wealth, Gage became a generous philanthropist; he established, for instance, several free hospitals and sanatoria for consumptives.

Because of his philanthropies, he was created in 1918 a knight bachelor. He died at Toronto, Ontario, on January 14, 1921.

[*Can. who was who*, vol. 2; Morgan, *Can. men* (1912).]

Gagen, Robert Ford (1847-1926), painter, was born in London, England, on May 10, 1847, the eldest son of John J. Gagen, an architect. He came to Canada with his parents in 1865, and settled in Seaforth, Huron county, Ontario. Later he moved to Toronto, and entered the employ of Notman and Fraser, photographers. He studied painting under John A. Fraser (q.v.); and in 1872 he became a charter member of the Ontario Society of Artists. In 1880 he was elected an associate of the Royal Canadian Academy of Arts, and in 1915 a member. He was particularly successful as a painter of seascapes, though he did many excellent landscapes, including some paintings of the Rocky Mountains. In 1889 he was elected secretary of the Ontario Society of Artists, and he held this position until his death, at Toronto, on March 2, 1926. In 1873 he married Jane, daughter of John Palmer, of Scarborough, Ontario; and by her he had two daughters.

[*Who's who in Canada*, 1926; *Can. who was who*, vol. 1; N. MacTavish, *The fine arts in Canada* (Toronto, 1925); A. H. Robson, *Canadian landscape painters* (Toronto, 1932).]

Gagnon, Alphonse (1851-1932), author and journalist, was born at St. Jean Port-Joli, Quebec, on June 23, 1851, the son of Charles Gagnon. He became a journalist on the staff of *Le Canadien* at Quebec, then an official stenographer, and lastly a civil servant. In 1907 he was appointed secretary of the department of public works at Quebec. He died at Quebec on October 4, 1932. He was the author of *Études archéologiques et variétés* (Quebec, 1894; new ed., Montreal, 1913), *L'Amérique précolombienne* (Quebec, 1908), *Notes sur les sauvages du Canada* (Proceedings 18th Session, Am. Congress of Americanists, 1913), *Questions d'hier et d'aujourd'hui* (Lille, 1913),

La lumière visible (Montreal, 1920), and *La vieille Angleterre* (Montreal, 1925).
[*Bull. rech. hist.*, 1933.]

Gagnon, Clarence A. (1881-1942), etcher and painter, was born in Montreal, Quebec, on November 8, 1881. He studied art at the Montreal Art Gallery and at the Académie Julien, in Paris, France; and he achieved his first successes as an etcher. In later years he turned to painting; and he became famous for his pictures of winter landscapes in Quebec. He was elected an associate of the Royal Canadian Academy in 1910, and an academician in 1921. He died at Montreal, Quebec, on January 5, 1942.
[*Can. who's who*, 1936-37; N. MacTavish, *The fine arts in Canada* (Toronto, 1925); A. H. Robson, *Clarence A. Gagnon* (Toronto, 1938).]

Gagnon, Ernest (1834-1915), author and musician, was born at Louiseville, Lower Canada, on November 7, 1834, the son of Charles Edouard Gagnon and Julie Jane Durand. He was educated at Joliette College, and studied music in Europe. From 1864 to 1909 he was organist of the Quebec Basilica; and for over thirty years he was secretary of the department of agriculture and public works in Quebec. He died in Quebec on September 15, 1915. Apart from a large number of musical compositions, he published *Chansons populaires du Canada* (Quebec, 1865; 2nd ed., 1880; 3rd ed., 1894; 4th ed., 1900; 5th ed., Montreal, 1908; 6th ed., 1913), *Lettres de voyage* (Quebec, 1876), *Le comte de Paris à Québec* (Quebec, 1895), *Le fort et le château Saint-Louis* (Quebec, 1895), *Le palais législatif à Québec* (Quebec, 1897), *Louis Jolliet* (Quebec, 1902; 2nd ed., Montreal, 1913), *Choses d'autrefois* (Quebec, 1905), *Feuilles volantes et pages d'histoire* (Quebec, 1910), and *Hommes et choses d'autrefois* (Quebec, 1917). He also printed for private circulation *Famille Charles-Edouard Gagnon* (Quebec, 1898; new ed., 1914).
[*Proc. Roy. Soc. Can.*, 1916; Morgan, *Can. men* (1912); *Bull. rech. hist.*, 1916; Le Jeune, *Dict. gén.*]

Gagnon, Philéas (1854-1915), bibliographer, was born at Quebec in 1854, the son of Charles Gagnon and Hortense Caron. He was for many years a merchant in Quebec, and sat in the city council. He made a collection of Canadiana, superior probably to any other private collection, which he sold in 1910 to the city of Montreal. Of this he issued an annotated catalogue, under the title *Essai de bibliographie canadienne* (Quebec, 1895); and a second and supplementary volume was issued later by the city of Montreal under the same title (Montreal, 1913). He was the author also of *Québec il y a cent ans* (Quebec, 1909). He died at Quebec on March 25, 1915.

[*Bull. rech. hist.*, 1927; Morgan, *Can. men* (1912); Le Jeune, *Dict. gén.*]

Gagnon, Wilfrid (1898-1963), industrialist, was born in Montreal, Quebec, September 15, 1898. He was educated at Ste. Marie College, Montreal (B.A., 1918). He joined the firm of Aird and Son Limited after graduation and held various positions, rising to president in 1926. He was chairman of the board of Dow Breweries, chairman of Canadian Aviation Electronics, president of Narwil Shoes Limited, and Wilmont Shoes Limited. He was also director of some twenty industrial and financial companies. In 1936 he was minister of trade and commerce in the Godbout (Liberal) government of the province of Quebec. He died at Montreal on June 10, 1963.
[*Can. who's who*, 1955-57; C. M. de Boissonnault, *Histoire politique de la province de Québec* (Quebec, 1935).]

Galbraith, John (1846-1914), educationist, was born at Montreal on September 5, 1846. He was educated at the University of Toronto (B.A., 1868; M.A., 1875; LL.D., 1902), and became a civil engineer. In 1878 he was appointed to the chair of engineering in the School of Practical Science, Toronto; and in 1889 he became principal of the School. When the School of Practical Science was absorbed by the University of Toronto in 1906, he became dean of the faculty of applied science in the university. He died at Go-Home Bay, Ontario, on July 22, 1914. In 1903 he was made an LL.D. of Queen's University, Kingston.
[Morgan, *Can. men* (1912); *Univ. of Toronto monthly*, 1914.]

Gale, George (1857-1940), journalist, was born at Quebec, Canada East, on July 13, 1857; and died at Montreal, Quebec, on March 9, 1940. He was the author of *Quebec 'twixt old and new* (Quebec, 1915) and *Historic tales of old Quebec* (Quebec, 1923).
[Montreal *Gazette*, March 10, 1940.]

Gale, Samuel (1747-1826), loyalist, was born in England in 1747, and came to America in 1770 as a paymaster in the British army. He emigrated to Canada during the American Revolution, and he eventually became secretary to General Prescott (q.v.). He died at Farnham, Lower Canada, on June 27, 1826. He was the author of *An essay on the nature and principles of public credit* (London, 1784), as well as a *Second essay* (London, 1785), a *Third essay* (London, 1786), and a *Fourth essay* (London, 1786).
[Morgan, *Bib. can.*]

Gale, Samuel (1783-1865), judge and author, was born at St. Augustine, Florida, in 1783, the son of Samuel Gale (q.v.), assistant paymaster of the British forces in America. He was admitted to the bar of Lower Canada in

1808; and in 1817 he was retained as counsel by Lord Selkirk (q.v.) in his contest with the North West Company. In 1834 he was appointed a judge of the Court of King's Bench in Montreal; he retired from the bench in 1848, and he died in June, 1865. He was the author of *Nerva*; *or, a collection of papers published in the Montreal Herald* (Montreal, 1814), in which he made an attack on the administration of Sir George Prevost (q.v.) during the War of 1812.

[P. G. Roy, *Les juges de la province de Québec* (Quebec, 1933).]

Galinée, René de Bréhant de (1645?-1678), priest and explorer, was a native of Brittany. He came to Canada as a Sulpician missionary in 1668, and in the following year was sent with Dollier de Casson (q.v.) and La Salle (q.v.) to try to reach the Mississippi and pave the way for Sulpician missions among the western tribes. The party left Montreal on July 6, 1669, and the two priests, having been abandoned by La Salle, spent the winter on the northern shore of Lake Erie, where they took possession of the country in the name of Louis XIV. Owing to various misfortunes they gave up the attempt to reach the Mississippi, and having visited Sault Ste. Marie, returned to Montreal in the spring of 1670. Galinée made a map of the Great Lakes, and wrote a *Récit de voyage de MM. Dollier et Galinée* (1669-1670). He died on August 16, 1678, on his way to Rome.

[Le Jeune, *Dict. gén.*; J. H. Coyne, *Exploration of the great lakes* (Ontario Hist. Soc., papers and records, 1903); R. G. Thwaites (ed.), *The Jesuit relations*, vol. I (Cleveland, Ohio, 1899); *Dict. Can. biog.*, vol. 1.]

Gallifet, François de (1666-1746), governor of Three Rivers (1710-20), was born at Aix-en-Provence, France, in 1666. He entered the army, and in 1688 he was sent to Canada. He held various posts in the colony, and from 1710 to 1720 he was governor of Three Rivers. He died at Avignon, France, in 1746.

[Le Jeune, *Dict. gén.*; *Dict. Can. biog.*, vol. 3.]

Galt, Sir Alexander Tilloch (1817-1893), Canadian minister of finance (1858-62 and 1864-68), and Canadian high commissioner in London (1880-83), was born in Chelsea, London, on September 6, 1817, the youngest son of John Galt (q.v.), the Scottish novelist. He came to Canada in 1835 as a clerk in the office of the British American Land Company at Sherbrooke, Lower Canada, and from 1844 to 1855 he was commissioner of the company. He became interested in railway development; and he was one of the Canadian promoters of the Grand Trunk Railway. In 1849 he was elected to the Legislative Assembly of Canada for Sherbrooke county as an independent member; but he resigned in 1850. He was returned for Sherbrooke town in 1853; and he continued to represent this constituency in the Assembly until 1867, and in the House of Commons until 1872. He came to be regarded as the leader of the English-speaking members from Lower Canada; and in 1858 he became minister of finance in the Cartier-Macdonald administration, joining the government on the condition that the federation of British North America was to be a plank in its platform. With George E. Cartier (q.v.) and John Ross (q.v.), he went to England to urge Confederation on the British government, but without success. In 1862 he resigned office with his colleagues; but in 1864 he became again minister of finance, and he continued in this office until 1866. He was a delegate to the Charlottetown and Quebec Conferences of 1864 and to the Westminster Conference of 1866; and he was one of the chief architects of the British North America Act. In 1867 he became the first finance minister of the Dominion; but in 1868 he retired from office because of a disagreement with Sir John Macdonald (q.v.).

Galt never again held cabinet office. He severed his connection with political parties, pronounced himself a believer in the future independence of Canada, and in 1872 retired from parliament. In 1875 he was appointed a member of the Halifax Fisheries Commission, under the Treaty of Washington; and the next few years of his life were mainly devoted to diplomatic or semi-diplomatic work. In 1880 he was appointed the first Canadian high commissioner in London; and he held this post until 1883. His last ten years were devoted to the development of various enterprises he had launched in the Canadian North West; but after 1890 his health rapidly failed, and he died at Montreal on September 19, 1893.

He was twice married, (1) in 1848 to Elliott (d. 1850), daughter of John Torrance, of Montreal, and (2) in 1851 to her younger sister, Amy Gordon. By his first wife he had one son; and by his second wife two sons and eight daughters. He declined the C.B. (civil) in 1867, but was created a K.C.M.G. in 1869, and a G.C.M.G. in 1878. He was the author of several pamphlets: *Canada, 1849 to 1859* (London and Quebec, 1860), *The political situation* (Montreal, 1875), *Church and state* (Montreal, 1876), *Civil liberty in Lower Canada* (Montreal, 1876), *The relations of the colonies to the Empire* (London, 1881), and *Future of the Dominion of Canada* (London, 1881).

[O. D. Skelton, *The life and times of Sir A. T. Galt* (Toronto, 1920); C. A. Magrath, *The Galts, father and son* (Lethbridge, Alta., n.d.); *Dict. nat. biog.*; *Cyc. Am. biog.*; Dent, *Can. port.*, vol. 2; E. M. Chadwick, *Ontarian families* (2 vols., Toronto, 1894-98).]

Galt, Elliott Torrance (1850-1928), financier, was born at Sherbrooke, Canada East, on

May 24, 1850, the eldest son of Sir Alexander Tilloch Galt (q.v.). He was educated at Bishop's College School, Lennoxville, and at Harrow, England; and in 1881 he went to the North West Territories as an Indian commissioner. He became a pioneer in railway and irrigation projects in the Canadian West; and in 1903 he became president of the Alberta Railway and Irrigation Company, one of the early railway mergers in the West. He died at New York, N.Y., on May 14, 1928.

[C. A. Magrath, *The Galts, father and son* (Lethbridge, Alta., n.d.); Morgan, *Can. men* (1912).]

Galt, John (1779-1839), novelist, was born in Irvine, Ayrshire, Scotland, on May 2, 1779, the son of John Galt, the captain of a West Indiaman. He was educated at Greenock, went to London in 1804, spent the years 1809-11 in the Near East, and then returned to England to support himself by writing. He tried journalism, biography, drama, and finally fiction. His stories of Scottish life, which he began to publish in 1820, established his reputation as a novelist. At the same time he began his connection with Canada. In 1820 he was appointed London agent for the Canadian claimants for compensation in connection with losses sustained during the War of 1812; and in 1824 he was the promoter of the Canada Company, and was appointed secretary of the board of directors. As a commissioner of the company he visited Canada in 1825, and again in 1826. On the latter occasion, he was appointed superintendent, and he remained in Canada until 1829. He founded in 1827 the town of Guelph, Upper Canada; and the town of Galt, Upper Canada, was named after him. To him belongs the honour of opening up the Huron Tract; but in doing so he did not succeed in carrying his board of directors with him, and he was recalled. The last ten years of his life were spent in England and Scotland, in poverty, ill-health, and bookmaking. In 1834 he interested himself in the formation of the British American Land Company, for the exploitation of the Eastern Townships of Lower Canada, and he was appointed superintendent of this company; but his health prevented him coming out again to Canada, and he died at Greenock, Scotland, on April 11, 1839. In 1813 he married Elizabeth, daughter of Dr. Tilloch, editor of the *Philosophical Magazine* and by her he had three sons.

His most famous novels were *Annals of the parish* (Edinburgh, 1821), *The Ayrshire legatees* (Edinburgh, 1821), *The provost* (Edinburgh, 1822), *Sir Andrew Wylie* (Edinburgh, 1822), *The entail* (Edinburgh, 1823), *The last of the lairds* (Edinburgh, 1826), and *Laurie Todd* (London, 1830). Very few of his writings deal with Canada. He was the author of papers entitled *Statistical account of Upper Canada* (Philosophical magazine, 1807), and *Colonial discontent* (Blackwood's magazine, 1829), of a story entitled *The Hurons, a Canadian tale* (Fraser's magazine, 1830), and *The Canadas from original documents furnished by John Galt*, by A. Picken (London, 1832). His *Autobiography* London, 1833) contains information about his life in Canada; and to him is sometimes attributed "The Canadian boat song", which appeared in *Blackwood's* in September, 1829.

[Jennie W. Aberdein, *John Galt* (Oxford, 1936); R. K. Gordon, *John Galt* (Toronto, 1920), with bibliography; R. and K. M. Lizars, *In the days of the Canada Company* (Toronto, 1896); *Dict. nat. biog.*; E. M. Chadwick, *Ontarian families* (2 vols., Toronto, 1894-98).]

Galt, John (1856-1933), merchant and financier, was born in Montreal in 1856, the son of Sir A. T. Galt (q.v.). He was educated at the Montreal High School; and in 1882, he went to Winnipeg, where he became a wholesale grocer. For several years he was president of the Union Bank of Canada. He died at Victoria, British Columbia, on April 8, 1933.

[Morgan, *Can. men* (1912).]

Galt, Sir Thomas (1815-1901), chief justice of the Court of Common Pleas, Ontario (1887-94), was born in London, England, on August 17, 1815, the son of John Galt (q.v.). He was educated in England and Scotland, and came to Canada in 1833, as a clerk in the service of the Canada Company. Six years later, he entered the public service, as a clerk in the office of the attorney-general for Upper Canada; but in 1845 he was called to the bar (Q.C., 1858), and went into private practice in Toronto. In 1869 he was appointed a puisne judge of the Court of Common Pleas, and in 1887 he became chief justice of the court. He retired from the bench in 1894, and he died in Toronto on June 29, 1901. In 1847 he married Frances Louisa, daughter of Lieut. James Marshall Perkins, R.N.; and by her he had four sons and four daughters. He was created a knight bachelor in 1888.

[Morgan, *Can. men* (1898); *Morang's annual register*, 1901; W. J. Rattray, *The Scot in British North America* (4 vols., Toronto, 1881); Dent, *Can. port.*, vol. 3; E. M. Chadwick, *Ontarian families* (2 vols., Toronto, 1894-98).]

Gamache, Louis Olivier (1784-1854), pirate of Anticosti, was born at L'Islet, Quebec, in 1784. He became a cabin-boy in the Royal Navy; but after many years spent in the service he returned to Canada, and settled on the island of Anticosti. Here he acquired the reputation of a pirate. He died on the island of Anticosti in September, 1854.

[J. B. A. Ferland, *Opuscules* (Quebec, 1877).]

Gamelin, Emilie, *née* **Tavernier** (1800-1851), founder and first mother superior of the

Sisters of Charity in Montreal, was born at Montreal, on February 19, 1800, the younger daughter of Antoine Tavernier. In 1823 she married Jean-Baptiste Gamelin; but within four years she lost by death her husband and three infant children. In 1828 she opened a refuge in Montreal for the old and infirm; and in 1831, she founded a society of "Ladies of Charity". This became in 1844 the order of Sisters of Charity, of which she was the first mother superior. She died, of cholera, on September 23, 1851.

[*Vie de Mère Gamelin* (Montreal, 1900); Le Jeune, *Dict. gén.*]

Gamey, Robert Roswell (1865-1917), politician, was born in Maxwell, Grey county, Ontario, on August 20, 1865. He became a mining speculator and insurance agent; in 1902 he was elected to represent Manitoulin as a Conservative in the Ontario legislature, and he continued to represent this constituency until his death. In 1903 he brought against the Ross government charges of bribery and corruption which caused a great sensation, and were partly responsible for the defeat of the government. He died at Toronto on March 19, 1917.

[*Can. parl. comp.*]

Gammell, Isaac (1861?-1932), educationist and author, was born about 1861, and became a school-teacher in the province of Quebec. He became president of the Association of Protestant School Teachers in Quebec; and he died at Morrin Heights, Quebec, on May 24, 1932. He was the author of an *Elementary history of Canada* (Toronto, 1907).

[*Can. ann. review*, 1932.]

Gandier, Alfred (1861-1932), clergyman and educationist, was born in Hastings county, Canada West, on November 29, 1861. He was educated at Queen's University, Kingston (B.A., 1884; M.A., 1887) and at Edinburgh University (B.D., 1889), and was ordained a minister of the Presbyterian Church in Canada in 1889. After holding charges at Brampton, Ontario, at Halifax, Nova Scotia, and Toronto, Ontario, he was appointed in 1908 principal of Knox College, Toronto; and he held this post until his death, at Toronto, on June 13, 1932. He was the author of *The Son of Man coming in His Kingdom* (New York, 1922).

[Morgan, *Can. men* (1912).]

Gane, William Law (1815-1879), journalist, was born in Harwich, England, in 1815, and became a well-known journalist in London, as well as a contributor to *Blackwood's*, *Fraser's*, and the *Gentleman's Magazine*. He came to Canada in 1860, and settled in the township of Lowe, Ottawa county, Lower Canada. Hence his *nom de plume* of "The Lowe Farmer", which was attached to his Canadian

articles. He became a sessional clerk on the staff of the Canadian House of Commons; and he died at Ottawa, Ontario, on September 17, 1879.

[*Dom. ann. reg.*, 1879.]

Ganong, Gilbert White (1851-1917), lieutenant-governor of New Brunswick (1917), was born at Springfield, in Kings county, New Brunswick, in 1851, of United Empire Loyalist stock. He became a prosperous manufacturer of confectionery; and from 1900 to 1908 he represented Charlotte county in the Canadian House of Commons. On June 29, 1917, he was appointed lieutenant-governor of New Brunswick; but he died on October 23 following. In 1876 he married Marie, daughter of John B. Robinson.

[*Can. parl. comp.*]

Ganong, William Francis (1864-1941), botanist and historian, was born at Saint John, New Brunswick, on February 19, 1864. He was educated at the University of New Brunswick (B.A., 1884; M.A., 1886; Ph.D., 1898; LL.D., 1920), at Harvard University (B.A., 1887), and at the University of Munich (Ph.D., 1894). In 1894 he was appointed professor of botany in Smith College, Northampton, Massachusetts; and this position he held until his retirement in 1932. He died at Saint John, New Brunswick, on September 7, 1941. He was for many years a corresponding member of the Royal Society of Canada; and he contributed to the *Transactions* of this society a long series of papers dealing with the history and cartography of New Brunswick. He was elected president of the Botanical Society of America in 1908; and he was the author of several standard books on botany: *The teaching botanist* (New York, 1899), *A laboratory course in plant physiology* (New York, 1901), *The living plant* (New York, 1913), and *A text book of botany for colleges* (New York, 1916). He was also the editor of Nicolas Denys's *Description of the natural history of the coasts of North America* (Toronto, 1908) and Chrestien Le Clercq's *New relation of Gaspesia* (Toronto, 1910), and joint editor, with H. H. Langton, of Patrick Campbell's *Travels* (Toronto, 1937).

[*Proc. Roy. Soc. Can.*, 1942; *Who's who in America*, 1940-41; *Can. who's who*, 1936-37.]

Gard, Anson Albert (b. 1849), author, was born near Tremont City, Ohio, on September 9, 1849. He was educated at Ohio Wesleyan University; and, after a chequered business career in the United States, he came to Canada in 1901. Before coming to Canada he had published *Gard's log book* (New York, 1888) and *My friend Bill* (New York, 1900); but while in Canada he became a somewhat prolific author. He wrote *The Yankee in Quebec* (New York, 1901), *The wandering Yankee* (New York, 1902), *Montreal as seen by the wandering Yankee* (Montreal, 1903), *The hub and the spokes;*

or, The capital and its environs (Ottawa, 1904), *Pioneers of the upper Ottawa and the humors of the valley* (Ottawa, 1906), *The real Cobalt* (Toronto, 1908), *North Bay, the gateway to Silverland* (Toronto, 1909), and *Silverland and its stories* (Toronto, 1909). He died some time after 1915.

[Morgan, *Can. men* (1912).]

Gardiner, Herbert Fairbairn (1849-1924), author and journalist, was born at Brockville, Ontario, on August 21, 1849, the son of the Rev. James Gardiner and Matilda Fairbairn. He was educated at Albert College (B.A., 1869; M.D., 1870), and became a journalist. He was successively editor of the Brantford *Expositor*, the Hamilton *Spectator*, and the Hamilton *Times*. In 1903 he was appointed principal of the Ontario Institute for the Education of the Blind at Brantford; but he resigned this position in 1916, and he died at Hamilton, Ontario, on October 27, 1924. He was the author of *Nothing but names: An inquiry into the origin of the names of the counties and townships of Ontario* (Toronto, 1899).

[Morgan, *Can. men* (1912).]

Gardiner, James Garfield (1883-1962), statesman, was born at Farquhar, Ontario, on November 30, 1883. When he was five years old his family moved to Lincoln, Nebraska, because of the depression in Canada. He attended school at Lincoln and at Alpena, Michigan, before returning with his parents to Ontario in 1895. For the next five years James Gardiner worked on various farms in Huron county. In 1901 he went to Clearwater, Manitoba, on a harvest excursion train, and began to work for his uncle and to attend school. He received his high school certificate and a "non-professional" teacher's certificate in 1904. He attended Regina, Saskatchewan, Normal School (1905) and Manitoba College (B.A., 1911). He became principal of the Continuation School at Lemburg, Saskatchewan, in 1911 and was immediately involved in the reciprocity election of that year. In 1914 he was elected to the Saskatchewan legislature, being re-elected in 1917, 1919, 1922, and 1925. He was minister of highways from 1922, and premier from 1926 to 1929, when his government was defeated by the Conservatives under Dr. J. T. M. Anderson (q.v.). He was returned to power in the 1934 election in which Anderson's Conservatives won no seats and the Co-operative Commonwealth Federation, contesting its first Saskatchewan election, won five. In 1935 he became minister of agriculture in the federal cabinet of Mackenzie King, being elected in 1936 and in every subsequent election until 1957. He was minister of agriculture from 1935 to 1957 and minister of National War Services from July, 1940, to June, 1941. He was responsible for the Prairie Farm Rehabilitation Act and its offshoots designed to soften the blows of drought on the prairie. Provision was made for the construction of dams and dugouts to collect water, the reseeding of abandoned land, the establishment of community pastures and arrangements for a postponement of mortgage payments, and for payments for food and clothing in areas of crop failure. Gardiner began farming near Lemburg, Saskatchewan, in 1916 and his life was devoted to farming and the interests of farmers. He died at Balcarres, Saskatchewan, on January 12, 1962.

[*Can. who's who*, 1955-57; N. A. Benson, *None of it came easy* (Toronto, 1955); *Can. parl. guide.*]

Gariépy, Charles Napoléon (1868-1932), priest and educationist, was born at Château-Richer, Quebec, on June 4, 1868. He was ordained a priest of the Roman Catholic Church in 1892; and in 1893 he was appointed a professor of theology in Laval University. He became in 1906 rector of the university, and an apostolic protonotary. He died at Quebec, on July 29, 1932. He was the author of *De jure et justitia* (Quebec, 1911) and *Commentaires sur le nouveau code de droit canonique* (Quebec, 1919).

[Allaire, *Dict. biog.*; *Bull. rech. hist.*, (1932).]

Garneau, Alfred (1836-1904), poet, was born in Quebec, Lower Canada, on December 20, 1836, the eldest son of François-Xavier Garneau (q.v.). He was educated at the Quebec Seminary, and was called to the bar in 1860. In 1861 he entered the civil service of Canada, and in 1873 he was appointed chief French translator to the Senate of Canada, a position which he occupied until his death at Ottawa in 1904. In his youth he contributed some striking verse to *Le Foyer Canadien* (1863-66) and other periodicals; and he published a fourth edition of his father's *Histoire du Canada*, with a memoir of the author by P. J. O. Chauveau (q.v.). After his death, his son Hector published a collection of his poems, under the title *Poésies* (Montreal, 1906).

[P. G. Roy, *Fils de Québec*, vol. 4 (Lévis, Que., 1933); Le Jeune, *Dict. gén.*]

Garneau, François-Xavier (1809-1866), historian, was born at Quebec, Lower Canada, on June 15, 1809. He was educated at the Quebec Seminary, and became a notary public. In 1831 he accompanied D. B. Viger (q.v.) to England and France as his secretary, and met many literary notabilities. In 1840 he was stimulated to write a history of Canada by Lord Durham's remark that the French Canadians were a people "without a history and without a literature". The first volume of his *Histoire du Canada* appeared in Quebec in 1845; the second in 1846; the third in 1848; and the fourth at Montreal in 1852. A second edition was published at Quebec in 1852, and a third in 1859. A fourth edition was published at Montreal in 1882, under the direction of Alfred Garneau (q.v.), and a fifth at Paris in 1913-20 under the editorship of Hector Garneau. An English translation, by A. Bell, was published in Montreal in 1860. Garneau died at Quebec, on February 3, 1866. He married Esther Bilodeau, and by her he had several children.

[G. Lanctot, *François-Xavier Garneau* (Toronto, 1927); H. R. Casgrain, *F.-X. Garneau* (Quebec, 1866); P. J. O. Chauveau, *François-Xavier Garneau, sa vie et ses oeuvres* (Montreal, 1884); L. M. Darveau, *Nos hommes de lettres* (Montreal, 1873); H. d'Arles, *Nos historiens* (Montreal, 1921); P. G. Roy, *Fils de Québec*, vol. 3 (Lévis, Que., 1933); Le Jeune, *Dict. gén.*]

Garneau, Hector de Saint-Denys- (1912-1943), poet, was born at Montreal, Quebec, on June 13, 1912, and died suddenly near the village of Ste. Catherine de Fossambault, north of Quebec, Quebec, on October 24, 1943. He was educated at the Collège Ste. Marie in Montreal; but a heart condition prevented him from taking up a profession, and he turned to painting and poetry. He published only one volume of poetry, *Regards et jeux dans l'espace* (Montreal, 1937); but after his death his *Poésies complètes* (Montreal, 1949) appeared, and also his *Journal* (Montreal, 1954).

[Romain Légaré, *L'aventure poétique et spirituelle de Saint-Denys-Garneau* (Montreal, 1957); M. B. Ellis, *De Saint-Denys-Garneau: art et réalisme* (Montreal, 1949); E. Kushner, *Saint-Denys-Garneau* (Montreal, 1967).]

Garneau, Sir John George (1864-1944), civil engineer and merchant, was born at Quebec, Canada East, on November 19, 1864, the son of Pierre Garneau (q.v.). He was educated at Laval University (B.A.Sc., 1884), and became a civil engineer. Later, he went into the wholesale dry goods business founded by his father, and became in 1911 its president. In 1908 he was appointed chairman of the National Battlefields Commission; and he was knighted by the Prince of Wales (later King George V) in person at the time of the tercentennial celebration of the founding of Quebec. He was an honorary LL.D. of the University of Toronto (1917), of McGill University (1921), and of Bishop's College, Lennoxville (1931). He died at Quebec, Que., on February 6, 1944.

[*Can. who's who*, 1936-37.]

Garneau, Pierre (1823-1905), merchant and politician, was born at Cap Santé, Lower Canada, on May 8, 1823. He became head of an extensive wholesale dry goods firm, and president of the Quebec Steamship Company and the Quebec Street Railway Company. He represented Quebec county in the Quebec Legislative Assembly from 1873 to 1878, and from 1881 to 1886; and in 1887 he was appointed a member of the Quebec Legislative Council. He was a member of the Quebec government, holding various portfolios, from 1874 to 1878 and from 1887 to 1891. He died at Quebec, Que., on June 23, 1905.

[Morgan, *Can. men* (1898); *Can. parl. comp.*]

Garnier, Charles (1606-1649), missionary and martyr, was born in Paris, France, on May 25, 1606, of "a rich and noble family", and was educated at the Collège de Clermont. In 1624 he entered the Jesuit novitiate; and in 1636 he was sent to Quebec. He went as a missionary to the Hurons in 1637; and in 1639 he began, with Father Isaac Jogues (q.v.), the evangelization of the Petun nation. He laboured among these Indians for ten years; and on December 7, 1649, he was massacred by the Iroquois at the Indian village of St. Jean. He was canonized in 1930.

[Le Jeune, *Dict. gén.*; R. G. Thwaites (ed.), *The Jesuit relations* (73 vols., Cleveland, Ohio, 1899-1901); F. Larivière, *La vie ardente de Saint Charles Garnier* (Montreal, 1957); *Dict. Can. biog.*, vol. 1.]

Garnier, John Hutchison (1810?-1898), physician and poet, was born in Scotland of Irish parentage about 1810, and was educated at Dublin. He came to Canada about 1850, and practised as a physician, first at Hagersville, Ontario, and then at Lucknow, Ontario. He died at Lucknow on February 1, 1898. He was the author of *Prince Pedro: a tragedy* (Toronto, 1877).

[C. C. James, *A bibliography of Canadian poetry* (Toronto, 1899).]

Garrioch, Alfred Campbell (1848-1934), clergyman and author, was born at Kildonan, Assiniboia, on February 10, 1848, and died at Winnipeg, Manitoba, on December 3, 1934. He was educated at St. John's College, Winnipeg, and was ordained a priest of the Church of England in 1875. He became a missionary in the Peace River country, and later was incumbent of several parishes in Manitoba. He retired from parochial work in 1905; and in his later years was the author of four books: *First furrows* (Winnipeg, 1923), *The far and furry north* (Winnipeg, 1925), *A hatchet mark in duplicate* (Toronto, 1929), and *The correction line* (Winnipeg, 1933).

[Morgan, *Can. men* (1912); *Encyc. Can.*]

Garry, Nicholas (1782?-1856), deputy governor of the Hudson's Bay Company (1822-35), was born in England about 1782, the natural son of Nicholas Langley (d. 1783) and Isabella Garry, whose name he took. He was brought up by his uncle, Thomas Langley, who became a director of the Hudson's Bay Company in 1807; and he himself became a director in 1817. In 1821 he was selected to visit Canada to supervise the amalgamation of the Hudson's Bay Company with the North West Company; and the *Diary* of his journey has been printed in the *Transactions* of the Royal Society of Canada for 1900. From 1822 to 1835 he was deputy-governor of the Hudson's Bay Company; but in 1835 he became of unsound mind, and his affairs were administered by the master in chancery from about 1839 until his death at Claygate, Surrey, England, on December 24, 1856. Fort Garry and other places in western Canada were named after him.

[E. E. Rich (ed.), *Journal of occurrences in the Athabasca department, by George Simpson* (Toronto: The Champlain Society, 1938).]

Garvin, Mrs. Amelia Beers, *née* **Warnock** (1878-1956), author, was born at Galt, Ontario, in 1878, and died at Toronto, Ontario, on September 7, 1956. She became a journalist, and, prior to her marriage in 1912 to John W. Garvin (q.v.), she was literary editor of the Toronto *Mail and Empire*. She published several small volumes of verse: *Grey knitting and other poems* (Toronto, 1914), *The white comrade and other poems* (Toronto, 1916), *The new Joan and other poems* (Toronto, 1917), *Morning in the west* (Toronto, 1923), *The island and other poems* (Toronto, 1934), and *The flute and other poems* (Toronto, 1950). She was also the author of the following prose works: *Isabella Valancy Crawford* (Toronto, 1923), *Legends of the St. Lawrence* (Montreal, 1926), *Canadian houses of romance* (Toronto, 1926), republished in a revised and enlarged edition under the title *Historic houses of Canada* (Toronto, 1952), *Canadian cities of romance* (Toronto, 1933), *This is Ontario* (Toronto, 1937), and *Toronto: Romance of a great city* (Toronto, 1956). She wrote under the *nom de plume* of "Katherine Hale".

[*Can. who's who*, 1952-54; *Encyc. Can.*; W. P. Percival, *Leading Canadian poets* (Toronto, 1948).]

Garvin, John William (1859-1935), editor and publisher, was born at Lynden, Ontario, on March 19, 1859. He was educated at the University of Toronto (B.A., 1892), and became a school-teacher. Later, he entered the insurance business. He died at Toronto on August 19, 1935. An enthusiastic student of Canadian literature, he edited *The collected poems of Isabella Valancy Crawford* (Toronto, 1905), *Canadian poets* (Toronto, 1916; new and rev. ed., 1926), *Canadian poems of the great war* (Toronto, 1918), *Canadian verse for boys and girls* (Toronto, 1930), *Cap and bells: An anthology of light verse by Canadian poets* (Toronto, 1936), and a series of books entitled *Master-works of Canadian literature*, only a few of which, however, were actually published. In 1912 he married Amelia Beers Warnock.

[L. Pierce, "Foreword" to J. W. Garvin,

Cap and bells (Toronto, 1936); Morgan, *Can. men* (1912).]

Gaspé, Philippe Aubert de. See **Aubert de Gaspé, Philippe.**

Gates, Horatio (1777-1834), merchant and banker, was born in Barre, Massachusetts, on October 30, 1777, the son of Captain Benjamin Gates, who had served in the army of the Continental Congress. Early in life he came to Canada, by way of Vermont, and founded in Montreal the firm of Horatio Gates and Co., importers of groceries and liquors. He was allowed to remain unmolested during the War of 1812, and in 1814 became a Canadian citizen. He was one of the founders of the Bank of Montreal, and from 1832 to 1834 was its president. From 1832 to 1834 he was also a member of the Legislative Council of Lower Canada. He died at Montreal on April 11, 1834.

[A. Shortt, *Founders of Canadian banking; Horatio Gates* (Journal of the Can. Bankers' Association, 1922.]

Gaudet, Placide (1850-1930), genealogist, was born at Dupuis Corner, near Shediac, New Brunswick, on November 19, 1850, the son of Placide F. Gaudet and Marie Vienneau. For twenty-five years he was on the staff of the Public Archives of Canada at Ottawa; and he died at Shediac, New Brunswick, on November 9, 1930. He was the author of *Généalogies des familles acadiennes*, printed in the Public Archives Report for 1905, *Le grand dérangement* (Montreal, 1922), and many articles on genealogical and historical subjects.

[*Bull. rech. hist.*, 1931.]

Gauvreau, Charles Arthur (1860-1924), politician and author, was born at Isle Verte, Canada East, on September 29, 1860. He was educated at Laval University, and was admitted to practice as a notary public in 1885. From 1897 to his death he represented Témiscouata in the Canadian House of Commons. He died at Rivière-du-Loup, Quebec, on October 9, 1924. He was the author of *Nos paroisses: L'Isle-Verte* (Lévis, Que., 1889), *Nos paroisses: Trois-Pistoles* (Lévis, Que., 1890), and *Au bord du Saint-Laurent* (Rivière-du-Loup, Que., 1923).

[*Can. parl. comp.*]

Gay, James (1810-1891), poetaster, was born on March 24, 1810, at Clovelly, Devonshire, England. He emigrated to Canada in 1834, and settled in Guelph, Upper Canada. Here he was in succession a carpenter, a waggon-maker, a gun-smith, a hotel-keeper, and finally an umbrella-mender and saw-sharpener. He died at Guelph on February 23, 1891. He described himself as "the poet laureate of Canada"; and he wrote to Lord Tennyson on one occasion, "Dear Sir, now

Longfellow has gone there are only two of us left." He was the author of *Poems* (Guelph, Ontario, 1883), and *Canada's poet* (London, 1885?).

[W. A. Deacon, *The four Jameses* (1927; new edition, Toronto, 1974).]

Geddie, John (1815-1872), missionary, was born in Scotland in 1815, but came to Nova Scotia when young, and was educated at Pictou Academy. He was licensed by the presbytery of Pictou in 1837, and for seven years was in charge of a church in Prince Edward Island. In 1845, however, he was sent out as a missionary to the New Hebrides; and here he spent the rest of his life. He died in Australia, on December 14, 1872.

[G. Patterson, *Missionary life among the cannibals: Being the life of the Rev. John Geddie* (Toronto, 1882); *Dict. Can. biog.*, vol. 10.]

Geikie, Walter Bayne (1830-1917), dean of the faculty of medicine in Trinity University, Toronto (1878-1903), was born in Edinburgh, Scotland, on May 8, 1830, the son of the Rev. Archibald Geikie. He came to Canada, and was licensed as a medical practitioner by the Medical Board of Upper Canada in 1851. From 1856 to 1870 he was on the medical staff of Victoria University, Cobourg; and from 1878 to 1903 he was dean of the medical faculty of Trinity University, Toronto. He died in Toronto on January 12, 1917.

[*Can. who was who*, vol. 1; Morgan, *Can. men* (1912).]

Gélinas, Joseph Gérin (1874-1927), priest and author, was born at Louiseville, Quebec, on February 8, 1874, was ordained a priest of the Roman Catholic Church in 1889, and was on the staff of the Three Rivers Seminary from that date until his death on January 24, 1927. He was the author of *Arthur Beaulac* (Three Rivers, Que., 1914), *Au foyer* (Montreal, 1917), and *En veillant* (Montreal, 1919).

[Allaire, *Dict. biog.*]

Gemmill, John Alexander (1847-1905), lawyer and author, was born at Ramsay, Lanark county, Canada West, on March 20, 1847. He was educated at Glasgow University, and was called to the bar in Ontario in 1871 (Q.C., 1896). He practised law, first in Almonte, and then in Ottawa. In 1881 he became the proprietor and editor of the *Canadian parliamentary companion*. He died at Ottawa on November 7, 1905. In 1883 he married Emily Helen, daughter of the Hon. Alexander Walker Ogilvie (q.v.). He was the author of *The practice of the parliament of Canada upon bills of divorce* (Toronto, 1889), and *The Ogilvies of Montreal* (Montreal, 1904).

[Morgan, *Can. men* (1898).]

Geoffrion, Christophe Alphonse (1843-1899), lawyer and politician, was born at Va-

rennes, Quebec, on November 23, 1843, the son of Félix Geoffrion and Catherine Brodeur. He was educated at St. Hyacinthe College and at McGill University (B.C.L., 1866; D.C.L., 1893). He practised law in Montreal in partnership with Sir A. A. Dorion (q.v.), was created a Q.C. in 1879, and was elected *bâtonnier* of the Montreal bar in 1885. In 1895 he was elected to the Canadian House of Commons as a Liberal, to fill the vacancy in Verchères caused by the death of his brother, Félix Geoffrion (q.v.), the sitting member. In 1896 he was included in the Laurier government as a minister without portfolio, and he continued as such until his death on July 18, 1899. In 1870 he married Eulalie, eldest daughter of Sir A. A. Dorion (q.v.).

[Morgan, *Can. men* (1898); Le Jeune, *Dict. gén.*; *Can. parl. comp.*; *Can. who was who*, vol. 1.]

Geoffrion, Félix (1832-1894), notary public and politician, was born at Varennes, Quebec, on October 4, 1832, the son of Félix Geoffrion and Catherine Brodeur. From 1854 to 1863 he was registrar of Verchères. In 1863 he was elected to the Legislative Assembly of Canada as member for Verchères; in 1867 he was elected to the Canadian House of Commons for the same constituency, and he continued to be re-elected at every general election until his death. On July 8, 1874, he was sworn of the privy council as minister of inland revenue in the Mackenzie administration; but in December, 1876, ill-health compelled the resignation of his portfolio. He died at Quebec on August 7, 1894. In October, 1856, he married Almaide, youngest daughter of Lieut.-Colonel Joseph Dansereau of Verchères.

[Dent, *Can. port.*, vol. 3; Bibaud, *Panth. can.*; Le Jeune, *Dict. gén.*; *Can. parl. comp.*]

Geoffrion, Louis Philippe (1875-1942), lawyer and lexicographer, was born near Varennes, Quebec, on Feburary 24, 1875, and was educated at Laval University in Montreal. He was called to the bar, and practised law in Montreal until 1903. He then became private secretary to Sir Lomer Gouin (q.v.); and in 1912 he was appointed clerk of the Legislative Assembly of the province of Quebec. This position he held until his death at Quebec, Que., on September 3, 1942. In his official capacity, he edited *Règlements de la Chambre* (Quebec, 1915); but his most important work was done as a student of the French language in Canada. He was the author of *Zigzags autour de nos parlers* (3 vols., Quebec, 1924-27), and joint author, with Adjutor Rivard, of a *Glossaire du parler français au Canada* (Quebec, 1930). He was elected in 1927 a fellow of the Royal Society of Canada.

[*Proc. Roy. Soc. Can.*, 1943; *Can. who's who*, 1936-37.]

George, James (1801?-1870), clergyman and author, was born in Perthshire about

1801, and was educated at St. Andrew's University and at Glasgow University (D.D., 1855). In 1829 he emigrated to the United States, and was licensed to preach by the Saratoga Presbytery of the Associate Reformed Church. In 1833 he came to Canada, and became minister of the Presbyterian church at Scarborough, near Toronto. In 1853 he was appointed professor of mental and moral philosophy in Queen's College, Kingston; but in 1862 he returned to pastoral work, and during his later years he was minister of the Presbyterian church in Stratford, Ontario. He died in Stratford on August 26, 1870. He was the author of a large number of pamphlets, containing mostly lectures and sermons, as well as *The Sabbath school of the fireside* (Kingston, 1859); and a collection of his sermons was published posthumously, under the title, *Thoughts on high themes* (Toronto, 1874).

[W. Gregg, *History of the Presbyterian Church in the Dominion of Canada* (Toronto, 1885).]

Gérin, Léon (1863-1951), social scientist, was born at Quebec on May 17, 1863, the son of Antoine Gérin-Lajoie and the grandson of Etienne Parent (qq.v.). He was educated at Laval University in Montreal, and later studied sociology in Paris. He was called to the Quebec bar in 1885, but practised law for only a short time. He became chief translator for the House of Commons in Ottawa; and retired from the civil service only in 1936. Meanwhile he continued his sociological studies, and was undoubtedly the pioneer social scientist in the province of Quebec. After retirement he brought together some of his studies in two books, *Le type économique et social des Canadiens* (Montreal, 1938) and *Aux sources de notre histoire* (Montreal, 1946). In 1925 he published a life of his father; and after his retirement he published, also the result of his years as a translator, *Vocabulaire pratique de l'anglais au français* (Montreal, 1937). He was elected a fellow of the Royal Society of Canada in 1898, and its president in 1933; and he received honorary degrees from Laval University and the University of Montreal. He died at Montreal on January 17, 1951.

[*Proc. Roy. Soc. Can.*, 1951; *Encyc. Can.*; *Can. who's who*, 1948.]

Gérin-Lajoie, Antoine (1824-1882), journalist and author, was born at Yamachiche, Lower Canada, on August 4, 1824. He was educated at the College of Nicolet, and while still at school wrote "Un Canadien errant", a famous French-Canadian song, and a play entitled *Le jeune Latour* (Montreal, 1884). He was called to the bar of Lower Canada in 1848, but did not practise law. From 1845 to 1852 he was editor of *La Minerve*; then he became French translator to the Legislative Assembly; and finally he was appointed assistant

librarian in the Library of Parliament, a post which he held until his retirement on pension in 1880. He died at Ottawa on August 4, 1882. He was one of the founders of the Institut Canadien at Montreal, and was twice its president. In the establishment of the *Soirées canadiennes* (Quebec, 1861-65) and the *Foyer canadien* (Quebec, 1863-66) he took a prominent part; and he was the author of a *Catéchisme politique* (Montreal, 1851) and of two well-known novels, *Jean Rivard le défricheur* (Montreal, 1874) and *Jean Rivard l'économiste* (Montreal, 1876). After his death appeared his *Dix ans au Canada, de 1840 à 1850* (Quebec, 1888), a history of the establishment of responsible government in Canada.

[L. de Montigny, *Antoine Gérin-Lajoie* (Toronto, 1926); L. Gérin, *Antoine Gérin-Lajoie* (Montreal, 1925); H. R. Casgrain, *Biographie de Gérin-Lajoie* (Trans. Roy. Soc. Can., 1885), and *Biographies canadiennes* (Montreal, 1885); Le Jeune, *Dict. gén.*]

Gérin-Lajoie, Mme. Marie, *née* **Lacoste** (1867-1945), feminist, was born at Montreal, Quebec, on October 19, 1867, the daughter of Sir Alexander Lacoste (q.v.). In 1887 she married Henri Gérin-Lajoie, a son of Antoine Gérin-Lajoie (q.v.); and she became a champion of women's rights in the province of Quebec. It was her influence that was decisive in bringing about female suffrage in French Canada. She was the author of two legal treatises: *Traité de droit usuel* (Montreal, 1902) and *La femme et le code civil* (Montreal, 1929). She died at Montreal on November 1, 1945.

[C. L. Cleverdon, *The woman suffrage movement in Canada* (Toronto, 1956); *Encyc. Can.*]

Gerrard, Samuel (1767-1857), merchant, was born in Ireland in 1767, and came to Canada about 1787. He entered business in Montreal, and became a partner in the firm of Parker, Gerrard, and Ogilvy, later Gerrard, Gillespie and Co. This was one of the firms which financed the XY Company between the years 1797 and 1804; and through it Samuel Gerrard acquired after 1804 an indirect interest in the North West Company. When the firm of McTavish, McGillivrays and Co. failed in 1825, Samuel Gerrard was appointed one of the trustees; and it largely fell to him to unravel the tangled finances of the North West Company. His papers, which are now in the Sulpician Library in Montreal, naturally contain a vast amount of material of interest to the historian of the fur-trade. Gerrard died in Montreal on March 24, 1857, aged 90 years; and his wife, Ann Grant, who was the granddaughter of Richard Dobie (q.v.), died in Montreal on October 18, 1854, aged 81 years. Their only surviving child, Samuel Henry Gerrard, died in Germany in 1858.

[Charles Drisard, *L'honorable Samuel Gerrard* (Bull. rech. hist., 1928).]

Gesner, Abraham (1797-1864), geologist, was born at Cornwallis, Nova Scotia, on May 2, 1797, the son of Colonel Henry Gesner, a United Empire Loyalist. He studied medicine at St. Bartholomew's and Guy's hospitals, London, England, and after receiving the degree of M.D., returned to Nova Scotia in 1824. While practising his profession, he gradually turned to scientific studies. In 1838 he was commissioned to make a geological survey of New Brunswick, and in 1846 of Prince Edward Island. In 1852 he discovered kerosene oil, and in 1853 he went to live in New York. He returned to Canada in 1862, having sold his patents for the manufacture of kerosene; and he died at Halifax, Nova Scotia, on April 19, 1864. Besides numerous scientific papers and reports, he was the author of *Remarks on the geology and mineralogy of Nova Scotia* (Halifax and London, 1836), *New Brunswick, with notes for emigrants* (London, 1847), *The industrial resources of Nova Scotia* (Halifax, 1849), *A practical treatise on coal, petroleum, and other distilled oils* (New York and London, 1861; 2nd ed., 1865), and *The gold fields of Nova Scotia* (Halifax, 1862).

[Morgan, *Bib. can.*; *Cyc. Am. biog.*; W. G. MacFarlane, *New Brunswick bibliography* (Saint John, N.B., 1895).]

Ghent, Percy (1888-1952), radiologist and author, was born in England in 1888, and died at Winnipeg, Manitoba, on September 21, 1952. He came to Canada, and for thirty years was a radiologist in the Toronto General Hospital. He also conducted a column of literary and historical interest in the Toronto *Telegram*; and he was the author of *John Reade and his friends* (Toronto, 1925), *Literary and historical fragments of Canadian interest* (Toronto, 1927), and *Roentgen, a brief biography* (Toronto, 1929).

[Toronto *Globe and Mail*, Sept. 23, 1952; *Can. who's who*, 1949-51.]

Giasson, Jacques (1747-1808), fur-trader, was born in Montreal in 1747, the son of Jacques Giasson and Marie Angélique Hubert. Following his father, who had been a fur-trader at Green Bay in the French period, he was engaged all his life in the south-west trade. He was elected a member of the Beaver Club of Montreal in 1791; and he died at Montreal on January 30, 1808.

[M. M. Quaife (ed.), *The John Askin papers*, vol. 2 (Detroit, Mich., 1931).]

Gibb, David (1884-1971), painter, was born in 1884. He was guided by Homer Watson to study at the Ontario College of Art. In 1904 he studied at the Art Students' League in New York for four months. He served in the Canadian army in the First World War and was gassed. He spent a year in hospital and then returned to his art studies on a rehabilitation grant. Settling at Galt, he painted landscapes and gave some instructions to students. He also continued his own studies with Carl Ahrens and Marion Mattice. He died in 1971.

[C. S. MacDonald, *A Dictionary of Canadian artists*, vol. 2 (1968).]

Gibbon, John Murray (1875-1952), publicity agent and author, was born in Ceylon on April 12, 1875; and was educated at King's College, Aberdeen, Christ Church, Oxford, and the University of Göttingen. He became a journalist in London, and for a time was editor of *Black and White*. In 1907 he was invited to supervise the European publicity work of the Canadian Pacific Railway; and in 1913 he was brought to Canada as the general publicity agent of the railway, a position he held until his retirement in 1945. He wrote the history of the C.P.R. under the title *Steel of empire* (Toronto, 1935); but the range of his literary output was much wider. He was the author of five novels: *Hearts and faces* (London, 1916), *Drums afar* (Toronto, 1918), *The conquering hero* (New York, 1920), *Pagan love* (Toronto, 1922), and *The eyes of a gypsy* (London, 1926). Among his historical works were *Scots in Canada* (London, 1911), *Canadian mosaic* (Toronto, 1938), *Three centuries of Canadian nursing* (Ottawa, 1947), *Our old Montreal* (Toronto, 1947), and *The romance of the Canadian canoe* (Toronto, 1951). He edited *Canadian folk-songs, old and new* (London, 1927), and he was the author of *Melody and the lyric* (London, 1930) and *The magic of melody* (London, 1933). He died at Montreal on July 2, 1952. He was the founder and first president of the Canadian Authors' Association in 1921; and he was elected a fellow of the Royal Society of Canada in 1922. In 1946 the degree of LL.D. was conferred on him by the University of Montreal.

[*Proc. Roy. Soc. Can.*, 1953; *Can. who's who*, 1949-51; *Encyc. Can.*]

Gibbons, Sir George Christie (1848-1918), chairman of the Canadian section of the International Waterways Commission (1905-11), was born at St. Catharines, Upper Canada, on July 2, 1848, the son of William Gibbons. He was educated at Upper Canada College, was called to the Ontario bar in 1869 (Q.C., 1891), and practised law in London, Ontario. Though never a member of parliament, he was a prominent Liberal; and from 1905 to 1911 he was chairman of the Canadian section of the International Waterways Commission. He died at Montreal on August 8, 1918. In 1876 he married Elizabeth Campbell, daughter of Hugh Craig of Montreal; and by her he had several children. In 1911 he was created a knight bachelor.

[H. E. Whitney, *Sir George C. Gibbons* (Am. Rev. of Cdn. Studies, 1973); *Who was* who, 1916-28; Can. parl. comp.; Morgan, Can. men (1912); Rose, Cyc. Can. biog. (1886).]

Gibbs, Thomas Nicholson (1821-1883), minister of inland revenue for Canada (1873), was born at Terrebonne, Lower Canada, on March 11, 1821. With his brother, he entered business as a produce merchant, and he became one of the most successful businessmen in Canada. He was president of the Dominion Telegraph Company, of the Standard Bank, of the Ontario Loan and Savings Co., and chairman in Canada of the English and Scottish Investment Co. He was elected in 1865 to the Legislative Assembly of Canada for South Ontario, and in 1867 to the Canadian House of Commons, on this occasion defeating George Brown (q.v.). For five months in 1873 he was a member of the Dominion government of Sir John Macdonald (q.v.), first as secretary of state for the provinces, and then as minister of inland revenue. He was defeated in South Ontario in the general elections of 1874, was again elected to the Commons in a by-election in 1876, and was a second time defeated in 1878. In 1880 he was called to the Senate; and he died at Ellesmere Hall, Oshawa, Ontario, on April 7, 1883.

[Dom. ann. reg., 1883; Can. parl. comp.]

Gibson, George Herbert Rae (1881-1932), physician and author, was born in Edinburgh, Scotland, in 1881, and died there on July 16, 1932. He was a graduate of Edinburgh University in medicine; and prior to the outbreak of the First World War, he practised medicine in Vancouver, British Columbia. He went overseas with the first Canadian contingent as medical officer with the 7th Canadian Infantry Battalion; and was awarded the D.S.O. in 1918. Under the nom de plume of "Herbert Rae", he was the author of Maple leaves in Flanders fields (Toronto, 1916).

[Who was who, 1928-40.]

Gibson, Sir John Morison (1842-1929), lieutenant-governor of Ontario (1908-14), was born in the township of Toronto, Upper Canada, on January 1, 1842, the son of William Gibson and Mary Sinclair. He was educated at the University of Toronto (B.A., 1863; LL.B., 1869; LL.D., 1902), and was called to the bar of Ontario in 1867 (Q.C., 1890). He joined the Canadian militia in 1860, and rose to be a major-general in the reserve of officers; and he was a member of the team of Canadian marksmen who went to Wimbledon in 1874, 1875, and 1879. In 1879 he won the Prince of Wales prize at Wimbledon. From 1879 to 1898 he represented Hamilton in the Legislative Assembly of Ontario, and from 1898 to 1905 East Wellington; and he was successively provincial secretary, commissioner of crown lands, and attorney-general in the Mowat, Hardy, and Ross governments. From 1908 to

1914 he was lieutenant-governor of Ontario; and in 1912 he was created a K.C.M.G. He died at Hamilton, Ontario, on June 3, 1929. He was thrice married (1) in 1869 to Emily Annie (d. 1874), daughter of Ralph Birrell, (2) in 1876 to Caroline (d. 1877), daughter of the Hon. Adam Hope, and (3) in 1881, to Eliza, daughter of Judge Malloch, Brockville, by whom he had several children.

[Who was who, 1928-40; Can. who was who, vol. 1; Morgan, Can. men (1912); Can. parl. comp.]

Gibson, William (1849-1914), senator of Canada, was born at Peterhead, Scotland, on August 7, 1849, the eldest son of William Gibson and Lucretia Gilzean. He emigrated to Canada in 1870, and became a contractor. He owned and operated two of the most extensive limestone quarries in Canada, at Beamsville and at Crookston, Ontario. From 1891 to 1900 he represented Lincoln in the Canadian House of Commons, as a Liberal; and in 1902 he was called to the Senate of Canada. He died at Beamsville, Ontario, on May 4, 1914. At the time of his death he was president of the Bank of Hamilton.

[Morgan, Can. men (1912); Can. parl. comp.]

Giffard, Robert (1587-1668), pioneer, was born at Mortange-au-Perche, France, in 1587. He became a surgeon and an apothecary; and in 1634 he emigrated with his family to New France, having been granted the seigniory of Notre Dame de Beauport, near Quebec. He played an important part in the colonization of New France, and was for some years a member of the Council of Quebec. He died at Quebec on April 14, 1668. In 1628 he married Marie Regnouard; and by her he had two sons and four daughters.

[A. Cambray, Robert Giffard, premier seigneur de Beauport (Cap de la Madeleine, Que., 1932); J. Besnard, Les diverses professions de Robert Giffard (Nova Francia, 1929); Le Jeune, Dict. gén.; Dict. Can. biog., vol. 1.]

Gilbert, Sir Humphrey (1537?-1583), adventurer, was born near Dartmouth, Devonshire, about 1539, the son of Otto Gilbert and the step-brother of Sir Walter Raleigh. He was educated at Eton and Oxford, where he studied mathematics and navigation; and when still a young man he petitioned Queen Elizabeth to be allowed to search for the north-west passage to China. In 1576 he published his well-known Discourse advocating a voyage of discovery to the north-west; and in 1578 he was granted a charter by Queen Elizabeth. His first voyage was a failure, but in 1583 he left Plymouth with five ships and reached the harbour of St. John's, Newfoundland. He took possession of the island in the name of Queen Elizabeth; and he began to plan the plantation here of the first English colony in North America. On his return voyage, he and his ship were lost in a storm off the Azores on September 8, 1583.

[D. B. Quinn, (ed.,) *The voyages and colonizing enterprises of Sir Humphrey Gilbert* (2 vols., London, 1940); D. B. Chidsey, *Sir Humphrey Gilbert, Elizabeth's racketeer* (New York, 1932); W. G. Gosling, *The life of Sir Humphrey Gilbert* (London, 1911); *Dict. nat. biog.*; *Encyc. Can.*; *Dict. Can. biog.*, vol. 1]

Gilkison, William (1777-1833), sailor and colonizer, was born in Irvine, Ayrshire, Scotland, on March 9, 1777. He came to America in 1796, and was given command of a schooner on Lake Erie, in the service of the North West Company. He took part in the War of 1812; but after the war he returned to Scotland with his family. He came back to Canada in 1832, with John Galt (q.v.), and he was the founder of the town of Elora. He died at Onondaga, on the banks of the Grand River, near Brantford, Ontario, on April 23, 1833. In 1803 he married Isabella (d. 1826), daughter of Commodore Alexander Grant (q.v.); and he had by her several children.

[John R. Connon, *Elora* (Elora, Ont., 1930).]

Gill, Charles Ignace Adélard (1871-1918), poet, was born at Sorel, Quebec, on October 21, 1871, the son of the Hon. Charles Gill, a judge of the Superior Court at Montreal. He was educated at St. Laurent College; and he studied painting under Gérome at the Ecole des Beaux Arts in Paris, France. He returned to Canada, and for twenty-five years he was professor of design at the Jacques Cartier Normal School, Montreal. He died in Montreal on October 16, 1918. In his leisure hours he wrote poetry; and some of his verse was published in *Les soirées du Château de Ramezay* (Montreal, 1900), issued by the "École Littéraire de Montréal". After his death a volume of his poems was published, with a preface by Albert Lozeau (q.v.), under the title *Le Cap Eternité, poème suivi des étoiles filantes* (Montreal, 1919).

[E. S. Caswell, *Canadian singers and their songs* (3rd ed., Toronto, 1925); C. ab der Halden, *Nouvelles études de littérature canadienne française* (Paris, 1907); Le Jeune, *Dict. gén.*; *Revue canadienne*, 1919.]

Gill, Edward Anthony Wharton (1858-1944), clergyman and novelist, was born in England in 1858, and died in Winnipeg, Manitoba, in 1944. He was educated at the University of London and the University of Manitoba (M.A., 1889), and was ordained a priest of the Church of England. He was made an honorary canon of St. John's Cathedral, Winnipeg, in 1907; and in 1920 he was appointed professor of pastoral theology at St. John's College,

Winnipeg. He was the author of two novels: *Love in Manitoba* (Toronto, 1912) and *An Irishman's luck* (Toronto, 1914). He was the author also of *A Manitoba chore boy* (London, 1912). He retired in 1934.

[*Can. who's who*, 1936-37.]

Gillespie, George (1772-1842), merchant, was born in Scotland in 1772, one of a family of fourteen children. He came to Canada about 1790, and seems to have been for a time in the service of the North West Company. In 1798 he was in charge of the house of the North West Company at St. Joseph's; and in 1799 he was elected a member of the Beaver Club, of Montreal. He became a partner in the firm of Parker, Gerrard, Ogilvy and Co., later Gillespie, Moffatt and Co.; and for a number of years represented this firm at Michilimackinac. He returned to Scotland shortly after 1812; and he spent the remainder of his life at Biggar Park, Lanarkshire. Here he died in 1842.

[W. S. Wallace (ed.), *Documents relating to the North West Company* (Toronto: The Champlain Society, 1934).]

Gillespie, Robert (1785-1863), merchant, was born in Scotland in 1785, a younger brother of George Gillespie (q.v.). He came to Canada about the year 1800; and ultimately became a partner in the firm of Gillespie, Moffatt and Co. He returned to England in 1822; and was until 1856 at the head of the English branch of Gillespie, Moffatt and Co. He died in 1863. He married (1) Anna Agnes, daughter of Dr. Robert Kerr, formerly surgeon of Sir John Johnson's "Royal Greens", by whom he had at least one son, Sir Robert Gillespie (1818-1901); and (2) Caroline Matilda (d. 1879), second daughter of Dr. Daniel Arnoldi, of Montreal.

[W. S. Wallace (ed.), *Documents relating to the North West Company* (Toronto: The Champlain Society, 1934).]

Gillespy, William (1824-1886), poet and journalist, was born at Little Corby, near Carlisle, England, in 1824, and emigrated to Canada in 1842. He became a journalist, and was on the editorial staff of the Brantford *Courier*, the Hamilton *Spectator*, and the London *Times*. He died at Hamilton, Ontario, on April 19, 1886. He was the author of a volume of *Fugitive poetry* (Hamilton, 1846).

[*Dom. ann. reg.*, 1886; C. C. James, *A bibliography of Canadian poetry* (Toronto, 1899).]

Gillies, Archibald C. (1834-1887), clergyman, was born at Lotbinière, Lower Canada, in 1834. He became a Presbyterian minister, and held charges in Canada West and in Nova Scotia. He died at Dunedin, New Zealand, in October, 1887. He was the author of *Daily meditations, a collection of poems* (Kingston, C.W., 1860) and *Popery dissected* (Pictou, N.S., 1874).

[Morgan, *Bib. can.*]

Gilmour, George Peel (1900-1963), university president, was born in Hamilton, Ontario, March 14, 1900. His great-grandfather was the first Baptist minister in Montreal and one of the founders of the Canada Baptist College in Montreal in 1838; and his father was professor of church history at McMaster University. He was educated at McMaster (B.A., 1921; B.Th., 1923), Oxford and Yale universities (M.A., 1929). After a period in the pastorate he joined the faculty of McMaster University in 1929 as lecturer in Biblical literature and church history. In 1941 he was appointed administrative head of McMaster, becoming president in 1950. During his presidency, McMaster changed from a denominational to a publicly supported institution free of church control and expanded both in size and in the diversification of its teaching and research areas. He was president of the Canadian Council of Churches (1946-48). In 1951 he became president of the National Conference of Canadian Universities. He was chairman of the Baptist publications committee, and a fellow of the Royal Society of Canada. He received many honorary degrees. His writings include *The university and its neighbours* (Toronto, 1955); *The Bible and the Christian religion* (Toronto, 1936); *A handbook of the Gospels* (Toronto, 1944); *Canada's tomorrow* (ed., Toronto, 1954); *The memoirs called Gospels* (Toronto, 1959); and he was an editor of *The hymnary* used by the Baptist and United churches. He died at Hamilton, Ontario, on July 12, 1963.

[*Proc. Roy. Soc. Can.* (1964).]

Gilpin, Edwin (1821-1906), clergyman, was born at Aylesford, Nova Scotia, on June 10, 1821. He was educated at King's College, Windsor (B.A., 1847; M.A., 1850; B.D., 1853; D.D., 1863; D.C.L., 1890), and was ordained a priest of the Church of England in 1848. After having been a master in the Halifax Grammar School and the Halifax High School, and principal of the Halifax Academy, he was inducted canon of St. Luke's Cathedral, Halifax, in 1864, became archdeacon of Nova Scotia in 1874, and dean of Nova Scotia in 1889. He died at Halifax, Nova Scotia, on January 29, 1906. In 1850 he married Amelia, daughter of the Hon. T. C. Haliburton (q.v.), the author of *Sam Slick*.

[Morgan, *Can. men* (1898).]

Gingras, Joseph Apollinaire (1847-1935), priest and poet, was born at St. Antoine de Tilly, Canada East, on March 7, 1847; and was ordained a priest of the Roman Catholic Church in 1873. He served in various parishes in the province of Quebec; and he died at Chicoutimi, Quebec, in 1935. He was the author of *Au foyer de mon presbytère: Poèmes et chansons* (Quebec, 1881).

[A. Lacasse, *L'Abbé Apollinaire Gingras*

et son oeuvre (Trans. Roy. Soc. Can., 1936); Allaire, *Dict. biog.*]

Gingras, Léon (1808-1860), priest, was born at Quebec, Lower Canada, on August 5, 1808; and was ordained a priest of the Roman Catholic Church in 1831. He was a professor of theology at the Quebec Seminary from 1831 to 1858; and he died at Paris, France, on February 18, 1860. He was the author of *L'Orient; ou, Voyage en Egypte, en Arabie, en Terre-Sainte, en Turquie, et en Grèce* (2 vols., Quebec, 1847).

[Allaire, *Dict. biog.*; Morgan, *Bib. can.*]

Girard, Marc Amable (1822-1892), prime minister of Manitoba (1874), was born at Varennes, Lower Canada, on April 25, 1822, and was educated at the College of St. Hyacinthe. He became a notary public; and in 1871 he was called to the bar of Manitoba. He went to Manitoba in 1870 with Archbishop Taché (q.v.) and Joseph Royal (q.v.); and he represented St. Boniface in the Legislative Assembly of the province from 1870 to 1878 and from 1879 to 1883. From 1870 to 1872 he was provincial treasurer of Manitoba; from July to December, 1874, he was prime minister of the province; and from 1879 to 1883 he was a member of the Norquay government, first as provincial secretary, and then as minister of agriculture. In 1871, on the entrance of Manitoba into the Dominion, he was called to the Senate of Canada; and in 1872 he was appointed senior member of the council of the North West Territories. He died at St. Boniface, Manitoba, on September 12, 1892. In 1878 he married Aurélie Lamoth, widow of Alfred Versailles, Montreal.

[J. P. Robertson, *Political manual of Manitoba* (Winnipeg, 1887); A. G. Morice, *Dictionnaire historique des canadiens de l'ouest* (Kamloops, B.C., 1908); Rose, *Cyc. Can. biog.* (1886); *Can. parl. comp.*; Le Jeune, *Dict. gén.*]

Girod, Amury (d. 1837), adventurer, was born in France (not in Switzerland, as is usually stated), and spent his youth on a model farm. He served, it is said, as a cavalry officer in the Mexican army; and he came to Canada about 1828. He established a model farm near Quebec, under the patronage of Joseph François Perrault (q.v.); he farmed for a time near St. Charles, in the Richelieu valley; and he finally settled near Varennes, Lower Canada. He became an ardent *patriote*; and in 1837 he headed the insurgents in the St. Eustache district. He fled from the field of action; and, when recognized and in danger of apprehension, committed suicide near Pointe-aux-Trembles, Lower Canada, toward the end of December, 1837. In 1833 he married Zoé Ainse, of Varennes; she died in 1842. Girod published *Notes diverses sur le Canada* (Village Debartzch, L.C., 1835).

[L. A. Huguet-Latour and L. E. de Belle-feuille, *Amury Girod* (Bull. rech. hist., 1902); Wm. McLennan, *Amury Girod* (Canadian antiquarian and numismatic journal, 1879).]

Girouard, Désiré (1836-1911), judge, was born at St. Timothée, Lower Canada, on July 7, 1836, the son of Jérémie Girouard and Hypolite Picard. He was educated at Montreal College and at McGill University (B.C.L., 1860; D.C.L., 1874); and was called to the bar in 1860 (Q.C., 1880). From 1878 to 1895 he represented Jacques Cartier in the Canadian House of Commons as a Conservative. In 1895 he was appointed a judge of the Supreme Court of Canada; and he occupied this post until his death at Ottawa on March 22, 1911. He was thrice married, (1) in 1862 to Marie Matilde (d. 1863), daughter of John Pratt, of Montreal, (2) in 1865 to Essie (d. 1879), daughter of Dr. Joseph Cranwill, of Ballynamoney, Ireland, and (3) in 1881 to Edith Bertha, daughter of Dr. John Beaty, of Cobourg, Ontario. Apart from a number of legal treatises, he published *Lake St. Louis, old and new* (Montreal, 1893), *Supplement to "Lake St. Louis"* (Montreal, 1903), and several works on the history of the Girouard family.

[*Dict. nat. biog.*, supp. II; Morgan, *Can. men* (1898); J. Tassé, *Le 38ème fauteuil* (Montreal, 1891); *Bull. rech. hist.*, 1898, 1901, and 1916; Le Jeune, *Dict. gén.*; *Can. parl. comp.*]

Girouard, Sir Percy (1867-1932), soldier, was born in Montreal, Quebec, on January 26, 1867, the son of the Hon. Désiré Girouard (q.v.). He was educated at the Royal Military College, Kingston, and in 1888 he obtained a commission in the Royal Engineers. He served in the Dongola Expeditionary Force of 1896, in the Nile expedition of 1897, and in the South African War from 1899 to 1902. From 1907 to 1908 he was high commissioner of Northern Nigeria; from 1908 to 1909, governor of Northern Nigeria; and from 1909 to 1912, governor of East Africa. In 1915 he became director-general of munitions supply at the British War Office. He died in London, England, on September 26, 1932. In 1903 he married Mary Gwendolyn (d. 1915), daughter of the Hon. Sir Richard Solomon; and by her he had one son. He was awarded the D.S.O. in 1896, and he was created a K.C.M.G. in 1900.

[*Who was who*, 1928-40.]

Girty, Simon (1741-1818), frontiersman, was born near Harrisburg, Pennsylvania, in 1741. He became an Indian interpreter; and in the later stages of the War of the American Revolution he played an important part on the British side in the struggle for the Old North West. He acquired, however, among the Americans an unhappy reputation for savage atrocities. After the Revolution, he settled near Amherstburg, Upper Canada; and he died near Amherstburg on February 18, 1818.

[C. W. Butterfield, *History of the Girtys* (Cincinnati, 1890); T. Boyd, *Simon Girty, the white savage* (New York, 1928).]

Gisborne, Frederick Newton (1824-1892), inventor, was born at Broughton, Lancashire, England, on March 8, 1824, the son of Hartley P. Gisborne, of Darley Dale, Derbyshire. He emigrated to Canada in 1845, and for two years farmed near St. Eustache, Lower Canada. He then became a telegraph operator, in the employ of the Montreal Telegraph Company; and he was a pioneer in the development of telegraphy in North America. In 1879 he was appointed superintendent of the Canadian government telegraph and signal service. He died at Ottawa, on August 30, 1892. In 1882 he became a charter member of the Royal Society of Canada; and he was the inventor of many electrical and signalling devices.

[Sir J. Grant, *F. N. Gisborne: In memoriam* (Trans. Roy. Soc. Can., 1893); *Cyc. Am. biog.*; Rose, *Cyc. Can. biog.* (1886); Le Jeune, *Dict. gén.*]

Gissing, Ronald (1895-1967), painter, was born in England in 1895 and educated at Edinburgh, where he received art instruction. He came to Canada in 1913 and worked as a cowhand in Alberta and later in Montana, Nebraska, and Arizona. He made sketches of ranch scenes and he was urged to take formal art training. He held his first show in Calgary in 1929 and opened a studio there. However, hard times forced him to return to Cochrane, Alberta, but he continued to paint. His home and paintings were destroyed by fire in 1944 but he rebuilt and continued painting, amid growing recognition of his ability. He was influenced in his early work by Leonard Richmond and A. C. Leighton, but developed his own distinctive style. His paintings, many of which are of mountain regions, are clear and radiant. Much of his work has been reproduced in calendars, Christmas cards, and illustrations. Examples of his work may be found in the Edmonton Museum of Art, the University of Alberta, and the Vancouver Art Gallery. He died at Okotoks, Alberta, September 29, 1967.

[C. S. MacDonald, *A dictionary of Canadian artists*, vol. 2 (Ottawa, 1968).]

Givins, James (1759?-1846), chief superintendent of Indian affairs for Upper Canada, was born about 1759, and came to Canada as a young man. He was first employed as a clerk of the North West Company in the West; but later left the fur-trade, and obtained a commission in the British army. In 1791 he was a subaltern in the Queen's Rangers at Niagara; and he accompanied Simcoe (q.v.) on many of his journeys about Upper Canada. He settled in York (Toronto) about 1798. He saw service in the War of 1812, as an A.D.C. to Sir Isaac

Brock (q.v.), with the rank of major; and later he was appointed chief superintendent of Indian affairs for Upper Canada. He resigned this post in 1842; and he died at Toronto on March 7, 1846.

[J. Ross Robertson, *Landmarks of Canada* (Toronto, 1917); L. H. Irving, *Officers of the British forces in Canada during the War of 1812-15* (Welland, Ont., 1908).]

Glackemeyer, Charles (1820-1892), lawyer, was born at Montreal, Lower Canada, on June 22, 1820. He was called to the bar of Lower Canada in 1843; and in 1859 he was appointed clerk of the city of Montreal. He died on April 9, 1892. He compiled *The charter and by-laws of the city of Montreal* (Montreal, 1865), with *Appendix* (Montreal, 1870).

[P. G. Roy, *La famille Glackemeyer* (Bull. rech. hist., 1916).]

Glackemeyer, Édouard Claude (1826-1910), civil servant, was born at Quebec, Lower Canada, on February 5, 1826. He was admitted to practice as a notary public in 1847; but he did not practise his profession long. Most of his life was spent as an assistant registrar in the registry office of the province of Quebec. He died at Quebec City on February 5, 1910. He was the author of *Alphabetical table of the cities, towns, villages, parishes, and townships in each county of the province of Quebec* (Quebec, 1889).

[P. G. Roy, *La famille Glackemeyer* (Bull. rech. hist., 1916).]

Gladman, George (1800-1863), fur-trader and explorer, was born at Brunswick House, a Hudson's Bay Company post on Brunswick Lake, on June 23, 1800. He became a clerk of the Hudson's Bay Company and was stationed successively at Moose Factory, at Cumberland House, at York Factory, and elsewhere; and he was promoted to the rank of chief trader in 1837. In 1857-58 he had charge of the expedition appointed by the Canadian government to explore the country between the head of Lake Superior and the Red River Settlement; and he was, with other members of the expedition, the author of the subsequent *Report on the exploration of the country between lake Superior and the Red River Settlement* (Toronto, 1858). He died at Port Hope, Canada West, on September 24, 1863.

[Morgan, *Bib. can.*; G. P. de T. Glazebrook (ed.), *The Hargrave correspondence* (Toronto: The Champlain Society, 1938).]

Gladstone, James (1887-1971), senator, was born at Mountain Hill, Alberta, May 21, 1887, and educated at St. Paul's Anglican Mission School and at the Calgary Indian Industrial School (1903-05). Gladstone had a varied life, beginning as an employee of the Mission School on the Blood Indian reserve (1905-06), drayman at Fort Macleod, Alberta (1906-07), ranch hand (1907-11), scout for the Royal North-West Mounted Police (1911), mail-carrier for the Blood Indian reserve (1912-14), and ranch hand on the Blood Reserve (1914-18); he was self-employed as rancher and farmer from 1920 to his retirement. He was a delegate to Ottawa in 1947, 1951, and 1953 to discuss Indian problems with the federal government and to the Winnipeg meeting of 1951 with federal ministers. He became president of the Indian Association of Alberta in 1948 and remained in office for nine years, becoming honorary president in 1957. The following year he was called to the Senate of Canada, being the first Indian senator in Canada's history. He died at Fernie, British Columbia, September 4, 1971.

[*Can. who's who*, 1967-69; *Can. ann. rev.*, 1971.]

Glasgow, Robert (1875-1922), publisher, was born at Danville, Quebec, on September 3, 1875. He became a book-salesman; and it was his experience in selling the *Makers of Canada* series of volumes that convinced him there was an opportunity awaiting anyone who would publish a first-class history of Canada written by specialists. He formed the publishing firm of Glasgow, Brook and Co.; and this firm published in 1914, under the editorship of Adam Shortt (q.v.) and A. G. Doughty (q.v.), a history of Canada in 23 volumes, entitled *Canada and its provinces*. This was followed by the *Chronicles of Canada*, a series of thirty-two monographs, each dealing with a particular phase of Canadian history. The success of this venture persuaded him to launch in the United States a similar series, the *Chronicles of America*, which eventually ran to 50 volumes; and the remainder of his life was spent chiefly in the United States. He died at New York, N.Y., on April 5, 1922. In 1920 Yale University conferred on him the honorary degree of M.A.

[*Can. who was who*, vol. 1.]

Glashan, John Cadenhead (1844-1932), educationist, was born in Aberdeenshire, Scotland, in 1844, and came to Canada with his parents in 1853. He became a school-teacher, and in 1871 he was appointed inspector of public schools for the county of Middlesex, Ontario. Later, in 1876, he became inspector of public schools for the city of Ottawa. He was an advanced student of higher mathematics; and in 1899 the University of Toronto conferred on him the honorary degree of LL.D. He was elected a fellow of the Royal Society of Canada in 1902. His death took place at Ottawa, Ontario, on March 14, 1932. He was the author of *Arithmetic for high schools* (Toronto, 1890), and joint author, with others, of *Algebraic analysis* (Boston, 1889).

[*Proc. Roy. Soc. Can.*, 1932; Morgan, *Can. men* (1912).]

Glasier, John B. (1809-1894), senator of Canada, was born in Lincoln, Sunbury, New Brunswick, on September 3, 1809. He became a lumber merchant, and before Confederation sat for some years for Sunbury in the New Brunswick House of Assembly. In 1868 he was called to the Senate of Canada; and he sat in the Senate until his death at Ottawa, Ontario, in 1894.

[R. G. Riddell (ed.), *Canadian portraits* (Toronto, 1940); *Can. parl. comp.*]

Glass, David (1829-1906), speaker of the Legislative Assembly of Manitoba (1887-88), was born in the township of Westminster, Upper Canada, on July 20, 1829, the son of Samuel Glass. He was educated at the London grammar school; and in 1864 he was called to the bar of Upper Canada (Q.C., 1876). From 1872 to 1874 he represented Middlesex in the Canadian House of Commons, as a Conservative. In 1882 he removed to Winnipeg; and in 1886 he was elected to represent St. Clements in the Legislative Assembly of Manitoba. From 1887 to 1888 he was speaker of the Assembly; but ill-health compelled in 1888 his retirement from politics. During his later years he spent much of his time on the Pacific slope, where he had acquired considerable interests; and he died at Spokane, Washington, on July 17, 1906. In 1852 he married Sara, daughter of Henry Dalton; and by her he had one son and one daughter.

[S. F. Glass, *Biographical sketch of the life and times of the Hon. David Glass* (Trans. London and Middlesex Hist. Soc., 1919); *Can. parl. comp.*]

Glazebrook, Arthur James (1859-1940), publicist, was born in London, England, in 1859, the son of Michael Glazebrook, a wine merchant. He was educated at Haileybury College; but in 1876 he came out with his family to Canada. In 1883 he entered the service of the Bank of British North America, afterwards absorbed by the Bank of Montreal; and he continued in the service of this bank until 1900. He then became an exchange broker in Toronto, and he retired from business only in 1934. He was one of the founders of the Round Table movement in Canada in 1910; and for many years he contributed to the periodical entitled the *Round Table*. He died at Toronto, Ontario, on November 28, 1940.

[*Round Table*, March, 1941.]

Glenie, James (1750-1817), politician, was born in Fifeshire, Scotland, in 1750. He was educated at St. Andrew's University and the Royal Military Academy at Woolwich; and in 1775 he was given a commission in the army. He was sent to America, and he saw service in Canada during the American Revolution; but in 1780 he was court-martialled for insubordination, and was cashiered. The finding of the court-martial was quashed in England, and Glenie's commission was restored to him; but he resigned his commission in 1787, and settled in New Brunswick. From 1789 to 1803 he represented Sunbury county in the House of Assembly of New Brunswick; and in the Assembly he took a leading part in attacking the administration of the province. In 1805 Glenie returned to England; and he died at Chelsea on November 23, 1817. Several of his mathematical treatises were presented to the Royal Society of London on his behalf by Francis Maseres (q.v.); and in 1779 he was elected a fellow of the Royal Society.

[*Dict. nat. biog.*; G. F. G. Stanley, *James Glenie, a study in early colonial radicalism* (Coll. Nova Scotia Hist. Soc., vol. 25, 1942).]

Globensky, Charles Auguste Maximilien (1830-1906), author, was born at St. Eustache, Lower Canada, on November 15, 1830, the son of Maximilien Globensky and Elizabeth Lemaire St. Germain. From 1875 to 1876 he represented the constituency of Two Mountains in the Canadian House of Commons; and by his marriage with Virginie-Marguerite Lambert-Dumont, he became seignior of Mille-Iles. He died at St. Eustache on February 12, 1906. He was the author of *La rebellion de 1837 à Saint-Eustache* (Quebec, 1883).

[*Bull. rech. hist.*, 1928.]

Glover, Sir John Hawley (1829-1885), governor of Newfoundland (1875-81 and 1883-85), was born in 1829, and died in London, England, on September 30, 1885. He entered the Royal Navy in 1841, and rose to the rank of captain. During the latter part of his life, however, he served in various administrative capacities. In 1873 he was appointed a commissioner, under Sir Garnet Wolseley, to deal with the natives on the Gold Coast; and he distinguished himself during the Ashanti War of 1873-74. In 1874 he was created a G.C.M.G.; and in 1875 he was appointed governor of Newfoundland. He was transferred to the Leeward Islands in 1881, but was reappointed as governor of Newfoundland in 1883.

[*Dict. nat. biog.*; *Dom. ann. reg.*, 1885; *Encyc. Can.*]

Godbout, Joseph Adélard (1892-1956), prime minister of Quebec (1936 and 1939-44), was born at St. Eloi, Témiscouata county, Quebec, on September 24, 1892. He was educated at the Seminary at Rimouski (B.A., 1912) and at the Agricultural School of Ste. Anne de la Pocatière (B.S.A., 1918), and afterwards did post-graduate work at the Massachusetts Agricultural College. He taught agriculture at Ste. Anne de la Pocatière from 1918 to 1930; but in 1929 he was elected to represent L'Islet in the Quebec legislature as a Liberal, and he continued to represent this constituency until his defeat in the election of 1948. In 1930 he became minister of agriculture in the Taschereau administration; and on the retirement of L. A. Taschereau (q.v.) in 1936, he became prime minister of Quebec. He held office on this occasion for only two months, since in the elections of 1936 the Liberals were defeated by the Union Nationale under Maurice Duplessis (q.v.). Three years later, however, the Union Nationale was defeated, and Godbout again became prime minister and minister of agriculture. His party was again defeated in 1944, and he continued as leader of the opposition until 1948. In 1949 he was appointed a member of the Senate of Canada. In 1956 he suffered a severe fall at his farm, near Quebec, and he died in hospital at Montreal on September 18, 1956. He received honorary degrees from Laval University, the University of Montreal, and McGill University.

[*Can. who's who*, 1954-56; *Encyc. Can.*]

Goddard, James Stanley (d. 1795), furtrader, was one of the earliest traders from Montreal to reach the upper country. He was at Michilimackinac as early as 1761; and he was at Green Bay, Lake Michigan, when the Conspiracy of Pontiac broke out in 1763. In 1766 he was appointed by Robert Rogers (q.v.) as second-in-command, under James Tute of the expedition from the Mississippi to Grand Portage, on Lake Superior, described by Jonathan Carver (q.v.). He was engaged in the western fur-trade as late as 1778; but about that year he was appointed storekeeper of the Indian department at Montreal, and he retained this position until his death at Montreal in 1795. In 1780 he married in Montreal Mrs. Margaret Sunderland; and by her he had one son and five daughters.

[L. P. Kellogg, *The mission of Jonathan Carver* (Wisconsin magazine of history, 1928-29); *Collections, State Historical Society of Wisconsin*, vol. xviii (1908).]

Godsell, Philip Henry (1889-1961), furtrader and author, was born in England in 1889. He came to Canada as a Hudson's Bay Company apprentice in 1906 and spent thirty years in Northern Canada. Much of his time was spent as a post inspector, which meant that he travelled over the whole of Northern Canada. He was part of the North at a time of rapid change and wrote about it in a number of books — *Arctic trader: The account of twenty years with the Hudson's Bay Company* (1934); *Red hunters of the snow: An account of thirty years' experience with the primitive Indian and Eskimo tribes of the Canadian North-west and Arctic coast, with a brief history of the early contact between the white fur trader and the aborigines* (1938); *The vanishing frontier: A saga of traders, Mounties and men of the last north-west* (1939); *They got their man: On patrol with the North-West Mounted Police* (1941); *The romance of the Alaska Highway* (1944); and *Pilots of the purple twilight* (1955). He died at Calgary, Alberta, October 27, 1961.

[Norah Story, *The Oxford companion to Canadian history and literature* (Toronto, 1967); V.B. Rhodenizer, *Canadian literature in English* (Montreal, 1965).]

Goforth, Jonathan (1859-1936), missionary, was born near Thorndale, Canada West, on February 10, 1859. He was educated at Knox College, Toronto, and was ordained a minister of the Presbyterian Church in 1886. The following year he was appointed a missionary to China; and he devoted almost the whole of his life to mission work in China, even after he had lost his sight. He was superannuated in 1934; and he died at Wallaceburg, Ontario, on October 8, 1936.

[Rosalind Goforth, *Goforth of China* (Toronto, 1937); Morgan, *Can. men* (1912).]

Goforth, Mrs. Rosalind, *née* **Bell-Smith** (1864-1942), author, was born in 1864, and died in 1942. In 1887 she married the Rev. Jonathan Goforth (q.v.); and she was the author of her husband's biography, *Goforth of China* (Toronto, 1937), as well as of *How I know God answers prayer* (Toronto, 1939) and *Climbing: Memoirs of a missionary's wife* (Toronto, 1940).

[Private information.]

Goldberg, Eric (1890-1969), artist, was born in Berlin, Germany, October 28, 1890. He was educated at the Ecole des Beaux Arts, Paris, and later taught at the Berlin Academy. He spent some time in Palestine as a teacher of arts and crafts prior to the First World War. After the war he emigrated to Chicago. He married the Montreal artist Regina Serden in Paris, where they lived for seven years, and then came to Canada. He conducted his own art school in Montreal for twenty years and was a member of the Eastern Group of artists and the Contemporary Arts Society. His paintings of people are graceful and charming and they cover a great range of human activity. Examples are to be found in the Montreal Museum of Fine Arts, the Joliette Seminary Museum, the Edmonton Museum of Arts, and at Vancouver and Fredericton. He died at Montreal, February, 1969.

[*Who's who in Canadian Jewry* (Montreal, 1967); C. S. MacDonald, *A dictionary of Canadian artists,* vol. 2 (Ottawa, 1968); Montreal *Gazette* (February 20, 1969).]

Goldie, John (1793-1886), naturalist, was born at Kirkoswald, Ayrshire, Scotland, on March 21, 1793. He studied botany under Sir William Hooker, who was in charge of the Botanic Gardens, Glasgow, Scotland; and in 1817 and 1819 he visited Canada and the United States for the purpose of botanical fieldwork. He then conducted a series of botanical researches in Russia and Siberia, but in 1844 he returned to Canada with his family, and settled near Ayr, Upper Canada. Here he continued to live until his death at Ayr, Ontario, on July 23, 1886. In 1815 he married Margaret Dunlop, daughter of James Smith, of Monkwood Grove, Ayrshire; and three sons and two daughters survived him. The *Aspidium goldianum*, a fern which he identified and described in Canada, was named after him. His *Diary of a journey through Upper Canada and some of the New England states, 1819*, has been published (Toronto, 1897).

[*Dom. ann. reg.*, 1886.]

Goldsmith, Oliver (1794-1861), poet, was born at St. Andrew's, New Brunswick, in 1794, the son of Henry Goldsmith, a nephew of Oliver Goldsmith, the English poet. He held a post in the commissariat department in Saint John, New Brunswick, and became worthy master of the Albion lodge of Freemasons in Saint John. In 1844 he removed to Hong Kong, and he died at Liverpool, England, in July, 1861. He wrote, in imitation of his great-uncle, a poem entitled *The rising village* (London, 1825), and this was later reprinted, with other verses (Saint John, N.B., 1834).

[W. E. Myatt (ed.), *The autobiography of Oliver Goldsmith* (Toronto, 1943); W. G. MacFarlane, *New Brunswick bibliography* (Saint John, N.B., 1895).]

Gooderham, Sir Albert Edward (1861-1935), philanthropist, was born in Toronto, Ontario, on June 2, 1861, the son of George Gooderham (q.v.). He was educated at the Toronto Model School, and began business in his father's office in Gooderham and Worts, distillers. Of this business he ultimately became vice-president and managing director. He was a member of the board of governors of the University of Toronto; and the establishment of the Connaught Laboratories and the Anti-Toxine Farm was largely owing to his generosity. Among his other philanthropies were the establishment and equipment of a Preventorium in Toronto for tubercular children and a hospital for officers in London, England, during the First World War. He died in Toronto on April 26, 1935. He married in 1888 Mary Redford Duncanson; and he had two sons and three daughters. He was created a K.C.M.G. in 1934.

[*Can. who was who*, vol. 2; Morgan, *Can. men* (1912); *Who was who*, 1928-40.]

Gooderham, George (1820-1905), president of the Bank of Toronto (1882-1905), was born in York (Toronto), Upper Canada, on March 14, 1820, the third son of William Gooderham and Harriet Herring. He entered the employ of Gooderham and Worts, millers and distillers, a firm founded by his father; and he ultimately became president of the company of Gooderham and Worts, Ltd. In 1882 he was elected president of the Bank of Toronto; and he retained this position until his death, at Toronto, on May 1, 1905. He married Harriet,

daughter of Joseph Kay Dean; and by her he had several children.

[E. B. Shuttleworth, *The windmill and its times* (Toronto, 1924).]

Goodridge, Augustus Frederick (1839-1920), prime minister of Newfoundland (1894), was born at Paignton, Devonshire, England, in 1839, and died at St. John's, Newfoundland, on February 16, 1920. He came to Newfoundland in 1852, and became a fish merchant in St. John's. He entered politics as a Conservative, and represented first Ferryland and then Twillingate in the House of Assembly from 1880 to 1890, lost his seat in the latter year, but recovered it in 1893. He was minister without portfolio in the Thorburn administration of 1885-89; and on the resignation of the Whiteway government of April, 1894, he became prime minister. He resigned, however, in December, 1894. In 1913 he was appointed a member of the Legislative Council.

[*Encyc. Can.*; *Newfoundland supp.*]

Goodspeed, Calvin (1842-1912), clergyman and educationist, was born at Nashwaak, New Brunswick, on May 5, 1842; and was educated at the University of New Brunswick (B.A., 1866; M.A., 1872; LL.D., 1900), at the Newton Theological Seminary, Massachusetts, and at Leipzig University, Germany. He was a professor at McMaster University, Toronto, from 1891 to 1905, and at Baylor University, Texas, from 1905 to 1909. He died at Paradise, Nova Scotia, on July 6, 1912. He was the author of *The Messiah's second advent* (Toronto, 1900).

[Morgan, *Can. men* (1912).]

Gordon, Andrew Robertson (1896-1967), chemist and university administrator, was born on June 26, 1896. After three years' service in the Canadian Field Artillery in the First World War he entered the University of Toronto (B.A., 1922; M.A., 1923; Ph.D., 1925), and was appointed lecturer on his graduation. He was a pioneer in the application of wave mechanics and statistical mechanics to chemical problems. Data originating in his laboratory on vapour pressures, electrical conductivities, transference numbers, diffusion coefficients, and electromotive force measurements have stood the test of time. Dr. Gordon became head of the department of chemistry in 1944 and dean of the school of Graduate Studies in 1953. He retired in 1964, having directed the school through a period of rapid expansion while retaining a high standard of scholarship. During the Second World War he was on the advisory committee on chemical warfare and became a member of the Defence Research Board. He was a member of the National Research Council and a director of Atomic Energy of Canada from 1952 to 1966. He was awarded the O.B.E. (1946) and the medal of the Chemical Institute of Canada

(1955). He was a fellow of the Royal Society of Canada. He died at Toronto, 1967.

[*Proc. Roy. Soc. Can.*, 1968; *Can. who's who*, 1955-57.]

Gordon, Sir Arthur Hamilton, afterwards Baron Stanmore (1819-1912), lieutenant-governor of New Brunswick (1861-66), was born in 1819, the youngest son of the fourth Earl of Aberdeen. He was private secretary to his father when prime minister of Great Britain (1852-55), and was for a time private secretary to William Ewart Gladstone in 1858. In 1861 he was appointed lieutenant-governor of New Brunswick; and, while in favour of the union of the Maritime provinces, opposed at first the union of British North America. Under pressure from the Colonial Office he was compelled to withdraw his opposition; and he retired from office in New Brunswick in 1866. He was subsequently governor of Trinidad (1866-70), of Mauritius (1871-74), of Fiji (1875-80), of New Zealand (1880-82), and of Ceylon (1883-90). He died at Ascot, England, on January 30, 1912. In 1865 he married Rachel Emily, daughter of Sir John Shaw-Lefèvre; and by her he had one son and one daughter. In 1878 he was created a G.C.M.G., and in 1893 Baron Stanmore in the peerage of the United Kingdom. He was the author of *Wilderness journeys in New Brunswick* (Saint John, New Brunswick, 1846), *The story of a little war* (London, 1879), *The life of Lord Aberdeen* (London, 1905), and *Memoirs of Sidney Herbert* (2 vols., London, 1906).

[*Burke's peerage*; *Who was who*, 1897-1916; J. Hannay, *History of New Brunswick* (Saint John, N.B., 1909); W. G. MacFarlane, *New Brunswick bibliography* (Saint John, N.B., 1895); J. K. Chapman, *The career of Arthur Hamilton Gordon, First Lord Stanmore, 1819-1912* (Toronto, 1964).]

Gordon, Sir Charles Blair (1867-1939), financier and industrialist, was born at Montreal, Quebec, on November 22, 1867. He was educated at the Montreal High School, and entered the textile business in Montreal. In 1909 he was elected president of the Dominion Textile Company; in 1912 he was elected a director of the Bank of Montreal; and in 1927 he became president of this bank. From 1915 to 1917 he was vice-chairman of the Imperial Munitions Board in Canada; and in 1917-18 he was director-general of war supplies for Great Britain, with headquarters at Washington, D.C. He was created an O.B.E. in 1917 and a G.B.E. in 1918. He died at Montreal, Quebec, on July 30, 1939.

[*Who was who*, 1928-40; *Can. who's who*, 1936-37.]

Gordon, Charles William (1860-1937), clergyman and novelist, was born at Indian Lands, Glengarry county, Canada West, on September 13, 1860, the son of the Rev. Daniel Gordon and Mary Robertson. He was educated

at the University of Toronto (B.A., 1883) and at Knox College, Toronto (D.D., 1906); and he was ordained a minister of the Presbyterian Church in 1890. For three years he served as a missionary to the miners and lumbermen of the North West Territories; and in 1894 he was called to St. Stephen's Church, Winnipeg, of which he remained pastor for the rest of his life. In 1897 he contributed to the *Westminster*, a Presbyterian Church periodical, a series of stories about missionary work among the miners of the Rocky Mountains; and when these stories were published as a book they achieved a great success. He became a popular novelist whose sales soared into the hundreds of thousands; and though his books were open to the charge of didacticism and sentimentalism, they had qualities which made him perhaps the most popular novelist Canada has produced. In the First World War he served as a chaplain with the Canadian Expeditionary Force, and was mentioned in dispatches. In 1922 he was elected moderator of the Presbyterian Church in Canada. He died in Winnipeg, Manitoba, on October 31, 1937. In 1899 he married Helen Skinner, daughter of the Reverend John M. King (q.v.); and by her he had one son and six daughters. In 1904 he was elected a fellow of the Royal Society of Canada; he received honorary degrees from the University of Glasgow and Queen's University, Kingston; and in 1935 he was awarded the C.M.G.

Under the nom-de-plume of "Ralph Connor", he was the author of *Beyond the marshes* (Toronto, 1897), *Black Rock* (Chicago, 1898), *The sky pilot* (Chicago, 1899), *The man from Glengarry* (New York, 1901), *Glengarry school days* (New York, 1902), *Breaking the record* (New York, 1903), *The prospector* (New York, 1904), *The doctor* (New York, 1906), *The life of James Robertson* (New York, 1908), *The angel and the star* (New York, 1908), *The foreigner* (New York, 1909), *The dawn of Galilee* (New York, 1909), *The recall of love* (New York, 1910), *Corporal Cameron* (New York, 1912), *The patrol of the Sundance Trail* (New York, 1914), *The major* (New York, 1917), *The sky pilot in no man's land* (New York, 1919), *To him that hath* (New York, 1921), *The Gaspards of Pine Croft* (New York, 1921), *Treading the wine-press* (New York, 1925), *The friendly four* (New York, 1926), *The runner* (Garden City, N.Y., 1929), *The rock and the river* (New York, 1931), *The arm of gold* (New York, 1932), *The Glengarry girl* (New York, 1933), *Torches through the bush* (New York, 1934), *The rebel loyalist* (New York, 1935), *He dwelt among us* (New York, 1936), and *Postscript to adventure: the autobiography of Ralph Connor* (New York, 1938).

[*Can. who's who*, 1936-37; *Americana annual*, 1938.]

Gordon, Daniel Miner (1845-1925), principal of Queen's University (1902-17), was born at Pictou, Nova Scotia, on January 30, 1845, the son of William Gordon and Amelia Miner. He was educated at Pictou Academy, at Glasgow University (M.A., 1863; B.D., 1866; D.D., 1895), and at Berlin University. He was ordained a minister of the Presbyterian Church in Canada in 1866, and he served successively in charges at Truro, Ottawa, Winnipeg, and Halifax. From 1894 to 1902 he was professor of systematic theology and apologetics at the Halifax Presbyterian College; and in 1902 he was appointed principal and vice-chancellor of Queen's University, Kingston. He retired from this position, because of ill-health, in 1917. He served as a chaplain in the North West Rebellion of 1885; and in 1896 he was elected moderator of the General Assembly of the Presbyterian Church in Canada. In 1915 he was created a C.M.G.; and he held the honorary degree of LL.D. from Dalhousie University (1904), the University of Toronto (1911), and St. Andrew's University (1911). He died at Kingston, Ontario, on September 1, 1925. He was the author of *Mountain and prairie* (Montreal, 1880), an account of a journey made in 1879 from Victoria, Vancouver Island, to Winnipeg, by way of the Peace River pass.

[Wilhelmina Gordon, *Daniel M. Gordon, his life* (Toronto, 1941); *Can. who was who*, vol. 1; Morgan, *Can. men* (1912).]

Gordon, Donald (1901-1969), banker, C.N.R. president, was born in Oldmeldrum, Scotland, December 11, 1901. He joined the Bank of Nova Scotia in 1916, rising to become assistant manager, Toronto Branch, by 1930. In 1935 he became secretary of the new Bank of Canada, becoming deputy governor in 1938. During the Second World War he was chairman of the Wartime Prices and Trade Board, a position which he retained from 1941 to 1947. He was appointed director of the industrial development bank, a federal government operation, upon its creation in 1944, and became executive director of the International Bank for Reconstruction and Development in 1948. Gordon was appointed president of the Canadian National Railway system in 1950, although he had no previous experience with railroads. His wide training in finance and his knowledge of the country helped prepare the railway for the heavy demands of the next twenty years. He retired from the C.N.R. in 1966 to become president of the British Newfoundland Corporation. He received honours from many universities; he was made C.M.G. (1944) and K.G. He died at Montreal, Quebec, May 3, 1969.

[*Can. who's who*, 1964-66; *Encyc. can.* (1972); and numerous articles by and about him in Canadian magazines of the period.]

Gordon, Hortense Crompton (1887-1961), artist, was born Hortense Mattice in Hamilton, Ontario, in 1887. She began to study in Saturday morning classes in Hamilton and later attended the School of Design in Detroit, Michigan, but was basically self-taught.

In 1916 she began teaching in the art department at Hamilton Technical Institute, becoming head of the department on the retirement of her husband, J. S. Gordon, in 1934. She became interested in the painting of the Group of Seven and in the impressionist style which she studied during several visits to Europe. She produced her first abstract paintings in the 1930s and in 1952 held her first solo exhibition in New York. She joined a Toronto group calling themselves Painters Eleven, which held a joint exhibition in 1955 in Toronto. Hortense Gordon developed a distinctive style, founded on the reduction of complex concepts to simple strong colours, which was recognized as invitations came to exhibit her works both in Europe and in America. Besides painting she was also a leader in textile design and in art as applied to industry. She was made an associate of the Royal Canadian Academy of Arts in 1928 and was a member of the International Federation of Art. She died in Hamilton, November 6, 1961.

[*Can. who's who*, 1955-57; C.S. MacDonald, *A dictionary of Canadian artists*, vol. 2, (Toronto, 1967).]

Gordon, James D. (1832-1872), missionary, was born at Cascumpeque, Prince Edward Island, the younger brother of the Rev. George N. Gordon, a missionary of the Presbyterian Church in Nova Scotia, who was killed, with his wife, by the natives of Erromanga, in the New Hebrides. He published an account of the life and death of his brother and his brother's wife, under the title, *The last martyrs of Erromanga* (Halifax, N.S., 1863), and in 1864 he followed his brother to Erromanga as a missionary. He too was killed by the natives on Erromanga in the early part of 1872.

[G. Patterson, *Missionary life among the cannibals* (Toronto, 1882); Morgan, *Bib. can.*; *Dict. Can. biog.*, vol. 10.]

Gordon, Wesley Ashton (1884-1943), minister of immigration and colonization for Canada (1930-35), was born at Owen Sound, Ontario, on February 11, 1884. He was educated at Osgoode Hall Law School, Toronto, and was called to the bar of Ontario in 1908 (K.C., 1928). From 1930 to 1935 he represented Temiskaming South in the Canadian House of Commons; and during this period he was a member of the Bennett government, holding at first the portfolio of minister of immigration and colonization, and later, in addition to this, the portfolios of minister of mines and minister of labour. He died at Toronto, Ontario, on February 9, 1943.

[*Can. who's who*, 1936-37; *Can. parl. comp.*]

Gore, Sir Charles Stephen (1793-1869), soldier, was born in 1793, the third son of the second Earl of Arran. He entered the British Army in 1808, and fought throughout the later stages of the Napoleonic Wars. He was in Canada as deputy quartermaster-general during the rebellion of 1837, and he was in command of the column repulsed at St. Denis on November 25, 1837. In 1854 he became a lieutenant-general; and in his last years he was lieutenant-governor of Chelsea Hospital, London. Here he died on September 4, 1869. In 1824 he married Sarah Rachel, daughter of Hon. James Fraser, a legislative councillor of Nova Scotia. He was created a K.H. in 1836, a K.C.M.G. in 1860, and a G.C.B. in 1867.

[*Dict. nat. biog.*]

Gore, Francis (1769-1852), lieutenant-governor of Upper Canada (1806-17), was born at Blackheath, Kent, England, in 1769. In 1787 he obtained a commission in an infantry regiment; but in 1795 he was transferred to the 17th Lancers, and in 1802 he retired from the army with the rank of major. In 1804 he was appointed lieutenant-governor of Bermuda, and in 1806 of Upper Canada. His term of office in Upper Canada lasted until 1817; but from 1811 to 1815 he was absent from the province on leave, and the duties of his office were performed by administrators. From the first he had trouble with the Reform element in the province; and his high-handed behaviour did not tend to allay discontent. In 1817 he prorogued the legislature in a fit of anger, and a month later sailed for England, whence he did not return. In 1818 he was appointed a deputy teller of the Exchequer; and this post he held until 1836. He died at Brighton, England, on November 3, 1852. In 1803 he married Arabella, sister of Sir Charles Wentworth.

[D. B. Read, *The lieutenant-governors of Upper Canada* (Toronto, 1900).]

Gosford, Archibald Acheson, second Earl of (1776-1849), governor-in-chief of British North America (1835-37), was born on August 1, 1776, the son of Arthur, first Earl of Gosford, and Millicent Pole. He was educated at Christ Church, Oxford (M.A., *honoris causa*, 1797); and he entered political life in 1798 as member for Armagh in the Irish parliament. In 1801, under the terms of the union of Great Britain and Ireland, he became member for Armagh in the British House of Commons, and he continued to represent this constituency until he succeeded his father as Earl of Gosford, in the Irish peerage, in 1807. In 1811 he was elected a representative peer for Ireland; and he became in the House of Lords an exponent of the Whig policy of conciliation in Ireland. In 1832 he was appointed lord lieutenant of Armagh, and his success in this office was such that in 1835 he was appointed by the Melbourne government governor-in-chief of British North America (except Newfoundland), and a royal commissioner to inquire into the state of affairs in Lower Canada. As governor, he adopted toward Louis Joseph Papineau (q.v.) and the French-Canadian *patriotes* a policy of "conciliation without concession"; and in so doing he alienated the good-will of the English element in the colony, without winning over the French extremists. He was at last compelled, in the autumn of 1837, to recognize the failure of his policy; and his resignation was accepted on November 14, only a few days before the outbreak of rebellion. After his return to England, he opposed vigorously in the House of Lords the Act of Union of 1840, but without success. His later years were devoted to his estates in Ireland; and he died at his residence, Market Hill, Armagh, Ireland, on March 27, 1849. In 1805 he married Mary (d. 1841), daughter of Robert Sparrow, of Worlingham Hall, Suffolk; and by her he had one son and four daughters. In 1835 he was created Baron Worlingham in the peerage of the United Kingdom; and in 1838 he received the G.C.B. on the civil side.

[*Dict. nat. biog.*, supp. I; *Cyc. Am. biog.*; Le Jeune, *Dict. gén.*; Morgan, *Cel. Can.*; R. Christie, *History of Lower Canada* (6 vols., Montreal and Quebec, 1848-56); F. X. Garneau, *Histoire du Canada* (5th ed., Paris, 1913-20).]

Gosling, William Gilbert (1863-1930), historian, was born in Bermuda on September 8, 1863, and died at Hamilton, Bermuda, on November 5, 1930. He went to Newfoundland in 1881, and became a successful businessman. He was mayor of St. John's from 1916 to 1919. A student of history, he was the author of *A history of Labrador* (London, 1910) and *The life of Sir Humphrey Gilbert* (London, 1911). He left his library to the Public Library of St. John's, now known as the Gosling Memorial Library.

[Morgan, *Can. men* (1912); *Encyc. Can.*; *Newfoundland supp.*]

Gosnell, R. Edward (1860-1931), author and journalist, was born at Lake Beauport, Quebec, in 1860. He was educated in Ontario, was first a school-teacher, and then a journalist, and in 1888 went to British Columbia. He became librarian of the British Columbia legislature, then editor of the Victoria *Colonist*, then provincial archivist. In his later years he was a free-lance journalist. He died at Vancouver, British Columbia, on August 5, 1931. He was the author of *Some practical phases of a great question* (n.p., 1901), and *The story of Confederation* (n.p., 1918); he collaborated with R. H. Coats in *Sir James Douglas* (Toronto, Makers of Canada, 1910; new ed., 1926), and with E. O. S. Scholefield in *A history of British Columbia* (Vancouver, 1913); and he was the editor of *The year-book* of British Columbia (Victoria, 1897; 2nd ed., 1903; 3rd ed., 1911; 4th ed., 1914).

[Morgan, Can. men (1912); E. O. S. Scholefield and F. W. Howay, British Columbia (4 vols., Vancouver, B.C., 1941).]

Gosselin, Amédée Edmond (1863-1941), priest and historian, was born at St. Charles de Bellechasse, Canada East, on September 30, 1863. He was educated at the Quebec Seminary, and was ordained a priest of the Roman Catholic Church in 1890. He was appointed a professor in the Seminary, and he spent in the Seminary the rest of his life. In 1904 he was appointed archivist of the Seminary; and in 1911 he was elected a fellow of the Royal Society of Canada. He died at Quebec, Que., on December 20, 1941. He was the author of Notes sur la famille de Coulon de Villiers (Lévis, Que., 1906) and L'instruction au Canada sous le régime français (Quebec, 1911).

[Proc. Roy. Soc. Can., 1942; Allaire, Dict. biog.]

Gosselin, Auguste Honoré (1843-1918), ecclesiastical historian, was born at St. Charles de Bellechasse, Lower Canada, on December 29, 1843, the son of Joseph Gosselin and Angèle Labrie. He was educated at the Quebec Seminary and at Laval University (B.A., 1863; Litt.D., 1890), and was ordained a priest of the Roman Catholic Church in 1866. He was engaged in parochial work until 1893; from that date he devoted himself wholly to historical research. He died on August 14, 1918. In 1892 he was elected a member of the Royal Society of Canada; and in 1897 he was made an LL.D. of Ottawa University. He was the author of La vie de Mgr. de Laval (2 vols., Quebec, 1890), Les Normands au Canada (5 vols., Evreux, 1892-1904), Henri de Bernières (Evreux, 1898), Le vénérable François de Montmorency-Laval (Quebec, 1901), Le docteur Labrie (Quebec, 1903), Jean Nicolet (Quebec, 1905), La mission du Canada avant Mgr. de Laval (Evreux, 1909), Au pays de Mgr. de Laval (Quebec, 1910), and a series of volumes on the history of the Roman Catholic Church in Canada, entitled L'Église du Canada (4 vols., Quebec, 1911-17).

[Proc. Roy. Soc. Can., 1919; Le Jeune, Dict. gén.; Allaire, Dict. biog.; Morgan, Can. men; D. Gosselin, Généalogie de la famille Gosselin (Quebec, 1902); bibliography in A. Gosselin, Carnet bibliographique des publications (Quebec, 1916).]

Gosselin, David (1846-1926), priest and historian, was born at St. Laurent, Island of Orleans, Quebec, on November 22, 1846, the son of Joseph Gosselin and Soulange Lapierre. He was educated at Quebec, and was ordained a priest of the Roman Catholic Church in 1872. He served in various parishes, but in 1920 retired to the Franciscan Monastery at Quebec; and he died here on March 2, 1926. In 1922 he

was created apostolic notary, was made an LL.D. of Laval University, and was elected a member of the Royal Society of Canada. He was the author of Manuel de pèlerin de la bonne Ste. Anne (Quebec, 1879), Abrégé de l'histoire sainte (Quebec, 1887), Tablettes chronologiques et alphabétiques des principaux évènements et de l'histoire du Canada (Quebec, 1887), Histoire populaire de l'Église du Canada (Quebec, 1887), Catéchisme populaire de la lettre encyclique de ... Léon XIII (Quebec, 1891), Histoire du Cap-Santé (Quebec, 1899), Généalogie de la famille Gosselin (Quebec, 1902), Pages d'histoire ancienne et contemporaine de ma paroisse natale (Quebec, 1904), Dictionnaire généalogique des familles de Charlesbourg (Quebec, 1906), Neuvaine de Saint-Esprit (Quebec, 1907), Les étapes d'une classe (Quebec, 1924), and Autour du concile du Vatican (Quebec, 1924).

[Proc. Roy. Soc. Can., 1926; Le Jeune, Dict. gén.; Allaire, Dict. biog.]

Gouin, Sir Jean Lomer (1861-1929), prime minister of Quebec (1905-20), was born at Grondines, Quebec, on March 19, 1861, the son of Dr. J. N. Gouin. He was educated at Laval University (LL.B., 1884; LL.D., 1902), and was called to the Quebec bar in 1884. He was elected Bâtonnier-général of the Quebec bar in 1910. From 1897 to 1908 he represented the St. James division of Montreal, and from 1908 to 1920 Portneuf, in the Legislative Assembly of Quebec. From 1900 to 1904 he was minister of public works in the Parent administration; and from 1905 to 1920 he was prime minister and attorney-general of Quebec. From 1921 to 1925 he represented Laurier-Outremont in the Canadian House of Commons; and from 1921 to 1924 he was minister of justice in the Mackenzie King government. On January 10, 1929, he was appointed lieutenant-governor of the province of Quebec; and he died, in office, on March 28, 1929. He married (1) in 1888, Eliza (d. 1904), daughter of the Hon. Honoré Mercier (q.v.), and (2) in 1911, Alice, daughter of Auguste Amos, Montreal; and he had two sons by his first wife. He was created a knight bachelor in 1908, and a K.C.M.G. in 1913.

[Can. parl. comp.; Le Jeune, Dict. gén.; H. Charlesworth (ed.), A cyclopaedia of Canadian biography (Toronto, 1919); Morgan, Can. men (1912).]

Gould, Charles Henry (1855-1919), librarian, was born in Montreal, Quebec, on December 6, 1855, the son of Joseph Gould and Abigail De Witt. He was educated at McGill University (B.A., 1877); and after spending several years in business was appointed in 1892 librarian of McGill University. In 1904 he founded at McGill the first library school in Canada. He died at Montreal on July 30, 1919.

[Morgan, Can. men (1912).]

Gourlay, John Lowry (1821-1904), clergyman and author, was born in county Tyrone,

Ireland, in 1821, and came to Canada in 1834. He was educated at Knox College, Toronto (B.A., 1848) and Princeton University (M.A., 1852); and was ordained a minister of the Presbyterian Church in 1851. He held various charges in the United States; and in his later years he was stationed at Aylmer, Quebec. He died at Ottawa, Ontario, in 1904. He was the author of *The history of the Ottawa valley* (n.p., 1896).

[Private information.]

Gourlay, Robert Fleming (1778-1863), author and agitator, was born in the parish of Ceres, Fifeshire, Scotland, on March 24, 1778. He was educated at St. Andrews University; and became interested in the reform of the poor laws. In 1817 he came to Canada, and set up in Kingston as a land agent. By his outspoken criticism of conditions in Upper Canada, he very soon fell foul of the "Family Compact", or ruling clique in the province at that time. He was arrested as a seditious alien, was tried and found guilty, and was banished from the province. He returned to Scotland, and there prepared his valuable *Statistical account of Upper Canada* (3 vols., London, 1822). About 1836 he went to live in the United States, and in 1837-38 he was influential in dissuading American sympathizers from giving aid to William Lyon Mackenzie (q.v.). In 1842 the parliament of United Canada declared the sentence passed on him null and void; but he did not return to Canada until 1856. In 1860 he unsuccessfully contested Oxford county as a candidate for the Legislative Assembly of Canada; and shortly afterward he returned to Scotland. He died at Edinburgh on August 1, 1863. His autobiography was published by him in a curious work entitled *The banished Briton and Neptunian*, issued in thirty-eight parts (Boston, 1843); and he was the author of a number of pamphlets.

[W. R. Riddell, *Robert (Fleming) Gourlay* (Ont. Hist. Soc., papers and records, 1916); W. Smith, *Robert Gourlay* (Queen's quarterly, 1926); E. A. Cruikshank, *The government of Upper Canada and Robert Gourlay* (Ont. Hist. Soc., papers and records, 1926); L. D. Milani, *Robert Gourlay, Gadfly* (Toronto, 1971); *Cyc. Am. biog.*; Morgan, *Cel. Can.* and *Bib. can.*; J. C. Dent, *The Upper Canadian rebellion* (2 vols., 1885); W. S. Wallace, *The family compact* (Toronto, 1915).]

Gow, John Milne (1844-1898), author, was born in Perth, Scotland, on June 16, 1844, and was educated at Dalhousie University, Halifax, Nova Scotia. He became first a school-teacher, and then a journalist; and he died at Lower La Have, Nova Scotia, in 1898. He was the author of *Cape Breton illustrated* (Toronto, 1893).

[Morgan, *Can. men* (1898).]

Gowan, Sir James Robert (1815-1909), judge and senator of Canada, was born at Cahore, county Wexford, Ireland, on December 22, 1815, the son of Henry Galton Gowan and Elizabeth Burkitt. He came to Canada in 1832, and settled in what is now Peel county, Upper Canada. He studied law under the Hon. J. E. Small (q.v.), and was called to the bar of Upper Canada in 1839 (Q.C., 1889). In 1843 he was appointed judge of the county court of Simcoe; and he presided over this court until 1883, when he resumed private practice. As a judge, he was in great demand for special commissions; and in 1873 he was one of the royal commissioners appointed to investigate the "Pacific Scandal". From 1885 to 1907 he was a member of the Senate of Canada, and for half of this period he was chairman of the divorce committee of the Senate. He died at Barrie, Ontario, on March 18, 1909. In 1853 he married Anna, daughter of the Rev. S. B. Ardagh, rector of Barrie, Ontario. He was created a C.M.G. in 1893, and a K.C.M.G. in 1905; and in 1883 Queen's University, Kingston, conferred on him the degree of LL.D.

[H. H. Ardagh, *Life of Sir James Robert Gowan* (Toronto, 1911); A. H. U. Colquhoun (ed.), *The Hon. James R. Gowan, a memoir* (Toronto, 1894); Morgan, *Can. men* (1898); Rose, *Cyc. Can. biog.* (1886); Dent, *Can. port.*, vol. 3; *Can. parl. comp.*; *Cyc. Am. biog.*]

Gowan, Ogle Robert (1803-1876), journalist and politician, was born at Mount Nebo, Wexford county, Ireland, on July 13, 1803. From 1822 to 1829 he was a journalist in Dublin; and in 1829 he came to Canada, and established the Brockville *Statesman*, a weekly newspaper which he edited until 1852. He then came to Toronto, and was for a time editor of the *Patriot*. He was one of the founders, and for many years the grand master, of the Orange Association of British America; and he played an active part in suppressing the rebellion of 1837 in Upper Canada. He represented Leeds in the Legislative Assembly of Upper Canada from 1836 to 1841, and in that of United Canada from 1844 to 1847, and the north riding of Leeds and Grenville from 1858 to 1861. He died at Toronto on August 21, 1876. He was the author of *Responsible or parliamentary government* (Toronto, 1839), an early pamphlet advocating responsible government, and *Orangeism, its origin and history* (3 vols., Toronto, 1859).

[W. B. Kerr, *When Orange and Green united* (Ont. Hist. Soc., papers and records, 1942); Morgan, *Cel. Can.* and *Bib. can.*; J. C. Dent, *The last forty years* (2 vols., Toronto, 1881); W. Kingsford, *The early bibliography of Ontario* (Toronto, 1892); *Dict. Can. biog.*, vol. 10.]

Grace, Nathaniel Hew (1902-1961), scientist, was born at Allahabad, India, November 10, 1902, the son of a missionary. He attended school in California and in Saskatchewan and entered the University of Saskatchewan in 1921, where he earned his B.Sc. (1925) and M.Sc. (1927). He then studied at McGill under Dr. Otto Maass (q.v.) and received his Ph.D. in physical chemistry in 1931. On graduation he joined the staff of the Division of Chemistry of the National Research Council where he was a pioneer investigator on plant hormones or growth regulators. During the Second World War he was a senior research officer with responsibility for studies connected with wartime shortages of starch, rubber, resins, and vegetable oils. In 1951 he left Ottawa and became director of the Research Council of Alberta, where he initiated a program of expansion which increased the staff five-fold, and permitted the council to begin a number of new studies. Much of the new work was related to soil, weather, and water-resource studies and involved co-operation with departments of the national government. Dr. Grace was awarded an M.B.E. in 1946, was made a fellow of the Royal Society in 1948 and a fellow of the Chemical Institute of Canada in 1948. He died at Edmonton in 1961.

[*Trans. Roy. Soc. Can.* (1962).]

Graham, Mrs. Emma, *née* **Jeffers** (d. 1922), author, was born in Wilton, Ontario, the elder daughter of the Rev. Wellington Jeffers, D.D. At an early age, she contributed to the *Christian Guardian*, when her father was editor; and in her later years she was a contributor to the Toronto *Globe*. She married the Rev. James Graham, and lived with him successively in Clinton, Goderich, London, Dundas, Windsor, Strathroy, and Toronto. She had three sons and three daughters. Her death took place in Toronto on August 20, 1922. She was the author of *Etchings from a parsonage verandah* (Toronto, 1895).

[Private information.]

Graham, Felix (d. 1787), merchant, was an Albany trader who was engaged as early as 1767 in the trade about Michilimackinac. He was an early partner of Peter Pond (q.v.). During the American Revolution, he removed from Albany to Montreal; and he died in Montreal on February 4, 1787.

[M. M. Quaife (ed.), *The John Askin papers*, vol. 1 (Detroit, Mich., 1928); H. A. Innis, *Peter Pond* (Toronto, 1930).]

Graham, George Perry (1859-1943), journalist and politician, was born at Eganville, Canada West, on March 31, 1859. He was educated at the Iroquois high school and the Morrisburg Collegiate Institute; and he became a school-teacher. In 1880, however, he entered journalism as editor of the Morrisburg *Herald*; and eventually he became editor and proprietor of the Brockville *Recorder*. From 1898 to 1907 he represented Brockville in the Legis-

lative Assembly of Ontario; and from 1904 to 1905 he was provincial secretary in the administration of Sir George Ross (q.v.). For two years after the defeat of the Ross government, he was leader of the Liberal opposition in the legislature; but in 1907 he was appointed minister of railways and canals in the Dominion administration of Sir Wilfrid Laurier (q.v.), and he retained this portfolio until the defeat of the government in 1911. He was elected to represent Brockville in the Canadian House of Commons from 1907 to 1911, South Renfrew from 1912 to 1917, and South Essex from 1921 to 1925. He was not a candidate for election in 1917, but he declined to join the Union government of that year, and he gave to Sir Wilfrid Laurier a general support. In the first King administration (1921-25), he was first minister of militia and defence (1921-23) and then minister of railways and canals (1923-26). In 1926 he was summoned to the Senate, where he became a much respected "elder statesman". He died at Brockville, Ontario, on January 1, 1943. In 1925 he had the honour of being sworn of the Imperial Privy Council.

[*Can. who's who*, 1936-37; *Can. parl. comp.*; H. Charlesworth (ed.), *A cyclopaedia of Canadian biography* (Toronto, 1919),]

Graham, Gwethalyn (1913-1965), novelist, was born in Toronto, Ontario, January 18, 1913, daughter of Frank Erichsen-Brown (q.v.). She attended Rosedale Public School; Havergal College, Toronto; a Swiss boarding school; and Smith College in Massachusetts. Married at nineteen, she was later divorced and married David Yalden-Thomson in 1947. She began her first novel at twenty-one, about a Swiss boarding school. It was published in 1938 as *Swiss sonata* and won the Governor General's Award. Her second, *Earth and high heaven* (1944), deals with anti-Semitism and also won the Governor General's Award. It was made into a motion picture and was translated into ten languages. She also collaborated with Solange Chaput-Rolland in *Dear enemies* (1963), an exchange of views on English-French relations in Canada. She was a frequent contributor to *Saturday Night* and *Maclean's* magazine. She died at Montreal, Quebec, November 25, 1965.

[*Can. who's who*, 1955-57; Clara Thomas, *Canadian novelists* (Toronto, 1948); Norah Story, *The Oxford companion to Canadian history and literature* (Toronto, 1967); V.B. Rhodenizer, *Canadian literature in English* (Montreal, 1965).]

Graham, Hugh (1758-1829), clergyman, was born at Hench, West Calder, Scotland, in 1758; and was educated at Edinburgh University. He came to Nova Scotia in 1785, as one of the first Presbyterian ministers in the province; and he died at Stewiacke, Nova Scotia, in 1829. He was the author of *Sermon and ad-*

dresses (Halifax, N.S., 1799) and *A warning to youth* (Pictou, N.S., 1824).

[R. J. Long, *Nova Scotia authors* (East Orange, N.J., 1918); Morgan, *Bib. can.*]

Graham, Hugh. See **Atholstan, Hugh Graham, Baron.**

Graham, Sir Wallace (1848-1917), chief justice of Nova Scotia (1915-17), was born at Antigonish, Nova Scotia, on January 15, 1848, the son of David Graham and Mary Elizabeth Bigelow. He was educated at Acadia College (B.A., 1867), and was admitted to the bar in Nova Scotia in 1871 (Q.C., 1881). He practised law in Halifax; and in 1887-88 he was one of the associate counsel in the British case before the Fishery Commission at Washington. In 1889 he was appointed a puisne judge of the Supreme Court of Nova Scotia; and in 1915 he became chief justice of this court. He died on October 12, 1917. He was created a knight bachelor in 1916.

[Morgan, *Can. men* (1912); *Who was who*, 1916-28.]

Grandin, Vital Justin (1829-1902), Roman Catholic bishop of St. Albert (1871-1902), was born in France on February 8, 1829. In 1851 he entered the Oblate order, and in 1854 he was ordained a priest. He was sent to Canada and in 1855 he established a mission at Lake Isle à la Crosse, in the North West. In 1869 he transferred this mission to St. Albert; and when the diocese of St. Albert was created in 1871, he became the first bishop of St. Albert. He died at St. Albert on June 3, 1902.

[E. Jonquet, *Mgr. Grandin* (Montreal, 1903); Rev. Br. Memorian, *Vital Justin Grandin* (Can. Cath. Hist. Assoc. report, 1935-36); Le Jeune, *Dict. gén.*]

Grant, Alexander (1734-1813), president and administrator of Upper Canada (1805-06), was born in 1734, the second son of Patrick Grant, eighth laird of Glenmoriston, Inverness-shire, Scotland. He served in the merchant marine and in the Royal Navy, and in 1757 came to America as an officer in a Highland regiment. In the Seven Years' War he commanded a sloop on Lake Champlain; and later he was appointed commodore of the western lakes, with headquarters at Detroit. In 1792 he became a member of the first Executive Council and of the first Legislative Council of Upper Canada; and in 1805-06, after the death of General Hunter (q.v.) he was administrator of the government of the province. He died at Castle Grant, his place at Grosse Point, on Lake St. Clair, in May, 1813. In 1774 he married Thérèse Barthe; and by her he had one son and nine daughters.

[G. F. Macdonald, *Commodore Alexander Grant* (Ont. Hist. Soc., papers and records, 1925).]

Grant, Charles (*fl.* 1780-1784), merchant, was a son of James Grant, laird of Kincorth, and a cousin of Robert Grant the Nor'Wester (q.v.). He became a merchant of Quebec, and in 1780 he made for General Haldimand a well-known report on the fur-trade. He married Jane Holmes, and had by her two sons and two daughters. One of the sons was Charles Grant the younger (q.v.), and the other was Frederick, who was a merchant in Quebec, and afterwards purchased the estate of Ecclesgreig in Scotland, where the Forsyth-Grants still live. One daughter, Jane, married Capt. Kenelm Conner Chandler, of the 60th Regiment, seignior of Nicolet; and the other, Margaret, married the Hon. John Forsyth (q.v.). Charles Grant died in December, 1784; and in 1793 his widow married in Quebec the Hon. John Blackwood.

[W. S. Wallace, *Strathspey in the Canadian fur-trade*, in R. Flenley (ed.), *Essays in Canadian history* (Toronto, 1939).]

Grant, Charles (1784-1843), fur-trader, was born probably in Quebec, about September, 1784, the younger son of Charles Grant of Quebec (q.v.). He entered the service of the North West Company as a clerk; and in 1816 he was stationed at Rainy Lake. He was at Grand Portage in 1821, but seems to have retired from the fur-trade at that time. In 1815 he was elected a member of the Beaver Club, and in 1827 he was its acting secretary. He acquired the ownership of the fief Bruères; and during his later years he lived on a farm at Côte Ste. Catherine (now Outremont), near Montreal. About 1828 he married Amelia Williams; and by her he had four sons and five daughters, several of whom have left descendants. He died on May 21, 1843. His sister Margaret (d. 1818) married the Hon. John Forsyth (q.v.); and her son William, on succeeding to the estate of his maternal uncle, Frederick Grant, in Scotland, assumed the name of Forsyth-Grant.

[W. S. Wallace (ed.), *Documents relating to the North West Company* (Toronto: The Champlain Society, 1934).]

Grant, Charles William, Baron de Longueuil (1782-1848), legislative councillor of Lower Canada, was born at Quebec on February 4, 1782, the son of Capt. David Alexander Grant and Marie Charles Joseph, Baronne de Longueuil, daughter of Charles Jacques, third Baron de Longueuil. He was appointed a member of the Legislative Council of Lower Canada in 1811; and he died at Alwington House, near Kingston, Upper Canada, on July 5, 1848.

[A. Jodoin and J. L. Vincent, *Histoire de Longueuil et de la famille de Longueuil* (Montreal, 1880); Bibaud, *Panth. can.*]

Grant, Cuthbert (d. 1799), fur-trader, was probably the son of David Grant of Lethendry, in the parish of Cromdale, Strathspey, Scotland, and his wife Margaret, third daughter of Robert Grant of Glenbeg, and a younger brother of Robert Grant (q.v.). Certainly Robert Grant had a younger brother named Cuthbert who was a "merchant in Canada". The difficulty is that there was another Cuthbert Grant, a merchant of Quebec, who died in Quebec in 1792. At any rate the Cuthbert Grant who was a fur-trader appears in the North West as early as 1785 when, with Laurent Leroux (q.v.) in opposition, he led the way to the Great Slave Lake. In 1787-88 he was with Alexander Mackenzie (q.v.) in the Athabaska department; but his later years were spent chiefly on the Red River, where his "favourite residence" appears to have been at River Tremblante. He was made a partner of the North West Company about 1795; and he died in the North West in 1799. His shares in the North West Company lapsed in 1805.

[W. S. Wallace, *Strathspey in the Canadian fur-trade*, in R. Flenley (ed.), *Essays in Canadian history* (Toronto, 1939).]

Grant, Cuthbert James (1796?-1854), warden of the plains, was a half-breed son of Cuthbert Grant (q.v.), and was born in the North West about 1796. He was baptized in the Scotch Presbyterian Church in Montreal in 1798, and was educated in Montreal. He returned to the North West about 1815, and in 1816 he was one of the leaders of the *Bois-Brulés* in the affair at Seven Oaks. In 1817 he was arrested by Colonel Coltman (q.v.), but he was later released on bail at Quebec. In 1823-24 he was employed as a clerk by the Hudson's Bay Company, but was discharged. In 1828 he was given the nominal post of "Warden of the Plains", and he retained this until 1848. He died at White Horse Plain, Manitoba, on July 15, 1854. He was survived by his wife, Mary McGillis.

[Mrs. M. A. MacLeod, *Cuthbert Grant of Grantown* (Can. hist. rev., 1940); F. J. Audet, *Cuthbert-James Grant* (Bull. rech. hist., 1935); M. Complin, *The warden of the plains* (Canadian geographical journal, 1934); M. A. MacLeod and W. L. Morton, *Cuthbert Grant of Grantown* (Toronto, 1963).]

Grant, George Monro (1835-1902), principal of Queen's University, Kingston (1877-1902), was born at Albion Mines, Nova Scotia, on December 22, 1835, the son of James Grant and Mary Monro. He was educated at Pictou Academy, at the West River Seminary, and at Glasgow University; and was ordained a minister of the Church of Scotland in 1860. From 1863 to 1877 he was minister of St. Matthew's Church, Halifax, Nova Scotia; and in 1877 he was appointed principal of Queen's University, Kingston, Ontario. Through his energy in raising an endowment fund, he placed this university in a greatly improved financial position; and he became an outstand-

ing figure, not only in educational matters, but in the political world as well. An ardent imperialist, but a believer in the future of Canada, a vigorous and fearless controversialist, but a man of generous and liberal instincts, he won for himself a position as a publicist not equalled by that of the head of any other Canadian university at that time. He died at Kingston, Ontario, on May 10, 1902. In 1872 he married Jessie, daughter of William Lawson, of Halifax; and by her he had one son.

In 1877 he was made a D.D. of Glasgow University, and in 1892 an LL.D. of Dalhousie University. In 1899 he was elected moderator of the Presbyterian Church in Canada, and in 1901 president of the Royal Society of Canada. His most notable publication was *Ocean to ocean* (Toronto, 1873; new ed., 1925); but he was also the author of *New year sermons* (Halifax, 1865-66), *Our five foreign missions* (Kingston, 1887), *Advantages of imperial federation* (London, 1889-91), *Our national objects and aims* (Toronto, 1890-91), and *The religions of the world* (London and Toronto, 1894), as well as numerous articles in English, American, and Canadian periodicals. He was also the editor and part author of *Picturesque Canada* (2 vols., Toronto, 1882).

[W. L. Grant and F. Hamilton, *Principal Grant* (Toronto, 1904); R. C. Wallace (ed.), *Some great men of Queen's* (Toronto, 1941); *Dict. nat. biog.*, supp. II; Dent, *Can. port.*, vol. 1; Taché, *Men of the day*; Rose, *Cyc. Can. biog.* (1886); Morgan, *Can. men* (1898).]

Grant, Harold T. (1899-1965), admiral, was born in Halifax, Nova Scotia, March, 1899. He was educated at the Royal Naval College of Canada and served at sea during the First World War. A career officer, he was in command of H.M.C.S. *Skeena* in 1938 and became staff officer of operations with Atlantic command in 1939. He was chief of naval personnel at Naval Headquarters in 1940 and on loan to the Royal Navy, in command of H.M.S. *Enterprise* in 1943, and of the Canadian cruiser *Ontario*, 1944. He was senior officer, Canadian warships, operating in the Pacific Ocean (1945) and chief of naval administration and supply (1946). He was made chief of naval staff from 1947 to 1951 when he retired with the rank of vice-admiral. He was president of Homes Lines Steamship Agency of Canada. He was awarded the D.S.O. (1944) and C.B.E. (1946). He died at Ottawa, Ontario, May 8, 1965.

[*Can. who's who*, 1955-57.]

Grant, James (d. 1798?) fur-trader, appears first in the fur-trade licences in 1777, as trading to Lake Timiskaming. From that date to 1783 he was associated with John Porteous and then Daniel Sutherland (q.v.) in the Timiskaming trade. In 1795 he became a partner in the North West Company; and he was dead by 1799, as appears from McTavish,

Frobisher and Co.'s agreement of 1799, where he is described as "the late". A "J. Grant" died in Montreal on December 26, 1798, and this may have been James Grant.

[W. S. Wallace, *Strathspey in the Canadian fur-trade*, in R. Flenley (ed.), *Essays in Canadian history* (Toronto, 1939).]

Grant, James (*fl.* 1805-1827), fur-trader, was a clerk of the North West Company at Fond du Lac in 1805, and continued in charge of this post until 1813. From 1814 to 1815 he was at the Pic, on Lake Superior, but in 1816 he was back at Fond du Lac, as he was there arrested by Lord Selkirk (q.v.). He was made a partner of the North West Company in 1816, and in 1817 Ross Cox (q.v.) met him at Fort William. He retired from the fur-trade in 1821, and in 1827 he was the guest of Charles Grant, Jr. (q.v.) at the Beaver Club in Montreal. After that, he disappears from view.

[W. S. Wallace (ed.), *Documents relating to the North West Company* (Toronto: The Champlain Society, 1934).]

Grant, Sir James Alexander (1831-1920), physician, was born in Inverness, Scotland, in 1831, the son of Dr. James Grant and Jane Ord. He came to Canada with his parents when only a few weeks old, and was educated at Martintown, Upper Canada, at Queen's College, Kingston, and at McGill University, Montreal (M.D., 1854). He entered on the practice of medicine at Ottawa, and was from 1867 to 1905 physician to the governor-general. He sat in the Canadian House of Commons from 1867 to 1874 as the member for Russell, and from 1892 to 1896 as the member for Ottawa. In 1872 he was elected president of the Canadian Medical Association; in 1882 he was selected as one of the charter members of the Royal Society of Canada, and in 1909 he was elected president of this society. He died in Ottawa on February 5, 1920. In 1856 he married Maria, daughter of Edward Malloch; and by her he had several children. He was created a K.C.M.G. in 1887.

[*Proc. Roy. Soc. Can.*, 1920; Morgan, *Can. men* (1912) and *Bib. can.*; Rose, *Cyc. Can. biog.* (1886); W. J. Rattray, *The Scot in British North America* (4 vols., Toronto, 1880).]

Grant, James Miller (1853-1940), author, was born at Grantown, Scotland, in 1853; and died at Toronto, Ontario, on March 15, 1940. He was the author, under the nom-de-plume of "Grant Balfour", of *The fairy school of Castle Frank* (Toronto, 1899), *Canada my home, and other poems* (Toronto, 1910), and *On golden wings through wonderland* (Toronto, 1927).

[Morgan, *Can. men* (1912).]

Grant, John, of Montreal (d. 1809), was apparently a brother of William Grant of St. Roch (q.v.). He appears to have come to Canada as early as 1764; and he married before

1774 Anne Freeman, the illegitimate daughter of Richard Dobie (q.v.). By her he had at least five daughters, one of whom, Ann, married Samuel Gerrard (q.v.), and another, Elizabeth, married in 1798 James Finlay, Jr. (q.v.). From 1779 to 1785 John Grant was engaged in company with Gabriel Cotté and Maurice Blondeau (q.v.), in trading to Lake Superior, but in 1798 he is described as "at present absent from this province". He died in 1809, and his will is in the Montreal Court House.

[W. S. Wallace (ed.), *Documents relating to the North West Company* (Toronto: The Champlain Society, 1934).]

Grant, John, of Lachine (1749-1817), merchant, was born in Glenmoriston, near Inverness, Scotland, in 1749. He came to Canada in 1771, and established himself at Lachine, where he engaged in the business of forwarding. In the fur-trade licences, his name appears as trading to Oswegatchie, Cataraqui, Niagara, and Detroit between 1777 and 1785. In 1804 he was an agent of Quetton de St. George at York (Toronto). The Rev. R. Campbell, in his *History of the Scotch Presbyterian Church, St. Gabriel Street, Montreal* (Montreal, 1887), p. 230, says that he was "agent for the North West Company, and attended to the forwarding and supplies from Montreal". On July 30, 1777, he married in Montreal Margaret Beattie; and one of his daughters married in Lachine in 1806 Thomas Blackwood. His son, James C. Grant, became a prominent member of the Lower Canada bar. He died at Lachine on August 23, 1817. He does not appear to have been related to the other Grants in the fur-trade, but was more probably connected with Commodore Alexander Grant (q.v.), administrator of the province of Upper Canada in 1805-06, who came also from Glenmoriston.

[W. S. Wallace (ed.), *Documents relating to the North West Company* (Toronto: The Champlain Society, 1934).]

Grant, MacCallum (1845-1928), lieutenant-governor of Nova Scotia (1916-25), was born in Hants county, Nova Scotia, on May 17, 1845, the son of John Nutting Grant and Margaret MacCallum. He was privately educated, and began his business career in Halifax in 1873. In 1916 he was appointed lieutenant-governor of Nova Scotia, and he continued in office until 1925. He died at Halifax, Nova Scotia, on February 23, 1928. In 1887 he married Laura McNeill, daughter of the Hon. Daniel McNeill Parker (q.v.); and by her he had five sons and one daughter.

[*Can. who was who*, vol. 1; Le Jeune, *Dict. gén.*; *Can. parl. comp.*]

Grant, Peter (1764-1848), fur-trader, was born, apparently in Scotland, in 1764. He came to Canada, and entered the service of the

North West Company in 1784, at the same time as Edward Umfreville (q.v.). In 1789 he was at Lac Rouge; in 1793 he was at the forks of the river Qu'Appelle; he was met by David Thompson (q.v.) near Grand Portage in July, 1797; and in 1799 he was proprietor of the post at Rainy Lake. He was made a partner of the North West Company after 1795, and was for several years in charge of the Red River department. In 1802 he was sent as an agent of the North West Company to deal with the military authorities of Sault Ste. Marie. He relinquished one of his shares in the Company in 1805, but was still apparently a partner in 1808, when William McGillivray (q.v.) signed for him at Fort William. He seems to have retired from the fur-trade before 1807, when he was made a member of the Beaver Club at Montreal; and he settled at Ste. Anne, Bout de l'Isle. He died at Lachine on July 20, 1848.

[W. S. Wallace (ed.), *Documents relating to the North West Company* (Toronto: The Champlain Society, 1934).]

Grant, Richard (1793-1862), fur-trader, was born in Montreal in 1793, the son of William Grant of Three Rivers (q.v.). He entered the service of the North West Company in 1816, and in 1821, when the North West Company was merged with the Hudson's Bay Company, was stationed on the Saskatchewan. He became a clerk in the Hudson's Bay Company, and in 1836 he was promoted to the rank of chief trader. He retired in 1853, and he died in 1862.

[T. C. Elliott, *Richard ("Captain Johnny") Grant* (Oregon historical quarterly, 1935).]

Grant, Robert (1752-1801), fur-trader, was born in 1752, the grandson of Donald Grant of Easter Lethendry, in the parish of Cromdale, Strathspey, Scotland, and the second son of David Grant of Lethendry and Margaret, third daughter of Robert Grant of Glenbeg, in the same parish. He came to Canada, and entered the fur-trade. In 1778 John Askin (q.v.) noted that he and his partner, William Holmes (q.v.), whom he described as "deserving young men", were embarking in the North West trade. In 1779 Holmes and Grant appear as one of the partnerships in the original sixteen-share North West Company of that year; and they appear also in the twenty-share company of 1783. Robert Grant seems to have spent most of his time in the West in the Red River district. Roderick Mackenzie in his *Reminiscences* says that he wintered on the Red River in 1785-86, and he was again there in 1790. In 1787 he is reputed to have founded Fort Esperance on the Qu'Appelle River. His partner Holmes sold out in 1790; and in 1793 Robert Grant retired, and returned to Scotland. On December 5, 1795, he married Anne, second daughter of the Rev. Lewis Grant of Cromdale; and by her he had two sons and two daughters, the youngest of whom, Davina, married on

November 9, 1819, Frederick Grant, a son of Charles Grant the elder (q.v.), who purchased the estate of Mount Cyrus or Ecclesgreig, near Montrose, where the Forsyth-Grant family still lives. In 1797 Robert Grant acquired the estate of Kincorth, and there he lived until his death on August 16, 1801.

[W. S. Wallace, *Strathspey in the Canadian fur-trade*, in R. Flenley (ed.), *Essays in Canadian history* (Toronto, 1939).]

Grant, William, of St. Roch (1741-1805), merchant, was born in Scotland in 1741, and came to Canada in 1763, an agent of the London firm of Robert Grant and Co., which had engaged in the trade with Canada. In 1763 he purchased from the Marquis de Vaudreuil a grant of the fur-trading rights in La Baye, Lake Michigan; but this grant was voided, and William Grant appears to have taken no direct part subsequently in the fur-trade. But most of the Grants who embarked in the fur-trade appear to have been related to him, though the exact relationship is difficult to determine. He himself concentrated his energies about Quebec and the lower St. Lawrence. In 1777 he was appointed deputy receiver-general of Quebec; and in 1778 he was appointed a member of the Legislative Council of the province. In 1784 he was relieved of his duties as deputy receiver-general, because of serious deficiencies in his accounts; and he was not appointed to the Legislative Council of Lower Canada on its creation in 1791. From 1792 to his death, however, he represented the upper town of Quebec in the Legislative Assembly of Lower Canada. He purchased a large number of seigniories along the banks of the St. Lawrence, and he had extensive interests in Quebec, near which, at St. Roch, he had a large house. But he evidently died insolvent, for after his death his seigniories were put up to auction. He died at Quebec on October 5, 1805. In 1770 he married the widow of Charles Jacques Le Moyne, third Baron de Longueuil; and his nephew, Capt. David Alexander Grant, married her daughter, who was heiress to the title.

[R. La Roque de Roquebrune, *M. William Grant* (Nova Francia, 1927); W. S. Wallace, *Strathspey in the Canadian fur-trade*, in R. Flenley (ed.), *Essays in Canadian history* (Toronto, 1939).]

Grant, William, of Three Rivers (1743-1810), fur-trader, was born at Blairfindie, in the parish of Kirkmichael, in Scotland, in 1743. He first appears in the fur-trade in 1777, when he goes security for five canoes sent to Nipigon. In 1778 he was at Michilimackinac; and from that date until 1788 he appears to have been associated with George McBeath (q.v.) in the firm of McBeath, Grant and Co., sending canoes to Michilimackinac. His business associates, to judge from the fur-trade licences, were Richard Dobie (q.v.), John Grant of Montreal (q.v.), and Etienne Campion (q.v.). About 1795 the firm of Grant, Campion and Company, in which he was the senior partner, acquired one share in the North West Company; but the firm appears to have dissolved shortly afterwards. In 1788 he purchased a property in Three Rivers, and thenceforward he was known as William Grant of Three Rivers. In his later years, he was engaged in small business in Nicolet and Sorel; and he died at or near Sorel on November 20, 1810.

[W. S. Wallace, *Strathspey in the Canadian fur-trade*, in R. Flenley (ed.), *Essays in Canadian history* (Toronto, 1939).]

Grant, Sir William (1752-1832), attorney-general of Quebec (1776-77), was born at Elchies, Scotland, on October 13, 1752, the son of James Grant, a farmer. He was educated at King's College, Aberdeen, and in 1774 he was called to the bar from Lincoln's Inn. He came to Canada in 1775, and took part in the defence of Quebec against the Americans. On May 10, 1776, he was appointed attorney-general of the province; and he held this office until his departure from Canada in 1777. In 1790 he was returned to the British parliament as one of the members for Shaftesbury; and he continued a member of parliament until 1812. From 1799 to 1801 he was solicitor-general in the Pitt administration; and from 1802 to 1817 he was master of the rolls. He died at Barton House, Dawlish, on May 23, 1832. He was knighted in 1799; in 1809 he was elected lord rector of the University of Aberdeen; and in 1820 he was made a D.C.L. of Oxford University. He was not married.

[*Dict. nat. biog.*; Morgan, *Cel. Can.*]

Grant, William Lawson (1872-1935), historian and educationist, was born at Halifax, Nova Scotia, on November 2, 1872, the son of the Rev. George Monro Grant (q.v.) and Jessie, daughter of William Lawson. He was educated at Queen's University, Kingston, and at Balliol College, Oxford (B.A., 1898). He taught at Upper Canada College and St. Andrew's College, Toronto, from 1898 to 1904. From 1904 to 1910 he was Beit lecturer in colonial history at Oxford; and from 1910 to 1917 he was professor of colonial history at Queen's University, Kingston. In 1917 he was appointed headmaster of Upper Canada College, and he retained this post until his death at Toronto on February 3, 1935. In 1911 he married Maude, daughter of Sir George Parkin (q.v.). He was elected a fellow of the Royal Society of Canada in 1911; and in 1929 he was made an LL.D. of the University of Toronto. He was the author of *The Ontario high school history of Canada* (Toronto, 1914), and *The tribune of Nova Scotia* (Toronto, 1915); and he was joint author with C. F. Hamilton of *Principal Grant, a biography* (Toronto, 1904). He edited the *Voyages of Samuel de Champlain* (New York, 1907); with H. E. Egerton, he edited *Canadian constitu-*

tional development (London, 1908); with J. Munro, he edited *Acts of the Privy Council, Colonial Series* (London, 1907-10); and he edited and translated Lescarbot's *History of New France* (3 vols., Toronto, Champlain Society, 1907-14).

[*Can. hist. rev.*, 1935; *Proc. Roy. Soc. Can.*, 1935; Morgan, *Can. men* (1912).]

Gray, John Hamilton (1812-1887), prime minister of Prince Edward Island (1863-65), and one of the Fathers of Confederation, was born in Prince Edward Island in 1812, and was educated at Charlottetown, Prince Edward Island. From 1831 to 1852 he saw service in the British army as a cavalry officer, chiefly in India and South Africa; and he returned to Prince Edward Island about 1856. In 1858 he was elected to represent the fourth district of Queen's county, in the Island Assembly, and he was re-elected in 1863. From 1863 to 1865 he was prime minister of the Island and president of the executive council; and he took a leading part in the Confederation negotiations of 1864. He was chairman of the Charlottetown conference on maritime union; and he was a delegate to the Quebec conference on British North American union. On the rejection of the Quebec Resolutions by the Prince Edward Island legislature, he retired from political life and devoted himself to military duties. He had been since 1862 officer commanding the volunteer brigade of the Island, with the rank of colonel; and in 1867 he was appointed adjutant-general of the militia of the Island. In 1873 he was appointed deputy adjutant-general of Military District No. 10 of the Dominion. He died at "Inkerman House", in the Royalty of Charlottetown, on August 13, 1887. In 1871 he was created a C.M.G.

[Taylor, *Brit. Am.*, vol. 2; J. B. Pollard, *Historical sketch of Prince Edward Island* (Charlottetown, P.E.I., 1898); D. Campbell, *History of Prince Edward Island* (Charlottetown, P.E.I., 1865).]

Gray, John Hamilton (1814-1889), one of the Fathers of Confederation, was born at St. George's, Bermuda, in 1814, the son of William Gray, British consul in Virginia. He was educated at King's College, Windsor, Nova Scotia (B.A., 1833), and in 1837 he was called to the bar of New Brunswick (Q.C., 1853). From 1850 to 1867 he represented Saint John in the Legislative Assembly of New Brunswick; and he was a member of the executive council from 1851 to 1854, and from 1856 to 1857, holding on the latter occasion the portfolio of attorney-general. In 1864 he was one of the appointees of the Conservative opposition in New Brunswick at the Charlottetown and Quebec Conferences; and at these conferences he was a strong advocate of Confederation. From 1866 to 1867 he was speaker of the Legislative Assembly of New Brunswick. In 1867 he was elected to repre-

313

sent Saint John in the Canadian House of Commons; and during the first session of the House he was chairman of the committee of supply. In 1872 he resigned from parliament to accept appointment as a puisne judge of the Supreme Court of British Columbia; and this office he held until his death at Victoria, British Columbia, on June 5, 1889. He married in Dublin in 1845 Eliza, eldest daughter of Lieut.-Col. Harry Ormond, of the 13th Foot; and by her he had seven children. In 1854 he was promoted lieutenant-colonel commanding the Queen's Rangers of New Brunswick. He was the author of *Confederation; or the political and parliamentary history of Canada from the conference at Quebec in October, 1864, to the admission of British Columbia in July, 1871*, vol. i (Toronto, 1872). The second volume was never published.

[*Can. parl. comp.*; J. B. Kerr, *Biographical dictionary of well-known British Columbians* (Vancouver, B.C., 1890); E. O. S. Scholefield and F. W. Howay, *British Columbia* (4 vols., Vancouver, B.C., 1914); J. Hannay, *History of New Brunswick* (2 vols., Saint John, N.B., 1909); W. G. MacFarlane, *New Brunswick bibliography* (Saint John, N.B., 1895).]

Gray, John William Dering (1797-1868), clergyman, was born at Preston, near Halifax, Nova Scotia, on July 23, 1797; and was educated at King's College, Windsor (B.A., 1818). He was ordained a priest of the Church of England, and was rector successively at Amherst, Nova Scotia, and Saint John, New Brunswick. He died on February 1, 1868. In addition to a number of sermons that were published, he was the author of *A brief view of the scriptural authority and historical evidence of infant baptism* (Halifax, N.S., 1837) and *A letter to members of the Church of England in reply to a letter from Edward Maturin* (Saint John, N.B., 1859).

[W. G. MacFarlane, *New Brunswick bibliography* (Saint John, N.B., 1895).]

Gray, Joseph Alexander (1884-1966), nuclear scientist and professor of physics, was born in Melbourne, Australia, February 7, 1884. He graduated from the University of Melbourne in 1907 and the following year he went to England and worked for a year on radioactivity at the Imperial College of Science. From 1909 to 1912 he studied under Professor Rutherford at the University of Manchester. He was awarded the M.Sc. degree in 1912 and joined the physics department at McGill University in Montreal. For the five years of the First World War he was an officer, first in the Artillery and then in the Engineering Corps. During this time he perfected a system of locating enemy guns by sound ranging. He was twice mentioned in dispatches and awarded an O.B.E. for his work. He returned to McGill University in 1919 as associate pro-

fessor of physics and in 1924 went to Queen's University at Kingston as Chown Research professor of physics, a position he held until retirement in 1952. During his period as a student of Rutherford at Manchester he studied the interaction of beta particles and of X and gamma rays with atoms. He continued his studies at McGill and Queen's of the gamma-rays of radium D and radium E, and in 1927 published the first significant measurements of the scattering of X-rays by gases. During the decade preceeding the Second World War, Dr. Gray tried unsuccessfully to raise funds for the installation of a charged-particle accelerator at Queen's University. However, with the explosion of the atomic bomb in 1945 interest in nuclear science revived and a synchrotron and laboratory were installed in 1950 at Queen's University. A complete list of his papers is appended to his biography in *Biographical memoirs of fellows of the Royal Society of London*, vol. 13 (November, 1967). He was a fellow of the Royal Society and of the Royal Society of Canada and a fellow of the American Physical Society. He was a member of the National Research Council of Canada and chairman of the selection committee for Nuffield Fellowships. He died in London, England, March 5, 1966.

[*Proc. Roy. Soc. Can.*, 1968.]

Gray, Robert Isaac Dey (1772?-1804), solicitor-general of Upper Canada (1794-1804), was born about 1772, the son of Major James Gray and Elizabeth Low. At the outbreak of the American Revolution, in 1776, his parents came to Canada; and his father served throughout the revolution as a field officer in the 1st battalion of the King's Royal Regiment of New York ("Johnson's Royal Greens"). In 1884 he settled with his parents at Gray's Creek, near Cornwall; and after some schooling at Quebec, he began at Cornwall the study and practice of law. In 1794 he was appointed by Simcoe (q.v.) acting solicitor-general of Upper Canada, and the appointment was confirmed in 1796. In 1796 he was elected to represent Stormont in the Legislative Assembly of the province, and in 1800 he was re-elected for Stormont and Russell. He was drowned in the loss of the *Speedy* on Lake Ontario on October 8, 1804.

[W. R. Riddell, *Robert Isaac Dey Gray* (Canadian law times, 1921).]

Green, Anson (1801-1879), clergyman, was born at Middleburgh, Schoharie county, New York, on September 27, 1801. He came to Upper Canada in 1823, and in 1824 was admitted a probationer of the Methodist Church. In 1830 he was ordained a minister; and in 1842 he was elected president of the Canadian conference. From 1844 to 1853, and again from 1859 to 1862 he was book steward of the Methodist Church. He was superannuated in 1865, and he died at Toronto on February 19, 1879. He married Rachel, daughter of Caleb

Hopkins (q.v.); and had by her one son and one daughter. He edited *The minutes of the Wesleyan conference* (2 vols., Toronto, 1858) and he was the author of *The life and times of the Rev. Anson Green, written by himself* (Toronto, 1877).

[*Dom. ann. reg.*, 1879; E. M. Chadwick, *Ontarian families*, vol. 1 (Toronto, 1894); *Dict. Can. biog.*, vol. 10.]

Green, Benjamin (1713-1772), administrator of Nova Scotia (1771), was born at Salem, Massachusetts, the youngest son of the Reverend Joseph Green. He was educated at Harvard University; but did not graduate. In 1745 he was secretary to Sir William Pepperell (q.v.) in the expedition against Louisbourg; and remained there as government secretary until 1749. He then settled in Halifax, Nova Scotia, and was appointed in 1750 secretary of the Executive Council and treasurer of the province. He resigned the treasurership in 1768; but retained his seat in the Council, and in 1771 he acted as administrator of the province. He died at Halifax, Nova Scotia, on October 14, 1772.

[B. Murdoch, *A history of Nova Scotia* (3 vols., Halifax, N.S., 1866).]

Green, Ernest (1882-1947), statistician and historian, was born in Stamford township, Ontario, in 1882, and died at Niagara Falls, Ontario, on November 4, 1947. He was first a journalist, and then he became a statistician in the Trade and Commerce department of the Canadian government, and later in the Dominion Bureau of Statistics. He retired on pension in 1943. He was interested in the history of the Niagara Peninsula, and he was the author of *Lincoln at bay: A sketch of 1814* (Welland, Ont., 1923) and of a number of valuable papers contributed to the *Papers and Records* of the Ontario Historical Society.

[Toronto *Globe and Mail*, Nov. 5, 1947.]

Green, Francis (1742-1809), loyalist, was born in Boston, Massachusetts, on August 21, 1742, the second son of Benjamin Green (q.v.). He was educated at Harvard University (B.A., 1760); but during most of his academic course he was absent on active duty. He joined his regiment at Halifax, Nova Scotia, in 1757, and was at the siege of Louisbourg in 1758, and at Quebec in 1760. Later, he saw service in the West Indies; but in 1766 he sold his commission, and returned to Boston. He took the Loyalist side in the American Revolution; and in 1784 he settled in Nova Scotia. Here he served first as sheriff of Halifax, and later as senior judge of the Court of Common Pleas. In 1797 he returned to the United States, and he died at Medford, Massachusetts, on April 21, 1809. He was much interested in the education of deaf mutes, and was the first American writer on the subject. His chief publication was an anonymous treatise entitled *Vox oculis subjecta* (London, 1783).

[*Dict. Am. biog.; Cyc. Am. biog.*]

Greene, Daniel Joseph (1850-1911), prime minister of Newfoundland (1894-95), was born at St. John's, Newfoundland, in 1850, and died there on December 12, 1911. He was educated at St. Bonaventure College, St. John's, and Laval University, where he studied law. Having been called to the bar in 1874 (Q.C., 1889), he returned to Newfoundland to practise law. Elected to represent Ferryland in the Newfoundland House of Assembly, he became leader of the opposition in 1887, and on the defeat of Prime Minister Goodridge (q.v.) in December, 1894, he became prime minister and attorney-general. Within two months, however, he was compelled to relinquish office; and he retired from active politics in 1897, though he was appointed a member of the Legislative Council that year.

[*Encyc. Can.; Newfoundland supp.*]

Greenfield, Herbert (1865-1949), prime minister of Alberta (1921-25), was born in Winchester, England, on November 26, 1865. He came to Canada in 1892, and eventually became a homesteader in Alberta. He was one of the founders of the United Farmers of Alberta, and later was elected vice-president. When the United Farmers of Alberta swept the province in the general election of 1921, the leading figure in the movement, Henry Wise Wood (q.v.), declined the invitation to form a government, and Greenfield undertook to do so. He was sworn in as prime minister on August 31, 1921; and was elected to represent Peace River in a by-election a few months later. He retired from office in 1925; and from 1927 to 1931 he was agent-general of Alberta in London. On his return to Alberta he became interested in the petroleum industry. He died at Calgary, Alberta, on August 23, 1949.

[*New York Times*, Aug. 24, 1949; *Encyc. Can.; Can. parl. comp.*, 1925).]

Greenshields, Robert Alfred Ernest (1861-1942), jurist, was born at Danville, Canada East, on February 2, 1861. He was educated at McGill University (B.A., 1883; B.C.L., 1885), and was called to the bar of Quebec in 1885 (Q.C., 1896). He practised law in Montreal; and in 1910 he was appointed a puisne judge of the Superior Court of Quebec. He became chief justice of this court in 1933, and continued as such until his death at Montreal, Quebec, on September 28, 1942.

[*Can. who's who*, 1936-37; P. G. Roy, *Les juges de la province de Québec* (Quebec, 1933).]

Greenway, Thomas (1838-1908), prime minister of Manitoba (1888-1900), was born in Cornwall, England, on March 25, 1838, the eldest son of Thomas Greenway and Elizabeth

Heard. He came to Canada with his parents in 1844, and was educated in the public schools of Huron county, Upper Canada. For many years he was a general merchant at Centralia, Ontario; and for ten years he was reeve of the township. From 1875 to 1878 he represented South Huron in the Canadian House of Commons, as an independent; but in 1878 he removed to Manitoba, where he took up farming; and in 1879 he was elected to represent Mountain in the Legislative Assembly of Manitoba. He continued to represent this constituency as a Liberal until 1904; and from 1888 to 1900 he was prime minister of the province. It was during his ministry that the Manitoba separate school controversy was settled. In 1904 he was elected to represent Lisgar in the Canadian House of Commons; but he did not take a prominent place in the House, and in 1908 he retired to accept an appointment as a member of the Board of Railway Commissioners. Shortly afterwards, on October 30, 1908, he died at Ottawa. He was twice married, (1) in 1860 to Annie Hicks (d. 1875), and (2) in 1877 to Emma Essery.

[*Can. parl. comp.*; Morgan, *Can. men* (1898); J. P. Robertson, *Political manual of Manitoba* (Winnipeg, 1887); A. Begg, *History of the north west* (3 vols., Toronto, 1894).]

Gregg, William (1817-1909), ecclesiastical historian was born at Killycreen, near Ramelton, county Donegal, Ireland, on July 5, 1817, the son of Daniel Gregg and Jane Graham. He was educated at Glasgow University (B.A., 1843) and at Edinburgh University (M.A., 1844). In 1846 he was licensed to preach in the Free Church of Scotland, and came to Canada as a missionary. From 1847 to 1857 he was minister of St. John's Presbyterian Church, Belleville; and from 1857 to 1872 of Cooke's Church, Toronto. In 1864 he was appointed lecturer in apologetics in Knox College, Toronto; and he remained on the staff of this college, first as professor of apologetics, and later as professor of apologetics and church history, until his retirement in 1895. He died at Toronto on May 26, 1909. In 1849 he married Phoebe, eldest daughter of Dr. Rufus Holden, of Belleville; and by her he had several children. He was a D.D. of Hanover University (1878); and he was the author of a *History of the Presbyterian Church in Canada* (Toronto, 1885).

[Morgan, *Can. men* (1898).]

Grégoire, Georges Stanislas (1845-1928), physician and poet, was born at Restigouche, Bonaventure county, Canada East, on November 6, 1845. He became a physician, and practised medicine at Lake Megantic. From 1912 to 1923 he represented Frontenac in the Legislative Assembly of Quebec. He died at Sherbrooke, Quebec, on April 6, 1928. He was the author of *De Cheops à Eiffel; ou, Le*

cycle *du matérialisme: Essai poétique inédit* (Sherbrooke, Que., 1893).

[*Bull. rech. hist.*, 1928.]

Gregory, Claudius Jabez (1879?-1944), journalist and author, was born in England about 1879, and came to Canada when a young man. He became a journalist, and later an advertising expert; and he died at Burlington, Ontario, on October 1, 1944. He was the author of three novels, *Forgotten men* (Hamilton, Ont., 1933), *Valerie Hathaway* (Toronto, 1933), and *Solomon Levi* (New York, 1935).

[Toronto *Globe and Mail*, Oct. 2, 1944.]

Gregory, John (1751?-1817), merchant, was a native of England who came to Canada about 1773. He may have been connected with the London firm of Mark and Thomas Gregory, which was engaged in the trade with Canada in the early days of British rule. He entered into partnership with James Finlay (q.v.), and from 1773 to 1783 the firm of Finlay and Gregory continued to send canoes to the West. On Finlay's retirement in 1784, Gregory took into partnership Normand McLeod (q.v.), and the firm of Gregory and McLeod was the backbone of the opposition to the North West Company from 1783 to 1787. In 1787 he became a partner in the North West Company, and later a member of the firm of McTavish, Frobisher and Co. In 1791 he was elected a member of the Beaver Club. He retired from the firm of McTavish, Frobisher and Co. on May 31, 1806; and he died in Montreal on February 22, 1817. In 1779 he married Isabella Ferguson (d. 1819); and by her he had several children. His son George (d. 1850) married a daughter of the Hon. John Forsyth (q.v.); and his youngest daughter married, in 1806, David Mitchell. He had a brother George who lived for many years in Quebec.

[W. S. Wallace (ed.), *Documents relating to the North West Company* (Toronto: The Champlain Society, 1934).]

Gregory, John Uriah (1830-1913), civil servant, was born at Troy, New York, on November 7, 1830. He entered the Canadian civil service; and for many years he was the representative of the department of marine and fisheries at Quebec. He died at Quebec on May 30, 1913. He was the author of *En racontant: Récits de voyage en Floride, au Labrador, et sur le fleuve St-Laurent* (Quebec, 1886).

[Morgan, *Can. men* (1898).]

Gregory, William (*fl.* 1764-1767), judge, was a barrister who came to Quebec from England in 1764, and was appointed first chief justice of Quebec. He was removed from office in 1766, and for a time practised law in Montreal. It is possible that he is identical with the William Gregory who was appointed a judge of the Superior Court of South Carolina in 1775. The date and place of his death is not known.

[F. J. Audet, *Les juges en chef de la province de Québec* (Quebec, 1927); P. G. Roy, *Les juges de la province de Québec* (Quebec, 1933); A. W. P. Buchanan, *The bench and bar of Lower Canada* (Montreal, 1925); Le Jeune, *Dict. gén.*]

Grenfell, Sir Wilfred Thomason (1865-1940), medical missionary and author, was born near Chester, England, on February 28, 1865. He was educated at Marlborough College and at Oxford University (M.D., 1889); and in 1890 he accepted the position of superintendent of the Mission to Deep-Sea Fishermen. He sailed for Labrador in 1892; and he devoted the rest of his life to the Labrador Mission. At the time of his death, the mission included five hospitals, seven nursing stations, and three orphanages. In recognition of his work, he received honorary degrees from many universities, and in 1927 he was created a K.C.M.G. He died at Charlotte, Vermont, on October 9, 1940. He was the author of *Vikings of to-day* (London, 1895), *The harvest of the sea* (New York, 1905), *Off the rocks* (Philadelphia, 1906), *A man's faith* (Boston, 1908), *Adrift on an ice-pan* (Boston, 1909), *Down to the sea* (New York, 1910), *A man's helpers* (Boston, 1910), *Down north on the Labrador* (New York, 1911), *The adventure of life* (Boston, 1912), *Tales of the Labrador* (Boston, 1916), *Labrador days* (Boston, 1919), *A Labrador doctor* (Boston, 1919), *Northern neighbors* (Boston, 1923), *Yourself and your body* (New York, 1924), *Labrador looks at the Orient* (Boston, 1928), *Forty years for Labrador* (Boston, 1932), and *The romance of Labrador* (New York, 1934); he was joint author, with others, of *Labrador, the country and the people* (New York, 1909), and he compiled *A Labrador logbook* (Boston, 1938).

[J. Reason, *Deep-sea doctor* (London, 1942); E. H. Hayes, *Forty years on the Labrador* (New York, 1930); F. L. Waldo, *With Grenfell on the Labrador* (New York, 1920); J. Johnston, *Grenfell of Labrador* (London, n.d.); A. G. Hall, *Doctor Wilfred Grenfell* (London, n.d.); *Who was who*, 1929-40 (London, 1941); *Can. who's who*, 1936-37; Morgan, *Can. men* (1912).]

Grey, Albert Henry George Grey, fourth Earl (1851-1917), governor-general of Canada (1904-11), was born in St. James's Palace, London, England, on November 28, 1851, the son of General Charles Grey, private secretary to Prince Albert, and afterwards to Queen Victoria. He was educated at Harrow and at Trinity College, Cambridge (B.A., 1873); and in 1880 he was elected, as a Liberal, to represent South Northumberland in the British House of Commons. He succeeded his uncle, Henry, third Earl Grey, in the earldom in 1894; and from 1894 to 1897 he was administrator of

Rhodesia. In 1904 he was appointed governor-general of Canada; and he proved to be one of the most popular governors Canada has had. His term of office was twice extended, at the request of the Canadian government; and he left Canada only in the autumn of 1911. His later years were occupied with work of a public-spirited character, such as appealed to him; and he was also president of Armstrong College, Newcastle-on-Tyne. He died on August 29, 1917. In 1877 he married Alice, daughter of Robert Stayner Holford, M.P.; and by her he had one son and two daughters. In 1916 he became chancellor of the order of St. Michael and St. George; and he was an honorary LL.D. of Cambridge University, McGill University, and Queen's University, Kingston, and an honorary D.C.L. of Oxford University.

[Harold Begbie, *Albert, fourth Earl Grey* (London, 1918); Sir A. MacPhail, *Lord Grey in Canada* (Canadian century, 1911); *Dict. nat. biog.*, supp. III; *Annual register*, 1917; O. D. Skelton, *The life and letters of Sir Wilfrid Laurier* (2 vols., Toronto, 1922).]

Grey Owl (pseud.). See **Belaney, Archibald Stansfeld.**

Grier, Sir Edmund Wyly (1862-1957), painter, was born in Melbourne, Australia, on November 26, 1862. He came to Canada in 1876, and was educated at Upper Canada College, Toronto. Later he studied art in London at the Slade School of Art under Legros, in Rome at the Scuola Libera, and in Paris at the Académie Julien under Bouguereau and Robert-Fleury. He returned to Canada in 1891, opened a studio in Toronto, and embarked on a long and very successful career as a portrait-painter. He painted the portraits of a large number of Canadian celebrities contemporaneous with him. He became a member of the Ontario Society of Artists in 1896, and was its president from 1908 to 1913; he was elected an A.R.C.A. in 1893, and an R.C.A. in 1894; and he was president of the Academy from 1929 to 1939. The honorary degree of D.C.L. was conferred on him by Bishop's University in 1935; and the same year he was created a knight bachelor, on the recommendation of the Canadian government. He died at Toronto, on December 7, 1957. Several of his paintings are in the National Gallery at Ottawa, including a self-portrait. His memoirs, which he wrote during his last years, are being prepared for publication.

[*Can. who's who*, 1955-57; *Encyc. Can.*; A. Bridle, *Sons of Canada* (Toronto, 1916); Toronto *Globe and Mail*, Dec. 8, 1957.]

Griesbach, William Antrobus (1878-1945), soldier and senator, was born at Fort Qu'Appelle, North West Territories, on January 3, 1878, the son of one of the original officers of the Royal Canadian Mounted Police.

He was educated at St. John's College, Winnipeg; and after having been called to the bar in 1901 (K.C., 1919), practised law in Edmonton. He interrupted his education to serve as a private during the South African War; and he interrupted his legal career to serve throughout the First World War, first with the cavalry, and later with the infantry. He rose to the rank of brigadier-general, and was awarded the D.S.O. in 1916, the C.M.G. in 1918, and the C.B. in 1919. After the war he became inspector-general of the Canadian Army for Western Canada, with the rank of major-general. He was appointed to the Canadian Senate in 1921. He died at Edmonton, Alberta, on January 21, 1945. His reminiscences were published posthumously under the title *I remember* (Toronto, 1946).

[*Can. who's who*, 1938-39; *Can. parl. comp.*, 1944.]

Griffin, Frederick (1889-1946), journalist and author, was born at Castle Blaney, county Down, Ireland, in 1889, and died at Toronto, Ontario, on January 15, 1946. He came to Canada in 1912. In 1916 he obtained employment with the Toronto *Daily Star*, and he continued on the staff of the *Star* and the *Star Weekly*, as reporter and special writer, for the rest of his life. He covered outstanding events all over the world; and he was the author of *Soviet scene* (Toronto, 1932) and *Variety show* (Toronto, 1936).

[Toronto *Globe and Mail*, Jan. 16, 1946.]

Griffin, Martin Joseph (1847-1921), journalist and librarian, was born at St. John's, Newfoundland, on August 7, 1847, the son of Capt. P. Griffin, of the merchant marine. He came to Nova Scotia in 1854, and was educated at St. Mary's College, Halifax. He was called to the bar of Nova Scotia in 1868, and practised law in Halifax. From 1868 to 1874 he was editor of the Halifax *Express*; and from 1881 to 1885 he was editor of the Toronto *Mail*. He was then appointed one of the librarians of parliament at Ottawa, and he held this post until shortly before his death at Ottawa, on March 19, 1921. During his later years he contributed a weekly column of literary criticism to the Montreal *Gazette*, under the caption, "At Dodsley's". He was created a C.M.G. in 1907; and he was an LL.D. of Dalhousie University (1902) and of McGill University (1909).

[*Can. who was who*, vol. 2; Morgan, *Can. men* (1912); *Can. parl. comp.*; Rose, *Cyc. Can. biog.* (1888).]

Griffin, Watson (1860-1952), publicist and author, was born at Hamilton, Ontario, on November 4, 1860, and died at Toronto, Ontario, on January 10, 1952. He was educated in Hamilton, and became a journalist successively in Hamilton, Buffalo, Toronto, and Montreal. In 1916 he entered the service of the Canadian government as superintendent of its

commercial intelligence service, a position from which he retired in 1921. He published two novels: *Twok* (Hamilton, 1887) and *The gulf of years* (Toronto, 1927); and he was the author of *The provinces and the states* (Toronto, 1884), *Canada, the land of waterways* (New York, 1890), and *Canada, the country of the twentieth century* (Ottawa, 1915).

[*Can. who's who*, 1948; Morgan, *Can. men* (1912); Toronto *Globe and Mail*, Jan. 11, 1952.]

Griffiths, James (1825-1896), painter, was born in Newcastle, Staffordshire, England, in 1825; and during the early part of his life worked as a painter of china. He emigrated to Canada in 1854, and for many years lived at London, Ontario. He specialized in painting flowers. He joined the Ontario Society of Artists in 1873; and he became a charter member of the Royal Canadian Academy in 1886. He died on August 10, 1896.

[H. G. Jones and E. Dyonnet, *History of the Royal Canadian Academy of Arts* (Montreal, 1934).]

Grouard, Emile Jean Baptiste Marie (1840-1931), missionary, was born at Brûlon, a small town in the department of La Sarthe, France, on February 2, 1840. He was educated in France and at Laval University, Quebec, having come to Canada in 1860; he joined the Oblate order; and he was ordained a priest of the Roman Catholic Church in 1862. He was sent as a missionary to Fort Chipewyan, Lake Athabaska; and he spent his life ministering to the Indians of the Far North West. He introduced the first printing press into the Peace River district; and he published many hymn books, prayer books, and catechisms, in the languages of the various Indian tribes. He was made titular bishop of Ibora; and from 1910 to 1930 he was vicar apostolic of Athabaska. He died on March 7, 1931, at Grouard, Alberta, a town at the west end of Lesser Slave Lake, called after him. He was the author of *Souvenirs de mes soixante ans d'apostolat dans l'Athabaska Mackenzie* (Lyon, France, 1923).

[Le Jeune, *Dict. gén.*; Allaire, *Dict. biog.*]

Groulx, Lionel Adolphe (1878-1967), historian, was born January 13, 1878, at Chenaux, near Montreal, the son of a lumberjack. He was educated at the Seminary at Ste.Thérèse-de-Blainville and at the Grand Seminary of Montreal and was ordained in 1903. He taught at Valleyfield Seminary before going to Europe for further study in Rome, at the University of Fribourg, in Switzerland, and in Paris. On his return he resumed his teaching at Valleyfield until appointed professor of Canadian history at the University of Montreal in 1915. While at Valleyfield he organized a youth movement which became l'Action Catholique, later part of l'Association de la Jeunesse under the slogan *Notre Maître le* passé. His early writings, *Croisade d'adolescents* (1912); *Le rapaillages — vieilles choses, vieilles gens* (1916); and *Chez nos ancêtres* (1920), were based on his love for the religious and social virtues of the past. He sought to build up the self-esteem of his countryman also by espousing the cause of Dollard des Ormeaux, the legendary hero of the early days of the French settlement, in *Si Dollard revient* (1919). He did not espouse separatism as a cause but rather emphasized the French and Catholic destiny of Francophones in the St. Lawrence Valley and saw Canadian history as a constant struggle of the French to survive the overwhelming pressure and animosity of the British conquerors. He was the founder of a school of historical writing based on the theme of survival. Among his most important works are *Nos lettres constitutionnelles* (five parts, 1915-16); *La Confédération canadienne, ses origines* (1918). *Histoire du Canada français depuis la découverte* (4 parts, 1950-52) was his major work. He also wrote two novels, *L'appel de la race* (1922) and *Au Cap Blomidon* (1932), under the pseudonym "Alonie de Lestres". He was the founder of the Institut d'Histoire de l'Amérique Française (1946) and the *Revue d'Histoire de l'Amerique française* (1947). He was elected to the Royal Society of Canada in 1918, was awarded the Tyrrell Medal of the society in 1948, and resigned in 1952. He died at Montreal, Quebec, May 23, 1967.

[*Can. who's who*, 1955-57; *Encyc. Can.* (1972); N. Story, *The Oxford companion to Canadian history and literature* (Toronto, 1967); A. Laurendeau, *L'Abbé Groulx* (Montreal, 1939).]

Grove, Frederick Philip (1879-1948), writer and teacher, included in a number of his books references to his early life which were considered to be autobiographical. However, research by Douglas Spettigue of Queen's University has made it almost certain that Grove was born Felix Paul Greve, of German parentage, at Radomno on the German-Polish border on February 14, 1879. He grew up in Hamburg, attended the University of Bonn, and travelled as a student to Munich and to Rome. He worked as a freelance writer and translator from 1902 until he came to Canada in 1909 or 1910. He began teaching in rural Manitoba in 1912 and became principal of Gladstone High School at Gladstone, Manitoba. His wife taught at Falmouth, thirty miles away, and Grove, who made the journey between the towns each week-end, was inspired to write of his experience in *Over prairie trails* (1922) and *The turn of the year* (1923). He moved to Ottawa in 1929 to become for a year editor of the Graphic Press. He then bought a farm at Simcoe, Ontario, where he lived until his death in 1948. He received the Lorne Pierce Medal of the Royal Society in 1934 and became a Fellow of the Royal Society in 1941. His *In search of myself* won a Gov-

ernor General's Award, and the Universities of Manitoba and Western Ontario conferred honorary degrees on him. He published eight novels, *Settlers of the marsh* (New York, 1925), *A search for America* (Ottawa, 1927), *Our daily bread* (Toronto, 1930), *The Yoke of Life* (1930), *Fruits of the earth* (Toronto, 1933), *Two generations* (Toronto, 1939), *The Master of the mill* (Toronto, 1944), and *Consider her ways* (Toronto, 1947), as well as three books of essays, *Over prairie trails* (Toronto, 1922), *The turn of the year* (Toronto, 1923), and *It needs to be said* (Toronto, 1929), and a semi-autobiographical work, *In search of myself* (Toronto, 1946).

[D. Pacey, *Frederick Philip Grove* (Toronto, 1945); D. Pacey (ed.), *Frederick Philip Grove* (Toronto, 1970); D. O. Spettigue, *Frederick Philip Grove* (Toronto, 1969); D. O. Spettigue, *F.P.G.: The European Years* (Ottawa, 1973).]

Guèvremont, Germaine *née* **Grignon** (1900-1968), novelist, was born at St. Jérôme, Quebec. She was educated in Quebec and at Loretto Abbey in Toronto. After her marriage to Hyacinthe Guèvremont she lived at Sorel, Quebec, where she became a correspondent for the Montreal *Gazette*. She also wrote short stories with a Sorel background. In 1935 she moved to Montreal and published a book of her stories as *En plein terre* (1942); she followed this with a novel, *Le survenant* (1945), and a sequel, *Marie-Didace* (1947). The two novels were translated into English as one book, *The outlander* (Toronto, 1950), and known as *Monk's reach* in the English edition. She received the Governor General's award for *The outlander* in 1950 and was elected a fellow of the Royal Society of Canada in 1961. She died at Montreal, August 21, 1968.

[R. Leclerc, *Germaine Guèvremont* (1963); *Can. who's who*, 1961-63; *Encyc. Can.* (1972); *Proc. and Trans. Roy. Soc. Can.* (1969).]

Gugy, Bartholomew Conrad Augustus (1796-1876), soldier and politician, was born at Three Rivers, Lower Canada, on November 6, 1796, the son of the Hon. Louis Gugy (q.v.). He was an officer in the Canadian Fencibles during the War of 1812, and was present at the battle of Châteauguay. In 1822 he was called to the bar of Lower Canada; and from 1831 to 1838 he sat in the Legislative Assembly of the province as member for Sherbrooke. He was a vigorous champion of the government; and he played a prominent part in crushing the rebellion of 1837. In 1838 he was appointed police magistrate of Montreal, and in 1841 adjutant-general of the militia of Lower Canada. From 1848 to 1851 he again represented Sherbrooke in the Legislative Assembly, and he was a bitter opponent of Lord Elgin (q.v.). In 1853 he removed from Montreal to Quebec; and he died at Beauport, near Quebec, on June

11, 1876. Up to the time of the abolition of the seigniorial tenure in 1854, he was seignior of Yamachiche, Rivière du Loup, Grandpré, Grosbois, and Dumontier.

[P. G. Roy, *B.-C.-A. Gugy* (Bull. rech. hist., 1904); D. R. Barry, *An eminent Quebec lawyer of the last century* (Canadian law times, 1912); *Dict. Can. biog.*, vol. 10.]

Gugy, Conrad (1730-1786), legislative councillor of Quebec, was born at The Hague, Holland, in 1730, the eldest son of a Swiss officer in the Dutch army. He obtained a commission in the British army, and took part in the conquest of Canada in 1759-60. He settled in Canada after the conquest, and in 1764, purchased several seigniories. In 1775 he was appointed a member of the Legislative Council; and during the later years of the American Revolution he had charge of the Loyalists' concentration camp at Yamachiche. He died in 1786, and left his estates to his younger brother, Barthélemi Gugy, an officer in the French army.

[N. Caron, *Les Gugy au Canada* (Bull. rech. hist., 1900).]

Gugy, Louis (1770-1840), legislative councillor of Lower Canada, was born in Paris, France, in 1770, the son of Barthélemi Gugy, an officer in the Swiss Guard of the French army. He came to Canada with his father about 1786, on the death of his uncle Conrad Gugy (q.v.), whose properties his father inherited. In the War of 1812 he commanded the third battalion of the incorporated militia of Lower Canada. From 1816 to 1818 he was a member of the Legislative Assembly of Lower Canada; and in 1818 he was appointed a member of the Legislative Council. In his later years he was sheriff of Montreal. He died on July 17, 1840.

[N. Caron, *Les Gugy au Canada* (Bull. rech. hist., 1900).]

Guibord, Joseph (d. 1869), printer, was a member of the Canadian Institute of Montreal who died in Montreal on November 19, 1869. Since the members of the Canadian Institute were at this time under excommunication by the Roman Catholic bishop, the priest of the parish of Notre Dame refused Guibord burial in consecrated ground. Guibord's widow, Henriette Brown, at the instance of the Canadian Institute, brought action in the courts to compel the church to grant her husband burial in the plot belonging to him. The action became a *cause célèbre*, and ran the gamut of the courts until in 1874 the Judicial Committee of the Privy Council found finally in favour of the widow.

[T. Hudon, *L'Institut canadien de Montréal et l'affaire Guibord* (Montreal, 1938); *History of the Guibord case* (Montréal, 1875); J. S. Willison, *Sir Wilfrid Laurier and the Liberal party* (2 vols., To-

ronto, 1903); Le Jeune, *Dict. gén.*; L. C. Clark, *The Guibord affair* (Toronto, 1971).]

Guigues, Joseph Eugène Bruno (1805-1874), first Roman Catholic bishop of Ottawa, was born in France on August 26, 1805. He entered the Oblate order, and was ordained a priest in 1828. In 1844 he was sent to Canada as acting superior. In 1847 he was appointed the first bishop of Bytown (Ottawa); and in 1856 he was appointed as provincial in charge of missions. He died at Ottawa on February 8, 1874.

[R. P. Alexis, *Histoire du diocèse d'Ottawa* (2 vols., Ottawa, 1898); Le Jeune, *Dict. gén.*; Allaire, *Dict. biog.*; *Bull. rech. hist.*, 1926; *Dict. Can. biog.*, vol. 10.]

Guillet, Edwin Clarence (1898-1975), historian, was born at Cobourg, Ontario, September 29, 1898, and educated at the University of Toronto (B.A., 1922) and at McMaster University (B.A., 1926; M.A., 1927). He joined the staff of Lindsay Collegiate in 1923 and of the Central Technical School in Toronto in 1926, remaining until 1934. From 1958 to 1962 he served as research historian with the Ontario Department of Public Records and Archives. In 1963 he was appointed consultant on Canadiana to the Library of Trent University, a position he held until his death. Guillet began *Early life in Upper Canada* (1933) in order to provide teaching material for courses in Ontario history. He followed this with *Toronto: from trading post to great city* (1934); *The great migration* (1937); *Lives and times of the patriots* (1938); *The pathfinders of North America* (1939); *Pioneer travel* (1939); *Pioneer arts and crafts* (1940); *This man hanged himself* (1944); *Life insurance without exploitation* (1946); *Pioneer life in the county of York* (1946); *Pioneer inns and taverns* (1954-56); *Pioneer Cobourg, 1780-1948* (1948); *Centennial history of the Ontario Educational Association* (1960); and many others. He died on June 27, 1975, in Toronto, Ontario

[M. Clogg (ed.), *A Bio-bibliography of Dr. Edwin C. Guillet* (Kingston: Douglas Library, Queen's University, 1970).]

Gunn, Donald (1797-1878), fur-trader and historian, was born in Halkirk, Caithnessshire, Scotland, in September, 1797. He entered the service of the Hudson's Bay Company in 1813, and was stationed successively at York Factory, at Severn, and at Oxford House. He left the service of the Company in 1823, and settled in the Red River colony. For about twenty years he was one of the judges of the court of petty sessions in Assiniboia, and for a time he was president of the court. In 1871 he was appointed a member of the Legislative Council of Manitoba, and he sat in the council until its abolition in 1876. He died at St. Andrew's, Manitoba, on November 30, 1878. In 1819 he married Margaret, daughter of James Swain, of York Factory. He contributed a number of papers on the natural history of the North West to the *Miscellaneous collections* of the Smithsonian Institution; and he collaborated with C. R. Tuttle in a *History of Manitoba from the earliest times* (Ottawa, 1880).

[Isabel E. Henderson, *Donald Gunn on the Red River Settlement* (Can. mag., April, 1922); *Dom. ann. reg.; Can. parl. comp.; Cyc. Am. biog.*; A. Begg, *History of the north-west* (3 vols., Toronto, 1894); *Dict. Can. biog.*, vol. 10.]

Gurd, Norman St. Clair (1870-1943), lawyer and author, was born at Sarnia, Ontario, on November 27, 1870. He was educated at Trinity University, Toronto (LL.B., 1896), and was called to the bar of Ontario in 1894. He practised law in Sarnia; but took an interest in literary matters, and was in 1906-08 president of the Ontario Library Association. He died at Sarnia, Ontario, on July 16, 1943. He was the author of *The story of Tecumseh* (Toronto, 1912).

[*Can. who's who*, 1936-37; Morgan, *Can. men* (1912).]

Gurnett, George (1792?-1861), journalist, was born at Horsham, Sussex, England, about 1792. He came to America as a young man, and prior to 1826 lived in Richmond, Virginia. About 1826 he settled in Ancaster, Upper Canada; and there he published from 1827 to 1828 the *Gore Gazette*. In 1829 he founded in York (Toronto) the *Courier of Upper Canada*; and he continued publication of this paper until 1837. In 1837, and again in 1848, 1849, and 1850, he was mayor of Toronto; and in 1851 he became police magistrate of Toronto. He died at Toronto on November 7, 1861.

[J. E. Middleton, *The municipality of Toronto: a history* (3 vols., Toronto, 1923); W. S. Wallace, *The periodical literature of Upper Canada* (Can. hist. rev., 1931).]

Gussow, Hans Theodor (1879-1961), botanist, was born at Breslau, Germany, August 24, 1879. He was educated at Breslau and at Queen's University, Kingston, Ontario. He came to Canada in 1909 and became a botanist at the Dominion Experimental Farm, Ottawa, in 1909 and Dominion botanist in 1911, a post which he held until his retirement in 1944. He was a fellow of the Royal Society of Canada and of many international horticultural and botanical societies. He died at Victoria, British Columbia, June 15, 1961. He wrote *Mushrooms and toadstools*, with W. S. Odell (Ottawa, 1927).

[*Can who's who*, 1955-57.]

Guthrie, Hugh (1866-1939), minister of justice for Canada (1930-35), was born at Guelph, Ontario, on August 13, 1866, the son of Donald Guthrie. He was educated at Os-

goode Hall Law School, Toronto, and was called to the Ontario bar in 1888 (K.C., 1902). He represented South Wellington in the Canadian House of Commons continuously from 1900 to 1935, at first as a Liberal, but after 1917 as a Unionist or Conservative. He was appointed solicitor-general of Canada in the Union government of 1917; and from 1920 to 1921 he was minister of militia and defence. He was minister of national defence in the short-lived Meighen administration of 1926; and in 1930 he was appointed minister of justice in the Bennett administration. He retired from this post in 1935, to accept appointment as chief commissioner of the Board of Railway Commissioners for Canada. He died at Ottawa, Ontario, on November 3, 1939.

[*Can. who's who*, 1938-39; *Can. parl. comp.*; Morgan, *Can. men* (1912).]

Guthrie, Norman Gregor (1877-1929), poet, was born in Guelph, Ontario, in 1877, the son of Donald Guthrie, and brother of the Hon. Hugh Guthrie (q.v.). He was educated at McGill University (B.A., 1897) and at Osgoode Hall, Toronto; and was called to the bar in 1902. He practised law in Ottawa, and he died at Ottawa on December 1, 1929. He was the author of *The poetry of Archibald Lampman* (Toronto, 1927), and under the pen-name of "John Crichton" he published four volumes of poetry, *A vista* (Montreal, 1921), *Flower and flame* (Toronto, 1924), *Pillar of smoke* (Toronto, 1925), and *Flake and petal* (Toronto, 1928).

[*Canadian bookman*, 1930.]

Guy, John (d. 1628?), colonizer, was a citizen of Bristol, England, and was sheriff of Bristol in 1605-06 and mayor in 1618-19. He represented Bristol in the House of Commons for two terms, 1620-22, 1624-25. In 1609 he published an appeal for the colonization of Newfoundland, and persuaded James I to grant a charter to the "Company of Adventurers and Planters of London and Bristol", authorizing it to found a colony in the eastern and southern parts of Newfoundland. In 1610 Guy took out a party of thirty-nine colonists, and established a colony at Cupid's, Newfoundland. He made a second visit to Newfoundland in 1612; but in 1613 he returned to England, leaving the colony to perish.

[*Dict. nat. biog.; Encyc. Can.; Newfoundland supp.*; J. R. Smallwood (ed.), *The book of Newfoundland* (2 vols., St. John's, 1937; *Dict. Can. biog.*, vol. 1.]

Guy, Louis (1768-1850), legislative councillor of Lower Canada, was born in Montreal on June 28, 1768. He studied law, and became in 1801 a notary public. From 1830 to 1838 he was a member of the Legislative Council of Lower Canada. He died at Montreal on February 17, 1850.

[*Notice sur la famille Guy* (Montreal, 1867).]

Guyard, Marie. See **Marie de l'Incarnation.**

Gwynne, John Wellington (1814-1902), judge, was born at Castleknock, county Dublin, Ireland, on March 30, 1814, the eldest son of the Rev. William Gwynne, D.D. He was educated at Castleknock school and at Trinity College, Dublin, and came to Canada in 1832. He was called to the bar of Upper Canada in 1837 (Q.C., 1850), and practised law in Toronto. In 1868 he was appointed a puisne judge of the Court of Common Pleas, and in 1879 a puisne judge of the Supreme Court of Canada. He died at Ottawa on January 7, 1902. In 1852 he married Julia, daughter of Dr. William Durie; and by her he had one son.

[D. B. Read, *Lives of the judges* (Toronto, 1888).]

Gye, Mme. Marie Louise Emma Cécile, alias **Albani,** *née* **Lajeunesse** (1847-1930), prima donna, was born at Chambly, Quebec, on September 24, 1847, the daughter of Joseph Lajeunesse and Melina Mignault. She was educated at the Convent of the Sacred Heart, Montreal, and studied singing in Paris, France, and Milan, Italy. She made her *début* at Messina in 1870, under the name of "Albani"; and she became an opera-singer of world-wide repute. She died at London, England, on April 1, 1930. In 1878 she married Ernest Gye, impresario; and she had one son. She was the subject of some famous verses by W. H. Drummond (q.v.), entitled "When Albani Sang".

[H. Charbonneau, *L'Albani* (Montreal, 1938); *Americana annual*, 1930; *Bull. rech. hist.*, 1931.]

Gzowski, Sir Casimir Stanislaus (1813-1898), civil engineer and financier, was born in St. Petersburg, Russia, on March 5, 1813, the son of Stanislaus, Count Gzowski, a Polish officer in the Imperial Russian Guard. He studied military engineering in Russia, and entered the Russian army; but in November, 1830, he joined the Poles in the expulsion of the Grand Duke Constantine, Governor of Poland, from Warsaw. He was wounded, captured, imprisoned, and exiled. In 1833 he arrived in New York; and the next eight years he spent in the United States. In 1841 he came to Toronto, Upper Canada, and received employment as an engineer with the Canadian department of public works. In 1848 he left the government service, and in 1853 he organized the firm of Gzowski and Company, which obtained the contract for building the Grand Trunk from Toronto to Sarnia. At a later date (1871-73) he built the international bridge at Niagara. He died at Toronto, on August 24, 1898. In 1839 he married Maria Beebe, daughter of an American physician; and by her had five sons and three daughters. He was a lieutenant-colonel in the militia, and in 1879 he was appointed honorary A.D.C. to the Queen, with the rank of colonel. In 1890 he was created a K.C.M.G. He was the first president of the Canadian Society of Civil Engineers.

[*Can. who was who*, vol. 2; Morgan, *Can. men* (1898); Rose, *Cyc. Can. biog.* (1886); Dent, *Can. port.*, vol. 3; O. D. Skelton, *The life and times of Sir A. T. Galt* (Toronto, 1920); L. Kos-Rabcewicz-Zubhowski and W. E. Greening, *Sir Casimir Stanislaus Gzowski: a biography* (Toronto, 1959).]

Haanel, Eugene Emil Felix Richard (1841-1927), scientist, was born at Breslau, Silesia, in 1841. He was educated at Breslau University (Ph.D., 1872), and came to America as a young man. From 1872 to 1890 he was professor of natural history at Victoria University, Cobourg; and he founded, at Cobourg, Faraday Hall, the first science hall in Canada. He was subsequently for twenty years superintendent and then director of mines at Ottawa; and he died at Ottawa on June 26, 1927. He was a charter member of the Royal Society of Canada; and he was the author of *Peat as a source of fuel* (Ottawa, 1918), as well as of numerous contributions to scientific journals.

[*Proc. Roy. Soc. Can.*, 1928; Morgan, *Can. men* (1912).]

HacKenley, John (1877-1943), Anglican archbishop of Halifax, was born at Colne, Lancashire, England, on August 4, 1877; and was educated at King's College, Windsor, Nova Scotia. He was ordained a priest of the Church of England in Canada in 1905; and, after serving in several parishes in Nova Scotia, was elected bishop of Nova Scotia in 1925. Later, he became archbishop of Nova Scotia and metropolitan of the ecclesiastical province of Canada. He died at La Have, Nova Scotia, on November 15, 1943. He was not married.

[*Can. who's who*, 1938-39.]

Hagarty, Sir John Hawkins (1816-1900), chief justice of Ontario (1884-97), was born in Dublin, Ireland, on December 17, 1816, the son of Matthew Hagarty. He was educated at Trinity College, Dublin, but came to Canada before graduation, and settled in Toronto in 1835. He was called to the bar of Upper Canada in 1840 (Q.C., 1850); and in 1856 he was raised to the bench as a puisne judge of the Court of Common Pleas. In 1862 he was appointed a judge of the Court of Queen's Bench; in 1868, chief justice of the Common Pleas; in 1878, chief justice of the Queen's Bench; and in 1884, president of the Court of Appeal, with the title of chief justice of Ontario. He retired from the bench in 1897; and he died at Toronto on April 26, 1900. In 1897 he was created a knight bachelor. He married in 1843, Anne Elizabeth, daughter of

Dr. Henry Grasett, of Toronto. He was a writer of occasional verses, some of which appeared in the *Maple leaf*, an annual founded by the Rev. John McCaul (q.v.) in 1847. Later in life a poem by him, entitled *A legend of Marathon*, was printed for private circulation (Toronto, 1888).

[Morgan, *Can. men* (1898); Rose, *Cyc. Can. biog.* (1886); Dent, *Can. port.*, vol. 4; N. F. Davin, *The Irishman in Canada* (Toronto, 1877); *Can. law review*, 1900.]

Hagel, Nathaniel Francis (1846-1915), lawyer, was born at Hagel's Corner, near Ingersoll, Canada West, on February 9, 1846. He was called to the bar in 1873, and for eight years practised law in Toronto, Ontario; then he removed to Winnipeg, Manitoba, and here he became one of the most successful criminal lawyers in Canada. Of seventy-six prisoners accused of murder who were defended by him, only one was convicted. He died at Winnipeg, Manitoba, on January 17, 1915.

[R. St. G. Stubbs, *Lawyers and laymen of western Canada* (Toronto, 1939).]

Hagerman, Christopher Alexander (1792-1847), judge, was born at Adolphustown, Upper Canada, on March 28, 1792, the son of Nicholas Hagerman, a United Empire Loyalist. He was educated at Kingston, Upper Canada, and was called to the bar of Upper Canada in 1815. During the War of 1812 he was an aide-de-camp of the governor-general; and in 1815 he was appointed a member of the Executive Council of Upper Canada. From 1819 to 1840 he was almost continuously a member of the Legislative Assembly. In 1828 he was appointed a judge of the Court of King's Bench; but the appointment was not confirmed, and in 1829 he was compensated with the appointment of solicitor-general of Upper Canada. In 1837 he was appointed attorney-general of the province; and in 1840 he received his patent as a judge of the Court of Queen's Bench. He died at Toronto on May 14, 1847. He was three times married, (1) to Elizabeth Macaulay, sister of Sir James B. Macaulay (q.v.), by whom he had one daughter, (2) to Emily Merry, by whom he had one daughter, and (3) to Caroline Tysen. He was regarded as one of the pillars of the "Family Compact".

[D. B. Read, *The lives of the judges of Upper Canada* (Toronto, 1888); J. C. Dent, *The Upper Canadian rebellion* (2 vols., Toronto, 1885).]

Haggart, John Graham (1836-1913), postmaster-general of Canada (1888-92) and minister of railways and canals (1892-96), was born in Perth, Upper Canada, on November 14, 1836, the son of John Haggart and Isabella Graham. He was educated in Perth, and entered his father's milling business. In 1872 he was elected as Conservative member for South Lanark in the Canadian House of Commons, and he continued to represent this constituency until his death. In 1888 he became postmaster-general in the Macdonald government, and he held this portfolio until 1892; he then became minister of railways and canals, and this office he held, except for a few days in January, 1896, until the resignation of the Tupper government in July, 1896. In 1892, on the appointment of Sir Mackenzie Bowell (q.v.) to the Senate, he became leader of the Ontario Conservatives in the House; and he was in 1896 one of the "bolters" who resigned from the Bowell cabinet. Throughout the period of the Laurier administration he was a prominent member of the Conservative opposition in parliament; and he died at Ottawa on March 13, 1913. He married Caroline, daughter of Robert Douglas, of Perth.

[Morgan, *Can. men* (1912); *Can. who's who* (1910); *Can. parl. comp.*; J. Castell Hopkins, *Life and work of the Rt. Hon. Sir John Thompson* (Brantford, Ont., 1895); Sir J. Pope (ed.), *Correspondence of Sir John Macdonald* (Toronto, 1921).]

Hague, Dyson (1857-1935), clergyman and author, was born in Toronto on April 20, 1857, the second son of George Hague (q.v.). He was educated at the University of Toronto (B.A., 1880; M.A., 1881), and at Wycliffe College, Toronto; and was ordained a priest of the Church of England in 1883. He was successively rector of churches in Brockville, Ontario, in Halifax, Nova Scotia, in London, Ontario, and in Toronto, Ontario. He retired from parochial work in 1933, and he died in hospital at Galt, Ontario, on May 6, 1935. In 1884 he married May, daughter of Robert Baldwin, and granddaughter of the Hon. Robert Baldwin (q.v.). He was the author of *The protestantism of the Prayer Book* (Toronto, 1890), *The Church of England before the Reformation* (London, 1897), *The story of the English Prayer Book* (London, 1926; 2nd ed., London, 1930), *Through the Prayer Book* (London, 1932), and a number of pamphlets on religious subjects.

[*Who's who in Canada*, 1934-35; Morgan, *Can. men* (1912).]

Hague, George (1825-1915), general manager of the Merchants Bank of Canada (1877-

1902), was born at Rotherham, Yorkshire, England, on January 13, 1825, the son of John Hague. He came to Canada in 1854, and entered the service of the Bank of Toronto. From 1863 to 1876 he was cashier of the Bank of Toronto; and from 1877 to 1902 he was general manager of the Merchants Bank. He died at Montreal, Quebec, on August 26, 1915. He was the author of *The banking of Canada* (Ottawa, 1897), *Practical studies from the Old Testament* (Toronto, n.d.), and *Banking and commerce* (New York, 1908).

[Morgan, *Can. men* (1912).]

Hague, John (1829-1906), author and journalist, was born at Rotherham, England, on March 3, 1829, the younger brother of George Hague (q.v.). He came to Canada as a young man, and was appointed secretary of the Interoceanic Railway. He later became a journalist, and in his later days was editor of the *Trade Review* and the *Financial Chronicle*, Montreal. He died at Montreal on August 19, 1906. He was the author of *Canada for the Canadians* (Toronto, 1889).

[Morgan, *Can. men* (1898).]

Hahn, Emanuel Otto (1881-1957), sculptor, was born in Württemberg, Germany, on May 30, 1881, and came to Canada with his parents in 1888. He was educated in Toronto at the local schools, and received his first training in art at the Central Ontario School of Art in Toronto. Later he studied at Stuttgart in Germany. He opened a studio in Toronto, and became perhaps the best-known sculptor in Canada. He was elected a member of the Ontario Society of Artists in 1925, an A.R.C.A. in 1927, and an R.C.A. in 1930. He executed the memorials to Edward Hanlan and Sir Adam Beck (qq.v.) in Toronto; and examples of his sculpture are to be found in the National Gallery at Ottawa, in the Toronto Art Gallery, and in the Royal Ontario Museum. He died at Toronto on February 14, 1957.

[Charles Comfort, *Emanuel Otto Hahn* (Canadian Art, Summer, 1957); *Can. who's who*, 1955-57; *Encyc. Can.*; Toronto *Globe and Mail*, Feb. 15, 1957.]

Hahn, Gustav (1866-1962), artist, was born in Germany, July 27, 1866. He studied at Stuttgart, Munich, and in Italy. He came to Canada in 1888. He was for many years a teacher and head of the Department of Interior Design at the Ontario College of Art, retiring in 1946. He also conducted classes at the Royal Ontario Museum. He was a member of the Royal Academy (A.R.C.A., 1901; R.C.A., 1905); and of the Ontario Society of Artists. He died at Toronto, Ontario, December 4, 1962.

[C. S. MacDonald, *A dictionary of Canadian artists,* vol. 2 (Ottawa, 1968).]

Hahn, James Emanuel (1892-1955), soldier and industrialist, was born in New York

City on July 30, 1892, of German-speaking parents. He came to Ontario with his parents in 1898, and was educated in Berlin (later Kitchener) and at the University of Toronto. He served as an intelligence officer in the First World War, was twice wounded, and was awarded the M.C. in 1915, and the D.S.O. in 1918. He was called to the bar in Ontario in 1920, but he soon turned from law to business. He became the president of the John Inglis Company in Toronto, which supplied munitions, such as the Bren gun, for the Canadian army in the Second World War. He died at his summer home at Campbellton, New Brunswick, on August 31, 1955. He was the author of two books: *The intelligence service within the Canadian Corps* (Toronto, 1930), and an autobiography entitled *For action* (Toronto, 1954).

[Toronto *Globe and Mail*, Sept. 1., 1955; *Can. who's who*, 1952-54.]

Hahn, Paul (1875-1962), ornithologist, was born in 1875 in Stuttgart, Germany. He was a brother of Emanuel Otto Hahn (q.v.) and Gustav Hahn (q.v.). He joined the Nordheimer Piano Company when he came to Canada in 1888 and was also a professional cellist. From 1928 to 1934 he was Canadian representative for Steinway pianos and remained chairman of this company until his death. An ardent naturalist, he lectured at the Royal Ontario Museum on extinct and vanishing birds. He died at Balsam Lake, Ontario, July 20, 1962.

[Metropolitan Toronto Library Board, *Biographical scrapbooks*, vol. 20.]

Haight, Canniff (1825-1901), author, was born at Adolphustown, Upper Canada, on June 4, 1825, the son of Shadrick Ricketson Haight and Mary Canniff. He was educated at the Picton grammar school and at Victoria College, Cobourg, and for a time studied medicine. He became, however, a chemist and bookseller in Picton, Ontario. Later, he removed to Toronto; and he was employed to copy at the Library of Congress in Washington the manuscript reports of the royal commissioners on United Empire Loyalist claims. He died in Toronto on June 25, 1901. In 1852 he married Jane Casey, daughter of Isaac Ingersoll, of Fredericksburg; and by her he had several children. He published *Country life in Canada fifty years ago* (Toronto, 1885), *Here and there in the home land* (Toronto, 1895), and *A genealogical narrative of the Daniel Haight family* (Toronto, 1899).

[Morgan, *Can. men* (1898); *United Empire Loyalists' Association, Transactions*, vol. 4.]

Haines, Frederick Stanley (1879-1960), painter and gallery director, was born at Meaford, Ontario, in 1879. He attended the Central Ontario School of Art under William Cruikshank (q.v.) and George A. Reid (q.v.); studied at Antwerp under Jules de Vrient; and

won a gold medal in figure painting. He became secretary of the department of graphic art at the Canadian National Exhibition in 1919 and commissioner in 1924. He was curator of the Art Gallery of Toronto from 1928 until his appointment as principal of the Ontario College of Art in 1932, a post which he retained until his retirement in 1951. Haines did not work in abstract or non-objective styles himself but retained an open mind towards all kinds of painting. He brought the work of Dali and Picasso to the Canadian National Exhibition in the 1930s and during the Second World War was responsible for having Canadian paintings reproduced for servicemen's hostels and lounges. He was a man who enjoyed life whether it was expressed in music, art, golf, or in conversations with his friends. He is represented by paintings in the National Gallery of Canada, at Hart House in the University of Toronto, at Meaford High School (18 paintings) and Thornhill High School (14 paintings), the I.B.M. collection, and others. He died at Toronto, Ontario, in November, 1960.

[C. S. MacDonald, *A dictionary of Canadian artists*, vol. 2 (Ottawa, 1968); J. A. B. McLeish, *September gale* (Toronto, 1956).]

Haldane, John (d. 1857), fur-trader, was a native of Scotland who entered the service of the XY Company about 1798; and he was one of the XY traders who became partners of the North West Company in 1804. In 1804 he was at Red Lake and Lac Seul; from 1806 to 1812 he was at Monontagué; from 1812 to 1813 at the Pic; from 1813 to 1814 on the Athabaska River; and from 1814 to 1815 on the Churchill River. In 1817 Ross Cox (q.v.) met him at Fort William. In 1821, on the union of the North West and Hudson's Bay companies, he was made a chief factor, and was placed in charge of the Columbia district, to which he had already been transferred. In 1823 he was brought east to take charge of the Lake Superior district, and he remained in charge of this district until his retirement from the fur-trade in 1827. He died in Edinburgh, Scotland, on October 11, 1857.

[W. S. Wallace (ed.), *Documents relating to the North West Company* (Toronto: The Champlain Society, 1934).]

Haldimand, Sir Frederick (1718-1791), governor-in-chief of the province of Quebec (1778-86), was born in the canton of Neuchâtel, Switzerland, on August 11, 1718, the son of François Louis Haldimand and Marie Madelaine de Trytorrens. He became a soldier of fortune in various armies in Europe, among others in the army of Frederick the Great of Prussia; and in 1756 he took service in the British army, as a lieutenant-colonel in the Royal Americans. He served in America throughout the Seven Years' War; and from 1762 to 1764 was military lieutenant-governor of the district of Three Rivers in

Canada. In 1767 he was appointed to command the southern district of North America, and for the next six years his headquarters were in Florida. In 1773-74 he was commander-in-chief at Boston, but his foreign birth rendered him unsuitable for high command in America during the Revolution, and in 1774 he was recalled to England.

He succeeded Sir Guy Carleton (q.v.) as governor of the province of Quebec in 1778. His period of office in Canada, coinciding as it did with the alliance between Old France and the American revolutionists, was one of especial difficulty, and some of the measures he was forced to adopt in coping with disaffection in Canada were somewhat arbitrary. But his measures for the defence of the province were eminently successful; and his arrangements for placing on the land the loyalists who flocked into Canada at the close of the American Revolution were a model of efficient organization. At the end of 1784 Haldimand returned to England on leave of absence; and in 1786 he was succeeded as governor by Sir Guy Carleton (q.v.). He died at Yverdun, Switzerland, near his birthplace, on June 5, 1791.

In 1772 he was promoted to be a major-general in America, and in 1776 to be a general in America; in 1777 he became lieutenant-general in the army; and in 1785 he was created a K.B. He was not married.

[Jean N. McIlwraith, *Sir Frederick Haldimand* (Toronto, 1904); J. M. LeMoine, *Le général Sir Frederick Haldimand à Québec* (Trans. Roy. Soc. Can., 1888); W. Smith, *The struggle over the laws of Canada, 1763-1783* (Can. hist. rev., 1920); F. J. Audet, *Sir Frédéric Haldimand* (Trans. Roy. Soc. Can., 1923). The Haldimand papers are in the British Museum (Addit. MSS., 21661-21892); and copies of them are in the Canadian Archives, and are calendared in the Archives Reports, 1884-89.]

Hale, Edward (1800-1875), legislative councillor of Quebec, was born in Quebec on December 6, 1800, the second son of the Hon. John Hale (q.v.). He was educated in England, and from 1823 to 1828 was military secretary to his uncle, Lord Amherst, the governor-general of India. On his return to Canada, he settled at Sherbrooke, Lower Canada. He was appointed a member of the Special Council of Lower Canada in 1839, and from 1841 to 1847 he represented Sherbrooke in the Legislative Assembly of United Canada. In 1867 he was appointed a member of the Legislative Council of the province of Quebec, and he retained his seat until his death at Quebec on April 26, 1875. In 1831 he married Eliza Cecilia, daughter of the Hon. Edward Bowen (q.v.), and by her he had seven children. He must be distinguished from Edward Hale, of Portneuf, who was also a member of the Special Council of 1839, and who died in 1862.

[*Can. parl. comp.*; *Dict. Can. biog.*, vol. 10.]

Hale, Horatio (1817-1896), ethnologist, was born at Newport, New Hampshire, on May 3, 1817, the son of David and Sara Josepha Hale. He was educated at Harvard University (B.A., 1837), and in 1837 was appointed philologist of the Wilkes expedition to the Pacific Islands. In 1856 he came to Canada, and settled at Clinton, Canada West; and here he died on December 28, 1896. In 1886 he was elected president of the anthropological section of the American Association for the Advancement of Science; and he published, in addition to many papers contributed to learned periodicals, *The Iroquois book of rites* (Philadelphia, 1883) and *An international idiom, a manual of the Oregon trade-language or Chinook jargon* (London, 1890). In 1854 he married Margaret, daughter of William Pugh, sometime of Goderich township, Huron county, Upper Canada.

[*Cyc. Am. biog*; Rose, *Cyc. Can. biog.* (1886); *Proc. Roy. Soc. Can.*, 1897.]

Hale, Jeffrey (1803-1864), philanthropist, was born at Quebec, Lower Canada, on April 19, 1803, the son of the Hon. John Hale (q.v.). He entered the Royal Navy, but retired with the rank of captain, and founded in Quebec the Quebec Savings Bank. He died at Tunbridge Wells, Kent, England, in November, 1864; and by his will he left a bequest for the foundation of the Jeffrey Hale Hospital in Quebec.

[*La famille Hale* (Bull. rech. hist., 1932).]

Hale, John (1765-1838), receiver-general of Lower Canada (1824-38), was born in England in 1765, the son of General John Hale, who had been with Wolfe (q.v.) at Quebec. He came to Canada in 1793 as military secretary to the Duke of Kent, and in 1799 he was appointed paymaster-general of the forces in Canada. In 1808 he was sworn of the Legislative Council of Lower Canada, and in 1820 of the Executive Council. From 1824 to his death he was receiver-general of Lower Canada. He died at Quebec on December 24, 1838. In 1798 he married, in London, Elizabeth Frances, daughter of General William Amherst, and sister of Earl Amherst, governor-general of India in 1825; and by her he had eight sons and four daughters.

[J. Desjardins, *Guide parlementaire historique de la province de Québec* (Quebec, 1902); *La famille Hale* (Bull. rech. hist., 1932).]

Hale, Katherine (pseud.). See **Garvin, Mrs. Amelia Beers,** *née* **Warnock.**

Haliburton, Robert Grant (1831-1901), lawyer and author, was born at Windsor, Nova Scotia, on June 3, 1831, the son of the Hon. Thomas Chandler Haliburton (q.v.). He was educated at King's College, Windsor (M.A., 1852; D.C.L., 1876), and was called to the bar of Nova Scotia in 1853 (Q.C., 1876). He practised law in Halifax until 1877, and in Ottawa from 1877 to 1881. Ill health then compelled him to give up the practice of law, and to spend his winters in tropical or semi-tropical climates. He was one of the founders of the "Canada First" party; and his pamphlet on *Intercolonial trade* (Ottawa, 1868) foreshadowed the adoption of the National Policy. In his later years he became interested in anthropology and ethnology; and in 1887 he discovered the existence of a race of pigmies in North Africa, an account of which was published by him under the title, *The dwarfs of mount Atlas* (London, 1891). He was the author of numerous papers and lectures on political, economic, and scientific subjects, and he published a small volume of poems, entitled *Voices from the Street* (Halifax, N.S.). He died, unmarried, at Pass Christian, Missouri, on March 7, 1901.

[Morgan, *Bib. can.* and *Can. men* (1898); C. C. James, *A bibliography of Canadian poetry* (Toronto, 1899); W. S. Wallace, *The growth of Canadian national feeling* (Toronto, 1927).]

Haliburton, Thomas Chandler (1796-1865), judge and author, was born at Windsor, Nova Scotia, on December 17, 1796, the son of the Hon. William Otis Haliburton and Lucy Grant. He was educated at King's College, Windsor (B.A., 1815), and was called to the bar of Nova Scotia in 1820. He began the practice of law in Annapolis, and in 1826 he was elected to represent Annapolis in the Legislative Assembly of Nova Scotia. In 1829 he was appointed a judge of the Court of Common Pleas, and in 1841 a judge of the Supreme Court of the province. In 1856 he retired from the bench, and removed to England. In 1859 he was elected to represent Launceston in the British House of Commons; and he represented this constituency until his death at Gordon House, Isleworth, on the Thames, England, on August 27, 1865. In 1816 he married Louisa (d. 1840), daughter of Captain Lawrence Neville, of the 19th Light Dragoons; and in 1856 Sarah Harriet, daughter of William Mostyn Owen, of Woodhouse, Shropshire, and widow of Edward Hosier Williams, of Eaton Mascott, Shrewsbury. In 1858 he was made an honorary D.C.L. of Oxford University.

As an author, Haliburton's first efforts were historical. His first book was his *Historical and statistical account of Nova Scotia* (2 vols., Halifax, 1829). In 1835, however, he turned to the writing of humorous fiction, in a series of papers contributed to the *Nova Scotian*, under the pseudonym of "Sam Slick". These were republished in book form in three series, under the title *The clockmaker; or, The sayings and doings of Sam Slick of Slickville* (Halifax, 1836; London, 1838; London, 1840); and became widely popular, being pirated under various titles in the United States, and translated into several languages. These volumes were followed by *The attaché; or, Sam Slick in En-*

gland (4 vols., London, 1843-44) and *Sam Slick's wise saws and modern instances* (2 vols., London, 1853). Other humorous works published by him were *The letter-bag of the Great Western; or, Life in a steamer* (Halifax, 1840), *Traits of American humour by native authors* (3 vols., London, 1852), *The old judge; or, Life in a colony* (2 vols., London, 1849), *The Americans at home; or, Bye-ways, backwoods, and prairies* (3 vols., London, 1854, *Nature and human nature* 2 vols., London, 1855), and *The season ticket* (London, 1860). Among his more serious publications, mostly political in character, were *The bubbles of Canada* (London, 1839), *A reply to the report of the Earl of Durham* (London and Halifax, 1840), and *Rule and misrule of the English in America* (2 vols., London, 1851).

[V. L. O. Chittick, *Thomas Chandler Haliburton* (New York, 1924); J. D. Logan, *Thomas Chandler Haliburton* (Toronto, 1925); *Haliburton, a centenary chaplet* (Toronto, 1897); F. Blake Crofton, *Haliburton, the man and the writer* (Windsor, N.S., 1889); A. H. O'Brien, *Haliburton, a sketch and bibliography* (Trans. Roy. Soc. Can., 1908); *Dict. nat. biog.*; *Cyc. Am. biog*; Rose, *Cyc. Can. biog.* (1888).]

Halkett, John (1768-1852), author, was born, probably in Scotland, in 1768. He was elected a member of the Committee of the Hudson's Bay Company; and in 1815 he married Lady Katherine Douglas, sister of the Earl of Selkirk (q.v.). He was Lord Selkirk's personal representative in England during Lord Selkirk's absence in Canada from 1815 to 1818; and he published the *Statement respecting the Earl of Selkirk's settlement of Kildonan* (London, 1917), as well as the *Correspondence in the years 1817, 1818, and 1819 between Earl Bathurst and J. Halkett, Esq., on the subject of Lord Selkirk's settlement at the Red River* (London, 1819) and *The narratives of John Pritchard, Pierre Chrysologue Pambrun, and Frederick Damien Huerter, respecting the aggressions of the North-West Company, against the Earl of Selkirk's settlement upon Red River* (London, 1819). In 1822 he visited Canada as the representative of the Selkirk estate; and he presided at a meeting of the Council of the Northern Department of Rupert's Land, held at York Factory in 1822. On his return to England, he published *Historical notes respecting the Indians of North America* (London, 1825); and he continued for many years to serve on the committee of the Hudson's Bay company. He died at Brighton, England, on November 12, 1852. Fort Halkett, on the Liard River in the North West Territories, and Cape Halkett, in Alaska, were named after him.

[W. S. Wallace, *Lord Selkirk's ghost writer* (Beaver, 1940); E. E. Rich (ed.), *Journal of occurrences in the Athabasca department, by George Simpson* (Toronto: The Champlain Society, 1938).]

Hall, Frank (1895-1972), labour leader, was born in Norfolk, England. He came to Canada in 1913 and worked in Montreal as a labourer before becoming a freight checker with the Canadian Pacific Railway. He organized a union among the checkers in 1918. In 1925 he became international vice-president of the Brotherhood of Railway and Steamship Clerks. He was well known as a union negotiator and was elected general chairman of the Conference Committee representing fifteen non-operating and three operating railway unions in 1947. In 1952 he was elected a member of the General Council of the International Transport Workers Federation and became a member of the executive in Berne, Switzerland, in 1960. He led the fight for a job freeze on Canadian Railways in the 1960s when it was recognized that technological change would result in a reduction in railway jobs, and this resulted in the establishment of a job security fund to lessen the impact of a technological change on workers. He died at Montreal, Quebec, May 18, 1972.

[*Can. who's who*, 1967-69; *Canadian Labour*, vol. 17, number 6 (June, 1972).]

Hallam, Douglas (1883-1948), airman and author, was born in Toronto, Ontario, on October 10, 1883, and died there on December 10, 1948. He was educated at Upper Canada College; and he served in the First World War, first as a private in a machine-gun battery, and then as a commissioned officer in the R.N.A.S. and the R.A.F. He was awarded the D.F.C., with two bars, was mentioned in dispatches five times, and was wounded at Gallipoli. Under the pseudonym "P.I.X.", he was the author of *The spider web: The romance of a flying-boat war flight* (Edinburgh, 1919). After the war he was for many years secretary of a mercantile association in Toronto.

[Toronto *Globe and Mail*, Dec. 15, 1948; *Can. who's who*, 1948.]

Hallett, Henry (1772?-1844), fur-trader, was born in England about 1772, and was a nephew of Philip Turnor (q.v.). He entered the service of the Hudson's Bay Company as a writer in 1793, but was dismissed from the Company's service in 1810 because of his "atrocious cowardly murder of an Indian". He then entered the service of the North West Company as a clerk; and he was taken over as a clerk by the Hudson's Bay Company at the union of 1821. He retired from the fur-trade in 1822, and he lived at the Red River settlement until 1843. He died in March, 1844.

[W. S. Wallace (ed.), *Documents relating to the North West Company* (Toronto: The Champlain Society, 1934).]

Halliburton, Sir Brenton (1775-1860), chief justice of Nova Scotia (1833-60), was born in Rhode Island on December 3, 1775, the son of John Halliburton, a loyalist who settled in Nova Scotia during the American Revolution. He studied law in England and was called to the bar of Nova Scotia in 1803. In 1807 he was appointed to the bench; in 1816 he became a member of the Council of Twelve in Nova Scotia; and in 1833 he was promoted to be chief justice of the province. He died near Halifax, Nova Scotia, on July 15, 1860. In 1799 he married the eldest daughter of the Right Rev. Charles Inglis (q.v.). He was created a knight bachelor in 1859. A frequent contributor to the press, his most notable publication was a series of letters on the War of 1812, published in 1813 in the Halifax *Recorder*, under the pseudonym "Anglo-American", and he was the author also of *Observations on the importance of the North American colonies to Great Britain* (Halifax, 1825; London, 1831), and *Reflections on passing events: A poem* (Halifax, privately printed, 1856).

[Rev. G. W. Hill, *Memoir of Sir Brenton Halliburton* (Halifax, 1864); D. Campbell, *Nova Scotia* (Montreal, 1873); Peter Lynch, *Early reminiscences of Halifax* (Coll. Nova Scotia Hist. Soc., 1912); Morgan, *Bib. can.*]

Halliburton, John Croke (1806-1884), clerk of the Legislative Council of Nova Scotia (1838-84), was born in Halifax, Nova Scotia, in 1806, the eldest son of Sir Brenton Halliburton (q.v.). He was called to the bar of Nova Scotia in 1829, and in 1838 he was appointed clerk of the Legislative Council—a position he held for the rest of his life. As a young man, he fought a bloodless duel in the Tower Woods, near Halifax, with Joseph Howe (q.v.). He died at Halifax on November 7, 1884.

[*Dom. Ann. reg.*, 1884.]

Hallowell, James (1778-1816), merchant, was the second son of James Hallowell (q.v.), and was born in 1778, probably in England. He came to Canada with his parents as an infant; and became connected, like his father and elder brother William (q.v.), with the firm of McTavish, Frobisher and Co. He died at Brooklyn, Long Island, in the United States, on November 29, 1816. He married a daughter of Daniel Sutherland (q.v.); and William Hallowell, M.D. (1814-1863), of Toronto, of whom there is a sketch in William Canniff, *The medical profession in Upper Canada* (Toronto, 1894), would appear to have been his son.

[W. S. Wallace (ed.), *Documents relating to the North West Company* (Toronto: The Champlain Society, 1934).]

Hallowell, James (1748?-1830), merchant, was born in England about 1748. He was a relative, and probably a cousin, of the Benjamin Hallowell who died in York, Upper Canada, in 1799, and after whom Hallowell (now Picton) was named. He came to Canada about 1780; and in 1787 he became a partner in the firm of McTavish, Frobisher and Co. He continued to be a partner in this firm, and consequently a member of the North West Company, until about 1810, when he had a disagreement with his partners, and withdrew. He died at Bedford, England, on April 20, 1830, at the age of 82. He had seven children, all of whom died young, except two, William (q.v.) and James (q.v.).

[W. S. Wallace (ed.), *Documents relating to the North West Company* (Toronto: The Champlain Society, 1934).]

Hallowell, William (1771-1838), merchant, was the eldest son of James Hallowell (q.v.), and was born, probably in England, on August 17, 1771. He came to Canada with his parents about 1780; and in 1802 he became a junior partner in the firm of McTavish, McGillivrays and Co., and a partner in the North West Company. About 1810, he had, with his father, a disagreement with his partners in McTavish, McGillivrays and Co., and withdrew from the fur-trade. He died at Montreal in September, 1838. He married in Albany, New York, on February 8, 1798, Martha Henry; and by her he had three sons and two daughters. His eldest son, James (1796-1858), became a member of the Montreal bar, and practised law at Sherbooke, in the Eastern Townships; and his elder daughter, Elizabeth (1799-1866), married the Rev. John Bethune, dean of Montreal, and brother of Angus Bethune (q.v.).

[W. S. Wallace (ed.), *Documents relating to the North West Company* (Toronto: The Champlain Society, 1934).]

Halton, Matthew (1904-1956), journalist and broadcaster, was born at Pincher Creek, Alberta, on September 7, 1904, and died at London, England, on December 3, 1956. He was educated at the University of Alberta (B.A., 1929) and at the University of London. He became a journalist with the Toronto *Daily Star*, and reported for it the events of the Second World War. From 1944 to his death he was the European correspondent for the Canadian Broadcasting Corporation. In 1945 he was awarded the O.B.E. for his services as a war correspondent. He was the author of *Ten years to Alamein* (Toronto, 1944).

[*Can. who's who*, 1952-54; *Encyc. Can.*; Toronto *Globe and Mail*, Dec. 4, 1956.]

Halton, William (d. 1821), provincial agent for Upper Canada in London (1816-21), was secretary to Francis Gore (q.v.), when lieutenant-governor of Upper Canada, from 1806 to 1811 and from 1815 to 1816. On his return to England in 1816, he was appointed agent for Upper Canada. He died in London, England, in 1821.

[H. F. Gardiner, *Nothing but names* (Toronto, 1899).]

Ham, Albert (1858-1940), musician, was born at Bath, England, on June 7, 1858. He was educated at Trinity College, Dublin (Mus.D., 1894), and he came to Canada in 1897 as organist and choirmaster of St. James Cathedral, Toronto. He retained this position until his return to England in 1933; and while he was in Canada, he was an outstanding figure in the musical world. He was the founder and conductor of the National Chorus; and he was for many years on the staff of the Toronto Conservatory of Music. He died at Brighton, England, on February 7, 1940. In 1906 he received the degree of Mus.D. from the University of Toronto; and in 1934 that of D.C.L. from Bishop's University, Lennoxville. He was the author of *Outlines of musical form* (London, 1920) and *The rudiments of music and elementary harmony* (London, 1920).

[*Can. who's who*, 1938-39.]

Ham, George Henry (1847-1926), journalist and author, was born at Trenton, Canada West, on August 23, 1847, the son of Dr. J. V. Ham. He was educated at the Whitby Grammar School, and he began life as a journalist on the staff of the Whitby *Chronicle* in 1865. In 1875 he went to Winnipeg, and he was a journalist there until 1891. He then entered the service of the Canadian Pacific Railway as advertising manager; and he spent the rest of his life in the employ of the Canadian Pacific. He died at Montreal on April 16, 1926. He was the author of *The new west* (Winnipeg, 1888), *The flitting of the gods* (Toronto, 1906), *Reminiscences of a raconteur* (Toronto, 1921), and *The miracle man of Montreal* (Toronto, 1922).

Can. who was who, vol. 1; Morgan, *Can. men* (1912).]

Hamber, Eric Werge (1880-1960), lieutenant-governor of British Columbia (1936-41), was born in Winnipeg, Manitoba, on April 21, 1880, and died at Vancouver, British Columbia, on January 10, 1960. He was educated at St. John's College, Winnipeg, and at the University of Manitoba (B.A., 1898). He entered the Dominion Bank, and became manager successively at Calgary, Vancouver, and London, England. In 1913 he left the bank and went into business in British Columbia. He became a director of the Canadian Pacific Railway and other corporations. From 1936 to 1941 he was lieutenant-governor of British Columbia. He was chancellor of the University of British Columbia from 1944 to 1951; and he was created a C.M.G. in 1946.

[*Can. who's who*, 1958-60; *Encyc. Can.*]

Hambleton, Jack (1901-1961), author, was born in Staffordshire, England, in 1901. His family came to Canada in 1902 and settled at Valleyfield, Quebec, where Jack began his schooling. He left school at 13 and worked at Detroit as a machinist before joining the U.S. Expeditionary Force to Siberia in 1919. He was later stationed in the Philippines and Hawaii with the United States Marines. He returned to Canada in 1921 and became a dock worker at Sarnia. He worked his way through business college and then joined the Canadian Press as a reporter. In 1934 he became director of the Ontario Travel and Publicity Bureau. In 1938 he joined the Toronto *Star*, and later worked as a columnist for the *Globe and Mail*. An outdoorsman, Hambleton wrote eleven books for juveniles. His last book, *Fire in the valley* (1960), was included as one of a hundred best books for juveniles selected by the *New York Times*. He died at Toronto, Ontario, October 25, 1961.

[Metropolitan Toronto Library Board, *Biographical scrapbooks*, vol. 18.]

Hamel, Théophile (1817-1870), painter, was born at Ste. Foy, Lower Canada, on November 8, 1817, and studied drawing at Quebec under Antoine Plamondon (q.v.). In 1844 he went to Europe, and studied in Italy. On his return to Canada he was in great demand as a portrait-painter, and executed portraits of the members of the Baldwin-Lafontaine ministry, and of the speakers of the Legislative Council and Legislative Assembly, both before and after the union, as well as many others. He painted also a number of church pictures and some compositions from Canadian history. His work marked a distinct advance on that of his predecessors. He died at Quebec, on December 23, 1870.

[*Bull. rech. hist.*, 1913; Bibaud, *Panth. can.*; E. Morris, *Art in Canada: The early painters* (Toronto, 1911).]

Hamel, Thomas Etienne (1830-1913), priest, was born at Quebec, Lower Canada, on December 28, 1830, the son of Victor Hamel and Thérèse De Foy. He was educated at Quebec, and was ordained a priest of the Roman Catholic Church in 1854. From 1871 to 1880 and from 1883 to 1886 he was rector of Laval University, Quebec; and later was librarian. In 1886 he was appointed an apostolic prothonotary in the diocese of Quebec. He died in Quebec on July 16, 1913. He was a charter member of the Royal Society of Canada; and he was the author of *Le premier cardinal canadien* (Quebec, 1888) and *Un cours d'éloquence parlée* (Quebec, 1906).

[*Proc. Roy. Soc. Can.*, 1914; Morgan, *Can. men* (1912); Allaire, *Dict. biog.*; Le Jeune, *Dict. gén.*]

Hamil, Frederick Coyne (1903-1968), historian, was born at Ridgetown, Ontario, January 20, 1903. He was educated at Queen's University (B.A., 1925; M.A., 1926), Columbia University (B.S., 1927), and the University of Michigan (M.A., 1931; Ph.D. 1933). He served as library assistant at the University of Michigan (1927-36) and as assistant librarian at Carleton College (1936-37). He began teaching at Wayne State University in 1937, becoming a full professor in 1956. He died December 24, 1968. His publications included, *The valley of the lower Thames, 1640-1850* (Toronto, 1951), *Lake Erie baron: The story of Colonel Talbot* (Toronto, 1955).

[*Can. hist. rev.*, vol. L.]

Hamilton, Sir Charles, Bart. (1767-1849), governor of Newfoundland (1818-24), was born on July 6, 1767, the son of John Hamilton, who was created a baronet for his gallant conduct at the siege of Quebec in 1774. He was educated at the Royal Naval Academy at Portsmouth, entered the Royal Navy, and rose to the rank of admiral in 1830. In 1784, on his father's death, he succeeded to the baronetcy, and in 1833, he was created a K.C.B. From 1818 to 1824 he was governor of Newfoundland, and it was during his régime that Newfoundland was given colonial status.

[*Dict. nat. biog.*; *Encyc. Can.*; *Newfoundland supp.*]

Hamilton, Charles (1834-1919), Anglican archbishop of Ottawa and metropolitan of Canada (1909-15), was born at Hawkesbury, Upper Canada, on January 6, 1834, the fourth son of Lieut.-Col. George Hamilton and Lucy Craigie. He was educated at the Montreal High School, and at University College, Oxford (B.A., 1856; M.A., 1859); and he was ordained a deacon of the Church of England in 1857, and a priest in 1858. From 1885 to 1896 he was bishop of Niagara; and from 1896 to 1909, first bishop of Ottawa; and from 1909 to 1915, archbishop of Ottawa and metropolitan of Canada. He died at La Jolla, California, on March 14, 1919. He was a D.D. of Lennoxville University (1885), a D.C.L. of Trinity University, Toronto (1885), and a D.D. of the University of King's College, Nova Scotia. In 1862 he married Frances Louisa Hume, daughter of Tannatt Houston Thomson; and by her he had four sons and five daughters.

[C. H. Mockridge, *The bishops of the Church of England in Canada* (Toronto, 1896); W. H. Bradley, *The life of the Most Rev. Charles Hamilton* (Journal of the Canadian Church Historical Society, 1961); *Can. who was who*, vol. 1; Morgan, *Can. men* (1912); *Who's who and why* (1917-18); E. M. Chadwick, *Ontarian families*, vol. 1 (Toronto, 1894).]

Hamilton, Charles Frederick (1869-1933), journalist and author, was born at Roslin, Ontario, on December 7, 1869, the son of Charles Samuel Hamilton, M.D., C.M., and Alice, daughter of G. E. Jacques, of Montreal. He was educated at Queen's University (M.A., 1890), and in 1891 became a journalist. He served successively on the Toronto *World, Star, Globe,* and *News*; and in 1899-1900 he acted as war correspondent of the Toronto *Globe* in South Africa. During the later years of his life he was on the staff of the Royal Canadian Mounted Police. He died at Ottawa on December 4, 1933. He collaborated with W. L. Grant in *The life of Principal Grant* (Toronto, 1904); and he contributed accounts of the military history of Canada to A. Shortt and A. G. Doughty (eds.), *Canada and its provinces* (23 vols., Toronto, 1913), and to the *Canadian Defence Quarterly*, 1928.

[Morgan, *Can. men* (1912).]

Hamilton, Henry (d. 1796), lieutenant-governor of Quebec (1782-85), was a British army officer of Irish descent who entered the army in 1754. He served throughout the Seven Years' War; and in 1775 he was appointed lieutenant-governor of Detroit. He was captured by George Rogers Clark at Vincennes in 1779, and was sent as a prisoner to Virginia, but was exchanged in 1780. In 1782 he was appointed lieutenant-governor of Quebec, and in 1784 on Haldimand's departure for England, he became administrator of the province, and reversed Haldimand's policy in regard to the introduction of English laws. In 1785 he was superseded by Henry Hope (q.v.), and he left Canada. He was later governor of the Bermudas and of Dominica; and he died at Antigua on September 29, 1796.

[N. V. Russell, *The Indian policy of Henry Hamilton* (Can. hist. rev., 1930); *Cyc. Am. biog.*; Morgan, *Cel. Can.*]

Hamilton, James Cleland (1836-1907), author, was born at Belfast, Ireland, on May 21, 1836, the son of the Rev. William Hamilton and Anna Patterson, and the nephew of the Hon. Christopher Salmon Patterson (q.v.). He was educated at Hanover College and Rutgers College, and at the University of Toronto (LL.B., 1861), and he was called to the bar of Upper Canada in 1861. He practised law in Toronto for many years; and he died in Toronto in February, 1907. He was the author of *The prairie province* (Toronto, 1876) and *The Georgian bay* (Toronto, 1893), as well as of a number of papers contributed to the proceedings of the Royal Canadian Institute, of which he was an active member.

[Morgan, *Can. men* (1898).]

Hamilton, John (1802-1882), senator and ship-owner, was born at Queenston, Upper Canada, in 1802, the youngest son of Robert Hamilton (q.v.) and Mary Herkimer. He was educated in Edinburgh, Scotland; and he went into business in Canada, first in Montreal, and after 1840 in Kingston. He was the pioneer, and for many years the dominant figure, in the business of steam navigation on Lake Ontario and the upper St. Lawrence. In 1831 he was called to the Legislative Council of Upper Canada; in 1841 to the Legislative Council of United Canada; and in 1867 to the Senate of Canada, of which he was for fifteen years the senior member. He died at Kingston, Ontario, on October 10, 1882. He married Frances Pasia, daughter of David Macpherson; and by

her he had seven sons and four daughters.

[*Dom. ann. reg.*, 1882; *Can. parl. comp.*; Rose, *Cyc. Can. biog.* (1886); E. M. Chadwick, *Ontarian families,* vol. 1 (Toronto, 1894).]

Hamilton, John (1827-1888), senator and lumberman, was born near Quebec in 1827, the third son of Lieut.-Col. George Hamilton of Hawkesbury and Lucy Susannah Christiana Craigie. He was educated at Montreal; and he became the head of the lumbering firm of Hamilton Brothers, and proprietor of the Hawkesbury mills. In 1860 he was elected to the Legislative Council of Canada for the "Inkerman" district; and in 1867 he was called to the Senate of Canada. He resigned from the Senate in May, 1887; and he died on April 3, 1888. He married (1) Rebecca, daughter of John Lewis, (2) Ellen Marion, daughter of William Wood, and (3) Jean, daughter of Charles Cambie, and widow of John Major. By his first wife he had two sons and two daughters; and by his second wife two sons and three daughters.

[Rose, *Cyc. Can. biog.* (1886); *Can. parl. comp.*; Taylor, *Brit. Am.*, vol. 3; E. M. Chadwick, *Ontarian families*, vol. 1 (Toronto, 1894).]

Hamilton, Pierce Stevens (1826-1893), journalist and author, was born at Brookfield, Colchester county, Nova Scotia, on January 23, 1826. He was educated at Acadia College, Wolfville; and in 1852 he was called to the bar of Nova Scotia. He drifted from law to journalism, and from 1853 to 1861 he was the editor of the Halifax *Acadian Recorder*. In 1863 he was appointed gold commissioner, and in 1864 chief commissioner of mines for Nova Scotia. He died on February 22, 1893. He was a foremost advocate in Nova Scotia of the union of the British North American provinces, and he published a number of brochures which helped to prepare in Nova Scotia the way for Confederation: *Observations upon a union of the colonies of British North America* (Halifax, N.S., 1855), *A union of the colonies of British North America considered rationally* (Halifax, N.S., 1856), *Letter to his grace the duke of Newcastle upon a union of the colonies of British North America* (Halifax, N.S., 1860), *Union of the colonies of British North America* (Halifax, N.S., 1861), and *A review of Hon. Joseph Howe's essay entitled "Confederation considered in relation to the interest of the Empire"* (Halifax, N.S., 1866). He published also a volume of verse, *The feast of Ste. Anne, and other poems* (Montreal, 1878 and 1890).

[Morgan, *Bib. can.*; C. C. James, *A bibliography of Canadian poetry* (Toronto, 1899); M. Josephine Shannon, *Two forgotten patriots* (Dalhousie review, 1934); W. B. Hamilton, *P. S. Hamilton, the forgotten confederate* (Coll. Nova Scotia Hist. Soc., 1968).]

Hamilton, Robert (1750-1809), merchant and legislative councillor, was born on February 25, 1750, the son of the Rev. John Hamilton (1714-97), minister of Bolton, Scotland, and Jane Wright. He came to Canada during the American Revolutionary War and settled first at Carleton Island, near Kingston, and then on the Niagara River. For a time he was in partnership with Richard Cartwright (q.v.); and he became a general merchant near Queenston, of which he was the founder. He was appointed a member of the Legislative Council of Upper Canada in 1792; and he died at Niagara on March 8, 1809. He married (1) Catherine Askin (d. 1796), widow of John Robertson, and (2) Mary Herkimer, widow of Neil McLean; by his first wife he had five sons, and by his second three sons. The city of Hamilton, Ontario, was named after his son George (1787-1835), who bought in 1813 a tract of land at the head of Lake Ontario.

[H. F. Gardiner, *The Hamiltons of Queenston, Kingston, and Hamilton* (Ont. Hist. Soc., papers and records, 1907); E. M. Chadwick, *Ontarian families*, vol. 1 (Toronto, 1894).]

Hammond, Melvin Ormond (1876-1934), journalist and author, was born at Clarkson, Peel county, Ontario, on July 17, 1876. He joined the staff of the Toronto *Globe* in 1895, and he served on this paper until his death at Toronto on October 7, 1934. He was the author of *Confederation and its leaders* (Toronto, 1917) and *Canadian footprints* (Toronto, 1926).

[*Can. who was who*, vol. 2; Morgan, *Can. men* (1912).]

Hamond, Sir Andrew Snape, Bart. (1738-1828), lieutenant-governor of Nova Scotia, was born at Blackheath, England, on December 17, 1738; and he died at Lynn, Norfolk, on October 12, 1828. He entered the Royal Navy, and rose to the rank of commodore. From 1780 to 1782 he was lieutenant-governor of Nova Scotia; and in 1783 he was created a baronet.

[*Dict. nat. biog.*]

Hanbury, David Theophilus (1864-1910), explorer and author, was born at East Barnet, near London, England, in 1864, and died near San Francisco, California, in 1910. He was educated at Clifton College, and later studied surveying and geology under the auspices of the Royal Geographical Society. He lived a roving life until a few years before his death, when he purchased an island in San Francisco bay. His most important journeys were in northern Canada. He twice made the journey between Great Slave Lake and Chesterfield Inlet; and his last important journey was from Chesterfield Inlet by the Coppermine River to the Arctic coast, and thence to Great Bear Lake. These journeys he described in his *Sport* and *travel in the Northland of Canada* (London, 1904).

[*Geographical Journal*, vol. 36, p. 738; *Encyc. Can.*]

Hanington, Daniel (1804-1889), speaker of the Legislative Council of New Brunswick (1882-86), was born at Shediac, New Brunswick, in 1804, the son of William Hanington. From 1833 to 1862 he represented Westmorland in the Legislative Assembly of New Brunswick; and in 1850-51 he was a member of the Executive Council. In 1867 he was appointed a member of the Legislative Council of New Brunswick, and from 1882 to 1886 he was its speaker. He died at Shediac, New Brunswick, on May 5, 1889.

[*Can. parl. comp.*]

Hanington, Daniel Lionel (1835-1909), prime minister of New Brunswick (1882-83), was born at Shediac, New Brunswick, on June 27, 1835, the son of Daniel Hanington (q.v.). He was educated at the Sackville Academy, and in 1861 was called to the bar of New Brunswick (Q.C., 1881). From 1870 to 1874, and from 1878 to 1892, he represented Westmorland in the House of Assembly of New Brunswick; in 1878 he became a minister without portfolio in the Fraser administration; and from May, 1882, to February, 1883, he was prime minister of the province. In 1892, he was appointed a puisne judge of the Supreme Court of New Brunswick; and he died at Dorchester, New Brunswick., on May 5, 1909. In 1861 he married Emily Myers, daughter of Thomas Robert Wetmore, Gagetown, New Brunswick; and by her he had three sons and four daughters.

[J. Hannay, *Premiers of New Brunswick* (Can. mag., 1897); Morgan, *Can. men* (1898); Rose, *Cyc. Can. biog.* (1888); *Can. parl. comp.*; *Can. who was who*, vol. 1.]

Hanlan (properly **Hanlon**), **Edward** (1855-1908), oarsman, was born in Toronto, Upper Canada, on July 12, 1855, the son of John Hanlon and Mary Gibbs. He was educated at the public schools, Toronto, and in 1873 he became amateur champion oarsman of Toronto bay. He turned professional in 1876, and defeated all competitors in the Philadelphia races of that year. In 1876 he became champion of Canada, and in 1878 champion of America; and the following year he went to England, where he established a record on the Tyne. In 1880 he won the world's championship on the Thames, and he retained the title until 1884, when he lost it to William Beach, of Australia. Though he continued to race for several years, he did not again win the world's championship. He won, during his career, over 150 races, and was unsurpassed for his finish and style. He died at Toronto on January 4, 1908, and was buried with civic honours. He married on December 17, 1877, Margaret Gordon Sutherland, of Pictou, Nova Scotia, and by her he had two sons and six daughters.

[*Dict. nat. biog.*, supp. II; *Can. who was who*, vol. 2; Morgan, *Can. men* (1912).]

Hanna, David Blythe (1858-1938), railway-builder, was born at Thornliebank, Scotland, on December 20, 1858. He emigrated to Canada in 1882, and entered the employ of the Grand Trunk Railway. Later he joined Sir William Mackenzie (q.v.) and Sir Donald Mann (q.v.) in their first railway enterprise; and in 1902 he was elected third vice-president of the Canadian Northern Railway. In 1918, when the Canadian Northern Railway was taken over by the Canadian government, and incorporated in the Canadian National Railways, he was appointed first president of the board of directors of the Canadian National Railways; and he held this position until 1922. From 1927 to 1928 he was first chairman of the Liquor Control Board of Ontario. He died at Toronto, Ontario, on December 1, 1938. He was the author of an autobiography, *Trains of recollection* (Toronto, 1924).

[*Can. who's who*, 1936-37; Morgan, *Can. men* (1912).]

Hanna, William John (1862-1919), provincial secretary of Ontario (1905-14) and food controller of Canada (1917-18), was born in the township of Adelaide, Middlesex county, Upper Canada, on October 13, 1862, the son of George Hanna, a farmer, and Jane Murdock. He was educated at the public schools and at Osgoode Hall, Toronto, and in 1890 he was called to the Ontario bar (K.C., 1908). He became solicitor for the Imperial Oil Company of Canada, and ultimately its president. In 1902 he was elected to represent West Lambton in the Legislative Assembly of Ontario; and in 1905 he became provincial secretary in the Whitney administration. He held this portfolio until the death of Sir James Whitney (q.v.) in 1914. He then became a minister without portfolio in the Hearst administration. In 1917 he was appointed food controller of Canada by the Dominion government; but ill health compelled his retirement from office in 1918, and he died at Augusta, Georgia, on March 20, 1919. His period of office in Ontario was notable for his work in connection with prison reform. He was twice married, (1) to Jean G. Neil (d. 1891), by whom he had one son, and (2) to Maud McAdams, by whom he had two daughters.

[*Can. parl. comp.*; Morgan, *Can. men* (1912); H. Charlesworth (ed.), *A cyclopaedia of Canadian biography* (Toronto, 1919); *Can. who was who*, vol. 2.]

Hannaford, Michael (1832-1891), painter, was born at Stoke Gabriel, Devon, England, in 1832. He went as a young man to New Zealand, and was there employed in a bank. He came to Canada in 1875, and he spent his later years in Toronto, where he devoted himself chiefly to the painting of landscapes. His best known picture is "Toronto from Norway", now in the Toronto Public Library. He died suddenly in Toronto, on May 7, 1891. He was a member of the Ontario Society of Artists.

[Private information.]

Hannam, Herbert Henry (1898-1963), agriculturalist, was born at Swinton Park, Grey county, Ontario, September 27, 1898. He was educated at the University of Toronto (B.S.A., 1926). Dr. Hannam taught school in northern Saskatchewan in the summer while attending the agricultural college, and while in Saskatchewan he attended the organization meetings of the Saskatchewan wheat pools and became interested in the co-operative movement. On graduation from university he became livestock editor for *Canadian Countryman* and became in succession editorial secretary of the United Farmers of Ontario and then secretary-treasurer of the United Farmers in 1933. In 1935 he was elected first vice-president of the Canadian Chamber of Agriculture at its inaugural meeting and became also the president of the Ontario Federation. In 1940 the Chamber of Agriculture became the Canadian Federation of Agriculture; Hannam had been elected president in 1939. In 1936 he became secretary of the United Farmers' Co-operative and editor of *The Rural Co-operator*. In 1946 he led the Canadian delegation to the first World Farmers' Conference in London, England, which inaugurated the International Federation of Agricultural Producers, and he became the first president. He was a delegate to meetings of the Food and Agricultural Organization of the United Nations and promoted the co-operative idea both in Canada and abroad. He wrote *Co-operation; the plan for tomorrow which works today* (Toronto, 1938), and *Pulling together for twenty-five years* (Toronto, 1940), a brief story of events and people in the United Farmers movement in Ontario during the quarter-century 1914-39. He died at Ottawa on July 12, 1963.

[*Can. who's who*, 1961-63; *Saturday Night*, Dec. 6, 1949.]

Hannan, Michael (1821-1882), Roman Catholic archbishop of Halifax (1877-82), was born at Killmallock, county Limerick, Ireland, on July 20, 1821. He came to Nova Scotia in 1840; and in 1845 he was ordained a priest of the Roman Catholic Church. He became vicar-general of Halifax; and, on the death of Archbishop Connolly (q.v.), he was appointed archbishop of Halifax. He administered the see until his death at Halifax, Nova Scotia, on April 17, 1882.

[*Dom. ann. reg.*, 1882; Dent, *Can. port.*, vol. 3; N. F. Davin, *The Irishman in Canada* (Toronto, 1877); *Can. who was who*, vol. 2.]

Hannay, James (1842-1910), journalist and historian, was born at Richibucto, New Brunswick, on April 22, 1842, the son of the Rev. James Hannay and Jane Salter. He was called to the bar of New Brunswick in 1867, and from 1867 to 1871 he was reporter of the Supreme Court of New Brunswick. He drifted, however, into journalism, and was successively on the editorial staff of the Saint John *Telegraph* (1872-83), the Montreal *Herald* (1883-85), and the Brooklyn *Eagle* (1885-88). He then became editor of the Saint John *Gazette* (1888-93), and of the Saint John *Telegraph* (1893-1901). It is, however, as a historian that he is best known. His first publication was an edition, with introduction and notes, of *Nine years a captive, or John Gyles' experiences among the Melicete Indians from 1689 to 1698* (Saint John, 1875). This was followed by *The history of Acadia* (Saint John, 1879), *The life and times of Sir Leonard Tilley* (Saint John, 1896), *History of the War of 1812* (Toronto, 1905), published also under the title *How Canada was held for the Empire* (London, 1905), *Wilmot and Tilley* (Toronto, 1907), *History of the Queen's Rangers* (Trans. Roy. Soc. Can., 1909), *The history of New Brunswick* (2 vols., Saint John, 1909), and *The heroine of Acadia* (Saint John, 1910). He died at Saint John, New Brunswick, on January 12, 1910. In 1864 he married Margaret, daughter of Elias T. Ross of Saint John. In 1899 he was made a D.C.L. of Acadia University; and in 1906 he was elected a fellow of the Royal Society of Canada.

[*Proc. Roy. Soc. Can.*, 1910; Morgan, *Can. men* (1898); W. G. MacFarlane, *New Brunswick bibliography* (Saint John, N.B., 1895).]

Hanson, Richard Burpee (1879-1948), politician, was born at Bocabec, New Brunswick, on March 20, 1879, and died at Fredericton, New Brunswick, on July 14, 1948. He was educated at Mount Allison University (B.A., 1899) and Dalhousie University (LL.B., 1901), and was called to the bar in 1902 (K.C., 1917). He practised law in Fredericton, and was mayor of Fredericton from 1918 to 1920. He was elected to represent York-Sunbury in the Canadian House of Commons from 1925 to 1935, and from 1940 to 1945; and in 1934-35 he was minister of trade and commerce in the Bennett government. In 1940 he was elected leader of the Conservative opposition in parliament, after the defeat of R. J. Manion (q.v.), but he resigned as leader in 1943.

[*Can. who's who*, 1948; *Can. parl. comp.*, 1942; *Encyc. Can.*]

Hardisty, Richard (1831-1889), senator of Canada, was born in the Upper Ottawa valley, on March 3, 1831, the son and grandson of chief factors of the Hudson's Bay Company. He himself entered the service of the Company,

and for many years was chief factor in charge of the Edmonton district. He was called to the Senate of Canada on February 23, 1888; but he died at Winnipeg, Manitoba, on October 18, 1889.

[E. Taylor, *Hon. Richard Hardisty* (Beaver, Feb., 1924).]

Hardy, Arthur Sturgis (1837-1901), prime minister of Ontario (1896-99), was born at Mount Pleasant, near Brantford, Upper Canada, on December 14, 1837, the son of Russell Hardy and Julietta Sturgis, both of United Empire Loyalist stock. He was educated at the Brant county grammar school and at Rockwood Academy, near Guelph; and he read law in offices in Brantford and Toronto. In 1865 he was called to the bar of Upper Canada, and he practised law in Brantford with much success. From 1873 to 1899 he represented South Brant in the Legislative Assembly of Ontario; and in 1877 he entered the Mowat government as provincial secretary. In 1889 he became commissioner of crown lands, and in 1896, on the resignation of Sir Oliver Mowat (q.v.), prime minister and attorney-general. Ill health compelled his retirement from office in 1899; and he died at Toronto on June 13, 1901. In 1870 he married Mary, daughter of the Hon. J. C. Morrison (q.v.), of Toronto; and by her he had four children.

[*Can. parl. comp.*; *Cyc. Am. biog.*; Dent, *Can. port.*, vol. 2; Rose, *Cyc. Can. biog.* (1886); Morgan, *Can. men* (1898); *Can. who was who*, vol. 1.]

Hardy, Edwin Austin (1867-1952), educationist, was born in New Hampshire on August 30, 1867, and died at Toronto, Ontario, on October 31, 1952. He came to Ontario with his parents in 1869; and he was educated at the schools in Uxbridge and at the University of Toronto (B.A., 1888; D.Paed., 1912). He became a school-teacher, and for ten years before his retirement in 1936 was head of the English department in the Jarvis St. Collegiate in Toronto. He took a wide interest in all phases of education; he was a founder of the Ontario Library Association, and its secretary for a quarter of a century. He was the author of *The public library* (Toronto, 1912) and *Talks on education* (Toronto, 1923). For his services he was awarded the O.B.E. in 1939.

[*Can. who's who*, 1949-51; Toronto *Globe and Mail*, Nov. 1, 1952.]

Hardy, Elias (1744-1798), Loyalist, was born at Farnham, Surrey, England, in 1744. He was called to the bar in 1770, and in 1775 he emigrated to Virginia. He set up in New York as an agent for attending to the claims of the Loyalists; and in 1783 he went in this capacity to Saint John, New Brunswick. He became the leader of the popular or "Lower Cove" party in Saint John; and he died at Saint John on December 25, 1798.

[W. O. Raymond, *A biographical sketch of Elias Hardy* (Trans. Roy. Soc. Can., 1919).]

Hargrave, James (1798-1865), fur-trader, was born in Roxburghshire, Scotland, in 1798. He entered the service of the North West Company in 1820, and was taken over by the Hudson's Bay Company in 1821 as a clerk. He was promoted to the rank of chief trader in 1833, and to that of chief factor in 1844. Most of his service was spent at York Factory. He retired from the service of the Company in 1859, and he died at Burnside House, Brockville, Upper Canada, on or about May 16, 1865. In 1840 he married Letitia Mactavish (d. 1854), a niece of John George McTavish (q.v.), and a sister of William Mactavish, governor of Rupert's Land from 1864 to 1870; and after her death he married, secondly, Margaret Alcock. His son, Joseph James Hargrave (d. 1894), who was also a servant of the Hudson's Bay Company, published a volume entitled *Red River* (Montreal, 1871), in which he made use of the copious papers which his father had preserved.

[G. de T. Glazebrook (ed.), *The Hargrave correspondence* (Toronto: The Champlain Society, 1938).]

Harmon, Daniel Williams (1778-1845), fur-trader and author, was born in Vermont in 1778. He entered the service of the North West Company in 1800; and the next nineteen years he spent in the North West. When he returned to the East in 1819, he brought with him his journals; and these were edited and published by the Rev. Daniel Haskel, of Andover, Massachusetts, under the title *Journal of voyages and travels in the interior of North America* (Andover, 1820). In his later years he settled on the shores of Lake Champlain; and he died in 1845. In 1805 he married in the West a French halfbreed, and by her he had fourteen children. One of his daughters afterwards conducted in Ottawa, Canada, a fashionable girls' boarding-school.

[G. Bryce, *The remarkable history of the Hudson's Bay Company* (London, 1900); L. J. Burpee, *The search for the western sea* (London, 1908); W. S. Wallace (ed.), *Documents relating to the North West Company* (Toronto: The Champlain Society, 1934); *Encyclopedia Americana.*]

Harpe, Charles Eugène (1909-1952), poet, was born in 1909, and died suddenly at Kamouraska, Quebec, on July 31, 1952. He was the author of *Les croix de chair* (Montmagny, 1945) and *Les oiseaux dans la brume* (Montmagny, 1948).

[Montreal *Gazette*, Aug. 1, 1952.]

Harper, John Murdoch (1845-1919), educationist and author, was born at Johnstone, Scotland, on February 10, 1845, the son of Robert M. Harper and Marion Henderson. He was educated in Scotland, and at Queen's University, Kingston, Canada (B.A., 1882), and at the University of Illinois (Ph.D., 1881). He taught school in the Maritime provinces of Canada; and from 1880 to 1886 he was rector of the Quebec Grammar School. From 1886 to 1903 he was inspector of superior schools in the province of Quebec. He then resigned, and devoted himself to literary work. He was a voluminous writer; and among other works he published *Translations in verse from Homer and Virgil* (Montreal, 1888), *The battle of the plains* (Quebec, 1895), *The earliest beginnings of Canada* (Toronto and Quebec, 1901), *The little sergeant* (Quebec, 1905), *Champlain, a drama* (Toronto, 1908), and *The greatest event in Canadian history* (Toronto, 1909). He died at Quebec on March 1, 1919. He was married (1) to Agnes (d. 1883), daughter of William Kirkwood, of Paisley, Scotland; and (2) to Elizabeth, daughter of Andrew Hastings, of Saint John, New Brunswick.

[Morgan, *Can. men* (1912); Rose, *Cyc. Can. biog.* (1888).]

Harper, William Edmund (1878-1940), astronomer, was born at Dobbington, Ontario, on March 20, 1878. He was educated at the University of Toronto (B.A., 1906; M.A., 1907; D.Sc., 1935), and on graduation obtained an appointment on the staff of the Dominion Observatory. In 1924 he was appointed assistant director, and in 1935 director, of the Dominion Astrophysical Observatory at Victoria, British Columbia; and he died at Victoria on June 4, 1940. He was elected a fellow of the Royal Society of Canada in 1924.

[*Proc. Roy. Soc. Can.*, 1941; *Can. who's who*, 1935-37.]

Harrington, Bernard James (1848-1907), mineralogist, was born at St. Andrews, Lower Canada, on August 5, 1848. He was educated at McGill University (B.A., 1869), and at the Sheffield Scientific School of Yale University (Ph.D., 1871); and in 1871 he was appointed lecturer in mining and chemistry at McGill University. He was on the staff of McGill University for thirty-six years; and from 1872 to 1879 he was also on the staff of the Geological Survey of Canada. He died at Montreal on November 29, 1907. In 1876 he married Anna Lois, eldest daughter of Sir J. W. Dawson (q.v.). In addition to a large number of scientific papers, he was the author of *The life of Sir William Logan* (Montreal, 1883).

[*Proc. Roy. Soc. Can.*, 1908; *Can. who was who*, vol. 1; Morgan, *Can. men* (1898).]

Harrington, Gordon Sidney (1883-1943), prime minister of Nova Scotia (1930-33), was born at Halifax, Nova Scotia, on August 7, 1883. He was educated at Dalhousie University (LL.B., 1904), and was called to the bar of Nova Scotia in 1904 (K.C., 1915). He served with the Canadian Expeditionary Force from 1915 to 1920; and from 1918 to 1920 was deputy minister of the Overseas Military Forces of Canada in London, England. He represented Cape Breton in the Legislative Assembly of Nova Scotia from 1925 to 1937. From 1925 to 1930 he was minister of public works and mines in the Rhodes government; from 1930 to 1933 he was prime minister of Nova Scotia; and from 1933 to 1937 he was leader of the Conservative Opposition. He died at Halifax, Nova Scotia, on July 4, 1943.

[*Can. who's who*, 1938-39; *Can. parl. comp.*]

Harriott, John Edward (1797-1866), furtrader, was born in London, England, in 1797, and entered the service of the Hudson's Bay Company in 1809. He was promoted to the rank of chief trader in 1829, and to that of chief factor in 1846. He died at Montreal on February 7, 1866.

[E. E. Rich (ed.), *Colin Robertson's correspondence book* (Toronto: The Champlain Society, 1939).]

Harris, Sir Charles Alexander (1855-1947), governor of Newfoundland (1917-22), was born at Wrexham, Wales, on June 28, 1855, and died on March 26, 1947. He was educated at Christ's College, Cambridge, and read law at Lincoln's Inn. In 1879, however, he entered the British colonial service in which he had a brilliant career. He became chief clerk of the Colonial Office in 1909; and was made governor of Newfoundland in 1917, at the same time being created a K.C.M.G. His period of office ended in 1922; and he retired to private life. He contributed some chapters on Newfoundland to the *Cambridge history of the British Empire*, vol. vi (London, 1930).

[*Who was who*, 1941-50; *Encyc. Can.*; *Newfoundland supp.*]

Harris, Edward William (1832-1925), lawyer and author, was born at Long Point Bay, Lake Erie, Upper Canada, in 1832. He was called to the bar in 1854, and practised law in London, Ontario. He died in London, Ontario, on October 1, 1925. He took an active interest in public affairs; and was the author of *History and historiettes: United Empire Loyalists* (Toronto, 1897), *The quail* (Toronto, 1905), *Canada, the making of a nation* (Toronto, 1907), *A review of civic ownership* (Toronto, 1908), and *Recollections of Long Point* (Toronto, 1918).

[Morgan, *Can. men* (1912).]

Harris, Elmore (1854-1911), clergyman, was born at Brantford, Canada West, on February 23, 1854, the son of John Harris, of the Massey-Harris Company. He was educated at the University of Toronto (B.A., 1877), and became a Baptist minister. He was the pastor of churches in St. Thomas and Toronto, Ontario;

and in 1895 he became president of the Toronto Bible Training College. In 1899 he received the degree of D.D. from McMaster University. He died at Delhi, India, in December, 1911.

[Morgan, *Can. men* (1912).]

Harris, Joseph Hemington (1800-1881), first principal of Upper Canada College, was born in England in 1800, and was educated at Clare College, Cambridge (B.A., 1822; M.A., 1825; D.D., 1829). He was elected a fellow of Clare College, and in 1829 he came to Canada, at the instance of his brother-in-law, Sir J. Colborne (q.v.), as principal of Upper Canada College. He returned to England in 1838; and from 1848 to 1879 he was vicar of Tormohun, Devonshire, England. He died at Torquay, England, on June 29, 1881. While in Canada, he published *A letter to the Hon. and Ven. Archdeacon Strachan* (York [Toronto], 1833) and *Observations on Upper Canada College* (Toronto, 1836).

[*Dom. ann. reg.*, 1880-81.]

Harris, Lawren Stewart (1885-1970), painter, was born at Brantford, Ontario, in 1885, a grandson of Alanson Harris. He was educated at St. Andrew's College, Toronto, and at the University of Toronto. He studied art in Berlin from 1904 to 1908 and travelled in Arabia and Palestine before returning to America, where he did illustrations for *Harper's* magazine. He opened a studio in Toronto in 1910 and upset tradition by using a number of old houses as his models. When he exhibited one of these in 1912 it was considered to be in questionable taste. In 1913, he and J. E. H. MacDonald (q.v.), whom he had met at the Toronto Arts and Letters Club, visited an exhibition of Scandinavian art in Buffalo which impressed them both, and in the summer they went sketching together in the Laurentians. Through the Arts and Letters Club of Toronto he also met F. Johnston, Tom Thomson (q.v.), Tom Maclean, Frank Carmichael (q.v.), F. H. Varley, Arthur Lismer, and later A. Y. Jackson (q.v.). Harris and Dr. James MacCallum co-operated in building the Studio Building, where artists were able to devote their whole time to painting. MacDonald, Thomson, Beatty, Jackson, Harris and others moved into the building in 1914. The outbreak of the war and enlistments in the army broke up the group and Harris was posted to Camp Borden as a musketry instructor, but before the end of 1918 most of the group had reassembled, and, using a box car fitted with a stove and bunks, had ventured into the Algoma region of Ontario on a sketching trip. By 1920 the painters had become loosely organized as the Group of Seven— Harris, MacDonald, Lismer, Varley, Carmichael, Franz Johnston, and A. Y. Jackson. Harris wrote the text for the catalogue of their first joint exhibition at the Art Museum of Toronto in 1920. He stated that the artists here represented "are all imbued with the idea that an art must grow and flower in the land before the country will be a real home for its people". As successive sketching trips took Harris and his friends to the north shore of Lake Superior and to the Rockies, his painting became more spacious, dramatic, stark, and abstract. His paintings of the Canadian Arctic have an awesome quality which may, in part, be attributed to his continuing interest in the metaphysical. He moved to Vancouver in 1942 and continued his fine painting and teaching and was in part responsible for bringing the work of Emily Carr (q.v.) before Canadians. He was the moving force behind the original Group of Seven and of its successor, the Canadian Group of Painters. From 1944 to 1947 he was president of the Federation of Canadian Artists. He died at Vancouver in January, 1970. His paintings are to be found in the National Gallery of Canada, the Art Gallery of Ontario, the Winnipeg Art Gallery, the Art Gallery of Hamilton, the Vancouver Art Gallery, the McMichael Collection at Kleinburg, Ontario, and the Yale University Art Gallery, and in private collections.

[C. S. MacDonald, *A dictionary of Canadian artists*, vol. 2 (Ottawa, 1968); *Lawren Harris paintings, 1910-1948*, biographical introduction by A. Y. Jackson (Art Gallery of Toronto, 1948); R.G.P. Colgrove and Bess Harris (eds.), *Lawren Harris* (Toronto, 1969).]

Harris, Robert (1849-1919), portrait painter, was born in the Vale of Conway, North Wales, on September 17, 1849, the son of William Critchlow Harris and Sarah Stretch. He came with his parents to Prince Edward Island in 1856, and was educated at the Prince of Wales College, Charlottetown. He studied painting in the Slade School, London, England, and under Bonnat in Paris, France. In 1882 he was a charter member of the Royal Canadian Academy, and from 1893 to 1906 he was president of the Academy. His best-known picture was "The fathers of Confederation", which depicts the members of the Quebec Conference of 1864 in session. He painted the portraits of most of the outstanding Canadians of his day, and at the time of his death was regarded as the dean of Canadian artists. He died at Montreal on February 27, 1919. In 1885 he married Elizabeth, daughter of L. N. Putnam, of Montreal. He was created a C.M.G. in 1902.

[*Can. who was who*, vol. 2; Morgan, *Can. men* (1912); *Can. who's who* (1910); N. MacTavish, *The fine arts in Canada* (Toronto, 1925).]

Harris, William Richard (1847-1923), priest and author, was born in Cork, Ireland, on March 3, 1847, and came to Canada with his parents at an early age. He was educated at St.

Michael's College, Toronto, and at Ste. Anne's College, Quebec; and in 1869 he was appointed secretary to Archbishop Lynch (q.v.). He was ordained a priest of the Roman Catholic Church in 1870; and he served successively in parishes in Toronto, Newmarket, and St. Catharines, Ontario. In 1884 he became dean of St. Catharines. He retired from active parochial work in 1904; and he died at Toronto on March 5, 1923. He published *The history of early missions in western Canada* (Toronto, 1893), *The Catholic church in the Niagara peninsula* (Toronto, 1895), *The pioneers of the cross in Canada* (Toronto, 1912), and *The cross-bearers of the Saguenay* (Toronto, 1920).

[Morgan, *Can. men* (1912); Rose, *Cyc. Can. biog.* (1888); Le Jeune, *Dict. gén.*]

Harrison, David Howard (1843-1905), prime minister of Manitoba (1887-88), was born in the township of London, Upper Canada, on June 1, 1843, the son of Milner Harrison. He was educated at the University of Toronto and McGill University (M.D., 1864); and he practised medicine in St. Mary's, Ontario, until 1882. He then retired from practice, and settled in Manitoba. In 1883 he was elected to represent Minnedosa West in the Legislative Assembly of Manitoba; in 1886 he was sworn in as minister of agriculture; and in 1887 he became prime minister. He resigned after holding office for less than a month, and retired from political life. He died at Vancouver, British Columbia, on September 8, 1905. In 1866 he married Kate, daughter of George Stevenson, of Sarnia, Ontario.

[*Can. parl. comp.*; J. P. Robertson, *A political manual of the province of Manitoba* (Winnipeg, 1887).]

Harrison, Robert Alexander (1833-1878), chief justice of Ontario (1875-78), was born in Montreal, Lower Canada, on August 3, 1833, the eldest son of Richard Harrison and Frances Butler. He was educated at Upper Canada College and at Trinity University, Toronto (B.C.L., 1855; D.C.L., 1859); and he was called to the bar of Upper Canada in 1855 (Q.C., 1867). From 1854 to 1859 he occupied a post in the Canadian civil service; he then began the practice of law, and rapidly acquired a brilliant reputation. From 1867 to 1872 he represented West Toronto in the Canadian House of Commons; and in 1875 he was appointed chief justice of the Court of Queen's Bench in Ontario. Under stress of work, his health broke down; and he died at Toronto on November 1, 1878. He married (1) in 1859 Anna (d. 1866), daughter of John McClure Muckle, of Quebec; and (2) in 1868 Kennithina Johana Mackay, daughter of Hugh Scobie (q.v.), of Toronto. He was the author of many legal works, including a *Sketch of the growth and importance of the legal profession in Upper Canada* (Toronto, 1857); and in 1859-60 he edited *Poker*, a humorous journal.

[D. B. Read, *Lives of the judges of Upper Canada and Ontario* (Toronto, 1888); *Dom. ann. reg.*, 1878; *Cyc. Am. biog.*; Morgan, *Cel. Can.* and *Bib. can.*; *Dict. Can. biog.*, vol. 10.]

Harrison, Samuel Bealey (1802-1867), provincial secretary of Canada (1841-43), was born in Manchester, England, on March 2, 1802. He studied law, and was called to the English bar, but shortly before the Canadian rebellion of 1837 he emigrated to Upper Canada. He became private secretary to Sir George Arthur (q.v.), the last lieutenant-governor of Upper Canada; and in 1841 he was appointed by Lord Sydenham (q.v.) provincial secretary for Upper Canada in the first administration after the union, and one of the commissioners of public works. He retired from the government in 1843, and from the board of public works in 1844. He represented Kingston in the Legislative Assembly of Canada from 1841 to 1844, and Kent from 1844 to 1845. In 1845 he was appointed a judge of the surrogate court, and in 1848 a judge of the county court of York. He died on July 23, 1867.

[*Cyc. Am. biog.*; J. C. Dent, *The last forty years* (2 vols., Toronto, 1881).]

Harrison, Mrs. Susie Frances, *née* Riley (1859-1935), author, was born in Toronto in 1859, and was educated there and in Montreal. In 1879 she married John W. F. Harrison, organist and choirmaster; but before this she had already begun her literary career. She died in Toronto on May 8, 1935. She was the author of several works of fiction, *Crowded out and other sketches* (Ottawa, 1886), *The forest of Bourg-Marie* (Toronto, 1898), and *Ringfield* (Toronto, 1914). Her reputation rests chiefly, however, on her poems, and especially on her mastery of the difficult villanelle form. Her chief volumes of verse were *Pine, rose, and fleur-de-lis* (Toronto, 1891; 2nd ed., 1896), *In northern skies, and other poems* (Toronto, 1912), *Songs of love and labour* (Toronto, 1925), *Penelope, and other poems* (Toronto, 1932), and *Four ballads and a play* (Toronto, n.d.). She published also *The Canadian birthday book* (Toronto, 1887). Frequently she wrote under the pen-name "Seranus".

[Morgan, *Can. men and women* (1912); L. Pierce, *An outline of Canadian literature* (Toronto, 1927).]

Harrison, Thomas (1839-1906), educationist, was born at Sheffield, New Brunswick, on October 24, 1839; and was educated at Trinity College, Dublin (B.A., 1864; LL.B., 1864; M.A., 1873). In 1870 he was appointed professor of English and philosophy in the University of New Brunswick; and from 1885 to 1892 he was president of this university. In 1892 he was appointed chancellor of the university. He died at Fredericton, New Brunswick, on September 18, 1906.

[Morgan, *Can. men* (1898).]

Harriss, Charles Albert Edward (1862-1929), musician, was born in London, England, on December 17, 1862. He was educated at St. Michael's College, Tenbury, England; and he came to Canada in 1882 as organist of the church of St. Alban the Martyr in Ottawa. He organized and directed many concerts and musical festivals, not only in Canada, but throughout the British Empire, and became a figure in the musical world of international reputation. He was made a Mus. Doc. (Cantuar) and a freeman of the Worshipful Company of Musicians, London. He died at Ottawa on July 30, 1929. In 1897 he married Ella Beatty, widow of George K. Shoenberger, of Cincinnati. He was the author of the following musical compositions: *Daniel before the king, Torquid, Festival mass, Coronation mass (Edward VII), Pan, The sands of Dee, The crowning of the king,* and many choruses, songs, and pianoforte and organ pieces.

[*Who was who*, 1929-40; *Can. who was who*, vol. 1.]

Harrold, Ernest William (1889-1945), journalist, was born in Warwickshire, England, on May 7, 1889. He came to Canada in 1913, and joined the staff of the Ottawa *Citizen*. Except for service in the Canadian army during the First World War, when he was gassed, he remained with the *Citizen* until his death at Ottawa on October 23, 1945. He was appointed associate editor in 1923; and for the last fifteen years of his life he conducted a weekly column entitled "The diary of our own Pepys". After his death, extracts from this column were published under the same title, edited by I. Norman Smith (Toronto, 1947).

[Toronto *Globe and Mail*, Oct. 25, 1945.]

Hart, Aaron (1724-1800), merchant, was an English Jew who came to Canada in 1759-60 as a commissary in the British army, and who settled as a merchant in Three Rivers. Here he established a prosperous business, and founded a family that has played a notable part in commerce and literature. He died at Three Rivers, Lower Canada, on December 28, 1800.

[R. Douville, *Aaron Hart* (Three Rivers, Que., 1938); *Encyc. Can.*]

Hart, Adolphus Mordecai (1814-1879), author, was born in Three Rivers, Lower Canada, on April 11, 1814. He was called to the bar of Lower Canada; and later he practised law in St. Louis, Missouri. He returned to Canada in 1857, and lived in Montreal until his death on March 23, 1879. He was the author of a *History of the issues of paper money in the American colonies* (St. Louis, 1851), a *History of the discovery of the valley of the Mississippi* (St. Louis, 1852), *Life in the far west* (Cincinnati, 1850), and *Practical suggestions on mining rights and privileges in Lower Canada* (Montreal, 1867).

[*Dom. ann. reg.*, 1879; *Dict. Can. biog.*, vol. 10.]

Hart, Charles Desmond (1935-1972), historian, was born in Cornwall, Ontario, on June 8, 1935. He was educated at Queen's University (B.A., 1960), at the University of Toronto, and at the University of Washington in Seattle. He taught American history at Washington University, was visiting lecturer at Queen's University (1963), and was appointed to the staff of York University, Toronto, in 1965. He died at Toronto on September 18, 1972. He published a number of articles on American Civil War history.

[*Can. hist. rev.*, vol. LIV.]

Hart, Ezekiel (d. 1843), merchant, was the son of Aaron Hart (q.v.). In 1807 he was elected to represent Three Rivers in the Legislative Assembly of Lower Canada, but, being a Jew, was declared ineligible to sit; re-elected in 1808, he was again refused his seat; and he was nominated again in 1809, but withdrew from the contest at the last moment, though he had the support of Sir James Craig (q.v.). He died on September 16, 1843.

[J. J. Price (ed.), *Proceedings relating to the expulsion of Ezekiel Hart from the House of Assembly of Lower Canada* (Publications of the American Jewish Historical Society, No. 23); R. Douville, *Aaron Hart* (Three Rivers, Que., 1938).]

Hart, Gerald Ephraim (1849-1936), historian, was born at Montreal, Canada East, on March 26, 1849, the son of Adolphus Mordecai Hart (q.v.). He became a well-known numismatist; and was a prominent member of the Antiquarian and Numismatic Society of Montreal. He died at Montreal, Quebec, on July 13, 1936. He was the author of *The fall of New France* (Montreal, 1888) and *The Quebec Act, 1774* (Montreal, 1891).

[Morgan, *Can. men* (1912).]

Hart, John (1879-1957), prime minister of British Columbia (1941-47), was born in county Leitrim, Ireland, on March 31, 1879, and died at Victoria, British Columbia, on April 7, 1957. He came to Canada in 1898, became a successful broker and financial agent in Victoria. He was elected a member of the British Columbia legislature in 1916, and was minister of finance in the Liberal government from 1917 to 1924. He then retired temporarily from political life; but he was re-elected to the legislature in 1933, and from 1941 to 1947 he was prime minister and minister of finance. He did much to put the finances of British Columbia on a sound footing.

[*Can. who's who*, 1955-57; *Can. parl. comp.*, 1947; *Encyc. Can.*]

Hart, Julia Catherine, *née* **Beckwith** (1796-1867), novelist, was born in Fredericton,

New Brunswick, on March 10, 1796, the eldest daughter of Nehemiah Beckwith and Julie-Louise Le Brun de Duplessis. In 1820 she removed with her family to Kingston, Upper Canada. Here she married in 1822 George Henry Hart, and here too she published, in 1824, a novel entitled *St. Ursula's convent*. This appears to be the first novel published by a Canadian in Canada. In 1826 she went to live in the United States, and there she published *Tonnewonte, or the adopted son of America* (Exeter, 1831). About 1831 she returned to Fredericton, and there she died on November 28, 1867.

[P. Gagnon, *Le premier roman canadien* (Trans. Roy. Soc. Can., 1900); W. G. MacFarlane, *New Brunswick bibliography* (Saint John, N.B., 1895); *Bull. rech. hist.*, vols. I and VII.]

Hart-McHarg, William (1869-1915), soldier and author, was born at Kilkenny Barracks, Ireland, in 1869, and came to Canada in 1885. He was called to the bar in Manitoba in 1895, and in British Columbia in 1897; and practised law in Vancouver, British Columbia. He served with the Royal Canadian Regiment in the South African War from 1899 to 1900; and in the First World War he commanded the 7th Battalion of the Canadian Expeditionary Force. He was killed at the battle of St. Julien, in April, 1915. He was the author of *From Quebec to Pretoria* (Toronto, 1902).

[Morgan, *Can. men* (1912); E. O. S. Scholefield and F. W. Howay, *British Columbia* (4 vols., Vancouver, B.C., 1914).]

Harvard, William Martin (1790-1857), clergyman and author, was born in 1790, and became a Wesleyan Methodist missionary in British India and Ceylon. After his return to England, he was sent out in 1836 to Canada as president of the Wesleyan Methodist Conference in Upper Canada; and from 1839 to 1844 he was chairman of the Canada Eastern District. He returned to England in 1847, and he died at Richmond, England, on December 15, 1857. He was the author of *Remarks and suggestions respectfully offered on that portion of the clergy reserve property (landed and funded) of Upper Canada, "not specifically appropriated to any particular church"* (Quebec, 1838), and *Five defensive letters in behalf of the British Wesleyan Conference, and their missionary society, and its agents and congregations, in western Canada* (Toronto, 1846).

[Morgan, *Bib. can.*]

Harvey, Arthur (1834-1905), statistician, was born at Halesworth, Suffolk, England, in 1834, and was educated at Trinity College, Dublin, but did not graduate. He emigrated to Canada in 1856, and for several years was engaged in journalism. In 1862 he was appointed chief statistical clerk in the auditor-general's department of the Canadian government; and in 1867 he founded the *Year book and almanac of British North America*, the predecessor of the *Canada year book*. Though he resigned from the civil service in 1870, and went into business in Toronto, he kept up his interest in statistical work. He was a fellow of the Royal Statistical Society; and from 1890 to 1893 he was president of the Canadian Institute. In 1892 he was elected a member of the Royal Society of Canada. He died at Toronto on April 7, 1905. In 1858 he married Jane, daughter of John Grist, Quebec.

[S. Blackburn, *The late Arthur Harvey* (Trans. Roy. Soc. Can., 1905); Morgan *Can. men* (1898); Rose, *Cyc. Can. biog.* (1886); *Cyc. Am. biog.*]

Harvey, Athelstan George (1884-1950), biographer, was born in 1884, became a barrister in Vancouver, British Columbia, and died there on January 15, 1950. He became interested in the history of British Columbia, and was the author of *Douglas of the fir* (Cambridge, Mass., 1947), a biography of David Douglas (q.v.) after whom the Douglas fir was named.

[Private information.]

Harvey, Daniel Cobb (1886-1966), archivist, was born in Cape Traverse, Prince Edward Island, of United Empire Loyalist stock on January 10, 1886. He was educated at Prince of Wales College, and then at Dalhousie University, from which he graduated in 1910, being chosen as Rhodes scholar for that year. He entered Oxford University, where he obtained a B.A. (1913) and M.A. (1917) in modern history. He began his academic career in McGill University in 1913 as lecturer in history. From 1915 to 1931 he taught in Manitoba, first at Wesley College, until 1920, and then at the University of Manitoba. In 1931 he assumed the newly created position of archivist of Nova Scotia where he remained until retirement in 1956. He died in Halifax on August 7, 1966. He was elected Fellow of the Royal Society of Canada in 1928 and won the Tyrrell medal in 1942. He was author of *The French regime in Prince Edward Island* (New Haven, 1926), *Joseph Howe* (Toronto, 1927), *The colonization of Canada* (Toronto, 1936), *The heart of Howe* (Toronto, 1939). He also edited vol. II of the *Diary of Simeon Perkins* (Champlain Society, 1958), *Whelan's union of the British Provinces* (Toronto, 1927) and *Journeys to the Island of St. John* (Toronto, 1955).

[*Can. hist. rev.*, vol. XLVII.]

Harvey, Jean-Charles (1891-1967), writer, was born at La Malbaie, Quebec, November 10, 1891, and educated at the University of Montreal. In 1916 he joined the editorial staff of *La patrie*; he later went to *La presse* and from 1919 to 1922 was employed in the publicity department of the National Farm Machin-

ery Company at Montmagny. He then became a member of the editorial staff of *Le soleil* of Quebec, becoming editor in 1926. He was a critic of the development policies of the Taschereau government, which gave large concessions to outside capital without obtaining compensating benefits for Quebec residents. His novel *Marcel Faure* (1922) deals with this theme. He also attacked the educational system and its domination by clinical influence which restricted freedom of thought and the training of students for an industrial society. Two books, *L'homme qui va* (1929) and *Les demi-civilisés* (1934), which was translated as *Sackcloth for banner* (1938), dealt with the search for personal freedom and were condemned by many clerics and laymen. Harvey lost his position at *Le soleil* and became chief of the Bureau of Provincial Statistics. He wrote *Nouvelles* (1935) in a continuing campaign for freedom of thought. In 1937 he founded *Le jour* at Montreal and continued to edit it until it ceased publication in 1946. In it he attacked separatism and the facism which was represented by Adrien Arcand. A collection of these editorials was published as *Les grenouilles demandent un roi* (1942) and translated as *The eternal struggle: The truceless conflict between the rights of the individual and the forces of despotism* (1953). He became manager of *Le petit journal* and *Photo-journal* of Montreal in 1953 after a period of employment (1946-52) with the Canadian Broadcasting Corporation. His literary criticism was collected as *Pages de critique* (1926) and *Art et combat* (1938), and his poetry as *La fille du silence* (1958). He died at Montreal, Quebec, January 3, 1967.

[N. Story, *The Oxford Companion to Canadian History and Literature* (Toronto, 1967).]

Harvey, Sir John (1778-1852), lieutenant-governor of Nova Scotia (1846-52), was born in 1778, and entered the British army as an ensign in the 80th Regiment in 1794. He served throughout the Revolutionary and Napoleonic wars; and in 1812 he was appointed deputy-adjutant-general to the forces in Canada, with the rank of lieutenant-colonel. He served in Canada throughout the War of 1812, and was in command at the engagement at Stoney Creek, Upper Canada, in 1813. During the latter part of his life he was employed in official positions in British North America. From 1837 to 1841 he was lieutenant-governor of New Brunswick; from 1841 to 1846 he was governor of Newfoundland; and from 1846 to 1852 he was lieutenant-governor of Nova Scotia. In this last capacity it fell to him to introduce, in its full form, the principle of responsible government in the Maritime provinces. He died at Halifax, Nova Scotia, on March 22, 1852. In 1806 he married the Hon. Elizabeth Lake, daughter of Gerard, first Viscount Lake. He was created a K.C.H. in 1824, and a K.C.B. in 1838; and in 1844 he was appointed to the colonelcy of the 59th Foot. At the time of his death, he had risen to the rank of lieutenant-general; and had served in the army longer, with one exception, than any other officer in British North America.

[Morgan, *Cel. Can.*; D. Campbell, *History of Nova Scotia* (Montreal, 1873), J. Hannay, *History of New Brunswick* (2 vols., Saint John, N.B., 1909); Sir C. Lucas, *The Canadian war of 1812* (Oxford, 1906).]

Harvey, Moses (1820-1901), clergyman and author, was born in Armagh, Ireland, in 1820, and died at St. John's, Newfoundland, on September 3, 1901. He was educated at the Royal College, Belfast, and in 1844 was ordained a Presbyterian minister. He came to Newfoundland in 1852, and for twenty-five years was pastor of St. Andrew's Free Presbyterian Church at St. John's. He became an authority on the history and resources of Newfoundland, and was the author of *Lectures, literary and biographical* (Edinburgh, 1864), *This Newfoundland of ours* (St. John's, 1878), *Across the island with Sir John Glover* (St. John's, 1879), *Newfoundland, the oldest British colony* (London, 1883), *Text book of Newfoundland history* (Boston, 1885), *A short history of Newfoundland* (London, 1890), *Newfoundland as it is in 1894* (St. John's, 1894), *Newfoundland in the jubilee year* (St. John's, 1897), and *Newfoundland at the beginning of the 20th century* (New York, 1902). He was also joint author, with Joseph Hatton, of *Newfoundland, its history* (Boston, 1883). He was elected a fellow of the Royal Society of Canada in 1891.

[Morgan, *Can. men* (1898); *Newfoundland supp.*; *Who was who*, 1897-1916).]

Harvie, Eric Lafferty (1892-1975), business executive and lawyer, was born in Orillia, Ontario, April 2, 1892. He was educated in Orillia and at Osgoode Hall Law School and the University of Alberta. He read law with T.L. Mulcahy in Orillia and James Short in Calgary and was called to the bar of Alberta in 1915. He served in the First World War with the 15th Light Horse, and the 103rd Calgary Regiment. He was overseas with the 56th and 49th battalions and later transferred to the R.F.C. as captain. He was president and chairman of the Harvie Foundation; chairman and director of the Glenbow Foundation, Glenbow Investments Limited, Managers Limited, Luxton Museum Limited, Weston Minerals, and Ace Foundation; vice-president and director of Belvedere Foundation and Belvedere Securities Limited; director of Glenbow Ranching Limited, and Riske Creek Ranching Limited. He was awarded the Order of Canada (1967), was a fellow of the Royal Society of the Arts, and was a patron of historic and philanthropic organizations. He died at Calgary, Alberta, January 11, 1975.

[*Can. who's who*, 1970-72.]

Harwood, Robert Unwin (d. 1863), legislative councillor of Lower Canada, was born in Sheffield, England, and came to Canada in 1822 to found in Montreal a branch of the family business. In 1823 he married Marie, daughter of the Hon. M. E. G. Alain Chartier de Lotbinière (q.v.), who had inherited the seigniory and manor-house of Vaudreuil; and after his marriage, he retired from business, and devoted himself to looking after his wife's interests. In 1832 he was appointed a member of the Legislative Council of Lower Canada; and he was a member of the Special Council of the province from 1839 to 1841. He was elected a member of the Legislative Assembly of United Canada for Vaudreuil from 1858 to 1860, and of the Legislative Council for Rigaud from 1860 to his death on April 12, 1863.

[J. D. Borthwick, *History and biographical gazetteer of Montreal* (Montreal, 1892); J. Desjardins, *Guide parlementaire historique de la province de Québec* (Quebec, 1902).]

Haskins, James (1805-1845), poet, was born in Dublin, Ireland, in 1805. He was educated at Trinity College, Dublin (A.B., 1824; M.B., 1833), and emigrated to Canada in 1834. He practised medicine in Belleville, Canada West, and its neighbourhood; and he died at the village of Frankford, in the Trent valley, in the autumn of 1845. His *Poetical works* were published posthumously by his friend Henry Baldwin (Hartford, 1848), with a memoir.

[Morgan, *Bib. can.*]

Hassard, Albert Richard (1873-1940), lawyer and author, was born at Petigo, county Fermanagh, Ireland, in 1873. He was educated at Trinity University, Toronto (B.C.L., 1895), and was called to the Ontario bar in 1895. He practised law in Toronto; and he died there on June 26, 1940. He was the author of *Canadian constitutional history and law* (Toronto, 1900), *A new light on Lord Macaulay* (Toronto, 1918), *Famous Canadian trials* (Toronto, 1924), and *Not guilty, and other trials* (Toronto, 1926).

[Morgan, *Can. men* (1912).]

Hathaway, Ernest Jackson (1871-1930), author, was born in Toronto, Ontario, in 1871, the son of James Hathaway. He was educated in Toronto, and was for many years secretary of the wholesale stationery firm of Warwick Bros. and Rutter. He died in Toronto on March 3, 1930. He was the author of *Jesse Ketchum and his times* (Toronto, 1929).

[*Canadian bookman*, 1930.]

Hathaway, Rufus H. (1869-1933), bibliophile, was born in Toronto, Ontario, on September 26, 1869, the son of James Hathaway, and the brother of Ernest Jackson Hathaway (q.v.). He entered the service of the Great North Western Telegraph Company, which was later absorbed by the Canadian National

Railways; and he ultimately became superintendent of the commercial news department of the Canadian National Railways. He retired in 1932, and he died in Toronto, Ontario, on March 7, 1933. He was an outstanding collector of the works of Canadian authors; and his collection of Canadian literature was after his death presented to the Library of the University of New Brunswick.

[*A catalogue of the Rufus Hathaway collection of Canadian literature, University of New Brunswick* (Fredericton, N.B., 1935).]

Hatheway, Calvin (1796-1866), author, was born in Burton, Sunbury county, New Brunswick, on September 17, 1796, and died at Saint John, New Brunswick, on August 20, 1866. He published *Sketches of New Brunswick* (Saint John, N.B., 1825), and a *History of New Brunswick* (Saint John, N.B., 1846).

[W. G. MacFarlane, *New Brunswick bibliography* (Saint John, N.B., 1895).]

Hatheway, George Luther (1813-1872), prime minister of New Brunswick (1871-72), was born in New Brunswick on August 4, 1813, of Loyalist stock. He was educated in Saint John, New Brunswick, and became a farmer. He represented York in the House of Assembly of New Brunswick from 1850 to 1857; and from 1861 to 1865 he was a member of the Executive Council, and chief commissioner of public works. He was opposed to Confederation, and in 1865 he was called upon to form a government pledged to withdraw New Brunswick from union; but in 1866 he deserted the anti-Confederation party, and contributed largely to its defeat. In 1871 he was again invited to form a provincial government, in which he took the portfolio of provincial secretary; but he had been in office only a little over a year when he died suddenly, from blood poisoning, at Fredericton, on July 5, 1872. In 1840 he married Martha Slason.

[*Can. parl. comp.*; J. Hannay, *Premiers of New Brunswick since Confederation* (Can. mag., 1897), and *History of New Brunswick* (2 vols., Saint John, N.B., 1909); *Dict. Can. biog.*, vol. 10.]

Hatheway, Warren Franklin (1850-1923), merchant and author, was born at Saint John, New Brunswick, on September 16, 1850. He was head of a firm of wholesale grocers, and he represented Saint John in the New Brunswick Legislative Assembly from 1908 to 1912. He died at Saint John, New Brunswick, on October 29, 1923. In addition to a number of articles contributed to journals in Canada, Great Britain, and the United States, he was the author of *Canadian nationality: The cry of liberty, and other essays* (Toronto, 1906) and *Why France lost Canada, and other essays and poems* (Toronto, 1915).

[Morgan, *Can. men* (1912).]

Hatt, Samuel (d. 1842), legislative councillor of Lower Canada, was born in England, and settled in Ancaster, Upper Canada, in 1798. With his brother Richard (1769-1819), he established one of the earliest mills at the head of Lake Ontario; but after the death of his brother he removed to Chambly, Lower Canada, and became an influential figure in the lower province. In 1829 he was appointed a member of the Legislative Council of Lower Canada. He died at Chambly, Lower Canada, on July 8, 1842.

[J. Desjardins, *Guide parlementaire historique* (Quebec, 1902).]

Haultain, Sir Frederick William (1857-1942), chief justice of the Court of Appeal, Saskatchewan (1917-38), was born at Woolwich, England, on November 25, 1857, the son of Lieut.-Col. F. W. Haultain, R.A. He was educated at the University of Toronto (B.A., 1879; LL.D., 1915), and was called to the bar of Ontario in 1882, and of Saskatchewan in 1884 (K.C., 1902). He sat in the legislature of the North West Territories for Macleod from 1888 to 1905, and was president of the Executive Council from 1897 to 1905. When the province of Saskatchewan was formed in 1905, he was elected to represent South Qu'Appelle in the Legislative Council, and from 1905 to 1912 he was leader of the Provincial Rights party. In 1912 he was appointed chief justice of the Superior Court of Saskatchewan, and in 1917 of the Court of Appeal. He retired from the bench in 1938; and he died at Montreal, Quebec, on January 30, 1942. In 1916 he was created a K.B.

[L. H. Thomas, *The political and private life of F. W. G. Haultain* (Saskatchewan History, 1970); *Can. who's who*, 1938-39; *Who's who*, 1941; *Can. parl. comp.*; Le Jeune, *Dict. gén.*]

Haultain, Theodore Arnold (1857-1941), author, was born at Cannanore, India, on November 3, 1857, the son of Major-Gen. F. M. Haultain. He was educated at the University of Toronto (B.A., 1879; M.A., 1880), and for many years he was private secretary to Goldwin Smith (q.v.). He was Goldwin Smith's literary executor and biographer. His later years were spent in England; and he died in England on June 11, 1941. He was the author of *The war in the Soudan* (Toronto, 1885), *Versiculi* (Toronto, 1893), *Two country walks in Canada* (Toronto, 1903), *The mystery of golf* (Boston, 1908), *Hints for lovers* (Boston, 1909), and *Goldwin Smith, his life and opinions* (London, 1913); and he edited *Goldwin Smith's Reminiscences* (London, 1910) and *A selection from Goldwin Smith's correspondence* (London, 1913).

[Morgan, *Can. men* (1912).]

Haviland, Thomas Heath (1822-1895), lieutenant-governor of Prince Edward Island

(1879-84), was born in Charlottetown, Prince Edward Island, on November 13, 1822, the son of the Hon. Thomas Haviland. He was educated in Brussels, Belgium; and, on his return to Prince Edward Island, was called to the bar in 1846. The following year he was elected a member of the Legislative Assembly of the Island for Georgetown; and this constituency he represented continuously until 1870. From 1859 to 1862 he was a member of the Executive Council, as colonial secretary; from 1863 to 1864 he was speaker of the Assembly; in 1865 he was solicitor-general; and from 1866 to 1867 he was again colonial secretary. In 1870 he was elected to the Legislative Council; and from 1870 to 1872, and again from 1873 to 1876, he once more filled the post of colonial secretary. He was one of the delegates from Prince Edward Island to the Quebec Conference in 1864; and he was one of the three delegates who went to Ottawa in 1873 to arrange the terms on which Prince Edward Island was finally admitted into Confederation. When Prince Edward Island was included in the Dominion, he was called to the Canadian Senate; but in 1879, he resigned from the Senate on his appointment as lieutenant-governor of Prince Edward Island. This post he occupied until 1884. He died in Charlottetown on September 11, 1895. In 1847 he married Annie Elizabeth, daughter of John Grubbe, of Horsenden House, Buckinghamshire, England.

[*Cyc. Am. biog.*; Dent, *Can. port.*, vol. 4; D. Campbell, *History of Prince Edward Island* (Charlottetown, 1875); D. A. MacKinnon and A. B. Warburton (eds.), *Past and present of Prince Edward Island* (Charlottetown, n.d.).]

Hawkes, Arthur (1871-1933), journalist and author, was born in Aylesford, Kent, England, in 1871. He became a journalist, and in 1905 settled in Toronto, Canada, as managing editor of the Toronto *World*. Later he was in charge of publicity for the Canadian Northern Railway; and he aided in founding the Amalgamated Press Service of Canada, out of which the Canadian Press developed. He died in Toronto on October 12, 1933. He was the author of *An appeal to the British-born* (Toronto, 1911) and *The birthright* (Toronto, 1919).

[Morgan, *Can. men* (1912).]

Hawkins, Alfred (1802?-1854), author, was born at Bridgeport, England, about 1802, and became a wine merchant. After emigrating to Canada, he was appointed shipping master of the port of Quebec; and he died at Quebec of cholera on June 30, 1854. He was an ardent collector of "Canadiana"; and he published several works of real historical value: *Picture of Quebec with historical recollections* (Quebec, 1834), *The plan of the naval and military operations before Quebec, and Death*

of Wolfe (London, 1842), and the *Quebec directory* for 1843-44 and 1847-48.

[*Bull. rech. hist.*, 1935.]

Hawkins, Ernest (1802-1868), clergyman and author, was born in the parish of Kimpton, Hertfordshire, on January 25, 1802, and was educated at Balliol College, Oxford (B.A., 1824; M.A., 1827; B.D., 1839). He took holy orders in the Church of England, and from 1838 to 1864 he was secretary of the Society for the Propagation of the Gospel. He was then appointed to a canonry at Westminster; and he died at Westminster on October 5, 1868. He was the author, among other works, of the following books relating especially to Canada: *Documents relative to the erection and endowment of additional bishoprics in the colonies* (London, 1844), *Historical notices of the missions of the Church of England in the North American colonies* (London, 1845), *Annals of the diocese of Fredericton* (London, 1847), *Annals of the diocese of Toronto* (London, 1848), and *Annals of the diocese of Quebec* (London, 1849).

[*Dict. nat. biog.*]

Hawley, James Edwin (1897-1965), geologist and professor, was born at Kingston, Ontario, September 27, 1897. He was educated at Queen's University (B.A., 1918; M.A., 1920), and at the University of Wisconsin (Ph.D., 1926). He worked with Imperial Oil in Alberta, with the Ontario Bureau of Mines, and with Whitehall Petroleum Corporation of London, England, in Alberta, Ecuador, India, and Burma, before assuming an academic position at the University of Wisconsin in 1927. In 1929 he became professor, and head, of the department of mineralogy at Queen's University. He became head of the department of geological sciences in 1950 and remained head until his retirement in 1962. He contributed to the Canadian Institute of Mining and Metallurgy's volume *Structural geology of Canadian ore deposits* and published *The Sudbury ores: their mineralogy and origin* in 1962 besides some sixty other scientific papers. In 1933 he was awarded the Barlow memorial prize for a paper on *The Siscoe metal deposit*, in 1951 he received the Willet G. Miller medal in geology from the Royal Society of Canada and in 1964 he was awarded the Logan medal of the Geological Association of Canada. He was a fellow of the Royal Society, the Geological Society of America, the Mineralogical Society of America, the Geological Society of Canada, the Canadian Institute of Mining and Metallurgy, and the Mineralogical Association of Canada. He died at Tucson, Arizona, on April 20, 1965.

[*Proc. Roy. Soc. Can.* (1965); *Can. who's who*, 1955-57.]

Hawley, William Fitz (1804-1855), poet, was born in 1804, and died at Laprairie, Canada East, in January, 1855. He was the author of *Quebec, the harp, and other poems* (Montreal, 1829) and *The unknown, or Lays of the forest* (Montreal, 1831).

[Morgan, *Bib. can.*]

Hay, Charles C. (1902-1973), business man, was born at Kingston, Ontario, June 28, 1902. He attended public school in Saskatoon, Saskatchewan, and graduated from the engineering school of the University of Saskatchewan (B.A.Sc., 1925). He was employed in the engineering department of the Canadian Pacific Railway (1928-29), became a member of the contracting firm of Gibbs Brothers and Hay (1930-32), and a founder of Hi-Way Refineries in Saskatchewan and Alberta (1932). He became president of Royalite Company after it had bought Hi-Way Refineries, president of Gulf Oil (1964-69), and president of Hockey Canada (1969-73). Mr. Hay was a director of Canada Permanent Mortgage Corporation, Canada Permanent Trust, and Gulf Oil of Canada. He was a director of the Canadian Nuclear Association, the Engineering Institute of Canada, and the Association of Professional Engineers of Alberta, and had been on the Senate and the Board of Governors of the University of Alberta. He died at Toronto, Ontario, October 24, 1973.

[*Can. who's who*, 1970-72.]

Hay, William (1818-1888), architect, was born in Peterhead, Scotland, on May 27, 1818. In 1847 he was sent out by the British government to St. John's, Newfoundland, and Halifax, Nova Scotia, to design government buildings; and from about 1850 to 1860 he practised his profession in Toronto. He was the architect of some of the finest buildings of that period in Ontario, notably the city hall and court house at Kingston, and St. Michael's College in Toronto. In 1860, he returned to Scotland, and resumed the practice of his profession in Edinburgh. He died at his house "Rabbit Hall", in Portobello, near Edinburgh, on May 30, 1888.

[G. P. Ure, *A handbook of Toronto* (Toronto, 1858); private information.]

Haydon, Andrew (1867-1932), politician and author, was born at Pakenham, Ontario, on June 28, 1867, the son of James Haydon and Eleanor Sadler. He was educated at Queen's University, Kingston (M.A., 1893; LL.B., 1895), and at Osgoode Hall; and he was called to the bar in 1897. He practised law in Ottawa, and became an influential figure in the Liberal party. He was secretary of the National Liberal Convention held at Ottawa in 1919; and from 1919 to 1922 he was secretary of the Liberal organization committee. In 1924 he was called to the Senate of Canada; and he was one of the senators against whom charges were made in connection with the Beauharnois Canal. He died in Ottawa on November 10,

1932. He was the author of *Pioneer sketches in the district of Bathurst* (Toronto, 1925) and *Mackenzie King and the Liberal party* (Toronto, 1930).

[*Can. parl. comp.*]

Hayman, Robert (1575-1629), colonizer and author, was born in Devonshire, England, in 1575 and died at Guiana in 1629. He was educated at Exeter College, Oxford, and studied law at Lincoln's Inn. About 1618 he became governor of Bristol's colony in Newfoundland, and during the next ten years he visited the colony fairly often. He returned to England shortly before 1628, and he then published, under the title *Quodlibets lately come over from New Britaniola, anciently called Newfoundland* (London, 1628), some epigrams, verses, and odds and ends he had written at Harbour Grace. Later, he went to found a colony in Guiana, and he died there.

[*Dict. nat. biog; Encyc. Can.; Newfoundland supp.; Dict. Can. biog.*, vol. 1.]

Hays, Charles Melville (1856-1912), president of the Grand Trunk Railway Company (1909-12), was born at Rock Island, Illinois, on May 16, 1856. He was educated at the public schools of Rock Island, and at the age of seventeen entered the service of the Atlantic and Pacific Railway, in St. Louis, Missouri. He rose in the railway world until in 1889 he was appointed general manager of the reorganized Wabash system. In 1896 he came to Canada as general manager of the Grand Trunk Railway, and, with the exception of part of the year 1901, when he was president of the Southern Pacific Railway, he continued to manage the Grand Trunk Railway until 1909, when he was appointed president of the company. In 1905 he was elected president also of the Grand Trunk Pacific Railway, which was to a large extent his creation. He was drowned in the *Titanic* disaster of April 15, 1912. He married Clare, daughter of William H. Gregg, of St. Louis, Missouri; and by her he had four daughters.

[*Can. who was who*, vol. 1; Morgan, *Can. men* (1912); *Can. who's who*, 1910; H. A. Lovett, *Canada and the Grand Trunk* (Montreal, 1924); D. B. Hanna, *Trains of recollection* (Toronto, 1924).]

Haythorne, Robert Poore (1815-1891), prime minister of Prince Edward Island, was born in Bristol, England, on December 2, 1815, and emigrated to Prince Edward Island in 1842. He sat in the elective Legislative Council of Prince Edward Island from 1867 to 1874; and in 1867 he was appointed a member of the Executive Council. From 1872 to 1873 he was prime minister of the province, but was defeated on the question of Confederation with Canada. On the admission of the province into Confederation later in 1873, he was called to the Senate of Canada. He died in 1891.

[*Can. parl. comp.*]

Hazen, Sir John Douglas (1860-1937), prime minister of New Brunswick (1908-11), minister of marine and fisheries for Canada (1911-17), and chief justice of New Brunswick (1917-35), was born at Oromocto, New Brunswick, on June 5, 1860. He was educated at the University of New Brunswick (B.A., 1879; B.C.L., 1890; LL.D., 1908), and was called to the bar in New Brunswick in 1883 (Q.C., 1894). He practised law, first at Fredericton, and then at Saint John, New Brunswick; and he made his first entrance into politics as member for Saint John City in the Canadian House of Commons from 1891 to 1896. He later sat for Sunbury in the Legislative Assembly of New Brunswick from 1899 to 1911; and from 1908 to 1911 he was prime minister of the province. In 1911 he entered the Dominion government of Robert Borden (q.v.), as minister of marine and fisheries, and was elected by acclamation to represent Saint John City and County in the Canadian House of Commons. He held this portfolio until his appointment in 1917 as chief justice of New Brunswick; in 1918 he was awarded the K.C.M.G. in recognition of his services. He retired from the bench in 1935; and he died at Saint John, New Brunswick, on December 27, 1937.

[*Can. who's who*, 1936-37; *Who was who*, 1928-40; *Can. parl. comp.*]

Hazen, Moses (1733-1803), rebel, was born at Haverhill, Massachusetts, in 1733, of Jewish parentage. He was with the British army at Louisbourg in 1758, and at Quebec in 1759; and he settled at St. John, near Montreal. Here, in 1775, he took the part of the American invaders of Canada; and he was forced in 1776 to flee to Vermont. He died at Troy, New York, in 1803.

[*Dict. Am. biog.*; *Cyc. Am. biog.*]

Hazen, Robert Leonard (1808-1874), senator of Canada, was born at Fredericton, New Brunswick, in 1808, the son of William Hazen, Jr., and the grandson of the Hon. William Hazen (q.v.). He was called to the bar in New Brunswick in 1831 (Q.C., 1843), and became a leader of the bar. From 1843 to 1854 and from 1856 to 1857 he was a member of the Executive Council of New Brunswick; and he sat in the Legislative Assembly of the province for Saint John City from 1837 to 1848 when he was appointed a member of the Legislative Council. In 1867 he was called by proclamation to the Senate of Canada. He died at Saint John on August 15, 1873.

[*Can. parl. comp.*; *Dict. Can. biog.*, vol. 10.]

Hazen, William (1738-1814), loyalist, was born in Massachusetts in 1738, and in 1762 became one of the earliest grantees of land on the St. John River. Unlike most of the settlers on the St. John, he remained loyal during the American Revolution; and when New Brunswick was created a province in 1783, he was appointed a member of the first Executive Council. He died at Saint John, New Brunswick, in 1814.

[*New Brunswick magazine*, 1898.]

Head, Sir Edmund Walker, Bart. (1805-1868), governor-in-chief of Canada (1854-61), was born in 1805, the only son of the Rev. Sir John Head, Bart, rector of Rayleigh, Essex, England. He was educated at Winchester and at Oriel College, Oxford (B.A., 1827; M.A., 1830). From 1830 to 1837 he was a fellow of Merton College, Oxford; and in 1841 he was appointed a poor-law commissioner. From 1848 to 1854 he was lieutenant-governor of New Brunswick; and such was his success in this post that in 1854 he was appointed governor-in-chief of Canada. His period of office in Canada was full of difficulties, chiefly owing to the antagonism between Upper and Lower Canada; and he was called upon to deal with the crisis connected with the "Double Shuffle" of 1858. His refusal to grant a dissolution to George Brown (q.v.) on this occasion earned for him the hostility of the Liberal party. He retired from office in 1861, before the political deadlock in Canada became acute; and in 1862 he was appointed a civil service commissioner. He died in London, England, on January 28, 1868. In 1838 he married Anna Maria, daughter of the Rev. John Yorke; and by her he had one son and two daughters. He succeeded to the baronetcy, on the death of his father, in 1838; in 1857 he was sworn of the privy council; and in 1860 he was created a K.C.B. An accomplished scholar, he was elected a fellow of the Royal Society, and in 1862 he was made a D.C.L. of Oxford. He was the author of a translation of Kugler's *Handbook of painting of the German, Dutch, Spanish, and French schools* (London, 1848), a grammatical essay entitled *Shall and will* (London, 1856; 2nd ed., London, 1858), a translation from the Icelandic of *The story of Viga Glum* (London, 1866), and a posthumous volume of *Ballads and other poems* (London, 1868).

[*Dict. nat. biog.*; Morgan, *Cel. Can.*; Dent, *Can. port*, vol. 4, and *The last forty years* (2 vols., Toronto, 1881); W. G. MacFarlane, *New Brunswick bibliography* (Saint John, N.B., 1895); D. G. Kerr, *Sir Edmund Head* (Toronto, 1954).]

Head, Sir Francis Bond, Bart. (1793-1875), lieutenant-governor of Upper Canada (1835-38), was born at the Hermitage, Higham, Kent, England, in 1793, the son of James Roper Head. He was educated at the Royal Military Academy, Woolwich, and in 1811 obtained a commission in the Royal Engineers. He was present at Waterloo, and he remained in the army until 1825. He then retired on half-pay, to accept the post of manager of the Rio Plata Mining Association. He went to South America, but the mining venture proved a fiasco, and in 1826 he returned to England. In 1834 he was appointed assistant poor law commissioner for Kent; and in 1835 he was offered the lieutenant-governorship of Upper Canada. Though professedly a Liberal, he pursued in Canada a reactionary policy, and his attitude had not a little to do with the outbreak of the Rebellion of 1837. As the result of a dispute with the Home government over the appointment of a Reformer to a public office, he resigned in September, 1837; but he was not relieved until January, 1838; and it therefore fell to him to deal with the rebellion in Upper Canada. Though he succeeded, with the aid of the loyal inhabitants, in crushing the rebels, his conduct was so erratic and irresponsible that he was never again given public employment. He died at his residence, Duppas Hall, Croydon, England, on July 20, 1875. In 1816 he married his cousin, Julia Valenza (d. 1879), daughter of the Hon. Hugh Somerville. He was created a K.C.H. in 1835, a baronet in 1837, and a privy councillor in 1867.

A vivacious and versatile writer, he published a considerable number of books. His Canadian experiences are dealt with in *A narrative* (London, 1839), and *The emigrant* (London, 1846); but he wrote also *Rough notes of journeys in the Pampas and Andes* (London, 1828), *Bubbles from the Brunnens of Nassau*, by "an Old Man" (London, 1834), *Highways and dryways* (London, 1849), *Stokers and pokers* (London, 1849), *A faggot of French sticks* (London, 1852), *The horse and his rider* (London, 1860), *The royal engineer* (London, 1869), and *Sketch of the life of Sir J. M. Burgoyne* (London, 1872). He was for many years a contributor to the *Quarterly Review*; and two volumes of his *Quarterly* essays were republished under the title, *Descriptive essays* (London, 1857).

[W. Smith, *Sir Francis Bond Head* (Report of the Canadian Historical Association, 1930); *Dict. nat. biog.*; D. B. Read, *The lieutenant-governors of Upper Canada* (Toronto, 1900); Morgan, *Cel. Can.*; J. C. Dent, *The Upper Canadian rebellion* (2 vols., Toronto, 1885); W. S. Wallace, *The Family Compact* (Toronto, 1915); S. W. Jackman, *Galloping Head* (London, 1958); *Dict. nat. biog.*, vol. 10.]

Head, Sir George (1782-1855), soldier and author, was born at the Hermitage, Higham, Kent, England, in 1782, the son of James Roper Head, and brother of Sir Francis Bond Head (q.v.). He was educated at the Charterhouse; and in 1809 he became a clerk of the commissariat department of the British army. In 1814 he was sent to Canada, and was stationed successively at Halifax, at Quebec, on Lake Huron, and again at Halifax. In 1823 he was placed on half-pay; and in 1830 he acted as deputy knight-marshal at the coronation of William IV. He was also deputy knight-marshal to Queen Victoria. He died near Charing Cross, London, on May 2, 1855, unmarried.

He was knighted in 1831. Like his brother, he was a graphic and popular writer; and, among other works, he published his Canadian reminiscences under the title *Forest scenes and incidents in the wilds of North America* (London, 1829).

[*Dict. nat. biog.*]

Heagerty, John Joseph (1879-1946), physician and historian, was born at Montreal, Quebec, on December 26, 1879, and died at Ottawa, Ontario, on February 5, 1946. He was educated at McGill University (M.D., C.M., 1905; D.P.H., 1912); and from 1905 to 1911 was in general practice. He then entered the civil service in Ottawa, and at the time of his death was executive assistant in the department of pensions and national health. He became an authority on the history of medicine in Canada, and was the author of *Four centuries of medical history in Canada* (2 vols., Toronto, 1928) and *The romance of medicine in Canada* (Toronto, 1940).

[*Can. who's who*, 1938-39.]

Healy, William Joseph (1867-1950), journalist, librarian, and author, was born in Belleville, Ontario, on April 15, 1867, and died at San Francisco, California, on August 24, 1950. He was educated at the University of Toronto (B.A., 1890), and became a journalist. In 1899 he became associate editor of the *Manitoba Free Press*; and in 1920 he was appointed provincial librarian of Manitoba. He retired in 1937, and went to live with a daughter in San Francisco. He was the author of *Women of Red River* (Winnipeg, 1923) and *Winnipeg's early days* (Winnipeg, 1927).

[B. B. Peel, comp., *A bibliography of the prairie provinces* (Toronto, 1956); *Can. who's who*, 1936-37.]

Hearne, Samuel (1745-1792), explorer, was born in London, England, in 1745. His father having died when he was young, his mother removed to Bimmester, Dorsetshire, and he was there educated. At the age of eleven years, he became a midshipman in the Royal Navy; but about the age of twenty he entered the service of the Hudson's Bay Company, and was sent out to Fort Prince of Wales, at the mouth of the Churchill River. In 1769, 1770, and in 1771-72, he made journeys of exploration into the interior; and on the third journey he reached the Arctic Ocean at the mouth of the Coppermine River — being the first white man to reach the Arctic overland from Hudson Bay. In 1774 he built Cumberland House, the first inland post of the Hudson's Bay Company; and in 1775 he was appointed governor of Fort Prince of Wales. He was in charge of this fort when it was captured by the French under Admiral de la Pérouse in 1782, and was carried a captive to France; but he was sent back to Churchill in 1783, and he remained there until 1787. He then returned to England, and he died there in November, 1792. His last years were apparently spent in the preparation of his posthumously published *Journey from Prince of Wales's Fort in Hudson's Bay to the Northern Ocean* (London, 1795; new ed., by J. B. Tyrrell, Toronto, Champlain Society, 1911; tr. into French by Lallement, Paris, 1799). Some of his journals have been published under the title *Journals of Samuel Hearne and Philip Turnor*, by J. B. Tyrrell (Toronto: The Champlain Society, 1934).

[W. S. Wallace, *By star and compass* (Toronto, 1922); S. Leacock, *Adventurers of the far north* (Toronto, 1914); L. J. Burpee, *The search for the western sea* (Toronto, 1908); Agnes Laut, *The pathfinders of the west* (Toronto, 1904) and *The conquest of the great north-west* (2 vols., New York, 1908); G. Bryce, *The remarkable history of the Hudson's Bay Company* (London, 1900); B. Willson, *The great company* (2 vols., London, 1899).]

Hearst, Sir William Howard (1864-1941), prime minister of Ontario (1914-19), was born in Bruce county, Canada West, on February 15, 1864. He was educated at Osgoode Hall Law School, Toronto, and was called to the Ontario bar in 1888 (K.C., 1908). He practised law in Sault Ste. Marie, Ontario; and he represented Sault Ste. Marie in the Ontario legislature from 1900 to 1919. He became minister of lands, forests, and mines in the Whitney administration; and, on the death of Sir James Whitney (q.v.), he became prime minister of the province. He remained prime minister during the whole of the First World War; but was defeated in 1919, and retired to private life. He then practised law in Toronto; and he died at Toronto, on September 29, 1941. He was created a K.C.M.G. in 1917.

[*Can. who's who*, 1936-37; H. Charlesworth (ed.), *A cyclopaedia of Canadian biography* (Toronto, 1919); *Can. parl. comp.*; Morgan, *Can. men* (1912).]

Heatherington, Alexander (d. 1878), geologist and author, was born in Russia, but emigrated to Nova Scotia, where he interested himself in gold-mining. He died in Toronto, Ontario, on March 8, 1878. He was the author of *A practical guide for tourists, miners and investors ... in the gold fields of Nova Scotia* (Montreal, 1868), *Mining industries of Nova Scotia* (London, 1874), and three pamphlets on *The gold yield of Nova Scotia* (London and Halifax, 1871-76).

[*Dom. ann. reg.*, 1878.]

Heavysege, Charles (1816-1876), poet and dramatist, was born in England on May 2, 1816. He came to Canada in 1853, and settled in Montreal as a woodcarver. Later he became a reporter on the staff of the Montreal *Witness*. Just before coming to Canada he published anonymously his first poem, *The revolt of Tar-*

tarus (London, 1852); and this was followed in Canada by *Sonnets* (Montreal, 1855), *Saul, a drama in three parts* (Montreal, 1857; 2nd. ed., 1859; 3rd ed., Boston, 1869), *Count Filippo, or the unequal marriage* (Montreal, 1860), *Jephthah's daughter* (Montreal and London, 1865), and *Jezebel* (New Dominion Monthly, Montreal, 1867). He published also a novel, *The advocate* (Montreal, 1865); but this was far below the level of his poetry. He died in Montreal on July 14, 1876.

[L. J. Burpee, *Charles Heavysege* (Trans. Roy. Soc. Can., 1901); *Can. who was who*, vol. 2.; Rose, *Cyc. Can. biog.* (1888); Morgan, *Bib. can.*; C. C. James, *A bibliography of Canadian poetry* (Toronto, 1899); R. P. Baker, *English-Canadian literature to the Confederation* (Cambridge, Mass., 1920); *Dict. Can. biog.*, vol. 10.]

Hébert, Adrien (1890-1967), painter, was born in Paris, France, April 12, 1890, the son of Louis Philippe Hébert (q.v.), one of Canada's most famous sculptors. He began his elementary schooling in France but travelled between France and Montreal during his childhood as his father worked on sculptures on both sides of the Atlantic. In 1904 he began study at the Monument National with Joseph St. Charles, Edmond Dyonnet, Joseph Franchère, and Jobson Paradis. From 1907 to 1911 he studied with William Brymner at the Art Association of Montreal. In Paris in 1912 he enrolled in the classes of Fernand Cormon. It was not until he discovered Monet, Sisley, and other impressionists that he became really interested in painting. On his return to Montreal in 1914, he taught drawing five half-days a week for thirty-five years for the Academic Commission of Montreal. In the afternoons he worked in his own studio. He did a number of portraits in his early years which were considered audacious and cruel, and by 1925 he had turned to painting his city, particularly the harbour and port of Montreal. He exhibited these works in Paris in 1930 and in Montreal in 1931. He continued to explore ships, streets, and locomotive works, and the *Gazette* noted "these things give him ample opportunity to portray activity and to work out complicated substantial designs". He was elected A.R.C.A. in 1932 and won the Jessie Dow prize for painting in 1936 and 1940. His paintings combine an impressionist flavour with a Canadian approach to actuality. His work is included in the National Gallery; Le Havre Museum, France; the Montreal Museum of Fine Arts; the Museum of the Province of Quebec; the Art Association of Montreal; and in private collections. He died at Montreal, 1967.

[*Can. who's who*, 1955-57; C. S. MacDonald, *A dictionary of Canadian artists*, vol. 2 (Ottawa, 1968).]

Hébert, Louis (d. 1627), colonist, was a native of Paris, France. He was an apothecary at the court of the French king; and in 1604 he accompanied the expedition of Monts (q.v.) to Acadia. His interest in herbs led to attempts at agriculture in Port Royal; and he deserves the title of the first Canadian farmer. He returned to France in 1614, but was persuaded by his friend Champlain (q.v.) to settle at Quebec in 1617. In 1623 he was granted land on the site of what is now the Upper Town of Quebec; and here he commenced farming. He died at Quebec on January 25, 1627, as the result of a fall. By his wife, Marie Rollet, he had one son and two daughters; and many families of French Canada trace their descent to him.

[A. Couillard-Després, *Louis Hébert et sa famille* (Paris, 1913) and *La première famille française au Canada* (Montreal, 1907); N. E. Dionne, *Louis Hébert* (Bull. rech. hist., 1900); C. W. Colby, *Canadian types of the old régime* (New York, 1908); M. J. and G. Ahern, *Notes pour servir à l'histoire de la médecine dans le Bas-Canada* (Quebec, 1923); Le Jeune, *Dict. gén.*; *Dict. Can. biog.*, vol. 1.]

Hébert, Louis Philippe (1850-1917), sculptor, was born at Ste. Sophie d'Halifax, Megantic county, Lower Canada, on January 27, 1850, the son of Théophile Hébert and Julie Bourgeois. He studied art at Montreal under Napoléon Bourassa (q.v.), and afterwards in France. In 1883 he was elected a member of the Royal Canadian Academy; and he became the most notable Canadian sculptor and designer of monuments of his day. He died at Westmount, Quebec, on June 13, 1917. In 1901 he was created chevalier of the Legion of Honour in France; and in 1903 he was made a C.M.G.

[*Can. who was who*, vol. 1; Morgan, *Can. men* (1912); Le Jeune, *Dict. gén.*; N. Mac-Tavish, *The fine arts in Canada* (Toronto, 1925).]

Hébert, Maurice (1888-1960), literary critic, was born at Quebec City, on January 21, 1888, and died there in 1960. He was educated at the Quebec Seminary and Laval University; and for many years he was the literary critic of *Le Canada Français*. Latterly, he was director of the Quebec Tourist and Publicity Bureau. He was elected a fellow of the Royal Society of Canada in 1935; and he was the author of *De livres en livres* (Montreal, 1929), *Et d'un livre à l'autre* (Montreal, 1932), and *Les lettres au Canada français* (Montreal, 1936).

[*Proc. Roy. Soc. Can.*, 1960; *Encyc. Can.*]

Heck, Mrs. Barbara, *née* **Ruckle** (1734-1804), "the mother of Methodism in America", was born at Ballingrame, Ireland, in 1734. She married Paul Heck, and in 1760 she and her husband emigrated to New York. Here she founded the first Methodist Society in America. She and her husband came north to Canada during the American Revolution; and

they eventually settled in the township of Augusta in the "New Settlements" on the St. Lawrence. Here again she formed a pioneer Methodist Society. She died in the township of Augusta, Upper Canada, in 1804.

[B. Hume, *Barbara Heck* (Toronto, 1930); F. H. Wooding, *Barbara Heck* (Canadian geographical journal, 1935); W. Canniff, *History of the settlement of Upper Canada* (Toronto, 1869).]

Hector, Sir James (1834-1907), geologist, was born in Edinburgh, Scotland, on March 16, 1834, the son of Alexander Hector, writer to the signet, and Margaret Macrostie. He was educated at Edinburgh University (M.D., 1856), and in 1857 he was appointed surgeon and geologist to accompany the exploring expedition to the western parts of British North America, under the command of Captain John Palliser (q.v.). He made many important observations in regard to the geology and ethnology of the Canadian west and the Rocky Mountains; and he discovered the pass through the Rocky Mountains which to-day bears his name. In 1861 he was appointed geologist to the government of New Zealand; and in 1866 he became director of the meteorological department of the New Zealand Institute, and of the colonial museum and the botanical gardens at Wellington. He retired from his position in 1903, and he died at Wellington, New Zealand, on November 5, 1907. He was created a C.M.G. in 1875 and a K.C.M.G. in 1887.

[*Dict. nat. biog.*, supp. II.]

Heenan, Peter (1875-1948), politician, was born at Tullaree, county Down, Ireland, on February 19, 1875, and died at Toronto, Ontario, on May 12, 1948. He came to Canada in 1902, and became a locomotive engineer. In 1919 he was elected to represent Kenora in the Ontario legislature, and was re-elected in 1923; but he resigned his seat in order to stand for the constituency in the Dominion House of Commons. He was elected, and was minister of labour in the Mackenzie King government from 1926 to 1934. In 1934 he was appointed minister of lands and forests in the Hepburn government in Ontario, and was elected to the Ontario legislature by acclamation. He was defeated at the polls in 1943, and resigned with the Hepburn government.

[*Who was who*, 1941-50; *Can. who's who*, 1948; *Can. parl. comp.*, 1942; Toronto *Globe and Mail*, May 13, 1948.]

Heeney, Arnold Danford Patrick (1902-1970), diplomat, was born in Montreal, Quebec, April 5, 1902, where his father was a clergyman of the Church of England. He was educated at St. John's College School in Winnipeg and at the University of Manitoba, where he was awarded a Rhodes scholarship (1923). He spent two years at St. John's College, Oxford (B.A., 1925), and returned to

McGill to study law (B.C.L., 1929). He was called to the bar in Quebec in 1929 and was created King's Counsel in 1941. He practised law in Montreal until 1938 and was also a part-time lecturer in the faculty of law at McGill. He became principal secretary to Prime Minister Mackenzie King in 1938 and Clerk of the Privy Council and Secretary to the Cabinet from 1940 until 1949. From 1949 to 1952 he was Under Secretary of State for External Affairs and from 1952 to 1953 was Canada's representative to the North Atlantic Council and the Organization for European Economic Cooperation. He was chairman of the Civil Service Commission of Canada (1957-1959), and served twice (1953-57 and 1959-62) as Canadian Ambassador to the United States. He was awarded the Vanier Medal of the Institute of Public Administration in 1963, and was made a Companion of the Order of Canada (1968). At the time of his death in Ottawa, Ontario, on December 20, 1970, he was chairman of the Canadian sections of the International Joint Commission and the Canada-United States Permanent Joint Board on Defence.

[*Can. who's who,* 1967-69; *External Affairs,* vol. 4 (October, 1952), pp. 341-5; *Financial Post,* Oct. 22, 1955; Dec. 7, 1957; Feb. 21, 1959.]

Heeney, William Bertal (1873-1955), clergyman and author, was born at Danford Lake, Quebec, on February 18, 1873, and died at Ottawa, Ontario, on April 14, 1955. He was educated at McGill University (B.A., 1899) and the Montreal Diocesan College, and was ordained a priest of the Church of England. From 1909 until his retirement he was rector of St. Luke's Church, Winnipeg. He was the author of two novels, *Pickanock* (London, 1912) and *D'Arcy Conyers* (Toronto, 1922), and a biography of Bishop Stewart (q.v.), entitled *I walk with a bishop* (Toronto, 1937). He was also the editor of *Leaders of the Canadian Church* (3 vols., Toronto, 1918-43).

[*Can. who's who,* 1952-54.]

Heighington, Wilfred (1897-1945), lawyer and author, was born in Toronto, Ontario, in 1897, and died there on March 24, 1945. He was educated at the Royal Military College, Kingston, and Osgoode Hall, and practised law in Toronto. He served overseas with the Canadian Corps during the First World War; and he represented St. David's in the Ontario legislature as a Conservative from 1929 to 1943. A frequent contributor of *jeux d'esprit* to Canadian periodicals, he was the author of *Whereas and whatnot* (Toronto, 1934) and *The cannon's mouth* (Toronto, 1943).

[Toronto *Globe and Mail,* March 25, 1945; *Can. who's who,* 1938-39.]

Hellmuth, Isaac (1817-1901), Anglican bishop of Huron (1872-83), was born near Warsaw, Poland, of Jewish parents, on December 14, 1817. He was educated at the University of Breslau, and here he was converted to Christianity. He went to England in 1841, and studied for the ministry of the Church of England. In 1844 he emigrated to Canada, and in 1846 was ordained at Quebec a priest of the Church of England. He first became a professor at Bishop's College, Lennoxville; and was then appointed superintendent of the Colonial and Continental Church Society in British North America. In 1861 he was instrumental in founding Huron College, at London, Canada West; and in 1863 he became its first principal. In 1865 he founded also the Hellmuth Boys' College, and in 1869 the Hellmuth Ladies' College, at London. In 1871 he became coadjutor bishop, and in 1872 bishop, of Huron. In 1878 he was the prime mover in the foundation of the Western University, in connection with Huron College; and the University was opened by him in 1881. He resigned the bishopric of Huron in 1883, and went to England. He died at Weston-super-Mare on May 28, 1901. He was twice married, (1) in 1847 to Catherine (d. 1884), daughter of General Thomas Evans, C.B., by whom he had two sons and one surviving daughter; and (2) in 1886 to Mary, daughter of Admiral the Hon. Arthur Duncombe and widow of the Hon. Ashley Carr-Glynn, by whom he had no issue. He was a D.D. of Lennoxville University (1854) and a D.C.L. of Trinity University, Toronto (1854). He was the author of a number of theological books and pamphlets.

[C. H. Mockridge, *Bishops of the Church of England in Canada* (Toronto, 1896); A. H. Crowfoot, *This dreamer, Life of Isaac Hellmuth, Second Bishop of Huron* (Toronto, 1963); *Dict. nat. biog.; Cyc. Am. biog;* Dent, *Can. port,* vol. 2; Morgan, *Can. men* (1898).]

Helmcken, John Sebastian (1824-1920), speaker of the Legislative Assembly of Vancouver Island, was born in London, England, on June 5, 1824, of German parentage. He was educated at St. George's school and at the Apothecaries' Hall (M.R.C.S., 1848). In 1850 he emigrated to Vancouver Island as a surgeon in the employ of the Hudson's Bay Company; and from 1855 to 1871 he was a member of the Assemblies of Vancouver Island and British Columbia, and speaker of these bodies. He was at first an opponent of Confederation; but was a member of the delegation sent to Ottawa in 1870 to arrange the terms of union, and it was largely through him that the building of a transcontinental railway was made a condition of union. In 1871 he declined appointment to the Senate of Canada, and retired to private life. He died at Victoria, British Columbia, on September 1, 1920. In 1852 he married the daughter of Sir James Douglas (q.v.).

[J. B. Kerr, *Biographical dictionary of well-known British Columbians* (Vancouver, B.C., 1890); Morgan, *Can. men*

(1912); F. W. Howay and E. O. S. Scholefield, *British Columbia* (Vancouver, B.C., 1914).]

Heming, Arthur (1870-1940), artist and author, was born in Paris, Ontario, on January 17, 1870. He studied art in New York and London; and on his return to Canada he specialized in drawings, and later paintings, of wilderness life in Canada. He was elected an associate of the Canadian Royal Academy of Arts; and he achieved a wide reputation as a delineator of "the colour, romance, and beauty of Canadian wild life". He was the author of three books, which he himself illustrated: *Spirit Lake* (New York, 1907), *The drama of the forests* (Garden City, N.Y., 1921), and *The living forest* (Garden City, N.Y., 1925). He died at Hamilton, Ontario, on October 31, 1940.

[W. J. Phillips, *The art of Arthur Heming* (Beaver, 1940); *Can. who's who*, 1936-37.]

Hemmeon, Joseph Clarence (1880-1963), economist and professor, was born at Parrsboro, Nova Scotia, in 1880, and was educated at Acadia (B.A., 1898; M.A., 1904) and at Harvard (Ph.D., 1906). He taught at Illinois University before his appointment to McGill University in 1907, where he became the other half of a department of economics and political science whose head was Stephen Leacock (q.v.). He succeeded Leacock as department head on his retirement in 1936 and retained the post until 1945. His particular interests were politics and labour problems, and he approached them from a liberal, non-dogmatic point of view. He died on December 27, 1963, at Wolfville, Nova Scotia. He wrote *Organization and development of the British Post Office to 1840* (1912); *Economic relations of British American provinces before Confederation* (1934); and *The Canadian railway worker* (1936).

[*Can. journ. ec. pol. sc.*, vol. XXX; V. B. Rhodenizer, *Canadian literature in English* (Montreal, 1965).]

Hemmeon, Morley De Wolfe (1868-1919), educationist, was born at Saint John, New Brunswick, on April 7, 1868. He was educated at Acadia University (B.A., 1888), and Harvard University (M.A., 1906; Ph.D., 1908); and he became principal of the Academy at Guysboro, Nova Scotia. He died at Wolfville, Nova Scotia, on August 22, 1919. He was the author of *Burgage tenure in mediaeval England* (Cambridge, Mass., 1914).

[*Records of the graduates of Acadia University* (Wolfville, N.S., 1926).]

Hemsley, Richard (1846-1931), merchant, was born in Cirencester, Gloucestershire, England, on July 16, 1846, and he died at Montreal, Quebec, in 1931. He emigrated to Canada in 1867, and became a jeweller and watchmaker in Montreal. Shortly before his death he published his reminiscences, under the title *Looking back* (Montreal, 1930).

[Private information.]

Henday, Anthony (*fl.* 1748-1762), fur-trader, was a native of the Isle of Wight, England. Having been outlawed in 1748 for smuggling, he entered in 1750 the service of the Hudson's Bay Company, and was sent out to York Factory. In 1754-55 he made a famous journey inland, in the course of which he visited the French post of Pasquia on the Saskatchewan, and spent the winter among the Blackfoot Indians, of whose customs he left us our first account. His journal has been published, with introduction and notes by L. J. Burpee, under the title *York Factory to the Blackfeet country* (Trans. Roy. Soc. Can., 1907).

[A. S. Morton, *A history of the Canadian west* (Toronto, 1939); J. G. MacGregor, *Behold the Shining Mountains, being an account of the travels of Anthony Henday, 1754-55, the first white man to enter Alberta* (Edmonton, 1954); *Dict. Can. biog.*, vol. 3.]

Henderson, James (1849-1924), Methodist minister, was born at Airdrie, near Glasgow, Scotland, on March 1, 1849. He emigrated to Canada in 1870, and became one of the most outstanding preachers in the Methodist Church. He died at Montreal on November 21, 1924.

[Salem G. Bland, *James Henderson, D.D.* (Toronto, 1926); Morgan, *Can. men* (1912).]

Henderson, James (1871-1951), painter, was born in Glasgow, Scotland, in 1871, and died in Regina, Saskatchewan, on July 6, 1951. He studied art at the Glasgow School of Art and in London. He came to Canada in 1910, and in 1916 he opened a studio at Fort Qu'Appelle; he devoted himself to painting western landscapes and Indian subjects in a traditional manner. Three of his paintings are in the National Gallery at Ottawa.

[*Encyc. Can.*]

Henderson, John Lanceley Hodge (1917-1973), historian, was born in Montreal, Quebec, on July 19, 1917. The Hendersons moved to London, Ontario, in 1928, where John completed his secondary education in evening classes. He graduated from the University of Western Ontario in 1940 (B.A.), Huron College (L.Th., 1943; B.D., 1947; D.D., 1955). After serving in various parishes he became dean of residence at Huron College and a member of the history department (1955) and librarian (1956). He died at Venice, Italy, on May 24, 1973. He wrote *John Strachan 1787-1867* (Toronto, 1969), *John Strachan: Documents and opinions* (Toronto, 1969), and many articles on related subjects.

[*Can. hist. rev.*, vol. LIV.]

Henderson, Velyien Ewart (1877-1945), pharmacologist, was born at Cobourg, Ontario, on June 27, 1877, and died at his summer cottage on Georgian Bay on August 6, 1945. He was educated at Upper Canada College and the University of Toronto (B.A., 1899; M.A. and M.B., 1902), and after two years of post-graduate study at the University of Pennsylvania and in Germany and England, he was appointed to the staff of the faculty of medicine in the University of Toronto. He served overseas in the First World War both as a combatant officer and as a medical officer, and on his return in 1919 he was appointed professor of pharmacology at Toronto. He was elected a fellow of the Royal Society of Canada in 1927, and was president of Section V in 1937-38. He was the author of *Materia medica and pharmacy* (Toronto, 1932), which went into six editions, and a booklet entitled *Air crew in their element* (Toronto, 1942). He was also joint author, with Miss W. L. Chute, of a *Materia medica* (Toronto, 1943).

[*Proc. Roy. Soc. Can.*, 1946; *Can. who's who*, 1938-39.]

Hendrie, Sir John Strathearn (1857-1923), lieutenant-governor of Ontario (1914-19), was born in Hamilton, Upper Canada, on August 15, 1857, the son of William Hendrie and Margaret Walker. He was educated at the Hamilton Grammar School and Upper Canada College, Toronto; and became a railway contractor. He promoted the Hamilton Bridge Works Company, and was for some years its general manager. In 1902 he was elected to represent Hamilton in the Legislative Assembly of Ontario, and he sat continuously for this seat until 1914. In 1905 he became a minister without portfolio in the Whitney administration, and in 1906 he was appointed a member of the Ontario Hydro-Electric Commission. In 1914 he was appointed lieutenant-governor of Ontario, and his period of office ended in 1919. He died at Baltimore, Maryland, on July 18, 1923. In 1885 he married Lena Maude, daughter of P. R. Henderson, of Kingston, Ontario; and by her he had one son and one daughter. He was created a knight bachelor in 1915, and in 1907 was gazetted a C.V.O. He held the long service ribbon in the Canadian militia, and from 1903 to 1909 he was lieutenant-colonel commanding the 2nd Brigade, Canadian Field Artillery. The owner of a famous racing stable, he won the King's plate, Toronto, in 1910.

[Morgan, *Can. men* (1912); *Can. who's who*, 1910; *Can. parl. comp.*; *Can. ann. review*, 1902-19.]

Hendrie, Lilian Margaret (1870-1952), educationist and author, was born in Montreal in 1870, and died there on May 12, 1952. She was the headmistress of the Montreal High School for Girls from 1911 to 1930; and she was the author of *Early days in Montreal, and rambles in the neighbourhood* (Montreal, 1932).

[Montreal *Gazette*, May 14, 1952.]

Hendry, Anthony. See **Henday, Anthony.**

Heney, Hugues (1789-1844), executive councillor of Lower Canada, was born on September 9, 1789. He was educated at Montreal, and became for a short time a clerk in the service of the North West Company. In 1804 he was stationed on the upper Red River, and in 1805 he accompanied F. A. Larocque (q.v.) to the Mandan country. In 1811 he was called to the bar of Lower Canada. From 1820 to 1830 he was a member of the Legislative Assembly of Lower Canada for Montreal East; and in the Assembly he opposed the extremists under L. J. Papineau (q.v.). In 1833 he was appointed a member of the Executive Council of Lower Canada, and he continued in the council until 1841. In 1842 he was appointed a commissioner for the revision of the statutes of Lower Canada; but he died, before the completion of this work, at Three Rivers, Lower Canada, on January 15, 1844. He was the author of a *Commentaire sur l'acte constitutionel du Haut et du Bas-Canada* (Montreal, 1832); and in 1818 he took part in the Selkirk controversy by translating into French John Halkett's *Statement respecting the Earl of Selkirk's settlement of Kildonan* (London, 1817) and S. H. Wilcocke's *Narrative of occurrences in the Indian countries of North America* (London, 1817).

[Morgan, *Bib. can.*; Bibaud, *Panth. can.*; Le Jeune, *Dict. gén.*; F. J. Audet, *Les députés de Montréal* (Montreal, 1943).]

Hennepin, Louis (1626-1705?), Recollect friar, explorer, and author, was born in Belgium on May 12, 1626. He entered the Recollect order as a novice while still a youth; and, after a varied career in Europe, came as a missionary to New France in 1675. He was stationed first at Quebec, and then at Fort Frontenac; and in 1678 he was selected to accompany La Salle (q.v.) on his journey of discovery to the Mississippi. In 1680 he was dispatched by La Salle, with two companions, to push on from Fort Crèvecoeur to the Mississippi to report on the country; but he and his companions were captured by the Sioux, and were compelled to spend several months with their captors wandering through the country of the Upper Mississippi. They were rescued by the *coureur-de-bois* Du Lhut (q.v.), and Hennepin made his way back to Quebec in the summer of 1681. Thence he returned, probably in the following autumn, to France. The remainder of his life was passed in Europe; and the last glimpse we have of him is in a convent in Rome in 1701. The date and place of his death are not known.

Hennepin's reputation rests on his writings, about which much controversy has raged. In

351

1683 he published at Paris his *Description de la Louisiane*, in which he gave a fairly veracious account of his travels. The success of the book, of which new editions were published in 1684 and 1688, and which was translated into Dutch, German, and Italian, led him, however, to bring out, after the death of La Salle (q.v.), a new book entitled *Nouvelle découverte d'un très grand pays* (Utrecht, 1697), which was marked by gross fabrications and plagiarisms, and in which he claimed credit for La Salle's discoveries. This was followed by a third book, *Nouveau voyage d'un pais plus grand que l'Europe* (Utrecht, 1698), and by an English version of Hennepin's travels entitled *A new discovery of a vast country in America* (London, 1698), both of which contained the falsifications of the *Nouvelle découverte*. All of these publications reached new editions; and Hennepin must have been one of the most widely read authors of his day.

[R. G. Thwaites (ed.), *Hennepin's A new discovery* (2 vols., Chicago, 1903), with bibliography by V. H. Paltsits; N. E. Dionne, *Hennepin, ses Voyages et ses oeuvres* (Quebec, 1897), Jérome Goyens, *Le P. Louis Hennepin* (Quaracchi, 1925); and L. Hennepin, *A description of Louisiana*, tr. by J. G. Shea (New York, 1880), with bibliography; *Dict. Can. biog.*, vol. 2.]

Hennessey, Frank (1893-1941), painter, was born in Ottawa, Ontario, in 1893. Though he acquired an international reputation as an artist, he was largely self-taught, and drew his inspiration from the Gatineau country near Ottawa. He achieved a brilliant success both with crayon and with oils. In 1932 he was elected a member of the Ontario Society of Artists; in 1934, an associate of the Royal Canadian Academy; and in 1941, shortly before his death, an academician. He died, by his own hand, in Ottawa, Ontario, on November 8, 1941.

[W. Colgate, *Canadian art* (Toronto, 1944).]

Henry, Alexander (1739-1824), fur-trader and author, was born in New Jersey in August, 1739. He was one of the first English traders to reach Michilimackinac after the British conquest of Canada; and he narrowly escaped being murdered by the Indians during Pontiac's Conspiracy in 1763. From that date to 1780 he was one of the pioneers of the Canadian fur-trade. For several years he was a trader on Lake Superior; but on March 9, 1776, he reached Cumberland House, in the valley of the Saskatchewan and he wintered on Beaver Lake. He was not included in the original North West Company in 1779; and in 1781 he settled in Montreal as a general merchant. Some time after 1787, however, he sold out his interests in the Indian country to the North West Company, and became (according to a statement made in the biography of him in the *Canadian magazine* for April and May, 1824) "a dormant partner in that firm, where he continued until 1796". In 1796 he and Alexander Henry, Jr., sold their shares to William Hallowell. He died at Montreal on April 4, 1824. The story of his career as a fur-trader is told in his *Travels and adventures in Canada and the Indian countries* (New York, 1809; new ed., by James Bain, Toronto, 1901).

[Morgan, *Bib. can.*; *Cyc. Am. biog.*; *Canadian magazine and literary repository*, 1824; L. J. Burpee, *The search for the western sea* (London, 1908).]

Henry, Alexander (d.1813?), fur-trader, was the second son of Alexander Henry the elder (q.v.), the author of *Travels and adventures*. He was born after 1785, and became a clerk in the North West Company. He was murdered by the Indians at Fort Nelson, on the Liard River, in the Mackenzie River department, either at the end of 1812 or the beginning of 1813.

[W. S. Wallace (ed.), *Documents relating to the North West Company* (Toronto: The Champlain Society, 1934).]

Henry, Alexander (d. 1814), fur-trader, was a nephew of Alexander Henry the elder (q.v.), the author of *Travels and adventures*. He entered the service of the North West Company as a clerk about 1792; and during the next twenty-two years he travelled all over the North West, from the Great Lakes to the Pacific. His journals, which he kept from day to day, have been published by Elliott Coues under the title, *New light on the early history of the greater North-West* (3 vols., New York, 1897). He became a partner of the North West Company between 1799 and 1802; and he was drowned off Fort George, on the Pacific coast, on May 22, 1814.

[*Cyc. Am. biog.*; L. J. Burpee, *The search for the western sea* (London, 1908).]

Henry, Edme (1760-1841), notary public, soldier, and banker, was born at Longueuil, Canada, on November 15, 1760, the son of Edme Henry, surgeon-major of the Royal Roussillon regiment, and a Canadian, Geneviève Fournier. His father left Canada before he was born, and settled later in the Islands of St. Pierre and Miquelon; but he was brought up in Canada, and in 1783 received a commission as notary public from Sir Frederick Haldimand (q.v.). From 1786 to 1793 he lived in the Island of Miquelon; but in the latter years he returned to Canada, and resumed practice as a notary public at Laprairie, Lower Canada. He saw active service in the War of 1812 as a major in the 2nd battalion of the Beauharnois militia; and he commanded this battalion at the battle of Châteauguay. From 1810 to 1814 he also represented the county of Huntingdon in the Legislative Assembly of Lower Canada. Later, he was the founder of

Henry's Bank, a private banking venture which failed during the troubles of 1837. He died at Laprairie, Lower Canada, on September 14, 1841.

[*Bull. rech. hist.*, 1927.]

Henry, George Stewart (1871-1958), prime minister of Ontario, was born in King township, Ontario, on July 16, 1871, and died near Toronto, Ontario, on September 2, 1958. He was educated at Upper Canada College, the University of Toronto (B.A., 1896), and the Ontario Agricultural College, and became a farmer near Toronto. He represented East York in the Legislative Assembly of Ontario from 1913 to 1943 as a Conservative. He was minister of agriculture in the Hearst government from 1918 to 1919, and minister of public works and highways in the Ferguson government from 1923 to 1930; and he succeeded G. H. Ferguson (q.v.) as prime minister in 1930. His government was defeated in the elections of 1934, after which he was leader of the opposition until 1937, when he retired from political life. In 1931 the University of Toronto conferred on him the LL.D. degree.

[*Can. who's who*, 1955-57; *Can. parl. comp*, 1956; *Encyc. Can.*]

Henry, John (*fl.* 1776-1820), adventurer, was born in Ireland about 1776, and emigrated to New York about 1792. In 1807, after a chequered career, he appeared in Montreal, and here he ingratiated himself with the heads of the North West Company. He appears to have been the author of the pamphlet *On the origin and progress of the North West Company of Canada* (London, 1811). In 1808-09 he was employed by Sir James Craig (q.v.) to sound public opinion in the United States, and to open negotiations with the Federalist party. Dissatisfied with the reward he received for his services, he sold his letters to the United States government in 1811 for $50,000; and their publication had not a little to do with the outbreak of the War of 1812. Before the letters were published, however, Henry was smuggled out of the United States; and the rest of his life he spent in Europe. The last glimpse of him was in 1820, when he was sent to Italy as a paid informer to obtain evidence against Queen Caroline of Great Britain.

[E. A. Cruikshank, *The political adventures of John Henry* (Toronto, 1936); C. S. Blue, *John Henry, the spy* (Can. mag., 1916); *Dict. Am. biog.*]

Henry, Robert (1778?-1859), fur-trader and banker, was an adopted nephew of Alexander Henry the elder (q.v.), and was born about 1778. He entered the service of the North West Company as a clerk, and became a partner of the Company in 1810. From 1810 to 1811 he was on the Churchill River, and from 1811 to 1815 he was in the Athabaska department. He "went down" on rotation in 1815; and

in that year he was elected a member of the Beaver Club in Montreal. In 1817 he retired from the fur-trade, and settled in Cobourg, Upper Canada. Here he pursued for many years the business of banking; and here he died on May 10, 1859, aged 81 years. On November 2, 1817, he married Christine, daughter of the Rev. John Bethune (q.v.), and sister of Angus Bethune (q.v.); and by her he had two daughters.

[W. S. Wallace (ed.), *Documents relating to the North West Company* (Toronto: The Champlain Society, 1934); E. E. Rich (ed.), *Journal of occurrences in the Athabasca department, by George Simpson* (Toronto: The Champlain Society, 1938).]

Henry, Walter (1791-1860), army surgeon and author, was born at Donegal, Ireland, on January 1, 1791. He was educated at Trinity College, Dublin, Ireland, and studied surgery in London, England. In 1811 he entered the British army as a hospital assistant; and he saw service in the Peninsular War, the Nepalese War of 1816-17, and the Canadian rebellions of 1837 and 1838. He was stationed in Canada as a staff surgeon from 1827 to 1841; and in 1852 he returned to Canada as inspector-general of hospitals. He retired on half-pay in 1856, and settled in Belleville, Upper Canada, where he died on June 27, 1860. While in Canada he published, under the *nom de plume* of "A Staff Surgeon", *Trifles from my portfolio* (2 vols., Quebec, 1839; 2nd ed., under the title, *Henry's military life*, London, 1843); and he contributed to the New York *Albion* a number of papers under the pseudonyms, "Miles", "Scrutator", and "Piscator". To the *Transactions* of the Literary and Historical Society of Quebec he contributed also a paper, *Observations on the habits of the salmon family* (Quebec, 1837).

[Morgan, *Bib. can.*]

Henry, William (1783?-1846?) fur-trader, was the eldest son of Alexander Henry the elder (q.v.), and was born about 1783. He entered the service of the North West Company as a clerk in 1801; and from 1801 to 1809 he was employed in the Red River district. In 1810 he was at Cumberland House; and in 1811 he was on the Athabaska River. In 1812 he was transferred to the Columbia department, and until 1816 he was in charge of a post on the Willamette River. In 1817 he returned to Fort William; and he was then sent to Lesser Slave Lake. He was retained as a clerk in this district on the union of the North West and Hudson's Bay Companies in 1821; but in 1823 he appears to have retired to Canada. Here he became a surveyor and civil engineer. About 1848 he settled in Newmarket, Upper Canada; and here he died about 1864. In Montreal, after 1823, he married the sister of John Felton, who had been the signal midshipman on Nelson's flagship, the *Victory*, at the battle of

Trafalgar; and by her he had several children. One of his sons, Charles, died, after a most adventurous career, in Barrie, Ontario, in June, 1897.

[W. S. Wallace (ed.), *Documents relating to the North West Company* (Toronto: The Champlain Society, 1934).]

Henry, William Alexander (1816-1888), one of the Fathers of Confederation, was born in Halifax, Nova Scotia, on December 30, 1816, the son of Robert N. Henry and Margaret Hendricksen. He was educated at the High School in Halifax, and in 1840 was called to the bar of Nova Scotia (Q.C., 1849). From 1841 to 1867 he represented Antigonish in the Legislative Assembly of Nova Scotia, first as a Liberal, and after 1857 as a Conservative. He became a member of the provincial government in 1849, and he continued a member of successive administrations until 1867. He was one of the leading advocates of Confederation in Nova Scotia, and was a member of the Charlottetown and Quebec Conferences in 1864 and of the London Conference in 1866. At the latter he was one of the two members who framed the original draft of the British North America Act. In 1867 he was defeated at the polls, as a result of his advocacy of Confederation; and from 1867 to 1875 he resumed the practice of law in Halifax. In 1875 he was appointed a judge of the Supreme Court of Canada; and this post he held until his death at Ottawa on May 3, 1888. He was twice married, (1) in 1841 to Sophia Caroline McDonald (d. 1845), and (2) in 1850 to Christiana McDonald; and he had several children.

[Rose, *Cyc. Can. biog.* (1886); *Cyc. Am. biog.*; Dent, *Can. port.*, vol. 2; *Can. parl. comp.*, 1867; D. Campbell, *History of Nova Scotia* (Montreal, 1873); P. R. Blakeley, *William Alexander Henry: A father of confederation from Nova Scotia* (Coll. Nova Scotia Hist. Soc., 1968).]

Henshaw, Mrs. Julia Wilmotte, *née* **Henderson** (1869-1937), author, was born at Durham, England, in 1869. She married in 1887 Charles Grant Henshaw, of Montreal; and for most of the rest of her life she lived in Vancouver, British Columbia. She died in Vancouver on November 18, 1937. She was the author of *Hypnotized?* (Toronto, 1898), *Why not, sweetheart?* (Toronto, 1901), *Mountain wild-flowers of Canada* (Toronto, 1906), *Mountain wild-flowers of America* (Boston, 1906), and *Wild-flowers of the North American mountains* (New York, 1915).

[*Who's who among North American authors*, 1935; Morgan, *Can. men and women* (1912); *Can. who's who*, 1936-37.]

Henson, Josiah (1789-1883), an escaped slave who was reputed to be the original of the character of "Uncle Tom" in Mrs. H. B. Stowe's *Uncle Tom's cabin.* He was born at Port To-

bacco, Maryland, on June 15, 1789; and he escaped to Canada in 1830. He lived for the rest of his life at Dresden, Ontario; and he became here the pastor of a negro church. He died at Dresden on May 18, 1883. He was the author of *The life of Josiah Henson, formerly a slave* (Boston, 1849), later republished under varying titles.

[Jessie Louise Beattie, *Black Moses* (Toronto, 1957); *Cyc. Am. biog.*]

Hepburn, Mitchell Frederick (1896-1953), prime minister of Ontario (1934-42), was born at St. Thomas, Ontario, on August 12, 1896, and died at his farm, near St. Thomas, on January 5, 1953. After several years as a bank clerk, and after a brief service with the armed forces during the First World War, he became an onion farmer. In 1926 he was elected to represent West Elgin in the Canadian House of Commons, and in 1930 he was chosen leader of the Liberal party in Ontario. In 1934 he resigned his seat in the House of Commons to lead the Liberal party in the provincial elections in Ontario, and he won one of the most decisive victories in the history of Ontario. He became prime minister of Ontario and provincial treasurer, and embarked on a period of office that was full of controversy. In particular, he waged a bitter war on the Liberal prime minister of Canada, Mackenzie King (q.v.), for reasons that were never wholly clear; and this split in the Liberal party was ultimately the cause of his undoing. He resigned as prime minister in 1942; and though he became leader of the Liberal opposition in the legislature, he was defeated in the election of 1945, and retired "to watch the grass grow" on his farm.

[N. McKenty, *Mitch Hepburn* (Toronto, 1967); Toronto *Globe and Mail*, Jan. 6, 1953; *Can. who's who*, 1949-51; *Can. parl. comp.*, 1944; *Encyc. Can.*]

Herbert, Mary E. (*fl.* 1859-1865), journalist, was born in Ireland, emigrated to Nova Scotia, and died in Halifax, Nova Scotia. She contributed to a number of Maritime province journals; and she was the author of *Scenes in the life of a Halifax belle* (Halifax, N.S., 1859), *Woman as she should be; or, Agnes Wiltshire* (Halifax, N.S., 1861), and *Flowers by the wayside* (Halifax, N.S., 1865).

[R. J. Long, *Nova Scotia authors* (East Orange, N.J., 1918); Morgan, *Bib. can.*]

Herbin, John Frederic (1860-1923), author, was born at Windsor, Nova Scotia, on February 8, 1860, of French and Acadian parentage. He was educated at Acadia College (B.A., 1890). He died at Wolfville, Nova Scotia, on December 29, 1923. Among his publications were *The marshlands* (Windsor, N.S., 1893), *The history of Grand Pré* (Toronto, 1903), *The heir to Grand Pré* (Toronto, 1907), *Jen of the* *marshes* (Toronto, 1922), and *The land of Evangeline* (Toronto, 1923).

[Morgan, *Can. men* (1912); R. J. Long, *Nova Scotia authors* (East Orange, N.J., 1918).]

Herchmer, Lawrence William (1840-1915), commissioner of the Royal North West Mounted Police (1886-1900), was born in Oxfordshire, England, on April 25, 1840. In 1858 he was gazetted an ensign in the 46th Foot, and he saw service with his regiment in India and elsewhere. On his retirement from the army, he came to Canada, and in 1878 he was appointed inspector of Indian agencies in the North West Territories. In 1886 he was appointed commissioner of the Royal North West Mounted Police; and he commanded this force until his retirement in 1900. He died at Vancouver, British Columbia, on February 17, 1915. In 1868 he married Mary Helen, daughter of the Hon. Henry Sherwood (q.v.).

[Morgan, *Can. men* (1898); B. Deane, *Mounted police life in Canada* (London, 1916); A. L. Haydon, *The riders of the plains* (Toronto, 1910).]

Heriot or **Herriot, Frederick George** (1786-1843), soldier, was born in the Island of Jersey on January 11, 1786, the third son of Roger Heriot and Anne Nugent. He entered the British army in 1801, and came to Canada in 1802. He was second in command of the Canadian Voltigeurs during the War of 1812 in Canada, and was present at the battle of Crysler's Farm. In 1816 he founded the town of Drummondville, in the Eastern Townships; and from 1829 to 1833 he represented Drummond in the Legislative Assembly of Lower Canada. In 1840 he was appointed a member of the Special Council of Lower Canada. He rose to the rank of major-general in the army; and he died at Comfort Hall, Drummondville, on December 29, 1843. For his services in the War of 1812 he was created a C.B. He was unmarried.

[J. C. A. Heriot, *Major-general the Hon. Frederick George Heriot* (Can. antiq. and num. journal, 1911); J. C. St. Amant, *L'hon. Fréderic-George Herriot* (Bull. rech. hist., 1902).]

Heriot, George (1766-1844), deputy postmaster-general of British North America, was born at Haddington, Scotland, 1766, the son of the sheriff-clerk of East Lothian. He is said to have been a cousin of Frederick George Heriot (q.v.). He came to Canada, and for a number of years was a clerk in the ordnance department at Quebec. In 1800 he was appointed deputy postmaster-general of British North America. He resigned this post in 1816, and he died in England, unmarried, in 1844. He was the author of a *History of Canada* (2 vols., London, 1804), and *Travels through the Canadas* (London, 1807), the latter illustrated by himself.

[J. C. A. Heriot, *George Heriot* (pamphlet, n.p., n.d.); W. Smith, *A history of the post-office in British North America* (Toronto, 1920); Morgan, *Bib. can.*]

Herkimer, Johan Jost (1733?-1795), loyalist, was born on the Mohawk River, in the province of New York, about 1733. He took the loyalist side in the American Revolution; and in 1777 made his way overland to the English post at Niagara. He was given a commission as captain in the Indian department; and he served in Canada throughout the remainder of the revolutionary war. He settled in Cataraqui (Kingston), on the Bay of Quinte in 1784 or 1785; and he died there in August, 1795.

[W. D. Reid, *Johan Jost Herkimer, U.E., and his family* (Ont. Hist. Soc., papers and records, 1936).]

Heron, Francis (1794-1840), fur-trader, was born in Donegal, Ireland, in 1794, and was a brother of James Heron (q.v.). He entered the service of the Hudson's Bay Company in 1812; and in 1814 was the steward at York Factory. From 1815 to 1818 he was at Fort Cumberland; from 1818 to 1821, at Fort Edmonton; from 1821 to 1822, at Fort Cumberland; from 1822 to 1823, on the South Branch expedition; from 1823 to 1824, in the Mackenzie River district; from 1824 to 1828, at Fort Garry; from 1828 to 1829, at Brandon House; from 1829 to 1835, at Fort Colville, in the Columbian district; and from 1835 to 1839 he was in Europe on furlough. He was promoted to the rank of chief trader in 1828; and he retired from the Company's service in 1839. He died in April, 1840.

[E. E. Rich (ed.), *Journal of occurrences in the Athabasca department, by George Simpson* (Toronto: The Champlain Society, 1938).]

Heron, James (*fl.* 1812-1857), was a native of Rathmelon, county Donegal, Ireland, and was a brother of Francis Heron (q.v.). He entered the service of the Hudson's Bay Company in 1812; and was first stationed in the Winnipeg district. In 1815 he deserted to the North West Company, "because of bad treatment"; and in 1817 Ross Cox (q.v.) met him at Fort Alexander. From 1821 to 1827 he was on the Churchill River, and from 1828 to 1831 at Fort Chipewyan. In 1832, however, he was discharged from the Company's service, and retired to Canada. He settled at what came to be known as Heron's Isle, in the parish of St. Martin, Lower Canada; but the date of his death is not known. He was still living in 1857. He married Fanny, the eldest daughter of George Keith (q.v.); and she died on Heron's Isle on December 30, 1850.

[E. E. Rich (ed.), *Journal of occurrences in the Athabasca department, by George Simp-*

son (Toronto: The Champlain Society, 1938).]

Herridge, Herbert Wilfred (1895-1973), forest farmer and politician, was born in South Kensington, England, February 28, 1895. He came to Canada in 1906 and was educated in British Columbia and at the Ontario Agricultural College. He served with the 54th Kootenay battalion in the First World War and was wounded (1916). He entered politics in 1941 as the C.C.F. member for Kootenay in the British Columbia legislature. He resigned in 1945 and was expelled from the C.C.F. movement by action of the British Columbia provincial executive. In 1945 he accepted the nomination of C.C.F. clubs as the candidate for the federal riding of Kootenay and was elected and continued to represent Kootenay until his retirement in 1968. He became parliamentary leader of the New Democratic Party in 1962 and was a leader in the fight against the Columbia River development treaty of 1964. An ardent conservationist, he was a member of the Agricultural Institute of Canada, and president of the Canadian Tree Farmer's Association. He died at Nakusp, British Columbia, October 19, 1973.

[*Can. who's who*, 1970-72.]

Herridge, William Thomas (1857-1929), clergyman and author, was born at Reading, England, on January 14, 1857, the son of the Rev. William Herridge. He came to Canada with his parents as a child, and was educated at the University of Toronto (B.A., 1880) and at the Montreal Presbyterian College (B.D., 1883; D.D., 1899). From 1883 to his death he was pastor of St. Andrew's Church, Ottawa; and in 1914 he was moderator of the Presbyterian Church in Canada. He died at Ottawa, on November 17, 1929. In 1885 he married Marjorie, daughter of the Rev. Thomas Duncan, D.D.; and by her he had two sons and two daughters. He was the author of *The orbit of life* (New York, 1906) and *The coign of vantage* (New York, 1908).

[*Can. who was who*, vol. 1; Morgan, *Can. men* (1912).]

Herrington, Walter Stevens (1860-1947), lawyer and historian, was born of United Empire Loyalist stock in the township of Ameliasburg, Prince Edward county, Ontario, on July 14, 1860, and died at Napanee, Ontario, on July 16, 1947. He was educated at Victoria University, then at Cobourg (B.A., 1883), and at Osgoode Hall. He was called to the bar in 1887, and for the rest of his life he practised law in Napanee. He also devoted much time to the study of Canadian history. He was the founder and, for many years, the president of the Lennox and Addington Historical Society; and he was the author of *The heroines of Canadian history* (Toronto, 1909), *Martyrs of New France* (Toronto, 1909), *The*

evolution of the prairie provinces (Toronto, 1911), *The history of the county of Lennox and Addington* (Toronto, 1913), *Pioneer life among the Loyalists of Upper Canada* (Toronto, 1915), and *The history of the Grand Lodge of Canada in the province of Ontario* (Hamilton, 1930). With the Rev. A. J. Wilson, he was also joint author of *The war work of the county of Lennox and Addington* (Napanee, 1922). He was elected a fellow of the Royal Society of Canada in 1919.

[*Proc. Roy. Soc. Can.*, 1948; *Can. who's who*, 1938-39; Morgan, *Can. men* (1912).]

Hertel de la Fresnière, Joseph François (1642-1722), soldier, was born in Three Rivers, Canada, on July 3, 1642. In 1690 he commanded the raiding-party which fell upon the English village of Salmon Falls, New Hampshire, and massacred its inhabitants; and he later commanded part of the French force besieging Casco Bay. In 1716 he was granted, for his military services, letters of nobility by Louis XV. He died at Boucherville, Canada, on May 22, 1722.

[*Cyc. Am. biog.*; Le Jeune, *Dict. gén.*; F. Parkman, *Count Frontenac and New France* (Boston, 1877); *Dict. Can. biog.*, vol. 2.]

Heward, Prudence (1896-1947), painter, was born in Montreal, Quebec, in 1896, and died in Los Angeles, California, where she had gone because of her health, on March 19, 1947. She studied painting at the Art Association of Montreal under William Brymner (q.v.) and Randolph Hewton, and at the Académie Colarossi in Paris under Charles Guérin. She was mainly notable for her figure painting; she became a member of the Canadian Group of Painters in 1933 and of the Contemporary Arts Society in 1939. Four of her oil paintings are in the National Gallery at Ottawa.

[Montreal *Gazette*, March 20, 1947; *Encyc. Can.*]

Hewitt, Charles Gordon (1885-1920), zoölogist, was born near Macclesfield, England, on February 23, 1885, the son of Thomas Henry Hewitt and Rachel Frost. He was educated at the grammar school, Macclesfield, and at Manchester University (B.Sc., 1902; M.Sc., 1903; D.Sc., 1909). In 1909 he came to Canada, having been appointed Dominion entomologist; and this office he held until his death at Ottawa on February 29, 1920. In 1913 he was elected a fellow of the Royal Society of Canada. He was the author of *The house-fly* (Manchester, 1910), *House-flies and how they spread disease* (New York, 1912), and *Conservation of the wild life of Canada* (New York, 1921).

[*Proc. Roy. Soc. Can.*, 1920.]

Hey, William (1733-1797), chief justice of Quebec, was an English barrister who was in 1766 appointed chief justice of Quebec, *vice*

William Gregory (q.v.), dismissed. He discharged the duties of his office until 1773, when he returned to England on leave of absence. His advice, with that of Guy Carleton (q.v.), had much to do with the form of the Quebec Act of 1774. In 1775 he returned to Canada for a few months; but in 1776 his resignation as chief justice was accepted. While in England he had been elected to represent Sandwich in the House of Commons; and in 1777 he obtained a post as commissioner of customs. This post he retained until his death on March 3, 1797. Two of his papers on the administration of justice in Canada have been printed in *The Lower Canada Jurist* (Montreal, 1857).

[W. S. Wallace (ed.), *The Maseres letters* (Toronto, 1919); A. Shortt and A. G. Doughty (eds.), *Documents relating to the constitutional history of Canada* (2 vols., Ottawa, 1918); *Cyc. Am. biog.*]

Hickman, William Albert (1875-1957?), author, was born at Pictou, Nova Scotia, in 1875, and is said to have died in 1957, though this date has not been verified. He was the author of two novels, *The sacrifice of the Shannon* (New York, 1903), and *An unofficial love story* (New York, 1907), and a book of short stories, *Canadian nights* (New York, 1914). He also wrote a *Handbook of New Brunswick* (Fredericton, 1900).

[Morgan, *Can. men* (1912).]

Hickson, Sir Joseph (1830-1897), general manager of the Grand Trunk Railway (1874-91), was born in Otterburn, Northumberland, England, in 1830, the son of Thomas Hickson. He entered the service of the North Eastern Railway, and later of the Manchester, Sheffield, and Lincolnshire Railway; and in 1854 he was appointed chief accountant of the Grand Trunk Railway Company of Canada. In 1874 he became general manager of the Grand Trunk Railway, and he filled this position until 1891. He died at Montreal, Quebec, on January 4, 1897. In 1869 he married Catherine, daughter of Andrew Dow, of Montreal; and by her he had six children. In 1890 he was created a knight bachelor.

[*Annual register*, 1897; Taché, *Men of the day*; Rose, *Cyc. Can. biog.* (1886); H. A. Lovett, *Canada and the Grand Trunk* (Montreal, 1924).]

Higgins, David William (1834-1917), journalist and author, was born at Halifax, Nova Scotia, on November 30, 1834, the son of William B. Higgins. He was educated in Brooklyn, New York; and in 1856 he went to California. In 1858 he took part in the gold rush to the Fraser; and in 1860 he settled in Victoria, Vancouver Island. He joined the staff of the *Colonist* newspaper, and for many years he was the editor of the *Colonist*. Later, he became editor of the Vancouver *World*, from

which he retired in 1907. From 1886 to 1898 he represented Esquimalt in the Legislative Assembly of British Columbia; and from 1890 to 1898 he was speaker of the Assembly. He died at Victoria on November 30, 1917. He was the author of *The mystic spring* (Toronto, 1904; New York, 1908), and *The passing of a race* (Toronto, 1905).

[Morgan, *Can. men* (1912); *Can. parl. comp.*]

Higgins, Thomas Alfred (1823-1905), clergyman, was born at Rawdon, Nova Scotia, on February 17, 1823. He was educated at Acadia College (B.A., 1854; M.A., 1857; D.D., 1885), and was ordained a minister of the Baptist Church in 1857. He died at Wolfville, Nova Scotia, on May 9, 1905. He was author of *The life of John Cramp Mockett* (Montreal, 1887).

[Morgan, *Can. men* (1898); R. J. Long, *Nova Scotia authors* (East Orange, N.J., 1918).]

Hill, Allan Massie (1876-1943), clergyman, was born at Halifax, Nova Scotia, in 1876. He was educated at Dalhousie University (B.A., 1896; M.A., 1899), at Pine Hill College, Halifax (B.D., 1900), and at the University of Illinois (Ph.D., 1907), and was ordained a minister of the Presbyterian Church in 1899. He was the pastor of churches in Saint John, New Brunswick, in Yarmouth, Nova Scotia, and in Montreal, Quebec. He died in Montreal, Quebec, on October 9, 1943. He was the author of *Sweepings frae the curling rink* (Yarmouth, N.S., 1910).

[Morgan, *Can. men* (1912); R. J. Long, *Nova Scotia authors* (East Orange, N.J., 1918).]

Hill, George William (1824-1906), clergyman and author, was born at Halifax, Nova Scotia, on November 9, 1824, the brother of the Hon. P. C. Hill (q.v.). He was educated at Acadia College and at King's College, Windsor (B.A., 1847), and became a clergyman of the Church of England. He was for many years rector of St. Paul's Church, Halifax, and also chaplain to the Legislative Council. He resigned in 1885 to accept the charge of an English church in Switzerland; and in his later years he was rector of Gravely, Hertfordshire, England. He died in England in 1906. He was the author of *Old Testament history* (Halifax, N.S., 1855), *Nova Scotia and Nova Scotians* (Halifax, N.S., 1858), *Review of the rise and progress of the Church of England in Nova Scotia* (Halifax, N.S., 1858), *Records of the Church of England in Newport* (Halifax, N.S., 1858), *Records of the Church of England in Rawdon* (Halifax, N.S., 1858), *The school of the prophets* (Halifax, N.S., 1860), *Memoir of Sir Brenton Halliburton* (Halifax, N.S., 1864), and *Letter to the parishioners of St. Paul's* (Halifax, N.S., 1866), as well as some sermons and two papers contributed to the *Collections* of the Nova Scotia Historical Society, of which he was twice president.

[Morgan, *Can. men* (1898); R. J. Long, *Nova Scotia authors* (East Orange, N.J., 1918).]

Hill, George William (1862-1934), sculptor, was born in Shipton township, Canada East, in 1862. He was educated at St. Francis College, Richmond, Quebec; and he studied art at the Académie Julien and the École Nationale des Beaux-Arts in Paris, France. He returned to Montreal in 1900; and he successfully practised there for forty years his profession as sculptor. He was elected an associate of the Royal Canadian Academy in 1908, and an academician in 1915. He was especially in demand as a designer and sculptor of war memorials; but he was also the sculptor of some notable busts of famous Canadians. He died at Montreal, Quebec, on July 17, 1934.

[Morgan, *Can. men* (1912); N. MacTavish, *The fine arts in Canada* (Toronto, 1925).]

Hill, Hamnett Pinhey (1876-1942), lawyer, was born in Ottawa, Ontario, on December 18, 1876, the son of Hamnett Pinhey Hill and Margaret Christie, and the grandson of Alexander James Christie (q.v.). He was educated at the University of Toronto (B.A.,1898) and at Osgoode Hall Law School, and was called to the bar of Ontario in 1903 (K.C., 1921). He practised law in Ottawa; and he represented Ottawa in the Ontario legislature from 1919 to 1923. He was an authority on the history of Ottawa, and the author of *John Randall and the Le Breton flats* (Ottawa, 1918) and *The history of Christ Church Cathedral, Ottawa, 1832-1932* (Ottawa, 1932). He died at Ottawa on December 15, 1942.

[*Can. who's who*, 1936-37; H. Charlesworth (ed.), *A cyclopaedia of Canadian biography* (Toronto, 1919).]

Hill, James Edgar (1842-1911), clergyman, was born in Glasgow, Scotland, on October 18, 1842. He was educated at Edinburgh University (M.A., 1868; B.D., 1872), and was licensed to preach by the presbytery of Edinburgh in 1872. In 1882 he came to Canada as minister of St. Andrew's Church, Montreal; and he remained in this charge until his death at Montreal, on March 3, 1911. He was the author of *Queen Charity and other sermons* (Montreal, 1891).

[Morgan, *Can. men* (1898).]

Hill, James Jerome (1838-1916), railway magnate, was born near Guelph, Upper Canada, on September 16, 1838, the son of James Hill and Anne Dunbar. Early in life he settled in Minnesota. In 1870 he organized the Red River Transportation Company, which first opened communication between St. Paul and Winnipeg; and in 1879 he became general manager; and in 1883 president, of the St.

Paul, Minneapolis, and Manitoba Railway Co. In 1893 he became president of the Great Northern Railway system. He died at St. Paul, Minnesota, on May 29, 1916. In 1867 he married Mary Theresa Mehegan, of St. Paul.

[J. G. Pyle, *Life of James J. Hill* (2 vols., Garden City, N.Y., 1917); N. Patterson, *James Jerome Hill* (Can. mag., 1906).]

Hill, Philip Carteret (1821-1894), prime minister of Nova Scotia (1875-78), was born in Halifax, Nova Scotia, in 1821, the son of Capt. N. T. Hill, of the Royal Staff Corps. He was educated at King's College, Windsor (D.C.L., 1858), and was called to the bar of Nova Scotia in 1844. In 1867 he was a member of the first government of Nova Scotia under Confederation, but he failed of election to the legislature, and resigned with his colleagues in November of that year. From 1870 to 1878 he represented Halifax in the Legislative Assembly; in 1874 he was sworn in as provincial secretary, and in 1875 he became prime minister of the province, on the platform of complete severance of federal and provincial politics. In 1878 both he himself and his administration were defeated at the polls, and he retired from public life. His later years were spent in England, at Tunbridge Wells; and he died in England on September 13, 1894. He married a daughter of the Hon. Enos Collins (q.v.). He published several pamphlets and lectures, most of which were on theological subjects.

[J. W. Longley, *Premiers of Nova Scotia since 1867* (Can. mag., 1897); *Can. parl. comp.*; *Statistical year book of Canada for 1894.*]

Hill, Robert Brown (1843-1900), historian, was born in Scotland in 1843, and died in 1900. He settled at Portage la Prairie, Manitoba, in the early seventies, and became first a carriage-maker and then a journalist. He was the author of *Manitoba: History of its early settlement, development, and resources* (Toronto, 1890).

[B. B. Peel, comp., *A bibliography of the prairie provinces* (Toronto, 1953).]

Hill, Sir Stephen John (1809-1891), governor of Newfoundland (1869-1876), was born on June 10, 1809, and died in London, England, on October 20, 1891. He entered the British army, and was successively governor of the Gold Coast, Sierra Leone, the Leeward and Caribbean Islands, and Newfoundland. He came to Newfoundland as governor at the time when the question of Confederation was referred to the electors, but he was not successful in his attempt to influence the electors to vote for Confederation. After his period of office in Newfoundland he retired from the colonial service. He was created a K.C.M.G. in 1874.

[*Dict. nat. biog.*, supp. 2; *Encyc. Can.*; *Newfoundland supp.*]

Hill, Thomas (d. 1860), journalist and author, came to New Brunswick about 1842 and established there the *Loyalist and Conservative Advocate*. His early life is wrapped in mystery, but he appears to have been born in London, and to have served for a time in the United States army, from which he ultimately deserted. He was connected in New Brunswick with various short-lived newspapers, and he played an important part in the discussions over the introduction of responsible government. He died at Fredericton, New Brunswick, in October, 1860. He was the author of *The provincial association: A tragic-comedy in verse* (Fredericton, N.B., 1845) and of *The constitutional lyrist* (Fredericton, N.B., 1845), and he compiled *A book of Orange songs* (Fredericton, N.B., 1850).

[W. G. MacFarlane, *New Brunswick bibliography* (Saint John, N.B., 1895).]

Hilliard, Anna Marion (1902-1958), physician and author, was born at Morrisburg, Ontario, in 1902, and died at Toronto, Ontario, on July 15, 1958. She was educated at the University of Toronto (B.A., 1924; M.B., 1927), and went into medical practice in Toronto. From 1947 to 1957 she was chief of obstetrics and gynaecology at the Women's College Hospital in Toronto. She was the author of *A woman doctor looks at love and life* (Toronto, 1957).

[*Can. who's who*, 1955-57.]

Hill-Tout, Charles (1858-1944), anthropologist, was born at Buckland, Devonshire, England, on September 28, 1858. He emigrated to Canada when a young man, and became a school principal in Vancouver, British Columbia. He made a special study of the native tribes of British Columbia; and in 1913 was elected a fellow of the Royal Society of Canada. He died in Vancouver, British Columbia, on June 30, 1944. He was the author of *The native races of British North America: The far west* (London, 1907).

[*Can. who's who*, 1936-37; *Proc. Roy. Soc. Can.*, 1945.]

Hilts, Joseph Henry (1819-1903), clergyman and author, was born near Niagara, Upper Canada, on May 4, 1819. He joined the Methodist Church in 1841, and in 1856 he became a minister of the Methodist Episcopal Church. For many years he was a travelling missionary in Ontario. He died at Dundas, Ontario, in 1903. In 1843 he married Eliza Jane Griffin, of Grimsby. He was the author of *The experiences of a backwoods preacher* (Toronto, 1887), *Among the forest trees; or, How the Bushman family got their homes* (Toronto, 1888), and *Clothed with the sun* (Toronto, 1891).

[Morgan, *Can. men* (1898).]

Hincks, Clarence Meredith (1885-1964), psychiatrist, was born in St. Mary's, Ontario,

April 8, 1885, and educated at the University of Toronto (B.A., 1905; M.D., 1907). He began practice in Toronto and in 1913 became a school doctor and introduced an intelligence testing program which led to special classes for children with problems. Five years later he led a crusade for mental health and founded the Canadian Association for Mental Health. He established the first mental health clinic in Canada and helped organize the school for child studies at the University of Toronto. A man who suffered from mental illness himself, Dr. Hincks not only organized many of the innovative measures taken on behalf of the mentally ill but went on extensive crusades to raise money to finance them. He once raised $100,000 at a luncheon given in his honour in Montreal. He was a recognized world authority on the treatment of mental problems and travelled extensively for study and teaching. He held the gold medal of the Comité d'Honneur of the World Federation for Mental Health. He died at Toronto, Ontario, December 17, 1964.

[*Can. who's who*, 1961-63; Metropolitan Toronto Library Board, *Biographical scrapbooks*, vol. 7, 22, 25.]

Hincks, Sir Francis (1807-1885), statesman, was born in Cork, Ireland, on December 14, 1807, the youngest son of the Rev. Thomas Dix Hincks, the founder of the Royal Cork Institution. He was educated at the Royal Belfast Academical Institution; and from 1824 to 1829 he served an apprenticeship in a counting-house in Belfast. In 1832 he came to Canada, and settled in York, Upper Canada. In 1835 he became cashier or manager of the People's Bank, which was established by some of the Reformers in opposition to the Bank of Upper Canada; and in 1839 he founded the *Examiner* newspaper as an organ of moderate Liberal opinion. In 1841 he was elected to the first Legislative Assembly of united Canada for Oxford; and in 1842 was appointed receiver-general and a member of the Executive Council by Sir Charles Bagot (q.v.). He continued as receiver-general in the first Baldwin-Lafontaine administration, and retired from office with his colleagues in November, 1843. In 1848 he resumed office as inspector-general in the second Baldwin-Lafontaine government; and on the retirement of Robert Baldwin (q.v.) and Louis Lafontaine (q.v.) in 1851, he became prime minister in the Hincks-Morin administration. His government rendered important services in connection with railway-building and the negotiation of the reciprocity agreement with the United States in 1854; but it failed to deal with the thorny questions of the secularization of the clergy reserves and the abolition of the seigniorial tenure of Lower Canada, and in September, 1854, it was obliged to resign.

In 1855 Hincks was appointed by the Colonial Office governor-in-chief of Barbados and the Windward Islands; and in 1862 he became governor of British Guiana. On relinquishing this post in 1869, he returned to Canada, and was immediately pressed into service by Sir John Macdonald (q.v.) as finance minister of the Dominion. He was elected to the House of Commons for North Renfrew, and in the second parliament of Canada he sat for Vancouver. His "resurrection", as it was termed, proved, however, a disappointment, since he had, in his fifteen years' absence, lost touch with Canadian politics, and he did not bring to Macdonald the strength anticipated. In February, 1873, therefore, he resigned from the cabinet, and in 1874 he retired from active politics. From 1873 to 1879 he was president of the ill-fated City Bank of Montreal; and during his last years he was the editor of the Montreal *Journal of Commerce*. He died in Montreal on August 18, 1885.

He married (1) in 1832, Martha Anne Stewart (d. 1874), of Belfast; and (2) in 1875 Emily Louisa Delatre (d. 1879), widow of the Hon. R. B. Sullivan (q.v.). He was created a C.B. in 1862, and a K.C.M.G. in 1869. He published his *Reminiscences* (Montreal, 1884), and some pamphlets, *Canada, its financial position and resources* (London, 1849), *The political history of Canada between 1840 and 1855* (Montreal, 1877), and *The boundaries formerly in dispute between Great Britain and the United States* (Montreal, 1885).

[R. S. Longley, *Sir Francis Hincks* (Toronto, 1943); *Dict. nat. biog.*; Dent, *Can. port.*, vol. 1; Taylor, *Brit. Am.*; Rose, *Cyc. Can. biog.* (1886); *Dom. ann. reg.*, 1885; Sir R. Cartwright, *Reminiscences* (Toronto, 1912). *Dict. Can. biog.*, vol. 10.]

Hincks, William (1794-1871), educationist, was born at Cork, Ireland, on April 16, 1794, the second son of the Rev. Thomas Dix Hincks, and brother of Sir Francis Hincks (q.v.). He entered the ministry of the Presbyterian Church in Ireland, and was successively stationed at Cork, at Exeter, and at Liverpool. From 1827 to 1834 he was professor of natural philosophy at Manchester College, York; from 1842 to 1847 he was editor of the *Inquirer*; from 1849 to 1853 he was professor of natural history at Queen's College, Cork; and in 1853 he was appointed professor of natural history at University College, Toronto. This post he occupied until his death at Toronto, on September 10, 1871. He was the author of a number of scientific papers.

[*Dict. nat. biog.*; J. King, *McCaul, Croft, Forneri* (Toronto, 1914); *Canadian journal*, 1873; Morgan, *Bib. can*; *Dict. Can. biog.*, vol. 10.]

Hind, Ella Cora (1861-1942), journalist, was born in Toronto, Canada West, on September 18, 1861, and died at Winnipeg, Manitoba, on October 6, 1942. She joined the staff of the Winnipeg *Free Press* in 1906, and became its agricultural editor, famous for her crop estimates. She was the author of *Red River jottings* (1905), *Seeing for myself* (Toronto, 1937), and *My travels and findings* (Toronto, 1939).

[K. M. Haig, *Brave harvest: The life story of E. Cora Hind* (Toronto, 1945); *Can. who's who*, 1936-37; *Encyc. Can.*]

Hind, Henry Youle (1823-1908), geologist and explorer, was born at Nottingham, England, on June 1, 1823, the third son of Thomas Hind and Sarah Youle. He was educated at Queen's College, Cambridge, but did not graduate; and in 1846 he emigrated to Canada. From 1848 to 1853 he was lecturer in chemistry and mathematics at the provincial normal school, Toronto; and from 1853 to 1864 he was professor of chemistry and geology in the University of Trinity College, Toronto. During this period he was employed by the Canadian government as geologist on the Red River expedition of 1857, and he was in command of the Assiniboine and Saskatchewan exploring expedition of 1858, and of the Labrador expedition of 1861. In 1864 he was engaged to make a geological survey of New Brunswick; and in 1869-71 he made a survey of the goldfields of Nova Scotia. In 1877 he was employed in connection with the international fisheries commission sitting at Halifax, Nova Scotia, to deal with disputes between Canada and the United States. In 1890 he was appointed president of a church school of Edgehill, Nova Scotia; and he died at Windsor, Nova Scotia, on August 9, 1908. In 1850 he married Katherine, daughter of Lieut.-Col. Duncan Cameron (q.v.), of the 79th Highlanders; and by her he had two sons and two daughters. In 1853 he received the degree of M.A. from Trinity University, Toronto, and in 1890 that of D.C.L. from King's College, Windsor, Nova Scotia. He was the editor of the *Canadian Journal* from 1852 to 1855, of the *Journal of the Board of Arts and Manufactures for Upper Canada* from 1861 to 1863, and of the *British American Magazine* (Toronto, 1863). Among his publications were the *Narrative of the Canadian Red River exploring expedition of 1857, and of the Assiniboine and Saskatchewan exploring expedition of 1858* (2 vols., Toronto, 1859; London, 1860), *Explorations in the interior of the Labrador peninsula* (2 vols., London, 1863), *Notes on the northern Labrador fishing ground* (Newfoundland, 1876), and *The effect of the fishery clauses of the treaty of Washington on the fisheries and fisherman of British North America* (Halifax, N.S., 1877).

[*Dict. nat. biog.*, supp. II; *Cyc. Am. biog.*; Rose, *Cyc. Can. biog.* (1888); Morgan, *Can. men* (1898) and *Bib. can.*]

Hind, William George Richardson (1833-1888), painter, was born in Nottingham, England, in 1833, the brother of Henry Youle

Hind (q.v.). He studied art in London and on the continent, and came to Canada in 1852. For two years he taught drawing in Toronto. He then went back to England, but in 1861 he came again to Canada, and joined his brother as artist on an expedition to Labrador. In 1863-64 and on later occasions he visited the North West and British Columbia, and he specialized in water-colour paintings of Indian life. During his later years he lived in New Brunswick; and he died at Sussex, New Brunswick, in 1888. A number of his drawings and paintings are in the John Ross Robertson collection in the Toronto Public Library.

[J. Ross Robertson, *Landmarks of Canada* (Toronto, 1917).]

Hingston, Sir William Hales (1829-1907), surgeon, was born at Hinchinbrook, Huntingdon, Lower Canada, on June 29, 1829, the eldest son of Lieut.-Col. Samuel James Hingston and Eleanor McGrath. He was educated at the grammar school in Huntingdon, under John (afterwards Sir John) Rose (q.v.), and at the Sulpician College in Montreal. He was apprenticed to a chemist for a time, and then he studied medicine at McGill University (M.D., 1851) and at Edinburgh (L.R.C.S., 1852). After further study in London, Dublin, Paris, Berlin, Heidelberg, and Vienna, he returned to Montreal in 1854, and commenced practice. He won a high reputation as a surgeon in Montreal, and in 1886 he was elected president of the College of Physicians and Surgeons of Quebec. He was mayor of Montreal in 1875-76; and in 1896 he was appointed a member of the Senate of Canada. He died at Montreal on February 19, 1907. In 1875 he married Margaret Josephine, daughter of the Hon. Donald Alexander Macdonald (q.v.); and by her he had four sons and one daughter. In 1895 he was created a knight bachelor; and he was a D.C.L. of Bishop's College, Lennoxville, and an LL.D. of Victoria University, Toronto. In addition to contributions to medical periodicals, he was the author of *The climate of Canada and its relation to life and health* (Montreal, 1884).

[*Dict. nat. biog.,* supp. II; Morgan, *Can. men* (1898); Rose, *Cyc. Can. biog.* (1888); *Can. parl. comp.*; *Can. who was who,* vol. 1.]

Hingston, William Hales (1877-1964), Jesuit Provincial, was born in Montreal in 1877, the son of Sir William Hales Hingston (q.v.). He entered the Jesuit order in 1896 and was ordained in 1911. He taught humanities and philosophy at Loyola College in Montreal and at Ignatius College in Guelph, Ontario, before becoming a chaplain in the First World War. He was rector of Loyola College from 1919 to 1925 and provincial from 1928 to 1934. During this term the Jesuit order took direction of St. Paul's High School and College in Winnipeg and Regiopolis College in Kingston and founded Regis College in Toronto. From 1934 to 1947 he was engaged in parish work and from that time until his death on November 30, 1964, he was a spiritual director at Regis College, Toronto.

[Metropolitan Toronto Library Board, *Biographical scrapbooks*, vol. 22.]

Hirschfelder, Jacob Maier (1819-1902), educationist, was born in Baden-Baden, Germany, in 1819, and was educated at the University of Heidelberg. He came to Canada about 1837; and after living for a time in Quebec and Montreal he came to Toronto in 1844 as tutor in Hebrew at King's College (afterwards the University of Toronto). In 1853 he was appointed lecturer in Oriental languages in University College, Toronto; and he retired from this position in 1888. He died at Toronto on August 2, 1902. He was the author of *A key to German conversation* (Toronto, 1845), *An essay on the spirit and characteristics of Hebrew poetry* (Toronto, 1855), *The Biblical expositor* (Toronto, 1855; new ed., 2 vols., Toronto, 1882-85), *The Scriptures defended: Being a reply to Bishop Colenso's book on the Pentateuch and the Book of Joshua* (Toronto, 1863), and *A wife to her sister* (Toronto, 1878).

[Morgan, *Bib. can.*]

Hitchins, Fred Harvey (1904-1972), historian, was born in London, Ontario, on July 10, 1904. He was educated at London Collegiate Institute and the University of Western Ontario (B.A., 1923; M.A., 1924). He then went to the University of Pennsylvania (Ph.D., 1930), and his doctoral thesis, *The colonial land and emigration commission,* was published in Philadelphia in 1931. He taught at New York University from 1928 to 1941 when he entered the Royal Canadian Air Force. He became a member of the Air Historical Section in 1941 and spent two years in Britain with the British Air Ministry's Historical Branch. He returned to Ottawa in November, 1943. In 1945 he was promoted to the rank of wing commander and became Air Historian. He played a major role in the production of the three-volume history *The R.C.A.F. overseas 1939-44.* He also wrote *Among the few* (1948), *The R.C.A.F. logbook* (1949), and *Air Board, C.A.F. and R.C.A.F., 1919-1939.* He rejoined the history department of the University of Western Ontario in 1960. He died at London, Ontario, November 3, 1972.

[*Can. hist. rev.,* vol. LIV.]

Hitsman, John Mackay (1917-1970), military historian, was born at Kingston, Ontario, April 19, 1917. He attended Kingston Collegiate and entered Queen's University in 1935 (M.A., 1940). While at Queen's he was a member of the Canadian Officers' Training Corps and enlisted in the Canadian Army Active Service Force in 1941. He was posted to Canadian Military Headquarters, London,

England, in 1943 as a member of the Army Historical Section. He became Captain in 1944 and transferred to the Canadian Army Interim Force in 1946. He was released in 1947, already suffering from the crippling disease which caused his death. He was employed in the Army Historical Section in Ottawa. He was the author of *Military inspection services in Canada, 1855-1950* (Ottawa, 1962); *The incredible war of 1812* (Toronto, 1965); and *Safeguarding Canada* (Toronto, 1968). He died at Ottawa, Ontario, February 11, 1970.

[*Can. hist. rev.*, vol. LI (1970); *Dept. National Defence* (1975).]

Hobson, Richmond P. (1907-1966), author, was born in Washington, D.C., and lived in various parts of the United States. In 1934 he and three companions set out to explore the interior of British Columbia beyond the Itcha, Algak, and Fawnie Mountain ranges. They discovered a large area of grassland which has become ranching country. Hobson told their story in *Grass beyond the mountains* (1951) and *The rancher takes a wife* (1961). He died at Vanderhoof, British Columbia in August, 1966.

[V.B. Rhodenizer, *Canadian literature in English* (Montreal, 1965); N. Story, *Oxford companion to Canadian history and literature* (Toronto, 1967); *Canadian author and bookman*, Autumn, 1961.]

Hoch, James (1827-1878), painter, was born at St. Kitts, West Indies, on November 7, 1827, the son of the Rev. Samuel Hoch, a Moravian missionary from southern Germany. He came to Canada in 1870, and having had an art education in England, became art teacher at Trinity University and Bishop Strachan School, Toronto. He was one of the founders of the Ontario Society of Artists in 1872; and he became noted for his painting of trees. He died at Toronto, Ontario, on May 1, 1878.

[N. MacTavish, *The fine arts in Canada* (Toronto, 1925).]

Hocquart, Gilles (1694-1783), intendant of New France (1731-48), was the third son of Jean-Hyacinthe Hocquart, seignior of Essenlis and of Muscourt. He held the post of commissary of marine, and on March 8, 1729, he received the commission of commissary-general of New France. He arrived at Quebec at the end of August, and on February 21, 1731, he was appointed intendant. In September, 1748, he was replaced by Bigot (q.v.), and returned to France, where he became intendant of Brest and a councillor of state. He died in April, 1783.

[R. Roy, *Les intendants de la Nouvelle-France* (Trans. Roy. Soc. Can., 1903), with portrait; R. Roy, *Gilles Hocquart* (Bull. rech. hist., vol. vii); A. Shortt (ed.), *Documents relating to Canadian currency, exchange, and finance during the French period* (2 vols., Ottawa, 1925).]

Hodder, Edward Mulberry (1810-1878), surgeon and yachtsman, was born at Sandgate, Kent, England, on December 30, 1810. He passed the examination of the Royal College of Surgeons in 1834, and he moved to Canada in 1838. After spending five years in the Niagara district, he set up in practice in Toronto. From 1850 to 1856 he was professor of obstetrics in Trinity University, Toronto; and in 1871 he was appointed dean of the medical faculty in this university. He died at Toronto on December 20, 1878. An enthusiastic yachtsman, he was for many years commodore of the Royal Canadian Yacht Club; and he was the author of *The harbours and ports of lake Ontario* (Toronto, 1857).

[*Dom. ann. reg.*, 1878; W. Canniff, *The medical profession in Upper Canada* (Toronto, 1894); *Dict. Can. biog.*, vol. 10.]

Hodgins, James Cobourg (1866-1953), clergyman and author, was born in Toronto, Ontario, in 1866, and died there on December 29, 1953. He was educated at the University of Toronto and Knox College, and soon after graduation became a Unitarian minister. He was the pastor of the Unitarian Church in Toronto from 1916 to 1942; and he was the author of a novel entitled *The wilderness campers* (Toronto, 1921).

[Toronto *Globe and Mail*, Dec. 30, 1953.]

Hodgins, John George (1821-1912), educationist and historian, was born in Dublin, Ireland, on August 21, 1821, the son of William Hodgins and Frances Doyle. He came to Canada in 1833, and was educated at Upper Canada Academy and at Victoria College, Cobourg (M.A., 1856). In 1844 he entered the department of education for Upper Canada as a clerk; in 1855 he became deputy superintendent of education, under the Rev. Egerton Ryerson (q.v.); and from 1876 to 1889 he was deputy minister of education for Ontario. He was then appointed librarian and historiographer to the department, and this position he retained until his death at Toronto, on December 23, 1912. He was twice married, (1) in 1849 to Frances Rachel (d. 1883), daughter of James Doyle, of Cloyne, county Cork, Ireland; and (2) in 1889 to Helen Fortescue, daughter of John Scoble. In 1870 he was made an LL.D. of the University of Toronto; and in 1885 he was awarded the Confederation medal. For many years he edited the *Upper Canada Journal of Education*; and he was the author of many school textbooks. His chief works, however, were his *Documentary history of education in Upper Canada* (28 vols., Toronto, 1894-1910), *The establishment of schools and colleges in Ontario* (3 vols., Toronto, 1910), and *Historical and other papers and documents illustrative of* *the educational system of Ontario* (3 vols., Toronto, 1911).

[Morgan, *Can. men* (1912); Rose, *Cyc. Can. biog.* (1886).]

Hodgins, Thomas (1828-1910), lawyer, was born in Dublin, Ireland, on October 6, 1828, the fourth son of William Hodgins, and brother of John George Hodgins (q.v.). He was educated at the University of Toronto (B.A., 1856; LL.B., 1858; M.A., 1860), and was called to the bar of Upper Canada in 1858 (Q.C., 1873). He practised law in Toronto; and from 1871 to 1879 he represented West Elgin in the Legislative Assembly of Ontario as a Liberal. In 1883 he was appointed master-in-ordinary of the Supreme Court of Ontario; and in 1903 he was appointed a judge of the Court of Admiralty. He died in Toronto on January 14, 1910. In 1858 he married Maria Burgoyne, daughter of John Scoble. In 1906 he was made an LL.D. of the University of Toronto. In addition to a number of law books, chiefly relating to municipal and election law, he published *The Canadian educational directory* (Toronto, 1857), *British and American diplomacy affecting Canada* (Toronto, 1900), and *The Alaska boundary dispute* (Toronto, 1902).

[Morgan, *Bib. can.* and *Can. men* (1898).]

Hodgson, Sir Robert (1798-1880), lieutenant-governor of Prince Edward Island (1874-79), was born in Charlottetown, Prince Edward Island, in 1798, the son of Robert Hodgson and Rebecca Robinson. He was educated at the Collegiate School, Windsor, Nova Scotia, and was called to the bar of Nova Scotia in 1819. In 1828 he was appointed attorney-general of Prince Edward Island; in 1840, president of the Legislative Council; and in 1841, acting chief justice. He resigned this office, on the introduction of responsible government, in 1851; but in 1852 was reappointed chief justice, and he held this post until 1874. From 1874 to 1879 he was lieutenant-governor of the island; and he died at Charlottetown, Prince Edward Island, on September 15, 1880. In 1827 he married Fanny, daughter of Capt. Ranald Macdonald, of the Glengarry Light Infantry. He was created a knight bachelor in 1869.

[*Cyc. Am. biog.*; *Can. parl. comp.*; *Dom. ann. reg.,* 1880-81; D. A. MacKinnon and A. B. Warburton (eds.), *Past and present of Prince Edward Island* (Charlottetown, P.E.I., 1906); *Dict. Can. biog.*, vol. 10.]

Hogan, John Sheridan (1815-1859), journalist, was born in 1815 near Dublin, Ireland, and came to Canada about 1827. He entered a printing office in Hamilton, Upper Canada, and became a journalist on the staff of the *Canadian Wesleyan*. He studied law in the office of Sir Allan MacNab (q.v.), but was never called to the bar. In 1842 he was arrested at Rochester, New York, on a charge of complic-

ity in the burning of the steamer *Caroline* in 1838; but was acquitted. Later he became the editor-in-chief of the Toronto *Colonist*. In 1857 he was returned to the Legislative Assembly of Canada, as a Reformer, for the county of Grey; but his career was cut short by his murder by bandits, near Toronto, in December, 1859. He published a prize essay on *Canada* (Montreal, 1855).

[*Cyc. Am. biog.*; Morgan, *Cel. Can.* and *Bib. can.*; N. F. Davin, *The Irishman in Canada* (Toronto, 1877); W. S. Wallace, *Murders and mysteries* (Toronto, 1931).]

Hogg, James (1800-1866), journalist and poet, was born in Leitrim, Ireland, on September 14, 1800. He came to New Brunswick in 1819, and settled first in Saint John, and then in Fredericton. In 1844 he founded the *New Brunswick Reporter* (Fredericton), which he edited until his death at Fredericton on June 12, 1866. He published two volumes of verse, *Poems* (Saint John, 1825), and *Poems, religious, moral and sentimental* (Fredericton, n.d.).

[Morgan, *Bib. can.*; C. C. James, *A bibliography of Canadian poetry* (Toronto, 1899); W. C. MacFarlane, *New Brunswick bibliography* (Saint John, N.B., 1895).]

Holbrook, John Howard (1876-1958), physician, was born in southern Ontario in 1876, and died at Hamilton, Ontario, on March 14, 1958. He was educated at the University of Toronto (M.B., 1906), and from 1908 to 1945 he was medical superintendent of the Mountain Sanatorium at Hamilton.

[Marjorie Freeman Campbell, *Holbrook of the San* (Toronto, 1953); *Canadian Medical Association Journal,* 1958.]

Holdstock, Alfred Worsley (1820-1901), artist, was born at Bath, England, in 1820, and came to Canada in 1850. He became a master in the National School on Bonsecours Street in Montreal, and he also taught drawing. He specialized in water-scapes, and most of his work was in pastel, though he did also a few oil paintings. He died in 1901.

[Private information.]

Holland, Norah Mary (1876-1925), poet, was born in Collingwood, Ontario, on January 10, 1876; was educated in Toronto; and married Lionel Claxton. She died in Toronto on April 27, 1925. Under her maiden name she published two volumes of verse, *Spun yarn and spindrift* (Toronto, 1919) and *When half-gods go, and other poems* (Toronto, 1924).

[J. W. Garvin (ed.), *Canadian poets* (Toronto, 1926); *Can. who was who*, vol. 1.]

Holland, Samuel (1728?-1801), surveyor-general (1764-1801), was born at or near Nijmegen, eastern Holland, about 1728. He entered the Dutch army at the age of seventeen; and in 1754 he joined the British army. He was sent to America in 1756. He served in America during the Seven Years' War, and was with Wolfe (q.v.) when he died on the Plains of Abraham. In 1764 he was appointed surveyor-general of the province of Quebec and the northern district of North America; and during the remaining years of his life he carried out extensive surveys in the Maritime provinces and Canada. During the American Revolution, he was for a time attached with the rank of major to the German mercenary troops serving with the British; but in 1780 he settled at Quebec, and supervised the surveys for the new Loyalist settlements. In 1779 he was appointed a member of the Council for the affairs of the province; but was not reappointed to the Legislative Council of Lower Canada in 1791, probably on account of failing health. He died at Quebec on December 27, 1801. In 1749 he married, in Holland, Gertrude Hasse, but he left her in 1754; and about 1764 he married Marie Josephte Rolette, of Quebec. By her he had ten children. He contributed several papers to the *Proceedings* of the Royal Society of London.

[Willis Chipman, *The life and times of Samuel Holland* (Ont. Hist. Soc., papers and records, 1924); F. J. Audet, *Samuel Holland* (Les Cahiers des Dix, 1958); Morgan, *Bib. can.*]

Holmes, Andrew Fernando (1797-1860), dean of the faculty of medicine in McGill University (1854-60), was born in 1797 at Cadiz, Spain, whither his parents had been taken after being captured by a French frigate on their way from England to Canada. He came to Canada eventually, with his parents, in 1801. He studied medicine in Edinburgh and in Paris; and, on his return to Canada in 1819, he practised medicine in Montreal. In 1824 he was one of the founders of the Montreal School of Medicine, which was in 1828 absorbed by the University of McGill College; and he was a prominent member of the medical faculty of that university from that date to his death. In 1854 he was appointed dean of the faculty. He died at Montreal in September, 1860.

[Morgan, *Cel. Can.* and *Bib. can.*; C. Macmillan, *McGill and its story* (Toronto, 1921).]

Holmes, George (1861-1912), Anglican bishop of Moosonee and of Athabaska, was born in Westmorland, England, in 1861. He was educated at the Church Missionary College, Islington, London, and was ordained a deacon of the Church of England in 1887, and a priest in 1888. From 1887 to 1905 he was a missionary at Great Slave Lake, in the North West Territories of Canada; in 1903 he was elected Anglican bishop of Moosonee; and in 1909 he was translated to the bishopric of Athabaska. He died at London, England, on February 3, 1912. In 1905 he received the degree of D.D. from St. John's College, Winnipeg.

[Morgan, *Can. men* (1912).]

Holmes, John or **Jean** (1799-1852), priest and educationist, was born at Windsor, Vermont, in 1799. He was educated for the ministry of the Wesleyan Church, but became a convert to Roman Catholicism, and was ordained a priest in 1823. He joined the staff of the Quebec Seminary in 1828, became director of the *Petit Séminaire*, and introduced revolutionary changes in the curriculum — notably the introduction of Greek, the teaching of history and geography by improved methods, and the devotion of greater attention to natural history, music, and drawing. His influence on the history of education in Lower Canada was profound. In his later years he went into retirement at Lorette, Lower Canada; and here he died in 1852. He was the author of an *Histoire ancienne des Egyptiens* (Quebec, 1831), a *Nouvel abrégé de géographie moderne* (Quebec, 1832), and a volume of *Conférences* (Quebec, 1850; new ed., 1876).

[Abbé A. Gosselin, *L'abbé Holmes et l'instruction publique* (Trans. Roy. Soc. Can., 1907); P. J. O. Chauveau, *L'abbé Holmes et ses conférences* (pamphlet, Quebec, 1876); L. M. Darveau, *Nos hommes de lettres* (Montreal, 1873); Morgan, *Cel. Can.* and *Bib. can.*; Bibaud, *Panth. can.*; Le Jeune, *Dict. gén.*]

Holmes, Robert (1860-1930), painter, was born at Cannington, Ontario, on June 25, 1860. He studied art at the Toronto Art School and at the Royal College of Art, London, England; and for many years he was drawing master at Upper Canada College, Toronto. He was one of the founders of the Ontario College of Art, and for many years had charge of the elementary work in the College. He specialized in the painting of flowers, and painted over one hundred varieties of Canadian wild flowers. He became a member of the Ontario Society of Artists in 1909, and was its president from 1919 to 1923; he was a member of the Society of Graphic Art, Toronto, and was its president from 1909 to 1911; and he was elected an associate of the Royal Canadian Academy in 1909, and an academician in 1919. He died suddenly at Toronto on May 14, 1930, while addressing the students in the Ontario College of Art.

[*Can. who was who*, vol. 1; Morgan, *Can. men* (1912); N. MacTavish, *The fine arts in Canada* (Toronto, 1925); A. H. Robson, *Canadian landscape painters* (Toronto, 1932).]

Holmes, Simon Hugh (1831-1919), prime minister of Nova Scotia (1878-82), was born at East River, Pictou, Nova Scotia, on July 30, 1831, the son of the Hon. John Holmes, later a senator of Canada, and Christina Fraser. He was educated at Pictou Academy; and was called to the bar of Nova Scotia in 1864 (Q.C., 1880). From 1862 to 1882 he was editor and proprietor of the Pictou *Colonial Standard*, and in 1871 he was elected to represent Pictou as a Conservative in the Legislative Assembly of Nova Scotia. In 1878 he became prime minister and provincial secretary of the province; but he resigned office in 1882, and accepted an appointment as prothonotary and clerk of the crown in the county of Halifax. This position he held until his death at Halifax on October 14, 1919. In 1874 he married Isabella, eldest daughter of James Little, of Haliburton Stream, Pictou, Nova Scotia.

[J. W. Longley, *Premiers of Nova Scotia since 1867* (Can. mag., 1897); Morgan, *Can. men* (1912); Rose, *Cyc. Can. biog.* (1888); Dent, *Can. port.*, vol. 4; *Can. parl. comp.*; J. Castell Hopkins, *The life and work of the Rt. Hon. Sir John Thompson* (Brantford, Ont., 1895).]

Holmes, William (d. 1792), fur-trader, was a native of Ireland, and was probably a brother of the Jane Holmes who married Charles Grant (q.v.), and a half-brother of John King (d. 1806), of the firm of King and McCord of Montreal. He came to Canada a few years after the British conquest, and engaged in the fur-trade. He was on the Saskatchewan in 1774, and again in 1776; and in 1778 he formed a partnership with Robert Grant (q.v.). He became an original member of the North West Company in 1779. He was at Sturgeon River Fort on the Saskatchewan in 1779-80, and on the Red Deer River in 1782-83; and he was at Cumberland House in May, 1784, on his way to Grand Portage. He was on the North Saskatchewan again in 1787-88; but in 1790 he sold his share in the North West Company to John Gregory (q.v.), and retired from the fur-trade. He died at Montreal on August 17, 1792.

[W. S. Wallace (ed.), *Documents relating to the North West Company* (Toronto: The Champlain Society, 1934).]

Holmested, George Smith (1841-1928), lawyer and author, was born in London, England, on March 15, 1841. He came to Canada in 1858, and was called to the bar of Upper Canada in 1866. In 1872 he was appointed referee in chambers at Osgoode Hall, Toronto; in 1877 he became registrar in chancery, and later registrar in bankruptcy. He completed fifty-five years of service in Osgoode Hall; and he died at Toronto on January 25, 1928. With Thomas Langton, he was joint author of *The Judicature Act of Ontario and rules of practice* (Toronto, 1898); and he published a number of other legal treatises.

[Morgan, *Can. men* (1912).]

Holt, Sir Herbert Samuel (1856-1941), financier, was born in Dublin, Ireland, on February 12, 1856. He studied civil engineering in Ireland, and came to Canada in 1875. For several years he was employed on the staffs of several railways in Ontario and Quebec as an engineer; and in 1883-84 he was engineer and superintendent of construction on the prairie and mountain divisions of the Canadian Pacific Railway. He then became a railway contractor, and between 1884 and 1892 he carried out several contracts in different parts of Canada, the last in partnership with Messrs Mackenzie and Mann. After 1892 he turned his attention to banking and finance; and he was president of the Sovereign Bank from 1902 to 1904, and of the Royal Bank from 1907 to 1934. He then became chairman of the board of the Royal Bank; and he retained this position until his death at Montreal, Quebec, on September 29, 1941. He was created a knight bachelor in 1915.

[*Can. who's who*, 1938-39; *Who's who*, 1941; Morgan, *Can. men* (1912).]

Holton, Luther Hamilton (1817-1880), politician, was born in Leeds county, Upper Canada, in 1817, the son of Ezra Holton and Anna Phillips. He was educated in Montreal; and in 1836 he entered the mercantile firm of Henderson and Hooker, forwarders. Later he became a partner in the firm, which took the name of Hooker and Holton. He was one of the incorporators of the Grand Trunk Railway; from 1852 to 1857 he was one of the government directors of that railway; and he was a member of the firm of contractors, Gzowski and Co., which built the Toronto-Sarnia section of the railway. From 1854 to 1857 he represented Montreal in the Legislative Assembly of Canada; and in 1862 he was elected to the Legislative Council of Canada for the Victoria division, but he resigned in 1863 from the Council, and was elected to the Assembly for Châteauguay. He continued to represent this constituency in the Assembly until Confederation, and then in the Canadian House of Commons until his death. From 1871 to 1874 he sat also for Montreal Centre in the Legislative Assembly of Quebec. He was twice a member of the government. In the short-lived Brown government of August, 1858, he was commissioner of public works; and he was minister of finance in the S. Macdonald-Dorion government of 1863-64. An advanced Liberal, he opposed the coalition government of 1864; and in 1865 he opposed the adoption of the Quebec Resolutions in the Canadian legislature. In 1873 he declined to join the Mackenzie administration, though he gave it loyal support. He died at Ottawa on March 14, 1880. In 1839 he married Eliza, daughter of William Forbes of Montreal, and by her he had six children.

[Dent, *Can. port.*, vol. 2; Rose, *Cyc. Can. biog.* (1886); *Can. biog. dict.*, Quebec vol. (Chicago, 1881); F. R. E. Campeau, *Illustrated guide* (Ottawa, 1879); A. Mackenzie, *The life and speeches of George Brown* (Toronto, 1882); J. S. Willison, *Sir Wilfrid Laurier and the Liberal party* (2 vols., Toronto, 1903); Sir R. Cartwright, *Reminiscences* (Toronto, 1914); *Dict. Can. biog.*, vol. 10.]

Hope, Henry (d. 1789), lieutenant-governor of Quebec (1785-89), was the fifth son of the Hon. Charles Hope, of Craigiehall, Linlithgowshire, Scotland, and grandson of Charles, first Earl of Hopetown. He entered the British army, and rose to the rank of brigadier-general. In 1785 he was commissary-general of the troops in Canada, and was appointed to succeed Henry Hamilton (q.v.) as lieutenant-governor of Quebec. He administered the government of the province until the arrival of Lord Dorchester (q.v.) as governor in 1786, and he continued to perform the duties of lieutenant-governor until his death at Quebec on April 13, 1789. He married Sarah, daughter of the Rev. John Jones, prebendary of Mullaghbrack; and she erected a monument to him in Westminster Abbey.

[Sir J. B. Paul (ed.), *The Scots peerage*, vol. 4 (Edinburgh, 1907); W. Kingsford, *History of Canada*, vol. 7 (Toronto, 1894).]

Hope, William (1863-1931), painter, was born in Montreal, Canada East, in 1863, the son of John H. Hope. He studied art in Paris, France; and afterwards opened a studio in Montreal. He specialized in landscapes and marines; and his work was characterized by a mastery of atmosphere. He was elected an associate of the Royal Canadian Academy in 1895, and a member in 1902. During the First World War he was an official artist with the Canadian forces. He died at Montreal on February 5, 1931.

[H. G. Jones and E. Dyonnet, *History of the Royal Canadian Academy of Arts* (Montreal, 1934); N. MacTavish, *The fine arts in Canada* (Toronto, 1925); Morgan, *Can. men* (1912).]

Hopkins, Caleb (1786-1880), politician, was born in New Jersey in 1786, and came to Upper Canada with his father, who was a "late loyalist", in 1798. He became a farmer in the township of Nelson, Halton county, Upper Canada. He represented Halton in the Legislative Assembly of Upper Canada from 1828 to 1830 and from 1834 to 1836. He represented the eastern riding of this constituency in the Legislative Assembly of united Canada from 1841 to 1844 and from 1850 to 1851; and he was a member of the "Clear Grit" party. He died in Toronto on October 8, 1880.

[*Dom. ann. reg.*, 1880-81; J. C. Dent, *The last forty years* (2 vols., Toronto, 1881); *Dict. Can. biog.*, vol. 10.]

Hopkins, John Castell (1864-1923), publicist, was born at Dyersville, Iowa, on April 1, 1864, the son of John C. Hopkins and Phelia Heudebourck. He was educated at Bowmanville, Ontario, and entered the employ of the Imperial Bank. He then became a journalist and publicist. He contributed copiously to magazines and encyclopaedias in England, the United States, and Canada; he edited *Canada, an encyclopaedia of the country* (6 vols., Toronto, 1897-1900); in 1901 he edited *Morang's annual register of Canadian affairs*, and from 1902 to 1922 he wrote the *Canadian annual review*. In addition to a large number of pamphlets, he was the author of *Toronto, an historical sketch* (Toronto, 1893), *The life and work of the Rt. Hon. Sir John Thompson* (Brantford, Ont., 1895), *The story of the Dominion* (Toronto, 1899; new ed., 1922), *The progress of Canada in the nineteenth century* (Edinburgh, 1900), *Canada at war* (Toronto, 1919), and *The province of Ontario in the war* (Toronto, 1919). Though much of his work was done under the pressure of circumstances, it has much value for reference purposes. He died at Toronto on November 5, 1923. In 1906 he married Annie Beatrice Mary, daughter of J. J. Bonner, Toronto; and by her he had two daughters.

[J. E. Middleton, *The municipality of Toronto* (3 vols., Toronto, 1923); Morgan, *Can. men* (1912); *Can. who was who*, vol. 2.]

Hopson, Peregrine Thomas (d. 1759), governor of Nova Scotia (1752-56), was a British army officer who commanded a regiment of foot, and became first governor of Cape Breton. In 1749 he was sworn a member of the Council of Nova Scotia; and in 1752 he succeeded Cornwallis (q.v.) as governor. On November 1, 1753, he left for England, on account of ill health, leaving Charles Lawrence (q.v.) as lieutenant-governor. He resigned his office in 1755, and he died in 1759.

[D. Campbell, *Nova Scotia* (Montreal, 1873); B. Murdoch, *History of Nova Scotia* (3 vols., Halifax, N.S., 1865); Le Jeune, *Dict. gén.*; *Dict. Can. biog.*, vol. 3.]

Horden, John (1828-1893), first Anglican bishop of Moosonee, was born at Exeter, England, in 1828. He was educated at St. John's School, Exeter, and was for a time apprenticed to a trade. In 1850 he offered himself to the Church Missionary Society as a foreign missionary; and in 1851 he was sent to Moose Factory, on Hudson Bay, to work among the Indians. Here he spent the rest of his life. He baptized thousands of Indians; and he translated the Gospels into the Indian sign language, printing the translation with his own hands. In 1872 he was consecrated first bishop of Moosonee; and he died at Moose Factory on January 12, 1893. In 1851 he married Elizabeth Oke; and she accompanied him to his missionary field.

[A. R. Buckland, *John Horden* (London, 1895); B. Batty, *Forty-two years among the Indians and Eskimo* (London, 1893).]

Horning, Lewis Emerson (1858-1928), educationist, was born at Norwich, Ontario, on

April 2, 1858, the son of James Horning and Eliza Macklem. He was educated at Victoria University, Cobourg (B.A., 1884) and at the University of Göttingen (Ph.D., 1891). From 1886 to 1891 he was assistant professor of classics and modern languages at Victoria University; from 1891 to 1905, professor of German and Old English; and from 1905 to his death, professor of Teutonic philology. He died at Toronto on January 6, 1925. He made a special study of Canadian literature; and he collaborated with L. J. Burpee in a *Bibliography of Canadian fiction* (Toronto, 1904).

[Morgan, *Can. men* (1912).]

Hornyansky, Nicholas (1896-1965), painter and etcher, was born in Budapest, Hungary, in 1896. He studied at the University of Budapest, the Academy of Fine Arts, Budapest, and in Vienna, Munich, Antwerp, and Paris. He served as an artillery officer in the Hungarian army on the Russian front from 1915 to 1917, where he was wounded. In 1919 he went to Belgium, where he worked with Franz Hens doing landscape painting. He came to Canada in 1929 and settled in Toronto. He exhibited with the Royal Canadian Academy and with the Ontario Society of Artists, and taught printmaking at the Ontario College of Art from 1945 to 1958. Hornyansky was influenced by Van Eyck, Breughel (the younger), El Greco, and Diego Rivera. However, he developed his own distinctive style marked by unusually fine and colourful work. As manager of the touring exhibitions of the Royal Society of Canadian Painters, Etchers, and Engravers he did much to make these works known throughout Canada and the United States. He was elected an A.R.C.A. in 1943, and was a member of the American Colour Print Society and the Ontario Society of Artists. His works have been exhibited throughout the world and he is represented in the National Gallery of Canada, the Royal Ontario Museum, the National Print Collection (U.S.A.), Antwerp, and Ghent. He died at Toronto, 1965.

[*Can. who's who*, 1955-57; C. S. MacDonald, *A dictionary of Canadian artists*, vol. 2 (Ottawa, 1968); P. Duval, *Canadian drawings and prints*.]

Houde, Camillien (1889-1958), politician, was born at Montreal, Quebec, on August 13, 1889, and died there on September 11, 1958. He first became a bank clerk, but later turned to politics. In 1923 he was elected a member of the Quebec Legislative Assembly as a Conservative, and in 1929 he became leader of the Conservative party, but was defeated at the polls in 1931. In 1928, however, he had been elected mayor of Montreal, and he held this office almost continuously until 1954. During the Second World War he took a strong stand against the National Registration Act, and was in consequence interned from 1940 to 1944. In 1949 he was elected as an independent member of the House of Commons, but he took little part in the proceedings of the House. He retired from political life in 1954.

[Hertel La Roque, *Camillien Houde* (Montreal, 1961); *Who was who*, 1951-60; *Can. who's who*, 1955-57.]

Houde, Frédéric (1847-1884), journalist, was born at Rivière-du-Loup (en haut), Canada East, on September 23, 1847. He became a journalist, and became eventually the proprietor of the Montreal newspaper, *Le Monde*. In 1878 he was elected to represent Maskinongé in the Canadian House of Commons; and he sat for this constituency until his death at Louiseville, Quebec, on November 15, 1884. He published in his newspaper a novel entitled *Le manoir mystérieux*, which was later republished in book form by Casimir Hébert (Montreal, 1913).

[*Bull. rech. hist*, 1927; *Dom. ann. reg.*, 1884.]

Housser, Frederick Broughton (1889-1936), journalist, was born at Winnipeg, Manitoba, on June 2, 1889. From 1923 to 1927 and from 1934 to 1936 he was financial editor of the Toronto *Daily Star*; and he was at the same time an art critic. He died at Toronto, Ontario, on December 24, 1936. He was the author of *A Canadian art movement: The story of the Group of Seven* (Toronto, 1926, reprinted 1974).

[*Can. who's who*, 1936-37.]

Houston, William (1844-1931), journalist and author, was born in Lanark, Canada West, on September 9, 1844, the son of James Houston and Janet Young. He was educated at the University of Toronto (B.A., 1872; M.A., 1874), and became a journalist. He was on the staff of the Toronto *Globe*, under George Brown (q.v.); and later he was on the staff of the Saint John *Daily Telegraph* and the Toronto *Liberal*. From 1883 to 1892 he was librarian of the Legislative Library, Toronto; and from 1892 to 1904 he was a public school inspector. In his later days he was again employed on the Toronto *Globe*. He died in Hamilton, Ontario, on October 16, 1931. In 1883, he married Jane Hood, daughter of James Ewing, and by her he had one daughter; but both his wife and daughter predeceased him. He was the editor of *Documents illustrative of the Canadian constitution* (Toronto, 1891).

[Morgan, *Can. men* (1912).]

Houston, William Robert (1866-1940), publisher and herbalist, was born at Mount Forest, Ontario, on October 2, 1866, the son of the Rev. Stuart Houston. He was educated at Trinity College School, Port Hope; and he founded in 1901 Houston's Publications, which issued the *Annual financial review* and the *Bank directory of Canada*. He was a pioneer in the cultivation of culinary herbs in Canada, and the author of *The herbal of culinary herbs* (Toronto, 1933). He died at Toronto, Ontario, on January 21, 1940.

[*Can. who's who*, 1936-37.]

How, Henry (1828-1879), author and scientist, was born at London, England, on July 11, 1828. He was educated at a private school in Beaconsfield and at the Royal College of Chemistry. In 1854 he was appointed professor of chemistry and natural history in the University of King's College, Windsor, Nova Scotia. He died on September 27, 1879. In addition to a large number of scientific papers, he was the author of *The mineralogy of Nova Scotia* (Halifax, 1869).

[*Dom. ann. reg.*, 1879; Morgan, *Bib. can.*; R. J. Long, *Nova Scotia authors* (East Orange, N.J., 1918); *Dict. Can. biog.*, vol. 10.]

Howard, Alfred H. (1854-1916), artist, was born at Liverpool, England, on July 12, 1854; and he was employed in Liverpool as a lithographer. He settled in Toronto in 1876, and though he had never attended an art school, he was elected an A.R.C.A. in 1881, and an R.C.A. in 1883, and won the Marquis of Lorne's bronze medal for design in 1884. For many years he took a leading place in decorative art, and he was noted as a creator of beautiful illuminated addresses. He died at Toronto on February 17, 1916.

[H. G. Jones and E. Dyonnet, *History of the Royal Canadian Academy of Arts* (Montreal, 1934); N. MacTavish, *The fine arts in Canada* (Toronto, 1925).]

Howard, John George (1803-1890), architect, was born near London, England, on July 27, 1803, and became a surveyor and architect. He emigrated to Canada in 1832, and settled in York (Toronto). As surveyor, architect, and engineer he played a conspicuous part in the development of Toronto; and in 1883 he was made a charter member of the Royal Canadian Academy of Art. He died at Toronto on February 3, 1890. By his will his estate, now known as High Park, was bequeathed to the city of Toronto.

[Toronto Public Library, *Landmarks of Canada* (Toronto, 1917); H. G. Jones and E. Dyonnet, *History of the Royal Canadian Academy of Arts* (Montreal, 1934).]

Howard, Joseph (d. 1797), merchant, came to Canada, and settled in Montreal, in the early days of British rule. He was prominent in attempting to break in on the monopoly of the trade at the King's Posts acquired by Gray and Dunn in 1765; and in 1766 he was one of those arrested on suspicion of having been concerned in the assault on Thomas Walker (q.v.). He was prominent in the fur-trade at Michilimackinac about 1778,

but was not included in the North West Company in 1779. In his later years he was a merchant at Berthier; and here he died in December, 1797.

[W. S. Wallace (ed.), *The Maseres letters* (Toronto, 1919).]

Howe, Jonas (1840-1913), manufacturer and historian, was born at Saint John, New Brunswick, in 1840. He was educated in Saint John, lived there all his life, and died there on December 15, 1913. He was one of the founders of the New Brunswick Historical Society, and was from 1901 to 1903 its president; and he contributed to its transactions many historical papers.

[Morgan, *Can. men* (1912).]

Howe, Joseph (1804-1873), statesman, was born in Halifax, Nova Scotia, on December 13, 1804, the son of John Howe, a loyalist of the American Revolution, and Mary, daughter of Captain Edes. He had little formal education, and at the age of thirteen became a "printer's devil" in his father's printing-shop. In 1828 he became proprietor and editor of the Halifax *Nova Scotian*, and this paper he continued to edit until 1841. In 1835 he was prosecuted for libel on account of his attacks on the government, and won his case, which he pleaded himself. This incident brought him into the political arena. In 1836 he was elected to the Legislative Assembly of Nova Scotia as one of the members for Halifax; and he sat in the Assembly, first for Halifax (1836-51), then for Cumberland (1851-55), and lastly, for Windsor (1856-63), almost without intermission until his appointment as imperial fishery commissioner in 1863. He became the foremost advocate in Nova Scotia of responsible government. In 1840 he was included by Lord Falkland (q.v.) in the Executive Council; but he resigned from it in 1843, returned to the *Nova Scotian*, and for several years he waged a war upon Lord Falkland with a view to the granting of full responsible government. In 1848 the long fight ended in the defeat of the government; Sir John Harvey (q.v.), who had become governor in 1846, invited James Boyle Uniacke (q.v.) to form an administration; and in this government Howe became provincial secretary (1848-54). From 1854 to 1857 he was chairman of the Railway Board; and from 1857 to 1860 he was in opposition. In 1860 he again became provincial secretary, in the administration formed by William Young (q.v.); and, on the elevation of Young to the bench later in the year, he became prime minister of Nova Scotia.

In 1863 he retired from provincial politics to become fishery commissioner for Great Britain under the Reciprocity Treaty of 1854; and consequently he had no share in the negotiations for Confederation in 1864. He had long been an advocate of British American union; but, perhaps for personal reasons, he opposed the federation proposals, and on his retirement from the post of fishery commissioner in 1866, he put himself at the head of the anti-Confederation forces in Nova Scotia. In 1867 he went to London in the hope of persuading the British government to repeal Confederation; but his mission was unsuccessful, and in 1868 he was induced to cease his agitation, and to accept the union. In 1869, on the offer of "better terms" to Nova Scotia, he accepted office first as president of the council, and then as secretary of state, in the Dominion government under Sir John Macdonald (q.v.), and was elected to the Canadian House of Commons as member for Hants.

At Ottawa he did not add to his reputation. His health was poor, and he felt that he was in a false position. In May, 1873, he therefore retired from politics, and accepted the office of lieutenant-governor of Nova Scotia; but this office he held for only a few weeks. On June 1, 1873, he died at Halifax. In 1828 he married Catherine Susan Ann, daughter of Captain John McNab, Royal Nova Scotia Fencibles; and by her he had ten children.

Howe was a speaker and writer of great natural powers. Though he never overcame some of the deficiencies of his early education, he gained an unparalleled hold on the affections of the electors of Nova Scotia, and was not unfairly known as "the tribune of the people". His *Speeches and public letters* were collected and edited, nominally by William Annand (q.v.), but really by himself (2 vols., Halifax, 1858); and a new and enlarged edition of them has been published by J. A. Chisholm (2 vols., Halifax, 1909). His *Poems and essays* were collected and published shortly after his death (Montreal, 1874). A more recent collection of speeches and letters is by J. M. Beck, *Joseph Howe: Voice of Nova Scotia* (Toronto, 1964).

[J. A. Roy, *Joseph Howe; A study in achievement and frustration* (Toronto, 1935); J. W. Longley, *Joseph Howe* (Toronto, 1904); W. L. Grant, *The tribune of Nova Scotia* (Toronto, 1914); Rev. G. M. Grant, *The late Hon. Joseph Howe* (Canadian monthly, 1875); E. M. Saunders, *Three premiers of Nova Scotia* (Toronto, 1909); G. E. Fenety, *Life and times of Joseph Howe* (Saint John, 1896); L. J. Burpee, *Joseph Howe and the Anti-Confederation League* (Trans. Roy. Soc. Can., 1916); *Dict. nat. biog.*; Dent, *Can. port.*, vol. 2; Rose, *Cyc. Can. biog.* (1886); Taylor, *Brit. Am.*; Morgan, *Bib. can.*; R. P. Baker, *History of English-Canadian literature to the Confederation* (Cambridge, Mass., 1920); *Dict. Can. biog.*, vol. 10.]

Howell, Alfred (1836-1911), lawyer, was born near Toronto, Upper Canada, on July 3, 1836. He was called to the bar of Ontario in 1875, and practised law in Toronto. He died at Toronto on July 10, 1911. He was the author of

Naturalization and nationality (Toronto, 1884), *Admiralty law* (Toronto, 1893), and *Probate, administration, and guardianship* (Toronto, 1895).

[Morgan, *Can. men* (1898).]

Howell, Henry Spencer (1857-1912), author, was born at Galt, Ontario, on July 5, 1857; and died at Galt on August 6, 1912. Besides some pamphlets he published *An island paradise, and reminiscences of travel* (Toronto, 1892; 2nd ed., 1911).

[Morgan, *Can. men* (1912).]

Howlan, George William (1835-1901), lieutenant-governor of Prince Edward Island (1894-99), was born at Waterford, Ireland, on May 19, 1835. His parents emigrated to Prince Edward Island in 1839, and he was educated at the Central Academy, Charlottetown. He became a merchant and shipowner, interested in the fisheries. From 1862 to 1873 he sat for Queen's in the Legislative Assembly of Prince Edward Island; and from 1866 to 1873 he was, almost without interruption, a member of the Executive Council. In 1873 he was one of the delegates sent to Ottawa to arrange the terms of Prince Edward Island's entrance into Confederation; and on the completion of the union he was called, in November, 1873, to the Senate of Canada. From 1894 to 1899 he was lieutenant-governor of Prince Edward Island; and he died at Charlottetown on May 11, 1901.

[Morgan, *Can. men* (1898); *Can. parl. comp.*; Le Jeune, *Dict. gén.*]

Howland, Oliver Aiken (1847-1905), politician and author, was born at Lambton Mills, Canada West, on April 18, 1847, the son of Sir W. P. Howland (q.v.) and his first wife, Marianne Blyth. He was educated at Upper Canada College and at the University of Toronto; and he was called to the Ontario bar in 1875 (Q.C., 1896). From 1894 to 1898 he represented South Toronto in the Legislative Assembly of Ontario; and from 1901 to 1902 he was mayor of Toronto. He died at Toronto, on March 9, 1905, unmarried. He was the author of *The Irish problem* (London, 1887) and *The new empire* (Toronto, 1891).

[Morgan, *Can. men* (1898); *Can. parl. comp.*]

Howland, Sir William Pearce (1811-1907), minister of inland revenue for Canada (1867-68) and lieutenant-governor of Ontario (1868-73), was born at Paulings, New York, on May 29, 1811, the second son of Jonathan Howland, of Dutchess county, New York, and of Lydia Pearce. He was educated at the Kinderhook Academy; and in 1830 he came to Upper Canada. He settled first at Cooksville, near York (Toronto), where he went into business with his brother. In 1840 he purchased the Lambton mills in York county; and shortly afterwards he established a wholesale grocery business in Toronto. Though he was in sympathy with the Reform movement, he refused to implicate himself in the Rebellion of 1837; and after the union of 1841 he became a naturalized Canadian. In 1857 he was elected as a Reformer to represent West York in the Legislative Assembly of Canada; and he continued to represent this constituency, first in the Assembly, and then in the House of Commons until 1868. In 1862-63 he was minister of finance in the S. Macdonald-Sicotte government and in 1863-64 he was receiver-general in the S. Macdonald-Dorion government. In November, 1864, he entered the Great Coalition, with the portfolio of postmaster-general, succeeding Oliver Mowat (q.v.), who had been raised to the bench. When George Brown (q.v.) retired from the cabinet in 1865, Howland, with William McDougall (q.v.), declined to follow him. In 1866 his portfolio was changed to that of finance; and he was one of the Canadian delegates who went the same year to Westminster to discuss with the British government the terms of the British North America Act. In 1867 he was appointed minister of inland revenue in the first cabinet of the Dominion; but his political usefulness was impaired by the rejection of McDougall and himself at the Reform convention in Toronto in June, 1867, and in 1868 he retired from office to accept the lieutenant-governorship of Ontario. His term of office in Ontario lasted until 1873, and he then retired from public life. He continued in business until 1894, and he died at Toronto on January 1, 1907. He was thrice married, (1) in 1843 to Mrs. Webb, *née* Blyth, of Toronto, (2) in 1866 to Susannah Julia, widow of Capt. Hunt, of Toronto, and (3) to Elizabeth May Rattray, widow of James Bethune, Q.C., of Toronto. In 1867 he was created a C.B. (civil), and in 1879 a K.C.M.G.

[*Dict. nat. biog.*; Morgan, *Can. men* (1898); Rose, *Cyc. Can. biog.* (1886); *Can. biog. dict.*, Ont. vol. (Toronto, 1880); Dent, *Can. port.*, vol. 3; D. B. Read, *Lieutenant-governors of Upper Canada and Ontario* (Toronto, 1900); J. Young, *Public men and public life in Canada* (2 vols., Toronto, 1912).]

Howley, Michael Francis (1843-1914), Roman Catholic archbishop and historian, was born at St. John's, Newfoundland, on September 25, 1843. He was educated for the priesthood at the College of the Propaganda, Rome, and was ordained a priest in 1868. He returned to Newfoundland in 1870; and in 1892 he was the first Newfoundlander to be raised to the episcopate when he was made bishop of St. George's, West Newfoundland, in 1892. In 1894 he was transferred to the see of St. John's; and in 1904 he was made archbishop. He died on October 15, 1914. In 1902 he was elected a fellow of the Royal Society of Canada, in view of the publication of his *Ecclesiastical history of Newfoundland* (Bos-

ton, 1888). He was the author also of *Poems and other verses* (New York, 1903).

[*Proc. Roy. Soc. Can.*, 1915; *Who was who, 1897-1916.*]

Howse, Joseph (1773-1852), explorer and fur-trader, was born in England in 1773, and became a clerk in the service of the Hudson's Bay Company. In 1810 he crossed the Rocky Mountains by the pass named after him, and built on the west side of the mountains the first and only trading-post constructed by the Hudson's Bay Company prior to 1821. He retired from the service of the Hudson's Bay Company after twenty years' service; and he died at Cirencester, England, in 1852. He was the author of *A grammar of the Cree language* (London, 1844; 2nd ed., 1865).

[E. E. Rich (ed.), *Colin Robertson's correspondence book* (Toronto: The Champlain Society, 1939).]

Huard, Victor Alphonse (1853-1929), priest and author, was born at St. Roch, near Quebec, on February 22, 1853, the son of Laurent Huard. He was educated at the Quebec Seminary, and was ordained a priest of the Roman Catholic Church in 1876. He became a professor, and ultimately superior, of the Chicoutimi Seminary. In 1901 he returned to Quebec City, and became the editor of *La semaine religieuse*, as well as of *Le naturaliste canadien*, which he had edited since 1894. He died on October 15, 1929. He was the author of *L'apôtre du Saguenay* (Quebec, 1895), *Labrador et Anticosti* (Montreal, 1897), *Traité élémentaire de zoologie et d'hygiene* (Quebec, 1906), *Abrégée de zoologie* (Quebec, 1907), and *La vie et l'oeuvre de l'Abbé Provancher* (Quebec, 1926).

[Allaire, *Dict. biog.*; Le Jeune, *Dict. gén.*]

Hubert, Jean François (1739-1797), Roman Catholic bishop of Quebec (1788-97), was born at Quebec on February 23, 1739, the son of Jacques François Hubert, a baker, and Marie-Louise Maranda. He was educated at Quebec, and was ordained a priest by Mgr. Briand (q.v.) in 1766. From 1774 to 1778 he was superior of the Quebec Seminary; from 1781 to 1785 he was a missionary among the Hurons of the Detroit district; and in 1786 he was consecrated coadjutor of the bishop of Quebec, with the title of bishop of Almyra. In 1788 he became bishop of Quebec, and he administered the diocese until a few months before his death, which took place at Quebec on October 17, 1797.

[Allaire, *Dict. biog.*, Le Jeune, *Dict. gén.*; A. Gosselin, *L'église du Canada après la conquête* (2 vols., Quebec, 1916-17).]

Hubert, Petrus (1810-1882), notary public, was born at Yamachiche, Lower Canada, on August 19, 1810; and died at Three Rivers, Quebec, April 1, 1882. He was the author of

Lois organiques et la jurisprudence sur le notariat actuel en la province de Québec (Three Rivers, Que., 1870).

[*Bull. rech. hist.*, 1925.]

Hudon, Maxime (1841-1914), priest and poet, was born at St. Denis, Canada East, on December 19, 1841; and died at Berthier-en-bas, Quebec, on October 6, 1914. He was the author of *Sentiments et souvenirs* (2 vols., Quebec, 1907).

[Allaire, *Dict. biog.*]

Hudson, Henry (d. 1611), explorer, was an English sea-captain about whose early life nothing is known. He comes into the pages of history only in 1607, when he appears as the captain of a ship sent out by the Muscovy Company, in an endeavour to find a passage to Asia by the north of Europe. In this, and in another expedition the following year, Hudson was turned back by the ice. In 1609, in an attempt to find a westward route to Asia, he crossed the Atlantic in the service of the Dutch East India Company, entered New York harbour, and discovered and explored the Hudson River. For his next voyage he obtained the support of some English merchants; and in 1610 he set sail for Hudson Strait in the *Discovery*, a small vessel of only 55 tons, with a crew of 21 men. He made his way through Hudson Strait, and discovered and explored Hudson Bay. He wintered on the shores of James Bay; but as he was returning the following summer, his crew mutinied; and Hudson, his young son John, and eight of the crew who were ill and useless, were, on or about June 23, cast adrift in an open boat. Their fate is unknown. The *Discovery* succeeded in getting back to the British Isles, with eight of the mutineers still alive; and it was from these that the world learned of the discovery of Hudson Bay.

[L. Powys, *Henry Hudson* (London, 1927); Alice E. Cate, *Henry Hudson* (Boston, 1932); T. A. Janvier, *Henry Hudson* (New York, 1909); *Dict. nat. biog.*; *Cyc. Am. biog.*; *Dict. Am. biog.*; L. J. Burpee, *The search for the western sea* (2 vols., Toronto, 1935); *Dict. Can. biog.*, vol. 1.]

Hughes, James (1772-1853), fur-trader, was born in Montreal on October 3, 1772, probably the son of Capt. James Hughes (1738-1825), town major of Montreal. He entered the service of the North West Company about 1791, and in 1793 was a clerk at Fort de l'Isle on the Saskatchewan. From 1798 to 1817 he was almost continuously in the Fort des Prairies department; and he was made a partner of the North West Company between 1799 and 1802. He retired from the fur-trade in 1821; but during the next nine years he ran through his savings, and in 1830 he was engaged as a clerk by the Hudson's Bay Company, when nearly sixty years of age. He re-tired to Canada again in 1833; and he was in his later years an officer of the Indian department, with the rank of major. He was killed near Lachine, on the Island of Montreal, on July 13, 1853, when his horse bolted into a Grand Trunk Railway train. John McDonald of Garth (q.v.) described him as being "as brave a fellow as ever treaded the earth".

[W. S. Wallace (ed.), *Documents relating to the North West Company* (Toronto: The Champlain Society, 1934).]

Hughes, James Laughlin (1846-1935), educationist and author, was born near Bowmanville, Ontario, on February 20, 1846, the son of John Hughes, and the brother of Sir Sam Hughes (q.v.). He was educated at the Toronto Normal School, and became a school-teacher. From 1902 to 1913 he was chief inspector of schools in Toronto. He died at Toronto on January 3, 1935. He was the author of a number of educational books: *Mistakes in teaching* (Toronto, 1877; new ed., 1880), *How to secure and retain attention* (Toronto, 1879), *School history of Canada* (Toronto, 1884), *Froebel's educational laws* (New York, 1898), *Dickens as an educator* (New York, 1900), *Teaching to read* (New York, 1901), *Training the children* (New York, 1913), and *Adult and child* (Syracuse, 1917). He published also an edition of the *Poems* of Robert Burns (New York, 1920), as well as a volume entitled *The real Robert Burns* (Edinburgh, 1922); and he was the author of seven volumes of verse: *Songs of gladness and growth* (Toronto, 1916), *Rainbows on war clouds* (Syracuse, 1917), *The child's paradise* (Toronto, 1919), *Love memories* (Toronto, 1920), *In nature's temple shrines* (Toronto, 1921), *God made them good* (Toronto, 1922), and *My sunshine book* (Toronto, 1923).

[L. Pierce, *Fifty years of public service: A life of James L. Hughes* (Toronto, 1924); Morgan, *Can. men* (1912); *Who's who among North American authors*, 1933-35.]

Hughes, John (1849-1932), merchant and soldier, was born in Darlington township, Durham county, Canada West, on December 18, 1849, the second son of John Hughes and Caroline Laughlin, and the brother of Sir Samuel Hughes (q.v.). He became a village merchant; but he took also an active interest in the Orange order, in which he became in 1911 the grand master of the grand lodge of Ontario East, and in the Canadian militia, in which he rose to the rank of major-general. He saw service in the North West Rebellion of 1885; and in the First World War was, first, commandant of the mobilization camp at Valcartier and, later, inspector-general of military camps in Canada. He died at Bowmanville, Ontario, on April 13, 1932.

[*Can. who was who*, vol. 1; Morgan, *Can. men* (1912).]

Hughes, Katherine (d. 1925), author, was born at Melbourne, Prince Edward Island, the daughter of John Wellington Hughes and Annie Laurie O'Brien. She was educated at Notre Dame Convent and Prince of Wales College, Charlottetown, and became a journalist. She joined the staff of the Montreal *Star* in 1903, and of the Edmonton *Bulletin* in 1906. In 1908 she was appointed provincial archivist for Alberta. She died at New York on April 27, 1925. She was the author of *Archbishop O'Brien, man and churchman* (Ottawa, 1906) and *Father Lacombe, the black-robe voyageur* (Toronto, 1911).

[Morgan, *Can. men and women* (1912).]

Hughes, Sir Richard, Bart. (1729?-1812), lieutenant-governor of Nova Scotia (1778-81), is said to have been born in 1729, the son of Sir Richard Hughes, first baronet. He was educated at the Royal Academy at Portsmouth, and in 1742 entered the Royal Navy. In 1778 he was sent out to Halifax, Nova Scotia, as resident commissioner of the navy; and later in the same year was appointed lieutenant-governor of Nova Scotia. In 1780 he was promoted to be rear-admiral of the blue; and in 1781 he was transferred from Halifax to become commander-in-chief of the squadron in the Downs. From 1789 to 1791 he was again commander-in-chief at the port of Halifax; and he retired from service in 1794. He died on January 5, 1812. He succeeded to the baronetcy in 1780, on the death of his father.

[*Dict. nat. biog.*]

Hughes, Sir Samuel (1853-1921), minister of militia and defence for Canada (1911-16), was born at Darlington, Canada West, on January 8, 1853, the third son of John Hughes and Caroline Laughlin. He was educated at the Toronto Normal School and at the University of Toronto; and until 1885 he was a school-teacher. From 1885 to 1897 he was editor and proprietor of the Lindsay *Warder*; and in 1892 he was elected as a Conservative to represent North Victoria in the Canadian House of Commons. He sat for this constituency continuously until 1904; and from 1904 to 1921 he represented Victoria and Haliburton. Early in life he entered the volunteer militia, and in 1897 he became lieutenant-colonel commanding the 45th Regiment. He served in various capacities with the imperial troops in the South African War in 1899-1900; and in 1902 he was promoted to be colonel. He came to be regarded as a leading parliamentary authority on militia matters, and in 1911 he was appointed minister of militia and defence in the Borden government. He held this portfolio during the first half of the First World War; and in the organization and dispatch of the Canadian Expeditionary Force he showed great energy. In 1916, however, he came into conflict with Sir Robert Borden; and on November 9, 1916, the prime minister requested his resignation. An administrator of great driving force, he was at the same time lacking in discretion and good judgment; and both before and after his retirement from the cabinet, he was an outspoken critic of everyone with whom he did not agree. He died at Lindsay, Ontario, on August 24, 1921. He was twice married, (1) in 1872 to Caroline Preston, and (2) in 1875 to Mary, daughter of H. W. Burk, M.P.; and he had one son and two daughters. In 1915 he was created, for his services in connection with the war, a K.C.B.; and he was at the time of his death a lieutenant-general in the militia.

[C. F. Winter, *Lieutenant-general the Hon. Sir Sam Hughes* (Toronto, 1931); B. B. Cooke, *Major-general Sir Sam Hughes* (Can. mag., 1915); *Who was who,* 1916-28; Morgan, *Can. men* (1912); H. Charlesworth (ed.), *A cyclopaedia of Canadian biography* (Toronto, 1919); *Can. ann. review,* 1901-21.]

Hughes, William St. Pierre (1863-1940), soldier and civil servant, was born in Durham county, Canada West, on June 2, 1863, the son of John Hughes and Caroline Laughlin, and the younger brother of Sir Samuel Hughes (q.v.). In 1893 he was appointed secretary to the warden of the Kingston penitentiary, and in 1913 he became inspector of penitentiaries, and in 1919 superintendent of penitentiaries. During the First World War he raised and commanded the 21st Battalion of the Canadian Expeditionary Force; and from 1916 to 1917 he commanded the 10th Canadian Infantry Brigade, with the rank of brigadier-general. He was awarded the D.S.O., and was twice mentioned in dispatches. He died at Ottawa, Ontario, on June 1, 1940.

[H. Charlesworth (ed.), *A cyclopaedia of Canadian biography* (Toronto, 1919).]

Hugolin, Rév. Père. See **Lemay, Hugolin Marie**

Huguet-Latour, Louis Adolphe (1821-1904), author, was born in Lower Canada on December 31, 1821, and became a notary public. He died at Montreal, Quebec, on May 2, 1904. He was the author of *Annales de la tempérance* (Montreal, 1854) and *Annuaire de Ville-Marie* (Montreal 1864).

[*Cyc. Am. biog.*; Morgan, *Bib. can.*; E. Z. Massicotte, *L'archéologue Huguet-Latour* (Bull. rech. hist., 1940).]

Humbert, Stephen (1762?-1849), loyalist and author, was born in New Jersey about 1767, and settled in Saint John, New Brunswick, in 1783. He became a member of the House of Assembly; and was influential in introducing Methodism into New Brunswick. He died on January 16, 1849. He published *The union harmony; or, British America's sacred vocal music* (Saint John, N.B., 1801), and *The rise and progress of Methodism in the pro-*

vince of New Brunswick (Saint John, N.B., 1836).

[W. G. MacFarlane, *New Brunswick bibliography* (Saint John, N.B., 1895).]

Hume, George Sherwood (1893-1965), geologist, was born in Milton, Ontario, in 1893 and began his long career in geology along the Niagara escarpment. He graduated from the University of Toronto in 1915, spent some time on overseas military service, and returned to Canada in 1919. In 1920 he graduated from Yale University with a Ph.D. degree in geology. He joined the Geological Survey of Canada in 1921 and was directed to make a study of the petroleum and natural gas resources of Canada. During the next thirty-five years, until his retirement, he was regarded as the principal Canadian government expert on petroleum exploration and resources. During the Second World War he was advisor to the oil controller for Canada. He became chief of the Bureau of Geology in 1947 and in 1949 was made director of the mines, forests and scientific services branch of the department of mines and resources and acting deputy minister of mines. On retirement from the government service he became chief geologist and vice-president of Westcoast Transmission Company. He was a fellow of the Royal Society of Canada, the Geological Association of Canada, and the Geological Society of America, as well as the winner of a number of medals for his work on the geology of oil and gas in both southern and northern Alberta. He died at Calgary in 1965.

[*Proc. & Trans. Roy. Soc. Can.* (series four, vol. IV, 1966).]

Humphrey, Jack Weldon (1901-1967), painter, was born in Saint John, New Brunswick, in 1901. He studied at the Boston Museum School (1920-23), and with Charles Hawthorne of the National Academy of Design in New York (1924-29). While in Europe in 1930 he studied for a short time with Hans Hoffman in Munich. In 1938 he travelled to Mexico and in 1952 returned to study in France on a Royal Society of Canada Fellowship. His studio was in Saint John, New Brunswick, and by 1935 he had begun to receive national recognition as a painter. His earlier works include a number of remarkable natural portraits of children. He worked in many mediums including oil on canvas, on board, on masonite; charcoal, chalk, pastel, and pencil drawings; water colours; gouache; and acrylic. After his return from Europe in 1953 he broke from figurative painting and carried abstraction almost to the limit. In 1938 he became a member of the Eastern Group of Painters, which later became the Contemporary Art Society. He first exhibited in 1929 and thereafter in many exhibitions including a retrospective of sixty-eight of his works which travelled across Canada in 1967. His

paintings are to be found in the National Gallery of Canada; the Art Gallery of Ontario; Hart House, Toronto; the New Brunswick Museum; the Art Museum, London, Ontario; the Beaverbrook Gallery; the Edmonton Art Gallery; the Winnipeg Art Gallery; and the Confederation Art Gallery at Charlottetown, Prince Edward Island; as well as in university and private collections. He died at Saint John, New Brunswick, in 1967.

[C. S. MacDonald, *Dictionary of Canadian artists*, vol. 2 (Ottawa, 1968); *Atlantic advocate*, March, 1958; *Canadian art*, 1948, 1966; *artscanada*, Feb., 1967.]

Hunt, Thomas Sterry (1826-1892), geologist and chemist, was born at Norwich, Connecticut, on September 5, 1826. He was educated at Yale University (M.A., 1852), and in 1846 he was appointed to the staff of the Geological Survey of Canada. He was connected with the Survey until 1872; from 1856 to 1862 he was professor of chemistry at Laval University, Quebec, and from 1862 to 1868 at McGill University, Montreal. From 1872 to 1878 he was professor of geology at the Massachusetts Institute of Technology, Boston. He then returned to Canada, and devoted himself to geological and chemical researches; and he died in New York on February 12, 1892. In 1878 he married the eldest daughter of Mr. Justice Gale, of Montreal; but had no children. In 1859 he was made a fellow of the Royal Society of London; in 1882 he became a charter member of the Royal Society of Canada, and in 1884 he was its president. He was president of the American Institute of Mining Engineers in 1877, and of the American Chemical Society in 1880. He was an LL.D. of Cambridge (1881). Apart from a great number of scientific and technical papers, he was the author of *A new basis for chemistry* (Boston, 1887), *Chemical and geological essays* (Boston, 1875; 2nd ed., Salem, 1878), *Mineral physiology and physiography* (Boston, 1886; new ed., 1890), and *Systematic mineralogy* (New York, 1891).

[J. Douglas, *Memoir of Thomas Sterry Hunt* (Philadelphia, 1898), with bibliography; *Proc. Roy. Soc. Can.*, 1892; Rose, *Cyc. Can. biog.* (1888); Morgan, *Cel. Can.*; *Cyc. Am. biog.*]

Hunter, Andrew Frederick (1863-1940), journalist and archaeologist, was born in Innisfil township, Canada West, on December 31, 1863; and was educated at the University of Toronto (B.A., 1889; M.A., 1892). He became a journalist, and from 1889 to 1895 was editor of the Barrie *Examiner*. Later he became for many years secretary of the Ontario Historical Society. He died at Toronto, Ontario, on October 19, 1940. He was the author of *A history of Simcoe county* (2 vols., Barrie, Ont., 1909); and he was joint editor, with E. A. Cruikshank (q.v.), of *The correspondence of the Honourable*

Peter Russell (3 vols., Toronto, 1932-36).
[Morgan, *Can. men* (1912).]

Hunter, Horace Talmadge (1881-1961), publisher, was born at Meadowvale, Ontario, May 15, 1881. He was educated at the University of Toronto (B.A., 1903). He joined the MacLean Publishing Company on graduation and was appointed general manager in 1911, becoming president in 1933 and chairman in 1952. During this period the company published *Maclean's* magazine, *Chatelaine, Canadian Homes and Gardens,* the *Financial Post,* and thirty-four business newspapers in Canada, the United States, and Great Britain. He died at Toronto, November 1, 1961.
[*Can. who's who*, 1958-60.]

Hunter, James (1817-1881), missionary, was born in England in 1817, and was sent out by the Church Missionary Society to the Hudson's Bay Company's territories as a missionary to the Indians in 1844. For ten years he was stationed at The Pas, on the Saskatchewan River; and later he was in charge of St. Andrew's Church, in the Red River Settlement. While in this charge, he was appointed archdeacon of Cumberland and in 1859 he was instrumental in beginning the missionary work of the Church of England in the Mackenzie River district. He returned to England in 1864, and became vicar of St. Matthew's, Bayswater, London. This charge he held until his death in 1881. He was the author of *A lecture on the grammatical construction of the Cree language* (London, 1875).
[W. B. Heeney (ed.), *Leaders of the Canadian Church: Second series* (Toronto, 1920).]

Hunter, John Edwin (1856-1919), evangelist, was born in Durham county, Canada West, on July 19, 1856. After spending some years as an itinerant preacher, he entered Victoria University, and was ordained a minister of the Methodist Church in 1882. For ten years he was stationed in Manitoba; then he returned to eastern Canada, and for some years he was associated with the Rev. Hugh Thomas Crossley in evangelistic and revival work. The names of Crossley and Hunter — Crossley specializing in the singing, and Hunter in the preaching — became famous as revivalists all over Canada. Hunter died at Toronto, Ontario, on May 17, 1919.
[Morgan, *Can. men* (1898).]

Hunter, John Howard (1839-1911), educationist and civil servant, was born at Bandon, Ireland, on December 22, 1839; and was educated at the University of Toronto (B.A., 1861; M.A., 1862). He became a schoolteacher; but in 1881 was appointed head of the insurance branch of the Ontario government. He died in Toronto, Ontario, in November, 1911. He was the author of *The Upper Canada*

College question (Toronto, 1868) and *A manual of insurance law* (Toronto, 1881).
[*Cyc. Am. biog.*; Morgan, *Can. men* (1898).]

Hunter, Peter (1746-1805), lieutenant-governor of Upper Canada (1799-1805) was born in 1746 of a Scottish family of Auchterarder, Perthshire, the brother of the celebrated John Hunter, M.D. (d. 1809). He entered the British army, became colonel of the 60th Rifle Regiment, and ultimately rose to the rank of lieutenant-general. In 1799 he was appointed commander-in-chief of the forces in Canada; and at the same time he became lieutenant-governor of Upper Canada. During a large part of his tenure of office his duties as commander-in-chief necessitated his absence from York (Toronto), and in these absences the government was left in the hands of a commission of executive councillors. From this fact has arisen the statement that it was under Hunter that the "Family Compact" originated. He died suddenly at Quebec, while on a tour of inspection, on August 21, 1805. He was unmarried. No portrait of him is known to exist.
[E. A. Cruikshank, *A memoir of Lieutenant-General Peter Hunter* (Ont. Hist. Soc., papers and records, 1934); D. B. Read, *The lieutenant-governors of Upper Canada* (Toronto, 1900).]

Hunter-Duvar, John (1830-1899), author, was born in Scotland on August 29, 1830. He spent a good deal of his life in the Maritime provinces of Canada; and from 1879 to 1889 he was Dominion inspector of fisheries for Prince Edward Island. His later years were spent in retirement at his place "Hernewood", Alberton, Prince Edward Island; and here he died on January 25, 1899. He wrote both poetry and prose of a fanciful and romantic character, including *The enamorado, a drama* (Summerside, P.E.I., 1879), *De Roberval, a drama* (Saint John, N.B., 1888), *Stone, bronze, and iron ages* (London, 1892), and *Annals of the court of Oberon* (London, 1895).
[Morgan, *Can. men* (1898); *Can. who was who*, vol. 2; A. MacMurchy, *Handbook of Canadian literature* (Toronto, 1906); C. C. James, *Bibliography of Canadian poetry* (Toronto, 1899); W. G. MacFarlane, *New Brunswick bibliography* (Saint John, N.B., 1895).]

Huntington, Lucius Seth (1827-1886), politician and author, was born at Compton, Lower Canada, on May 26, 1827, the son of Seth Huntington, of Waterville, Lower Canada. He was educated at the common schools, and in 1853 was called to the Canadian bar. In 1861 he was elected as a Liberal to the Legislative Assembly of Canada for the county of Shefford; and this constituency he represented until 1882, first in the Assembly of united Canada, and then in the Canadian House of

Commons. In 1863-64 he was solicitor-general for Lower Canada in the Sandfield Macdonald government; and in 1864-65 he was a vigorous opponent of Confederation. In 1873 he preferred against the Macdonald government the charges in connection with the granting of the Canadian Pacific Railway charter which led to the fall of the government; and in 1874 he was included in the Mackenzie administration as president of the council. He became postmaster-general in 1875, and in 1878 he resigned with the rest of the Mackenzie government. In 1882 he was defeated at the polls in Shefford, and retired from active political life. He removed to New York, and there he died on May 19, 1886. He was twice married, (1) to Miriam Jane (d. 1871), daughter of Major Wood of Shefford, and (2) in 1877 to Mrs. Marsh, of New York. In 1884 he published a novel, *Professor Conant* (Toronto).

[*Cyc. Am. biog.*; *Dom. ann. reg.*, 1886; Rose, *Cyc. Can. biog.* (1886); Dent, *Can. port.*, vol. 4; *Can. parl. comp.*]

Huntley, Sir Henry Vere (1795-1864), lieutenant-governor of Prince Edward Island (1841-47), was the third son of the Rev. Richard Huntley of Gloucestershire. He entered the navy in 1809, and in 1839 he was appointed lieutenant-governor of the settlements on the River Gambia. In August, 1841, he became lieutenant-governor of Prince Edward Island, and he held office until 1847. He died in Santos, Brazil, on May 7, 1864. In 1841 he was created a knight bachelor. He published several not very important works, among them *Peregrine Scramble; or, Thirty years' adventures of a blue-jacket* (2 vols., London, 1849), *Observations upon the free trade policy of England in connection with the Sugar Act of 1846* (London, 1849), *Seven years' service on the slave coast of western Africa* (2 vols., London, 1850), and *California, its gold and its inhabitants* (2 vols., London, 1856).

[*Dict. nat. biog.*]

Huot, Antonio (1877-1929), priest and author, was born at Quebec on March 22, 1877, the son of Emmanuel Huot. He studied in Rome, Italy, and became in 1900 professor of philosophy at the Quebec Seminary. Ill health compelled his resignation, however, in 1901; and he then became almoner to a private family. He died at Quebec on April 7, 1929. He was the author of *Le fléau maçonnique* (Quebec, 1906), *Le poison maçonnique* (Quebec, 1911), *Le bien paternal* (Quebec, 1912), *L'oeuvre de la réconstruction* (Quebec, 1919), *France et Italie, impressions de voyage* (Quebec, 1924), *La question juive chez-nous* (Quebec, 1926; Eng. trans., 1926), and, under the pseudonym "Jean Duterroir", *La question juive* (Quebec, 1914).

[*Bull. rech. hist.*, 1929; Allaire, *Dict. biog.*]

Huot, Charles (1855-1930), painter, was born at Quebec, Canada East, on March 26,

1855. He studied art in France and Germany for several years, and then returned to Canada. He died at Sillery, near Quebec, on January 27, 1930.

[H. Magnan, *Charles Huot, sa vie, sa carrière* (Quebec, 1932); Le Jeune, *Dict. gén.*]

Hurlbert, Jesse Beaufort (1812?-1891), author, was born about 1812, in Augusta township, Grenville county, Upper Canada, of United Empire Loyalist descent. He was educated at the Wesleyan University, Middletown, Connecticut (A.B., 1835); and from 1839 to 1841 he was acting principal of Upper Canada Academy, Cobourg, Upper Canada. When Victoria College was organized in 1841, he became its first professor of natural science. In 1847 he resigned this chair, and with his wife opened the Adelaide Academy for Young Ladies in Toronto. In his later years he held a post in the civil service in Ottawa; and he died at Ottawa on May 12, 1891. He was the author of *Collection of the products of the waters and forests of Upper Canada* (Montreal, 1862), *Britain and her colonies* (London, 1865), *Field and factory side by side; or, How to establish and develop native industries* (Montreal, 1870), *The climates, productions, and resources of Canada* (Montreal, 1872), *Physical atlas ... of the Dominion of Canada* (n.p., 1880), *Currents of air and ocean in connection with climates* (Salem, Mass., 1883), *Food zones of Canada* (n.p., 1884), *Jesuit teaching on the Ten Commandments* (Montreal, 1890), and *The end justifies the means* (Montreal, 1890).

[*Morgan, Bib. can.*]

Hurley, James Joseph (1898-1963), soldier and diplomat, was born in Brantford, Ontario, August 13, 1898. He was educated in Brantford schools. He served in the First World War (1916-19), and in the Second World War (1940-46), and was awarded the O.B.E. From 1920 to 1940 he was employed in the family firm, Hurley Printing Company Limited, rising to president and managing director. He was Canadian consul at Detroit, Michigan, from 1946 until 1951, when he became Canadian high commissioner to Ceylon. In 1958 he was appointed Canadian ambassador to South Africa. He died at Brantford, Ontario, December 29, 1963.

[*Can. who's who*, 1961-63; Metropolitan Toronto Library Board, *Biographical scrapbooks*, vol. 21.]

Hurley, Maisie (1888-1964), editor and publisher, was born in Swansea, Wales, in 1888. She travelled to India and then to Canada with her father, a mining engineer, and became interested in the Indian life and languages of British Columbia. She founded and edited the first Indian newspaper, *Native Voice*, in 1946, and was a strong advocate of native rights. She often appeared in court and at one time was jailed for her support of a client's rights. She married Michael Murphy, a boxing promoter, with whom she had eloped, and secondly, in 1951, Tom Hurley, a Vancouver lawyer, to whom she was legal secretary, and who, like Maisie, was a defender of Indian claims. She died at Vancouver, British Columbia, October 3, 1964.

[Metropolitan Toronto Library Board, *Biographical scrapbooks*, vol. 22.]

Huston, James (1820-1854), *littérateur*, was born in Lower Canada on August 21, 1820. He became assistant French translator to the Legislative Assembly of united Canada; and he was one of the original members of the Institut Canadien of Montreal. He made a collection of the most important contributions to French-Canadian literature, both in prose and poetry, published between 1777 and 1850, and he republished these under the title *Le répertoire national, ou recueil de littérature canadienne* (4 vols., Montreal, 1848-50; new ed., Montreal, 1893). His own contributions to this collection were *Visite à un village français* (1842) and *De la position et des besoins de la jeunesse canadienne-française* (1847). He died at Quebec on September 21, 1854.

[Morgan, *Bib. can.*; Le Jeune, *Dict. gén.*; E. Lareau, *Histoire de la littérature canadienne* (Montreal, 1874); *Le répertoire national* (new ed., Montreal, 1893), vol. 2, pp. 328-29; *Le Pays,* Montreal, Sept. 21, 1854.]

Hutchison, Alexander Cowper (1838-1922), architect, was born at Montreal, Lower Canada, on April 2, 1838. In his early years he was a stone-cutter; and he was in charge of the stone-cutting required for the Parliament Buildings at Ottawa prior to 1865. Later, he became an architect in Montreal; and many of the principal buildings in Montreal were designed by him. He was a charter member of the Royal Canadian Academy of Arts, and was for some years its vice-president. He died at Montreal, Quebec, on January 1, 1922.

[Morgan, *Can. men* (1912); H. G. Jones and E. Dyonnet, *History of the Royal Canadian Academy of Arts* (Montreal, 1934).]

Hutton, Maurice (1856-1940), educationist, was born in Manchester, England, in 1856, the son of the Rev. Joseph Henry Hutton, and the nephew of Richard Hutton, the editor of the London *Spectator*. He was educated at Magdalen College School and at Worcester College, Oxford (B.A., 1879; M.A., 1883); and he was elected in 1879 a fellow of Merton College, Oxford. In 1880 he was appointed professor of classics in University College, Toronto; and in 1901 he became principal of the college. In 1906-07 he was acting president of the University of Toronto. He retired on pension in 1929; and he died at Toronto, Ontario, on April 5, 1940. He was throughout his life in Canada an outstanding exponent, both by example and

by precept, of the value of a classical education. In 1913 he was elected a fellow of the Royal Society of Canada; and he received the honorary degree of LL.D. from several universities. Though for many years he published nothing save occasional essays and addresses, he was the author during his later years of several notable books: *The Greek point of view* (London, 1925), *Many minds* (Toronto, 1927), *All the rivers run into the sea* (Toronto, 1928), and *The sisters Jest and Earnest* (Toronto, 1930). In 1885 he married Annie Margaret, daughter of the Reverend John McCaul (q.v.), first president of the University of Toronto.

[*Who was who,* 1928-40; *Proc. Roy. Soc. Can.,* 1941; *University of Toronto monthly,* 1940; Morgan, *Can. men* (1912).]

Hutton, William (d. 1861), author, was from 1853 to his death on July 19, 1861, secretary of the Bureau of Agriculture in Canada. He published *Canada, a brief outline of her geographical position, productions, climate, capabilities, educational and municipal institutions, etc.* (3rd ed., Quebec, 1861), *Caird's erroneous view of Canada answered and refuted* (Toronto, 1858), and *Le Canada et l'Illinois comparés* (Quebec, 1860).

[Morgan, *Bib. can.*]

Hyman, Charles Smith (1854-1926), minister of public works for Canada (1904-07), was born in London, Canada West, in 1854, the son of Ellis Walton Hyman. He was educated at Hellmuth College, London; and became a manufacturer. He was elected to represent London in the Canadian House of Commons in 1891, and again in 1900 and 1904; and in 1904 he became acting minister, and in 1905 minister of public works in the Laurier government. He resigned both his portfolio and his seat in parliament in 1907. He died at London, Ontario, on October 8, 1926.

[Morgan, *Can. men* (1912); *Can. parl. comp.*; *Who was who,* 1916-28.]

Hynes, Leonard (1911-1975), industrialist, was born in Toronto, Ontario, July 3, 1911. He was educated at St. Michael's College, University of Toronto (B.A., 1932; M.A., 1933). He joined Canadian Industries Limited in 1933 and rose to become vice-president and director in 1954, president from 1960 to 1971, and then chairman of the board. He was a director of the Bank of Montreal, and Pilkington Brothers (Canada). He was a member of the executive council of the Canadian Chamber of Commerce, chairman (1964) of the joint committee of the Canada and United States Chamber of Commerce, and a member of the Chemical Institute of Canada. He was interested in health and education in the Montreal area. He died at Kingston, Ontario, March 1, 1975.

[*Can. who's who,* 1970-72.]

I

Iberville, Pierre Le Moyne, Sieur d' (1661-1706), soldier and colonizer of Louisiana, was born at Montreal on July 20, 1661, the third son of Charles Le Moyne, Sieur de Longueuil, and Catherine Thierry Primot. He was educated at the Sulpician Seminary at Montreal, and in 1673 entered the French navy. He returned to Canada in 1683, and three years later accompanied the Sieur de Troyes (q.v.) on his expedition against the English in Hudson Bay. On Troyes's return to Quebec, Iberville was left in command of the expedition; and during the following years he was repeatedly active in Hudson Bay. In 1690 he was given command of two ships with which to cruise in Hudson Bay, and with these captured Fort Severn. In 1694 he again visited Hudson Bay, and took York Fort. In 1696 he commanded an attack on Pemaquid, Acadia, and captured St. John's, Newfoundland. In 1697 he sailed for Hudson Bay, defeated a superior English fleet, and recaptured York Fort. In 1698 he set out from Brest in command of an expedition to discover the mouth of the Mississippi, and there he planted a colony, and in 1700 built a fort on the site of New Orleans. In 1706 he took the islands of Nevis and St. Christopher. While preparing an expedition against the English colonies on the Atlantic sea-board, he died at Havana of yellow fever, on July 9, 1706. He married, in 1693, Marie Thérèse Pollet de la Combe Pocatière, by whom he had several children.

[P. Daviault, *La grande aventure de Le Moyne d'Iberville* (Montreal, 1937); L. Le Jeune, *Le Chevalier Pierre Le Moyne d'Iberville* (Ottawa, 1937); Charles B. Reed, *The first great Canadian* (Chicago, 1910), with portrait and bibliography; Abbé Desmazures, *Histoire du chevalier d'Iberville* (Montreal, 1890); E. Rousseau, *Les exploits d'Iberville* (Quebec, 1888); Abbé Daniel, *D'Iberville, ou le Jean-Bart canadien, et la baie d'Hudson* (Montreal, 1868); J. B. Tyrrell (ed.), *Documents relating to the early history of Hudson bay* (Toronto, Champlain Society, 1931); N. M. Crouse, *Le Moyne d'Iberville* (Ithaca, 1954); G. Frégault, *Iberville le conquérant* (Montreal, 1944); *Dict. Can. biog.*, vol. 2.]

Idington, John (1840-1928), judge of the Supreme Court of Canada, was born near Morriston, Upper Canada, on October 14, 1840. He was educated at the University of Toronto (LL.B., 1864), and was called to the bar in 1864 (Q.C., 1876). He was appointed a judge of the High Court of Justice in Ontario; and in 1905 he became a judge of the Supreme Court of Canada. He died at Ottawa on February 7, 1928.

[Morgan, *Can. men* (1912); *Can. parl. comp.*]

Ignatieff, Nicholas (1904-1952), educationist and author, was born in St. Petersburg, Russia, on March 7, 1904, and died at Toronto, Ontario, on March 28, 1952. He was educated at the University of London (B.Sc., 1925), and on graduation came to Canada. For a time he was a teacher in Upper Canada College. He served overseas with the Canadian forces in the Second World War, rising to the rank of lieutenant-colonel. In 1947 he was appointed warden of Hart House, in the University of Toronto. He was the author of *The Russian emerges* (Toronto, 1932).

[*Can. who's who*, 1949-51; *Encyc. Can.*]

Iles, George (1852-1942), author, was born in Gibraltar on June 20, 1852, and came to Canada with his parents when a child. He was educated in Montreal; and for some years prior to 1887 he was manager of the Windsor Hotel in Montreal. The latter part of his life he spent in New York, engaged in literary work; and he died in New York on October 3, 1942. In 1928 McGill University conferred on him the honorary degree of LL.D. He was the author of *A class in geometry* (New York, 1894), *Flame, electricity, and the camera* (New York, 1900), *Inventors at work* (New York, 1906), *Leading American inventors* (New York, 1912), and *Canadian stories* (New York, 1918); and he was the editor of *Little masterpieces of science* (6 vols., New York, 1902) and *Little masterpieces of autobiography* (6 vols., New York, 1908).

[*Who's who in America*, 1940-41; Morgan, *Can. men* (1910).]

Ilsley, James Lorimer (1894-1967), judge and cabinet minister, was born in Somerset county, Nova Scotia, January 3, 1894, and educated at Acadia University (B.A., 1913) and Dalhousie University (LL.B., 1916). He was first elected to the House of Commons in 1926 and was re-elected four times, retiring in 1948 to return to his law practice. In 1935 he was appointed minister of national revenue and in 1940 became minister of finance with responsibility for directing Canada's support for the Second World War. Despite his austere approach and because of his qualities of courage and integrity, he was a popular finance minister. In 1944 he was one of the five ministers who persuaded Mackenzie King to undertake conscription. He left his post as minister of finance in 1946 and became minister of justice, a position which he held until he retired from political life in 1948 to return to legal practice in the firm of Ilsley, Duquet, and MacKay of Montreal. He was appointed a puisne judge of the Supreme Court of Nova Scotia in 1949 and was chief justice of Nova Scotia from 1950 until his death on January 14, 1967.

[Metropolitan Toronto Central Library, *Biographical scrapbooks*, vols. 33, 58; *Can. who's who*, 1964-66.]

Imrie, John (1846-1902), poet, was born in Glasgow, Scotland, in 1846. He came to Canada in 1871, and settled in Toronto, Ontario. Here he founded a printing establishment; and in 1890 he began the publication of a periodical entitled *The Scottish-Canadian*. He died in Toronto on November 10, 1902. He was a writer of Scottish dialect verse; and he published *Songs and miscellaneous poems* (Toronto, 1888; new and enlarged edition, with introduction by G. Mercer Adam, 1891).

[*Can. who was who*, vol. 1; Morgan, *Can. men* (1898).]

Imrie, John Mills (1883-1942), journalist and publisher, was born in Toronto, Ontario, on October 21, 1883, the son of John Imrie (q.v.). He was educated in Toronto, and became editor of *Printer and publisher* and *Bookseller and stationer*, two trade papers. From 1913 to 1919 he was secretary-manager of the Canadian Press Association; and in 1921 he became managing director of the *Edmonton Journal*. He was vice-president of the Canadian Institute of International Affairs from 1934 to 1936; and he was interested in the Boy Scouts' Association and the St. John Ambulance Association. He died at Edmonton, Alberta, on June 19, 1942.

[*Can. who's who*, 1936-37.]

Inch, James Robert (1835-1912), educationist, was born at Petersville, Queen's county, New Brunswick, on April 29, 1835. He was educated at Mount Allison University (A.B., 1864; A.M., 1867; LL.D., 1878), and be-

came a school-teacher. From 1864 to 1878 he was principal of Mount Allison Ladies' College; and from 1878 to 1909 he was president of the University of New Brunswick. From 1891 to 1909 he was also superintendent of education in New Brunswick. He died at Amherst, Nova Scotia, on October 14, 1912.

[Morgan, *Can. men* (1912); Rose, *Cyc. Can. biog.* (1888).]

Inglis, Charles (1734-1816), first Anglican bishop of Nova Scotia, was born in Glen and Kilcarr, Ireland, in 1734, the son of the Rev. Archibald Inglis. He was educated in Ireland, and was in 1757 a master in a church school in Lancaster, Pennsylvania. He returned to England in 1758 to take holy orders; and was ordained deacon and priest in the same year, and sent out to Dover, Delaware. In 1765 he was appointed assistant to the rector of Trinity Church, New York. During the American Revolution, he was well known for his loyalty to the Crown; and his church was burnt, his congregation scattered, and his property confiscated. He went to Nova Scotia in 1783, and to England in the following year. In 1787 he was consecrated first bishop of Nova Scotia, and to his charge was added also Newfoundland, Prince Edward Island, and Quebec; but in 1793 Quebec was made a separate diocese. In 1788 he founded a church academy at Windsor; and in 1802 it was granted a royal charter as the University of King's College. In 1796, on account of his failing health, he moved to "Clermont", a farm near Halifax, and spent much of his time writing. In 1809 he was made a member of the Council of Nova Scotia, ranking next to the chief justice of the province. He died on February 24, 1816. He married (1) in 1764, Mary Vining of Dover (d. 1764), and (2) Mary Crooke of Ulster county, New York (d. 1783), by whom he had two sons and two daughters. In 1767 he received the honorary degree of M.A. from King's College, New York; and in 1778 the honorary degree of D.D. from the University of Oxford. A number of his sermons and essays were published in New York, Halifax, and London.

[R. V. Harris, *Charles Inglis* (Toronto, 1937); J. W. Lydekker, *The life and letters of Charles Inglis* (London, 1936); W. F. Vroom, *Charles Inglis* (Coll. Nova Scotia Hist. Soc., 1933); R. S. Rayson, *Charles Inglis* (Queen's quarterly, 1925); C. H. Mockridge, *The bishops of the Church of England in Canada* (Toronto, 1896); J. Fingard, *Charles Inglis* (Can. hist. rev., 1968); *Dict. nat. biog.*; Morgan, *Bib. can.*]

Inglis, David (d. 1877), clergyman, was born in the parish of Greenlaw, Berwickshire, Scotland, and was educated at the University of Edinburgh. He was licensed to preach by the presbytery of Carlisle, England; but in 1846 he emigrated to the United States. Here he served several charges until, in 1852, he was called to Montreal to become pastor of the St. Gabriel Street Presbyterian church. In 1865 he removed to Hamilton, to become pastor of the McNab Street Church; and from 1871 to 1872 he was professor of systematic theology in Knox College, Toronto. In 1872, however, he returned to the United States; and he died at Brooklyn, New York, on December 15, 1877. He was the author of *Crown jewels* (Montreal, 1854).

[R. Campbell, *A history of the Scotch Presbyterian Church, St. Gabriel Street, Montreal* (Montreal, 1887).]

Inglis, John (1777-1850), third Anglican bishop of Nova Scotia (1825-50), was born in New York in 1777, the son of Charles Inglis (q.v.), first bishop of Nova Scotia, and Mary Crooke. He was educated at the church academy founded by his father at Windsor, and also at King's College, Windsor. He was ordained deacon by his father in 1801, and was his commissary until his death in 1816. Upon his father's death he went to England, expecting to be appointed to the bishopric, but the Rev. Robert Stanser received the appointment; and it was not until the resignation of the latter in 1825 that he was appointed bishop. He was instrumental in having the "Church tests" removed from King's College, but opposed its union with Dalhousie College at Halifax. He formed a Diocesan Church Society, which was the first of what are now called synods. In 1839 part of his see was divided into two new dioceses, one for Upper Canada, and the other for Newfoundland and Bermuda; and in 1845 New Brunswick was formed into the separate diocese of Fredericton. Inglis died on October 27, 1850, in London, England. He married a daughter of the Hon. Thomas Cochran, and by her he had three sons and three daughters. A number of his sermons and addresses were published in Halifax and London; and his correspondence is in the Public Archives at Ottawa.

[C. H. Mockridge, *The bishops of the Church of England in Canada* (Toronto, 1896); Morgan, *Bib. can.*]

Inglis, Walter (1815-1884), missionary, was born in Scotland in 1815, was educated at Edinburgh and Glasgow universities, and was ordained a Presbyterian minister in 1842. In 1842 he was sent by the London Missionary Society to South Africa, and here he was associated with David Livingstone. He was expelled from the Transvaal by the Boers, however; and in 1855 he was sent to Canada as a missionary by the United Presbyterian Church in Scotland. He occupied various charges in Ontario; and he died at Ayr, Ontario, on October 18, 1884.

[W. Cochrane, *Memoirs and remains of the Rev. Walter Inglis, African missionary and Canadian pastor* (Toronto, 1887); *Dom. ann. reg.*, 1884.]

Inkster, Colin (1843-1934), politician and civil servant, was born at the Red River Settlement on August 3, 1843. He was appointed a member of the Legislative Council of Manitoba in 1871; and in 1874 he became minister of agriculture and president of the Council in the provincial administration. In 1876 he was appointed speaker of the Legislative Council of Manitoba; and it was by his casting vote that the Council was then abolished. From 1876 to 1928 he was sheriff of the eastern judicial district of Manitoba. He died near Winnipeg, Manitoba, on September 29, 1934.

[J. P. Robertson, *A political manual of the province of Manitoba* (Winnipeg, 1887).]

Innes, John (1864-1941), painter, was born at London, Ontario, in 1864, and died at Vancouver, British Columbia, on January 13, 1941. He went to the Canadian West before the building of the Canadian Pacific Railway, and he spent the last thirty years of his life in Vancouver, painting colourful pictures of pioneer days in the West.

[J. B. Cowan, *John Innes, painter of the Canadian West* (Vancouver, 1945); A. H. Robson, *Canadian landscape painters* (Toronto, 1932).]

Innis, Harold Adams (1894-1952), economist and historian, was born near Otterville, Ontario, on November 5, 1894, and was educated at McMaster University, then in Toronto (B.A., 1916; M.A., 1918), and at the University of Chicago (Ph.D., 1920). He enlisted in the Canadian army in 1916, and was wounded in France in 1917. In 1920 he was appointed lecturer in the department of political science in the University of Toronto, and he continued in this department for the rest of his life. He became head of the department in 1937, and in 1947 he became dean of the School of Graduate Studies as well. He was elected a fellow of the Royal Society of Canada in 1934, and its president in 1946; and he became the president of the Canadian Political Science Association in 1937, and of the American Economic Association in 1951. Honorary degrees were conferred on him by the University of New Brunswick, the University of Manitoba, McMaster University, Glasgow University, and Laval University. His sadly premature death occurred at Toronto on November 8, 1952.

He was the author of *A history of the Canadian Pacific Railway* (London, 1923), *Peter Pond* (Toronto 1930), *The fur trade in Canada* (New Haven, Conn., 1930; new ed., Toronto, 1951), *Problems of staple production in Canada* (Toronto, 1933), *The cod fisheries* (New Haven, Conn., 1940; new ed., Toronto, 1954), *Political economy in the modern state* (Toronto, 1946), *Empire and communications* (Toronto, 1950), *The bias of communication* (Toronto, 1951), and *Changing concepts of time* (Toronto, 1952). After his death his widow edited his *Essays in Canadian economic his-*

tory (Toronto, 1956). He was the editor of the first volume of *Select documents in Canadian economic history* (Toronto, 1929), and joint editor, with A. R. M. Lower, of the second (Toronto, 1933). He also edited *Essays in political science* (Toronto, 1938), *The diary of Alexander James McPhail* (Toronto, 1940), and *The diary of Simeon Perkins* (Toronto, 1948). A bibliography of his publications is printed in the *Canadian journal of economic and political science*, May, 1953.

[D. G. Creighton, *Harold Adams Innis: Portrait of a scholar* (Toronto, 1957); *Proc. Roy. Soc. Can.*, 1953; *Can. who's who*, 1949-51; *Encyc. Can.*]

Irvine, Acheson Gosford (1837-1916), commissioner of the North-West Mounted Police (1880-86), was born at Quebec, Lower Canada, on December 7, 1837, the son of Lieut.-Col. J. G. Irvine and Annie, daughter of the Hon. Matthew Bell. He was gazetted a lieutenant in the militia in 1864, and later served as major in the 2nd Battalion of the Quebec Rifles in the Red River expeditionary force of 1870. In 1871 he was appointed commanding officer of the Provisional Battalion of Rifles left in Manitoba after the collapse of the Red River rebellion; and on the formation of the North-West Mounted Police in 1875 he was appointed assistant commissioner of the Police. He became commissioner in 1880, and was in command of the police during the North-West rebellion of 1885. He retired from this post in 1886; and in 1892 he was appointed warden of the Stony Mountain penitentiary in Manitoba. He held this position until shortly before his death at Quebec City, on January 9, 1916. In 1902 he was decorated with the Imperial Service Order. He was not married.

[Morgan, *Can. men* (1912); P. G. Roy, *Fils de Québec*, vol. 2 (Lévis, Que., 1933); A. L. Haydon, *The riders of the plains* (London, 1910).]

Irvine, George (1826-1897), lawyer and politician, was born at Quebec, Lower Canada, on November 16, 1826, the son of Lieut.-Col. John George Irvine, and the grandson of the Hon. James Irvine (q.v.). He was called to the bar of Lower Canada in 1848 (Q.C., 1867), and he became one of the outstanding lawyers of Quebec. He represented Megantic in the Legislative Assembly of united Canada from 1863 to 1867, in the Canadian House of Commons from 1867 to 1872, and in the Legislative Assembly of Quebec from 1867 to 1876 and from 1878 to 1884. He was then appointed judge of the Court of Vice-Admiralty at Quebec; but was permitted to practise his profession as a barrister before the other courts, and continued to have one of the most lucrative practices in the province. He died at Quebec City on February 24, 1897.

[P. C. Roy, *Fils de Québec,* vol. 3 (Lévis, Que., 1933); *Can. parl. comp.*]

Irvine, James (d. 1829), executive and legislative councillor of Lower Canada, was a Quebec merchant who came to Canada prior to 1785. He was a member of the Executive Council of Lower Canada from 1809 to 1822; he represented at the same time the upper town of Quebec in the Legislative Assembly of Lower Canada from 1810 to 1814; and he was a member of the Legislative Council of Lower Canada from 1818 to his death, at Quebec, on September 27, 1829.

[J. Desjardins, *Guide parlementaire historique* (Quebec, 1902).]

Irvine, William (1885-1962), political evangelist, was born in Gletness, in the Shetland Islands, April 21, 1885. He came to Canada in 1908 at the urging of the Reverend James Woodsworth (q.v.) to assist in the missionary work of the Methodist Church. He was educated at Wesley (Methodist) and Manitoba (Presbyterian) colleges in Winnipeg and ordained to the Methodist ministry. While serving in Calgary he edited *The nutcracker*, a newspaper, which became the *Alberta non-partisan* in 1917 when Irvine became a supporter of the Alberta non-partisan league, a farmer's political action league. In 1919 the league joined the United Farmers of Alberta, and Irvine's paper was re-named the *Western independent*. He was associate editor of the *People's weekly* (1935-45). He was elected, along with J. S. Woodsworth (q.v.), as a labour member of the House of Commons in 1921. Defeated in 1925 he was re-elected in 1926 and became one of the "Ginger Group" of Progressives. He was defeated in the 1935 election, but re-elected in 1945. He retired from politics in 1949 to his home in Wetaskiwin, Alberta. Irvine was a founding member of the Co-operative Commonwealth Federation. The development of his political thought may be followed in his writings: *The farmer in politics* (Toronto, 1920), in which he explains the political philosophy of Henry Wise Wood; *Cooperative government* (Ottawa, 1929), in which he discusses the failures evident to him in parliamentary democracy and foreshadows some of the ideas adopted by the C.C.F. party; *The people must choose; Cooperation or catastrophe: An interpretation of the C.C.F. and its policy* (Ottawa, 1934); *Forces of reconstruction* (Ottawa, 1934); *Is socialism the answer? An intelligent man's guide to basic democracy* (Ottawa, 1945); *Live or die with Russia* (Edmonton, 1958); and *The twain shall meet* (ed.) (Edmonton, 1960), a symposium on China. He also wrote two political plays, *In brains we trust*, a play in three acts (Toronto, 1935); *You can't do that*, a play in three acts (Toronto, 1936). He died at Edmonton, October 26, 1962.

[*Can. who's who*, 1955-57; N. Story, *The Oxford companion to Canadian history and literature* (Toronto, 1967); V.B. Rhodenizer, *Canadian literature in English* (Montreal,

1965); K.W. McNaught, *A prophet in politics: A biography of J. S. Woodsworth* (Toronto, 1959).]

Irving, Sir Aemilius (1823-1913), lawyer and member of the Canadian House of Commons, was born in Leamington, England, in 1823, the son of the Hon. Jacob Aemilius Irving (q.v.) and Catherine Diana, daughter of Sir Jere Homfray, of Llandaff House, Glamorganshire. He came to Canada with his parents in 1834, was educated at Upper Canada College, Toronto, and was called to the bar of Upper Canada (Q.C., 1863). From 1893 to his death he was treasurer of the Law Society of Upper Canada; and he represented Hamilton in the Canadian House of Commons as a Liberal from 1874 to 1878. He died in Toronto on November 27, 1913. In 1851 he married Augusta Louisa, daughter of Colonel Gugy, of Quebec; and by her he had five sons and two daughters. In 1905 he was made an LL.D. of the University of Toronto, and in 1907 he was created a knight bachelor.

[Morgan, *Can. men* (1912); *Can. who's who*, 1910; *Can. law review*, 1913.]

Irving, Jacob Aemilius (1797-1856), legislative councillor, was born at Charleston, South Carolina, on January 29, 1797, the eldest son of Jacob Aemilius Irving, of Ironshore, Jamaica, and of Liverpool, and the grandnephew of Paulus Aemilius Irving (q.v.). He entered the British army, fought in the Waterloo campaign in 1815, and became a captain in the 13th Hussars. In 1834 he came to Upper Canada, and settled in the Niagara peninsula. On the introduction of municipal government, he was appointed the first warden for the district of Simcoe; and in 1843 he was called to the Legislative Council of Canada. In the Council he was a supporter of the administration of Baldwin and Lafontaine. He died at Niagara Falls, Upper Canada, on October 7, 1856. In 1821 he married Catherine Diana (d. 1858), daughter of Sir Jere Homfray, of Llandaff House, Glamorganshire; and by her he had several children.

[Morgan, *Cel. Can.*; *Cyc. Am. biog.*]

Irving, Lukin Homfray (1855-1942), civil servant, was born at Galt, Canada West, on October 19, 1855, the second son of Sir Aemilius Irving (q.v.). He was educated at the Galt grammar school and at the Royal Military College, Kingston; and he entered the Ontario civil service in 1880. He died at Toronto, Ontario, on December 22, 1942. He was the author of *Officers of the British forces in Canada during the war of 1812-15* (Toronto, 1908).

[Morgan, *Can. men* (1912).]

Irving, Paulus Aemilius (1714-1796), president and administrator of the province of Quebec (1766), was born near Dumfries, Scotland, on September 23, 1714, the son of William Irving, laird of Bonshaw. He entered the British army at an early age, and in 1759 he commanded the 15th Regiment at the battle of the Plains of Abraham. In 1764 he was appointed a member of the first Council of the province of Quebec; and from June to September, 1766, he administered the government of the province in the absence of General Murray (q.v.). In December, 1766, he was dismissed from Council by Carleton (q.v.); and in 1771 he was appointed lieutenant-governor of Guernsey. He died in England on April 22, 1796. He married Judith, daughter of Capt. William Westfield, of Dover; and by her he had one son and two daughters.

[Morgan, *Cel. Can.*; *Cyc. Am. biog.*; A. G. Doughty (ed.), *The journal of Captain John Knox* (3 vols., Toronto: The Champlain Society, 1914-16); A. Shortt and A. G. Doughty (eds.), *Documents relating to the constitutional history of Canada, 1759-1791* (2 vols., Ottawa, 1918).]

Irving, Paulus Aemilius (1857-1916), jurist, was born at Hamilton, Canada West, on April 3, 1857, the third son of Sir Aemilius Irving (q.v.). He was educated at Trinity University (B.A., 1877; M.A., 1881; B.C.L., 1881; D.C.L., 1902); and was called to the bar of Ontario in 1880, and to that of British Columbia in 1882. From 1883 to 1890 he was deputy attorney-general in British Columbia; in 1897 he was appointed a puisne judge of the Superior Court of British Columbia; and in 1909 he became a judge of the Court of Appeal. He died at Victoria, British Columbia, on April 9, 1916.

[Morgan, *Can. men* (1912).]

Irwin, Benoni (1840-1896), painter, was born at Newmarket, Upper Canada, on June 29, 1840. He studied art at Toronto, at the National Academy of Design in New York, and in Paris under Carolus Duran. On his return to America, he lived successively in New York, Baltimore, and San Francisco. One of his most notable pictures was his "Study in brown", which was shown at the World's Fair in Chicago in 1893. He died at South Coventry, Connecticut, on August 25, 1896.

[M. Fielding, *A dictionary of American painters* (Philadelphia, n.d.).]

Irwin, Robert (1865-1941), lieutenant-governor of Nova Scotia (1937-40), was born in 1865, and engaged in the lumber business in Nova Scotia. From 1906 to 1925 he represented Shelburne county in the Legislative Assembly of Nova Scotia; and from 1917 to 1925 he was speaker of the Assembly. In 1937 he was appointed lieutenant-governor of Nova Scotia; but he retired from office in 1940, and he died at Shelburne, Nova Scotia, on May 16, 1941.

[*Can. who's who*, 1938-39; *Can. parl. comp.*]

Isbister, Alexander Kennedy (1822-1883), educationist and author, was born at Cumberland House, North West Territories, in 1822, the half-breed son of Thomas Isbister, an officer of the Hudson's Bay Company. He was educated in Scotland; and in 1837 he returned to Canada, and entered the service of the Hudson's Bay Company. After several years in the North West he went back, however, to Scotland, and studied at Aberdeen University and at Edinburgh University (M.A., 1858). He became a school-teacher, and from 1858 to 1882 was master of the Stationers' Company's School, London, England. In 1862 he was appointed editor of the *Educational Times*; and in 1872 he became dean of the College of Preceptors, Bloomsbury. He studied law, and in 1864 was admitted to the bar at the Middle Temple (LL.B., University of London, 1866). He played an important part in 1870 as a champion in London of the rights of the *Métis* or half-breeds of Manitoba; and he was an early advocate of the inclusion of the North West in Confederation. He died at Islington, London, on May 28, 1883. He published, besides a number of school books, *A proposal for a new penal settlement in the uninhabited districts of British North America* (London, 1850).

[*Dict. nat. biog.*; *Dom. ann. reg.*, 1883; G. Bryce, *The remarkable history of the Hudson's Bay Company* (London, 1900).]

Ives, William Bullock (1841-1899), minister of trade and commerce for Canada (1894-96), was born in Compton township, Lower Canada, on November 17, 1841, the son of Eli Ives and Artemissa Bullock. He was educated at Compton Academy; and in 1867 was called to the Quebec bar (Q.C., 1880). He took an active part in railway and industrial development in the Eastern Townships, and was president of the Hereford Railway Company. From 1878 to 1891 he represented Richmond and Wolfe as a Conservative in the Canadian House of Commons; and from 1891 to his death he represented Sherbrooke. From 1892 to 1894 he was president of the council in the administration of Sir John Thompson (q.v.); and in the administration of Sir Mackenzie Bowell (q.v.) he became minister of trade and commerce. He was one of the "bolters" who left the government on January 6, 1896; but he was reappointed to office nine days later, and continued in office until the defeat of the Tupper government later in the year. He died at Sherbrooke on July 15, 1899. In 1869 he married Elizabeth, only daughter of the Hon. John Henry Pope (q.v.). He was a D.C.L. of Bishop's College, Lennoxville (1898).

[Morgan, *Can. men* (1898); *Can. parl. comp.*; N. S. Garland, *Parliamentary directory* (Ottawa, 1885); J. Castell Hopkins, *The life and work of the Rt. Hon. Sir John Thompson* (Brantford, Ont., 1895).]

$\mathcal{J}$

Jack, Mrs. Annie L., *née* **Hayr** (1839-1912), author, was born in Northamptonshire, England, on January 1, 1839, the daughter of John Hayr. She came to America in 1852, and was educated at Troy, New York. She married Robert Jack (d. 1900), a fruitgrower; and after her marriage settled near Châteauguay, Quebec. Here she died on February 15, 1912. She was the author of *The little organist of St. Jérôme, and other stories* (Châteauguay Basin, Quebec, 1902), *The Canadian garden* (Châteauguay Basin, Quebec, 1903; new ed., Montreal, 1911), *Rhyme thoughts for a Canadian year* (Châteauguay Basin, Quebec, 1904), and *Maple lore* (Montreal, 1911).

[Morgan, *Can. men and women* (1912).]

Jack, David Russell (1864-1913), journalist and historian, was born at Saint John, New Brunswick, on May 5, 1864, the son of Henry Jack and Annie Johnston. He was educated at Saint John; and in 1884 became vice-consul for Spain at Saint John. In 1901 he founded *Acadiensis*, a monthly journal devoted to the history of the Maritime provinces; and he edited this journal until it ceased publication in 1909. He died at Clifton Springs, New York, unmarried, on December 2, 1913. He was the author of a *Centennial prize essay on the history of the city and county of St. John* (Saint John, N.B., 1883), and a *History of Saint Andrew's church, St. John* (Saint John, N.B., 1913).

[*Can. who was who*, vol. 1; Morgan, *Can. men* (1912).]

Jack, Isaac Allen (1843-1903), lawyer, was born at Saint John, New Brunswick, on June 26, 1843. He was called to the bar of New Brunswick, and became recorder of Saint John. He was the author of *The memoirs of a Canadian secretary* ("Toronto, 1928" [Saint John, N.B., about 1883]) and *History of St. Andrew's Society of St. John* (Saint John, N.B., 1903); and he was editor of *Biographical review* (Boston, 1900). He died on April 5, 1903.

[W. G. MacFarlane, *New Brunswick bibliography* (Saint John, N.B., 1895); private information.]

Jack, William Brydone (1819-1886), president of the University of New Brunswick (1861-85), was born at Tinwald, Dumfries-shire, Scotland, on November 23, 1819. He was educated at St. Andrew's University (M.A., 1840); and in 1840 was appointed professor of mathematics and natural philosophy in King's College, Fredericton, New Brunswick. When this college received its charter as the University of New Brunswick, he was appointed president, and he held this office until ill health compelled his retirement in 1885. He died at Fredericton on November 23, 1886.

[*Dom. ann. reg.*, 1886; Dent, *Can. port.*, vol. 4, under "Brydone-Jack".]

Jackman, William T. (1872-1951), educationist, was born at Kilsyth, Ontario, on January 8, 1872, and died at Toronto, Ontario, on November 8, 1951. He was educated at the University of Toronto (B.A., 1896; M.A., 1900), and took post-graduate work at the University of Pennsylvania and the University of London. He taught for several years in the United States; then in 1915 he was appointed professor of rural economics at the University of Toronto, and in 1931 professor of transportation. He retired in 1941. His publications include *The development of transportation in modern England* (2 vols., Cambridge, 1916), *Economics of transportation* (Chicago, 1926), and *Economic principles of transportation* (Toronto, 1935).

[H. A. Innis, *William T. Jackman* (Canadian journal of economics and political science, May, 1952), with bibliography; *Can. who's who*, 1948.]

Jackson, Alexander Young (1882-1974), Canada's best-known painter, member of the Group of Seven, was born in Montreal, October 3, 1882. He left school at the age of twelve to work as an office boy in a lithographing company. There his ability brought him to the attention of his employer, who transferred him to the Art Department under Arthur Nantel. He worked at photo-engraving and printing while attending the Monument National in Montreal as an evening student. In 1905 he worked his way to Europe on a cattle-boat and went to Paris, where he visited art galleries and museums. On his return to North America he attended the Art Institute of Chicago for evening classes with Clute and Richardson while he worked for a firm of designers in the city. He returned to Paris to study in 1907 and travelled extensively in Italy and France, living for a time at Episy and painting the French countryside. In 1910 he came back to Canada and in Sweetsburg, Quebec, he painted "Edge of Maple Wood". In 1911 he again spent most of the year in France and England. At this period Jackson was strongly influenced by French Impressionist painting, and the canvases which he exhibited on his return to Montreal were not easy to sell. In 1912 he met J. E. H. MacDonald of Toronto as he was passing through the city on his way to Berlin (now Kitchener) and was introduced to Arthur Lismer, Frederick Varley, and other members of the Arts and Letters Club. In Berlin he met Lawren Harris, and at Georgian Bay Dr. James MacCallum. MacCallum and Harris were then building the Studio Building in Toronto and offered Jackson a studio and a year's expenses. In 1914 he and Tom Thomson moved into the Studio Building, which they used as headquarters while they travelled into the Algonquin region, sketching and painting. In 1915, Jackson joined the Canadian Army as a private and was wounded in action. On his recovery he was transferred to Canadian War Records as a lieutenant. He painted many war scenes during his time with the army and was discharged in April, 1919. That autumn he went sketching in Northern Ontario with J. E. H. MacDonald, Lawren Harris, and Franz Johnston. The following year the Group of Seven — Harris, Lismer, MacDonald, Carmichael, Johnston, Varley, and Jackson — held its first exhibition in Toronto. The exhibition aroused a great deal of controversy, and the painters were accused of being garish, crude, and freakish. The Group continued to exhibit until 1931 amid extensive criticism, although their paintings were well received in England at the Wembley exhibition of 1924. In 1927 and 1930 Jackson travelled to the Arctic with the supply steamer and in 1931 his Arctic sketches were exhibited at the National Gallery in Ottawa, and in Montreal and Toronto. He became a founding member of the Canadian Group of Painters in 1933 which included over forty members. Alone or in company with friends he painted in every part of Canada. He left Toronto to live in Manotick, Ontario, in 1955 but returned in 1968 to the Toronto area and lived at Kleinburg in an apartment at the McMichael Gallery, where dozens of his paintings are housed. He died at Kleinburg, April 5, 1974. He wrote *A Painter's Country*, his autobiography, in 1958 and numerous articles on Canadian painting.

[C. S. MacDonald, *A dictionary of Canadian artists*, vol. 2 (Ottawa, 1968); T. MacDonald, *The Group of Seven* (Toronto, 1944); F. B. Housser, *A Canadian art movement* (Toronto, 1926); P. Duval, *The Group of Seven drawings* (Toronto, 1965); P. Duval, *The McMichael Conservation Collection* (Toronto, 1967).]

Jackson, Gilbert (1890-1959), economist, was born at Hedon, Yorkshire, England, on March 2, 1890, and died at Toronto, Ontario, on June 16, 1959. He was educated at St. John's College, Cambridge, and came to Canada in 1911 as a lecturer in economics at the University of Toronto. He was promoted to the rank of professor in 1927, but almost immediately left the university to become economist to the Bank of Nova Scotia. In 1935 he went to England as adviser to the Governors of the Bank of England. He returned to Toronto in 1939 and became a general economic consultant under the business name of "Gilbert Jackson and Associates". In this capacity he exerted a very considerable influence. He was the author of *An economist's confession of faith* (Toronto, 1935).

[Toronto *Globe and Mail*, June 17, 1959; *Can. who's who*, 1958-60.]

Jackson, John Mills (1764?-1836), settler and author, was born about 1764, the son of Josiah Jackson, of the Isle of St. Vincent; and was educated at Balliol College, Oxford (matric., 1783). He came to Upper Canada in 1806, quarrelled with the government, and in 1809 published in London *A view of the political situation of the province of Upper Canada*. He later settled on the south shore of Lake Simcoe, at what is now known as Jackson's Point; and his daughter married Admiral Augustus Baldwin (q.v.). He died while in England in 1836. Because of his political opinions, he was nicknamed "Jacobin Jackson".

[J. Ross Robertson, *Landmarks of Toronto*, vol. 2 (Toronto, 1896); W. S. Wallace, *The family compact* (Toronto, 1915); J. Foster, *Alumni oxonienses* (Oxford, n.d.); *Can. arch. report*, 1892, note D.]

Jackson, Sir Richard Downes (1777-1845), administrator of the government of Lower Canada (1839-40), was a veteran of the Peninsular War who had entered the army in 1794. In 1838 he attained the rank of lieutenant-general; and in 1839 he was appointed commander-in-chief of the British forces in North America. As such, he twice administered the government of Lower Canada in the absence of the governor-in-chief, Charles Poulett Thomson (q.v.). He died of apoplexy in Montreal on June 9, 1845.

[Morgan, *Cel. Can.*; F. J. Audet, *Gouverneurs, lieut.-gouverneurs, et administrateurs du Canada* (Trans. Roy. Soc. Can., 1908).]

Jacob, Edward Frederick Fulford (1882-1928), journalist and author, was born in Elora, Ontario, in 1882. He became a journalist, and for many years was literary and dramatic critic on the staff of the Toronto *Mail* and *Empire*. He died at Toronto on June 3, 1928. He was the author of several one-act plays, five of which were published in a volume entitled *One-third of a bill* (Toronto, 1925), and he wrote two novels, *The day before yesterday* (Toronto, 1925) and *Pee Vee* (Toronto, 1928).

[Toronto *Mail and Empire*, June 4, 1928.]

Jacob, Edwin (1795?-1868), educationist, was born in Gloucestershire, England, about 1795; and was educated at Corpus Christi College, Oxford (B.A., 1815; M.A., 1818; D.D., 1829). He was ordained a priest of the Church of England, and from 1827 to 1829 was rector of St. Pancras, Chichester, England. In 1829, however, he came to New Brunswick as vice-president and principal of King's College, Fredericton; and he retained this position until 1861. He died at Cardigan, York county, New Brunswick, on May 31, 1868. He was the author of *Sermons intended for the propagation of the Gospel* (Fredericton, N.B., 1835).

[W. G. MacFarlane, *New Brunswick bibliography* (Saint John, N.B., 1895); J. Foster, *Alumni oxonienses* (8 vols., Oxford, 1887-92).]

Jacobi, Otto Reinhold (1812-1901), landscape-painter, was born at Königsberg, Prussia, on February 27, 1812. He studied art at the Academy of Berlin, and in 1832 won a prize entitling him to three years of study at Düsseldorf. He was appointed by the Grand Duke of Nassau court painter at Wiesbaden, and this post he held for twenty years. In 1860 he came to Canada in order to paint a picture of Shawinigan Falls; and he was so attracted by the country that he stayed in Canada. He devoted himself to painting landscapes, and for many years he had a studio in Toronto. He was a charter member of the Royal Canadian Academy of Arts, and from 1890 to 1893 he was its president. The last years of his life he spent with his son on a ranch near Taiva, Dakota, United States; and here he died on February 20, 1901. His pictures are much prized, especially for the quality of their colour.

[E. Morris, *Art in Canada: The early painters* (Toronto, 1911); N. MacTavish, *The fine arts in Canada* (Toronto, 1925); *Can. who was who*, vol. 2; Morgan, *Can. men* (1898); Le Jeune, *Dict. gén.*]

Jacobs, Samuel William (1871-1938), lawyer and politician, was born at Lancaster, Ontario, on May 6, 1871. He was educated at McGill University (B.C.L., 1893) and at Laval University, Montreal (LL.M., 1894), and was called to the Quebec bar in 1894 (K.C., 1906). He practised law in Montreal, and was employed as counsel in a wide variety of criminal cases. He represented Montreal-Cartier in the Canadian House of Commons from 1917 to his death, which took place at Montreal, Quebec,

on August 21, 1938. He was the author of *The railway law of Canada* (Montreal, 1909).

[*Can. who's who*, 1936-37; *Can. parl. comp.*]

Jaffray, Robert (1832-1914), senator (1906-14), was born near Bannockburn, Scotland, on January 23, 1832, the son of William Jaffray and Margaret Heugh. He was educated at Stirling Academy, and came to Canada in 1852. He founded a retail and wholesale grocery business in Toronto, and carried it on successfully until 1883. He then retired to devote himself to the numerous other financial interests of which he was a director; and among these was the Toronto *Globe*. In 1888 he became president of the Globe Printing Co., and until his death he retained a controlling interest in the company. In 1906 he was called to the Senate of Canada; and he continued a senator until his death in Toronto on December 16, 1914. In 1860 he married Sarah, daughter of John Bugg, of Toronto; and by her he had two sons and two daughters.

[Morgan, *Can. men* (1912); *Can. parl. comp.*; Rose, *Cyc. Can. biog.* (1888); *Commemorative biographical record of the county of York* (Toronto, 1907).]

Jakeway, Charles Edwin (1847-1906), physician and poet, was born at Holland Landing, Upper Canada, in 1847. He was educated at the University of Toronto (M.D., 1871), and practised medicine at Stayner, Ontario. Here he died in 1906. He was the author of *The lion and the lilies: A tale of the conquest, and other poems* (Toronto, 1897).

[C. M. Whyte-Edgar, *A wreath of Canadian song* (Toronto, 1910).]

Jamay, Denis. See **Jamet, Denis.**

James, Charles Canniff (1863-1916), civil servant and bibliographer, was born at Napanee, Ontario, on June 14, 1863, the son of Charles James and Ellen Canniff, both of United Empire Loyalist stock. He was educated at the Napanee High School and at Victoria University, Cobourg (B.A., 1883; M.A., 1886). In 1886 he became professor of chemistry in the Guelph Agricultural College; and in 1891 he was appointed deputy minister of agriculture for Ontario. This position he held until his appointment in 1912 as commissioner to administer the Dominion Agricultural Instruction Act. He was an authority on certain phases of Canadian literature and history. He published a valuable *Bibliography of Canadian poetry (English)* (Toronto, 1899), and a number of papers on the early history of Ontario, notably *The first legislature of Upper Canada* (Trans. Roy. Soc. Can., 1902), *The second legislature of Upper Canada* (Trans. Roy. Soc. Can., 1903), *The downfall of the Huron nation* (Trans. Roy. Soc. Can., 1907), *William Dummer Powell* (Trans. Roy. Soc. Can., 1912), and *David Wil-*

liam Smith (Trans. Roy. Soc. Can., 1913). He died at St. Catharines, Ontario, on June 23, 1916. In 1887 he married Frances, daughter of James Crossen, of Cobourg; and by her he had one son. He was elected a fellow of the Royal Society of Canada in 1905; in 1911 he was created a C.M.G.; and in 1912 he was made an LL.D. of the University of Toronto.

[*Proc. Roy. Soc. Can.*, 1917; Morgan, *Can. men* (1912).]

James, Cyril Frank (1903-1973), university principal, was born October 8, 1903, in London, England, and educated at the University of London (B.Comm., 1923) and the University of Pennsylvania (M.A., 1924; Ph.D., 1926). While attending the University of London he worked with Barclay's Bank (1921-23), and later joined the Wharton School of Finance and Commerce at the University of Pennsylvania, where he rose to be professor of finance (1935-39). He came to McGill University as director of the school of commerce in 1939; he became principal and vice-chancellor in 1940. He was chairman of the Canadian Government Advisory Committee on Reconstruction (1941-43), and a member of the Department of Veterans Affairs University Committee from 1945. He was president of the National Conference of Canadian Universities (1948-50), and chairman of the Association of Universities of the British Commonwealth in 1949. Among his writings are *The economics of money, credit, and banking* (1930, 1935, 1941), *The growth of Chicago banks* (2 vols., 1938), and a contribution to *Economic problems in a changing world* (1939). He was a fellow of the Royal Society of Canada, and chairman of Oxfam (1971). He died at London, England, May 3, 1973.

[*Can. who's who*, 1970-72; *Encyc. Can.* (1972).]

James, Thomas (1593?-1635), navigator, was born in Bristol, England, about 1593. He studied law, but later took to the sea. In 1631 he commanded an expedition to Hudson Bay which resulted in the re-discovery of James Bay, named after him; and he wintered on Charlton Island. He died, apparently, in 1635. *The strange and dangerous voyage of Captain Thomas James* was first published in London by royal command in 1635; a second edition was printed in 1740; and the narrative was reprinted by the Hakluyt Society in 1894.

[R. B. Bodilly, *The voyage of Captain Thomas James for the discovery of the Northwest passage, 1631* (London, 1928); *Dict. nat. biog.*; Le Jeune, *Dict. gén.*; *Dict. Can. biog.*, vol. 1.]

Jameson, Mrs. Anna Brownell, *née* **Murphy** (1794-1860), author, was born in Dublin, Ireland, on May 17, 1794, the eldest daughter of Brownell Murphy, a miniature painter. Until she was thirty years of age she was a gov-

erness; but in 1826 she married Robert Sympson Jameson (q.v.). The marriage was not happy; and in 1829 Jameson went to Dominica, as a puisne judge, leaving his wife behind. In 1833 he was appointed attorney-general of Upper Canada; and in 1836, in answer to his request, she joined him in Toronto. Two years later, however, she left him, and returned to England: and when he died in 1854 he made no provision for her in his will. She devoted herself to writing for the remainder of her life; and she died at Ealing, Middlesex, on March 17, 1860. The fruit of her two years in Canada appeared in her *Winter studies and summer rambles in Canada* (London, 1838), but she wrote also *The diary of an ennuyée* (London, 1826), *Loves of the poets* (London, 1829), *Celebrated female sovereigns* (2 vols., London, 1831), *Characteristics of women* (2 vols., London, 1832), *Visits and sketches* (London, 1834), *Companion to the public picture galleries of London* (London, 1842), *Memoirs of the early Italian painters* (London, 1845), *Sacred and legendary art* (4 vols., London, 1852-61), and *A commonplace book of thoughts, memories, and fancies* (London, 1854).

[Mrs. Stewart Erskine, *Anna Jameson* (London, 1915); Gerardine Macpherson, *Memoirs of the life of Anna Jameson* (London, 1878); Clara Thomas, *The life of Anna Jameson* (Toronto, 1967); Blanche Macdonald, *Mrs. Jameson in Canada* (Univ. mag., 1912); *Dict. nat. biog.*; Dent, *Can. port.*, vol. 2.]

Jameson, Robert Sympson (1798-1854), vice-chancellor of Upper Canada (1837-54), was born in the Lake district in England, the son of Thomas Jameson. He read law at the Middle Temple, was called to the bar, and in 1824 became a reporter in the court of his patron, Lord Eldon. In 1826 he married Anna Murphy (q.v.); but the marriage was not a success, and in 1829 he separated from her, and accepted appointment as a puisne judge in the island of Dominica, in the West Indies. In 1833 he was appointed attorney-general of Upper Canada, and he spent the rest of his life in this province. From 1835 to 1837 he represented Leeds in the Legislative Assembly of Upper Canada; and in 1837 he was appointed first vice-chancellor of the newly established Court of Equity in the province. This position he occupied without interruption until his death at Toronto in 1854. His wife spent a year or more with him in Toronto in 1836-38; but they then separated finally, and never again saw each other.

[D. B. Read, *The lives of the judges of Upper Canada* (Toronto, 1888); Clara Thomas, *Vice-Chancellor Robert Sympson Jameson* (Ont. Hist., 1964).]

Jamet, Albert (d. 1948), monk and historian, was born in Tours, France, and died at Quebec, Quebec, on August 23, 1948. He joined the Benedictine order, and became interested in the religious history of New France. He was the author of *Marguerite Bourgeoys, 1620-1700* (Montreal, 1942), and he edited *Les annales de l'Hôtel-Dieu de Québec* (Quebec, 1939) and *Marie de l'Incarnation . . . Ecrits spirituels et historiques* (4 vols., Paris, 1939-49).

[*New York Times*, Aug. 25, 1948.]

Jamet, Denis (d. 1625), Recollet missionary, was commissary or superior of the Recollet mission sent to Canada in 1615, and it was he who, on June 24, 1615, celebrated the first mass ever sung in New France. He became superior of the Franciscan friary at Quebec; and he died in France in 1625.

[O. M. Jouve, *Les Franciscains et le Canada*, vol. 1 (Quebec, 1915); Le Jeune, *Dict. gén.*; *Dict. Can. biog.*, vol. 1.]

Jamieson, Mrs. Nina, *née* **Moore** (d. 1932), was the daughter of W. F. Moore (q.v.), of Dundas, and was for many years a contributor of occasional papers on rural life to the Toronto *Mail and Empire*. She died at St. George, Ontario, on November 6, 1932. She was the author of *The hickory stick* (Toronto, 1921) and *The cattle in the stall* (Toronto, 1932).

[Toronto *Mail and Empire*, Nov. 7, 1932.]

Jamot, Jean François (1828-1886), Roman Catholic bishop of Peterborough, was born at Châtelard, France, on June 23, 1828. He was educated at Limoges, and was ordained a priest of the Roman Catholic Church in 1853. In 1855 he was sent to Canada, and became the first Roman Catholic parish priest at Barrie, Canada West. In 1863 he became rector of St. Michael's Cathedral, Toronto; in 1865 he was appointed vicar-general of the diocese; and in 1874 he was raised to the episcopate as bishop of Sarepta and vicar apostolic of northern Ontario. He was transferred in 1882 to the newly erected diocese of Peterborough; and he remained in charge of this diocese until his death at Peterborough, Ontario, on May 4, 1886.

[*Dom. ann. reg.*, 1886; Allaire, *Dict. biog.*]

Jardine, Robert (b. 1840), clergyman and author, was born in Augusta, Upper Canada, in 1840; and was educated at Queen's University, Kingston (B.A., 1863; M.A., 1866) and at Edinburgh University (D.Sc., 1867). He was professor of English literature and philosophy at the University of New Brunswick from 1867 to 1869; and he was ordained a minister of the Church of Scotland, and spent seven years in India as a missionary. In 1877 he returned to Canada, and became a minister of the Presbyterian Church in Canada. He held charges at Chatham, New Brunswick, at Brockville, Ontario, and at Prince Albert, North West Territories. In 1893 he left the Presbyterian Church, and went to Chicago, where he became the pastor of the Church of Our Father,

and an exponent of "Liberal Christianity". His later history has not been ascertained. He was the author of *The elements of the psychology of cognition* (London, 1874).

[Morgan, *Can. men* (1898); Rose, *Cyc. Can. biog.* (1880).]

Jarvis, Alan Hepburn (1915-1972), National Gallery director and sculptor, was born in Brantford, Ontario, July 26, 1915. He was educated at the University of Toronto (B. A., 1938); Oxford University (Rhodes scholar, 1938-39); and the New York University Graduate School of Fine Arts (1940-41). In 1936 he travelled through Europe by car photographing Romanesque church sculpture and while in New York he studied museology, and early Christian and eighteenth-century English art. In 1941 he worked in the personnel department of Parnall aircraft in England, manufacturers of the Lancaster bomber, and became, in succession, special assistant and then private secretary to Sir Stafford Cripps, the minister of aircraft production; director of public relations of the Council of Industrial Design, England; director of Pilgrim pictures (1947-50); head of Oxford House; chairman of London's Group Theatre; and director of the British Handcraft Export Corporation. In 1955 he was appointed director of the National Gallery of Canada. Here he began a program of lectures, television programs, and travelling exhibitions to bring art out of the galleries and into public consciousness. His idea, he said, was, "rather than 'elevating' public taste, to increase people's enjoyment in looking at everything around them: landscapes, houses, everyday things embodying industrial design, and finally the fine arts — painting, drawing, sculpture". He resigned his position at the National Gallery in 1959 after a disagreement on purchasing policy with the Diefenbaker government and became editor of *Canadian Art* and chairman of the Society for Art Publication. In 1961 he assisted in organizing the first Canadian Conference of the Arts. He completed many sculptured heads, including those of Sir Stafford Cripps, Peter Ustinov, Sir Eric Bowater, Dr. Cyril James, and others. Among his written works are *The things we see* (Penguin, 1946); *Douglas Duncan: A memorial portrait* (Toronto, 1974); *David Brown Milne — 1822-1953* (Toronto, 1955); *Frances Loring — Florence Wyle* (Toronto, 1969); and many articles in *artscanada*. He died at Toronto, December 2, 1972.

[*Can. who's who*, 1955-57; MacDonald, *A dictionary of Canadian artists* (vol. 2, Ottawa, 1968); Peter C. Newman, *Is Jarvis misspending our art millions?* (Maclean's magazine, Nov. 22, 1958).]

Jarvis, Edward James (1788-1852), chief justice of Prince Edward Island (1827-52), was born in Saint John, New Brunswick, in 1788, the youngest son of Munson Jarvis. He studied law in England; and in 1816 was called to the bar of New Brunswick. In 1822 he was appointed a judge of the Supreme Court of New Brunswick, but the appointment was not confirmed; and he obtained instead, first an appointment as a judge in Malta, and then, in 1827, an appointment as chief justice of Prince Edward Island. This position he held until his death at Charlottetown, Prince Edward Island, on May 9, 1852.

[J. W. Lawrence, *The judges of New Brunswick* (Saint John, N.B., 1907); G. A. Jarvis and others, *The Jarvis family* (Hartford, Conn., 1879).]

Jarvis, George Stephen (1797-1878), judge, was born in Fredericton, New Brunswick, on April 21, 1797, the son of Stephen Jarvis (q.v.). He was educated at Fredericton, and removed to Upper Canada with his parents in 1809. He served throughout the War of 1812 in Upper Canada, and was in 1815 gazetted a lieutenant of the 104th Regiment. On the disbandment of this regiment, he returned to civilian life, studied law under Jonas Jones (q.v.), and was called to the bar of Upper Canada in 1823. From 1836 to 1840 he represented Cornwall in the Legislative Assembly of Upper Canada; and in 1825 he was appointed judge of the Ottawa district. For the remainder of his life he served in a series of appointments as a judge. He died at Cornwall, Ontario, on April 15, 1878. He was twice married, (1) to Julia (d. 1842), daughter of Sheriff Sherwood, and (2) to Anna Mary, daughter of the Rev. Salter Mountain (q.v.).

[G. A. Jarvis and others, *The Jarvis family* (Hartford, Conn., 1879); E. M. Chadwick, *Ontarian families*, vol. 1 (Toronto, 1894); *Dom. ann. reg.*, 1878; *Dict. Can. biog.*, vol. 10.]

Jarvis, Harold Augustus (1864-1924), singer, was born in Toronto, Canada West, on December 27, 1864, the son of Arthur M. Jarvis. He was educated in Toronto, and became for a time an officer on transoceanic liners. He then studied singing at the Academy of Music in London, England; and he became a tenor of international reputation. He sang on the operatic stage with Albani and other distinguished artists. In his later years he lived in Detroit, Michigan; and he died there on April 1, 1924.

[Morgan, *Can. men* (1912).]

Jarvis, Samuel Peters (1792-1857), soldier and civil servant, was born in Niagara, Upper Canada, on November 15, 1792, the eldest son of William Jarvis (q.v.). He served throughout the War of 1812, and in 1837 he raised and commanded a loyalist regiment, the Queen's Rangers. He was called to the bar in Upper Canada, was appointed clerk of the Crown in chancery, and ultimately became chief superintendent of Indian affairs. In 1818

he married Mary Boyles, daughter of William Dummer Powell (q.v.); and by her he had five sons and four daughters. He died at Toronto on September 6, 1857.

[G. A. Jarvis and others, *The Jarvis family* (Hartford, Conn., 1879); E. M. Chadwick, *Ontarian families*, vol. 1 (Toronto, 1894); J. Ross Robertson, *Landmarks of Toronto*, vol. 1 (Toronto, 1894).]

Jarvis, Stephen (1756-1840), loyalist, was born in Danbury, Connecticut, on November 6, 1756, the son of Stephen Jarvis and Rachel Starr, and the first cousin of William Jarvis (q.v.). He served throughout the American Revolutionary War; and in 1784 settled with his family in Fredericton, New Brunswick. In 1809 he removed to York, Upper Canada. He became registrar of deeds for the Home district, and in 1833 gentleman usher of the black rod in the Legislative Assembly. During the War of 1812 he was adjutant-general of militia. He died at Toronto on April 12, 1840; and by his wife, Amelia Glover, of Danbury, Connecticut, he had three sons and three daughters. His *Reminiscences of a loyalist* were published by Thomas Stinson Jarvis (q.v.) in the *Canadian Magazine* in 1906.

[G. A. Jarvis and others, *The Jarvis family* (Hartford, Conn., 1879); E. M. Chadwick, *Ontarian families*, vol. 1 (Toronto, 1894); J. Ross Robertson, *The history of freemasonry in Canada* (2 vols., Toronto, 1900).]

Jarvis, Thomas Stinson (1854-1926), lawyer and novelist, was born at Toronto, Canada West, on May 31, 1854, the son of Stephen Maule Jarvis. He was educated at Upper Canada College and at Osgoode Hall, and was called to the Ontario bar in 1880. In 1891 he went to the United States, and engaged in literary work. He died at Los Angeles, California, on January 1, 1926. He was the author of *Letters from east longitudes* (Toronto, 1875), *Geoffrey Hampstead* (New York, 1890), *Dr. Perdue* (Chicago, 1892), *The ascent of life* (Boston, 1894), *She lived in New York* (New York, 1894), and *The price of peace* (Los Angeles, 1921).

[Morgan, *Can. men* (1898); E. M. Chadwick, *Ontarian families*, vol. 1 (Toronto, 1894).]

Jarvis, William (1756-1817), provincial secretary of Upper Canada, was the fifth son of Samuel Jarvis of Norwalk, Connecticut, and Martha Seymour, and was born at Stamford, Connecticut, on September 11, 1756. In 1782 he became a cornet in the Queen's Rangers (1st American Regiment) under Lieut.-Col. John Graves Simcoe (q.v.); and when Simcoe was appointed lieutenant-governor of Upper Canada in 1791, Jarvis came to Upper Canada with him as secretary of the province. This position he occupied until his death at York, Upper Canada, on August 13, 1817. At the time of his death he was also grand master of Freemasons in Upper Canada. He married, in 1785, at St. George's, Hanover Square, London, Hannah Owen, daughter of the Rev. Samuel Peters, D.D.; and by her he had three sons and four daughters.

[G. A. Jarvis and others, *The Jarvis family* (Hartford, Connecticut, 1879); E. M. Chadwick, *Ontarian families*, vol. 1 (Toronto, 1894); J. Ross Robertson, *The history of freemasonry in Canada*, vol. 1 (Toronto, 1900) and *The diary of Mrs. John Graves Simcoe* (Toronto, 1912).]

Jarvis, William Botsford (1799-1864), sheriff of the Home district, Upper Canada, was born in York (Toronto) on May 4, 1799, the third son of Stephen Jarvis (q.v.). He was appointed sheriff of the Home district in 1827, and in 1837-38 he commanded a regiment of militia. He married Mary Boyles (d. 1852), daughter of William Powell; and by her he had two sons and three daughters.

[Mrs. Alden G. Meredith, *Mary's Rosedale and gossip of Little York* (Ottawa, 1928); G. A. Jarvis and others, *The Jarvis family* (Hartford, Conn., 1879); E. M. Chadwick, *Ontarian families*, vol. 1 (Toronto, 1894); J. C. Dent, *The Upper Canadian rebellion* (2 vols., Toronto, 1885).]

Jarvis, William Henry Pope (1876-1944), journalist and author, was born at Summerside, Prince Edward Island, on May 23, 1876, and died at Canton, Ontario, on December 14, 1944. He became a journalist, and he was the author of *Trails and tales in Cobalt* (Toronto, 1907), *The letters of a remittance man to his mother* (London, 1908), and *The great gold rush* (Toronto, 1913).

[*Can. who's who*, 1936-37; Morgan, *Can men* (1912).]

Jeanneret, François Charles Achille (1890-1967), university chancellor, was born in Elmira, Ontario, November 18, 1890, and educated at the University of Toronto (B.A., 1912). After teaching for a year at Upper Canada College he joined the staff of the University of Toronto as a lecturer in French, becoming department head in 1926 and head of the humanities and social sciences division of the school of graduate studies from 1947 to 1951. He was principal of University College for eight years and chancellor of the university from 1957 to 1965, when he retired from the university. Dr. Jeanneret directed a summer school in Sillery, Quebec, for fifteen years, which thousands of Ontario teachers attended; and he wrote a number of French text-books. He was honoured by Laval University for his promotion of Anglo-French understanding in Canada. He died at Toronto, Ontario, January 15, 1967.

[*Can. who's who*, 1961-63; Metropolitan Toronto Central Library, *Biographical scrapbooks*, vol. 33.]

Jefferys, Charles William (1869-1951), artist, was born in Rochester, England, on August 25, 1869, and came to Canada in 1879. He became apprenticed to a lithographic firm in Toronto, and studied art under C. M. Manly and G. A. Reid (qq.v.). Except for the years from 1893 to 1900, when he was an artist on the staff of the New York *Herald*, he remained in Toronto for the rest of his life. He first engaged in book and magazine illustration, and he became an unrivalled authority on the pictorial side of Canadian history. From 1912 to 1939 he was an instructor in drawing and painting in the department of architecture in the University of Toronto. He became a member of the Ontario Society of Artists in 1902, and was its president from 1913 to 1919; he was the first president of the Canadian Society of Graphic Arts in 1903; he was elected an A.R.C.A. in 1912, and an R.C.A. in 1925; and in 1934 Queen's University conferred on him the honorary degree of LL.D. He died at Toronto, Ontario, on October 8, 1951. Several of his paintings are in the National Gallery at Ottawa. He published *Dramatic episodes in Canadian history* (Toronto, 1930), *Canada's past in pictures* (Toronto, 1934), and *The picture gallery of Canadian history* (3 vols., Toronto, 1942-45).

[W. Colgate, *C. W. Jefferys* (Toronto, 1945); *Can. who's who*, 1949-51; *Encyc. Can.*]

Jenkins, Charles Christopher (1882-1943), journalist and novelist, was born at Hamilton, Ontario, on August 11, 1882. He became a journalist and was for many years on the staff of the Toronto *Globe*. He died at Toronto, Ontario, on November 22, 1943. He was the author of two novels, *The timber pirate* (Toronto, 1922) and *The reign of brass* (Toronto, 1927).

[*Can. who's who*, 1936-37.]

Jenkins, John (1813-1898), clergyman, was born in Exeter, England, in 1813, and was educated at Mount Radford College, Exeter, and the Hoxton Theological Institution, London. He was ordained to the ministry of the Wesleyan Methodist Church in 1837, and for some years was a missionary in India. He accepted later the charge of a Methodist Church in Montreal, Canada; but in 1853 he joined the Presbyterian Church, and after spending ten years in Philadelphia, he became pastor of St. Paul's Presbyterian Church, Montreal. In 1878 he was elected moderator of the Presbyterian Church in Canada. He retired from parochial work in 1881; and he died in 1898. He was the author of *A Protestant's appeal to the Douai Bible and other Roman Catholic standards* (Montreal, 1853), *The faithful minister: A memorial of the late Rev. William*

Squire (Montreal, 1853), *Pauperism in great cities* (Philadelphia, 1854), *Thoughts on the crisis* (Philadelphia, 1860), and *Canada's thanksgiving for national blessings* (Montreal, 1865).

[Morgan, *Can. men* (1898) and *Bib. can.*]

Jenkins, John Edward (1838-1910), politician and author, was born at Bangalore, Mysore, India, on July 28, 1838, the eldest son of the Rev. John Jenkins (q.v.) and Harriette Shepstone. He came to Canada with his parents at an early age, and was educated at McGill University and at the University of Pennsylvania. He studied law in England, and was called to the bar at Lincoln's Inn in 1864. In 1874 he was appointed the first agent-general for Canada in London; but this appointment he held for only two years. From 1874 to 1880 he represented Dundee as a radical in the British House of Commons; but when he attempted to recover the seat in 1885 and in 1896 as a Conservative, he was defeated. After suffering for some years from paralysis, he died in London, England, on June 4, 1910. In 1867 he married Hannah Matilda Johnstone, of Belfast, Ireland; and by her he had five sons and two daughters. He was especially famous as the author of a satire entitled *Ginx's baby* (London, 1870); but he wrote also *Lord Bantam* (London, 1871), *Barney Geoghegan, M.P.* (London, 1872), and the following works of fiction: *Little Hodge* (London, 1873), *The devil's chain* (London, 1876), *Lutchmee and billoo* (3 vols., London, 1877), *A paladin of finance* (London, 1882), *A week of passion* (3 vols., London, 1884), *A secret of two lives* (London, 1886), and *Pantalas* (London, 1897). In 1886 he became editor of the *Overland Mail* and the *Homeward Mail*, newspapers of which his brother-in-law, Sir Henry Seymour King, was the proprietor.

[*Dict. nat. biog.*, supp. II; *Cyc. Am. biog.*; Morgan, *Can. men* (1898); *Can. who was who*, vol. 2.]

Jenkins, Robert Smith (1870-1931), educationist and poet, was born at Rosemont, Ontario, on December 26, 1870. He was educated at the University of Toronto (B.A., 1893; M.A., 1896) and at Chicago University, where he was a fellow in Romance languages in 1901-02. He became a school-teacher, first in Ontario, then in Alberta, and later in eastern Canada; and he died at Toronto, Ontario, on November 12, 1931. He was the author of *Poems of the new century* (Toronto, 1903), *Canadian civics* (Toronto, 1908), *The heir from New York* (Toronto, 1911) and *Canadian poems* (Toronto, 1938).

[Morgan, *Can. men* (1912); *University of Toronto monthly*, 1932.]

Jenness, Diamond (1886-1969), anthropologist, was born in Wellington, New Zealand, in 1886. He was educated at the Uni-

versity of New Zealand and at Oxford, which sponsored his first field study on the d'Entrecasteaux group of islands near New Guinea in 1911-12. The following year he was invited to join the Canadian Arctic Expedition under V. Stefansson (q.v.). The expedition met with early disaster: the death of Jenness's fellow anthropologist, Henri Beuchat, and the loss of the principal ship. However, Jenness continued the study of the Eskimos of Coronation Gulf until 1916, when the expedition heard of the First World War and many members returned south. Jenness served as a gunner in the Canadian Army from 1917 to 1919 and during the Second World War as deputy director of intelligence for the Royal Canadian Air Force. From 1919 to 1947 he was on the staff of the National Museum of Canada and was chief of the division of anthropology from 1926 until his retirement. His book *People of the twilight* (New York, 1928), based on his study of the Coronation Gulf Eskimos, is regarded as one of the best narratives of life with a nomadic people; and his *Indians of Canada* (Ottawa, 1932) is a monumental ethnographic survey. Jenness prepared nine volumes as part of the official reports of the Canadian Arctic Expedition, 1913-19, and many papers and bulletins as a member of the staff of the National Museum. Among his most fascinating studies were "Ethnology and archaeology", suggesting places for arctic studies, in *Arctic Institute of North America Bulletin* (March, 1946); "Prehistoric culture waves from Asia to America" in *Washington Academy of Sciences Journal* (1940); and studies of Eskimo administration under American (Alaska) and Canadian auspices, published by the Arctic Institute of North America from 1962 to 1969; *The economics of Cyprus* (Montreal, 1962) is a study of land-use on the island. Jenness made a notable contribution to the understanding of Canadian aboriginal inhabitants. He was a fellow of the Royal Society of Canada, a companion of the Order of Canada, and a vice-president of the American Association for the Advancement of Science. In 1938 he was president of the American Anthropological Association. He died at Ottawa, November 29, 1969.

[*Proc. and Trans. Roy. Soc. Can.*, vol. VIII, 1970; *Can. who's who*, 1955-57.]

Jennings, Clotilda (d. 1895), poet, was born in Nova Scotia, and died in Montreal, Quebec, in 1895. She was the author, under the pseudonym of "Maude", of a book of verse, *Linden rhymes* (Halifax, 1854), and of a book of fiction and verse, *The white rose in Acadia, and Autumn in Nova Scotia* (Halifax, 1855).

[Morgan, *Bib. can.*; C. C. James, *A bibliography of Canadian poetry* (Toronto, 1899).]

Jennings, John (1814-1876), clergyman and author, was born in Glasgow, Scotland, on

October 8, 1814. He was educated at St. Andrew's University and the Theological Hall of the United Associate Synod; and in 1838 was sent to Canada as a missionary by the United Presbyterian Church. He became the pastor of a church in Toronto, and he remained its pastor for 36 years. He was prominent in the agitation for the secularization of King's College, Toronto, and of the clergy reserves. He died in Toronto in February, 1876. From 1851 to 1854 he was the editor of the *Canadian Presbyterian Magazine*; and he was the author of two pamphlets, *Reason or revelation* (Toronto, 1852) and *Say no* (Toronto, 1865).

[Morgan, *Bib. can.*; W. Gregg, *A history of the Presbyterian church in the Dominion of Canada* (Toronto, 1885); *Dict. Can. biog.*, vol. 10.]

Jérémie, Nicolas (1669-1732), fur-trader and author, was born at Quebec in 1669, and became a fur-trader. From 1694 to 1714 he was employed almost continuously in the fur-trade at the posts on Hudson Bay; and his account of his life on Hudson Bay, originally published in French in a collection of northern voyages issued at Amsterdam by J. F. Bernard in 1720, has been translated, with introduction and notes, by R. Douglas and J. N. Wallace, under the title of *Twenty years of York Factory, 1694-1714* (Ottawa, 1926). He died at Quebec on October 19, 1732.

[J. B. Tyrrell (ed.), *Documents relating to the early history of Hudson bay* (Toronto: The Champlain Society, 1931); Le Jeune, *Dict. gén.*; *Dict. Can. biog.*, vol. 2.]

Jessup, Edward (1735-1816), loyalist, was born in Stamford, Connecticut, in 1735. He became a prosperous landowner in Albany, New York; and on the outbreak of the American Revolutionary War, he raised a corps of rangers, known as "the Loyal Rangers" or "Jessup's Corps", which he himself commanded. After the war, he settled in the township of Augusta, on the north shore of the St. Lawrence; and in 1810 he founded here the town of Prescott. He died at Prescott in February, 1816.

[T. W. H. Leavitt, *History of Leeds and Grenville* (Brockville, Ont., 1879); A. Couillard-Després, *Histoire de Sorel* (Montreal, 1926).]

Jetté, Sir Louis Amable (1836-1920), lieutenant-governor of Quebec (1898-1908) and chief justice of the Court of King's Bench in Quebec (1909-11), was born at L'Assomption, Lower Canada, on January 15, 1836, the son of Amable Jetté, a merchant, and Caroline Gauffreau. He was educated at L'Assomption College, and was called to the bar in Lower Canada in 1857. He practised law in Montreal, and in 1870 distinguished himself in the famous Guibord case. In 1872 he was elected to the Canadian House of Commons in the Lib-

eral interest for Montreal East, defeating Sir George Cartier (q.v.). He represented this constituency until 1878, when he was appointed a puisne judge of the Superior Court of Quebec. In 1898 he retired from the bench to accept appointment as lieutenant-governor of Quebec; and this post he held until 1908, being reappointed for a second term. During this period he was a member of the Alaska Boundary Tribunal in 1903, and he was one of the commissioners who dissented from the award of the tribunal. In 1908 he was re-appointed to the bench, and in 1909 he became chief justice of the Court of King's Bench in Quebec. He retired from the bench finally in 1911, and he died at Quebec on May 5, 1920. In 1862 he married Berthe, daughter of Toussaint Laflamme, of Montreal; and by her he had one son. He was an LL.D. of Laval University (1878) and of the University of Toronto (1908), and a D.C.L. of Bishop's College, Lennoxville (1899). In 1901 he was created a K.C.M.G.

[H. Charlesworth (ed.), *A cyclopaedia of Canadian biography* (Toronto, 1919); Morgan, *Can. men* (1912); *Can. who's who*, 1910; Rose, *Cyc. Can. biog.* (1888); F. J. Audet, *Les juges en chef de la province de Québec* (Quebec, 1927); L. O. David, *Mes contemporains* (Montreal, 1894) and *Souvenirs et biographies* (Montreal, 1911); Le Jeune, *Dict. gén.*]

Jewitt, John R. (1783-1821), author, was born in 1783, and was armourer on board the *Boston*, an American trading vessel, when it arrived at Nootka Sound, Vancouver Island, in 1803. The crew of the *Boston* were massacred by the Indians, but Jewitt and one other of the crew were taken captive. Jewitt remained in the hands of the Indians from March, 1803, to July, 1805; and during this period he kept a journal of his experiences. This *Journal* was published by him (Boston, 1807), and has been several times republished. He died at Hartford, Conn., January 7, 1821.

[E. S. Meany, Jr., *The later life of John R. Jewitt* (British Columbia historical quarterly, 1940).]

Jobin, Louis (1845-1928), sculptor in wood, was born in 1845, and spent his life at Quebec and Ste. Anne de Beaupré, carving statues for churches, in the best manner of the old Canadian school of wood-carvers dating from early in the French régime. He died at Ste. Anne de Beaupré, Quebec, in 1928.

[D. Potvin, *Les Ilets-Jérémie: Louis Jobin, sculpteur sur bois* (Quebec, 1928); R. G. Riddell (ed.), *Canadian portraits* (Toronto, 1940).]

Jobin, Raoul (1906-1974), musician and singer, was born in Quebec City and educated at Laval University. He made his debut with the Paris Grand Opera in 1930 and was a member of the company until 1940 and from

1947 to 1949. He also sang with the Paris Opéra Comique and with the Metropolitan Opera in New York (1940-50), making his debut there in *Manon* in 1940. He appeared with various opera companies in Europe and in North and South America and as a concert artist. He died at Quebec City, Quebec, January 13, 1974.

[*Can. who's who*, 1970-72; *Creative Canada* (vol. 1).]

Jodoin, Alexandre (d. 1915), lawyer, died at Longueuil, Quebec, in January, 1915. He was joint author, with J. L. Vincent, of *L'histoire de Longueuil et de la famille de Longueuil* (Montreal, 1889).

[*Bull. rech. hist.*, index, vol. 4, p. 273.]

Jodoin, Claude (1913-1975), labour leader, was born in Westmount, Quebec, May 25, 1913. He was educated at St. Mary's College, and Jean-de-Brébeuf College, Montreal. He represented the International Ladies' Garment Workers' Union (A.F.L. – T.L.C., 1937). He became assistant manager of the Montreal joint board of the Dressmakers' Union (1941), and manager in 1947. He was a member of the executive board of the International Confederation of Free Trade Unions (1949) and Canadian Workers' delegate to the International Labour Office in Geneva (1950-54). He was a city councillor of Montreal (1940-42 and 1947-54) and a member of the Quebec Legislative Assembly (1942-44). He served in the Second World War as captain in the Mont Royal Fusiliers. He was a member of the National Research Council, the Economic Council of Canada, and the Canadian Institute of International Affairs. He was awarded the Order of Canada in 1967. He died at Ottawa, Ontario, March 1, 1975.

[*Can. who's who*, 1970-72.]

Jogues, Isaac (1607-1646), missionary and martyr, was born at Orléans, France, on January 10, 1607. He was educated at the Jesuit college, and entered the Society of Jesus as a novice in 1624. He was ordained a priest in 1636, and in the same year sailed for Quebec. He was employed in the Huron mission, and in 1642 he was captured by the Iroquois, and brutally tortured and maimed; but he was rescued by the Dutch of Fort Orange, and returned to France by way of New Amsterdam (New York). In 1644 he sailed again for Canada; and in 1646 he undertook a mission to the heart of the Iroquois country. Here he was massacred on October 18, 1646. He was canonized in 1930.

[F. Martin, *Vie du Père Jogues* (Montreal, 1873); M. J. Scott, *Isaac Jogues* (New York, 1927); F. Talbot, *Saint among savages* (New York, 1935); R. G. Thwaites (ed.), *The Jesuit relations* (73 vols., Cleveland, 1897-1901); Le Jeune, *Dict. gén.*; *Dict. Can. biog.*; vol. 1.]

Johnson, Daniel (1915-1968), premier of Quebec, was born at Danville, Quebec, April 9, 1915. He was educated at the Seminary of St. Hyacinthe (B.A., 1935); and at the University of Montreal (L.C.B., 1940). He represented Bagotville in the Quebec legislature from 1946 until his death in 1968. In 1955 he became parliamentary secretary to the Hon. Maurice Duplessis, who was premier and head of the Union Nationale party. He became minister of hydraulic resources in 1958. After the defeat of the Union Nationale in 1960 Johnson was chosen party leader, and led his followers to victory in 1966, when he became premier, minister of federal-provincial affairs, and minister of national resources. He pursued a strong Quebec nationalist program. He died suddenly while visiting a hydro-electric project at Manicouagan, Quebec, September 26, 1968.

[*Can. who's who*, 1964-66; *Can. parl. guide* (1968).]

Johnson, Edward (1881-1959), singer and opera manager, was born in Guelph, Ontario, on August 22, 1881, and died there on April 20, 1959. He had a highly successful career as an operatic tenor in Italy, Spain, Portugal, South America, Chicago, and New York; and in 1935 he became the general director of the Metropolitan Opera Association in New York. On his retirement from this position in 1950, he returned to Canada and became chairman of the Royal Conservatory of Music in Toronto. The University of Western Ontario conferred on him the degree of LL.D. in 1929, and the University of Toronto that of Mus.D. in 1934. He was created a C.B.E. in recognition of his services to music.

[Toronto *Globe and Mail*, April 21, 1959; Ruby Mercer, *The tenor of his time: Edward Johnson of the Met* (Toronto, 1976); *Can. who's who*, 1958-60; *Encyc. Can.*]

Johnson, Emily Pauline (1862-1913), poet, was born at "Chiefswood", Six Nation Indian Reserve, Ontario, in 1862, the second daughter of George Henry Martin Johnson, chief of the Six Nation Indians, and Emily Howells of Bristol, England. She was educated at the Brantford Model School, and at an early age contributed verses to periodicals. Her first volume of verse was *White wampum* (London, 1895), and this was followed by *Canadian born* (Toronto, 1903). She was the author also of *Legends of Vancouver* (Toronto, 1911), *The moccasin-maker* (Toronto, 1913), and *The Shagganappi* (Toronto, 1913). She died at Vancouver, British Columbia, on March 7, 1913. Her collected poems have been issued under the title of *Flint and feather* (Toronto, n.d.), with a biographical sketch.

[Mrs. W. Garland Foster, *The Mohawk princess* (Vancouver, B.C., 1931); Morgan, *Can. men and women* (1912); A. MacMurchy, *Handbook of Canadian literature* (Toronto, 1906); J. D. Logan and D. French,

Highways of Canadian literature (Toronto, 1924); L. Pierce, *Outlines of Canadian literature* (Toronto, 1927).]

Johnson, Sir Francis Godschall (1819-1894), governor of Assiniboia (1855-58), was born at Oakley House, Bedfordshire, England, on January 1, 1819, the son of Godschall Johnson, of the 10th Royal Hussars, and Lucy Bisshopp. He was educated at St. Omer, France, and at Bruges, Belgium, and came to Canada in 1834. He was called to the bar of Lower Canada (Q.C., 1848). In 1854 he was appointed recorder of Rupert's Land, and in 1855 governor of Assiniboia. In 1858 he returned to practise law in Montreal; and in 1865 he was appointed a judge of the Superior Court of Montreal. From 1870 to 1872 he assisted in the organization of the government of Manitoba, as a special commissioner. He was appointed chief justice of the Superior Court of the province of Quebec in 1889; and in 1890 he was knighted. He died on May 27, 1894. He was twice married, (1) in 1840 to Mary Gates Jones, of Montreal (d. 1853), and (2) in 1857 to Mary Mills, of Somersetshire, England. By each wife he had three children.

[Rose, *Cyc. Can. biog.* (1888); L. O. David, *Mes contemporains* (Montreal, 1894); E. H. Oliver, *The Canadian north west* (2 vols., Ottawa, 1914); P. G. Roy, *Les juges de la province de Québec* (Lévis, Que., 1933).]

Johnson, George (1837-1911), statistician, was born at Annapolis Royal, Nova Scotia, on October 29, 1837. He was educated at the Sackville Academy, New Brunswick; and was for many years engaged in journalism, first as editor of the *Halifax Reporter*, and then as Ottawa correspondent of the Toronto *Mail*. In 1887 he was appointed statistician of the Department of Agriculture at Ottawa, and in 1891 Dominion statistician. He retired from this position in 1904, and he died at Grand Pré, Nova Scotia, on January 17, 1911. He was the author of a *Handbook of Canada* (Ottawa, 1886), *Graphic statistics of Canada* (Ottawa, 1887), *Alphabet of first things in Canada* (Ottawa, 1889), and *A report on the forest wealth of Canada* (Ottawa, 1895).

[*Can. parl. comp.*]

Johnson, George Washington (1839-1917), author, was born at Binbrook, Upper Canada, in 1839. In 1864 he went to Cleveland, Ohio, and he was for a time on the staff of the Cleveland *Plain Dealer*. He then returned to Canada, and became a school-teacher in Hamilton, Ontario. From 1891 to 1906 he was on the staff of Upper Canada College, Toronto. He died at Pasadena, California, on January 4, 1917. He was the author of a volume of verse, entitled *Maple leaves* (Hamilton, 1864), and two novels, *The Mente's secret; or, The vengeance of Madra* (Cleveland, 1864) and *The belle of Bladen's brook* (Cleveland, 1865). He

was also the author of a popular song entitled "When you and I were young, Maggie".

[C. C. James, *A bibliography of Canadian poetry* (Toronto, 1899); L. E. Horning and L. J. Burpee, *A bibliography of Canadian fiction* (Toronto, 1904); private information.]

Johnson, Guy (1740-1788), loyalist, was born in county Meath, Ireland, in 1740, the nephew of Sir William Johnson, Bart. (q.v.). In 1774 he succeeded his uncle as superintendent of Indian affairs for New York; but in 1775 he fled to Montreal, and thence he sailed for England. In 1776 he was in New York; and in 1778 he took part in the raids on the Mohawk valley. He died in London, England, on March 5, 1788. He married his first cousin, Mary, daughter of Sir William Johnson, Bart.

[*Dict. nat. biog.*; *Cyc. Am. biog.*; A. L. Gibb, *Colonel Guy Johnson* (Papers of the Michigan Academy of Sciences, Arts, and Letters, 1941).]

Johnson, Helen Mar (1835-1863), poet, was born at Magog, Lower Canada, in 1835, and died at the same place on March 3, 1863. She published a volume of *Poems* (Boston, 1855), and another volume of her verse was published posthumously, with a biographical sketch, under the title *Canadian wild flowers* (Boston, 1884).

[C. M. Whyte-Edgar, *A wreath of Canadian song* (Toronto, 1910); C. C. James, *A bibliography of Canadian poetry* (Toronto, 1899).]

Johnson, Sir John, Bart. (1742-1830), loyalist, was born in the Mohawk valley on November 5, 1742, the only son of Sir William Johnson, Bart. (q.v.). He succeeded to his father's estates in the Mohawk valley in 1774; but in 1776 he was compelled to flee, with a large number of his tenants, to Canada, because of his loyalist sympathies. In Canada he organized and commanded two battalions of the King's Royal Regiment of New York; and he played an important part in the border forays which marked the later stages of the War of the Revolution. His estates in New York having been confiscated, he settled in Canada after the war, and was appointed in 1783 superintendent-general of Indian affairs in British North America. He was regarded as the most outstanding of the United Empire Loyalists in Canada, and was an unsuccessful candidate for the position of lieutenant-governor of Upper Canada in 1791. In 1787 he was appointed a member of the Legislative Council of Quebec, and in 1796 of that of Lower Canada; and he sat in this Council until his death at Mount Johnson, near Montreal, on January 4, 1830. In 1773 he married Mary, daughter of John Watts, of New York; and by her he had eight sons and three daughters. He was knighted in 1765, and he succeeded to his father's baronetcy in 1774.

[J. Watts de Peyster, *The life and misfortunes and the military career of Brig.-Gen. Sir John Johnson, Bart.* (New York, 1882); Mabel G. Walker, *Sir John Johnson, loyalist* (Mississippi valley historical review, December, 1916); Morgan, *Cel. Can.*; *Cyc. Am. biog.*; *Dict. Am. biog.*]

Johnson, John Mercer (1818-1868), one of the Fathers of Confederation, was born in Liverpool, England, in October, 1818. He came with his father to New Brunswick at an early age, was educated in the Northumberland county grammar school, and was admitted to the bar in 1840. In 1850 he was elected a member of the Legislative Assembly of New Brunswick for Northumberland; and in 1854 he became solicitor-general. He was subsequently postmaster-general, speaker of the Assembly and attorney-general in succession. In 1864 he was a delegate to the Quebec Conference; and in 1866 he was a delegate to the London Conference, at which the details of the British North America Act were settled. In 1867 he was elected to represent Northumberland in the Canadian House of Commons; but he died, soon afterward, in Northumberland county, New Brunswick, on November 9, 1868.

[*Cyc. Am. biog.*; *Can. parl. comp.*; J. Hannay, *History of New Brunswick* (Saint John, N.B., 1909).]

Johnson, John Smoke (1792-1886), Indian chief, was born at the Mohawk village, Upper Canada, on December 2, 1792. During the War of 1812 he was the leader of the Six Nation Indians on the British side. He died on the Six Nation Reserve, near Brantford, Ontario, on August 26, 1886.

[Evelyn H. C. Johnson, *Chief John Smoke Johnson* (Ont. Hist. Soc., papers and records, 1914).]

Johnson, John W. Fordham (1866-1938), lieutenant-governor of British Columbia (1931-36), was born at Spalding, Lincolnshire, England, on November 28, 1866, and emigrated to British Columbia in 1888. He became president of the British Columbia Sugar Refining Company in 1920; and from 1931 to 1936 he was lieutenant-governor of British Columbia. He died at Vancouver, British Columbia, on November 28, 1938.

[*Can. who's who*, 1936-37.]

Johnson, Phelps (1850-1926), civil engineer, was born in the United States in 1850, and came to Canada in his early days as engineer for the Toronto Bridge Company. He rose to be an outstanding bridge-builder, and he was the architect of the famous Quebec City bridge. He died at Montreal on February 20, 1926.

[Morgan, *Can. men* (1912).]

Johnson, Sir William, Bart. (1715-1774), superintendent of Indian affairs for New York, was born in Smithtown, county Meath, Ireland, in 1715. He was adopted by his relative, Admiral Sir Peter Warren, and accompanied the latter to America in 1738. He was placed in charge of Sir Peter Warren's estates in the Mohawk valley, and in 1752 inherited them. He gained a great hold over the Indians, and in 1755 he was appointed superintendent of Indian affairs for New York. In 1755 he commanded the expedition against Crown Point, and defeated and captured Baron Dieskau (q.v.) at Lake George. In 1759 he commanded the provincial troops under General Prideaux in the expedition against Niagara, and was chiefly responsible for the success of the expedition. He died at Johnson Hall, near Schenectady, New York, on July 11, 1774. In 1755 he was created a baronet of the United Kingdom. By his wife, Catherine Wisenberg, he left one son and two daughters. His *Papers* have been edited by A. C. Flick (9 vols., Albany, N.Y., 1921-33).

[A. C. Buell, *Sir William Johnson* (New York, 1903); W. L. Stone, *Life and times of Sir William Johnson* (2 vols., Albany, 1865); A. Pound and R. E. Day, *Johnson of the Mohawks* (New York, 1930); *Dict. nat. biog.*; *Dict. Am. biog.*; *Cyc. Am. biog.*]

Johnston, Ebenezer Forsyth Blackie (1850-1919), lawyer and art connoisseur, was born in Haddingtonshire, Scotland, on December 20, 1850. He came to Canada as a young man, studied law at Osgoode Hall, Toronto, and was called to the bar of Ontario in 1880 (Q.C., 1890). He practised law at Guelph, Ontario, until 1885; he then removed to Toronto, and, after serving four years as deputy attorney-general of Ontario, he became an outstanding criminal lawyer. He died in Toronto on January 29, 1919. In 1886 he married Sara, daughter of W. C. Schreiber, of Barrie, Ontario; and by her he had one daughter. A well-known authority on painting and other fine arts, he was the author of the chapters on "Painting and sculpture in Canada" in A. Shortt and A. G. Doughty (eds.), *Canada and its provinces* (23 vols., Toronto, 1914).

[Morgan, *Can. men* (1912); H. Charlesworth, *Candid chronicles* (Toronto, 1925).]

Johnston, Hugh (1840-1922), clergyman, was born in Elgin county, Upper Canada, on January 5, 1840. He was educated at Victoria University, Cobourg (B.A., 1865; M.A., 1869; B.D., 1874; D.D., 1889), and he was ordained a minister of the Methodist Church in 1865. He held various charges in Hamilton, Montreal, and Toronto, in Canada, and in Washington and Baltimore, in the United States; and he died at Baltimore, Maryland, on September 24, 1922. He was the author of *Toward the sunrise* (Toronto, 1893), *A merchant prince* (Toronto, 1893), *Beyond death* (New York,

1903), and *Travel films* (Baltimore, Md., 1913).

[*Who's who in America; Cyc. Am. biog.*; Morgan, *Can. men* (1912).]

Johnston, or Johnstone, James William (1792-1873), prime minister of Nova Scotia (1844-48 and 1857-60), was born in Jamaica, West Indies, on August 29, 1792. He was educated in Scotland; and studied law in Annapolis, Nova Scotia, where his parents had settled. He was called to the bar of Nova Scotia in 1813; and he practised law, first in Kentville, Kings county, and then in Halifax. In 1834 he was appointed solicitor-general of the province, and in 1837 he was appointed a member of the Legislative Council. In 1841 he was appointed attorney-general, and at the general elections of 1843, having resigned from the Legislative Council, he was elected to represent the county of Annapolis in the Legislative Assembly. This constituency he represented continuously for twenty years. He became the leader of the Conservative party in Nova Scotia, and from 1844 to 1848, and from 1857 to 1860 he was first minister of the province. In 1864 he was appointed a judge in equity, and this position he held until his death in Cheltenham, England, on November 21, 1873. He was twice married, (1) to Amelia Elizabeth, daughter of William James Almon, by whom he had three sons and three daughters, and (2) to Louise, widow of Capt. Wentworth, R.A., by whom he had three sons and one daughter.

[A. Calnek, *Memoir of J. W. Johnstone* (Halifax, 1884); J. W. Payzant, *James William Johnstone* (Coll. Nova Scotia Hist. Soc., 1912); E. M. Saunders, *Three premiers of Nova Scotia* (Toronto, 1909); A. W. Savary, *Three premiers* (Can. mag., 1909); Rose, *Cyc. Can. biog.* (1888); *Trans. Roy. Soc. Can.*, 1899; *Dict. Can. biog.*, vol. 10.]

Johnston, Mrs. Mabel Annesley, *née* **Sullivan** (1870-1945), author, was born in Toronto, Ontario, in 1870, and died there on April 1, 1945. She was a grand-daughter of the Rev. Henry Scadding and of the Hon. Robert Baldwin Sullivan (qq.v.), and she married W.R. Johnston, a Toronto merchant. She was the author of *A Canadian book of months* (Toronto, 1908) and, under the *nom de plume* of "Susanne Marny", of *Tales of old Toronto* (Toronto, 1909).

[Toronto *Telegram*, April 3, 1945.]

Johnston, William (1840-1917), historian, was born at Airdsgreen Farm, Glenbuck, near Muirkirk, Ayrshire, Scotland, on March 6, 1840. He came to Canada about 1859, and settled in Blanshard township, in the Huron Tract. In 1873 he became township clerk of Blanshard. He died at St. Mary's, Ontario, on January 13, 1917. He was the author of *The pioneers of Blanshard* (Toronto, 1899), *The*

history of the county of Perth (Stratford, Ont., 1903), and *Canadian melodies* (Stratford, Ont., 1909).

[Private information.]

Johnstone, James, Chevalier de (1719-1800?), soldier, was born in Edinburgh, Scotland, in 1719, the son of James Johnstone, a merchant. He took part in the Jacobite rebellion of 1745, and was an aide-de-camp of Prince Charles Edward Stewart. In 1746 he escaped to Paris, and in 1750 he entered the French army. From 1752 to 1758 he was stationed at Louisbourg, and in 1758 he escaped to Canada and became aide-de-camp, first of Lévis (q.v.), and then of Montcalm (q.v.). He was present at the battle of the Plains of Abraham; and after the capitulation of Montreal was allowed by Murray (q.v.) to return to France, his real nationality being generously ignored. He obtained a pension from the French government; but this was stopped at the outbreak of the French Revolution, and in his last days he was reduced to poverty. He died about 1800, but the exact date is not known. In 1762 he was created a chevalier of St. Louis. He left behind him in manuscript his memoirs of the rebellion of 1745 and of the campaign in Canada; and these were published, in translation, under the title *Memoirs of the rebellion in 1745-46* (London, 1820), and under the title *Memoirs of the chevalier de Johnstone* (Aberdeen, 1870-71). Three manuscripts dealing with the Seven Years' War in Canada, attributed to Johnstone, have been published in the *Historical documents* of the Literary and Historical Society of Quebec, 2nd series (Quebec, 1868), and his *Memoirs* have been published in the 9th series (Quebec, 1915).

[P. B. Casgrain, *Les Mémoires de Chevalier Johnstone* (Bull. rech. hist., 1905); Hon. E. Fabre Surveyer, *Le Chevalier Johnstone* (Transactions of the Franco-Scottish Society, vol. viii, Edinburgh, 1935).]

Johnstone, John Young (1887-1930), painter, was born in Montreal, Quebec, on November 12, 1887. He studied art in Montreal and in Paris, France, where he was a pupil of Pau, Casteluche, Simon, and Menard. His early work showed much promise, and in 1920 he was elected an A.R.C.A. His later work was less successful. He died at Havana, Cuba, in destitution, on February 13, 1930.

[N. MacTavish, *The fine arts in Canada* (Toronto, 1925).]

Jolliet, Louis (1645-1700), discoverer of the Mississippi, was born in Quebec in 1645, the son of Jean Jollyet, a wheelwright in the employ of the Company of New France, and Marie d'Abancourt. He was educated at the Jesuit college at Quebec, and took minor orders; but in 1669 he abandoned ecclesiastical life, and engaged in the fur-trade. In 1672 Frontenac sent him, in company with Marquette (q.v.), to explore the Mississippi. He set out in May, 1673, and descended this river past the mouths of the Illinois, Missouri, Ohio, and Arkansas rivers, but turned back from a village of the Arkansas Indians on July 17. Unfortunately the records of this journey were lost by Jolliet on his return. In 1679 he made a voyage to Hudson Bay; and the following year received a grant of the Island of Anticosti, where he settled with his family. In 1694 he explored the coast of Labrador. In 1697 he obtained the seigniory of Jolliet in Beauce county, Quebec, and in 1697 he was appointed royal hydrographer and royal pilot for the St. Lawrence. He died on one of the islands of the St. Lawrence, between May 4 and September 15, 1700. He married, in October, 1675, Claire Françoise Byssot, by whom he had seven children.

[E. Gagnon, *Louis Jolliet* (Quebec, 1902) and *Où est mort Louis Jolliet* (Bull. rech. hist., vol. viii); F. B. Steck, *The Jolliet-Marquette expedition* (Washington, D.C., 1927); P. G. Roy, *Fils de Québec*, vol. 1 (Lévis, P.Q., 1933); Le Jeune, *Dict. gén.*; J. Delanglez, *Life and voyages of Louis Jolliet* (Chicago, 1948); *Dict. Can. biog.*, vol. 1.]

Joly de Lotbinière, Sir Henri Gustave (1829-1908), prime minister of Quebec (1878-79), minister of inland revenue for Canada (1897-1900), and lieutenant-governor of British Columbia (1900-06), was born in Epernay, France, on December 5, 1829, the son of Gaspard Pierre Gustave Joly, seignior of Lotbinière, and Julie Christine, daughter of the Hon. M. E. G. A. Chartier de Lotbinière. He was educated in Paris, France; but returned to Canada with his parents early in life and was called to the bar of Lower Canada in 1855 (Q.C., 1878). In 1861 he was elected to represent Lotbinière in the Legislative Assembly of Canada; and this constituency he represented continuously until 1885, first in the Assembly of United Canada (1861-67), then in both the Canadian House of Commons and the Legislative Assembly of Quebec (1867-74), and finally, after the abolition of dual representation, in the Quebec Assembly (1874-85). From 1867 to 1878 he was the leader of the Liberal opposition in Quebec; and, on the dismissal of the Boucherville administration in 1878, he was appointed prime minister of the province. He was defeated and resigned office in 1879, and in 1885 he retired from the legislature, declining to unite with his political associates in the agitation over the execution of Louis Riel (q.v.). For a time he retired from public life; but in 1896 he was elected to the Canadian House of Commons for Portneuf, and in 1897 he became minister of inland revenue in the Laurier government. In 1900 he retired from parliament to accept appointment as lieutenant-governor of British Columbia. This office he relinquished in 1906, and he died at

Quebec on November 15, 1908. In 1856 he married Margaretta Josepha (d. 1904), daughter of Hammond Gowen, Quebec; and by her he had three sons and three daughters. In 1888 he assumed his mother's surname of Lotbinière with the consent of the Quebec legislature. In 1895 he was created a K.C.M.G.

[*Dict. nat. biog.*, supp. II; Le Jeune, *Dict. gén.*; Dent, *Can. port.*, vol. 3; *Can. parl. comp.*; *Can. who was who*, vol. 1.]

Jolys, Jean Marie Arthur (d. 1926), priest and local historian, died at St. Pierre-Jolys, Manitoba, on June 14, 1926. He wrote the history of the parish, under the title *Pages de souvenirs et d'histoire* (n.p., 1914?).

[Private information.]

Joncaire, Louis Thomas de (1670-1739), seignior of Chabert, and commandant at Niagara (1720-30), was born in St. Rémi, Provence, France, in 1670. He was sent out to Canada in 1687 as an officer in the marine troops; and he was shortly afterwards taken prisoner by the Seneca Indians. He became one of the most trusted and successful officers of the French government in dealing with the Indians; and most of his service was on the Niagara frontier. From 1720 to 1726 he was commandant at Niagara. He died at Niagara on June 29, 1739.

[Frank H. Severance, *The story of Joncaire: His life and times on the Niagara* (Publications of the Buffalo Historical Society, 1906); Le Jeune, *Dict. gén.*; *Dict. Can. biog.*, vol. 2.]

Joncas, Louis Zépherin (1846-1903), politician and civil servant, was born at Grand River, Gaspé, Canada East, on July 26, 1846. He was educated at Masson College, Terrebonne; and became manager of the Gaspé Fishing Company. He represented Gaspé in the Canadian House of Commons from 1887 to 1896; and in 1896 he was appointed superintendent of fish and game in the Quebec civil service. He died on March 28, 1903. He was the author of *The fisheries of Canada* (Ottawa, 1885), and was joint author, with E. T. D. Chambers (q.v.), of *The sportsman's companion* (Quebec, 1899).

[Faucher de Saint-Maurice, *Louis Zéphirin Joncas* (Revue d'histoire de la Gaspésie, 1968); Morgan, *Can. men* (1898); *Can. parl. comp.*]

Jones, Alfred Gilpin (1824-1906), lieutenant-governor of Nova Scotia (1900-06), was born at Weymouth, Nova Scotia, on September 28, 1824, the son of Guy Carleton Jones. He was educated at Yarmouth Academy, and entered business. He founded, and was for many years the head of, the West Indian importing firm of A. G. Jones and Co. He entered politics as an opponent of Confederation in 1864-67; and in 1867 he was elected a member of the

Canadian House of Commons for Halifax. He was defeated in 1872, but sat again for Halifax in the Commons from 1874 to 1878; and in 1878 he became minister of militia in the Mackenzie government. Defeated in 1878 and in 1882, he was again elected in 1887, and sat until 1891. In 1900 he was appointed lieutenant-governor of Nova Scotia; and he died in office, at Halifax, on March 15, 1906. In 1850 he married Margaret Wiseman (d. 1865), daughter of the Hon. W. J. Stairs, Halifax; and in 1876 Emma, daughter of Edward Albro, Halifax.

[Morgan, *Can. men* (1898); Rose, *Cyc. Can. biog.* (1888); Dent, *Can. port*, vol. 3; *Can. parl. comp.*]

Jones, Alice (1853-1933), novelist, was born in Halifax, Nova Scotia, on August 26, 1853, the daughter of the Hon. A. G. Jones (q.v.). She lived in Halifax for many years; but during the last twenty-eight years of her life she lived at Mentone, France. Here she died on February 27, 1933. She wrote sometimes under the pseudonym "Alix John"; and she was the author of *The night hawk* (Toronto and New York, 1901), *Bubbles we buy* (Toronto, 1903), *Gabriel Praed's castle* (Boston, 1904), *Marcus Holbeach's daughter* (New York, 1912), and *Flame of frost* (n.p., 1918).

[Morgan, *Can. men and women* (1912).]

Jones, Arthur Edward (1838-1918), priest and archaeologist, was born at Brockville, Upper Canada, on November 17, 1838, the son of Henry Jones and Lucy Catherine Macdonell. He was educated at St. Mary's College, Montreal; and in 1857 joined the Society of Jesus. He was ordained a priest of the Roman Catholic Church in 1873; and in 1882 he was appointed archivist of St. Mary's College, Montreal. In addition to some controversial pamphlets dealing with the Jesuits, he published the *Aulneau collection: Rare or unpublished documents (1734-45)* (Montreal, 1893), and *Old Huronia* (5th Report of the Bureau of Archives, Ontario, 1908). He died at Montreal on January 19, 1918. In 1910 he was elected a member of the Royal Society of Canada.

[*Proc. Roy. Soc. Can.*, 1918; Morgan, *Can. men* (1912); Le Jeune, *Dict. gén.*; *Bull. rech. hist.*, 1926; *Can. who was who*, vol. 1.]

Jones, Cecil Charles (1872-1943), educationist, was born at Boundary Creek, New Brunswick, on February 11, 1872; and was educated at the University of New Brunswick (B.A., 1897; M.A., 1899; Ph.D., 1902) and at Harvard University (B.A., 1898). From 1898 to 1906 he was professor of mathematics at Acadia University; and in 1906 he became professor of mathematics in the University of New Brunswick, and also chancellor of the university. He was appointed president of the university in 1931, and he retired from this post in 1941. He died at Fredericton, New Brunswick, on August 19, 1943. He was an honorary LL.D. of the University of Toronto (1907), of Bates University (1920), and of McMaster University (1923), and an honorary D.C.L. of Acadia University (1934).

[*Can. who's who*, 1936-37; Morgan, *Can. men* (1912).]

Jones, Charles (1781-1840), legislative councillor of Upper Canada, was born in 1781, the second son of Ephraim Jones (q.v.). He was educated at Cornwall, Upper Canada, under John Strachan (q.v.), and became one of the founders of Brockville, Upper Canada. From 1821 to 1828 he represented Leeds in the Legislative Assembly of the province, and from 1829 to 1840 he sat in the Legislative Council. He died at Brockville on August 21, 1840. He married (1) in 1807 Mary (d. 1812), daughter of the Rev. John Stuart (q.v.), and (2) in 1820 Florella Smith (d. 1877). By his first wife he had three sons, and by his second three sons and two daughters.

[A. H. Young (ed.), *The parish register of Kingston, Upper Canada* (Kingston, Ont., 1921); E. M. Chadwick, *Ontarian families* (2 vols., Toronto, 1894-98).]

Jones, Chilion (1835-1912), civil engineer and architect, was born in Brockville, Upper Canada, on October 10, 1835, the sixth son of the Hon. Jonas Jones (q.v.). He became a civil engineer and architect; and he designed the Parliament Buildings at Ottawa. In later life he was a manufacturer in Gananoque, Ontario. He died in Bermuda on April 1, 1912.

[E. M. Chadwick, *Ontarian families*, vol. 1 (Toronto, 1894).]

Jones, Sir Daniel (1794-1838), was born in 1794, the son of Daniel Jones, a loyalist. In 1835 he visited England as the agent of a Canadian Loan and Trust Company; and in 1836 he was created a knight bachelor by William IV at Windsor Castle, the first native-born Canadian to be thus honoured. He died at Brockville, Upper Canada, on August 23, 1838.

[Morgan, *Cel. Can.*, under "Sir David [*sic*] Jones"; C. C. James, *The second legislature of Upper Canada* (Trans. Roy. Soc. Can., 1904).]

Jones, Ephraim (1750-1812), loyalist, was born in the Mohawk valley on April 27, 1750, the son of Col. Elisha Jones. He came to Canada after the American Revolution, and settled in Elizabethtown. He represented Grenville in the first Legislative Assembly of Upper Canada (1792-96); and he died on January 21, 1812. He married (1) Charlotte (d. 1803), daughter of Michel Coursolles, of Verchères, Lower Canada, and (2) Margaret S. Beek (d. 1852); and he had six sons.

[A. H. Young (ed.), *The parish register of Kingston, Upper Canada* (Kingston, Ont., 1921); E. M. Chadwick, *Ontarian families* (2 vols., Toronto, 1894-98).]

Jones, George Mallory (1873-1940), educationist, was born at Port Perry, Ontario, on September 13, 1873. He was educated at the University of Toronto (B.A., 1896), and became a school-teacher, first at Whitby, then at Hagersville, and finally at Toronto, Ontario. In 1915 he was appointed a lecturer on the staff of the Ontario College of Education, in the University of Toronto; and in 1929 he became professor of methods in English and history in this institution. In 1935 he became also managing editor of *The School*. He died at Toronto, Ontario, on January 4, 1940. He was joint author, with C. D. Allin (q.v.), of *Annexation, preferential trade, and reciprocity* (Toronto, 1911), with L. E. Horning and J. D. Morrow, of *A high school grammar* (Toronto, 1921), and with A. Yates, of *Practical and literary English* (Toronto, 1928).

[*Can. who's who*, 1936-37.]

Jones, Herbert Chilion (1836-1923), lawyer, was born at Brockville, Upper Canada, on May 6, 1836. He was educated at the University of Trinity College, Toronto (B.A., 1855; M.A., 1858); and was called to the bar of Upper Canada in 1859. He practised law in Toronto; and he died at Toronto, Ontario, on January 30, 1923. He was the author of *Jones on prescription* (Toronto, 1878) and *The "Torrens system" of transfer of land* (Toronto, 1886).

[Morgan, *Can. men* (1912); E. M. Chadwick, *Ontarian families* (2 vols., Toronto, 1894-98).]

Jones, James Edmund (1866-1939), police magistrate, naturalist, musician, and author, was born at Belleville, Ontario, on June 24, 1866, the son of the Rev. Septimus Jones. He was educated at Upper Canada College and at the University of Toronto (B.A., 1888), was called to the bar of Ontario in 1891, and practised law in Toronto until 1920. He was then appointed police magistrate of the city of Toronto, and he retained this position until his death at Toronto on June 13, 1939. A man of varied interests, he was the author of *Camping and canoeing* (Toronto, 1903), *Pioneer crimes and punishments in Toronto and the Home district* (Toronto, 1924), *Some familiar wild flowers* (Toronto, 1930), and *Mushrooms, ferns, and grasses* (Toronto, 1930); and he was the compiler of *The University of Toronto song book* (Toronto, 1887; new ed., 1916), *The book of common praise* (Toronto, 1909), and *Campfire choruses* (Toronto, 1916).

[*Can. who's who*, 1936-37.]

Jones, James Thomas (pseud.). See **Leslie, Mary.**

Jones, John Walter (1878-1954), prime minister of Prince Edward Island (1943-53), was born at Pownal, Prince Edward Island, on April 14, 1878, and died at Ottawa, Ontario, on March 31, 1954. He was educated at Prince of Wales College, the Ontario Agricultural College (B.S.A., 1909), and Acadia University (B.A., 1904; M.A., 1914). He became an outstanding farmer in Prince Edward Island; he sat in the legislature of the province as a Liberal from 1935 to 1953; and he was prime minister from 1943 to 1953, when he accepted appointment to the Senate of Canada. He was the author of *Fur-farming in Canada* (Montreal, 1913).

[*Can. who's who*, 1952-54; *Can. parl. comp.*, 1953; *Encyc. Can.*]

Jones, Jonas (1791-1848), judge, was born in Elizabethtown, Upper Canada, on May 19, 1791, the fifth son of Ephraim Jones (q.v.). He was educated at Cornwall, Upper Canada, under John Strachan (q.v.), and he fought on the British side throughout the War of 1812. He was called to the bar of Upper Canada in 1815, and practised law in Brockville, Upper Canada. From 1816 to 1828 he was a member of the Legislative Assembly of Upper Canada for Grenville, and again from 1836 to 1837 for Leeds. In 1837 he was appointed a judge of the Court of Queen's Bench, and in 1839 he was appointed speaker of the Legislative Council of Upper Canada. He sat on the bench until his death at Toronto on July 8, 1848. He was regarded as one of the leading members of the "Family Compact". He married Mary Elizabeth, daughter of David Ford of Morristown, New York; and had by her eight sons and three daughters.

[D. B. Read, *Lives of the judges* (Toronto, 1888); E. M. Chadwick, *Ontarian families* (2 vols., Toronto, 1894-98).]

Jones, Llewellyn (1840-1918), Anglican bishop of Newfoundland (1878-1917), was born in Liverpool, England, on October 11, 1840, and died at St. John's, Newfoundland, on January 9, 1918. He was educated at Harrow and Trinity College, Cambridge (M.A., 1866), and was ordained a priest of the Church of England in 1864. After serving for some years as rector of Little Hereford, he was appointed bishop of Newfoundland and Bermuda in 1878; he continued in this office until failing health forced his resignation in 1917.

[*Who was who*, 1916-28; *Encyc. Can.*; *Newfoundland supp.*]

Jones, Sir Lyman Melvin (1843-1917), senator of Canada, was born in York county, Upper Canada, on September 21, 1843, the son of Norman Jones and Theresa Jane Patterson. He entered the employ of A. Harris and Sons, manufacturers of agricultural implements, Brantford, Ontario, and in 1872 was admitted a partner. On the formation of the Massey-Harris Company in 1891, he was appointed general manager; and in 1902 he became president. In 1888, while western manager of A. Harris and Sons, he was elected to represent North Winnipeg in the Legislative Assembly of Manitoba; and from 1888 to 1889 he was a member of the Greenway government. In 1901 he was called to the Senate of Canada; and in 1911 he was created a K.C.M.G. He died at Toronto on April 15, 1917. In 1872 he married Louisa, daughter of Thomas Irwin, Tecumseh, Ontario; and by her he had one daughter.

[Morgan, *Can. men* (1912); *Can. parl. comp.*]

Jones, Peter (1802-1856), Indian missionary, was born at Burlington Heights, near Hamilton, Upper Canada, in 1802, the son of Augustus Jones, a surveyor, and an Ojibway woman. His Indian name was Kahkewaguonaby. In 1883 he was ordained a minister of the Wesleyan Methodist Church; and he served as a missionary among the Ojibway Indians for over twenty years. He died at Brantford, Upper Canada, on June 29, 1856. He published an *Ojebway spelling book* (1828), an *Ojebway hymn book* (New York, 1829), *The gospel of St. Matthew, translated into the Ojebway language* (York, Upper Canada, 1829), *The gospel according to St. John, translated into the Chippeway language* (York, Upper Canada, 1831); and his *History of the Ojibway Indians* was published posthumously (London, 1861).

[*Life and Journals of the Rev. Peter Jones* (Toronto, 1860); Morgan, *Bib. can.*]

Jones, Robert Vonclure (1835-1917), educationist, was born at Pownal, Prince Edward Island, on June 25, 1835. He was educated at Prince of Wales College, Charlottetown, and at Acadia University (B.A., 1860; M.A., 1863; Ph.D., 1886); and he was professor of Greek and Latin in Acadia University from 1864 to 1913. He died at Wolfville, Nova Scotia, on October 25, 1917.

[*Records of the graduates of Acadia University* (Wolfville, N.S., 1926).]

Jones, Solomon (1756-1822), loyalist and physician, was born in the province of New Jersey in 1756, and was educated for the medical profession in Albany, New York. He was a surgeon's mate with the Loyalist forces during the American Revolutionary War; and in 1784 settled in Augusta township, near Cornwall, on the St. Lawrence River. He was one of the first physicians in what became Upper Canada, and he was also one of the first magistrates. From 1796 to 1800 he represented Leeds and Frontenac in the Legislative Assembly of Upper Canada. His death took place at his place, "Old Homewood" (which is still standing), on September 22, 1822. He married Mary Tunnacliffe, of Richmond, New York; and by her he had four sons and three daughters.

[L. Pierce, *Doctor Solomon Jones* (Queen's quarterly, 1929).]

Jones, William (1838-1907), educationist, was born at Toronto, Upper Canada, on October 13, 1838, the seventh son of the Hon. Jonas Jones (q.v.). He was educated at Upper

Canada College and at St. John's College, Cambridge (M.A., 1862), and in 1863 he was appointed professor of mathematics in the University of Trinity College, Toronto. In 1868 he was ordained a priest of the Church of England, and subsequently he became dean of Trinity College and acting provost. He retired from the chair of mathematics in 1895, and during his later years was bursar and registrar of the college. He died at Toronto, Ontario, on October 7, 1907.

[Morgan, *Can. men* (1898); E. M. Chadwick, *Ontarian families* (2 vols., Toronto, 1894-98).]

Jordan, Jacob (d. 1796), merchant, was an English merchant who came to Canada in the early days of British rule, and settled in Montreal. He became one of the leading merchants of Montreal; and he represented the county of Effingham in the Legislative Assembly of Lower Canada from 1792 to his death on February 24, 1796. He married in Montreal in 1767 Ann Livingston; and by her he had several children. His son, Jacob Jordan, Jr., succeeded him in 1796 in the representation of the county of Effingham.

[J. Desjardins, *Guide parlementaire de la province de Québec* (Quebec, 1902).]

Jordan, John A. (1843-1917), journalist, was born at Quebec, Canada East, on March 27, 1843, was called to the bar in 1865, but later turned to journalism. He died at Quebec, on October 13, 1917. He was the author of *The Gross-Isle tragedy and the monument to the Irish fever victims* (Quebec, 1909).

[P. G. Roy, *Les avocats de la région de Québec* (Lévis, Que., 1936).]

Jordan, Louis Henry (1855-1923), clergyman, was born at Halifax, Nova Scotia, on July 27, 1855; and was educated at Dalhousie University (B.A., 1875; M.A., 1878), at Princeton University, at Edinburgh University (B.D., 1882), at Oxford, and in Germany. He was ordained a minister of the Presbyterian Church in 1882; and he was the pastor of churches in Halifax, Montreal, and Toronto. He retired from parochial work in 1900; and he devoted the rest of his life to travel and study. He died on October 4, 1923. He was the author of *Comparative religion, its genesis and growth* (Edinburgh, 1905), *Comparative religion: A survey of its recent literature* (Edinburgh, 1909), *Modernism in Italy* (London, 1909), and *Comparative religion, its adjuncts and allies* (London, 1915); and he was joint author, with B. Labanca, of *The study of religion in the Italian universities* (London, 1909).

[*Who was who*, 1916-28; Morgan, *Can. men* (1912).]

Jordan, William George (1852-1939), clergyman and educationist, was born at Whitby, England, in 1852. He was educated at London University (B.A., 1885), and was ordained a minister of the Presbyterian Church in England. He came to Canada in 1889, served as minister of St. Andrew's Church, Strathroy, Ontario, and in 1899 was appointed professor of Hebrew and Old Testament exegesis in Queen's University, Kingston. This post he filled with distinction for thirty years, until his retirement in 1929. He died at Toronto, Ontario, on May 31, 1939. He was the author of *Prophetic ideas and ideals* (New York, 1902), *The Philippian gospel* (New York, 1904), *Biblical criticism and modern thought* (Edinburgh, 1909), *Commentary on the book of Deuteronomy* (New York, 1911), *The song and the soil* (New York, 1913), *Religion in song* (London, 1916), *The challenge of the book* (New York, 1921), *Ancient Hebrew stories and their modern interpretation* (London, 1922), *Songs of service and sacrifice* (London, 1924), *History and revelation* (London, 1926), and *The book of Job* (New York, 1929).

[R. C. Wallace (ed.), *Some great men of Queen's* (Toronto, 1941); *Can. who's who*, 1936-37; Morgan, *Can. men* (1912).]

Joseph, Henry (1775-1832), merchant, was born in England in 1775, and in early youth was persuaded to settle in Canada by his uncle, Aaron Hart. He became a merchant, first in Berthier-en-haut, Lower Canada, and later in Montreal; and he was the first merchant, it is said, to charter Canadian ships for Canadian trade with Great Britain. He was thus one of the founders of the Canadian merchant marine. One of the ships he controlled was the famous *Eweretta*, which was employed by the North West Company. He died of cholera at Berthier-en-haut, Lower Canada, on June 21, 1832. He married Rachel, daughter of Levi Solomons (q.v.); and by her he had five sons and four daughters.

[J. D. Borthwick, *History and biographical gazetteer of Montreal* (Montreal, 1892).]

Juchereau-Duchesnay. See **Duchesnay.**

Judah, Henry Hague (1808-1883), lawyer, was born in London, England, on April 28, 1808. He came to Canada in early life, and was called to the bar of Lower Canada in 1829 (Q.C., 1854). He represented Champlain in the Legislative Assembly of United Canada from 1843 to 1844; and in 1854 he was appointed one of the commissioners for determining the compensation due the *seigneurs* under the Act abolishing seigniorial tenure. For several years he was president of the Montreal City and District Savings Bank. He died at Montreal, Quebec, on February 10, 1883.

[*Dom. ann. reg.*, 1883.]

Jukes, Joseph Beete (1811-1869), geologist, was born in Birmingham, England, in 1811; and died in Dublin, Ireland, on July 29, 1869. He was educated at Cambridge University (B.A., 1836), and came to be recognized as one of the outstanding geologists of his time. In 1839-40 he carried out the first geological sur-

vey of Newfoundland; and he published a *Report on the geology of Newfoundland* (London, 1839) and *Excursions in and about Newfoundland* (2 vols., London, 1842). Later he was employed on survey work in Australia, North Wales, and Ireland.

[*Dict. nat. biog.*; *Encyc. Can.*]

Julien, Henri (1854-1908), cartoonist, was born at Quebec City, in 1854. In 1869 he removed to Montreal, and was apprenticed an engraver with the firm of Leggo and Co. He entered the employment of G. E. Desbarats (q.v.), the publisher of the *Canadian Illustrated News*, and he became one of the artists on the staff of this journal. Later he became a cartoonist on the staff of the Montreal *Star*, and a contributor of caricatures to *L'Illustration*, of Paris, and the *Graphic*, of London. Although he was a distinguished draughtsman and painter, it is chiefly on his cartoons and caricatures that his fame rests. He died at Montreal on September 18, 1908.

[M. Barbeau, *Henri Julien* (Toronto, 1941); *Can. who was who*, vol. 2; A. H. Robson, *Canadian landscape painters* (Toronto, 1932).]

Jumonville, Joseph Coulon de Villiers, Sieur de (1718-1754), soldier, was born at Verchères, New France, on September 8, 1718, the son of Nicolas Antoine Coulon de Villiers and Angélique Jarret de Verchères. At an early age he went west with his father to the Illinois country, and in 1739 he was sent on an expedition against the Indians of Louisiana. He became one of the French officers employed particularly with the Indians; and after some years spent in Acadia he was sent with Contrecoeur (q.v.) to the Ohio. After the capture of Fort Duquesne by the French, he was sent with a small party to watch the Virginians under George Washington, and on the morning of May 28, 1754, he and his party were surprised by Washington's force. Jumonville, with 9 of his men, was killed; and the rest of his men, with one exception, were taken prisoners.

[G. Robitaille, *Washington et Jumonville: Étude critique* (Montreal, 1933); Le Jeune, *Dict. gén.*; *Dict. Can. biog., vol. 3.*]

Juneau, Félix Emmanuel (1816-1886), educationist, was born at Quebec, Lower Canada, on May 27, 1816; and was educated at the Quebec Seminary and the College of Ste. Anne. He became a school-teacher, and in 1859 was appointed an inspector of schools. He died at Quebec, Que., on February 17, 1886. Among the books published by him were *Dissertation sur les méthodes d'enseignement primaire* (Quebec, 1846), *Nouvelle méthode pour apprendre à bien lire* (Quebec, 1847), *Nouvel alphabet, ou Lectures graduées* (Quebec, 1858), and *Ode à mon âme* (Quebec, 1874).

[P. G. Roy, *Fils de Québec*, vol. 3 (Lévis, Que., 1933); *Bull. rech. hist.*, 1942.]

Kaiser, Thomas Erlin (1863-1940), physician, politician, and author, was born near Weston, Canada West, in 1863. He was educated at the University of Toronto (M.D., 1890), and he practised medicine in Oshawa, Ontario. He represented Ontario county in the Canadian House of Commons from 1925 to 1930. He was the author of *Historic sketches of Oshawa* (Oshawa, Ont., 1921); and he edited *A history of the medical profession of the county of Ontario* (Oshawa, Ont., 1934).

[*Can. who's who*, 1936-37; *Can. parl. comp.*]

Kalm, Peter (1716-1779), botanist and author, was born in Sweden in 1716, and was educated at the universities of Abo and Upsala. He became a botanist of some distinction, and was a friend of Linnaeus. In 1748 he was sent by the Swedish government to North America, to make investigations into the natural history of the New World. He remained in North America for three years, and part of this time was spent in Canada. He was the first really scientific observer of natural phenomena in Canada. On his return to Sweden, he became professor of botany in the University of Abo; and he died in 1779. He was the author of a number of scientific works; and he wrote an account of his *Travels into North America*, which was translated into English by John Reinhold Forster (3 vols., London, 1770; 2nd ed., 2 vols., 1772).

[Martti Kerkkonen, *Peter Kalm's North American Journey* (Helsinki, 1959); *Cyc. Am. biog.*; Le Jeune, *Dict. gén.*]

Kane, Jack (1924-1962), musician and conductor, was born in England in 1924 and came to Canada at the age of six. He began studying the clarinet at an early age and by the time he was fifteen was playing with a cabaret orchestra. He joined the Canadian Army in 1942 and on discharge became a student at the Royal Conservatory of Music of Toronto. On graduation he began conducting for the Canadian Broadcasting Corporation in 1949. He became conductor-arranger for CBC television in 1952. He continued with his "big band" programs until his death at Toronto, Ontario, March 22, 1962.

[Metropolitan Toronto Library Board, *Biographical scrapbooks*, vol. 18.]

Kane, Paul (1810-1871), painter, was born in Mallow, county Cork, Ireland, on September 3, 1810, the son of Michael Kane, a discharged soldier. He came to Canada with his family in 1818 or 1819, and settled in York (Toronto), where his father opened a wine and spirit shop. He was educated at the Home District Grammar School, and was for a time employed in a furniture factory. In 1836 he went to the United States, and in 1841 to France and Italy, as an art student. He returned to Canada in 1845, and devoted himself to depicting the life of the Indians of the North West. He travelled many thousands of miles in canoe, on horseback, or on snowshoe, in order to study his subject; and the result was a series of pictures which had both artistic and historical value. Most of his pictures are now in the Royal Ontario Museum at Toronto or in the Parliament Buildings at Ottawa. He published an account of his travels in the North West under the title *Wanderings of an artist among the Indians of North America* (London, 1859). He died at Toronto, Ontario, on February 20, 1871.

[A. H. Robson, *Paul Kane* (Toronto, 1938); L. J. Burpee (ed.), *Paul Kane's wanderings* (Toronto, 1925); Sir D. Wilson, *Paul Kane* (Canadian journal, 1871); E. Morris, *Art in Canada: The early painters* (Toronto, 1911); N. MacTavish, *The fine arts in Canada* (Toronto, 1925); Morgan, *Cel. Can.*; N. F. Davin, *The Irishman in Canada* (Toronto, 1877); *Dict. Can. biog.*, vol. 10.]

Karr, William John (d. 1938), educationist, was a school-teacher on the staff of the Normal School, Ottawa, Ontario, who became director of professional training in the Normal schools of the province of Ontario. He died at Toronto, Ontario, on December 18, 1938. He was the author of *Explorers, soldiers, and statesmen: A history of Canada through biography* (Toronto, 1939).

[*Can. who's who*, 1936-37.]

Kasahara, Yoshiko (1912-1966), sociologist and statistician, was born in Tokyo on

March 25, 1912. She was educated at Tsuda Women's College, and in 1950 received a scholarship to the University of Texas, where she received an M.A. degree. She continued her studies at the University of Michigan, receiving an M.A. in mathematics and a Ph.D. in sociology (1958). Dr. Kasahara joined the census division of the Dominion Bureau of Statistics in 1956, specializing in demographic research. She died at Ottawa on December 6, 1966. Among her papers and articles are "Mobility of Canada's population, 1956-1961" in *Canada Year Book* (1966); "Population trends in Canada", *Canadian journal of public health* (1966); "Population projection for Canada, 1963-1970", *Economic council of Canada* (Ottawa, 1966), and many others.

[*Can. journ. ec. pol. sc.*, vol. XXXIII.]

Kay, William Frederic (1876-1942), politician, was born at Montreal, Quebec, on May 18, 1876; and was educated at McGill University (B.C.L., 1901). He became a farmer at Sweetsburg, Quebec; and he represented Brome-Missisquoi in the Canadian House of Commons from 1911 to 1930. In June, 1930, he was sworn in as a minister without portfolio in the Mackenzie King government; but he was defeated in the general elections later in 1930, and he then retired to private life. He died at Sweetsburg, Quebec, on May 8, 1942.

[*Can. parl. comp.*; *Can. who's who*, 1936-37.]

Kean, Abram (1855-1945), master mariner, was born at Flowers Island, Bonavista Bay, Newfoundland, on July 8, 1855, and died at St. John's on May 18, 1945. For nearly fifty years he commanded ships in the seal fishery; and he is said to have brought in more than a million seals. A vast amount of information regarding the seal and other fisheries is to be found in his autobiography, *Old and young ahead: A millionaire in seals* (London, 1935).

[*Encyc. Can.*; *Newfoundland supp.*]

Keats, Sir Richard Goodwin (1757-1834), governor of Newfoundland (1813-16), was born at Chalton, Hampshire, England, on January 16, 1757, and died at Greenwich, England, on April 5, 1834. He entered the Royal Navy in 1770, and rose to the rank of admiral in 1825. During his period of office as governor of Newfoundland, from 1813 to 1816, the first grants were made of land for agricultural purposes. He was created a K.B. in 1808.

[*Dict. nat. biog.*; *Encyc. Can.*; *Newfoundland supp.*]

Keefer, George (1773-1858), loyalist and pioneer, was born at Pepper Cotton Creek, near Newton, New Jersey, in 1773; and he came to Canada with his widowed mother in 1792. He settled in the Niagara peninsula, and was the founder of the town of Thorold. During the War of 1812 he served as an officer in the Lincoln militia. Later, he joined with William Hamilton Merritt (q.v.) in promoting the Welland Canal, and he was the first president of the Welland Canal Company. He died at Thorold, Canada West, on June 26, 1858. He was twice married, (1) to Catherine, daughter of Peter Lampman, and (2) to Jane, daughter of Edward McBride.

[Rose, *Cyc. Can. biog.* (1886); Morgan, *Cel. Can.*]

Keefer, George Alexander (1836-1912), civil engineer, was born at Cornwall, Upper Canada, on September 10, 1836, the son of George Keefer, Jr., and the nephew of Thomas Coltrin Keefer (q.v.). He was educated at Upper Canada College, Toronto, and became a civil engineer. He was employed on the surveys for the Grand Trunk Railway in Ontario and on the surveys for the Canadian Pacific Railway in the Rockies. In 1900 he became resident engineer for the Canadian government in British Columbia; and he died at Victoria, British Columbia, on May 17, 1912.

[Morgan, *Can. men* (1912).]

Keefer, Samuel (1811-1890), civil engineer, was born at Thorold, Upper Canada, on January 20, 1811, the fourth son of George Keefer (q.v.), a Loyalist, and his first wife, Catherine, daughter of Peter Lampman. In 1841 he was appointed chief engineer to the department of public works in Canada, and he held this position until 1853. Later he became government inspector of railways and deputy commissioner of public works; and in this latter capacity he prepared the plans for the erection of the Parliament Building at Ottawa. In 1864 he retired to private practice, and in 1869 he achieved much fame on account of his construction of the suspension bridge across the Niagara River. He died at Brockville, Ontario, on January 7, 1890. He was twice married, (1) to Anne (d. 1876), daughter of the Hon. George Crawford, a senator of Canada, and (2) in 1883 to Rosalie, eldest daughter of Captain C. A. B. Pocock, R. N., of Brockville.

[Rose, *Cyc. Can. biog.* (1886); *Cyc. Am. biog.*; R. Keefer, *Memoirs of the Keefer family* (Norwood, Ont., 1935).]

Keefer, Thomas Coltrin (1821-1915), civil engineer, was born at Thorold, Upper Canada, on November 4, 1821, the son of George Keefer (q.v.), a Loyalist, and his second wife, Jane, daughter of Edward McBride. He was educated at Upper Canada College, Toronto, and became a civil engineer. He was employed on the Erie and Welland canals and on the Ottawa and St. Lawrence river works; and he became one of the leading hydraulic engineers of the continent. He died at Ottawa on January 7, 1915. He was twice married, (1) in 1848 to Elizabeth (d. 1870), daughter of the Hon.

Thomas McKay, and (2) to her sister Annie (d. 1906), widow of John McKinnon, of Ottawa. In 1891 he was elected a member of the Royal Society of Canada, and in 1898 he was its president. In 1905 he was made an LL.D. of McGill University. He was the author of *The philosophy of railways* (Montreal, 1849, new ed. 1972), *The influence of the canals of Canada on her agriculture* (Toronto, 1850), and numerous technical reports.

[*Proc. Roy. Soc. Can.*, 1915; Morgan, *Can. men* (1912); Rose, *Cyc. Can. biog.* (1886); R. Keefer, *Memoirs of the Keefer family* (Norwood, Ont., 1935).]

Keele, William Conway (1798-1872), legal author, was born in England on February 2, 1798, and emigrated to Canada prior to 1835. He settled near Toronto, at what afterwards came to be known as Toronto Junction; and he practised law in Toronto. He died on July 11, 1872. He was the author of *The provincial justice, or magistrate's manual* (Toronto, 1835; 5th ed., 1864), *The district law manual* (Toronto, 1844), and *A brief view of the laws of Upper Canada* (Toronto, 1844).

[Morgan, *Bib. can.*; private information.]

Keen, George (1869-1953), journalist, was born at Stoke-on-Trent, England, on May 8, 1869, and died at Brantford, Ontario, on December 4, 1953. He came to Canada in 1904, and soon became interested in the co-operative movement. In 1908 he organized the Co-operative Union of Canada, of which he was general secretary for many years; and he was editor of the *Canadian Co-operator* from 1909 until it ceased publication in 1947. He was the author of *The birth of a movement: Reminiscences of a co-operator* (n.p., 1950). Shortly before his death, St. Francis Xavier University conferred on him the honorary degree of LL.D.

[Toronto *Globe and Mail*, Dec. 5, 1953; *Encyc. Can.*]

Keith, George (d. 1859), fur-trader, was a native of Scotland who entered the service of the North West Company between 1799 and 1806, when he appears as a clerk in the Athabaska department. From 1806 to 1815 he was in the Mackenzie River department; and in 1813 he was made a partner of the North West Company. From 1817 to 1821 he was in charge of the Athabaska department; and at the union of 1821 he was made a chief factor of the Hudson's Bay Company. For several years after 1821 he was in charge of the English River department. He went on furlough to England, with his brother James (q.v.), in 1843; and he retired from the service of the Hudson's Bay Company in 1845. He died in Aberdeen, Scotland, on January 22, 1859.

[E. E. Rich (ed.), *Journal of occurrences in the Athabasca department, by George Simpson* (Toronto: The Champlain Society, 1938).]

Keith, James (1784-1851), fur-trader, was a younger brother of George Keith (q.v.), and was born in Scotland in 1784. He entered the service of the North West Company about the beginning of the nineteenth century; and became a partner in 1814. From 1813 to 1816 he was on the Columbia. In 1821 he was made a chief factor of the Hudson's Bay Company, and was placed in charge of the English River department. Later he was transferred to Fort Chipewyan. In 1826 he was placed in charge of the Montreal department, with headquarters at Lachine; and here he remained until 1843. He was then granted furlough, returned to Scotland, and retired from the service of the Hudson's Bay Company in 1845. He died in Aberdeen, Scotland, on January 27, 1851. He was a brother-in-law of Sir George Simpson (q.v.), having married a sister of Lady Simpson.

[E. E. Rich (ed.), *Journal of occurrences in the Athabasca department, by George Simpson* (Toronto: The Champlain Society, 1938).]

Kelly, Edward (1875-1937), priest, was born on May 31, 1875, and was ordained a priest of the Roman Catholic Church in 1905. He died at Toronto, Ontario, on September 6, 1937. He was the author of *The story of St. Paul's parish, Toronto* (Toronto, 1923).

[Private information.]

Kelly, John David (1861-1958), artist, was born at Gore's Landing, Rice Lake, Canada West, in 1861, and died at Toronto, Ontario, on December 28, 1958. He received his training at the old Ontario School of Art in Toronto; and after a year with the Grip Publishing Company, entered the service of the Stone Lithographing Company (later Rolph, Clark, Stone Ltd.) as a commercial artist. He remained with this firm for over seventy years, and became famous for the Canadian historical scenes with which he illustrated the firm's calendars.

[Toronto *Globe and Mail*, Dec. 29, 1958.]

Kelly, John Hall (1879-1941), Canadian high commissioner to Eire (1939-41), was born at St. Godefroy, Quebec, on September 1, 1879. He was educated at St. Joseph's College, Westmoreland, New Brunswick (B.A., 1900; M.A., 1925) and at Laval University (LL.L., 1903; LL.D., 1933). He was called to the Quebec bar in 1903; and he represented Bonaventure in the Legislative Assembly of Quebec from 1904 to 1914. In 1914 he was appointed a member of the Legislative Council of Quebec; and in 1939 he was appointed by the Dominion government Canadian high commissioner to Eire. He died at Dublin, Ireland, on March 10, 1941.

[*Can. who's who*, 1938-39; *Can. parl. comp.*]

Kelly, Leroy Victor (1880-1956), journalist and author, was born in 1880, and died at Vancouver, British Columbia, on January 6, 1956. After homesteading for several years in Alberta, he became a journalist. From 1905 to 1910 he was on the staff of the Calgary *Herald*, and from 1915 to 1949 he was marine editor of the Vancouver *Daily Province*. He was the author of *The range men* (Toronto, 1913).

[B. B. Peel (comp.), *A bibliography of the prairie provinces* (Toronto, 1956).]

Kelly, Michael Vincent (1863-1942), priest, was born in Adjala township, Simcoe county, Canada West, in 1863; and was educated at St.Michael's College and the University of Toronto (B.A., 1887). He joined the congregation of St. Basil, and was ordained a priest of the Roman Catholic Church in 1891. He served in a number of parishes in Ontario, and finally in a parish in Detroit, Michigan. He died at Toronto, Ontario, on July 24, 1942. He compiled *The frequent communicant's prayer-book* (Chicago, 1931).

[*Guide to Catholic literature* (Detroit, Mich., 1940).]

Kelsey, Henry (c. 1667-1724), explorer, was a native of London, England, who was apprenticed to the Hudson's Bay Company about 1684. During 1690-92 he made an expedition into the interior from Hudson Bay, which brought him to the plains of northern Saskatchewan; and he was probably the first white man in America to see the bison and the grizzly bear. He became in 1717 governor of York Factory; and he died in 1724.

[J. F. Kenney, *The career of Henry Kelsey* (Trans. Roy. Soc. Can., 1929); C. N. Bell (ed.), *The journal of Henry Kelsey* (Hist. and Sci. Soc. of Manitoba, trans. no. 4, new series, 1928); C. Martin and A. G. Doughty (eds.), *The Kelsey papers* (Ottawa, 1929); J. W. Whillans, *First in the West: The story of Henry Kelsey* (Edmonton, 1955); *Dict. Can. biog.*, vol. 2.]

Kemble, William (1781-1845), journalist, was born in England in 1781. From 1823 to 1842 he was editor of the *Quebec Mercury*; and he died at Quebec on February 25, 1845.

[Morgan, *Cel. Can.*; *Bull. rech. hist.*, 1936.]

Kemp, Sir Albert Edward (1858-1929), manufacturer and politician, was born at Clarenceville, Quebec, on August 11, 1858. Beginning life as a book-keeper, he became one of the leading manufacturers in Canada, as president of the Kemp Manufacturing Co. of Toronto, makers of sheet-metal wares; and he was president of the Canadian Manufacturers' Association in 1895-97. In 1900 he was elected Conservative member for East Toronto, in the Canadian House of Commons; and he continued to represent this constituency continuously, except for the years 1908-11, until 1921. In 1911 he became a minister without portfolio in the Borden government; and during the First World War he played an increasingly important part in the government of Canada. In 1915 he was appointed chairman of the War Purchasing Commission; in 1916, he succeeded Sir Sam Hughes (q.v.) as minister of militia and defence; and in 1917 he went to London as minister of the overseas military forces, a portfolio which he retained until the demobilization of the Canadian overseas forces was completed. In 1918 he was a member of the Imperial War Cabinet; and in 1919 he was one of the commissioners and plenipotentiaries representing Canada at the Peace Conference in Paris. In the formation of the Meighen government in 1920, he took office, but without portfolio; and in 1921 he was called to the Senate of Canada. In 1927 he retired from business, and he died at Pigeon Lake, Ontario, on August 12, 1929. In 1917 he was created, in recognition of his war services, a K.C.M.G. He was twice married; first, in 1879, to Miss Wilson (d. 1924), by whom he had three daughters; and second, in 1925, to Mrs. Norman Copping, by whom he had one daughter.

[*Can. who was who*, vol. 1; *Can. parl. comp.*; H. Charlesworth (ed.), *A cyclopaedia of Canadian biography* (Toronto, 1919); Morgan, *Can. men* (1912).]

Kemp, Alexander Ferrie (1822-1884), clergyman and author, was born in Greenock, Scotland, in 1822. He was educated at Edinburgh University and at the Presbyterian College, London; and having been ordained to the ministry, became chaplain to the 26th Cameronian Regiment, then stationed in Bermuda. In 1855 he was invited to become the pastor of St. Gabriel Street Church, Montreal; and he remained in this charge until 1865. He was subsequently a professor in Olivet College, Michigan, and in Knox College, Galesburg; and in his later years he was principal of ladies' colleges in Brantford and in Ottawa. He died on May 4, 1884. With the Rev. Donald Fraser (q.v.), he was editor of the *Canadian Presbyter* (Montreal, 1857-58); and he was the author of a *Digest of the minutes of the Synod of the Presbyterian Church of Canada* (Montreal, 1861), and *Rules and forms of procedure in the church courts* (Montreal, 1865), as well as of a number of contributions to the *Canadian Naturalist*.

[*Dom. ann. reg.*, 1884.]

Kempt, Sir James (1764-1854), administrator of the government of Canada (1828-30), was born in 1764, the son of Gavin Kempt, of Botley Hill, Southampton, and of Edinburgh. In 1783 he was gazetted an ensign in the 101st Foot; and he rose in rank until he became a general in 1841. He served throughout the Revolutionary and Napoleonic wars, except for the years 1807-11, when he was quartermaster-general in North America; and he commanded a division at Waterloo. In 1819 he was appointed governor of Portsmouth; and in 1820 he was sent out to America as lieutenant-governor of Nova Scotia. He governed this province, with intervals of leave of absence, until 1828; and he then became administrator of the government of Canada until 1830. He died in London, England, on December 20, 1854. He was created a G.C.B. in 1815, a G.C.H. in 1816, and a privy councillor in 1830.

[*Dict. nat. biog.*; Le Jeune, *Dict. gén.*]

Kendall, Henry Ernest (1864-1949), lieutenant-governor of Nova Scotia (1942-47), was born in Sydney, Nova Scotia, on April 29, 1864, and died at Windsor, Nova Scotia, on September 2, 1949. He was educated at Mount Allison University (B.A., 1884) and McGill University (M.D., 1887), and for many years practised medicine in Sydney. During the First World War he served, with the rank of lieutenant-colonel, in the C.A.M.C.; and after the war he became a highly successful farmer at Windsor, Nova Scotia. In 1942 he was appointed lieutenant-governor of Nova Scotia, but retired in 1947 because of ill health.

[*Can. who's who*, 1948; *Can. parl. guide*, 1945; *Encyc. Can.*]

Kenderdine, Augustus Frederick La Fosse (1870-1947), painter, was born near Blackpool, England, in 1870, and died at Saskatoon, Saskatchewan, on August 3, 1947. He studied art at the Manchester School of Art and the Julien Academy in Paris. About 1907 he came to Canada, and for twelve years he farmed in northern Saskatchewan. About 1920, however, he resumed painting, and he became a well-known painter of western landscapes. From 1934 to 1947 he was director of the department of fine arts at the University of Saskatchewan. One of his landscapes is in the National Gallery at Ottawa.

[*Encyc. Can.*]

Kennedy, Alexander (1781?-1832), fur-trader, was born in the Orkney Islands about 1781. He entered the service of the Hudson's Bay Company in 1798 as a writer. He was employed at various posts in the Hudson's Bay Company's territories during the following years; and from 1813 to 1819 he was in charge of Cumberland House. On the union of the Hudson's Bay and North West companies in 1821, he was made a chief factor; and from 1822 to 1825 he was employed in the Columbia River district. He retired in 1829; and he died at London, England, on June 6, 1832.

[E. E. Rich (ed.), *Colin Robertson's correspondence book* (Toronto: The Champlain Society, 1939).]

Kennedy, Sir Arthur Edward (1810-1883), governor of Vancouver Island (1863-67), was born on April 9, 1810, the fourth son of Hugh Kennedy, of Cultra, county Down, Ireland. He was educated at Trinity College, Dublin. He entered the army in 1827 as an ensign in the 27th Foot, and retired from the army in 1848. In 1851 he was appointed governor of Gambia, and in 1852 governor of Sierra Leone. From 1854 to 1862 he was governor of Western Australia; and in 1863 he was appointed governor of Vancouver Island. He administered the government of the island until 1867; and in 1868 he was knighted. Subsequently he was governor, successively, of Hong Kong (1872-77) and of Queensland (1877-83). He died on board ship off Aden in the Red Sea on June 13, 1883. In 1839 he married Georgina Mildred, daughter of Joseph Macartney, of St. Helen's, county Dublin, Ireland; and by her he had one son and two daughters.

[*Dict. nat. biog.*; E. O. S. Scholefield and F. W. Howay, *British Columbia* (4 vols., Vancouver, B.C., 1914); *Dom. ann. reg.*, 1883.]

Kennedy, David (1828-1903), pioneer, was born in Ayrshire, Scotland, on April 20, 1828, and died at Tara, Ontario, on July 31, 1903. He was the author of *Incidents of pioneer days at Guelph and the county of Bruce* (Toronto, 1903).

[N. Robertson, *The history of the county of Bruce* (Toronto, 1906).]

Kennedy, Henry Dawson (1869-1925), evangelist, was born in 1869, and became an evangelist. He conducted evangelical campaigns in both Canada and the United States; and he died at Peterborough, Ontario, on October 9, 1925. He was the author of *Misunderstood* (Toronto, 1903) and *Does God care?* (New York, 1927).

[*New York Times*, Oct. 15, 1925.]

Kennedy, Howard Angus (1861-1938), journalist and author, was born in London, England, on December 27, 1861. He was educated at the City of London School, and emigrated to Canada in 1881. He was on the staff of the Montreal *Daily Witness* from 1881 to 1890; and was the war correspondent of this newspaper during the North West Rebellion. He returned to England in 1890, and from 1891 to 1910 he was the editor of *The Times Weekly*; but he returned to Canada in 1912; and during the remainder of his life was a free-lance journalist. In 1929 he was elected national secretary of the Canadian Authors' Association; and he occupied this position until his death at Montreal, Quebec, on February 15, 1938. He was the author of *Professor Blackie, his sayings and doings* (London, 1895), *The story of Canada* (London, 1897), *Old highland days* (London, 1901), *The new world fairy book* (London, 1904), *New Canada* and the new Canadians (London, 1907), *The book of the west* (Toronto, 1925), *Unsought adventure* (New York, 1929), and *The red man's wonder book* (New York, 1931).

[*Can. who's who*, 1936-37.]

Kennedy, Sir John (1838-1921), engineer, was born at Spencerville, Upper Canada, in 1838, the son of William Kennedy. He was educated at McGill University, and began his career as civil engineer under T. C. Keefer (q.v.). From 1871 to 1875 he was chief engineer of the Great Western Railway; and from 1875 to 1907 he was chief engineer of the Montreal Harbour Commission. He then became a consulting engineer; and he died at Montreal on October 25, 1921. He was created a knight bachelor in 1916.

[*Who was who*, 1916-28; *Can. who was who*, vol. 1; Morgan, *Can. men* (1912).]

Kennedy, Roderick Stuart (1889-1953), journalist and author, was born in Montreal, Quebec, on December 16, 1889, the son of Howard Angus Kennedy (q.v.), and died at Montreal on May 18, 1953. He was educated at Macdonald College (B.S.A., 1912); but, after farming for a year or two in Alberta, he served in the First World War, and on his return to Canada became a journalist. From 1922 to 1939 he was advertising manager of the *Montreal Star*; and from 1939 to 1953 he was editor-in-chief of the *Family Herald and Weekly Star*. He was the author of a novel, *The road south* (Toronto, 1947).

[*Can. who's who*, 1949-51.]

Kennedy, Thomas Laird (1878-1959), prime minister of Ontario (1948-49), was born at Dixie, Ontario (near Toronto), on August 15, 1878, and died there on February 13, 1959. He became a farmer, and represented the rural constituency of Peel in the Ontario legislature from 1919 to 1934 and from 1937 to 1958. He was minister of agriculture from 1930 to 1934 in the Henry administration, and from 1943 to 1948 in the Drew administration. In 1948 he became prime minister of Ontario, but resigned in 1949, though he continued as minister of agriculture in the Frost administration until 1952. He retired from politics in 1958. He served overseas during the First World War with the rank of colonel; and he rose in the militia to the rank of brigadier-general.

[*Can. who's who*, 1952-54; *Can. parl. guide*, 1957; *Encyc. Can.*]

Kennedy, William (1814-1890), explorer, was born at Cumberland House in 1814, the half-breed son of Chief Factor Alexander Kennedy (q.v.) of the Hudson's Bay Company. He became a clerk in the Hudson's Bay Company; and in 1851 was sent out in command of the *Prince Albert* to search for Sir John Franklin (q.v.). He published an account of his experiences in *A short narrative of the second voyage*

of the *Prince Albert, in search of Sir John Franklin* (London, 1853). He spent the later years of his life in the Red River Settlement; he died in 1890.

[*Encyc. Can.*]

Kennedy, William Costello (1868-1923), minister of railways and canals for Canada (1921-23), was born at Ottawa, Ontario, on August 27, 1868, the son of William Kennedy and Julia Costello. He was educated in the separate schools of Toronto, and became a clerk in a loan company in Toronto. In 1897 he removed to Windsor, Ontario, and from 1903 to 1917 he was president of the Windsor Gas Company. In 1917 he was elected member of the Canadian House of Commons for North Essex as an anti-conscriptionist Liberal; and in 1921 he became minister of railways and canals in the Mackenzie King government. Under him was carried out the consolidation of the component elements of the Canadian National Railways; and his administration gave great promise. It was cut short, however, by his death in Florida, U.S.A., on January 18, 1923. He married in 1907 Glencora, daughter of George W. Bolton of Detroit, Michigan.

[H. Charlesworth (ed.), *A cyclopaedia of Canadian biography* (Toronto, 1919); *Can. parl. comp.*]

Kennedy, William Paul McClure (1879-1963), historian and jurist, was born January 8, 1879, in Shankill, county Dublin, Ireland. He was educated at Trinity College, Dublin, where he achieved first-class honours and the university gold medal in 1900. In 1913 he came to Canada and taught English at St. Francis Xavier University and in 1915 joined the faculty of the University of Toronto as lecturer in English and history. In 1922 he was appointed a special lecturer in federal constitutional law in the department of political economy; in 1926 he became professor of law and political institutions. Under his direction a department of law was established at the University of Toronto in 1930, which developed into a School of Law in 1941 and a Faculty of Law three years later. Dr. Kennedy was founder-editor of the *University of Toronto Law Journal*; and in his articles and books he exerted a lasting influence on the study of constitutional and public law. He wrote *The life of Archbishop Parker* (London, 1908); *The interpretations of the Bishops and their influence on Elizabethan episcopal policy* (London, 1908); *Visitation articles and injunctions of the period of the Reformation, 1535-1575* (3 vols., London, 1910); *Parish life under Queen Elizabeth* (London, 1916); *Documents of the Canadian constitution — 1759-1915* (Toronto, 1918); *Constitution of Canada* (London, 1922); *Lord Elgin* (Toronto, 1926); *Some aspects of the theories and workings of constitutional law* (New York, 1932); *Reports on the law of Quebec, 1767-1770* (with G. Lanctot, Ottawa,

1931); *The law of the taxing power in Canada* (with D.C. Wells, Toronto, 1931); *The right to trade* (with J. Finkleman, Toronto, 1933); *The law and custom of the South African constitution* (with H. J. Schlosberg and H. J. H. Joshua, London, 1935); *Essays on constitutional law* (London, 1934). He died at Toronto, Ontario, August 12, 1963.

[*Proc. Roy. Can. Soc.*, 1964.]

Kenney, James Francis (1884-1946), archivist and historian, was born at Marysville, Ontario, on December 6, 1884, and died at Ottawa, Ontario, on June 4, 1946. He was educated at the University of Toronto (B.A., 1907), the University of Wisconsin (M.A., 1908), and Columbia University (Ph.D., 1910); and in 1912 he joined the staff of the Public Archives of Canada at Ottawa. There he became director of historical research, and for a short time, acting archivist. He was the compiler of *The catalogue of pictures . . . in the Public Archives of Canada* (Ottawa, 1925); and he edited *The sources of the early history of Ireland* (New York, 1929) and *The founding of Churchill: Being the journal of Captain James Knight* (Toronto, 1932). He was elected a fellow of the Royal Society of Canada in 1934; and the University of Ottawa and the National University of Ireland conferred on him honorary degrees.

[*Proc. Roy. Soc. Can.*, 1946; *Can. who's who*, 1938-39.]

Kenny, Sir Edward (1800-1891), receiver-general of Canada (1867-69), was born in Kerry county, Ireland, in July, 1800. He came to Halifax, Nova Scotia, in 1824, and entered the service of a firm of wholesale dry-goods merchants. In 1828 he and his brother established the firm of T. and E. Kenny. In 1841 he was appointed a member of the Legislative Council of Nova Scotia, and from 1856 to 1867 he was president of that body. In 1867 he was called to the Senate of Canada, and at the same time he was appointed receiver-general in the first government of the Dominion of Canada. His appointment was largely due to the fact that he combined the qualifications of coming, like Charles Tupper (q.v.), from Nova Scotia, and of being, like D'Arcy McGee (q.v.), an Irish Roman Catholic. There being no room for both Tupper and McGee in the cabinet, they both stood aside in favour of Kenny. In 1869 he exchanged his portfolio for that of president of the council; and in 1870 he resigned from the cabinet to accept appointment as administrator of the government of Nova Scotia. He was administrator of the province for a few months, and was then created a knight bachelor. In 1876 he vacated his seat in the Canadian Senate, having been absent from parliament during two consecutive sessions; and he died at Halifax, Nova Scotia, on May 16, 1891. In 1832 he married Anne, daughter of Michael Forrestell, and by her he had several children.

[*Cyc. Am. biog.*; *Can. parl. comp.*; Rose, *Cyc. Can. biog.* (1888); Sir J. G. Bourinot, *Builders of Nova Scotia* (Trans. Roy. Soc. Can., 1899); Sir C. Tupper, *Recollections of sixty years in Canada* (London, 1914).]

Kent, John (1805-1872), prime minister of Newfoundland (1858-61), was born at Waterford, Ireland, in 1805, and died at St. John's, Newfoundland, in 1872. He settled in Newfoundland in 1820; and took a leading part in the struggle for representative institutions and responsible government. He was elected to the House of Assembly in 1832 to represent St. John's as a Liberal, and he played a prominent part in politics until his retirement in 1869. He was prime minister from 1858 to 1861, when he was dismissed from office by the governor.

[*Encyc. Can.*; *Newfoundland supp.*; *Dict. Can. biog.*, vol. 10.]

Kent, John (*fl.* 1807-1888), schoolmaster and journalist, was born in England in 1807, and came to Canada in 1833, as headmaster of the preparatory school of Upper Canada College. Shortly after his arrival he became the editor of the *Canadian Literary Magazine* (York [Toronto], U.C.), of which only three numbers appear to have been published. He resigned his post in Upper Canada College in 1838; and, after acting for a short time as secretary to Sir George Arthur (q.v.), he became in 1840 editor of the *Church*. He wrote under the pen-name of "Alan Fairford". In 1843 he returned to England, and became tutor and later the secretary of the fourth Earl of Carnarvon. He spent his later years in Madeira and the Azores; and he died some time after 1888.

[A. H. Young, *John Kent* (pamphlet, Toronto, 1927); W. S. Wallace, *The periodical literature of Upper Canada* (Can. hist. rev., 1931); Sir A. H. Hardinge, *The life of Henry Howard Molyneux Herbert, fourth Earl of Carnarvon* (3 vols., Oxford, 1925); H. Scadding, *Some Canadian nom-de-plumes identified* (Toronto, 1877); A. H. Young, *The roll of pupils of Upper Canada College, Toronto* (Kingston, Ont., 1917).]

Kent and Strathern, Edward Augustus, Duke of (1767-1820), soldier, was born at Buckingham Palace, London, England, on November 2, 1767, the fourth son of King George III and Queen Charlotte. He was educated in Germany and in Switzerland; and in 1790 he was placed in command of the 7th Regiment of Foot (Royal Fusiliers) at Gibraltar. In 1791 he was sent with his regiment to Canada, and was stationed for two years at Quebec. In 1792 he visited Lieut.-Col. Simcoe (q.v.) at Niagara. In 1793 he was promoted to be a major-general, and was sent at his own request to the West Indies, where he saw active service under Sir Charles (afterwards Lord) Grey, in command of a brigade of grenadiers, in the reduction of Martinique and St. Lucia. At the close of the operations, he returned to Canada, and in 1796 was promoted to be lieutenant-general. In 1798 he was invalided to England, as the result of a fall from his horse; and in 1799 he was raised to the peerage as Duke of Kent and Strathern and Earl of Dublin. At the same time he was raised to the rank of general, and was appointed commander-in-chief of the forces in British North America. This appointment, however, he retained for only a little over a year, when ill-health once more compelled him to return to England. During his years in Canada he established especially friendly relations with the French Canadians, and especially with the Salaberry family, with whom he kept up a correspondence for the rest of his life. In 1802 he was appointed governor of Gibraltar; but his rigid discipline caused a mutiny, and he was recalled to England. Though he was gazetted a field-marshal in 1805, he was never again actively employed in the army. He died at Sidmouth, England, on January 23, 1820. In 1818 he married, for reasons of state, Victoria Mary Louisa, widow of Emich Charles, prince of Leiningen; and by her he had one child, afterwards Queen Victoria. During his stay in Canada he was accompanied by a Madame de St-Laurent, with whom he was said to have contracted a morganatic marriage. In 1799 the Island of St. John was re-named Prince Edward Island in his honour.

[E. Neale, *The life of his Royal Highness, Edward, Duke of Kent* (London, 1850); W. J. Anderson, *The life of F.M., H.R.H. Edward Duke of Kent* (Toronto, 1870); *Dict. nat. biog.*; Le Jeune, *Dict. gén.*; P. G. Roy, *Les petites choses de notre histoire* (6 vols., Lévis, Que., 1919-31); M. Porter, *Overture to Victoria* (Toronto, 1961).]

Keough, William James (1913-1971), legislator, was born in St. John's, Newfoundland, October 30, 1913. He was educated at St. Patrick's Hall School and at St. Bonaventure's College. He was an editor of the *Labour Herald* and a Co-op fieldworker and auditor. He was elected a member of the National Convention for St. George's in 1946 and was appointed minister of natural resources in the Smallwood interim government. He was elected to the first provincial legislature for St. George's in 1949 and became minister of fisheries and co-operatives. He was a delegate to the conference with Britain on Newfoundland's future in 1947 and a member of the Newfoundland delegation to the Dominion-Provincial Conference at Ottawa in January, 1950, and at Quebec in September, 1950. He became minister of mines and resources in 1956, of mines, agriculture and resources in 1961, and of labour in 1967. He died at St. John's, Newfoundland, March 2, 1971.

[*Can. who's who*, 1967-69.]

Kerby, George W. (1860-1944), clergyman and educationist, was born in Lambton county, Canada West, on July 18, 1860. He was educated at Victoria University, Cobourg (B.A., 1888), and was ordained in 1888 a minister of the Methodist Church. He was the pastor of churches in Woodstock, Hamilton, St. Catharines, Brantford, Montreal, and Calgary; and from 1910 to 1942 he was principal of Mount Royal College, Calgary. He died at Calgary, Alberta, on February 9, 1944. He was the author of *The broken trail* (Toronto, 1909).

[*Canadian author and bookman*, 1944; *Can. who's who*, 1936-37; Morgan, *Can. men* (1912).]

Kernighan, Robert Kirkland (1857-1926), poet and journalist, was born at Rushdale Farm, near Hamilton, Ontario, on April 25, 1857, the son of Andrew Kernighan and Jane Kirkland. He was educated in the common schools, and as a young man he served an apprenticeship in journalism on the staff of the Hamilton *Spectator*. Later he was for a time editor of the *Winnipeg Sun*. But most of his life he spent at "The Wigwam", the log-cabin which his grandfather had built on the land granted to him by the Crown. From this retreat he contributed for many years both prose and verse to Toronto newspapers, and especially to the *Evening Telegram*, under the nom-de-plume of "The Khan". He published *The Tattleton papers* (Hamilton, 1894), *The Khan's canticles* (Hamilton, 1896), and *The Khan's book of verse* (Toronto, 1925). Two of his most famous verses, which were set to music, were "The Men of the Northern Zone" and "When Daddy Comes Home with his Wages". He died at Rushdale Farm, Rockton, Ontario, on November 3, 1926. He was not married.

[Morgan, *Can. men* (1912).]

Kerr, James (1765?-1846), executive and legislative councillor of Lower Canada, was born at Leith, Scotland, about 1765; was educated at the University of Glasgow; and was called to the English bar in 1785. In 1793 he came to Canada, and began the practice of law in Quebec; and in 1797 he was appointed a judge of the Vice-Admiralty Court of Quebec. In 1807 he was appointed a judge of the Court of King's Bench; from 1812 to 1831 he was a member of the Executive Council of Lower Canada; from 1821 to 1838 he was a member of the Legislative Council of Lower Canada; and from 1827 to 1831 he was president of the Legislative Council. In 1834 he was removed from the bench by Lord Aylmer (q.v.), as the result of charges made against him in the House of Assembly; and he died at Quebec on May 5, 1846.

[P. G. Roy, *Les juges de la province de Québec* (Quebec, 1933); Morgan, *Cel. Can.*]

Kerr, James Kirkpatrick (1841-1916), speaker of the Senate of Canada (1909-11), was born near Guelph, Upper Canada, on August 1, 1841, the eldest son of Robert Warren

Kerr and Jane Hamilton Kirkpatrick. He was educated at the Galt Grammar School under Dr. Tassie (q.v.), and was called to the bar of Upper Canada in 1862 (Q.C., 1874). A prominent Ontario Liberal, he was called to the Senate in 1903, and from 1909 to 1911 he was speaker of the Senate. He died at Toronto on December 4, 1916. He was twice married, (1) in 1864 to Anne Margaret, daughter of the Hon. William Hume Blake (q.v.), and (2) in 1883 to Adelaide Cecil Staveley, daughter of the Rev. George Stanley-Pinhorne, by whom he had several daughters and one son. From 1875 to 1877 he was grand master of the Masonic Grand Lodge of Canada.

[Morgan, *Can. men* (1912); *Can. who's who*, 1910; *Can. parl. comp.*]

Kerr, Robert (1764?-1824), military surgeon, was born about 1764, and was surgeon to the 2nd Battalion of Sir John Johnson's "Royal Greens" (King's Royal Regiment of New York) during the American Revolution. After the war he was appointed surgeon to the Indian department, and was stationed at Newark (Niagara), Upper Canada. This appointment he retained until his death at Niagara in March, 1824. He married a sister of Joseph Brant (q.v.); and one of his sons, Simcoe Kerr, became chief of the Mohawks.

[W. Canniff, *The medical profession in Upper Canada* (Toronto, 1894).]

Kerr, Wilfred Brenton (1896-1950), historian, was born at Seaforth, Ontario, in 1896, and died at Kenmore, New York, on January 12, 1950. After serving overseas in the First World War with the artillery, he obtained his university education at Oxford (B.A., 1921) and the University of Toronto (M.A., 1923; Ph.D., 1925). In 1925 he was appointed a member of the department of history and government in the University of Buffalo; and he remained a member of this department for the rest of his life. He was the author of two books about his war-time experiences, *Shrieks and crashes* (Toronto, 1924) and *Arms and the maple leaf* (Seaforth, Ont., 1943); and his historical publications included *The reign of terror* (Toronto, 1927), *Bermuda and the American Revolution* (Princeton, 1936), and *The maritime provinces of British North America and the American Revolution* (Sackville, N.B., 1941).

[*Can. hist. rev.*, 1950.]

Kerr, William Alexander Robb (1875-1945), president of the University of Alberta (1935-41), was born at Toronto, Ontario, in 1875, and died at Edmonton, Alberta, on January 21, 1945. He was educated at the University of Toronto (B.A., 1899; M.A., 1902); and Harvard University (Ph.D., 1904). From 1904 to 1909 he was professor of Romance languages and literature at Adelphi College, Brooklyn; and then he was invited to become professor of modern languages in the newly-founded University of Alberta at Edmonton; he became dean of the faculty of arts and science in 1914, and president of the University in 1936. He retired from the presidency because of ill-health in 1941. Among other publications, he was the editor of *A short anthology of French Canadian prose* (Toronto, 1927).

[*Proc. Roy. Soc. Can.*, 1946; *Can. who's who*, 1938-39.]

Kerr, William Henry Corrie (d. 1891), lawyer and scholar, was educated at the University of Toronto (B.A., 1859; M.A., 1864), and was called to the Upper Canada bar in 1863. He practised law, first in Brantford, and then in Toronto, Ontario; and he died on March 29, 1891, in New York, whither he had gone for medical treatment. He edited *The Heroides of Ovid* (Toronto, 1865).

[Morgan, *Bib. can.*; Toronto *Empire*, March 30, 1891.]

Kerr, William Warren Hastings (1826-1888), lawyer, was born at Three Rivers, Lower Canada, in 1826, the son of James Hastings Kerr, and the grandson of the Hon. James Kerr (q.v.). He was educated at Lundy's College, Quebec, and at Queen's University, Kingston; and was called to the bar of Lower Canada in 1854 (Q.C., 1873). He practised law, first at Quebec, and then at Montreal; and he was for many years professor of international law and dean of the faculty of law in McGill University. He became a foremost counsel at the Lower Canada bar; and was counsel in several notable cases, such as those of the St. Alban's raiders and the Consolidated Bank. He died at Montreal, Quebec, on February 12, 1888.

[Rose, *Cyc. Can. biog.* (1888).]

Kerwin, Patrick (1889-1963), chief justice of Canada, was born in Sarnia, Ontario, October 25, 1899, and educated at Osgoode Hall, which he entered at age sixteen. He was called to the bar in 1911. He practised in Guelph and was city solicitor and solicitor for Wellington county. In 1932 he was made a justice of the Supreme Court of Ontario and in 1935 a justice of the Supreme Court of Canada. He became chief justice in 1954. The fact that appeals to the judicial committee of the Privy Council in London were abolished in 1949 gave the Supreme Court of Canada more work and responsibility in Canadian legal matters. Chief Justice Kerwin, always jealous of individual freedom, was respected as an outstanding jurist. Notable cases which came before him were those which concerned the Quebec "padlock law" and Jehovah's Witnesses. He died at Ottawa, Ontario, February 2, 1963.

[*Can. who's who*, 1955-57; Metropolitan Toronto Library Board, *Biographical scrapbooks*, vol. 11, 21, 70.]

Ketchum, Jesse (1782-1867), philanthropist, was born in Spencertown, New York, in 1782, and came to Upper Canada in 1799. He established a tannery at York (Toronto), and became wealthy. From 1830 to 1834 he was one of the members for the county of Durham in the Legislative Assembly of Upper Canada, and he was a prominent Reformer; but he took no part in the rebellion of 1837. In 1845 he returned to the United States, and for the rest of his life he lived in Buffalo, New York. Here he died on September 7, 1867. Both before and after he left Toronto he made many gifts of land and money to religious and philanthropic projects.

[E. J. Hathaway, *Jesse Ketchum and his times* (Toronto, 1929).]

Ketchum, John Davidson (1893-1962), professor of psychology, was born at Cobourg, Ontario, on June 10, 1893. He was educated at St. Alban's Cathedral School, Toronto; Trinity College School, Port Hope; and the University of Toronto. He was a student of piano in Germany in 1914 and was interned at Ruhleben prison camp for the duration of the war along with 4,000 other prisoners. On his return to Canada he completed his studies in arts in the University of Toronto (B.A., 1922; M.A., 1926), and later enrolled at the University of Chicago's school of graduate studies. He became a lecturer in psychology at the University of Toronto in 1926 and became a full professor in 1950. He was editor of the *Canadian Journal of Psychology* (1953-58) and author of *Ruhleben: A prison camp society* (Toronto, 1965) published after his death. He maintained his interest in classical music and psychology throughout his teaching career until his retirement in 1961. He died April 24, 1962, at Toronto.

[*Can. who's who*, 1955-57; *Trans. Roy. Soc. Can.* (1962).]

Ketchum, Thomas Carleton Lee (1862?-1927), journalist and author, was born about 1862, and died at Woodstock, New Brunswick, on February 27, 1927. He was an original member of the staff of the Toronto *Empire*, and at the time of his death was editor of the Woodstock *Despatch*. He was the author of *A short history of Carleton county, New Brunswick* (Woodstock, N.B., 1922), and *High spots of Canadian history* (Saint John, N.B., 1926).

[Private information.]

Ketchum, William Quintard (1818-1901), clergyman, was born at Woodstock, New Brunswick, on August 3, 1818. He was educated at King's College, Fredericton (B.A., 1846; M.A., 1849), and was ordained a priest of the Church of England in 1846. He was curate at Fredericton, New Brunswick, from 1845 to 1859, and rector at St. Andrews, New Brunswick, from 1859 to his death at St. Andrews on August 9, 1901. He was the author of *Lectures on the missions of the church in the United States* (Saint John, N.B., 1872) and *The*

life and work of the Most Reverend John Medley (Saint John, N.B., 1893).

[Morgan, *Can. men* (1898); W. G. MacFarlane, *New Brunswick bibliography* (Saint John, N.B., 1895).]

Keveny, Owen (d. 1816), colonizer, was a native of Sligo, Ireland, and was the leader of the second party sent out by Lord Selkirk (q.v.) to the Red River Settlement in 1812. He became in 1815 a servant of the Hudson's Bay Company, and in September, 1816, he was murdered by a small party of Nor'Westers on the Winnipeg River. His murderer was brought to trial in Quebec, in May, 1818; but escaped punishment because of doubts regarding the jurisdiction of the courts of Lower Canada in the Indian country.

[E. E. Rich (ed.), *Colin Robertson's correspondence book* (Toronto: The Champlain Society, 1939).]

Keys, David Reid (1856-1939), educationist, was born at Louisville, Kentucky, in 1856, of Irish parents, and died at Toronto, Ontario, on July 11, 1939. He was educated at Upper Canada College and the University of Toronto (B.A., 1878; M.A., 1889), and did post-graduate work at Columbia University and at Leipzig, Geneva, and Munich. He was a member of the teaching staff of University College, Toronto, from 1882 to 1923, latterly as professor of Anglo-Saxon. He was the author of *Toronto, an historical and descriptive sketch* (Toronto, 1913).

[Toronto *Globe and Mail*, July 12, 1939.]

Khan, The (pseud.). See **Kernighan, Robert Kirkland.**

Kidd, Adam (1802-1831), poet, was born in Ireland in 1802. He came to Canada, and here he published a volume entitled *The Huron chief, and other poems* (Montreal, 1830). He died in Quebec on July 5, 1831.

[Morgan, *Bib. can.*; C. C. James, *A bibliography of Canadian poetry* (Toronto, 1899).]

Kierzkowski, Alexandre Edouard (1816-1870), politician and author, was born in the Grand Duchy of Posen in 1816. He fought in the Polish national cause in 1830-31, and was forced to exile himself in Paris. Here he studied civil engineering; and in 1841 he emigrated to Canada. He took an active part in politics; and in 1858 he was elected to the Legislative Council, and in 1861 to the Legislative Assembly, but on both occasions was unseated. In 1867, however, he was elected to the Canadian House of Commons for St. Hyacinthe; and he remained a member of the House until his death at St. Ours, Quebec, on August 4, 1870. He was twice married, (1) to Louise, daughter of the Hon. P. D. Debartzch (q.v.), and (2) to Caroline Virginie, daughter of the Hon. Roch François de St. Ours. He was the author of a pamphlet entitled *La question de la tenure seigneuriale du Bas-Canada* (Montreal, 1852).

[*Bull. rech. hist.*, 1904; Le Jeune, *Dict. gén.*]

Kilgour, David Eckford (1912-1973), business consultant, was born at Brandon, Manitoba, December 26, 1912. He was educated in Brandon, at St. Andrew's College, in Aurora, Ontario, and at the University of Manitoba. He joined the Great West Life Assurance Company in 1933, became general manager in 1955, and was president from 1959 to 1971. He was chairman of the Canada Committee of the Hudson's Bay Company and a governor of the University of Manitoba. He died at Winnipeg, Manitoba, March 13, 1973.

[*Can. who's who*, 1970-72.]

Killaly, Hamilton Hartley (1800-1874), chairman of the board of works for Canada (1841-46), was born in Dublin, Ireland, in 1800, the son of John A. Killaly and Alicia Hamilton. He was educated at Trinity College, Dublin (B.A., 1819; M.A., 1832), and at the Royal Academy of Science; and he became a civil engineer. For a number of years he was employed under his father, who was government engineer for the Irish board of works. He emigrated to Canada in 1834, and took up land near London, Upper Canada. In 1838 he was appointed engineer in charge of the Welland Canal; and in 1841, on the union of Upper and Lower Canada, he became chairman of the board of works of the united province. From 1841 to 1844 he represented London in the Legislative Assembly of Canada; and from 1841 to 1843 he was a member of the Executive Council. He ceased to be chairman of the board of works in 1846; but in 1848 he was appointed to take charge of the Welland Canal and the western works, and from 1851 to 1859 he was assistant commissioner of public works for Canada, and a member of the board of railway commissioners. From 1859 to 1862 he was inspector of railways; and in 1862 he was appointed a member of a royal commission to report on the defences and fortifications of Canada. During his later years he lived at Toronto; and he died suddenly, at Picton, Ontario, on March 28, 1874. In 1833 he married Martha Handy, of Dublin, Ireland; and by her he had several children. In *Salmon fishing in Canada* (London, 1860), by W. A. Adamson (q.v.), there is a racy description of him under the name of "The Commissioner".

[J. C. Dent, *The last forty years* (2 vols., Toronto, 1881); N. F. Davin, *The Irishman in Canada* (Toronto, 1877); S. Leacock, *Baldwin* (Toronto, 1907); private information; *Dict. Can. biog.*, vol. 10.]

Killam, Albert Clements (1849-1908), jurist, was born at Yarmouth, Nova Scotia, on September 18, 1849. He was educated at the University of Toronto (B.A., 1872), and was called to the Ontario bar in 1877 (Q.C., 1884). He practised law first at Windsor, Ontario, and then in Winnipeg, Manitoba; and he represented South Winnipeg in the legislature of Manitoba from 1883 to 1885. He was then appointed a judge of the Court of Queen's Bench in Manitoba; in 1899 he became chief justice of Manitoba; and in 1903 he became a judge of the Supreme Court of Canada. In 1905 he left the bench to become first chief commissioner of the Board of Railway Commissioners for Canada; but his occupancy of this post was cut short by his death at Ottawa, Ontario, on March 1, 1908.

[*Can. parl. comp.*; Morgan, *Can. men* (1898).]

Killins, Ada Gladys (1901-1963), painter, was born in Caistor township, Lincoln county, Ontario, in 1901. She attended Teachers' College, and began teaching art at Memorial School, Niagara Falls, in 1924. She studied with Franz Johnston and in the summer (1935-38) with Carl Schaefer at Geneva Park, Lake Couchiching. In 1947 she gave up teaching to devote all her time to painting. She moved to Glen Cross in 1955. She died in 1963 and was buried at Smithville, Ontario. Her work is "individual and personal". She exhibited at the Art Gallery of Toronto in 1938 with the Canadian Society of Painters in Water Colour, of which she was a member; in 1942 she contributed fifteen paintings to the exhibition "Four Canadian Painters" which included Brigden, Phillips, and Thoreau MacDonald. At her death, a memorial exhibition with a catalogue was held at Oak Hall, Niagara Falls. Her paintings are in the Niagara Falls Public Library; Memorial School, Niagara Falls; Canada Packers, Toronto; and in private collections.

[C. S. MacDonald, *A dictionary of Canadian artists,* vol. 3 (Ottawa, 1971).]

Kilpatrick, Thomas Buchanan (1858-1930), clergyman and author, was born in Glasgow, Scotland, in 1858. He was educated at Glasgow University (B.A., 1877; B.D., 1880), and was ordained a minister of the Free Church of Scotland in 1882. In 1889 he came to Canada as professor of systematic theology in Manitoba College, Winnipeg; in 1905 he became professor of systematic theology in Knox College, Toronto; and in 1925, at the time of church union, he transferred to Emmanuel College, Toronto. He died in Toronto on May 20, 1930. He was the author of *A tract about tracts* (Toronto, 1906), *New Testament evangelism* (Toronto, 1911), and *Our common faith* (Toronto, 1928).

[*Can. who was who*, vol. 2; Morgan, *Can. men* (1912).]

Kimber, Harry Goldring (1892-1966), newspaper proprietor, was born in Toronto,

Ontario, in 1892 and was educated in Toronto schools. He began his life work as a newspaper man when he became a junior in the *Globe* business office in 1912. For three years during the First World War he served with the Red Cross, but devoted the rest of his working life to the newspaper world. He was circulation manager of the *Globe* from 1919 to 1930, when he became general manager of the London, Ontario, *Advertiser*. He returned to the *Globe* at the urging of George McCullagh (q.v.) in 1936 and became its general manager. He continued in this position when the *Globe* and the *Mail* were amalgamated in 1938. In 1951 he became assistant publisher and on McCullagh's death in 1952 became publisher. He was also named publisher of the newly acquired *Telegram* at that time. He retired as president and publisher in 1957 and retired from the company in 1958. He was a director of the Canadian National Exhibition, a keen yachtsman, and a member of the Toronto Harbour Commission. He was a former president of the Canadian Daily Newspaper Publishers' Association. He died at Toronto, Ontario, February 4, 1966.

[*Can. who's who*, 1961-63; Metropolitan Toronto Library Board, *Biographical scrapbooks*, vol. 26.]

Kimber, Joseph René (1786-1843), physician and politician, was born at Quebec on November 26, 1786, the eldest son of René Kimber and Marie-Josephte Robitaille. He was admitted to practice as a physician in 1811; and he played a prominent part in Lower Canadian politics before the rebellion of 1837. He represented Three Rivers in the Legislative Assembly of Lower Canada from 1832 to 1838, and was one of Papineau's lieutenants. In the Legislative Assembly of United Canada he represented Champlain from 1841 to 1843; and he was appointed to the Legislative Council only a short time before his death at Montreal on December 22, 1843. He married Apolline Berthelot; and by her he had a son and a daughter.

[*La famille Jékimbert ou Kimber* (Bull. rech. hist., 1915); *Bull. rech. hist.*, 1935.]

Kindle, Edward Martin (1869-1940), geologist and palaeontologist, was born in Johnson county, Indiana, on March 10, 1869. He was educated at the University of Indiana (A.B., 1893), at Cornell University (M.S., 1896), and at Yale University (Ph.D., 1899); and after serving on the staff of the Indiana Geological Survey and the United States Geological Survey, he was appointed in 1912 a member of the Canadian Geological Survey, and in 1918 he became chief of the division of palaeontology in the Canadian Geological Survey. He retired from this post in 1938; and he died in Ottawa, Ontario, on August 28, 1940. He had carried out extensive investigations all along the sub-Arctic of the western

hemisphere from Alaska to Labrador; and he contributed many valuable papers to scientific periodicals. He was elected a fellow of the Royal Society of Canada in 1920.

[*Proc. Roy. Soc. Can.*, 1941; *Can. who's who*, 1936-37.]

King, Dougall Macdougall (1878-1922), physician, was born at Berlin (now Kitchener), Ontario, on November 11, 1878, the son of John King (q.v.), and the brother of the Right Hon. W. L. Mackenzie King. He was educated at the University of Toronto (M.B., 1902); and until 1913 practised medicine in Ottawa. He was then compelled by ill-health to remove to Colorado; and he died at Denver, Colorado, on March 18, 1922. He was the author of *The battle with tuberculosis, and how to win it* (Philadelphia, 1917) and *Nerves and personal power* (New York, 1922).

[*Who was who in America.*]

King, Edwin H. (1828-1896), president of the Bank of Montreal (1869-73), was born in Ireland in 1828, and came to Canada about 1850. He entered the Bank of British North America; but in 1857 he joined the Bank of Montreal, and in 1863 he became its general manager, and in 1869 its president. He exercised an important influence on Canadian affairs during the negotiations leading to Confederation. In 1873 he retired from office, and went to live in England. He died at Monte Carlo on April 14, 1896.

[*The centenary of the Bank of Montreal* (Montreal, 1917).]

King, George Edwin (1839-1904), prime minister of New Brunswick (1872-78), was born at Saint John, New Brunswick, on October 8, 1839, the second son of George King, a shipbuilder. He was educated at Mount Allison College, Sackville, New Brunswick, and at the Wesleyan University, Connecticut (B.A., 1859; M.A., 1862). In 1865 he was called to the bar of New Brunswick (Q.C., 1873), and he practised law at Saint John. From 1867 to 1878 he represented Saint John in the House of Assembly of New Brunswick. In 1869 he became a member of the Wetmore administration without portfolio; in 1870 he became attorney-general; and in 1872, prime minister. He retired from office in 1878, and was defeated in Saint John as a candidate for election to the Canadian House of Commons. In 1880 he was appointed a judge of the Supreme Court of New Brunswick; and in 1893 a judge of the Supreme Court of Canada. He died at Ottawa on May 7, 1901. In 1866 he married Lydia, daughter of Aaron Eaton, of Saint John, New Brunswick. He was an LL.D. of the University of New Brunswick (1886), and a D.C.L. of Mount Allison University (1893).

[J. Hannay, *Premiers of New Brunswick*

(Can. mag., 1897); Morgan, *Can. men* (1898); *Can. parl. comp.*]

King, George Gerald (1836-1928), senator of Canada, was born at Springfield, New Brunswick, on December 11, 1836. He became the head of a prosperous lumber company; and he represented Queens, as a Liberal, in the Canadian House of Commons from 1878 to 1887, and from 1891 to 1896. In 1896 he was called to the Senate, and he sat in the Senate until his death on April 28, 1928.
[*Can. Parl. comp.*; Morgan, *Can. men* (1912).]

King, James Horace (1873-1955), cabinet minister and senator, was born at Chipman, New Brunswick, on January 18, 1873, the son of the Hon. George King (q.v.), and died at Ottawa, Ontario, on July 14, 1955. He was educated at McGill University (M.D., C.M., 1895), and practised medicine first in New Brunswick and then in British Columbia. From 1903 to 1909 and from 1915 to 1922 he represented Cranbrook in the British Columbia legislature, and during the latter period was minister of public works in the Brewster and Oliver governments. In 1922 he was offered the portfolio of public works in the Mackenzie King administration at Ottawa, and was elected to represent Kootenay in the Canadian House of Commons. He later became minister of soldiers' civil re-establishment, and then minister of pensions and national health. He was appointed a senator in 1930, and was government leader in the Senate from 1942 to 1945, and speaker of the Senate from 1945 to 1949.
[*Can. who's who*, 1952-54; *Can. parl. guide*, 1954; *Encyc. Can.*]

King, John (1843-1916), lawyer and author, was born in Toronto, Canada, on September 12, 1843, the son of Lieut. John King, R.H.A., and Christina, daughter of Alexander Macdougall. He was educated at the University of Toronto (B.A., 1865; M.A., 1865), and was called to the bar of Ontario in 1869 (Q.C., 1890). He practised law in Berlin (Kitchener), Ontario, and in Toronto; and he was a lecturer at Osgoode Hall, the law school of the Law Society of Upper Canada. He died at Toronto on August 30, 1916. In 1872 he married Isabel Grace, youngest daughter of William Lyon Mackenzie (q.v.); and by her he had several children, one of whom was the Right Hon. W. L. Mackenzie King (q.v.). He was the author of *The other side of the story* (Toronto, 1886), *A decade in the history of newspaper libel* (Woodstock, 1892), *The law of defamation* (Toronto, 1907), and *McCaul: Croft: Forneri* (Toronto, 1914).
[Morgan, *Can. men* (1912).]

King, John Mark (1829-1899), clergyman and scholar, was born at Yetholm, Roxburgh-

shire, Scotland, on May 25, 1829, the son of Ralph King and Mary Scott. He was educated at Edinburgh University (M.A., 1854) and at the University of Halle. In 1856 he emigrated to Canada, and he was ordained a minister of the Presbyterian Church in 1857. From 1863 to 1883 he was in charge of churches in Toronto; and from 1883 to his death on March 5, 1899, he was principal of Manitoba College, Winnipeg. In 1873 he married Janet Macpherson, daughter of Hugh Skinner. He received the degree of D.D. from Knox College in 1882; and in 1883 he was moderator of the General Assembly of the Presbyterian Church in Canada. He published *A critical study of "In Memoriam"* (Toronto, 1898).
[Morgan, *Can. men* (1898).]

King, Thomas Davies (1819-1884), Shakespearian student, was born in Bristol, England, in 1819. He came to Canada in 1858, and was for a time in the employ of the Grand Trunk Railway. In his later years he devoted himself to literature and art, and was described as "the father of Shakespearian study in Montreal". He died at Montreal on November 8, 1884. He was the author of *Bacon versus Shakspere* (Montreal, 1875).
[*Dom. ann. reg.*, 1884.]

King, William (1812-1895), missionary and abolitionist, was born near Newton Limavady, Londonderry county, Ireland. He was educated at Glasgow University (B.A., 1833), and he then emigrated to the United States. In 1846 he was sent as a missionary to Canada, and he founded in Elgin county, Canada West, a colony for escaped negro slaves. He died at Chatham, Ontario, on January 5, 1895.
[Annie Straith Jamieson, *William King, friend and champion of slaves* (Toronto, 1925).]

King, William Benjamin Basil (1859-1928), novelist, was born at Charlottetown, Prince Edward Island, on February 26, 1859; and was educated at King's College, Windsor (B.A., 1881). He took orders in the Church of England, and was rector successively of St. Luke's pro-cathedral in Halifax and of Christ Church, Cambridge, Massachusetts. He lost his eyesight, and turned to the writing of novels, in which he achieved a considerable success. He died at Cambridge, Massachusetts, on June 22, 1928. His novels included *Griselda* (Chicago, 1900), *Let not man put asunder* (New York, 1901), *In the garden of charity* (New York, 1903), *The steps of honor* (New York, 1904), *The giant's strength* (New York, 1907), *The inner shrine* (New York, 1909), *Wild olive* (New York, 1910), *The street called straight* (New York, 1912), *The side of the angels* (New York, 1916), *The high heart* (New York, 1917), *The lifted veil* (New York, 1917), *The city of comrades* (New York, 1919), *The thread of flame* (New York, 1920), *The* *empty sack* (New York, 1921), *The happy isles* (New York, 1923), *High forfeit* (New York, 1925), and *Pluck* (New York, 1928); and he was the author of several books on religion and spiritualism.

[*Dict. Am. biog.*; *Who's who in Am.*; *Can. who was who*, vol. 2.]

King, William Lyon Mackenzie (1874-1950), prime minister of Canada (1921-26, 1926-30, and 1935-48), was born in Berlin (now Kitchener), Ontario, on December 17, 1874, the son of John King and the grandson of William Lyon Mackenzie (qq.v.). He was educated at the University of Toronto (B.A., 1895; M.A., 1897), and did post-graduate work in sociology at Harvard University (A.M., 1898; Ph.D., 1909). In 1900 he was invited by Sir William Mulock (q.v.) to become Canada's first deputy minister of labour; and in 1909 he was persuaded by Sir Wilfrid Laurier (q.v.) to enter politics, was elected to represent Waterloo in the Canadian House of Commons, and became Canada's first minister of labour not holding a separate portfolio. His ideas in regard to the solution of labour problems were enunciated in his books, *The secret of heroism* (Toronto, 1906) and *Industry and humanity* (Toronto, 1918; rev. eds., 1935 and 1947).

He was out of parliament from 1911 to 1921; and during the war he obtained employment with the Rockefeller Foundation. But in 1919 he was chosen to succeed Laurier as leader of the Liberal party; and in 1921 he was elected to represent North York in the House of Commons, and became prime minister and minister for external affairs. Except for a period of a few months in 1926, when Arthur Meighen (q.v.) held office with a shadow cabinet, he remained prime minister until he was defeated by R. B. Bennett (q.v.) in the elections of 1930. He came back to power, however, in 1935; and from that time until his retirement in 1948 he held the reins of government firmly in his hands. In fact, when he retired, he had held office longer than any previous prime minister in the British commonwealth.

How he achieved this miracle is difficult to explain. He was by no means a glamorous leader; and his period of office was filled with controversies. On two separate occasions he split the Liberal party over the conscription issue; he fell foul of the governor-general, Lord Byng (q.v.), in 1926; and he himself described the revelations made in 1931-32 with regard to the Beauharnois Power Corporation and the Liberal party as "the valley of humiliation". Yet there can be no doubt that he was a very adroit politician. A striking illustration of this was the way in which, in 1942, he brought about the resignation of the Liberal prime minister of Ontario, Mitchell Hepburn (q.v.), who had launched a full-fledged attack against him. His greatest achievement, however, was undoubtedly his success in preventing a breach between the English and the French in Canada during the Second World War.

He died, unmarried, near Ottawa, Ontario, on July 22, 1950.

[R. M. Dawson and H. Blair Neatby, *William Lyon Mackenzie King: A political biography*, 3 vols. (Toronto, 1958-77); F. A. McGregor, *The fall and rise of Mackenzie King 1911-1919* (Toronto, 1962); J. W. Pickersgill and D. F. Forster (eds.), *The Mackenzie King record*, 4 vols. (Toronto, 1960-70); A. S. Ferns and B. Ostry, *The age of Mackenzie King* (Toronto, 1955); B. Hutchison, *The incredible Canadian* (Toronto, 1952); H. R. Hardy, *Mackenzie King of Canada* (Toronto, 1949); C. P. Stacey, *A very double life: The private world of Mackenzie King* (Toronto, 1976); *Encyc. Can.*; *Can. who's who*, 1948; *Can. parl. guide*, 1947.]

Kingdon, Hollingworth Tully (d. 1907), Anglican bishop of Fredericton, was born in London, England, and was educated at Trinity College, Cambridge (B.A., 1858; M.A., 1861; D.D., 1881). He was ordained a priest of the Church of England in 1859; and, after occupying several charges in England, he came to Canada in 1881 as coadjutor of Bishop Medley (q.v.) in the see of Fredericton. He remained in this post until his death at Fredericton, New Brunswick, on October 11, 1907. He was a D.D. of King's College, Windsor (1890) and a D.C.L. of Trinity University, Toronto (1893).

[Morgan, *Can. men* (1898).]

Kingsford, Rupert Etherege (1849-1920), lawyer, was born at Montreal, Canada East, on October 20, 1849, the son of William Kingsford (q.v.). He was educated at the University of Toronto (B.A., 1869; M.A., 1871; LL.B., 1873), and was called to the bar in Ontario in 1873. He practised law in Toronto; and in 1894 he was appointed deputy police magistrate in Toronto, and in 1902 second police magistrate. He died at Toronto, Ontario, on October 6, 1920. He was the author of *A manual of evidence in civil cases* (Toronto, 1889), *Manual of the law of landlord and tenant* (Toronto, 1896), *Commentaries on the law of Ontario* (Toronto, 1896), and *The law relating to executors and administrators* (Toronto, 1900).

[Morgan, *Can. men* (1912).]

Kingsford, William (1819-1898), historian, was born in London, England, on December 23, 1819, the son of William Kingsford, of Lad Lane. He was educated at Nicholas Wanostracht's school in Camberwell, and in 1836 enlisted in the 1st Dragoon Guards. He came with his regiment to Canada in 1837, and in 1840 was offered a commission, but preferred to obtain his discharge. He entered in 1841 the office of the city surveyor of Montreal; and in due course he qualified as a civil engineer. He had a chequered career as an engineer, and was employed successively on the Hudson River Railway, on the Panama Isthmus Railway, and on the Grand Trunk Railway. In 1873 he was appointed by the Canadian government engineer in charge of the harbours of the Great Lakes and the St. Lawrence; but in 1879 he was summarily dismissed by Sir Hector Langevin (q.v.), minister of public works. He reviewed his dismissal in a pamphlet entitled *Mr. Kingsford and Sir Hector Langevin* (Toronto, 1882); but he did not succeed in obtaining redress, and the remainder of his life he devoted to historical research. He had already published a number of pamphlets of a semi-historical nature: *The history, structure, and statistics of plank roads* (Philadelphia, 1852), *The Canadian canals* (Toronto, 1865), and *A political coin* (Toronto, n.d.). He now applied himself, at the age of sixty, to writing a history of Canada. The first-fruit of his labour was an essay on *Canadian archaeology* (Montreal, 1886), followed by *The early bibliography of Ontario* (Toronto, 1892). The first volume of his *History of Canada* appeared in 1887, and the tenth and last volume in 1898; and while the work is not without defects, it was a remarkable achievement for a septuagenarian, and in many ways has not been superseded. He survived the completion of his *History* only a few months, dying in Toronto on September 28, 1898. In 1848 he married Maria Margaret, daughter of William Burns Lindsay, clerk of the Legislative Assembly of Canada. In 1886 he was elected a member of the Royal Society of Canada; and he was an honorary LL.D. of Queen's University, Kingston, and Dalhousie University, Halifax.

[*Dict. nat. biog.*, supp. I; Morgan, *Can. men* (1898); *Proc. Roy. Soc. Can.*, 1894 and 1899; Le Jeune, *Dict. gén.*]

Kingsmill, Sir Charles Edmund (1855-1935), naval officer, was born at Guelph, Canada West, on July 7, 1855, the son of John Juchereau Kingsmill and Ellen Diana Grange, and the grandson of Colonel William Kingsmill (q.v.). He served in the Royal Navy until 1908, when he was appointed director of the naval service of Canada. He retired from this post in 1920; and he died at Portland, Ontario, on July 15, 1935. He was promoted to be admiral on the retired list of the Royal Navy in 1917; and he was created a knight bachelor in 1918.

[*Who was who*, 1928-40; Morgan, *Can. men* (1912).]

Kingsmill, George (1799-1852), soldier, was born at Eliogarty, county Tipperary, Ireland, in 1799, the son of Parr Kingsmill. He purchased a commission as a subaltern in the Enniskillen Dragoons in 1815, and saw active service at Waterloo. He resigned his commission in 1828, with the rank of captain; and in 1829 he emigrated to Canada, and settled in York (Toronto). He was high constable of To-

ronto from 1835 to 1846; and in the rebellion of 1837 he served as an aide-de-camp of Sir Francis Bond Head (q.v.). He died of cholera at Galt, Canada West, in 1852.

[J. Ross Robertson, *What art has done for Canadian history* (Toronto, 1917); private information.]

Kingsmill, William (1794?-1876), soldier, was born in England about 1794, and became an officer in the 66th Regiment of Foot. He came to Canada about 1825, and was later appointed sheriff of the Niagara district. He died in Toronto, Ontario, on May 6, 1876. He was the author of *The Greenwood tragedy: Three addresses delivered to the prisoners in Toronto gaol* (Guelph, C.W., 1864).

[Private information.]

Kingston, George Allen (1870-1943), lawyer and poet, was born in Hastings county, Ontario, in 1870. He was educated at the Osgoode Hall Law School, and was called to the bar of Ontario in 1892. From 1914 to 1935 he was one of the commissioners of the Workmen's Compensation Board of Ontario. He died at Toronto, Ontario, on April 11, 1943. He was the author of *Legendary lyrics* (Picton, Ont., 1938).

[Toronto *Globe and Mail*, April 12, 1943.]

Kingston, George Templeman (1817-1886), meteorologist, was born at Oporto, Portugal, in 1817, and was a brother of W. H. G. Kingston, the novelist. He was educated at Cambridge University (B.A., 1846; M.A., 1849), and emigrated to Canada. For some time he had charge of the Naval School at Quebec; and in 1855 he was appointed professor of meteorology in the University of Toronto, and director of the magnetic observatory at Toronto. He died at Toronto on January 21, 1886. He published an *Abstract of magnetical observations made at the Magnetical Observatory, Canada West, during the years 1856 to 1862 inclusive, and during parts of the years 1853, 1854, and 1855* (Toronto, 1863), and a number of papers in the *Canadian Journal* and the *British American Magazine*.

[*Dom. ann. reg.*, 1886; Morgan, *Bib. can.*]

Kingston, Harold Reynolds (1886-1963), educator, was born in Picton, Ontario, June 26, 1886, and educated at Queen's University (M.A., 1908) and the University of Chicago (Ph.D., 1914). He taught public school (1903-06) and high school (1908-12) before being appointed to the department of mathematics and astronomy at the University of Manitoba (1913-21). He became professor of mathematics and astronomy and head of the department at the University of Western Ontario in 1921. He was dean of arts and science from 1947 to 1952 and principal of University College from 1950 to 1952, when he retired. He was president of the Royal Astronomical Society of Canada (1930-31) and a member of international mathematical and astronomical societies. He published *Metric properties of nets of plane curves* (1916); *The constancy of solar wavelengths and the possibility of determining the solar distance therefrom* (1920) with R. E. Delury; *An easy pocket guide to the stars* (1925); *A new geometry* (1936) with J.E. Durrant; and *A new course in analytic geometry* (1940); as well as numerous articles. He died at London, Ontario, February 10, 1963.

[*Can. who's who*, 1955-57.]

Kinnear, David (1807?-1862), journalist, was born at Edinburgh, Scotland, about 1807. He was admitted a member of the Scottish bar; but did not take up the practice of law. He emigrated to America in 1835, and ultimately settled as a farmer at Drummondville, Lower Canada. He served with the loyalist troops during the rebellion of 1837; and after the rebellion he became editor of the Montreal *Gazette*, and later of the Montreal *Herald*. The latter post he held until his death at Montreal on November 20, 1862.

[Morgan, *Bib. can.*]

Kirby, William (1817-1906), author, was born at Kingston-upon-Hull, England, on October 13, 1817, and came to Canada with his parents in 1832. He settled in Niagara, Upper Canada, in 1839, and for more than twenty years edited the Niagara *Mail*. From 1871 to 1895 he was collector of customs at Niagara. His first important publication was *The U. E.* (Niagara, 1859), a poem in Spenserian stanzas. His reputation rests mainly, however, on a novel, *The golden dog* (New York and Montreal, 1877; new ed., 1896), which was translated into French by Pamphile LeMay (q.v.) and L. H. Fréchette (q.v.). He published also *Memoirs of the Servos family* (Toronto, 1884), *Canadian idyls* (Welland, Ontario, 1894), *Annals of Niagara* (Lundy's Lane Historical Society, 1896), and a number of less important works. He died at Niagara on June 23, 1906. He married the daughter of John Whitmore, Niagara, and had two sons. In 1883 he became a charter member of the Royal Society of Canada.

[Lorne Pierce, *William Kirby* (Toronto, 1929); W. R. Riddell, *William Kirby* (Toronto, 1923); J. Carnochan, *Reminiscences* (Transactions of the U.E. Loyalists' association, 1914); *Proc. Roy. Soc. Can.*, 1907; Morgan, *Can. men* (1898); Rose, *Cyc. Can. biog.* (1886).]

Kirchhoffer, John Nesbitt (1848-1914), senator of Canada, was born at Ballyvourney, county Cork, Ireland, on May 5, 1848; and was educated at Marlborough College, England. He came to Canada in 1864, and was called to the bar of Ontario in 1871, and that of Manitoba in 1884. He practised law first at Port Hope, Ontario, and after 1884 at Brandon, Manitoba. He was a member of the Manitoba legislature from 1886 to 1889; and in 1892 he was called to the Senate of Canada. He served in the volunteer militia during the Fenian raids and the North West rebellion; and on several occasions he was captain of Canadian teams in international cricket. He died on December 22, 1914.

[Morgan, *Can. men* (1912); *Can. parl. comp.*]

Kirk, Lawrence Eldred (1886-1969), agriculturalist, was born at Bracebridge, Ontario, May 27, 1886. His parents were farmers and moved from Bracebridge to Belmont, Manitoba, in 1892, to a 320-acre farm. He worked on the farm and had four or five months of school each year in the off season. In 1903 the family moved to Arcola, Saskatchewan, to another farm. Here, Kirk was able to earn enough money off the farm to pay his way to the Free Methodist Seminary at Jackson, Michigan. After a year he returned to Canada and enrolled in Moose Jaw High School, where he obtained his senior matriculation and a $150 scholarship. By alternately working and studying he graduated from the University of Saskatchewan in 1917 with a combined degree in arts and agriculture. He obtained a Ph.D. from the University of Minnesota in 1927, and was especially successful in introducing the plant-breeding techniques which had been successful with field corn to other forage crops. He was appointed Dominion Agrostologist in the Dominion Experimental Farms branch in 1931 and directed experiments for the improvement of forage crops. From 1937 to 1947 he was dean of agriculture at the University of Saskatchewan. He became chief of the plant production and plant protection branch of the Food and Agriculture Organization of the United Nations in 1947. Among the undertakings of the branch during his period of office were the development of hybrid field corn in the European and Mediterranean area; rice, wheat, and barley breeding; the cataloguing of genetic stocks of wheat and rice; the distribution of seed for experimental purposes; and the control of infestation in stored products. He undertook several missions for the Food and Agriculture Organization dealing with food requirements of Arab refugees (1948), a United Nations mission to the Near East (1949), a United Nations Mission to Afghanistan (1950), and an International Bank Mission to Turkey (1950). Kirk was a strong believer in co-operative effort and introduced many of his plans on a regional rather than a national basis despite objections from the United Nations' Food and Agriculture Organization. He was largely successful because he was able to encourage co-operation among nations with similar problems and because of his dedication to improving the lot of the less fortunate people of the world. He returned to the University of Saskatchewan in 1956. He died November 28, 1969. He was a fellow of the Royal Society of Canada, of the Agricultural Institute of Canada, and of the American Society of Agronomists. Among his publications are *Industrial utilization of farm products in Saskatchewan* (Regina, 1944).

[*Proc. and Trans. Roy. Soc. Can.*, vol. VIII (1970); *Can. who's who*, 1955-57.]

Kirkconnell, Thomas Allison (1862-1934), educationist, was born in 1862, and was educated at Queen's University (B.A., 1884). He became a school-teacher, and from 1908 to 1932 was principal of the Lindsay Collegiate Institute. He died at Milton, Ontario, on April 6, 1934.

[W. Kirkconnell, *A Canadian headmaster* (Toronto, 1935).]

Kirke, Sir David (1597-1654), adventurer, was born in Dieppe, France, in 1597, the son of a Scottish merchant. In 1627 he was given by Charles I of England command of an expedition against Canada, and in 1629 he captured Quebec. He was knighted by Charles I in 1633, and in 1637 he was appointed governor of Newfoundland; but in 1651 he was recalled by Cromwell's Council of State, on suspicion of complicity with the royalists. He died in 1654, probably in an English prison, where he was detained at the suit of Lord Baltimore, who laid claim to Newfoundland. His wife, sister, and children were still living at Ferryland, in Newfoundland, in 1673, and his son at Renewse in 1680.

[H. Kirke, *The first English conquest of Canada* (2nd ed., London, 1908); L. D. Scisco, *Kirke's memorial on Newfoundland* (Can. hist. rev., 1926); Le Jeune, *Dict. gén.*; *Dict. Can. biog.*, vol. 1.]

Kirke, Sir Lewis (*fl.* 1599-1660), adventurer, was a brother of Sir David Kirke (q.v.), and accompanied his brother to Canada in 1627. He was left in charge of Quebec when it was captured by the English in 1629, and surrendered it to the French in 1632. He fought on the royalist side in the Great Rebellion in England, and was knighted by Charles I in 1643. After the Restoration of 1660 he was appointed captain and paymaster of the corps of gentlemen-at-arms.

[H. Kirke, *The first English conquest of Canada* (2nd ed., London, 1908); Le Jeune, *Dict. gén.*; *Dict. Can. biog.*, vol. 1.]

Kirkpatrick, Frank Home (1875-1940), educationist, was born in Gwillimbury township, Ontario, in 1875. He was educated at the Ottawa Normal School and at Hiram College, Ohio; and he was for a time professor of oratory in Wooster University and Hiram College. He returned to Canada to become principal of the Toronto Conservatory School of Expression; and he was in his later years employed by various educational institutions as an instructor in public speaking. He died near Toronto, Ontario, on April 4, 1940. He was the author of *Public speaking* (Toronto, 1923).

[Toronto *Globe and Mail*, April 5, 1940.]

Kirkpatrick, Sir George Airey (1841-1899), lieutenant-governor of Ontario (1892-97), was born at Kingston, Upper Canada, on September 13, 1841, the son of Thomas Kirkpatrick and Helen, daughter of Alexander Fisher. He was educated at the grammar school in Kingston, at the high school in St. Johns, Lower Canada, and at Trinity College, Dublin (B.A., and LL.B., 1861). He was called to the bar of Upper Canada in 1865 (Q.C., 1880); and in 1870 he was elected to succeed his father in the representation of the county of Frontenac in the Canadian House of Commons. This seat he retained without interruption until his appointment as lieutenant-governor of Ontario in 1892. His term of office expired in 1897; and he died at Toronto, Ontario, after a long illness, on December 13, 1899. He was twice married, (1) in 1865 to Frances Jane (d. 1877), daughter of the Hon. John Macaulay (q.v.) of Kingston; and (2) in 1883 to Isabel Louise, daughter of Sir David Lewis Macpherson (q.v.). By his first wife he had four sons and one daughter; and by his second wife one son. He was created a K.C.M.G. in 1897.

[D. B. Read, *The lieutenant-governors of Upper Canada and Ontario* (Toronto, 1900); D. Swainson, *George Airey Kirkpatrick* (Historic Kingston, 1970); E. M. Chadwick, *Ontarian families* (2 vols., Toronto, 1894-98); Morgan, *Can. men* (1898); Rose, *Cyc. Can. biog.* (1886); Taché, *Men of the day*; *Can. parl. comp.*]

Kirkwood, Kenneth Porter (1899-1968), diplomat and author, was born in Brampton, Ontario, April 14, 1899, and educated at the University of Toronto (B.A., 1922), at British universities, and at Columbia University (M.A., 1927). He was employed by the Student Christian Movement (1922-23), and was a teacher in Smyrna, Turkey (1925-26), and at Columbia University. He joined the department of external affairs at Ottawa in 1928 and was stationed in Washington, Tokyo, the Hague, Rio de Janeiro, Buenos Aires, Santiago, and Warsaw. From 1952 to 1954 he was High Commissioner to Pakistan. He then went to Egypt as ambassador. In 1956 he became High Commissioner to New Zealand, returning to Ottawa in 1957. He retired in 1959. Kirkwood was co-author with Arnold Toynbee of *Turkey* (1927) in the Modern World series. He also wrote *Unfamiliar Lafcadio Hearn* (1936); *Lafcadio Hearn's ancestors* (1938); *Renaissance in Japan* (Tokyo, 1938); *Under Argentine skies* (Buenos Aires, 1945); *Abstractions, philosophical notes* (1937); and verses published as *In Gardens of Proserpine* (Yedo, 1930); *Song in my heart* (1932); *Travel dust*

(Tokyo, 1935); *Lyrics and sonnets* (1934); *Time's Tavern* (1937); *Excursions among books* (essays) (Buenos Aires, 1945). He died September 26, 1968, at Ottawa.

[*Can. who's who,* 1955-57; V.B. Rhodenizer, *Canadian literature in English* (Montreal, 1965).]

Kittson, Henry (1848-1925), clergyman, was born at Pembina, Minnesota, on November 15, 1848, the son of Norman W. Kittson (q.v.). He was educated at the University of Bishop's College, Lennoxville (B.A., 1870; M.A., 1871), and was ordained a priest of the Church of England in 1873. After serving as a missionary for several years, and as rector of churches in St. Paul, Minnesota, and in Philadelphia, Penn., he returned to Canada, and was rector of churches at Montreal and Ottawa. In 1903 he was made a canon of Christ Church Cathedral, Ottawa. He died at Berthierville, Quebec, on July 23, 1925. He was the author of *Church history from the archives* (Kingston, 1911).

[Morgan, *Can. men* (1912).]

Kittson, Norman Wolfred (1814-1888), fur-trader, was born at Chambly, Lower Canada, in 1814, the son of George Kittson and Nancy Tucker. His paternal grandmother's second husband was Alexander Henry (q.v.), the author of *Travels and Adventures.* In 1830 he was apprenticed to the American Fur Company for three years, and went west. In 1843 he became an agent of the American Fur Company, in charge of the valleys of the Upper Minnesota River and the Red River; and he established himself at Pembina, in opposition to the Hudson's Bay Company. He withdrew from the fur-trade in 1854; and went into the general supply business for the Indian trade. In the sixties he developed a line of steamers and barges on the Red River that came to be known as the Red River Transportation Company. In his later years he was associated with James J. Hill in his railway enterprises. He died in 1888.

[C. W. Rife, *Norman W. Kittson* (Minnesota history, 1925).]

Kittson, William (d. 1841), fur-trader, was an adopted son of George Kittson, a merchant of Sorel, Lower Canada. He served with the Canadian Voltigeurs in the War of 1812, and retired after the war as a second lieutenant. He then entered the service of the North West Company as an apprentice clerk. He was sent to the Pacific slope in 1818; and here he spent the rest of his life. He assisted in the founding of Fort Colvile and Fort Nisqually; and in 1840 he was in charge at Fort Nisqually. He died at Fort Vancouver on December 25, 1841. His first wife was a woman of the Walla Walla tribe; and his second was Helene, daughter of Finan McDonald (q.v.).

[Private information.]

Klein, Abraham Moses (1909-1972), poet, was born at Montreal, Quebec, February 14, 1909. He was educated at McGill University (B.A., 1930), and the University of Montreal (Law, 1933). He was a strong Zionist, and was editor of the *Canadian Zionist* (1936-37). The style of his poetry is strongly influenced by his Hebraic background, and its content by the experience of the Jewish people in his lifetime. His poetic works include *Hath not a Jew* (New York, 1940); *Poems* (Philadelphia, 1944); *The Hitleriad* (New York, 1944); *The rocking chair and other poems* (Toronto, 1948); and poems published in *The Canadian Forum,* the *Menorah Journal, The Nation,* and *Poetry* (Chicago). His *The rocking chair and other poems* won the Lorne Pierce Medal in 1957. He also wrote a novel, *The Second Scroll* (New York, 1951), a parable in the form of a pilgrimage to Israel. He died at Montreal, Quebec, August 21, 1972.

[*Can. who's who,* 1967-69; N. Story, *The Oxford companion to Canadian history and literature* (Toronto, 1967).]

Klengenberg, Kris (1869-1931), Arctic explorer, was born in Denmark, on December 21, 1869. His baptismal name was Christian Klengenberg Jorgensen; but after leaving Denmark at the age of fifteen, he dropped the name Jorgensen. He became a sailor; and in 1893 he married an Eskimo girl at Port Hope, Alaska. Thenceforth most of his life was spent as a trader and explorer in the Canadian Arctic. He established a trading-post at Rymer Point on Victoria Land; and it is said that his occupation of this post, after he had become a naturalized Canadian, strengthened Canada's claim to the Arctic islands. He had several children; and these carried on his work of amelioration among the Eskimo. He died at Vancouver, British Columbia, on May 4, 1931.

[T. MacInnes, *Klengenberg of the Arctic* (London, 1932); *Can. who was who,* vol. 1.]

Klinck, Leonard Sylvanus (1877-1969), educational pioneer, served for five years as the first dean of agriculture at the University of British Columbia and for twenty-five years as its president. He was born at Victoria Square, Ontario, on January 20, 1877. He attended elementary and secondary schools in Markham township and was a farmer and teacher before he entered the Agricultural College of the University of Toronto, graduating with a B.Sc. in 1903. He then went to the University of Minnesota and Iowa State College where he continued his studies in plant breeding (M.S.A., 1905; D.Sc., 1920). He was for nine years professor and head of the department of cereal husbandry at Macdonald College, McGill University. Here he began the experiments which later produced *Rhizoma* alfalfa. He came to the University of British Columbia in 1914 as a planner, intending to return to McGill, but he remained as professor of agronomy and dean of agriculture. In 1919, on the death of president Wesbrook, he became the second president of the University of British Columbia. He retired in 1944. Dr. Klinck was an advocate of university extension programs and a promoter of adult education. He was first president of the Agricultural Institute of Canada, which established the L.S. Klinck lectureship series in his honour in 1966. He was a fellow of the Royal Society of Canada, president of the British Columbia branch of the British and Foreign Bible Society, a governor of Union College, and a member of the board of the Y.M.C.A. He died at Vancouver, British Columbia, March 27, 1969.

[*Proc. and Trans. Roy. Soc. Can.* (fourth series, vol. VII, 1969); *Can. who's who*, 1961-63; *The Klinck family* (Stouffville, 1955).]

Klotz, Oscar (1878-1936), pathologist, was born at Preston, Ontario, on January 21, 1878, the son of Otto Julius Klotz (q.v.). He was educated at the University of Toronto (M.B., 1903), at McGill University (M.D., C.M., 1906), and at the universities of Bonn, Freiburg, and Marburg. He was lecturer in pathology at McGill University from 1907 to 1910, professor of pathology at the University of Pittsburgh from 1910 to 1920, professor of pathology in the faculty of medicine at Sao Paulo, Brazil, from 1920 to 1923, and professor of pathology in the University of Toronto from 1923 until his death, at Toronto, on November 3, 1936. He was the author of monographs on *Arterio-sclerosis* (Lancaster, Pa., 1911), *Influenza* (Pittsburgh, Pa., 1919), and *Concerning aneurysms* (Toronto, 1926).

[*Can. who's who*, 1936-37.]

Klotz, Otto Julius (1852-1923), astronomer, was born at Preston, Canada West, on March 31, 1852, the son of Otto Klotz, a native of Kiel, Holstein. He was educated at the Galt grammar school, at the University of Toronto (LL.D., 1904), and at the University of Michigan (C.E., 1872). In 1879 he entered the topographical surveys branch of the department of the interior at Ottawa; and during the subsequent thirty years he was engaged in surveys in the Canadian North-West, in British Columbia, and in Alaska. In 1908 he was appointed assistant chief astronomer to the department of the interior, and in 1917 director of the Dominion observatory. He died at Ottawa on December 28, 1923. In 1873 he married Mary Widenmann, daughter of the German consul in Michigan. In 1910 he was elected a fellow of the Royal Society of Canada; and he was the author of a number of pamphlets on astronomical and geographical subjects.

[R. M. Stewart, *Dr. Otto Klotz* (Journal of the Royal Astronomical Society of Canada,

1924); *Proc. Roy. Soc. Can.*, 1925; Morgan, *Can. men* (1912).]

Kneller, Henry (d. 1776), attorney-general of Canada (1769-75), came to Canada shortly after the British conquest. He was first deputy clerk of the Council and then clerk of the Crown; and from 1769 to 1775 he was attorney-general. He left Canada in 1775 with Chief Justice Hey (q.v.), and he died in England in March, 1776.

[P. G. Roy, *Les avocats de la région de Québec* (Lévis, Que., 1936).]

Knight, Archibald Patterson (1849-1935), biologist, was born near Renfrew, Canada West, in 1849. He was educated at Queen's University, Kingston (B.A., 1872; M.A., 1874), and at Victoria University (M.D., C.M., 1889); and for many years was a schoolmaster. In 1892 he was appointed professor of biology and physiology at Queen's University; and he retired from this post only in 1919. He died at Kingston on October 19, 1935. He was the author of a *High school chemistry* (Toronto, 1887), *Introductory physiology and hygiene* (Toronto, 1905), and *Hygiene for younger people* (Toronto, 1911).

[*Can. who's who*, 1936-37; Morgan, *Can. men* (1912).]

Knight, Cyril Workman (1879-1960), mining geologist, was born at Kingston, Ontario, November 28, 1879. His father was principal of Kingston Collegiate and Victoria Institute. Knight entered Queen's University in 1898 in the school of mining. He was awarded a B.Sc. in mining and geology in 1903 and then enrolled at Columbia University, where in 1905 he and William Campbell published a paper in *Economic Geology*, entitled "The paragenesis of the cobalt-nickel arsenides and silver deposits of Temiskaming, Ontario". This paper formed the basis for the branch of geology known as mineralography. In 1907 he joined the staff of the Ontario Bureau of Mines, where he worked until 1923, publishing thirty-six papers as a result of his investigations of Ontario mineral deposits. From 1923 to 1928 he was chief geologist for the Nipissing Mining Company, and in 1928 he established the Cyril Knight Prospecting Company. In 1930 he published a paper announcing the discovery, by Gilbert Labine, of pitchblende ore at Great Bear Lake. He was president of North Rankin Nickel Mines Limited from 1941 until his retirement in 1955. This company was formed to exploit the nickel deposits which his prospecting company had discovered at Rankin Inlet on Hudson Bay. He was a fellow of the Royal Society, a fellow of the Geological Society of America, and a primary organizer of the Geological Association of Canada in 1947. He died at Toronto in October, 1960.

[*Can. who's who*, 1955-57; *Trans. Roy. Soc. Can.* (1962).]

Knight, James (1640?-1720?), governor-in-chief in Hudson Bay (1713-18), was born in England, possibly in Berkshire, about the middle of the seventeenth century. He entered the service of the Hudson's Bay Company as a shipwright in 1676, and rose in the service of the Company until he was made in 1713 governor-in-chief of the posts in Hudson Bay. He returned to England in 1718; and in 1719 he was given command of an expedition "to find out the Streight of Anian, in order to discover gold, and other valuable commodities, to the northward". The expedition miscarried; and Knight and his crews perished on Marble Island in Hudson Bay, in 1720-21.

[J. F. Kenney (ed.), *The founding of Churchill: Being the journal of Captain James Knight, governor-in-chief in Hudson Bay, from the 14th of July to the 13th of September, 1717* (London, 1932); J. B. Tyrrell (ed.), *Documents relating to the early history of Hudson Bay* (Toronto: The Champlain Society, 1931); *Dict. Can. biog.*, vol. 2.]

Knister, Raymond (1900-1932), novelist, was born in Essex county, Ontario, in 1900. He devoted himself to writing, and was just beginning to make a name for himself when he was drowned, off Stoney Point, on Lake St. Clair, on August 30, 1932. He was the author of a novel entitled *White narcissus* (Toronto, 1929), and of a prize novel, *My star predominant*, which, owing to the failure of the firm of publishers which offered the prize, and the author's subsequent death, was not published until 1934. He also edited a volume of *Canadian short stories* (Toronto, 1928); and a volume of his *Collected poems*, with a memoir by Dorothy Livesay, was published after his death (Toronto, 1949).

[*Canadian author*, 1932.]

Knowles, Mrs. Elizabeth Annie McGillivray, *née* **Beach** (1866-1928), painter, was born at Ottawa, Canada, on January 8, 1866, the daughter of William Godkin Beach, of Brockville. She studied art under F. McGillivray Knowles (q.v.), and in 1890 married him. She made a specialty of nature studies; and in 1908 she was elected an associate of the Royal Canadian Academy of Art. Most of her professional life she spent in Toronto, but a few years before her death she and her husband opened a studio at Riverton, New Hampshire, and she died at Lancaster, New Hampshire, on October 4, 1928.

[*Can. who was who*, vol. 2; Morgan, *Can. men and women* (1912); N. MacTavish, *The fine arts in Canada* (Toronto, 1925).]

Knowles, Farquhar McGillivray Strachan Stewart (1860-1932), painter, was born at Syracuse, New York, on May 22, 1860, of English parentage. He studied art in Toronto, Canada, in Philadelphia, Pennsylvania, in London, England, and at the Académie Ju-

lien, Paris, France. He returned to Canada, and was elected an A.R.C.A. in 1889 and R.C.A. in 1899. During the latter half of his life he had a studio in Toronto, and he became one of the leading exponents in Canada of the classical school of landscape-painting. He died at Toronto on April 9, 1932. In 1890 he married Elizabeth Annie (q.v.), daughter of William Godkin Beach, of Brockville, Ontario, and she also became a painter of some distinction.

[*Can. who was who*, vol. 2; Morgan, *Can. men* (1912); A. H. Robson, *Canadian landscape painters* (Toronto, 1932); N. MacTavish, *The fine arts in Canada* (Toronto, 1925).]

Knowles, Robert Edward (1868-1946), clergyman and novelist, was born in Grey county, Ontario, on March 30, 1868, and died at Galt, Ontario, on November 15, 1946. He was educated at Manitoba College (B.A., 1890) and at Queen's University; and in 1891 was ordained a minister of the Presbyterian Church. He was for many years the minister of Knox Church, Galt. In later life, after an illness, he became a special writer for the Toronto *Daily Star*. He was the author of seven novels: *St. Cuthbert's* (Toronto, 1905), *The undertow* (Toronto, 1906), *The dawn at Shanty Bay* (Toronto, 1907), *The web of time* (Toronto, 1908), *The attic guest* (Toronto, 1909), *The handicap* (Toronto, 1910), and *The singer of the Kootenay* (Toronto, 1911).

[Toronto *Globe and Mail*, Nov. 16, 1946; *Can. who's who*, 1938-39; *Encyc. Can.*]

Knowlton, Paul Holland (d. 1863), pioneer, was the son of Silas Knowlton, a native of Massachusetts, who settled in Stukely, Lower Canada, in 1796. He began farming about 1810 on the shores of Lake Brome, and later, about 1832, founded the town of Knowlton, in Shefford county, Lower Canada. He represented Shefford county in the Legislative Assembly of Lower Canada from 1830 to 1834; he was a member of the Special Council of Lower Canada from 1838 to 1841; and he was a member of the Legislative Council of United Canada from 1841 to his death on August 28, 1863.

[E. M. Taylor, *History of Brome county* (2 vols., Montreal, 1908-37).]

Knox, Ellen Mary (1858-1924), educationist, was born at Wadden, Surrey, England, on October 4, 1858. She was educated at St. Hugh's Hall, Oxford; and, after some time on the staff of the Cheltenham Ladies College, she came to Canada in 1894 to assume the principalship of Havergal Ladies' College, Toronto. She continued in charge of this school until her death at Toronto on January 24, 1924. She was the author of *Bible lessons for schools* (3 vols., London, 1907-08) and *The girl of the new day* (Toronto, 1919).

[*Ellen Mary Knox* (Toronto: Havergal College, 1925); A. R. Collins, *Real people* (Walkerton, Ont., n.d.); Morgan, *Can. men and women* (1912).]

Knox, John (d. 1778), soldier and author, was born in Ireland, the third son of John Knox, a merchant of Sligo. He served as a volunteer in the war that ended in 1748, and in 1749 was rewarded with an ensigncy in the 43rd Regiment of Foot. He went to America as a lieutenant in 1757, and he served throughout the Seven Years' War until after the capitulation of Montreal in 1760. Appointed in 1761 captain of an independent company that later became the 99th Foot, Knox retired on half pay in 1763 when the regiment was disbanded. From 1775 until his death on February 8, 1778, he was in command of the garrison at Berwick, England. He was the author of *An historical journal of the campaigns in North America for the years 1757, 1758, 1759, and 1760* (2 vols., London, 1769; new ed., by A. G. Doughty, with introduction, notes, and appendix, 3 vols., Toronto, The Champlain Society, 1914-15).
[Le Jeune, *Dict. gén.*]

Kolaut, Pacome (1926-1968), Eskimo sculptor, was born in the Eastern Arctic at Igloolik. He was an outstanding hunter and a leader in his community and became president of the Igloolik Cooperative when it was founded in 1963. He became a fine carver and is represented by *Bear Hunt* in the National Museum of Canada. He was drowned in Foxe Basin in June, 1968, as he and two friends attempted to bring heavy earth-moving equipment from Bray Island to Igloolik.
[C. S. MacDonald, *Dictionary of Canadian Artists*, vol. 3 (1971); Van der Velde, "Pacome Kolaut and the Igloolik Cooperative" in *North*, vol. 15, no. 5. (1968).]

Konantz, Margaret McTavish (1899-1967), international welfare organizer, was born in Winnipeg, Manitoba, April 30, 1899, and educated in Winnipeg and Toronto private schools. Mrs. Konantz began her work as president of the Junior League of Winnipeg in 1929, and became Canadian representative to the Junior Leagues of America in 1933. She was chairman of the Manitoba campaign of the child-care division of the Canadian Welfare Council in 1936. During the Second World War she was active in wartime volunteer work and organized a co-ordinating board for war and welfare services. She became active in United Nations support as president of the Winnipeg Branch of the United Nations Association from 1957 to 1961. During this period she visited Asia for UNICEF and became national chairman of the UNICEF Committee in 1965. Mrs. Konantz was a member of the Canadian delegation to the 18th United Nations General Assembly in 1963 and the representative of Canada at the 20th General Assembly. She

was elected a member of the House of Commons in 1963 but was defeated in the 1965 election. In 1946 she received the O.B.E. for her war work. She died in Fredericton, New Brunswick, May 11, 1967, while on a speaking tour for UNICEF.
[*Can. who's who*, 1964-66.]

Kribs, Louis P. (1857-1898), journalist, was born at Hespeler, Canada West, on February 27, 1857. He became a journalist, and was employed successively on the staffs of the Toronto *Globe, Mail, News, World*, and *Empire*. In 1891, while parliamentary correspondent of the *Empire*, he was elected president of the Press Gallery at Ottawa. In 1894 he founded the *Advocate*, a journal devoted to the defence of the spirits, wine, and beer trade. He died on March 24, 1898. An ardent Conservative, he was the author of *The Manitoba school question, considered historically, legally, and controversially* (Toronto, 1895).
[Morgan, *Can. men* (1898).]

Krieghoff, Cornelius (1815-1872), painter, was born at Amsterdam, Holland, in 1815, the son of Johann Krieghoff. He first travelled about Europe, and then came to America. He joined the United States army, and took part in the Seminole Indian war in Florida. Drawings which he made of episodes in this war led the United States government to commission him to make replicas for the War Department. From Rochester, New York, where he executed this work, he came to Toronto, Canada, where his brother Ernest was living. He then removed to Montreal, and in 1853 he went to Quebec. About 1864 he was persuaded to go to Chicago; and here he died in 1872. He had a studio successively in Toronto, in Montreal, and in Quebec; and many of his pictures are still in these places. Perhaps his most important work was "After the Ball at Jolifous-Montmorency".
[M. Barbeau, *Cornelius Krieghoff* (Toronto, 1934); A. H. Robson, *Cornelius Krieghoff* (Toronto, 1937); *Dict. Can. biog.*, vol. 10.]

Krotkov, Gleb Paul (1901-1968), plant biologist, was born in Moscow, Russia, in 1901, the son of a university professor. His family fled to southern Russia during the revolution and he enlisted in the White Russian Navy. His ship escaped the defeat of the other ships in the flotilla by sailing to Bizerte in Tunis, where he was discharged. He worked for a year as a mule driver before making his way to Marseilles as a stowaway. He made his way to Czechoslovakia, where he won a scholarship at the agricultural college. He graduated *cum laude* in 1925 as an agricultural engineer; and with the money he saved by completing the four-year course in three years he and a companion from Bizerte emigrated to London, Ontario. Here he worked on a farm before getting employment as a labourer at the Horticultural Station in Vineland, Ontario. In 1927 he enrolled as a graduate student in plant physiology at the University of Toronto. He completed his M.A. in 1931 and his Ph.D. in 1934. From 1931 until 1963 he was a member of the department of biology at Queen's University, rising from lecturer to head of the department in 1958. During the Second World War he undertook extensive investigation of Russian research into rubber plant substitutes. He and his students did extensive work on photosynthetic metabolism in marine algae, the occurrence of nucleic acids and phosphate esters in algae and higher plants, and the translocation of assimilates in coniferous trees. He was a fellow of the Royal Society of Canada and received its highest prize for biological research, the Flavelle Medal, in 1964. He was a member of the National Research Council. He died at Kingston, Ontario, January 29, 1968.

[*Proc. Roy. Soc. Can.*, vol. VI (1968).]

Kylie, Edward Joseph (1880-1916), historian, was born in Lindsay, Ontario, on September 19, 1880. He was educated at the University of Toronto (B.A., 1901) and Balliol College, Oxford (B.A., 1903; M.A., 1906). In 1904 he was appointed lecturer in history at the University of Toronto, and in 1908 associate professor. In 1915 he was appointed adjutant of the 147th Battalion, Canadian Expeditionary Force; and he died at Owen Sound, Ontario, on May 14, 1916. He translated and edited *The English correspondence of St. Boniface* (London, 1911).

[*Can. who was who*, vol. 1; *University of Toronto monthly*, 1916; Morgan, *Can. men* (1912).]

Labadie, Louis (1765-1824), school-teacher, was born at Quebec on May 18, 1765, and was educated at the Quebec Seminary. He became a school-teacher, and had schools successively at Beauport, Rivière-Ouelle, Kamouraska, Berthier-en-haut, Verchères, St. Eustache, and Varennes. He achieved a considerable reputation, and was known as "le maître d'école patriotique". He died at Verchères, Lower Canada, on June 19, 1824.

[Mgr. Amédée Gosselin, *Louis Labadie* (Trans. Roy. Soc. Can., 1913); P. G. Roy, *Fils de Québec*, vol. 2 (Lévis, Que., 1933).]

La Barre, Joseph-Antoine Lefebvre de (1622-1688), governor of New France (1682-84), was the son of Antoine Lefebvre, Sieur de la Barre, and Madeleine Belin, and was born in 1622. He was successively royal intendant at Paris, at Bourbonnais, at Auvergne, and at Dauphiné. In 1664 he was made governor of Guiana; and in 1666 he became lieutenant-general. On returning to France in 1671, he published a *Journal du voyage de Sieur de la Barre en la terre ferme et Isle de Cayenne*. In 1682 he was appointed governor of New France, and he arrived at Quebec in the month of August. He was recalled after his disastrous campaign against the Iroquois, in 1684. He died in Paris in May, 1688. He married on September 20, 1645, Marie Mandat (d. December, 1689), and he had one son.

[J. E. Roy, *La famille Lefebvre de la Barre* (Bull. rech. hist., vol. ii); R. Roy, *Joseph-Antoine Lefebvre, sieur de la Barre, gouverneur de la Nouvelle-France en 1682* (Bull. rech. hist., vol. xx); Le Jeune, *Dict. gén.*; *Dict. Can. biog.*, vol. 1.]

Labat, Gaston P. (1843-1908), journalist, was born in France, of Polish origin, in 1843. After serving in the French army, he emigrated to Canada, and became a journalist. He served on the staffs of several newspapers in Quebec and Montreal; and he died at Montreal on February 9, 1908. He was the author of *Les Voyageurs canadiens à l'expédition du Soudan* (Quebec, 1886) and *Le livre d'or des contingents canadiens dans l'Afrique sud* (Montreal, 1901).

[*Bull. rech. hist.*, 1924.]

Labelle, François Xavier Antoine (1833-1891), priest and colonizer, was born at Ste. Rose, Laval county, Quebec, on November 24, 1833. He was educated at the College of Ste. Thérèse, and was ordained a priest of the Roman Catholic Church in 1856. From 1868 to his death, he was parish priest of St. Jérôme; and he devoted great zeal to the colonization of the townships north of Montreal. He came, in fact, to be known as the "Apostle of Colonization". In 1888 he was appointed deputy-minister of agriculture and colonization under the Mercier government in Quebec; and in 1889 he was created by the Pope an apostolic prothonotary. He died at Quebec on January 4, 1891.

[Abbé E.-J. Auclair, *Le curé Labelle* (Montreal, 1930); Allaire, *Dict. biog.*; Le Jeune, *Dict. gén.*]

Laberge, Charles Joseph (1827-1874), lawyer, journalist, and politician, was born at Montreal, Lower Canada, on October 21, 1827, and was educated at St. Hyacinthe College. He was called to the bar of Lower Canada in 1848 (Q.C., 1858), and became a member of the *parti rouge*. From 1854 to 1861 he represented Iberville in the Legislative Assembly of Canada; and in 1858 he was solicitor-general for Lower Canada in the short-lived Brown-Dorion administration. In 1872 he was appointed editor-in-chief of *Le National*. He died on August 3, 1874. In 1859 he married Hélène Olive, daughter of the Hon. J. O. Turgeon; and by her he had several children.

[H. Mercier, *Charles Laberge* (pamphlet, Montreal, 1884); L. O. David, *Mes contemporains* (Montreal, 1894) and *Souvenirs et portraits* (Montreal, 1911); *Cyc. Am. biog.*; Bibaud, *Panth. can.*; Le Jeune, *Dict. gén.*; *Dict. Can. biog.*, vol. 10.]

Labrecque, Michel Thomas (1849-1932), Roman Catholic bishop of Chicoutimi (1892-1928), was born at St. Antoine, Canada East, on December 30, 1849. He was ordained a priest in 1876, and became a professor in the Quebec Seminary. After three years of study in Rome, where he received the degree of D. Theol. (1883), he was appointed professor of moral theology in Laval University, and later he became director of the *grande séminaire*. In 1892 he was elected bishop of Chicoutimi, and he continued in charge of this diocese until his retirement in 1928, when he became titular bishop of Heliopolis. He died at Chicoutimi, Quebec, on June 3, 1932.

[Allaire, *Dict. biog.*]

Labrie, Jacques (1784-1831), physician, politician, and author, was born at St. Charles de Bellechasse, Quebec, on January 4, 1784, the son of Jacques Nau dit Labrie and Marie Louise Brousseau. He was educated at the Quebec Seminary, and studied medicine at Quebec and at Edinburgh, Scotland. He was one of the founders and editors of the *Courrier de Québec* (1806-08); but in 1808 he left Quebec, and settled at St. Eustache, in the Two Mountains district, as a country doctor. Here he took a great interest in education and political reform; and in 1827 he was elected to represent the county of York (later the county of Two Mountains) in the Legislative Assembly of Lower Canada. He was re-elected in 1830; but died on October 6, 1831. In 1809 he married Marie Marguerite Gagnier, daughter of the notary of St. Eustache; and by her he had nine children, the eldest of whom married Dr. Jean Olivier Chénier (q.v.). His only publication was a popular treatise on *Les premiers rudiments de la constitution britannique* (Montreal, 1827); but he wrote also a history of Canada which was burnt, in manuscript, in the destruction by fire of the village of St. Benoît in 1838.

[Abbé A. Gosselin, *Un historien canadien oublié* (Trans. Roy. Soc. Can., 1893) and *Le docteur Labrie* (Quebec, 1907); *Cyc. Am. biog.*; Bibaud, *Panth. can.*; Morgan, *Bib. can.*; *Bull. rech. hist.*, 1930.]

Lacasse, Pierre Zacharie (1845-1921), missionary and author, was born at St. Jacques de l'Achigan, Quebec, on March 9, 1845, the son of Joseph Lacasse and Marguerite Mirault. He entered the Oblate order, and was ordained a priest in 1873. From 1875 to 1881 he was a missionary on the Labrador coast; then he was engaged in looking after colonization about Lake St. John and in preaching. In 1896 he was sent to the North West; and for twenty-five years he was a missionary among the French-speaking population of Manitoba and Saskatchewan. He died at Gravelbourg, Saskatchewan, on February 28, 1921. He was the author of *Une mine produisant l'or et l'argent* (Quebec, 1880), *Une mine de pierres détachées* (Quebec, 1881), *Trois contes sauvages* (Quebec, 1882), *Une nouvelle mine: Le prêtre et ses détracteurs* (Montreal, 1892), *Dans le camp ennemi* (Montreal, 1893), *Autour du drapeau* (Montreal, 1895), *Difficultés scolaires de Manitoba* (Montreal, 1895), and, under the pseudonym of "Jean Desprairies", *Une visite dans les écoles du Manitoba* (Montreal, 1897).

[Majella Quinn, *Zacharie Lacasse* (Recherches Sociographiques, 1969); Allaire, *Dict. biog.*; Le Jeune, *Dict. gén.*]

La Colombière, Joseph de (1651-1723), vicar-general of Quebec, was born in France in 1651, was ordained a priest in 1681, and was sent to Canada as a Sulpician missionary in 1682. He became vicar-general of Quebec, and a member of the Superior Council. He died at Quebec on July 18, 1723.

[Mgr. A. Gosselin, *Essai de biographie de l'abbé Joseph de la Colombière* (Trans. Roy. Soc. Can., 1935); *Dict. Can. biog.*, vol. 2]

Lacombe, Albert (1827-1916), missionary, was born at St. Sulpice, L'Assomption county, Lower Canada, on February 28, 1827, the son of Albert Lacombe and Agatha Duhamel. He was educated at L'Assomption College, joined the Oblate order, and was ordained a priest in 1849. He was one of the first Roman Catholic missionaries sent to the North West; and he spent his life in the service of the Indians and half-breeds in the North West Territories. During the rebellion of 1885 he rendered valuable aid to the authorities. He died near Calgary on December 11, 1916. Among other works, he was the author of a *Dictionnaire de la langue des Cris* (Montreal, 1874) and a *Grammaire de la langue des Cris* (Montreal, 1874).

[Katherine Hughes, *Father Lacombe, the black-robe voyageur* (Toronto, 1911); Une soeur de la Providence, *Le Père Lacombe* (Montreal, 1916); Gaston Carrière, *Le père Albert Lacombe* (Revue de l'Université d'Ottawa, 1967-68); Ray Bagley, *Lacombe in the nineties* (Alta. hist. rev., 1962); J. G. MacGregor, *Father Lacombe* (Edmonton, 1975); Le Jeune, *Dict. gén.*; Morgan, *Can. men* (1912); Allaire, *Dict. biog.*]

Lacorne, Louis de Chapt, Sieur de (1696-1762), seignior, was born in Montreal in 1696, was married in 1740 to Elizabeth de Ramezay, and died at his seigniory of Terrebonne in 1762. He is sometimes confused with his younger and more famous brothers.

[A. Fauteux, *Le chevalier de Lacorne* (Bull. rech. hist., 1920); Le Jeune, *Dict. gén.*]

Lacorne, Louis François de (1703-1761), soldier, was born on June 6, 1703, at Fort Frontenac, the son of Jean Louis de Lacorne. He was gazetted a captain in the French army in 1744, and fought under Ramezay (q.v.) in Acadia in 1747. In 1753 he was appointed commandant of the posts of the West, rebuilt Fort Paskoyac on the Saskatchewan, established a post on the site of the later Fort Cumberland, and explored the Carrot River valley of the Saskatchewan. Here he made some experiments in the growing of wheat; and he may thus be described as the first agriculturist of the Canadian West. He left the western country about 1755, and he played a brilliant part in the Seven Years' War. In 1761 he was drowned in the wreck of the *Auguste,* while emigrating from Canada. He married in 1728 Marie-Anne Hubert Lacroix, widow of Charles de Couagne; but he left no posterity. In 1749 he was created a chevalier de St. Louis. He is often confused with his younger brother, St. Luc de Lacorne.

[A. Fauteux, *Le chevalier de Lacorne* (Bull. rech. hist., 1920); L.A. Prud'homme, *Les successeurs de La Vérendrye* (Trans. Roy. Soc. Can., 1906); Le Jeune, *Dict. gén.*; *Dict. Can. biog.* vol. 3.]

Lacorne, St. Luc de (1712-1784), legislative councillor of Quebec, was born in 1712, the younger brother of the Chevalier Louis François de Lacorne (q.v.). He was an officer in the French army during the Seven Years' War, and in 1761, when leaving Canada, was shipwrecked on the *Auguste* off Cape Breton. He was one of seven survivors of the shipwreck; and he returned to Canada, and spent there the remainder of his life. In 1765 he was arrested on a charge of complicity in the attack on Thomas Walker (q.v.) in Montreal. He took part in the defence of the province against the Americans in 1775-76; and he commanded the Canadians and the Indians in the campaign of 1778, under Burgoyne. In 1775 he was appointed a member of the Legislative Council of Quebec; and he continued a member of the Council until his death in 1784. In his later years he was known as "Lacorne St. Luc". His *Journal de voyage . . . dans le navire l'Auguste en 1761* (Montreal, 1778) is one of the earliest of Canadian imprints.

[W. D. Lighthall, *La Corne St. Luc* (Montreal, 1908); A. Fauteux, *Le chevalier de Lacorne* (Bull. rech. hist., 1920); Le Jeune, *Dict. gén.*; Bibaud, *Panth. can.*]

La Corne de Chapt de St. Luc, Joseph Marie (1714-1779), priest and diplomat, was born at Verchères, New France, in 1714. He became a priest of the Roman Catholic Church, and in 1763 was sent to England to negotiate with the British government the appointment of a Roman Catholic bishop of Quebec. He succeeded in obtaining the appointment of Briand (q.v.). He died on December 8, 1779, at the abbey of Maubec, in France.

[R. La Roque de Roquebrune, *Un grand diplomate canadien: L'Abbé de la Corne* (Nova Francia, 1925); Le Jeune, *Dict. gén.*]

Lacoste, Sir Alexandre (1842-1923), chief justice of Quebec (1891-1907), was born at Boucherville, Lower Canada, on January 12, 1842, the son of the Hon. Louis Lacoste (q.v.), and Marie Antoinette Thaïs Proulx. He was educated at the College of St. Hyacinthe and at Laval University, was called to the bar of Lower Canada in 1863 (Q.C., 1876), and practised law in Montreal. In 1882 he was ap-

pointed a legislative councillor of Quebec, and in 1884 a senator of Canada. In 1891 he was appointed speaker of the Senate; but later in the same year he was appointed chief justice of the province of Quebec, and he occupied this position until his retirement on pension in 1907. In his later years he practised law in Montreal as a consultant; and he died at Montreal on August 17, 1923. In 1886 he married Marie Louise, daughter of Léon Globensky, of Montreal. He was an LL.D. of Laval University (1879) and a D.C.L. of Bishop's College, Lennoxville (1895). In 1892 he was appointed a privy councillor and was created a knight bachelor.

[E. F. Surveyer, *Sir Alexandre Lacoste* (Canadian bar review, 1923); Morgan, *Can. men* (1912); Taché, *Men of the day*; Le Jeune, *Dict. gén.*; *Can. parl. comp.*]

Lacoste, Louis (1798-1878), senator of Canada, was born at Boucherville, Lower Canada, on April 3, 1798. He was educated at the Sulpician College, Montreal; and in 1821 was admitted to practice as a notary public of Lower Canada. From 1834 to 1838 he sat in the Legislative Assembly of Lower Canada for Chambly; and he represented Chambly in the legislature of United Canada for much of the period from 1843 to 1861. He was then elected to represent the Montarville division in the Legislative Council; and in 1867 he was called to the Senate of the Dominion by royal proclamation. He died at Boucherville, Quebec, on November 26, 1878.

[*Dom. ann. reg.*, 1878; *Can parl. comp.*; J. C. Dent, *The last forty years* (2 vols., Toronto, 1881); *Dict. Can. biog.*, vol. 10.]

Lacroix, Henri Olivier (1826-1897), author, was born at Monroe, Michigan, on August 10, 1826, the son of Dominique Lacroix and Henriette Lalumière. He came to Canada before 1850; and in his later years he was employed in the customs house at Montreal. Apart from a number of pamphlets, in both French and English, he was the author of *Spiritisme américain: Mes expériences avec les esprits* (Paris, 1889). He died at Montreal on February 26, 1897.

[E. Z. Massicotte, *Un spirite canadien-français* (Bull. rech. hist., 1917).]

Lafitau, Joseph-François (1681-1746), missionary and author, was born in Bordeaux, France, and entered the Society of Jesus. He came to Canada in 1712 as a missionary, and was stationed for a time at the Sault St. Louis, where his portrait is still preserved. On his return to France he published a *Mémoire concernant la précieuse plante ginseng de Tartarie* (Paris, 1718), which gave rise to the trade with Canada in ginseng. Later he published his *Moeurs des sauvages américains* (2 vols., Paris, 1723; 4 vols., Rouen, 1724). He died in France on July 3, 1746.

[H. Verreau, "Notice biographique", in *Mémoire concernant la précieuse plante ginseng* (Montreal, 1855); *Cyc. Am. biog.*; Morgan, *Cel. Can.*; R. G. Thwaites (ed.), *The Jesuit relations* (73 vols., Cleveland, 1897-1901); *Dict. Can. biog.*, vol. 3.]

Laflamme, Joseph Clovis Kemner (1849-1910), priest and geologist, was born at St. Anselme, Canada East, on September 18, 1849. He was educated at the Quebec Seminary, and was ordained a priest of the Roman Catholic Church in 1872. From 1870 to 1909 he was professor of geology and mineralogy at Laval University; from 1875 to 1893 he was also professor of physics; and in 1893 he became rector of the University. He was a charter member of the Royal Society of Canada, and in 1891 was elected its president. He died at Quebec, Que., on July 6, 1910. He was the author of *Éléments de minéralogie et de géologie* (Quebec, 1881), *Notions sur l'électricité et le magnetisme* (Quebec, 1893), and *Éléments de minéralogie, de géologie, et de paléontologie* (Quebec, 1898).

[*Proc. Roy. Soc. Can.*, 1911; Le Jeune, *Dict. gén.*; Allaire, *Dict. biog.*; Morgan, *Can. men* (1898).]

Laflamme, Napoléon Kemner (1865-1929), lawyer and senator of Canada, was born at Lyster, Megantic county, Quebec, on October 22, 1865. He was educated at the Quebec Seminary and Laval University (LL.B., 1890), and was called to the bar of Quebec in 1893 (K.C., 1909). He became one of the leaders of the Montreal bar, and was employed as an advocate in several famous cases, both civil and criminal. In 1925 he was elected *bâtonnier* of the Montreal bar, and also *bâtonnier-général* of the bar of the province of Quebec. From 1921 to 1925 he represented Drummond-Arthabaska in the Canadian House of Commons; and in 1927 he was called to the Senate of Canada. He died at St. Mathias, Quebec, on August 10, 1929.

[*Can. who was who*, vol. 1; Morgan, *Can. men* (1912).]

Laflamme, Toussaint Antoine Rodolphe (1827-1893), lawyer and politician, was born at Montreal on May 15, 1827, the son of Toussaint Laflamme, a merchant, and Marguerite Suzanne Thibaudeau. He was educated at the College of St. Sulpice and at McGill University (B.C.L., 1856; D.C.L., 1873); and he was called to the bar of Lower Canada in 1849 (Q.C., 1863). In 1844 he was one of the founders of the Institut Canadien of Montreal; in 1847 he was its president; and in 1852, one of its incorporators. From 1872 to 1878 he represented Jacques Cartier in the Canadian House of Commons; and from 1876 to 1878 he was a member of the Mackenzie administration, first as minister of inland revenue (1876-77), and then as minister of justice (1877-78). In

1878 he retired from active politics; and he died on December 7, 1893. He was not married.

[*Can. who was who*, vol. 2; Le Jeune, *Dict. gén.*; Dent, *Can. port.*, vol. 1; Rose, *Cyc. Can. biog.* (1886); Bibaud, *Panth. can.*; *Can. parl. comp.*; J. D. Borthwick, *Montreal, its history* (Montreal, 1875); L. O. David, *Mes contemporains* (Montreal, 1894).]

La Flèche, Leo Richer (1888-1956), soldier and diplomat, was born in Concordia, Kansas, on April 15, 1888, and died in Montreal, Quebec, on March 7, 1956. He came to Canada with his parents as an infant; and after an apprenticeship in banking, entered the civil service. He served overseas during the First World War, was severely wounded, was promoted to the rank of lieutenant-colonel, and was awarded the D.S.O. After the war he was one of those who founded the Canadian Legion, and he was its president from 1928 to 1931. From 1932 to 1940 he served as deputy minister of national defence; and in 1938 he was promoted to the rank of major-general. After the war he entered the diplomatic service, and was successively Canadian ambassador to Greece (1945-49), high commissioner to Australia (1949-51), and ambassador to Uruguay and Argentina (1951-55).

[*Can. who's who*, 1952-54; *Can. parl. guide*, 1944; *Encyc. Can.*]

Laflèche, Louis François Richer (1818-1898), Roman Catholic bishop of Three Rivers (1870-98), was born at Ste. Anne de la Pérade, Lower Canada, on September 4, 1818. He was educated at the College of Nicolet, and was ordained a priest in 1844. From 1844 to 1856 he was a missionary in the North West; he was then successively a professor in the college of Nicolet, vicar-general of Three Rivers, coadjutor to the bishop of Three Rivers, and in 1870 bishop of Three Rivers. He administered this see until his death on July 14, 1898. He was the author of *Quelques considérations sur les rapports de la société civile avec la religion et la famille* (Montreal, 1866) and *Conférences* (Three Rivers, 1885).

[R. Rumilly, *Mgr Laflèche et son temps* (Montreal, 1938); A. G. Morice, *Dictionnaire biographique* (Quebec, 1908); Allaire, *Dict. biog.*; Le Jeune, *Dict. gén.*]

Lafleur, Eugene (1856-1930), lawyer and author, was born at Longueuil, Quebec, in 1856. He was educated at McGill University (B.A., 1877; B.C.L., 1877; D.C.L., 1900), and was called to the Quebec bar in 1881 (Q.C., 1899). From 1890 to 1909 he was professor of international law at McGill University; and he became an outstanding jurist. He died at Ottawa on April 29, 1930. Besides numerous papers on legal subjects, he was the author of *The conflict of laws in the province of Quebec* (Montreal, 1898).

[*Who's who in Canada*, 1930-31; Morgan, *Can. men* (1912).]

Lafleur, Paul Theodore (d. 1924), educationist, was born at Montreal, Quebec, the brother of Eugene Lafleur (q.v.). He was educated at McGill University (B.A., 1880; M.A., 1887), and was for many years a member of the teaching staff of this university. He died at Luxor, Egypt, on February 9, 1924. He was the author of *Illustrations of logic* (Boston, 1899).
[Morgan, *Can. men* (1912).]

Lafontaine, Sir Louis Hippolyte, Bart. (1807-1864), prime minister of Canada (1848-51), was born near Boucherville, Chambly county, Lower Canada, on October 4, 1807, the third son of Antoine Ménard dit La Fontaine, a farmer, and the grandson of Antoine Ménard La Fontaine, a member of the Legislative Assembly of Lower Canada from 1796 to 1804. He was educated at the College of Montreal, was called to the bar of Lower Canada, and practised law in Montreal. From 1830 to 1837 he was a member of the Legislative Assembly of Lower Canada for Terrebonne; and he was a supporter, though by no means a blind follower, of Louis Joseph Papineau (q.v.). He opposed the appeal to arms by the *patriotes* in 1837; but he deemed it wise to leave Canada, and on his return to Canada in 1838 was arrested. He was released, however, without trial; and when the union of 1841 was brought about, he became the leader of the French-Canadian Reformers. In the elections of 1841 he was defeated in Terrebonne, but found a seat, through the offices of Robert Baldwin (q.v.), in the fourth riding of York, Upper Canada. Thereafter he sat continuously in the Assembly until 1851, first for the fourth riding of York (1841-44), next for Terrebonne (1844-48), and lastly for the city of Montreal (1848-51).

During this period he was twice a member of the government of Canada. In 1842 he joined with Robert Baldwin in the formation of the first Baldwin-Lafontaine administration, holding the portfolio of attorney-general for Lower Canada; and it was as a result of a disagreement between himself and Sir Charles Metcalfe (q.v.) that the government resigned in November, 1843. He remained in opposition until the defeat of the Draper administration in 1848, and he was then called upon by Lord Elgin (q.v.) to form what is called the second Baldwin-Lafontaine administration. In this he again held the portfolio of attorney-general for Lower Canada; and it was he who introduced into parliament the famous Rebellion Losses Bill of 1848, the passage of which finally demonstrated the triumph of the principle of responsible or parliamentary government in Canada. This episode marked the zenith of his political career. Henceforth he grew more and more conservative in his attitude, especially in regard to the burning questions of the abolition of the seigniorial tenures and the secularization of the clergy reserves; and, shortly after the retirement of Robert Baldwin in 1851, he resigned from the government and withdrew from public life. In 1853 he was appointed chief justice of Lower Canada, and this position he occupied until his death at Montreal on February 26, 1864.

He was twice married, (1) to Adèle, daughter of Amable Berthelot, of Montreal, and (2) to Jane, daughter of Charles Morrison, of Berthier, and widow of Thomas Kinton, of Montreal; and by his second wife he had two sons, both of whom died in infancy. In 1854 he was created a baronet of the United Kingdom, but the title became extinct on his death. He was the author of *Les deux girouettes, ou l'hypocrisie démasquée* (pamphlet, Montreal, 1834), *Notes sur l'amovibilité des curés dans le Bas Canada* (pamphlet, Montreal, 1837), *Analyse de l'ordonnance du Conseil Spécial sur les bureaux d'hypothèques* (Montreal, 1842), and, with Jacques Viger (q.v.), the joint author of *Du l'esclavage en Canada* (Montreal, 1859). Lafontaine's papers were left to the Société Historique de Montréal, and a selection from them was printed and edited by M. de la Bruère in the *Revue canadienne*, 1916.

[Stephen Leacock, *Baldwin, Lafontaine, Hincks* (Toronto, 1907); L. O. David, *Biographies et portraits* (Montreal, 1876); E. Z. Massicotte, *Notes sur Sir Louis Hippolyte Lafontaine* (Bull. rech. hist., 1916); *Sir L.-H. Lafontaine* (Bull. rech. hist., 1917); *Dict. nat. biog.*; Le Jeune, *Dict. gén.*; Dent, *Can. port.*, vol. 3; Taylor, *Brit. Am.*, vol. 1; Morgan, *Cel. Can.* and *Bib. can.*; Bibaud, *Panth. can.*]

Lafrance, Charles Joseph Lévesque dit (1833-1921), educationist, was born at Quebec, Lower Canada, on November 13, 1833. He became a school-teacher, and from 1859 to 1876 he conducted a commercial academy at Quebec. From 1878 to 1914 he was treasurer of the city of Quebec; and he died at Quebec on December 12, 1921. He was the author of *Abrégé de grammaire française* (Quebec, 1865) and *Nouvelle arithmétique commerciale et pratique* (Quebec, 1867).
[*Bull. rech. hist.*, 1927; P.G. Roy, *Fils de Québec*, vol. 4 (Lévis, Que., 1933).]

Lafrance, François Xavier (1814-1867), priest, was born at Quebec, Lower Canada, on February 16, 1814, and was educated at the Quebec Seminary. He was ordained a priest of the Roman Catholic Church in 1841. He became a missionary among the Acadians of New Brunswick, and was the founder of the College of St. Joseph at Memramcook, New Brunswick. He died at Barachois, near Shediac, New Brunswick, on November 27, 1867.
[P.F. Bourgeois, *Vie de l'abbé François Xavier Lafrance* (Montreal, 1925); P. G. Roy, *Fils de Québec*, vol. 3 (Lévis, Que., 1933).]

Lagacé, Pierre Minier (1830-1884), priest, was born at Ste. Anne de la Pocatière, Lower Canada, October 17, 1830. He was ordained a priest of the Roman Catholic Church in 1854; and was first a professor, and then superior, at the College of Ste. Anne de la Pocatière. In his later years he was principal of the Normal School at Quebec; and he died at Quebec on December 6, 1884. He was the author of *Les chants d'église harmonisés* (Quebec, 1859) and *Cours de lecture à haute voix* (Quebec, 1875).

[Allaire, *Dict. biog.*; Bull rech. hist., 1932.]

La Galissonière, Roland Michel Barrin, Comte de (1693-1756), governor of New France (1747-49), was the son of a lieutenant-general of the navy, and was born in Rochefort on November 11, 1693. He was educated at the college of Beauvais, and in 1710 he entered the Royal Navy. In 1738 he was made a captain, and in 1747 was appointed administrator of Canada during the captivity of La Jonquière (q.v.) in England. He returned to France in 1749, and became head of the department of nautical charts at Paris. In 1755 he became lieutenant-general of the naval forces; and in the next year he commanded the French fleet at Minorca, and defeated the British under Admiral Byng. He died on October 26, 1756, at Montereau.

[C. de Bonnault, *M. de la Galissonière* (Franco-American review, 1937); Edouard Goepp, *Roland-Michel Barrin, Marquis de La Galissonière* (Bull. rech. hist., vol. viii); P. G. R., *Le Comte de la Galissonière et la Nouvelle-France* (Bull. rech. hist., vol. iii); *Dict. Can. biog.*, vol. 3.]

Lagemodière, Mme. Marie Anne, *née* **Gaboury** (1780-1875), the first French-Canadian woman in the Canadian West, was born at Maskinongé, Que., on August 2, 1780, the daughter of Charles Gaboury. In 1806 she married Jean-Baptiste Lagemodière, a western fur-trader, and accompanied him to the Red River. She died in 1875 at St. Boniface, Manitoba.

[G. Dugas, *La première canadienne du Nord-Ouest* (Montreal, 1883); *Dict. Can. biog.*, vol. 10.]

La Hontan, Louis-Armand de Lom d'Arce, Baron de (1666-1715), soldier and author, was the son of the Baron Isaac de Lom d'Arce and Jeanne-Françoise Le Fascheux de Couttes, and was born on June 9, 1666. He early entered the army as a lieutenant in the Bourbon regiment, and came to Canada in 1683 as an officer in the marines, arriving at Quebec on November 8. In 1684 he took part in La Barre's unsuccessful march against the Senecas, and in 1687, during Denonville's expedition against the Iroquois, he commanded Fort St. Joseph. In 1688-89 he made a voyage down the Wisconsin and the Mississippi into unexplored territory. In 1690 he left Quebec

for France carrying despatches to Louis XIV, and before returning in 1691, his rank was raised to that of captain. In 1692 he made another voyage to France to propose plans for a fleet on the Great Lakes, and was named king's lieutenant at Plaisance. Here he came into disagreement with the governor, who complained of his insubordination, and in 1693 he sailed for Portugal to escape arrest. He then visited Denmark, and finally took up his residence in Holland. He died in Hanover in 1715. From 1694 to 1703 he was engaged in writing his memoirs, which were published at The Hague in 1703, under the title, *Nouveaux voyages de M. le Baron de La Hontan dans l'Amérique Septentrionale*. This work had an immediate vogue, went through twelve French editions in less than half a century, and was translated into English, Dutch, and German.

[F. C. B. Crompton, *Glimpses of early Canadians: Lahontan* (Toronto, 1925); J. E. Roy, *Le Baron de Lahonton* (Trans. Roy. Soc. Can., 1894); R. G. Thwaites (ed.), *New voyages to North America, by the Baron de Lahontan* (2 vols., Chicago, 1905); *Dict. Am. biog.*; *Cyc. Am. biog.*; Le Jeune, *Dict. gén.*; *Dict. Can. biog.*, vol. 2.]

Laidlaw, George (1828?-1889), railway builder, was born in Scotland about 1828, the son of George Laidlaw, of Comar, Ross-shire, and nephew of William Laidlaw, factor to Sir Walter Scott, at Abbotsford. He came to Canada in youth, and engaged first in the grain business. Then he turned to railway-building, and he took a foremost part in building the Toronto, Grey, and Bruce Railway, the Toronto and Nipissing Railway, and the Credit Valley Railway – lines which were ultimately absorbed by the Canadian Pacific and Grand Trunk Railways, but which in earlier days made a network of communications about Toronto. In his later days, he lived on his farm near Coboconk, on Balsam Lake, Ontario; and he died here on August 6, 1889. He was the author of *Cheap railways: A letter to the people of Grey and Bruce* (Toronto, 1867), and the compiler of *Reports and letters on light narrow gauge railways* (Toronto, 1867; 2nd ed., with appendix, 1868).

[Private information.]

Laing, Arthur (1904-1975), senator, was born at Eburne, British Columbia, September 9, 1904. He graduated from the University of British Columbia (B.S.A., 1925), and worked with Vancouver Milling and Grain Company (1926-33) and as manager of the agricultural chemical division of Buckerfield's Limited (1933-51). He was an unsuccessful candidate in the provincial elections of 1937 and 1941, but was elected to the House of Commons in the general election of 1949. He resigned in 1953 to lead the British Columbia Liberal party and was a member of the British Columbia Assembly from 1953 to 1956. He resigned his leadership in 1959 after his defeat in the 1956 provincial election but was returned to Ottawa in 1962, for Vancouver South. He became minister of northern affairs and national resources (1963-66); Indian affairs and northern development (1966-68); public works (1968); and veterans affairs (1972). He was summoned to the Senate in 1972. He was a member of the Agricultural Institute of Canada. He died at Vancouver, British Columbia, February 13, 1975.

[*Can. who's who*, 1970-72.]

Laird, David (1833-1914), journalist and politician, was born at New Glasgow, Prince Edward Island, on March 12, 1833, the son of the Hon. Alexander Laird, an executive councillor of Prince Edward Island. He was educated at the Presbyterian Theological Seminary, Truro, Nova Scotia; but became a journalist, and was the founder, and for many years the editor and publisher, of the Charlottetown *Patriot*. In 1871 he was elected for Belfast in the Legislative Assembly of Prince Edward Island; and in 1872 he became a member of the Hawthorne administration in the Island. He had opposed Confederation on the basis of the Quebec Resolutions in 1864; but in 1873 he was one of the delegates sent to Ottawa to arrange for the admission of Prince Edward Island into the Dominion. In 1873 he was elected for Queen's county, Prince Edward Island, in the Canadian House of Commons, and was regarded as the leader of the Prince Edward Island members in the House. His refusal to support Sir John Macdonald (q.v.) in the "Pacific Scandal" crisis in 1873 was one of the chief factors in the fall of the Macdonald government. From 1873 to 1876 he was minister of the interior in the Mackenzie administration; and in 1876 he was appointed lieutenant-governor of the North West Territories. On the termination of his period of office as lieutenant-governor, he returned to Charlottetown, and resumed the control of the *Patriot*. In 1898, however, he was appointed Indian commissioner for the North West Territories, Manitoba, and Keewatin; and he held this post until his death at Ottawa on January 12, 1914. In 1864 he married Mary Louisa, daughter of Thomas Owen, postmaster-general of Prince Edward Island; and by her he had four sons and two daughters.

[M. O. Hammond, *Confederation and its leaders* (Toronto, 1917); *Can. who was who*, vol. 2; Morgan, *Can. men* (1912); Dent, *Can. port.*, vol. 3; *Cyc. Am. biog.*; *Can. parl. comp.*; A. Morris, *Treaties of Canada with the Indians* (Toronto, 1880).]

Lajoie, Antoine Gérin. See **Gérin-Lajoie, Antoine.**

La Jonquière, Jacques Pierre Taffanel, Marquis de (1685-1752), governor of New France (1749-52), was born at the Château of Lasgraïsses, near Albi, France, in 1685. He served in the war against the Protestant Cévennes peasants in France, and in the defence of Toulon against the British admiral Thomas Mathews. In 1746 he was a rear-admiral under the Duc d'Anville in the expedition against Acadia; and in 1749 he was appointed governor of New France. He administered the government of New France until his death, at Quebec, on March 17, 1752. In 1721 he married Marie Angélique de la Valette; and by her he had one daughter.

[Marquis de la Jonquière, *Le chef d'escadre Marquis de la Jonquière et le Canada* (Paris, n.d.); P. G. R., *La mort du gouverneur de la Jonquière* (Bull. rech. hist., 1897); A. Gosselin, *Les de la Jonquière au Canada* (Bull. rech. hist., 1898); P.G.R., *A-t-on calomnié M. de la Jonquière?* (Bull. rech. hist., 1920); *Cyc. Am. biog.*; Le Jeune, *Dict. gén.*; *Dict. Can. biog.*, vol. 3.]

Lake, Sir Percy Henry Noel (1855-1940), soldier, was born at Tenby, Wales, on June 29, 1855; and was educated at Uppingham School. He entered the British army as a subaltern in the 59th Regiment in 1873; and he rose to the rank of lieutenant-general. He saw active service in Afghanistan, in the Soudan, and in Mesopotamia; and he was created a C.B. in 1902, a C.M.G. in 1905, a K.C.M.G. in 1908, and a K.C.B. in 1916. From 1905 to 1908 he was chief of the general staff in the Canadian militia; and from 1908 to 1910 he was inspector-general of the Canadian militia, and chief military adviser to the minister of militia. He retired from the army in 1919; and he died at Victoria, British Columbia, on November 16, 1940.

[*Who was who*, 1928-40; *Can. who's who*, 1936-37.]

Lake, Sir Richard Stuart (1860-1950), lieutenant-governor of Saskatchewan (1915-21), was born in Preston, Lancashire, England, on July 10, 1860, and died at Victoria, British Columbia, on April 23, 1950. He came to Canada in 1883, and became a farmer in Saskatchewan. He was a member of the Legislative Assembly of the North West Territories from 1898 to 1904, he represented Qu'Appelle in the Canadian House of Commons as a Conservative from 1904 to 1911, and he was lieutenant-governor of Saskatchewan from 1915 to 1921. In 1918 he was created a K.C.M.G. From 1931 to his death he lived in Victoria, British Columbia.

[*Can. who's who*, 1936-37; *Can. parl. guide*, 1920; *Encyc. Can.*]

Lalande, Louis (1869-1944), priest and author, was born at St. Hermas, Quebec, on December 25, 1869, and died at Montreal, Quebec, on October 20, 1944. He joined the Society of Jesus, and was ordained a priest of the Roman Catholic Church in 1894. From 1895 to 1906 he was a professor at the Collège Ste. Marie in Montreal, and at the time of his death he was the *doyen* of the Jesuit order in Canada. He was the author of *Une vieille seigneurie, Boucherville* (Montreal, 1890), *Causons* (Montreal, 1915), *Silhouettes paroissiales* (Montreal, 1920), and *Leurs profils et leur gestes* (Montreal, 1932), as well as of some works of edification.

[Allaire, *Dict. biog.*]

Lalemant, Charles (1587-1674), first superior of Jesuit missions in Canada, was born in Paris on November 17, 1587. On July 29, 1607, he became a novice of the Society of Jesus at Rouen. From 1612 to 1615 he was instructor in the college of Nevers, from 1620 to 1622 professor in the college at Bourges, and for three years principal of the boarding school of Clermont, Paris. In March, 1625, he was appointed superior of the mission at Quebec; and he arrived at Quebec with Enemond Massé and Jean de Brébeuf, in June of that year. In November, 1627, he went to France to secure supplies, and on returning in the following May, his ship was captured by D. Kirke (q.v.), and he was sent to Belgium and later to France. Upon returning to France in 1629, he was made rector of the college at Eu, and later of that at Rouen. In April, 1634, he again went to Canada, but he finally returned to France in 1638 and became agent for the Canadian missions. He died in Paris on November 18, 1674. He was the author of the *Relation* of 1625, which affords a graphic picture of the life of the little settlement at Quebec, and the beginnings of the Jesuit missions.

[R. G. Thwaites (ed.), *The Jesuit relations* (73 vols., Cleveland, 1897-1901); T. J. Campbell, *Pioneer priests of North America* (3 vols., New York, 1908-11); Le Jeune, *Dict. gén.*; *Cyc. Am. biog.*; *Dict. Can. biog.*, vol. 1.]

Lalemant, Gabriel (1610-1649), Jesuit missionary, was the nephew of Jérôme and Charles Lalemant (q.v.), and was born in Paris on October 3, 1610. On March 24, 1630, he became a Jesuit novice. From 1632 to 1635, he was instructor at Moulins, and again from 1641 to 1644, the intervening time being spent at Bourges and La Flèche; and later he was prefect of the college at Bourges and at La Flèche. He came to Canada in September, 1646, and laboured with Brébeuf (q.v.) at the mission of St. Ignace, among the Hurons. Here he was tortured to death by the Iroquois on March 17, 1649.

[R. G. Thwaites (ed.), *The Jesuit relations* (73 vols., Cleveland, 1897-1901); T. J. Campbell, *Pioneer priests of North America* (3 vols., New York, 1908-11); Le Jeune, *Dict. gén.*; *Cyc. Am. biog.*; *Dict. Can. biog.*, vol. 1.]

Lalemant, Jérôme (1593-1673), superior of Jesuit missions in Canada, was born in Paris on July 27, 1593. He entered the Jesuit novitiate on October 20, 1610, and after completing his probation, filled various positions in the colleges. In 1638 he was sent to Canada as a missionary to the Hurons, and he remained in the Huron country until 1645. In September, 1645, he went to Quebec to assume the office of superior of the missions in New France, and this position he held until November, 1650, when he returned to France. In 1658 he was made rector of the college at La Flèche, and in September, 1659, he was again appointed superior of the missions of New France. He died at Quebec on January 26, 1673. He wrote the *Relations* of the Huron missions (1639-1644), and those of New France (1646-48 and 1660-64).

[R. G. Thwaites (ed.), *The Jesuit relations* (73 vols., Cleveland, 1897-1901); T. J. Campbell, *Pioneer priests of North America* (3 vols., New York, 1908-11); Le Jeune, *Dict. gén.*; *Cyc. Am. biog.*; *Dict. Can. biog.*, vol. 1.]

Lambton, John George. See Durham, **Earl of.**

Lamont, John Henderson (1865-1936), jurist, was born at Horning's Mills, Canada West, in 1865; and was educated at the University of Toronto (B.A., 1892; LL.B., 1893). He was called to the bar of Ontario in 1893 (K.C., 1907); and practised law in Toronto until 1899. He then went to Prince Albert, in the North West Territories, to practise law; and in 1904 he was elected a member of the House of Commons for Saskatchewan. He resigned in 1905 to accept office as the first attorney-general of the province of Saskatchewan; and he sat in the Saskatchewan legislature for Prince Albert from 1905 to 1907. In 1907 he was appointed a judge of the Supreme Court of Saskatchewan; in 1918 he was transferred to the Court of Appeal; and in 1927 he was appointed a judge of the Supreme Court of Canada. He died in Ottawa, Ontario, on March 10, 1936.

[*Can. parl. comp.*; Morgan, *Can. men* (1912).]

La Mothe Cadillac, Antoine de. See **Cadillac, Antoine de La Mothe.**

Lampman, Archibald (1861-1899), poet, was born in the village of Morpeth, in western Ontario, on November 17, 1861, the son of the Rev. Archibald Lampman and Susannah Gesner. He was educated at Trinity University, Toronto (B.A., 1882); and in 1883 he obtained a post in the civil service at Ottawa. This post he retained until his death at Ottawa on February 10, 1899. He published three volumes of poetry, *Among the millet* (Ottawa, 1888), *Lyrics of earth* (Boston, 1893), and *Alcyone* (Edinburgh, 1899). A collected edition of his poems was published, with a memoir by Duncan Campbell Scott, after his death (Toronto, 1900); and a supplementary selection, entitled *At the Long Sault, and other poems*, has been edited by E. K. Brown (Toronto, 1943). He has been described as "the Canadian Keats"; and he is perhaps the most outstanding exponent of the Canadian school of nature poets. In 1895 he was elected a fellow of the Royal Society of Canada. In 1887 he married Emma Maud, daughter of Edward Playter, M.D., of Toronto; and by her he had one son and one daughter.

[C. Y. Connor, *Archibald Lampman* (Montreal, 1929); N. G. Guthrie, *The poetry of Archibald Lampman* (Toronto, 1927); O. J. Stevenson, *A people's best* (Toronto, 1927); A. MacMurchy, *A handbook of Canadian literature* (Toronto, 1906); Morgan, *Can. men* (1898).]

Lanaudière, Charles François Xavier Tarieu de (1710-1776), legislative councillor of Quebec, was born at Ste. Anne de la Pérade, New France, on November 4, 1710, the son of Pierre Thomas Tarieu de Lanaudière, seigneur de la Pérade. He entered the *troupes de la marine* in 1726 as an ensign, and he rose to the rank of captain. He served throughout the Seven Years' War, and became a prisoner of war at the capitulation of Montreal in 1760. He returned to France, but in 1763 he came back to Canada, and accepted the British régime. In 1775 he was appointed a member of the Legislative Council of the province of Quebec; but he died shortly afterwards, at Quebec, on February 1, 1776.

[P. G. Roy, *La famille Tarieu de Lanaudière* (Lévis, Que., 1922); Le Jeune, *Dict. gén.*]

Lanaudière, Charles Louis Tarieu de (1743-1811), legislative councillor of Lower Canada, was born at Quebec, New France, on October 14, 1743, the son of Charles François Xavier Tarieu de Lanaudière (q.v.). He obtained a commission in the *troupes de la marine*, and saw service at the battles of the Plains of Abraham and Ste. Foy. After the capitulation of Montreal, he returned with his regiment to France, and served there until 1767. He then came back to Canada; and he distinguished himself in the defence of Canada during the American Revolution. In 1792 he was appointed a legislative councillor of Lower Canada; and he sat in the Council until his death, at Quebec, Lower Canada, on October 2, 1811. He was known as the "Chevalier de Lanaudière".

[P. G. Roy, *La famille Tarieu de Lanaudière* (Lévis, Que., 1922); Le Jeune, *Dict. gén.*]

Lancefield, Richard Thomas (1854-1911), librarian and author, was born in London, England, on August 10, 1854, the son of Charles James Lancefield. He came to Canada with his parents in 1859, and was educated in the public schools of Hamilton, Ontario. In 1888 he became the librarian of the Hamilton Public Library; and about the same time he founded the *Canadian Bookseller*, of which he was the first editor. He died in Toronto, Ontario, on September 21, 1911. In 1878 he married Christina, daughter of Samuel McNair; and by her he had several children. He was the author of *Why I joined the new crusade: A plea for the placing of taxes on land values only* (Toronto, 1888), *Notes on copyright* (Hamilton, 1896; 2nd ed., 1897), *Tim and Mrs. Tim, a story* (Toronto, 1897), and *Victoria, sixty years a queen* (Toronto, 1897).

[Morgan, *Can. men* (1898).]

Lanceley, John Ellis (1848-1900), clergyman, was born in Birkenhead, England, on January 10, 1848. He came to Canada in early youth, and was educated at Victoria University, Cobourg. He entered the Methodist ministry in 1870, and was the pastor of churches in many parts of Ontario. He died at Toronto, Ontario, on March 5, 1900. He was the author of *The Virgin Mary, and other sermons* (Toronto, 1891) and *The devil of names, and other lectures and sermons* (Toronto, 1900).

[Morgan, *Can. men* (1898); G. H. Cornish, *Cyclopaedia of Methodism in Canada* (2 vols., Toronto, 1881-1903).]

Land, Robert Ernest Augustus (1847-1927), author, was born at Hamilton, Canada West, on January 2, 1847; and died at Santa Monica, California, on January 31, 1927. He was for several years grand commander of the Knights of Malta in America; and he was the author of *Fifty years in the Malta order* (2 vols., Toronto, 1928).

[Morgan, *Can. men* (1912).]

Landerkin, George (1839-1903), senator of Canada, was born in West Gwillimbury, Upper Canada, in 1839, the son of James Landerkin. He was educated at Victoria College, Cobourg (M.D., 1862), and he practised medicine for many years at Hanover, Ontario. He represented South Grey, as a Liberal, in the Canadian House of Commons from 1872 to 1878, and from 1882 to 1901, when he was called to the Senate of Canada. A man of much native humour, he was known as "the wit of the House". He died on October 4, 1903. In 1870 he married Mary, daughter of Joseph Kirkendall, of Elora, Ontario.

[*Can. parl. comp.*; Morgan, *Can. men* (1898).]

Landmann, George Thomas (1779-1854), soldier, was born at Woolwich, England, in 1779. He was educated at the Royal Military Academy, and obtained a commission in the Royal Engineers in 1795. He was sent to Canada in 1797, and was employed first in the construction of fortifications at St. Joseph's Island, in Lake Huron, and then in the cutting of a new canal at the Cascades in the St. Lawrence River. He returned to England in 1802. He served throughout the Napoleonic Wars; and he retired from the army, with the rank of lieutenant-colonel, in 1824. He died at Shacklewell, near Hackney, London, on August 24, 1854. An account of his years in Canada will be found in his *Adventures and recollections* (2 vols., London, 1852).

[*Dict. nat. biog.*]

Landon, Fred (1880-1969), historian and librarian, was born in London, Ontario, on November 5, 1880. He was educated at the University of Western Ontario (B.A., 1906). He joined the editorial staff of the London *Free Press* in 1906 and was for a time a member of the Parliamentary Press Gallery, Ottawa. He became librarian of the London Public Library in 1916, and while there taught United States history at the University of Western Ontario from 1917 to 1947. He secured the 40,000-volume Barnett collection for the university library in 1918. In 1923 he became director of libraries at the university, becoming also in later years vice-president and dean of the faculty of graduate studies. He was very interested in the Great Lakes area and was assistant editor of *Inland Seas*. He encouraged the study of local history. He died on August 1, 1969. Among his publications are *Western Ontario and the American frontier* (Toronto, 1941); *Lake Huron* (Indianapolis, 1944); and *An exile from Canada to Van Diemen's land* (Toronto, 1960).

[*Can. hist. rev.*, vol. L, 1969.]

Landry, Auguste Charles Philippe Robert (1846-1919), speaker of the Senate of Canada (1911-17), was born at Quebec on January 15, 1846, the son of Dr. J. E. Landry and Caroline Lelièvre. He was educated at the Quebec Seminary and at the Agricultural College at St. Anne's; and he became a gentleman farmer. In 1875 he was elected to represent Montmagny as a Conservative in the Legislative Assembly of Quebec; and from 1878 to 1887 he represented this constituency in the Canadian House of Commons. In 1892 he was summoned to the Senate of Canada; and from 1911 to 1917 he was its speaker. He died on December 20, 1919. In 1868 he married Wilhelmina (d. 1903), daughter of Etienne Couture; and in 1908 he married Amélie, daughter of Elisée Dionne, and widow of Edouard Taschereau. He was the author of *Traité populaire d'agriculture théorique et pratique* (Montreal, 1878) and of several pamphlets.

[*Can. parl. comp.*; *Cyc. Am. biog.*]

Landry, Sir Pierre Armand (1846-1916), chief justice of New Brunswick, was born in Dorchester, New Brunswick, on May 1, 1846, the son of Armand Landry and Pelagi Casey.

He was educated at St. Joseph's College, Memramcook, New Brunswick, and was called to the bar in 1870 (Q.C., 1881). From 1878 to 1883 he represented Westmorland in the Legislative Assembly of New Brunswick, and he was commissioner of public works in the Fraser administration and provincial secretary in the Hanington administration. From 1883 to 1890 he represented Westmorland in the Canadian House of Commons; and in 1890 he was appointed a county court judge. In 1893 he was made a puisne judge of the Supreme Court of New Brunswick; and in 1913 he became chief justice of the King's Bench. He was created a knight bachelor on June 3, 1916; and he died on July 28, 1916.

[Raymond Mailhot, *Sir Pierre A. Landry* (Société historique acadienne, 1972); *Can. parl. comp.*; Morgan, *Can. men* (1912).]

Lane, William Fletcher (*fl.*1794-1863), fur-trader, was born in Ireland about 1794. He entered the service of the North West Company as a constable in 1820. At the union of 1821 he became a clerk of the Hudson's Bay Company; and he was employed first on the Ottawa River, and later in New Caledonia. He retired from the service of the Company, still with the rank of clerk, in 1863, and was granted a pension. He married a daughter of Simon McGillivray, Jr. (q.v.).

[E. E. Rich (ed.), *Colin Robertson's correspondence book* (Toronto: The Champlain Society, 1939).]

Lang, Byllee Fay (1908-1963), sculptor, was born in Didsbury, Alberta, in 1908, and grew up on her father's ranch there. Her art education was begun at the Winnipeg School of Art, but because it had no sculpture courses she moved to Toronto and studied at the Ontario College of Art with Emanuel Hahn (q.v.). She also studied in Munich and with Baldfitsch in Berlin. Returning to Canada, she established a private school of sculpture in Winnipeg in 1936 and three years later joined the staff of the Winnipeg School of Art. She lived in Montreal in 1945 and from 1946 to her death in 1963 she was resident in Bermuda. One of her most important works is the figures of Christ and the Apostles she did for Bermuda Cathedral. Her work has been characterized as "rugged, honest, and straightforward". She was a member of the Manitoba Society of Artists (1938); the Sculptors' Society of Canada (1942); and the Federation of Canadian Artists (1942). She is represented in the Winnipeg Art Gallery and in private collections. She died in Bermuda in 1963.

[G. McInnes, *Canadian art* (Toronto, 1950); C. S. MacDonald, *A dictionary of Canadian artists*, vol. 3 (Ottawa, 1971).]

Lang, Louis LaCourse (1880-1965), industrialist, was born in Kitchener, Ontario, in 1880, and educated in Kitchener separate schools and at LaSalle Institute, Chicago. He was associated with Lang Tanning of Kitchener, of which he became president, from an early age. He had been senior vice-president of the Bank of Montreal; president of the Mutual Life of Canada; honorary president of the Ontario division of the Canadian Cancer Society; member of the board of governors of the University of Western Ontario; and was a Knight Commander of St. Gregory. He died at Galt, Ontario, February 25, 1965.

[*Can. who's who*, 1955-57.]

Lang, William Robert (1870-1925), chemist and soldier, was born in Glasgow, Scotland, on July 29, 1870. He was educated at Glasgow University (B.Sc., 1890; D.Sc., 1899) and at the University of Paris. He was a lecturer in chemistry at Glasgow University from 1890 to 1900; and in 1900 he came to Canada as professor of chemistry in the University of Toronto. In 1911 he was elected a fellow of the Royal Society of Canada. In 1902 he organized the 2nd Field Co., Canadian Engineers; and in 1914 he became the officer commanding the University of Toronto contingent, Canadian Officers' Training Corps. He became a general staff officer in Canada during the First World War; and he commanded the University of Toronto contingent, C.O.T.C., and remained professor of chemistry in this university until his death, at Toronto, Ontario, on November 20, 1925. He was the author of *Chemical industries of the Dominion* (Toronto, 1905) and *Organization, administration, and equipment of His Majesty's land forces in peace and war* (Toronto, 1916).

[Morgan, *Can. men* (1912); *Univ. of Toronto monthly*, 1925.]

Langelier, Charles (1851-1920), politician and judge, was born at Ste. Rosalie, Lower Canada, on August 23, 1851, the son of Louis Sébastien Langelier and the younger brother of Sir François Langelier (q.v.). He was educated at the Quebec Seminary and at Laval University (LL.B., 1875; LL.D., 1902), and was called to the bar of Quebec in 1875 (Q.C., 1880). He represented Montmorency in the Legislative Assembly of Quebec from 1878 to 1881, in the Canadian House of Commons from 1886 to 1890, and again in the Legislative Assembly of Quebec from 1890 to 1892. During the last period he was successively president of the council and provincial secretary in the Mercier administration. From 1898 to 1901 he represented Lévis in the Legislative Assembly of Quebec; and in 1901 he was appointed sheriff of Quebec. In 1910 he was raised to the bench as a judge of the sessions of the peace in Quebec; and this position he held until his death at Quebec on February 7, 1920. In 1882 he married Marie Louise Lucile LaRue, of Quebec. In addition to a number of pamphlets, he was the author of *Souvenirs*

politiques de 1878 à 1900 (2 vols., Quebec, 1908).

[Morgan, *Can. men* (1912); Le Jeune, *Dict. gén.*; Bibaud, *Panth. can.*; *Can. parl. comp.*]

Langelier, Sir François Charles Stanislas (1838-1915), lieutenant-governor of Quebec (1911-15), was born at Ste. Rosalie, Lower Canada, on December 24, 1838, the son of Louis Sébastien Langelier and Julie Esther Casault. He was educated at the Seminary of St. Hyacinthe and at Laval University (LL.B., 1860), and in 1861 he was called to the bar of Lower Canada (Q.C., 1878). In 1863 he was appointed a member of the law faculty of Laval University, Quebec, and in 1892 dean of the faculty. He represented Montmagny in the Legislative Assembly of Quebec from 1873 to 1875, and Portneuf from 1878 to 1881; and he held the portfolios of commissioner of lands and provincial treasurer in the Joly administration of 1878-80. From 1884 to 1887 he represented Megantic in the Canadian House of Commons, and from 1887 to 1898 Quebec Centre. In 1898 he was appointed a judge of the Superior Court of Quebec, and from 1906 to 1911 he was acting chief justice of this court. In 1911 he became lieutenant-governor of Quebec; and he died in office, at Spencerwood, near Quebec, on February 8, 1915. He was twice married, (1) in 1864 to Virginie Sarah Sophie Legaré (d. 1891), and (2) in 1892 to Marie Louise Adelaide Braun; and he had two sons and two daughters. In 1909 he was elected a member of the Royal Society of Canada; and in 1911 he was created a knight bachelor. He was the author of several legal treatises.

[*Proc. Roy. Soc. Can.*, 1915; Morgan, *Can. men* (1912); Rose, *Cyc. Can. biog.* (1886); *Can. parl. comp.*; Le Jeune, *Dict. gén.*]

Langelier, Jean Chrysostome (d. 1910), author, was a civil servant of the province of Quebec, who died at New Carlisle, New Brunswick, on May 7, 1910. He published *Étude sur les territoires du Nord-Ouest du Canada* (Montreal, 1873), *The Quebec and Lower St. Lawrence tourist's guide* (Quebec, 1875), *Biographie de Frs. Vézina* (Quebec, 1876), *Manuel de tenue des livres* (Quebec, 1877), *Cours d'arithmétique* (Quebec, 1878), *Le Nord* (Quebec, 1882), *Esquisse sur la Gaspésie* (Lévis, Que., 1884), *Notes on Gaspésia* (Quebec, 1885), *Esquisse générale du Nord-Ouest du Canada* (Three Rivers, Que., 1886), *Le bassin méridional de la Baie d'Hudson* (Quebec, 1887), *Description des cantons arpentés et des territoires explorés de la province de Québec* (Quebec, 1889), *Traité d'agriculture* (Quebec, 1890), *Liste des terrains concédés par la couronne dans la province de Québec* (Quebec, 1891), *Guide pratique de l'ensilage* (Quebec, 1891), and *Les arbres de commerce de la province de Québec* (Quebec, 1906).

[*Bull. rech. hist.*, vol. 15 and index vols.]

Langevin, Edmond Charles Hippolyte (1824-1889), priest, was born at Quebec, Lower Canada, on August 30, 1824; and was ordained a priest of the Roman Catholic Church in 1847. He became vicar-general of the bishop of Rimouski; and he died at Rimouski, Quebec, on June 2, 1889. He was the author of *Notice biographique sur François de Laval de Montmorency* (Montreal, 1874).

[Allaire, *Dict. biog.*; *Bull. rech. hist.*, 1929; *Cyc. Am. Biog.*]

Langevin, Sir Hector Louis (1826-1906), minister of public works for Canada (1869-73 and 1879-91), was born at Quebec, Lower Canada, on August 25, 1826, the son of Lieut.-Col. Jean Langevin and Sophie Scholastique La Force. He was educated at the Quebec Seminary and studied law in Montreal in the office of George-Etienne Cartier (q.v.), whose political successor he became. He was called to the bar of Lower Canada in 1850 (Q.C., 1864), and practised law in Quebec. From 1857 to 1867 he represented Dorchester in the Legislative Assembly of Canada; and from 1864 to 1866 was solicitor-general for Lower Canada in the "Great Coalition" and from 1866 to 1867 postmaster-general. After Confederation he represented Dorchester in the Canadian House of Commons from 1867 to 1874, and Three Rivers from 1878 to 1896. In the first Dominion government he filled the offices of secretary of state (1867-69) and minister of public works (1869-73); on the death of Sir George Cartier (q.v.) in 1873, he became the recognized leader of the French-Canadian Conservatives; and on the return of the Conservatives to power in 1878, he first became postmaster-general (1878-79), and then he resumed the portfolio of public works (1879-91). In 1891 he was impelled to resign from the government as the result of charges of corruption made against his department; he was personally exonerated from the charges, but was found guilty of negligence. He retired from public life in 1896, and he died at Quebec on June 11, 1906. In 1854 he married Marie Justine (d. 1882), daughter of Lieut.-Col. Charles H. Têtu, of Quebec; and by her he had nine children. He was created a C.B. in 1868, and a K.C.M.G. in 1881; and he was an honorary LL.D. of Laval University (1882).

[Andrée Désilets, *Hector Louis Langevin* (Quebec, 1972); Barbara Fraser, *The political career of Sir Hector Louis Langevin* (Can. hist. rev., 1961); *Dict. nat. biog.*, supp. 2; *Cyc. Am. biog.*; Rose, *Cyc. Can. biog.* (1888); Dent, *Can. port.*, vol. 2; Taylor, *Brit. Am.*, vol. 2; Le Jeune, *Dict. gén.*; Bibaud, *Panth. can.*; Morgan, *Bib. can.* and *Can. men* (1898); *Can. parl. comp.*]

Langevin, Jean Pierre François LaForce (1821-1892), Roman Catholic bishop, was born at Quebec on September 22, 1821, the son of Lieut.-Col. Jean Langevin,

and elder brother of Sir Hector Louis Langevin (q.v.). He was educated at the Quebec Seminary, and was ordained a priest in 1844. From 1844 to 1849 he was professor of mathematics at the Quebec Seminary, and from 1858 to 1867 he was principal of the Laval normal school. In 1867 he was consecrated bishop of St. Germain de Rimouski; and he administered this diocese until shortly before his death on January 26, 1892. He was the author of a *Traité de calcul différentiel* (Quebec, 1848), *Notes sur les archives de Notre Dame de Beauport* (Quebec, 1860), and *Cours de pédagogie* (Quebec, 1865).

[*Cyc. Am. biog.*; Allaire, *Dict. biog.*; Le Jeune, *Dict. gén.*]

Langevin, Louis Philippe Adélard (1855-1915), Roman Catholic archbishop of St. Boniface (1895-1915), was born at St. Isidore, Quebec, on August 23, 1855, the son of François Théophile Langevin and Mary Pamela Racicot. He was educated at the Jesuit College in Montreal, and in 1881 joined the Oblate order. He was ordained a priest in 1882. From 1885 to 1893 he was a professor of theology in Ottawa University; and in 1893 he went to Manitoba, at the invitation of Archbishop Taché (q.v.), and became rector of St. Mary's Church, Winnipeg. In 1895 he was consecrated archbishop of St. Boniface, in succession to Archbishop Taché, and he took a prominent part in the controversy over separate schools in Manitoba. He administered the archdiocese for twenty years, and he died at Montreal on June 16, 1915. In 1892 he received the degree of D.D. from the Vatican.

[A. G. Morice, *Vie de Mgr Langevin* (St. Boniface, 1916); P. H. Barabé, *Mgr Adélard Langevin* (Revue de l'Université d'Ottawa, 1941); Le Jeune, *Dict. gén.*; Allaire, *Dict. biog.*; *Can. who was who*, vol. 2.]

Langhorn, John (d. 1813), missionary, was born in Wales, and was educated at St. Bees College, Cumberland, England. He took holy orders in the Church of England, and in 1786 he was sent to Upper Canada as a missionary by the Society for the Propagation of the Gospel. He served in the Bay of Quinte district until 1813; he then returned to England, but the vessel on which he was returning is said to have been lost with all on board. His *Registers* have been printed in *Papers and Records* of the Ontario Historical Society, vol. 1 (Toronto, 1899).

[*Ont. Hist. Soc., papers and records*, 1899.]

Langlade, Charles Michel de (1729-1800), fur-trader, was born at Michilimackinac in May, 1729, the son of Augustine Langlade, who had come to Michilimackinac to engage in the fur-trade in 1727. He engaged with his father in the fur-trade at Green Bay and elsewhere; and in 1755 he was in command of the Indians and *coureurs-de-bois* at the battle of the Monongahéla. In 1758 he was appointed second-in-command at Michilimackinac; and in 1759 he led an Indian contingent from the West to Quebec, and fought with them at the Plains of Abraham. After the capture of Montreal, he returned to Michilimackinac; but during the American invasion of Canada, he led another contingent of Indians to Montreal, and he fought under Burgoyne in 1777. After the American Revolution, he was appointed an officer of the Indian department at Green Bay; and he died there in January, 1800. In 1754 he married at Michilimackinac Charlotte Bourassa, and by her he had two daughters; but before this he had by an Ottawa woman a son named Charles, who was educated at Montreal, and who took part in the capture of Michilimackinac in 1812. This son married an Ottawa woman, and had by her two sons, Charles and Louis. Louis became an officer of the Indian department, and was a subaltern under Dominique Ducharme (q.v.) at the battle of Beaver Dams in 1813.

[S. Tassé, *Les canadiens de l'ouest* (Montreal, 1878); A. G. Morice, *Dictionnaire historique des canadiens et des métis français* (Quebec, 1908).]

Langlois, Joseph Godefroy (1866-1928), journalist, was born at Ste. Scholastique, Quebec, on December 26, 1866. He was educated at Laval University (B.L., 1886), and became a journalist. He was successively editor-in-chief of *La Patrie*, of *Le Canada*, and of *Le pays*. From 1904 to 1910 he represented the St. Louis division of Montreal in the Legislative Assembly of Quebec; and in 1914 he was appointed Canadian commissioner at Brussels, Belgium. He discharged the duties of this post until his death at Brussels, on April 6, 1928. He was the author of *La république de 1848* (Montreal, 1897), *Sus au Sénat* (Montreal, 1898), and *L'uniformité des livres* (Montreal, 1908).

[*Bull. rech. hist.*, 1928; Morgan, *Can. men* (1912); *Can. parl. comp.*]

Langstroth, George Otty (1905-1964), physicist, was born at Hampton, New Brunswick, on August 9, 1905. He was educated at Dalhousie University (B.A., 1925), and at McGill University (Ph.D., 1930), and did post-graduate research at King's College, London (1930-32), and Rijks University, Holland (1932-33). He was research associate at McGill (1934-38) and at the Massachusetts Institute of Technology (1938-39), and became associate professor of physics at the University of Manitoba in 1939, and professor of physics at the University of Alberta in 1945. From 1948 to 1952 he was head of physics and meteorology at the Suffield Experimental Station and in 1952 became chief superintendent of the station, transferring to the same position at the Naval Research Establishment at Dartmouth, Nova Scotia, in 1957, a position he

held until his death on May 22, 1964. Dr. Langstroth contributed to the study of medical physics "A method for the determination of lead in cerebrospinal fluid" and a number of other papers, and was an expert on toxicological warfare. He was a fellow of the Royal Society of Canada.

[*Proc. Roy. Soc. Can.* (1965).]

Langton, Hugh Hornby (1862-1953), librarian and author, was born at Quebec, Canada East, on August 29, 1862, the son of John Langton (q.v.), and died at Toronto, Ontario, on September 30, 1953. He was educated at the University of Toronto (B.A., 1883; M.A., 1905), and was called to the bar in Ontario, but did not practise law. He became registrar of the University of Toronto from 1887 to 1912, and librarian from 1892 to 1923. He was a charter member of the Champlain Society, and was its treasurer from 1911 to 1934, and its president from 1934 to 1936. With Professor G. M. Wrong (q.v.), he was joint editor of the *Review of Historical Publications relating to Canada* (1897-1918), which preceded the *Canadian Historical Review*. For the Champlain Society he translated a large part of *The works of Samuel Champlain* (6 vols., Toronto, 1922-1936) and the whole of Sagard's *Grand voyage du pays des Hurons* (Toronto, 1939); and he edited Patrick Campbell's *Travels in North America* (Toronto, 1937). After his retirement, he published several biographies: *Sir Daniel Wilson* (Toronto, 1929), *Sir John Cunningham McLennan* (Toronto, 1939), and *James Douglas* (Toronto, 1949); and he edited the letters and journals of his aunt, Anne Langton, under the title *A gentlewoman in Upper Canada* (Toronto, 1950).

[*Can. hist. rev.*, 1953; *Can. who's who*, 1948; *Encyc. Can.*]

Langton, John (1808-1894), auditor-general of Canada (1855-78), was born in England, in April, 1808, and was educated at Trinity College, Cambridge (M.A., 1832). He came to Canada in 1833, and settled near Peterborough, Upper Canada. From 1851 to 1855 he represented Peterborough in the Legislative Assembly of Canada; and in 1855 he was appointed by the MacNab-Taché government first auditor of public accounts. At Confederation he was appointed auditor-general of the Dominion, and he held this post until 1878. He died at Toronto, on March 19, 1894. In 1845 he married Lydia, daughter of James Hartley Dunsford; and by her he had five sons and two daughters.

[W. A. Langton (ed.), *Early days in Upper Canada* (Toronto, 1926) and *The letters of John Langton* (Can. hist. rev., 1924); H. R. Balls, *John Langton and the Canadian audit office* (Can. hist. rev., 1940); *Can. parl. comp.*]

Langton, Thomas (1849-1914), lawyer, was born at Blyth, Canada West, on May 5, 1849, the son of John Langton (q.v.). He was educated at Upper Canada College and at the University of Toronto (B.A., 1869; M.A., 1871; LL.B., 1874), and was called to the Ontario bar in 1872 (Q.C., 1890). He was for many years a law partner of Sir Oliver Mowat (q.v.); and in 1882 he married Laura, second daughter of Sir Oliver Mowat. He died at Toronto, Ontario, on December 10, 1914. He was joint author, with G. S. Holmested (q.v.), of *The Judicature Act of Ontario* (2 vols., Toronto, 1898) and *Forms and precedents of proceedings in the Supreme Court of Judicature for Ontario, and the Supreme Court of Canada* (Toronto, 1904).
[Morgan, *Can. men* (1912).]

Langton, William Alexander (1854-1933), architect, was born at Peterborough, Canada West, on June 8, 1854, the son of John Langton (q.v.). He became an architect, practised his profession in Toronto, Ontario, and died in Toronto on April 3, 1933. He edited a collection of his father's letters under the title *Early days in Upper Canada* (Toronto, 1926).
[Private information.]

Langtry, John (1834-1906), clergyman and author, was born near Burlington, Ontario, on January 21, 1834, the son of William Langtry, a farmer. He was educated at Trinity University, Toronto (B.A., 1854; M.A., 1857; D.C.L., 1892), and was the first graduate of that institution to be admitted to holy orders. He was stationed successively at Collingwood, Yorkville, and Toronto; and for many years he was rector of St. Luke's Church, Toronto. He died at Toronto on August 22, 1906. In 1856 he married Sarah, daughter of Henry Bonslaw, of St. George, Ontario; and by her he had several children. He was the author of *Catholic versus Roman* (Toronto, 1886), *History of the Church in Eastern Canada and Newfoundland* (London, 1892), and *Presbyterianism: A lecture* (Toronto, 1889).
[Morgan, *Can. men* (1912).]

Lanigan, George Thomas (1845-1886), journalist, was born at St. Charles, Lower Canada, on December 10, 1845. He began life as a telegrapher, but drifted into journalism, and in 1869 became editor-in-chief of the *Montreal Star*. He went later to the United States, and served in turn on newspapers in Chicago, New York, Rochester, and Philadelphia. He died at Philadelphia, while on the staff of the *Daily Record*, on February 5, 1886. Under the pseudonym of "Allid", he published *National ballads of Canada, imitated and translated from the originals* (Montreal, 1865); and he was the author of *Fables of G. Washington Aesop* (New York, 1878).
[*Dom. ann. reg.*, 1886; *Can. who was who*, vol. 2; *Cyc. Am. biog.*; E. S. Caswell (ed.), *Canadian singers and their songs* (3rd ed., Toronto, 1925).]

Lansdowne, Henry Charles Keith Petty-Fitzmaurice, fifth Marquess of (1845-1927), governor-general of Canada (1883-88), was born on January 14, 1845, the eldest son of the fourth Marquess. He was educated at Eton and at Balliol College, Oxford; and he succeeded his father in the peerage in 1866. From 1868 to 1872 he was one of the lords of the Treasury; from 1872 to 1874 he was under-secretary for India. He was appointed governor-general of Canada on August 24, 1883; and he retained this post until May 30, 1888. He was then appointed governor-general of India, and this post he held until 1893. On his return to England, he re-entered politics; and he was secretary of state for war from 1895 to 1900, foreign secretary from 1900 to 1905, and minister without portfolio from 1915 to 1916. He was described by Sir John Macdonald as "the ablest governor under whom I have served, with possibly the exception of Lord Lisgar." He died at Clonmore, in Ireland, on June 4, 1927. In 1869 he married Lady Maud Evelyn Hamilton, daughter of the Duke of Abercorn; and by her he had one son, the Earl of Kerry, and two daughters. He was made in 1895 a Knight of the Garter; in 1917 he became chancellor of the Order of St. Michael and St. George; and he was a D.C.L. of Oxford University.
[Lord Newton, *Lord Lansdowne: A biography* (London, 1929); *Who was who*, 1928-40.]

Lanton, Henry (1809?-1888), clergyman, was born about 1809 in England, and came to Canada in 1838. He was ordained at Quebec a minister of the Wesleyan Methodist Church; and he occupied many charges in both Quebec and Ontario. He died at Hamilton, Ontario, on September 21, 1888. He was the author of *Lectures on the second advent of Christ* (Montreal, 1855).
[Morgan, *Bib. can.*; G. H. Cornish, *Cyclopaedia of Methodism in Canada* (2 vols., Toronto, 1881-1903).]

La Palme, Beatrice (1881-1921), singer, was born in Montreal, Quebec, in 1881. She studied music at the Royal College of Music, London, England; and she made her début at Montreal in 1900. Later, she sang in grand opera in Brussels and at the Covent Garden Theatre, London, and became a *prima donna*. In 1908 she married Salvator Issaury, of the Opéra Comique, Paris; and she died at Montreal, Quebec, on January 10, 1921.
[Morgan, *Can. men and women* (1912).]

La Peltrie, Marie Madeleine de (1603-1671), founder of the Ursuline convent at Quebec, was the daughter of M. de Chauvigny, seignior of Vaubougon, and a native of Alençon, and was born in 1603. At an early age she resolved to embrace the religious life; but, when she was only seventeen, her father forced her to marry M. de La Peltrie. After the death of her husband in 1625, she decided to go to New France to found a school for Indian girls, and in May, 1639, she sailed for Canada with three Ursuline nuns, with whom she founded a convent of that order in Quebec. There she maintained until 1642 a school for girls, in which both Indian and French children were received. In May, 1642, she joined the little band of colonists under Maisonneuve (q.v.), which set out to found Montreal. In 1646 she returned to Quebec, and became a novice in the Ursuline order there. She died in Quebec on November 16, 1671.

[Le Jeune, *Dict. gén.*; *Les Ursulines de Québec* (4 vols., Quebec, 1864-66); R. G. Thwaites (ed.), *The Jesuit relations* (73 vols., Cleveland, 1897-1901); *Dict. Can. biog.*, vol. 1.]

Laperrière, Augustin (1829-1903), librarian and author, was born on December 28, 1829, and became in 1850 a clerk in the Library of Parliament. He rose to be senior French clerk in the Library; and he died at Ottawa, Ontario, on April 20, 1903. He was the author of *Decisions of the speakers of the Legislative Assembly and House of Commons of Canada from 1841 to June 1872* (Ottawa, 1872) and two plays, *Les pauvres de Paris* (Ottawa, 1877) and *Une partie de plaisir à la caverne de Wakefield* (Ottawa, 1881); and he was compiler and editor of *Les guêpes canadiennes, annotées* (2 vols., Ottawa, 1881-83).

[Morgan, *Bib. Can.*]

Lapointe, Ernest (1876-1941), minister of justice for Canada (1924-30 and 1935-41), was born at St. Eloi, Quebec, on October 6, 1876. He was educated at Rimouski College and Laval University, and was called to the bar in 1898 (K.C., 1908). He practised law, first in Rivière-du-Loup, and later in Quebec; and he represented Kamouraska as a Liberal in the Canadian House of Commons from 1904 to 1919, and Quebec East from 1919 to 1941. In 1921 he was appointed minister of marine and fisheries in the first Mackenzie King government; and in this capacity he signed in 1923 the so-called "Halibut treaty" between Canada and the United States, which was the first treaty signed by a Canadian alone, with full authority from the Crown. In 1924 he became minister of justice; and he continued to occupy this post for the rest of his life, except for the years 1930-35, when the Liberals were in opposition. He was one of the Canadian representatives at the Imperial Conference of 1926; and he was the head of the Canadian delegation to the Imperial Conference of 1929. After the death of Sir Wilfrid Laurier (q.v.), he became the chief protagonist of the Liberal party in French Canada. When Canada declared war on Germany in 1939, he opposed conscription, but supported strongly the entrance of Canada into the war, and in the province of Quebec he won a bitter political fight against the forces of French-Canadian isolationism, led by Maurice Duplessis, then prime minister of Quebec. He died at Montreal, Quebec, on November 26, 1941. In 1937 he was created an imperial privy councillor.

[*Americana annual*, 1941; *Can. who's who*, 1936-37.]

Laporte, Sir Hormisdas (1850-1934), merchant and financier, was born at Lachine, Canada East, on November 7, 1850. He became the head of a large firm of wholesale grocers in Montreal, Quebec, and the president of the Banque Provinciale du Canada. During the First World War he was chairman of the War Purchasing Commission; and in recognition of his services he was created a privy councillor in 1917, and a knight bachelor in 1918. He died in Montreal, Quebec, on February 20, 1934.

[*Who was who*, 1928-40.]

La Potherie, Claude Charles Le Roy de (1663-1736), author and soldier, was born at Paris, France, on May 15, 1663. His first post was as chief writer in the Marine at Brest in 1691. In March, 1697, he was made commissary of the fleet, which, under Iberville (q.v.), set out from La Rochelle, on April 8, to attack Fort Nelson, an English trading-post on Hudson Bay. In May, 1698, he was appointed comptroller of the Marine and of fortifications in Canada, and arrived at Quebec on November 28. In 1705 he appears as assistant major at Guadeloupe; and he died there on April 18, 1736. It was in 1702 that he sent to the printer in Paris his *Histoire de l'Amérique septentrionale*, but the work did not appear until 1716 (new eds., Paris, 1722, and Amsterdam, 1723). He married on March 11, 1700, Elisabeth de Saint-Ours, daughter of Pierre de Saint-Ours, and by her he had three children.

[J.-E. Roy, *Claude-Charles Le Roy de La Potherie* (Trans. Roy. Soc. Can., 1897); *L'historien Le Roy de La Potherie* (Bull. rech. hist., vol. ix); J. B. Tyrrell (ed.), *Documents relating to the early history of Hudson Bay* (Toronto: The Champlain Society, 1931); Le Jeune, *Dict. gén.*; *Dict. Can. biog.*, vol. 2.]

Larcombe, Samuel (1852-1937), agriculturist, was born at Musbury, Devonshire, England, on April 9, 1852. He emigrated to Canada with his wife in 1889, and settled at Birtle, Manitoba. He came eventually to be known as "Western Canada's Wheat King". He died at Birtle, Manitoba, on October 20, 1937.

[R. St. G. Stubbs, *Lawyers and laymen of western Canada* (Toronto, 1939).]

Lareau, Edmond (1848-1890), journalist and historian, was born at St. Grégoire, Lower Canada, in 1848, and was educated at McGill University (B.C.L., 1864). In 1870 he became editor of *Le Pays*, and in 1872 of *Le National*. He was the author of an *Histoire de la littérature canadienne* (Montreal, 1874), and he supplemented this with a volume of *Mélanges historiques et littéraires* (Montreal, 1879). With Gonzalve Doutre, he was joint author of *Le droit civil canadien* (Montreal, 1872); he published later in two volumes an *Histoire du droit canadien* (Montreal, 1888-89); and during his later years he was a professor of civil law at McGill University. In 1886 he was elected, as a Liberal, to the Legislative Assembly of Quebec for the county of Rouville; and he sat in the Assembly until his death on April 22, 1890.

[*Cyc. Am. biog.*; Le Jeune, *Dict. gén.*; Bibaud, *Panth. can.*; J. D. Borthwick, *Montreal, its history* (Montreal, 1875).]

Larkin, John (1801-1858), priest and educationist, was born at Newcastle-on-Tyne, England, on February 2, 1801, and was ordained a priest of the Roman Catholic Church in 1827. On ordination he came to Canada; and from 1827 to 1840 he was a professor at the College of Montreal. He then went to the United States, where he joined the Society of Jesus; and he died on December 11, 1858. He was the author of *Grammaire grecque à l'usage du Collège de Montréal* (Montreal, 1837).

[*Bull. rech. hist.*, 1930.]

Larkin, Peter Charles (1856-1930), high commissioner for Canada in the United Kingdom (1922-30), was born in Montreal, Quebec, on May 13, 1856. He was educated at Montreal and Toronto, and went into business as a tea merchant. He originated the idea of selling tea to the public in sealed lead packets, and he built up the Salada Tea Company, of which he was the president. He was known as "The Tea King of America". For many years he was treasurer of the Ontario Liberal Association; and in 1922 he was sworn of the King's Privy Council for Canada, and appointed Canadian high commissioner in London. This post he retained until his death in London on February 3, 1930. By his wife, Jean Ross, he had one son and one daughter.

[*Who was who*, 1928-40; *Can. parl. comp.*]

La Rochefoucauld-Liancourt, François Alexandre Frédéric, Duc de (1747-1827), traveller and author, was born on January 11, 1747, the son of the Duc d'Estissac, master of the robes to the king of France. He was elected to the States-General of France in 1789, and he became president of the National Assembly; but in 1792 he was compelled by the revolutionists to take refuge in England, and his cousin Louis Alexandre having been assassinated, he assumed the title of Duc de la Rochefoucauld. In 1795 he visited the United States and he spent the years 1795-97 travelling in the United States and Upper Canada. He returned to France in 1799, but failed to win the favour of Napoleon; and though he took his place in the House of Peers at the Restoration in 1814, he never took a prominent part in public life. He died on March 27, 1827. A voluminous writer, he was the author of a work of some importance for Canadian history, *Voyage dans les Etats-unis d'Amérique fait en 1795, 1796, et 1797* (8 vols., Paris, 1799), translated into English by Henry Newman, and published under the title *Travels through the United States of North America, the country of the Iroquois, and Upper Canada in the years 1795, 1796, and 1797*, in quarto (2 vols., London, 1799), and in octavo (London, 1799; 2nd ed., 1800). That part of the book relating to Canada has been republished, with annotations by Sir David William Smyth (q.v.), and with notes by the Hon. W. R. Riddell, in the *Thirteenth Report of the Bureau of Archives for the province of Ontario* (Toronto, 1917).

[A. de Castellane, *Gentilhommes démocrates: Les deux La Rochefoucauld* (Paris, 1891); H. Clergue, *Phases of France on the eve of the revolution* (London, 1922); *Encyclopedia Americana*.]

Larocque, Charles (1809-1875), Roman Catholic bishop of St. Hyacinthe, was born at Chambly, Lower Canada, on November 15, 1809. He was educated at the Seminary of St. Hyacinthe, and he was ordained a priest in 1832. In 1866 he was elected bishop of St. Hyacinthe; and he died on July 15, 1875.

[Allaire, *Dict. biog.*; Le Jeune, *Dict. gén.*; *Dict. Can. biog.*, vol. 10.]

Larocque, François Antoine (*fl.* 1801-1815), fur-trader, was a brother of Joseph Larocque (q.v.). He entered the service of the XY Company as a clerk in 1801, and was stationed successively on the Churchill River, at Fort des Prairies, and on the Red River. He was a clerk on the Red River when the union of the XY and the North West companies took place in 1804; and in the autumn of that year he made, with Charles McKenzie (q.v.), a journey to the Mandans. His journal of this expedition has been edited, with introduction and notes, by L. J. Burpee, under the title *Journal of Larocque from the Assiniboine to the Yellowstone* (Publications of the Canadian Archives, No. 3, Ottawa, 1910). He retired from the fur-trade before 1815, and settled in Montreal, where he was elected a member of the Beaver Club. He was unfortunate in business; and he spent his last days, at an advanced age, in the convent of the Grey Nuns at St. Hyacinthe, Lower Canada. He married a daughter of Gabriel Cotté, a merchant of Michilimackinac; and by her he had one son.

[A. G. Morice, *Dictionnaire historique des canadiens et des métis français de l'ouest* (Kamloops, B.C., 1908).]

Larocque, Joseph (1787?-1866), fur-trader, was born in Canada about 1787, the younger brother of François Antoine Larocque (q.v.). He entered the service of the XY Company in 1801, and in 1804 he was a clerk of the North West Company on the Churchill River. Later he was transferred to the Pacific slope; and in 1813 he was with John George McTavish (q.v.) when the latter received the surrender of Astoria. He remained for several years on the Pacific slope, where Ross Cox (q.v.) frequently met him; but he was back at Fort William in the summer of 1817. Between 1817 and 1820 he was made a partner of the North West Company; and at the time of the union of 1821, he became a chief trader in the Hudson's Bay Company. In 1825 he left the West; and for several years he was in charge at Mingan, on the lower St. Lawrence. He resigned from the service of the Company about 1830; and in 1833 he married Archange Guillon (d. 1863). From 1837 to 1851 he lived in France; then he spent several years at Montreal; and in 1857 he went to spend his last years with the Grey Nuns in Ottawa. Here he died on December 1, 1866.

[J. Tassé, *Les canadiens de l'ouest* (2 vols., Montreal, 1878); A. G. Morice, *Dictionnaire historique des canadiens et des métis français de l'ouest* (Kamloops, B.C., 1908).]

Larocque, Joseph (1808-1887), Roman Catholic bishop of St. Hyacinthe (1860-65), was born at Chambly, Lower Canada, on August 28, 1808, and was a cousin of the Right Rev. Charles Larocque (q.v.). He was educated at the College of St. Hyacinthe, and in 1835 he was ordained a priest. He became superior of the College of St. Hyacinthe; and in 1847 he was appointed coadjutor bishop of Montreal, with the title of bishop of Cydonia. In 1860 he became bishop of St. Hyacinthe, but he resigned this charge in 1865 and was appointed bishop of Germanicopolis. He died on November 18, 1887.

[Allaire, *Dict. biog.*; Le Jeune, *Dict. gén.*]

Larocque, Paul (1846-1926), Roman Catholic bishop of Sherbrooke (1893-1926), was born at Ste. Marie de Monnoir, Quebec, on October 27, 1846. He was educated at the colleges of Ste. Thérèse and St. Hyacinthe, and was ordained a priest in 1869. He became rector of the cathedral at St. Hyacinthe in 1884; and in 1893 he was made bishop of Sherbrooke. He died at Sherbrooke, Quebec, on August 15, 1926.

[Morgan, *Can. men* (1912); Le Jeune, *Dict. gén.*; Allaire, *Dict. biog.*]

Larose, Wilfrid (1863-1936), lawyer and author, was born in 1863, and died at Ottawa, Ontario, on August 24, 1936. He was the author of *Variétés canadiennes* (Montreal, 1898).

[*Ottawa Journal*, Aug. 25, 1936.]

Larsen, Henry Asbjorn (1899-1964), seaman, was born in Fredrikstad, Norway, September 30, 1899. When he was an adolescent the tradition of Norwegian Arctic exploration was at its height. He served in the Norwegian navy and on discharge entered the merchant navy and was trained at navigation school, where he earned a mate's certificate. After some time in Norwegian vessels he took a navigator's berth in *Old Maid* of Seattle, a schooner trading in the Western Arctic. In April of 1928 Larsen joined the R.C.M.P. as a constable and took command of the *St. Roch*, the R.C.M.P. patrol vessel, on her commissioning at Vancouver in that year. Between 1928 and 1939 he and the *St. Roch* spent twelve summers and seven winters in the Arctic. In 1940-42 he completed a west-to-east trip through the Northwest Passage following the route of Amundsen's Gjöa. In 1942 the return journey was completed in one season through Lancaster and Viscount Wellington sounds and through Prince of Wales Strait to the Beaufort Sea. Henry Larsen was commissioned sub-inspector in September, 1944, inspector, 1946, and superintendent, 1953. From 1949 until his retirement in 1961 he was stationed at Ottawa in command of "G" division, R.C.M.P. Following retirement he lived for a time in Lunenburg, Nova Scotia, before moving to Vancouver, British Columbia, where he died October 29, 1964. He was a fellow of the Royal Canadian Geographical Society and a fellow of the Arctic Institute of North America. In 1943 he and his crew were awarded the Polar Medal and in 1946 the Patron's Gold Medal of the Royal Geographic Society of London. He was awarded the Massey Medal in 1959.

[*Arctic*, vol. 18 (March, 1965), pp. 67 ff.; *North*, vol. 14, no. 5 (September-October, 1967), pp. 40 ff.; *Can. Geog. Journal*, vol. 83 (September, 1971), p. 81, vol. 86 (May, 1973), p. 177. The official report of the voyages is in the R.C.M.P. "Blue Book", published at Ottawa in 1945.]

Lartigue, Jean Jacques (1777-1840), first Roman Catholic bishop of Montreal, was born at Montreal, Quebec, on June 30, 1777. He was ordained a priest of the Roman Catholic Church in 1800; and in 1806 he joined the Sulpician order. He was created bishop of Telmesse in 1820, with oversight over the district of Montreal; and in 1836 he was created bishop of Montreal. He died at Montreal, Lower Canada, on April 19, 1840.

[Allaire, *Dict. biog.*; Le Jeune, *Dict. gén.*]

LaRue, François Alexandre Hubert (1833-1881), author, was born at St. Jean, Island of Orleans, Lower Canada, on March 25, 1833. He was educated at the Quebec Seminary, and studied medicine at the universities of Louvain and Paris. In 1859 he was appointed a professor of medicine in Laval University; and this position he retained until his death at Quebec on September 25, 1881. He was one of the founders of *Les soirées canadiennes* (Quebec, 1861-65), and he was the author of a number of books and pamphlets on various subjects. Chief among these were *Les chansons historiques du Canada* (Quebec, 1863), *Mélanges historiques, littéraires, et d'économie politique* (2 vols., Quebec, 1870-81), *Histoire populaire du Canada* (Quebec, 1875), *De la manière d'élever les jeunes enfants du Canada* (Quebec, 1876), *Petit manuel d'agriculture, d'horticulture, et d'arboriculture* (Quebec, 1878), and *Voyage sentimental sur la rue St. Jean* (Quebec, 1879).

[Jean Du Sol, *Le Dr. Hubert LaRue* (Quebec, 1912); *Nouvelles soirées canadiennes*, January, 1882; *Dom. ann. reg.*, 1880-81; *Bull. rech. hist.*, 1906.]

LaSalle, René-Robert Cavelier, Sieur de (1643-1687), explorer, was born in Rouen, France, on November 21, 1643. He came to Canada in 1667, and obtained the grant of a seigniory at Lachine, on the Island of Montreal. In 1669 he began his attempts to find the route to the Western sea. He first explored the Ohio River; then he penetrated into Lake Michigan, and discovered the upper Illinois. In 1673 he was placed in command of Fort Frontenac, on Lake Ontario; and from here he set out in 1678 to explore the Mississippi. After many trials he succeeded in 1682 in descending the Mississippi from its junction with the Illinois to its mouth. He next attempted to found a colony at the mouth of the Mississippi; but his ships failed to find the Mississippi, and the colonists were landed on what is now the coast of Texas. In an attempt to reach the Mississippi, and bring back relief from Canada, LaSalle was shot by mutineers on March 19, 1687.

[G. Gravier, *Découvertes et établissements de Cavelier de la Salle* (Paris, 1870); I. J. Cox (ed.), *The journeys of René Robert Cavelier, Sieur de la Salle* (2 vols., New York, 1905); H. R. Stiles (ed.), *La Salle's last voyage* (Albany, 1906); F. Parkman, *LaSalle and the discovery of the Great West* (Boston, 1869); D. Girouard, *Lake St. Louis, old and new, and Cavelier de la Salle* (2 vols., Montreal, 1893-1903); M. Constantin-Weyer, *Cavelier de la Salle* (Paris, 1927); R. F. Lockridge, *La Salle* (New York, 1931); F. Gaither, *The fatal river* (New York, 1931); L. V. Jacks, *La Salle* (New York, 1931); A. Chesnel, *History of Cavelier de la Salle* (New York, 1932); C. de la Roncière, *Le père de la Louisiane* (Paris, 1936); *Dict. Am. biog.*; *Cyc. Am. biog.*; *Dict. Can. biog.*, vol. 1.]

Lash, Zebulon Aiton (1846-1920), lawyer, was born in Newfoundland in September, 1846, and was educated there. He came to Canada as a youth, and was called to the bar of Upper Canada in 1868. From 1872 to 1876 he was deputy minister of justice at Ottawa. He then entered into partnership with Edward

Blake (q.v.) in Toronto, and he became one of the outstanding commercial lawyers of the country. He was chief legal counsel for the Canadian Bankers' Association, the Canadian Bank of Commerce, the Canadian Northern Railway, and other important corporations. Though a Liberal in politics, he opposed the reciprocity agreement of 1911, and was not without influence in securing the defeat of the Laurier government in that year. He was the author of an important pamphlet entitled *Defence and foreign affairs* (Toronto, 1917) and of a valuable survey of constitutional development in Canada since 1867 in *The federation of Canada* (Toronto, 1917), by George M. Wrong and others. He died in Toronto on January 24, 1920. He married Elizabeth Ann, daughter of Judge Miller, of Milton, Ontario; and by her he had three sons and one daughter. In 1909 he was given the honorary degree of LL.D. by the University of Toronto.

[Morgan, *Can. men* (1912); *Who was who*, 1916-28.]

Laskey, John K. (*fl.* 1835-1840), journalist, poet, and novelist, was in 1835 the editor, at St. Stephen, New Brunswick, of the *Plow and Anvil*, an agricultural journal. Soon afterwards he removed to Saint John, New Brunswick; and while there he published two volumes of poetry, *Mars Hill and other poems* (Saint John, N.B., 1838) and *Leisure hours* (Saint John, N.B., 1838), and a novel, *Alethes; or, The Roman exile* (Saint John, N.B., 1840). The date of his death has not been ascertained.

[C. C. James, *A bibliography of Canadian poetry* (Toronto, 1899); W. G. MacFarlane, *New Brunswick bibliography* (Saint John, N.B., 1895).]

Lasnier, Raymond (1924-1968), painter, was born in Quebec City. He began his study with a correspondence course in drawing and later studied with Mrs. Geraldine Bourbeau in Montreal, and with Jordi Bonet and Léon Bellefleur, and received a diploma from the Ecole des Beaux-Arts of Quebec. Although paralysed in both legs by poliomyelitis at four years of age, he led an active and independent life. After his schooling he settled at Trois Rivières, where he was a member of the Cultural Centre Commission and a teacher of art history at the Centre for University Studies. He was a keen sailor and many of his paintings are about boating and boats. For a brief period before his death he did non-figurative acrylic canvases. His large "Madonna" is on permanent display at Chenaux Park at Cap-de-la-Madeleine and he is represented in the Museum of the Province of Quebec. He did many paintings for Christmas cards and tourist advertisements. He died at Trois Rivières, Quebec, in 1968.

[C. S. MacDonald, *A dictionary of Canadian artists*, vol. 3 (Ottawa, 1971).]

Lasserre, Henri (1875-1945), educationist, was born in Geneva, Switzerland, on July 4, 1875, and died at Toronto, Ontario, on May 26, 1945. He became a lawyer, but gave up the practice of law in order to administer a short-lived co-operative colony in Switzerland. He emigrated to Canada in 1921, and was appointed first a lecturer and then an assistant professor in French at Victoria College in Toronto. His chief interest still centred in the idea of the co-operative community. He established the Canadian Fellowship for Co-operation Communities and the Robert Owen Foundation, to which he turned over his personal fortune.

[W. Thomson, *Pioneer in community: Henri Lasserre's contribution to the fully co-operative society* (Toronto, 1949); *Encyc. Can.*]

Latchford, Francis Robert (1854-1938), jurist, was born at Aylmer, Canada East, on April 30, 1854. He was educated at the University of Ottawa (B.A., 1882), and was called to the bar of Ontario in 1885. He practised law in Toronto and Ottawa; from 1899 to 1905 he represented South Renfrew in the Ontario legislature; and from 1899 to 1904 he was commissioner of public works, and from 1904 to 1905 attorney-general in the Ross administration. In 1908 he was appointed a judge of the Supreme Court of Ontario; and in 1923 he became chief justice in appeal in this court. He died at Toronto, Ontario, on August 13, 1938.

[*Can. who's who*, 1936-37.]

Laterrière, Marc Pascal de Sales (1792-1872), legislative councillor of Canada, was born at Baie-du-Febvre, Lower Canada, in 1792, the second son of Jean-Pierre de Sales Laterrière (q.v.). He was educated at the Quebec Seminary, and studied medicine at Philadelphia, under Dr. Benjamin Rush. He began the practice of medicine in Quebec in 1812, and during the War of 1812 he was surgeon-general of the militia of Lower Canada. In 1816 he sold his practice at Quebec, and went to live at his seigniory of Les Eboulements. From 1824 to 1830 he represented Northumberland in the Legislative Assembly of Lower Canada, and from 1830 to 1832 Saguenay. In 1832 he was appointed a member of the Legislative Council of Lower Canada, and in 1838 a member of the Special Council of the province. From 1845 to 1854 he again represented Saguenay in the Legislative Assembly of Canada; and in 1856 he was elected to represent the Laurentides division in the Legislative Council. He opposed Confederation, and in 1867 he was defeated at the polls as a candidate for the House of Commons. He died at Les Eboulements, Quebec, on March 29, 1872.

[H. R. Casgrain, *Biographies canadiennes* (Montreal, 1885); M. J. and G. Ahern, *Notes pour servir à l'histoire de la médecine dans le Bas-Canada* (Quebec, 1923); *Can. parl. comp.*, 1864-67; *Dict. Can. biog.*, vol. 10.]

Laterrière, Jean-Pierre de Sales (1747-1815), physician and author, was said by himself to have been born at St. Salvy, in the parish of Bonneval, France, on September 23, 1747, the son of Jean-Pierre de Sales Laterrière and Marie Delargue. Doubts, however, have been cast on this fact. He is said to have studied medicine in Paris; and he came to Canada in 1766. He became the manager, and later part proprietor, of the St. Maurice Forges. In 1779 he was arrested by the British on a charge of complicity with the Americans; and he spent three years in prison. After the American Revolution, he went to Harvard University to study medicine; and in 1789 he was officially admitted to the practice of medicine in Quebec. He retired from active practice in 1810, and went to live at his seigniory of Les Eboulements. He died at Quebec on June 8, 1815. He married Marie Catherine Delzène, widow of Christophe Pélissier, of Three Rivers; and by her he had one daughter and two sons. He was the author of a *Dissertation on puerperal fever* (Boston, 1789); and he left in manuscript an autobiography, which was later published privately by Alfred Garneau (q.v.) under the title, *Mémoires de Pierre de Sales Laterrière et de ses traverses* (Quebec, 1873).

[H. R. Casgrain, *Biographies canadiennes* (Montreal, 1885); M. J. and G. Ahern, *Notes pour servir à l'histoire de la médecine dans le Bas-Canada* (Quebec, 1923); P. Gagnon, *Essai de bibliographie canadienne* (Quebec, 1895).]

Laterrière, Pierre de Sales (1785-1834), physician, was born in June, 1785, the son of Jean-Pierre de Sales Laterrière (q.v.). He was educated at the Quebec Seminary, and studied medicine in London, England, under Sir Astley Cooper. He succeeded to his father's practice in Quebec; and during the War of 1812 he served as medical officer of the Canadian *Voltigeurs*. In 1823 he went to live in England, and he returned to Canada only a short time before his death at Les Eboulements, Lower Canada, on December 15, 1834. In 1815 he married, in London, Mary Anne, only daughter of Sir Fenwick Bulmer; and by her he had several children. He published, under the pseudonym of "A Canadian", *A political and historical account of Lower Canada, with remarks on the present situation of the people* (London, 1830).

[H. R. Casgrain, *Biographies canadiennes* (Montreal, 1885); M. J. and G. Ahern, *Notes pour servir à l'histoire de la médecine dans le Bas-Canada* (Quebec, 1923); Morgan, *Bib. can.*; P. A. de Gaspé, *Mémoires* (Ottawa, 1866).]

Lathern, John (1831-1905), clergyman and author, was born near Alston, Cumberland, England, on July 31, 1831. He was educated at the local grammar school; and in 1859 he was ordained a minister of the Methodist Church. The same year he came to New Brunswick as pastor of the Methodist Church in Fredericton; and he spent the rest of his life in the Maritime provinces. For many years he was editor of the *Wesleyan*, the Methodist church paper. He died at Halifax, Nova Scotia, on January 8, 1905. In 1859 he married Mary Elizabeth, daughter of John Simpson, King's Printer, New Brunswick. In 1883 he received the degree of D.D. from Mount Allison University; and he was the author of *Institute lectures* (Halifax, 1871), *The Macedonian cry* (Halifax, 1874), *Baptism* (Halifax, 1879), and *The Hon. Judge Wilmot* (Toronto, 1881).

[*Can. who was who*, vol. 1; Morgan, *Can. men* (1898).]

La Tour, Charles de Saint-Etienne de (1593-1666), governor of Acadia, was the son of Claude de La Tour (q.v.), and in 1610 came with his father to Acadia in the service of Poutrincourt (q.v.). After the destruction of the French establishments by Argall in 1613, he followed Biencourt (q.v.), Poutrincourt's son, into the forests, and with him lived the wild life of the Indians. In 1621 Biencourt returned to France, and La Tour, to whom he left in 1623 all his property and rights in Acadia, became virtually ruler of the country. In 1628, after his father's alliance with the English, he was made a baronet of Nova Scotia, but refused to transfer his allegiance, and was rewarded by Louis XIII with the governorship of part of Acadia. In 1636 Charnisay (q.v.) succeeded Rasilly (q.v.) as governor, and a bitter feud began between Charnisay and La Tour. In 1645 Charnisay, taking advantage of his enemy's absence, attacked Fort St. John, La Tour's headquarters, and in spite of the heroic resistance of Madame La Tour, captured the stronghold and put the defenders to death. La Tour left the country, and took refuge in Canada until the death of Charnisay in 1650. He then proceeded to France, and succeeded in persuading the king to appoint him governor of Acadia. In 1654, when the country fell into the hands of the English, he was permitted to remain and received a grant of land from Cromwell. He died at Cap de Sable in 1666. He married first, in 1640, Françoise Marie Jacquelins (d. June 15, 1645), the daughter of a barber of Le Mans, and secondly, in 1653, the widow of his old enemy, Charnisay; and he had several children.

[A. Couillard-Després, *Charles de Saint-Etienne de la Tour* (Arthabaska, Quebec, 1930), and *Charles de Saint-Etienne de la Tour* (pamphlet, St. Hyacinthe, Quebec, 1932); G. O. Bent, *Fortunes of La Tour* (University magazine, vol. xi); A. G. Doughty, *The Acadian exiles* (Toronto, 1916); F.

Parkman, *The old régime in Canada* (Boston, 1892); Le Jeune, *Dict. gén.*; *Dict. Can. biog.*, vol. 1.]

La Tour, Claude de (*fl.* 1610-1635), adventurer and trader, was of the St. Etienne family which belonged to the neighbourhood of Evreux, in Normandy, and is described as a Huguenot nobleman whom poverty had forced to seek his fortune in the New World. On February 26, 1610, he sailed from Dieppe in the service of Poutrincourt (q.v.). He established a trading-post at the mouth of the Penobscot, but was later driven away by a party from the English colony of Plymouth. In 1627 he sailed for France to procure stores and ammunition for the defence of Acadia, and while returning with a fleet in 1628, his ship was captured by the English and he himself was carried to London. Here he insinuated himself into favour at the court, married one of the queen's French maids of honour, and had himself and his son created baronets of Nova Scotia. He then returned to Acadia, where he undertook to win over his son to the side of the English. The latter, however, proved loyal, and induced his father to renew his allegiance to France. Claude de La Tour lived for some time at Port La Tour, and his later years were spent at Cape Sable, where he died in 1635 or 1636.

[G. O. Bent, *Fortunes of La Tour* (University magazine, vol. xi); A. G. Doughty, *The Acadian exiles* (Toronto, 1916); *Dict. Can. biog.*, vol. 1.]

Latour, Louis A. Huguet. See **Huguet-Latour, Louis A.**

La Tour, Louis Bertrand de (1700?-1780), priest and author, was born at Toulouse, France, about 1700, and was ordained a priest of the Roman Catholic Church about 1725. He was sent to New France in 1729 as grand vicar of the bishop of Quebec, and was appointed a member of the Superior Council. He returned to France, however, in 1731, and remained there for the rest of his life. He died at Montauban, in Gascony, on January 19, 1780. Among other works, he wrote *Mémoires sur la vie de M. de Laval, premier évêque de Québec* (Cologne, 1761), and an *Histoire de l'Hôtel-Dieu de Québec* (Montauban, n.d.) is attributed to him. His *Oeuvres complètes* have been published by the Abbé J. P. Migne (7 vols., Petit-Montrouge, 1855).

[P. J. O. Chauveau, *Bertrand de la Tour* (Lévis, 1898); Allaire, *Dict. biog.*; Le Jeune, *Dict. gén.*]

Latulipe, Elie Anicet (1859-1922), first Roman Catholic bishop of Haileybury, was born at St. Anicet, Lower Canada, on August 3, 1859. He was educated at the College of Montreal, and was ordained a priest in 1885. After serving as chaplain to two religious orders, he became in 1894 rector of Pembroke

Cathedral, and in 1908 he was appointed vicar apostolic of Temiskaming, with the title of bishop of Catenna *in partibus*. In 1915 he became first bishop of Haileybury, and he presided over this diocese until the destruction of Haileybury by fire in 1922. Shortly afterwards, he died at Cobalt, Ontario, on December 14, 1922.

[Allaire, *Dict. biog.*; Morgan, *Can. men* (1912); Élie J. Auclair, *Figures canadiennes: Première série* (Montreal, 1933).]

Lauberivière, François Louis Pourroy de (1711-1740), fifth Roman Catholic bishop of Quebec, was born at Grenoble, France, on June 16, 1711; and was ordained a priest in 1735. In 1739 he was named bishop of Quebec, and he arrived at Quebec in the later summer of 1740; but he died, only a few days after his arrival, on August 20, 1740.

[Comte de Quinsonas, *Un dauphinois* (Paris, 1936); Le Jeune, *Dict. gén.*; Allaire, *Dict. biog.*; *Dict. Can. biog.*, vol.2.]

Laumet, Antoine, dit de Lamothe Cadillac (1658-1730), founder of Detroit, was born at Les Laumets in France. His baptismal name was Antoine Laumet, and he assumed the noble alias de Lamothe Cadillac and a noble pedigree probably to advance himself socially and financially. He came to Canada about 1683 and engaged in various enterprises. In 1694 he was appointed to the command of the post at Michilimackinac. In 1701 he founded the fur-trading post of Detroit, and remained in command there until 1710. From 1710 to 1717 he was governor of Louisiana. He then returned to France, and in 1723 became governor of Castelsarrasin, a small town in France. He died there on October 15, 1730.

[A. C. Laut, *Cadillac* (Indianapolis, 1931); N. Saint-Pierre, *Lamothe-Cadillac et la fondation de Détroit* (Bull. rech. hist., 1913); C. M. Burton, *A sketch of the life of Antoine de la Mothe Cadillac* (Detroit, 1895); *Dict. Can. biog.*, vol. 2.]

Laure, Pierre (1688-1738), missionary, was born at Orléans, France, on September 17, 1688. He entered the Society of Jesus as a novice in 1707, and in 1711 was sent to Canada. In 1720 he was sent as a missionary to the Saguenay country, with headquarters at Chicoutimi; and he remained in this mission until 1737. He then was appointed parish priest at Les Eboulements; and he died here on November 22, 1738. He was the author of a dictionary and grammar of the Montagnais language, which have unfortunately been lost; but the journal of his Saguenay mission from 1720 to 1730 was found nine times in a garret in Quebec. It has been edited by A. E. Jones under the title, *Mission du Saguenay* (Montreal, 1889).

[A. E. Jones (ed.), *P. Laure: Mission du Saguenay, précédée de quelques notes biog-*

raphiques sur ce missionaire (Montreal, 1889); *Dict. Can. biog.*, vol. 2.]

Laurendeau, André (1912-1968), journalist and politician, was born at Montreal, March 21, 1912, and educated at the University of Montreal, and in Paris, France. On his return to Montreal in 1937 he became director of l'Action Nationale; and in 1942 he formed the League for the Defence of Canada, to oppose conscription in Canada. He joined the Bloc Populaire as secretary, became chief of the provincial wing of the party, and sat in the Quebec Legislative Assembly from 1944 to 1947. In 1947 he joined the staff of *Le Devoir* and in 1957 became editor-in-chief. At his urging, a Royal Commission on bilingualism and biculturalism was established by the Canadian government in 1963 under the co-chairmanship of A. Davidson Dunton and himself. After twenty-three regional meetings, and thirty-four days of public hearings in which some four hundred briefs were presented, it issued its preliminary report in 1965. As co-chairman of the commission he was deeply committed to working out the means of achieving an equitable relationship between the two main racial and linguistic groups in Canada. He was a fellow of the Royal Society of Canada. He died at Ottawa, June 1, 1968.

[*Proc. and Trans. Roy. Soc. Can.* (1968); *Can. Forum*, vol. 48 (1968-69); A. Laurendeau, *Witness for Quebec* (Toronto, 1973).]

Laureys, Henry (1882-1958), economist and diplomat, was born in Belgium, on October 3, 1882, and died in Montreal, Quebec, on April 26, 1958. He was educated at the University of Louvain, and came to Canada in 1911 as a professor in the Ecole des Hautes Etudes Commerciales in Montreal. He became dean of this school in 1916, and continued as such for many years; but in 1940 he entered the Canadian diplomatic service. He was Canadian high commissioner in South Africa from 1940 to 1944, ambassador to Peru from 1944 to 1947, and minister to Denmark from 1947 till his retirement in 1950. He was the author of *Essai de géographie économique du Canada* (Brussels, 1914), *Le conquête des marchés extérieurs* (Montreal, 1927), translated into English under the title, *The foreign trade of Canada* (Toronto, 1930), and *La technique de l'exportation* (Montreal, 1935).

[*Can. who's who*, 1955-57.]

Laurie, John Wimburn (1835-1912), soldier and politician, was born in London, England, on October 1, 1835, the eldest son of John Laurie, M.P., and Eliza Helen, daughter of Kenrick Collet. He was educated at Harrow and Sandhurst, and was gazetted an ensign in the 2nd Queen's Royals in 1853. He served in the Crimean War and in the Indian Mutiny; and he came to Canada in 1861 at the time of the *Trent* affair. He served in the Fenian raids of 1866 and 1870; and in 1885 he was second-in-command of the force despatched by the Canadian government to deal with the second North West rebellion. He retired from the army, with the rank of lieutenant-general, in 1887; and from 1887 to 1891 he represented Shelburne, Nova Scotia, as a Conservative in the Canadian House of Commons. During his later years he lived in England; and from 1895 to 1906 he represented Pembroke Boroughs in the British House of Commons. He died in London, England, on May 19, 1912. In 1863 he married Frances, daughter of the Hon. Enos Collins (q.v.); and by her he had two sons and three daughters. He was a D.C.L. of King's College, Nova Scotia (1883); and in 1902 he was created a C.B. (civil).

[M. Laurie, *Oakfield and its founder* (Coll. Nova Scotia Hist. Soc., 1938); Morgan, *Can. men* (1912); *Can. who was who*, vol. 1; *Who was who*, 1897-1916; *Can. parl. comp.*; Rose, *Cyc. Can. biog.* (1888); C. P. Mulvaney, *History of the North West rebellion of 1885* (Toronto, 1885).]

Laurier, Sir Wilfrid (1841-1919), prime minister of Canada (1896-1911), was born at St. Lin, in the county of L'Assomption, Lower Canada, on November 20, 1841, the son of Carolus Laurier, a land surveyor, and Marcelle Martineau. He was educated at L'Assomption College and at McGill University (B.C.L., 1864), and was called to the bar of Lower Canada in 1864. While a law student in Montreal, in the office of Rodolphe Laflamme (q.v.), he joined the Institut Canadien, and became a member of the *parti rouge*. After practising law in Montreal for two years, he assumed the editorship of *Le Défricheur* of Arthabaskaville; but this journal ceased publication in 1867, and Laurier then devoted himself to the practice of law in Arthabaskaville. In 1871 he was elected to represent Drummond and Arthabaska in the Legislative Assembly of Quebec; but in 1874 he resigned in order to contest this seat in the Canadian House of Commons. He was successful, and he continued to sit in the Commons until his death in 1919, first for Drummond and Arthabaska (1874-77), and then for Quebec East (1877-1919).

He first attained cabinet rank in 1877, when he was appointed minister of inland revenue in the Mackenzie administration. He retired from office with his colleagues in 1878, and went into opposition. In 1887 he was chosen leader of the Liberal opposition in parliament in succession to Edward Blake (q.v.), and he led the Liberal party from this time to his death. In 1896, on the defeat of the Tupper government over the Manitoba schools question, he became prime minister of Canada, with the portfolio of president of the council. He formed a strong administration, described at the time as a "ministry of all the talents";

and his government remained in power until its defeat in the general elections of 1911 on the issue of reciprocity with the United States. In 1913 he was instrumental in defeating, by means of his majority in the Senate, the Navy bill of the Borden government, by which it was proposed to contribute three dreadnoughts to the British Navy; but in 1914, at the outbreak of the European war, he proclaimed a political truce, and gave the government complete support. It is possible that if, at this time, the government had invited him to join in the formation of a national or coalition government, he might have accepted the invitation; but unfortunately the offer was postponed until 1917, and was then declined. In the general elections of 1917, which were fought on the issue of compulsory military service, Laurier carried Quebec with him, but was defeated in every other province. About his last years there was a touch of tragedy. The issues of 1917 split the Liberal party in twain; and he saw many of his former allies estranged from him. His fine equipoise, however, did not forsake him, and when he died at Ottawa on February 17, 1919, he had long established himself in the estimation of even his bitterest political opponents.

As prime minister of Canada, he left a deep impress on the history of the country. One feature of his régime, his railway policy, proved in the end disastrous; and his fiscal policy of 1911 was rejected by the electors. But during his régime Canada enjoyed a period of unparalleled prosperity; and for this the aggressive immigration policy of his government was in part responsible. His most notable contribution to Canadian development, however, was along constitutional lines. Though thoroughly loyal to Great Britain, as was shown by his course during the Boer War and at the outbreak of the European war of 1914, he was a pronounced nationalist, and Canada really achieved a national status under his guidance. It was under him that the last British troops were withdrawn from Canada, and that the Canadian militia ceased to be commanded by an imperial officer; it was under him that the policy of a Canadian navy was inaugurated, and that Canada undertook responsibility for the defence of her own shores; it was under him that Canada acquired the right to negotiate separate commercial treaties, and to contract herself out of other treaties. His theory that the British Empire was "a galaxy of free states" was championed at successive meetings of the Imperial Conference; and at these he successfully resisted all attempts to place any limitations on Canadian autonomy.

In 1868 he married Zoë, daughter of G. N. R. Lafontaine, of Montreal; but he had no children. Many honours came to him. He was an LL.D. of the University of Toronto (1897), of McGill University (1898), and of Glasgow University (1911), a D.C.L. of Oxford University (1897), of Cambridge University (1897), of Queen's University (1898), of Edinburgh University (1902), and a Litt.D. of Laval University (1902). In 1897 he was created a G.C.M.G. and a privy councillor, and the same year he was created a grand officer of the Legion of Honour of France.

His only publication was a famous *Lecture on political liberalism* (Quebec, 1877). But many of his speeches, which touched the high-water mark of Canadian oratory both in English and in French, are collected in Ulric Barthe (comp.), *Wilfrid Laurier on the platform* (Quebec, 1890) and in Sir W. Laurier, *Discours à l'étranger et au Canada* (Montreal, 1910). Some of his letters have been published in L. Pacaud, *Sir Wilfrid Laurier: Lettres à mon père et à ma mère* (Arthabaska, Que., 1935).

[O. D. Skelton, *The life and letters of Sir Wilfrid Laurier* (2 vols., Toronto, 1921) and *The day of Sir Wilfrid Laurier* (Toronto, 1915); J. W. Dafoe, *Laurier* (Toronto, 1922); J. Willison, *Sir Wilfrid Laurier and the Liberal party* (2 vols., Toronto, 1903; new and enlarged ed., Toronto, 1926); U. Barthe (comp.), *Wilfrid Laurier on the platform* (Quebec, 1890); J. Schull, *Laurier* (Toronto, 1965); *Dict. nat. biog.*, supp. 3; Morgan, *Can. men* (1912).]

Lauriston, Victor (1881-1973), writer and journalist, was born at Fletcher, Ontario, October 16, 1881, and educated in Goderich, Chatham, and at Osgoode Hall, Toronto. He was a journalist with the Chatham *Planet* and *News* (1904-08), and was editor of the *News* from 1908 to 1913, when he resigned to become a freelance journalist. He was Canadian correspondent for the *Oil and Gas Journal* and he was the author of *The twenty-first burr* (New York, 1922); *Inglorious Milton* (Chatham, Ontario, 1934); *Arthur Stringer* (Toronto 1941); *Postscript to a poet* (Chatham, Ontario, 1941); *Lambton's hundred years* (Sarnia, 1949); *Romantic Kent* (Chatham, Ontario, 1952); and *Blue flames of service* (1961). He was a chairman of the board of education at Chatham (1929) and an alderman of the city (1921-22). He was recognized as Canada's columnist of the year in 1965. He died at Chatham, Ontario, October 18, 1973.

[*Can. who's who,* 1970-72.]

Laut, Agnes Christina (1871-1936), journalist and author, was born at Stanley, Ontario, on February 11, 1871, the daughter of John Laut and Eliza George, and the granddaughter of the Rev. James George (q.v.). She was educated at the University of Manitoba, and she began her journalistic career on the staff of the *Manitoba Free Press* in Winnipeg. Then she went to the United States, and most of her life was spent there; but she continued throughout life to write about Canada. She died at Wassaic, New York, on November 15, 1936. She was the author of *Lords of the north* (New York, 1900), *Heralds of empire* (New York, 1902), *The story of the trapper* (New York, 1902), *Pathfinders of the west* (New York, 1904), *Vikings of the Pacific* (New York, 1905), *The conquest of the great north west* (2 vols., New York, 1908), *Canada, the empire of the north* (Boston, 1909), *Freebooters of the wilderness* (New York, 1910), *The new dawn* (New York, 1913), *Through our unknown southwest* (New York, 1913), *The "Adventurers of England"* on Hudson Bay (Toronto, 1914), *The Canadian commonwealth* (Indianapolis, 1915), *Pioneers of the Pacific coast* (Toronto, 1915), *The Cariboo trail* (Toronto, 1916), *Canada at the crossroads* (Toronto, 1921), *The fur-trade of America* (New York, 1921), *The quenchless light* (New York, 1924), *The blazed trail of the old frontier* (New York, 1926), *Enchanted trails of Glacier park* (New York, 1926), *The conquest of our western empire* (New York, 1927), *The romance of the rails* (2 vols., New York, 1929), *The overland trail* (New York, 1929), *Cadillac, knight errant of the wilderness* (Indianapolis, 1931), and *Pilgrims of the Santa Fé* (New York, 1931).

[*Who was who in America*; *Can. who's who,* 1936-37.]

Lauzon, Gilles (1631-1687), colonist, was born at Caën, Normandy, in 1631, and emigrated to Canada with Marguerite Bourgeoys (q.v.) in 1653. He settled in Montreal, and died there on September 21, 1687. In 1656 he married Marie Archambault; and he has to-day a large number of descendants in Canada. He was not related in any way to Jean de Lauzon (q.v.).

[L. Lauzon, *Un pionnier de Ville-Marie: Gilles Lauzon et sa posterité* (Quebec, 1926); *Dict. Can. biog.*, vol. 1.]

Lauzon, Jean de (1584-1666), governor of New France (1651-56), was the son of François de Lauzon and Isabelle Lotin, and was born in 1584. In 1627 he was a member of both the state and privy councils, president of the grand council, and intendant of Guyenne. On April 29, 1627, he became a member of the Company of One Hundred Associates. In January, 1651, he was appointed governor of New France. His administration, which lasted until 1656, was marked by quarrels with the Montreal colony, and by general disaffection among the residents of Canada. He returned to France, and he died there on February 16, 1666. He married first, Marie Gaudard, and second, in 1651, Anne Després, sister-in-law of the Sieur Duplessis-Bochart, and he had four sons.

[J. E. Roy, *La seigneurie de Lauzon* (6 vols., Lévis, 1897); Le Jeune, *Dict. gén.*; *Dict. Can. biog.*, vol. 1.]

La Valinière, Pierre Huet de (1732-1806), priest, was born in France on January 10, 1732, and entered the Sulpician order. He was sent to Canada, and was ordained a priest at Montreal in 1755. He served as a parish priest in Canada from 1755 to 1779, and in various capacities in the United States from 1785 to 1798. He then returned to Canada; and he died at L'Assomption, Lower Canada, on June 29, 1806. He was the author of *Vraie histoire; ou, Simple précis des infortunes, pour ne pas dire des persécutions, qu'a souffert et souffre encore le Rév. P. H. de la V.* (Albany, N.Y., 1792).

[*Cyc. Am. biog.*; Allaire, *Dict. biog.*]

Lavallée, Calixa (1842-1891), musician, was born at Verchères, Canada East, on December 28, 1842. He studied music in the United States and in Europe; and, on his return to America, he lived in Montreal, Quebec, and Boston. He died at Boston on February 21, 1891; and in 1933 his remains were transferred from Boston to Montreal. In 1867 he married at Lowell, Massachusetts, Josephine Gentilly; and by her he had one son. His chief title to fame is that he was the composer of the Canadian national anthem, *O Canada*.

[E. Lapierre, *Calixa Lavallée* (Montreal, 1937); H. Magnan, *Calixa Lavallée* (Bull. rech. hist., 1927); R. G. Riddell (ed.), *Canadian portraits* (Toronto, 1940).]

Laval-Montmorency, François Xavier (1623-1708), first bishop of Quebec, was born at Montigny-sur-Avre, France, on April 30, 1623, the son of Hugues de Laval, seignior of Montigny, and Michelle de Péricard. He was educated at the Jesuit college of La Flèche and at the Collège de Clermont in Paris, and he was ordained a priest in 1647. In 1658 he was consecrated bishop of Petraea *in partibus*, and was appointed by the Pope apostolic vicar in New France. He arrived in Quebec in 1659, and from that date until 1688 he had oversight of the spiritual life of the colony. In 1674 he was given the title of bishop of Quebec; from 1663 he was a member of the Sovereign or Supreme Council; and at all stages he exerted a powerful influence in the affairs of the colony. Several governors who crossed his path were recalled, notably Avaugour (q.v.), Mézy (q.v.), and Frontenac (q.v.). He waged a bitter warfare on the sale of spirituous liquors to the Indians; he organized the parochial system of New France; and he founded at Quebec the seminary which, in 1852, became Laval University. In 1688 ill-health compelled him to hand over the charge of the see to his successor, Bishop de St. Vallier (q.v.); but he continued to live at Quebec in the seminary which he had founded, placing himself humbly under the authority of the father superior, and here he died on May 6, 1708. A man of illustrious and aristocratic origin, he could brook no opposition, and his tenure of the bishopric was far from peaceful; but his personal piety and disinterestedness were complete.

[H. A. Scott, *Bishop Laval* (Toronto, 1926); A. Leblond de Brumath, *Bishop Laval* (Toronto, 1906); A. Gosselin, *François de Montmorency-Laval* (Quebec, 1890; new ed.,

1906); Mgr H. Têtu, *Mgr de Laval* (Quebec, 1887) and *Les évêques de Québec* (Quebec, 1889); C. Roy, *Mgr de Laval* (Quebec, 1923); E. Bégin, *François de Laval* (Quebec, 1959); *Catholic encyclopedia*; Le Jeune, *Dict. gén.*; *Dict. Can. biog.*, vol. 2.]

Lavaltrie, Pierre Paul Margane, Sieur de (1743-1810), soldier and seignior, was born at Montreal, New France, on August 14, 1743, the son of Pierre Margane, Sieur des Forêts et de Lavaltrie (1678-1766). He was enrolled in the *troupes de la marine* at the early age of thirteen; and he served throughout the later stages of the Seven Years' War in Canada. At the end of the war he went to France and served in the French army until 1765, when he was recalled to Canada by his father to take charge of the seigniory of Lavaltrie. In 1775 he served, with the rank of captain, in the British forces defending Canada against the Americans; and he rose to the rank of colonel in the Canadian militia. From 1792 to 1796 he represented the county of Warwick in the Legislative Assembly of Lower Canada. He died at Lavaltrie, Lower Canada, on September 10, 1810.

[Le Jeune, *Dict. gén.*]

Laverdière, Charles Honoré (1826-1873), priest and historian, was born at Château Richer, Lower Canada, on October 23, 1826. He was educated at the Quebec Seminary, and in 1851 was ordained a priest of the Roman Catholic Church. He became a professor in the Quebec Seminary in 1851; and he was appointed later librarian of Laval University. He died at Quebec on March 11, 1873. He was the author of an *Histoire du Canada* (Quebec, 1869), and he edited *Les relations des Jésuites* (3 vols., Quebec, 1858), *Les oeuvres de Champlain* (6 vols., Quebec, 1870), and *Le journal des Jésuites* (Quebec, 1871).

[Faucher de St. Maurice, *L'Abbé C. H. Laverdière* (Quebec, 1873); *Cyc. Am. biog.*; Allaire, *Dict. biog.*; Le Jeune, *Dict. gén.*; *Dict. Can. biog.*, vol. 10.]

La Vérendrye, François, Chevalier de (1715-1794), explorer, was born at Sorel, Canada, on December 22, 1715, the third son of Pierre Gaultier de Varennes, Sieur de La Vérendrye (q.v.). He joined his father in the West about 1736, and in 1738 he accompanied his father on the expedition to the Mandan country. In 1739 he discovered the Saskatchewan River, and in 1742-43 he made an expedition to the south-west in company with his younger brother, Louis Joseph (q.v.), which resulted, apparently, in the discovery of the foothills of the Rocky Mountains. He remained in the West until 1749; then he returned to Canada, and obtained a commission in the army. He served in Canada during the Seven Years' War; and after the conquest he lived in Montreal. Here he died on July 31, 1794. As early as 1738 he enjoyed the use of the title "Chevalier", possibly as a *chevalier banneret*; and after he inherited from his brother in 1762 the seigniory of Tremblay, he became known as the Sieur du Tremblay. He was unmarried, and with him the name of La Vérendrye became extinct.

[Abbé I. Caron, *Pierre Gaultier de Varennes de La Vérendrye et ses fils* (Bull. rech. hist., 1917); A. H. de Trémaudan, *Who was the Chevalier de La Vérendrye?* (Can. hist. rev., 1920); L. J. Burpee (ed.), *Journals and letters of Pierre Gaultier de Varennes de La Vérendrye and his sons* (Toronto: The Champlain Society, 1927); Le Jeune, *Dict. gén.*]

La Vérendrye, Jean Baptiste de (1713-1736), fur-trader, was born at Sorel, Canada, on September 3, 1713, the eldest son of Pierre Gaultier de Varennes, Sieur de La Vérendrye (q.v.). He accompanied his father to the West in 1731, and in 1734 he founded Fort Maurepas on the Red River. On June 6, 1736, he met his death at the hands of the Indians on an island in Lake Superior.

[T. J. Campbell, *Out of the grave, the discovery of Fort St. Charles in 1908* (Bulletin de la Société Historique de Saint Boniface, vol. v, pt. 3); L. J. Burpee (ed.), *Journals and letters of Pierre Gaultier de Varennes de La Vérendrye and his sons* (Toronto: The Champlain Society, 1927); Le Jeune, *Dict. gén.*; *Dict. Can. biog.*, vol. 2.]

La Vérendrye, Louis Joseph de (1717-1761), explorer, was born at Île aux Vaches, on Lac Saint-Pierre, Canada, on November 9, 1717, the fourth son of Pierre Gaultier de Varennes, Sieur de La Vérendrye (q.v.). He joined his father in the West about 1735, accompanied him on the trip to the Mandans in 1738, and was with his brother, Pierre Gaultier de La Vérendrye (q.v.) on the expedition to the Rocky Mountains in 1742-43. In 1753 he received a commission as ensign on the active list; and in 1755 he took his place in the Montreal garrison. He served in Canada during the Seven Years' War; and was drowned, in November, 1761, in the wreck of the *Auguste*, while returning to France.

[Abbé I. Caron, *Pierre Gaultier de Varennes de La Vérendrye et ses fils* (Bull. rech. hist., 1917); A. H. de Trémaudan, *Who was the Chevalier de La Vérendrye?* (Can. hist. rev., 1920); L. J. Burpee (ed.), *Journals and letters of Pierre Gaultier de Varennes de La Vérendrye and his sons* (Toronto: The Champlain Society, 1927); Le Jeune, *Dict. gén.*; N. M. Crouse, *La Vérendrye, fur trader and explorer* (Toronto, 1956); *Dict. Can. biog.*, vol. 3.]

La Vérendrye, Pierre Gaultier de Varennes, Sieur de (1685-1749), explorer and fur-trader, was born at Three Rivers,

Canada, on November 17, 1685, the son of René Gaultier de Varennes, governor of Three Rivers. He entered the French army, and after serving in Canada and in Newfoundland took part in the campaigns in Flanders. He was severely wounded at the battle of Malplaquet in 1709; and shortly afterwards returned to Canada. He then engaged in the fur-trade, first at St. Maurice and later at Lake Nipigon. Here he conceived the idea of pushing westward in search of the Western Sea. He left Montreal for the West in 1731, and in the succeeding years he built a chain of fur-trading posts at Rainy Lake, at the Lake of the Woods, at Lake Winnipeg, at the Red River, and on the Assiniboine River. In 1738 he visited the Mandan villages on the Missouri. In 1742 two of his sons penetrated far to the south-west, and possibly reached the foothills of the Rocky Mountains. His operations, however, were not successful from a financial point of view; and in 1743, broken in health and burdened with debt, he was compelled to return to Montreal to face the creditors. He died in Montreal on December 5, 1749. In 1712 he married Marie-Anne, daughter of Louis Dandonneau du Sablé, sieur de l'Ile du Pas, and Jeanne Lenoir; and by her he had four sons and two daughters. In September, 1749, he received a belated acknowledgment of his services, was created a chevalier of St. Louis, and was promoted to the rank of a captain in the Marine troops.

[L. J. Burpee (ed.), *Journals and letters of Pierre Gaultier de Varennes de La Vérendrye and his sons* (Toronto: The Champlain Society, 1927); N. M. Crouse, *La Vérendrye, fur trader and explorer* (Toronto, 1956); A. Champagne, *Les La Vérendrye et le poste de l'Ouest* (Quebec, 1968); A. S. Morton, *La Vérendrye* (Can. hist. rev., 1928); Le Jeune, *Dict. gén.*; *Dict. Can. biog.*, vol. 3.]

La Vérendrye, Pierre Gaultier de (1714-1755), fur-trader and soldier, was born at Sorel, Canada, on December 1, 1714, the second son of Pierre Gaultier de Varennes, Sieur de La Vérendrye (q.v.). He accompanied his father to the West in 1731; and in 1741 he founded Fort Dauphin, on Lake Dauphin. After his father's return to Montreal in 1743, he remained in the West until 1749. He then returned to Canada and obtained a commission in the army as an ensign of foot. He died at Quebec on September 13, 1755.

[Abbé I. Caron, *Pierre Gaultier de Varennes de La Vérendrye et ses fils* (Bull. rech. hist., 1917); L. J. Burpee (ed.), *Journals and letters of Pierre Gaultier de Varennes de La Vérendrye and his sons* (Toronto: The Champlain Society, 1927); Le Jeune, *Dict. gén.*; *Dict. Can. biog.*, vol. 3.]

Lavergne, Armand Renaud (1880-1935), deputy speaker of the Canadian House of Commons (1930-35), was born at Arthabaskaville, Quebec, on February 21, 1880. He was educated at Laval University (B.L., 1899; LL.B., 1903), and was called to the bar in Quebec in 1903. He represented Montmagny in the House of Commons from 1904 to 1908, as a Liberal; and he was successively a Liberal, a Nationalist, and a Conservative. From 1908 to 1912 he sat in the Legislative Assembly of Quebec as a lieutenant of Henri Bourassa. In 1930 he was elected to represent Montmagny in the Canadian House of Commons, and he was deputy speaker of the House from 1930 to his death in Ottawa, Ontario, on March 6, 1935. He was the author of *Trente ans de vie nationale* (Montreal, 1934).

[*Un patriote: Armand La Vergne* (Montreal, 1935); Marc LaTerreur, *Armand Lavergne* (R.H.A.F., 1963); *Can. parl. comp.*; Morgan, *Can. men* (1912).]

Laverlochère, Jean Nicolas (1812-1884), missionary, was born in France in 1812. He entered the Oblate order, and was ordained a priest at Montreal, Canada, in 1844. He was a missionary in the Saguenay district from 1844 to 1847, in the North West from 1847 to 1863, at Plattsburg, New York, from 1863 to 1868, and on Lake Timiskaming from 1868 to his death on September 4, 1884. He was the author of *Mission de la Baie d'Hudson: Lettre à Mgr l'Evêque de Bytown* (n.p., 1848).

[Allaire, *Dict. biog.*; Le Jeune, *Dict. gén.*]

Law, Robert (1860-1919), clergyman and educationist, was born in West Lothian, Scotland, in 1860, and was educated at Edinburgh University (D.D., 1911) and at Tübingen University. He held several pastoral charges in Scotland, and in 1909 he came to Canada as professor of New Testament literature and exegesis in Knox College, Toronto. He died in Toronto on April 7, 1919. He was the author of *The test of life* (Edinburgh, 1909), *The emotions of Jesus* (New York, 1914), *The grand adventure, and other sermons* (New York, 1916), and *The hope of our calling* (New York, 1918).

[*Who was who*, 1916-28; Morgan, *Can. men* (1912).]

Lawrence, Charles (1709-1760), governor of Nova Scotia (1756-60); was born in England in 1709. He entered the British army in 1727 as an ensign in Montague's Foot, and joined the 45th Foot in Nova Scotia in 1747 as a major. In 1749 he was appointed a member of the council of Nova Scotia; in 1754 he became lieutenant-governor of the province, and in 1756 governor. It was during his régime, and mainly by his orders, that the deportation of the Acadians took place in 1755. In 1757 he was promoted brigadier-general, and he commanded a brigade at the siege of Louisburg in 1759. He died at Halifax, Nova Scotia, on October 19, 1760.

[J. S. Macdonald, *Life and administration of Governor Charles Lawrence* (Coll. Nova Scotia Hist. Soc., 1905); J. F. Kenney, *The genealogy of Charles Lawrence* (Can. Hist. Assoc. report, 1932); *Dict. nat. biog.*; *Cyc. Am. biog.*; Le Jeune, *Dict. gén.*; J. C. Webster, *The forts of Chignecto* (Shediac, N.B., 1930); *Dict. Can. biog.*, vol. 3.]

Lawrence, Joseph Wilson (1818-1892), historian, was born at Saint John, New Brunswick, on February 28, 1818, the son of a manufacturer. He inherited his father's business, but took also an active interest in the politics and history of New Brunswick. He was twice elected to represent Saint John in the Legislative Assembly of the province before Confederation, and he made a valuable collection of material relating to the history of New Brunswick. He died on November 6, 1892. During his lifetime he published, in addition to a number of pamphlets, *Footprints, or incidents in the early history of New Brunswick* (Saint John, N.B., 1883), and *The Loyalists' centennial souvenir* (Saint John, N.B., 1887). After his death a committee arranged for the publication of his chief work, *The judges of New Brunswick and their times* (Saint John, N.B., 1907).

[W. G. MacFarlane, *New Brunswick bibliography* (Saint John, N.B., 1895).]

Lawson, George (1827-1895), botanist, was born at Newport, in the parish of Forgan, Fifeshire, Scotland, on October 12, 1827, the son of Alexander Lawson and Margaret McEwen. He was educated at Edinburgh University; and in 1858 he came to Canada on his appointment as professor of chemistry and natural history at Queen's University, Kingston. In 1863 he went to Dalhousie University, Halifax, as professor of chemistry; and this position he retained until his death at Halifax, on November 10, 1895. Apart from a great number of papers contributed to scientific periodicals, he was the author of *The royal water-lily of South America and the water-lilies of our own land* (Edinburgh, 1849), *British agriculture* (Edinburgh, 1858), and *The fern flora of Canada* (Halifax, N.S., 1888). He was a Ph.D. of Giessen University (1857) and an LL.D. of McGill University (1863). In 1882 he was selected as a charter member of the Royal Society of Canada, and in 1888 he was elected president of the Society. He was twice married, (1) to Lucy (d.1871), daughter of Charles Stapley, of Tunbridge Wells, Kent; and (2) in 1876 to Caroline Matilda, daughter of William Jordan, of Halifax, and widow of George Alexander Knox. By his first wife he had two daughters.

[A. H. Mackay, *Memoir of the late Professor Lawson* (Proc. Roy. Soc. Can., 1896, App. B.); *Cyc. Am. biog.*; Rose, *Cyc. Can. biog.* (1888); R. J. Long, *Nova Scotia authors* (East Orange, N.J., 1918).]

Lawson, J. Murray (1848-1925), journalist, was born at Yarmouth, Nova Scotia, on

January 13, 1848. He became the editor of the Yarmouth *Herald*, which had been founded by his father; and he died at Yarmouth on May 27, 1925. He was the author of *Record of the shipping of Yarmouth, N.S.* (Yarmouth, N.S., 1876) and *Yarmouth past and present* (Yarmouth, N.S., 1902).
[Private information.]

Lawson, Mrs. Jessie Kerr (1839?-1917), journalist and author, was born in Fifeshire, Scotland, about 1839. She came to Canada in middle age, and became a journalist in Toronto. Later she returned to Scotland, and was a journalist in Dundee. In 1911 she settled a second time in Toronto; and here she died on July 30, 1917. She married in Scotland William Lawson; and she had eight children. She was the author of *The epistles o' Hugh Airlie* (Toronto, 1888), *Dr. Bruno's wife* (Toronto, 1893), *The harvest of Moloch* (London, 1908), and *Lays and lyrics* (Toronto, 1913).
[Private information.]

Lawson, Mrs. Mary Jane, *née* **Katzmann** (1828-1890), poet, was born near Dartmouth, Nova Scotia, in 1828; and she died at Halifax, Nova Scotia, in 1890. She married William Lawson, of Halifax. After her death, some of her fugitive verse was collected and published under the title *Frankincense and myrrh* (Halifax, N.S., 1893); and H. Piers edited her *History of the townships of Dartmouth, Preston, and Lawrencetown, Halifax county, N.S.* (Halifax, N.S., 1893).
[C. M. Whyte-Edgar, *A wreath of Canadian song* (Toronto, 1910).]

Lea, Walter Maxfield (1874-1936), prime minister of Prince Edward Island, was born on February 10, 1874; and died at Charlottetown, Prince Edward Island, on January 10, 1936. He was a breeder of Holstein cattle and Percheron horses; and he entered the legislature of the Island in 1915, as member for the fourth district of Prince. In 1927 he became minister of agriculture in the Saunders cabinet; and from 1930 to 1931 he was prime minister of the province. From 1931 to 1935 he was leader of the Liberal opposition; but in the summer of 1935 he was returned to power as prime minister with an unprecedented majority of 30 members behind him, not one opposition candidate having been elected.
[*Can. parl. comp.*]

Leach, William Turnbull (1805-1886), clergyman and educationist, was born at Berwick-on-Tweed, England, in March, 1805. He was educated at Edinburgh University (M.A., 1827), and in 1831 was ordained a minister of the Church of Scotland. In 1832 he came to Canada, as minister of St. Andrew's Church, York, Upper Canada; but in 1841, he joined the Church of England, and became the first rector of St. George's Church, Montreal, a position which he occupied for twenty years. In

1854 he became a canon of Christ Church Cathedral, Montreal, and in 1865 archdeacon of Montreal. For over thirty years he was on the staff of McGill College and University, and he ultimately became dean of the faculty of arts and vice-principal of the college. He retired from active academic work in 1881; and he died at Montreal on October 13, 1886. His only publications were some sermons and addresses.
[*Dom. ann. reg.*, 1886; *Cyc. Am. biog.*; Morgan, *Bib. can.*; C. Macmillan, *McGill and its story* (London, 1921).]

Leacock, Stephen Butler (1869-1944), educationist and author, was born at Swanmore, Hampshire, England, on December 30, 1869. He came to Canada at an early age; and was educated at Upper Canada College, at the University of Toronto (B.A.), and at the University of Chicago (Ph.D., 1903). From 1889 to 1899 he was a master at Upper Canada College; and in 1903 he was appointed a lecturer in political science at McGill University. He was appointed professor of political science, and head of the department, in 1908; and he continued in this position until his retirement in 1936. He was the author of a number of books dealing with history, economics, and political science: *Elements of political science* (Boston, 1906), *Baldwin, Lafontaine, Hincks* (Toronto, 1907), *Adventurers of the far north* (Toronto, 1914), *The dawn of Canadian history* (Toronto, 1914), *The mariner of St. Malo* (Toronto, 1914), *Essays and literary studies* (New York, 1916), *The British empire* (New York, 1940), *Canada* (Montreal, 1941), and *Montreal, seaport and city* (Garden City, N.Y., 1942). But it was as a humorist that he achieved his greatest reputation. He became perhaps the best-known humorist in the English-speaking world. In this field, he was the author of the following books: *Literary lapses* (London, 1910), *Nonsense novels* (London, 1911), *Sunshine sketches of a little town* (London, 1912), *Behind the beyond* (London, 1913), *Arcadian adventures with the idle rich* (London, 1914), *Moonbeams from the larger lunacy* (New York, 1915), *Further foolishness* (New York, 1916), *Frenzied fiction* (New York, 1918), *The Hohenzollerns in America* (New York, 1919), *Winsome Winnie, and other new nonsense novels* (New York, 1920), *My discovery of England* (London, 1922), *Over the footlights, and other fancies* (London, 1923), *College days* (New York, 1923), *The garden of folly* (New York, 1924), *Winnowed wisdom* (New York, 1926), *Short circuits* (New York, 1928), *The iron man and the tin woman* (New York, 1929), *Laugh with Leacock* (New York, 1930), *Wet wit and dry humour* (New York, 1931), *Afternoons in Utopia* (New York, 1932), *The dry Pickwick, and other incongruities* (London, 1932), *Humor, its theory and technique* (New York, 1935), *The greatest pages of American humor* (Garden City, N.Y., 1936), *Hellements*

449

of *hickonomics* (New York, 1936), *Funny pieces* (New York, 1936), *Here are my lectures and stories* (New York, 1937), *My discovery of the West* (Toronto, 1937), *Humour and humanity* (London, 1937), *Model memoirs, and other sketches* (New York, 1938), *Too much college* (New York, 1939), *Laugh parade* (New York, 1940), *My remarkable uncle, and other sketches* (New York, 1942), *Happy stories* (New York, 1943), and *How to write* (New York, 1943). He was the author also of two biographies of humorists, *Mark Twain* (London, 1932) and *Charles Dickens* (London, 1933). He was elected a fellow of the Royal Society of Canada in 1910; and he received honorary degrees from Brown University, Queen's University, the University of Toronto, the University of Bishop's College, and McGill University. He died at Toronto, Ontario, on March 28, 1944.

[Peter McArthur, *Stephen Leacock* (Toronto, 1923); C. K. Allen, *Oh, Mr. Leacock!* (Toronto, 1925); O. J. Stevenson, *A people's best* (Toronto, 1927); S. J. Kunitz and H. Haycraft (eds.), *Twentieth century authors* (New York, 1942); R. L. Curry, *Stephen Leacock* (New York, 1959); C. Berger, *The other Mr. Leacock* (Can. Lit., 1973); D. Cameron, *Faces of Leacock* (Toronto, 1967); F. W. Watt, *Critic or entertainer* (Can. Lit., 1960).]

Leavitt, Thaddeus W. H. (1844?-1909), author, was born in Leeds county, Ontario, about 1844. He began life as a school-teacher; but as a young man he went prospecting for gold in South Africa, Australia, and New Zealand. While in Australia, he wrote *The history of Victoria and Melbourne, The history of Tasmania*, and *Australian representative men*, according to the title-page of one of his later books. On his return to Canada, he became the editor of the *Brockville Recorder*; and he later founded and edited the *Brockville Times*. He then occupied for some time a position in the civil service in Ottawa; and from 1899 to 1905 he was organizer for the Conservative party in Ontario. In 1905 he was appointed inspector of public libraries in Ontario; and he died at Bancroft, Ontario, on June 21, 1909. He was the author of *The witch of Plum Hollow* (Detroit, 1898), and *Kaffir, Kangaroo, Klondyke: Tales of the gold fields* (Toronto, 1898); but the book by which he is mainly remembered is his *History of Leeds and Grenville* (Brockville, 1879).

[Private information.]

LeBer, Pierre (1669-1707), painter, was born in Montreal in 1669. He built a chapel at Point St. Charles, and adorned it with his pictures. A portrait of Marguerite Bourgeoys (q.v.) is attributed to him. He is thus one of the earliest Canadian artists. He died at Point St. Charles on October 1, 1707.

[Le Jeune, *Dict. gén.*; *Dict. Can. biog.*, vol. 2.]

LeBlanc, Sir Pierre Laurent Damase Evariste (1853-1918), lieutenant-governor of Quebec (1915-18), was born at St. Martin, Lower Canada, on August 10, 1853, the son of Joseph LeBlanc and Adèle Bélanger. He was educated at the Jacques Cartier Normal School and McGill University, Montreal, and was called to the Quebec bar in 1879 (Q.C., 1893). From 1882 to 1908 he represented Laval in the Legislative Assembly of Quebec, and under the Boucherville, Taillon, and Flynn administrations he was speaker of the Assembly. In 1915 he was appointed lieutenant-governor of Quebec; and he died in office at Quebec on October 18, 1918. In 1886 he married Hermine, daughter of Théodore Beaudry; and by her he had one son and two daughters. He was created a K.C.M.G. in 1916.

[E. Z. Massicotte, *Les ancêtres de Sir Evariste Le Blanc* (Bull. rech. hist., 1921); H. Charlesworth (ed.), *A cyclopaedia of Canadian biography* (Toronto, 1919); Morgan, *Can. men* (1912); *Can. parl. comp.*]

Leblanc de Marconnay, Hyacinthe (*fl.* 1834-1851), journalist, was a native of France who came to Canada in 1834, and was editor successively of *La Minerve, Le Populaire*, and *L'Ami du Peuple*, all journals published in Montreal. He returned to France in 1845, and in 1851 was living in Paris. While in Canada he published a comedy, *Valentine; ou, La Nina canadienne* (Montreal, 1836).

[B. Sulte, *Leblanc de Marconnay* (Bull. rech. hist., 1912); E. Z. Massicotte, *Leblanc de Marconnay* (Bull. rech. hist., 1920).]

Leblond de Brumath, Adrien (1854-1939), educationist, was born at Schlestadt, Alsace, on April 16, 1854. He came to Canada, and was for many years principal of a commercial academy in Montreal. He died in Montreal on May 3, 1939. He was the author of *Vie de Mademoiselle Mance et commencements de la colonie de Montréal* (Montreal, 1883), *Mgr Ignace Bourget* (Montreal, 1885), *Histoire populaire de Montréal* (Montreal, 1890), *Manuel du baccalauréat* (Montreal, 1899), and *Bishop Laval* (Toronto, 1906).

[*Bull. rech. hist.*, index vols., 1895-1925.]

LeBourdais, Donat Marc (1887-1964), writer, was born at Clinton, British Columbia, April 25, 1887. From 1904 to 1909 he was a telegrapher in the Yukon Telegraph Service. He was a Calgary real estate salesman from 1913 to 1919, when he founded the journal *The Canadian nation,* which he published in Ottawa until 1921. He was a freelance journalist and a correspondent for the North American Newspaper Alliance until appointed editor of *Mental health* (1927-33). He continued writing magazine articles, and he was the author of *Northward on the new frontier* (1931); *Stefansson, the explorer* (1951); *Canada's cen-*

tury (1951); *Why be a sucker* (1952); *Nations of the North* (1953); *Sudbury Basin* (1953); *Metals and men* (1957); *Canada and the atomic revolution* (1959); *Stefansson: Ambassador of the north* (1963). He died at Toronto, Ontario, November 8, 1964.

[*Can. who's who*, 1949; Metropolitan Toronto Library Board, *Biographical scrapbooks*, vol. 23.]

Leckie, Robert Gilmour Edwards (1869-1923), soldier, was born at Halifax, Nova Scotia, on June 4, 1869, the son of Major Robert Gilmour Leckie and Sarah, daughter of the Rev. John Edwards. He was educated at the Royal Military College, Kingston, and at King's College, Windsor, Nova Scotia (B.Sc., 1895). He practised civil engineering, first in the Maritime provinces and after 1898 in British Columbia. He entered the Canadian militia as a subaltern in 1890; and he commanded a squadron of the 2nd Canadian Mounted Rifles in the South African War. In 1910 he was gazetted lieutenant-colonel commanding the 72nd Highlanders of Canada; and in 1914 he was given command of the 16th Battalion in the First Canadian contingent. He served in France from 1915 to 1916, when he was wounded and invalided to Canada. He died at Vancouver, British Columbia, on June 22, 1923. In 1915 he was created a C.M.G., and he had attained the rank of major-general when he retired from the Canadian army.

[Morgan, *Can. men* (1912); *Can. ann. review*, 1912-18.]

LeClercq, Chrestien (1641-1700?), Recollet missionary and author, was born at Bapaume, France, in 1641. He became a member of the Recollet order, and in 1675 came to Canada as a missionary. From 1675 to 1679 and from 1682 to 1686 he laboured among the Indians of the Gaspé Peninsula and northern New Brunswick, and he invented the hieroglyphic characters which are still in use among the Micmac Indians. He returned to France in 1687, and became superior of the Recollet monastery at Lens. In 1691 he published two books, the *Nouvelle relation de la Gaspésie* (Paris) and the *Etablissement de la foy dans la Nouvelle France* (Paris). The first has been edited and translated by W. F. Ganong (Toronto: Champlain Society, 1910), and the second by J. G. Shea (2 vols., New York, 1881). The date of LeClercq's death is not certain.

[W. F. Ganong (ed.), *Le Clercq: New relation of Gaspesia* (Toronto: The Champlain Society, 1910); J. G. Shea (ed.), *First establishment of the faith in New France* (2 vols., New York, 1881); F. Parkman, *Pioneers of New France in the new world* (Boston, 1865); H. Harrisse, *Notes pour servir à l'histoire de la Nouvelle France* (Paris, 1870); H. P. Biggar, *Early trading companies of New France* (Toronto, 1901); Le Jeune, *Dict. gén.*; *Dict. Can. biog.*, vol. 1.]

Lecompte, Edouard (1856-1929), priest and author, was born at Côte des Neiges, near Montreal, Canada East, on February 24, 1856, the son of Hubert Lecompte and Marguerite Lauzon. He was educated at the College of Montreal, and entered the Society of Jesus in 1876. After studying in France and England, he was ordained a priest of the Roman Catholic Church in 1887. In 1907 he became provincial of the Society of Jesus in Canada. He died at Montreal, Quebec, on December 30, 1929. He was the author of *Les Jésuites au Canada au XIXe siècle* (Montreal, 1920), *Nos voyageurs* (Quebec, 1920), *Un grand Chrétien, Sir Joseph Dubuc* (Montreal, 1923), *Les anciennes missions de la Compagnie de Jésus dans la Nouvelle France* (Montreal, 1925), *Les missions modernes de la Compagnie de Jésus au Canada* (Montreal, 1925), *Catherine Tekakwitha* (Montreal, 1927), and *Le Père Louis Leboeuf* (Montreal, 1928).

[Allaire, *Dict. biog.*; Le Jeune, *Dict. gén.*; Morgan, *Can. men* (1912).]

Le Compte Dupré, Jean Baptiste (1731-1820), legislative councillor, was born at Montreal, Canada, on February 25, 1731. In 1758 he married Marie Catherine, daughter of François Martel de Brouage, commandant of the Labrador coast; and some years later he removed to Quebec to attend to his wife's interests. He was an officer in the militia, and he took a prominent part in the defence of Quebec in 1775. In 1785 he was appointed a member of the Legislative Council of Quebec; but was not appointed a member of the Legislative Council of Lower Canada in 1792. He died at Quebec, Lower Canada, on May 7, 1820.

[P. G. Roy, *La famille LeCompte Dupré* (Lévis, Que., 1941).]

Ledingham, George Aleck (1903-1962), plant pathologist and editor, was born at Dornoch, Ontario, October 23, 1903. He was raised on a farm at Hawarden, Saskatchewan, and was a graduate of the University of Saskatchewan (B.Sc., 1927; M.Sc., 1928). In 1932 he graduated from the University of Toronto as a Ph.D. and after a short time at the laboratory of Cryptogamic Botany at Harvard University he joined the National Research Council of Canada as an editor of the *Canadian journal of research*. Dr. Ledingham did extensive studies of the effects of fumes on vegetation at Trail, British Columbia, both during his year as a graduate student and after his transfer to the Division of Applied Biology of the National Research Council in 1934.

During the Second World War he did research on the production of synthetic rubber and industrial chemicals. In 1947 he was appointed director of the National Research Council's Prairie Regional Laboratory at Saskatoon, Saskatchewan. Here he undertook the study of chemical characteristics of host-parasite relationships of wheat and other plant rusts. He was made a member of the Order of the British Empire in 1948. He was a fellow of the Royal Society of Canada, a member of the Chemical Institute of Canada, and in 1956, president of the Canadian Society of Microbiologists. He was editor of the *Canadian journal of technology* (1951-57), and associate editor of the *Canadian journal of microbiology* from 1958 until his death. In addition he published some sixty-five research papers. He died on August 13, 1962.

[*Proc. Roy. Soc. Can.* (1963).]

Lee, George Herbert (1854-1905), lawyer and author, was born at Springhill, York county, New Brunswick, on April 8, 1854. He was educated at the University of New Brunswick (B.A., 1872; M.A., 1875), and was admitted an attorney-at-law in New Brunswick in 1876. He practised law in Saint John, New Brunswick, until 1893. He then went to Boston, Massachusetts; and he died in Boston on August 25, 1905. He was the author of *An historical sketch of the first fifty years of the Church of England in the province of New Brunswick* (Saint John, N.B., 1880).

[Private information.]

Leeming, Ralph (1788-1872), clergyman, was born at Blackburn, Lancashire, England, in 1788. He was educated at St. Bee's College, Cumberland, and was ordained a clergyman of the Church of England. In 1816 he was sent to Canada by the Society for the Propagation of the Gospel in Foreign Parts, and became the first rector at Ancaster, Upper Canada. He retired from active parochial work about 1834, and he died at Dundas, Ontario, in 1872.

[T. D. J. Farmer, *A history of the parish of St. John's Church, Ancaster* (Guelph, Ont., 1924); *Dict. Can. biog.*, vol. 10.]

Leeming, William (1787-1863), clergyman, was born in Yorkshire, England, on January 25, 1787, and was educated at St. Bee's College, Cumberland. He came to Canada in 1820, and was rector of Trinity Church, Chippawa, Upper Canada, from 1820 to his death on June 1, 1863.

[W. B. and A. B. Kerr, *Reverend William Leeming* (Ontario Hist. Soc., papers and records, 1936).]

Lees, John (*fl.* 1764-1775), merchant, was a native of Scotland who settled in Quebec as early as 1764. He engaged in the Indian trade; and his journal of a journey made by him in 1768 from Boston to Detroit, and from Detroit to Montreal, has been edited by C. M. and M. A. Burton, and published by the Society of Colonial Wars of the State of Michigan (Detroit, Mich., 1911). He was one of the group of Quebec merchants who pressed in 1774 for a Legislative Assembly; but he returned to England before 1778, and became a collector of excise in Scotland.

[C. M. and M. A. Burton (eds.), *Journal of J. L., of Quebec, merchant* (Detroit, 1911).]

Lees, John (d. 1807), executive councillor of Lower Canada, was the son of John Lees (q.v.), merchant of Quebec. He served as a captain of British militia during the American Revolution; in 1792 he was elected to represent Three Rivers in the Legislative Assembly of Lower Canada, and in 1794 he was appointed a member of the Executive Council of the province. In April, 1795, he received the appointment of storekeeper to the Indian Department, and he retained this post until his death on March 2, 1807, when he left his accounts in much confusion.

[M. M. Quaife, *The John Askin papers*, vol. II (Detroit, 1931); J. Desjardins, *Guide parlementaire historique* (Quebec, 1902).]

Lefroy, Augustus Henry Frazer (1852-1919), lawyer and author, was born in Toronto, on June 21, 1852, the son of General Sir John Henry Lefroy (q.v.), and Emily Merry, daughter of Sir John Beverley Robinson, Bart. (q.v.). He was educated at Rugby and at New College, Oxford (B.A., 1875; M.A., 1880); and was called to the English bar in 1877, and to the Ontario bar in 1878 (K.C., 1908). He practised law in Toronto, and became a leading authority on constitutional questions. In 1900 he was appointed professor of Roman law, jurisprudence, and the history of English law in the University of Toronto; and he continued to occupy a chair of law in this university until his death at Ottawa on March 7, 1919. In 1884 he married Mary Theodora, daughter of Henry Seton Strathy, of Toronto; and by her he had three sons. He was the author of *The law of legislative power in Canada* (Toronto, 1897), *Canada's federal system* (Toronto, 1913), *Leading cases in Canadian constitutional law* (Toronto, 1914), *A short treatise on Canadian constitutional law* (Toronto, 1918), and a number of pamphlets on law and government.

[Morgan, *Can. men* (1912); *Canadian law times*, 1919.]

Lefroy, Sir John Henry (1817-1890), soldier and scientist, was born at Crondall, Hampshire, England, on January 28, 1817, the third son of the Rev. John Henry George Lefroy. In 1834 he obtained a commission in the Royal Artillery; and in 1839 he was sent to St. Helena as director of the magnetical observatory there. In 1842-43 he made a magnetic survey of British North America, the results of which were later published by him in his *Diary of a magnetic survey of a portion of the Dominion of Canada, chiefly in the North West Territories* (London, 1883). From 1844 to 1853 he was in charge of the magnetic observatory at Toronto. He then returned to England, and occupied a series of appointments in the British army, until his retirement with the rank of general in 1882. In 1871 he was appointed governor of the Bermudas; and in 1880 he became for a short period governor of Tasmania. He died at Lewarne, near Liskeard, Cornwall, England, on April 11, 1890. In 1848 he married Emily Merry (d. 1859), daughter of Sir John Beverley Robinson, Bart. (q.v.); and in 1860 Charolotte, daughter of Lieut.-Col. Thomas Dundas, of Carron Hall, Stirlingshire, Scotland. He was created a K.C.M.G. in 1877; and in 1883 McGill University conferred on him the degree of LL.D. He was the author of *Memorials of the discovery of the Bermudas* (2 vols., London, 1877-79) and *The botany of Bermuda* (London, 1884), and after his death his widow published privately his *Autobiography*.

[A. H. F. Lefroy, *General Sir J. H. Lefroy* (Trans. Can. Inst., 1890-91); *Dict. nat. biog.*; E. M. Chadwick, *Ontarian families* (2 vols., Toronto, 1894-98).]

Légal, Emile Joseph (1849-1920), first Roman Catholic archbishop of Edmonton, was born in France on October 9, 1849. He was educated at Nantes, and was ordained a priest in 1874. He emigrated to Canada and joined the Oblate order in 1880. From 1881 to 1897 he was a missionary among the Indians of Alberta; and in 1897 he became coadjutor of the bishop of St. Albert, with the title bishop of Pogla *in partibus*. He succeeded to the bishopric of St. Albert in 1902; and in 1912 he was chosen first archbishop of the ecclesiastical province of Edmonton. He died at Edmonton, Alberta, on March 10, 1920. He was the author of *Les Indiens dans les plaines* (Lyons, 1891), *Règlements et usages du diocèse* (Montreal, 1903), and a series of *Mandements* from 1905 to 1915. He compiled also *Short sketches of the history of the Catholic churches and missions in central Alberta* (Winnipeg, 1914).

[Allaire, *Dict. biog.*; Le Jeune, *Dict. gén.*; Morgan, *Can. men* (1912).]

LeGardeur de St. Pierre, Jacques (1701-1755), soldier, was born in 1701 at the seigniory of Repentigny near Montreal, the son of Jean Paul LeGardeur, Sieur de St. Pierre, and Josette Le Neuf de la Vallière. In 1750 he was appointed to the command of an expedition which was to continue the explorations of La Vérendrye (q.v.) in the West, but penetrated only to the valley of the Saskatchewan. In 1753 he returned to Montreal, and at the end of the year he was in command of Fort Le Boeuf, on the Ohio, when its evacuation was demanded by George Washington. In 1755 he commanded the Indians in the Dieskau expedition, and he was killed in the first engagement at Lake George on September 8.

[E. Mallet, *Jacques Le Gardeur de Saint Pierre* (Bull. rech. hist., 1898); L. A. Prud'homme, *Les successeurs de La Vérendrye* (Trans. Roy. Soc. Can., 1906); Le Jeune, *Dict. gén.*; *Dict. Can. biog.*, vol. 3.]

Légaré, Joseph (1789-1855), artist, was born at Quebec on March 10, 1789. Beginning as a copyist of religious paintings, he became a painter of landscapes, portraits, and scenes of Indian and Canadian life. A number of his pictures are owned by Laval University. In politics, he was a partisan of Louis-Joseph Papineau (q.v.); and he was arrested as a suspect after the rebellion of 1837 in Lower Canada. On February 8, 1855, he was appointed by the MacNab-Taché government a member of the Legislative Council of United Canada; but he died only a few months later on June 21, 1855.

[G. Bellerive, *Artistes-peintres canadiens-français* (Quebec, 1925).]

Legendre, Napoléon (1841-1907), author, was born at Nicolet, Lower Canada, on February 13, 1841, the son of François Félix Legendre and Marie Renée Turcotte. He was educated under the Jesuits in Montreal, and was called to the bar of Lower Canada in 1865. In 1876 he accepted a position in the Quebec public service, and this he held until his death at Quebec on December 16, 1907. In 1867 he married Marie-Louise Dupré, of Quebec. He was a charter member of the Royal Society of Canada; and in 1890 he was made a Litt.D. of Laval University. He was the author of a novel entitled *Sabre et scalpel*, published in the *Album de la Minerve* (1872), and of the following books: *A nos enfants* (Quebec, 1875), *Echos de Québec* (2 vols., Quebec, 1877), *Les perce-neige, premières poésies* (Quebec, 1886), *La langue française au Canada* (Quebec, 1890), *Mélanges, prose et vers* (Quebec, 1891). He contributed a number of papers to the *Transactions* of the Royal Society of Canada.

[*Proc. Roy. Soc. Can.*, 1908; Morgan, *Can. men* (1898); Le Jeune, *Dict. gén.*]

Legge, Charles (1829-1881), civil engineer, was born at Gananoque, Upper Canada, on September 29, 1829. He was educated at Queen's College, Kingston, and studied civil engineering under Samuel Keefer (q.v.). He played an important part in the building of canals and railways in Canada; and he was engineer in charge of the construction of the Victoria Bridge, Montreal. He died at Toronto, Ontario, on April 12, 1881. Besides many reports on the construction of railways and canals, he was the author of *A glance at the Victoria bridge and the men who built it* (Montreal, 1860) and *Harbour improvements at foot of Lachine canal* (Montreal, 1864).

[*Dom. ann. reg.*, 1880-81.]

Legge, Francis (1719-1783), governor of Nova Scotia, was born in England in 1719, a relative of William, second Earl of Dartmouth, one of his Majesty's principal secretaries of state. In 1773 he was appointed governor of Nova Scotia, and he remained in the colony until 1776. He embroiled himself with nearly everyone in the colony; and in 1776 he was recalled, but he continued to draw the salary attached to the office of governor of Nova Scotia until 1782. He died on May 15, 1783.

[Viola F. Barnes, *Francis Legge, governor of Nova Scotia* (New England quarterly, 1931); D. Campbell, *History of Nova Scotia* (Montreal, 1873); B. Murdoch, *History of Nova Scotia* (3 vols., Halifax N.S., 1867).]

Leggett, William Martin (b. 1813), clergyman and poet, was born at Sussex Vale, New Brunswick, in 1813. He became a Methodist minister; but in 1845 he joined the Church of England, and later he went to England to live. He apparently died in England, at some date not ascertained. When only about twenty years of age, he published *The forest wreath: A collection of lyrics* (Saint John, N.B., 1833).

[W. G. MacFarlane, *New Brunswick bibliography* (Saint John, N.B., 1895).]

Leggo, William (1822-1888), lawyer and author, was born in Perth, Upper Canada, on January 23, 1822. He was called to the bar in Ontario in 1870, and practised law at first in Hamilton, Ontario. He then removed to Winnipeg, where he became master in chancery for Manitoba; and he died in Winnipeg on March 31, 1888. He was the author of *Forms and precedents of pleadings and proceedings in the court of chancery for Ontario* (Hamilton, Ont., 1872) and *The history of the administration of the Right Honorable Frederick Temple, Earl of Dufferin* (Montreal, 1878).

[Private information.]

Leighton, A. C. (1901-1965), painter, was born in Hastings, England, and was educated at Hastings and at the Hornsey School, London. He had no formal art training but began painting for a commission firm. E. Leslie Badham saw his work at Mansion House, London, and advised him to try for the Royal Society of British Artists exhibit. He entered two pictures and was elected to the Academy. In 1928 he was commissioned by the Canadian Pacific Railway to paint scenes of the prairies and the Rockies. He travelled across Canada and exhibited the paintings he made at the Leyland Gallery, Vancouver, in 1928. From 1930 to 1938 he was a teacher at the Institute of Technology and Art at Calgary, Alberta. He also conducted summer school classes at the Brewster Dude Ranch near Banff, beginning in 1934. He organized the Calgary Sketch Club and lectured at the University of Alberta. He was a founder of the Alberta Society of Artists (1931). His works were exhibited in Calgary (1930), at the Royal Academy, London, England (1934), and at Montreal (1936). His paintings are to be found in the National Gallery, Ottawa, the Vancouver Art Gallery, the Winnipeg Art Gallery, the Edmonton Art Gallery, New York Central Reference Library, I.B.M., the Seagram Collection, and in Britain

at Eastbourne, Hastings, Brighton, Hull, and Glasgow, as well as in private collections. He was a member of the Royal Society of British Artists (1929) and an associate of the Royal Canadian Academy (1935). He died at Calgary. Alberta, in 1965

[C. S. MacDonald, *A dictionary of Canadian artists*, vol. 3 (Ottawa, 1971); J. R. Harper, *Painting in Canada* (Toronto, 1966).]

Leitch, John S. (1880-1963), shipbuilder, was born in Scotland in 1880 and studied naval architecture and shipbuilding before coming to Canada in 1912. He became manager of the shipyards in Collingwood and at Kingston. During the First World War he organized the production of explosive shells and supervised the construction of trawlers and cargo vessels for the Imperial Munitions Board. In the Second World War he organized work in four Canadian shipbuilding yards and the construction of Bangor and Algerine minesweepers, trawlers, and corvettes. China coasters and warrior tugs were under his direction. He was president of Canadian Shipbuilding and Engineering Limited, and of Collingwood Shipyards, Port Arthur Shipyards, and Midland Shipyards. He was a member of the Institute of Naval Architects of London, and the Society of Engineers, New York; and a fellow of the Royal Society of Arts. He died at Collingwood, Ontario, December 2, 1963.

[Metropolitan Toronto Library Board, *Biographical scrapbooks*, vol. 21.]

Leitch, William (1814-1864), principal of Queen's University (1859-64), was born at Rothesay, in the Island of Bute, in 1814. He was educated at Glasgow University (B.A., 1837; M.A., 1838; D.D., 1860); and in 1838 he was licensed as a minister of the Church of Scotland. He was appointed principal of Queen's University, Kingston, in 1859, and he held this office until his death at Kingston on May 9, 1864. He published *God's glory in the heavens* (London, 1862), and some papers in the *Transactions* of the Botanical Society of Canada.

[Taylor, *Brit. Am.*, vol. 1; Morgan, *Bib. can.*; W. I. Addison (comp.), *Roll of the graduates of the University of Glasgow* (Glasgow, 1898).]

Leith, James (1777-1838), fur-trader, was born in August, 1777, in Aberdeenshire, Scotland, the son of Alexander Leith, a graduate of King's College, Aberdeen. He emigrated to Canada about 1797, at the instance of Edward Ellice (q.v.), and in 1798 entered the service of the XY Company. He appears to have been a relative of George Leith (d. 1801), senior partner in the Montreal firm of Leith, Jameson and Co. He was one of the six wintering partners of the XY Company absorbed as wintering partners by the North West Company in 1804;

and at the time of the union of the North West and Hudson's Bay companies in 1821, he was made a chief factor. From 1806 to 1807 he was at Folle Avoine; from 1807 to 1810, at Michipicoten; from 1810 to 1811, at Rainy Lake; from 1811 to 1812, at the Red River; from 1812 to 1815, at Monontagué and Lake Nipigon; in 1816 at Rainy Lake; and in 1817 he was sent to the Red River to arrest some of Selkirk's men. In 1821 he was in charge of the Athabaska district; and from 1822 to 1829 he was in charge of the Cumberland House district. He retired from the Company's service in 1830; and he died at Torquay, England, unmarried, on June 19, 1838. By his will he left half his estate for the propagation of the Protestant religion among the Indians.

[E. E. Rich (ed.), *Journal of occurrences in the Athabasca department, by George Simpson* (Toronto: The Champlain Society, 1938).]

Le Jeune, Louis (1857-1935), priest and author, was born at Pleybert-Christ, Brittany, France, on November 12, 1857. He entered the Oblate order in 1877; and in 1896 he was sent to Canada as a missionary and preacher. From 1898 to 1913 he was professor of French literature at the University of Ottawa; and from 1900 to 1907 he was the editor of *La Revue Littéraire*. He died at Ottawa on February 4, 1935. He published a devotional book, *La beauté de l'âme* (Montreal, 1922), and several books intended for use in schools; but his chief work was his *Dictionnaire général du Canada* (2 vols., Paris, 1931).

[E. Richard, *Le Père Le Jeune* (La Bannière de Marie Immaculée, 1936); Allaire, *Dict. biog.*]

Le Jeune, Paul (1591-1664), missionary, was born at Châlons-sur-Marne, France, in July, 1591, of Huguenot parentage. In 1613, having been converted to Roman Catholicism, he entered the Jesuit novitiate; and he became in 1630 superior of the Jesuit residence at Dieppe. In 1632 he went to Quebec as superior of the Canadian mission; and he was superior of the mission until 1639. He remained in Canada until 1649; then he returned to France, and became procurator of foreign missions. He died in France on August 7, 1664. Beside the Jesuit *Relations* for the years 1632-39 he wrote some religious works, one of which, *A ten days' retreat*, has been reprinted (Rennes, 1843).

[*Cyc. Am. biog.*; R. G. Thwaites (ed.), *The Jesuit relations*, vol. 5 (Cleveland, 1897); C. de Rochemonteix, *Les Jésuites de la Nouvelle France* (3 vols., Paris, 1895-96); T. J. Campbell, *Pioneer priests of North America* (New York, 1908); Le Jeune, *Dict. gén.*; *Dict. Can. biog.*, vol. 1.]

Le Loutre, Jean Louis (1709-1772), priest, was born at Morlaix, France, on September 26, 1709, the son of Jean Maurice Le Loutre, Sieur

Despré, and of Catherine Huet. He studied at the Seminary of St. Esprit, Paris, and was ordained a priest of the Roman Catholic Church. In 1737 he went to Louisbourg, and in 1738 he became a missionary to the Micmacs. He gained an ascendancy over both the Indians and the Acadians; and is said to have made use of this to incite them against the English. The latter placed a price on his head; and when Fort Beauséjour was captured by the English in 1755, he escaped to Miramichi. Thence he sailed for Quebec, but he was captured by an English trading-ship, and was taken to Portsmouth. From 1755 to 1763 he was held a prisoner in the Island of Jersey; and he was released only after the signing of the Treaty of Paris. On his return to France, he interested himself in arranging for the settlement of the Acadians at Belle-isle-en-mer. He died at Nantes in 1772. About 1753 he received the title of vicar-general from the bishop of Quebec.

[N. McL. Rogers, *The Abbé Le Loutre* (Can. hist. rev., 1930); A. G. Doughty (ed.), *The journal of Captain John Knox*, vol. 1 (Toronto: The Champlain Society, 1914); T. B. Akins (ed.), *Selections from the public documents of Nova Scotia* (Halifax, N.S., 1869); F. Parkman, *Montcalm and Wolfe* (2 vols., Boston, 1884); Le Jeune, *Dict. gén.*; J. C. Webster, *The career of the Abbé Le Loutre in Nova Scotia* (Shediac, N.B., 1933)]

Le Marchant, Sir John Gaspard (1803-1874), lieutenant-governor of Nova Scotia (1852-58), was born in 1803, the third son of Major-General John Gaspard Le Marchant. He was gazetted an ensign in the 10th Foot in 1820; and he rose in the British army to the rank of lieutenant-general in 1864. He served with the British Auxiliary Legion in Spain in 1835-37; and in 1838 he was created, for his services, a knight bachelor. From 1847 to 1852 he was governor of Newfoundland; and from 1852 to 1858 he was lieutenant-governor of Nova Scotia. He was subsequently governor of Malta and commander-in-chief of Madras. He died at London, England, on February 6, 1874. In 1839 he married the third daughter of the Rev. Robert Taylor, of Clifton Campbell, Staffordshire. He was created a G.C.M.G. in 1860, and a K.C.B. (civil) in 1865.

[*Dict. nat. biog.*; D. Campbell, *Nova Scotia* (Montreal, 1873); *Dict. Can. biog.*, vol. 10.]

Lemay, Georges (1857-1902), journalist, was born at St. Paul, Minnesota, on January 1, 1857, and was educated at the College of St. Boniface and the Quebec Seminary. He became a journalist, and was on the staff of several newspapers in the province of Quebec; but in 1887 he went to New York, and became a music teacher and organist. He died in New York, N.Y., on April 17, 1902. While in Canada, he published *Petites fantaisies littéraires* (Quebec, 1884).

[*Bull. rech. hist.*, 1926.]

Lemay, Hugolin Marie (1877-1938), priest and bibliographer, was born at Knowlton, Quebec, on September 20, 1877, and was baptized Stanislas. He was educated at the College of St. Hyacinthe, and in 1902 joined the Franciscan order. He was ordained a priest in 1903, and took the name of Hugolin. He became the historian and bibliographer of the Franciscans, as well as a vigorous advocate of temperance. In 1928 he was elected a fellow of the Royal Society of Canada. He died at Montreal, Quebec, on June 25, 1938. He was the author of *Si femme savait! Si femme voulait! Femme contre intempérance* (Montreal, 1907), *Au fond du verre: Histoires d'ivrognes* (Montreal, 1908), *De l'enseignement antialcoolique* (Montreal, 1909), *Par la lutte et par l'amour* (Montreal, 1909), *Les manifestes electoraux* (Montreal, 1909), *N'en buvons plus: Histoires de tempérance* (Montreal, 1909), *Bibliographie des ouvrages concernant la tempérance* (Quebec, 1910), *Catalogue de l'exposition anti-alcoolique du premier congrès de tempérance du diocèse de Québec* (Quebec, 1910), *L'invincible obstacle* (Montreal, 1912), *La lutte antialcoolique dans la province de Québec* (Montreal, 1912), *Les vacances du jeune tempérant* (Montreal, 1913), *Inventaire des travaux, livres, brochures, feuillets, et autres écrits concernant la tempérance, publiés par les Pères Franciscains du Canada* (Montreal, 1915), *Les Franciscains et la croisade antialcoolique dans la province de Québec* (Montreal, 1915), *Pour les treize mardis* (Montreal, 1915), *De la mort à la vie* (Montreal, 1916), *De Québec à Percé* (Montreal, 1916), *Bibliographie franciscaine* (Quebec, 1916), *Bibliographie du tiers-ordre séculier de Saint François au Canada* (Montreal, 1921), *Pieuse union en l'honneur de Saint Joseph* (Lille, 1923), *Horizons et pensées* (Montreal 1925), *Dans la cloître et par le monde* (Montreal, 1925), *Le père Joseph Denis* (2 vols., Quebec, 1926), *Notes bibliographiques pour servir à l'histoire des Récollets du Canada* (6 parts, Montreal and Quebec, 1932-33), and *Vieux papiers, vieux chansons* (Montreal, 1936).

[*Proc. Roy. Soc. Can.*, 1939; *Bibliographie du R. P. Hugolin, o.f.m.* (Montreal, 1932).]

Lemay, Léon Pamphile (1837-1918), poet and novelist, was born at Lotbinière, Lower Canada, on January 5, 1837, the son of Léon Lemay and Marie Louise Auger. He was educated at the Quebec Seminary, and studied theology at the University of Ottawa, but he abandoned theology for law, and was called to the bar of Lower Canada in 1865. In 1867 he was appointed librarian to the Quebec legislature; and he occupied this position until his retirement in 1892. He died at St. Jean-Deschaillons, Quebec, on June 11, 1918. In 1863 he married Selina Robitaille, of Quebec; and by her he had four sons and seven daughters. He was a charter member of the Royal Society of Canada, and a Litt.D. of Laval University. As a poet his first work was *Essais poetiques* (Quebec, 1865), and this was followed by *Evangéline*, a translation in verse of Longfellow's poem (Quebec, 1870), *Deux poèmes couronnés* (Quebec, 1870), *Les vengeances* (Quebec, 1875), *Fables canadiennes* (Quebec, 1881), *Petits poèmes* (Quebec, 1883), *Tonkourou* (Quebec, 1888), *Les gouttelettes* (Quebec, 1904), *Evangéline et autres poèmes de Longfellow* (Montreal, 1912), *Les Epis* (Montreal, 1914), and *Reflets d'antan* (Montreal, 1916). In fiction he was the author of *Le pèlerin de Sainte Anne* (2 vols., Quebec, 1877), *Picounoc-le-maudit* (2 vols., Quebec, 1878), *L'affaire Sougraine* (Quebec, 1884), *Contes vrais* (Quebec, 1899), and a translation of William Kirby's *The golden dog*, under the title *Le chien d'or* (Quebec, 1884). He published also some plays, *Les vengeances, drame en six actes* (Quebec, 1876) and *Rouge et bleu, comédies* (Quebec, 1891).

[C. Roy, *Pamphile Lemay* (Canada français, 1918); *Cyc. Am. biog.*; Morgan, *Can. men* (1912); Rose, *Cyc. Can. biog.* (1888); Le Jeune, *Dict. gén.*; C. ab der Halden, *Nouvelles études de littérature canadienne-française* (Paris, 1907).]

Lemieux, François Xavier (1811-1864), chief commissioner of public works for Canada (1855-57), was born at Lévis, Lower Canada, on February 9, 1811, the son of Gabriel Lemieux and Judith Bonneville. He was educated at the Quebec Seminary, and was called to the bar of Lower Canada in 1839. He sat in the Legislative Assembly of Canada for Dorchester from 1847 to 1854, and for Lévis from 1854 to 1861; and he was chief commissioner of public works in the MacNab-Taché and Taché-Macdonald cabinets from 1855 to 1857. He was also receiver-general in the short-lived Brown-Dorion administration of 1858. Defeated for the Assembly in 1861, he was elected to the Legislative Council in 1862. He died at Lévis, Lower Canada, on May 16, 1864.

[L. Lemieux, *L'hon. François-Xavier Lemieux* (Bull. rech. hist., 1904); Soeur Andrée Désilets, *Une figure politique du 19ᵉ siècle* (R.H.A.F., 1967-68); Le Jeune, *Dict. gén.*]

Lemieux, Sir François Xavier (1851-1933), chief justice of Quebec, was born at Lévis, Canada East, on April 9, 1851, the son of Antoine Lemieux. He was educated at Laval University (LL.B., 1872; LL.D., 1900), and was called to the bar in 1872. He became famous as a criminal lawyer, and was the counsel for Louis Riel (q.v.) at Regina in 1885, and for Honoré Mercier (q.v.) before the Royal Commission of 1892. From 1883 to 1892 he represented Lévis, and from 1894 to 1897 Bonaventure, in the Legislative Assembly of Quebec; and in 1897 he was appointed a puisne judge of the Supreme Court of the province of Quebec. In 1911 he was made chief justice of this court, and he retained this position until his death at Quebec on July 18, 1933. In 1874 he married Diana, daughter of the Hon. M. A. Plamondon; and by her he had six sons and six daughters. He was created a knight bachelor in 1914.

[F. J. Audet, *Les juges en chef de la province de Québec* (Quebec, 1927); P. G. Roy, *Les juges de la province de Québec* (Lévis, 1933); *Can. parl. comp.*; Morgan, *Can. men* (1912); Le Jeune, *Dict. gén.*]

Lemieux, Rodolphe (1866-1937), postmaster-general of Canada (1906-11), was born at Montreal, Quebec, on November 1, 1866. He was educated at the College of Nicolet and at Laval University (B.C.L., 1891; LL.D., 1896), and was called to the bar of Quebec in 1891 (K.C., 1898). He was a law partner of the Hon. Honoré Mercier (q.v.) and of Sir Lomer Gouin (q.v.), and was a professor of law at Laval University from 1896 to 1926. He was elected a member of the Canadian House of Commons for Gaspé in 1896, and he continued a member of the House until he was called to the Senate of Canada in 1930; and he was solicitor-general of Canada from 1904 to 1906, postmaster-general from 1906 to August 11, 1911, and minister of marine and fisheries from August 11 to October 6, 1911. He was elected a fellow of the Royal Society of Canada in 1908 (president, section 1, 1909-10); and he was created a knight commander of the order of St. Gregory in 1924 (Grand Cross, 1930). He died at Montreal, Quebec, on September 28, 1937. He was the author of *De la contrainte par corps* (Montreal, 1895) and *Les origines du droit franco-canadien* (Montreal, 1900).

[*Proc. Roy. Soc. Can.*, 1938; *Can. who's who*, 1936-37; *Can. parl. comp.*]

Le Moine, Sir James MacPherson (1825-1912), author, was born at Quebec, Lower Canada, on January 24, 1825, the son of Benjamin Le Moine, a merchant, and Julia Ann, daughter of Daniel MacPherson, seignior of Crane Island. He was educated at the Quebec Seminary, and in 1850 was called to the bar of Lower Canada. He practised law in Quebec; and from 1869 to 1899 he was inspector of inland revenue for the district of Quebec. He died at Quebec on February 5, 1912. In 1850 he married Harriet Mary (d. 1900), daughter of Edward Atkinson, Yorkshire, England; and by her he had two daughters. He was a D.C.L. of Bishop's College, Lennoxville (1901); and in 1894 he was president of the Royal Society of Canada. In 1897 he was created a knight bachelor. He was a most voluminous writer, and wrote in both French and English. His first publication was a popular work entitled *Ornithologie du Canada* (2 vols., Quebec, 1860-61); and his most important work was a series of miscellanies entitled *Maple leaves* (6 vols., Quebec, 1863-1906). He published also a number of books on Quebec

and the lower St. Lawrence, *The lower St. Lawrence; or, Quebec to Halifax* (Quebec, 1862), *The tourist's note-book for Quebec* (Quebec, 1870), *Quebec past and present* (Quebec, 1876), *The chronicles of the St. Lawrence* (Montreal and Quebec, 1878), *Picturesque Quebec* (1882), *Monographies et esquisses* (Quebec, 1885), *The explorations of Jonathan Oldbuck* (Quebec, 1889), *The legends of the St. Lawrence* (Quebec, 1898), and *The port of Quebec* (Quebec, 1901).

[Mrs. D. H. McLean, *Sir J. M. Le Moine* (Trans. Women's Canadian Historical Society of Ottawa, 1911); B. Muddiman, *Grape festivals of Spencer Grange* (Can. mag., 1913); *Proc. Roy. Soc. Can.*, 1912; Le Jeune, *Dict. gén.*; bibliography in *Bull. rech. hist.*, 1918, and in R. Renault, *Bibliographie de Sir James M. Le Moine* (Quebec, 1897).]

Le Moyne, Charles (1626-1685), seignior, came to Canada from Normandy in 1641, and became an interpreter at Montreal. He acquired several seigniories, notably those of Longueuil and Châteauguay; and he died at Montreal in February, 1685. He was the father of twelve sons, many of whom became famous.

[A. Jodoin and J. L. Vincent, *Histoire de Longueuil* (Montreal, 1889); Le Jeune, *Dict. gén.*; Bibaud, *Panth. can.*; *Bull. rech. hist.*, 1907; *Dict. Can. biog.*, vol. 1.]

Le Moyne, Charles, Baron de Longueuil. See **Longueuil, Charles Le Moyne, Baron de.**

Le Moyne, Jacques, Sieur de Sainte-Hélène. See **Sainte-Hélène, Jacques Le Moyne, Sieur de.**

Le Moyne, Jean Baptiste, Sieur de Bienville. See **Bienville, Jean Baptiste Le Moyne, Sieur de.**

Le Moyne, Paul, Sieur de Maricourt. See **Maricourt, Paul Le Moyne, Sieur de.**

Le Moyne, Paul Joseph, Chevalier de Longueuil. See **Longueuil, Paul Joseph Le Moyne, Chevalier de.**

Le Moyne, Pierre, Sieur d'Iberville. See **Iberville, Pierre Le Moyne, Sieur d'.**

Lennox, Charles Gordon, Duke of Richmond. See **Richmond, Charles Gordon Lennox, Duke of.**

Lenoir, Joseph (1822-1861), poet, was born at St. Henri, near Montreal, Lower Canada, in 1822. He was educated at the College of Montreal, and was called to the bar of Lower Canada in 1847. He was assistant editor of the *Journal de l'instruction publique* when he died, on April 3, 1861. His poems, originally published in various periodicals of his time, have been collected and edited by Casimir Hébert under the title *Poèmes épars* (Montreal, 1916).

[*Bull. rech. hist.*, 1929; Le Jeune, *Dict. gén.*]

Leonard, Reuben Wells (1860-1930), engineer, financier, and philanthropist, was born at Brantford, Ontario, on February 21, 1860, the son of Francis Henry Leonard and Elizabeth Catton. He was educated at the Royal Military College, Kingston, from which he graduated with the silver medal in 1883. He joined the engineering staff of the Canadian Pacific Railway, and in 1885 he was a staff officer in charge of transport during the North West Rebellion. From 1886 to 1906 he was successively engineer in charge or construction manager of various Canadian railways, hydro-electric power developments, and iron and nickel ore developments; in 1892-93, for example, he was in charge of the construction of the first hydro-electric power development at Niagara Falls. In 1906, he promoted, and became the president of, the Coniagas mine in northern Ontario; and this mine became the source of his large fortune. From 1911 to 1914 he was chairman of the Canadian National Transcontinental Railway Commission; in 1919 he was president of the Engineering Institute of Canada; and he was for many years lieutenant-colonel commanding the Corps of Guides in No. 2 Military District. During his latter years he became noted for his generous benefactions. In 1922, he and his wife presented Chatham House in London to the Royal Institute of International Affairs, to serve as a centre for the study of the problems of the British Empire; and in 1916 he established a number of scholarships, under the Leonard Foundation, for the education of the sons of clergymen, school-teachers, soldiers, and others. He died, after a lingering illness, at St. Catharines, Ontario, on December 17, 1930.

[*Who was who*, 1929-40; *Can. who was who*, vol. 2; Morgan, *Can. men* (1912); H. Charlesworth (ed.), *A cyclopaedia of Canadian biography* (Toronto, 1919).]

Lepage, John (d. 1885), poet, was a schoolteacher in Charlottetown, Prince Edward Island, who was known as "the island minstrel". He died at Charlottetown in January, 1885. He was the author of *The island minstrel* (2 vols., Charlottetown, P.E.I., 1860-67).

[*Dom. ann. reg.*, 1885; C. C. James, *A bibliography of Canadian poetry* (Toronto, 1899).]

Lépine, Ambroise Dydime (1834?-1923), rebel, was born in the Red River valley about 1834, the son of a French-Canadian father and a half-breed mother. During the Red River rebellion of 1869-70 he was adjutant-general in the provincial government of Louis Riel (q.v.); and he was president of the court-martial

which condemned to death Thomas Scott. After the rebellion he took refuge in the United States, but soon returned to Canada, and in 1873 was arrested and tried on the charge of complicity in the murder of Scott. He was found guilty, and condemned to death; but his sentence was commuted to two years' imprisonment and the loss of his civil rights. On his release from prison, he settled first near Batoche, Saskatchewan, and then near Forget, Saskatchewan; and a few years before his death, which occurred on June 8, 1923, his civil rights were restored to him.

[L. A. Prud'homme, *Ambroise Dydime Lépine* (Trans. Roy. Soc. Can., 1925); B. Cooke, *The trial of Lépine* (Can. mag., 1915); A. G. Morice, *Dictionnaire historique des canadiens et des métis français de l'ouest* (Quebec, 1908); Le Jeune, *Dict. gén.*; *Can. who was who*, vol. 1.]

Leprohon, Mrs. Rosanna Eleanora, *née* **Mullins** (1829-1879), novelist, was born in Montreal in 1829. She became a contributor to the *Literary Garland* (Montreal, 1838-52), and in this periodical appeared her first novels: *Ida Beresford* (1848), *Florence FitzHardinge* (1849), *Eva Huntingdon* (1850), and *Clarence FitzClarence* (1851). In 1859 she published *Eveleen O'Donnell* in the Boston *Pilot* and *The manor house of de Villerai* in the Montreal *Family Herald*. Her first story to appear in book form was *Antoinette de Mirecourt* (Montreal, 1864; tr. into French by J. A. Genand, Montreal, 1864); and this was followed by *Clive Weston's wedding anniversary* (Montreal, 1872), and *Armand Durand* (Montreal, 1868; tr. into French by J. A. Genand, 1869). She died at Montreal on September 20, 1879. In 1851 she married Dr. Leprohon, who became a prominent medical doctor in Montreal. After her death there was published *The poetical works of Mrs. Leprohon (Miss R. E. Mullins)* (Montreal, 1881).

[*Dom. ann. reg.*, 1879; Morgan, *Bib. can.*; *Cyc. Am. biog.*; L. E. Horning and L. J. Burpee, *A bibliography of Canadian fiction* (Toronto, 1904); C. C. James, *A bibliography of Canadian poetry* (Toronto, 1899); *Dict. Can. biog.*, vol. 10.]

Leroux, Laurent (1758?-1855), fur-trader, was born in Canada about 1758, and first appears in the fur-trade as a clerk in the service of Gregory, McLeod and Co. in 1784. On the union of this company with the North Company in 1787, he became a clerk in the service of the North West Company, and was chiefly employed in the Athabaska district. In 1791 he was employed on the Great Slave Lake. He returned to Lower Canada in 1796, and settled at L'Assomption. From 1827 to 1830 he represented the constituency of Leinster in the Legislative Assembly of Lower Canada. He died in 1855, aged 97 years. After 1796, he married Esther Loiselle.

[A. G. Morice, *Dictionnaire historique des canadiens et des métis français de l'ouest* (Kamloops, B.C., 1908).]

Léry, Charles Etienne Chaussegros de (1774-1842), executive councillor of Lower Canada, was born on September 30, 1774, the youngest son of the Hon. Joseph Gaspard Chaussegros de Léry (q.v.). From 1826 to 1837 he was a member of the Executive Council of Lower Canada, and from 1838 to 1841 a member of the Special Council of the province. He died on February 17, 1842.

[P. G. Roy, *La famille Chaussegros de Léry* (Lévis, Que., 1934); F. Daniel, *Le Vicomte C. de Léry . . . et sa famille* (Montreal, 1867); Le Jeune, *Dict. gén.*]

Léry, François Joseph Chaussegros, Vicomte de (1754-1824), military engineer, was born at Quebec on September 11, 1754, the eldest son of the Hon. Joseph Gaspard Chaussegros de Léry (q.v.). He was educated at Paris, France, and became a lieutenant of engineers in the French army in 1773. He served in America in 1781-82; and he rose to high rank in the army of Napoleon. In 1811 he was created a baron of the Empire; and at the restoration he was created a viscount, and promoted to the rank of lieutenant-general. He retired from the army in 1818, and he died at Chartrettes, near Melun, France, on September 5, 1824. He married the daughter of the Duke of Valmy.

[Vicomte de Léry, *Notice biographique du lieutenant-général vicomte de Léry* (Paris, 1824); F. Daniel, *Le Vicomte C. de Léry . . . et sa famille* (Montreal, 1867); P. G. Roy, *La famille Chaussegros de Léry* (Lévis, Que., 1934); Le Jeune, *Dict. gén.*]

Léry, Joseph Gaspard Chaussegros de (1682-1756), military engineer, was born in France in 1682. He came to Canada in 1716, and was employed in fortifying Quebec and Montreal. His death took place at Quebec on March 23, 1756. He married Marie-Renée Le Gardeur de Beauvais, and by her he had eleven children.

[P. G. Roy, *La famille Chaussegros de Léry* (Lévis, Que., 1934); F. Daniel, *Le Vicomte C. de Léry . . . et sa famille* (Montreal, 1867); Le Jeune, *Dict. gén.*; *Dict. Can. biog.*, vol. 3.]

Léry, Joseph Gaspard (or **Gaspard Joseph**) **Chaussegros de** (1721-1797), legislative councillor of Quebec and of Lower Canada, was born at Quebec on July 21, 1721, the son of Joseph Gaspard Chaussegros de Léry (q.v.). A military engineer like his father, he built Fort Beauséjour in Acadia; and he fought as an officer in the *troupes de la marine* throughout the Seven Years' War. In 1761 he emigrated to France, but he returned to Canada a few years later, and in 1768 was appointed *grand voyer* of the province. In 1778 he

was appointed a member of the Legislative Council of Quebec, and in 1792 of the Legislative Council of Lower Canada. He died on December 11, 1797. He married Louise Madeline, daughter of François Martel de Brouage. During the French régime he was created a chevalier de St. Louis.

[P. G. Roy, *La famille Chaussegros de Léry* (Lévis, Que., 1934); F. Daniel, *Le Vicomte C. de Léry . . . et sa famille* (Montreal, 1867); Le Jeune, *Dict. gén.*]

Léry, Louis René Chaussegros de (1762-1833), legislative councillor of Lower Canada, was born in Paris, France, on October 13, 1762, the son of the Hon. Joseph Gaspard Chaussegros de Léry (q.v.), and the younger brother of the Vicomte de Léry (q.v.). From 1784 to 1794 he served as an officer in the French army; then he returned to Canada, and became *grand voyer* of the district of Montreal. He was gazetted in 1813 a lieutenant-colonel in the Canadian militia, and he fought throughout the War of 1812. In 1818 he was appointed a member of the Legislative Council, and he sat in the Council until his death at Boucherville, Lower Canada, on October 28, 1833. He married Charlotte Boucher de Boucherville.

[P. G. Roy, *La famille Chaussegros de Léry* (Lévis, Que., 1934); F. Daniel, *Le Vicomte C. de Léry . . . et sa famille* (Montreal, 1867); Le Jeune, *Dict. gén.*]

Lescarbot, Marc (*fl.* 1570-1642), lawyer, poet, and historian, was born at Vervins, near Laon, France, about 1570. He studied law, and was called to the bar in Paris, in 1599. In 1606-07 he accompanied Poutrincourt (q.v.) to Port Royal in Acadia; and in 1609 he published in Paris a most entertaining account of the discoveries in the New World, under the title *Histoire de la Nouvelle France*. A second edition was published in 1611, and a third, much enlarged and revised, in 1618. This third edition has been reprinted by the Champlain Society with an English translation by W. L. Grant (3 vols., Toronto, 1907-14). Lescarbot published also a small volume of poems, dealing with the New World, *Les muses de la Nouvelle France* (Paris, 1609). He died in 1642.

[H. P. Biggar, Introduction to Lescarbot, *History of New France*, vol. 1 (Toronto: The Champlain Society, 1907) and *The French Hakluyt* (American historical review, 1901); Le Jeune, *Dict. gén.*; *Dict. Can. biog.*, vol. 1.]

Lesieur, Toussaint (*fl.* 1784-1799), furtrader, was a native of New France who became a clerk in the service of Gregory, McLeod and Co. about 1784. In 1787 he was in opposition to Cuthbert Grant (q.v.) in the Athabaska district. In 1789 he was in partnership with Simon Fraser, of St. Anne's (q.v.), in charge of a post at Rivière des Trembles and Portage de l'Isle. This partnership apparently continued until Simon Fraser became a partner of the

North West Company, and Lesieur returned to Canada. According to the accounts of McTavish, Frobisher and Co., he was still living in 1799.

[A. G. Morice, *Dictionnaire historique des canadiens et des métis français de l'ouest* (Kamloops, B.C., 1908).]

Leslie, James (1786-1873), merchant and politician, was born at Kair, Kincardineshire, Scotland, on September 4, 1786, the son of Capt. James Leslie, who had been Wolfe's assistant quartermaster-general at Quebec in 1759. He was educated at the University of Aberdeen, and came to Canada in 1804. During the War of 1812-15 he held a commission in the Canadian militia; and he retained his connection with the militia until his retirement with the rank of lieutenant-colonel in 1862. He was for many years a successful merchant in Montreal; and he represented Montreal East in the Legislative Assembly of Lower Canada from 1824 to the rebellion of 1837. From 1841 to 1848 he sat in the Legislative Assembly of United Canada for Verchères, and in 1848 he was appointed a member of the Legislative Council. From 1848 to 1851 he was a member of the second Baldwin-Lafontaine administration, first as president of the Council (1848), and then as provincial secretary (1848-51). In 1867 he was called to the Senate of Canada, and he continued to sit in this chamber until his death at Montreal on December 6, 1873, having been a member of Canadian legislatures almost continuously for nearly fifty years. In 1815 he married Julia, daughter of Patrick Langan, seignior of Bourchemin, Lower Canada.

[*Cyc. Am. biog.*; *Can. parl. comp.*; J. M. Le Moine, *The Scot in New France* (Montreal, 1881), App. C.; J. C. Dent, *The last forty years* (2 vols., Toronto, 1881); J. D. Borthwick, *Montreal, its history* (Montreal, 1875); R. Campbell, *History of the St. Gabriel Street Church, Montreal* (Montreal, 1887); *Dict. Can. biog.*, vol. 10.]

Leslie, Kenneth (1892-1974), poet, was born in Pictou, Nova Scotia, November 1, 1892. He was educated at Dalhousie University (B.A., 1912), at the University of Nebraska (M.A., 1914), and at Harvard. He became editor of the New York *Protestant*. "His poetry combines imaginative, impersonal expression with pictures drawn from Nova Scotia life, and his varying rhythms are frequently those of the sea." He won the Governor-General's Award for his collection of poems, *By stubborn stars and other poems* (1938). His other collections include *Windward rock* (1934); *Such a din* (1935); and *Lowlands low* (1936). He died at Halifax, Nova Scotia, October 7, 1974.

[*Can. who's who*, 1970-72; N. Story, *The Oxford companion to Canadian history and literature* (Toronto, 1967).]

Leslie, Mary (1842-1920), novelist and versifier, was born at Leslie's Corners, Wellington county, Canada West, on June 11, 1842. She studied art in Canada and Holland, and gave lessons in drawing. She died in Toronto, Ontario, on March 1, 1920. She was the author of *The Cromaboo mail-carrier* (Guelph, Ont., 1878), *Rhymes of the kings and queens of England* (Toronto, 1896), and *Historical sketches of Scotland* (Toronto, 1905).

[Morgan, *Can. men and women* (1912).]

Lesperance, Jean Talon (1838-1891), journalist and author, was born at St. Louis, Missouri, in 1838, of a family originally Canadian. He was educated at the Ecole Polytechnique in Paris and at the University of Heidelberg. During the American Civil War he fought in the army of the South; and after the war, his family having lost its fortune, he came to Canada. He settled first at St. Johns, Quebec, and became a journalist. He founded the *News* at St. Johns; in 1872 he joined the staff of the Montreal *Gazette*; in 1873 he became the editor of the *Canadian Illustrated News*; and in 1888, after a second period on the staff of the *Gazette*, he became editor of the *Dominion Illustrated News*. He died at the Hôtel Dieu in Montreal on March 10, 1891. He was a charter member of the Royal Society of Canada; and he contributed a number of papers to its transactions. His chief publications were, however, two novels, *The Bastonnais* (Toronto, 1877) and *Tuque bleu* (Montreal, 1882), and a volume of verse, *The book of honour* (privately printed, n.d.).

[*Bull. rech. hist.*, 1924; A. MacMurchy, *Handbook of Canadian literature* (Toronto, 1906); C. C. James, *A bibliography of Canadian poetry* (Toronto, 1899); L. E. Horning and L. J. Burpee, *A bibliography of Canadian fiction* (Toronto, 1904); C. M. Whyte Edgar, *A wreath of Canadian song* (Toronto, 1910).]

Lessard, François Louis (1860-1927), soldier, was born at Quebec, Canada East, on December 9, 1860. He entered the Canadian militia in 1880, and served in the North West Rebellion of 1885 as a subaltern. In 1888 he was gazetted a captain in the Royal Canadian Dragoons, in 1894 major, and in 1898 lieutenant-colonel. He commanded the Royal Canadian Dragoons in the South African War, and was mentioned in despatches. In 1907 he was appointed adjutant-general of the Canadian militia, with the rank of colonel, and he was promoted to be brigadier-general in 1911 and major-general in 1912. During the First World War he occupied important posts in Canada, but was not permitted to serve overseas. He died at Meadowvale, Ontario, on August 7, 1927.

[*Who was who*, 1916-28; Morgan, *Can. men* (1912).]

Lesseps, Comte Jacques de (1883-1927), aviator, was born in 1883, the son of Comte Ferdinand de Lesseps, the creator of the Suez canal. He became a pioneer in aviation; and his flights in an airplane over Montreal in June and July, 1910, were among the first flights made in Canada. During the First World War, he commanded a squadron in the French Air Force, and he was decorated with the Legion of Honour. He lost his life in an airplane crash near Matane, in the Gaspé Peninsula, on October 18, 1927, while engaged in making a map of the peninsula from the air. In 1910 he married Grace, daughter of Sir William Mackenzie (q.v.); and by her he had two sons and two daughters.

[E. Z. Massicotte, *L'aviateur Jacques de Lesseps* (Bull. rech. hist., 1941).]

Lesslie, James (1800-1885), journalist, was born at Dundee, Scotland, in 1800, the son of Edward Lesslie. He came to Canada with his parents in 1822, and settled at Dundas, Upper Canada. Here, under the name of Lesslie and Sons, the family opened a shop. Later, after the father's death in 1828, the business was moved to Toronto. In 1834 James Lesslie was elected an alderman of Toronto; and subsequently he became president of the People's Bank. An advanced Reformer, and a political ally of William Lyon Mackenzie (q.v.), he was accused of being implicated in the Rebellion of 1837, and was imprisoned. Sir F. B. Head (q.v.) described him as a "notorious rebel". About 1844 he purchased the Toronto *Examiner* from Francis Hincks (q.v.); and this paper became later the mouthpiece of the "Clear Grit" wing of the Liberal party. In 1854 he sold his paper to George Brown (q.v.), and it was amalgamated with the *Globe*. In 1857 he retired to Eglinton, near Toronto; and there he died on April 19, 1885.

[*Cyc. Am. biog.*; *Dom. ann. reg.*, 1885; W. J. Rattray, *The Scot in British North America* (4 vols., Toronto, 1880); J. C. Dent, *The Upper Canadian rebellion* (2 vols., Toronto, 1885) and *The last forty years* (2 vols., Toronto, 1881).]

LeSueur, William Dawson (1840-1917), civil servant and author, was born at Quebec, Lower Canada, on February 19, 1840, the son of Peter LeSueur and Barbara Dawson. He was educated at the Montreal High School, the Ontario Law School, and the University of Toronto (B.A., 1863). He entered the Canadian civil service, and from 1888 until his retirement from the service in 1902 he was secretary of the post office department. For many years he wrote regularly for the Montreal *Gazette*, and then for the *Montreal Star*; and he gained a high reputation as an essayist by literary, scientific, and philosophical papers contributed to English, American, and Canadian periodicals. In his later days he became interested in Canadian history. He published a

life of *Count Frontenac* (Toronto, 1906); and he wrote a life of William Lyon Mackenzie which he was restrained from publishing by an injunction obtained in the courts by Mackenzie's heirs. He died at Ottawa on September 28, 1917. In 1867 he married Anne Jane, daughter of James Foster, of Montreal; and by her he had one son and one daughter. In 1900 he was made an LL.D. of Queen's University, Kingston; and in 1913 he was elected president of the Royal Society of Canada.

[*Proc. Roy. Soc. Can.*, 1918; P. G. Roy, *Fils de Québec*, vol. 4 (Quebec, 1933); Morgan, *Can. men* (1912); *Can. who's who* (1910).]

Le Tac, Xiste (Sixte) (1650-1718), missionary and historian, was born at Rouen, Normandy, in 1650. He entered the Recollet order in 1668, and was ordained a priest about 1674. In 1676 he was sent to Canada, and he was stationed successively at Charlesbourg, at Three Rivers, and at Quebec. In 1689 he was sent to Plaisance, Newfoundland, as superior of the Recollet mission there; but within a few months he returned to France, and he died at Rouen on April 10, 1718. After his return to France, he wrote an *Histoire chronologique de la Nouvelle France*, which was published, with notes, by Eugène Réveillaud (Paris, 1888).

[Allaire, *Dict. biog.*; Le Jeune, *Dict. gén.*; *Dict. Can. biog.*, vol. 2.]

Letellier, Blaise Ferdinand (1862-1930), jurist, was born at Lévis, Canada East, on June 22, 1862. He was educated at Laval University (LL.B., 1886; LL.D., 1911), and was called to the bar of Quebec in 1886 (K.C., 1903). He practised law in St. Joseph de la Beauce and Quebec; and from 1905 to 1910 he was a member of the Legislative Council of the province of Quebec. In 1910 he was appointed a judge of the Superior Court of Quebec for the district of Chicoutimi-Saguenay; and he sat on the bench until his death, at Montreal, Quebec, on December 15, 1930.

[Morgan, *Can. men* (1912); P. G. Roy, *Les juges de la province de Québec* (Quebec, 1933).]

Letellier de St. Just, Luc (1820-1881), lieutenant-governor of Quebec (1876-79), was born at Rivière Ouelle, Lower Canada, on May 12, 1820, the son of François Letellier and Marie, daughter of Charles Casgrain, seignior of Rivière Ouelle. He was educated at the College of Ste. Anne, and was admitted a notary public in 1841. From 1851 to 1852 he represented Kamouraska in the Legislative Assembly of Canada; in 1860 he was elected to the Legislative Council for the "Granville" division; and in 1867 he was called to the Senate of Canada. He was minister of agriculture in the S. Macdonald-Dorion administration of 1863-64, and in the Mackenzie government from 1873 to 1876. In 1876 he was appointed lieutenant-governor of Quebec, and in 1878 he took the extreme course of dismissing from office the Conservative administration of Boucher de Boucherville (q.v.). In 1879 he was dismissed from office by the governor-general on the advice of the Macdonald government, and he died at Rivière Ouelle, Quebec, on January 28, 1881. He married Eugénie, daughter of F. Laurent, of Quebec.

[P. B. Casgrain, *Letellier de St. Just et son temps* (Quebec, 1885); *Dom. ann. reg.*, 1878-81; Dent, *Can. port.*, vol. 1; Le Jeune, *Dict. gén.*; J. E. Collins, *Canada under the administration of Lord Lorne* (Toronto, 1884); Sir J. Pope (ed.), *Correspondence of Sir John Macdonald* (Toronto, 1921); Sir J. Willison, *Sir Wilfrid Laurier and the Liberal party* (2 vols., Toronto, 1903); R. MacG. Dawson, *The principle of official independence* (London, 1922).]

Lett, Benjamin (1814?-1858), filibusterer, was born in Ireland about 1814, and came to Canada with his parents in 1819. The family settled first on the Ottawa River, near Montreal; but after the death of the father, they moved in 1833 to Darlington township, in Upper Canada. "Ben" Lett (as he was invariably known) joined the "patriot" forces on Navy Island at the end of 1837; and he took part in many of the incidents which kept the border between Canada and the United States in a ferment during the years 1838-41. He was reputed to have been concerned in the destruction, on April 17, 1840, of the monument erected to Isaac Brock (q.v.) on Queenston Heights. He was arrested in Buffalo, New York, in September, 1841, and was sentenced to four years in prison. After his release from prison, he went to Illinois, and thence to Wisconsin; and he died at Milwaukee, Wisconsin, on December 9, 1858.

[E. C. Guillet, *The lives and times of the patriots* (Toronto, 1938); J. Squair, *The townships of Darlington and Clarke* (Toronto, 1927).]

Lett, Sherwood (1895-1964), judge, was born in Iroquois, Ontario, August 1, 1895, and educated at the University of British Columbia (B.A., 1916) and at Oxford University (B.A. [Juris.], 1922). During the First World War he served in Europe, where he won the Military Cross at Amiens; in the Second World War he was wounded at Dieppe in 1942 and at Caen in Normandy in 1944. In 1942 he was awarded the D.S.O. He was called to the bar of British Columbia in 1922 and practised law in Vancouver. He became chancellor of the University of British Columbia in 1951 and in 1955 was made chief justice of the Supreme Court of British Columbia. In 1963 he declared unconstitutional the expropriation of B.C. Electric by the British Columbia government, a decision of great constitutional significance. He died at Vancouver, British Columbia, July 2, 1964.

[*Can. who's who*, 1961-63; The Metropolitan Toronto Library Board, *Biographical scrapbooks*, vol. 23.]

Lett, William Pittman (1819-1892), journalist and poet, was born in Wexford county, Ireland, in 1819, the son of Capt. Andrews Lett, of the 26th Cameronian Highlanders. He was brought to Canada in 1820, and he was one of the earliest inhabitants of Ottawa (then Bytown). From 1855 to his death on August 15, 1892, he was city clerk of Ottawa. He was the author of *Recollections of Bytown and its oldest inhabitants* (Ottawa, 1874) in verse; and *The city of Ottawa and its surroundings* (Ottawa, 1884) and *Annexation and British connection* (Ottawa, 1889) in prose.

[A. H. D. Ross, *Ottawa past and present* (Toronto, 1927).]

LeVasseur, Nazaire (1848-1927), journalist, was born at Quebec, Canada East, on February 8, 1848. He became a journalist, and was for ten years on the staff of *L'Evénement*, Quebec; later he was a civil servant. He died at Quebec, Que., on November 8, 1927. He was the author of *Têtes et figures* (Quebec, 1920) and *Réminiscences d'antan: Québec il y a 70 ans* (Quebec, 1926).

[*Bull. rech. hist.*, 1928.]

Levasseur-Borgia, Joseph (1773-1839), politician, was born at Quebec on January 13, 1773, the son of Louis Levasseur-Borgia and Marie Anne Trudel. He was educated at the Quebec Seminary, and was called to the bar of Lower Canada in 1800. He was one of the founders of the newspaper *Le Canadien*, and had his commission as lieutenant in the militia cancelled by Sir James Craig (q.v.) in 1808, but was reinstated by Sir George Prevost (q.v.) in 1812, with the rank of captain. From 1808 to 1820 and from 1824 to 1830 he represented Cornwallis county in the Legislative Assembly of Lower Canada; and he was one of the most active of Papineau's supporters. He died on June 27, 1839.

[Francis-J. Audet, *Joseph Le Vasseur-Borgia* (Trans. Roy. Soc. Can., 1925); Le Jeune, *Dict. gén.*]

Lévis, François Gaston, Duc de (1720-1787), commander-in-chief of the French forces in Canada (1759-60), was born on August 23, 1720, at the Château d'Ajac, near Limours, Languedoc, France, the son of Jean de Lévis, Marquis d'Ajac, and Jeanne Maguelonne. He entered the French army in 1735, and during the next twenty years saw active service in various parts of Europe. He was created a chevalier de St. Louis in 1748; and in 1756 he was sent to Canada as second-in-command under the Marquis de Montcalm (q.v.), with the rank of brigadier. He played a distinguished part during the Seven Years' War in Canada; and after the death of

Montcalm in 1759 he succeeded to the command of the French troops in Canada. He fell back on Montreal, but in the spring of 1760 he advanced against the British in Quebec, and on April 28 he defeated the British under Murray (q.v.) at Ste. Foy. He was compelled, however, to retreat to Montreal a second time by the arrival of British men-of-war at Quebec; and he was compelled to capitulate at Montreal on September 8, 1760. He returned to France, and was created a lieutenant-general in 1761. He served under the Duc de Condé in 1761-62; in 1766, he was appointed governor of Artois; and in 1780, governor of Arras. He was created a marshal of France in 1783, and he was made Duc de Lévis in 1784. He died at Arras on November 26, 1787. His papers have been collected and edited by the Abbé H. R. Casgrain, under the title *Collection des manuscrits du Maréchal de Lévis* (12 vols., Montreal and Quebec, 1889-96).

[G. de Hautecloque, *Le Maréchal de Lévis* (Arras, 1901); H. R. Casgrain, *Montcalm et Lévis* (Tours, 1889); Le Jeune, *Dict. gén.*]

Lewis, John (1858-1935), senator of Canada, was born in Toronto on January 17, 1858. He became a journalist, and was for many years on the staff of the Toronto *Globe*. In 1925 he was summoned to the Senate of Canada. He died at Toronto on May 18, 1935. He was the author of *George Brown* (in "The Makers of Canada" series, Toronto, 1910), of the chapters on the political history of Canada from 1867 to 1912 in A. Shortt and A. G. Doughty (eds.), *Canada and its provinces* (23 vols., Toronto, 1914), and of *Mackenzie King, the man, his achievements* (Toronto, 1925; new ed., revised by N. M. Rogers, Toronto, 1933).

[*Can. parl. comp.*; Morgan, *Can. men* (1912).]

Lewis, John Travers (1825-1901), Anglican archbishop of Ontario and metropolitan of Canada, was born at Garrycloyne Castle, Cork, Ireland, on June 20, 1825, the eldest son of Rev. John Lewis and Rebecca Olivia Lawless. He was educated at Trinity College, Dublin (B.A., 1848), and in 1849 was ordained a priest of the Church of England. He came to Canada in 1850, and in 1854 he became rector of St. Peter's Church, Brockville, Upper Canada. In 1862 he was consecrated bishop of Ontario; in 1893 he was elevated to the dignity of metropolitan of Canada; and in 1894 he became archbishop. He died at sea on May 4, 1901. In 1851 he married Annie Henrietta Marguerite (d. 1886), daughter of the Hon. Henry Sherwood; and in 1889 Ada Maria, daughter of Evan Leigh, of Manchester, England. He was an LL.D. and D.D. of Trinity College, Dublin, an hon. D.D. of Oxford University, and an LL.D. of Bishop's College, Lennoxville, and Trinity University, Toronto. He was the originator of the idea of holding the Lambeth conferences, at which all the bishops

of the Anglican communion might be present.

[Ada L. Lewis, *Life of John Travers Lewis* (London, 1930); *Cyc. Am. biog.*; Morgan, *Can. men* (1898); Rose, *Cyc. Can. biog.* (1886); Dent, *Can. port.*]

Lewis, Nellie Margaret (1892-1956), author, was born at Orangeville, Ontario, in 1892, and died at Toronto, Ontario, on May 18, 1956. She was on the staff of the Ontario Council of Christian Education for forty years, and became an authority on recreational work. She was the author of *Games and parties the year round* (Toronto, 1938), *Boys and girls at play* (Toronto, 1946), and *More games and parties* (Toronto, 1951).

[Toronto *Globe and Mail*, May 19, 1956.]

Lewis, Thaddeus (b. 1793), Methodist minister, was born in Lennox and Addington county, Upper Canada, in 1793. He served in the War of 1812, and afterwards was first a farmer, and then a school-teacher. In 1823 he was licensed as a preacher in the Methodist Episcopal Church, and he was for many years employed in the Bay of Quinte circuit. After his retirement, he published his *Autobiography* (Picton, C.W., 1865).

[F. M. Staton and M. Tremaine (eds.), *A bibliography of Canadiana* (Toronto, 1934).]

Libby, Walter (1867-1955), educationist, was born at Port Hope, Ontario, on March 2, 1867, and died at Toronto, Ontario, on November 29, 1955. He was educated at Victoria College, Cobourg (B.A., 1887), the University of Toronto (M.A., 1902), and Clark University (Ph.D., 1905); and for many years he was a teacher in secondary schools in Ontario. Subsequently, he served on the teaching staff of several institutions in the United States: Northwestern University, the Carnegie Institute of Technology, and the University of Pittsburgh. He retired from teaching in 1924; and during the later years of his life lived in Toronto. He was the author of *An introduction to the history of science* (Boston, 1917), *The history of medicine in its salient features* (Boston, 1922), and *Introduction to contemporary civilization* (New York, 1929).

[*Can. who's who*, 1948.]

Liddell, Thomas (1800-1880), principal of Queen's College, Kingston (1841-46), was born in Scotland in 1800, the son of John Liddle or Liddell. He was educated at Glasgow and Edinburgh universities, and became a minister of the Church of Scotland. From 1829 to 1831 he was minister of the Montrose Chapel of Ease, and from 1831 to 1841 of Lady Glenorchy's parish, Edinburgh. In 1841 he came to Canada to assume the principalship of the newly organized Queen's College, at Kingston, Upper Canada; and he retained this position until 1846. He then returned to Scotland; and he was minister of Lochmaben from 1850 until his death on June 11, 1880.

[W. I. Addison (ed.), *The matriculation albums of the University of Glasgow from 1728 to 1858* (Glasgow, 1913); *Dict. Can. biog.*, vol. 10.]

Lighthall, William Douw (1857-1954), lawyer and author, was born at Hamilton, Canada West, on December 27, 1857, and died at Montreal, Quebec, on August 3, 1954. He was educated at McGill University (B.A., 1879; B.C.L., 1881; M.A., 1889; D.C.L., 1921), was called to the bar in 1881 (K.C., 1905), and practised law in Montreal until his retirement in 1944. A prolific writer in various fields, he was elected a fellow of the Royal Society of Canada in 1902, and its president in 1918. He was the author of three works of fiction: *The young seigneur* (Montreal, 1888), *The false chevalier* (Montreal, 1898), and *The master of life* (Toronto, 1908), the last under the pseudonym of "Wilfred Chateauclair"; his occasional verse was brought together by him under the title *Old measures* (Montreal, 1922); and he edited an early anthology of Canadian verse, *Songs of the Great Dominion* (Toronto, 1889), which ran into several editions. He was also an authority on the history of Montreal, and wrote *Montreal after 250 years* (Montreal, 1892) and *Sights and shrines of Montreal* (Montreal, 1903).

[*Proc. Roy. Soc. Can.*, 1955; *Can. who's who*, 1936-37; Morgan, *Can. men* (1912).]

Lillie, Adam (1803-1869), clergyman and author, was born in Glasgow, Scotland, on June 18, 1803. He was educated at Glasgow University, and became a Congregationalist minister. In 1834 he emigrated to Canada, and he became the pastor of churches in Brantford and Dundas, Upper Canada. He was the father of a movement which resulted in the formation, in Toronto, of a Theological Institute for the training of Congregationalist ministers; and when this institute was opened in 1840, he became a professor in it. He died suddenly at Montreal on October 19, 1869. He was the author of *Ministerial education* (Toronto, 1840), *Canada: Its growth and prospects* (Brockville, 1852), and *Canada: Physical, economic, and social* (Toronto, 1855).

[Morgan, *Bib. can.*]

Lind, Carl Werner (1891-1961), painter, was born in Sweden in 1891. At age fifteen he left home and went to sea, settling in the United States in 1907. He moved to Prince Albert, Saskatchewan, in 1910, and the following year took up a homestead nearby. During the First World War he was a member of the Royal Canadian Mounted Police on overseas service and on his return took employment with the Hudson's Bay Company as a purchasing agent. His travels through the north country inspired his wildlife paintings and scenes of the wilderness. He died at his home at St. Walburg, Saskatchewan, in 1961. Most of his works are privately owned in the Battleford and St. Walburg areas.

[C. S. MacDonald, *A dictionary of Canadian artists*, vol. 3 (Ottawa, 1971).]

Lindsay, Sir Charles William (1856-1939), merchant and philanthropist, was born at Montreal, Canada West, on April 6, 1856. He was educated at the Montreal High School and the Perkins Institute for the Blind, Watertown, Massachusetts. He lost his eyesight at the age of nineteen; yet, despite this handicap, he built up one of the largest businesses in Canada in musical instruments, and took part in a wide range of public philanthropies. He was created a K.B.E. in 1935; and he died at Westmount, Quebec, on November 7, 1939.

[*Can. who's who*, 1936-37.]

Lindsay, Lionel St. Georges (1849-1921), priest and historian, was born at Montreal, Canada East, on May 1, 1849, the son of William Burns Lindsay (q.v.) and Marie Henriette Bourret. He was educated at Laval University and the Gregorian University, Rome (Ph.D., 1883; D.D., 1885), and was ordained a priest of the Roman Catholic Church in 1875. After serving on the staff of Lévis College, as an almoner of the Ursulines, and as a school inspector, he was appointed in 1907 archivist of the diocese of Quebec. He died at Quebec City on February 10, 1921. He was the author of *Pèlerinages d'outre-mer* (Quebec, 1890), *Notre Dame de la Jeune Lorette en la Nouvelle France* (Quebec, 1900), and *Le centenaire de l'archevêché de Québec* (Quebec, 1919).

[Le Jeune, *Dict. gén.*; Allaire, *Dict. biog.*; Morgan, *Can. men* (1912); *Bull. rech. hist.* 1932.]

Lindsay, William Bethune (1880-1933), soldier, was born on November 3, 1880, the son of Dr. W. B. Lindsay, of Strathroy, Ontario. He was educated at the Royal Military College; and was appointed in 1900 assistant engineer of the department of marine and fisheries, Ottawa. In 1904 he was gazetted a subaltern in the Royal Canadian Engineers; and in 1914 he organized the 1st Canadian Divisional Engineers, with the rank of major. In 1915, he was appointed commandant of the Royal Engineers of the 1st Canadian Division, with the rank of lieutenant-colonel; in 1916, chief engineer of the Canadian Army Corps, with the rank of brigadier-general; and in 1918, general officer commanding the Canadian Engineers, with the rank of major-general. He was mentioned in despatches seven times, and was awarded the C.B., the C.M.G., and the D.S.O. He retired from the army in 1920, on account of ill-health; and he died on June 27, 1933, at Toronto.

[*Can. ann. rev.*, 1933.]

Lindsay, William Burns (1824-1872), civil servant, was born at Quebec, Lower Canada, on February 11, 1824, the son of William Burns Lindsay. He was called to the bar in 1844, but never practised law. He was employed about the Legislative Assembly of Canada, of which his father was clerk. He was first assistant clerk, and then in 1862 he succeeded his father as clerk of the Legislative Assembly. He became in 1867 the first clerk of the Canadian House of Commons; and he died in Ottawa, Ontario, on September 2, 1872.

[P. G. Roy, *Les avocats de la région de Québec* (Lévis, Que., 1936).]

Lindsey, Charles (1820-1908), journalist and author, was born in Lincolnshire, England, in 1820, and came to Canada in 1841. In 1846 he joined the editorial staff of the Toronto *Examiner*, and in 1853 he became editor-in-chief of the Toronto *Leader*. He was appointed registrar of deeds for Toronto in 1867, and this position he occupied until his death at Toronto, on April 12, 1908. In 1852 he married Janet, daughter of William Lyon Mackenzie (q.v.). His chief work was *The life and letters of Wm. Lyon Mackenzie* (2 vols., Toronto, 1862; new and revised ed., by G. G. S. Lindsey, Toronto, 1908); but he was also the author of *The clergy reserves* (Toronto, 1851), *Prohibitory laws* (Toronto, 1855), *The prairies of the western states* (Toronto, 1860), *An investigation of the unsettled boundaries of Ontario* (Toronto, 1873), and *Rome in Canada* (Toronto, 1878). In 1882 he was chosen a charter member of the Royal Society of Canada.

[L. A. M. Lovekin, *Charles Lindsey* (Can. mag., 1920); *Can. who was who*, vol. 2; Morgan, *Cel. Can., Bib. can.*, and *Can. men* (1898).]

Lindsey, George Goldwin Smith (1860-1920), lawyer, was born in Toronto, Canada West, on March 19, 1860, the son of Charles Lindsey (q.v.) and Janet, daughter of William Lyon Mackenzie (q.v.). He was educated at Upper Canada College and at the University of Toronto (B.A., 1882), and was called to the bar of Ontario in 1886 (Q.C., 1899). He practised law in Toronto; and from 1899 to 1901 he was president of the Toronto Reform Association. He was a cricket enthusiast; and in 1887 he was captain of a Canadian team of cricketers that played in England. He died in Toronto, Ontario, on May 27, 1920. He inherited the papers of his father and his maternal grandfather, which were deposited after his death in the University of Toronto Library; and he published a revised and abbreviated edition of his father's *William Lyon Mackenzie* (Toronto, 1908).

[Morgan, *Can. men* (1912).]

Line, John (1885-1970), university professor and theologian, was born at High Wycombe, England, March 3, 1885. He was educated in English schools and at the University of Toronto (B.A., 1913; M.A., 1916; B.D., 1916); at Montreal Wesleyan College (S.T.D., 1922); and Pine Hill Divinity Hall, Halifax (D.D., 1934). He became professor of systematic theology at Mount Allison University in 1916. He was later professor of systematic theology at Pine Hill Divinity Hall and then at the University of Toronto (Emmanuel College) until his retirement in 1952. He was the author of *Inspiration and modern criticism* (1925); *The doctrine of Christ in history* (1924).

[*Can. who's who*, 1964-66.]

Ling, George Herbert (1874-1942), educationist, was born at Wallacetown, Ontario, on January 15, 1874, and was educated at the University of Toronto (B.A., 1893; LL.D., 1927) and at Columbia University (M.A., 1894; Ph.D., 1896). He became professor of mathematics at the University of Saskatchewan; and from 1911 to 1938 was dean of arts in this university. He died at Toronto, Ontario, on October 21, 1942. He was joint author, with G. Wentworth and D. E. Smith, of *Elements of projective geometry* (Boston, 1922).

[*Can. who's who*, 1938-39; Morgan, *Can. men* (1912).]

Linscott, Thomas S. (1846-1919), clergyman, author, and publisher, was born in Devonshire, England, on June 19, 1846. He came to America, and in 1875 was ordained a minister of the Methodist Episcopal Church. In 1879 he retired from the ministry, and became head of the publishing business of Bradley, Garretson and Co. in Brantford, Ontario. He died at Quebec City on March 1, 1919. He was the author of *The heart of Christianity* (2 vols., Philadelphia, 1906-07).

[Morgan, *Can. men* (1912).]

Linton, John James Edmonstoune (1804-1869), author, was born at Rothesay, Isle of Bute, Scotland, in 1804, and emigrated to Canada in 1833. He settled on the Canada Company's lands near Stratford, Upper Canada; and in 1849 he was appointed clerk of the peace for the county of Perth. He died on January 23, 1869. Under the pen-name of "A settler, at Stratford, Huron district, Canada West", he published *The life of a backwoodsman* (London, 1843; 2nd ed., 1850); and he was the author of *A prohibitory liquor law for Upper Canada, with remarks* (Toronto, 1860).

[W. Johnston, *History of the county of Perth* (Stratford, Ont., 1903).]

Lisgar, Sir John Young, Bart., Baron (1807-1876), governor-general of Canada, was born at Bombay, India, on August 31, 1807, the eldest son of Sir William Young, first baronet, by his wife, Lucy, youngest daughter of Lieut.-Col. Charles Frederick. He was educated at Eton and at Corpus Christi College, Oxford (B.A., 1829), and in 1834 he was called to the English bar at Lincoln's Inn. From 1831 to 1855 he represented the county of Cavan in the House of Commons in the Conservative interest. From 1841 to 1844 he was one of the lords of the Treasury in the administration of Sir Robert Peel, and from 1844 to 1846 he was a secretary of the Treasury. In the Aberdeen administration, he was chief secretary for Ireland from 1852 to 1855. He then resigned to accept appointment as lord high commissioner of the Ionian islands, and he held this post until his recall in 1859. From 1861 to 1867 he was governor-general of New South Wales; and in 1869 he was appointed governor-general of Canada. His period of office coincided with the first Riel Rebellion; and he acquired in Canada a reputation for ability and sound judgment. He resigned office in June, 1872, and returned to Ireland. He died at Lisgar House, Baillieborough, Ireland, on October 6, 1876. In 1835 he married Adelaide Annabella, daughter of Edward Tuite Dalton; but he left no issue. He succeeded to his father's baronetcy on the death of the latter in 1848; he was created a G.C.M.G. in 1855, a K.C.B. in 1859, and a G.C.B. in 1868; and in 1870 he was raised to the peerage as Baron Lisgar of Lisgar and Baillieborough.

[*Dict. nat. biog.*; Dent, *Can. port.*, vol. 4; Sir J. Pope, *Memoirs of Sir John Alexander Macdonald* (2 vols., Ottawa, 1894) and *Correspondence of Sir John Macdonald* (Toronto, 1921); *Dict. Can. biog.*, vol. 10.]

Liston, James Knox (*fl.* 1843-1868), poet, was at one time a resident of Clinton, Upper Canada. He was the author of *Niagara Falls: A poem, in three cantos* (Toronto, 1843) and *Poetry for the Dominion of Canada* (Toronto, 1868).

[Morgan, *Bib. can.*; C. C. James, *A bibliography of Canadian poetry* (Toronto, 1899).]

Little, Sir Joseph Ignatius (1835-1902), chief justice of the Supreme Court of Newfoundland (1898-1902), was born in Prince Edward Island in 1835, and died at St. John's, Newfoundland, on July 14, 1902. He moved to Newfoundland at an early age, studied law in the office of his brother, Philip Francis Little (q.v.), and was called to the bar in 1859. He sat in the House of Assembly from 1869 to 1883, was attorney-general in the Bennett administration from 1870 to 1874, and was a minister without portfolio in the Whiteway administration from 1882 to 1883. He was appointed a puisne judge in 1883, and became chief justice in 1898; and he was created a knight bachelor in 1901.

[*Who was who*, 1898-1918; *Newfoundland supp.*; *Encyc. Can.*]

Little, Philip Francis (1824-1897), prime minister of Newfoundland (1855-58), was born in Prince Edward Island in 1824, and died in

Ireland on October 22, 1897. He studied law in Charlottetown, was called to the bar, and in 1844 began practice in St. John's, Newfoundland. In 1850 he was elected to the Newfoundland House of Assembly, soon became the leader of the Liberal party, and in 1855 became the first prime minister of Newfoundland under responsible government. In 1858 he retired from office in order to accept appointment as a judge of the Supreme Court. He retired from the bench in 1866, and went to live in Ireland.

[D. W. Prowse, *History of Newfoundland* (London, 1895); *Newfoundland supp.*; *Encyc. Can.*]

Livesay, Mrs. Florence, *née* **Randal** (1874-1953), journalist and author, was born in Compton, Quebec, on November 3, 1874; and died at Toronto, Ontario, on July 28, 1953. She was educated at the Compton Ladies' College, and in 1908 married John Frederick Bligh Livesay (q.v.). She became a journalist, first in Ottawa, and then in Winnipeg. She was the author of a volume of verse entitled *Shepherd's purse* (Toronto, 1923) and a work of fiction entitled *Savour of salt* (Toronto, 1927). She translated from the Ukrainian *Songs of Ukraina* (Toronto, 1916) and a novel, *Marusia* (Toronto, 1940); and after her husband's death she edited his *The making of a Canadian* (Toronto, 1947).

[*Can. who's who*, 1952-54; *Encyc. Can.*]

Livesay, John Frederick Bligh (1875-1944), journalist, was born on the Isle of Wight, England, in 1875. He came to Canada in 1895 and became a journalist. In 1918 he served as a war correspondent for the Canadian Press; and from 1920 to 1940 he was general manager of the Canadian Press. He died at Clarkson, Ontario, on June 15, 1944. He was the author of *Canada's hundred days* (Toronto, 1919) and *Peggy's Cove* (Toronto, 1944). After his death, his autobiography was edited with a memoir by his wife, under the title *The making of a Canadian* (Toronto, 1947).

[*Can. who's who*, 1938-39.]

Livingston, Stuart (1865-1923), author, was born in Hamilton, Ontario, in 1865, the son of T. C. Livingston. He was educated at Osgoode Hall and the University of Toronto (LL.B., 1889), and was called to the bar in 1889 (Q.C., 1896). He practised law, first in Hamilton, and later in Vancouver, British Columbia; and he died at Vancouver on November 13, 1923. He was the author of a volume of poems, entitled *In various moods* (Toronto, 1894), and a novel, *The history of Professor Paul* (Hamilton, n.d.).

[Morgan, *Can. men* (1898).]

Livius, Peter (1727?-1795), chief justice of Quebec (1777-86), was born in Bedford, England, about 1727. He first appears as "one of his Majesty's Council" in New Hampshire in 1773; and in 1774 he was appointed chief justice of New Hampshire. On the outbreak of the American Revolution, he was appointed a judge of the Court of Common Pleas in Montreal; and in 1777 he became chief justice of Quebec. He came into conflict with Sir Guy Carleton (q.v.), and was dismissed from office by Carleton in 1778, but was reinstated by the Privy Council, to which he had appealed. He held the office of chief justice of Quebec until 1786, though after 1778 he was an absentee official; and he died in England on July 23, 1795.

[W. Smith, *The struggle over the laws of Canada* (Can. hist. review, 1920); Morgan, *Cel. Can.* and *Bib. can.*; A. Shortt and A. G. Doughty (eds.), *Documents relating to the constitutional history of Canada* (2nd ed., Ottawa, 1918).]

Lizars, Kathleen Macfarlane (d. 1931), historian, was born in Stratford, Ontario, and was educated in Toronto and in Scotland. For some years she was private secretary to the Hon. John Robson (q.v.), when he was prime minister of British Columbia. With her sister Robina (afterwards Mrs. Robert Smith), she was joint author of *In the days of the Canada Company* (Toronto, 1896), *Humours of '37* (Toronto, 1897) and *Committed to his charge* (Toronto, 1900); and she was later the author of *The valley of the Humber* (Toronto, 1913). She died at Toronto, Ontario, on April 20, 1931.

[Morgan, *Can. men and women* (1912).]

Lizars, Robina (d. 1918), historian, was the sister of Kathleen Macfarlane Lizars (q.v.), and with her was joint author of *In the days of the Canada Company* (Toronto, 1896), *Humours of '37* (Toronto, 1897), and *Committed to his charge* (Toronto, 1900). She married Robert Smith; and she died at Toronto, Ontario, on August 26, 1918.

[Private information.]

Lloyd, Cecil Francis (1884-1938), poet, was born at Stonelea House, Herefordshire, England, on November 22, 1884. He came to Canada in 1896, and was educated at Queen's University, Kingston, and at London University. He was employed from 1917 to 1930 in a business firm in Winnipeg, Manitoba; but during his last years he tried to make a living by writing. He died in Winnipeg on July 13, 1938. He was the author of *Landfall: The collected poems of Cecil Francis Lloyd* (Toronto, 1935).

[*Can. who's who*, 1936-37.]

Lloyd, George Exton (1861-1940), bishop, was born in London, England, on January 6, 1861, and was educated at the University of New Brunswick (M.A., 1894) and at Wycliffe College, Toronto. He was ordained a clergyman of the Church of England while serving as chaplain of the Queen's Own Rifles of Toronto

during the North West Rebellion of 1885; and during the engagement at Cut Knife Creek he was severely wounded. In 1890 he became rector of Rothesay, New Brunswick; and in 1891 he founded the Rothesay College for boys. In 1903 he became chaplain of the Barr colonists in Saskatchewan; and he was later elected head of the colony, the centre of which, Lloydminster, was named after him. From 1905 to 1909 he was archdeacon of Prince Albert; and from 1922 to 1931 he was bishop of Saskatchewan. He died at Victoria, British Columbia, on December 8, 1940. He was D.D. of Wycliffe College, Toronto, St. John's College, Winnipeg, and Emmanuel College, Saskatoon; and an LL.D. of the University of Saskatchewan.

[*Can. who's who*, 1936-37; Morgan, *Can. men* (1912).]

Lloyd, Wallace (pseud.). See **Algie, James.**

Lloyd, Sir William Frederick (1864-1937), prime minister of Newfoundland (1918-19), was born at Stockport, Devonshire, England, on December 17, 1864, and died at St. John's, Newfoundland, on June 13, 1937. He came to Newfoundland as a school-teacher, and later became first a journalist and then a lawyer (LL.B., 1894). He represented Port de Grave in the Newfoundland House of Assembly from 1904 to 1909, and Trinity from 1909 to 1919. In 1915 he became leader of the Liberal opposition, and in 1917 minister of justice in the coalition administration of Sir Edward Morris (q.v.). When Morris was raised to the peerage in 1918, he became prime minister; but he was defeated in 1919 by a vote of no-confidence, and retired from politics to accept appointment as registrar of the Supreme Court of Newfoundland. He was created a K.C.M.G. in 1919.

[*Who was who*, 1928-40; *Newfoundland supp.; Encyc. Can.*]

Lloyd, Woodrow Stanley (1913-1972), political leader, was born at Webb, Saskatchewan, July 16, 1913. He enrolled in the engineering school of the University of Saskatchewan but decided to become a teacher instead and graduated with a B.A. He was active in Home and School clubs and was president of the Saskatchewan Teachers' Federation from 1940 to 1944. He was elected to the Saskatchewan legislature in the general election of that year when the Co-operative Commonwealth Federation (C.C.F.) won power in Saskatchewan for the first time. He was minister of education for Saskatchewan from 1944 to 1960 and provincial treasurer in 1960-61. He became leader of the party and premier of Saskatchewan on November 7, 1961, and retained this position until the defeat of his government in the election of 1964, when he became leader of the opposition. He was premier of Saskatchewan during the introduction of a government health-care program in 1962, when the medical profession initially boycotted the legislation. In 1971 he accepted the position of representative of the United Nations in South Korea for the United Nations development program. He died at Seoul, Korea, on April 7, 1972.

[*Can. who's who*, 1967-69; *Encyc. Can.* (Toronto, 1972); *Canadian Labour*, vol. 17, no. 4 (April, 1972).]

Llwyd, John Plummer Derwent (1861-1933), clergyman and author, was born at Manchester, England, in 1861. He was educated at Trinity University, Toronto (B.D., 1905; D.D., 1908), and at Oxford and Berlin; and he was ordained a priest of the Church of England in 1885. He was successively rector of churches in Illinois, Nebraska, and Washington; but in 1909 he was appointed vice-provost of Trinity University, Toronto, and he retained this post until 1912, when he became dean of Nova Scotia. He died at Halifax, Nova Scotia, on February 22, 1933. In 1915 he was made a D.C.L. of King's College, Nova Scotia. He was the author of *The vestal virgin: A dramatic poem* (Halifax, N.S., 1920), *Poems of nature, childhood, and religion* (Toronto, 1928), and *Son of thunder: A study of the life and work of John of Bethsaida* (New York, 1932).

[Morgan, *Can. men* (1912).]

Loblaw, Theodore Pringle (1872-1933), merchant and philanthropist, was born at Elm Grove, Simcoe county, Ontario, on July 1, 1872. At the age of fifteen, he was an orphan, and had to make his way in the world. He became a grocery clerk in Toronto, and by 1900 was the owner of a grocery store. In 1910 he opened the first of a chain of stores, and by 1919 he had nineteen stores in Toronto. He then conceived the idea of the "groceteria"; and in 1919 he organized the Loblaw Groceterias Company. In 1924 he opened a chain of groceterias in Buffalo, New York, and in 1928 one in Chicago, Illinois. The success of the Loblaw Groceterias worked a revolution in retail merchandising. Shortly before his death in Toronto, on April 2, 1933, T. P. Loblaw became a convert to the doctrines of the Oxford Group; and in his later years his benefactions to hospitals and other charitable organizations were on a princely scale.

[*Who's who in Canada*, 1930-31.]

Lochhead, William (1864-1927), educationist, was born in Perth county, Canada West, on April 3, 1864. He was educated at McGill University (B.A., 1885) and at Cornell University (M.Sc., 1895); and after serving as science master in several secondary schools in Ontario, he was appointed in 1898 professor of biology in the Ontario Agricultural College, at Guelph, Ontario. In 1905 he became professor of biology at Macdonald College, Ste. Anne de Bellevue, Quebec; and he died at Ste. Anne de Bellevue on March 26, 1927. He was the author of *Modern biological laws and theories relating to animal and plant breeding* (Montreal, 1911), *Class book of economic entomology* (Philadelphia, 1919), and *An introduction to heredity and genetics* (Ste. Anne de Bellevue, Que., 1927).

[Morgan, *Can. men* (1912).]

Locke, George Herbert (1870-1937), librarian, was born at Beamsville, Ontario, on March 29, 1870, the son of the Rev. Joseph H. Locke. He was educated at Victoria College, University of Toronto (B.A., 1893; B. Paed., 1896; M.A., 1895; LL.D., 1927); and during his earlier years he held various academic posts on the staffs of Chicago University, Harvard University, and Macdonald College, Ste. Anne de Bellevue, Quebec, as well as the post of editor of the *School Review* from 1900 to 1906. In 1908 he was appointed chief librarian of the Toronto Public Library, in succession to James Bain (q.v.); and he built up in Toronto one of the great public library systems of the North American continent. In 1927 he was elected president of the American Library Association. He died at Toronto, Ontario, on January 28, 1937. In addition to numerous contributions to Canadian bibliography, issued by the Toronto Public Library during his period of office, of which he was the supervising editor, he was the author of *When Canada was New France* (Toronto, 1919) and *Builders of the Canadian commonwealth* (Toronto, 1923).

[*Can. who's who*, 1936-37; Morgan, *Can. men* (1912).]

Locke, Mahlon William (1881-1942), physician and surgeon, was born at Williamsburg, Ontario, in 1881; and was educated at Queen's University, Kingston (M.D., 1904). He did postgraduate work at the University of Edinburgh and Glasgow University, specializing in manipulative surgery and orthopaedics; and he returned to Canada to practise in his native town. He achieved a reputation for the cure of arthritis and other ailments by means of foot treatment that brought patients to Williamsburg from all parts of North America. He died at Williamsburg on February 9, 1942.

[J. Smyth Carter, *Dr. M. W. Locke and the Williamsburg scene* (Toronto, 1933); E. May Merkley, *Our doctor* (Morrisburg, Ont., 1933); Rex Beach, *The hands of Dr. Locke* (New York, 1934); *Can. who's who*, 1938-39).]

Lockhart, Arthur John (1850-1926), clergyman and author, was born in Lockhartville, Kings county, Nova Scotia, on May 5, 1850, and was ordained a minister of the Methodist Episcopal Church in 1872. He was stationed for many years in Maine; and he died at Springfield, Massachusetts, on June 29, 1926. He wrote under the nom-de-plume of "Pastor

Felix"; and was the author of *The masque of minstrels* (in collaboration with his brother, Bangor, Me., 1887), *Beside the Narraguagus, and other poems* (Buffalo, N.Y., 1892), *The papers of Pastor Felix* (Toronto, 1903), and *The birds of the cross, and other poems* (Winterport, Me., 1909).

[R. J. Long, *Nova Scotia authors* (East Orange, N.J., 1918); Morgan, *Can. men* (1912).]

Lodge, Rupert Clendon (1886-1961), philosopher, was born in Manchester, England, in 1886. He was educated at Oxford, Marburg, and Berlin universities. He taught at the University of Minnesota and at the University of Alberta between 1914 and 1920, when he was appointed professor of logic and the history of philosophy as well as, along with Professor A.W. Wright, joint head of the department of philosophy at the University of Manitoba. From 1934 until his retirement in 1947 he was head of the department of philosophy. He developed a theory of "comparativism" in which he recognized the possibility of several major points of view, each of which had something to contribute. He wrote many articles and thirteen books, among which the best known are, *Plato's theory of ethics* (New York, 1928); *The great thinkers* (London, 1949); *Plato's theory of education* (London, 1947); *The questioning mind* (London, 1937); *The philosophy of education* (New York, 1937); and *Applied philosophy* (London, 1951). He was elected to the presidency of the western section of the American Philosophical Association in 1926, and made a fellow of the Royal Society of Canada in 1946. He died at St. Petersburg, Florida, March 1, 1961.

[*Proc. Roy. Soc. Can., 1964.*]

Lofthouse, Joseph (1855-1933), first Anglican bishop of Keewatin, was born at Wadsley, Yorkshire, England, on December 18, 1855. He was trained for foreign missionary work at the C.M.S. College, Islington; and was sent in 1882 as a missionary to Hudson Bay. He served at Fort York and Fort Churchill, and in 1899 was appointed archdeacon of York, Moosonee. In 1902, when the new see of Keewatin was formed, comprising the southeastern portion of Rupert's Land and the west coast of Hudson Bay, he was appointed its first bishop; and he resigned his see, and returned to England, only in 1921. He died at Dawlish, England, on December 16, 1933. He was a D.D. of St. John's College, Winnipeg; and he was the author of *A thousand miles from a post office; or, Twenty years' life and travel in the Hudson's Bay regions* (Toronto, 1922).

[*Who was who*, 1929-40; Morgan, *Can. men* (1912).]

Logan, Hance James (1869-1944), senator of Canada, was born at Amherst Point, Nova Scotia, on April 26, 1869. He was educated at Dalhousie University (LL.B., 1891), and was called to the bar of Nova Scotia in 1891 (K.C., 1910). He practised law in Amherst, Nova Scotia; and from 1896 to 1908, and again from 1921 to 1929, he represented Cumberland in the Canadian House of Commons. In 1929 he was called to the Senate of Canada. He died at Ottawa, Ontario, on December 26, 1944.

[*Can. who's who*, 1936-37; *Can. parl. comp.*; Morgan, *Can. men* (1912).]

Logan, John Daniel (1869-1929), scholar and author, was born at Antigonish, Nova Scotia, on May 2, 1869, the son of Charles Logan and Elizabeth Gordon Rankin. He was educated at Dalhousie University (B.A., 1893; M.A., 1894) and at Harvard University (B.A., 1894; M.A., 1895; Ph.D., 1896). He occupied a great variety of positions in academic life, in advertising, and in journalism; and at the time of his death, which took place at Milwaukee, Wisconsin, on January 24, 1929, he was head of the English department of Marquette University. He was the author of *The structural principles of style* (Vermilion, S.D., 1900), *The religious functions of a comedy* (Toronto, 1907), *Quantitative punctuation* (Toronto, 1907), *Democracy, education, and the new dispensation* (Toronto, 1908), *The making of the new Ireland* (Toronto, 1909), *Aesthetic criticism in Canada* (Toronto, 1917), *Marjorie Pickthall* (Halifax, 1922), *Thomas Chandler Haliburton* (Toronto, 1924), and the following volumes of verse: *Preludes, sonnets, and other verses* (Toronto, 1907), *Songs of the makers of Canada* (Toronto, 1911), and *Insulters of death* (Toronto, 1916). With Donald G. French he wrote *Highways of Canadian literature* (Toronto, 1925).

[*Harvard College, Class of 1894: Thirty-fifth anniversary report, 1894-1929* (Norwood, Mass., 1930); Morgan, *Can. men* (1912); R. J. Long, *Nova Scotia authors* (East Orange, N.J., 1918).]

Logan, John Edward (d. 1915), poet, lived for many years in Montreal, and died there in 1915. He wrote poetry under the pseudonym "Barry Dane"; and after his death his friends of the Pen and Pencil Club of Montreal published a selection of his poems under the title *Verses* (Montreal, 1916).

[Preface to John E. Logan, *Verses* (Montreal, 1916).]

Logan, Joseph (1878-1961), Indian chief, was born on the Grand River Reserve in 1878. He was chosen chief at the age of twenty-four and spent his life in the service of his tribe. He was convinced that the treaty known as the Haldimand Deed of 1784 had been violated and Indian rights ignored. He travelled to England in 1929 and 1931 to press his case and carried it to the League of Nations and the United Nations at its founding in San Francisco. Ousted from his hereditary position by the government of Canada, his position was partially restored in 1959 by the recognition of his own people. He died at Brantford, Ontario, December 11, 1961.

[Metropolitan Toronto Library Board, *Biographical scrapbooks*, vol. 18.]

Logan, Robert (d. 1866), fur-trader, was the son of a West India merchant in London, England, who became a clerk in the North West Company. From 1806 to 1814 he was stationed at Sault Ste. Marie. In 1814 he was persuaded by Colin Robertson (q.v.) to join the Hudson's Bay Company; and he took part in the struggle between Lord Selkirk (q.v.) and the North West Company in 1814-19. In 1819 he was appointed to look after Lord Selkirk's interests at Red River during the absence of Alexander Macdonell (q.v.). He settled in the Red River Settlement, and he was a councillor of Assiniboia from 1823 to 1839. He died on May 26, 1866; and his will is on file in the archives of the Hudson's Bay Company.

[E. E. Rich (ed.), *Colin Robertson's correspondence* (Toronto: The Champlain Society, 1939).]

Logan, Sir William Edmond (1798-1875), geologist, was born in Montreal, Lower Canada, on April 20, 1798, the son of William Logan and Janet Edmond. He was educated at the High School, Edinburgh, Scotland, and he attended Edinburgh University for one year. In 1818 he entered the business of his uncle, Hart Logan, in London, England, and in 1831 he became manager of some of his uncle's coal and copper-smelting interests in South Wales. Here he devoted himself to the study of the Welsh coal-beds, and acquired a reputation as a geologist. In 1843, when the Canadian Geological Survey was organized, he was appointed its director; and he continued to direct its activities until 1869, only a few years before his death in Wales on June 22, 1875. He revolutionized the current conceptions of Canadian geology; and in 1851 he was, in recognition of his work, elected a fellow of the Royal Society of London. In 1856 he was created a knight bachelor; and he was a D.C.L. of Bishop's College, Lennoxville (1855), and an LL.D. of McGill University (1856). He was not married.

[B. J. Harrington, *Life of Sir Wm. E. Logan* (London, 1883); Rose, *Cyc. Can. biog.* (1886); Taylor, *Brit. Am.*, vol. 2; Morgan, *Cel. Can.* and *Bib. can.*; Bibaud, *Panth. can.*; Le Jeune, *Dict. gén.*; *Dict. Can. biog.*, vol. 10.]

Long, John (*fl.* 1768-1791), fur-trader and author, was apparently a native of England. He was sent to Canada in 1768 as a merchant's clerk, and he became so conversant with the Indian languages that he was employed as an interpreter. He took part in the War of the American Revolution; and he was later em-

ployed as a fur-trader in the Nipigon country and in what is now northern Quebec. After some time spent in the Loyalist settlements about the Bay of Quinte, he returned to England in 1788. In 1791 he published his *Voyages and travels of an Indian interpreter and trader* (London, 1791). This was translated into German by B. G. Hoffmann in 1791, and by G. Forster in 1792; and into French by J. Billecocq in 1794 (2nd ed., 1810), but without the Indian vocabularies contained in the English edition. The English edition has been edited, with notes and introduction, by R. G. Thwaites (Cleveland, Ohio, 1904), and by M. M. Quaife (Chicago, 1922). After 1791 he disappears from view.

[M. M. Quaife (ed.), *John Long's Voyages and travels* (Chicago, 1922).]

Long, John Alexander (1891-1957), educationist, was born at Walkerton, Ontario, on July 17, 1891, and died at Toronto, Ontario, on March 18, 1957. He was educated at McMaster University (B.A., 1915), the University of Toronto, and Columbia University (Ph.D., 1932); and during his later years was director of educational research at the Ontario College of Education. He was for several years editor of the *Canadian journal of psychology*; and he was the author of *Motor abilities of deaf children* (New York, 1932), *The validation of test items* (Toronto, 1935) and *Conducting and reporting research in education* (Toronto, 1936).

[*Can. who's who*, 1955-57.]

Long, Marion (1882-1970), painter, was born in Toronto, Ontario, in 1882. She studied at the Ontario College of Art under G. A. Reid and Laura Muntz, and in New York with Charles Hawthorne. She opened a studio in Toronto in 1913. In 1922 she was elected an associate of the Royal Canadian Academy and in 1933 was the first woman in fifty years to become a full member. A portrait painter, Miss Long painted many well-known Canadians, but she was also noted for her scenes of Toronto streets. She was a member of the Ontario Society of Artists and the Ontario Institute of Painters. She is represented in the National Gallery of Canada, the Art Gallery of Ontario, the University of Saskatchewan (Saskatoon), the Regina Public Library and Art Gallery, St. Hilda's College (Toronto), and Queen's University. She died at Toronto, Ontario, in August, 1970.

[C. S. MacDonald, *A dictionary of Canadian artists*, vol. 4 (Ottawa, 1974).]

Long, Morden Heaton (1886-1965), historian, was born in Brantford, Ontario, September 24, 1886. He was educated at McMaster University (B.A., 1908); Oxford (B.A., 1912; M.A., 1924). He became history master at Victoria High School, Edmonton, in 1913, and in 1918 became a lecturer in history at the University of Alberta, becoming a full professor in 1935 and head of the department in 1946. He began publication in 1920 with *Knights errant of the wilderness*, which dealt with the lives of seven explorers of the Canadian West. In 1943 he published *A history of the Canadian people, Vol. 1, New France*, an incisive analysis of the old régime written with logic, clarity, and sympathetic appreciation of the problems that faced the struggling French colony. He was a member of the Historic Sites and Monuments Board and was from 1946 to 1965 chairman of the Geographic Board of Alberta. He was a fellow of the Royal Society of Canada. He died at Edmonton, May 14, 1965.

[*Proc. Roy. Soc. Can.*, 1965; *Can. hist. rev.*, vol. XLVI (1965); *Can. who's who*, 1955-57.]

Long, Robert James (1849-1933), printer and bibliographer, was born at Liverpool, Nova Scotia, in 1849, and became a printer and journalist. He spent most of his life in the United States; but he was an indefatigable student of the history and literature of Nova Scotia, and he was the author of *Nova Scotia authors and their work* (East Orange, N.J., 1918), of which only a few copies were printed. He died at Boston, Massachusetts, on November 3, 1933.

[Private information.]

Longley, James Wilberforce (1849-1922), judge and historian, was born in Paradise, Nova Scotia, on January 4, 1849, the son of Israel Longley and Frances Manning. He was educated at Acadia University, Wolfville, Nova Scotia (B.A., 1871; M.A., 1875; D.C.L., 1897); and he was called to the bar of Nova Scotia in 1875 (Q.C., 1890). From 1873 to 1887 he was chief editorial writer on the *Acadian Recorder*, and later he became managing editor of the Halifax *Chronicle*. From 1882 to 1905 he represented Annapolis in the Legislative Assembly of Nova Scotia, and from 1884 to 1905 he was a member of the Executive Council, first as minister without portfolio, then as attorney-general (1884-96) in the Fielding administration, and finally as commissioner of crown lands (1896-1905) in the Murray administration. In 1905 he was appointed a puisne judge of the Supreme Court of Nova Scotia, and he sat in this court until his death at Halifax on March 16, 1922. He was an LL.D. of St. Francis Xavier College, Nova Scotia; and in 1898 he was elected a member of the Royal Society of Canada. He contributed to periodical literature numerous papers on the history of Nova Scotia, and he was the author of two biographies, *Joseph Howe* (Toronto, 1904) and *Sir Charles Tupper* (Toronto, 1916).

[*Proc. Roy. Soc. Can.*, 1922; H. Charlesworth (ed.), *A cyclopaedia of Canadian biography* (Toronto, 1919); Morgan, *Can. men* (1912); Rose, *Cyc. Can. biog.* (1888).]

Longley, Ronald Stewart (1896-1967), historian and administrator, was born in Paradise, Nova Scotia, on February 16, 1896. He attended Acadia University (B.Sc., 1921), and Harvard University (M.A., 1924; Ph.D., 1934). He became principal of Queen's County Academy, Liverpool, Nova Scotia (1925-27); an instructor in social sciences at Horton Academy (1927-29); joined the department of history of Acadia University (1929); became dean of arts and science, Acadia University (1947), and dean of arts in 1961. He was in the Canadian artillery in the First World War. He was mayor of Wolfville (1956-61), president of the Maritime Baptist Convention (1940-41), and president of the Canadian Authors' Association (1964-66), and was elected fellow of the Royal Society of Canada (1954). He retired from the university in 1964. He was author of *Acadia University 1839-1938* (Wolfville, 1939), *Sir Francis Hincks* (Toronto, 1943), and numerous historical articles. He died at Wolfville, Nova Scotia, on January 7, 1967.

[*Can. hist. rev.*, vol. XLVIII (1967).]

Longstaff, Frederick Victor (1879-1961), naval historian and architect, was born at Ilkley, Yorkshire, England, on June 15, 1879. He was educated at Eton, and at Cambridge University. He was trained as an architect in London. He was in the British army from 1899 until 1909, and in 1911 came to Victoria, British Columbia, where he began to practise architecture. He returned to the army during the First World War, retiring because of ill health in 1915. He did extensive studies of British Columbia's maritime history and was a fellow of the Royal Geographic Society. He died at Victoria, British Columbia, on October 4, 1961. He wrote *The book of the machine gun*, with Captain Attridge (London, 1917), *Esquimalt Naval Base: A history of its work and its defences* (Victoria, 1941), *History of Christ Church cathedral, Victoria* (Victoria, 1951), and a number of articles on the geography of British Columbia.

[*Can. who's who*, 1958-60.]

Longueuil, Charles LeMoyne, Baron de (1656-1729), governor of Montreal (1724-29), was born at Montreal on December 10, 1656, the eldest son of Charles Le Moyne (q.v.). He took part in the defence of Quebec in 1690, was appointed governor of Trois-Rivières in 1720, and from 1724 to 1729 was governor of Montreal. In 1725-26 he was also for a short time administrator of the government of New France. He died at Montreal on June 7, 1729. In 1700 the seigniory of Longueuil, which he inherited from his father, was erected into a barony. He married in 1681 Elisabeth Souart d'Adoncourt.

[A. Jodoin and J. L. Vincent, *Histoire de Longueuil* (Montreal, 1889); Le Jeune, *Dict. gén.*; *Dict. Can. biog.*, vol. 2.]

Longueuil, Charles LeMoyne, Baron de (1687-1755), governor of Montreal (1749-55), was born at the château of Longueuil, near Montreal, on October 18, 1687, the son of Charles LeMoyne, first Baron de Longueuil (q.v.). From 1749 to his death he was governor of Montreal; and in 1752 he was for a few months administrator of the government of New France. He died at Montreal on January 17, 1755.

[A. Jodoin and J. L. Vincent, *Histoire de Longueuil* (Montreal, 1889); Le Jeune, *Dict. gén.*; *Dict. Can. biog.*, vol. 3.]

Longueuil, Joseph Dominique Emmanuel de (1738-1807), legislative councillor of Quebec and Lower Canada, was born at the manor house of Soulanges, Canada, on May 2, 1738, the son of Paul Joseph LeMoyne, Chevalier de Longueuil (q.v.). He fought under Montcalm (q.v.) in the Seven Years' War, and unlike his father, remained in Canada after the conquest. He took part in the defence of Canada in 1775-76, and was taken prisoner by the Americans. From 1778 to 1791 he was a member of the Legislative Council of Quebec, and from 1791 to 1807 of the Legislative Council of Lower Canada. He died at Montreal on January 19, 1807.

[Le Jeune, *Dict. gén.*; *Les barons de Longueuil* (Nova Francia, 1929).]

Longueuil, Paul Joseph LeMoyne, Chevalier de (1701-1778), governor of Three Rivers (1757-60), was born at the château of Longueuil, near Montreal, on September 17, 1701, the son of Charles LeMoyne, first Baron de Longueuil (q.v.). From 1743 to 1749 he was commandant at Detroit, and from 1757 to 1760 governor of Three Rivers. At the conquest, he emigrated to France, and his later years were spent at Tours. He died on May 12, 1778, at Port-Louis, France. In 1744 he was created a chevalier de St. Louis. He married Marie Geneviève Joybert, daughter of the Chevalier de Soulanges.

[Le Jeune, *Dict. gén.*; *Les barons de Longueuil* (Nova Francia, 1929).]

Loomis, Sir Frederick Oscar Warren (1870-1937), soldier, was born in Sherbrooke, Que., on February 1, 1870. He was educated at the University of Bishop's College, and became a general contractor. He enlisted in the Canadian militia as a private in 1886; and in 1914 he was given command of the 13th Battalion, Canadian Expeditionary Force. He was promoted brigadier-general in 1916; and in 1918 major-general, commanding the 3rd Canadian Division. He was awarded the D.S.O. in 1915 (bar in 1918), as well as several foreign decorations; he was created a C.M.G. in 1917, and a K.C.B. in 1919. He retired to civilian life in 1919; and he died at Montreal, Que., on February 15, 1937.

[*Can. who's who*, 1936-37.]

Loranger, Thomas Jean Jacques (1823-1885), politician and judge, was born at Ste.

Anne d'Yamachiche, Lower Canada, on February 2, 1823. He was educated at Nicolet College; and in 1844 he was called to the bar of Lower Canada (Q.C., 1854). From 1854 to 1863 he represented Laprairie in the Legislative Assembly of United Canada; and from 1857 to 1858 he held office in the Macdonald-Cartier government. From 1863 to 1883 he was a judge of the Supreme Court of Quebec; and he was the author of a *Commentaire sur le code civil du Bas-Canada* (Montreal, 1880), as well as of a number of pamphlets on legal and constitutional subjects. He died on the Island of Orleans, Quebec, on August 18, 1885.

[*Dom. ann. reg.*, 1885; *Cyc. Am. biog.*; Le Jeune, *Dict. gén.*; P. G. Roy, *Les juges de la province de Québec* (Lévis, Que., 1933); L. O. David, *Souvenirs et biographies* (Montreal, 1911).]

Lord, John Keast (1818-1872), naturalist and author, was born in 1818, and became a veterinary surgeon. He served in the Crimean War, and was present at the battle of Balaklava. After the war he came to Canada and worked from 1858 to 1862 as veterinary surgeon and assistant naturalist to the British North American Boundary Commission. During the last years of his life he was manager of the Brighton Aquarium in England; and he died at Brighton on December 9, 1872. He was not married. Among other works, he was the author of *The naturalist in Vancouver island and British Columbia* (2 vols., London, 1866) and *At home in the wilderness* (London, 1867; 3rd ed., 1872).

[*Dict. nat. biog.*; *Dict. Can. biog.*, vol. 10.]

Lorimer, John G. (1807-1897), journalist and author, was born in St. John's, Newfoundland, on May 10, 1807. He was educated in Nova Scotia; and became a journalist in New Brunswick. He was also for a time official reporter to the New Brunswick legislature. He died at Cambridgeport, Massachusetts, in November, 1897. He was the author of *The recluse of New Brunswick ... a poem* (Saint John, N.B., 1842) and *History of islands and islets in the Bay of Fundy, Charlotte county, New Brunswick* (St. Stephen, N.B., 1876).

[Morgan, *Can. men* (1898); W. G. MacFarlane, *New Brunswick bibliography* (Saint John, N.B., 1895).]

Lorimier, Charles Chamilly de (1842-1919), jurist, was born at Dubuque, Iowa, on September 13, 1842. He was educated at St. Mary's College, Montreal, and was called to the bar of Lower Canada in 1865 (Q.C., 1879). In 1889 he was appointed a judge of the Superior Court of Quebec for the district of Joliette, and in 1899 he was transferred to the district of Montreal. He retired from the bench in 1914; and he died at Montreal, Quebec, on May 24, 1919. He was the compiler of *La bib-*

liothèque du code civil de la province de Québec (21 vols., Montreal, 1871-90).

[P. G. Roy, *Les juges de la province de Québec* (Quebec, 1933).

Lorimier, François Marie Thomas, Chevalier de (1803-1839), *patriote* leader, was born at St. Cuthbert, Lower Canada, in 1803. He was admitted to practice as a notary public in 1829, and espoused the *patriote* cause. In 1838 he acted as "brigadier-general" of the rebel forces at Lacolle Mill, and was taken prisoner. He was tried by court-martial, condemned to death, and hanged on February 15, 1839. In 1832 he married Marguerite Henriette Cadieux (d. 1891); and by her he had one son and four daughters.

[H. Fabre, *Esquisse biographique sur Chevalier de Lorimier* (Montreal, 1856); E. Z. Massicotte, *La famille de Lorimer* (Bull. rech. hist., 1915); Le Jeune, *Dict. gén.*]

Loring, Frances Norma (1887-1968), sculptor, was born in Wardner, Idaho, October 14, 1887. She was educated in Switzerland, Germany, and Paris. She studied art at the Beaux Arts, Geneva; the Académie Colorassi, Paris; the Art Institute of Chicago; the Art Students League, New York; and the Academy of Fine Arts, Boston. She and Florence Wyle (q.v.) set up a studio in New York (1909-1912). When her family moved to Canada in 1912 she decided to go to Toronto, where in 1913 she took a studio on Church Street. She was joined by Miss Wyle the following year. Miss Loring did a number of statuettes of wartime workers for the Canadian government which are in the National Gallery. In 1920 Misses Loring and Wyle moved to a new and larger studio, which soon became a social as well as artistic centre for Toronto musicians, architects, writers, painters, and sculptors. Frances Loring was a sculptor whose phenomenal output was of a singularly high standard, uncluttered, flowing, and expressive. Her works are to be found in many private collections as well as in the National Gallery of Canada, in the Art Gallery of Ontario, at the Rainbow Bridge (Niagara Falls), and in the grounds of the Parliament Buildings in Ottawa. She did war memorials for Galt, Ontario; St. Stephen, New Brunswick; Augusta, Maine; and Peterborough, Ontario. Frances Loring was a co-founder of the Sculptors' Society of Canada (1928); a member of the Royal Canadian Academy (1947) and the Ontario Society of Artists; and a chief organizer of the Federation of Canadian Artists and the National Arts Council. She died at Newmarket, Ontario, on February 5, 1968.

[*Canadian who's who*, 1955-57; C. S. MacDonald, *A dictionary of Canadian artists*, vol. 4 (Ottawa, 1974); R. Sisler, *The girls* (Toronto, 1972).]

Lorne, Sir John Douglas Sutherland Campbell, Marquis of, afterwards ninth Duke of Argyll (1845-1914), governor-general of Canada (1878-83), was born at Stafford House, London, England, on August 6, 1845, the eldest son of George, eighth Duke of Argyll, and Elizabeth, eldest daughter of the second Duke of Sutherland. He was educated at Edinburgh Academy, at Eton, at St. Andrew's University, and at Trinity College, Cambridge. From 1868 to 1871 he was private secretary to his father, then secretary of state for India; and from 1868 to 1878 he sat in the House of Commons at Westminster as Liberal member for Argyllshire. He sat also in the House of Commons, as Unionist member for South Manchester, from 1895 to 1900. Then he succeeded to the dukedom of Argyll, and took his seat in the House of Lords. In 1871 he married Princess Louise, fourth daughter of Queen Victoria; and in 1878 he was appointed governor-general of Canada. His period of office was marked at one stage by strained relations between himself and Sir John Macdonald (q.v.), who had been returned to power in 1878; but the difficulties between them were later smoothed over, and Lord Lorne proved one of the most popular governors Canada has had. He died on May 2, 1914, and was succeeded in the dukedom by his nephew. He wrote a number of books, both of prose and poetry; and those which have reference to Canada are *Memories of Canada and Scotland* (Montreal, 1884), *Imperial federation* (London, 1885), *Canadian pictures* (London, 1885), *Passages from the past* (2 vols., London, 1907), and *Yesterday and to-day in Canada* (London, 1910).

[J. E. Collins, *Canada under the administration of Lord Lorne* (Toronto, 1884); *Who was who*, 1897-1916; Dent, *Can. port.*, vol. 1; Le Jeune, *Dict. gén.*; Sir J. Pope (ed.), *Correspondence of Sir John Macdonald* (Toronto, 1921); W. S. MacNutt, *Days of Lorne* (Fredericton, 1955).]

Lorrain, Léon (1852?-1892), poet, was born about 1852, and became a lawyer in St. Johns, Quebec. He was drowned in a mysterious way in the Richelieu River on January 29, 1892. He was the author of *Les fleurs poétiques* (Montreal, 1890).

[*Bull. rech. hist.*, 1923.]

Lortie, Stanislas Alfred (1869-1912), priest and author, was born at Quebec City, on November 14, 1869, the son of Henri Lortie and Marie Ursule Drolet. He was ordained a priest of the Roman Catholic Church in 1892; and for many years he was a professor of theology and philosophy at Laval University, Quebec. He died at Curran, Ontario, on August 19, 1912. Besides a three-volume work embodying his lectures on philosophy, he was the author of *Un compositeur typographe de Québec* (Paris, 1901) and *L'origine et le parler des canadiens-français* (Paris, 1904).

[Allaire, *Dict. biog.*; Le Jeune, *Dict. gén.*]

Lotbinière, Sir Henri Gustave Joly de. See **Joly de Lotbinière, Sir Henri Gustave.**

Lotbinière, Michel Eustache Gaspard Alain Chartier de (1748-1822), legislative councillor of Lower Canada, was born on August 31, 1748, the son of the Marquis Michel Gaspard Chartier de Lotbinière (1723-99), and inherited from his father the seigniories of Vaudreuil, Rigaud, and Lotbinière, as well as the title of marquis, which he never used. In 1775 he fought on the British side against the Americans. From 1792 to 1796 he was one of the members for the county of York in the Legislative Assembly of Lower Canada; and in 1793 he was elected speaker of the Assembly. In 1796 he was appointed a member of the Legislative Council; and he died at Montreal on January 1, 1822.

[Abbé Daniel, *L'Hon. M. E. G. Alain Chartier de Lotbinière* (Bull. rech. hist., 1903); P. G. Roy, *Fils de Québec*, vol. 2 (Lévis, Que., 1933); Le Jeune, *Dict. gén.*]

Loudon, James (1841-1916), president of the University of Toronto (1892-1906), was born at Toronto, Upper Canada, in 1841, the son of William Loudon. He was educated at the Toronto Grammar School, Upper Canada College, and the University of Toronto (B.A., 1862; M.A., 1864; LL.D., 1894). In 1864 he became classical tutor in University College, Toronto, and later mathematical tutor. In 1875 he was appointed professor of mathematics and physics; and in 1887 professor of physics alone. He was appointed president of the university in 1892, and continued to preside over the affairs of the university until his resignation in 1906. He then retired on a pension, and he died in Toronto on December 29, 1916. In 1872 he married Julia, daughter of John Lorn McDougall (q.v.); and by her he had three sons and one daughter. From 1876 to 1878 he was president of the Canadian Institute; and in 1901 he was elected president of the Royal Society of Canada, of which he was a charter member.

[H. H. Langton, *James Loudon and the University of Toronto* (Toronto, 1927); *Proc. Roy. Soc. Can.*, 1917; *University of Toronto monthly*, 1917; Morgan, *Can. men* (1912); W. S. Wallace, *A history of the University of Toronto* (Toronto, 1927).]

Loudon, Thomas Richardson (1883-1962), university professor, was born in Toronto, Ontario, September 1, 1883. He was educated at the University of Toronto (B.A.Sc. Hon.). He was a member of the firm of James, Loudon, and Hertzberg from 1912 to 1919. Meanwhile, he served in the First World War with the Canadian Engineers in France and was invalided to Canada in 1918. He maintained his connection with the C.O.T.C. at the University of Toronto from 1919 to 1939, being in command of the unit from 1926 to 1931.

During the Second World War he was in command of the Test and Development Establishment of the R.C.A.F. He was professor of civil engineering and aeronautics at the University of Toronto until his retirement in 1954. He was mentioned in despatches in the First World War and awarded the volunteer officer's decoration in the Second World War. He was a member of the Professional Engineers' Institute and the Royal Canadian Institute, and was involved in amateur athletic organization for many years. He died at Toronto, Ontario, in 1962.

[*Can. who's who*, 1955-57.]

Loudon, William James (1860-1951), educationist and author, was born in Toronto, Ontario, on June 25, 1860, and died there on September 27, 1951. He was educated at the University of Toronto (B.A., 1880), and was appointed a demonstrator in the department of physics at Toronto in 1881. He retired as emeritus professor of mechanics in 1930. Besides two or three scientific treatises, he was the author of *The small-mouthed bass* (Toronto, 1910), *Studies of student life* (8 vols., Toronto, 1923-40), *A Canadian geologist: Biography of Joseph B. Tyrrell* (Toronto, 1930), and *Sir William Mulock* (Toronto, 1932).

[Toronto *Globe and Mail*, Sept. 29, 1951; *Can. who's who*, 1948.]

Lougheed, Sir James Alexander (1854-1925), minister of soldiers' civil re-establishment for Canada (1918-21), was born at Brampton, Ontario, on September 1, 1854. He was educated at Toronto, and was called to the bar of Ontario in 1877. In 1883 he removed to Calgary, and was called to the bar of the North West Territories (Q.C., 1889). In 1889 he was called to the Senate of Canada; and in 1906 he became Conservative leader in the Senate. He became a minister without portfolio in the Borden government in 1911, and government leader in the Senate; and during the War of 1914-18 he was chairman of the Military Hospitals Commission. In 1918 he became head of the newly created department of soldiers' civil re-establishment, and he retained this post in the short-lived Meighen administration of 1920-21. He died at Ottawa on November 3, 1925. In 1884 he married Belle, daughter of William Hardisty, of the Hudson's Bay Company. In 1916 he was created a K.C.M.G.

[*Can. parl. comp.*; *Who was who*, 1916-28; Morgan, *Can. men* (1912).]

Lougheed, William Foster (1910-1962), economist, was born in Toronto, Ontario, in 1910, son of Professor William James Lougheed. He was a graduate of Upper Canada College, McMaster University (M.A., 1936), and the University of Chicago. He taught at Wayne University (1939), Dalhousie University (1940), and the University of Manitoba until he became adviser to the Wartime

Prices and Trade Board during the Second World War. From 1944 to 1954 he was chief economist for the Canadian Bank of Commerce. He then formed his own consulting company. He was the author of *Labour government and management relations* (1943); *Municipal finance* (1950); *The gold mining community* (1958); and *Secondary manufacturing industry in the Canadian economy* (1962). He was a member of the American Economists' Association, Canadian Economics and Political Science Association, and the Royal Economists' Association of England. He died at Toronto, Ontario, November 18, 1962.

[Metropolitan Toronto Library Board, *Biographical scrapbooks*, vol. 20.]

Lount, Samuel (1791-1838), rebel, was born on the banks of the Susquehanna River, in Pennsylvania, on September 24, 1791, the son of Gabriel Lount, a native of Bristol, England. He came with his father to Upper Canada in 1811; settled in the township of Whitchurch, Simcoe county; and became a prosperous blacksmith at Holland Landing. In 1834 he was elected one of the representatives of Simcoe in the Legislative Assembly of Upper Canada, as a Reformer; but he was defeated in 1836, and he joined with William Lyon Mackenzie (q.v.) in the rebellion of 1837. He was captured, was tried on the charge of high treason, was condemned to death, and was hanged at Toronto on April 12, 1838.

[J. C. Dent, *The Upper Canadian rebellion* (2 vols., Toronto, 1885); E. C. Guillet, *The lives and times of the patriots* (Toronto, 1938).]

Lount, William (1840-1903), jurist, was born at Holland Landing, Upper Canada, on March 3, 1840, the son of George Lount, and the nephew of Samuel Lount (q.v.). He was educated at the University of Toronto, and was called to the bar of Upper Canada in 1863 (Q.C., 1876). He practised law, first in Barrie, and then in Toronto, Ontario; and acquired an outstanding reputation as a lawyer in criminal cases. From 1867 to 1871 he represented North Simcoe in the Legislative Assembly of Ontario; and from 1896 to 1897 he represented Centre Toronto in the Canadian House of Commons. He was appointed a judge of the High Court of Justice of Ontario in 1901; and he died on April 24, 1903.

[Morgan, *Can. men* (1898).]

Lovell, John (d. 1893), publisher, was born in Ireland, and came to Canada in 1820. He became a publisher in Montreal, and became especially known as a publisher of directories, gazetteers, geographies, and school-books. He died in Montreal on July 1, 1893.

[J. D. Borthwick, *History of the diocese of Montreal* (Montreal, 1910).]

Lovett, Henry Almon (1866-1944), lawyer and author, was born at Brooklyn, Nova Scotia, on May 10, 1866. He was educated at Acadia University (B.A., 1886), at the University of Michigan, and at Dalhousie University (LL.B., 1889); and was called to the bar of Nova Scotia in 1890 (K.C., 1907) and to that of Quebec in 1909. He practised law in Halifax until 1908, and thereafter in Montreal. He became a prominent corporation lawyer, and was employed as counsel for the Canadian government in the Grand Trunk Railway arbitration of 1921. He died at Winnipeg, Manitoba, on June 29, 1944. He was the author of *Canada and the Grand Trunk* (Montreal, 1924).

[*Can. who's who*, 1936-37.]

Low, Albert Peter (1861-1942), geologist, was born in Montreal, Canada East, on May 24, 1861, and died at Ottawa, Ontario, on October 9, 1942. He was educated at McGill University (B.A.Sc., 1882) and joined the staff of the Geological Survey of Canada. He was appointed director of the Geological Survey in 1906; but a year and a half later became deputy minister of the department of mines. He retired from the civil service in 1913. He was the author of a large number of geological reports, and he wrote the story of an expedition to the Arctic that he commanded in 1903-04, under the title *The cruise of the Neptune* (Ottawa, 1906). In 1905 he was elected a fellow of the Geological Society of America.

[*Proceedings of the Geological Society of America*, April, 1944; Morgan, *Can. men* (1912); *Encyc. Can.*]

Low, George Jacobs (1836-1906), clergyman, was born in Calcutta, India, on April 11, 1836. He came to Canada as a young man, and was educated at Trinity University, Toronto, and at Huron College, London, Ontario; and he was ordained a priest of the Church of England in 1865. He was incumbent successively at Merrickville, Carleton Place, Brockville, and Almonte, in Ontario; and he was made a canon of the diocese of Ottawa in 1897. He died at Ottawa, Ontario, on December 14, 1906. He was the author of *Papers on prohibition* (New York, 1887) and *The old faith and the new philosophy* (Toronto, 1900).

[Morgan, *Can. men* (1898).]

Low, Solon Earl (1900-1962), national Social Credit leader, was born at Cardston, Alberta, son of James Low, who had been a member of the Constitutional Convention of the state of Utah. Solon was educated at Cardston schools, the Calgary Normal College, the University of Alberta, and the University of Southern California, where he majored in social science, economics, and physical education. He taught at Raymond, Alberta, and was made principal of the Stirling, Alberta, school in 1934. He was elected to the Alberta legislature in 1935 in the landslide victory which gave the newly formed Social

Credit party of William Aberhart (q.v.) fifty-six of the sixty-three seats. He was provincial treasurer (1937-44), minister of education (1943-44), and minister without portfolio (1944-45). He became president and national leader of the Social Credit Association of Canada at the national convention in Toronto in 1944, succeeding John Blackmore, and was re-elected in Regina in 1946 and in 1950. He was elected to the House of Commons for Peace River in 1945 and again in 1949. He became the member for Warner in 1953 and again for Peace River in 1957. He was defeated and his party left without representation in the House of Commons in the Diefenbaker victory of 1958. Low retired as national leader in favour of Robert Thompson in 1961. He died at Shelby, Montana, on December 22, 1962.

[*Can. who's who*, 1955-57; *Can. parl. guide*, 1958; *Can. Dir. of Parliament*, 1867-1967.]

Low, Thomas Andrew (1871-1931), minister of trade and commerce for Canada (1923-25), was born on March 12, 1871, at Quebec, the son of Alexander George Low and Margaret Henderson. He became a manufacturer in Renfrew, Ontario, and was president of the Renfrew Flour Mills and other companies. From 1908 to 1912 he represented South Renfrew in the Canadian House of Commons; he then resigned his seat, but was re-elected for this constituency in 1921, and became a minister without portfolio in the King government. In 1923 he was made minister of trade and commerce, but was defeated in the general elections of 1925, and retired to private life. He died at Renfrew on February 9, 1931. In 1904 he married Mary, daughter of Noble Dean, of Renfrew; and by her he had one son.

[*Can. parl. comp.*]

Lowe, John (1899-1960), clergyman and educationist, was born at Calgary, Alberta, on January 9, 1899, and died at Oxford, England, on August 15, 1960. He was educated at Trinity College, University of Toronto (B.A., 1921; M.A., 1922), was chosen a Rhodes scholar for Ontario in 1922, and spent two years at Christ Church, Oxford (B.A., 1924; M.A., 1929). He was ordained a priest of the Church of England in 1925, and in 1926 he was appointed a fellow and tutor in the General Theological Seminary in New York. In 1927 he returned to Toronto, and became first a lecturer, then a professor, and finally dean, in the faculty of theology in Trinity College. In 1939 he was offered and accepted the post of dean of Christ Church, Oxford; he resigned from this position only in 1959, because of ill-health. He was vice-chancellor of Oxford University from 1948 to 1951; and he was made an honorary D.D. of Trinity College in 1939, and an honorary LL.D. of the University of Toronto in 1949.

He was the author of a volume of lectures entitled *Saint Peter* (New York, 1956).

[*Can. who's who*, 1958-59; *Who's who*, 1959; *Crockford's clerical directory* (Oxford, 1959).]

Lowry, Malcolm (1909-1957), author, was born in England in 1909, and died there in 1957. He lived in Canada, however, for twenty-five years, from 1939 to 1954; and he did most of his writing in a squatter's cabin at Dollarton, on Burrard Inlet, in British Columbia. It was here he wrote the final draft of his novel, *Under the volcano* (New York, 1947), and most of the stories in his posthumously published *Hear us O Lord from heaven thy dwelling-place* (Philadelphia, 1961).

[*Canadian Literature*, Spring, 1961, with bibliography.]

Lozeau, Albert (1878-1924), journalist and poet, was born in Montreal, on June 23, 1878, and died at Montreal on March 24, 1924. He was an invalid from the age of eighteen; but he found energy to contribute to the Montreal *Devoir*, and to publish several volumes of verse, *L'âme solitaire* (Montreal, 1907), *Le Miroir des jours* (Montreal, 1912), and *Lauriers et feuilles d'érables* (Montreal, 1916). He was also the author of a volume of essays, *Billets du soir* (Montreal, 1911). In 1911 he was elected a fellow of the Royal Society of Canada.

[C. Roy, *Sur le tombe d'Albert Lozeau* (Canada français, 1924); C. ab der Halden, *Nouvelles études de littérature canadienne française* (Paris, 1907); Morgan, *Can. men* (1912); Le Jeune, *Dict. gén.*; *Proc. Roy. Soc. Can.*, 1925; *Can. who was who*, vol. 1.]

Lucas, Daniel Vannorman (1834-1911), clergyman and author, was born near Niagara Falls, Upper Canada, on July 12, 1834. He was educated at Victoria University, Cobourg, and was ordained a minister of the Methodist Church in 1862. After serving for two years as a missionary in British Columbia, he held various pastorates in Quebec and Ontario. In his later years, he devoted himself exclusively to temperance work. He died at Hamilton, Ontario, on June 10, 1911. He was the author of *Australia and homeward* (Toronto, 1888), *Canaan and Canada* (Toronto, 1904), and *The Maoris of New Zealand* (Toronto, 1910).

[Morgan, *Can. men* (1912).]

Lucas, James Richard (1867-1938), Anglican bishop of Mackenzie River, was born at Brighton, England, on August 20, 1867; and was educated at the Church Missionary College, Islington, England. He was sent out to the North West Territories of Canada as a missionary in 1891; and he was ordained a priest of the Church of England in 1893. From 1891 to 1899 he was stationed at Fort Chipewyan, and from 1900 to 1913 at Fort Simpson. He became archdeacon of Mackenzie River in 1906, and bishop in 1913. He resigned from this see in 1926; and from 1929 to 1934 he was warden of the Church Army in Canada. He died at Worthing, England, on October 7, 1938. In 1913 he was made an honorary D.D. of St. John's College, Winnipeg.

[*Can. who's who*, 1936-37; Morgan, *Can. men* (1912); O. R. Rowley, *The Anglican episcopate of Canada and Newfoundland* (Milwaukee, Wis., 1928).]

Ludlow, Gabriel George (1736-1808), administrator of the province of New Brunswick (1803-08), was born in New York on April 10, 1736, the son of Gabriel Ludlow. He served as a colonel in a Loyalist regiment during the American Revolution; and he came to Canada with his brother, George Duncan Ludlow (q.v.), at the same time as Governor Thomas Carleton (q.v.), in 1784, and was appointed to the Council. He was the first mayor of the city of Saint John, and he held this office for ten years. In 1803, in the absence of Carleton, he was appointed president and administrator of the province, and he discharged the duties of this office until his death on February 12, 1808.

[J. W. Lawrence, *Lives of the judges of New Brunswick* (Saint John, N.B., 1907); *Collections of the New Brunswick Historical Society*, vols. 1-2.]

Ludlow, George Duncan (1734?-1808), chief justice of New Brunswick (1784-1808), was born in New York about 1734, the son of Gabriel Ludlow. In 1768 he was appointed a member of the Council of New York, and in 1769 a puisne judge of the Supreme Court of New York. In 1778 he was appointed master of the rolls, and superintendent of police at Long Island. Upon the evacuation of New York in 1783 he went to England; and he accompanied Thomas Carleton (q.v.) to New Brunswick in 1784. He was appointed to the Council, and was made first chief justice of New Brunswick. He died at his home "Springhill", near Fredericton, New Brunswick, on November 13, 1808. He married a daughter of Thomas Duncan of New York.

[J. W. Lawrence, *Lives of the judges of New Brunswick* (Saint John, N.B., 1907).]

Lugrin, Charles Henry (1846-1917), journalist, was born at Fredericton, New Brunswick, in 1846. He was educated at the University of New Brunswick (B.A., 1865; M.A., 1886), and was called to the bar in 1870. He practised law in New Brunswick, in the state of Washington, and in British Columbia; and in all these places he combined law with journalism. From 1897 to 1902 he was editor of the Victoria *Colonist*. He died in Victoria, British Columbia, on June 14, 1917. He was the author of *New Brunswick, its resources, prog-*

ress, and advantages (Fredericton, N.B., 1886).

[Morgan, *Can. men 1912).*]

Lusignan, Alphonse (1843-1892), author, was born on September 27, 1843, the son of Jean-Baptiste Lusignan. He was educated at the College of St. Hyacinthe and at the Montreal Seminary. He was admitted to the bar of Quebec in 1872; and in 1874 he entered the civil service at Ottawa. He died in Ottawa on January 5, 1892. In 1885 he was elected a fellow of the Royal Society of Canada; and in 1887 he was appointed an officer of the French Academy. He was the author of *Recueil de chansons canadiennes et françaises* (Montreal, 1859), *L'école militaire de Québec* (Montreal, 1864), *Décisions judiciaires* (Montreal, 1872), *Coups d'oeil et coups de plume* (Ottawa, 1884), and *A la presse française du Canada: Fautes à corriger* (Quebec, 1890).

[*A la mémoire de Alphonse Lusignan: Hommages de ses amis et confrères* (Montreal, 1892); *Cyc. Am. Biog.*; Le Jeune, *Dict. gén.*; *Bull. rech. hist.*, 1924.]

Lyall, Mrs. Laura, *née* **Muntz** (1860-1930), painter, was born at Radford, Warwickshire, England, on June 18, 1860, a daughter of Eugene Gustavus Muntz. She came to Canada with her parents at the age of nine, and was brought up on a backwoods farm in Muskoka. In 1887 she went to England to study painting, and several years later she studied in France, Holland, and Italy. She was especially successful with her portraits of children; and she was elected an associate of the Royal Canadian Academy in 1895. In 1915 she married Charles W. B. Lyall; and she died at Toronto, on December 9, 1930.

[N. MacTavish, *The fine arts in Canada* (Toronto, 1925); Morgan, *Can. men and women* (1912), under "Muntz, Laura".]

Lyall, William (1811-1890), clergyman and educationist, was born in Paisley, Scotland, on June 11, 1811, and was educated at Glasgow and Edinburgh universities. He became a minister of the Free Church of Scotland; and in 1848 he came to Canada as a tutor in Knox College, Toronto. From 1850 to 1860 he was professor of classics and mental philosophy in the Free Church College, Halifax, Nova Scotia, and from 1860 to 1863 in the united Free and United Presbyterian College, at Truro, Nova Scotia. In 1863 he became professor of logic and psychology in Dalhousie University; and he held this chair until his death at Halifax, Nova Scotia, on January 17, 1890. In 1864 he received the degree of LL.D. from McGill University; and 1882 he became a charter member of the Royal Society of Canada. He was the author of *The intellect, the emotions, and the moral nature* (Edinburgh, 1855).

[Morgan, *Bib. can.*; Rose, *Cyc. Can. biog.* (1888).]

477

Lyman, John (1886-1967), artist, was born September 29, 1886, at Biddeford, Maine. He came to Canada as an infant and was educated in Montreal and at the Hotchkiss School, Lakeville, Connecticut. He entered McGill University, Montreal, in 1905, and in 1907 went to France and then to England, where he was a student at the Royal College of Art in London. He also studied with Jean-Paul Laurens (Paris, 1908-09) and Henri Matisse (Paris, 1909-10). After travelling and studying in Europe and the United States he settled in Montreal in 1931, where he established the Atelier in co-operation with Hazen Sise, Georgie Holt, and André Biéler and wrote reviews for the *The Montrealer*. He became a member of the department of fine arts at McGill University in 1948 and became chairman of the department in 1951, retiring in 1957. Lyman, whose art was condemned as garish in 1913, became acceptable by 1927 and after his return to Montreal founded the Eastern Group of Painters (1939) with six other artists, and the Contemporary Art Society for Artists and Laymen. Lyman's work has been compared with that of his friend Morrice and his teacher, Matisse, but although there is similarity of subject his style is his own. He is "the creator of a classic land where light reveals form through colour". His work is to be found in the National Gallery of Canada; Musée du Québec; Montreal Museum of Fine Arts; University of Manitoba; McGill University; Art Gallery of Hamilton; Beaverbrook Gallery, Fredericton; and Musée d'art, Montreal. He also wrote a biography, *J. W. Morrice* (1945), and a number of periodical articles. He died in Barbados, May 26, 1967.

[*Creative Canada*, vol. 2 (1972); *John Lyman, octogenarian: A retrospective tribute* (Ministère des Affaires Culturelles, 1966); G. Viau, *La peinture moderne au Canada français* (Quebec, 1964).]

Lymburner, Adam (1745?-1836), merchant, was born at Kilmarnock, Ayrshire, Scotland, about 1745. He came to Canada in 1770 to take charge of the business at Quebec of his brother, John, who was lost at sea in the autumn of 1775. He took a prominent part in opposing the Constitutional Act of 1791, and in 1790 appeared at the bar of the House of Commons at Westminster in opposition to the measure. In 1791 he was appointed an executive councillor of Lower Canada, but he did not present himself for admission to the Council until 1799, when he was refused permission to take the oath on the ground of non-attendance. He died at London, England, on January 10, 1836.

[*Cyc. Am. biog.*; *Bull. rech. hist.*, 1931; R. Christie, *History of Lower Canada*, vol. 1 (Quebec, 1848).]

Lynch, John Joseph (1816-1888), first Roman Catholic archbishop of Toronto, was born near Clones, county Monaghan, Ireland, on February 6, 1816. He was educated at the College of Castleknock, Ireland, and at the Seminary of St. Lazare, Paris, France; and in 1843 he was ordained a priest of the Roman Catholic Church. From 1844 to 1846 he was a missionary in Ireland; in 1846 he emigrated to Texas; and from 1848 to 1856 he was professor in the Seminary of St. Mary of the Barrens in Texas. In 1856 he founded the Seminary of Our Lady of the Angels at Niagara Falls, New York; and in 1859 he was consecrated bishop of Toronto. In 1870 he was raised to the dignity of archbishop of Toronto; and his period of office was marked by a great development of the Roman Catholic Church in Ontario. He died at Toronto on May 12, 1888.

[H. C. McKeown, *The life and labours of Most Rev. John Joseph Lynch, D.D.* (Montreal and Toronto, 1886); *Cyc. Am. biog.*; Dent, *Can. port.*, vol. 1; Rose, *Cyc. Can. biog.* (1886); *Can. who was who*, vol. 2; Le Jeune, *Dict. gén.*]

Lynch-Staunton, George (1858-1940), lawyer and senator of Canada, was born at Southampton, Canada West, on September 9, 1858. He was educated at St. Mary's College, Montreal, and at Upper Canada College, Toronto; studied law; and was called to the bar in Ontario in 1882 (Q.C., 1899). He practised law in Hamilton, Ontario, and distinguished himself in several famous criminal cases. He was summoned to the Senate of Canada in 1917; and he remained a senator until his death on March 19, 1940.

[*Can. parl. comp.*; *Can. who's who*, 1936-37.]

Lyon, George Seymour (1858-1938), golf champion, was born at Richmond, Canada West, on July 27, 1858. In his earlier years he was a noted cricketer; but in his later years he turned to golf, and he became a famous figure on Canadian golf links. He won the Canadian amateur golf championship six times between 1898 and 1907, and he won the Olympic golf championship at St. Louis, Mo., in 1904. Later he won repeatedly the amateur senior golf championship in Canada. He died at Toronto, Ontario, on May 11, 1938. His son, George Seymour Lyon, Jr., who was also a notable golfer, died in Toronto, Ontario, as the result of war service, on October 20, 1925.

[*Can. who's who*, 1936-37; Morgan, *Can. men* (1912).]

Lyon, Laurance (1875-1932), author, was born in Toronto, Ontario, in 1875, the son of John Laurance Lyon and Lucy, daughter of Sir Samuel Henry Strong (q.v.). He was educated at Trinity College School, Port Hope, and Osgoode Hall, Toronto, and was called to the bar in Ontario in 1898, and the bar in Quebec in 1900. He practised law in Montreal from 1900 to 1905; but after that date he lived in France and England. He was the proprietor of the *Outlook* (London) from 1916 to 1919; and from 1918 to 1921 he was Conservative member for Hastings in the British House of Commons. He was the author of *The pomp of power* (London, 1922), *The path to peace* (London, 1923), *Where freedom falters* (London, 1927), *The fruits of folly* (London, 1929), and an autobiography entitled *By the waters of Babylon* (London, 1930), all of which were published anonymously. He died in the Sacred Heart Hospital in Montreal on November 11, 1932. In 1901 he married Yvonne, daughter of Sir Henry Taschereau (q.v.); and by her he had two daughters.

[*Who was who*, 1929-40.]

Lysons, Sir Daniel (1816-1898), soldier, was born at Rodmarton, Gloucestershire, England, on August 1, 1816, the son of the Rev. Daniel Lysons. He was educated at Shrewsbury College, and entered the British army in 1834. He served throughout the Canadian rebellion of 1837-38; and in 1862 he returned to Canada to reorganize the Canadian militia. He was promoted to be a general in 1879; and he was created a K.C.B. in 1877 and a G.C.B. in 1886. Among other publications, he was the author of *Parting words on the rejected militia bill* (Quebec, 1862), and *Early reminiscences* (London, 1896), the latter dealing with the rebellion of 1837-38.

[*Dict. nat. biog.*, supp. III.]

Maass, Otto (1890-1961), chemist, was born in New York City, July 8, 1890. His family moved to Montreal when Otto was about six years of age. He was educated at Montreal High School and entered McGill University in 1907 (B.A., 1911). He then worked as a demonstrator at McGill and received his M.Sc. in 1912. He enrolled in Frederick William University in Berlin in 1913 on an 1851 Exhibition Fellowship. When the First World War broke out he escaped internment in Germany by going to Switzerland and then returning to Montreal. In 1919 he was awarded a Ph.D. from Harvard University. He had been a lecturer at McGill since 1917 and became a professor in 1923. He was chairman of the chemistry department from 1937 to 1955, when he retired. Among his early interests was an automatic Toepler pump (1915), which he then used in succeeding experiments. During the Second World War he was director of chemical warfare in the department of national defence and played a major part in the establishment of the experimental station at Suffield, Alberta. In 1940 he became assistant to the director of the National Research Council and spent much of his time in co-ordinating the research work in Canadian universities and among the western allies. One of the results of this work was the production of the explosive RDX in the McGill laboratories. In 1955, on retirement from McGill, he accepted the post of principal research officer for the National Research Council in Ottawa. Ill-health forced his resignation in 1958, but he became associated again with McGill as a research associate, a position he filled until his death on July 3, 1961.

He was a fellow of the Royal Society, of the Royal Society of Canada, and of the Chemical Institute of Canada, and was a member of the Order of the British Empire (1947). Dr. Maass was one of the first to insist on the importance of doing research in Canadian universities. He was the author of an *Introduction to physical chemistry* with E. W. R. Steacie (New York, 1931), and a large number of scientific papers.

[*Can. who's who*, 1955-57; *Proc. Roy. Soc. Can.*, 1962.]

Mabane, Adam (1734-1792), legislative councillor of the province of Quebec, was born in Edinburgh, Scotland, in 1734, and was a cousin of James Thomson, the poet. He studied medicine at Edinburgh University, and came to Canada as a surgeon's mate in Wolfe's expedition against Quebec. During the period of military rule (1760-64) he was attached to the military hospital at Quebec; and in 1764 he was appointed a member of the Council and a judge of the Court of Common Pleas. In 1766 he was dismissed from the Council by Guy Carleton (q.v.); but he was re-appointed to the Council in 1775, and he became the friend and confidant of Haldimand (q.v.). In 1791 he was appointed a member of the Executive Council of Lower Canada; but he did not take his seat, as his death occurred on January 3, 1792.

[Mrs. F. C. Warren and Hon. E. Fabre Surveyer, *From surgeon's mate to chief justice: Adam Mabane* (Trans. Roy. Soc. Can., 1930); Hilda Neatby, *The political career of Adam Mabane* (Can. hist. rev., 1935); Abbé L. Bois, *Le juge Adam Mabane* (Quebec, 1881); *Bull. rech. hist.*, 1901.]

Mabee, James Pitt (1859-1912), chairman of the board of railway commissioners for Canada (1908-12), was born at Port Rowan, Ontario, on November 5, 1859, the son of Simon Pitt Mabee and Frances Leaton. He was educated at the St. Thomas High School, and was called to the Ontario bar in 1882 (Q.C., 1899). In 1905 he was appointed a judge of the High Court of Justice in Ontario; and in 1908 he became chairman of the board of railway commissioners for Canada. He died at Toronto on May 6, 1912. In 1884 he married Marie, daughter of William Thorold, of Mount Williams, Ontario; and by her he had one son and one daughter.

[Morgan, *Can. men* (1912).]

Macallum, Archibald Byron (1859-1934), biochemist, was born at Belmont, Canada West, in 1859; and was educated at the University of Toronto (B.A., 1880; M.B., 1889; M.A., 1899) and at Johns Hopkins University (Ph.D., 1888). He was appointed lecturer in physiology in the University of Toronto in 1887, and became head of this department in

1901; in 1908 he became professor of biochemistry, and he retained this chair until 1918. From 1920 to 1929 he was professor of biochemistry at McGill University. He was elected a fellow of the Royal Society of Canada in 1901, and in 1916 its president; in 1906 he was elected a fellow of the Royal Society of London. He was a pioneer in scientific medicine in Canada; and he received, in recognition of this fact, honorary degrees from several universities in Great Britain and the United States. He died at London, Ontario, on April 5, 1934.

[*Proc. Roy. Soc. Can.*, 1934; *Univ. of Toronto monthly*, 1934; *Who was who*, 1929-40; Morgan, *Can. men* (1912).]

Macara, John (1813-1882), lawyer, was born in Edinburgh, Scotland, in 1813. He became a writer to the Signet; but emigrated to Canada about 1843, and was for some time employed on the staff of the Toronto *Globe*. He was called to the bar of Upper Canada in 1848; and for many years practised law at Goderich, Ontario. He died at Goderich on February 20, 1882. He was the author of *The origin, history, and management of the University of King's College* (Toronto, 1844).

[*Dom. ann. reg.*, 1882.]

McAree, John Verner (1876-1958), journalist, was born at Toronto, Ontario, in 1876, and died there on March 22, 1958. He was educated in the public schools of Toronto, and in 1898 became a journalist on the staff of the Toronto *Mail and Empire*. For many years he conducted a column, first in the *Mail and Empire*, and later in the *Globe and Mail*; and some of his contributions to this were reprinted in book form under the titles *The fourth column* (Toronto, 1934) and *Culled from our columns* (Toronto, 1962). He also wrote *Cabbagetown store* (Toronto, 1953).

[*Can. who's who*, 1955-57.]

McArthur, David Carmen (1897-1967), executive, was born in Brooklyn, New York, August 12, 1897. He was educated in Ontario high schools and at the Ontario Agricultural College, Guelph (B.S.A., 1921). He began his career with the *Globe*, Toronto, in 1922 and also worked for the *Farmer's Sun*, Toronto, and as publicity director for the Royal Winter Fair, Toronto. He was Canadian manager for Chilean Nitrate from 1928 to 1931, when he joined Maclean Publishing Company. He left Maclean's to become Ontario director of press and information for the Canadian Broadcasting Corporation and in 1940 was given the responsibility of organizing the Canadian Broadcasting Corporation National News Service, which he served as chief editor until 1953. He established high non-political standards for the government-owned broadcasting service and attracted top correspondents to the C.B.C. news. He became special projects direc-

tor for the C.B.C. in 1953 and retired in 1962. During the First World War, McArthur served with the 55th battalion, Canadian Field Artillery, from 1916 to 1919, and subsequently wrote the history of the unit. He died in Ottawa, Ontario, March 17, 1967.

[*Can. who's who*, 1964-66; *Globe and Mail*, Toronto (March 20, 1967).]

McArthur, Duncan (1885-1943), historian and politician, was born at Dutton, Ontario, on March 17, 1885. He was educated at Queen's University, Kingston (B.A., 1907; M.A., 1908; LL.D., 1935); and from 1907 to 1912 he was employed in the Public Archives of Canada. He then studied law at Osgoode Hall, Toronto, and was called to the bar in 1915. From 1919 to 1922 he was assistant general manager of the London and Western Trusts Company, at London, Ontario; but in 1922 he was appointed head of the department of history at Queen's University, and he served in this position until, in 1934, he was made deputy minister of education for Ontario. In 1940 he was made minister of education for Ontario, and was elected to represent Simcoe Centre in the Legislative Assembly of Ontario. During the latter part of his period of office, he suffered from ill-health; and he died at Grand Bend, Ontario, on July 20, 1943, during the provincial elections of that year. He was the author of a *History of Canada* (Toronto, 1927); and he was joint editor, with Sir Arthur Doughty (q.v.), of *Documents relating to the constitutional history of Canada, 1791-1818* (Ottawa, 1914).

[*Can. who's who*, 1938-39; *Can. parl. comp.*; *Can. hist. rev.*, 1943.]

McArthur, James Joseph (1856-1925), surveyor, was born at Aylmer, Canada East, on May 9, 1856. He became a Dominion land surveyor in 1879, and he entered the service of the Canadian government in 1881. He introduced the system of phototopography for the survey of the Rocky Mountains in 1887; and he was employed in explorations in the Yukon Territory in 1897-99. He was employed also in the final definition of the boundaries between Canada and Alaska and between Canada and the United States; and he was geographer and topographical expert on the staff of the British representatives before the Alaska Boundary Tribunal in 1903. He died at Ottawa, Ontario, on October 14, 1925.

[Morgan, *Can. men* (1912).]

McArthur, Peter (1866-1924), journalist and author, was born in Middlesex county, Ontario, on March 10, 1866, the son of Peter McArthur and Catherine McLennan. He was educated at the Strathroy High School; and in 1887 he matriculated at the University of Toronto. In 1889, however, he left the University, and became a journalist. From 1890 to 1908 he was a journalist in New York, with the exception of the years 1902-04, which he spent in London, England. In 1908 he returned to the family homestead in Ekfrid township, Middlesex county, Ontario; and here he spent the rest of his life. During this period he contributed to the Toronto *Globe* a series of weekly or semi-weekly articles describing the activities of his little farm. He died at the Victoria Hospital, London, Ontario, on October 28, 1924. In 1895 he married Mabel Waters, of Niagara-on-the-Lake, Ontario; and by her he had four sons and one daughter. Apart from innumerable contributions to periodicals, he was the author of *To be taken with salt: Being an essay on teaching one's grandmother to suck eggs* (London, 1903), *The prodigal and other poems* (New York, 1907), *In pastures green* (Toronto, 1915), *The red cow and her friends* (Toronto, 1919), *Sir Wilfrid Laurier* (Toronto, 1919), *The affable stranger* (Toronto, 1920), *Stephen Leacock* (Toronto, 1923), and *Around home* (Toronto, 1925). From 1910 to 1911 he wrote and published at St. Thomas, Ontario, a little periodical entitled *Ourselves*.

[W. A. Deacon, *Peter McArthur* (Toronto, 1924); J. W. Garvin (ed.), *Canadian poets* (Toronto, 1916); Morgan, *Can. men* (1912).]

Macaulay, Sir James Buchanan (1793-1859), chief justice of the Court of Common Pleas for Upper Canada, was born in Niagara, Upper Canada, on December 3, 1793, the second son of James Macaulay, M.D., and Elizabeth Hayter. He was educated under John Strachan (q.v.) at Cornwall, and obtained a commission in the 98th Regiment. During the War of 1812 he was an officer in the Glengarry Fencibles, and was present at the capture of Ogdensburg, at the battle of Lundy's Lane, and at the attack on Fort Erie. In 1822 he was called to the bar of Upper Canada; and in 1829 he was made a puisne judge of the Court of King's Bench. He sat in this court until 1849, when he was appointed chief justice of the Court of Common Pleas. He retired from the bench in 1856, and was made treasurer of the Law Society of Upper Canada. In 1857 he was appointed a judge of the Court of Error and Appeal; and he held this position until within a few months of his death, at Toronto, on November 26, 1859. In 1821 he married Rachel Crookshank, daughter of John Gamble; and by her he had one son and four daughters. He was created a knight bachelor in 1859.

[D. B. Read, *Lives of the judges* (Toronto, 1888); *Dict. nat. biog.*; E. M. Chadwick, *Ontarian families* (2 vols., Toronto, 1894-98).]

Macaulay, John (1792-1857), legislative councillor, was born in Kingston, Upper Canada, on October 17, 1792, the eldest son of Robert Macaulay and Ann Kirby. In 1836 he was appointed a member of the Legislative Council of Upper Canada; in 1841 he became a member of the Legislative Council of united Canada; and from 1841 to 1842 he was receiver-general for Upper Canada. He died in 1857.

[A. H. Young (ed.), *The parish register of Kingston, Upper Canada* (Kingston, Ont., 1921).]

Macaulay, John Simcoe (1791-1855), soldier, was born in England on October 13, 1791, the eldest son of James Macaulay, M.D., and Elizabeth Hayter. He came to Canada with his parents as an infant; but was educated in England, and became an officer in the Royal Engineers. He returned to Canada, and settled in Toronto, in 1835; and in 1837 he commanded a militia battalion, with the militia rank of colonel. In 1839 he was appointed a member of the Legislative Council of Upper Canada; but he was not appointed in 1841 a member of the Legislative Council of united Canada. In 1842 he was defeated as a candidate for the Legislative Assembly of Canada in the 3rd riding of York; and in 1843 he went to live in England. He died at his country place, near Rochester, Kent, England, on December 22, 1855. In 1825 he married Ann Gee, daughter of the Hon. John Elmsley (q.v.); and by her he had four sons and five daughters. He was the author of a *Treatise on field fortification* (London, 1834), which ran into many editions, and of a *Description of Chasseloup de Loubat's system of fortification* (London, 1851).

[W. Canniff, *The medical profession in Upper Canada* (Toronto, 1894), p. 487; E. M. Chadwick, *Ontarian families* (2 vols., Toronto, 1894-98).]

Macaulay, Robertson (1833-1915), insurance executive, was born in Fraserburgh, Aberdeenshire, Scotland, in 1833. He came to Canada in 1854, and entered the service of the Canada Life Assurance Company. In 1874 he became secretary of the Sun Life Assurance Company, in Montreal; and he rose in the service of this company until he became general manager in 1887, and president in 1889. The amazing growth of this insurance company was largely his work. He resigned the general managership of the company to his son, Thomas Bassett Macaulay (q.v.), in 1906; and he died at Montreal, Quebec, on September 27, 1915.

[Morgan, *Can. men* (1912); J. Schull, *The Century of the Sun* (Toronto, 1971).]

Macaulay, Thomas Bassett (1860-1942), insurance executive, was born at Hamilton, Canada West, on June 6, 1860, the son of Robertson Macaulay (q.v.). He was educated at the Montreal High School, and entered the service of the Sun Life Assurance Company of Canada in 1877. In the service of this company he rose until he became managing director in 1906, president in 1915, and chairman of the board of directors in 1934. He was a fellow, by examination, of the Institute of Actuaries of Great Britain; and a charter member, and in

1899-1901 president, of the Actuarial Society of America. He was an LL.D. of McGill University (1930), of Edinburgh University (1930), and of Aberdeen University (1930). He maintained a private experimental farm at Hudson Heights, Quebec; and it was there he died on April 3, 1942.

[*Can. who's who*, 1936-37; J. Schull, *The Century of the Sun* (Toronto, 1971).]

Macaulay, Zachary (*fl.* 1758-1786), merchant, came to Canada in 1758 as an ensign on board the British man-of-war *Princess of Orange*. He was present at the capture of Louisbourg in 1758 and of Quebec in 1759; and after the peace established himself as a merchant at Quebec. In 1773 he accompanied Thomas Walker (q.v.) to London as a delegate of the Quebec merchants in their demand for a house of assembly. His name appears in many of the petitions of the period, but disappears after 1786. The statement that he was the Zachary Macaulay who was the father of Lord Macaulay is erroneous.

[D. Brymner, *Zachary Macaulay* (Bull. rech. hist., 1896).]

McBeath, George (1740?-1812), furtrader, was born in Scotland about 1740, and came to Canada soon after the British conquest. He engaged in the fur-trade, and spent his first winter in the Indian country in 1766-67. He was interested in some of the earliest ventures to the North-West, and in 1775 was in partnership with Simon McTavish (q.v.). In 1779 and 1783 he was one of the partners in the original sixteen-share North West Company. In 1787 he sold one of his shares to McTavish, Frobisher and Co.; and in 1792 he sold the second share to Alexander (later Sir Alexander) Mackenzie (q.v.). In 1785 he was one of the founders of the Beaver Club of Montreal. In his later years he was a victim of financial reverses; and in 1785 he went to live at L'Assomption. From 1793 to 1796 he represented Leinster in the first legislature of Lower Canada. He died at Montreal on December 3, 1812. He was, apparently, twice married. By his first wife, Jane Graham, who died in 1787, he had one son and one daughter; and in 1801 he married secondly, at Pointe-aux-Trembles, Erie Smyth, widow of David McCrae, of L'Assomption.

[E. Fabre Surveyer, *George McBeath* (La Presse, Montreal, 1927); M. M. Quaife (ed.), *The John Askin papers*, vol. 1 (Detroit, Mich., 1928).]

Macbeth, Madge Hamilton Lyons (1878-1965), novelist, was born in Philadelphia, Pennsylvania, in 1878, and educated in Hellmuth Ladies' College, London, Ontario. She lived in Ottawa and travelled a great deal. Left a widow, she supported her two small children by her writing. She wrote *The winning game* (1910); *Kleath* (1917); *The Patter-*

son limit (1923); *The land of afternoon* (1924), about Ottawa life; *Shackles* (1927), an early women's liberation book; *Beggar your neighbour* (1929) with E. L. M. Burns; *Wings in the West* (1932); and some others. Her autobiography, *Over my shoulder*, appeared in 1953 and *Boulevard career* in 1957. She also wrote a number of travel books, *Over the gangplank to Spain* (1931); and *Three Elysian islands: Grand Canary, Lanzarote, Fuerteventura* (1956). She died at Ottawa, Ontario, September 20, 1965.

[*Can. who's who*, 1949-51; Norah Story, *Oxford companion to Canadian history and literature* (Toronto, 1967); V. B. Rhodenizer, *Canadian literature in English* (Montreal, 1965).]

MacBeth, Roderick George (1858-1934), clergyman and author, was born at Kildonan, near Winnipeg, Manitoba, on December 21, 1858, the son of Robert MacBeth and Mary MacLean. He was educated at the University of Manitoba (B.A., 1882; M.A., 1885), and was called to the bar of Manitoba in 1886; but he deserted law for the church, and after studying at Princeton Seminary he was ordained a minister of the Presbyterian Church in 1891. He occupied pastorates in Carman and Winnipeg, Manitoba, in Vancouver, British Columbia, in Paris, Ontario, and again in Vancouver; and he died at Vancouver on February 28, 1934. A descendant of one of the Selkirk settlers at Kildonan, he was greatly interested in the early history of the Canadian west; and he was the author of *The Selkirk settlers in real life* (Toronto, 1897), *The making of the Canadian west* (Toronto, 1898; 2nd ed., 1905), *The romance of western Canada* (Toronto, 1918), *Policing the plains* (Toronto, 1922), and *The romance of the Canadian Pacific Railway* (Toronto, 1924). He wrote also *Our task in Canada* (Toronto, 1912), a book on church work entitled *The burning bush and Canada* (Toronto, 1926), and a biography of Sir Augustus Nanton (Toronto, 1931).

[Morgan, *Can. men* (1912); *Presbyterian record*, 1934.]

McBride, Sir Richard (1870-1917), prime minister of British Columbia (1903-15), was born at New Westminster, British Columbia, on December 15, 1870, the son of Arthur Hill McBride and Mary D'Arcy. He was educated at Dalhousie University, Halifax (LL.B., 1890), and was called to the bar in British Columbia in 1892 (K.C., 1905). In 1898 he was elected to the legislature of British Columbia as a Liberal-Conservative; and he sat in the legislature continuously until 1915, first for Dewdney (1898-1907), and then for Victoria (1907-15). In 1900 he became minister of mines in the Dunsmuir administration; from 1902 to 1903 he was leader of the opposition; and in June, 1903, he became prime minister of the province of British Columbia. He retained power until the end of 1915, when he resigned to accept the post of agent-general of British Columbia in London. He died in England on August 8, 1917. In 1912 he was created a K.C.M.G.; and in 1913 he was made an LL.D. of the University of California. He married, in 1896, Margaret, daughter of Neil McGillivray, of New Westminster, British Columbia; and by her he had six daughters.

[*Can. who was who*, vol. 1; *Who was who*, 1916-28; *Can. parl. comp.*; Morgan, *Can. men* (1912); R. E. Gosnell, *The yearbook of British Columbia* (Victoria, B.C., 1911); E. O. S. Scholefield and F. W. Howay, *British Columbia* (4 vols., Vancouver, B.C., 1914).]

MacBrien, Sir James Howden (1878-1938), soldier, was born at Myrtle, Ontario, on June 30, 1878. He was educated at the Port Perry High School, and saw service in the South African War from 1900 to 1902. In the First World War he commanded the 12th Infantry Brigade, with the rank of brigadier-general; he was awarded the D.S.O. in 1915 (with bar, 1918) and the C.M.G. in 1918; and in 1919 he was promoted major-general. From 1919 to 1920 he was chief of the general staff of the overseas military forces of Canada; and from 1920 to 1928 he was chief of the general staff at Ottawa. In 1931 he was appointed commissioner of the Royal Canadian Mounted Police; and he held this post until his death at Toronto, Ontario, on March 5, 1938. He was created a K.C.B. in 1935.

[*Can. who's who*, 1936-37; *Can. parl. comp.*]

MacCabe, John Alexander (1842-1902), educationist, was born in county Cavan, Ireland, on January 9, 1842, and was educated at the Catholic University of Ireland, Dublin. He came to Canada in 1869 as a master at the Normal School, Truro, Nova Scotia; and in 1875 he was appointed principal of the Normal School, Ottawa, Ontario. He died at Ottawa on November 30, 1902. He was the author of *An English grammar for the use of schools* (Halifax, N.S., 1873).

[Morgan, *Can. men* (1898); R. J. Long, *Nova Scotia authors* (East Orange, N.J., 1918).]

McCaig, Donald (1832-1905), poet, was born in Cape Breton, Nova Scotia, on May 15, 1832. He was educated at the Toronto Normal School, and became a school-teacher, and ultimately a public school inspector in the district of Algoma, Ontario. He died at Collingwood, Ontario, on July 28, 1905. He was the author of a volume of poems, *Milestone moods and memories* (Toronto, 1894).

[Morgan, *Can. men* (1898).]

McCallum, Sir Henry Edward (1852-1919), governor of Newfoundland (1898-1901), was born at Yeovil, Somersetshire, England, on October 28, 1852, and died on November 24, 1919. He was educated at the Royal Military Academy, Woolwich, and was commissioned in the Royal Engineers. He became successively governor of Lagos, Newfoundland, and Natal; and he was created a K.C.M.G. in 1898.

[*Annual register*, 1919; *Who was who*, 1916-28; *Encyc. Can.*]

MacCallum, Henry Reid (1897-1949), philosopher, was born in Turkey, of missionary parents, in 1897, and died at Toronto, Ontario, on May 1, 1949. He was educated at Queen's University, Kingston, and at Oxford University; and he did post-graduate work at Harvard University. After teaching for a time at Queen's University, he became a professor of philosophy in the University of Toronto in 1927. After his death, some of his writings were published under the title *Imitation and design, and other essays* (Toronto, 1953), edited by William Blissett.

[Toronto *Globe and Mail*, May 2, 1949.]

McCarroll, James (1815-1896), poet and humorist, was born in Lanesboro, county Longford, Ireland, on August 3, 1815. He came to Canada with his family in 1831, and became a journalist. In 1843 he became editor and proprietor of the Peterborough *Chronicle*, and in 1847 of the *Newcastle Courier* (Cobourg). Later he established a humorous weekly, the *Latchkey*; and in this appeared first his *Letters of Terry Finnegan to the Hon. T. D. McGee* (Toronto, 1864). His poems were collected and published under the title *Madeline and other poems* (Chicago, 1889). He died at Buffalo, New York, in 1896.

[*Cyc. Am. biog.*; Morgan, *Bib. can.*; A. MacMurchy, *Handbook of Canadian literature* (Toronto, 1906).]

McCarthy, D'Alton (1836-1898), lawyer and politician, was born at Oakley Park, Blackrock, near Dublin, Ireland, on October 10, 1836, the son of D'Alton McCarthy and Charleszina Hope Manners. He came to Canada with his parents in 1847, and was educated at the grammar school in Barrie, Canada West. In 1858 he was called to the bar of Upper Canada (Q.C., 1872), and he won a high reputation as a barrister. In 1876 he was returned to the Canadian House of Commons as a Conservative for the constituency of Cardwell; in the general elections of 1878 he was returned to North Simcoe, and this constituency he represented continuously until his death. For many years he occupied a high place in the councils of the Conservative party; but in 1889 he broke with his party on the issue of the Jesuits' Estates Act, and placed himself at the head of the "Equal Rights" movement. Henceforward he sat in parliament as an independent, and he gave a partial support to the Laurier government formed in 1896. He died at Toronto on May 11, 1898. He was twice married, (1) to Emma Catharine (d. 1890), daughter of E. G. Lally, and (2) to her sister, Agnes Elizabeth, widow of R. B. Bernard.

[Amicus (pseud.), *The late D'Alton McCarthy* (Can. mag., 1903); Taché, *Men of the day*; Rose, *Cyc. Can. biog.* (1886); Morgan, *Can. men* (1898); *Can. parl. comp.*; Sir J. Pope (ed.), *The correspondence of Sir John Macdonald* (Toronto, 1921); Sir J. Willison, *Sir Wilfrid Laurier and the Liberal party* (2 vols., Toronto, 1903); J. Castell Hopkins, *The life and work of the Rt. Hon. Sir John Thompson* (Brantford, Ont., 1895); Toronto *Globe*, May 12, 1898.]

McCarthy, D'Alton Lally (1870-1963), lawyer, was born at Barrie, Ontario, December 5, 1870, and was educated in Canada and Scotland, graduating from Trinity College, Toronto (B.A., 1892). He was called to the bar of Ontario in 1895, and joined his father's firm. Later he became Toronto counsel for the Grand Trunk Railway. In 1920 he was the Ontario government prosecutor in the Home Bank case. He was a bencher of the Upper Canada Law Society and its treasurer (1939-44). He was a past president of the Canadian Bar Association. He played polo and rode to the hounds until he was seventy-five. He died at Toronto, Ontario, September 3, 1963.

[*Can. who's who*, 1955-57; Metropolitan Toronto Library Board, *Biographical scrapbooks*, vol. 21.]

McCarthy, Edward Joseph (1850-1931), Roman Catholic archbishop of Halifax, was born at Halifax, Nova Scotia, on January 25, 1850, the son of Patrick McCarthy. He was educated at Halifax and Montreal, and was ordained a priest in 1874. After serving as parish priest in various parts of the Maritime provinces, he was appointed archbishop of Halifax in 1906, and he retained this position until his death at Halifax on January 26, 1931.

[*Can. who was who*, vol. 1.]

MacCarthy, Hamilton Thomas Carleton Plantagenet (1847-1939), sculptor, was born in London, England, in 1847, the son of Hamilton Wright MacCarthy, a noted English sculptor. He studied art in his father's studio, and on the continent of Europe; and in 1885 he came to Canada. He had a studio first in Toronto, and then in Ottawa; and he was for many years in great demand as a sculptor of busts of public men and a designer of public monuments. He was elected a member of the Royal Canadian Academy of Arts in 1886; and he remained an active member until 1916. He died at Ottawa, Ontario, on October 24, 1939.

[*Can. who's who*, 1936-37; Morgan, *Can. men* (1912); W. Colgate, *Canadian art* (Toronto, 1943); N. MacTavish, *The fine arts in Canada* (Toronto, 1925).]

McCarthy, Justin (1786-1832), lawyer and author, was born at Montmagny, Quebec, on April 7, 1786; and was admitted to the bar of Lower Canada in 1812. While still a law student, he published a *Dictionnaire de l'ancien droit du Canada* (Quebec, 1809). In 1820 he announced the forthcoming publication of a *Dictionnaire des lois du Canada*; but this work never appeared. He died at Quebec in June, 1832.

[P. G. Roy, *Les avocats de la région de Québec* (Lévis, Que., 1936); Morgan, *Bib. can.*]

McCarthy, Leighton Goldie (1869-1952), lawyer and diplomat, was born at Walkerton, Ontario, on December 15, 1869, and died at his summer home, Longuissa, on Georgian Bay, on October 3, 1952. He read law in Barrie, Ontario, was called to the bar in 1892 (K.C., 1902), and became an outstanding lawyer in Toronto. He represented North Simcoe as a Liberal in the Canadian House of Commons from 1898 to 1908. He was a personal friend of President Roosevelt, and in 1941 the Mackenzie King government appointed him Canadian minister to the United States. In 1943 he was promoted to the rank of ambassador, being the first Canadian ambassador. He retired in 1945, at the end of the Second World War.

[*Can. who was who*, 1948; *Can. who's who*, 1949-51; *Encyc. Can.*]

McCarthy, Pearl (1895-1964), art critic, was born in Toronto, Ontario, in 1895 and educated at the University of Toronto (B.A., 1917), and at Oxford University (B. Litt., 1927). She married Colin Sabiston in 1937. She became art critic for the Toronto *Globe and Mail* in 1937 after a career as a reporter with the Montreal *Gazette* and the *Mail and Empire* of Toronto. She was a friend and champion of the Group of Seven but her interest reached out to European and Eskimo art. She wrote *Leo Smith: A biographical sketch* (1956) and collaborated in a number of other books. She died March 25, 1964, at Toronto.

[*Can. who's who*, 1961-63; Metropolitan Toronto Library Board, *Biographical scrapbooks*, vol. 22; V. B. Rhodenizer, *Canadian literature in English* (Montreal, 1965).]

McCarty, Charles Justin (d. 1790), Methodist martyr, was a local preacher in the United Empire Loyalist settlements about the Bay of Quinte. He was arraigned before the court of quarter sessions in Kingston in 1790 as a "vagabond, imposture, and disturber of the peace". He was ordered to leave the district, but returned, and was arrested and confined to jail until he could be sent across the American border. While being deported, he disappeared; and it was conjectured that he died, either by foul means, or by misadventure.

[C. B. Sissons, *The martyrdom of McCarty*

(Canadian journal of religious thought, 1927).]

McCaul, John (1807-1886), president of University College, Toronto (1853-80), was born in Dublin, Ireland, on March 7, 1807. He was educated at Trinity College, Dublin (B.A., 1824; M.A., 1828; LL.D., 1835), and from 1828 to 1838 he was a university examiner in classics. In 1833 he was admitted to holy orders in the Church of Ireland; but most of his time was given during this period to classical scholarship. In 1839 he was appointed principal of Upper Canada College, Toronto; and in 1842 professor of classics and vice-president of King's College (University of Toronto). In 1849 he became president of King's College; and in 1853 president of the reorganized University College. He held this position until age compelled his retirement in 1880; and he died at Toronto on April 16, 1886. In 1839 he married Emily, daughter of the Hon. Jonas Jones (q.v.); and by her he had three sons and four daughters. Most of his publications dealt with Greek and Roman literature and epigraphy; and notable among them were his *Britanno-Roman inscriptions* (Toronto, 1863), and *Christian epitaphs of the first six centuries* (Toronto, 1869). He was a frequent contributor to the periodicals of his day, and he was the editor of the *Maple Leaf*, a pioneer Canadian literary annual.
    [J. King, *McCaul: Croft: Forneri* (Toronto, 1914); *Cyc. Am. biog.*; Rose, *Cyc. Can. biog.* (1888); Morgan, *Bib. can.*; W. S. Wallace, *A history of the University of Toronto* (Toronto, 1927).]

McCawley, George (1802-1878), president of King's College, Nova Scotia, was born at St. John's, Newfoundland, in 1802. He was educated at King's College, Nova Scotia (B.A., 1821; M.A., 1824; D.D., 1835), and from 1822 to 1828 was headmaster of the grammar school at Fredericton, New Brunswick. In 1826 he was ordained a priest of the Church of England; and in 1828 he was appointed professor of mathematics, Hebrew, and logic in the University of New Brunswick. In 1835 he became president of King's College, Windsor, Nova Scotia; and he retained this position until 1875. He died at Halifax, Nova Scotia, on December 21, 1878.
    [*Dict. Can. biog.*, vol. 10; *Dom. ann. reg.*, 1878.]

McCharles, Aeneas (1844-1906), mining pioneer, was born at Middle River, Cape Breton, Nova Scotia, on October 17, 1844. He became a mining prospector in the Algoma district of Ontario, and was the discoverer of the North Star mine. He died at Sudbury, Ontario, on August 5, 1906. Under the terms of his will, his executors published his autobiography, entitled *Bemocked of destiny* (Toronto, 1908).
    [*Can. ann. rev.*, 1906.]

McClelan, Abner Reid (1831-1917), lieutenant-governor of New Brunswick (1896-1902), was born at Hopewell, New Brunswick, on January 4, 1831, the son of Peter McClelan. He was educated at Hopewell Academy and at Mount Allison Academy, and became a successful merchant. From 1854 to 1867 he sat for Albert in the New Brunswick Legislative Assembly; and from 1866 to 1867 he was chief commissioner of public works in the Mitchell government. He was one of the chief supporters of Confederation in New Brunswick; and in 1867 he was called to the Senate of Canada by royal proclamation. In 1896 he was appointed lieutenant-governor of New Brunswick, and he held this position until 1902. He then retired to private life, and died at Moncton, New Brunswick, on January 30, 1917. He was a D.C.L. of Mount Allison University (1898) and an LL.D. of the University of New Brunswick (1900). In 1876 he married Anna, daughter of William J. Reid, of Harvey, New Brunswick.
    [*Can. parl. comp.*; Morgan, *Can. men* (1912); Rose, *Cyc. Can. biog.* (1888).]

McClelland, John (1877-1968), publisher, was born in Glasgow, Scotland, March 10, 1877. He was educated in Toronto, and at the age of thirteen left school to work in the Methodist Book Room. He opened his own shop on King Street, April 6, 1906, and later became a publisher in his own right. He was chairman of the Toronto Board of Education in 1921-22. His firm launched many Canadian writers, and one autumn published thirty-five different new Canadian books. John McClelland died at Toronto, Ontario, May 7, 1968.
    [*Can. who's who*, 1955-57; Toronto *Saturday Night*, May, 1956.]

McClung, Mrs. Nellie Letitia, *née* **Mooney** (1873-1951), author and feminist, was born at Chatsworth, Ontario, on October 20, 1873, and died at Victoria, British Columbia, on September 1, 1951. She moved with her parents to Manitoba when a child, was educated at the Winnipeg Normal School, and became a school-teacher. She married Robert Wesley McClung, a Manitoba druggist, in 1898, and she brought up a family of five children. Her first novel, *Sowing seeds in Danny* (New York, 1908), proved a great success, and was followed by *The second chance* (New York, 1910), *The Black Creek stopping-house and other stories* (Toronto, 1912), *Purple springs* (Toronto, 1921), *When Christmas crossed the Peace* (Toronto, 1923), *The beauty of Martha* (London, 1923), *Painted fires* (New York, 1925), *All we like sheep, and other stories* (Toronto, 1926), *Be good to yourself* (Toronto, 1930), *Flowers for the living* (Toronto, 1931), *Leaves from Lantern Lane* (Toronto, 1936), and *More leaves from Lantern Lane* (Toronto, 1937). She also published two volumes of essays and addresses: *In times like these* (New

York, 1913) and *The next of kin* (Boston, 1917); and two books of an autobiographical nature: *Clearing in the West* (Toronto, 1935) and *The stream runs fast* (Toronto, 1945). She became a champion of women's rights, and she sat in the Alberta legislature as a Liberal for Edmonton from 1921 to 1926.

[Clara Thomas, *Canadian novelists* (Toronto, 1940); E. McCourt, *The Canadian West in fiction* (Toronto, 1949); *Can. who's who*, 1948; *Encyc. Can.*]

MacColl, Evan (1808-1898), poet, was born at Kenmore, Lochfyneside, Scotland, on September 21, 1808. His family came to Canada in 1831, but he did not follow them until 1850. He became a customs officer at Kingston, Upper Canada, and held this position until he retired on pension. Before coming to Canada he published *Clàrsach nam beann; or, Poems and songs in Gaelic* (Glasgow, 1838), and *The mountain minstrel; or, Poems and songs in English* (Glasgow, 1838). In Canada, he published *Poems and songs, chiefly written in Canada* (Toronto, 1883; new and enlarged ed., Kingston, Ontario, 1888). In 1883 he was selected as one of the charter members of the Royal Society of Canada; and for many years he was the bard of the St. Andrew's Society in Kingston. He died in Toronto on July 25, 1898.

[A. Mackenzie, "A biographical sketch", in *Poems and songs* (2nd ed., Kingston, 1888); *Cyc. Am. biog.*; Morgan, *Can. men* (1898); Rose, *Cyc. Can. biog.* (1888); A. MacMurchy, *Handbook of Canadian literature* (Toronto, 1906); bibliography in *Proc. Roy. Soc. Can.*, 1894).]

McConachie, George William Grant (1909-1965), airline president, was born in Hamilton, Ontario, April 24, 1909. He was educated at the University of Alberta. He began flying with Independent Airways in 1930 and in 1931 became president of the company. He formed his own company, United Air Transport, in 1934, and in 1937 formed Yukon Southern Airways and was president from 1937 to 1941. During the Second World War he was involved in the air training program as manager of the Portage La Prairie observer school but was also supervising the opening of a northwest route to supply planes to Russia via Siberia. He became general manager of Canadian Pacific Airlines on its formation in 1942 as a result of the amalgamation of a number of smaller lines, and president in 1947. He guided it to the status of a world airline. He won the McKee aviation trophy in 1945 for outstanding contribution to aviation in Canada. He died in California, June 29, 1965.

[*Can. who's who*, 1961-63; *Canadian Aviation*, vol. 38 (August, 1965); Metropolitan Toronto Library Board, *Biographical scrapbooks*, vol. 71.]

McConnell, George Newton (1894-1962) farmer, was born at McConnell, Manitoba, 1894. He was educated in Manitoba public schools and at the University of Manitoba (B.S.A., 1912). He began farming after graduation and raised grain and Aberdeen Angus cattle. For over forty years he was involved in farm organization and farmers' movements in the province of Manitoba. He was a member of the Board of Grain Commissioners for Canada; vice-president of Manitoba Pool Elevators; director of the Canadian Co-operative Wheat Producers, and of the Pool Insurance Co. He was a delegate to the International Federation of Agricultural Producers, Paris, France, 1948. He became chief commissioner of the Board of Grain Commissioners of Canada in 1961. He died at Winnipeg on November 21, 1962.

[*Can. who's who*, 1961-63).]

McConnell, Richard George (1857-1942), geologist and explorer, was born at Chatham, Canada East, on March 26, 1857, and was educated at McGill University (B.A., 1879). In 1880 he joined the staff of the Geological Survey of Canada; and until his appointment as deputy minister of mines at Ottawa in 1914, he was engaged in the exploration of the Canadian north-west. In 1887-88 he made one of the longest exploratory trips on record in the Geological Survey, travelling from Wrangell in Alaska, by way of Telegraph Creek, Dease River, and Liard River to the delta of the Mackenzie, and returning by way of the Porcupine and Yukon rivers to Skagway — incidentally demonstrating the fact that the Rocky Mountain system ended at latitude 60° north. He retired from the civil service of Canada in 1921; and he died at Ottawa, Ontario, on April 1, 1942. In 1913 he was elected a fellow of the Royal Society of Canada.

[*Proc. Roy. Soc. Can.*, 1942; *Can. who's who*, 1936-37).]

McCord, David Ross (1844-1930), founder of the McCord National Museum, was born in Montreal on March 18, 1844, the son of the Hon. John Samuel McCord and Anne, daughter of David Ross, Q.C. He was educated at McGill University (B.A., 1863; M.A., 1867; B.C.L., 1867); and he was called to the bar of Lower Canada in 1868 (Q.C., 1895). He was an enthusiastic collector of everything of interest to the student of Canadian history; and in 1919 he presented his valuable collection of material to McGill University, with the result that the McCord National Museum was opened to the public in 1921. He died on April 12, 1930; and was the last of his branch of the McCord family in Montreal.

[P. G. Roy, *Les avocats de la région de Québec* (Lévis, Que., 1936).]

McCord, Frederick Augustus (1856-1908), author, was born in Aylmer, Quebec, in

1856, the son of the Hon. Thomas McCord. He was educated at Laval University, Montreal (LL.B., 1852), and was called to the Quebec bar in 1884. In 1887 he became assistant law clerk of the House of Commons, and in 1890 law clerk. He died at Ottawa on July 23, 1908. He was the author of *Errors in Canadian history* (Montreal, 1880) and *Handbook of Canadian dates* (Montreal, 1888).

[Morgan, *Can. men* (1898); P. G. Roy, *Les avocats de la région de Québec* (Lévis, Que., 1936).]

McCord, Thomas (1828-1886), judge and author, was born in Montreal, Lower Canada, on October 17, 1828, the son of the Hon. William King McCord. He was educated at McGill College, and was called to the bar in 1850. In 1873 he was appointed a puisne judge of the Superior Court of Quebec; and he died at Quebec on February 19, 1886. He was the author of *A synopsis of the changes in the law effected by the Civil Code of Lower Canada* (Ottawa, 1866), and he issued three successive annotated editions of the *Civil Code of Lower Canada* (Montreal, 1867, 1870, and 1880).

[P. G. Roy, *Les juges de la province de Québec* (Quebec, 1933).]

McCorkill, Charles Joseph Sarsfield (1854-1920), jurist, was born at Farnham, Canada East, on August 31, 1854. He was educated at McGill University (B.C.L., 1877), and was called to the bar of Quebec in 1878 (Q.C., 1899). He practised law, first in Montreal, and then in Cowansville, Quebec. From 1897 to 1898 he was a member of the Legislative Assembly of Quebec, and from 1898 to 1906 a member of the Legislative Council; and from 1903 to 1906 he was provincial treasurer in the Parent and Gouin administrations. In 1906 he was appointed a judge of the Superior Court for the district of Quebec. He retired from the bench in 1918, and he died at Quebec City on March 10, 1920.

[P. G. Roy, *Les juges de la province de Québec* (Quebec, 1933); *Can. parl. comp.*; Morgan, *Can. men* (1912).]

MacCormac, John Patrick (1895-1958), journalist, was born in Ottawa, Ontario, in 1895, and died in Norway, while on holiday, in July 1958. He served in the Canadian artillery during the First World War, and was awarded the M.C. In 1924 he joined the staff of the *New York Times*, and was a correspondent for this paper at Ottawa from 1933 to 1939. He was the author of *Canada: America's problem* (New York, 1940), *America and world mastery* (New York, 1942), and *This time for keeps* (New York, 1943).

[*New York Times*, July 7, 1958.]

McCormick, Charles (d. 1790), fur-trader, was one of the early English "pedlars" on the Saskatchewan. E. M. Chadwick *(Ontarian*

families, 1, 120) identifies him with the Lieut. McCormick who was with Major Robert Rogers (q.v.) when he took possession of the western posts in 1760; but this is doubtful. William Tomison, the Hudson's Bay officer at Cumberland House, described him, on March 15, 1779, as "going about sword in hand threatening the natives to make them trade with him"; and he was not included in the North West partnership of 1779. He died at St. Laurent, near Montreal, in 1790, and his will, which is preserved in the Court House at Montreal, and is in French, describes him as "cydevant marchand". In October 1779, he married in Christ Church, Montreal, Marguerite (d. 1854), daughter of John Peter Arnoldi of Montreal; and by her he had two sons, the elder of whom, John Johnson Dease, died young, and the second of whom, Thomas, became for many years manager of the Bank of Upper Canada at Niagara. Sir John Johnson (q.v.), was named tutor of his son, in case his wife remarried.

[E. M. Chadwick, *Ontarian families,* vol. 1 (Toronto, 1894).]

McCourt, Edward Alexander (1907-1972), novelist and teacher, was born in Westmeath, Ireland, October 10, 1907. He came to Canada in 1909, attended primary schools in rural Alberta, completed his high school education by means of correspondence courses, enrolled at the University of Alberta (B.A., 1932), and then went to Merton College, Oxford, as the Alberta Rhodes scholar for 1932. He taught at Ridley College (Ontario) in 1935-36; at Upper Canada College, 1936-38; at Queen's University, 1938-39; and at the University of New Brunswick, 1939-44, before becoming professor of English at the University of Saskatchewan in 1944, a position which he held until his death in 1972. McCourt won the All Canada Fiction Award for *Music at the close* (1947). He also wrote *The flaming hour* (1947); *Home is the stranger* (1950); *Buckskin brigadier,* the story of the Alberta field force (1955); *The wooden sword* (1956); *Revolt in the west: The story of the Riel Rebellion* (1958); *Walk through the valley* (1958); *Fasting friar* (1963); *The road across Canada* (1965); *Remember Butler: The story of William Butler* (1967); *Saskatchewan* (1968); and *The Yukon and Northwest Territories* (1969). He died January 6, 1972, at Saskatoon, Saskatchewan.

[*Can. who's who,* 1955-57; *Creative Canada* vol. 2; W. Toye, *Supplement to the Oxford companion to Canadian history and literature* (Toronto, 1973).]

McCowan, Daniel (1882-1956), naturalist, was born at Crieff, Scotland, on January 20, 1882, and died at Cloverdale, British Columbia, on February 19, 1956. He was educated in Scotland, but came to Canada when a young man, and became an authority on the flora and fauna of the Canadian Rockies and an expert photographer. He was the author of *Animals of* *the Canadian Rockies* (Toronto, 1936), *A naturalist in Canada* (Toronto, 1941), *Outdoors with a camera in Canada* (Toronto, 1945), *Hill-top tales* (Toronto, 1948), *Tidewater to timberline* (Toronto, 1951), and *Upland trails in Canada* (Toronto, 1955), all illustrated with his own photographs.

[*Encyc. Can.*]

McCrae, John (1872-1918), physician and poet, was born at Guelph, Ontario, on November 30, 1872, the son of Lieut.-Col. David McCrae and Janet Simpson Eckford. He was educated at the University of Toronto (B.A., 1894; M.B., 1898); and in 1900 he was appointed fellow in pathology at McGill University, Montreal, and pathologist to the Montreal General Hospital. Later he was appointed physician to the Alexandra Hospital, Montreal, and assistant physician to the Royal Victoria Hospital. In 1899-1900 he served as an artillery subaltern in the Canadian contingent in the South African War; and in 1914 he enlisted as a medical officer in the First Canadian Contingent in the First World War. In 1915 he was posted to No. 3 General Hospital at Boulogne, as officer in charge of medicine; and there he remained until his death on January 28, 1918, of pneumonia. For many years before the war he contributed occasional verses to the *University Magazine* and other periodicals; and in 1915 he published in *Punch* a poem, entitled "In Flanders Fields", which was perhaps the most famous set of verses written in English during the First World War. His verses were collected and published posthumously under the title *In Flanders fields, and other poems* (Toronto, 1919).

[Sir A. Macphail, "An essay in character", in J. McCrae, *In Flanders fields* (Toronto, 1919); Morgan, *Can. men* (1912); A. E. Byerly, *The McCraes of Guelph* (Elora, Ont., 1932).]

McCreight, John Foster (d. 1913), prime minister of British Columbia (1871-72), was a native of Ireland who came to British Columbia by way of Australia, and began the practice of law in Victoria, Vancouver Island, in 1860. In 1871 he was selected by Joseph Trutch (q.v.), the lieutenant-governor of British Columbia, to head the first provincial administration as prime minister and attorney-general. He resigned at the end of 1872; and from 1880 to 1897 he was a justice of the Supreme Court of British Columbia. After his retirement from the bench, he lived in England; and he died at Hastings, England, on November 18, 1913.

[W. N. Sage, *John Foster McCreight* (Trans. Roy. Soc. Can., 1940).]

McCrimmon, Abraham Lincoln (1865-1935), educationist, was born at Delhi, Canada West, in 1865. He was educated at the University of Toronto (B.A., 1890; M.A., 1891) and at the University of Chicago; and from 1891 to 1904 he was on the staff of Woodstock College. In 1904 he was appointed professor of political economy and sociology in McMaster University; and he was chancellor of McMaster University from 1911 to 1923. He then resumed his former position as professor of sociology; and he died at Hamilton, Ontario, on April 16, 1935. He was the author of *The woman movement* (Philadelphia, 1915).

[*McMaster University monthly*, 1935; Morgan, *Can. men* (1912).]

McCullagh, George Clement (1905-1952), newspaper proprietor, was born at London, Ontario, on March 16, 1905, and died in Toronto, Ontario, on August 5, 1952. After being employed in a bank, he was the assistant financial editor of the Toronto *Globe* from 1921 to 1928. He then entered the employ of a Toronto brokerage firm; and while with them he amassed sufficient capital to enable him, with the assistance of W. H. Wright (q.v.), to buy both the Toronto *Globe* and the Toronto *Mail and Empire*, and to merge them in the *Globe and Mail*, of which he became president in 1936. In 1949 he bought also the Toronto *Telegram*.

[Toronto *Globe and Mail*, Aug. 6, 1952; Pierre Berton, *The amazing career of George McCullagh* (Maclean's, Jan. 15, 1949); B. J. Young, *C. George McCullagh and the Leadership League* (Can. hist. rev., 1966); *Can. who's who*, 1948; *Encyc. Can.*]

McCulloch, Robert Osborne (1864-1943), industrialist, was born at Galt, Canada West, on April 2, 1864. He was educated at the University of Toronto (B.A., 1885) and at the Osgoode Hall Law School, and was called to the bar of Ontario in 1888. He retired from the practice of law in 1898, and became secretary-treasurer of the firm of Goldie and McCulloch in Galt, Ontario. In 1917 he became president of this company, and in 1931 chairman of the board. He died at Galt, Ontario, on May 5, 1943. In his younger days he was a cricket player of some note; and he was joint author, with John E. Hall, of *Sixty years of Canadian cricket* (Toronto, 1895).

[*Can. who's who*, 1936-37; Morgan, *Can. men* (1912).]

McCulloch, Thomas (1777-1843), clergyman and educationist, was born in the parish of Neilston, Renfrewshire, Scotland, in 1777. He was educated at Glasgow University, and became a minister of the Presbyterian Church. In 1803 he emigrated to Nova Scotia, and became pastor of the Presbyterian Church at Pictou. He was foremost in the establishment of Pictou Academy, the first non-sectarian school for higher education in Nova Scotia, and became its first president. In 1838 he became the first principal of Dalhousie College in Halifax; and he died at Halifax in 1843. In addition to a number of theological works, he was the author of *Colonial gleanings* (Edinburgh, 1826) and the *Letters of Mephibosheth Stepsure*, reprinted from the *Acadian Recorder* of 1821-22 (Halifax, 1860).

[Rev. W. McCulloch, *The life of Dr. McCulloch* (Truro, Nova Scotia, 1920); F. C. MacIntosh, *Some Nova Scotian scientists* (Dalhousie review, 1930); R. G. Riddell (ed.), *Canadian portraits* (Toronto, 1940); Morgan, *Bib. can.*]

McCullough, Charles Robert (1865-1947), educationist, was born at Bowmanville, Canada West, on February 18, 1865, and died at Hamilton, Ontario, on April 2, 1947. From 1888 to 1902 he was principal of the Hamilton Business College; and in his later years he was managing director of the Hamilton Conservatory of Music. In 1892 he founded in Hamilton the first Canadian Club, and was its president until 1910. For many years he was a regular contributor to the Hamilton *Spectator*.

[Nina L. Edwards, *The story of the first Canadian Club* (Hamilton, 1953); *Can. who's who*, 1936-37; *Encyc. Can.*]

McCully, Jonathan (1809-1877), one of the Fathers of Confederation, was born in Cumberland county, Nova Scotia, in 1809. He became a school-teacher in Cumberland county, and Charles Tupper (q.v.) was one of his pupils. In 1837 he was called to the bar of Nova Scotia, and entered on the practice of law at Amherst, Nova Scotia. In 1847 he was appointed a member of the Legislative Council of Nova Scotia; and from 1860 to 1862 he was solicitor-general and chief commissioner for railways, as well as government leader in the Upper House. In 1849 he moved to Halifax, and there he drifted into journalism. From 1857 to 1865 he edited William Annand's *Morning Chronicle and Nova Scotian*; and in it he advocated the union of the British North American provinces. In 1865 he was replaced as editor by Joseph Howe (q.v.), and he then became editor of the *Morning Journal*, which he renamed the *Unionist*, and in which he continued to advocate Confederation. In 1864 he was a delegate to the Charlottetown and Quebec conferences; and in 1866 he was a delegate to the final conference at Westminster. In 1867 he was called to the Senate of Canada; and in 1870 he was made a puisne judge of the Supreme Court of Nova Scotia. This post he held until his death at Halifax on January 2, 1877. He was the author of a pamphlet entitled *British America: Arguments against a union of the provinces reviewed* (London, 1867).

[N. H. Meagher, *Life of the Hon. Jonathan McCully* (Coll. Nova Scotia Hist. Soc., 1927); *Cyc. Am biog.*; *Can. parl. comp.*; Morgan, *Bib. can.*; E. M. Saunders, *Three premiers of Nova Scotia* (Toronto, 1909); *Dict. Can. biog.*, vol. 10.]

McCully, Laura Elizabeth (1886-1924), poet, was born in Toronto, Ontario, on March 17, 1886, the daughter of S. E. McCully, M.D. She was educated at the University of Toronto (B.A., 1907; M.A., 1909), and became a poet and journalist. She died at Toronto on July 8, 1924. She published *Mary Magdalene and other poems* (Toronto, 1914).

[Morgan, *Can. men and women* (1912); *Can. who was who*, vol. 1.]

McCurdy, James Frederick (1847-1935), orientalist, was born at Chatham, New Brunswick, on February 18, 1847. He was educated at the University of New Brunswick (B.A., 1866; LL.D., 1894) and at the Princeton Theological Seminary (Ph.D., 1878). From 1873 to 1882 he was assistant professor of Oriental languages at Princeton University; in 1886 he became lecturer in Oriental languages, and in 1888 professor at the University of Toronto; and he retired from this post only in 1913. He died at Toronto, on March 31, 1935. He was the author of *Argosemitic speech* (Andover, 1881), *History, prophecy, and the monuments* (3 vols., New York, 1894-1901), and *Life and work of D. J. Macdonnell* (Toronto, 1897).

[*University of Toronto monthly*, 1935; Morgan, *Can. men* (1912); *Can. who was who*, vol. 2.]

McCurdy, John Alexander Douglas (1886-1961), air pioneer, was born at Baddeck, Nova Scotia, on August 2, 1886. He was educated at the University of Toronto (M.E.), and at Nova Scotia Technical College (D. Eng.). He worked with Dr. Alexander Graham Bell (q.v.) and made the first airplane flight in the British Empire at Baddeck Bay, Nova Scotia, in 1909 in the *Silver Dart*, an aircraft of his own design. He was associated with Dr. Bell, Glen Curtiss, Thomas Selfridge, and F. W. "Casey" Baldwin in the Aerial Experiment Association, Halifax, in 1907. During the Second World War he served as assistant director-general of aircraft production in the Department of Munitions and Supply. He was lieutenant-governor of Nova Scotia (1947-52). He died at Montreal on June 25, 1961.

[*Can. who's who*, 1955-57.]

McCurry, Harry Orr (1889-1964), art gallery director, was born in Ottawa, Ontario, August 21, 1889. He was educated in Ottawa. He became associated with the National Gallery of Canada in 1922, becoming assistant director and secretary in 1927. From 1939 to 1955 he was director of the Gallery. He directed the Gallery during a period of rapid growth; and besides writing extensively on art he encouraged travelling exhibits of Gallery works throughout Canada. During the First World War he served in the Canadian army. He was a past president of the Canadian Museums' Association, and a director of the

National Film Society of Canada. He died at Ottawa, Ontario, May 14, 1964.

[*Can. who's who*, 1961-63.]

MacDermot, Terence William Leighton (1896-1966), diplomat and educator, was born in Jamaica in 1896, and educated in Montreal at Montreal High School and McGill University, where he was Rhodes scholar (Oxford, B.A., M.A., 1922). He began teaching at Lower Canada College, Montreal, in 1923 and became assistant professor of history at McGill University in 1935. He was principal of Upper Canada College from 1935 to 1942. He was on active service in the Second World War (1942-44). In 1944 he joined the department of external affairs and was loaned to the United Nations in 1946 for special organizational duties. He was Canadian High Commissioner to South Africa from 1950 to 1954 and ambassador to Greece and Israel from 1954 to 1957. He then became High Commissioner to Australia, a post which he relinquished on retirement in 1961. He joined the staff of Bishop's University in 1961 as associate professor and head of the department of political science. He died at Sherbrooke, Quebec, on January 28, 1966.

[*Can. who's who*, 1961-63; Metropolitan Toronto Library Board, *Biographical scrapbooks*, vol. 26.]

Macdonald, Andrew Archibald (1829-1912), lieutenant-governor of Prince Edward Island (1884-89), was born at Three Rivers, Prince Edward Island, on February 14, 1829, the son of Hugh Macdonald. He was educated at the county grammar school, and became a merchant and shipowner. He was a member of the Legislative Assembly of the Island from 1853 to 1858, and in 1863 he was elected to the Legislative Council. He was a delegate from Prince Edward Island to the Quebec Conference of 1864; and from 1867 to 1872 he was a member of the Executive Council of Prince Edward Island. On the inclusion of the Island in the Dominion in 1873, he became postmaster-general in the provincial cabinet; and he retained this portfolio until his appointment as lieutenant-governor of the province in 1884, an appointment which he held until 1889. In 1891 he was called to the Senate of Canada, and his seat in the Senate he retained until his death at Ottawa on March 21, 1912. In 1863 he married Elizabeth, third daughter of the Hon. Thomas Owen; and by her he had four sons. An account of the Quebec Conference, drawn up by him from notes taken at the time, is printed in the *Canadian Historical Review*, vol. i (1920).

[*Cyc. Am. biog.*; Morgan, *Can. men* (1912); Rose, *Cyc. Can. biog.* (1888).]

Macdonald, Angus Lewis (1890-1954), prime minister of Nova Scotia (1933-40 and 1945-54), was born at Dunvegan, Inverness county, Nova Scotia, on August 10, 1890, and died at Halifax, Nova Scotia, on April 13, 1954. He was educated at St. Francis Xavier University (B.A., 1914), Dalhousie University (LL.B., 1921), and Columbia and Harvard universities (S.J.D., 1929); and was called to the bar in Nova Scotia in 1921 (K.C., 1936). He was a member of the staff of the Dalhousie Law School from 1922 to 1929; then in 1930 he was elected leader of the Liberal party in Nova Scotia. In 1933 he was elected to represent Halifax South in the legislature, and became prime minister. In 1940, at the request of the Canadian prime minister, Mackenzie King (q.v.), he resigned, to become minister of national defence for naval services in the Canadian government. He discharged the duties of this portfolio with great success until the end of the Second World War, when he resumed his position as prime minister of Nova Scotia, and continued as such until overwork brought about his sudden death. His *Speeches*, with a biographical note by T. A. Crerar, were published after his death (Toronto, 1960).

[*Can. who's who*, 1952-54; *Can. parl. guide*, 1953; *Encyc. Can.*]

McDonald, Archibald (1790-1853), furtrader, was born at Leechkentium Glenco Appin, Argyllshire, Scotland, on February 3, 1790, and came out to the Red River in 1813, in charge of a party of Lord Selkirk's colonists. He was deputy governor of the Red River Settlement under Miles Macdonell (q.v.). He wrote a *Narrative respecting the destruction of the Earl of Selkirk's settlement upon the Red River in 1815* (Montreal, 1816), and a *Reply to the letter recently addressed to the Earl of Selkirk by the Hon. and Rev. J. Strachan* (Montreal, 1816). After the Red River troubles, he entered the service of the Hudson's Bay Company; and shortly after the union of the Hudson's Bay and North West companies in 1821, he was sent to the Columbia. In 1828 he accompanied Governor Simpson (q.v.) on a journey from York Factory to the Columbia; and his diary of this journey has been published by Malcolm McLeod, under the title *Peace River* (Ottawa, 1872). He was promoted to the rank of chief trader in 1828; and from 1828 to 1833 he was in charge at Fort Langley. From 1834 to 1844 he was in charge at Fort Colvile; and in 1842 he was made a chief factor. When he retired from the Company's service, he settled at St. Andrew's, Lower Canada; and here he died on January 15, 1853. In 1823 he married a daughter of Chief Comcomly, of the Chinook tribe; and by her he had one son, Ranald McDonald, whose reminiscences have been edited by W. S. Lewis and N. Murakami, under the title *Ranald MacDonald* (Spokane, Wash., 1923).

[W. S. Lewis, *Archibald McDonald* (Washington historical quarterly, 1915); E. E. Rich (ed.), *Journal of occurrences in the Athabasca country, by George Simpson* (Toronto: The Champlain Society, 1938).]

Macdonald, Augustine Colin (1837-1919), lieutenant-governor of Prince Edward Island (1915-19), was born at Panmure, Prince Edward Island, on June 30, 1837, the son of Hugh Macdonald and brother of Andrew Archibald Macdonald (q.v.). He was educated at the Central Academy, Charlottetown, and became a merchant. In 1870 he was elected to the Legislative Assembly of Prince Edward Island for the third electoral district of King's county; and in 1873, on the inclusion of the Island in the Dominion, he was elected to the Canadian House of Commons as a Liberal-Conservative. He was defeated in 1874, but was re-elected in 1878, and he continued to sit for King's county in the Commons, with the exception of the years 1887-91, until 1896. In 1915 he was appointed lieutenant-governor of Prince Edward Island; and he died in office on July 16, 1919. In 1865 he married Mary Elizabeth, sixth daughter of the Hon. John Small Macdonald; and by her he had a family of seven children.
[*Can. parl. comp.*; Rose, *Cyc. Can. biog.* (1888).]

Macdonald, Charles (1828?-1901), educationist, was born in Aberdeen, Scotland, about 1828, and was educated at Aberdeen University (B.A., 1850). He was licensed to be a minister of the Presbyterian Church in 1856; but he became a teacher rather than a preacher, and taught for several years in the Aberdeen grammar school. In 1863 he came to America as professor of mathematics in Dalhousie University, Halifax, Nova Scotia; and he occupied this post until his death at Halifax on March 11, 1901.
[J. W. Logan, *Charles Macdonald* (Dalhousie review, 1942).]

MacDonald, David Keith Chalmers (1920-1963), was born in Glasgow, Scotland, in 1920 and was educated in Glasgow and Edinburgh. He entered Edinburgh University in 1937 and was granted his M.A. degree in 1941. After service with the army in the Military College of Science he returned to Edinburgh, receiving his Ph.D. in 1946. He then spent some time at Oxford University. He joined the National Research Council of Canada in 1951. He was one of the world's foremost physicists in the low temperature and solid state field, and became head of the division of pure physics. Crippled by muscular dystrophy, he was able to carry on his work with increasing difficulty until a week before his death. He was awarded the Gold Medal of the Canadian Association of Physicists in 1960. He was a fellow of the Royal Society (London); of the Royal Society (Edinburgh); and of the Royal Society of Canada. He was a good teacher and was able to explain physics in popular terms on television and radio, and in films. He died at Ottawa, Ontario, July 28, 1963.
[*Proc. and Trans. Roy. Soc. Can.*, 1964; Metropolitan Toronto Library Board, *Biographical scrapbooks*, vol. 21.]

McDonald, Donald (1783-1867), clergyman, was born in Perthshire, Scotland, in 1783. He was educated at St. Andrew's University, and was ordained a minister of the Presbyterian Church. He emigrated to America in 1824; and for forty years he was a minister in Prince Edward Island. He died at Southport, Prince Edward Island, in 1867. He was the author of *Spiritual hymns* (Charlottetown, P.E.I., 1835; new ed., 1840), *A treatise on baptism* (Charlottetown, P.E.I., 1845), *The subjects of the millennium* (Charlottetown, P.E.I., 1849), and *The plan of salvation* (Charlottetown, P.E.I., 1874).
[M. Lamont, *Life of Rev. D. McDonald* (Charlottetown, P.E.I., 1902); R. J. Long, *Nova Scotia authors* (East Orange, N.J., 1918).]

McDonald, Donald (1816-1879), senator of Canada, was born in Caledonia, New York, in 1816, the son of Alexander McDonald, a native of Inverness-shire, Scotland. He came with his parents to Canada in 1823, and was educated at Upper Canada College, Toronto. He became a civil engineer and surveyor, in the service of the Canada Company, and many of the early maps of the western part of Upper Canada were prepared by him. In 1858 he was elected to represent the Tecumseh division of Upper Canada in the Liberal interest; and in 1867 he was called by royal proclamation to the Senate of Canada. He died at Toronto, Ontario, on January 20, 1879.
[*Cyc. Am. biog.*; *Dom. ann. reg.*, 1879; *Can. parl. comp.*; *Dict. Can. biog.*, vol. 10.]

Macdonald, Donald Alexander (1817-1896), postmaster-general for Canada (1873-75), and lieutenant-governor of Ontario (1875-80), was born at St. Raphael, Upper Canada, on February 17, 1817, the son of Alexander Macdonald, and the younger brother of John Sandfield Macdonald (q.v.). He was educated at St. Raphael's College; and became a railway contractor. He represented Glengarry in the Legislative Assembly of Canada from 1857 to 1867; and in the Canadian House of Commons from 1867 to 1875. From 1873 to 1875 he was postmaster-general in the Mackenzie administration. In 1875 he resigned to become lieutenant-governor of Ontario; and this position he held until 1880. He then retired from public life, and he died at Montreal on June 10, 1896. He was twice married, (1) in 1843 to Margaret Josephine (d. 1844), eldest daughter of Duncan Macdonell of Cornwall, and (2) to Catherine (d. 1869), second daughter of Colonel the Hon. Alexander Fraser of Fraserfield, Glengarry.
[D. B. Read, *Lives of the lieutenant-governors of Upper Canada and Ontario* (Toronto, 1900); *Canadian biographical dictionary*, Ontario vol. (Toronto, 1880); *Cyc. Am. biog.*; *Can. parl. comp.*]

Macdonald, Sir Donald Alexander (1845-1920), soldier, was born at Cornwall, Upper Canada, on October 31, 1845, the son of Alexander Eugene Macdonald. He was educated at the county high school, and in 1863 was commissioned an ensign in the Canadian militia. He served in the Fenian raid of 1866, in the Red River expedition of 1870, and in the North West Rebellion of 1885. In 1904 he was appointed quartermaster-general of the Canadian militia, and he held this appointment until 1918. He was thus responsible for the equipment of the Canadian forces at the outbreak of the First World War, and during almost the whole of its duration. He was placed on the retired list in 1918, and he died at Ottawa on May 4, 1920. In 1918 he was created a K.C.M.G. for his services during the war. In 1876 he married Mary, second daughter of the Hon. Hugh Richardson; and by her he had one daughter.

[H. Charlesworth (ed.), *A cyclopaedia of Canadian biography* (Toronto, 1919); *Who was who*, 1916-28; *Can. who was who*, vol. 2.]

Macdonald, Edward Mortimer (1865-1940), minister of national defence for Canada (1923-25), was born at Pictou, Nova Scotia, on August 16, 1865. He was educated at Pictou Academy and Dalhousie University (LL.B., 1887), and was called to the bar of Nova Scotia in 1887 (K.C., 1904). He practised law in Pictou; and he sat for Pictou in the Legislative Assembly of Nova Scotia from 1897 to 1904. He represented Pictou in the Canadian House of Commons from 1904 to 1917 and from 1921 to 1925, and Antigonish-Guysboro from 1925 to 1926; and from 1923 to 1925 he was minister of national defence in the first Mackenzie King administration. He retired from political life in 1926; and he died at Pictou, Nova Scotia, on May 25, 1940. He was the author of *Reminiscences, political and personal* (Toronto, 1938).

[*Can. who's who*, 1936-37; *Can. parl. comp.*; Morgan, *Can. men* (1912).]

Macdonald, Mrs. Ewan. See **Montgomery, Lucy Maud.**

McDonald, Finan (1782-1851), fur-trader, was born in Aberdeenshire, Scotland, in 1782, the son of Angus Ban McDonald and Nelly McDonell, and the younger brother of John McDonald le Borgne (q.v.). He entered the service of the North West Company in 1804; and was with David Thompson on the Columbia from 1807 to 1812. In 1813 Ross Cox (q.v.) met him among the Flatheads. He was taken over as a clerk by the Hudson's Bay Company in 1821; and he remained in the Columbia department until his retirement in 1827, when he settled in Upper Canada. He died at Charlottenburg, Glengarry, Upper Canada, on December 3, 1851, and was buried in the Roman Catholic cemetery in St. Raphael's, Ontario.

He married a Spokane wife, and by her had two children.

[J. A. Meyers, *Finan McDonald* (Washington historical quarterly, 1922).]

McDonald, Hugh (1827-1899), politician and judge, was born in Antigonish, Nova Scotia, in 1827. He was called to the bar of Nova Scotia in 1855 (Q.C., 1872), and in 1859 he was elected to represent Inverness in the House of Assembly of Nova Scotia. He opposed Confederation, and in 1866 went to England, with Joseph Howe (q.v.) and William Annand (q.v.), to protest against it. In 1867 he was elected to represent Antigonish in the Canadian House of Commons; and in 1873 he became president of the council in the Mackenzie administration. Later in 1873, however, he retired from politics, and was appointed a judge of the Supreme Court of Nova Scotia. He resigned from the bench in 1893, and he died on February 28, 1899.

[*Can. parl. comp.*]

Macdonald, Sir Hugh John (1850-1929), prime minister of Manitoba (1900), was born at Kingston, Ontario, on March 13, 1850, the only surviving son of Sir John A. Macdonald (q.v.). He was educated at the University of Toronto (B.A., 1869), and was called to the bar in 1872 (Q.C., 1890). He practised law first in Toronto, and after 1882 in Winnipeg. He represented Winnipeg in the Canadian House of Commons from 1891 to 1893 and from 1896 to 1897; and he was minister of the interior in the short-lived Tupper administration of 1896. In 1899 he was appointed leader of the Conservative party in Manitoba, and was elected to represent South Winnipeg in the Legislative Assembly of Manitoba; and in 1900 he became prime minister of the province, with the portfolio of attorney-general. Later in the same year he resigned office to contest Brandon in the general elections for the House of Commons; and on his defeat he retired to private life. In 1911 he was appointed police magistrate of Winnipeg, and this position he retained, until his death at Winnipeg, on March 29, 1929. In 1913 he was created a knight bachelor. He was twice married, (1) to Jean King (d. 1881), daughter of W. A. Murray, Toronto, and (2) to Agnes Gertrude, daughter of E. J. Vankoughnet, Q.C., Toronto.

[*Can. who was who*, vol. 1; Morgan, *Can. men* (1912); *Can. parl. comp.*; R. St. G. Stubbs, *Lawyers and laymen of western Canada* (Toronto, 1939).]

McDonald, James (1828-1912), politician and judge, was born at East River, Pictou county, Nova Scotia, on July 1, 1828. He was educated at New Glasgow, Nova Scotia, and was called to the bar of Nova Scotia in 1851 (Q.C., 1867). From 1859 to 1867 he represented Pictou county in the Legislative Assembly of Nova Scotia; and in 1864 he became financial secretary in the Tupper government. He was defeated as a Confederation candidate in Pictou for the Canadian House of Commons in 1867; but he was elected to the House of Commons in 1872, and though defeated in 1874, he was re-elected in 1878. From 1878 to 1881 he was minister of justice in the government of Sir John Macdonald (q.v.). In 1881 he was appointed chief justice of the Supreme Court of Nova Scotia, and this position he occupied until his retirement in 1904. He died at Halifax, Nova Scotia, on October 3, 1912. In 1856 he married Jane, daughter of William Mortimer of Pictou; and by her he had several sons and daughters.

[*Cyc. Am. biog.*; Morgan, *Can. men* (1912); Rose, *Cyc. Can. biog.* (1888); Dent, *Can. port.*, vol. 4; *Can. parl. comp.*]

MacDonald, James Alexander (1862-1923), clergyman and journalist, was born in the township of East Williams, Middlesex county, Ontario, on January 22, 1862, the son of John Alexander MacDonald, a native of Pictou, Nova Scotia. He was educated at Knox College, Toronto; and in 1891 was ordained a minister of the Presbyterian Church in Canada. From 1891 to 1896 he was pastor of Knox Church, St. Thomas, Ontario. In 1896 he founded in Toronto the *Westminster*, a religious journal; and in 1902 he was appointed managing editor of the Toronto *Globe*. In this position he exercised a notable influence in Canadian politics for many years. A breakdown in health compelled his retirement from active journalism in 1916; and he died at Toronto on May 13, 1923. In 1890 he married Grace Lumsden, daughter of William Christian; and by her he had two sons and one daughter. He was an LL.D. of Glasgow University (1909) and of Birmingham University (1911). He edited *From far Formosa* (Toronto, 1895), an account of the work of a Canadian missionary, as well as a volume in memory of Principal Caven (Toronto, 1908); and he published a number of his papers and addresses in *Democracy and the nations* (Toronto, 1915) and *The North American idea* (Toronto, 1917).

[*J. A. MacDonald* (Outlook, 1923); *University of Toronto monthly*, 1923; Morgan, *Can. men* (1912); A. Bridle, *Sons of Canada* (Toronto, 1916).]

MacDonald, James Edward Hervey (1874-1932), painter and poet, was born at Durham, England, in 1874, and emigrated to Canada in 1887. He studied painting at the Hamilton Art School and at the Ontario School of Art, Toronto; and was elected a member of the Ontario Society of Artists in 1909, an A.R.C.A. in 1912, and an R.C.A. in 1929. From 1929 to 1932 he was principal of the Ontario College of Art; and he was one of the original members of the Group of Seven. He died at Toronto on November 26, 1932. A volume of his poems, entitled *West by east*, was published posthumously (Toronto, 1933).

[E. R. Hunter, *J. E. H. MacDonald* (Toronto, 1940); N. MacTavish, *The fine arts in Canada* (Toronto, 1925), A. H. Robson, *J. E. H. MacDonald* (Toronto, 1937); *Can. who was who*, vol. 2.]

Macdonald, James Simon (1837-1914), historian, was born at Halifax, Nova Scotia, on May 7, 1837. Though primarily a successful business man, he was a serious student of the history of Nova Scotia, and was one of the founders, and later the president, of the Nova Scotia Historical Society. He died at Halifax, Nova Scotia, in 1914. He was the author of *Annals, North British Society, Halifax, Nova Scotia* (Halifax, N.S., 1868; 3rd ed., 1905), and many valuable papers contributed to the *Proceedings of the Nova Scotia Historical Society*.

[Morgan, *Can. men* (1912).]

Macdonald, James Williamson Galloway (1897-1960), painter, was born in Thurso, Scotland, on May 31, 1897, and died at Toronto, Ontario, on December 3, 1960. He studied at the Edinburgh College of Art, and came to Canada in 1927. After some years as an art instructor in Vancouver and Calgary, he became an instructor in the Ontario College of Art in Toronto in 1947. In 1933 he was one of the original members of the Canadian Group of Painters. Examples of his painting are to be found in the National Gallery at Ottawa and the Art Gallery of Ontario.

[Toronto *Globe and Mail*, Dec. 5, 1960; *Can. who's who*, 1958-60.]

MacDonald, Mrs. Jane Elizabeth Gostwycke, *née* **Roberts** (1864-1922), poet, was born at Westcock, New Brunswick, on Feb. 17, 1864, the daughter of the Rev. G. Goodridge Roberts and the sister of Sir Charles G. D. Roberts (q.v.). In 1896 she married her cousin, Samuel Archibald Roberts MacDonald; and they lived in Fredericton, New Brunswick, until 1912. She and her family then removed to the west; and finally they lived in Ottawa. Here she died on November 8, 1922. She was the author of *Our little Canadian cousin* (Boston, 1904) and *Dream verses and others* (Boston, 1906); and was joint author, with W. C. Roberts and T. G. Roberts, of *Northland lyrics* (Boston, 1899).

[*Can. who was who*, vol. 1; L. Roberts, *The book of Roberts* (Toronto, 1923).]

McDonald, John (1770-1828), fur-trader, known as "McDonald le Borgne", was born in 1770 at Munial Farm, at the east end of Loch Hourne, Inverness-shire, Scotland, the son of Angus Ban McDonald. With his father and mother and brothers and sisters, he emigrated to Glengarry, Canada, in 1786. He was a clerk at Lachine in 1791, and in 1798 he became a wintering partner in the XY Company. He was one of the six wintering partners of the XY Company who became partners of the North West Company in 1804; and in 1806 he was stationed in the Fort des Prairies district. He was distinguished by the letters "A McK Co" after his name, whereas John McDonald of Garth (q.v.) was described as "John McDonald N.W.". In 1816 he was one of the partners arrested by Lord Selkirk at Fort William, and he afterwards stood trial at York (Toronto), but was acquitted. In 1821, on the union of the North West and Hudson's Bay companies, he was made a chief factor. From 1821 to 1822 he was in charge of the upper Red River; and from 1823 to 1826, of the Winnipeg River district at Fort Alexander. He was granted furlough in 1827; and he died on February 8, 1828, and was buried in the Church of England cemetery at Newmarket, Upper Canada. He married a half-breed, Marie Poitras; and by her he had at least one daughter, who married Angus Grant, and some of whose descendants are said to be still living at Midland, Ontario. About 1825 he bought a property on the north side of Kempenfeldt Bay on Lake Simcoe; and it is probable that he died here.

[E. E. Rich (ed.), *Journal of occurrences in the Athabasca department, by George Simpson* (Toronto: The Champlain Society, 1938).]

McDonald, John (1782-1834), fur-trader, known as "McDonald le Grand", was born in Inverness-shire, Scotland, in 1782, and entered the service of the North West Company in 1801. Ross Cox (q.v.) met him in New Caledonia in 1814; and he seems to have spent most of his service as a clerk in this department. From 1831 to 1833 he was stationed at Great Slave Lake; and he retired from the Company's service in 1834. He died at St. Andrew's, Lower Canada, on December 1, 1834; and his will is filed in Hudson's Bay House in London.

[W. S. Wallace (ed.), *Documents relating to the North West Company* (Toronto: The Champlain Society, 1934).]

Macdonald, John (1824-1890), senator of Canada, was born in Perth, Scotland, on December 27, 1824, the son of John Macdonald and Elizabeth Neilson. He came to Canada in 1838 with his father, who was a non-commissioned officer in the Sutherland Highlanders. In 1849 he established in Toronto a dry-goods business which laid the foundation of a large fortune. In 1863 he was elected for the western division of Toronto in the parliament of Canada, as an independent Liberal; but was defeated in 1867. From 1875 to 1878 he was again a member of the Canadian parliament, this time for Centre Toronto. In 1887 he was made a senator of Canada, the only Liberal ever appointed to the upper house on the nomination of Sir John Macdonald. He died at Toronto, on February 4, 1890. He was

twice married, and by his second wife he had five sons and five daughters.

[H. Johnston, *A merchant prince: Life of the Hon. Senator John Macdonald* (Toronto, 1893); *Cyc. Am. biog.*; Rose, *Cyc. Can. biog.* (1886); *Can. parl. comp.*]

Macdonald, Sir John Alexander (1815-1891), statesman, was born on January 11, 1815, in Glasgow, Scotland, the eldest son of Hugh Macdonald and Helen Shaw. He came to Canada with his parents in 1820, and his youth was spent in Kingston, Upper Canada, and its vicinity. Educated at the Royal Grammar School in Kingston, he was called to the bar of Upper Canada in 1836. In 1844 he was elected to represent Kingston in the Legislative Assembly of Canada, and he sat almost continuously for Kingston in parliament from that day to his death in 1891. His first tenure of office was in 1847-48, when he was for ten months receiver-general in the Draper administration. In 1854 he was mainly instrumental in forming the coalition of parties which resulted in the creation of the Liberal-Conservative party; and he became attorney-general for Upper Canada in the MacNab-Morin government. In 1856 he became Upper Canadian leader in the Taché-Macdonald ministry; and in 1857 prime minister in the Macdonald-Cartier ministry. Defeated in 1858, he resumed office after four days in the Cartier-Macdonald administration, first as postmaster-general and then as attorney-general for Upper Canada, this change of portfolios being incidental to the "Double Shuffle". In 1862 his government was defeated, and he was in opposition until the formation of the second Taché-Macdonald administration of March-June, 1864.

The defeat of this administration and the consequent deadlock in government resulted in the formation of the "Great Coalition" which brought about the confederation of the British North American provinces. In the formation of this coalition Macdonald played a leading part; and he came to be regarded, especially after the resignation of George Brown (q.v.) from the government in 1865, as the chief architect of Confederation. He took a foremost part both in the Quebec Conference of 1864 and in the London Conference of 1866, at which the details of the British North America Act were worked out. In 1867, therefore, he was selected as first prime minister of the Dominion of Canada; and he continued to fill this office, except for the period of the Mackenzie administration (1873-78), until his death. His defeat in 1873 was the result of the so-called "Pacific Scandal", and it was thought that his eclipse on this occasion would be permanent; but in 1878 he came back to power on the "National Policy" of high protection, and in the three subsequent general elections, in 1882, in 1886, and in 1891, he proved invincible at the polls. The elections of 1891, however, were too great a strain on his health; and on June 6, 1891, he died at Ottawa.

Macdonald had not perhaps a high code of political ethics, and he at times raised opportunism almost to the level of a political principle, yet it may be doubted whether a statesman of stricter views could have guided the destinies of Canada during the difficult period of his prime ministry as successfully as he did. In the art of managing men he was unrivalled; and there were some points, such as the safeguarding of law and order and the continuance of the British connection, on which he knew no compromise. To his initiative were due, also, the inclusion in the Dominion of British Columbia and the North West, and the building of the Canadian Pacific Railway. In many ways, the Dominion of Canada is to-day the creature of his statesmanship.

For his services in connection with Confederation, he was created in 1867 a K.C.B. In 1879 he was sworn of the privy council, and in 1884 he became a G.C.B. He was a D.C.L. of Oxford (1865), and in 1886 he was offered by Cambridge the degree of LL.D. He was twice married, first in 1843 to his cousin Isabelle Clark (d. 1858), and second to Susan Agnes Bernard, who was, after his death, created Baroness Macdonald of Earnscliffe. By his first wife he had two sons, one of whom died in infancy; and by his second wife one daughter.

[The chief authorities are Sir J. Pope, *Memoirs of Sir J. A. Macdonald* (2 vols., Ottawa, 1895; new ed., Toronto, 1930), *The day of Sir John Macdonald* (Toronto, 1915), *Correspondence of Sir John Macdonald* (Toronto, 1921), and D. G. Creighton, *John A. Macdonald* (2 vols., Toronto, 1952-55). There are a number of other biographies, but none of these are of much original value except G. R. Parkin, *Sir John A. Macdonald* (Toronto, 1910); Donald Swainson, *John A. Macdonald: The man and the politician* (Toronto, 1971); and E. B. Biggar, *Anecdotal life of Sir John Macdonald* (Montreal, 1891). Useful materials are to be found in Sir R. Cartwright, *Reminiscences* (Toronto, 1912), to which Sir J. Pope issued a rejoinder; in Goldwin Smith, *Reminiscences* (New York, 1910); in J. K. Johnson, *Affectionately yours: The letters of Sir John A. Macdonald and his family* (Toronto, 1969); and in biographies of such contemporaries of Macdonald as Brown, Cartier, Galt, Mackenzie, Tupper, and Laurier. General historical works covering the period of Macdonald's political career are J. C. Dent, *The last forty years* (2 vols., Toronto, 1881) and J. S. Willison, *Sir Wilfrid Laurier and the Liberal party* (2 vols., Toronto, 1903).]

MacDonald, John Alexander (1846-1922), journalist and civil servant, was born in 1846, and saw active service during the Fenian raid of 1866. He was a journalist later in Arnprior, Ontario; and during his later years he was a clerk in the Bureau of Archives, at Toronto. He died at Toronto on August 22, 1922. He was the author of *Troublous times in Canada* (Toronto, 1910).

[Private information.]

Macdonald, John Sandfield (1812-1872), prime minister of Canada (1862-64) and prime minister of Ontario (1867-71), was born at St. Raphael, Upper Canada, on December 12, 1812, the son of Alexander Macdonald. He was educated at the grammar school in Cornwall, Upper Canada; and in 1840 he was called to the bar of Upper Canada. In 1841 he was elected to represent Glengarry in the Legislative Assembly of Canada, and he sat for this constituency continuously until 1857, and from 1857 to 1867 he sat for Cornwall. His course in politics was independent and somewhat erratic. He leaned at first toward Conservatism, but in 1844 he sided with the Reform leaders against Sir Charles Metcalfe (q.v.), and he was henceforth rated as a Reformer. From 1849 to 1851 he was solicitor-general in the second Baldwin-Lafontaine administration; but he was not included in the Hincks-Morin government, and was relegated in 1852-54 to the position of speaker of the Assembly. He opposed the MacNab-Taché and succeeding Liberal-Conservative governments; but, being a Roman Catholic and an advocate of the "double-majority" principle, he was not in harmony with the wing of the Reform party led by George Brown (q.v.). He was included in 1858 in the short-lived Brown-Dorion administration as attorney-general west; but this was merely a temporary *rapprochement*, and when Sandfield Macdonald was invited to form a government in 1862, George Brown was not a member of it. As first minister in the Macdonald-Sicotte government (1862-63), and in the Macdonald-Dorion government (1863-64), he carried on the administration with considerable adroitness under difficult circumstances; but his defeat in March, 1864, and the subsequent defeat of the Taché-Macdonald ministry in June, 1864, brought about the deadlock from which issued Confederation. Sandfield Macdonald opposed Confederation, and fought against it vigorously; but once it had become an accomplished fact, he accepted it, and in 1867 he was persuaded by Sir John Macdonald (q.v.) to undertake the prime ministry of Ontario. He formed in Ontario a coalition government, known as "the Patent Combination"; and for over four years he administered the affairs of the province with great prudence and economy. At the end of 1871, however, he was defeated in the House by the Liberals under Edward Blake (q.v.), and resigned. His health, never robust, had given way; and he died soon afterwards at Cornwall, Ontario, on June 1, 1872. In 1840 he married a daughter of the Hon. George Waggoman, United States senator from Louisiana; and had three sons and four daughters.

[M. O. Hammond, *Confederation and its leaders* (Toronto, 1917); *Proceedings at the unveiling of the statue of John Sandfield Macdonald* (pamphlet, Toronto, 1909); Morgan, *Cel. Can.*; Taylor, *Brit. Am.*, vol. 1; Dent, *Can. port.*, vol. 4; Rose, *Cyc. Can. biog.* (1886); C. Clarke, *Sixty years in Upper Canada* (Toronto, 1908); Sir J. Pope, *Memoirs of the Rt. Hon. Sir J. A. Macdonald* (2 vols., Ottawa, 1895); J. C. Dent, *The last forty years* (2 vols., Toronto, 1881); Goldwin Smith, *Reminiscences* (Toronto, 1910); W. S. Wallace, "Political History of Ontario", in Shortt and Doughty (eds.), *Canada and its provinces*, vol. 17 (Toronto, 1914); B. W. Hodgins, *John Sandfield Macdonald, 1812-1872* (Toronto, 1971); *Dict. Can. biog.*, vol. 10.]

Macdonald, Mrs. Lucy Maud, *née* **Montgomery.** See **Montgomery, Lucy Maud.**

McDonald, Robert (1829-1913), missionary, was born at the Red River Settlement, Hudson's Bay Territories, in 1829, the son of Neil McDonald, a former servant of the Hudson's Bay Company. He was educated at St. John's Collegiate School, in the Red River Settlement, and was ordained a priest of the Church of England in 1852. After serving an apprenticeship among the Cree Indians of the White Dog Mission, on the Winnipeg River, he was sent in 1862 to the Yukon, and he spent forty years as a missionary among the natives of the Yukon and the Mackenzie River district. He translated the Gospels and the Book of Common Prayer into Tudukh; and these translations were published by the British and Foreign Bible Society in 1873. In 1876 he became archdeacon of Mackenzie River; and he retired from this position only in 1906. He died at Winnipeg, Manitoba, on August 28, 1913.

[W. B. Heeney (ed.), *Leaders of the Canadian church: Second series* (Toronto, 1920).]

MacDonald, Robert Gear (1874-1943), poet, was born in St. John's, Newfoundland, on August 5, 1874, and died there in 1943. Besides contributing both prose and verse to periodicals, he was the author of a volume of poems entitled *From the isle of Avalon* (1908).

[*Newfoundland supp.*]

MacDonald, Ronald (1798?-1854), journalist, was a native of Prince Edward Island, and was born about 1798. He was educated at the Quebec Seminary, was for a number of years a teacher of deaf-mutes in Quebec, and became the editor of the *Gazette de Québec* and of *Le Canadien*. He died on October 14, 1854, at Quebec.

[P. G. Roy, *Le journaliste Ronald MacDonald* (Bull. rech. hist., 1936).]

McDonald, William (1837-1916), senator of Canada, was born at River Dennis Mountain, Nova Scotia, on October 7, 1837. He was educated at St. Francis Xavier College, Antigonish, and became first a school-teacher. Later he became postmaster at Glace Bay, Nova Scotia. He represented Cape Breton in the Canadian House of Commons from 1872 to 1884, and was one of the "old guard" of Sir John Macdonald (q.v.). In 1884 he was summoned to the Senate of Canada; and he sat in the Senate until his death at Glace Bay, Nova Scotia, on July 4, 1916.

[Morgan, *Can. men* (1912); *Can. parl. comp.*]

Macdonald, Sir William Christopher (1831-1917), manufacturer and philanthropist, was born in 1831 at Glenaladale, Prince Edward Island, the son of the Hon. Donald Macdonald, president of the Legislative Council of Prince Edward Island, and Ann Matilda Brecken. He was educated at the Central Academy, Charlottetown, Prince Edward Island, and in 1854 began business as a commission merchant in Montreal, Canada. He later became a tobacco manufacturer, and acquired a very large fortune. He was a generous benefactor of McGill University, Montreal, and the Ontario Agricultural College, Guelph, Ontario; and he founded and endowed the Macdonald Agricultural College at Ste. Anne de Bellevue, Quebec. He died, unmarried, at Montreal on June 9, 1917. For many years he was chancellor of McGill University. He was created a knight bachelor in 1898.

[J. F. Snell, *Sir William Macdonald and his kin* (Dalhousie review, 1943); *Who was who*, 1916-28; Morgan, *Can. men* (1912); *Can. who's who* (1910); C. Macmillan, *McGill and its story* (Toronto, 1920).]

Macdonald, William John (1832-1916), senator of Canada, was born in the Isle of Skye on November 29, 1832, the third son of Major Alexander Macdonald and Flora McRae. He was privately educated, and went to Vancouver Island, in the service of the Hudson's Bay Company, in 1851. From 1859 to 1866 he sat in the Legislative Assembly of Vancouver Island, and from 1866 to 1871 in the Legislative Council of British Columbia. On the entrance of British Columbia into Confederation in 1871, he was appointed to the Senate of Canada, and he continued a senator until 1915. He died at Victoria, British Columbia, on October 25, 1916. In 1857 he married Catherine Balfour, daughter of Capt. Murray Reid of the Hudson's Bay Company; and by her he had three sons and three daughters. He published his reminiscences in a pamphlet entitled *A pioneer* (Victoria, 1915).

[Morgan, *Can. men* (1912); *Can. who's who* (1910); *Can. parl. comp.*; J. B. Kerr, *Biographical dictionary of well-known British Columbians* (Vancouver, B.C., 1890).]

Macdonald, William Peter (1771-1847), priest and journalist, was born in the parish of Eberlow, Banffshire, Scotland, on March 25, 1771. He was educated at the College of Douai, France, and at the Royal Scots College, in Valladolid, Spain; and was ordained a priest of the Roman Catholic Church in 1796. After a varied career, he was in 1826 invited by Bishop Macdonell (q.v.) to come to Upper Canada. Bishop Macdonell made him his vicar-general; and he had charge of the parishes of Kingston, Toronto, Prescott, Hamilton, and Bytown. While at Kingston he began the publication of the *Catholic*, the first English Roman Catholic newspaper in Canada. He died at Toronto on April 2, 1847. He was the author of a controversial pamphlet entitled *Remarks on Doctor Strachan's pamphlet against the Catholic doctrine of the real presence of Christ's body and blood in the Eucharist* (Kingston, 1834).

[P. F. Cronin, *Early Catholic journalism in Canada* (Canadian Catholic Historical Association, report, 1935-36).]

MacDonald, Wilson Pugsley (1880-1967), controversial Canadian lyric poet, was born in Cheapside, Ontario, May 5, 1880, the son of a Baptist minister, and was educated at Woodstock Collegiate and McMaster University, Hamilton. His first poem was published in 1899 and he continued writing poetry for over fifty years. He worked as an advertising man and newspaper reporter in the United States and Canada before returning to Toronto in 1906 to devote his life to poetry. His style was related more closely to the nineteenth-century lyric poets than to twentieth-century developments; and although he received great praise from some critics he remained a controversial figure on the Canadian literary scene. He claimed that he was better known in Russia, which he visited in 1957 as part of a Canada–Russia cultural exchange, than he was in Canada.

He published eleven volumes of verse — mostly at his own expense and in his own handwriting. Among his works are *Songs of the prairie land* (1918); *Out of the wilderness* (1926); *The miracle songs of Jesus* (1921); *Confederation ode* (1927); *Caw caw ballads* (1930); *A flagon of beauty* (1931); *Paul Marchand* (1933); *Song of the undertow* (1935); *Comber Cove* (1937); *Greater poems of the Bible* (1943); *The lyric year* (1952); as well as a number of plays and magazine articles. He died at Toronto, Ontario, April 8, 1967.

[*Can. who's who*, 1961-63; *Canadian Author and Bookman* (Spring, 1958); Metropolitan Toronto Library Board, *Biographical scrapbooks*, vols. 33 & 36; Toronto *Globe and Mail*, April 10, 1967.]

McDonald of Garth, John (1774?-1860), fur-trader, was born in Scotland about 1774, and came to Canada, in the service of the North West Company, in 1791. From this date until 1816 he served almost continuously in the western country; and in 1813 he received the surrender of Fort Astoria. In 1816 he settled at Gray's Creek, Glengarry, Canada; and here he died in 1860. He left several children. His "Autobiographical notes" have been published in L. R. Masson, *Les bourgeois de la compagnie du Nord Ouest*, vol. ii (Quebec, 1890).

[R. Campbell, *History of the Scotch Presbyterian Church, St. Gabriel St., Montreal* (Montreal, 1887); G. Bryce, *The remarkable history of the Hudson's Bay Company* (London, 1900).]

Macdonell, Alexander, of Aberchalder (d. 1790?), soldier, was a native of Aberchalder, Scotland. He is said to have been an aide-de-camp of the Pretender, Prince Charles Stewart, in 1745. Elsewhere he is described as having been "principal tackman on the estate". He emigrated to America in 1773, settled in Tryon county, New York, and during the American Revolution was a captain in the King's Royal Regiment of New York. Against him many inhumanities were charged by the revolutionists. In 1784 he settled in the township of Charlottenburg, on the St. Lawrence River, and his place was known as Glengarry House. He appears to have died in the beginning of 1790.

[E. M. Chadwick, *Ontarian families* (2 vols., Toronto, 1894-98); W. Canniff, *History of the settlement of Upper Canada* (Toronto, 1869); J. A. Macdonell, *Sketches of the early settlement and history of Glengarry* (Montreal, 1893); W. L. Scott, *The Macdonells of Leek, Collachie, and Aberchalder* Canadian Catholic Historical Association, report, 1934-1935).]

Macdonell, Alexander, of Greenfield, (d. 1819), soldier, was a native of Scotland who emigrated to Canada about 1792. He settled in Glengarry county, Upper Canada, and in the War of 1812 he commanded the 2nd battalion of the Glengarry militia. He died in 1819. His wife was Janet, daughter of Alexander Macdonell of Aberchalder (q.v.), and sister of Lieut.-Col. John Macdonell (q.v.), first speaker of the Legislative Assembly of Upper Canada. By her he had six sons and four daughters.

[E. M. Chadwick, *Ontarian families* (2 vols., Toronto, 1894-98); J. A. Macdonell, *Sketches illustrating the early settlement and history of Glengarry* (Montreal, 1893); W. J. Rattray, *The Scot in British North America* (4 vols., Toronto, 1880).]

McDonell, Alexander (fl. 1815-1823), acting governor of the Red River colony, was sheriff of the Red River colony under Governor Semple (q.v.) in 1815-16, and succeeded to the command in the settlement on Semple's death at Seven Oaks in 1816. Lord Selkirk appointed him his agent in 1818, and he administered the affairs of the settlement until the arrival of Governor Bulger (q.v.) in 1822. He was thereafter for a short time a councillor of Assiniboia; but appears to have been removed from office in 1823. He was known as the "Grasshopper Governor", from the fact that a pest of grasshoppers visited the colony during his period of office.

[E. H. Oliver, *The Canadian north-west*, vol. 1 (Ottawa, 1914); C. Martin, *Lord Selkirk's work in Canada* (Oxford, 1916); A. Begg, *History of the north-west* (3 vols. Toronto, 1894); J. P. Pritchett, *The Red River Valley: 1811-1849* (Toronto, 1942).]

Macdonell, Alexander (1762-1840), Roman Catholic bishop of Kingston (1826-40), was born at Glen Urquhart, Scotland, on July 17, 1762. He became a priest in the Roman Catholic Church and the organizer and chaplain of the Glengarry Fencibles, a Roman Catholic Highland regiment which saw service in Ireland in 1798. When the regiment was disbanded in 1802, Macdonell obtained grants of land in Canada for as many of the men of the regiment as desired them; and in 1804 he came to Canada with several hundred Highland settlers. He and his flock settled in Glengarry, Upper Canada; and in the War of 1812 he served as chaplain of the Glengarry Light Infantry. In 1826 he was raised to the episcopate as bishop of Kingston or Regiopolis; and in 1831 he was appointed a member of the Legislative Council of Upper Canada. He died on January 14, 1840, at Dumfries, Scotland. The town of Alexandria, in the county of Glengarry, Upper Canada, is named in his honour. His *Reminiscences* were published posthumously (Toronto, 1888).

[H. J. Somers, *The life and times of the Hon. and Rt. Rev. Alexander Macdonell* (Washington, D.C., 1931); J. A. Macdonell, *A sketch of the life of the Hon. and Rt. Rev. Alexander Macdonell* (Alexandria, Ontario, 1890) and *Sketches illustrating the early settlement and history of Glengarry* (Montreal, 1893); *Dict. nat. biog.*; *Cyc. Am. biog.*; Morgan, *Cel. Can.*; E. M. Chadwick, *Ontarian families* (2 vols., Toronto, 1894-98).]

Macdonell, Alexander (1833-1905), Roman Catholic bishop of Alexandria (1890-1905), was born in the township of Lochiel, Glengarry county, Upper Canada, on November 1, 1833, the son of James Macdonell and Christina Macdonell. He was educated at St. Joseph's College, Ottawa, and was ordained a priest of the Roman Catholic Church in 1862. In 1886 he was appointed vicar-general of the diocese of Kingston, and in 1890 he was raised to the episcopate as the first bishop of the newly created diocese of Alexandria. He died on May 29, 1905.

[*Can. who was who*, vol. 1; Morgan, *Can. men* (1898).]

Macdonell, Alexander C. (1762-1842), legislative councillor of Upper Canada, was born at Fort Augustus, in Glengarry, Scotland, in 1762, the second son of Allan Macdonell (q.v.), of Collachie. During the American Revolution he was a subaltern in Butler's Rangers, and in 1784 he settled in Canada. From 1800 to 1812, and from 1820 to 1823 he represented Glengarry in the Legislative Assembly of Upper Canada; and in 1804 he was elected speaker of the Assembly. From 1792 to 1805 he was sheriff of the Home district of Upper Canada; and from 1805 to 1812 he acted as the agent of Lord Selkirk (q.v.) in connection with the Baldoon settlement in the western district of Upper Canada. During the War of 1812 he was a colonel of militia and deputy paymaster-general; and after the war he was superintendent of the settlement of disbanded soldiers at Perth, Upper Canada. In 1831 he was appointed a member of the Legislative Council of the province. He died at Toronto on March 18, 1842. He married Anne, daughter of James Smith, and sister of the Hon. Samuel Smith (q.v.); and by her he had five sons and two daughters. His *Journal* for 1793 has been printed in the *Transactions* of the Canadian Institute, 1890; and that for 1799 in J. E. Middleton and F. Landon, *The province of Ontario* (4 vols., Toronto, 1927).

[Brother Alfred, *Hon. Alexander McDonell (Collachie)* (pamphlet, Toronto, n.d.); E. M. Chadwick, *Ontarian families* (2 vols., Toronto, 1894-98); J. A. Macdonell, *Sketches illustrating the early settlement and history of Glengarry* (Montreal, 1893).]

Macdonell, Alexander Greenfield (d. 1835), fur-trader, was the sixth son of Alexander Macdonell of Greenfield, and a second cousin of John Macdonell (q.v.) and Miles Macdonell (q.v.). He entered the service of the North West Company, and in 1808 was a clerk in the Red River department, under John McDonald of Garth (q.v.). He was made a partner of the North West Company in 1814, was placed in charge of the Red River department, and played a prominent part in the Selkirk troubles of the years immediately following. In 1820 he was in charge of the English River department; but at the union of the North West and Hudson's Bay companies, he retired from the fur-trade. He was elected to represent the county of Glengarry in the Legislative Assembly of Upper Canada in 1821; and for a number of years he was sheriff of the Ottawa district. In 1834 he was elected to represent Prescott and Russell in the Legislative Assembly of Upper Canada; and he died in Toronto, in February, 1835, while attending the first session of the Assembly. He was the author of a *Narrative of the transactions in the Red River country, from the commencement of the operations of the Earl of Selkirk till the summer of 1816* (London, 1819).

[J. A. Macdonell, *Sketches illustrating the*

early settlement and history of Glengarry (Montreal, 1893); C. Martin, Lord Selkirk's work in Canada (Oxford, 1916).]

Macdonell, Allan (d. 1792), soldier, was a native of Collachie, Scotland. He fought under the Pretender, Prince Charles Stewart, at Culloden in 1745; and he came to America in 1773. He settled in the Mohawk valley; and in the American Revolution he was a captain in the 84th Royal Highland Emigrants. In 1784 he came to Canada, and settled in Glengarry county, on the St. Lawrence. He died in 1792. He married Helen, daughter of The MacNab; and by her he had three sons and two daughters.
[E. M. Chadwick, *Ontarian families* (2 vols., Toronto, 1894-98); J. A. Macdonell, *Sketches illustrating the early settlement and history of Glengarry* (Montreal, 1893).]

McDonell, Allan (*fl.* 1799-1843), furtrader, entered the service of the XY Company in 1799; and in 1804 he is listed as a clerk in the North West Company at Fort Dauphin. He was for many years employed in the Swan River or Red River departments; and in 1806 took part in an expedition to the Mandans. He took a prominent part in the Selkirk troubles; and was one of the officers of the North West Company arrested by Lord Selkirk in 1816, and tried at York (Toronto) in 1818. In 1816 he was made a partner of the North West Company; and at the union of 1821 he became a chief trader of the Hudson's Bay Company. From 1821 to 1826 he was in charge of the Swan River department, with headquarters, first, at Fort Dauphin, and, secondly, at Fort Pelly; and from 1826 to 1834 he was in charge of the Timiskaming district. He was promoted to the rank of chief factor in 1828. From 1835 to 1841 he was in charge of the Rainy Lake district; and in 1839 he was made a councillor of Rupert's Land. He was granted furlough in 1841; and he retired from the service of the Hudson's Bay Company in 1843.
[W. S. Wallace (ed.), *Documents relating to the North West Company* (Toronto: The Champlain Society, 1934); R. H. Fleming (ed.), *Minutes of Council, Northern Department of Rupert Land*, 1821-31 (Toronto: The Champlain Society, 1940).]

McDonell, Allan (1808-1888), lawyer and prospector, was born at York, Upper Canada, on November 5, 1808, the son of the Hon. Alexander McDonell of Collachie (q.v.), and died at Toronto, Ontario, on September 9, 1888. He was called to the bar of Upper Canada in 1832, and for a time was a partner of Sir Allan MacNab (q.v.). He was then sheriff of the Gore District for some years. In his later years he devoted himself to exploring the mining possibilities of the Lake Superior region; and he proposed the building of a railway to the Pacific as early as 1852. He published a paper

entitled *Observations upon the construction of a railroad from Lake Superior to the Pacific*, in the *Eighth report of the standing committee on railways and telegraphs* (Toronto, 1852).
[W. J. Rattray, *The Scot in British North America*, vol. iv (Toronto, 1880).]

Macdonell, Angus (d. 1804), lawyer, was the eldest son of Allan Macdonell (q.v.), of Collachie. In 1792 he was appointed the first clerk of the Legislative Assembly of Upper Canada; and from 1801 to 1804 he represented Glengarry and Prescott in the Assembly. From 1801 to 1804 he was also treasurer of the Law Society of Upper Canada. He was drowned in the loss of the *Speedy* on Lake Ontario on October 7, 1804. He was not married.
[E. M. Chadwick, *Ontarian families* (2 vols., Toronto, 1894-98); W. R. Riddell, *Upper Canada sketches* (Toronto, 1922) and *Old province tales* (Toronto, 1920).]

Macdonell, Sir Archibald Cameron (1864-1941), soldier, was born at Windsor, Canada West, on October 6, 1864, the son of Samuel Smith Macdonell. He graduated from the Royal Military College, Kingston, in 1886; and, after serving for two or three years in the Canadian permanent militia, he transferred to the Royal North West Mounted Police. He served in the South African War with the Canadian Mounted Rifles, and rose to the rank of lieutenant-colonel. He became a superintendent of the Royal North West Mounted Police in 1903; and he was given command of Lord Strathcona's Horse when the First World War broke out. In 1915 he was given command of the 7th Canadian Infantry Brigade, with the rank of brigadier-general; in 1917 he was appointed to command the First Canadian Division, with the rank of major-general; and from 1919 to 1925 he was commandant of the Royal Military College, Kingston. He was awarded the D.S.O. in 1901, the C.M.G. in 1916, the C.B. in 1917, and the K.C.B. in 1919; and on retirement he was promoted lieutenant-general. He died at Kingston, Ontario, on December 23, 1941.
[*Who's who*, 1941; *Can. who's who*, 1936-37.]

Macdonell, Blanche Lucile (1853-1924), novelist, was born in 1853; was educated in Toronto, Ontario; and died in Montreal, Quebec, on November 24, 1924. Besides several serial stories which she contributed to periodicals, she was the author of a novel entitled *Diane of Ville Marie* (Toronto, 1896).
[Morgan, *Can. men and women* (1912).]

Macdonell, George (1779?-1870), soldier, was born in Scotland about 1779, the son of John Macdonell of Leek, who had fought under Prince Charles Stewart at Culloden in 1745, under Wolfe at Quebec in 1759, and had later commanded a veteran corps in Newfoundland.

He entered the British army, and became a captain in the King's Regiment; in 1812 he raised the Glengarry Light Infantry, and played as its commanding officer an important part in the battle of Châteauguay in 1813. After the war he returned to the British army, and he rose in it to the rank of major-general. He died in 1870. In 1820 he married the Hon. Laura, daughter of Lord Arundel of Wardour; and by her he had one son. In 1818 he was created a C.B. for his services at Châteauguay. He was familiarly known as "Red George".

[W. S. Buell, *"Red George" — one of the Macdonells* (Can. hist. review, 1923); E. M. Chadwick, *Ontarian families* (2 vols., Toronto, 1894-98); J. A. Macdonell, *Sketches illustrating the early settlement and history of Glengarry* (Montreal, 1893).]

Macdonell, John (d. 1809), first speaker of the Legislative Assembly of Upper Canada, was the eldest son of Alexander Macdonell of Aberchalder (q.v.). During the American Revolutionary War he was a captain in Butler's Rangers. From 1792 to 1800 he represented Glengarry in the Legislative Assembly of Upper Canada; and from 1792 to 1796 he was its speaker. From 1796 to 1802 he commanded the 2nd battalion of the Royal Canadian Volunteer Regiment; and in 1807 he was appointed paymaster of the 10th Royal Veteran Battalion. He died at Quebec on November 21, 1809. He married Helen, daughter of Henry Yates, sometime governor of New York State; and by her he had one son.

[E. A. Cruikshank, *A memoir of Lieutenant-Colonel John Macdonell* (Ont. Hist. Soc. papers and records, vol. xxii); C. C. James, *The first legislators of Upper Canada* (Trans. Roy. Soc. Can., 1902); W. Canniff, *History of the settlement of Upper Canada* (Toronto, 1869), pp. 114-16; E. M. Chadwick, *Ontarian families* (2 vols., Toronto, 1894-98); J. Ross Robertson (ed.), *Mrs. Simcoe's diary* (Toronto, 1911).]

Macdonell, John, of Scotus (1728-1810), soldier, was a native of Scotland who came to America in 1773, and settled in Schoharie county, New York. He came to Canada after the American Revolution, and settled at St. Andrew's, near Cornwall, on the St. Lawrence River. He died on April 15, 1810; and he had three sons and one daughter.

[*A narrative of the early life of Col. John McDonell of Scottos* (Canadian magazine, Montreal, 1825); Rev. A. G. Morice, *A Canadian pioneer, Spanish John* (Can. hist. rev., 1929); E. M. Chadwick, *Ontarian families* (2 vols., Toronto, 1894-98).]

Macdonell, John (1768-1850), fur-trader, was born in Scotland on November 30, 1768, the eldest son of John Macdonell of Scotus, commonly known as "Spanish John", and the elder brother of Miles Macdonell (q.v.). He

came to America with his father in 1773; and at the close of the American Revolution came to Canada. Between 1788, when he was gazetted an ensign in the militia battalion of Cornwall and Osnabruck, and 1793, he became a clerk in the service of the North West Company. His journal for the years 1793-97 has been printed in L. R. Masson, *Les bourgeois de la Compagnie du Nord-Ouest*, vol. i (Quebec, 1889). He was made a partner of the North West Company about 1796; and in 1799 he was in charge of the Upper Red River department. He was employed in this department almost continuously until 1809, when he was placed in charge of the Athabaska River department. In 1808 he was elected a member of the Beaver Club of Montreal. He retired as a partner of the North West Company in 1812, and returned to Canada. He settled at Point Fortune, on the Ottawa River; and here he opened a store, and for many years ran a boat service on the Ottawa River. He died at Point Fortune on April 17, 1850, and was buried in the Roman Catholic cemetery at St. Andrews, Quebec. He married Magdeleine Poitras (d. 1871); and by her he had six sons and two daughters.

[Rev. A. G. Morice, *Miles Macdonell and his brothers* (Can. hist. rev., 1929); C. M. Gates (ed.), *Five fur-traders of the north-west* (Minneapolis, Minn., 1933); E. M. Chadwick, *Ontarian families* (2 vols., Toronto, 1894-98).]

Macdonell, John (1785-1812), attorney-general of Upper Canada, was born at Greenfield, Inverness, Scotland, on April 19, 1785, the fourth son of Alexander Macdonell of Greenfield (q.v.). He came to Upper Canada with his father about 1792. He was called to the bar of Upper Canada in 1808, and in 1812 was appointed attorney-general of the province. In 1812 he was also elected to represent Glengarry in the Legislative Assembly of Upper Canada. On the outbreak of the War of 1812 he became provincial aide-de-camp to General Brock (q.v.), and he negotiated the terms of the capture of Detroit. He fell with Brock at the battle of Queenston Heights on October 12, 1812. He was unmarried.

[E. M. Chadwick, *Ontarian families* (2 vols., Toronto, 1894-98); J. A. Macdonell, *Sketches illustrating the early settlement and history of Glengarry* (Montreal, 1893); W. Caniff, *History of the Settlement of Upper Canada* (Toronto, 1869).]

Macdonell, John Alexander (1851-1930), author, was born at Kingston, Ontario, on June 26, 1851, the son of Archibald John Macdonell and Mary Long-Innes. He was educated at Queen's College School, Kingston, and was called to the bar of Ontario in 1875 (Q.C., 1890). For a number of years he was, under Sir John Macdonald (q.v.), organizer for the Conservative party. He died at Alexandria, Ontario, on April 25, 1930. He was the author of *A sketch of the life of the Hon. and Rt. Rev. Alexander Macdonell* (Alexandria, Ontario, 1890) and *Sketches illustrating the early settlement and history of Glengarry* (Montreal, 1893).

[Morgan, *Can. men* (1912).]

Macdonell, Miles (1769-1828), governor of Assiniboia, was born in Scotland in 1769, the second son of John Macdonell (q.v.), of Scotus, otherwise known as "Spanish John". He came to America with his father in 1773, and about 1783 he settled with his father and a number of his relations at Rivière aux Raisins, on the upper St. Lawrence, in Canada. In 1794 he was gazetted a lieutenant, and in 1796 a captain, in the Royal Canadian Volunteers; and in 1800 he was an unsuccessful candidate for election to the Legislative Assembly of Upper Canada for the county of Glengarry. In 1811 Lord Selkirk (q.v.) made him his agent in the establishment of the Red River colony; and he was appointed by the Hudson's Bay Company the first governor of Assiniboia. He came into conflict with the Nor'Westers, was arrested by them, and was carried a prisoner to Montreal in 1815. He returned to the Red River with Selkirk in 1817, but only for a short time; and his later years were spent mainly on his farm at Osnaburgh, Upper Canada. He died at the house of his brother, John Macdonell (q.v.), at Point Fortune, on the Ottawa River, on June 28, 1828.

[A. G. Morice, *Sidelights on the careers of Miles Macdonell and his brothers* (Can. hist. rev., 1929); *Cyc. Am. biog.*; E. H. Oliver, *The Canadian north-west* (2 vols., Ottawa, 1914); C. Martin, *Lord Selkirk's work in Canada* (Oxford, 1916); G. Bryce, *The remarkable history of the Hudson's Bay Company* (London, 1900); E. M. Chadwick, *Ontarian families* (2 vols., Toronto, 1894-98).]

Macdonnell, Daniel James (1843-1896), clergyman, was born at Bathurst, New Brunswick, on January 15, 1843, the eldest son of the Rev. George Macdonnell (q.v.). He came with his parents to Canada West in 1852, and he was educated at Queen's University, Kingston (B.A., 1858). After several years of teaching school, he went to Scotland and Germany to study theology; and on his return to Canada in 1866 he was inducted the pastor of St. Andrew's Church, Peterborough. In 1870 he was called to be the minister of St. Andrew's Church, Toronto; and he remained in charge of this congregation until his death, at Fergus, Ontario, on February 19, 1896. A courageous and original thinker, he was compelled to face in 1886-88 a prolonged trial for heresy in the church courts; but he triumphed in the end over his opponents. In 1868 he married Elizabeth Logie, daughter of the Rev. George Smellie, of Fergus, Ontario; and by her he had five sons and two daughters.

[J. F. McCurdy, *Life and work of D. J. Macdonnell* (Toronto, 1897); Rose, *Cyc. Can. biog.* (1888).]

Macdonnell, George (1812?-1871), clergyman and author, was born in Fifeshire, Scotland, about 1812, and came with his parents to Halifax, Nova Scotia, in early youth. He was educated at Edinburgh University; and in 1840 became Presbyterian minister at Bathurst, New Brunswick. In 1852 he removed to Canada West; and from 1855 to 1869 he was pastor of St. Andrew's Church, Fergus. He died at Milton, Ontario, on April 25, 1871. He was the author of *Book of devotions and sermons* (Montreal, 1851) and *Aid to sacramental communion* (Montreal, 1864).

[A. E. Byerly, *Fergus* (Elora, Ont., 1934).]

MacDonnell, Sir Richard Graves (1814-1881), lieutenant-governor of Nova Scotia (1864-65), was born in Dublin, Ireland, on September 3, 1814, the eldest son of Richard MacDonnell, D.D., provost of Trinity College, Dublin. He was educated at Trinity College (B.A., 1835; M.A., 1836; LL.B., 1845; LL.D., 1862), and was called to the Irish bar in 1838, and to the English bar in 1841. In 1843 he was appointed chief justice, and in 1847 governor, of the British settlements on the Gambia. From 1855 to 1862 he was governor of South Australia; from 1864 to 1865 he was lieutenant-governor of Nova Scotia, during the period of the first negotiations looking toward Confederation; and from 1865 to 1872 he was governor of Hong Kong. He then retired from the public service on a pension; and he died at Hyères, France, on February 5, 1881. He was created a C.B. in 1852, a knight bachelor in 1856, and a K.C.M.G. in 1871.

[*Dict. nat. biog.*; *Can. who was who*, vol. 2; Taylor, *Brit. Am.*, vol. 1.]

Macdonnell, Ronald Macalister (1909-1973), diplomat, was born in Vernon, British Columbia, May 11, 1909, and educated at the University of Manitoba (B.A. (Hons.), 1930), and at Oxford University (B.A. (Hons.), 1932). He entered the department of external affairs as third secretary in 1934 and served in Ottawa, Washington, and Moscow. He was appointed chargé d'affaires in Czechoslovakia (1947), and opened the first Canadian legation there. He was minister in the Canadian Embassy at Paris (1950-52) and assistant undersecretary of state in Ottawa (1952-54). He was first Canadian commissioner in the International Supervisory Commission in Vietnam and Cambodia. He was ambassador to Egypt and minister to Lebanon (1957-58) and deputy undersecretary of state for external affairs (1959). He became secretary general of the International Civil Aviation Organization, Montreal, in 1959. He was successively ambassador to Indonesia (1963); high commissioner to New Zealand (1966-70); and high

commissioner to Sri Lanka (1970-73). He died at Colombo, Sri Lanka, May 19, 1973.
[*Can. who's who*, 1970-72.]

McDonnell, William (1814-1900), author, was born in Cork, Ireland, in 1814, and settled in Canada about 1830. He first lived in Peterborough, Upper Canada, and about 1840 moved to Lindsay, where he founded a tannery and later a store. From 1866 to 1868 he was mayor of Lindsay. He died at Lindsay, Ontario, on June 20, 1900. He was the author of the following novels, *Exeter Hall* (Boston, 1869), *Heathens of the heath* (New York, 1874; 2nd ed., 1875), and *Family creeds* (Toronto, 1879). He published also two long narrative poems, *Manita* (Lindsay, n.d.) and *Cleopa* (Lindsay, n.d.); and he wrote both libretto and music for a three-act operatic romance, *Marina, the fisherman's daughter* (Toronto, 1884).
[Private information.]

McDouall, Robert (d. 1848), soldier, entered the British army as a cornet in 1796, and saw service in Canada during the War of 1812. He was present at the battle of Stoney Creek, and was mentioned in despatches. He was promoted to the rank of lieutenant-colonel in 1813; and in the summer of 1814 he was in command at Michilimackinac, during its successful defence against the Americans. He retired from the army on half-pay in 1816; and was awarded the C.B. in 1817. He was promoted to the rank of major-general in 1841; and he died at Stranraer, Scotland, on November 15, 1848.
[L. H. Irving, *Officers of the British forces in Canada during the war of 1812-15* (Welland, Ont., 1908); W. Wood (ed.), *Select British documents of the Canadian war of 1812* (3 vols., Toronto, 1920-28); Morgan, *Cel. Can.*]

McDougall, Alexander (*fl.* 1799-1814), fur-trader, became a partner of the North West Company prior to 1799. He signed the agreements of 1802 and 1804 by attorney; and he does not appear to have been ever at Grand Portage or Fort William. Probably he was in charge of some district, such as the Timiskaming or Abitibi district, dependent on Montreal. A "Mr. M'gdougle" is said by J. B. Perrault (q.v.) to have been in charge of a fort at the lower end of Lake Abitibi in 1812. He seems to have retired from the fur-trade about 1813; and in 1814 he was elected a member of the Beaver Club of Montreal. He was dead by 1825.
[W. S. Wallace (ed.), *Documents relating to the North West Company* (Toronto: The Champlain Society, 1934).]

McDougall, Duncan (*fl.* 1810-1817), fur-trader, joined the Pacific Fur Company of J. J. Astor (q.v.) as a partner in 1810, and took part in the founding of Fort Astoria in 1811. He was in charge of Fort Astoria when it was handed over to the Nor'Westers in 1813; and he then entered the service of the North West Company, apparently as a partner. He remained on the Pacific coast until 1817, when he went east to Fort William, and when Ross Cox (q.v.) met him on his way to his winter quarters, Franchère (q.v.) says he died "a miserable death" at Bas de la Rivière, Lake Winnipeg; but does not say when. He married in 1813 a daughter of Comcomly, chief of the Chinooks.
[E. Coues (ed.), *New light on the early history of the greater northwest* (3 vols., New York, 1897).]

McDougall, George (*fl.* 1815-1843), fur-trader, was a brother of James McDougall (q.v.). D. W. Harmon (q.v.), who met him in New Caledonia in 1816, says that he had come out to the Peace River in 1815, as a clerk in the Hudson's Bay Company party commanded by John Clarke (q.v.). He left the Hudson's Bay Company at Fort Vermilion, and crossed the mountains to visit his brother James. At Stuart's Lake, in 1816, he took service with the North West Company; and he remained in New Caledonia until after 1825. He was taken over as a clerk by the Hudson's Bay Company in 1821; and most of his later service was at Lesser Slave Lake. He was still a clerk in 1843.
[E. E. Rich (ed.), *Journal of occurrences in the Athabasca department, by George Simpson* (Toronto: The Champlain Society, 1938).]

McDougall, George Millward (1821-1876), missionary, was born in Kingston, Upper Canada, September 9, 1821. He was educated at Victoria College, Cobourg; and in 1851 was sent as a missionary to Garden River, near Sault Ste. Marie. From there he went to the West in 1860, and was stationed at Rossville, in the Hudson's Bay Territories. About January 25, 1876, he perished in a snow-storm near Calgary, North West Territories.
[Rev. J. McDougall, *George Millward McDougall, the pioneer, patriot and missionary* (Toronto, 1888); Rev. J. McLean, *The hero of the Saskatchewan* (Barrie, Ont., 1891); *Dict. Can. biog.*, vol. 10.]

McDougall, James (1783?-1851), fur-trader, was born about 1783, and entered the service of the North West Company in 1798. He was a clerk in the Athabaska department in 1799; and from 1808 to 1816 he was employed either in New Caledonia or on the Peace River. He was taken over as a clerk by the Hudson's Bay Company in 1821; and the rest of his service was spent entirely in New Caledonia. He was "superannuated" in 1832; and John McLean (q.v.) described him as, in 1841, "still struggling with adversity". He died at Montreal, on August 17, 1851, aged 67 years.

[W. S. Wallace (ed.), *Documents relating to the North West Company* (Toronto: The Champlain Society, 1934).]

MacDougall, James Brown (1871-1950), educationist and author, was born in Scotland, on June 1, 1871, and died at Toronto, Ontario, on May 28, 1950. He came to Canada at an early age, and was educated at Queen's University (B.A., 1896) and the University of Toronto (D. Paed., 1918). He became a schoolteacher, and from 1919 to 1942 was assistant chief inspector of the public and separate schools of Ontario, with special charge of the schools in northern and eastern Ontario. He was the author of *Rural life in Canada* (Toronto, 1913), *Building the north* (Toronto, 1919), *The real Mother Goose* (Toronto, 1940), and *Ten thousand miles of gold* (Toronto, 1946).

[*Can. who's who*, 1948.]

McDougall, John (1842-1917), missionary and author, was born at Owen Sound, Ontario, on December 27, 1842, the son of the Rev. George Millward McDougall (q.v.). He was educated at Victoria University (D.D., 1903), and was ordained a minister of the Methodist Church in 1874. He was for many years a missionary among the Indians of the Canadian North West; and he rendered valuable services to the government in connection with both of the North West rebellions. He was superannuated in 1906; and he died at Calgary, Alberta, on January 15, 1917. He was the author of *George Millward McDougall* (Toronto, 1888), *Forest, lake, and prairie* (Toronto, 1895), *Saddle, sled, and snowshoe* (Toronto, 1896), *Pathfinding on plain and prairie* (Toronto, 1898), *"Wa-pee Moostooch" or White Buffalo* (Calgary, 1908), *In the days of the Red River rebellion* (Toronto, 1911), and *On western trails in the early seventies* (Toronto, 1911).

[Morgan, *Can. men* (1912).]

McDougall, John Lorn (1838-1909), auditor-general of Canada (1878-1905), was born at Renfrew, Upper Canada, on November 6, 1838, the son of John Lorn McDougall, a lumber merchant, and Catherine Cameron. He was educated at the Montreal High School and at the University of Toronto (B.A., 1859; M.A., 1882; LL.D., 1904). Until 1878 he managed the lumber business established by his father at Renfrew. From 1867 to 1871 he was the representative of South Renfrew in the Legislative Assembly of Ontario, and he represented the same constituency in the Canadian House of Commons from 1869 to 1872, and again from 1874 to 1878. In 1878 he was appointed auditor-general of Canada; and he held this office until his retirement in 1905. He died at Ottawa on January 15, 1909. In 1870 he married Marion, daughter of P. Morris, of Ottawa; and by her he had several children. He was created a C.M.G. in 1897.

[*Can. who was who*, vol. 1; *Can. parl. comp.*; Morgan, *Can. men* (1898); Rose, *Cyc. Can. biog.* (1886); *Canadian biographical dictionary*, Ontario vol. (Toronto, 1880).]

McDougall, John Malcolm (1858-1924), jurist, was born at Three Rivers, Canada East, on January 5, 1858, the son of the Hon. William McDougall (q.v.), of Three Rivers. He was educated at McGill University, and was called to the bar of Quebec in 1879; and he practised law, first at Three Rivers, then at Aylmer, and finally at Hull, Quebec. He contested unsuccessfully the county of Wright in the elections for the Legislative Assembly of Quebec in 1891, the county of Wright in 1896, in 1897, and in 1905, and the county of Argenteuil in 1911; and in 1911 he was appointed, like his father, a judge of the Superior Court for the district of Ottawa. He retired from the bench in 1922; and he died at Montreal, Quebec, on August 5, 1924.

[P. G. Roy, *Les juges de la province de Québec* (Quebec, 1933); Morgan, *Can. men* (1912).]

McDougall, Mrs. Margaret (1826?-1898), author, was born about 1826, and lived in later life, first, at White River, Ontario, and secondly at Bay City, Michigan. She died in 1898. She published, under the pseudonym "Nora", two books: *Verses and rhymes by the way* (Pembroke, Ont., 1880) and *The days of a life* (Almonte, Ont., 1883).

[M. K. Goodrich, *A bibliography of Michigan authors* (Richmond, Va., 1928); C. C. James, *A bibliography of Canadian poetry* (Toronto, 1899).]

McDougall, William (1822-1905), one of the Fathers of Confederation, was born near York (Toronto), Upper Canada, on January 25, 1822, the son of Daniel McDougall and Hannah Matthews. He was educated at Victoria College, Cobourg; and in 1847 he was admitted to practice as an attorney and solicitor in Upper Canada. Later, in 1862, he was called to the bar of Upper Canada (Q.C., 1881). He became one of the leaders of the "Clear Grit" or radical wing of the Reform party; and in 1850 he founded the *North American*, the organ of this faction. In 1857, however, the *North American* was absorbed by the *Globe*, and McDougall became an associate of George Brown (q.v.). In 1858 he was elected to the Legislative Assembly of Canada, and he was a member of parliament almost continuously until 1882. In the Canadian Assembly he sat for North Oxford from 1858 to 1863, for North Ontario from 1863 to 1864, and for North Lanark from 1864 to 1867; in the Canadian House of Commons he sat for North Lanark from 1867 to 1872, and for Halton from 1878 to 1882; and in the Legislative Assembly of Ontario he sat for South Simcoe from 1875 to 1878.

From 1862 to 1864 he was commissioner of crown lands in the Macdonald-Sicotte and Macdonald-Dorion administrations; and in 1864, with George Brown, he entered the "Great Coalition" as provincial secretary. He was a delegate to the Charlottetown and Quebec conferences of 1864, and to the Confederation Conference at Westminster in 1866. He parted company with George Brown when Brown resigned from the coalition government in 1865; and in 1867 he became one of the leading Liberals in the first government of the Dominion. He was minister of public works from 1867 to 1869; in 1868 he went to England with Sir George Cartier (q.v.) to arrange for the acquisition by the Dominion of the Hudson's Bay Company's territories; and in 1869 he was appointed lieutenant-governor of Rupert's Land and the North West Territories. His attempt to enter upon his duties in the North West resulted in an unfortunate fiasco, when he was turned back by the Red River rebels at Pembina; and he was immediately removed from office. This episode, together with the fact that he had been repudiated by the Liberals under George Brown, destroyed his political influence; and he gradually retired from public life. In 1873 he resumed his legal practice; and he died at Ottawa on May 29, 1905. He was twice married, (1) in 1845 to Amelia Caroline, daughter of Joseph Easton, Millbank, Upper Canada; and (2) in 1872 to Mary Adelaide, daughter of John Beatty, M.D., professor in Victoria College, Cobourg. In 1867 he was created a C.B. (civil).

He was the author of *Eight letters to the Hon. Joseph Howe on the Red River rebellion* (Toronto, 1870), *Six letters to the Hon. O. Mowat on the amendment of the provincial constitution* (Toronto, 1875), and *An open letter to the Hon. H. Mercier on the federalism of the federal constitution of 1867* (Toronto, 1887).

[M. O. Hammond, *Confederation and its leaders* (Toronto, 1917); Morgan, *Can. men* (1898) and *Bib. can.*; Rose, *Cyc. Can. biog.* (1886); Dent, *Can. port.*, vol. 4; *Can. parl. comp.*; Sir J. Pope, *Memoirs of the Rt. Hon. J. A. Macdonald* (2 vols., Ottawa, 1894) and *Correspondence of Sir John Macdonald* (Toronto, 1921); Sir G. W. Ross, *Getting into parliament and after* (Toronto, 1913); C. Clarke, *Sixty years in Upper Canada* (Toronto, 1908); O. D. Skelton, *The life and times of Sir A. T. Galt* (Toronto, 1920).]

McDougall, William (1831-1886), jurist, was born in Scotland in 1831, and came to Canada with his parents in 1842. His father, John McDougall, became a leading industrialist in the region of Three Rivers; but the son studied law, and was called to the bar of Lower Canada in 1854. From 1868 to 1880 he represented Three Rivers in the Canadian House of Commons; and in 1880 he was appointed a judge of the Superior Court for the district of Ottawa. He died at Aylmer, Quebec, on March 3, 1886.

[P. G. Roy, *Les juges de la province de Québec* (Quebec, 1933); *Dom. ann. reg.*, 1886; *Can. parl. comp.*]

McDowall, Robert (1769?-1841), clergyman, was born in what is now the United States, of Scottish parentage, about 1769. He was licensed to preach by the Dutch Reformed Church in 1790, and in 1798 he came to Upper Canada as a missionary. In 1800 he accepted a call from the congregations at Adolphustown, Ernestown, and Fredericksburgh, on the Bay of Quinte; and he remained in this charge, first as a minister of the Dutch Reformed Church, but later as a minister in connection with the Church of Scotland, until his death at Fredericksburgh, on August 3, 1841. He was the author of *A sermon on the nature of justification through the imputed righteousness of the Redeemer* (York, 1805), which was one of the earliest examples of a printed pamphlet in Upper Canada; and he published a volume of *Discourses* (Albany, 1806).

[W. Gregg, *A history of the Presbyterian Church in Canada* (Toronto, 1885).]

McDunnough, James Halliday (1877-1962), insect taxonomist and builder of insect collections, was born in Toronto, May 10, 1877. He received his early education in Toronto, and in 1897 went to Germany, where he studied languages and music with Josef Joachim. He began his study of entomology at the University of Berlin in 1904, at the same time as he was taking an "extramural" course in moderns at Queen's University. He was granted an M.A. by Queen's and a Ph.D. by Berlin in 1909. He returned to North America in 1909 and became associated with the marine biological laboratory at Wood's Hole, Massachusetts. In 1910 he became the first curator of the Barnes collection of lepidoptera and began the publication with Dr. Barnes of an extensive series of papers on butterflies and moths. He came to Ottawa in 1919 as chief of the newly created division of systematic entomology, becoming the first officer appointed to develop a national collection of insects and an insect identification service. From this he developed one of the most important collections of North American insects during his twenty-eight years with the department and published 199 taxonomic papers on moths, butterflies, and mayflies. Dr. McDunnough left Ottawa in 1946 to join the American Museum of Natural History in New York as research associate but, on the death of his wife in 1950, he moved to Halifax, where, in addition to his association with the American Museum, he became a research associate of the Nova Scotia Museum of Science and continued his researches in entomology. He was a fellow of the Entomological Society of America and of the Royal Society of Canada and an honorary member of the New York Entomological Society and the Lepidopterists' Society. From 1921 until 1938 he edited *The Canadian entomologist*. He was an indefatigable collector and the Canadian National Collection of Insects and its supporting library are his memorials. He died at Halifax, Nova Scotia, February 23, 1962.

[*Proc. Roy. Soc. Can.*, 1962.]

McEachren, Duncan McNab (1841-1924), veterinary surgeon, was born at Campbelltown, Argyllshire, Scotland, on October 27, 1841. He graduated from the Edinburgh Veterinary College in 1861; and emigrated to Canada shortly afterwards. In 1866 he founded the Montreal Veterinary College, which became in 1890 a faculty in McGill University; and he was professor of veterinary science in this institution from 1866 to his retirement in 1903. From 1876 to 1902 he was also chief inspector of livestock for Canada; and after 1902 he became honorary consulting veterinarian to the government of Canada. McGill University conferred on him the degrees of D.V.S. (1890) and LL.D. (1909). He died at Ormstown, Quebec, on October 13, 1924. With A. Smith, he was joint author of *The Canadian horse and his diseases* (Toronto, 1867).

[Morgan, *Can. men* (1912); Rose, *Cyc. Can. biog.* (1888).]

McElheran, Robert Benjamin (1877-1939), clergyman and educationist, was born at London, Ontario, in 1877, and died at Toronto, Ontario, on August 12, 1939. He was educated at the University of Toronto (B.A., 1906; M.A., 1908) and Wycliffe College, and was ordained a priest of the Church of England. From 1907 to 1930 he was rector of St. Matthew's Anglican Church in Winnipeg, and from 1930 to his death he was principal of Wycliffe College.

[Mrs. R. B. McElheran, *That's what I'm here for: Robert B. McElheran, his days and his ways* (Toronto, 1955); *Can. who's who*, 1936-37; Toronto *Globe and Mail*, Aug. 14, 1939.]

McEvay, Fergus Patrick (1852-1911), Roman Catholic archbishop of Toronto (1908-11), was born at Lindsay, Canada West, on December 8, 1852, the son of Michael McEvay and Mary Lehane. He was educated at St. Michael's College, Toronto, at the St. Francis Seminary, Milwaukee, and at the Jesuits' College, Montreal; and he was ordained a priest in 1882. He served successively at Fenelon Falls, Peterborough, and Hamilton, in Ontario; and in 1899 he was consecrated bishop of London. In 1908 he became archbishop of Toronto; and he died at Toronto on May 10, 1911.

[Morgan, *Can. men* (1912); *Can. who was who*, vol. 2.]

McEvoy, Bernard (1842-1932), journalist and author, was born in Birmingham, England, on February 7, 1842, the son of Henry McEvoy. He was educated in Birmingham, and became a journalist. He came to Canada in 1888, and for ten years was on the staff of the Toronto *Mail and Empire*. In 1901 he went to British Columbia, and for many years he was on the staff of the Vancouver *Province*. He died at Vancouver on February 16, 1932. He married Susan Isabelle, daughter of W. J. Holmden, Plymouth, England; and by her he had four sons. He was the author of *A way from newspaperdom and other poems* (Toronto, 1897; 2nd ed., 1898), *The feast of the dead* (Toronto, 1899), *From the Great Lakes to the wide west* (Toronto, 1902), *Verses for my friends* (Vancouver, B.C., 1924), and *Elvira and Fernando* (Toronto, 1927); and he was joint author, with A. H. Finlay, of *History of the 72nd Seaforth Highlanders of Canada* (Vancouver, B.C., n.d.).

[*Can. who was who*, vol. 2; Morgan, *Can. men* (1912).]

McEvoy, John Millar (1864-1935), judge and author, was born at Caradoc, Ontario, in 1864. He was educated at the University of Toronto (B.A., 1890; LL.B., 1892), and was for a time lecturer in political science in this university. He was called to the bar in 1893, and for many years practised law in London, Ontario. He was appointed a judge of the Supreme Court of Ontario in 1927; and he died in Toronto on April 16, 1935. He was the author of *The Ontario township: A history of the growth of municipal institutions in the province* (Toronto, 1889), *Essay on Canadian banking and currency* (Toronto, n.d.), and *Karl Marx's theory of value* (Toronto, n.d.).

[*University of Toronto monthly*, 1935; Morgan, *Can. men* (1912); *Fortnightly law journal*, Toronto, 1935.]

Macfarlane, Alexander (1818-1898), senator of Canada, was born at Wallace, Nova Scotia, on June 17, 1818, the son of the Hon. Donald Macfarlane. He was called to the bar of Nova Scotia in 1844 (Q.C., 1867); and he represented Cumberland in the House of Assembly of Nova Scotia from 1856 to 1867. From 1865 to 1867 he was a member of the Executive Council of the province; and in 1866-67 he was one of the delegates of Nova Scotia at the London Conference for the completion of Confederation. In 1870 he was called to the Senate of Canada, and he sat in the Senate until his death on December 13, 1898. He married Anne, daughter of Amos Seaman, of Minudie, Nova Scotia.

[*Cyc. Am. biog.*; *Can. parl. comp.*; Rose, *Cyc. Can. biog.* (1886).]

Macfarlane, John (1857-1914), poet, was born at Abington, Lanarkshire, Scotland, in May, 1857. He came to Canada about 1890, and settled in Montreal, where he became a journalist. He died in Montreal on September 7, 1914. He edited an anthology entitled *The harp of the Scottish covenant* (London, 1895); and he was the author of *Heather and harebell* (Montreal, 1892) and *Songs of the thistle and maple* (Toronto, 1913).

[Morgan, *Can. men* (1912).]

Macfarlane, Thomas (1834-1907), mining engineer and author, was born at Pollokshaws, Renfrewshire, Scotland, on March 5, 1834, the son of Thomas Macfarlane. He was educated at Glasgow and at the Royal Mining School, Freiburg, Germany; and came to Canada in 1860 as a mining engineer. He discovered the famous Silver Islet mine, on Lake Superior. In 1886 he was appointed chief analyst to the department of inland revenue at Ottawa; and this office he held until his death on June 10, 1907. In 1858 he married Margaret Skelly, of Pollokshaws; and by her he had several children. In 1882 he was appointed a charter member of the Royal Society of Canada; and he published, in addition to many contributions to scientific periodicals, *Within the Empire* (Ottawa, 1891), an essay on imperial federation.

[*Proc. Roy. Soc. Can.*, 1908; Morgan, *Can. men* (1898).]

McGee, Thomas D'Arcy (1825-1868), one of the Fathers of Confederation, was born at Carlingford, county Louth, Ireland, on April 13, 1825, the son of James McGee, a coast guardsman, and Dorcas Catherine Morgan. He was educated at a day-school in Wexford, Ireland; and in 1842 he emigrated to America. He joined the staff of the Boston *Pilot*, a weekly journal for Irish-Americans, and became its editor. In 1845 he returned to Ireland, and became the editor of *Freeman's Journal* in Dublin. The policy of this newspaper proved too moderate for him, and he transferred his services to the *Nation*, the organ of the "Young Ireland" party. Though not actually in arms, he was implicated in the rebellion of 1848, and escaped to America in the disguise of a priest. In New York he founded in 1848 the *New York Nation*, a short-lived weekly newspaper; in 1850 he moved to Boston, and founded the *American Celt*, and in 1852 he moved to Buffalo, where he published the *American Celt* for five years.

In 1857 he moved from Buffalo to Montreal, Lower Canada, at the invitation of some leading Irish-Canadians. In Montreal he founded a newspaper called the *New Era* (1857-58), and in 1858 he was elected, as an Irish Roman Catholic, to the Legislative Assembly of Canada for Montreal West. This constituency he represented until 1867; and he was re-elected for it to the first House of Commons of the new Dominion. He first aligned himself with the Reformers, and in 1862-63 he was president of the council, and later provincial secretary, in the S. Macdonald-Sicotte administration. When the government was reorganized in 1863, however, he was omitted from it; and he then transferred his allegiance to the Conservatives. He became minister of agriculture in the second Taché-Macdonald government of 1864, and he continued to hold this portfolio in the "Great Coalition" until 1867. He was a delegate to the Charlottetown and Quebec conferences in 1864, and he contributed in a peculiar degree to the success of the Confederation movement. From the moment of his arrival in Canada, he had preached the doctrine of "the new nationality"; and his eloquent advocacy did more than anything else to create the psychological basis for union. In 1867, when the first cabinet of the Dominion of Canada was being formed, he stood aside, with Charles Tupper (q.v.), in a spirit of rare self-abnegation, in order that the claims of the Irish Roman Catholics and the people of Nova Scotia might be combined in the appointment to office of Edward Kenny (q.v.). In the first parliament of the Dominion, therefore, he was merely a private member of the House of Commons. But his claim to the title of having been the chief apostle of Canadian national unity was even then secure.

Even before he came to Canada, he had begun to shed many of his youthful anti-British ideas; and in Canada he became a loyal subject of the Crown. In 1866 he condemned with vehemence the Irish-American Fenians who invaded Canada; and in so doing he incurred the enmity of the Fenian organization in the United States. As a result, he was assassinated at Ottawa, in the early morning of April 7, 1868, by a Fenian named Whalen, as he was returning from a late session of the House.

One of the most brilliant orators who have graced Canadian public life, McGee was also a writer and poet of no mean order. Before coming to Canada he published several books dealing with Irish affairs, notably *A history of the Irish settlers in North America* (Boston, 1852) and *Historical sketches of O'Connell and his friends* (Boston, 1854); and in Canada he published *A popular history of Ireland* (New York, 1863) and *The Irish position in British and in republican North America* (pamphlet, Montreal, 1866). In connection with Confederation he published *Speeches and addresses, chiefly on the subject of British American union* (London, Montreal, 1865; tr. into French by L. G. Gladu, St. Hyacinthe, 1865), and *The mental outfit of the new Dominion* (pamphlet, 1867). He was also the author of *Canadian ballads, and occasional verses* (Montreal, 1858). After his death his poetical work was collected by Mrs. J. Sadlier under the title *The poems of Thomas D'Arcy McGee* (New York, 1869), with a biographical sketch; and the Hon. Charles Murphy edited *D'Arcy McGee: A collection of his speeches and addresses* (Toronto, 1937).

[Isabel Skelton, *The life of Thomas D'Arcy McGee* (Gardenvale, Quebec, 1925);

A. Brady, *D'Arcy McGee* (Toronto, 1925); H. J. O'C. French, *Life of the Hon. T. D. McGee* (pamphlet, Montreal, 1868); M. O. Hammond, *Confederation and its leaders* (Toronto, 1917); W. S. Wallace, *The growth of the Canadian national feeling* (Can. hist. rev., 1920); K. O'Donnell, *D'Arcy McGee's Canadian ballads* (Rev. de L'Univ. d'Ottawa, 1971); T. Slattery, *Assassination of D'Arcy McGee* (Toronto, 1968); *Dict. nat. biog.*; *Cyc. Am. biog.*; Morgan, *Bib. Can.*; Taylor, *Brit. Am.*; Josephine Phelan, *The ardent exile* (Toronto, 1951).]

MacGeorge, Robert Jackson (1811?-1884), clergyman and author, was born near Glasgow, Scotland, about 1811. He was educated at Glasgow and Edinburgh universities, and was ordained a priest of the Church of England in 1840. In 1841 he came to Canada, and became the incumbent of Christ Church, Streetsville, Upper Canada. While here he edited the *Streetsville Review* (1848-58), in which he wrote under the pseudonym of "Solomon of Streetsville". He was also editor of the *Anglo-American Magazine* (Toronto, 1852-55), and to this periodical he contributed a number of interesting papers. In 1854 he returned to Scotland, and he became dean of Argyll and of the Isles. He died at Orcadia, Rothesay, Scotland, on May 14, 1884. He was the editor of *The Canadian Christian offering* (Toronto, 1848), and the author of *Tales, sketches, and lyrics* (Toronto, 1858).

[*Dom. ann. reg.*, 1884; *Cyc. Am. biog.*; C. C.James, *A bibliography of Canadian poetry* (Toronto, 1899); A. MacMurchy, *Handbook of Canadian literature* (Toronto, 1906).]

MacGibbon, Duncan Alexander (1882-1969), economist, was born at Lochaber Bay, Quebec, March 12, 1882. He worked as a printer and a reporter before enrolling at McMaster University, where he obtained a B.A. in 1908 and M.A. in 1911. After teaching at Brandon College, Manitoba, he became a graduate student at the University of Chicago (Ph.D., 1915). On graduation he began teaching at McMaster University, but this was interrupted by his enlistment in the First Canadian Tank Battalion in the First World War. At the end of the war he taught at Khaki College, Ripon, Yorkshire, for a year before returning to Canada as professor and head of the department of political economy at the University of Alberta. In 1929 he left the university to become a member of the Canadian Board of Grain Commissioners, where he served until his retirement in 1949. He then returned to Hamilton and taught, part-time, at McMaster University. He produced two definitive books on the grain trade, *The Canadian grain trade* (Toronto, 1932), and a second volume, *The Canadian grain trade, 1931-1951* (Toronto, 1952). He was a member of the edito-

rial board of the *Canadian Journal of Economics and Political Science*. His experience with the wheat economy during the depression of the 1930s gave him a perspective on production and economic problems which went beyond the consideration of monetary and fiscal policies as tools for attacking world-wide problems related to population and food production. He was a fellow of the Royal Society of Canada, a fellow of the Royal Economic Society, a member of the Canadian Political Science Association (president, 1935), and of the Canadian Institute of International Affairs. He died at Hamilton, Ontario, on October 10, 1969.

[*Proc. and Trans. Roy. Soc. Can.*, vol. VIII.]

McGibbon, Robert Davidson (1857-1906), lawyer, was born in Montreal, Canada East, in 1857, and was educated at McGill University (B.A., 1877; B.C.L., 1879). He was called to the bar in 1879, and practised law in Montreal. He died in Montreal on April 18, 1906. He was the author of *A complete synopsis of the great pew case* (Montreal, 1877).

[Morgan, *Can. men* (1898).]

McGill, Andrew (1756-1805), merchant, was born in Glasgow, Scotland, in 1756, the fifth son of James McGill, a merchant of Glasgow, and a younger brother of James McGill (q.v.) of Montreal. He matriculated into Glasgow University in 1765 at the early age of ten years. He joined his brothers James and John (q.v.) in Montreal about 1775, and became a junior partner in the firm of Todd and McGill. He died in Montreal on August 1, 1805, aged 49 years. He married Anne, daughter of Dr. Wood of Cornwall; and she married in 1807 the Rev. John Strachan (q.v.), afterwards first bishop of Toronto.

[W. D. Lighthall, *The newly discovered "James and Andrew McGill Journal, 1797"* (Trans. Roy. Soc. Can., 1935).]

McGill, Anthony (1847-1929), chemist, was born at Rothesay, Scotland, and came to Canada in early youth. He was educated at the University of Toronto (B.A., 1880) and at Victoria University, Cobourg (B.Sc., 1882); and was for some years a school-teacher. In 1887 he was appointed assistant chief analyst in the department of inland revenue at Ottawa; and in 1907 he became chief analyst. In 1900 he was elected a fellow of the Royal Society of Canada; and he contributed a number of papers to its *Transactions*. He retired from the civil service in 1918; and died at Berkeley, California, on January 1, 1929.

[Morgan, *Can. men* (1912).]

McGill, Mrs. Helen Emma, née Gregory (1864-1947), judge, was born in Hamilton, Canada West, on January 7, 1864, and died in Chicago, Illinois, on February 27, 1947. She was educated at Trinity College, Toronto (Mus. B., 1886; B.A., 1889; M.A., 1890); and during the first part of her life was a journalist in the United States. After the death of her first husband in 1901, and her marriage to her second husband in 1903, she went to live in Vancouver, British Columbia; and there in 1917 she was appointed judge of the Juvenile Court, an office she held, with an interval of only five years, until her retirement in 1945.

[Elsie MacGill, *My mother the judge* (Toronto, 1955); *Can. who's who*, 1938-39; *Encyc. Can.*]

McGill, James (1744-1813), merchant and philanthropist, was born in Glasgow, Scotland, on October 6, 1744, the eldest son of James McGill, a merchant of Glasgow. He matriculated into Glasgow University in 1756, but it does not appear that he graduated from the University. He emigrated to the American colonies, and engaged in the fur-trade. He later became a charter member of the Beaver Club of Montreal; and the date of his Beaver Club medal reveals the fact that he first wintered in the Indian country in 1766. He spent the winter of 1771 at Crow Wing River, west of Fond du Lac. He made Montreal his headquarters about 1774; and he was a party to the joint stock arrangement of the western traders in 1775. He entered into partnership with Isaac Todd, and played for many years a foremost part in the Canadian fur-trade. He was never, as has been sometimes stated, a member of the North West Company; but after 1779 confined himself to the south-west trade. From 1792 to 1796, and from 1800 to 1804, he represented the West Ward of Montreal in the Legislative Assembly of Lower Canada; and in 1793 he was appointed a member of the Executive Council of the province. He died at Montreal on December 12, 1813; and a large part of his estate was left by will to found McGill University. In 1776 he married Charlotte, daughter of Guillaume Guillemin, and widow of François des Rivères.

[J. W. Dawson, *A biographical sketch of James McGill* (Barnard's American journal of education, 1859); C. Macmillan, *McGill and its story* (Toronto, 1921); R. Campbell, *A history of the Scotch Presbyterian Church, St. Gabriel St., Montreal* (Montreal, 1887); W. D. Lighthall, *The newly discovered "James and Andrew McGill Journal, 1797"* (Trans. Roy. Soc. Can., 1935).]

McGill, John (1746-1797), merchant, was born in 1746, a son of James McGill, a merchant of Glasgow, Scotland, and a younger brother of James McGill (q.v.), of Montreal. He came to Canada as early as 1770, for his name appears in the fur-trade licences of that date; and the date on his Beaver Club medal reveals the fact that he wintered in the Indian country in 1770. In 1773 he appears in the fur-trade licences as a partner of his brother James, and in 1774 as a partner of Charles Paterson (q.v.). He became a member of the firm of Todd and McGill, and he died in Montreal on December 1, 1797.

[W. S. Wallace (ed.), *Documents relating to the North West Company* (Toronto: The Champlain Society, 1934).]

McGill, John (1752-1834), executive councillor of Upper Canada, was born in Auckland, Wigtonshire, Scotland, in March, 1752. In 1773 he emigrated to Virginia, and he served in the loyalist forces throughout the American Revolution. In the later stages of the war he was a captain in the Queen's Rangers under Simcoe (q.v.). In 1783 he settled in Saint John, New Brunswick; but in 1792 he came to Upper Canada with Simcoe as commissary of stores. In 1796 he was appointed a member of the Executive Council of Upper Canada, and in 1797 a member of the Legislative Council. In 1801 he was made inspector-general of accounts, and in 1813 receiver-general. He retired on a pension in 1822, and he died at York (Toronto), on December 31, 1834. In New Brunswick he married Catherine, sister of the Hon. George Crookshank; but she died in 1819, and McGill's estate passed to his nephew, Peter McCutcheon, who thereupon assumed the name of Peter McGill (q.v.).

[*Cyc. Am. biog.*; W. J. Rattray, *The Scot in British North America* (4 vols., Toronto, 1881); J. Ross Robertson (ed.), *The diary of Mrs. Simcoe* (Toronto, 1911).]

McGill, Peter (1789-1860), speaker of the Legislative Council of Canada (1847-48), was born at Cree Bridge, Wigtonshire, Scotland, in August, 1789, the son of John McCutcheon, of Newton Stewart in Galloway. He emigrated to Canada in 1809, and engaged in business in Montreal. He assumed the name of McGill at the request of his uncle, the Hon. John McGill (q.v.), whose heir he became in 1835, and was later the head of the firm of Peter McGill and Co. From 1834 to 1860 he was president of the Bank of Montreal; and in 1834 he became chairman of the first railway company in Canada, the St. Lawrence and Champlain. In 1841, he was appointed to the Legislative Council of Canada, and in 1847-48 he was speaker of the Council, with a seat in the Executive Council. He died at Beaver Hall Place, his house in Montreal, on September 28, 1860.

[A. Shortt, *Founders of Canadian banking: The Hon. Peter McGill* (Journal of the Can. Bankers' Assoc., 1924); Rev. W. Snodgrass, *The night of death: A Sermon on the occasion of the death of Hon. Peter McGill* (Montreal, 1860); Taylor, *Brit. Am.*, vol. 2; Morgan, *Cel. Can.*; W. J. Rattray, *The Scot in British North America* (4 vols., Toronto, 1881); J. C. Dent, *The last forty years* (2 vols., Toronto, 1881).]

McGill, Robert (1798-1856), clergyman and author, was born in Ayrshire, Scotland, in 1798; and was ordained a minister of the Church of Scotland in 1829. The same year he was sent to Canada as minister of the Presbyterian Church at Niagara, Upper Canada. He remained in this charge until 1845; and from 1837 to 1840 he edited here the *Canadian Christian Examiner*, a monthly periodical. In 1845 he became minister of St. Paul's Church, Montreal; and he died at Montreal on February 4, 1856. In 1853 he was made a D.D. of Glasgow University. He was the author of *Brief notes on the relation of the synod of Canada to the Church of Scotland* (Niagara, 1844), *Letters on the condition and prospects of Queen's College, Kingston* (Montreal, 1846), and *Discourses preached on various occasions* (Montreal, 1853).

[W. Gregg, *A history of the Presbyterian Church in the Dominion of Canada* (Toronto, 1885); R. Campbell, *A history of the Scotch Presbyterian Church, St. Gabriel Street, Montreal* (Montreal, 1887).]

McGillicuddy, Owen Ernest (1888-1954), journalist and poet, was born in Goderich, Ont., in 1888; and died at Toronto, Ont., on August 11, 1954. He was at first a reporter on the Toronto *Star*; but in 1927 he joined the staff of the *Mail and Empire*, later the *Globe and Mail*. He was the author of *The little marshal, and other poems* (Toronto, 1918) and of a sketch of the early life of Mackenzie King (q.v.), entitled *The making of a premier* (Toronto, 1922).

[Toronto *Globe and Mail*, Aug. 12, 1954.]

McGillicuddy, Paul Clark (1918-1942), airman and author, was born in Toronto, Ontario, on February 12, 1918, and was educated at the University of Toronto (B.A., 1940). While still an under-graduate, he published a book entitled *Between lectures* (Toronto, 1939). Soon after graduation, he enlisted in the Royal Canadian Air Force, and became a pilot. He was shot down during the raid on Dieppe on August 19, 1942; and he died at Littlehampton, England, two days later, on August 21, 1942.

[*University of Toronto monthly*, 1942.]

McGillis, Angus (d. 1811), fur-trader, was the second son of Donald McGillis, a United Empire Loyalist who settled in Charlottenburgh, Glengarry, Upper Canada, and his wife Mary, daughter of Ranald McDonell, Lundy. He entered the service of the North West Company, and was a clerk at Fort Dauphin in 1805. He died in 1811; and his will is preserved in the Sulpician Library at Montreal. He married an Indian wife, and by her had four children. One of these was probably the Angus McGillis who was a clerk at the time of the union of the North West and Hudson's Bay companies in 1821, and who died at

the Red River on January 23, 1843. Another was a daughter who married one Grant, and lived afterwards in St. Paul, Minnesota.

[W. S. Wallace (ed.), *Documents relating to the North West Company* (Toronto: The Champlain Society, 1934).]

McGillis, Donald (*fl.* 1786-1817), fur-trader, was a son of John McGillis, the eldest brother of Hugh McGillis (q.v.), and was born probably in Cape Breton in 1786, but afterwards came to Glengarry, Upper Canada. In 1811 he went out on the *Tonquin* with the expedition of J. J. Astor (q.v.) that founded Astoria. When Astoria was captured by the Nor'Westers in 1813, he took service with the North West Company. He did not, however, remain long in the Company's service, for in 1817 Ross Cox (q.v.) found him living on the Ottawa River. Later, he lived in Alexandria, Upper Canada, where he was for a time deputy registrar of deeds for Glengarry. He married Ruby Rutherford, of Middleboro, Vermont.

[W. S. Wallace (ed.), *Documents relating to the North West Company* (Toronto: The Champlain Society, 1934).]

McGillis, Hugh (1767?-1848), fur-trader, was born at Muneraghie, Inverness-shire, Scotland, about 1767, the fifth son of Donald McGillis, afterwards a United Empire Loyalist, who settled in Charlottenburgh, Upper Canada, and his wife Mary, daughter of Ranald McDonell, Lundy. He came to America with his parents in 1773, and after the American Revolution came north with them to Glengarry, Upper Canada. He entered the service of the North West Company as a clerk in 1790; and in 1801 he became a partner of the Company. He was at Fort Dauphin in 1799; and in 1802 he succeeded Archibald Norman McLeod (q.v.) in charge at this post. From 1806 to 1812 he was at Fond du Lac; from 1812 to 1813, at Fort William; from 1813 to 1814, at Michipicoten; and from 1814 to 1815, at the Lesser Slave Lake. In 1816 he was one of the partners of the North West Company arrested by Lord Selkirk (q.v.) at Fort William, and he was afterwards tried at York (Toronto), but acquitted. He retired from the fur-trade in 1816; and in 1818 he purchased Sir John Johnson's property at Williamstown, Upper Canada. Here he resided until his death, at Williamstown, on July 23, 1848, aged 81. There is a tablet to his memory in the Roman Catholic Church at Williamstown. He married in the West an Indian woman, by whom he had seven children, and whom he sent back to the West after he settled in Williamstown. All his children died without issue; and he left his property to his nephew, John McGillis, son of his brother Duncan.

[W. S. Wallace (ed.), *Documents relating to the North West Company* (Toronto: The Champlain Society, 1934).]

McGillivray, Carrie Holmes (d. 1949), novelist, was born near Williamstown, Ontario, and died at Toronto, Ontario, on May 16, 1949. She was for some years employed in the Ontario Bureau of Archives in Toronto; and she was the author of an historical novel, *The shadow of tradition: A tale of old Glengarry* (Ottawa, 1927; new ed., Toronto, 1945).

[Toronto *Globe and Mail*, May 18, 1949.]

MacGillivray, Donald (1862-1931), missionary and linguist, was born in Bruce county, Ontario, in 1862, and was educated at the University of Toronto (B.A., 1882; LL.D., 1919). For forty-three years he was a Presbyterian missionary in China; and because of his linguistic gifts, he was appointed general secretary of the Christian Literature Society of China. He translated St. John's Gospel into Chinese; and he compiled a "Mandarin-Romanized" Chinese dictionary. He died in London, England, on May 28, 1931, on his way home to Canada on furlough.

[*Who was who*, 1929-40.]

McGillivray, Duncan (d. 1808), fur-trader, was the second son of Donald McGillivray, "a small tenant of the Lovat Estate in Inverness-shire", and his wife, Anne McTavish, a sister of Simon McTavish (q.v.). He entered the service of the North West Company some time prior to 1793, and in 1793-95 he was stationed in the Upper Fort des Prairies department. His *Journal* for 1794-95 has been published, with valuable notes and introduction, by A. S. Morton (Toronto, 1929). He remained in this department until 1799, when he returned to Montreal, was elected a member of the Beaver Club, and became a partner in the firm of McTavish, Frobisher, and Co. As such, he returned to the West in 1800, and the statement has been made that he crossed the Rocky Mountains in 1801. This statement, however, has been definitely disproved. He left the West finally in 1802; and from 1802 to 1807 he was one of the agents of the North West Company at Fort William. He died, unmarried, in Montreal, on April 9, 1808.

[A. S. Morton, *The history of the Canadian west* (Toronto, 1940), *Under western skies* (Toronto, 1937), and *Did Duncan McGillivray and David Thompson cross the Rockies in 1801?* (Can. hist. rev., 1937); J. B. Tyrrell, *David Thompson and the Columbia River* (Can. hist. rev., 1937) and *Duncan McGillivray's movements in 1801* (Can. hist. rev., 1939).]

McGillivray, John (1777?-1855), fur-trader, was born near Inverness, Scotland, about the year 1777, the second son of Farquhar McGillivray, who is reputed to have led the remnant of the Clan Chattan from the field of Culloden. With his elder brother Duncan, he came to Canada and entered the service of the North West Company about 1796. His brother (who must be distinguished from the Duncan McGillivray who was a brother of the Hon.

William McGillivray) died soon afterwards; but John McGillivray rose rapidly in the service of the North West Company. He was made a partner of the Company in 1801; and he was in charge at Athabaska River from 1806 to 1810, and at Dunvegan from 1810 to 1815. He was one of the partners of the Company arrested by Lord Selkirk (q.v.) in 1816, and tried at York (Toronto) in 1817. He retired from the fur-trade in 1818, and settled in Williamstown, Upper Canada. From 1839 to 1841 he was a member of the Legislative Council of Upper Canada; and in 1852 he fell heir to the estate of Dunmaglass, near Inverness, Scotland, the home of the head of the clan. He never actually came into possession of the estate, for there was prolonged litigation over it; and he died at Williamstown, Upper Canada, in October, 1855. In 1819 he married at St. Andrews, Upper Canada, Isabelle, daughter of Colonel the Hon. Neil McLean; and by her he had four sons.

[W. S. Wallace (ed.), *Documents relating to the North West Company* (Toronto: The Champlain Society, 1934); J. N. Wallace, *The wintering partners on Peace River* (Ottawa, 1929).]

McGillivray, Joseph (1790?-1832), fur-trader, was born about 1790, a son of the Hon. William McGillivray (q.v.). He was made a partner of the North West Company in 1813, and from 1813 to 1817 was at Fort Okanagan. He was at Fort William in the summer of 1817; but evidently returned to the Columbia department, where he remained until 1828. In 1821 he was promoted to the rank of chief trader. In 1828 he was transferred to New Caledonia; and he retired from the fur-trade in 1831. He died at Montreal on April 22, 1832, aged 42.

[Ross Cox, *Adventures on the Columbia River* (2 vols., London, 1831).]

McGillivray, Simon (1783-1840), merchant, was born in Stratherrick in Inverness-shire, Scotland, in 1783, the youngest son of Donald McGillivray and Anne McTavish, a sister of Simon McTavish (q.v.). He was educated at his uncle's expense; but lameness precluded him from entering the fur-trade, like his brothers William and Duncan (q.v.). In 1805 he became a partner in the London firm of McTavish, Fraser and Co.; and in 1813 he became also a partner in the Montreal house of McTavish, McGillivrays and Co. He played a leading part in bringing about the union of the Hudson's Bay and North West companies in 1821, and in the summer of 1821 he made a journey to Fort William to oversee the details of the union. In 1822 he became a member of the new firm of McGillivrays, Thain, and Co.; and from 1821 to 1824 he was one of the special joint committee in London for the oversight of the fur-trade. In 1824, he and his brother William accepted stock in the Hudson's Bay Company in lieu of their rights; but in 1825 the firms of McTavish, McGillivrays, and Co. and McGillivrays, Thain, and Co. were declared insolvent, and Simon McGillivray was forced to go to Montreal to attempt to straighten out their tangled finances. In this, however, he was unsuccessful; and in 1830 he accepted an appointment as one of the commissioners appointed by the United Mexican Silver Mining Company to reorganize the management of their silver mines. He was in Mexico from 1830 to 1835. On his return to London, he became one of the proprietors of the *Morning Chronicle*; and in 1837 he married the eldest daughter of Sir John Easthope, his fellow proprietor. He died at his residence, Dartmouth Row, Blackheath, London; and was buried in Norwood cemetery, near London. He was survived by his widow, and one daughter, Mary, who afterwards married Rear-Admiral Richard Dawkins. From 1822 to 1840 he was grand master of the second Provincial Grand Lodge of Upper Canada.

[J. Ross Robertson, *The history of freemasonry in Canada* (2 vols., Toronto, 1899); W. S. Wallace (ed.), *Documents relating to the North West Company* (Toronto: The Champlain Society, 1934); *Diary of Nicholas Garry* (Trans. Roy. Soc. Can., 1900).]

McGillivray, Simon (d. 1840), fur-trader, was a son of the Hon. William McGillivray (q.v.), and a younger brother of Joseph McGillivray (q.v.). He entered the service of the North West Company as a clerk about 1803. He was for a number of years employed in the Athabaska department; and he was made a partner of the North West Company before the union of 1821. He was made a chief trader of the Hudson's Bay Company in 1821; and he spent most of the rest of his life at Hamilton Inlet, on the Labrador coast. In 1839, however, he was ordered to return to the Athabaska district; and he died, on his way thither, in the summer of 1840. His will is on file at Somerset House, in London. He married Theresa Roy; and by her he had four sons and five daughters.

[W. S. Wallace (ed.), *Documents relating to the North West Company* (Toronto: The Champlain Society, 1934).]

McGillivray, William (1764?-1825), furtrader, was born about 1764 in Scotland, probably in Stratherrick, Inverness-shire, and was the son of Donald McGillivray and Anne McTavish, sister of Simon McTavish (q.v.). He was educated at his uncle's expense; and in 1784 he came to Canada, and entered the service of the North West Company as a clerk. In 1785-86 he was in the Red River department; and in 1786-87 he was in charge of the post at Lac des Serpents, and with Roderick McKenzie (q.v.) was mainly responsible for bringing about the union of the North West Company and Gregory, McLeod and Company in 1787. He became a partner in the North West Com-

pany in 1790, and a member of the firm of McTavish, Frobisher and Co. in 1793; and on the death of his uncle, Simon McTavish (q.v.), in 1804, he became the chief director of the North West Company. Fort William was named after him in 1807. In 1812 he commanded the *Voyageurs* with Brock (q.v.) at Detroit; and in 1814 he was created, in recognition of his services, a legislative councillor of Lower Canada. He directed the policy of the North West Company in regard to the Selkirk settlement at the Red River; and in 1816 he was arrested by Lord Selkirk (q.v.) at Fort William and sent down to Canada for trial. With his brother Simon (q.v.), he helped to negotiate the union of the North West Company and the Hudson's Bay Company in 1821; and after the union he became one of the joint board for consulting and advising on the management of the fur-trade. He bought the estate of Peineau-Ghael, in the isle of Mull, Scotland; but does not appear to have lived there. He died at St. John's Wood, London, on October 16, 1825, aged 61. He married in 1800 Magdeleine (d. 1810), the daughter of Capt. John McDonald of Garth and Magdeleine Small, and the sister of John McDonald of Garth (q.v.); and by her had two daughters. By an Indian woman, he had before this two sons, Joseph (q.v.) and Simon (q.v.), and a daughter, Elizabeth, who married one Jourdain, of Berthier, Lower Canada.

[W. S. Wallace (ed.), *Documents relating to the North West Company* (Toronto: The Champlain Society, 1934); R. Campbell, *A history of the Scotch Presbyterian Church, St. Gabriel Street, Montreal* (Montreal, 1887); Le Jeune, *Dict. gén.*; Marjorie Wilkins Campbell, *McGillivray, lord of the Northwest* (Toronto, 1962).]

McGiverin, Harold Buchanan (1870-1931), minister without portfolio in the Dominion government (1924-25), was born in Hamilton, Ontario, on August 4, 1870, the son of Lieut.-Col. William McGiverin, M.P., and Emma Counsell. He was educated at Upper Canada College and the Osgoode Hall Law School, and was called to the bar of Ontario in 1893. He was a famous cricketer and football player, was captain of the Ottawa "Rough Riders" when they won the Dominion rugby football championship, and in 1908 was president of the Canadian Cricket Association. From 1908 to 1911 and from 1921 to 1925 he represented Ottawa in the Canadian House of Commons, and from 1924 to 1925 he was a minister without portfolio in the King government. He died at Victoria, British Columbia, on February 4, 1931. In 1898 he married Maude, daughter of the Hon. C. H. Mackintosh (q.v.), and by her he had one son.

[*Can. parl. comp.*; *Can. who was who*, vol. 2; Morgan, *Can. men* (1912).]

McGoun, Archibald (1853-1921), lawyer, was born at Montreal, Canada East, on December 15, 1853, and was educated at McGill University (B.A., 1876; LL.B., 1878; M.A., 1889). He was called to the bar of Quebec in 1878 (Q.C., 1899), and he practised law in Montreal. In 1888 he was appointed professor of civil law in McGill University. He died at Montreal, Quebec, on June 5, 1921. An advocate of imperial federation, he published *A federal parliament of the British people* (Toronto, 1890) and several pamphlets on imperial relations.

[Morgan, *Can. men* (1912).]

McGoun, Lachlan (1837-1896), songwriter, was born in Glasgow, Scotland, in 1837, and came to Canada about 1857. After living successively in Montreal and Port Hope, he settled in Napanee, Ontario, in 1867; and was employed as a painter and decorator. He served with the artillery during the Fenian raid in 1866, and while on active service composed the song, "Tramp, tramp, tramp, the boys are marching". He died in Napanee, Ontario, on November 11, 1896, as the result of a fall from a scaffold while painting the public school building.

[C. C. James, *A bibliography of Canadian poetry* (Toronto, 1899).]

McGrath, Sir Patrick Thomas (1868-1929), journalist, politician, and author, was born in St. John's, Newfoundland, on December 16, 1868. He was educated in the Christian Brothers' School in St. John's, and eventually became a journalist. He was appointed a member of the Legislative Council of Newfoundland in 1912, and was president of the Council from 1915 to 1919 and from 1925 to his death at St. John's, Newfoundland, on June 14, 1929. He was created a K.C.E. in 1918. In addition to numerous books, pamphlets, and articles on Newfoundland, he was the author of *From ocean to ocean: An account of a trip across Canada* (London, 1911).

[W. S. Wallace (ed.), *The encyclopaedia of Canada*, vol. 4 (Toronto, 1936); *Dict. nat. biog.*, supp. 4; *Who was who*, 1929-40.]

McGreevy, Thomas (1827-1897), politician, was born in Quebec, Lower Canada, on July 27, 1827, of Irish parentage. He became a contractor, and was president of the Richelieu and Ontario Navigation Company. From 1858 to 1864 he was a member of the city council of Quebec; and in 1867 he was appointed a member of the Legislative Council of Quebec, and was elected a member of the Canadian House of Commons for Quebec West. He resigned from the Legislative Council of Quebec in 1874, as a result of the abolition of dual representation; but he represented Quebec West in the Commons until 1892. In 1892 he was implicated in some serious charges of political corruption, and was expelled from the House. He died at Quebec, on January 2, 1897.

[*Can. parl. comp.*; N. F. Davin, *The*

Irishman in Canada (Toronto, 1877); Sir R. Cartwright, *Reminiscences* (Toronto, 1912); P. G. Roy, *Fils de Québec*, vol. 4.]

McGregor, Gordon (1901-1971), transportation executive, was born in Montreal, Quebec, September 26, 1901. He was educated at St. Andrew's College, Toronto, and at McGill University. He began his career in the engineering department of the Bell Telephone Company (1923-39). He joined Air Canada (Trans-Canada Air Lines) in 1945 as general traffic manager and rose to become president (1948-68). During the Second World War he served with the R.C.A.F. as Squadron Commander of 401 and 402 squadrons (1941); director of Air Staff, R.C.A.F. Overseas headquarters (1941-42); Commanding Officer of "X" wing, R.C.A.F., Anchorage, Alaska (1942-43); R.C.A.F. Station Commander, Patricia Bay, British Columbia (1943-44); Headquarters Staff, 83rd Group, Normandy (1944); and Commanding Officer, 126 Wing, 2nd Tactical Air Force in Europe (1944-45). He was a Commander, Order of Orange-Nassau, French Croix de Guerre, Czechoslovakian War Cross, Distinguished Flying Cross, and Order of the British Empire. He died at Montreal, Quebec, March 8, 1971.

[*Can. who's who*, 1955-57 and 1967-69).]

McGregor, James (1759-1820), clergyman, was born in the parish of Comrie, Perthshire, Scotland, in 1759. He was educated at Edinburgh University, and was ordained a minister of the Presbyterian Church in 1786. In 1787 he became a pastor of the Presbyterian church in Pictou, Nova Scotia; and this charge he served until his death, at Pictou, in 1830. He published *A letter to a clergyman, urging him to set free a black girl he held in slavery* (Halifax, 1788), *Letter to the General Associate Synod* (Paisley, Scotland, 1793), and *Dain a Chomnadh Crabdiudh* (Glasgow, 1818), a volume of Gaelic poetry.

[G. Patterson, *Remains of the Rev. James McGregor* (Philadelphia and Edinburgh, 1859), and *A memoir of Dr. McGregor* (Philadelphia and Edinburgh, 1859); Morgan, *Bib. can.*; R. J. Long, *Nova Scotia authors* (East Orange, N.J., 1918).]

McGregor, James Drummond (1838-1918), lieutenant-governor of Nova Scotia (1910-15), was born at New Glasgow, Nova Scotia, on September 1, 1838, the son of Roderick McGregor and Janet Chisholm, and the grandson of the Rev. James McGregor (q.v.). He became a merchant and ship-owner, and was senior partner in the firms of R. McGregor and Sons and J. D. and P. A. McGregor. He was a member of the Legislative Assembly of Nova Scotia from 1898 to 1901. In 1903 he was summoned to the Senate of Canada; and in 1910 he was appointed lieutenant-governor of Nova Scotia. His term of office ended in 1915; and he died at New Glasgow, Nova Scotia, on March 4, 1918. He was twice married, (1) in 1867 to Elizabeth McColl, of Guysboro' (d. 1891), and (2) in 1894 to Roberta Ridley, of Peterborough, Ontario.

[*Can. parl. comp.*; Morgan, *Can. men* (1912).]

McGregor, James Duncan (1860-1935), lieutenant-governor of Manitoba (1929-34), was born at Amherstburg, Canada West, on August 29, 1860. He was educated at Windsor, Ontario; but went to the west when a young man. From 1897 to 1899 he was mine inspector of the Yukon territory; and later he became president of the Glen Carnoch Farms in Manitoba. He was appointed lieutenant-governor of Manitoba in 1929; and he retired from office in 1934. He died at Winnipeg, Manitoba, on March 15, 1935.

[*Winnipeg Free Press*, Mar. 16, 1935; *Can. parl. comp.*]

MacGregor, James Gordon (1852-1913), scientist, was born at Halifax, Nova Scotia, on March 31, 1852, the son of the Rev. Peter G. MacGregor and Caroline McColl, and the grandson of the Rev. James McGregor (q.v.). He was educated at Dalhousie University (B.A., 1871; M.A., 1874), at Edinburgh and Leipzig universities, and at the University of London (D.Sc., 1876). From 1879 to 1901 he was professor of physics at Dalhousie University; and he was then appointed professor of natural philosophy at Edinburgh University. He died at Edinburgh, Scotland, on May 21, 1913. He was a charter member of the Royal Society of Canada, an LL.D. of Glasgow University, and the author of *An elementary treatise on kinematics and dynamics* (London, 1887; new ed., 1902), and *Physical laws and observations* (London, n.d.), as well as of many contributions to scientific periodicals.

[*Who was who*, 1897-1916; *Can. who was who*, vol. 2; Morgan, *Can. men* (1912); *Proc. Roy. Soc. Can.*, 1914; R. J. Long, *Nova Scotia authors* (East Orange, N.J., 1918).]

MacGregor, John (1797-1857), author and statistician, was born at Drynie, near Stornoway, Scotland, in 1797, the son of David MacGregor. As a young man he emigrated to America, and settled in Prince Edward Island. Here he became a member of the House of Assembly, and in 1823 he was appointed high sheriff of the island. He returned to England about 1828, and for a time devoted himself to the publication of his statistical researches. From 1840 to 1847 he was one of the secretaries of the Board of Trade; and from 1847 to 1856 he represented Glasgow in the British House of Commons. In 1856 the Royal British Bank, of which he had been the chief promoter, failed; and he absconded to the continent. He died at Boulogne, France, on April 23, 1857. He was the author of a large number of publi-

cations, of which those dealing with British North America were *Historical and descriptive sketches of the maritime colonies of British America* (London, 1828), *Observations on emigration to British America* (London, 1829), *British America* (2 vols., Edinburgh, 1832), and *The progress of America from the discovery by Columbus to the year 1846* (London, 1847).

[*Dict. nat. biog.*; *Cyc. Am. biog.*; A. B. Warburton, *The history of Prince Edward Island* (Saint John, N.B., 1923).]

MacGregor, Patrick (1816-1882), lawyer, was born in Perthshire, Scotland, in 1816. He came to Canada in 1833, and was for a time a master in the grammar school at Kingston, Upper Canada. He returned to Scotland to graduate at Edinburgh University (M.A., 1841); and after spending a few years in the United States, he once more settled in Canada. He was called to the bar of Upper Canada in 1857; and practised law in Toronto until his death, on January 25, 1882. He was the author of *A system of logic* (New York, 1862); and he translated into English *The genuine remains of Ossian* (London, 1841).

[*Dom. ann. reg.*, 1882; Morgan, *Bib. can.*]

MacGregor, Sir William (1846-1919), governor of Newfoundland (1904-09), was born in Aberdeenshire, Scotland, on October 20, 1846, and died in Aberdeen on July 3, 1919. He studied medicine at Glasgow and Aberdeen universities (M.D., 1874), and for a time practised medicine in Scotland. He then served as a medical officer in the South Pacific, and came to occupy various posts in the British colonial service. From 1888 to 1898 he was chief administrator of British New Guinea, and from 1899 to 1904 governor of Lagos. Then for five years he was governor of Newfoundland; and finally he served as governor of Queensland. While governor of Newfoundland, he published a *Report on the trade and commerce of Newfoundland* (St. John's, 1907). In 1889 he was created a K.C.M.G., and in 1907 a G.C.M.G.; and he received honorary degrees from several universities.

[*Who was who*, 1915-28; *Encyc. Can.*; *Newfoundland supp.*]

McGuckin, James M. (1835-1903), priest and educationist, was born at Cooleystown, county Tyrone, Ireland, in 1835. He entered the novitiate of the Oblate order in England in 1860; and in 1863 he was sent as a missionary to British Columbia. He was ordained a priest by Bishop Demers (q.v.) in 1863; and for more than twenty years he laboured in the missions to the Indians and the miners of British Columbia. He became president of the Oblate College, New Westminster; and from 1889 to 1899 he was rector of the University of Ottawa. He returned to British Columbia, however, as superior of the Oblates in Vancouver; and he died on April 7, 1903.

[Morgan, *Can. men* (1898).]

McGuigan, James Charles (1894-1974), cardinal and archbishop, was born in Hunter River, Prince Edward Island, November 26, 1894. He was educated at Prince of Wales College, Charlottetown; St. Dunstan's College, Charlottetown; Laval University (Hon. B.A., 1914); and the Grand Seminary of Quebec (doctorate in theology, 1918); with postgraduate study at the Catholic University of America (1927). He was ordained priest in 1918 and taught for a year at St. Dunstan's before becoming secretary to Bishop O'Leary of Charlottetown, whom he accompanied to Edmonton in 1920. He was chancellor of the Edmonton diocese (1923-25); vicar-general (1923-30); rector of St. Joseph's Cathedral, Edmonton (1925-27), and of St. Joseph's Seminary, Edmonton (1927-39). He was consecrated archbishop of Regina in 1930 and was transferred to Toronto in 1934, where he became archbishop in 1935, a position which he held until 1971. He was created cardinal on December 23, 1945, and was consecrated in February, 1946, the first English-speaking Canadian to be named to the Sacred College. He died at Toronto, Ontario, on April 8, 1974.

[*Can. who's who*, 1967-69; Metropolitan Toronto Library Board, *Biographical scrapbooks*, vol. 85.]

Machar, Agnes Maule (1837-1927), poet and novelist, was born in Kingston, Upper Canada, on January 23, 1837, the daughter of the Rev. John Machar (q.v.). She was educated in Kingston, and she lived there throughout her life. Both under her own name and under the pen-name of "Fidelis", she obtained a considerable reputation as a writer. She was the author of the following novels: *Katie Johnston's cross* (Toronto, 1870), *For king and country* (Toronto, 1874), *Marjorie's Canadian winter* (Boston, 1892), *Roland Graeme, knight* (Montreal, 1894), *Down the river to the sea* (New York, 1894), *The heir of Fairmount Grange* (London, 1895) and *The quest of the fatal river* (Toronto, 1904); and she published a volume of verse under the title *Lays of the true north* (London, 1899; new ed., 1902). She was the author also of *The story of old Kingston* (Toronto, 1908) and *Stories of the British Empire* (Toronto, 1913). She collaborated with her mother in publishing *The memorials of the Rev. John Machar* (Toronto, 1873), and with T. G. Marquis (q.v.) in writing *Stories of New France* (Boston, 1890). She died in Kingston, unmarried, on January 24, 1927.

[R. W. Cumberland, *Agnes Maule Machar* (Queen's quarterly, 1927); *Can. who was who*, vol. 1; Morgan, *Can. men* (1912); A. MacMurchy, *Handbook of Canadian literature* (Toronto, 1906); L. E. Horning and L. J. Burpee, *A bibliography of Canadian fiction* (Toronto, 1904).]

Machar, John (1796-1863), principal of Queen's University, Kingston, was born in December, 1796, in the parish of Tannadice, Forfarshire, Scotland. He was educated at King's College, Aberdeen (M.A., 1813), and studied theology at Edinburgh University. He was licensed to preach in the Church of Scotland in 1819, and in 1827 he came to Canada as minister of St. Andrew's Church, Kingston, Upper Canada. In 1846 he was appointed principal of Queen's College, Kingston; and this post he occupied until 1854. He died in Kingston on February 7, 1863. In 1847 he received the degree of D.D. from the University of Glasgow.

[*Memorials of the life and ministry of the Rev. John Machar* (Toronto, 1873).]

Machray, Robert (1831-1904), Anglican archbishop of Rupert's Land, was born in Aberdeen, Scotland, on May 17, 1831, the son of Robert Machray, advocate, and Christian Macallum. He was educated at King's College, Aberdeen (M.A., 1851) and Sidney Sussex College, Cambridge (B.A., 1855; M.A., 1858; D.D., 1865); and in 1855 he was elected to a fellowship in this college. Though brought up as a Presbyterian, he joined the Church of England while at Cambridge, and in 1856 he took holy orders. In 1862 he became vicar of Madingley, near Cambridge; and in 1865 he was appointed bishop of Rupert's Land. He arrived in Winnipeg in 1866, and for nearly forty years he presided over the destinies of the Church of England in western Canada. In 1875 he became metropolitan of Canada, and in 1893 archbishop of Rupert's Land and primate of all Canada. He revived and reorganized St. John's College, Winnipeg; and he became in 1877 the first chancellor of the University of Manitoba, of which St. John's was a constituent college. This position he retained until his death at Winnipeg on March 9, 1904. He was unmarried. He was a D.D. of the University of Manitoba (1883) and of Durham University (1888), and a D.C.L. of Trinity University, Toronto.

[R. Machray, *Life of Archbishop Machray* (Toronto, 1909); *Dict. nat. biog.*, supp. II; *Cyc. Am. biog.*; Morgan, *Can. men* (1898); Dent, *Can. port.*, vol. 2; C. H. Mockridge, *The bishops of the Church of England in Canada* (Toronto, 1896); B. Heeney, *Leaders of the Canadian church* (Toronto, 1920).]

McIlwraith, Jean Newton (1859-1938), author, was born at Hamilton, Canada West, in 1859, the daughter of Thomas McIlwraith (q.v.). She became for a time a publisher's reader in New York; but she devoted the greater part of her life to writing. She was the author of *The making of Mary* (New York, 1895), *A book about Shakespeare* (New York, 1898), *Canada* (New York, 1899), *A book about Longfellow* (New York, 1900), *The curious career of Roderick Campbell* (Toronto, 1901), *Sir Frederick Haldimand* (Toronto, 1904), *A Diana of Quebec* (Toronto, 1912), *The little admiral* (Toronto, 1924), and *Kinsmen at war*

(Ottawa, 1927); and she was joint author, with William McLennan, of *The span o' life* (New York, 1899). She died at Burlington, Ontario, on November 17, 1938.

[*Who's who among North American authors*, 1933-35; Morgan, *Can. men and women* (1912); *Can. hist. rev.*, 1939.]

McIlwraith, Thomas (1824-1903), ornithologist, was born at Newton, Ayr, Scotland, on December 25, 1824. He came to Canada in 1853 to take the position of superintendent of the gas works at Hamilton, Canada West; and in 1871 he went into business for himself in Hamilton, as a coal merchant. He was a pioneer in the study of Canadian ornithology; and he published *The birds of Ontario* (Hamilton, Ontario, 1886; new and rev. ed., Toronto, 1894). He died on January 31, 1903. In 1853 he married in Scotland Mary, daughter of Hugh Park; and by her he had four sons and three daughters.

[Morgan, *Can. men* (1898); Rose, *Cyc. Can. biog.*, (1888).]

McIlwraith, Thomas Forsyth (1899-1964), anthropologist, was born at Hamilton, Ontario, April 9, 1899, and educated at McGill University. After service with the King's Own Scottish Borderers in the First World War he entered Cambridge University (B.A., 1921; M.A., 1924) in Anthropological Tripos. He lectured at Cambridge and while there undertook, with the support of the National Museum of Canada, a study of the Bella Coola Indians of British Columbia — the first comprehensive study of an Indian tribe ever carried out in Canada and published as *The Bella Coola Indians* (Toronto, 1948). After a one-year term at Yale University he was appointed in 1925 to be lecturer in anthropology at the University of Toronto, the first anthropologist to be appointed to the staff of any Canadian university. In 1936 he was made professor and became head of the department of anthropology. Throughout his life he was concerned with the preservation of archaeological sites and discoveries, particularly in Ontario. He was a fellow of the Royal Society of Canada and had been president of the Canadian Social Science Research Council and of the Royal Canadian Institute. He died at Toronto, March 29, 1964.

[*Proc. Roy. Soc. Can.*, 1964.]

McInerney, Ralph George (1897-1972), industrialist, was born in Richibucto, New Brunswick, December 14, 1897. He was educated at St. Thomas' College, Chatham, New Brunswick, and at St. Dunstan's University, Charlottetown, Prince Edward Island. He was a graduate in law from King's College law school. He served as a pilot in the First World War from 1917 to the end of the war. He worked as an editor on the Saint John *Telegraph-Journal*, and edited the *Business Review* and the *Maritime Retailer*. He was a

member of the Saint John city council from 1928 to 1935 and was elected to the New Brunswick legislature in 1939. He was appointed chairman of the Board of New Brunswick Public Utilities in 1953. He was president of Ralph G. McInerney Company and the E. R. Machun Company. He died at Saint John, New Brunswick, November 25, 1972.

[*Can. who's who*, 1955-57.]

MacInnes, Charles Malcolm (1891-1971), historian, was born in Calgary, Alberta, on December 21, 1891. He was educated at Dalhousie University (B.A., 1915) and at Balliol College, Oxford (B.A., 1919; M.A., 1926). From 1919 to 1957 he taught history at the University of Bristol. He was a founder member of the British Empire Society for the Blind. He wrote *In the shadow of the Rockies* (London, 1935), *An introduction to the economic history of the British Empire* (London, 1935), *The British Commonwealth and its unsolved problems* (London, 1925), *The early English tobacco trade* (London, 1926), *England and slavery* (Bristol, 1934), *Gateway of Empire* (Bristol, 1939), and *The British Commonwealth and Empire 1815-1949* (London, 1951).

[*Can. hist. rev.*, vol. 52.]

McInnes, Donald (1824-1900), senator of Canada, was born in Oban, Scotland, on May 26, 1824. He emigrated to Canada in 1840, and settled first in Dundas, and then in Hamilton, Upper Canada. He became president of the Bank of Hamilton, and a very successful merchant and manufacturer. In 1880 he was appointed chairman of the royal commission appointed to inquire into the organization of the civil service of Canada; and in 1881 he was called to the Senate. He died at Hamilton, Ontario, on December 9, 1900. In 1863 he married Mary Amelia, fourth daughter of Sir John Beverley Robinson, Bart. (q.v.).

[*Cyc. Am. biog.*; *Can. parl. comp.*; Morgan, *Can. men* (1898).]

McInnes, Graham Campbell (1912-1970), public servant and writer, was born in London, England, February 18, 1912. He was educated in London, in Hobart, Tasmania, and at the University of Melbourne (B.A., 1933; M.A., 1935). He was art editor of the Toronto *Saturday Night* (1935-41), a commentator for the Canadian Broadcasting Corporation (1937-39), and a script writer, director, and head of graphics with the National Film Board in Ottawa (1940-48). He joined the department of external affairs in 1948, serving in Ottawa until 1952; in India, 1952-53; in New Zealand, 1954-55; as chief of Protocol, Ottawa, 1957; at Imperial Defence College, 1958; at Canada House, London, 1959-62; and as High Commissioner to Jamaica, 1962-65. He became minister and permanent delegate of Canada to the United Nations Educational Scientific and Cultural Organization in 1965. His autobiographical writings are: *The road to Gundagai* (London, 1965); *Humping my bluey* (London, 1966); *Finding a father* (London, 1967); *Goodbye, Melbourne Town* (London, 1968). He also wrote *A short history of Canadian art* (Toronto, 1939) and *Canadian art* (Toronto, 1950) as well as the novels *Lost Island* (London, 1954), and *Sushila* (London, 1957). He also produced films on Canadian artists Tom Thomson (q.v.), A. Y. Jackson (q.v.), and Emily Carr (q.v.), and a series of "War Industry" films. He died February 28, 1970.

[*Can. who's who*, 1967-69; *The road to Gundagai* (London, 1965); *Humping my bluey* (London, 1966); *Finding a father* (London, 1967).]

McInnes, Thomas Robert (1840-1904), lieutenant-governor of British Columbia (1897-1900), was born at Lake Ainslie, Nova Scotia, on November 5, 1840, the son of John McInnes and Mary Hamilton. He was educated at the Normal School, Truro, Nova Scotia, at Harvard University, and at the Rush Medical College, Chicago (M.D., 1869). For five years he practised medicine at Dresden, Ontario; but in 1874 he moved to New Westminster, British Columbia, and here he built up a large practice. He represented New Westminster in the Canadian House of Commons as an independent from 1878 to 1881; and in 1881 he was called to the Senate of Canada. In 1897 he was appointed lieutenant-governor of British Columbia; but he was dismissed from office in 1900. He died on March 15, 1904.

[*Cyc. Am. biog.*; *Can. who was who*, vol. 1; *Can. parl. comp.*; Morgan, *Can. men* (1898).]

McInnes, Thomas Robert Edward (1867-1951), poet, was born at Dresden, Ontario, on October 29, 1867, the son of Thomas Robert McInnes (q.v.), and died at Vancouver, British Columbia, on February 11, 1951. He was educated at the University of Toronto (B.A., 1889) and Osgoode Hall, and was called to the bar, but he did not practise law. He spent some years in the civil service, took part in the Yukon gold rush, lived for a few years in China, and lived latterly in British Columbia. He is chiefly remembered for his poetry, especially for *A romance of the lost* (Montreal, 1908), of which a second edition appeared under the title *Lonesome bar* (Montreal, 1909), *In amber lands* (New York, 1910), *Rhymes of a rounder* (New York, 1913), *Roundabout rhymes* (Toronto, 1923), and *Complete poems* (Toronto, 1923); but he was also the author of *Chinook days* (Vancouver, 1926), *The teaching of the old boy* (London, 1927), and *Oriental occupation of British Columbia* (Vancouver, 1927). He wrote under the *nom de plume* of "Tom MacInnes".

[*Can. who's who*, 1948; *Encyc. Can.*; D. Pacey, *Creative writing in Canada* (Toronto, 1952).]

McInnis, Edgar Wardwell (1899-1973), historian, was born in Charlottetown, Prince Edward Island, July 26, 1899. He served in the First World War with the Canadian Artillery and on the cessation of hostilities he entered the University of Toronto. A Rhodes scholar in 1923, he studied with Keith Feiling at Oxford. While at Oxford he won the Newdigate Prize for poetry. On graduation from Oxford he taught at Oberlin College, Ohio, before being appointed to the University of Toronto in 1928. McInnis's interest in international affairs led him to publish *The unguarded frontier: A history of American-Canadian relations* (New York, 1942) and to produce an account of the Second World War while it was in progress and which came out in annual instalments. He also wrote *North America and the modern world* (Toronto, 1945) and *Canada: A political and social history* (New York, Toronto, 1947). He was given leave by the university in 1951 and in the same year was elected president of the Canadian Institute of International Affairs, for which he lectured and arranged many conferences. In 1960 he joined the department of history at the newly formed York University, at Toronto, becoming chairman in 1962, and dean of graduate studies in 1963. He retired in 1968. He wrote *The Atlantic triangle and the cold war* (Toronto, 1959); and collaborated in the writing of *Canada and the United Nations* (Toronto, 1956), and *The shaping of postwar Germany* (Toronto, 1960).

In 1966 he received the Tyrrell Medal of the Royal Society, its highest award for history. His contribution to the study of international affairs was immense and his writings reached thousands outside as well as within the universities. He died at Toronto, Ontario, September 27, 1973.

[*Can. hist. rev.*, vol. 55 (1974).]

McIntosh, Angus (1756?-1833), legislative councillor of Upper Canada, was born near Inverness, Scotland, about 1756, the son of the head of the McIntosh clan. He emigrated to Canada as a young man, and settled in Detroit prior to 1787. In 1796, on the American occupation of Detroit, he removed to Sandwich, Upper Canada. He was, for a number of years, agent for the North West Company at Detroit and Sandwich, though he never became a partner in the Company. In 1820 he was appointed a member of the Legislative Council of Upper Canada; but in 1831 he returned to Scotland to take possession of his ancestral estate at Moy Hall, Inverness-shire; and he died at Inverness, on January 25, 1833. He married in 1788 Mary (d. 1827), daughter of Jacques Baudry dit Desbuttes dit St. Martin; and by her he had several sons, who returned with him to Scotland.

[M. M. Quaife (ed.), *The John Askin papers*, vol. 1 (Detroit, Mich., 1928).]

McIntosh, Donald (1773?-1845), fur-trader, was born about 1773, and entered the service of the North West Company. He was in charge at Michipicoten in 1816, when he was arrested by Lord Selkirk (q.v.). He was appointed a chief trader in 1821; and he spent the remainder of his service in the Lake Superior district. From 1830 to 1838 he was in charge at Fort William; and in 1840 he retired, and settled at St. Polycarpe, near Montreal. Here he died on November 15, 1845, aged 72 years.

[W. S. Wallace (ed.), *Documents relating to the North West Company* (Toronto: The Champlain Society, 1934).]

McIntosh or **Mackintosh, William** (1784-1842), fur-trader, was born in 1784, and entered the service of the North West Company. He was stationed at Lesser Slave Lake in 1803. In 1805 he was transferred to the Peace River; and in 1815 he made a successful defence of Fort Vermilion against the Hudson's Bay men under John Clarke (q.v.). He was made a partner of the North West Company in 1816; and in 1819 he was one of the Nor'Westers arrested by William Williams (q.v.). At the time of the union of 1821, he was made a chief trader; and he was promoted to the rank of chief factor in 1823. From 1825 to 1829 he was in charge at Nelson House; from 1829 to 1832, at Cumberland House; and from 1832 to 1834, at Dunvegan. He retired from the fur-trade in 1837, and he died on February 16, 1842.

[E. E. Rich (ed.), *Journal of occurrences in the Athabasca department, by George Simpson* (Toronto: The Champlain Society, 1938).]

McIntyre, James (1827-1906), poetaster, was born in Forres, Scotland, in 1827. He came to Canada in 1841, and lived successively in St. Catharines and Ingersoll, Ontario. In his later years he was an undertaker. He died at Ingersoll on March 5, 1906. He was the author of *Musings on the bank of the Canadian Thames* (Ingersoll, 1884) and *Poems* (Ingersoll, 1889).

[W. A. Deacon, *The four Jameses* (1927, new ed., Toronto, 1974); R. G. Riddell (ed.), *Canadian portraits* (Toronto, 1940).]

McIntyre, Willard Ezra (1852-1915), clergyman, was born at Cumberland Point, New Brunswick, on September 4, 1852. He was educated at the University of New Brunswick (B.A., 1877), and was ordained a Baptist minister in 1884. He occupied several pastorates in New Brunswick; and in 1903 he was appointed superintendent of Baptist missions in New Brunswick. He died at Saint John, New Brunswick, on September 28, 1915. Just before his death he began the publication of a Baptist bibliography, entitled *Baptist authors: A manual of bibliography, 1500-1914*

(Montreal, 1914-15); but of this only the first three parts or numbers appeared.

[Morgan, *Can. men* (1912).]

McKay, Alexander (d. 1811), fur-trader, was the son of Donald McKay and Elspeth Kennedy, United Empire Loyalists who settled in the township of Charlottenburg, Glengarry county, Upper Canada. He entered the service of the North West Company before 1791, and accompanied Sir Alexander Mackenzie (q.v.) on his overland journey to the Pacific Ocean in 1793. He was at Portage la Prairie in 1794-95, and he was made a partner of the North West Company in 1799. He was in charge at Lake Winnipeg, in 1799, and again in 1806; and he retired from the Company in 1808. In 1807 he was elected a member of the Beaver Club of Montreal. In 1810 he became a partner in the Pacific Fur Company of J. J. Astor (q.v.), and sailed to Astoria with Gabriel Franchère (q.v.). He was murdered by the Indians on the *Tonquin*, near Nootka, in the summer of 1811. He married a half-breed, by whom he had at least one son, Thomas (q.v.); and his wife afterwards married Dr. John McLoughlin (q.v.). His sister Catherine married in 1804 Simon Fraser (q.v.), of Ste. Anne's, Bout de l'Isle.

[W. S. Wallace (ed.), *Documents relating to the North West Company* (Toronto: The Champlain Society, 1934).]

Mackay, Alexander Bisset (1842-1901), clergyman and author, was born at Montrose, Scotland, on March 22, 1842. He was educated at Edinburgh University and at the Presbyterian College, London, England; and was ordained a minister of the Presbyterian Church in 1869. After holding charges at Worcester and at Brighton, in England, he came to Canada in 1879 as minister of the Crescent Street Church, Montreal; and he remained pastor of this church until his death, which took place on a yachting trip, on July 25, 1901. He was the author of *Gospel rays on the law of Moses* (London, 1875), *The glory of the Cross* (London, 1877), *The story of Naaman* (London, 1882), *The conquest of Canaan* (London, 1884), and *Apples of gold on salvers of silver* (London, 1890).

[Morgan, *Can. men* (1898).]

MacKay, Alexander Grant (1860-1920), politician, was born in Sydenham township, Grey county, Canada West, on March 7, 1860, the son of Hugh MacKay and Catherine McInnis. He was educated at the University of Toronto (B.A., 1883; M.A., 1885), and in 1891 he was called to the bar in Ontario (K.C., 1902). From 1903 to 1912 he represented North Grey in the Legislative Assembly of Ontario; from 1904 to 1905 he was commissioner of crown lands in the Ross administration; and from 1907 to 1911 he was leader of the Liberal opposition in Ontario. In 1912 he removed to

Edmonton, Alberta; and was called to the bar in Alberta. In 1913 he was elected to represent Athabaska in the Legislative Assembly of Alberta; and, in 1918 he became minister of health and municipal affairs in the government of Alberta. He died at Edmonton, Alberta, on April 25, 1920. He was not married.
[Morgan, *Can. men* (1912); *Can. parl. comp.*]

MacKay, Alexander Howard (1848-1929), educationist, was born at Mount Dalhousie, Pictou county, Nova Scotia, on May 19, 1848. He was educated at Dalhousie University (B.A., 1873; LL.D., 1892) and at the University of Halifax (B.Sc., 1880); and was principal of the Pictou Academy, from 1873 to 1889. In 1890 he was appointed superintendent of education in Nova Scotia, and he retired from this post only in 1925. In 1888 he was elected a fellow of the Royal Society of Canada; and in 1905 St. Francis Xavier University conferred on him the degree of LL.D. He died at Dartmouth, Nova Scotia, on May 19, 1929.
[*Proc. Roy. Soc. Can.*, 1929; Morgan, *Can. men* (1912); R. J. Long, *Nova Scotia authors* (East Orange, N.J., 1918).]

Mackay, Angus (1841-1931), agriculturist, was born in Pickering township, Upper Canada, on January 10, 1841. He became one of the pioneers of the Indian Head district of Saskatchewan in 1882; and in 1889 he was appointed superintendent of the first Dominion experimental farm in the Canadian West, established that year at Indian Head. In this capacity he had a profound influence on the development of agriculture in the Canadian West. He retired from this post in 1914; and during his later years he was inspector of western farms. He died at Indian Head, Saskatchewan, on June 10, 1931.
[R. G. Riddell (ed.), *Canadian portraits* (Toronto, 1940); Morgan, *Can. men* (1912).]

McKay, Donald (*fl.* 1786-1810), fur-trader, was a brother of Alexander and William McKay (q.v.). He entered the service of the North West Company and was on the Saskatchewan in 1786, when he passed Cumberland House. He entered the service of the Hudson's Bay Company in 1790. He was stationed at Osnaburgh House in 1792, and on the Red River in 1794. In 1799 he left York Factory for England, on board the *King George*; and he died, according to a record in the possession of the McKay family, in 1810. He was known as "Mad McKay". Another Donald McKay, possibly a half-breed son of the older Donald, entered the service of the Hudson's Bay Company as a clerk in 1806, retired from the service in 1836, and died in Canada in 1838.
[W. S. Wallace (ed.), *Documents relating to the North West Company* (Toronto: The Champlain Society, 1934).]

MacKay, Douglas (1900-1938), journalist, was born at Woodstock, Ontario, on December 6, 1900. He was educated at Woodstock College and Columbia University (B.A., 1923), and became a journalist. For several years he was a member of the parliamentary bureau of the Canadian Press at Ottawa; and he was then successively publicity director for the Canadian Steamship Lines, for the Seigniory Club, and for the Canadian Committee of the Hudson's Bay Company. In the last capacity, he was editor of the *Beaver* from 1933 to 1938. He died in an airplane crash in the United States on January 10, 1938. He was the author of *The honourable company: A history of the Hudson's Bay Company* (Indianapolis, 1936).
[*Can. who's who*, 1936-37.]

Mackay, George Leslie (1844-1901), missionary, was born in Zorra, Oxford county, Canada West, on March 22, 1844. He was educated at the University of Toronto and Knox College, Toronto, at Princeton Theological Seminary, and at Edinburgh University; and was ordained a minister of the Presbyterian Church in 1871. He spent his life as a missionary in Formosa, China; and he died on the Island of Formosa on June 2, 1901. In 1880 he was made an honorary doctor of divinity of Queen's University, Kingston; and in 1894 he was elected moderator of the General Assembly of the Presbyterian Church in Canada. He was the author of a Chinese Romanized dictionary of the Formosan vernacular and of *From far Formosa: The island, its people and missions* (New York, 1896).
[Marian Keith, *The black-bearded barbarian* (New York, 1912); Morgan, *Can. men* (1898).]

Mackay, Hugh (1751?-1848), loyalist, was born in Scotland about 1751, and came to America before the American Revolution. He served throughout the revolutionary war as a subaltern in the Queen's Rangers; and in 1783 he settled in Charlotte county, New Brunswick. In 1792 he was elected a member of the New Brunswick House of Assembly; and continued to sit in the Assembly for thirty years. In 1793 he was gazetted a colonel of militia; and in his later years he was a judge of the Court of Common Pleas for Charlotte county. He died at St. George, Charlotte county, New Brunswick, in 1848.
[L. Sabine, *The American loyalists* (Boston, 1849); W. O. Raymond (ed.), *The Winslow papers* (Saint John, N.B., 1901).]

McKay, Hugh (1844?-1928), missionary, was born about 1844, and was educated at Knox College, Toronto (D.D., 1907). He was ordained a minister of the Presbyterian Church in Canada in 1877; and he spent most of his life as a missionary among the Indians of Manitoba and the North West Territories. He died at Winnipeg, Manitoba, on September 20, 1928.

[Morgan, *Can. men* (1912).]

MacKay, Mrs. Isabel Ecclestone, *née* **Macpherson** (1875-1928), author, was born at Woodstock, Ontario, on November 25, 1875, the daughter of Donald McLeod Macpherson and Priscilla Ecclestone. She was educated at the Woodstock Collegiate Institute, and in 1895 married Peter J. MacKay, a court stenographer. In 1909 she removed to Vancouver, British Columbia; and she died in Vancouver on August 15, 1928. She first achieved reputation as a poet; and she published several volumes of verse: *Between the lights* (Toronto, 1904), *The shining ships and other verse* (Toronto, 1918), and *Fires of driftwood* (Toronto, 1922). But she also wrote many short stories; and she published several novels: *The house of windows* (Toronto, 1912), *Up the hill and over* (Toronto, 1917), *Mist of morning* (Toronto, 1919), *The window-gazer* (Toronto, 1921), and *Blencarrow* (Toronto, 1926), as well as two plays, *Treasure* (New York, 1926) and *The cache* (New York, 1927), and a book of folklore, entitled *Indian nights* (Toronto, 1930). Her *Complete poems* were published after her death (Toronto, 1930).

[*Who's who among North American authors*, 1927-28; Morgan, *Can. men* (1912); L. Pierce, *An outline of Canadian literature* (Toronto, 1927); J. W. Garvin (ed.), *Canadian poets* (Toronto, 1926).]

McKay, James (1828-1879), president of the Executive Council of Manitoba (1871-74), was born at Edmonton House, Saskatchewan, North West Territories, the eldest son of James McKay, a servant of the Hudson's Bay Company. He was educated at Red River, and became a member of the Council of Assiniboia and of the North West Council. From 1871 to 1876 he was a member of the Legislative Council of Manitoba; from 1871 to 1874 he was president of the Executive Council; and from 1874 to 1878 minister of agriculture. Failing health compelled him to retire from political life in 1878, and he died at Deer Lodge, near Winnipeg, on December 3, 1879. In 1859 he married Margaret, daughter of Chief Factor Rowand (q.v.), of the Hudson's Bay Company.

[*Cyc. Am. biog.*; *Can. parl. comp.*; *Dom. ann. reg.*, 1879; *Dict. Can. biog.*, vol. 10.]

MacKay, John (1870-1938), educationist, was born at Kintore, Ontario, on June 1, 1870. He was educated at the University of Toronto (B.A., 1901) and at the United Free Church College, Glasgow, Scotland; and was ordained a minister of the Presbyterian Church in Canada in 1902. From 1902 to 1908 he was pastor of Crescent Street Presbyterian Church, Montreal; from 1908 to 1919 he was principal of Westminster Hall, Vancouver; and from 1919 to his death at Winnipeg, on May 16,

1938, he was principal of the Manitoba Theological College, Winnipeg. He was a D.D. of the Presbyterian Theological College, Montreal.

[*Can. who's who*, 1936-37; Morgan, *Can. men* (1912).]

McKay, John George (1886-1923), poet, was born at Little Branch, New Brunswick, on January 15, 1886; and was educated at Acadia University (B.A., 1915). He served in the First World War as a Y.M.C.A. officer, was wounded at the battle of Amiens in 1918, and was awarded the M.C. After the war, he served as Y.M.C.A. secretary at McGill University, Montreal; and he died at Montreal, Quebec, on August 7, 1923. After his death his poems were collected and edited by N. C. Hannay under the title *Après la guerre* (Boston, 1925).

[*Records of the graduates of Acadia University* (Wolfville, N.S., 1926).]

MacKay, John Keiller (1888-1970), lieutenant-governor of Ontario, was born in Pictou county, Nova Scotia, July 11, 1888. He was educated at St. Francis Xavier University (B.A., 1912); Royal Military College, Kingston, Ontario; and Dalhousie University (LL.B., 1922). He was called to the Nova Scotia bar in 1922 and was a partner of MacKay, Matheson and Martin of Toronto before being appointed a justice of the Supreme Court of Ontario in 1935 and of the Court of Appeal in 1950. He became lieutenant-governor of Ontario in 1957 and remained in office until his retirement in 1963. He was chairman of Bramalea Consolidated Developments Limited, Toronto; director of Canada Permanent Trust; a member of the Board of Governors, University of Toronto; and chancellor of the University of Windsor. During the First World War he served with the Canadian Artillery and was three times mentioned in despatches and awarded the D.S.C. (1916). He was a member and patron of a number of Scottish societies in Canada and was honoured by eight Canadian universities with honorary degrees. He died at Toronto, June 12, 1970.

[*Can. who's who*, 1967-69.]

McKay, Joseph William (1829-1900), fur-trader, was born at Rupert House, on Hudson Bay, on January 31, 1829. He crossed the Rocky Mountains to Fort Vancouver, in the Columbia department, in 1844; and he spent the rest of his life on the Pacific slope. He made many exploratory journeys in what is now British Columbia; and he was a pioneer in the development of the coal mines of the province. From 1855 to 1859 he was one of the members of the Legislative Assembly of Vancouver Island. He retired from the service of the Hudson's Bay Company in 1879, with the rank of chief trader; and in 1883 he entered the service of the Indian department of the Canadian government. He died at Victoria, British Columbia, on December 21, 1900.

[J. T. Walbran, *British Columbia coast names* (Ottawa, 1909).]

Mackay, Robert (1840-1916), senator of Canada, was born in Caithness, Scotland, in 1840, the son of Angus Mackay. He came to Canada in 1855, and entered the wholesale dry-goods business in Montreal. He became wealthy, and in 1893 he retired from active business to devote himself to his many financial interests. In 1896 and in 1900 he unsuccessfully contested Montreal West as a Liberal for the Canadian House of Commons; and in 1901 he was called to the Senate of Canada. He sat in this house until his death at Montreal on December 25, 1916.

[*Can. who was who*, vol. 1; *Can. parl. comp.*; Morgan, *Can. men* (1912).]

MacKay, Robert Peter (1847-1929), clergyman, was born in East Zorra, Canada West, on April 24, 1847. He was educated at the University of Toronto (B.A., 1875) and Knox College (D.D., 1900); and was ordained a minister of the Presbyterian Church in Canada in 1877. In 1892 he was appointed secretary of the board of foreign missions of the church; and during the rest of his life he was actively engaged in the direction of missionary work. In 1911 he was elected moderator of the Presbyterian Church in Canada; and he was one of the leaders of the movement that led to the union of the Presbyterian, the Methodist, and the Congregational churches in Canada in 1925. He died at Woodstock, Ontario, on May 27, 1929. He was the author of a handbook on the missions of the Presbyterian Church in Canada.

[A. Thomson, *The life and letters of Rev. R. P. MacKay* (Toronto, 1932); Morgan, *Can. men* (1912).]

Mackay, Robert Walter Stuart (1809?-1854), publisher, was born in Scotland about 1809, the son of an officer in the Black Watch. He came to Canada when a young man, and entered the publishing business. In 1842 he founded the *Montreal Directory* (Montreal, 1842-54), and in 1848 the *Quebec Directory* (Quebec, 1848-52). In 1851 he issued also the *Canada Directory* (Montreal, 1851). Other publications by him were a *Stranger's guide to the island and city of Montreal* (Montreal, 1848), a *Stranger's guide to the cities of Montreal and Quebec* (Montreal, 1852), and a *Stranger's guide to the cities and principal towns of Canada* (Montreal, 1854). He died at Montreal on October 9, 1854.

[Morgan, *Bib. can.*]

McKay, Thomas (1792-1855), legislative councillor, was born at Perth, Scotland, in 1792; and in 1817 he emigrated to Canada. He became one of the contractors for the Lachine Canal in 1821, and the Rideau Canal afterwards; and in 1826 he settled near Bytown, on the Ottawa River. From 1834 to 1841 he represented Russell in the Legislative Assembly of Upper Canada; and in 1841 he was appointed a member of the Legislative Council of United Canada. He died at Rideau Hall, Ottawa, on October 9, 1855. In 1813 he married at Perth, Scotland, Ann Crichton; and by her he had sixteen children.

[Francis J. Audet, *The honourable Thomas McKay*, M.L.C. (Canadian Historical Association, annual report, 1932).]

McKay, Thomas (1797?-1850?), fur-trader, was born in the Indian country about 1797, the half-breed son of Alexander McKay (q.v.), and was baptized in the Scotch Presbyterian church at Williamstown, Glengarry, on November 9, 1804, aged 6 years. He entered the service of the Pacific Fur Company in 1810, and accompanied his father to Astoria. On the capture of Astoria in 1813, he took service with the North West Company; and he remained a clerk in the Columbia department, first with the North West Company and, after 1821, with the Hudson's Bay Company, almost continuously for about twenty-five years. He seems to have left the service of the latter between 1836 and 1839; and in 1839 Townsend met him near the Great Salt Lake, Utah. He appears to have settled on a farm in Oregon, to have become a citizen of the United States, and to have taken part in the Cayuse War of 1848. He died about 1850.

[E. E. Rich (ed.), *The letters of John McLoughlin*, 1st series (Toronto: The Champlain Society, 1941).]

McKay, William (1772-1832), fur-trader and soldier, was born in 1772, the son of Donald McKay and Elspeth Kennedy, and was a brother of Alexander McKay (q.v.). He entered the service of the North West Company in 1790, and was made a partner in 1796. He was in charge at Lake Winnipeg in 1799, and in 1805 was at Portage la Prairie. He retired from the fur-trade in 1807, and was elected a member of the Beaver Club of Montreal. In the War of 1812 he commanded the British force which captured Prairie-du-Chien; and after the war he became an officer of the Indian department, with the rank of lieutenant-colonel. He died in Montreal in 1832. In 1808 he married Eliza, daughter of the Hon. Mr. Justice Davidson; and by her he had a son, Robert, who became a judge of the Superior Court of Quebec. McKay street, in Montreal, is named after him.

[W. S. Wallace (ed.), *Documents relating to the North West Company* (Toronto: The Champlain Society, 1934); R. Campbell, *A history of the Scotch Presbyterian Church, St. Gabriel Street, Montreal* (Montreal, 1893).]

MacKay, William Alexander (1842-1905), clergyman and author, was born in Zorra township, Oxford county, Upper Canada, on March 15, 1842, of Highland Scottish parentage. He was educated at the University of Toronto (B.A., 1869) and at Knox College, Toronto; and he was ordained a minister of the Presbyterian Church. He held at first several country pastorates; but in 1878 he was called to Chalmers Church, Woodstock, Ontario, and this charge he served until his death at Woodstock on November 28, 1905. He was the author of *Immersion proved to be a scriptural mode of baptism* (Toronto, 1881), *Baptism: Its mode and meaning at the time of our Lord* (Toronto, 1892), *Pioneer life in Zorra* (Toronto, 1899), and *Zorra boys at home and abroad* (Toronto, 1900).

[Morgan, *Can. men* (1898).]

McKechnie, Neil Kenneth (1873-1951), artist and author, was born in England in 1873, and died at Birch Cliff, Ontario, on June 5, 1951. He was the author of *The heir of all the ages* (Indianapolis, 1926) and *The saddleroom murder* (Philadelphia, 1927), and joint author, with R. H. King, of *Classical mythology in song and story* (2 vols., Toronto, 1937-39).

[Toronto *Globe and Mail*, June 6, 1951.]

McKee, Alexander (d. 1799), Indian agent, was born in Pennsylvania, and was appointed in 1772 deputy agent for Indian affairs at Fort Pitt. He took the Loyalist side in the American Revolution, and in 1778 escaped with Simon Girty (q.v.) to Detroit. Here he became superintendent of Indian affairs. On the American occupation of Detroit in 1796, he removed to the mouth of the River Thames; and here he died on January 13, 1799.

[W. R. Hoberg, *Early history of Colonel Alexander McKee* (Pennsylvania magazine of history and biography, 1934); M. M. Quaife (ed.), *The John Askin papers*, vol. I (Detroit, Mich., 1928).]

MacKeen, David (1839-1916), lieutenant-governor of Nova Scotia (1915-16), was born at Mabou, Nova Scotia, on September 20, 1839, the son of the Hon. William MacKeen, M.L.C. For many years he was general manager of the Dominion Coal Company. From 1887 to 1896 he represented Cape Breton as a Conservative in the Canadian House of Commons; and in 1896 he was called to the Senate of Canada. In 1915 he resigned from the Senate to become lieutenant-governor of Nova Scotia; but he died at Halifax, Nova Scotia, on November 13, 1916. He was thrice married, (1) in 1867 to Isabel, daughter of Henry Poole, of Derby, England, (2) in 1877 to Frances, daughter of William Lawson of Halifax, Nova Scotia, and (3) in 1888 to Jane, daughter of John Crerar, of Halifax, Nova Scotia.

[Morgan, *Can. men* (1912); *Can. parl. comp.*]

McKellar, Archibald (1816-1894), politician, was born near Inverary Castle, Argyllshire, Scotland, on February 3, 1816, the son of Peter McKellar and Flora MacNab, and came to Canada with his parents in 1817. He was brought up on a farm in Aldborough township, in the London district of Upper Canada, and later removed with his family to Raleigh township, in Kent county. He represented Kent in the Legislative Assembly of United Canada from 1857 to 1867, and in the Legislative Assembly of Ontario from 1867 to 1875; and from 1871 to 1875 he was commissioner of public works, minister of agriculture, and provincial secretary in the Blake and Mowat administrations. In 1875 he was appointed sheriff of the county of Wentworth; and he retained this position until his death at Hamilton on February 12, 1894. In 1836 he married his second cousin, Lucy MacNab (d. 1857), by whom he had nine children; and in 1874 he married, secondly, Catherine Mary, widow of Lawrence William Mercer, and daughter of Dr. Grant Powell, Toronto.

[*Can. parl. comp.*; Rose, *Cyc. Can. biog.* (1886).]

McKelvie, Bruce Alastair (1889-1960), journalist and author, was born at Vancouver, British Columbia, on November 19, 1889, and died at Victoria, British Columbia, on April 17, 1960. He became a journalist and for many years was managing editor of the Victoria *Colonist*. He was the author of several books relating to local history: *The early history of the province of British Columbia* (Toronto, 1926), *Maquinna the magnificent* (Vancouver, 1946), *Fort Langley* (Vancouver, 1947), *Tales of conflict* (Vancouver, 1950), and *Pageant of B.C.* (Toronto, 1955); and he also wrote a novel, entitled *Huldowget* (Toronto, 1926), and two books for juveniles: *The black canyon* (London, 1927) and *Pelts and powder* (Toronto, 1929).

[*Can. who's who*, 1958-60; *Encyc. Can.*]

MacKendrick, William Gordon (1864-1959), soldier and author, was born at Galt, Ontario, in 1864, and died at Oakville, Ontario, on September 22, 1959. During the First World War he served overseas with the Canadian Expeditionary Force, and during the latter part of the war he was seconded to the British Fifth Army, with the rank of lieutenant-colonel, in charge of roads. After the war he wrote a number of books, most of them under the *nom de plume* of "The Road-builder": *The destiny of America* (Toronto, 1921), *God's commonwealth, British and American* (Toronto, 1928), *The freedom of the seas* (Toronto, 1929), *God's economic plan* (Toronto, 1932), and *This is Armageddon* (Toronto, 1942).

[*Can. who's who*, 1948.]

Mackenzie, Sir Alexander (1764-1820), fur-trader and explorer, was born near Stornoway, in the Island of Lewis, the second son of Kenneth Mackenzie and Isabella Maciver. In

1774, he emigrated with his father and two of his maternal aunts to New York, where his maternal uncle, John Maciver, known as "Ready Money John", was established in business. On the outbreak of the American Revolution, Kenneth Mackenzie, with his older brother John, obtained commissions in Sir John Johnson's "Royal Greens"; and the young Alexander was sent north, later, to school in Montreal. Kenneth Mackenzie died on service in 1780 at Carleton Island, in Lake Ontario; but his brother John, who probably became Alexander's guardian, settled in 1784 in Glengarry, and died, unmarried, in 1795. The young Alexander entered about 1779 the service of the firm of Finlay, Gregory and Co., afterwards Gregory, McLeod, and Co., as a clerk; and in 1784 he was sent to Detroit. In 1785 he was sent to the West, as a wintering partner of the firm; and when the firm was absorbed by the North West Company in 1787 he became a partner of this Company. In 1788 he was placed in charge of Fort Chipewyan on Lake Athabaska; and in 1789 he made from this post the expedition to the Arctic Ocean which has given his name to the Mackenzie River. In 1793 he followed this up with his epoch-making journey to the Pacific Ocean. In 1799, because of disagreements with Simon McTavish (q.v.) and William McGillivray (q.v.), he announced his intention of severing his connection with the North West Company, and went to England. Here he published his *Voyages* (London, 1801), and in 1802 received the honour of knight bachelor. He returned to Canada in 1802; and became the leading partner in the XY Company. On the union of the XY and North West companies in 1804, he again acquired an interest in the North West Company, but was "excluded from any interference", and organized the firm of Sir Alexander Mackenzie and Co. to look after his interests in the North West Company. In 1805 he was elected a member of the Legislative Assembly of Lower Canada for the county of Huntingdon; but in 1808 he returned to Scotland, and there he spent his remaining years. In 1812 he married Geddes, the daughter of George Mackenzie of Avoch, a merchant of Tower Hill, London, by whom he had two sons and one daughter; and the same year he purchased her father's estate of Avoch, in Ross-shire. He died in a wayside inn on his way from Edinburgh to Avoch, on March 12, 1820. For many years he had received nothing from his interest in the North West Company; and on the failure of McTavish, McGillivrays and Co. in 1825, his estate was a heavy creditor of this firm. In 1830, after some litigation, Lady Mackenzie received from Edward Ellice (q.v.), one of those who had brought about the union of the North West and Hudson's Bay companies in 1821, the sum of £10,000.

[M. S. Wade, *Mackenzie of Canada* (Edinburgh, 1927); A. P. Woollacott, *Mackenzie and his voyageurs* (London, 1927); Hume Wrong, *Sir Alexander Mackenzie* (Toronto, 1927); R. H. Fleming, *The origin of "Sir Alexander Mackenzie and Company"* (Can. hist. rev., 1928); W. K. Lamb, ed., *Journals and letters of Sir Alexander Mackenzie* (Toronto, 1970); R. Daniells, *Alexander Mackenzie and the North West* (Toronto, 1969); Dict. nat. biog.; Cyc. Am. biog.; Morgan, *Bib. can.* and *Cel. Can.*]

McKenzie, Alexander (1767?-1830), fur-trader, was a nephew of Sir Alexander Mackenzie (q.v.), and was born, probably in Scotland, about 1767. From 1790 to 1796 he was a trader near Detroit; and in 1798 he entered the service of the XY Company as a wintering partner. He became a partner of the North West Company on the union of the two companies in 1804; and from 1804 to 1808 he was in charge of the Athabaska department. From 1809 to 1810 he was at the Pic, on Lake Superior; and from 1811 to 1812 he was agent of the Company at Fort William. He was one of the North West partners arrested by Lord Selkirk (q.v.) in 1816, and was tried at the assizes in York in 1818, but was acquitted. He appears to have become a retired partner about this time; but he was at Fort William in the summer of 1821, as an agent of McTavish, McGillivrays, and Co. He died in Montreal on July 23, 1830; and his will is on file at the Court House in Montreal. He married Isabella Latour; and by her he had two children, John George McKenzie, who was born at Long Lake, and died at Berthier, Lower Canada, on January 17, 1838, and Ann (Nancy), who was born at Grand Portage, and married in 1829 William Cowie at Sault Ste. Marie. His widow married John McBean. On the Athabaska he was known by the nickname "The Emperor"; and in his obituary notice in the *Canadian Courant* he is described as a "Major on the staff of the militia of this province".

[W. S. Wallace (ed.), *Documents relating to the North West Company* (Toronto: The Champlain Society, 1934).]

Mackenzie, Alexander (1822-1892), prime minister of Canada (1873-78), was born near Dunkeld, Perthshire, Scotland, on January 28, 1822, the son of Alexander Mackenzie of Logierait, Perthshire, and Mary, daughter of Donald Fleming. He came to Canada in 1842, and settled first at Kingston, Upper Canada, and then at Sarnia, Upper Canada, as a builder and contractor. From 1852 to 1854 he edited the *Lambton Shield*, a Reform newspaper, and he became a supporter and friend of George Brown (q.v.). He was elected to the Legislative Assembly of Canada for the county of Lambton in 1861, and he supported Confederation; but in 1865 he refused the office of president of the Council in the coalition government, on the withdrawal of Brown. In 1867 he was elected both to the Canadian House of Commons and to the Legislative Assembly of Ontario. He continued a member of the Ontario house until "dual representation" was abolished in 1872; and he was a member of the Dominion house continuously until his death. In 1873, on the fall of Sir John Macdonald (q.v.), he was called upon to form the first Liberal administration of the Dominion; and his government, sustained in the general elections of 1874, remained in power until its defeat at the polls in 1878. In 1880 he resigned the leadership of the Liberal party, and was succeeded by Edward Blake (q.v.). Thereafter he took a comparatively minor part in politics; and he died at Toronto on April 17, 1892.

He was a man of strict integrity and great industry. While prime minister he filled the arduous post of minister of public works; and his defeat in 1878 was partly due to the attention which he gave to his departmental duties. Though an effective parliamentary speaker, he was without the personal magnetism of Sir John Macdonald (q.v.); and he was lacking in boldness and imagination.

He was twice married, (1) to Helen (d. 1852), daughter of William Neil, of Irvine, Scotland, and (2) to Jane, eldest daughter of Robert Sym, of Perthshire, Scotland. By his first wife he had one daughter. He wrote a biography of his friend George Brown, *The life and speeches of George Brown* (Toronto, 1882); and a volume of his speeches was published under the title *Speeches in Scotland and Canada* (Toronto, 1876).

[W. Buckingham and G. W. Ross, *The Hon. Alexander Mackenzie, his life and times* (Toronto, 1892); *Dict. nat. biog.*; Dent, *Can. port.*, vol. 1; Rose, *Cyc. Can. biog.* (1886); *Cyc. Am. biog.*; *Dom. ann. reg.*, 1878; J. Young, *Public men and public life in Canada* (2 vols., Toronto, 1912); Sir J. Willison, *Reminiscences* (Toronto, 1919); Sir G. W. Ross, *Getting into parliament and after* (Toronto, 1913); D. C. Thomson, *Alexander Mackenzie, clear grit* (Toronto, 1960).]

Mackenzie, Sir Alexander (1860-1943), lawyer and financier, was born in Kincardine, Canada West, on June 30, 1860. He was called to the bar in Ontario in 1883, and became a partner in the law firm of Blake, Lash, and Cassels in Toronto. From law he passed to finance; and he became president of the Brazilian Traction, Light, and Power Company and other South American enterprises in which Canadians were interested. For his financial services in the First World War he was created a K.B.E. In his later years he lived in Italy; but on the entrance of Italy into the Second World War, he returned to Canada, and he died at Kincardine, Ontario, on July 12, 1943. In 1908 he married Mabel, daughter of the Hon. S. H. Blake (q.v.).

[*Who's who*, 1943.]

Mackenzie, Arthur Stanley (1865-1938), educationist, was born at Pictou, Nova Scotia,

on September 20, 1865. He was educated at Dalhousie University (B.A., 1885) and at Johns Hopkins University (Ph.D., 1894). From 1891 to 1905 he taught physics at Bryn Mawr College; from 1905 to 1910 he was professor of physics at Dalhousie University; and from 1911 to 1931 he was president of Dalhousie University. He retired from academic life in 1931; and he died at Halifax, Nova Scotia, on October 2, 1938. In 1913 he was elected a fellow of the Royal Society of Canada; and in 1937 he was appointed president of the Nova Scotia Economic Council. He was the editor of *The laws of gravitation: Memoirs by Newton, Bouguer, and Cavendish, together with abstracts of other important memoirs* (New York, 1900).

[W. C. Murray, *Stanley Mackenzie of Dalhousie* (Dalhousie review, 1939); *Proc. Roy. Soc. Can.*, 1939; *Can. who's who*, 1936-37.]

McKenzie, Charles (1774-1855), fur-trader, was born at Farintosh, in Scotland, in 1774, and was probably a relative of the Hon. Roderick McKenzie (q.v.). He entered the service of the North West Company in 1803; and in 1804 he was a clerk on the Assiniboine. His account of the Missouri Indians, to whom he made four trading expeditions in the years 1804 to 1806, has been published by L. R. Masson, in his *Bourgeois de la Compagnie du Nord-Ouest*, vol. 1 (Quebec, 1889). In 1807 he was transferred to the region between Rainy Lake and Albany; and here he spent most of the rest of his service. He was taken over as a clerk by the Hudson's Bay Company in 1821; and he was still a clerk when he retired from the service in 1854. He died at the Red River Settlement on March 3, 1855; and his will is on record at Hudson's Bay House in London. He married an Indian woman; and by her he had one son, Hector, and three daughters.

[W. S. Wallace (ed.), *Documents relating to the North West Company* (Toronto: The Champlain Society, 1934).]

McKenzie, Daniel (1769?-1832), fur-trader, was born, probably in Scotland, about 1769. He entered the service of the North West Company about 1790, and in 1791 was at Fort Chipewyan, on Lake Athabaska. He was at Upper Fort des Prairies and Rocky Mountains in 1799; and he became a partner of the North West Company in 1796. In 1806 he was in charge of the Athabaska district; from 1808 to 1809 he was on the Lower Red River; from 1809 to 1812 he was in the English River department; and from 1813 to 1815 he was at Fond-du-Lac. He was one of the North West Company partners arrested by Lord Selkirk (q.v.) in 1816, but was released, and was at Ste. Anne's, in the Island of Montreal, in 1817. In 1818 he published *A letter to the Rt. Hon. the Earl of Selkirk in answer to a pamphlet entitled "A postscript in answer to the Statement re-*

specting the Earl of Selkirk's settlement on the Red River in North America", which was written, but not printed, at Sandwich, Upper Canada, and is one of the rarest items in the literature relating to the Selkirk controversy. He retired from the fur-trade about this time; and, because of his intemperate habits, a trust fund was established for his support. He died at Brockville, Upper Canada, on May 8, 1832, aged 63 years, and is described in his obituary notice as "of Augusta, North Carolina".

[W. S. Wallace (ed.), Documents relating to the North West Company (Toronto: The Champlain Society, 1934).]

McKenzie, Daniel Duncan (1859-1927), politician and judge, was born at Lake Ainslie, Cape Breton, on January 9, 1859, the son of Duncan McKenzie and Jessie McMillan. He was educated at the Sydney Academy, and was called to the bar of Nova Scotia in 1889 (K.C., 1908). From 1904 to 1906, and from 1908 to 1923, he represented Cape Breton North in the Canadian House of Commons; and on the death of Sir Wilfrid Laurier (q.v.) in 1919 he was chosen House leader of the Liberal opposition. From 1921 to 1923 he was solicitor-general in the King administration; and in 1923 he was appointed a judge of the Supreme Court of Nova Scotia. He died at Halifax, Nova Scotia, on June 9, 1927. In 1891 he married Florence McDonald; and by her he had one son.

[Can. parl. comp.]

McKenzie, Donald (1783-1851), governor of Assiniboia, was born in Scotland in 1783, and was a younger brother of the Hon. Roderick McKenzie (q.v.). He emigrated to Canada in 1800, and entered the service of the North West Company as a clerk. In 1809 he entered the service of J. J. Astor's American Fur Company; and in 1811 he made the overland journey to Astoria. Here he remained until the capture of Astoria by the Nor'Westers in 1813, when he re-entered the service of the North West Company. He became a partner of the North West Company; and at the union of 1821 he became a chief factor of the Hudson's Bay Company. In 1822 he was appointed a member of the Council of the North West Territories; and from 1825 to 1833 he was governor of Assiniboia. He then retired from the fur-trade, and settled in Mayville, Chautauqua county, New York. Here he died on January 20, 1851.

[C. W. Mackenzie, Donald Mackenzie, king of the northwest (Los Angeles, Cal., 1937); E. Cawcroft, Donald Mackenzie (Can. mag., 1918); E. E. Rich (ed.), Colin Robertson's correspondence book (Toronto: The Champlain Society, 1939).]

Mackenzie, Frederick A. (1869-1931), war correspondent, was born at Quebec, Canada, on September 17, 1869. He was war correspondent of the London Daily Mail from 1900

to 1910; editor of The Times Weekly Edition from 1910 to 1914; and a war correspondent on the western front during the First World War. From 1921 to 1926 he was a special correspondent in Russia. He died at Zeist, Holland, on July 31, 1931. He was the author of Through the Hindenburg line (London, 1919), Russia before dawn (London, 1923), World-famous crimes (London, 1927), The authentic biography of the Rt. Hon. Lord Beaverbrook (London, 1931).

[Who was who, 1929-40.]

McKenzie, Henry (1781?-1832), merchant, was born in Scotland about 1781, and was a younger brother of the Hon. Roderick McKenzie (q.v.). He came to Canada about 1800, and in 1803 was at Kaministikwia (Fort William). On the death of Simon McTavish (q.v.), he was appointed to manage his seigniory and mills at Terrebonne; and when Sir Alexander Mackenzie (q.v.) left Canada in 1808, he was appointed to manage his affairs in Canada. In 1814 he became a member of the firm of McTavish, McGillivrays and Co. of Montreal; and during the Selkirk controversy of 1814-18 he was particularly charged with the publicity campaign of the North West Company. After the union of 1821, however, his relations with his partners in the firm of McTavish, McGillivrays and Co. became strained, and he was denied access to the books of the Company. After the failure of the Company in 1825 he published a Letter to Simon McGillivray (Montreal, 1827), which is a review of his relations with it. In 1815 he was elected a member of the Beaver Club of Montreal, and in 1819 he became an elder, and afterwards clerk of session, in the St. Gabriel Street Presbyterian Church in Montreal. He died of cholera in Montreal on June 28, 1832. In 1815 he married Anne, youngest daughter of the Rev. John Bethune, and sister of Angus Bethune (q.v.), and by her he had two children.

[R. Campbell, A history of the Scotch Presbyterian Church, St. Gabriel Street, Montreal (Montreal, 1887).]

McKenzie, James (d. 1849), fur-trader, was a younger brother of the Hon. Roderick McKenzie (q.v.), and entered the service of the North West Company as a clerk in 1794. He was in the Athabaska department in 1795, and remained there until 1806. In 1802 he became a partner of the North West Company; and in 1806 he was appointed to the King's Posts in the Lower St. Lawrence. His Athabaska journal of 1799-1800 and his account of the King's Posts in 1808 have been published by Masson in his Bourgeois de la Compagnie du Nord-Ouest, vol. ii (Quebec, 1890). He seems to have retired from the management of the King's Posts prior to the union of 1821, for at that time they were managed by James C. McTavish (q.v.); but he evidently retained some connection with them, for in the notice of his death, which took place at Quebec on July

18, 1849, "of the prevailing malady", he is described as "agent of the Hudson's Bay Company". His wife died at Quebec on October 19, 1850. He had two sons and two daughters.

[W. S. Wallace (ed.), *Documents relating to the North West Company* (Toronto: The Champlain Society, 1934).]

Mackenzie, James Bovell (1851-1919), poet, was born in 1851, and died in Toronto, Ontario, on January 7, 1919. He was the author of *The Six Nation Indians of Canada* (Toronto, 1896), *Thayendanegea, an historico-military drama* (Toronto, 1898), and *Alfred the great, and other poems* (Toronto, 1902).

[Toronto *Globe*, Jan. 8, 1919.]

Mackenzie, John Joseph (1865-1922), pathologist, was born at St. Thomas, Ontario, in 1865. He was educated at the University of Toronto (B.A., 1886; M.B., 1899), and at Leipzig and Berlin universities. In 1900 he was appointed professor of pathology and bacteriology in the University of Toronto; and he occupied this chair until his death in Muskoka, Ontario, on August 1, 1922. From 1915 to 1918 he served as a medical officer with No. 4 Canadian Hospital at Salonika; and his letters from Salonika have been edited, with a memoir, by his wife under the title *Number 4 Canadian Hospital: The letters of Professor J. J. Mackenzie from the Salonika front* (Toronto, 1933).

[Morgan, *Can. men* (1912); *University of Toronto monthly*, 1922.]

McKenzie, Kenneth (d. 1817), fur-trader, would appear to have been a relative of the Hon. Roderick McKenzie (q.v.), since his will is preserved among the Masson papers in the Canadian Archives, which came from the Hon. Roderick McKenzie's estate. He entered the service of the North West Company, at a date not ascertained. He was made a partner in 1805; and from 1806 to 1816 he was in charge at Fort William. In 1813 he was elected a member of the Beaver Club in Montreal; and in 1816 he was, with William McGillivray (q.v.), one of the agents of the North West Company at Fort William. He was arrested by Lord Selkirk (q.v.) at Fort William in 1816; and he was drowned, while still a prisoner, on Lake Superior in 1817. He is to be distinguished from the Kenneth Mackenzie (1801-61), who is described as a relative of Sir Alexander Mackenzie (q.v.), who was a clerk in the service of the North West Company in 1820, and whose later career in the American fur-trade is described in H. M. Chittenden, *History of the fur-trade of the far west* (3 vols., New York, 1902).

[W. S. Wallace (ed.), *Documents relating to the North West Company* (Toronto: The Champlain Society, 1934).]

McKenzie, Nathaniel Murdoch William John (1856-1943), fur-trader, was born near Stromness, Orkney, Scotland, on December 5, 1856. He entered the employ of the Hudson's Bay Company in 1876, and saw forty years of service in northern Canada, from Labrador to Athabaska. He died at Winnipeg, Manitoba, on February 15, 1943. He published his autobiography under the title *The men of the Hudson's Bay Company* (Fort William, Ont., 1921).

[*Beaver*, 1943.]

McKenzie, Robert Tait (1867-1938), physician and sculptor, was born at Almonte, Ontario, on May 26, 1867. He was educated at McGill University (B.A., 1889; M.D., C.M., 1892; LL.D., 1919) and at Springfield College (M.P.E., 1914). From 1894 to 1904 he was medical director of physical training at McGill University, and a member of the teaching staff in anatomy; and in 1904 he was appointed professor and director of the department of physical education at the University of Pennsylvania. About 1902 he began to contribute sculpture, chiefly of an athletic character, to the exhibitions of the Royal Academy and other art exhibitions in England and America; and he became one of the most famous of living sculptors. In 1928 he was elected a fellow of the Royal Canadian Academy. He died at Philadelphia, Pennsylvania, on April 28, 1938. Among his publications were *Exercise in education and medicine* (Philadelphia, Pa., 1909) and *Reclaiming the maimed* (New York, 1918).

[C. Hussey, *Tait McKenzie, a sculptor of youth* (London, 1929); *Who's who in America*; *Can. who's who*, 1936-37; O. J. Stevenson, *A people's best* (Toronto, 1927).]

McKenzie, Roderick (1761?-1844), fur-trader, was born in Scotland, about 1761, a first cousin of Sir Alexander Mackenzie (q.v.), and came to Canada in 1784. He entered the service of Gregory, McLeod and Co., and in 1785 was sent to the West as a clerk. In 1788 he built Fort Chipewyan, on Lake Athabaska; and in 1789 and 1792 he was in charge at this post during his cousin's expeditions to the Arctic and Pacific oceans. He declined to follow his cousin when he joined the XY Company in 1800; and the relations between them were strained for many years. He was made a partner of McTavish, Frobisher and Co. in 1800; and was one of the agents of the Company at Grand Portage in that year. He retired from active participation in the fur-trade in 1801, resigning one of his two shares in the Company; and he resigned the other share in 1805. He continued, however, to be a dormant partner in the firm of McTavish, Frobisher and Co. (later McTavish, McGillivrays and Co.) until its failure in 1825; and in 1827 he brought action against the trustees appointed by Simon McGillivray (q.v.) to recover his share of the assets of the firm. In 1804 he purchased from the estate of Simon McTavish (q.v.) the seigniory of Terrebonne; and here he lived till his death on August 15, 1844. In his later years he devoted himself to gathering material for the history of the fur-trade; and much of this material was afterwards published by his son-in-law, the Hon. L. R. Masson, in his *Bourgeois de la Compagnie du Nord-Ouest* (2 vols., Quebec, 1889-90). From 1817 to 1838 he was a member of the Legislative Council of Lower Canada. In 1803 he married Marie Louise Rachel, daughter of Charles Jean Baptiste Chaboillez (q.v.); and by her he had several children.

[W. S. Wallace (ed.), *Documents relating to the North West Company* (Toronto: The Champlain Society, 1934).]

McKenzie, Roderick (1772?-1859), fur-trader, was born in Scotland, about 1772, and entered the service of the Hudson's Bay Company. He was a clerk at Fort Wedderburn, on Lake Athabaska, during the Selkirk troubles of 1816-17. In 1821 he was made a chief trader; and in 1830 he was promoted to the rank of chief factor. From 1830 to 1843 he was in charge of the English River department at Isle à la Crosse; but he must have retired soon after this date. He died on January 2, 1859, at Caberleigh Cottage, Red River Settlement, aged 87 years. He was usually known as "Roderick McKenzie, senior".

[W. S. Wallace (ed.), *Documents relating to the North West Company* (Toronto: The Champlain Society, 1934).]

Mackenzie, Sir William (1849-1923), railway builder, was born at Kirkfield, Upper Canada, on October 30, 1849, the son of John Mackenzie. He was educated at the Lindsay grammar school, and in his early years was a school teacher. He entered the lumber business, and ultimately became a railway contractor. In 1888 he entered into partnership with Sir Donald Mann; and with him he projected and built the Canadian Northern Railway system. He was president of the Canadian Northern Railway Company, and of a large number of subsidiary companies. In his later years he saw many of his enterprises threatened by disaster; and in 1918 the Canadian Northern Railway was taken over by the Canadian government in a state of insolvency. He died at Toronto on December 4, 1923. In 1872 he married Margaret, daughter of John Merry, of Kirkfield, Ontario; and by her he had several children. He was created a knight bachelor in 1911.

[T. D. Regehr, *The Canadian Northern Railway* (Toronto, 1976); *Can. who was who*, vol. 2; *Who was who*, 1916-28; H. Charlesworth (ed.), *A cyclopaedia of Canadian biography* (Toronto, 1919); Morgan, *Can. men* (1912).]

Mackenzie, William Lyon (1795-1861), politician and rebel, was born at Springfield,

Dundee, Scotland, on March 12, 1795, the only son of Daniel Mackenzie and Elizabeth Mackenzie, both natives of Kirkmichael, Perthshire. He was educated at the parish school, and at an early age went into trade. He came to Canada in 1820, and went into business as a shop-keeper, first in York (Toronto), then in Dundas, and lastly in Queenston. In Queenston he founded in 1824 the *Colonial Advocate*, a political journal which after November, 1824, he published in York (Toronto). In this journal he attacked the so-called "Family Compact" or governing clique with such virulence that on June 8, 1826, a number of young men connected with the "Family Compact" raided his printing-press, broke up the forms, and deposited some of the type in Toronto Bay. This incident, on account of which Mackenzie was awarded in the courts substantial damages, made him a popular hero; and he came to be regarded as the leader of the radical wing of the Reform party in the province.

In 1828 he was elected to the Legislative Assembly of Upper Canada as one of the members for the county of York; and from the outset he took an active part in the House. In 1831 he was expelled from the Assembly for "a libel constituting a breach of the privileges of this House"; and though five times re-elected by his constituents, he was five times expelled, and was even declared incapable of sitting. In 1835 he was elected the first mayor of the newly incorporated city of Toronto; and in the Assembly of 1835, in which the Reformers were in a majority, he once more took his seat as one of the members for the county of York. To a large extent he dominated the House; and the *Seventh report of the committee on grievances* (Toronto, 1835), in which the case of the Reformers was summed up, was mainly his handiwork.

Up to this point, Mackenzie's agitation for reform had been conducted on constitutional lines; but the dissolution of the Assembly by Sir Francis Bond Head (q.v.) in 1836, and the subsequent defeat of Mackenzie and the Reformers in the country, as well as the rejection of the demands of the Reformers by the British parliament in the Russell Resolutions of 1837, embittered him and drove him into a course culminating in armed rebellion. Of the rebellion of December, 1837, in Upper Canada, he was the chief organizer; and there is reason for believing that, during that unfortunate episode, his mind was unbalanced. The revolt proved a fiasco; and Mackenzie escaped to the United States. He first set up a provisional government on Navy Island in the Niagara River; and he was at last imprisoned for a breach of the United States neutrality laws. In the United States he supported himself and his family by journalism and hack-writing, in which a strong anti-British bias was displayed.

In 1849 he was permitted to return to Canada under an amnesty Act of the Canadian legislature; and in 1851 he was elected to the Legislative Assembly for the county of Haldimand, his principal opponent being George Brown (q.v.). In the House he proved, however, to be a negligible quantity; and in August, 1858, he resigned his seat, and retired to private life. He continued to publish, at irregular intervals, a paper which he had established in 1853, entitled *Mackenzie's Message*; but in 1860 he ceased even the publication of this journal, and on August 28, 1861, he died at Toronto. In 1822 he married Isabel (d. 1873), daughter of Peter Baxter of Dundee, Scotland; and by her he had thirteen children.

Mackenzie was not, as is commonly supposed, an advocate of responsible government. His panacea for the ills of Upper Canada before 1837 was the application of the elective principle to the Legislative Council; and his *Seventh report on grievances* specifically rejected the idea of responsible government. Even after his return to Canada in 1849 he did not appear to grasp the underlying conventions of responsible government, but was completely out of sympathy with the new order of things.

In addition to his journalistic work, Mackenzie published the following books and pamphlets: *The history of the destruction of the Colonial Advocate press* (York, 1827); *The legislative black list of Upper Canada* (York, 1828); *Catechism of education* (York, 1830); *Poor Richard or the Yorkshire almanack* (York, probably 1830-34); *Sketches of Canada and the United States* (London, 1833); *Mackenzie's own narrative of the late rebellion* (Toronto, 1838); *The Caroline almanac* (Rochester, New York, 1842); *Trial of Rev. Washington Van Zandt, for seduction of Sophia Murdock* (Rochester, New York, 1842); *The sons of the emerald isle* (New York, 1844); *The lives and opinions of Benj. Franklin Butler and Jesse Hoyt* (Boston, 1845); and *The life and times of Martin Van Buren* (Boston, 1846).

[C. Lindsey, *The life and times of Wm. Lyon Mackenzie* (2 vols., Toronto, 1862), edited with numerous additions by G. G. S. Lindsey, under the title *William Lyon Mackenzie* (Toronto, 1908); J. C. Dent, *The story of the Upper Canadian rebellion* (2 vols., Toronto, 1885); J. King, *The other side of the story* (Toronto, 1886); W. S. Wallace, *The family compact* (Toronto, 1915); Morgan, *Cel. Can.* and *Bib. can.*; W. Smith, *Political leaders of Upper Canada* (Toronto, 1931); D. Flint, *William Lyon Mackenzie: Rebel against authority* (Toronto, 1971); F. H. Armstrong, *William Lyon Mackenzie, first mayor of Toronto* (Can. hist. rev., 1967); L. F. Gates, *Mackenzie's Gazette* (Can. hist. rev., 1965); F. H. Armstrong, *William Lyon Mackenzie: The persistent hero* (Jour. Can. stud., 1971); W. Kilbourn, *The firebrand* (Toronto, 1956). A biography of Mackenzie was written by W. D. Lesueur (q.v.) from the Tory point of view;but its publication was prevented by a legal injunction obtained by Mackenzie's descendants.]

McKenzie, William Patrick (1861-1942), clergyman and poet, was born in Almonte, Canada West, in 1861. He was educated at Upper Canada College, Toronto, at the University of Toronto (B.A., 1884), at Knox College, Toronto, and at the Auburn Theological Seminary; and was ordained in 1889 a clergyman of the Presbyterian Church in Canada. In 1895 he left the Presbyterian Church, to become a leader in the Christian Science movement in the United States; and in 1909 he became president of the board of directors of the Mother Church of Christian Science in Boston. He died at Cambridge, Massachusetts, on September 8, 1942. Throughout life he continued to publish booklets of verse: *A song of trust, and other thoughts in verse* (Toronto, 1887), *Voices and undertones, in song and poem* (Toronto, 1889), *Songs of the human* (Toronto, 1892), *Hearts-ease hymns, and some other verses* (Toronto, 1895), *The sower, and other poems* (Cambridge, Mass., 1903), *Fields of bloom* (Cambridge, Mass., 1930), and *Prelude poems for the new day* (Chicago, 1942).

[*Who's who in America*, 1940-41; Morgan, *Can. men* (1912); C. C. James, *A bibliography of Canadian poetry* (Toronto, 1899).]

McKeown, Hugh Charles (1841-1889), lawyer, was born in St. Catharines, Upper Canada, on March 21, 1841. He was called to the bar of Upper Canada in 1860, and practised law first in Hamilton, and then in New York. On retiring from legal practice, he returned to St. Catharines; and he died there on March 24, 1889. He was the author of *The life and labors of Most Rev. John Joseph Lynch* (Montreal, 1886).

[Private information.]

MacKeracher, William Mackay (1871-1913), poet and journalist, was born at Châteauguay, Quebec, on July 28, 1871, the son of the Rev. C. M. MacKeracher and Dolina Mackay. He was educated at McGill University (B.A., 1894), and at the Montreal Presbyterian College; and in 1897 he was ordained a minister of the Presbyterian Church, but he did not take up pastoral work. He became a journalist and for many years was on the staff of the Montreal *Daily Witness*. He died at Montreal on April 6, 1913. In 1899 he married Bertha Gledhill, of New York. The author of much occasional verse, he published two volumes of poetry, *Canada my land* (Toronto, 1908) and *Sonnets and other verse* (Toronto, 1909).

[Morgan, *Can. men* (1912).]

Mackerras, John Hugh (1832-1880), educationist, was born at Nairn, Scotland, in 1832. He came to Canada at an early age, and was educated at Queen's College, Kingston (B.A., 1850; M.A., 1852). He was ordained a minister of the Presbyterian Church in 1853, and for ten years was pastor of the Presbyterian church in Belleville, Canada West. In 1864 he was appointed professor of classical literature in Queen's University, Kingston; and he held this post until his death, at Peterborough, Ontario, on January 9, 1880.

[*Dom. ann. reg.,* 1880-81; Dent, *Can. port.,* vol. 1.]

McKibbin, Archibald (1863-1925), clergyman and author, was born in Stanley township, Huron county, Ontario, on April 12, 1863. He was educated at Victoria University (B.A., 1896), and was ordained a minister of the Methodist Church. He died at London, Ontario, on November 18, 1925. He wrote under the pseudonym "Mack Cloie"; and he was the author of *The old orchard* (Toronto, 1903) and *The pancake preacher* (Toronto, 1906).

[Morgan, *Can. men* (1912).]

McKim, Anson (1855-1917), pioneer in advertising, was born at Napanee, Canada West, on May 2, 1855. When a young man, he joined the staff of the *Mail* newspaper in Toronto; and from 1879 to 1889 he was the representative of this newspaper in Montreal. He then resigned to open in Montreal an advertising agency, A. McKim and Company. He was a pioneer in general advertising in Canada; and the McKim Advertising Agency, as the firm was known after 1907, became one of the largest advertising businesses in the country, with branches in Toronto, Winnipeg, and London, England. In 1892 McKim began publication of the *Canadian newspaper directory*, as a guide for advertisers. He was killed by a train at Coteau Junction, Quebec, on January 25, 1917.

[*Can. who was who,* vol. 2.]

McKindsey, George Crawford (1829-1901), senator of Canada, was born in Halton county, Upper Canada, of Irish parentage, on March 29, 1829. He was educated in the common schools; and from 1859 to 1882 was sheriff of Halton. He was called to the Senate of Canada in 1884; and he died in 1901.

[*Can. parl. comp.*]

Mackinnon, Clarence (1868-1937), clergyman and educationist, was born at Hopewell, Nova Scotia, on March 11, 1868. He was educated at Edinburgh University (M.A., 1889; B.D., 1894), and was ordained a minister of the Presbyterian Church in 1892. After serving as pastor of churches in Nova Scotia and Manitoba, he was appointed in 1909 principal of the Presbyterian Theological College, Halifax, and in 1927 of Pine Hill Divinity Hall, Halifax. During the First World War, he served as a chaplain; and in 1924 he was elected moderator of the Presbyterian Church in

Canada. He died at Halifax, Nova Scotia, on October 9, 1937. He was a D.D. of the University of Manitoba, and an LL.D. of Dalhousie University and Mount Allison University. He was the author of *The life of Principal Oliver* (Toronto, 1936), and *Reminiscences* (Toronto, 1938).

[*Can. who's who,* 1936-37; Morgan, *Can. men* (1912).]

MacKinnon, Colin Francis (1810-1879), Roman Catholic archbishop, was born at Williams Point, near Antigonish, Nova Scotia, on July 20, 1810. He was educated at Urban College, Rome, and was ordained a priest in 1837. He became parish priest at St. Andrew's, Antigonish county, Nova Scotia; and in 1852 he was raised to the episcopate as bishop of Arichat. He resigned this see in 1877, and was appointed archbishop of Amida *in partibus*. He died on September 26, 1879.

[*Can. who was who,* vol. 2; Le Jeune, *Dict. gén.; Dict. Can. biog.,* vol. 10.]

McKinnon, Murdoch (1865-1944), lieutenant-governor of Prince Edward Island (1919-24), was born at Brooklin, King's county, Prince Edward Island, on March 15, 1865. He became a farmer; and represented 4th King's in the legislature of Prince Edward Island from 1897 to 1919. From 1911 to 1917 he was provincial secretary-treasurer and commissioner of agriculture in the Mathieson administration; and from 1919 to 1924 he was lieutenant-governor of Prince Edward Island. As lieutenant-governor, he made constitutional history in the province by refusing his assent to the Church Union bill of 1923. He died at Charlottetown, Prince Edward Island, on October 12, 1944.

[*Can. who's who,* 1936-37; *Can. parl. comp.*]

McKinnon, Neil John (1911-1975), banker, was born in Cobalt, Ontario, January 17, 1911. He entered the Canadian Bank of Commerce at age fourteen and continued his high school and business education in evening classes and by correspondence courses. In 1929 he began work in the head office of the bank in Toronto, becoming inspector, branch manager, and chief inspector; he became president in 1956, and chairman of the board and president in 1959. After the amalgamation of the Imperial Bank of Canada and the Canadian Bank of Commerce in June, 1961, he became chairman of the board and chief executive officer in 1963, and chairman of the Canadian Imperial Bank of Commerce in 1965. He retired in 1973.

He was a director of ten Canadian companies and was president of the Toronto Board of Trade in 1953. He was active in behalf of the Community Chest and other charitable causes. He died at Port Carling, Ontario, August 4, 1975.

[*Can. who's who*, 1970-72; Toronto *Globe and Mail*, August 4, 1975; Metropolitan Toronto Library Board, *Biographical scrapbooks*, vol. 71.]

McKinnon, William Charles (d. 1862), clergyman and author, was born in Cape Breton, Nova Scotia, and became first a journalist in Sydney, Cape Breton. He then became a Wesleyan Methodist clergyman; and he died in Nova Scotia in 1862. He was the author of *St. Castine: A legend of Cape Breton* (Sydney, N.S., 1850), *Frances; or, Pirate Cove* (Halifax, N.S., 1851), *St. George; or, The Canadian League* (2 vols., Halifax, N.S., 1852), and some other tales not printed in book form, such as *The midnight murder* and *The pirates of the Gulf*.

[Morgan, *Bib. can.*; R. J. Long, *Nova Scotia authors* (East Orange, N.J., 1918).]

Mackintosh, Charles Herbert (1843-1931), lieutenant-governor of the North West Territories (1893-98), was born in London, Upper Canada, in 1843, the son off Capt. William Mackintosh. He was educated at the Galt Grammar School and Caradoc Academy, and became a journalist. From 1874 to 1892 he was the proprietor and editor of the Ottawa *Daily Citizen*; and from 1877 to 1882 he was also proprietor and editor of the *Canadian Parliamentary Companion*. He represented Ottawa in the Canadian House of Commons from 1882 to 1887 and from 1890 to 1893; and from 1893 to 1898 he was lieutenant-governor of the North West Territories. On his retirement from this office, he became a financial broker and agent in Victoria, British Columbia; and he died at Ottawa on December 22, 1931. He was the author of *The Chicago fire* (Chicago, 1871) and *The Liberal-Conservative handbook* (Toronto, 1876).

[*Can. parl. comp.*; H. Charlesworth (ed.) *A cyclopaedia of Canadian biography* (Toronto, 1919); Morgan, *Can. men* (1912); Rose, *Cyc. Can. biog.* (1886).]

McKishnie, Archibald P. (1876-1946), novelist, was born at New Scotland, Ontario, in 1876, and died at Toronto, Ontario, on July 7, 1946. For many years he was a journalist in Toronto and Montreal, and he wrote a number of successful novels: *Gaff Linkum* (Toronto, 1907), *Love of the wild* (Toronto, 1910), *Willow, the wisp* (Toronto, 1918), *A son of courage* (Toronto, 1920), *Openway* (Toronto, 1922), *Big John Wallace* (Toronto, 1922), *Mates of the tangle* (Toronto, 1924), *Brains, Limited* (Toronto, 1925), and *Dwellers of the marsh realm* (Chicago, 1937). He was a brother of Jean Blewett (q.v.).

[Toronto *Globe and Mail*, July 8, 1946; *Can. who's who*, 1936-37; *Encyc. Can.*]

Macklem, Thomas Clark Street (1862-1944), clergyman and educationist, was born at Chippawa, Canada West, on November 25, 1862, the son of Oliver Tiffany Macklem and Julia A. Street. He was educated at Upper Canada College, Toronto, and at St. John's College, Cambridge (B.A., 1885; M.A., 1886), and was ordained a priest of the Church of England in 1885. From 1900 to 1921 he was provost and vice-chancellor of the University of Trinity College, Toronto; and it was under him that the federation of this university with the University of Toronto was consummated. He died in Toronto, Ontario, on June 17, 1944. He was the recipient of honorary degrees from Trinity University, the University of Toronto, the University of New Brunswick, and the University of Bishop's College.

[*Can. who's who*, 1936-37; Morgan, *Can. men* (1912).]

McLachlan, Alexander (1818-1896), poet, was born in 1818 in Johnstone, Renfrewshire, Scotland, the son of Charles McLachlan and Jane Sutherland. He came to Canada in 1840, and most of his life was spent in farming in various parts of Ontario. He published *The spirit of love and other poems* (Toronto, 1846), *Poems* (Toronto, 1856), *Lyrics* (Toronto, 1858), *The emigrant and other poems* (Toronto, 1861), and *Poems and songs* (Toronto, 1874; 2nd ed., 1888). After his death, *The poetical works of Alexander McLachlan* (Toronto, 1900) was published by a committee of admirers. Much of his best verse was in Scottish dialect. He died at Orangeville, Ontario, on March 30, 1896. About 1841, he married his first cousin, Clamina McLachlan; and by her he had eleven children.

["Biographical sketch" in *The poetical works of Alexander McLachlan* (Toronto, 1900); *Can. who was who*, vol. 2; *Cyc. Am. biog.*; Morgan, *Bib. can.*; C. C. James, *A bibliography of Canadian poetry* (Toronto, 1899); A. MacMurchy, *A handbook of Canadian literature* (Toronto, 1906).]

McLachlan, Robert Wallace (1845-1926), antiquarian and numismatist, was born at Montreal, Canada East, on March 9, 1845, the son of William McLachlan and Ann Stephen. He was educated at McGill University, and first went into business, but ultimately became an official in the Montreal Court House. He began to collect coins as a boy; and he became the leading authority on numismatics in Canada. For many years he was editor of the *Journal* of the Antiquarian and Numismatic Society of Montreal; and he was one of the founders of the Château de Ramezay Museum, to which he bequeathed his collection of upwards of 10,000 coins. He was elected a fellow of the Royal Society of Canada in 1914. He died at Montreal on May 10, 1926. He published a large number of brochures on antiquarian and numismatic subjects, among which the more important were *Canadian temperance medals* (Montreal, 1879), *Money and medals of Can-*

ada under the old régime (Montreal, 1885), Canadian numismatics (Montreal, 1886), The Louisbourg medals (Montreal, 1886), Canadian communion tokens (Montreal, 1891), Coins struck in Canada previous to 1840 (Brussels, 1892), The Nova Scotian treasury notes (Montreal, 1898), Medals awarded to Canadian Indians (Montreal, 1899), The copper currency of the Canadian banks (Ottawa, 1903), and Fleury Mesplet, the first printer of Montreal (Ottawa, 1907).

[Proc. Roy. Soc. Can., 1926; Morgan, Can. men (1912).]

McLagan, Thomas Rodgie (1897-1972), transportation executive, was born in Westmount, Quebec, January 22, 1897. He was educated at Lower Canada College and, after a period of service in the First World War as a gunner with the 11th Battery Canadian Field Artillery, he completed his education at McGill University in 1923. He joined the Laurentide Company in 1923, was with Dufresne, McLagan and Associates from 1932 to 1939, and was vice-president and general manager of Canadian Vickers Limited from 1939 to 1951. He became president and general manager of Canada Steamship Lines in 1951, and chairman of the board in 1966. He held directorships in twenty-two Canadian companies, was president of the Canadian Manufacturers Association (1960-61), and was a member of the Montreal Board of Trade. He was made an officer of the Order of the British Empire (O.B.E.) in 1946. He died at Montreal, Quebec, September 2, 1972.

[Can. who's who, 1967-69.]

MacLaren, David Lawrence (1893-1960), lieutenant-governor of New Brunswick (1945-60), was born in Saint John, New Brunswick, on October 27, 1893, and died there on September 7, 1960. During the First World War he served overseas with the Royal Canadian Artillery, and lost a leg at Vimy Ridge. He was elected mayor of Saint John in 1936; and in 1945 he was appointed minister of national revenue in the Mackenzie King government, but failed to find a seat in the Canadian House of Commons in the election of that year. He was then appointed lieutenant-governor of New Brunswick, was re-appointed to serve a second and a third term, and died in office.

[Can. parl. comp., 1959; Can. who's who, 1958-60; Encyc. Can.]

Maclaren, John James (1842-1926), lawyer and judge, was born at Lachute, Canada East, on July 1, 1842, the son of John Maclaren and Janet Mackintosh. He was educated at Victoria University, Cobourg (B.A., 1862; M.A., 1866; LL.B., 1868; LL.D., 1888), and at McGill University (B.C.L., 1868; D.C.L., 1888). He was called to the bar in Quebec in 1868 (Q.C., 1878), and he practised law in Montreal until 1884, when he removed to To-

ronto. In 1902 he was appointed a judge of the Supreme Court of Ontario. He died at Toronto on July 8, 1926. He was the author of Roman law in English jurisprudence (Toronto, 1888), Bills, notes, and cheques (Toronto, 1892; 5th ed., 1916), Banks and banking (Toronto, 1894; 8th ed., 1928), and International arbitration (Toronto, 1909).

[Canadian law times, 1926; Morgan, Can. men (1912).]

MacLaren, Murray (1861-1942), minister of pensions and national health for Canada (1930-34) and lieutenant-governor of New Brunswick (1935-40), was born at Richibucto, New Brunswick, on April 30, 1861. He was educated at the University of New Brunswick (B.A., 1880; LL.D., 1916) and at Edinburgh University (M.B., C.M., 1884; M.D., 1888); and he practised medicine in Saint John, New Brunswick, for many years. During the First World War he commanded No. 1 Canadian General Hospital, Canadian Overseas Military Forces of Canada; and he was awarded in 1916 the C.M.G. From 1921 to 1934 he represented Saint John in the Canadian House of Commons; and from 1930 to 1934 he was minister of pensions and national health in the Bennett government. He resigned to accept appointment as lieutenant-governor of New Brunswick; and he retained this position until 1940. He died at Saint John, New Brunswick, on December 24, 1942.

[Can. who's who, 1936-37; Morgan, Can. men (1912); Can. parl. comp.]

McLaren, Peter (d. 1919), senator of Canada, was born in Lanark, Upper Canada, the son of James McLaren. He became a wealthy lumberman of the Ottawa valley; and in 1881-83 he was concerned in a long-drawn-out lawsuit with Boyd Caldwell and Co., a rival lumbering firm, that ended in a victory for the cause of provincial rights. In 1890 he was called to the Senate, on the advice of Sir John Macdonald (q.v.); and he sat in the Senate until his death, at Perth, Ontario, on May 3, 1919.

[Can. parl. comp.]

McLarty, Norman Alexander (1889-1945), lawyer and politician, was born at St. Thomas, Ontario, on February 18, 1889, and died at Ottawa, Ontario, on September 16, 1945. He was educated at the University of Toronto (B.A., 1910) and Osgoode Hall, and was called to the bar in 1913 (K.C., 1935). He practised law, first at Medicine Hat, Alberta, and later at Windsor, Ontario. He was elected to represent Essex West as a Liberal in 1935; and he held in succession the portfolios of postmaster-general, minister of labour, and secretary of state in the Mackenzie King government. Ill-health caused his resignation a few months before his death.

[Can. parl. comp., 1944; Can. who's who, 1938-39; Encyc. Can.]

McLaughlin, Robert Samuel (1871-1972), manufacturer, president of General Motors of Canada, was born at Enniskillen, Ontario, September 8, 1871. He was educated in Oshawa public and high schools, and joined his father's carriage business in 1887, becoming a partner in 1895. He was responsible for the founding of the McLaughlin Motor Car Company in Oshawa in 1907 which produced a car designed in Canada with an American Buick engine and called first the McLaughlin and later the McLaughlin-Buick. He became director and treasurer of the Chevrolet Motor Company of Canada on its establishment in 1915. McLaughlin Motor Car Company became part of General Motors of Canada in 1918, and Mr. McLaughlin was president of General Motors of Canada until 1945 and chairman of the board until his death. As a wealthy philanthropist, R. S. McLaughlin made gifts of a library, parks, playgrounds, and hospital facilities to Oshawa. He made large gifts to Queen's University at Kingston, and the Ontario Agricultural College at Guelph. He died at Oshawa, Ontario, January 6, 1972.

[*Can. who's who*, 1967-69; *Encyc. Can.* (1972); R. S. McLaughlin, "My first century on wheels", *Weekend* magazine (Toronto, November 13, 1971).]

Maclean, Alexander (1822-1916), clergyman, was born at Hopewell, Nova Scotia, in 1822, and was ordained a minister of the Presbyterian Church in 1852. He died at Eureka, Nova Scotia, on August 17, 1916. He was the author of *The story of the kirk* (Halifax, N.S., 1911).

[R. J. Long, *Nova Scotia authors* (East Orange, N.J., 1918).]

McLean, Alexander (1827-1864), clergyman and author, was born on the island of North Uist, Scotland, in 1827. He became a Presbyterian minister in Canada; and he died at Morriston, Ontario, on May 24, 1864. He was the author of *The more priests the more crime* (Toronto, 1854) and *The tricentenary of the Scottish reformation* (Toronto, 1861).

[Morgan, *Bib. can.*]

McLean, Alexander Daniel (1896-1969), aviation pioneer, was born at Maxville, Ontario, January 31, 1896, and was educated in Ontario schools and the University of Alberta. He served in the Royal Flying Corps during the First World War as a flying instructor in England, and on his return to Canada joined the Royal Canadian Air Force Reserve. During 1927 and 1928 he undertook mapping and aerial photography in eastern Canada for the Royal Canadian Air Force, and on January 29, 1929, he flew the inaugural flight of the airmail service from Ottawa to Saint John, New Brunswick. He was appointed inspector of western airways for the Civil Aviation Branch in 1929, where he did aerial and mapping sur-

veys and laid out the first airway system in Canada. In 1931 he was transferred to Ottawa as acting superintendent of airways and airports and by 1937 had completed the Trans Canada Airway System, together with its administration. He also surveyed a possible system through the Canadian Northwest to Alaska in 1935. During the Second World War he was responsible for the selection, survey, and development of airports for the British Commonwealth Air Training Plan. He was appointed controller of Civil Aviation in 1941 and was awarded the McKee Trophy for his service to aviation. He was awarded the O.B.E. in 1946. He retired from government service in 1950. He died at Ottawa, Ontario, May 16, 1969.

[*Canadian Aviation*, vol. 24 (February, 1951); *Can. who's who*, 1955-57.]

Maclean, Alexander K. (1869-1942), politician and jurist, was born at Upper North Sydney, Nova Scotia, on October 18, 1869, and was educated at Dalhousie University (LL.B., 1892). He was called to the bar of Nova Scotia in 1892; and he practised law for many years, first in Lunenburg, Nova Scotia, and later in Halifax, Nova Scotia. He represented Lunenburg in the Nova Scotia legislature from 1901 to 1904, in the Canadian House of Commons from 1904 to 1909, and in the Nova Scotia legislature from 1909 to 1911; and from 1909 to 1911 he was attorney-general in the Murray administration. From 1911 to 1923 he represented Halifax county in the Canadian House of Commons; and from 1917 to 1920 he was minister without portfolio in the Union government of Sir Robert Borden (q.v.). In 1923 he was appointed president of the Exchequer Court of Canada; and he occupied this position until his death at Ottawa, on July 31, 1942.

[*Can. who's who*, 1936-37; Morgan, *Can. men* (1912); *Can. parl. comp.*]

Maclean, Allan (1725-1784), soldier, was born in the Island of Mull in 1725, the son of Maclean of Torloisk. He served as a subaltern in the Scots brigade in the Dutch service from 1747 to 1757; and he was then gazetted a captain in Montgomery's Highlanders (77th Foot), and was sent to America. He served in Canada during the later stages of the Seven Years' War; and during the American Revolution he commanded the Royal Highland Emigrants (84th Foot). He appears to have died in 1784.

[J. P. MacLean, *Renascence of the Clan Maclean* (Cleveland, Ohio, 1913) and *The family of Maclean* (Franklin, Ohio, 1915); *Dict. nat. biog.*; *Cyc. Am. biog.*]

McLean, Archibald (1791-1865), chief justice of Upper Canada (1862-65), was born at St. Andrews, Upper Canada, on April 5, 1791, the second son of Lieut.-Col. Neil McLean. He was educated at Cornwall, Upper Canada, under John Strachan (q.v.), and in 1808 he was entered as a student of law in the books of the Law Society of Upper Canada. He served in the War of 1812 as a subaltern in the 3rd York Militia, was wounded at the battle of Queenston Heights, and was taken prisoner at the battle of Lundy's Lane. In 1815, at the close of the war, he was called to the bar of Upper Canada; and he began the practice of law in Cornwall. From 1820 to 1836 he represented Stormont in the Legislative Assembly of Upper Canada, and he was twice elected speaker of the House. In 1836 he was commissioned a member of the Legislative Council of Upper Canada; and in 1837 he was appointed a puisne judge of the Court of Queen's Bench. In 1850 he became a puisne judge of the Court of Common Pleas; and in 1856 he went back to the Queen's Bench. In 1862 he was appointed chief justice of the Queen's Bench, and in 1863 president of the Court of Appeal. He died at Toronto on October 24, 1865. He married a daughter of John McPherson, of Three Rivers.

[D. B. Read, *The lives of the judges of Upper Canada* (Toronto, 1888).]

McLean, Hugh Havelock (1854-1938), lieutenant-governor of New Brunswick (1928-33), was born at Fredericton, New Brunswick, on March 22, 1854. He was called to the bar of New Brunswick in 1874 (Q.C., 1900), and practised law for many years in Saint John, New Brunswick. He joined the Canadian militia at the time of the Fenian raids, and he saw service in the North West Rebellion of 1885. He retired to the reserve of officers in 1911, with the rank of colonel; but in the First World War he served, first as a brigadier-general commanding the 7th Infantry Brigade, and then as general officer commanding all troops in New Brunswick, with the rank of major-general. From 1908 to 1917 he represented Queens-Sunbury, and from 1917 to 1921 Kings and Queens county, in the Canadian House of Commons; and from 1928 to 1933 he was lieutenant-governor of New Brunswick. He died at Saint John, New Brunswick, on November 22, 1938.

[*Can. who's who*, 1936-37; *Can. parl. comp.*; Morgan, *Can. men* (1912).]

MacLean, James Alexander (1868-1945), educationist, was born at Mayfair, Ontario, on August 2, 1868, and died at London, Ontario, on January 18, 1945. He was educated at the University of Toronto (B.A., 1892) and Cornell University (M.A., 1893; Ph.D., 1894). He was professor of political economy at the University of Colorado from 1898 to 1900, president of the University of Idaho from 1900 to 1912, and president of the University of Manitoba from 1913 to his retirement in 1934. He was the author of *Essays on the financial history of Canada* (New York, 1894).

[*Can. who's who*, 1936-37; *Encyc. Can.*]

McLean, John (1797?-1890), fur-trader and explorer, was born in Argyllshire, Scotland, toward the end of 1797, or the beginning of 1798. He entered the service of the Hudson's Bay Company at Montreal in 1821, and he remained in the service of the company until 1845. He was stationed in various places in eastern and western Canada, and from 1837 to 1842 was in charge of Fort Ungava in Labrador. It was while here, in 1838, that he set out on the first overland journey across the Labrador peninsula, in the course of which he discovered the Great Falls of Labrador. After his retirement in 1845, he settled in Guelph, Canada West, and for many years he was clerk of the division court at Elora, Ontario. His last years he spent with his youngest daughter in Victoria, British Columbia; and here he died on March 8, 1890. He was twice married, in the second place to the daughter of the Rev. James Evans (q.v.); and he had two sons and three daughters. He was the author of *Notes of a twenty-five years' service in the Hudson's Bay Territory* (2 vols., London, 1849).

[W. S. Wallace (ed.), *Notes of a twenty-five years' service in the Hudson's Bay Territory*, by John McLean (Toronto: The Champlain Society, 1932); D. Boyle, *Notes on the discoverer of the Great Falls of Labrador* (Transactions of the Canadian Institute, 1890-91).]

Maclean, John (1828-1886), first Anglican bishop of Saskatchewan, was born on November 17, 1828, the son of Charles Maclean, of Portsoy, Banffshire, Scotland. He was educated at King's College, Aberdeen (M.A., 1851), and at first was employed in a counting-house in London, England. In 1858 he was ordained a priest of the Church of England, and came to Canada under the auspices of the Colonial and Continental Church Society. For several years he was assistant to the bishop of Huron, at London, Canada West; but in 1866 he went to the North West as rector of St. John's Cathedral, Winnipeg, archdeacon of Assiniboia, and warden of St. John's College, Winnipeg. In 1874 he was consecrated first bishop of Saskatchewan, and he had oversight of this diocese until his death on November 7, 1886. In 1871 he received the degree of D.C.L. from Trinity University, Toronto, and from Bishop's College, Lennoxville; and that of D.D. from Kenyon College, Ohio.

[*Dict. nat. biog.*; *Dom. ann. reg.*, 1886; C. H. Mockridge, *The bishops of the Church of England in Canada* (Toronto, 1896); W. B. Heeney, *Leaders of the Canadian church* (Toronto, 1920).]

Maclean, John (1851-1928), missionary and author, was born at Kilmarnock, Scotland, on October 30, 1851. He came to Canada as a youth, and was educated at Victoria University, Cobourg (B.A., 1882; M.A., 1887), and at the Wesleyan University, Bloomington, Illinois (Ph.D., 1888). He was ordained a minister of the Methodist Church in 1880; and from 1880 to 1889 he served as a missionary among the Blood Indians, near Macleod, Alberta. After 1889 he was Methodist minister at various places in the Canadian West. He died at Winnipeg, Manitoba, on March 7, 1928. He wrote sometimes under the *nom de plume* of "Robin Rustler"; and he was the author of *Lone land lights* (Toronto, 1882), *The Indians, their manners and customs* (Toronto, 1889), *James Evans, the inventor of the syllabic system of the Cree language* (Toronto, 1890), *The hero of the Saskatchewan* (Barrie, Ont., 1891), *Canadian savage folk, the native tribes of Canada* (Toronto, 1896), *The warden of the plains, and other stories* (Toronto, 1896), *The great northwest* (Toronto, 1902), *The life of William Black* (Halifax, 1907), *James Evans* (Toronto, 1924), and *McDougall of Alberta* (Toronto, 1926).

[Morgan, *Can. men* (1912); L. E. Horning and L. J. Burpee, *A bibliography of Canadian fiction* (Toronto, 1904).]

Maclean, Quentin Morvaren (1896-1962), musician, was born in London, England, in 1896. He was a pupil of Sir Richard Terry and of Max Regar at Leipzig. He gave his first recital at thirteen, and at eighteen was soloist at the Leipzig Bach festival. He became a theatre organist in England in 1926 and gave regular weekly concerts for the B.B.C. Mr. Maclean came to Canada in 1939 and played as a theatre organist and for the C.B.C. He was organist at Holy Rosary Church in Toronto for twenty years. He wrote *Organ tone and terminology*. He died at Toronto, Ontario, July 9, 1962.

[Metropolitan Toronto Library Board, *Biographical scrapbooks*, vol. 20.]

McLean, Simon James (1871-1946), economist, was born at Quebec City, on June 14, 1871, and died at Ottawa, Ontario, on November 5, 1946. He was educated at the University of Toronto (B.A., 1894), Columbia University (M.A., 1896), and the University of Chicago (Ph.D., 1897); and he held teaching positions successively in the University of Arkansas, Leland Stanford University, and the University of Toronto. He became an outstanding authority on transportation, and in 1908 was appointed a member of the Board of Railway Commissioners at Ottawa. He became assistant chief commissioner of the Board in 1918, and continued as such until his retirement in 1938. He was the author of *The tariff history of Canada* (Toronto, 1895) and *Inland traffic* (New York, 1917).

[*Can. who's who*, 1936-37.]

Maclean, William Findlay (1854-1929), journalist, was born at Ancaster, Ontario, on August 10, 1854, the son of John Maclean and Isabella Findlay. He was educated at the University of Toronto (B.A., 1880), and in 1880 founded the *World* newspaper in Toronto, of which he was the proprietor and editor until its discontinuance in 1921. From 1892 to 1904 he represented East York, and from 1904 to 1926 South York, in the Canadian House of Commons; and at the time of his retirement from parliament was "dean of the House". Nominally a Conservative, he was never a strict party man, and frequently took an independent course. He died at his home "Donlands", near Toronto, on December 7, 1929.

[*Can. parl. comp.*; Morgan, *Can. men* (1912).]

McLean, William John (1841-1929), furtrader, was born in the isle of Lewis, Scotland, on October 27, 1841. He entered the service of the Hudson's Bay Company in 1859, and was employed first in the Mackenzie and Swan River districts. In 1885, when the North West rebellion broke out, he was in charge of Fort Pitt; and he and his family were for over two months prisoners in the hands of Big Bear. He retired from the Company's service in 1892, with the rank of chief trader; and in his later years he was an officer of the department of Indian Affairs. He died on November 12, 1929.

[R. Watson, *Late Chief Trader W. J. McLean* (Beaver, 1929).]

Maclear, Thomas (d. 1898), publisher, was a native of Scotland who came to Canada shortly before 1850 as the representative of the Edinburgh publishing house of Blackie and Company. He was a bookseller and publisher in Toronto from 1850 to 1887; and he died at Montreal, Quebec, on January 2, 1898.

[Private information.]

McLelan, Abner Reid (1831-1917), lieutenant-governor of New Brunswick (1897-1902), was born at Hopewell, New Brunswick, on January 4, 1831, the son of Peter McLelan. He was educated at Mount Allison Academy; and he sat in the Legislative Assembly of New Brunswick as member for Albert from 1854 to 1867. From 1866 to 1867 he was commissioner for public works in the New Brunswick government; and in 1867 he was called to the Canadian Senate. In 1897 he was appointed lieutenant-governor of New Brunswick; and he held this office until 1902. He died at Moncton, New Brunswick, on January 30, 1917.

[*Can. parl. comp.*; Morgan, *Can. men* (1912).]

McLelan, Archibald Woodbury (1824-1890), lieutenant-governor of Nova Scotia (1888-90), was born at Londonderry, Nova Scotia, on December 24, 1824, the son of G. W. McLelan, for many years a member of the Legislative Assembly of Nova Scotia. He was educated at the Mount Allison Academy, New Brunswick, and became a lumber merchant and ship-builder. He was a member of the Legislative Assembly of Nova Scotia for Colchester from 1858 to 1867, and of the Canadian House of Commons from 1867 to 1869. From 1869 to 1881 he was a senator of Canada; but in 1881 he resigned from the Senate in order to re-enter the House of Commons, and from that date until 1888 he was again the member for Colchester in the Dominion House. He opposed the entrance of Nova Scotia into Confederation on the basis of the Quebec Resolutions of 1864; but, with Joseph Howe (q.v.), he accepted the union when "better terms" were granted in 1869. In 1869 he was one of the commissioners for the construction of the Intercolonial Railway; and in 1881 he entered the Dominion cabinet of Sir John Macdonald (q.v.). In this government he was successively president of the Council (1881-82), minister of marine and fisheries (1882-85), minister of finance (1885-87), and postmaster-general (1887-88). In 1888 he was appointed lieutenant-governor of Nova Scotia; and he died in office, at Halifax, on June 26, 1890. In 1854 he married Caroline Metzler, of Halifax.

[*Cyc. Am. biog.*; *Can. parl. comp.*; Bibaud, *Panth. can.*; Rose, *Cyc. Can. biog.* (1886); *Canadian biographical dictionary*, Quebec vol. (Chicago, 1881).]

McLellan, Archibald (d. 1820), fur-trader, entered the service of the North West Company in 1792, and in 1795 he appears as a clerk at Bas de la Rivière House. He was at Rainy Lake in 1799, and he seems to have remained there until 1810. He was admitted a partner of the North West Company in 1805, to begin with the outfit of 1808. Between 1810 and 1815 he was at Michipicoten; and in 1815 he was sent to Lake Athabaska. He took a prominent part in the Selkirk troubles; and in 1818 he was, with Charles de Reinhard, tried at Quebec for murder, but was acquitted. For an account of the trial, see S. H. Wilcocke (ed.), *Report of the trials of Charles de Reinhard and Archibald McLellan for murder* (Montreal, 1818). He retired from the fur-trade in 1819; and he died in Glengarry, Upper Canada, on January 15, 1820.

[W. S. Wallace (ed.), *Documents relating to the North West Company* (Toronto: The Champlain Society, 1934).]

McLellan, James Alexander (1832-1907), educationist, was born at Shubenacadie, Nova Scotia, in 1832, and was educated at the University of Toronto (B.A., 1862; M.A., 1853; LL.B., 1872; LL.D., 1873). He became a school-teacher; and, after teaching in St. Mary's, Ontario, in Yarmouth, Nova Scotia, and at Upper Canada College, Toronto, he was appointed in 1871 a high school inspector for Ontario, in 1875 director of normal schools for Ontario, and in 1885 principal of the Ontario Normal College in Hamilton, Ontario. He died at Toronto, Ontario, on August 11, 1907. He was the author of *The teacher's handbook of algebra* (Toronto, 1879), *Elements of algebra*

(Toronto, 1886), and *Applied psychology* (Toronto, 1889); and he was joint author, with A. F. Ames, of *The public school arithmetic* (New York, 1898), and *Primary arithmetic* (New York, 1898), and, with John Dewey, of *The psychology of number* (New York, 1903).

[Morgan, *Can. men* (1898).]

McLennan, Sir John Cunningham (1867-1935), physicist, was born at Ingersoll, Ontario, on April 14, 1867, the son of David McLennan and Barbara Cunningham. He was educated at the University of Toronto (B.A., 1892; Ph.D., 1900; LL.D., 1919) and at Cambridge University. He was appointed a demonstrator in physics at the University of Toronto; and he became professor of physics in 1907. He made important advances in the fields of radio-activity, low temperature research, spectroscopy, and the treatment of cancer by radium; and during the First World War his work on the magnetic detection of submarines aided greatly in reducing this menace to British shipping. In 1915 he was elected a fellow of the Royal Society; and in 1928 he was awarded the royal medal of the Royal Society and the Bakerian lectureship. In 1924 he was elected president of the Royal Society of Canada; and in 1926 he was awarded the Society's Flavelle medal. He retired from his chair in the University of Toronto in 1932, and went to live in England. He died suddenly on October 9, 1935, while travelling on the train from Paris to Boulogne, in France. In June, 1935, he was made a knight commander of the British Empire for "fundamental discoveries in physics and scientific work in peace and war".

[H. H. Langton, *Sir John Cunningham McLennan: A memoir* (Toronto, 1939); *Who was who*, 1928-40; *Proc. Roy. Soc. Can.*, 1936; *University of Toronto monthly*, 1935; Morgan, *Can. men* (1912).]

McLennan, John Stewart (1853-1939), journalist, historian, and senator of Canada, was born in Montreal, Canada East, on November 5, 1853, the son of Hugh McLennan and Isabella Stewart. He was educated at the Montreal High School, McGill University (B.A., 1870), and Trinity Hall, Cambridge (B.A., 1875). He became the manager of a coal company in Cape Breton, and later of an iron and steel company; but in 1900 he retired from the iron and steel business, and in 1904 he became proprietor of the Sydney *Post* (later the *Post-Record*). In 1916 he was appointed a member of the Canadian Senate; and he remained a member of the Senate until his death in Ottawa, Ontario, on September 15, 1939. He was the author of *Louisburg from its foundation to its fall* (London, 1918); and the publication of this book brought about his election to the Royal Society of Canada in 1926.

[*Proc. Roy. Soc. Can.*, 1940; *Can. parl. comp.*; *Can. who's who*, 1936-37.]

McLennan, Roderick R. (1842-1907), politician and banker, was born at Glen Donald, Charlottenburg, Glengarry, Canada West, on January 1, 1842. He became a railway contractor, and was responsible for the construction of some of the most difficult parts of the Canadian Pacific Railway north of Lake Superior. Later he became a private banker in Glengarry, Ontario; and he represented Glengarry in the Canadian House of Commons from 1891 to 1904. In 1905 he was one of the founders of the ill-fated Farmers' Bank. He died at Cornwall, Ontario, on March 8, 1907.
[Morgan, *Can. men* (1898); *Can. parl. comp.*]

McLennan, William (1856-1904), author, was born in Montreal, Canada East, on May 8, 1856, the son of Hugh McLennan and the younger brother of the Hon. John Stewart McLennan (q.v.). He was educated at the Montreal High School and at McGill University (LL.B., 1880), and in 1881 was admitted a notary public of the province of Quebec. His first publication, apart from contributions to periodicals, was *Songs of Old Canada* (Montreal, 1886), a volume of translations from the French. His reputation rests mainly, however, on his works of fiction, *Spanish John* (Toronto, 1898), *The span o' life* (Toronto, 1899), written in collaboration with Miss Jean McIlwraith, and *In Old France and New* (Toronto, 1900). These are all books of exceptional merit. He died at Montreal on July 28, 1904. In 1899 he was elected a fellow of the Royal Society of Canada.
[Morgan, *Can. men* (1898); A. MacMurchy, *Handbook of Canadian literature* (Toronto, 1906); L. E. Horning and L. J. Burpee, *A bibliography of Canadian fiction* (Toronto, 1904); *Trans. Roy. Soc. Can.*, 1905.]

McLeod, Alexander (d. 1809), fur-trader, was a native of the parish of Deurinish in Scotland, and was a nephew of Normand McLeod (q.v.), of Gregory, McLeod and Co. He entered the service of the North West Company before 1787, and in 1791 was at Fort Chipewyan, on Lake Athabaska. He became a wintering partner of the Company in 1795; but he left the Peace River district, where he had been stationed, in 1799, and in 1802 he was at Grand Portage. He retired from the fur-trade about this time, and in 1805 he relinquished his two shares in the Company. He settled in Montreal, and here he died in 1809.
[W. S. Wallace (ed.), *Documents relating to the North West Company* (Toronto: The Champlain Society, 1934).]

McLeod, Alexander (*fl.* 1825-1841), deputy-sheriff of the Niagara district, was born in Forfarshire, Scotland, and emigrated to Canada about 1825. When the rebellion of 1837 broke out, he was deputy sheriff of the Niagara district; and he was reputed to have played a

part in the cutting-out of the *Caroline*. Three years later, while in the United States, he was arrested on charges of murder and arson; and his arrest caused a diplomatic incident of some acuteness. He was, however, acquitted of the charges brought against him; and he was awarded a pension of £200 per annum by the British government.
[A. H. U. Colquhoun, *Famous Canadian trials* (Can. mag., 1915); A. Watt, *The case of Alexander McLeod* (Can. hist. rev., 1931); M. L. Bonham, *Alexander McLeod* (New York history, 1937); *Dict. Can. biog.*, vol. 10.]

McLeod, Alexander Roderick (d. 1840), fur-trader, entered the service of the North West Company in 1802, and was a clerk on the Peace River in 1806. His journal for 1806 has been printed by J. N. Wallace, in his *Wintering partners on the Peace River* (Ottawa, 1929). In 1809 he was at Rocky Mountain House, and again in 1811. He was at Grand Portage in the summer of 1821, and was made a chief trader in the Hudson's Bay Company. From 1821 to 1823 he was stationed in the Athabaska district; from 1823 to 1825, in the Mackenzie River district; in 1825, at Fort Vancouver; from 1831 to 1833, at Fort Simpson; in 1833 to 1835, with Back's expedition; from 1835 to 1836, at Great Slave Lake; from 1838 to 1839, at Fort Dunvegan. In 1839 he went to Canada on furlough; and he died on June 11, 1840.
[R. Harvey Fleming (ed.), *Minutes of council, Northern Department of Rupert Land* (Toronto: The Champlain Society, 1940).]

McLeod, Archibald Norman (*fl.* 1796-1837), fur-trader, entered the service of the North West Company prior to 1796, for D. W. Harmon (q.v.) says that Alexander McLeod, a half-breed son by a Rapid River woman, was in his fifth year in July, 1801. It is probable that he was a relative of Normand McLeod (q.v.), of Gregory, McLeod and Co. He was made a partner of the North West Company before 1799, when he was "proprietor at Fort Dauphin". His journal for 1800-01 has been printed in C. M. Gates (ed.), *Five fur-traders of the North-west* (Minneapolis, 1933). He went to the Athabaska country in 1802, and he remained there until 1808. He became a partner in McTavish, McGillivrays and Co., and a member of the Beaver Club in 1808; and in 1809 he retired as a wintering partner of the North West Company. He took a prominent part in the Selkirk troubles of 1815-18, and he was at Fort William in 1821; but on the union of the North West Company and the Hudson's Bay Company in that year, he withdrew from the fur-trade, and went to live in Scotland. In 1826 he was described as living "at Sunnybank, in the county of Aberdeen"; and in 1837 he was barrack-master at Belfast, Ireland. His death occurred between 1837 and 1845, since his widow died at Coley Parsonage,

Halifax, Yorkshire, on March 12, 1845. Possibly he died in 1838, as a new barrack-master at Belfast was appointed in that year.

[W. S. Wallace (ed.), *Documents relating to the North West Company* (Toronto: The Champlain Society, 1934).]

McLeod, Arthur James (b. 1836), lawyer and author, was born at Westfield, Queens county, Nova Scotia, in 1836. He was educated at Harvard University, but did not graduate. He studied law, and practised it in Boston for many years. The date of his death has not been ascertained. He was the author of *The notary of Grand Pré* (Boston, 1901).

[R. J. Long, *Nova Scotia authors* (East Orange, N.J., 1918).]

McLeod, Clement Henry (1851-1917), educationist, was born at Strathlorn, Cape Breton, Nova Scotia, on January 20, 1851. He was educated at McGill University (B.A.Sc., 1873; M.E., 1878), and became an engineer. He was employed in the construction of the Intercolonial Railway; and in 1874 he was appointed superintendent of the observatory at McGill University. In 1888 he became professor of geodesy at McGill, and in 1908 vice-dean of the faculty of applied science at McGill. He was elected a fellow of the Royal Society of Canada in 1893. He died at Montreal, Quebec, on December 26, 1917. He was the author of *Elementary descriptive geometry* (New York, 1905).

[*Proc. Roy. Soc. Can.,* 1918; Morgan *Can. men* (1912).]

McLeod, Donald (1779-1879), "patriot" general, was born in Aberdeen, Scotland, on January 1, 1779. He was educated at Aberdeen University, and served from 1803 to 1808 in the British navy. He then enlisted in the army, fought under Sir John Moore at Corunna, was transferred to Canada, where he fought at Queenston Heights, Chrysler's Farm, and Lundy's Lane, and returned to Europe in time to be present at the battle of Waterloo. Having been discharged from the army, he settled in Canada in 1816, and a little later opened a classical school at Prescott. Here he founded the *Grenville Gazette*, a Reform newspaper. In 1838 he became "general commanding the western division of the patriot army", and was active in filibustering on the frontier. He was arrested and tried at Detroit, Michigan, for breach of the neutrality laws of the United States; but was acquitted, and settled in Cleveland, Ohio. Here he died on July 22, 1879. He published a *History of the Canadian insurrection* (Cleveland, Ohio, 1841), *History of Wiskonsin* (Buffalo, N.Y., 1846), and *Biography of Hon. Fernando Wood* (New York, 1856).

[*Dom. ann. reg.*, 1879; J. C. Dent, *The Upper Canadian rebellion* (2 vols., Toronto, 1885).]

MacLeod, Mrs. Elizabeth Susan, *née* **MacQueen** (1842-1939), poet, was born in Edinburgh, Scotland, on February 23, 1842; and died at Charlottetown, Prince Edward Island, on January 14, 1939. She was the author of *Carols of Canada* (Charlottetown, P.E.I., 1893).

[Private information.]

McLeod, Sir Ezekiel (1840-1920), chief justice of New Brunswick (1914-17), was born at Cardwell, New Brunswick, on October 29, 1840, the son of John McLeod and Mary McCready. He was educated at Harvard University (LL.B., 1867), and was called to the bar of New Brunswick in 1868 (Q.C., 1882). He represented Saint John in the Legislative Assembly of New Brunswick from 1882 to 1886, and in the Canadian House of Commons from 1891 to 1896. During 1882-83 he was attorney-general in the Hanington administration. In 1896 he was appointed a puisne judge of the Supreme Court of New Brunswick, and in 1914 he was made chief justice of New Brunswick. He died at Hampton, New Brunswick, on June 11, 1920. He was knighted in 1917.

[*Who was who*, 1916-28; Morgan, *Can. men* (1912); *Can. parl. comp.*]

Macleod, James Farquharson (1836-1894), soldier, was born in 1836, the son of a British army officer, and was educated at Upper Canada College, Toronto, and Queen's University, Kingston (B.A., 1854). In 1860 he was admitted to the bar of Upper Canada. He served during the North West rebellion of 1869-70 as a brigade-major of militia, was mentioned in despatches, and was created in 1870 a C.M.G. In 1873 he was commissioned a captain of the North-West Mounted Police; in 1874 he became assistant commissioner, and in 1877 commissioner, in command of the Police. In 1880 he was appointed stipendiary magistrate, with jurisdiction in all cases, civil and criminal, in the North West Territories; and in 1887 a puisne judge of the Supreme Court of the North West Territories. He died at Calgary, N.W.T., on September 5, 1894.

[*Cyc. Am. biog.*; S. B. Steele, *Forty years in Canada* (Toronto, 1915); A. L. Haydon, *The riders of the plains* (Toronto, 1910); Capt. B. Deane, *Mounted police life in Canada* (London, 1916); R. G. MacBeth, *Policing the plains* (Toronto, 1923).]

McLeod, John (1788-1849), fur-trader, was born at Stornoway, Scotland, in 1788, and entered the service of the Hudson's Bay Company in 1811. In 1814 he was in charge of the post at the forks of the Red River, and his diary describing his defence of the post against the Nor'Westers has been printed in the *Collections of the State Historical Society of North Dakota*, vol. 2 (Bismarck, N.D., 1908). He played a prominent part in the Selkirk troubles; and in 1821 he was promoted to the rank of chief trader. From 1822 to 1826 he was in the Columbia department. He retired from the service of the Hudson's Bay Company in 1848; and he died at Hochelaga, Lower Canada, on July 24, 1849.

[W. S. Wallace (ed.), *Documents relating to the North West Company* (Toronto: The Champlain Society, 1934).]

MacLeod, John M. (b. 1825), clergyman, was born at West River, Nova Scotia, on August 21, 1825. He was educated at Pictou Academy, the West River Seminary, and the theological hall of the Presbyterian Church in the Maritime provinces; and was ordained a minister of the Presbyterian Church in 1853. He was the pastor successively of churches at Richmond Bay, Prince Edward Island, at New Glasgow, Nova Scotia, at Charlottetown, Prince Edward Island, and at Vancouver, British Columbia. In his later years, he published a *History of Presbyterianism on Prince Edward Island* (Chicago, 1904). The date of his death has not been ascertained.

[R. J. Long, *Nova Scotia authors* (East Orange, N.J., 1918); Morgan, *Can. men* (1912).]

McLeod, Malcolm (1821-1899), author, was born at Green Lake, Beaver River, Hudson's Bay Territories, on October 21, 1821, the son of John McLeod (q.v.), a factor of the Hudson's Bay Company. He was educated at Edinburgh, studied law in Montreal, and was called to the bar in 1845. From 1874 to 1876 he was district judge for the counties of Ottawa and Pontiac; but apart from this, he spent his life as a practising barrister (Q.C., 1887). He died in Ottawa in 1899. He edited A. McDonald's *Peace River* (Ottawa, 1872), and wrote five pamphlets on *The Pacific Railway* (1874-80), under the pen name of "Britannicus", and *The problem of Canada* (Ottawa, 1880).

[*Cyc. Am. biog.*; private information.]

McLeod, Neil (1842-1915), prime minister of Prince Edward Island (1889-91), was born at Uigg, Prince Edward Island, on December 15, 1842; and was educated at Acadia University (B.A., 1869; M.A., 1870). He was called to the bar in 1872 (Q.C., 1891); and practised law in Charlottetown. He represented Charlottetown in the Legislative Assembly of the Island from 1879 to 1893; from 1879 to 1880 he was provincial secretary and treasurer; and from 1889 to 1891 he was attorney-general and prime minister. In 1893 he was appointed county court judge for Prince county. He died on October 19, 1915.

[*Can. parl. comp.*; *Records of the graduates of Acadia University* (Wolfville, N.S., 1926).]

McLeod, Normand (d. 1796), fur-trader and merchant, was a native of the Island of Skye, Scotland. In a letter dated Detroit, January 6, 1770, he refers to "faithful services from the beginning of the year 1747 in Holland, Brabant, and North America, to the end of the year 1764" (*Mich. Pion. Coll.*, X, 374-75); and it is probable that he is the Captain Normand McLeod who was a friend and correspondent of Sir William Johnson (see *The Johnson papers*, 8 vols., Albany, New York, 1921-36). He was for a time an officer of the Indian department, but by 1776 he was established as a trader in Detroit. In 1783 he became a partner of John Gregory (q.v.), in the firm of Gregory, McLeod and Co., which succeeded to that of Finlay, Gregory and Co. In 1787, when Gregory, McLeod and Co. was absorbed in the North West Company, he became a dormant partner. He sold out his interest in the Company in 1790, and he died in Montreal in 1796. He married, probably in Detroit, Cécile Robert; but he seems to have had no children.

[W. S. Wallace (ed.), *Documents relating to the North West Company* (Toronto: The Champlain Society, 1934).]

McLeod, Robert Randall (1839-1909), author, was born at Brookfield, Queens county, Nova Scotia, in 1839. He was educated at Horton Academy and at Harvard University; and he became a Unitarian preacher, with charges in Maine and Massachusetts. Later he went to Mexico, where he was interested in mining; and ultimately he returned to Nova Scotia. He died at Brookfield, Nova Scotia, on February 12, 1909. He was the author of *In the Acadian land; Nature studies* (Brookfield, N.S., 1899), *Markland or Nova Scotia* (Toronto, 1903), *Further nature studies* (Halifax, N.S., 1910), and a number of historical papers contributed to *Acadiensis*.

[R. J. Long, *Nova Scotia authors* (East Orange, N.J., 1918).]

McLoughlin, John (1784-1857), fur-trader, was born at Rivière du Loup, Canada, on October 19, 1784. The son of John McLoughlin and Angélique, eldest daughter of Malcolm Fraser (q.v.) of Murray Bay. He studied medicine in Quebec and became a qualified physician. About 1806 he entered the service of the North West Company, probably through the influence of his uncle, Alexander Fraser (q.v.); and in the summer of 1807 he was at Sturgeon Lake in the Nipigon department, when D. W. Harmon (q.v.) was sent to him for medical attention. The following winter he was at Vermilion Lake, near Rainy Lake; and he seems to have been employed in the Rainy Lake district for a number of years. In 1814, when he was made a partner of the North West Company, he was placed in charge of the Rainy Lake district. In 1820 he went, with Angus Bethune (q.v.), to London as a representative of the wintering partners, to arrange a union with the North West Company;

but the Hudson's Bay Company declined to negotiate separately with Bethune and himself, and the union was concluded with the McGillivrays (q.v.) and Edward Ellice (q.v.). McLoughlin was very much discontented with the terms of the union of the North West Company and the Hudson's Bay Company in 1821; but accepted a commission in the Hudson's Bay Company as chief factor. In 1823 he was sent to the Columbia department; and in 1824 he was in charge at Fort George (Astoria), but in 1826 he removed his headquarters to Fort Vancouver, which he built. Here he remained until 1846. He then resigned from the Hudson's Bay Company, and during his last years he kept a general store in Oregon City. He came to be known as "the father of Oregon". He died at Oregon City on September 3, 1857. He married the widow of Alexander McKay (q.v.); and by her he had two sons and two daughters.

[R. C. Johnson, *John McLoughlin* (Portland, Ore., 1935); B. B. Barker, *The Financial papers of Dr. John McLoughlin* (Portland, Ore., 1949); R. G. Montgomery, *The white-headed eagle, John McLoughlin* (New York, 1935); F. V. Holman, *Dr. John McLoughlin* (Cleveland, Ohio, 1907); T. C. Elliott, *Marguerite Wadin McKay McLoughlin* (Oregon historical quarterly, December, 1935). McLoughlin's letters to the Governor and Company of the Hudson's Bay Company have been edited by E. E. Rich under the title *The letters of John McLoughlin* (3 vols., Toronto: The Champlain Society, 1941-44).]

MacMahon, Hugh (1836-1911), jurist, was born in Guelph, Upper Canada, on March 6, 1836, the son of Hugh MacMahon, a land surveyor. He was educated by his father as an engineer, and was first employed on the surveys for the proposed Ottawa ship canal. He resigned from this employment in 1857, and entered on the study of law. He was called to the bar in 1864 (Q.C., 1876), and practised law first in Brantford, then in London, and finally in Toronto, Ontario. He distinguished himself as a criminal lawyer, especially in the famous Biddulph murder trial. In 1887 he was appointed a judge of common pleas division of the High Court of Ontario; and he presided over the trial of Reginald Birchall (q.v.). He died in Toronto, Ontario, on January 18, 1911.

[*Can. who's who*, 1910; Morgan, *Can. men* (1898).]

MacMaster, Sir Donald, Bart. (1846-1922), lawyer, was born at Williamstown, Upper Canada, on September 3, 1846, the son of Donald MacMaster and Mary Cameron. He was educated at McGill University (B.C.L., 1871; D.C.L., 1874); and was called to the Quebec bar in 1871 (Q.C., 1882). From 1879 to 1882 he represented Glengarry in the Legislative Assembly of Ontario; and from 1882 to 1886 in the Canadian House of Commons. In

1905 he went to live in England, in order to specialize in appeals before the Judicial Committee of the Privy Council; and from 1910 to 1918 he represented the Chertsey division of Surrey in the British House of Commons. He died in London, England, on March 3, 1922. In 1880 he married Janet (d. 1883), daughter of Ronald Sandfield Macdonald; and in 1890 Ella Virginia, daughter of Isaac De Ford, Baltimore, Maryland. He was created a baronet of the United Kingdom in 1921.

[*Who was who*, 1916-28; *Can. who was who*, vol. 1; *Can. parl. comp.*; Morgan, *Can. men* (1912).]

McMaster, William (1811-1887), president of the Canadian Bank of Commerce (1867-86), was born in county Tyrone, Ireland, on December 24, 1811, the son of William McMaster, a linen merchant. He came to Canada in 1833, and settled in York (Toronto), Upper Canada. He entered here the wholesale dry-goods business, and became eventually the head of the prosperous house of Wm. McMaster and Nephews. Gradually his activities became mainly financial. In 1867 he founded, and became the first president of, the Canadian Bank of Commerce; and he retained the presidency of this bank until the year before his death. In 1862 he was elected to the Legislative Council of united Canada for the Midland division; and in 1867 he was called to the Senate of Canada. He died at Toronto on September 22, 1887. In 1851 he married Mary Henderson (d. 1868), of New York, and in 1871 Susan Moulton, widow of James Fraser, of Newburgh, New York; but there was no issue of either marriage. The bulk of his estate went by his will to the endowment of McMaster University, which he had been chiefly instrumental in founding.

[O. C. Masters, *William McMaster* (Canadian banker, 1942); *Cyc. Am. biog.*; *Can. parl. comp.*; Rose, *Cyc. Can. biog.* (1886); Dent, *Can. port.*, vol. 3; V. Ross, *A history of the Canadian Bank of Commerce* (2 vols., Toronto, 1922).]

MacMechan, Archibald McKellar (1862-1933), scholar and author, was born at Berlin (now Kitchener), Ontario, on June 21, 1862, the son of the Rev. John MacMechan and Mary Jean, daughter of Archibald McKellar (q.v.). He was educated at the University of Toronto (B.A., 1884), and at Johns Hopkins University (Ph.D., 1889). In 1889 he was appointed professor of English language and literature at Dalhousie University, Halifax, Nova Scotia; and he retained this post until shortly before his death at Halifax, on August 7, 1933. He was the author of *The relation of Hans Sachs to the Decameron* (Halifax, 1889), *The porter of Bagdad* (Toronto, 1901), *The life of a little college* (Boston, 1914), *The winning of responsible government* (Toronto, 1915), *Sagas of the sea* (Toronto, 1923), *Old province tales* (Toronto, 1924), *Headwaters of Canadian lit-*

erature (Toronto, 1924), *The book of Ultima Thule* (Toronto, 1927), *There go the ships* (Toronto, 1928), and *Red snow on Grand Pré* (Toronto, 1931), as well as of a series of *Nova Scotia chap-books*, published in 1920-27. He edited Thomas Carlyle's *Sartor Resartus* (1897) and *Heroes and hero-worship* (1901), *Select poems of Lord Tennyson* (1907), and vols. 2 and 3 of *Nova Scotia Archives* (Halifax, 1901-08). A volume of poems, entitled *Late harvest* (Toronto, 1934), was published posthumously.

[W. Gordon, *Archibald MacMechan* (Queen's quarterly, 1933); Morgan, *Can. men* (1912).]

McMicken, Gilbert (1813-1891), speaker of the Legislative Assembly of Manitoba (1880-83), was born in London, England, in 1813, of Scottish parentage. He came to Canada in 1832, and went into business as a forwarding agent at Chippawa, Upper Canada. From 1857 to 1861 he represented Welland in the Legislative Assembly of Canada; and during the American Civil War he was appointed stipendiary magistrate for Canada West. At the time of the Fenian raids he was commissioner of police for the Dominion; and he did much to forewarn the government of the Fenian designs both in the east and in the North West. He remained in the service of the Dominion government in various capacities until 1877, when he retired on a pension. In 1879 he was elected to represent Cartier in the Legislative Assembly of Manitoba; and in 1880 he was chosen speaker of the Assembly. He retired from political life in 1883; and he died at Winnipeg, Manitoba, on March 6, 1891. In 1835 he married Ann Theresa, daughter of Alexander Duff, and grand-daughter of Commodore Grant (q.v.).

[*Cyc. Am. biog.*; *Can. parl. comp.*; Rose, *Cyc. Can. biog.* (1888); J. P. Robertson, *A political manual of Manitoba* (Winnipeg, 1887).]

MacMillan, Alexander Stirling (1871-1955), prime minister of Nova Scotia (1940-45), was born in Antigonish county, Nova Scotia, on November 1, 1871, and died at Halifax, Nova Scotia, on August 7, 1955. He was a member of the Legislative Council of Nova Scotia from 1924 until its abolition in 1928; and in 1928 he was elected to the Nova Scotia legislature as a Liberal. He sat in the legislature until 1945; in 1933 he became minister of highways; and from 1940 to his resignation in 1945 he was prime minister.

[*Can. who's who*, 1952-54; *Can. parl. guide*, 1944; *Encyc. Can.*]

McMillan, Sir Daniel Hunter (1846-1933), lieutenant-governor of Manitoba (1900-11), was born at Whitby, Ontario, in January, 1846, the son of James McMillan. He was educated at Whitby and at Collingwood, Ontario;

and in his earlier years saw service on the Niagara frontier in 1864, in the Fenian raid of 1866, and in the torth West rebellions of 1870 and 1885. He settled in Winnipeg in 1870; and from 1880 to 1900 he represented Centre Winnipeg in the Legislative Assembly of Manitoba. From 1889 to 1900 he was provincial treasurer in the Greenway administration; and from 1900 to 1911 he was lieutenant-governor of Manitoba. He died at Winnipeg on April 14, 1933. In 1877 he married Mary (d. 1923), daughter of James Lindsay, Collingwood. He was created a K.C.M.G. in 1902; and he was made an LL.D. of the University of Manitoba in 1911.

[*Can. who was who*, vol. 2; *Who was who*, 1929-40; Morgan, *Can. men* (1912); *Can. parl. comp.*]

MacMillan, Sir Ernest Campbell (1893-1973), musician, was born at Mimico, Ontario, August 18, 1893. He was educated in Toronto at Jarvis Collegiate and in Scotland before becoming a student at the University of Toronto (B.A., Honours History, 1915). He studied music in Edinburgh, Scotland, with Frederick Niecks, Alfred Hollins, and W. B. Ross. He also studied in Paris and at Oxford University (Mus. D., 1918). MacMillan, a child prodigy, gave a public organ recital in Massey Hall at the age of ten. When he was thirteen he became an associate of the Royal College of Organists; at seventeen he became a fellow of the society and received the LaFontaine prize for highest standing; he received his Bachelor of Music degree from Oxford University in the same year. When the First World War broke out MacMillan was studying in Paris and had travelled to Bayreuth, Germany. He was interned for four years, during which he composed the music for the work based on Swinburne's *Ode to England*, and on the basis of his composition was granted a Mus. D. from Oxford University. MacMillan was conductor of the Toronto Mendelssohn Choir (1942-57); conductor of the Toronto Symphony Orchestra (1931-56); dean of the Faculty of Music, University of Toronto (1927-52); principal of the Toronto Conservatory of Music (1926-42); and president of the Composers, Authors and Publishers Association of Canada. He appeared both as guest conductor and as organ soloist in Canada and the United States and was an adjudicator at musical festivals in Canada and the United Kingdom. In 1935 he was knighted by George V. Among his compositions are a number of folksongs as well as works for orchestral groups, choirs, and orchestras. He died at Toronto, Ontario, May 6, 1973.

[*Can. who's who*, 1967-69; Metropolitan Toronto Library Board, *Biographical scrapbooks*, vols. 71, 85.]

McMillan, James (d. 1858), fur-trader, was born in Scotland, and entered the service of the North West Company prior to 1804, when he appears as a clerk at Fort des Prairies. With David Thompson (q.v.), he was one of the pioneers of the fur-trade on the Columbia. Ross Cox (q.v.) met him on the Spokane River in 1813. In 1821 he became a chief trader of the Hudson's Bay Company; and in 1827 he was promoted to the rank of chief factor. He explored the lower part of the Fraser River in 1824, and he built Fort Langley at the mouth of the Fraser in 1827. He left the Columbia department in 1829; and from 1830 to 1834 he was placed in charge of the experimental farm at the Red River Settlement. He was granted furlough in 1837, and he retired from the Company's service in 1839. He died in 1858.

[R. Harvey Fleming (ed.), *Minutes of council, Northern department of Rupert Land* (Toronto: The Champlain Society, 1940).]

Macmillan, John C. (1862-1926), priest, was born at Dundas, Prince Edward Island, on July 25, 1862, was ordained a priest of the Roman Catholic Church, and died at Charlottetown, Prince Edward Island, on April 18, 1926. He was the author of *The history of the Catholic church in Prince Edward Island from 1835 to 1891* (Quebec, 1913).

[Private information.]

Macmillan, John Walker (1868-1932), clergyman and author, was born at Mount Forest, Ontario, on September 26, 1868; and was educated at the University of Toronto and Union Seminary, New York. He was ordained a minister of the Presbyterian Church in Canada in 1891; and he held successive charges in Vancouver, Lindsay, Winnipeg, and Halifax. In 1916 he was appointed professor of social ethics in Manitoba College, Winnipeg; and in 1919 he became professor of sociology in Victoria College, Toronto. Later, he was appointed also chairman of the Minimum Wage Board of the province of Ontario. He died at Toronto on April 16, 1932. He was the author of *Happiness and goodwill* (Toronto, 1922) and *The limits of social legislation* (Toronto, 1933).

[Morgan, *Can. men* (1912); *University of Toronto monthly*, 1932.]

McMullen, James (1836-1913), senator of Canada, was born at Monaghan, Ireland, on November 29, 1836, and came to Canada with his parents in 1846. He became a merchant in Mount Forest, Ontario; and from 1882 to 1900 he represented North Wellington as a Liberal in the Canadian House of Commons. In 1902 he was called to the Senate of Canada, and he sat in the Senate until his death at Mount Forest, Ontario, on March 18, 1913.

[Morgan, *Can. men* (1912); *Can. parl. comp.*]

McMullen, John Mercier (1820-1907), journalist and historian, was born in the north of Ireland in 1820. He came to Canada in 1849,

and in 1857 he became the editor and proprietor of the Brockville *Monitor*. His chief work was a *History of Canada*, the first edition of which appeared in Brockville in 1855; a second and enlarged edition appeared in 1867; and a third and final edition, which brings the narrative down to 1891, in 1892. He died at Brockville, Ontario, on February 9, 1907.

[Morgan, *Cel. Can.* and *Can. men* (1898); *Can. ann. review*, 1907.]

MacMurchy, Archibald (1832-1912), schoolmaster, was born at Clachan, Kintyre, Argyllshire, in 1832. He came to Canada with his parents in 1840, and was educated at Rockwood Academy, Upper Canada, and at the University of Toronto (B.A., 1861; M.A., 1868; LL.D., 1907). In 1858 he was appointed mathematical master of the Toronto Grammar School; and he remained on the staff of this school, after 1872 as rector or principal, until his retirement in 1900. He died at Toronto on April 27, 1912. In 1859 he married Marjory Jardine, daughter of James Ramsay, of Linlithgow, Scotland; and by her he had three sons and three daughters. For many years he was editor of the *Canada Educational Monthly*; and he wrote, in addition to a number of schoolbooks, a useful *Handbook of Canadian literature* (Toronto, 1906).

[Morgan, *Can. men* (1912).]

MacMurchy, Helen (1862-1953), physician and author, was born in Toronto, Ontario, on January 7, 1862, the daughter of Archibald MacMurchy (q.v.), and died there on October 8, 1953. She was educated in the public schools of Toronto, obtained a certificate in the Toronto Normal School, and was at first a schoolteacher. She then studied medicine at the University of Toronto (M.D., 1901), and took post-graduate work at Johns Hopkins and at Philadelphia; and she was in private practice in Toronto until 1913. The latter part of her life was devoted to welfare work under government auspices. She was the author of *The almosts: A study of the feeble-minded* (Boston, 1920) and of numerous booklets and government documents relating to social welfare. In 1934 she was awarded the C.B.E.

[*Can. who's who*, 1938-39; *Encyc. Can.*]

MacMurchy, Marjory. See Willison, Marjory, Lady, *née* **MacMurchy.**

McMurray, Thomas (d. 1795), merchant, was a trader who settled in Montreal about 1772. He appears to have been at Michilimackinac between 1769 and 1772. His name occurs in the fur-trade licences for 1778, and that of his son Samuel (d. 1795) for 1790. He died in the early part of 1795, apparently at the same time as his son. In September, 1772, he married, first, Jane (d. 1778), widow of Tobias Izenhoult; and in January, 1782, he married, secondly, Helen Peacock, of Montreal.

[W. S. Wallace (ed.), *Documents relating to the North West Company* (Toronto: The Champlain Society, 1934).]

McMurray, Thomas (1779?-1849), fur-trader, would appear to have been a younger son of Thomas McMurray (d. 1795), and to have been born in Montreal in 1779. He entered the service of the XY Company, and in 1803-04 was in charge of the XY post at Fort Dauphin. On the union of the XY and the North West companies, he was sent as a clerk to Rainy Lake. In 1817 Ross Cox (q.v.) met him at Isle à la Crosse, and it was at Isle à la Crosse that he was arrested by John Clarke (q.v.) in 1820. He was elected a member of the Beaver Club of Montreal in 1815, and he was made a partner of the North West Company in 1816. At the time of the union of 1821, he was made a chief trader. In 1821 he was stationed at Winnipeg River; in 1823 at Fort Dauphin; in 1824 at Rainy Lake; from 1825 to 1831 at the Lake of the Woods; and from 1831 to 1834 at the Pic. He was granted furlough in 1841, and he retired from the Company's service in 1843. He died near Brighton, in the township of Cramahé, Upper Canada, on January 15, 1849. He was married; and had at least two sons, William (q.v.) and Samuel.
[E. E. Rich (ed.), *Journal of occurrences in the Athabasca department, by George Simpson* (Toronto: The Champlain Society, 1938).]

McMurray, William (d. 1877), fur-trader, was born in the North West, the son of Thomas McMurray (q.v.), a chief trader of the Hudson's Bay Company. He was educated at the Red River Academy, and about 1837 was apprenticed to the Hudson's Bay Company as a postmaster. He rose in the service of the Company until he was made a chief factor in 1866; and later he became inspecting chief factor for the northern district. He died suddenly at Winnipeg on March 7, 1877.
[Private information.]

McMurray, William (1810-1894), clergyman, was born at Seagoe, near Portadown, Ireland, on September 19, 1810. He was brought to Canada as an infant; and was educated in York (Toronto). In 1832 he was sent as an Indian missionary to Sault Ste. Marie; and in 1833 he was ordained a priest of the Church of England. He became rector of Ancaster in 1840; and in 1875 he was made archdeacon of Niagara. He died at the rectory, Niagara, on May 19, 1894. He was a D.D. and D.C.L. of Trinity College, Toronto. He was twice married, (1) in 1833 to Charlotte (or Ogenebugakwa, *i.e.,* "Wild Rose") Johnston, daughter of John Johnston, of Sault Ste Marie, and (2) to Amelia, daughter of Capt. James Baxter, of the Royal Canadian Rifles. By his first wife he had three sons and one daughter.
[T. D. J. Farmer, *A history of the parish of St. John's church, Ancaster* (Guelph, Ont., 1924).]

McMurrich, James Playfair (1859-1939), biologist, was born at Toronto, Canada West, on October 16, 1859, the son of the Hon. John McMurrich (q.v.). He was educated at the University of Toronto (B.A., 1879; M.A., 1881; LL.D., 1931) and at Johns Hopkins University (Ph.D., 1885); and he held teaching positions on the staff of the Ontario Agricultural College, Johns Hopkins University, Haverford College, Clark University, Cincinnati University, and the University of Michigan. In 1907 he was appointed professor of anatomy in the University of Toronto; and he held this position until his retirement in 1930. From 1922 to 1930 he was also dean of the School of Graduate Studies in this University. In 1909 he was elected a fellow of the Royal Society of Canada; in 1916 he was elected president of the Society; and in 1939 he was awarded posthumously the Society's Flavelle medal. He was president of the American Society of Naturalists in 1907, of the American Association for the Advancement of Science in 1922; and he received honorary degrees from the University of Michigan and Cincinnati University. He died at Toronto, Ontario, on February 9, 1939. Besides numerous scientific papers, he was the author of *A text-book of invertebrate morphology* (New York, 1894), *The development of the human body* (Philadelphia, 1902), and *Leonardo da Vinci, the anatomist* (Baltimore, 1930); he edited J. Sobotta's *Atlas and text-book of human anatomy* (3 vols., Philadelphia, 1906-07), of which a fourth edition was published in 1936; and he was joint editor, with H. Morris, of *Human anatomy* (Philadelphia, 1906).
[*Proc. Roy. Soc. Can.*, 1939; *Can. who's who*, 1936-37; Morgan, *Can. men* (1912).]

McMurrich, John (1804-1883), legislative councillor of Canada, was born near Paisley, Scotland, in 1804. He came to Canada in 1833 as representative of a Glasgow firm of wholesale merchants; and he founded branches of the business in Toronto, Kingston, and Hamilton. From 1862 to 1864 he sat in the Legislative Council of Canada as an elected member for the Saugeen division; and from 1867 to 1871 he represented North York in the Legislative Assembly of Ontario. He died at Toronto, Ontario, on February 13, 1883.
[*Dom. ann. reg.*, 1883; *Can. parl. comp.*]

Macnab, Alexander (1811-1891), clergyman and educationist, was born in Upper Canada in 1811, and was educated at Union College, Schenectady (D.D., 1848). He was ordained a minister of the Wesleyan Methodist Church in 1834; and in 1845 was appointed principal of Victoria College, Cobourg, in succession to the Rev. Egerton Ryerson (q.v.). He resigned from this position, however, in 1849, and left the Methodist Church. He was ordained in 1851 a priest of the Church of England; and he was rector of St. John's Church, Bowmanville, from 1853 to his death on November 15, 1891.

[J. Squair, *The townships of Darlington and Clarke* (Toronto, 1927); W. Canniff, *The medical profession in Upper Canada* (Toronto, 1894).]

MacNab, Sir Allan Napier, Bart. (1798-1862), prime minister of Canada (1854-56), was born at Niagara, Upper Canada, on February 19, 1798, the son of Lieut. Allan MacNab, formerly of the Queen's Rangers, and Anne Napier. He was educated at the Home District Grammar School; and, though still in his teens, fought throughout the campaigns of 1813 and 1814. He was called to the bar of Upper Canada in 1826, and is said to have been the first Q.C. appointed in the province. In 1830 he was elected to the Legislative Assembly for Wentworth, and he continued to sit in the Assembly until the union. From 1837 to 1840 he was its speaker. During the rebellion of 1837 he commanded "the men of Gore", and later was placed in command of the loyal forces on the Niagara frontier. For his services he was in 1838 created a knight bachelor.

In the Legislative Assembly of United Canada he represented Hamilton continuously from 1841 to 1857. From 1841 to 1844 he was leader of the Tory opposition; from 1844 to 1848 he was again speaker of the Assembly; and from 1848 to 1854 he was again leader of the opposition. In 1854 he became prime minister of the province, in the so-called MacNab-Morin and MacNab-Taché administrations; but in 1856 discontent with his leadership forced his resignation. With him disappeared from Canadian politics the last trace of the ascendancy of the "Family Compact". From 1857 to 1860 he lived in England; but in 1860 he returned to Canada, and was elected to the Legislative Council for the Western division. In the spring of 1862 he was elected speaker of the Legislative Council; but his health was unequal to the duties of the office, and he died at Dundurn, Hamilton, on August 8, 1862.

He was twice married, (1) in 1821 to Elizabeth (d. 1825), daughter of Lieut. Daniel Brooke, by whom he had one son and one daughter, and (2) in 1831 to Mary (d. 1846), daughter of John Stuart, of Brockville. He was created a baronet in 1858; but the baronetcy became extinct on his death. In 1860 he was appointed an honorary A.D.C. to Queen Victoria, with the honorary rank of colonel in the British army.

[Sir J. G. Bourinot, *Some memories of Dundurn and Burlington Heights* (Trans. Roy. Soc. Can., 1900); *Dict. nat. biog.*; *Cyc. Am. biog.*; Morgan, *Cel. Can.*; Taylor, *Brit. Am.*, vol. 2; J. C. Dent, *Can. port.*, vol. 4, *The Upper Canadian rebellion* (2 vols., Toronto,

1885), and *The last forty years* (2 vols., Toronto, 1881); Sir J. Pope, *Memoirs of the Right Hon. Sir J. A. Macdonald* (2 vols., Ottawa, 1894); A. H. Young, *The Rev. John Stuart and his family* (Kingston, 1920); W. S. Wallace, *The knight of Dundurn* (Toronto, 1960).]

MacNab, Archibald, Chief of (1781?-1860), colonizer, was born in Scotland about 1781, the son and heir of Francis, twelfth Chief of MacNab. He fled from Scotland to Canada in 1823, in order to avoid the service on him of a writ of caption; and in Canada he was granted a township (named after him MacNab) on the Ottawa River, on which he settled a number of his clansmen. He became embroiled with the settlers, however, and in 1843 he returned to Scotland. He came into a small estate in the Orkneys, and here he lived until 1859, when he retired to France on a small pension granted him by his wife, from whom he had separated in 1819. He died at the fishing-village of Lanion, near Boulogne, on April 22, 1860.

[R. Wild, *Macnab, the last laird* (London, 1938); A. Fraser, *The last laird of MacNab* (Toronto, 1889).]

McNab, Archibald Peter (1864-1945), lieutenant-governor of Saskatchewan (1936-45), was born in Glengarry, Canada West, on May 29, 1864, and died at Regina, Saskatchewan, on April 30, 1945. He went to the West with his family in 1882, farmed in southern Manitoba for twenty years, and then went into the grain business in Saskatchewan. From 1908 to 1926 he was a member of the Saskatchewan legislature, and held several portfolios. In 1936 he was appointed lieutenant-governor of Saskatchewan, and continued in this post until his death.

[*Can. who's who*, 1938-39; *Can. parl. guide*, 1944; *Encyc. Can.*]

McNab, James (1792-1871), legislative councillor of Nova Scotia, was born in Halifax, Nova Scotia, on November 30, 1792, the son of the Hon. Peter McNab (q.v.). In 1840 he was elected to represent Halifax in the House of Assembly of Nova Scotia; in 1848 he was appointed to the Legislative Council; and he was on three occasions a member of the executive council of the province before Confederation. He favoured Confederation, and in 1867 he became provincial treasurer in the Blanchard administration. He resigned from office with his colleagues at the end of 1867; and he died at Halifax on October 17, 1871.

[D. Campbell, *Nova Scotia* (Montreal, 1873); E. M. Saunders, *Three premiers of Nova Scotia* (Toronto, 1909); *Can. parl. comp.*]

McNab, Peter (1767?-1847), executive councillor of Nova Scotia, was born in Halifax,

Nova Scotia, about 1767, the son of Peter McNab, a naval officer who settled in Halifax about 1758. He inherited from his father McNab's Island, in Halifax harbour; and he became a member of the Legislative Council of Nova Scotia, and of the old Council of Twelve. He died on June 1, 1847. In 1789 he married Joanna Cullerton; and by her he had several children.

[E. M. Chadwick, *Ontarian families* (2 vols., Toronto, 1894-98).]

McNaught, William Carlton (1888-1963), author, was born in Toronto, Ontario, February 13, 1888, and educated in Toronto schools and the University of Toronto (B.A., 1911), where he was the editor of the *Varsity*. He joined the Calgary *Herald* in 1912 and the Toronto *News* in 1914. From 1919 to 1936 he was a writer and executive with J. J. Gibbons advertising agency, and he later worked in the editorial department at Ryerson Press, the United Church of Canada's publishing house. In 1940 he wrote *Canada gets the news* for the Canadian Institute of International Affairs, and, with H. E. Stephenson, *The story of advertising in Canada* ; in 1953 he wrote *What time the tempest*. Mr. McNaught was secretary treasurer of the *Canadian Forum* from 1936 to 1948 as well as being director of the company and an editor of the magazine. He served with the Canadian army in the First World War in the 84th battalion with the rank of captain. He was a member of the staff of McKim Advertising Limited from 1937 to 1952. He died at Toronto, Ontario, February 26, 1963.

[*Can. who's who*, 1955-57; Metropolitan Toronto Library Board, *Biographical scrapbooks*, vol. 21; *Canadian Forum* (April, 1963).]

McNaught, William Kirkpatrick (1845-1919), manufacturer and politician, was born at Fergus, Canada West, on September 6, 1845. He spent his early years on a farm; but later went into business in Toronto, and became the president of the American Watch Company. From 1906 to 1915 he represented North-West Toronto in the Ontario legislature; and he died at Toronto, Ontario, on February 2, 1919. He was the author of *Lacrosse and how to play it* (Toronto, 1873), and some pamphlets on commercial subjects.

[Morgan, *Can. men* (1912); *Can. parl. comp.*]

McNaughton, Andrew George Latta (1887-1966), soldier and diplomat, was born in Moosomin, Saskatchewan, February 25, 1887. He received his education in engineering at McGill University (B.Sc., 1910; M.Sc., 1912) and joined the faculty of engineering at that university. He had been a member of the Canadian Militia since 1909, and after the outbreak of war in 1914 he was attached to the 2nd Brigade, Canadian Field Artillery, and

went overseas. He won the D.S.O. and was three times mentioned in despatches. He was wounded twice. Before the end of the war he became a brigadier-general in command of the Canadian Corps Heavy Artillery. He remained in the military service after the war, holding staff and command appointments, and attended the Staff College at Camberley in England and the Imperial Defence College. He became Chief of the Canadian General Staff in 1929, with the rank of major-general, continuing in this post until 1935, when he became president of the National Research Council. On the outbreak of the Second World War he returned to the army as Commander of the First Canadian Division. He became Corps Commander in 1940, with the rank of lieutenant-general. When an army headquarters with two corps was formed in 1942 he became Commander of the First Canadian Army. He gave up his command in December, 1943, and returned to Canada early in 1944, retiring from the army with the rank of general in September of 1944. He became Minister of National Defence in November, replacing J. L. Ralston (q.v.), who had resigned over the issue of conscription. In August, 1945, he left the cabinet and became Chairman of the Canadian section of the Canadian-U.S. Permanent Joint Board on Defence until 1959. He was Chairman (Canadian section) of the International Joint Commission from 1950 to 1962; Canadian representative on the United Nations Atomic Energy Commission (1946); president of the Atomic Energy Control Board of Canada (1946-48); and Canadian permanent delegate to the United Nations and representative on the Security Council (1948-49). He was created C.M.G. (1919), C.B. (1935), and C.H. 1946.

[J. Swettenham, *McNaughton*, 3 vols. (Toronto, 1968-69); Metropolitan Toronto Library Board, *Biographical Scrapbooks*, vol. 24.]

Macnaughton, John (1858-1943), educationist, was born near Kenmore, Perthshire, Scotland, in 1858, was educated at the University of Aberdeen, and at the Edinburgh Theological College, and was ordained a minister of the Church of Scotland. He came to Canada in 1889 as professor of Greek in Queen's University, Kingston; and though he spent the years 1908-19 at McGill University and the years 1919-25 at the University of Toronto, his best work was done at Queen's. Though he wrote little, he was a most stimulating teacher and one of the most strikingly original personalities in academic life in Canada in his day. He retired on pension in 1925; and most of his later years were spent in England, but he died at Montreal, Quebec, on February 5, 1943. His only book was *Lord Strathcona* (Toronto, 1926), but a volume of his *Essays and addresses* was published after his death (Kingston, 1946).

[W. D. Woodhead, *John Macnaughton* (Queen's quarterly, 1943); D. D. Calvin, *Queen's University at Kingston* (Kingston, Ont., 1941); T. R. Glover and D. D. Calvin, *A corner of empire* (Toronto, 1937); *University of Toronto monthly*, 1919 and 1925.]

MacNeil, Donald Jonathan (1903-1968), geologist and university professor, was born in Sydney, Nova Scotia, April 20, 1903. He studied engineering and geology at St. Francis Xavier University (B.Sc., 1930). He worked with Dr. W. T. Thom of Princeton University in 1931 on a geological survey in New Brunswick, and became a teaching fellow at Princeton, receiving a Ph.D. in 1935. He spent some years as an oil and gas prospector in Alberta, Oklahoma, and Texas before returning to St. Francis Xavier as head of the department of geology in 1943. He was instrumental in the establishment of the Crystal Cliffs co-operative geological institute with the Massachusetts Institute of Technology and the Nova Scotia government in 1948. He was head of the department of geology at St. Francis Xavier University for twenty-five years, and mayor of Antigonish, Nova Scotia, for six years. He had a deep interest in extending the benefits of education as widely as possible and in using his geological knowledge for the advancement of Nova Scotia and Canada. Among his writings on Nova Scotia are *Petroleum possibilities of Nova Scotia* (Transactions of the Mining Society of Nova Scotia, 1945); *The application of geology in the development of Nova Scotia coalfields* (Transactions of the Mining Society of Nova Scotia, 1948); and *The transverse trough of Cabot strait* (Trans. Roy. Soc. Can., 1956). He died at Antigonish, Nova Scotia, November 21, 1968.

[*Proc. and Trans. Roy. Soc. Can.*, vol. VII.]

McNeil, Neil (1851-1934), Roman Catholic archbishop of Toronto (1912-34), was born at Mabou, Nova Scotia, on November 23, 1851. He was educated at St. Xavier's College, Antigonish, Nova Scotia, and was ordained a priest of the Roman Catholic Church in 1879. From 1884 to 1891 he was rector of St. Xavier's College; and from 1895 to 1910 he was Vicar apostolic of St. John's, Newfoundland, with the title of bishop of Nilopolis. In 1912 he became archbishop of Toronto; and he died at Toronto on May 25, 1934.

[Morgan, *Can. men* (1912); *Can. who was who*, vol. 2.]

MacNeill, John (1874-1937), clergyman and educationist, was born near Paisley, Bruce county, Ontario, on March 5, 1874. He was educated at McMaster University, Toronto (B.A., 1896; D.D., 1918), and was ordained a minister of the Baptist Church in 1889. From 1899 to 1930 he was the pastor of churches in Winnipeg and Toronto; and in 1930 he was appointed principal of the faculty of theology in McMaster University, which had removed to Hamilton, Ontario. He died at Hamilton, on February 10, 1937. He was the author of *World power* (Toronto, 1914), *Many mansions* (Toronto, 1926), and *Reality in religion* (Philadelphia, 1934).

[*Can. who's who*, 1936-37.]

McNicoll, David (1852-1916), railway executive, was born at Arbroath, Scotland, in 1852. He entered the service of the North British Railway in 1866; and in 1874 he came to Canada, as a clerk first in the Northern Railway of Canada, and then in the Toronto, Grey, and Bruce Railway. In 1883 he entered the service of the Canadian Pacific Railway, and in 1900 he became general manager of this railway, and second vice-president. In 1903 he became first vice-president, and he continued as such until his retirement in 1915. He died at Guelph, Ontario, on November 25, 1915.

[Morgan, *Can. men* (1912).]

McNicoll, Helen (1879-1915), painter, was born in Canada in 1879, and studied art in Montreal, London, and Cornwall. She specialized in landscape and figure painting, and was notable as a "painter of sunlight". She was elected an associate of the Royal Canadian Academy in 1914. She died in England on June 27, 1915.

[H. G. Jones and E. Dyonnet, *History of the Royal Canadian Academy of Arts* (Montreal, 1934).]

McNutt, Alexander (1725?-1811), colonizer, was born in Ireland, of Scottish ancestry, about 1725. He emigrated to Virginia before 1753, and was present at the defeat of Braddock (q.v.) on the Monongahela in 1756 and at the capture of Louisbourg in 1758. In 1760 and later he interested himself in promoting immigration into Nova Scotia; and a considerable part of the pre-Loyalist settlement of the province was the result of his efforts. During the American Revolution he returned to Virginia; and he died at Lexington, Virginia, in 1811.

[W. O. Raymond, *Colonel Alexander McNutt and the pre-Loyalist settlements of Nova Scotia* (Trans. Roy. Soc. Can., 1911 and 1912).]

Macoun, James Melville (1862-1920), biologist, was born at Belleville, Canada West, on November 7, 1862, the eldest son of John Macoun (q.v.). He was educated at Albert University, Belleville; and entered the service of the Geological Survey of Canada in 1883. He rose in the service of the Geological Survey until he became in 1917 head of the biological division. He was awarded the C.M.G. in 1912; and he was elected a fellow of the Linnaean Society of London in 1914. He died at Ottawa, Ontario, on January 8, 1920. With his father, he was joint author of a *Catalogue of Canadian birds* (Ottawa, 1909).

[*Who was who*, 1916-28; Morgan, *Can. men* (1912).]

Macoun, John (1832-1920), botanist, was born at Maralin, county Down, Ireland, on April 17, 1832. He emigrated to Canada in 1850, and became a farmer. While farming, he picked up a practical knowledge of botany and geology; and in 1868 he was appointed professor of botany and geology in Albert College, Belleville, Ontario. In 1872 he was included in Sandford Fleming's expedition to the Pacific; in 1879 he was appointed explorer for the Canadian government in the North West Territories; and in 1882 he became botanist to the Geological Survey of Canada. In 1885 he was promoted to be assistant director and naturalist to the Survey; and this position he occupied until his death. He died at Ottawa on July 18, 1920. He was a charter member of the Royal Society of Canada; and he published, in addition to several catalogues of Canadian plants and birds, *Manitoba and the great north west* (Guelph, Ontario, 1882) and *The forests of Canada and their distribution* (Ottawa, 1895). His *Autobiography* (Ottawa, 1922) was published posthumously by the Ottawa Field Naturalist' Club.

[Morgan, *Can. men* (1912); G. M. Grant, *From ocean to ocean* (Toronto, 1873); *Proc. Roy. Soc. Can.*, 1894 and 1921.]

Macoun, William Tyrrell (1869-1933), horticulturist, was born at Belleville, Ontario, on January 27, 1869, a younger son of John Macoun (q.v.). He was educated at Albert University, Belleville, and entered the service of the Canadian government as a horticulturist at the Central Experimental Farm at Ottawa. Ultimately he became Dominion horticulturist. He died at Ottawa, Ontario, on August 13, 1933.

[Morgan, *Can. men* (1912).]

Macphail, Agnes Campbell (1890-1954), legislator, was born in Grey county, Ontario, on March 24, 1890, and died at Toronto, Ontario, on February 12, 1954. She attended the Stratford Normal School and became a school-teacher. In 1921 she was elected to the Canadian House of Commons as the candidate of the United Farmers of Ontario for Southeast Grey — the first woman in Canada to be elected a member of parliament. She sat for South-east Grey from 1921 to 1935, and for Grey-Bruce from 1935 to 1940. She was defeated in the federal elections of 1940; but was elected a member of the Ontario legislature in 1943, supporting the C.C.F. She retired from political life in 1951, and died in 1954.

[M. Stewart and D. French, *Ask no quarter: A biography of Agnes Macphail* (Toronto, 1959); *Can. who's who*, 1949-51; *Can. parl. guide*, 1950; *Encyc. Can.*]

McPhail, Alexander James (1883-1931), president of the Canadian wheat pool, was born in Paisley, Ontario, on December 23, 1883. He went to Manitoba in 1899, and to Saskatchewan in 1907; and attended the Manitoba Agricultural College in 1908-09. From 1913 to 1918 he was employed by the department of agriculture in Saskatchewan; and in 1922 he was elected secretary of the Saskatchewan Graingrowers' Association. In 1924 he became president of the Saskatchewan Wheat Pool Board, and of the Central Sales Agency of the western wheat pools; and he retained this position until his death at Regina, Saskatchewan, on October 21, 1931. His chief contribution to the farmers' movement in western Canada was the amalgamation of farmers' organizations in Saskatchewan and the formation of the Central Sales Agency operating for the three prairie provinces. In 1927 he married Marion Baird; and by her he had one son. He was the author of various speeches on the activities of the wheat pools.

[H. A. Innis (ed.), *The diary of Alexander James McPhail* (Toronto, 1940).]

Macphail, Sir Andrew (1864-1938), physician and author, was born at Orwell, Prince Edward Island, on November 24, 1864. He was educated at Prince of Wales College, Charlottetown, and at McGill University (B.A., 1888; M.D., C.M., 1891; LL.D., 1921); and he practised medicine in Montreal. From 1907 to 1937 he was professor of the history of medicine in McGill University; and he served as a medical officer in the First World War. From 1907 to 1920 he was editor of the *University Magazine*; and he became an outstanding figure in the literary life of Canada. He was elected a fellow of the Royal Society of Canada in 1910; and in 1918 he was created a knight bachelor. He died at Montreal, Quebec, on September 23, 1938. He was the author of *Essays in Puritanism* (Boston, 1905), *The vine of Sibmah* (New York, 1906), *Essays in politics* (New York, 1909), *Essays in fallacy* (New York, 1910), *Official history of the Canadian forces in the Great War; The medical services* (Ottawa, 1925), *Three persons* (Montreal, 1929), *The Bible in Scotland* (London, 1931), and *The master's wife* (Montreal, 1939); he was the compiler of *The book of sorrow* (New York, 1916); and he was the translator of Louis Hémon's *Maria Chapdelaine* (Toronto, 1921).

[*Proc. Roy. Soc. Can.*, 1939; *Can. who's who*, 1936-37; Morgan, *Can. men* (1912).]

McPhedran, Alexander (1847-1934), physician and educationist, was born in Halton county, Canada West, in 1847. He was educated at the University of Toronto (M.B., 1876); and from 1900 to 1919 he was professor of medicine in the University of Toronto. In 1905 and 1906 he was president of the Canadian Medical Association; and in 1915 he was elected a fellow of the Royal Society of Canada, a rare honour for a practising physician. He died at Toronto, Ontario, on December 19, 1934.

[*University of Toronto monthly*, 1934; Morgan, *Can. men* (1912).]

Macpherson, Mrs. Charlotte Holt, *née* **Gethings** (*fl.* 1828-1890), chronicler, was born in Quebec, Lower Canada, the daughter of Charles Gethings, manager of the Bank of Quebec. At the age of eighteen years, she married Daniel Macpherson (1822-1889), a notary public of Quebec. After her husband's death, she went to Montreal, and there she published two volumes of reminiscences, *Reminiscences of old Quebec* (Montreal, 1890) and *Old memories* (Montreal, 1890). The date of her death has not been ascertained.

[P. G. Roy, *Fils de Québec*, vol. 4 (Lévis, Que., 1933).]

Macpherson, Cluny (1879-1966), medical doctor and inventor, was born in St. John's, Newfoundland, in 1879. He graduated in medicine in 1901 from McGill University and began practice as a medical missionary in Labrador with Dr. Wilfred Grenfell. During the Second World War he was a medical officer with the Newfoundland Regiment and was assigned as one of a team of doctors in the British War Office attempting to develop an effective gas mask. Cluny Macpherson's prototype was the first successful respiratory protection against poison gas. He saw service as a medical officer in France, Belgium, Egypt, Gallipoli, and Salonika. After the war he returned to Newfoundland and carried on his medical practice until 1965. He was a director of the Grenfell Mission. He died at St. John's, Newfoundland, November 16, 1966.

[Metropolitan Toronto Library Board, *Biographical scrapbooks*, vol. 26.]

Macpherson, Mrs. Daniel. See Macpherson, Mrs. Charlotte Holt, *née* **Gethings.**

Macpherson, Sir David Lewis (1818-1896), minister of the interior (1883-85), was born at Castle Leathers, near Inverness, Scotland, on September 12, 1818, the youngest son of David Macpherson. He was educated at the Royal Academy of Inverness, and came to Canada in 1835. He entered the service of a firm of forwarding agents in Montreal, of which his elder brother was senior partner; and he eventually became a successful railway contractor, in association with Casimir Gzowski (q.v.). In 1864 he was elected as a Conservative to the Legislative Council of Canada for the "Saugeen" division; and in 1867 he was called to the Senate of Canada. In 1871 he was a rival of Sir Hugh Allan (q.v.) for the charter for the building of the Canadian Pacific Railway, and his failure to obtain the charter somewhat chilled his party loyalty. But in 1880 he was appointed speaker of the Senate and a minister without portfolio in the Macdonald government; and from 1883 to 1885 he was minister of the interior. Failing health and charges of incapacity against him arising from the North West Rebellion of 1885 brought about his retirement from the cabinet; and during the remainder of his life he took little part in public affairs. He died in mid-Atlantic on August 16, 1896. In 1844 he married Elizabeth Sarah, eldest daughter of William Molson of Montreal, and grand-daughter of John Molson (q.v.). In 1884 he was created a K.C.M.G. He published several pamphlets on finance: *Banking and currency* (Toronto, 1869), *Letter on the increasing public expenditure of Ontario* (Toronto, 1879), and *Letters showing the decrease in the controllable public expenditure under the present administration* (Toronto, 1881).

[*Cyc. Am. biog.*; Rose, *Cyc. Can. biog.* (1886); Dent, *Can. port.*, vol. 3; Taylor, *Brit. Am.*, vol. 3; Sir J. Pope, *Memoirs of the Rt. Hon. Sir J. A. Macdonald* (2 vols., Ottawa, 1894) and *Correspondence of Sir John Macdonald* (Toronto, 1921).]

Macpherson, Harold (1884-1963), merchant, was born in St. John's, Newfoundland, and educated at the Methodist College in that city. He was a member of the Upper House of the Newfoundland Assembly at its dissolution in 1934 when commission government was introduced. He was a noted breeder of Newfoundland dogs and Ayrshire cattle. Macpherson was chairman of the Royalstores Limited and T. McMurdo and Company; a director of the Dominion Atlantic Insurance and Equitable Life; and was vice-president of Riverside Woolen Mills. He died at St. John's, Newfoundland, July 15, 1963.

[*Can. who's who*, 1955-57; Metropolitan Toronto Library Board, *Biographical scrapbooks*, vol. 21.]

Macpherson, James Pennington (1839-1916), lawyer and civil servant, was born at Kingston, Upper Canada, on May 29, 1839, the son of an officer in the British army, and a nephew of Sir John A. Macdonald (q.v.). He was educated at Queen's University (B.A., 1857; M.A., 1865), and was called to the bar in 1861. He practised law in Cobourg and Ottawa; and during his later years he held a position in the Canadian civil service at Ottawa. He retired on pension in 1895; and he died at Ottawa, Ontario, on February 9, 1916. He was the author of *Life of the Right Hon. Sir John A. Macdonald* (2 vols., Saint John, N.B., 1891).

[Morgan, *Can. men* (1912).]

McPherson, John (1817-1845), poet, was born at Liverpool, Nova Scotia, on February 4, 1817; and died at Brookfield, Nova Scotia, on July 26, 1845. He was a school-teacher who styled himself "the Harp of Acadia". He wrote *The praise of water: A prize poem* (Halifax,

1843), and his literary remains were published after his death, with a memoir of him, under the title *Harp of Acadia: Poems, descriptive and moral* (Halifax, 1862).

[C. M. Whyte-Edgar, *A wreath of Canadian song* (Toronto, 1910); C. C. James, *A bibliography of Canadian poetry* (Toronto, 1899); R. J. Long, *Nova Scotia authors* (East Orange, N.J., 1918).]

McPherson, Murdock (1796?-1863), fur-trader, was born at Gairloch, Ross-shire, Scotland, about 1796, and entered the service of the North West Company in 1816. Ross Cox (q.v.) met him when he was *en route* to the Athabaska district in 1817. He was taken over as a clerk by the Hudson's Bay Company at the union of 1821; and in 1823 he was transferred to the Mackenzie River department. He remained here until 1848, with the exception of the years 1840-43, which he spent on furlough and at Tadoussac. He was promoted to be a chief trader in 1834, and a chief factor in 1847. He was granted two years' furlough in 1849, and he retired in 1851. He died in 1863.

[W. S. Wallace (ed.), *Documents relating to the North West Company* (Toronto: The Champlain Society, 1934).]

McPherson, William David (1863-1929), lawyer and politician, was born in Lambton county, Canada West, on August 22, 1863. He was educated at the Osgoode Hall Law School, and was called to the Ontario bar in 1885 (K.C., 1908). He practised law in Toronto; and from 1908 to 1919 he represented North-West Toronto in the Ontario legislature. From 1916 to 1919 he was provincial secretary in the Hearst administration. He was a member of the Masonic order, and was grand master of the Grand Lodge of Canada in 1913-14, and grand master of the Grand Orange Lodge of North America in 1922. He died at Toronto, Ontario, on May 2, 1929. He was the author of *The law of elections in Canada* (Toronto, 1905), and joint author, with J. M. Clark, of *The law of mines in Canada* (Toronto, 1898).

[*Can. who was who*, vol. 1; Morgan, *Can. men* (1912).]

McQueen, David George (1854-1930), clergyman, was born near Kirkwall, Ontario, on December 25, 1854. He was educated at the University of Toronto (B.A., 1884), and at Knox College (D.D., 1905); and he was ordained a minister of the Presbyterian Church in 1887. He was sent to Edmonton as a pioneer pastor; and he remained in Edmonton as a pastor until his death on October 22, 1930.

[E. A. Corbett, *McQueen of Edmonton* (Toronto, 1934).]

Macqueen, Thomas (1803-1861), journalist and poet, was born in the parish of Kilbirnie, Ayrshire, Scotland, on October 9, 1803. He became a stone-mason; and in 1842 he emi-

grated to Canada. He settled first in Fitzroy township, in the district of Bathurst, Canada West; but in 1848 he removed to Goderich, Canada West, and became the editor of the *Huron Signal*, a Reform newspaper. He died on his farm near Goderich on June 25, 1861. Before coming to Canada he published three volumes of verse; and in Canada he frequently wrote verses, notable among which was a poem on Lake Huron, entitled "Our Own Broad Lake". His Canadian verses were, however, never collected in book form.

[A. Haydon, *Pioneer sketches of the district of Bathurst* (Toronto, 1925); Morgan, *Bib. can.*]

McTavish, Alexander (1784?-1832), fur-trader, was born about 1784, and was probably a relative of Donald McTavish (q.v.). He came out to Astoria on the *Isaac Todd* in 1813, as a clerk in the service of the North West Company. In 1817 he was at Fort William, and in 1821, when he was taken over as a clerk by the Hudson's Bay Company, he was stationed at the Pic, on Lake Superior. From 1824 to 1832 he was in charge at Lake Nipigon; and in 1828 he was promoted to the rank of chief trader. He died at Lake Nipigon on December 9, 1832, of apoplexy, aged about 48 years.

[W. S. Wallace (ed.), *Documents relating to the North West Company* (Toronto: The Champlain Society, 1934).]

McTavish, Donald (d. 1814), fur-trader, was born in Stratherrick, Inverness-shire, Scotland, and was a son of Alexander McTavish, and a first cousin of Simon McTavish (q.v.). He must have entered the service of the North West Company as a clerk prior to 1790, since his obituary notice in the *Quebec Gazette*, of December 14, 1815, describes him as having been employed in the West upwards of twenty-five years. He was made a partner of the North West Company prior to 1799, for in that year he was "proprietor" on the Upper English River. He was in charge of the English River department until 1808; and from 1808 to 1811 he was in charge at Fort Dunvegan, in the Athabaska department. He returned to Great Britain in 1812; and in 1813 he commanded the expedition which sailed on the *Isaac Todd* for Fort Astoria. He was drowned near the mouth of the Columbia on May 22, 1814. In 1814, before the news of his death reached Montreal, he was made a partner in the firm of McTavish, McGillivrays, and Co.

[E. Coues (ed.), *New light on the early history of the greater north-west* (3 vols., New York, 1897).]

Mactavish, Dugald (1817-1871), fur-trader, was born at Kilchrist, Argyllshire, Scotland, in 1817, and was a nephew of John George McTavish (q.v.). He entered the service of the Hudson's Bay Company as an apprentice clerk at Moose Factory in 1833. In 1835 he was at Michipicoten, and in 1837 at Lachine; but in 1839 he was transferred to the Columbia; and here, except for a period spent in Hawaii about 1847, he remained until 1859. He was promoted to the rank of chief trader in 1851; and he died at Montreal, of heart disease, on May 24, 1871.

[G. P. de T. Glazebrook (ed.), *The Hargrave correspondence* (Toronto: The Champlain Society, 1938); *Dict. Can. biog.*, vol. 10.]

McTavish, James Chisholm (d. 1827), fur-trader, was probably a relative of Donald McTavish (q.v.), and sailed with him for Astoria in the *Isaac Todd* in 1813. He was at Fort William, when that place was captured by Lord Selkirk (q.v.) in 1816. Prior to 1821, he was employed in the management of the King's Posts, on the lower St. Lawrence; and he was continued in that capacity, after the union of the North West and Hudson's Bay companies, until 1827, when he was dismissed from the service. He died, shortly afterwards, on the Island of Orleans, Lower Canada, on December 16, 1827.

[W. S. Wallace (ed.), *Documents relating to the North West Company* (Toronto: The Champlain Society, 1934).]

McTavish, John (d. 1852), merchant, was born in Scotland, a son of Alexander McTavish, and a nephew of Simon McTavish (q.v.). He came to Canada about 1808; and in 1814 he became a partner in McTavish, McGillivrays, and Co., in charge of the accounting department. He did not prove a success in this capacity, however, and in 1816 he went to the United States. There he married in 1816, Emily, youngest daughter of Richard Caton, of Doughoregon Manor House, near Baltimore, Maryland, who was connected with the Carrolls of Carrolltown. In 1834 he was appointed British consul at Baltimore; and he died on June 21, 1852.

[W. S. Wallace (ed.), *Documents relating to the North West Company* (Toronto: The Champlain Society, 1934).]

McTavish, John George (d. 1847), fur-trader, was the second son of the chief of the Clan Tavish, and was introduced into the fur-trade in Canada through the friendship of Simon McTavish (q.v.) with his father. Apparently Simon McTavish, while in Scotland, introduced himself to the head of the clan, somewhat dazzled him with his wealth, persuaded him to have his arms registered (as well as those of Simon McTavish himself, as a distant kinsman), and in 1798 took his son John George into the North West Company as a clerk. The latter was at Grand Portage in 1802; he was stationed in the Athabaska district in 1808; and he was with John McDonald of Garth (q.v.) when he went to the relief of

David Thompson (q.v.) in 1811. In 1813 he was on the Columbia, and received the surrender of Fort Astoria. He was made a partner of the North West Company in 1813; and in 1819 he was arrested by William Williams (q.v.), of the Hudson's Bay Company, in connection with the Selkirk troubles. He was sent to England for trial; but was released in 1821, and was appointed a chief factor of the Hudson's Bay Company. He was in charge at York Factory from 1821 to 1828, and at Moose Factory from 1831 to 1834. From 1836 to 1847 he was in charge at the Lake of Two Mountains, near Montreal. He retired from the Company in 1847; and he died on July 20, 1847.

[W. S. Wallace (ed.), *Documents relating to the North West Company* (Toronto: The Champlain Society, 1934); E. E. Rich (ed.), *Journal of occurrences in the Athabasca department, by George Simpson* (Toronto: The Champlain Society, 1938).]

MacTavish, Newton McFaul (1877-1941), journalist, was born at Staffa, Ontario, on February 17, 1877. He was on the staff of the Toronto *Globe* from 1898 to 1906; and from 1906 to 1926 he was editor of the *Canadian Magazine*. From 1926 to 1932 he was a member of the Canadian Civil Service Commission; and from 1920 to 1932 he was a trustee of the National Gallery. He died at Toronto, Ontario, on August 17, 1941. He was the author of *Thrown in* (Toronto, 1923), *The fine arts in Canada* (Toronto, 1925), and *Ars longa* (Toronto, 1938).

[*Can. who's who*, 1936-37; Morgan, *Can. men* (1912).]

McTavish, Simon (1750-1804), merchant, was born in 1750, probably in Stratherrick, Inverness-shire. He belonged to a branch of the Clan Tavish which had fled from Argyllshire, and settled in Inverness-shire several generations before he was born. He emigrated to America before 1772, and engaged in the fur-trade from Albany. He was in Detroit as early as 1772; and in 1775 he transferred his headquarters to Montreal. He was trading at Grand Portage in 1776, in partnership with James Bannerman; and in 1779 he was one of the partners in the original sixteen-share North West Company of that year. He seems to have been one of the prime movers in bringing about the renewed agreement of 1783; and in 1787 he formed a partnership with Joseph Frobisher, known as McTavish, Frobisher and Co., which became the supply house and virtual directorate of the North West Company. As the head of this house, he became in fact, if not in name, the director of the Company; and for many years he visited Grand Portage in the summer to superintend the trade. He became perhaps the richest man in Montreal. In 1793 Sir Alured Clarke (q.v.) recommended that he should be appointed a member of the Legislative Council; but for some reason this recommendation was never acted on. In 1800 he purchased the estate of Dunardary in Argyllshire, which was the home of the chief of Clan Tavish, and which had recently come into the market; and in 1803 he commenced the building of a mansion on the side of the mountain in Montreal. This house was not yet completed when he died in Montreal, on July 6, 1804. His will is on file in Somerset House, London. On February 27, 1793, he married Marguerite, daughter of Charles Jean Baptiste Chaboillez (q.v.), "a handsome young lady with a *plum*"; and by her he had two sons, William and Simon, Jr., and two daughters, Ann and Mary. The widow married, a few years after McTavish's death, William Smith Plenderleath, an officer in the British army. Over McTavish's will a good deal of litigation resulted; and the final distribution did not take place until 1839. His Montreal property, on which he was buried, finally reverted to his eldest nephew, John McTavish (q.v.), whose executors ultimately sold it. Before it was sold, however, one of the executors had Simon McTavish's tomb covered with a mound of earth, to prevent vandals breaking in.

[W. S. Wallace, *The pedlars from Quebec* (Toronto, 1954).]

Mactavish, William (d. 1870), governor of Assiniboia (1858-70) and of Rupert's Land (1864-70), was born in Scotland, and was the nephew of John George McTavish (q.v.). He came to Rupert's Land in 1833 as a clerk in the service of the Hudson's Bay Company. He became a chief factor in 1851, and in 1858 he was appointed governor of Assiniboia. Six years later he became also governor of Rupert's Land. His illness during the critical period of the North West Rebellion of 1869-70 unfitted him to cope with the troubles attending the transfer of Rupert's Land to Canada; and he died at Liverpool, England, in 1870, while on his way to the south of France.

[E. H. Oliver (ed.), *The Canadian northwest* (2 vols., Ottawa, 1914); J. P. Robertson, *A political manual of the province of Manitoba* (Winnipeg, 1887); G. Bryce, *The remarkable history of the Hudson's Bay Company* (London, 1900); G. P. de T. Glazebrook (ed.), *The Hargrave correspondence* (Toronto: The Champlain Society, 1938).]

McTavish, William Sharpe (1858-1932), clergyman and author, was born in Nassagaweya township, Halton county, Canada West, on April 16, 1858. He was educated at the University of Toronto, at Knox College, Toronto (B.D., 1887), and at Union Theological Seminary, New York. He was ordained a minister of the Presbyterian Church in Canada in 1885; and he was the pastor of churches at St. George, Deseronto, Kingston, and Madoc, in Ontario. He died at Belleville, Ontario, on October 4, 1932. He was the author of

Reapers in many fields (Toronto, 1904) and *Harvests in many lands* (Toronto, 1908).

[Morgan, *Can. men* (1912); *Union Theological Seminary, Alumni catalogue* (New York, 1937).]

MacVannell, John Angus (1871-1915), educationist, was born at St. Mary's, Ontario, on October 5, 1871; and was educated at the University of Toronto (B.A., 1893; M.A., 1894) and at Columbia University (Ph.D., 1898). He was for many years on the staff of Columbia University; and he was the author of *Hegel's doctrine of the will* (New York, 1896) and *The educational theories of Herbart and Froebel* (New York, 1905). He died at St. Mary's, Ontario, on November 10, 1915.

[Morgan, *Can. men* (1912).]

MacVicar, Donald Harvey (1831-1902), principal of the Presbyterian College, Montreal, was born in Dunglass, Argyllshire, Scotland, on November 29, 1831, the son of John MacVicar and Janet MacTavish. His parents came to Canada when he was a child, and he was educated at the University of Toronto and Knox College, Toronto. In 1859 he was licensed to preach in the Presbyterian Church; and in 1868 he became head of the Presbyterian College at Montreal. This position he occupied until his death on December 15, 1902. In 1860 he married Eleanor, daughter of Robert Goulding, of Toronto; and by her he had five children. He was an LL.D. of McGill University (1870) and a D.D. of Knox College (1883); and in 1881 he was moderator of the general assembly of the Presbyterian Church in Canada.

[J. H. MacVicar, *Life and work of Donald H. MacVicar* (Toronto, 1904); Morgan, *Can. men* (1912); Rose, *Cyc. Can. biog.* (1886); *Cyc. Am. biog.*]

MacVicar, Malcolm (1829-1904), first chancellor of McMaster University, was born in Dunglass, Argyllshire, Scotland, on September 30, 1829, the son of John MacVicar and Janet MacTavish. He came to Canada with his parents as a child, and was educated at Rochester University (B.A., 1859). He held various academic positions in the United States until 1881, when he was appointed a professor in the Baptist College, Toronto. When this college became McMaster University in 1887, he was appointed its first chancellor. In 1890 he resigned his post, and returned to the United States. Here he died, at Cato, New York, on May 18, 1904. He was the inventor of the MacVicar tellurian globe; and in 1870 he received the degree of Ph.D. from the University of the State of New York, and that of LL.D. from the University of Rochester.

[A. L. McCrimmon, *Malcolm MacVicar* (McMaster University monthly, 1905); *Cyc. Am. biog.*]

MacVicar, William Mortimer (1851-1928), educationist, was born at Port Medway, Nova Scotia, on March 22, 1851. He was educated at Acadia University (B.A., 1872; M.A., 1876), and became a school-teacher, first in Nova Scotia, and later in Boston, Massachusetts. He died at Watertown, Massachusetts, in 1928. He was the author of *A short history of Annapolis Royal* (Toronto, 1897).

[*Acadia University, Records of the graduates* (Wolfville, N.S., 1926).]

McWilliams, Mrs. Margaret May, *née* Stovel (1875-1952), author, was born in Toronto, Ontario, in 1875, and died at Winnipeg, Manitoba, on April 12, 1952. She was educated at the University of Toronto (B.A., 1898), and became a journalist. In 1903 she married Roland Fairbairn McWilliams (q.v.), and moved with him to Winnipeg in 1910; when he became lieutenant-governor of Manitoba in 1940, she became the chatelaine of Government House. She was the author of *Manitoba milestones* (Toronto, 1928) and *This new Canada* (London, 1948); and with her husband was joint author, under the pseudonym of "Oliver Stowell", of *If I were king of Canada* (Toronto, 1931). She was the founder and first president of the Canadian Federation of University Women.

[*Encyc. Can.*]

McWilliams, Roland Fairbairn (1874-1957), lieutenant-governor of Manitoba (1940-53), was born at Peterborough, Ontario, on October 10, 1874, and died at Winnipeg, Manitoba, on December 9, 1957. He was educated at the University of Toronto (B.A., 1896; LL.B., 1897), was called to the bar in 1899, and first practised law in Peterborough. He then moved to Winnipeg; and in 1940 he was appointed lieutenant-governor of Manitoba. This position he held until 1953. With his first wife, Margaret, (q.v.) he was joint author, under the pseudonym "Oliver Stowell", of *If I were king of Canada* (Toronto, 1931).

[*Can. who's who*, 1955-59; *Can. parl. guide*, 1952; *Encyc. Can.*]

Madsen, Marius Krestian (1901-1967), prospector and mine-owner, was born in Jutland in 1901. As a young man of nineteen he joined the Danish East Greenland Company in 1920 to explore and establish trading posts along the coast of Greenland. Their ship was crushed in the Arctic ice and the party survived on polar bear and seal for almost a year before the relief ship arrived. Madsen joined the new exploring party and remained another year in a station on Sabine Island. He came to Canada in 1925 and went prospecting in the Red Lake area, where he staked claims which led to the establishment of Madsen Red Lake Gold Mines in 1938 and the opening up of the Patricia Red Lake mining region. He was president of Madsen Construction; Marius Mining and Developments; Advance Red Lake Gold Mines; Superior Sand and Gravel; Belmar Realty Company; Belmar Farms; Madsen Red Lake Gold Mines; Casa Maria Hotel, Jamaica; Honey Pot Ski Lodge, Ontario. He died at Toronto, Ontario, February 16, 1967.

[*Can. who's who*, 1964-66; Toronto *Globe and Mail*, February 20, 1967.]

Magann, George Loranger (1892-1963), ambassador, was born in Toronto, Ontario, in May, 1892, and educated at the Oratory School in Edgbaston, England; Loyola College, Montreal; Ecole des Roches, Verneuil, France; Trinity College School, Port Hope; and Royal Military College, Kingston. He served in the First World War (1914-18) and was wounded and mentioned in despatches. He began work with G. P. Magann, Toronto, railway contractors, in 1919, and on his father's death reorganized the company as G. L. Magann and Company. He joined the department of external affairs in 1941 and during the closing days of the Second World War was in charge of an exchange of prisoners in Switzerland. In 1950 he headed the Canadian delegation to the International Refugee Organization meeting at Geneva. He was ambassador to Greece (1949-54) and to Switzerland (1954-57), as well as being Canadian minister to Austria. He died at Toronto, Ontario, February 26, 1963.

[*Can. who's who*, 1955-57; Metropolitan Toronto Library Board, *Biographical scrapbooks*, vol. 21.]

Magee, Knox (1877-1934), journalist and novelist, was born in South Gower, Grenville county, Ontario, on November 6, 1877, and died at Winnipeg, Manitoba, on May 9, 1934. He was the author of two historical romances, *With ring of shield* (Toronto, 1900) and *Mark Everard* (Toronto, 1901), and he was the editor of the *Moon*, a short-lived humorous journal published in Toronto in 1902-03. In 1907 he went to Winnipeg, and became editor of the Winnipeg *Saturday Post*.

[Morgan, *Can. men* (1912).]

Magnan, Aristide (1863-1929), priest and author, was born at Ste. Ursule de Maskinongé, Canada East, on September 28, 1863; and was ordained a priest of the Roman Catholic Church in 1886. He served in various parishes in Canada and the United States; and he died at St. Désiré du Lac-Noir, Quebec, on February 22, 1929. He was the author of *A la recherche de la vérité* (Quebec, 1902), *Histoire de la race française aux Etats-Unis* (Paris, 1912), *Rimes et raisons* (Quebec, 1923), and *Histoire de la paroisse de Notre-Dame de Lourdes de Fall-River* (New Bedford, Mass., 1926).

[Allaire, *Dict. biog.*; *Bull. rech. hist.*, 1929.]

Magnan, Charles Joseph (1865-1942), educationist, was born at Ste. Ursule, Canada East, on November 11, 1865, and was educated at the Ecole Normale at Quebec. He became a school-teacher, and in 1889 was appointed a professor on the staff of the Ecole Normale. In 1911 he was appointed inspector-general of Catholic schools; and in 1929, inspector-general of Catholic normal schools. In 1922 he was elected a fellow of the Royal Society of Canada, and he received honorary degrees from Laval University and the University of Ottawa. He died at Portneuf, Quebec, on June 2, 1942. He was the author of *L'enseignement primaire* (Three Rivers, Que., 1888), *Manuel de droit civique* (Quebec, 1895), *Mémorial sur l'éducation au Canada* (Quebec, 1903), *A propos d'instruction obligatoire* (Quebec, 1919), *Eclairons la route* (Quebec, 1922), *L'instruction publique dans la province de Québec* (Quebec, 1932), *Sur les routes de France* (Montreal, 1934), and *Le carillon-sacré-coeur* (Quebec, 1939); and he was joint author, with J. Ahern, of *Mon premier livre* (Quebec, 1900).

[*Proc. Roy. Soc. Can.*, 1943; Morgan, *Can. men* (1912).]

Magnan, Joseph Roch (1857-1904), priest, was born at L'Assomption, Canada East, in 1857, and was ordained a priest of the Roman Catholic Church in 1881. For many years he was curé of Muskegon, Michigan. He died at Rome, Italy, on June 12, 1904. He was the author of *Cour français de lectures graduées* (3 vols., Montreal, 1902).

[Allaire, *Dict. biog.*; *Bull. rech. hist.*, 1927.]

Magrath, Charles Alexander (1860-1949), public servant and politician, was born in North Augusta, Canada West, on April 22, 1860, and died at Victoria, British Columbia, on October 30, 1949. He went to the North West in 1878, and became a land surveyor and irrigation engineer. He entered public life early. From 1891 to 1902 he represented Lethbridge in the legislature of the North West Territories, and from 1898 to 1901 was a minister without portfolio in the Haultain administration. From 1908 to 1911 he represented Medicine Hat in the Canadian House of Commons as a Conservative; but in the latter part of his life he devoted himself to public service of an administrative kind. From 1914 to 1935 he was chairman of the Canadian section of the International Joint Commission, and from 1925 to 1931 chairman of the Ontario Hydro-Electric Power Commission. In 1927 he was elected a fellow of the Royal Society of Canada; and he was the author of *Canada's growth and some problems affecting it* (Ottawa, 1910) and *The Galts, father and son, pioneers in the development of Southern Alberta* (Lethbridge, Alta., 1935).

[*Proc. Roy. Soc. Can.*, 1950; *Can. who's who*, 1948; *Encyc. Can.*]

Magrath, James (1766-1851), clergyman, was born in Ireland in 1766, and was educated at Trinity College, Dublin. He was ordained a priest of the Church of England, and was rector, first of the parish of Castlerea, county Roscommon, and then of the parish of Shankill, diocese of Leighlin. In 1827 he emigrated to Canada with his family, and was appointed rector of the township of Toronto, Upper Canada. He named his home Erindale; and he lived there until his death on June 14, 1851. An account of the settlement of the Magrath family at Erindale will be found in T. W. Magrath, *Authentic letters from Upper Canada, with an account of Canadian field sports* (Dublin, 1833).

[John Banks, *The Reverend James Magrath* (Ont. His., 1963); Morgan, *Cel. Can.*]

Maguire, Thomas (1776-1854), priest and author, was born in Philadelphia, Pennsylvania, on May 9, 1776. He was educated at the Quebec Seminary, and was ordained a priest of the Roman Catholic Church in 1799. He occupied various ecclesiastical posts in Lower Canada; and he died at Quebec, Canada East, on July 17, 1854. He was the author of *Recueil des notes diverses sur le gouvernement d'une paroisse* (Paris, 1830) and *Manuel des difficultés les plus communes de la langue française* (Quebec, 1841).

[*Cyc. Am. biog.*; Allaire, *Dict. biog.*; Le Jeune, *Dict. gén.*]

Maheux, Joseph Thomas Arthur (1884-1963), historian, was born at Ste. Julie de Megantic, Quebec, June 22, 1884. He was educated at the Grand Séminaire, Quebec, and ordained to the priesthood in 1908. He spent three years teaching at the Séminaire and then went on to the Sorbonne in Paris (L. Litt., 1915; Dip. Philol., 1917). He returned to the Séminaire in Quebec as professor of rhetoric in 1918, but continued his studies in music, astronomy, botany, and ornithology for his own pleasure. He was secretary of the Faculty of Arts at Laval University from 1924 to 1932, and bursar from 1927 to 1930. From 1930 to 1939 he was engaged in organizing secondary education for girls in the Province of Quebec. He was professor of history at Laval from 1938 to 1952 and became head of the department of history and geography in 1945. He was awarded an O.B.E. (1944) for his work with the C.O.T.C. at Laval. He was considered an opponent of Abbé Groulx's historical emphasis on Quebec separatism because of his writings, particularly those dealing with national themes: *French Canada: a new interpretation* (1942); *French Canada and Britain* (1942); *What keeps us apart* (1944); and *Problems of Canadian unity* (1944). He also wrote *l'Histoire de la Compagnie Price au Canada* (1955); *Propos sur l'Education* (1941); *Recherches sur l'Université de Laval* (1949); *Nos débuts sous le Régime anglais* (1940); *L'histoire de la médi-*

cine à Québec (1950); as well as numerous articles and reviews.

He was a fellow of the Royal Society of Canada and received an honorary degree from the University of New Brunswick. He died at Quebec, August 30, 1963.

[*Proc. and Trans. Roy. Soc. Can.*, 1968; *Can. who's who*, 1955-57.]

Mahon, Alexander Wylie (1853-1930), clergyman, was born in Londonderry, Nova Scotia, on November 6, 1853. He was educated at Dalhousie University and at Princeton Theological College (B.D., 1893), and was ordained a minister of the Presbyterian Church in Canada in 1883. He held charges at St. Peter's Road, Prince Edward Island, and at St. Andrews, New Brunswick; and from 1918 to 1924 he was assistant pastor of St. Andrew's Church, Toronto. He died at Toronto, Ontario, on August 3, 1930. He was the author of *Canadian hymns and hymn-writers* (St. Andrews-by-the-Sea, N.B., 1908).

[R. J. Long, *Nova Scotia authors* (East Orange, N.J., 1918); *Biographical catalogue of the Princeton Theological Seminary* (Princeton, N.J., 1933).]

Maillard, Pierre (1710?-1762), missionary, was born in the diocese of Chartres, France, probably in 1710, and was sent in 1735 from the Seminary of the Society of Foreign Missions in Paris to Cape Breton (Ile Royale) as a missionary. He quickly mastered the Micmac language, and, for the next twenty-five years, he proved to be one of the most influential missionaries in Nova Scotia. He died at Halifax, on August 12, 1762.

[N. M. Rogers, *Apostle to the Micmacs* (Dalhousie review, 1926); A. David, *Messire Pierre Maillard* (Bull. rech. hist., 1929); J. E. Burns, *The Abbé Maillard and Halifax* (Canadian Catholic Historical Association, report, 1936-37); Le Jeune, *Dict. gén.*; *Dict. Can. biog.*, vol. 3.]

Mailloux, Alexis (1801-1877), priest and author, was born at Ile aux Coudres, Lower Canada, on January 8, 1801, was educated at the Quebec Seminary, and was ordained a priest in 1825. He was grand vicar of the bishop of Quebec from 1838 to 1877, and from 1847 to 1875 he was employed as a temperance lecturer. He died at St. Henri de Lauzon, Quebec, on August 4, 1877. He was the author of *La croix présentée aux membres de la Société de tempérance* (Quebec, 1850), *Manuel des fabriques* (Quebec, 1855), *L'ivrognerie est l'oeuvre du démon* (Quebec, 1867), *Histoire de l'Ile aux Coudres* (Montreal, 1879), and *Promenade autour de l'Ile aux Coudres* (Ste. Anne de la Pocatière, Que., 1880).

[Allaire, *Dict. biog.*; *Dict. Can. biog.*, vol. 10.]

Mair, Charles (1838-1927), poet, was born at Lanark, Upper Canada, on September 21, 1838, the son of James Mair and Margaret Holmes. He was educated at Queen's University, Kingston; but did not proceed to a degree. He became first a journalist, and was one of the originators of the "Canada First" movement in 1868. In 1870 he represented the Montreal *Gazette* during the first Riel rebellion, and was imprisoned and narrowly escaped being shot by the rebels. He spent the rest of his life in the West, either on the prairies or in British Columbia, was an officer of the Governor-General's Body Guard during the second Riel Rebellion in 1885, and was later employed in the Canadian civil service in the West. He died at Victoria, British Columbia, on July 7, 1927. In 1868 he married Elizabeth Louise Mac-Kenny (d. 1906), a niece of Sir John Schultz (q.v.). He was elected a fellow of the Royal Society of Canada in 1889, and was made an LL.D. of Queen's University, Kingston, in 1926. He was the author of *Dreamland and other poems* (Montreal, 1868), *Tecumseh, a drama* (Toronto, 1886; 2nd ed., Toronto, 1901), and *Through the Mackenzie basin* (Toronto, 1908). These works, with a paper on *The American bison*, originally published in the *Transactions* of the Royal Society of Canada, and some *Memoirs and Reminiscences*, contributed to a weekly newspaper in 1925, were republished by John W. Garvin (q.v.) in vol. xiv of a series entitled *Master works of Canadian authors* (Toronto, the Radisson Society, 1926).

[A. Ermatinger Fraser, *A poet-pioneer of Canada* (Queen's quarterly, 1928); Norman Shrive, *Charles Mair* (Toronto, 1965); *Can. who was who*, vol. 1; *Proc. Roy. Soc. Can.*, 1928; Morgan, *Can. men* (1912); Rose, *Cyc. Can. biog.* (1886); G. T. Denison, *The struggle for imperial unity* (Toronto, 1909).]

Maisonneuve, Paul de Chomedey, Sieur de (1612-1676), founder and first governor of Montreal (1642-65), was born in February, 1612, at Neuville-sur-Vanne, Aube, France. He saw much service in European wars before he was appointed first governor of Montreal by the Société de Notre-Dame de Montréal, which had obtained a grant of the Island of Montreal from Lauzon (q.v.) and the Company of New France. He sailed from La Rochelle in 1641, with a company of soldiers and artisans, and arrived at Quebec on August 20. The winter he spent at Sillery, and on May 18, 1642, he landed on the Island of Montreal, and laid the foundations of the future city of Montreal. He was governor of Montreal for twenty-two years; but in 1665 he was removed from office by Tracy (q.v.), and he returned to France. He died in obscurity in Paris on September 9, 1676.

[P. G. Roy, *Les gouverneurs de Montréal* (Bull. rech. hist., 1905); E.-Z. Massicotte, *Les juges de Montréal sous le régime français* (Bull. rech. hist., 1921); P. G. Roy, *Notes et documents sur le fondateur de Montréal* (Bull. rech. hist., 1916); P. Rousseau, *Histoire de la vie de M. Paul de Chomedey, sieur de Maisonneuve* (Montreal, 1886); H. J. J. B. Chouinard, *Paul de Chomedey, sieur de Maisonneuve* (Quebec, 1882); Le Jeune, *Dict. gén.; Dict. Can. biog.*, vol. 1.]

Maitland, George H. (1881-1965), newspaper editor, was born in Stratford, Ontario, in 1881. He was educated in Stratford schools and joined the *Stratford Herald* as a reporter. After seven years he left for the Toronto *Star*, where he worked as reporter and editor until his retirement in 1954. He crusaded for the public ownership of the Toronto Street Railway and was an early supporter of Ontario Hydro. Under his guidance the *Star* grew from a small city paper to one of Canada's largest dailies. He died at Toronto, Ontario, June 22, 1965.

[Toronto *Star*, June 23, 1965; *Can. who's who*, 1955-57.]

Maitland, Sir Peregrine (1777-1854), lieutenant-governor of Upper Canada (1818-28) and of Nova Scotia (1828-32), was born at Long Parish, Hants, England, in 1777, the son of Thomas Maitland, of Shrubs Hall, in the New Forest. He entered the British army in 1792 as an ensign in the Foot Guards, and he served throughout the Revolutionary and Napoleonic wars. At the battle of Waterloo he commanded the First Brigade of the First Division; and in 1815 he was created a K.C.B. In 1818 he was appointed lieutenant-governor of Upper Canada, and he retained this post for ten years. A man of high character, he was at the same time seized with the narrow and reactionary ideas of his day; and his régime was marked by a persecution of the Reformers in the province which occasionally descended to pettiness. He was removed from office in 1828; but was compensated with an appointment as lieutenant-governor of Nova Scotia. He retired from this post in 1832; and in 1836 he was appointed commander-in-chief of the Madras army, and in 1843 governor and commander-in-chief at the Cape of Good Hope. In 1843 he attained the rank of general, and in 1853 he was created a G.C.B. He died at London, England, on May 30, 1854. He was twice married, (1) in 1803 to the Hon. Louisa (d. 1805), daughter of Sir Edward Crofton, Bart., and Anne, Baroness Crofton, and (2) in 1815 to Lady Sarah Lennox, daughter of Charles, fourth Duke of Richmond and Lennox (q.v.).

[D. B. Read, *The lieutenant-governors of Upper Canada* (Toronto, 1900); *Dict. nat. biog.*; Morgan, *Cel. Can.*; J. C. Dent, *The Upper Canadian rebellion* (2 vols., Toronto, 1885); W. S. Wallace, *The family compact* (Toronto, 1915).]

Malartic, Anne Joseph Hippolyte de Maurès, Comte de (1730-1800), soldier, was born at Montauban, France, in 1730. He entered the army, and saw service in Flanders and Italy. In 1755 he was sent to Canada, and he served under Dieskau (q.v.) and Montcalm (q.v.) throughout the Seven Years' War. He was one of Montcalm's *aides-de-camp* at the battle of the Plains of Abraham. After the conquest of Canada he returned to France, and he rose to the rank of lieutenant-general in the French army. He died in France on July 28, 1800. His *Journal des campagnes au Canada* was published by the Comte Gabriel de Maurès de Malartic and P. Gaffarel (Dijon, 1890).

[*Bull. rech. hist.*, 1899; Le Jeune, *Dict. gén.*]

Malcolm, Sir James (1767-1850), soldier, was born in 1767. He entered the Royal Marines at the age of thirteen, and saw nearly half a century of service. He served in America during the last stages of the Revolution and during the the War of 1812. In 1814 he distinguished himself at the storming of Fort Oswego; and for his services on this occasion he was mentioned in the *Gazette* of July 5, 1814, and was created a K.C.B. in 1815. He died at his home, Minholm, Dumfriesshire, Scotland, on January 17, 1850.

[*Annual register*, 1850.]

Malcolm, James (1880-1935), minister of trade and commerce for Canada (1926-30), was born at Kincardine, Ontario, on July 14, 1880. He was educated at Upper Canada College, Toronto; and entered his father's furniture-manufacturing business, of which he later became president. He represented North Bruce in the Canadian House of Commons from 1921 to 1935; and he was minister of trade and commerce in the Mackenzie King government from 1926 to 1930. He died at Kincardine on December 6, 1935.

[*Can. parl. comp.*]

Malhiot, François Victor (1776-1840), fur-trader, was born in 1776, and entered the service of the North West Company as a clerk about 1791. He was a cousin of Jacques Porlier (q.v.). From 1796 to 1804 he was in the Upper Red River department; and from 1804 to 1807 he was in charge of a post at Lac aux Flambeaux. His journal for 1804-05 has been printed in the *Wisconsin Historical Collections*, xix, 1910. In 1807 he retired from the fur-trade, and settled at Contrecoeur, Lower Canada, with his half-breed son. Here he died in 1840. D. W. Harmon (q.v.) describes his marriage to an Indian woman on August 8, 1800, at Fort Alexandria.

[A. G. Morice, *Dictionnaire historique des canadiens ... de l'ouest* (Kamloops, B.C., 1908).]

Malhiot, Henri Gédéon (1837-1909), jurist, was born at St. Pierre-les-Becquets,

Lower Canada, on March 6, 1837. He was educated at Nicolet and Chambly, Lower Canada, and was called to the bar of Lower Canada in 1858. He practised law at Three Rivers; and from 1871 to 1876 he represented Three Rivers in the Legislative Assembly of Quebec. From 1874 to 1876 he was minister of crown lands in the Boucherville administration. In 1888 he was appointed a judge of the Superior Court for the district of Ottawa; and he retired from the bench in 1897. He died at St. Pierre-les-Becquets, Quebec, on October 21, 1909.

[P. G. Roy, *Les juges de la province de Québec* (Quebec, 1933).]

Mallet, Mère Marie Anne Marcelle (1805-1871), founder of the Institute of the Sisters of Charity of Quebec, was born near Montreal, Lower Canada, on March 26, 1805. She entered the Hôpital Général at Montreal as a novice in 1824, and she took the veil in 1826. In 1849 she founded at Quebec the Institute of the Sisters of Charity; and she became the first superior of this Institute. She died at Quebec on April 9, 1871.

[*Une fondatrice et son oeuvre: Mère Mallet* (Quebec, 1939); *Dict. Can. biog.*, vol. 10.]

Malloch, Archibald (1887-1953), physician and author, was born in Hamilton, Ontario, on August 10, 1887, and died at White Plains, New York, on September 18, 1953. He was educated at Queen's University (B.A., 1908) and McGill University (M.D., C.M., 1913), and did post-graduate work in medicine in London. He practised medicine in Montreal for some years, and occupied various positions on the teaching staff at McGill. In 1926, however, for reasons of health, he accepted the position of librarian of the New York Academy of Medicine; and this post he held until shortly before his death. He was the author of *Finch and Baines, a seventeenth century friendship* (New York, 1917), *William Harvey* (New York, 1929), and *Short years: The life and letters of John Bruce MacCallum* (Chicago, 1938).

[*Can. who's who*, 1949-51; *New York Times*, Sept. 20, 1953.]

Mallory, Benajah (*fl.* 1798-1814), traitor, was an American settler who came to Upper Canada prior to 1798, and obtained grants amounting to 1,400 acres in and about Burford, Oxford county, Upper Canada. In 1798 he was commissioned captain of the Burford militia; and from 1805 to 1812 he represented Oxford county in the Legislative Assembly of Upper Canada. In 1813 he went over to the Americans, and became second-in-command of the "Canadian Volunteers", commanded by Joseph Willcocks (q.v.). After the death of Willcocks in 1814, he succeeded to the command of this corps; but was soon relieved of his command. His subsequent career does not appear to be known.

[W. R. Riddell, *Benajah Mallory, traitor*

(Ont. Hist. Soc., papers and records, 1930); R. C. Muir, *The early political and military history of Burford* (Quebec, 1913).]

Mance, Jeanne (1606-1673), foundress of the Hôtel-Dieu at Montreal, was born at Langres in Champagne, France, in 1606. In 1641 she came to Canada with Maisonneuve (q.v.), and in 1642 she founded at Montreal the Hôtel-Dieu. Here she spent the rest of her life, and here she died in 1673.

[J. K. Foran, *Jeanne Mance* (Montreal, 1931); P. Benoit, *La vie inspirée de Jeanne Mance* (Montreal, 1934); Abbé E. M. Faillon, *Vie de Mademoiselle Mance* (2 vols., Paris, 1854); Abbé Rambouillet, *Vie de Jeanne Mance* (Langres, 1877); A. LeBlond de Brumath, *Vie de Mademoiselle Mance* (Montreal, 1883); Le Jeune, *Dict. gén.*; *Dict. Can. biog.*, vol. 1.]

Manigault, Gabriel (1809-1888), author, was born in Charleston, South Carolina, in 1809. After the American Civil War, he removed with his family to London, Ontario; and while living in London, he wrote and published three books: a novel entitled *Saint Cecilia* (Philadelphia, 1871), *The United States unmasked* (London, 1879), and *A political creed* (New York, 1884). He died in London, Ontario, on January 20, 1888.

[Private information.]

Manion, Robert James (1881-1943), minister of railways and canals for Canada (1930-35), was born at Pembroke, Ontario, on November 19, 1881. He was educated at Trinity University, Toronto (M.D., C.M., 1904), and practised medicine at Fort William, Ontario. He served as a medical officer in the Canadian Expeditionary Force in the First World War, and in 1917 was awarded the military cross for gallantry at Vimy Ridge. He represented Fort William in the Canadian House of Commons from 1917 to 1935; and he was minister of soldiers' civil re-establishment in the first Meighen administration in 1921, postmaster-general in the second Meighen administration in 1926, and minister of railways and canals in the Bennett administration of 1930-35. In 1933 he was the head of the Canadian delegation to the League of Nations at Geneva. In 1938 he was elected leader of the National Conservative party at a convention held in Toronto; but he and his party were defeated in the general elections of 1940. He died at Ottawa, Ontario, on July 2, 1943. In 1906 he married Yvonne, daughter of D. L. Desaulniers; and by her he had three sons. He was the author of two books of an autobiographical character, *A surgeon in arms* (New York, 1918) and *Life is an adventure* (Toronto, 1936).

[*Can. who's who*, 1938-39; *Can. parl. comp.*]

555

Manly, Charles Macdonald (1855-1924), painter, was born at Englefield Green, Surrey, England, in 1855, the son of the Rev. John G. Manly (q.v.). He came to Canada with his parents at an early age, and was educated in Canada. He studied painting in Toronto, in London, England, and in Dublin, Ireland. In 1902 he was elected an associate of the Royal Canadian Academy of Arts, and from 1903 to 1905 he was president of the Ontario Society of Artists. He painted both landscapes and figures, in oils and water-colours. He died in Toronto on April 4, 1924.

[Morgan, *Can. men* (1912); N. MacTavish, *The fine arts in Canada* (Toronto, 1925).]

Manly, John G. (1814-1908), clergyman and author, was born in 1814, and became in 1834 a Methodist preacher in Upper Canada. He served in various places in Canada, Jamaica, England, and Ireland; and he died at Toronto, Ontario, in 1908. He was the author of *The nature, origin, progress, present state, and character of Wesleyan Methodism* (Kingston, 1840), *Canada: Its geography, scenery, produce, population, institutions, and condition* (London and Dublin, 1860), and *The religion of life; or, Christ and Nicodemus* (Toronto, 1875).

[G. H. Cornish (ed.), *A cyclopaedia of Methodism in Canada* (2 vols., Toronto, 1881-1903).]

Mann, Sir Donald (1853-1934), railway-builder, was born at Acton, Ontario, on March 23, 1853, the son of Hugh Mann and Helen Macdonell. He became in 1880 a railway contractor; and he became the associate of Sir William Mackenzie (q.v.) in the building of the Canadian Northern Railway system. After the purchase of the Canadian Northern Railway by the Canadian government in 1917-23, he retired to private life; and he died at Toronto, Ontario, on November 10, 1934. In 1887 he married, in Winnipeg, Jennie E. Williams; and by her he had one son. He was created a knight bachelor in 1911.

[T.D. Regehr, *The Canadian Northern Railway* (Toronto, 1976); *Who was who*, 1929-40; *Can. who was who*, vol. 2.]

Mann, Gother (1747-1830), military engineer, was born at Plumstead, Kent, England, on December 21, 1747, and was educated at the Woolwich Military Academy. He entered the British army as an ensign in 1763, and became a general in 1821. From 1785 to 1791 and from 1794 to 1804 he was in command of the Royal Engineers in Canada; and he made many reports on, and plans for, the improvement of the fortifications and lines of communication in Canada. Especially note-worthy was his report on the Cascades and the Mill Rapid Cascades on the St. Lawrence, made in 1800. Most of the works he recommended were carried out, and completed by 1805. He was

inspector-general of fortifications in England from 1811 to his death on March 27, 1830. In 1767 he married Ann, second daughter of Peter Wade, of Eythorne, Kent, England; and by her he had five sons and three daughters. Many of his plans and reports are preserved in the British Museum and the Public Archives of Canada.

[*Dict. nat. biog.*; A. Shortt and A. G. Doughty (eds.), *Canada and its provinces* (23 vols., Toronto, 1914).]

Manners-Sutton, Sir John Henry Thomas, afterwards third **Viscount Canterbury** (1814-1877), lieutenant-governor of New Brunswick (1854-61), was born in London on May 27, 1814, the son of Charles Manners-Sutton, first Viscount Canterbury, by his first wife Lucy Maria Charlotte, daughter of John Denison. He was educated at Eton and Cambridge (M.A., 1835), and he studied law, but was never called to the bar. He was from 1841 to 1847 member for Cambridge in the British House of Commons, and on July 1, 1854, was appointed lieutenant-governor of New Brunswick. He arrived in New Brunswick at a time of political crisis, when there was a great cry for reform; and it was during his term of office that responsible government was firmly established in New Brunswick. He returned to England in October, 1861, and was appointed governor of Trinidad (1864), and then governor of Victoria (1866). On the death of his brother he took his seat in the House of Lords as Viscount Canterbury in 1873. He died in London on June 24, 1877. He married, on July 5, 1838, Georgina, daughter of Charles Thompson of Norfolk; and by her he had five sons and two daughters.

[*Dict. nat. biog.*; J. Hannay, *History of New Brunswick* (Saint John, N.B., 1909); *Dict. Can. biog.*, vol. 10.]

Manning, James Harold (1897-1924), poet, was born at Saint John, New Brunswick, on February 15, 1897. He was educated at Acadia University (B.A., 1919), and at Harvard University. He entered the employ of the Standard Oil Company; and died at Maturin, Venezuela, on October 27, 1924. He edited the *Poems* of his brother, Frederick Charles Manning, who was killed on active service in France on April 14, 1917; and after his own death his own verses were published, under the title *Courcelette and other poems* (Saint John, N.B., 1925).

[*Records of the graduates of Acadia University* (Wolfville, N.S., 1926).]

Manseau, Joseph Amable (1837-1887), educationist, was born at St. Polycarpe de Soulanges, Lower Canada, on September 6, 1837. He became a teacher of stenography in Montreal; and he died at Montreal on October 31, 1887. He was the author of *Phonography made easy* (Montreal, 1878) and *Dictionnaire* *des locutions vicieuses du Canada* (Quebec, 1881).

[*Bull. rech. hist.*, 1929.]

Manson, Donald (1796-1880), fur-trader, was born in Thurso, Caithness, Scotland, in 1796; and entered the service of the Hudson's Bay Company in 1817. He was employed at first in the English River district and on the South Saskatchewan; but in 1827 he was transferred to the Columbia district, and he remained on the western side of the Rocky Mountains until his retirement in 1858. He was promoted to the rank of chief trader in 1837, and from 1844 to 1857 he was in charge of the New Caledonia district, with headquarters at Stuart Lake. He died on January 7, 1880, at Champoeg, Oregon.

[E. E. Rich (ed.), *Journal of occurrences in the Athabasca department, by George Simpson* (Toronto: The Champlain Society, 1938); *Dic. Can. biog.*, vol. 10.]

Manson, Jane Sproule (1878-1961), physician, was born in Britton in Perth county, Ontario, August 29, 1878. She was educated at the University of Toronto (M.B., 1907). After teaching school for several years she returned to the Toronto General Hospital, and studied in London, Vienna, and Berlin. She became the first Canadian woman to sit for the primary examinations of the Royal College in London, was admitted to the Royal College of Surgeons, and became Licentiate of the Royal College of Physicians, London, in 1911. Dr. Manson returned to practise otolaryngology in Toronto, and was appointed to the staff of the University of Toronto in 1912. She served during the First World War in London. She became chief of the nose, throat, and ear department, Women's College Hospital, Toronto, in 1924.

[*Can. who's who*, 1955-57.]

Marchand, Félix Gabriel (1832-1900), prime minister of Quebec (1897-1900), was born at St. John's, Lower Canada, on January 9, 1832, the son of Gabriel Marchand, a merchant, and Mary McNider. He was educated at the college of St. Hyacinthe, and was admitted a notary public in 1855. From 1867 to 1900 he represented St. John's in the Legislative Assembly of Quebec. He was a member of the Joly administration in Quebec from 1878 to 1879, holding successively the portfolios of provincial secretary and commissioner of crown lands; and he was prime minister and provincial treasurer of Quebec from 1897 to 1900. He was hardly less notable as a journalist and *littérateur* than as a politician. In 1860 he founded, with Charles Laberge (q.v.), *Le Franco-Canadien* at St. John's, and in 1883 he became editor-in-chief of *Le Temps* of Montreal. In 1882 he was selected as a charter member of the Royal Society of Canada, and in 1897 he was its president. In his earlier days

he wrote poetry, much of which appeared in the *Ruche littéraire et politique* (1853-54), in the *Foyer canadien*, and in the *Revue canadienne*. Later, he turned to the writing of comedies, *Fatenville* (Revue canadienne, 1869), *Erreur n'est pas compte* (Montreal, 1872), *Un bonheur en attire un autre* (Montreal, 1884), and *Les faux brillants* (Montreal, 1885). He published also *Manuel et formulaire général et complet du notariat de la province de Québec* (Montreal, 1892). He died at St. Johns, Quebec, on September 16, 1900. In 1854 he married Marie Herselie, daughter of Louis Turgeon of Terrebonne, and by her he had eleven children. In 1891 he was made an LL.D. of Laval University.

[*Dict. nat. biog.*; *Proc. Roy. Soc. Can.*, 1901; Morgan, *Can. men* (1898); Bibaud, *Panth. can.*; Le Jeune, *Dict. gén.*; Rose, *Cyc. can. biog.* (1886); *Canadian biographical dictionary*, Quebec vol. (Chicago, 1881); E. Lareau, *Histoire de la littérature canadienne* (Montreal, 1873).]

Marcoux, Joseph (1791-1855), priest and linguist, was born on March 16, 1791, the son of Joseph Marcoux and Marie Vallière. He was for forty years a Roman Catholic missionary among the Iroquois of the Sault St. Louis. He published an Iroquois grammar and dictionary, and several books of edification in the Iroquois language. The *Lettres de feu M. Jos. Marcoux* were published posthumously (Montreal, 1869). He died on May 29, 1855.

[Allaire, *Dict. biog.*; Le Jeune, *Dict. gén*; *Bull. rech. hist.*, 1919.]

Maricourt, Paul le Moyne, Sieur de (1663-1704), soldier, was born in 1663, the fourth son of Charles Le Moyne, Sieur de Longueuil (q.v.), and Catherine Thierry Primot. In 1686 he accompanied Troyes (q.v.) and his brother Iberville (q.v.) on their expedition against the English forts on Hudson Bay, and, for his performance on the expedition, he was promoted to second lieutenant of the troops. He took part in the capture of the *Hampshire* on the bay in 1689, and in the following year led a party of *voyageurs* to Quebec to aid in the defence of the city. In 1694 he again accompanied Iberville to Hudson Bay, and took part in the taking of Fort Nelson. In 1701 he negotiated an important treaty with the Iroquois; and he died at Montreal on March 21, 1704. He married, first, Marie-Madeleine Dupont, and, second, Françoise Aubert.

[Charles B. Reed, *The first great Canadian* (Chicago, 1910); Agnes C. Laut, *The conquest of the great north west* (2 vols., Chicago, 1908); A. Jodoin and J. L. Vincent, *Histoire de Longueuil* (Montreal, 1889); Le Jeune, *Dict. gén.*; *Dict. Can. biog.*, vol. 2.]

Marie-Anne, Mère (1809-1890), founder of the Sisters of Ste. Anne de Lachine, was born at Terrebonne, Lower Canada, on April 18,

1809, the daughter of Jean Baptiste Sureau dit Blondin; and was christened Marie Esther. She became a school-teacher; and in 1849 she founded a house of teaching nuns, and took the name of Mère Marie-Anne. The mother-house of the order was opened first at Ste. Geneviève; but after several removals it was in 1864 fixed at Lachine. Mère Marie-Anne died at Lachine, Quebec, on January 2, 1890.

[F. Langevin, *Mère Marie-Anne* (Montreal, 1935); E. J. Auclair, *Histoire des soeurs de Sainte-Anne* (Montreal, 1922); Le Jeune, *Dict. gén.*]

Marie de l'Incarnation (1599-1672), first superior of the Ursuline convent at Quebec, was born at Tours, France, on October 28, 1599. At the age of seventeen, she was married to Claude Martin, a silk manufacturer of Tours; but her husband died in 1619, leaving her with an infant son, to whose education she devoted herself for twelve years. In 1632 she entered the Ursuline convent at Tours; and in 1639 she accompanied Madame de la Peltrie to Canada to found an Ursuline convent at Quebec. Of this convent she became the first superior, and she retained the position until her death on April 30, 1672. Her *Lettres spirituelles et historiques*, written to her son Claude, were collected and published by him in 1681 (2nd ed., 2 vols., Paris, 1876; 3rd ed., by Dom Albert Jamet, 3 vols., Paris, 1929-36), and form a valuable source for the history of the period. She also composed a catechism in Huron, three catechisms in Algonkian, and a dictionary of French and Algonkian. She received beatification by papal decree in 1877.

[C. Martin, *Histoire de la Vénérable Mère Marie de l'Incarnation* (2 vols., Paris, 1892); *Marie de l'Incarnation,* by an Ursuline nun of Quebec (Quebec, 1935); A. Repplier, *Mère Marie de l'Incarnation* (New York, 1931); G. Robitaille, *Telle qu'elle fut: Études critiques sur Marie de l'Incarnation* (Montreal, 1939); *Dict. Can. biog.*, vol. 1.]

Marie-Rose, Mère (1811-1849), founder in Canada of the Congregation of Sisters of the Holy Names of Jesus and of Mary, was born at St. Antoine sur Richelieu, Lower Canada, on October 6, 1811, the daughter of Olivier Durocher, and was christened Eulalie. In 1844 she founded, and became the first mother superior of, the Congregation of Sisters of the Holy Names of Jesus and of Mary, at Longueuil, near Montreal; and at the same time she took the name in religion of "Marie-Rose". "I am called Marie-Rose," she said. "May I be a rose of agreeable odour to Jesus Christ!" She died at Longueuil on October 6, 1849.

[R. P. Duchaussois, *Rose du Canada* (Montreal, 1931); R. P. Archambault, *Sur les pas de Marthe et de Marie* (Montreal, 1929); Le Jeune, *Dict. gén.*]

Marie-Victorin, Frère (1885-1944), priest and botanist, was born at Kingsey Falls, Quebec, on April 3, 1885, the son of Cyrille Kirouac, and was christened Conrad Kirouac. He was educated at the University of Montreal (D.Sc., 1922), and he entered the Order of the Christian Brothers, taking the name in religion of Marie-Victorin. He became director of the Botanical Institute in the University of Montreal, and one of the most distinguished scientists in Canada. In 1924 he was elected a fellow of the Royal Society of Canada; and in 1933 he was elected president of Section Five of the Royal Society of Canada. He died near St. Hyacinthe, Quebec, on July 15, 1944. A voluminous writer, he was the author of *Croquis laurentiens* (Montreal, 1920), *Les filicinées de Québec* (Montreal, 1923), *Etudes floristiques sur la région du lac Saint-Jean* (Montreal, 1925), *Les équisétinées du Québec* (Montreal, 1927), *Le dynamisme dans la flore de Québec* (Montreal, 1929), *Flore laurentienne* (Montreal, 1935), and *Histoire de l'Institut botanique de l'Université de Montréal* (Montreal, 1941).

[L. P. Audet, *Le Frère Marie-Victorin* (Quebec, 1942); M. Gauvreau, *Le président de l'ACFAS* (Montreal, 1938), *Proc. Roy. Soc. Can.*, 1945; *Can. who's who*, 1936-37.]

Markland, George Herchmer or **Herkimer** (1790?-1862), executive and legislative councillor and inspector-general of Upper Canada, was born in Kingston, Upper Canada, about 1790, the son of Thomas Markland. He was educated under John Strachan (q.v.), and in 1810 was described as "a good, indeed an excellent young man" who wished to study for the ministry. He did not take holy orders; but he became a protégé of Strachan, and in 1820 was appointed a member of the Legislative Council of the province. In 1822 he was commissioned an honorary member of the Executive Council, and in 1827 a regular member. In 1828 he was appointed registrar of King's College, and in 1833 he became inspector-general of Upper Canada. In 1838 charges were made against him that his habits were "derogatory to his character as a public officer". He had already resigned, with his colleagues, from the Executive Council in 1836; now he resigned the inspector-generalship, and he ceased to attend the meetings of the Legislative Council. In 1841 defalcations were discovered in his accounts; and he was held responsible. He returned to Kingston; and he was buried there on May 19, 1862.

[W. S. Wallace, *A history of the University of Toronto* (Toronto, 1927).]

Marler, Sir Herbert Meredith (1876-1940), diplomat, was born at Montreal, Quebec, on March 7, 1876, the son of William de Montmollin Marler. He was educated at McGill University (B.C.L., 1898), was called to the bar, and for many years practised law in

Montreal in association with his father. From 1921 to 1925 he represented the St. Lawrence-St. George constituency in the Canadian House of Commons; and in September, 1925, he was sworn of the Privy Council for Canada and appointed minister without portfolio in the Mackenzie King administration, but on his defeat in the general elections of 1925, he resigned from the cabinet. He was appointed the first envoy extraordinary and minister plenipotentiary from Canada to Japan; and he represented Canada at Tokyo from 1929 to 1936. In 1936 he was appointed Canadian minister at Washington. He died at Montreal, Quebec, on January 31, 1940. In 1932 he was made an honorary LL.D. of the University of British Columbia; and in 1935 he was created, in recognition of his services in Japan, a K.C.M.G.

[*Who was who*, 1929-40; *Can. who's who*, 1938-39; *Can. parl. comp.*]

Marling, Alexander (1832-1890), educationist, was born at Ebley, Gloucestershire, England, on April 11, 1832. He came to Canada with his parents in 1842, and was educated at Upper Canada College, Toronto, and at the University of Toronto (LL.B., 1862). He became a clerk in the department of education, under Egerton Ryerson (q.v.), in 1854, and he rose until he became first secretary of the department, and then deputy minister. He died at Toronto, Ontario, on April 12, 1890. He was the author of *A brief history of public and high school text-books authorized for the province of Ontario* (Toronto, 1890).

[Rose, *Cyc. Can. biog.* (1886).]

Marmette, Joseph Etienne Eugène (1844-1895), author, was born at St. Thomas de Montmagny, Lower Canada, on October 25, 1844, the son of Dr. Joseph Marmette and Claire Geneviève Elizabeth, daughter of Sir Etienne P. Taché (q.v.). He was educated at Laval University, and entered the Canadian civil service as a clerk in the Treasury department. In 1883 he was attached to the Public Archives of Canada, and in his later years he spent much time in France making researches into the materials relating to Canadian history contained in the French archives. He died at Ottawa on May 7, 1895. In 1868 he married Marie Esther Josephine, daughter of François-Xavier Garneau (q.v.); and by her he had four children. He was the author of the following novels: *Charles et Eva* (Revue canadienne, 1866), *François de Bienville* (Quebec, 1870), *L'intendant Bigot* (Montreal, 1872), *Le chevalier de Mornac* (Montreal, 1873), *La fiancée du rebelle* (Revue canadienne, 1875), *Le tomahawk et l'épée* (Quebec, 1877), and *A travers la vie* (Revue nationale, 1895). He was also the author of *Les Machabées de la Nouvelle-France* (Quebec, 1878), *Héroisme et trahison* (Quebec, 1878), and *Récits et souvenirs* (Quebec, 1891).

[M. Brodeur, *Joseph Marmette* (Canada français, 1938); O. Maurault, *Joseph Marmette* (Revue trimestrielle canadienne, 1927); R. LeMoine, *Joseph Marmette* (Quebec, 1968); *Cyc. Am. biog.*; Taché, *Men of the day*; P. G. Roy, *La famille Taché* (Lévis, Que., 1904); Le Jeune, *Dict. gén.*]

Marquette, Jacques (1637-1675), missionary and explorer, was born at Laon, France, on June 10, 1637. He entered the Jesuit novitiate in 1654 at Nancy; and in 1666 he was sent to Canada as a missionary. In 1669 he replaced Allouez at Chequamegon, in the Ottawa mission; and in 1671 he founded the mission of St. Ignace among the Hurons at Michilimackinac. In 1673 he set out with Louis Jolliet (q.v.) on the voyage of exploration which resulted in the discovery of the Mississippi, and its exploration as far south as the mouth of the Arkansas. In 1674, after his return to Green Bay, he went to found a mission among the Kaskaskia Indians in Illinois, but ill-health compelled him to abandon the project, and he died on his way back to the straits of Mackinac, on May 18, 1675. Just before his death he wrote an account of his expedition to the Mississippi; and this journal has been published in R. G. Thwaites (ed.), *The Jesuit relations* (73 vols., Cleveland, 1898) and in J. G. Shea, *Discovery and exploration of the Mississippi valley* (New York, 1852).

[A. Repplier, *Père Marquette* (Garden City, N.Y., 1929); G. J. Garraghan, *Some hitherto unpublished Marquettiana* (Mid-America, 1936); R.G. Thwaites, *Father Marquette* (New York, 1902); Rev. S. Hedges, *Father Marquette* (New York, 1903); F. B. Steck, *The Jolliet-Marquette expedition* (Glendale, Calif., 1928); J. L. H. Neilson, *Facsimile of Père Marquette's Illinois prayer book* (Quebec, 1908); *Dict. Am. biog.*; *Cyc. Am. biog.*; Le Jeune, *Dict. gén.*; *Dict. Can. biog.*, vol. 1.]

Marquis, Thomas Guthrie (1864-1936), author, was born in Chatham, New Brunswick, on July 4, 1864. He was educated at Queen's University, Kingston (B.A., 1889), and until 1901 was a school-teacher. In the later years of his life he was a free-lance journalist, and occupied various positions in the book-trade. He died in Toronto on April 1, 1936. He was the author of *Marguerite de Roberval: A romance of the days of Jacques Cartier* (Toronto, 1899), *Presidents of the United States* (Philadelphia, 1903), *Canada's sons on kopje and veldt* (Toronto, 1900), *Brock, the hero of Upper Canada* (Toronto, 1912), *The Jesuit missions* (Toronto, 1916), and *The war chief of the Ottawas* (Toronto, 1915). He edited *Builders of Canada from Cartier to Laurier* (Toronto, 1903); and he collaborated with Agnes Maule Machar (q.v.) in *Stories of New France* (Boston, 1890).

[Morgan, *Can. men*; private information.]

Marsden, Joshua (1777-1837), missionary and author, was born near Liverpool, England, in 1777. After serving in the British navy, he became a local Methodist preacher; and in 1800 he was sent to Nova Scotia as a missionary. In 1808 he went to Bermuda, and in 1814 he returned to England. Here he died in 1837. He was the author of *Grace displayed: An interesting narrative of the life, conversion, Christian ministry, and missionary labours of Joshua Marsden* (New York, 1814), *The narrative of a mission to Nova Scotia, New Brunswick, and the Somers islands, with a tour to lake Ontario* (Plymouth Dock, 1816; 2nd ed., 1827), and *The back-slider, a descriptive moral poem, in four books* (Plymouth Dock, 1815).

[R. J. Long, *Nova Scotia authors* (East Orange, N.J., 1918).]

Marsh, Alfred Henry (1851-1909), lawyer and author, was born near Brighton, Ontario, on May 30, 1851. He was educated at the University of Toronto (B.A., 1874), and was called to the bar in 1877 (Q.C., 1889). For some years he was a law partner of Sir John Macdonald (q.v.). He died at Toronto, on September 6, 1909. In 1880 he married Augusta, daughter of the Hon. William Proudfoot. He was the author of a *History of the Court of Chancery and of the rise and development of the doctrines of equity* (Toronto, 1888).

[Morgan, *Can. men* (1898).]

Marsh, Edith Louise (d. 1960), local historian, died at "Peasemarsh Farm", near Clarksburg, Ontario, on July 10, 1960. She was the author of *Where the buffalo roamed* (Toronto, 1908), *Birds of Peasemarsh* (Toronto, 1919), *The story of Canada* (London, 1919), *A history of the County of Grey* (Owen Sound, Ont., 1931), and *With the birds* (Toronto, 1935).

[*Who's who among North American authors*, 1936-39.]

Marshall, John George (1786-1880), judge and author, was born at Country Harbour, Nova Scotia, in 1786. Educated at the Halifax grammar school, he was called to the bar of Nova Scotia in 1810, and he represented Sydney in the Legislative Assembly of Nova Scotia from 1811 to 1823. From 1823 to 1841 he was chief justice of the common pleas in Cape Breton; then, on the abolition of this court, he retired on pension. He died in Halifax, Nova Scotia, on April 7, 1880. A voluminous writer on religious and political subjects, he was the author, among other books and pamphlets, of *A patriotic call to prepare in a season of peace from political danger* (Halifax, 1819), *The justice of the peace, and county and township officer for Nova Scotia* (Halifax, 1837; 2nd ed., 1845), *Impartial view of causes and effects in the present social condition of the United Kingdom* (Halifax, 1851), *The strong drink delusion* (Halifax, 1855), *On the moral condition of British society* (Liverpool, 1857), *Errors reviewed and fallacies exposed* (Halifax, 1859), *Sermons* (Halifax, 1862), *Answers to "Essays and reviews"* (Halifax, 1862), *A full review and exposure of Bishop Colenso's errors* (London, 1863), *A full review of Bishop Colenso's profane fictions and fallacies* (London, 1864), *An examination of the proposed union of the North American provinces* (Halifax, 1865), *Fictions and errors* (Halifax, 1877), *Reflections during a visit to my native place* (Halifax, 1881), and *A brief history of public proceedings and events, legal, parliamentary, and miscellaneous, in the province of Nova Scotia during the earliest years of the present century* (Halifax, 1879). Under the nom-de-plume of "A Nova Scotian" he published *Remarks upon the proposed federation of the provinces* (Halifax, 1864), and *Confederation considered on its merits* (Halifax, 1867).

[*Dom. ann. reg.*, 1880-81; Morgan, *Bib. can.*; R. J. Long, *Nova Scotia authors* (East Orange, N.J., 1918); *Dict. Can. biog.*, vol. 10.]

Marshall, William Edward (1859-1923), poet, was born at Liverpool, Nova Scotia, on April 1, 1859. He was called to the Nova Scotia bar in 1881; and for many years practised law in Bridgewater, Nova Scotia. In 1898 he was appointed registrar of deeds for the district of Lunenburg; and he occupied this position until his death at Bridgewater on May 23, 1923. He was the author of only two small volumes, *A book of verse* (Montreal, 1909) and *Brookfield and other poems* (Montreal, 1919).

[*Can. who was who*, vol. 2; J. W. Garvin (ed.), *Canadian poets* (Toronto, 1926).]

Marsile, Moïse Joseph (1846-1933), priest and poet, was born at Longueuil, Canada East, on November 19, 1846; entered the order of Clerics of St. Viateur; and was ordained a priest in 1875. He spent most of his life in the United States; but he returned for a time to Canada on his retirement. He died at Bourbonnais, near Chicago, Illinois, on March 10, 1933. He was the author of five volumes of verse: *Épines et fleurs* (Bourbonnais, Ill., 1889), *Liola, ou Légende indienne* (Montreal, 1893), *Lévis, ou Abandon de la Nouvelle France* (Montreal, 1903), *Les Laurentiades* (Montreal, 1925), and *Au lond de ma route* (Luçon, 1929).

[Allaire, *Dict. biog.*]

Marten, Humphrey (b. 1729?), fur-trader, was born in England about 1729, and was engaged by the Hudson's Bay Company in 1750 as a "writer". He reached York Factory in the summer of that year; and from 1762 to 1786 he was, with a number of brief intervals, in command at York Factory. It was he who surrendered the fort to La Pérouse, in 1782; and he was then taken a prisoner to France, but returned to Hudson Bay in 1783. In 1787 he severed his connection with the Hudson's Bay Company; and thereafter he passes from view.

[J. B. Tyrrell (ed.), *The journals of Samuel Hearne and Philip Turnor* (Toronto: The Champlain Society, 1934).]

Marter, George Frederick (1840-1907), politician, was born at Brantford, Upper Canada, on June 6, 1840, the eldest son of Dr. Peter Marter and Augusta, daughter of the Hon. Harris Hatch, of St. Andrews, New Brunswick. He was educated at the Brantford grammar school, and went into commerce. Later he removed to Muskoka; and in 1886 he was elected to represent Muskoka in the Legislative Assembly of Ontario. This constituency he represented until 1894, when he was elected for North Toronto; and from 1894 to 1896 he was leader of the Conservative opposition in the Assembly. He retired from the Assembly in 1902, having been defeated as an independent candidate; and he died at Toronto on May 10, 1907. In 1862, he married Mary A. Green, of Windham, Ontario.

[*Can. parl. comp.*; Morgan, *Can. men* (1898).]

Martin, Abraham (1589-1664), nicknamed "L'Ecossais" (the Scot), was born in 1589 in France. He came to Canada about 1620, and for many years was an *engagé* of the Company of One Hundred Associates, who granted him the lands, on the heights of Quebec, afterwards known as the Plains of Abraham. He was one of the few French settlers who remained in Quebec after its surrender to the English in 1628. In 1647 he is mentioned as a "royal pilot". He died in Quebec on September 8, 1664. He married in 1613, before coming to Canada, Marguerite Langlois, by whom he had numerous children.

[P. G. R., *Abraham Martin dit l'Ecossais et les plaines d'Abraham* (Bull. rech. hist., 1928); J. M. Le Moine, *The Scot in New France* (Quebec, 1880); R. G. Thwaites (ed.), *The Jesuit relations*, vol. 32 (Cleveland, Ohio, 1900); W. Wood, *The fight for Canada* (London, 1904); *Dict. Can. biog.*, vol. 1.]

Martin, Archer (1865-1941), jurist, was born in Hamilton, Canada West, on May 6, 1865. He was educated at Trinity College School, Port Hope, Ontario; and he was called to the bar of Manitoba in 1887 and of British Columbia in 1894. He was appointed a judge of the Supreme Court of British Columbia in 1898, a judge in admiralty in 1902, and a judge of the Appeal Court of British Columbia in 1909. He died at Victoria, British Columbia, on September 1, 1941. He was the author of *The Hudson's Bay Company's land tenures* (London, 1898).

[*Can. who's who*, 1936-37; Morgan *Can. men* (1912).]

Martin, Chester (1882-1958), historian, was born in Kings county, Nova Scotia, on June 22, 1882, and died at Toronto, Ontario, on April 2, 1958. He was educated at the University of New Brunswick (B.A., 1902) and Balliol College, Oxford (M.A., 1907), which he entered as the first Rhodes scholar from North America. After working for some time in the Public Archives at Ottawa, he was appointed professor of modern history at the University of Manitoba in 1909; and in 1929 he became head of the department of history at the University of Toronto, a position he held for twenty-three years, until his retirement in 1952. He was elected a fellow of the Royal Society of Canada in 1920, and was president of the Canadian Historical Association in 1928. He was the author of *Lord Selkirk's work in Canada* (Oxford, 1916), *The natural resources question* (Winnipeg, 1920), *Empire and commonwealth* (Oxford, 1929), *"Dominion land" policy* (Toronto, 1938), and *Foundations of Canadian nationhood* (Toronto, 1955); he was editor of *Canada in peace and war* (London, 1941), and joint editor, with A. G. Doughty (q.v.), of *The Kelsey papers* (Ottawa, 1929).

[*Proc. Roy. Soc. Can.*, 1958; *Can. who's who*, 1955-57; *Encyc. Can.*]

Martin, Clara Brett (d. 1923), the first woman lawyer in Canada, was born in Toronto, and was educated at Trinity University (B.A., 1890; B.C.L., 1897). She was called to the bar in 1897, and was the first woman in Canada to be admitted to practise law. For several years she was a member of the Board of Education in Toronto. She died in Toronto on October 30, 1923.

[Morgan, *Can. men and women* (1912); *Canadian law times*, 1923.]

Martin, George (1822-1900), poet, was born at Kilrae, county Derry, Ireland, in 1822, the son of James Martin. He came to Canada in 1832, and was educated at the Black River Literary Institute, Watertown, New York. In 1835 he settled in Montreal, where he followed the business of photography. He was a friend of Charles Heavysege (q.v.), and in 1887 he published a volume of verse, *Marguerite, and other poems* (Montreal). He died in Montreal in 1900.

[Morgan, *Can. men* (1898); *Can. who was who*, vol. 2; A. MacMurchy, *Handbook of Canadian literature* (Toronto, 1906).]

Martin, Horace Tassie (1859-1905?), author, was born in Montreal, Canada East, on May 30, 1859. He was educated in Montreal, and became a partner in the firm of John Martin, Sons & Co., military outfitters, Montreal. He was interested in zoology; and he was the author of *Castorologia; or, The history and traditions of the Canadian beaver* (Montreal, 1892). He died about 1905.

[Morgan, *Can. men* (1898).]

Martin, John Patrick (1886-1969), writer, was born in 1886 and taught school in

Dartmouth, Nova Scotia, where he compiled a history of the town. He was appointed town historian in 1957 and published *The Story of Dartmouth* the same year. He died at Dartmouth, May 11, 1969.

[*Atlantic Advocate,* May, 1957.]

Martin, Joseph (1852-1923), prime minister of British Columbia (1900), was born in Milton, Canada West, on September 24, 1852, the son of Edward Martin and Mary Ann Fleming. He was educated at the Toronto Normal School and at the University of Toronto; and in early life was a school-teacher. In 1882 he was called to the bar in Manitoba, and in 1897 in British Columbia (Q.C., 1899). He practised law in Portage la Prairie and in Winnipeg; and from 1883 to 1892 he represented Portage la Prairie in the Legislative Assembly of Manitoba. From 1888 to 1891 he was attorney-general in the Greenway administration, and he fathered the measure abolishing separate schools in Manitoba. From 1893 to 1896 he represented Winnipeg in the Canadian House of Commons; but was defeated in the general elections of 1896. From 1897 to 1908 he practised law in Vancouver; and from 1898 to 1903 he represented Vancouver in the Legislative Assembly of British Columbia. From 1898 to 1899 he was attorney-general in the Semlin administration, and in 1900 he was for a short time prime minister of British Columbia. In 1908 he went to England, and from 1910 to 1918, he represented East St. Pancras in the British House of Commons. He died at Vancouver, British Columbia, on March 2, 1923. In 1881 he married Eliza, daughter of Edward Reilly, Richmond, Ontario, and widow of George W. Eaton, Ottawa, Ontario.

[*Who was who,*1916-28; *Can. parl. comp.*; Morgan, *Can. men* (1912); J. P. Robertson, *Political manual of Manitoba* (Winnipeg, 1887).]

Martin, Mungo (1879-1962), carver, was born at Fort Rupert on Vancouver Island in 1879. He was trained as an artist by Yakotglasami, a famous carver of the Kwakiutl Indians and by his stepfather, Charlie James. His first totem pole, commissioned for a potlatch at Alert Bay, now stands on the campus of the University of British Columbia. Martin supported himself by his painting and carving during the early years of the twentieth century, but as the life of the Indians changed, totems and other artifacts lost their appeal. For many years he earned his livelihood as a fisherman. In 1947 under the direction of Professor Hunter Lewis, Martin came to the University of British Columbia to restore some recently purchased totem poles. He then went on to design and carve new totem poles using traditional tools and to add to the knowledge of Kwakiutl Indians by producing masks, paintings, and utensils in the old style. He spent the

last years of his life working at the Provincial Museum, Victoria. He died at Victoria on August 16, 1962. Examples of his painting are reproduced in *The Beaver* (Summer, 1964).

[*The Beaver*, March, 1952; *Canadian art*, Spring, 1955; *The Beaver*, Summer, 1964.]

Martin, Thomas Mower (1838-1934), painter, was born in London, England, on October 5, 1838, the son of Edward H. Martin, of the Inner Temple. He came to Canada in 1862, and settled in Toronto. He became one of the founders of the Royal Canadian Academy and the Ontario Society of Artists; and he was well-known for his Canadian landscapes. He died at Toronto on March 16, 1934. Seventy-seven of his landscapes were reproduced in colour in T. Mower Martin and W. W. Campbell, *Canada* (London, 1907).

[N. MacTavish, *The fine arts in Canada* (Toronto, 1925); H. G. Jones and E. Dyonnet, *History of the Royal Canadian Academy of Arts* (Montreal, 1934); Morgan, *Can. men* (1912).]

Martin, William Melville (1876-1970), judge, was born in Norwich, Ontario, August 23, 1876. He was educated at Clinton Collegiate Institute and at the University of Toronto (B.A., 1898). He read law with Robinette and Godfrey in Toronto and was called to the bar in Saskatchewan in 1904. He practised law in Regina until 1916. He had been elected a member of the House of Commons in 1908 and 1911, but resigned in 1916 to become premier of Saskatchewan. He resigned from the legislature in 1922 to become a judge of the Court of Appeal for Saskatchewan. He held this position until he became chief justice of Saskatchewan in 1941, and retired in 1961. He was affectionately known as Saskatchewan's "grand old man". He was active as president of the Canadian Red Cross Society, the Jubilee Cancer Fund, and the Canadian National Institute for the Blind. He died at Saskatoon, Saskatchewan, June 22, 1970.

[*Can. who's who*, 1967-69.]

Martineau, Flavien (1830-1887), priest and poet, was born at Chauché, La Vendée, France, on June 17, 1830; was ordained a priest of the Roman Catholic Church in 1854; and joined the Sulpician order in 1865. He came to Canada in 1865; and was stationed in Montreal, Quebec, until his death on December 14, 1887. After his death his poems were collected and published under the title, *Une voix d'outre-tombe* (Montreal, 1888).

[Allaire, *Dict. biog.*]

Martineau, Marcel (1847-1923), priest and genealogist, was born in Montreal, Canada East, on January 16, 1847; was ordained a priest of the Roman Catholic Church in 1871; and died at Montreal, Quebec, on April 25, 1923. He was the author of *Généalogie de la* *famille Martineau-Lormière* (Montreal, 1902). [Allaire, *Dict. biog.*]

Marty, Aletta Élise (1865-1929), educationist, was born in Mitchell, Ontario, and was educated at Queen's University (B.A., 1893; M.A., 1895; LL.D., 1921). She became a school-teacher, and eventually she was appointed inspector of public schools in Toronto, Ontario, the first woman to occupy such a post. She died at Pretoria, South Africa, on May 10, 1929. She was the author of *The principles and practice of oral reading* (Toronto, 1904) and *An educational creed* (Toronto, 1921); and editor of *Creative young Canada* (Toronto, 1928).

[H. M. Ridley, *Canada's first woman inspector* (Can. mag., 1923); *Can. who's who*, 1910.]

Mascarene, Paul (1684-1760), acting governor of Nova Scotia (1740-49), was born in Castras, in the south of France, in 1684. His father was a Huguenot who was obliged to flee from France, leaving his son in the care of his grandmother. He was educated at Geneva, and afterwards went to England. In 1706 he was gazetted a lieutenant in the British army, and in 1709 he was sent to America to assist in the taking of Port Royal. In 1740 he succeeded Lawrence Armstrong (q.v.) as lieutenant-governor of Annapolis. He administered the affairs of the province until the arrival of Governor Cornwallis (q.v.) in 1749. He defended Annapolis against Du Vivier in 1744. In 1758 he retired from active service, with the rank of brevet colonel; and he died at Boston, Massachusetts, on January 22, 1760.

[J. B. Brebner, *Paul Mascarene of Annapolis Royal* (Dalhousie review, 1929); J. C. Webster, *The forts of Chignecto* (Shediac, N.B., 1930); *Dict. nat. biog.*; Le Jeune, *Dict. gén.*; *Dict. Can. biog.*, vol. 3.]

Maseres, Francis (1731-1824), attorney-general of Quebec (1766-69), was born in London on December 15, 1731, the son of Peter Abraham Maseres and Magdalene, daughter of Francis du Pratt du Clareau, both of Huguenot origin. He was educated at Clare College, Cambridge (B.A., 1752; M.A., 1755); and in 1758 he was called to the bar from the Inner Temple. In 1766 he was attorney-general of Quebec, and he held this office until 1769. He then returned to England, and in 1773 he was made a cursitor baron of the exchequer, a sinecure post which he held until his death at Reigate, Surrey, on May 19, 1824. He published, during his long life, a large number of books and papers in mathematics, law, history, and politics; but those which deal chiefly with Canada are *Considerations on the expediency of procuring an act of parliament for the settlement of the province of Quebeck* (London, 1766), *A collection of several commissions and other public instruments relating to the province of Quebeck* (London, 1770),

Mémoire à la défence d'un plan d'acte de parlement pour l'éstablissement des loix de la province de Québec (London, 1773), *An account of the proceedings of the British and other inhabitants of the province of Quebeck, in North America, in order to obtain a house of assembly* (London, 1775), *Additional papers concerning the province of Quebeck* (London, 1776), *The Canadian freeholder* (3 vols., 1777-79), and two papers in *Occasional essays* (London, 1809). After his return to England he acted on several occasions, also, as the agent of the British minority in Quebec. He was not married.

[W. S. Wallace (ed.), *The Maseres letters* (Toronto, 1919); *Dict. nat. biog.*; *Cyc. Am. biog.*; J. M. LeMoine, *Maple leaves* (Quebec, 1894); Le Jeune, *Dict. gén.*; Morgan, *Bib. can.*]

Mason, James (1843-1918), senator of Canada, was born in Toronto, Canada West, on August 25, 1843. He was educated at the Toronto Model School, and entered the service of the Toronto Savings Bank, which became ultimately the Home Bank of Canada; and of this bank he became general manager and president. He saw active service in the Fenian Raids and in the North West Rebellion of 1885; and he rose in the militia to the rank of brigadier-general. He was called to the Senate of Canada in 1913; and he died in Toronto, Ontario, on July 16, 1918.

[Morgan, *Can. men* (1912); *Can. parl. comp.*]

Mason, James Cooper (1875-1923), soldier and banker, was born in Toronto, Ontario, on January 11, 1875, the son of the Hon. James Mason (q.v.). He was educated in Toronto, and entered the service of the Home Bank of Canada. He served in the South African War as an officer in the Royal Canadian Regiment, was wounded, and was awarded the D.S.O. He ultimately became general manager of the Home Bank; and he died at Toronto, Ontario, on August 6, 1923, shortly before the Home Bank closed its doors.

[Morgan, *Can. men* (1912).]

Mason, John (1586-1635), governor of Guy's colony in Newfoundland, was born at King's Lynn, Norfolk, England, in 1586, and died in England early in December, 1635. He was educated at Magdalen College, Oxford; and in 1615 he was appointed to succeed John Guy (q.v.) as governor of the colony Guy had founded in Newfoundland. He remained in Newfoundland for six years, and during this time he seems to have carried out a thorough exploration of the island. By 1619 he had completed the first English map of Newfoundland; and this was prefixed to Sir William Vaughan's *Cambrensium Caroleia* (London, 1625). He was also the author of an extremely rare pamphlet entitled *A briefe discourse of the*

Newfoundland (Edinburgh, 1620), of which there is a copy in the British Museum. Later, Mason took part in the colonization of New England, and is regarded as the founder of New Hampshire.

[*Captain John Mason, the founder of New Hampshire* (Boston: The Prince Society, 1887); *Dict. nat. biog.; Dict. Can. biog.*, vol. 1.]

Massé, Enemond (1575-1646), Jesuit missionary, was born at Lyons, France, in 1575. He entered the Jesuit novitiate in 1595, and was ordained a priest in 1603. In 1611 he accompanied Father Biard (q.v.) to Acadia as a missionary. He returned to France in 1613; but in 1625 he was sent to Quebec as a missionary, and he remained in Canada, with the exception of the years 1629 to 1633, until his death at the residence of St. Joseph de Sillery on May 12, 1646.

[T. J. Campbell, *Pioneer priests of North America*, vol. i (New York, 1910); R. G. Thwaites (ed.), *The Jesuit relations* (73 vols., Cleveland, Ohio, 1897-1901); Le Jeune, *Dict. gén.; Dict. Can. biog.*, vol. 1.]'

Massey, Mrs. Alice Stuart, *née* **Parkin** (d. 1950), author, was born in Fredericton, New Brunswick, the daughter of Sir George Parkin (q.v.), and died at Batterwood House, near Port Hope, Ontario, on July 29, 1950. In 1915 she married Vincent Massey, later governor-general of Canada (1952-59); and she was the very hospitable hostess of the Canadian Embassy in Washington and of Canada House in London when her husband was first Canadian minister to the United States and high commissioner for Canada in Great Britain. She was the author of *Occupations for trained women in Canada* (London, 1920).

[Toronto *Globe and Mail*, July 31, 1950.]

Massey, Charles Vincent (1887-1967), governor-general of Canada, was born in Toronto, Ontario, February 20, 1887. He was educated at the University of Toronto (B.A., 1910), and Balliol College, Oxford (B.A., 1913; M.A., 1918). He was lecturer in history and dean of residence at Victoria College, University of Toronto, from 1913 to 1915, when he joined the army as a staff officer in military district No. 2 (1915-18). He was president of Massey-Harris Company from 1921 to 1925, when he was appointed to the Mackenzie King cabinet; however, he did not obtain an electoral mandate. He attended the Imperial Conference in London in 1926 and was appointed first Canadian minister to the United States (1926-30). He was president of the National Liberal Federation (1932-35), and was appointed Canadian high commissioner in London, England, in 1935, a position which he filled with distinction through the years of the Second World War. He returned to Canada in 1946. In 1949 he became chairman of the Royal Commission on National Development in the Arts, Letters and Sciences, popularly known as the Massey Commission, and in 1951 presented its report, which did much to promote "a vigorous and distinctive cultural life". Vincent Massey was appointed governor-general of Canada in 1952 for a five-year term which was subsequently extended to 1959. As governor-general he travelled far and wide in Canada. He was a patron of the arts, of education, and of literature. In his person he seemed to embody the best English influences in Canadian life; yet he saw Canada and Canadians as having the potential to make a unique contribution to the world of arts and letters. He was chancellor of the University of Toronto (1947-53), and trustee of the British National Gallery (1941-46), and of the National Gallery of Canada (1948-52). He was made a Companion of Honour (1946), and an Honourable Fellow of the Royal Society of Canada, and was awarded the Canada Council Medal (1961). He wrote his memoirs, *What's past is prologue* (Toronto, 1963), and published several volumes of his speeches. His best literary monument is the *Report of the royal commission on national development in the arts, letters and sciences*. He died at London, December 30, 1967.

[*Can. who's who*, 1964-66; *Encyc. Can.* (1972).]

Massey, Chester Daniel (1850-1926), philanthropist, was born near Newcastle, Ontario, on June 17, 1850, the eldest son of Hart Almerrin Massey (q.v.). As a boy he entered his father's implement works, which were later merged with A. Harris and Son to form the Massey-Harris Company, with head office in Toronto; and of this company he became in 1901 the president, and later the honorary president. He is chiefly remembered, however, for his generous benefactions. He made large gifts to Victoria College, the Toronto General Hospital, Massey Hall, Toronto, the Toronto Art Gallery, and many other institutions; and in his later years he was chairman of the Hart A. Massey Foundation, which gave to the University of Toronto the magnificent building known as Hart House. He died in Toronto, on June 2, 1926. He was twice married, first in 1888 to Anna Dobbins (d. 1903), by whom he had two sons, and secondly in 1907 to Margaret Phelps.

[Morgan, *Can. men* (1912).]

Massey, Hart Almerrin (1823-1896), manufacturer and philanthropist, was born in the township of Haldimand, Northumberland county, Upper Canada, on April 29, 1823, the son of Daniel Massey, a farmer. He was educated at Victoria College, Cobourg. In 1851 he became manager, and in 1855 sole proprietor, of the factory for agricultural implements established by his father at Newcastle, Upper Canada. In 1870 he became president of the

Massey Manufacturing Company, and in 1891 of the Massey-Harris Company. He died at Toronto on February 20, 1896. In 1847 he married Eliza Ann Phelps, of Johnstown, New York, and by her he had several children. He was a munificent philanthropist, and the Massey Music Hall, Toronto, was founded by him. Hart House, in the University of Toronto, built and endowed by the Massey Foundation, was named after him.

[*Hart Almerrin Massey* (pamphlet, Toronto, 1896); Mollie Gillen, *The Masseys* (Toronto, 1966); *Cyc. Am. biog.*; Rose, *Cyc. Can. biog.* (1886).]

Massicotte, Edmond Joseph (1875-1929), artist, was born at Montreal, Quebec, on December 1, 1875. He studied art in Montreal, and about 1892 he began to contribute illustrations to *Le Monde illustré*, to *La Presse*, to *Le Passe-Temps*, and to *Le Samedi*. But his chief work was a series of scenes of Canadian manners and customs which constituted a sort of picture gallery of national life. A number of these pictures were published in an album entitled *Nos canadiens d'autrefois*. Seventeen of his pictures were purchased by the government of Quebec. He died at Montreal on March 1, 1929. He married in 1914 Aldine Émond.

[Morgan, *Can. men* (1912); private information.]

Massicotte, Edouard Zotique (1867-1947), archivist and historian, was born in Montreal, Quebec, on December 24, 1867, and died there on November 8, 1947. He was educated at Laval University (LL.B., 1895), and practised law for a short time in Montreal. He then turned to journalism, and became editor of *Le Monde illustré*; and in 1911 the Quebec government appointed him chief archivist of the judicial district of Montreal. He continued to make known and available to the public the rich collection of historical materials under his care until only a few years before his death. When appointed archivist, he already had several books to his credit: *La Cité de Sainte-Cunégonde de Montréal* (Montreal, 1892), *Le droit civil canadien* (Montreal, 1896), *Monographie de plantes canadiennes* (Montreal, 1899) and *La famille Massicotte* (Montreal, 1904). After his appointment, he wrote *Conteurs canadien-français du xixe siècle* (3 vols., Montreal, 1912), *Moeurs, coutumes, et industries canadiens-français* (Montreal, 1913), *Montréal sous le régime français* (Montreal, 1919), *Dollard des Ormeaux et ses compagnons* (Montreal, 1920), *Faits curieux de l'histoire de Montréal* (Montreal, 1922), *Miettes d'histoire canadienne* (Montreal, 1924), *Récits d'histoire canadiens* (Montreal, 1924), *Sainte-Geneviève de Batiscan* (Trois-Rivières, 1936), and several genealogies. He was also joint author, with R. Roy, of *Armorial du Canada français* (2 vols., Montreal, 1915-18). He was elected a fellow of the Royal Society of Canada in 1920; and in

1936 the University of Montreal conferred on him the honorary degree of Litt.D.

[V. Morin, *Trois docteurs* (Montreal, 1936); *Proc. Roy. Soc. Can.*, 1948; *Can. who's who*, 1938-39; *Encyc. Can.*]

Masson, Louis François Rodrigue (1833-1903), lieutenant-governor of Quebec (1884-87), was born at Terrebonne, Lower Canada, on November 7, 1833, the fourth son of the Hon. Joseph Masson, a member of the Legislative Council, and Marie Geneviève Sophie Raymond. He was educated at the Jesuit College, Georgetown, district of Columbia, U.S.A., at the Seminary of the Holy Cross, Worcester, Mass., and at the College of St. Hyacinthe, Lower Canada. He was called to the bar of Lower Canada in 1859, but did not seriously devote himself to law. In 1867 he was elected for Terrebonne as a Conservative in the Canadian House of Commons, and this constituency he represented continuously until 1882. From 1878 to 1880 he was minister of militia in the government of Sir John Macdonald (q.v.), and for six months in 1880 he was president of the council; but ill-health compelled his retirement from the cabinet. In 1882 he was appointed a member of the Senate of Canada; but in 1884 he resigned to become lieutenant-governor of Quebec. Ill-health again intervened to compel his retirement from this post in 1887, and in 1890 he was a second time called to the Senate. In his later years he devoted much attention to gathering materials for the history of the western fur-trade; and he published, under the title *Les bourgeois de la Compagnie du Nord-ouest* (2 vols., Montreal, 1889-90), a valuable collection of journals, letters, and other documents relating to the history of the North West Company. He died at Montreal on November 8, 1903. He was twice married, (1) in 1856 to Louisa Rachel (d. 1880), eldest daughter of Lieut.-Col. Alexander Mackenzie, and (2) in 1883 to Cecile, daughter of John H. Burroughs, of Quebec. He was an LL.D. of Laval University (1886) and a D.C.L. of Bishop's College, Lennoxville (1887). In 1885 Pamphile Lemay (q.v.) published in his honour some lines entitled *Les derniers seront les premiers* (Trans. Roy. Soc. Can.).

[*Cyc. Am. biog.*; *Can. parl comp.*; Morgan, *Can. men* (1898); Taché, *Men of the day*; Le Jeune, *Dict. gén.*; J. Tassé, *Le 38ème fauteuil* (Montreal, 1891); L. O. David, *Souvenirs et biographies* (Montreal, 1911).]

Massue, Louis Joseph (1786-1869), legislative councillor of Canada, was born at Varennes, Quebec, on April 4, 1786, the son of Gaspard Massue and Marie-Joseph Huet. He became a wealthy merchant of Quebec, and in 1843 he was called to the Legislative Council of Canada. He resigned in 1851 to accept the post of controller of customs at the port of

Quebec; and he died at Quebec on July 4, 1869.
[Le Jeune, *Dict. gén.*; *Bull. rech. hist.*, 1919.]

Masten, Cornelius Arthur (1857-1942), jurist, was born at La Colle, Canada East, on December 16, 1857. He was educated at Victoria University, Cobourg (B.A., 1879), and was called to the bar of Ontario in 1883 (K.C., 1908). He practised law in Toronto; and in 1915 he was appointed a judge of the Supreme Court of Ontario. He died at Toronto, Ontario, on July 31, 1942. He was the author of *Canadian company law* (Toronto, 1901).
[*Can. who's who*, 1936-37; *Fortnightly law journal*, 1942; *University of Toronto monthly*, 1942.]

Masters, Charles Harding (1852-1931), lawyer and author, was born at Amherst, Nova Scotia, on March 26, 1852. He was educated at Acadia University (B.A., 1871; M.A., 1876), and was called to the bar of New Brunswick in 1877. He practised law in Saint John, New Brunswick, for several years; then he was appointed in 1885 assistant reporter, and in 1895 chief reporter, to the Supreme Court of Canada. He died at Ottawa, Ontario, on February 10, 1931. He was the author of *Canadian appeals* (Toronto, 1894), and *The practice of the Supreme Court of Canada* (Ottawa, 1899).
[Morgan, *Can. men* (1912).]

Mather, William Allen (1885-1961), railwayman, was born in Oshawa, Ontario, September 12, 1885. He was educated at McGill University (B.Sc., 1908). He began work as an axeman on the Canadian Pacific Railway in 1903; he became superintendent at Kenora in 1913, and general superintendent at Moose Jaw in 1918, and at Calgary in 1932. He was made assistant to the vice-president of the Canadian Pacific Railway at Montreal (1933), general manager of the western lines, Winnipeg (1934), vice-president of western lines (1942), vice-president of the Prairies region (1947), and company president (1948). He retired in 1955.
[*Can. who's who*, 1955-57.]

Matheson, Samuel Pritchard (1852-1942), Anglican primate of all Canada (1909-30), was born at Kildonan, Manitoba, on September 20, 1852. He was educated at St. John's College, Winnipeg (B.D., 1880; D.D., 1903), and was ordained a priest of the Church of England in 1876. He served for many years on the staff of St. John's College and St. John's College School; and from 1883 to 1902 he was secretary of the provincial synod of Rupert's Land. In 1903 he became coadjutor bishop of Rupert's Land, and in 1905 bishop of Rupert's Land and metropolitan of the ecclesiastical province of Rupert's Land, with the title of archbishop. In 1909 he was elected primate of

all Canada; and he retired from this position only in 1930. He was for many years chancellor of the University of Manitoba; and he received honorary degrees from Cambridge University, Durham University, and the University of King's College, Windsor, Nova Scotia.
[*Can. who's who*, 1936-37; Morgan, *Can. men* (1912); O. R. Rowley, *The Anglican episcopate of Canada and Newfoundland* (Milwaukee, Wis., 1928).]

Mathews, Jehu (d. 1902), author and journalist, was for many years on the editorial staff of the Toronto *Mail*. He was a contributor to the *Canadian Monthly and National Review* (Toronto, 1872-78); and he published *A colonial on the colonial question* (London, 1872), in which he advocated colonial representation in the British parliament. In 1890 he wrote a series of papers for the Imperial Federation League under the title, *What is imperial federation?* He died in Toronto on January 16, 1902.
[Morgan, *Can. men* (1898).]

Mathews, Peter (1786-1838), rebel, was born in 1786, the son of a United Empire Loyalist who settled in the township of Pickering, Upper Canada, after the American Revolution. He became a supporter of William Lyon Mackenzie (q.v.), and took a prominent part in the rebellion of 1837. Captured after the skirmish at Montgomery's Tavern, he was tried for treason, was condemned, and was hanged at Toronto on April 12, 1838.
[E. C. Guillet, *The lives and times of the patriots* (Toronto, 1938); J. C. Dent, *The Upper Canadian rebellion* (2 vols., Toronto, 1885).]

Mathieson, Alexander (1795-1870), clergyman, was born at Renton, Dumbartonshire, Scotland, on October 1, 1795; and was educated at the University of Glasgow (M.A., 1815; D.D., 1832). He was licensed to preach in the Church of Scotland in 1823; and in 1826 he came to Canada as minister of St. Andrew's Church, Montreal. He remained in charge of this church until his death at Montreal on February 14, 1870. A number of his sermons were printed. He was the author of *The moral and religious influence of autumn: A sermon in three parts* (Montreal, 1849).
[J. Croil, *Life of the Rev. Alex. Mathieson* (Montreal, 1870); R. Campbell, *A history of the Scotch Presbyterian church, St. Gabriel Street, Montreal* (Montreal, 1887); *Brit. Am.*, vol. 1; Morgan, *Bib. can.*]

Mathieson, John Alexander (1863-1947), prime minister of Prince Edward Island (1911-17), was born at Harrington, Prince Edward Island, on May 19, 1863, and died at Charlottetown, Prince Edward Island, on January 7, 1947. He was educated at Prince of Wales College, and became at first a school-teacher. In 1894 he was called to the bar, and he practised law in Georgetown and in Charlottetown. He was elected a member of the provincial legislature in 1901, and in 1902 he was chosen leader of the Conservative opposition. In the elections of 1911 he led his party to victory, and he was prime minister and attorney-general until 1917, when he became chief justice. He retired from the bench in 1943.

[Morgan, *Can. men* (1912); *Can. who's who*, 1938-39; *Can. parl. guide*, 1916; *Encyc. Can.*]

Mathieu, Michel (1838-1916), jurist, was born at Sorel, Lower Canada, on December 20, 1838. He was admitted a notary public in 1864, and was called to the bar of Lower Canada in 1865. From 1865 to 1872 he was sheriff of the Richelieu district; and he represented Richelieu in the Canadian House of Commons from 1872 to 1874, and in the Legislative Assembly of Quebec from 1875 to 1881. In 1881 he was appointed a judge of the Superior Court of the province of Quebec; and he retired from the bench in 1909. He died at Montreal, Quebec, on July 30, 1916. He was the author of *Rapports judiciaires revisés de la province de Québec* (23 vols., Montreal, 1891-1903) and *Table alphabétique des causes de la province de Québec* (2 vols., Montreal, 1901-02), and he was editor of *The municipal code of the province of Quebec* (Montreal, 1887).

[P. G. Roy, *Les juges de la province de Québec* (Quebec, 1933); Morgan, *Can. men* (1912).]

Mathieu, Olivier Elzéar (1853-1929), first Roman Catholic archbishop of Regina, was born at St. Roch, Quebec, on December 24, 1853. He was educated at the Quebec Seminary, and was ordained a priest in 1878. Except for a year spent in study at Rome, he was on the staff of Laval University from 1878 to 1908; and he was rector of the University from 1899 to 1908. In 1911 he was raised to the archiepiscopate. He was the founder of seminaries of learning at Gravelbourg and at Regina; and he was the author of numerous pastoral letters and works of edification. He died at Regina, Saskatchewan, on October 26, 1929.

[Raymond Huel, *Mgr. Olivier Elzéar Mathieu* (Rev. de l'Univ. d'Ottawa, 1972); Allaire, *Dict. biog.*; Le Jeune, *Dict. gén.*]

Matthew, George Frederick (1837-1923), geologist, was born at Saint John, New Brunswick, on August 12, 1837. He was educated at the Saint John grammar school; and in 1853 he became a clerk in the customs house at Saint John. He became chief clerk and surveyor in the customs house; but his chief interests were scientific, and he became a pioneer in the study of the geology and natural history of the Maritime provinces. When the Royal Society of Canada was formed in 1882,

he became one of its charter members; and he contributed a number of important papers to its *Transactions*. He received the honorary degree of D.Sc. from Laval University in 1894, and that of LL.D. from the University of New Brunswick in 1897. He died at Hastings-on-Hudson, New York, on April 14, 1923.

[*Proc. Roy. Soc. Can.*, 1923; Morgan, *Can. men* (1912).]

Matthews, Albert (1873-1949), lieutenant-governor of Ontario (1937-46), was born at Lindsay, Ontario, on May 17, 1873, and died at Windermere, Ontario, on August 13, 1949. He became a highly successful investment broker, and was a director of several financial institutions. He was also chairman of the board of governors of McMaster University. He was appointed lieutenant-governor of Ontario in 1937, and continued in this position until 1946. He received honorary degrees from McMaster University, the University of Western Ontario, Queen's University, the University of Toronto, and Acadia University.

[*Can. who's who*, 1948; *Can. parl. guide*, 1945.]

Matthews, Marmaduke (1837-1913), painter, was born in Warwickshire, England, in 1837. He was educated at the Cowley Diocesan School, Oxford, and came to Canada in 1860. He was an original member of the Ontario Society of Artists, and in 1894 he was elected its president. In 1880 he was chosen also a charter member of the Royal Canadian Academy of Arts, and became its secretary. He was especially successful in landscape painting. He died in Toronto on September 13, 1913.

[*Can. who was who*, vol. 2; Morgan, *Can. men* (1912); N. MacTavish, *The fine arts in Canada* (Toronto, 1925); H. G. Jones and E. Dyonnet, *The Royal Canadian Academy of Arts* (Montreal, 1934).]

Maura, Sister [Mary Power] (1881-1957), educationist and author, was born in 1881, and died at Halifax, Nova Scotia, on January 16, 1957. She was educated at Dalhousie University (M.A.) and Notre Dame University (Ph.D.), and became a Sister of Charity of Halifax Congregation. From 1925 to her death she was professor of English at Mount Saint Vincent College, outside Halifax. She was the author of *Shakespeare's Catholicism* (Cambridge, Mass., 1924), several small volumes of verse, and two or three short miracle or mystery plays.

[*Can. who's who*, 1955-57.]

Maurault, Joseph Pierre Anselme (1819-1871), priest and historian, was born at Kamouraska, Lower Canada, on December 17, 1819. He was educated at the college of Ste. Anne de la Pocatière and at the Quebec Seminary; and he was ordained a priest of the Roman Catholic Church in 1842. He was a parish priest successively at St. François du Lac and St. Thomas de Pierreville, Quebec. He died on July 5, 1871. He was the author of *L'histoire des Abénakis depuis 1605 jusqu'à nos jours* (Quebec, 1866).

[Allaire, *Dict. biog.*; Le Jeune, *Dict. gén.*; *Bull. rech. hist.*, 1927.]

Mavor, James (1854-1925), political economist, was born at Stranraer, Scotland, on December 8, 1854, the son of the Rev. James Mavor and Mary Ann Bridie. He was educated at the University of Glasgow, and became professor of political economy at St. Mungo's College, Glasgow. He became also the editor of the *Scottish Art Review* (Glasgow). In 1892 he was appointed professor of political economy at the University of Toronto; and he occupied this chair until his retirement on pension in 1923. In 1914 he was elected a fellow of the Royal Society of Canada. He died in Glasgow, Scotland, on October 31, 1925. He was the author of a number of government reports, dealing with immigration, with the wheat-producing capacity of the Canadian North West, and with workmen's compensation; and he published, among other works, *An economic history of Russia* (2 vols., London, 1914), an autobiography entitled *My windows on the street of the world* (2 vols., London, 1923), and *Niagara in politics* (New York, 1925).

[*Who was who*, 1916-28; *University of Toronto monthly*, 1925; Morgan, *Can. men* (1912); *Proc. Roy. Soc. Can.*, 1926.]

Mawdsley, James Buckland (1894-1964), geologist, was born near Sienna, Italy, on July 22, 1894, of British-American parents. In 1904 his family settled near Gainsborough, Saskatchewan, where he had his early education. In 1913 he entered McGill University, Montreal. His education was interrupted by a period of service in the Princess Patricia's Canadian Light Infantry and the Royal Flying Corps. He returned to McGill in 1919, graduating in mining engineering in 1921. He then went to Princeton University, where he received his Ph.D. degree in 1924. For five years he worked on geologic surveys in northern Quebec and his work was published as *Geology and ore deposits of Rouyn-Harricanaw region, Quebec*, being memoir 166 of the Geological Survey of Canada, and memoir 185, *Chibougamau Lake map area*, by Mawdsley and Norman. He was appointed professor and head of the department of geology at the University of Saskatchewan in 1929 and held this position until 1961, when he became dean of the College of Engineering. He was also director of the Institute of Northern Studies for the University of Saskatchewan. He was past president of the Geological Association of Canada and of the Canadian Institute of Mining and Metallurgy. He was awarded the Barlow medal in 1953 for his paper *Uranium-bearing deposits, Charlebois Lake area, North-*

ern *Saskatchewan*. He was a fellow of the Royal Society of Canada, of the Royal Canadian Geographical Society, and of the Geological Society of America, and a charter associate of the Arctic Institute. He died at Edmonton on December 3, 1964.

[*Proc. and Trans. Roy. Soc. Can.*, 1965.]

Maxse, Sir Henry Berkeley Fitzhardinge (1832-1883), governor of Newfoundland (1881-83), was born in 1832, and died at Government House, St. John's, Newfoundland, on September 8, 1883. He entered the British army in 1849 as a subaltern in the Guards, served throughout the Crimean War as aide-de-camp to the Earl of Cardigan, and was one of the "immortal six hundred" in the charge of the Light Brigade at Balaclava. He was governor of Heligoland from 1864 to 1881; and he was then appointed governor of Newfoundland, but his term of office was cut short by death. He was created a K.C.M.G. in 1877.

[*Dict. nat. biog.*; *Dom. ann. reg.*; *Encyc. Can.*]

Mayne, Daniel Hayden (*fl.* 1837-1838), school-teacher and author, is described in the Toronto directory of 1837 as employed at the "East York district school"; but his name does not appear in subsequent directories. He was the author of *Poems and fragments* (Toronto, 1838).

[C. C. James, *A bibliography of Canadian poetry* (Toronto, 1899).]

Mazari, Frank (1938-1971), historian, was born in Italy on August 1, 1938, and came to Canada in 1953. He was educated at the University of Toronto and at the London School of Economics (Ph.D., 1966). He was interested in European history and strategic studies and published articles in the *Historical Journal, Middle Eastern Studies, Canadian Slavonic papers*, and the *International Journal*. He had been a reporter for the Toronto *Globe and Mail* and national editor for the C.B.C. radio news. He was associate professor of history at the University of British Columbia. He died in September, 1971.

[*Can. hist. rev.*, vol. LIII.]

Mazurette, Salomon (1848-1910), musician, was born at Montreal on June 26, 1848, the son of Salomon Mazurette and Mathilde Collin. He studied music in Paris; and, on his return to America in 1870, became famous as a violinist, a pianist, and a composer. He was the author of "Home, sweet home", as well as many other musical compositions. He died at Detroit, Michigan, in September, 1910.

[*Bull. rech. hist.*, 1934; Le Jeune, *Dict. gén.*]

Mazzoleni, Ettore (1905-1968), conductor, was born in Brusio, Switzerland, June 18, 1905. He was educated in England at Oxford

University (B.A., 1927), at the Royal College of Music, and at the University of Rochester in the United States (Mus. D., 1949). In 1929 he joined the staff of Upper Canada College and was appointed soon thereafter as lecturer in music history at the Toronto Conservatory of Music. He became conductor of the Conservatory Orchestra, and in 1945 was appointed principal of the Conservatory. From 1943 to 1948 he was associate conductor of the Toronto Symphony Orchestra. He made frequent appearances as guest conductor, particularly with the Concerts Symphoniques at Montreal. His compositions include songs, incidental music for plays, and folksong arrangements. His best-known orchestral works are his transcriptions of Bach's *Passacaglia and Fugue* and *Fugue in C Minor*. He died at Toronto, Ontario, June 1, 1968.

[Grove, *Dictionary of Music and Musicians*, vol. V; *Can. who's who*, 1955-57; *Encyc. Can.* (1972).]

Meagher, Nicholas Hogan (1842-1932), jurist, was born at Mabou, Nova Scotia, on October 25, 1842. He was called to the bar of Nova Scotia in 1872; and in 1890 he was appointed a puisne judge of the Supreme Court of Nova Scotia. He died at Halifax, Nova Scotia, on August 26, 1932. He was the author of *The religious warfare in Nova Scotia, 1855-1860* (Halifax, N.S., 1928).

[Morgan, *Can. men* (1912).]

Medley, John (1804-1892), first Anglican bishop of Fredericton, was born on December 19, 1804, the son of George Medley, of Grosvenor Place, Chelsea, England. He was educated at Wadham College, Oxford (B.A., 1826; M.A., 1830), and in 1829 he was ordained a priest of the Church of England. In 1845 he was consecrated bishop of Fredericton, New Brunswick; and he administered this diocese for nearly half a century. In 1879 as the senior bishop of the Church of England in Canada he became metropolitan of Canada. He died at Fredericton, New Brunswick, on September 9, 1892. He was a D.D. of Oxford and Durham universities, and an LL.D. of Cambridge University. He published a number of sermons and theological commentaries and translations; and he composed several anthems.

[W. Q. Ketchum, *Life of Bishop Medley* (Saint John, N.B., 1893); L. N. Harding, *John Medley and the Church in New Brunswick* (Journal of the Cdn. Church Hist. Soc., 1966); *Dict. nat. biog.*; *Cyc. Am. biog.*; Dent, *Can. port.*, vol. 2; Morgan, *Bib. can.*; C. H. Mockridge, *Bishops of the Church of England in Canada* (Toronto, 1896); W. G. MacFarlane, *New Brunswick bibliography* (Saint John, N.B., 1895).]

Meek, Theophile James (1881-1966), Semitic scholar, was born near Port Stanley, Ontario, November 17, 1881. He was educated at the University of Toronto (B.A., 1903), McCormick Theological Seminary, Chicago, in Germany, and in Palestine. From 1909 to 1918 he was professor of biblical history and literature at James Millikin University, Decatur, Illinois. After teaching at Meadville Theological School and at Bryn Mawr College he joined the department of oriental languages at University College at the University of Toronto, of which he became head in 1950, two years before his retirement. His most outstanding contribution to Mesopotamian studies was his translation of the ancient Near Eastern law codes; the code of Hammurabi, middle Assyrian laws, Neo-Babylonian laws, and other legal documents included in the book, *Ancient Near Eastern texts* (Princeton, 1950); he also published *Cuneiform bilingual hymns, prayers and penitential psalms* (Leipzig, 1913), and *Old Akkadian, Sumerian and Cappadocian texts from Nuzi* (Cambridge, Mass., 1935). His most popular work was *Hebrew Origins* (1936), which went through three editions. He was one of four scholars commissioned to do a new translation of the Old Testament, which appeared in 1927 as *The Old Testament, an American translation*, and he also did commentaries on the Book of Lamentations and the Song of Songs for *The Interpreter's Bible*, which appeared in 1956. Professor Meek headed a number of expeditions to the Near East and was recognized by the American Oriental Society and the Society of Biblical Literature and Exegesis and was associate editor of the *American Journal of Semitic Languages* for eleven years. He was a fellow of the Royal Society of Canada. A selected bibliography of his writings is included in *The seed of wisdom*, W. S. McCullough, ed. (Toronto, 1964). He died at Toronto on February 19, 1966.

[*Proc. and Trans. Roy. Soc. Can.*, 1966.]

Meighen, Arthur (1874-1960), prime minister of Canada (1920-21 and 1926), was born near Anderson, Perth county, Ontario, on June 16, 1874. He was educated at the University of Toronto (B.A., 1896), and taught school for a year; but in 1898 he went to Winnipeg where he began the study of law. He was called to the bar in Manitoba in 1903; and began to practise law in Portage la Prairie.

In 1908 he was elected to represent Portage la Prairie in the Canadian House of Commons as a Liberal-Conservative; and thus began his long political career, which began brilliantly, but was repeatedly interrupted by tragic disappointments. He continued to represent Portage la Prairie until 1921; and his striking ability as a debater soon brought him into prominence. He became solicitor-general in 1913, was sworn in as a member of the Privy Council in 1915, was appointed successively secretary of state and minister of the interior in 1917, and on the resignation of Sir Robert Borden (q.v.) in 1920 became prime minister of

Canada. Then the fates turned against him. In the election of 1921 the government was defeated at the polls, and Meighen himself was defeated in Portage la Prairie. He found a seat elsewhere in a by-election, and continued to lead the Liberal-Conservative party in the House of Commons; and in the election of 1925 he regained his seat in Portage la Prairie, but failed to obtain an over-all majority in the Commons. As a result of the refusal of the governor-general, Lord Byng (q.v.), to grant Mackenzie King (q.v.) a dissolution in 1926, and King's resignation, Meighen was invited to form a government in June, 1926. But his government was short-lived, for in the elections that followed a stalemate in the House, the Liberals were returned to power. Meighen thereupon resigned in favour of R. B. Bennett (q.v.), and in 1932 was appointed a member of the Senate. In 1941 he resigned from the Senate to seek election to the House of Commons for North York; but in the by-election that followed he was defeated, and retired definitely from political life. Seldom has a statesman of such ability and integrity been treated so unkindly by the Canadian electorate.

In his later years, Meighen engaged in business in Toronto; and he died at Toronto on August 5, 1960. He was the author of *Oversea addresses* (Toronto, 1921), *The greatest Englishman in history* (Toronto, 1936; reprinted, Fort Erie, 1954), and *Unrevised and unrepented: Debating speeches and others* (Toronto, 1949).

[R. Graham, *Arthur Meighen: A biography*, 3 vols. (Toronto, 1960-65); *Can. who's who*, 1958-60; *Encyc. Can.*]

Meighen, Robert (1838-1911), capitalist, was born at Dungiven, Ireland, on April 18, 1838. He came to Canada in early youth, and lived in Perth, Canada West. In 1879 he removed to Montreal; and he was one of the founders, and later became the president and managing director, of the Lake of the Woods Milling Company. He died in Montreal, Quebec, on July 13, 1911. In 1868 he married Elsie, daughter of William Stephen, Montreal, and sister of Lord Mountstephen (q.v.).

[Morgan, *Can. men* (1912).]

Meilleur, Jean Baptiste (1796-1878), superintendent of education for Lower Canada (1842-55), was born at St. Laurent, Montreal Island, Lower Canada, on May 8, 1796. He was educated at Montreal College, at Castleton Academy of Medicine, Vermont (M.D., 1825), and at Middlebury College, Vermont. In 1834 he founded L'Assomption College, Lower Canada. In 1842 he was appointed first superintendent of education for Lower Canada, and in the years that followed he laid the foundations of the educational system of the province of Quebec. In 1855 he was superseded by P. J. O. Chauveau (q.v.), and was appointed inspector of post-offices, Montreal. He died in Montreal on December 6, 1878. In 1855 he was made an LL.D. of St. John College, New York. Besides a number of text-books, he published *Court traité sur l'art épistolaire* (Montreal, 1853) and *Mémorial de l'éducation du Bas-Canada* (Montreal, 1860). Collections of his letters have been published by L. Pouliot in the *Bulletin des recherches historiques*, 1937, and by L. Lortie in the *Revue trimestrielle canadienne*, 1938.

[*Dict. nat. biog.*; *Cyc. Am. biog.*; Bibaud, *Panth. can.*; Le Jeune, *Dict. gén.*; *Dom. ann. reg.*, 1878; Morgan, *Cel. Can.* and *Bib. can.*; E. Lareau, *Histoire de la littérature canadienne* (Montreal, 1873); *Dict. Can. biog.*, vol. 10.]

Melanson, Louis Joseph Arthur (1879-1941), first Roman Catholic archbishop of Moncton, was born at Three Rivers, Quebec, on March 25, 1879, and was ordained a priest in 1905. From 1933 to 1936 he was bishop of Gravelbourg, Saskatchewan; and in 1936 he was consecrated first archbishop of Moncton. He died at Campbellton, New Brunswick, on October 23, 1941.

[R. P. Albert, *Mgr. Louis-Joseph-Arthur Melanson* (Montreal, 1941); *Can. who's who*, 1938-39; Allaire, *Dict. biog.*]

Mellish, Henry Frederick (1828-1899), clergyman and author, was born on April 22, 1828. He was ordained a clergyman of the Church of England in 1860; and in 1875 he became rector of St. Paul's Church, Caledonia, Ontario. He died at Caledonia on September 30, 1899. He was the author of *No popery; or, A defence of the Book of Common Prayer* (Caledonia, Ont., 1878).

[Private information.]

Mellish, John Thomas (1841-1924), educationist and lawyer, was born at Pownel, Prince Edward Island, on January 26, 1841. He was educated at Prince of Wales College, Charlottetown, at Mount Allison University (B.A., 1869; M.A., 1872), at Victoria University (LL.B., 1890), and at King's College, Windsor (B.C.L., 1903; D.C.L., 1909); and for many years he was a school-teacher in the Maritime provinces. In 1888 he was called to the bar of Nova Scotia and of Prince Edward Island; and he practised law in Charlottetown, Prince Edward Island. He died at Vancouver, British Columbia, on March 30, 1924. He was the author of *Outlines of the history of Methodism in Charlottetown, P.E.I.* (Charlottetown, 1888).

[Morgan, *Can. men* (1912); W. G. MacFarlane, *New Brunswick bibliography* (Saint John, N.B., 1895).]

Melville, Henry (d. 1868), surgeon and author, was a graduate of Edinburgh University who came to Canada, by way of the West Indies, prior to 1846. He practised medicine, first in Niagara, and then in Toronto; and in 1850 he became one of the founders of the Upper Canada School of Medicine, which became in 1851 the medical faculty of the University of Trinity College. For several years he was professor of surgery in this university. He then went to New York, where he associated himself with Dr. R. Hunter, who was not regarded as a regularly qualified practitioner. From New York he returned to England; and he died in London, England, on March 25, 1868. He was the author, while in Canada, of *The rise and progress of Trinity College, Toronto* (Toronto, 1852).

[W. Canniff, *The medical profession in Upper Canada* (Toronto, 1894).]

Ménard, René (1605-1661), Jesuit missionary, was born in Paris, France, on March 2, 1605, entered the Society of Jesus in 1624, and was ordained a priest in 1637. He was sent to Canada in 1640. He was a missionary first among the Nipissings, and later among the Iroquois; and in 1660 he was sent to the western end of Lake Superior to found the first mission in this region. Here he lost his way in the woods, and either died of starvation, or was murdered by the Indians, in 1661.

[Allaire, *Dict. biog.*; Le Jeune, *Dict. gén.*; *Dict. Can. biog.*, vol. 1.]

Meneval, Louis Alexandre des Friches, Chevalier de (d. 1709), governor of Acadia (1687-90), was an officer in the French army who was appointed in 1687 governor of Acadia. He rebuilt Port Royal, but in 1690 surrendered the place to Sir William Phips (q.v.). He was taken a prisoner to England in 1691; and he died in France in 1709.

[J. C. Webster, *Acadia at the end of the seventeenth century* (Saint John, N.B., 1934); Le Jeune, *Dict. gén.*; *Dict. Can. biog.*, vol. 2.]

Menzies, George (d. 1847), journalist and poet, was born in Scotland, and on coming to Canada became a journalist. In 1840 he founded the *Herald* in Woodstock, Upper Canada, the first newspaper published in the county of Oxford; and he died at Woodstock on March 4, 1847. He was the editor of *Album of the table rock, Niagara Falls, C.W., and sketches of the falls* (Niagara, C.W., 1846); and his widow published *The posthumous works of the late George Menzies, being a collection of poems, sonnets, etc.* (Woodstock, 1850).

[Morgan, *Bib. can.*]

Merchant, Francis Walter (1855-1937), educationist, was born at Oil Springs, Canada West, on November 25, 1855. He was educated at Albert College (B.A., 1878; M.A., 1880) and at the University of Toronto (D.Paed., 1901). He became a school-teacher, and in 1908 was appointed chief inspector of public and separate schools in Ontario. In 1911 he became director of industrial and technical education; in

1923, chief director of education; and in 1930, chief adviser to the minister of education. In 1911 he was asked to make a report on bilingual schools in Ontario; and his report resulted in the issuance of the famous Regulation 17, which roused great opposition among the French-Canadian population in Ontario. He died at Toronto, Ontario, on January 29, 1937. He was the author of *Elementary mechanics* (Toronto, 1906); and he was joint author, with C. Fessenden, of *High school physical science* (2 parts, Toronto, 1895-96) and, with C. A. Chant, of *Elements of physics* (New York, 1924).

[*Can. who's who*, 1936-37; *University of Toronto monthly*, 1937; Morgan, *Can. men* (1912).]

Mercier, Honoré (1840-1894), prime minister of Quebec (1887-91), was born at St. Athanase, Lower Canada, on October 15, 1840, the son of an *habitant*. He was educated at the Jesuits' College, Montreal, and in 1862 became for a time editor of *Le Courrier de St. Hyacinthe*. In 1865 he was called to the bar of Lower Canada, and in 1866 he abandoned journalism for law. In 1871 he was one of the founders of the *Parti national*; and from 1872 to 1874 he sat in the Canadian House of Commons for Rouville. He was out of parliament from 1874 to 1879; but in 1879 he was elected to represent St. Hyacinthe in the Legislative Assembly of Quebec, and became for a few months solicitor-general in the Joly administration. In 1883 Joly (q.v.) resigned the leadership of the Liberal party in the province of Quebec, and Mercier was chosen to succeed him. As leader of the opposition, his energy resulted in 1886 in the defeat of the Conservatives, and he was called upon to form an administration. His tenure of the premiership, which lasted four years, was marked by boldness and originality. It was, however, a distinct embarrassment to the Liberal party in the other provinces. Mercier's nationalist ideas and his policy in regard to the Jesuit estates roused great opposition among English-speaking Canadians; and some scandals in connection with his disbursement of public moneys detracted greatly from the force of the Liberal charges of corruption levelled against Sir John Macdonald (q.v.). In 1891 the lieutenant-governor of Quebec took the extreme step of dismissing Mercier from office, and in the general elections that followed he was overwhelmingly defeated. He died at Montreal on October 30, 1894.

He was twice married, (1) to Léopoldine Boivin, of St. Hyacinthe, by whom he had one daughter, and (2) to Virginie St. Denis, of St. Hyacinthe. His speeches, which are among the finest examples of French-Canadian oratory, were collected by J. O. Pelland under the title *Biographie, discours, conférences de l'honorable Honoré Mercier* (Montreal, 1890). Shortly before his death he published an interesting brochure, *L'avenir du Canada* (Montreal, 1893).

[R. Rumilly, *Mercier* (Montreal, 1936); *L'honorable M. Mercier, sa vie, ses oeuvres, sa fin* (Montreal, 1896); J. O. Pelland (ed.), *Biographie, discours, conférences de l'honorable Honoré Mercier* (Montreal, 1890); *Dict. nat. biog.*, supp. I; *Cyc. Am. biog.*; Taché, *Men of the day*; Bibaud, *Panth. can.*; Le Jeune, *Dict. gén.*; Rose, *Cyc. Can. biog.* (1888); *Can. parl. comp.*; C. Langelier, *Souvenirs politiques* (2 vols., Quebec, 1909-12).]

Mercier, Honoré (1875-1937), lawyer and politician, was born at St. Hyacinthe, Quebec, in 1875, the son of the Hon. Honoré Mercier (q.v.). He was educated at Laval University (LL.B., 1900); was called to the bar in 1900; and practised law in Montreal. He represented Châteauguay in the Legislative Assembly of Quebec from 1907 to 1936; and he was minister of colonization, mines, and fisheries in the Quebec government from 1914 to 1919, and minister of lands and forests from 1919 to 1936. He retired from political life in 1936; and he died at Châteauguay, Quebec, on June 20, 1937.

[*Can. who's who*, 1936-37; *Can. parl. comp.*]

Meredith, Edmund Allen (1817-1898), civil servant and author, was born at Ardtrea, county Tyrone, Ireland, on October 7, 1817, the son of the Rev. Thomas Meredith, fellow of Trinity College, Dublin, and brother of Sir William Collis Meredith (q.v.). He was educated at Trinity College, Dublin (B.A., 1837), and came to Canada in 1842. He was called to the bar in 1844, but did not practise. In 1846 he was appointed principal of McGill College, Montreal; but he resigned this position in 1847 to accept appointment as assistant provincial secretary for Upper Canada. In 1867 he became under-secretary of state for the provinces in the Dominion government, and in 1873 he was appointed first deputy minister of the newly created Department of the Interior. He retired from the civil service in 1878; and he died in Toronto, where he had spent his retirement, on November 12, 1898. In 1851 he married Anne Frances, daughter of Sheriff W. B. Jarvis, of York county. He was the author of *An essay on the Oregon question* (Montreal, 1846) and of a number of papers and pamphlets on prison reform. He was an honorary M.A. of Bishop's College, Lennoxville, and an LL.D. of the University of McGill College; and he was for two years president of the Literary and Historical Society of Quebec.

[Morgan, *Can. men* (1898) and *Bib. can.*]

Meredith, Sir Vincent, Bart. (1850-1929), president of the Bank of Montreal (1913-28), was born at London, Ontario, on February 28, 1850, the son of John Walsingham Cooke Meredith. He was educated at Hellmuth College, London, and entered the service of the Bank of Montreal in 1867. He was appointed general manager of the bank in 1911, vice-president in 1912, president in 1913, and chairman of the board in 1928. He was created a baronet of the United Kingdom in 1916. In 1888 he married Isobel Brenda, daughter of Andrew Allan (q.v.), but died without issue.

[*Can. who was who*, vol. I; *Who was who*, 1929-40; Morgan, *Can. men* (1912).]

Meredith, Sir William Collis (1812-1894), jurist, was born in Dublin, Ireland, on May 13, 1812, the son of the Rev. Thomas Meredith. He emigrated to Canada, studied law, and in 1836 was called to the bar of Lower Canada (Q.C., 1844). He was a judge of the Superior Court of Lower Canada from 1852 to 1859, and of the Court of Queen's Bench from 1859 to 1866. From 1866 to 1884 he was chief justice of the Superior Court of Quebec. In 1886 he was knighted; and he died at Quebec on February 26, 1894. In 1854 he was made a D.C.L. of Bishop's College, Lennoxville, and in 1880 an LL.D. of Laval University. In 1847 he married Sophia Holmes, of Quebec, and by her he had several children.

[*Cyc. Am. biog.*; Rose, *Cyc. Can. biog.* (1888); P. G. Roy, *Les juges de la province de Québec* (Quebec, 1933).]

Meredith, Sir William Ralph (1840-1923), chief justice of Ontario (1894-1923), was born in the township of Westminster, Middlesex county, Upper Canada, on March 31, 1840, the son of John Cooke Meredith and Sarah Pegler. He was educated at the London District Grammar School and at the University of Toronto (LL.B., 1872; LL.D., 1889); and he called to the bar of Upper Canada in 1861 (Q.C., 1875). He practised law first in London, Ontario, and then in Toronto. In 1872 he was elected to represent London in the Legislative Assembly of Ontario, and in 1878 he succeeded Sir M. C. Cameron (q.v.) as leader of the Conservative opposition in the Assembly. In 1894 he retired from politics and was appointed chief justice of the common pleas division of the High Court of Justice in Ontario. In 1896 he was knighted; and in 1900 he was elected chancellor of the University of Toronto, a position he occupied until his death. He died at Toronto on August 21, 1923. In 1862 he married Mary, daughter of Marcus Holmes of London, Ontario, and by her he had several children.

[*Who was who*, 1916-28; *University of Toronto monthly*, 1923; Morgan, *Can. men* (1912); H. Charlesworth (ed.), *A cyclopaedia of Canadian biography* (Toronto, 1919); Taché, *Men of the day*; C. Clarke, *Sixty years in Upper Canada* (Toronto, 1908).]

Merkel, Andrew Doane (1884-1954), journalist and author, was born at Morley, New York, on December 15, 1884, of Canadian parents, and died at Halifax, Nova Scotia, on June 25, 1954. He was educated at King's College, Windsor, and became a journalist. From 1918 to his retirement in 1946 he was Atlantic superintendent of the Canadian Press. He was the editor of *Letters from the front* (Halifax, 1914) and author of *Schooner Bluenose* (Toronto, 1948) and two narrative poems, *Tallahassee* (Halifax, 1945) and *The order of good cheer* (Lower Granville, N.S., 1946).

[*Can. who's who*, 1949-51; *Encyc. Can.*]

Merner, Samuel (1823-1908), senator of Canada, was born at Reichenboch, Switzerland, on January 18, 1823. He came to Canada in 1837, and settled in Waterloo county, Upper Canada. He represented South Waterloo in the Canadian House of Commons from 1877 to 1882; and he was called to the Senate in 1887. He died in Berlin (Kitchener), Ontario, on August 11, 1908.

[*Can. parl. comp.*]

Merritt, Jedediah Prendergast (1820-1901), author, was born on June 1, 1820, the son of the Hon. William Hamilton Merritt (q.v.), and died at St. Catharines, Ontario, on November 18, 1901. He was the author of the *Biography of the Hon. W. H. Merritt* (St. Catharines, 1875), and he edited the *Biography of William H. Merritt, Jun., principally by himself, with correspondence* (St. Catharines, 1876).

[E. M. Chadwick, *Ontarian families* (2 vols., Toronto, 1894-98); Rose, *Cyc. Can. biog.* (1888).]

Merritt, Thomas (1759-1842), loyalist, was born in New England in 1759, the son of Thomas Merritt and Amy Purdy. During the American Revolutionary War he was an officer in the mounted corps of the Queen's Rangers. In 1783 he settled in New Brunswick, but later he came to Upper Canada and took up land in the Niagara Peninsula. From 1803 to 1820 he was sheriff of Lincoln county, and he was a cavalry officer in the War of 1812. He died on May 12, 1842. In 1779 he married Mary Hamilton, of South Carolina; and by her he had one son and five daughters.

[W. H. Merritt, *Memoirs of Major Thomas Merritt, U.E.L.* (Annual Transactions of the United Empire Loyalists' Association, 1914); E. M. Chadwick, *Ontarian families* (2 vols., Toronto, 1894-98).]

Merritt, Thomas Rodman (1824-1906), president of the Imperial Bank of Canada, was born at Mayville, New York, on October 17, 1824, the son of the Hon. William Hamilton Merritt (q.v.). He was educated at Upper Canada College, and entered the business of milling and shipping. He represented Lincoln in the Canadian House of Commons from 1868 to 1874; but then declined nomination. For many years he was president of the Niagara District

Bank; and in 1902 he became president of the Imperial Bank of Canada. He died at St. Catharines, Ontario, on January 11, 1906. In 1853 he married Mary, eldest daughter of Thomas Benson.

[Morgan, *Can. men* (1898); E. M. Chadwick, *Ontarian families* (2 vols., Toronto, 1894-98).]

Merritt, William Hamilton (1793-1862), president of the Executive Council of Canada (1848-50), was born at Bedford, New York, on July 3, 1793, the son of Thomas Merritt (q.v.). He came to Upper Canada with his parents, and in 1812 became an ensign in the Lincoln militia. In the War of 1812, he was present at the capture of Detroit, commanded a troop of cavalry in the later stages of the war, and was taken prisoner at the battle of Lundy's Lane. He became the promoter of the Welland Canal. From 1832 to 1841 he represented Haldimand in the Legislative Assembly of Upper Canada; and from 1841 to 1860 he represented Lincoln in the Legislative Assembly of united Canada. In 1848 he became president of the council in the second Baldwin-Lafontaine administration, and in 1850 he was transferred to the commissionership of public works. Early in 1851, however, he retired from the cabinet; and thenceforth he served as a private member. In 1860 he was elected to the Legislative Council; and he died on July 5, 1862. In 1815 he married Catherine Rodman, daughter of Jedediah Prendergast, M.D., of Dutchess county, New York; and by her he had four sons and two daughters.

[J. P. Merritt, *Biography of the Hon. W. J. Merritt* (St. Catharines, Ontario, 1875); T. C. Keefer, *The old Welland canal and the man who made it* (Ottawa, 1911); D. C. Masters, *W. H. Merritt and the expansion of Canadian railways* (Can. hist. rev., 1931); A. R. M. Lower, *A half-forgotten builder of Canada* (Queen's quarterly, 1939); Dent, *Can. port.*, vol. 4; Taylor, *Brit. Am.*, vol. 2; Morgan, *Bib. can.*; E. M. Chadwick, *Ontarian families* (2 vols., Toronto, 1894-98); J. C. Dent, *The last forty years* (2 vols., Toronto, 1881).]

Merritt, William Hamilton (1855-1918), mining engineer and militia officer, was born at St. Catharines, Ontario, on June 8, 1855, the son of William Hamilton Merritt, barrister, of St. Catharines, and Janet Lang, daughter of the Hon. James Morris (q.v.). He was the grandson of the Hon. William Merritt (q.v.). He was educated at Upper Canada College, at Clifton College in England, and at the Royal School of Mines in England; and he became one of the most prominent mining engineers in Canada. He entered the militia in 1884, and served throughout the North West Rebellion of 1885 and the South African War. From 1903 to 1908 he commanded the Governor-General's Bodyguard, and in 1911 was appointed to command the 1st Cavalry

Brigade. He was president of the Canadian Defence League, and he published a book entitled *Canada and national defence* (Toronto, 1917), in which he advocated the adoption of compulsory military service. He died at Toronto on October 26, 1918. He married Margaret, daughter of Robert Simpson, of Toronto.

[*Can. who was who*, vol. 2; Morgan, *Can. men* (1912); E. M. Chadwick, *Ontarian families* (2 vols., Toronto, 1894-98).]

Merritt, William Hamilton (1865-1924), physician, was born on June 13, 1865, the eldest son of Jedediah Prendergast Merritt, of St. Catharines, Ontario. He was educated at Trinity University, Toronto (M.D., 1888); and he practised medicine in St. Catharines. He served in France in command of the 14th Battery of the Canadian Corps; and he died at St. Catharines on April 22, 1924. He married Maud Cloudman, daughter of Judge Haynes Hudson, of Memphis, Tennessee.

[E. M. Chadwick, *Ontarian families* (2 vols., Toronto, 1894-98).]

Mesplet, Fleury (1735?-1794), printer, was born in the parish of St. Vizier, diocese of Lyon, France, about 1735, the son of Jean Baptiste Mesplet and Marie-Antoinette Capeau. He became a printer, and in 1774 migrated to America. He settled first at Philadelphia, but in 1776 he removed to Montreal. Here he set up the first printing office in Montreal, and his productions are among the earliest examples of the art of printing in Canada. After a chequered career he died in Montreal on January 22, 1794.

[R. W. McLachlan, *Fleury Mesplet, the first printer at Montreal* (Trans. Roy. Soc. Can., 1906), and *Some unpublished documents relating to Fleury Mesplet* (Trans. Roy. Soc. Can., 1920); A. Fauteux, *Fleury Mesplet: Une étude sur les commencements de l'imprimerie dans la ville de Montréal* (Papers of the Biographical Society of America, vol. xxviii, part 2, 1934); V. Morin, *Fleury Mesplet* (Montreal, 1939); Le Jeune, *Dict. gén.*]

Metcalfe, Sir Charles Theophilus Metcalfe, first Baron (1785-1846), governor-general of Canada (1843-45), was born at the Lecture House, Calcutta, India, on January 30, 1785, the second son of Thomas Theophilus Metcalfe, a major in the Bengal army. He was educated at Eton, and in 1801 entered the Indian civil service. He rose rapidly, and in 1833 was appointed provisional governor-general of India. In 1838 he retired from the Indian civil service; and in 1839 he was appointed governor of Jamaica. In this office he was remarkably successful; and in 1843 he was appointed governor-general of Canada. His period of office in Canada was a critical period. His predecessor, Sir Charles Bagot (q.v.), had conceded, in effect, the demands of the Reformers

for "responsible government"; but the Colonial Office was as yet not prepared to accept the principle without reservations. Metcalfe took up virtually the position which had been adopted by Lord Sydenham (q.v.); and in November, 1843, his ministers, headed by Robert Baldwin (q.v.) and Louis Lafontaine (q.v.), resigned as a protest against his failure to consult them in regard to an official appointment. For nine months he carried on the government without the assistance of a single secretary of state; and then, having formed a Conservative administration, he appealed to the country in November, 1844, and was sustained at the polls. This triumph, however, he did not long survive. He was already the victim of a malignant disease, and in 1845 he was compelled to ask for his recall. He died at Malshanger, near Basingstoke, Hampshire, England, on September 5, 1846. In 1822, on the death of his elder brother, he succeeded to the baronetcy which his father had acquired in 1802; in 1836 he was invested with the G.C.B.; and in 1845, as "a mark of the Queen's entire approbation and favour", he was created Baron Metcalfe of Fern Hill in the county of Berks. He was not married, and on his death the barony became extinct. As an administrator he was exceptionally able and upright; and in Canada justice has never been done to his self-sacrificing zeal and integrity.

[E. Thompson, *The life of Charles, Lord Metcalfe* (London, 1937); Sir J. W. Kaye, *Life and correspondence of Charles, Lord Metcalfe* (new and revised ed., London, 1858); E. G. Wakefield, *View of Sir Charles Metcalfe's government of Canada* (London, 1844); J. C. Dent, *The last forty years* (2 vols., Toronto, 1881); J. L. Morison, *British supremacy and Canadian self-government* (Toronto, 1919); *Dict. nat. biog.*; Morgan, *Cel. Can.* and *Bib. can.*]

Méthot, Michel Edouard (1826-1892), priest and educationist, was born at Ste. Croix de Lotbinière, Lower Canada, on July 28, 1826. He was ordained a priest of the Roman Catholic Church in 1849; and he passed his whole life in the seminary at Quebec. He was first a professor, then prefect of studies, and finally rector of Laval University. He died at Quebec on February 8, 1892. He was the author of a pamphlet entitled *La terre et l'univers* (Quebec, 1869).

[*Bull. rech. hist.*, 1933; Allaire, *Dict. biog.*]

Meulles, Jacques de (*fl.* 1682-1686), intendant of New France (1682-86), was the son of François de Meulles, seignior of the forest of Montpensier, in Poitou. Before coming to Canada he held the office of grand bailiff of Orléans. He was named intendant of New France on May 1, 1682, and he arrived at Quebec on October 9, of that year. His period of office was uneventful, except for his quarrels with the governors. His complaints against La Barre (q.v.) were mainly instrumental in procuring La Barre's recall; and he himself was succeeded by Champigny (q.v.), in 1686, owing to his opposition to Denonville (q.v.). He sailed for France during the first week of October, 1686. He married a sister of Michel Bégon, intendant of Rochefort, and father of Michel Bégon (q.v.), intendant of New France.

[R. Roy, *Jacques de Meulles* (Bull. rech. hist., vol. viii), and *Intendants of New France* (Trans. Roy. Soc. Can., 1903); Le Jeune, *Dict. gén.*]

Mewburn, Sydney Chilton (1863-1956), soldier and politician, was born in Hamilton, Canada West, on December 4, 1863, and died there on August 11, 1956. He was called to the bar in Ontario in 1885 (K.C., 1910), and practised law in Hamilton. In 1910 he became commanding officer of the 13th Royal Regiment of Hamilton; and on the outbreak of the First World War he served in an administrative capacity in the department of militia and defence, rising to the rank of major-general in 1917. During the conscription crisis of 1917, however, he retired from the army and successfully carried East Hamilton as a Unionist in support of Sir Robert Borden (q.v.). He became minister of militia and defence in the Borden government, and resigned this portfolio only in 1920, when demobilization had been completed. He continued to represent East Hamilton in the House of Commons until 1925. He was created a C.M.G. in 1916.

[*Can. who's who*, 1952-54; *Can. parl. guide*, 1920; *Encyc. Can.*]

Meyer, Hoppner (*fl.* 1842-1860), painter and engraver, was born in London, England, in the early years of the nineteenth century, the son of Henry Meyer (1782-1847), a painter and engraver of German extraction. He came to Canada about 1842; and he was a "professor of painting" in Toronto from 1842 to 1860. During this time he did a number of small portraits in water-colour. He is said to have returned to England, and to have died there; but the date of his death has not been ascertained.

[W. Colgate, *Hoppner Meyer, a painter and engraver of Upper Canada* (Ont. Hist. Soc., papers and records, 1945).]

Mézy, Augustin de Saffray, Chevalier de (d. 1665), governor of New France (1663-65), was town major of Caën, Normandy, and the principal member of the company of devotees formed at Caën by Bernières (q.v.). His piety so delighted Bishop Laval (q.v.) that the latter had him appointed governor of New France in 1663, believing that he would prove a willing tool in his hands. Laval and Mézy reached Quebec on September 15, 1663, and for a time all went well. Mézy, however, in the following year, gave evidence of a strong will of his own, removed from the council at Quebec those members who were Laval's creatures, and reconstructed the council by his own authority. Laval preferred charges against him at court, and an inquiry was ordered. Before this could take place, Mézy died at Quebec, on May 6, 1665.

[F. Parkman, *The old régime in Canada* (Boston, 1880); R. G. Thwaites (ed.), *The Jesuit relations*, vol. 47 (Cleveland, Ohio, 1899); *Bull. rech. hist.*, vol. 5; Le Jeune, *Dict. gén.*; *Dict. Can. biog.*, vol. 1.]

Michel, Sir John (1804-1886), administrator of the government of Canada (1865-66 and 1866-67), was born in Dorsetshire, England, on September 1, 1804, the son of Lieutenant-General John Michel. He was educated at Eton, and entered the army in 1823. In 1858 he was gazetted major-general; in 1866, lieutenant-general; in 1874, general; and in 1885, field-marshal. From 1865 to 1867 he was commander-in-chief of the British forces in North America; and during the absence of Lord Monck (q.v.) in England from September 30, 1865, to February 12, 1866, and from December 10, 1866, to June 25, 1867, he was administrator of the government of Canada. From 1875 to 1880 he was commander of the forces in Ireland; and he died at Dawlish, Dorsetshire, England, on May 23, 1886. He was created a K.C.B. in 1858 and a G.C.B. in 1865.

[*Dict. nat. biog.*; *Cyc. Am. biog.*; Taylor, *Brit. Am.*, vol. 2; *Dom. ann. reg.*, 1886.]

Michell, Humfrey (1883-1970), economist, was born in London, England, February 21, 1883, and graduated in 1905 from Oxford University. In 1910 he came to Canada as a teacher at St. John's College, Winnipeg, and, while there, completed the requirements for his M.A. degree at the University of Manitoba. He joined the staff of Queen's University, Kingston, Ontario, in 1913 as assistant director of the correspondence course in banking which Queen's administered for the Canadian Bankers' Association. In 1919 he moved to McMaster University and remained there as professor of political economy until his retirement in 1948. After retirement he went to Lennoxville, P.Q., where he taught for some years at Bishop's College. His early publications dealt with co-operative institutions and agricultural problems. His "Caisses Populaires", published in *Queen's Quarterly* (1914), was the earliest study, in English, of this co-operative banking venture. He also published, in the same journal, "The Grange in Canada" (1914); "The problem of agricultural credit in Canada" (1914); "The co-operative store in Canada" (1916); and "Profit-sharing and producers' co-operatives in Canada" (1918). He contributed "A survey of prices in Canada from 1848" to *Statistical contributions to Canadian economic history to 1931*, ed. W. A. Mackintosh (Toronto, 1931). From 1927 to 1931 he published *The Canadian Economic*

Service, but was forced to discontinue because of lack of money. During the thirties he worked on *The Economics of ancient Greece*, which was published at Cambridge in 1940. He published a further study under the title *Sparta* (Cambridge, 1953). His studies of prices and business cycles in Canada and his encouragement of the statistical approach to economic studies are among his lasting contributions to learning. He was elected a fellow of the Royal Society of Canada in 1942. He died at Lennoxville, P.Q., May 5, 1970.

[*Proc. and Trans. Roy. Soc. Can.*, 1970; *Can. who's who*, 1955-57.]

Middlemiss, James (1823-1907), clergyman and author, was born at Duns, Berwickshire, Scotland, on February 24, 1823. He was educated at Edinburgh University and at the Free Church College, Edinburgh; and he was licensed as a candidate for the ministry of the Free Church of Scotland in 1849. He came to Canada in 1855, and from 1856 until his resignation in 1893 he was the minister of the Presbyterian church in Elora, Ontario. He died at Guelph, Ontario, on March 10, 1907. In 1886 he received the degree of D.D. from Knox Church, Toronto. He was the author of *Letters on the union with the Church of Scotland* (Toronto, 1874), *A plea for popular instruction in the evidences of Christianity* (Toronto, 1883), *Misconception of Calvinism* (Toronto, n.d.), and *Christian instruction in the public schools of Ontario* (Toronto, 1901).

[Morgan, *Can. men* (1898); John R. Connon, *Elora* (Elora, Ont., 1930).]

Middleton, Sir Frederick Dobson (1825-1898), soldier, was born at Belfast, Ireland, on November 2, 1825, the son of Major General Charles Middleton and Fanny, daughter of Francis Wheatley, R.A. He was educated at Sandhurst, and entered the British army in 1842. He saw service in the Indian Mutiny; and in 1868 he was stationed in Canada. In 1884 he was appointed to the command of the Canadian militia, with the rank of major-general; and he commanded the expedition sent to the North West Territories to suppress the Riel Rebellion in 1885. For his services in suppressing the rebellion he was granted a pension, and created a K.C.M.G. In 1887 he was retired with the rank of lieutenant-general; but he continued to command the Canadian militia until 1890. In 1896 he was appointed Keeper of the Crown Jewels at the Tower of London; and he died at London on January 25, 1898. He was twice married, (1) to Emily, daughter of T. Hassall, and (2) in 1870 to Eugénie Marie, daughter of Théodore Doucet, of Montreal. He contributed an account of the North West Rebellion to the *United Service Magazine*, and this has been republished, with notes and an introduction, by G. H. Needler (Toronto, 1948).

[*Who was who*, 1897-1916; Morgan, *Can.*

men (1898); Rose, *Cyc. Can. biog.* (1886); *Dom. ann. reg.*, 1885; G. T. Denison, *Soldiering in Canada* (Toronto, 1901).]

Middleton, Jesse Edgar (1872-1960), journalist and author, was born in Pilkington township, Wellington county, Ontario, on November 3, 1872, and died at Toronto, Ontario, on May 27, 1960. He was educated at the Ottawa Normal School, and for a few years taught school. He then turned to journalism, and for most of his life was a special writer on Toronto newspapers. He was a most versatile author. He first published a volume of poetry, *Sea-dogs and men-at-arms* (Toronto, 1918); he then turned to local history and wrote *The municipality of Toronto* (3 vols., Toronto, 1923), *The romance of Ontario* (Toronto, 1931), and *Toronto's hundred years* (Toronto, 1934); and he was the author of two novels, *Green plush* (London, 1932) and *The clever ones* (London, 1936). With Fred Landon, he was joint author of *The province of Ontario: A history* (4 vols., Toronto, 1927); with E. L. Morrison, of *William Tyrrell of Weston* (Toronto, n.d.); and with his wife, of *Green fields afar* (Toronto, 1947).

[*Can. who's who*, 1948.]

Middleton, Sir John (1870-1954), governor of Newfoundland (1928-32), was born in Scotland in 1870, and died at Bath, England, on November 5, 1954. He was educated at Edinburgh University, and entered the British colonial service. After occupying various positions, he was governor of Newfoundland from 1928 to 1932. He was created a K.B.E. in 1924, and a K.C.M.G. in 1931.

[*Encyc. Can.*; *Newfoundland supp.*]

Mignault, Pierre Basil (1854-1945), jurist, was born at Worcester, Massachusetts, on September 30, 1854, and died at Montreal, Quebec, on October 15, 1945. He studied law at McGill University (B.C.L., 1878), and was called to the bar in 1878. He practised law in Montreal, and in 1906 became *bâtonnier* of the Montreal bar. From 1918 to 1929 he was a justice of the Supreme Court of Canada. He was the author of *Manuel de droit parlementaire* (Montreal, 1889), *Droit paroissial* (Montreal, 1893), and *Le droit civil canadien* (9 vols., Montreal, 1895-1916). He was elected a fellow of the Royal Society of Canada in 1908; and he received honorary degrees from several universities, including the University of Paris.

[*Proc. Roy. Soc. Can.*, 1946; *Can. who's who*, 1936-37.]

Mikel, William Charles (1867-1950), lawyer and local historian, was born in Belleville, Ontario, in 1867, and died there in October, 1950. He was educated at the University of Trinity College (B.C.L., 1897) and Osgoode Hall, and became a prominent lawyer in

Belleville. He was the author of *City of Belleville history* (Picton, Ont., 1943).

[*Can. who's who*, 1948.]

Miles, Henry Hopper (1818-1895), author and educationist, was born in London, England, on October 18, 1818, the son of Lieut. Richard Miles, R.N. He was educated at the universities of Edinburgh and Aberdeen; and in 1845 he came to Canada as vice-principal and professor of mathematics in the University of Bishop's College, Lennoxville. In 1867 he was appointed secretary of the department of public instruction in the province of Quebec, and this post he occupied until only a few years before his death on August 4, 1895. In 1847 he married Elizabeth, daughter of William Wilson, M.D., of Ripon, Yorkshire; and by her he had two sons and two daughters. He was an LL.D. of the University of Aberdeen (1863) and of McGill University (1866), and a D.C.L. of Bishop's College (1866). He was the author of *On the ventilation of dwelling-houses and schools* (Montreal, 1858), *The Canadian archives* (Quebec, 1870), *A school history of Canada* (Montreal, 1870), *The history of Canada under the French régime* (Montreal, 1872), and *The child's history of Canada* (Montreal, 1876), as well as of some papers in the *Transactions* of the Literary and Historical Society of Quebec.

[J. D. Borthwick, *History of the diocese of Montreal* (Montreal, 1910).]

Miles, John C. (d. 1911), painter, was born and educated in Saint John, New Brunswick, of loyalist descent. He studied painting and drawing in Boston, and in 1871, he opened a studio in Boston, and was elected a member of the Boston Art Club. In 1882 he was chosen an associate of the Royal Canadian Academy of Arts; and later he returned to live in Saint John. He was mainly notable for his landscapes of the Maritime provinces; but he was also a successful portrait painter. He died in Saint John, New Brunswick, on December 2, 1911.

[W. P. Dole, *Some fine art* (Acadiensis, 1903); Morgan, *Can. men* (1912).]

Miles, Robert Seaborn (1795?-1870), furtrader, was born about 1795 at Fairford, Oxfordshire, England. He entered the service of the Hudson's Bay Company as an accountant and writer; and from 1821 to 1833 he was accountant at York Factory. He was promoted to the rank of chief trader in 1828, and to that of chief factor in 1844. From 1844 to 1857, he was in charge at Moose Factory; and from 1858 to 1860, in the Lake Huron district. He retired in 1861; and he died at Horning Toft, near Brockville, Ontario, on May 3, 1870.

[E. E. Rich (ed.), *Journal of occurrences in the Athabasca department, by George Simpson* (Toronto: The Champlain Society, 1938).]

Miles, Stephen (1789-1870), journalist and clergyman, was born at Royalton, Vermont, on October 19, 1789, of English and Welsh extraction. In 1805 he became an apprentice in the printing office of Nahum Mower at Windsor, Vermont; and in 1807 he accompanied Mower when he moved his printing press to Montreal, Lower Canada. In 1810 he founded in Kingston the *Kingston Gazette*, the first newspaper published in the eastern part of Upper Canada. He sold his press in 1819, and for nine years he was the printer of the *Upper Canada Herald*, owned and edited by Hugh C. Thomson (q.v.). From 1828 to 1830 he published the *Kingston Gazette and Religious Advocate*; and from 1832 to 1833 he published in Prescott the *Grenville Gazette*. In 1835 his career as a printer and journalist came to an end, and he entered the Wesleyan ministry. After serving for many years as an itinerant preacher, he was superannuated about 1854. He died at Ernestown, Ontario, on December 13, 1870; and he was buried at Camden East, Ontario.

[W. Canniff, *History of the settlement of Upper Canada* (Toronto, 1869), pp. 352-55; J. Carroll, *Case and his contemporaries* (5 vols., Toronto, 1867-77).]

Millar, John (d. 1905), educationist and author, was born in Ireland, but came to Canada at an early age, and was educated at the Toronto Normal School and at the University of Toronto (B.A., 1872). He became a highly successful teacher, and in 1890 he was appointed deputy minister of education for Ontario. He died at Toronto on October 3, 1905. He was the author of *School management* (Toronto, 1896), *Books, a guide to good reading* (Toronto, 1897), *The school system of the state of New York* (Toronto, 1898), and *Canadian citizenship* (Toronto, 1899).

[Morgan, *Can. men* (1898).]

Miller, Andrew Howard (1886-1962), geophysicist, was born on a farm near Teulon, Manitoba, June 13, 1886. He attended local schools and St. John's College in Winnipeg, where he received his B.A. degree and the Rhodes scholarship for Manitoba in 1906. He went to Oxford University (B.A., 1910), and then to the School of Engineering at McGill in Montreal. He was appointed lecturer at the University of Wisconsin, but left after two years to join the Canadian Field Artillery on the outbreak of the First World War. He served in France for three years, re-entering Oxford in 1918 for graduate studies in applied science (M.A., 1919). On his return to Canada he joined the staff of the Dominion Observatory, where he served until his retirement in 1951. His main interests were the measurement and interpretation of the earth's gravitational field, and the application of physical methods to problems of prospecting for minerals and of structural geology. He initiated gravity surveys to cover Canada systematically. Early surveys of the lower reaches of the Mackenzie River made by him in 1921 and 1922 demanded long trips by barge, wagon, pack-horse, and on foot with more than two tons of equipment. In 1928 he completed a series of pendulum observations to link the important gravity reference stations on Europe and North America. He published twelve articles dealing with the fundamental and practical aspects of both magnetic and gravitational methods of prospecting. During the Second World War he worked with the National Research Council in the establishment of a standard gauge-testing laboratory for the use of war industries throughout Canada. Post-war gravimeters made it possible to demonstrate the power of gravimetry in delineating earth structure. Miller supervised the establishment of some 5,000 gravimeter stations between 1945 and 1951. He published thirty scientific papers on earth physics. He was a member of the Royal Astronomical Society of Canada and of the Royal Society of Canada. He died at Ottawa, March 11, 1962.

[*Proc. Roy. Soc. Can.*, 1962.]

Miller, Emile (1885-1922), educationist, was born at St. Placide, Quebec, in 1885. He became professor of geography at the University of Montreal, and secretary of the Société Saint-Jean-Baptiste of Montreal. He was drowned at Contrecoeur, Quebec, on August 3, 1922, while trying to save his small son. He was the author of *Terres et peuples du Canada* (Montreal, 1913), *Pour qu'on aime la géographie* (Montreal, 1921), and *Mon voyage autour du monde* (Montreal, 1926).

[*Bulletin de la Société de Géographie de Québec*, septembre-octobre, 1922.]

Miller, James Collins (1880-1940), educationist, was born in Wellington county, Ontario, on June 18, 1880. He was educated at Throop College, Pasadena, Cal. (B.S., 1907); and at Columbia University (M.A., 1910; Ph.D., 1913). He became an expert in technical education, and served in the departments of education in both Alberta and Ontario in this capacity. During the First World War he was employed in both Canada and the United States as an expert in vocational rehabilitation. In 1921 he was appointed professor of education at Indiana University; and in 1925, professor of educational administration at the University of Pennsylvania. He died at Philadelphia, Pa., on September 30, 1940. He was the author of *Rural schools in Canada* (New York, 1913) and *National government and education in federated democracies: The Dominion of Canada* (New York, 1940).

[*Who was who in America.*]

Miller, John Ormsby (1861-1936), clergyman and educationist, was born in Liverpool, England, in 1861. He came to Canada as a young man, and was educated at the University of Toronto (B.A., 1888; M.A., 1890). He was ordained a priest of the Church of England in 1888, and in 1889 he was appointed headmaster of Ridley College, at St. Catharines, Ontario. He continued as headmaster of this school until his retirement in 1921; and he died at Toronto, Ontario, on November 17, 1936. He was the author of *Short studies in ethics* (Toronto, 1895), and the editor of *The new era in Canada* (Toronto, 1917).

[Morgan, *Can. men* (1912).]

Miller, Mrs. Maria, *née* **Morris** (1813-1875), artist, was born in Halifax, Nova Scotia, in 1813, and made a specialty of painting the flowers of Nova Scotia. She published a series of her paintings in *The wild flowers of Nova Scotia* (London, 1840; 2nd series, 1853). She died at Halifax, Nova Scotia, on October 28, 1875.

[Morgan, *Bib. can.*; *Dict. Can. biog.*, vol. 10.]

Miller, Willet Green (1866-1925), geologist, was born at Forrestville, Norfolk county, Ontario, on July 19, 1866. He was educated at the University of Toronto (B.A., 1890), and later he held junior appointments in the University of Toronto and Queen's University, and at Chicago, Harvard, and Heidelberg universities. In 1896 he entered the employ of the government of Ontario as a geologist, and in 1902 he was appointed provincial geologist. He had a great deal to do with the development of mining in Ontario in the period that followed; and he received many honours in recognition of his services. He was given the honorary degree of LL.D. from Queen's University in 1907 and from the University of Toronto in 1913; and in 1914 he was awarded the gold medal of the Institute of Mining and Metallurgy. He was elected a fellow of the Royal Society of Canada; and after his death the Royal Society of Canada established the Willet Green Miller medal in his honour. He died at Toronto, Ontario, on February 4, 1925. He was the author of *Minerals and how they occur* (Toronto, 1906).

[*Can. who was who*, vol. 1; *Proc. Roy. Soc. Can.*, 1925; Le Jeune, *Dict. gén.*; Morgan, *Can. men* (1912).]

Miller, William (1835-1912), speaker of the Senate of Canada, was born in Antigonish, Nova Scotia, on February 12, 1835, the son of Charles Miller. He was educated at the Antigonish Academy, and was called to the bar of Nova Scotia in 1860 (Q.C., 1872). He sat in the House of Assembly of Nova Scotia from 1863 to 1867; and was a prominent advocate of Confederation. He was called to the Senate of Canada in 1867, and from 1883 to 1887 was its speaker. He died on February 23, 1912. In 1891 he was appointed a member of the Privy Council for Canada.

[*Cyc. Am. biog.*; *Can. parl. comp.*; Morgan,

Can. men (1912); Rose, *Cyc. Can. biog.* (1886).]

Miller, William Lash (1866-1940), chemist, was born at Galt, Ontario, in 1866; and was educated at the University of Toronto (B.A., 1887) and at Munich University (Ph.D., 1890). He returned to the University of Toronto as a demonstrator in chemistry; and from 1907 to 1938 he was professor of physical chemistry in this university. He was elected a fellow of the Royal Society of Canada in 1899, and its president in 1934. In 1935 he was awarded, in recognition of his scientific researches, the C.B.E. He died at Toronto, Ontario, on September 1, 1940.

[*Proc. Roy. Soc. Can.*, 1941; *Can. who's who*, 1936-37; Morgan, *Can. men* (1912).]

Milligan, James Lewis (1876-1961), poet and dramatist, was born in Liverpool, England, in 1876. A graduate of the University of Liverpool, he came to Canada in 1911. He had already published some poetry and had won the Henman's prize medal for poetry. A lay preacher in the Methodist church, he became editor of the Peterborough *Review*. In 1914 he joined the Toronto *Globe* as a military correspondent and editorial writer. He left in 1922 to do publicity for the Church Union Movement. In 1925 he became a member of the *Mail and Empire* staff and later did public-relations work for the Ontario department of mines. His last editorial position was with the *Stratford Beacon-Herald*, from which he retired in 1937. In addition to his newspaper writing, Mr. Milligan wrote hymns; a play, *Judas Iscariot*; the lyrics for a light opera, *The Dream Pedlar*; and several volumes of verse. He died at Toronto, Ontario, on May 1, 1961.

[Toronto *Globe and Mail*, May 2, 1961.]

Mills, David (1831-1903), minister of the interior (1876-78) and minister of justice for Canada (1897-1902), was born in the township of Oxford, Kent county, Upper Canada, on March 18, 1831, the son of Nathaniel Mills and Mary Guggerty. He was educated at the common schools and at the University of Michigan (LL.B., 1855). From 1856 to 1865 he was superintendent of schools for the county of Kent. In 1867 he was elected as a Reformer to the Canadian House of Commons for Bothwell; and he represented this constituency continuously until 1896. Having been defeated in the general elections of that year, he was appointed to the Senate, and he continued a member of the Senate until 1902. From 1876 to 1878 he was minister of the interior in the Mackenzie administration; and from 1897 to 1902 he was minister of justice in the Laurier government. In 1872 he was commissioned by the government of Ontario to report upon the boundaries of Ontario; and he published a report embodying the results of his investigations (Toronto, 1873). From 1882 to 1887 he

was chief editorial writer on the London *Advertiser*; and in 1883 he was called to the bar of Ontario (Q.C., 1890). He came to be regarded as an authority on constitutional law; and in 1888 was appointed to the chair of constitutional and international law in the University of Toronto. In 1902 he was appointed a judge of the Supreme Court of Canada; but he held this position for only one year. He died at Ottawa on May 8, 1903. In 1860 he married Mary J. Brown of Chatham, Ontario; and by her he had three sons and four daughters.

[F. Landon, *David Mills* (Willison's monthly, 1929); Morgan, *Can. men* (1898); Rose, *Cyc. Can. biog.* (1886); *Can. parl. comp.*; J. S. Willison, *Sir Wilfrid Laurier and the Liberal party* (2 vols., Toronto, 1903).]

Mills, James (1840-1924), educationist and railway commissioner, was born near Bond Head, Upper Canada, on November 24, 1840. He was educated at Victoria University (B.A., 1868; M.A., 1871; LL.D., 1892); and became a school-teacher. In 1879 he was appointed president of the Ontario Agricultural College, and he continued in this position until his appointment in 1904 as a member of the Board of Railway Commissioners for Canada. He died at Ottawa, Ontario, on April 4, 1924. With T. Shaw, he was joint author of *The first principles of agriculture* (Toronto, 1890).

[Morgan, *Can. men* (1912); Rose, *Cyc. Can. biog.* (1886); *Can. parl. comp.*]

Mills, Thomas Wesley (1847-1915), physiologist, was born at Brockville, Canada West, on February 22, 1847. He was educated at the University of Toronto (B.A., 1871); M.A., 1872) and at McGill University (M.D., C.M., 1878; D.V.S., 1890). He became a demonstrator in physiology at McGill University in 1882; and from 1886 to 1910 he was professor of physiology. He was elected a fellow of the Royal Society of Canada in 1890. He died in London, England, on February 13, 1915. He wrote *A text-book of animal physiology* (New York, 1889), *A text-book of comparative physiology* (New York, 1890), *The dog in health and in disease* (New York, 1892), *The nature and development of animal intelligence* (London, 1898), and *Voice production in singing and speaking* (Philadelphia, 1906).

[Morgan, *Can. men* (1912).]

Mills, William Lennox (1846-1917), Anglican bishop of Ontario (1901-17), was born at Woodstock, Canada West, on January 27, 1846. He was educated at Huron College, London (B.D., 1884) and at Trinity University (B.D., 1884; D.D., 1894; D.C.L., 1901), and was ordained a priest of the Church of England in 1873. After serving as rector of several parishes in Ontario and Quebec, he was in 1900 elected coadjutor-bishop of Ontario, with the title of bishop of Kingston; and he became bishop of Ontario in 1901. He died at Kingston, Ontario, on May 4, 1917. In 1901 Queen's University conferred on him the honorary degree of LL.D.

[Morgan, *Can. men* (1912).]

Milne, David Bruce (1882-1953), painter, was born in Bruce county, Ontario, in 1882, and died at Toronto, Ontario, on December 26, 1953. He studied art at the Art Students' League in New York; and in 1918 he was appointed official artist for the Canadian War Memorials. After the war he painted in the Berkshire Hills; but he returned to Canada in 1929, and settled in Muskoka. His painting was highly individual and impressionistic, and he gained recognition only slowly. He was a member of the Canadian Group of Painters.

[D. W. Buchanan, *The growth of Canadian painting* (Toronto, 1950); G. Elliott, *David Milne* (Canadian Art, Spring 1954); *Encyc. Can.*]

Milner, William Stafford (1861-1931), educationist, was born at Toronto, Canada West, on March 28, 1861, and was educated at the University of Toronto (B.A., 1881; M.A., 1895). After teaching for some time in secondary schools, he was appointed in 1891 associate professor of classics in University College, Toronto, and in 1907 professor of Greek and Roman history. He retired on pension in 1929, and he died at Toronto on April 27, 1931. As a teacher, he exerted a profound influence on successive generations of students; but he published little, his chief publication being a pamphlet entitled *Greek, Roman, English, and American conceptions of liberty* (Toronto, 1903).

[*Can. who was who*, vol. 1; Morgan, *Can. men* (1912); *University of Toronto monthly*, 1929.]

Milnes, Sir Robert Shore, Bart. (1746-1837), lieutenant-governor of Lower Canada (1797-1808), was born in England in 1746, the son of John Milnes of Wakefield. He obtained a commission in the Royal Horse Guards; and in 1795 he was appointed governor of Martinique. In 1797 he came to Canada as lieutenant-governor of Lower Canada, and from 1799 to 1805 he was administrator of the government. He returned to England in 1805, and he ceased to be lieutenant-governor of Lower Canada in 1808. He died in 1837. In 1801 he was created a baronet of the United Kingdom.

[F. J. Audet, *Gouverneurs, lieutenant-gouverneurs de la province de Québec* (Trans. Roy. Soc. Can., 1908); R. Christie, *History of Lower Canada* (6 vols., Montreal and Quebec, 1848-56); Morgan, *Cel. Can.*; Le Jeune, *Dict. gén.*]

Miner, Jack (1865-1944), naturalist, was born at Dover Centre, Ohio, on April 10, 1865.

He came to Canada with his parents in 1878, and settled in Essex county, Ontario. Here he established in 1904 a bird sanctuary at Kingsville; and this bird sanctuary achieved world-wide fame. Wild geese and other migratory birds were caught and tagged, with a view to the study of their migrations; and great advances were made in the conservation of the wild bird life of North America. The Jack Miner Migratory Bird Foundation was created for the purpose of ensuring the continuance of the work of the bird sanctuary; and its founder came to be known as the chief of bird lovers and conservationists in North America. In 1943 he was created an O.B.E. He died at Kingsville, Ontario, on November 3, 1944. He was the author of *Jack Miner and the birds* (Toronto, 1934) and *Jack Miner on current topics* (Toronto, 1929).

[J. B. Tigrett, *Duck's best friend is Jack Miner* (Saturday evening post, March 18, 1944); *Can. who's who*, 1936-37; *Who's who among North American authors*, vol. 7.]

Minto, Gilbert John Elliot, fourth Earl of (1845-1914), governor-general of Canada (1898-1904), was born on July 9, 1845, the eldest son of William Hugh, third Earl of Minto, and Emma Eleanor Elizabeth Hislop. He was educated at Eton and at Trinity College, Cambridge (B.A., 1866; Hon. LL.D., 1911), and obtained a commission in the Scots Guards. He was attached to the Turkish army during the Russo-Turkish War of 1877, served in the Afghan campaign of 1879 and in the Egyptian campaign of 1882, and was chief of staff under General Middleton (q.v.) in the Canadian North West Rebellion of 1885. From 1883 to 1885 he was also military secretary to Lord Lansdowne (q.v.), governor-general of Canada. He succeeded to the earldom of Minto in 1891; and in 1898 he was appointed governor-general of Canada. His period of office, which lasted until 1904, coincided with the earlier part of the administration of Sir Wilfrid Laurier (q.v.), when considerable advances were made toward Canadian autonomy; and the difficulties which he encountered were handled with exceptional tact, though it cannot be said that he was a popular governor. In 1905 he was appointed viceroy of India, and he remained in India until 1910. He died at Hawick, Scotland, on March 1, 1914. In 1883 he married Mary Caroline, daughter of General the Hon. Charles Grey; and by her he had two sons and three daughters. He was created a G.C.M.G. in 1898, a privy councillor in 1902, and a K.G. in 1910. In 1911 he was elected Lord Rector of Edinburgh University.

[John Buchan, *Lord Minto, a memoir* (London, 1924); *Dict. nat. biog.*, 3rd supp.; *Who was who*, 1897-1916; Morgan, *Can. men* (1912); O. D. Skelton, *The life and letters of Sir Wilfrid Laurier* (2 vols., Toronto, 1921).]

Misener, Robert Scott (1878-1963), shipowner, was born in Port Colborne, Ontario, in 1878. He first sailed on a lake ship at fifteen as a deck-hand on a lumber-hauler. Nine years later he had his master's papers; and soon afterward he bought a wooden steamer and went into the shipping business. He and J. O. McKellar operated a number of ships under the name Sarnia Steamships Limited. After the Second World War, and with the opening of the St. Lawrence Seaway, the company bought larger ships and became Scott Misener Steamships. Mr. Misener remained president and general manager of the line which operated twelve ships until his death at Port Colborne, June 3, 1963.

[Metropolitan Toronto Library Board, *Biographical scrapbooks*, vol. 21.]

Mitchell, Charles Hamilton (1872-1941), civil engineer, soldier, and educationist, was born at Petrolia, Ontario, on February 18, 1872. He was educated at the University of Toronto (B.A.Sc., 1894; C.E., 1898; LL.D., 1918); and for many years practised in Niagara Falls and Toronto as a civil engineer. He joined the Canadian militia in 1899; and he served in the First World War as an intelligence officer in France, Belgium, and Italy. He rose to the rank of brigadier-general; and he was awarded the D.S.O. in 1916, the C.M.G. in 1917, and the C.B. in 1918. In 1919 he was appointed dean of the faculty of applied science in the University of Toronto; and he retained this post until his death at Toronto, Ontario, on August 26, 1941.

[*Americana annual*, 1942; *Can. who's who*, 1936-37; *University of Toronto monthly*, 1941.]

Mitchell, Humphrey (1894-1950), minister of labour for Canada (1941-50), was born in Old Shoreham, Sussex, England, on September 9, 1894, and died at Ottawa, Ontario, on August 1, 1950. He came to Canada in 1912, and settled in Hamilton, Ontario. He served in the Royal Navy from 1914 to 1918, but returned to Hamilton after the war, and took an active part in trade union affairs. In 1931 he was elected Labour member of the Canadian House of Commons for East Hamilton; and, though he was defeated in 1935, he was appointed minister of labour in the King government in 1941, and was elected in a by-election for Welland. He held the portfolio of minister of labour until his death in 1950.

[*Can. who's who*, 1948; *Can. parl. guide*, 1949; *Encyc. Can.*]

Mitchell, James (1843-1897), prime minister of New Brunswick (1896-97), was born at the Scotch settlement, York county, New Brunswick, on March 16, 1843, the son of William Mitchell and Ann Dobie. He was educated at the University of New Brunswick (B.A., 1867; M.A., 1869; LL.D., 1897); he was called to the bar of New Brunswick in 1870 (Q.C.,

1891); and he practised law at St. Stephen, New Brunswick. He was a member of the Legislative Assembly of New Brunswick for Charlotte county from 1882 to 1897; and from 1883 to 1897 he was a member of the Executive Council, holding successively the portfolios of surveyor-general (1883-90), provincial secretary, receiver-general, commissioner of agriculture (1890-96), and attorney-general (1896-97). From 1896 to 1897 he was prime minister of New Brunswick; but in October, 1897, he was forced to resign through ill-health, and he died at St. Stephen, New Brunswick, on December 15, 1897. In 1873 he married Mary Anne, daughter of L. Ryder of St. Stephen.

[J. Hannay, *Premier of New Brunswick* (Can. mag., 1897); Morgan, *Can. men* (1898); Rose, *Cyc. Can. biog.* (1888); *Can. parl. comp.*]

Mitchell, John (1882-1951), author, was born in 1882, and died at Toronto, Ontario, on October 18, 1951. He became a lawyer, and got himself into trouble with the law; and his trial and conviction roused a good deal of public interest. But his chief claim to fame is that he was the author, under the pseudonym of "Patrick Slater", of two novels, *The yellow briar* (Toronto, 1933), and *Robert Harding* (Toronto, 1938), and a volume of verse, *The waterdrinker* (Toronto, 1938). He also wrote *The settlement of York County* (Toronto, 1952), which was published posthumously.

[Toronto *Globe and Mail*, Oct. 20, 1951; *Encyc. Can.*]

Mitchell, Peter (1824-1899), prime minister of New Brunswick (1866-67) and one of the Fathers of Confederation, was born at Newcastle, New Brunswick, on January 4, 1824. He was educated at the Newcastle grammar school, and was called to the bar of New Brunswick in 1848. From 1856 to 1860 he was a member of the Legislative Assembly of New Brunswick, and from 1860 to 1867 a member of the Legislative Council. He was a member of the Tilley administration from 1858 to 1865, and a delegate to the Quebec Conference in 1864. On the defeat of the anti-Confederation government of 1864-65 in New Brunswick, he became prime minister and president of the Council; and it fell to him to make the final arrangements for the entrance of the province into Confederation. At the Westminster conference of 1866 he joined with Sir George Cartier (q.v.) in pressing for a federal rather than a unitary type of government in Canada. In 1867 he was called to the Senate of Canada, and became minister of marine and fisheries in the first Dominion government. In 1872 he resigned from the Senate, and was elected to the House of Commons for his old constituency of Northumberland; and this constituency he represented as an independent Liberal from 1872 to 1878, and from 1882 to 1891. In 1873, on the defeat of the Macdonald government, he became editor of the Montreal *Herald*, and in 1885 he became its proprietor. He died at Montreal, on October 25, 1899. In 1853 he married Mrs. Gough, of Saint John, New Brunswick. He was the author of *A review of President Grant's recent message to the U.S. Congress* (Ottawa, 1870) and *Notes on a holiday trip* (Montreal, 1880), the latter an account of a visit to the North-West. Some of his political reminiscences are contained in an article in the Toronto *News*, February 15, 1894.

[M. O. Hammond, *Confederation and its leaders* (Toronto, 1917); *Dict. nat. biog.*, supp. I; Morgan, *Can. men* (1898); E. M. Saunders, *Three premiers of Nova Scotia* (Toronto, 1909); J. Hannay, *History of New Brunswick* (2 vols., Saint John, N.B., 1909); J. C. Dent, *The last forty years* (2 vols., Toronto, 1881); W. G. MacFarlane, *New Brunswick bibliography* (Saint John, N.B., 1895).]

Mitchell, Roy (1884-1944), theatrical director, was born at Fort Gratiot, Michigan, in 1884. He was educated at the University of Toronto (B.A., 1906), and first became a newspaper reporter. When Hart House theatre was opened in Toronto in 1919, he was appointed its first director; and throughout life he was interested in the Little Theatre movement. In his later years he was professor of the drama department in New York University. He died, while on a holiday, at New Canaan, Connecticut, on July 27, 1944. He was the author of *Shakespeare for community players* (Toronto, 1919), *The school theatre* (New York, 1925), and *Creative theatre* (New York, 1929).

[Toronto *Globe and Mail*, July 28, 1944.]

Moberly, Walter (1832-1915), civil engineer, was born at Steeple Orton, Oxfordshire, England, on August 15, 1832, the second son of Captain John Moberly, R.N. He came to Canada when a child, and was educated at Barrie, Ontario. He studied engineering under F. W. Cumberland (q.v.); and in 1859 he was appointed superintendent of public works in British Columbia. In 1862-63 he was engaged in the construction of the Yale-Cariboo wagon road; and in 1864-66 he was assistant surveyor-general of British Columbia. In 1864 he was elected to the Legislative Council of British Columbia; but in 1866 he went to the United States, and for four years was engaged there in exploration and railway-building. In 1871 he returned to Canada to take charge of the Rocky Mountain and British Columbia surveys for the Canadian Pacific Railway. He was then employed as an engineer in Manitoba; and he died at Vancouver, British Columbia, on May 14, 1915. He was the author of *The rocks and rivers of British Columbia* (London, 1885; reprinted, Ottawa, 1926), and of two papers of an autobiographical character, *History of Cariboo wagon road* (Vancouver, 1908)

and *The early history of the Canadian Pacific Railway* (Vancouver, 1909).

[*Can. who was who*, vol. 1; Morgan, *Can. men* (1898); H. Palmer, *Early explorations in British Columbia for the Canadian Pacific Railway* (Bulletin of the Geographical Society of Philadelphia, vol. 16).]

Mockridge, Charles Henry (1844-1913), ecclesiastical historian, was born at Brantford, Canada West, on December 15, 1844, the son of the Rev. James Mockridge. He was educated at Trinity University, Toronto (B.A., 1865; M.A., 1869; B.D., 1877; D.D., 1882), and was ordained a priest of the Church of England in 1869. He was successively rector of a number of parishes in Canada and the United States; and he died at Louisville, Kentucky, on February 25, 1913. He was the author of *The bishops of the Church of England in Canada and Newfoundland* (Toronto, 1896) and *Twenty-five years of the Church in Canada* (Toronto, 1898).

[Morgan, *Can. men* (1912); *Can. who was who*, vol. 1.]

Moffatt, George (1787-1865), merchant and legislative councillor, was born at Sidehead, Durham, England, on August 13, 1787, and came to Canada in 1801. He entered the service of the XY Company; and appears to have remained in the western country, as a clerk, first of the XY Company, and then of the North West Company, until about 1810. In 1811 he appears in Montreal, in partnership with a young merchant named Dowie, who was a nephew of Sir Alexander Mackenzie (q.v.). Shortly afterwards he entered the firm of Parker, Gerrard, and Ogilvy, which had been the supply house of the XY Company, and had an interest in the North West Company; and in time he acquired a controlling interest in this firm, which came to be known as Gerrard, Gillespie, Moffatt, and Co., and then as Gillespie, Moffatt, and Co. He was elected a member of the Beaver Club in 1814. In 1830 he was called to the Legislative Council of Lower Canada; and in 1839 he was sworn of the Executive Council. On the union of Upper and Lower Canada in 1841, he was elected to represent Montreal in the Legislative Assembly of Canada; and he held this seat until 1847, when he withdrew from active politics. In 1849 he was elected first president of the British American League. He died at Montreal on February 25, 1865. In 1809, while in the Indian country, he had born to him a son, Lewis, afterwards a merchant in Toronto; but in 1816 he married Sophia, daughter of David McCrae, of St. John's, who was himself an old Indian trader, and a member of the Beaver Club. By her he had three sons, George, John Ogilvy, and Kenneth Mackenzie.

[Adam Shortt, *The Honourable George Moffatt* (Journal of the Canadian Bankers' Association, 1925); Taylor, *Brit. Am.*, vol. 1:

J. D. Borthwick, *History and biographical gazetteer of Montreal* (Montreal, 1892); E. E. Rich (ed.), *Colin Robertson's correspondence book* (Toronto: The Champlain Society, 1939).]

Moffatt, Mrs. Gertrude, *née* **MacGregor** (1884-1923), poet, was born on May 13, 1884, at Stratford, Ontario, the daughter of the Rev. Daniel Arthur MacGregor. She was educated at McMaster University (B.A., 1906), and in 1909 was married to Thomas E. Moffatt, later principal of the public school at Tweed, Ontario. She died at Ottawa on October 8, 1923. After her death her collected poems were edited by B. K. Sandwell, under the title *A book of verses* (Toronto, 1924).
[*Can. who was who*, vol. 1.]

Molson, Herbert (1875-1938), brewer and financier, was born at Montreal, Quebec, on March 29, 1875, the son of John Thomas Molson. He was educated at McGill University (B.A.Sc., 1894); and he rose in the Molson brewery business until he became president of the firm. He served in the First World War with the 42nd Battalion of the Canadian Expeditionary Force, was wounded and mentioned in despatches, and was awarded the M.C. and the C.M.G. In his later years he was a governor of McGill University and president of the Montreal General Hospital. He died at Montreal, Quebec, on March 26, 1938.
[*Can. who's who*, 1936-37; B. K. Sandwell, *The Molson family* (Montreal, 1933); M. Denison, *The barley and the stream* (Toronto, 1955).]

Molson, John (1764-1836), capitalist, was born in Lincolnshire, England, in 1764. He emigrated to Canada in 1782, and established a brewery in Montreal. In 1809 he became the pioneer in steam navigation on the St. Lawrence, when he placed on the river the steamship *Accommodation*. From 1816 to 1820 he represented Montreal East in the Legislative Assembly of Lower Canada; and in 1832 he was appointed a member of the Legislative Council. From 1826 to 1834 he was president of the Bank of Montreal. He died in Montreal on January 11, 1836.
[B. K. Sandwell, *The Molson family* (Montreal, 1933); M. Denison, *The barley and the stream* (Toronto, 1955); *Cyc. Am. biog.*; Morgan, *Cel. Can.*; R. Campbell, *History of the Scotch Presbyterian church, St. Gabriel Street, Montreal* (Montreal, 1887).]

Molson, John (1787-1860), capitalist, was born at Montreal on October 14, 1787, the son of the Hon. John Molson (q.v.). He entered his father's business, and became in 1837 the president of the first railway in Canada, the St. Lawrence and Champlain. In 1853 he joined with his brother William (q.v.) in organizing Molson's Bank. He died in Montreal on July 12, 1860. He avoided politics, but was a member of the Special Council of Lower Canada in 1838, and he was one of the signatories of the annexation manifesto of 1849.
[B. K. Sandwell, *The Molson family* (Montreal, 1933); M. Denison, *The barley and the stream* (Toronto, 1955); *Cyc. Am. biog.*; Morgan, *Cel. Can.*]

Molson, William (1793-1875), capitalist, was born in Montreal on November 5, 1793, the son of the Hon. John Molson (q.v.). He was for many years a brewer and distiller in Montreal; and in 1855 he became first president of Molson's Bank. He was also president of the Champlain Railway Company, and a local director of the Grand Trunk Railway. He died in Montreal on February 18, 1875. He was a governor of McGill University, and was one of its principal benefactors.
[B. K. Sandwell, *The Molson family* (Montreal, 1933); M. Denison, *The barley and the stream* (Toronto, 1955); *Dict. Can. biog.*, vol. 10.]

Monck, Sir Charles Stanley, fourth Viscount (1819-1894), governor-general of British North America (1861-67), and of the Dominion of Canada (1867-68), was born at Templemore, Tipperary county, Ireland, the eldest son of Charles Joseph Kelly, third Viscount Monck, and Bridget, youngest daughter of John Wellington of Tipperary county, Ireland. He was educated at Trinity College, Dublin, and was called to the Irish bar in 1841. He succeeded his father in the peerage in 1849; but, since the peerage was Irish, he did not have a seat in the House of Lords, and in 1852 he was elected to the British House of Commons as Liberal member for Portsmouth. From 1855 to 1857 he was a lord of the treasury in the Palmerston administration; and in 1861 he was appointed governor-general of British North America. His period of office was notable for his successful efforts to maintain peace between Great Britain and the United States during and after the American Civil War, and for the energetic, though constitutional, part which he played in bringing about the federation of British North America. In 1867 he was the first governor-general of the Dominion of Canada; but he resigned in 1868, and returned to Ireland. From 1874 to 1892 he was lord-lieutenant of Dublin county, Ireland; and he died on November 30, 1894. In 1844 he married his cousin, the Lady Elizabeth Louise Mary Monck, fourth daughter of Henry Stanley, first Earl of Rathdowne; and by her he had two sons and two daughters. In 1866 he was created Baron Monck of Ballytrammon, in the peerage of the United Kingdom; and in 1869 he was created a G.C.M.G., and was called to the Privy Council.
[R. G. Trotter, *Lord Monck and the great coalition of 1864* (Can. hist. rev., 1922) and *Canadian federation* (London, 1924); *Dict.*

nat. biog., supp. I; Annual register, 1894; Dent, Can. port., vol. 4; Taylor, Brit. Am., vol. 1; Morgan, Cel. Can.; Sir J. Pope, Memoirs of the Rt. Hon. Sir. J. A. Macdonald (2 vols., Ottawa, 1894) and Correspondence of Sir John Macdonald (Toronto, 1921); J. B. Cowan, Canada's governors-general (Toronto, 1952).]

Monckton, Robert (1726-1782), soldier, was born on June 24, 1726, the second son of John Monckton, created Viscount Galway in 1727, and Lady Elizabeth Manners, daughter of the Duke of Rutland. He entered the British army, and rose to the rank of lieutenant-general in 1770. He was sent to Nova Scotia in 1752, and in 1754 was made lieutenant-governor of Annapolis Royal. In 1755 he was in command of the expedition against Fort Beauséjour; and his journal of this expedition has been printed in J. C. Webster, The forts of Chignecto (Shediac, N.B., 1930). In December, 1755, he was appointed lieutenant-governor of Nova Scotia. In 1759 he was senior brigadier-general under Wolfe (q.v.) at Quebec, and was severely wounded at the battle of the Plains of Abraham. He was appointed governor of New York in 1761, and thereafter his connection with Canada ceased. He returned to England in 1763, and was successively governor of Berwick-on-Tweed and of Portsmouth. In 1779 he was elected also member of parliament for Portsmouth. He died on May 3, 1782, and was buried at Kensington parish church. He was not married. Moncton, New Brunswick, was named after him.

[Dict. nat. biog.; Cyc. Am. biog.; J. C. Webster, The forts of Chignecto (Shediac, N.B., 1930).]

Mondelet, Charles Joseph Elzéar (1801-1876), judge, was born at St. Charles, Lower Canada, on December 28, 1801, the son of Jean Marie Mondelet, notary public. He was educated at the College of Nicolet and the College of Montreal, and was called to the bar of Lower Canada in 1822. He practised law, first in Three Rivers, and then in Montreal, until 1842, when he was appointed district judge for Terrebonne, L'Assomption, and Berthier. In 1844 he was appointed a circuit judge at Montreal; in 1849 a judge of the Superior Court of Lower Canada; and in 1859 an assistant judge in appeals of the Court of Queen's Bench. He died at Montreal on December 31, 1876. His Letters on elementary and practical education (Montreal, 1841) are said to have influenced the school law passed in the first parliament after the union of 1841.

[P. G. Roy, Les juges de la province de Québec (Quebec, 1933); Le Jeune, Dict. gén.; Morgan, Bib. can. and Cel. Can.; J. D. Borthwick, History and biographical gazetteer of Montreal (Montreal, 1892); F. J. Audet, Les Mondelet (Les Cahiers des Dix, 1938); Dict. Can. Biog., vol. 10.]

Mondelet, Dominique (1799-1863), executive councillor of Lower Canada, was born at St. Marc, Lower Canada, on January 23, 1799, the son of Jean Marie Mondelet, notary public. He was called to the bar of Lower Canada, and practised law in Montreal. In 1831 he was elected to represent the county of Montreal in the Legislative Assembly of Lower Canada; and in 1832 he was appointed a member of the Executive Council of the province. The Assembly thereupon declared his seat vacant; and in the elections of 1834 he was defeated by Louis Joseph Papineau (q.v.). He continued to be an executive councillor until 1841, and he was a member of the Special Council of 1838. In 1842 he was appointed a judge of the Court of Queen's Bench at Three Rivers, and in 1849 a judge of the Superior Court. He died at Three Rivers on February 19, 1863.

[F. J. Audet, Les Mondelet (Les Cahiers des Dix, 1938); P. G. Roy, Les juges de la province de Québec (Quebec, 1933); J. D. Borthwick, History and biographical gazetteer of Montreal (Montreal, 1892); Le Jeune, Dict. gén.]

Monet, Dominique (1865-1923), jurist, was born at Napierville, Canada East, on January 2, 1865. He was educated at L'Assomption College and the Quebec Seminary, and was called to the bar of Lower Canada in 1889. From 1891 to 1904 he represented Napierville in the Canadian House of Commons; and from 1904 to 1905, in the Legislative Assembly of Quebec. In 1905 he was for a short time a member of the Parent administration. From 1905 to 1908 he was protonotary of the district of Montreal; and in 1908 he was appointed a judge of the Superior Court for the district of Iberville. He died at sea, near Puerto Rico, on February 6, 1923.

[P. G. Roy, Les juges de la province de Québec (Quebec, 1933); Morgan, Can. men (1912); Can. parl. comp.]

Monk, Frederick Debartzch (1856-1914), minister of public works for Canada (1911-12), was born at Montreal, Lower Canada, on April 6, 1856, the fourth son of the Hon. S. C. Monk and Rosalie Caroline, daughter of the Hon. P. D. Debartzch (q.v.). He was educated at McGill University (B.C.L., 1877), and was called to the Quebec bar in 1878 (Q.C., 1893). From 1896 to 1914 he represented Jacques Cartier in the Canadian House of Commons; from 1900 to 1904 he was leader of the Liberal-Conservative party in the province of Quebec; and in 1911 he was given the portfolio of public works in the Borden administration. He had by this time, however, developed strong Nationalist leanings; and in 1912 he resigned from the cabinet as the result of a disagreement with his colleagues over the naval policy of the government. He died at Montreal on May 15, 1914. In 1879 he married Marie

Louise, daughter of D. H. Sénécal, of Montreal. He was an LL.D. of Laval University (1890).

[*Can. parl. comp.*; Morgan, *Can. men* (1912); *Can. ann. review*, 1912.]

Monk, Sir James (1745-1826), chief justice of Lower Canada, was born at Boston, Massachusetts, in 1745, the son of James Monk and Anne Dering. He was educated at Halifax, Nova Scotia, where his father had settled in 1749, and was called to the bar of Nova Scotia. In 1770 he went to England, and in 1774 he was called to the English bar from the Middle Temple. The same year he was appointed solicitor-general of Nova Scotia, and was elected to represent Yarmouth in the Legislative Assembly of the province. In 1776 he was appointed attorney-general of the province of Quebec; and this post he occupied until 1789, when he was suspended from office. In 1792, however, he was appointed attorney-general of Lower Canada; and in 1794 he was made chief justice of the Court of King's Bench for Montreal. The same year he was appointed a member of the Executive and Legislative Councils, and he was three times speaker of the Legislative Council. From 1819 to 1820 he was also administrator of the government of Lower Canada. In 1824 he retired from the bench, and went to live in England; and he died at Cheltenham, England, on November 18, 1826. In 1825 he was created a knight bachelor. He was the anonymous author of *State of the present form of government of the province of Quebec* (London, 1789).

[F. J. Audet, *Les juges en chef de la province de Québec* (Quebec, 1927); P. G. Roy, *Les juges de la province de Québec* (Quebec, 1933); R. Christie, *History of Lower Canada* (6 vols., Quebec and Montreal, 1848-54).]

Monk, Samuel Wentworth (1792-1865), protonotary of the Court of Queen's Bench, Montreal (1815-65), was born at Windsor, Nova Scotia, on May 3, 1792, the third son of Major Monk and his wife, Elizabeth Wentworth and the nephew of Sir James Monk (q.v.). He was called to the bar of Nova Scotia in 1813; but in 1815 he was appointed, through the influence of his uncle, protonotary of the Court of King's Bench, Montreal, and this post he occupied until his death, at Montreal, on March 13, 1865, fifty years later.

[Taylor, *Brit. Am.*, vol. 1.]

Monro, Alexander (1813-1896), civil engineer and author, was born in Banff, Scotland, in 1813. He emigrated to New Brunswick when a youth, and he was for many years engaged in surveys in New Brunswick and Nova Scotia. He lived at Baie Verte, New Brunswick; and he died there on December 26, 1896. He was the author of *A treatise on theoretical and practical land surveying* (Pictou, N.S., 1844), *New Brunswick, with a brief outline of Nova Scotia and Prince Edward Is-*land (Halifax, N.S., 1855), *Statistics of British North America* (Halifax, N.S., 1862), *History, geography and statistics of British North America* (Montreal, 1864), and *The United States and the Dominion of Canada* (Saint John, N.B., 1879).

[W. G. MacFarlane, *New Brunswick bibliography* (Saint John, N.B., 1895).]

Monroe, Walter Stanley (1871-1952), prime minister of Newfoundland (1924-28), was born in Dublin, Ireland, on May 14, 1871, and died at St. John's, Newfoundland, on October 6, 1952. He was educated at Harrow, and came to Newfoundland in 1888. Here he entered the business of his uncle, Moses Monroe; and in 1909 he established his own business, the Monroe Export Company. He was elected to represent Bonavista in the Newfoundland House of Assembly in 1923, and in 1924 he became a minister without portfolio in the Warren administration. Later, in the election of 1924, he led the Conservatives to victory, and became prime minister. He retired as prime minister in 1928, and on his subsequent defeat in the election of 1928, retired from active politics. In 1929 he was appointed a member of the Legislative Council.

[*Newfoundland supp.*; *Encyc. Can.*]

Montague, Percival John (1882-1966), soldier and judge, was born at Dunnville, Ontario, November 10, 1882. He was educated at Upper Canada College, Toronto, and at the University of Toronto (B.A., 1904). He studied law and was called to the bars of Ontario (1907) and Manitoba (1907). He joined a law firm in Winnipeg and practised there until 1932, when he was appointed a justice of the Court of Queen's Bench in Manitoba. He served in the First World War, receiving five mentions in despatches. He was officer commanding the Fort Garry Horse (1920-25) and the Sixth Mounted Brigade (1928-36). He served in the Second World War as D.A.G.; as major-general in charge of administration and chief of staff at Canadian Military Headquarters, London; and as judge advocate general of the Canadian army overseas. He was awarded the C.B. (1943); the C.M.G.; the D.S.O.; the M.C.; and the V.D. In 1951 he was appointed justice of the Court of Appeal in Manitoba. He died at Winnipeg, Manitoba, June 11, 1966.

[*Can. who's who*, 1955-57.]

Montague, Walter Humphries (1858-1915), minister of agriculture for Canada (1896), was born in Adelaide, Middlesex county, Ontario, on November 21, 1858, the son of Joseph Montague, a farmer. He was educated at the School of Medicine, Toronto, and at Victoria University, Cobourg (M.D., 1882), and he practised medicine at Dunnville, Ontario. In 1890 he was elected to represent Haldimand in the Canadian House of Commons. In 1895 he became, for a few months, secretary of state in the Bowell administration, and at the end of that year he was appointed minister of agriculture. He was one of the "nest of traitors" charged by Mackenzie Bowell (q.v.) with conspiring against him in 1896, and he became a member of the Tupper administration of that year. He retired from office on the defeat of the Tupper government in July, 1896, and he was defeated in the general elections for the House of Commons in 1900. In 1913 he was elected to represent Kildonan in the Legislative Assembly of Manitoba and at the same time he was appointed minister of public works in the Roblin government. He died at Winnipeg, where he had lived since 1908, on November 14, 1915.

[*Can. parl. comp.*; Morgan, *Can. men* (1898).]

Montcalm, Louis Joseph de Montcalm-Gozon, Marquis de (1712-1759), lieutenant-general and commander-in-chief of the French forces in Canada (1756-59), was born at the château of Candiac, near Nîmes, France, on February 28, 1712, the son of Louis Daniel de Montcalm, seigneur de Saint-Véran, and Marie-Thérèse de Castellane-Dampus. He received an excellent private education, and in 1721 entered the army as an ensign. In 1756 he was sent to Canada as major-general, and in 1758 he was raised to lieutenant-general and commander-in-chief of the French forces. He opened his campaign with the capture of Oswego in August, 1756; and in 1757 he took and demolished Fort William Henry. His greatest success was, however, the defeat of Abercromby's invading army at Ticonderoga (Carillon) in 1758. In 1759 he defended Quebec against the army of Wolfe (q.v.), until defeated at the battle of the Plains of Abraham on September 13, 1759. During the battle he was mortally wounded, and he died in Quebec the following day, before the surrender of the citadel. He represented the French régime in Canada at its best. In 1736 he married Angélique Louise Talon du Boulay, daughter of the Marquis du Boulay, and he had by her five children.

[T. Chapais, *Le Marquis de Montcalm* (Quebec, 1911); Abbé H. R. Casgrain, *Wolfe and Montcalm* (Toronto, 1905); F. Parkman, *Montcalm and Wolfe* (Boston, 1884); C. P. Stacey, *Quebec, 1759* (Toronto, 1959); A. G. Doughty and G. W. Parmalee, *The siege of Quebec and the battle of the plains of Abraham* (6 vols., Quebec, 1901); Abbé H. R. Casgrain (ed.), *Collection des manuscrits du Maréchal de Lévis* (12 vols., Montreal and Quebec, 1889-95); M. Sautai, *Montcalm au combat de Carillon* (Paris, 1909); A. G. Doughty (ed.), *An historical journal of the campaigns in North America, by Capt. John Knox* (3 vols., Toronto, 1914-16); C. Winchester (tr.), *Memoirs of the Chevalier de Johnstone* (3 vols., Aberdeen, 1870-71); G. Robitaille, *Montcalm et ses historiens* (Montreal, 1936); *Dict. Can. biog.*, vol. 3.]

Montgolfier, Etienne (1712-1791), priest, was born at Vidalon-les-Annonay, France, on December 24, 1712. He entered the Sulpician order in 1734, and was ordained a priest in 1741. He was sent to Canada in 1751, and became vicar-general of the Montreal district. In 1759 he was appointed superior of the Sulpician order in Canada; and after the British conquest he was nominated as successor to Bishop de Pontbriand (q.v.), but the appointment of a bishop was not approved by the British government, and eventually Mgr. Briand (q.v.) was made superintendent of the Roman Catholic Church. Mgr.Montgolfier continued, however, superior of the Sulpicians in Canada until his death at Montreal on August 27, 1791. He was reputed to be the author of a posthumously published *Vie de Soeur Bourgeoys* (Ville-Marie [Montreal], 1818).

[Allaire, *Dict. biog.*; Le Jeune, *Dict. gén.*; A. Gosselin, *L'Eglise du Canada* (4 vols., Quebec, 1911-17).]

Montgomery, John (1788-1879), rebel, was born at Gagetown, New Brunswick, on February 29, 1788. He came to Upper Canada in early youth, and settled in York (Toronto). He served in the York Volunteers in the War of 1812; but in 1837 his tavern on Yonge Street was the *rendezvous* of William Lyon Mackenzie (q.v.) and his insurgents. Montgomery was arrested, tried for high treason, convicted, and sentenced to be hanged; but his sentence was commuted to banishment; and while awaiting banishment at Fort Henry, near Kingston, Upper Canada, he escaped to the United States. He returned to Canada in 1843, under the Amnesty Act. His later years were spent in Barrie, Ontario; and here he died on October 31, 1879.

[*Dom. ann. reg.*, 1879; *Dict. Can. biog.*, vol. 10.]

Montgomery, Lucy Maud (1874-1942) novelist, was born at Clifton, Prince Edward Island, on November 30, 1874. She was educated at Prince of Wales College, Charlottetown, and at Dalhousie University; and for a short time was a school-teacher. In 1911 she married the Reverend Ewan MacDonald, a Presbyterian clergyman; and by him she had two children. She died at Toronto, Ontario, on April 24, 1942. She was the author of *Anne of Green Gables* (Boston, 1908), *Anne of Avonlea* (Boston, 1909), *Kilmeny of the orchard* (Boston, 1910), *The story girl* (Boston, 1911), *Chronicles of Avonlea* (Boston, 1912), *The golden road* (Boston, 1913), *Anne of the island* (Boston, 1915), *The watchman, and other poems* (Toronto, 1917), *Anne's house of dreams* (New York, 1917), *Rainbow valley* (New York, 1919), *Further chronicles of Avonlea* (Boston, 1920), *Rilla of Ingleside* (New York, 1921), *Emily of New Moon* (New York, 1923), *Emily climbs* (New York, 1925), *The blue castle* (New York, 1926), *Emily's quest* (New York, 1928),

Magic for Marigold (New York, 1929), *A tangled web* (New York, 1931), *Pat of Silver Bush* (New York, 1933), *Mistress Pat* (New York, 1935), *Anne of Windy Poplars* (New York, 1936), *Jane of Lantern Hill* (New York, 1937), and *Anne of Ingleside* (New York, 1939).

[*Can. who's who*, 1936-47; Morgan, *Can. men* (1912); Hilda M. Ridley, *The story of L. M. Montgomery* (Toronto, 1956).]

Montgomery, Richard (1736-1775), soldier, was born in Dublin, Ireland, on December 2, 1736. In 1755 he obtained a commission in the British army, and in 1757 he was sent to America. He served at the capture of Louisbourg in 1758 and on Lake Champlain in 1759, and was present at the capitulation of Montreal in 1760. In 1771, after his return to England, he sold his commission, and emigrated to New York. Here he married, in 1773, Janet, daughter of the Hon. Robert Livingston, one of the judges of the Court of King's Bench; and with the Livingston family he took the revolutionary side in the War of American Independence. In 1775 he was appointed by Washington a brigadier-general in the revolutionary army; and he commanded the expedition which captured Montreal in November, 1775. At the beginning of December, he effected a junction with the forces of Benedict Arnold (q.v.) before Quebec; and he was killed in an attack on Quebec on New Year's Eve, 1775.

[Faucher de St. Maurice, *Quelques notes sur le général Richard Montgomery* (Trans. Roy. Soc. Can., 1891); Louise Livingston Hunt, *Biographical notes* (Poughkeepsie, N.Y., 1876); *Dict. Am. biog.*; *Cyc. Am. biog.*; Le Jeune, *Dict. gén.*]

Montigny, Benjamin Antoine Testard de (1838-1899), lawyer, was born at St. Jérôme, Lower Canada, on October 6, 1838. He was educated at the College of Joliette, and was called to the bar in 1859. He served as a papal zouave in 1861-62; and on his return to Canada in 1863 he entered on the practice of law. In 1873 he was appointed stipendiary magistrate of the district of Terrebonne; and in 1880 he became recorder of Montreal. He died at Montreal on August 15, 1899. He was throughout life a frequent contributor to the newspapers; and he was the author of *Histoire du droit canadien* (Montreal, 1869), *Catéchisme politique* (Montreal, 1878), *Droit criminel: Des arrestations* (Montreal, 1882), *La colonisation: Le nord* (Montreal, 1886), and *Manuel d'économie domestique* (Montreal, 1896).

[Jeune, *Dict. gén.*]

Montigny, Henry Gaston Testard de (1870-1914), journalist, was born at St. Jérôme, Quebec, on May, 27, 1870, the eldest son of Benjamin Antoine Testard de Montigny (q.v.). He became a journalist in Montreal; and he died at Montreal on October 30, 1914. He was the author of *L'étoffe du pays* (published posthumously, Montreal, 1951).

[Le Jeune, *Dict. gén*; *Bull. rech. hist.*, 1921.]

Montigny, Louvigny Testard de (1876-1955), author, was born at St. Jérôme de Terrebonne, Quebec, on December 1, 1876, the son of Benjamin Antoine Testard de Montigny (q.v.), and died at Ottawa, Ontario, on May 20, 1955. He was educated at St. Mary's College and Laval University in Montreal, and became a journalist in Montreal. In 1910 he was appointed a translator to the Senate of Canada, and in 1915 chief translator, a post he held until his death. He was the author of *La langue française au Canada* (Ottawa, 1916), *Antoine Gérin-Lajoie* (Toronto, 1925), *Le bouquet de Mélusine* (Montreal, 1937), *Au pays de Québec* (Montreal, 1945), *Ecrasons le perroquet!* (Montreal, 1948), and *L'épi rouge* (Montreal, 1953). In 1925 he was created a Chevalier de la Légion d'Honneur.

[*Can. who's who*, 1952-54; *Encyc. Can.*]

Montizambert, Frederick (1843-1929), physician, was born at Quebec, Canada East, on February 3, 1843. He was educated at Laval University, at Edinburgh University (M.D., 1864), and at Johns Hopkins University. He entered the public health service of Canada in 1866; and in 1899 became director-general of public health and sanitary adviser of the Canadian government, with the rank of deputy minister. He was a pioneer in the field of public health in Canada; and was made, in recognition of his services, an I.S.O. (1903) and a C.M.G. (1916) In 1888 the University of Bishop's College conferred on him the degree of D.C.L. He died at Ottawa, Ontario, on November 2, 1929. He was the author of numerous reports and papers bearing on public health.

[Morgan, *Can. men* (1912); *Can. parl. comp.*]

Montmagny, Charles Jacques Huault de (*fl.* 1622-1653), governor of New France (1636-48), was the son of Charles Huault, seigneur de Montmagny, and Antoinette du Drac. He was educated by the Jesuits, and in August, 1622, was admitted to the Order of Malta. He served his apprenticeship as a soldier by fighting against the Turks and Moors. In 1632 he appears as administrator of the affairs of the Company of New France; and on January 15, 1636, he was appointed governor to succeeed Champlain (q.v.). He arrived at Quebec on June 11, 1636. During his administration, he restored Fort St. Louis, and built a fort at the mouth of the Richelieu River to check the inroads of the Iroquois; and in 1645 he arranged a peace with the Iroquois. He was recalled from the governorship in early 1648, and sailed for France on September 23. In 1652 he was made attorney-general of the Order of Malta, and sent to the island of Saint-Christophe, as commander. There he died some time in 1653.

[J.-E. Roy, *M. de Montmagny* (La Nouvelle-France, 1906); Le Jeune, *Dict. gén.*; *Dict. Can. biog.*, vol. 1.]

Montminy, Théophile (1842-1899), priest and author, was born at St. Jean Chrysostôme, Canada East, on February 24, 1842, and was ordained a priest of the Roman Catholic Church in 1870. He was parish priest successively at several places in the province of Quebec; and he died suddenly in Quebec, City, on December 17, 1899. He was the author of *Québec aux Antilles: Notes de voyage* (Quebec, 1888).

[Allaire, *Dict. biog.*; *Bull. rech. hist.*, 1929.]

Montmollin, David Francis de (1721?-1803), clergyman, was born at Neufchâtel, Switzerland, about 1721, and is said to have been a son of the Comte de Montmollin. He lived in England from about 1748 to 1768; and in 1768 he was appointed by royal mandamus minister of the Church of England at Quebec, Canada. He retained this charge until his death at Quebec, on December 17, 1803.

[*Bull. rech. hist.*, 1936.]

Montour, Nicolas (1760?-1808), fur-trader, was born about 1760, and went to the West, apparently in 1777, as clerk to Barthélemi Blondeau (q.v.). Later, in 1782, he was described as "clerk to the Messrs. Frobisher". He became a partner in the North West Company in 1784, when he seems to have been given two shares in the sixteen-share concern of that year. Most of his time in the West he spent on the Saskatchewan. He retired from the fur-trade about 1790; and in 1795 he bought the seigniory of La Pointe-du-Lac, Lower Canada, where he built a manor house likened to "the Château of the Middle Ages". He was elected a member of the Beaver Club in 1790; and from 1796 to 1800 he represented the county of St. Maurice in the Legislative Assembly of Lower Canada, where he generally voted with the English party. He died "at his manor of Woodlands" on August 6, 1808; and he was buried "in the new cemetery of Three Rivers". He left behind him in the West a half-breed son, named also Nicolas Montour, who was a clerk at Fort des Prairies in 1804-06, was stationed in the Kootenay country in 1813, and was discharged on the Saskatchewan by Sir George Simpson (q.v.) in 1823. After his return to Lower Canada, the elder Montour married in 1798 Geneviève Wills, who died on April 2, 1832, aged 64 years; and by her he had three daughters.

[A. Tessier, *Deux enrichis* (Les Cahiers des Dix, 1938); E. Fabre Surveyer and F. J. Audet, *Les députés de Saint-Maurice et de*

Buckinghamshire (Three Rivers, Que., 1934); W. S. Wallace (ed.), *Documents relating to the North West Company* (Toronto: The Champlain Society, 1932).]

Montpetit, André Napoléon (1840-1898), author, was born at Beauharnois, Lower Canada, on July 4, 1840. He was educated at the College of St. Hyacinthe, and was called to the bar in 1862. He became a journalist, and in 1870 he was appointed editor of *L'Opinion Publique*. In this journal he published his *Histoire des Hurons de Lorette*. He died at Montreal on May 26, 1898. In 1866 he married Adèle, daughter of Professor J. B. Labelle; and by her he had four sons and three daughters. He was the author of *Abrégé de géographie moderne à l'usage de la jeunesse* (Quebec, 1870), *Colonie française de Metgermette* (Quebec, 1874), *Major L. N. Voyer* (Montreal, 1876), *L'amiante, c'est le million* (Quebec, 1884), *Nos hommes forts* (Quebec, 1884), *Louis Riel à la Rivière du Loup* (Lévis, 1885), and *Les poissons de l'eau douce du Canada* (Montreal, 1897).

[L. O. David, *Biographies et portraits* (Montreal, 1876), and *Souvenirs et biographies* (Montreal, 1911); Le Jeune, *Dict. gén.*]

Montpetit, Edouard (1882-1954), political economist, was born at Montmagny, Quebec, in 1882, the son of André Napoléon Montpetit (q.v.), and died at Montreal, Quebec, on March 27, 1954. He was educated at the Collège de Montréal (B.A., 1899) and at the Ecole des Sciences Politiques in Paris; and in 1910 he was appointed professor of political science in the University of Montreal. He became director of the School of Social, Economic, and Political Science in 1920, and at the same time secretary-general of the University. In 1914 he was elected a fellow of the Royal Society of Canada. In the course of his long and distinguished academic career, he published *Les survivances françaises au Canada* (Montreal, 1914), *Au service de la tradition française* (Montreal, 1920), *Sous le signe de l'oe* (Montreal, 1932), *Les cordons de la bourse* (Montreal, 1935), *Le front contre la vitre* (Montreal, 1936), *La conquête économique* (3 vols., Montreal, 1938-42), *Reflets d'Amérique* (Montreal, 1941), *Propos sur la montagne* (Montreal, 1946), and *Souvenirs* (3 vols., 1944-55).

[*Proc. Roy. Soc. Can.*, 1954; *Can. who's who*, 1952-54; *Encyc. Can.*]

Montplaisir, Hippolite (1840-1927), senator of Canada, was born at Cap de la Madeleine, Lower Canada, on May 7, 1840. He was educated at the Three Rivers Academy, and became a farmer. He was mayor of his native parish for twenty-five years consecutively; and he was summoned to the Senate of Canada in 1891. He sat in the Senate until his death at Three Rivers, Quebec, on June 20, 1927.

[*Can. parl. comp.*]

Montrésor, John (1736-1799), military engineer, was born at Gibraltar on April 6, 1736, the son of James Gabriel Montrésor, a British engineer officer. He went with his father to America in 1754, and obtained a commission in the British army under Braddock (q.v.). He was wounded at the Monongahela in 1756, was present at the capture of Louisbourg in 1758, and of Quebec in 1759, and served in the campaign that led to the capitulation of Montreal in 1760. For two years he was engaged intermittently on a survey of the St. Lawrence River; and in 1763 he was employed to carry dispatches from Amherst (q.v.) to the commander of the garrison at Detroit. In 1764 he was employed in strengthening the defences on the Niagara River, where he built Fort Erie, and at Detroit; and he was later employed as an engineer officer in New York. He was commissioned chief engineer in America in 1775, and served throughout the American Revolutionary War until 1778, when he was recalled to England. He resigned from the army; and his later years were embittered by disputes with the British Treasury over his accounts. He died in Maidstone prison, while under surveillance, on June 26, 1799.

[J. C. Webster, *The life of John Montrésor* (Trans. Roy. Soc. Can., 1928); F. M. Montrésor, *Captain John Montrésor in Canada* (Can. hist. rev., 1924); *Dict. Am. biog.*; *Cyc. Am. biog.*]

Monts, Pierre Du Gua or **Guast, Sieur de** (1558?-1628), colonizer, was born in Saintonge, France, about 1558. He fought on the Protestant side in the French wars of religion, and was rewarded by Henri IV with the governorship of Pons in Saintonge. He seems to have made several voyages to Canada, and was a passenger in Chauvin's expedition of 1600. In 1603 he obtained a monopoly of the trade in New France, and founded the settlement at St. Croix, transferred in 1605 to Port Royal; but this monopoly was revoked in 1607. He obtained, however, a new one-year monopoly, and sent out Champlain to found the post of Quebec on the St. Lawrence. For some years he was the proprietor of the post at Quebec; but after the death of Henri IV in 1610, he lost his influence at court, and within a few years withdrew from active interest in the Canadian trade. He died apparently in 1628, not (as has been frequently stated) in 1611.

[W. Inglis Morse, *Pierre Du Gua, Sieur de Monts* (London, 1939); H. P. Biggar, *The early trading companies of New France* (Toronto, 1901); M. Lescarbot, *The history of New France* (3 vols., Toronto: The Cham-

plain Society, 1907-14); *Cyc. Am. biog.*; Le Jeune, *Dict. gén.*; *Dict. Can. biog.*, vol. 1.]

Monty, Rodolphe (1874-1928), secretary of state for Canada (1921), was born in Montreal, Quebec, on November 30, 1874, and was educated at Laval and McGill universities. He was called to the bar of Quebec in 1897 (K.C., 1909), and was in 1829 *bâtonnier* of the bar in Montreal. From September to December, 1921, he was secretary of state in the Meighen administration. He died at St. Hyacinthe, Quebec, on December 1, 1928.

[*Can. parl. comp.*]

Moodie, Robert (d. 1837), soldier, was a native of Dunfermline, Fifeshire, Scotland. He obtained a subaltern's commission in the 28th Foot in 1796, and he saw service in the Peninsular War. He came to New Brunswick with the 104th Regiment, and he served with this regiment in Upper Canada in the War of 1812. In 1814 he was placed on half-pay, with the rank of lieutenant-colonel. About 1822 he returned to Scotland, and he lived at St. Andrews until 1835. He then settled in Upper Canada, north of Toronto; and he was killed by the rebels when riding south to give warning of the Mackenzie rising, on December 4, 1837. In 1811 he married at Fredericton, New Brunswick, Frances, daughter of the Hon. George Sproule, surveyor-general of New Brunswick.

[C. Ward, *Colonel Robert Moodie* (Acadiensis, 1901); Morgan, *Cel. Can.*; J. C. Dent, *The Upper Canadian rebellion* (2 vols., Toronto, 1885).]

Moodie, Mrs. Susanna, *née* **Strickland** (1803-1885), author, was born at Bungay, Suffolk, England, on December 6, 1803, the daughter of Thomas Strickland, of Reydon Hall, and the sister of Agnes Strickland and Mrs. Catherine Parr Traill (q.v.). In 1831 she married Lieut. J. W. D. Moodie, of the 21st Fusiliers; and in 1832 she and her husband emigrated to Canada. They settled first near Cobourg, Upper Canada, and then north of Peterborough, where they underwent all the hardships of pioneer life in Canada at that time. In 1839 she moved to Belleville, Upper Canada, her husband having been appointed sheriff of Hastings county. After her husband's death in 1869, she lived in Toronto, and here she died on April 8, 1885. Her best-known book is *Roughing it in the bush* (London, 1852), in which she describes her experiences as a settler in Upper Canada, and which appeared first in the *Literary Garland* (Montreal, 1838-52); but she wrote also *Enthusiasm and other poems* (London, 1830), *Life in the clearings* (London, 1853), *Mark Hurdlestone* (London, 1853), *Flora Lindsay* (London, 1854), *Matrimonial speculations* (London, 1854), *Geoffrey Moncton* (London, 1856), and *Dorothy Chance*, a serial published in the Montreal *Daily News*, 1867.

[*Dom. ann. reg.*, 1885; Rose, *Cyc. Can. biog.* (1886); Morgan, *Bib. can.*; A. MacMurchy, *Handbook of Canadian literature* (Toronto, 1906); R. P. Baker, *History of English-Canadian literature to the Confederation* (Cambridge, Mass., 1920); E. A. McCourt, *Roughing it with the Moodies* (Queen's Quarterly, 1945); G. H. Needler, *Otonabee pioneers* (Toronto, 1953).]

Moody, Richard Clement (1813-1887), engineer, was born in Barbados in 1813, the younger son of Colonel Thomas Moody, R.E. He was educated at Woolwich Military Academy, and in 1830 obtained a commission in the Royal Engineers. He rose to the rank of colonel in 1858, and major-general in 1866. In 1858 he was sent to British Columbia as commissioner of lands and public works, armed with a commission as lieutenant-governor, to be used in case of the governor's death; and he remained in British Columbia until 1863. In 1859 he selected the site for New Westminster, the first capital of the colony. He died in England on March 31, 1887.

[*Dict. nat. biog.*]

Moore, Elwood S. (1878-1966), geologist and university professor, was born near Heathcote, Ontario, August 3, 1878. He attended Meaford High School and was admitted to the University of Toronto in 1900. On graduation in 1904 he became house master at Pickering College and later taught at Collingwood Collegiate. He entered the University of Chicago in 1907 as a fellow in geology and received his Ph.D. *magna cum laude* in 1909. He was professor at the school of mines of Pennsylvania State College from 1909 until 1922, by which time he was dean of the school. He came to the University of Toronto in 1922 as professor of economic geology and director of geology at the Royal Ontario Museum. By 1945 the departments of mineralogy, petrography, and geology were combined as a department of geological sciences; and Dr. Moore continued as head of the new department until his retirement in 1949. As a student he had assisted Dr. A. P. Coleman in a pioneer geological survey of the Sudbury Basin and after graduation he undertook geological surveys for the Ontario department of mines and the Geological Survey of Canada. His work spanned the period from "reconnaissance" surveys to specialized and detailed geology. After his retirement from university teaching Dr. Moore did a re-study of the McIntyre and Hollinger mine areas and the Gowganda silver area. He was a fellow of the Royal Society of Canada and its president in 1945. He was a charter member of the American Mineralogical Society and a fellow of the Geological Society of America. He was a member of the National Geographic Society, the Canadian Geo-

graphical Society, and the Royal Canadian Institute. He published *Coal, its properties, analysis, geology classification, uses, and distribution* (New York, 1922), *The mineral resources of Canada* (Toronto, 1929), *American influence on Canadian mining* (Toronto, 1941), and *Elementary geology for Canada* (Toronto, 1944), as well as numerous papers and lectures. He died at Toronto, Ontario, March 26, 1966.

[*Proc. and Trans. Roy. Soc. Can.*, 1968; *Can. who's who*, 1955-57.]

Moore, Henry Napier (1893-1963), editor, was born at Newcastle-on-Tyne, England, in 1893. He became a reporter for the *Newcastle Daily Journal* in 1910, and two years later went to Victoria, British Columbia, as a reporter for the *Vancouver News Advertiser*. He joined the staff of the *Montreal Daily Mail* in 1915, becoming news editor. He then moved to the *Montreal Star* and was for a time their New York correspondent. He was appointed editor of *Maclean's* magazine in 1926. He is credited with encouraging the development of much Canadian literary talent. He was editorial director of Maclean-Hunter Publishing Co. until 1954, when he became consultant to the firm. He died at Nassau, April 4, 1963.

[*Can. who's who*, 1955-57; Metropolitan Toronto Library Board, *Biographical scrapbooks*, vol. 21.]

Moore, Philip Henry (1799-1880), legislative councillor of Canada (1841-67), was born in 1799, and belonged to the family after which Moore's Corners, Missisquoi county, Lower Canada, was named. He was an officer in the militia detachment that drove back the rebels at Moore's Corners in 1838; and for some years he was registrar of the county of Missisquoi. He was called to the Legislative Council of Canada after the Union of 1841, and he sat in the Council until Confederation in 1867. He was omitted from the list of those called to the Senate of Canada in 1867, and he was unsuccessful when he ran as an opposition candidate for the House of Commons in Missisquoi in the first Dominion elections. He then retired to private life; and he died at St. Armand Station (formerly Moore's Corners) on November 21, 1880.

[*Dom. ann. reg.*, 1880-81; *Dict. Can. biog.*, vol. 10.]

Moore, William Francis (1851-1935), educationist and author, was born in Durham county, Ontario, in 1851, and became a school teacher. From 1894 to 1927 he was principal of the Dundas High School; and he died in Hamilton, Ontario, on August 29, 1935. He was the author of *Indian place-names in Ontario* (Toronto, 1930).

[Private information.]

Moore, William Henry (1872-1960), politician and author, was born at Stouffville, Ontario, on October 19, 1872, and died at his farm, near Dunbarton, Ontario, on August 16, 1960. He was educated at Woodstock College and the University of Toronto (B.A., 1894), and became a lawyer. Later he became a farmer. From 1930 to 1945 he represented Ontario county in the Canadian House of Commons. An old-fashioned Liberal, he was the author of many books and pamphlets setting forth his ideas on current affairs, among them being *The irresponsible five* (Toronto, 1917), *Railway nationalization* (Toronto, 1917), *The clash* (London, 1918), *The commandments of men* (Toronto, 1925), *The definite national purpose* (Toronto, 1935), *Underneath it all* (Pickering, Ont., 1942), *When the iron is hot* (Pickering, Ont., 1943), *Grey days* (Pickering, Ont., 1945), and *By their fruits* (Pickering, Ont., 1949). He was the author also of a political novel, *Polly Masson* (London, 1919).

[*Can. who's who*, 1958-60; *Can. parl. guide*, 1944; Morgan, *Can. men* (1912).]

Moorsom, William Scarth (1804-1863), soldier, was born near Whitby, Yorkshire, England, in 1804, the son of Admiral Sir Robert Moorsom, K.C.B. He was educated at the Royal Military College, Sandhurst, and in 1821 entered the British army as an ensign. In 1826 he was sent to Nova Scotia, as a captain in the 52nd Light Infantry; and while in Nova Scotia he was for a time deputy quartermaster-general. He sold his commission in 1832, and during the remainder of his life was a civil engineer, employed mainly in railway surveying. He died at Westminster, England, on June 3, 1843. He was the author of a book describing his life in Nova Scotia, entitled *Letters from Nova Scotia* (London, 1830).

[*Dict. nat. biog.*; *Gentleman's magazine*, 1863.]

Morang, George Nathaniel (1866-1937), publisher, was born at Eastport, Maine, on March 10, 1866. He came to Canada in 1888, and became the agent in Canada of United States publishers. Eventually, he formed in Canada a publishing house of his own; and he was the publisher of the series of biographies known as *The makers of Canada* (21 vols., Toronto, 1904-11). He died near Uxbridge, Ontario, on October 5, 1937.

[*Can. who's who*, 1936-37; Morgan, *Can. men* (1912).]

Moreau, Charles Henri (1835-1867), caricaturist and humorist, was born in Paris, France, in 1835, and studied art in Paris. He emigrated to America, and saw active service in the army of the Potomac during the American Civil War. Toward the end of the war he came to Canada, and established in Montreal in 1865 an early, though short-lived, French-Canadian comic pictorial weekly named *Le Perroquet*. He died in France in 1867.

[Morgan, *Bib. can.*]

Moreau, Louis Edmond (1834-1895), priest and author, was born at Repentigny, Lower Canada, on August 18, 1834, was ordained a priest of the Roman Catholic Church in 1859, and died at St. Barthélemi, Quebec, on April 28, 1895. In 1868 he was chaplain of the Pontifical Zouaves who went from Canada to the aid of Pope Pius IX; and he was the author of *Nos croisés, ou L'histoire anecdotique de l'expédition des volontaires canadiens à Rome pour la défense de l'Eglise* (1871).

[Allaire, *Dict. biog.*; *Bull. rech. hist.*, 1929.]

Moreau, Louis Zéphirin (1824-1901), Roman Catholic bishop of St. Hyacinthe, was born at Bécancourt, Lower Canada, on April 1, 1824; and was ordained a priest at Montreal in 1846. After holding a great variety of posts, first at Montreal, and then at St. Hyacinthe, he became in 1876 bishop of St. Hyacinthe, and he presided over this see for twenty-five years. He died at St. Hyacinthe, Quebec, on May 24, 1901.

[Allaire, *Dict. biog.*]

Moreau, Stanislas Albert (1854-1913), priest, was born at St. Luc-sur-Richelieu, Canada East, on March 6, 1854. He was admitted to the priesthood in 1882; and he served as parish priest in several parts of the province of Quebec. He died at Montreal, Quebec, on January 25, 1913. He was the author of *Précis de l'histoire de la seigneurie, de la paroisse, et du comté de Berthier* (Berthier, Que., 1889), *Histoire de St. Luc* (Montreal, 1901), and *Histoire de l'Acadie, province de Québec* (Montreal, 1908).

[Allaire, *Dict. biog.*]

Moreton, Julian (1825-1900), clergyman and author, was born in England in 1825, and died there in 1900. He was ordained a clergyman of the Church of England in 1848, and from 1849 to 1861 he was a missionary in Newfoundland. From 1862 to 1874 he was a chaplain in India; and in 1878 he became vicar of Saltash, Cornwall, England. He was the author of *Life and work in Newfoundland: Reminiscences of thirteen years spent there* (London, 1863).

[H. J. Morgan, *Bibliotheca canadensis* (Ottawa, 1867); S. A. Allibone, *Dictionary of authors*, supplement, vol. ii (Philadelphia, 1908).]

Morgan, Henry James (1842-1913), civil servant and author, was born in Quebec on November 14, 1842, the son of a veteran of the Napoleonic wars who had come to Canada in 1838, and who died about 1847. He entered the civil service of Canada at the age of eleven years; and, except for a short period following 1861, when he resigned in order to attend Morrin College, Quebec, he continued in the civil service until his retirement on pension in 1895. He was one of the founders of the "Canada First" movement of 1868-75; and he originated the idea of a medal for long service in the militia. It is chiefly, however, by his literary work that he is remembered. His first book was *The tour of H.R.H. the Prince of Wales in Canada and the United States* (Montreal, 1860). This was followed by a biographical dictionary entitled *Celebrated Canadians* (Quebec, 1862), the first-fruits of biographical studies which culminated in the publication of *Canadian men and women of the time* (Toronto, 1898; new and revised edition, 1912) and *Types of Canadian women* (Toronto, 1901). In 1867 he published the *Bibliotheca canadensis* (Ottawa), a contribution to Canadian bibliography which, with all its imperfections, was a notable performance at that time. In 1862 he founded the annual *Canadian parliamentary companion*; having sold his rights in this, he founded in 1878 the *Dominion annual register* (1878-86); and the same year he published *The Canadian legal directory*. In 1865 he edited *Speeches and addresses of the Hon. Thomas D'Arcy McGee on the British American Union* (London), and in 1895 he published, in collaboration with L. J. Burpee, *Canadian life in town and country* (Toronto). He died at Brockville, Ontario, on December 27, 1913. In 1873 he married Emily, second daughter of the Hon. A. N. Richards (q.v.). He was an LL.D. of the University of Ottawa (1903) and a D.C.L. of King's College, Windsor, Nova Scotia (1905); and he was elected a fellow of the Royal Society of Canada in 1904.

[*Proc. Roy. Soc. Can.*, 1914; *Cyc. Am. biog.*; Dent, *Can. port.*, vol. 4; Rose, *Cyc. Can. biog.* (1886); G. T. Denison, *The struggle for imperial unity* (Toronto, 1909).]

Morgan-Powell, Samuel (1867-1962), journalist, was born at Highbury Park, London, England, in 1867. He was educated at Ellesmere, and at the University of London. He began his newspaper career as an office boy with the *Yorkshire Post*. He became, in turn, sports writer and music and drama critic on the paper. In 1900, after a period of free-lance writing, he went to British Guiana as subeditor of the Demerara *Daily Chronicle*. He came to Canada in 1905, and worked on the Montreal *Witness* and the *Herald*. He joined the staff of the *Montreal Star* as news editor in 1908. He became editor of the paper in 1941, retiring in 1946. Morgan-Powell travelled extensively in Europe and in Central and South America. As a young man he had served with the Royal Warwicks (1896-1900). While in Canada he was interested in promoting music and drama and was secretary of the Earle Grey music and drama competition (1908). He wrote *Memories that live* (Toronto, 1929), *Down the*

years (Toronto, 1938), *Night thoughts* (poems, second edition, 1895), *The devil in heaven, Love in the hands of fate, Where dark souls go,* and *This Canadian literature* (Toronto, 1940). He died at Montreal, June 4, 1962.

[*Can. who's who*, 1955-57.]

Morgann, Maurice (1726-1802), civil servant and author, was born in London, England, in 1726, of Welsh descent. He became a clerk in the office of the secretary of state, and was private secretary to the Earl of Shelburne. In 1767 he was chosen to go to Canada to confer with Carleton (q.v.) concerning the laws of Canada. He was in Canada from August, 1768, to January, 1770; and he was largely responsible for Carleton's report, as printed in W. P. M. Kennedy and G. Lanctot (eds.), *Reports on the laws of Quebec, 1767-1770* (Ottawa, Public Archives, 1931). He died at Knightsbridge on March 28, 1802. Although the author of several pamphlets, he is chiefly remembered for his *Essay on the dramatic character of Sir John Falstaff* (London, 1777).

[*Dict. nat. biog.*]

Morice, Adrien Gabriel (1859-1938), priest and historian, was born at St. Marssur-Colmont, France, on August 27, 1859. He joined the Oblate order, and was ordained a priest in 1882. He was for many years a missionary among the Indians of British Columbia. In his later years he lived in Manitoba; and he died at St. Boniface, Manitoba, on April 21, 1938. He was the author of *Le petit catéchisme à l'usage des sauvages Porteurs* (Mission du Lac Stuart, B.C., 1891), *Au pays de l'ours noir* (Paris, 1897), *The history of the northern interior of British Columbia* (Toronto, 1904), *Dictionnaire historique des canadiens et des métis français de l'ouest* (Quebec, 1908), *History of the Catholic church in western Canada* (2 vols., Toronto, 1910), *Histoire abrégé de l'ouest canadien* (St. Boniface, Man., 1914), *Fifty years in Western Canada* (Toronto, 1930), *The Carrier language* (2 vols., Winnipeg, 1932), *Souvenirs d'un missionnaire en Colombie Britannique* (St. Boniface, Man., 1933), *Croquois anthropologiques* (Winnipeg, 1934), *Monseigneur Turquetil* (Winnipeg, 1935), and *A critical history of the Red River insurrection* (Winnipeg, 1935).

[T. O'Hagan, *Father Morice* (Toronto, 1928); Raymond Huel, *Adrien Gabriel Morice* (Rev. de l'Univ. d'Ottawa, 1971-73); Allaire, *Dict. biog.*]

Morin, Augustin Norbert (1803-1865), politician and judge, was born at St. Michel, Lower Canada, on October 12, 1803. He was educated at the Quebec Seminary; and in 1828 he was called to the bar of Lower Canada. In 1830 he was elected to the Legislative Assembly of Lower Canada for the county of Bellechasse, and became a supporter of Louis Joseph Papineau (q.v.). He was reputed to have been, in part, the author of the Ninety-Two Resolutions of 1834; and the same year he was deputed, with Denis Benjamin Viger (q.v.), to lay before the British parliament the views of the Lower Canadian Assembly. Though he was not actually under arms during the rebellion of 1837, a warrant was issued for his arrest on the charge of high treason; and he spent the winter of 1837-38 in hiding. In 1841 he was returned to the Legislative Assembly of Canada for Nicolet, and he continued to sit in the Assembly, first for Nicolet (1841-44), secondly for Bellechasse (1844-51), then for Terrebonne (1851-54), and finally for Chicoutimi and Tadoussac (1854-55), until his elevation to the bench. In 1842-43 he was commissioner of crown lands in the first Baldwin-Lafontaine administration; from 1848 to 1851 he was speaker of the Assembly; and in 1851 he became the chief colleague of Francis Hincks (q.v.) in the Hincks-Morin administration, holding the portfolio of provincial secretary. On the collapse of this government in 1854 he became the chief colleague of Sir Allan MacNab in the MacNab-Morin administration, with the portfolio of crown lands. But in 1855 he resigned from the government, and was appointed a judge of the Superior Court of Lower Canada. He died at St. Hyacinthe, Lower Canada, on July 27, 1865.

[A. Béchard, *L'honorable A. N. Morin* (Quebec, 1885); L. O. David, *L'hon. A. N. Morin* (Montreal, 1872) and *Biographies et portraits* (Montreal, 1876); Morgan, *Cel. Can.* and *Bib. can.*; Le Jeune, *Dict. gén.*; J. C. Dent, *The last forty years* (2 vols., Toronto, 1881); Sir F. Hincks, *Reminiscences* (Montreal, 1884).]

Morin, Louis Siméon (1831-1879), solicitor-general for Lower Canada (1860-63), was born at Lavaltrie, Lower Canada, on January 20, 1831, the son of Joseph Morin and Félicité Pelletier. He was called to the bar of Lower Canada in 1853, and in 1857 was elected to the Legislative Assembly of Canada for Terrebonne. In 1860 he was appointed attorney-general for Canada East in the Cartier-Macdonald government; but in 1863 he retired from the government, having been twice defeated in Terrebonne. In 1865 he was appointed one of the secretaries to the commission for the codification of the laws of Lower Canada, and he then became joint protonotary and clerk of the crown for the district of Joliette. He died at Lavaltrie, Quebec, on May 7, 1879. "No man ever sat in the Canadian parliament from whom so much was expected, and who so utterly disappointed the hopes of his friends."

[*Dom. ann. reg.*, 1879; Le Jeune, *Dict. gén.*; Morgan, *Cel. Can.*; L. O. David, *Souvenirs et biographies* (Montreal, 1911) and *Mes contemporains* (Montreal, 1894); J. C. Dent, *The last forty years* (2 vols., Toronto, 1881); *Dict. Can. biog.*, vol. 10.]

Morin, Marie (1649-1730), nun, was born in Quebec, New France, in 1649, and was the first native-born Canadian to take the veil. She became a sister in the Hôtel Dieu of Montreal, and in 1697 was charged with compiling the annals of the Hôtel Dieu. Her manuscript has been published by Victor Morin under the title *Annales de l'Hôtel-Dieu de Montréal* (Montreal, 1921). She died at Montreal on April 8, 1730.

[Le Jeune, *Dict. gén.*; *Dict. Can. biog.*, vol. 2.]

Morin, Victor (1865-1960), author and notary, was born in St. Hyacinthe, Quebec, on August 15, 1865. He was educated at Girouard Academy and St. Hyacinthe Seminary (B.A., 1884) and Laval University (LL.B., 1888; LL.D., 1910). He became a notary in 1888 and practised his profession until he was past ninety. When he attended Laval University in Montreal, classes were held in the old Château de Ramezay built in 1705 and saved from destruction by the Archeological Society of Montreal, of which Morin became president in 1927. He did not enter politics but served on many boards and committees. He was on the National and Historic Sites and Monuments Board (1921-24) and on the Provincial Commission for the Preservation of Historic Monuments from 1922. He was president of the St. Jean Baptiste Society (1915-24) and a member of the Antiquarian and Numismatic Society. He was elected a fellow of the Royal Society of Canada in 1916. For thirty-three years he was treasurer of the Board of Notaries and until his seventieth year he lectured on civil law at the University of Montreal. As a young man he was associated with the Independent Order of Foresters and was for a time its chief executive officer. As president of the Historical Society of Montreal he had an opportunity to promote better understanding between French and English Canadians, and his wide knowledge of Canadian history made him a popular interpreter of French culture and folklore. He was author of *Vingt ans après*, *Les Médailles décernées aux Indiens* (1916), *Trait d'art héraldique* (Montreal, 1919), *La ville aux clochers dans la verdure*—translated as *The city of spires in the green* (Montreal, 1923), *La Chanson canadienne* (Montreal, 1928), *Croquis Montréalais* — translated as *Old Montreal with pen and pencil* (Montreal, 1929), *Dîner en musique* (Montreal, 1930), *Le Ramezay et leur château* — translated as *De Ramezay family and château* (Montreal, 1939), *Seigneur et censitaires* (Montreal, 1941), *Le vieux Montréal* (Montreal, 1942), *Légende dorée de Montréal* (Montreal, 1949). He died at Montreal in 1960.

[Renée Morin, *Victor Morin* (Montreal, 1967); *Can. who's who*, 1958-60; *Proc. Roy. Soc. Can.*, 1961; *Food for thought* (Nov., 1958); *Encyc. Can.* (1966).]

Morine, Sir Alfred Bishop (1857-1944), lawyer and politician, was born at Port Medway, Nova Scotia, on March 31, 1857. He was educated at Dalhousie University (LL.B., 1892), and was called to the bar, first in Nova Scotia, and then in Newfoundland, in 1894, and in Ontario in 1906 (K.C., 1908). He practised law in St. John's, Newfoundland, except for the years 1906-12 and 1930-44, when he practised law in Toronto, Ontario; and he represented Bonavista in the Newfoundland House of Assembly from 1886 to 1906, and again from 1914 to 1919. He was successively colonial secretary, minister of finance and customs, minister of marine and fisheries, and minister of justice in the government of Newfoundland; and from 1924 to 1928 he was a member of the Legislative Council of Newfoundland, and government leader in the Council, with a seat in the cabinet without portfolio. In 1928 he was created a knight bachelor. He died in Toronto, Ontario, on December 18, 1944. He was the author of *The mining law of Canada* (Toronto, 1909).

[*Who's who*, 1944; *Can. who's who*, 1938-39; Morgan, *Can. men* (1912).]

Morley, Percival Fellman (1884?-1936), author, was born about 1884, and became an analyst in the department of health in Ontario. He retired from the civil service of Ontario in December, 1933, because of ill-health; and his dead body was found in the Back River near Montreal in September, 1936, over four months after his disappearance in Toronto in May, 1936. He was the author of *Bridging the chasm: A study of the Ontario-Quebec question* (Toronto, 1919).

[Private information.]

Mornay, Louis François de (1663-1741), third Roman Catholic bishop of Quebec, was born in Brittany in 1663, the fourth son of Charles de Mornay, seignior of Mesnil-Théribus. He entered the Capuchin order in 1682, and in 1713 became coadjutor to the bishop of Quebec. He succeeded to the see in 1727 on the death of Bishop St. Valier (q.v.), and he resigned in 1733. He was accidentally killed in the streets of Paris on November 28, 1741.

[R. Roy, *Mgr. François de Mornay* (Bull. rech. hist., 1904); Allaire, *Dict. biog.*; Le Jeune, *Dict. gén.*; Abbé C. Tanguay, *Répertoire général du clergé canadien* (Quebec, 1868).]

Morrice, James Wilson (1864-1924), painter, was born in Montreal, Quebec, on August 14, 1864, the son of David Morrice, a merchant and manufacturer. He was educated at the University of Toronto (B.A., 1886), and studied painting in Paris, France. He became an exponent of the French impressionist school of painting; and most of his life was spent in France. He died at Tunis, Algiers, on January 24, 1924.

[D. W. Buchanan, *James Wilson Morrice* (Toronto, 1936); *Can. who was who*, vol. 1; Morgan, *Can. men* (1912); N. MacTavish, *The fine arts in Canada* (Toronto, 1925).]

Morrin, Joseph (1792-1861), physician and philanthropist, was born in Dumfriesshire, Scotland, in 1792. He was brought to Canada by his parents at an early age, was educated in Quebec, and studied medicine in Edinburgh and London. He practised medicine in Quebec, and became the first president of the medical board of Lower Canada. A short time before his death he gave a large sum of money for the erection of a Presbyterian College in Quebec, to be known as Morrin College. He died at Quebec on August 29, 1861.

[*Cyc. Am. biog.*; M. J. and G. Ahern, *Notes pour servir à l'histoire de la médecine dans le bas-Canada* (Quebec, 1923).]

Morris, Alexander (1826-1889), lieutenant-governor of Manitoba and the North West Territories (1872-77), was born at Perth, Upper Canada, on March 17, 1826, the eldest son of the Hon. William Morris (q.v.). He was educated at the Perth grammar school, at Madras College, St. Andrews, Scotland, at the University of Glasgow, and later at McGill University, Montreal, where he was the first graduate in arts. He was called to the bar of Upper Canada in 1851; and to the bar of Lower Canada in the same year. In 1861 he was elected as a Conservative for Lanark in the Legislative Assembly of Canada, and this seat he held, first under the Union, and then after Confederation, until 1872. He advocated Confederation in two published lectures, *Nova Britannia* (Montreal, 1858) and *The Hudson's Bay and Pacific Territories* (Montreal, 1859), which were republished later under the title *Nova Britannia* (Toronto, 1884); and he played an important part in the *pourparlers* which led to the formation of the coalition of 1864 which preceded Confederation. From 1869 to 1872 he was minister of inland revenue in the government of Sir John Macdonald (q.v.); in 1872 he was appointed chief justice of the Court of Queen's Bench in Manitoba; and later in the same year he became lieutenant-governor of Manitoba and the North West Territories. When his term of office ended, he returned to Ontario, and from 1878 to 1886 he represented East Toronto in the Legislative Assembly of Ontario. He died on October 28, 1889. In 1851 he married Margaret, daughter of William Cline of Cornwall, and niece of the Hon. Philip Vankoughnet (q.v.). He published, in addition to the papers mentioned above, *The treaties of Canada with the Indians of the North-west* (Toronto, 1880), and a prize essay entitled *Canada and her resources* (Montreal, 1855).

[L. Staples, *The Hon. Alexander Morris* (Canadian Historical Association, report,

1928); *Cyc. Am. biog.*; Dent, *Can. port.*, vol. 3; Rose, *Cyc. Can. biog.* (1886); Morgan, *Bib. can.*; E. M. Chadwick, *Ontarian families*, vol. 1 (Toronto, 1894).]

Morris, Charles (1711-1781), chief justice of Nova Scotia, was born in Boston, Massachusetts, on June 8, 1711, the son of Charles Morris and Esther Rainstorpe. He surveyed the whole of Nova Scotia in 1745-46, and helped to lay out the town of Halifax in 1749. He was appointed a member of the Executive Council of Nova Scotia in 1755; and in 1764, though a layman, he was made an assistant justice to the chief justice. From 1776 to 1778 he was chief justice of the Supreme Court of the province. He died in 1781. In 1735 he married Mary, daughter of the Hon. John Read, attorney-general of Massachusetts.

[*Catalogue of portraits of the judges of the Supreme Court of Nova Scotia* (Halifax, N.S., 1929).]

Morris, Edmund Montague (1871-1913), painter, was born at Perth, Ontario, in 1871, the youngest son of the Hon. Alexander Morris (q.v.). He studied painting at the Art Students' League in New York, and under Laurens and Constant in Paris; and returned to Canada in 1896. In 1897 he was elected an associate of the Royal Canadian Academy; and he won a reputation as a painter of Indian portraits. In 1908 he was one of the founders of the Canadian Art Club, and he became its honorary secretary. He was drowned at Portneuf, Quebec, on August 21, 1913. Some of his paintings are in the National Gallery at Ottawa; and he was the author of a valuable pamphlet entitled *Art in Canada: The early painters* (Toronto, 1911). He was not married.

[W. M. Boultbee, *Edmund Morris* (Can. mag., 1908); Morgan, *Can. men* (1912); N. MacTavish, *The fine arts in Canada* (Toronto, 1925).]

Morris, Edward Patrick, first Baron (1859-1935), prime minister of Newfoundland (1909-18), was born at St. John's, Newfoundland, on May 8, 1859, and died at London, England, on October 24, 1935. He was educated at St. Bonaventure's College in St. John's and the University of Ottawa. He was articled to Sir James Winter (q.v.), and was called to the bar in Newfoundland in 1885 (Q.C., 1896). From 1885 to 1918 he represented St. John's West in the Newfoundland House of Assembly; he served as minister without portfolio in the Whiteway and Bond administrations, and was minister of justice in the Bond government from 1902 to 1907; and he was prime minister of Newfoundland from 1909 to 1918. He had been created a knight bachelor in 1904, and a K.C.M.G. in 1913; but in 1918 he was created a peer, and resigned as prime minister. He went to live in London, and remained there until his death. He received honorary degrees from several British universities.

[*Dict. nat. biog.*, 5th supp.; *Who was who*, 1928-40; *Encyc. Can.*; *Newfoundland supp.*]

Morris, James (1798-1865), legislative councillor, was born at Paisley, Scotland, in 1798, the son of Alexander Morris, and came to Canada with his parents in 1801. His father settled first in Montreal, Lower Canada, and then in Brockville, Upper Canada; and he was educated at an academy in Sorel, Lower Canada, kept by the father of Dr. Wolfred Nelson (q.v.). He went into business at Brockville; and in 1837 he was elected a member of the Legislative Assembly of Upper Canada for Leeds. In 1841 he was returned to the Legislative Assembly of united Canada for Leeds; and in 1844 he was appointed to the Legislative Council. From 1851 to 1853 he was postmaster-general in the Hincks-Morin administration, and from 1853 to 1854 he was speaker of the Legislative Council. He was again speaker of the Legislative Council in the short-lived Brown-Dorion administration of 1858; and in the Macdonald-Sicotte government he was receiver-general from 1862 to 1863. He died at Brockville on September 29, 1865. He married in 1827 Emily Rosamond, daughter of Henry Murney of Kingston, and had by her four sons and four daughters.

[*Cyc. Am. biog.*; Morgan, *Cel. Can.*; Taylor, *Brit. Am.*, vol. 3; J. C. Dent, *The last forty years* (2 vols., Toronto, 1881); Sir F. Hincks, *Reminiscences* (Montreal, 1884); E. M. Chadwick, *Ontarian families*, vol. 1 (Toronto, 1894).]

Morris, James Lewis (1862-1946), engineer and author, was born near Renfrew, Canada West, in 1862, and died at Toronto, Ontario, on February 21, 1946. He was the first graduate of the School of Practical Science, at Toronto (C.E., 1885), and for many years was a civil engineer in Pembroke. In his later years he was inspector of surveys in the Ontario department of lands and forests; and it was while employed in this department that he published *The Indians of Ontario* (Toronto, 1943). In 1927 the University of Toronto conferred on him the honorary degree of D.Eng.

[Toronto *Globe and Mail*, Feb. 22, 1946.]

Morris, Leslie (1904-1964), communist party chief, was born in Somerset, England, in 1904. He began working in the coal mines at thirteen and when he was seventeen came to Canada with his parents. He was employed on the railway in Winnipeg and helped found the Young Workers League in 1922. At the founding National Convention a year later he became National Secretary and spent the remainder of his life, except for a short period in 1925, as an officer of the Communist Party of Canada. He was an editor and writer for *The Worker*, the *Daily Clarion*, the *Tribune*, and the *Daily Tribune*, all party publications. He held almost every key position in the party during his long association and became federal leader in 1962 on the retirement of Tim Buck. He adhered to the Soviet line in his policies and was active in subduing the 1955 revolt which split the party during the Sino-Soviet dispute of that year. He ran unsuccessfully in six federal, three provincial, and four civic elections despite his popularity within his own party. He died at Toronto, November 14, 1964.

[Metropolitan Toronto Library Board, *Biographical scrapbooks*, vol. 22.]

Morris, Patrick (1789-1849), reformer, was born in Waterford, Ireland, in 1789, and came to Newfoundland in 1800. He became a leader in the agitation in Newfoundland for representative government; and in 1828 he published in London a pamphlet entitled *Arguments to prove the policy and necessity of granting to Newfoundland a constitutional government*. After an Assembly had been granted, he was elected to represent St. John's, and in 1840 was appointed colonial secretary. This position he held until his death on August 22, 1849. Shortly before his death he published *A short review of the history, government, constitution, fishing and agriculture of Newfoundland* (St. John's, Newfoundland, 1847), a copy of which is in the British Museum.

[*Newfoundland supp.*]

Morris, Robert Schofield (1898-1964), architect, was born in Hamilton, Ontario, November 14, 1898, and was educated there. He entered the Royal Military College in 1915 and a year later was commissioned in the artillery. He served in France and Belgium with the 70th Brigade, 15th Scottish division, was wounded at Ypres, and returned to Canada in 1918. In 1923 he graduated from the school of architecture at McGill University and worked and studied in New York, in Britain, and in Europe. He became a partner in the firm of Marani, Lawson and Morris, Toronto, in 1929. He was involved in the construction of the Manufacturers Life building, the Metropolitan Toronto Courthouse, and the Fort York Armoury in Toronto. He was awarded the Royal Institute of British Architects' gold medal in 1958 for services to the profession, and was a fellow of the Royal Architectural Institute of Canada and a former president of the Ontario Association of Architects. He died at Ottawa, June 5, 1964.

[Metropolitan Toronto Library Board, *Biographical scrapbooks*, vol. 22.]

Morris, William (1786-1858), legislative councillor, was born at Paisley, Scotland, on October 31, 1786, the son of Alexander Morris, and came to Canada with his parents in 1801. His father settled first in Montreal, Lower Canada, and then at Brockville, Upper Canada. He served throughout the greater part of the War of 1812 as a militia officer; and in 1816 he founded a mercantile business at Perth, Upper Canada. In 1820 he was elected to the Legislative Assembly of Upper Canada as a member for Lanark, and he represented this constituency continuously in the Assembly until 1836. He took a prominent part in pressing the claims of the Church of Scotland to a share in the Clergy Reserves. In 1836 he was appointed to the Legislative Council of Upper Canada; and in 1841 to the Legislative Council of Canada. From 1844 to 1846 he was receiver-general in the Draper administration, and from 1846 to 1848 president of the Executive Council. In 1853 failing health compelled him to retire from public life, and he died at Montreal on June 29, 1858. In 1823 he married Elizabeth, daughter of John Cochran, of Kirkcudbright, Scotland; and had by her three sons and four daughters. His correspondence is in the Public Archives at Ottawa; and the *Journal* of his mission to England in 1837 has been edited by E. C. Kyte (Ont. Hist. Soc., papers and records, 1934). He was the author of *A letter on the subject of the clergy reserves* (Toronto, 1838), and *Reply to six letters addressed to him by John Strachan* (Toronto, 1838).

[*Cyc. Am. biog.*; Morgan, *Cel. Can. and Bib. can.*; Dent, *Can. port.*; Taylor, *Brit. Am.*, vol. 1; J. C. Dent, *The last forty years* (2 vols., Toronto, 1881); E. M. Chadwick, *Ontarian families*, vol. 1 (Toronto, 1894).]

Morrison, Angus (1822-1882), lawyer and politician, was born in Edinburgh, Scotland, on January 20, 1822, the son of Hugh Morrison, of the 42nd Highlanders. He came to Canada with his parents in 1832, and was educated at Upper Canada College. He was called to the bar of Upper Canada in 1846 (Q.C., 1873). From 1854 to 1863 he represented North Simcoe in the Legislative Assembly of Canada, and from 1864 to 1874 he represented Niagara in the Legislative Assembly of Canada and in the Canadian House of Commons. He died in Toronto, Ontario, on June 10, 1882.

[A. MacMurchy, *Sketch of the life and times of Joseph Curran Morrison and Angus Morrison* (Toronto, 1918); *Dom. ann. reg.*, 1882; *Cyc. Am. biog.*]

Morrison, Aulay MacAulay (1863-1942), jurist, was born at Baddeck, Nova Scotia, on June 15, 1863. He was educated at Dalhousie University (LL.B., 1888; M.A., 1929), and was called to the bar of Nova Scotia in 1888, and to that of British Columbia in 1890. He practised law at New Westminster, British Columbia, from 1890 to 1904; from 1896 to 1904 he represented New Westminster in the Canadian House of Commons; and in 1904 he was appointed a judge of the Supreme Court of British Columbia. In 1928 he became chief justice of this court; and he died on February 27, 1942.

[*Can. who's who*, 1938-39; *Can. parl. comp.*]

Morrison, Sir Edward Whipple Bancroft (1867-1925), journalist and soldier, was born at London, Ontario, on July 6, 1867. He was educated at the Galt Collegiate Institute under Dr. Tassie (q.v.), and he became a journalist, first in Hamilton, Ontario, and then in Ottawa. Here he became editor-in-chief of the Ottawa *Citizen*, a post from which he retired only in 1912. He joined the Canadian militia as an artillery subaltern in 1898; and from 1899 to 1901 he saw service in South Africa. In 1913 he was gazetted a lieutenant-colonel in the Canadian Permanent Militia; and in 1914 he proceeded overseas with the First Canadian Contingent. He served throughout the whole of the First World War, and from 1916 to 1919 he was general officer commanding the Canadian artillery. After the war he was appointed successively inspector-general of artillery in the Canadian militia, master-general of ordnance, and adjutant-general. He retired on pension in 1924; and he died at Ottawa on May 28, 1925. He received the D.S.O. in 1901, the C.M.G. in 1917, the C.B. in 1918, and the K.C.M.G. in 1919. He was the author of *With the guns in South Africa* (Hamilton, Ont., 1901).

[*Can. who was who*, vol. 2; *Who was who*, 1916-28; Morgan, *Can. men* (1912).]

Morrison, James J. (1861-1936), farmer and politician, was born in Peel township, Wellington county, Canada West, in July, 1861. In 1915 he organized and became the secretary-treasurer of the United Farmers of Ontario; and in 1919, on the success of the U.F.O. at the polls, he was invited to form a government, but declined. It was he who advised the lieutenant-governor to call on E. C. Drury to form a Farmers' Government. He died on March 17, 1936. His baptismal name was merely James Morrison, but he added the initial "J", to distinguish himself from another James Morrison who lived in his neighbourhood.

[Private information.]

Morrison, Joseph Curran (1816-1885), politician and judge, was born in the north of Ireland on August 20, 1816, the son of Hugh Morrison, of the 42nd Highlanders. He came with his parents to Canada in 1832, and was educated at Upper Canada College. He was called to the bar of Upper Canada in 1839, entered into partnership with William Hume Blake (q.v.), and in 1853 was created a Q.C. In 1850 he was elected as a "Baldwin Reformer" to the Legislative Assembly of Canada for the west riding of York, and in 1851 for Niagara. From 1853 to 1854 he was solicitor-general for Upper Canada in the Hincks-Morin administration; and from 1856 to 1857 was receiver-general in the Taché-Macdonald government. In 1857 he failed of election to the Assembly; but in 1860 he returned to the House, and from 1860 to 1862 he was solicitor-general in the

Cartier-Macdonald government. In 1862 he was appointed a puisne judge of the Court of Common Pleas; in 1863 he was promoted to the Queen's Bench; and in 1877 he was transferred to the Court of Appeal. He died in Toronto on December 6, 1885. In 1845 he married Elizabeth, daughter of Joseph Bloor, of Toronto. For fourteen years (1863-76) he was chancellor of the University of Toronto.

[A. MacMurchy, *Sketch of the life and times of Joseph Curran Morrison and Angus Morrison* (Toronto, 1918); *Dom. ann. reg.*, 1885; *Cyc. Am. biog.*; Dent, *Can. port.*, vol. 4; D. B. Read, *Lives of the judges* (Toronto, 1888).]

Morrison, Thomas David (1796?-1856), physician and politician, was born in Quebec, Lower Canada, about 1796. He settled in York (Toronto) about 1816, and was for a time employed in the surveyor-general's office. In 1824 he was admitted to practice as a physician by the Upper Canada Medical Board; and he became a prominent figure in the life of York. In 1834 he was returned as a Reformer to the Legislative Assembly of Upper Canada in the third riding of York; and in 1836 he was elected mayor of Toronto. In 1837 he took no active part in the rebellion headed by William Lyon Mackenzie (q.v.), but he was to such an extent implicated in it that he was arrested and tried on a charge of high treason. He was acquitted by the jury; but, fearing a second indictment, he fled to Rochester, New York, and he did not return to Toronto until 1843. He died in Toronto on March 19, 1856.

[W. Canniff, *The medical profession in Upper Canada* (Toronto, 1894); J. C. Dent, *The Upper Canadian rebellion* (2 vols., Toronto, 1885).]

Morrison, William (1785-1866), fur-trader, was born in Montreal in 1785, the son of Alan Morrison and Josepha, the daughter of Jean Etienne Wadden (q.v.). He entered the service of the XY Company about 1802; and for a number of years after the union of 1804 he was a clerk in the service of the North West Company in the Fond du Lac and Nipigon departments, where he encountered Jean Baptiste Perrault (q.v.). In 1816 he entered the service of the South West Company, and was for many years in charge of the Fond du Lac department. He retired from the fur-trade about 1826, and settled on Morrison's Island, near Berthier, Lower Canada. He died on Morrison's Island on August 7, 1866. He married an Indian wife; and by her he had several children.

[*Cyc. Am. biog.*]

Morrow, Ernest Lloyd (1884-1951), clergyman and author, was born at Millbrook, Ontario, on September 2, 1884, and died at Toronto, Ontario, on February 3, 1951. He was educated at the University of Toronto (B.A.,

1909; M.A., 1910) and Edinburgh University (Ph.D., 1923). He was ordained a minister of the Presbyterian Church, was pastor of several churches in Ontario, and from 1926 to 1936 was professor of systematic theology in Knox College, Toronto. He was the author of *Church union in Canada* (Toronto, 1923).

[*Can. who's who*, 1948).]

Morse, William Inglis (1874-1952), historian and bibliographer, was born at Paradise, Nova Scotia, on June 4, 1874, and died at Cambridge, Massachusetts, on June 5, 1952. He was educated at Acadia University (B.A., 1897) and at the Episcopal Theological School in Cambridge, Massachusetts (B.D., 1900). He was ordained a minister of the Protestant Episcopal Church in 1901; and from 1905 to 1930 he was rector of the Church of the Incarnation at Lynn, Massachusetts. He was the author of a number of books relating to the early history of Nova Scotia, notably *Gravestones of Acadia, and other essays on Nova Scotia* (London, 1929), *The land of the new adventure* (London, 1932), *Acadiensia Nova* (2 vols., London, 1935), and *Pierre Du Gua, Sieur de Monts* (London, 1939). He was also the compiler of *Bliss Carman: Bibliography* (Windham, Conn., 1941) and of *The Canadian collection at Harvard University* (6 vols., Cambridge, Mass., 1944-1949). He received honorary degrees from Acadia and Dalhousie universities.

[*Can. who's who*, 1949-51; *Can. hist. rev.*, 1952.]

Mortimer, George (1784-1844), clergyman, was born in London, England, on May 20, 1784; and was educated at Queen's College, Cambridge (B.A., 1811; M.A., 1814). He was ordained a priest of the Church of England in 1812. He emigrated to Canada with his family in 1832; and he was rector of Thornhill, near Toronto, Upper Canada, from 1832 to his death on June 15, 1844. After his death, the Reverend J. Armstrong published his *Life and letters* (London, 1847).

[J. Armstrong, *The life and letters of the Rev. George Mortimer* (London, 1847).]

Morton, Arthur Silver (1870-1945), historian, was born in Trinidad, British West Indies, on May 16, 1870, the son of the Rev. John Morton. He was educated at Edinburgh University (M.A., 1894; B.D., 1896) and at the University of Berlin; and in 1896 he was ordained a minister of the Presbyterian Church in New Brunswick. He was the pastor of churches at Shediac, Fairville, and St. Stephen, New Brunswick; and from 1904 to 1907 he was lecturer in church history at the Presbyterian College, Halifax, Nova Scotia. In 1912 he was appointed interim professor of church history at Knox College, Toronto; and in 1914 he became professor of history and librarian at the University of Saskatchewan.

He retired from these posts in 1940, when he was appointed archivist of the province of Saskatchewan; and he died at Saskatoon, Saskatchewan, on January 26, 1945. He was elected a fellow of the Royal Society of Canada in 1932; and he was awarded the Society's Tyrrell medal in 1941. In 1922 he was made a D.D. of Pine Hill College, Halifax, and in 1941 an LL.D. of the University of Saskatchewan. He was the author of *The way to union* (Toronto, 1912), *Under western skies* (Toronto, 1937), *History of prairie settlement* (Toronto, 1938), *A history of the Canadian west to 1870-71* (London, 1939), and *The life of Sir George Simpson* (Toronto, 1945); he was joint author, with Sarah E. Morton, of *John Morton of Trinidad* (Toronto, 1916); and he was the editor of *Narratives of Saskatoon* (Saskatoon, Sask., 1927) and *The journal of Duncan McGillivray* (Toronto, 1929).

[*Arthur Silver Morton, M.A., B.D., D.D., LL.D., F.R.S.C., professor of history and librarian in the University of Saskatchewan, 1914-1940* (pamphlet, Saskatoon, Sask., 1943).]

Morton, Guy Eugene (1884-1948), journalist and novelist, was born in North Gwillimbury, Ontario, in 1884, and died at Toronto, Ontario, on February 26, 1948. He became a journalist in Toronto, latterly on the staff of the *Globe and Mail*; but he was also a successful writer of mystery stories. He was the author of *The enemy within* (Baltimore, 1918), *Rangy Pete* (Boston, 1922), *Black gold* (Boston, 1924), *Wards of the azure hills* (London, 1926), *King of the world* (London, 1927), *The black robe* (New York, 1927), *The forbidden road* (London, 1928), *The Perrin murder case* (London, 1930), *Zola's thirteen* (London, 1930), *The scarlet thumbprint* (London, 1931), *The red lady* (London, 1931), *Mystery at Hermit's End* (London, 1932), *3-7-9- murder* (London, 1935), *The ragged robin murders* (London, 1935), *Ashes of murder* (London, 1936), *Silver-voiced red murder* (London, 1937), and *Mystery at Hardacres* (London, 1937).

[Clara Thomas, *Canadian novelists, 1920-1945* (Toronto, 1946).]

Mosher, Aaron Roland (1881-1959), trade union leader, was born in Halifax county, Nova Scotia, May 10, 1881. He began work at the age of fifteen and was employed on the Intercolonial Railway from 1903 to 1907, when he led a week-long strike for improved wages and working conditions. In 1908 he was a founder of the Canadian Brotherhood of Railway Employees and was its president for forty-four years. It became the largest transport union and largest non-international union in Canada. In 1927 he helped establish the All-Canadian Congress of Labour and was its president until it merged with Canadian branches of the Congress of Industrial Organizations (C.I.O.) to become the Canadian Congress of Labour. He was the only president of the C.C.L. until its merger with the Trades and Labour Congress to form the Canadian Labour Congress in 1956. During the Second World War he served on the National Wartime Labour Relations Board, the National Employment Committee, and the Canadian Welfare Council. He died at Ottawa, September 26, 1959.

[*Can. who's who*, 1955-57; *Encyc. Can.* (1972); Metropolitan Toronto Library Board, *Biographical scrapbooks*, vol. 22.]

Moss, Sir Charles (1840-1912), chief justice of Ontario (1902-12), was born in Cobourg, Upper Canada, on March 8, 1840, the son of John Moss, brewer, and Ann Quigley. After several years in his father's business, he entered the Upper Canada Law School, Toronto, and was called to the bar of Ontario in 1869 (Q.C., 1881). In 1897 he was appointed a judge of the Ontario Court of Appeals, and in 1902 he became chief justice. From 1900 to 1906 he was vice-chancellor of the University of Toronto. He died at Toronto on October 11, 1912. In 1871 he married Emily, second daughter of the Hon. Robert Baldwin Sullivan (q.v.); and by her he had three sons and two daughters. In 1900 he was made an LL.D. of the University of Toronto; and in 1907 he was created a knight bachelor.

[Morgan, *Can. men* (1912); *Can. who's who* (1910); Rose, *Cyc. Can. biog.* (1886).]

Moss, Charles Eugene (1860-1901), painter, was born in Ohio, United States, in 1860. He studied art at St. Louis, Missouri, and later at the Julian Academy in Paris under Bougereau, Gérôme, Ferrier, and Bonnat. He was then appointed headmaster of the Ottawa Art School. In 1887 he settled in Orange, New Jersey; but in 1896 he returned to Ottawa, and he was elected an A.R.C.A. in 1897 and an R.C.A. in 1898. During his later years he devoted himself mainly to landscape painting in water-colours; but he was also a painter of portraits and figures. He died in 1901.

[N. MacTavish, *The fine arts in Canada* (Toronto, 1925); H. G. Jones and E. Dyonnet, *History of the Royal Canadian Academy of Arts* (Montreal, 1934).]

Moss, Ezra Henry (1892-1967), botanist, was born at London, Ontario, April 11, 1892, and educated at the University of Toronto (B.A., 1916; M.A., 1920; Ph.D., 1925). He served for three years with the Royal Canadian Corps of Signals and was awarded the Military Medal in 1918. He joined the staff of the department of botany at the University of Alberta in 1921 and became head of the department in 1938, a position which he held until his retirement in 1957. His contribution to botanical science was that of a detail-seeker, a tester, and a patient gatherer of evidence, who provides the basis for botanical theory. As part

of his study of the plants, he collected and identified the vascular plants known to occur within the boundaries of Alberta and published, as a result of this work, the definitive volume *The flora of Alberta* (Toronto, 1959). He was a fellow of the Royal Society of Canada. He died in Edmonton in 1967.

[*Proc. Roy. Soc. Can.*, 1964.]

Moss, Thomas (1836-1881), chief justice of Ontario (1878-81), was born at Cobourg, Upper Canada, on August 20, 1836, the eldest son of John Moss, brewer, of Toronto. He was educated at Upper Canada College and at the University of Toronto (B.A., 1858; M.A., 1859), and was called to the bar of Upper Canada in 1861 (Q.C., 1872). In 1873 he was elected to represent West Toronto in the Canadian House of Commons, as a Liberal with the support of the "Canada First" party; and he was re-elected in the general elections of 1874. In 1875, however, he resigned from parliament on being appointed a judge of the Court of Appeal for Ontario. In 1877 he became chief justice of the Court of Appeal; and in 1878 chief justice of Ontario. He died at Nice, France, on January 4, 1881. In 1863 he married Amy, eldest daughter of the Hon. Robert Baldwin Sullivan (q.v.). From 1874 to his death he was vice-chancellor of the University of Toronto.

[D. B. Read, *Lives of the judges* (Toronto, 1888); *Dom. ann. reg.*, 1880-81; Dent, *Can. port.*, vol. 1; Rose, *Cyc. Can. biog.* (1886); *Canadian biographical dictionary*, Ontario vol. (Toronto, 1881); H. J. Morgan, *Legal directory*, 1878; *Canada law journal*, 1881.]

Motherwell, William Richard (1860-1943), minister of agriculture for Canada (1921-26 and 1926-30), was born in Perth, Canada West, on January 6, 1860. He was educated at the Ontario Agricultural College, Guelph, Ontario, and began farming near Abernethy, Saskatchewan, in 1882. He sat in the Legislative Assembly of Saskatchewan from 1905 to 1918, for North Qu'Appelle, Humboldt, and Kindersley successively; and during the whole of this period he occupied the posts of minister of agriculture and provincial secretary in the provincial government. From 1921 to 1925 he represented Regina, and from 1925 to 1935 Melville, in the Canadian House of Commons; and during the years from 1921 to 1930 he was minister of agriculture in the first and second Mackenzie King administrations. He died at Regina, Saskatchewan, on May 24, 1943.

[*Can. who's who*, 1936-37; *Can. parl. comp.*]

Moulton, Ebenezer (1709-1783), pioneer Baptist preacher, was born at Windham, Connecticut on December 25, 1709, and settled in Brimfield (now Wales), Massachusetts. In 1741 he was ordained an elder of the Baptist Church; and, when he removed to Nova Scotia in 1761, he became the pioneer Baptist preacher in that province. He lived at Yarmouth, Nova Scotia, from 1761 to 1771. He then returned to Brimfield, Massachusetts; and he died there in 1783.

[M. W. Armstrong, *"Elder Moulton" and the Nova Scotia Baptists* (Dalhousie review, 1944).]

Mounier, François (d. 1769), merchant and executive councillor of Quebec, was a Huguenot from La Rochelle, France. He came to Canada in the late 1740s, and became a merchant at Quebec. In 1764 General Murray appointed him a member of the Executive Council of Quebec, and he became a judge of the Court of Common Pleas in 1765. He died at Quebec on June 17, 1769.

[*Bull. rech. hist.*, 1896, 1898, and 1901; P. Gagnon, *Essai de bibliographie canadienne*, vol. 2 (Montreal, 1913), p. 354; W. S. Wallace (ed.), *The Maseres letters* (Toronto, 1919); *Dict. Can. biog.*, vol. 3.]

Mountain, Armine Simcoe Henry (1797-1854), soldier, was born at Quebec, Lower Canada, on February 4, 1797, the son of the Right Rev. Jacob Mountain (q.v.). He was educated in England, and in 1815 obtained a commission in the British Army. He saw active service in China and India, and rose to the rank of colonel. He died at Futtyghur, India, on January 29, 1854.

[Mrs. A. S. H. Mountain (ed.), *Memoirs and letters of the late Colonel A. S. H. Mountain* (London, 1857); P. G. Roy, *Fils de Québec*, vol. 3 (Lévis, Que., 1933).]

Mountain, Armine Wale (1823-1885), clergyman, was born in Quebec, Lower Canada, in 1823, the eldest son of the Right Rev. G. J. Mountain (q.v.). He was educated at Lundy's School, Quebec, and at University College, Oxford (B.A., 1845; M.A., 1854), and he was ordained a priest of the Church of England in 1846. He became the first incumbent of St. Michael's Church, Bergerville, near Quebec; but in 1869 he went to England, and became the vicar of St. Mary's, Stoney Stratford, Buckinghamshire. He died at Stoney Stratford on January 31, 1885. He was the author of *A memoir of George Jehoshaphat Mountain* (Montreal, 1866).

[*Dom. ann. reg.*, 1885.]

Mountain, George Jehoshaphat (1789-1863), third Anglican bishop of Quebec (1837-63), was born at Norwich, England, on July 27, 1789, the second son of the Right Rev. Jacob Mountain (q.v.). He was educated at Trinity College, Cambridge (B.A., 1810; D.D., 1819), and in 1811 became secretary to his father at Quebec. He was admitted to holy orders in the Church of England in 1814, and was appointed rector of Fredericton in New Brunswick. He returned to Quebec in 1816,

and in 1821 he was appointed rector of Quebec and archdeacon of Lower Canada. In 1836 he was appointed bishop of Montreal, and in 1837 bishop of Quebec. This see he administered until his death at Quebec on January 6, 1863. In 1814 he married Mary Hume, third daughter of Deputy Commissioner-General Thompson; and by her he had several children. In 1853 he was made a D.C.L. of Oxford University; and, apart from his published sermons and journals, he was the author of a volume of poems, *Songs of the wilderness* (London, 1846).

[A. W. Mountain, *A memoir* (Montreal, 1866); F. Taylor, *The last three bishops appointed by the Crown in Canada* (Montreal, 1870); *Dict. nat. biog.*; Taylor, *Brit. Am.*, vol. 3; Morgan, *Bib. can.* and *Cel. Can.*; C. H. Mockridge, *The bishops of the Church of England in Canada* (Toronto, 1896).]

Mountain, Jacob (1749-1825), first Anglican bishop of Quebec, was born at Thwaite Hall, Norfolk, on December 30, 1749, the third son of Jacob Mountain and Ann, daughter of Jehoshaphat Postle of Wymondham. He was educated at Caius College, Cambridge (B.A., 1774; M.A., 1777; D.D., 1793), and in 1779 he was elected a fellow of the college. After holding several livings in England, he was appointed in 1793 first Protestant bishop of Quebec. This see he administered for over thirty years; and he died at Quebec on June 16, 1825. He married a daughter of John Kentish of Bardfield Hall, Essex; and by her he had five sons and two daughters. Besides a number of sermons and charges, he published *Poetical reveries* (London, 1777).

[C. H. Mockridge, *The bishops of the Church of England in Canada* (Toronto, 1896); *Les Mountain au Canada* (Bull. rech. hist., 1914); *Dict. nat. biog.*; *Cyc. Am. biog.*; Morgan, *Bib. can.* and *Cel. Can.*; T. R. Millman, *Jacob Mountain, first Lord Bishop of Quebec* (Toronto, 1947).]

Mountain, Jehoshaphat (d. 1817), clergyman, was the elder brother of the Right Rev. Jacob Mountain (q.v.), and came with him to Canada in 1793. In 1794 he was appointed assistant to the Anglican rector of Three Rivers, and in 1800 he succeeded to the charge of the parish. In 1803 he became rector of Christ Church, Montreal, and he died in Montreal on April 10, 1817, aged seventy. By his wife, Mary (d. 1833), he had three children.

[*Les Mountain au Canada* (Bull. rech. hist., 1914).]

Mountain, Salter Jehoshaphat (1770?-1830), clergyman, was born at Felmingham, Norfolk, England, about 1770, the son of the Rev. Jehoshaphat Mountain (q.v.). He was educated at Cambridge University, took holy orders, and came to Canada in 1793 as chaplain to his uncle, the Right Rev. Jacob Mountain (q.v.), first bishop of Quebec. From 1797 to

1817 he was rector at Quebec, and from 1817 to 1830 at Cornwall, Upper Canada. He died at Cornwall on September 18, 1830. In 1811 he married Anna Maria, daughter of Matthew Scott, merchant; and his wife and six children survived him.

[*Les Mountain au Canada* (Bull. rech. hist., 1914).]

Mount Stephen, Sir George Stephen, Bart., first Baron. See Stephen, Sir George, Bart.

Mousseau, Joseph Alfred (1838-1886), prime minister of Quebec (1882-84), was born at Berthier-en-haut, Lower Canada, in July, 1838, the son of Louis Mousseau and Sophie Duteau de Grand Pré. He was educated at Berthier Academy, and was called to the bar of Lower Canada in 1860 (Q.C., 1873). He was one of the founders and editors of *Le Colonisateur* in 1862 and *L'Opinion Publique* in 1870. From 1874 to 1882 he represented the county of Bagot in the Canadian House of Commons. From 1880 to 1881 he was president of the council and from 1881 to 1882 secretary of state in the government of Sir John Macdonald (q.v.). In 1882 he resigned in order to assume the prime-ministry of Quebec; but in 1884 he retired from politics and was appointed a puisne judge of the Superior Court of Quebec. He died in Montreal on March 30, 1886. He married Marie Louise Hersetie, eldest daughter of Léopold Des Rosiers, notary public of Berthier.

[*Dom. ann. reg.*, 1886; *Cyc. Am. biog.*; *Can. parl. comp.*; Dent, *Can. port.*, vol. 4; Le Jeune, *Dict. gén.*; J. Tassé, *Le 38ème fauteuil* (Montreal, 1891).]

Mowat, Herbert Macdonald (1862-1928), jurist, was born at Kingston, Canada West, on April 11, 1862, the son of the Reverend J. B. Mowat, and the nephew of Sir Oliver Mowat (q.v.). He was educated at Queen's University, Kingston (B.A., 1881; LL.B., 1886), and was called to the bar in Ontario in 1886 (Q.C., 1899). He practised law in Toronto; and from 1917 to 1921 he represented the Parkdale division of Toronto in the Canadian House of Commons as a Liberal-Unionist. In 1921 he was appointed a justice of the Supreme Court of Ontario; and he retained this post until his death at Toronto on April 24, 1928.

[*Can. who was who*, vol. 1; *Can. parl comp.*; Morgan, *Can. men* (1912).]

Mowat, James Gordon (1851-1906), journalist, was born at Galt, Canada West, on March 20, 1851. He became a journalist, and from 1874 to 1881 was editor and proprietor of the Galt *Reformer*. He then joined the staff of the Toronto *Globe*; and in 1893 he became the founder and first editor of the *Canadian magazine*. He died at Toronto, Ontario, on April 21, 1906.

[Private information.]

Mowat, Sir Oliver (1820-1903), statesman, was born in Kingston, Upper Canada, the eldest son of John Mowat and Helen Levack, natives of Caithness-shire, Scotland. He was educated at private schools in Kingston, and in 1841 was called to the bar of Upper Canada (Q.C., 1856). In the general elections of 1857 he was returned as a Liberal for South Ontario in the Legislative Assembly of Canada; and in the short-lived Brown-Dorion administration of 1858 he occupied the position of provincial secretary. In 1863-64 he was postmaster-general in the Macdonald-Dorion government; and in the "Great Coalition" of June, 1864, he held the same portfolio. He attended the Quebec Conference as one of the delegates from Upper Canada; but on November 14, 1864, he was appointed vice-chancellor of Upper Canada, and temporarily retired from politics.

His return to political life occurred in 1872, when Edward Blake (q.v.) resigned the premiership of Ontario. Blake advised the lieutenant-governor to call upon Mowat to form an administration, and Mowat, retiring from the bench, accepted the invitation. He was elected for North Oxford, and he continued to be prime minister and attorney-general of Ontario from 1872 to 1896, a period of office unparalleled in the history of British parliamentary government. During this period he played a foremost part in the fight for "provincial rights"; and his administration was marked by a gradual, but noteworthy, extension of the franchise. Though cautious and even conservative, he was actuated by high ideals; at the same time, he was a practical politician, and the description of "Christian statesman" which he once applied to himself was sometimes thrown back in his face. "The leopard does not change his spots," observed Goldwin Smith (q.v.), with reference to Mowat, "even when he becomes a Christian statesman."

In 1896 Mowat was appointed to the Senate, where he became the government leader, and he was included in Laurier's "ministry of all the talents" as minister of justice. In 1897, however, he found that his new duties were too heavy for him, at his advanced age, and he retired to accept the lieutenant-governorship of Ontario. This post he occupied until his death on April 19, 1903.

He married in 1846 Jane, second daughter of John Ewart, of Toronto; and by her he had three sons and four daughters. He was created a K.C.M.G. in 1892, and a G.C.M.G. in 1897.

[C. R. W. Biggar, *Sir Oliver Mowat* (2 vols., Toronto, 1905); W. S. Wallace, "Political History of Ontario", in A. Shortt and A. G. Doughty (eds.), *Canada and its provinces*, vol. xvii (Toronto, 1914); G. W. Ross, *Getting into parliament and after* (Toronto, 1913); C. Clarke, *Sixty years in Upper Canada* (Toronto, 1908); Margaret Evans, *Oliver Mowat* (Ont. hist., 1970); *Dict. nat. biog.*, supp. II; Dent, *Can. port.*, vol. 1; Morgan, *Can. men* (1898); Rose, *Cyc. Can. biog.* (1886); *Can. parl. comp.*]

Mowatt, Andrew Joseph (1838-1911), clergyman, was born at Woodstock, New Brunswick, on February 11, 1838. He was educated at the Presbyterian Seminary in Truro, Nova Scotia; and was ordained a minister of the Presbyterian Church in 1866. He was the pastor successively of churches at Stellarton and at Windsor, Nova Scotia, at Fredericton, New Brunswick, and at Montreal, Quebec. He died at Montreal on February 19, 1911. He was the author of *Words of life* (Fredericton, N.B., 1900).

[*Can. who was who*, vol. 2; Morgan, *Can. men* (1898).]

Mower, Nahum (1779?-1830), printer and journalist, was born in Worcester, Massachusetts, about 1779. In 1807 he came to Montreal, and founded there the *Canadian Courant*, of which he was proprietor for over twenty-two years. He died at Montreal on March 7, 1830.

[A. Fauteux, *The introduction of printing into Canada* (Montreal, 1930).]

Moyen, Jean (1828-1899), priest and educationist, was born in France on August 10, 1828. He entered the Sulpician order in 1848, was ordained a priest in 1852, and from 1858 to 1874 was on the staff of the Seminary of St. Sulpice in Montreal. He died in France on January 8, 1899. While in Canada, he published *Cours élémentaire de botanique et flore du Canada* (Montreal, 1871).

[*Bull. rech. hist.*, 1930.]

Moyse, Charles Ebenezer (1852-1924), educationist, was born at Torquay, Devonshire, England, on March 9, 1852, and was educated at University College, London (B.A., 1872). He became for a time headmaster of St. Mary's College, Peckham; and in 1879 he came to Canada as professor of English literature at McGill University, Montreal. He retired from this position in 1920; and he died at Montreal on June 28, 1924. He was the author of *Shakespeare's skull and Falstaff's nose* (London, 1889), under the *nom-de-plume* of "Belgrave Titmarsh", and *Ella Lee: Glimpses of child life* (London, 1910).

[*Can. who was who*, vol. 1; Morgan, *Can. men* (1912).]

Muchall, Mrs. Mary Elizabeth, *née* **Traill** (1841-1892), author, was born at Ashburnham, Peterborough county, Upper Canada, on November 7, 1841, the fourth daughter of Thomas and Catherine Parr Traill (q.v.). In 1863 she married Thomas William Muchall; and she died on May 28, 1892. She was the author of a little book of verse entitled *Step by*

step; or, The shadow on a Canadian home (Toronto, 1876).

[C. C. James, *A bibliography of Canadian poetry* (Toronto, 1899).]

Muckle, Joseph Thomas (1887-1967), philologist, was born in Middlesex, New York, January 22, 1887. He was educated in New York and at St. Michael's College, Toronto. He entered St. Basil's Novitiate in 1907 and was ordained to the priesthood in 1915. After ordination he continued his study of the classics, receiving his M.A. from the Catholic University of America, Washington, in 1916. He taught classics at St. Michael's College, Toronto, from 1916 to 1919, and from 1919 to 1923 was Superior of Assumption College, Windsor. From 1923 to 1926 he taught in Texas, returning to St. Michael's in Toronto at the time that negotiations were being undertaken to establish an institute devoted to the study of the thought of the middle ages. Muckle went to Chicago, Harvard, and Europe to study and begin gathering a library for the new Institute of Mediaeval Studies which was founded in 1929 and was granted a pontifical charter in 1939. He introduced palaeography and mediaeval Latin studies and developed a program for the serious study of patristic and mediaeval culture at the Institute. He was a demanding teacher and an outstanding mediaevalist. In 1946 he became a fellow of the Royal Society of Canada, and was awarded honorary degrees by Assumption University and the University of Western Ontario. He died in Florida, May 9, 1967. He edited *Abelard's letter of consolation to a friend* (Mediaeval Studies, vol. 12, 1964); the treatise *De Anima of Dominicus Gundissalinus* (Mediaeval Studies, vol. 2, 1940), and Algazel's *Metaphysics* (St. Michael's Mediaeval Studies, 1933).

[*Proc. Roy. Soc. Can.*, 1967.]

Mudroch, Vaclav (1924-1969), historian, was born in Prague, Czechoslavakia, on April 4, 1924. He graduated from Charles University, Prague (LL.D., 1949); the University of British Columbia (B.A., 1954); and the University of Toronto (M.A., 1956; Ph.D., 1960). He fled from Czechoslavakia to West Germany and came to Canada in 1951. He taught at the University of Saskatchewan (1958), the University of Kansas (1958-63), and Carleton University (1963-69). He died on November 24, 1969.

[Information from Carleton University.]

Muir, Alexander (1830-1906), song-writer, was born at Lesmahagow, Lanarkshire, Scotland, on April 5, 1830, the son of John Muir. He was brought to Canada in 1833 by his father, and was educated at Queen's University, Kingston (B.A., 1851). He became a public-school teacher, chiefly in Toronto. In 1867 he composed the words and music of the patriotic song "The Maple Leaf Forever". He died at Toronto, Ontario, on June 26, 1906.

[Morgan, *Can. men* (1898); E. S. Caswell, *Canadian singers and their songs* (3rd ed., Toronto, 1925).]

Muir, Robert Cuthbertson (1856-1935), historian, was born in Burford, Canada West, in 1856, the son of Robert Muir. He entered the grain business, first at Burford, and later at Quebec; but on retirement from business in 1914, he returned to Burford, and he died there on June 19, 1935. He entered the Canadian militia in 1874, and was gazetted a major in 1902. He was the author of *The early political and military history of Burford* (Quebec, 1913).

[Private information.]

Muldrew, William Hawthorne (1867-1904), educationist, was born in 1867, and was educated at Queen's University. He became a school-teacher, and in 1903 was appointed dean of the Macdonald Institute of the Ontario Agricultural College. He died at Guelph, Ontario, on October 7, 1904. He was the author of *Sylvan Ontario* (Toronto, 1901).

[*The educational record of Canada*, 1904.]

Mulgrave, George Augustus Constantine Phipps, Earl of, afterwards **Marquis of Normanby** (1819-1890), lieutenant-governor of Nova Scotia (1858-63), was born on July 23, 1819, the son of the first Marquis of Normanby, and Maria Liddell, eldest daughter of Thomas Henry, Lord Ravensworth. From 1831 to 1838 he was known as the Viscount Normanby, and from 1838 to his father's death as the Earl of Mulgrave. From 1847 to 1858 he represented Scarborough as a Liberal in the British House of Commons; and in 1851 he became comptroller of the royal household, and was sworn of the Privy Council. In 1858 he was appointed lieutenant-governor of Nova Scotia; and he held this office until 1863, when he returned to England on succeeding to his father's title as Marquis of Normanby. He was subsequently governor of Queensland (1871-73), of New Zealand (1874-79), and of Victoria (1879-84). In 1884 he retired from public life, and he died at Brighton, England, on April 3, 1890. In 1844 he married Laura (d. 1885), daughter of Capt. Robert Russell, R.N.; and by her he had several children. He was created a K.C.M.G. in 1874, a G.C.M.G. in 1877, and a G.C.B. in 1885.

[*Dict. nat. biog.*; *Can. who was who*, vol. 2; D. Campbell, *Nova Scotia* (Montreal, 1873).]

Mullock, John Thomas (1807-1869), Roman Catholic bishop of Newfoundland, was born at Limerick, Ireland, in 1807, and died at St. John's, Newfoundland, on March 29, 1869. A member of the Franciscan order, educated at Seville and Rome, he came to Newfoundland in 1848, as coadjutor to Bishop Fleming (q.v.), whom he succeeded in 1850. He completed the Roman Catholic cathedral at St. John's, founded St. Bonaventure's College, and built two convents. He was the author of *Two lectures on Newfoundland* (St. John's, 1850).

[J. R. Smallwood, ed., *The book of Newfoundland* (2 vols., St. John's, 1937); *Newfoundland supp.*; *Encyc. Can.*]

Mulock, Cawthra (1884-1918), capitalist and financier, was born in Toronto, Ontario, in 1884, the second son of Sir William Mulock (q.v.). He was educated at Upper Canada College and at the University of Toronto; and in 1909 he inherited from his aunt, Mrs. Cawthra Murray, the widow of William Cawthra (q.v.), a fortune variously estimated at from four to eight million dollars. He was a benefactor of the Toronto General Hospital and the Hospital for Sick Children. He died at New York, N.Y., on December 1, 1918. In 1903 he married Adèle Baldwin, daughter of Sir W. G. Falconbridge (q.v.).

[Morgan, *Can. men* (1912).]

Mulock, Sir William (1844-1944), politician and jurist, was born at Bondhead, Canada West, on January 19, 1844, the son of Thomas Homan Mulock, M.D., and Mary Cawthra. He was educated at the University of Toronto (B.A., 1863; M.A., 1871; LL.D., 1894), and was called to the bar of Ontario in 1868 (Q.C., 1890); and he early became one of the leaders of the Ontario bar. In 1882 he was elected to represent North York in the Canadian House of Commons in the Liberal interest; and he continued to represent this constituency without a break until 1905. In 1896 he was appointed postmaster-general in Sir Wilfrid Laurier's "ministry of all the talents"; and in 1898 he was responsible for the introduction of "imperial penny postage" within the British Empire. In 1900 he became minister responsible for the newly established department of labour; and in this capacity he introduced into public life the Right Hon. W. L. Mackenzie King as his first deputy minister of labour. In 1905 he retired from political life to become chief justice of the Exchequer division of the Supreme Court of Canada; and in 1923 he became chief justice of Ontario. He retired from the bench in 1936. From 1881 to 1900 he was vice-chancellor of the University of Toronto; and in this capacity he took a leading part in bringing about university federation in Ontario. In 1924 he was elected chancellor of the University of Toronto; and he continued in this position until his death at Toronto, Ontario, on October 1, 1944. In 1870 he married Sarah (d. 1912), daughter of James Crowther; and by her he had two sons and two daughters. He was created a K.C.M.G. in 1902, and an imperial privy councillor in 1925. He retained to his hundredth year an amazing possession of all his faculties; and in his later years he was known as "Canada's grand old man".

[W. J. Loudon, *Sir William Mulock* (Toronto, 1932); *Who's who*, 1944; *Can. who's who*, 1938-39; Morgan, *Can. men* (1912); Rose, *Cyc. Can. biog.* (1886); *Can. parl. comp.*; *Univ. of Toronto monthly*, 1944; W. S. Wallace, *A history of the University of Toronto* (Toronto, 1927).]

Mulvany, Charles Pelham (1835-1885), clergyman and author, was born in Dublin, Ireland, on May 20, 1835, and was educated at Trinity College, Dublin. For several years he was a surgeon in the Royal Navy; but in 1872 he was ordained a priest of the Church of England in Canada. He taught classics at Bishop's College, Lennoxville, and served as missionary or curate in various rural parishes in Canada. During the latter years of his life he supported himself by his pen; and he published *Toronto past and present* (Toronto, 1884), and *The history of the North West rebellion* (Toronto, 1885). With Amos Henry Chandler, he was also joint author of *Lyrics, songs, and sonnets* (Toronto, 1880). He died in Toronto, on May 31, 1885, leaving unfinished a *History of liberalism in Canada*.

[*Dom. ann. reg.*, 1885; *Cyc. Am. biog.*; Mrs. C. M. Whyte-Edgar, *A wreath of Canadian song* (Montreal, 1910).]

Mulvey, Thomas (1863-1935), civil servant and author, was born at Toronto, Ontario, on August 18, 1863. He was educated at the University of Toronto (B.A., 1884), and was called to the bar in Ontario in 1889 (K.C., 1902). From 1903 to 1909 he was assistant provincial secretary in Ontario; and from 1909 to 1933 he was under-secretary of state for Canada. He died at Ottawa, Ontario, on December 1, 1935. He was the author of the chapters on *The judicial system of Ontario* in A. Shortt and A. G. Doughty (eds.), *Canada and its provinces*, vol. xviii (Toronto, 1914); and he was the editor of *Canadian company law* (Montreal, 1913).

[*Can. parl. comp.*; Morgan, *Can. men* (1912).]

Munday, Walter Alfred Don (1890-1950), mountain-climber and author, was born in Manitoba on March 16, 1890, and died at Vancouver, British Columbia, on June 12, 1950. He was educated in Portage la Prairie, but moved to Vancouver in 1909. He served with the Canadians in France during the First World War, and was awarded the M.M. After the war he and his wife joined the Alpine Club of Canada, and became pioneers in mountaineering in the Rockies. He contributed many papers to the *Canadian Alpine Journal*, and was the author of *The unknown mountain* (London, 1948). Mount Munday in the Rockies was named after him.

[*Canadian Alpine Journal*, 1951.]

Munro, Bruce Weston (1860-1900?), humorist, was born near Newcastle, Durham county, Canada West, in 1860, and died about 1900. He was the author of *Splinters; or, A grist of giggles* (Toronto, 1886), *A blundering boy* (Toronto, 1887), and *Groans and grins of one who survived* (Toronto, 1889).

[L. E. Horning and L. J. Burpee, *A bibliography of Canadian fiction* (Toronto, 1904).]

Munro, David Ransom (1828-1890), author, was born in Saint John, New Brunswick, in 1828. He exhibited a collection of the woods of his native province at the World's Exhibition in London, England, in 1862; and he published at the same time a pamphlet entitled *Forest and ornamental trees of New Brunswick* (Saint John, N.B., 1862). He died at Roanoke, Va., on July 9, 1890.

[W. G. MacFarlane, *New Brunswick bibliography* (Saint John, N.B., 1895).]

Munro, Henry (1770?-1854), fur-trader, was a son of the Hon. John Munro (q.v.), one of the members of the first Legislative Council of Upper Canada, and became a surgeon in the service of the North West Company in 1796. For several years he was stationed at, or near, Grand Portage. In 1805, he was sent to succeed J. B. Perrault (q.v.), at the Pic, on Lake Superior; and in 1812 he was appointed surgeon's mate in the Corps of Canadian Voyageurs raised by the North West Company. He died at Lachenaie, Lower Canada, on August 20, 1854, and was buried in the old Protestant cemetery at Macouche.

[W. S. Wallace (ed.), *Documents relating to the North West Company* (Toronto: The Champlain Society, 1934).]

Munro, John (1731-1800), legislative councillor of Upper Canada, was born in Scotland in 1731. He served in America in the Seven Years' War; and later settled near Albany, New York, where he acquired considerable property. In the American Revolutionary War, he was a captain in the King's Royal Regiment of New York; and after the war he settled in the new settlements on the north bank of the St. Lawrence River. He became the sheriff of the Lunenburg district, and a member of the Land Board; and in 1792 he was appointed a member of the Legislative Council of Upper Canada. He died at Dickenson's Landing, Upper Canada, in October, 1800.

[A. Ewart and J. Jarvis, *The personnel of the Family Compact* (Can. hist. rev., 1926); H. H. Langton (ed.), *Travels . . . by P. Campbell* (Toronto: The Champlain Society, 1937); E. A. Cruickshank, *The King's Royal Regiment of New York* (Ont. Hist. Soc., papers and records, 1931).]

Munro, William Bennett (1875-1957), political scientist, was born at Almonte, Ontario, on January 5, 1875, and died at Pasadena, California, on September 4, 1957. He was educated at Queen's University (B.A., 1895; M.A., 1896; LL.B., 1898), Harvard University (M.A., 1899; Ph.D., 1900), and the University of Berlin. From 1901 to 1904 he was instructor in history at Williams College; from 1904 to 1929 professor of government at Harvard University; and from 1929 to 1945 professor of history and government at the California Institute of Technology. In 1927 he was elected president of the American Political Science Association, and in 1929 president of the American Association of University Professors. Honorary degrees were conferred on him by Queen's University and by several universities in the United States. He was the author of a large number of books on history and government; those relating to Canada were *The seigniorial system in Canada* (Cambridge, Mass., 1907), *Documents relating to the seigniorial tenure in Canada* (Toronto: The Champlain Society, 1908), *The seigneurs of old Canada* (Toronto, 1914), *The crusaders of New France* (New Haven, 1918), and *American influences on Canadian government* (Toronto, 1929).

[*Who's who in America*, 1956-57; *Can. who's who*, 1948; *Encyc. Can.*]

Munroe, Hugh Edwin (1878-1947), lieutenant-governor of Saskatchewan (1930-36), was born at St. Elmo, Ontario, on June 16, 1878, and died at St. Petersburg, Florida, on March 12, 1947. He was educated at McGill University (M.D., C.M., 1903) and at Edinburgh University (L.R.C.P. and S., 1905). He practised as a surgeon in Saskatoon, Saskatchewan, for thirty years; and he served with distinction as a medical officer in the First World War. He was a Conservative candidate in the provincial elections of 1905 and 1912, but was not elected; and for a time he was president of the Saskatchewan Conservative Association. He was appointed lieutenant-governor of Saskatchewan in 1930 by the Bennett government.

[*Can. who's who*, 1938-39; *Can. parl. guide*, 1936; *Encyc. Can.*]

Muntz, Laura. See **Lyall, Mrs. Laura,** *née* **Muntz.**

Murchie, John Carl (1895-1966), soldier, was born in Edmundston, New Brunswick, June 7, 1895. He graduated from Royal Military College, Kingston, in 1915, and went overseas as a junior artillery officer. He was seriously wounded in France but recovered and returned to battle before the end of the war. He was a career military officer and held various military appointments in Canada and Britain before the Second World War. He attended a gunnery course at Camberley and spent two years at the War Office, London. He was appointed chief of the Canadian General Staff in 1944 and left the command in August, 1945, with the rank of lieutenant-general. He retired from the army in 1947 and he died at Ottawa, Ontario, March 5, 1966.

[*Encyc. Can.* (1972); Metropolitan Toronto Library Board, *Biographical scrapbooks*, vol. 26.]

Murdoch, Beamish (1800-1876), historian, was born at Halifax, Nova Scotia, in 1800. He was called to the bar of Nova Scotia in 1822; and from 1826 to 1830 he represented Halifax in the House of Assembly. For a number of years he was editor of the *Acadian Recorder*; and from 1852 to 1860 he was recorder of Halifax. He died at Lunenburg, Nova Scotia, on February 9, 1876. His chief work was his *History of Nova Scotia* (3 vols., Halifax, 1865-67), but he was also the author of a *Narrative of the late fires at Miramichi, New Brunswick* (Halifax, 1825), an *Essay on the mischievous tendency of imprisoning for debt* (Halifax, 1831), and an *Epitome of the laws of Nova Scotia* (4 vols., Halifax, 1832-33).

[Morgan, *Bib. can.*; R. J. Long, *Nova Scotia authors* (East Orange, N.J., 1918); W. G. MacFarlane, *New Brunswick bibliography* (Saint John, N.B., 1895); *Nova Scotia Historical Society Collections*, 1918; *Dict. Can. biog.*, vol. 10.]

Murdoch, James Young (1890-1962), industrialist, was born in Toronto, Ontario, July 29, 1890, and was educated there. He was called to the bar of Ontario in 1913. He was associated with Holden, Murdoch, Walton, Finlay, Robinson and Pepall from 1913 until his death. In 1922 he became interested in the mining field and was first president of Noranda Mines, a position which he held until 1956. He was a director of thirty-five companies. He was created King's Counsel in 1929 and received the O.B.E. following the Second World War for his work with the National War Service Funds Advisory Board. He died at Toronto, Ontario, April 18, 1962.

[Metropolitan Toronto Library Board, *Biographical scrapbooks*, vol. 20.]

Murdoch, William (1823-1887), poet, was born in Paisley, Scotland, on February 24, 1823. He came to New Brunswick in 1854, and was appointed to the staff of the marine station at Partridge Island. In 1865 he became a journalist on the staff of the *Morning News* in Saint John, New Brunswick. He died on May 4, 1887. He published *Poems and songs* (Saint John, N.B., 1860) and *Discursory ruminations, a fireside drama, etc.* (Saint John, N.B., 1876).

[Morgan, *Bib. can.*; W. G. MacFarlane, *New Brunswick bibliography* (Saint John, N.B., 1895).]

Mure, John (d. 1823), merchant, was a resident of Quebec who became in 1798 one of the partners in the XY Company; and on the union of the XY and North West companies in 1804, he became a partner in Sir Alexander Mackenzie and Co., which controlled a quarter interest in the new organization. From 1804 to

1810 he represented the county of York in the Legislative Assembly of Lower Canada, and from 1810 to 1814, the lower town of Quebec; and in 1812 he was appointed a member of the Executive Council of the province. He died in Scotland on January 17, 1823.

[*Bull. rech. hist.*, 1935.]

Murison, Ross George (1866?-1905), educationist, was born at Mintlaw, Aberdeenshire, Scotland, about 1866; and emigrated to Canada in 1882. After working on a farm in Glengarry, Ontario, and teaching school for several years, he received his higher education at the University of Toronto (B.A., 1893; M.A., 1894; Ph.D., 1902) and at Knox College (B.D., 1896). He was appointed assistant professor in Oriental languages in University College, Toronto; but died at Toronto after only a brief academic career, on September 4, 1905. He was the author of *Babylonia and Syria* (Edinburgh, 1901) and *History of Egypt* (Edinburgh, 1903).

[*Varsity*, 1905.]

Murphy, Anna. See **Jameson, Mrs. Anna.**

Murphy, Charles (1863-1935), secretary of state for Canada (1908-11) and a postmaster-general (1921-26), was born at Ottawa, Ontario, on December 8, 1863, and was educated at the University of Ottawa (B.A., 1886). He was called to the bar in Ontario in 1891. From 1908 to 1925 he represented Russell in the Canadian House of Commons; and from 1908 to 1911 he was secretary of state in the Laurier government, and from 1921 to 1926 post-master-general in the Mackenzie King government. In 1925 he was appointed a member of the Senate of Canada, and thereafter he took a less active part in politics. He died at Ottawa on November 24, 1935. He was not married.

[*Can. parl. comp.*; Morgan, *Can. men* (1912).]

Murphy, Mrs. Emily Cowan, *née* **Ferguson** (1868-1933), author, was born in Cookstown, Ontario, on March 14, 1868, the daughter of Isaac Ferguson, and granddaughter of Ogle R. Gowan (q.v.). She was educated at Bishop Strachan School, Toronto; and in 1887 she married the Rev. Arthur Murphy, rector of Chatham, Ontario, by whom she had two daughters. In 1904 she went to western Canada; and for many years she played a prominent part in philanthropic and humanitarian affairs in Alberta. She became judge of the Juvenile Court at Edmonton; and in 1925 she was appointed official visitor to the jails and mental hospitals of Alberta. She died at Edmonton on October 27, 1933. Under the pen-name of "Janey Canuck", she was the author of *Janey Canuck in the west* (Toronto, 1910), *Open trails* (Toronto, 1912), *Seeds of pine* (Toronto, 1914), *The black candle*

(Toronto, 1922), and *Our little Canadian cousin of the great northwest* (Boston, 1923).

[*Can. who was who*, vol. 2; Morgan, *Can. men and women* (1912); *Who's who among North American authors*, vol. 6; B. H. Sanders, *Emily Murphy: Crusader* (Toronto, 1945).]

Murphy, Michael (d. 1868), Fenian leader, was a saloon-keeper of Toronto, Canada West, who became president in 1858 of "the Hibernian Benevolent Society of Canada" — an organization with Fenian leanings. In 1866, just before the Fenian raid of that year, he was arrested at Cornwall with six accomplices; but he succeeded with his companions in breaking jail, and in reaching the safety of the United States. He died in Buffalo, New York, on April 11, 1868.

[C. P. Stacey, *A Fenian interlude: The story of Michael Murphy* (Can. hist. rev., 1934).]

Murray, Alexander Hunter (1818-1874), fur-trader and explorer, was born at Kilmun, Argyllshire, Scotland, in 1818. As a young man, he emigrated to the United States, and entered the service of the American Fur Company. About 1846, he came up to Fort Garry from Missouri, and took service with the Hudson's Bay Company; and he rose in this company to the rank of chief trader. His fame rests chiefly on his expedition to the Yukon, whither he was sent by the Hudson's Bay Company in 1847, to open Fort Yukon, in Russian Alaska. He retired from the fur-trade in 1867; and he died at his home, "Bellevue", near Lower Fort Garry, in April, 1874. He married Anne, daughter of Colin Campbell (q.v.); and by her he had three sons and five daughters. His *Journal of the Yukon*, 1847-48, has been edited by L. J. Burpee (Ottawa, Public Archives, 1910).

[R. Watson, *Chief Trader Alexander Hunter Murray and Fort Youcon* (Beaver, 1929); Martha M. Black, *Alexander Hunter Murray* (Beaver, 1934); *Dict. Can. biog.*, vol. 10.]

Murray, Daniel Alexander (1862-1934), educationist, was born at Scotsburn, Nova Scotia, on May 23, 1862. He was educated at Dalhousie University (B.A., 1884), and at Johns Hopkins University (Ph.D., 1893); and, after holding academic posts at Dalhousie University, New York University, and Cornell University, he was appointed in 1907 professor of applied mathematics at McGill University. He retired on pension in 1930; and he died at Montreal, Quebec, on October 19, 1934. He was the author of *An elementary course in the integral calculus* (New York, 1898), *Plane trigonometry* (New York, 1899), *Spherical trigonometry* (New York, 1900), *Atoms and energies* (New York, 1901), *A first course in infinitesimal calculus* (New York, 1903), *Practi-*

cal mathematics (New York, 1905), *Introductory course in differential equations* (New York, 1906), *Differential and integral calculus* (New York, 1908), and *Elements of plane trigonometry* (New York, 1911).

[*American men of science*, 5th ed.; Morgan, *Can. men* (1912).]

Murray, Sir George (1772-1846), provisional lieutenant-governor of Upper Canada (April-July, 1815), was born at Crieff, Perthshire, Scotland, on February 6, 1772, the second son of Sir William Murray, Bart., and Lady Augusta Mackenzie, daughter of George, third Earl of Cromarty. He was educated at the University of Edinburgh; and he entered the British army as an ensign in the 71st Regiment in 1789. He served throughout the Revolutionary and Napoleonic wars; and in 1814 he attained the rank of local lieutenant-general. In 1815 he was sent to Canada, with orders for the recall of Sir George Prevost (q.v.); and in April, 1815, he was appointed by Sir Gordon Drummond (q.v.) provisional lieutenant-governor of Upper Canada. In July, 1815, he returned to England to join the army in Flanders; and for three years he was chief of staff of the army of occupation in France. In 1823 he was elected to the British House of Commons to represent Perth; and from 1828 to 1830 he was secretary of state for war and the colonies in the administration of the Duke of Wellington. He died at London, England, on July 28, 1846. In 1826 he married Lady Louisa Erskine, sister of the Marquis of Anglesey, and widow of Sir James Erskine; and by her he had one daughter. In 1813 he was created a K.C.B., and in 1815 a G.C.B. In 1820 he received the degree of LL.D. from Oxford University; and in 1824 he was elected a fellow of the Royal Society. He edited *The letters and despatches of John Churchill, first Duke of Marlborough* (5 vols., London 1845); and some of his papers have been published by M. R. Dobie in the *Journal of the Society for Army Historical Research*, January, 1931.

[D. B. Read, *The lieutenant-governors of Upper Canada* (Toronto, 1900); *Dict. nat. biog.*; Morgan, *Cel. Can.*]

Murray, George (1830-1910), scholar and *littérateur*, was born in London, England, on March 23, 1830, the son of James Murray, a foreign correspondent of *The Times*. He was educated at King's College, London, and at Hertford College, Oxford (B.A., 1854); and in 1859 he emigrated to Canada. In 1862 he was appointed classical master in the Montreal High School; and this position he retained until 1892. In 1882 he took charge of the literary department of the *Montreal Star*; and after 1892 he devoted himself wholly to journalism and literature. He died at Montreal on March 13, 1910. He was a member of the Royal Society of Canada; and he was the author of *Verses and versions* (Montreal, 1891).

[*Proc. Roy. Soc. Can.*, 1910; Morgan, *Can. men* (1898); A. MacMurchy, *Handbook of Canadian literature* (Toronto, 1906); *Can. who was who*, vol. 1.]

Murray, George Henry (1861-1929), prime minister of Nova Scotia (1896-1923), was born at Grand Narrows, Cape Breton, on June 7, 1861, the son of William Murray. He was educated at Boston University, and was called to the bar of Nova Scotia in 1883 (Q.C., 1895). From 1889 to 1896 he was a member of the Legislative Council of New Brunswick; and from 1897 to 1923 he represented Victoria in the Legislative Assembly. From 1891 to 1896 he was a member of the Executive Council of the province without portfolio; and in 1896 he succeeded W. S. Fielding (q.v.) as prime minister of the province. He retained power in Nova Scotia for over a quarter of a century, and resigned from the government and the legislature only in 1923. He died at Montreal, Quebec, on January 9, 1929. In 1889 he married Grace, daughter of John B. Moore, North Sydney, Cape Breton; and by her he had three children. He was an LL.D. of St. Francis Xavier College (1905) and of Dalhousie University (1908).

[J. D. Logan, *A political Bayard* (Can. mag., 1919); *Can. who was who*, vol. 2; *Can. parl. comp.*; Morgan, *Can. men* (1912).]

Murray, Sir Herbert Harley (1829-1904), governor of Newfoundland (1895-98), was born in Bromley, Kent, England, in 1829, and died on March 22, 1904. He was educated at Christ Church, Oxford (B.A., 1851; M.A., 1856). In 1890 he became chairman of the Board of Customs in Great Britain; and he was governor of Newfoundland from 1895 to 1898. He was created a K.C.B. in 1895.

[*Who was who*, 1897-1916; *Encyc. Can.*]

Murray, Howard (1859-1930), educationist, was born at New Glasgow, Nova Scotia, on June 27, 1859; and was educated at Dalhousie University, at University College, London (B.A., 1883), and at Edinburgh University. In 1887 he was appointed tutor in classics at Dalhousie University, lecturer in 1890, and professor in 1894; and in 1901 he became dean of the university. In 1906 he was appointed a member of the Advisory Board of Education in Nova Scotia; and later he became its chairman. He died at Halifax, Nova Scotia, on September 9, 1930.

[Morgan, *Can. men* (1912).]

Murray, James (1721-1794), governor of Quebec (1760-68), was born at Ballencrief, Scotland, on January 21, 1721, the fifth and youngest son of Alexander, fourth Lord Elibank, and Elizabeth Stirling. He entered the army in 1740, as a second lieutenant in Wynyard's Marines; and during the next twenty years saw much active service in both

Europe and America. In 1751 he purchased the lieutenant-colonelcy of the 15th Foot; and in 1758 he commanded a brigade at the capture of Louisbourg, Cape Breton. He was one of Wolfe's brigadiers in 1759 during the siege of Quebec; and he commanded the left wing of the British army at the battle of the Plains of Abraham. On the death of Wolfe (q.v.), and the departure of the other brigadiers, he succeeded to the command of the British force in Quebec; and though defeated at the battle of St. Foy in the spring of 1760, he retained Quebec until the arrival of reinforcements by sea. In the summer of 1760 he took part in the movements which led to the surrender of the French troops in Canada; and in the autumn of 1760 he was appointed military governor of Quebec. He commanded the troops in this area during the period of military rule; and in 1764 he was appointed first civil governor of the province of Quebec. He distinguished himself by his opposition to the repressive measures first proposed by the British government in regard to the French Canadians; and he inaugurated the policy of conciliation of the French afterwards embodied in the Quebec Act. In doing so, he fell foul of the English mercantile element which had invaded the colony; and in 1766 he was recalled to meet the charges made against him. After full inquiry, the charges made against him by the English element were dismissed, and he continued to hold the office of governor of Quebec until 1768; but he did not return to Canada.

In 1774 he was appointed governor of Minorca, and in 1782 he was compelled, after a long siege, to surrender Minorca to a combined French and Spanish force. He was court-martialled, but the charges against him were dismissed. In 1772 he was promoted to be lieutenant-general; and in 1783 full general. He died at Beauport House, near Battle, Sussex, on June 18, 1794. He was twice married, (1) to Cordelia Collier (d. 1779), by whom he had no issue; and (2) to Anne, daughter of Abraham Witham, by whom he had three daughters and one son.

[Major-Gen. R. H. Mahon, *Life of General the Hon. James Murray, a builder of Canada* (London, 1921); A. C. Murray, *The five sons of "Bare Betty"* (London, 1936); J. M. Le Moine, *Le premier gouverneur anglais de Québec* (Trans. Roy. Soc. Can., 1890); *Dict. nat. biog.*; Morgan, *Cel. Can.*; Le Jeune, *Dict. gén.*]

Murray, Sir John (1841-1914), naturalist, was born at Cobourg, Upper Canada, on March 3, 1841, the second son of Robert Murray. He was educated at Victoria University, Cobourg, and at Edinburgh University. In 1868 he visited the Arctic as a naturalist on board a whaler; and from 1872 to 1876 he was a naturalist attached to the *Challenger* expedition for the investigation of the physical and biological features of the great ocean basins. He edited the report of the *Challenger* expedition (50 vols., Edinburgh, 1880-95); and he was the author of *A summary of the scientific results of the Challenger expedition* (Edinburgh, 1895), *The depths of the ocean* (London, 1912), and *The ocean* (London, 1913). He died at Edinburgh, Scotland, on March 16, 1914. He was created a K.C.B. in 1898; and he was a fellow of the Royal Society. He was a Ph.D. of the University of Jena (1885), an LL.D. of Edinburgh University (1888) and of the University of Toronto (1899), and a D.Sc., of Cambridge University (1895).

[*Can. who was who*, vol. 1; *Who was who, 1897-1916*; Morgan, *Can. men* (1912).]

Murray, John Clark (1836-1917), philosopher, was born at Paisley, Scotland, on March 19, 1836, the son of Provost David Murray, of Paisley. He was educated at Glasgow, Edinburgh, Heidelberg, and Göttingen universities; and in 1862 was appointed professor of mental and moral philosophy at Queen's University, Kingston. In 1872 he was appointed to the chair of philosophy in McGill University, and he became professor *emeritus* in this university in 1903. He died at Montreal, Quebec, on November 20, 1917. In 1882 he became a charter member of the Royal Society of Canada; and he was an LL.D. of the University of Glasgow. He was the author of *Outline of Sir William Hamilton's philosophy* (Boston, 1870), *The ballads and songs of Scotland* (London, 1874), *A handbook of psychology* (London, 1885), *An introduction to ethics* (Boston, 1891), *He that had received the five talents* (London, 1904), and *A handbook of Christian ethics* (Edinburgh, 1908).

[*Proc. Roy. Soc. Can.*, 1918; Morgan, *Can. men* (1912); *Cyc. Am. biog.*; *Can. who was who*, vol. 1.]

Murray, John Lovell (1874-1955), clergyman and author, was born at Woodville, Ontario, in 1874, and died at Toronto, Ontario, on April 30, 1955. He was educated at the University of Toronto (B.A., 1895); in 1897 he graduated from Knox College, Toronto; and he was ordained a minister of the Presbyterian Church. Most of his life was spent in Y.M.C.A. and missionary work; and in 1921 he founded in Toronto the Canadian School of Missions, of which he was for many years the director. He was the author of *World Friendship, Inc.* (New York, 1921) and *Nation-builders* (Toronto, 1933).

[Toronto *Globe and Mail*, May 1, 1955.]

Murray, John Wilson (1840-1906), detective, was born in Edinburgh, Scotland, on June 25, 1840, the son of Daniel Duncan Murray, a sea captain. At the age of five, he came with his parents to America; and, after serving in the United States navy during the civil war, entered the United States secret service. In 1875 he entered the service of the government of Ontario as a detective; and he continued in this service until shortly before his death at Toronto, Ontario, on June 13, 1906.

[*Memoirs of a great detective: Incidents in the life of John Wilson Murray* (London, 1904).]

Murray, Louisa (1818-1894), novelist, was born at Carisbrooke, Isle of Wight, on May 24, 1818, the daughter of Lieut. Edward Murray, 100th Regiment, and Louisa Rose, daughter of Major Charles Lyons, 7th Fusiliers. She spent her early years with her father's family in county Wicklow, Ireland, and was educated there. In 1844 she removed with her relatives to Canada, and lived first at Wolfe Island, and later at Stamford, Ontario. She died at Stamford on July 27, 1894. In 1851 she published in the *Literary Garland* her first novel, *Fauna; or, The red flower of Leafy Hollow*; and this was followed by *The settlers of Long Arrow*, published in *Once a Week* (1861), *The cited curate*, published in the *British American Magazine* (1863), and several other stories. None of her novels appear to have been published in book form. In her later years she contributed occasionally to the *Nation*, the *Canadian Monthly*, and the *Week*.

[H. J. Morgan, *Types of Canadian women* (Toronto, 1903).]

Murray, Mrs. Margaret, *née* **Polson** (d. 1927), organizer, was born in Paisley, Scotland, the daughter of William Polson, a manufacturer. In 1865 she married Professor John Clark Murray (q.v.), and lived first in Kingston, and later in Montreal. In 1900 she founded in Canada the Imperial Order of Daughters of the Empire. She died in Montreal, Quebec, on January 27, 1927.

[*Echoes*, 1927.]

Murray, Robert (d. 1853), clergyman and educationist, was a native of Scotland who was ordained a minister of the Church of Scotland. He came to Canada, and was for a time a Presbyterian minister at Oakville, Upper Canada. From 1842 to 1844 he was assistant superintendent of common schools for Upper Canada; and in 1844 he was appointed professor of mathematics and moral philosophy in King's College, Toronto. After some years of declining health, he died at Port Albert, Ashfield township, Canada West, on March 13, 1853.

[J. G. Hodgins (ed.), *Documentary history of education in Upper Canada*, vol. II (Toronto, 1904); R. D. Gidney, *The Rev. Robert Murray* (Ont. hist., 1971).]

Murray, Robert (1832-1910), clergyman and hymn-writer, was born at Earltown, Nova Scotia, in 1832; and was educated at the Free Church College, Halifax, Nova Scotia. He was ordained a minister of the Presbyterian

Church; and for forty-four years he was editor of the *Presbyterian Witness*. He was the author of many hymns, some of which are included in the official hymnaries of the Presbyterian Church and of the Church of England; and he was the author of a verse which is, in Canada, sometimes added to the national anthem. He died at Halifax, Nova Scotia, on December 12, 1910.

[R. J. Long, *Nova Scotia authors* (East Orange, N.J., 1918).]

Murray, Sinclair (pseud.). See **Sullivan, Alan.**

Murray, Walter Charles (1866-1945), president of the University of Saskatchewan (1908-37), was born at Studholm, Kings county, New Brunswick, on May 12, 1866. He was educated at the University of New Brunswick (B.A., 1886), at Edinburgh University (M.D., 1891), and at Berlin; and he was professor of philosophy at the University of New Brunswick from 1891 to 1892, and at Dalhousie University from 1892 to 1908. In 1908 he was appointed president of the University of Saskatchewan; and he presided over the destinies of this university until his retirement in 1937. He died at Saskatoon, Saskatchewan, on March 23, 1945. He was an honorary LL.D. of Queen's University, the University of Alberta, McGill University, the University of Manitoba, McMaster University, and the University of Wisconsin; and he was elected a fellow of the Royal Society of Canada in 1918.

[*Can. who's who*, 1938-39; Morgan, *Can. men* (1912); *Proc. Roy. Soc. Can.*, 1945.]

Murray, William Waldie (1891-1956), soldier and author, was born in Hawick, Scotland, in 1891, and died at Ottawa, Ontario, on August 2, 1956. He served overseas with the 2nd Battalion of the Canadian Expeditionary Force in the First World War; and he was the author of *The history of the 2nd Canadian Battalion* (Ottawa, 1947). He was also the author, under the pseudonym of "The Orderly Sergeant", of *Five nines and whiz bangs* (Ottawa, 1937).

[Private information.]

Musgrave, Sir Anthony (1828-1888), governor of British Columbia (1869-71), was born in Antigua, West Indies, in 1828, the son of Anthony Musgrave, M.D. He entered the colonial service of Great Britain; and, after holding various positions in the West Indies, became in 1864 governor of Newfoundland. He had something to do with the negotiations of 1864 regarding the entrance of Newfoundland into Confederation; and in 1869 he was appointed governor of British Columbia, with instructions to expedite the entrance of British Columbia into Confederation. This he did, and his term of office in British Columbia ended with the completion of his task. In 1872 he was appointed lieutenant-governor of Natal; in 1873, governor of South Australia; in 1877, governor of Jamaica; and in 1888 governor of Queensland, Australia. He died at Brisbane, Queensland, Australia, in October, 1888. He was created a C.M.G. in 1871, and a K.C.M.G. in 1875. He was the author of *Studies in political economy* (London, 1875), and of several pamphlets.

[F. W. Howay, *Governor Musgrave and Confederation* (Trans. Roy. Soc. Can., 1921); *Dict. nat. biog.*; *Cyc. Am. biog.*; *Can. who was who*, vol. 2.]

Myrand, Ernest (1854-1921), historian, was born at Quebec, Lower Canada, on June 29, 1854, the son of Louis Japhet Myrand and Marie Anne Adelaide Marmette, a sister of Joseph Marmette (q.v.). He was educated at the Quebec Seminary and at Laval University, and first became a journalist on the staff of *Le Canadien*, under Israel Tarte (q.v.). He then entered the civil service of the province of Quebec; in 1902 he was appointed registrar in the provincial secretary's office; and in 1912 he became librarian of the Legislative Library at Quebec. His first book was *Une fête de Noël sous Jacques Cartier* (Quebec, 1888); and this was followed by *Sir William Phips devant Québec* (Quebec, 1893), *Monsieur de la Colombière, orateur* (Montreal, 1898), *Noëls anciens de la Nouvelle-France* (Quebec, 1899; new and revised ed., 1907), and *Frontenac et ses amis* (Quebec, 1901). In 1909 he was elected a fellow of the Royal Society of Canada. He died at Quebec on May 21, 1921.

[*Proc. Roy. Soc. Can.*, 1922; Le Jeune, *Dict. gén.*; Morgan, *Can. men* (1912).]

Nadeau, Jean Marie (1906-1960), advocate and professor, was born at Saint Césaire, Quebec, on December 8, 1906. He graduated from the University of Rennes, France (Lic. in Letters), and the University of Paris (Diploma in Law, 1934). He was called to the Quebec bar in 1930 and in partnership with his brother was a member of the legal firm of Nadeau and Nadeau. In 1937 he was appointed to the political economy department of the University of Montreal, becoming a full professor in 1945, and remaining until 1950. He was responsible for the restoration of the Bibliothèque St. Sulpice (1942-44) at the request of the Quebec government. He was author of *La canalisation du St-Laurent* (Montreal, 1942), *Le Sénat et le problème des chemins de fer canadiens* (Montreal, 1939), *Horizons d'après-guerre* (Montreal, 1944), and *Enterprise privée et socialisme* (Montreal, 1944). He was a member of the Royal Society of Canada. He died on October 5, 1960.

[*Proc. Roy. Soc. Can.,* 1961; *Can. who's who,* 1955-57.]

Nairne, John (1731-1802), soldier and seignior, was born in Scotland on March 1, 1731. He came of Jacobite stock, and not long after the rising of 1745 he took service with the "Scots brigade" in Holland. In 1757 he returned to Scotland, and obtained a commission in the 78th Regiment (Fraser's Highlanders). He was present at the capture of Louisbourg in 1758 and of Quebec in 1759; and in 1761 he purchased the seigniory of Murray Bay, on the north shore of the St. Lawrence. Here he lived for the rest of his life; and he died at Quebec on July 14, 1802. In 1766 he married in Canada Christiana Emery, a native of Scotland.

[G. M. Wrong, *A Canadian manor and its seigneurs* (Toronto, 1908; new ed., 1926).]

Nankevill, Benjamin (1799-1856), clergyman, was born in 1799, and was ordained a Methodist minister in Upper Canada in 1839. He died at Cooksville, Canada West, on October 9, 1856. He was the author of *A series of letters to the Rev. J. A. Mulock, presbyter, of the Church of England: Being a reply to certain charges against the Methodists* (Carleton Place, C.W., 1850).

[G. H. Cornish, *Cyclopaedia of Canadian Methodism* (Toronto, 1881).]

Nantel, Antonin (1839-1929), priest and author, was born at St. Jérôme, Lower Canada, on September 17, 1839, the son of Guillaume Nantel and Adelaide Desjardins. He was educated at Laval University (B.A., 1859; M.A., 1867; LL.D., 1902), and was ordained a priest of the Roman Catholic Church. In 1871 he became the superior of the Ste. Thérèse Seminary, and he retired from this position only a few years before his death, at Ste. Thérèse de Blainville, Quebec, on July 30, 1929. He was the author of *Les fleurs de la poésie canadienne* (Montreal, 1869), of a school geography (Montreal, 1871), and of *Pages historiques et littéraires* (Montreal, 1928).

[Allaire, *Dict. biog.*; Le Jeune, *Dict. gén.*]

Nantel, Guillaume Alphonse (1852-1909), lawyer, politician, and author, was born at St. Jérôme, Canada East, on November 4, 1852, the brother of the Rev. Antonin Nantel (q.v.) and the Hon. W. B. Nantel (q.v.). He was called to the bar of Quebec, and for a time practised law; but eventually drifted into journalism and politics. He represented Terrebonne in the Legislative Assembly of Quebec from 1882 to 1897; and he was minister of public works in the Boucherville and Taillon governments from 1891 to 1896, and minister of crown lands in the Flynn government from 1896 to 1897. He died at Montreal, Quebec, on June 3, 1909. He was the author of *Notre nord-ouest provincial: Étude sur la vallée d'Ottawa* (Montreal, 1887) and *La métropole de demain* (Montreal, 1910).

[Morgan, *Can. men* (1898); *Can. parl. comp.*]

Nantel, Wilfrid Bruno (1857-1940), minister of inland revenue for Canada (1911-14) and minister of mines (1911-12), was born at St. Jérôme, Canada East, on November 8, 1857. He was educated at the Seminary of Ste. Thérèse de Blainville, and was called to the bar of Quebec. He practised law at St. Jérôme, and was repeatedly elected mayor of St. Jérôme. From 1908 to 1914 he represented Terrebonne in the Canadian House of Commons; and he was minister of inland revenue (1911-14) and minister of mines (1911-12) in the Borden administration. He resigned from the cabinet in 1914 to accept appointment as deputy chief commissioner of the Board of Railway Commissioners for Canada; and he held this position until 1924. He died at St. Jérôme, Quebec, on May 23, 1940.

[*Can. who's who*, 1936-37; *Can. parl. comp.*; Morgan, *Can. men* (1912).]

Nanton, Sir Augustus (1860-1925), financier, was born in Toronto, Canada West, May 7, 1860, the son of Daniel Augustus Nanton and Mary Louisa, daughter of William Botsford Jarvis (q.v.). At the age of thirteen he entered the service of the brokerage firm of Pellatt and Osler, Toronto; and in 1884 he was sent west to represent this firm in Winnipeg. He became one of the outstanding figures in the financial life of Canada; and he was knighted in 1917 for his services in connection with the financing of Canada's part in the First World War. In 1924, on his election as president of the Dominion Bank, he returned to live in Toronto; and he died in Toronto, on April 24, 1925.

[R. G. MacBeth, *Sir Augustus Nanton, a biography* (Toronto, 1931); *Who was who*, 1916-28; Morgan, *Can. men* (1912).]

Narbonne, Charles Henri (1627?-1681), buccaneer, was born in Canada about 1627, the son of a French officer and an Indian woman, and took the name of his father's native city. He began life as a soldier in Canada, but in 1660 went to the West Indies, and there became famous as a buccaneer. In 1670 he joined Sir Henry Morgan in the expedition against Panama. He amassed a large fortune, settled in Tortugas, West Indies, and in 1677 became deputy lieutenant of the French king. He died at Tortugas in 1681.

[*Cyc. Am. biog.*]

Narbonne, Edouard (b. 1849?), author, was born about 1849 at St. Rémi, Canada East. A score of years later, some members of his family claimed descent from the Counts of Narbonne-Lara; and he assumed the style of "M. le Comte de Narbonne-Lara". It was under this name that he published his *Esquisses poétiques* (Montreal, 1875) and his *L'aimable compagnon: Anecdotes, traits de satire, etc.* (Montreal, 1876). Shortly after the publication of these volumes, he went to live in the United States, and was apparently still living there in 1915.

[*Bull. rech. hist.*, 1915.]

Narbonne, Pierre Rémi (1806-1839), rebel, was born at St. Rémi, Lower Canada, in 1806. He was active in the rebellions of 1837 and 1838, and was captured at Napierville, Lower Canada, in the late autumn of 1838. He was tried at Montreal on a charge of high treason, and was hanged on January 26, 1839.

[*Cyc. Am. biog.*; *Dict. nat. biog.*; Le Jeune, *Dict. gén.*; L. O. David, *Les patriotes de 1837-1838* (Montreal, 1884).]

Narbonne-Lara, Edouard, Comte de. See **Narbonne, Edouard.**

Nash, Charles William (1848-1926), naturalist, was born at Bognor, Sussex, England, on August 15, 1848. He came to Canada in 1869, and became a farmer. In 1899 he was appointed lecturer on biology to the Farmers' Institutes in Ontario, and later biologist to the Provincial Museum, to which he presented his collection of the birds and fishes of Ontario. He died at Toronto, Ontario, on February 12, 1926. He wrote a number of books and papers on the birds and fishes of Ontario, and the results of his life-work were summed up in his *Manual of the vertebrates of Ontario* (Toronto, 1908).

[Morgan, *Can. men* (1912).]

Nault, André (1829-1924), rebel, was born at Point Douglas, in the Red River Settlement, in 1829, the son of Amable Nault and Josette Lagimodière, daughter of the first Canadian woman in the West. Since his life was passed among the *métis*, he came to be regarded as one of them, though he had no strain of Indian blood in his veins. He commanded the *métis* who seized Fort Garry at the time of the Riel Rebellion in 1870; and it was he who commanded the firing party at the execution of Thomas Scott (q.v.). He took refuge in the United States, but returned to Canada in 1874; and he died at St. Vital, Manitoba, in 1924.

[A. G. Morice, *Dictionnaire historique des canadiens ... de l'ouest* (Kamloops, B.C., 1908); A. H. De Trémaudan (ed.), *The execution of Thomas Scott* (Can. hist. rev., 1925).]

Naylor, Albert Enos (1895-1963), financier, was born at Chatham, Ontario, January 23, 1895. He was educated in Winnipeg, Manitoba, and served in the Royal Air Force and the Royal Flying Corps during the First World War. After discharge he joined the Ford Motor Company's sales staff in Winnipeg. In 1922 he became a branch manager of Trader's Finance, where he rose to be president and general manager (1944-56). He was a director of Canadian General Securities; Canadian Insurance Shares Limited; Canadian General Insurance Company; Trader's General Insurance; Trader's Properties; and Trader's Leasing Company. During the Second World War he was a member of the Maritime Prices and Trade Board, and was awarded the O.B.E. in 1945. He died at Toronto, Ontario, January 24, 1963.

[*Can. who's who*, 1955-57; Metropolitan Toronto Library Board, *Biographical scrapbooks*, vol. 21.]

Need, Thomas (b. 1808), author, was born in England in 1808, and was educated at University College, Oxford (B.A., 1830). He emigrated to Upper Canada in 1832, and settled in Verulam township, near the site of the present town of Bobcaygeon, Ontario. He remained in Canada over ten years; but when still a young man returned to England. He was living in Nottingham as late as 1870, and his widow was living in Ashby-de-la-Zouche in 1904; but the date of his death has not been ascertained. While still living in Canada, he published an account of his experiences as a settler in Upper Canada, under the title *Six years in the bush* (London, 1838).

[*Burke's landed gentry* (London, 1939) under "Need of Winthorpe Hall"; J. Foster, *Alumni Oxonienses* (8 vols., Oxford, 1887-92); W. A. Langton (ed.), *Early days in Upper Canada* (Toronto, 1926); T. W. Poole, *A sketch of the early settlement and subsequent progress of the town of Peterborough* (Peterborough, C. W., 1867).]

Needler, George Henry (1866-1962), university professor, was born at Millbrook, Ontario, in 1866. He was educated at Port Hope and at the University of Toronto (B.A., 1889) and the University of Leipzig (Ph.D., 1891). He served with the Queen's Own Rifles in the Riel Rebellion of 1885. During the First World War he commanded a training school for officers. He joined the staff of the University of Toronto in modern languages in 1891 and retired in 1936. He wrote *Otonabee pioneers* (1953); *The Battleford column: Versified memoirs of a Queen's Own Corporal in the Northwest Rebellion* (1948); *Louis Riel: The rebellion of 1885* (1957). He died at Toronto, Ontario, January 1, 1962.

[Metropolitan Toronto Library Board, *Biographical scrapbooks*, vols. 20 & 71; *Can. who's who*, 1948; *Dalhousie Review* (Autumn, 1958).]

Neil, James Stephen (1877-1947), novelist, was born in Toronto, Ontario, in 1877, and died at his home in Markham township, Ontario, on May 29, 1947. He was the author of an historical novel, *All the king's men* (Toronto, 1924).

[Toronto *Globe and Mail*, May 30, 1947.]

Neilson, Henry Ivan (1865-1931), painter and etcher, was born at Quebec, on June 27, 1865, the youngest of thirteen children of John Neilson, D.L.S., and grandson of the Hon. John Neilson (q.v.). He became a marine engineer, and was for a number of years in the service of the Canadian Pacific Ocean Steamships. He turned to painting, however, in 1897, and studied art at the Glasgow School of Fine Arts, at the Académie de la Clausse, Paris, and at St. Giles Academy, Brussels. He lived in Scotland until 1910, when he returned to Canada, and was elected an A.R.C.A. While primarily a landscape painter, he also used many figure subjects; and in his later years he devoted much attention to etching. He is represented by many etchings both in the National Gallery, Ottawa, and in the Quebec Museum. He became a member of the teaching staff of the New School of Fine Arts at Quebec in 1921, and in 1929 he was appointed its principal. He died at Quebec on April 27, 1931.

[N. MacTavish, *The fine arts in Canada* (Toronto, 1925); Morgan, *Can. men* (1912).]

Neilson, John (1776-1848), journalist and politician, was born in Balmaghie, Kirkcudbrightshire, Scotland, on July 17, 1776, the son of William Neilson and Isabel Brown. At the age of fourteen he was sent to Canada; his elder brother Samuel (q.v.) had preceded him, to join his uncle, William Brown, proprietor of the *Quebec Gazette*. He succeeded to the ownership of the paper in 1797, and conducted it for over fifty years. From 1818 to 1834 he represented Quebec county in the Legislative Assembly of Lower Canada; and in 1822 and in 1828 he was one of the delegates sent to London to represent the views of the Lower Canada Reformers. In 1834 he parted company with the extreme Reformers, headed by Louis Joseph Papineau (q.v.); and in 1835 he went, for a third time, to London, as a representative of the "Constitutional Associations" of Lower Canada. In 1841 he was again elected to represent Quebec county, in the Legislative Assembly of Canada; and in 1844 he was appointed a member of the Legislative Council. He died at Quebec on February 1, 1848. The Neilson papers are in the Public Archives of Canada.

[*Dict. nat. biog.*; *Cyc. Am. biog.*; Morgan, *Cel. Can.* and *Bib. can.*; Le Jeune, *Dict. gén.*; R. Christie, *History of Lower Canada* (6 vols., Quebec and Montreal, 1848-56); J. C. Dent, *The last forty years* (2 vols., Toronto, 1881).]

Neilson, John Louis Hubert (1845-1925), medical officer, was born near Quebec, Canada East, on March 24, 1845, the eldest son of John Neilson and Laura Moorehead, and the grandson of the Hon. John Neilson (q.v.). He was educated at St. Mary's College, Montreal, at Laval University (M.L., 1869), and at the Royal Army Medical School, Netley, England; and he became in 1869 a medical officer in the Canadian permanent militia. He rose to the rank of surgeon-colonel, and in 1898 he was appointed director-general of medical services in the Canadian militia. He retired on pension in 1903; and he died at Quebec City on June 5, 1925. He was the author of a pamphlet on *The Royal Canadian Volunteers* (Montreal, 1895), and the editor of *Fac-simile of Père Marquette's Illinois prayer book* (Quebec, 1908).

[Morgan, *Can. men* (1912).]

Neilson, Samuel (1771-1793), printer, was born in Balmaghie, Kirkcudbrightshire, Scotland, in 1771, the son of William Neilson and Isabel Brown, and the elder brother of John Neilson (q.v.). He was sent to Canada, at an early age, to learn the trade of printer and journalist with his uncle, William Brown, who had founded the *Quebec Gazette*. William Brown died suddenly on March 22, 1789; and Samuel Neilson then became proprietor of the *Quebec Gazette*. He continued its publication until his own death, which took place at Quebec on January 12, 1793.

[*Bull. rech. hist.*, 1935.]

Nelles, Samuel Sobieski (1823-1887), president of Victoria University (1850-87), was born at Mount Pleasant, Upper Canada, on October 17, 1823. He was educated at Lewiston Academy, New York, at the Genesee Wesleyan Seminary, at Victoria University, Cobourg, and at the Wesleyan University, Middletown, Connecticut (B.A., 1846). In 1847 he entered the ministry of the Methodist Church in Canada; and in 1850 he was appointed president of Victoria University. He died at Cobourg, Ontario, on October 17, 1887. By his wife, a daughter of the Rev. Enoch Wood (q.v.), he had one son and three daughters. In 1860 he was made a D.D. of Queen's University, Kingston, and in 1873 an LL.D. of Victoria University. He was the editor of a textbook on logic (Toronto, 1870).

[*Cyc. Am. biog.*; Rose, *Cyc. Can. biog.* (1888); Dent, *Can. port.*, vol. 3.]

Nelligan, Emile (1879-1941), poet, was born in Montreal, Quebec, December 24, 1879, the son of an Irish father and a French-Canadian mother. While still a youth in his teens, he evinced an extraordinary genius as a poet; but his work was cut short in 1900 by insanity. He died in an asylum in Montreal on November 18, 1941. His work was collected and published, with an introduction by Louis Dantin, under the title *Emile Nelligan et son oeuvre* (Montreal, 1903).

[L. Lacourcière (ed.), *Introduction to Nelligan's Poésies complètes, 1896-1899* (Montreal, 1952); C. Roy, *Histoire de la littérature française-canadienne* (Quebec, 1930); *Saturday night*, Dec. 13, 1941; Paul Wuczynski, *Emile Nelligan* (Ottawa, 1960); *Nelligan et la musique* (Rev. de l'Univ. d'Ottawa, 1969).]

Nelson, Horatio (d. 1863), physician, was the son of Dr. Wolfred Nelson (q.v.). He was educated at New York University (M.D., 1842); and he became the editor of *Nelson's American Lancet*, a periodical published at Plattsburg, New York, from 1850 to 1856. From 1853 to 1854 he was also professor of surgery at the University of Vermont. Later he returned to Canada; and he died at Montreal, Canada East, in January, 1863. He was the author of *Strictures of the rectum* (Montreal, 1861).

[Morgan, *Bib. can.*]

Nelson, Hugh (1830-1893), lieutenant-governor of British Columbia (1887-92), was born in Larne, county Antrim, Ireland, on May 25, 1830, the son of Robert Nelson. He settled in British Columbia in 1858, and ultimately engaged in the lumber business. From 1870 to 1871 he was a member of the Legislative Assembly of British Columbia for New Westminster; and he was one of the chief advocates of the entrance of British Columbia into federation. From 1871 to 1873 he represented New Westminster in the Canadian House of Commons. In 1879 he was appointed to the Senate of Canada; and in 1887 he became lieutenant-governor of British Columbia. His term of office came to an end in 1892; and he died in London, England, March 3, 1893. In 1885 he married Emily, daughter of J. B. Stanton, of the Canadian civil service.

[*Cyc. Am. biog.*; Rose, *Cyc. Can. biog.* (1888); *Can. parl. comp.*; J. B. Kerr, *Biographical dictionary of well-known British Columbians* (Vancouver, B.C., 1890).]

Nelson, John (1873-1936), journalist and author, was born at Paisley, Ontario, on March 8, 1873. He became a journalist, and from 1898 to 1921 he was on the staff of various newspapers in Victoria and Vancouver, British Columbia. In 1925 he became supervisor of public relations in the Sun Life Assurance Company in Montreal. He was honorary secretary of the Canadian Institute of International Affairs; and in 1933-34 he was president of Rotary International. He died in Chicago, Illinois, on January 24, 1936. He was the author of *The Canadian provinces: Their problems and policies* (Toronto, 1924).

[*New York Times*, January 25, 1936; Morgan, *Can. men* (1912).]

Nelson, Robert (1794-1873), rebel, was born in Montreal, Lower Canada, in January, 1794, the son of William Nelson, and brother of Wolfred Nelson (q.v.). He studied medicine, and served in the War of 1812 as a regimental surgeon. In 1827 he was elected, with Louis Joseph Papineau (q.v.), to represent Montreal in the Legislative Assembly of Lower Canada; and he supported Papineau in his demand for reforms. He took no active part in the rebellion of 1837; but in 1838 he went to the United States, and organized a force of filibusters, with which he invaded Canada. He proclaimed Canada a republic, and styled himself "president of the provisional government". He was defeated at Lacolle and Odelltown by the loyalist forces, and fled to the United States. For a time he lived in California, but during the last eleven years of his life he practised as a consulting surgeon in New York. He died at Gifford's, Staten Island, on March 1, 1873. He was the author of a number of papers on medical subjects.

[C. E. Nelson, *Robert Nelson* (New York medical register, 1873); *Cyc. Am. biog.*;

Morgan, *Cel. Can.*; Le Jeune, *Dict. gén.*; R. Christie, *History of Lower Canada* (6 vols., Quebec and Montreal, 1848-55); L. O. David, *Les patriotes de 1837-1838* (Montreal, 1884); *Dict. Can. biog.*, vol. 10.]

Nelson, Wolfred (1791-1863), rebel, was born in Montreal, Lower Canada, on July 10, 1791, the son of William Nelson. He studied medicine, and in the War of 1812 served as a regimental surgeon. In 1827 he was elected to represent Sorel in the Legislative Assembly of Lower Canada; and during the next ten years was one of the chief lieutenants of Louis Joseph Papineau (q.v.). He took a leading part in organizing the rebellion of 1837, and was present at the engagements of St. Denis and St. Charles. He was captured, and was one of the eight insurgents banished by Lord Durham (q.v.) to the Bermudas in 1838. He was released, however, later in the same year; and in 1843 he took advantage of the amnesty to return to Canada, and resumed the practice of his profession in Montreal. From 1844 to 1851 he represented Richelieu in the Legislative Assembly of Canada; but in 1851 he withdrew from political life, and was appointed an inspector of prisons. In 1859 he became chairman of the board of prison inspectors; and he died at Montreal on June 17, 1863.

[*Cyc. Am. biog.*; Morgan, *Cel. Can.*; Le Jeune, *Dict. gén.*; R. Christie, *History of Lower Canada* (6 vols., Quebec and Montreal, 1848-55); L. O. David, *Les patriotes de 1837-1838* (Montreal, 1884); W. Nelson, *Wolfred Nelson et son temps* (Montreal, 1946).]

Nercam, André (1814-1890), priest, was born at Bordeaux, France, in 1814, entered the Sulpician order, and was ordained a priest in 1840. He came to Canada in 1848, and served in Montreal until his death there on January 22, 1890. He was the author of *Vie d'Adèle Coulombe, religieuse hospitalière de l'Hôtel-Dieu de Montréal* (Tours, 1863).

[Allaire, *Dict. biog.*]

Nesbitt, Wallace (1858-1930), lawyer, was born at Woodstock, Ontario, on May 13, 1858, the son of John W. Nesbitt and Mary Wallace. He was educated at Woodstock College and Osgoode Hall, Toronto, and was called to the bar in Ontario in 1881 (Q.C., 1899). In 1903 he was appointed a judge of the Supreme Court of Canada, but he resigned from the bench in 1905 to resume practice. He became a leader of the Ontario bar; in 1927 he was elected treasurer of the Law Society of Upper Canada, and in 1928 president of the Canadian Bar Association. He died at Toronto, Ontario, on April 7, 1930.

[*Can. who was who*, vol. 1; Morgan, *Can. men* (1912).]

Nesbitt, William (d. 1784), speaker of the House of Representatives of Nova Scotia (1759-83), came to Nova Scotia about 1750, and was first employed as a clerk in the office of the provincial secretary. He was dismissed from this post by the governor in 1752; but later received the appointment of attorney-general of the province. From 1758 to 1784 he represented Halifax county in the House of Representatives of Nova Scotia; and from 1759 to 1783 he was speaker of the House, as well as attorney-general. He died at Halifax, Nova Scotia, in 1784.

[T. B. Akins (ed.), *Selections from the public documents of Nova Scotia* (Halifax, N.S., 1869); B. Murdoch, *History of Nova Scotia* (3 vols., Halifax, 1865).]

Nesbitt, William Beattie (1866-1913), physician, politician, and financier, was born at Vandecar, Oxford county, Ontario, on May 23, 1866; and was educated at the University of Toronto (B.A., 1887) and Trinity University (M.D., 1887). He practised medicine in Toronto for several years; and he represented North Toronto as a Conservative in the Legislative Assembly of Ontario from 1902 to 1908. In 1906 he became first president of the ill-starred Farmers' Bank; but he resigned from this position in 1908. He died at Toronto, Ontario, on January 31, 1913.

[*Can. who's who*, 1910.]

Nettle, Richard (1815-1905), author, was born in Devonport, England, on June 29, 1815. He took service in the Royal Navy; but in 1842 left the Navy to come to Canada. In 1857 he was appointed superintendent of fisheries for Lower Canada; and he was a pioneer in establishing fish hatcheries in Canada. In 1864 he was transferred to the inland revenue department; he was retired on pension in 1898; and he died at Ottawa, Ontario, on May 22, 1905. His portrait is in the rooms of the Literary and Historical Society of Quebec. He was the author of *The salmon fisheries of the St. Lawrence and its tributaries* (Montreal, 1857).

[Ottawa *Morning Citizen*, May 24, 1905; private information.]

Nevers, Edmond Boisvert de (1862-1906), author and journalist, was born at La Baie-du-Febvre, Canada East, in 1862. He was educated at the Seminary of Nicolet, and in 1888 he went to Europe. Here he studied for a time under the historian Mommsen at Berlin. He travelled extensively in Germany, Italy, Spain, and Portugal; and he finally settled down in Paris as a journalist in connection with the Havas agency. Failing health brought about his return to Canada; and he obtained an appointment in the civil service of the province of Quebec. He died at Central Falls, Rhode Island, on April 15, 1906. He was the author of *L'avenir du peuple canadien-*

français (Paris, 1896) and *L'âme américaine* (2 vols., Paris, 1900).

[J. Bruchési, *Edmond de Nevers* (Canada français, 1935); C. Galarneau, *Edmond de Nevers: Essayist* (Laval, 1960); Le Jeune, *Dict. gén.*]

New, Chester William (1882-1960), historian, was born at Montreal, Quebec, on October 9, 1882, and died at Hamilton, Ontario, on August 31, 1960. He was educated at the University of Toronto (B.A., 1903), McMaster University (B.D., 1907), and the University of Chicago (Ph.D., 1913). From 1913 to 1920 he was professor of history at Brandon College, and from 1920 to 1951 professor of history at McMaster University. He was the author of *History of the alien priories in England* (Chicago, 1916), *Lord Durham* (Oxford, 1929), and *The Life of Henry Brougham* (Oxford, 1961); and he was joint author, with C. E. Phillips, of *Ancient and mediaeval history* (Toronto, 1941; new and rev. ed., 1954), and, with R. G. Trotter, of *A world history from 1760 to the present* (Toronto, 1954). He was elected a fellow of the Royal Society of Canada in 1937 and of the Royal Society in 1948.

[*Proc. Roy. Soc. Can.*, 1961; *Can. who's who*, 1958-60; *Can. hist. rev.*, 1960.]

Newcombe, Edmund Leslie (1859-1931), judge of the Supreme Court of Canada, was born at Cornwallis, Nova Scotia. He was educated at Dalhousie University (B.A., 1878; M.A., 1881; LL.B., 1882; LL.D., 1911). In 1883 he was called to the bar; and in 1893 he was appointed deputy minister of justice for Canada, a position which he held for over thirty years. In 1924 he was appointed a judge of the Supreme Court of Canada; and he died at Ottawa on December 9, 1931.

[*Can. parl. comp.*; Morgan, *Can. men* (1912).]

Newell, John Robert (1853-1912), clergyman and poet, was born at Springfield, Canada West, on August 7, 1853. He was educated at Huron College, London, Ontario, and was ordained a priest of the Church of England in 1885. He was the rector of various churches in Ontario; and he died on October 14, 1912, at Sarnia, Ontario. He was the author of *The times, and other poems* (Toronto, 1881) and *Poems and songs* (Toronto, 1904).

[Morgan, *Can. men* (1912).]

Newhall, Mrs. Georgina Alexandrina, *née* **Fraser** (1859-1932), journalist and poet, was born at Galt, Canada West, on September 2, 1859, the daughter of James G. Fraser. She became a journalist, and was the first editor of the women's page in the Toronto *News*. In 1884 she married Eugene Pierre Newhall, of Minneapolis, Minnesota; and she died in Calgary, Alberta, on November 11, 1932. Some of her verses were collected in *Selections from Scottish Canadian poets* (Toronto, 1900).

[Morgan, *Can. men and women* (1898).]

Newnham, Jervois Arthur (1852-1941), Anglican bishop of Moosonee (1893-1904) and of Saskatchewan (1904-21), was born on October 15, 1852, near Bath, England. He came to Canada as a young man, and was educated at McGill University, Montreal (B.A., 1878; M.A., 1883; LL.D., 1921). He was ordained a priest of the Church of England in 1880; and after serving as curate of Christ Church Cathedral in Montreal and rector of a church in Westmount, Quebec, he became in 1890 a missionary at Moose Factory. He was elected bishop of Moosonee in 1893; and he exercised oversight of this vast diocese until he was translated to the see of Saskatchewan in 1904. He retired from the episcopate in 1921; and for several years he served as rector of a church in Clifton, England. His later days, however, were spent in retirement at Hamilton, Ontario; and here he died on January 11, 1941.

[Mrs. F. P. Shearwood, *By water and the word* (Toronto, 1943); *Can. who's who*, 1936-37; Morgan, *Can. men* (1912).]

Newton, Gilbert Stuart (1794-1835), painter, was born in Halifax, Nova Scotia, on September 20, 1794, the twelfth and youngest son of the Hon. Henry Newton, collector of customs at Halifax. About 1820 he went to Italy to study painting, and later he settled in England. He was elected a member of the Royal Academy in 1834; and he died at Chelsea on August 5, 1835.

[*Dict. nat. biog.*; *Encyclopedia Americana.*]

Newton, William (1828-1910), missionary and author, was a clergyman of the Church of England, stationed in a parish in the diocese of Toronto, who was in 1875 sent to the West as a missionary by the Society for the Propagation of the Gospel. He was the first Anglican missionary at Edmonton, North West Territories; and he had his headquarters at Edmonton for over thirty years. He died at Victoria, British Columbia, on February 11, 1910. He was the author of *Twenty years on the Saskatchewan, N.W. Canada* (London, 1897).

[Private information.]

Nichol, Robert (1774?-1824), soldier and legislator, was born in Dumfries-shire, Scotland, about 1774. He was a relative of the Hon. Robert Hamilton (q.v.), and came to Canada before 1795. He settled in Norfolk county, Upper Canada, and here he became the local agent of Col. Thomas Talbot (q.v.). In 1812 he was appointed by General Brock quartermaster-general of the militia of Upper Canada, and he served in this capacity during the War of 1812-15. In 1812 he was also elected to represent Norfolk in the Legislative Assembly of the province, and he continued to represent this constituency until 1821. He then became judge of the Surrogate Court of the district of Niagara; and on May 3, 1824, he met his death near Queenston, Upper Canada, when driving in a snow storm from Niagara to his home in Stamford township. His horses having missed their way, he was precipitated over the bank of the Niagara gorge, and was "literally dashed to pieces".

[E. A. Cruikshank, *A sketch of the public life and services of Robert Nichol* (Ont. Hist. Soc., papers and records, 1922) and *Some letters of Robert Nichol* (Ont. Hist. Soc., papers and records, 1923); Morgan, *Cel. Can.*]

Nichol, Walter Cameron (1866-1928), lieutenant-governor of British Columbia (1921-26), was born at Goderich, Ontario, on October 15, 1866, the son of Robert Nichol, barrister, and grandson of Col. Robert Nichol (q.v.). He was educated in Hamilton, Ontario, and in 1881 joined the staff of the Hamilton *Spectator*. From 1888 to 1896 he was editor of the Hamilton *Herald*. In 1897 he went to British Columbia, and became editor of the Victoria *Province*, then a weekly newspaper. In 1898 he removed the *Province* to Vancouver, and made it a daily paper, with great success. From 1921 to 1926 he was lieutenant-governor of British Columbia; and he died at Victoria, British Columbia, on December 19, 1928. In 1897 he married Quita, daughter of Charles Greenwood Moore, M.D., of London, Ontario.

[*Can. who was who*, vol. 2; Morgan, *Can. men* (1912); Le Jeune, *Dict. gén.*; *Can. parl. comp.*]

Nicholls, Frederic (1856-1921), senator of Canada, was born in England on November 23, 1856. He was educated in Germany, and came to Canada in 1874. He was a pioneer in electrical development in Canada, and became president of the Canadian General Electric Company, as well as of many other corporations. In 1917 he was called to the Senate of Canada; and he died at Battle Creek, Michigan, on October 25, 1921. In 1875 he married Florence (d. 1909), daughter of Commander Graburn, R.N.; and by her he had several children.

[H. Charlesworth (ed.), *A cyclopaedia of Canadian biography* (Toronto, 1919); *Can. parl. comp.*; Morgan, *Can. men* (1912).]

Nichols, Mark Edgar (1873-1961), journalist, was born in Halton county, Ontario, in 1873. He was educated in Oakville. He began his newspaper career on the Toronto *Telegram* as parliamentary correspondent. He became editor of the Toronto *World* in 1903, resigning to become president and editor of the Winnipeg *Telegram* in 1905. He was managing editor of the *Winnipeg Tribune* (1920-35) and the Vancouver *Province* (1935-45). He retired to write *The story of the Canadian Press* (To-

ronto, 1948). During the First World War he was director of public information (1917-18).

[*Can. who's who*, 1955-57.]

Nicholson, Byron (1857-1916), journalist and civil servant, was born at Hamilton, Canada West, on January 27, 1857. He became a journalist, and was for many years editor and publisher of the Barrie *Examiner*. In 1891 he was appointed collector of crown timber dues at the port of Quebec; and in 1909 he accepted a clerical position on the staff of the Senate of Canada. He died at Ottawa, Ontario, in June, 1916. He was the author of *The French-Canadian* (Toronto, 1902) and *In old Quebec, and other sketches* (Quebec, 1908).

[Morgan, *Can. men* (1912).]

Nicholson, Francis (1655-1728), governor of Nova Scotia (1713-15), was born November 12, 1655, at Downholme, near Richmond, Yorkshire, England, and entered the British army in 1678. He was appointed lieutenant-governor of New York in 1686, and of Virginia in 1696, governor of Maryland in 1694, and of Virginia in 1698. He was an advocate of a vigorous policy against Canada; and in 1710 he was in command of the expedition that captured Port Royal. In 1713 he was made governor of Nova Scotia, but he left the colony in 1715; and in 1719 he was appointed governor of South Carolina. He held this nominal post until his death in London on March 5, 1728. The *Dictionary of national biography* states that he was knighted in 1720; but no confirmation of this statement has been found. He was the author of the *Journal of an expedition for the reduction of Port Royal* (London, 1711; reprinted by the Nova Scotia Historical Society, 1879) and *An apology or vindication of Francis Nicholson, governor of South Carolina* (London, 1724).

[*Dict. Am. biog.*; Le Jeune, *Dict. gén.*; *Dict. nat. biog.*; *Cyc. Am. biog.*; *Dict. Can. biog.*, vol. 2.]

Nicholson, Patrick Joseph (1885-1965), scholar and university president, was born at Beaver Cove, Cape Breton Island, September 8, 1887. He was educated at St. Francis Xavier College (B.A., 1909); Johns Hopkins University (M.A., 1911; Ph.D., 1913); the Grand Séminaire, Montreal; and St. Augustine's Seminary in Toronto. Dr. Nicholson was a noted Gaelic scholar and received an award from Aberdeen University for his assistance in maintaining Scottish culture in the New World. A physicist, he was professor of physics at St. Francis Xavier University and president of the university from 1944 to 1954. He was president of the Conference of Canadian Universities (1950-51). He was a member of the board of governors of the Nova Scotia Research Foundation and a fellow of the American Association for the Advancement of Science and the American Physics Society. He became monsignor in 1946 and vicar-general of Antigonish diocese in 1950. He died at Antigonish, Nova Scotia, November 4, 1965.

[*Can. who's who*, 1961-63; Metropolitan Toronto Library Board, *Biographical scrapbooks*, vol. 23.]

Nickerson, Moses Hardy (1846-1943), journalist and poet, was born at Newelton, Nova Scotia, on September 10, 1846. After teaching school for many years, he became a journalist; and from 1897 to 1911 he was editor and proprietor of the *Coast Guard*, a weekly newspaper, with offices at Clarke's Harbour, Nova Scotia. From 1902 to 1912 he also represented Shelburne in the Legislative Assembly of Nova Scotia. He died at Clarke's Harbour, Nova Scotia, on March 23, 1943. He was the author of a volume of verse, entitled *Carols of the coast* (Halifax, N.S., 1892).

[R. J. Long, *Nova Scotia authors* (East Orange, N.J., 1918); C. C. James, *A bibliography of Canadian poetry* (Toronto, 1899); Morgan, *Can. men* (1912); *Can. who's who* (1910); *Can. parl. comp.*]

Nickinson, John (1808-1864), actor-manager, was born in London, England, in 1808. In early youth he enlisted in the 28th Regiment; but he obtained his discharge in 1835, with the rank of colour-sergeant, and emigrated to the United States. Here he became an actor; and from 1848 to 1852 he played at the Olympic Theatre, New York. In 1852 he came to Toronto, Canada, and from 1853 to 1858 he was manager of the Royal Lyceum Theatre in Toronto. He was a pioneer in theatrical management in Canada; and his daughter Charlotte (Mrs. Daniel Morrison) became a distinguished actress. He died in Cincinnati, Ohio, in 1864.

[J. Ross Robertson, *Landmarks of Canada: What art has done for Canadian history* (Toronto, 1917).]

Nicol, William Bulmer (1812-1886), physician and educationist, was born at Stockwell, Middlesex, England, on November 11, 1812. He was educated at Christ's College, Cambridge (B.A.), and studied medicine at the University of King's College, London. He came to Canada in 1836, and practised medicine first at Bowmanville, Upper Canada, and then at Toronto. In 1843 he was appointed professor of materia medica in King's College, Toronto; and he continued in this post until King's College became the University of Toronto in 1850. He occupied an outstanding position in the history of the medical profession in Ontario; and he died at Toronto, Ontario, on December 24, 1886.

[W. Canniff, *The medical profession in Upper Canada* (Toronto, 1894).]

Nicollet, Jean (1598?-1642), explorer, was born at Cherbourg, France, about 1598, the son of Thomas Nicollet and Marguerite Delamer. He came to Canada in 1618 in the service of the fur-trading company, and immediately on his arrival, was sent to l'Ile des Allumettes to learn the Algonkian language, and here he spent two years. The next eight or nine years were spent among the Nipissings. After the capture of Quebec in 1629, Nicollet remained loyal to the French, and returned to the country of the Nipissings, where he stayed until July, 1633. He was then recalled to Quebec, and became clerk and interpreter of the Company of One Hundred Associates. In 1634, under Champlain's instructions, he explored Lake Michigan as far as Green Bay, ascended Green Bay and Fox River to an Indian village west of Lake Winnebago, and made a treaty of peace with the tribes. In October, 1642, he was named *commis général* of the Company of One Hundred Associates during the absence of Le Tardif. On October 27, 1642, he was drowned while hastening to Three Rivers to prevent the death of a captive, belonging to a tribe in alliance with the Iroquois, whom the Algonkians were torturing. He married on October 7, 1642, Marguerite Couillard, by whom he had one daughter.

[A. Gosselin, *Jean Nicolet et le Canada de son temps* (Quebec, 1905); B. Sulte, *Jean Nicolet et la découverte du Wisconsin* (Revue canadienne, 1910); C. W. Butterfield, *History of the discovery of the North-West by John Nicolet in 1634, with a sketch of his life* (Cincinnati, 1881); *Dict. Am. biog.*; *Cyc. Am. biog.*; Le Jeune, *Dict. gén.*; *Dict. Can. biog.*, vol. 1.]

Nicolson, Alexander Wylie (d. 1903), clergyman, was a native of the Maritime provinces who was ordained a minister of the Methodist Church in 1860, and served for many years in the Maritime provinces. He died at Halifax, Nova Scotia, on June 28, 1903. He was the author of *Memories of James Bain Morrow* (Toronto, 1881).

[G. H. Cornish, *Cyclopaedia of Methodism in Canada* (2 vols., Toronto, 1881-1904).]

Nisbet, James (1823-1874), missionary, was born at Hutchisontown, Glasgow, Scotland, on September 8, 1823. He became a minister of the Canada Presbyterian Church, and was its first missionary in the Canadian West. He founded the town of Prince Albert in 1866; and he died at Kildonan, Manitoba, on September 30, 1874.

[E. H. Oliver, *The Presbyterian Church in Saskatchewan, 1866-1881* (Trans. Roy. Soc. Can., 1934); *Dict. Can. biog.*, vol. 10.]

Niven, Charles David (1897-1968), physicist, was born in Aberdeen, Scotland, July 16, 1897. He graduated from the University of Aberdeen (B.Sc., 1918) and the University of Toronto (Ph.D., 1929). He worked on the problems of thermo-conductivity at the National Research Council in Ottawa, which he joined in 1930. During the Second World War he experimented with the concept of a huge artificial iceberg to be used as a floating landing-ground in mid-Atlantic. He was a founder of the Eastern Ontario (rural) Society for the Prevention of Cruelty to Animals (S.P.C.A.) and author of *A history of the humane movement* (New York, 1967) selected by the American Library Association as one of the twelve best books published in 1967. He also wrote *The magic surface*, a book about ice, and numerous scientific papers as well as publications relating to cruelty to animals. He died at Quarries, Ontario, in 1969. He was a fellow of the Royal Society of Canada.

[*Proc. and Trans. Roy. Soc. Can.*, 1969.]

Niven, Frederick John (1878-1944), novelist, was born at Valparaiso, Chile, of Scottish parents, on March 31, 1878; and was educated in Glasgow, Scotland. He became first a library assistant and then a journalist; and it was while still employed as a journalist that he wrote his first novel. During the First World War he was employed in the Ministry of Information in Great Britain; but after the war he left England, and settled in British Columbia. Here he lived during the latter part of his life; and he died at Vancouver, British Columbia, on January 30, 1944. He was the author of the following novels: *The lost cabin mine* (London, 1909), *The island Providence* (London, 1910), *A wilderness of monkeys* (London, 1911), *Above your heads* (London, 1911), *Dead men's bells* (London, 1912), *The porcelain lady* (London, 1913), *Hands up!* (London, 1913), *Ellen Adair* (London, 1913), *Justice of the peace* (London, 1914), *The S.S. Glory* (London, 1915), *Two generations* (London, 1916), *Cinderella of Skookum creek* (London, 1916), *Sage-brush stories* (London, 1917), *Penny Scot's treasure* (London, 1918), *The lady of the crossing* (London, 1919), *A tale that is told* (London, 1920), *Treasure trail* (London, 1923), *The wolfer* (London, 1923), *Queer fellows* (London, 1927), *The three Marys* (London, 1930), *The Paisley shawl* (London, 1931), *The rich wife* (London, 1932), *Mrs. Barry* (London, 1933), *Triumph* (London, 1934), *The flying years* (London, 1935), *Old soldier* (London, 1936), *The staff at Simson's* (London, 1937), *Mine inheritance* (London, 1940), *Brothers-in-arms* (London, 1942), and *Under which king?* (London, 1943). He was the author also of two volumes of verse, *Maple-leaf songs* (London, 1917) and *A lover of the land, and other poems* (London, 1925), a descriptive volume, *Canada West* (Toronto, 1930), an autobiography, *Coloured spectacles* (London, 1938), and *The transplanted* (Toronto, 1944); and, with W. J. Phillips, he was joint author of *Colour in the Canadian Rockies* (Toronto, 1937).

[L. J. Burpee, *Frederick Niven* (Dalhousie

review, 1944); *Who's who,* 1943; *Can. who's who,* 1938-39; *Who's who among North American authors*, vol. 6; S. J. Kunitz and H. Haycraft, *Twentieth century authors* (New York, 1942); W. H. New, *Life and four landscapes: Frederick John Niven* (Canadian Literature, 1967).]

Nivert, Désiré Amable Chrétien (1605?-1661), missionary, was born at Calais, France, about 1605. He became a Recollet, and came to Canada, where he took part in the mission to the Hurons. He died in Canada in 1661.

[*Cyc. Am. biog.*]

Niverville, Joseph Claude Boucher de. See **Boucher de Niverville, Joseph Claude.**

Noel, Mrs. John Vavasour (1815-1873), novelist, was born in Ireland on December 22, 1815. She emigrated to America in 1832, and for a number of years conducted a seminary for young ladies in Savannah, Georgia. In 1847 she removed to Canada, and settled in Kingston. There she died on June 21, 1873. She was the author of *The abbey of Rathmore, and other tales* (Kingston, C.W., 1859), *The cross of pride* (Canadian Illustrated News, 1863), and *The secret of Stanley Hall* (Saturday Reader, Montreal, 1865).

[L. E. Horning and L. J. Burpee, *A bibliography of Canadian fiction* (Toronto, 1904); Morgan, *Bib. can.*]

Noiseux, François Xavier (1748-1834), priest, was born at Ste. Foy, near Quebec, Canada, on November 17, 1748. He was educated at the Quebec Seminary, and was ordained a priest of the Roman Catholic Church in 1774. He was parish priest successively at Pointe-aux-Trembles, at Beloeil, at St. Hyacinthe, and at Three Rivers. He retired from parochial work in 1812; and he died at Three Rivers, Lower Canada, on November 18, 1834. Not long before his death he compiled and published a *Liste chronologique des évêques et des prêtres, tant séculiers que réguliers, employés au service de l'église du Canada* (Quebec, 1834).

[H. Vallée, *M. l'abbé F.-X. Noiseux* (Three Rivers, 1931); Allaire, *Dict. biog.*; A. Godbout, *La liste chronologique de l'abbé Noiseux* (Culture, 1941).]

Nolan, Patrick James (1864-1913), lawyer, was born in Limerick, Ireland, on March 17, 1864. He was educated at Dublin University and the Royal University of Ireland (B.A., 1884; LL.B., 1885), and was called to the Irish bar in 1885. He emigrated to the Canadian north-west in 1889, and was called to the bar of the North West Territories (K.C., 1907). During the rest of his life he practised law in Calgary; and he became one of the most famous trial lawyers in Canada. He died at Calgary, Alberta, on February 11, 1913.

[R. St. G. Stubbs, *Lawyers and laymen of western Canada* (Toronto, 1939); Morgan *Can. men* (1912).]

Nordheimer, Samuel (1824-1912), capitalist, was born at Memelsdorf, Germany, in 1824, of Jewish parentage. He emigrated to the United States about 1839; and later he founded, with his brother Abraham, the firm of A. and S. Nordheimer, dealers in musical supplies, at Kingston, and then at Toronto, Ontario. He became president of the Federal Bank of Canada, and director of many financial corporations. In 1887 he was appointed German consul for Ontario; and in 1904 he was decorated with the order of the Red Eagle. He died at Toronto on June 29, 1912. In 1871 he married Edith Louise, daughter of James Boulton, of Toronto, and for many years president for Canada of the Imperial Order of the Daughters of the Empire; and by her he had one son and seven daughters.

[Morgan, *Can. men* (1912); Rose, *Cyc. Can. biog.* (1886).]

Norman, Richard Whitmore (1829-1906), clergyman, was born at Southborough, Kent, England, on April 24, 1829. He was educated at King's College, London, and at Exeter College, Oxford (B.A., 1851; M.A., 1853), and was ordained a priest of the Church of England in 1853. He was successively principal of St. Michael's College, Tenbury, and of Radley College, near Oxford; but in 1866 he came to Canada. After spending over twenty years in parochial work in Montreal, he was appointed rector of Quebec in 1888, and dean of the cathedral. In 1896 and 1897 he was elected president of the Literary and Historical Society of Quebec; and he received the honorary degrees of D.C.L. and D.D. from Bishop's College, Lennoxville. He died at Toronto, Ontario, on March 3, 1906. He was the author of *Confession and absolution: Three sermons* (Montreal, 1873).

[Morgan, *Can. men* (1898); Rose, *Cyc. Can. biog.* (1888).]

Normanby, Marquis of. See **Mulgrave, George Augustus Constantine, Earl of.**

Normand, Louis Philippe (1863-1928), president of the Privy Council of Canada (1921), was born at Three Rivers, Quebec, on September 21, 1863. He was educated at Laval University (M.D., 1886), and practised medicine at Three Rivers, of which he was repeatedly mayor. From September to December, 1921, he was president of the Privy Council in the Meighen administration. In 1922 he was elected president of the Medical Council of Canada. He died at Three Rivers on June 27, 1928.

[*Can. parl. comp.*; Morgan, *Can. men* (1912).]

Norquay, John (1841-1889), prime minister of Manitoba (1878-87), was born in the Red River Settlement, Assiniboia, on May 8, 1841. He was educated at St. John's Academy, Winnipeg, under the Right Rev. David Anderson (q.v.); and in 1871 he was elected to represent High Bluff in the first Legislative Assembly of Manitoba. He continued a member of the Assembly until his death. He was appointed minister of public works in the first administration of Manitoba in 1871; he became provincial secretary in 1875, and minister of public works again in 1876; and in 1878 he was called upon, with Joseph Royal (q.v.), to form a government. He was prime minister from 1878 to 1887, when he resigned to become a railway commissioner. He died at Winnipeg, on July 5, 1889. In 1862 he married Elizabeth, daughter of George Setter, of Poplar Point, Manitoba.

[*Can. who was who*, vol.2; *Cyc. Am. biog.*; Rose, *Cyc. Can. biog.* (1888); *Can. parl. comp.*; Dent, *Can. port.*, vol. 3; J. P. Robertson, *Political manual of Manitoba* (Winnipeg, 1887); A. Begg, *History of the north-west* (Toronto, 1894); W.L. Morton, *Manitoba, a history* (rev. ed., Toronto, 1967).]

Norris, Tobias Crawford (1861-1936), prime minister of Manitoba (1915-22), was born in Brampton, Ontario, on September 5, 1861. He went to the North West as a youth, with his parents, and became a farmer. In 1896 he was elected to the Legislative Assembly of Manitoba; in 1909 he became leader of the Liberal opposition; and in 1915 he became prime minister of the province. He was defeated in the general elections of 1922; and in 1927 he resigned the leadership of the Liberal party in Manitoba to contest a seat in the Canadian House of Commons. In 1929 he was appointed a member of the Board of Railway Commissioners for Canada; and he died in Toronto on October 29, 1936. His term of office as prime minister of Manitoba saw the introduction into the province of female suffrage, minimum wage laws, and prohibition.

[*Can. parl. comp.*; Morgan, *Can. men* (1912).]

Northrup, William Barton (1856-1925), lawyer and politician, was born at Belleville, Canada West, on October 19, 1856. He was educated at Upper Canada College and the University of Toronto (B.A., 1877; M.A., 1878), and was called to the Ontario bar in 1878 (K.C., 1902). He practised law in Belleville, Ontario; and from 1892 to 1896 and from 1900 to 1917 he represented East Hastings in the Canadian House of Commons. Though never a minister of the Crown, he was an outstanding member of the Conservative party. In 1918 he was appointed clerk of the House of Commons; but he resigned this position in 1924, and he died at Ottawa, Ontario, on October 22, 1925.

[H. Charlesworth (ed.), *A cyclopaedia of*

Canadian biography (Toronto, 1919); Morgan, *Can. men* (1912); *Can. parl. comp.*]

Norwood, Gilbert (1880-1954), classical scholar, was born in Sheffield, England, on November 23, 1880, and died at Toronto, Ontario, on October 18, 1954. He was educated at St. John's College, Cambridge (B.A., 1903; M.A., 1904), and was elected a fellow of the College in 1903. He taught classics at the University of Manchester from 1903 to 1908, and from 1908 to 1926 was professor of Greek at University College, Cardiff. In 1926 he came to the University of Toronto as professor of Latin in University College; and in 1928 he became director of classical studies, which position he held until his retirement in 1951. He was the author of *The riddle of the Bacchae* (Manchester, 1908), *Greek tragedy* (London, 1921), *Euripides and Shaw, with other essays* (London, 1921), *The art of Terence* (Oxford, 1923), *The writers of Greece* (London, 1925), *The wooden man, with other stories and essays* (New York, 1926), *Greek comedy* (London, 1931), *Plautus and Terence* (New York, 1932), *Spoken in jest* (Toronto, 1938), *Pindar* (Berkeley, Calif., 1945), and *Essays on Euripidean drama* (Berkeley, Calif., 1954). A full bibliography will be found in M. E. White, ed., *Studies in honour of Gilbert Norwood* (Toronto, 1952). In 1933 the University of Wales conferred on him the degree of D.Litt.; and in 1943 he was elected a fellow of the Royal Society of Canada.

[*Proc. Roy. Soc. Can.*, 1955; *Can. who's who*, 1952-54.]

Norwood, Robert Winkworth (1874-1932), clergyman and poet, was born at New Ross, Lunenburg county, Nova Scotia, on March 27, 1874, the son of the Rev. Joseph W. Norwood and Edith, daughter of Capt. Harding. He was educated at King's College, Windsor, Nova Scotia (B.A., 1897; D.C.L., 1921), and was ordained a priest of the Church of England in 1898. He was rector successively of charges in Bridgewater, Nova Scotia, in London, Ontario, in Philadelphia, Pennsylvania, and in New York. He died at New York on September 28, 1932. He was the author of several volumes of poetry: *His lady of the sonnets* (Boston, 1915), *The witch of Endor* (Toronto, 1916), *The piper and the reed* (Toronto, 1917), *The modernists* (New York, 1918), *The man of Kerioth* (New York, 1918), *Bill Boram* (New York, 1921), *Mother and son* (New York, 1925), and *Issa* (New York, 1931). He was also the author of four volumes of prose: *The heresy of Antioch* (New York, 1928), *The steep ascent* (New York, 1928), *The man who dared to be God* (New York, 1929), and *His glorious body* (New York, 1930).

[A. D. Watson, *Robert Norwood* (Toronto, 1924); *Canadian bookman*, 1927 and 1932; *Can. who was who*, vol. 2.]

Notman, William (1826-1891), photographer, was born in Paisley, Scotland, on March 8, 1826, and died in Montreal, Quebec, on November 25, 1891. He came to Canada in 1856, and became the leading photographer in Montreal. He published *Portraits of British Canadians* (3 vols., Montreal, 1865-8), with letterpress by John Fennings Taylor (q.v.).

[*How the fabulous Mr. Notman achieved the impossible* (Maclean's magazine, May 11, 1957); *Encyc. Can.*]

Noyelles de Fleurimont, Nicolas Joseph de (1695-1761), soldier and explorer, was born in Brittany, France, on October 13, 1695. He entered the French army, and came to Canada in 1710. He was commandant at Detroit in 1720, in 1728, and again in 1738-41. In 1743 he was charged with the task of continuing the discoveries of La Vérendrye (q.v.) in the West; and in 1748 he took possession of Fort La Reine, and sent the sons of La Vérendrye (q.v.) to found Fort Bourbon and Fort Pasquia. In 1750 he was recalled, and replaced by Legardeur de St. Pierre (q.v.), and in 1751 he was named town major of Three Rivers. He died at Rochefort, France, on August 16, 1761.

[L. A. Prud'homme, *Les successeurs de la Vérendrye* (Trans. Roy. Soc. Can., 1906); Le Jeune, *Dict. gén.*; *Dict. Can. biog.*, vol. 3.]

Noyes, John Powell (1842-1923), lawyer and local historian, was born at Potton, Brome, Canada East, in 1842, and died in 1923. He was educated at St. Mary's College, Montreal, was called to the bar in 1866 (Q.C., 1879); and practised law in the Eastern Townships. He was the author of *Canadian loyalists and early pioneers in the district of Bedford* (Cowanville, 1901) and *Sketches of some early Shefford pioneers* (Montreal, 1905).

[Morgan, *Can. men* (1912).]

Nursey, Walter R. (1847-1927), author, was born in Crostwick, Norfolk, England, in 1847, the son of the Rev. P. F. Nursey. He emigrated to Canada in 1865, and was successively a farmer, a banker, a civil servant, a fur-trader, and an organizer for the Conservative party. In 1909 he was appointed inspector of public libraries in Ontario; and he died in Toronto on March 14, 1927. He was the author of *The story of Isaac Brock* (Toronto, 1908), and with Alexander Begg (q.v.) joint author of *Ten years in Winnipeg* (Winnipeg, 1879).

[Morgan, *Can. men* (1912).]

Oakes, Forrest (d. 1783), fur-trader, was an English merchant who came to Canada in the earliest days of British rule. He was a partner in the firm of Mackenzie and Oakes in Quebec in 1761; and he was in Montreal in February, 1762, when he ran foul of the soldiers, during the period of military rule, and was tried by court-martial. He is said to have been a son of Sir Hildebrand Oakes (see *Dict. Nat. Biog*.); but this is impossible, though there was evidently some relationship between them. He engaged in the Indian trade; and in 1779 he became one of the parties to the formation of the original North West Company; but his firm was not included in the agreement of 1783-84, for he died in Montreal in 1783. His will is preserved in the Court House at Montreal; and it reveals the fact that he left property in the parish of Handsworth, Staffordshire, England. He left one son, John Meticamish Oakes, evidently a half-breed, who was a minor, and two sisters, Jemima (d. 1809), the wife of Lawrence Ermatinger (q.v.), and Margaret, who had married in 1767 Edward William Gray, afterwards sheriff of Montreal. Another sister, who would appear to have predeceased him, married in 1770 Edward Chinn, an early Indian trader at Michilimackinac.

[A. S. Morton, *Forrest Oakes ... in the North-west* (Trans. Roy. Soc. Can., 1937).]

Oakes, Sir Harry, Bart. (1874-1943), mining executive, was born at Sangerville, Maine, on December 23, 1874, and was educated at Bowdoin College (B.A., 1896). He became interested in mining; and after spending a number of years as a miner and prospector in Alaska, New Zealand, and California, he came to northern Ontario. Here he staked out in 1912 the Tough-Oakes property and what later became the Lake Shore mine. From these mines he derived a large fortune; and for some years he lived on a large estate near Niagara Falls, Ontario. In 1935, however, he removed to Nassau in the Bahamas, reputedly because of the Canadian income tax. At his place near Nassau, he was murdered on July 8, 1943. In 1939, in recognition of his benefactions in England, he was created a baronet of the United Kingdom.

[*Who's who,* 1943; *Can. who's who,* 1938-39; G. Bocca, *The life and death of Sir Harry Oakes* (New York, 1959); B. Moon, *The murdered Midas of Lake Shore* (Maclean's magazine, Sept. 1, 1950); M. Houts, *King's X: Common law and the death of Sir Harry Oakes* (New York, Toronto, 1972).]

Obalski, Joseph (1852-1915), mining engineer, was born in France in 1852, and was educated at L'Ecole des Mines, Paris, France. He came to Canada in 1881, as superintendent of mines under the Quebec government; and he continued in this position until his resignation in 1909. He then became a consulting engineer in Montreal; and he died at Montreal, Quebec, on March 25, 1915. He was a charter member of the Canadian Institute of Mining and Metallurgy, and became its vice-president; and he was the author of *Mines et minéraux de la province de Québec* (Quebec, 1889).

[Morgan, *Can. men* (1912); *Canadian mining bulletin,* April, 1915.]

O'Brien, Arthur Henry (1865-1957), lawyer and bibliographer, was born at Toronto, Ontario, on August 2, 1865, and died there on October 11, 1957. He was educated at Trinity University (B.A., 1887; M.A., 1888), and was called to the bar of Ontario in 1890. From 1908 to 1913 he was law clerk of the House of Commons at Ottawa; in his later days he practised law in Toronto. He compiled several law digests, covering conveyancing, chattel mortgages and bills of sale, fish and game laws, and railway cases; and he was the author of *Haliburton ("Sam Slick"): A sketch and bibliography* (Montreal, 1909).

[Morgan, *Can. men* (1912); *Can. who's who,* 1948.]

O'Brien, Cornelius (1843-1906), Roman Catholic archbishop of Halifax (1882-1906), was born in Prince Edward Island on May 4, 1843. He was educated at St. Dunstan's College, Charlottetown, and at the College of the Propaganda, Rome, Italy, and in 1871 he was ordained a priest of the Roman Catholic Church. From 1871 to 1873 he was a teacher in St. Dunstan's College; from 1873 to 1874 he was principal priest at the cathedral at Charlottetown; and from 1874 to 1882 he was parish priest at Indian River. In 1882 he succeeded Archbishop Hannan (q.v.) as archbishop of Halifax; and he remained in oversight of the see until his death at Halifax on March 9, 1906. In 1882 he was chosen a charter member of the Royal Society of Canada, and in 1896 he was its president. He was the author of *Philosophy of the Bible vindicated* (Charlottetown, 1876), *Mater admirabilis* (Montreal, 1882), a novel entitled *After weary years* (Baltimore, 1885), *Saint Agnes, virgin and martyr* (Halifax, 1887), *Aminta, a modern life drama* (New York, 1890), and *Memoirs of the Right Rev. Edmund Burke* (Ottawa, 1894).

[Katherine Hughes, *Archbishop O'Brien* (Ottawa, 1906); *Dict. nat. biog.*, supp. II; *Can. who was who*, vol. 1; *Cyc. Am. biog.*; *Proc. Roy. Soc. Can.*, 1906; Morgan, *Can. men* (1898); Le Jeune, *Dict. gén.*; A. MacMurchy, *Handbook of Canadian literature* (Toronto, 1906).]

O'Brien, Edward George (1799?-1875), pioneer settler, was born at Woolwich, England, probably on January 8, 1799. He first served as a midshipman in the navy, and then as an officer in the army. About 1830 he came to Canada, and settled at Shanty Bay, on Lake Simcoe, Upper Canada. He became a justice of the peace and a lieutenant-colonel in the militia, and was active in suppressing the rebellion of 1837. He died on September 8, 1875. He married Mary Sophia, daughter of the Rev. Edward Gapper; and by her he had several children.

[W. R. Riddell, *Old province tales* (Toronto, 1920); N. F. Davin, *The Irishman in Canada* (Toronto, 1877); A. F. Hunter, *A history of Simcoe county* (2 vols., Barrie, Ont., 1909); A. S. Miller, *The journals of Mary O'Brien* (Toronto, 1968); *Dict. Can. biog.*, vol. 10.]

O'Brien, Henry (1836-1931), lawyer, was born at Shanty Bay, Upper Canada, in 1836, the third son of Lieut.-Col. E. G. O'Brien (q.v.). He was educated at the Church Grammar School, Toronto, and was called to the bar in 1861 (Q.C., 1899). He practised law in Toronto, and was for many years editor of the *Canadian Law Journal*. He was the founder of the Argonaut Rowing Club, Toronto, and was for sixteen years its president; and he was the first president of the Canadian Association of Amateur Oarsmen. He died at Toronto, Ontario, on September 3, 1931. He was the editor of *The Ontario Division Courts Act* (Toronto, 1880).

[Morgan, *Can. men* (1912).]

O'Brien, James (1836-1903), senator of Canada, was born at Aughnagar, county Tyrone, Ireland, on August 3, 1836. He emigrated to Canada in 1850, and in 1858 entered in Montreal the wholesale clothing and dry goods trade. He built up a successful business; and in 1893 was able to retire with a large fortune. In 1895 he was called to the Senate of Canada; and he sat in the Senate until his death on May 28, 1903.

[Morgan, *Can. men* (1898); *Can. parl. comp.*]

O'Brien, Lucius James (1796-1870), surgeon, was born in Woolwich, England, in 1796, and became a surgeon in the British army. Soon after his brother, Edward George O'Brien (q.v.), he came to Canada in 1832, and settled at Thornhill, Upper Canada. In 1837-38 he was chief military surgeon at Toronto, and from 1845 to 1853 he was professor of medical jurisprudence in King's College (University of Toronto). From 1848 to 1856 he was also editor of the *Patriot* of Toronto. Later, having lost his money, he became secretary to the Hon. William Cayley (q.v.), and obtained an appointment in the office of the receiver-general of Canada. He died in Ottawa, Ontario, on August 14, 1870.

[N. F. Davin, *The Irishman in Canada* (Toronto, 1877); W. Canniff, *The medical profession in Upper Canada* (Toronto, 1894).]

O'Brien, Lucius Richard (1832-1899), president of the Royal Canadian Academy of Arts (1880-90), was born at Shanty Bay, Upper Canada, on August 15, 1832, the son of Lieut.-Col. E. G. O'Brien (q.v.). He was educated at Upper Canada College, and in 1847 entered an architect's office. He became a civil engineer; and also a painter in water-colours. In 1872 he became a member of the Ontario Society of Artists, and from 1873 to 1880 was vice-president of this society. In 1880 he was selected as a charter member of the Royal Canadian Academy of Arts, and he was elected its first president, holding office from 1880 to 1890. Chiefly a landscape artist, he was especially noted for his pictures of scenery in the Rocky Mountains. He died on December 13, 1899. He was twice married, (1) in 1860 to Margaret, eldest daughter of Capt. Andrew St. John of Orillia, Upper Canada; and (2) in 1888 to Katherine Jane, third daughter of the Ven. Archdeacon Brough, of London, Ontario.

[*Cyc. Am. biog.*; Morgan, *Can. men* (1898); Rose, *Cyc. Can. biog.* (1886); E. Morris, *Art in Canada: The early painters* (Toronto, 1906); W. Colgate, *Canadian Art, 1820-1940* (Toronto, 1943); P. Duval, *Canadian Water Colour Painting* (Toronto, 1954).]

O'Brien, Michael John (1851-1940), senator of Canada, was born at Lochaber, Nova Scotia, on September 19, 1851. He became a railway contractor, and played a conspicuous part in building a considerable part of the present mileage of the railway lines of Canada. No fewer than 800 miles of the National Transcontinental Railway were built by him. He played a prominent part in developing the mines of northern Ontario and Quebec; and he became one of Canada's leading capitalists. In 1918, although a Liberal in politics, he was called to the Senate of Canada by the government of Sir Robert Borden (q.v.). He died at Renfrew, Ontario, on November 26, 1940. In 1925 he was created by the Pope a knight commander of St. Gregory the Great.

[*Can. parl. comp.; Can. who's who*, 1936-37.]

O'Brien, Murrough Charles (1868-1955), physician and author, was born in Delhi, India, on May 2, 1868, and died in North Battleford, Saskatchewan, on December 5, 1955. He was educated at Dover College and St. Mary's Hospital Medical School in England, and later completed his medical studies at the Manitoba Medical College (M.D., 1897). He began the practice of medicine and surgery at Dominion City, Manitoba; and, with the exception of some months when he was a medical officer during the First World War, he spent his long life as a country doctor, often visiting patients in outlying places in Manitoba and Saskatchewan on horseback. With R. Tyre, he was the author of an autobiography, *Saddle-bag surgeon* (Toronto, 1954).

[*Encyc. Can.*]

O'Brien, Sir Terence (1830-1903), governor of Newfoundland (1889-96), was born in 1830, and died on February 25, 1903. He was educated at Sandhurst, and entered the British Army. He served in India during the Indian mutiny, and remained in India until 1867, when he was appointed inspector-general of police at Mauritius. From 1881 to 1889 he was governor of Heligoland, and from 1889 to 1896 governor of Newfoundland. He was created a K.C.M.G. in 1887.

[*Who was who*, 1897-1915; *Annual register*, 1903; *Encyc. Can.*]

O'Brien, William Edward (1831-1914), politician, was born at Thornhill, Upper Canada, on March 10, 1831, the eldest son of Lieut.-Col. E. G. O'Brien (q.v.). He was educated at Upper Canada College; and became a farmer. He was called to the bar of Upper Canada in 1874, but never practised law. In 1882 he was elected to represent Muskoka in the Canadian House of Commons as a Conservative, and he retained his seat until 1896. He was a prominent member of the Equal Rights Association, and was one of the "noble thirteen" who voted for the disallowance of the Jesuits' Estates Act in 1888. He opposed also the Manitoba School Bill of the Tupper government in 1896. He died at Shanty Bay, Ontario, on December 22, 1914. In 1864 he married Elizabeth, only daughter of Col. R. R. Loring, and widow of J. F. Harris, London, Ontario. In 1882 he became lieutenant-colonel

commanding the 35th Battalion (Simcoe Foresters) of the Canadian militia; and during the North West Rebellion of 1885 he commanded the York and Simcoe regiment.

[Morgan, *Can. men* (1912); *Can. parl. comp.*]

O'Callaghan, Edmund Bailey (1797-1880), journalist and historian, was born at Mallow, Ireland, on February 27, 1797. He was educated in Paris, France, and came to Canada in 1823. He studied medicine at Quebec, Lower Canada, and was admitted to practice in 1827. From 1834 to 1837 he represented Yamaska in the Legislative Assembly of Lower Canada, and during the same period he was the editor of the Montreal *Vindicator*, the organ of the Society of Friends of Ireland. He was actively implicated in the rebellion of 1837, and escaped to the United States. He there became the historian and archivist of the state of New York. In this capacity, he compiled *The documentary history of the state of New York* (4 vols., Albany, 1850-51), and edited *Documents relating to the colonial history of the state of New York* (11 vols., 1856-61). He published also *The late session of the provincial parliament of Lower Canada* (Montreal, 1836), *Jesuit relations of discoveries and other occurrences* (pamphlet, New York, 1847; French translation, Montreal, 1850), and *The history of the New Netherlands* (New York, 1846; 2nd ed., 2 vols., 1848). He died in New York on May 29, 1880.

[F. S. Guy, *Edmund Bailey O'Callaghan* (Washington, D.C., 1934); *Dict. nat. biog.*; *Cyc. Am. biog.*; *Dom. ann. reg.*, 1880-81; *Magazine of American history*, July, 1880; Le Jeune, *Dict. gén.*; *Can. who was who*, vol. 2.; *Dict. Can. biog.*, vol. 10.]

O'Connor, Dennis (1841-1911), Roman Catholic archbishop of Toronto (1899-1908), was born in the township of Pickering, Upper Canada, on March 28, 1841. He was educated at St. Michael's College, Toronto, and in France; and was ordained a priest of the Roman Catholic Church in 1863. From 1863 to 1870 he was a professor in St. Michael's College, Toronto, and from 1870 to 1890 he was superior of L'Assomption College, Sandwich, Ontario. In 1890 he was consecrated bishop of London, Ontario; and in 1899 he became third archbishop of Toronto. He retired from the archiepiscopate in 1908, and he died at Toronto, Ontario, on June 30, 1911.

[*Can. who was who*, vol. 1; Morgan, *Can. men* (1912).]

O'Connor, Frank P. (1885-1939), senator of Canada, was born at Deseronto, Ontario, on April 9, 1885. He founded in 1913 the Laura Secord Candy Shops, Ltd., a highly successful business, of which he remained president. In 1935 he was called to the Senate of Canada; and he became an influential figure in the

Liberal party. He died at Toronto, Ontario, on August 21, 1939.

[*Can. who's who*, 1936-37; *Can. parl. comp.*]

O'Connor, John (1824-1887), politician and jurist, was born in January, 1824, at Boston, Massachusetts. His parents, who had come to the United States in 1823, removed to Canada in 1828, and settled in Essex county, Upper Canada. He was called to the bar of Upper Canada in 1854 (Q.C., 1872). He sat for Essex in the Legislative Assembly of Canada from 1863 to 1864, and in the Canadian House of Commons from 1867 to 1874. In 1878 he was elected to the Commons for Russell, and he represented this constituency until 1884. In 1873 he was president of the privy council and in 1873 he was minister of inland revenue, and then postmaster-general, in the Macdonald government; in 1878 he again became president of the council; in 1880 he was re-appointed postmaster-general; and later in the same year he became secretary of state. In 1884 he was appointed a puisne judge of the Court of Queen's Bench in Ontario; and he sat on the bench until his death at Cobourg, Ontario, on November 3, 1887. In 1849 he married Mary, daughter of Richard Barrett, formerly of Killarney, Ireland; and by her he had nine children. He was the author of *Letters addressed to the governor-general on the subject of Fenianism* (1870).

[D. B. Read, *Lives of the judges* (Toronto, 1888); *Cyc. Am. biog.*; Rose, *Cyc. Can. biog.* (1888); Dent, *Can. port*, vol. 4; *Canadian biographical dictionary*, Ontario vol. (Toronto, 1880); N. F. Davin, *The Irishman in Canada* (Toronto, 1877).]

O'Connor, Richard Alphonsus (1838-1913), Roman Catholic bishop of Peterborough (1889-1913), was born at Listowel, county Kerry, Ireland, on April 15, 1838; and came to Canada with his parents as a child. He was educated at St. Michael's College, Toronto, and the Grand Seminary, Montreal; and was ordained a priest in 1861. He was successively parish priest at the Gore of Toronto, at Niagara Falls, and at Adjala, Ontario; and in 1870 he became dean of Barrie. He was raised to the episcopacy as bishop of Peterborough in 1889; and he retained oversight of this see until his death at Peterborough, Ontario, on January 23, 1913.

[Morgan, *Can. men* (1912).]

Odell, Jonathan (1737-1818), clergyman, physician, author, and provincial secretary of New Brunswick (1784-1818), was born in Newark, New Jersey, on September 25, 1737, the son of John Odell and Temperance, daughter of Jonathan Dickinson, president of Princeton College. He was educated at the College of New Jersey, and then at Newark; and after graduating (M.A., 1754) he studied

medicine, and became a surgeon in the British army. While in the West Indies, he resigned his commission; and went to England to study for holy orders. He was ordained deacon in 1766 and priest in 1767, and was appointed rector in Burlington, New Jersey. After the American Revolution, in which he served as a captain in a loyal New Jersey regiment, he accompanied Sir Guy Carleton (q.v.) to England; and in 1784 he came out to New Brunswick, where he was appointed provincial secretary, registrar of records, and clerk of the council. These offices he held continuously until 1812, when his only son, William Franklin (q.v.), succeeded him. He died in Fredericton, New Brunswick, on November 25, 1818. He married Anne DeCou on May 6, 1772; and by her he had one son and three daughters. He wrote a number of patriotic verses which were very popular among the Loyalists, and were collected and published by Winthrop Sargent under the title *Loyal verses of Stansbury and Odell* (Albany, N.Y. 1860).

[*Dict. Am. biog.*; *Cyc. Am. biog.*; W. G. MacFarlane, *New Brunswick bibliography* (Saint John, N.B., 1895); J. W. Lawrence, *The judges of New Brunswick* (Saint John, N.B., 1907); M. A. Pool (comp.), *Odell genealogy* (Monroe, Wis., 1935).]

Odell, William Franklin (1774-1844), provincial secretary of New Brunswick (1812-44), was born in Burlington, New Jersey, on October 19, 1774, the only son of the Rev. Jonathan Odell (q.v.) and Anne DeCou. He studied law, and was called to the bar of New Brunswick in 1806. He succeeded his father as provincial secretary of New Brunswick in 1812, and he held this office for thirty-two years until his death. In 1817 he was appointed one of the commissioners to inquire into the boundary between New Brunswick and the United States. He died at Fredericton, New Brunswick, on December 25, 1844. He married Elizabeth, daughter of the Rev. Elisha Newell, of New Jersey; and by her he had three daughters and one son.

[J. W. Lawrence, *Judges of New Brunswick and their times* (Saint John, N.B., 1907); *Cyc. Am. biog.*; M. A. Pool (comp.), *Odell genealogy* (Monroe, Wis., 1935).]

Odell, William Hunter (1811-1891), senator of Canada, was born at Fredericton, New Brunswick, on November 26, 1811, the only son of William Franklin Odell (q.v.). He was educated at King's College, Fredericton (B.A., 1832), and in 1838 was called to the bar of New Brunswick. The same year he was appointed deputy provincial secretary, registrar, and clerk of the executive council; and in 1847 he was made a judge of the Court of Common Pleas in New Brunswick. From 1850 to 1867 he was a member of the Legislative Council of the province; and in 1865-66 he was postmaster-general in the government formed in opposition to Confederation. In 1867 he was appointed by royal proclamation a senator of the Dominion of Canada; and he sat in the Senate until his death, at Halifax, Nova Scotia, on July 26, 1891. He married the eldest daughter of the Hon. Henry Bliss, of Halifax.

[J. W. Lawrence, *The judges of New Brunswick and their times* (Saint John, N.B., 1907); *Can. who was who*, vol. 1; *Cyc. Am. biog.*; *Can. parl. comp.*; M. A. Pool (comp.), *Odell genealogy* (Monroe, Wis., 1935).]

O'Donel, James Louis (1737-1811), first Roman Catholic bishop of Newfoundland, was born in Tipperary, Ireland, in 1737, and died at Waterford, Ireland, on April 15, 1811. He entered the Franciscan order; and in 1784 he was appointed prefect apostolic of Newfoundland, and in 1796 bishop. He returned to Ireland on his retirement in 1806.

[*Newfoundland supp.*; *Encyc. Can.*]

O'Donnell, John Harrison (1844-1912), physician and author, was born at Simcoe, Canada West, in 1844. He went to Manitoba in 1869, and from 1871 to 1875 he was a member of the Legislative Council of Manitoba. He graduated from the medical school of Trinity University, Toronto, with the degree of M.D. in 1888; and he practised medicine for many years in Winnipeg, Manitoba. He died at Winnipeg, Manitoba, on October 26, 1912. He was the author of *Manitoba as I saw it* (Toronto, 1909).

[Morgan, *Can. men* (1912); *Can. parl. comp.*]

O'Donoghue, William B. (1843-1878), rebel, was born in 1843 in county Sligo, Ireland. He was, at the outbreak of the Red River Rebellion of 1869-70, a teacher in St. Boniface College, Winnipeg. He was "secretary to the treasury" in Riel's provisional government; and on the arrival of the troops he escaped to the United States. He was not included in the amnesty granted to Riel (q.v.) and Lépine (q.v.), on account of his supposed connection with a projected Fenian invasion of Manitoba; but the clemency of the Crown was extended to him in 1877. He died at St. Paul, Minnesota, on March 16, 1878.

[J. P. Robertson, *Political manual of Manitoba* (Winnipeg, 1887); *Dom. ann. reg.*, 1878; A. Begg, *The creation of Manitoba* (Toronto, 1871); *Can. who was who*, vol. 2; Le Jeune, *Dict. gén.*; *Dict. Can. biog.*, vol. 10.]

O'Donohue, John (1824-1902), senator of Canada, was born at Tuam, Galway, Ireland, on April 18, 1824. He emigrated to Canada in 1839, and engaged in mercantile pursuits in Toronto. He studied law, and was called to the bar in Ontario in 1869 (Q.C., 1880). In 1874 he was elected to represent Toronto East in the Canadian House of Commons, but was unseated on petition, and defeated. In 1882 he was called to the Senate of Canada; and he sat in this House until his death on December 7, 1902. In 1848 he married Charlotte Josephine, daughter of Dr. Bradley, of Toronto.

[Morgan, *Can. men* (1898); *Can. parl. comp.*; *Cyc. Am. biog.*]

Ogden, Charles Richard (1791-1866), attorney-general of Lower Canada (1833-42), was born on February 6, 1791, the son of the Hon. Isaac Ogden (q.v.) and Sarah Hanson. He was educated at Three Rivers and at Montreal, and he was called to the bar of Lower Canada in 1812 (K.C., 1816). From 1814 to 1824, and from 1830 to 1833, he represented Three Rivers in the Legislative Assembly of Lower Canada; in 1823 he was appointed solicitor-general of Lower Canada, and in 1833 attorney-general. As such it was his duty to deal with the rebels of 1837 and 1838; and he incurred, on account of his activity during this period, the hostility of the French Canadians. In 1840 he was appointed a member of the Special Council of Lower Canada; and in 1841 he countersigned, as attorney-general, the proclamation bringing into effect the union of Upper and Lower Canada. In 1841 he was again elected to represent Three Rivers in the Legislative Assembly; and he entered the first government of the Union as attorney-general for Lower Canada. In 1842, however, while he was on leave of absence, the government resigned; and though he protested that he had been appointed "during good behaviour", and not "during pleasure", he ceased to be attorney-general — the first victim of the new theory of responsible government. In 1844 he went to live in England, and was called to the English bar. He eventually obtained an appointment as attorney-general of the Isle of Man, and later, in 1857, as district registrar at Liverpool. Both these offices he held until his death in February, 1866. He was twice married, (1) to Mary, daughter of General Coffin, and (2) to Susan, daughter of Isaac Winslow Clarke. By his second wife he had four sons and one daughter.

[W. Ogden Wheeler, *The Odgen family in America* (Philadelphia, 1907); Taylor, *Brit. Am.*, vol. 3; J. C. Dent, *The last forty years* (2 vols., Toronto, 1881); R. Christie, *History of Lower Canada* (6 vols., Quebec and Montreal, 1848-56).]

Ogden, Isaac (1739-1824), jurist, was born in New Jersey in 1739, the son of the Hon. David Ogden. During the American Revolution he adhered to the loyalist cause, and the property of his family was confiscated. He went to England, on the evacuation of New York, in 1783; and in 1788 came to Canada. Here he was appointed a judge of the Admiralty Court at Quebec. In 1796 he became a puisne judge of the Court of King's Bench at

Montreal; and he retained this post until failing health compelled his resignation in 1818. He died in England in 1824.

[W. Ogden Wheeler, *The Ogden family in America* (Philadelphia, 1907); L. Sabine, *American loyalists* (Boston, 1847).]

Ogden, Peter Skene (1794-1854), fur-trader, was born in Quebec, Lower Canada, in 1794, the son of the Hon. Isaac Ogden (q.v.) and Sarah Hanson. He entered the service of the North West Company as a clerk in 1811; and from 1811 to 1818 he was stationed at Isle à la Crosse. He was transferred to the Columbia department in 1818; and in 1820 he was made a partner of the Company. In 1823, after the union of 1821, he was given the rank of a chief trader in the Hudson's Bay Company; and in 1835 he became a chief factor. He spent most of his life, after 1818, on the Pacific slope; and he died near Oregon City on September 27, 1854. It has been said that he was the anonymous author of *Traits of American Indian life and character* (London, 1853); but this is not certain. His *Snake country journals* have been edited by E. E. Rich and A. M. Johnson for the Hudson's Bay Record Society (London, 1950).

[T. C. Elliott, *Peter Skene Ogden* (Quarterly of the Oregon Historical Society, 1910); E. E. Rich (ed.), *Peter Skene Ogden's Snake country journals, 1824-25 and 1825-26* (London, 1950); Archie Binns, *Peter Skene Ogden, fur trader* (1967).]

Ogden, Uzziel (1828-1910), physician, was born in Toronto township, Peel county, Upper Canada, on March 6, 1828. He studied medicine under Dr. John Rolph (q.v.), and was licensed to practise medicine in 1849. He practised medicine in Toronto, and in 1855 was appointed professor of midwifery in the Toronto School of Medicine. In 1887 he became professor of gynaecology in the University of Toronto; and he was the founder of the *Canadian Journal of Medical Science*. He died in Toronto, Ontario, on January 4, 1910.

[(Morgan, *Can. men* (1898).]

Ogden, William Winslow (1837-1915), physician, was born in Toronto township, Peel county, Upper Canada, on July 3, 1837, a brother of Dr. Uzziel Ogden (q.v.); and was educated at the University of Toronto (M.B., 1860) and at Victoria University (M.D., 1878). He practised medicine in Toronto; and from 1887 to 1912 was professor of forensic medicine in the University of Toronto. He was also for forty-four years a member of the Toronto school board, and in 1908-09 was its chairman. He died at Toronto, Ontario, on April 22, 1915.

[Morgan, *Can. men* (1912).]

Ogilvie, Alexander Walker (1829-1902), senator of Canada, was born at St. Michel,

near Montreal, Lower Canada, on May 7, 1829, the son of Alexander Ogilvie. In 1854 he founded the firm of A. W. Ogilvie and Co., millers and grain merchants. From 1867 to 1871, and from 1875 to 1878, he represented Montreal West in the Legislative Assembly of Quebec; and in 1881 he was called to the Senate of Canada. He sat in the Senate until shortly before his death in Montreal, on March 31, 1902. In 1854 he married Sarah, daughter of William Leney, of Longue Pointe; and by her he had several children.

[J. A. Gemmill, *The Ogilvies of Montreal* (Montreal, 1904); *Can. who was who*, vol. 1; Morgan, *Can. men* (1898); Rose, *Cyc. Can. biog.* (1888); *Cyc. Am. biog.*; *Can. parl. comp.*]

Ogilvie, James (1741?-1813), administrator of Cape Breton (1797-99), was born about 1741, and entered the British army in 1757. He rose in the army until he reached in 1803 the rank of general; and from 1790 to 1797 he was in command of the British troops at Halifax. From 1797 to 1799 he was also civil administrator of Cape Breton, which was at that time a province separate from Nova Scotia. He died on February 24, 1813.

[R. Brown, *History of the island of Cape Breton* (London, 1869); Le Jeune, *Dict. gén.*]

Ogilvie, John (1722-1774), clergyman, was born in New York in 1722, and was educated at Yale University (B.A., 1748; M.A., 1751). He was ordained a priest of the Church of England, and became a chaplain with the colonial forces in the Seven Years' War. From 1760 to 1764 he was stationed at Montreal, and he was the first Protestant clergyman in Montreal. His register of births, deaths, and marriages in Montreal from 1760 to 1763 is still in existence. He died in New York on November 26, 1774.

[A. H. Young, *The Reverend John Ogilvie* (Ont. Hist. Soc., papers and records, 1925); *Bull. rech. hist.*, 1936.]

Ogilvie, William (1846-1912), commissioner of the Yukon (1898-1901), was born at Ottawa, Upper Canada, on April 7, 1846, the son of James Ogilvie and Margaret Halliday. He was educated in Ottawa, and in 1869 was admitted to practice as a provincial and Dominion land surveyor. Between 1875 and 1898 he carried out many surveys and explorations in the Canadian West, and notably in the Mackenzie River and Yukon districts. He was in the Yukon Territory at the time of the "gold rush" of 1898; and from 1898 to 1901 he was commissioner in the Yukon for the Dominion government. He died in Winnipeg on November 13, 1912. His reminiscences were published posthumously under the title *Early days on the Yukon* (Toronto, 1913).

[Morgan, *Can. men* (1912); *Can. who's who*, 1910.]

Ogilvie, William Watson (1835-1900), miller, was born at Côte St. Michel, near Montreal, Lower Canada, on February 14, 1835, the younger brother of the Hon. A. W. Ogilvie (q.v.). He was educated at the Montreal High School; and in 1860 he was taken into the firm of A. W. Ogilvie and Co. as a junior partner. After the retirement of A. W. Ogilvie and the death of John Ogilvie in 1888, he succeeded as head of the business and became "the largest individual miller in the world". He died at Montreal, Quebec, on January 12, 1900.

[J. A. Gemmill (ed.), *The Ogilvies of Montreal* (Montreal, 1904); Morgan, *Can. men* (1898); *Can. who was who*, vol. 1.]

Ogilvy, John (1769?-1819), merchant, was born in Scotland about 1769. He came to Canada about 1790, and became a partner in the firm of Parker, Gerrard, and Ogilvy. This was the firm that joined with Forsyth, Richardson, and Co. to form the XY Company, and John McDonald of Garth (q.v.) says in his autobiography that in 1798 John Ogilvy was "at the head of the XY Co." He signed the agreement of 1804, by which the XY and North West companies were amalgamated; and thus acquired in the North West Company an indirect interest. In 1817 he was appointed a commissioner, under the Treaty of Ghent, for determining the boundaries of British North America; and he died, while engaged in this capacity, at Sandwich, Upper Canada, on September 28, 1819. A portrait of him is in the McCord National Museum, in Montreal.

[W. S. Wallace (ed.), *Documents relating to the North West Company* (Toronto: The Champlain Society, 1934).]

O'Grady, Standish (*fl.* 1793-1841), poet, was the author of an early volume of Canadian poetry, entitled *The emigrant* (Montreal, 1841). The author describes himself on the title-page as a graduate of Trinity College, Dublin; and in his notes he says that he was a class-mate at Trinity College of the famous Robert Emmet. But there is in G. D. Burtchaell and T. U. Sadleir (eds.), *Alumni Dublinenses* (London, 1924), no Standish O'Grady who graduated from Trinity College at the same period as Robert Emmet, though there were several of that name who graduated later. The author says in his notes that he had been a Protestant clergyman in Ireland, had come to Canada in 1836, and had tried farming near Sorel, but with disastrous results. After the publication of his book, he disappears from view.

[C. C. James, *A bibliography of Canadian poetry* (Toronto, 1899).]

O'Grady, William John (d. 1840), priest and journalist, was born in Ireland, and was ordained a priest of the Roman Catholic Church in the diocese of Cork. He went to Brazil with a party of Irish immigrants; and later he came to Upper Canada in 1828. He was given charge of the mission at York (Toronto), but he came into conflict with the bishops, and he became one of the leaders of the advanced wing of the Reform party. In 1832 he became the editor of the *Canadian Correspondent*; and in 1834 this paper was merged with W. L. Mackenzie's *Colonial Advocate*, under the name of *Correspondent and Advocate*. O'Grady died in Whitby, Upper Canada, in 1840.

[E. Kelly, *The story of St. Paul's parish, Toronto* (Toronto, 1922).]

O'Hagan, Thomas (1855-1939), educationist, journalist, and poet, was born near Toronto, Canada West, on March 6, 1855. He was educated at St. Michael's College, Toronto, at the University of Ottawa (B.A. 1882; M.A., 1885), and at Syracuse University (Ph. D., 1889). He became a school-teacher, and taught in many separate Roman Catholic schools in the province of Ontario, as well as in several secondary schools. From 1910 to 1913 he was editor of the *New World* in Chicago; but he returned to Canada later, and devoted his later years to writing. He died in Toronto, unmarried, on March 2, 1939. He was the author of *A gate of flowers* (Toronto, 1887), *In dreamland, and other poems* (Toronto, 1893), *Songs of the settlement and other poems* (Toronto, 1899), *Studies in poetry* (Boston, 1900), *Canadian essays* (Toronto, 1901), *Essays, literary, critical, and historical* (Toronto, 1909), *Chats by the fireside* (Somerset, Ohio, 1911), *In the heart of the meadow* (Toronto, 1914), *Essays on Catholic life* (Baltimore, Md., 1916), *Songs of heroic days* (Toronto, 1916), *Collected poems* (Toronto, 1922), *With staff and scrip* (Toronto, 1924), *Dean Harris* (Toronto, 1924), *The genesis of Christian art* (New York, 1926), *Intimacies in Canadian life and letters* (Ottawa, 1927), *Spain and her daughters* (Toronto, 1931), and *What Shakespeare is not* (Toronto, 1936).

[*Can. who's who*, 1936-37; *Who's who among North American authors*, vol. 7; *Who was who in America*; Morgan, *Can. men* (1912).]

O'Hanly, John Lawrence Power (1829-1912), civil engineer and author, was born at Waterford, Ireland, on June 24, 1829, the son of Patrick O'Hanly and Bridget Power. He came to Canada as a young man, and became a land surveyor and civil engineer. He was employed on the Intercolonial Railway, the Southern Railway, the Canadian Pacific Railway, the Ottawa and Gatineau Railway, and the Ontario Pacific Railway; and on the Ontario and Quebec boundary survey, and on surveys in Manitoba and the North-West. He died at Ottawa on March 22, 1912. He was the author of *The Intercolonial Railway* (Ottawa,

1868), and *The political standing of Irish Catholics in Canada* (Ottawa, 1872).

[Morgan, *Can. men* (1912).]

O'Higgins, Harvey Jerrold (1876-1929), author, was born at London, Ontario, on November 14, 1876. He was educated at the University of Toronto, but did not graduate. He was at first a journalist in Toronto; but he soon obtained an entrée into the best American periodicals, and he then removed to the United States. He died at Martinsville, New Jersey, on February 28, 1929. His chief publications were *The smoke-eaters* (New York, 1905), *Don-o'-dreams* (New York, 1906), *A grand army man* (New York, 1908), *Old clinkers* (Boston, 1909), *The adventures of detective Barney* (New York, 1915), *The secret springs* (New York, 1920), *Some distinguished Americans* (New York, 1922), *Julie Crane* (New York, 1924), and *Clara Barron* (New York, 1926). He collaborated also in a number of works — with Judge B. Lindsey in *The beast* (New York, 1910), with F. J. Cannon in *Under the prophet in Utah* (New York, 1911), with Judge Lindsey in *The doughboy's religion* (New York, 1920), with E. H. Reade in *The American mind in action* (New York, 1924), and with Harriet Ford in the following plays: *On the hiring line* (New York, 1909), *The Argyle case* (1912), *The dummy* (1913), *Polygamy* (1914), and *Main street* (1921).

[*Who was who in America*; *Who's who among North American authors*, vol. 4; Morgan, *Can. men* (1912).]

O'Keefe, Eugene (1827-1913), brewer and banker, was born at Bandon, county Cork, Ireland, on December 10, 1827, and came to Upper Canada with his parents in 1832. He was educated in Toronto; and for some years was employed as a book-keeper in the Toronto Savings Bank. In 1861 he founded the Victoria Brewery, which became the O'Keefe Brewery Company; and of this company he became president. In 1904 he was elected president of the Home Bank; and he continued in this position until his death, at Toronto, Ontario, on September 30, 1913. In recognition of his benefactions, he was appointed in 1909 a private chamberlain to the Pope.

[Morgan, *Can. men* (1912).]

Oldright, William (d. 1917), physician and educationist, was born at St. Kitts, West Indies; and was educated at the University of Toronto (B.A., 1863; M.B., 1865; M.D., 1867). He practised medicine in Toronto, Ontario; and from 1887 to 1910 he was professor of hygiene in the medical faculty of the University of Toronto. He died at Chicago, Ill., on January 4, 1917.

[Morgan, *Can. men* (1912).]

O'Leary, Frank M. (1894-1963), commission merchant, was born in St. John's, New-

foundland, October 10, 1894, and educated at St. Patrick's Hall School in St. John's. He served overseas in the First World War, and in the Second World War was director of civil defence at St. John's. He was president of F. M. O'Leary Limited, a building supplies firm and vice-president of Newfoundland Fire and General Insurance. He was director of Eastern Provincial Airways, United Towns Electric Company, Avalon Telephone Company, and Eastern Trust. He died September 2, 1963, at St. John's, Newfoundland.

[Metropolitan Toronto Library Board, *Biographical scrapbooks*, vol. 21.]

O'Leary, Henry Joseph (1879-1938), Roman Catholic archbishop of Edmonton, was born at Richibucto, New Brunswick, on March 13, 1879. He was educated at the Canadian College in Rome, Italy, was ordained a priest in 1901, and in 1902 received the degree of D.D. from the University of the Propaganda. In 1913 he was made bishop of Charlottetown; and in 1920 archbishop of Edmonton. He died at Victoria, British Columbia, on March 5, 1938.

[G. Brassard, *Armorial des évêques du Canada* (Montreal, 1940); *Can. who's who*, 1936-37; Morgan, *Can. men* (1912).]

O'Leary, Thomas (1842-1925), museum curator, was born at Quebec, Canada East, on May 15, 1842. In 1894 he was appointed curator of the Château de Ramezay at Montreal; and he continued in this post until his death at Montreal on July 24, 1925. He published a guide to the museum and portrait gallery of the Château de Ramezay, of which repeated editions were published; and he contributed several historical papers to the *Journal* of the Antiquarian and Numismatic Society of Montreal.

[P. G. Roy, *Fils de Québec*, vol. 4 (Lévis, Que., 1933).]

Oleson, Tryggvi Julius (1912-1963), historian, was born at Glenboro, Manitoba, on May 4, 1912. He was educated at the University of Manitoba (B.A., 1934; M.A., 1936), the University of Toronto (Ph.D., 1950), and the Pontifical Institute of Mediaeval Studies (Toronto). He held teaching posts at the University of British Columbia and the University of Manitoba. He was a member of the Mediaeval Academy and the Renaissance Society of America, and fellow of the Royal Society of Canada. He died October 9, 1963, at Winnipeg, Manitoba. He was author of *The Witenagemot in the reign of Edward the Confessor* (London, 1955), and *Early voyages and northern approaches: A history of Canada from 1000 to 1632* (Toronto, 1964).

[*Can. hist. rev.*, vol. XLV (1964).]

Olier de Verneuil, Jean Jacques (1608-1657), priest, was born in Paris, France, on

September 20, 1608. He was for many years *curé* of the parish of St. Sulpice in Paris; and in 1640 he took a leading part in forming the company which established the Sulpician settlement at Montreal. He continued to be interested in the missions of Canada until his death, which took place in Paris on April 2, 1657; and his letters, which contain a narrative of the Sulpician missions in Canada, were published posthumously under the title, *Lettres et correspondance du Père Olier de Verneuil sur les établissements de la foi dans la Nouvelle France* (Paris, 1674).

[Abbé Faillon, *La vie et les oeuvres de Jean Jacques Olier de Verneuil* (Paris, 1855); P. Pourrat, *Jean Jacques Olier* (Paris, 1932); *Cyc. Am. biog.*; Le Jeune, *Dict. gén.*]

Oliver, Edmund Henry (1882-1935), educationist and historian, was born at Eberts, Kent county, Ontario, on February 8, 1882, and was educated at the University of Toronto (B.A., 1902; M.A., 1903) and at Columbia University (Ph.D., 1905). From 1905 to 1909 he was lecturer in history in McMaster University, Toronto; from 1909 to 1914 he was professor of history and economics in the University of Saskatchewan; and from 1914 to his death he was principal of St. Andrew's College, Saskatoon. In 1930 he was elected moderator of the United Church of Canada. He died at Round Lake, Saskatchewan, on July 11, 1935. He was a doctor of divinity of Emmanuel College, Toronto, of Queen's University, Kingston, and of the Union College of British Columbia. In 1921 he was elected a fellow of the Royal Society of Canada, and in 1934 president of Section Two. He was the author of *Roman economic conditions* (Toronto, 1907), *The Canadian North West, its early development and legislative records* (2 vols., Ottawa, 1914), *The winning of the frontier* (Toronto, 1930), *The social achievements of the Christian church* (Toronto, 1930), *Tracts for difficult times* (New York, 1933), and a series of papers on the history of Saskatchewan in the *Transactions* of the Royal Society of Canada.

[C. Mackinnon, *Life of Principal Oliver* (Toronto, 1936); *Proc. Roy. Soc. Can.*, 1936; Morgan, *Can. men* (1912).]

Oliver, Frank (1853-1933), minister of the interior for Canada (1905-11), was born in Peel county, Ontario, in 1853, the son of Allan Bowsfield. As a young man, he adopted his mother's maiden name, and went west in 1873 to Winnipeg, and in 1876 to Edmonton, where he founded the *Edmonton Bulletin* in 1880. Of this journal he remained the proprietor until 1923. He was elected to the North West Council in 1883 and to the Legislative Assembly of the North West Territories; and he represented first Alberta, and then Edmonton, in the Canadian House of Commons from 1896 to 1917. From 1905 to 1911 he was minister of the interior in the Laurier administration. From

1923 to 1928 he was a member of the Board of Railway Commissioners for Canada. He died at Ottawa on March 31, 1933. In 1881 he married Harriet, daughter of Thomas Dunlop, of Prairie Grove, Manitoba; and by her he had one son and four daughters. In 1930 he was made an LL.D. of the University of Alberta.

[*Can. parl. comp.*; Morgan, *Can. men* (1912); *Who was who*, 1929-40.]

Oliver, John (1856-1927), prime minister of British Columbia (1918-27), was born at Hartington, Derbyshire, England, on July 31, 1856, the son of Robert Oliver and Emma Lomas. He came to Canada with his parents in 1870; and in 1877 he went to British Columbia, where he became a rancher. He was elected to represent Delta in the Legislative Assembly of British Columbia in 1900, and was chosen leader of the Liberal opposition in 1905. He was defeated in 1909, and did not return to the legislature until 1916, when he became minister of railways and agriculture in the Brewster cabinet. On the death of Brewster (q.v.) in 1918, he succeeded to the prime-ministry; and he retained power until his death at Victoria, British Columbia, on August 17, 1927. In 1886 he married Elizabeth Woodward, of Mud Bay, British Columbia, and by her he had five sons and three daughters.

[James Morton, *Honest John Oliver* (London, 1933); *Can. parl. comp.*; H. Charlesworth (ed.) *A cyclopaedia of Canadian biography* (Toronto, 1919); Morgan, *Can. men* (1912).]

Oliver, William (1848-1937), mariner and missionary, was born at Bishopton on the Clyde, Scotland, on March 19, 1848. He became a sailor, and by the age of thirty-five had secured his master's certificate. He came to British Columbia about 1880; and for nearly half a century he was a leading figure in the Methodist (later United) Church marine missions, as the builder and skipper of a succession of mission boats. He died on January 3, 1937, in New Westminster, B.C.

[W. H. Morris, *Captain William Oliver, a fisher of men* (Trujillo, Peru, 1941); R. C. Scott, *My captain Oliver* (Toronto, 1947).]

Olivier, Louis Auguste (1816-1881), jurist and author, was born at Berthier-en-haut, Lower Canada, in 1816. He was called to the bar of Lower Canada in 1839 (Q.C., 1864). From 1863 to 1867 he represented the Lanaudière division in the Legislative Council of Canada; and in 1867 he was called to the Senate of Canada. In 1873 he was appointed a judge of the Superior Court of Quebec for the district of Joliette; and he sat in this court until his death, at Joliette, Quebec, on September 18, 1881. He contributed to *Le répertoire national* (Montreal, 1848-50) an *Essai sur la littérature du Canada* and some poetry.

[P. E. Roy, *L. A. Olivier* (Lévis, Que.,

1891); *Can. parl. comp.*; *Bull. rech. hist.*, 1901; Morgan, *Bib. can.*; P. G. Roy, *Les juges de la province de Québec* (Quebec, 1933).]

Ollivier, Nazaire Nicolas (1860-1898), lawyer and politician, was born at St. Nicolas, Canada East, in 1860, and was educated at Laval University. He was called to the bar of Quebec in 1888; and in 1897 he was elected to represent Lévis in the Legislative Assembly of Quebec. After sitting for this constituency for only a few months, he died suddenly at Lévis, Quebec, on May 2, 1898. He was the author of *De la nullité des contrats* (Quebec, 1890).

[P. G. Roy, *Dates Lévisiennes*, vol. 4 (Lévis, Que., 1933).]

O'Malley, Andrew (1863-1921), priest and author, was born in Rochester, New York, on November 8, 1863; and was educated at St. Michael's College, Toronto, and at the Grand Seminary, Montreal. He was ordained a priest of the Roman Catholic Church in 1893; and after serving in several parishes in Ontario, he became in 1915 pastor of Barrie, Ontario, and dean. He died at Toronto, Ontario, on November 8, 1921. He was the author of *Essays and lectures* (Barrie, Ont., 1916) and a poem, *Joan of Arc* (Barrie, Ont., 1920).

[E. Kelly, *The story of St. Paul's parish, Toronto* (Toronto, 1922).]

O'Meara, Arthur Eugene (1861?-1928), missionary, was born at Georgetown, Canada West, about 1861, the son of the Rev. Canon F. A. O'Meara (q.v.). He was educated at the University of Toronto (B.A., 1883), and was called to the bar of Ontario in 1886. He practised law in Toronto for some years; but in 1906 he was ordained a priest of the Church of England, and he became a missionary among the Indians of British Columbia. He died at Chilliwack, British Columbia, on April 2, 1928.

[Morgan, *Can. men* (1912).]

O'Meara, Frederick Augustus (1814-1888), clergyman and translator, was born in Wexford, Ireland, in 1814, and educated at Trinity College, Dublin (B.A., 1837). He took holy orders in the Church of Ireland, and in 1838 was sent as a missionary to Canada. For twenty years he was a missionary among the Ojibwa Indians on Manitoulin Island; and in his later years he was rector of Port Hope, Ontario. He died at Port Hope, suddenly, on December 17, 1888. He translated into Ojibwa the *Book of Common Prayer* (Toronto, 1853), the *New Testament* (Toronto, 1854), and (with the Rev. Peter Jacobs) the *Pentateuch* (Toronto, n.d.). With Peter Jacobs, he also compiled a *Hymn book for the use of Ojibway Indian congregations* (Toronto, n.d.).

[Morgan, *Bib. can.*; W. A. Craick, *Port Hope historical sketches* (Port Hope, Ont., 1901).]

O'Meara, James Dallas (1849-1901), clergyman, was born at Manitowaning, Manitoulin Island, Canada West, on March 15, 1849, the son of the Rev. Canon F. A. O'Meara (q.v.). He was educated at the University of Toronto (B.A., 1870; M.A., 1874) and at Huron College, London, Ontario. He was ordained a priest of the Church of England in 1873, and was appointed shortly afterwards a professor of theology in St. John's College, Winnipeg. He was made a canon of the cathedral chapter in 1876, and dean of Rupert's Land in 1897. He died at Winnipeg, Manitoba, on December 6, 1901.

[Morgan, *Can. men* (1898).]

O'Meara, Thomas Robert (1864-1930), principal of Wycliffe College, Toronto, was born in Georgetown, Ontario, on October 16, 1864, the son of the Rev. F. A. O'Meara (q.v.). He was educated at the University of Toronto and at Wycliffe College, Toronto; and was ordained a priest of the Church of England in 1888. From 1887 to 1906 he was engaged in parochial work in Toronto; and in 1906 he was appointed second principal of Wycliffe College. He died at Toronto on January 10, 1930.

[*The jubilee volume of Wycliffe College* (Toronto, 1927); *Can. who was who*, vol. 1; Morgan, *Can. men* (1912).]

O'Neil, John (1834-1878), Fenian leader, was born at Drumgallon, county Monaghan, Ireland, on March 8, 1834. He emigrated to the United States in 1848; and after a varied career served as a cavalry officer in the American Civil War. He joined the Fenian brotherhood, and in May, 1866, he was the leader of the Fenian force which crossed the Niagara River, captured Fort Erie, and fought at Ridgeway. He was later appointed "inspector-general" of the Fenian forces; and in May, 1870, he again attempted an invasion of Canada, but was turned back at Eccles Hill near the Vermont border. Finally, in October, 1871, he invaded Canadian territory a third time, but without the support of the Fenian council, when he seized Pembina on the Red River. He was, however, arrested by United States troops, and the invasion came to nought. In his later years, he was the agent for a firm of land speculators in Nebraska; and he died at Omaha, Nebraska, on January 7, 1878. He was the author of an *Address . . . to the officers and members of the Fenian brotherhood* (1868) and an *Offical report . . . on the attempt to invade Canada* (1870).

[*Dict. Am. biog.*]

O'Neill, John Johnston (1886-1966), geologist and university administrator, was born at Port Colborne, Ontario, November 12, 1886. He was educated at McGill University (B.Sc., 1909; M.Sc. 1910), and at Yale University (Ph.D., in structural geology and petrology, 1912). He was geologist with the Canadian

Arctic expedition, southern party, under V. Stefansson (q.v.) (1913-16), and on the staff of the Geological Survey of Canada (1914-20). He did petroleum research in Kashmir and British India in 1920 and returned in the autumn of 1921 to McGill as assistant professor of geology. He was head of the department from 1929 to 1952. From 1948 to 1952 he was vice-principal of the university. He was responsible in large measure for the rapid expansion of graduate programs to meet post-war demands while carrying on his geological studies in Quebec. His work is recorded in some twenty published works as well as in private reports. He was a fellow of the Royal Society of Canada (1925) and a fellow of the Geographic Society of America. He died at Ottawa, Ontario, June 1, 1966.

[*Proc. and Trans. Roy. Soc. Can.*, 1967; *Can. who's who*, 1955-57.]

Orchard, William John (1869-1948), author, was born in Ontario in 1869, became a school-teacher in Indian Head, Saskatchewan, and later farmed for many years at Tregarva. He was an amateur archaeologist, gathered a large collection of Indian artifacts, and was the author of *The stone age on the prairies* (Regina, 1942) and *Prehistoric campsites of Saskatchewan* (Regina, 1946).

[B. B. Peel (comp.), *A bibliography of the prairie provinces* (Toronto, 1956).]

Ord, Lewis Craven (1881-1952), consulting engineer and author, was born in Toronto, Ontario, in 1881, the nephew of Lewis Redman Ord (q.v.), and died in England, in June, 1952. He was educated at Upper Canada College, and became an industrial consultant. During the Second World War he was employed as a consulting engineer by various departments of the British government. He was the author of *Secrets of industry* (London, 1950) and *Industrial frustration* (London, 1953).

[Toronto *Globe and Mail*, July 5, 1952.]

Ord, Lewis Redman (1856-1942), land surveyor and author, was born in Toronto, Canada West, on October 17, 1856, and died in Toronto on December 22, 1942. He was for many years engaged in topographical surveys in the Canadian West, and organized the Dominion Land Surveyors' Corps during the Riel Rebellion in 1885. In his later years he was employed by the Ontario Hydro-Electric Commission. He was the anonymous author of an attack on the inefficiency of the higher command of the Canadian forces during the Riel Rebellion, entitled *Reminiscences of a bungle, by one of the bunglers* (Toronto, 1887).

[*Association of Ontario Land Surveyors, annual report*, 1943.]

Orde, John Fosbery (1870-1932), jurist, was born at Great Village, Nova Scotia, on May 8, 1870. He was called to the bar in Ontario in 1891 (K.C., 1908), and practised law in Ottawa. In 1923 he was appointed a judge of the court of appeal of the Supreme Court of Ontario; and he sat on the bench until his death, at Toronto, Ontario, on August 1, 1932.

[Morgan, *Can. men* (1912).]

O'Reilly, Charles (1846-1920), physician and hospital superintendent, was born at Hamilton, Canada West, on June 19, 1846. He was educated at McGill University (M.D., C.M., 1867), and was resident physician at the Hamilton City Hospital from 1867 to 1875. In 1875 he became medical superintendent of the Toronto General Hospital, and he retired from this position only in 1905. He came to be known as one of the leading experts on hospital administration in North America; and in 1890 received from Trinity University the honorary degree of M.D., C.M. He died at Toronto, Ontario, on May 3, 1920.

[Morgan, *Can. men* (1912); C. K. Clarke, *A history of the Toronto General Hospital* (Toronto, 1913).]

Ormiston, William (1821-1899), clergyman and educationist, was born at Symington, Lanarkshire, Scotland, on April 23, 1821; and came to Canada with his parents in 1834. He was educated at Victoria University, Cobourg (B.A., 1848; M.A., 1856; LL.D., 1867); and from 1848 to 1849 was professor of mental and moral philosophy in this university. In 1849 he was ordained a minister of the Presbyterian Church; and after serving as a school-teacher and school inspector, he became in 1857 pastor of the Central Presbyterian Church in Hamilton, Canada West. In 1870 he went to the United States, as pastor of a Dutch Reformed church in New York; and he died at Gladstone, California, on March 9, 1899.

[*National cyclopaedia of American biography,* vol. 13 (New York, 1906); *Brit. Am.,* vol. 3.]

Oronhyatekha (1841-1907), supreme chief ranger of the Independent Order of Foresters, was born on the Six Nations Indian reservation, near Brantford, Upper Canada, on August 10, 1841. He was educated at the Industrial School on the reservation, at the Wesleyan Academy, Wilbraham, Massachusetts, at Kenyon College, Ohio, and at the University of Toronto. The Prince of Wales, on his visit to Canada in 1860, was so interested in him that he was invited to continue his studies at Oxford University; and here he qualified himself as a physician. On his return to Canada he practised, first, at Frankford, Ontario, and then at London, Ontario. He was here initiated into the Order of Foresters, and in this order he rapidly rose to the position of chief executive. In 1881 he was elected supreme chief ranger of the order, and this position he continued to occupy until his death. In 1889 the head office of the order was moved to Toronto, and here Oronhyatekha lived during his later years. He died at Savannah, Georgia, on March 3, 1907. In 1863 he married Ellen Hill, a great-granddaughter of Joseph Brant (q.v.). He was the author of a *History of the Independent Order of Foresters* (Toronto, 1894).

[Morgan, *Can. men* (1898).]

Orr, Rowland Beatty (1852-1933), physician and archaeologist, was born at Kleinburg, Ontario, on March 16, 1852, of Irish parentage. He was educated at the University of Toronto (M.B., 1877), and studied medicine in London and Edinburgh. He practised medicine in Toronto; and was prominent in local politics. In 1911 he was appointed curator of the Provincial Museum in Toronto; and from 1911 to 1924 he edited the *Annual Archaeological Report*, printed as an appendix to the report of the minister of education in Ontario. He died in Toronto on May 28, 1933.

[Toronto *Globe*, May 29, 1933.]

Orsonnens, Eraste d' (*fl.* 1856-1860), journalist, was a son of Capt. Prothais d'Odet d'Orsonnens (q.v.), and became a contributor to the French-Canadian periodical literature of the middle of the last century. He was the author of two small volumes, *Felluna, la vierge iroquoise* (Montreal, 1856), and *Une apparition: Episode de l'émigration irlandaise au Canada* (Montreal, 1860).

[Morgan, *Bib. can.*]

Orsonnens, Prothais d'Odet d' (d. 1834), soldier, was a native of Fribourg, Switzerland, who came to Canada about 1810 as captain of the grenadier company of a regiment of Swiss mercenaries called, after their commanding officer, the Meurons. When the regiment was disbanded after the War of 1812, he was engaged by Lord Selkirk (q.v) to command the party of Meurons that accompanied Selkirk to the West in 1816, and captured Fort William and Fort Douglas. On his return from the West, he settled at St. Roch de l'Achigan, Lower Canada; and he died there on March 16, 1834. He married Sophie Rocher; and by her he had two sons and two daughters.

[F. J. Audet, *Odet d'Orsonnens* (Bull. rech. hist., 1930); Le Jeune, *Dict. gén.*]

Orth, Bertrand (1848-1931), Roman Catholic archbishop of Victoria (1903-08), was born at Algert, near Cologne, Germany, on December 6, 1848. He was ordained a priest at Brussels, Belgium, in 1872; and became a missionary in the diocese of Vancouver. In 1900 he became bishop of Victoria, British Columbia; and in 1903 he was created an archbishop. He resigned his see in 1908, and became titular archbishop of Amasée. He died near Florence, Italy, on February 10, 1931.

[G. Brassard, *Armorial des évêques du Canada* (Montreal, 1940); Le Jeune, *Dict. gén.*]

Osborne, Mrs. Marion, *née* **Francis** (1871-1931), poet and dramatist, was born at Montreal, Quebec, on May 14, 1871, the daughter of George Grant Francis. In 1892 she married Charles Lambert Bath (d. 1897), and in 1902 Colonel Henry Campbell Osborne. For many years she lived in Toronto; but from 1920 to her death she lived in Ottawa. There she died on September 5, 1931. She was the author of *Poems* (London, Chiswick Press, 1914), *The song of Israfel and other poems* (Toronto and London, 1923), *Flight Commander Stork* (Toronto, 1925), a lyrical drama entitled *Sappho and Phaon* (Toronto, 1926), and a prose comedy, *The point of view,* included in V. Massey (ed.), *Canadian plays from Hart House Theatre,* vol. i (Toronto, 1926).

[*Can. who was who,* vol. 1; J. W. Garvin (ed.), *Canadian poets* (Toronto, 1926).]

Osborne, William Frederick (1873-1950), educationist, was born at Quyon, Quebec, on September 8, 1873, and died at Montreal, Quebec, on February 4, 1950. He was educated at the University of Toronto (B.A., 1893; M.A., 1901), and was for many years a professor of French language and literature at the University of Manitoba. He was the author of *The genius of Shakespeare, and other essays* (Toronto, 1908), *The faith of a layman* (London, 1910), and *America at war* (New York, 1917).

[*Can. who's who,* 1948.]

Osgoode, William (1754-1824), jurist, was born in England in March, 1754. He was educated at Christ Church, Oxford (M.A., 1777), and was called to the bar from the Inner Temple. In 1792 he was appointed first chief justice of Upper Canada, was commissioned a member of the Legislative Council, and was appointed speaker of the Council. In 1794 he became chief justice of Lower Canada. In 1801 he retired from the bench on a pension, and returned to England; and he died in London on January 17, 1824. He was the author of a pamphlet on *The laws of descent* (London, 1779).

[W. R. Riddell, *William Osgoode* (Canadian law times, 1921); D. B. Read, *The lives of the judges of Upper Canada* (Toronto, 1888); F. J. Audet, *Les juges en chef de la province de Québec* (Quebec, 1927); *Cyc. Am. biog.*; Dent, *Can. port.,* vol. 3; Le Jeune, *Dict. gén.*]

Osler, Britton Bath (1839-1901), lawyer, was born in the township of Tecumseth, Simcoe county, Upper Canada, on June 19, 1839, the second son of the Rev. Featherstone Lake Osler and Ellen Free Picton. He was educated at the Barrie Grammar School, and in 1862 obtained the degree of LL.B. at the University of Toronto. He was called to the bar of Upper Canada in 1862 (Q.C., 1876), and practised law, first in Dundas, then in Hamilton, and lastly in Toronto. From 1874 to 1880 he was crown attorney for the county of Wentworth;

and after moving to Toronto in 1882 he rapidly acquired a reputation as the foremost criminal lawyer in Canada. He was prosecuting counsel in the trials at Regina arising out of the Riel Rebellion in 1885, and in the trials of McGreevy (q.v.) and Connolly in 1891. He died at Atlantic City, New Jersey, on February 5, 1901. He was twice married, (1) in 1863 to Caroline (d. 1895), daughter of Capt. Henry Smith, H.E.I.C.S., and (2) in 1897 to Elizabeth Mary, eldest daughter of A. G. Ramsay, of Hamilton.

[Morgan, *Can. men* (1898); H. Charlesworth, *Candid chronicles* (Toronto, 1925).]

Osler, Sir Edmund Boyd (1845-1924), financier, was born in the township of Tecumseth, Simcoe county, Upper Canada, on November 20, 1845, the son of the Rev. Featherstone Lake Osler and Ellen Free Picton. He was educated at the Dundas Grammar School, and began his career as a clerk in the Bank of Upper Canada. When that bank failed in 1866, he became a stock-broker; and he was a member of the Toronto Stock Exchange until 1903. In 1901 he was elected president of the Dominion Bank; and he was a director of the Canadian Pacific Railway. From 1896 to 1917 he represented West Toronto as a Conservative in the Canadian House of Commons. He died at Toronto on August 4, 1924. In 1872 he married Annie Farquharson (d. 1910), daughter of James L. Cochran, of Aberdeen, Scotland; and by her he had several children. He was created a knight bachelor in 1912.

[*Who was who*, 1916-28; *Can. who was who*, vol. 1; M. Abbott (ed.), *Sir William Osler memorial volume* (Toronto, 1926); H. Charlesworth (ed.), *A cyclopaedia of Canadian biography* (Toronto, 1919); Morgan, *Can. men* (1912); *Can. parl. comp.*; O. D. Skelton and others, *The Dominion Bank* (Toronto, 1921).]

Osler, Featherston (1838-1924), jurist, was born at Newmarket, Upper Canada, in 1838, the eldest son of the Rev. Featherstone Lake Osler and Ellen Free Picton. He was educated at the Barrie and Bond Head Grammar Schools, and was called to the bar of Upper Canada in 1860 (Q.C., 1879). He practised law in Toronto, and in 1879 he was appointed a puisne judge of the Court of Common Pleas in Ontario. In 1883 he became a judge of the Court of Appeal in Ontario; and this post he retained until his retirement from the bench in 1910. From 1910 to his death he was president of the Toronto General Trusts Corporation. He died at Toronto on January 16, 1924. In 1861 he married Henrietta (d. 1902), daughter of Captain Henry Smith, H.E.I.C.S.

[*Can. who was who*, vol. 1; *Who was who*, 1916-28; Morgan, *Can. men* (1912).]

Osler, Sir William, Bart. (1849-1919), physician and author, was born at Bond Head,

Upper Canada, on July 12, 1849, the youngest son of the Rev. Featherstone Lake Osler and Ellen Free Picton. He was educated at Trinity College School, Port Hope, at Trinity University, Toronto, at McGill University (M.D., 1872); and he studied in London, Berlin, and Vienna. From 1874 to 1884 he was on the staff of the medical school at McGill University; from 1884 to 1889 he was professor of clinical medicine at the University of Philadelphia; from 1889 to 1905 he was professor of medicine at Johns Hopkins University, Baltimore; and from 1905 to his death he was regius professor of medicine at Oxford University. He died at Oxford on December 29, 1919. In 1892 he married Grace Lindsee Revere, widow of Dr. S. W. Gross, of Philadelphia. He was an LL.D. of McGill University (1895), of Aberdeen University (1898), of Edinburgh University (1898), of the University of Toronto (1899), of Yale University (1901), of Harvard University (1904), of Johns Hopkins University (1905); a D.C.L. of Trinity University (1902); and a D.Sc. of Oxford University (1904) and Leeds University (1910). In 1898 he was elected a fellow of the Royal Society, and in 1911 he was created a baronet of the United Kingdom.

He published numerous monographs and papers on medical subjects, including a work on *The principles and practice of medicine* (New York, 1892), which went into many editions, and he edited a medical encyclopaedia entitled *The system of medicine* (7 vols., London, 1907-10). But his reputation rests chiefly on his addresses and less technical publications: *Science and immortality* (London, 1904), *Aequanimitas, and other addresses* (London, 1904), *Counsels and ideals* (Oxford, 1905), *Thomas Linacre* (Oxford, 1908), *An Alabama student, and other essays* (Oxford, 1908), *A way of life* (Oxford, 1914), and *The student life, and other essays* (Boston, 1931).

[H. Cushing, *The life of Sir William Osler* (2 vols., Oxford, 1925); E. G. Reid, *The great physician* (Oxford, 1931); *Contributions to medical and biological research, dedicated to Sir William Osler . . . by his pupils and co-workers* (2 vols., New York, 1919); *Dict. Am. biog.*; *Encyclopedia Americana*; *Who was who*, 1916-28; Morgan, *Can. men* (1912); Maude E. Abbott, *Classified and annotated bibliography of Sir William Osler* (Montreal, 1939); I. McNeill, *The scamp who became the great physician* (Maclean's Magazine, June 1, 1951); I. Noble, *The doctor who dared* (Toronto, 1959).]

O'Sullivan, Dennis Ambrose (1848-1892), lawyer, was born in Northumberland county, Canada West, on February 21, 1848. He was educated at the University of Toronto (B.A., 1872; M.A., 1876; LL.B., 1877), and was called to the bar in Ontario in 1875. He practised law in Toronto; and he died in Toronto in 1892. He was the author of *A manual of government in Canada* (Toronto, 1879), *Practical conveyanc-*

ing (Toronto, 1881), *How to draw a will* (Toronto, 1881), and *Essays on the church in Canada* (Toronto, 1890). In 1887 the honorary degree of LL.D. was conferred on him by Laval University.

[Rose, *Cyc. Can. biog.* (1888).]

O'Sullivan, Michael (1784-1839), jurist, was born at Cahir, Lismore, Ireland, on May 4, 1784, the son of John O'Sullivan and Eleanor O'Donell. He came to Canada at an early age, and was educated at the College of Montreal. He studied law under Denis Benjamin Viger (q.v.), and was called to the bar of Lower Canada in 1811 (K.C., 1831). He served in the militia during the War of 1812-14, and distinguished himself at the battle of Châteauguay. He was one of the first editors of *Le Canadien*; and from 1814 to 1824 he represented Huntingdon in the Legislative Assembly of Lower Canada. In 1833 he was appointed solicitor-general of Lower Canada; and in 1838 he became chief justice of the Court of King's Bench at Montreal. He died at Montreal on March 7, 1839. In 1809 he married Cécile, daughter of Pierre Berthelet.

[F. J. Audet, *Les juges en chef de la province de Québec* (Quebec, 1927); P. G. Roy, *Les juges de la province de Québec* (Lévis, Que., 1933); Le Jeune, *Dict. gén.*]

Otter, Sir William Dillon (1843-1929), soldier, was born near Clinton, Ontario, on December 3, 1843, the son of Alfred William Otter and Anna de la Hooke. He was educated at the Toronto Model School and Upper Canada College; and entered the volunteer militia in 1861. He was adjutant of the Queen's Own Rifles during the Fenian raid of 1866, and became lieutenant-colonel commanding the regiment in 1874. He entered the permanent militia in 1883; and during the North West Rebellion of 1885 he commanded the column which marched on Battleford. Later he captured the Indian chief Poundmaker (q.v.). He commanded the first contingent of troops sent to the South African War in 1899, and was wounded in action in 1900. From 1908 to 1910 he was chief of the general staff at Ottawa, with the rank of brigadier-general; from 1910 to 1912 he was inspector-general, with the rank of major-general; and during the First World War he was director of internment operations. He died at Toronto on May 6, 1929. Created a C.B. in 1900 and a C.V.O. in 1908, he was made a K.C.B. in 1913; and he was made an LL.D. of the University of Toronto in 1922. He was the author of *The guide* (Toronto, 1880), a military manual which went into many editions.

[*Who was who*, 1929-40; *Can. who was who*, vol. 1; Morgan, *Can. men* (1912).]

Ouimet, Adolphe (1840-1910), lawyer and journalist, was born near Montreal, Lower Canada, on April 25, 1840; and was called to

the bar of Lower Canada in 1861. After practising law for several years, he became a journalist. He died at Montreal, Quebec, on March 13, 1910. He was the author of *Les contemporains canadiens* (Three Rivers, 1858), and joint author, with the Abbé Villeneuve, of *La comédie infernale* (Montreal, 1871), and, with B. A. T. de Montigny, of *La vérité sur la question métisse au Nord-ouest* (Montreal, 1889).

[E.-Z. Massicotte, *Adolphe Ouimet* (Bull. rech. hist., 1926).]

Ouimet, Gédéon (1823-1905), prime minister of Quebec (1873-74), was born at Ste. Rose, Lower Canada, on June 3, 1823, the son of Jean Ouimet and Marie Boutron *dit* Major. He was educated at the colleges of St. Hyacinthe and Montreal, and was called to the bar of Lower Canada in 1844 (Q.C., 1867). From 1857 to 1861 he was Conservative member for Beauharnois in the Legislative Assembly of Canada; and from 1867 to 1875 he sat for Two Mountains in the Legislative Assembly of Quebec. He was attorney-general in the Chauveau administration in Quebec from 1867 to 1873; and from 1873 to 1874 he was prime minister of Quebec, with the portfolios of minister of public instruction and provincial secretary. In 1876 he was appointed superintendent of education for Quebec; and this post he held for twenty years, after which he retired on a pension. He was appointed also in 1895 to the Legislative Council of Quebec. He died at Quebec on April 23, 1905. In 1850 he married Jane, daughter of Alexis Pellant, of Montreal; and by her he had six children. He was a D.C.L. of Bishop's College, Lennoxville, and an LL.D. of Laval University.

[Morgan, *Can. men* (1898); *Can. parl. comp.*; Rose, *Cyc. Can. biog.* (1888); *Cyc. Am. biog.*; *Canadian biographical dictionary*, Quebec vol. (Chicago, 1881); Bibaud, *Panth. can.*; Le Jeune, *Dict. gén.*; J. D. Borthwick, *Montreal, its history* (Montreal, 1875).]

Ouimet, Joseph Alderic (1848-1916), politician and jurist, was born at Ste. Rose, Lower Canada, on May 20, 1848, the son of Michel Ouimet, J.P., and Elizabeth Filiatrault St. Louis. He was educated at the College of Ste. Thérèse and at Victoria University, Cobourg, Ontario (LL.B., 1869) and was called to the Quebec bar in 1870 (Q.C., 1880). He became head of the law firm of Ouimet, Emard, and Maurault, of Montreal. From 1873 to 1896 he represented Laval as a Liberal-Conservative in the Canadian House of Commons; and from 1887 to 1891 he was the speaker of the House. He was sworn of the King's Privy Council for Canada in 1891, and from 1892 to 1896 he was minister of public works in the successive Abbott, Thompson, and Bowell cabinets. In 1896 he was appointed a puisne judge of the Court of King's Bench of Quebec; and he retired from the bench in 1906. He died at Montreal on May 12, 1916. In 1874 he married Marie Thérèse, daughter of Alfred Chartier La Rocque, of Montreal; and by her he had several children. From 1879 to 1889 he was lieutenant-colonel commanding the 65th Mount Royal Rifles. He saw service in the Fenian raids of 1870 and in the North West Rebellion of 1885; and in 1888 he was president of the Dominion Rifle Association.

[P. G. Roy, *Les juges de la province de Québec* (Quebec, 1933); A. W. G. Macalister, *Bench and bar of Quebec, Nova Scotia and New Brunswick* (Montreal, 1907); Morgan, *Can. men* (1912); Rose, *Cyc. Can. biog.* (1888); *Canadian biographical dictionary*, Quebec vol. (Chicago, 1881); Bibaud, *Panth. can.*; Taché, *Men of the day*; *Cy. Am. biog.*]

Ouimet, Joseph Alphonse (1845-1900), jurist, was born at St. Eustache, Lower Canada, on November 17, 1845, the son of Louis Ouimet and Marguerite Goulet. He was educated at St. Mary's Jesuit College and at the College of Montreal, and was called to the bar of Lower Canada in 1868. For a number of years he practised law in Montreal in partnership with his cousin, Joseph Alderic Ouimet (q.v.); and he became professor of administrative law in Laval University, Montreal. In 1885 he was appointed a special commissioner to report on the causes of the North West Rebellion; and in 1886 he was chairman of the royal commission to examine into claims for compensation arising out of the rebellion. The same year he was appointed a puisne judge of the Superior Court of Quebec; and in 1894 he was made a judge of the Court of Queen's Bench in Quebec. He died on December 19, 1900. He married, in 1868, Elmina, daughter of F. Poirier, Montreal. In 1878 he was made an LL.D. of Laval University, Montreal.

[P. G. Roy, *Les juges de la province de Québec* (Quebec, 1933); A. W. G. Macalister, *Bench and bar of Quebec, Nova Scotia, and New Brunswick* (Montreal, 1907); Morgan, *Can. men* (1898).]

Outerbridge, Herbert Arthur (1883-1963), merchant, was born in St. John's, Newfoundland, March 7, 1883, and educated in England and France. During the First World War he served with the Newfoundland Regiment, was wounded, and was awarded the M.B.E. He joined Harvey and Company as a junior clerk in 1903, became a director in 1910, and twenty years later was president of the firm. He was one of Newfoundland's best-known businessmen. He was president of Harvey Estates Limited and Harvey Lumber and Hardware Limited, and a director of Marine Agencies Limited and Browning-Harvey Limited. He died at St. John's, Newfoundland, February 22, 1963.

[*Can. who's who*, 1961-63; Metropolitan Toronto Library Board, *Biographical scrapbooks*, vol. 21.]

Outram, Sir James, Bart. (1864-1925), clergyman, explorer, and author, was born in London, England, on October 13, 1864, the eldest son of Sir Francis Boyd Outram, Bart., and the grandson of Sir James Outram, Bart., a famous figure in the Indian Mutiny. He was educated at Pembroke College, Cambridge (B.A., 1888; M.A., 1893); and was ordained a priest of the Church of England in 1890. After serving as a curate, he was from 1896 to 1900 the vicar of a parish in Ipswich; but in 1900 he retired from active parochial work, because of ill health. In 1901 he became interested in mountaineering in the Canadian Rockies; and in subsequent years he climbed for the first time some of the highest peaks in the Rockies. Mount Outram, the highest peak on the west branch of the north fork of the Saskatchewan, was named after him. He succeeded to the baronetcy on the death of his father in 1912; and he died at Victoria, British Columbia, on March 12, 1925. He was the author of *In the heart of the Canadian Rockies* (London, 1905).

[*Who was who*, 1916-28; Morgan, *Can. men* (1912); *Canadian alpine journal*, 1925.]

Outram, Joseph (1803-1885), author, was born on the Clyde, near Glasgow, Scotland, in 1803, settled in Nova Scotia in 1861, and died at Halifax, Nova Scotia, in 1885. He was the author of *Nova Scotia, its condition and resources* (Edinburgh, 1850) and *A handbook of information for emigrants to Nova Scotia* (Halifax, N.S., 1864).

[R. J. Long, *Nova Scotia authors* (East Orange, N.J., 1918).]

Owen, Charles Boidman (d. 1878), lawyer and author, was born in Lunenburg, Nova Scotia. He was called to the bar of Nova Scotia (Q.C., 1873); and was for a time a member of the Nova Scotia legislature. He died at Yarmouth, Nova Scotia, on October 23, 1878. Under the pen-name of "A Nova-Scotian", he published *An epitome of the history, statistics, etc., of Nova Scotia* (Halifax, N.S., 1842).

[R. J. Long, *Nova Scotia authors* (East Orange, N.J., 1918); *Dom. ann. reg.*, 1878.]

Owen, Derwyn Trevor (1876-1947), primate of the Church of England in Canada, was born at Twickenham, England, on July 29, 1876, and died at Toronto, Ontario, on April 14, 1947. He came to Canada in early youth with his parents, and was educated at local schools and at Trinity College, Toronto (L.Th., 1907). He was ordained a priest of the Church of England in 1901, and after serving several parishes, was elected bishop of Niagara in 1925. In 1932 he was elected bishop of Toronto, and in 1934 archbishop of Toronto and primate of all Canada. Honorary degrees were conferred on him by several universities.

[Charles Edward Riley, *Derwyn Trevor Owen, primate of all Canada* (Toronto,

1966); *Who was who*, 1941-50; *Can. who's who*, 1938-39.]

Owen, Egbert Americus (d. 1908), local historian, was born in Vittoria, Norfolk county, Canada West; and died at Hamilton, Ontario, on May 2, 1908. He was the author of *Pioneer sketches of Long Point settlement* (Toronto, 1898).

[Private information.]

Owen, Eric Trevor (1882-1948), educationist, was born in England in 1882, a younger brother of Archbishop Derwyn Trevor Owen (q.v.), and died at Toronto, Ontario, on March 2, 1948. He was educated at the University of Trinity College (B.A., 1902), and, after post-graduate work at Oxford, was appointed to the staff of Trinity College in classics. In 1923 he was appointed professor of Greek in University College, Toronto. He was the author of *The story of the Iliad* (Toronto, 1946) and *The harmony of Aeschylus* (Toronto, 1952), the latter published posthumously.

[Toronto *Globe and Mail*, March 3, 1948.]

Owen, Lemuel Cambridge (1822-1912), prime minister of Prince Edward Island (1873-76), was born November 1, 1822, and died at Charlottetown, Prince Edward Island, on November 26, 1912. He was a ship-builder; and he became a member of the Island's House of Assembly from 1860 to 1866, and of its Legislative Council from 1873 to 1876. During the latter period he was prime minister.

[*Encyc. Can.*]

Owens, William (1840-1917), senator of Canada, was born in Argenteuil county, Lower Canada, on May 15, 1840. He became postmaster and mayor of the township of Chatham, Quebec; and he represented Argenteuil in the Legislative Assembly of Quebec from 1881 to 1891. He was called to the Senate of Canada in 1896; and he sat in the Senate until his death, at Montreal, Quebec, on June 8, 1917.

[*Can. parl. comp.*]

Oxenden, Ashton (1808-1892), Anglican bishop of Montreal, and metropolitan of Canada (1869-78), was born at Broome Park, Canterbury, England, on September 20, 1808, the fifth son of Sir Henry Oxenden, Bart. He was educated at Harrow and at University College, Oxford (B.A, 1831; M.A, 1859; D.D., 1869), and was ordained a priest of the Church of England in 1833. For twenty years he was vicar of Pluckley in Kent; and in 1869 he was elected bishop of Montreal and metropolitan of Can-

ada. Ill health compelled his retirement from this bishopric in 1878; and he died at Biarritz, France, on February 22, 1892. He was the author of numerous theological and devotional works; but the only books by him which have special reference to his life in Canada are *My first year in Canada* (London, 1871) and *The history of my life: An autobiography* (London, 1891). After his death there was published his *Plain sermons, with a memoir of the author* (London, 1893).

[*Dict. nat. biog.*; *Cyc. Am. biog.*; C. H. Mockridge, *The bishops of the Church of England in Canada* (Toronto, 1896).]

Oxley, James Macdonald (1855-1907), writer of books for boys, was born at Halifax, Nova Scotia, on October 22, 1855, the son of James Black Oxley, a merchant, and Ellen Macdonald. He was educated at the Halifax Grammar School, at Dalhousie University (B.A., 1874), and at Harvard University. He was called to the bar of Nova Scotia in 1878, and for five years he practised law in Halifax. From 1883 to 1891 he was legal adviser to the department of marine and fisheries at Ottawa; and he then entered the service of the Sun Life Assurance Company at Montreal. During his last years he lived in Toronto; and he died there on September 9, 1907. He was a successful writer of books for boys, and was the author of *Bert Lloyd's boyhood* (Philadelphia, 1889), *Up among the ice floes* (Philadelphia, 1890), *The chore boy of Camp Kippewa* (Philadelphia, 1891), *The wreckers of Sable Island* (Philadelphia, 1891), *Donald Grant's development* (Philadelphia, 1892), *Fergus MacTavish; or, Portage and prairie* (Philadelphia, 1892), *Archie of Athabasca* (Boston, 1893), *The good ship Gryphon* (Philadelphia, 1893), *In the wilds of the west coast* (New York, 1894), *My strange rescue; and other stories of sport and adventure in Canada* (New York, 1895), *Baffling the blockade* (New York, 1896), *The romance of commerce* (New York, 1896), *The boy tramps; or, Across Canada* (New York, 1896), *The hero of Start Point, and other stories* (Philadelphia, 1896), *On the world's roof* (Philadelphia, 1897), *In the swing of the sea* (Philadelphia, 1898), *Fife and drum at Louisbourg* (Boston, 1899), *Terry's trials and triumphs* (New York, 1899), *L'Hasa at last* (Philadelphia, 1900), *North overland with Franklin* (Boston, 1901), *With Rogers on the frontier* (New York, 1902), and *The family on wheels* (New York, 1905).

[Morgan, *Can. men* (1898); Rose, *Cyc. Can. biog.* (1886); *Cyc. Am. biog.*; A. MacMurchy, *A handbook of Canadian literature* (Toronto, 1906).]

𝒫

Pacey, William Cyril Desmond (1917-1975), literary critic, was born in Dunedin, New Zealand, May 1, 1917. He was educated in Canada, at Victoria College (B.A., 1938), and in England, at Trinity College, Cambridge (1938-40; Ph.D., 1941). He became professor of English at Brandon College, University of Manitoba, in 1940, leaving in 1943 to join the Wartime Information Board. In 1944 he joined the English department of the University of New Brunswick, becoming acting dean of arts in 1955, dean of graduate studies in 1960, and vice-president of the university in 1970. He was the author of *Frederick Philip Grove* (1945), *The picnic and other stories* (1958), *Ethel Wilson* (1968), *Essays in Canadian criticism* (1969), and *Frederick Philip Grove* (1970); as well as editing several collections of prose and verse. He became a fellow of the Royal Society of Canada (1955). He died at Fredericton, New Brunswick, July 4, 1975.

[*Can. who's who*, 1970-72.]

Pacifique de Valigny, Rev. Père (1863-1943), missionary and author, was born at Valigny, Poitiers, France, on September 7, 1863, under the secular name of Henri-Joseph-Louis Buisson, and died at Montreal, Quebec, on September 29, 1943. He joined the Capuchin order in 1880, and came to Canada in 1894 as missionary to the Micmacs of Ste. Anne de Restigouche. For practically the rest of his life he devoted himself to this mission; and in doing so he made himself not only a master of the Micmac language, but also an authority on the history and geography of Northern New Brunswick and the Gaspé peninsula. He was the author of *Leçons grammaticales, théoriques et pratiques, de la langue Micmaque* (Ste. Anne de Restigouche, 1939), *Etudes historiques et géographiques* (15 nos., n.p., 1922-32), and *Chronique des plus anciennes églises de l'Acadie* (Montreal, 1944).

[Biographical sketch prefixed to *Chronique des plus anciennes églises de l'Acadie* (Montreal, 1944).]

Pack, Rowland (1927-1964), musician, was born in London, Ontario, July 15, 1927. He began his professional career at thirteen when he became a church organist. He entered the Royal Conservatory of Music of Toronto as a scholarship cello student at age eighteen, and studied with Isaac Mamott. Three years later, in 1948, he joined the Toronto Symphony Orchestra, and by age twenty-six was first cellist of the orchestra as well as of the C.B.C. Symphony on the retirement of Mr. Mamott. He played the organ at St. Anne's Church in Toronto and also founded and conducted the Rowland Pack Chamber Singers. His interest in ancient music led him to revitalize many antique scores and revive many half-forgotten instruments. He was responsible for much of the re-awakened interest in performing ancient music. He died at Toronto, Ontario, January 3, 1964.

[Metropolitan Toronto Library Board, *Biographical scrapbooks*, vol. 22.]

Packard, Frank Lucius (1877-1942), novelist, was born at Montreal, Quebec, on February 2, 1877. He was educated at McGill University (B.A.Sc., 1897), and at the University of Liège, Belgium; and he was for a number of years employed on engineering work in the United States. He began to contribute to popular periodicals in 1906; and he published his first book in 1911. He became a highly successful writer of "thrillers", and was one of the few Canadian writers who made a good livelihood by writing, while living in Canada. He died at Lachine, Quebec, on February 17, 1942. He was the author of *On the iron at Big Cloud* (New York, 1911), *Greater love hath no man* (New York, 1913), *The miracle man* (New York, 1914), *The beloved traitor* (New York, 1916), *The sin that was his* (New York, 1917), *The adventures of Jimmie Dale* (New York, 1917), *The wire devils* (New York, 1918), *The further adventures of Jimmie Dale* (New York, 1918), *From now on* (New York, 1919), *The night operator* (New York, 1919), *The white moll* (New York, 1920), *Pawned* (New York, 1921), *Doors of the night* (New York, 1922), *Jimmie Dale and the phantom clue* (New York, 1922), *The four stragglers* (New York, 1923), *The locked book* (New York, 1924), *Running special* (New York, 1925), *Broken waters* (New York, 1925), *The red ledger* (New York, 1926), *Two stolen idols* (New York, 1927), *The devil's mantle* (New

York, 1927), *Shanghai Jim* (Garden City, N.Y., 1928), *Tiger claws* (Garden City, N.Y., 1928), *The big shot* (Garden City, N.Y., 1929), *Jimmie Dale and the blue envelope murder* (Garden City, N.Y., 1930), *The gold skull murders* (Garden City, N.Y., 1931), *The hidden door* (Garden City, N.Y., 1932), *The purple ball* (Garden City, N.Y., 1933), *Jimmie Dale and the missing hour* (Garden City, N.Y., 1935), *The dragon's jaws* (Garden City, N.Y., 1937), and *More knaves than one* (New York, 1938).

[*Who's who in America*; *Can. who's who*, 1936-37.]

Pagan, Robert (1750?-1821), merchant, was born in Scotland about 1750, and emigrated to America in 1769. He settled in Falmouth (now Portland), Massachusetts, as the representative of a firm of Glasgow merchants; but he was driven out of the town as a loyalist in 1778, and in 1784 he settled at St. Andrews, New Brunswick. He became a prominent figure in early New Brunswick; and he represented Charlotte county in the House of Assembly for several years. He died at St. Andrews, New Brunswick, on November 23, 1821.

[D. R. Jack, *Robert and Miriam Pagan* (Acadiensis, 1902).]

Page, Rhoda Ann (1826-1863), poet, was born in Hackney, England, in 1826, and came to Canada in 1832. In 1856 she married a Mr. Faulkner, and went to live near Rice Lake, Ontario. Here she died in 1863. She was the author of a volume of verse entitled *Wild notes from the backwoods* (Cobourg, C.W., 1850).

[C. C. James, *A bibliography of Canadian poetry* (Toronto, 1899).]

Paget, Mrs. Amelia M. (1867-1922), author, was born at Fort Simpson, North West Territories, in 1867, and died on July 10, 1922. She was the author of *The people of the plains* (Toronto, 1909).

[Private information.]

Paget, Edward Clarence (1851-1927), clergyman and author, was born at Swithland Rectory, Leicestershire, England, on August 14, 1851, the son of the Rev. E. J. Paget and the grandson of Vice-Admiral Sir Charles Paget. He was educated at Keble College, Oxford (B.A., 1874; M.A., 1877), and at Cuddesden College; and was ordained a clergyman of the Church of England in 1875. He came to America in 1886 as assistant minister of Davenport Cathedral, Iowa; in 1887 he became rector of Holy Trinity Church, Muscatine, Iowa; and in 1899 he came to Canada as vicar of Revelstoke, British Columbia. In 1900 he was appointed rector, and in 1901 dean, of Calgary, Alberta; and he remained in this post until his death, at Calgary, Alberta, on March

26, 1927. He was the author of *Memoir of the Honble. Sir Charles Paget* (London, 1913).

[*Who was who*, 1916-28; Morgan, *Can. men* (1912).]

Pagnuelo, Siméon (1840-1915), jurist, was born at Laprairie, Lower Canada, on January 5, 1840, and was called to the bar of Lower Canada in 1861. He practised law, first at Napierville, and then, after 1866, at Montreal; and in 1889 he was appointed a judge of the Superior Court for the district of Montreal. He retired from the bench in 1912; and he died at Montreal on May 14, 1915. He was the author of *Etudes historiques et légales sur la liberté religieuse en Canada* (Montreal, 1872) and *Lettres sur la réforme judiciare* (Montreal, 1880).

[P. G. Roy, *Les juges de la province de Québec* (Quebec, 1933).]

Painchaud, Charles François (1782-1838), priest and educationist, was born at the Ile aux Grues, Quebec, on September 9, 1782, the son of François Painchaud and of Marie-Angélique Drouin. He was educated at Quebec, and was ordained a priest in 1805. From 1806 to 1814 he was a parish priest on the shores of the Bay of Chaleurs; and in 1814 he went to Ste. Anne de la Pocatière. Here he founded, in 1829, the classical college of Ste. Anne de la Pocatière; and he had a profound influence on education in French Canada. He died at Ste. Anne de la Pocatière on February 8, 1838.

[N. E. Dionne, *Vie de C. F. Painchaud* (Quebec, 1894); C. Bacon, *Eloge de messire C. F. Painchaud* (Ste. Anne de la Pocatière, Que., 1864); H. Têtu, *Souvenirs inédits sur l'abbé Painchaud* (Quebec, 1893); Allaire, *Dict. biog.*; Le Jeune, *Dict. gén.*]

Palliser, Sir Hugh, Bart. (1723-1796), governor of Newfoundland (1764-69), was born at Kirk Deighton, Yorkshire, on February 26, 1723, and died at Vach, Buckinghamshire, on March 19, 1796. He entered the Royal Navy in 1735, and in 1759 took part in the operations on the St. Lawrence that led to the capture of Quebec. For five years after the cession of Canada to the British he was governor of Newfoundland, and during his period of office he did everything he could to discourage settlement in Newfoundland, maintaining that the island should be preserved as a training-ground for British sailors and fishermen. His views were afterwards embodied in what was known as "the Palliser Act" (1774). It was during his period of office also that James Cook (q.v.) carried out his survey of Newfoundland. He was created a baronet in 1773; and was promoted to the rank of rear-admiral in 1775, vice-admiral in 1778, and admiral in 1787.

[R. M. Hunt, *Life of Sir Hugh Palliser* (London, 1844); W. H. Whiteley, *Governor*

Hugh Palliser and the Newfoundland and Labrador fishery, 1764-1768 (Can. hist. rev., 1969); *Dict. nat. biog.*; *Encyc. Can.*]

Palliser, John (1807-1887), explorer, was born on January 29, 1807, the eldest son of Wray Palliser, of county Waterford, Ireland. In 1847 he set out on a hunting expedition in north-western America; and he later described his experiences in *Solitary rambles and adventures of a hunter in the prairies* (London, 1853). In 1857 he was appointed to command an expedition sent out by the British government to explore British North America between the parallels of 49° and 50° north latitude and 100° and 115° west longitude. He spent the years 1857-1861 in discharging this commission; and his report was issued in the British parliamentary papers for 1863. He died unmarried at Comragh, county Waterford, Ireland, on August 18, 1887. In 1877 he was created a C.M.G.

[Irene M. Spry, ed., *The papers of the Palliser expedition, 1857-1860* (The Champlain Society, 1968), *The Palliser expedition: An account of John Palliser's British North American exploring expeditions, 1857-1860* (Toronto, 1964); *Dict. nat. biog.*; *Cyc. Am. biog.*; *Beaver*, March, 1937.]

Palmer, David (1789-1866), poet, was born at Grand Lake, Queens county, New Brunswick, on February 28, 1789, of loyalist stock; and he died on June 1, 1866. He was the author of *New Brunswick, and other poems* (Saint John, N.B., 1869).

[W. G. MacFarlane, *New Brunswick bibliography* (Saint John, N.B., 1895).]

Palmer, Edward (1809-1889), politician and jurist, was born at Charlottetown, Prince Edward Island, on September 1, 1809, the son of James B. Palmer, a barrister, and Millicent, daughter of Benjamin Jones, of London, England. He was educated at Charlottetown, studied law under his father, and was called to the bar in 1831 (Q.C., 1857). From 1835 to 1860 he was a member of the Legislative Assembly of Prince Edward Island for Charlottetown and Royalty; and from 1860 to 1873 he was a member of the Legislative Council. He repeatedly held office in the Island administration. From 1848 to 1851 he was solicitor-general; for some months in 1854 he was attorney-general; in 1859 he became president of the council; and he was again attorney-general from 1863 to 1869, and from 1872 to 1873. He was a delegate to the Charlottetown conference on the union of the Maritime provinces in 1864, and to the Quebec conference later in the same year. He opposed Confederation on the basis of the Quebec Resolutions; but in 1873 threw his influence in favour of union. In 1873 he was appointed a judge of the Queen's County Court, Prince Edward Island; and in 1874 he was appointed chief justice of

the Supreme Court of the Island. This office he held until his death on November 4, 1889. He married Isabella, daughter of Benjamin Tremain, of Quebec; and by her he had nine children.

[*Canadian biographical dictionary, Quebec and Maritime provinces vol.* (Quebec, 1881); J. H. Gray, *Confederation* (Toronto, 1872); Le Jeune, *Dict. gén.*]

Palmer, Herbert James (1851-1939), prime minister of Prince Edward Island (May-December, 1911), was born at Charlottetown, Prince Edward Island, on August 25, 1851. He was educated at King's College, Windsor, Nova Scotia; and was called to the bar in Prince Edward Island in 1877 (Q.C., 1898). He represented the 3rd district of Queen's in the local legislature from 1900 to 1904 and from 1908 to 1911; and he was attorney-general of the province for a few months in 1908, and prime minister for a few months in 1911. He died in Charlottetown on December 22, 1939.

[*Can. parl. comp.*; Morgan, *Can. men* (1912).]

Pambrun, Pierre Chrysologue (1792-1841), fur-trader, was born at L'Islet, below Quebec, Lower Canada, on December 17, 1792, the son of André Dominique Pambrun. He served in the Canadian *Voltigeurs* under Salaberry in the War of 1812, and took part in the battle of Châteauguay. After the war, in 1815, he entered the service of the Hudson's Bay Company; and in 1816 he was taken prisoner by the *bois-brûlés* of the North West Company on the Qu'Appelle River. In 1821 he was stationed at Cumberland House; and in 1824 he was transferred to the Pacific slope. Here he spent the remainder of his life. He died at Fort Walla Walla, in the Oregon country, in 1841, as the result of injuries received when breaking in a wild horse. Just before his death, in 1840, he had been promoted to the rank of chief trader. About 1821, at Cumberland House, he married the half-breed daughter of Edward Umfreville (q.v.); and she was still living, in the state of Washington, in 1878. One of his sons, Pierre Chrysologue, entered the service of the Hudson's Bay Company, and was met by Lord Milton and Dr. Cheadle in the foothills of the Rocky Mountains in 1868.

[J. Tassé, *Les Canadiens de l'ouest* (2 vols., Montreal, 1878); A. G. Morice, *Dictionnaire historique des canadiens et des métis français de l'ouest* (Quebec, 1908); Le Jeune, *Dict. gén.*]

Pampalon, Pierre (1861-1921), priest, was born at Lévis, Canada East, on July 13, 1861, and died at Montreal, Quebec, on January 22, 1921. He was the author of *Une fleur canadienne de l'Institut de Saint-Alphonse* (Montreal, 1902).

[Allaire, *Dict. biog.*]

Panet, Bernard Claude (1753-1833), Roman Catholic bishop of Quebec (1825-33), was born in Quebec on January 9, 1753, the second son of Jean Claude Panet (q.v.). He was educated at the Quebec Seminary, and in 1778 was ordained a priest of the Roman Catholic Church. In 1781 he became *curé* of the parish of Rivière-Ouelle; and served in this parish for nearly forty-five years. In 1806 he was appointed coadjutor to Bishop Plessis (q.v.) with the title of bishop of Saldes *in partibus*; and in 1825 he became bishop of Quebec. He died at Quebec on February 14, 1833.

[P. G. Roy, *La famille Panet* (Lévis, 1906); H. Têtu, *Les Evêques de Québec* (Quebec, 1889); Allaire, *Dict. biog.*; Le Jeune, *Dict. gén.*]

Panet, Charles Eugène (1829-1898), deputy minister of militia and defence (1875-98), was born at Quebec on November 27, 1829, the son of the Hon. Philippe Panet (q.v.). He was educated at the Quebec Seminary and at the Jesuit College, Georgetown; and in 1854 he was called to the bar of Lower Canada. In 1874 he was called to the Senate of Canada; but in 1875 he resigned his seat in the Senate to accept the position of deputy minister of militia and defence, and he retained this position until shortly before his death at Ottawa on November 22, 1898. He was thrice married; and he had sixteen children. In 1886 he was gazetted a colonel in the Canadian militia.

[P. G. Roy, *La famille Panet* (Lévis, 1906); Morgan, *Can. men* (1898); P. G. Roy, *Fils de Québec*, vol. 4 (Lévis, Que., 1933).]

Panet, Jean Antoine (1751-1815), speaker of the Legislative Assembly of Lower Canada (1792-1814), was born at Quebec on June 8, 1751, the eldest son of Jean Claude Panet (q.v.). In 1772 he was admitted to practice as a notary public, and in 1773 as a barrister. In 1792 he was elected to represent the upper town of Quebec in the Legislative Assembly of Lower Canada; and he was a member of the Assembly continuously until 1814, for the upper town of Quebec until 1808, for Huntingdon until 1814, and again for the upper town of Quebec in 1814. During the whole of this period, except for about two years between 1794 and 1797 when he was a judge of the Court of Common Pleas, he was speaker of the Assembly, being elected in all seven times. At the beginning of 1815 he was appointed a member of the Legislative Council; but he survived his appointment only a few months, dying at Quebec on May 17, 1815. In 1779 he married Louise Philippe, daughter of surgeon-major Philippe Louis François Badelard; and by her he had fifteen children.

[P. G. Roy, *La famille Panet* (Lévis, 1906) and *Les juges de la province de Québec* (Québec, 1933); Le Jeune, *Dict. gén.*; Bibaud, *Panth. can.*]

Panet, Jean Claude (1720-1778), jurist, was born in Paris, France, in 1720, the son of Jean Nicolas Panet and Marie Madeleine Françoise Foucher. He emigrated to Canada as a soldier in the troops of the Marine, and in 1741 was admitted to practice as an attorney. In 1744 he was appointed royal notary in Quebec, and in 1751 an assessor of the Sovereign Council. He was present at Quebec during the siege of 1759, and remained in the city after its capture. In 1760 he was appointed by General Murray (q.v.) chief clerk of the Superior Court of Quebec, and in 1765 clerk of the Court of Common Pleas in Quebec. In 1766 he resigned this post, and the next year he was admitted to practise as a barrister. In 1775 he was named a justice of the peace for Quebec, and in 1776 a judge of the Court of Common Pleas for Quebec. He was thus the first French-Canadian judge under British rule. He died at Quebec on February 28, 1778. In 1747 he married Marie-Louise, daughter of Claude Barolet; and by her he had fourteen children. He was the author of a *Journal du siège de Québec*, published by the Literary and Historical Society of Quebec in its *Manuscripts*, fourth series (Quebec, 1875).

[P. G. Roy, *La famille Panet* (Lévis, 1906) and *Les juges de la province de Québec* (Quebec, 1933); Le Jeune, *Dict. gén.*; Bibaud, *Panth. can.*]

Panet, Louis (1794-1884), senator of Canada, was born at Quebec on March 19, 1794, the third son of the Hon. Jean Antoine Panet (q.v.). He was admitted to practice as a notary public in Lower Canada in 1819. In 1852 he was appointed a member of the Legislative Council of Canada, in 1867 of the Legislative Council of Quebec, and in 1871 of the Senate of Canada. He resigned from the Senate, on account of ill health, in 1874; and he died at Quebec on May 15, 1884. In 1820 he married Marie Louise, daughter of Dr. Frederic W. Oliva; and by her he had five children.

[P. G. Roy, *La famille Panet* (Lévis, 1906); *Dom. ann. reg.*, 1884; *Can. parl. comp.*]

Panet, Philippe (1791-1855), jurist, was born at Quebec on February 28, 1791, the second son of the Hon. Jean Antoine Panet (q.v.). He served in the Canadian *Voltigeurs* during the War of 1812, and was present at the battle of Châteauguay. In 1817 he was called to the bar of Lower Canada; and from 1816 to 1824 and from 1830 to 1832 he represented Northumberland in the Legislative Assembly of the province. In 1831 he was appointed by Lord Aylmer (q.v.) a member of the executive council of Lower Canada; and in 1832 he was gazetted a judge of the Court of King's Bench for the district of Quebec. In 1838 he was suspended from the bench by Sir John Colborne (q.v.); but he resumed his seat in 1840, and continued to occupy a seat on the bench until his death at Quebec on January 15, 1855. In 1819 he married Marie Luce, daughter of Pierre Casgrain; and by her he had twelve children.

[P. G. Roy, *La famille Panet* (Lévis, 1906) and *Les juges de la province de Québec* (Quebec, 1933); Le Jeune, *Dict. gén.*]

Panet, Pierre Louis (1761-1812), jurist, was born in Montreal on August 2, 1761, the eldest son of the Hon. Pierre Méru Panet (q.v.). In 1780 he was admitted to practice as a notary public and barrister in Montreal; and in 1783 he was appointed clerk of the Court of Common Pleas in Quebec. In 1792 he was elected to represent Cornwallis in the Legislative Assembly of Lower Canada, and he opposed the election of his cousin, Jean Antoine Panet (q.v.), as speaker of the House. In 1795 he was appointed a judge of the Court of King's Bench at Montreal, in succession to his cousin, Jean Antoine Panet, and he sat on the bench in this court until his death. In 1800 he was elected to represent Montreal East in the Legislative Assembly; but in 1801 he was appointed a member of the Executive Council. He died at Montreal on December 2, 1812. In 1781 he married Marie Anne Cerré; and by her he had twelve children.

[P. G. Roy, *Le famille Panet* (Lévis, 1906) and *Les juges de la province de Québec* (Quebec, 1933); Morgan, *Cel. Can.*; Le Jeune, *Dict. gén.*; Bibaud, *Panth. can.*]

Panet, Pierre Méru (1731-1804), executive councillor of Lower Canada, was born in Paris, France, in 1731, the fourth child of Jean Nicolas Panet and Marie Françoise Foucher, and brother of Jean Claude Panet (q.v.). He joined his brother in Quebec in 1746, and in 1754 he was appointed royal notary for Montreal. In 1761 he was named clerk of the court of captains of militia in Montreal, during the period of military rule; and in 1768 he became a notary public and barrister in Montreal. In 1778 he succeeded his brother as a judge of the Court of Common Pleas for Quebec, and he sat on the bench until his retirement in 1784. In 1791 he was appointed a member of the Executive Council of Lower Canada; and he died at Montreal on June 15, 1804. In 1754 he married Marie Anne Trefflé Rottot, and by her he had seventeen children.

[P. G. Roy, *La famille Panet* (Lévis, 1906) and *Les juges de la province de Québec* (Quebec, 1933).]

Pangman, John (1808-1867), legislative councillor of Lower Canada, was the son of Peter Pangman (q.v.), and was born on November 13, 1808. He inherited his father's estate at Mascouche, Lower Canada, and was the seignior of Lachenaie. In 1837-38 he was a member of the Legislative Council of Lower Canada. He died on January 5, 1867. He was twice married, (1) in 1835 to Marie Henriette, daughter of the Hon. Janvier Lacroix, by whom he had three sons and two daughters,

and (2) in 1857 to Georgiana, daughter of Dr. Robertson, of Montreal, by whom he had one son.

[J. D. Borthwick, *Montreal, its history* (Montreal, 1875).]

Pangman, Peter (1744?-1819), fur-trader, was born in New England, of German descent, about 1744. He engaged in the fur-trade; and in 1767 his name appears in the Michilimackinac licences as trading to the Mississippi. In 1774 he transferred his energies to the Saskatchewan; and he was engaged in the fur-trade on the Saskatchewan almost continuously until 1790. In 1783 he joined Gregory, McLeod, and Co.; and in 1787, when this firm was absorbed by the North West Company, he became a partner in the North West Company. He retired from the fur-trade about 1794; and in that year he purchased the seigniory of Lachenaie, in Lower Canada; and here he died on August 28, 1819. He had a half-breed son, commonly known after him as "Bastonnais Pangman", who was prominent in the Seven Oaks affair on the Red River in 1816; and in 1796 he married Grace MacTier, by whom he had one son (q.v.) and one daughter.

[A. S. Morton, *Forrest Oakes, Charles Boyer, Joseph Fulton, and Peter Pangman in the North-West* (Trans. Roy. Soc. Can., 1937); R. Campbell, *History of the Scotch Presbyterian Church, St. Gabriel Street, Montreal* (Montreal, 1887).]

Panneton, Joseph Elie (1835-1910), priest, was born at Three Rivers, Lower Canada, on June 11, 1835, and died at Montreal, Quebec, on December 1, 1910. He was the author of *Un sanctuaire canadien* (Montreal, 1897).

[Allaire, *Dict. biog.*]

Panneton, Philippe (1895-1960), physician, author, and diplomat, was born at Three Rivers, Quebec, on April 30, 1895, and died in Portugal on December 29, 1960. He was educated at the University of Montreal (M.D., 1920), took post-graduate work in Paris, and practised medicine in Montreal. In 1956 he was appointed Canadian ambassador to Portugal. Under the *nom de plume* of "Ringuet", he was the author of *Trente arpents* (Paris, 1938), which was translated into English, German, and Dutch, *Un monde était leur empire* (Montreal, 1943), *L'héritage et autres contes* (Montreal, 1946), *Fausse monnaie* (Montreal, 1947), *Le poids du jour* (Montreal, 1948), and *L'amiral et le facteur* (Montreal, 1954). He was also joint author, with L. Francoeur, of *Littératures* (Montreal, 1924).

[*Can. who's who*, 1958-60; *Encyc. Can.*]

Panton, James Hoyes (1847-1898), educationist, was born in the Cupar of Fife, Scotland, on May 7, 1847. He came to Canada when a child, and was educated at the University of Toronto (B.A., 1877; M.A., 1878). Except for the years 1883-84, which he spent in Winnipeg, Manitoba, he was on the staff of the Ontario Agricultural College, Guelph, from 1878 to his death at Guelph, Ontario, on February 2, 1898. He was the author of *Rambles in the north-west* (Guelph, Ont., 1885); and while in Winnipeg he contributed a number of papers to the *Transactions* of the Literary and Scientific Society of Manitoba.

[Morgan, *Can. men* (1898).]

Panton, Lawrence Arthur Colley (1894-1954), painter, was born at Egremont, Cheshire, England, on June 15, 1894, and died at Toronto, Ontario, on November 22, 1954. He came to Canada in 1911, and studied art at the Ontario College of Art. From 1924 to 1950 he taught art in secondary schools in Toronto, and from 1951 to his death he was principal of the Ontario College of Art. He was a member of the Ontario Society of Artists, and its president from 1930 to 1937; he was elected an A.R.C.A. in 1934 and an R.C.A. in 1943; and from 1952 to his death he was vice-president of the Royal Canadian Academy. Two of his oil paintings are in the National Gallery at Ottawa. He was the author of *The story of the Canadian Society of Artists* (Toronto, 1947).

[P. Duvall, *Canadian water colour painting* (Toronto, 1954); *Can. who's who*, 1952-54.]

Papin, Joseph (1825-1862), lawyer and politician, was born at L'Assomption, Lower Canada, on December 14, 1825, was educated at L'Assomption College, and studied law in Montreal. He was one of the early members of the Institut Canadien of Montreal, of which he was president in 1847, and he was described as the "Danton" of the *Parti rouge*. From 1854 to 1857 he represented L'Assomption in the Legislative Assembly of Canada. He was then appointed counsel to the corporation of Montreal; and he died at L'Assomption on February 23, 1862.

[J. D. Borthwick, *Montreal, its history* (Montreal, 1875); Morgan, *Bib. can.*; Bibaud, *Panth. can.*; A. Fauteux, *Le mystérieux Joseph Papin* (Bull. rech. hist., 1932); E. Z. Massicotte, *Le mystérieux negociant-notaire Joseph Papin* (Bull. rech. hist., 1932).]

Papineau, Auguste Cyrille (1828-1915), jurist, was born at La Petite Nation (now Papineauville), Lower Canada, on March 4, 1828, the son of the Hon. Denis Benjamin Papineau (q.v.). He was educated at the College of St. Hyacinthe, and was called to the bar of Lower Canada in 1861. He practised law, first in St. Hyacinthe, and later in Montreal; and in 1876 he was appointed a judge of the Superior Court for the district of Montreal. He

retired from the bench in 1889; and he died at Montreal, Quebec, on May 27, 1915.

[P. G. Roy, *Les juges de la province de Québec* (Quebec, 1933).]

Papineau, Denis Benjamin (1789-1854), commissioner of crown lands for Canada (1844-47), was born in Montreal on November 13, 1789, the son of Joseph Papineau (q.v.) and Marie-Rosalie Cherrier, and the younger brother of Louis Joseph Papineau (q.v.). He did not share his brother's political views, and took no part in the rebellions of 1837-38. In 1842 he was elected to represent Ottawa county in the Legislative Assembly of Canada; and in 1844, at the invitation of Sir Charles Metcalfe (q.v.), he entered the Executive Council as commissioner of crown lands. It was he who introduced the bill authorizing the official use of the French language in the Assembly; though the bill did not become law until 1848, under the Baldwin-Lafontaine administration. He failed, however, to win over the support of any considerable number of French Canadians, and his partial deafness hindered his effectiveness both in the Assembly and in the cabinet. In 1847, therefore, he was persuaded to retire from office; and later in the same year he withdrew from the Assembly. Until his brother, Louis Joseph, returned from exile in 1846, he devoted his energies to the development of his father's seigniory of La Petite Nation, to which he had gone as a settler in 1809, and he was its directing spirit. In 1853 he founded Papineauville. He died at Plaisance, Canada East, on January 20, 1854. In 1813 he married Louise Angélique, daughter of Michel Cornud, a merchant of Quebec; and he had by her five sons and four daughters. The best-known of his sons were Denis Emery Papineau (1819-98), a notary public who represented Ottawa county in the Legislative Assembly of Canada from 1858 to 1861, and the Hon. Auguste Cyrille Papineau (q.v.).

[J. C. Dent, *The last forty years* (2 vols., Toronto, 1881); *Bull. rech. hist.*, 1933; Le Jeune, *Dict. gén.*]

Papineau, Joseph (1752-1841), notary public and politician, was born at Montreal, on October 16, 1752, the son of Joseph Papineau and Marie-Josèphe Beaudry. He was educated at the Montreal and Quebec seminaries, and was commissioned a surveyor in 1773 and a notary public in 1780. In 1776 he was one of two volunteers who carried dispatches from Montreal to Sir Guy Carleton (q.v.) at Quebec, through the American lines. He sat in the Legislative Assembly of Lower Canada from 1792 to 1804, and from 1809 to 1814, for Montreal county or Montreal East. In 1801 he bought the seigniory of La Petite Nation, on the Ottawa River; and here he lived until 1818, when he sold the seigniory to his son Louis Joseph (q.v.), and went to live in Montreal. Here he died on July 8, 1841. In

1779 he married Marie-Rosalie Cherrier; and by her he had seven sons and three daughters.

[L. O. David, *Les deux Papineau* (Montreal, 1896) and *Biographies et portraits* (Montreal, 1876); Bibaud, *Panth. can.*; Le Jeune, *Dict. gén.*; *Bull. rech. hist.*, 1933.]

Papineau, Louis Joseph (1786-1871), *patriote* leader, was born in Montreal on October 7, 1786, the son of Joseph Papineau (q.v.) and Marie-Rosalie Cherrier. He was educated at the Quebec Seminary, and was called to the bar of Lower Canada in 1811. He served as an officer in the Canadian militia during the War of 1812, and was present at the capture of Detroit. In 1814 he was elected to represent Montreal West in the Legislative Assembly of Lower Canada; in 1815 he was chosen speaker of the Assembly; and he sat for Montreal West continuously, and he occupied the speaker's chair almost continuously, until the rebellion of 1837-38. During this period he came to be regarded as the leader of the French-Canadian reformers or *patriotes*, and their chief spokesman. In 1820 Lord Dalhousie (q.v.) induced him to accept a seat in the Executive Council; but he found his advice disregarded, and soon resigned from the council. In 1822 he took a leading part in opposing the abortive union bill of that year, and went to London with John Neilson (q.v.) to protest against it. After this he became bitterly hostile to the British government in Canada; and not even Lord Gosford (q.v.) was able to conciliate him. His policy resulted in the rebellion of 1837, though he himself took no active part in the rebellion, and fled to the United States soon after the outbreak of hostilities. He remained in the United States until 1839, vainly endeavouring to bring about American intervention in the Canadian struggle; and then he went to France. He lived in Paris until, in 1844, the Canadian government granted an amnesty to the rebels of 1837; and under the amnesty he returned to Canada. Here he re-entered politics; and from 1848 to 1851 he represented Saint Maurice, and from 1852 to 1854 Deux-Montagnes, in the Legislative Assembly of Canada. But he did not regain his former commanding position in the House; and in 1854 he retired to private life, on his seigniory of La Petite Nation, on the Ottawa River. Here he died, at his manor-house of Montebello, on September 25, 1871. In 1818 he married Julie Bruneau; and by her he had several children. One of his daughters was the mother of Henri Bourassa (q.v.), noted politician and publicist, and former director of *Le Devoir*.

Papineau's place in Canadian history is difficult to define. Though he was regarded as the leader of the *patriotes* for so many years before 1837, he was, as the historian Christie has pointed out, a man who followed, rather than led, public opinion. Nor were his political views enlightened. He was not an advocate of responsible government; but his solution of the difficulties of Lower Canada lay in an elective upper house. His apparent vacillation and pusillanimity at the time of the rebellion of 1837 brought much discredit on him; and in his later days he lost almost entirely his hold on his compatriots. He lent his support to the Institut Canadien, and he may be regarded as having been a sort of godfather to the *Parti rouge*. Herein lies, perhaps, his chief importance in Canadian history.

[L.-J. Papineau, *Histoire de l'insurrection du Canada* (Montreal, 1968); F. Ouillet, *Louis Joseph Papineau: A divided soul* (Ottawa, 1961); A. D. DeCelles, *Papineau* (Montreal, 1905), and *Papineau Cartier* (Toronto, 1904); E. Circé-Côté, *Papineau, son influence* (Montreal, 1924); L. O. David, *Les deux Papineau* (Montreal, 1896); N. Story, *Papineau in exile* (Can. hist. rev., 1929); R. Rumilly, *Papineau* (Paris, 1934); *Dict. nat. biog.*; *Cyc. Am. biog.*; Rose, *Cyc. Can. biog.* (1888); Morgan, *Cel. Can.*; Dent, *Can. port.*, vol. 2; Taylor, *Brit. Am.*, vol. 3; Bibaud, *Panth. can.*; Le Jeune, *Dict. gén.*; *Dict. Can. biog.*, vol. 10.]

Papineau, Samuel (1670-1737), pioneer, was born in Montigny, Poitou, near Bordeaux, France, in 1670. He was a soldier, and came to Canada in 1695. In 1699 he obtained a grant of land from the Sulpicians in the seigniory of Ville Marie (Montreal), at Côte St. Michel; and he died at Sault-au-Recollet, Montreal, in 1737. In 1704 he married Catherine Quevillon, of Rivière des Prairies; and he became the founder of the Papineau family in Canada. His descendants are to be found, not only in the different provinces of Canada, but also in the United States and in England. He was surnamed Montigny, after his place of origin, to distinguish him from others who had taken the name of Papineau, like the Papineau surnamed Deslauriers and the Papineau surnamed Fortville. These had taken the name Papineau, as some of their people had married into the Papineau family. Even to-day some of the Papineaus are known by the name of Montigny.

[*Bull. rech. hist.*, 1933; *Dict. Can. biog.*, vol. 2.]

Papineau, Talbot Mercer (1883-1917), lawyer and soldier, was born at the manor-house of Montebello on March 25, 1883, the son of Louis Joseph Papineau and Caroline Rogers, of Philadelphia, and the great-grandson of the Hon. Louis Joseph Papineau (q.v.). He was educated at Oxford University (B.A., 1908), and on his return to Canada was called to the Quebec bar. In August, 1914, he joined the Princess Patricia's Canadian Light Infantry; he won the Military Cross in France, and rose to the rank of major. He was killed at Passchendaele on October 30, 1917. He was the author of "An open letter to Mr. Henri Bourassa" in *Canadian nationalism and the* *war* (Montreal, 1916). With his death, a career of much promise was cut short.

[Private information.]

Pâquet, Benjamin (1832-1900), priest and educationist, was born at St. Nicolas, Lower Canada, on March 27, 1832, and was ordained a priest of the Roman Catholic Church. He became a professor in Laval University, and from 1887 to 1893 was rector of the university. He died at Quebec, Que., on February 25, 1900. He was author of *Le libéralisme* (Quebec, 1872) and some pamphlets.

[Allaire, *Dict. biog.*]

Pâquet, Etienne Théodore (1850-1916), notary public and politician, was born at St. Nicolas, Canada East, on January 8, 1850, and was educated at the Quebec Seminary and Laval University. He was admitted a notary public in 1872, and he practised his profession in his native parish. He represented Lévis in the Legislative Assembly of Quebec from 1875 to 1885; and he was provincial secretary in the Chapleau administration from 1879 to 1882. He died at Quebec on May 23, 1916. He was the author of *Fragments d'histoire religieuse et civile de la paroisse de Saint-Nicolas* (Lévis, Que., 1894).

[*Bull. rech. hist.*, 1934; *Can. parl. comp.*]

Pâquet, Louis Adolphe (1859-1942), priest and educationist, was born at St. Nicolas, Canada East, on August 4, 1859, and was ordained a priest of the Roman Catholic Church. He became dean of the faculty of theology in Laval University; and in 1903 he was elected a fellow of the Royal Society of Canada. He died at Quebec City on February 24, 1942. A voluminous writer, he published *La foi et la raison* (Quebec, 1890), *Droit publique de l'église* (4 vols., Quebec, 1908-20), *Discours et allocutions* (Quebec, 1915), *Etudes et appréciations* (6 vols., Quebec, 1918-36), *Commentaria in summam theologicam St. Thomas* (6 vols., Quebec, 1920-23), *Cours d'éloquence sacrée* (2 vols., Quebec, 1925), and *La prière dans l'oeuvre de salut* (Quebec, 1931).

[*Proc. Roy. Soc. Can.*, 1942; G. Simard, *Monseigneur Louis-Adolphe Pâquet* (Trans. Roy. Soc. Can., 1942); C. O. Garant, *Louis-Adolphe Pâquet* (Canada français, 1942); *Can. who's who*, 1936-37.]

Paquet, Zéphirin (1818-1905), merchant, was born near Pointe-aux-Trembles, Lower Canada, on December 20, 1818. He was the founder and for many years the proprietor of an extensive wholesale drygoods business in Quebec. He died at Quebec City on February 26, 1905.

[Rév. Frère Alcas, *Zéphirin Paquet: Sa famille, sa vie, son oeuvre* (Quebec, 1927).]

Paquin, Elzéar (1850-1947), physician and author, was born at Ile Bizard, Canada East, in 1850, and died at Montreal, Quebec, on January 17, 1947. He graduated in medicine from Laval University, Montreal, and for many years he practised medicine in Chicago, Illinois. He returned to Montreal about the turn of the century, and became known as a pronounced French-Canadian nationalist. He was the author of *Le livre des mères* (Montreal, 1881), *Riel: Tragédie en quatre actes* (Montreal, 1886), and *La colonie canadienne-française de Chicago* (Chicago, 1893).

[Montreal *Gazette*, Jan. 19, 1947.]

Paquin, Jacques (1791-1847), priest, was born at Deschambault, Lower Canada, on September 19, 1791, and was ordained a priest of the Roman Catholic Church in 1814. He was the parish priest at St. Eustache during the rebellion of 1837; and he was probably the author of the *Journal historique des évènements arrivés à Saint-Eustache, pendant la rebellion du comté du Lac des deux Montagnes* (Montreal, 1838). He died at St. Eustache on December 7, 1847.

[Allaire, *Dict. biog.*]

Paquin, Julien (1858-1938), priest, was born at St. André, Canada East, on April 24, 1858, entered the Society of Jesus, and was ordained a priest in 1886. He was stationed at Wikwemikong, on Manitoulin Island, from 1892 to 1898 and from 1902 to 1907; and he died at Wikwemikong on May 11, 1938. He was the author of *The tragedy of old Huronia* (Fort Ste. Marie, near Midland, Ont., 1932).

[Allaire, *Dict. biog.*]

Paradis, Émilien Zéphirin (1841-1908), jurist, was born at L'Acadie, Canada East, on December 24, 1841, and practised law at St. Johns, Quebec. In 1901 he was appointed a judge of the Superior Court for the district of Iberville; and he continued on the bench until his death at St. Johns, Quebec, on May 10, 1908.

[P. G. Roy, *Les juges de la province de Québec* (Quebec, 1933).]

Paradis, J. Gaudiose (1860-1924), physician and author, was born in 1860, and was educated at Laval University. He became a country doctor, and published his reminiscences under the title, *Feuilles de journal: Souvenirs d'un médecin de campagne* (Quebec, 1923). He died at Quebec City on December 1, 1924.

[Private information.]

Paradis, Jobson (1871-1926), painter, was born at St. Johns, Quebec, in 1871, the son of the Hon. E. Z. Paradis (q.v.). He was educated at the University of Ottawa and at Notre Dame University, in Indiana; and later he studied painting in Paris under Gérome and Grégori. On his return to Canada, he obtained a post as a translator in the civil service at

Ottawa. He died at Guelph, Ontario, on May 11, 1926.

[*Bull. rech. hist.*, 1926.]

Paradis, Louis Laurent (1859-1938), priest, was born at Quebec, Canada East, on February 28, 1859, and was ordained a priest of the Roman Catholic Church in 1882. For many years he was parish priest at Lotbinière, Quebec; and he was the author of *Les annales de Lotbinière* (Quebec, 1933). He died at Quebec on May 26, 1938.

[Allaire, *Dict. biog.*]

Paradis, Odilon (1829-1889), priest, was born at Quebec, Lower Canada, on June 29, 1829, and was ordained a priest of the Roman Catholic Church in 1852. He spent his life as a parish priest in various parishes in the province of Quebec; and he died at Quebec City on March 1, 1889. He was the author of *Notes historiques sur la paroisse et les curés de Sainte-Anne de la Pocatière* (Ste. Anne de la Pocatière, Que., 1869).

[Allaire, *Dict. biog.*; *Bull. rech. hist.*, 1929.]

Paré, Edmond (1857-1897), lawyer and journalist, was born at Quebec, Canada East, in 1857, and was educated at Laval University. He was called to the Quebec bar in 1884, and he practised law in Quebec until his death on November 24, 1897. He contributed articles and sketches to various periodicals; and these were collected after his death by L. Brunet in a volume entitled *Lettres et opuscules* (Quebec, 1899).

[N. E. Dionne, *Inventaire chronologique des livres, brochures, journaux, et revues publiés dans la province de Québec de 1764 à 1904* (Trans. Roy. Soc. Can., 1904).]

Parent, Amand (1818-1907), clergyman, was born at Quebec, Lower Canada, in 1818, the son of French-Canadian Roman Catholic parents. In 1840 he was converted to Protestantism, and in 1856 he became a missionary of the Methodist Church, the first French Canadian to be ordained in this denomination. He died at Waterloo, Quebec, on February 18, 1907. He wrote an autobiography, entitled *The life of the Rev. Amand Parent* (Toronto, 1887), describing "fifty-seven years' experience in the evangelical work in Canada, thirty-one years in connection with the [Methodist] Conference, and eight years among the Oka Indians."

[G. H. Cornish (comp.), *Cyclopaedia of Methodism in Canada* (2 vols., Toronto, 1881-1903).]

Parent, Etienne (1802-1874), journalist, was born at Beauport, near Quebec, Lower Canada, on May 2, 1802, and was educated at the College of Nicolet and the Quebec Seminary. From 1822 to 1825 he was editor of *Le Canadien* in Quebec; and in 1831, after several years devoted to the study of law, he revived this journal, and again became its editor. In this position he achieved an unrivalled place in French-Canadian journalism. He supported L. J. Papineau (q.v.) up to the outbreak of the rebellion of 1837; and, though he did not take part in the rebellion, he was arrested in 1837 and imprisoned. In 1841 he was elected for the county of Saguenay to the first Legislative Assembly of united Canada; but in 1842 a serious deafness, contracted in prison, compelled him to resign his seat. In the same year he gave up the editorship of *Le Canadien*, and accepted the post of clerk of the Executive Council. In 1847 he was appointed under-secretary for Lower Canada; in 1867 he became under-secretary of state for the Dominion; and he retired from office in 1872. He died at Ottawa on December 22, 1874. After his entrance into the civil service, he exerted an influence through public lectures which he delivered before the Institut Canadien and elsewhere; and these were collected and published after his death under the title *Discours* (Quebec, 1878).

[P. E. Gosselin, ed., *Etienne Parent* (Montreal, 1964); B. Sulte, *Mélanges historiques* (Montreal, 1928); *Dict. nat. biog.*; *Cyc. Am. biog.*; Morgan, *Bib. can.*; Bibaud, *Panth. can.*; Le Jeune, *Dict. gén.*; E. Lareau, *Histoire de la littérature canadienne* (Quebec, 1873); *Dict. Can. biog.*, vol. 10.]

Parent, Georges (1879-1942), speaker of the Senate of Canada (1940-42), was born at Quebec City on December 15, 1879, the son of the Hon. Simon Napoléon Parent (q.v.). He was educated at Laval University, and was called to the bar of Quebec in 1904. He represented Montmorency in the Canadian House of Commons from 1904 to 1911, and Quebec West from 1917 to 1930. He was called to the Senate of Canada in 1930; and in 1940 he was appointed speaker of the Senate. He died at Montreal, Quebec, on December 14, 1942.

[*Can. parl. comp.*; *Can. who's who*, 1938-39.]

Parent, Simon Napoléon (1855-1920), prime minister of Quebec (1900-05), was born at Beauport, near Quebec, Lower Canada, on September 12, 1855, the son of Simon Polycarpe Parent and Lucie Bélanger. He was educated at Laval University (LL.L., 1881; LL.D., 1902), and was called to the bar of Quebec in 1881 (Q.C., 1899). From 1890 to 1905 he represented St. Sauveur as a Liberal in the Legislative Assembly of Quebec; from 1894 to 1905 he was mayor of Quebec; from 1897 to 1900 he was commissioner of lands, mines, and forests in the Marchand administration; and from 1900 to 1905 he was prime minister of Quebec. In 1905 he was appointed chairman of the National Transcontinental Railway Commission, and this position he retained until the defeat of the Laurier government in 1911. He was then appointed chairman of the Quebec Streams Commission; and he died at Montreal on September 7, 1920. In 1877 he married Clara, daughter of Ambroise Gendron; and by her he had a family of four sons and four daughters. In 1902 he was made an LL.D. of Bishop's College, Lennoxville, Quebec.

[H. Charlesworth (ed.), *A cyclopaedia of Canadian biography* (Toronto, 1919); Morgan, *Can. men* (1912); *Can. who's who* (1910); *Can. parl. comp.*]

Paris, Firmin (pseud.). See **Hudon, Maxime.**

Parke, Thomas (d. 1864), surveyor-general of Canada (1841-45), was a native of Wicklow county, Ireland, who came to Canada in 1820, and became a builder and architect. From 1834 to 1840 he represented Middlesex in the Legislative Assembly of Upper Canada; and from 1841 to 1844 in the Assembly of united Canada. From 1841 to 1845 he was surveyor-general of Canada, but without a seat in the Executive Council. He died at St. Catharines, Canada West, on January 29, 1864.

[Rose, *Cyc. Can. biog.* (1886), under "E. Jones Parke"; J. C. Dent, *The last forty years* (2 vols., Toronto, 1881).]

Parker, Daniel McNeill (1822-1907), physician and politician, was born at Windsor, Nova Scotia, on April 28, 1822, the son of Francis Parker. He was educated at Windsor and at Horton Academy, and he studied medicine at Edinburgh University. He practised medicine and surgery for many years in Halifax; and his name became a household word in Nova Scotia. In 1867 he was called to the Legislative Council of Nova Scotia; and he sat in the Council until 1898. He died at Halifax, Nova Scotia, on November 4, 1907.

[W. F. Parker, *Daniel McNeill Parker, M.D.: His ancestry and a memoir of his life* (Toronto, 1910); *Can. who was who*, vol. 1.]

Parker, Sir Horatio Gilbert, Bart. (1862-1932), author, was born at Camden East, Canada West, on November 23, 1862, the eldest son of Joseph Parker. He was educated at the Ottawa Normal School and at Trinity University, Toronto; and was ordained in 1882 a deacon of the Church of England, but did not take orders. In 1885 he went to Australia, and there engaged in journalism. In 1889 he went to England, and turned to the writing of fiction. He achieved a great success as an historical novelist, and entered politics in England. From 1900 to 1918 he represented Gravesend in the British House of Commons, and he became a leading figure in the Unionist party. He was created a knight bachelor in 1902, a baronet in 1915, and a privy councillor in 1916. He died in London, England, on September 6, 1932. In 1895 he married Amy (d. 1925),

daughter of Ashley Van Tine, New York. He was the author of the following novels and collections of short stories: *Pierre and his people* (London, 1892), *The chief factor* (New York, 1893), *The trespasser* (London, 1893), *Mrs. Falchion* (London, 1893), *The translation of a savage* (London, 1894), *The trail of the sword* (London, 1895), *When Valmond came to Pontiac* (London, 1895), *An adventurer of the north* (London, 1895), *A Romany of the snows* (New York, 1896), *The pomp of the Lavilettes* (Boston, 1896), *The seats of the mighty* (London, 1896), *The battle of the strong* (London, 1898), *The liar* (Boston, 1899), *The hill of pains* (Boston, 1899), *The lane that had no turning* (London, 1900), *The right of way* (London, 1901), *A pardonable liar* (Boston, 1902), *Donovan Pasha* (London, 1902), *A ladder of swords* (London, 1904), *The march of the white guard* (New York, 1906), *The weavers* (London, 1907), *Northern lights* (London, 1909), *Cumner's son* (London, 1910), *The going of the white swan* (New York, 1912), *The judgement house* (London, 1913), *The money master* (London, 1915), *You never know your luck* (London, 1915), *The world for sale* (London, 1916), *Wild youth and another* (London, 1919), *No defence* (London, 1920), *Carnac's folly* (London, 1922), *The power and the glory* (London, 1925), *Tarboe* (London, 1927), and *The promised land* (London, 1928). He was also the author of two books of verse, *A lover's diary* (Chicago, 1894; new ed., London, 1901) and *Embers* (London, privately printed, 1908), a book of travel, *Round the compass in Australia* (London, 1892), and a book on the First World War, *The world in the crucible* (London, 1915). With Claude G. Bryan, he wrote *Old Quebec* (London, 1903), and with Richard Dawson, *The land, the people, and the state* (London, 1910). In 1913 a collected edition of his works was published in New York.

[J. W. Garvin, *Sir Gilbert Parker and Canadian Literature* (Canadian bookman, 1932); Sir A. Macphail, *Sir Gilbert Parker* (Trans. Roy. Soc. Can., 1939); *Who was who*, 1929-40; O. J. Stevenson, *A people's best* (Toronto, 1927); L. Pierce, *An outline of Canadian literature* (Toronto, 1927); Morgan, *Can. men* (1912); *Dict. nat. biog.*]

Parker, Reginald John Marsden (1881-1948), lieutenant-governor of Saskatchewan (1945-48), was born at Liskeard, Cornwall, England, on February 7, 1881, and died at Regina, Saskatchewan, on March 23, 1948. He came to Canada in 1898, and was for many years a farmer near Togo, Saskatchewan. He was a member of the Saskatchewan legislature from 1929 to 1944, and was minister of municipal affairs in the Patterson government from 1934 to 1944. In 1945 he was appointed lieutenant-governor of the province, but died during his term of office.

[*Can. who's who*, 1948; *Can. parl. guide*, 1947; *Encyc. Can.*]

Parker, Stuart Crawford (1888-1950), clergyman and author, was born in Glasgow, Scotland, on November 21, 1888, and died at Richmond Hill, Ontario, on January 15, 1950. He was educated at the University of Glasgow (M.A., 1909; B.D., 1912), and became a minister of the Church of Scotland. He came to Canada in 1923 as minister of St. Andrew's Presbyterian Church, Toronto; and in 1939 he was elected moderator of the Presbyterian Church in Canada. He was the author of *The book of St. Andrew's* (Toronto, 1930), *Little tales of Jesus* (Toronto, 1935), *Jesus asks a question* (Toronto, 1937), *The guest chamber* (Toronto, 1938), and *Yet not consumed* (Toronto, 1947). In 1927, Knox College, Toronto, conferred on him the degree of D.D.

[*Can. who's who*, 1948.]

Parker, William Frederick (1860-1918), lawyer and biographer, was born at Halifax, Nova Scotia, on September 10, 1860, the son of Dr. Daniel McNeill Parker (q.v.); and died at Wolfville, Nova Scotia, on March 10, 1918. He was the author of *Daniel McNeill Parker, M.D.: His ancestry and a memoir of his life* (Toronto, 1910).

[*Records of the graduates of Acadia University* (Wolfville, N.S., 1926).]

Parker, William Ruston Percival (1872-1936), lawyer, was born in Brantford, Ontario, on July 5, 1872; and was educated at the University of Toronto (B.A., 1893; LL.B., 1896). He was called to the bar of Ontario in 1896, and practised law in Toronto. He died on April 21, 1936. He was the author of *Frauds on creditors and assignments for the benefit of creditors* (Toronto, 1903), and joint author, with George M. Clark, of *Company law* (Toronto, 1909).

[*Who's who in Canada,* 1934-35; Morgan, *Can. men* (1912).]

Parkin, Sir George Robert (1846-1922), educationist and author, was born at Salisbury, New Brunswick, on February 8, 1846, the son of John Parkin. He was educated at the University of New Brunswick (B.A., 1868; M.A., 1873; LL.D., 1894), and at Oxford University. From 1868 to 1872 he was headmaster of the Bathurst Grammar School; from 1874 to 1889 of the Collegiate School, Fredericton; and from 1895 to 1902 of Upper Canada College, Toronto. In 1889 he made a lecture tour of the Empire, at the request of the Imperial Federation League; and in 1902 he was appointed organizing representative of the Rhodes Scholarship Trust. This position he held until his death at London, England, on June 25, 1922. In 1878 he married Annie Connell, daughter of William Fisher, of Fredericton, New Brunswick; and by her he had one son and four daughters. In 1898 he was created a C.M.G., and in 1920 a K.C.M.G. He was a D.C.L. of Trinity University, Toronto (1898),

and an LL.D. of McGill University (1903). His chief publications were *Reorganization of the British Empire* (London, 1882), *Round the Empire* (London, 1892), *Imperial federation* (London, 1892), *The great Dominion* (London, 1895), *Edward Thring, headmaster of Uppingham school* (London, 1898), *Sir John Macdonald* (Toronto, Makers of Canada, 1908), and *The Rhodes scholarships* (Toronto, 1912).

[Sir J. Willison, *Sir George Parkin* (London, 1929); Sir C. Lucas, *Sir George Parkin* (United Empire, 1922); *Can. who was who*, vol. 1; *Who was who*, 1916-28; W. G. MacFarlane, *New Brunswick bibliography* (Saint John, N.B., 1895).]

Parkin, John Buckworth (1816-1875), criminal lawyer, was born at Dewsbury, Yorkshire, England, in 1816, the son of the Rev. Edward Parkin. He came to Canada in 1818, with his father, who was appointed rector of the Church of England at Chambly, Lower Canada; and he was called to the bar of Lower Canada in 1837. He became perhaps the most famous criminal lawyer of his day in Canada; and he died at Quebec on December 16, 1875.

[C. Langelier, *J. B. Parkin* (Bull. rech. hist., 1897); *Dict. Can. biog.*, vol. 10.]

Parkinson, Amy (1859?-1938), poet, was born in Liverpool, England, about 1859, and emigrated to Canada as a child. She lived for the rest of her life in Toronto, Ontario; and for more than sixty years she was a bedridden invalid. From her sick room she issued numerous poems and some booklets of verse, notably *Love through all* (Toronto, 1893) and *Best* (Toronto, 1902). She died in Toronto on February 12, 1938.

[C. C. James, *A bibliography of Canadian poetry* (Toronto, 1899).]

Parks, William Arthur (1868-1936), palaeontologist, was born at Hamilton, Ontario, on December 11, 1868. He was educated at the University of Toronto (B.A., 1892; Ph.D., 1900; LL.D., 1936); and he became a fellow in geology at this university in 1893. He became head of the department of geology, and director of the Royal Ontario Museum of Palaeontology; and he retained these positions until shortly before his death at Toronto on October 3, 1936. He was a fellow of the Royal Society of London and of the Royal Society of Canada, and was elected president of the latter in 1926. In 1925 he was elected president of the geological section of the British Association for the Advancement of Science, and in 1927 president of the Palaeontological Society of America. He was the author of *Building and ornamental stones of Canada* (2 vols., Ottawa, 1912-14), and co-author, with A. P. Coleman, of *Elementary geology, with special reference to Canada* (London, 1922); and he was especially noted for the work he did on the dinosaurs of Alberta, with regard to which he published several studies.

[M. A. Fritz, *William Arthur Parks, Ph.D., LL.D., F.R.S., 1868-1936* (Toronto, 1971); *Proc. Roy. Soc. Can.*, 1937; *Can. who's who*, 1936-37; Morgan, *Can. men* (1912).]

Parlow, Kathleen (1890-1963), musician, was born in Calgary, Alberta, in 1890. She studied violin with Henry Holmes of San Francisco as a child, and later with Leopold Aur, at the Imperial Conservatory, St. Petersburg, Russia. At fifteen she played for Queen Alexandra in London and she made her formal debut in Berlin in 1908. She appeared as guest soloist with European and North American orchestras and toured extensively in Europe and the Far East. She returned to Canada, and during the 1940s was co-founder of the Canadian Trio, and of the Parlow string quartette. She continued to give concert recitals until 1959, and was active in the Royal Conservatory of Music at Toronto. She died at Oakville, Ontario, August 19, 1963.

[*Creative Canada*, vol. 2.]

Parmelee, George William (1860-1941), educationist and historian, was born at Waterloo, Canada East, in 1860. He was educated at Queen's University, Kingston (B.A., 1889), and in 1891 he was appointed English secretary of the Council of Public Instruction of the province of Quebec. He held this post with distinction for nearly forty years; and he was honoured with the degree of D.C.L. from Bishop's College, Lennoxville, in 1902, and that of LL.D. from McGill University in 1911. He retired on pension in 1930; and he died at Quebec City on September 9, 1941. He was joint editor, with Sir Arthur Doughty (q.v.), of *The siege of Quebec and the battle of the Plains of Abraham* (6 vols., Quebec, 1901); and he compiled *The school law of the province of Quebec* (Quebec, 1899).

[Morgan, *Can. men* (1912).]

Parr, John (1725-1791), governor of Nova Scotia (1782-91), was born in Dublin, Ireland, on December 20, 1725, the son of John Parr, of Belturbet, county Cavan. He was educated at Trinity High School, and entered the British army as an ensign in 1744. In 1771 he reached the rank of lieutenant-colonel; and in 1782 he was appointed governor of Nova Scotia. It was during his period of office that the Loyalist migration to Nova Scotia took place, and that New Brunswick was made a separate province; and Saint John, New Brunswick, was first named Parrtown in his honour. His commission was changed in 1786 to that of lieutenant-governor of Nova Scotia, instead of governor; and he was thus the last to hold the post of governor and commander-in-chief of Nova Scotia. He died at Halifax, Nova Scotia, on November 25, 1791. In 1761 he married Sara, daughter of Richard Walmesley, of Lan-

cashire; and by her he had three sons and two daughters.

[J. S. Macdonald, *Memoir of Governor John Parr* (Coll. Nova Scotia Hist. Soc., 1910); Le Jeune, *Dict. gén.*]

Parry, Sir William Edward (1790-1855), sailor and explorer, was born at Bath, England, on December 19, 1790. He entered the British navy as a midshipman in 1803, and served throughout the Napoleonic wars. In 1818 he accompanied Capt. (afterwards Sir John) Ross (q.v.) on his expedition to the Arctic; in 1819-20 he commanded another expedition, which penetrated to Melville Island; in 1821-23 he was in command of an expedition which reached the western end of Fury and Hecla straits; and in 1824-25 he commanded a fourth expedition, but had the misfortune to lose one of his ships in Prince Regent Inlet. From 1825 to 1829 he was hydrographer to the admiralty; and in his later years he held a variety of positions. He died at Ems, Germany, where he had gone for medical treatment, on July 8, 1855. He was knighted in 1829, and was promoted to the rank of rear-admiral in 1852. He was the author of a *Journal of a voyage for the discovery of a north-west passage from the Atlantic to the Pacific, performed in the years 1819-20* (London, 1821), *Journal of a second voyage for the discovery of a north-west passage, performed in the years 1821-3* (London, 1824), *Journal of a third voyage for the discovery of a north-west passage, performed in the years 1824-5* (London, 1826), and *A narrative of an attempt to reach the North Pole in boats fitted for that purpose, and attached to H.M. ship Hecla, in the year 1827* (London, 1828). An abridgement of the three volumes relating to the north-west passage was published in 5 vols. (London, 1828).

[A. Parry, *Parry of the Arctic* (London, Toronto, 1963); E. Parry, *Memoirs of Rear-Admiral Sir W. Edward Parry, Kt.* (London, 1857); *Dict. nat. biog.*; *Encyclopedia Americana*; Le Jeune, *Dict. gén.*]

Pascal, Albert (1848-1920), first Roman Catholic bishop of Prince Albert, was born at St. Genest de Bauzon, France, on August 3, 1848. He came to Canada as a youth; was educated at the Montreal Seminary; and was ordained a priest in 1873. He became a missionary, first in the lumber camps of the upper Ottawa Valley, and then in the far north-west. In 1891 he was appointed apostolic vicar of Saskatchewan, with the title of bishop of Mosynopolis; and in 1907 he became first bishop of Prince Albert. He died at Aix-en-Provence, France, on July 14, 1920.

[Allaire, *Dict. biog.*; Le Jeune, *Dict. gén.*]

Patenaude, Esioff Léon (1875-1963), politician, was born in St. Isadore, Quebec, February 12, 1875. He was educated at Montreal College and at Laval University

(B.A., 1899). He became an advocate in 1899. He was first elected to the Quebec Legislative Assembly in 1908 and re-elected in 1912, resigning in 1915 on being appointed minister of inland revenue in the federal government of Sir Robert Borden (q.v.). He resigned in 1917 on the conscription issue. In 1923 he re-entered political life as a member of the Quebec legislature; he ran and was defeated in the federal election of 1925. In 1926 Arthur Meighen (q.v.) appointed him to his cabinet, but he was defeated along with the Meighen government in the general election of 1926. From 1934 to 1939 he was lieutenant-governor of Quebec. He was president of Alliance Nationale; vice-president of Crédit Foncier Franco-Canadien; director of McColl-Frontenac Oil, Commerce Mutual Fire Insurance, and Canadian Mercantile Insurance Company. He died at Montreal, Quebec, February 7, 1963.

[*Can. who's who*, 1955-57; Metropolitan Toronto Library Board, *Biographical scrapbooks*, vols. 5 & 21.]

Paterson, Charles (d. 1788), fur-trader, was a trader from Montreal whose name first appears in the fur-trade licences in 1770. He appears on the Saskatchewan in 1774, and in the winter of 1775-76 he made, with Alexander Henry (q.v.) and William Holmes (q.v.), an overland journey to the Assiniboine. He formed a partnership with John McGill (q.v.), and the firm of McGill and Paterson held two shares in the sixteen-share North West Company formed in 1779. About 1783, however, he withdrew from the North West trade, for his name is not found among the partners of the North West Company of that year; and shortly afterward he became the director for the trade of the Michilimackinac Company in Lake Michigan. He was drowned in Lake Michigan, off a point still known as Paterson's Point, on September 10, 1788; and a vivid account of his death has been left us by J. B. Perrault (q.v.), who was an eyewitness. He had a brother, Allan, who was in partnership with him after 1780, but who retired from the fur-trade after his death, and who married in 1784 Cornelia, the daughter of Capt. John Munro (q.v.), of Matilda.

[W. S. Wallace (ed.), *Documents relating to the North West Company* (Toronto: The Champlain Society, 1934).]

Paterson, Thomas William (1852-1921), lieutenant-governor of British Columbia (1909-14), was born at Darvel, Ayrshire, Scotland, on December 6, 1852, the son of William Paterson and Margaret Pearson. He came to Canada with his parents in 1855, and was educated in Oxford county, Ontario. He became a railway contractor, built a section of the Canadian Pacific Railway north of Lake Superior, and later built a number of railways in British Columbia. From 1902 to 1903 he represented North Victoria in the Legislative Assembly of British Columbia, and from 1903 to 1907 he represented the Islands. In 1909 he was appointed lieutenant-governor of British Columbia; and his term of office expired in 1914. He died at Victoria, British Columbia, on August 29, 1921. In 1886 he married Emma, daughter of the Hon. George Riley, a senator of Canada.

[Morgan, *Can. men* (1912); *Can. parl. comp.*]

Paterson, William (1839-1914), minister of customs for Canada (1897-1911), was born in Hamilton, Upper Canada, on September 19, 1839, the son of James and Martha Paterson, of Aberdeen, Scotland. His parents died from cholera in 1849, and he was adopted by the Rev. Dr. Ferrier, a Presbyterian minister. He was educated at Hamilton and Caledonia, Haldimand county, Upper Canada, and he went into business in Brantford, Upper Canada. Here he established himself in 1863 as a manufacturer of biscuits and confectionery, and built up a successful business. From 1872 to 1896 he represented South Brant in the Canadian House of Commons; and during the latter part of this period he became one of the leaders of the Liberal party in the House. In 1896 he was defeated for South Brant, but was returned for North Grey, and was appointed controller of customs, and in 1897 minister of customs, in the Laurier administration. This department he administered continuously until the defeat of the Laurier government in 1911, sitting successively for North Grey (1896-1900), for North Wentworth (1900-04), and for Brant (1904-11). In 1902 he was a delegate to the Imperial Conference; and in 1911 he was one of the ministers who negotiated the abortive reciprocity agreement at Washington. He died at Picton, Ontario, on March 18, 1914. In 1863 he married Lucy Olive, daughter of T. C. Davies, of Brantford.

[Morgan, *Can. men* (1912); *Can. parl. comp.*; Rose, *Cyc. Can. biog.* (1886); O. D. Skelton, *Life and letters of Sir Wilfrid Laurier* (2 vols., Toronto, 1921); J. Young, *Public men and public life in Canada* (2 vols., Toronto, 1912); Sir G. Ross, *Getting into parliament and after* (Toronto, 1913).]

Paterson-Smyth, John. See **Smyth, John Paterson.**

Paton, John Lewis Alexander (1863-1946), educationist, was born in Sheffield, England, on August 13, 1863, and died at Beckenham, Kent, England, in May, 1946. He was educated at St. John's College, Cambridge (B.A., 1886; M.A., 1890); and became a schoolmaster. After being successively headmaster of University College School, London, and of the Manchester Grammar School, he was appointed the first president of Memorial University College, in St. John's, Newfoundland, in 1928, and he held this position until 1933.

[J. A. Venn, *Alumni Cantabrigienses*, Part II (Cambridge, 1953).]

Patrick, Alfred (1811-1892), civil servant and author, was born in Kingston, Upper Canada, in 1811, and was educated at York (Toronto) under the Rev. John Strachan (q.v.). He entered the civil service in 1827, and in 1873 was appointed clerk of the House of Commons. He retired on pension in 1880; and he died at Niagara-on-the-Lake, Ontario, on July 18, 1892. He was the author of a *Digest of "Precedents or decisions" by the select committees appointed to try the merits of Upper Canada contested elections, from 1824 to 1849* (Montreal, 1849).

[*Can. parl. comp.*]

Patrick, William (1852-1911), clergyman and educationist, was born in Glasgow, Scotland, on September 6, 1852, and was educated at Glasgow University (M.A., 1875) and at the Free Church College in Glasgow. He was ordained a clergyman of the Free Church of Scotland in 1878; and from 1878 to 1892 was minister of Free St. David's Church, Kirkintilloch, and from 1892 to 1900 minister of Free St. Paul's, Dundee. In 1900 he came to Canada as principal of Manitoba College, Winnipeg; and he retained this position until his death at Kirkintilloch, Scotland, on September 28, 1911. He was the author of *James, the Lord's brother* (Edinburgh, 1906).

[Morgan, *Can. men* (1912).]

Patterson, Andrew Dickson (1854-1930), portrait painter, was born in Picton, Ontario, on June 30, 1854, the son of the Hon. Christopher Salmon Patterson (q.v.). He was educated at Upper Canada College, Toronto, and he studied painting in England. He became a portrait-painter in much demand for the painting of Canadian public men; and his work was exhibited at the Chicago and St. Louis World's Fairs and at the Pan-American Exhibition at Buffalo in 1901. In 1886 he was elected a fellow of the Royal Canadian Academy. He died at Montreal, Quebec, on July 31, 1930.

[N. MacTavish, *The fine arts in Canada* (Toronto, 1925); Morgan, *Can. men* (1912).]

Patterson, Christopher Salmon (1823-1893), jurist, was born in London, England in 1823, of Irish parentage, and was educated at the Royal Academical Institution, Belfast, Ireland. He came to Canada in 1845, and in 1851 was called to the bar of Upper Canada (Q.C., 1872). In 1874 he was appointed a judge of the Court of Appeal in Ontario; and in 1888 a judge of the Supreme Court of Canada. He died on July 24, 1893. In 1853 he married the daughter of Andrew Dickson, of Glenconway, Antrim, Ireland.

[*Can. parl. comp.*; Dent, *Can. port.*, vol. 4.]

Patterson, Edward Lloyd Stewart (1869-1932), banker and author, was born in Strathroy, Ontario, in 1869, the son of the Rev. Robert Stewart Patterson. He was educated at Gibraltar and in England; but in 1888 returned to Canada, and entered the service of the Eastern Townships Bank at Sherbrooke. In this bank, which was absorbed by the Canadian Bank of Commerce in 1912, he rose to the rank of assistant general manager; and in the Canadian Bank of Commerce he became superintendent of the Eastern Townships branches. He retired on pension in 1930; and he died at Toronto, Ontario, on September 4, 1932. He was the author of *Notes on foreign exchange* (Toronto, 1916), *Banking principles and practice* (New York, 1917), *Domestic and foreign exchange* (New York, 1918), *International exchange* (New York, 1921), and *Canadian banking* (Toronto, 1932), and, with M. B. Foster, he was co-author of a volume on *Banking* (New York, 1931).

[*Journal of the Canadian Bankers' Association*, vol. 40, 1932-33.]

Patterson, Frederic William (1877-1965), educationist, was born in Saint John, New Brunswick, July 18, 1877. He was educated at Woodstock and Fredericton in New Brunswick and at McMaster University in Ontario, being ordained into the ministry of the Baptist Church in 1899. He held pastorates in western Canada at Calgary, Edmonton, and Winnipeg, and was general secretary of the Baptist Union of Western Canada before being appointed president of Acadia University at Wolfville, Nova Scotia, in 1923, a post which he held until 1947. During his tenure the university grew from 300 to 900 students and the value of its buildings rose from $500,000 to $4 million. He died at Wolfville, Nova Scotia, February 10, 1965.

[*Can. who's who*, 1961-63.]

Patterson, George (1824-1897), clergyman and historian, was born at Pictou, Nova Scotia, on April 30, 1824, the son of Abraham Patterson and Christiana, daughter of the Rev. James MacGregor (q.v.). He was educated at Pictou Academy and at Dalhousie University (LL.D., 1896); and he was ordained a minister at the Presbyterian Church in 1849. For twenty-seven years he was minister of Green Hill, Pictou; and then he became minister at New Glasgow, Nova Scotia. He died at New Glasgow, Nova Scotia, on October 26, 1897. In 1851 he married Margaret, daughter of Hugh McDonald (q.v.), of Antigonish, Nova Scotia. In addition to a number of historical contributions to the Transactions of the Royal Society of Canada, of which he was elected a member in 1889, he was the author of a *History of the county of Pictou* (Montreal, 1877), and of the following biographies: *Memoir of the Rev. James MacGregor* (Halifax, N.S., 1859), *Memoirs of the Revds. S. F. Johnston and J. W.*

Matheson and Mrs. Mary J. Matheson (Pictou, N.S., 1864), *Missionary life among the cannibals, being the life of the Rev. John Geddie* (Toronto, 1882), and *Sketch of the life and labours of the Rev. John Campbell* (New Glasgow, N.S., 1889).

[Morgan, *Can. men* (1898); *Cyc. Am: biog.*; *Proc. Roy. Soc. Can.*, 1898.]

Patterson, George Geddie (d. 1951), jurist and historian, was born at Green Hill, Pictou county, Nova Scotia, the son of the Rev. George Patterson (q.v.), and died at New Glasgow, Nova Scotia, on September 10, 1951. He was educated at Dalhousie College, and was called to the bar of Nova Scotia in 1889. He practised law in New Glasgow; and from 1901 to 1906 he represented Pictou county in the Legislative Assembly of Nova Scotia. In 1907 he was appointed judge of the county court for Pictou and Cumberland counties. He was the author of *The history of Dalhousie College and University* (Halifax, N.S., 1887), *Studies in Nova Scotia history* (Halifax, N.S., 1940), and *More studies in Nova Scotia history* (Halifax, N.S., 1941).

[*Who's who in Canada*, 1950.]

Patterson, James Colebrooke (1839-1929), lieutenant-governor of Manitoba (1895-1900), was born in Armagh, Ireland, in 1839, the son of the Rev. James Patterson. He was educated in Dublin, and came to Canada in 1857. After teaching school for a number of years, he was called to the bar of Ontario in 1876, and practised law in Windsor, Ontario. From 1874 to 1878 he represented North Essex in the Legislative Assembly of Ontario; and from 1878 to 1895 he represented successively the constituencies of Essex, North Essex, and West Huron in the Canadian House of Commons. From 1891 to 1895 he was a member of the Abbott, Thompson, and Bowell administrations, holding in turn the portfolios of secretary of state and minister of militia and defence. From 1895 to 1900 he was lieutenant-governor of Manitoba. He then retired to private life, and he died at Ottawa on February 17, 1929.

[*Can. parl. comp.*; Morgan, *Can. men* (1912).]

Patterson, John (1872-1956), meteorologist, was born in Oxford county, Ontario, on January 3, 1872, and died at Clarkson, Ontario, on February 22, 1956. He was educated at the University of Toronto (B.A., 1890), and did post-graduate work at Cambridge University. In 1903 he was appointed professor of physics in the University of Allahabad, and in 1905 meteorologist for the government of India. In 1910 he returned to Canada to join the staff of the Meteorological Service of Canada; and from 1929 to 1946 he was its director or controller. He was elected a fellow of the Royal Society of Canada in 1918; he was secretary of

the Society from 1921 to 1935; and editor of its *Transactions* from 1923 to 1939. He compiled and edited also the *General index to publications of the Canadian Institute, 1852-1912* (Toronto, 1914).

[*Proc. Roy. Soc. Can.*, 1956; *Can. who's who*, 1952-54.]

Patterson, Walter (d. 1798), governor-in-chief of the Island of St. John (1769-84) and then lieutenant-governor (1784-87), was born in Ireland, the son of William Patterson, of Foxhall, county Donegal. He entered the British army, and saw service in America with the 8th Regiment. In 1769 he was appointed governor-in-chief and captain-general of the Island of St. John (Prince Edward Island); and, except for the years 1775-80, which he spent on leave in England, he administered the affairs of the island until 1787. In 1784, however, his commission as governor was withdrawn, and he was appointed lieutenant-governor; and in 1787 he was recalled to answer "serious and secret charges" against him. He was succeeded in the government by Edmund Fanning (q.v.), but did not return to England until 1789. He died in London, England, on September 6, 1798, in great poverty. In 1770 he married in England Hester Warren; and by her he had "at least four children." By Margaret Hyde, who was ostensibly his wife in Charlottetown, he had two daughters.

[A. B. Warburton, *A history of Prince Edward Island* (Saint John, N.B., 1923); *Canadian Archives report*, 1895.]

Patterson, William John (1815-1886), author, was born in Glasgow, Scotland, in 1815; and after some time spent in journalism in the United States, he settled in Montreal. In 1863 he was appointed joint secretary of the Board of Trade and Corn Exchange Association in Montreal, and he held this post until his death in Montreal on June 12, 1886. He was the author of a large number of pamphlets and trade reports, notably *Commercial relations of the British North American provinces* (Montreal, 1866), *Some plain statements about immigration, and its results* (Ottawa, 1872), *Descriptive statement of the great water highways of the Dominion of Canada* (Montreal, 1874), *Brief notes relating to the resources, industries, commerce, and prospects of Newfoundland* (Montreal, 1876), *Two trade letters* (Montreal, 1876), *Another trade letter* (Montreal, 1876), *Trade letter No. IV* (Montreal, 1880), and *The Dominion of Canada* (Montreal, 1883). He published *Annual reports on the commerce of Montreal* from 1863 to 1882; and also a series of *Statements relating to the home and foreign trade of Canada.*

[*Dom. ann. reg.*, 1886.]

Patteson, Thomas Charles (1836-1907), journalist and civil servant, was born at Patney, Wiltshire, England, on October 5, 1836, the son of the Rev. Thomas Patteson. He was educated at Eton and at Merton College, Oxford (B.A., 1858). He then came to Canada, and in 1863 he was called to the bar of Upper Canada, and entered into partnership with the Hon. John Ross (q.v.). In 1872, when the Toronto *Mail* was established as the organ of the Conservative party, he was appointed its managing editor; and he conducted the *Mail* until 1879. He was then appointed postmaster of Toronto; and this post he held until his death at Toronto on September 21, 1907. In 1867 he married Marie Louise, daughter of Ralph Jones, of Port Hope, Ontario. He was the founder of the Ontario Jockey Club, and was the author of a number of pamphlets, notably *Sporting intelligence* (Toronto, 1866) and *Observations on riding* (Toronto, 1901).

[Morgan, *Can. men* (1898); *Canadian biographical dictionary*, Ontario vol. (Toronto, 1890).]

Pattillo, Thomas Richard (1833-1910), sportsman, was born at Liverpool, Nova Scotia, in 1833, and was educated at Acadia University (B.A., 1856). He became a schoolteacher, and later a school inspector; but in his later years he was in business at Bridgewater, Nova Scotia. He died at Halifax, Nova Scotia, on July 8, 1910. He was the author of *Moose-hunting, salmon-fishing, and other sketches of sport* (London, 1902).

[*Records of the graduates of Acadia University, 1843-1926* (Wolfville, N.S., 1926).]

Patton, Harald Smith (1889-1945), economist, was born at Minnedosa, Manitoba, on January 4, 1889, and died at Washington, D.C., on December 1, 1945. He was educated at the University of Toronto (B.A., 1912) and Harvard University (M.A., 1921; Ph.D., 1926), and was a lecturer in economics at the University of Alberta from 1921 to 1925, a professor in economics at the University of Cincinnati from 1925 to 1929, and professor of economics and head of the department at the Michigan State College from 1929 to his death. He was the author of *Grain growers' cooperation in Western Canada* (Cambridge, Mass., 1928).

[*Can. who's who*, 1948.]

Patton, James (1824-1888), solicitor-general for Upper Canada (1862), was born at Prescott, Upper Canada, on June 10, 1824, the son of Major Andrew Patton, a native of St. Andrew's, Fifeshire, Scotland. He was educated at Upper Canada College and King's College, Toronto (LL.D., 1858). He was called to the bar of Upper Canada in 1845 (Q.C., 1862), and he began the practice of law at Barrie, Upper Canada. In 1860 he opened an office in Toronto, and he later became head of the firm of Patton, Osler, and Moss. In 1856 he was elected a member of the Legislative Council of Canada for an eight-year term; but on seeking re-election in 1862, after being appointed

solicitor-general for Upper Canada in the Cartier-Macdonald government, he was defeated, resigned his portfolio, and retired from political life. In 1878 he ceased to practise law, and from 1881 to his death he was collector of customs at Toronto. He died at Toronto on October 12, 1888. In 1853 he married Martha Marietta, daughter of Alfred Hooker, of Prescott. From 1860 to 1864 he was vice-chancellor of the University of Toronto; and he was the author of the *Canadian constable's assistant* (Toronto, 1852).

[*Cyc. Am. biog.*; Rose, *Cyc. Can. biog.* (1888); *Can. parl. comp.*, 1862; *Canadian biographical dictionary*, Ontario vol. (Toronto, 1880); Morgan, *Cel. Can. and Bib. can.*; J. C. Dent, *The last forty years* (2 vols., Toronto, 1881).]

Pattullo, Thomas Dufferin (1873-1956), prime minister of British Columbia (1933-41), was born in Woodstock, Ontario, on January 19, 1873, and died at Victoria, British Columbia, on March 29, 1956. He became first a journalist, and for a time he edited the Galt *Reformer*. In 1897 he went to the Yukon as secretary to the Yukon Commission, and from 1898 to 1901 was an assistant gold commissioner. He then moved to Prince Rupert, where he set up in business for himself, and where he became successively alderman and mayor. In 1916 he was elected to represent Prince Rupert in the British Columbia legislature as a Liberal, and he was minister of lands from 1916 to 1928. From 1928 to 1933 he was leader of the Liberal opposition in the legislature, and in 1933 he became prime minister. When his party failed to obtain a majority in the election of 1941, he resigned his seat and retired from politics. In 1937 the University of British Columbia conferred on him the honorary degree of LL.D.

[M. A. Ormsby, *T. Dufferin Pattullo and the Little new deal* (Can. hist. rev., 1962); *Can. who's who*, 1952-54; *Can. parl. guide*, 1940; *Encyc. Can.*]

Payzant, John Young (1837-1920), lawyer and financier, was born at Falmouth, Nova Scotia, on February 9, 1837. He was educated at Acadia University (B.A., 1860; M.A., 1863; D.C.L., 1915), and was called to the bar of Nova Scotia (Q.C., 1890). He practised law in Halifax, Nova Scotia; and he became president of the Bank of Nova Scotia. He died at Los Angeles, California, on November 18, 1920.

[Halifax *Morning Chronicle*, Nov. 20, 1920; Morgan, *Can. men* (1912); *Records of the graduates of Acadia University* (Wolfville, N.S., 1926).]

Peacock, Sir Edward Robert (1871-1962), merchant banker, was born at St. Elmo, Glengarry county, Ontario, August 2, 1871. He was educated at Almonte High School and Queen's University, Kingston (M.A., 1894), where he won the University medals in English and political science. He was English master and senior house master at Upper Canada College (1895-1902). He became private secretary to E. R. Wood, president of Dominion Securities Corporation, in 1902 and manager of the Corporation in London, England, in 1907. He was director of Brazilian Traction; Barcelona Power; Mexican Light and Power Company; the Canadian Pacific Railway; Harris and Partners; Baring Brothers; and the Bank of England (1921-46). He was a Rhodes trustee, and chairman of the Imperial War Graves Commission. He was knighted in 1934. He was author of *Trusts, combines and monopolies* (Toronto, 1898) and *Canada* (Toronto, 1900). He died in England on November 19, 1962.

[*Can. who's who*, 1955-57; *Who was who*, 1961-70.]

Péan, Michel Jean Hugues (1723-1782) soldier and public official, was born at St. Ours, New France, on May 18, 1723, the eldest son of Jacques Hugues Péan, Sieur de Livandière. He entered the Marine forces of Canada as an ensign in 1738, and reached the rank of captain in 1750. In 1756 he was appointed brevet major at Quebec; and he was one of the group of public officials about the intendant Bigot (q.v.) who plundered New France in the dying days of the French régime. After the fall of Quebec, he retired to France. He was thrown into the Bastille, and in 1764 was condemned to make restitution to the French exchequer to the extent of 600,000 livres. He died at Cangy, France, on August 21, 1782.

[P. G. Roy, *Les petites choses de notre histoire*, vol. 3 (Lévis, Que., 1922); A. Shortt (ed.), *Documents relating to Canadian currency, exchange, and finance during the French period* (2 vols., Ottawa, 1925); Le Jeune, *Dict. gén.*]

Pearce, William (1848-1930), civil engineer and land surveyor, was born in Elgin county, Canada West, on February 1, 1848; and was educated at the School of Practical Science, Toronto. He became a land surveyor, and was in charge of surveys for the Canadian government in Manitoba and the North West Territories from 1873 to 1881. In later years he served in various capacities in the Canadian North-West as an officer of the Canadian government; and he played an important part in the development of the West in regard to settlement, mining, irrigation, and railways. He died at East Calgary, Alberta, on March 3, 1930. He left behind him, in manuscript, a valuable account of his service in the West, which has not yet been published.

[Morgan, *Can. men* (1912).]

Pearson, Lester Bowles (1897-1972), diplomat and prime minister, was born in Toronto, Ontario, April 23, 1897, the son of a Methodist minister. He was educated in Peterborough and Hamilton, and at Victoria College, Toronto (B.A., 1919) and St. John's College, Oxford (B.A., 1923). He entered the Canadian army as a private and served in the Dardanelles with the R.C.A.M.C. He transferred to the Royal Flying Corps in 1917 and was invalided home after an injury. He joined the department of external affairs in 1928 after teaching for four years in the department of history of the University of Toronto. He served as first secretary in the department of external affairs from 1928 to 1935, then in the office of the Canadian High Commissioner in London, England, from 1938 to 1941. He became assistant under-secretary of state for external affairs in Ottawa in 1941 and was appointed minister-counsellor to the Canadian legation in Washington in 1942, becoming minister plenipotentiary in July, 1944, and ambassador to the United States, January, 1945. He returned to Canada to become under-secretary of state for external affairs in September, 1946, and remained in that post until joining the St. Laurent (q.v.) government as secretary of state for external affairs in 1948. He was elected for Algoma East in 1948 and re-elected in succeeding elections. In 1958 he became leader of the Liberal party and leader of the opposition in the House of Commons. He became prime minister of Canada on the defeat of the Diefenbaker government in 1963. The new Liberal government lacked an absolute majority in the House of Commons, and the election of November, 1965, resulted in a slight improvement in its position. In 1968 Lester Pearson resigned as prime minister and leader of the party. Pierre Trudeau was elected as his successor to the party leadership and became prime minister after the 1968 general election. Lester Pearson was chairman of the NATO Council (1951-52) and was active in the United Nations from its formation, becoming president of the 7th General Assembly (1952-53). He signed the North Atlantic Treaty for Canada and led the Canadian delegations to the Commonwealth Colombo Conference of 1950, the Japanese Peace Treaty Conference at San Francisco, 1951, and the conference on German rearmament in 1954. On his retirement from active political life he became chairman of international development for the World Bank. He was also chancellor of Carleton University; chairman of the Commission of International Development; member of the Advisory Committee of the Woodrow Wilson International Centre for Scholars; president of the International Institute for Strategic Studies; chairman of the Board of Governors of the International Development Research Centre; chairman of the Board of Sports Participation Canada; and chairman of the International Broadcast Institute. Lester Pearson was prime minister during Canada's centennial year (1967) and was host to visitors from all over the world. He was responsible for Canada's flag and introduced a new bilingual character into Canadian federalism. He was the first Canadian to receive the Nobel Peace Prize and the Gold Medal Award of the National Institute of Social Sciences of the United States. His awards and honours range from honorary membership in the Royal Architectural Society to the Theodore Herzl award of the Zionist Organization of America.

His writings include *Democracy and world politics* (1955); *Diplomacy in the nuclear age* (1959); *The four faces of peace* (1964); *Peace in the family of man* (1968); *The crisis of development* (1970); *Words and occasions* (1970); *Mike: The memoirs of the Right Honourable L. B. Pearson*, 3 vols. (1972-4). He was co-author of *Partners in development* (1969).

He married Maryon Elspeth Moody in 1925; they had one son and one daughter. He died at Ottawa, Ontario, December 27, 1972.

[*Can. who's who*, 1967-69; A. W. Burton, *Mr. Pearson and Canada's revolution by diplomacy* (1966); J. R. Beal, *The Pearson phenomenon* (1964); P. N. L. Nicholson, *Vision and indecision* (1968); Winterlee and Cramer, *Portraits of Nobel laureates in peace* (1971).]

Pearson, William Henry (1831-1920), author, was born at Brixton, England, on November 9, 1831, and came to Canada in 1835. From 1847 to 1854 he was employed in the Toronto Post Office; and from 1854 to 1908 he was in the employ of the Consumers' Gas Company of Toronto, of which he became general manager. He died at Toronto, Ontario, on April 5, 1920. He published his reminiscences under the title *Recollections and records of Toronto of old* (Toronto, 1914).

[Rose, *Cyc. Can. biog.* (1886).]

Peat, Harold Reginald (1893-1960), soldier and author, was born in 1893, and died in Jamaica, on May 30, 1960. He enlisted in the First Canadian Contingent in the First World War, and later recounted his experiences in a book entitled *Private Peat* (Indianapolis, 1917). His wife followed this with a book entitled *Mrs. Private Peat* (Indianapolis, 1918).

[*New York Times*, May 31, 1960.]

Peck, Edmund James (1850-1924), missionary and grammarian, was born at Rusholme, near Manchester, England, on April 15, 1850. He spent over ten years in the British navy; but in 1875 he entered the training institute of the Church Missionary Society, and in 1876 was sent as a missionary to the Eskimo in Hudson Bay. Here he remained for the greater part of his life. He died in Toronto, Ontario, on September 10, 1924. His *Eskimo grammar* was published by the Geographic Board of Canada (Ottawa, 1919; new ed., 1931).

[A. Lewis, *The life and work of E. J. Peck among the Eskimos* (London, 1904).]

Pedley, Charles (1820-1872), clergyman, was born in Hanley, England, on August 6, 1820. He became a Congregational minister; and after serving as pastor of a church at Chester-le-Street, Durham, England, he became pastor of a church at St. John's, Newfoundland, in 1857. In 1864 he removed to Canada; and he died at Coldsprings, Ontario, on February 22, 1872. He was the author of *The history of Newfoundland* (London, 1863).

[*Cyc. Am. biog.*; Morgan, *Bib. can.*; *Dict. Can. biog.*, vol. 10.]

Pedley, Hugh (1852-1923), clergyman, was born at Chester-le-Street, Durham, England, in 1852, the son of the Rev. Charles Pedley (q.v.). He was educated at McGill University (B.A., 1876), and became a Congregational minister. He was pastor of churches in Cobourg, Ontario, in Winnipeg, Manitoba, and in Montreal, Quebec; and he died at Knowlton, Quebec, on July 26, 1923. He was the author of *Looking forward* (Toronto, 1913).

[Morgan, *Can. men* (1912).]

Pedley, James Henry (1892-1945), soldier and author, was born in Vancouver, British Columbia, in 1892, the son of the Rev. James William Pedley (q.v.), and died in Toronto, Ontario, on December 26, 1945. He was educated at the University of Toronto (B.A., 1913), and Osgoode Hall, but his legal education was interrupted by the First World War and he was called to the bar only in 1919. He served during the war in the Canadian Corps, and was awarded the M.C. He was the author of *Only this: A war retrospect* (Ottawa, 1927).

[Toronto *Globe and Mail*, Dec. 27, 1945.]

Pedley, James William (1856-1933), clergyman and author, was born at Chester-le-Street, Durham, England, in 1856, the son of the Rev. Charles Pedley (q.v.). He was educated at McGill University (B.A., 1884), and became a Congregationalist minister. He was the pastor of churches in Georgetown, Ontario, in Vancouver, British Columbia, and in London and Toronto, Ontario. He died in Toronto on May 24, 1933. He was the author of a *Biography of Lord Strathcona and Mount Royal* (Toronto, 1915).

[Morgan, *Can. men* (1912).]

Peel, Paul (1859-1892), painter, was born in London, Ontario, in 1859, the son of John Peel. He studied art at the Pennsylvania Academy of Fine Arts in Philadelphia; and in 1880 he went to London, England, and entered the Royal Academy. In 1887 he went to Paris, where he studied under Gérôme, Boulanger, and Constant; and here he worked for the rest of his short life. In 1889 his picture, "Life is bitter," was awarded honourable mention at the Salon; and in 1890 his famous "After the bath," representing the slender nude figures of children before a fire, was awarded a gold medal. In 1890 he came to Canada, and held a sale of his pictures in Toronto; but he returned to France, and he died at Paris on October 25, 1892. In 1890 he was elected a fellow of the Royal Canadian Academy of Arts.

[N. MacTavish, *The fine arts in Canada* (Toronto, 1925); E. Morris, *Art in Canada: The early painters* (Toronto, 1911); Le Jeune, *Dict. gén.*]

Pelland, Joseph Alfred (1873-1915), civil servant and author, was born at Chambly, Quebec, in 1873. He was educated at St. Mary's College, Montreal, and at Laval and McGill universities; and became a journalist. Later he became the publicist of the department of colonization in the province of Quebec; and he served in this capacity until his death at Quebec City on January 27, 1915. He was the author of *Le nouveau Québec* (Quebec, 1906), *La province de Québec* (Quebec, 1908), *La colonisation dans la province de Québec* (Quebec, 1910), and *Vastes champs offerts à la colonisation et à l'industrie* (5 vols., Quebec, 1910-14).

[Morgan, *Can. men* (1912).]

Pelland, Joseph Octave (1861-1924), lawyer, was born in 1861, was called to the bar of Quebec, and died at Montreal, Quebec, on September 16, 1924. He was the author and compiler of *Biographie, discours, conférences de l'honorable Honoré Mercier* (Montreal, 1890).

[Montreal *Gazette*, Sept. 17, 1924.]

Pellatt, Sir Henry Mill (1860-1939), financier and soldier, was born at Toronto, Canada West, on January 16, 1860. He became a stockbroker and financier; and his financial career was marked by spectacular vicissitudes. In his youth he was a notable athlete, and won in 1879 the amateur championship of America for the mile running race. In 1880 he joined the Queen's Own Rifles of Canada as a subaltern; and throughout life he took an active interest in the Canadian militia. He became a lieutenant-colonel in 1901, a colonel in 1907, a brigadier-general in 1912, and a major-general in 1918. In 1902 he took the bugle band of the Queen's Own Rifles to England, at his own expense, to attend the coronation of King Edward VII; and in 1910 he took the regiment to England, at his own expense, to take part in the annual manoeuvres of the British army at Aldershot. In 1905, in recognition of his services in the militia, he was created a knight bachelor. His palatial Toronto residence, Casa Loma, is one of the city's landmarks. He died at Toronto, Ontario, on March 8, 1939.

[F. Griffin, *Sir Henry Mill Pellatt* (Toronto, 1939); *Who was who*, 1929-40; *Can. who's who*, 1936-37; Morgan, *Can. men* (1912).]

Pelletier, Alexis (1837-1910), priest, was born at St. Arsène de Témiscouata, Lower Canada, on April 26, 1937, and was ordained a priest of the Roman Catholic Church in 1863. He was a professor first in the Quebec Seminary, and then in the College of Ste. Anne de la Pocatière; and in his later years he was parish priest at St. Bruno and at Valleyfield, Quebec. He died in Montreal, Quebec, on June 25, 1910. He was the author of *Le Don Quichotte montréalais sur sa Rossinante; ou, M. Dessaulles et la grande guerre ecclésiastique* (Montreal, 1873) and a number of other controversial pamphlets.

[*Bull. rech. hist.*, 1929; Allaire, *Dict. biog.*]

Pelletier, Sir Charles Alphonse Pantaléon (1837-1911), lieutenant-governor of Quebec (1908-11), was born at Rivière Ouelle, Lower Canada, on January 22, 1837, the youngest son of J. M. Pelletier and Julie Painchaud. He was educated at the College of Ste. Anne de la Pocatière and at Laval University (B.L., 1858), and was called to the bar of Lower Canada in 1860 (Q.C., 1879). From 1869 to 1877 he sat for Kamouraska as a Liberal in the Canadian House of Commons; and he represented Quebec East in the Legislative Assembly of Quebec from 1873 to the abolition of dual representation in 1874. In 1872 he was one of the founders of the *parti national*. In 1877 he was called to the Senate of Canada, and from 1877 to 1878 he was minister of agriculture in the Mackenzie administration. From 1896 to 1901 he was speaker of the Senate; but in 1904 he resigned from the Senate, and was appointed a judge of the Superior Court of Quebec. This position, in turn, he resigned in 1908, to accept appointment as lieutenant-governor of Quebec. He died in office, at Quebec, on April 29, 1911. He was twice married, (1) in 1862 to Suzanne, daughter of the Hon. C. E. Casgrain, and (2) in 1866 to Virginie, daughter of the Hon. M. P. de Sales La Terrière; and he had one son. In 1878 he was created a C.M.G.; and in 1898 a K.C.M.G.

[*Can. who's who*, 1910; Morgan, *Can. men* (1898); Rose, *Cyc. Can. biog.* (1886); Dent. *Can. port.*, vol. 3; *Can. parl. comp.*; *Cyc. Am. biog.*; P. G. Roy, *Les juges de la province de Québec* (Quebec, 1933); Le Jeune, *Dict. gén.*]

Pelletier, Louis Philippe (1857-1921), postmaster-general of Canada (1911-14), was born at Trois Pistoles, Quebec, on February 2, 1857, the son of Thomas Philippe Pelletier and Caroline, sister of Sir Louis Napoléon Casault (q.v.). He was educated at the College of Ste. Anne de la Pocatière and at Laval University, Quebec, and was called to the bar in 1880. He was a member of the Quebec legislature from 1888 to 1904; and he was provincial secretary in the Boucherville and Taillon governments from 1891 to 1896, and attorney-general in the Flynn government from 1896 to 1897. In 1911 he was elected to represent Quebec county in the Canadian House of Commons; and from 1911 to 1914 he was postmaster-general in the Borden government. He retired from office, because of ill-health, in 1914, and was appointed a judge of the Supreme Court of the province of Quebec. He died at Quebec on February 8, 1921.

[P. G. Roy, *Les juges de la province de Québec* (Quebec, 1933); *Can. parl. comp.*; Morgan, *Can. men* (1912); Le Jeune, *Dict. gén.*]

Pelly, Sir John Henry, Bart. (1777-1852), governor of the Hudson's Bay Company, was born on March 31, 1777, the eldest son of Henry Hinde Pelly, of Upton House, Essex, England. He became a director of the Hudson's Bay Company in 1806, deputy-governor in 1812, and governor in 1822. He died at Upton House on August 13, 1852. In 1840 he was created a baronet of the United Kingdom. In 1807 he married Emma, daughter of Henry Bouldon, of Thorncroft, Surrey; and by her he had a large family. Several places in the Hudson's Bay Territories were named after him.

[D. R. Pelly, *The Pelly family in England*, printed for private circulation (1912).]

Pelly, Robert Parker (*fl.* 1790-1825), governor of Assiniboia (1823-25), was born in England on January 10, 1790, and was a cousin of Sir John Henry Pelly, Bart. (q.v.). He was a captain in the East India Company's service; but from 1823 to 1825 he was governor of Assiniboia in the Hudson's Bay Company's territories. The date of his death does not appear to be known.

[D. R. Pelly, *The Pelly family in England*, printed for private circulation (1912).]

Pemberton, George (d. 1868), executive and legislative councillor, was a merchant of Quebec who was from 1838 to 1841 president of the chamber of commerce in Quebec. From 1837 to 1841 he was a member of the Executive Council of Lower Canada; and from 1841 to 1849 he was a member of the Legislative Council of united Canada. He died on February 21, 1868.

[J. Desjardins, *Guide parlementaire historique de la province de Québec* (Quebec, 1902).]

Pemberton, Joseph Despard (1821-1893), first surveyor-general of British Columbia, was born near Dublin, Ireland, on July 23, 1821, and was educated at Trinity College, Dublin. He became a civil engineer, and was for several years professor of engineering at the Royal Agricultural College in Cirencester, Gloucestershire, England. In 1851 he was sent out to America by the Hudson's Bay Company as surveyor-general of British Columbia. He was elected a member of the first Legislative Assembly of Vancouver Island in 1856; and he sat in the Executive

Council of the Island from 1863 to 1866. He died at Victoria, British Columbia, on November 11, 1893. He was the author of *Facts and figures relating to Vancouver Island and British Columbia* (London, 1860).

[Harriet S. Sampson, *Joseph Despard Pemberton* (British Columbia historical quarterly, 1944); J. B. Kerr, *Biographical dictionary of well-known British Columbians* (Vancouver, B.C., 1890).]

Pénard, Jean Marie (1864-1939), missionary to the Indians, was born in Brittany, France, in 1864, and was ordained a priest of the Roman Catholic Church in 1887. He came to Canada the following year; and he spent the rest of his life as a missionary among the Chipewyan Indians in northern Saskatchewan. He died at The Pas, Manitoba, on November 13, 1939. He was the author of *Mgr Charlebois* (Montreal, 1937).

[*New York Times*, Nov. 15, 1939.]

Penhallow, David Pearce (1854-1910), botanist, was born at Kittery Point, Maine, on May 25, 1854; and was educated at Boston University (B.Sc., 1875). From 1876 to 1880 he was professor of botany and chemistry in the Imperial College of Agriculture in Japan. After his return to America, he was appointed in 1883 professor of botany in McGill University, Montreal; and the same year he was elected a fellow of the Royal Society of Canada. He became an outstanding authority on the palaeobotany of Canada; and he contributed many papers on this subject to the *Transactions* of the Royal Society of Canada and other periodicals. He died at sea, while on his way to England, on October 20, 1910. He was the author of *The botany of Montreal* (Montreal, 1891) and *The botanical collector's guide* (Montreal, 1891).

[*Proc. Roy. Soc. Can.*, 1911; *Can. who's who*, 1910.]

Pennington, Myles (1814-1898), railwayman, was born in Lancaster, England, on May 13, 1814. He entered the service of the Great Western Railway; and in 1853 he was sent to Canada as first general freight agent of the Grand Trunk Railway. His active life coincided with the railway development of Canada in the latter half of the nineteenth century; and his reminiscences, which he published under the title *Railways and other ways* (Toronto, 1896), are a valuable contribution to the history of Canadian railways. He died in Toronto, Ontario, in 1898.

[Private information.]

Penny, Edward Goff (1820-1881), journalist, was born in Hornsey, London, England, on May 15, 1820, and came to Canada in 1842. He joined the staff of the Montreal *Herald*, and eventually became its editor and one of its proprietors. He was an opponent of Confederation, and published a pamphlet entitled *The proposed British North American confederation: Why it should not be imposed upon the colonies* (Montreal, 1867). In 1874 he was called to the Senate of Canada; and he died at Montreal on October 11, 1881. In 1857 he married Eleanor (d. 1881), daughter of Oliver Smith, of Montreal.

[A. G. Penny (ed.), *The annexation movement* (Can. hist. rev., 1924); *Dom. ann. reg.*, 1880-81; Morgan, *Bib. can.*; *Can. parl. comp.*; J. D. Borthwick, *History and biographical gazetteer of Montreal* (Montreal, 1892).]

Pepperrell, Sir William, Bart. (1696-1759), soldier, was born at Kittery Point, Maine, on June 27, 1696. For many years he was a member of the Council of Massachusetts; and in 1744 he was appointed to command the expedition sent by the English colonies to reduce Louisbourg. In fitting out this expedition, he engaged his whole fortune. He succeeded, with the aid of the British fleet, in capturing Louisbourg in 1745; and in 1746 he was created a baronet. He died on July 6, 1759.

[Usher Parsons, *The life of Sir William Pepperrell, Bart.* (Boston, 1855); *Dict. nat. biog.*; *Dict. Am. biog.*; Le Jeune, *Dict. gén.*; *Dict. Can. biog.*, vol. 3.]

Perkins, Simeon (1735-1812), merchant and diarist, was born at Norwich, Connecticut, on February 24, 1735. He settled in Liverpool, Nova Scotia, in 1762; and for fifty years was a prominent merchant in this place. For thirty-four years he was a member of the House of Assembly of Nova Scotia; and for thirty years he was a judge of probate. He died at Liverpool, Nova Scotia, on May 9, 1812. From 1766 to his death he kept a diary, which has been preserved, and which is a valuable mine of information regarding the early history of Nova Scotia. The first part of the diary has been published by the Champlain Society in three volumes, the first (1766-1780) edited by H. A. Innis (Toronto, 1948), the second (1780-1789) edited by D. C . Harvey and C. B. Fergusson (Toronto, 1958), and the third (1790-1796) edited by C. B. Fergusson (Toronto, 1961). It has also published the diary covering the period 1797 to 1803, edited by C. B. Fergusson (Toronto, 1967).

[R. J. Long, *Nova Scotia authors* (East Orange, N.J., 1918); J. F. More, *The history of Queens county, N.S.* (Halifax, 1873).]

Perley, Sir George Halsey (1857-1938), acting prime minister of Canada on several occasions, was born at Lebanon, New Hampshire, on September 12, 1857, the son of William G. Perley and Mabel Ticknor Stevens. He was educated at the grammar school in Ottawa, where his father had engaged in the lumber trade, and at Harvard University

(B.A., 1878). He carried on the lumber business founded by his father in the Ottawa Valley; and in 1904 he was elected to represent Argenteuil in the Canadian House of Commons. He continued to represent this constituency in the Commons from that date until his death at Ottawa, on January 4, 1938, with the exception of the years from 1917 to 1925, during most of which he was in England. In 1911 he was appointed a minister without portfolio in the Borden government; from 1914 to 1922 he was high commissioner of Canada in London; and in 1916-17 he was minister of the overseas military forces of Canada. He was secretary of state in the short-lived Meighen administration of 1926; and he was a minister without portfolio in the Bennett administration formed in 1930. As senior privy councillor, he was repeatedly, during the years 1930-35, acting prime minister. In 1884 he married Annie Hespeler (d. 1910), daughter of Ward H. Bowlby, K.C., Berlin (Kitchener), Ontario, by whom he had one daughter; and in 1913 he married, secondly, Emily Colby, daughter of the Hon. Thomas White (q.v.). He was created a K.C.M.G. in 1915, and a G.C.M.G. in 1933; and in 1932 he was appointed an imperial privy councillor.

[*Who was who*, 1929-40; *Can. who's who*, 1936-37; *Can. parl. comp.*; Morgan, *Can. men* (1912); Sir R. Borden, *Memoirs* (2 vols., Toronto, 1938).]

Perley, Moses Henry (1804-1862), writer on the natural history of the Maritime provinces, was born at Maugerville, New Brunswick, on December 31, 1804, the son of Moses Perley and Mary Perley. He was educated at Saint John, New Brunswick, and in 1830 was called to the bar, but practised law only for a short time. He had a varied career. For several years he was engaged in the lumbering business; in 1841 he was appointed special commissioner for Indian affairs in New Brunswick; in 1847 he was sent to England to secure aid in railway-building; he was then employed in investigating the fishery grounds of New Brunswick; from 1851 to 1853 he was engaged in the compilation of trade statistics in connection with the Reciprocity Treaty of 1854; in 1854 he was a commissioner for carrying out the terms of this treaty; and in 1861 he became the editor of the *Colonial Empire* of Saint John, New Brunswick. He died on board H.M.S. *Desperate* off Forteau, Labrador, on August 17, 1862. In 1829 he married Jane, daughter of Isaac Ketchum; and by her he had eight children. He founded the Natural History Society of New Brunswick; and, besides many articles in periodicals, he published the following: *Report on the condition ... of the Indian tribes of New Brunswick* (Fredericton, n.d.); *Report on the forest trees of New Brunswick* (Fredericton, 1847); *Report on the fisheries of the gulf of St. Lawrence* (Fredericton, 1849); *Report on the fisheries of the bay of*

Fundy (Fredericton, 1851); *Catalogue of fishes of New Brunswick and Nova Scotia* (Fredericton, 1851); *Report on the sea and river fisheries of New Brunswick* (Fredericton, 1852); and *Handbook of information for emigrants to New Brunswick* (Saint John, N.B., 1854). A lecture *On the early history of New Brunswick*, delivered by him at Saint John in 1841, was edited with notes by W. F. Ganong (Saint John, N.B., 1891).

[*Dict. nat. biog.*; Morgan, *Bib. can.*; Le Jeune, *Dict. gén.*; W. G. MacFarlane, *New Brunswick bibliography* (Saint John, N.B., 1895).]

Perley, William Dell (1838-1902), senator of Canada, was born at Gladstone, Sunbury county, New Brunswick, on February 6, 1838, the son of the Hon. W. E. Perley. He was educated at Sackville Academy and the Baptist Seminary in New Brunswick, and became a farmer. After farming for a number of years in New Brunswick, he went west, and began farming at Wolseley in the North West Territories. He sat in the North West Council from 1885 to 1887; he represented East Assiniboia in the Canadian House of Commons from 1887 to 1888, and in 1888 he was called to the Senate of Canada. He died at Wolseley, Saskatchewan, on July 15, 1909.

[*Can. parl. comp.*]

Perodeau, Narcisse (1851-1932), lieutenant-governor of Quebec (1924-29), was born at St. Ours, Canada East, on March 26, 1851. He was educated at McGill University (B.C.L., 1876), and was admitted a notary public of the province of Quebec in 1876. In 1897 he was appointed a member of the Legislative Council of Quebec; and in 1910 he became a minister without portfolio in the Gouin administration, and government leader in the upper house. In 1924 he succeeded the Hon. L. P. Brodeur (q.v.) as lieutenant-governor of the province; and he remained in this post until 1929. He was then re-appointed government leader in the Legislative Council; but he did not long perform the duties of this office. He died at Montreal, Quebec, on November 18, 1932. In 1900 he was made a D.C.L. of Laval University in Montreal.

[*Can. who was who*, vol. 1; Le Jeune, *Dict. gén.*; *Can. parl. comp.*; Morgan, *Can. men* (1912).]

Perold, John Gabriel (1877-1944), clergyman and economist, was born at Paarl, Cape Colony, South Africa, on July 18, 1877, of Dutch descent. He was educated in South Africa, and at Princeton Theological Seminary, Princeton, New Jersey (B.D., 1905). He was ordained a minister of the Dutch Reformed Church of South Africa in 1906; and for seventeen years he was pastor of churches in Cape Colony and the Transvaal. He came to Canada in 1924; and, after taking his M.A. at

the University of Toronto, he was appointed a member of the teaching staff in economics in this university. He died at Toronto, Ontario, on October 19, 1944. He was the author of *Credit unions* (5 pts., Toronto, 1943).

[Toronto *Globe and Mail*, Oct. 21, 1944.]

Perrault, Antonio (1880-1955), lawyer, was born at Murray Bay, Quebec, on September 15, 1880, and died at Montreal, Quebec, on January 19, 1955. He was educated at Laval University (LL.D., 1916) and was called to the bar in Quebec in 1906. From 1912 to 1940 he was professor of law at the University of Montreal; and in 1944 he was elected *bâtonnier* of the Montreal bar. He was the author of *Traité de droit commercial* (3 vols., Montreal, 1940); and in 1940 he became the chief editor of *La Revue du Barreau*. He was elected a fellow of the Royal Society of Canada in 1917.

[*Proc. Roy. Soc. Can.*, 1955; *Can. who's who*, 1952-54.]

Perrault, Charles Ovide (1809-1837), *patriote* leader, was born in Montreal, Lower Canada, in September, 1809. He was called to the bar of Lower Canada in 1832; and in 1834 he was elected to represent the county of Vaudreuil in the Legislative Assembly of Lower Canada. He became one of the leaders of the younger *patriotes*; and he was mortally wounded at the battle of St. Denis on November 23, 1837. He died the following day.

[E. Fabre-Surveyer, *Charles-Ovide Perrault* (Trans. Roy. Soc. Can., 1937).]

Perrault, Jean Baptiste (1761-1844), furtrader, was born at Three Rivers, Canada, in 1761, the son of Jean Baptiste Perrault and Marie LeMaitre. He was educated at Quebec, and entered the fur-trade about 1783. For ten years he was a trader in the Illinois country; but in 1793 he entered the service of the North West Company as a clerk. He was stationed in the Fond du Lac department until 1799; and from 1799 to 1805 he was in charge at the Pic, on Lake Superior. From 1805 to 1806 he was on the St. Maurice and Ottawa rivers; and in 1806 he left the employ of the North West Company. He was subsequently employed by the Pacific Fur Company, by an independent trader, and by the Hudson's Bay Company; but he retired from the service of the Hudson's Bay Company in 1821, and settled at Sault Ste. Marie. Here he died in 1844. He married an Indian woman; and by her he had at least nine children. His *Narrative*, a translation of which has been published in the *Michigan Pioneer and Historical Collections*, vol. 37, 1909-10, is one of the most interesting and valuable documents relating to the history of the fur-trade.

[A. G. Morice, *Dictionnaire historique des canadiens et des métis français de l'ouest* (Kamloops, B.C., 1908).]

Perrault, Jean Baptiste Olivier (1773-1827), executive and legislative councillor of

Lower Canada, was born at Quebec on July 22, 1773. He was called to the bar of Lower Canada in 1799, and in 1808 was appointed advocate-general of the province. In 1812 he was appointed a judge of the Court of King's Bench for the district of Quebec, and the same year he was sworn of the Executive Council of Lower Canada. In 1818 he became also a member of the Legislative Council. He died at Quebec on March 19, 1827.

[P. G. Roy, *Les juges de la province de Québec* (Quebec, 1933); Le Jeune, *Dict. gén.*; *Bull. rech. hist.*, 1902).]

Perrault, Joseph François (1753-1844), author and educationist, was born in Quebec, on June 1, 1753, the son of a fur-trader. He was educated at the Quebec Seminary; and he was engaged in the western fur-trade until 1781. He then began business by himself in Montreal, but he did not prosper, and he turned instead to the study of law. He was called to the bar in 1790; in 1795 he was appointed clerk of the peace at Quebec; and in 1802 he became prothonotary at Quebec. This position he held for the rest of his life. Though largely self-educated, he took a great interest in education and scientific agriculture, and he established at his own expense model schools and experimental farms. He published a large number of books and pamphlets, mainly of a legal or educational character; among them, however, were an *Abrégé de l'histoire du Canada* (5 vols., Quebec, 1832-36) and an autobiography, entitled *Biographie de Joseph-François Perrault ... écrite par lui-même, à l'âge de quatre-vingt ans, sans lunettes, à la suggestion de Lord Aylmer* (Quebec, 1834). He died at Quebec, on April 4, 1844. In 1783 he married Ursule, daughter of Major Richard McCarthy; and by her he had two sons and three daughters.

[P. B. Casgrain, *La vie de Joseph François Perrault* (Quebec, 1898); J.-J. Jolois, *Joseph François Perrault (1753-1844) et les origines de l'enseignement laïque au Bas-Canada* (Montreal, 1969); L. P. Cormier, *Quatres lettres inédites de Joseph-François Perrault* (Rev. de l'Univ. de Laval, 1963); P. Bender, *Old and new Canada* (Montreal, 1882); *Cyc. Am. biog.*; Morgan, *Bib. can.*; Le Jeune, *Dict. gén.*; *Bull. rech. hist.*, 1914.]

Perrault, Joseph Xavier (1838-1905), agriculturist, was born in Quebec, Lower Canada, on May 28, 1838, the son of Lieut.-Col. Joseph Xavier Perrault, and the grandson of Joseph François Perrault (q.v.). He was educated at the Quebec Seminary; and he studied agriculture at the University of Durham and at the Royal College at Cirencester, England, and at the National School of Agriculture, Grignon, France. He returned to Canada, and in 1857 he was appointed secretary of the Board of Agriculture. In 1863 he was returned to the Legislative Assembly of Canada for

Richelieu; but he opposed Confederation, and was defeated in 1867. In 1887 he founded the Chamber of Commerce at Montreal; and he was the first farmer in Quebec to import Ayrshire cattle and Percheron stallions. He occupied various temporary official positions; and in 1903 he was appointed a secretary of the Royal Transportation Commission. He died on April 9, 1905. In 1866 he married C. F. Couillard, of Montreal. He was an officer of the Legion of Honour of France; and he was the author of a number of books and pamphlets on agricultural and political subjects, notably of a *Traité d'agriculture pratique* (Montreal, 1865).

[Morgan, *Bib. can.* and *Can. men* (1898); Le Jeune, *Dict. gén.*]

Perré, Henri (1828-1890), painter, was born at Strasbourg, Alsace, in 1828. He took part in the insurrection of 1849 in Saxony, and afterwards fled to the United States. His later years were spent in Canada, and he was for a time on the staff of the Ontario School of Art, the first art school in Toronto. In 1880 he became a charter member of the Royal Canadian Academy; and he died in Toronto in 1890. He painted in a conventional manner, but he did some important work as a landscape-painter.

[N. MacTavish, *The fine arts in Canada* (Toronto, 1925).]

Perrin, William Willcox (1848-1934), Anglican bishop of Columbia (1893-1911), was born in Gloucestershire, England, on August 11, 1848. He was educated at King's College, London, and Trinity College, Oxford (B.A., 1870; M.A., 1873; D.D., 1893), and was ordained a priest of the Church of England in 1872. After serving as curate and then vicar in Southampton, he was in 1893 appointed bishop of Columbia, in British Columbia; and he presided over this see, at Victoria, until 1911. He then returned to England as suffragan bishop of Willesden; and later, in 1929, he became assistant bishop of London. He died in London, England, on June 27, 1934.

[*Who was who*, 1929-40; Morgan, *Can. men* (1912).]

Perrot, François Marie (1644?-1691), governor of Montreal (1669-84), was born about 1644 in Paris, France, and became a captain in a regiment of Auvergne. In 1669 he was named governor of Montreal by the Sulpicians, and came to Canada with Talon (q.v.) in 1670, arriving at Quebec on August 18. In 1672 he obtained the concession of Ile Perrot above Montreal, where he established a trading-post, and carried on an illegal traffic with the Indians, exchanging brandy for furs. He encouraged and protected the lawless bands of *coureurs de bois*, and his conduct became so tyrannical that Frontenac (q.v.) had him arrested, imprisoned, and tried before the Superior Council at Quebec in 1674. He was then sent to France and kept for three months in the Bastille; but on his release the governorship of Montreal was restored to him. In 1684, he was appointed governor of Acadia. His malpractices continued here, and, in 1687, he was succeeded by Menneval (q.v.). He remained at Port Royal as a trader; in 1690 he was taken prisoner by Phips (q.v.); and he lost his life at Martinique in 1691. He married, in 1669, Madeleine Laguide Meynier, the niece of Jean Talon (q.v.); and he had by her six children.

[A. Malchelosse, *François-Marie Perrot* (Montreal, 1942); P. G. Roy, *François Marie Perrot* (Bull. rech. hist., 1896; Le Jeune, *Dict. gén.*; *Dict. Can. biog.*, vol. 1.]

Perrot, Nicolas (1644?-1717), voyageur, was born in France by 1644. He came to Canada as a child, and was employed by the Jesuits from 1660 to 1665, and, a year later, by the Sulpicians. For the next ten years he was engaged in the fur-trade, and often acted as interpreter for the Algonkin. He became one of the best-known figures of the Upper Lake region. In 1684 he induced a number of the western tribes to join La Barre (q.v.) in his campaign against the Iroquois; and his influence was later of great service to Denonville (q.v.) and Vaudreuil (q.v.). About 1693 he discovered the lead mines of the Mississippi. Because of the decree which abolished all trading privileges, the last ten years of his life were spent in poverty. During this period he composed his memoirs, which were published in 1864 under the title of *Mémoire sur les moeurs, coustumes et relligion des sauvages de l'Amérique septentrionale*, with notes by the Jesuit Tailhan; and the book affords an interesting picture of the life of the tribes in the North West. Perrot died on August 13, 1717. He married, some time after 1665, Madeleine Raclot, by whom he had nine children.

[R. G. Thwaites (ed.), *The Jesuit relations*, vol. lv (Cleveland, 1900); Le Jeune, *Dict. gén.*; *Dict. Can. biog.*, vol. 2.]

Perry, Charles Ebenezer (1835-1917), clergyman, was born in Clarke township, Upper Canada, in 1835. He became a Methodist preacher in 1862; and he served in many charges in Ontario. He was superannuated in 1902; and he died at Toronto, Ontario, on February 20, 1917. He was the author of *Hon. N. Clarke Wallace, grand master Loyal Orange Association of British America* (Toronto, 1897).

[G. H. Cornish, *The cyclopaedia of Methodism in Canada* (2 vols., Toronto, 1880-1903).]

Perry, James Black (1845-1936), broker and author, was born in Fergus, Canada West, on February 27, 1845. He became a broker in Toronto; and he died in Toronto, Ontario, on January 19, 1936. Under the pseudonym of

"Logan Weir", he was the author of *Yon toon o' mine* (Toronto, 1924).

[Private information.]

Perry, James Roy (1874-1902), economist, was born in 1874, the eldest son of James Black Perry (q.v.). He was educated at the University of Toronto (B.A., 1896); and after a year spent in post-graduate work, he entered the employ of a firm of investment brokers in Toronto. He died in Toronto, Ontario, on February 2, 1902. He was the author of *Public debts in Canada* (Toronto: University of Toronto Studies, Economic series, no. 1, 1898).

[Private information.]

Perry, Peter (1793-1851), politician, was born at Ernestown, near Kingston, Upper Canada, in 1793, the son of Robert Perry, a United Empire Loyalist. He had little education, but by force of character early became an outstanding member of the Reform party in Upper Canada. In 1824 he was elected, with M. S. Bidwell (q.v.), to represent Lennox and Addington in the Legislative Assembly, and he continued to represent this constituency until his defeat in the elections of 1836, partly as the result of the dissemination of a pamphlet by Egerton Ryerson (q.v.) entitled *Peter Perry picked to pieces*. He then left the Bay of Quinte region, and opened a general store at a place henceforth known as "Perry's Corners" (now Whitby, Ontario). He did not re-enter public life until 1849, when he became one of the founders of the "Clear Grit" party, and was elected to the Legislative Assembly of united Canada for the east riding of York. He died not long afterwards at Saratoga Springs, New York, on August 24, 1851.

[G. M. Jones, *The Peter Perry election and the rise of the Clear Grit party* (Ont. Hist. Soc., papers and records, 1914); Dent, *Can. port.*, vol. 3, and *The last forty years* (2 vols., Toronto, 1881); E. Ryerson, *The story of my life* (Toronto, 1883).]

Peters, Frederick (1852-1919), prime minister of Prince Edward Island (1891-97), was born in Charlottetown, Prince Edward Island, on April 8, 1852, the son of the Hon. James Horsfield Peters and Mary, daughter of Sir Samuel Cunard, Bart. (q.v.). He was educated at King's College, Windsor, Nova Scotia (B.A., 1871), and was called to the bar at the Inner Temple, London, in 1876, and to the bar of Prince Edward Island and of Nova Scotia the same year (Q.C., 1894). He was elected to represent Charlottetown as a Liberal in the Island Assembly in 1890; and from 1891 to 1897 he was prime minister and attorney-general. In the latter year he resigned, and removed to British Columbia. Here he practised law until his death at Prince Rupert, British Columbia, on July 29, 1919. In 1888 he married the youngest daughter of the Hon. J. H. Gray (q.v.), of Charlottetown.

[Morgan, *Can. men* (1912); *Can. parl. comp.*]

Peterson, Sir William (1856-1921), principal of McGill University (1895-1919), was born at Edinburgh, Scotland, on May 29, 1856, the fifth son of John Peterson and Grace Anderson. He was educated at Edinburgh University (B.A., 1875), at the University of Göttingen, and at Corpus Christi College, Oxford (M.A., 1883); and in 1879 he was appointed assistant professor of humanity in Edinburgh University. From 1882 to 1895 he was principal of University College, Dundee; and in 1895 he was appointed principal of McGill University, Montreal. This post he occupied until his retirement in 1919, and he died in London, England, on January 4, 1921. In 1885 he married Lisa, daughter of William Ross, of Glenearn, Perthshire, Scotland. In 1901 he was created a C.M.G., and in 1915 a K.C.M.G. He was an LL.D. of St. Andrew's University (1885), of Princeton University (1896), of the University of New Brunswick (1900), of Yale University (1901), of Johns Hopkins University (1902), of Queen's University, Kingston (1903), of Aberdeen University (1906), of the University of Toronto (1907), and of Harvard University (1909). He was the author of *Canadian essays and addresses* (London, 1915), and the editor of a number of Latin texts.

[C. Macmillan, *McGill and its story* (Toronto, 1921); *Who was who*, 1916-28; *Can. who was who*, vol. 2; Morgan, *Can. men* (1912); London, *Canadian Gazette*, Jan. 13, 1921.]

Petitclair, Pierre (1813-1860), poet and dramatist, was born at Quebec in 1813. His later years were spent on the Labrador coast. He was the author of three comedies, *Griphon, ou la vengeance d'un valet* (Quebec, 1837), *La donation* (Répertoire nationale, 1848), and *Une partie de campagne* (Quebec, 1865). Some of his verses are printed in J. Huston (ed.), *Le répertoire national* (Montreal, 1848-50). He died at Pointe-au-Pot, Labrador, on August 15, 1860.

[L. M. Darveau, *Nos hommes de lettres* (Montreal, 1873); E. Lareau, *Histoire de la littérature canadienne* (Montreal, 1874); Morgan, *Bib. can.*; *Bull. rech. hist.*, 1915; Le Jeune, *Dict. gén.*]

Petitot, Emile Fortuné Stanislas Joseph (1838-1917), missionary and geographer, was born at Grancey-le-Château, near Marseilles, France, in 1838. He became a priest in the Oblate order; and in 1862 he was sent to the Canadian North West as a missionary. He served as a missionary in various parts of what are now the provinces of Alberta and Saskatchewan until 1882. He then returned to

France, and in 1886 he became the parish priest of Mareuil-les-Meaux. Here he died on May 29, 1917. He published a number of valuable works dealing with the geography, anthropology, and linguistics of the Canadian North West: *Dictionnaire de la langue Déné-Dindjié* (Paris, 1876), *Vocabulaire français-esquimau* (Paris, 1876), *Monographie des Esquimaux Tchiglit du Mackenzie et de l'Anderson* (Paris, 1876), *Monographie des Déné-Dindjié* (Paris, 1876), *Traditions indiennes du Canada Nord-ouest* (Paris, 1886), *Les Grands Esquimaux* (Paris, 1887), *En route pour la mer glaciale* (Paris, 1888), *Quinze ans sous le cercle polaire* (Paris, 1889), *Origine Asiatique des Esquimaux* (Rouen, 1890), *Autour du grand lac des Esclaves* (Paris, 1891), and *Exploration de la région du grand lac des Ours* (Paris, 1893).

[A. G. Morice, *L'abbé Emile Petitot et les découvertes géographiques au Canada* (Le Canada français, 1921); Le Jeune, *Dict. gén.*]

Petrie, Robert Methven (1906-1966), astronomer, was born in St. Andrews, Scotland, on May 15, 1906. He came to Canada with his parents in 1911 and lived in British Columbia. He graduated in physics in 1928 and received his Ph.D degree from the University of Michigan in 1932. Dr. Petrie was on the staff of the University of Michigan until his appointment to the Dominion Astrophysical Observatory in Ottawa in 1935. He became the director of the Observatory in 1951 and Dominion astronomer in 1964. During his studies of the radial velocities of spectroscopic binaries, Petrie became convinced that in order to achieve results of the highest accuracy it was necessary to obtain improved wavelengths for the atomic absorption lines that occur in the different types of stellar spectra. Since many of the observed features are blends of lines of several atoms, the wavelengths to be used must be determined for each spectral type and for spectograms of each dispersal used. His work in solving this problem, based on observations of both hot and cold stars, was accepted as the basis for such radial-velocity measurements by the International Astronomical Union in 1955. Realizing the need for a more powerful telescope, Dr. Petrie drew the plans for the 48-inch reflecting telescope built by Grubb Parsons and Company and put into operation in 1962. He directed the development of the 150-inch so-called "Queen Elizabeth II" telescope which was to have been set up on Mount Kobau, British Columbia, but which was abandoned as a government economy measure.

Dr. Petrie was a fellow of the Royal Society of Canada and recipient of the Tory Medal in 1961. He was a member of the International Astronomical Union and active on commissions relating to radial velocities, stellar spectography, photometric double stars, and galactic structure.

He was awarded the M.B.E. in 1945 for his wartime work in submarine detection. He died at Vancouver, British Columbia, April 8, 1966.

[*Proc. and Trans. Roy. Soc. Can.*, vol. IV (1966); *Can. who's who*, 1961-63.]

Phair, Robert (1837-1931), missionary, was born in county Tyrone, Ireland, in 1837; and was educated at the Church Missionary College, Islington, England. He was ordained a priest of the Church of England in 1866, and came to Canada as a missionary among the Indians in Manitoba. From 1888 to 1915 he was superintendent of Indian missions in the Anglican diocese of Rupert's Land. He died at San Diego, California, on November 11, 1931.

[Morgan, *Can. men* (1912).]

Phelan, Gerald Bernard (1892-1965), philosopher, was born in Halifax, Nova Scotia, August 26, 1892, and educated at St. Mary's College and Holy Heart Seminary, being ordained a priest in 1914. After a series of parochial appointments he went to Europe in 1922 and at Louvain he received the Ph.D. degree in psychology in 1924. He came to St. Michael's College, University of Toronto, in 1925 as professor of psychology and became professor of philosophy in 1926. He assumed responsibility for the library of the newly formed Institute of Mediaeval Studies, and in 1939 when it became the Pontifical Institute of Mediaeval Studies he became president. From 1946 to 1952 he was at the University of Notre Dame, Indiana, where he organized a Mediaeval Institute. He returned to Toronto in 1952 as professor of philosophy at St. Michael's College. He retired in 1962.

He was an excellent linguist and an able musicologist but philosophy was his first love. He insisted on the fundamentally sapiential character of philosophy in contrast to the methodology and knowledge within the positive and social sciences.

He was a fellow of the Royal Society of Canada; fellow of the Canadian Academy of St. Thomas; and member, and at one time president, of the American Catholic Philosophical Association. He was a member of the Humanities Research Council of Canada, of the British Psychological Society, and the British Institute of Philosophy.

Monsignor Phelan died on May 30, 1965, at Toronto, Ontario. He wrote *Feeling — experience and its modalities* (Louvain, 1925), *Jacques Maritain* (London, 1937), *St. Thomas and analogy* (Milwaukee, 1948), *The wisdom of St. Anselm* (Latrobe, 1960).

[*Proc. Roy. Soc. Can.*, 1965.]

Philipps, Richard (1661?-1750), governor of Nova Scotia (1719-49), was born about 1661, the second son of Richard Philipps and Frances Noel. At the Revolution of 1688 he entered the service of William of Orange, and was present at the battle of the Boyne in 1690. In 1712 he became colonel of the 12th Regiment of Foot, and in 1717 of the 40th Regiment. In 1719 he was appointed governor of Placentia and captain-general of Nova Scotia. From 1720 to 1722 he administered in person the affairs of Nova Scotia; but he then returned to England, and, with the exception of the years 1729-31, his duties were performed by deputies. He ceased to draw his salary as governor in 1749, and he died on October 14, 1750.

[*Dict. nat. biog.*; B. Murdoch, *History of Nova Scotia* (3 vols., Halifax, N.S., 1866); D. Campbell, *History of Nova Scotia* (Montreal, 1873); *Coll. Nova Scotia Hist. Soc.*, vols. 2 and 5; *Dict. Can. biog.*, vol. 3.]

Phillipps-Wolley, Sir Clive Oldnall Long (1854-1918), author, was born at Wimborne, Dorsetshire, England, on April 3, 1854, the son of R. A. L. Phillipps, F.R.G.S. He was educated at Rossall School, England; and, after serving for some years as British consul at Kertch, Russia, he studied law, and was called to the bar from the Middle Temple in 1884. In 1876 he inherited the Wolley estate at Woodhall, Hamwood, Shropshire, and assumed the Wolley arms and name. In 1896 he removed to British Columbia; and he lived at Victoria, Vancouver Island, for the rest of his life. He died at Somenos, British Columbia, on July 8, 1918. He was created a knight bachelor in 1915; and in 1913 he was elected a fellow of the Royal Society of Canada. Among other books, he published *Sport in the Crimea and Caucasus* (London, 1881), *Savage Svânetia* (London, 1883), *The trottings of a tenderfoot* (London, 1884), *A sportsman's Eden* (London, 1888), *Snap* (London, 1890), *Gold, gold in Cariboo* (London, 1893), *Big game shooting* (London, 1894), *The Queensberry cup* (London, 1895), *One of the broken brigade* (London, 1897), *The Chicamon stone* (London, 1900), *Songs of an English Esau* (London, 1902), and *Songs from a young man's land* (London, 1920).

[*Proc. Roy. Soc. Can.*, 1919; *Who was who*, 1916-28; *Can. who's who*, 1912.]

Phillips, John Arthur (1842-1907), journalist and author, was born in Liverpool, England, on February 25, 1842, the son of Arthur Phillips, of Barbados, West Indies, and Mary Ann Griffith. He was educated in Barbados; but became a journalist in New York in 1865 and in Canada in 1870. He lived first in Montreal, and after 1878 in Ottawa. Here he died on January 8, 1907. In 1875 he married Ivy Sarah Parsons. He was the author of *Thompson's turkey, and other Christmas tales* (Montreal, 1873), *From bad to worse* (Montreal, 1877), *The ghost of a dog* (Ottawa, 1885), and *Out of the snow, and other stories* (Ottawa, 1886); and he collaborated with C. R.

Tuttle in his *Illustrated history of the Dominion* (Boston, 1878).

[Morgan, *Can. men* (1898); L. E. Horning and L. J. Burpee, *A bibliography of Canadian fiction* (Toronto, 1904).]

Phillips, Samuel G. (1831-1892), clergyman, was born in 1831, and was received on trial as a preacher of the Wesleyan Methodist Church in 1854. He was ordained in 1857, and occupied many charges in Quebec and eastern Ontario. He died at Brockville, Ontario, on March 3, 1892. He was the author of *The need of the world* (Toronto, 1882) and other pamphlets; and he was the editor of *The Canadian Methodist pulpit*.

[G. H. Cornish, *Cyclopaedia of Methodism in Canada* (2 vols., Toronto, 1881-1903).]

Phillips, Walter Joseph (1884-1963), artist, was born at Barton-on-Humber, England, October 25, 1884. He studied at Bourne College, Birmingham (1896-1902), and with Edward Taylor of the Municipal School of Art, Birmingham. He taught Latin and arithmetic at Yarmouth College for a year and then went to South Africa, where his uncle was a schoolmaster. He returned to England in 1908. He tried freelance commercial art for a year but then took a position as art master at Bishop Woodsworth School, Salisbury. Here he met Ernest Carlos, an artist, who shared his technical knowledge and training. Phillips was married to Gladys Kate Pitcher in 1912 and he and his wife and son emigrated to Winnipeg, Manitoba, in 1913. From 1913 to 1924 he was art master at the newly opened St. John's Technical School in Winnipeg. He formed a friendship with the etcher Cyril Barrand, who taught him that art. However, he was more interested in woodcuts and began working in colour woodcuts. In all, he made some 160 colour woodcuts of central and western Canadian subjects. He also was a skilled water-colour painter. From 1914 to 1924 he painted mostly at Lake of the Woods, from 1924 to 1935 he painted the prairies, and from 1936, particularly after his association with the Banff School of Fine Arts in 1940, he painted the Rockies. Although he was a superb colourist, Phillips himself said "colour exists only by virtue of light: form is eternal."

He published several books of woodcuts: *Ten Canadian colour prints* (1927), *The Canadian scene*, *Essays in wood*, *Winter woodcuts*, and *Ten woodcuts*; illustrated Watson's *Dreams of Fort Garry*; and provided 32 pen-drawings and 32 colour illustrations for Frederick Niven's *Colour in the Canadian Rockies* (1927). He wrote about his art, *The technique of the colour wood-cut* (1926), as well as a number of articles in magazines and a weekly column, *Art and Artists*, in the *Winnipeg Tribune* (1926-42). He died at Victoria, British Columbia, June 11, 1963. He was elected A.R.C.A. (1921) and R.C.A. (1933); was a founder member of the Canadian Society of Painters in Water Colour; and was a member of the Society of Canadian Painter-Etchers.

[D. C. Scott, *W. J. Phillips* (Toronto, 1947); *Encyc. Can.*]

Phillips, William Eric (1893-1964), manufacturer, was born in Toronto, Ontario, in 1893 and educated at Upper Canada College and the University of Toronto (B.A.Sc., 1914) as a chemist. He went to Germany for further study but left just before war was declared. He served with the Leinster Regiment and the Royal Warwickshire Regiment in France, being commissioned and becoming a lieutenant-colonel by the age of twenty-three. He was wounded in France and subsequently loaned to the French government for post-war work in Poland. He resigned his commission in 1920 and returned to Canada. He worked with his father in the glass business in Kingston before founding his own firm, W. E. Phillips Limited, in Oshawa, to supply glass for the automotive trade. During the Second World War he headed Research Enterprises Limited for the government and received the O.B.E. for making it a model war industry. He was chairman of the Board of Governors of the University of Toronto (1945-63) and helped guide the post-war expansion of the university. He was chairman of Massey-Ferguson, Argus Corporation, Duplate Canada, Canadian Pittsburgh Industries, and Standard Chemical, and director of the Royal Bank, Canadair, Brazilian Traction, and many other companies. He was on the Board of Trustees of the Toronto General Hospital and the Ontario Cancer Society, and a member of the Chemical Institute of Canada, and the Engineering Institute of Canada. He had been awarded, besides the O.B.E., the D.S.O. and the M.C. He died in Palm Beach, Florida, December 25, 1964.

[Metropolitan Toronto Library Board, *Biographical scrapbooks*, vols. 22, 23, 72; *Can. who's who*, 1961-63.]

Phipps, George Augustus Constantine, Earl of Mulgrave. See **Mulgrave, George Augustus Constantine, Earl of.**

Phips, Sir William (1651-1695), governor of Massachusetts, was born in Maine on February 2, 1651, of humble parents. He became a ship's carpenter in Boston, married a wealthy widow, became a ship-owner, and in 1687 he succeeded in raising a Spanish treasure-ship off Haiti, an exploit for which he was knighted. In 1690 he was given command of a New England expedition against Port Royal in Acadia. He captured Port Royal; and later in the year he proceeded against Quebec. He made his way up the St. Lawrence to the basin of Quebec; but he was not able to capture the citadel. In 1692 he was appointed first royal governor of Massachusetts; but he was recalled in 1694 to London to meet charges of maladministration, and he died in London, on February 18, 1695, during the hearing of these charges.

[Carl Van Doren (ed.), *The life of Sir William Phips* (New York, 1929); H. O. Thayer, *Sir William Phips* (New York, 1927); E. Myrand, *Sir William Phips devant Québec: Histoire d'un siège* (Quebec, 1893); Alice Lounsbury, *Sir William Phips* (New York, 1941); Cotton Mather, *Life of Sir William Phips* (New York, 1971); C. L. Alderman, *Stormy knight: The life of Sir William Phips* (Philadelphia, Penn., 1964); *Dict. Am. biog.*; Le Jeune, *Dict. gén.*; *Dict. Can. biog.*, vol. 1.]

Phyn, James (1742-1821), merchant, was born on March 12, 1742, a son of George Phyn, of the Corse of Monelly, in Scotland, and his wife, Janet Simpson. He was thus an uncle of the Hon. John Forsyth (q.v.) and his brothers, and of the Hon. John Richardson (q.v.). He came to America before 1763, for in that year he became a partner of John Duncan, an Indian trader of Schenectady, in a firm which came to be known in 1767 as Phyn, Ellice, and Co. In 1774 he left for England, to found in London the firm of Phyn, Ellice, and Co., which was destined to play for many years an important role in the history of the Canadian fur-trade. It was a party to the formation of the XY Company in 1798; and on the union of the XY and North West Companies in 1804, it became one of the regular supply houses of the North West Company. Phyn died on November 2, 1821. About 1768 he married in Schenectady the daughter of Dr. John Constable, a friend of Sir William Johnson; and by her he had at least two sons.

[R. H. Fleming, *Phyn, Ellice and Company of Schenectady* (Contributions to Canadian economics, IV, 1932).]

Pichon, Thomas (1700-1781), traitor and author, was born at Vire, Calvados, France, on March 30, 1700. He became a lawyer, and then entered the service of the French king. In 1751 he came to Cape Breton as secretary to the governor; and in 1755 his treason in providing the English with military information resulted in the capture by the English of Fort Beauséjour. He went in 1756 to live in England; he died on the island of Jersey, November 22, 1781. He was the anonymous author of *Lettres et mémoires pour servir à l'histoire naturelle, civile, et politique du Cap Breton* (The Hague, 1760), translated into English under the title, *Genuine letters and memoirs relating to the natural, civil, and commercial history of the islands of Cape Breton and Saint John* (London, 1760).

[G. Lanctot, *Le traître Pichon* (Bull. rech. hist., 1930); J. C. Webster, *Thomas Pichon* (Halifax, N.S., 1937); Le Jeune, *Dict. gén.*]

Pickthall, Marjorie Lowry Christie (1883-1922), author, was born at Gunnersbury, near Chiswick, London, England, on September 14, 1883, the daughter of Arthur C. Pickthall and Helen Mallard. She came to Canada with her parents in 1889, settled in Toronto, and was educated at Bishop Strachan School. From an early age she contributed poems and stories to the magazines and newspapers; and before her first book appeared, her genius was recognized. In 1912 she went to England, and she remained there until 1919. Then she went to live in British Columbia, first in Victoria, and then in Vancouver. Here she died suddenly on April 19, 1922. Her first book was a little volume of poetry, entitled *Drift of pinions* (Montreal, 1912); and this was followed by *The lamp of poor souls, and other poems* (Toronto, 1917), *The wood carver's wife, and later poems* (Toronto, 1922), *Little songs* (Toronto, 1925), and *Complete poems* (Toronto, 1936). In addition to some juvenile stories, she published two novels, *Little hearts* (London, 1915) and *The bridge* (London and New York, 1922), and a collection of her short stories was published posthumously under the title *Angels' shoes and other stories* (London, 1923).

[L. Pierce, *Marjorie Pickthall: A book of remembrance* (Toronto, 1925); J. D. Logan, *Marjorie Pickthall* (Halifax, N.S., 1922); E. J. Pratt, *Marjorie Pickthall* (Canadian Forum, 1933); *Canadian bookman*, May, 1922; *Can. who was who*, vol. 2; Le Jeune, *Dict. gén.*; A. MacMechan, *Headwaters of Canadian literature* (Toronto, 1924).]

Picquet, François (1708-1781), missionary, was born in Bourg-en-Bresse, France, on December 4, 1708, the son of humble parents. He joined the congregation of St. Sulpice in 1729, was ordained a priest, and in 1735 was sent to Canada as a missionary. He obtained a great influence with the Algonkin and Nipissing Indians; and in 1749 he built a fort at La Présentation (now Ogdensburg, N.Y.). He fought at the head of his Indians during the Seven Years' War, and was wounded at the siege of Quebec in 1759. A price having been placed on his head by the English, he escaped in Indian dress after the battle of the Plains of Abraham, and made his way overland to New Orleans. In 1763 he returned to France, and he died in poverty at the home of his sister, a peasant woman of the village of Verjon, on July 15, 1781.

[A. Chagny, *Un défenseur de la Nouvelle-France: François Picquet, "le Canadien"* (Montreal, 1913); *Cyc. Am. biog.*; Le Jeune, *Dict. gén.*]

Pidgeon, George Campbell (1872-1971), minister, was born in Maria, Quebec, March 2, 1872. He was educated at Morrin College, Quebec; at McGill University (B.A., 1891); and at the Presbyterian Theological College at Montreal (B.D., 1895; D.D., 1905). He began his ministry in Montreal and held charges in Ontario and British Columbia. He was professor of practical theology at Westminster Hall, Vancouver, from 1909 to 1915. He was minister of Bloor Street United Church from 1915 to 1948. He was the last moderator of the Presbyterian Church in Canada before union (1925) and the first moderator of the United Church of Canada.

He was first chairman of the Presbyterian Churches Committee on moral and social reform (1907) and president of the Social Service Council of British Columbia (1909) and of Canada (1918).

He served with the Y.M.C.A. in the First World War in England and France (1917-18). He died at Toronto, Ontario, on June 15, 1971.

[*Can. who's who*, 1964-66; J. W. Grant, *George Pidgeon* (Toronto, 1962).]

Pierce, Lorne (1890-1961), editor and litterateur, was born at Delta, Ontario, August 3, 1890. He attended Queen's University (B.A., 1912; LL.D., 1928); Union Theological Seminary, New York (B.D., 1916); New York University (M.A., 1916); Victoria College, University of Toronto (B.D., 1917); and United Theological College, Montreal (Th.D., 1920). He was ordained into the ministry of the Methodist Church in 1916. He became editor of the Ryerson Press in 1920, remaining in this position until retirement in 1960. In 1926 he donated the Lorne Pierce medal for Canadian literature to be awarded by the Royal Society of Canada. He was a Canadian cultural nationalist who was able to encourage Canadian poets and writers by giving them an opportunity to publish their works. He believed in developing a distinctive Canadian culture to which both founding races and all groups and cultures could contribute. He established the series *Makers of Canadian literature* in 1923 to provide short biographies of Canadian writers. The Ryerson Chapbooks were launched in 1925 to publish Canadian poets. In 1927 he published *An outline of Canadian literature* in both French and English. Other works were *Marjorie Pickthall: A book of remembrance* (Toronto, 1925), *William Kirby: A portrait of a Loyalist* (Toronto, 1929), *Three Fredericton poets* (Toronto, 1933), *The chronicle of a century, 1829-1929: The record of one hundred years of progress in the publishing concerns of the Methodist, Presbyterian and Congregational churches in Canada* (Toronto, 1929), *In conference with the best minds* (Toronto, 1927), *Primitive Methodism and the new Catholicism* (Toronto, 1923), *English Canadian literature* (Ottawa, 1932). He was a supporter of church union in 1925 and continued to be a strong churchman as well as an advocate of a comprehensive Canadian literary development. His collection of Canadiana is housed at the Douglas Library at Queen's University, Kingston. He died at Toronto, November 28, 1961.

[*Can. who's who*, 1955-57; C. H. Dickinson, *Lorne Pierce, A profile* (Toronto, 1965).]

Pierce, William Henry (1856-1948), missionary to the Indians and author, was born at what is now Prince Rupert, British Columbia, in 1856, of a Scottish father and an Indian mother, and died at Prince Rupert, on April 10, 1948. His mother having died three weeks after his birth, he was brought up by his Indian grandfather. He came under the influence of missionaries who had been sent to British Columbia to evangelize the Indians, and he himself became a missionary. When an old man, he told the story of his life in a book entitled *From potlatch to pulpit* (Vancouver, 1933), edited by the Rev. J. P. Hicks.

[Private information.]

Piers, Harry (1870-1940), museum curator, was born at Halifax, Nova Scotia, on February 12, 1870. In 1899 he was appointed curator of the provincial museum at Halifax; and he retained this position until his death at Halifax, on January 24, 1940. He was the author of *Robert Field, portrait painter* (New York, 1927).

[*Can. who's who*, 1936-37; Morgan, *Can. men* (1912).]

Pike, Warburton (1861?-1915), explorer and author, was born at Wareham, Dorsetshire, England, about 1861. He matriculated at Brasenose College, Oxford, in 1880; but did not graduate. He came to Canada and made some notable explorations in the far north, which he described in two books: *The barren ground of northern Canada* (London, 1892) and *Through the sub-arctic forest* (London, 1896). He died at Vancouver, British Columbia, on October 20, 1915.

[Private information.]

Pilkington, Robert (1765-1834), soldier, was born at Chelsfield, Kent, England, on November 7, 1765. He was educated at the Royal Military Academy at Woolwich; and obtained a commission in the Royal Artillery in 1787. In 1789 he transferred to the engineers, and in 1790 he was sent to Canada. He was at first stationed at Quebec; but from 1793 to 1796 he was on the staff of Lieut.-Col. Simcoe (q.v.) in Upper Canada. He accompanied Simcoe on some of his journeys about the province, and made some maps and sketches. In 1794 he was sent to establish a fort on the Miami River. He returned to England in 1803; and he rose in the Army until he became inspector-general of fortifications, with the rank of major-general.

[*Dict. nat. biog.*; J. Ross Robertson (ed.), *The diary of Mrs. John Graves Simcoe* (Toronto, 1911); P. J. Robinson, *Toronto during the French régime* (Toronto, 1933).]

Pilot, Robert Wakeham (1898-1967), artist, was born in St. John's, Newfoundland, October 9, 1898. He studied at the Monument National, Montreal, under Maurice Cullen, Edmond Dyonnet, and William Brymner; at the Art Association of Montreal; at the Académie Julien in Paris with Pierre Laurens; and at the Société Nationale des Beaux-Arts in Paris. Much of his work was done in Nova Scotia and New Brunswick. He is represented in the National Gallery of Canada and the Quebec Provincial Museum as well as by murals in Montreal and book illustrations for *Storied streets of Quebec* and *The patriot* by J. Guyon. He served in the First World War with the Canadian Army, and in the Second World War (1940-45). He became A.R.C.A. (1935) and was president of the Academy (1952-54). He died at Montreal, Quebec, December 17, 1967.

[*Can. who's who*, 1955-57.]

Pilot, William (1841-1913), clergyman and educationist, was born in Bristol, England, on December 30, 1841, and died on September 25, 1913. In 1867 he was ordained a clergyman of the Church of England, and came to Newfoundland as vice-principal of Queen's College, in St. John's. He became principal of the college in 1878; and from 1875 to 1908 he was superintendent of Church of England schools in Newfoundland. In 1893 he became also president of the Council of Higher Education. He is said to have published a text-book on the geography of Newfoundland, but the exact title of this publication has proved difficult to ascertain.

[*Encyc. Can.*; *Newfoundland supp.*]

Pinhey, John Charles (1860-1912), artist, was born at Ottawa, Canada, on August 24, 1860, the son of John Hamnet Pinhey and Constance Pinhey. He studied art at the Central School of Art, Toronto, and later at the Académie Julien and the Ecole des Beaux-Arts in Paris. On his return to Canada, he had his studio for many years at Hudson Heights, Quebec, on the lower Ottawa River; and he achieved a considerable reputation as a painter of figure studies. In 1897 he was elected a member of the Royal Canadian Academy of Arts; and he died at Montreal on September 7, 1912.

[*Morgan, Can. men* (1912); N. MacTavish, *The fine arts in Canada* (Toronto, 1925).]

Pinkham, William Cyprian (1844-1928), Anglican bishop of Calgary (1888-1928), was born at St. John's, Newfoundland, on November 11, 1844, the son of William Pinkham. He was educated at the Church of England Academy, St. John's, Newfoundland, and at St. Augustine's College, Canterbury, England; and was ordained a priest of the Church of England in 1869. In 1887 he was elected bishop of Saskatchewan, and in 1888 bishop of Calgary. This latter position he held for forty years. He died at Calgary, Alberta, on

July 18, 1928. In 1887 he was made a D.C.L. of Trinity University, Toronto, and a D.D. of St. John's College, Winnipeg.

[*Morgan, Can. men* (1912).]

Pinsonnault, Adolphe (1815-1883), first Roman Catholic bishop of London, Ontario, was born at Laprairie, Lower Canada, on November 23, 1815, and was ordained a priest in 1840. In 1856 he became first Roman Catholic bishop of London, Ontario; and he presided over this diocese until 1866. He then retired, with the title of bishop of Birtha; and he died at Montreal, Quebec, on January 30, 1883. He was the author of a pamphlet entitled *Le dernier chant de cygne sur le tumulus du gallicanisme* (Montreal, 1870).

[Allaire, *Dict. biog.*; Le Jeune, *Dict. gén.*; *Dom. ann. reg.*, 1883.]

Pipes, William Thomas (1850-1909), prime minister of Nova Scotia (1882-84), was born at Amherst, Nova Scotia, on April 15, 1850, the son of Jonathan Pipes of Amherst Point. He was educated at Amherst, and at Acadia College, and became headmaster of the Sydney academy. He was called to the bar in 1875 (Q.C., 1890), and was elected to the Legislative Assembly of Nova Scotia in the Liberal interest for Cumberland in 1882. He became the leader of the government without office and without salary, on August 3, 1882, and resigned on July 15, 1884. In 1887 he was made judge of probates for Cumberland. In 1898, he was appointed to the Legislative Council, and entered the Murray administration without portfolio. He became commissioner of public works and mines for Nova Scotia in 1905, and attorney-general in 1907. In 1906 he retired from the Legislative Council, and was elected to the Legislative Assembly for Cumberland. He died in Boston on October 7, 1909. He married Ruth Eliza (d. 1894), daughter of David McElmon, on November 23, 1876.

[*Morgan, Can. men* (1898); *Can. parl. comp.*; J. Hannay, *Premiers of Nova Scotia since 1867* (Can. mag., 1897).]

Piquefort, Jean (pseud.). See **Routhier, Sir Adolphe Basile.**

Pirie, Alexander Fraser (1849-1903), journalist, was born in Guelph, Canada West, in 1849. He became a journalist on the staff of the Toronto *Sun*, the Toronto *Telegram*, and the Montreal *Star*; and was one of the first columnists in Canadian journalism. In 1889 he purchased the Dundas *Banner*, and he edited this paper until his death on August 8, 1903. In 1893 he was elected president of the Canadian Press Association; and he was the author of *Picturesque Dundas* (Dundas, Ont., 1896).

[*Morgan, Can. men* (1898).]

Pitblado, Isaac (1867-1964), lawyer, was born in Glenelg, Nova Scotia, March 15, 1867, and educated in Halifax schools and at the University of Manitoba (B.A., 1886; LL.B., 1889; M.A., 1893), and at Dalhousie University (LL.D., 1919). He arrived in Winnipeg in 1882 and was called to the bar of Manitoba in 1890. He was an expert in the complexities of freight rates and he appeared at numerous hearings of the Board of Railway Commissioners on behalf of the railways and the province of Manitoba. He was a founder of the Canadian Bar Association. He continued practice until he was 93, and at age 80 was retained by the C.P.R. to present its application for increased freight charges. He was a director of a number of Western Canadian companies, was registrar of the University of Manitoba (1893-1900), and was chairman of the Board of Governors (1917-24). He died at Winnipeg, Manitoba, December 6, 1964.

[*Can. who's who*, 1961-63; Metropolitan Toronto Library Board, *Biographical scrapbooks*, vols. 22 & 72.]

Piuze, Liveright (1754-1813), physician, was born in Warsaw, Poland, on February 2, 1754, and emigrated to America in his youth. He became a medical officer in the American army during the War of the Revolution, was afterwards kidnapped by Indians, was handed over to the English at Niagara, and ultimately settled as a licensed surgeon and apothecary at Rivière-Ouelle, on the south shore of the St. Lawrence. There he died on April 22, 1813. His autobiography was translated into French by J. R. Piuze, and was published, under the title *Récit des aventures de Liveright Piuze*, in the *Bulletin des recherches historiques*, 1919.

[Le Jeune, *Dict. gén.*]

Plamondon, Antoine (1804-1895), painter, was born at Lorette, near Quebec, Lower Canada, on February 28, 1804. He went to Paris to study painting in 1826, and became a pupil of Guérin. On his return to Quebec, he painted many portraits and numerous pictures for churches. He became a member of the Royal Canadian Academy of Arts in 1880; and he died at Pointe-aux-Trembles, Quebec, on September 4, 1895.

[G. Bellerive, *Artistes-peintres canadiens-français* (Quebec, 1925); E. Morris, *Art in Canada: The early painters* (Toronto, 1911); N. MacTavish, *The fine arts in Canada* (Toronto, 1925); William Colgate, *Canadian Art, 1820-1940* (Toronto, 1943); *Bull. rech. hist.*, 1926.]

Plamondon, Marc Aurèle (1823-1900), journalist, politician, and jurist, was born in Quebec, Lower Canada, the son of Pierre Plamondon and Aimée Mondion, on October 16, 1823. He was educated at the Quebec Seminary, and was called to the bar in 1846. In 1848 he was one of the founders of the Institut Canadien of Quebec, and its first president; and in 1855 he was one of the founders and the editor of *Le National*, the organ of the Reform party in Lower Canada. In 1874 he was made a puisne judge of the Superior Court of Quebec; and he retired on pension in 1897. He died on August 4, 1900. In 1859 he married Mathilde L'Ecuyer, of Quebec.

[Morgan, *Can. men* (1898); P. G. Roy, *Les juges de la province de Québec* (Quebec, 1933).]

Planté, Joseph Bernard (1768-1826), politician, was born at Pointe-aux-Trembles, near Quebec, on December 19, 1768. He was educated at the Quebec Seminary, and became a notary public. He represented Hampshire in the Legislative Assembly of Lower Canada from 1796 to 1808; and he was one of the founders of *Le Canadien*. From 1809 to 1826 he represented Kent in the Legislative Assembly of the province. He died at Quebec on February 13, 1826.

[F. J. Audet, *Joseph-Bernard Planté* (Trans. Roy. Soc. Can., 1933).]

Plaskett, John Stanley (1865-1941), astronomer, was born at Woodstock, Canada West, on November 17, 1865. He was educated at the University of Toronto (B.A., 1899; D.Sc., 1923), and entered the service of the astronomical branch of the department of the interior at Ottawa in 1903. In 1918 he was made director of the Dominion Astro-physical Observatory at Victoria, British Columbia; and he remained in this post until his retirement in 1935. He was elected a fellow of the Royal Society of Canada in 1910; and in 1932 he was awarded the Society's Flavelle medal. He was an honorary D.Sc. of the University of Pittsburgh (1913) and an honorary LL.D. of the University of British Columbia (1925), of McGill University (1932), and of Queen's University (1934); and he was created a C.B.E. in 1935. He was the author of a large number of papers contributed to the *Transactions* of the Royal Society of Canada and various astronomical journals. He died at Esquimalt, British Columbia, on October 17, 1941.

[*Proc. Roy. Soc. Can.*, 1942; *Can. who's who*, 1936-37; Morgan, *Can. men* (1912).]

Playter, George Frederick (1811?-1866), clergyman and author, was born about 1811, and became a minister of the Wesleyan Methodist Church in Upper Canada in 1833. From 1844 to 1846 he was editor of the *Christian Guardian*, Toronto, and from 1847 to 1849 he edited the *Prince Edward Gazette*, Picton. He died at Frankford, Canada West, on October 24, 1866. He was the author of *The history of Methodism in Canada* (Toronto, 1862), of which only Vol. I was published.

[Morgan, *Bib. can.*; G. H. Cornish, *A cyclopaedia of Methodism in Canada* (2 vols., Toronto, 1880-1903).]

Plessis, Joseph Octave (1763-1825), Roman Catholic bishop of Quebec (1806-25), was born near Montreal, Quebec, on March 3,

1763, the son of humble parents. He was educated in the College of Montreal and the Seminary of Quebec. He became secretary to Bishop Briand (q.v.), and in 1786 he was ordained a priest. In 1788 he became secretary to Bishop Hubert; in 1792 he was appointed curé of Quebec; and in 1801 he was consecrated a bishop and made coadjutor to Bishop Denault. In 1806 he succeeded the latter as bishop of Quebec; and he opposed vigorously the policy adopted by Sir James Craig (q.v.), in regard to the French Canadians. He came to an agreement, however, with Sir George Prevost (q.v.), and during the War of 1812 he played an important part in ensuring the loyalty of the French Canadians. In 1818 he was nominated archbishop of Quebec, but he did not assume the title. In the same year he was appointed a member of the Legislative Council of Lower Canada; and in 1822 he opposed the projected union of Upper and Lower Canada. He interested himself in education; and the colleges of Nicolet and St. Hyacinthe were founded under his régime. He died at Quebec on December 4, 1825. A sermon which he preached on the occasion of the naval victory of the British in the Mediterranean in 1798 was printed during his lifetime (Quebec, 1799); and his *Journal de deux voyages apostoliques dans le Golfe Saint-Laurent et les provinces d'en bas, en 1811 et 1812* was published in the *Foyer canadien*, 1865.

[J. B. A. Ferland, *Notice biographique sur Mgr J. O. Plessis* (Foyer canadien, 1863), tr. by T. B. French (Quebec, 1864; 2nd ed., 1878); I. Caron, *Mgr Joseph Octave Plessis* (Trans. Roy. Soc. Can., 1937); L. Laurent, *Québec et l'Eglise aux Etats-Unis sous Mgr Briand et Mgr Plessis* (Montreal, 1945); *Dict. nat. biog.*; *Cyc. Am. biog.*; Morgan, *Bib. can.*; Le Jeune, *Dict. gén.*]

Plumb, Josiah Burr (1816-1888), speaker of the Senate of Canada (1887-88), was born at East Haven, Connecticut, in 1816, the son of the Rev. Elijah Griswold Plumb and Grace Hubbard Burr. He was for many years manager of the State Bank of Albany, New York. At the end of the American Civil War he settled in Canada; and in 1874 he was elected to represent Niagara in the Canadian House of Commons, as a Conservative. He became a friend and confidant of Sir John Macdonald (q.v.); and when defeated for North Wellington in 1882, he was appointed a member of the Senate of Canada. In 1887 he was made speaker of the Senate, and he presided over the Senate until his death at Niagara, Ontario, on March 12, 1888. In 1849 he married the youngest daughter of the Hon. Samuel Street, of Niagara Falls, Upper Canada; and by her he had three sons and three daughters.

[*Cyc. Am. biog.*; Rose, *Cyc. Can. biog.* (1886); *Can. parl. comp.*; Sir J. Pope (ed.), *Correspondence of Sir John Macdonald* (Toronto, 1921).]

Poirier, Pascal (1852-1933), senator and author, was born at Shediac, New Brunswick, on February 15, 1852, of French-Acadian descent. He was educated at St. Joseph's College, Memramcook (B.A., 1872), and was called to the bar of Quebec in 1877, and that of New Brunswick in 1887. From 1872 to 1885 he was postmaster of the House of Commons, Ottawa; and in 1885 he was called to the Senate of Canada. He remained a member of the Senate until his death at Shediac on September 25, 1933. In 1879 he married Anna, sister of Alphonse Lusignan (q.v.). In 1899 he was elected a member of the Royal Society of Canada; and he was the author of *L'origine des Acadiens* (Montreal, 1874), *Le Père Lefebvre et l'Acadie* (Montreal, 1898), *Le parler Franco-Acadien et ses origines* (Quebec, 1928), and a number of historical papers contributed to the *Transactions* of the Royal Society of Canada.

[*Proc. Roy. Soc. Can.*, 1934; *Can. parl. comp.*; Morgan, *Can. men* (1912); Le Jeune, *Dict. gén.*]

Poisson, Adolphe (1849-1922), poet, was born at Gentilly, Canada East, on March 14, 1849. He was educated at the Quebec Seminary and at the College of Nicolet; and in 1874 he was called to the bar of Quebec, and was appointed registrar of the county of Arthabaska. He published four volumes of poetry: *Chants canadiens* (Quebec, 1880), *Heures perdues* (Quebec, 1894), *Sous les pins* (Montreal, 1902), and *Chants de soir* (Arthabaska, 1917). He died at Arthabaska, Quebec, on April 22, 1922. In 1882 he married Amélie, daughter of A. Côté, Quebec.

[Morgan, *Can. men* (1912); P. G. Roy, *Les avocats de la région de Québec* (Lévis, Que., 1936); Le Jeune, *Dict. gén.*; *Bull. rech. hist.*, 1926.]

Pollard, Richard (1752-1824), missionary, was born in 1752. He came to Canada in 1775, and in 1787 he settled on the Detroit River. He became the sheriff of the Western district of Upper Canada; but in 1802, owing to the scarcity of clergymen coming from the Mother Country, he took holy orders in the Church of England; and he was missionary at Sandwich, Upper Canada, from 1802 to his death on November 6, 1824.

[A. H. Young, *The Revd. Richard Pollard* (Ont. Hist. Soc., papers and records, 1929).]

Pollok, Allan (1829-1918), clergyman and educationist, was born at Buckhaven, Scotland, on October 19, 1829. He was educated at Glasgow University, and was licensed as a minister of the Church of Scotland in 1852. He came to Nova Scotia in that year, and became the pastor of St. Andrew's Church, New Glasgow. In 1873 he was appointed professor of church history and practical theology in Pine Hill College, Halifax; and in 1894 he became principal of the College. He was made a D.D. of

Glasgow University in 1900, and of Dalhousie University in 1902. He retired in 1904; and he died at Halifax, Nova Scotia, on July 7, 1918. He was the author of *Studies in practical theology* (Edinburgh, 1907).

[*Can. who was who*, vol. 1; Morgan, *Can. men* (1912).]

Pond, Peter (1740-1807?), fur-trader and explorer, was born in Milford, Connecticut, on January 18, 1740. After serving as a soldier in the French and Indian wars, he became a fur-trader at Detroit, and was for ten years or more engaged in the fur-trade on the upper Mississippi. In 1775 he made his first expedition to the Canadian North West; and in the development of the fur-trade here he played an important part. In 1778 he established the first post in the Athabaska country; and he appears to have reached later Great Slave Lake. In 1783 he became one of the partners in the North West Company; but the murder of John Ross (q.v.) by some of his men in 1787, being the second murder with which he had been connected in the West, brought about his retirement from the fur-trade, and in 1790 he sold his share in the company to William McGillivray (q.v.). He returned to the United States, and became for a time a special agent of the American government in its dealings with the Indians. In his later years he returned to New England, and he died about 1807 a poverty-stricken and forgotten old man. The maps he drew of his explorations in the North West were among the first which exercised an influence over future events. The most recent edition of the fragment of his *Narrative* which has come down to us is in C. M. Gates (ed.), *Five fur-traders of the North West* (Minneapolis, 1933).

[H. A. Innis, *Peter Pond, fur-trader and adventurer* (Toronto, 1930); G. C. Davidson, *The North West Company* (Berkeley, Calif., 1918); L. J. Burpee, *The search for the western sea* (Toronto, 1908); W. S. Wallace (ed.), *Documents relating to the North West Company* (Toronto: The Champlain Society, 1934); H. R. Wagner, *Peter Pond, fur-trader and explorer* (New Haven, 1955).]

Pontbriand, Henri Marie Dubreuil de (1708-1760), Roman Catholic bishop of Quebec (1741-60), was born in Vannes, France, in January, 1708. He was ordained a priest of the Roman Catholic Church, about 1732, and in 1741 he was consecrated in Paris bishop of Quebec. He came out to Canada the same year, and he administered the affairs of the diocese of Quebec until the capture of Quebec in 1759. He then retired to Montreal; and here he died on June 8, 1760.

[A. Gosselin, *L'église du Canada depuis Mgr de Laval jusqu'à la conquête, 3e partie* (Quebec, 1914); *Cyc. Am. biog.*; Allaire, *Dict. biog.*; Le Jeune, *Dict. gén.*; *Dict. Can. biog.*, vol. 3.]

Pont-Gravé, François, Sieur de. See **Du Pont, François Gravé, Sieur.**

Poole, Thomas Wesley (1831?-1905), physician and journalist, was born about 1831, a younger brother of William Henry Poole (q.v.), and was educated at Victoria University (M.D., 1856). He practised medicine in Norwood, Canada West; but in 1864 removed to Peterborough, and became the editor of the Peterborough *Weekly Review*. Later he went back to the practice of medicine, and practised in Lindsay, Ontario. He died in Lindsay on August 27, 1905. He was the author of *A sketch of the early settlement and subsequent progress of the town of Peterborough, and of each township in the county of Peterborough* (Peterborough, Ont., 1867).

[F. H. Dobbin, "Notes on the history of the Medical Association of Peterborough" (MSS. in the Peterborough Public Library).]

Poole, William Henry (1820-1896), clergyman, was born in Kilkenny county, Ireland, on April 3, 1820, and came to Upper Canada with his parents in 1831. He was brought up in Carleton Place, attended Victoria University for several sessions, and became a school-teacher. In 1846, however, he entered the ministry of the Wesleyan Methodist Church; and he ministered to various congregations in Canada until in 1879 he received and accepted a call to a Methodist Episcopal Church in Detroit, Michigan. He died on August 7, 1896. He was known as "Anglo-Israel" Poole, from the fact that he was the author of *Anglo-Israel; or, The Saxon race proved to be the lost tribes of Israel* (Toronto, 1889).

[Rose, *Cyc. Can. biog.* (1886).]

Pope, James Colledge (1826-1885), prime minister of Prince Edward Island (1865-67 and 1870-72) and minister of marine and fisheries for Canada (1878-82), was born at Bedeque, Prince Edward Island, on June 11, 1826, the second son of the Hon. Joseph Pope, of Charlottetown, and Lucy, daughter of Captain Colledge. He was educated in England; and in 1849 he went to California during the "gold rush". He returned to Prince Edward Island, however, and there engaged in shipbuilding and other mercantile enterprises. He was a member of the Legislative Assembly of Prince Edward Island, for Prince county from 1857 to 1867, and for Charlottetown from 1872 to 1873; he became a minister without portfolio in the Palmer administration in 1859, colonial secretary in the Gray administration from 1863 to 1865, prime minister of Prince Edward Island from 1865 to 1867, from 1870 to 1872, and again for a few months in 1873. He opposed the entrance of the Island into Confederation, both on the basis of the Quebec Resolutions of 1864 and on the terms secured by the Haythorne government in 1873; but in 1873 he succeeded in bringing about federation on more favourable terms, and was elected a member of the Canadian House of Commons for Prince county. He was defeated in 1874, and from 1875 to 1876 he again represented Prince county in the provincial Assembly; but in 1876 he was re-elected to the House of Commons, this time for Queen's county, and he continued to represent this constituency until 1882. From 1878 to 1882 he was minister of marine and fisheries in the Macdonald government; but owing to ill-health he ceased to administer his department in 1881. He died at Summerside, Prince Edward Island, on May 18, 1885. In 1852 he married Eliza, daughter of Thomas Pethick, of Charlottetown; and by her he had eight children.

[*Dom. ann. reg.*, 1885; Rose, *Cyc. Can. biog.* (1888); Dent, *Can. port.*, vol. 4; *Canadian biographical dictionary*, Quebec and Maritime provinces vol. (Chicago, 1881); *Cyc. Am. biog.*; *Can. parl. comp.*; D. A. MacKinnon and A. B. Warburton (eds.), *Past and present of Prince Edward Island* (Charlottetown, n.d.).]

Pope, John Henry (1824-1889), minister of agriculture for Canada (1871-73 and 1878-85) and minister of railways and canals (1885-89), was born in the Eastern Townships, Lower Canada, in 1824, the son of John Pope and Sophia Lahern. He was educated at the Compton High School, in the Eastern Townships, and first devoted himself to agriculture. In 1857 he was elected to represent Compton as a Liberal-Conservative in the Legislative Assembly of Canada, and this constituency he represented continuously, first in the Assembly, and then in the House of Commons, until his death thirty-two years later. In 1864 he was one of those who conducted the *pourparlers* which brought about the great coalition; and in 1871 he was sworn of the privy council and became minister of agriculture in the Macdonald government. He resigned with his colleagues at the time of the "Pacific Scandal" in 1873; but he was one of the chief lieutenants of Sir John Macdonald (q.v.) in opposition, and in 1878, when Macdonald came back to power, he resumed his old portfolio. In 1885 he exchanged it for that of minister of railways and canals, and this portfolio he held until his death at Ottawa on April 1, 1889. In 1880 he went to England with Macdonald and Tupper in connection with the contract for the building of the Canadian Pacific Railway; and it was partly through his influence on Macdonald that the government saw the contractors through the financial difficulties that several times threatened to overwhelm them. Though not an orator, he was an exceedingly shrewd practical politician.

[*Cyc. Am. biog.*; Rose, *Cyc. Can. biog.* (1888); *Can. parl. comp.*; Dent, *Can. port.*, vol. 4; *Canadian biographical dictionary*, Quebec and Maritime provinces vol. (Chicago, 1881); Sir J. Pope (ed.), *The correspondence of Sir John Macdonald* (Toronto, 1921); O. D. Skelton, *Life and Times of Sir A. T. Galt* (Toronto, 1920) and *Life and letters of Sir Wilfrid Laurier* (2 vols., Toronto, 1922).]

Pope, Sir Joseph (1854-1926), undersecretary of state for Canada (1896-1909) and under-secretary of state for External Affairs (1909-1926), was born at Charlottetown, Prince Edward Island, on August 16, 1854, the son of the Hon. William Henry Pope (q.v.), one of the Fathers of Confederation. He was educated at Charlottetown, but removed to Ottawa in 1878. From 1882 to 1891 he was private secretary to Sir John Macdonald (q.v.), and he was appointed Macdonald's literary executor. In 1896 he was appointed under-secretary of state for Canada, and for thirty years he was a distinguished figure in the public life of Canada. In 1903 he was associate secretary to the Alaska Boundary Tribunal, and in 1906 he was British plenipotentiary at the Pelagic Sealing Conference in Washington. He was made a C.M.G. in 1901, a C.V.O. in 1908, and a K.C.M.G. in 1912. He died at Ottawa on December 2, 1926. In 1884 he married Henriette, daughter of Sir Henri Taschereau (q.v.); and by her he had five sons and one daughter. He was the author of *Jacques Cartier, his life and voyages* (Ottawa, 1890), *Memoirs of the Right Hon. Sir John Alexander Macdonald* (2 vols., Ottawa, 1894; new ed., Toronto, 1930), *The royal tour of 1901* (Ottawa, 1903), and *The day of Sir John Macdonald* (Toronto, 1915); and he edited *Confederation documents* (Toronto, 1895) and *The correspondence of Sir John Macdonald* (Toronto, 1921). His memoirs have been edited by his son, Maurice Pope, under the title *Public servant* (Toronto, 1960).

[*Can. who was who*, vol. 1; *Who was who*, 1916-28; Morgan, *Can. men* (1912).]

Pope, Rufus Henry (1857-1944), senator of Canada, was born at Cookshire, Canada East, on September 13, 1857, the son of the Hon. J. H. Pope (q.v.). He was educated at Cookshire and Sherbrooke, Quebec; and became a farmer and stock-raiser. In 1889 he succeeded his father as the representative of Compton in the Canadian House of Commons; and he continued to represent this constituency in the Commons until 1904. He was called to the Senate of Canada in 1911; and he sat in the Senate until his death in Cookshire, Quebec, on May 16, 1944.

[*Can. who's who*, 1938-39; Morgan, *Can. men* (1898); *Can. parl. comp.*]

Pope, William Henry (1825-1879), politician and jurist, was born at Bedeque, Prince Edward Island, on May 29, 1825, the eldest son of the Hon. Joseph Pope, of Charlottetown, and Lucy, daughter of Captain Colledge. He was educated in England, studied law under Edward Palmer (q.v.) in Charlottetown, and was called to the bar of Prince Edward Island in 1847. In 1859 he was appointed colonial secretary of the Island, though without a seat in the Executive Council; and from 1863 to 1873 he represented Belfast in the Legislative Assembly of the Island. He was an advocate of Confederation, and was in 1864 a delegate to both the Charlottetown and Quebec conferences. In 1873 he was appointed judge of the county court of Prince county, Prince Edward Island; and this office he held until his death at Summerside, Prince Edward Island, on October 7, 1879. In 1851 he married Helen, daughter of Thomas Desbrisay, of Charlottetown; and by her he had eight children, of whom Sir Joseph Pope, the biographer and literary executor of Sir John Macdonald (q.v.), was the eldest. He was the author of *The confederation question considered from the P.E.I. point of view* (Charlottetown, 1866).

[*Dom. ann. reg.*, 1879; Morgan, *Bib. can.*; *Canadian biographical dictionary*, Quebec and Maritime provinces vol. (Chicago, 1881); *Dict. Can. biog.*, vol. 10.]

Porlier, Jacques (1765-1839), fur-trader, was born in Montreal, and was educated there. He went to Green Bay, on Lake Michigan, and engaged in the fur-trade about 1791. He was elected a member of the Beaver Club of Montreal in 1801; and he became a partner of the South West Company. He died at Green Bay on July 12, 1839.

[J. Tassé, *Les Canadiens de l'Ouest*, vol. i (Montreal, 1878).]

Porlier, Pierre Antoine (1725-1789), priest, was born in Montreal, New France, on May 19, 1725, and was ordained a priest in 1748. From 1749 to 1778 he was parish priest of Ste. Anne de la Pocatière; and from 1778 to 1789, of St. Ours. He died at St. Ours, Quebec, on August 17, 1789. He left behind a *Mémoire*, which is preserved in the archives of the archbishopric of Quebec, describing the events of the American invasion in 1775-76.

[Allaire, *Dict. biog.*; *Bull. rech. hist.*, 1900.]

Porter, William Henry (1840-1928), clergyman, was born at Port Medway, Nova Scotia, on December 20, 1840. He was educated at Acadia University (B.A., 1861; M.A., 1864), and became a Baptist minister. He died at New Westminster, British Columbia, on June 1, 1928. He was the author of *Canadian scenes, and other poems* (Toronto, 1907), and compiler of *Converse with the King* (Brantford, Ont., 1892).

[*Records of the graduates of Acadia University* (Wolfville, N.S., 1926).]

Portlock, Mrs. Rosa, *née* **Elliott** (1839-1928), Bible-woman, was born in England in 1839, and came to Canada about 1871. She married William Portlock, a labourer, who died in 1893; and she lived for many years in Woodstock, Ontario. Her last days were spent in an Old Ladies' Home in Hamilton, Ontario; and she died there in 1928. She was the author of two autobiographical works, *The head keeper* (Toronto, 1898) and *Twenty-five years of Canadian life* (Toronto, 1901).

[Private information.]

Portneuf, Pierre Robineau, Chevalier de (1708-1761), soldier, was born at Montreal, New France, on August 9, 1708, the second son of René Robineau, third Baron de Portneuf. He obtained a commission as ensign in the *troupes de la marine*; and in 1750 he was sent to Toronto to build the first fort at this place, at the mouth of the Humber River. He saw service in the Ohio Valley during the Seven Years' War, and was in command at Presqu'ile from 1756 to 1759. In 1761 he surrendered to the British; and in the autumn of 1761 he embarked for France. But the vessel in which he sailed, the *Auguste*, was wrecked on November 15, 1761, on the coast of Cape Breton; and Portneuf, with most of the rest of the passengers, was drowned.

[P. J. Robinson, *Toronto during the French régime* (Toronto, 1933); E. Z. Massicotte, *Les Montréalais et les deux forts de Toronto* (Bull. rech. hist., 1933); *Dict. Can. biog.*, vol. 3.]

Pothier, Jean Baptiste Toussaint (1771-1845), legislative and executive councillor of Lower Canada, was born at Montreal, on May 16, 1771, the son of Louis Toussaint Pothier, a fur-trader, and Louise Courault. In 1812 he organized and commanded a corps of voyageurs for the defence of the lakes. From 1824 to 1838 he was a member of the Legislative Council of Lower Canada; from 1838 to 1839 of the Executive Council; and from 1838 to 1841, of the Special Council. He died at Montreal on October 22, 1845. In 1820 he married Anne Françoise, daughter of Lieut.-Col. Ralph Henry Bruyères, R. E.

[E. Z. Massicotte, *L'honorable Toussaint Pothier* (Bull. rech. hist., 1920); Le Jeune, *Dict. gén.*]

Potier, Pierre (1708-1781), Jesuit missionary and grammarian, was born at Blandain, Belgium, on April 2, 1708; and entered the Society of Jesus as a novice in 1729. He was ordained a priest in 1742; and in 1743 he was sent to Canada as a missionary. After a year at Ancienne Lorette, near Quebec, he was sent to the Huron mission opposite Detroit, on the Detroit River, in 1744; and here he spent the rest of his life. He died at what is now Sandwich, on the Detroit River, on July 16, 1781. He was a scientific student of the Huron language; and a number of his manuscripts, dealing with Huron grammar and etymology, have been preserved at St. Mary's College, Montreal. The more important of these have been reproduced in facsimile, under the title, "Huron manuscripts from Rev. Pierre Potier's collection", in the *Fifteenth report of the Bureau of Archives for the province of Ontario* (Toronto, 1920). Selections from Potier's diary, covering the years 1743-81, have been published by E. R. Ott (Mid-America, 1936).

[G. Paré, *The Catholic church in Detroit, 1701-1888* (Detroit, 1951); Allaire, *Dict. biog.*]

Potter, Austin (d. 1913), clergyman, was ordained a minister of the Methodist Church in Canada in 1874, and was stationed at various places in Ontario. He died on January 16, 1913. He was the author of *From wealth to poverty; or, The tricks of the traffic: A story of the drink curse* (Toronto, 1884).

[G. H. Cornish, *Cyclopaedia of Methodism in Canada* (2 vols., Toronto, 1881-1903).]

Potts, John (1838-1907), general secretary of education for the Methodist Church (1886-1907), was born at Maguire's Bridge, county Fermanagh, Ireland, in 1838. He came to Canada in 1855, and was educated at Victoria University, Cobourg. In 1861 he was ordained a minister of the Methodist Church, and he held successive charges in many parts of Ontario. In 1886 he was appointed general educational secretary of the Methodist Church, and he held this position until his death at Toronto on October 16, 1907. Early in life he married Margaret, daughter of John Breden, of Kingston. He was a D.D. of the Wesleyan University of Ohio (1878) and of Victoria University (1894).

[Morgan, *Can. men* (1898); Rose, *Cyc. Can. biog.* (1886); *Cyc. Am. biog.*; N. F. Davin, *The Irishman in Canada* (Toronto, 1877).]

Pouchot, Pierre (1712-1769), soldier, was born at Grenoble, France, on April 8, 1712; and entered the French army in 1733 as an engineer officer. After having seen service in Italy, Flanders, Germany, and Austria, he accompanied his regiment to Canada in 1755; and he served with distinction in the Seven Years' War in America. He was in command of Fort Niagara when it was captured by the British in 1759, and was taken prisoner; but, having been exchanged, he was placed in command of Fort Lévis in 1760, and vigorously opposed the advance of Amherst (q.v.) on Montreal. After his return to France, he was employed in the island of Corsica; and he was killed there on May 8, 1769. His *Mémoires sur la dernière guerre de l'Amérique septentrionale entre la France et l'Angleterre* were published posthumously (3 vols., Yverdon, Switzerland, 1781).

[Le Jeune, *Dict. gén.*; A. G. Doughty (ed.), *The journal of Captain John Knox* (3 vols., Toronto: The Champlain Society, 1914-16); T. Chapais, *Le marquis de Montcalm* (Quebec, 1911); *Dict. Can. biog.*, vol. 3.]

Pouliot, Jean-François (1890-1969), senator, was born at Rivière-du-Loup, Quebec, in 1890, son, grandson, and great-grandson of members of the Legislative Assembly of Quebec. He entered the House of Commons in 1924 and was re-elected at each general election until he was called to the Senate in 1955. During the Second World War he was a leading anti-conscriptionist and broke with his party on the issue. He supported the Quebec anti-communist "padlock law". He wrote extensively on Quebec parish law and was a correspondent for *La Presse* of Montreal, a position which he used to good effect in his anti-conscription fight. He had the reputation of being the wordiest member of the House of Commons. He died July 6, 1969, at Rivière-du-Loup.

[*Can. who's who*, 1955-57; *Maclean's magazine*, vol. 67.]

Pouliot, Joseph Camille (1865-1935), jurist and author, was born at Rivière-du-Loup, Canada East, on August 1, 1865. He was called to the bar of Quebec in 1888, and practised law in Rivière-du-Loup. In 1910 he was appointed a judge of the Superior Court for the district of Arthabaska; and he died at Rivière-du-Loup, Quebec, on December 20, 1935. He was the author of *Vie de la Vénérable Mère Marie-Crescence* (Fraserville, Que., 1895), *Glanures historiques et légales* (Quebec, 1925), *Québec et l'Ile d'Orléans* (Quebec, 1927), and *Glanures historiques et familiales* (Quebec, 1927).

[P. G. Roy, *Les juges de la province de Québec* (Quebec, 1933), and *Les avocats de la région de Québec* (Lévis, Que., 1936).]

Pouliot, Joseph Elzéar (1838-1906), lawyer, was born at Rimouski, Lower Canada, on April 15, 1838, and was called to the bar in 1862. He died at Rivière-du-Loup, Quebec, on July 3, 1906. He was the author of *Notions d'agriculture* (Quebec, 1891).

[P. G. Roy, *Les avocats de la région de Québec* (Lévis, Que., 1936).]

Poundmaker (1826-1886), Indian chief, was born near Battleford, North West Territories, in 1826. In 1881, as a chief of the Cree nation, he acted as guide of the Marquis of Lorne (q.v.) and his party from Battleford to Calgary, during the vice-regal tour of the North-West; and in 1885 he was persuaded by Louis Riel (q.v.) to take part in the second North-West Rebellion. He commanded the Indians at the skirmish of Cut Knife Creek and at Batoche. After the capture of Riel, he surrendered himself to General Middleton (q.v.), was tried at Regina, and was sentenced to three years' imprisonment. He was released after a year's confinement; but he died shortly afterward, on July 4, 1886, while on a visit to Crowfoot, chief of the Blackfoot Indians, at Gleichen, near Calgary.

[*Can. who was who*, vol. 2; *Cyc. Am. biog.*; C. P. Mulvaney, *The history of the North-West rebellion of 1885* (Toronto, 1885); Major Boulton, *Reminiscences of the North-West rebellions* (Toronto, 1886); N. Sluman, *Poundmaker* (Toronto, 1967).]

Poutré, Félix (1816?-1885), patriot or spy, was born in Lower Canada about 1816, and is reputed to have taken some part in the patriot rebellion of 1837-38. He was imprisoned at Montreal, probably as a government agent employed to spy upon his fellow-prisoners, and he is said to have escaped punishment by feigning madness. He later published a pamphlet giving an account of his experiences, under the title *Échappé de la potence* (Montreal, 1862; 2nd ed., Montreal, 1884), and this was translated into English under the title *Escaped from the gallows* (Montreal, 1862). He became a popular hero; and Louis Fréchette (q.v.) embodied his story in an historical drama entitled *Félix Poutré*. His claims to fame as a patriot have, however, been seriously questioned; and it is probable that he was an *agent provocateur*. He died in Montreal, February 24, 1885.

[L. A. Lapointe, *Documents inédits sur Félix Poutré* (Bull. rech. hist., 1927); G. Lanctot, *La fin d'une légende* (Revue franco-americaine, 1913); E. Blondel, *Félix Poutré* (Bull. rech. hist., 1926); A. Fauteux, *Les patriotes de 1837-1838* (Montreal, 1950); *Dom. ann. reg.*, 1885.]

Poutrincourt, Jean de Biencourt de. See Biencourt de Poutrincourt, Jean de.

Powell, Grant (1819-1904), under-secretary of state for Canada, was born in York (Toronto), Upper Canada, on September 2, 1819, the third son of Grant Powell, M.D., and Elizabeth Bleeker, and grandson of the Hon. William Dummer Powell (q.v.). He was educated at Upper Canada College; and in 1839 he entered the office of the civil secretary of Upper Canada. In 1883 he was appointed under-secretary of state for Canada; and he retired on pension in 1896. He died at Ottawa on January 28, 1904.

[Rose, *Cyc. Can. biog.* (1886).]

Powell, Henry Watson (1733-1814), soldier, was born in England in 1733, and entered the British army. He came to Canada in 1776 in command of the 53rd Foot, became a brigadier-general, and was successively in command at Ticonderoga, Montreal, Niagara, and Quebec. He returned to England at the close of the American Revolutionary War, and in 1801 became a general. He died at Lyme, England, on July 14, 1814.

[*Cyc. Am. biog.*; J. M. LeMoine, *Picturesque Quebec* (Montreal, 1882).]

Powell, Ray Edwin (1887-1973), business executive, was born in Tablegrove, Illinois, December 7, 1887. He was educated at Monmouth College, Monmouth, Illinois, and at the University of Illinois. He served in the United States Army in 1917. He was senior vice-president and director of the Aluminum Company of Canada and a director of twenty other companies, most of which were associated with the aluminum industry. He was chancellor of McGill University, a governor of Laval University, and a governor of the Montreal General Hospital. He died at Montreal, Quebec, November 9, 1973.

[*Can. who's who*, 1967-69.]

Powell, Robert Henry Wynyard (1856-1935), physician and author, was born in Toronto, Canada West, on February 16, 1856, and died at Ottawa, Ontario, on April 4, 1935. He was educated at McGill University (M.D., C.M., 1876); and he practised medicine in Ottawa for the rest of his life. In 1900 he was elected president of the Canadian Medical Association. He was the author of *The doctor in Canada* (Montreal, 1890).

[*Canadian Medical Association Journal*, May, 1935; E. M. Chadwick, *Ontarian families*, vol. 1 (Toronto, 1894).]

Powell, Walker (1828-1915), soldier, was born at Waterford, Upper Canada, on May 20, 1828, the son of Israel Wood Powell and Melinda Boss. He was educated at Victoria University, Cobourg. From 1857 to 1861 he represented Norfolk in the Legislative Assembly of Canada; and in 1862 he became deputy adjutant-general of Upper Canada. In 1868 he was appointed deputy adjutant-general of Canada, and in 1875 adjutant-general, with the rank of colonel in the militia. He held this office until his retirement on pension in 1896; and he had much to do with the organization of the militia system of the Dominion. He died at Ottawa on May 6, 1915. He married (1) in 1853 Catherine Emma Culver (d. 1855), and (2) in 1857 Mary Ursula Bowlby; and he had six children. In 1885 he was created a C.M.G.

[Morgan, *Can. men* (1912); Rose, *Cyc. Can. biog.* (1886); *Cyc. Am. biog.*]

Powell, William Dummer (1755-1834), chief justice of Upper Canada, was born in Boston, Massachusetts, in 1755, the son of John Powell and Jane Grant. He was educated in England and in Holland, and in 1779 he was called to the English bar from the Middle Temple. The same year he came to Canada, and was admitted to practise as an attorney in the province of Quebec. He practised law in Montreal, and in 1783 was one of the delegates sent to England to petition for the repeal of the Quebec Act. In 1789 he was appointed the first judge of the Court of Common Pleas in the district of Hesse. In 1794 he was appointed a judge of the Court of King's Bench in Upper

Canada; and in 1816 he became chief justice of this court. At the same time he was appointed speaker of the Legislative Council of the province. He retired from the bench in 1825; and he died at Toronto on September 6, 1834. In 1773 he married Anne, daughter of Dr. J. Murray, of Norwich, England; and by her he had five sons and three daughters.

[W. R. Riddell, *The life of William Dummer Powell* (Lansing, Mich., 1924); C. C. James, *William Dummer Powell, a critical incident* (Trans. Roy. Soc. Can., 1912); D. B. Read, *Lives of the judges* (Toronto, 1888); E. M. Chadwick, *Ontarian families* (2 vols., Toronto, 1894-98).]

Power, Charles Gavan (1888-1968), senator, was born at Sillery, Quebec, January 18, 1888, and educated at Loyola College, Montreal, and Laval University, Quebec (B.A., 1907; LL.L., 1910).

He served in the First World War, was wounded twice, and was awarded the Military Cross. He rose from batman to major and thereafter was generally known by his prewar hockey nickname "Chubby" and his wartime military title. He was first elected for the riding of Quebec South in 1917, in a riding which his father had won first in 1901. He was re-elected in every general election until 1955, when he was called to the Senate. Power was appointed minister of pensions and national health in the King government of 1935 and pressed for greater pension benefits for veterans of the First World War; in 1939 he was made postmaster general and a year later, in May, 1940, was made minister of national defence for air and associate minister of national defence (July, 1940), and was given the responsibility for putting the British Commonwealth Air Training plan into operation. He was extremely competent and managed to keep the plan operating to the satisfaction of the Commonwealth countries involved. He resigned from the cabinet on the conscription issue in 1944. Power believed that the disunity which would be caused by the introduction of conscription would be more destructive than the alternative which he envisaged as a delay in bringing the war, which was now virtually won, to a conclusion.

Before his resignation and after, Power continued his efforts to make the transition from service to civilian life easier for the veterans of the Second World War than it had been for his contemporaries in 1919.

He died at Quebec City, May 30, 1968.

[*Can. who's who*, 1955-57; Norman Ward (ed.), *A party politician, The memoirs of Chubby Power* (Toronto, 1966); Metropolitan Toronto Library Board, *Biographical scrapbooks*, vol. 87.]

Power, Lawrence Geoffrey (1841-1921), speaker of the Senate of Canada (1901-05), was born at Halifax, Nova Scotia, on August 9, 1841, the son of Patrick Power (q.v.) and Ellen Gaul. He was educated at St. Mary's College, Halifax (B.A., 1858), and at Harvard University (LL.B., 1866); and was called to the bar of Nova Scotia in 1866 (K.C., 1905). From 1867 to 1877 he was clerk of the House of Assembly of Nova Scotia; and in 1877 he was called to the Senate of Canada. From 1901 to 1905 he was speaker of the Senate; and in 1905 he was sworn of the Imperial privy council. He died at Halifax on September 12, 1921. In 1880 he married Susan O'Leary, of West Quoddy, Nova Scotia. He received the honorary degree of LL.D. from Ottawa University in 1901.

[Morgan, *Can. men* (1912); *Cyc. Am. biog.*; Rose, *Cyc. Can. biog.* (1888); *Can. parl. comp.*; *Can. who was who*, vol. 1.]

Power, Mary. See **Maura, Sister**

Power, Michael (1804-1847), Roman Catholic bishop of Toronto (1842-47), was born in Halifax, Nova Scotia, on October 17, 1804. He became a priest of the Roman Catholic Church, and was curé of La Prairie, Lower Canada, until 1841. In that year he was nominated bishop of the western part of the diocese of Kingston; and in 1842 he was consecrated first bishop of Toronto. He espoused the cause of the Jesuits in Upper Canada; and for a time he was chairman of the council of public instruction in Upper Canada. He died in Toronto, on October 1, 1847.

[*Cyc. Am. biog.*; Le Jeune, *Dict. gén.*]

Power, Patrick (1815-1881), politician, was born in the county of Waterford, Ireland, on March 17, 1815, the son of Lawrence Power. He emigrated to Nova Scotia with his father in 1823, and was educated in Halifax. He went into business in Halifax, and became a supporter of Joseph Howe (q.v.). In 1867 he was elected as an anti-confederation candidate in Halifax county in the Canadian House of Commons; and he sat in the House of Commons from 1867 to 1872, and from 1874 to 1878. He died at Halifax, on February 23, 1881.

[*Dom. ann. reg.*, 1880-81; Rose, *Cyc. Can. biog.* (1886); *Can. parl. comp.*]

Pownall, Sir George (1755-1834), provincial secretary of Quebec and Lower Canada (1755-1803?), was born in England in 1755, the son of John Pownall, M.P., and the nephew of Thomas Pownall, later governor of Massachusetts. He came to Canada with Chief Justice Hey (q.v.) in 1775, and was appointed secretary and registrar of the province of Quebec and a member of the Legislative Council. In 1791 he became provincial secretary of Lower Canada, and a member of the Legislative Council of Lower Canada. He returned to England about 1803; and in 1804 he fell heir to the estates of his uncle, Thomas Pownall. He died on October 17, 1834. In 1796 he was created a knight bachelor.

[C. A. W. Pownall, *Thomas Pownall* (London, 1908); *Bull. rech. hist.*, 1925.]

Pozer, Christian Henry (1835-1884), senator of Canada, was born at the manor of Aubert-Gallion, St. Georges de la Beauce, Lower Canada, on December 26, 1835, the son of William Pozer (1787-1861), seignior of Aubert-Gallion, and grandson of Jean Georges Pozer, or Pfotzer (1752-1848), a German loyalist who settled in Quebec in 1785, and who became an early Canadian millionaire. He studied law at Quebec, and was called to the bar of Lower Canada in 1860. He represented Beauce in the Canadian House of Commons from 1867 to 1876; and in 1876 he was called to the Senate of Canada. He died at St. Georges de la Beauce, Quebec, on July 18, 1884.

[P. Angers, *Les seigneurs et premiers censitaires de St. Georges-Beauce et la famille Pozer* (Beauceville, Que., 1927); *Dom. ann. reg.*, 1884; *Can. parl. comp.*]

Pratt, Calvert Coates (1888-1963), senator and merchant, was born at Blackhead, Newfoundland, October 6, 1888. He was educated at Grand Bank Academy. At twenty-eight he became a director and secretary-treasurer of A. E. Hickman Company. During the Second World War he was active in instituting a ship-building program for Newfoundland. He was awarded an O.B.E. and in 1951 was appointed to the Senate of Canada. He was president of Purity Factories Limited; and a director of the Canadian Bank of Commerce, the British Newfoundland Corporation, Canadian Power and Paper Securities, Newfoundland Light and Power, and a number of other companies. Mr. Pratt was past president of the Newfoundland Board of Trade. He was a brother of the poet E. J. Pratt (q.v.). He died at St. John's, Newfoundland, November 13, 1963.

[*Can. who's who*, 1955-57; Metropolitan Toronto Library Board, *Biographical scrapbooks*, vol. 21.]

Pratt, Edwin John (1882-1964), poet, was born in Western Bay, Newfoundland, February 4, 1883. He was educated at St. John's Methodist College in Newfoundland, and after a period as a preacher and a teacher he enrolled at Victoria College, University of Toronto (B.A., 1911; M.A., 1912; B.D., 1913; Ph.D., in theology, 1916). He was a demonstrator in psychology at University College until 1920, when he joined the department of English at Victoria College. Here he remained until his retirement in 1951.

Pratt's first poem, *Rachael*, was privately published in 1917. His earliest success, *The Titans* (1926), is an epic tale of the whale fishery. Generally acknowledged to be Canada's greatest poet in English, Pratt brought a breadth of perspective and at the same time a close observation of individual and group reaction to great themes, often related to the effects of natural and man-made calamity. In his poems, nature is vast and powerful and man strong and enduring. He stands for the mental as well as the physical exuberance of Canadian life. He worked on a broad canvas with epic themes and soon was recognized as a major contemporary poet. It has been said that he was a master of language and narrative verse who had a democratic vision and a zest for the heroic in man as he faces fate, the elements, and brute force. Besides poems related to the sea and its forces, Pratt also wrote of the heroic in Canadian historic and contemporary events. He died at Toronto, Ontario, April 26, 1964.

His published works include: *Newfoundland verse* (1926); *The witches' brew* (1925); *The titans* (1926); *The iron door* (1928); *The Roosevelt and the Antinoe* (1930); *Verses of the sea* (1930); *Many moods* (1932); *The Titanic* (1935); *The fable of the goats* (1937); *Brébeuf and his brethren* (1940); *Dunkirk* (1941); *Collected poems* (1944, 1958); *They are returning* (1945); *Behind the log* (1947); *Toward the last spike* (1952); *Here the tides flow* (1962). His collected poems appeared in 1944 and in a second edition in 1958. He received three Governor-General's awards for poetry, the Canada Council medal, and the Royal Society's Lorne Pierce medal (1940). He was a fellow of the Royal Society of Canada.

[Metropolitan Toronto Library Board, *Biographical scrapbooks*, vol. 22; *Can. who's who*, 1961-63; *Encyc. Can.* (1972); W. Toye, *Supplement to the Oxford companion to Canadian history and literature* (Toronto, 1973); H. W. Wells and C. F. Klinck, *Edwin J. Pratt: The man and his poetry* (Toronto, 1947); M. Ross, ed., *Our sense of identity* (Toronto, 1954); J. Sutherland, *The poetry of E. J. Pratt* (Toronto, 1956); D. Pacey, *Ten Canadian poets* (Toronto, 1958).]

Préfontaine, Joseph Raymond Fournier (1850-1905), minister of marine and fisheries for Canada (1902-05), was born at Longueuil, Lower Canada, on September 16, 1850, and was educated at St. Mary's College, Montreal, and at McGill University (B.C.L., 1873). He was called to the bar of Quebec in 1873 (Q.C., 1893), and practised law for many years in Montreal. He represented Chambly in the Legislative Assembly of Quebec from 1875 to 1881, and in the Canadian House of Commons from 1886 to 1896. In 1896 he was returned to the Commons for Maisonneuve; in 1898 he was elected mayor of Montreal; and in 1902 he was appointed minister of marine and fisheries in the Laurier government. He died at Paris, France, on December 26, 1905. In 1876 he married Hermantine, daughter of the Hon. J. B. Rolland, a senator of Canada.

[Morgan, *Can. men* (1898); *Can. parl. comp.*; W. H. Atherton, *Montreal* (3 vols., Montreal, 1914).]

Prendergast, James Emile Pierre, (1858-1945), chief justice of Manitoba (1930-44), was born at Quebec, Canada East, on March 22, 1858, the son of James Prendergast and Emilie Gauvreau. He was educated at Laval University (B.A., 1878; LL.B., 1881; LL.D., 1910), and was called to the bar in 1881. In 1882 he removed to Manitoba. He was elected to represent La Vérendrye in the Legislative Assembly of Manitoba in 1885; and he sat in the Assembly, with the exception of a brief interval in 1888-89, until his retirement in 1897. In 1888-89 he was provincial secretary in the first Greenway administration. In 1897 he was appointed a county court judge in Manitoba; in 1902, a judge of the Superior Court of the North West Territories; in 1905, a judge of the Supreme Court of the province of Saskatchewan; in 1910, a judge of the Court of King's Bench in Manitoba; in 1920, a judge of the Court of Appeal in Manitoba; and in 1930, chief justice of Manitoba. He retired from the bench in 1944; and he died at Winnipeg, Manitoba, on April 18, 1945.

[*Can. who's who*, 1938-39; *Who's who in Canada*, 1944.]

Prescott, Sir Henry (1783-1874), governor of Newfoundland (1834-41), was born at Kew, England, on May 4, 1783, and died at London, England, on November 18, 1874. He entered the Royal Navy as a midshipman in 1796, and rose in rank until he became vice-admiral in 1854, and an admiral in 1860. His period of office as governor of Newfoundland was filled with squabbles and controversies, in dealing with which he was not conspicuously successful. He was created a K.C.B. in 1856, and a G.C.B. in 1869.

[*Dict. nat. biog.*; *Encyc. Can.*; *Newfoundland supp.*; *Dict. Can. biog.*, vol. 10.]

Prescott, Robert (1725-1816), governor-in-chief of Canada (1797-1807), was born in 1725 in Lancashire, England. He entered the British army, and in 1757 served in the expedition against Rochefort, as a captain in the 15th Foot. In 1758 he took part in the expedition against Louisbourg; and in 1759 he was aide-de-camp to General Amherst (q.v.). He served in America during the War of the American Revolution, and was present at the battle of the Brandywine. He then served in the West Indies, and in 1794 he was appointed governor of Martinique; but his health failed, and he returned to England in 1795. In 1796 he was sent to Canada as lieutenant-governor of Lower Canada, and administrator of the government of Canada. In 1797 he was appointed governor-in-chief, in succession to Lord Dorchester (q.v.), and in 1798 he was promoted to be full general. He returned to England in

1799; but he retained his appointment as governor until 1807, and his duties were performed by deputies. He settled at Rosegreen, near Battle, Sussex, England; and here he died on December 21, 1816.

[*Dict. nat. biog.*; *Cyc. Am. biog.*; Morgan, *Cel. Can.*; R. Christie, *History of Lower Canada* (6 vols., Quebec and Montreal, 1848-54).]

Preston, Sydney Herman (1858-1931), humorist, was born at Ottawa, Canada West, in 1858, and was educated in Ottawa. From 1882 to 1900 he was a teacher of music in the Toronto Normal and Model School; and in his later years he lived on a farm near Clarkson, Ontario. He died at Clarkson, Ontario, on January 6, 1931. He acquired a reputation as a humorist, through his contributions to American periodicals; and he published two volumes: *The abandoned farmer* (New York, 1901) and *On common ground* (New York, 1906).

[Morgan, *Can. men* (1912).]

Preston, William Thomas Rochester (1851-1942), politician and civil servant, was born at Ottawa, Canada West, on September 6, 1851. He became a journalist; and from 1883 to 1893 he was secretary of the Ontario Liberal Association. In 1893 he was appointed librarian of the Ontario Legislative Library; and in 1899 he was appointed inspector of Canadian immigration agencies in Europe. In 1902 he became commissioner of emigration for Canada in London; and during the following years he played an important part in directing toward Canada the flood of immigration that preceded the First World War. He died at Croydon, England, on November 2, 1942. He was the author of *The life and times of Lord Strathcona* (London, 1914) and *My generation of politics and politicians* (Toronto, 1927).

[Morgan, *Can. men* (1912); *New York Times*, Nov. 4, 1942.]

Prévost, François. See **Provost, François.**

Prevost, Sir George, Bart. (1767-1816), governor-in-chief of Canada (1811-15), was born on May 19, 1767, the eldest son of Major-General Augustine Prevost. He entered the British army, was gazetted a captain in the 25th Foot in 1784, and became a major in the Royal Americans in 1790. In 1794-96 he saw active service in St. Vincent, West Indies; and in 1798 he was appointed military governor of St. Lucia, with the rank of brigadier-general. He was so successful in conciliating the good will of the French population of the island that, in 1801, he was appointed civil governor. In 1802 he became governor of Dominica, and in 1805 he drove the French from this island. In 1808 he was appointed lieutenant-governor of Nova Scotia, with the rank of lieutenant-general; and he administered the affairs of this province with general approval until, in 1811, he was transferred to Quebec as administrator of the government of Lower Canada. Later in the same year he became governor-in-chief of the Canadas; and he was commander-in-chief of the British forces in Canada during the War of 1812. As governor, he performed a signal service in conciliating the good will of the French Canadians, who had been roused to hostility by the conduct of Sir James Craig (q.v.); but as commander-in-chief he was personally responsible for two of the most humiliating episodes of the War of 1812, the withdrawal after the successful attack on Sackett's Harbour in 1813, and the defeat at Plattsburg in 1814. In 1815 he was recalled to face court-martial in connection with the Plattsburg episode; but he died at London, England, on January 5, 1816, a week before the court-martial was due to be held. In 1789 he married Catherine Anne, daughter of Major-General John Phipps, R.E.; and by her he had one son and two daughters. In 1805 he was created, for his services in the West Indies, a baronet of the United Kingdom.

[R. Christie, *Memoirs of the administration of the colonial government of Lower Canada by Sir J. Craig and Sir G. Prevost* (Quebec, 1818); *The letters of Veritas* (Montreal, 1815); *The Canadian inspector* (Montreal, 1815); E. B. Breton, *Some account of the public life of the late Lieut.-Gen. Sir G. Prevost, Bart.* (London, 1823); *Dict. nat. biog.*; Morgan, *Cel. Can.* and *Bib. can.*]

Prévost, Jules Edouard (1871-1943), senator of Canada, was born at St. Jérôme, Quebec, on November 21, 1871. He was educated at the Sulpician College, Montreal, and in Paris, France, and Rome, Italy; and became a journalist. He represented Terrebonne in the Canadian House of Commons from 1917 to 1930; and he sat in the Canadian Senate from 1930 to his death, at Montreal, Quebec, on October 13, 1943.

[*Can. who's who*, 1936-37; *Can. parl. comp.*]

Price, David Edward (1826-1883), senator of Canada, was born in Quebec in 1826, the eldest son of William Price (q.v.), founder of Chicoutimi. He became the senior partner of the firm of Price Brothers and Co. From 1855 to 1864 he represented Chicoutimi and Saguenay in the Legislative Assembly of Canada; in 1864 he was elected to the Legislative Council; and in 1867 he was called to the Senate. He died at Quebec on August 22, 1883.

[*Dom. ann. reg.*, 1883.]

Price, Evan John (1840-1899), senator of Canada, was born at Quebec, Lower Canada, on May 8, 1840, the fourth son of William Price (q.v.). He was educated in England; but returned to Canada to take part, with his brothers, in the direction of the lumber busi-

ness founded by his father. In 1888 he was called to the Senate of Canada; and he sat in the Senate until his death, at Wolfesfield, near Quebec, on August 30, 1899.

[P. G. Roy, *Fils de Québec*, vol. 4 (Lévis, Que., 1933); *Bull. rech. hist.*, 1932.]

Price, James Hervey (1797-1882), commissioner of crown lands for Canada (1848-51), was born in Cumberland, England, in 1797. He came to Canada in 1828, and was called to the bar of Upper Canada in 1833. He allied himself with the advanced Reformers, but held aloof from the Rebellion of 1837. From 1841 to 1851 he represented the first riding of York in the Legislative Assembly of Canada, and from 1848 to 1851 he was commissioner of crown lands in the second Baldwin-Lafontaine administration. In 1851 he was defeated in South York; and shortly afterward he returned to England, where he spent the remainder of his days. He died at Shirley, near Southampton, England, on July 13, 1882.

[*Dom. ann. reg.*, 1882; J. C. Dent, *The Upper Canadian rebellion* (2 vols., Toronto, 1885) and *The last forty years* (2 vols., Toronto, 1881).]

Price, William (1789-1867), lumber merchant, was born at Hornsey, Middlesex, England, on September 17, 1789. He entered the employ of a London mercantile house; and in 1810 was sent to Canada to obtain lumber. He visited the Saguenay River and the region of Lake St. John; and eventually he went into the lumber business in Canada on his own account. His lumbering operations extended from Quebec to the Saguenay, as well as up the Ottawa River; and he was known as "the father of the Saguenay". He died at Wolfesfield, near Quebec, on March 14, 1867.

[L. Duchêne, *Les enterprises de William Price, 1810-1850* (Histoire sociale/Social history, vol. 1, 1968); Taylor, *Brit. Am.*, vol. 3; *Bull. rech. hist.*, 1932.]

Price, Sir William (1867-1924), manufacturer and politician, was born at Talca, Chile, on August 30, 1867, the son of Henry Ferrier Price and Florence Rogerson. He was educated at Bishop's College School, Lennoxville, Quebec, and at St. Mark's School, Windsor, England; and in 1886 he entered the firm of Price Brothers and Co., lumber and paper manufacturers, Quebec. In 1889 he became president, managing director, and sole partner of this company; and he conducted the business until his death. From 1908 to 1911 he represented Quebec West in the Canadian House of Commons; and in 1912 he was appointed chairman of the Quebec Harbour Commission. He was created a knight bachelor in 1915. He was accidentally killed on October 2, 1924, while inspecting his timber-limits at Kenogami, Quebec. In 1894 he married Aemilia Blanche, daughter of R. Herbert

Smith; and by her he had six children.

[*Who was who*, 1916-28; Morgan, *Can. men* (1912); *Can. parl. comp.*; *Bull. rech. hist.*, 1932.]

Price-Brown, John (1844-1938), physician and novelist, was born at Manchester, England, in 1844, and came to Canada in his youth. He was educated at the University of Toronto (M.B., 1868; M.D., 1869), and practised medicine, first in Galt, Ontario, and then in Toronto. He retired from practice in 1914, and he died at Toronto on April 3, 1938. He was the author of several novels, some of them under the *nom-de-plume* of "Eric Bohn": *How Hartman won* (Toronto, 1903), *Hickory, a tale of the lakes* (Toronto, 1904), *The Mac's of '37* (Toronto, 1910), and *Laura the undaunted* (Toronto, 1930).

[*Can. who's who*, 1936-37.]

Prideaux, John (1718-1759), soldier, was born in Devonshire, England, in 1718, the son of Sir John Prideaux, Bart. He entered the British army, and rose to the rank of brigadier-general. He commanded the expedition sent in 1759 to capture Fort Niagara from the French; and he was killed during the siege of the fort, on July 19, 1759, a few days before the fort surrendered. He was buried in the chapel of the fort on July 28.

[*Dict. nat. biog.*]

Prieur, François Xavier (1814-1891), rebel, was born at The Cedars, Soulanges county, Lower Canada, on May 8, 1814, and became a merchant at St. Timothée, Lower Canada. He took part in the insurrection near Beauharnois, Lower Canada, in 1838, was taken prisoner, was tried, and was condemned to be hanged. His sentence was commuted to deportation to Australia; and he returned to Canada only in 1846. In his later years he was warden of the St. Vincent de Paul Penitentiary. He died at Montreal, Quebec, on February 1, 1891. A few years before his death he published his reminiscences, under the title of *Notes d'un condamné politique de 1838* (Montreal, 1884).

[Émile Falardeau, *Prieur l'idéaliste* (Montreal, 1943).]

Primrose, Alexander (1861-1944), surgeon and educationist, was born at Pictou, Nova Scotia, on April 5, 1861, the son of Howard Primrose. He was educated at Pictou Academy and at Edinburgh University (M.B., C.M., 1886); and was an interne at the Middlesex Hospital, London (M.R.C.S., 1887). He began practice as a surgeon in Toronto, Ontario; and from 1896 to 1907 he was professor of anatomy in the University of Toronto, from 1918 to 1931 professor of clinical surgery, and from 1920 to 1932 dean of the faculty of medicine. In the First World War he served as lieutenant-colonel of No. 4 Canadian General Hospital and as a consulting surgeon in the Canadian forces in England, with the rank of colonel; and in 1919 he was created a C.B. He died in Toronto, Ontario, on February 8, 1944.

[*Can. who's who*, 1936-37; *Univ. of Toronto monthly*, 1943.]

Primrose, Clarence (1830-1902), senator of Canada, was born at Pictou, Nova Scotia, on October 5, 1830, the son of James Primrose. He was educated at Pictou Academy and Edinburgh University; and became eventually head of the firm of Primrose Brothers, general merchants and agents for Lloyds, England. He was called to the Senate of Canada in 1892; and he died on December 22, 1902.

[Morgan, *Can. men* (1898); *Can. parl. comp.*]

Primrose, Philip Carteret Hill (1865-1937), lieutenant-governor of Alberta (1935-37), was born at Pictou, Nova Scotia, in 1865. He was educated at the Royal Military College, Kingston, Ontario; and shortly after graduation joined the Royal North West Mounted Police. He rose to the rank of superintendent; but resigned in 1915 to accept appointment as stipendiary magistrate at Edmonton, Alberta. This post he occupied for twenty years, until his appointment in 1935 as lieutenant-governor of Alberta. He died, in office, at Edmonton, on March 17, 1937.

[*Can. who's who*, 1936-37; *Can. parl. comp.*]

Prince, Jean Charles (1804-1860), first Roman Catholic bishop of St. Hyacinthe, was born at Nicolet, Lower Canada, on February 13, 1804, of Acadian parentage. He was educated at the Seminaries of Nicolet and of St. Hyacinthe, and was ordained a priest in 1826. From 1830 to 1840 he was a professor on the staff of the St. Hyacinthe Seminary. In 1844 he was made bishop coadjutor of Montreal, with the title of bishop of Martyropolis; and when the diocese of St. Hyacinthe was created in 1852, he became its first bishop. He died at St. Hyacinthe, Canada East, on May 5, 1860.

[G. Brassard, *Armorial des évêques du Canada* (Montreal, 1940).]

Prince, John (1796-1870), soldier and politician, was born in England in March, 1796. He was educated at Hereford, and in 1813 obtained a commission as a subaltern in the 1st Regiment of Herefordshire militia. In 1815 he began the study of law and in 1821 he was called to the English bar. He emigrated to Canada in 1833, and settled at Sandwich, Upper Canada. During the disturbances on the Canadian border following the rebellion of 1837, he was active in repelling American filibusters; and on December 4, 1838, he commanded the force of Canadian militia which repelled a body of invaders which crossed from Detroit to Windsor. Five prisoners taken by him were shot as outlaws. In 1836 he was elected to represent Essex in the Legislative Assembly of Upper Canada; and after 1841 he represented this constituency in the Legislative Assembly of united Canada until 1854, and the Western division in the Legislative Council from 1856 to 1860. Never a party man, his political course was erratic; and in his later days he was an advocate of Canadian independence. In 1860 he was appointed judge of the district of Algoma; and he died at Sault Ste. Marie, Ontario, on November 30, 1870.

[Taylor, *Brit. Am.*, vol. 2; J. C. Dent, *The Upper Canadian rebellion* (2 vols., Toronto, 1885) and *The last forty years* (2 vols., Toronto, 1881).]

Prince, Joseph Evariste (1851-1923), lawyer, was born at Nicolet, Canada East, on May 15, 1851. He was called to the Quebec bar in 1879, and practised law in Quebec. In 1899 he was appointed professor of Roman law in Laval University; and later he taught political economy. He was appointed postmaster of St. Roch, near Quebec, in 1920; and he died at Quebec on June 6, 1923. He was the author of *Le Séminaire de Nicolet: Souvenir des fêtes du centenaire* (Quebec, 1903).

[P. G. Roy, *Les avocats de la région de Québec* (Lévis, Que., 1936); *Bull. rech. hist.*, 1924.]

Prince, Sadie O. (1861-1905), poet, was born at Springfield, Lunenburg county, Nova Scotia, in 1861; and died in 1905. She was the author of a volume of *Poems* (Toronto, 1900).

[R. J. Long, *Nova Scotia authors* (East Orange, N.J., 1918).]

Pringle, George Charles Fraser (1873-1949), clergyman and author, was born in 1873, and died at Vancouver, British Columbia, on February 20, 1949. He was educated at the University of Toronto (B.A., 1898) and at Knox College, and was ordained a minister of the Presbyterian Church in Canada. In his early days he served as a missionary in the Klondike; and during the First World War he was a chaplain with the Canadian forces in France. He was the author of *Tillicums of the trail: Being Klondike yarns told to Canadian soldiers overseas by a sourdough padre* (Toronto, 1922), *In great waters: The story of the United Church Marine Mission* (Toronto, 1928), and *Adventures in service* (Toronto, 1929).

[Private information.]

Pringle, Jacob Farrand (1816-1901), jurist and historian, was born in Valenciennes, France, on June 27, 1816, the son of Lieut. James Pringle of the 81st Foot and his wife, Ann Margaret Anderson, who later settled in Cornwall, Upper Canada. He was educated at the Cornwall grammar school; and was called to the bar of Upper Canada in 1838. From 1866 to within a short time before his death, he was county judge of Stormont, Dundas, and Glengarry. He died at Cornwall on February 1, 1901. In 1844 he married Isabella, daughter of Colonel the Hon. Alexander Fraser, of Fraserfield; and by her he had five sons and five daughters. He was the author of a valuable local history, *Lunenburgh, or the old Eastern District* (Cornwall, Ont., 1890).

[Morgan, *Can. men* (1898); J. F. Pringle, *The genealogy of Jacob Farrand Pringle and his wife* (Cornwall, Ont., 1892).]

Pringle, John (1852-1935), clergyman, was born in Prince Edward Island in 1852, and was educated at Queen's University, Kingston (B.A., 1875; D.D., 1904). He was ordained a minister of the Presbyterian Church, and he became famous as a missionary in the Yukon at the time of the Klondike "gold-rush" in 1897-98, and afterwards. In 1908 he accepted a charge at Sydney, Cape Breton; and he was a chaplain with the Canadian Expeditionary Force overseas during the First World War. He died at Lowell, Massachusetts, on April 20, 1935.

[Morgan, *Can. men* (1912); *New York Times*, April 21, 1935.]

Prior, Edward Gawler (1853-1920), prime minister of British Columbia (1902-03), was born on May 21, 1853, at Dallaghgill, near Ripon, Yorkshire, England, the son of the Rev. Henry Prior and of Hannah Mouncey Kendell. He studied mining engineering at Wakefield, England; and in 1873 he came to Vancouver Island as mining engineer for the Vancouver Coal Mining and Land Co. From 1878 to 1880 he was provincial inspector of mines; and he then established himself as a hardware merchant at Victoria. He represented Victoria as a Conservative in the Legislative Assembly of British Columbia from 1886 to 1888, and in the Canadian House of Commons from 1888 to 1902. From December 17, 1895, to July 8, 1896, he was controller of inland revenue in the Dominion government; and in 1902 he became minister of mines in the Dunsmuir ministry of British Columbia. He was again elected to represent Victoria in the provincial Assembly; and on November 21, 1902, he succeeded Dunsmuir (q.v.) as prime minister of British Columbia. On June 1, 1903, however, he was dismissed from office, following the break-up of his cabinet and personal charges levelled against himself; and he thereupon retired to private life. In 1919 he was appointed lieutenant-governor of British Columbia; and he died in office at Victoria, British Columbia, on December 12, 1920. He was twice married, (1) in 1878 to Suzette, daughter of the Hon. John Work (q.v.), by whom he had one son and three daughters, and (2) in 1899 to Genevieve, daughter of Capt. Thomas Wright of San Francisco. For many years he was lieutenant-colonel commanding the 5th Regiment of Garrison Artillery; and he was twice president of the Dominion Artillery Association.

[*Can. who was who*, vol. 2; *Can. parl. comp.*; Morgan, *Can. men* (1912); J. B. Kerr, *Biographical dictionary of well-known British Columbians* (Vancouver, B.C., 1890).]

Pritchard, John (1777-1856), fur-trader, was born in Shropshire, England, in 1777. He came to Canada about 1800, and became a clerk in the XY Company. In 1804 he was stationed at Lake Nipigon. He became a clerk in the North West Company in 1805, and from 1808 to 1814 he was in charge of the Souris River post. In 1815 he took service with Lord Selkirk (q.v.), and was appointed a councillor of Assiniboia. He was present at the affair of Seven Oaks in 1816, and was made a prisoner by the half-breeds. Taken to Montreal, he gave evidence in the Selkirk trials. Afterwards he settled on the Red River, and in 1822 he organized the Buffalo Wool Company. He died at the Red River Settlement in 1856. His narrative of the struggle between Selkirk and the North West Company was published in J. Halkett (ed.), *Narratives of John Pritchard, Pierre Chrysologue Pambrun, and Frederick Damien Heurter* (London, 1819); and some of his letters, written between the years 1805 and 1836 were published by George Bryce (q.v.), under the title *Glimpses of the past* (Middlechurch, Manitoba, 1892).

[E. E. Rich (ed.), *Colin Robertson's correspondence book* (Toronto: The Champlain Society, 1939).]

Procter, Henry Adolphus (1787-1859), soldier, was born in Wales in 1787, and entered the British army. He came to Canada before the outbreak of the War of 1812 as officer commanding the 41st Regiment. In the campaigns of 1812 and in 1813 he was in command in the Amherstburg sector, and he inflicted some reverses on the Americans. In the autumn of 1813, however, he was compelled to retreat, and at the battle of Moraviantown, on October 5, he was defeated by General Harrison. He was court-martialled for his behaviour on this occasion, and was suspended for six months from rank and pay; but he later resumed service in the army, was made a C.B., and rose to the rank of lieutenant-general. He died at his home in Montgomeryshire, Wales, on May 13, 1859.

[E. A. Cruikshank, *Harrison and Procter* (Trans. Roy. Soc. Can., 1911); *Cyc. Am. biog.*]

Proctor, John James (1838-1909), journalist and author, was born in Liverpool, England, in 1838, and was educated at Sedburgh in Yorkshire. He came to Canada in 1856, and for several years taught on the staff of Bishop's College, Lennoxville. He then became a journalist, and at the time of his death on December 17, 1909, he was editor of the Quebec *Morning Chronicle*. He was the author of a volume of verse, *Voices of the night and other poems* (Montreal, 1861), and a novel entitled *The philosopher in the clearing* (Quebec, 1897).

[C. M. Whyte-Edgar, *A wreath of Canadian song* (Toronto, 1910).]

Proudfoot, John James Aitchison (1821-1903), clergyman was born in Perthshire, Scotland, in 1821, the second son of the Rev. William Proudfoot (q.v.). He came to Canada with his parents in 1832; and in 1847 he was ordained a minister of the United Presbyterian Church. From 1851 to 1889 he was minister of the First Presbyterian Church in London, Ontario; and from 1889 to 1901 he was professor of homiletics, church government, and pastoral theology in Knox College, Toronto. He died at London, Ontario, on January 14, 1903. Under the editorship of A. J. MacGillivray and J. A. Turnbull, his collected works were published posthumously under the title *Systematic homiletics* (Chicago, 1903).

[*Can. who was who*, vol. 1; Morgan, *Can. men* (1898).]

Proudfoot, William (1788?-1851), clergyman, was born in Scotland about 1788, and was educated at Edinburgh University. He was ordained a minister of the United Presbyterian Church; and in 1813 was ordained to the charge of Pitrodie, in Perthshire. In 1832 he came to Canada as a missionary, and settled at London, Upper Canada. Here he died on February 10, 1851. On his arrival in Canada, he kept a diary; and his diary and letters are one of the most valuable sources for the social history of Upper Canada at this period. Portions of these have been published in the *Transactions* of the London and Middlesex Historical Society for 1915, 1917, and 1922, and in the *Papers and records* of the Ontario Historical Society for 1931, 1932, 1933, 1934, 1936, and 1937.

[W. Gregg, *History of the Presbyterian Church in the Dominion of Canada* (Toronto, 1885).]

Proudfoot, William (1823-1903), jurist, was born near Errol, Perthshire, Scotland, on November 9, 1823, the son of the Rev. William Proudfoot (q.v.). He came to Canada with his parents in 1832, and was educated by his father at London, Upper Canada. In 1849 he was called to the bar of Upper Canada, and became an outstanding equity lawyer. In 1874 he was appointed a vice-chancellor of the Court of Chancery of Ontario; and he held this position until his retirement from the bench in 1890. In 1884 he was appointed professor of Roman law, jurisprudence, and the history of English law in the University of Toronto. He died on August 4, 1903. In 1853 he married the daughter of John Thomson, Toronto; and on her death in 1871 Emily, daughter of Adam Cook, Hamilton, Ontario.

[Morgan, *Can. men* (1898); Dent, *Can. port.*, vol. 3.]

Proudfoot, William (1859-1922), senator of Canada, was born in Colborne township, Huron county, Canada West, on February 21, 1859, the son of Robert Proudfoot and Margaret Darlington, and a nephew of the Hon. William Proudfoot (q.v.). He was educated at Goderich, Ontario, and at Osgoode Hall, Toronto; and was called to the Ontario bar in 1881 (K.C., 1902). From 1908 to 1919 he represented Huron Centre in the Legislative Assembly of Ontario; and from 1917 to 1919 he was leader of the Liberal opposition in the Assembly. Defeated in the elections of 1919, he was called to the Senate of Canada; and he sat in the Senate until his death at Toronto on December 3, 1922. In 1886 he married Marion F. Dickson; and by her he had one son and one daughter.

[Morgan, *Can. men* (1912); *Can. parl. comp.*; H. Charlesworth (ed.), *A cyclopaedia of Canadian biography* (Toronto, 1919).]

Proulx dit Clément, Jean Baptiste (1846-1904), priest and author, was born at Ste. Anne, Lower Canada, on January 7, 1846, the son of J. B. Proulx dit Clément and Adeline Lauzon. He was educated at the College of Ste. Thérèse de Blainville, and was ordained a priest of the Roman Catholic Church in 1869. From 1870 to 1874 he was a missionary in Manitoba. In 1889 he was appointed vice-rector of Laval University, Montreal; and he died at Ottawa on March 1, 1904. He was the author of several dramatic works, published under the pseudonym "Joannes Iovhanné," of which the best known was *L'enfant perdu et retrouvé, ou Pierre Cholet* (Mile-End, 1887; 2nd ed., Montreal, 1892); he was the author of *Au lac Abbitibi* (Montreal, 1882; 2nd ed., 1885), *A la baie Hudson* (Montreal, 1886), *Cinq mois en Europe* (Montreal, 1888), *Mémoire sur l'union de la faculté de médecine de l'Université de Laval à Montréal et de l'École de médecine et de chirurgie de Montréal* (Rome, 1890), *Ma justification pour avoir faire triompher civilement les décrets romains au Canada* (Montreal, 1891), *En Europe, par ci par là* (Joliette, Que., 1892), *A Rome pour la troisième fois* (Joliette, Que., 1893), *Journal de mes pas et démarches dans le diocèse de Hartford* (Rome, 1896), and *Dans la ville éternelle* (Montreal, 1897); and he edited several volumes of documents relating to the university question in Montreal.

[Morgan, *Can. men* (1898); Allaire, *Dict. biog.*; Le Jeune, *Dict. gén.*; *Bull. rech. hist.*, 1930; E. J. Auclair, *Figures canadiennes* (Montreal, 1933).]

Provancher, Léon (1820-1892), priest and naturalist, was born March 10, 1820, at the village of Courtnoyer, Lower Canada, the son

of Joseph-Etienne Provancher and Geneviève Hébert. He was educated at the College of Nicolet, and was ordained a priest of the Roman Catholic Church in 1844. In 1868 he founded *Le Naturaliste Canadienne*, which he edited until his death, and in 1888 he founded also *La Semaine Religieuse de Québec*. In 1879 the French government made him an officer of the French Academy; in 1880 Laval University conferred on him the degree of D.Sc.; and in 1887 he was elected a member of the Royal Society of Canada. He died at Cap Rouge, near Quebec, on March 23, 1892. He was the author of an *Essai sur les insectes et les maladies qui affectent le blé* (Montreal, 1857), a *Traité élémentaire de botanique* (Quebec, 1858), *La flore canadienne* (2 vols., Quebec, 1862), *Le verger canadien* (Quebec, 1862), *Les oiseaux du Canada* (Quebec, 1874), *L'echo du Calvaire* (Quebec, 1883), *Histoire du Canada* (Quebec, 1884), and *De Québec à Jerusalem* (Quebec, 1884).

[V. A. Huard, *La vie et l'oeuvre de l'Abbé Provancher* (Paris, 1926); Allaire, *Dict. biog.*; Le Jeune, *Dict. gén.*]

Provencher, Joseph Alfred Norbert (1843-1887), journalist and Indian agent, was born at La Baie du Febvre, Lower Canada, on January 6, 1843. He was educated at the Nicolet Seminary, and was called to the bar of Lower Canada in 1864. In 1866 he became editor of *La Minerve*, the chief Conservative journal in Montreal. In 1869 he was appointed a member of the provincial council of the North West Territories; and he was an intermediary between the Métis and the Canadian authorities during the first Riel Rebellion. From 1870 to 1876 he was an Indian commissioner in the North West Territories. He returned to Montreal in 1881, and in 1884-85 was editor-in-chief of *La Presse*. He died in Montreal on October 28, 1887. He was one of the founders of the *Revue Canadienne*; and in the early volumes of this periodical appeared a number of essays by him.

[J. P. Robertson, *Political manual of Manitoba* (Winnipeg, 1887); A. G. Morice, *Dictionnaire historique des canadiens et des métis francais de l'ouest* (Quebec, 1908); Morgan, *Bib. can.*; Le Jeune, *Dict. gén.*]

Provencher, Joseph Norbert (1787-1853), Roman Catholic bishop of St. Boniface (1847-53), was born at Nicolet, province of Quebec, on February 12, 1787. He was educated at the Nicolet Seminary, and in 1811 was ordained a priest of the Roman Catholic Church. In 1818 he was sent as a missionary to the North West; and in 1820 he was appointed bishop of Judiopolis *in partibus*, and apostolic vicar of the North West. In 1847 he was designated bishop of St. Boniface; and he died near Winnipeg on June 7, 1853. In 1818 he founded the College of St. Boniface. His letters have been published in the *Bulletin de la*

Société de St. Boniface, vol. iii (St. Boniface, Manitoba, 1913).

[D. Frémont, *Mgr Provencher et son temps* (Winnipeg, 1935); J. P. Robertson, *Political manual of Manitoba* (Winnipeg, 1887); A. G. Morice, *Dictionnaire historique des canadiens et des métis français de l'ouest* (Quebec, 1908); Allaire, *Dict. biog.*; Le Jeune, *Dict. gén.*]

Provost, François (1638-1702), governor of Three Rivers, was born in Paris, France, in 1638. He entered the French army, and came to Canada in 1665, as an officer in the Carignan-Salières regiment. In 1669 he was appointed town major of Quebec; and he distinguished himself in the defence of Quebec against the English in 1690. In 1699 he succeeded Claude de Ramezay (q.v.) as governor of Three Rivers, and he held this post until his death at Quebec on June 1, 1702.

[Le Jeune, *Dict. gén.*; *Bull. rech. hist.*, 1905, 1921; *Dict. Can. biog.*, vol. 2.]

Provost, Théophile Stanislas (1835-1904), priest and author, was born at Varennes, Lower Canada, on July 31, 1835; and was ordained a priest of the Roman Catholic Church in 1857. He was parish priest of a number of places in the province of Quebec; and he died at Joliette, Quebec, on May 3, 1904. He was the author of *La bourse ou la vie* (Joliette, Que., 1883) and *Histoire d'un établissement paroissial de colonisation* (Joliette, Que., 1888).

[Allaire, *Dict. biog.*]

Prowse, Daniel Woodley (1834-1914), jurist and historian, was born in Newfoundland in 1834. He was educated in England, and was called to the bar in Newfoundland in 1858 (Q.C., 1870). He became a judge of the Central District Court in 1869, and he remained on the bench until 1898. He became an outstanding authority on the history of Newfoundland and the Gulf of St. Lawrence; and in 1902 he was created a C.M.G. He died at St. John's, Newfoundland, on March 16, 1914. He was the author of *A manual for magistrates in Newfoundland* (St. John's, Nfld., 1877) and *A history of Newfoundland from the English, colonial, and foreign records* (London, 1895); and he edited *The Newfoundland guide book* (London, 1895).

[G. M. Story, *Judge Prowse (1834-1914)* (Newfoundland Quarterly, LXVIII (1), 1971); *Who was who*, 1897-1916; Morgan, *Can. men* (1912).]

Prowse, Samuel (1835-1902), senator of Canada, was born at Charlottetown, Prince Edward Island, on August 28, 1835. He was a member of the House of Assembly of Prince Edward Island, with brief intervals, from 1867 to 1889; and he was a member of the Executive Council, without portfolio, of the Island from 1876 to 1878 and from 1879 to 1889. He was

called to the Senate of Canada in 1889; and he died on January 14, 1902.

[*Can. parl. comp.*]

Pruden, John Peter (1778?-1868), furtrader, was born at Edmonton, Middlesex, England, about 1778. He entered the service of the Hudson's Bay Company in 1791, as an apprentice, and later as a writer, at York Factory. From 1798 to 1808 he was on the Saskatchewan; and from 1809 to 1824 he was in charge of Carlton House. In 1821 he was made a chief trader. He was in charge of Norway House in 1825-26, but later returned to command at Carlton House. He was promoted to the rank of chief factor in 1836; and he retired from the Company's service in 1837. After his retirement, he lived at the Red River; and here he died on May 30, 1868. His daughter married Chief Trader John McLeod (q.v.).

[E. E. Rich (ed.), *Journal of occurrences in the Athabasca department, by George Simpson* (Toronto: The Champlain Society, 1938).]

Prud'homme, Louis Arthur (1853-1941), jurist and historian, was born at St. Urbain de Châteauguay, Canada East, on November 21, 1853. He was educated at the Montreal College, and was called to the bar in Quebec in 1879, and in Manitoba in 1881. He was appointed a county court judge in Manitoba in 1885, and he served in this capacity until his retirement in 1925. He was a diligent student of the history of the Canadian west; and in 1903 he was elected a fellow of the Royal Society of Canada. He died at St. Boniface, Manitoba, on March 1, 1941. He was the author of a large number of historical papers contributed to the *Transactions* of the Royal Society of Canada and to other periodicals.

[*Proc. Roy. Soc. Can.*, 1941; Morgan, *Can. men* (1912); Le Jeune, *Dict. gén.*]

Pugsley, William (1850-1925), minister of public works for Canada (1907-11), was born September 27, 1850 at Sussex, New Brunswick, the son of William Pugsley. He was educated at the University of New Brunswick (B.A., 1868; B.C.L., 1879; D.C.L., 1884), and was called to the bar in 1872 (Q.C., 1891). For ten years he was reporter to the Supreme Court of Nova Scotia. He represented Kings county in the Legislative Assembly of New Brunswick from 1885 to 1892 and from 1899 to 1907; and was solicitor-general of New Brunswick from 1889 to 1892, and attorney-general from 1900 to 1907. In 1907 he became prime minister of New Brunswick, but after a few months of office resigned, and became minister of public works in the Laurier government at Ottawa. He represented Saint John city and county in the Canadian House of Commons from 1907 to 1911, and Saint John city from 1911 to 1918. In 1918 he was appointed lieutenant-governor of New Brunswick; he retired from office in 1923, and was then appointed chairman of the Reparations Commission. He died in Toronto on March 3, 1925. He was twice married, (1) in 1876 to Fannie (d. 1914), daughter of Thomas Parks, Saint John, New Brunswick, and (2) in 1915 to Miss Macdonald, Saint John, New Brunswick.

[*Can. parl. comp.*; Morgan, *Can. men* (1912); Le Jeune, *Dict. gén.*]

Puisaye, Joseph Geneviève, Comte de (1755-1827), French royalist, was born at Mortagne-au-Perche, France, in 1755, the son of André Louis Charles de Puisaye, marquis de Puisaye. Though, at the outbreak of the French Revolution in 1789, he was numbered among the Reform noblesse, he later became one of the chief royalist leaders. He took refuge in England, and commanded the ill-fated Quiberon expedition in 1795. In 1798 he obtained from the British government a concession of land in the townships of Markham and Vaughan, Upper Canada; and in 1799 he came out with a number of other royalists to found a settlement. The settlement proved a failure, however, and in 1802 Puisaye returned to England. He died at Hammersmith, near London, England, on October 13, 1827. On his return to England he published his *Mémoires* (6 vols., London, 1803-08).

[Lucy E. Textor, *A colony of émigrés in Canada* (Toronto, 1904); Janet Carnochan, *The Count de Puisaye* (Niagara Historical Society, No. 15, 1907); Abbé A. P. Gaulier, *Joseph-Geneviève de Puisaye* (Bull. rech. hist., 1913).]

Punshon, William Morley (1824-1881), Methodist minister, was born at Doncaster, England, in 1824. He became a minister of the Wesleyan Methodist Church; and in 1868 he came to Canada. As pastor of the Metropolitan Church in Toronto, he assumed an outstanding position as a pulpit orator; and he played an important part in bringing about the union of the Methodist Churches in Canada. In 1873 he returned to England, and he died at Brixton, London, England, on April 14, 1881.

[F. W. Macdonald, *Life of W. M. Punshon* (London, 1887); *Dom. ann. reg.*, 1880-81; Dent, *Can. port.*, vol. 3.]

Purdom, Thomas Hunter (1853-1923), lawyer, was born in London, Canada West, on July 25, 1853. He was called to the bar of Ontario in 1876 (Q.C., 1899), and he practised law in London until his death on November 14, 1923. With Judge D. J. Hughes of St. Thomas,

he was joint author of *The history of the Middlesex bar* (London, Ont., 1912).

[*Can. who was who*, vol. 1; Morgan, *Can. men* (1912).]

Putman, John Harold (1866-1940), educationist and author, was born in Lincoln county, Ontario, on September 17, 1866, and died at Ottawa, Ontario, on September 12, 1940. He was educated at Queen's University (B.A., 1899; B. Paed., 1907; D. Paed., 1909), and he taught in various schools in different parts of Ontario. In 1910 he became chief inspector of schools in Ottawa; and in 1936 the University of Toronto conferred on him the honorary degree of LL.D. He was the author of *Britain and the Empire* (Toronto, 1904), *Egerton Ryerson and education in Upper Canada* (Toronto, 1912), *Schoolmasters abroad* (Toronto, 1937), and *Fifty years at school* (Toronto, 1938).

[*Can. who's who*, 1935-37.]

Puyjalon, Henry de (1839-1905), author, was born in France in 1839, of an ancient and noble family. He came to Canada in 1872; and he spent most of the rest of his life on the Quebec Labrador coast, the last years as a recluse on Ile-à-la-Chasse, one of the Mingan Islands. He died here on August 17, 1905. He was the author of *Petit guide du chercheur des minéraux* (Montreal, 1892), *Petit guide du chasseur de pelleterie* (Montreal, 1893), *Récits du Labrador* (Quebec, 1894), and *Histoire naturelle à l'usage des chasseurs canadiens et des éleveurs d'animaux à fourrure* (Quebec, 1900).

[D. Potvin, *Puyjalon, le solitaire de l'Ile-à-la-Chasse* (Quebec, 1938).]

Pyke, George (1775-1851), jurist, was born at Halifax, Nova Scotia, in 1775, and was called to the bar of Nova Scotia, and then to the bar of Lower Canada, in 1796. He represented Gaspé in the House of Assembly of Lower Canada from 1804 to 1814; and in 1812 he was appointed attorney-general of the province. In 1816 he became law clerk of the Legislative Council of Lower Canada; and in 1818 he was made a judge of the Court of King's Bench for the district of Montreal. He retired from the bench in 1842; and he died at Pointe-à-Cavagnal (Vaudreuil), Canada East, on February 3, 1851. He was the author of *Pyke's Reports* (Quebec, 1811), a collection of judicial decisions in the Canadian courts.

[P. G. Roy, *Les juges de la province de Québec* (Quebec, 1933).]

Quesnel, Frédéric Auguste (1785-1866), politician, was born at Montreal, in 1785, the eldest son of Joseph Quesnel (q.v.). He was called to the bar of Lower Canada, and from 1826 to 1834 he was a member of the Legislative Assembly of Lower Canada. A supporter of Papineau during his earlier career, he broke with his leader over the Ninety-Two Resolutions, and in 1835 failed of re-election to the Assembly. In 1837 he was appointed a member of the Executive Council of the province; and he served as an executive councillor until the Union of 1841. From 1841 to 1844 he sat as the representative of Montmorency in the Legislative Assembly of united Canada. He died on July 28, 1866. In 1813 he married Marguerite Denaut (d. 1820); and by her he had two sons and three daughters, all of whom predeceased him. He acquired a fortune in the fur-trade and by speculation, and the bulk of this fortune he left to his nephew, the Hon. Charles Joseph Coursol (q.v.).

[E. Z. Massicotte, *La famille du poète Quesnel* (Bull. rech. hist., 1917), C. S. Cherrier, *L'honorable F. A. Quesnel* (pamphlet, Montreal, 1878); F. J. Audet, *L'hon. Frédéric-Auguste Quesnel* (Bull. rech. hist., 1927); Le Jeune, *Dict. gén.*]

Quesnel, Joseph (1749-1809), poet and dramatist, was born at St. Malo, France, on November 15, 1749, the son of Isaac Quesnel de la Rivaudais and Pélagie-Jeanne-Marguerite Duguen. He came to Canada in 1779, and took out letters of naturalization a few years later. He was a merchant, but in his leisure moments he wrote poems, epistles, hymns, epigrams, songs, and comedies. His chief compositions were a dialogue in verse, entitled *Le rimeur dépité*, and the following comedies: *Colas et Colinette, Les républicains français*, and *L'Anglomanie*. Of these none was published in his lifetime, except *Les républicains français*, which Bibaud says was printed in Paris; but many of his writings were printed posthumously in the *Bibliothèque canadienne* (9 vols., Montreal, 1825-30) and in the *Répertoire national* (4 vols., Montreal, 1848-50). He died at Montreal on July 3, 1809. In 1770 he married Marie-Josephte Deslandes; and by her he had thirteen children.

[E. Z. Massicotte, *La famille du poète Quesnel* (Bull. rech. hist., 1917); *Cyc. Am. biog.*; Le Jeune, *Dict. gén.*; Bibaud, *Panth. can.*; Morgan, *Bib. can.*; E. Lareau, *La littérature canadienne* (Montreal, 1874).]

Quesnel, Jules Maurice (1786-1842), fur-trader, was born in Montreal in 1786, the second son of Joseph Quesnel (q.v.). He entered the service of the North West Company, and in 1804 was stationed at Edmonton. In 1808 he accompanied Simon Fraser (q.v.) in his exploration of the Fraser River. He left the service of the North West Company in 1811, and returned to Canada. In 1838 he was appointed a member of the Special Council of Lower Canada; and in 1841 a member of the Legislative Council under the union. He died at Montreal on May 20, 1842. In 1816 he married Marie Josephte Cotté, the daughter of a fur-trader of the North West.

[E. Z. Massicotte, *La famille du poète Quesnel* (Bull. rech. hist., 1917); A. G. Morice, *Dictionnaire historique des canadiens et des métis français de l'ouest* (Quebec, 1908); W. S. Wallace (ed.), *Documents relating to the North West Company* (Toronto: The Champlain Society, 1934).]

Quetton de St. George, Laurent. See **St. George, Laurent Quetton de.**

Quevillon, Louis Amable (1749-1823), wood-carver and architect, was born in 1749 at St. Vincent de Paul, Canada. He was a self-taught artist; but he gathered about him a number of apprentices, and their work is an illustration of one of the first native impulses in Canadian art. He died at St. Vincent de Paul on March 9, 1823.

[E. Vaillancourt, *Une maîtrise d'art en Canada* (Montreal, 1920); Bibaud, *Panth. can.*; Le Jeune, *Dict. gén.*]

Queylus, Gabriel de Thubière de Lévy de (1612-1677), superior of the Sulpician missions in Canada (1657-61 and 1668-71), was born in the diocese of Rodez in France in 1612. He entered the Sulpician order, was ordained a priest in 1645, and in 1657 he came to Canada as first superior of the Sulpician missions in

Canada. He returned to France in 1661, and he remained there until 1668; but in 1668 he became for a second time superior of the Sulpicians in Canada. Though he had quarrelled with Bishop Laval (q.v.) during his earlier stay in Canada, he now became grand vicar to Laval. He returned to France finally in 1671; and he died at Paris on March 20, 1677.

[Allaire, *Dict. biog.*; Le Jeune, *Dict. gén.*; Bibaud, *Panth. can.*; A. Gosselin, *Le vénérable François de Montmorency Laval* (Quebec, 1906).]

Quiblier, Joseph Vincent (1796-1852), priest and educationist, was born at St. Julien, in the diocese of Lyon, France, on May 24, 1796, and was ordained a priest of the Roman Catholic Church in 1819. He entered the Sulpician order in 1825, and was sent to Canada. From 1831 to 1846 he was superior of the Seminary at Montreal; and he is generally regarded as the organizer of primary education among the French Roman Catholics in Montreal. In 1846 he left Canada, to assume the charge of a parish in London, England; and he died at Issy, France, on September 17, 1852.

[Allaire, *Dict. biog.*; Le Jeune, *Dict. gén.*]

Quigley, Richard Francis (d. 1918), lawyer and author, was born at Newcastle, New Brunswick; and was educated at Harvard University (LL.B., 1874) and at Boston University (LL.B., 1875). He was called to the bar of New Brunswick in 1876 (Q.C., 1894), and practised law in Saint John, New Brunswick. He received the degree of Ph.D. from the Pope in recognition of his defence of the Roman Catholic Church in a series of letters published under the title *Ipse, ipsa, ipsum: which?* (New York, 1890), later republished under the title *Mary, the Mother of Christ, in prophecy and fulfillment* (New York, 1907). He received also the degree of LL.D. from Laval University in 1894. He died in Saint John, New Brunswick, in 1918.

[Morgan, *Can. men* (1912); *Guide to Catholic literature* (Detroit, Mich., 1940); W. G. MacFarlane, *New Brunswick bibliography* (Saint John, N.B., 1895).]

Quinpool, John (pseud.). See **Regan, John William.**

R

Raby, Augustin (1702-1782), pilot, was born at Quebec in 1702, and became a pilot and navigator. It was he who piloted the British fleet up the St. Lawrence to Quebec in June, 1759. He died at Quebec on December 19, 1782.

[P. G. Roy, *Les petites choses de notre histoire*, vol. 1 (Lévis, Que., 1919); Le Jeune, *Dict. gén.*]

Racine, Antoine (1822-1893), first Roman Catholic bishop of Sherbrooke, was born at Jeune Lorette, near Quebec, Lower Canada, on January 26, 1822; was educated at Quebec; and was ordained a priest in 1844. After serving in several parishes in French Canada, he was made first bishop of Sherbrooke, in 1874; and he presided over this see until his death, at Sherbrooke, Quebec, on July 17, 1893.

[*Mgr A. Racine, premier évêque de Sherbrooke: Notice biographique* (Sherbrooke, Que., 1893); Le Jeune, *Dict. gén.*; Allaire, *Dict. biog.*]

Racine, Dominique (1828-1888), first Roman Catholic bishop of Chicoutimi, was born at Jeune Lorette, near Quebec, Lower Canada, on January 24, 1828. He was educated at Quebec, and was ordained a priest of the Roman Catholic Church in 1853. In 1862 he went to Chicoutimi as parish priest, and in 1878 he was elected first bishop of Chicoutimi. He died at Chicoutimi on January 28, 1888.

[V. A. Huard, *L'apôtre du Saguenay* (Quebec, 1895); Allaire, *Dict. biog.*; Le Jeune, *Dict. gén.*]

Radcliffe, Thomas (1794-1841), legislative councillor of Upper Canada, was born in Castle Coote, Roscommon county, Ireland, on April 17, 1794, the eldest son of the Rev. Thomas Radcliffe, of Dublin, Ireland. He entered the British army in 1811, and served as a subaltern in the Peninsular War and in the War of 1812 in Canada. In 1816 he was placed on half-pay, and in 1836 he came to Upper Canada and settled in Adelaide, near London. He commanded a body of militia during the rebellion of 1837; and in 1839 he was appointed a member of the Legislative Council of Upper Canada. He died on Amherst Island, Upper Canada, on June 6, 1841.

[A. Ewart and J. Jarvis, *The personnel of the Family Compact* (Can. hist. rev., 1926); Rose, *Cyc. Can. biog.* (1886).]

Radisson, Pierre Esprit (1636?-1710), explorer and fur-trader, was born in Paris, France, about 1636. He came to Canada in 1651, and settled at Three Rivers. In 1652 he was captured by the Iroquois, but he escaped from them in 1653 and returned to Canada by way of New York, Holland, and France. Between 1654 and 1660 he made, with his brother-in-law Chouart des Groseilliers (q.v.), either one or two voyages to the country west of the Great Lakes. His own account of these voyages, which was first discovered and printed in 1885, seems to suggest that he reached the Mississippi on one journey and Hudson Bay on the other; but grave doubt has been cast on these extravagant claims. It is probable, however, that Radisson was the first white man to penetrate to the old North-West.

In 1665 Radisson, as the result of a disagreement with the French authorities, went to England, and offered to lead a trading expedition to Hudson Bay. The outcome of this was the foundation in 1670 of the Hudson's Bay Company. In the service of this company Radisson remained until 1676; then he reverted to his French allegiance, returned to Canada, and in 1682 led an expedition against the English on Hudson Bay. In 1684, however, he once more entered the service of the Hudson's Bay Company; and for the rest of his life he was either a servant or a pensioner of the company. He died in England in 1710. His account of his journeys has been published by the Prince Society under the title *Voyages of Pierre Esprit Radisson* (Boston, 1885), and in the Canadian Archives Report for 1895 under the title *Relation du voiage du Sieur Pierre Esprit Radisson*; and a more recent version has been edited by Arthur T. Adams, under the title *The explorations of Pierre Esprit Radisson* (Minneapolis, 1961).

[Grace L. Nute, *Caesars of the wilderness* (New York, 1943); S. Vestal, *King of the fur-traders* (Boston, 1940); D. Frémont, *Pierre Radisson* (Montreal, 1933); N. E. Dionne,

Chouart and Radisson (Quebec, 1910); W. Upham, *Groseilliers and Radisson* (Minnesota Historical Collections, 1905); B. Sulte, *Radisson in the north-west* (Trans. Roy. Soc. Can., 1904); G. Bryce, *The remarkable history of the Hudson's Bay Company* (Toronto, 1900) and *Further history of Pierre Esprit Radisson* (Trans. Roy. Soc. Can., 1898); A. T. Adams, *A new interpretation of the voyages of Radisson* (Minnesota history, 1925) and *The Radisson problems* (Minnesota history, 1934); *Dict. Am. biog.*; Le Jeune, *Dict. gén.*; *Dict. Can. biog.*, vol. 2.]

Rae, John (1796-1872), economist, was born at Footdee, a suburb of Aberdeen, Scotland, on June 1, 1796. He was educated at Aberdeen University (M.A., 1815) and at Edinburgh University, where he studied medicine. In 1822 he emigrated to Canada; and he taught school first at Williamstown, Upper Canada, then at Quebec and Montreal, and finally at Hamilton, Upper Canada. He was dismissed from his school in Hamilton in 1848 as a free-thinker; and drifted from there to the United States, and from the United States to the Hawaiian Islands. He returned to the United States in 1871, and he died on Staten Island, New York, at the home of a former pupil, Sir Roderick Cameron, on July 12, 1872. He was the author of an important contribution to the science of political economy, entitled *Statement of some new principles on the subject of political economy, exposing the fallacies of the system of free trade, and of some other doctrines maintained in the "Wealth of Nations"* (Boston, 1834).

[R. W. James, *John Rae, political economist* (Toronto, 1965); C. W. Mixter (ed.), *The sociological theory of capital* (New York, 1905); *Dict. Am. biog.*; H. Higgs (ed.), *Palgrave's dictionary of political economy* (3 vols., London, 1925-26); *Dict. Can. biog.*, vol. 10.]

Rae, John (1813-1893), explorer, was born near Stromness in the Orkney Islands, on September 30, 1813. He studied medicine at Edinburgh University; and in 1833 he was appointed surgeon to the Hudson's Bay Company's ship which visited annually Moose Factory. From 1835 to 1845 he was resident surgeon at Moose Factory; and in 1846 he was sent on his first journey of exploration, which resulted in the survey of the shores of Committee Bay. In 1847 he joined the first land expedition in search of Sir John Franklin (q.v.), under Sir John Richardson (q.v.); and in 1851 he undertook another search for Franklin, in the course of which he covered 5,380 miles, 700 of which were newly discovered coast-line. On his return to England, he proposed yet another expedition in search of Franklin; and this expedition, which set out in 1853, resulted in the discovery of Franklin's fate. In his later years Rae lived in London, England; and in 1880 he was elected a fellow of the Royal Society. He died in London on July 22, 1893. In 1860 he married Catharine Jane Alicia, daughter of Major George Ash Thompson, of Ardkill, Londonderry, Ireland; but he left no children. He was the author of *A narrative of an expedition to the shores of the Arctic sea in 1846 and 1847* (London, 1850); and his *Report ... of the proceedings of the Arctic searching expedition* was printed by order of the House of Commons (London, 1852). Recently E. E. Rich and A. M. Johnson have edited for the Hudson's Bay Record Society *John Rae's correspondence with the Hudson's Bay Company on Artic exploration* (London, 1953).

[R. Mitchell, *Dr. John Rae* (Canadian Medical Association journal, 1933) and *Physician, fur-trader, and explorer* (Beaver, 1936); *Dict. nat. biog.*; Le Jeune, *Dict. gén.*]

Raffeix, Pierre (1635-1724), priest and cartographer, was born in Auvergne, France, January 15, 1635, and entered the Jesuit novitiate in 1653. He was sent to Canada in 1663, and became a missionary to the Iroquois. He died at Quebec on August 29, 1724. He was the maker of three early maps of Canada: one, dated 1676, describing "the westernmost parts of Canada"; another, dated 1688, describing Lake Ontario and the territories of the Five Nations; and a third covering the whole of New France to Lake Erie on the west and New England on the south.

[Rev. T. J. Campbell, *Pioneer priests of North America*, vol. i (New York, 1908); R. G. Thwaites (ed.), *The Jesuit relations*, vol. 47 (Cleveland, Ohio, 1899); Le Jeune, *Dict. gén.*; *Dict. Can. biog.*, vol. 2.]

Ragueneau, Paul (1608-1680), missionary, was born in Paris, France, on March 18, 1608. He joined the Society of Jesus, and was sent to Canada as a missionary in 1636. He joined the Jesuit mission among the Hurons, and he was superior of the mission when it was attacked by the Iroquois in 1649. He brought the remnant of the Huron tribe to Quebec, and he laboured among them until 1662. He then returned to France, and for the rest of his life he acted as agent for the Jesuit missions in Canada. He died at Paris on September 3, 1680. He was the author of *Vie de la Mère Catherine de St. Augustin, religieuse hospitalière de Québec, en la Nouvelle France* (Paris, 1672), *Relation de ce qui s'est passé de plus remarquable ès missions des pères de la Compagnie en la Nouvelle France* (7 vols., Paris, 1647-57), and *Mémoires touchant les vertus des Pères de Noue, Jogues, Daniel, Brébeuf, Lallement, Garnier et Chabanel* (Paris, n.d.).

[*Cyc. Am. biog.*; Allaire, *Dict. biog.*; Le Jeune, *Dict. gén.*; R. G. Thwaites (ed.), *The Jesuit relations* (73 vols., Cleveland, Ohio, 1897-1901); *Dict. Can. biog.*, vol. 1.]

Raimbault, Jean (1770-1841), priest, was born at Orléans, France, on February 7, 1770. He came to Canada as a young man, and was ordained a priest of the Roman Catholic Church in Canada in 1795. He was parish priest of Nicolet, Lower Canada, from 1806 to his death at Nicolet on February 16, 1841.

[L. E. Bois, *L'abbé Raimbault, archi-prêtre, curé de Nicolet: Étude biographique* (Quebec, 1869); Allaire, *Dict. biog.*]

Raine, Walter (1861-1934), naturalist, was born in Leeds, England, in 1861. He came to Canada in youth, settled in Toronto, and became an authority on Canadian birds. He was the author of *Bird-nesting in north-west Canada* (Toronto, 1892), and he presented his collection of birds' eggs to the Royal Ontario Museum. He died in Toronto on July 29, 1934.

[Private information.]

Rainville, Joseph Hormisdas (1875-1942), senator of Canada, was born at Ste. Angèle, Quebec, on March 8, 1875. He was educated at Laval University (B.A., 1897), and became an advocate. He represented Chambly-Verchères in the Canadian House of Commons from 1911 to 1917; and he was called to the Senate of Canada in 1932. In 1928 he acted as chief organizer for the Liberal-Conservative party in the province of Quebec; and from 1930 to 1932 he was chairman of the Montreal Harbour Board. He died at St. Lambert, near Montreal, Quebec, on April 14, 1942.

[*Can. parl. comp.*; *Can. who's who*, 1936-37.]

Rainville, Paul (1887-1952), museum director, was born at Arthabaska, Quebec, on September 15, 1887, and died at Quebec, Quebec, on May 15, 1952. From 1931 until his death he was director of the Quebec Provincial Museum; and he was the author of *"Tibi", Carnet de Sanatorium* (Beauceville, Que., 1925).

[*Can. who's who*, 1948.]

Rale (Rasles), Sébastien (1657-1724), missionary, was born at Pontarlier, France, on January 4, 1657, and entered the Society of Jesus. He was sent to Canada as a missionary in 1689; and was stationed for a year or two, first at the Abenaki mission near Quebec, and then in the Illinois country. In 1693, he was recalled to Quebec, and sent south to take charge of the Abenaki mission on the Kennebec River; and here he spent the last thirty years of his life. He became the temporal, as well as the spiritual, adviser of his flock; and thus incurred the hostility of the English. A reward of £10,000 was placed on his head; and on August 23, 1724, a party of New England militia fell on his mission station, and shot him down in front of his chapel. He was the author of *A dictionary of the Abnaki language*, published a century or more after his death, with a memoir and notes by John Pickering (Cambridge, Mass., 1833).

[N. E. Dionne, *Le Père Sébastien Rasles* (Trans. Roy. Soc. Can., 1903); J. F. Sprague, *Sébastian Ralé* (Boston, 1906); T. J. Campbell, *Pioneer priests of North America*, vol. iii (New York, 1911); A. Beauchesne, *Le martyre du Père Rasle* (Trans. Roy. Soc. Can., 1935); Le Jeune, *Dict. gén.*; *Dict. Can. biog.*, vol. 2.]

Ralston, James Layton (1881-1948), minister of national defence for Canada (1926-30 and 1940-44), was born at Amherst, Nova Scotia, on September 27, 1881, and died at Montreal, Quebec, on May 21, 1948. He was educated at the Dalhousie Law School, and was called to the bar in 1903 (K.C., 1914). During the First World War, he served overseas with the 85th Highland Battalion — of which he became the commanding officer — was wounded, and was awarded the D.S.O., with bar. From 1911 to 1920 he represented Cumberland in the Nova Scotia legislature. He represented Shelburne-Yarmouth in the Canadian House of Commons from 1925 to 1935, and was minister of national defence in the Mackenzie King government. He was not a candidate for re-election in 1935; but he was pressed into service as finance minister in 1939, and minister of national defence in 1940. In 1944 he broke with Mackenzie King (q.v.) on the question of conscription for overseas service, and retired from political life.

[Montreal *Gazette*, May 24, 1948; *Can. who's who*, 1948; *Encyc. Can.*]

Rambau, Alfred Xavier (1810-1856), journalist, was born in the department of the Loire, France, on February 22, 1810. He came to America when a young man, and in 1833 was engaged by P. D. Debartzch (q.v.) to edit *L'Echo du pays*, at St. Charles, Lower Canada. He was called to the bar in 1848; but he did not practise law. In 1854 he founded in Montreal *La Patrie*; but his editorship was cut short by death on October 30, 1856. He was the author of a pamphlet entitled *Le Bill seigneurial* (Montreal, 1855).

[E. Z. Massicotte, *Le Journaliste-avocat Rambau* (Bull. rech. hist., 1940).]

Rameau de Saint-Père, François Edme (1820-1899), historian, was born at Adon, France, in 1820. He became a journalist and man of letters in Paris; and he was the author of two works on the history of Acadia, *La France aux colonies: Acadiens et Canadiens* (Paris, 1859) and *Une colonie féodale* (2 vols., Paris, 1877-89). In 1884 he was elected a corresponding member of the Royal Society of Canada; and in 1889 he was made an LL.D. of Laval University. He died, suddenly, at Adon, France, on December 15, 1899.

[Le Jeune, *Dict. gén.*]

Ramezay, Claude de (1659-1724), governor of Montreal (1704-24), was born at LaGesse, France, June 15, 1659, the son of Timothé de Ramezay, a descendant of the Scottish family of Ramsay, and Catherine Tribouillard. He came to Canada in 1685 as a lieutenant in the *troupes de la Marine*, took part in 1686 in Denonville's expedition against the Iroquois, and in 1690 was present at the siege of Quebec. On July 1, 1690, he was appointed governor of Three Rivers; and on May 28, 1699, he was named commander of the royal troops in the colony. In June, 1703, he was made a chevalier of St. Louis, and on May 15, 1704, was appointed governor of Montreal. From 1714 to 1716 he was administrator of New France. He died at Montreal on August 1, 1724. He married, on November 8, 1690, Marie Charlotte Denys, and by her he had sixteen children.

[V. Morin, *Les Ramezay et leur château* (Montreal, 1939); R. Roy, *De Ramezay* (Bull. rech. hist., 1899); *La famille de Ramezay* (Bull. rech. hist., 1910 and 1911); Le Jeune, *Dict. gén.*; *Dict. Can. biog.*, vol. 2.]

Ramezay, Jean Baptiste Nicolas Roch de (1708-1771?), commandant of Quebec (1758-59), was born in Montreal on September 4, 1708, the son of Claude de Ramezay (q.v.) and Marie Charlotte Denys. In 1720 he became an ensign, in 1726 a lieutenant, and in 1734 a captain. In 1742 he was given the command of Fort Nipigon on Hudson Bay, and in 1746 he was sent to Acadia. On his return to Quebec in 1748, he was made a chevalier of St. Louis; and in the following year was named town major of Quebec. In 1758 he was promoted to the post of King's lieutenant. In 1759, after the flight of Vaudreuil (q.v.), following Montcalm's defeat, he made every effort to save Quebec from the English, but was obliged to capitulate on September 18. He returned to France soon afterward, and lived in Paris. He died about 1771. He married, on December 6, 1728, Louise Godefroy de Tonnancour, and by her he had six children.

[V. Morin, *Les Ramezay et leur château* (Montreal, 1939); *La famille de Ramezay* (Bull. rech. hist., 1910 and 1911); Le Jeune, *Dict. gén.*]

Ramsay, Andrew John (d. 1907), schoolteacher and versifier, was "a half-cut schoolmaster and quarter-cut poet", who apparently lived most of his life in Ontario. In 1899, he was living in Westover, Ontario; and he died in 1907. He was the author of *The Canadian lyre* (Hamilton, C.W., 1859), *Win-on-ah; or, The forest light, and other poems* (Toronto, 1869), *One quiet day* (Hamilton, Ont., 1873), and *Muriel the foundling, and other original poems* (Toronto, 1886).

[C. C. James, *A bibliography of Canadian poetry* (Toronto, 1899); Morgan, *Bib. can.*; R. Davies, *A harp that once* (Queen's quarterly, 1943).]

Ramsay, David Shaw (d. 1906), priest, was born in Edinburgh, Scotland, and was educated at Edinburgh University. He came to Canada as a young man, and in 1867 he was ordained a priest of the Roman Catholic Church. After serving for a time in England, he returned to Canada and became parish priest at Magog, Quebec. He died at Montreal, Quebec, on February 23, 1906. He was the author of *The life of the Venerable Marie Marguerite Dufrost de Lajemmerais, Madame d'Youville* (Montreal, 1896).

[Morgan, *Can. men* (1898).]

Ramsay, George, ninth Earl of Dalhousie. See **Dalhousie, George Ramsay, ninth Earl of.**

Ramsay, J. R. (pseud.). See **Ramsay, Andrew John.**

Ramsay, Thomas Kennedy (1826-1886), jurist, was born in Ayr, Scotland, on September 2, 1826. He came to Canada, was called to the bar, and was appointed an assistant judge of the Superior Court of Quebec in 1870, and a puisne judge of the Court of Queen's Bench in 1873. He died at St. Hugues, Quebec, on December 22, 1886. In 1857 he founded the *Lower Canada Jurist*; and he was the author of *Notes sur la coutûme de Paris* (Montreal, 1863; 2nd ed., 1864), *Government commissions of inquiry* (Montreal, 1863), and a *Digested index to the reported cases in Lower Canada* (Quebec, 1865).

[P. G. Roy, *Les juges de la province de Québec* (Quebec, 1933); *Dom. ann. reg.*, 1886.]

Rand, Ivan Cleland (1884-1969), Supreme Court justice, was born in Moncton, New Brunswick, April 27, 1884. He was educated at Mount Allison University (B.A., 1909), and at Harvard Law School (LL.B., 1912). He was called to the bar in New Brunswick in 1912 but practised in Medicine Hat, Alberta (1912-20), returning to Moncton where he practised with Senator C. W. Robinson from 1920 to 1926. He was elected to the New Brunswick legislature in 1925 and became attorney-general of the province. He resigned his portfolio on the defeat of the government in September, 1925. He was employed as counsel for the Canadian National Railways at Moncton and Montreal from 1926. He became a judge of the Supreme Court of Canada in 1943. In 1945 he acted as arbiter in the Ford labour dispute and established what has been known as the Rand formula for the settlement of labour disputes. This formula denied the demand for a union shop but granted the check-off of dues for all employees whether members or not. It also laid on the union the responsibility for repudiating all strikes not called by the union, and for not calling a strike before obtaining a majority vote of all employees to whom the agreement applied. It also provided for fines and loss of seniority for employees participating in illegal strikes.

He was a member of the United Nations committee on Palestine in 1947 and supported the recommendation for partition. In 1959 he conducted an inquiry into the Canadian coal industry and in 1968 an inquiry into Newfoundland labour laws; in the same year he headed a Royal Commission on Ontario labour disputes. He was dean of law at the University of Western Ontario from 1959 to 1964. He was a companion of the Order of Canada. He died January 2, 1969.

[*Encyc. Can.* (1972); *Can. who's who*, 1967-69; *Report of Royal Commission Inquiry into Labour Disputes* (August, 1968); H. A. Logan, *Trade Unions in Canada* (Toronto, 1948).]

Rand, Silas Tertius (1810-1889), clergyman and philologist, was born in Cornwallis, Nova Scotia, on May 17, 1810. He was ordained to the Baptist ministry in 1834, and in 1846 he became a missionary among the Micmac Indians of New Brunswick and Nova Scotia. He became an authority on the linguistics and folk-lore of the Micmac, and actually rescued their language from oblivion. Besides translating into Micmac a good part of the Old and New Testaments, he compiled a Micmac grammar (Halifax, N.S., 1875) and a Micmac dictionary (Halifax, N.S., 1888). He wrote also *A short statement of facts relating to the history, manners, customs, language, and literature of the Micmac tribe of Indians* (Halifax, N.S., 1850) and *Legends of the Micmacs* (New York and London, 1894). He died at Hantsport, Nova Scotia, on October 4, 1889. He was a D.D. of Acadia University, and an LL.D. of Queen's University, Kingston.

[J. S. Clark, *Rand and the Micmacs* (Charlottetown, P.E.I., 1899); *Can. who was who*, vol. 2; *Cyc. Am. biog.*; W. G. MacFarlane, *New Brunswick bibliography* (Saint John, N.B., 1895).]

Rand, Theodore Harding (1835-1900), chancellor of McMaster University (1891-95), was born in Cornwallis, Nova Scotia, in 1835. He was the son of a cousin of Silas Tertius Rand (q.v.). He was educated at Acadia College (B.A., 1860; M.A., 1863; hon. LL.D., 1874), and from 1860 to 1864 he taught in the provincial normal school at Truro, Nova Scotia. From 1864 to 1870 he was superintendent of education for Nova Scotia, and from 1871 to 1883 superintendent of education for New Brunswick. From 1883 to 1885 he was on the staff of Acadia University; and in 1885 he was appointed to the staff of the Baptist College (later McMaster University), Toronto. In 1891 he became the chancellor of this institution; but ill-health compelled his withdrawal from administrative work in 1895; and he died at Fredericton, New Brunswick, on May 29,

1900. He was the author of *At Minas basin, and other poems* (Toronto, 1897) and *Song waves, and other poems* (Toronto, 1900); and he was the editor of an excellent *Treasury of Canadian verse* (Toronto, 1900).

[*Can. who was who*, vol. 1; *Cyc. Am. biog.*; Morgan, *Can. men* (1898); Dent, *Can. port.*, vol. 3; W. G. MacFarlane, *New Brunswick bibliography* (Saint John, N.B., 1895); A. MacMurchy, *Handbook of Canadian literature* (Toronto, 1906).]

Randal, Stephen (1804-1841), journalist, was born in Vermont on January 1, 1804, and was educated in the Eastern Townships, Lower Canada. He came to Upper Canada when a young man, as a protégé of the bishop of Quebec. In 1828 he was teaching school in Hamilton, Upper Canada; and about 1832 he became editor of the *Hamilton Free Press*. In 1832-33 he edited also in Hamilton a semi-monthly literary journal, named the *Voyager*. About 1836 he went to Hallowell (Picton), and he published there a short-lived periodical named *Randal's Magazine*. He died at Stanstead, Lower Canada, on April 27, 1841.

[W. S. Wallace, *The periodical literature of Upper Canada* (Can. hist. rev., 1931).]

Randall, Robert (1766-1834), pioneer, was born in Maryland in 1766. He came to Upper Canada in 1798, and settled at Niagara Falls. Here he built a saw and flour mill, in which was ground the first flour sent from Upper Canada to the British market, and a foundry for the manufacture of the first bar and cast iron made in Upper Canada. He established also a mercantile business at Cornwall. In various parts of the province he acquired valuable lands, including the site of what is now a large part of the city of Ottawa. In 1809, owing to the failure of his British agents, he was arrested and imprisoned for debt; and he lost his various properties. There were irregularities in the disposal of these properties; and for many years he strove, though in vain, to obtain justice from the courts of the province. In 1820 he was elected to the Legislative Assembly of Upper Canada for Niagara; and in 1825 he was elected for Lincoln. During this period he gained the friendship of William Lyon Mackenzie (q.v.), and the latter made Randall's treatment a political issue against the "Family Compact." Randall died near Niagara Falls, Upper Canada, on May 1, 1834; and in his will Mackenzie was named his executor. He was buried at Lundy's Lane.

[H. P. Hill, *Robert Randall and the Le Breton Flats* (Ottawa, 1919).]

Raney, William Edgar (1859-1933), politician and jurist, was born near Aultville, Stormont county, Ontario, on December 8, 1859. He was educated at Trinity University (B.C.L., 1886), and Osgoode Hall, Toronto, was called to the bar of Ontario in 1886 (K.C.,

1906), and practised law in Toronto. He became a leading advocate of the prohibition of the sale of spirituous liquors in Ontario; and in 1919 he was appointed attorney-general in the Drury administration in the province. He was elected in 1920 to represent Wellington East in the Legislative Assembly of Ontario; and he sat in the legislature until 1927, but resigned his portfolio on the defeat of the government in 1923. In 1927 he was appointed a judge of the High Court division of the Supreme Court of Ontario; and he continued on the bench until his death, at Toronto, Ontario, on September 24, 1933.

[*Can. parl. comp.*; *Who's who in Canada* , 1932-33.]

Ranken, George (1828-1856), soldier and author, was born in London, England, on January 4, 1828. He was educated at the Royal Military Academy, Woolwich; and in 1847 he was commissioned a second lieutenant in the Royal Engineers. From 1850 to 1854 he was stationed in Canada; in 1855 he was sent to the Crimea; and on February 28, 1856 he was killed by the explosion of a mine at Sebastopol. He was the author of *The experiment: A farce, in one act* (Quebec, 1854); and his journal and correspondence were later published by his brother under the title *Canada and the Crimea, or Sketches of a soldier's life* (London, 1862).

[*Dict. nat. biog.*]

Rankin, Arthur McKee (1844-1914), actor, was born in Sandwich, Canada West, on February 6, 1844. He was educated at Upper Canada College, Toronto; but ran away from school to join a theatrical company. He was brought back to Canada, and was employed for a time in the civil service at Ottawa; but, on the advice of Sir John Macdonald (q.v.), he returned to the stage, and became an outstanding actor. He wrote one play, *True to life*; and he played in a play written by his brother, George Cameron Rankin (q.v.), entitled *The Canucks*. He died at San Francisco, California, on April 17, 1914.

[A. H. Young (ed.), *The roll of pupils of Upper Canada College* (Kingston, Ont., 1917); Morgan, *Can. men* (1912).]

Rankin, George Cameron (1841-1903), novelist and playwright, was born at Sandwich, Canada West, on August 11, 1841. He was educated at Upper Canada College, and lived for many years at Windsor, Ontario. He died on January 6, 1903. He was the author of a novel entitled *Border Canucks* (Detroit, Mich., 1890), which was later dramatized.

[L. E. Horning and L. J. Burpee, *A bibliography of Canadian fiction* (Toronto, 1904).]

Rankin, John Ireland (1879-1961), industrialist, was born at Lindsay, Ontario, May 28, 1879, and educated at the Lindsay Collegiate Institute. He joined the Bank of Ottawa in 1896 and was for a time the manager of the Haileybury, Ontario, branch. He left the bank in 1914 to join the N. A. Timmins Corporation and rose to become the president of the company. He was chairman of the St. Lawrence Paper Mills and the Lake St. John Power and Paper Company; president of St. Lawrence Corporation; director of the Iron Ore Company; vice-president of Labrador Mining Exploration; and director of eight other companies. He died at Montreal, Quebec, September 4, 1961.

[*Can. who's who*, 1949-51.]

Raphael, William (1833-1914), painter, was born in West Prussia in 1833. He graduated from the Royal School of Art in Berlin, and in 1860 he emigrated to Canada. At Montreal, where he lived for the rest of his life, he conducted a large drawing and painting class for artists. He was one of the original members of the Royal Canadian Academy on its formation in 1880; and in 1904 he was appointed a member of the Council of Arts and Manufactures of Quebec. He died in Montreal in 1914. There are several portraits by him in the Parliament Buildings at Ottawa.

[N. MacTavish, *The fine arts in Canada* (Toronto, 1925).]

Rapin, François Xavier Aldéric (1868-1901), painter, was born at St. Timothée, Quebec, on October 25, 1868. He studied painting in Paris, France, and returned to Canada about 1893. He did some portraits and some church paintings that were full of great promise; but he died, prematurely, at Montreal, Quebec, in May, 1901.

[E. Falardeau, *Artistes et artisans du Canada*, series 3 (Montreal, 1943); *Bull. rech. hist.*, 1925.]

Rasilly, Isaac de (1587-1635), governor of Acadia (1632-35), was born in Touraine, France, in 1587. He became a renowned seaman, and took part in several important naval engagements. In 1626 he presented to Richelieu a memoir relating to the colonies, which resulted in the formation of the Company of New France in the following year. He was one of the members of the Company of One Hundred Associates, and after 1628 was their naval commander. In 1632 he was commissioned to receive Acadia from the English in accordance with the treaty of Saint Germain, and arrived in Acadia in August, 1632. He established himself at La Hêve, and became the head of an organization to colonize Port Royal and La Hêve. He died in November, 1635.

[G. O. Bent, *The fortunes of La Tour* (University magazine, vol. 11); F. Parkman, *The old régime in Canada* (Boston, 1892); P. Margry (ed.), *Découvertes et établissements des français*, vol. 1 (Paris, 1879); R. G. Thwaites (ed.), *The Jesuit relations*, vol. 8

(Cleveland, 1897); Le Jeune, *Dict. gén.*; *Dict. Can. biog.*, vol. 1.]

Rasles, Sébastien. See **Rale (Rasles), Sébastien.**

Rattray, William Jordan (1835-1883), journalist and author, was born in London, England, in 1835, the son of Alexander Rattray. His father came to Canada, and set up in business in Toronto as a baker in 1848; and he was educated at the University of Toronto (B.A., 1858). He became a journalist, and was a contributor to the Toronto *Grumbler*, and to the *Canadian Monthly* (1872-78). In his later years he was on the editorial staff of the Toronto *Mail*. He died at Toronto on September 19, 1883. His only separate publication was *The Scot in British North America* (4 vols., Toronto, 1880-84), a compilation that hardly reflects his best qualities.
[*Dom. ann. reg.*, 1883.]

Raudot, Jacques (1638-1728), intendant of New France (1705-11), was born in 1638, the son of Jean Raudot, seignior of Bazarne and Coudray, and Marguerite Talon. In 1674 he was councillor in the parliament of Metz, and on May 26, 1678, he became councillor at the Cour des Aides, Paris. On January 1, 1705, he was made intendant of New France, and this post he held until 1711, devoting himself to the welfare of the colony. He returned to France and was appointed councillor of marine. He died February 20, 1728.
[R. Roy, *Les intendants de la Nouvelle-France* (Trans. Roy. Soc. Can., 1903); *Jacques et Antoine-Denis Raudot* (Bull. rech. hist., vol. ix); Le Jeune, *Dict. gén.*; *Dict. Can. biog.*, vol. 2.]

Ravenhill, Alice (1859-1954), educationist and author, was born in Epping Forest, Essex, England, on March 31, 1859, and died at Victoria, British Columbia, on May 27, 1954. She was educated in London, and became a lecturer on public health. She was the author of *Lessons in practical hygiene* (Leeds and Glasgow, 1907) and, with Catherine Schiff, joint editor of *Household administration* (New York, 1911). In 1910 she came to live in Victoria, British Columbia, where she became interested in welfare work among the Indians of the Pacific slope. She was the author of *The native tribes of British Columbia* (Victoria, B.C., 1938), *A corner stone of Canadian culture: An outline of the arts and crafts of the Indian tribes of British Columbia* (Victoria, B.C., 1944), and *Folklore of the Far West* (Victoria, B.C., 1953); and she told the story of her life in *Alice Ravenhill: The memoirs of an educational pioneer* (Toronto, 1951). In 1948 the University of British Columbia conferred on her an honorary degree.
[*Encyc. Can.*]

Rawson, Donald Strathearn (1905-1961), limnobiologist, was born at Claremont, Ontario, on May 19, 1905. He entered the University of Toronto in 1922, receiving his Ph.D. degree in 1929. On graduation he joined the staff of the department of biology of the University of Saskatchewan. From 1928 to 1934 he did extensive work on the lakes of the newly established Prince Albert National Park. From 1935 to 1941 his work was extended to include the national parks of the Canadian Rockies and Riding Mountain National Park in Manitoba. In 1942 he began work on the great northern lakes, Reindeer, Athabaska, and Great Slave; after 1947 he worked on the Churchill drainage system, Lac la Ronge, and Amisk Lake. Through all these studies and some sixty publications the northern Canadian lakes have become familiar to students of limnology all over the world. He played an important role in the founding of the Canadian Society of Wildlife and Fishery Biologists. At his death he was head of the department of biology at the University of Saskatchewan. He died at Saskatoon on February 16, 1961.
[*Proc. Roy. Soc. Can.*, 1961.]

Ray, George R. (d. 1935), fur-trader, was a former employee of the Hudson's Bay Company who was elected in 1914 to represent Fort Nelson in the Legislative Assembly of Manitoba. He died at Edmonton, Alberta, on October 13, 1935. He was the author of *Kasba (White Partridge), a story of Hudson Bay* (Toronto, 1915).
[*Can. parl. comp.*, 1915.]

Raymond, Adélard (1889-1962), air vice-marshal, was born in St. Stanislas de Kosta, Quebec, on July 10, 1889, and educated at Valleyfield College. He was a lieutenant in the Royal Flying Corps in the First World War, and on demobilization opened a flying field at Cartierville, Quebec. In 1926 he sold his interest and went into the hotel business in Montreal. At the outbreak of the Second World War he was made commander of 118th Bomber Squadron. In 1940 he was one of a group of Canadian instructors serving with the French Air Force, and, after escaping internment, he returned to Canada on the fall of France. After commanding Lachine Manning Depot, No. 2, Service Flying Training School, he became commander of No. 3 Training Command, Montreal. In 1944 he became air vice-marshal in command of No. 1 Air Command, Trenton, Ontario. He retired in 1945 and at the time of his death was president of Queen's Hotel Limited, Montreal, and director of Canadair, Gleneagles Investments Limited, Crown Trust, and Imperial Life. He died at Montreal, Quebec, February 24, 1962.
[Metropolitan Toronto Library Board, *Biographical scrapbooks*, vol. 20.]

Raymond, Joseph Sabin (1810-1887), priest, was born at St. Hyacinthe, Lower Canada, on March 13, 1810; and was ordained a priest of the Roman Catholic Church in 1832. He became in 1832 a professor on the staff of the St. Hyacinthe Seminary; for three separate periods he was superior of the Seminary; and from 1852 to 1887 he was grand vicar of St. Hyacinthe. He died at St. Hyacinthe, Quebec, on July 3, 1887. He was the author of *Entretien sur les études classiques* (Montreal, 1872), *Devoirs du citoyen* (St. Hyacinthe, Que., 1875), and a number of other pamphlets.

[Allaire, *Dict. biog.*; Le Jeune, *Dict. gén.*; Rose, *Cyc. Can. biog.* (1888).]

Raymond, William Odber (1853-1923), clergyman and historian, was born at Woodstock, New Brunswick, on February 3, 1853, the second son of Lieut.-Col. Charles W. Raymond. He was educated at the Woodstock grammar school and at the University of New Brunswick (B.A., 1876; M.A., 1891; LL.D., 1901); and he was ordained a priest of the Church of England in 1879. From 1878 to 1884 he was stationed at Stanley, New Brunswick; and from 1884 to 1920 he was rector of St. Mary's Church, Saint John, New Brunswick. In 1908 he became archdeacon of Saint John. After retirement from active parochial work, he removed to Toronto; and here he died on November 23, 1923. In 1879 he married Julia Nelson, of Saint John; and by her he had one son and one daughter. He was elected a fellow of the Royal Society of Canada in 1906; and he was an outstanding authority on the history of the Maritime provinces of Canada. In addition to numerous papers contributed to the *Transactions* of the Royal Society of Canada, the *Collections* of the New Brunswick Historical Society, and other periodicals, he wrote *The history of the river St. John* (Saint John, N.B., 1905), and he edited the valuable *Winslow papers* (Saint John, N.B., 1901).

[*Proc. Roy. Soc. Can.*, 1924; Morgan, *Can. men* (1912); *Can. who's who*, 1910.]

Read, David Breakenridge (1823-1904), lawyer and historian, was born at Augusta, Upper Canada, on June 13, 1823, the third son of John Landon Read, merchant, and Janet, daughter of David Breakenridge. He was educated at Upper Canada College, Toronto; and was called to the bar of Upper Canada in 1845 (Q.C., 1858). For thirty years he was a bencher of the Law Society of Upper Canada, and he was the author of *Lectures on the Judicature Act* (Toronto, 1881). In 1858 he was mayor of Toronto. During his later years he devoted himself to historical and biographical research; and he published *The lives of the judges of Upper Canada* (Toronto, 1888), *The life and times of General John Graves Simcoe* (Toronto, 1890), *The life and times of Major-General Sir Isaac Brock* (Toronto, 1894), *The rebellion of 1837* (Toronto, 1897), and *The lieutenant-governors of Upper Canada and Ontario* (Toronto, 1900). He died in Toronto on May 11, 1904. He married Emily, daughter of Norman Ballard, of Picton, Ontario; and by her he had three daughters and one son.

[Morgan, *Can. men* (1898); *Commemorative biographical record of the county of York, Ontario* (Toronto, 1907).]

Read, John Erskine (1888-1973), jurist, was born in Halifax, Nova Scotia, July 5, 1888, educated at Dalhousie University (B.A., 1909), Columbia University, and University College, Oxford (B.A., 1912; B.C.L., 1913). He was called to the bar of Nova Scotia in 1913 and became a K.C. in 1925. He served in the First World War with the Canadian Field Artillery (1914-18) and was wounded. He was professor of law at Dalhousie from 1920 and dean of the law school from 1924 to 1929. He was a legal advisor to the department of external affairs from 1919 to 1946, a delegate to the Imperial Conferences of 1930 and 1937, and deputy secretary of the Imperial Economic Conference of 1932. He represented Canada at the Committee of Jurists in Washington in 1945 and was Canadian alternate to the United Nations' first General Assembly in 1946. He was a judge of the International Court of Justice from 1946 to 1958. On his retirement from the International Court he lectured at the University of Ottawa. He wrote *The origins and nature of the law* (Toronto, 1955); and *The rule of law on the international plane* (Toronto, 1961). He died at Toronto, Ontario, December 23, 1973.

[*Can. who's who*, 1967-69.]

Reade, John (1837-1919), journalist and poet, was born at Ballyshannon, county Donegal, Ireland, on November 13, 1837, the son of Joseph Reade and Frances Smyth. He was educated at Queen's College, Belfast, and came to Canada in 1856. He first studied law, and then theology; and in 1864 was ordained a clergyman of the Church of England. He had, however, before this interested himself in journalism; and in 1870 he left the church to become literary editor of the Montreal *Gazette*. This position he held for the rest of his life, conducting for many years a column entitled "Old and New", under the initials "R.V." In 1870 he published a volume of verse, *The prophecy of Merlin, and other poems* (Montreal); and he contributed to literary periodicals and to the transaction of learned societies a large number of papers on a great variety of subjects. In 1882 he was appointed one of the charter members of the Royal Society of Canada; and in 1896 he was elected a fellow of the Royal Society of Literature of Great Britain. In 1906 he was made an LL.D. of the University of Ottawa. He died, unmarried, at Montreal, on March 26, 1919.

[*Proc. Roy. Soc. Can.*, 1919; *Can. who was who*, vol. 1; Morgan, *Can. men* (1912); Rose,

Cyc. Can. biog. (1886); A. MacMurchy, *A handbook of Canadian literature* (Toronto, 1906).]

Reade, John Collingwood (1905-1963), news analyst and writer, was born in Fairfield, England, in 1905, and educated at Oundel School and at Saanich, Vancouver Island, where he went with his family as a child. He had a varied career before coming to radio and newscasting. He had been a mounted policeman, a merchant seaman, and an advertising and brokerage executive, and had travelled widely in North and South America and in Europe. He joined the Hamilton *Spectator* as a reporter in 1929 and later was advertising manager for Dominion Canners and for Mutual Life of Waterloo before founding his own advertising firm. His first broadcast was an assignment to cover the abdication crisis of 1936 for the Columbia Broadcasting System. During the Second World War he acted as war correspondent for the Toronto *Globe and Mail* and radio station CFRB. He was for eight months in 1944 press secretary for John Bracken (q.v.), leader of the opposition. He was an editorial writer for the *Globe and Mail* in 1946 and 1947. He became a freelance broadcaster in 1948 and continued his radio and television work until his accidental death on January 13, 1963.

[Metropolitan Toronto Library Board, *Biographical scrapbooks*, vol. 21.]

Ready, John (d. 1845), lieutenant-governor of Prince Edward Island (1824-31), was a British army officer who was in 1820 appointed a member of the Executive Council of Lower Canada, and in 1824 lieutenant-governor of Prince Edward Island. His tenure of office, which lasted until 1831, was very popular and successful; and after his return to England he became a major-general and governor of the Isle of Man. It was while holding this position that he died, on July 10, 1845.

[A. B. Warburton, *A history of Prince Edward Island* (Saint John, N.B., 1923).]

Reaman, George Elmore (1889-1969), author, was born at Concord, Ontario, July 22, 1889, and educated at Victoria College (B.A., 1911; M.A., 1913), McMaster University (M.A., 1916), Queen's University (B. Paed., 1917), and Cornell University (Ph.D., 1920). He began teaching at Moose Jaw in 1913, moved to Woodstock Collegiate in 1915, and became educational director for the Toronto Y.M.C.A. in 1920. From 1925 to 1932 he was superintendent of the Training School for Boys at Bowmanville, Ontario. He became head of the department of English at the Ontario Agricultural College at Guelph in 1939, a position he held until 1954. He was founder and first president of the Pennsylvania German Folklore Society (1951). He wrote *English for new Canadians* (1919); *The new citizen* (1921);

Our Canada: A Canadian citizenship primer (1923); *English grammar for new Canadians* (1923); *History of the Holstein-Frisian Breed in Canada* (1946); *The Trail of the black walnut* (1956); *The Trail of the Huguenots* (1963); *History of Dominion Life Assurance Company* (1965); *The Trail of the Iroquois Indians* (1967); *History of agriculture in Ontario* (1969). He died at Toronto, December 7, 1969.

[*Can. who's who*, 1967-69.]

Redpath, Peter (1821-1894), merchant and philanthropist, was born at Montreal, Lower Canada, on August 1, 1821, the son of John Redpath, a sugar manufacturer. He was educated in Montreal, studied business methods in England, and entered his father's sugar refinery. In 1864 he was appointed a member of the board of governors of McGill University; and his gifts to McGill University were on a princely scale. He endowed a chair of natural philosophy; he presented to the university a museum and a library building; and he made gifts to the library of much valuable historical material. He was also for some years president of the Montreal General Hospital. In 1879 he retired from business, and went to live in England. Here he died, at Chislehurst Manor House, on February 1, 1894. In 1847 he married Grace, daughter of William Wood, of Bowden, Manchester, England. He left no children.

[Sir J. W. Dawson, *Peter Redpath* (Montreal, 1894); *Can. who was who*, vol. 2; *Dict. nat. biog.*; Toronto *Globe*, Feb. 3, 1894.]

Reed, Thomas Arthur (1871-1958), author, was born in Toronto, Ontario, on September 25, 1871, and died there on March 13, 1958. He graduated in music from Trinity University (Mus.B., 1901), and was secretary of the Mendelssohn Choir in Toronto from 1902 to 1929. He was financial secretary of the University of Toronto Athletic Association from 1914 to 1947, and paymaster of the University of Toronto C.O.T.C. from 1914 to 1943. He became a leading authority on the history of Toronto, and was joint author of *Our royal town of York* (Toronto, 1929). He also wrote *The blue and white* (Toronto, 1944), a history of athletics at the University of Toronto, and edited *A history of the University of Trinity College* (Toronto, 1952).

[*Can. who's who*, 1955-57.]

Reesor, David (1823-1902), senator of Canada, was born at Markham, Upper Canada, on January 18, 1823, of German descent. He was the founder, and for a number of years the editor, of the Markham *Economist*. In 1860 he was elected to represent the division of King's in the Legislative Council of Canada; and in 1867 he was summoned by royal proclamation to the Senate of Canada. He sat in the Senate until his death on April 27, 1902. He married Emily, daughter of Daniel

McDougall, and sister of the Hon. William McDougall (q.v.); and by her he had one son and four daughters.

[*Can. parl. comp.*; Rose, *Cyc. Can. biog.* (1888).]

Reeves, John (1752?-1829), chief justice of the Supreme Court of Newfoundland (1791-92), was born in London, England, about 1752, and died there on August 7, 1829. He was educated at Eton and Merton College, Oxford (B.A., 1775; M.A., 1778), and was called to the bar at the Middle Temple in 1779. In 1791 he was appointed chief justice of the Supreme Court of Newfoundland for one year, and did much to reform the legal system in the colony. Among his voluminous writings was his *History of the government of the island of Newfoundland* (London, 1793). In 1790 he was elected a fellow of the Royal Society.

[J. Foster, *Alumni Oxonienses, 1715-1886* (Oxford and London, 1888); *Dict. nat. biog.*; *Encyc. Can.*]

Reford, Robert (1831-1913), merchant and capitalist, was born in county Antrim, Ireland, in 1831, and came to Canada with his family in 1845. He lived in Toronto until 1865, and after that in Montreal, as a general merchant; and in 1870 he founded in Montreal a steamship agency business, the Robert Reford Company, which became the agent for the Donaldson Line to Glasgow, the Thomson Line to London, Hull, and Newcastle, and other lines. He became president, not only of this company, but of a variety of other businesses; and before his death became one of the outstanding capitalists of Montreal. He died at Montreal on March 16, 1913.

[Morgan, *Can. men* (1912); *Can. who was who*, vol. 2.]

Regan, John William (1873-1945), journalist and author, was born in 1873 and died at Halifax, Nova Scotia, on February 11, 1945. He became a journalist, and was for some years the correspondent in Halifax of the Associated Press. He became an authority on the history of Halifax, and was the author of *Sketches and traditions of the North West Arm* (Halifax, N.S., 1908). He was also, under the *nom de plume* of "John Quinpool", the author of *First things in Acadia* (Halifax, N.S., 1936).

[*New York Times*, Feb. 12, 1945.]

Reid, George Agnew (1860-1947), painter, was born near Wingham, Canada West, on July 25, 1860, and died at Toronto, Ontario, on August 23, 1947. He studied painting at the Central Ontario School of Art, at the Pennsylvania Academy, and in Paris and Madrid; and he opened a studio in Toronto. He became a member of the Ontario Society of Artists in 1885, and was its president from 1897 to 1902; he was elected an A.R.C.A. in 1885 and an R.C.A. in 1890, and was president of the Royal Canadian Academy from 1906 to 1909; and he was principal of the Ontario College of Art from 1912 to 1926. Several of his paintings are in the National Gallery in Ottawa, and there are some good examples of his mural paintings in the Royal Ontario Museum.

[M. M. Miner, *G. A. Reid, Canadian artist* (Toronto, 1946); Morgan, *Can. men* (1912); *Can. who's who*, 1938-39; *Encyc. Can.*]

Reid, James (1769-1848), chief justice, was born in Scotland in 1769, and came to Canada about 1788. He studied law in the office of John Reid, clerk of the Court of Common Pleas at Montreal, and was called to the bar of Lower Canada in 1794. In 1807, he was appointed a judge of the Court of King's Bench at Montreal; and in 1825 he became chief justice of this court. In June, 1838, he became a member of the Executive Council of Lower Canada; but a few months later he resigned both from the Council and from the bench, on pension. He died at Montreal on January 19, 1848.

[F. J. Audet, *Les juges en chef de la province de Québec* (Quebec, 1927); P. G. Roy, *Les juges de la province de Québec* (Quebec, 1933); Morgan, *Cel. Can.*]

Reid, James (1832-1904), senator of Canada, was born at the Cascades, Wakefield, Lower Canada, on August 1, 1832. He was educated at Fraser's Academy, Ottawa; and when a young man went to British Columbia by way of Panama, and engaged in mining. In 1871 he founded at Quesnel, British Columbia, a general mercantile business; and from 1881 to 1888 he represented Cariboo as a Conservative in the Canadian House of Commons. In 1888 he was called to the Senate of Canada; and he sat in the Senate until his death on May 3, 1904.

[J. B. Kerr, *Biographical dictionary of well-known British Columbians* (Vancouver, B.C., 1890); Morgan, *Can. men* (1898); *Can. parl. comp.*]

Reid, John Dowsley (1859-1929), minister of customs for Canada (1911-21), was born at Prescott, Ontario, on January 1, 1859, the son of John Reid. He was educated at Queen's University, Kingston (M.D., C.M., 1890), but practised medicine for only a short time, and became eventually the manager of the Imperial Starch Company, Prescott. From 1891 to 1921 he represented Grenville in the Canadian House of Commons; and he was minister of customs in the Borden cabinet from 1911 to 1917, and minister of railways and canals from 1917 to 1921. In 1921 he was appointed to the Senate of Canada. He died at Prescott on August 26, 1929. In 1899 he married Ephie, daughter of John Labatt, of Hamilton, Ontario; and by her he had one son and one daughter.

[*Can. parl. comp.*; Morgan, *Can. men* (1912).]

Reid, John Hotchkiss Stewart (1909-1963), historian, was born in Glasgow, Scotland, in 1909. He came to Canada as a boy and graduated from the University of British Columbia in 1929. During the depression he was a school-teacher, newspaper reporter, and camp cook. He returned to the University of British Columbia, obtaining his M.A. in English in 1942. He was a flight-lieutenant in the R.C.A.F. in the Second World War. After the war he entered the University of Toronto, where he received his Ph.D. in 1946. In 1947 he was appointed to the staff of United College, Winnipeg. He resigned in 1959 to accept an appointment as executive secretary of the Canadian Association of University teachers. He died after a lengthy illness at Ottawa on December 13, 1963. He was author of *Mountains, men and rivers* (Toronto, 1954), *The origins of the British Labor Party* (Minneapolis, 1955), *A sourcebook of Canadian history* (with K. McNaught and H. Crowe, Toronto, 1964), and *Our modern world* (with E. McInnes, Toronto, 1963).

[*Can. hist. rev.*, vol. XLV, 1964.]

Reid, Mary Augusta, *née* **Hiester** (1854-1921), painter, was born at Reading, Pennsylvania, in 1854, the daughter of Dr. Hiester. In 1885 she married George A. Reid (q.v.), a Canadian artist, and in 1886 she came to Canada. She had studied painting in Philadelphia and in Paris, France; and in 1888 she was elected a member of the Ontario Society of Artists. In 1896 she became an associate of the Royal Canadian Academy. Beginning as a painter of flowers and still life, she achieved success also in landscapes, gardens, interiors, and mural decoration. She died at Toronto on October 4, 1921. A memorial exhibition of her work was held in Toronto after her death.

[Morgan, *Can. men and women* (1912); N. MacTavish, *The fine arts in Canada* (Toronto, 1925).]

Reid, Robert (1850-1922), poet, was born at Wanlockhead, Dumfriesshire, Scotland, on June 8, 1850. He was employed in mercantile houses in Glasgow and Belfast until 1877, when he came to Canada and took a position with the firm of Henry Morgan and Company, Montreal. He rose in the service of this company until he became a director. He retired about 1914; and he died at Montreal, Quebec, on June 1, 1922. Under the pseudonym of "Rob Wanlock" he wrote Scottish dialect verse; and he was the author of *Poems, songs, and sonnets* (Paisley, Scotland, 1894).

[Morgan, *Can. men* (1912); C. C. James, *A bibliography of Canadian poetry* (Toronto, 1899).]

Reid, Sir Robert Gillespie (1842-1908), contractor and financier, was born at Coupar Angus, Perthshire, Scotland, in 1842. He became a contractor, and in 1865 went to Australia, where he engaged in gold mining and the construction of public works. In 1871 he came to Canada, and here he made a reputation first as a bridge-builder. He built the international bridge across the Niagara River, the bridge of Sault Ste. Marie, and the Lachine bridge, at Montreal, as well as the international bridge across the Rio Grande between Mexico and Texas and the bridges across the Colorado at Austin, Texas, and across the Delaware at the famous water gap in Pennsylvania. He also took part in the building of the Canadian Pacific Railway; and the Jackfish Bay section of this railway, north of Lake Superior, was his work. In 1890 he transferred his energies to Newfoundland, and here he engaged in railway-building, in the operation of telegraphs and steamships, and in the exploitation of natural resources on a scale which amounted to the acquisition by him of the "whole realizable assets" of the island. In 1901 he became president of the "Reid-Newfoundland Company"; but his health broke down under the strain of his labours, and during his later years his work was carried on by his sons. He died at Montreal, Quebec, on June 3, 1908. In 1865 he married Harriet Duff; and by her he had three sons and one daughter. In 1907 he was created a knight bachelor.

[*Who was who*, 1897-1916; J. R. Smallwood (ed.), *The book of Newfoundland* (2 vols., St. John's, Newfoundland, 1937).]

Reid, Robie Lewis (1866-1945), lawyer and historian, was born at Cornwallis, Kings county, Nova Scotia, on November 3, 1866. He was educated at Dalhousie University and at the University of Michigan (LL.B., 1899); and was called to the bar of British Columbia in 1893 (K.C., 1907). He practised law first in New Westminster, and then in Vancouver; and was elected a bencher of the Law Society of British Columbia. A diligent student of the history of British Columbia, he was in 1936 elected a fellow of the Royal Society of Canada, and made an LL.D. of the University of British Columbia. He died in Vancouver on February 6, 1945. He was the author of *The assay office and the proposed mint at New Westminster* (Victoria, B.C., 1926).

[*Proc. Roy. Soc. Can.*, 1935; *British Columbia historical quarterly*, 1935; *Can. who's who*, 1938-39.]

Reid, William (1816-1896), clergyman, was born at Kildrummy, Aberdeenshire, Scotland, on December 10, 1816, and was educated at King's College, Aberdeen. He came to Canada in 1840, and was ordained a minister of the Presbyterian Church. He was elected moderator of the Presbyterian Church in Canada in 1879; and he was for many years clerk of the General Assembly. In 1876 Queen's University conferred on him the honorary degree of D.D. He died at Toronto, Ontario, on January 19, 1896.

[R. Campbell, *A History of the Scotch Presbyterian Church, St. Gabriel Street, Montreal* (Montreal, 1887); Rose, *Cyc. Can. biog.* (1886); *Cyc. Am. biog.*]

Reid, William Angus (1895-1961), executive, was born in St. John's, Newfoundland, on November 30, 1895. He was educated at Bishop Field College in St. John's and at Harrow in England. He was managing director of Reid Newfoundland Company Limited, a director of Bowaters Newfoundland Pulp and Paper Mills, director of the British Newfoundland Corporation Limited, and agent in Newfoundland for a number of insurance companies. He was past president of the Newfoundland Board of Trade. He died at St. John's on May 27, 1961.

[*Can. who's who*, 1955-57.]

Reiffenstein, John C. (1784?-1840), soldier and merchant, was born at Frankfort-on-the-Main, Germany, about 1784. He entered the British army, and came to Halifax, Nova Scotia, about 1806 as ensign and adjutant in the 98th Regiment. He was appointed a staff adjutant in 1812, and he saw service during the War of 1812 at Miami, Fort Stephenson, and at Moraviantown. It was he who brought the report of Procter's defeat at Moraviantown to headquarters. After the war he resigned from the army, and became a prominent merchant in Quebec. He died in 1840. In 1807 he married in Halifax a Miss Carr; and by her he had several children.

[B. Sulte, *Mélanges historiques*, vol. xiv (Montreal, 1928).]

Rémy, Daniel de, Sieur de Courcelle. See Courcelle, Daniel de Rémy, Sieur de.

Renaud, Emiliano (1875-1932), pianist and composer, was born at St. Jean de Matha, Quebec, on June 26, 1875. He studied music in Montreal, Vienna, and Berlin; and in 1904 he returned to Montreal, where, with an interval spent in the United States, he lived until his death on October 3, 1932. He was the composer of a large number of musical works, chiefly concert pieces.

[*Soeurs de Ste. Anne, Dictionnaire biographique des musiciens canadiens* (Lachine, Quebec, 1935).]

Renison, Robert John (1875-1957), archbishop, was born at Cashel, Tipperary, Ireland, on September 8, 1875, and died at Toronto, Ontario, on October 6, 1957. He came to Canada with his parents in 1883, and was educated at Trinity College School, Port Hope, the University of Toronto (B.A., 1896; M.A., 1897), and Wycliffe College. He was ordained a priest of the Church of England in 1896; and in 1898 he went as a missionary to the Indians of James Bay. He spent fourteen years in this capacity, and became an authority on the Indian languages. He served overseas as a chaplain in the First World War; and he was the rector of churches in Hamilton, Vancouver, and Toronto. In 1931 he was elected bishop of Athabaska; and in 1943 he returned to the James Bay region as bishop of Moosonee. In 1952 he was elected archbishop of Moosonee and metropolitan of Ontario; and he retired in 1954. He was the author of *Wednesday morning* (Toronto, 1944), *For such a time as this* (Toronto, 1947), and an autobiography, entitled *One day at a time*, published posthumously (Toronto, 1957). He was also joint author, with J. C. Hopkins, of *Canada at war* (Toronto, 1919). Honorary degrees were conferred on him by several universities.

[*Can. who's who*, 1955-57; *Encyc. Can.*]

Renouf, Edward Michael (1860-1941), publisher, was born at St. John's, Newfoundland, on April 9, 1860. He was educated in Newfoundland, and settled in Montreal in 1880. He entered the publishing business under S. E. Dawson (q.v.), and later founded the Renouf Publishing Company. He rose in the militia to the command of the 2nd Regiment, Montreal Artillery; and in 1911 became president of the Dominion Artillery Association. He died at Montreal, on April 20, 1941.

[*Can. who's who*, 1936-37.]

Reppen, John Richard (Jack) (1933-1964), artist, was born in Toronto, Ontario, July 17, 1933, and educated at Northern Vocational High School in Toronto. He studied electricity in high school and after graduation began attending the Ontario College of Art, in evening classes. He sold his first drawings, which were caricatures of athletes, to Toronto newspapers, but he was soon to be recognized as a serious artist. His paintings of Yucatan ruins using many materials have been widely acclaimed. His paintings were among the Canadian works chosen for the fifth biennial showing of Canadian painting in London. He died at Toronto, Ontario, June 2, 1964.

He is represented in the CIL Collection, Montreal; in collections at Queen's University; Hart House, at the University of Toronto; the London Art Museum, London, Ontario; and the Montreal Museum of Fine Arts; and in many private collections.

[Metropolitan Toronto Libarary Board, *Biographical scrapbooks*, vol. 22.]

Retty, Joseph Arlington (1904-1961), geologist, was born at Fort Coulonge, Quebec, on June 3, 1904. He was educated at Ottawa University (B.A., 1926) and at Princeton University (Ph.D. in geology, 1931). In 1936 he headed a party sent out by the Labrador Mining and Exploration Company to do a geological survey of the Quebec-Labrador border country; the last maps had been made in 1893. After two years a rich deposit of iron was located in Ungava near the Labrador boundary.

The party mapped an area one-quarter the size of the United States. At Havre St. Pierre, 420 miles downriver from Quebec City, a rich deposit of ilmenite was also discovered. He worked for the Iron Ore Company as chief geologist from 1946 to 1952, when he resigned to become a consultant and a professor at the University of Montreal. He worked also for the Quebec Department of Mines and the Geological Survey of Canada. He was a fellow of the Geological Association of Canada and the Arctic Institute of North America. He died at Montreal, March 15, 1961.

[*Can. who's who*, 1955-57; *Saturday Night*, Mar. 27, 1951, Aug. 3, 1957.]

Reville, Frederick Douglas (1866-1944), journalist, was born at Witney, Oxfordshire, England, on October 8, 1866, and came to Canada in 1881. He became joint proprietor of the Brantford *Daily Courier*, and was its editor until it was amalgamated in 1918 with the Brantford *Expositor*. He died at Brantford, Ontario, on August 11, 1944. He was the author of *A rebellion* (Brantford, Ont., 1912) and *History of the county of Brant* (2 vols., Brantford, 1920).

[*Can. who's who*, 1936-37.]

Reynolds, Henry Dunbar (1820-1864), clergyman, was born in Dublin, Ireland, in 1820. He was called to the Irish bar in 1842, but came to Canada later, studied divinity at Bishop's College, Lennoxville, and was admitted to holy orders in the Church of England in 1854. He became curate at St. Mark's Church, Niagara, and in 1856 came into conflict with the rector and with Bishop Strachan (q.v.). He was removed from his curacy; and published in defence of himself a volume entitled *The Niagara church case* (Toronto, 1857). Later he left the church, and was called to the bar of Upper Canada. He died at Greenock, Scotland, on July 23, 1864.

[Morgan, *Bib. can.*]

Reynolds, William Kilby (1848-1902), journalist and author, was born in Saint John, New Brunswick, on June 19, 1848. He studied law, but turned to journalism, and he was employed on the staff of newspapers in Saint John, Sackville, Moncton, and Boston. He died at Saint John, New Brunswick, on December 2, 1902. He was the author of *An intercolonial outing* (Ottawa, 1883), *Some facts about St. John* (Saint John, N.B., 1889), and *Annals of the provinces: No. 1, Old time tragedies* (Saint John, N.B., 1895).

[W. G. MacFarlane, *New Brunswick bibliography* (Saint John, N.B., 1895); Morgan, *Can. men* (1898).]

Rhinewine, Abraham (1887-1932), journalist and author, was born in Poland in 1887. He came to Canada, by way of England, in 1907; and in 1912 he joined the staff of the *Toronto Hebrew Journal*, a Yiddish daily news-

paper. In 1915 he became the editor of this paper; and he continued to edit the paper until his death in Toronto, Ontario, in 1932. In addition to a number of books in Yiddish, dealing chiefly with historical themes, he was the author of *Looking back a century, on the centennial of Jewish political equality in Canada*, edited by I. Goldstick (Toronto, 1932).

[Private information.]

Rho, Joseph Adolphe (1835-1905), artist, was born at Gentilly, Lower Canada, on April 1, 1835, the son of Alexis Rho and Herménégilde St. Germain. Little is known of his early years; but in middle age he acquired a reputation as a sculptor and painter of religious subjects. He also painted portraits. He died at Bécancour, Quebec, on August 6, 1905. He was twice married; and by his first wife he had seven children.

[G. Bellerive, *Artistes-peintres canadiens-français* (Quebec, 1925); *Bull. rech. hist.*, 1932.]

Rhodes, Edgar Nelson (1877-1942), prime minister of Nova Scotia (1925-30), and minister of finance for Canada (1932-35), was born at Amherst, Nova Scotia, on January 5, 1877. He was educated at Acadia University (B.A., 1900; D.C.L., 1922) and Dalhousie University (LL.B., 1902; LL.D., 1932); and he was called to the bar of Nova Scotia in 1902 (K.C., 1916). He practised law at Amherst, Nova Scotia; and he represented Cumberland county in the Canadian House of Commons from 1908 to 1925. In 1916 he was elected deputy speaker of the House of Commons, and in 1917 speaker; and in 1921 he was sworn of the Privy Council. In 1925 he became prime minister of Nova Scotia, having been for some years the leader of the Conservative party in the province; and he retained this post until 1930, when he returned to the federal arena first as minister of fisheries and then as minister of finance in the Bennett administration. From 1930 to 1935 he represented Richmond West-Cape Breton in the House of Commons; and in 1935 he was called to the Senate of Canada. He died at Ottawa, Ontario, on March 15, 1942.

[*Can. who's who*, 1936-37; *Can. parl. comp.*; H. Charlesworth (ed.), *A cyclopaedia of Canadian biography* (Toronto, 1919).]

Richard, Edouard (1844-1904), historian, was born at Princeville, Lower Canada, on March 14, 1844, the son of the Hon. Louis Richard and Hermine Prince. He was educated at the College of Nicolet and at McGill University, and was called to the bar in Quebec in 1868. For seven years he practised law in Arthabaskaville, Quebec, in partnership with Sir Wilfrid Laurier (q.v.); and from 1872 to 1878 he represented Megantic in the Canadian House of Commons. From 1878 to 1883 he was sheriff of the North West Territories; and for a number of years thereafter he lived in Winnipeg. He devoted much time to the study of the history of the Acadians, and in 1895 he published two volumes of his work on *Acadia*. A French translation of this work was published by H. d'Arles (q.v.) in three volumes in 1916-21. In 1897 he was employed by the Canadian government to undertake historical research in Paris, France, the results of which were published in the Canadian Archives Reports for 1899, 1904, and 1905. He died at Battleford, North West Territories, on March 27, 1904. In 1896 he was elected a fellow of the Royal Society of Canada, and was made a Litt.D. of Laval University.

[*Proc. Roy. Soc. Can.*, 1904; Morgan, *Can. men* (1898); *Can. parl. comp.*; *Can. who was who*, vol. 1; Le Jeune, *Dict. gén.*]

Richard, Louis (1838-1908), priest and educationist, was born at Nicolet, Lower Canada, on November 28, 1838, and was ordained a priest of the Roman Catholic Church on September 25, 1864. He became first a professor, and then superior, of the Three Rivers Seminary; and in 1900 was made an apostolic protonotary. He died at Three Rivers, Quebec, on January 6, 1908. He was the author of *Histoire du collège des Trois-Rivières* (Three Rivers, Que., 1885).

[Allaire, *Dict. biog.*; *Bull. rech. hist.*, 1930.]

Richards, Albert Norton (1822-1897), lieutenant-governor of British Columbia (1876-81), was born at Brockville, Upper Canada, on December 8, 1822, the youngest son of Stephen Richards and Phoebe Buell. He was educated at the district grammar school, and was called to the bar of Upper Canada in 1848 (Q.C., 1863). He represented South Leeds in the Legislative Assembly of Canada from 1863 to 1864, and in the Canadian House of Commons from 1872 to 1874; and from December, 1863, to January, 1864, he was solicitor-general for Upper Canada in the Sandfield Macdonald administration. In 1869 he was appointed attorney-general of Manitoba, and accompanied the Hon. William McDougall (q.v.) in his abortive attempt to assume the government of Manitoba. He then went to British Columbia, and in 1871 was called to the bar in that province. For several years he was legal agent of the Dominion government in British Columbia; and in 1876 he was appointed lieutenant-governor of the province. His period of office terminated in 1881; and he then retired to private life. He died at Victoria, British Columbia, on March 6, 1897. He married (1) in 1849 Frances (d. 1853), daughter of Benjamin Chaffey, of Somersetshire, England; and (2) in 1854 Ellen Chaffey, daughter of John Cheslett, of Somersetshire.

[J. B. Kerr, *Biographical dictionary of well-known British Columbians* (Vancouver, B.C., 1892); Dent, *Can. port.*, vol. 4; *Can. parl. comp.*]

Richards, Charles Dow (1879-1956), prime minister of New Brunswick, was born in York county, New Brunswick, on June 12, 1879, and died at Fredericton, New Brunswick, on September 15, 1956. He was educated at the University of New Brunswick (B.A., 1904), and became a school-teacher. In 1911, however, he was called to the bar, and he practised law in Fredericton from 1912 to 1933. In 1920 he was elected to the legislature of New Brunswick as a Conservative, and was chosen leader of the opposition. In 1925 he became minister of lands and mines in the Baxter government; and when J. B. M. Baxter (q.v.) resigned in 1931, he succeeded him as prime minister. In 1933 he himself resigned, to accept appointment to the Supreme Court of New Brunswick, and in 1948 he became chief justice of the province.

[*Can. who's who*, 1952-54; *Can. parl. guide*, 1932; *Encyc. Can.*]

Richards, Stephen (1820-1894), lawyer and politician, was born at Brockville, Upper Canada, in 1820, the second son of Stephen Richards and Phoebe Buell. He was educated at the Johnstown district grammar school and at Potsdam Academy, New York; and was called to the bar of Upper Canada in 1844 (Q.C., 1858). From 1867 to 1875 he represented Niagara in the Legislative Assembly of Ontario; and from 1867 to 1871 he was first commissioner of crown lands and then provincial secretary in the Sandfield Macdonald administration in Ontario. From 1876 to 1879 he was treasurer of the Law Society of Upper Canada. He died at Toronto on October 4, 1894, and was buried in Brockville. He was married to Susan, daughter of Benjamin Chaffey, of Somersetshire, England.

[*Can. parl. comp.*; Toronto *Globe*, Oct. 5, 1894.]

Richards, Sir William Buell (1815-1889), chief justice of the Supreme Court of Canada (1875-79), was born at Brockville, Upper Canada, on May 2, 1815, the eldest son of Stephen Richards and Phoebe Buell. He was educated at the Johnstown district grammar school and at Potsdam Academy, New York; and was called to the bar of Upper Canada in 1837 (Q.C., 1850). From 1848 to 1853 he represented Leeds in the Legislative Assembly of Canada; and from 1851 to 1853 he was attorney-general for Upper Canada in the Hincks-Baldwin administration. In 1853 he was appointed a puisne judge of the Court of Common Pleas in Upper Canada; and in 1873 he became chief justice of this court. In 1875, when the Supreme Court of Canada was formed, he became its first chief justice; and from July to October, 1876, he was deputy governor of Canada, during the absence of Lord Dufferin (q.v.) in British Columbia. He retired from the bench in 1879; and he died at Ottawa on January 26, 1889. In 1846 he married

Deborah Catharine (d. 1869), daughter of John Muirhead, of Niagara. He was created a knight bachelor in 1877; and in 1885 he was awarded the Confederation medal.

[*Cyc. Am. biog.*; Dent, *Can. port.*, vol. 1; *Can. parl. comp.*]

Richardson, Hugh (1784-1870), mariner, was born in London, England, in 1784, the son of a West India merchant, and came to Canada in 1820. He became the captain of the *Canada*, an early steamship on Lake Ontario, which was built by himself. He died in Toronto, Ontario, on August 2, 1870. He was the author of a pamphlet entitled *York Harbour* (York, U.C., 1833).

[J. Ross Robertson, *Landmarks of Canada* (Toronto, 1917).]

Richardson, Hugh (1826-1913), administrator of the North West Territories, was born at London, Upper Canada, in 1826, the son of Richard Richardson and Elizabeth Sara Miller. He studied law and was admitted to the bar of Upper Canada in 1847. Later, he went to the West, and became legal adviser of the lieutenant-governor of the North West Territories from 1876 to 1887. From 1887 to 1903 he was one of the judges of the Supreme Court of the North West Territories; and from 1897 to 1898 he was administrator of the North West Territories. He died at Ottawa on July 15, 1913.

[Morgan, *Can. men* (1912).]

Richardson, James (1791-1875), bishop of the Methodist Episcopal Church in Canada (1858-75), was born at Kingston, Upper Canada, on January 29, 1791, the son of Captain James Richardson, of the provincial marine. He served in the provincial marine during the War of 1812, and lost an arm at Sackett's Harbour. In 1818 he joined the Methodist Episcopal Church, and became a local preacher. In 1824 he became an itinerant minister; in 1832 he was appointed editor of the *Christian Guardian*; and in 1858 he was elected bishop of the Methodist Episcopal Church of Canada. He died at Clover Hill, Toronto, on March 9, 1875. In 1813 he married Rebecca Dennis, of Kingston; and by her he had several children.

[T. Webster, *Life of Rev. James Richardson* (Toronto, 1876); A. H. Young (ed.), *The parish register of Kingston, Upper Canada* (Kingston, Ont., 1921); *Dict. Can. biog.*, vol. 10.]

Richardson, James (1810-1883), geologist, was born in Perthshire, Scotland, on March 29, 1810, and came to Canada early in life. He became a farmer in Beauharnois county, Lower Canada; and interested himself in geology. He was persuaded by Sir William Logan (q.v.) to join the Geological Survey of Canada; and he was one of the first practical geologists to make a survey of the Canadian

north-west. He was on the staff of the Geological Survey for thirty-six years; and in his later years he was cabinet keeper of the Survey. He died at Matane, Quebec, on November 18, 1883. Richardson Inlet, in the Queen Charlotte Islands, was named after him by G. M. Dawson (q.v.) in 1878.

[J. T. Walbran, *British Columbia coast names* (Ottawa, 1909).]

Richardson, James Armstrong (1885-1939), chancellor of Queen's University (1929-39), was born in Kingston, Ontario, on August 21, 1885; and was educated at Queen's University (B.A., 1906; LL.D.). He became president of James Richardson and Sons, grain merchants, and an outstanding Canadian financier and capitalist. In 1929 he succeeded Sir R. Borden (q.v.) as chancellor of Queen's University. He was a pioneer in the development of Canadian aviation. He died at Winnipeg, Manitoba, on June 27, 1939.

[*Can. who's who*, 1936-37; *Canadian aviation*, July, 1939; *Saturday night*, July 8, 1939.]

Richardson, John (1755?-1831), merchant and executive councillor of Lower Canada, was born at Portsoy, Banffshire, Scotland, about 1755, the son of John Richardson and a daughter of George Phyn, of the Corse of Monelly. He was thus, through his mother, a first cousin of both James Phyn (q.v.) and John Forsyth (q.v.). He came to America in 1773, and entered the employ of Phyn and Ellice at Schenectady. During the American Revolution he saw service on a privateer. In 1787 he removed to Canada and entered the employ of Robert Ellice and Co. This firm, however, was dissolved in 1790; and Richardson became a partner in its successor, which was known as Forsyth, Richardson and Co. This firm became one of the firms that supplied the XY Company; and on the union of the XY and North West companies in 1804, its members became partners in the North West Company. He represented Montreal in the Legislative Assembly of Lower Canada from 1792 to 1796, and from 1804 to 1808; in 1804 he was appointed a member of the Executive Council of the province; and in 1816, a member of the Legislative Council. In 1817 he was one of the founders of the Bank of Montreal. He died at Montreal on May 18, 1831. Some of his letters have been published by E. A. Cruikshank in the *Papers and Records* of the Ontario Historical Society, 1905.

[Adam Shortt, *The Hon. John Richardson* (Journal of the Canadian Bankers Association, 1921); R. Campbell, *A history of the Scotch Presbyterian Church, St. Gabriel Street, Montreal* (Montreal, 1887).]

Richardson, Sir John (1787-1865), explorer and author, was born at Nith Place, Dumfries, Scotland, on November 5, 1787. He was educated at Edinburgh University (M.D., 1816); and in 1807 he qualified as a member of the Royal College of Surgeons. From 1807 to 1815 he served as a naval surgeon in the Napoleonic Wars; but in 1815 went on half-pay. He accompanied Sir John Franklin (q.v.) on his journeys of discovery in north-western America in 1819-22 and in 1825-27; and on the latter occasion, he was in charge of the party that explored the shores of the Arctic Ocean from the mouth of the Mackenzie to the mouth of the Coppermine. He contributed the natural history notes to Franklin's *Narrative* of his first expedition, and an account of his discoveries, as well as other matters, to Franklin's *Narrative* of his second expedition. In 1848, when it was decided to send a search expedition after that of Franklin, he was appointed to command it, with Dr. John Rae (q.v.) as second-in-command; but he returned to England in 1849, leaving Rae in charge. He died at Grasmere, England, on June 5, 1865. He was elected a fellow of the Royal Society in 1825, and he was knighted in 1846. Besides many scientific publications, he was the author of *An Arctic searching expedition* (2 vols., London, 1851).

[J. McIlraith, *Life of Sir John Richardson* (London, 1868); *Dict. nat. biog.*]

Richardson, John (1796-1852), soldier and author, was born at Queenston, Upper Canada, on October 4, 1796, the eldest son of Dr. Robert Richardson and Madeleine, daughter of Col. John Askin, of Detroit. He was educated at Detroit and Amherstburg. He served as a cadet during the earlier part of of the War of 1812, but was taken prisoner at Moraviantown in 1813, and spent a year in captivity in the United States. He then obtained a commission in the British army, and went to England. In 1818 he was placed on half pay; and he lived in London until 1834, devoting part of his time to literary work. From 1834 to 1837 he served with the British Auxiliary Legion in Spain, attaining his majority, and winning the cross of the military order of St. Ferdinand. In 1838 he returned to Canada; and in 1840 he settled at Brockville, Upper Canada. Here he edited successively *The New Era, or Canadian Chronicle* (1840-42), and *The Canadian Loyalist* (1843-44). In 1845 he was appointed superintendent of police of the Welland Canal; but this post was abolished in 1846. For several years he lived in Montreal; and about 1850 he went to New York. Here he died, in lonely poverty, on May 12, 1852. About 1830 he married in England a wife whose Christian names were Maria Caroline; she died at St. Catharines, Canada West, on August 16, 1845.

As an author, Richardson tried his hand at various types of literature. His first publication was a poem, *Tecumseh, or The warrior of the west* (London, 1828). He then wrote several works of fiction, *Écarté, or The salons of Paris* (3 vols., London, 1829), *Kensington gardens in*

1830 (London, 1830), *Wacousta, or The prophecy: A tale of the Canadas* (3 vols., London, 1832), and *The Canadian brothers, or The prophecy fulfilled* (2 vols., Montreal, 1840), the latter republished under the title *Matilda Montgomerie* (New York, 1851). His most valuable works, however, were autobiographical and historical: *Movements of the British Legion* (London, 1837), *Personal memoirs* (Montreal, 1838), *The war of 1812* (Brockville, 1842; new ed., by A. C. Casselman, Toronto, 1902), *Eight years in Canada* (Montreal, 1847), and *The Guards in Canada* (Montreal, 1848). After going to New York he published a number of cheap novels, *Hardscrabble* (New York, 1850), *Wau-nan-gee, or The massacre of Chicago* (New York, 1850), *The monk knight of St. John* (New York, 1850), and *Westbrook, or The outlaw* (New York, n.d.). An anonymous article published by him in 1849, entitled *A trip to Walpole island and Port Sarnia*, has been republished, with notes, by A. H. U. Colquhoun (Toronto, 1923).

[W. R. Riddell, *John Richardson* (Toronto, 1923); A. C. Casselman (ed.), *Richardson's War of 1812* (Toronto, 1902); *Dict. nat. biog.*; *Cyc. Am. biog.*; Morgan, *Cel. Can.* and *Bib. can.*; R. P. Baker, *History of English-Canadian literature to the Confederation* (Cambridge, Mass., 1920); A. MacMechan, *Headwaters of Canadian literature* (Toronto, 1924).]

Richardson, Robert Lorne (1860-1921), journalist and author, was born at Balderson, Lanark county, Ontario, on June 2, 1860, the son of Joseph Richardson and Harriet Thompson. In 1882 he went to Winnipeg and in 1889 he became the founder and editor of the Winnipeg *Tribune*. From 1896 to 1900 he represented Lisgar in the Canadian House of Commons. He died at Winnipeg on November 6, 1921. He was the author of two novels, *Colin of the ninth concession* (Toronto, 1903) and *The Camerons of Bruce* (Toronto, 1906).

[Morgan, *Can. men* (1912).]

Richey, Matthew (1803-1883), Methodist preacher, was born in Ramelton, in the north of Ireland, on May 25, 1803. His parents were Presbyterians, but at the age of fourteen he became converted to Methodism, and shortly afterward sailed to Canada. He was ordained a minister of the Methodist Church in 1825, and in 1836 he was appointed principal of Upper Canada Academy in Cobourg, Upper Canada. From 1841 to 1843 he was in Toronto, and thence he was moved successively to Kingston and Montreal. In 1849 he was appointed acting president of the Canada Methodist Conference, and in 1851 president. In 1856 he was chosen president of the "Methodist Conference of Eastern British America." He died in Halifax, Nova Scotia, on October 24, 1883. He published *The internal witness of the Spirit the common privilege of Christian believers* (Charlottetown, P.E.I., 1829); *Sermon preached for the benefit of the poor* (Halifax, N.S., 1833); *Sermon on the death of the Rev. William McDonald* (Halifax, N.S., 1834); *Short and scriptural method with Antipedo-baptists* (Halifax); *Memoir of the late Rev. William Black* (Halifax, N.S., 1839); *Sermons delivered on various occasions* (Toronto, 1840); *Two letters addressed to the "Church" exposing the intolerance and bigotry of that journal* (Toronto, 1843); *An address at the inauguration of the Young Men's Christian Association* (Halifax, N.S., 1854); *Britain's refuge, a discourse on the fall of Sebastopol* (Halifax, N.S., 1855); *Sermon on the death of Rev. Wm. Bennett* (Halifax, N.S., 1858); *Sermon on the death of Rev. W. Croscombe* (Halifax, N.S., 1860); and *Plea for the confederation of the colonies of British North America* (Charlottetown, P.E.I., 1867).

[*Dom. ann. reg.*, 1883; *Cyc. Am. biog.*; Taylor, *Brit. Am.*, vol. 3; W. G. MacFarlane, *New Brunswick bibliography* (Saint John, N.B., 1895).]

Richey, Matthew Henry (1828-1911), lieutenant-governor of Nova Scotia (1883-88), was born at Windsor, Nova Scotia, on June 10, 1828, the eldest son of the Rev. Matthew Richey (q.v.) and Louisa Matilda Nicholls. He was educated at the College School, Windsor, at Upper Canada College, and elsewhere, and was called to the bar in 1850 (Q.C., 1873). He was elected to the city council of Halifax in 1858, and held the office of mayor from 1864 to 1867, and from 1875 to 1878. In 1878 he was returned to the Canadian House of Commons in the Conservative interest for Halifax city and county, and was re-elected in 1882. On July 4, 1883, he was appointed lieutenant-governor of Nova Scotia, and his term of office lasted until 1888. He died in Halifax, Nova Scotia, on February 21, 1911. In June, 1854, he married Sarah Lavina, daughter of the Hon. J. H. Anderson. For several years he was a governor of Dalhousie College; and he was president of the Nova Scotia Historical Society (1893-95). In 1884 he received the honorary degree of D.C.L. from Mount Allison University.

[Morgan, *Can. men* (1912); *Can. parl. comp.*]

Richmond, Charles Gordon Lennox, fourth Duke of (1764-1819), governor-general of Canada (1818-19), was born in 1764, the only son of Lord George Henry Lennox and Louisa, daughter of the fourth Marquis of Lothian. From 1790 to 1806 he represented Sussex in the British House of Commons; and in 1806 he succeeded his uncle in the dukedom. From 1807 to 1813 he was lord-lieutenant of Ireland; and in 1818 he was appointed governor-general of Canada. He died of hydrophobia, contracted from the bite of a pet fox, near Richmond, Upper Canada, on August 28, 1819. In 1789 he married Lady Charlotte,

daughter of Alexander, fourth Duke of Gordon; and by her he had several children.

[E. A. Cruikshank, *Charles Lennox, the fourth Duke of Richmond* (Ont. Hist. Soc., papers and records, 1927); *Dict. nat. biog.*; Dent, *Can. port.*, vol. 3; Morgan, *Cel. Can.*]

Richter, John George (1854-1932), insurance expert, was born near Hespeler, Ontario, on September 18, 1854. In 1883 he became general manager of the London Life Insurance Company, and in 1920 its president; and he had not a little to do with the development of life insurance in Canada. He died in London, Ontario, on October 11, 1932. In 1890 he was elected a fellow of the Actuarial Society of America.

[F. Landon, *John George Richter* (London, Ont., 1935); *Can. who was who*, vol. 1.]

Riddell, John Henry (1863-1952), clergyman and educationist, was born near Bolton, Canada West, on November 1, 1863, and died at Carleton Place, Ontario, on November 9, 1952. He was educated at Victoria University (B.A., 1890; B.D., 1892), and became a minister of the Methodist Church. He was pastor of several churches in Manitoba, and then, in 1896, he became professor of classics in Wesley College, Winnipeg. In 1903 he left Winnipeg to found Alberta College in Edmonton; and in 1917 he returned to Winnipeg as president of Wesley College. He retired in 1938. Victoria University conferred on him the degree of D.D. in 1906, and the University of Alberta that of LL.D. He was the author of *Methodism in the middle West* (Toronto, 1946).

[*Can. who's who*, 1948.]

Riddell, Robert Gerald (1908-1951), educationist and diplomat, was born at Edmonton, Alberta, on May 4, 1908, the son of the Rev. John Henry Riddell (q.v.), and died at Virginia Beach, Virginia, on March 16, 1951. He was educated at the University of Manitoba (B.A., 1930), the University of Toronto (M.A., 1931), and New College, Oxford (B.A., 1933; B.Litt., 1934). He taught history at the University of Toronto from 1934 to 1942; but in 1943 he entered the department of external affairs at Ottawa. He rose rapidly in this department, and in 1950 he was appointed Canada's permanent delegate to the United Nations, with the rank of ambassador. A brilliant career was cut short by his sudden and untimely death. He was the author of *Canadian portraits* (Toronto, 1940).

[Toronto *Globe and Mail*, March 17, 1951; *Encyc. Can.*]

Riddell, Walter Alexander (1881-1963), diplomat, was born at Stratford, Ontario, August 5, 1881. He was educated at Manitoba College, University of Manitoba (B.A., 1907), at Columbia University (M.A., 1908; Ph.D., 1916), and at the Union Theological Seminary (B.D., 1912). He did graduate research in Ottawa, Paris, and London. He then undertook social surveys for the Presbyterian and Methodist churches (1913). He became superintendent of trades and labour for the Ontario government in 1916 and was Ontario's first deputy minister of labour in 1919, during which time he drafted the mother's allowance and minimum wage acts of 1920. He was with the International Labour office from 1920 to 1925 under the League of Nations. He was advisory officer to the Canadian delegation to the League of Nations from 1925 to 1927, and counsellor at the Canadian legation at Washington (1937-40). He was Canadian High Commissioner to New Zealand from 1940 until 1946, when he retired from public service and became professor of international relations at the University of Toronto until his retirement in 1952.

Dr. Riddell wrote *The rise of ecclesiastical control in Quebec* (1916); *World security by conference* (1947); *Documents on Canadian foreign policy, 1917-1939* (Toronto, 1962); as well as numerous other articles and surveys.

As Canada's representative at the League of Nations meeting in 1935, he moved that sanctions be applied against Italy because of her invasion of Ethiopia. His move was repudiated by the Canadian government and he was soon recalled from the League position. On his retirement from the University of Toronto, Dr. Riddell was employed as a labour conciliation officer for the Ontario government. He died at Algonquin Park, Ontario, July 27, 1963.

[*Can. who's who*, 1961-63; Metropolitan Toronto Library Board, *Biographical scrapbooks*, vols. 3, 21.]

Riddell, William Renwick (1852-1945), jurist and historian, was born in the township of Hamilton, Canada West, on April 6, 1852. He was educated at Victoria University, Cobourg (B.A., 1874; B.Sc., 1876; LL.B., 1878), and at Osgoode Hall, Toronto; and was called to the Ontario bar in 1883 (Q.C., 1894). He practised law first in Cobourg, Ontario, and then in Toronto; and in 1906 he was appointed a judge of the King's Bench division of the High Court of Justice of Ontario. In 1925 he was transferred to the Appellate division of the Supreme Court of Ontario; and he retained this position until his death at Toronto, Ontario, on February 18, 1945. He was an LL.D. of Lafayette College (1912), McMaster University (1915), the University of Toronto (1916), Northwestern University (1917), the University of Rochester (1917), Wesleyan University (1918), Yale University (1918), and Boston University (1920), an L.A.D. of Syracuse University (1911), a J.U.D. of Trinity College, Hartford (1913), and a D.C.L. of Colby College (1925); and in 1917 he was elected a fellow of the Royal Society of Canada. He was the author of *The legal profession in Upper Canada in its early periods* (Toronto, 1916), *Robert (Fleming) Gourlay* (Toronto, 1916),

The constitution of Canada in its history and practical working (New Haven, Conn., 1917), *Old province tales* (Toronto, 1920), *Upper Canada sketches* (Toronto, 1922), *The Canadian constitution in form and fact* (New York, 1923), *William Kirby* (Toronto, 1923), *John Richardson* (Toronto, 1923), *The life of William Dummer Powell* (Lansing, Mich., 1924), *The life of John Graves Simcoe* (Toronto, 1926), *Michigan under British rule* (Lansing, Mich., 1926), *The bar and courts of the province of Upper Canada, or Ontario* (Toronto, 1928), and a large number of papers on legal and historical subjects, published in a great variety of periodicals, of which a complete collection is to be found in the Riddell Library in Osgoode Hall, Toronto.

[*Proc. Roy. Soc. Can.*, 1945; *Can. who's who*, 1936-37; *Who's who among North American authors*, vol. 6; *Who's who*, 1944.]

Ridout, John Gibbs (1840-1911), lawyer, was born at Toronto, Upper Canada, on August 22, 1840, the son of Thomas Gibbs Ridout (q.v.). He joined the Prince of Wales Royal Canadian Regiment in 1858 as an ensign, and was promoted to the rank of lieutenant in 1862. In 1871, however, he retired from the army, and was called to the bar of Ontario. He became an authority on patent law, and was the author of a *Treatise on the patent law of the Dominion of Canada* (Toronto, 1894). He died at Toronto, Ontario, on August 22, 1911.

[Morgan, *Can. men* (1912).]

Ridout, Thomas (1754-1829), surveyor-general of Upper Canada (1810-29), was born at Sherborne, Dorsetshire, England, on March 17, 1754, the son of George Ridout. He emigrated to Maryland in 1774; and spent the period of the American Revolution trading with the West Indies and France. In 1787 he was captured by the Indians and was brought to Canada. He obtained employment in 1792 in the commissariat department of Upper Canada, and in 1793 in the surveyor-general's office. In 1799 he was appointed joint acting surveyor-general of the province; and in 1810 surveyor-general. From 1812 to 1816 he was a member of the Legislative Assembly for the east riding of York and Simcoe county; in 1825 he was appointed a member of the Legislative Council of Upper Canada; and he sat in the Council until his death, at York (Toronto), on February 8, 1829. He was twice married, (1) in 1776 to Isabella, sister-in-law of John Donovan, postmaster of Hancock, Virginia, by whom he had one son; and (2) in 1789 to Mary, daughter of Alexander Campbell, a United Empire Loyalist, of Fort Edward, Bay of Quinte, by whom he had seven sons and five daughters.

[Matilda Edgar, *Ten years of Upper Canada* (Toronto, 1890); E. M. Chadwick, *Ontarian families* (2 vols., Toronto, 1894-98).]

Ridout, Thomas Gibbs (1792-1861), cashier of the Bank of Upper Canada (1822-61), was born near Sorel, Lower Canada, on October 10, 1792, the third son of Thomas Ridout (q.v.). He came with his parents to Newark (Niagara), and then to York (Toronto), when his father entered the service of the government of Upper Canada; and he was educated under the Rev. John Strachan (q.v.) at Cornwall, Upper Canada. During the War of 1812 he was deputy assistant commissary general for Upper Canada, and he remained in the commissariat until 1820. In 1822 he was appointed cashier (or general manager) of the Bank of Upper Canada, and he continued in this position until shortly before his death on July 29, 1861. He was twice married, (1) in 1825 to Anne Maria Louisa, daughter of Daniel Sullivan, by whom he had two sons and one daughter; and (2) in 1834 to Matilda Ann, daughter of Hollingsworth Bramley, of Yorkshire, England, and by her he had six sons and five daughters.

[Matilda Edgar, *Ten years of Upper Canada* (Toronto, 1890); E. M. Chadwick, *Ontarian families* (2 vols., Toronto, 1894-98); Morgan, *Cel. Can.*]

Riedesel, Friedrich Adolphus, Baron von (1738-1800), soldier, was born at his ancestral castle of Lauterbach, in Hesse, Germany, on June 3, 1738. He became an officer in the army of the Duke of Brunswick; and in 1776 he was sent to America, with the rank of major-general, in command of the force of German mercenaries lent to the British government by the Duke of Brunswick. He commanded this force throughout the remainder of the American revolutionary war; and he returned to Europe, with the remnants of his force, in 1783. He continued in Europe his military career, and in 1787 was promoted to the rank of lieutenant-general. In 1794 he was appointed commandant of the city of Brunswick; and here he died on January 6, 1800. His papers were published by Marc von Eelking under the title *Leben und Wirken des herzoglich braunschweig'schen General-Leutnants Friedrich Adolph Riedesel, Freiherrn zu Eisenbach* (3 vols., Leipzig, 1856), and were partially translated into English by W. L. Stone under the title *Memoirs and letters and journals during his residence in America* (2 vols., Albany, 1868). His wife, Friederike Charlotte Luise, Freifrau von Riedesel (1764-1808), who accompanied him to America, published *Die Berufs-Reise nach America* (Berlin, 1801), and this has been twice translated, first under the title *Letters and memoirs relating to the war of American independence* (New York, 1827), and secondly, by W. L. Stone, under the title *Letters and journals relating to the war of the American Revolution* (Albany, 1867).

[G. Monarque, *Un général allemand au Canada: Le Baron Friedrich Adolphus von Riedesel* (Montreal, 1927); *Cyc. Am. biog.*]

Riel, Louis (1844-1885), leader in the North West rebellions of 1870 and 1885, was born at St. Boniface, Manitoba, on October 22, 1844, the son of Louis Riel and Julie Lagimonière, and grandson of Jean Baptiste Riel, a native of Berthier, Lower Canada. He was educated at the Seminary in Montreal, and then returned to the West. In 1869 he became secretary of the *Comité national des Métis*, an organization formed to resist the establishment of Canadian authority in the North West. Later in the same year he was elected president of the provisional government set up by the rebels. He escaped from the country in August, 1870, on the arrival of the expeditionary force under Wolseley; but in 1873, and again in 1874, he was elected to represent Provencher, in the Canadian House of Commons. In 1874, on taking the oath, he was expelled from the House; and in 1875 a warrant of outlawry was issued against him. He took refuge in Montana, and there he remained until, in the summer of 1884, he was invited to return to Canada to organize the half-breeds of the North West Territories so as to obtain redress of their grievances. The outcome of his visit to Canada was a second rebellion in the North West. On the defeat of the rebels at Batoche, on May 12, 1885, by General Middleton (q.v.), Riel was captured. He was tried at Regina, in July, on the charge of high treason, was found guilty, and on November 16, 1885, was hanged in the Mounted Police barracks at Regina. Riel was a man of some ability, but of an unbalanced mind; and over the question of his sanity opinions are still divided. After his death some poems he had written were published under the title *Poésies religieuses et politiques* (Montreal, 1886).

[Sir J. Pope, *Correspondence of Sir John Macdonald* (Toronto, 1921); A. G. Morice, *Dictionnaire historique des Canadiens et des Métis français de l'ouest* (Quebec, 1908), and *A critical history of the Red River rebellion* (Winnipeg, 1935); *Can. who was who*, vol. 2; Le Jeune, *Dict. gén.*; E. B. Osler, *The man who had to hang* (Toronto, 1961); G. H. Needler, *Louis Riel* (Toronto, 1957); W. M. Davidson, *The life and times of Louis Riel* (Calgary, 1952); H. Bowsfield, *Louis Riel, the rebel and the hero* (Don Mills, 1971); G. F. G. Stanley, *The birth of western Canada: A history of the Riel rebellions* (London, 1936); J. K. Howard, *Strange empire, a narrative of the north-west* (New York, 1952).]

Rinfret, Fernand (1883-1939), secretary of state for Canada (1926-30 and 1935-39), was born in Montreal, Quebec, on February 28, 1883. He became a journalist, and from 1909 to 1926 was editor of *Le Canada*, a Montreal newspaper. From 1920 to 1939 he represented the St. James division of Montreal in the Canadian House of Commons; and from 1926 to 1930, and again from 1935 to 1939, he was secretary of state in the Canadian government. From 1932 to 1934 he was also mayor of Montreal. He died at Los Angeles, California, on July 12, 1939. A man of scholarly and literary tastes, he was elected in 1920 a fellow of the Royal Society of Canada; and he was the author of *Louis Fréchette* (St. Jérôme, Que., 1906), *Octave Crémazie* (St. Jérôme, Que., 1906), and *Pensées et souvenirs* (Montreal, 1942).

[*Can. who's who*, 1936-37; *Can. parl. comp.*]

Rinfret, Thibaudeau (1879-1962), chief justice, was born in Montreal, Quebec, June 22, 1879. He was educated at St. Mary's College, Montreal (B.A., 1897), Laval University, and McGill University (B.C.L., 1900). He became an advocate in 1901 and King's Counsel in 1912. He practised law in St. Jérôme and Montreal. In 1922 he became a judge of the Superior Court of Quebec and in 1924 was appointed to the Supreme Court of Canada. He was a law professor at McGill University for ten years and a justice of the Supreme Court for thirty years, ten years as chief justice.

An expert on constitutional law, he was a member of the court when it ruled that a provincial government could not delegate its powers to the federal government or vice-versa.

He was a lover of sports events and opera. He was a regent of the University of Ottawa and, after his retirement from the Supreme Court in 1954, he worked on a revision of the Civil Code of Quebec. He died at Montreal, Quebec, July 25, 1962.

[Metropolitan Toronto Library Board, *Biographical scrapbooks*, vols. 20, 86; *Can. who's who*, 1949-51.]

Ringuet (pseud.). See **Panneton, Philippe.**

Rintoul, William (1797-1851), clergyman, was born at Kincardine, Scotland, on October 30, 1797, and was educated at Edinburgh and Glasgow universities. He was ordained a minister of the Presbyterian Church in England in 1821; and in 1831 he was sent to Canada by the Glasgow Colonial Society as the first minister of St. Andrew's Church, York (Toronto). In 1834 he was transferred to Streetsville, Upper Canada; and in 1836 he was elected moderator of the synod of the Presbyterian Church of Canada, in connection with the Church of Scotland. In 1844, however, he threw in his lot with the Free Church; and he was the first professor of Hebrew in Knox College, Toronto. In 1850 he accepted a call to the Scotch Presbyterian Church in Montreal; and he died on September 13, 1851, at Trois Pistoles, Canada East, while on a missionary visit to Métis, on the lower St. Lawrence.

[R. Campbell, *A history of the Scotch Presbyterian Church, St. Gabriel Street, Montreal* (Montreal, 1887).]

Riordan, Charles (1847-1931), paper-manufacturer, was born at Ballybunnion, county Kerry, Ireland, on November 28, 1847. He came with his parents to America in 1850, and in 1863 he came to Canada to join his brother John, who had started a paper mill at St. Catharines, Canada West. He became one of the pioneers of the pulp and paper industry in Canada, and was president of the Riordan Paper Company from 1882 to 1921. On the death of his brother John in 1884, he became president of the *Mail* Printing Company of Toronto; and in 1895 he bought the *Empire* newspaper, and amalgamated it with the *Mail*, thus forming the Toronto *Mail and Empire*. He died in Montreal, Quebec, on August 17, 1931.

[*Can. who was who*, vol. 1; *Pulp and paper magazine*, Sept., 1931.]

Riquart, Jean (d. 1726), pioneer, was a native of France, and probably emigrated to Canada in 1664. In 1667 he became the first settler in what became later Ste. Anne de la Pérade; and he died near Ste. Anne de la Pérade on July 8, 1726. He was the ancestor of the families in the province of Quebec which to-day bear the name "Ricard".

[R. Douville, *Jean Riquart, premier colon de Sainte-Anne de la Pérade* (Three Rivers, Que., 1943).]

Ritchie, John William (1808-1890), jurist, was born at Annapolis, Nova Scotia, on March 26, 1808, the son of the Hon. Thomas Ritchie. He was educated privately, and in 1831 was called to the bar of Nova Scotia. In 1839 he was appointed law clerk of the Legislative Council of Nova Scotia; and this position he held until 1860. In 1864 he was appointed a member of the Legislative Council, and from 1864 to 1867 he was solicitor-general of the province. In 1866 he was a representative of Nova Scotia at the conference in London which resulted in the framing of the British North America Act; and in 1867 he was called by royal proclamation to the Senate of Canada. In 1870 he was appointed a judge of the Supreme Court of Nova Scotia; and in 1873 he became a judge in equity. He resigned from the bench in 1882; and he died at his home at Belmont on December 18, 1890. In 1838 he married Amelia, daughter of the Hon. W. B. Almon. In 1878 he was elected first president of the Nova Scotia Historical Society.

[L. G. Power, *Our first president: The Hon. J. W. Ritchie* (Coll. Nova Scotia Hist. Soc., 1918); Charles St. C. Stayner, *John William Ritchie: One of the Fathers of Confederation* (Coll. Nova Scotia Hist. Soc., 1968); *Cyc. Am. biog.*]

Ritchie, Sir William Johnstone (1813-1892), chief justice of Canada (1879-92), was born in Annapolis, Nova Scotia, on October 28, 1813, the son of the Hon. Thomas Ritchie and

Elizabeth Wildman Johnstone. He was educated at Pictou Academy, and was called to the bar of New Brunswick in 1838 (Q.C., 1854). From 1847 to 1851 he represented the city and county of Saint John in the House of Assembly of New Brunswick. In 1855 he was made a puisne judge of the Supreme Court of New Brunswick, and in 1865 he became chief justice of the province. On October 8, 1875, he was appointed a puisne judge of the Supreme Court of Canada, and in 1879 he was made chief justice of Canada. From July 6, 1881, to January, 1882, he acted as deputy governor of Canada during the absence of Lord Lorne (q.v.) in England, and again from September 6 to December, 1882. On March 5, 1884, he was appointed deputy to the governor-general, Lord Lansdowne (q.v.). He died at Ottawa on September 25, 1892. He married (1) in 1843, Martha Strang of St. Andrew's (d. 1847), and (2) in 1854, Grace Vernon, daughter of Thomas Nicholson of Saint John. He was created a knight bachelor in 1881. He published *The Chesapeake; before Mr. Justice Ritchie, with his decision thereon* (Saint John, N.B., 1864), and *Observations of the Chief Justice of New Brunswick on a bill entitled "An Act to Establish a Supreme Court for the Dominion of Canada," presented to parliament on May 21, 1869, by the Hon. Sir John A. Macdonald, K.C.B.* (Saint John, N.B., 1870).

[*Cyc. Am. biog.*; *Can. parl. comp.*; Dent, *Can. port.*, vol. 2; J. W. Lawrence, *The judges of New Brunswick* (Saint John, N.B., 1907); W. G. MacFarlane, *New Brunswick bibliography* (Saint John, N.B., 1895).]

Ritchot, Joseph Noël (1825-1905), priest, was born at L'Assomption, Lower Canada, on December 25, 1825, and was ordained a priest of the Roman Catholic Church in 1855. After serving at Berthierville and Ste. Agathe des Monts in Canada East, he went west in 1862 and became the first parish priest at Qu'Appelle on the Saskatchewan, and later, from 1870 to his death, the parish priest at St. Norbert, Manitoba. In 1870 he exerted a moderating influence on Louis Riel (q.v.) and the rebels at Red River, and was one of the intermediaries sent by the rebels to Ottawa to arrange for the setting up of the province of Manitoba. In 1898 he was created an apostolic prothonotary. He died at St. Norbert, Manitoba, on March 16, 1905.

[A. M. Morice, *Dictionnaire historique des canadiens et des Métis français de l'ouest* (Kamloops, B.C., 1908); Allaire, *Dict. biog.*]

Ritter, Henry (1816-1853), painter, was born in Montreal, Lower Canada, in 1816. He studied painting in Hamburg and Düsseldorf, Germany; and he was notable especially for his pictures of the sea. He died on December 21, 1853.

[*Cyc. Am. biog.*]

Rivard, Adjutor (1868-1945), jurist and author, was born at St. Grégoire de Nicolet, Quebec, on January 22, 1868, and died at Quebec City, on July 17, 1945. He was educated at Laval University, and was called to the bar in 1891 (K.C., 1910). He practised law, first at Chicoutimi, and then at Quebec. He was appointed a judge of the Court of King's Bench in 1921, and remained on the bench until ill-health compelled his retirement in 1942. He published two legal treatises, *De la liberté de la presse* (Quebec, 1923) and *Manuel de la Cour d'Appel* (Quebec, 1941); but he was also a keen student of linguistics, and he was the author of *L'art de dire* (Quebec, 1899), *Manuel de la parole* (Quebec, 1902), *Etudes sur les parlers de France au Canada* (Quebec, 1914), *Chez nous* (Quebec, 1914), *Chez nos gens* (Quebec, 1918), and *Contes et propos divers* (Quebec, 1944). With L. P. Geoffrion (q.v.), he was joint author of *Le glossaire du parler français au Canada* (Quebec, 1930). He was elected a fellow of the Royal Society of Canada in 1908; and Laval University conferred on him the degree of D. Litt.

[*Proc. Roy. Soc. Can.*, 1946; *Can. who's who*, 1938-39; *Encyc. Can.*]

Robb, James Alexander (1859-1929), minister of finance for Canada (1925 and 1926-29), was born at Huntingdon, Quebec, on August 10, 1859, the son of Alexander Robb and Jenny Smith. He was educated at the Huntingdon Academy and became a prosperous flour-miller. From 1906 to 1908 he was mayor of Valleyfield, Quebec; and from 1908 to his death he represented Huntingdon and Châteauguay-Huntingdon in the Canadian House of Commons. In 1921 he became minister of trade and commerce in the King administration; in 1923 he was transferred to the portfolio of immigration and colonization, and in 1925 to that of finance. This portfolio he resumed on the return to power of the King government in 1926, and he held it until his death at Toronto on November 11, 1929.

[*Can. who was who*, vol. 1; *Can. parl. comp.*; Morgan, *Can. men* (1912).]

Robert, Joseph Arthur (1876-1939), priest and educationist, was born at Beauport, Quebec, on October 22, 1876. He was educated at the Quebec Seminary, and was ordained a priest of the Roman Catholic Church in 1902. After studying at Rome and at Louvain, he became in 1907 a professor of philosophy at Laval University; and he occupied this position until his death at Quebec, on March 21, 1939. He was the author of *Histoire de la philosophie* (Quebec, 1912), *Leçons de logique* (Quebec, 1914), *Leçons de morale* (Quebec, 1915), and *Leçons de psychologie* (Quebec, 1916).

[Allaire, *Dict. biog.*]

Roberton, Thomas Beattie (1879-1936), journalist and author, was born in Glasgow,

Scotland, on October 20, 1879. He emigrated to Canada in 1910; and in 1918 he joined the staff of the *Winnipeg Free Press*. He became associate editor-in-chief of this newspaper; and he died in Winnipeg on January 13, 1936. He was the author of a volume of historical essays entitled *The fighting bishop* (Ottawa, 1926), and after his death some of his fugitive journalistic writings were collected and published under the titles, *T.B.R.: Newspaper pieces* (Toronto, 1936) and *A second helping of newspaper pieces* (Toronto, 1937).

[*New York Times*, Jan. 15, 1936.]

Roberts, Sir Charles George Douglas (1860-1943), poet and novelist, was born at Douglas, York county, New Brunswick, on January 10, 1860, the son of the Rev. George Goodridge Roberts. He was educated at the University of New Brunswick (B.A., 1879; M.A., 1881; LL.D., 1906); and from 1885 to 1895 he was professor of English literature at King's College, Windsor. In 1897 he went to New York, and he lived and wrote there until 1907, when he went abroad. In 1911 he settled in England; and he saw service, first with the British, and then with the Canadian army, in the First World War. In 1925 he returned to Canada, and settled in Toronto, Ontario. Here he died on November 26, 1943. In 1890 he was elected a fellow of the Royal Society of Canada; and in 1926 he was the first recipient of the Society's Lorne Pierce medal for "the most outstanding contribution to Canadian literature". In 1935 he was created a knight bachelor on the recommendation of the Canadian government. In poetry, he published the following volumes: *Orion, and other poems* (Philadelphia, 1880), *In divers tones* (Boston, 1886), *Ave* (Toronto, 1892), *Songs of the common day* (Toronto, 1893), *The book of the native* (Boston, 1896), *New York nocturnes, and other poems* (Boston, 1898), *Poems* (New York, 1901), *The book of the rose* (Boston, 1903), *Poems* (Boston, 1907), *New poems* (London, 1919), *The sweet o' the year, and other poems* (Toronto, 1925), *The vagrant of time* (Toronto, 1927), *The iceberg, and other poems* (Toronto, 1934), *Selected poems* (Toronto, 1936), and *Canada speaks of Britain* (Toronto, 1941). In fiction, he was the author of the following books: *The raid from Beauséjour* (New York, 1894), *Reuben Dare's shad boat* (New York, 1895), *The forge in the forest* (Boston, 1896), *Earth's enigmas* (Boston, 1896), *Around the camp fire* (New York, 1896), *A sister to Evangeline* (Boston, 1898), *By the marshes of Minas* (Boston, 1900), *The heart of the ancient wood* (New York, 1900), *The kindred of the wild* (Boston, 1902), *Barbara Ladd* (Boston, 1902), *The watchers of the trails* (Boston, 1904), *Red Fox* (Boston, 1905), *The heart that knows* (Boston, 1906), *The haunters of the silences* (Boston, 1907), *The house in the water* (Boston, 1908), *The red oxen of Bonval* (New York, 1909), *The backwoodsmen* (London,

1909), *Kings in exile* (London, 1909), *More kindred of the wild* (London, 1911), *Neighbours unknown* (London, 1911), *Babes of the wild* (London, 1912), *The feet of the furtive* (London, 1912), *Hoof and claw* (London, 1913), *A Balkan prince* (London, 1913), *The secret trails* (London, 1916), *The ledge on Bald Face* (London, 1918), *In the morning of time* (London, 1919), *Wisdom of the wilderness* (London, 1922), *They that walk in the wild* (London, 1924), and *Eyes of the wilderness* (London, 1933). He was the author also of *The Canadian guide-book* (New York, 1891), *The land of Evangeline* (Kentville, N.S., 1895), *A history of Canada* (Boston, 1897), and *Canada in Flanders*, Vol. III (London, 1918); he translated P. A. de Gaspé's *The Canadians of old* (New York, 1890); and he edited *Poems of wild life* (London, 1888), *Northland lyrics* (Boston, 1899), and *Flying colours* (Toronto, 1942).

[E. M. Pomeroy, *Sir Charles G. D. Roberts* (Toronto, 1943); J. Cappon, *Charles G. D. Roberts* (Toronto, 1923) and *Roberts and the influences of his time* (Toronto, 1905); W. J. Keith, *Charles G. D. Roberts* (Toronto, 1969); *Proc. Roy. Soc. Can.*, 1944; *Can. who's who*, 1936-37; Morgan, *Can. men* (1912).]

Roberts, George Edward Theodore Goodridge (1877-1953), poet and novelist, was born in Fredericton, New Brunswick, on July 7, 1877, and died at Digby, Nova Scotia, on February 24, 1953. He was educated at the University of New Brunswick, and became a journalist. He was a war correspondent during the Spanish-American war, and served in the Canadian army during the First World War. He lived in many parts of the world; but despite his peripatetic life, he published thirty novels and several volumes of poetry. None of his novels achieved a great success, but his poetry attracted more attention, especially *The leather bottle* (Toronto, 1934). He was also joint author, with others, of *Northland lyrics* (Boston, 1899).

[Goodridge Macdonald, *Theodore Goodridge Roberts, poet and novelist* (Canadian Author and Bookman, Spring 1953); *Can. who's who*, 1948; *Encyc. Can.*]

Roberts, Jane Elizabeth Gostwycke. See **Macdonald, Mrs. Jane Elizabeth Gostwycke,** *née* **Roberts.**

Roberts, Richard (1874-1945), clergyman and author, was born in North Wales, on May 31, 1874; and was educated at the University of Wales and at the Theological College, Bala, North Wales. He was ordained a minister of the Presbyterian Church; and after serving in various charges in England, he came to America in 1917 as pastor of the church of the Pilgrims in Brooklyn, N.Y. In 1922 he came to Canada as pastor of the American Presbyterian Church in Montreal; and from 1928 to 1938 he was pastor of the Sherbourne Street

United Church in Toronto. From 1934 to 1936 he was moderator of the United Church of Canada. He died in New York, N.Y., on April 11, 1945. He was the author of *The renascence of faith* (London, 1912), *Personality and nationality* (London, 1914), *The church in the commonwealth* (London, 1917), *The red cap on the cross* (London, 1918), *The unfinished programme of democracy* (London, 1919), *That one face* (New York, 1919), *The Jesus of poets and prophets* (London, 1919), *The untried door* (New York, 1921), *What's best worth saying* (New York, 1922), *The Gospel at Corinth* (New York, 1924), *The ascending life* (New York, 1924), *The new man and the divine society* (New York, 1926), *Florence Simms* (New York, 1926), *The Christian God* (New York, 1929), *The spirit of God and the faith of to-day* (Chicago, 1930), *The preacher as man of letters* (New York, 1931), *That strange man upon his cross* (New York, 1934), and *The contemporary Christ* (New York, 1938).

[*Can. who's who*, 1936-37; *Who's who in America*, 1944-45.]

Roberts, William Goodridge (1904-1974), painter, was born in Barbados, British West Indies, September 24, 1904. He studied at the Beaux-Arts in Montreal and the Art Students League of New York.

A prolific painter, he was influenced by Matisse. He has been called Canada's first modern artist, introducing new ideas into Canadian art. He continued painting landscapes, still life, and nudes and did not move into the field of non-figurative painting. He was resident artist at Queen's University (1933-36) and the University of New Brunswick (1959-60). During the Second World War he was an official war artist with the R.C.A.F. He was an instructor with the Montreal Museum of Fine Arts (1939-43 and 1945-53) and is represented in the National Gallery of Canada, the Quebec Museum, and the Art Gallery of Ontario; he has exhibited in Europe, Mexico, South America, and throughout Canada and the United States. He was a member of the Canadian Group of Painters, the Society of Painters in Water Colour, the Society of Graphic Arts, and the Contemporary Art Society. He died at Montreal, Quebec, January 28, 1974.

[*Can. who's who,* 1970-72.]

Roberts, William Harris Lloyd (1884-1966), author and poet, was born in Fredericton, New Brunswick, October 21, 1884, and attended King's College School at Windsor, Nova Scotia, and schools in Fredericton. He began writing as a reporter for the *News* at Nelson, British Columbia, in 1911, and did writing and editing for the Canadian Immigration Service. After 1920 he devoted his time to writing. Among his works are *England over the seas* (poems, 1914); *The book of Roberts* (essays, 1923); *Along the Ottawa*

(poems, 1927); and *I sing of life* (poems, 1937). He was parliamentary correspondent for the *Christian Science Monitor* (1925-39). He died at Toronto, Ontario, June 28, 1966.

[*Can. who's who*, 1955-57.]

Robertson, Colin (1779?-1842), fur-trader, was born about 1779, and entered the service of the North West Company as a clerk prior to 1804. He was employed mainly in the English river department; but in September, 1809, he was dismissed from the service by John McDonald of Garth (q.v.). In 1814 he entered the employ of Lord Selkirk (q.v.) and the Hudson's Bay Company; and in 1818 he was the chief officer of the Hudson's Bay Company in the Athabaska district. In 1819 he was arrested by the Nor'Westers, but escaped, it was said, by breaking his parole. In 1820, he went to England, and was in London when the negotiations in regard to the union of the North West and Hudson's Bay companies were in progress; and his letters, preserved in Hudson's Bay House, are one of our chief sources for the history of these negotiations. In 1821 he was made a chief factor of the Hudson's Bay Company, and was placed in charge at Norway House. In 1824 he was transferred to Fort Churchill; in 1826, to Island Lake; and in 1830, to Swan River. He had leave of absence from 1832 to 1837; but from 1837 to 1839 he had charge of the New Brunswick district. He retired in 1840, with a pension. In 1841 he was elected to represent the Lake of Two Mountains in the first Legislative Assembly of united Canada; but he died at Montreal on February 3, 1842, from the effects of being thrown from his cariole the preceding day. His eldest son, Colin Robertson, Jr., died at Montreal, on November 29, 1844, aged 23.

[E. E. Rich (ed.), *Colin Robertson's correspondence book* (Toronto: The Champlain Society, 1939).]

Robertson, Gideon Decker (1874-1933), minister of labour for Canada (1918-21 and 1930-33), was born at Welland, Ontario, on August 26, 1874. He became a railway telegrapher and station agent, and from 1907 to 1914 was chairman of the telegraphers' organization of the Canadian Pacific Railway. In 1914 he was elected a vice-president of the Order of Railway Telegraphers. He was appointed a member of the Canadian Senate and was sworn of the Privy Council in 1917 as minister without portfolio, and in 1918 became minister of labour in the Borden government. He retired from office on the defeat of the Meighen government in 1921, but was reappointed minister of labour in the Bennett government in 1930. He died on August 5, 1933.

[*Can. parl. comp.*]

Robertson, Henry Hyndman (1859-1913), lawyer, was born near Dundas, Canada

West, on September 5, 1859, the son of the Hon. Thomas Robertson (q.v.), and the grandson of Colonel Titus Geer Simons (q.v.). He was educated at Upper Canada College and Osgoode Hall, Toronto, and was called to the bar in 1886 (K.C., 1908). He practised law in Hamilton, Ontario; and in 1906 was elected president of the Wentworth Historical Society. He died at Toronto, Ontario, on December 23, 1913. He was the author of *The Gore district militia* (Hamilton, Ont., 1904) and a number of papers contributed to the publications of the Ontario Historical Society and the Wentworth Historical Society.

[Morgan, *Can. men* (1912).]

Robertson, James (1800?-1878), clergyman and author, was born in Scotland about 1800, and was educated at the University of Aberdeen. He was ordained a priest of the Church of England in 1826, and was sent to Nova Scotia in 1829, as a missionary of the Society for the Propagation of the Gospel in Foreign Parts. He was for many years rector of Wilmot, Nova Scotia; and he was a voluminous contributor to the religious periodicals of the Maritime provinces. He died at Middleton, Nova Scotia, on January 19, 1878. His chief publication was *A treatise on infant baptism* (Halifax, N.S., 1836).

[*Dom. ann. reg.*, 1878.]

Robertson, James (1839-1902), superintendent of Presbyterian home missions (1881-1902), was born in the village of Dull, Perthshire, Scotland, on April 24, 1839, the son of James Robertson and Christina McCallum. He came to Canada with his parents in 1855 and was educated at the University of Toronto, at Princeton University, and at the Union Theological Seminary, New York. In 1869 he was ordained a minister of the Canada Presbyterian Church; and from 1869 to 1874 he was stationed at Norwich, Ontario. In 1874 he accepted the charge of Knox Church, Winnipeg; and in 1881 he was appointed superintendent of missions in Western Canada. This post he continued to fill until his death, at Toronto, on January 4, 1902; and "the story of his work is the history of the Presbyterian Church in Western Canada." In 1888 he was made a D.D. of the Presbyterian College of Montreal; and in 1895 he was elected moderator of the Presbyterian Church in Canada. In 1869 he married Mary Anne Cowing, of Blandford, Oxford county, Ontario; and by her he had two daughters.

[C. W. Gordon, *The life of James Robertson* (Toronto, 1908); Morgan, *Can. men* (1898); J. T. McNeill, *The Presbyterian church in Canada* (Toronto, 1925).]

Robertson, James Wilson (1857-1930), educationist and agricultural expert, was born at Dunlop, Ayrshire, Scotland, on November 2, 1857, and came to Canada with his parents in 1875. He became a farmer, and from 1886 to 1890 was professor of dairying in the Ontario Agricultural College. In 1890 he was appointed dairy commissioner for Canada, and agriculturist on the staff of the Central Experimental Farm in Ottawa; and from 1895 to 1904 he was commissioner of agriculture and dairying for Canada. From 1905 to 1910 he was principal of Macdonald College at Ste. Anne de Bellevue, Quebec. In 1919 he was appointed Canadian director of food supplies, and represented Canada on the food section of the Supreme Economic Council in Paris. He received the honorary degree of LL.D. from the University of Toronto (1903), from Queen's University (1903), from the University of New Brunswick (1904), and from McGill University (1909), and the degree of D.Sc. from Iowa University; and in 1905 he was created a C.M.G. He died at Ottawa, Ontario, on March 20, 1930.

[*Who's who in Canada*, 1930-31; Morgan, *Can. men* (1912); *Can. who's who*, 1910.]

Robertson, John Charles (1864-1956), educationist, was born at Brampton, Canada West, on April 2, 1864, and died at Toronto, Ontario, on February 24, 1956. He was educated at the University of Toronto (B.A., 1883; M.A., 1904) and Johns Hopkins University. He taught Greek at Victoria College, Toronto, from 1894 until his retirement in 1932. He was the author of a number of classical text-books and a volume of essays, entitled *Mixed company* (Toronto, 1939). With his son, H. G. Robertson, he was joint author of *The story of Greece and Rome* (London, 1928). He was also the compiler of *Latin songs, old and new* (Toronto, 1934). In 1938 he received from the University of Toronto the degree of LL.D.

[*Can. who's who*, 1948.]

Robertson, John Kellock (1885-1958), physicist, was born at Perth, Ontario, on January 2, 1885, and died in London, England, on June 24, 1958. He was educated at the University of Toronto (B.A., 1907; M.A., 1908); in 1909 he was appointed a lecturer in physics at Queen's University, Kingston; and from 1943 until his retirement in 1951 he was head of the department. He was the author of *X-rays and X-ray apparatus* (Toronto, 1924), *Introduction to physical optics* (New York, 1929), *Atomic artillery* (New York, 1937), and *Radiological physics* (New York, 1941), all of which ran into several editions. He was the author also of a picture of Perth during his boyhood, entitled *Tayville* (Toronto, 1932). He was elected a fellow of the Royal Society of Canada in 1926; and Queen's University conferred on him the honorary degree of LL.D. in 1951.

[*Proc. Roy. Soc. Can.*, 1959; *Can. who's who*, 1955-57.]

Robertson, John Palmerston (1841-1919), librarian, was born at Fortingal, Perthshire, Scotland, on May 23, 1841, and came to Canada with his parents in 1845. He became first a school-teacher, and then a journalist; and finally, in 1884, he was appointed provincial librarian of Manitoba. He died at Los Angeles, California, on April 11, 1919. He was the author of *A political manual of the province of Manitoba and the North West Territories* (Winnipeg, 1887).

[Morgan, *Can. men* (1912).]

Robertson, John Ross (1841-1918), journalist, historian, and philanthropist, was born in Toronto, on December 28, 1841, the son of John Robertson, of Toronto, and Margaret, daughter of Hector Sinclair, of Stornoway, Isle of Lewis, Scotland. He was educated at Upper Canada College, and early entered journalism. In 1866 he founded the *Daily Telegraph* (1866-71) in Toronto; and in 1876 he founded the *Evening Telegram*. The success of this paper laid the foundation of a large fortune, and enabled its proprietor to indulge his passion for philanthropy and for historical collections. He was the founder and benefactor of the Hospital for Sick Children, Toronto; and the John Ross Robertson collection of Canadian historical pictures in the Toronto Public Library was his creation. From 1896 to 1900 he sat in the Dominion House of Commons for East Toronto; and he rose to high rank in the Masonic order. He wrote *The history of freemasonry in Canada* (2 vols., Toronto, 1900); and he published *Robertson's Landmarks of Toronto* (6 vols., Toronto, 1894-1914), and *The diary of Mrs. John Graves Simcoe* (Toronto, 1912). In 1914 he was elected a fellow of the Royal Society of Canada; and he died in Toronto on May 30, 1918. He was twice married, (1) to Maria Louisa Gilbee (d. 1886), and (2) to Jessie Elizabeth Holland. By his first wife he had two sons.

[R. Poulton, *The paper tyrant: John Ross Robertson of the Toronto Telegram* (Toronto, 1971); *Proc. Roy. Soc. Can.*, 1919; Morgan, *Can. men* (1912); J. E. Middleton, *The municipality of Toronto* (3 vols., Toronto, 1923); *Can. who was who*, vol. 1.]

Robertson, Norman (1845-1936), local historian, was born in Belleville, Canada West, on June 27, 1845. In 1887 he was appointed treasurer of the county of Bruce in Ontario; and in 1901 he was elected first secretary of the Bruce County Historical Society. He was the author of *The history of the county of Bruce* (Toronto, 1906). He died at Walkerton, Ontario, on June 21, 1936.

[Rose, *Cyc. Can. biog.* (1888).]

Robertson, Norman Alexander (1904-1968), diplomat, was born in Vancouver, British Columbia, March 4, 1904, and educated at the University of British Columbia, Oxford University, and the Brookings Graduate School in Washington, U.S.A. Before joining the Canadian public service he taught at the University of British Columbia and at Harvard University. He began his diplomatic career in 1920 as third secretary in the department of external affairs and was stationed in Washington. After a period in Ottawa he was promoted first secretary in 1935 and counsellor in 1940. In 1941 he became under-secretary of state for external affairs and in 1946 was appointed High Commissioner for Canada in the United Kingdom. He was senior advisor to the Canadian delegation at the United Nations Organizing Conference in 1945 and attended the Paris Peace Conference in 1946. He became clerk of the Privy Council and secretary to the Cabinet in March, 1949; was again appointed High Commissioner to the United Kingdom in 1952; and in 1957 became ambassador to the United States. In 1958 he again became under-secretary of state for external affairs, a position which he held until 1964, when he was appointed Canada's chief negotiator in the Kennedy round of tariff negotiations at Geneva. Norman Robertson, along with Hume Wrong (q.v.) and Oscar Skelton (q.v.), was largely responsible for laying the foundations of the Canadian department of external affairs, in the 1920s and 1930s. During the Second World War he was the closest advisor of Prime Minister Mackenzie King and after the war was one of those most responsible for the respect in which Canadian foreign policy was held throughout the world. He constantly amazed his colleagues with his fund of knowledge and his calm good judgement. He died at Ottawa, Ontario, July 16, 1968.

[*Can. who's who*, 1961-63; *External Affairs*, vol. 20 (1968).]

Robertson, Thomas (1827-1905), jurist, was born at Ancaster, Upper Canada, on January 25, 1827, the son of Alexander Robertson and Matilda, daughter of Col. Titus Geer Simons (q.v.). He was educated at King's College, Toronto, and was called to the bar in 1852 (Q.C., 1873). He practised law in Hamilton, Ontario; and from 1878 to 1887 he represented Hamilton in the Canadian House of Commons. He was appointed a judge of the chancery divisions of the High Court of Justice in Ontario in 1887; and he remained on the bench until his resignation in 1903. He died at Hamilton, Ontario, on September 6, 1905.

[Morgan, *Can. men* (1898).]

Roberval, Jean François de la Rocque, Sieur de (1500?-1560), colonizer, was born either in Languedoc or in Picardy, about 1500. In 1541 he was commissioned by the king of France viceroy and lieutenant-general of New France, and appointed to command an expedition to follow up the discoveries of Jacques Cartier (q.v.). He set sail in 1542, and spent the winter of 1542-43 at Cartier's former headquarters near Quebec. In 1543, however, he returned with his colonists to France. He died in Paris in 1560.

[N. E. Dionne, *Jean François de la Rocque, Seigneur de Roberval* (Trans. Roy. Soc. Can., 1899); H. P. Biggar, *A collection of documents relating to Jacques Cartier and the Sieur de Roberval* (Ottawa, 1830); R. La Roque de Roquebrune, *Roberval* (Revue des questions historiques, 1934); S. E. Dawson, *The Saint Lawrence basin* (London, 1905); Le Jeune, *Dict. gén.*; *Dict. Can. biog.*, vol. 1.]

Robidoux, Joseph Emery (1843-1929), politician and jurist, was born at Laprairie, Canada East, on March 10, 1843. He was educated at St. Mary's College, Montreal, and at McGill University (D.C.L., 1887), and was called to the bar of Lower Canada in 1866. In 1877 he was appointed professor of civil law at McGill University. He represented Châteauguay in the Legislative Assembly of Quebec from 1884 to 1892 and from 1897 to 1900; and he was provincial secretary, and later attorney-general, in the Mercier administration, and provincial secretary in the Marchand administration. In 1900 he was appointed a judge of the Superior Court of Quebec; and he remained on the bench until 1926. He died at Montreal, Quebec, on March 15, 1929.

[P. G. Roy, *Les juges de la province de Québec* (Quebec, 1933); Morgan, *Can. men* (1912); *Can. parl. comp.*]

Robie, Simon Bradstreet (1770-1858), president of the Legislative Council of Nova Scotia (1827-38), was born at Marble Head, Massachusetts, in 1770, the son of Thomas Robie. Early in the American Revolution he was brought to Halifax, Nova Scotia, by his parents, who were loyalists; and he was educated at Halifax. About 1790 he was called to the bar of Nova Scotia; and in 1799 he was elected to represent Truro in the General Assembly of the province. In 1806 he was elected to represent Halifax county, and this seat he retained in the Assembly until 1824. In 1815 he was appointed solicitor-general of the province, and in 1817 he was elected speaker of the Assembly. Both these offices he held until 1824, when he was appointed master of the rolls in Nova Scotia. At the same time he became a member of both the Executive and Legislative councils; and in 1827 he was appointed president of the Legislative Council. He resigned from the bench in 1834; he ceased to preside over the Legislative Council in 1838; and he resigned from the Council in 1848. The rest of his life he spent in retirement, and he died at Halifax on January 3, 1858.

[I. Longworth, *Honorable Judge Robie* (Acadiensis, 1901).]

Robins, John Daniel (1884-1952), educationist and humorist, was born at Windsor, Ontario, on September 8, 1884, and died at To-

ronto, Ontario, on December 18, 1952. He was educated at Victoria College, University of Toronto (B.A., 1913; M.A., 1922), the University of Marburg, and the University of Chicago (Ph.D., 1927). He joined the staff of Victoria College in 1914, first in the department of German, and later in the department of English. From 1938 until his death he was professor of English and head of the department. He was the author of *The incomplete anglers* (Toronto, 1943) and *Cottage cheese* (Toronto, 1951), and he was editor of *A pocketful of Canada* (Toronto, 1946) and joint editor, with Margaret V. Ray, of *A book of Canadian humour* (Toronto, 1951).

[*Can. who's who*, 1948; *Encyc. Can.*]

Robinson, Albert Henry (1881-1956), painter, was born in Hamilton, Ontario, on January 2, 1881, and died at Montreal, Quebec, on October 7, 1956. He studied at the Hamilton Art School and at the Académie Julien and the Ecole des Beaux-Arts in Paris. He became an instructor in the Hamilton Art School, but in 1909 removed to Montreal and devoted his whole time to painting. Many of his landscapes are in the National Gallery at Ottawa, the Montreal Museum of Art, the Toronto Art Gallery, and other collections. He was elected an A.R.C.A. in 1911 and an R.C.A. in 1914; and in 1933 he was one of the founders of the Canadian Group of Painters.

[T. R. Lee, *Albert H. Robinson, "the painter's painter"* (Montreal, 1956); *Can. who's who*, 1952-54; *Encyc. Can.*]

Robinson, Beverley (1723-1792), loyalist, was born in Virginia in 1723, the son of the Hon. John Robinson, speaker of the House of Burgesses of Virginia. He served under Wolfe (q.v.) at the capture of Quebec in 1759; and at the outbreak of the American Revolution he raised the Loyal American Regiment. This regiment he commanded throughout the war. In 1784 he went to New Brunswick, and was appointed a member of the first Council of the province; but he did not take his seat, as he very soon went to England. He lived at Thornbury, near Bath, until his death in 1792. He married Susanna, daughter of Frederick Philipse; and by her he had several sons.

[*Cyc. Am. biog.*; L. Sabine, *The American loyalists* (Boston, 1864).]

Robinson, Sir Charles Walker (1836-1924), soldier and author, was born at Beverley House, Toronto, on April 3, 1836, the fourth and youngest son of Sir John Beverley Robinson, Bart. (q.v.). He was educated at Upper Canada College and at Trinity University, Toronto (D.C.L., 1879); and in 1857 he obtained a commission as a second lieutenant in the Rifle Brigade. He served in the Crimean War, in the Ashanti War, and in the Zulu War; and from 1892 to 1895 he was commander of the forces in Mauritius, with the rank of major-general. He retired from the army in 1898; and he died in London, England, on May 20, 1924. In 1884 he married Margaret Frances, daughter of Lieut.-Gen. Sir Archibald Alison, Bart.; and by her he had two daughters. He was the author of *Wellington's campaigns* (3 vols., London, 1905-08), *Canada and Canadian defence* (London, 1910), and *The life of Sir John Beverley Robinson, Bart.* (London, 1904). He was created a K.C.B. in 1923.

[*Who was who*, 1916-28; Morgan, *Can. men* (1912).]

Robinson, Christopher (1763?-1798), loyalist, was born in Westmorland county, Virginia, about 1763. He was educated at the College of William and Mary; and early in the American Revolution he took refuge in New York, and obtained a commission in the Queen's Rangers (1st American Regiment), commanded by Lieut. Col. John Graves Simcoe (q.v.). In 1783 he went to Nova Scotia, and took up land in Wilmot; but in 1788 he removed to Lower Canada, and in 1792 he settled in Upper Canada. In 1796 he was elected to represent Lennox and Addington in the Legislative Assembly of Upper Canada; and he died at York (Toronto), on November 2, 1798. In 1784 he married Esther, daughter of the Rev. John Sayre, formerly of Fairfield, Connecticut; and by her he had three sons and two daughters.

[*Cyc. Am. biog.*; C. W. Robinson, *Life of Sir John Beverley Robinson* (London, 1904); E. M. Chadwick, *Ontarian families* (2 vols., Toronto, 1894-98).]

Robinson, Christopher (1828-1905), lawyer, was born at Beverley House, Toronto, on January 21, 1828, the third son of Sir John Beverley Robinson, Bart. (q.v.). He was educated at Upper Canada College and at King's College, Toronto (B.A., 1846), and in 1850 was called to the bar of Upper Canada (Q.C., 1863). From 1856 to 1872 he was reporter of the Court of Queen's Bench; and from 1872 to 1885 he was editor of the *Law reports*. He was counsel in many of the most famous cases in Canadian legal history, and in several international arbitrations; and he occupied an outstanding position at the Canadian bar. He repeatedly declined judicial preferment, and in 1894 he declined the honour of knighthood. He died at Toronto on October 21, 1905. In 1879 he married Elizabeth Street, daughter of the Hon. Josiah Burr Plumb (q.v.); and by her he had three sons and one daughter. In 1902 he was elected chancellor of Trinity University, Toronto; and from the University of Toronto he received in 1903 the degree of D.C.L.

[*Canadian law review*, 1905; Morgan, *Can. men* (1898); E. M. Chadwick, *Ontarian families* (2 vols., Toronto, 1894-98).]

Robinson, Christopher Blackett (1837-1923), editor and publisher, was born at Thorah, Upper Canada, on November 2, 1837. He began his career in 1857 as editor and publisher of the Beaverton *Post*, which he published later in Lindsay, Ontario. He removed in 1871 to Toronto, and began the publication of the *Canada Presbyterian*, a church paper that was in 1907 amalgamated with the *Westminster*. For many years he was associated also with Goldwin Smith (q.v.) in the publication of the *Week* (1883-92). In his later years he lived in Ottawa, where he published the *Dominion Presbyterian*; and he died in Ottawa, Ontario, on June 11, 1923.

[Morgan, *Can. men* (1912); Rose, *Cyc. Can. biog.* (1886).]

Robinson, Clifford William (1866-1944), prime minister of New Brunswick (1907-08) and senator of Canada (1924-44), was born at Moncton, New Brunswick, on September 1, 1866. He was educated at Mount Allison University (B.A., 1886), and was called to the bar of New Brunswick in 1893. He practised law in Moncton; and he represented Moncton in the Legislative Assembly of New Brunswick from 1897 to 1908, and from 1917 to 1924. On the resignation of the Hon. William Pugsley (q.v.) in 1907, he became prime minister of New Brunswick, and he remained prime minister until the defeat of his government in 1908. Later, he became first, in 1917, minister without portfolio, and then minister of lands and mines in the administration of the Hon. W. E. Foster; but he retired from this position on his appointment in 1924 to the Senate of Canada. He sat in the Senate until his death, at Montreal, Quebec, on July 27, 1944.

[*Can. who's who*, 1936-37; Morgan, *Can. men* (1912); *Can. parl. comp.*]

Robinson, Sir Frederick Philipse (1763-1852), provisional lieutenant-governor of Upper Canada (July-September, 1815), was born near New York in September, 1763, the fourth son of Colonel Beverley Robinson (q.v.). He became an ensign in his father's regiment, the Loyal Americans, in 1777, and he served throughout the American Revolutionary War. Toward the end of the war he transferred to a British regiment; and in 1794-95 he served with distinction in the West Indies. He was a senior staff officer during the Peninsular War; and in 1814 he returned to America as commander of the forces in Upper Canada. In July, 1815, he was appointed provisional lieutenant-governor of Upper Canada; and he held this position until the arrival in Canada, in September, 1815, of Francis Gore (q.v.). From 1816 to 1821 he held appointments in the West Indies; in 1825 he was promoted to be lieutenant-general, and in 1841 general. He died at Brighton, England, on January 1, 1852. In 1815 he was created a K.C.B., and in 1838 a G.C.B. His journal of the expedition to Plattsburg in 1814 has been published in the

Journal of the Royal United Service Institution, August, 1916.

[D. B. Read, *The lieutenant-governors of Upper Canada* (Toronto, 1900); *Dict. nat. biog.*; Morgan, *Cel. Can.*; C. W. Robinson, *Life of Sir John Beverley Robinson* (London, 1904).]

Robinson, Sir John Beverley, Bart. (1791-1863), chief justice of Upper Canada, was born at Berthier, Lower Canada, on July 26, 1791, the second son of Christopher Robinson (q.v.), an officer of the Queen's Rangers, and Esther, daughter of the Rev. John Sayre. He was educated at Kingston and at Cornwall, Upper Canada, under John Strachan (q.v.), who became his friend and patron; and he entered upon the study of law. In the campaign of 1812 he served under Isaac Brock (q.v.) as a militia officer; and in 1813 he was appointed acting attorney-general of the province. On the conclusion of peace he was appointed solicitor-general, and in 1818 attorney-general. In 1821 he was elected to the Legislative Assembly of Upper Canada for the town of York, and he continued to sit in the House, and act as attorney-general, until he was, in 1829, appointed chief justice of Upper Canada, speaker of the Legislative Council, and president of the Executive Council. He resigned the presidency of the Executive Council about 1832; and he ceased to be a member of the Legislative Council at the Union of 1841; but he held the office of chief justice until, in 1862, he was appointed first president of the Court of Error and Appeal. Shortly after this, on January 30, 1863, he died at Beverley House, Toronto.

He was a man of great ability and scrupulous integrity. During the period of his political career (1821-41), he was one of the guiding spirits of what came to be known as the "Family Compact"; and no more striking refutation could be found of the traditional view of the "Family Compact" than his connection with it. As a judge he has had few equals in the history of Canadian judicature.

In 1817 he married in London, England, Emma, daughter of Charles Walker, of Harlesden, Middlesex, England; and by her he had four sons and four daughters. He was made a C.B. in 1850; and he was created a baronet of the United Kingdom in 1854. In 1853 he was elected the first chancellor of the University of Trinity College, Toronto. His only important publication, outside the sphere of law, was *Canada and the Canada bill* (London, 1840).

[C. W. Robinson, *Life of Sir John Beverley Robinson, Bart.* (London, 1904); J. Jarvis, *Three centuries of Robinsons* (Toronto, 1953); *Dict. nat. biog.*; Morgan, *Cel. Can.*; Taylor, *Brit. Am.*; D. B. Read, *Lives of the judges* (Toronto, 1888); J. C. Dent, *The story of the upper Canadian rebellion* (2 vols., Toronto, 1885).]

Robinson, John Beverley (1821-1896), lieutenant-governor of Ontario (1880-87), was born in York (Toronto), Upper Canada, on February 21, 1821, the second son of Sir John Beverley Robinson, Bart. (q.v.). He was educated at Upper Canada College; and he was aide-de-camp to Sir Francis Bond Head (q.v.) during the rebellion of 1837. He was called to the bar of Upper Canada in 1844. In 1857 he was elected mayor of Toronto; and in 1858 he was elected to the Legislative Assembly of Canada as one of the members for Toronto. He represented Toronto in the Legislative Assembly and in the Canadian House of Commons until 1872; from 1872 to 1874 he represented Algoma; and from 1878 to 1880 West Toronto. From March to May, 1862, he was president of the council in the Cartier-Macdonald ministry; but this was the sole occasion on which he held a cabinet position. From 1880 to 1887 he was lieutenant-governor of Ontario. He died at Toronto on June 10, 1896. In 1847 he married Mary Jane, second daughter of the Hon. Christopher Alexander Hagerman; and by her he had five children, of whom the eldest, John Beverley, succeeded to the baronetcy.

[D. B. Read, *Lieutenant-governors of Upper Canada and Ontario* (Toronto, 1900); Dent, *Can. port.*, vol. 3; Rose, *Cyc. Can. biog.* (1886); E. M. Chadwick, *Ontarian families* (2 vols., Toronto, 1894-98); C. W. Robinson, *Life of Sir John Beverley Robinson* (London, 1904).]

Robinson, Percy James (1873-1953), educationist and historian, was born at Whitby, Ontario, on October 18, 1873, and died at Toronto, Ontario, on June 19, 1953. He was educated at the University of Toronto (B.A., 1897; M.A., 1902). In 1899 he joined the staff of St. Andrew's College as classical master, and he continued in this post until his retirement in 1946. He became interested in the study of the Indian languages, and this led him to the study of various phases of early Canadian history. This bore fruit in the publication of his *Toronto during the French régime* (Toronto, 1934) and his translation for the Champlain Society of Du Creux's *Historia Canadensis* (2 vols., Toronto, 1951-52). He was elected a fellow of the Royal Society of Canada in 1937; and in 1934 the University of Toronto conferred on him the degree of LL.D.

[*Proc. Roy. Soc. Can.*, 1954; *Can. hist. rev.*, Sept., 1953; *Can. who's who*, 1952-54.]

Robinson, Peter (1785-1838), executive councillor of Upper Canada, was born in New Brunswick in 1785, the eldest son of Christopher Robinson (q.v.), an officer of the Queen's Rangers, and Esther, daughter of the Rev. John Sayre. His parents came to Upper Canada in 1792, settling first at Kingston, and then in 1798 at York. In the War of 1812 he commanded a rifle company at the capture of

Detroit; and in 1813 he distinguished himself in the defence of Michilimackinac. In 1817 he was elected to the Legislative Assembly of Upper Canada for the east riding of York; and in 1824-25 he was instrumental in settling a large number of Irish immigrants in the neighbourhood of Peterborough, which was named after him. He was appointed commissioner of crown lands, with a seat in the Executive and Legislative councils, in 1827; and he continued in this office until the resignation of the whole Executive Council, as the result of a disagreement with Sir Francis Bond Head (q.v.), in 1836. He died, unmarried, in Toronto, on July 8, 1838.

[C. W. Robinson, *Life of Sir John Beverley Robinson* (London, 1904); E. M. Chadwick, *Ontarian families* (2 vols., Toronto, 1894-98).]

Robinson, William Benjamin (1797-1873), executive councillor of Canada, was born at Kingston, Upper Canada, on December 22, 1797, the third son of Christopher Robinson (q.v.), an officer of the Queen's Rangers, and Esther, daughter of the Rev. John Sayre. From 1830 to 1857, with the exception of the years 1841-44, he represented the county of Simcoe in the Legislative Assembly of Upper Canada and united Canada; and in 1844-45 he was for a short time inspector-general, with a seat in the Executive Council, and in 1846-47 chief commissioner of public works. He was also one of the commissioners of the Canada Company. He died at Toronto on July 18, 1873. He married Ann Elizabeth (or Eliza Ann), daughter of William Jarvis (q.v.); but had no children.

[C. W. Robinson, *Life of Sir John Beverley Robinson* (London, 1904); E. M. Chadwick, *Ontarian families* (2 vols., Toronto, 1894-98); A. F. Hunter, *A history of Simcoe county* (2 vols., Barrie, Ont., 1909); *Dict. Can. biog.*, vol. 10.]

Robinson, Sir William Cleaver Francis (1834-1897), governor of Prince Edward Island (1870-73), was born on January 14, 1834, the fifth son of Admiral Hercules Robinson. He entered the service of the Colonial Office in 1858 as private secretary to his elder brother, Sir Hercules Robinson, afterwards first Baron Rosmead, who was lieutenant-governor of St. Kitts. In 1866 he himself was appointed governor of the Falkland Islands, and from 1870 to 1873 he was governor of Prince Edward Island. It was during his administration, and partly as a result of his judicious counsels, that the inclusion of Prince Edward Island in the Canadian confederation took place in 1873. After leaving Prince Edward Island he occupied successively important posts as governor in Western Australia, the Straits Settlements, South Australia, and Victoria; and he retired from active service in 1895. He died in South Kensington, London, England, on May 2, 1897. In 1862 he married Olivia Edith Dean, daughter of the Right Rev. Thomas Stewart Townsend, bishop of Meath, and by her he had three sons and two daughters. He was created a C.M.G. in 1873, a K.C.M.G. in 1877, and a G.C.M.G. in 1887. He was a musical composer of some note, and was the author of a number of well-known songs.

[*Dict. nat. biog.*]

Robitaille, Georges (1883-1950), priest and historian, was born at Joliette, Quebec, on June 13, 1883, and died at L'Epiphanie, Quebec, in June, 1950. He was educated at the Collège de Joliette (B.A., 1903), at the Grande Séminaire de Montréal, and at the University of Propaganda, in Rome (Ph.D., 1907; D.Th., 1909). He was ordained a priest in 1906; and from 1909 to 1927 he was on the teaching staff of Joliette Seminary. From 1927 to 1937 he was rector of the parish of St. Alexis de Montcalm, and from 1937 until his death he was rector of the parish of L'Epiphanie. A careful student of Canadian history, he was the author of *Etudes sur Garneau* (Montreal, 1929), *Washington et Jumonville* (Montreal, 1933), *Montcalm et ses historiens* (Montreal, 1936), *Telle qu'elle fut* (Montreal, 1939), and *Marie de l'Incarnation et nos martyres* (Montreal, 1941). At the time of his death he was working on a history of the Seven Years' War; but this has not been published. He was elected a fellow of the Royal Society of Canada in 1937.

[*Proc. Roy. Soc. Can.,* 1951; *Can. who's who*, 1948.]

Robitaille, Theodore (1834-1897), lieutenant-governor of the province of Quebec (1879-84), was born at Varennes, Lower Canada, on January 29, 1834, the son of Louis Adolphe Robitaille, notary public. He was educated at the Seminary of Ste. Thérèse, at Laval University, and at the University of McGill College (M.D., 1858). He practised for many years as a physician and surgeon at New Carlisle, Bonaventure county, Quebec; and in 1861 he was elected the representative of Bonaventure county in the Legislative Assembly of Canada. This constituency he represented, first in the Assembly, and after 1867 in the House of Commons, continuously until 1879. In 1873 he became receiver-general in the Macdonald government, but held office for only a few months, when the government resigned. From 1874 to 1878 he was one of Sir John Macdonald's "Old Guard" in the House; and when, in 1879, Letellier de St. Just (q.v.) was dismissed from the lieutenant-governorship of Quebec, he was appointed to the vacant post. His term of office lasted until 1884; and in 1885 he was appointed to the Senate of Canada. He died at New Carlisle, Quebec, on August 18, 1897. In 1867 he married Marie Josephine Charlotte Emma, daughter of P. A. Quesnel, and granddaughter of the Hon. F. A. Quesnel (q.v.).

[*Cyc. Am. biog.*; *Can. parl comp.*; Dent, *Can. port.*, vol. 3; Rose, *Cyc. Can. biog.* (1886); Le Jeune, *Dict. gén.*]

Roblin, Sir Rodmond Palen (1853-1937), prime minister of Manitoba (1900-15), was born in Sophiasburgh, Prince Edward county, Canada West, on February 15, 1853, of United Empire Loyalist descent. He was educated at Albert College, Belleville. In 1877 he migrated to Manitoba, and he became a successful farmer on a large scale at Carman, Manitoba. In 1889 he was elected to represent Dufferin in the Manitoba legislature; and from 1889 to 1899 he was leader of the Conservative opposition. In 1900 he succeeded Sir Hugh John Macdonald (q.v.) as prime minister of Manitoba; and he held power until 1915, when he was compelled to resign as the result of charges of political corruption brought against his government in connection with the building of the parliament buildings in Winnipeg. He retired from public life; and he died at Hot Springs, Arkansas, on February 16, 1937. Ir 1875 he married Adelaide Demill (d. 1928); and by her he had four sons. He was created a K.C.M.G. in 1912.

[A. R. Ross, *Thirty-five years in the limelight: Sir Rodmond P. Roblin and his times* (Winnipeg, 1936); *Can. parl. comp.*; *Can. who's who*, 1936-37.]

Robson, Albert Henry (1882-1939), art connoisseur, was born at Lindsay, Ontario, on January 7, 1882. He was educated at the Toronto College of Art; and in 1915 he became art director of Rous and Mann, a firm of printers and publishers. He died at Toronto, Ontario, on March 6, 1939. He was the author of *Canadian landscape painters* (Toronto, 1932) and a series of booklets on Canadian painters in the "Canadian Artists series".

[C. W. Jefferys, *Albert H. Robson* (Canadian bookman, 1939); *Can. who's who*, 1936-37.]

Robson, John (1824-1892), prime minister of British Columbia (1889-92), was born at Perth, Upper Canada, on March 14, 1824, the son of John Robson and Euphemia Richardson. He was educated at the Perth grammar school; and in 1859 he emigrated to British Columbia. In 1861 he founded at New Westminster the *British Columbian*, the first newspaper on the mainland of British Columbia; and in its columns he waged the battle for constitutional government in the province. In 1867 he was elected to represent New Westminster in the Legislative Council of British Columbia; and he was one of the foremost advocates of Confederation. In 1869 he removed to Victoria, and became editor of the Victoria *Colonist*. From 1871 to 1875 he represented Nanaimo as a Liberal in the provincial legislature, and from 1882 to 1892 he represented again New Westminster, where he had resumed in 1879

publication of the *British Columbian*. In 1883 he was appointed provincial secretary and minister of mines, finance, and agriculture in the Smithe administration; and in 1889 he became prime minister of the province. He died in London, England, on June 29, 1892. In 1854 he married Susan, daughter of Captain Longworth, of Goderich, Upper Canada.

[J. B. Kerr, *Biographical dictionary of well-known British Columbians* (Vancouver, B.C., 1892); *Can. parl. comp.*]

Roche, Nicholas (1870-1930), priest and educationist, was born at Wexford, Ireland, in 1870. He came to Canada, was educated at St. Michael's College, Toronto, and became a member of the Basilian order. From 1906 to 1910 he was president of St. Michael's College; and from 1911 to 1924 he was provincial of the Basilian order in Canada. He died at Owen Sound, Ontario, on May 16, 1932.

[Morgan, *Can. men* (1912).]

Roche, William (1842-1925), senator of Canada, was born in Halifax, Nova Scotia, in 1842, and was educated there. He became a merchant in Halifax; and he represented Halifax in the House of Assembly of Nova Scotia from 1886 to 1897, and in the Canadian House of Commons from 1900 to 1908. From 1896 to 1897 he was a member of the Murray administration in Nova Scotia, without portfolio. In 1910 he was summoned to the Senate of Canada; and he sat in the Senate until his death, at Halifax, Nova Scotia, on October 19, 1925.

[Morgan, *Can. men* (1912); *Can. parl. comp.*]

Roche, William James (1859-1937), minister of the interior for Canada (1912-17), was born at Clandeboye, Canada West, on November 30, 1859. He was educated at Trinity Medical College, Toronto, and the Western University, London, Ontario (M.D., C.M., 1883; LL.D., 1916), and he practised medicine for many years at Minnedosa, Manitoba. He represented Marquette in the Canadian House of Commons from 1896 to 1917; and he was sworn of the Privy Council and became secretary of state in the Borden administration in 1911. In 1912 he became minister of the interior; and in 1917 he was appointed chairman of the Civil Service Commission. He held this position until 1925; and he died at Ottawa, Ontario, on September 30, 1937. From 1916 to 1929 he was chancellor of the University of Western Ontario, of which he was the first medical graduate.

[*Can. who's who*, 1936-37; *Can. parl. comp.*]

Rocheblave, Philippe François de Rastel, Chevalier de (1727-1802), soldier, was born in 1727, at Savournon, Franche-Comté, France, the son of the Marquis de Rocheblave, and entered the French army. He was retired on half-pay after the peace of 1748, and afterwards came to Canada. He became an officer in the colonial troops, and served throughout the Seven Years' War. At the end of the war he retired to the Illinois country; and from 1765 to 1773 he seems to have been in the Spanish service. He returned to the British Illinois in 1773, however, and in 1776 he was left in command at Kaskaskia. Here he was captured, on July 4, 1778, by George Rogers Clark, and was sent a prisoner to Virginia. In 1780 he joined the British forces in New York, and in 1781 he was back in Quebec. At the close of the American Revolution, he settled with his family at Varennes, near Montreal. He represented the county of Surrey in the Legislative Assembly of Lower Canada from 1792 until his death, which took place on April 3, 1802.

[D. Girouard, *La famille de Rocheblave* (Bull. rech. hist., 1898); Percy J. Robinson, *Toronto during the French régime* (Toronto, 1933) and *The Chevalier de Rocheblave and the Toronto purchase* (Trans. Roy. Soc. Can., 1937).]

Rocheblave, Pierre Rastel de (1764?-1840), fur-trader, was born about 1764, the son of Philippe François Rastel de Rocheblave (q.v.). He became a wintering partner of the XY Company in 1798; and in 1802 was in opposition to John McDonald of Garth (q.v.) at Fort Augustus. On the union of the XY and North West companies in 1804, he became a wintering partner of the North West Company, and was placed in charge of the Assiniboine district. From 1807 to 1810 he was again in the Athabaska department; and from 1810 to 1812 he was in charge of the Pic, on Lake Superior; and in 1814 he was appointed agent of the North West Company in regard to the southwest trade. In 1816 he became a partner in McTavish, McGillivrays, and Co.; and from 1816 to 1821 he was one of the agents of the North West Company at the annual meetings at Fort William. In 1821 he retired from the fur-trade; but on the failure of McTavish, McGillivrays, and Co. in 1825, and the subsequent return of Simon McGillivray (q.v.), he was placed in temporary charge of the Montreal office, until the Hudson's Bay Company took charge of it. From 1824 to 1827 he represented Montreal West in the Legislative Assembly of Lower Canada; in 1832 he was appointed a member of the Legislative Council of Lower Canada, and in 1838 of the Special Council; and from 1838 to his death he was a member of the Executive Council of the province. He died at Montreal on October 5, 1840. In 1819 he married Elmire (d. 1886), daughter of Jean Bouthillier; and by her he had two daughters.

[D. Girouard, *La famille de Rocheblave* (Bull. rech. hist., 1898); W. S. Wallace (ed.), *Documents relating to the North West Com-*

pany (Toronto: The Champlain Society, 1934).]

Roddick, Sir Thomas George (1846-1923), surgeon, was born at Harbour Grace, Newfoundland, on July 31, 1846, the son of John Irvine Roddick and Emma Jane Martin. He was educated at Truro, Nova Scotia, and at McGill University (M.D., 1868), and practised surgery in Montreal. In 1875 he was appointed professor of clinical surgery in McGill University; and from 1901 to 1908 he was dean of the faculty of medicine in this university. From 1896 to 1898 he was president of the British Medical Association; and in 1900 he was made an honorary F.R.C.S. (Eng.). He entered the Canadian militia in 1868, saw service in the Fenian Raid of 1807, and was deputy surgeon-general in the North West expeditionary force of 1885. From 1896 to 1904 he represented Montreal West, as a Conservative, in the Canadian House of Commons. He died at Montreal on February 20, 1923. He was twice married, (1) in 1880 to Marion (d. 1890), daughter of William McKinnon, and (2) in 1906 to Amy, daughter of J. J. Redpath, of Chislehurst, England. He was an LL.D. of Edinburgh University (1898) and of Queen's University, Kingston (1903), and a D.Sc. of Oxford University (1904); and in 1914 he was created a knight bachelor.

[H. E. MacDermot, *Sir Thomas Roddick* (Toronto, 1938); *Can. who was who*, vol. 1; *Who was who*, 1916-28; Morgan, *Can. men* (1912).]

Rodier, Charles Séraphin (1797-1876), legislative councillor of Quebec, was born in Montreal, Lower Canada, in 1797, and became a successful wholesale merchant in Montreal. He was mayor of Montreal from 1857 to 1861; and in 1867 he was called to the Legislative Council of the province of Quebec. He died in February, 1876.

[E. Z. Massicotte, *Deux Rodier* (Bull. rech. hist., 1938); *Can. parl. comp.*; *Dict. Can. biog.*, vol. 10.]

Rodier, Charles Séraphin (1818-1890), senator of Canada, was born in Montreal in 1818, and became an outstanding merchant and capitalist. He was called to the Senate of Canada in 1888; and he died in 1890.

[E. Z. Massicotte, *Deux Rodier* (Bull. rech. hist., 1938); *Can. parl. comp.*]

Rodier, Edouard Etienne (1805-1840), *patriote* leader, was born in 1805, and was called to the bar of Lower Canada in 1826. In 1832 he was elected to represent L'Assomption in the Legislative Assembly of Lower Canada; and he became one of the leaders of the *patriote* party. He was a principal in two famous duels of pre-Rebellion days; and when the Rebellion of 1837 broke out, he fled to the United States to escape arrest. He returned to Canada, however, in 1838; and he died at Montreal, Lower Canada, on February 10, 1840.

[L. O. David, *Les patriotes de 1837-1838* (Montreal, 1884); A. Fauteux, *Le duel au Canada* (Montreal, 1935).]

Rodomar, Oleg Wladimir (1900-1961), industrialist, was born in Kiev, Ukraine, September 23, 1900. He was educated at the Imperial Corps of Cadets, Odessa (1909-16), and the Officers' Training School, Simbirsk, Russia (1916-18). He also studied at Columbia University, New York (1920-21). On leaving university he became assistant manager of Standard Oil of New York at Smyrna and Salonica (1921-24). He came to Canada in 1924. After undertaking training in the Ford Motor Company factory in Detroit he became district sales manager, Ford Motor Company of Canada Limited (1926-29) and subsequently moved to the Chrysler Corporation of Canada (1929-47). He was deputy administrator of ration administration for the Wartime Prices and Trade Board (1942-47). He joined Philips Industries in 1947, becoming president in 1956. He was formerly captain in the 3rd Hussars, Russian Imperial Army. He died at Toronto, January 30, 1961.

[*Can. who's who*, 1955-57; *National reference book* (1956).]

Roe, Henry (1829-1909), clergyman and author, was born at Henryville, Lower Canada, on February 22, 1829, the son of Dr. John Hill Roe and Jane Ardagh; and was educated at Bishop's College, Lennoxville (B.A., 1855; M.A., 1867; D.D., 1879; LL.D., 1896). In 1873 he became professor of divinity in Bishop's College, and from 1882 to 1891 he was dean of the faculty and vice-principal. He died at Richmond, Quebec, on August 3, 1909. In 1854 he married Julia, daughter of Assistant Commissary-General John George Smith. For many years he was the Canadian correspondent of the London *Guardian*; and he was the author of a number of books and pamphlets, including *Bicentenary sermons* (Montreal, 1862), *Purgatory, trans-substantiation, and the mass examined* (Quebec and Montreal, 1863), *Advantages and means of keeping up reading among the clergy* (Montreal, 1864), and *The story of the first hundred years of the diocese of Quebec* (Quebec, 1893).

[Morgan, *Can. men* (1898).]

Roger, Charles (1819-1878?), journalist, was born in Dundee, Scotland, on April 14, 1819. He came to Canada in 1842, and became a journalist. Eventually, he accepted a position in the civil service in Ottawa; and he died in Ottawa, perhaps in 1878. He was the author of *The rise of Canada from barbarism to wealth* (Quebec, 1856) and *Ottawa, past and present* (Ottawa, 1871).

[Morgan, *Bib. can.*; *Dict. Can. biog.*, vol. 10.]

Rogers, Benjamin (1837-1923), lieutenant-governor of Prince Edward Island (1910-15), was born at Bedeque, Prince Edward Island, in 1837, and became an export merchant. From 1878 to 1893 he was a member of the Legislative Assembly of the island, and was several times a member of the Executive Council. From 1910 to 1915 he was lieutenant-governor of Prince Edward Island. He died at Alberton, Prince Edward Island, on May 16, 1923.

[*Can. parl. comp.*; Morgan, *Can. men* (1912).]

Rogers, David McGregor (1772-1824), member of the Legislative Assembly of Upper Canada, was born on November 23, 1772, the second son of James Rogers (q.v.). He came with his father to Fredericksburgh on the Bay of Quinte in 1784, and took up later a large military grant at West Lake. In 1796 and in 1800 he was elected a member of the Legislative Assembly for Prince Edward county, and from 1804 to 1816 he sat for the county of Northumberland, to which he had removed. He was out of the legislature from 1816 to 1820; but in 1820 was again elected for Northumberland. He died on July 13, 1824. In 1802 he married Sarah Playter (d. 1810), of York (Toronto), and in 1811 Elizabeth Playter (d. 1825); and of his first marriage he had two sons and two daughters.

[Morgan, *Cel. Can.*; W. Rogers, *Rogers, ranger and loyalist* (Trans. Roy. Soc. Can., 1900); E. M. Chadwick, *Ontarian families* (2 vols., Toronto, 1894-98).]

Rogers, Grace Dean, *née* **McLeod** (1865-1958), author, was born at Westfield, Nova Scotia, in 1865, and died at Toronto, Ontario, on October 20, 1958. She was educated at Dalhousie University and Acadia University (M.A., 1911). In 1891 she married H. W. Rogers, a barrister of Amherst, Nova Scotia; the Hon. Norman McLeod Rogers (q.v.) was her son. She was the author of *Stories of the land of Evangeline* (Boston, 1891; new ed. Toronto, 1923) and a novel, *Joan at Halfway* (Toronto, 1919).

[Morgan, *Can. men* (1912).]

Rogers, James (1726?-1792), loyalist, was born in New Hampshire about 1726, the third son of James Rogers and Mary McFatridge. During the Seven Years' War he was a captain in Rogers' Rangers, and was present at the captures of Louisbourg, Quebec, and Montreal. He then settled in Vermont; but he took up arms again during the American Revolution, and in 1778 was gazetted a major in the King's Rangers. During the later stages of the war he was in command at St. John's. In 1784 he settled at Fredericksburgh on the Bay of Quinte with a number of his Rangers; and here he died in 1792. In 1763 he married Margaret, daughter of the Rev. David McGregor,

ROGERS

Londonderry, New Hampshire; and by her he had two sons and three daughters.

[W. Rogers, *Rogers, ranger and loyalist* (Trans. Roy. Soc. Can., 1900); E. M. Chadwick, *Ontarian families* (2 vols., Toronto, 1894-98); W. Canniff, *History of the early settlement of Upper Canada* (Toronto, 1869).]

Rogers, James (1826-1903), first Roman Catholic bishop of Chatham, was born in Ireland on July 11, 1826. He was educated at Halifax, Nova Scotia, and at the Montreal Seminary; and was ordained a priest at Halifax in 1851. After serving as a missionary in Nova Scotia, he became in 1860 first Roman Catholic bishop of Chatham, in New Brunswick. He retired from the episcopate in 1902; and he died at Chatham, New Brunswick, on March 22, 1903.

[Allaire, *Dict. biog.*]

Rogers, Norman McLeod (1894-1940), minister of labour for Canada (1935-39) and minister of national defence (1939-40), was born at Amherst, Nova Scotia, on July 25, 1894. He was educated at Acadia University (B.A., 1919), and at Oxford University (M.A., 1920; B.Litt., 1921; B.C.L., 1922), and he was called to the bar of Nova Scotia in 1924. From 1922 to 1927 he was professor of history at Acadia University; from 1927 to 1929 he was secretary to the prime minister of Canada, the Right Hon. W. L. Mackenzie King; and from 1929 to 1935 he was professor of political science at Queen's University, Kingston. In 1935 he was elected to represent Kingston in the Canadian House of Commons, and became minister of labour in the third Mackenzie King administration. Two weeks after the outbreak of the Second World War in 1939, he exchanged this portfolio for that of minister of national defence; and it fell to him to lay down the lines along which the war effort of Canada was to develop. His career was, however, cut short by his death in an airplane crash, when he was proceeding from Ottawa to Toronto, on June 10, 1940. While still an undergraduate, he had served in the ranks of the First World War in 1914-18. He was the author of a campaign biography entitled *Mackenzie King* (Toronto, 1935).

[*Canadian journal of political and economic science*, August, 1941; *Can. who's who*, 1938-39; *Can. parl. comp.*]

Rogers, Robert (1731-1795), soldier, was born in Dumbarton, New Hampshire, on November 7, 1731, the second son of James Rogers and Mary McFatridge. In 1755 he organized a company of scouts, known as Rogers' Rangers, for service against the French, and he served throughout the Seven Years' War. In 1760 he was commissioned to take possession of the western lake posts. At the outbreak of the American Revolution he organized the Queen's Rangers, and later, in 1779, the

King's Rangers. He died in London, England, on May 18, 1795. He published his *Journals* (London, 1765) and *A concise account of North America* (London, 1765; Dublin, 1770); and he was the author of *Ponteach, a tragedy* (London, 1776). His *Journals* have been republished by F. B. Hough (Albany, 1883). His journal of 1760-61 has been edited by V. H. Paltsits in the *Bulletin* of the New York Public Library for April, 1933.

[W. Rogers, *Rogers, ranger and loyalist* (Trans. Roy. Soc. Can., 1900); R. E. Day, *Robert Rogers* (Quarterly journal of the New York State Historical Association, 1928); J. J. Mayer, *Major Robert Rogers* (New York history, 1934); *Dict. Am. biog.*; *Dict. nat. biog.*; *Cyc. Am. biog.*; Morgan, *Bib. can.*; E. M. Chadwick, *Ontarian families* (2 vols., Toronto, 1894-98); J. R. Cuneo, *Robert Rogers of the rangers* (New York, 1959); H. M. Jackson, *Rogers' Rangers* (n.p., 1953).]

Rogers, Robert (1864-1936), minister of public works for Canada (1912-17), was born at Lachute, Quebec, on March 2, 1864, the son of Lieut.-Col. George Rogers. He was educated in Montreal, and in 1881 he went to Clearwater, Manitoba, where he became a storekeeper. In 1899 he was elected to represent Manitou in the Manitoba legislature, and he retained this seat until 1911. From 1900 to 1911 he was minister of public works in the Manitoba government; and in 1911 he was for a time acting prime minister of the province. Later in 1911 he resigned his provincial portfolio to become minister of the interior in the Borden government at Ottawa, and was elected to represent Winnipeg in the Canadian House of Commons. In 1912 he became minister of public works, and he retained this portfolio until the formation of the Union government in 1917, when he retired temporarily to private life. He was re-elected to represent Lisgar in the Canadian House of Commons in 1925 and in 1930; but never again held office under the Crown. He died in a sanitarium at Guelph, Ontario, on July 21, 1936. In 1888 he married Aurelia Regina Widmeyer; and by her he had one son.

[*Can. parl. comp.*; *Who was who*, 1929-40; Morgan, *Can. men* (1912).]

Rogers, Robert David (1809-1885), militia officer, was born in Haldimand township, Northumberland county, Upper Canada, in 1809. He saw active service during the Rebellion of 1837, and was one of those who cut out the steamer *Caroline*; he saw service also in the Fenian Raid of 1866, and rose to the rank of lieutenant-colonel. He died at Ashburnham, near Peterborough, Ontario, on February 17, 1885. His diary covering the cutting out of the *Caroline* has been printed by F. M. de la Fosse (Can. hist. rev., 1932).

[*Dom. ann. reg.*, 1885.]

Rogers, Robert Vashon (1843-1911), lawyer and author, was born in Kingston, Canada West, in 1843, the youngest son of the Rev. R. Vashon Rogers, headmaster of the Kingston Grammar School. He was educated at Queen's University, Kingston (B.A., 1861; hon. LL.D., 1895), and was called to the bar in 1865 (Q.C., 1889). He died at Kingston on May 2, 1911. He was the author of *Wrongs and rights of a traveller* (Toronto, 1875; new ed., under title, *The law of the road,* Edinburgh, 1881), and *The law and medical men* (Toronto, 1884).

[Morgan, *Can. men* (1912).]

Roland, Walpole (d. 1931), civil engineer, was a land valuator for the Canadian Pacific Railway and a surveyor who reported on mining locations in northern Ontario during the last quarter of the nineteenth century. He died at Detroit, Michigan, on March 30, 1931. He was the author of *Algoma West* (Toronto, 1887).

[Private information.]

Rolette, Frédéric (1785-1831), naval officer, was born in Quebec on September 23, 1785. He enlisted in the Royal Navy, and saw service at the battles of the Nile and Trafalgar. After the battle of Trafalgar, he returned to Canada, and in 1807 was commissioned a second lieutenant in the provincial marine. He distinguished himself greatly during the War of 1812, especially at the battle of Lake Erie on September 10, 1813, in which he commanded the *Lady Prevost.* He died at St. Roch de Québec, Lower Canada, on March 17, 1831.

[P. G. Roy, *Fils de Québec,* vol. 3 (Lévis, Que., 1933).]

Rolland, Jean Baptiste (1815-1888), senator of Canada, was born at Verchères, Lower Canada, on January 2, 1815. In 1842 he founded in Montreal the book, paper, and fancy goods business that developed into the firm of J. B. Rolland & Fils, with large paper mills at St. Jérôme. In 1887 he was called to the Senate of Canada; but he died less than a year later, on March 22, 1888, at Montreal. In 1839 he married Esther Dufresne; and by her he had six sons and six daughters.

[Rose, *Cyc. Can. biog.* (1888).]

Rolland, Jean Damien (1841-1912), legislative councillor of Quebec, was born in Montreal, Lower Canada, on February 23, 1841, the eldest son of Jean Baptiste Rolland. He was educated at the Christian Brothers' Academy and St. Mary's College, in Montreal; and entered his father's business. On his father's death in 1888, he succeeded to the direction of the business. He became later also president of the Banque d'Hochelaga, and of the Canadian Manufacturers' Association. In 1896 he was appointed a member of the Legislative Council of Quebec. He died at Montreal, Quebec, on November 16, 1912.

[Morgan, *Can. men* (1912); *Can. parl. comp.*]

Rolland, Jean Roch (1785-1862), jurist, was born at Montreal, Quebec, on May 11, 1785, and was called to the bar of Lower Canada in 1806. He practised law in Montreal, and became one of the leaders of the Lower Canadian bar. From June 28 to November 2, 1838, he was a member of the Executive Council of the province; and in 1838 he was appointed a judge of the Court of King's Bench for Three Rivers. He became chief justice of the Court of King's Bench in 1847, and of the Court of Appeal in 1850. He retired from the bench in 1855; and he died at his manor-house at Ste. Marie de Monnoir, Canada East, on August 5, 1862. In 1821 he married Marguerite, daughter of Colonel Jean Baptiste Philippe Charles d'Estimauville, Baron de Beaumouchel.

[P. G. Roy, *Les juges de la province de Québec* (Quebec, 1933); Le Jeune, *Dict. gén.*; *Bull. rech. hist.,* 1904.]

Rolph, John (1793-1870), physician and politician, was born at Thornbury, Gloucestershire, England, on March 4, 1793, the son of Dr. Thomas Rolph and Frances Petty. His father emigrated to Upper Canada about 1810, and he followed his family in 1812, but later returned to England to study law and medicine. He remained in England until 1821, was called to the bar at the Inner Temple, and became a member of the Royal College of Surgeons. On his return to Canada he settled at Charlotteville, Norfolk county, Upper Canada, was called to the bar of Upper Canada, and practised concurrently law and medicine. In 1828, dissatisfied with a decision of Mr. Justice Sherwood (q.v.), he threw off his gown, and ceased to practise law; and in 1829 he was officially licensed to practise medicine. In 1831 he settled in York (Toronto), and he played henceforth an important part in the history of medicine in Upper Canada. From the first he undertook the instruction of medical students, and in 1843 he founded in Toronto a medical school, known as the Toronto School of Medicine, which later became the medical school of Victoria University, and was an important rival of the medical department of King's College.

Law and medicine, however, did not suffice to exhaust his energies. From 1824 to 1830 he represented Middlesex, and from 1836 to 1837 he represented Norfolk in the Legislative Assembly of Upper Canada; and he became one of the leaders of the Reform party in the province. In 1836 he accepted the invitation of Sir F. Bond Head (q.v.) to become, with Robert Baldwin (q.v.), a member of the Executive Council of Upper Canada; but two weeks later he resigned with all his colleagues, both Tory and Reform. In 1837 he was implicated in the Mackenzie rebellion, and was compelled to flee the province. He went to Rochester, New York, and there practised medicine until 1843, when the amnesty granted by the Canadian legislature permitted him to return to Toronto. He became one of the founders of the "Clear Grit" party; and in 1851 he was elected to represent Norfolk in the Legislative Assembly of Canada. In 1851 he became commissioner of crown lands in the Hincks-Morin administration, and in 1853 president of the council; but in 1854 he voted in the House against his colleagues, and precipitated the fall of the government. In 1857 he retired from parliament and from political life; and he died at Mitchell, Ontario, on October 19, 1870. In 1834 he married at Kingston, Upper Canada, Grace, daughter of George Henry Haines, formerly of Leicester, England; and by her he had three sons and one daughter.

[W. Canniff, *The medical profession in Upper Canada* (Toronto, 1894); *Dict. nat. biog.*; *Cyc. Am. biog.*; J. C. Dent, *The Upper Canadian rebellion* (2 vols., Toronto, 1885) and *The last forty years* (2 vols., Toronto, 1881).]

Rolph, Thomas (*fl.* 1833-1844), physician and author, came to Canada from England in 1833. He was a member of the Royal College of Surgeons in England, and in 1835 he began practice as a physician in Ancaster, Upper Canada. In 1839 he was appointed a Canadian immigration agent in the British Isles; and he retained this position until 1843. He settled in Portsmouth, England, where he died. He was the author of *A brief account, together with observations made during a visit to the West Indies, and a tour through the United States of America, in parts of the years 1823-33; together with a statistical account of Upper Canada* (Dundas, Upper Canada, 1836; 2nd ed., London, 1842), and *Emigration and colonization* (London, 1844).

[W. Canniff, *The medical profession in Upper Canada* (Toronto, 1894); Morgan, *Bib. can.*]

Rolph, William Kirby (1917-1953), biographer, was born in Toronto, Ontario, in 1917, and died at Canberra, Australia, on December 22, 1953. He was educated at the University of Toronto (B.A., 1940) and Brown University (M.A., 1941; Ph.D., 1943); and he taught history successively at the University of Western Ontario, New York University, the University of Saskatchewan, and Tulane University. While at the University of Saskatchewan, he made a study of the co-operative movement among the western farmers, and published *Henry Wise Wood of Alberta* (Toronto, 1950). In 1952 he received a research fellowship from the National University of Australia to make a similar study of the Australian country party, but his work was cut short by his early death.

[*Can. hist. rev.*, March, 1954.]

Roper, John Charles (1858-1940), Anglican archbishop of Ottawa, was born at Frant, Sussex, England, on November 8, 1858. He was educated at Keble and Brasenose colleges, Oxford (B.A., 1881; M.A., 1884), and was ordained a priest of the Church of England in 1883. He came to Canada in 1886, and from 1886 to 1889 he was a professor of theology in Trinity University, Toronto. He was then rector of St. Thomas's Church, Toronto, until 1897; and after serving for fifteen years as a professor in the General Theological Seminary in New York, he was elected in 1912 bishop of British Columbia. In 1915 he was transferred to the archiepiscopal see of Ottawa; and in 1933 he became metropolitan of the ecclesiastical province of Ontario. He died at Toronto, Ontario, on January 26, 1940. He received honorary degrees from Trinity University, Hobart College, the General Theological Seminary, Bishop's College, Lennoxville, and King's College, Windsor.

[*Can. who's who*, 1936-37; Morgan, *Can. men* (1912).]

Rordans, Joshua Long (1824-1888), law stationer and author, was born in London, England, in 1824. He came to Canada in 1847, and established himself in Toronto as a law stationer and publisher. He died in Toronto, Ontario, in 1888. He was the author of *The Canadian conveyancer* (Toronto, 1859); and he compiled *The Upper Canada law directory*, which appeared in 1858, 1860-61, and 1862.

[*Commemorative biographical record of the county of York, Ontario* (Toronto, 1907).]

Rorke, Louise Richardson (d. 1949), writer of books for children, was born at Thornbury, Ontario, and died at Pickering, Ontario, on July 23, 1949. She became a school-teacher; but joined the staff of *The Canadian Teacher*, and was its editor for many years before her retirement in 1945. She was the author of *Lefty: The story of a boy and a dog* (Toronto, 1931), which went into several editions, *Sugar Shanty* (New York, 1941), and *Lefty's adventures* (Toronto, 1945).

[Toronto *Globe and Mail*, July 24, 1949.]

Rosa, Narcisse (1823-1907), ship-builder and author, was born in 1823; and became a ship-builder at Quebec. In his later years he published a book entitled *La construction des navires à Québec et ses environs, grèves et naufrages* (Quebec, 1897). He died at Quebec City on November 3, 1907.

[Private information.]

Rosaire, Arthur D. (1879-1922), landscape painter, was born in Canada, and studied art in Montreal. He exhibited in the Royal Canadian Academy between 1910 and 1920; and he was elected an associate of the Academy in 1915. He died in 1922.

[H. G. Jones and E. Dyonnet, *History of the*

Royal Canadian Academy of Arts (Montreal, 1934).]

Rose, George MacLean (1829-1898), publisher, was born in Wick, Caithness-shire, Scotland, on March 14, 1829. He was educated at the Wick Academy, and was apprenticed as a printer in the office of the *John o' Groat Journal*. He came to Canada in 1851, and established a printing shop in Montreal. In 1856 he removed to Upper Canada, and for two years was a journalist. In 1858 he entered the publishing business, and in 1865 he became a partner in the firm of Hunter, Rose, and Co., Ottawa. In 1871 this firm moved from Ottawa to Toronto, and for many years was one of the most enterprising of Canadian publishing houses. It published the *Canadian Monthly* (1872-78), and its successor, *Rose-Belford's Canadian Monthly* (1878-82). In 1886-88 Rose brought out also two volumes of a *Cyclopedia of Canadian biography*. He died at Toronto on February 10, 1898. In 1856 he married Margaret, daughter of William Manson, of Oxford county, Upper Canada; and by her he had several children.

[Morgan, *Can. men* (1898); *Cyc. Am. biog.*; Rose, *Cyc. Can. biog.* (1886).]

Rose, Sir John, Bart. (1820-1888), minister of finance for Canada (1868-69), was born at Turiff, Aberdeenshire, Scotland, on August 2, 1820, the son of William Rose and Elizabeth Fyfe. He was educated at King's College, Aberdeen; and in 1836 he came with his parents to Canada. He served as a volunteer in the loyalist forces in the rebellion of 1837. In 1842 he was called to the bar of Lower Canada (Q.C., 1848); and he built up a large practice in Montreal. In 1857 he was elected to represent Montreal in the Legislative Assembly of Canada and became solicitor-general for Lower Canada in the Macdonald-Cartier administration. In 1858 he became minister of public works in the Cartier-Macdonald government; but in 1861 he retired from office, though he continued to sit for Montreal. He was a delegate at the London Conference of 1866-67, at which the final arrangements in regard to the Canadian Confederation were made; and in 1868 he became the second finance minister of the Dominion, representing Huntingdon in the Canadian House of Commons. In 1869 he resigned to join the banking firm of Morton, Rose, and Co., of London, England; and he left Canada, though he continued to act as an unofficial representative of Canada in London. He became a well-known figure in London society; and in 1883 the Prince of Wales appointed him receiver-general of the duchy of Lancaster. He died suddenly on August 24, 1888, while a guest of the Duke of Portland, at Langwell, Caithness. He married (1) in 1843 Charlotte (d. 1883), widow of Robert Sweeny (q.v.), and daughter of Robert Emmett Temple, of Rutland, Vermont, by whom he had five children;

and (2) in 1887 Julia, daughter of Keith Stewart Mackenzie, of Seaforth, and widow of the ninth Marquis of Tweeddale. He was created a baronet of the United Kingdom in 1870, a K.C.M.G. in 1872, a G.C.M.G. in 1878, and a privy councillor in 1886.

[M. H. Long, *Sir John Rose and the high commissionership* (Can. hist. rev., 1931); *Dict. nat. biog.*; Rose, *Cyc. Can. biog.* (1886); Morgan, *Cel. Can.*; Sir J. Pope, *Memoirs of Sir J. A. Macdonald* (2 vols., Ottawa, 1894).]

Rose, John Edward (1844-1901), jurist, was born at Willowdale, Canada West, on October 4, 1844. He was educated at Victoria University, Cobourg (B.A., 1864; M.A., 1867; LL.B., 1867; LL.D., 1885). He was called to the bar in Ontario in 1867 (Q.C., 1881), and he became one of the leaders of the Ontario bar. He was appointed a judge of the common pleas division of the High Court of Justice in Ontario in 1883. He died in Toronto, Ontario, on January 19, 1901. He was the author of *The Canadian conveyancer and handy book of property law* (Toronto, 1884).

[Morgan, *Can. men* (1898); Rose, *Cyc. Can. biog.* (1888).]

Rose, William John (1885-1968), professor of Polish literature and history, University of London, was born in Minnedosa, Manitoba, on August 7, 1885. He entered Wesley College, University of Manitoba, in 1901 and graduated (B.A.) in 1905. He spent the next three years at Magdalen College, Oxford, as Manitoba Rhodes Scholar, before returning to Wesley College as lecturer in classics. He went to Europe in 1912 to do graduate studies at the University of Leipzig. After the outbreak of the First World War, Rose and his wife spent four years as prisoners of war in Austrian Silesia, but he was able to continue studying courses in Polish literature from the University of Cracow. From 1919 to 1927 he was Y.M.C.A. secretary in charge of student relief in Cracow and Warsaw. He returned to North America in 1927, and from 1927 to 1936 he was assistant professor of sociology at Dartmouth College, Hanover, New Hampshire. He then assumed the position of professor of Polish literature and history in the school of Slavonic and East European studies at the University of London. In 1939 he became director of the school, succeeding Sir Bernard Pares. He was deeply involved during the Second World War in the foreign research and press service of the British Foreign Office. He retired from his University of London post in 1950 and on his return to Canada became "visiting professor" at the University of British Columbia for the next six years.

His numerous writings were related to his Christian life and to his long interest in Poland. He wrote *Duch i Praca Y.M.C.A. w Ameryce* (1921, in Polish); translated *Danzig and Poland* by S. Askenzy (1922); *Stanislas*

Konarski, preceptor of Poland (London, 1929); The drama of Upper Silesia (London, 1936); The Polish tradition (London, 1936); Poland (Harmondsworth, 1939); The rise of Polish democracy (London, 1944); Poland, old and new (London, 1948); he also contributed to the Cambridge history of Poland (Cambridge, 1941). In his honour the Canadian Polish Congress issued a Festschrift volume, The Polish past in Canada (Toronto, 1960). He died in Vancouver, British Columbia, March 10, 1968.

[Can. who's who, 1955-57; Proc. Trans. Roy. Soc. Can., vol. VII.]

Rosebrugh, Abner Mulholland (1835-1914), physician and author, was born near Galt, Upper Canada, on November 8, 1835. He was educated at Victoria College, Cobourg (M.D., 1859), and practised medicine in Toronto. He devoted himself chiefly to the study of ophthalmology and medical electricity; and he invented various electrical devices. He died in Toronto on November 6, 1914. He was the author of An introduction to the study of the optical defects of the eye (Toronto, 1866), Chloroform, and a new way of administering it (Toronto, 1869), A handbook of medical electricity (Toronto, 1885), and Recent advances in electro-therapeutics (Toronto, 1887).

[Morgan, Can. men (1912).]

Ross, Alexander (1783-1856), fur-trader and author, was born in Nairnshire, Scotland, on May 9, 1783. He emigrated to Canada in 1805, and for several years he taught school in Glengarry, Upper Canada. In 1810 he entered the service of the Pacific Fur Company, and he took part in the founding of Fort Astoria. In 1813, when Astoria was handed over to the Nor'-Westers, he became a clerk in the North West Company; and he remained on the Pacific slope until after the union of the North West and Hudson's Bay companies in 1821. He retired from the fur-trade in 1825, and settled in the Red River district. He became sheriff of Assiniboia; and from 1835 to 1850 he was a member of the Council of Assiniboia. He died at the Red River Settlement on October 23, 1856. He was the author of Adventures of the first settlers on the Oregon or Columbia river (London, 1849), The fur-hunters of the far West (2 vols., London, 1855), and The Red River settlement (London, 1856). Some of his letters have been published in Transaction No. 63 of the Manitoba Historical and Scientific Society.

[G. Bryce, Alexander Ross (Can. mag., 1917), and Alexander Ross, fur-trader, author, and philanthropist (Queen's quarterly, 1903); Dict. nat. biog.; Cyc. Am. biog.; Morgan, Bib. can.; E. H. Oliver, The Canadian North West (2 vols., Ottawa, 1914).]

Ross, Alexander Herbert Douglas (d. 1950), local historian, died at Toronto, Ontario, on April 6, 1950. In his later years he was a civil servant in the Parliament Buildings in Toronto. He was the author of A short history of the Arnprior High School (Ottawa, 1922) and of Ottawa, past and present (Ottawa, 1927).

[Private information.]

Ross, Alexander McLagan (1829-1900), provincial treasurer of Ontario, was born in Dundee, Scotland, on April 20, 1829, the son of Colin Ross and Elizabeth McLagan. He came with his parents to Canada in 1834, and was educated at Goderich, Upper Canada. He entered the Bank of Upper Canada, and was later an officer of the Royal Canadian Bank and the Canadian Bank of Commerce. From 1875 to 1890 he represented West Huron in the Legislative Assembly of Ontario; and from 1883 to 1890 he was provincial treasurer. In 1890 he was appointed clerk of the county court, York county, Ontario; and he died at Toronto on September 29, 1900.

[Morgan, Can. men (1898); Can. parl. comp.; Rose, Cyc. Can. biog. (1886).]

Ross, Alexander Milton (1832-1897), naturalist, was born at Belleville, Upper Canada, on December 13, 1832, the son of William Ross and Frederika Grant. He was educated at the common school of Belleville, but at the age of eleven had to leave school to earn a livelihood. He went to New York, and became a compositor on the Evening Post, then edited by William Cullen Bryant, the poet. At the same time he studied medicine, and in 1855 he obtained the degree of M.D., and was admitted a member of the College of Physicians and Surgeons. He became actively interested in the anti-slavery campaign, and was a personal friend of John Brown, the abolitionist. He served as a surgeon in the American Civil War; and after the war he took service as a surgeon in the Mexican army. About 1870 he returned to Canada, and devoted himself to the study of Canadian flora and fauna. He died at Detroit, Michigan, on October 27, 1897. In 1857 he married Hester Harrington; and by her he had one son. He published the following books and pamphlets: Recollections of an abolitionist (Montreal, 1867); The birds of Canada (Toronto, 1871); Butterflies and moths of Canada (Toronto, 1873); The flora of Canada (Toronto, 1875); The forest trees of Canada (Toronto, 1875); Catalogue to illustrate the animal resources of the Dominion (Toronto, 1876); Ferns and wild flowers of Canada (Toronto, 1877); Mammals, reptiles, and fresh water fishes of Canada (Montreal, 1878); and Memoirs of a reformer (Toronto, 1893).

[F. Landon, A daring Canadian abolitionist (Michigan history magazine, 1921); Cyc. Am. biog.; Morgan, Can. men (1898); Rose, Cyc. Can. biog. (1888).]

Ross, Bernard Rogan (1827-1874), fur-trader, was a servant of the Hudson's Bay

Company who was born September 25, 1827, at Londonderry, Ireland, and was employed in the Mackenzie River district about the middle of the nineteenth century. He retired from the Company's service, settled at Fort Garry, Manitoba, and died at Toronto, Ontario, on June 21, 1874. He contributed some valuable papers on the Mackenzie River district to the *Canadian Naturalist* for 1861-62.

[Morgan, *Bib. can.*; *Dict. Can. biog.*, vol. 10.]

Ross, Charles (1794?-1844), fur-trader, was born at Kingcraig, Inverness-shire, Scotland, about 1794. The statement is made in N. de B. Lugrin, *The pioneer women of Vancouver Island* (Victoria, B.C., 1928), that "according to Bishop Ridge, he was the son of a Scottish nobleman." He entered the service of the North West Company as a clerk in 1818; and was stationed first at Norway House. After the union of the North West and Hudson's Bay companies, he was stationed at Rainy Lake; and here, apparently, he married his wife, whose name was Isabella Melville (or Merilia). In 1824 he was transferred to New Caledonia; and he was promoted to the rank of chief trader in 1831. He was in charge of the building of Fort Victoria in 1843; and he died there on June 27, 1844. He is to be distinguished from the Charles Ross who was in charge of Fort Vermilion in 1833, was afterwards transferred to the Columbia department, and was commissioned a chief trader in 1843.

[W. K. L., *Five letters of Charles Ross* (British Columbia historical quarterly, 1943).]

Ross, Dudley E. (1898-1967), surgeon, was born in Toronto, Ontario, January 21, 1898. He was educated at McGill University (M.D., 1921). During the First World War he served as a private with the McGill Hospital in France (1915-16) and as surgeon probationer with the Royal Naval Volunteer Reserve (1916-19). He maintained his connection with the army and was a lieutenant-colonel with the Royal Canadian Army Medical Corps in the Second World War. Dr. Ross was appointed surgeon at the Montreal Children's Hospital in 1930 and surgeon-in-chief in 1937. In 1940 he performed the hospital's first operation on a child with a congenital heart abnormality. He wrote a number of articles on such subjects as the causes of lung abnormalities and procedures in congenital heart conditions. He died at Montreal, Quebec, February 4, 1967.

[*Can. who's who*, 1949-51; Metropolitan Toronto Library Board, *Biographical scrapbooks*, vol. 33.]

Ross, Dunbar (1800?-1865), solicitor-general for Lower Canada (1853-57), was born at Clonakilty, Ireland, about 1800. He emigrated to Canada in youth, was called to the bar of Lower Canada (Q.C., 1853), and prac-

tised law in Quebec. From 1850 to 1851 he represented Megantic in the Legislative Assembly of Canada, and Beauce from 1854 to 1861. From 1853 to 1857 he was solicitor-general for Lower Canada. He died at Quebec on May 16, 1865. Under the *nom-de-plume* of "Zeno" he published a pamphlet entitled *The "Crise" Metcalfe, and the Lafontaine-Baldwin cabinet defended* (Montreal, 1844), and under his own name *The seat of government of Canada, its Legislative Council, and "double majority" question* (Quebec, 1858).

[Morgan, *Bib. can.*; *Bull. rech. hist.*, 1929; J. Desjardins, *Guide parlementaire historique* (Quebec, 1902).]

Ross, Duncan (d. 1834), clergyman, was born in Tarbert, Ross-shire, Scotland, and was educated at Edinburgh University. He was ordained as a missionary to Nova Scotia in 1795; and for nearly forty years he was stationed at West River, Nova Scotia. He died at West River on October 25, 1834. He was the author of *The subject and mode of baptism ascertained from the Scripture* (Edinburgh, 1810), and several pamphlets printed at Pictou, Nova Scotia, between 1824 and 1832.

[R. J. Long, *Nova Scotia authors* (East Orange, N.J., 1918); Morgan, *Bib. can.*]

Ross, Mrs. Ellen, *née* **McGregor** (d. 1892), author, was born in Banff, Scotland, the daughter of Capt. McGregor. She married first a journalist of Inverness named Stalker; and after his death she married, secondly, a banker of Inverness named Alexander Ross. With her second husband she emigrated to Canada, and settled in Montreal. Left a widow in Montreal, she turned to writing for support. In addition to a number of stories contributed to American magazines and newspapers, she published *Violet Keith* (Montreal, 1868), *The wreck of the White Bear* (Montreal, 1871), *A legend of the Grand Gordons* (Montreal, 1873), and *The legend of the holy stones* (Montreal, 1878). She died in Montreal in 1892.

[Private information.]

Ross, Eustace William Wrighton (1894-1966), poet and physicist, was born in Peterborough, Ontario, in 1894. He was educated at the University of Toronto. During the First World War he did research for the British Admiralty in England. His poetry was first published in *The Dial*, a poetry magazine of the 1920s, and in *Poetry*, a Chicago magazine. He had two volumes of poems published, *Laconics* (1930), and *Sonnets* (1932), and is represented by poems in the *Oxford book of Canadian verse*. In 1956 a collection of his verse was published under the title *Experiment 1923-29*, and in 1957 he was included in A. J. M. Smith, ed., *The book of Canadian poetry*.

He is regarded as Canada's first modern poet and a superb imagist. He was director of the magnetic division of the Dominion Observatory at Agincourt, Ontario, until his retirement in 1959. He died at Toronto, Ontario, August 27, 1966.

[N. Story, *Oxford companion to Canadian history and literature* (Toronto, 1967); Metropolitan Toronto Library Board, *Biographical scrapbooks*, vol. 26.]

Ross, François Xavier (1869-1945), first Roman Catholic bishop of Gaspé, was born at Grosses-Roches, Matane county, Quebec, on March 6, 1869. He was educated at the Quebec Seminary and at Rimouski, and was ordained a priest in 1894. After serving as parish priest in several places, and after studying in Rome, he became principal of the normal school at Rimouski in 1906, and he remained in this position until he was made first bishop of Gaspé in 1923. In 1920 he was elected a fellow of the Royal Society of Canada. He died at Quebec City on July 5, 1945. He was the author of *Louis Veuillot et la presse catholique* (Quebec, 1913), *Manuel de pédagogie* (Quebec, 1915), *Noces d'argent de Mgr Blais* (Quebec, 1918), and *Questions scolaires* (Quebec, 1920).

[Allaire, *Dict. biog.*; *Proc. Roy. Soc. Can.*, 1946.]

Ross, Frank Mackenzie (1891-1971), businessman, was born in Glasgow, Scotland, April 14, 1891, and educated at the Royal Academy, Tain, Scotland. He came to Canada at the age of nineteen and worked in Toronto, joining the 48th Highlanders on the outbreak of the First World War. He received the Military Cross and Bar. During the Second World War he was director-general of the armament, supply, and naval equipment branch, and on the restoration of peace became co-ordinator of reconstruction councils. He moved to British Columbia after his marriage in 1945.

Frank Ross was director of 35 companies, and from 1955 to 1960 was lieutenant-governor of British Columbia. He died at Vancouver, British Columbia, December 11, 1971.

[*Can. who's who*, 1967-69.]

Ross, Sir George William (1841-1914), prime minister of Ontario (1899-1905), born near Nairn, Middlesex county, Ontario, on September 18, 1841, the son of James Ross and Ellen McKinnon. He was educated at the Toronto Normal School and at Albert University, Belleville (LL.B., 1883). For many years he was a teacher and school inspector. From 1872 to 1883 he represented West Middlesex in the Canadian House of Commons; he then entered the Mowat administration in Ontario as minister of education, and was elected to the Legislative Assembly for West Middlesex. On the retirement of A. S. Hardy (q.v.), he became prime minister of Ontario, and held office until the government was defeated at the polls in 1905. He continued to sit in the legislature, as leader of the opposition, until 1907, when he was appointed a senator of Canada. In 1910 he

was chosen as Liberal leader in the Senate; and he held this position until his death in Toronto on March 7, 1914. He was thrice married, (1) in 1862 to Christina (d. 1872), daughter of Duncan Campbell, (2) in 1875 to Catharine (d. 1902), daughter of William Boston, and (3) in 1907 to Mildred, daughter of John Robert Peel. In 1910 he was created a knight bachelor. He was an LL.D. of St. Andrew's University (1888), of Victoria University (1892), of the University of Toronto (1894), of McMaster University (1902), and of Queen's University (1903); and in 1896 he was elected a fellow of the Royal Society of Canada. With William Buckingham (q.v.) he collaborated in *The life and times of the Hon. Alexander Mackenzie* (Toronto, 1892), and he was the author of *The school system of Ontario* (New York, 1896), *The senate of Canada* (Toronto, 1914), and a large number of pamphlets and public addresses. As a public speaker he was almost unrivalled among Canadians of his day. His reminiscences were published under the title *Getting into parliament, and after* (Toronto, 1913).

[Margaret Ross, *Sir George W. Ross, a biographical study* (Toronto, 1924); *Who was who*, 1898-1916; Morgan, *Can. men* (1912); Rose, *Cyc. Can. biog.* (1886); *Can. parl. comp.*; C. R. W. Biggar, *Sir Oliver Mowat* (2 vols., Toronto, 1905); C. Clarke, *Sixty years in Upper Canada* (Toronto, 1908).]

Ross, Hugh Robert (1870-1937), author, was a Winnipeg insurance agent who wrote *Thirty-five years in the limelight: Sir Rodmond P. Roblin and his times* (Winnipeg, 1936).

[B. B. Peel, *A bibliography of the prairie provinces* (Toronto, 1956).]

Ross, James (1811-1886), principal of Dalhousie College and University (1864-85), was born at West River, Pictou, Nova Scotia, on July 28, 1811, the son of the Rev. Duncan Ross. He was ordained a minister of the Presbyterian Church in 1835; in 1842 he became editor of the *Presbyterian Banner*; and later he became principal of the Presbyterian Theological Seminary at West River, and after 1858 at Truro. When this college was merged with Dalhousie College in 1863, he was appointed principal of Dalhousie, and professor of ethics and political economy. He resigned in 1885, and he died at Dartmouth, Nova Scotia, on March 15, 1886.

[*Dom. ann. reg.*, 1886.]

Ross, James (1835-1871), journalist, was born in the Red River Settlement, in the North West, on May 9, 1835, the son of Alexander Ross (q.v.). He was educated at St. John's College, Winnipeg, and at the University of Toronto (B.A., 1857). In 1857-8 he was assistant classical master at Upper Canada College; but in 1858 he returned to the North West, and from 1860 to 1864 he was editor and proprietor of the *Nor' Wester*, the only newspaper at that time in the Canadian West. After serving for a time on the editorial staff, first of the Hamilton *Spectator*, and then of the Toronto *Globe*, he returned a second time to the West, and was admitted to the bar of the North West Territories. In 1870 he was appointed chief justice under the provisional government set up by Louis Riel (q.v.). He died at Winnipeg on September 20, 1871.

[*Cyc. Am. biog.*; Morgan, *Bib. can.*; *Dict. Can. biog.*, vol. 10.]

Ross, James (1848-1913), contractor, was born at Cromarty, Scotland, in 1848, the son of Captain John Ross, a shipowner, and Mary McKeddie. He was educated at Inverness Academy, and emigrated to the United States in 1868. He held positions as a resident engineer on various railways in the United States, and later in Canada. In 1883 he took charge of the construction of the Canadian Pacific Railway west of Winnipeg; and he became one of the most successful railway contractors in Canada. He became an associate of Sir William Mackenzie (q.v.), and installed electric railway systems in Montreal, Toronto, London, and Winnipeg. He was president of the Dominion Coal Company, the Dominion Iron and Steel Company, the Dominion Bridge Company, and other important corporations. He died in Montreal on March 20, 1913. In 1872 he married Annie, daughter of John Kerr, Kingston, Ontario.

[Morgan, *Can. men* (1912).]

Ross, Sir James Clark (1800-1862), naval explorer, was born in Wigtonshire, Scotland, on April 15, 1800, the son of George Ross of Balsarroch, and the nephew of Sir John Ross (q.v.). He entered the Royal Navy in 1812; and in 1819-20, in 1821-23, and in 1824-25 he accompanied Parry (q.v.) on his Arctic explorations. In 1829-33 he accompanied his uncle, Sir John Ross (q.v.), on his second expedition to the Arctic; and he discovered the magnetic pole on June 1, 1831. In 1839-43 he made a successful voyage of discovery in the Antarctic; and in 1843 he was knighted. In 1848-49 he commanded an expedition sent out in search of Sir John Franklin; and in his later years he was regarded as "the first authority on all matters relating to Arctic navigation". He died at Aylesbury, England, on April 3, 1862. In 1828 he was elected a fellow of the Royal Society; and he was the author of *A voyage of discovery in the southern and antarctic seas* (2 vols., London, 1847).

[E. S. Dodge, *The polar Rosses* (London, 1973); *Encyc. Can.*, 1968; *Dict. nat. biog.*]

Ross, James Hamilton (1856-1932), senator of Canada, was born at London, Canada West, on May 12, 1856. He was educated in London, but went to the North West Ter-

ritories as a young man, and became a rancher near Moose Jaw. He was elected a member of the North West Assembly in 1883, and retained his seat until 1901; and during this period he was successively treasurer, commissioner of public works, and territorial secretary of the Executive Council. In 1901 he was appointed commissioner of the Yukon Territory; but he resigned this post on his election in 1902 as the first member from the Yukon in the Canadian House of Commons. He was summoned to the Senate of Canada in 1904; and he sat in the Senate until his death, at Victoria, British Columbia, on December 14, 1932.

[*Can. parl. comp.*]

Ross, John (d. 1787), fur-trader, first appears in the fur-trade licences in Canada in 1779. In 1780 he was in partnership with Peter Pangman (q.v.). He became a partner in the venture organized by Gregory, McLeod, and Co. in 1783, and was placed in charge of the Athabaska district. In the spring of 1787 he was killed in a scuffle with some of the men of Peter Pond (q.v.), the North West Company partner who was opposed to him.

[W. S. Wallace (ed.), *Documents relating to the North West Company* (Toronto: The Champlain Society, 1934); J. B. Tyrrell, *Journals of Samuel Hearne and Philip Turnor* (Toronto: The Champlain Society, 1934).]

Ross, Sir John (1777-1856), explorer, was born on June 24, 1777, the fourth son of the Rev. Andrew Ross, minister of Inch, Wigtonshire, Scotland, and Elizabeth, daughter of Robert Corsane, provost of Dumfries. He entered the Royal Navy in 1790, but served in the merchant marine until 1799, when he returned to the Navy. He was on active service during the remainder of the Napoleonic Wars; and in 1812 he was promoted to the rank of commander. In 1818 he was appointed to the command of an expedition for the discovery of the north-west passage, which resulted in the re-discovery of Baffin's Bay. In 1829 he made another attempt to discover the north-west passage; and on this occasion he was ice-bound for four years. On his return to England, he was created a knight bachelor; and in 1839 he was appointed British consul at Stockholm. He returned to England in 1846, and in 1847 he urged on the Admiralty the immediate dispatch of an expedition for the relief of Sir John Franklin (q.v.), but his advice was rejected. In 1850-51 he himself made an expedition for the relief of Franklin, but he did not penetrate farther than Lancaster Sound. He died at London, England, on August 30, 1856. He published *A voyage of discovery* (London, 1819), *Narrative of a second voyage in search of a north-west passage* (2 vols., London, 1835), and *Rear-admiral Sir John Franklin: A narrative of the circumstances and causes which led to* *the failure of the searching expeditions sent by government and others* (London, 1855), as well as other works on naval subjects.

[E. S. Dodge, *The polar Rosses* (London, 1973); *Dict. nat. biog.*; *Cyc. Am. biog.*]

Ross, John (1818-1871), senator of Canada, was born in county Antrim, Ireland, on March 10, 1818. He came to Canada with his parents as a child, and was educated in the district school at Brockville, Upper Canada. He was called to the bar of Upper Canada in 1839, and practised law in Toronto. In 1848 he was appointed a legislative councillor of Canada; and during the fifteen years preceding Confederation he repeatedly held office in the government. From 1851 to 1853 he was solicitor-general for Upper Canada, and from 1853 to 1854 attorney-general; from 1854 to 1856 he was speaker of the Legislative Council; in 1858 he was for a few months receiver-general; and from 1858 to 1862 he was president of the Council and minister of agriculture. In 1867 he was called to the Senate of Canada by royal proclamation; and in 1869 he became speaker of the Senate. He died near Toronto, Ontario, on January 31, 1871. Early in 1847 he married Margaret, daughter of George Crawford. She died before the year was out. In 1851, he married Augusta Elizabeth, daughter of the Hon. Robert Baldwin (q.v.). From 1852 to 1857 he was a government director of the Grand Trunk Railway, and for a time he was president of the railway.

[Morgan, *Cel. Can.*; *Cyc. Am. biog.*; *Can. parl. comp.*; J. C. Dent, *The last forty years* (2 vols., Toronto, 1881); *Dict. Can. biog.*, vol. 10.]

Ross, John Jones (1832-1901), prime minister of Quebec (1884-87), was born at Quebec, Lower Canada, on August 16, 1832, the son of G. McIntosh Ross and Marie Louise Gouin. He was educated at the Quebec Seminary, and in 1853 was admitted to practice as a physician. He represented Champlain in the Legislative Assembly of Canada from 1861 to 1867, and in the Canadian House of Commons from 1867 to 1874. In 1867 he was elected also to represent Champlain in the Legislative Assembly of Quebec; but later in 1867 he was appointed to the Legislative Council of the province. From 1873 to 1884 he was a member of successive governments in the province of Quebec, and from 1884 to 1887 he was prime minister. In 1887 he was appointed a senator of Canada; from 1891 to 1893 he was speaker of the Senate; and in 1896 he was a member of the Tupper administration without portfolio. He died on May 4, 1901. In 1856 he married Arline, daughter of Lieut.-Col. Lanouette, of Champlain, Lower Canada.

[Morgan, *Can. men* (1898); *Can. parl. comp.*]

Ross, Margaret (1845-1935), biographer, was born in Middlesex county, Canada West,

on July 5, 1845, and died at Toronto, Ontario, on February 9, 1935. She was a sister of Sir George W. Ross (q.v.), and was the author of *Sir George W. Ross: A biographical study* (Toronto, 1923).

[Private information.]

Ross, Philip Dansken (1858-1949), journalist, was born in Montreal, Canada East, on January 1, 1858, and died at Ottawa, Ontario, on July 5, 1949. He was educated at McGill University (B.A.Sc., 1878), and became a journalist. After serving an apprenticeship on newspapers in Montreal and Toronto, he became managing editor of the *Ottawa Journal* in 1886, and president of the Journal Publishing Company in 1891. Queen's University conferred on him the honorary degree of LL.D. in 1919, and McGill University in 1935. He was the author of an autobiography entitled *Retrospects of a newspaper person* (Toronto, 1931).

[I. N. Smith, *The Journal men* (Toronto, 1974); *Can. who's who*, 1948; *Encyc. Can.*]

Ross, Victor Harold (1878-1934), business man and author, was born in Walkerton, Bruce county, Ontario, in 1878, the son of Donald Wilson Ross. He was educated in the public schools of Walkerton and Windsor, and became a journalist in Toronto. For many years he was financial editor of the Toronto *Globe*; but in 1917 he joined the staff of the Standard Oil Company. In 1919 he was elected a director of Imperial Oil Limited; and he became ultimately vice-president of this company. He died in Toronto on February 23, 1934. He was the author of *Petroleum in Canada* (Toronto, 1927) and *A history of the Canadian Bank of Commerce* (2 vols., Toronto, 1920-22).

[Toronto *Globe*, Feb. 24, 1934.]

Ross, William (1780?-1855), fur-trader, was born in Ross-shire, Scotland, about 1780. For several years he served as an ensign in the 11th Regiment of Foot. Then he entered the service of the Hudson's Bay Company, and was successively in charge at Oxford House, at Nelson House, and at Fort Churchill. After his retirement, he lived at Ottawa, Canada West; and there he died on January 12, 1855.

[W. S. Wallace (ed.), *Documents relating to the North West Company* (Toronto: The Champlain Society, 1934).]

Ross, William (1825-1912), minister of militia and defence for Canada (1873-74), was born at Boularderie Island, Nova Scotia, on December 20, 1825, the son of John Ross and Robina McKenzie. He was educated at the village school, and became a village postmaster. From 1859 to 1867 he sat for Victoria in the Legislative Assembly of Nova Scotia, and from 1867 to 1874 in the Canadian House of Commons. In 1873 he was appointed minister of militia and defence in the Mackenzie government; but he resigned in 1874 to accept the post of collector of customs at Halifax, Nova Scotia. He re-entered the House of Commons as member for Victoria in 1900; and in 1905 he was called to the Senate. He died at Ottawa on March 17, 1912. In 1855 he married Eliza (d. 1910), daughter of Peter Moore, North Sydney, Nova Scotia. He was a lieutenant-colonel in the Canadian militia; and he was a grand master of the Freemasons of Nova Scotia.

[Morgan, *Can. men* (1912); *Can. parl. comp.*; Rose, *Cyc. Can. biog.* (1888).]

Ross, William Benjamin (1854-1929), leader of the Conservative party in the Senate of Canada (1926-29), was born in Prince Edward Island in 1854. He was educated at Dalhousie University, and was called to the bar of Nova Scotia in 1878. He was called to the Senate of Canada in 1912, and was appointed leader of the Conservative party in the Senate in 1926. He died at Guelph, Ontario, on January 10, 1929.

[*Can. parl. comp.*]

Ross, William Donald (1869-1947), lieutenant-governor of Ontario (1927-32), was born at Little Bras d'Or, Nova Scotia, on June 20, 1869, and died at Toronto, Ontario, on June 25, 1947. He entered the employ of the Bank of Nova Scotia at the age of fourteen, and rose until he became a director. From 1903 to 1914 he was general manager of the Metropolitan Bank of Toronto; and he then became a leading financier. In 1927 he became lieutenant-governor of Ontario for the full term of five years.

[Morgan, *Can. men* (1912); *Can. who's who*, 1936-37; *Can. parl. guide*, 1932.]

Ross, William Wilson (1838-1884), clergyman and author, was born in 1838, and was ordained a minister of the Wesleyan Methodist Church in Canada in 1861. He was the pastor of various churches in Ontario and Quebec; and he died at Ingersoll, Ontario, on March 28, 1884. He was the author of *10,000 miles by land and sea* (Toronto, 1876).

[G. H. Cornish, *Cyclopaedia of Methodism in Canada* (2 vols., Toronto, 1881-1903); *Dom. ann. reg.*, 1884.]

Rothwell, Mrs. Annie. See Christie, Mrs. Annie Rothwell.

Rottenburg, Francis, Baron de (1757-1832), president and administrator of Upper Canada (1813), was born on November 14, 1757, at Danzig in Poland. From 1782 to 1791 he served as an officer in the French army; and from 1791 to 1794 he commanded a battalion of infantry under Kosciusko, the Polish patriot. He then entered the British army; and in 1810 he was sent to Canada. In 1811, with the rank of major-general, he was appointed commander of the forces in Lower Canada; and he commanded the left division of the British army in Canada throughout the War of 1812. From June 19 to December 12, 1813, he was president and administrator of Upper Canada. He returned to England in 1815, and he died at Portsmouth, England, on April 24, 1832. He was knighted in 1818, and was promoted to the rank of lieutenant-general in 1819. In 1799 he published a book entitled *Regulations for the exercise of riflemen and light infantry* (War Office, London).

[D. B. Read, *The lieutenant-governors of Upper Canada and Ontario* (Toronto, 1900); *Lieut.-general Baron Francis de Rottenburg* (Journal of the Society for Army Historical Research, 1931).]

Rottermund, E. S., Comte de (1813-1858), a European geologist who was for many years employed as chemist or inspector of mines on the staff of the crown lands department of united Canada. He died near Geneva, Switzerland, in 1858. His wife was a daughter of the Hon. P. D. Debartzch (q.v.). He was the author of several reports on the geology and minerals of Canada, notably a report on the geological exploration of lakes Huron and Superior (Toronto, 1857).

[Morgan, *Cel. Can.*]

Roubaud, Pierre Antoine (*fl.* 1742-1787), adventurer, was a native of Avignon, France, who entered the Society of Jesus, and came to Canada in 1742 as a missionary. He served for many years among the Abnaki at St. François du Lac. After the Conquest, he ingratiated himself with General Murray (q.v.); and was used by the British authorities as a secret agent. In 1764, having been repudiated by the Jesuits, he was sent by Murray to London, where he seems to have been of service to the government. In 1782-84 he assisted Ducalvet (q.v.) in his negotiations with the British government, and then betrayed to the authorities the information thus acquired. It is said that in 1785 he reverted to Roman Catholicism, took refuge with the Sulpicians in Paris, and died in Paris in 1787 or shortly afterwards. He was described by Sir Guy Carleton (q.v.) as "a man of genius ... but void of truth, without one spark of honour or of honesty."

[G. Lanctot, *La vie scandaleuse d'un faussaire* (Trans. Roy. Soc. Can., 1956); D. Brymner, *Report on Canadian archives, 1885* (Ottawa, 1886); Allaire, *Dict. biog.*; P. Gagnon, *Essai de bibliographie canadienne* (Quebec, 1895), no. 4299.]

Roue, William James (1879-1970), marine architect, was born at Halifax, Nova Scotia, April 27, 1879. He left high school at seventeen and went to work as a junior clerk in a wholesale grocers, studying mechanical drafting at night. Although he had been sailing from childhood, his training in ship design came from a borrowed copy of Dixon and Kemp's *Yacht Architecture*. The first yacht built to his design was launched in 1909. In 1920 he was asked to submit a design for a fast schooner. The ship *Bluenose* was built at the Smith and Rhuland yard in Lunenburg and became champion of the Atlantic fishing fleet, retaining her title until she was wrecked in the West Indies in 1946. The *Bluenose* appeared on the fifty-cent Canadian stamp in 1929 and the ten-cent coin in 1937. In later years he designed the Roue 20's, the eight-metre *Norseman*, a Great Lakes champion from 1956 to 1959, and the *Acadia*, "R" class. A replica of *Bluenose* known as *Bluenose II* was launched in 1963. He designed working ships and ferries for the maritime governments and during the Second World War designed wooden landing craft and tugs. He died at Halifax, Nova Scotia, January 14, 1970.

[*Atlantic Advocate*, vol. 51, no. 5.]

Rouillard, Eugène (1851-1926), geographer, was born at Quebec, Canada East, on June 4, 1851, the son of Nicolas Rouillard and Marie Elisa Legris dit Lépine. He was educated at Laval University (LL.B., 1875; LL.D., 1916), and was admitted a notary public in 1876. Until 1893 he was prominent in the journalism and politics of Quebec; but in 1894 he was appointed an inspector of crown lands in the province of Quebec, and he retained this post until shortly before his death at Quebec on October 16, 1926. In 1907 he was instrumental in reviving the Société de Géographie de Québec, became its secretary-treasurer, and contributed many articles to its *Bulletin*; and in 1915 he was elected a fellow of the Royal Society of Canada. He was the author of *Les bibliothèques populaires* (Quebec, 1890), *Étude sur la colonisation dans les cantons de Témiscouata, Matane, Rimouski, Bonaventure, et Gaspé* (Quebec, 1899); *Noms géographiques de la province de Québec et des provinces maritimes empruntés aux langues sauvages* (Quebec, 1906), *La côte nord du Saint-Laurent et le Labrador canadien* (Quebec, 1908), and *Dictionnaire des rivières et des lacs de la province de Québec* (Quebec, 1914).

[*In memoriam Eugène Rouillard* (Bulletin de la Société de la Géographie du Québec, 1926); *Bull. rech. hist.*, 1927; Le Jeune, *Dict. gén.*; Morgan, *Can. men* (1912); *Proc. Roy. Soc. Can.*, 1927.]

Rouleau, Charles Borromée (1840-1901), jurist, was born at Isle Verte, Lower Canada, on December 13, 1840. After teaching school, he studied law, and in 1868 was called to the bar of Quebec. From 1876 to 1883 he was police magistrate of the district of Ottawa, and from 1883 to 1887 he was a police magistrate for the North West Territories. In 1887 he was appointed a judge of the Supreme Court of the North West Territories; and he remained on the bench until his death on August 25, 1901.

He was the author of *Notre système judiciaire* (Ottawa, 1888).

[*Bull. rech. hist.*, 1934.]

Rouleau, Charles Edmond (1841-1926), soldier and author, was born at Ste. Anne de la Pocatière, Lower Canada, on September 18, 1841, the son of Charles Rouleau and Sophie Lebrun. In 1865 he served in the Canadian militia during the Fenian raids; and from 1868 to 1870 he was a zouave in the Papal army at Rome. On his return to Canada, he became a journalist. He died at Quebec on December 24, 1926. He was the author of *Souvenirs de voyage d'un soldat de Pie IX* (Quebec, 1881), *Rome et le Canada* (Quebec, 1885), *Le guide du cultivateur* (Quebec, 1890), *L'émigration, les principales causes* (Quebec, 1896), *Légendes canadiennes* (Quebec, 1901), *La Papauté et les zouaves pontificaux* (Quebec, 1905), and *Les zouaves canadiens* (Quebec, 1924).

[*Bull. rech. hist.*, 1927.]

Rouleau, Raymond Marie (1866-1931), cardinal of the Roman Catholic Church, was born at Isle Verte, Quebec, in 1866. He was educated at the Seminary of Rimouski, entered the Dominican Order in 1886, and was ordained a priest in 1892. He became the first prior of the house of the Dominicans in Ottawa in 1900; and in 1923 he was elected bishop of Valleyfield, Quebec. In 1926 he became archbishop of Quebec, and in 1927 he was made a cardinal, the third Canadian to be thus honoured. He died at Quebec on May 31, 1931.

[Allaire, *Dict. biog.*; Le Jeune, *Dict. gén.*; *Can. who was who*, vol. 1.]

Rous, John (1700?-1760), naval officer, was in command of a Boston privateer which raided the French posts on the coast of Newfoundland in 1744. He took part in the capture of Louisbourg in 1745, and was given the rank of captain in the Royal Navy. He was engaged in the defence of the coast of Nova Scotia in 1749; was in command of the squadron sent against Beauséjour in 1755; and took part in the expedition against Cape Breton under Lord Loudon in 1756. He commanded the *Sutherland* at the capture of Louisbourg in 1758; and in 1759 was with Admiral Saunders at the siege of Quebec. He settled at Halifax, and was sworn a member of the Council of Nova Scotia in 1754. He died in 1760.

[B. Murdoch, *History of Nova Scotia* (Halifax, N.S., 1867); T. B. Akins (ed.), *Public documents of Nova Scotia* (Halifax, N.S., 1869); *Dict. Can. biog.*, vol. 3.]

Rousseau, Dominique (1755-1825), jeweller and trader, was born at Quebec, Canada, on November 9, 1755, and became a jeweller in Montreal. He became interested in the trade with Michilimackinac and the West; and in 1801 and again in 1806 he tried to invade the monopoly of the North West Company at

Grand Portage, without success. He died on February 27, 1825.

[E. Z. Massicotte, *Dominique Rousseau* (Bull. rech. hist., 1943); Earl of Selkirk, *Sketch of the British fur-trade in North America* (London, 1816).]

Rousseau, Edmond (d. 1909), archivist and historian, was an officer of the judicial archives of Quebec. He died at Quebec on March 8, 1909. He was the author of a novel, *Le Château de Beaumanoir* (Lévis, Que., 1886), several historical works, *Les exploits d'Iberville* (Quebec, 1888), *La Monongahéla* (Quebec, 1890), and *Deux récits* (Montreal, 1903), and two books on temperance, *Alcool et alcoolisme* (Quebec, 1905), and *Petit catéchisme de tempérance et de tuberculose* (Quebec, 1909).

[*Bull. rech. hist.*, 1914, and supplement to index vols.]

Rousseau, Jean Baptiste (1758-1812), fur-trader, was born in 1758, the son of Jean Bonaventure Rousseau, who received in 1770 a licence to trade "at Toronto". The son, following the father, became a fur-trader at the mouth of the Humber River, near Toronto, and was "the last citizen of the old French Toronto, and the first of the new English York". In 1795, however, he removed to Ancaster, Upper Canada; and he died, while on a visit to Niagara, on November 16, 1812.

[Percy J. Robinson, *Toronto during the French régime* (Toronto, 1933).]

Rousseau, Pierre (1827-1912), priest and author, was born at Nantes, France, on February 11, 1827, entered the Sulpician order, and was ordained a priest in 1852. He came to Canada in 1854, and spent most of his life in Montreal, where he died on February 8, 1912. He was the author of *Vie de M. Pierre-Louis Billaudèle, grand-vicaire et dixième supérieur du séminaire de Montréal* (Montreal, 1885), and *Histoire de la vie de M. Paul de Chomedey, sieur de Maisonneuve* (Montreal, 1886).

[Allaire, *Dict. biog.*; *Bull. rech. hist.*, 1928.]

Routh, Sir Randolph Isham (1787-1858), executive councillor of Lower Canada, was born at Poole, Dorsetshire, England, in 1787, the son of the Hon. Richard Routh, sometime chief justice of Newfoundland. He entered the British army, served in the Peninsular War and at Waterloo, and in 1826 was appointed commissary general in Canada. From 1838 to 1841 he was a member of the Executive Council of Lower Canada formed by Lord Durham (q.v.). He died in London, England, on November 29, 1858. In 1841 he was made, for his services in Canada, a knight bachelor, and later he received the decoration of K.C.B. His second wife, whom he married in Quebec in 1830, was Maria Louise, daughter of the Hon. Jean Thomas Tashereau (q.v.).

[*Dict. nat. biog.*; Le Jeune, *Dict. gén.*]

Routhier, Sir Adolphe Basile (1839-1920), jurist and author, was born at St. Placide, Lower Canada, on May 8, 1839, the son of Charles Routhier, a veteran of the War of 1812, and Angélique Lafleur. He was educated at the Seminary of Ste. Thérèse and at Laval University, Quebec (B.A., 1858; B.C.L., 1860; Litt. D., 1880; LL.D., 1883; and he was called to the bar of Lower Canada in 1861 (Q.C., 1873). In 1873 he was appointed a puisne judge of the Superior Court of Lower Canada, and in 1904 he became chief justice. He retired from the bench in 1906, and he died at St. Irénée-les-Bains, Quebec, on June 27, 1920. As an author, he displayed the greatest versatility. In prose, he published the following: *Causeries du dimanche* (Montreal, 1871), *En canot* (Quebec, 1881), *Les grand drames* (Montreal, 1889), *Conférences et discours* (2 vols., Montreal, 1889 and 1905), *De Québec à Victoria* (Quebec, 1893), *La reine Victoria et son jubilé* (Quebec, 1898), *Québec et Lévis* (Montreal, 1900), *Quebec* (Montreal, 1904), an historical drama entitled *Montcalm et Lévis* (Quebec, 1918), and two novels, *Le centurion* (Quebec, 1909), translated into English by Lucille P. Borden (St. Louis, 1910), and *Paulina* (Quebec, 1918). Under the pseudonym of "Jean Piquefort", he published also *Portraits et pastels littéraires* (Quebec, 1873). In poetry he published a volume entitled *Les échos* (Quebec, 1873); but his chief production was the national anthem, "O Canada". In 1862 he married Marie Clorinde, daughter of J. O. Mondelet, Montreal. In 1882 he was chosen a charter member of the Royal Society of Canada, and he was president of the society in 1915-16. In 1911 he was created a knight bachelor.

[Abbé E. J. Auclair, *Sir Adolphe Routhier* (Revue canadienne, 1920); *Proc. Roy. Soc. Can.*, 1921; Taché, *Men of the day*; Le Jeune, *Dict. gén.*; Rose, *Cyc. Can. biog.* (1888); Morgan, *Can. men* (1912).]

Rouville, Jean Baptiste Melchior Hertel de (1748-1817), legislative councillor of Lower Canada, was born at Three Rivers in 1748, the son of René Ovide Hertel de Rouville (q.v.). In 1761 he went with his father to France; but he returned to Canada in 1772. In 1775 he took part in the defence of Fort St. John against the Americans, was taken prisoner, and spent a year and a half in captivity. From 1792 to 1796 he represented the county of Bedford in the Legislative Assembly of Lower Canada; and in 1812 he was appointed to the Legislative Council. He died at Chambly, Lower Canada, on November 30, 1817. By his wife, Marie-Anne Hervieux, he had eight children, of whom six died young.

[P. G. R., *René-Ovide Hertel de Rouville* (Bull. rech. hist., 1915); Le Jeune, *Dict. gén.*]

Rouville, Jean Baptiste René Hertel de (d. 1859), legislative councillor of Lower Canada, was the son of the Hon. Jean Baptiste Melchior Hertel de Rouville (q.v.). He was an officer in the Canadian Voltigeurs, and fought at Châteauguay in 1813. From 1824 to 1830 he represented Bedford in the Legislative Assembly of Lower Canada, and from 1837 to 1838 he sat in the Legislative Council. He died at Beloeil, Lower Canada, on January 14, 1859. In 1816 he married Anne-Charlotte Boucher de la Broquerie; and by her he had several children.

[P. G. Roy, *René Ovide Hertel de Rouville* (Bull. rech. hist., 1915); Le Jeune, *Dict. gén.*]

Rouville, René Ovide Hertel de (1720-1793), jurist, was born at Port Toulouse, Ile Royale (Cape Breton), on September 6, 1720, the son of Jean-Baptiste Hertel de Rouville, commandant at Port Toulouse, and Marie-Anne Beaudoin. From 1747 to 1760 he was the sub-delegate of the intendant at the St. Maurice forges. He left for France in 1761, but returned soon afterwards to Canada, and was appointed in 1765 grand-voyer for the district of Montreal. In 1775 he was appointed a civil judge at Montreal, and in 1779 a judge of the Court of Common Pleas. This post he held until his death at Montreal on August 12, 1793. He was twice married, (1) in 1741 to Marie-Louise-Catherine André de Leigne (d. 1766), by whom he had five children, and (2) in 1767 to Charlotte-Gabrielle Jarret de Verchères (d. 1808), widow of Pierre-Joseph Raimbault de Saint-Blin.

[P. G. Roy, *L'hon. René Ovide Hertel de Rouville* (Bull. rech. hist., 1906 and 1915); Le Jeune, *Dict. gén.*]

Roux, Jean Henri Auguste (1760-1831), priest and author, was born in the diocese of Aix, in Provence, France, on February 5, 1760. He was ordained a priest of the Roman Catholic Church in 1784, and entered the order of St. Sulpice. He went to England in 1791, at the height of the French Revolution; and in 1794 he was sent to Canada as assistant superior of the Sulpicians. In 1798 he became superior of the Sulpicians in Canada; and he continued in this position until his death at Montreal, Lower Canada, on April 7, 1831. He is said to have been the author of the anonymous *Vie de la vénérable Soeur Marguerite Bourgeois* (Montreal, 1818).

[Allaire, *Dict. biog.*]

Rowan, Sir William (1789-1879), administrator of Canada (1853-54), was born in the Isle of Man, June 18, 1789, the eighth son of Robert Rowan, of Mullens and Garry, county Antrim. He entered the British army in 1803, and saw service in the Peninsular War, at Waterloo, and in Canada. From 1832 to 1839 he was civil and military secretary to Sir John Colborne (q.v.); and in 1849 he was appointed commander-in-chief of the British forces in North America. From August, 1853, to June 1854, he was administrator of the government of Canada, during the absence of Lord Elgin (q.v.); and in 1855 he returned to England. He rose to the rank of field-marshal; and he died in Bath, England, on September 26, 1879. He was knighted in 1856.

[*Dict. nat. biog.*; *Cyc. Am. biog.*; *Dom. ann. reg.*, 1879; Morgan, *Cel. Can.*; *Dict. Can. biog.*, vol. 10.]

Rowan, William (1891-1957), zoologist, was born at Basle, Switzerland, on July 29, 1891, and died at Edmonton, Alberta, on June 30, 1957. He was educated at University College, London (B.Sc., 1917); in 1919 he was appointed lecturer in zoology in the University of Manitoba; and in 1920 he became the first professor of zoology in the University of Alberta, a position he retained until his retirement in 1956. It was for his work as an ornithologist that he was especially notable; and he was the author of *The riddle of migration* (Baltimore, 1931). He was elected a fellow of the Royal Society of Canada in 1934; and in 1946 he was awarded the Society's Flavelle medal.

[*Proc. Roy. Soc. Can.*, 1958; *Encyc. Can.*]

Rowand, John (1787-1854), fur-trader, was born in Montreal, Canada, in 1787, the son of an assistant surgeon in the Montreal General Hospital. He entered the service of the North West Company as an apprentice clerk, and was stationed in 1804 and 1805 at Fort des Prairies, and in 1806 on the lower Red River. In 1807 he returned to the Saskatchewan; and in 1808 he built a fort on the site of what is now the city of Edmonton. Here he remained, with brief intervals, for most of the rest of his life. He was made a partner of the North West Company shortly before the union of 1821; and in 1821 he became a chief trader in the Hudson's Bay Company. In 1823 he was placed in charge of Fort Edmonton; and in 1826 he was promoted to the rank of chief factor. He died at Fort Pitt on the Saskatchewan on June 1, 1854. He married an Indian girl who saved his life when he was thrown from his horse on the prairies in his early days in the West; and by her he had several children. One of his sons entered the service of the North West Company; and another, who was educated at Edinburgh University, became a successful physician at Quebec.

[R. Mitchell, *John Rowand, chief factor* (Beaver, 1935); I. Allan, *John Rowand, fur trader* (Toronto, 1963); E. E. Rich (ed.), *Colin Robertson's correspondence book* (Toronto: The Champlain Society, 1939).]

Rowe, Peter Trimble (1856-1942), Anglican bishop of Alaska, was born at Meadowville, Canada West, on November 20, 1856. He was educated at the University of Trinity College, Toronto (B.A., 1880; M.A., 1889; D.D., 1895), and was ordained a priest of the Church of England in 1880. From 1882 to 1895 he was rector of St. James's Church, Sault Ste. Marie, Michigan; and in 1895 he was elected first missionary bishop of Alaska. He discharged the duties of this post until his death at Victoria, British Columbia, on June 1, 1942.

[T. Jenkins, *Man of Alaska* (New York, 1943); *Who's who in America*, 1941-42; *Can. who's who*, 1936-37; Morgan, *Can. men* (1912).]

Rowell, Newton Wesley (1867-1941), president of the council for Canada (1917-20) and chief justice of Ontario (1936-37), was born in London township, Middlesex county, Ontario, on November 1, 1867. He was educated at Osgoode Hall Law School, Toronto, and was called to the Ontario bar in 1891 (K.C., 1902). He practised law in Toronto, and soon became a leader of the Ontario bar. In 1911 he was elected to represent North Oxford in the Ontario Legislature, and was chosen leader of the Liberal party in Ontario. In 1917 he became president of the council in the Union government formed by Sir Robert Borden (q.v.), and was elected to represent Durham in the Canadian House of Commons. He was a prominent member of the Union government, and was a member of the Imperial War Cabinet. He resigned his portfolio in the government in 1920, and his seat in the House of Commons in 1921. In 1936 he was appointed chief justice of Ontario; and in 1937 he was appointed chairman of the Royal Commission on Dominion-Provincial Relations, but ill-health compelled his resignation from this commission in 1938. After three years of illness, he died at Toronto, Ontario, on November 22, 1941. He was the author of *The British Empire and world peace* (Toronto, 1922); and in 1937 he was elected a fellow of the Royal Society of Canada. Several universities conferred on him honorary degrees.

[M. E. Prang, *N. W. Rowell, Ontario nationalist* (Toronto, 1975); *Proc. Roy. Soc. Can.*, 1942; *Can. who's who*, 1938-39; *Can. parl. comp.*]

Rowley, Owsley Robert (1868-1949), banker and author, was born at Yarmouth, Nova Scotia, on January 12, 1868, and died at Toronto, Ontario, on November 24, 1949. He became a banker, and on his retirement in 1932 was an inspector of branches in the Bank of Montreal. Actively interested in the work of the Church of England, he was the author of *The house of bishops* (Montreal, 1907), and *The Anglican episcopate of Canada and Newfoundland* (Milwaukee, 1928).

[*Can. who's who*, 1948.]

Rowsell, Henry (1806-1890), printer and publisher, was born in London, England, in February, 1806. He emigrated to Canada in 1833, and established a printing and publishing business in Toronto, Upper Canada. For many years he was printer to the University of Toronto. He retired from business in 1880; and he died in Toronto on July 29, 1890.

[J. Ross Robertson, *The landmarks of Canada* (Toronto, 1917).]

Roy, Camille (1870-1943), priest and educationist, was born at Berthier-en-Bas, Quebec, on October 22, 1870. He was educated at the Quebec Seminary (B.A., 1890), the Catholic University of Paris (Ph.D., 1896), and at the Sorbonne (M.A. and L. ès L., 1900); and was ordained a priest of the Roman Catholic Church in 1894. He became professor of French literature in Laval University, Quebec, and after 1926 professor of Canadian literature. From 1924 to 1927, and again from 1932 to his death, he was rector of Laval University. In 1904 he was elected a fellow of the Royal Society of Canada; in 1928 he was elected its president; and in 1929 he was the recipient of the Society's Lorne Pierce medal for distinguished work in Canadian literature. He received the honorary degree of LL.D. from the universities of Toronto and Ottawa; and in 1928 he was created an officer of the Legion of Honour. He died at Quebec City on June 24, 1943.

He was an outstanding authority on the literature of French Canada; and was the author of the following books: *L'Université Laval et les fêtes du cinquantenaire* (Quebec, 1903), *Essais sur la littérature canadienne* (Quebec, 1907), *Nos origines littéraires* (Quebec, 1909), *Les fêtes du troisième centenaire de Québec* (Quebec, 1911), *Propos canadiens* (Quebec, 1912), *Nouveaux essais sur la littérature canadienne* (Quebec, 1914), *La critique littéraire au XIXe siècle* (Quebec, 1918), *Manuel d'histoire de la littérature canadienne* (Quebec, 1918), *Mgr de Laval* (Quebec, 1923), *Érables en fleurs* (Quebec, 1924), *A l'ombre d'érables* (Quebec, 1924), *L'abbé Henri Raymond Casgrain* (Montreal, 1925), *Études et croquis* (Montreal, 1928), *Les leçons de notre histoire* (Quebec, 1929), *Regards sur les lettres* (Quebec, 1931), *Poètes de chez nous* (Montreal, 1934), *Romanciers de chez nous* (Montreal, 1935), *Nos problèmes d'enseignement* (Montreal, 1935), *Pour conserver notre héritage français* (Montreal, 1937), *Pour former des hommes nouveaux* (Montreal, 1941), *Du fleuve aux océans* (Montreal, 1943), and *Semences de vie* (Quebec, 1943). He was also the compiler of *Morceaux choisis d'auteurs canadiens* (Montreal, 1934).

[J. E. B., *Monseigneur Camille Roy* (Canada français, 1943); *Proc. Roy. Soc. Can.*, 1944; *Can. who's who*, 1938-39; Morgan, *Can. men* (1912); Fr. Ludovic, *Bio-*

bibliographie de Mgr Camille Roy (Quebec, 1941).]

Roy, Charles (d. 1844), printer, was the son of a French soldier who settled in Canada after the British conquest. He was an apprentice in the printing shop of John Neilson (q.v.), proprietor of the *Quebec Gazette*; and in 1806 he was the printer of the famous *Le Canadien* newspaper at Quebec. He died at Quebec, on December 3, 1844.

[*L'imprimeur Louis Roy* (Bull. rech. hist., 1918).]

Roy, Ernest (1871-1928), politician and jurist, was born at St. Vallier, Quebec, on October 3, 1871, and was educated at the Quebec Seminary. He was called to the bar in 1898, and practised law in Quebec. He represented Montmagny in the Legislative Assembly of Quebec from 1900 to 1908, and Dorchester in the Canadian House of Commons from 1908 to 1911. In 1923 he was appointed a judge of the Superior Court of Quebec; and he remained on the bench until his death, at St. Michel de Bellechasse, on August 17, 1928.

[P. G. Roy, *Les juges de la province de Québec* (Quebec, 1933); *Can. parl. comp.*; *Can. who's who*, 1910.]

Roy, James (1834-1922), clergyman, was born at Montreal, Lower Canada, on November 12, 1834; and was educated at Victoria University (B.A., 1868; M.A., 1871) and at McGill University (M.A., 1879; LL.D., 1883). He was ordained a Methodist minister in 1854, a Congregationalist in 1877, and an Anglican in 1882. He held various pastoral and academic charges in Canada and in the United States; he died at Montreal, Quebec, on May 25, 1922. He was the author of *Catholicity and Methodism* (Montreal, 1877) and *How to interpret our Bible* (New York, 1911).

[Morgan, *Can. men* (1912).]

Roy, Joseph Camille. See Roy, Camille.

Roy, Joseph Edmond (1858-1913), historian, was born at Lévis, Quebec, on December 7, 1858, the son of Léon Roy, N.P., and Marguerite Lavoye. He was educated at Laval University (LL.B., 1880; Lit.D., 1898), and was admitted to practice as a notary public in 1880. From 1908 to his death he was attached to the Public Archives of Canada; and he made an important *Report on the archives of France relating to Canadian history* (Ottawa, 1911). He died at Quebec, on May 8, 1913. In 1885 he married Lucienne Carrier, of Lévis, Quebec. In 1891 he was elected a fellow of the Royal Society of Canada, and in 1908 he was its president. His chief publications were *Le premier colon de Lévis* (Lévis, 1884), *Histoire de la seigneurie de Lauzon* (5 vols., Lévis, 1897-1904), *Histoire du notariat au Canada* (4 vols., Lévis, 1899-1902), and a number of papers in

the transactions of the Royal Society of Canada. From 1898 to 1913 he edited *La Revue de Notariat* (Lévis).

[*Proc. Roy. Soc. Can.*, 1913; Morgan, *Can. men* (1912); Le Jeune, *Dict. gén.*]

Roy, Louis (d. 1799), printer, was the son of a French soldier who settled in Canada after the conquest. He was apprenticed as a printer in the printing office of John Neilson (q.v.), proprietor of the *Quebec Gazette*; and in 1793 he came to Newark (Niagara), Upper Canada, and for two years published the *Upper Canada Gazette or American Oracle*, an official journal. In 1795 he went to Montreal, and published there the *Gazette de Montréal*. He died in New York on September 22, 1799.

[W. Kingsford, *The early bibliography of the province of Ontario* (Toronto, 1892); *Bull. rech. hist.*, 1918; P. G. Roy, *Fils de Québec*, vol. 2 (Lévis, Que., 1933); W. Colgate, *Louis Roy* (Ont. hist. soc., papers and records, vol. 43).]

Roy, Louis Rodolphe (1858-1925), politician and jurist, was born at St. Vallier, Canada East, on February 7, 1858. He was educated at the Quebec Seminary and Laval University (LL.B., 1883; LL.D., 1908), and was called to the bar of Quebec in 1883 (K.C., 1903). He represented Kamouraska in the Legislative Assembly of Quebec from 1897 to 1909; and from 1905 to 1909 was provincial secretary. He was appointed a judge of the Superior Court for the district of Rimouski in 1909; and he retired from the bench because of illness in 1923. He died at Quebec City on May 14, 1925.

[P. G. Roy, *Les juges de la province de Québec* (Quebec, 1933); Morgan, *Can. men* (1912).]

Roy, Paul Eugène (1859-1926), Roman Catholic archbishop of Quebec (1925-26), was born at Berthier, Quebec, on November 9, 1859, and was educated at Quebec and at Paris, France. He was ordained a priest of the Roman Catholic Church in 1886, and in 1908 was appointed coadjutor bishop of Quebec. In 1920 he became coadjutor to Cardinal Bégin, and archbishop in 1925; and he died at Quebec on February 20, 1926. He was the author of a biographical sketch of *L. A. Olivier* (Lévis, 1891); and a collection of his addresses was published under the title *Discours religieux et patriotiques* (Quebec, 1927).

[Allaire, *Dict. biog.*; Le Jeune, *Dict. gén.*; *Can. who was who*, vol. 1.]

Roy, Pierre Georges (1870-1953), archivist, was born at Lévis, Quebec, on October 23, 1870, and died there on November 4, 1953. He was educated at the Quebec Seminary and became a journalist. In 1895 he began the publication of the *Bulletin des Recherches Historiques*, which he edited for more than fifty years. In 1920 he was appointed the first archivist of the province of Quebec, a post that he held for over twenty years, during which he published a series of valuable annual reports, as well as many collections of original documents relating to the province of Quebec. He was the author of a number of genealogical studies of French-Canadian families; and among his other publications might be mentioned his *Petites choses de notre histoire* (7 vols., Lévis, 1919-44), *Le vieux Québec* (2 vols., Lévis, 1923-31), and *Fils de Québec* (4 vols., Lévis, 1933). Most of his publications, which numbered over three hundred, are listed in the bibliography by his son, Antoine Roy, *L'oeuvre historique de Pierre Georges Roy* (Paris, 1928). He was elected a fellow of the Royal Society of Canada in 1911; and in 1932 he was awarded the Society's Tyrrell medal for historical research.

[*Proc. Roy. Soc. Can.*, 1954; *Can. who's who*, 1948; *Encyc. Can.*]

Royal, Joseph (1837-1902), journalist, historian, and lieutenant-governor of the North West Territories (1888-93), was born at Repentigny, Lower Canada, on May 7, 1837, of humble parentage. He was educated at St. Mary's Jesuit College, Montreal, and in 1857 joined the staff of *La Minerve*, Montreal. The next year he founded the short-lived *L'Ordre*, Montreal; in 1864 he was one of the originators of the *Revue Canadienne*; and in 1867 he founded *Le Nouveau Monde* (1867-81). In 1864 he was called to the bar; and in 1870 he went to the North West. Here he established in 1870 *Le Métis* (afterwards *Le Manitoba*); and the same year he was elected to the first Legislative Assembly of Manitoba for St. François-Xavier West. He continued a member of this House until 1879, and was successively speaker of the Assembly (1871-72), provincial secretary (1872-74), provincial secretary and minister of public works (1874-76), attorney-general (1876-78), and minister of public works (1878). From 1879 to 1888 he was a member of the Canadian House of Commons for Provencher; and in 1888 he was appointed lieutenant-governor of the North West Territories. On the expiration of his term of office in 1893 he returned to Montreal, and became editor of *La Minerve*. He died in Montreal, on August 23, 1902. In 1894 he was elected a member of the Royal Society of Canada. Most of his literary work appeared in fugitive form in periodicals; but he published separately *La vallée de la Mantawa* (Montreal, 1869) and *Le Canada, république ou colonie?* (Montreal, 1894), and there was published posthumously an *Histoire du Canada 1841 à 1867* (Montreal, 1909).

[Abbé G. Dugas, *L'Hon. M. Joseph Royal* (Revue canadienne, 1902); L. A. Prud'-homme, *L'honorable Joseph Royal* (Trans. Roy. Soc. Can., 1904); J. Tassé, *Le 38me fauteuil* (Montreal, 1891); Rose, *Cyc. Can.*

biog. (1886); *Can. parl. comp.*; Morgan, *Can. men* (1898); Le Jeune, *Dict. gén.*]

Ruark, Fletcher (1879-1952), poet, was born at Southport, North Carolina, in 1879, and died at Windsor, Ontario, on January 1, 1952. He was the author of *Poems* (Windsor, Ont., 1931), *Jecila and other poems* (Windsor, Ont., 1934), *Red wind and other poems* (New York, 1940), and *Mosaic and other poems* (Windsor, Ont., 1948). He also published a prose work entitled *Sketches from life* (Windsor, Ont., 1942).

[Private information.]

Russell, Alexander Jamieson (1807-1887), civil servant and author, was born in Glasgow, Scotland, on April 29, 1807. He came to Canada with his parents in 1822, and settled in Megantic county, Lower Canada, where his father became crown lands agent. He became a surveyor and engineer, was employed on the construction of the Rideau Canal and the building of roads and bridges in Lower Canada; and eventually became an official in the crown lands office of the Canadian government. He died at Ottawa, Ontario, in 1887. He was the author of *The Red River country, Hudson's Bay, and North West territories considered in relation to Canada* (Ottawa, 1869) and of an important pamphlet, *On Champlain's astrolabe* (Montreal, 1879).

[J. G. Wilson and J. Fiske (eds.), *Appleton's Cyclopaedia of American biography*, vol. 5 (New York, 1888).]

Russell, Benjamin (1849-1935), jurist and author, was born at Dartmouth, Nova Scotia, on January 10, 1849, the son of Nathaniel Russell. He was educated at Mount Allison University (B.A., 1868; M.A., 1871; D.C.L., 1893), and was called to the bar in Nova Scotia in 1872. He was elected to represent Halifax in the Canadian House of Commons in 1896, and Hants in 1900; and in 1904 he was appointed a puisne judge of the Supreme Court of Nova Scotia. This post he held for over thirty years; and he died in office at Halifax on September 21, 1935. He was the author of several legal works and of an *Autobiography* (Halifax, N.S., 1932).

Russell, George Horne (1861-1933), painter, was born at Banff, Scotland, in 1861. He studied art in London, and came to Canada in 1890. He specialized in portrait-painting; but he was also a painter of landscapes and marines. Elected an associate of the Royal Canadian Academy of Arts in 1909, he became a fellow in 1918; and from 1922 to 1926 he was president of the Academy. He died at St. Stephen, New Brunswick, on June 25, 1933.

[*Can. who was who*, vol. 2; Morgan, *Can. men* (1912); N. MacTavish, *The fine arts in Canada* (Toronto, 1925).]

Russell, George Stanley (1883-1957), clergyman and author, was born at Great

Grimsby, Lincolnshire, England, on March 31, 1883, and died at Toronto, Ontario, on June 21, 1957. He was educated at Aberdeen University and Bradford Theological College, and became a Congregational minister. After serving in several charges in England, he came to Canada in 1929 as minister of the Deer Park United Church in Toronto; and he continued as minister of this church until his death. Aberdeen University conferred on him the honorary degree of D.D. in 1937, and Victoria College in 1940. He was the author of *The faith of a man to-day* (London, 1923), *The monastery by the river* (New York, 1930), *The church in the modern world* (Toronto, 1931), *The face of God, and other sermons* (New York, 1935), and an autobiography, *The road behind me* (Toronto, 1936).

[*Can. who's who*, 1952-54.]

Russell, Peter (1733-1808), president and administrator of Upper Canada (1796-99), was born at Cork, Ireland, June 11, 1733, the son of Capt. Richard Russell, 14th Foot. He entered the army at an early age, but in 1772 sold his commission and came to America as one of the secretaries of Sir Henry Clinton. At the close of the American Revolutionary War he returned to England; and in 1791 he came out to Canada with Simcoe (q.v.) as inspector-general of Upper Canada. In 1792 he was appointed a member of the Executive and Legislative councils of the province; and from 1796 to 1799 he was the administrator of the government, with the title of president. He died at York (Toronto), on September 30, 1808; and his property was willed to his sister, Elizabeth Russell, who left it to William Warren Baldwin (q.v.). His *Correspondence* has been collected and edited for the Ontario Historical Society by E. A. Cruikshank and A. F. Hunter (3 vols., Toronto, 1932-36).

[Dorothy R. Plaunt, *The Honourable Peter Russell* (Can. hist. rev., 1939); E. A. Cruikshank, *The early life and letters of the Honourable Peter Russell* (Ontario Historical Society, papers and records, 1933); D. B. Read, *The lieutenant-governors of Upper Canada* (Toronto, 1900); E. M. Chadwick, *Ontarian families* (2 vols., Toronto, 1894-98).]

Russell, Willis (1814-1887), hotel proprietor and author, was born in New England in 1814. He came to Canada about 1844, and became the proprietor of a succession of hotels in Quebec. In his later days he was the proprietor of the St. Louis hotel. He died in Quebec on October 16, 1887. He was the author of *Quebec, as it was, and as it is* (Quebec, 1857).

[Rose, *Cyc. Can. biog.* (1888).]

Rutherford, Alexander Cameron (1858-1941), prime minister of Alberta (1905-10), was born at Osgoode, Carleton county, Canada West, on February 2, 1858. He was educated at McGill University (B.A. and B.C.L., 1881; LL.D., 1932), and was called to the bar of Ontario in 1885, and to that of the North West Territories in 1895 (K.C., 1910). From 1902 to 1905 he represented Strathcona in the legislature of the North West Territories; and from 1905, on the creation of Alberta, to 1913 he represented Strathcona in the legislature of Alberta. He was called upon to form the first administration in the province; and from 1905 to 1910 he was prime minister, provincial treasurer, and minister of education. On his defeat in the elections of 1913, he retired to private life. He died at Edmonton, Alberta, on June 11, 1941.

[*Can. who's who*, 1936-37; *Can. parl. comp.*; Morgan, *Can. men* (1912).]

Rutherford, John Gunion (1857-1923), veterinary surgeon, was born at Mountain Bank, Peeblesshire, Scotland, on December 25, 1857, the son of the Rev. Robert Rutherford. He was educated at the Glasgow High School, came to Canada in 1875, and studied at the Ontario Agricultural College and at the Ontario Veterinary College (V.S., 1879). In 1884 he settled at Portage la Prairie, Manitoba; and in 1885 he served as veterinary officer with the North West field force during the Riel rebellion. From 1892 to 1896 he represented Lakeside in the Legislative Assembly of Manitoba; and from 1897 to 1900 he represented Macdonald in the Canadian House of Commons. In 1902 he was appointed veterinary director-general for Canada, and in 1906 live-stock commissioner. In 1918 he became a member of the board of railway commissioners, and this post he held until his death at Ottawa, on July 24, 1923. In 1887 he married Edith, daughter of Washington Boultbee, of Ancaster, Ontario. He was created a C.M.G. in 1910.

[H. Charlesworth (ed.), *A cyclopaedia of Canadian biography* (Toronto, 1919); Morgan, *Can. men* (1912); *Can. who's who* (1910); *Can. parl. comp.*]

Rutledge, Joseph Lister (1885-1957), editor and historian, was born in Winnipeg, Manitoba, in 1885, and died at Toronto, Ontario, on March 12, 1957. He was educated at Victoria College, University of Toronto (B.A., 1907), and became a journalist on the staff of the London *Advertiser*. Later he was successively editor of *Maclean's* magazine, the *Canadian Magazine*, *Liberty*, and the *Canadian Author and Bookman*. He was the author of *Century of conflict* (Toronto, 1956), in the "Canadian History Series" edited by T. B. Costain.

[Toronto *Globe and Mail*, March 13, 1957; *Can. who's who*, 1952-54.]

Ruttan, Henry (1792-1871), author, was born at Adolphustown, Upper Canada, in

1792, the son of William Ruttan, a United Empire Loyalist. From 1820 to 1824 and from 1836 to 1841 he represented Northumberland in the Legislative Assembly of Upper Canada; and in 1837 he was elected for a short time speaker of the Assembly. From 1827 to 1857 he was sheriff of the Newcastle district; and in his later years he devoted much attention to the subject of ventilation. He died at Cobourg, Ontario, on July 31, 1871. He was the author of *Lectures on the ventilation of buildings* (Cobourg, C.W., 1848) and *Ventilation and warming of buildings* (New York, 1862).

[C. E. Thompson (ed.), *Autobiography of the Honourable Henry Ruttan, of Cobourg, Upper Canada* (United Empire Loyalists' Association, annual transactions, 1899); Morgan, *Bib. can.*; *Dict. Can. biog.*, vol. 10.]

Ruttan, Robert Fulford (1856-1930), educationist, was born at Newburgh, Canada West, on July 15, 1856, the son of Dr. Allan Ruttan. He was educated at the University of Toronto (B.A., 1881; D.Sc., 1914), at McGill University (M.D., C.M., 1884), and at Berlin University; and in 1887 he was appointed lecturer in chemistry in the medical faculty of McGill University. He became professor of chemistry in 1891, professor of organic and biological chemistry in 1902, director of the department of chemistry in 1912, and dean of the faculty of graduate studies in 1924. In 1896 he was elected a fellow of the Royal Society of Canada, and in 1919 he was elected president of this Society. He retired from teaching in 1928; and he died at Montreal on February 19, 1930. For several years he was president of the Royal Montreal Golf Club.

[*Proc. Roy. Soc. Can.*, 1930; *Who was who*, 1929-40; Morgan, *Can. men* (1912).]

Ryan, Thomas (d. 1889), senator of Canada, was born at Balinakill, county Kildare, Ireland, and was educated at Clongowes College. He came to Canada at an early age, and went into business in Montreal. In 1863 he retired from business, and was elected to represent the Victoria division in the Legislative Council of united Canada; and in 1867 he was called to the Senate of Canada. He sat in the Senate until his death on May 25, 1889.

[Rose, *Cyc. Can. biog.* (1886); *Can. parl. comp.*]

Ryan, William Thomas Carroll (1839-1910), poet, was born in Toronto, Canada, on February 3, 1839, the son of Thomas Ryan and Honor Carroll. He was educated at St. Michael's College, Toronto, and served as a volunteer in the Crimean War when still in his teens. From 1859 to 1867 he was enlisted in the 100th Regiment (Royal Canadians). He then returned to Canada, and engaged in journalism, first at Ottawa, then at Saint John, and then at Montreal. He died at Montreal on March 24, 1910. In 1870 he married Mary Ann

McIver, of Ottawa, the author of a volume of *Poems* (Ottawa, 1870). He published *Oscar, and other poems* (Hamilton, 1857), *Songs of a wanderer* (Ottawa, 1867), *Picture poems* (Ottawa, 1884), and *Poems, songs, ballads* (Montreal, 1903).

[*Can. who was who*, vol. 2; Morgan, *Can. men* (1898); *Cyc. Am. biog.*; A. MacMurchy, *Handbook of Canadian literature* (Toronto, 1906); C. C. James, *A bibliography of Canadian poetry* (Toronto, 1899).]

Ryckman, Edmond Baird (1866-1934), minister of national revenue (1930-33), was born at Huntingdon, Quebec, on April 16, 1866, the son of the Rev. Edward Bradshaw Ryckman and Emmaline Baird. He was educated at Victoria University, Cobourg (B.A., 1887; M.A., 1889; LL.B., 1890) and at Osgoode Hall, Toronto; and was called to the bar in 1890 (K.C., 1908). He practised law in Toronto, and from 1921 to his death he represented East Toronto in the Canadian House of Commons. He was minister of public works in the short-lived Meighen administration of 1926; and from 1930 to 1933 he was minister of national revenue in the Bennett government. He died at Toronto, on January 11, 1934. In 1895 he married Mabel Louise, daughter of Edward Gurney; and by her he had two sons and two daughters.

[*Can. parl. comp.*; Morgan, *Can. men* (1912).]

Ryerse (or **Ryerson**), **Samuel** (1752-1812), loyalist, was born in New Jersey in 1752, the third son of Luykas Ryerson. He was a captain in the 4th New Jersey Volunteers (Loyalists) during the American Revolutionary War; and in 1783 he took refuge in New Brunswick. In 1794 he removed to Upper Canada, where he obtained a large grant of land near Long Point on Lake Erie. Port Ryerse, Norfolk county, is named after him. He became lieutenant of the county of Norfolk, judge of the London district court, and a lieutenant-colonel of the militia. He died in June, 1812. In 1783 he married Sarah Underhill, widow of Capt. Davenport; and by her he had two sons and one daughter. The form of his name was changed from Ryerson to Ryerse as a result of its having been so spelt in his militia commission.

[A. W. Ryerson, *The Ryerson genealogy* (Chicago, 1916); L. J. Ryerson, *The genealogy of the Ryerson family in America* (New York, 1902); E. M. Chadwick, *Ontarian families* (2 vols., Toronto, 1894-98); L. H. Tasker, *The United Empire Loyalist settlement at Long Point, Lake Erie* (Ont. Hist. Soc., papers and records, 1900).]

Ryerson, Adolphus Egerton (1803-1882), clergyman, controversialist, and educationist, was born in the township of Charlotteville, Norfolk county, Upper Canada, on March 24, 1803, the fourth son of Colonel Joseph Ryerson (q.v.), a United Empire Loyalist, and Mehetabel Stickney. He was educated at the district grammar school; and in 1825 he entered the ministry of the Methodist Church. After serving in various places as a Methodist preacher, he was in 1829 chosen editor of the *Christian Guardian*, the organ of the Wesleyan Methodist Church, and, except for the years 1831-33 and 1837-38, he continued to edit this journal until 1840. He became known as a powerful controversialist, attacking especially the exclusive claims of the Church of England to the Clergy Reserves; and he acquired a great influence over the Methodist electors of the province. He leaned at first toward the Reform party; but in 1833 he came out in opposition to William Lyon Mackenzie (q.v.), of whose extreme course he disapproved, and in 1837 his influence was a powerful factor on the loyalist side. He was also influential in securing in 1844 the victory of the administration formed by Sir Charles Metcalfe (q.v.).

In 1841 he was appointed the first president of the University of Victoria College, at Cobourg; and in 1844 he accepted the position of chief superintendent of education for Upper Canada. This position he retained until 1876; and the educational system of Ontario was largely his creation. In 1848 he established the *Journal of Education*; and this periodical he edited until his retirement in 1876.

He was twice married, (1) in 1828 to Hannah, daughter of John Aikman, and (2) in 1833 to Mary, daughter of James Rogers Armstrong, of Toronto. By his first wife he had two children, who died young; and by his second wife, one son and one daughter. He was a D.D. of the Wesleyan University, Middletown, Connecticut (1842) and an LL.D., from Victoria University, Cobourg (1861). An indefatigable controversialist, he published many pamphlets, of which the most notable were *Claims of the churchmen and dissenters of Upper Canada brought to a test* (Kingston, 1828), *The affairs of the Canadas* (London, 1837), *The clergy reserve question* (Toronto, 1839), *Sir Charles Metcalfe defended* (Toronto, 1844), *Letters in reply to the attacks of the Hon. George Brown* (Toronto, 1859), *University reform* (Toronto, 1861), and *The new Canadian dominion* (Toronto, 1867). His chief work was his history of *The loyalists of America, and their times* (2 vols., Toronto, 1882), and he was also the author of a history of *Canadian Methodism* (Toronto, 1882). His autobiography was published posthumously by J. G. Hodgins (Toronto, 1883).

[C. B. Sissons, *Egerton Ryerson, his life and letters* (2 vols., Toronto, 1937-47); Rev. E. Ryerson, *"The story of my life"*, ed. by J. George Hodgins (Toronto, 1883); N. Burwash, *Egerton Ryerson* (Toronto, 1903; new ed., revised by C. B. Sissons, 1926); C. Thomas, *Ryerson of Upper Canada* (Toronto, 1969); J. G. Hodgins, *Ryerson memorial volume* (Toronto, 1889); J. H. Putman,

Egerton Ryerson and education in Upper Canada (Toronto, 1912); L. J. Ryerson, *The genealogy of the Ryerson family in America* (New York, 1902); A. W. Ryerson, *The Ryerson genealogy* (Chicago, 1916); E. M. Chadwick, *Ontarian families* (2 vols., Toronto, 1894-98); *Dict. nat. biog.*; *Dom. ann. reg.*, 1882; Morgan, *Cel. can.* and *Bib. can.*; Dent, *Can. port.*, vol. 1.]

Ryerson, George (1792-1882), clergyman, was born near Fredericton, New Brunswick, on March 8, 1792, the eldest son of Colonel Joseph Ryerson (q.v.). He came to Upper Canada with his parents in 1799, and settled at Port Ryerse, on Lake Erie. He served as a sub-altern in the Norfolk militia during the War of 1812, and was severely wounded at the battle of Lundy's Lane. He was educated at Union College, in the United States. In 1819 he was ordained a minister of the Methodist Church; later he took orders in the Church of England; and finally he became a minister of the Catholic Apostolic Church. For many years he was the head of this body in America. He died at Toronto, Ontario, on December 19, 1882. He was thrice married, (1) about 1821 to Sarah, daughter of Thomas Rolph, M.D., by whom he had one son and two daughters; (2) to Sophia Symes, by whom he had one daughter; and (3) to Isabel Dorcas, daughter of the Hon. Ansel Sterling, of Connecticut, by whom he had one son.

[W. Canniff, *George Ryerson* (Belford's magazine, 1878; reprinted in *Annual Transactions* of the United Empire Loyalists' Association, vol. vi, 1914); E. Ryerson, *The story of my life* (Toronto, 1883); E. M. Chadwick, *Ontarian families* (2 vols., Toronto, 1894-98).]

Ryerson, George Ansel Sterling (1854-1925), physician and author, was born at Toronto on January 21, 1854, the son of the Rev. George Ryerson (q.v.). He was educated at the Galt Grammar School, at Trinity University, Toronto (M.B., 1875; M.D., 1876), and at Victoria University (M.D., C.M., 1892). In 1880 he was appointed professor of ophthalmology and otology in the Trinity Medical School; and he was a member of many medical societies, including the Royal College of Physicians and Surgeons, Edinburgh. He saw service in the Fenian Raid; he served as a medical officer in the North West Rebellion of 1885 and the South African War; and he rose to the rank of major-general in the Canadian militia. In 1896 he was one of the founders of the Canadian Red Cross Society; and from 1896 to 1898 he was president of the United Empire Loyalists' Association. From 1893 to 1898 he represented Toronto East in the Legislative Assembly of Ontario. He died in Toronto on May 20, 1925. He was the author of an autobiography entitled *Looking backward* (Toronto, 1924) and of a number of pamphlets on various subjects.

[Morgan, *Can. men* (1912); *Can. parl. comp.*]

Ryerson, John (1800-1878), clergyman, was born in the township of Charlotteville, Norfolk county, Upper Canada, on June 12, 1800, the fourth son of Colonel Joseph Ryerson (q.v.). In 1820 he was ordained a minister of the Wesleyan Methodist Church, and he continued in the ministry for fifty-eight years. In 1854 he visited the Hudson's Bay territories on a missionary tour, and he published a description of this expedition in *Hudson's Bay; or a missionary tour in the territory of the Hon. Hudson's Bay Company* (Toronto, 1855). He died at Simcoe, Ontario, on October 8, 1878. By his wife, Mary Lewis, he had one son and three daughters.

[*Cyc. Am. biog.*; *Dom. ann. reg.*, 1878; E. Ryerson, *The story of my life* (Toronto, 1883); E. M. Chadwick, *Ontarian families* (2 vols., Toronto, 1894-98); A. W. Ryerson, *The Ryerson genealogy* (Chicago, 1916); Morgan, *Bib. can.*; *Dict. Can. biog.*, vol. 10.]

Ryerson, Joseph (1761-1854), loyalist, was born in New Jersey on February 28, 1761, the second son of Luykas Ryerson. He fought throughout the American Revolutionary War on the British side, as an officer in the Prince of Wales Regiment (New Jersey); and in 1783 he settled in New Brunswick. Here he married, in 1784, Sophia Mehetabel Stickney, reputed to have been the first Englishwoman born in Canada after the British conquest; and by her he had six sons and two daughters. In 1799 he removed to Upper Canada, and settled in Charlotteville, Norfolk county. In 1810 he was appointed high sheriff of the London district,

and lieutenant of the county of Norfolk. He became a colonel in the militia; and, with his three eldest sons, fought in the War of 1812. He died on August 9, 1854.

[E. Ryerson, *The story of my life* (Toronto, 1883); E. M. Chadwick, *Ontarian families* (2 vols., Toronto, 1894-98); A. W. Ryerson, *The Ryerson genealogy* (Chicago, 1916).]

Ryland, Herman Witsius (1760-1838), clerk of the Executive Council of Lower Canada (1793-1838), was born in Northampton, England, in 1760. In 1781 he came to America as assistant deputy-paymaster-general of the British forces, and served throughout the last stages of the American Revolutionary War. On the evacuation of New York in 1784, he returned to England with Sir Guy Carleton (q.v.); and when Carleton, as Lord Dorchester, was appointed governor-general of British North America under the Act of 1791, Ryland came out to Canada in 1793 as his secretary. He was appointed both civil secretary and clerk of the Executive Council, and for many years he exercised a great influence on the government of Canada. He was the confidential adviser of Sir James Craig (q.v.), but was dismissed from office by Sir George Prevost (q.v.) as civil secretary in 1812. He continued, however, as clerk of the Executive Council until his death; and he was appointed in 1813 a member of the Legislative Council. He died at Beauport, near Quebec, on July 20, 1838. A selection of his papers is printed in R. Christie, *History of Lower Canada*, vol. vi (Quebec, 1854).

[F. J. Audet, *Herman Witsius Ryland* (Trans. Roy. Soc. Can., 1929); *Dict. nat. biog.*; Morgan, *Cel. can.*; Le Jeune, *Dict. gén.*]

Sabine, Sir Edward (1788-1883), soldier and author, was born in Dublin, Ireland, on October 14, 1788. He entered the British army as an artillery officer in 1803, and served in Canada during the War of 1812. He was astronomer in the first Arctic expedition of Sir John Ross (q.v.) in 1818, and in the expedition of Sir William Edward Parry (q.v.) in 1819-20. He made a series of voyages with the object of investigating the variations in the magnetic needle; and his researches resulted in the establishment of magnetic observatories throughout the British Empire, one of which was opened in Toronto in 1841. In 1818 he was made a fellow of the Royal Society, and from 1861 to 1871 he was its president. He died at Richmond, England, on June 26, 1883. He was created a knight of the Bath in 1869. He contributed the natural history notes to Sir W. E. Parry's *First Arctic voyage* (London, 1821); and he was the author of *An account of experiments to determine the figure of the earth* (London, 1825) and *The variability of the intensity of magnetism upon many parts of the globe* (London, 1838).

[*Dict. nat. biog.*]

Sabrevois de Bleury, Charles Clément (1798-1862), lawyer and politican, was born at Sorel, Lower Canada, on October 28, 1798. He was educated at the Montreal College, and was called to the bar of Lower Canada in 1819. He practised law in Montreal; and he represented Richelieu county in the House of Assembly of Lower Canada from 1832 to 1837; from 1837 to 1838 he was a member of the Legislative Council of the province; and from 1844 to 1847 he represented Montreal in the Legislative Assembly of united Canada. He died at his home at St. Vincent de Paul, Isle Jésus, near Montreal, on September 15, 1862. He is reputed to have been the author of *Refutation de l'écrit de Louis Joseph Papineau, ex-orateur de la Chambre d'assemblée du Bas-Canada, intitulé Histoire de l'insurrection du Canada* (Montreal, 1839).

[Le Jeune, *Dict. gén.*; *Bull. rech. hist.*, 1925.]

Sadlier, Mrs. Mary Anne, *née* **Madden** (1820-1903), author, was born at Cootehill,

county Cavan, Ireland, on December 21, 1820, the daughter of Francis Madden. She came to Canada in her youth, and in 1846 she married James Sadlier (d. 1869), a member of the firm of D. and J. Sadlier, publishers, New York, Boston, and Montreal. Most of her life was spent in New York, and there she became a friend of Thomas D'Arcy McGee (q.v.). In her later days she returned to Montreal; and there she died on April 5, 1903. She was the author of numerous romances of Irish life, in America and in Ireland; and she edited, with a biographical introduction, *The poems of Thomas D'Arcy McGee* (New York, 1869).

[*Dict. Am. biog.*; *Cyc. Am. biog.*; Morgan, *Can. men and women* (1898).]

Sagard-Théodat, Gabriel (d. 1650), missionary and author, was a lay brother in the Recollet order who came to Canada in 1623. He spent about one year in the Huron country, and then returned to France, where he wrote and published two books based on his experiences in Canada, *Grand voyage du pays des Hurons* (Paris, 1632) and *Histoire du Canada* (Paris, 1636), the latter of which was mainly an enlargement and revision of the former. Both works were reprinted in Paris by Tross in 1865-66; and the *Grand voyage* has been edited by G. M. Wrong (Toronto: The Champlain Society, 1939). Sagard died in 1650.

[Jean de la Croix Rioux, ed., *Gabriel Sagard-Théodat* (Montreal, 1964); R. G. Thwaites (ed.), *The Jesuit relations*, vol. 4 (Cleveland, Ohio, 1897); H. P. Biggar, *The early trading companies of New France* (Toronto, 1900); *Cyc. Am. biog.*; Le Jeune, *Dict. gén.*; *Dict. Can. biog.*, vol. 1.]

Sage, Walter Noble (1888-1963), historian, was born in London, Ontario, on August 9, 1888, the son of the Ven. George B. Sage. He was educated at Magdalen College School, Oxford, returning to Canada to enter the University of Toronto, from which he graduated in 1910 with honours in classics, history, and English. He graduated from Oxford in 1912 in modern history and in 1913 in economics and political science. He obtained a teaching position at Calgary College in 1913, and at Queen's University from 1915 to 1918. He joined the history department at the University of British Columbia in 1918, where he remained until his retirement in 1954. By his writing he drew attention to the unique features of British Columbia history. He was elected a Fellow of the Royal Historical Society (London) in 1933; and a Fellow of the Royal Society of Canada in 1937. He was the author of *Sir James Douglas and British Columbia* (Toronto, 1930), *The story of Canada*, with G. M. Wrong and Chester Martin (Toronto, 1929), and *British Columbia and the United States*, with F. W. Howay and H. F. Angus (New Haven, Toronto, 1942), and some forty papers and articles, mostly dealing with British Columbia history.

[*Can. hist. rev.*, vol. XLV, 1964.]

St. Aimé, Georges (pseud.). See **Pelletier, Alexis.**

St. Castin, Jean Vincent d'Abbadie, Baron de (1652-1707), soldier, was born in Béarn, France, in 1652, the son of Jean Jacques d'Abbadie de St. Castin, whose estate was made a barony in 1654. The son entered the army, and was sent to New France in 1665 as an ensign. In 1668 he returned to France, but in 1670 he was sent a second time to North America, this time as an officer in the garrison of the fort at Pentagoët (now Castine) at the mouth of the Penobscot River. Here he spent most of the rest of his life. About 1680 he married Mathilde Mataconando, the daughter of the chief of the Abnaki; and he obtained over these Indians an unrivalled influence. He died in France, whither he had returned on business, some time in 1707. His eldest son, Bernard Anselme d'Abbadie, Baron de St. Castin (1689-1720), succeeded him as chief military adviser of the Abnaki.

[R. Le Blant, *Un figure légendaire de l'histoire acadienne: Le baron de St. Castin* (Dix, 1934); P. Davioult, *Le Baron de Saint-Castin* (Montreal, 1939); Le Jeune, *Dict. gén.*; *Dict. Can. biog.*; vol. 2.]

St. Cyr, Joseph Fortunat (1875-1934), lawyer, was born at St. Johns, Quebec, on December 6, 1875. He was educated at the College of Montreal (B.A., 1897) and at Laval University (LL.L., 1900); and was called to the Quebec bar in 1900. He began the practice of law in St. Johns, Quebec; but in 1909 he was appointed magistrate for the district of Beauharnois and Iberville, and in 1917 he became judge of the sessions of the peace for the district of Montreal. In 1918 he resigned this office to take the post of chairman of the Montreal Tramways Commission. He died at Montreal, Quebec, on January 29, 1934. He compiled an *Index-digest to the Montreal law reports* (Montreal, 1905).

[H. Charlesworth (ed.), *A cyclopaedia of Canadian biography* (Toronto, 1919); *Who's who in Canada*, 1932-33.]

St. Cyr, Napoléon Dominique (1826-1899), naturalist, was born at Nicolet, Lower Canada, on August 4, 1826. He was educated at the Collège de Nicolet; and became a school-teacher. Later, in 1867, he was admitted a notary of the province of Quebec; and he practised his profession at Ste. Anne de la Pérade, Quebec. From 1875 to 1881 he represented Champlain county in the Legislative Assembly of Quebec; and in 1886 he was appointed curator of the museum of the department of public instruction at Quebec. He died at Quebec City on March 3, 1899. A diligent student of natural history, he was elected in 1881 a fellow of the Royal Society of Canada; and he was the author of *Catalogue des plantes et des oiseaux de la Côte Nord* (Quebec, 1886), as well as of numerous papers contributed to the *Naturaliste canadien*.

[*Bull. rech. hist.*, 1932.]

St. Denis, Joseph (1857-1927), priest and author, was born at Montreal, Canada East, on May 14, 1857. He was educated at the Montreal Seminary, and was ordained a priest of the Roman Catholic Church in 1884. He served as parish priest in various places in the province of Quebec until his retirement in 1905; and he died at Montreal, Quebec, on April 10, 1927. He was the author of *Cérémonies de la consécration d'une église à l'usage des fidèles* (Chambly, Que., 1907).

[Allaire, *Dict. biog.*]

St. George, Laurent Quetton de (d. 1821), soldier and merchant, was one of a number of French royalist officers who emigrated to Canada in 1798, and settled at Windham, in the township of Markham, north of York (Toronto), Upper Canada. He alone among his fellow colonists prospered. He engaged in the fur-trade, and in 1802 he opened a general store in York (Toronto). Later he opened branches of his business at Orillia, Niagara, Amherstburg, and elsewhere. He returned to France in 1815, and left his property to be administered by John Spread Baldwin. He died at Orléans, France, on June 8, 1821. He was twice married, (1) to the daughter of Jean Baptiste Vallière, the blacksmith of the Windham colony, and (2) after his return to France to Adèle de Barbeyrac de St. Maurice. By his first marriage he had one son and one daughter; and by his second marriage a son, Henri de St. George, who came to Canada in 1846 or 1847, and administered his father's Canadian property until his death at Oak Ridges, near Toronto, on January 6, 1896.

[N. E. Dionne, *Les ecclésiastiques et les royalistes français réfugiés au Canada* (Quebec, 1905); Lucy E. Textor, *A colony of émigrés in Canada* (Toronto, 1905); W. S. Wallace (ed.), *A merchant's clerk in Upper Canada* (Toronto, 1935).]

St. Germain, Hyacinthe (1838-1909), author, was born at Repentigny, Lower Canada, on September 23, 1838, the son of Pierre Venant St. Germain; and he died at Danville, Quebec, on December 8, 1909. He was the author of *Charles Héon, fondateur de la paroisse de St. Louis de Blandford* (Quebec, 1905) and *Souvenirs et impressions de voyage au Nord-ouest Canadien* (Arthabaska, Que., 1907).

[*Bull. rech. hist.*, 1928.]

St. Germain, Venant (or **Venance**) **Lemaire** (1751-1821), fur-trader, was born at the Lake of Two Mountains in 1751, the son of Bernardin Lemaire *dit* St. Germain and Marie-Joseph Lefèbvre. He became a fur-trader, and was trading to Grand Portage as early as 1777. In 1784 he was second-in-command under Edward Umfreville (q.v.) in the journey of exploration from Lake Nipigon to Lake Winnipeg. In 1790 he was elected a member of the Beaver Club in Montreal; but he was never apparently a partner of the North West Company, being rather a free trader under agreement with the Company. In 1795 he married Catherine Pichet; and by her he had several children. He died at Repentigny, Lower Canada, in 1821. He is not to be confused with the Venant St. Germain (probably his half-breed nephew), who was killed at Pembina in 1804.

[F. J. Audet, *Venant St. Germain* (Bull. rech. hist., 1932); R. Douglas, *Nipigon to Winnipeg* (Ottawa, 1929).]

Ste. Hélène, Jacques LeMoyne, Sieur de (1659-1690), soldier, was born on April 16, 1659, the second son of Charles LeMoyne de Longueuil (q.v.) and Catherine Primot. He accompanied his brothers Iberville (q.v.), and Maricourt (q.v.) on the expedition against the English posts on Hudson Bay in 1686; and in 1690 he was second-in-command of the raiding party which destroyed the village of Schenectady. He was mortally wounded on October 20, 1690, during the siege of Quebec; and he was buried at the Hôtel-Dieu in Quebec on December 4.

[C. B. Reed, *The first great Canadian* (Chicago, 1910); A. Jodoin and J. L. Vincent, *Histoire de Longueuil* (Montreal, 1889); Le Jeune, *Dict. gén; Dict. Can. Biog.*, vol. 1.]

St. Ignace, Jeanne Françoise Juchereau, Mère (1650-1723), mother superior and historian, was born at Quebec on July 7, 1650, the daughter of Jean Juchereau de La Ferté and Marie Gifford. She entered the Hôtel-Dieu of Quebec at the age of 12 years, and took the name of Soeur St. Ignace. She became mother superior of the Hôtel-Dieu; and she died on January 14, 1723. In her last years she compiled the history of the Hôtel-Dieu of Quebec; and this was later published in France under the title *Histoire de l'Hotel-Dieu de Québec* (Montauban, 1751).

[Le Jeune, *Dict. gén.*]

Saint-Jacques, Mme Henriette, *née* **Dessaulles** (1860-1946), journalist and author, was born at St. Hyacinthe, Quebec, on February 6, 1860, and died there on November 17, 1946. Under the pseudonym "Fadette", she contributed copiously to *Le Canada* and *Le Devoir*; some of her contributions were published in book form under the titles *Lettres de Fadette* (Montreal, 1918), *Les contes de la lune* (Montreal, 1932), and *Il était une fois* (Montreal, 1933).

[*Montreal Gazette*, Nov. 18, 1946.]

St. John, Frederick Edward Molyneux (1838-1904), journalist, was born in Newcastle, England, on November 28, 1838, and was educated at Rossall College. He entered the Royal Marines as a subaltern in 1855, and saw active service in China. After resigning his commission, he came to Canada in 1868, and became a journalist. As a special correspondent of the Toronto *Globe*, he accompanied Lord Wolseley on his expedition to the Red River in 1870; and in 1876 he accompanied Lord Dufferin (q.v.) on his mission to British Columbia. His account of this trip he published under the title, *The sea of mountains* (2 vols., London, 1877). In his later years he occupied a variety of positions; and shortly before his death he was appointed gentleman usher of the black rod at Ottawa. He died at Ottawa on January 30, 1904.

[Morgan, *Can. men* (1898).]

St. Laurent, Louis Stephen (1882-1973), Canadian prime minister, was born at Compton, Quebec, February 1, 1882, the son of a storekeeper. Completely bilingual from childhood, he was educated at St. Charles Seminary, Sherbrooke, Quebec, and at Laval University (B.A., 1902; LL.L., 1905). He was called to the bar of Quebec in 1905 (K.C., 1915). He became professor of law at Laval University in 1914. He was a member of the firm St. Laurent, Gagné, Devlin, and Tasherian, and had been bâtonnier of the Quebec City bar and bâtonnier-general of the Quebec provincial bar. He was president of the Canadian Bar Association (1930-32), and honorary life president. After representing both federal and provincial governments in constitutional cases before the Supreme Court of Canada and the Judicial Committee of the Privy Council in London, he was appointed joint counsel for the Rowell-Sirois Commission on Dominion-Provincial relations in 1937.

In 1941, at the age of fifty-nine, he was asked by Prime Minister Mackenzie King to enter public life as minister of justice and attorney-general of Canada. He was elected in a by-election in Quebec East in 1942 and became King's Quebec lieutenant, succeeding to the role of Ernest Lapointe (q.v.), who died in 1941. Mr. St. Laurent was re-elected at the general elections of 1945, 1949, 1953, and 1957 and retired from active politics in March,

1958. He was appointed secretary of state for external affairs in 1946. He was deputy chairman of the Canadian delegation to the United Nations Conference at San Francisco in 1945 and chairman of the Canadian delegations to the first and second sessions of the United Nations General Assembly in London in 1946 and again in 1947 in New York.

At the national Liberal leadership convention in August, 1948, he was chosen to succeed Mackenzie King. When illness prevented Mr. King from attending the meetings of the Commonwealth prime ministers in London in October, 1948, Mr. St. Laurent took his place and on November 15 of that year he became prime minister of Canada. His government was returned with large majorities in 1949 and 1953, but they lost the election of 1957, although he himself was re-elected. In September, 1957, he announced his retirement as Liberal leader and in January, 1959, Lester Bowles Pearson (q.v.) became leader of the Liberal party in Canada.

A constitutional lawyer by training, Louis St. Laurent played a leading role in the negotiations which led to the entry of Newfoundland into Confederation in 1949. As counsel for the Rowell-Sirois Commission, he helped interpret the delicate relationship which exists between Canada and its provinces. He was instrumental in abolishing appeals to the judicial committee of the Privy Council in London and the evolution of the Supreme Court of Canada as a court of final appeal. He was responsible for the appointment, in 1952, of Vincent Massey (q.v.), first Canadian-born governor-general. While he was secretary of state for external affairs and leader of the Canadian delegation to the United Nations, he enunciated the theory which led to the formation of the North Atlantic Treaty Organization.

Louis St. Laurent was a compassionate figure in Canadian public life, affectionately nicknamed "Uncle Louis" by thousands of Canadians. At the same time he was responsible for broadening Canada's vision of its responsibilities in the post-war world and for making his country known among the other nations of the world. He died at Quebec, July 25, 1973.

[*Can. who's who*, 1964-66; *Encyc. Can.* (1972); D. C. Thomson, *Louis St. Laurent: Canadian* (Toronto, 1967).]

St. Leger, Barry (1737-1789), soldier and author, was born in 1737, a nephew of Viscount Doneraile. He entered the British army in 1756 as an ensign in the 28th Regiment, and he served in America throughout the Seven Years' War. In the American Revolutionary War, he commanded the expedition against Fort Stanwix in 1777. He became commander-in-chief of the British forces in Canada, with the rank of brigadier-general, in 1784; but his name disappears from the army

lists in 1785. He died in England in 1789. He was the author of a valuable *Journal of occurrences in America* (London, 1780).

[*Cyc. Am. biog.*]

St. Luc, Lacorne. See **Lacorne, St. Luc de.**

St. Lusson, Simon François Daumont, Sieur de (d. 1673), French official, arrived in Canada in 1663, as a deputy of the intendant of New France. In 1670 Talon (q.v.) sent him to the west to search for copper mines and to establish friendly relations with the Indians. On June 14, 1671, he concluded a treaty with the western Indians at Sault Ste. Marie, and took possession of the western country in the name of the French king. He appears to have died in 1673.

[Le Jeune, *Dict. gén.*; B. Sulte, *Les français dans l'ouest en 1671* (Trans. Roy. Soc. Can., 1918); *Dict. Can. biog.*, vol. 1.]

St. Ours, Charles Louis Roch de (1753-1834), legislative councillor of Lower Canada, was born in New France on August 24, 1753. During the American Revolution he served as an officer in the Canadian militia, and for a time was aide-de-camp to Sir Guy Carleton (q.v.). In 1785 he travelled through Europe, and was received at the English, French, and Prussian courts. From 1808 to 1834 he was a member of the Legislative Council of Lower Canada. In 1792 he married Marie-Josephte Murray, and he died on November 11, 1834.

[*Cyc. Am. biog.*; C. Tanguay, *Dictionnaire généalogique* (Montreal, 1887); Le Jeune, *Dict. gén.*]

St. Ours, François Roch de (1800-1839), legislative councillor of Lower Canada, was born at the manor-house of St. Ours, Lower Canada, on October 23, 1800, the son of Charles Louis Roch de St. Ours (q.v.) and Marie-Josephte Murray. From 1824 to 1832 he represented the county of Richelieu in the Legislative Assembly of Lower Canada, and in 1832 he was appointed to the Legislative Council. In 1837 he was made sheriff of Montreal. He died at Montreal on September 11, 1839.

[E. Z. Massicotte, *Le shérif François-Roch de Saint-Ours* (Bull. rech. hist., 1919); *Bull. rech. hist.*, 1904; Le Jeune, *Dict. gén.*]

St. Ours, François Xavier de (1717-1759), soldier, was born in Canada on December 12, 1717, the son of Pierre de St. Ours and Hélène-Françoise Céloron. He entered the military service and rose rapidly in rank. He was one of the commanders of the militia in the attack on Fort George in 1757, and at the head of a few Canadians, drove back the forces of the English. After the battle of Ticonderoga in 1758, he was one of three officers specially mentioned by Montcalm for bravery. He commanded the right wing of the French army at the battle of the Plains of Abraham in 1759, and he was killed at the head of his troops. He married, in 1747, Thérèse Hertel de Cournoyer, and had by her nine children.

[*Cyc. Am. biog.*; F. Parkman, *Montcalm and Wolfe* (Boston, 1884); A. G. Doughty, *The siege of Quebec* (Quebec, 1901); C. Tanguay, *Dictionnaire généalogique* (Montreal, 1887); Le Jeune, *Dict. gén.*; *Dict. Can. biog.*, vol. 3.]

St. Ours, Paul Roch de (1747-1814), legislative councillor, was born in Canada on September 5, 1747, the son of Roch de St. Ours and Charlotte Deschamps. He became a member of the Legislative Council of Quebec in 1775, and in 1787 he introduced a bill limiting the application of French civil law. In 1792 he became a member of the first Executive Council of Lower Canada, and was a member until his death on August 11, 1814. He married Marie-Joseph Godfroy de Tonnancour.

[C. Tanguay, *Dictionnaire généalogique* (Montreal, 1887); R. Christie, *History of Lower Canada* (Montreal, 1866); Le Jeune, *Dict. gén.*]

St. Pierre, Henri Césaire Berryer (1842-1916), jurist, was born at Ste. Madeleine-de-Rigaud, on September 13, 1842. He was educated at the College of Montreal, and entered on the study of law; but while still a law student he enlisted in the 76th Regiment of New York during the American Civil War. He was wounded and taken prisoner by the Southern troops in 1863, and was released only in 1865. He then resumed the study of law, and was called to the bar of Quebec in 1870 (Q.C., 1889). He practised law in Montreal, and became an outstanding criminal lawyer. In 1902 he was appointed a judge of the Superior Court for the district of Beauharnois, and in 1909 he was transferred to the district of Montreal. He died at Montreal, Quebec, on January 8, 1916.

[P. G. Roy, *Les juges de la province de Québec* (Quebec, 1933); Morgan, *Can. men* (1912); Rose, *Cyc. Can. biog.* (1888).]

St. Pierre, Télesphore (1869-1912), journalist, was born at Lavaltrie, Quebec, on July 10, 1869. He became a printer and journalist; and he was engaged in journalism successively in the United States, in the province of Quebec, and in the Canadian North West. He died at St. Boniface, Manitoba, on October 25, 1912. He was the author of *Histoire des canadiens du Michigan et du comté d'Essex* (Montreal, 1895); and the compiler of *The Americans and Canada in 1837-38: Authentic documents* (Montreal, 1897).

[Morgan, *Can. men* (1912).]

St. Vallier, Jean Baptiste de la Croix Chevrières de (1653-1727), Roman Catholic bishop of Quebec (1688-1727), was born at Grenoble, France, on November 14, 1653. He took holy orders, and became one of the chaplains of Louis XIV. In 1685 he came to Canada as vicar-general of the diocese of Quebec; and in 1688 he succeeded Laval (q.v.) as bishop of Quebec. He administered the affairs of the diocese for forty years, and he died at Quebec on December 26, 1727. He was the author of *Estat présent de l'église et de la colonie française dans la Nouvelle-France* (Paris, 1688; reprinted, 1856).

[A. Gosselin, *Mgr de St. Vallier et son temps* (Evreux, 1899); Morgan, *Cel. Can.*; Allaire, *Dict. biog.*; C. Tanguay, *Répertoire général du clergé canadien* (Quebec, 1868); A. Gosselin, *L'Église du Canada depuis Mgr de Laval* (Quebec, 1911); Le Jeune, *Dict. gén.*; *Dict. Can. biog.*, vol. 2.]

Sait, Edward McChesney (1881-1943), educationist, was born at Montreal, Quebec, on August 24, 1881. He was educated at Upper Canada College, the University of Toronto (B.A., 1903; M.A., 1903), and Columbia University (Ph.D., 1911). He was a lecturer in history at Trinity College, Toronto, from 1903 to 1906; he then went to the United States, and was on the staff of Columbia University, the University of California, and Scripps College and Pomona College, California, successively. He died at Claremont, California, on October 27, 1943. He was the author of *Clerical control in Quebec* (Toronto, 1911), *Government and politics of France* (Yonkers-on-Hudson, N.Y., 1920), *American parties and elections* (New York, 1927), and *Democracy* (New York, 1929); and he was joint author, with D. P. Barrows, of *British politics in transition* (Yonkers-on-Hudson, N.Y., 1925).

[*Who's who in America*, 1942-43; *Who's who among North American authors*, vol. 6.]

Salaberry, Charles Michel d'Irumberry de (1778-1829), soldier, was born at Beauport, Lower Canada, on November 19, 1778, the son of Ignace Michel Louis Antoine d'Irumberry de Salaberry (q.v.). In 1794 he obtained a commission in the 60th Regiment, and he served in the British army throughout the Napoleonic Wars. In 1810 he came to Canada as aide-de-camp to General De Rottenburg; and in 1812 he was commissioned to raise among the French Canadians the Canadian Voltigeurs. In 1813 he defeated a superior American force at Châteauguay; and in 1817 he was created, in recognition of his services, a C.B. In 1818 he was appointed a member of the Legislative Council of Lower Canada, of which his father was already a member. He died at Chambly, Lower Canada, on February 27, 1829. In 1812 he married Marie-Anne-Julie, daughter of Jean-Baptiste-Melchior Hertel de Rouville, seignior of Chambly; and by her he had four sons and three daughters.

[P. G. Roy, *La famille d'Irumberry de Salaberry* (Lévis, 1905); F. Taylor, *L'hon.*

Chs. *Michel de Salaberry* (Revue canadienne, 1868); *Dict. nat. biog.*; *Cyc. Am. biog.*; Morgan, *Cel. Can.*; Le Jeune, *Dict. gén.*]

Salaberry, Charles René Léonidas d'Irumberry de (1820-1882), soldier and civil servant, was born at Chambly, Lower Canada, on August 27, 1820, the son of Lieut.-Col. Charles Michel d'Irumberry de Salaberry (q.v.). From 1855 to 1860 he was employed by the Hudson's Bay Company as an engineer in the North West; and in 1869 he was one of the commissioners appointed by the Dominion government to investigate the grievances of the *Métis* of the Red River district. With his fellow-commissioners he was arrested and imprisoned by Louis Riel (q.v.). He was the organizer and first lieutenant-colonel of the 9th Voltigeurs of Quebec; and in 1869 he was appointed a superintendent of woods and forests for the province of Quebec. He died at L'Assomption, Quebec, on March 25, 1882. He married (1) in 1849 Marie-Victorine Cordélia Franchère (d. 1855), (2) in 1869 Louise-Joséphine Allard (d. 1877), and (3) in 1880 Marie-Louise Baby. By his first marriage he had three children, and by his second, four.

[P. G. Roy, *La famille d'Irumberry de Salaberry* (Lévis, 1905); Le Jeune, *Dict. gén.*]

Salaberry, Ignace Michel Louis Antoine d'Irumberry de (1752-1828), legislative councillor of Lower Canada, was born at Beauport, near Quebec, on July 4, 1752, the youngest son of Michel d'Irumberry de Salaberry and Madeleine-Louise, daughter of Ignace Juchereau Duchesnay de Saint-Denys, seignior of Beauport. He was educated at the Quebec Seminary and in France. In 1755 he took part in the defence of Quebec against the Americans, and in 1777 he was with Burgoyne at Saratoga. He was a member of the Legislative Assembly of Lower Canada from 1792 to 1796. In 1808 he was appointed an honorary member of the Executive Council of Lower Canada; and in 1817 a member of the Legislative Council. He died at Quebec on March 22, 1828. In 1778 he married Françoise Catherine, daughter of Joseph Hertel de St. François, seignior of Pierreville; and by her he had eight children. He was popularly known as "Couronel Salumari".

[P. G. Roy, *La famille d'Irumberry de Salaberry* (Lévis, 1905); Le Jeune, *Dict. gén.*]

Sallans, George Herbert (1895-1960), journalist and novelist, was born at Horning's Mills, Ontario, in 1895, and died at Toronto, Ontario, on November 18, 1960. He was educated at Wesley College, Winnipeg; but his college course was interrupted by the First World War, in which he served overseas for three years with the Canadian Field Artillery. After the war he became a journalist; and during the last eleven years of his life he was a leader-writer on the staff of the Toronto *Globe and Mail*. He was the author of a novel, *Little man* (Toronto, 1942), which won the Ryerson fiction award.

[Toronto *Globe and Mail*, Nov. 19, 1960.]

Samuel, Sigmund (1868-1962), philanthropist and industrialist, was born in Toronto, Ontario, October 24, 1868. He was educated at Upper Canada College and the Toronto Model School. He entered the family metal business at fifteen years of age and shortly after the turn of the century became sole owner of Samuel and Son, Limited. Mr. Samuel moved to England before the First World War but returned to Canada in 1916, although he unsuccessfully stood for election to the British House of Commons in 1929 and 1931. An ardent student of Canadian history, he donated the Sigmund Samuel Library to the University of Toronto, the Sigmund Samuel Canadiana Gallery to the Ontario Provincial Archives, and a wing to house the 48,000 volumes of Chinese literature which he donated to the Royal Ontario Museum. He gave his home as a residence for the lieutenant-governor of Ontario. He was a member of the board of governors of the University of Toronto and the president of the board of governors of Toronto Western Hospital. He was a benefactor of Holy Blossom Synagogue, of which his father was a founder. He was a fellow of the Royal Historical Society and a fellow of the Royal Geographical Society. He died at Toronto, Ontario, April 2, 1962. He wrote *The seven years' war in Canada* (1935), and *In Return: The autobiography of Sigmund Samuel* (Toronto, 1963).

[Metropolitan Toronto Library Board, *Biographical scrapbooks*, vols. 20, 81 & 89; *Can. who's who*, 1955-57.]

Sanborn, John Sewall (1819-1877), politician and jurist, was born at Gilmanton, New Hampshire, on January 1, 1819; and was educated at Dartmouth College (B.A., 1842). He came to Canada in 1845, and was for a time a school-teacher at Sherbrooke, Canada East. He was called to the bar of Lower Canada in 1847; and for many years practised law in Sherbrooke. He represented Sherbrooke in the Legislative Assembly of united Canada from 1850 to 1854, and Compton from 1854 to 1857; he was a member of the Legislative Council for the division of Wellington from 1863 to 1867; and in 1867 he was called to the Senate of Canada. He was appointed a judge of the Superior Court of Quebec in 1872, and in 1874 he was promoted to the Court of Queen's Bench. He died July 17, 1877, at Ashbury Park, N.J. In July, 1847, he married Eleanor Hall Brooks, daughter of Samuel Brooks. She died in 1853, leaving three children; their only son died unmarried. His second wife, Nancy Judson Hasseltine, he married in 1856.

[P. G. Roy, *Les juges de la province de Québec* (Quebec, 1933); *Dict. Can. biog.*, vol. 10.]

Sanderson, Charles Rupert (1887-1956), librarian, was born at Bury, England, on May 19, 1887, and died at Toronto, Ontario, on July 24, 1956. He began library work at the John Ryland's Library in Manchester in 1909; and from 1914 to 1929 he was librarian of the Gladstone Library in London. In 1929 he came to Canada as deputy chief librarian of the Toronto Public Libraries. In 1937 he succeeded George H. Locke (q.v.) as chief librarian; and he remained in this post until his death. In 1941 he was chosen as the first chairman of the Canadian Library Council, out of which grew the Canadian Library Association. He was the author of a pamphlet on *Social credit* (Toronto, 1936), and he edited *The Arthur papers* (4 vols., 1943-58). In 1952 the University of Toronto conferred on him the degree of LL.D.

[*Can. who's who*, 1952-54; *Encyc. Can.*]

Sanderson, Joseph Edward (1830-1913), clergyman and historian, was born at York (Toronto), Upper Canada, on January 13, 1830, the son of John Sanderson and Margaret Crawford. He was educated at the University of Toronto (B.A., 1855; M.A., 1858), and in 1856 he was ordained a minister of the Methodist Church. He served in many charges in eastern Canada; and he was the founder and first principal of the Ontario Ladies' College, Whitby, Ontario. He died at Sault Ste. Marie, Ontario, on August 3, 1913. Among other works he published *The first century of Methodism in Canada* (2 vols., Toronto, 1908-10).

[Morgan, *Can. men* (1912); *Can. who was who*, vol. 1.]

Sandham, Alfred (1838-1910), historian and numismatist, was born in Montreal, Lower Canada, on November 19, 1838, the son of John Sandham and Elizabeth Tait. He was educated at the common schools, but left school at an early age, and was mainly self-educated. In 1864 he was appointed general secretary of the Young Men's Christian Association in Montreal; and this post he held for eleven years. In 1869 he was one of the founders of the Antiquarian and Numismatic Society of Montreal; and from 1872 to 1874 he was the editor of the *Canadian Antiquarian and Numismatic Journal*. In 1878 he removed to Toronto, and from 1878 to 1882 he was secretary of the Toronto Young Men's Christian Association. He then went into religious journalism, and started *The Christian Witness*, a journal that proved very successful from a financial point of view. He died in Toronto on December 25, 1910. His chief publications were *Coins, tokens, and medals of Canada*

(Montreal, 1869), with *Supplement* (Montreal, 1872), *McGill College and its medals* (Montreal, 1872), *Montreal past and present* (Montreal, 1872), and *History of Montreal Young Men's Christian Association* (Montreal, 1873). In 1857 he married Christina Houston, and he had by her several children.

[R. W. McLachlan, *Biographical notes on Alfred Sandham* (Canadian antiquarian and numismatic journal, 1911); *Can. who was who*, vol. 1; Morgan, *Can. men* (1898).]

Sandham, Henry (1842-1910), painter and illustrator, was born in Montreal, Lower Canada, on May 24, 1842, the son of John Sandham and Elizabeth Tait, and younger brother of Alfred Sandham (q.v.). He assisted his father, who was a house decorator, and taught himself the rudiments of painting. After some assistance from Jacobi (q.v.) and other Canadian artists, he went to Europe to study painting; and in 1880 he settled in Boston, Massachusetts. He executed illustrations for the American magazines, and at the same time he had great success as a painter of battle and historical scenes. "He was an excellent draughtsman" (E. Morris), and was a charter member of the Royal Canadian Academy of Arts in 1880. He died in London, England, on June 21, 1910; and a memorial exhibition of his chief paintings was held in the Imperial Institute, London, in June, 1911. In 1865 he married Agnes, daughter of John Fraser, a Canadian journalist; and by her he had six children, two of whom reached maturity.

[*Dict. nat. biog.*, Supp. 2; E. Morris, *Art in Canada: The early painters* (Toronto, 1911); Morgan, *Can. men* (1898); N. MacTavish, *The fine arts in Canada* (Toronto, 1925).]

Sandiford, Peter (1882-1941), educationist, was born at Little Hayfield, Derbyshire, England, on January 15, 1882. He was educated at the University of Manchester (B.Sc., 1904; M.Sc., 1907) and at Columbia University, New York (M.A., 1909; Ph.D., 1910). In 1913 he was appointed associate professor of education in the University of Toronto, and in 1919 professor of educational psychology. This position he retained until his death at Toronto, Ontario, on October 12, 1941. He was the author of *The training of teachers in England and Wales* (New York, 1910), *The mental and physical life of school-children* (New York, 1913), *Educational psychology* (New York, 1928), and *Foundations of educational psychology* (New York, 1938); he was also editor of *Comparative education* (Toronto, 1918).

[*Can. who's who*, 1936-37.]

Sandwell, Arnold Hugh (1892-1940), aviator, journalist, and author, was born in New Britain, Connecticut, on September 3, 1892. He was educated at the Mill Hill School in England, and came to Canada in 1911 as a reporter on the Montreal *Herald*. He served in the First World War as a flight commander in the Royal Naval Air Service and as a captain in the Royal Air Force; and later, after spending some years in British Columbia, he became in 1929 the editor of the weekly column on aviation in the Montreal *Daily Star*. He died at Montreal, Quebec, on March 10, 1940. He was the author of *Planes over Canada* (Toronto, 1938).

[*Can. who's who*, 1936-37.]

Sandwell, Bernard Keble (1876-1954), journalist and author, was born at Ipswich, England, in 1876, and died at Toronto, Ontario, on December 7, 1954. He was educated at Upper Canada College and at the University of Toronto (B.A., 1897). He became a journalist, and was dramatic editor of the Montreal *Herald* from 1905 to 1911, and editor of the Montreal *Financial Times* from 1911 to 1918. Later he was editor of Toronto *Saturday Night* from 1932 to 1951. He taught economics at McGill University from 1919 to 1923, and was head of the department of English at Queen's University from 1923 to 1925. In 1920 he became the first secretary of the Canadian Authors' Association; and in 1925 he was elected a fellow of the Royal Society of Canada. Queen's University conferred on him the degree of LL.D. in 1942, and Bishop's College that of D.C.L. in 1943. He was the author of *The privacity agent, and other modest proposals* (London, 1928), *The Molson family* (Montreal, 1933), *The Canadian people* (1941), and *The diversions of Duchesstown, and other essays* (Toronto, 1955).

[*Proc. Roy. Soc. Can.*, 1955; *Can. who's who*, 1952-54; *Encyc. Can.*]

Sanford, William Eli (1838-1899), senator of Canada, was born in New York, N.Y., in 1838. His father having died when he was a child, he was brought up and educated by an uncle in Hamilton, Canada West. In 1861 he founded in Hamilton the wholesale clothing firm of Sanford, McInnes & Co., and as its head he came to be known as the "Wool King of Canada". A personal friend of Sir John Macdonald (q.v.) and Sir John Thompson (q.v.), he was called to the Senate of Canada in 1887. He died, by drowning, at Windermere, Muskoka, Ontario, on July 10, 1899. He was a generous contributor to religious and philanthropic objects; and he was the founder and supporter of the Sanford Mission for the Chinese on the Pacific coast.

[Morgan, *Can. men* (1898); Rose, *Cyc. Can. biog.* (1886).]

Sangster, Charles (1822-1893), poet, was born at Kingston, Upper Canada, on July 16, 1822, the son of a shipwright at the Navy Yard. He had only a common school education, and from 1838 to 1849 was employed in the ordnance office, Kingston. He then engaged in journalism, and from 1850 to 1861 was sub-

editor of the Kingston *Whig*. In 1867 he obtained a post in the Canadian civil service at Ottawa, and this he held until his death at Kingston, on December 19, 1893. He published *The St. Lawrence and the Saguenay, and other poems* (Montreal, 1856); and *Hesperus, and other poems and lyrics* (Montreal, 1860). His manuscripts are now in the Library of McGill University.

[E. H. Dewart, *Charles Sangster* (Can. mag., 1896); *Can. who was who*, vol. 2; Rose, *Cyc. Can. biog.* (1888); Morgan, *Cel. Can.* and *Bib. can.*; R. P. Baker, *English-Canadian literature to the Confederation* (Cambridge, Mass., 1920); A. MacMurchy, *Handbook of Canadian literature* (Toronto, 1906).]

Sangster, John Herbert (1831-1904), educationist and physician, was born in London, England, on March 26, 1831, the son of John Alexander Sangster and Jane Hayes. He came to Canada in his youth, and was educated at Upper Canada College and at Victoria University, Cobourg (M.A., 1861; M.D., 1864). He became, first, a school-teacher; and from 1865 to 1871 he was headmaster of the Normal School in Toronto. In 1874 he was an unsuccessful candidate against Goldwin Smith (q.v.), for election to the Council of Public Instruction in Ontario. Soon afterward, he abandoned teaching for the practice of medicine; and became a country physician at Port Perry, Ontario. He died on January 27, 1904. He was the author of *Natural philosophy* (2 vols., Montreal, 1860), *Elementary arithmetic* (Montreal, 1860), *Elementary treatise on algebra* (Montreal, 1861), and *Student's note-book on inorganic chemistry* (Montreal, 1862).

[Morgan, *Bib. can.* and *Can. men* (1898); J. Squair, *John Seath and the school system of Ontario* (Toronto, 1920); Appleton's *Cyclopaedia of Canadian biography*, vol. 5 (New York, 1888).]

Sanguinet, Simon (1733-1790), jurist, was born in 1733, probably in the western country, the son of Simon Sanguinet, a notary of Varennes who was in his earlier years engaged in the fur-trade. He was one of the first notaries appointed after the British conquest, receiving his commission in 1764; and in 1768 he received a commission as a barrister. He practised law in Montreal; and in 1788 he was appointed a judge of the Court of Common Pleas for the district of Montreal. He died at Montreal, less than two years later, on March 16, 1790.

[P. G. Roy, *Les juges de la province de Québec* (Quebec, 1933).]

Santerre, Alec (1861-1911), a writer on agriculture and horticulture, whose real name was Alexandre Girard. He was born in 1861, and died in 1911. He was the author of *Le potager, jardin du cultivateur* (Quebec, 1902), *De*

SAUNDERS

la culture des arbres et des arbres fruitiers (Quebec, 1903), *La ruche canadienne: Culture des abeilles* (Quebec, 1903), *Le poulailler de la ferme* (Quebec, 1904), *The farmer's vegetable, fruit, and flower garden* (Quebec, 1905), and *The cultivation of fruit trees and shrubs* (Quebec, 1905).

[F. J. Audet and G. Malchelosse, *Pseudonymes canadiens* (Montreal, 1936).]

Sarrazin, Michel (1659-1734), physician, was born in Burgundy, France, September 5, 1659, and studied medicine. He emigrated to Canada in 1685, and in 1686 was appointed surgeon-major to the troops in the colony. In 1697 he was appointed physician to the king; and he played an important part in the early development of medicine in Canada, as well as in the early study of natural history. In 1707 he was appointed a member of the Superior Council; and he died at Quebec, September 8, 1734. In 1712 he married Marie-Anne Hazeur; and by her he had seven children.

[A. Vallée, *Michel Sarrazin* (Quebec, 1927); Le Jeune, *Dict. gén.*; *Dict. Can. biog.*, vol. 2.]

Saul, John Cameron (1869-1939), editor, was born at Ottawa, Ontario, on January 6, 1869; and was educated at the University of Manitoba (B.A., 1887; M.A., 1891). He was for some years a school-teacher; but in 1902 he became editor-in-chief of Morang and Company, publishers of *The Makers of Canada* series. In 1912 he became editor-in-chief of the Macmillan Company of Canada, and in 1919 editor-in-chief of W. J. Gage and Company. He died in Toronto, Ontario, on June 4, 1939. He was the editor of numerous text-books in use in Canadian schools.

[*Can. who's who*, 1936-37; Morgan, *Can. men* (1910).]

Saumarez, Sir Thomas (1760-1845), president and administrator of the province of New Brunswick (1813-14), was born in the island of Guernsey in 1760. He became a subaltern in the British army in 1776, distinguished himself as a junior officer in the War of the American Revolution, and rose to the rank of general in 1838. In 1812 he was appointed commandant of the British troops in Halifax; and from August 17, 1813, to August 13, 1814, he was president and administrator of the government of New Brunswick. He died in the island of Guernsey in 1845.

[*Dict. nat. biog.*; Le Jeune, *Dict. gén.*]

Saunby, John William (1858-1925), missionary, was born at Manotick, Canada West, on August 25, 1858. He was ordained a minister of the Methodist Church in 1886; and from 1887 to 1893, and again in 1910, he served as a missionary in Japan. He died at Victoria, British Columbia, on June 22, 1925. He was the author of *Japan, the land of the morning* (To-

ronto, 1894) and *The new chivalry in Japan* (Toronto, n.d.).

[Morgan, *Can. men* (1912).]

Saunders, Albert Charles (1874-1943), prime minister of Prince Edward Island (1927-1930), was born at Summerside, Prince Edward Island, on October 12, 1874. He was called to the bar of Prince Edward Island in 1900; and he was a member of the legislature of the province from 1919 to 1930. He became leader of the Liberal opposition, and in 1927 he was called upon to form an administration, in which he became prime minister and attorney-and advocate-general. He resigned office in 1930, and was appointed a justice of the Supreme Court of Prince Edward Island. He died at Summerside on October 18, 1943.

[*Can. who's who*, 1936-37; *Can. parl. comp.*]

Saunders, Sir Charles (1713?-1775), sailor, was born in Somersetshire, England, about 1713, and entered the Royal Navy in 1727. In 1759 he was promoted to be vice-admiral of the blue, and appointed commander-in-chief of the fleet which carried the army of James Wolfe (q.v.) to Quebec. To his efficiency and cordial co-operation the fall of Quebec in 1759 was in no small measure due. He was created a knight of the Bath in 1761; and in 1770 he was promoted to the rank of admiral. From 1754 to his death he represented Heydon in Yorkshire in the House of Commons. He died in London on December 7, 1775; and he was buried in Westminster Abbey.

[Edward Salmon, *Life of Admiral Sir Charles Saunders* (London, 1914); *Dict. nat. biog.*; Le Jeune, *Dict. gén.*]

Saunders, Sir Charles Edward (1867-1937), cerealist, was born at London, Ontario, on February 2, 1867, the son of William Saunders (q.v.) and Sarah Agnes Robinson. He was educated at the University of Toronto (B.A., 1888; D.Sc., 1922) and at Johns Hopkins University (Ph.D., 1891). In 1903 he was appointed Dominion cerealist at the Experimental Farms at Ottawa; and he discovered Marquis, Ruby, Garnet, and Reward wheats. He retired from the civil service, for reasons of health, in 1922. He was elected a fellow of the Royal Society of Canada in 1921; he was awarded the Flavelle medal of the Society in 1925; and he was created a knight bachelor in 1933. He died at Toronto, Ontario, on July 25, 1937. In 1892 he married Mary (d. 1936), daughter of John Blackwell, of Deer Park, Ontario, but he had no children. He was the author of *Essais et vers* (Montreal, 1928).

[*Proc. Roy. Soc. Can.*, 1938; *Can. who's who*, 1936-37; Elsie Pomeroy, *William Saunders and his five sons* (Toronto, 1956).]

Saunders, Edward Manning (1829-1916), clergyman and historian, was born in the An-

747

napolis Valley, Nova Scotia, on December 20, 1829, the son of David Saunders and Elizabeth Rhoades. He was educated at Acadia University (B.A., 1858; M.A., 1863; D.D., 1882) and at Newton Institute, Massachusetts. He was ordained a minister of the Baptist Church in 1858; and for many years he was the pastor of the First Baptist Church in Halifax. In his later years he was the pastor of the First Baptist Church in Ottawa. He died at Toronto on March 15, 1916. He was the author of several historical works, *The history of the Baptists of the Maritime provinces* (Halifax, 1902), *Three premiers of Nova Scotia* (Toronto, 1909), and *The life and letters of the Right Hon. Sir Charles Tupper* (2 vols., London, 1916).

[Morgan, *Can. men* (1912); Le Jeune, *Dict. gén.*]

Saunders, Henry Scholey (1864-1951), author, was born in 1864, a son of William Saunders (q.v.), and died at London, Ontario, on October 29, 1951. He was an admirer of Walt Whitman, was the author of *An introduction to Walt Whitman* (Toronto, 1934), and compiled a volume of *Parodies on Walt Whitman* (New York, 1923).

[Toronto *Globe and Mail*, Oct. 31, 1951; Elsie Pomeroy, *William Saunders and his five sons* (Toronto, 1956).]

Saunders, John (1754-1834), chief justice of New Brunswick (1822-34), was born in Virginia on June 1, 1754. He fought throughout the American Revolution on the loyalist side, as an officer in the Queen's Rangers, and in 1783 he went to England. Here he studied law at the Middle Temple, and in 1787 was called to the bar. In 1790 he was appointed an assistant judge of the Supreme Court of New Brunswick, and he took up his residence in Fredericton, New Brunswick, in 1791. In 1822 he was made chief justice of the Supreme Court; and he died at Fredericton on May 24, 1834. In 1790 he married Ariana Margaretta Jekkyl; and by her he had one son, the Hon. John Simcoe Saunders (q.v.), and two daughters.

[J. W. Lawrence, *The judges of New Brunswick and their times* (Saint John, N.B., 1907); L. Sabine, *American loyalists* (Boston, 1864); J. Hannay, *History of New Brunswick* (2 vols., Saint John, N.B., 1914).]

Saunders, John Simcoe (1795-1878), president of the Legislative Council of New Brunswick (1866-78), was born at Fredericton, New Brunswick, in 1795, the only son of Hon. John Saunders (q.v.). He was educated at Worcester College, Oxford (B.A., 1815), and was called to the bar of Nova Scotia in 1819, and to that of Lower Canada in 1820. In 1834 he was appointed advocate-general of New Brunswick, in 1840 surveyor-general, and in 1845 provincial secretary. He was made a member of the Legislative Council in 1833, and in 1866

he became its president. This position he occupied until his death at Fredericton on July 27, 1878. He married Elizabeth Sophia, daughter of the Rev. George Stone, rector of Stow Maries, Essex, England. He was the author of *The law of pleading and evidence in civil actions* (London, 1828).

[J. W. Lawrence, *The judges of New Brunswick* (Saint John, N.B., 1907); *Dom. ann. reg.*, 1878; *Can. parl. comp.*; J. Foster, *Alumni oxonienses* (Oxford, n.d.); *Dict. Can. biog.*, vol. 10.]

Saunders, Margaret Marshall (1861-1947), author, was born at Milton, Queens county, Nova Scotia, on April 13, 1861, the daughter of the Rev. E. M. Saunders (q.v.), and died at Toronto, Ontario, on February 15, 1947. She was educated in Edinburgh and in France, and became a successful writer of fiction, mostly of stories for children, about animals. These differed from the animal stories of Ernest Thompson Seton (q.v.) and Sir Charles G. D. Roberts (q.v.), however, in that they were all about tame, rather than wild, animals. Altogether she published about twenty-five books, of which the most famous was *Beautiful Joe* (Philadelphia, 1893), the autobiography of a dog, which ran into many editions, and was translated into several languages. Acadia University awarded her the honorary degree of M.A. in 1911; and in 1934 she was made a C.B.E.

[O. J. Stevenson, *A people's best* (Toronto, 1927); *Can. who's who*, 1936-37; *Who was who*, 1941-50; *Encyc. Can.*]

Saunders, William (1836-1914), agricultural scientist, was born in Devonshire, England, on June 16, 1836, and came to Canada with his parents in 1848. He became a manufacturing chemist at London, Upper Canada, and in 1868 he acquired a farm for the purpose of scientific experimentation. In 1886 he was appointed director of the newly formed Experimental Farms Branch of the Dominion Department of Agriculture; and he continued in charge of this branch until his retirement on pension in 1911. During this time he originated many promising varieties of fruit and grain; and in particular, he inaugurated the researches which resulted in the discovery by his son, Sir Charles Edward Saunders (q.v.), of the famous Marquis wheat, which is now the basis of the best wheat of the Canadian North West. He died at London, Ontario, on September 13, 1914. He married Sara Agnes, daughter of the Rev. J. H. Robinson; and by her he had several sons, one of whom, Sir Charles, carried on his work as a cerealist. In 1882 he was selected a charter member of the Royal Society of Canada, and in 1906 he was elected president of the Society. He was an LL.D. of Queen's University (1896) and of the University of Toronto (1904). He was the author of *Insects injurious to plants* (Philadelphia, 1883), and of a great number of scientific papers and reports.

[*Proc. Roy. Soc. Can.*, 1915; Morgan, *Can. men* (1912); A. H. R. Buller, *Essays on wheat* (Toronto, 1919); Elsie Pomeroy, *William Saunders and his five sons* (Toronto, 1956).]

Sauvelle, Paul Marc (1857-1920), journalist, civil servant, and author, was born at Le Havre, France, on February 21, 1857; and was educated at the University of France (B.Sc.) and the St. Cyr Military School. He came to America in 1880, and was for a time a journalist in Mexico. He came to Canada in 1884, and was for twenty-two years a journalist in Montreal. In 1906 he was appointed a translator on the staff of the department of mines at Ottawa; and he held this position until his death, at Ottawa, in April, 1920. He was the author of *Manuel des assemblées délibérantes* (Montreal, 1890), *Louisiane, Mexique, Canada* (Montreal, 1891), *Le lauréat manqué* (Montreal, 1894), *Napoléon 1er* (Montreal, 1898), *La loi de conciliation* (Montreal, 1899), and *Présidence des assemblées* (Montreal, 1914).

[Morgan, *Can. men* (1912).]

Sauvé, Arthur (1875-1944), postmaster-general of Canada (1930-35), was born at St. Hermas, Quebec, on October 1, 1875. He was educated at Laval University, Montreal, and became a journalist. He was successively editor-in-chief of *La Nation* and of *Le Canadien*, French-Canadian newspapers. From 1908 to 1930 he represented Two Mountains in the Quebec legislature, and from 1916 to 1930 he was leader of the Conservative opposition in the legislature. In 1930 he was elected to represent Two Mountains in the Canadian House of Commons; and from 1930 to 1935 he was postmaster-general in the Bennett government. In 1935 he was called to the Senate; and he died at Montreal, Quebec, on February 6, 1944.

[*Can. who's who*, 1936-37; *Can. parl. comp.*]

Sauvé, Joseph Mignault Paul (1907-1960), prime minister of Quebec (1959-1960), was born at St. Benoît, Quebec, on March 24, 1907, the son of the Hon. Arthur Sauvé (q.v.), and died at St. Eustache, Quebec, on January 2, 1960. He was educated at the University of Montreal, and was called to the Quebec bar in 1930. The same year he was elected to represent Two Mountains in the Quebec legislature, and he continued to represent this constituency until his death. He was speaker of the Legislative Assembly from 1936 to 1940, was appointed minister of youth and social welfare in the Duplessis cabinet, and in 1959 succeeded Duplessis (q.v.) as leader of the Union Nationale party and as prime minister. He went overseas during the Second World War as officer commanding the Fusiliers de Mont

Royal; and in 1947 he was promoted to the rank of brigadier.

[*Can. who's who*, 1958-60; *Encyc. Can.*]

Savary, Alfred William (1831-1920), jurist and historian, was born in Plympton, Digby county, Nova Scotia, in 1831. He was educated at King's College, Windsor (B.A., 1854; M.A., 1857), and was called to the bar of Nova Scotia in 1861. He represented Digby in the Canadian House of Commons from 1867 to 1872; and from 1876 to 1907 he was the county court judge for Annapolis, Digby, and Yarmouth. He died at Annapolis Royal, Nova Scotia, in 1920. He was the joint author, with W. A. Calnek, of a *History of the county of Annapolis* (1897), and he published a *Supplement* to this (1913); he was the author also of *The Savary families of America* (Boston, 1887); and he edited *David Fanning's narrative* (1908).

[T. C. Mellor, *Life of Judge Savary* (Annapolis Royal, 1922); Morgan, *Can. men* (1912).]

Savigny, Mrs. Annie Gregg (d. 1901), novelist, was the wife of Hugh P. Savigny, provincial land surveyor, of Toronto, Ontario, and died, a widow, at Toronto on July 10, 1901. She was the author of *A heart-song of to-day: A novel* (Toronto, 1886), *A romance of Toronto* (Toronto, 1888), *Lion, the mastiff* (Toronto, 1895), and *Three wedding rings* (Toronto, n.d.).

[Toronto *Globe*, July 11, 1901.]

Sawyer, Artemas Wyman (1827-1907), president of Acadia University (1869-96), was born in Rutland county, Vermont, on March 4, 1827, and was educated at Dartmouth College (A.B., 1847). From 1855 to 1860 he was professor of classics at Acadia University, Nova Scotia; from 1869 to 1896 he was president; and in his later years he remained as professor of psychology and Christian evidences. He died at Wolfville, Nova Scotia, on August 5, 1907.

[Morgan, *Can. men* (1898).]

Sawyer, William (1820-1889), portrait-painter, was born at Montreal, Lower Canada, in 1820, of English parents. He entered a law office in Montreal, but finding law distasteful, began to study art. In 1851 he went to study in New York, and later in London, Paris, and Antwerp. On his return to Canada, he settled in Kingston, Ontario, and became a successful portrait-painter. Several of his pictures are to be found in public buildings at Kingston and Ottawa — notable among them being his portrait of Sir John Macdonald (q.v.) in the Kingston City Hall. He died at Kingston, Ontario, on December 9, 1889.

[N. MacTavish, *The fine arts in Canada* (Toronto, 1925).]

Saxe, Mary Solace (1868-1942), librarian and author, was born in St. Albans, Vermont, in 1868. She came to Canada with her parents when a child; and from 1901 to 1931 she was librarian of the Westmount Public Library. She died at Montreal, Quebec, on May 27, 1942. She was the author of several one-act plays and a book for children, *Our little Quebec cousins* (Boston, 1919).

[Montreal *Gazette*, May 28, 1942.]

Sayer, John (1750?-1818), fur-trader, was born about 1750, and first appears in the fur-trade in 1780, when he was granted a licence to send one canoe to Michilimackinac. He engaged in the fur-trade in the Fond-du-Lac district; and as early as 1793 he was described by J. P. Perrault (q.v.) as "an agent of the [North West] Company" in this region. In 1799 he was "proprietor" in charge of the Fond-du-Lac department; but he retired from the fur-trade about 1806, and went to live at St. Annes, on the Island of Montreal. In 1810 he was elected a member of the Beaver Club of Montreal, though he does not appear to have attended any of its meetings. Ross Cox (q.v.) met him at St. Annes in September, 1817; and he died here on October 2, 1818, aged 68 years. He was apparently married to a French-Canadian half-breed; for he had a half-breed son, named Guillaume Sayer, who was the leader of a half-breed rising on the Red River in 1844.

[W. S. Wallace (ed.), *Documents relating to the North West Company* (Toronto: The Champlain Society, 1934).]

Scadding, Henry (1813-1901), clergyman and author, was born at Dunkeswell, Devonshire, England, on July 29, 1813, the son of John Scadding, at one time factor to Colonel John Graves Simcoe (q.v.). He came to join his parents in Canada in 1821, and was educated at Upper Canada College and St. John's College, Cambridge (B.A., 1837; M.A., 1840; D.D., 1852). In 1838 he was admitted to holy orders in the Church of England; and after teaching for several years in Upper Canada College, he became in 1847 rector of the Church of the Holy Trinity in Toronto. He retired from active parochial work in 1875, and devoted himself to literary and scholastic pursuits. He published a large number of pamphlets on historical, literary, and religious subjects; but his chief work was *Toronto of old* (Toronto, 1873), an admirable essay on local history. Later he collaborated with J. C. Dent (q.v.) in a volume entitled *Toronto, past and present* (Toronto, 1884), and with G. Mercer Adam (q.v.) in *Toronto, old and new* (Toronto, 1891). He died in Toronto on May 6, 1901. In 1841 he married Harriett Eugenia (d. 1843), daughter of John Spread Baldwin, Toronto. From 1870 to 1876 he was president of the Canadian Institute; and in 1885 he was awarded by the Canadian government the Confederation medal.

[T. A. Reed, *The Scaddings* (Ont. Hist. Soc., papers and records, 1944); Morgan, *Can. men* (1898) and *Bib. can.*; *Cyc. Am.*

biog.; A. H. Young (ed.), *The roll of pupils of Upper Canada College* (Toronto, 1917).]

Scatcherd, Thomas (1823-1876), politician, was born in Wyton, near London, Upper Canada, on November 10, 1823, the eldest son of John Scatcherd and Anne Farley. He was educated at the London grammar school; and he was called to the bar of Upper Canada in 1848. From 1861 to 1867 he represented West Middlesex in the Legislative Assembly of Canada, as a Reformer, and after 1867 he represented the riding of North Middlesex in the Canadian House of Commons until his death at Ottawa on April 15, 1876. In 1851 he married Isabella, daughter of Thomas Sprague; and by her he had two sons.

[W. Horton, *Memoir of the late Thomas Scatcherd* (London, Ont., 1878); *Can. parl. comp.*; *Dict. Can. biog.*, vol. 10.]

Schäffer, Mrs. Mary Townsend, *née* **Sharples** (1861-1939), author, was born at West Chester, Pennsylvania, in 1861. In 1889 she married Dr. Charles Schäffer, of Pennsylvania; but after his death in 1903, she removed to Canada, and became interested in the exploration of the Rocky Mountains of Canada. She died at Banff, Alberta, on January 23, 1939. She was the author of *Old Indian trails* (New York, 1911).

[*Who's who in America*, 1916-17.]

Schanck, John (1740-1823), admiral, was born in Scotland in 1740, and entered the British naval service in 1758. In 1777 he was placed in charge of the naval establishment on Lake Champlain and the Great Lakes with the rank of lieutenant; and he defeated the American flotilla on Lake Champlain on October 11-13, 1777. He was promoted to the rank of captain in 1783, to that of rear-admiral in 1805, vice-admiral in 1810, and admiral in 1821. He retired on half-pay, however, in 1802; and he died in the summer of 1823. He married a sister of Sir William Grant (q.v.), attorney-general of Quebec in 1776-77.

[*Dict. nat. biog.*]

Scherck, Michael Gonder. See **Sherk, Michael Gonder.**

Schofield, Frank Howard (1859-1929), educationist, was born at Black River, Nova Scotia, in 1859, and was educated at Acadia University (B.A., 1882). In 1889 he was appointed principal of the Winnipeg Collegiate Institute; and he occupied this position until 1909. He died at Victoria, British Columbia, on December 10, 1929. He was the author of *The story of Manitoba* (3 vols., Winnipeg, 1913).

[*Records of the graduates of Acadia University, 1843-1926* (Wolfville, N.S., 1926); Morgan, *Can. men* (1912).]

Scholefield, Ethelbert Olaf Stuart (1875-1919), librarian and historian, was born at St. Wilfrid's, Ryde, Isle of Wight, in 1875, the son of the Rev. Stuart Clement Scholefield. He came to British Columbia in 1887, on the appointment of his father as rector of St. Paul's Church, Esquimalt; and he was educated at Victoria, British Columbia. In 1901 he was appointed librarian and archivist to the Legislative Assembly of British Columbia; and he held this post until his death at Victoria, British Columbia, on December 24, 1919. With F. W. Howay, he was joint author of *British Columbia* (4 vols., Vancouver, 1914), and he published a series of valuable *Memoirs* of the provincial archives of British Columbia.

[Morgan, *Can. men* (1912); *Who's who and why*, 1915-16.]

Schreiber, Mrs. Charlotte Mount Brock, *née* **Morrell** (1834-1922), artist, was born at Woodham Mortimer, Essex, England, in 1834, the daughter of the Rev. Robert Price Morrell. She studied art in London, and exhibited at the Royal Academy. She became the second wife of Leymouth George Schreiber of Toronto in 1875, and with him came to live in Canada, first at Deer Park, near Toronto, and later at Springfield-on-the-Credit. She became a charter member of the Royal Canadian Academy of Art in 1880, and was a constant exhibitor at Canadian exhibitions, especially of figure studies. In 1898 she returned to England, and she lived at Paignton, South Devon, until her death in 1922.

[N. MacTavish, *The fine arts in Canada* (Toronto, 1925); Morgan, *Can. men* (1898).]

Schreiber, Sir Collingwood (1831-1918), civil engineer, was born in Essex, England, on December 14, 1831, the son of the Rev. Thomas Schreiber and Sarah, daughter of Admiral Bingham, R.N. He came to Canada in 1852, and engaged in railway engineering. In 1873 he became chief engineer of the government railways, and in 1880 he succeeded Sir Sandford Fleming (q.v.) as chief engineer of the Canadian Pacific Railway. These positions he held until 1892, when he was appointed chief engineer of the department of railways and canals. In 1905 he became general consulting engineer to the Dominion government; and he died at Ottawa on March 22, 1918. He was twice married, (1) to Caroline (d. 1892), daughter of Lieut.-Col. A. H. MacLean, 41st Regiment; and (2) in 1898 to Julia Maude, youngest daughter of Hon. Mr. Justice Gwynne, of the Supreme Court of Canada. He was created a C.M.G. in 1893, and a K.C.M.G. in 1916.

[Morgan, *Can. men* (1912); Rose, *Cyc. Can. biog.* (1886); *Cyc. Am. biog.*]

Schultz, Sir John Christian (1840-1896), lieutenant-governor of Manitoba (1888-95), was born at Amherstburg, Upper Canada, on January 1, 1840, the son of William Schultz and Eliza Riley. He was educated at Oberlin College, Ohio, at Queen's University, Kingston, and at Victoria University, Cobourg (M.D., 1860). He practised medicine at Fort Garry (Winnipeg). During the North West Rebellion of 1869-70 he was one of the leaders of the loyalist party, was seized and imprisoned by Louis Riel (q.v.), and was sentenced to death; but escaped. From 1871 to 1882 he represented Lisgar in the Canadian House of Commons, as a Liberal-Conservative. In 1882 he was called to the Senate of Canada; and in 1888 he became lieutenant-governor of Manitoba. His term of office came to an end in 1895; and he died on May 13, 1896. In 1894 he was elected a fellow of the Royal Society of Canada; and in 1895 he was created a K.C.M.G. He married, in 1868, at Winnipeg, Agnes Campbell Farquharson, of Georgetown, British Guiana.

[J. C. Hopkins, *J. C. Schultz* (Week, October, 1894); *Can. parl. comp.*; *Cyc. Am. biog.*; Rose, *Cyc. Can. biog.*; Dent, *Can. port.*, vol. 3; R. G. Riddell (ed.), *Canadian portraits* (Toronto, 1940).]

Sclater, John Robert Paterson (1876-1949), clergyman and author, was born in Manchester, England, on April 9, 1876, and died in Edinburgh, Scotland, on August 23, 1949. He was educated at Emmanuel College, Cambridge (B.A., 1898; M.A., 1900) and at Westminster Theological College, Cambridge. He was ordained a minister of the Presbyterian Church; and after serving as pastor of churches in Derby and Edinburgh, he came to Canada in 1923. From 1924 until his death he was minister of Old St. Andrew's Church in Toronto, which in 1925 joined the United Church; and he was moderator of the United Church of Canada from 1942 to 1944. Several universities conferred on him the degree of LL.D. He was the author of several books published before he came to Canada, and of *Modern fundamentalism* (New York, 1926) and *Public worship of God* (New York, 1927).

[*Can. who's who*, 1948.]

Scobie, Hugh (1811-1853), journalist, was born at Fort George, Inverness-shire, Scotland, on April 29, 1811. He was educated at the Tain Academy; and in 1832 he emigrated to Canada. In 1838 he founded the *British Colonist* newspaper at Toronto; and in 1850 he began the publication of the *Canadian Almanac*. He died at Toronto on December 4, 1853.

[Morgan, *Bib. can.*; J. Ross Robertson, *The landmarks of Canada* (Toronto, 1917).]

Scollard, David Joseph (1862-1934), Roman Catholic bishop, was born at Ennismore, Ontario, on November 4, 1862. He was educated at St. Michael's College, Toronto, and at Laval University; and was ordained a priest of the Roman Catholic Church in 1890. He was consecrated bishop of Sault Ste. Marie in 1905, and he administered this diocese until his death at North Bay, Ontario, on September 7, 1934.

[Morgan, *Can. men* (1912); *New York Times*, Sept. 8, 1934.]

Scott, Alexander Hugh (1853-1931), clergyman, was born at Charlottenburg, Glengarry county, Canada West, on April 20, 1853; and was educated at Queen's University (B.A., 1875; M.A., 1878). He was ordained a minister of the Presbyterian Church in Canada in 1878; and from 1878 to 1888 he was pastor of Knox Church, Owen Sound, Ontario. He then became pastor of St. Andrew's Church, Perth, Ontario; and here he remained for the rest of his life. He died at Perth, Ontario, on November 14, 1931. He was the author of *Ten years in my first charge* (Toronto, 1891).

[Morgan, *Can. men* (1912).]

Scott, David Lynch (1845-1924), jurist, was born at Brampton, Canada West, on August 21, 1845. He was educated at the Brampton grammar school, and was called to the bar in 1870 (Q.C., 1885). He practised law, first in Orangeville, Ontario, and after 1882 in Regina, North West Territories. He was one of the counsel for the Crown in the trial of Louis Riel (q.v.) in 1885; and in 1894 he was raised to the bench in the North West Territories. In 1905 he was transferred to the bench of Alberta; and in 1921 he became chief justice of the province. He died at South Cooking Lake, Alberta, on July 26, 1924.

[*Who was who*, 1917-28; Morgan, *Can. men* (1912).]

Scott, Duncan Campbell (1862-1947), civil servant and poet, was born at Ottawa, Canada West, on August 2, 1862, and died there on December 19, 1947. He was educated in the public schools of Ottawa and at Stanstead College, and at the age of seventeen became a clerk in the department of Indian Affairs in Ottawa. He rose in this department until, at the time of his retirement in 1932, he was its deputy superintendent general. He was a friend of Archibald Lampman (q.v.), who inspired him to become a poet; and he is generally regarded as one of that group of Canadian poets who grew up during "the Confederation era". He never achieved the popularity of Lampman, Roberts, and Carman; and recognition of his work was slow in coming. But he is now recognized as one of the outstanding figures in Canadian poetry. He was the author of *The magic house and other poems* (Ottawa, 1893), *Labour and the angel* (Boston, 1898), *New world lyrics and ballads* (Toronto, 1905), *Via borealis* (Toronto, 1906), *Lines in memory of Edmund Morris* (n.p., 1915), *Lundy's Lane and other poems* (New York, 1916), *Beauty and life* (Toronto, 1921), *Poems* (Toronto, 1926),

and *The green cloister: Later poems* (Toronto, 1935). He also wrote two volumes of short stories, *In the village of Viger* (Boston, 1896) and *The witching of Elspie* (New York, 1923), and he prefaced *The poems of Archibald Lampman* (Toronto, 1900) and Lampman's *Lyrics of earth, sonnets, and ballads* (Toronto, 1925) with excellent introductions. His last publication was a mixture of prose and verse, *The circle of affection* (Toronto, 1947). He was elected a fellow of the Royal Society of Canada in 1899, was its honorary secretary from 1911 to 1921, and its president for the year 1921-22. The University of Toronto conferred on him the degree of D.Litt. in 1922; and he was awarded the C.M.G. in 1934.

[E. K. Brown, *"Memoir"*, prefaced to *Selected poems of Duncan Campbell Scott* (Toronto, 1951); D. Pacey, *Ten Canadian poets* (Toronto, 1958); *Proc. Roy. Soc. Can.*, 1948; *Can. who's who*, 1938-39; Morgan, *Can. men* (1912); *Encyc. Can.*]

Scott, Ephraim (1845-1931), clergyman and editor, was born in Hants county, Nova Scotia, on January 29, 1845, and was educated at Dalhousie University (B.A., 1870; M.A., 1875) and at the Presbyterian College, Halifax (D.D., 1905), as well as at the Free Church College, Edinburgh. He was ordained a minister of the Presbyterian Church in 1875; and until 1891 he was engaged in pastoral work in Nova Scotia. He then became editor of *The Presbyterian Record*, published by the Presbyterian Church in Canada; and he conducted this periodical for 30 years. In 1921 he was elected moderator of the Presbyterian Church in Canada. He died at Montreal on August 7, 1931.

[*Can. who was who*, vol. 1; Morgan, *Can. men* (1912).]

Scott, Frederick George (1861-1944), clergyman and poet, was born at Montreal, Canada East, on April 7, 1861. He was educated at the University of Bishop's College, Lennoxville, Quebec (B.A., 1881; M.A., 1884; D.C.L., 1902), and was ordained a priest of the Church of England in 1886. From 1889 to 1934 he was rector of St. Matthew's Church, Quebec; from 1906 to 1925 he was a canon of the cathedral; and in 1925 he became archdeacon of Quebec. During the First World War he served as senior chaplain of the First Canadian Division, was wounded, was repeatedly mentioned in dispatches, and was awarded the C.M.G. in 1916 and the D.S.O. in 1918. In the post-war period he was elected Dominion chaplain of the Canadian Legion and the Army and Navy Veterans. He was elected a fellow of the Royal Society of Canada in 1900; and he received the honorary degree of LL.D. from McGill University, that of D.D. from King's College, London, England, and that of D.C.L. from King's College, Windsor, Nova Scotia. He died at Quebec City, on January

19, 1944. A poet of some note, he was the author of *The soul's quest and other poems* (London, 1888), *My lattice, and other poems* (Toronto, 1894), *The unnamed lake and other poems* (Toronto, 1897), *Poems, old and new* (Toronto, 1900), *The hymn of Empire, and other poems* (Toronto, 1906), *Poems* (London, 1910), *In the battle silences* (London, 1916), *In sun and shade* (Quebec, 1926), *New poems* (Quebec, 1929), *Selected poems* (Quebec, 1933), *Collected poems* (Vancouver, B.C., 1934), and *Poems* (London, 1936). In prose, he published a novel, *Elton Hazlewood* (New York, 1892), and *The great war as I saw it* (Toronto, 1922; 2nd and enl. ed., Vancouver, B.C., 1934).

[*Proc. Roy. Soc. Can.*, 1944; *Can. who's who*, 1938-39; *Who's who*, 1943; O. J. Stevenson, *A people's best* (Toronto, 1927).]

Scott, H. Percy (1856-1937), lawyer and author, was born at Windsor, Nova Scotia, in 1856. He was called to the bar of Nova Scotia, and practised law in Windsor. For some years he was lecturer in constitutional history in King's College, Windsor. He died at Windsor in 1937. He was the author of *Seeing Canada and the South* (Toronto, 1911) and *The new slavery* (Toronto, 1914).

[R. J. Long, *Nova Scotia authors* (East Orange, N.J., 1918).]

Scott, Henri Arthur (1858-1931), priest and historian, was born at St. Nicholas, Quebec, on September 3, 1858, the son of Maurice Scott and Lucie Guay. He was educated at Laval University (B.A., 1878; D.D., 1888; Litt.D., 1902), and he was ordained a priest of the Roman Catholic Church in 1882. He was parish priest at Ste. Foy, near Quebec, from 1893 to his death in 1931. He was the author of *Notre Dame de Sainte Foy* (Quebec, 1902), *Grands anniversaires: Souvenirs historiques et pensées utiles* (Quebec, 1919), *Bishop Laval* (Toronto, 1926), and *Nos anciens historiographes et autres études d'histoire canadienne* (Lévis, Que., 1930).

[Allaire, *Dict. biog.*; Le Jeune, *Dict. gén.*; Morgan, *Can. men* (1912).]

Scott, Sir Richard William (1825-1913), secretary of state for Canada (1874-78 and 1896-1908), was born at Prescott, Upper Canada, on February 24, 1825, the son of W. J. Scott, M.D., and Sarah Ann McDonell. He was privately educated, was called to the bar of Upper Canada in 1848 (Q.C., 1867), and practised law in Bytown (Ottawa). He represented Ottawa in the Legislative Assembly of Canada from 1857 to 1863, and in the Legislative Assembly of Ontario from 1867 to 1873. In 1871 he was elected speaker of the latter house; but on the fall of the Sandfield Macdonald government, he resigned this position and accepted the office of commissioner of crown lands in the Blake and Mowat administrations

(1871-73). In 1874 he was called to the Senate of Canada, and was appointed secretary of state in the Mackenzie administration. He retired from office with his colleagues in 1878, but in 1896 he resumed the secretaryship of state in the Laurier government, and retained it until his resignation in 1908. From 1902 to 1908 he was also government leader in the Senate. He was the father of the Separate School Act of 1863, and of the Canada Temperance Act, sometimes called the "Scott Act", of 1878. He died at Ottawa on April 23, 1913. In 1853 he married Mary (d. 1905), daughter of John Heron, of Dublin, Ireland. He was made an LL.D. of Ottawa University in 1889; and in 1909 he was created a knight bachelor.

[W. L. Scott, *Sir Richard Scott, K.C.* (Canadian Catholic Historical Association, report, 1936-37); *Can. who was who*, vol. 2; Morgan, *Can. men* (1912); Rose, *Cyc. Can. biog.* (1888); *Can. parl. comp.*; *Who was who*, 1897-1916).]

Scott, Thomas (1746-1824), chief justice of Upper Canada (1806-16), was born in Scotland in 1746, the son of the Rev. Thomas Scott, a clergyman of the Church of Scotland. He was educated for the ministry of the Church of Scotland, and became a "probationer"; but on the advice of Sir John Riddell, Bart., of Roxburghshire, in whose family he had been employed as tutor, he went to London to study law at Lincoln's Inn. He was called to the English bar in 1793; and in 1800 he received the appointment of attorney-general of Upper Canada. He arrived in York (Toronto) in 1801, and performed the duties of attorney-general until 1806. He was then appointed chief justice of the province, with a seat in the Executive and Legislative councils; and he retained this position until 1816. He died at York (Toronto), on July 29, 1824. He does not appear to have been married.

[W. R. Riddell, *Thomas Scott* (Ont. Hist. Soc., papers and records, 1923); D. B. Read, *Lives of the judges of Upper Canada* (Toronto, 1888).]

Scott, Thomas (1774-1823), soldier, was born in Edinburgh, Scotland, in 1774, the younger brother of Sir Walter Scott, the poet and novelist. He became paymaster of the 70th Regiment, and in 1814 came with his regiment to Canada. He was stationed successively at Cornwall and Kingston, Upper Canada, and at Quebec, Lower Canada; and he died at Quebec on February 4, 1823. He was at one time reputed to be the author of *Waverley*.

[P. G. Roy, *Un frère de Walter Scott à Québec* (Bull. rech. hist., 1896).]

Scott, Thomas (1846?-1870), loyalist, was an Orangeman from Ontario who went west before 1869, and was engaged for a time as a labourer under the Canadian government road superintendent. He was taken prisoner by the provisional government of Louis Riel (q.v.) on February 17, 1870, and after being tried by a sort of court martial, was shot at Fort Garry on March 4, 1870, at the early age of 24. His execution roused profound feeling in Ontario; and was one of the chief causes of the Wolseley expedition to the Red River.

[A. H. de Trémaudan (ed.), *The execution of Thomas Scott* (Can. hist. rev., 1925).]

Scott, Thomas Seaton (1836-1895), architect, was born at Birkenhead, England, in 1836, and studied architecture under his brother, Walter Scott. He came to Canada in 1863, and practised privately until 1871, when he was appointed Dominion architect. He became a charter member of the Royal Canadian Academy in 1880; and his chief works were the old Union station in Toronto and the old Bonaventure station in Montreal. He died in 1895.

[N. MacTavish, *The fine arts in Canada* (Toronto, 1925); H. G. Jones and E. Dyonnet, *History of the Royal Canadian Academy of Arts* (Montreal, 1834).]

Scott, Walter (1867-1938), prime minister of Saskatchewan (1905-16), was born in London township, Middlesex county, Ontario, on October 27, 1867. He became a journalist, and in 1895 became proprietor of the Regina *Leader*. From 1900 to 1905 he represented Assiniboia West in the Canadian House of Commons; and in 1905 he was invited to form the first government of the new province of Saskatchewan. He assumed the portfolios of president of the council and minister of public works, later substituting that of education for public works; and he sat in the Saskatchewan legislature for Lumsden district from 1905 to 1908, and for Swift Current from 1908 to 1916. In 1916 he was compelled by prolonged ill-health to retire from public life; and he died at Guelph, Ontario, on March 23, 1938.

[*Who's who in Canada*, 1936-37; *Can. parl. comp.*; Morgan, *Can. men* (1912).]

Scott, William (1812?-1891), clergyman and author, was born about 1812, and in 1839 was ordained a minister of the Wesleyan Methodist Conference in Upper Canada. He died at Ottawa on October 5, 1891. He was the author of *The teetotaller's handbook* (Toronto, 1860) and *Letters on superior education in its relation to the progress and permanence of Wesleyan Methodism* (Toronto, 1860).

[G. H. Cornish (ed.), *A cyclopaedia of Canadian Methodism* (2 vols., Toronto, 1884-1903).]

Scrimger, Francis Alexander Carron (1880-1937), surgeon and soldier, was born in Montreal, Quebec, on February 7, 1880. He was educated at McGill University (B.A., 1901; M.D., 1905), and entered on the practice of surgery in Montreal. In 1914 he went over-

seas as the medical officer of the 14th Battalion (Royal Montreal Regiment) of the Canadian Expeditionary Force; and he was awarded the Victoria Cross for his work at the second battle of Ypres in April, 1915. After the war, he resumed the practice of surgery in Montreal; and he became director of the department of surgery at the Royal Victoria Hospital and associate professor of surgery at McGill University. He died at Montreal on February 13, 1937.

[*Can. who was who*, vol. 2; *Can. who's who*, 1936-37).]

Scriven, Joseph Medlicott (1819-1886), hymn-writer, was born at Seapatrick (Bambridge), county Down, Ireland, on September 10, 1819, the son of Capt. James Scriven and Jane Medlicott. He was educated at Trinity College, Dublin (B.A., 1842) and at the Addiscombe Military College. In 1844 he emigrated to Canada. Here he taught school at Woodstock and Brantford, Canada West, and served as tutor in the family of Commander Pengelley, a retired naval officer, near Bewdley, on Rice Lake. He was a member of the Plymouth Brethren communion, and wrote hymns, one of which entitled "What a friend we have in Jesus", has become worldfamous. He died near Bewdley, Ontario, on August 10, 1886, and was buried in the Pengelley burial-ground. A collection of his verses was published under the title *Hymns and other verses* (Peterborough, Ont., 1869).

[E. S. Caswell, *Canadian singers and their songs* (3rd ed., Toronto, 1925); C. M. Whyte-Edgar, *A wreath of Canadian song* (Toronto, 1910); Le Jeune, *Dict. gén.*]

Scriver, Julius (1826-1907), legislator, was born in Hemmingford, Lower Canada, on February 5, 1826, of United Loyalist stock. He was educated at the University of Vermont; and he became a prosperous merchant in his native town. He represented the county of Huntingdon in the Canadian House of Commons from 1869 to 1900, and he was on his retirement from politics "the father of the House". He died at Quebec on September 5, 1907.

[*Can. parl. comp.*]

Seaborn, Edwin (1872-1951), physician and author, was born at Rawdon, Quebec, in 1872, and died at London, Ontario, in 1951. He was educated at the Western University, now the University of Western Ontario (M.D., 1895); and was for many years a member of its staff in medicine. He was the author of *The march of medicine in Western Ontario* (Toronto, 1944).

[*Can. who's who*, 1949-51.]

Seager, Charles (1844-1939), lawyer and author, was born at Wellington, Shropshire, England, on May 17, 1844, and came with his parents to Canada in 1845. He was educated at the grammar school, Port Dover, Canada West, and was called to the bar in Ontario in 1867. He practised law in Goderich, Ontario, was mayor of Goderich, and was later crown attorney for the county of Huron. He died in January, 1939. He was the author of *A handbook of procedure in criminal cases before justices of the peace* (Toronto, 1907).

[Morgan, *Can. men* (1912).]

Seager, Charles Allen (1872-1948), archbishop, was born at Goderich, Ontario, on July 9, 1872, and died at London, Ontario, on September 9, 1948. He was educated at the University of Trinity College, Toronto (B.A., 1895; M.A., 1896), and was ordained a priest of the Church of England in 1896. After serving as rector of several churches in Toronto and British Columbia, he was appointed provost of Trinity College, Toronto; and he retained this position until he was elected bishop of Ontario in 1926. In 1932 he was transferred to the see of Huron; and in 1945 he was chosen metropolitan archbishop of Ontario. He received honorary degrees from Trinity College and from the University of Western Ontario.

[*Can. who's who*, 1948.]

Seagram, Joseph Emm (1841-1919), distiller, horseman, and politician, was born in Galt, Ontario, in 1841, the son of Octavius Augustus Seagram and Amelia Styles. He was educated at the grammar school of Dr. Tassie (q.v.); and in 1870 entered the employ of a firm of millers and distillers in Waterloo, Ontario, of which he became sole proprietor in 1883. He was a devotee of the turf; in 1906 he became president of the Ontario Jockey Club; and he had a stable which on numerous occasions won the King's Plate in Ontario. From 1896 to 1908 he represented Waterloo in the Canadian House of Commons. He died at Waterloo, Ontario, on August 18, 1919. In 1869 he married Stephanie Erb (d. 1909); and by her he had several children.

[Morgan, *Can. men* (1912); *Can. parl. comp.*; *Can. who was who*, vol. 2.]

Seaman, Holly Skiff (1884?-1952), author, was born in Ontario about 1884, and died in Winnipeg, Manitoba, on April 7, 1952. He was an accountant in Winnipeg from 1903 to 1946; and he was the author of *Manitoba landmarks and red letter days* (Winnipeg, 1920).

[B. B. Peel, comp., *A bibliography of the prairie provinces* (Toronto, 1953).]

Seargeant, Lewis James (1825?-1905), general manager of the Grand Trunk Railway (1890-96), was born in England about 1825. He became connected with the South Wales Railway; and in 1874 he came to Canada as traffic manager of the Grand Trunk Railway. In 1890 he was appointed general manager of this railway; but in 1896 he retired, and was appointed a director. He died at London, England, on November 28, 1905.

[*Can. who was who*, vol. 2; *Railway and marine world*, January, 1906; Rose, *Cyc. Can. biog.* (1886); Taché, *Men of the day.*]

Seath, John (1844-1919), educationist, was born at Auchtermuchty, Fifeshire, Scotland, on January 6, 1844, the son of John Seath and Isabel Herkless. He was educated at Glasgow University and at Queen's University, Belfast, Ireland (B.A., 1861). In 1862 he came to Canada, and became a school-teacher. He taught successively at Brampton, Oshawa, Dundas, and St. Catharines, Ontario. In 1884 he was appointed an inspector of high schools in Ontario; and in 1906 he was appointed superintendent of education for Ontario. This post he occupied until his death, at Toronto, on March 17, 1919. In 1873 he married Caroline Louisa McKenzie, of Dundas, Ontario; and by her he had one son. He was an LL.D. of Queen's University, Kingston (1902) and of the University of Toronto (1905); and he was the author of a number of text-books and other educational publications.

[J. Squair, *John Seath and the school system of Ontario* (Toronto, 1920); *Can. who was who*, vol. 1; Morgan, *Can. men* (1912).]

Seaton, Sir John Colborne, first Baron. See **Colborne, Sir John, first Baron Seaton.**

Secord, Mrs. Laura, *née* **Ingersoll** (1775-1868), heroine, was born in Massachusetts in 1775, the daughter of Thomas Ingersoll and Sarah, daughter of Gen. John Whiting. After the American Revolution she came with her parents to Upper Canada, and here she married Sergeant James Secord, of the First Lincoln Militia. In the summer of 1813, while American troops were billeted in her house at Queenston, she came into possession of knowledge of American plans for a surprise attack on Beaver Dams; and she made her way through the American lines, and warned Lieut. James Fitzgibbon (q.v.), in command at Beaver Dams, of the projected attack. She lived for many years afterwards; and died at Chippawa, Ontario, on October 17, 1868.

[S. A. Curzon, *The story of Laura Secord* (pamphlet, Toronto, 1891); Mrs. E. J. Thompson, *Laura Secord* (Niagara hist. soc., no. 25, 1913); W. S. Wallace, *The story of Laura Secord* (Toronto, 1932).]

Secretan, James Henry Edward (1854-1926), civil engineer and author, was born in 1854, and for many years was on the surveying staff of the Canadian Pacific Railway. In his later years he was civil servant at Ottawa, and he died at Ottawa, suddenly, on December 22, 1926. He was the author of *To the Klondyke and back* (London, 1898), *Out west* (Ottawa,

1910), and *Canada's great highway: From the first stake to the last spike* (Toronto, 1924).

[Private information.]

Sedgewick, Garnet Gladwin (1882-1949), educationist, was born in Nova Scotia on May 20, 1882, and died at Vancouver, British Columbia, on September 4, 1949. He was educated at Dalhousie University (B.A., 1903) and Harvard University (M.A., 1911; Ph.D., 1913). From 1913 to 1918 he was on the staff of Washington University, St. Louis; but in 1918 he returned to Canada as professor of English in the University of British Columbia, and he was head of the department of English from 1930 until his retirement in 1948. He was elected a fellow of the Royal Society of Canada in 1946; and he was the author of a series of lectures entitled *Of irony, especially in drama* (Toronto, 1935). Dalhousie University conferred on him the honorary degree of LL.D. in 1948.

[*Proc. Roy. Soc. Can.*, 1950; *Can. who's who*, 1948; *Encyc. Can.*]

Sedgewick, George Herbert (1878-1939), chairman of the Tariff Board of Canada (1933-39), was born at Musquodoboit, Nova Scotia, on February 12, 1878, the son of William N. Sedgewick, and the nephew of the Hon. Robert Sedgewick (q.v.). He was educated at Dalhousie University, Halifax, and at the Osgoode Hall Law School, Toronto; and was called to the bar of Ontario in 1906 (K.C., 1928). He practised law in Toronto, and in 1930 was appointed a judge of the Supreme Court of Ontario. He retired from the bench in 1933 in order to accept the chairmanship of the Tariff Board at Ottawa; and he remained in this post until his death at Ottawa on March 14, 1939. In 1935 he was created a C.M.G.

[*Can. who's who*, 1936-37.]

Sedgwick, Robert (1848-1906), jurist, was born in Aberdeen, Scotland, on May 10, 1848, and came to Nova Scotia with his parents when a child. He was educated at Dalhousie College, Halifax (B.A., 1867; LL.D., 1893), and studied law under the Hon. John Sandfield Macdonald (q.v.). He was called to the bar of Ontario in 1872, and to that of Nova Scotia in 1873 (Q.C., 1880); and practised law in Halifax, Nova Scotia. In 1888 he became deputy minister of justice for Canada under the Hon. (later Sir) John S.D. Thompson (q.v.); and in 1893 he was appointed a puisne judge of the Supreme Court of Canada. He remained a judge in this court until his death on August 4, 1906.

[Morgan, *Can. men* (1898); Rose, *Cyc. Can. biog.* (1888).]

Sedgwick, Robert (1613?-1656), soldier, was born in Bedfordshire, England, about 1613, and emigrated to New England in 1636. He took a foremost part in organizing the militia of Massachusetts, and in 1652 was elected major-general of the colony. In 1653 he went to England, and was commissioned by Oliver Cromwell to command an expedition against the Dutch of Manhattan island; but before he was able to launch his attack, peace was signed with the Netherlands, and he therefore turned his expedition against the French in Acadia. In 1654 he captured the French forts at Port Royal and at the mouth of the St. John River. He was then sent by Cromwell on an expedition against the Spanish West Indies; and he died in Jamaica on May 24, 1656.

[*Dict. nat. biog.*; *Dict. Am. biog.*; Le Jeune, *Dict. gén.*; *Dict. Can. biog.*, vol. 1.]

Seers, Eugène (1865-1945), author, was born in Beauharnois, Canada East, in 1865, and died at Boston, Massachusetts, on January 17, 1945. He was educated at the Montreal Seminary and at the Sulpician Seminary near Paris, France. He became a member of the Order of the Blessed Sacrament, and spent thirteen years in Rome and Paris. He returned to Canada in 1894, and was placed in charge of the order's publications in Montreal. It was during this period that he edited, with an introduction, under the *nom de plume* "Louis Dantin", *Emile Nelligan et son oeuvre* (Montreal, 1903). Later, he left his religious order, and became a typographer with a Boston firm of printers and with the Harvard University Press. Here he resumed his literary work, and, still under the *nom de plume* of "Louis Dantin", wrote *Poètes de l'Amérique française* (2 vols., Montreal, 1928-34), *La vie en rêve* (Montreal, 1930), *Gloses critiques* (2 vols., Montreal, 1931-35), *Le coffret de Crusoé* (Montreal, 1932), and *Les enfances de Fanny* (Montreal, 1951).

[G. Nadeau, *Louis Dantin* (Manchester, N.H., 1948); *Encyc. Can.*]

Seghers, Charles John (1839-1886), Roman Catholic archbishop of Vancouver Island (1886), was born at Ghent, Belgium, on December 26, 1839. He was ordained a priest of the Roman Catholic Church in 1863, and was sent as a missionary to Vancouver Island. In 1873 he succeeded Bishop Demers (q.v.) as bishop of Vancouver Island; and in 1880 he became archbishop of Oregon City. In 1885, however, he returned to the see of Vancouver Island, and in 1886 he became once more archbishop. Later in 1886 he made an expedition to Alaska; and here, on November 28, 1886, he was murdered by a white companion.

[Sister Mary Annunciata, *Archbishop Seghers* (British Columbia historical quarterly, 1943); *Catholic encyclopedia.*]

Selby, Prideaux (d. 1813), receiver-general of Upper Canada, came to Canada as a subaltern in the 5th Regiment, and became assistant secretary of the department of Indian affairs. In 1804 he was appointed a judge of the district court of the Western district in Upper Canada; and in 1808 he became receiver-general of the province and a member of the Executive Council. He died on May 9, 1813.

[A. Ewart and J. Jarvis, *The personnel of the family compact* (Can. hist. rev., 1926).]

Selkirk, Thomas Douglas, fifth Earl of (1771-1820), philanthropist, was born at St. Mary's Isle, Kirkcudbrightshire, Scotland, on June 20, 1771, the seventh and youngest son of Dunbar Douglas, fourth Earl of Selkirk. He was educated at Edinburgh University; and here he was a member of a club for the discussion of social and political questions, of which Sir Walter Scott was also a member. In 1799, on the death of his father, all his brothers having died previously, he succeeded to the Scottish earldom of Selkirk; and he immediately began to formulate plans for relieving the distress consequent upon the economic revolution then in progress in the Highlands of Scotland. He proposed emigration of the evicted "crofters" to British North America; and in 1803 he planted his first colony of Highlanders in Prince Edward Island. At the same time he was connected with the establishment of a similar colony at Baldoon, near Lake St. Clair, in Upper Canada. His chief project, however, was the establishment of a settlement in the Red River valley, in what is now Manitoba. With a view to the founding of this colony, he acquired financial control of the Hudson's Bay Company, and obtained from the company in 1811 the cession of forty-five millions of acres in the Red River valley. In 1811 he sent out a party of settlers, under Miles Macdonell (q.v.), by way of Hudson Bay, and in 1812 a second party; and these established themselves near the site of the present city of Winnipeg—the first body of colonists in the North West.

In these proceedings Selkirk was actuated by the purest and most altruistic motives; but he failed to take into account the certain hostility of the North West Company to his plans for the colonization of the Red River valley. The Nor'Westers, who were the inheritors of the French fur-trade in the West, disputed the right of the Hudson's Bay Company to dispose of the territory in the Red River country; and they resolved to break up the Selkirk settlement. Twice they drove the settlers from their homes; and on June 19, 1816, a miniature battle took place at Seven Oaks, near Fort Douglas, between the Nor'Westers and the Selkirk settlers, under Robert Semple (q.v.), whom the Hudson's Bay Company had sent out as governor. In this skirmish Semple and twenty of his men were killed. Meanwhile, Selkirk was on his way to the Red River from Canada, with a force of disbanded soldiers; and when news reached him of the Seven Oaks affair, he seized the North West Company's headquarters at Fort William, on Lake Superior, arrested a

number of the officers of the North West Company, and sent them back to Canada for trial. The following spring he pushed on to the Red River, reinstated his colonists, and restored order. The battle was then transferred to the courts. The North West Company brought action against Selkirk for having conspired with others to ruin the company's trade in the West; and the trials, which took place in 1818, resulted in the defeat of Selkirk, who was ordered to pay heavy damages. Selkirk returned to England broken in health; and he died at Pau, in the south of France, on April 8, 1820. He was survived by his wife, Jean, daughter of James Wedderburn-Colvile, whom he married in 1807, and by whom he had one son and two daughters.

A clear and forceful writer, Selkirk published, in addition to several pamphlets on political subjects, the following works dealing with his emigration projects: *Observations on the present state of the highlands of Scotland* (London, 1805), *A sketch of the British fur-trade in North America, with observations relative to the North West Company of Montreal* (London, 1816; New York, 1818), and *A letter to the Earl of Liverpool . . . on the subject of the Red River settlement in North America* (privately printed, London, 1819). Two anonymous pamphlets on *The civilisation of the Indians of British North America* (London, 1807) have also been attributed to him. His *Diary* covering the years 1803-04 has been edited by Patrick C. T. White for the Champlain Society (Toronto, 1958).

[G. Bryce, *Life of Lord Selkirk* (Toronto, n.d.) and *Mackenzie, Selkirk, Simpson* (Toronto, 1905); C. Martin, *Lord Selkirk's work in Canada* (Oxford, 1916); Helen I. Cowan, *Selkirk's work in Canada* (Can. hist. rev., 1928); A. Macdonell, *A narrative of the transactions in the Red River country* (London, 1819); W. S. Wallace, *The literature relating to the Selkirk controversy* (Can. hist. rev., 1932); J. M. Gray, *Lord Selkirk of Red River* (Toronto, 1963); J. P. Pritchett, *The Red River Valley, 1811-1849* (Toronto, 1942).]

Sellar, Robert (1841-1919), journalist and author, was born in Glasgow, Scotland, on August 1, 1841, and came to Canada as a child. He became a journalist on the staff of the Toronto *Globe*; and in 1863 he founded the *Canadian Gleaner* at Huntingdon, Quebec. He retained the direction of this paper until his death at Huntingdon on November 30, 1919. He was the author of *The history of the county of Huntingdon* (Huntingdon, 1888), *Disabilities of Protestants in the province of Quebec* (Huntingdon, 1890), *Hemlock, a tale of the war of 1812* (Huntingdon, 1890), *Gleaner tales* (Huntingdon, 1895), *The tragedy of Quebec* (Huntingdon, 1907), *Morven* (Huntingdon, 1911), *The U.S. campaign of 1813* (Huntingdon, 1913), *True makers of Canada* (Huntingdon,

1915), and *George Brown and Confederation* (Toronto, 1917).

[G. Lanctot, *Un régionaliste anglais, Robert Sellar* (Bull. rech. hist., 1935); *Can. who was who*, vol. 1; Morgan, *Can. men* (1898); A. MacMurchy, *A handbook of Canadian literature* (Toronto, 1906).]

Selwyn, Alfred Richard Cecil (1824-1902), director of the Geological Survey of Canada (1869-95), was born at Kilmington, Somerset, England, on July 28, 1824, the son of the Rev. Townshend Selwyn, canon of Gloucester Cathedral, and Charlotte Sophia, daughter of Lord George Murray, bishop of St. David's. He was privately educated, and became an assistant geologist on the staff of the Geological Survey of Great Britain. From 1852 to 1869 he was director of the Geological Survey of Victoria, Australia; and from 1869 to his retirement on pension in 1895 he was director of the Geological Survey of Canada. He died at Vancouver, British Columbia, on October 18, 1902. In 1852 he married Matilda Charlotte (d. 1882), daughter of the Rev. Edward Selwyn, rector of Hemingford Abbots, Huntingdonshire. He was a fellow of the Royal Society, of the Geographical Society, and of the Royal Society of Canada. Of the last society he was president in 1896. In 1881 he was made an LL.D. of McGill University; and in 1886 he was created a C.M.G. A bibliography of his scientific papers and reports is to be found in *Trans. Roy. Soc. Can.*, 1894.

[*Dict. nat. biog.*, supp. II; Morgan, *Can. men* (1898); Rose, *Cyc. Can. biog.* (1888); *Proc. Roy. Soc. Can.*, 1903.]

Semlin, Charles Augustus (1836-1927), prime minister of British Columbia (1898-1900), was born in October, 1836, in Simcoe county, Upper Canada, of United Empire Loyalist descent. He became a school-teacher; but in 1862 he went to British Columbia, at the time of the Cariboo "gold fever", and settled at Cache Creek, British Columbia. From 1871 to 1876, and from 1882 to 1903, he represented Yale in the Legislative Assembly of British Columbia; and in 1898 he became prime minister of the province, with the portfolios of public works and agriculture. He was dismissed from office in 1900, and he retired from political life in 1903. He died, unmarried, at Ashcroft, British Columbia, on November 3, 1927.

[Morgan, *Can. men* (1912); *Can. parl. comp.*; J. B. Kerr, *Biographical dictionary of well-known British Columbians* (Vancouver, B.C., 1890).]

Semmens, John (d. 1921), missionary, was received on trial as a Methodist preacher at Chatham, Ontario, in 1871; and in 1872 he was sent to the North West as a missionary among the Indians. He spent most of his life at various mission stations in the North West;

and he died at Winnipeg, Manitoba, on February 1, 1921. He was the author of *The field and the work: Sketches of missionary life in the far north* (Toronto, 1884) and *The hand-book to Scripture truths*, translated into Cree by W. Isbister (Toronto, 1893).

[J. Carroll, *Cyclopaedia of Methodism in Canada* (2 vols., Toronto, 1881-1903).]

Semple, Robert (1777-1816), governor of the Hudson's Bay Company's territories (1815-16), was born on February 26, 1777, in Boston, Massachusetts. His parents espoused the loyalist cause during the American Revolution; and at the close of the Revolution he went into business in London, England. In the course of business he travelled extensively in South Africa, Spain, Italy, Asia Minor, the West Indies, Brazil, Venezuela and Germany; and he wrote *Walks and sketches at the Cape of Good Hope* (London, 1803), *Observations on a journey through Spain and Italy* (London, 1807), *A second journey in Spain* (London, 1810), *Sketch of the present state of Caracas* (London, 1812), and *Observations made on a tour from Hamburg through Berlin to Gothenburg* (London, 1814). He also wrote a novel, *Charles Ellis, or the friends* (London, 1814). In 1815 he obtained through the influence or Lord Selkirk (q.v.) an appointment as governor or chief agent of the Hudson's Bay Company in North America, in succession to Miles Macdonell (q.v.); and he arrived at the Red River Settlement in September of that year. In March, 1816, he seized and destroyed the fort of the North West Company at Red River; and on June 19 he came into armed collision with a party of Nor'Westers at Seven Oaks. In the fight which ensued he and twenty of his men were killed.

[*Dict. nat. biog.*; *Cyc. Am. biog.*; Le Jeune, *Dict. gén.*; G. Bryce, *The remarkable history of the Hudson's Bay Company* (London, 1900); C. Martin, *Lord Selkirk's work in Canada* (Oxford, 1916); E. E. Rich (ed.), *Colin Robertson's correspondence book* (Toronto: The Champlain Society, 1939).]

Sénécal, Louis Adélard (1829-1887), senator of Canada, was born at Varennes, Verchères county, Quebec, on July 10, 1829. He had a limited education, but became an important figure in the economic life of the province of Quebec. He built steamships, railways, saw-mills, and grist-mills; and he was interested in cotton-mills, pulp-factories, electric-light plants, and timber limits. He took also an active part in politics, first as a Liberal, and then as a Conservative; and he was a member of the Canadian House of Commons for Yamaska from 1867 to 1871, and for Drummond and Arthabaska from 1867 to 1872 — the only member to represent two constituencies at the same time in the history of the Dominion. On January 25, 1887, he was appointed to the Senate of Canada; but he died shortly afterwards, on October 11, 1887.

[*Can. parl. comp.*]

Seranus (pseud.). See **Harrison, Mrs. Susie Frances.**

Service, Robert William (1874-1958), poet and novelist, was born in Preston, England, on January 16, 1874, and died at Lancieux, France, on September 11, 1958. He was educated at Hill Head School in Glasgow, and entered the Commercial Bank of Scotland. He came to Canada in 1894, and entered the service of the Canadian Bank of Commerce. He was stationed at Vancouver, Victoria, Kamloops, and finally at Whitehorse and Dawson in the Yukon. It was while he was here that he published his first volume of verse, *Songs of a sourdough* (Toronto, 1907), which was an immediate success. This was followed by *Ballads of a cheechako* (Toronto, 1909), *Rhymes of a rolling stone* (Toronto, 1912), *The rhymes of a Red Cross man* (London, 1916), *Ballads of a bohemian* (New York, 1921), *Bar-room ballads* (New York, 1940), *Complete poems* (New York, 1940), *Songs of a sun-lover* (London, 1949), *Lyrics of a low brow* (New York, 1951), *Rhymes of a rebel* (New York, 1952), *Songs for my supper* (New York, 1953), *Carols of an old codger* (New York, 1954), *Rhymes for my rags* (New York, 1955), and *More collected verse* (New York, 1957). He also wrote six novels: *The trail of '98* (Toronto, 1911), *The pretender* (New York, 1914), *The poisoned paradise* (New York, 1922), *The roughneck* (New York, 1923), *The master of the microbe* (New York, 1926), and *The house of fear* (New York, 1927); but these did not achieve the popularity of his verse. He published his autobiography in two volumes, *The ploughman of the moon* (New York, 1945) and *Harper of heaven* (New York, 1948). He spent the latter part of his life in Monte Carlo.

[*Who's who in Am.*, 1958-59; *Can. who's who*, 1955-57; Morgan, *Can. men* (1912); *Encyc. Can.*]

Seton, Ernest Thompson (1860-1946), artist, naturalist, and author, was born at South Shields, Durham, England, on August 14, 1860, and died at Seton Village, Santa Fe, New Mexico, on October 23, 1946. He came to Canada with his parents in 1866, was educated in the public schools of Toronto, and studied art at the Ontario College of Art. Later he studied art in London, Paris, and New York. In 1890 he was appointed naturalist to the government of Manitoba, and began the study of animal life that was the basis of his later success as an author. He began writing animal stories as early as 1894; and between 1898 and his death he published more than forty books about wild animals, most of them illustrated by himself. Of these, the best-known are *Wild animals I have known* (New

York, 1898), *Lives of the hunted* (New York, 1901), *Two little savages* (New York, 1903), *Life histories of northern animals* (2 vols., New York, 1909), and *Lives of game animals* (4 vols., New York, 1925-28). He published several books about woodcraft, such as *Woodcraft and fable* (New York, 1905), and a valuable account of an expedition in northern Canada, entitled *The Arctic prairies* (New York, 1911). Towards the end of his life he published his autobiography, *Trail of an artist-naturalist* (New York, 1940). His baptismal name was Ernest Evan Thompson, but he changed it first to Ernest Seton Thompson, and then to Ernest Thompson Seton, because he believed he was the direct descendant of George Seton, last Earl of Winton.

[Julia Seton, "Memoir", in *Ernest Thompson Seton's America* (New York, 1954); *Encyc. Can.*; *Can. who's who*, 1938-39; Morgan, *Can. men* (1918).]

Sewell, Henry Fane (d. 1944), banker and poet, was born in India, the son of a British army officer. He came to Canada as a young man; and entered the service of the Bank of British Columbia, which was later absorbed by the Canadian Bank of Commerce. He was for many years a branch manager of the Canadian Bank of Commerce in Toronto. On retirement from the bank, he went to live in Vancouver, British Columbia; and he died there on October 5, 1944. He was much addicted to writing occasional verses; and he published a volume of his verses, under the title, *The King, Canada, and Empire* (Toronto, 1910).

[Toronto, *Globe and Mail*, Oct. 7, 1944.]

Sewell, Jonathan (1766-1839), chief justice of Lower Canada (1808-38), was born at Cambridge, Massachusetts, on June 6, 1766. He was educated at the grammar school in Bristol, England; and in 1785 he emigrated to New Brunswick, where he studied law in the office of Ward Chipman (q.v.). In 1789 he settled in Quebec, and was called to the bar of the province of Quebec. In 1793 he was appointed solicitor-general of Lower Canada, and in 1795 attorney-general; and he represented the borough of William Henry in the Legislative Assembly of the province from 1796 to 1808. In 1808 he was appointed chief justice of Lower Canada and president of the Executive Council; and in 1809 he became also speaker of the Legislative Council. He resigned the presidency of the Executive Council in 1829, and the office of chief justice in 1838; but he continued as speaker of the Legislative Council until his death at Quebec, on November 12, 1839. He was an LL.D. of Harvard University; and he published the following: *A plan for the federal union of the British provinces in North America* (London, 1814); *On the advantages of opening the river St. Lawrence to the commerce of the world* (London, 1814); *An essay on the* juridical history of France, so far as it relates to the law of the province of Lower Canada (Quebec, 1824); and, in collaboration with others, *Plan for a general legislative union of the British provinces in North America* (London, 1824). He was one of the earliest advocates of the federation of the British North American provinces.

[F. J. Audet, *Les juges en chef de la province de Québec* (Quebec, 1927); P. G. Roy, *Les juges de la province de Québec* (Quebec, 1933); Morgan, *Bib. can.* and *Cel. Can.*; Le Jeune, *Dict. gén.*; *Cyc. Am. biog.*; D. A. McArthur, *An early Canadian impeachment* (Kingston, Ont., 1913).]

Sewell, William George Grant (1829-1862), journalist and author, was born in Quebec on April 24, 1829, the grandson of the Hon. Jonathan Sewell (q.v.). He studied law, but in 1853 he became a journalist in New York. He died in Quebec on August 9, 1862. A few years before his death, he went to the West Indies in search of health; and while there he wrote *Ordeal of free labour in the British West Indies* (New York, 1861; 2nd ed., London, 1862).

[P. G. Roy, *Fils de Québec*, vol. 4 (Lévis, P.Q., 1933).]

Seymour, Benjamin (1806-1880), senator of Canada, was born at Fredericksburg, Upper Canada, in 1806; and was educated at the Royal Grammar School, Kingston. He represented Lennox and Addington in the Legislative Assembly of United Canada from 1844 to 1854; and in 1855 he was summoned to the Legislative Council. In 1867 he was appointed by royal proclamation a member of the Senate of Canada, and he sat in the Senate until his death at Port Hope, Ontario, on March 23, 1880.

[*Dom. ann. reg.*, 1880-81; *Can. parl. comp.*]

Seymour, Frederick (1820-1869), governor of British Columbia, was born on September 6, 1820, the fourth son of Henry Augustus Seymour, of Pembroke College, Cambridge. He entered the service of the Colonial Office; and was successively assistant colonial secretary of Tasmania, special magistrate of Antigua, president of Nevis, superintendent of Honduras and lieutenant-governor of the Bay Islands, and lieutenant-governor of Honduras. In 1864 he was appointed governor of the mainland of British Columbia; and he held this post until his death on June 10, 1869, on board H.M.S. *Sparrow Hawk*, off the coast of British Columbia. His régime was marked by his opposition to the union of British Columbia with Canada. In 1865 he married Florence Maria, daughter of the Hon. and Rev. Sir Francis Stapleton, Bart.

[F. W. Howay, *The attitude of Governor Seymour toward Confederation* (Trans. Roy. Soc. Can., 1920); Le Jeune, *Dict. gén.*; F. W.

Howay, *British Columbia*, vol. 2 (Vancouver, 1914).]

Seymour, James Cooke (1839-1902), clergyman and author, was born in Ulster, Ireland, on April 20, 1839, and came to Canada in 1857. He was received as a probationer in the Methodist Church in 1857. He served in various churches in Ontario; and he died at Paisley, Ontario, on September 1, 1902. He was the author of *The river of life* (Toronto, 1869), *Voices from the throne* (Toronto, 1881), *The temperance battlefield* (Toronto, 1882), *The gifts of the royal family; or, Systematic beneficence* (Toronto, 1888), and *Christ the apocalypse* (Toronto, 1902); and he edited *Humour, pith, and pathos* (Toronto, 1887).

[Morgan, *Can. men* (1898).]

Shank, David (d. 1831), soldier, was a loyalist who received in 1777 a commission in the Queen's Rangers. He served throughout the American Revolutionary War, and in 1783 returned to England on half-pay. When the Queen's Rangers were revived in 1791, on the appointment of Colonel Simcoe (q.v.) as lieutenant-governor of Upper Canada, he was employed in raising the regiment, and brought it out to Canada in 1792. He was gazetted major in 1794 and lieutenant-colonel in 1798; and remained in command of the regiment until his return to England in 1799. In 1803 he was appointed lieutenant-colonel of the Canadian Fencibles. He rose to the rank of lieutenant-general; and he died at Glasgow, Scotland, on October 16, 1831.

[J. Ross Robertson, *Landmarks of Canada* (Toronto, 1917); *Cyc. Am. biog.*]

Shank, John. See Schanck, John.

Shanly, Charles Dawson (1811-1875), poet and art critic, was born in Dublin, Ireland, on March 9, 1811, the son of James Shanly. He came to Canada with his parents in 1836, and settled in Middlesex county, Upper Canada. He was a writer of occasional verse, and he edited a short-lived periodical entitled *Punch in Canada*. In his later years he was an art critic in New York. He died at Arlington, Florida, whither he had gone in search of health, on April 15, 1875.

[*Cyc. Am. biog.*; T. H. Rand (ed.), *A treasury of Canadian verse* (Toronto, 1900); C. M. Whyte-Edgar, *A wreath of Canadian song* (Montreal, 1910); *Dict. Can. biog.*, vol. 10.]

Shanly, Francis (1820-1882), civil engineer, was born at Stradbally, Queen's county, Ireland, on October 29, 1820, the fifth son of James Shanly. He came to Canada with his parents in 1836, and settled in Middlesex county, Upper Canada. He became a civil engineer, and played an important part in the "railway era" in the Canadas. With his brother, Walter Shanly (q.v.), he built the

Hoosac tunnel in Massachusetts. In 1880 he was appointed chief engineer of the Intercolonial Railway. He died suddenly, in a sleeping car of the Grand Trunk Railway, between Kingston and Brockville, on September 13, 1882.

[F. N. Walker (ed.), *Daylight through the mountains: The letters and labours of Walter and Francis Shanly* (Toronto, 1957); *Dom. ann. reg.*, 1882.]

Shanly, Walter (1817-1899), civil engineer, was born at "The Abbey", Stradbally, Queen's county, Ireland, on October 11, 1817, the fourth son of James Shanly. He came to Canada in 1836 with his parents, settled in Middlesex county, Upper Canada, and became a civil engineer. From 1858 to 1862 he was general manager of the Grand Trunk Railway; and in 1869-75 he was engaged, with his brother, Francis Shanly (q.v.), in the construction of the Hoosac tunnel in Massachusetts. From 1863 to 1867 he represented South Grenville as a Conservative in the Legislative Assembly of Canada; and he sat in the Canadian House of Commons for this constituency, from 1867 to 1872, and from 1885 to 1891. He died in Montreal on December 17, 1899. He was not married.

[Taylor, *Brit. Am.*, vol. 3; *Cyc. Am. biog.*; N. F. Davin, *The Irishman in Canada* (Toronto, 1877); M. Pennington, *Railways and other ways* (Toronto, 1896); *Railroad gazette*, 1900; Morgan, *Bib. can.*; *Can. parl. comp.*; F. N. Walker (ed.), *Daylight through the mountains: The letters and labours of Walter and Francis Shanly* (Toronto, 1957).]

Shannon, William (*fl.* 1852-1876), Orangeman and anthologist, was for many years a clerk in the post-office, in Kingston, Ontario. He was chairman of the committee appointed by the Orangemen of Kingston and Belleville, Canada West, to receive the Prince of Wales (afterwards King Edward VII), on the occasion of his proposed visit to these towns in September, 1860. He published an account of the preparations made, and the refusal of the Prince of Wales to land at Kingston and Belleville if there were to be party demonstrations by the Orangemen, under the title *Narrative of the proceedings of the Loyal Orangemen of Kingston and Belleville, on the 4th, 5th, and 6th of September, 1860, in connection with the visit of H.R.H. the Prince of Wales to central Canada* (Belleville, C.W., 1861). He was also the compiler of two volumes of Orange songs and poems, *The United Empire minstrel* (Toronto, 1852) and *The Dominion Orange harmonist* (Toronto, 1876).

[F. M. Staton and M. Tremaine (eds.), *A bibliography of Canadiana* (Toronto, 1934).]

Shapiro, Lionel (1908-1958), journalist and author, was born in Montreal, Quebec, on February 12, 1908, and died there on May 27,

1958. He was educated at McGill University (B.A., 1929). He became a journalist, and during the Second World War achieved distinction as a war correspondent. He was the author of *They left the back door open* (London, 1944), an account of the Allied campaign in Sicily and at Salerno; and he followed this by three novels, *The sealed verdict* (New York, 1947), *Torch for a dark journey* (New York, 1950), and *The sixth of June* (New York, 1955).

[*Can. who's who*, 1955-57; *Encyc. Can.*]

Sharp, George (d. 1800), merchant, was a prominent trader of Detroit and the North West in the period subsequent to the American Revolution. In 1798 he became one of the original partners of the XY Company. He died at Montreal on January 17, 1800.

[M. M. Quaife (ed.); *The John Askin papers* (2 vols., Detroit, Mich., 1931).]

Sharpe, Samuel Simpson (1872-1918), politician and soldier, was born at Zephyr, Ontario, on March 13, 1872. He was educated at the University of Toronto (B.A., 1895) and at Osgoode Hall, and was called to the bar of Ontario in 1897. He practised law in Uxbridge, Ontario; and from 1908 to 1918 he represented Uxbridge in the Canadian House of Commons. He had held a commission in the 34th Regiment since 1894; and in 1915 he was given command of the 116th Battalion of the Canadian Expeditionary Force, which he raised and took overseas. He commanded the battalion at the front in France, was awarded the D.S.O., and was invalided home in 1918. He died on May 25, 1918.

[*Can. who was who*, vol. 1; H. Charlesworth (ed.), *A cyclopaedia of Canadian biography* (Toronto, 1919); Morgan, *Can. men* (1912); *Can. parl. comp.*]

Sharpe, William Henry (1868-1942), soldier and senator, was born in Scott township, Ontario county, Ontario, on April 19, 1868. He was educated at the Belleville Business College, and engaged in business as a general merchant in Manitou, Manitoba. He represented Lisgar in the Canadian House of Commons from 1908 to 1915; and in 1916 he was called to the Senate of Canada. During the First World War he raised and commanded, with the rank of lieutenant-colonel, the 184th Battalion of the Canadian Expeditionary Force. He died at Ottawa, Ontario, on April 19, 1942.

[*Can. who's who*, 1936-37; *Can. parl. comp.*]

Shatford, Allan Pearson (1873-1935), clergyman and author, was born at St. Margaret's Bay, Nova Scotia, on May 9, 1873. He was educated at King's College, Windsor (B.A., 1895; M.A., 1898; D.C.L. 1911), and was ordained a priest of the Church of England in 1896. After serving as rector of Bridgewater and North Sydney in Nova Scotia, he became assistant rector in 1906, and rector in 1912, of the Church of St. James the Apostle in Montreal. He served as chaplain to the 24th Battalion during the First World War, and was awarded the O.B.E. He died at his summer home in Nova Scotia on August 16, 1935. He was the author of a *Memoir of Herbert Symonds* (Montreal, 1921), *Six marks of a Christian* (Philadelphia, 1925), *He yet speaketh* (Toronto, 1938), and a number of Christmas brochures, one of which he published each year.

[R. J. Long, *Nova Scotia authors* (East Orange, N.J., 1918); Morgan, *Can. men* (1912).]

Shaughnessy, Thomas George Shaughnessy, first Baron (1853-1923), president of the Canadian Pacific Railway Company (1898-1918), was born at Milwaukee, Wisconsin, on October 6, 1853, the son of Thomas Shaughnessy, of Limerick, Ireland. He entered the employ of the Milwaukee and St. Paul Railway in 1869, and in 1882 he joined the staff of the Canadian Pacific Railway. He became president of this railway in 1898, and continued as such until 1918. He died at Montreal on December 9, 1923. In 1880 he married Elizabeth Bridget Nagle, of Milwaukee; and by her he had two sons and three daughters. In 1901 he was created a knight bachelor, and in 1907 a K.C.V.O.; and in 1916 he was created Baron Shaughnessy, in the peerage of the United Kingdom. He was a D.C.L. of Trinity College, Dublin, and an LL.D. of Dartmouth College and of McGill University.

[*Who was who*, 1916-28; A. Bridle, *Sons of Canada* (Toronto, 1916); Morgan, *Can. men* (1918); H. A. Innis, *A history of the Canadian Pacific Railway* (London, 1923).]

Shaughnessy, William James Shaughnessy, second Baron (1883-1938), lawyer and financier, was born in Montreal, Quebec, on September 29, 1883, the son of the first Baron Shaughnessy (q.v.). He was educated at McGill University, at Trinity College, Cambridge, and at Laval University (LL.M., 1910); and was called to the bar in 1910 (K.C., 1920). He served in the First World War as captain and adjutant of the Duchess of Connaught's Irish-Canadian Rangers, and afterwards as a staff officer in France. In 1920 he was promoted to command the Irish-Canadian Rangers, on amalgamation with the 199th Irish Rangers, and he retained command until 1926. He succeeded his father in the peerage in 1923; and he died in Montreal, Quebec, on October 4, 1938.

[*Who was who*, 1929-40; *Can. who's who*, 1936-37.]

Shaw, Aeneas (d. 1815), soldier, was the second son of Angus Shaw of Tordarroch, Scotland, and Anne Dallas. He served in the

Queen's Rangers under Simcoe (q.v.) in the American Revolutionary War; and in 1792 he came from New Brunswick to Upper Canada with his company of the reorganized Queen's Rangers. In 1794 he was appointed a member of the Legislative Council of Upper Canada, and later a member of the Executive Council. In 1803 he was placed on half-pay in the army, and he ceased to be a regular member of the Executive Council, though he remained an honorary councillor until 1807. In 1811 he was gazetted a major-general; and during the War of 1812 he was adjutant-general of the militia. He died near York (Toronto) on February 15, 1815. He was twice married, (1) to Ann Gosline (d. 1806), of Newton, New York, and (2) to Margaret Hickman, daughter of Capt. Poole Hickman, England, 47th Regiment. By his first marriage he had seven sons and six daughters.

[E. M. Chadwick, *Ontarian families*, vol. 1 (Toronto, 1894); J. Ross Robertson (ed.), *The diary of Mrs. Simcoe* (Toronto, 1911); W. J. Rattray, *The Scot in British North America* (4 vols., Toronto, 1880).]

Shaw, Angus (d. 1832), fur-trader, was a native of Scotland who entered the service of the North West Company as a clerk prior to 1787. In 1789 he was at Fort L'Orignal, near the source of the Fraser River; and in 1790 he was "at Moose Hill Lake, up the Beaver River from Isle à la Crosse". In 1791 he was back at Fort L'Orignal; and in 1792 he was at Fort George. He became a partner in the North West Company between 1795 and 1799; in 1797 he was elected a member of the Beaver Club of Montreal; and in 1799 he was proprietor in charge of the Upper English River district. In 1802 he was appointed agent in charge of the King's Posts, with headquarters at Quebec; and in 1808 he became a member of McTavish, McGillivrays, and Co. He was one of the agents of the North West Company at Fort William in 1810 and 1811; but thereafter he took little part in the fur-trade, until the struggle with Lord Selkirk (q.v.) reached its height, when he was one of the partners of the North West Company arrested by the Hudson's Bay men in 1819. He continued to be a partner in McTavish, McGillivrays, and Co. after the union of 1821, when they were made Montreal agents of the Hudson's Bay Company; and his estate, which was involved in the failure of that firm in 1825, was not settled until 1847. He became a victim of pulmonary tuberculosis; and he died at New Brunswick, New Jersey, on July 25, 1832, two days after his arrival at that place. He married a sister of the Hon. William McGillivray; and she died in London, England, on March 27, 1820.

[W. S. Wallace (ed.), *Documents relating to the North West Company* (Toronto: The Champlain Society, 1934).]

Shaw, Charles Lewis (1862-1911), war correspondent, was born at Perth, Canada

West, on February 7, 1862; and was educated at Trinity University, Toronto (B.A., 1881). He studied law, and was called to the bar of Manitoba in 1884; but became later a journalist and war correspondent. He accompanied Lord Wolseley's expedition to the Nile as a *voyageur* in 1884; and in 1899-1900 he served as a war correspondent with the Canadian troops in the South African War. He died at Winnipeg, Manitoba, on June 15, 1911.

[Morgan, *Can. men* (1912).]

Shaw, James (1798-1878), senator of Canada, was born in New Ross, county Wexford, Ireland, in 1798. He was educated in Dublin; and in 1820 he emigrated to Canada. For nine years he was clerk of the military settlement at Lanark, Upper Canada; and he was later an overseer, under Lieut.-Col. By (q.v.), in the construction of the Rideau Canal. He then settled in Smiths Falls as a merchant; and he represented the united counties of Lanark and Renfrew in the Legislative Assembly of Canada from 1851 to 1854, and the south riding of Lanark from 1854 to 1860. In 1860 he was elected to represent the Bathurst division in the Legislative Council; and he was called to the Senate of Canada in 1867. He died at Smiths Falls, Ontario, on February 6, 1878.

[Rose, *Cyc. Can. biog.* (1888); *Can. parl. comp.*; *Dom. ann. reg.*, 1878; *Dict. Can. biog.*, vol. 10.]

Shaw, James Eustace (1876-1962), professor, was born at Dewsbury, Yorkshire, on July 7, 1876. His father was called to the Baptist Mission Church of Rome in 1878 and the family spent eleven years in Rome. He took part of his education at King Henry VIII's School in Coventry, moved with his family to the United States in 1893 and entered Johns Hopkins University to study romance languages and literature. He remained at Johns Hopkins as a teacher for seventeen years before coming to Toronto in 1917 as professor of Italian, a post he held until his retirement in 1946. He was an inspiring teacher of Italian literature and philosophy of the thirteenth and fourteenth centuries. Besides doing much editorial work, he published *Essays on the "Vita Nuova"* (Princeton, 1929), *The lady philosophy in the "Convivio"* (Cambridge, Mass., 1938), and *Guido Cavalcanti's theory of love: The "Canzone d'Amore" and other related problems* (Toronto, 1949). He was a fellow of the Royal Society of Canada. He died at Toronto, November 10, 1962.

[*Proc. Roy. Soc. Can.*, 1964.]

Shaw, Marlow Alexander (1867-1929), educationist, was born in 1867, and was educated at the University of Toronto (B.A., 1896), and at Harvard University (Ph.D., 1903). He became in 1909 a professor of English at the University of Iowa; and he died at Iowa City, Iowa, on December 1, 1929. He was the author of *The happy islands: Stories and sketches of the Georgian bay* (Toronto, 1926).

[*University of Toronto monthly*, 1930.]

Shaw, William Isaac (1841-1911), clergyman and educationist, was born at Kingston, Upper Canada, on April 6, 1841; and was educated at Victoria University, Cobourg (B.A., 1861; M.A., 1864; LL.B., 1864) and at McGill University (LL.D., 1887). He was ordained a minister of the Methodist Church in 1868; and he held various charges in Ontario and Quebec. In 1877 he was appointed professor of Greek in the Wesleyan Theological College, Montreal; and in 1894 he became principal of this college. He became principal emeritus in 1899; and he died at Montreal, Quebec, on March 11, 1911. He was the author of *A digest of the doctrinal standards of the Methodist Church* (Toronto, 1895).

[Morgan, *Can. men* (1898); G. H. Cornish, *Cyclopaedia of Methodism in Canada* (2 vols., Toronto, 1881-1913).]

Shea, Sir Ambrose (1815-1905), politician, was born at St. John's, Newfoundland, on September 17, 1815, and died in London, England, on July 30, 1905. He was a member of the Newfoundland House of Assembly from 1848 almost continuously until 1882, was speaker of the House in 1855, a delegate to the Quebec Conference in 1864, and colonial secretary from 1865 to 1869. From 1887 to 1895 he was governor of the Bahamas. In 1883 he was created a K.C.M.G.

[*Newfoundland supp.*; *Encyc. Can.*]

Shea, Sir Edward Dalton (1820-1913), politician, was born at St. John's, Newfoundland, in 1820, a younger brother of Sir Ambrose Shea (q.v.). He represented Placentia in the Newfoundland House of Assembly from 1848 to 1855, and Ferryland from 1855 to 1865; and from 1866 to 1869 and from 1873 to 1913 he was a member of the Legislative Council. He was colonial secretary from 1874 to 1885, and president of the council from 1885 to 1912. He was created a K.B. in 1902.

[*Who was who*, 1897-1916; *Encyc. Can.*; *Newfoundland supp.*]

Sheaffe, Sir Roger Hale, Bart. (1763-1851), president and administrator of Upper Canada (1813), was born in Boston, Massachusetts, on July 15, 1763, the third son of William Sheaffe and Susannah Child. He obtained a commission in the British army in 1778, and served throughout the Revolutionary and Napoleonic wars. From 1787 to 1797, from 1802 to 1811, and again from 1812 to 1813 he was stationed in Canada. On the death of Brock (q.v.) at Queenston Heights, the command of the British forces devolved upon him; and he was commander-in-chief of the forces and president and administrator of Upper Canada until his recall to England in June,

1813. He rose to be a lieutenant-general in 1821, and a general in 1828. His death took place at Edinburgh, Scotland, on July 17, 1851. In 1810 he married Margaret, daughter of John Coffin, of Quebec. In 1813 he was created a baronet, in recognition of his services at Queenston Heights.

[D. B. Read, *The lieutenant-governors of Upper Canada* (Toronto, 1900); *Dict. nat. biog.*; Morgan, *Cel. Can.*]

Sheard, Mrs. Virna, *née* **Stanton** (d. 1943), novelist and poet, was born at Cobourg, Ontario, the daughter of Eldridge Stanton. In 1885 she married Dr. Charles Sheard (d. 1929), who was medical health officer of Toronto from 1893 to 1910, and represented Toronto South in the Canadian House of Commons from 1917 to 1925. She died in Toronto, Ontario, on February 22, 1943. She was the author of *Trevelyan's little daughter* (Toronto, 1898), *A maid of many moods* (Toronto, 1902), *By the queen's grace* (Toronto, 1904), *The man at Lone Lake* (London, 1912), *The miracle, and other poems* (Toronto, 1913), *The golden apple tree* (Toronto, 1920), *The ballad of the quest* (Toronto, 1922), *Candle flame* (Toronto, 1926), *Fortune turns her wheel* (Toronto, 1929), *Fairy doors* (Toronto, 1932), *Below the salt* (Toronto, 1936), and *Leaves in the wind* (Toronto, 1938).

[Morgan, *Can. men and women* (1912).]

Shedden, John (1825-1873), railway-builder, was born at Kilbirnie, Scotland, on November 5, 1825; and as a young man was an employee of the Glasgow and South Western Railway. He emigrated to America in 1855, and settled first in Virginia, where he obtained his first railway contract. Later, he came to Canada, and became cartage agent for the Grand Trunk Railway. He was the first president of the Toronto and Nipissing Railway, and vice-president of the Toronto, Grey, and Bruce Railway. He died, as the result of an accident, at Cannington, Ontario, on May 16, 1873.

[J. Ross Robertson, *Landmarks of Canada* (Toronto, 1917); *Dict. Can. biog.*, vol. 10.]

Sheepshanks, John (1834-1912), clergyman, was born in England in 1834, and was educated at Christ's College, Cambridge. He took holy orders in the Church of England; and from 1859 to 1867 he was the first rector of Holy Trinity Church, New Westminster, British Columbia. He then returned to England, and in 1893 he became bishop of Norwich. He died on June 3, 1912. The journal which he kept in British Columbia has been reproduced in part in the Rev. D. Wallace Duthie (ed.), *A bishop in the rough* (London, 1909).

[*Who was who*, 1897-1916.]

Shehyn, Joseph (1829-1918), acting prime minister of Quebec (1898), was born at Quebec, Lower Canada, on November 10, 1829, of Irish and French-Canadian parentage. He was educated at the Quebec Seminary; and he became a wholesale dry-goods merchant in Quebec. From 1875 to 1900 he was the representative of Quebec East as a Liberal in the Legislative Assembly of Quebec. From 1887 to 1891 he was provincial treasurer in the Mercier administration; from 1897 to 1900 he was minister without portfolio in the Marchand government; and in 1898 he was for some months acting prime minister. In 1900 he was summoned to the Senate of Canada, and he remained a member of the Senate until his death at Quebec on July 14, 1918. He was twice married, (1) in 1858 to Marie Zoé Virginie, daughter of Ambroise Verret, of Quebec, by whom he had several children, and (2) in 1902 to Mme Madeleine Josephine Leduc (*née* Beliveau), of Quebec. He was the author of *Railways vs. watercourses* (Quebec, 1884), a pamphlet in which he advocated the use of the railway to Quebec in shipping to Europe. For several years he was president of the Quebec Board of Trade.

[*Can. parl. comp.*; Morgan, *Can. men* (1912); Bibaud, *Panth. can.*; Rose, *Cyc. Can. biog.* (1888); Le Jeune, *Dict. gén.*]

Sheldrake, Sparham (1851-1903), schoolmaster and author, was born in England in 1851, the only son of Edward Sheldrake, of Inworth Priory, Suffolk. He was educated by private tutors, and went to Cambridge University, but did not graduate. When a young man, he emigrated to Canada, and he later founded at Lakefield, Ontario, the Grove School (now the Lakefield College School). He died in 1903. He was the author of *Curious facts: Prose and verse* (Toronto, 1895), and he contributed to the *Canadian magazine*.

[Private information.]

Shenston, Thomas Strahan (1822-1895), author, was born in London, England, on June 25, 1822. He came to Canada with his parents about 1831, and settled in the western part of Upper Canada. In 1841 he went into business in Woodstock, and about 1851 he was appointed county clerk and census commissioner of Oxford county. In 1853 he was appointed registrar of Brant county, and removed to Brantford. He died in Brantford, Ontario, on March 15, 1895. He was the author of *The county warden* (Brantford, C.W., 1851), *The Oxford gazetteer* (Hamilton, C.W., 1852), *The Berean* (Brantford, C.W., 1862), *The sinner and his Saviour* (London, 1879), *Teloogoo mission scrap book* (Brantford, Ont., 1888), and *A jubilee review of the First Baptist Church, Brantford* (Toronto, 1890).

[*The history of the county of Brant* (Toronto, 1883).]

Sheppard, Edmund Ernest (1855-1924), journalist and author, was born at South Dorchester, Elgin county, Canada West, on September 29, 1855. He was educated at Bethany College, West Virginia; and his early years were spent in Texas and Mexico. He returned to Canada in 1878, and became a journalist. From 1883 to 1887 he was editor-in-chief of the Toronto *News*; and in 1887 he founded *Saturday Night*, a weekly journal which achieved a great success. His contributions to this journal, under the pseudonym of "Don", brought him a national reputation. He retired from journalism in 1906, owing to ill health; and he died in California on November 6, 1924. In 1879 he married Melissa, daughter of Edwin Culver, of Mapleton, Ontario. He published three novels, *Dolly* (Toronto, 1886), *Widower Jones* (Toronto, 1888), and *A bad man's sweetheart* (Toronto, 1889), and he was the author also of *The thinking universe* (Los Angeles, Calif., 1915).

[*Can. who was who*, vol. 2; Morgan, *Can. men* (1912); H. Charlesworth, *Candid chronicles* (Toronto, 1925); L. E. Horning and L. J. Burpee, *A bibliography of Canadian fiction* (Toronto, 1904).]

Sheppard, George (1819-1912), journalist and author, was born at Newark-on-Trent, England, on January 5, 1819, and became a journalist. In 1850 he came to America; and from 1854 to 1857 he held a post in the actuarial department of the Canadian Life Assurance Company in Hamilton, Canada West. In 1857 he became editor of the Toronto *British Colonist*; and subsequently he was editor of the Toronto *Globe*, the Hamilton *Times*, the Quebec *Chronicle*, the Quebec *Mercury*, and chief political writer on the *New York Times*. He retired from active journalism in 1892; and he died at Jamaica Plain, Boston, Massachusetts, in 1912. He was the author of *The theory and practice of life assurance* (Hamilton, 1855), and he edited a *Cyclopedia of biography* (New York, 1865).

[Morgan, *Can. men* (1912).]

Sheppard, Peter Clapham (1882-1965), painter, was born in Toronto, Ontario, October 21, 1882. He was educated in Toronto schools and at the Ontario College of Art, where he studied with George Reid, J. W. Beatty, and William Cruickshank, graduating in 1912 with a scholarship in drawing and painting. He did most of his work in his studio in Toronto and is represented by works in the National Gallery of Canada and the Ontario Art Gallery at Toronto. He died at Newmarket, Ontario, April 24, 1965.

[*Can. who's who*, 1955-57.]

Sheppard, William (1783-1867), executive councillor of Lower Canada, was born at Quebec, on November 15, 1783. He made a fortune in the timber trade; and he was a member of the Executive Council of Lower Canada from 1837 to 1841. He died at Three Rivers, Quebec, on July 2, 1867. To the *Transactions* of

the Literary and Historical Society of Quebec he contributed *Observations on the plants of Canada described by Charlevoix in his History* (1829) and *Notes on the plants of Lower Canada* (1831), and to the *Annals* of the Botanical Society of Canada a paper on *The geographical distribution of the Coniferae in Canada* (1861). To the *Transactions* of the Literary and Historical Society of Quebec, his wife contributed a paper *On the recent shells which characterise Quebec and its environs* (1829), and *Notes on some of the song birds of Canada* (1837).

[P. G. Roy, *Fils de Québec*, vol. 3 (Lévis, Que., 1933).]

Sheraton, James Paterson (1841-1906), first principal of Wycliffe College, Toronto, was born in Saint John, New Brunswick, on November 29, 1841. He was educated at the University of New Brunswick (B.A., 1861), and he was ordained a priest of the Church of England in 1865. In 1877 he was appointed first principal of Wycliffe College, Toronto; and he continued as principal until his death at Toronto on January 24, 1906. He was the author of *Christian Science* (Toronto, 1891), *The inspiration and authority of the Holy Scriptures* (Toronto, 1893), *The higher criticism* (Toronto, 1904), and *Our Lord's teaching concerning himself* (Toronto, 1904).

[*In memoriam J. P. Sheraton* (Toronto, 1906); Morgan, *Can. men* (1898).]

Sherbrooke, Sir John Coape (1764-1830), governor-in-chief of Canada (1816-18), was born in England in 1764, the third son of William Coape, J.P., of Farnah in Duffield, Derbyshire, who took the name of Sherbrooke on his marriage in 1756 to Sarah, one of the co-heiresses of Henry Sherbrooke, of Oxton, Nottinghamshire. He entered the British army as an ensign in the 4th Foot in 1780; and he attained the rank of full general in 1825. In 1784-85 he was stationed in Cape Breton, Nova Scotia; and during the wars with France he saw service in the Netherlands, in India, in Sicily, in Egypt, and in the Peninsula. In 1809 he was second-in-command to Wellesley, and greatly distinguished himself at the battle of Talavera. In 1810 his health gave way, and he returned to England; and in 1811 he was appointed lieutenant-governor of Nova Scotia. During the War of 1812 the defence of Nova Scotia was conducted by him with great success; and in 1814 he led a military expedition up the Penobscot, which resulted in the capture of the port of Maine, and which to some extent offset the British failure at Plattsburg. In 1816 he became governor of Canada; but in 1818 he suffered a paralytic stroke, and was forced to send in his resignation. The rest of his life he spend in retirement at Calverton, Nottinghamshire; and he died there on February 14, 1830. In 1811 he married Katherine, daughter of the Rev. Reginald Pyndar, rector of Madresfield, Worcestershire; and she died in 1856 without issue. He was created a K.B. in 1809, and a G.C.B. in 1815. The Duke of Wellington described his as "a very good officer, but the most passionate man, I think, I ever knew."

[A. P. Martin, "Memoir of Sir J. C. Sherbrooke", appended to *Life and Letters of Viscount Sherbrooke* (2 vols., London, 1893); *Dict. nat. biog.*; Morgan, *Cel. Can.*; Le Jeune, *Dict. gén.*]

Sherk, Abraham Break (1832-1916), clergyman, was born in Waterloo county, Upper Canada, on November 6, 1832. He was educated at the Rockwood Academy and at Oberlin College, Ohio; and he became a minister of the United Brethren in 1854. He was the minister of churches first in Ontario, and then in the United States; but returned to Canada in 1897, and died in Toronto, Ontario, on November 27, 1916. He contributed several papers on the early history of Ontario to the *Papers and records* of the Ontario Historical Society.

[M. G. Sherk, *A memoir of Rev. A. B. Sherk* (Waterloo Historical Society, fourth annual report, 1916).]

Sherk, Michael Gonder (d. 1928), author, was a descendant of United Empire Loyalist families that settled in Upper Canada, and the son of the Rev. Abraham Break Sherk (q.v.). For many years he conducted a drug business in Toronto, Ontario. He died near Toronto in 1928. Under the pen-name of "A Canuck", he published a book entitled *Pen pictures of early pioneer life in Upper Canada* (Toronto, 1905).

[Private information.]

Sherman, Francis Joseph (1871-1926), poet and banker, was born on February 3, 1871, in Fredericton, New Brunswick, the eldest son of Louis Walsh Sherman and Alice Maxwell. He was educated at the University of New Brunswick; but did not proceed to a degree. He became a banker, and rose to be assistant general manager of the Merchants' Bank of Canada and, after the amalgamation in 1907, of the Royal Bank. He retired on pension in 1919; and he died at Atlantic City, New Jersey, on June 15, 1926. He published one volume of verse, *Matins* (Boston, 1896), and two booklets of verse, *In memorabilia mortis* (Boston, 1896) and *A prelude* (Boston, 1897); and he collaborated with Frank Day in *The deserted city* (Boston, 1899), and with John Bodkin in *Two songs at parting* (Boston, 1899).

[Charles G. D. Roberts, *Francis Sherman* (Trans. Roy. Soc. Can., 1934); *Can. who was who*, vol. 1.]

Sherwood, Adiel (1779-1874), sheriff of Leeds and Grenville (1829-64), was born near Montreal, May 16, 1779, the son of Thomas Sherwood, a loyalist. In 1784 his parents settled in Elizabethtown, Leeds county, Upper Canada; and from 1829 to 1864 he was sheriff of the united counties of Leeds and Grenville. He died at Brockville, Ontario, on March 25, 1874. In 1801 he married Mary, daughter of Stephen Baldwin, of Litchfield, Connecticut; and by her he had one son and seven daughters.

[*Canadian biographical dictionary*, Ontario vol. (Toronto, 1880); *Dict. Can. biog.*, vol. 10.]

Sherwood, Sir Arthur Percy (1854-1940), chief commissioner of police in Canada (1913-18), was born in Ottawa, Ontario, on March 18, 1854. He entered the militia as a private in the Governor-General's Foot Guards in 1877, and rose to command the 43rd Regiment, with the rank of lieutenant-colonel, in 1898. From 1879 to 1882 he was chief of police in Ottawa; and in 1882 he was commissioned a superintendent of the Dominion police. He was promoted to the rank of commissioner in 1885; and of chief commissioner in 1913. During the First World War he was also in charge of the secret service of Canada; and from 1910 to 1918 he was chief commissioner of the Boy Scouts Association of Canada. He died at Ottawa, Ontario, on October 15, 1940. He was created a C.M.G. in 1902, an M.V.O. in 1908, and a K.C.M.G. in 1916.

[*Who was who*, 1929-40; *Can. who's who*, 1936-37; Morgan, *Can. men* (1912).]

Sherwood, George (1811-1883), receiver-general of Canada (1858-62), was born in Augusta, Leeds county, Upper Canada, on May 29, 1811, the second son of the Hon. Levius Peters Sherwood (q.v.). He was educated at the Johnstown Grammar School, and was called to the bar of Upper Canada in 1833 (Q.C., 1856). He practised law at Prescott and Brockville; and he represented Brockville in the Legislative Assembly of Canada from 1841 to 1851, and from 1858 to 1863. From 1858 to 1862 he was receiver-general, and later, for a few months, commissioner of crown lands, in the Cartier-Macdonald government. In 1865 he was appointed judge of the county of Hastings; he retired from the bench in 1881; and he died at Toronto, Ontario, on February 7, 1883. In 1883 he married Marianne, daughter of Dr. Thomas G. Keegan, of Halifax, Nova Scotia; but he had no children.

[*Dom ann. reg.*, 1883; *Canadian biographical dictionary*, Ontario vol. (Toronto, 1880); *Can. parl. comp.*, 1863; J. C. Dent, *The last forty years* (2 vols., Toronto, 1881).]

Sherwood, Henry (1807-1855), solicitor-general for Upper Canada (1844-46) and attorney-general (1847-48), was born in Augusta, Leeds county, Upper Canada, in 1807, the eldest son of the Hon. Levius Peters Sherwood (q.v.). He was called to the bar of Upper Canada (Q.C., 1842), and practised law, first in Prescott, and then in Toronto. From 1837 to 1840 he was reporter of the Law Society of Upper Canada; and in 1841 he was elected to represent Toronto in the Legislative Assembly of United Canada. He held this seat continuously until 1854, and during this period came to be regarded as one of the leaders of the Conservative party in the House. In 1842, and again from 1844 to 1846, he was solicitor-general for Upper Canada; and on the retirement of the Hon. W. H. Draper (q.v.) in 1847, he became attorney-general for Upper Canada, and virtual leader of the government. Defeated in 1848, he went into opposition, and he took henceforth a somewhat subordinate part in politics. He died in Kissingen, Germany, in 1855.

[W. R. Riddell, *The legal profession in Upper Canada* (Toronto, 1916); J. C. Dent, *The last forty years* (2 vols., Toronto, 1881).]

Sherwood, Levius Peters (1777-1850), jurist, was born in St. Johns, Quebec, in 1777, the second son of Capt. Justus Sherwood, a loyalist from Connecticut. He was called to the bar of Upper Canada in 1803, and practised law in Brockville. From 1812 to 1816, and from 1820 to 1824, he represented Leeds in the Legislative Assembly of Upper Canada; and in 1821 he was elected speaker of the House. In 1825 he was appointed a judge of the Court of King's Bench in Upper Canada. He retired from the bench on pension in 1841; and in 1842 he was appointed a member of the Legislative Council of United Canada. He died in Toronto on May 19, 1850. He married Charlotte, daughter of Col. Ephraim Jones (q.v.), and by her he had four sons and three daughters.

[D. B. Read, *Lives of the judges of Upper Canada* (Toronto, 1888).]

Sherwood, William Albert (1859-1919), painter and poet, was born at Omemee, Canada West, on August 1, 1859, and died at Toronto, Ontario, on December 5, 1919. He was a member of the Ontario Society of Artists, and an associate of the Royal Canadian Academy of Arts. He acquired a considerable reputation, both as a portrait-painter, and as a painter of *genre* pictures, such as "The gold prospector", "The Canadian rancher", and "The Canadian backwoodsman". A frequent contributor to Canadian periodical literature, he was also the author of *Lays, lyrics, and legends* (Toronto, 1914).

[Morgan, *Can. men* (1912).]

Shiels, Andrew (1793-1879), poet, was born March 12, 1793, in the parish of Oxnam, Roxburghshire, Scotland, and became a stipendiary magistrate in Halifax, Nova Scotia. He died at Dartmouth, Nova Scotia, on November 5, 1879. He was the author of *The witch of the Westcot: A tale of Nova Scotia, in three cantos; and other waste leaves of literature* (Halifax, N.S., 1831); and he wrote occasional verse under the *nom de plume* of "Albyn".

[*Dom. ann. reg.*, 1879; R. J. Long, *Nova Scotia authors* (East Orange, N.J., 1918); *Dict. Can. biog.*, vol. 10.]

Shipley, John Wesley (1878-1943), chemist, was born at Stonewall, Manitoba, on February 14, 1878. He was educated at Wesley College, University of Manitoba (B.A., 1908) and Harvard University (M.A., 1911; Ph.D., 1913); and after holding a position in the Ohio State College and in the Manitoba Agricultural College, he was appointed in 1919 a member of the staff in chemistry in the University of Manitoba, and in 1930 head of the department of chemistry in the University of Alberta. He retired from the last position, because of ill health, in 1942; and he died at Edmonton, Alberta, on July 1, 1943. In 1925 he was elected a fellow of the Royal Society of Canada. He was the author of *Pulp and paper-making in Canada* (Toronto, 1929).

[*Proc. Roy. Soc. Can.*, 1944; *Can. who's who*, 1936-37.]

Short, Richard (*fl.* 1761), artist, was an officer in Wolfe's army who fought at the battle of the Plains of Abraham and Ste. Foy. While he was in garrison at Quebec in 1759-60, he executed a series of twelve engravings of Quebec which were published in London in 1761, and are now much sought after by collectors.

[*Bull. rech. hist.*, 1918; *Dict. Can. biog.*, vol. 3.]

Shortt, Adam (1859-1931), economist and historian, was born at Kilworth, near London, Ontario, on November 24, 1859, the son of George Shortt and Mary Shields. He was educated at Queen's University, Kingston (B.A., 1883; M.A., 1884; LL.D., 1911), and he studied at Glasgow and Edinburgh universities. In 1885 he was appointed assistant professor of philosophy in Queen's University; and in 1892 he became professor of political science. In 1908 he resigned to become a civil service commissioner at Ottawa, and he continued in this position until 1918. He was then appointed chairman of the Board of Historical Publications of the Public Archives of Canada. He died at Ottawa on January 14, 1931. He was created a C.M.G. in 1911; and in 1906 he was elected a fellow of the Royal Society of Canada. He was an outstanding authority on the economic history of Canada, and was the author of *Imperial preferential trade from a Canadian point of view* (Toronto, 1904), *Lord Sydenham* (Toronto, Makers of Canada, 1908; 2nd ed., 1926), and many valuable papers on the history of Canadian banking contributed to the *Journal* of the Canadian Bankers' Association. He edited *Documents relating to Canadian currency, exchange, and finance during the French period* (2 vols., Ottawa, 1926); and he was co-editor with A. G. Doughty of *Canada and its provinces* (23 vols., Toronto,

1914), and of *Documents relating to the constitutional history of Canada, 1759-1791* (Ottawa, 1907; new and revised ed., 2 vols., 1918).

[*Proc. Roy. Soc. Can.*, 1931; Morgan, *Can. men* (1912); R. C. Wallace (ed.), *Some great men of Queen's* (Toronto, 1941); W. A. Mackintosh, *Adam Shortt* (Canadian Journal of Economic and Political Science, 1938).]

Shotwell, James Thomson (1874-1965), historian, was born at Strathroy, Ontario, August 6, 1874. He attended the University of Toronto (B.A., 1898), and Columbia University. He began his public career as advisor to President Wilson in 1917. A staunch advocate of internationalism, he was a professor of history at Columbia University. He played a major role in drafting the Geneva protocol against aggressive war, the treaties of Locarno, the Kellogg-Briand Pact, and the United Nations' Charter. He was a strong advocate of United States participation in the League of Nations. His most monumental creative effort was a co-operative project undertaken in the six years after the First World War when he led 200 scholars in the production of a 150-volume study, "The Economic and Social History of the World War". During his long career he was involved in writing or editing over five hundred books. He died in New York, July 14, 1965.

[*Can. who's who*, 1955-57; Metropolitan Toronto Library Board, *Biographical scrapbooks*, vol. 23.]

Shreve, Charles J. (1808-1878), clergyman, was born at Lunenburg, Nova Scotia, in 1808. He was ordained a clergyman of the Church of England in 1833; and after serving as a missionary in Newfoundland, he was rector successively at Guysborough and Chester, Nova Scotia. He died at Halifax, Nova Scotia, in 1878. He was the author of *The divine origin and uninterrupted succession of episcopacy maintained* (Halifax, N.S., 1840).

[R. J. Long, *Nova Scotia authors* (East Orange, N.J., 1918); Morgan, *Bib. can.*]

Shutt, Frank Thomas (1859-1940), agricultural chemist, was born at Stoke Newington, London, England, on September 15, 1859. He was educated at the University of Toronto (B.A., 1885; M.A., 1886; D.Sc., 1914); and in 1887 he was appointed the first Dominion chemist, on the staff of the newly established Dominion Experimental Farms system. This position he occupied until his retirement in 1933. From 1912 to 1933 he was also assistant director of the Dominion Experimental Farms. "No one else in the history of Canada has made as great a contribution to agriculture through chemistry." He was elected a fellow of the Royal Society in 1899; and in 1935 he was awarded the Society's Flavelle medal. In 1935 he was awarded also the C.B.E. He died at Ottawa, Ontario, on January 5, 1940.

[*Proc. Roy. Soc. Can.*, 1940; *Can. who's who*, 1936-37.]

Sibbald, Mrs. Susan, *née* **Mein** (1783-1866), diarist, was born at Fowey, in Cornwall, on November 29, 1783. Her husband, Colonel Sibbald, whom she married in 1807, died in 1835; and after his death, she brought her family to Canada, and settled near Jackson's Point, on Lake Simcoe. She died in Toronto on July 9, 1866. Her *Memoirs* have been published by her great-grandson, F. Paget Hett (London, 1926), with a selection of letters covering the later years of her life in Canada.

[F. P. Hett, *Memoirs of Susan Sibbald* (London, 1926) and *Georgina* (Toronto, 1939).]

Sibbald, Thomas (1810-1890), naval officer, was born in Yorkshire, England, on September 21, 1810, the son of Mrs. Susan Sibbald (q.v.). He joined the Royal Navy, and rose in it to the rank of captain. He saw service in the Crimean War; but at the close of the war, in 1856, he retired from the Navy, and came to live with his mother at Jackson's Point in Canada. He died at Eildon Hall, near Jackson's Point, on March 4, 1890. After a brief visit to his mother in Canada in 1842, he wrote and published anonymously a little book entitled *A few days in the United States and Canada, with some hints to settlers* (London, 1843).

[F. P. Hett, *Georgina* (Toronto, 1939); S. Leacock, *A rare traveller's account* (Can. hist. rev., 1933).]

Sicotte, Louis Victor (1812-1889), politician and jurist, was born at Boucherville, Lower Canada, on November 6, 1812, the son of Toussaint Sicotte and Margaret St. Germain. He was educated at the College of St. Hyacinthe, and was called to the bar of Lower Canada in 1837 (Q.C., 1854). He was a member of the Legislative Assembly of Canada from 1851 to 1863; and from 1854 to 1857 he was speaker of the Assembly. He held office in the Taché-Macdonald administration as commissioner of crown lands from November 25, 1857, to July 29, 1858, and in the Macdonald-Cartier administration as chief commissioner of public works from August 6, 1858, to December 24, 1858. In 1862 he became, with John Sandfield Macdonald (q.v.), joint leader of the government, with the portfolio of attorney-general for Lower Canada; but, on the reorganization of the cabinet in 1863, he retired to accept the position of puisne judge of the Superior Court of Lower Canada. He retired from the bench in 1887, and he died at St. Hyacinthe, Quebec, on September 5, 1889. In 1837 he married Margaret Amelia, daughter of Benjamin Starnes, of Montreal; and by her he had eleven children.

[P. G. Roy, *Les juges de la province de Québec* (Quebec, 1933); *Cyc. Am. biog.*; Rose,

Cyc. Can. biog. (1886); *Canadian biographical dictionary,* Quebec vol. (Chicago, 1881); Le Jeune, *Dict. gén.*]

Siddons, J. H. (pseud.). See **Stocqueler, Joachim Hayward.**

Sifton, Arthur Lewis (1858-1921), jurist and politician, was born at St. John's, Middlesex county, Upper Canada, on October 26, 1858, the son of John Wright Sifton (q.v.). He was educated at Wesley College, Winnipeg, and at Victoria University, Cobourg (B.A., 1880; M.A., 1888), and was called to the bar of the North West Territories in 1883 (Q.C., 1892). From 1899 to 1903 he sat in the legislature of the North West Territories for Banff, and from 1901 to 1903 he was treasurer and commissioner of public works in the Haultain administration. In 1903 he was appointed chief justice of the Supreme Court of the North West Territories, and in 1905 of the Supreme Court of Alberta. In 1910 he retired from the bench, and became Liberal prime minister of Alberta, having been elected to the Legislative Assembly of Alberta for Vermilion. In 1917 he broke with the Liberal party, and entered the Dominion government as minister of customs under Sir R. Borden (q.v.). He was a member of the war committee of the Cabinet, and in 1918 he was one of the Canadian delegates to the peace conference at Versailles. In 1919 he became minister of public works and a few months later secretary of state, and he was made a member of the Imperial Privy Council; but he died at Ottawa on January 22, 1921. In 1882 he married Mary, daughter of William Deering, of Cobourg, Ontario; and by her he had one son and one daughter. He was an LL.D. of the University of Alberta (1908).

[*Who was who,* vol. 1; Hector Charlesworth (ed.), *A cyclopaedia of Canadian biography* (Toronto, 1919); *Can. parl. comp.*; Morgan, *Can. men* (1912).]

Sifton, Sir Clifford (1861-1929), minister of the interior for Canada (1896-1905), was born in Middlesex county, Ontario, on March 10, 1861, the son of John W. Sifton (q.v.), later speaker of the Legislative Assembly of Manitoba. He was educated at Victoria University, Cobourg (B.A., 1880), and was called to the Manitoba bar in 1882 (Q.C., 1895). He began the practice of law in Brandon, Manitoba; and from 1888 to 1896 he represented North Brandon in the Legislative Assembly of Manitoba. From 1891 to 1896 he was attorney-general and minister of education in the Greenway administration; and it fell to him to deal with the Dominion government in regard to the thorny question of separate schools in Manitoba. He represented Brandon in the Canadian House of Commons from 1896 to 1911; and from 1896 to 1905 he was minister of the interior in the Laurier administration. During these years he prosecuted a vigorous immigra-

tion policy, which resulted in filling the vacant spaces in the Canadian West. He resigned from office in 1905 because of disagreement with Sir Wilfrid Laurier (q.v.) over the educational clauses of the Acts which created the new provinces of Saskatchewan and Alberta. In 1909 he was appointed chairman of the Canadian Conservation Commission; and he retained this position until 1918. But in 1911 he opposed the proposals of Sir Wilfrid Laurier (q.v.) for reciprocity with the United States, and withdrew from parliament and from the Liberal party. For the rest of his life he pursued an independent, but influential, course in politics, mostly behind the scenes. He gave a general support to the war government of Sir Robert Borden (q.v.), but he never again held public office or sat in parliament. He died at New York on April 17, 1929. In 1884 he married Elizabeth Arma (d. 1925), daughter of H. T. Burrows, Ottawa; and by her he had four sons. In 1915 he was created a K.C.M.G.

[J. W. Dafoe, *Clifford Sifton in relation to his times* (Toronto, 1931); *Who was who,* 1929-40; *Can. parl. comp.*; Morgan, *Can. men* (1912); H. Charlesworth (ed.), *Cyclopaedia of Canadian biography* (Toronto, 1919).]

Sifton, John Wright (1833-1912), contractor and politician, was born in Middlesex county, Upper Canada, on August 10, 1833, the son of Bamlet Sifton, who came to Canada from Ireland in 1832. For many years a farmer and oil operator, he went to the North West in 1875 and became a contractor for the construction of telegraph and railway lines. In 1878 he was elected to represent St. Clements in the Legislative Assembly of Manitoba, and he was chosen speaker of the Assembly. Defeated in the next general election, he was re-elected for Brandon in 1881; but was defeated again in 1883, and in 1888. He then retired from politics, and occupied various positions in the civil service of Manitoba. He died at Winnipeg on September 19, 1912. In 1853 he married Kate (d. 1909), daughter of James Watkins, Parsonstown, King's county, Ireland; and by her he had two sons, the Rt. Hon. Arthur Lewis Sifton (q.v.) and the Hon. Sir Clifford Sifton (q.v.), and one daughter.

[Morgan, *Can. men* (1912); Rose, *Cyc. Can. biog.* (1888); J. P. Robertson, *A political manual of Manitoba* (Winnipeg, 1887).]

Sifton, Victor (1897-1961), publisher, was born in Ottawa, Ontario, March 17, 1897, the son of Sir Clifford Sifton (q.v.). He was educated in schools in Ottawa and at the University of Toronto, which he left to join the Canadian army in the First World War. He served with the 4th Canadian Mounted Rifles, was wounded in 1915, and was awarded the D.S.O. In the Second World War he was master-general of ordnance for Canada and was awarded the O.B.E. He became general manager of the *Winnipeg Free Press* in 1935 after serving as president of the Sifton family newspapers in Regina and Saskatoon. On the death of John W. Dafoe (q.v.) in 1944, he became president and publisher of the *Free Press* and in 1953 became sole owner. In 1959, he, with Max Bell (q.v.) of Calgary, incorporated F.P. Publications with ownership or control of the *Calgary Albertan*, the *Victoria Times*, the *Victoria Colonist*, the *Ottawa Journal*, the *Free Press*, and a part of the *Lethbridge Herald*. His brother Clifford owned the Regina *Leader-Post* and the Saskatoon *Star-Phoenix*. In 1938 Victor was president of the Canadian Daily Newspapers Association and, from 1948 to 1950, president of the Canadian Press. From 1947 to 1952 he was a member of the Board of Governors of the University of Manitoba and was chancellor of the university from 1952 to 1959. He was a keen horseman and hoɾse-breeder. He died at Winnipeg, Manitoba, April 22, 1961.

[Metropolitan Toronto Library Board, *Biographical scrapbooks*, vol. 18; *Winnipeg Free Press*, April 22, 1961.]

Signay, Joseph (1778-1850), first Roman Catholic archbishop of Quebec (1844-49), was born at Quebec on November 28, 1778. He was educated at the Quebec Seminary, and was ordained a priest in 1802. In 1826 he became coadjutor to the bishop of Quebec, with the title of bishop of Fusala; and in 1833 he succeeded as bishop of Quebec. In 1844 he became the first archbishop of Quebec; in 1849 he handed over the administration of the diocese to his coadjutor; and he died at Quebec on October 3, 1850. During the rebellions of 1837-38, he was noteworthy for the loyal attitude which he adopted; and his *mandements*, together with a biography of him, have been printed in H. Têtu and C. O. Gagnon, *Mandements, lettres pastorales, et circulaires des évêques de Québec* (6 vols. Quebec, 1887-90).

[*Cyc. Am. biog.*; Le Jeune, *Dict. gén.*; P. G. Roy, *Fils de Québec,* vol. 3 (Lévis, Que., 1933).]

Silcox, Claris Edwin (1888-1961), churchman, was born in Embro, Ontario, August 14, 1888. A graduate of the University of Toronto (B.A., 1908), he wrote "The blue and white", the university hymn. From Toronto he went to Brown University at Providence, Rhode Island (M.A., 1912), and Andover Newton Theological Seminary at Harvard. He served for eleven years in pastorates in New England before he joined the Rockefeller Foundation's Institute of Social and Religious Research in 1925. On his return to America he was a co-founder of the National Conference of Christians and Jews in 1929. He went to Toronto in 1930 to study the Church Union movement, publishing the result of his study, *Church union in Canada*, in 1932. In 1934, after two years in the United States, he became

general secretary of the Social Service Council of Canada, and on his resignation in 1940 he became director of the Canadian Conference of Christians and Jews. He wrote for the United Church *Observer* and *Saturday Night* and was an editor of *Canadian Commentator*. He died at Toronto, Ontario, May 9, 1961.

[Metropolitan Toronto Library Board, *Biographical scrapbooks*, vol. 18; *Can. who's who*, 1955-57.]

Sillitoe, Acton Windeyer (1841-1894), first Anglican bishop of New Westminster (1879-94), was born in Australia in 1841, and was educated at Pembroke College, Cambridge (B.A., 1862). He was ordained a priest of the Church of England in 1870; and in 1879 he was consecrated bishop of the new diocese of New Westminster, British Columbia. He reached New Westminster in 1880, and he administered the diocese until his death, at New Westminster, on June 9, 1894. He was a D.C.L. of the University of Trinity College, Toronto.

[H. H. Gowen, *Church work in British Columbia, being a memoir of the episcopate of Acton Windeyer Sillitoe* (London, 1899); C. H. Mockridge, *The bishops of the Church of England in Canada* (Toronto, 1896).]

Silvain, Timothée. See Sullivan, Timothy.

Silver, Arthur Peters (1851-1908), author, was born in Halifax, Nova Scotia, in 1851; and died near Halifax on February 14, 1908. He was the author of *Farm, cottage, camp, and canoe in maritime Canada* (London, 1908).

[Private information.]

Silvy, Antoine (1638-1711), missionary and author, was born at Aix-en-Provence, France, on October 16, 1638. In 1658 he entered the Society of Jesus as a novice, and in 1673 he was sent to Canada. He was employed as a missionary successively at Michilimackinac and Tadoussac from 1674 to 1684. In 1684 he accompanied a French expedition to Hudson Bay as chaplain; and in 1686 he accompanied Troyes (q.v.) as a chaplain on his overland journey to Hudson Bay. He remained at Fort Albany till 1693, when he returned to Quebec; and in his later years he taught mathematics at the Jesuit College in Quebec. He died at Quebec on May 8, 1711. His journal of the expedition to Hudson Bay in 1684-85 has been published by C. de Rochemonteix in the preface to his *Relation par lettres de l'Amérique septentrionale* (Paris, 1904), and has been republished, with English translation, in J. B. Tyrrell (ed.), *Documents relating to the early history of Hudson bay* (Toronto: The Champlain Society, 1931).

[Le Jeune, *Dict. gén.*; *Dict. Can. biog.*, vol. 2.]

Simard, Georges (1878-1956), priest and educationist, was born at Baie St. Paul, Quebec, on November 21, 1878, and died at Ottawa, Ontario, on November 2, 1956. He was educated at the University of Ottawa (D.Ph., 1903), was ordained a priest of the Roman Catholic Church in 1905, and spent almost his whole life on the teaching staff of the University of Ottawa. From 1932 to 1938 he was dean of the faculty of divinity. He was the author of *Les maîtres Chrétiens de nos pensées et de nos vies* (Ottawa, 1937), *Etudes canadiennes* (Montreal, 1938), *Les universités Catholiques* (Montreal, 1939), *Maux présents et foi chrétienne* (Montreal, 1941), *Les états Chrétiens et l'Eglise* (Montreal, 1942), and *Pour l'éducation dans un Canada souverain* (Ottawa, 1945). In 1942 the University of Montreal conferred on him an honorary doctorate.
[*Can. who's who*, 1952-54.]

Simard, Henri (1869-1927), priest and educationist, was born in Quebec City on March 4, 1869. He was ordained a priest of the Roman Catholic Church in 1891; but he passed his entire life as a professor in the Quebec Seminary and in Laval University. He taught especially physics and astronomy; and he was the author of *Traité élémentaire de physique* (Quebec, 1903), *Cours élémentaire de cosmographie* (Quebec, 1910), and *Propos scientifiques* (2 series, Quebec, 1920-27), as well as joint author, with Canon Huard (q.v.), of *Manuel de sciences usuelles* (Quebec, 1907). He was elected a fellow of the Royal Society of Canada in 1923. He died at Quebec on November 7, 1927.
[*Proc. Roy. Soc. Can.*, 1928; Allaire, *Dict. biog.*; *Bull. rech. hist.*, 1927.]

Simard, Joseph Arthur (1888-1963), ship-builder, was born at Baie St. Paul, Quebec, in 1888. At the age of fourteen he became a clerk with the Richelieu and Ontario Navigation Company. At twenty he became accountant for the city of Sorel and two years later was superintendent of Sorel Light and Power Company. In 1917 he became manager of the company. He founded a shipyard in Sorel with J. B. T. Lafrenière and Alcide Beaudet and in 1928 bought Sorel Mechanic's Workshops and General Dredging. He was president of United Towing, Sincennes McNaughton Line, Sorel Industries Limited, and La Société d'Administration et du Fiducie, and was a director of many other companies. He received the O.B.E. in 1942. He died in Florida on January 21, 1963.
[*Can. who's who*, 1955-57; Metropolitan Toronto Library Board, *Biographical scrapbooks*, vol. 21.]

Simcoe, John Graves (1752-1806), lieutenant-governor of Upper Canada (1791-96), was born at Cotterstock, Northamptonshire, England, on February 25, 1752, the son of Captain John Simcoe, R.N. He was educated at Eton and at Merton College, Oxford; and in 1771 he entered the British army as an ensign in the 35th Regiment. He served in America throughout the American Revolutionary War; and from 1777 to 1781 he commanded the Queen's Rangers, a corps of provincial troops, which he brought to a high state of efficiency. In 1781 he was invalided back to England; and for several years he lived on his estate at Wolford the life of a country gentleman. In 1790 he was elected to the House of Commons as member for St. Mawe's, Cornwall; and in 1791, on the passage of the Constitutional Act, he was appointed first lieutenant-governor of Upper Canada. He arrived in Canada in 1792, and chose Newark (Niagara) as the capital of his government. Later, in 1794, he moved the government offices to York (Toronto). His régime was notable for his efforts to open up the province by means of the building of roads and the encouragement of immigration; and in some ways his policy was remarkably farsighted. His views in regard to the relations of church and state, and his failure to allow for forces at work in a new country, contained, however, the seeds for future trouble. In 1794 he was promoted to be major-general; and, on leaving Canada in 1796, he was appointed governor and commander-in-chief of San Domingo, with the local rank of lieutenant-general. He returned to England in 1797, and in 1801 he was in command at Plymouth, when the French invasion of England was expected. In 1806 he was appointed commander-in-chief in India; but was directed first to proceed on a special mission to Lisbon. He was taken ill on the voyage, and returned home, but only to die at Exeter on October 26, 1806. In 1782 he married Elizabeth Posthuma, daughter of Lieut.-Col. Thomas Gwillim, of Old Court, Hereford; and by her he had two sons and seven daughters. He wrote and printed for private distribution a *History of the operations of a partisan corps called the Queen's Rangers* (Exeter, 1787; reprinted, with a memoir of the author, New York, 1844). His *Correspondence* has been edited for the Ontario Historical Society by Brig.-Gen. E. A. Cruikshank (4 vols., Toronto, 1921-26).
[M. Van Steen, *Governor Simcoe and his Lady* (Toronto, 1968); W. R. Riddell, *Life of John Graves Simcoe* (Toronto, 1926); D. C. Scott, *John Graves Simcoe* (Toronto, 1905); D. B. Read, *Life and times of Major-General John Graves Simcoe* (Toronto, 1890) and *The lieutenant-governors of Upper Canada* (Toronto, 1900); J. Ross Robertson, *The diary of Mrs. Simcoe* (Toronto, 1911); *Dict. nat. biog.*; *Cyc. Am. biog.*; Morgan, *Cel. Can.*; Dent, *Can. port.*]

Simons, Titus Geer (d. 1829), loyalist, was the son of Titus Simons (d. 1824), who had served as a quartermaster in Peters' Rangers in the American Revolutionary War. After the peace, the family settled first at Kingston, then at Niagara, later at York (Toronto), and finally at Flamboro, in Wentworth county, Upper Canada. From 1797 to 1801 the younger Simons was, first at Niagara, and then at York, the printer of the *Upper Canada Gazette*. He appears to have served as a boy in Peters' Rangers during the Revolutionary War; and he distinguished himself in command of militia detachments during the War of 1812. He was severely wounded at the battle of Lundy's Lane in 1813. After the close of the war, he became colonel of the Gore militia; and in 1816 he was appointed sheriff of the Gore district. He died at West Flamboro, Upper Canada, in August, 1829.

[H. H. Robertson, *Titus Simons* (United Empire Loyalists' Association, annual transactions, 1901 and 1902).]

Simpson, Charles Walter (1878-1942), painter, was born in Montreal, Quebec, in 1878. He studied art in Canada and the United States, and became a well-known illustrator. He was also noted for his landscape and marine paintings. He was elected an associate of the Royal Canadian Academy of Arts in 1913, and an academician in 1920. He died in Montreal on September 16, 1942.

[N. MacTavish, *The fine arts in Canada* (Toronto, 1925); H. G. Jones and E. Dyonnet, *History of the Royal Canadian Academy of Arts* (Montreal, 1934).]

Simpson, Sir George (1787?-1860), governor-in-chief of Rupert's Land, was born at Loch Broom, Ross-shire, Scotland, about 1787, the illegitimate son of George Simpson. In 1809 he entered the employ of a firm in London engaged in the West India trade; but in 1820 he took service with the Hudson's Bay Company, and was sent to Canada. He was influential in bringing about the union of the Hudson's Bay and North West companies in 1821, and was soon afterward appointed governor of the northern department of the united company. Later he became governor-in-chief of Rupert's Land, and general superintendent of the Hudson's Bay Company in North America. His administration of the affairs of the company was marked by great firmness; and he was notable also for the encouragement he gave to geographical exploration. In 1841-42 he crossed the continent, and made a trip around the world, an account of which is contained in his *Narrative of an overland journey around the world* (2 vols., London, 1847). During the later years of his life he lived at Lachine, near Montreal; and here he died, on September 7, 1860. He married, in 1827, Frances Ramsay, daughter of Geddes M. Simpson, of London; and by her he had one son and three daughters. In 1841 he was created a K.B.

[A. S. Morton, *Sir George Simpson* (Toronto, 1945); G. Bryce, *Mackenzie, Selkirk, Simpson* (Toronto, 1905); F. Merk (ed.), *Fur trade and empire: George Simpson's journal* (Cambridge, Mass., 1931); E. E. Rich (ed.), *Journal of occurrences in the Athabasca department, by George Simpson* (Toronto: The Champlain Society, 1938); J. S. Galbraith, *The Little Emperor* (Toronto, 1976) and *The Hudson's Bay Company as an imperial factor* (Berkeley, 1957); D. McKay, *The honourable company* (Toronto, 1936); *Dict. nat. biog.*; *Cyc. Am. biog.*; Morgan, *Cel. Can.* and *Bib. can.*; J. W. Chalmers, *Fur-trade governor: George Simpson* (Edmonton, 1960).]

Simpson, George Wilfred (1893-1969), historian, was born at Chatsworth, Ontario, March 24, 1893. He went to Saskatchewan as a young man and entered the University of Saskatchewan (B.A., 1919); he then went to the University of Toronto (M.A., 1920) and the University of London, where he was the first I.O.D.E. overseas fellow from Saskatchewan. He joined the history department at the University of Saskatchewan in 1922 as an instructor; he became professor in 1928, and head of the department of history in 1940. He is best known as a Ukrainian scholar. He learned the Ukrainian language and edited the first history of the Ukraine to be published in English. He introduced the first class in Slavic studies in 1937 and organized a department of Slavic studies in 1945. He was interested in the preservation of public and private papers of value for prairie history and helped develop the policy for the Saskatchewan Archives Act (1945). He became the first archivist (1945-48) and was the founder (1948) of *Saskatchewan history*, a publication of the Saskatchewan archives. He published *The Ukraine* (Toronto, 1941). He was a fellow of the Royal Society of Canada. He died in Saskatoon, Saskatchewan, March 6, 1969.

[*Proc. and Trans. Roy. Soc. Can.*, vol. VII, (1969).]

Simpson, John (1788-1873), member of parliament, was born in England in 1788, and emigrated to Canada in 1815 with his wife and the children she had had by a previous marriage. One of these children, John Arthur Roebuck (q.v.), was afterwards a member of the British House of Commons and agent of the Lower Canadian Assembly in London. In 1822 Simpson was appointed collector of customs at Coteau du Lac; and he retained this post for many years. From 1824 to 1827 he also represented the county of York in the Legislative Assembly of Lower Canada; and from 1841 to 1844 he represented Vaudreuil in the Legislative Assembly of United Canada. He died at Kingston, Ontario, in 1873.

[F. J. Audet, *John Simpson* (Can. Hist. Association, report, 1936); *Dict. Can. biog.*, vol. 10.]

Simpson, John (1807-1878), provincial secretary of Canada (1864), was born at Helmsley, Blackmoor, Yorkshire, England, on December 27, 1807. He carried on business as a linen-draper in London, England, for several years; but about 1835 he came to Canada, and settled at Niagara, Upper Canada. Here he established the *Chronicle*, a weekly newspaper, and kept a bookshop. Later he founded at Niagara a woollen factory. In 1857 he was elected to represent Niagara in the Legislative Assembly of Canada, and he continued to sit for this constituency until 1864. For three months in 1864 he was provincial secretary in the Taché-Macdonald government; but on the formation of the Brown-Macdonald coalition, he was appointed assistant auditor-general of Canada — a position which he held until his death at Ottawa, on September 19, 1878. He published *The Canadian forget-me-not for 1837* (Niagara, 1837) and *The Canadian mercantile almanack* (Niagara, 1844).

[*Dom. ann. reg.*, 1878; J. C. Dent, *The last forty years* (2 vols., Toronto, 1881); *Dict. Can. biog.*, vol. 10.]

Simpson, John (1812-1885), senator of Canada, was born at Rothes, near Elgin, Scotland, in May, 1812. He was brought to Canada by his parents in 1816, and began life in 1825 as a clerk at Darlington, Upper Canada. He became a successful general merchant; and in 1848 he opened a branch of the Bank of Montreal at Bowmanville, and later another branch at Whitby. In 1857 he was one of the founders of the Ontario Bank, and he became president of his bank. From 1856 to 1867 he represented the Queen's division as a Liberal in the Legislative Council of Canada; and in 1867 he was called to the Senate of Canada by royal proclamation. He died at Bowmanville, Ontario, on March 21, 1885.

[*Dom. ann. reg.*, 1885; *Can. parl. comp.*]

Simpson, Thomas (1808-1840), explorer, was born at Dingwall, Ross-shire, Scotland, on July 2, 1808, the son of Alexander Simpson, and a cousin of Sir George Simpson (q.v.). He was educated at the University of Aberdeen (B.A., 1828; M.A., 1829), and in 1829 he entered the service of the Hudson's Bay Company. In 1836-40 he commanded an important expedition which explored the Arctic coast of North America. On his return from this expedition, he was killed, or else committed suicide, near Turtle River, in the Hudson's Bay Company territories, on June 14, 1840. His *Narrative of the discoveries on the north coast of America ... during the years of 1836-39* was published posthumously (London, 1843).

[A. Simpson, *The life and travels of Thomas Simpson* (London, 1845); *Dict. nat. biog.*; *Cyc. Am. biog.*; D. MacKay and W. K. Lamb, *More light on Thomas Simpson* (Beaver, 1938).]

Sinclair, Alexander (1818-1897), pioneer and author, was born in Scotland in 1818, emigrated to Canada in 1831, settled in the western part of Upper Canada, and died near Ridgetown, Ontario, on December 17, 1897. He was the author of a pamphlet, *Pioneer reminiscences* (Toronto, 1898).

[A. Sinclair, *Pioneer reminiscences* (Toronto, 1898).]

Sinclair, Alexander Maclean (1840-1924), clergyman and Gaelic scholar, was born near Antigonish, Nova Scotia, in 1840. He was educated at Pictou Academy, and at the Presbyterian College, Halifax; and was ordained a minister of the Presbyterian Church in 1866. He held various pastoral charges in Nova Scotia and Prince Edward Island; and he came to be recognized in Canada as an outstanding authority on the Gaelic language and literature. Among the books published by him were *Peoples and languages of the world* (Charlottetown, P.E.I., 1894), *Clan Gillean* (Charlottetown, P.E.I., 1899), and *Mactalla nan tur* (Sydney, N.S., 1901), the last a collection of Gaelic poetry. In 1907 he was appointed lecturer on the Gaelic language and literature at Dalhousie University, Halifax. He died on February 14, 1924.

[C. W. Dunn, *Highland settler* (Toronto, 1953); Morgan, *Can. men* (1912).]

Sinclair, Samuel Bower (1855-1933), educationist and author, was born in Ridgetown, Canada West, in 1855. He was educated at Victoria University (B.A., 1889), at the University of Toronto (M.A., 1893), and at the University of Chicago (Ph.D., 1901). He was one of the pioneers in teacher-training in Canada, having been appointed principal of the Teachers' Training School in Hamilton in 1886. For many years he was dean of the Teachers' Training School at Macdonald College. He died in Toronto on December 20, 1933. He was the author of *First years at school* (New York, 1894), *The possibility of a science of education* (Toronto, 1903), *Brilliant and backward children* (Toronto, 1931), and, with Frederick Tracy, was joint author of *Introductory educational psychology* (Toronto, 1909).

[Morgan, *Can. men* (1922); Toronto *Globe*, Dec. 21, 1933.]

Sinnett, John Chester (1856-1928), priest and colonizer, was born at Ridgetown, Canada West, on August 7, 1856; and was educated at St. John's College, Fordham, New York. He entered the Society of Jesus, and was ordained a priest in 1884. He served as a professor in St. Mary's College, Montreal, and afterward at St. Boniface College, in Manitoba. During the South African War he was a Roman Catholic chaplain with the Canadian contingent; and after the war he returned to the Canadian West, and became the head of a large colony of English and French Roman Catholics near

Wetaskiwin, Alberta. In 1904 he was appointed vicar-general of the diocese of Prince Albert. He died at Guelph, Ontario, on March 16, 1928.

[Morgan, *Can. men* (1912).]

Sirois, Joseph (1881-1941), notary public, was born in Quebec City on October 2, 1881. He was educated at Laval University (B.A., 1900; LL.L., 1903; LL.D., 1907), and was admitted a notary public in 1903. He practised his profession in Quebec City; and from 1927 to 1930 was president of the Board of Notaries of the province. In 1937 he was appointed a member of the Royal Commission on Dominion-Provincial Relations; and, on the retirement of the Hon. N. W. Rowell (q.v.) in 1938, he became its chairman. The report of the commission was commonly known as "the Sirois report". His death took place at Quebec City on January 17, 1941.

[*Can. who's who*, 1938-39.]

Sirois, Joseph Napoléon Théodule (1835-1911), priest, was born in Kamouraska, Lower Canada, on March 23, 1835; and was ordained a priest of the Roman Catholic Church in 1859. He served in several parishes in the province of Quebec; and he died at St. Ignace du Cap St. Ignace, Quebec, on October 20, 1911. *He was the author of Monographie de Saint-Ignace du Cap Saint-Ignace* (Lévis, Que., 1903).

[Allaire, *Dict. biog.*; *Bull. rech. hist.*, 1930.]

Sise, Charles Fleetwood (1834-1918), founder of the Bell Telephone Company of Canada, was born at Portsmouth, New Hampshire, on October 9, 1834. He went to sea, and became a master mariner. In 1880, however, he left the sea, and came to Canada to organize the Bell Telephone Company of Canada. Of this company he became at first vice-president and managing director, and in 1890 president. In 1915 he retired as president, and became chairman of the board; and he died at Montreal, Quebec, on April 9, 1918.

[R. C. Featherstonhaugh, *Charles Fleetwood Sise* (Montreal, 1944); Morgan, *Can. men* (1912).]

Sissons, Charles Bruce (1879-1965), classical scholar and historian, was born at Crown Hill near Orillia, Ontario, in 1879. He graduated with the gold medal in classics from Victoria College in 1901. After teaching for a time in schools in Ontario and British Columbia he undertook further studies at Oxford University. On his return to Canada he was appointed lecturer at Victoria College in 1909, where he taught until his retirement in 1947. He was intensely devoted to the principles of liberalism and justice. He died at Toronto, May 27, 1965.

He was the author of *Bilingual schools in Ontario* (Toronto, 1917), *Egerton Ryerson, his life and letters* (Toronto, vol. I, 1937, vol. II, 1947), *A history of Victoria University* (Toronto, 1952), *My dearest Sophie: Letters from Egerton Ryerson to his daughter* (Toronto, 1955), *Church and state in Canadian education: A historical study* (Toronto, 1959), *Nil Alienum: The memoirs of Charles Bruce Sissons* (Toronto, 1964).

[*Can. hist. rev.*, 1965; *Can. who's who*, vol. IX.]

Siveright, John (1779?-1856), fur-trader, was born in Scotland about 1779, and entered the service of the XY Company in 1799, and that of the North West Company in 1805. Sir George Simpson (q.v.) wrote in 1832 that he "was promoted to the rank of clerk from being a gentleman's body servant." In 1815 he was at Portage la Prairie, and he became implicated in the Selkirk trials. From 1813 to 1823 he was in charge at Sault Ste. Marie; and from 1824 to 1847 he was in charge at Fort Coulonge on the Ottawa, and at Lake Timiskaming. He was promoted to the rank of chief trader in the Hudson's Bay Company in 1828, and to that of chief factor in 1846. He went on furlough in 1847; and he retired from the Company's service in 1849. He died at Edinburgh, Scotland, on September 4, 1856.

[G. P. de T. Glazebrook (ed.), *The Hargrave correspondence* (Toronto: The Champlain Society, 1938).]

Skakel, Alexander (1775?-1846), educationist, was born in Scotland about 1775. He was educated at King's College, Aberdeen; and came to Canada in the early years of the nineteenth century. He established a school in Montreal at which many distinguished Canadians received their education; and he was for many years secretary to the board of management of the Montreal General Hospital. In recognition of his services to education, the University of Aberdeen conferred on him the honorary degree of LL.D. He died at Montreal on August 13, 1846.

[R. Campbell, *A history of the Scotch Presbyterian Church, St. Gabriel Street, Montreal* (Montreal, 1887).]

Skead, James (1817-1884), senator of Canada, was born at Calder Hall, Moresby, Cumberland, England, on December 31, 1817. He came to Canada with his parents in 1832, and settled at Bytown (Ottawa), Upper Canada. Here he became a timber merchant and manufacturer. From 1862 to 1867 he represented the Rideau division of the Legislative Council of Canada as a Conservative; and in 1867 he was called to the Senate of Canada. He died at Ottawa on July 5, 1884.

[*Dom. ann. reg.*, 1884; *Can. parl. comp.*; *Cyc. Am. biog.*]

Skelton, Mrs. Isabel, *née* **Murphy** (d. 1956), author, was born in Carleton county,

Ontario, and died at Montreal, Quebec, on August 23, 1956. She was educated at Queen's University (M.A., 1901), and in 1904 she married Professor O. D. Skelton (q.v.). She was the author of *The backwoodswoman* (Toronto, 1924), *The life of Thomas D'Arcy McGee* (Gardenvale, Que., 1925), and *A man austere: William Bell, parson and pioneer* (Toronto, 1947).

[*Can. who's who*, 1952-54.]

Skelton, Oscar Douglas (1878-1941), economist and civil servant, was born at Orangeville, Ontario, on July 13, 1878. He was educated at Queen's University, Kingston (B.A., 1899; M.A., 1900) and at the University of Chicago (Ph.D., 1908). He was appointed in 1908 lecturer, and in 1909 professor, in political and economic science at Queen's University; and in 1919 he became dean of the faculty of arts. In 1925 he was appointed to succeed Sir Joseph Pope (q.v.) as under-secretary of state for foreign affairs at Ottawa; and he discharged, with conspicuous success, the duties of this post until his death at Ottawa on January 28, 1941. He won the confidence of successive prime ministers of both parties; and he exerted an influence on the course of public affairs in Canada from 1925 to 1941 greater than that of all but a few cabinet ministers. "He was," as one of his colleagues has testified, "the Deputy Prime Minister of Canada." In 1932 he was general secretary of the Imperial Conference held in Ottawa. He was the author of *Socialism: A critical analysis* (Boston, 1911), *The railway builders* (Toronto, 1915), *The Canadian dominion* (New Haven, Conn., 1919), *The life and times of Sir Alexander Tilloch Galt* (Toronto, 1920), *The life and letters of Sir Wilfrid Laurier* (2 vols., Toronto, 1921), and *Our generation, its gains and losses* (Chicago, 1938).

[*Proc. Roy. Soc. Can.*, 1941; *Can. who's who*, 1938-39; G. Dexter, *Oscar Douglas Skelton* (Queen's quarterly, 1941); W. A. Mackintosh, *O. D. Skelton* (Canadian banker, 1941); *Canadian journal of economic and political science*, May, 1941.]

Slater, Patrick (pseud.). See **Mitchell, John**.

Sleigh, Burrows Willcocks Arthur (1821-1869), soldier and author, was born in Canada in 1821, and joined the British army. He served at various times in Nova Scotia, New Brunswick, Prince Edward Island, and Canada East; and he rose to the rank of lieutenant-colonel in the 77th Regiment. He died in 1869. An account of his life in Canada will be found in his *Pine forests and hacmatack clearings; or, Travel, life, and adventure in the British North American provinces* (London, 1853).

[Frances M. Staton and Marie Tremaine (eds.), *A bibliography of Canadiana* (Toronto, 1934).]

Slight, Benjamin (1798?-1858), clergyman and author, was born about 1798, and was ordained in 1835 a minister of the Wesleyan Methodist Conference in Upper Canada. He died at Napanee, Canada West, on January 16, 1858. He was the author of *Indian researches, or facts concerning the North American Indians* (Montreal, 1844) and *The apocalypse explained* (Montreal, 1855).

[Morgan, *Bib. can.*]

Small, Ambrose (1867-1919?), theatre-owner, was born at Bradford, Ontario, on January 11, 1867. He became the manager of the Toronto Opera House, and later the owner of the Grand Opera House, Toronto; and eventually he came to control a chain of theatres throughout Canada. In 1919 he sold his theatrical interests to the Trans-Canada Theatres for one million dollars; and on the day on which he received payment of this amount, he disappeared. The probability is that he was murdered; but no trace of his body has ever been found, and his disappearance is one of the most intriguing mysteries in Canadian history.

[W. S. Wallace, *Murders and mysteries* (Toronto, 1931); R. T. Allen, *What really happened to Ambrose Small* (Maclean's Magazine, Jan. 15, 1951); F. McClement, *The strange case of Ambrose Small* (Toronto, 1974).]

Small, Henry Beaumont (1832-1919), civil servant and author, was born at Market Bosworth, Leicestershire, England, on October 31, 1832. He was educated at Lincoln College, Oxford; but did not graduate. He came to Canada as a young man, and was for a time a school-teacher, both in Canada and in the United States. In 1868 he obtained a position in the civil service of Canada at Ottawa; and he remained in the civil service until his retirement. He died in Bermuda, on February 8, 1919. He was the author of *The animals of North America* (2 series, Montreal, 1864-65), *The Canadian handbook and tourist's guide* (Montreal, 1866), *Chronicles of Canada* (Ottawa, 1868), *The products and manufactures of the new Dominion* (Ottawa, 1868), *Canadian forests: Forest trees, timber, and forest products* (Montreal, 1884), and *Botany of the Bermudas* (Hamilton, Bermuda, 1913).

[Rose, *Cyc. Can. biog.* (1886); Morgan, *Bib. can.*]

Small, James Edward (d. 1869), solicitor-general of Upper Canada (1842-43), was born in York, Upper Canada, before 1800, the second son of John Small (q.v.). He was called to the bar of Upper Canada in 1821, and practised law in York. He was counsel for the defendants in the suit which W. L. Mackenzie (q.v.) brought in 1826 against those who had destroyed his printing press. In 1836 he was a member of the Constitutional Reform Association; and in 1839 he was elected to represent the third riding of York in the Legislative Assembly of Upper Canada. He represented the same constituency from 1841 to 1848 in the Legislative Assembly of united Canada; and from 1842 to 1843 he was a member of the Executive Council and solicitor-general for Upper Canada in the first Baldwin-Lafontaine administration. In 1849 he was appointed county judge of Middlesex, and he held this post until his death in 1869.

[W. R. Riddell, *The legal profession in Upper Canada* (Toronto, 1916); J. C. Dent, *The Upper Canadian rebellion* (2 vols., Toronto, 1885) and *The last forty years* (2 vols., Toronto, 1881).]

Small, John (1726-1796), soldier, was born at Strath Ardle, Perthshire, Scotland, in 1726. He served with the Scotch brigade in Holland; and in 1747 obtained a commission in the 42nd Highlanders. He proceeded to America with his regiment, and took part in the attack on Ticonderoga and the capture of Montreal. In 1775 he was commissioned to raise a regiment of Highlanders in Nova Scotia; and he was present at the battle of Bunker Hill. He was appointed lieutenant-governor of Guernsey in 1793; and he died at Guernsey, having attained the rank of major-general, on October 3, 1794.

[*Dict. nat. biog.*; W. L. Calver, *Major-general John Small* (Fort Ticonderoga Museum bulletin, May, 1937).]

Small, John (1746-1831), clerk of the Executive Council of Upper Canada (1793-1831), was born in Gloucestershire, England, in 1746. He came to Canada in 1792; and in 1793 he was appointed clerk of the Executive Council of Upper Canada. This position he held until his death at York (Toronto) on July 18, 1831. He married Eliza Goldsmith, a native of Kent, England; and by her he had three sons.

[J. Ross Robertson, *Landmarks of Toronto*, vol. I (Toronto, 1894), and *Landmarks of Canada* (Toronto, 1917); *Commemorative biographical record of the county of York* (Toronto, 1907); E. S. Caswell, *A sketch of Major John Small* (York Pioneer and Historical Society report, 1933).]

Small, Patrick (d. 1810?), fur-trader, was born probably near Perth, Scotland, the son of John Small, and the grand-nephew of General John Small (q.v.). Through the influence of General Small, who was a friend of Simon McTavish (q.v.), he, like his relative, John McDonald of Garth (q.v.), became a clerk in the service of the North West Company. He first appears in the West in 1779, when he wintered on the Churchill River. For a number of years he was in charge at Isle à la Crosse. He became a partner in the North West Company in 1783; but he retired from the fur-trade in 1791, and returned to Great Britain. In 1794

he was adopted by his grand-uncle, General Small, and in 1796, at the latter's death, he was left by his will, a large part of his estate, including his property in Nova Scotia. He seems to have died about 1810. By a Cree woman at Isle à la Crosse he had one son, Patrick, and at least two daughters, one of whom married David Thompson (q.v.), and the other of whom was the "Indian wife" of John McDonald of Garth (q.v.).

[W. S. Wallace (ed.), *Documents relating to the North West Company* (Toronto: The Champlain Society, 1934).]

Smallwood, Charles (1812-1873), meteorologist, was born in Birmingham, England, in 1812. He became a physician, and in 1853 emigrated to Canada. He settled at St. Martin, Isle Jésus, Lower Canada, and acquired here a large medical practice. He established a meteorological observatory; and in 1858 he became professor of meteorology and astronomy at McGill University. He died at Montreal, Quebec, on December 22, 1873. He was an LL.D. of McGill University (1858).

[*Dict. Can. biog.*, vol. 10; *Dict. nat. biog.*; *Cyc. Am. biog.*]

Smart, William (1788-1876), clergyman, was born in Edinburgh, Scotland, on September 14, 1788. He was educated in England, and in 1811 he was ordained a minister of the Presbyterian Church. The same year he was sent by the London Missionary Society to Elizabethtown (Brockville), Upper Canada; and he was pastor of the First Presbyterian Church in that place until his resignation in 1849. He died at Gananoque, Ontario, on September 9, 1876. He was twice married, (1) in 1816 to Philena (d. 1855), widow of Israel Jones, of Brockville; and (2) in 1862 to Mrs. Bush, of Gananoque.

[Holly S. Seaman, *The Rev. William Smart* (Ont. Hist. Soc., papers and records, vol. v, 1904); *Dict. Can. biog.*, vol. 10.]

Smellie, Elizabeth Lawrie (1884-1968), nurse, was born in Port Arthur, Ontario, and educated in Toronto and at Johns Hopkins Training School for Nurses, graduating in 1909. Later, she entered Simmons College, Boston, where she undertook post-graduate studies in public-health nursing. During the First World War she served as a nursing sister with the Canadian Army Medical Corps and was matron of the Moore Barracks Hospital from 1915 to 1918. She was mentioned in despatches and awarded the Royal Red Cross (1917). On her return to Canada she was assistant matron-in-chief of the Canadian Army Nursing Service (1918-20) and assistant to the director of the McGill School of Graduate Nursing (1923-27). She was chief superintendent of the Victorian Order of Nurses for Canada (1924-47) and was responsible for the growth and development of the order. In 1940 she was appointed matron-in-chief, Royal Canadian Medical Corps, with the rank of major, and retired as colonel in 1944. She also supervised the organization of the Canadian Women's Army Corps in 1941. After the war she became nursing consultant to the department of veterans' affairs (1947-48). She died at Toronto, Ontario, March 5, 1968.

[*Can. who's who*, 1955-57; *Encyc. Can.* (1972).]

Smellie, George (1811-1896), clergyman, was born at St. Andrews, Orkney Islands, Scotland, on June 11, 1811, the son of the Rev. James Smellie. He was educated at Edinburgh University, and he was ordained a minister of the Church of Scotland in 1836. For several years he was assistant and successor to the minister in Lady Parish, North Isle; but in 1843 he came to Canada as minister of St. Andrew's Church, Fergus, Canada West. In 1844 he retired with the great part of the congregation to form the Free Church in Fergus, which was named Melville Church; and he continued as pastor of this church until his retirement in 1888. He died at Toronto, Ontario, on November 14, 1896. He was the author of *Memoir of the Rev. John Bayne, D.D., of Galt* (Toronto, 1871).

[A. E. Byerly, *Fergus* (Elora, Ont., 1934).]

Smet, Pierre Jean de (1801-1873), missionary, was born in Flanders in 1801, the son of Joost de Smet. He was educated by the Jesuits, and in 1821 emigrated to America, where he entered the novitiate of the Jesuits at Georgetown. In 1838 he went west as a missionary, and in 1841 he began his life's work among the Indians of Oregon. In 1842 he visited Fort Vancouver, and in 1845 Fort Edmonton. He died at St. Louis, Missouri, on May 23, 1873.

[R. P. Laveille, *Le Père de Smet* (Liège, 1913; 4th ed., Louvain and Paris, 1928); H. Magaret, *Father de Smet, pioneer priest of the Rockies* (New York, 1948); M. McHugh, *Giant of the Western Trail* (New York, 1958); L. Pfaller, *Father Smet in Dakota* (Richardton, N.D., 1962); J. U. Terrell, *Black Robe: The life of Pierre-Jean de Smet, missionary, explorer, pioneer* (Toronto, 1964); *Dict. Am. biog.*; Le Jeune, *Dict. gén.*]

Smillie, James (1807-1885), engraver, was born in Edinburgh, Scotland, on November 23, 1807. He came to Canada with his parents in 1821, and became an engraver in Quebec. A volume of his engravings of Quebec was published, with letterpress by the Reverend George Bourne (1780-1845), under the title, *The picture of Quebec* (Quebec, 1829). In 1830 he removed to the United States; and he became a successful engraver in New York. In 1839 he was elected an associate of the National Academy of Design, and in 1851 an

academician. He died at Poughkeepsie, New York, on December 4, 1885.

[*Dom. ann. reg.*, 1885.]

Smith, Sir Albert James (1822-1883), minister of marine and fisheries for Canada (1873-78), was born at Shediac, New Brunswick, on March 12, 1822, the son of T. E. Smith. He was educated at the Westmorland county grammar school; and was called to the bar of New Brunswick in 1847 (Q.C., 1861). From 1851 to 1867 he sat in the Legislative Assembly of New Brunswick for Westmorland; and from 1867 to 1868 he represented Westmorland in the Canadian House of Commons. In 1856 he became a member without portfolio of the first Liberal administration formed in New Brunswick; he was a member of several subsequent governments; and in 1865-66 he was president of the council in the Smith-Wilmot administration formed to oppose the inclusion of New Brunswick in Confederation. After Confederation he held for a time aloof from both parties; but in 1873 he became minister of marine and fisheries in the Mackenzie government, and he held this office until his defeat in the elections of 1878. He died at Dorchester, New Brunswick, on June 30, 1883. In 1868 he married June, daughter of J. W. Young, of Halifax, Nova Scotia. He was created a K.C.M.G. in 1878, in recognition of services rendered by him in connection with the Halifax Fishery Commission under the Treaty of Washington.

[*Dom. ann. reg.*, 1883; *Can. parl. comp.*; *Cyc. Am. biog.*; Dent, *Can. port.*, vol. 2; M. O. Hammond, *Confederation and its leaders* (Toronto, 1917).]

Smith, Andrew (d. 1910), principal of the Ontario Veterinary College (1862-1908), was a native of Ayrshire, Scotland, and graduated in 1861 from the Edinburgh Veterinary College. He came to Canada, and in 1862 founded in Toronto, Canada West, the Ontario Veterinary College as a proprietary school. He remained the principal of this college until 1908, when it was taken over by the Ontario government. He died in Toronto, Ontario, on August 15, 1910. He was a fellow of the Royal College of Veterinary Surgeons of England.

[Rose, *Cyc. Can. biog.* (1888).]

Smith, Benjamin Franklin (1864-1944), senator of Canada, was born in Jacksonville, New Brunswick, in 1864. He became the head of a large produce business in Florenceville, New Brunswick; and from 1903 to 1930 he represented Carleton county, with one brief interval, in the New Brunswick legislature. From 1912 to 1917 he was minister of public works in the New Brunswick government. From 1930 to 1935 he represented Victoria-Carleton in the Canadian House of Commons as a Conservative; and in 1935 he was called to the Senate of Canada. He sat in the Senate until his death at Ottawa, Ontario, on May 19, 1944.

[*Can. who's who*, 1936-37; *Can. parl. comp.*]

Smith, Charles Douglas (*fl.* 1812-1824) lieutenant-governor of Prince Edward Island, was a brother of Admiral Sir Sidney Smith (1764-1840). He was appointed lieutenant-governor of Prince Edward Island in 1812; and for over ten years he exercised in the colony an arbitrary and high-handed rule. In 1823 a largely signed petition for his recall was forwarded to London, and in 1824 he was replaced by Lieut.-Col. Ready (q.v.).

[D. Campbell, *History of Prince Edward Island* (Charlottetown, P.E.I., 1875); A. B. Warburton, *A history of Prince Edward Island* (Saint John, N.B., 1923).]

Smith, Clyde (pseud.). See **Smith, George.**

Smith, or Smyth, Sir David William, Bart. (1764-1837), surveyor-general of Upper Canada, was born in England on September 4, 1764, the only son of Major John Smith, of the 5th Regiment. He obtained a commission in his father's regiment, and came to Canada about 1790. In 1792 he was elected to the Legislative Assembly of Upper Canada, probably for Essex; and in 1796 he was elected to represent Lincoln. He was speaker of the second and third parliaments of Upper Canada. He was appointed also surveyor-general of the province; and in 1796 he was sworn of the Executive Council. In 1804 he went to England; and here he became agent for the Duke of Northumberland. He died in England, near Alnwick, on May 9, 1837. He married (1) in 1788 Anne (d. 1798), daughter of John O'Reilly, of Ballykilchrist, county Longford, Ireland, by whom he had eight children; and (2) in 1803 Mary, daughter of John Tylor, of Devizes, England, by whom he had one daughter. In 1821 he was created a baronet of the United Kingdom. He was the author of *A short topographical description of His Majesty's province of Upper Canada* (London, 1799; 2nd ed., 1813), the second edition of which is said to have been revised by Francis Gore (q.v.). His papers are in the Toronto Public Library.

[C. C. James, *The first legislators of Upper Canada* (Trans. Roy. Soc. Can., 1902), *The second legislature of Upper Canada* (Trans. Roy. Soc. Can., 1903), and *David William Smith* (Trans. Roy. Soc. Can., 1913); Morgan, *Cel. Can.*; *Cyc. Am. biog.*]

Smith, Sir Donald Alexander. See **Strathcona and Mount Royal, Baron.**

Smith, Edward (d. 1849), fur-trader, entered the service of the North West Company prior to 1806, when he appears as a clerk in the Athabaska department. He was employed for many years in the Athabaska

and Mackenzie River departments; and in 1814 he was made a partner of the North West Company. At the union of 1821, he was made a chief factor of the Hudson's Bay Company; and from 1821 to 1823 he was in charge at Fort Chipewyan, from 1823 to 1832 at Fort Simpson, and from 1834 to 1837 again at Fort Chipewyan. He was granted furlough in 1837, and shortly afterwards retired from the Company's service. He died in 1849.

[E. E. Rich (ed.), *Journal of occurrences in the Athabaska department, by George Simpson* (Toronto: The Champlain Society, 1938).]

Smith, Sir Frank (1822-1901), minister of public works for Canada (1891-92), was born at Richhill, Armagh, Ireland, in 1822, and came to Canada when ten years of age. In 1849 he set up in business as a grocer in London, Canada West, and in 1866 he was elected mayor of London. In 1867 he removed to Toronto, and he became there an outstanding merchant and capitalist. He was president of the Dominion Bank, of the Niagara Navigation Company, of the Northern Railway Company, of the Toronto Street Railway Company, and other companies. In 1871 he was called to the Senate of Canada; and from 1882 to 1896 he was almost continuously a member without portfolio of the successive Conservative governments. He was one of the founders of the Ontario Catholic League; and in 1891-92 he was for a few months minister of public works in the Abbott administration. He died at Toronto on January 17, 1901. He married the daughter of John O'Higgins, of Stratford, Ontario. In 1894 he was created a knight bachelor.

[*Who was who*, 1897-1916; Morgan, *Can. men* (1898); *Can. parl. comp.*]

Smith, Frank Clifford (1865-1937), journalist and novelist, was born at Kendal, England, in 1865. He came to Canada while a child, and was educated in Montreal. He became a journalist, and was employed, first on the staff of the Montreal *Daily Witness*, and later on that of the Montreal *Daily Star*. For some years he was private secretary to Lord Atholstan (q.v.). He died at Montreal, Quebec, on July 1, 1937. He was the author of *A lover in homespun, and other stories* (Toronto, 1896), *A daughter of patricians* (Toronto, 1900), and *The traitor* (Toronto, 1912).

[*Can. who's who*, 1936-37; Morgan, *Can. men* (1912).]

Smith, George (1852-1930), jurist and author, was born in Cambuslang, Lanarkshire, Scotland, on March 6, 1852. He came to Canada when a child, and was educated at the University of Toronto (B.A., 1879; M.A., 1880). He was called to the bar in Ontario in 1884, and practised law in Woodstock, Ontario. He represented North Oxford in the Canadian House of Commons from 1905 to 1908; and in 1909 he was appointed a county court judge in Essex county, Ontario. He died at Windsor, Ontario, on July 28, 1930. He was the author, under the pen-name of "Clyde Smith", of *The Amishman* (Toronto, 1912).

[Morgan, *Can. men* (1912).]

Smith, Goldwin (1823-1910), author and journalist, was born in Reading, Berkshire, England, on August 13, 1823, the son of Richard Pritchard Smith, M.D., and Elizabeth Breton. He was educated at Eton and at Magdalen College, Oxford (B.A., 1845; M.A., 1848). In 1846 he was elected Stowell law professor, and later tutor, of University College; in 1854 he was secretary of the Oxford University Commission; and from 1858 to 1866 he was regius professor of modern history at Oxford. During the American Civil War he visited the United States, and in 1868 he accepted the professorship of English and constitutional history at Cornell University, Ithaca, New York. He came to Canada in 1871, and settled in Toronto; and here he spent the remainder of his life.

He took a lively interest in Canadian affairs. He allied himself with the "Canada First" party, and in 1875 was the first president of the National Club in Toronto. Later he became an advocate of commercial union with the United States, and though he was never an advocate of "annexation", he did not conceal his view that political union with the United States was the ultimate destiny of Canada — a view that earned for him much unpopularity. In Canadian journalism he took an active part. In 1872 he contributed to the *Canadian Monthly* the first of a series of papers by "A Bystander"; and under this *nom de plume* he continued to write, at intervals, for over thirty years. He wrote, first, occasional papers for the *Canadian Monthly* (1872-78) and the *Nation* (1874-76); then he wrote and published himself a little journal entitled *The Bystander* (first series, monthly, January, 1880, to June, 1881; second series, quarterly, 1883; third series, monthly, October, 1889, to September, 1890); in 1884 he began contributing a weekly article to the *Week* (1883-90); and, lastly, he contributed for many years (1896-1909) a weekly *causerie* to the *Farmer's Sun* (later the *Weekly Sun*). To most of these journals he lent also his financial support.

Although a master of English style, Goldwin Smith did not fulfil in Canada his early promise of literary achievement. A bibliography of his writings would fill many pages; yet nothing he wrote is likely to occupy a permanent place in literature. His chief publications, apart from journalism, were *Lectures on modern history* (Oxford, 1861), republished as *Lectures on the study of history* (Toronto, 1883), *Irish history and Irish character* (Oxford, 1861), *Does the Bible sanction American slavery?* (Oxford, 1863), *The empire* (Oxford, 1863),

Three English statesmen (London, 1867), *Cowper* (London, 1881), *Lectures and essays* (New York, 1881), *Jane Austen* (London, 1890), *Canada and the Canadian question* (London, 1891), *William Lloyd Garrison* (Toronto, 1892), *Bay leaves* (New York, 1893), *Essays on questions of the day* (New York, 1893), *The United States, a political history* (New York, 1893), *Guesses at the riddle of existence* (New York, 1897), *Shakespeare the man* (Toronto, 1899), *The United Kingdom* (2 vols., London, 1899), *Commonwealth or empire* (New York, 1902), *In the court of history* (Toronto, 1902), *The founder of Christendom* (Toronto, 1903), *My memory of Gladstone* (London, 1904), *Irish history and the Irish question* (Toronto, 1905), *In quest of light* (Toronto, 1906), *Oxford and her colleges* (New York, 1906), and *No refuge but in truth* (Toronto, 1908). His *Reminiscences* were edited, after his death, by A. Haultain (Toronto, 1912).

He died at Toronto on June 7, 1910. In 1875 he married Harriet (d. 1909), daughter of Thomas Dixon, and widow of Henry Boulton of The Grange, Toronto. They had no children.

[Elizabeth Wallace, *Goldwin Smith, Victorian liberal* (Toronto, 1957); A. Haultain, *Goldwin Smith's correspondence* (Toronto, n.d.) and *Goldwin Smith, his life and opinions* (Toronto, n.d.); J. J. Cooper, *Goldwin Smith, D.C.L.* (pamphlet, Reading, 1912), with bibliography; W. L. Grant, *Goldwin Smith at Oxford* (Can. mag., 1910); A. H. U. Colquhoun, *Goldwin Smith in Canada* (Can. mag., 1910); W. S. Wallace, *The Bystander and Canadian journalism* (Can. mag., 1910); R. C. Brown, *Goldwin Smith and anti-imperialism* (Can. hist. rev., 1962); *Dict. nat. biog.*; *Can. who was who*, vol. 2.]

Smith, Harlan Ingersoll (1872-1940), archaeologist, was born at East Saginaw, Michigan, on February 17, 1872. He was educated at the University of Michigan (hon. M.A., 1929), and in 1891 obtained a position on the staff of the Peabody Museum, Cambridge, Massachusetts. From 1895 to 1911 he was on the staff of the American Museum of Natural History, New York. He came to Canada in 1911, and became the archaeologist of the Geological Survey of Canada. Later, in 1920, he became archaeologist to the National Museum of Canada. He died at Ottawa, Ontario, on June 28, 1940. He was the author of *An album of prehistoric Canadian art* (Ottawa, 1923) and numerous reports and contributions to scientific periodicals.

[*Can. who's who*, 1936-37.]

Smith, Sir Henry (1812-1868), solicitor-general for Upper Canada (1854-58), was born in London, England, on April 23, 1812. He emigrated to Canada with his parents about 1820, and was educated, first at an academy in Montreal, and then at the Royal Grammar

School in Kingston, Upper Canada. He was called to the bar of Upper Canada in 1836 (Q.C., 1846); and from 1841 to 1861 he represented Frontenac in the Legislative Assembly of Canada. From 1854 to 1858 he was solicitor-general west in successive Liberal-Conservative governments; and from 1858 to 1861 he was speaker of the Legislative Assembly. In 1867 he was elected to represent Frontenac in the Legislative Assembly of Ontario; but he died at Kingston, Ontario, in September, 1868. He was knighted on the occasion of the visit of the Prince of Wales to Canada in 1860.

[Morgan, *Cel. Can.*; J. C. Dent, *The last forty years* (2 vols., Toronto, 1881).]

Smith, James (1808-1868), attorney-general for Lower Canada (1844-47), was born in Montreal in 1808. He was educated in Scotland, but returned to Canada in 1823, and was called to the bar of Lower Canada in 1828. In 1844 he was elected to represent Missisquoi in the Legislative Assembly of Canada, and was appointed attorney-general for Lower Canada in the Viger-Draper administration. In 1847 he resigned office to accept appointment as a judge of the Court of Queen's Bench in Lower Canada; and in 1850 he was appointed a judge of the Superior Court. He died on November 29, 1868.

[P. G. Roy, *Les juges de la province de Québec* (Quebec, 1933); Morgan, *Cel. Can.*; *Cyc. Am. biog.*]

Smith, James (1821-1888), author, was born at Caraquet, New Brunswick, on September 5, 1821, and was educated at the Quebec Seminary. He was a school-teacher in Lower Canada, New Brunswick, and the United States; and for several years he was a farmer at Causapscal, New Brunswick. He died at St. Laurent de Matapédia on May 18, 1888. He published *Havre de refuge: Rimouski vs. Bic* (Quebec, 1856), *Les éléments d'agriculture* (Quebec, 1862), *Les soirées de la Baie de Chaleur* (1883), and *Un calomniateur démasqué par lui-même* (n.d.).

[*Bull. rech. hist.*, 1928.]

Smith, James (1832-1918), architect, was born at Macduff, Banffshire, Scotland, and came to Canada in 1851. He studied architecture in Toronto under W. Thomas (q.v.), and practised in Toronto. He became a charter member of the Royal Canadian Academy of Arts in 1880; and his chief works were the Metropolitan Church and old Knox College in Toronto. He died in 1918.

[N. MacTavish, *The fine arts in Canada* (Toronto, 1925); H. G. Jones and E. Dyonnet, *History of the Royal Canadian Academy of Arts* (Montreal, 1934).]

Smith, James Frazer (1858-1948), medical missionary, was born at Dornoch, Canada West, in 1858, and died at Edmonton, Alberta, on April 28, 1948. He graduated in theology and medicine at Queen's University, and became a medical missionary first in China, and then in India. He was the author of an autobiography entitled *Life's waking part* (Toronto, 1937).

[Private information.]

Smith, Joseph Henry (1839-1917), educationist, was born in the township of Flamborough West, Upper Canada, in 1839, of United Empire Loyalist stock. He became a school-teacher; and from 1870 until shortly before his death he was inspector of schools for the county of Wentworth. For some years he was president of the Wentworth Historical Society. He died at Hamilton, Ontario, in September, 1917. He was the author of *Historical sketch of the county of Wentworth and the head of the lake* (Hamilton, Ont., 1897) and *The Central School jubilee re-union* (Hamilton, Ont., 1905).

[Morgan, *Can. men* (1912); J. A. Griffin, *A backward look* (Papers and records of the Wentworth Historical Society, vol. 8, 1919).]

Smith, Joseph Leopold (1881-1952), musician and author, was born in Birmingham, England, in 1881, and died at Toronto, Ontario, on April 18, 1952. He was educated at Manchester University and the Royal Manchester College of Music, and in 1910 he came to Canada as a member of the teaching staff of the Conservatory of Music in Toronto. He became professor of music in the University of Toronto in 1938, and retired in 1950. He was the author of *Musical rudiments* (Boston, 1920) and *Music of the seventeenth and eighteenth centuries* (London, 1931).

[Pearl McCarthy, *Leo Smith: A biographical sketch* (Toronto, 1956); *Can. who's who*, 1949-51; *Encyc. Can.*]

Smith, Joshua (1881-1938), portrait-painter, was born in London, England, in 1881. He became a well-known portrait-painter, and was a member of the Royal Society of Artists. He came to Canada in 1920; and he painted the portraits of a number of persons prominent in public life in Canada. He died at Toronto, Ontario, on March 26, 1938.

[*Can. who's who*, 1936-37.]

Smith, Leo. See **Smith, Joseph Leopold.**

Smith, Lyman Cyrus (1850-1928), educationist and poet, was born in Wentworth county, Canada West, on September 8, 1850. He was educated at Victoria University, Cobourg (B.A., 1877), and became a secondary-school teacher. He died at Oshawa, Ontario, on January 30, 1928. He was the author of *Mabel Gray, and other poems* (Toronto, 1897) and *A blossom of the sea, and other poems* (Wilmington, Del., 1910).

[C. C. James, *A bibliography of Canadian poetry* (Toronto, 1899).]

Smith, Marcus (1815-1904), civil engineer, was born at Berwick-on-Tweed, England, on July 16, 1815. He became a civil engineer, and was employed in the survey and construction of some of the early English railways. He came to America in 1849; and between 1850 and 1860 he made plans and surveys of a number of cities and towns in Canada West, some of which were published, and he was employed as an engineer in the construction of the Great Western and the Niagara and Detroit Rivers Railway. From 1860 to 1868 he was in South Africa and Great Britain; but in 1868 he returned to Canada, and played an important part in the construction of the Intercolonial and Canadian Pacific railways. From 1886 to 1892 he was a consulting engineer in the service of the Canadian government. He died at Ottawa, Ontario, on August 14, 1904.

[Morgan, *Can. men* (1898).]

Smith, Mrs. Mary Ellen, *née* **Spear** (1861-1933), first woman in the British Empire to attain cabinet rank, was born at Tavistock, England, on October 11, 1861, the daughter of Richard Spear. In 1883 she married Ralph Smith, of Newcastle-on-Tyne, a student for the ministry of the Methodist Church, and later a lay reader. In 1891 they emigrated to British Columbia, and settled in Nanaimo. Ralph Smith went into politics in 1898, and became in 1916 minister of finance in the British Columbia administration; but he died in 1917, and his wife succeeded him in the legislature. In 1921 she was appointed minister without portfolio in the cabinet of the Hon. John Oliver (q.v.); and though she resigned her post in the cabinet in 1922, she continued a member of the legislature until 1928. She died at Vancouver, British Columbia, on May 3, 1933.

[*Can. who was who,* vol. 2; *Can. parl. comp.*]

Smith, Michael (*fl.* 1808-1814), author, was a native of Pennsylvania who became a Baptist minister, and emigrated to Upper Canada in 1808. In 1810 he obtained from Lieutenant-Governor Gore (q.v.) permission to prepare and print a gazetteer of Upper Canada; but on the outbreak of the War of 1812 he left Canada for the United States. His manuscript was confiscated; but he succeeded in preparing, from notes and from a part of the original manuscript sent to a printer in Buffalo, a work which appeared under the title *A geographical view of the province of Upper Canada, and promiscuous remarks upon the government* (Hartford, Conn., 1813). Subsequent editions, corrected and enlarged, appeared in New York (August, 1813), in Philadelphia (October, 1813), in Trenton, New Jersey (November, 1813), and in Baltimore (1814).

[F. M. Staton and M. Tremaine (eds.), *A bibliography of Canadiana* (Toronto, 1934).]

Smith, Paul Ernest (d. 1914), civil servant and author, was for many years clerk of the English journals of the Legislative Assembly of the province of Quebec. He was superannuated in 1897; and he died at Quebec City on September 4, 1914. He was the author of *Essai sur la rédaction des lois* (Quebec, 1878).

[Private information.]

Smith, Robert (1839-1885), jurist, was born at Loweswater, Cumberland, England, on June 19, 1839. He was educated at Trinity College, Cambridge, and at the University of Toronto (LL.B., 1861), and was called to the bar of Upper Canada in 1861 (Q.C., 1882). He practised law in Stratford, Ontario, for many years; but in 1883 he was appointed a justice of the Court of Queen's Bench in Manitoba, and removed to Winnipeg. He died at Winnipeg on January 19, 1885.

[*Dom. ann. reg.,* 1885; *Can. who was who,* vol. 2.]

Smith, Robert (1859-1942), jurist, was born in Lanark county, Canada West, on December 7, 1859. He was educated at the Osgoode Hall Law School, Toronto, and was called to the bar of Ontario in 1885. He practised law in Cornwall, Ontario; and from 1908 to 1911 he represented Stormont in the Canadian House of Commons. In 1922 he was appointed a justice of the Supreme Court of Ontario; and in 1927 he was transferred to the Supreme Court of Canada. He retired from the bench in 1933; and he died at Ottawa, Ontario, on March 18, 1942.

[*Can. who's who,* 1938-39; *Can. parl. comp.*; Morgan, *Can. men* (1912).]

Smith, Mrs. Robina, *née* **Lizars.** See **Lizars, Robina.**

Smith, Samuel (1756-1826), administrator of Upper Canada (1817-18 and 1820), was born at Hempstead, New York, on December 27, 1756. He served during the American Revolutionary War as an officer in the Queen's Rangers, under Simcoe (q.v.); and at the close of the war he settled in New Brunswick. After Simcoe was appointed lieutenant-governor of Upper Canada, he came to Upper Canada, and took up a grant of land. In 1815 he was appointed a member of the Executive Council of the province, and on two occasions (1817-18 and 1820) he was appointed administrator of the government. He died at York (Toronto) on October 20, 1826. In 1799 he married Jane Isabella Clarke (d. 1826); and by her he had two sons and six daughters.

[D. B. Read, *Lieutenant-governors of Upper Canada* (Toronto, 1900); Morgan, *Cel. Can.*; A. H. Young (ed.), *The parish register of Kingston* (Kingston, Ont., 1921); E. M.

Chadwick, *Ontarian families* (2 vols., Toronto, 1894-98).]

Smith, Sidney (1823-1889), postmaster-general of Canada (1858-62), was born in Port Hope, Upper Canada, on October 16, 1823. He was educated at Cobourg and Port Hope, Upper Canada, and was called to the bar in 1844. He began the practice of law in Cobourg; and in 1854 he was elected to represent the west riding of Northumberland in the Legislative Assembly. From 1858 to 1862 he was postmaster-general in the Cartier-Macdonald administration, and a member of the board of railway commissioners. In 1861 he was elected to the Legislative Council; but he resigned in 1863 to contest the constituency of Victoria in the Assembly. He was defeated, and thereupon retired from political life. In 1866 he was appointed inspector of registry offices for Upper Canada. He died on September 27, 1889.

[Morgan, *Cel. Can.*; *Cyc. Am. biog.*; Rose, *Cyc. Can. biog.* (1886); W. Cochrane, *Men of Canada,* vol. 4 (Brantford, Ont., 1895); J. C. Dent, *The last forty years* (2 vols., Toronto, 1881).]

Smith, Sidney Earle (1897-1959), educationist and cabinet minister, was born at Port Hood, Nova Scotia, on March 9, 1897, and died at Ottawa, Ontario, on March 17, 1959. He was educated at the University of King's College (B.A., 1915; M.A., 1919) and Dalhousie University (LL.B., 1920), and was called to the bar in Nova Scotia. After a year at Harvard, he was appointed a lecturer, and later an assistant professor, in the Dalhousie Law School; and after lecturing for four years in Osgoode Hall, Toronto, he returned to the Dalhousie Law School as dean. In 1934 he was appointed president of the University of Manitoba, and pulled the University through the financial catastrophe that nearly overwhelmed it; ten years later, in 1944, he accepted the principalship of University College in Toronto, on the understanding that in 1945 he was to assume the presidency of the University of Toronto. Here he remained president until 1957, when he was invited to join the Diefenbaker government as secretary of state for external affairs, and was later elected at a by-election to represent Hastings-Frontenac in the House of Commons. He held this portfolio for only a year and a half, and then died suddenly. He was the recipient of honorary degrees from many universities, was elected an honorary fellow of the Royal Society of Canada in 1950, and served as President of the National Conference of Canadian Universities and many other bodies. He was the author of *A selection of cases on the law of trusts* (Toronto, 1928); and joint author, with J. D. Falconbridge, of *A manual of Canadian business law* (Toronto, 1930), and, with H. E. Read, of *A selection of cases on equity* (Toronto, 1931).

[E. A. Corbett, *Sidney Earle Smith* (Toronto, 1961); *Proc. Roy. Soc. Can.*, 1959; *Can. who's who*, 1958-60; *Can. parl. guide*, 1958.]

Smith, Thomas Barlow (1839-1933), journalist, was born at Windsor, Nova Scotia, in 1839; and died on July 22, 1933. He was the author of *The young lion of the woods* (Halifax, N.S., 1889), *Rose Carney* (Halifax, N.S., 1889), *Backward glances* (Halifax, N.S., 1898), *Little Mayflower land* (Halifax, N.S., 1900), and *Nova Scotia: Trial and relief* (Windsor, N.S., 1929).

[R. J. Long, *Nova Scotia authors* (East Orange, N.J., 1918); *New York Times*, July 23, 1933.]

Smith, Thomas Watson (1835?-1902), clergyman and author, was born about 1835, and was ordained a minister of the Methodist Church in New Brunswick in 1857. From 1881 to 1886 he was the editor of the Halifax *Wesleyan*; and in 1890 he was president of the Nova Scotia Conference. He died on March 8, 1902, aged 66 years. In 1891 he received the degree of D.D. from Mount Allison University, and in 1901 the degree of LL.D. from Dalhousie University. He was the author of a *History of Methodism in Eastern British America* (2 vols., Halifax, 1877-90).

[G. H. Cornish, *A cyclopaedia of Methodism in Canada* (2 vols., Toronto, 1881-1903).]

Smith, William (1728-1793), chief justice of Quebec and of Lower Canada (1786-93), was born in New York on June 18, 1728, the son of William Smith, a judge of the Court of King's Bench for New York. He was educated at Yale College (B.A., 1745), and was called to the bar. In 1769 he was appointed a member of the Executive Council of New York, and in 1780 chief justice of the province. During the Revolution, he was a staunch loyalist, and in 1784 he left New York for England with Carleton (q.v.). When Carleton returned to Canada in 1786 as governor-in-chief of British North America, Smith came with him as chief justice of Quebec. As such, he had much to do with the framing of the Constitutional Act of 1791. Under the Act he became chief justice of Lower Canada, and speaker of the Legislative Council; but he died shortly afterwards at Quebec, on December 6, 1793. He married in 1752 Janet, daughter of James Livingston, of New York. He was the author of a *History of the province of New York* (London, 1757).

[L. F. S. Upton, *The diary and selected papers of Chief Justice William Smith, 1784-1793*, 2 vols. (Toronto, The Champlain Society, 1963-5) and *The loyal whig: William Smith of New York and Quebec* (Toronto, 1969); W. Smith, *Historical memoirs from 16 March 1763 to 25 July 1778*, ed. by H. W. Sabine (New York, 1969, 2 vols.); F. J. Audet, *Les juges en chef de la province de*

Québec (Quebec, 1927); P. G. Roy, *Les juges de la province de Québec* (Quebec, 1933); *Dict. Am. biog.*; *Cyc. Am. biog.*; Morgan, *Cel. Can.* and *Bib. can.*; L. Sabine, *American loyalists* (Boston, 1849).]

Smith, William (1769-1847), historian, was born in New York on February 7, 1769, the second son of William Smith (q.v.), afterwards chief justice of Quebec. He was educated at the Kensington Grammar School, London, England, and came to Canada with his father in 1786. In 1791 he was appointed clerk of the Legislative Assembly of Lower Canada, and later master in chancery for the province. From 1817 to 1837 he was a member of the Executive Council of Lower Canada. He was the author of a *History of Canada* (2 vols., Quebec, 1815 [actually 1826]), the first connected history of Canada in English. He died at Quebec on December 17, 1847. He married Susan, daughter of Admiral Charles Webber of Hampshire, England; and by her he had two sons and three daughters.

[J. M. Lemoine, *Picturesque Quebec* (Montreal, 1882); *Magazine of American history*, 1881; P. Gagnon, *Essai de bibliographie canadienne* (Quebec, 1895), no. 3337; *Bull. rech. hist.*, 1938.]

Smith, William (1859-1932), historian, was born in Hamilton, Ontario, on January 31, 1859, the son of Thomas Smith and Margaret Summerville. He was educated at the Hamilton Collegiate Institute and at the University of Toronto (B.A., 1883); and he entered the Canadian civil service. In 1902 he became secretary of the Post Office department; and in 1913 deputy keeper of public records in the Public Archives of Canada. He died in Ottawa on January 28, 1932. In 1911 he was invested with the Imperial Service Order. He was the author of a *History of the Post Office in British North America* (Cambridge, 1920), *The evolution of government in Canada* (Ottawa, 1928), and *Political leaders of Upper Canada* (Toronto, 1932).

[Morgan, *Can. men* (1912).]

Smith, William Alexander. See De Cosmos, Amor.

Smith, William Edward (1864-1944), missionary and author, was born in Kendal, Ontario, in 1864, and died at Toronto, Ontario, on January 28, 1944. He went to China in 1896 as a medical missionary, and he continued as such for forty years. A few years before his death he embodied the story of his life in a book entitled *A Canadian doctor in West China* (Toronto, 1939).

[*Toronto Globe and Mail*, Jan. 29, 1944.]

Smith, William George (1872-1943), educationist and author, was born in 1872, and died at Calgary, Alberta, on September 9, 1943. He was educated at Victoria College, University of Toronto (B.A., 1899), and became first a professor of sociology at the University of Toronto, and later director of the School of Social Work at the University of Manitoba. He was the author of *A Study in Canadian immigration* (Toronto, 1920) and *Building the nation* (Toronto, 1922).

[*University of Toronto Monthly*, Oct., 1943.]

Smith, William Henry (*fl.* 1846-1873), author, compiled *Smith's Canadian gazetteer* (Toronto, 1846) and *Canada: past, present, and future, being a historical, geographical, geological and statistical account of Canada West* (2 vols., Toronto, 1851). He appears to have been an English ship's surgeon who came to Canada, and became a travelling surgeon-dentist; and he apparently collected the information embodied in his books while making his professional journeys. He was evidently a man of excellent education; but his identity has remained, in spite of extensive research, a mystery.

[Morgan, *Bib. can.*; *Dict. Can. biog.*, vol. 10.]

Smith, William Loe (1855-1945), journalist and author, was born in 1855, and died at his summer home in Brooklin, Ontario, on July 15, 1945. He became a journalist, and was editor-in-chief of the Toronto *News* in the 1880s. In 1890 he became editor of the *Weekly Sun*, in which Goldwin Smith (q.v.) had an interest; this later became the *Farmer's Sun*. He was the author of *The pioneers of old Ontario* (Toronto, 1923).

[*Toronto Globe and Mail*, July 17, 1945.]

Smith, William Richmond (1868-1934), journalist, was born at Ottawa, Ontario, on February 26, 1868. He became a journalist, first in Ottawa, and then in Montreal, where he joined the staff of the *Montreal Star*. He went to South Africa as a war correspondent for that paper in 1899, with the first Canadian contingent. Later he saw service as a war correspondent in the Russo-Japanese War. His later years were spent in New York, N.Y.; and he died in New York on February 19, 1934. He was the author of *Municipal trading in Great Britain* (Toronto, 1904) and *The siege and fall of Port Arthur* (London, 1905).

[Morgan, *Can. men* (1912); *New York Times* (Feb. 20, 1934).]

Smith, William Wye (1827-1917), clergyman and poet, was born in Jedburgh, Scotland, on March 18, 1827, the son of John Smith and Sarah Veitch. He was brought by his parents to the United States in 1830, and to Canada in 1837. Educated in New York, he returned to Canada in 1849. He engaged successively in school-teaching, business, and journalism; and in 1865 he became a minister of the Congregational Church. He retired from active parochial work in 1907; and he died at Burford, Ontario, on January 6, 1917. He published several volumes of poetry, *Alazon and other poems* (Toronto, 1850), *Poems* (Toronto, 1888), and *Selected poems* (Toronto, 1908). He published also *The New Testament in braid Scots* (Toronto, 1896; new ed., 1901).

[Morgan, *Can. men* (1912); A. MacMurchy, *A handbook of Canadian literature* (Toronto, 1906).]

Smithers, Charles F. (1822-1887), banker, was born in London, England, on November 25, 1822. He emigrated to Canada in 1847, and entered the service of the Bank of British North America. In 1858 he entered the employ of the Bank of Montreal; and in 1879 he was appointed general manager of this bank. In 1881 he succeeded Sir George Stephen (q.v.) in the presidency of the bank; and he died at Montreal on May 20, 1887.

[J. D. Borthwick, *History and biographical gazetteer of Montreal* (Montreal, 1892).]

Smithurst, John (1807-1867), clergyman, was born in England in 1807. He was educated at a missionary church college at Islington, England, and in 1839 was ordained a priest of the Church of England. He was immediately sent by the Church Missionary Society as a missionary to Red River in the Hudson's Bay territories; and he remained at Red River until 1851. He then was appointed rector of St. John's Church at Elora, Canada West; and he died at Elora in 1867. Before coming to Canada, he was engaged to his cousin, Florence Nightingale; but the marriage was forbidden by their parents. Neither married.

[J. R. Connon, *Elora* (Fergus, Ont., 1930); Margaret MacLeod, *The lamp shines in Red River* (Beaver, 1936).]

Smyth, Sir David William, Bart. See **Smith, Sir David William, Bart**.

Smyth, George Strachey (1767?-1823), lieutenant-governor of New Brunswick (1817-23), was born in England about 1767, and at an early age he entered the British army. He attained the rank of major-general in 1812, and in that year he was appointed president and commander-in-chief of New Brunswick, in the absence of the lieutenant-governor, Thomas Carleton (q.v.); and on Carleton's death in 1817, he became himself lieutenant-governor of the province. He died at Government House, Fredericton, on March 27, 1823.

[J. W. Lawrence, *The judges of New Brunswick and their times* (Saint John, N.B., 1907); Le Jeune, *Dict. gén.*; J. Hannay, *History of New Brunswick* (2 vols., Saint John, N.B., 1909).]

Smyth, John Paterson (1852-1932), clergyman and author, was born in Ireland in 1852, and was educated at Trinity College, Dublin. He was ordained a priest of the Church of England in 1881. He came to Canada in 1907; and he was rector of St. George's Church, Montreal, from 1907 to 1926. He died in Montreal on February 14, 1932. In 1883 he married Annie Josephine, daughter of the Rev. Hugh Ferrar, fellow of Trinity College, Dublin; and by her he had three sons and three daughters. He was the author of *How we got our Bible* (London, 1886), *The old documents and the new Bible* (London, 1890), *How God inspired the Bible* (London, 1893), *Social service ideals* (London, 1900), *The Bible for the young* (London, 1901), *Truth and reality* (Edinburgh, 1901), *The gospel of the hereafter* (London, 1910), *The Bible in the making* (London, 1914), *A Syrian love story* (London, 1915), *God and the war* (London, 1915), *The story of St. Paul's life and letters* (London, 1917), *A people's life of Christ* (London, 1921), *On the rim of the world* (London, 1922), *The preacher and his sermon* (New York, 1922), *The Bible for school and home* (6 vols., New York, 1922-23), *God, conscience, and the Bible* (London, 1924), *Myself, and other problems* (New York, 1927), *A boy's and girl's life of Christ* (London, 1929), *The highlands of Galilee* (London, 1930), and *Marriage and romance* (London, 1930). A number of his books went into many editions, and were translated into several languages.

[*Who's who among North American authors*, vol. 5; *Who was who*, 1929-40; Morgan, *Can. men* (1912).]

Smythe, Albert Ernest Stafford (1861-1947), journalist and poet, was born in county Antrim, Ireland, on December 27, 1861, and died at Hamilton, Ontario, on October 2, 1947. He became a journalist in Belfast, then in Chicago, and finally in Toronto. In 1907 he was president of the Toronto Press Club. He was the author of *Poems, grave and gay* (Toronto, 1891) and *The garden of the sun* (Toronto, 1923).

[Morgan, *Can. men* (1912).]

Smythe, William (1842-1887), prime minister of British Columbia (1883-87), was born at Whittington, Northumberland, England, on June 30, 1842. He was educated at Whittington, England, and was for a time a merchant at Newcastle-upon-Tyne. He emigrated to British Columbia before Confederation in 1871, and was for a time a road commissioner of the colony. From 1871 to 1887 he represented Cowichan continuously in the legislature of British Columbia; and in 1875 he was chosen leader of the Conservative opposition. From 1876 to 1878 he was minister of finance and agriculture in the Elliott administration; and in 1883 he became prime minister of the province. He died in office, at Cowichan, British Columbia, on March 29, 1887. In 1873 he married Martha, daughter of A. R. Kier.

[*Can. parl. comp.*; F. W. Howay and E. O.

S. Scholefield, *British Columbia* (4 vols., Vancouver, B.C., 1914).]

Snelling, Richard (1834-1893), lawyer, was born in England in 1834, came to Canada as a young man, and was educated at the University of Toronto (LL.B., 1863; LL.D., 1873). He was called to the bar of Upper Canada, and became an outstanding lawyer in Toronto. In 1877 he was appointed registrar of the Anglican diocese of Toronto, and in 1890 chancellor. He died at Toronto, Ontario, on July 26, 1893. He was the author of *The Grand Trunk Railway of Canada: Proceedings of the preference bondholders historically, legally, and financially considered* (Toronto, 1862); and he was joint author, with Frederick T. Jones, of *The general orders and statutes relating to the practice, pleading, and jurisdiction of the court of chancery for Upper Canada* (Toronto, 1863).

[Morgan, *Bib. can.*; Toronto *Empire,* July 27, 1893.]

Snively, Mary Agnes (1847-1933), nurse, was born in St. Catharines, Ontario, on November 12, 1847, and was educated there and at the Bellevue Training School in New York. She was for many years a schoolteacher; but in 1884, she was appointed superintendent of the Training School for Nurses at the Toronto General Hospital. She remained in charge of this school until her retirement on pension in 1910; and she was the moving spirit in the organization of the Canadian Nurses Association, of which she was elected first president in 1911. She died at Toronto on September 26, 1933.

[Toronto *Globe*, Sept. 27, 1933.]

Snodgrass, William (1827-1906), principal of Queen's University, Kingston (1864-77), was born at Cardonald Mills, Paisley, Scotland, on September 4, 1827, the son of John Snodgrass. He was educated at the University of Glasgow (D.D., 1865); and became a clergyman of the Church of Scotland. From 1852 to 1856 he was minister of St. James Church, Charlottetown, Prince Edward Island; and from 1856 to 1864 of St. Paul's Church, Montreal. In 1864 he was appointed principal of Queen's University, Kingston, with the chair of divinity; and he retained this post until 1877. He then returned to Scotland; and for the remainder of his life he was minister of Canonbie, Dumfriesshire. He died at Riversdale, Kilmacolm, Scotland, on July 22, 1906. He published a number of sermons and addresses.

[*Can. who was who*, vol. 1; Morgan, *Bib. can.*; W. I. Addison, *The matriculation albums of the University of Glasgow* (Glasgow, 1913).]

Snow, Charles Hammett (1862-1931), pomologist, was born in 1862, and became a civil servant in the department of agriculture in Ottawa. He was responsible for the development of the "Snow" apple, a famous Canadian variety. He was an inspector in the fruit branch of the department of agriculture when he died at Ottawa on July 1, 1931.

[*Can. ann. review*, 1932.]

Snowball, Jabez Bunting (1837-1907), lieutenant-governor of New Brunswick (1902-07), was born at Lunenburg, Nova Scotia, on September 24, 1837, the son of the Rev. John Snowball. He was educated at Mount Allison College, Sackville, New Brunswick. He engaged in business and became president and general manager of the Canada Eastern Railway. From 1878 to 1882 he represented Northumberland in the Canadian House of Commons as an independent; and in 1891 he was called to the Senate of Canada. In 1902 he was appointed lieutenant-governor of New Brunswick; and he died in office, at Fredericton, New Brunswick, on February 24, 1907. He married (1) in 1858, Margaret, daughter of John McDougall, and (2) in 1873, Maggie, daughter of the Rev. Robert Archibald.

[*Can. who was who*, vol. 2; *Can. parl. comp.*]

Solomons, Levi (*fl.* 1760-1784), merchant, was one of the earliest Jewish traders in Canada. He was described by Francis Maseres (q.v.) as "a Jew of a very good character, who in partnership with three other Jews had carried on a large trade in North America, and had been much concerned in furnishing provisions to the army." He "had been ruined by unavoidable accidents that befell him in the Indian war in 1762 and 1763," and was declared a bankrupt in 1767. He continued in the fur-trade until 1782, the last date on which he appears to have obtained a fur-trade licence; and his name appears, with that of "Levy Solomons, Jr.", in the petition of the inhabitants of Montreal for a house of assembly in 1784. After that date, trace of him is lost. He would appear to have been a brother of Ezekiel Solomons, a Jewish trader who was captured by the Indians at Michilimackinac in 1763, and was afterwards taken by the Ottawa Indians to Montreal and ransomed, and many of whose half-breed descendants settled, first at Drummond Island, in Lake Huron, and afterwards at Penetanguishene, Upper Canada. Ezekiel Solomons was, according to his grandson, a native of Berlin, Germany; and no doubt Levi Solomons also was born in Germany.

[W. S. Wallace (ed.), *The Maseres letters* (Toronto, 1919); A. C. Osborne, *The migration of voyageurs from Drummond island to Penetanguishene in 1828* (Ont. Hist. Soc., papers and records, 1901).]

Somerville, Alexander (1811-1885), soldier and journalist, was born at Springfield, Oldhamstock, East Lothian, Scotland, on

March 15, 1811. In 1831 he enlisted in the Scots Greys; and from 1835 to 1838 he served with the British Auxiliary Legion in Spain. He then became a journalist, and wrote under the pen-name "The whistler at the plough". He came to Canada in 1858, and in 1863 he became the editor of the *Canadian illustrated news* (Hamilton). In 1866 he served in the militia during the Fenian invasion, and was present at the engagement at Ridgeway. He died in Toronto on June 17, 1885. He published *The autobiography of a workman* (London, 1849), *The whistler at the plough* (Manchester, 1852), *Conservative science of nations, being the first complete narrative of Somerville's diligent life in the service of public safety in Britain* (Montreal, 1860), *Canada a battleground* (Hamilton, 1862), and *A narrative of the Fenian invasion of Canada* (Hamilton, 1866).

[*Dom. ann. reg.*, 1885; Morgan, *Bib. can.*; *Cyc. Am. biog.*; W. J. Rattray, *The Scot in British North America* (4 vols., Toronto, 1883).]

Sommerville, William (1800-1878), clergyman and author, was born in Ireland in 1800, and was educated at Glasgow University (M.A., 1820). He was ordained a minister of the Reformed Presbyterian Church in 1831, and he was stationed in Kings county, Nova Scotia, from 1833 to his death in 1878. He was the author of *The Psalms of David designed for standing use in the church* (Halifax, N.S., 1834), *Antipedobaptism* (Halifax, N.S., 1838), *A dissertation of the nature and administration of the ordinance of baptism* (Halifax, N.S., 1845), *The exclusive claims of David's Psalms* (Saint John, N.B., 1855), *The study of the Bible* (Saint John, N.B., 1858), *The rule of faith* (Halifax, N.S., 1859), and *Southern slavery not founded on scripture warrant* (Saint John, N.B., 1864).

[R. J. Long, *Nova Scotia authors* (East Orange, N.J., 1918); W. G. MacFarlane, *New Brunswick bibliography* (Saint John, N.B., 1895).]

Southam, William (1843-1932), journalist, was born in Montreal, Canada East, on August 23, 1843, the son of William and Mercy Southam. He was educated in London, Ontario, and became first a printer and then a journalist. He became the president and founder of the Southam chain of newspapers in Canada. He died in Hamilton, Ontario, on February 27, 1932.

[*Can. who was who*, vol. 1; Morgan, *Can. men* (1912).]

Southesk, James Carnegie, Earl of (1827-1905), author, was born in Edinburgh, Scotland, on November 16, 1827, the eldest son of Sir James Carnegie, Bart. He was educated at the Edinburgh Academy and Sandhurst, and in 1849 succeeded his father in the baronetcy. In 1855 he obtained an Act of parliament reversing the attainder of his great-grandfather, James Carnegie, fifth Earl of Southesk, who had been implicated in the Jacobite Rebellion of 1715, and became sixth Earl of Southesk *de facto* and ninth *de jure*. In 1859-60 he undertook an expedition through some of the least-known parts of western Canada; and he published an account of this expedition under the title *Saskatchewan and the Rocky mountains* (Edinburgh, 1875). His later years were devoted to the writing of poetry and to antiquarian research. He died at Kinnaird Castle, Brechin, Scotland, on February 21, 1905. In 1869 he was made a K.T., and a peer of the United Kingdom, with the title Baron Balinhard of Farnell; and he was an LL.D. of St. Andrews University (1872) and of Aberdeen University (1875).

[J. N. Wallace, *Southesk's journey through the west* (Geographical journal, 1925); *Dict. nat. biog.*, supp. ii.]

Sower, Christopher (1754-1799), first printer in New Brunswick, was born at Germantown, Pennsylvania, on January 27, 1754, of German descent. He took the loyalist side in the American Revolution, and in 1784 was appointed king's printer and postmaster-general for New Brunswick. On October 11, 1785, he began in Saint John the publication of the *Royal Gazette and New Brunswick Advertiser*; and the same year he published the first almanac to appear in New Brunswick. In 1799 he went on a visit to Philadelphia and Baltimore, and had completed arrangements with his brother, Samuel Sower, for a co-partnership in a type foundry, when he died suddenly on July 2, 1799.

[A. Fauteux, *The introduction of printing into Canada* (Montreal, 1930); W. G. MacFarlane, *New Brunswick bibliography* (Saint John, N.B., 1895).]

Spark, Alexander (1762-1819), clergyman, was born in the parish of Marykirk, Scotland, in January, 1762, and was educated at the University of Aberdeen (LL.D., 1804). He came to Canada in 1780, and in 1784 became tutor to Sir John Caldwell (q.v.). In 1795 he became minister of St. Andrew's Church in Quebec; and he continued in this charge until his death on July 7, 1819. Between the years 1791 and 1819 he published in Quebec a number of sermons.

[W. Gregg, *History of the Presbyterian church in the Dominion of Canada* (Toronto, 1885).]

Sparling, Joseph Walter (1843-1912), clergyman and educationist, was born at Blanchard, Perth county, Canada West, on February 13, 1843. He was educated at Victoria University, Cobourg (B.A., 1871; M.A., 1874) and at Northwestern University, Evanston, Illinois (B.D., 1871; D.D., 1889); and was ordained a minister of the Methodist Church in 1871. From 1874 to 1883 he was financial secretary of the General Conference of the Methodist Church in Canada; and in 1888 he was appointed principal of Wesley College, Winnipeg. He remained the principal of this college until his death at Winnipeg, Manitoba, on June 16, 1912.

[Morgan, *Can. men* (1912); *Can. who was who*, vol. 2.]

Sparrow, Malcolm Weethie (1862-1936), dental surgeon and author, was born at Athens, Ohio, on August 11, 1862. He was educated at the Royal College of Dental Surgeons, Toronto (L.D.S., 1890), and at Trinity University, Toronto (D.D.S., 1901); and practised dental surgery in Toronto. Under the pseudonym of "Max Moineau", he contributed short stories to several periodicals; and he was the author of an historical romance, *The lady of Château Blanc* (Toronto, 1896). He died at Toronto, Ontario, on July 11, 1936.

[Morgan, *Can. men* (1912).]

Spedon, Andrew Learmont (1831-1884), author and journalist, was born in Edinburgh, Scotland, on August 21, 1831. He came to Canada with his parents in early life, and for a number of years taught school at Châteauguay, Lower Canada. He published *The woodland warbler* (Montreal, 1857), *Tales of the Canadian forest* (Montreal, 1861), *Rambles among the Blue Noses* (Montreal, 1863), *Canadian summer evening tales* (Montreal, 1867), *Sketches of a tour from Canada to Paris by way of the British Isles* (Montreal, 1868), and *The Canadian minstrel* (Montreal, 1870). His health failing, he removed to Bermuda; and there he died on September 26, 1884.

[*Dom. ann. reg.*, 1884; Morgan, *Bib. can.*]

Spence, Francis Stephens (1850-1917), journalist, was born in Donegal, Ireland, on March 29, 1850. He came to Canada in early youth, was educated at the Toronto Normal School, and was for some years a school-teacher. In 1882 he became a journalist; and during his later years he devoted much of his time to the advocacy of "prohibition". From 1886 to 1907 he was the secretary of the Ontario branch of the Dominion Alliance; and in 1908 he was elected its honorary president. He died in Toronto, Ontario, on March 8, 1917. He was the author of *The facts of the case: A summary of the most important evidence and argument presented in the report of the royal commission on the liquor traffic* (Toronto, 1896).

[Ruth E. Spence, *Prohibition in Canada: A memorial to Francis Stephens Spence* (Toronto, 1919); Morgan, *Can. men* (1912).]

Spence, Robert (1811-1868), postmaster-general of Canada (1854-58), was born at Dublin, Ireland, in 1811, and came to Canada at an early age. He was, successively, an auctioneer, a school-teacher, and a journalist. He edited a newspaper in Dundas, Upper Canada, which supported the Baldwin-Lafontaine and Hincks-Morin administrations; and in August, 1854, he was elected to the Legislative Assembly of Canada for North Wentworth. A month later he was included in the MacNab-Morin administration as postmaster-general; and he continued to be a member of the succeeding Liberal-Conservative governments until 1858. He was then compelled to resign from office because of the loss of his seat in the Assembly in November, 1857. At the same time he was appointed collector of customs at the port of Toronto; and this post he held until his death at Toronto on February 25, 1868.

[N. F. Davin, *The Irishman in Canada* (Toronto, 1877); J. C. Dent, *The last forty years* (2 vols., Toronto, 1881); J. Pope, *Memoirs of the Rt. Hon. Sir J. A. Macdonald* (2 vols., Ottawa, 1894).]

Spencer, Alexander Charles (1887-1970), soldier, industrialist, and engineer, was born at London, Ontario, November 19, 1887, and educated at the Central Collegiate Institute, and at the University of Toronto (B.A. Sc., 1908). He was employed by McClary Manufacturing Company at London (1909), by Hamilton Stove and Heater Company (1911-15), and by Imperial Oil of Sarnia (1919-29). He served with the C.M.R. and the Canadian Light Horse in the First World War (major, 1918), and was mentioned in despatches. He was lieutenant-colonel in command of the 1st Hussars, 1939, and was made commanding officer of 2nd Canadian Armoured Brigade in 1941; he was commander of Camp Borden, Ontario (1942-46), and became major-general in 1945.

He was president of Spenfield Securities Limited and of James Wright and Company Limited, and director of Canada Trust, Huron and Erie Mortgage Corporation, and of London Life Insurance Company. He was chancellor of Victoria University, Toronto, from 1944 to 1952. He was made C.B.E. in 1944, and was a member of the American Society of Professional Engineers and of the Association of Professional Engineers of Ontario. He died December 12, 1970.

[*Can. who's who*, 1955-57.]

Spencer, Hiram Ladd (1829-1915), journalist and poet, was born at Castleton, Vermont, on April 28, 1829. He became a journalist, and in 1857 he came to Saint John, New Brunswick, where he edited the *Maritime Monthly* (1863-70). He retired from journalistic work in 1903, and he died at Saint John, New Brunswick, on October 15, 1915. He was the author of *Poems* (Boston, 1848), *Summer saunterings away down east* (Boston, 1850), *A son of the years, and a memory of Acadia* (Saint John, N.B., 1889), *The inglenook philosopher of Kennebecasis bay* (Saint John, N.B., 1905), and *The fugitives, a sheaf of verses* (Saint John, N.B., 1909).

[Morgan, *Can. men* (1912); W. G. MacFarlane, *New Brunswick bibliography* (Saint John, N.B., 1895).]

Spetz, Theobald (d. 1921), priest and educationist, was a member of the Congregation of the Resurrection who became, in 1890, principal of St. Jerome's College, in Berlin (Kitchener), Ontario, a college for Roman Catholics of German extraction. He retired from the principalship in 1901; and he died at Kitchener, Ontario, on November 24, 1921. He was the author of *The Catholic Church in Waterloo county* (Toronto, 1916).

[Private information.]

Spilsbury, Francis B. (1756-1823), surgeon, was born in London, England, in 1756 the eldest son of Dr. Francis Spilsbury. He studied medicine at St. Bartholomew's Hospital, and entered the British navy as an assistant surgeon in 1778. He served throughout the Napoleonic Wars, and in 1813 he was sent to Canada as surgeon attached to the fleet of Sir James Yeo (q.v.). He took part in all the naval engagements on the Great Lakes during the later stages of the War of 1812; and in 1815 he retired on half-pay. He practised medicine in Kingston, Upper Canada, until his death there in 1823. In addition to some medical papers, he was the author of *The art of etching and aquatinting* (1794). His only son, Francis B. Spilsbury (1784-1830), also served in the British navy during the Napoleonic Wars and during the Canadian War of 1812. He returned to Canada in 1819, and settled near Colborne, Upper Canada, in 1821. He was the Tory candidate for the district of Newcastle in the House of Assembly of Upper Canada in 1830; but was defeated. Shortly afterwards, on October 6, 1830, he died at his residence, Osmondsthorpe Hall, near Colborne.

[W. Canniff, *The medical profession in Upper Canada* (Toronto, 1894).]

Spinks, William Ward (1851-1937), jurist, was born in England in 1851. He qualified as a solicitor, and began practice in Liverpool; but in 1884 he emigrated with his family to British Columbia. He practised law at Kamloops, British Columbia, from 1884 to 1889; and from 1889 to 1910 he was county court judge for Yale, British Columbia. He died in Victoria, British Columbia, on December 18, 1937. He was the author of *Tales of the British Columbia frontier* (Toronto, 1933).

[Morgan, *Can. men* (1912).]

Spinney, Edgar Keith (1851-1926), politician, was born at Argyle, Yarmouth county, Nova Scotia, on January 26, 1851, the son of Harvey Spinney. He became a merchant in Yarmouth, and in 1917 was elected to represent Yarmouth and Clare as a Liberal-Unionist in the Canadian House of Commons. In 1920 he was appointed a minister without portfolio in the Meighen government; but was defeated in the general elections of 1921. He died at Yarmouth, Nova Scotia, on May 13, 1926. In 1872 he married Emma, daughter of Capt. E. Anderson, of Annapolis; and by her he had four children.

[*Can. parl. comp.*; Morgan, *Can. men* (1912).]

Spotton, Henry Byron (1844-1933), botanist, was born at Port Hope, Ontario, in 1844, and was educated at the University of Toronto (B.A., 1864; M.A., 1865). He became a school-teacher, and in 1906 was appointed inspector of high schools in Ontario. He died at Galt, Ontario, on February 24, 1933. In 1879 he was elected a fellow of the Linnaean Society; and he was the author of *The commonly occurring wild plants of Canada* (Toronto, 1888), of which the most recently revised edition has appeared under the title *Wild plants of Canada: A flora* (Toronto, 1935).

[Morgan, *Can. men* (1912).]

Spragge, Mrs. Ellen Elizabeth, *née* **Cameron** (1854-1932), author, was born in Toronto, Canada West, in 1854, the daughter of the Hon. John Hillyard Cameron (q.v.). In 1878 she married Arthur Spragge (d. 1898). She became a water-colour artist and a freelance journalist. She died in Toronto, Ontario, on May 2, 1932. In 1886 she made a trip to the Pacific coast, when the Canadian Pacific Railway was opened, which she described in *From Ontario to the Pacific by the C.P.R.* (Toronto, 1887).

[Morgan, *Can. men and women* (1912).]

Spragge, John Godfrey (1806-1884), chief justice of Ontario (1881-84), was born at New Cross, Surrey, England, on September 16, 1806, the son of Joseph Spragge. He was brought to Canada by his parents at an early age, and was educated under his father, who became headmaster of a school in York (Toronto), and under the Rev. John Strachan (q.v.). He was called to the bar of Upper Canada in 1828, and in 1850 he became treasurer of the Law Society of the province. In 1851 he was appointed vice-chancellor of Upper Canada, and in 1869 chancellor. In 1881 he became chief justice of the province, and president of the Supreme Court. He died at Toronto on April 20, 1884. He married Catherine Rosamund, daughter of Dr. Alexander Thom, medical superintendent of the military settlements of the Rideau.

[D. B. Read, *The lives of the judges of Upper Canada and Ontario* (Toronto, 1888); *Dom. ann. reg.*, 1884; Dent, *Can. port.*, vol. 4.]

Sprague, James Sylvanus (1844-1920), physician, was born at Demorestville, Prince

Edward county, Canada West, on November 27, 1844. He was educated at Victoria University, Cobourg (M.D., 1869), and Trinity University, Toronto (M.D., C.M., 1890); and first practised medicine in Humboldt county, Iowa. He later returned to Canada, and practised first at Stirling, Ontario, and then at Perth, Ontario. He died at Belleville, Ontario, on April 23, 1920. He was the author of *Medical ethics and cognate subjects* (Toronto, 1902).

[Morgan, *Can. men* (1912).]

Spratt, Michael Joseph (1854-1938), Roman Catholic archbishop of Kingston, was born near Lindsay, Canada West, on April 16, 1854. He was educated at St. Michael's College, Toronto, at the College of Lévis, and at the Grand Seminary, Montreal; and was ordained a priest in 1882. He was the pastor of several parishes in Ontario; and in 1911 he was elevated to the episcopate as archbishop of Kingston. He was compelled by ill-health to hand over the administration of the diocese to a coadjutor in 1929; and he died at Kingston, Ontario, on February 23, 1938.

[G. Brassard, *Armorial des évêques du Canada* (Montreal, 1940).]

Sproat, Gilbert Malcolm (1834-1913), author, was born in Scotland, April 19, 1834, the son of Alexander Sproat and Hectorine Shaw; and was educated at Halton Hall, Dumfries, and at King's College, London. He was appointed in 1860 government agent on the west side of Vancouver Island, and for half a century was intimately connected with British Columbian affairs. From 1866 to 1870 he was chairman of the committee on British Columbian affairs in London; and from 1872 to 1875 he was the first agent-general for the province in London. From 1885 to 1890 he was government agent and gold commissioner in the Kootenay district; and later he was interested in real estate in British Columbia. He died at Victoria on June 4, 1913. He was the author of *Select odes of Horace in English lyrics* (London, n.d.), *Scenes and studies of savage life* (London, 1868), *The education of the rural poor in England* (London, 1870), *On the poetry of Sir Walter Scott* (London, 1871), and other books.

[T. A. Rickard, *Gilbert Malcolm Sproat* (British Columbia historical quarterly, 1937); Morgan, *Can. men* (1912).]

Sproatt, Henry (1866-1934), architect, was born in Toronto, Ontario, on June 14, 1866, and was educated in Collingwood, Ontario. He returned to Toronto, however, in 1882; and he studied architecture in New York, in France, and in Italy. He became the senior partner of the firm of Sproatt and Rolph, architects; and he designed such notable buildings as Hart House, Burwash Hall, and Trinity College, in the University of Toronto, Bishop Strachan School, Ridley College Chapel, the head office of the Manufacturer's Life in Toronto, and the

National Research Council Building in Ottawa. He was a widely recognized authority on Gothic architecture; and from 1926 to 1929 he was president of the Royal Canadian Academy of Arts. He died at Toronto on October 4, 1934. In 1920 the University of Toronto conferred on him the degree of LL.D.

[*Can. who was who*, vol. 2; *Who's who in Canada*, 1932-33; N. MacTavish, *The fine arts in Canada* (Toronto, 1925).]

Sprott, John (1780-1869), clergyman, was born at Caldon Park, Stoneykirk, Wigtownshire, Scotland, on February 3, 1780. He was educated at Edinburgh University and the Divinity Hall of the Reformed Presbyterians; and was licensed to preach in the Church of Scotland in 1809. In 1818 he sailed for America as a missionary; and he spent the rest of his life in Nova Scotia, first as minister at Windsor, Newport, and Rawdon, and after 1826 as minister at Musquodoboit. He died on September 15, 1869. He was thrice married; and by his third wife he had five children, one of whom, George Washington Sprott, became a distinguished minister of the Church of Scotland (see *Dict. nat. biog.*).

[G. W. Sprott (ed.), *Memorials of the Rev. John Sprott* (Edinburgh, 1906).]

Sproule, Dorothy (1868-1963), poet, was born in Dundas county, Ontario, November 4, 1868, and was educated at Albert College, Belleville, and at Stanstead College, Quebec. In 1894 she married the Reverend Frederic Sproule, who served in various eastern Ontario congregations until his death in 1924. She began to publish her poems in 1931, the best known being *Bread and roses* (1937). She received a Coronation Medal in 1937 for her Coronation ode. During her life she published a dozen volumes of poetry and contributed to many periodical publications. She was a member of the Canadian Authors' Association. Other volumes of poetry are *Poems of life*, *The mystic star*, *The golden goal*, and *Earth and stars*. She died at Montreal, Quebec, January 3, 1963.

[*Can. who's who*, 1955-57; Metropolitan Toronto Library Board, *Biographical scrapbooks*, vol. 21; Toronto *Saturday Night*, Jan. 5, 1952.]

Sproule, Robert Auchmuty (1799-1845), artist and draughtsman, was born in Tyrone, Ireland, in 1799. He was educated at Trinity College, Dublin (B.A., 1821; M.A., 1832); and came to Canada in the late twenties. He lived for some time in Montreal, and was married there; but he died at March, Canada West, in 1845. He did miniatures on ivory; and drawings of Quebec done by him were published as coloured lithographs in Montreal in 1832. He also supplied the illustrations for Hawkins's *Picture of Quebec* (Quebec, 1834).

[G. D. Burtchaell and T. U. Sadleir (eds.), *Alumni Dublinenses* (London, 1924).]

Sproule, Thomas Simpson (1843-1917), speaker of the Canadian House of Commons (1911-17), was born in the township of King, York county, Upper Canada, on October 25, 1843, the son of James Sproule, of Tyrone, Ireland. He was educated at the University of Michigan and at Victoria University, Cobourg (M.D., 1868). He practised medicine at Markdale, Ontario, and at the same time engaged in farming and stock-raising. In 1878 he was elected as a Conservative to represent East Grey in the Canadian House of Commons, and he represented this constituency continuously for the rest of his life. From 1901 to 1911 he was grand master of the Orange Association of British North America; and from 1911 to 1917 he was speaker of the House of Commons. He died at Markdale, Ontario, on November 10, 1917. In 1881 he married Mary Alice, second daughter of William Kingston Flesher, of Flesherton.

[*Can. parl. comp.*; Morgan, *Can. men* (1912).]

Squair, John (1850-1928), educationist and author, was born at Bowmanville, Ontario, in 1850. He was educated at the University of Toronto (B.A., 1883), and from 1883 to 1901 he was lecturer, and from 1901 to 1916 professor, in French in University College, Toronto. In 1924 the French government awarded him the cross of the chevalier of the Legion of Honour. He died at Toronto on February 15, 1928. He was the author of *The study of the French-Canadian dialect* (Toronto, 1888), *Problems in the study of language* (Toronto, 1924), *The history of the townships of Darlington and Clarke* (Toronto, 1927), and *The autobiography of a teacher of French* (Toronto, 1928); and with W. H. Fraser (q.v.) he was joint author of a *French grammar* (Toronto, 1900), which has gone into many editions.

[*Can. who was who*, vol. 1; Morgan, *Can. men* (1912).]

Squires, Sir Richard Anderson (1880-1940), prime minister of Newfoundland (1919-23 and 1928-32), was born at Harbour Grace, Newfoundland, on January 18, 1880, and died at St. John's, Newfoundland, on March 26, 1940. He was educated at Dalhousie University (LL.B., 1902), and was later called to the bar in Newfoundland. He represented Trinity in the House of Assembly in Newfoundland from 1909 to 1913; in 1914 he was appointed to the Legislative Council, and became first minister of justice and attorney-general, and then colonial secretary. In 1919 he resigned from the Legislative Council to become leader of the Liberal party, and he led his party to victory in the general election. He became prime minister from 1919 to 1923, and

again from 1928 to 1932. On his defeat in 1933, he retired from political life. He was created a K.C.M.G. in 1921.

[*Who was who*, 1929-40; *Can. who's who*, 1938-39; *Newfoundland supp.*; *Encyc. Can.*]

Stafford, Ezra Adams (1839-1891), clergyman and author, was born in Elgin county, Ontario, in 1839, and in 1860 entered the Methodist ministry. Later he graduated from Victoria University, Cobourg (B.A., 1880; M.A., 1883; LL.B., 1884; LL.D., 1890). He died at Hamilton, Ontario, on December 21, 1891. He was the author of *Recreations* (Toronto, 1883) and *Ecclesiastical law* (Toronto, 1888).

[G. H. Cornish, *Cyclopaedia of Methodism in Canada* (2 vols., Toronto, 1881-1903); C. C. James, *A bibliography of Canadian poetry* (Toronto, 1899).]

Stanfield, Frank (1872-1931), lieutenant-governor of Nova Scotia (1930-31), was born at Truro, Nova Scotia, on April 24, 1872. He was a member of the Legislative Assembly of Nova Scotia from 1911 to 1928; and in 1930 he was appointed lieutenant-governor of Nova Scotia. He died, soon after taking office, on September 25, 1931.

[*Can. who was who*, vol. 1; *Can. parl. comp.*]

Stanfield, John (1868-1934), senator of Canada, was born at Charlottetown, Prince Edward Island, on May 18, 1868. He was educated at Truro, Nova Scotia, and became a manufacturer of woollen goods. He was elected to represent Colchester in the Canadian House of Commons in 1907; and he represented this constituency until 1917, when he proceeded overseas in command of an infantry battalion from Nova Scotia. In 1921 he was called to the Senate of Canada; and he sat in the Senate until his death, at Truro, Nova Scotia, on January 22, 1934.

[Morgan, *Can. men* (1912); *Can. parl. comp.*]

Stanley, Sir Charles, fourth Viscount Monck. See **Monck, Sir Charles Stanley, fourth Viscount.**

Stanser, Robert (1760-1828), second Anglican bishop of Nova Scotia, was born at Harthill, Yorkshire, England, on March 16, 1760. He was educated at St. John's College, Cambridge (LL.B., 1788); and was ordained a priest of the Church of England in 1784. In 1791 he came to Nova Scotia as rector of St. Paul's Church, Halifax; and in 1816 he became bishop of Nova Scotia, in succession to the Right Rev. Charles Inglis (q.v.). He resigned from the see of Nova Scotia in 1824, having been absent from Nova Scotia through ill-health for several years; and he died at Hampton, Middlesex, England, on December 23, 1828. He was the author of *An examination* *of the Reverend Mr. Burke's letter of instruction to the Catholic missionaries of Nova-Scotia* (Halifax, N.S., 1804).

[O. R. Rowley, *The Anglican episcopate of Canada and Newfoundland* (Milwaukee, Wis., 1928); *Gentleman's magazine*, 1829.]

Stansfield, Alfred (1871-1944), metallurgist, was born at Bradford, Yorkshire, England, in 1871. He was educated at the Royal School of Mines, London, and at London University (B.Sc., 1894; D.Sc., 1898); and in 1901 he came to Canada as professor of metallurgy in McGill University. In 1913 he was elected a fellow of the Royal Society of Canada. He retired on pension from his position in McGill University in 1936; and he died at Westmount, Quebec, on February 5, 1944. He was the author of *The electric furnace* (New York, 1907) and *The electric furnace for iron and steel* (New York, 1923).

[*Proc. Roy. Soc. Can.*, 1944; *Can. who's who*, 1936-37.]

Stanton, Robert (1794-1866), printer and publisher, was born at St. John's, Lower Canada, on June 6, 1794, the son of William Stanton, afterwards deputy assistant commissary-general in Upper Canada. He was educated at the Home District Grammar School in York; and on August 19, 1826, he was appointed King's printer for Upper Canada. From 1826 to 1843 he was the editor and publisher of the *Upper Canada Gazette*; from 1843 to 1849 he was collector of customs at Toronto; and from 1849 to his death he was an officer of the law courts at Osgoode Hall, Toronto. He died in Toronto on February 24, 1866.

[W. S. Wallace, *The periodical literature of Upper Canada* (Can. hist. rev., 1931).]

Stark, Mark Young (1799-1866), clergyman, was born in Dunfermline, Scotland, on November 9, 1799, and was educated at the University of Glasgow. He was sent to Canada in 1833 by the Glasgow Colonial Society; and from 1833 to 1863 he was the Presbyterian minister at Ancaster and Dundas, Upper Canada. In 1844 he was elected moderator of the Presbyterian synod of Canada. He died on January 24, 1866. Some of his sermons were afterwards published, with a memoir by the Rev. William Reid (Toronto, 1871).

[W. Gregg, *History of the Presbyterian church in Canada* (Toronto, 1885).]

Starke, Richard Griffin (1831-1909), poet, was born in 1831, and died in Montreal, Quebec, on December 16, 1909. He was the author of *The lord of Lanoraie* (Montreal, 1898).

[Private information.]

Starnes, Cortlandt (1864-1934), commissioner of the Royal Canadian Mounted Police

(1923-31), was born in Montreal, Canada East, on January 31, 1864. He served with the 65th Montreal Regiment in the North West Rebellion of 1885; and in 1886 was appointed an inspector of the North West Mounted Police. In 1909 he was promoted to the rank of superintendent, in 1919 to that of assistant commissioner, and in 1923 to that of commissioner of the Royal Canadian Mounted Police, as the force had been renamed in 1920. He retired in 1931, and he died at St. Hilaire, Quebec, on May 28, 1934.

[*Who's who in Canada*, 1932-33.]

Starnes, Henry (1816-1896), politician and financier, was born in Kingston, Upper Canada, on October 13, 1816. He was educated at the Montreal College, and was for many years a merchant and banker in Montreal. From 1857 to 1863 he represented Châteauguay in the Legislative Assembly of united Canada; and in 1867 he was appointed a member of the Legislative Council of the province of Quebec. From 1878 to 1879 he was president of this Council. He died on March 3, 1896.

[Rose, *Cyc. Can. biog.* (1888); *Can. parl. comp.*; *Brit. Am.*, vol. 3.]

Starr, George Lothrop (1872-1925), clergyman and author, was born at Brockville, Ontario, in 1872, a grand-nephew of Sir Daniel Jones (q.v.). He was educated at Trinity University, Toronto (B.A., 1895; M.A., 1896), and was ordained a priest of the Church of England in 1896. In 1901 he became vicar of St. George's Church, Kingston, and later dean of Ontario. He died at Boston, Massachusetts, on November 19, 1925. He was the author of *Old St. George's* (Kingston, Ont., 1913).

[Morgan, *Can. men* (1912).]

Stavert, Sir William Ewen (1861-1937), banker, was born at Summerside, Prince Edward Island, on April 9, 1861. He entered the service of the Bank of Nova Scotia, and opened branches of the bank in Jamaica in 1889 and in Newfoundland in 1895. From 1901 to 1905 he was general manager of the Bank of New Brunswick; and he then entered the service of the Bank of Montreal. He was employed as curator or liquidator of banks and other corporations taken over by the Bank of Montreal; and during the First World War he was accounting officer to the British Treasury as a member of the British Ministry of Information. For his services in this position he was created in 1919 a K.B.E. After the war he was employed in various capacities in Canada as a financial expert; and he died at Montreal, Quebec, on December 30, 1937.

[*Who was who*, 1939-40; *Can. who's who*, 1936-37.]

Steacie, Edgar William Richard (1900-1962), chemist, was born in Westmount, Quebec, on December 25, 1900. He was educated at Royal Military College, Kingston, Ontario and at McGill University, Montreal, (B.Sc., 1923; Ph.D., 1926). On graduation he was appointed to the staff of McGill, becoming associate professor in 1937. In 1939 he became director of the division of chemistry of the National Research Council of Canada; he became vice-president (scientific) in 1950 and president in 1952, a position he held until his death. Dr. Steacie played a leading role in the Canada-United Kingdom Atomic Energy project from 1944 to 1946. His monograph *Atomic and free-radical reactions* published in 1946 became a standard work. He originated the idea of National Research Council postdoctoral fellowships to encourage young scientists from other parts of the world to work in Canadian laboratories. Dr. Steacie worked hard to strengthen the research programs in Canadian universities and to develop a government laboratory which would place a strong emphasis upon basic research. He was opposed to the continuation of measures of secrecy which were introduced to scientific affairs during the Second World War, and he spearheaded an agreement between the Soviet Academy of Sciences and the National Research Council for the exchange of scientists between the Soviet Union and Canada. He was at various times president of the Royal Society of Canada, the Chemical Institute of Canada, and the Farraday Society. In 1951-53 he was vice-president of the International Union of Pure and Applied Chemistry and in 1961 was elected president of the International Council of Scientific Unions. He endeavoured to organize and administer science so as to provide the maximum amount of freedom for scientists and to preserve the integrity of the scientific approach and method. His viewpoint is well described in *Science in Canada: Selections from the speeches of Dr. E. W. R. Steacie* (J. D. Babbitt (ed.), Toronto, 1965). He died at Ottawa, Ontario, in August, 1962.

[*Proc. Roy. Soc. Can.*, 1962.]

Stead, Robert James Campbell (1880-1959), poet and novelist, was born at Middleville, Lanark county, Ontario, on September 4, 1880, and died at Ottawa, Ontario, on June 26, 1959. He was brought up on a homestead in Manitoba, and became a journalist in the West. In 1913 he joined the colonization department of the Canadian Pacific Railway, and in 1919 he became a civil servant in the employ of the federal department of immigration and colonization at Ottawa. From 1936 until his retirement in 1946 he was superintendent of publicity for national parks and resources. He was the author of five volumes of poetry: *The empire builders and other poems* (Toronto, 1908), *Prairie born and other poems* (Toronto, 1911), *Songs of the prairie* (Toronto, 1911), *Kitchener and other poems* (Toronto, 1917), and *Why don't they cheer?*

Poems (Toronto, 1918); and he published the following novels: *The bail jumper* (Toronto, 1914), *The homesteaders* (Toronto, 1916), *The cow puncher* (New York, 1918), *Dennison Grant* (Toronto, 1920), *Neighbours* (Toronto, 1922), *The smoking flax* (Toronto, 1924), *Grain* (Toronto, 1926), and *The copper disc* (New York, 1931).

[Clara Thomas, *Canadian novelists* (Toronto, 1946); *Can. who's who*, 1958-60; *Encyc. Can.*]

Steele, Sir Samuel Benfield (1849-1919), soldier, was born at Purbrook, Simcoe county, Canada West, on January 5, 1849, the fourth son of Capt. Elmes Steele, R.N., and Anne Macdonald. He obtained a commission as an ensign in the 35th Regiment of Militia in 1866, and he served during the Fenian Raid of 1866, and in the Red River expedition of 1870. In 1873 he became a troop sergeant-major in the Royal North West Mounted Police; and in 1885 he became superintendent in command of this force. He commanded the cavalry during the North West Rebellion of 1885. During the South African War he commanded Strathcona's Horse; and from 1901 to 1906 he was in command of the South African constabulary. In 1907 he returned to Canada and in 1915 he was appointed to the command of the Second Canadian Contingent in the First World War, with the rank of major-general. In 1916 he was made general officer commanding in the Shorncliffe area; and he died at London, England, on January 30, 1919. In 1890 he married Marie Elizabeth, daughter of Robert W. Harwood, seignior of Vaudreuil. In 1900 he was created a C.B., and in 1917 a K.C.M.G. He published his reminiscences under the title *Forty years in Canada* (Toronto, 1915).

[R. G. MacBeth, *Sir Samuel Benfield Steele* (Can. mag., 1919); *Can. who was who, vol. 1; Morgan, Can. men* (1912).]

Steenwyck, Cornelis (d. 1684), Dutch governor of Nova Scotia and Acadia, was a native of Holland who emigrated to New Amsterdam (New York) about 1652. He became a prominent merchant, and in 1676 the Dutch West India Company appointed him "governor of Nova Scotia and Acadie", which had been overrun by a force under Dutch auspices in 1674-75, and re-named New Holland. He made no attempt to assert his authority, and in three or four years the French were again in occupation of Acadia. He died in New York in 1684.

[J. C. Webster, *Cornelis Steenwyck, Dutch governor of Acadie* (Shediac, N.B., 1929).]

Steeves, William Henry (1814-1873), one of the fathers of Confederation, was born at Hillsborough, New Brunswick, on May 20, 1814. He went into business, and became a member of the firm of Steeves Brothers. From 1846 to 1851 he represented Albert county as a Liberal in the Legislative Assembly of New

Brunswick, and from 1851 to 1867 he was a member of the Legislative Council of the province. He was a member of the Executive Council of New Brunswick almost continuously from 1857 to 1865, holding the portfolio of surveyor-general from 1854 to 1855, and that of commissioner of public works from 1855 to 1856 and from 1857 to 1863. He was a delegate from New Brunswick at the Intercolonial Railway conference in Quebec in 1862, at the Charlottetown Conference on maritime union in 1864, and at the Quebec Conference on British North American union later in the same year. On the completion of Confederation in 1867, he was called to the Senate of Canada; and he remained a member of the Senate until his death at Saint John, New Brunswick, on December 9, 1873.

[*Can. parl. comp.*, 1872; J. H. Gray, *Confederation* (Toronto, 1872); J. Hannay, *History of New Brunswick* (2 vols., Saint John, N.B., 1909); *Dict. Can. biog.*, vol. 10.]

Stefansson, Vilhjalmur (1879-1962), explorer, was born at Arnes, Manitoba, November 3, 1879. His parents were among Icelandic settlers who had arrived at Gimli, Manitoba, in 1875. In 1881 they moved to North Dakota, where he was educated, entering the preparatory school of the University of North Dakota in 1897. In 1902 he enrolled at Iowa University, graduating in 1903. He went to Harvard University the same year to study comparative religion but transferred to the Graduate School in Anthropology, remaining for two years. His first trip to the Arctic was with the Anglo-American Arctic Expedition of 1906. The expedition was abandoned because of shipwreck and loss of supplies, but Stefansson spent the winter of 1906-07 living with two Eskimo families. He returned to the Arctic with R. M. Anderson (q.v.) in 1908 as a two-man exploratory party under the sponsorship of the American Museum of Natural History and the Canadian government. They remained in the Arctic until June of 1912. In 1913 Stefansson went back to the Arctic in charge of a Canadian government expedition to explore the Beaufort Sea and the northern coast of Canada. This group remained in the Arctic until the summer of 1918, exploring new land masses in the little-known mid-Arctic and proving that southern man could live off the land in the Arctic. Stefansson, the last of the old school of Arctic explorers who worked with dog and sledge, was a controversial figure among his co-workers and sponsors because of his extremely independent attitude to his work and the way in which he contradicted the theories of Arctic exploration evolved over the previous three centuries. His findings, now more generally accepted, are described in his books. He was the author of *My life with the Eskimos* (New York, 1913); *Prehistoric and present commerce among the Arctic Eskimo* (New York, 1914); *Stefansson-*

Anderson Arctic expedition of the American Museum (New York, 1914); *The friendly Arctic* (New York, 1921); *Hunters of the great north* (New York, 1922); *The northward course of Empire* (New York, 1922); *Kak, the copper Eskimo*, with Violet Mary Irwin (New York, 1924); *The adventure of Wrangel Island*, with J. I. Knight (New York, 1925); *The standardization of error* (Toronto, 1927); *Adventures in error* (Detroit, 1936); *The three voyages of Martin Frobisher* (New York, 1938); *Iceland: The first American republic* (Westport, Connecticut, 1939); *The problem of Meighen Island* (New York, 1939); *Unsolved mysteries of the Arctic* (New York, 1939); *Ultima Thule* (New York, 1940); *Greenland* (New York, 1942); *Arctic Manual* (Washington, 1944); *The Arctic in fact and fable* (New York, 1945); *Not by bread alone* (New York, 1946); *Great adventures and explorations* (ed.) (New York, 1947). Stefansson promoted the importation of reindeer into the Arctic as a source of food for the Eskimos and Indians. This venture was not successful, nor was his effort to have the Canadian government assert sovereignty over Wrangel Island off the Asiatic coast. He continued as unofficial "ambassador of the north" until his death at Hanover, New Hampshire, on August 26, 1962.

[D.M. LeBourdais, *Stefansson, ambassador of the north* (Toronto, 1963); *Can. who's who*, 1955-57; N. Story, *The Oxford companion to Canadian history and literature* (Toronto, 1967).]

Steinhauer, Henry Bird (1804-1885), missionary, was born in the Rama Indian settlement, Lake Simcoe, Upper Canada, in 1804, a pure-blooded Indian of the Chippewa tribe. He received the name of Steinhauer from a German family that adopted and educated him. In 1840 he accompanied the Rev. James Evans (q.v.) to the North West, and settled at Norway House. Here he remained until 1855 assisting in the elaboration of the Cree syllabic characters. In 1858 he was ordained a minister of the Methodist Church, and was stationed at Whitefish Lake, North West Territories. Here he died on December 29, 1885. He translated into Cree a large part of the Old and the New Testaments.

[*Dom. ann. reg.*, 1885; *Cyc. Am. biog.*]

Stephansson, Stephan Gudmundsson (1853-1927), poet, was born in Iceland on October 3, 1853, and emigrated to the United States in 1873. He engaged in farming, first in Wisconsin, then in North Dakota, and finally in the Canadian North West. In 1889 he settled in what is now Alberta, near Innisfail; and here he lived until his death on August 10, 1927. He became a poet "unsurpassed by any other Icelandic poet since the Middle Ages". His first volume of verse was published in Reykjavik, Iceland, in 1898; and other volumes followed in 1900, in 1909-10, in 1914, in 1917, and in 1920. All his work was in Icelandic.

[Watson Kirkconnell, *Canada's leading poet: Stephan G. Stephansson* (University of Toronto quarterly, 1936).]

Stephen, Alexander Maitland (1882-1942), poet and novelist, was born near Hanover, Ontario, on May 8, 1882. He was educated at the Walkerton Collegiate Institute; and when a young man went west. He was successively a cowboy, a homesteader, a prospector, a school-teacher, and a lecturer. He was the author of the following volumes of verse: *The rosary of Pan* (Toronto, 1923), *The land of singing waters* (Toronto, 1927), *Brown earth and bunch grass* (Vancouver, B.C., 1931), and *Vérendrye, a poem of the new world* (Toronto, 1935). He was also the author of two novels, *The kingdom of the sun* (Toronto, 1927) and *The gleaming archway* (Toronto, 1929), and of two volumes of plays, *Class-room plays from Canadian history* (Toronto, 1929) and *Canadian industrial plays* (Toronto, 1931); and he compiled two anthologies, *The voice of Canada* (Toronto, 1926) and *The golden treasury of Canadian verse* (Toronto, 1929). He died in Vancouver, July 1, 1942.

[*Can. who's who*, 1936-37; *Who's who among North American authors*, vol. 5.]

Stephen, Sir George, Bart., afterwards **Baron Mount Stephen** (1829-1921), financier, was born at Dufftown, Banffshire, Scotland, on June 5, 1829, the son of William Stephen and Elspet Smith. He received a grammar school education, and emigrated to Canada in 1850. He entered the firm of William Stephen and Co., manufacturers of woollen goods, Montreal; and ultimately purchased a controlling interest. In 1873 he was elected a director of the Bank of Montreal, and from 1876 to 1881 he was its president. Together with his relative, Lord Strathcona (q.v.), he was a member of the syndicate which took over the St. Paul and Manitoba Railway, and in 1880 of the company which undertook the construction of the Canadian Pacific Railway. He was president of the Canadian Pacific Railway Company from 1881 to 1888. In 1888 he went to live in England, and his later years were largely occupied with philanthropy. He died at Brocket Hall, Hatfield, Herefordshire, England, on November 29, 1921. He was twice married, (1) in 1853 to Annie Charlotte (d. 1896), daughter of Benjamin Kane, London, England; and (2) in 1897 to Gian, daughter of Capt. Robert George Tufnell, R.N. In 1886 he was created a baronet of the United Kingdom; in 1891 Baron Mount Stephen, in the peerage of the United Kingdom; and in 1905 a G.C.V.O. In 1911 he was made an LL.D. of Aberdeen University.

[*Who was who*, 1916-28; *Debrett's Peerage* (1921); Morgan, *Can. men* (1912); Rose, *Cyc. Can. biog.* (1888); B. Wilson, *The life of Lord*

Strathcona (London, 1915); W. T. R. Preston, *The life and times of Lord Strathcona* (London, 1914); H. A. Innis, *The history of the Canadian Pacific Railway* (London, 1923); H. Gilbert, *The awakening continent, the life of Lord Mount Stephen* (vol. I, 1828-91, Aberdeen, 1965).

Stephens, Charles Henry (d. 1914), lawyer and author, was born in Montreal, Canada West, and was educated at McGill University (B.C.L., 1875). He was called to the bar of Quebec in 1876 (Q.C., 1893), and practised law in Montreal for many years. He died in Montreal, Quebec, on May 2, 1914. He was the author of *The Quebec law digest* (4 vols., Montreal, 1878-91) and *The law and practice of joint stock companies* (Toronto, 1881).

[Morgan, *Can. men* (1912).]

Stephens, George Washington (1866-1942), public official, was born in Montreal, Quebec, on August 3, 1866, the son of the Hon. G. W. Stephens. He was educated at McGill University and at universities in France, Germany, and Switzerland. He inherited a large estate from his father, and became an investment and real estate broker. From 1907 to 1912 he was chairman of the Montreal Harbour Commission; and in 1914 he was an unsuccessful candidate for the mayoralty of Montreal. In 1923 he was appointed a member of the Governing Commission of the Saar; and from 1924 to 1926 he was its president. He died at Los Angeles, California, on February 6, 1942. He was the author of *The St. Lawrence waterway project* (Montreal, 1929).

[*Can. who's who*, 1936-37; Morgan, *Can. men* (1912).]

Stephens, William A. (1809-1891), poet, was born in Belfast, Ireland, in 1809, and came to Canada in early youth. He contributed verse to many early Upper Canadian newspapers, and was one of the earliest writers of verse in the province. He died on March 21, 1891, at Owen Sound, Ontario, where he had been for many years collector of customs. He was the author of *Hamilton, and other poems* (Toronto, 1840), *A poetical geography, and Rhyming rules for spelling* (Toronto, 1848), *Hamilton, and other poems and lectures* (Toronto, 1871), and *The Centennial: An international poem* (Toronto, 1878).

[C. C. James, *A bibliography of Canadian poetry* (Toronto, 1899).]

Stevens, Dorothy (1889-1966), artist, was born in Toronto, Ontario, September 2, 1889. She was educated in Toronto, Vancouver, at the Slade School of Art, London, at the Colorossi Studio, and at the Grande Chaumière, Paris. She became a well-known portrait painter and etcher and exhibited in Europe and the United States as well as in Canada. She is represented in the National Gallery of

Canada, the Ontario Art Gallery, and the Edmonton Art Gallery. She became an associate of the Royal Canadian Academy in 1931 and a full member in 1949. She taught at the Women's Art Association and Artist's Workshop in Toronto, at the Doon School, and at Actinolite, Ontario. She was a member of the Canadian Society of Etchers and of the Society of American Etchers. In later years she was best known for her portraits of children of Mexico and the Caribbean, for although she maintained a Toronto studio she travelled extensively in Latin America. In 1930 she married R. de Bruno Austin. She died at Toronto, Ontario, June 5, 1966.

[Metropolitan Toronto Library Board, *Biographical scrapbooks*, vols. 16 and 60; *Can. who's who*, 1955-57.]

Stevens, Henry Herbert (1878-1973), cabinet minister and party leader, was born in Bristol, England, December 8, 1878. He came to Canada in 1887 and attended school at Peterborough, Ontario. The Stevens family moved to British Columbia in 1894. After serving with the American army in the Boxer Rebellion, Stevens returned to Vancouver and went into the grocery business; he later added real estate and insurance to his business interests and became involved in civic affairs. He was elected to the House of Commons for Vancouver (1911-30) and for East Kootenay (1930-40). He was minister of trade and commerce in the Meighen (q.v.) administration of 1921 and minister of customs and excise in the Meighen administration of 1926. From 1930 to 1934 he was minister of trade and commerce in the Bennett (q.v.) administration. He was chairman of the price-spreads commission (1934), and a disagreement with the Cabinet on his findings led to his resignation and the establishment of the Reconstruction party, which he led into the 1935 general election. As the only member of his party elected he rejoined the Conservative party in 1938. He was president of the Vancouver Board of Trade (1952-53) and was an unsuccessful candidate in the general election of 1953. He died at Vancouver, British Columbia, June 14, 1973.

[*Can. who's who*, 1967-69; *Encyc. Can.* (1972); Metropolitan Toronto Library Board, *Biographical scrapbooks*, vols. 2, 6, and 11.]

Stevens, James Gray (1822-1906), jurist, was born at Edinburgh, Scotland, on February 25, 1822. He emigrated to New Brunswick in 1840, and began the study of law in St. Stephen, New Brunswick. He was called to the bar in 1847 (Q.C., 1867); and he represented Charlotte county in the New Brunswick Assembly from 1861 to 1865 and from 1866 to 1867. In 1867 he was appointed a judge of the county court; and he sat on the bench until shortly before his death, at St. Stephen, New Brunswick, on October 16, 1906. He was the author of *Digest of the reported and unreported cases determined in the Supreme court of judicature of the province of New Brunswick* (Saint John, N.B., 1874). *Index to the statutes, rules, orders, regulations, treaties, and proclamations of the Dominion of Canada* (St. Stephen, N.B., 1876), and *Indictable offences and summary convictions* (Toronto, 1880).

[Morgan, *Can. men* (1898); W. G. MacFarlane, *New Brunswick bibliography* (Saint John, N.B., 1895).]

Stevens, Paul (1830-1882), author, was born in Belgium in 1830. He emigrated to Canada as a young man, and became the editor, first of *La Patrie*, and then of *L'Artiste*, in Montreal, Lower Canada. He published *Fables (en vers)* (Montreal, 1857) and *Contes populaires* (Ottawa, 1867). He died at Coteau du Lac, Lower Canada, where he was a tutor to the Beaujeu family, in 1882.

[Morgan, *Bib. can.*; *Cyc. Am. biog.*; E. Lareau, *Histoire de la littérature canadienne* (Montreal, 1873).]

Stevenson, John (1812-1884), speaker of the Legislative Assembly of Ontario (1867-71), was born in Hunterdon county, New Jersey, on August 12, 1812, the son of Edward Stevenson. He came to Canada with his parents at an early age, and went into business in the Bay of Quinte district. In 1863 he became the first warden of the united counties of Lennox and Addington; and in 1867 he was elected to represent Lennox in the Legislative Assembly of Ontario. Though without parliamentary experience, he was chosen the first speaker of the Assembly, and he presided over it until his defeat in the elections of 1871. He died at Napanee, Ontario, on April 1, 1884. In 1841 he married Phoebe Eliza Hall; and by her he had seven children, two of whom died in infancy.

[W. S. Herrington, *Some notes on the first Legislative Assembly of Ontario and its speaker, Hon. John Stevenson* (Trans. Roy. Soc. Can., 1915); *Dom. ann. reg.*, 1884.]

Stevenson, Orlando John (1869-1950), educationist and author, was born at Wardsville, Ontario, in 1869, and died at Guelph, Ontario, on August 15, 1950. He was educated at the University of Toronto (B.A., 1893; M.A., 1894; D.Paed., 1904); and he became a secondary-school teacher. In 1907 he was appointed an associate professor of education in Queen's University; and when in 1910 the teaching of pedagogy was discontinued at Queen's, he was appointed a lecturer in the Ontario College of Education in Toronto and head of the English department in the University of Toronto Schools. In 1916 he was appointed professor of English in the Ontario Agricultural College at Guelph; and this chair he held for nearly a quarter of a century. He was the author of a collection of biographical essays, entitled *A people's best* (Toronto, 1927), a small volume of verse, *The unconquerable north, and other poems* (Toronto, 1938), a biography of Alexander Graham Bell, entitled *The talking wire* (Toronto, 1947), and a number of school text-books, including the *Ontario high school grammar* (Toronto, 1911). After his death a selection of his contributions to the *O.A.C. Review* were edited for publication by his wife, under the title *Through the years* (Toronto, 1952). He was elected a fellow of the Royal Society of Canada in 1935.

[*Proc. Roy. Soc. Can.*, 1951; *Can. who's who*, 1948.]

Stewart, Alexander (d. 1840), fur-trader, entered the service of the North West Company as an apprentice clerk in 1796. In 1806 D.W. Harmon (q.v.) met him at Fort des Prairies. Later, he was placed in charge of a post on Lesser Slave Lake; and in 1812, though still a clerk, he was placed in charge of the Athabaska River department. He was made a partner of the North West Company in 1813; and was transferred to the Columbia, where he was present at the capture of Fort Astoria. In 1815 he returned to Lesser Slave Lake, and there he remained for several years. At the time of the union of 1821, he was made a chief factor of the Hudson's Bay Company. From 1821 to 1823 he was in charge at Fort William; from 1823 to 1826, at Island Lake; from 1826 to 1830, at Fort Chipewyan; and from 1831 to 1832, at Moose Factory. He was granted furlough in 1832; and he retired from the Company's service in 1833. He died in May, 1840. His name is frequently misspelled "Stuart".

[W. S. Wallace (ed.), *Documents relating to the North West Company* (Toronto: The Champlain Society, 1934).]

Stewart, Alexander (d. 1840), clergyman and author, was born in the Highlands of Scotland, and became a missionary among his fellow-countrymen. He came to Canada prior to 1827, and for several years he was minister of the first Baptist church in York (Toronto), Upper Canada. He resigned from this charge, however, in 1836; and he died at Toronto, Upper Canada, on June 19, 1840. He was the author of an early Upper Canada imprint, *Two essays: the first, on the Gospel; the second, on the Kingdom of Christ; and a sermon on baptism; with an appendix containing remarks on late publications of York* (York, U.C., 1827).

[J. Ross Robertson, *Landmarks of Toronto*, 4th series (Toronto, 1904).]

Stewart, Alexander (1794-1865), politician and jurist, was born in Halifax, Nova Scotia, on January 30, 1794, the son of the Rev. James Stewart. He was educated at the Halifax grammar school, and was admitted an attorney-at-law in Halifax in 1821. In 1826 he was elected to represent Cumberland in the Nova Scotia House of Assembly, and he sat in this House until he was appointed a member of the Legislative Council in 1837. Throughout his political career he was a prominent Reformer; but in 1840 he was sworn a member of the Executive Council of the province. In 1846 he resigned from the Legislative and Executive councils, to accept appointment as master of the rolls in Nova Scotia; and he occupied this position until the abolition of the Court of Chancery in 1855. He continued a judge of the Vice-Admiralty Court until his death at Halifax on January 1, 1865. In 1856 he was created a C.B.

[C. J. Townshend, *Life of Honorable Alexander Stewart, C.B.* (Coll. Nova Scotia Hist. Soc., vol. xv, 1911).]

Stewart, Alexander Charles (1867-1944), contractor and poet, was born in county Down, Ireland, on August 16, 1867. He came to Canada when a small child, and was educated in Pickering township, Ontario. He became a tunnel and bridge contractor at Fort William, Ontario; and in the intervals of contracting he wrote poetry. He died at Port Dover, Ontario, on June 12, 1944. He was the author of *The poetical works of A. C. Stewart* (Toronto, 1890), *The poetical review: A brief notice of Canadian poets and poetry* (Toronto, 1896), *Dust and ashes* (Toronto, 1910), *The shell* (Toronto, 1917), and *The beaver, and other odds and ends* (Toronto, 1918).

[J. W. Garvin (ed.), *Canadian poems of the great war* (Toronto, 1918); C. C. James, *A bibliography of Canadian poetry* (Toronto, 1899).]

Stewart, Andrew (1789?-1822), fur-trader, was born in Glasgow, Scotland, about 1789, and entered the service of the Hudson's Bay Company in 1811, as a writer at Moose Factory. In 1814-15 he was the master at Moose, and in 1815-16 at Missakami Lake. In 1816-17 he was at Kenogamissee; and from 1817 to 1821 he was at Michipicoten. He was promoted to the rank of chief trader in 1821; and he died at Osnaburgh House on May 24, 1822.

[E. E. Rich (ed.), *Colin Robertson's correspondence book* (Toronto: The Champlain Society, 1939).]

Stewart, Charles (1868-1946), prime minister of Alberta (1917-21), was born at Strabane, Ontario, on August 26, 1868, and died at Ottawa, Ontario, on December 6, 1946. He became a farmer in Alberta about 1900; and in 1909 he began his political career on election to the Legislative Assembly of Alberta as a Liberal. He became a member of the Sifton government in 1913, and in 1917 he succeeded A. L. Sifton (q.v.) as prime minister. He was defeated by the United Farmers of Alberta in 1921; but was later in the year appointed minister of the interior in the federal cabinet of Mackenzie King (q.v.). This portfolio he retained until 1930, except for a few months in

1926, when Arthur Meighen (q.v.) was prime minister. He was elected to represent Edmonton West in the elections of 1925, 1926, and 1930, but was defeated in 1935; and he was then appointed chairman of the Canadian section of the International Joint Commission, a post he held until his death.

[*Can. who's who*, 1938-39; *Can. parl. comp.*, 1934; *Encyc. Can.*]

Stewart, Charles James (1775-1837), Anglican bishop of Quebec (1826-37), was born in Scotland, on April 15, 1775, the fifth son of John Stewart, seventh Earl of Galloway. He was educated at Oxford University (M.A., 1799), and took holy orders in the Church of England. He came to Canada in 1808 as a missionary under the Society for the Propagation of the Gospel, and was stationed in St. Armand in the Eastern Townships. In 1819 he was appointed visiting missionary in the diocese of Quebec; and in 1826 he succeeded Bishop Mountain as bishop of Quebec. He died at London, England, on July 13, 1837. In 1817 he was made a D.D. of Oxford University. Besides several sermons and missionary reports, he published *A short view of the present state of the Eastern Townships* (Montreal, 1815) and a *Letter on the differences of opinion respecting the clergy reserves and other points* (Quebec, 1827). He was not married.

[J. N. Norton, *Life of Bishop Stewart of Quebec* (New York, 1859); W. J. D. Waddilove, *The Stewart missions* (London, 1838); C. H. Mockridge, *The bishops of the Church of England in Canada* (Toronto, 1896); Morgan, *Cel. Can.* and *Bib. can.*; *Cyc. Am. biog.*; T. R. Millman, *Life of the Rt. Rev. the Hon. Charles James Stewart* (London, Ont., 1953).]

Stewart, Elihu (1844-1935), land surveyor and author, was born at Sombra, Lambton county, Canada West, on November 17, 1844. He was educated at Toronto, and became a dominion and provincial land surveyor in 1872. From 1899 to 1907 he was superintendent of the Forestry Branch of the Department of the Interior, and was president of the Canadian Forestry Association in 1905. In his later days, he was engaged in business as a forestry expert. He died at Collingwood, Ontario, on July 9, 1935. He was the author of *Down the Mackenzie and up the Yukon* (Toronto, 1913).

[Morgan, *Can. men* (1912).]

Stewart, Mrs. Frances, *née* **Browne** (1794-1872), pioneer, was born in Dublin, Ireland, on May 24, 1794. In 1816 she married Thomas Alexander Stewart (d. 1847); and with him she emigrated to Upper Canada in 1822. She died at Peterborough, Ontario, on February 24, 1872. Extracts from her letters and journals were published by her daughter, Mrs. E. S. Dunlop, after her death, under the title *Our forest home* (Toronto, 1889; 2nd ed., Montreal, 1902).

[F. Stewart, *Our forest home* (2nd ed., Montreal, 1902).]

Stewart, George (1848-1906), journalist and author, was born in New York City, on November 26, 1848, the son of George Stewart and Elizabeth Dubuc. He came to Canada with his parents in 1851, was educated at London, Upper Canada, and at Saint John, New Brunswick, and became a journalist. In 1867 he founded and edited *Stewart's Literary Quarterly Magazine* (1867-72), and he was subsequently editor-in-chief of *Rose-Belford's Canadian Monthly* (Toronto, 1878). From 1879 to 1896 he was editor of the Quebec *Daily Chronicle*. He was a voluminous contributor to periodicals, encyclopaedias, and biographical dictionaries; and he was the author of the following books: *The story of the great fire in St. John, New Brunswick* (Montreal, 1877), *Canada under the administration of the Earl of Dufferin* (Toronto, 1878), *An account of the public dinner to H. E. the Count of Premio Real* (Quebec, 1881), *Essays from reviews* (Quebec, 1892; 2nd series, 1893). In 1882 he was made a charter member of the Royal Society of Canada; and he was the recipient of honorary degrees from Laval University, McGill University, Bishop's College, Lennoxville, and King's College, Nova Scotia. He died at Quebec on February 26, 1906.

[*Proc. Roy. Soc. Can.*, 1906; *Can. who was who*, vol. 1; Morgan, *Can. men* (1898); Rose, *Cyc. Can. biog.* (1888); W. G. MacFarlane, *New Brunswick bibliography* (Saint John, N.B., 1895).]

Stewart, Harriet (1862?-1931), feminist, was born about 1862, and was educated at Mount Allison University, New Brunswick (B.A., 1882). She was reputed to be the first woman in the British Empire to receive the degree of bachelor of arts. She died at Regina, Saskatchewan, on November 1, 1931.

[*Can. ann. rev.*, 1932.]

Stewart, Herbert Leslie (1882-1953), educationist and author, was born in Ireland on March 31, 1882, and died at Halifax, Nova Scotia, on September 19, 1953. He was educated at Lincoln College, Oxford (B.A., 1905), and the Royal University of Ireland (M.A., 1905; Ph.D., 1907). He was a lecturer in moral philosophy at the University of Belfast from 1909 to 1913; and in 1913 he came to Canada as professor of philosophy at Dalhousie University. This chair he held until his retirement in 1947. In 1921 he founded the *Dalhousie Review*; and he was its editor for twenty-six years. In 1920 he was elected a fellow of the Royal Society of Canada, and he was elected president of Section II in 1936. He was the author of *Questions of the day in philosophy and psychology* (London, 1912), *Nietzsche and* the ideals of modern Germany (London, 1915), Anatole France (New York, 1927), A century of Anglo-Catholicism (London, 1929), Modernism, past and present (London, 1932), From a library window (Toronto, 1940), The Irish in Nova Scotia (Halifax, 1949), and Winged words (Toronto, 1953).

[Proc. Roy. Soc. Can., 1954; Can. who's who, 1949-51; Encyc. Can.]

Stewart, Hugh Alexander (1871-1956), lawyer and politician, was born at Elizabethtown, Ontario, on September 29, 1871, and died at Brockville, Ontario, on September 4, 1956. He studied law at Osgoode Hall, Toronto, was called to the bar in 1893 (K.C., 1908), and practised law in Brockville. He became mayor of Brockville in 1905, and represented Leeds in the Canadian House of Commons as a Conservative from 1921 to 1940. He was minister of public works throughout the Bennett administration, from 1930 to 1935.

[Can. who's who, 1952-54; Can. parl. comp., 1940; Encyc. Can.]

Stewart, James David (1874-1933), prime minister of Prince Edward Island (1923-27 and 1931-33), was born at Lower Montague, Prince Edward Island, and was educated at Prince of Wales College, Charlottetown, and at Dalhousie University. He was called to the bar; and in 1917 he was elected a member of the Legislative Assembly of Prince Edward Island for South King's. He sat continuously in the Assembly until his death; and in 1921 he was elected leader of the Conservative opposition. From 1923 to 1927 and from 1931 to 1933 he was prime minister and attorney-general. He died on October 10, 1933.

[Can. parl. comp.]

Stewart, James G. (d. 1881), fur-trader and explorer, was a servant of the Hudson's Bay Company. He was the assistant of Robert Campbell (q.v.) in his exploration of the Yukon River in 1850; and the Stewart River, in the Yukon, was named after him. He was also one of the Hudson's Bay Company's expedition of 1855 in search of Sir John Franklin (q.v.). He was promoted to the rank of chief factor in 1869; but later left the service of the Hudson's Bay Company, and was appointed Indian agent at Edmonton, North West Territories. He died at Edmonton in 1881.

[Dom. ann. reg., 1880-81.]

Stewart, John (1758?-1834), author, was born about 1758, and settled in Prince Edward Island in 1778. He was speaker of the House of Assembly from 1795 to 1798, and again from 1824 to 1830; and he died on the island in 1834. He was the author of An account of Prince Edward Island, in the gulf of St. Lawrence (London, 1806).

[Morgan, Bib. can.; A. B. Warburton, History of Prince Edward Island (Saint John, N.B., 1923).]

Stewart, John (1794?-1858), legislative and executive councillor of Lower Canada, was born in Quebec about 1794. During the War of 1812 he was deputy paymaster-general of the Lower Canadian militia. In 1825 he was appointed a member of the Legislative Council of Lower Canada, and in 1826 a member of the Executive Council. At the time of the outbreak of the rebellion of 1837, he was acting as president of the Executive Council. He ceased to be a legislative councillor in 1838, and an executive councillor in 1841. He died at Quebec on January 5, 1858.

[Morgan, Cel. Can.]

Stewart, John Alexander (d. 1922), minister of railways and canals for Canada (1921), was born at Renfrew, Ontario, the son of Robert Stewart. He was educated at the University of Ottawa, studied law at Osgoode Hall, Toronto, and was called to the bar in Ontario. He practised law in Perth, Ontario; and from 1918 to 1922 he represented Lanark in the Canadian House of Commons. From September 21 to December 28, 1921, he was minister of railways and canals in the Meighen administration. He died at Montreal on October 7, 1922. In 1907 he married Jessie Mabel, daughter of J. T. Henderson, of Perth, Ontario.

[Can. parl. comp.; Can. who's who, 1910.]

Stewart, Louis Beaufort (1861-1937), surveyor and educationist, was born at Port Hope, Canada West, on January 27, 1861, the second son of George A. Stewart, C.E. He became a land surveyor, and with his father surveyed the Banff National Park. Mount Stewart and Stewart Canyon in the Rocky Mountains were named after him. Soon after the school of practical science was founded in Toronto, he was appointed lecturer in surveying; and when the school of practical science became the faculty of applied science in the University of Toronto, he was appointed professor of surveying and geodesy. He retired on pension in 1931; and he died at Toronto, Ontario, on March 15, 1937. He was the author of Practical astronomy and geodesy (Toronto, 1922).

[University of Toronto monthly, 1937; Morgan, Can. men (1912).]

Stewart, McLeod (1847-1926), lawyer and author, was born in Bytown (now Ottawa) on February 6, 1847, the eldest son of William Stewart, who represented Bytown in the Legislative Assembly of united Canada. He was educated at the University of Toronto (B.A., 1867; M.A., 1870), and was called to the Ontario bar in 1870. He practised law in Ottawa, and in 1887-88 he was mayor of Ottawa. He died at Ottawa on October 9, 1926. In 1874 he married Linnie Emma, eldest daughter of Colonel Walker Powell. He was the author of several pamphlets, *Ottawa an ocean port* (Ottawa, 1893), *Fifty years of the Ottawa Board of Trade* (Ottawa, 1908), and *The first half-century of Ottawa* (Ottawa, 1910).

[Rose, *Cyc. Can. biog.* (1886); A. H. D. Ross, *Ottawa past and present* (Toronto, 1927).]

Stewart, Neil McMartin (1902-1972), architect, was born in the North West Territories, September 19, 1902. He was educated at Ottawa Collegiate Institute (1917-18), the University of Alberta (B.A., 1923), and McGill University (B. Arch., 1927). He practised in New Brunswick and was the designer of the Beaverbrook Art Gallery at Fredericton, Lady Beaverbrook Arena, the Students' Centre at the University of New Brunswick, the Bank of Montreal, the Imperial Bank, the Federal Public Building in Fredericton, and one in Chatham, as well as regional high schools in Andover and Grand Falls. He served in the Second World War as commander of anti-submarine escort vessels and mine-sweepers. He was a member of the Atlantic Provinces economic councils and vice-president (1959-60) of the Royal Architectural Institute of Canada. He died at Fredericton, New Brunswick, November 12, 1972.

[*Can. who's who*, 1967-69.]

Stewart, Thomas Brown Phillips (1864-1892), poet, was born in Ontario, Canada, and was educated at the Brampton High School and at the University of Toronto (B.A., 1888; LL.B., 1891). He died at Toronto on February 2, 1892, leaving bequests to the Library of the University of Toronto and to the Library of Osgoode Hall. A writer of occasional verse, he published one volume of *Poems* (London, 1887).

[A. MacMurchy, *Handbook of Canadian literature* (Toronto, 1906); *Can. who was who*, vol. 2.]

Stewart, William (1835-1912), clergyman and editor, was born in Ecclefechan, Scotland, in 1835, and was educated at Glasgow University. He emigrated to Canada in 1856, and in 1859 he was ordained a minister of the Baptist Church. From 1894 to 1906 he was principal of the Toronto Bible Training School; and for several years he was editor of the *Canadian Baptist*. He died at Toronto on March 5, 1912.

[*Toronto Globe*, March 6, 1912.]

Stimson, Elam (1792-1869), physician and author, was born at Tolland, Connecticut, on October 4, 1792. He served in the American forces during the War of 1812, and later studied medicine at Yale University and at Dartmouth College, Hanover, New Hampshire (M.D., 1819). He came to Canada in 1823, and settled as a practitioner in Galt,

Upper Canada. Later, he removed to the London district, and then to the village of St. George, where he died on January 1, 1869. He was the author of one of the earliest medical treatises published in Canada, *The cholera beacon, being a treatise on the epidemic cholera as it appeared in Upper Canada in 1832-4* (Dundas, U.C., 1835).

[W. Canniff, *The medical profession in Upper Canada* (Toronto, 1894).]

Stimson, Elam Rush (1825?-1888), clergyman, was born about 1825, the second son of Dr. Elam Stimson (q.v.). He was ordained a priest of the Church of England about 1847, and was for some time a travelling missionary in the Talbot district. Later he was manager and treasurer of the Church Printing and Publishing Company, of Toronto, Ontario, which published the *Church Herald*. He died at Hamilton, Ontario, on August 5, 1888. He was the author of *History of the separation of church and state in Canada* (Toronto, 1887).

[*Western Ontario history nuggets*, no. 3 (London, Ont., 1944).]

Stinson, Joseph (1801?-1862), clergyman, was born in England about 1801, and came to Canada in 1823. He was ordained a minister of the Wesleyan Methodist Church, and he served in several charges in Upper and Lower Canada. From 1839 to 1840, and again from 1858 to 1861, he was president of the Wesleyan Methodist Conference of Canada; and in 1856 Victoria University conferred on him the degree of D.D. He died at Toronto, Canada West, on August 25, 1862. With M. Richey (q.v.), he was joint author of *A plain statement of facts, connected with the union and separation of the British Canadian conferences* (Toronto, 1840).

[G. H. Cornish, *Cyclopaedia of Methodism in Canada* (Toronto, 1881); J. Carroll, *Case and his contemporaries* (5 vols., Toronto, 1867-77).]

Stirling, Grote (1875-1953), civil engineer and politician, was born at Tunbridge Wells, England, on July 31, 1875, and died at Kelowna, British Columbia, on January 18, 1953. He was educated at the Crystal Palace Engineering School in London, came to Canada in 1911, and for many years was a civil engineer in Kelowna. He represented Yale in the Canadian House of Commons from 1924 to 1947, and from November, 1934, to October, 1935, was minister of national defence in the Bennett government.

[*Can. who's who*, 1949-51; *Can. parl. comp.*, 1935; *Encyc. Can.*]

Stirling, Sir William Alexander, Earl of (1567?-1640), poet and colonizer, was born at the manor house of Menstrie, in the parish of Logie, Scotland, about 1567, and was probably educated at the Stirling grammar school. He became tutor to the Earl of Argyll, and later to Prince Henry, son of James VI of Scotland and I of England. He became a distinguished poet of the time and a favourite with James I. In 1621 James made him a grant of Nova Scotia, or "New Scotland", and later this grant was extended to a large part of what is now Canada. This carried with it the right of creating baronets of Nova Scotia. In 1625 the grant was confirmed by Charles I; and in 1628 a band of Scottish colonists was sent out to Port Royal. The difficulties facing colonization proved, however, almost insuperable; and the Scottish colony in Acadia gradually died out. In 1626 Sir William Alexander was appointed secretary of state for Scotland; in 1630 he was created "Lord Alexander of Tullibody and Viscount Stirling", and in 1633 the Earl of Stirling, with the additional title of Viscount Canada. He died at London, in great pecuniary difficulties, on September 12, 1640; and was succeeded in the title by his infant grandson.

[T. H. McGrail, *Sir William Alexander* (Edinburgh, 1940); G. P. Insh, *Scottish colonial schemes* (Glasgow, 1922) and *Sir William Alexander's colony at Port Royal* (Dalhousie review, 1930); *Dict. Am. biog.*; *Dict. Can. biog.*, vol. 1.]

Stisted, Sir Henry William (1817-1875), lieutenant-governor of Ontario (1867-68), was born at St. Omer, France, in 1817, the son of Lieut.-Col. Charles Stisted, of the 3rd Hussars, and Eliza, daughter of Major-General Burn. He was educated at Sandhurst, entered the British army as an ensign in the 2nd Foot in 1835, and eventually rose to the rank of lieutenant-general. He saw service in Afghanistan and Persia; and in 1857 he commanded the advance guard of Havelock's force at the relief of Lucknow. In 1864 he became a major-general, and in 1866 he was appointed divisional commander of the troops in Upper Canada. In 1867 he was sworn in as first lieutenant-governor of Ontario; and he held this office until the appointment of Sir William Howland (q.v.) as lieutenant-governor in 1868. Shortly afterwards he returned to England; and he died at Wood House, Upper Norwood, Surrey, on December 10, 1875. In 1845 he married Maria, daughter of Lieut.-Col. Burton. He was created a C.B. in 1858, and a K.C.B. in 1871.

[*Dict. nat. biog.*; Le Jeune, *Dict. gén.*; *Dict. Can. biog.*, vol. 10.]

Stobo, Edward John (1838-1918), clergyman and author, was born in Glasgow, Scotland, on March 13, 1838; and was educated at Glasgow University and the Baptist Theological Hall, Glasgow. He was ordained a minister of the Baptist Church in 1866; and he came to Canada in 1872. He occupied a number of charges in Ontario and Quebec; and from 1886 to 1906 he was secretary of the Quebec auxiliary of the British and Foreign Bible Society.

He died at Quebec City on November 24, 1918. Under the pseudonym of "Aletheia", he was the author of *The o'erturn o' Botany bay; or, Dipper folk idyls* (Philadelphia, 1901).

[Morgan, *Can. men* (1912).]

Stobo, Edward John (1867-1922), clergyman and author, was born at Kilmarnock, Scotland, on January 26, 1867, the son of the Rev. Edward John Stobo (q.v.). He came to Canada with his parents, and was educated at the Western University (B.A., 1903), McMaster University (B.Th., 1896; B.D., 1899), and Temple University (D.S.T., 1907). He was ordained a Baptist minister in 1896, and served as the pastor of churches in Ontario and Manitoba. He died at Toronto, Ontario, on March 30, 1922. He was the author of *The glory of His robe* (New York, 1922).

[Morgan, *Can. men* (1912).]

Stobo, Robert (1726-1770), soldier, was born on October 7, 1726, the son of William Stobo, a merchant of Glasgow, Scotland. He emigrated to Virginia when a youth; and in 1754 he was appointed a captain in the Virginia regiment. When Washington was compelled to surrender Fort Necessity in 1755, Stobo was handed over to the French as a hostage. He was taken to Quebec, where he was condemned to death as a spy, having sent to the English a plan of Fort Duquesne. He escaped, however, in the spring of 1759, and made his way to Louisburg, whence he was sent back to Quebec to aid Wolfe (q.v.) in the capture of the fortress. He afterwards asserted that he gave Wolfe the idea of landing at Wolfe's Cove. In 1760 he was given a commission as captain in the 15th Regiment of Foot; and his name appears in the *Army List* as late as 1770. He died June 19, 1770, at Chatham, England. His own account of his life was afterwards published under the title *Memoirs of Major Robert Stobo, of the Virginia Regiment* (Pittsburgh, 1854); but the details of his story lack corroboration. His adventures were the basis of Sir Gilbert Parker's *Seats of the mighty* (London, 1896).

[R. C. Alberts, *The most extraordinary adventures of Major Robert Stobo* (Toronto, 1965); P. G. Roy, *Les petites choses de notre histoire*, vol. 1 (Lévis, Que., 1919); Le Jeune, *Dict. gén.*; *Dict. Am. biog.*; *Dict. Can. biog.*, vol. 3.]

Stockton, Alfred Augustus (1842-1907), lawyer and politician, was born at Studholme, Kings county, New Brunswick, on November 2, 1842. He was educated at Mount Allison University (B.A., 1864; M.A., 1867; D.C.L., 1884), and was called to the bar of New Brunswick in 1868. He practised law in Saint John, New Brunswick; and he represented Saint John county in the legislature of New Brunswick from 1883 to 1889, and Saint John city from 1890 to 1899. From 1892 to 1899 he was leader of the Conservative opposition. In 1904 he was elected to represent Saint John in the Canadian House of Commons, and he continued to represent this constituency until his death at Ottawa on March 15, 1907. He was the author of *The Monroe doctrine and other addresses* (Saint John, N.B., 1898); and he edited Joseph Lawrence's *The judges of New Brunswick and their times* (Saint John, N.B., 1907). He received the honorary degree of Ph.D. from the Illinois Wesleyan University in 1883, that of D.C.L. from King's College, Windsor, in 1884, and that of LL.D. from Victoria University, Cobourg, in 1887.

[*Can. who was who*, vol. 1; *Can. parl. comp.*; Morgan, *Can. men* (1898); Rose, *Cyc. Can. biog.* (1888).]

Stocqueler, Joachim Hayward (1800-1885), journalist, was born in London, England, of Portuguese extraction, in 1800. In 1821 he went to India, and he remained there for twenty years. He then lived for some years in England; but shortly before the outbreak of the American Civil War in 1860, he went to the United States, and he was employed during the war period as a newspaper correspondent in the United States and Canada. While in Canada he published, under the *nom de plume* of "J. H. Siddons", *The Canadian volunteers' hand-book* (Toronto, 1863). After the war he returned to England; and he died at Brighton, England, in 1885.

[*Dict. nat. biog.*]

Storgoff, Florence (1908-1964), leader, Sons of Freedom, Doukhobor sect, was born at Canora, Saskatchewan, in 1908. She lived for a short time with her parents in California before returning to Vancouver, where she married Fred Storgoff. They moved to the Kootenay Valley in southeastern British Columbia where a Doukhobor colony had been established whose peculiar social and religious beliefs led to clashes with the provincial authorities. The Storgoffs were sent to a special compound on Pier's Island near Victoria as a result of these activities. After their release Fanny Storgoff became acknowledged leader of the Sons of Freedom and spent three years in Kingston Penitentiary for arson. She led 900 followers to the lower British Columbia mainland in 1963, where some 400 camped outside Agassiz Mountain Prison in protest against the arrest of co-religionists. In 1964, while still involved in protest marches, she died of cancer at Vancouver, British Columbia, on September 11.

[Metropolitan Toronto Library Board, *Biographical scrapbooks*, vol. 22.]

Storm, William George (1826-1892), architect, was born in England in 1826, the son of Thomas Storm, a builder and contractor who came to Canada and settled in York (Toronto),

Upper Canada, in 1830. He studied architecture in Toronto, under William Thomas (q.v.), and in Europe; and he became an outstanding architect in Toronto. He was the architect of St. James Cathedral, Osgoode Hall, and University College, Toronto; and he was a charter member of the Royal Canadian Academy of Arts. He died in Toronto, Ontario, in 1892.

[N. MacTavish, *The fine arts in Canada* (Toronto, 1925); H. G. Jones and E. Dyonnet, *History of the Royal Canadian Academy of Arts* (Montreal, 1934).]

Stowe, Mrs. Emily Howard, *née* **Jennings** (1831-1903), physician and feminist, was born in South Norwich, Upper Canada, May, 1831. She became a school-teacher; but in 1856 she married John Stowe, of Norwich, and after her marriage she graduated from the New York College of Medicine for Women (M.D., 1867). She returned to Canada, and after a long fight was admitted in 1880 a member of the College of Physicians and Surgeons in Ontario. She was the first woman authorized to practise medicine in Canada. She became a leading female suffragist, and in 1893 she organized the Dominion Woman Suffrage Association, of which she became its first president. She died in Toronto on April 30, 1903.

[Morgan, *Can. men and women* (1898).]

Strachan, John (1778-1867), first Anglican bishop of Toronto (1839-67), was born at Aberdeen, Scotland, on April 12, 1778, the son of John Strachan and Elizabeth Findlayson. He was educated at the universities of Aberdeen (M.A., 1796) and St. Andrews, and for three years taught school. In 1799 he came to Canada, to take charge of a college projected by Simcoe (q.v.) in Upper Canada. The proposed college was not founded at that time; and for twelve years Strachan taught school at Kingston and Cornwall. In 1803 he took orders in the Church of England, and was appointed rector of Cornwall. In 1812 he became rector of York (Toronto), and in 1813 he played a conspicuous part during the American occupation of York. In 1818 he was appointed a member of the Executive Council, and in 1820 of the Legislative Council, of Upper Canada; and during the years that followed he was one of the pillars of the "Family Compact". In particular, he distinguished himself by his advocacy of the right of the Church of England to sole enjoyment of the Clergy Reserves. In 1836, however, he resigned from the Executive Council, and in 1841 he ceased to sit in the Legislative Council.

In 1825 he was appointed archdeacon of York, and in 1839 he became bishop of the newly created diocese of Toronto. Henceforth he took little part in politics, and devoted himself to religious and educational work. He became in 1827 the first president of King's College, Toronto; but when King's College was reorganized in 1850 as the University of Toronto, he withdrew from all connection with it, and founded, in 1851, the University of Trinity College, Toronto. Of this university he was the first chancellor.

He died at Toronto on November 2, 1867. In 1807 he married the widow of Andrew McGill of Montreal; and by her he had four sons and four daughters. In 1827 he was made an LL.D. of the University of St. Andrews, and in 1811 a D.D. of the University of Aberdeen.

His *Letter-book* for the years 1812-34 has been edited by G. W. Spragge (Toronto, 1946).

[T. B. Roberton, *The fighting bishop* (Ottawa, 1926); A. N. Bethune, *Memoir of the Right Rev. John Strachan* (Toronto, 1870); H. Scadding, *The first bishop of Toronto* (Toronto, 1868); S. Boorman, *John Toronto: A biography of Bishop Strachan* (Toronto, 1969); J. L. H. Henderson, *John Strachan, 1778-1867* (Toronto, 1969); D. Flint, *John Strachan: Pastor and politician* (Toronto, 1971); A. H. Young, *John Strachan* (Queen's quarterly, 1928); *Dict. nat. biog.*; *Cyc. Am. biog.*; Morgan, *Cel. Can. and Bib. can.*; Taylor, *Brit. Am.*, vol. 3; Dent, *Can. port.*, vol. 1; C. H. Mockridge, *The bishops of the Church of England in Canada* (Toronto, 1896); W. B. Heeney (ed.), *Leaders of the Canadian church* (Toronto, 1918).]

Straith, John (1826-1885), clergyman and author, was born in Aberdeenshire, Scotland, in 1826. He emigrated to Canada, and after studying theology at Knox College, Toronto, was ordained a minister of the Presbyterian Church in 1857. He died at Shelburne, Ontario, on January 10, 1885. He was the author of *Fidelity of the Bible* (Ingersoll, Ont., 1864).

[*Dom. ann. reg.*, 1885.]

Strange, Kathleen Redman (d. 1968), author, was born in London, England. She came to Canada with her husband in 1920. Without previous experience they took up farming near Fenn, Alberta, and three years later won the World Wheat Championship at Chicago. In 1924 she began magazine articles and in 1937, seven years after moving from the farm to Winnipeg, she won the Canadian Book Contest prize for non-fiction with *With the west in her eyes*, the story of the Stranges' farming experience in Alberta. In 1941 she published *Never a dull moment* in which she and her husband, Major H. G. L. Strange, collaborated in writing about her memoirs. In addition to her novels Mrs. Strange wrote sixty short stories for various magazines. They retired to England in 1958, returning to Victoria, British Columbia, in 1964. She died at Vancouver, British Columbia, January 9, 1968.

[Vancouver *Province,* Jan. 10, 1968; *Can. who's who*, 1955-57; *Canadian author and bookman*, vol. 42: 4 (1967).]

Strange, Sir Thomas Andrew Lumisden (1756-1841), chief justice of Nova Scotia (1789-98), was born on November 30, 1756, the second son of Sir Robert Strange, the engraver. He was educated at Christ Church, Oxford (B.A., 1778; M.A., 1782); and he was called to the bar at Lincoln's Inn in 1785. In 1789 he was appointed chief justice of Nova Scotia, and he retained this position until 1798, when he was appointed recorder and president of the court of the mayor and aldermen at Madras, India. In 1800 he became chief justice of the Supreme Court of the presidency of Madras; and he remained in India until 1817. He then returned to England, and devoted himself to the completion of his *Elements of Hindu law* (2 vols., London, 1825). He died at St. Leonard's, England, on July 16, 1841. He was knighted in 1798; and in 1818 he was made a D.C.L. of Oxford University. He was twice married; and by his second wife, Louisa, daughter of Sir William Burroughs, Bart., he had a numerous family.

[*Dict. nat. biog.*; B. Murdoch, *History of Nova Scotia* (3 vols., Halifax, N.S., 1867).]

Strange, Thomas Bland (1831-1925), soldier, was born at Meerut, India, on September 15, 1831, the second son of Colonel H. F. Strange and Letitia, daughter of Major N. Bland. He was educated at the Edinburgh Academy and at the Royal Military Academy, Woolwich; and he obtained a commission in the Royal Artillery. He served in the Indian Mutiny, and was present at the siege and capture of Lucknow. In 1871, he was appointed inspector of artillery in Canada; in 1882 he was placed on the reserve of officers, with the rank of major-general; and in 1885 he commanded the Albert field force in the second North West Rebellion, and was in command at the engagement of Frenchman's Butte. During his later years he lived in England. He died on July 9, 1925. He was twice married, (1) to Elinor Marie (d. 1917), daughter of Capt. Robert Taylor, and (2) in 1918 to Janet, daughter of the Rev. J. A. Fell, and widow of Col. F. C. Ruxton; and by his first wife he had two sons and three daughters. In addition to some publications on military subjects, he published his autobiography under the title *Gunner Jingo's jubilee* (London, 1894).

[*Who was who*, 1916-28; Morgan, *Can. men* (1912); *Cyc. Am. biog.*; C. P. Mulvaney, *The history of the North West rebellion of 1885* (Toronto, 1885).]

Strathcona, Sir Donald Alexander Smith, first Baron (1820-1914), Canadian high commissioner in England (1896-1914), was born at Forres, Morayshire, Scotland, the son of Alexander Smith, of Archieston, and Barbara, daughter of Donald Stuart, of Leanchoil. He was educated in Scotland; and in 1838 he entered the service of the Hudson's Bay Company. From 1838 to 1868 he was stationed on the Labrador coast. In 1869 he was appointed in charge of the Company's Montreal office, and here he rose in the service of the company until he became resident governor and chief commissioner in Canada. He first came into public notice in 1869, when he was appointed by the Canadian government a special commissioner to inquire into the troubles connected with the North West Rebellion of 1869-70; and his courage and tact had much to do with the settlement of these troubles. From 1870 to 1874 he represented Winnipeg in the Legislative Assembly of Manitoba, and from 1870 to 1880 he represented Selkirk in the Canadian House of Commons. In 1873, at the time of the "Pacific Scandal", his declaration that he could no longer "conscientiously" support the government, of which he had hitherto been a supporter, was partly responsible for the fall of the Macdonald administration. He was out of parliament from 1880 to 1887; but in 1887 he was elected to the House of Commons for Montreal West, and he continued to represent this constituency until 1896. During this period he gave the Conservative government an independent support. In 1896 he was appointed by the government of Sir Charles Tupper (q.v.) Canadian high commissioner in London; and this position he filled, with great acceptance, for the rest of his life.

A man of great wealth, the foundation of his fortune was laid in 1879, when he became, with George Stephen (q.v.), J. J. Hill (q.v.), and Norman Kittson (q.v.), one of the syndicate that purchased the St. Paul, Minneapolis, and Manitoba Railway, which first gave access by railway to the Canadian North West; and he continued for many years to be closely associated with railway development in Canada. In 1880 he was an important member of the group that organized the Canadian Pacific Railway Company; and during the years that followed it was mainly his courage and resource which enabled the company to survive the difficulties of the period of construction. In 1885 he was fittingly chosen to drive the last spike of the railway at Craigellachie, British Columbia. He was also an outstanding figure in Canadian finance. In 1887 he was elected president of the Bank of Montreal; and in 1905 he became its honorary president. For many years he was governor of the Hudson's Bay Company. His benefactions were almost without number. McGill University, the Royal Victoria Hospital, Montreal, Aberdeen University, the Young Men's Christian Association, and King Edward's Hospital Fund benefited especially from his munificence; and during the South African War he outfitted at his own expense a Canadian mounted force, known as "Strathcona's Horse".

He died in London, England, on January 21, 1914. In early life he married Isabella Sophia, daughter of Richard Hardisty, of the Hudson's Bay Company; and by her he had one daughter. He was created a K.C.M.G. in 1886, a G.C.M.G. in 1896, and a G.C.V.O. in 1908; and in 1897 he was raised to the peerage of the United Kingdom as Baron Strathcona and Mount Royal. In 1896 he was sworn of the Privy Council for Canada, and in 1904 of the Imperial Privy Council. He was a D.C.L. of Oxford, Dublin, and Durham universities, and an LL.D. of Cambridge, Yale, Aberdeen, Laval, Toronto, Queen's, Ottawa, Glasgow, and Manchester universities. In 1889 he was elected chancellor of McGill University, and in 1899 lord rector, and in 1903 chancellor, of Aberdeen University. In 1908 he was elected a fellow of the Royal Society.

[J. Macnaughton, *Lord Strathcona* (Toronto, 1926); B. Willson, *The life of Lord Strathcona and Mount Royal* (London, 1915) and *Lord Strathcona, the story of his life* (Toronto, 1902); W. T. R. Preston, *The life and times of Lord Strathcona* (London, 1914); J. W. Pedley, *Biography of Lord Strathcona and Mount Royal* (Toronto, 1915); G. Bryce, *The real Strathcona* (Can. mag., 1915); S. Macnaughton, *Lord Strathcona* (Living Age, 1914); *Who was who*, 1897-1916; Taché, *Men of the day*; Morgan, *Can. men* (1912); Rose, *Cyc. Can. biog.* (1886).]

Straton, Barry (1854-1901), poet, was born in Fredericton, New Brunswick, in 1854. He was educated at the Collegiate Institute, Fredericton; and studied law. But, finding law uncongenial, he turned to farming; and in the intervals of farming he wrote poetry. He published *Lays of love, and miscellaneous poems* (Saint John, N.B., 1884), *The building of the bridge: An idyll of the St. John* (Saint John, N.B., 1887), and *The hunter's handbook* (Boston, 1885). He died at Fredericton, New Brunswick, in 1901.

[*Can. who was who*, vol. 2.]

Stratton, James Robert (1857-1916), provincial secretary of Ontario (1900-05), was born at Millbrook, Canada West, on May 3, 1857, the son of James Stratton. He was educated at the Peterborough Collegiate Institute, became a journalist, and owned and published the Peterborough *Examiner*. From 1886 to 1905 he represented West Peterborough, as a Liberal, in the Legislative Assembly of Ontario; and from 1900 to 1905 he was provincial secretary in the Ross administration. Charges of political corruption made against him had much to do with the defeat of the Ross government in 1905. From 1908 to 1911 he represented West Peterborough in the Canadian House of Commons; but thereafter he retired to private life. He died at Hot Springs, Virginia, on April 19, 1916.

[Morgan, *Can. men* (1912); *Can. parl. comp.*]

Street, William Purvis Rochfort (1841-1906), jurist, was born in London, Canada

West, on November 13, 1841. He was called to the bar of Upper Canada in 1864 (K.C., 1883), and practised law in London, Ontario. In 1885 he was chairman of the commission sent to ascertain and settle the claims of the half-breeds in the North West; and in 1887 he was appointed a puisne judge of the Queen's Bench division of the High Court of Justice of Ontario. He remained on the bench until his death, at Toronto, Ontario, on July 31, 1906.

[Morgan, *Can. men* (1898); Rose, *Cyc. Can. biog.* (1886).]

Strickland, Edgar Harold (1889-1962), zoologist and professor, was born at Erith, Kent, England, on May 29, 1889. He studied at Wye Agricultural College, where his interest in insects was stimulated by F. V. Theobald. He came to Harvard University on a Carnegie studentship from 1911 to 1913 to prepare himself for service with the British Colonial Office in the control of sleeping sickness in Africa. He was loaned to Canada to obtain field experience, and opened a one-man field station in a barn at Lethbridge. He enlisted in the Canadian army and served as a lieutenant in the Canadian Machine Gun Corps until he was wounded in 1918. Returning to Canada, he began studies on the pale western cutworm and in 1922 was invited to join the faculty of the University of Alberta as professor of entomology and head of the one-man department. He remained at the University of Alberta until his retirement in 1954. From 1935 to 1940 he was commanding officer of the University of Alberta's Canadian Officer Training Corps; from 1936 to 1939 was aide-de-camp to the lieutenant-governor; and from 1942 to 1944 was commanding officer of the Canadian army basic training unit at Wetaskiwin, Alberta. He was an accomplished artist and illustrator, and published more than sixty papers covering such varied topics as the taxonomy and check lists of Alberta fauna; the comparative morphology of Diptera; the parasites of *Similium* species and their effect on hosts; the control of major groups of agricultural pests of western Canada; cutworms, grasshoppers, and wireworms; the influence of various factors on insect abundance; and the hazards of D.D.T. A complete bibliography appears in *The Canadian Entomologist* (vol. 95, March, 1963). He was a fellow of the Royal Society of Canada, a charter member of the Entomological Society of Alberta, an honorary member of the Entomological Society of Canada, and a fellow of the Entomological Society of America. He died at Victoria, British Columbia, May 31, 1962.

[*Proc. Roy. Soc. Can.*, 1962.]

Strickland, Samuel (1804-1867), author, was born at Reydon Hall, Suffolk, England, in 1804, the son of Thomas Strickland, and the brother of Mrs. Moodie (q.v.) and Mrs. Traill (q.v.). He came to Canada in 1825, entered the employ of the Canada Company, and ultimately settled at Lakefield, Upper Canada. Here he died in 1867. He was the author of *Twenty-seven years in Canada West* (2 vols., London, 1853).

[*Dict. nat. biog.*; *Cyc. Am. biog.*; Morgan, *Bib. can.*; A. MacMurchy, *Handbook of Canadian literature* (Toronto, 1906).]

Stringer, Arthur John Arbuthnott (1874-1950), poet and novelist, was born at Chatham, Ontario, on February 26, 1874, and died at Mountain Lakes, New Jersey, on September 13, 1950. He was educated at the University of Toronto, but did not graduate. After serving an apprenticeship as a journalist in Montreal, he became a free-lance writer in New York. Later he settled for some years on a fruit farm on the north shore of Lake Erie; and finally, in 1921, he went to live at Mountain Lakes in northern New Jersey. He was a most voluminous author. He published fifteen volumes of poetry, beginning with *Watchers of twilight, and other poems* (London, Ont., 1894) and ending with *New York nocturnes* (Toronto, 1948); and he was the author of no fewer than forty-five works of fiction, beginning with *The loom of destiny* (Boston, 1899) and ending with *The devastator* (Toronto, 1944). He first achieved success with his novels of crime, such as *The wire-tappers* (Boston, 1906) and *The gun-runner* (New York, 1909). Later, his trilogy describing life in the Canadian West, *The prairie wife* (New York, 1915), *The prairie mother* (New York, 1920), and *The prairie child* (New York, 1921), proved popular. His last book was a biography of Rupert Brooke, entitled *Red wine of youth* (Indianapolis, 1948).

[Victor Lauriston, *Arthur Stringer, son of the north* (Indianapolis, 1941), with bibliography; *Can. who's who*, 1948; *Encyc. Can.*]

Stringer, Isaac O. (1862-1934), archbishop of Rupertsland, was born near Kincardine, Canada West, in 1862, and was educated at the University of Toronto (B.A., 1891) and at Wycliffe College, Toronto. He was ordained a priest of the Church of England in 1893; and for ten years he was a missionary in the Mackenzie River diocese, first at Peel river, and then at Herschel Island. In 1905 he was elected bishop of Selkirk (later Yukon); and in 1931, archbishop of Rupertsland. He died at Winnipeg, Manitoba, on October 30, 1934.

[F. A. Peake, *The bishop who ate his boots: A biography of Isaac O. Stringer* (Toronto, 1966); B. Heeney (ed.), *Leaders of the Canadian church: Third series* (Toronto, 1943); Morgan, *Can. men* (1912).]

Strong, Sir Samuel Henry (1825-1909), chief justice of the Supreme Court of Canada (1892-1902), was born at Poole, Dorsetshire, England, on August 13, 1825, the son of the Rev. Samuel Spratt Strong and Jane

Elizabeth, daughter of John Gosse, of Poole. He came to Canada with his parents in 1836, and was educated at Quebec. He studied law at Bytown (Ottawa) and Toronto, Canada West, and was called to the bar of Upper Canada in 1849 (Q.C., 1863). From 1869 to 1874 he was a judge of the Court of Chancery of Ontario, and from 1874 to 1875 a judge of the Supreme Court of Ontario. In 1875 he was appointed a puisne judge of the Supreme Court of Canada, on its organization; and in 1892 he became chief justice of the Supreme Court. In 1897 he was sworn of the Imperial Privy Council, and became a member of the Judicial Committee of the Privy Council. He retired from the bench in 1902; and he died at Ottawa on August 31, 1909. In 1850 he married Elizabeth Charlotte Cane; and by her he had two children. He was created a K.B. in 1893.

[*Dict. nat. biog.*, supp. II; *Cyc. Am. biog.*; Rose, *Cyc. Can. biog.* (1886); Dent, *Can. port*, vol. 2; Morgan, *Can. men* (1898); *Can. parl. comp.*; *Who was who*, 1897-1916; *Canadian biographical dictionary*, Quebec vol. (Chicago, 1881).]

Stuart, Andrew (1785-1840), solicitor-general of Lower Canada (1837-40), was born in Kingston, Upper Canada, in 1785, the fifth son of the Rev. John Stuart (q.v.). He was educated at Kingston, under the Rev. John Strachan (q.v.), and was called to the bar of Lower Canada in 1807. From 1814 to 1837, except in 1835, he was one of the members for Quebec in the Legislative Assembly of Lower Canada. Though at first a member of the popular party, he broke with Papineau (q.v.) and became his chief antagonist in the Assembly. In 1837 he was appointed solicitor-general of Lower Canada; but he died, in office, at Quebec on February 21, 1840. He was twice married. By his first wife, Marguerite Dumoulin, he had two sons; and by his second wife, Jane Smith, he had three daughters and one son. He was the author of *Notes upon the south-west boundary line of the British provinces* (Quebec, 1830; 2nd ed., Montreal, 1832), *A review of the proceedings of the legislature of Lower Canada* (Montreal, 1832), and, with William Badgley, *An account of the endowments for education in Lower Canada* (London, 1838). He contributed also several papers to the *Transactions* of the Literary and Historical Society of Quebec.

[A. H. Young, *The Revd. John Stuart, D.D., U.E.L., of Kingston, U.C., and his family* (Kingston, Ont., 1921); Morgan, *Cel. Can. and Bib. can.*; R. Christie, *History of Lower Canada* (6 vols., Quebec and Montreal, 1848-54).]

Stuart, Sir Andrew (1812-1891), chief justice of the Superior Court of Quebec (1885-91), was born in Quebec on June 16, 1812, the eldest son of the Hon. Andrew Stuart (q.v.). He was educated at a private school at Chambly, Lower Canada, and was called to the bar of

Lower Canada in 1834 (Q.C., 1854). In 1860 he was appointed a puisne judge of the Superior Court of Lower Canada, and in 1885 he became chief justice of this court. He died in Quebec on June 9, 1891. In 1842 he married Elmire-Charlotte, third daughter of Philippe-Joseph Aubert de Gaspé; and by her he had five sons and five daughters. In 1887 he was created a knight bachelor.

[A. H. Young, *The Revd. John Stuart, D.D., U.E.L., of Kingston, U.C., and his family* (Kingston, Ont., 1921); Rose, *Cyc. Can. biog.* (1888); P. G. Roy, *Les juges de la province de Québec* (Quebec, 1933); F. J. Audet, *Les juges en chef de la province de Québec* (Quebec, 1927).]

Stuart, Charles (1783-1865), reformer, was born in Jamaica in 1783, the son of a British army officer. He became a commissioned officer in the British East India Company's forces in 1801, and retired on pension about 1814, with the rank of captain. He then emigrated to Canada, and took up a grant of land on Lake Simcoe, in Upper Canada. While living in Upper Canada, he published *The emigrant's guide to Upper Canada* (London, 1820). Later, he went to the United States, and became there one of the pioneers of the anti-slavery movement. He returned about 1842 to his property on Lake Simcoe in Upper Canada; and he died there in 1865.

[D. Malone (ed.), *Dictionary of American biography*, vol. 18 (New York, 1936).]

Stuart, Charles Allan (1864-1926), jurist, was born at Caradoc, Middlesex county, Canada West, on August 3, 1864. He was educated at the University of Toronto (LL.B., 1884), and for a short time was lecturer in constitutional history at the University of Toronto. In 1897 he moved to the North West Territories, and began the practice of law in Calgary. From 1905 to 1906 he represented Gleichen in the first legislature of Alberta; but in 1906 he was appointed a judge of the Supreme Court of the North West Territories. In 1907 he was appointed a judge of the newly formed Supreme Court of Alberta; and in 1908 he was elected chancellor of the University of Alberta. Both these positions he retained until his death on March 6, 1926.

[*Can. who was who*, vol. 1; Morgan, *Can. men* (1912); *Who was who*, 1916-28.]

Stuart, David (1765-1853), fur-trader, was born on December 22, 1765, at Balquhidder, Scotland. He is said to have been the son of that Alexander Stuart who was the successful opponent of the famous Rob Roy; and he was a cousin of John Stuart (q.v.) of the North West Company. He emigrated to Canada, and lived in Montreal before the close of the eighteenth century. His obituary notice in the *Detroit Daily Advertiser*, October 19, 1853, is authority for the statement that "for a time he was an agent of the Hudson Bay Company on the Atlantic Coast, in Nova Scotia, and elsewhere"; but this is almost certainly a mistake, for the Hudson's Bay Company had no posts in these districts at that time. It is possible that he was employed by the North West Company at the King's Posts or in the Maritime provinces. In 1810 he became a partner in John Jacob Astor's Pacific Fur Company; and he was one of the founders of Astoria. He remained with the Pacific Fur Company for many years; but he retired from the fur-trade about 1833, and went to live with his nephew, Robert Stuart (q.v.), in Detroit, Michigan. Here he died, at the house of his nephew's widow, on October 18, 1853.

[W. S. Wallace (ed.), *Documents relating to the North West Company* (Toronto: The Champlain Society, 1934).]

Stuart, George Okill (1776-1862), clergyman, was born at Fort Hunter, New York, on June 29, 1776, the eldest son of the Rev. John Stuart (q.v.). He was educated at King's College, Windsor, at Union College, Schenectady, and at Harvard University (B.A., 1801). He was ordained a priest of the Church of England; and was rector of York (Toronto) from 1801 to 1811, and of Kingston from 1811 to 1862. In 1821 he was made archdeacon of Upper Canada, in 1827 archdeacon of Kingston, and in 1862 dean of Ontario. He died on October 5, 1862.

[A. H. Young, *The Rev. George Okill Stuart* (Ont. Hist. Soc., papers and records, 1927) and *The Revd. John Stuart, D.D., U.E.L., of Kingston, U.C., and his family* (Kingston, Ont., 1921).]

Stuart, Henry Coleridge (1844-1909), clergyman and author, was born in London, England, on September 14, 1844. He came to Canada, and was educated at Bishop's College, Lennoxville (B.A., 1869; M.A., 1874). He was ordained a priest of the Church of England in 1871; and, after serving in several parishes in the province of Quebec, he was appointed in 1890 rector of the Crown parish of Three Rivers. He remained rector of this parish until his death, at Three Rivers, on February 24, 1909. He was the author of *The Church of England in Canada, 1759-1793* (Montreal, 1893); and some of his unpublished historical works are in the Quebec diocesan archives.

[Morgan, *Can. men* (1898).]

Stuart, Sir James, Bart. (1780-1853), chief justice of Lower Canada (1841-53), was born at Fort Hunter, New York, on March 2 (or 4), 1780, the third son of the Rev. John Stuart (q.v.). He was educated at Kingston, Upper Canada, under the Rev. John Strachan (q.v.), and at King's College, Windsor, Nova Scotia; and he was called to the bar of Lower Canada in 1801. In 1805 he was appointed solicitor-general of Lower Canada; and from 1808 to 1820 he was one of the members for Montreal in the Legislative Assembly of the province. From 1825 to 1827 he was also member for Sorel. In 1825 he was appointed attorney-general; but in 1831 he was suspended from office by Lord Aylmer (q.v.). In 1838 he was appointed by Lord Durham (q.v.) chief justice of the Court of Queen's Bench at Montreal; in 1839 he became president of the Special Council of Lower Canada; and he had much to do with the framing of the Act of Union, 1840. In 1841 he became chief justice of Lower Canada; and he occupied this position until his death at Quebec on July 14, 1853. In 1818 he married Elizabeth, daughter of Alexander Robinson of Montreal; and by her he had three sons and one daughter. In 1827 he was made a D.C.L. of King's College, Windsor; and in 1840 he was created a baronet. The baronetcy became extinct with the death of his third son in 1915.

[F. J. Audet, *Les juges en chef de la province de Québec* (Quebec, 1927); P. G. Roy, *Les juges de la province de Québec* (Quebec, 1933); *Dict. nat. biog.*; Morgan, *Cel. Can.*; A. H. Young, *The Revd. John Stuart, D.D., U.E.L., and his family* (Kingston, Ont., 1921).]

Stuart, John (1740-1811), clergyman, was born at Paxton, Pennsylvania, on March 10, 1740, the son of Andrew Stuart. He was educated at the College of Philadelphia, later the University of Pennsylvania (B.A., 1763; M.A., 1770; D.D., 1799), and was ordained a priest of the Church of England in 1770. The same year he was appointed missionary to the Mohawks at Fort Hunter, New York; and during the American Revolution he came to Canada. From 1781 to 1785 he taught school at Montreal; in 1785 he became the first Church of England missionary in the "Western Settlements", and from that date until his death at Kingston, Upper Canada, on August 15, 1811, he was rector of St. George's Church, Kingston. In 1775 he married in Philadelphia Jane Okill (d. 1821); and by her he had five sons and three daughters.

[A. H. Young, *The Revd. John Stuart, D.D., U.E.L., of Kingston, Upper Canada, and his family* (Kingston, Ont., 1921); Morgan, *Cel. Can.*; W. Canniff, *History of the settlement of Upper Canada* (Toronto, 1869).]

Stuart, John (1779-1847), fur-trader, was born in Strathspey, Scotland, in 1779, the son of Donald Stuart of Leanchoil. His sister Barbara was the mother of the first Lord Strathcona (q.v.). He entered the service of the North West Company in 1799, and was sent to the Peace River district. In 1806 he accompanied Simon Fraser (q.v.) on his descent of the Fraser River to the Pacific. He was placed in charge of New Caledonia in 1809; and in 1813 he became a partner of the North West Company. At the union of 1821, he was commissioned a chief factor of the Hudson's Bay

Company; and he remained in charge in New Caledonia until 1824. He retired from the service of the Hudson's Bay Company in 1839, and returned to Scotland. He died at his place, Springfield House, near Forres, Scotland, on January 14, 1847. His will is on file at Hudson's Bay House, in London. Stuart Lake, in British Columbia, is named after him.

[E. E. Rich (ed.), *Journal of occurrences in the Athabasca department by George Simpson* (Toronto: The Champlain Society, 1938).]

Stuart, Robert (1785-1848), fur-trader, was born in Callander, Perthshire, Scotland, on February 19, 1785, the nephew of David Stuart (q.v.). He emigrated to Canada in 1807, and in 1810 he joined John Jacob Astor's Pacific Fur Company. He was one of the founders of Astoria; and in 1812-13 he made the overland journey back from Astoria to St. Louis. In 1819 he went to Michilimackinac, as the agent of the American Fur Company; and he remained there until 1834. He then retired from the fur-trade, and settled in Detroit, Michigan. He died at Chicago, Illinois, on October 28, 1848. His son, David, born at Brooklyn, New York, in 1816, became a member of Congress for Detroit, and commanded a brigade under General W. T. Sherman in the American Civil War. Robert Stuart's narrative of his overland journey in 1812-13 has been edited by P. A. Rollins under the title *Discovery of the Oregon trail* (New York and London, 1935).

[*Dict. Am. biog.*]

Stuck, Hudson (1863-1920), missionary, was born in London, England, on November 11, 1863. He was educated at King's College, London, and in the Theological Department of the University of the South, at Sewanee, Tennessee. He was ordained a priest of the Protestant Episcopal Church in 1892, and for twelve years was rector of churches in Texas. In 1904 he became archdeacon of the Yukon, under the Right Rev. Peter Trimble Rowe (q.v.), first missionary bishop of Alaska; and the rest of his life was devoted to missionary work among the natives of the Yukon and Alaska. He died, unmarried, at Fort Yukon, Alaska, on October 10, 1920. He was the author of *Ten thousand miles with a dog sled* (New York, 1914), *Denali (Mount McKinley)* (New York, 1914), *Voyages on the Yukon and its tributaries* (New York, 1917), *The Alaskan missions of the Episcopal church* (New York, 1920), and *A winter circuit of our Arctic coast* (New York, 1920).

[*Dict. Am. biog.*; *Who was who in America*; *Who was who*, 1916-28.]

Stupart, Sir Robert Frederic (1857-1940), meteorologist, was born at Aurora, Canada West, on October 24, 1857, the son of Captain Robert Douglas Stupart, R.N. He was educated at Upper Canada College, Toronto, and entered the Canadian Meteorological Service in 1872. He rose to be director of the Meteorological Service of Canada and superintendent of the magnetic observatory at Toronto in 1894; and he continued in this position until his retirement in 1929. He was elected a fellow of the Royal Society of Canada in 1901; he was elected president of the Royal Astronomical Society of Canada in 1902, and of the Royal Canadian Institute in 1906; and he was created a K.B. in 1916. He died at Toronto, Ontario, on September 27, 1940.

[*Proc. Roy. Soc. Can.*, 1941; *Can. who's who*, 1936-37; Morgan, *Can. men* (1912).]

Stykolt, Stefan (1923-1962), journalist, was born in Zgierz, Poland, on October 12, 1923. He was educated in Poland and in France. He came to Canada in 1941 with his family and attended the University of Toronto (B.A., 1946), Harvard University, and Cambridge University. He returned to Canada in 1951 and accepted a teaching post in the department of economics and political science at the University of Toronto. Stykolt was an intelligent and penetrating economic journalist. He became managing editor of the *Canadian Forum* from 1954 to 1959, when he resigned to devote more of his time to academic life. He died, after a painful illness, on February 13, 1962. He wrote *Economic analysis and combines policy* (Toronto, 1965), *Efficiency in the open economy*, edited by Anthony Scott and James Rae (Oxford, 1969), *The tariff and competition in Canada*, with H. C. Eastman (Toronto, 1967), together with many articles and comments in the *Canadian Forum* and other journals.

[*Can. journ. ec. pol. sc.*, vol. XXIX.]

Subercase, Daniel d'Auger de (1661-1732), last French governor of Acadia (1706-10), was a native of Béarn, and in October, 1684, was a captain in Brittany. On February 3, 1687, he came to Canada with fifty soldiers. In 1690 he was commandant at Verdun, and in the same year he took part in the defence of Quebec. In 1694 he became a major, and took part in Frontenac's expedition against the Iroquois in 1696. On April 1, 1702, he was chosen to fill the governorship of Terre-Neuve, and in 1704-05 he destroyed the English habitations on the island. On April 10, 1706, he became governor of Acadia, and defended the province against several attacks by the British, but was compelled to yield in October, 1710, owing to lack of troops. Following the surrender of Port Royal, he returned to France, and arrived at Nantes on December 1, 1710. He died at Cannes, France, on November 19, 1732.

[B. G., *Daniel Auger, Sieur de Subercase* (Bull. rech. hist., 1910); *Cyc. Am. biog.*; Le Jeune, *Dict. gén.*; *Dict. Can. biog.*, vol. 2.]

Sullivan, Alan (1868-1947), novelist, was born at Montreal, Quebec, on November 29,

1868, the son of the Rt. Rev. Edward Sullivan (q.v.), and died at Tilford, England, on August 6, 1947. He was educated at the University of Toronto in engineering, but did not graduate. He entered the service of the Canadian Pacific Railway, and later was employed on a series of engineering jobs. During the First World War, though over forty years of age, he served with the Royal Air Force. In his later years he lived in England. He was the author of over forty novels, ten of them under the *nom de plume* of "Sinclair Murray". The most successful of his novels were probably those that dealt with Canada, such as *The rapids* (Toronto, 1920), *Under the northern lights* (London, 1926), *The great divide* (London, 1935), *The fur masters* (London, 1938), *Three came to Ville Marie* (Toronto, 1941), and *The Cariboo road* (London, 1946). He was also the author of *Aviation in Canada, 1917-1918* (Toronto, 1919).

[*Saturday Night*, Aug. 23, 1947; *Can. who's who*, 1938-39; *Encyc. Can.*; bibliography in R. E. Watters, *A check-list of Canadian literature* (Toronto, 1959).]

Sullivan, Edward (1832-1899), Anglican bishop of Algoma, was born at Lurgan, Ireland, on August 18, 1832. He was educated at Trinity College, Dublin (B.A., 1857), and emigrated to Canada in 1858. In 1859 he was ordained a priest of the Church of England; and he served successively in charges at London, Montreal, Chicago, and again at Montreal. In 1882 he was elected bishop of Algoma, and he remained in charge of this diocese until ill-health compelled his retirement in 1896. He was then appointed rector of St. James Church, Toronto; and he died in Toronto, on January 6, 1899. In 1866 he married Frances Mary, daughter of Edouard Renaud, of Neufchâtel, Switzerland; and by her he had several children. He was an S.T.D. of Chicago, a D.C.L. of Lennoxville, and a D.D. of Trinity University, Toronto.

[C. H. Mockridge, *The bishops of the Church of England in Canada* (Toronto, 1896); Morgan, *Can. men* (1898); *Cyc. Am. biog.*]

Sullivan, Michael (1838-1915), senator of Canada, was born in Killarney, Ireland, on February 13, 1838, and came to Canada with his parents in 1842. He was educated at Regiopolis College and at Queen's University; and he began the practice of surgery in Kingston, Canada West, in 1858. He was professor of anatomy in Queen's University from 1862 to 1870, and professor of surgery from 1870 to 1904. He was called to the Senate of Canada in 1884; and he died at Kingston, Ontario, on January 26, 1915.

[W. Gibson, *Senator the Hon. Michael Sullivan, M.D.* (Canadian Catholic Historical Association, report, 1938-39); Rose, *Cyc. Can. biog* (1886); *Can. parl. comp.*]

Sullivan, Robert Baldwin (1802-1853), politician and judge, was born at Bandon, near Cork, Ireland, on May 24, 1802, the second son of Daniel Sullivan and Barbara Baldwin, sister of William Warren Baldwin (q.v.). He came to Canada with his parents in 1819; and in 1828 he was called to the bar of Upper Canada. In 1835 he was elected mayor of Toronto, and in 1836 he was appointed by Sir F. Bond Head (q.v.) a member of the Executive Council of Upper Canada. In 1839 he was appointed also a member of the Legislative Council of the province, and as such he played an important part in helping Charles Poulett Thomson (q.v.) to bring about the union of Upper and Lower Canada in 1840. In 1841 he was appointed a member of the Legislative Council of united Canada; and he became president of the council in the first government of the united province. He continued to occupy this office in the first Baldwin-Lafontaine administration; but in 1844 he resigned with his colleagues, as a protest against the policy of Sir Charles Metcalfe (q.v.). In connection with the resignation of the ministry, he engaged in a newspaper controversy with the Rev. Egerton Ryerson (q.v.); and his contribution to the controversy was published under the pen-name of "Legion", with the title, *Letters on responsible government* (Toronto, 1844). In 1848 he was included in the second Baldwin-Lafontaine administration, as provincial secretary; but later in the same year he was appointed a puisne judge of the Court of Queen's Bench. In 1850 he was transferred to the Court of Common Pleas, and he sat in this court until his death at Toronto on April 14, 1853. He was twice married, (1) in 1829 to Cecelia Eliza (d. 1830), daughter of Capt. John Matthews, R.A., and (2) in 1833 to Emily Louisa, daughter of Lieut.-Col. Philip Delatre, of Stamford, Upper Canada, who survived him and who married secondly, in 1875, the Hon. Sir Francis Hincks (q.v.). By his second wife he had four sons and seven daughters.

[D. B. Read, *Lives of the judges of Upper Canada* (Toronto, 1888); Morgan, *Cel. Can. and Bib. can.*; J. C. Dent, *The Upper Canadian rebellion* (2 vols., Toronto, 1885) and *The last forty years* (2 vols., Toronto, 1881); E. M. Chadwick, *Ontarian families* (2 vols., Toronto, 1894-98).]

Sullivan, Timothy (or **Timothée Silvain**) (1696-1749), physician, was born in the parish of St. Philibert, Cork, the son of Daniel Sullivan, a lieutenant-general in the army of James II. He came to Canada in 1718, and practised medicine in Montreal for many years. He died at Montreal on June 16, 1749.

[Agidius Fauteux, *Un médecin irlandais à Montréal avant la conquête* (Bull. rech. hist., 1917); *Dict. Can biog.*, vol. 3.]

Sullivan, Sir William Wilfred (1843-1920), prime minister of Prince Edward Island

(1879-89), and chief justice (1889-1917), was born at New London, Prince Edward Island, on December 6, 1843. He was educated at St. Dunstan's College, and was called to the bar in 1867 (Q.C., 1876). From 1872 to 1889 he represented King's county in the Legislative Assembly of the Island; and from 1879 to 1889 he was the provincial prime minister. From 1889 to 1917 he was chief justice of Prince Edward Island; and in 1914 he was created a knight bachelor. He died at Memramcook, New Brunswick, on September 30, 1920.

[*Can. parl. comp.*; Morgan, *Can. men* (1912).]

Sulte, Benjamin (1841-1923), historian, was born at Three Rivers, Lower Canada, on September 17, 1841, the son of Benjamin Sulte and Marie Antoinette Lefebvre. He was educated at Three Rivers and at the Royal Military School, Quebec; and from 1860 to 1867 he was a journalist. He then entered the civil service of Canada, as an assistant translator in the House of Commons, and later he became an official in the department of militia and defence. In 1902 he retired from the civil service on pension; and he died at Ottawa on August 6, 1923. In 1871 he married Augustine, daughter of Etienne Parent (q.v.), under-secretary of state for Canada.

For over sixty years he was an indefatigable student of Canadian history. His most ambitious work was his *Histoire des canadiens-français* (8 vols., Montreal, 1882-84); but he published also the following works: *Histoire des Trois-Rivières* (Montreal, 1870), *Mélanges d'histoire et de littérature* (Ottawa, 1876), *Chronique trifluvienne* (Montreal, 1879), *La poésie française au Canada* (Montreal, 1881), *Album de l'histoire des Trois-Rivières* (Montreal, 1881), *Histoire de St. François-du-Lac* (Montreal, 1886), *Pages d'histoire du Canada* (Montreal, 1891), *Histoire de la milice canadienne-français* (Montreal, 1897), *La langue française au Canada* (Lévis, 1898), and *La bataille de Châteauguay* (Quebec, 1899). To newspapers and other periodicals he contributed innumerable articles on historical matters; and the more important of these have been collected and edited by Gérard Malchelosse under the title *Mélanges historiques* (21 vols., Montreal, 1918-34). He published also two volumes of verse, *Les Laurentiennes* (Montreal, 1870) and *Les chants nouveaux* (Ottawa, 1876); and he was the author of a French translation of "God Save the King". In 1882 he was appointed a charter member of the Royal Society of Canada, and in 1904 he was elected its president.

[G. Malchelosse, *Cinquante-six ans de vie littéraire* (Montreal, 1916); F. J. Audet, *Benjamin Sulte* (Bull. rech. hist., 1926); *Proc. Roy. Soc. Can.*, 1924; Morgan, *Can. men* (1912); Rose, *Cyc. Can. biog.* (1886); Le Jeune, *Dict. gén.*]

Surveyer, Edouard Fabre (1875-1957), jurist and historian, was born at Montreal, Quebec, on March 24, 1875, and died there on May 18, 1957. He was educated at Laval University (B.A., 1893; LL.M., 1896) and McGill University (B.C.L., 1896), and was called to the bar in 1896 (K.C., 1909). He practised law in Montreal; and in 1920 was appointed a judge of the Superior Court of the province of Quebec. In 1930 he was elected a fellow of Section II of the Royal Society of Canada; and he contributed a number of papers to the *Transactions* of the Society. He was the author of *The bench and bar of Montreal* (Montreal, 1907) and *The bench and bar of Quebec* (Montreal, 1931); and he was joint author, with F. J. Audet (q.v.), of *Les députés au premier parlement de Bas-Canada* (Montreal, 1946).

[*Can. who's who*, 1955-57; *Encyc. Can.*]

Sutherland, Alexander (1833-1910), clergyman and author, was born near Guelph, Upper Canada, on September 13, 1833. He was educated at Victoria College, Cobourg, and was ordained a minister of the Methodist Church in 1859. For 36 years he was foreign mission secretary of the Methodist Church in Canada. He died at Toronto on June 30, 1910. He was the author of *A summer in prairie land* (Toronto, 1882), *The Kingdom of God and problems of to-day* (Toronto, 1898), *Methodism in Canada* (London, 1903), and *The Methodist church and missions in Canada and Newfoundland* (Toronto, 1906).

[Morgan, *Can. men* (1898); *Cyc. Am. biog.*; Rose, *Cyc. Can. biog.* (1888).]

Sutherland, Daniel (1756?-1832), deputy postmaster-general of British North America (1817-28), was born in Scotland about 1756, and came to Canada as a young man. He appears as a merchant in Montreal as early as 1778, and for a number of years he was engaged in the fur-trade. He was one of the partners of the North West Company in 1790. In 1812 he was appointed postmaster at Montreal; and in 1817 he succeeded George Heriot (q.v.) as deputy postmaster-general of British North America. He retained this post until 1828, when he was succeeded by his son-in-law, T. A. Stayner (q.v.). He was a promoter of the Montreal Water Works Company in 1800, and of the Bank of Montreal in 1817. From 1818 to 1824 he was cashier of the Bank of Montreal at Quebec. He died of cholera at Quebec on August 19, 1832. In 1771 he married in Montreal Margaret Robertson; and by her he had several children.

[R. W. McLachlan, *Two Canadian golden wedding medals* (Canadian antiquarian and numismatic journal, 3rd series, vol. iii); W. S. Wallace (ed.), *Documents relating to the North West Company* (Toronto: The Champlain Society, 1934).]

Sutherland, George (1830-1893), clergyman and author, was born in New Glasgow, Nova Scotia, in 1830, and was educated at the Presbyterian College, Halifax. He was for many years pastor of the Presbyterian church in Charlottetown, Prince Edward Island; but in 1867 he went to New Zealand, and thence to Australia. He died at Sydney, New South Wales, in 1893. Besides a number of publications on religious subjects, he was the author of *A manual of the geography and natural and civil history of Prince Edward Island* (Charlottetown, P.E.I., 1861) and *The Magdalen islands* (Charlottetown, P.E.I., 1862).

[R. J. Long, *Nova Scotia authors* (East Orange, N.J., 1918).]

Sutherland, Hugh McKay (1843-1926), railway builder, was born at New London, Prince Edward Island, on February 22, 1843. He was educated in Oxford county, Canada West, whither his parents removed in 1849; and in 1878 he went to Winnipeg, and engaged there in the lumbering and contracting business. He was the chief organizer of the Winnipeg and Hudson's Bay Railway Company in 1887; and later he became one of the chief promoters of the Canadian Northern Railway. From 1882 to 1887 he represented Selkirk in the Canadian House of Commons. He died in England on August 14, 1926.

[Morgan, *Can. men* (1912); *Can. parl. comp.*]

Sutherland, James (1778-1844), fur-trader, was born at Ronaldsay, in the Orkney Islands, in 1778, and entered the service of the Hudson's Bay Company in 1797. He was first employed as a writer at York Factory. From 1808 to 1813 he was master at Cumberland House; and in 1816 he was made a prisoner by the Nor'Westers, during the Selkirk troubles. From 1819 to 1821 he was in charge of the Swan River district; and he was promoted to the rank of chief factor in 1821. He retired from the Company's service in 1827; and he died at the Red River Settlement on September 30, 1844. He is to be distinguished from an earlier servant of the Hudson's Bay Company, named James Sutherland, who died while in charge of Brandon House in 1797.

[E. E. Rich (ed.), *Journal of occurrences in the Athabasca department by George Simpson* (Toronto: The Champlain Society, 1938).]

Sutherland, James (1849-1905), minister of public works for Canada (1902-05), was born in the township of Ancaster, Upper Canada, on July 17, 1849, the son of Alexander Sutherland and Alison Renton. He was educated at the grammar school, Woodstock, Ontario, and entered business as a grocer and crockery merchant in Woodstock. From 1880 to 1905 he represented North Oxford in the Canadian House of Commons; in 1892 he was appointed chief "whip" for the Liberal party in the Commons; and in 1902 he became minister of public works in the Laurier government. He died at Woodstock, Ontario, on May 3, 1905. He was not married.

[Morgan, *Can. men* (1898); *Can. parl. comp.*]

Sutherland, John (1821-1899), senator of Canada, was born at the Red River Settlement on August 23, 1821, the son of Alexander Sutherland, and was educated at St. John's College. For several years he was a member of the Council of Assiniboia, and in 1870 he was appointed high sheriff of Manitoba; but he resigned this post in 1871, when he was called to the Senate of Canada. He sat in the Senate until his death on April 27, 1899.

[*Can. parl. comp.*]

Sutherland, John Campbell (1860-1936), author, was born in Galt, Canada West, on December 4, 1860. He was educated at the Galt Collegiate Institute under Dr. Tassie (q.v.) and at Queen's University, Kingston (B.A., 1901). In 1911 he was appointed inspector-general of Protestant schools in the province of Quebec; and he held this post until his death at Quebec on April 10, 1936. He was the author of *Canadian rural education* (Quebec, 1913), *The province of Quebec: Geographical and social studies* (Montreal, 1922), and *The romance of Quebec* (Toronto, 1934).

[*Educational record of the province of Quebec*, 1936; Morgan, *Can. men* (1912).]

Sutherland, Robert Franklin (1859-1922), speaker of the Canadian House of Commons (1905-09), was born at Newmarket, Ontario, on April 5, 1859, the son of Donald Sutherland and Jane Boddy. He was educated at the University of Toronto and Western University, and was called to the bar of Ontario in 1886 (Q.C., 1899). He practised law at Windsor, Ontario; and from 1900 to 1909 he represented North Essex in the Canadian House of Commons, as a Liberal. From 1905 to 1909 he was speaker of the House, and in 1909 he was sworn of the Canadian Privy Council. In 1909 he was appointed a judge of the High Court of Justice of Ontario; and he retained this position until his death, at Toronto, on May 23, 1922. In 1888 he married Mary Bartlett, of Windsor, Ontario.

[Morgan, *Can. men* (1912); *Can. parl. comp.*]

Sutherland, Thomas Jefferson (*fl.* 1837-1841), "patriot general", was a solicitor and journalist of Buffalo, New York, who was appointed by William Lyon Mackenzie (q.v.) second-in-command, under "General" Van Rensselaer (q.v.), of the "patriot" army gathered in 1837-38 on Navy Island in the Niagara River. He was sent from Navy Island to Detroit, and was in command of the filibusterers who captured Bois Blanc Island in 1838. Subsequently, he was captured, tried, and condemned to banishment to Van Diemen's Land; but, after several months' imprisonment at Quebec, he was released by orders of the British government, which regarded both his capture and his trial as irregular. He then returned to the United States, and published *Loose leaves from the portfolio of a late patriot prisoner in Canada* (New York, 1839), *Three political letters, addressed to Dr. Wolfred Nelson* (New York, 1840), and *A letter to her Majesty the British queen* (Albany, N.Y., 1841).

[E. C. Guillet, *The lives and times of the patriots* (Toronto, 1938); W. R. Riddell, *Old province tales* (Toronto, 1920).]

Suzor, Louis Théodore (1834-1866), soldier and author, was born in Lower Canada in 1834, and entered the Canadian volunteer militia in 1855. He rose to the rank of lieutenant-colonel; and at the time of his death at Quebec, on August 18, 1866, was deputy assistant adjutant-general of the militia. He was the author of *Aide-mémoire de carabinier-volontaire* (Quebec, 1862), *Tableau synoptique des mouvements d'une compagnie* (Quebec, 1863), *Tableau synoptique des mouvements de bataillon* (Quebec, 1863), *Exercices et évolutions d'infanterie* (Quebec, 1863), *Code militaire* (Quebec, 1864), *Maximes, conseils, et instructions sur l'art de la guerre* (Quebec, 1865), *Guide théorique et pratique des manoeuvres de l'infanterie* (Quebec, 1865), and *Traité d'art et d'histoire militaire* (Quebec, 1865).

[*Bull. rech. hist.*, 1927; Morgan, *Bib. can.*]

Sverdrup, Otto (1855-1930), Arctic explorer, was born at Harstad Farm, Helgeland, Norway, January 1, 1855. He went to sea in 1872; in 1888 he accompanied Nansen in his first crossing of Greenland; and from 1893 to 1896 was captain of the *Fram* on Nansen's famous attempt to reach the North Pole. In 1898 he took the *Fram* on a second expedition, this time as leader, with the object of exploring round the north of Greenland. He extricated himself from the ice only in 1902; but in the interval he discovered vast areas of unexpected new land west of Ellesmere Island — new land of almost greater area than that uncovered by the combined efforts of the Franklin search expeditions. In 1914-15 and in 1920 he led Arctic expeditions to the Kara Sea; but his fame as an explorer rests chiefly on his expedition of 1898-1902. He died in Oslo on November 26, 1930. His expedition of 1898-1902 was described in his *New land: Four years in Arctic regions* (tr. by H. H. Hearn, 2 vols., London, 1904).

[*Encyclopaedia Britannica; Americana.*]

Swabey, Maurice (d. 1902), clergyman and poet, was educated at King's College, Windsor

(B.A., 1852; M.A., 1859), and was ordained a priest of the Church of England in 1854. Between 1854 and 1875 he served in several parishes in Prince Edward Island and in Saint John, New Brunswick; and from 1875 to shortly before his death he was vicar of St. Thomas's Church, Exeter, England. He died at Exeter in 1902. Shortly after leaving New Brunswick, he published a volume of poetry, *Voices from Abegweet; or, The home on the wave* (London, 1878).

[*Acadiensis*, 1902.]

Swanson, William Walker (1879-1950), economist, was born in Scotland on December 15, 1879, and died at Saskatoon, Saskatchewan, on July 21, 1950. He was educated at Queen's University, Kingston (M.A., 1905) and the University of Chicago (Ph.D., 1908); and he was appointed professor of economics in the University of Saskatchewan. He was the author of *The establishment of the national banking system* (Kingson, 1910), *Depression and the way out* (Toronto, 1931), and *Rail, road, and river* (Toronto, 1937); and he was joint author, with P. C. Armstrong, of *Wheat* (Toronto, 1930).

[*Can. who's who*, 1948.]

Sweatman, Arthur (1834-1909), Anglican archbishop of Toronto (1906-09), was born in London, England, on November 19, 1834, the son of Dr. John Sweatman, of the Middlesex Hospital, London. He was educated at Christ's College, Cambridge (B.A., 1859; M.A., 1862; D.D., 1879), and was ordained a priest of the Church of England. He came to Canada in 1865 as headmaster of the Hellmuth Boys' College, London, Ontario; and in 1879 he was chosen bishop of Toronto. In 1906 he became archbishop of Toronto, and primate of All Canada; and he died at Toronto on January 24, 1909. He married Susanna, daughter of Robert Garland, of Islington, England; and by her he had several children.

[C. H. Mockridge, *The bishops of the Church of England in Canada* (Toronto, 1896); *Can. who was who*, vol. 2; Morgan, *Can. men* (1898); Dent, *Can. port.*]

Sweeney, James Fielding (1857-1940), Anglican archbishop of Toronto, was born in London, England, on November 15, 1857. He was educated at McGill University (B.A., 1878; M.A., 1881; LL.D., 1921), at the Montreal Diocesan College, and at Trinity University, Toronto (B.D., 1883; D.D., 1888); and he was ordained a priest of the Church of England in 1881. He became rector of St. Philip's Church, Toronto, in 1882; and in 1909 he was elected fourth Anglican bishop of Toronto. In 1932 he became archbishop and metropolitan of Ontario; but a few months later he resigned because of ill-health. He died at Toronto, Ontario, on September 17, 1940.

[*Can. who's who*, 1936-37; Morgan, *Can. men* (1912).]

Sweeney, John (1821-1901), Roman Catholic bishop of Saint John, New Brunswick, was born at Clones, Ireland, on May 12, 1821. He came with his parents to New Brunswick in early childhood, was educated at St. Andrew's College, Prince Edward Island, and at the Quebec Seminary, and was ordained a priest in 1844. He was consecrated bishop of Saint John, New Brunswick, in 1860; and he presided over this diocese until his death on March 25, 1901.

[Morgan, *Can. men* (1898); Le Jeune, *Dict. gén.*]

Sweeney, Robert (d. 1840), poet, was a native of Ireland who settled in Montreal about 1820. He was killed in a duel with Major Ward, of the Montreal garrison, in Montreal in 1840. He married Charlotte, daughter of Robert Emmett Temple, of Rutland, Vermont, afterwards the wife of Sir John Rose, Bart. (q.v.). He published in 1826 a small volume of verse entitled *Odds and ends*.

[A. Fauteux, *Le duel au Canada* (Montreal, 1934); C. M. Whyte-Edgar, *A wreath of Canadian song* (Toronto, 1910).]

Sydenham, Charles Poulett Thomson, first Baron (1799-1841), governor-general of Canada (1839-41), was born at Wimbledon, England, on September 13, 1799, the son of J. Poulett Thomson, a merchant. He was privately educated, and at the age of sixteen entered the St. Petersburg office of his father's firm, where he spent a number of years. From 1826 to 1830 he represented Dover in the House of Commons, and from 1830 to 1839 he represented Manchester. In 1830 he was appointed vice-president of the Board of Trade and treasurer of the navy in Earl Grey's administration; in 1834 he became president of the Board of Trade; and, except for an interval of a few months in 1834-35, he occupied this office until his appointment as governor-general of Canada in 1839, in succession to Lord Durham (q.v.).

A Liberal with a business training, he was sent to Canada to carry into effect Lord Durham's recommendations with regard to the union of the Canadas and the introduction of responsible government and municipal institutions. The union of the Canadas he achieved, with adroit diplomacy, by obtaining the assent of the Special Council of Lower Canada and the legislature of Upper Canada; and in 1840 the Act of Union passed the British parliament. Municipal institutions he succeeded in introducing into Upper Canada in 1841; and responsible government he introduced into the legislature of united Canada in a partial degree. He set up the machinery of responsible government with an executive council composed of heads of departments with seats in the legislature, and in harmony with the majority in the legislature. But he was his own prime minister; he himself presided over the meetings of council; and he took the view that "the Council was a council to be consulted, and no more." His régime was admirably suited for bridging over the period of transition to full responsible government; but it may be doubted whether it could have survived long, since it depended for its success on his finding a Council in harmony both with himself and with the majority in the Assembly.

It was perhaps, therefore, fortunate for his reputation that his period of office was cut short. On September 19, 1841, he died at Kingston, Upper Canada, as the result of a fall from his horse; and he was succeeded in office by Sir Charles Bagot (q.v.). In 1840 he had been created, for his services, Baron Sydenham of Kent in England and Toronto in Canada; and in 1841 he was made a G.C.B. But he died unmarried, and the peerage expired with him.

[G. Poulett Scrope, *Memoir of the life of Charles, Lord Sydenham* (London, 1844); A. Shortt, *Lord Sydenham* (Toronto, 1908); J. L. Morison, *British supremacy and Canadian self-government* (Toronto, 1919); *Dict. nat. biog.*; Morgan, *Cel. Can.*; W. P. M. Kennedy, *The constitution of Canada* (London, 1922).]

Sykes, Frederick Henry (1863-1917), educationist and author, was born at Queensville, Ontario, on October 21, 1863. He was educated at the University of Toronto (B.A., 1885; M.A., 1886), and at Johns Hopkins University (Ph.D., 1894). From 1895 to 1897 he was professor of English and history at the Western University, London, Ontario; but he then went to the United States, and, after occupying several academic positions, he became, in 1903, professor of English literature and director of extension teaching at Columbia University. From 1913 to 1917 he was president of the Connecticut College for Women. He died at Cambridge, Massachusetts, on October 14, 1917. In addition to editing a large number of college textbooks, he was the author of *French elements in middle English* (Oxford, 1899), *Elementary English composition* (Toronto, 1902), *Syllabus of lectures on Shakespeare* (New York, 1903), *Syllabus of lectures on the history of English literature in the nineteenth century* (New York, 1904), and *Public school English composition* (Toronto, 1908).

[*Who was who in America*; Morgan, *Can. men* (1912).]

Symington, Herbert James (1881-1965), lawyer and company director, was born at Sarnia, Ontario, November 22, 1881. He was educated at the University of Toronto and was called to the bar of Manitoba in 1905. He practised law in Winnipeg from 1905 until 1927. He was an expert on freight rates and represented the Western provinces in freight rate disputes. In 1927 he moved to Montreal, where he became solicitor and vice-president of Royal

Securities Corporation. In 1936 he became director of Canadian National Railways; he was on the board of Trans-Canada Air Lines at its formation in 1937, and was president from 1941 to 1947. He helped organize the International Civil Aviation Association and the International Air Transport Association and was the first president of the latter organization. During the Second World War he was power controller of the United States–Canada Raw Materials Board with responsibility for allocating electrical power. He was chairman and director of Price Brothers Company, and director of Canadian National Railways, Federal Grain, Canadian Marconi, International Power, Ottawa Valley Power, Bolivian Power, and Venezuelan Power. He died at Montreal, Quebec, September 28, 1965.

[*Can. who's who*, 1955-57; Metropolitan Toronto Library Board, *Biographical scrapbooks*, vol. 23.]

Symonds, Herbert (1860-1921), clergyman, was born in Suffolk, England, on December 28, 1860. He came to Canada as a young man, and was educated at Trinity University, Toronto (B.A., 1886; M.A., 1887). He was ordained a priest of the Church of England in 1887. From 1887 to 1892 he was a lecturer and then a professor of divinity on the staff of Trinity University; he was later rector of a church in Peterborough, Ontario; and from 1901 to 1903 he was headmaster of Trinity College School, Port Hope. In 1903 he was appointed vicar of Christ Church Cathedral, Montreal; and he continued in this position until his death at Montreal, Quebec, on May 24, 1921.

He was the author of *Lectures on Christian unity* (Toronto, 1899).

[*Herbert Symonds: A memoir* (Montreal, 1922); *Can. who was who*, vol. 1; Morgan, *Can. men* (1912).]

Symons, John (1808-1902), lawyer and financier, was born in Derby, England, on November 19, 1808. He studied law, was admitted a solicitor in 1832, and practised in London for twenty years. He then came to Canada, was admitted to the bar of Upper Canada, and for some years practised law in Toronto. In 1858 he founded the Canada Landed Credit Company, and he was its manager for many years. He died in Toronto, Ontario, in 1902. He was the author of *The battle of Queenston Heights* (Toronto, 1859).

[*Commemorative biographical record of the county of York, Ontario* (Toronto, 1907).]

Synge, Millington Henry (1823-1907), soldier and author, was born in Ireland on September 1, 1823. He became an officer in the Royal Engineers, and in 1848 was employed on the works at Bytown (Ottawa), Canada West. He rose to the rank of major-general in the British army; and he died on September 10, 1907. He was the author of several pamphlets relating to Canada: *Canada in 1848* (London, 1848?), *Great Britain one empire* (London, 1852), and *The colony of Rupert's Land* (London, 1863).

[F. M. Staton and M. Tremaine (eds.), *A bibliography of Canadiana* (Toronto, 1934); Burke's *Peerage and baronetage*.]

T

Tabaret, Joseph Henri (1828-1886), founder of the University of Ottawa, was born in France in 1828, and entered the Oblate order in 1845. He was sent to Canada, and was ordained a priest in 1850. In 1853 Mgr Guigues (q.v) placed him in charge of the college which he had established at Ottawa, as superior, and this college grew into the University of Ottawa. He died at Ottawa on February 28, 1886.

[G. Simard, *Le Père Tabaret et son oeuvre d'éducation* (Ottawa, 1928) and *Le fondateur de l'Université d'Ottawa* (Trans. Roy. Soc. Can., 1943); Le Jeune, *Dict. gén*; Allaire, *Dict. biog.*]

Taché, Alexandre Antonin (1823-1894), Roman Catholic archbishop of St. Boniface, was born at Rivière du Loup, Lower Canada, on July 23, 1823, the son of Charles Taché, eldest brother of Sir Etienne Paschal Taché (q.v.), and Henriette Boucher de la Broquerie. He was educated at the College of St. Hyacinthe and the Theological Seminary of Montreal; and in 1844 he became a novice in the Oblate order. In 1845 he went as a missionary to the Red River; in 1851 he was consecrated coadjutor bishop of St. Boniface; in 1853, on the death of Bishop Provencher (q.v.), he became second bishop of St. Boniface; and in 1871 he was created archbishop and metropolitan of St. Boniface. During the Red River rebellion of 1869 he was absent from the country; but he returned at the request of the Canadian government, and was greatly influential in restoring order. Unfortunately, his promises to the rebels, made in excess of his instructions, gave rise to much controversy. This controversy he dealt with in two pamphlets entitled *L'amnistie* (Montreal, 1874) and *Encore l'amnistie* (St. Boniface, 1875). He played also an important part in the earlier stages of the Manitoba separate schools controversy; and in this connection he published *Denominational or free Christian schools in Manitoba* (Winnipeg, 1877), *Les écoles séparées de Manitoba* (St. Boniface, 1890), *Une page d'histoire des écoles de Manitoba* (Montreal, 1894), and *Mémoire sur la question des écoles* (Montreal, 1894). He published also *Vingt années de missions dans le Nord-Ouest de L'Amérique* (Montreal, 1866), *Esquisse sur le Nord-Ouest de l'Amérique* (Montreal, 1869; tr. by Capt. D. R. Cameron, Montreal, 1870; new ed. by Mgr Langevin, Montreal, 1901), and *La situation au Nord-Ouest* (Quebec, 1885). He died at Winnipeg, Manitoba, on June 22, 1894.

[Dom Benoit, *Vie de Mgr Taché* (2 vols., Montreal, 1904); L. O. David, *Mgr A. A. Taché* (Montreal, 1883); *Vingt-cinquième anniversaire de l'épiscopat de Sa Grandeur Monseigneur Taché* (Montreal, 1875); *Dict. nat. biog.*; *Cyc. Am. biog.*; Dent, *Can. port.*, vol. 3; A. G. Morice, *History of the Catholic Church in western Canada* (2 vols., Toronto, 1910); P. G. Roy, *La famille Taché* (Lévis, Que., 1904); Le Jeune, *Dict. gén.*]

Taché, Sir Etienne Paschal (1795-1865), statesman, was born at St. Thomas, Lower Canada, in 1795, the third son of Charles Taché of Montmagny, and through his paternal grandmother was a descendant of Louis Jolliet (q.v.). He was educated at the Quebec Seminary; and he fought on the British side throughout the War of 1812. He then studied medicine, and for many years was a country doctor in his native parish. In 1841 he was elected to the Legislative Assembly of Canada for the county of L'Islet, and he sat for his county until 1846. From 1846 to 1848 he was deputy adjutant-general of militia for Lower Canada, with the rank of colonel; but in 1848 he re-entered political life as commissioner of public works in the Baldwin-Lafontaine administration, and was appointed a member of the Legislative Council. In 1849 he changed his portfolio for that of receiver-general; and this portfolio he retained in the successive Baldwin-Lafontaine, Hincks-Morin, MacNab-Morin, MacNab-Taché, and Taché-Macdonald administrations until his retirement from office in 1857. From 1856 to 1857 he was also technically prime minister, though the real head of the government was John A. Macdonald (q.v). From 1857 to 1864 Taché continued a member of the Legislative Council; and in 1858 he was created a knight bachelor, and in 1860 an aide-de-camp of the Queen, with the honorary rank of colonel in the British Army. In 1864, however, he was called from his retirement to become again prime minister in the second Taché-Macdonald administration; and, on the defeat of this government in June, 1864, he was pressed into service as the technical prime minister in the "Great Coalition". As such, he presided at the Quebec Conference; but before Confederation had been accomplished, he died at St. Thomas on July 30, 1865. He wrote *Quelques réflexions sur l'organisation de volontaires* (Quebec, 1863).

[M. O. Hammond, *Confederation and its leaders* (Toronto, 1917); *Dict. nat. biog.*; Dent, *Can. port.*, vol. 4; Taylor, *Brit. Am.*, vol. 1; Morgan, *Cel. Can.* and *Bib. can.*; P. G. Roy, *La famille Taché* (Lévis, Que., 1904); J. C. Dent, *The last forty years* (2 vols., Toronto, 1881).]

Taché, Joseph B. de la Broquerie (1858-1932), librarian, was born at St. Hyacinthe, Canada East, on March 22, 1858; and was educated at the St. Hyacinthe Seminary and at Laval University. From 1880 to 1882 he was private secretary to the Hon. J. A. Chapleau (q.v.), and from 1887 to 1892 to Sir A. R. Angers (q.v.). He then became a journalist, and from 1902 to 1914 he was editor and proprietor of *Le Courier de St. Hyacinthe*. In 1914 he was appointed King's Printer at Ottawa; and in 1920, general librarian of parliament. He died at Ottawa on March 21, 1932.

[*Can. parl. comp.*]

Taché, Joseph Charles (1820-1894), journalist and author, was born at Kamouraska, Lower Canada, on December 24, 1820, the son of Charles Taché and of Henriette Boucher de la Broquerie. He was educated at the Quebec Seminary, and became a physician and surgeon. From 1847 to 1857 he sat in the Legislative Assembly of Canada, first for Rimouski, and then for Témiscouata. From 1857 to 1859 he was editor of *Le Courrier du Canada*; in 1860 he became professor of physiology in Laval University; and in 1864 he was appointed deputy minister of agriculture for Canada. This office he continued to hold after Confederation until his retirement in 1888. He published many books and pamphlets on a wide variety of subjects; but his chief publications were *Esquisse sur le Canada* (Paris, 1855), *Des provinces de l'Amérique du Nord et d'une union fédérale* (Quebec, 1858), *Trois légendes de mon pays* (Montreal, 1876), *Forestiers et voyageurs* (Montreal, 1884), and *Les sablons* (Montreal, 1885). He died at Ottawa on April 16, 1894. In 1847 he married Françoise Lepage; and by her he had six children.

[P. G. Roy, *La famille Taché* (Lévis, 1904); Morgan, *Cel. Can.* and *Bib. can.*; Rose, *Cyc. Can. biog.* (1886); *Dict. nat. biog.*; Le Jeune, *Dict. gén.*]

Taché, Louis Hyppolite (1859-1927), author, was born at St. Hyacinthe, Quebec, on

August 30, 1859, the son of Antoine-Louis-Jean-Etienne Taché and Marie-Charlotte Beaudet. He was called to the Quebec bar in 1883, and for several years was private secretary to Sir J. A. Chapleau (q.v.). He died at Montreal on May 22, 1927. He was the author of *La poésie française au Canada* (St. Hyacinthe, 1881), *A legal hand-book and law-list for the Dominion of Canada* (Toronto, 1888), and the *Montreal citizen's directory* (Montreal, 1893); and he edited the *Nouvelles soirées canadiennes* (Quebec and Ottawa, 1882-88), and *Men of the day* (Ottawa and Montreal, 1890-94).

[*Bull. rech. hist.*, 1927.]

Taffanel, Jacques-Pierre, Marquis de La Jonquière. See **La Jonquière, Jacques-Pierre Taffanel, Marquis de.**

Taggart, William Stuart (1859-1925), portrait painter, was born at Stouffville, Canada West, in 1859. He was educated in the public and high schools of Ontario, and studied painting in England. He lived in Ottawa, Ontario, during the last thirty years of his life; and he executed portraits of Sir John Macdonald (q.v.), Sir John Thompson (q.v.), and Sir Wilfrid Laurier (q.v.). He died at Ottawa, Ontario, on December 17, 1925.

[Toronto *Globe*, December 18, 1925.]

Tailhan, Jules (1816-1891), priest and historian, was born in France in 1816, entered the Society of Jesus, and was ordained a priest about 1850. In 1858 he came to Canada as professor of philosophy at Laval University, Quebec; but he returned to France in 1860. He died in Paris on June 26, 1891. He edited and annotated the *Mémoire sur les moeurs, coûtumes, et religion des sauvages de l'Amérique septentrionale* of Nicolas Perrot (Paris, 1864).

[Allaire, *Dict. biog.*; Le Jeune, *Dict. gén.*]

Taillon, Sir Louis Olivier (1840-1923), prime minister of Quebec (1887 and 1893-96), was born at Terrebonne, Lower Canada, on September 26, 1840, the son of Aimé Taillon and Marie Josephte Daunais. He was educated at Masson College; and was called to the bar of Lower Canada in 1865 (Q.C., 1882). He practised law in Montreal, and in 1892 was *bâtonnier* of the Quebec bar. He represented Montreal East in the Legislative Assembly of Quebec from 1875 to 1886, Montcalm from 1886 to 1890, and Chambly from 1892 to 1896. From 1882 to 1883 he was speaker of the Legislative Assembly; from 1884 to 1886 he was attorney-general in the Ross administration; and in 1887, and again from 1893 to 1896, he was prime minister of the province. In 1896 he became postmaster-general in the Tupper administration at Ottawa; but he was defeated in the general elections later in the year, and thereupon retired to private life. He died at Montreal on April 25, 1923. He was a D.C.L. of

Bishop's College, Lennoxville (1895) and an LL.D. of Laval University (1901); and he was created a knight bachelor in 1917.

[Morgan, *Can. men* (1912); Taché, *Men of the day*; Rose, *Cyc. Can. biog.* (1886); *Who was who*, 1916-28; *Can. parl. comp.*; Le Jeune, *Dict. gén.*]

Tait, James (1829-1899), clergyman, was born in Scotland on April 6, 1829. He came to Canada with his parents as a child, and was educated at Knox College, Toronto, and at Edinburgh University. He was ordained a minister of the Presbyterian Church in 1866; and for eighteen years he was pastor of the Presbyterian church at Fitzroy Harbour, Ontario. He then retired from parochial work, and devoted himself to writing. He was the author of *Mind in matter* (London, 1884) and *Adrift in the breakers; or, The present dangers to religion* (Montreal, 1896). He died at Montreal, Quebec, on December 22, 1899.

[Morgan, *Can. men* (1898).]

Tait, Sir Melbourne McTaggart (1842-1917), chief justice of the Superior Court of Quebec (1906-12), was born at Melbourne, Lower Canada, on May 20, 1842. He was educated at McGill University (B.C.L., 1862), and was called to the bar of Lower Canada in 1863 (Q.C., 1882). He was for many years the law partner of Sir John Abbott (q.v.). In 1887 he was appointed a judge of the Superior Court of Quebec; from 1894 to 1906 he was assistant or acting chief justice of this court; and from 1906 to 1912 chief justice. He died in Montreal on February 10, 1917. He was twice married, (1) in 1863 to Monica, daughter of James Holmes, of Montreal, and (2) in 1878 to Lily, daughter of Henry B. Kaighn, of Newport, Rhode Island. He was a D.C.L. of McGill University (1891) and of Bishop's College, Lennoxville (1891).

[F. J. Audet, *Les juges en chef de la province de Québec* (Quebec, 1917); P. G. Roy, *Les juges de la province de Québec* (Quebec, 1933); Morgan, *Can. men* (1912); Rose, *Cyc. Can. biog.* (1886); *Can. who was who*, vol. 1.]

Tait, Sir Thomas (1864-1940), railway executive, was born at Melbourne, Canada East, on July 24, 1864, the son of Sir Melbourne Tait (q.v.). In 1880 he entered the service of the Grand Trunk Railway, and from 1882 to 1886 he was private secretary to Sir William Van Horne (q.v.). He rose to the post of manager of transportation; and in 1903 he was appointed chairman of the Board of Railway Commissioners of Victoria, Australia. He retired from this post and returned to Canada in 1910; and in 1916 he was appointed director-general of national service for Canada. He resigned this post, however, within a few weeks of accepting it; and he then retired to private life. He died at his summer home at

St. Andrews, New Brunswick, on July 25, 1940. In 1911 he was created a K.B.

[*Who was who*, 1929-40; *Can. who's who*, 1936-37.]

Talbot, Edward Allen (1801-1839), journalist and author, was born in Tipperary county, Ireland, in 1801, the son of Richard Talbot. He emigrated to Upper Canada with his father in 1818, and settled in the county of Middlesex. For a time he taught school, and then he became a journalist. In 1831 he founded the *London Sun*, and later the *Freeman's Journal*. He sympathized with the rebels of 1837, and in 1838 he left Canada for the United States. He died in the poor house at Lockport, New York, on January 9, 1839. He was the author of *Five years' residence in the Canadas, including a tour through part of the United States of America, in the year 1823* (2 vols., London, 1824).

[*Quebec Gazette*, Feb. 18, 1839; *History of the county of Middlesex, Canada* (Toronto, 1889).]

Talbot, Thomas (1771-1853), the founder of the Talbot settlement in Upper Canada, was born on July 17, 1771, at Castle Malahide, county Dublin, Ireland, the son of Richard Talbot of Malahide. He entered the British army in 1782, and in 1790 he came to Canada as a subaltern in the 24th Regiment. In 1792 he was appointed private secretary to Lieut.-Col. John Graves Simcoe (q.v.), lieutenant-governor of Upper Canada, and with Simcoe he visited the western part of the province. He returned to England in 1794, became lieutenant-colonel commanding the 5th Regiment of Foot, and spent several years in active service on the continent. On the conclusion of the Peace of Amiens, however, he sold his commission, and returned to Upper Canada. Here he obtained a grant of many thousand acres, with a view to founding a settlement. He established himself at Port Talbot, on Lake Erie, and here he lived, governing his settlers in almost patriarchal state, for nearly fifty years. From 1822 to 1832 he was a member of the Legislative Council of Upper Canada; but he took little interest in politics, and never attended the meetings of the Council. He died in London, Upper Canada, on February 6, 1853. He was a bachelor, and he bequeathed his estate to his servants.

[C. O. Ermatinger, *The Talbot régime* (St. Thomas, Ont., 1904); E. Ermatinger, *The life of Colonel Talbot* (St. Thomas, Ont., 1859); L. C. Kearney, *Life of Col. Thomas Talbot* (pamphlet, 1857); J. H. Coyne (ed.), *The Talbot papers* (Trans. Roy. Soc. Can., 1907 and 1909); Taylor, *Brit. Am.*, vol. 1; Dent, *Can. port.*, vol. 3; F. C. Hamil, *Lake Erie baron* (Toronto, 1955).]

Talling, Marshall P. (1857-1921), clergyman, was born at Bowmanville, Canada West, on February 22, 1857. He was educated at the University of Toronto (B.A., 1888), Knox College, Toronto, and the Presbyterian University, Wooster, Ohio (Ph.D., 1899); and he was ordained a minister of the Presbyterian Church in 1890. He was stationed successively at London, Peterborough, and Toronto, Ontario; and he died at Toronto on December 13, 1921. He was the author of *Communion with God* (Chicago, 1902) and *The science of spiritual life* (New York, 1912).

[Morgan, *Can. men* (1912).]

Talon, Jean Baptiste (1625?-1694), intendant of New France (1665-68 and 1670-72), was born at Châlons-sur-Marne, in Champagne, about 1625, the son of Philippe Talon and Anne Beuvy. He was educated by the Jesuits in Paris, and about 1653 he entered the French administrative service. After serving as commissary of war in Flanders, and as intendant of Hainault, he was appointed in 1665 intendant of New France. He came to Canada with Courcelles (q.v.), the first intendant under royal government who actually set foot in the colony; and he inaugurated a period of striking development. He encouraged immigration, so that the population of New France increased rapidly. He fostered the trade of New France: he was the first to build ships in the colony, and the first to establish a brewery; and he might almost be described as the first to give the colony a sound economic basis. His private affairs made necessary his return to France in 1668; but he resumed the intendancy in 1670, and held the post until 1672. On his return to France in the autumn of 1672, he was appointed *secrétaire du cabinet* and *valet de chambre* of the king; and he died in Paris on November 24, 1694.

[T. Chapais, *Jean Talon, intendant de la Nouvelle-France* (Quebec, 1904) and *The great intendant* (Toronto, 1914); R. Roy, *Jean Talon* (Bull. rech. hist., vol. vii) and *Les intendants de la Nouvelle-France* (Trans. Roy. Soc. Can., 1903); G. Parizeau, *Un grand intendant de la Nouvelle France* (Revue trimestrielle canadienne, 1927); Le Jeune, *Dict. gén.*; *Dict. Can. biog.*, vol. 1.]

Tamblyn, William Ferguson (1874-1956), educationist, was born at Oshawa, Ontario, in 1874, and died at Toronto, Ontario, on March 10, 1956. He was educated at the University of Toronto (B.A., 1895) and Columbia University (Ph.D., 1899); and he was professor of English at the University of Western Ontario from 1901 to 1947. He was the author of *The establishment of Roman power in Britain* (Hamilton, Ont., 1899) and a history of the University of Western Ontario entitled *These sixty years* (London, Ont., 1938). In 1944 the University of Western Ontario conferred on him the degree of Litt. D.

[*Can. who's who*, 1952-54.]

Tanguay, Cyprien (1819-1902), priest and genealogist, was born in Quebec, Lower Canada, on September 15, 1819, the son of Pierre Tanguay and Reine Barthell. He was educated at the Quebec Seminary, and was ordained a priest of the Roman Catholic Church in 1843. From 1843 to 1865 he served in various parishes in the province of Quebec. Then he entered the service of the Canadian government, and was employed in the department of agriculture until a few years before his death, when he was retired on pension. He died at Ottawa on April 28, 1902. In 1883 he was given the honorary degree of Litt.D. by Laval University; and in 1887 he was created a *prélat romain* by the Pope. He was one of the charter members of the Royal Society of Canada in 1882. The latter part of his life was devoted to the compilation of his monumental *Dictionnaire généalogique des familles canadiennes* (7 vols., Montreal, 1871-90). He published also a *Répertoire général du clergé canadien* (Quebec, 1868-69; new ed., 1893), *Monseigneur de l'Auberivière* (Montreal, 1885), and *A travers les régistres: Notes recueillies* (Montreal, 1886).

[Allaire, *Dict. biog.*; Le Jeune, *Dict. gén.*; *Cyc. Am. biog.*; Morgan, *Can. men* (1898); Rose, *Cyc. Can. biog.* (1886); *Proc. Roy. Soc. Can.*, 1894 and 1902.]

Tardivel, Jules Paul (1851-1905), author and journalist, was born at Covington, Kentucky, on September 2, 1851, the son of Claudius Tardivel and Isabella Brent. He came to Canada in 1868, and was educated at the College of St. Hyacinthe. In 1874 he joined the staff of *Le Canadien*; and in 1881 he founded *La Vérité* at Quebec. He was strongly clerical and ultramontane in politics, and advocated the independence of French Canada. He died at Quebec on April 24, 1905. In 1874 he married Henriette Brunelle, of St. Hyacinthe, Quebec. He was the author of a *Vie du Pape Pie IX* (Quebec, 1878), *Borrowed and stolen feathers* (Quebec, 1878), *L'anglicisme voilà l'ennemi* (Quebec, 1880), *Mélanges* (Quebec, 1887), *Notes de voyage* (Montreal, 1890), *La situation religieuse aux Etats-Unis* (Lille, 1900), *La langue française au Canada* (Montreal, 1901), and a novel entitled *Pour la patrie* (Montreal, 1895).

[Mgr. J. Fèvre, *Vie et travaux de J. P. Tardivel* (Paris, 1906); P. Savard, *Jules-Paul Tardivel, la France et les Etats-Unis; 1851-1905* (Quebec, 1967); Morgan, *Can. men* (1898); *Cyc. Am. biog.*; Le Jeune, *Dict. gén.*; P. G. Roy, *Fils de Québec*, vol. 4 (Quebec, 1933).]

Tarieu de Lanaudière, Charles François Xavier. See **Lanaudière, Charles François Xavier Tarieu de.**

Tarieu de Lanaudière, Charles Louis. See **Lanaudière, Charles Louis Tarieu de.**

Tarte, Joseph Israel (1848-1907), minister of public works for Canada (1896-1902), was born at Lanoraie, Berthier county, Lower Canada, on January 11, 1848, the son of Joseph Tarte, an *habitant*. He was educated at L'Assomption College, and was admitted to practice as a notary public in 1871. He very soon, however, drifted into journalism, and here he quickly made his mark. For over twenty years he was the editor of *L'Evènement* of Quebec; and in 1897 he acquired *La Patrie*, of Montreal. From 1877 to 1881 he represented Bonaventure in the Legislative Assembly of Quebec; and in 1891 he was elected to represent L'Islet in the Canadian House of Commons. Though elected as a Conservative, he took a foremost part in pressing the charges of corruption against Sir Hector Langevin (q.v.) and Thomas McGreevy (q.v.), and went over to the Liberal opposition. In 1896 he played an important part in determining the Liberal policy in regard to separate schools in Manitoba, and in organizing the Liberal forces in the province of Quebec. On the return of the Liberals to power, he was rewarded with the portfolio of public works in the Laurier government; and his administration of his department was most effective. He was, however, unlike his colleagues, a high protectionist; and his public advocacy of higher tariffs in 1902 brought about his dismissal from the government. He thereupon assumed the editorship of *La Patrie*, of Montreal; and he died in Montreal on December 18, 1907. He was twice married: by his first wife, Georgiana Sylvestre, he had three sons and three daughters; and by his second wife, Emma Laurencelle, he had one daughter.

[*Dict. nat. biog.*, supp. II; Morgan, *Can. men* (1898); *Can. parl. comp.*; Sir J. Willison, *Sir Wilfrid Laurier and the Liberal party* (2 vols., Toronto, 1903) and *Sir Wilfrid Laurier* (Toronto, 1926); O. D. Skelton, *Life and letters of Sir Wilfrid Laurier* (2 vols., Toronto. 1923); "Vieux-Rouge", *Les Contemporains* (Montreal, 1898).]

Taschereau, Antoine Charles (1797-1862), politician, was born at Quebec on October 26, 1797, the son of the Hon. Gabriel Elzéar Taschereau (q.v.) and his second wife, Louise-Françoise Juchereau Duchesnay. He represented Beauce in the Legislative Assembly of Lower Canada from 1830 to 1838; and in 1834, as chairman of the select committee appointed to report on the state of the province, he presented in the House the famous Ninety-two Resolutions. From 1841 to 1844 he represented Dorchester in the Legislative Assembly of United Canada. In 1849 he was appointed collector of customs at Quebec. He died at Deschambault, Lower Canada, on June 11, 1862. In 1819 he married Adelaide Elizabeth, daughter of Louis Fleury de la Gorgendière, seignior of Deschambault; and by her he had twelve children.

[P. G. Roy, *La famille Juchereau Duchesnay* (Lévis, 1903); Le Jeune, *Dict. gén.*]

Taschereau, Elzéar Alexandre (1820-1898), cardinal archbishop of Quebec, was born at Ste. Marie de la Beauce, Lower Canada, on February 17, 1820, the son of the Hon. Jean Thomas Taschereau (q.v.) and Marie, daughter of the Hon. Jean Antoine Panet (q.v.). He was educated at the Quebec Seminary, and was ordained a priest of the Roman Catholic Church in 1842. For nearly thirty years he was connected with the Quebec Seminary, first as a professor, then as director, and finally as superior. In 1862 he was chosen as vicar-general of the diocese of Quebec, and in 1871 was consecrated sixteenth bishop and sixth archbishop of Quebec. In 1886 he was created a cardinal of the Roman Catholic Church, being the first Canadian to attain this honour. He retired from the administration of his diocese in 1894; and he died at Quebec on April 12, 1898. He was the author of *Remarques sur les mémoires de l'évêque de Trois-Rivières sur les difficultés religieuses en Canada* (Quebec, 1882).

[T. E. Hamel, *Le premier cardinal canadien* (Quebec, 1886); H. Têtu, *S. E. le Cardinal Taschereau* (Quebec, 1898); *Can. who was who*, vol. 1; Morgan, *Can. men* (1898); *Cyc. Am. biog.*; Rose, *Cyc. Can. biog.* (1888); Taché, *Men of the day*; Le Jeune, *Dict. gén.*]

Taschereau, Gabriel Elzéar (1745-1809), legislative councillor of Lower Canada, was born at Quebec on March 27, 1745, the son of Thomas-Jacques Taschereau, a member of the Superior Council of New France, and Marie-Claire Fleury de la Gorgendière. He remained in Canada after the conquest, and took part in the defence of Quebec against the Americans in 1775. In 1777 he was appointed a judge of the Court of Common Pleas for Montreal, but resigned soon afterwards. From 1792 to 1796 he represented the county of Dorchester in the Legislative Assembly of Lower Canada; and in 1798 he was appointed to the Legislative Council. From 1794 to 1802 he was *grand voyer* of the district of Quebec; and in 1802 he was appointed deputy postmaster-general of the province, in succession to Hugh Finlay (q.v.). He died at his manor house at Ste. Marie de la Beauce, on September 18, 1809. He was twice married, (1) in 1773 to Marie-Louise-Elisabeth Bazin (d. 1783), by whom he had eight children, and (2) in 1789 to Louise-Françoise Juchereau Duchesnay (d. 1841), by whom he had three children.

[P. G. Roy, *L'hon. G. E. Taschereau* (Bull. rech. hist., 1902); Le Jeune, *Dict. gén.*]

Taschereau, Sir Henri Elzéar (1836-1911), chief justice of the Supreme Court of Canada (1902-06), was born at Ste. Marie de la Beauce, Lower Canada, on October 7, 1836, the son of Pierre Elzéar Taschereau and Catherine Hénédine, daughter of the Hon. Amable Dionne. He was educated at the Quebec Seminary, and was called to the bar of Lower Canada in 1857 (Q.C., 1867). He sat in the Legislative Assembly of Canada for Beauce county from 1861 to 1867. In 1871 he was appointed a judge of the Superior Court of Quebec; and in 1878 a judge of the Supreme Court of Canada. In 1902 he became chief justice of this court; and, as such, he was appointed for a short time in 1904 administrator of the government of Canada. He retired from the bench in 1906, and he died at Ottawa on April 14, 1911. He was twice married, (1) in 1857 to Marie Antoinette, daughter of the Hon. R. U. de Lotbinière Harwood, by whom he had two sons and three daughters; and (2) in 1897 to Marie Louise, daughter of Charles Panet, of Ottawa. He was created a knight bachelor in 1902, and a privy councillor in 1904. He was the author of several legal works.

[F. J. Audet, *Les juges en chef de la province de Québec* (Quebec, 1927); P. G. Roy, *Les juges de la province de Québec* (Quebec, 1933); *Dict. nat. biog.*, supp. II; *Can. who's who* (1910); Morgan, *Can. men* (1898); Rose, *Cyc. Am. biog.* (1888); *Can. parl. comp.*; Le Jeune, *Dict. gén.*]

Taschereau, Sir Henri Thomas (1841-1909), chief justice of the Court of King's Bench of Quebec, was born in Quebec on October 6, 1841, the son of the Hon. Jean Thomas Taschereau (q.v.) and Louise Adèle, daughter of the Hon. Amable Dionne. He was educated at the Quebec Seminary and at Laval University (B.L., 1861; B.C.L., 1862), and was called to the bar of Lower Canada in 1863. From 1872 to 1878 he represented Montmagny in the Canadian House of Commons; and in 1878 he was appointed a judge of the Superior Court of Quebec. In 1907 he was made chief justice of the Court of King's Bench at Quebec; and he died at Montmorency, near Paris, France, on October 11, 1909. He was twice married, (1) in 1864 to Marie Louise Séverine (d. 1883), daughter of E. L. Pacaud, of Arthabaska, and (2) in 1885 to Mme Marie Masson. By his first wife he had nine children. He was created a knight bachelor in 1908.

[F. J. Audet, *Les juges en chef de la province de Québec* (Quebec, 1927); P. G. Roy, *Les juges de la province de Québec* (Quebec, 1933); *Dict. nat. biog.*, supp. II; Rose, *Cyc. Can. biog.* (1888); *Can. parl. comp.*; Le Jeune, *Dict. gén.*]

Taschereau, Jean Thomas (1778-1832), judge of the Court of King's Bench at Quebec (1827-32), was the son of the Hon. Gabriel Elzéar Taschereau (q.v.). From 1800 to 1808, and from 1820 to 1827, he was a member of the Legislative Assembly of Lower Canada. In 1806 he was one of the founders of *Le Cana-*

dien, and in 1810 he was arrested and imprisoned by order of Sir. J. Craig (q.v.), but was released on promise of good behaviour. In 1827 he was appointed a judge of the Court of King's Bench at Quebec; and from 1828 to 1832 he was a member of the Legislative Council of Lower Canada. He died at Quebec on June 14, 1832. He married Marie, daughter of the Hon. Jean Antoine Panet (q.v.).

[P. G. Roy, *Les juges Taschereau* (Bull. rech. hist., 1897) and *Les juges de la province de Québec* (Quebec, 1933); Le Jeune, *Dict. gén.*; N. E. Dionne, *Pierre Bédard et ses fils* (Quebec, 1909); *Bull. rech. hist.*, 1903).]

Taschereau, Jean Thomas (1814-1893), judge of the Supreme Court of Canada (1875-78), was born at Quebec on December 12, 1814, the son of the Hon. Jean Thomas Taschereau (q.v.) and Marie, daughter of the Hon. Jean Antoine Panet (q.v.). He was educated at the Quebec Seminary, and was called to the bar of Lower Canada in 1836 (Q.C., 1860). He practised law in Quebec, and in 1865 was appointed a judge of the Superior Court of Quebec. In 1873 he was transferred to the Court of Queen's Bench in Quebec; and in 1875 he was appointed a judge of the newly formed Supreme Court of Canada. Ill-health compelled his retirement from the bench in 1878; and he died at Quebec on November 9, 1893. He was twice married, (1) in 1840 to Louise Adèle (d. 1861), daughter of the Hon. Amable Dionne, and (2) in 1862 to Marie Josephine, daughter of the Hon. René Edouard Caron (q.v.).

[P. G. Roy, *Les juges de la province de Québec* (Quebec, 1933); Le Jeune, *Dict. gén.*; Rose, *Cyc. Can. biog.* (1888).]

Taschereau, Joseph André (1806-1867), solicitor-general of Lower Canada, was born at Ste. Marie de la Beauce on November 30, 1806. He represented Beauce in the Legislative Assembly of Lower Canada from 1835 to 1838, and Dorchester in the Legislative Assembly of united Canada from 1845 to 1847; and during this latter period he was solicitor-general of Lower Canada, though without a seat in the Council. In 1847 he was appointed a judge of the Superior Court of Lower Canada for the district of Kamouraska; and he died at Kamouraska on March 30, 1867.

[J. C. Dent, *The last forty years* (2 vols., Toronto, 1881); *Bull. rech. hist.*, 1897; P. G. Roy, *Les juges de la province de Québec* (Quebec, 1933); Le Jeune, *Dict. gén.*]

Taschereau, Louis Alexandre (1867-1952), prime minister of Quebec (1920-36), was born at Quebec, Canada East, on March 5, 1867, and died at Quebec on July 6, 1952. He was educated at Laval University (LL.L., 1889), and was called to the bar in 1889 (K.C., 1903). He represented Montmorency in the Legislative Assembly of Quebec as a Liberal from 1900 to 1936; he was appointed minister of public works in 1907, and in 1920 he succeeded Sir Lomer Gouin (q.v.) as prime minister. In 1936 his government was defeated, and he retired from political life.

[*Can. who's who*, 1948; *Can. parl. comp.*, 1935; *Encyc. Can.*]

Tasker, Lawrence Hermon (1873-1945), educationist, was born at Mount Forest, Ontario, on July 20, 1873; and was educated at the University of Toronto (B.A., 1897; M.A., 1898). He became a school-teacher; and after 1902 he lived in the United States. He died at Yonkers, New York, on July 24, 1945. He was the author of *The United Empire Loyalist settlement at Long Point, Lake Erie*, published as volume 2 of the *Papers and records* of the Ontario Historical Society (Toronto, 1900).

[Morgan, *Can. men* (1912).]

Tassé, Joseph (1848-1895), author and politician, was born in Montreal on October 23, 1848. He was educated at Bourget College, Rigaud, Lower Canada, and became a journalist. From 1869 to 1872 he was associate editor of *La Minerve*, Montreal. Later he became editor of *La Minerve*. From 1878 to 1887 he sat in the Canadian House of Commons for Ottawa; and from 1891 to 1895 he sat in the Senate of Canada. He died at Montreal on January 18, 1895. He was a charter member of the Royal Society of Canada; and he was the author of *Philemon Wright; ou, Colonisation et commerce en bois* (Montreal, 1871), *Le chemin de fer Canadien Pacifique* (Montreal, 1872), *La vallée de l'Outaouais* (Montreal, 1873), *Les canadiens de l'ouest* (2 vols., Montreal, 1878), and *Le 38ème fauteuil; ou, Souvenirs parlementaires* (Montreal, 1891). He edited also the *Discours de Sir Georges Cartier* (Montreal, 1893).

[*Cyc. Am. biog.*; Rose, *Cyc. Can. biog.* (1886); *Can. parl. comp.*; Le Jeune, *Dict. gén.*]

Tassie, William (1815-1886), educationist, was born at Dublin, Ireland, on May 10, 1815. He emigrated to Canada with relatives in 1834, and was educated at University College, Toronto (M.A., 1858). In 1853 he became headmaster of the grammar school at Galt, Upper Canada, and under him the school acquired a national reputation. Later he was headmaster of the Collegiate Institute at Peterborough, Ontario; and here he died on December 15, 1886. In 1871 he was made an LL.D. of Queen's University, Kingston.

[*Dom. ann. reg.*, 1886; James E. Kerr, *Recollections of my schooldays at Tassie's* (Waterloo Historical Society, 3rd Ann. Report, 1915); J. C. Sutherland, *At Doctor Tassie's* (Can. mag., 1924); R. G. Riddell (ed.), *Canadian portraits* (Toronto, 1940).]

Taverner, Percy Algernon (1875-1947), ornithologist, was born at Guelph, Ontario, on June 10, 1875, and died at Ottawa, Ontario, on May 9, 1947. He was educated in schools at Port Huron and Ann Arbor, Michigan, and from 1900 to 1910 was employed in architects' offices in Chicago and Detroit. But from an early age his chief interest was in the study of bird life, and he became such an authority on Canadian birds that in 1910 he was appointed to the staff of the National Museum in Ottawa as an ornithologist. On his retirement in 1942 he was made honorary curator of birds at the Museum. He had no university degree, and it was strange that no university conferred on him an honorary degree; but in 1917 he was elected a fellow of the American Ornithologists' Union, and in 1935 he became a fellow of the Royal Society of Canada. He was the author of *Birds of Eastern Canada* (Ottawa, 1919), *Birds of Western Canada* (Ottawa, 1926), *Birds of Canada* (Ottawa, 1934), *Canadian land birds* (Toronto, 1939), and *Canadian water birds* (Toronto, 1939).

[*Proc. Roy. Soc. Can.*, 1947; *Can. who's who*, 1938-39; *Encyc. Can.*]

Taylor, Conyngham Crawford (1823-1898), author, was born at Manor Hamilton, county Leitrim, Ireland, on August 9, 1823. He emigrated to Canada in 1847, and went into the dry-goods business in Toronto. In 1883 he was given an appointment in the Customs House in Toronto; and he retained this post until his death at Toronto on August 5, 1898. He was the author of *Toronto "called back", from 1886 to 1850* (Toronto, 1886), of which new and revised editions, under varying titles, appeared in 1887, 1890, and 1892.

[Morgan, *Can. men* (1912).]

Taylor, Ernest Manly (1848-1941), clergyman, was born at Potton, Canada East, on January 29, 1848. He was educated at McGill University (B.A., 1875; M.A., 1882), and in 1877 was ordained a minister of the Methodist Church. In 1890 he was appointed government inspector of public schools in the district of Bedford; and he was for many years secretary of the Brome Historical Society. He died at Knowlton, Quebec, on March 27, 1941. He was the author of *History of Brome county, Quebec* (2 vols., Montreal, 1908-37).

[Morgan, *Can. men* (1912).]

Taylor, George (1840-1919), senator of Canada, was born at Lansdowne, Leeds county, Upper Canada, on March 31, 1840. He had a common school education, and became a manufacturer in Gananoque, Ontario; for many years he was president of the Ontario Wheel Company. From 1882 to 1911 he represented South Leeds in the Canadian House of Commons; and for twenty-five years he was chief whip of the Conservative party in the House of Commons. In 1911 he was called to the Senate of Canada; and he sat in the Senate until his death, at Ottawa, Ontario, on March 26, 1919. Though not a cabinet minister, he was for many years an influential and popular figure in Canadian politics.

[Morgan, *Can. men* (1912); *Can. parl. comp.*]

Taylor, Henry (*fl.* 1770-1860), author, was born in Quebec about 1770, and was at school in England about 1780 with Sir Isaac Brock (q.v.) and with James Hughes (q.v.), the Nor'Wester. He returned to Canada in 1819, and he wrote in Canada books which he himself peddled about the country. He must have been a very old man when he died. His death seems to have taken place between 1860 and 1866; H. J. Morgan (q.v.) says in his *Bibliotheca canadensis* (Ottawa, 1867) that he "died recently". He was the author of *Considerations on the past, present, and future condition of the Canadas* (Montreal, 1839), *An attempt to form a system of the creation of our globe* (Quebec, 1840), *Journal of a tour from Montreal, thro' Berthier and Sorel, to the eastern townships* (Quebec, 1840), *On the forthcoming union of the two Canadas* (Montreal, 1841), *A system of the creation of our globe, planets, and sun* (Quebec, 1841), *The present condition of united Canada* (Toronto, 1850), and *On the intention of the British government to unite the provinces of British North America* (Hamilton, 1857; new ed., Toronto, 1858).

[Morgan, *Bib. can.*]

Taylor, James P. (*fl.* 1851-1899), schoolteacher, was born in Cornwall, England, and emigrated to Canada in 1857. He became a school-teacher in Ontario; and in 1886, while teaching school in Uxbridge, Ontario, he became a convert to Roman Catholicism. Subsequently he taught school in Lindsay, Ontario. He was the author of *How a schoolmaster became a Catholic* (Lindsay, Ont., 1890) and *The cardinal facts of Canadian history* (Toronto, 1899). The date of his death has not been ascertained.

[Private information.]

Taylor, John Fennings (1817-1882), author, was born in London, England, on March 14, 1817, and was educated at Radley College, England. He came to Canada in 1836, and was appointed a clerk of the Legislative Council of Upper Canada. In 1841 he was transferred to the office of the Legislative Council of the united provinces, and in 1867 to that of the Senate of Canada. He was the author of *Portraits of British Americans* (3 vols., Montreal, 1867-68), *Thos. D'Arcy McGee, sketch of his life and death* (Montreal, 1868), *The last three bishops appointed by the Crown for the Anglican Church in Canada* (Montreal, 1870), and *Are legislatures parliaments?* (Montreal, 1879). He died at Old Point Comfort, Virginia, whither he had gone for his health, on May 4, 1882.

[*Dom. ann. reg.*, 1882; Morgan, *Bib. can.*]

Taylor, Robert Bruce (1869-1954), clergyman and educationist, was born at Cardross, Scotland, on October 22, 1869, and died at Cannes, France, on May 30, 1954. He was educated at Glasgow University (M.A., 1890), and was ordained a minister of the Free Church of Scotland. He came to Canada in 1911 as minister of St. Paul's Church, Montreal; and in 1917 he was appointed principal of Queen's University, Kingston. He resigned from his post in 1930, and for most of the rest of his life he lived abroad. Several universities conferred on him honorary degrees. He was the author of *Lands and peoples* (7 vols., Toronto, 1929-30), and he compiled *Ancient Hebrew literature* (4 vols., London, 1930).

[*Can. who's who*, 1948.]

Taylor, Thomas (1778-1838), jurist and law reporter, was born in St. Pancras, England, in 1778. He became an officer in the British army, and in 1809 was sent to Canada as an ensign in the 41st Regiment. He served on the Niagara frontier during the War of 1812, and was seriously wounded at the battle of Stoney Creek in 1813. He returned to England with his regiment in 1815, was placed on half-pay in 1817, and in 1819, having in the meantime been called to the bar by the Middle Temple, he came back to Canada, and was appointed judge of the Gore district court. In 1823 he was appointed official reporter for the Court of King's Bench in Upper Canada; and he was the author of the first volume of law reports issued in Upper Canada (York, Upper Canada, 1828; new ed., 1862).

[W. R. Riddell, *The first law reporter in Upper Canada and his reports: An address* (Toronto, 1916).]

Taylor, Sir Thomas Wardlaw (1833-1917), chief justice of Manitoba (1887-99), was born at Auchtermuchty, Fifeshire, Scotland, on March 25, 1833, the eldest son of the Rev. John Taylor, D.D., and Marion Antill, daughter of John Wardlaw, of Dalkeith, Scotland. He was educated at Edinburgh University (B.A., 1852) and at the University of Toronto (M.A., 1856); and he was called to the bar of Upper Canada in 1858 (Q.C., 1881). From 1872 to 1883 he was a master in chancery in Ontario; and in 1883 he was appointed a puisne judge of the Court of Queen's Bench in Manitoba. In 1887 he became chief justice of this court, and he presided over it until his retirement in 1899. He then returned to Ontario, and he died at Hamilton, Ontario, on March 2, 1917. He was twice married, (1) in 1858 to Jessie (d. 1863), daughter of John Cameron, of Wilmington, Delaware, and (2) to Margaret, daughter of Hugh Vallance, of Hamilton, Ontario. In 1897 he was created a knight bachelor. He was the author of several legal works.

[Morgan, *Can. men* (1912); *Can. who was who,* vol. 1.]

Taylor, William (1803-1876), clergyman and author, was born in the parish of Dennie, Scotland, in 1803, and was educated at the University of Glasgow. He was licensed to preach in 1827, and in 1831 was ordained the minister of a Secession church in Peebles. He was sent to Canada in 1833; and from that date to his death on September 5, 1876, in Portland, Maine, he was the minister of Erskine Presbyterian Church, in Montreal, Quebec. He was the author of *Hints on the proper employment of human life* (Montreal, 1838).

[W. Gregg, *History of the Presbyterian Church in the Dominion of Canada* (Toronto, 1885); *Dict. Can. biog.*, vol. 10.]

Taylor, William Robert (1882-1951), educationist, was born at Port Dover, Ontario, on April 12, 1882, and died at Toronto, Ontario, on February 24, 1951. He was educated at the University of Toronto (B.A., 1904; Ph.D., 1910), and Knox College, Toronto, and was ordained a minister of the Presbyterian Church. In 1914 he was appointed to the staff of the department of Oriental Languages in University College, Toronto, and in 1915 became head of the department. In 1945 he was appointed principal of University College, and he remained principal until his death. In 1948 he was elected a fellow of the Royal Society of Canada. He was joint editor, with W. S. MacCullough, of "The book of Psalms" in *The Interpreter's Bible* (vol. 4, 1955), published posthumously.

[*Proc. Roy. Soc. Can.,* 1951; *Can. who's who,* 1948.]

Taylor, Wilson (1861-1923), physicist, was born in Norfolk county, Canada West, on January 16, 1861, and was educated at the University of Toronto (B.A., 1892). He became a school-teacher, and taught in various secondary schools in Ontario. In 1919 he became a research assistant at the University of Toronto; but his researches were cut short by his death, at Toronto, Ontario, on October 3, 1923. He was the author of *An elementary treatise on arithmetic* (Toronto, 1898); and his scientific papers were published after his death by a group of his friends, under the title *A new view of surface forces* (Toronto, 1925).

[C. A. Chant, "Life of Wilson Taylor", in W. Taylor, *A new view of surface forces* (Toronto, 1925).]

Taylor-Bailey, Whitham (1891-1961), industrialist, was born at Montreal, Quebec, on March 7, 1891. He was educated at McGill University. He joined Dominion Bridge in 1908, becoming successively draftsman, designer, vice-president, and president. He was also closely associated with Robb Engineering, Sault Structural Steel, Dominion Engine Works, and numerous other enterprises. During the First World War he served with the Canadian army and was awarded the Military Cross. He died at Montreal, February 28, 1961.

[*Can. who's who,* 1955-57.]

Tecumseh (1768-1813), Indian chief, was born on the banks of the Mad River, a tributary of the Ohio River, in 1768, the son of Puckeshinwau, a chief of the Shawnee tribe. He gained a great ascendancy over the Indians of the Old North West; and in the War of 1812 he espoused, with his Indians, the British cause. He was present at the capture of Detroit in 1812; and he was with the British during the operations on the Detroit frontier in the spring and summer of 1813. He fell, however, in the battle of Moraviantown on October 6, 1813, and was buried by his braves in an unknown grave near the battlefield. He was a man of high ideals and statesmanlike views.

[J. M. Oskison, *Tecumseh and his times* (New York, 1938); E. Eggleston, *Tecumseh* (New York, 1918); N. S. Gurd, *The story of Tecumseh* (Toronto, 1912); Ethel T. Raymond, *Tecumseh* (Toronto, 1915); B. Drake, *Life of Tecumseh and of his brother the prophet* (Cincinnati, 1850); Glenn Tucker, *Tecumseh* (Indianapolis, 1956); B. Drake, *Life of Tecumseh* (New York, 1969); G. Tucker, *Tecumseh: Visions of glory* (New York, 1973).]

Teefy, John Reed (1848-1911), priest, was born at Richmond Hill, Canada West, on August 21, 1848. He was educated at the University of Toronto (B.A. 1871), and became a high-school teacher. Later, he joined the Basilian novitiate at Sandwich, Ontario; and in 1878 he was ordained a priest of the Roman Catholic Church. In 1878 he joined the staff of St. Michael's College, Toronto, and from 1889 to 1903 he was superior of the college. In 1903 he became pastor of Holy Rosary Church, Toronto; and in 1911 he was elected assistant superior-general of the Basilian Fathers. In 1896 he received the degree of LL.D. from the University of Toronto; and in 1906 he was appointed a member of the board of governors of the University. He died at Toronto, Ontario, on June 10, 1911. He was the author of *The worship of God, a course of seven Lenten sermons* (New York, 1902).

[H. Carr, *The Very Reverend J. R. Teefy, C.S.B.* (Canadian Catholic Historical Association, report, 1939-40); Morgan, *Can. men* (1912).]

Teeple, Peter (1762-1847), loyalist, was born near Trenton, New Jersey, on July 14, 1762, and served as an officer in the New Jersey Volunteers in the American Revolutionary War. He settled at Turkey Point (now

Charlotteville) on the north shore of Lake Erie in 1793; and in 1800 he was created a justice of the peace for the newly created London district. He died at Centreville, Oxford county, Ontario, in 1847.

[W. B. Waterbury, *Sketch of Peter Teeple, loyalist and pioneer* (Ont. Hist. Soc., papers and records, 1899).]

Teetzel, James Vernall (1853-1926), jurist, was born in Elgin county, Canada West, on March 6, 1853; and was educated at Woodstock College, the Galt Collegiate Institute, and Osgoode Hall Law School. He was called to the bar of Ontario in 1877 (Q.C., 1890), and practised law in Hamilton, Ontario. He was appointed a judge of the High Court of Justice in Ontario in 1903; and he sat on the bench until his death, at Barbados, British West Indies, on August 24, 1926. From 1910 to his death he was chairman of the Prison Parole Board of Ontario. He was an honorary LL.D. of McMaster University.

[Morgan, *Can. men* (1912).]

Tegakouitha, Catherine. See **Tekakwitha, Catherine.**

Tekakwitha, Catherine (1656-1680), the first Indian to be named venerable, was born in an Iroquois village in northern New York in 1656, the daughter of an Iroquois father and a Christian Algonkian mother. She was converted to Christianity and was compelled to flee to Canada, where she took the vows of a religious, and came to be regarded as a saint. She died at Caughnawaga, Canada, on April 17, 1680; and after her death her grave became a place of pilgrimage. Many miracles are said to have been wrought at her tomb or by her relics.

[Claude Chauchetière, *La vie de la B. Catherine Tegakoüita* (Manate, 1887); R. Rumilly, *Kateri Tekakwitha* (Paris, 1934); D. Sargent, *Catherine Tekakwitha* (New York, 1936); Sister Mary Immaculata, *Our Kateri* (New York, 1937); Le Jeune, *Dict. gén.*; M. C. Buehrle, *Kateri of the Mohawks* (Milwaukee, 1954), *Dict. Can. Biog.*, vol. 1.]

Telford, William (1828-1895), poet, was born at Leitholm, Berwickshire, Scotland, on January 6, 1828. He came to Canada in 1852, and settled first at Peterborough, Canada West. He then removed to a farm in Smith township, nearby; and he died there on April 13, 1895. He was the bard of the St. Andrew's Society of Peterborough; and his verses were published under the title *The poems of William Telford, bard of Peterboro' St. Andrew's Society* (Peterborough, Ont., 1887).

[D. Clark (ed.), *Selections from Scottish Canadian poets* (Toronto, 1900).]

Tellier, Sir Joseph Mathias (1861-1952), chief justice of Quebec (1932-42), was born at Joliette, Canada East, on January 15, 1861, and died at Joliette on October 18, 1952. He was educated at Laval (LL.L., 1884), was called to the bar in 1884 (Q.C., 1899), and practised law in Joliette. He represented Joliette in the Quebec Legislative Assembly from 1892 to 1916; and from 1908 to 1915 he was the leader of the Conservative opposition. In 1916 he was appointed a judge of the Superior Court of Quebec, in 1920 he was transferred to the Court of King's Bench, and in 1932 he became chief justice of Quebec; he resigned from the bench in 1942. He was created a knight bachelor in 1934.

[P. G. Roy, *Les juges de la province de Québec* (Quebec, 1933); *Can. who's who,* 1948; *Encyc. Can.*]

Temple, Sir Thomas, Bart. (1614-1674), governor of Nova Scotia (1657-70), was born at Stowe, Buckinghamshire, England, in January, 1614, the second son of Sir John Temple, of Stanton Bury, and grandson of Sir Thomas Temple, Bart., of Stowe. He seems to have taken the parliamentary side in the Civil War; and in 1657 he was appointed by Oliver Cromwell governor of Nova Scotia, which had been conquered by the English in 1654. He succeeded in retaining his governorship at the time of the restoration of Charles II in 1660; and in 1662 he was created a baronet of Nova Scotia. In 1667 Nova Scotia was ceded to France by the treaty of Breda; the actual surrender of the province did not take place until 1670, but with the cession Temple's commission ceased. He died in London on March 27, 1674.

[*Dict. nat. biog.*; Le Jeune, *Dict. gén.*; *Dict. Can. biog.*, vol. 1.]

Templeman, William (1844-1914), minister of inland revenue for Canada (1906-11), was born at Pakenham, Upper Canada, on September 28, 1844, the son of William Templeman and Helen Taylor. He was educated in the public schools, and became a printer and journalist. In 1867 he founded the Almonte *Gazette*, and in 1884 he removed to Victoria, British Columbia, and became connected with the Victoria *Times*. Of this paper he became editor and proprietor. In 1897 he was called to the Senate of Canada, and from 1902 to 1906 he was a member of the Laurier government without portfolio. In 1906 he became minister of inland revenue and the same year, having resigned from the Senate, he was elected to the House of Commons for Victoria. In 1909 he was elected for Comox-Atlin; but was defeated in 1911. He died at Victoria on November 15, 1914. In 1869 he married Eva Bond (d. 1914), of Almonte.

[Morgan, *Can. men* (1912); *Can. who's who,* 1910; *Can. parl. comp.*; O. D. Skelton, *Life and letters of Sir Wilfrid Laurier* (2 vols., Toronto, 1921).]

Ten Broeke, James (1859-1937), educationist, was born in Panton, Vermont, on October 13, 1859. He was educated at Middlebury College (B.A., 1884), at the Rochester Theological Seminary, and at Yale University (Ph.D., 1891); and was ordained a minister of the Baptist Church in 1887. After several years' pastoral work, he was appointed in 1895 professor of philosophy in McMaster University, Toronto; and he discharged the duties of this chair until his retirement in 1932. In 1924 McMaster University conferred on him the honorary degree of LL.D. He died at Middlebury, Vermont, on October 23, 1937. He was the author of two books, *A constructive basis for theology* (London, 1914) and *The moral life and religion* (New York, 1922).

[*Obituary record of graduates of Yale University deceased during the year 1937-1938* (New Haven, Conn., 1939).]

Terrill, Timothy Lee (1815-1879), provincial secretary for Canada (1856-57), was born in the township of Ascot, Lower Canada, on March 12, 1815, the son of Joseph Hazzard Terrill. He was called to the bar of Lower Canada in 1840 (Q.C., 1854), and from 1853 to 1861 he represented Stanstead in the Legislative Assembly of Canada. In 1856 he became provincial secretary in the Taché-Macdonald administration; but his health gave way, and he was compelled to resign in 1857. In his later years he devoted himself to farming in the Eastern Townships. He died on August 26, 1879, in Stanstead, Quebec.

[*Dom. ann. reg.,* 1879; *Dict. Can. biog.,* vol. 10.]

Teskey, Adeline Margaret (d. 1924), novelist, was born in Appleton, Ontario, and was educated at Genesee College, Lima, New York. She lived for many years in Welland, Ontario; and she died at Toronto, Ontario, on March 21, 1924. She was the author of *Where the sugar maple grows* (New York, 1901), *The village artist* (Toronto, 1905), *Alexander McBain, B.A.* (New York, 1906), *The yellow pearl* (New York, 1911), *The little celestial* (Toronto, 1912), and *Candlelight days* (Toronto, 1913).

[Morgan, *Can. men and women* (1912).]

Tessier, Auguste Maurice (1879-1932), jurist, was born at Rimouski, Quebec, on July 20, 1879, the son of the Hon. Auguste Tessier. He was called to the bar of Quebec in 1901, and practised law first in Richmond, Quebec, and then in Rimouski. From 1912 to 1922 he represented Rimouski in the Legislative Assembly of Quebec; and in 1922 he was appointed a judge of the Superior Court of Quebec. He died at Quebec City, on May 26, 1932.

[P. G. Roy, *Les juges de la province de Québec* (Quebec, 1933).]

Tessier, François Xavier (1800-1835), physician, was born at Quebec in 1800, and died at Quebec on December 24, 1835. He was educated at Quebec and at New York, and was admitted to practise medicine in Lower Canada in 1823. He founded the first medical journal published in Canada, *Le Journal de Médecine de Québec* (1826-27); and he was the author of *The French practice of medicine* (2 vols., New York, 1829).

[P. G. Roy, *Fils de Québec,* vol. 3 (Lévis, Que., 1933).]

Tessier, Jules (1852-1934), senator of Canada, was born at Quebec, Canada East, on April 16, 1852, the son of the Hon. U. J. Tessier (q.v.). He was educated at St. Mary's College, Montreal, and at Laval University (LL.B., 1874); and was called to the Quebec bar in 1874 (Q.C., 1899). He practised law in Quebec, and was for several years editor of the *Quebec law reports*. He represented Portneuf in the Legislative Assembly of Quebec from 1886 to 1903; and was a speaker of the Assembly from 1897 to 1900. He was called to the Senate of Canada in 1903; and he sat in the Senate until his death, at Montreal, Quebec, on January 6, 1934.

[*Can. parl. comp.*; Morgan, *Can. men* (1912); Rose, *Cyc. Can. biog.* (1888).]

Tessier, Ulric Joseph (1817-1892), jurist, was born at Quebec, Lower Canada, on May 4, 1817. He was admitted to the bar of Lower Canada as an advocate in 1839 (Q.C., 1863), and practised law in Quebec. From 1851 to 1854 he represented Portneuf in the Legislative Assembly of Canada, and from 1858 to 1867 he was an elected member of the Legislative Council. In 1861-62 he was commissioner of public works in the Macdonald-Sicotte government; and from 1863 to 1867 he was speaker of the Legislative Council. In 1867 he was called by royal proclamation to the Senate of Canada. He resigned from the Senate to accept appointment as a judge of the Superior Court of the province of Quebec in 1873, and in 1875 he was transferred to the Court of Queen's Bench. He died at Quebec on April 7, 1892. In 1859 he founded La Banque Nationale; and he was dean of the faculty of law in Laval University. He married in 1847 Adèle Drapeau Kelly, granddaughter of Joseph Drapeau, seignior of Rimouski and the Isle of Orleans.

[P. G. Roy, *Les juges de la province de Québec* (Quebec, 1933); Le Jeune, *Dict. gén.*; Morgan, *Bib. can.*; *Cyc. Am. biog.*]

Tessier, Yves (1800?-1847), painter, was born about 1800, and became a painter of portraits and of historical subjects in Montreal, Lower Canada. He died at Montreal on October 28, 1847.

[Montreal *Gazette*, Oct. 30, 1847.]

Têtu, Charles (1796-1864), notary public, was born at St. Thomas de Montmagny, Lower Canada, on December 14, 1796; and became a notary public. He died at Laprairie, Canada East, on December 12, 1864. He published a work entitled *Analyse et observations sur les droits relatifs aux évêques de Québec et de Montréal et au clergé du Canada* (Montreal, 1842).

[*Bull. rech. hist.*, 1927.]

Têtu, Henri (1849-1915), priest and historian, was born at Rivière Ouelle, Quebec, on October 24, 1849, the son of Dr. Ludger Têtu and Clémentine Dionne. He was educated at the College of Ste. Anne de la Pocatière, and was ordained a priest of the Roman Catholic Church in 1873. In 1887 he was appointed *camérier secret* to Pope Leo XIII, and in 1889 a prelate of the Holy See. He died at Quebec on June 15, 1915. He was the author of *Monseigneur de Laval* (Quebec, 1887), *Les évêques de Québec* (Quebec, 1889), *S. E. le Cardinal Taschereau* (Quebec, 1891), *David Têtu et les raiders de St. Alban* (Quebec, 1891), and *Histoire du palais épiscopal de Québec* (Quebec, 1896). He also edited, with Mgr C. O. Gagnon, *Les mandements des évêques de Québec* (8 vols., Quebec, 1887-96).

[Allaire, *Dict. biog.*; Morgan, *Can. men* (1912); Le Jeune, *Dict. gén.*; *Bull. rech. hist.*, 1915.]

Têtu, Horace (1842-1915), author, was born at Quebec, Lower Canada, on July 14, 1842, the son of Vital Têtu, M.P., and Virginie Ahier, and was educated at the Quebec Seminary. He died, unmarried, at Quebec on March 31, 1915. He devoted himself to the study of the history of journalism in the province of Quebec, and he published *Historique des journaux de Québec* (Quebec, 1875; new ed., 1889), *Journaux et revues de Québec* (Quebec, 1881; 3rd ed., 1883), *Journaux et revues de Montréal* (Quebec, 1881), and *Journaux de Lévis* (Quebec, 1890; 3rd ed., 1898). He published also *Souvenirs inédits de l'abbé Painchaud* (Quebec, 1894), *Doyens du clergé canadien de la province civile de Québec* (Quebec, 1896), *Résumé historique de l'industrie et du commerce de Québec* (Quebec, 1899), *Livre d'or du clergé canadien* (Quebec, 1903), *Édifices religieux érigés dans la province de Québec sous la domination française* (Quebec, 1903; new ed., 1910), and *Oiseaux de cage* (Quebec, 1906).

[P. G. Roy, *Fils de Québec*, vol. 4 (Quebec, 1933); Le Jeune, *Dict. gén.*; *Bull. rech. hist.*, 1915.]

Thain, Thomas (d. 1832), fur-trader, was born in Scotland, the son of a sister of the Hon. John Richardson (q.v.). Through his mother he was related to the Phyns, the Ellices, and the Forsyths. He came to Canada prior to 1804, for in that year Thomas Verchères de Boucherville met him on Lake Superior, evidently as a

clerk in the employ of the XY Company. In 1804 he was appointed, with John Ogilvy (q.v.), an agent to represent at Grand Portage the interests of Sir Alexander Mackenzie and Company in the reorganized North West Company; and in 1813 he became a partner in the firm of McTavish, McGillivrays, and Company. In 1822 he became also a partner in the firm of McGillivrays, Thain, and Company, which was formed to wind up the affairs of McTavish, McGillivrays, and Company. From 1821, when McTavish, McGillivrays, and Company became the Montreal agents of the Hudson's Bay Company, he was the virtual manager of the Montreal office and head of the Montreal department. Shortly before McTavish, McGillivrays, and Company and McGillivrays, Thain, and Company were forced into insolvency in 1825, he left Canada suddenly, in ill health, leaving the accounts of these firms in great confusion; and soon afterwards he was reported as being "confined as a lunatic in an asylum in Scotland". He died at Aberdeen, Scotland, on January 6, 1832.

[F. J. Audet, *Les députés de Montréal* (Montreal, 1943); W. S. Wallace (ed.), *Documents relating to the North West Company* (Toronto: The Champlain Society, 1934).]

Thatcher, Wilbert Ross (1917-1971), politician, was born in Neville, Saskatchewan, May 24, 1917, and educated at Moose Jaw Central Collegiate and Queen's University (B. Com., 1936). A member of the C.C.F. party, he was first elected to the House of Commons as the member for Moose Jaw in 1945. He was re-elected in 1949 and 1953, but he resigned from the party in 1955 and was defeated in the general elections of 1957 and 1958. He was elected to the Saskatchewan legislature in 1960 as leader of the Liberal party in Saskatchewan, becoming premier and provincial treasurer in 1964. He was re-elected in 1967 but his party failed to get a majority in the 1971 general election. He died on July 23, 1971.

[*Can. who's who*, 1967-69; *Can. ann. review*, 1971.]

Theller, Edward Alexander (1804-1859), filibuster, was born in Coleraine, county Kerry, Ireland, on January 13, 1804, and came to America when a young man. He studied and practised medicine in Montreal. He later went to the United States, and in 1838 he joined the American filibusterers along the Canadian border. He was captured on Lake Erie, while in command of a privateer, was tried, and was sentenced to imprisonment. He escaped from prison at Quebec, and fled to New York. In 1853 he went to California, where he was editor of several newspapers, and for a time was superintendent of public schools in San Francisco; and he died at Honitas, California, in 1859. He published *Canada in 1837-38, showing the causes of the late attempted revolu-*

tion and of its failure, together with personal adventures of the author (2 vols., Philadelphia, 1841).

[*Cyc. Am. biog.*; E. C. Guillet, *The lives and times of the patriots* (Toronto, 1938); J. C. Dent, *The Upper Canadian rebellion* (2 vols., Toronto, 1885); W. R. Riddell, *Old province tales* (Toronto, 1920).]

Thibaudeau, Isidore (1819-1893), president of the Executive Council of Canada (1863-64), was born at Cap Santé, Lower Canada, in 1819. He became head of the firm of Thibaudeau, Thomas, and Co., wholesale dry-goods merchants of Quebec and Montreal. From 1863 to 1867 he represented Quebec Centre in the Legislative Assembly of Canada; and from 1863 to 1864 he was president of the council in the Macdonald-Dorion administration. In 1867 he was appointed a member of the Legislative Council of Quebec; but he resigned in 1874, and was elected a member of the Canadian House of Commons for Quebec East. He resigned his seat in 1877, and retired to private life. He died in 1893. In 1847 he married Laura, daughter of Gaspard Drolet, of Quebec.

[*Les Thibaudeau* (Bull. rech. hist., 1933); *Can. parl. comp.*]

Thibaudeau, Joseph Elie (1822-1878), minister of agriculture for Canada (1858), was born on September 2, 1822, at Cap Santé, Lower Canada. He became a merchant; and from 1854 to 1861 he represented Portneuf in the Legislative Assembly of Canada. In 1858 he was president of the Council and minister of agriculture in the short-lived Brown-Dorion administration. In 1863 he was appointed registrar of the county of Portneuf; and this position he occupied until his death on January 5, 1878.

[D. Gosselin, *L'honorable Elie Thibaudeau* (Bull. rech. hist., 1900); *Bull. rech. hist.*, 1933; *Dict. Can. biog.*, vol. 10.]

Thibaudeau, Joseph Rosaire (1837-1910), senator of Canada, was born at Cap Santé, Lower Canada, on October 1, 1837. He became a member of the wholesale dry-goods firm of Thibaudeau, Thomas, and Co. (later Thibaudeau, Beliveau, and Archambault); and in 1878 he was called to the Senate of Canada. He was appointed sheriff of the district of Montreal in 1890, and this position he held until his death at Montreal on June 16, 1910. In 1873 he married Marguerite, daughter of Major G. LaMothe, postmaster of Montreal.

[*Les Thibaudeau* (Bull. rech. hist., 1933); *Can. parl. comp.*; *Can. who was who*, vol. 1.]

Thibault, Charles (1840-1905), lawyer, was born at St. Athanase d'Iberville, Lower Canada, on September 16, 1840; and was called to the bar of Lower Canada in 1865. In 1880 he was appointed secretary of the Board of Official Arbitrators of the Dominion. He was killed in a railway accident at Sutton, Quebec, on January 2, 1905. He was the author of *Biography of Sir Charles Tupper* (Montreal, 1883; French tr., 1884), *La croix, l'épée, et la charrue* (Montreal, 1886), and *Discours choisis* (Montreal, 1931).

[*Bull. rech. hist.*, 1924 and 1927.]

Thibault, Jean Baptiste (1810-1879), missionary, was born at Lévis, Lower Canada, on December 14, 1810, and was educated at the Quebec Seminary. In 1833 he went west to the Red River Settlement as a missionary, and was there ordained a priest of the Roman Catholic Church. He was a missionary in the West for nearly forty years; and in 1845 he was made vicar-general of the diocese of St. Boniface. During the Red River insurrection of 1869-70 he was a commissioner of the Canadian government, and did much by his influence to restrain the rebels. He returned to Canada in 1872; and he spent the last years of his life as parish priest at St. Denis, Quebec. He died there on April 4, 1879.

[A. G. Morice, *Dictionnaire historique des canadiens et des métis français de l'ouest* (Kamloops, B.C., 1908); *Dom. ann. reg.*, 1879; Allaire, *Dict. biog.*; *Dict. Can. biog.*, vol. 10.]

Thom, Adam (1802-1890), recorder of Rupert's Land (1838-49), was born in Scotland on August 30, 1802, and was educated at King's College, Aberdeen. He emigrated to Canada about 1832, studied law in Montreal, and was called to the bar of Lower Canada in 1837. While studying law, he engaged in journalism, and during the Rebellion of 1837 he was editor of the Montreal *Herald*. His attitude was so strongly anti-French that Lord Durham (q.v.) thought fit to attach him to his staff in 1838; and it was said that he was the author of parts of Lord Durham's *Report*. He accompanied Durham to England in 1838; but he was almost immediately appointed recorder of Rupert's Land, and he entered on his judicial duties at the Red River Settlement in 1839. He became unpopular with the French half-breeds; and in 1849 he was removed from the bench, though he continued to act as clerk of the Council of Assiniboia until 1854. He then resigned his appointments, and returned to Great Britain. He died in London, England, on February 21, 1890. He published, under various pen names, the following: *Letter to the Right Hon. E. G. Stanley, secretary of state for the colonies,* by an Emigrant (Montreal, 1834); *Remarks on the convention and on the petition of the constitutionalists,* by Anti-Bureaucrat (Montreal, 1835); *Review of the Report made in 1828 by the Canada Committee of the House of Commons* (Montreal, 1835); *Anti-Gallic Let-*

ters, addressed to his Excellency, the Earl of Gosford, by Camillus (Montreal, 1836); *The claims to the Oregon territory considered* (London, 1844); and *Chronology of prophecy* (London, 1848). He is said to have written for Sir George Simpson (q.v.) a large part of his *Narrative of a voyage round the world* (London, 1847).

[F. J. Audet, *Adam Thom* (Trans. Roy. Soc. Can., 1941); E. H. Oliver, *The Canadian north-west* (2 vols., Ottawa, 1914); *Can. who was who,* vol. 2; Le Jeune, *Dict. gén.*]

Thomas, Benjamin Daniel (1843-1917), clergyman and author, was born near Narberth, Wales, on January 23, 1843. He became a Baptist minister; and after serving as the pastor of a Baptist church in Wales, he went in 1868 to the United States. He was the pastor of churches in Pittston and Philadelphia, Pennsylvania; and in 1882 he came to Canada as the pastor of the Jarvis Street Baptist Church in Toronto. He remained in this charge until his retirement from pastoral work in 1903. He died at Grimsby, Ontario, on October 26, 1917. He was an honorary D.D. of Bucknell University (1896) and of McMaster University (1908); and he was the author of *The secret of the divine silence* (Toronto, 1903).

[Morgan, *Can. men* (1912); *Canadian Baptist,* Nov. 8, 1917.]

Thomas, Cyrus (1836-1908), author, was born in Troy, New York, on June 15, 1836. He became a school-teacher, and taught in various places in the Eastern Townships of the province of Quebec. He died at Richford, Vermont, on February 14, 1908. He was the author of *Contributions to the history of the Eastern Townships* (Montreal, 1866), *The history of Shefford* (Montreal, 1877), *The frontier schoolmaster* (Montreal, 1880), *History of the counties of Argenteuil, Que., and Prescott, Ont.* (Montreal, 1896), and *The Rev. John and a few philanthropists* (Montreal, 1903).

[Morgan, *Can. men* (1898).]

Thomas, Ernest (1865-1940), clergyman and author, was born in England in 1865, and was educated at McGill University and Queen's Theological College. He became a minister of the Methodist Church; and after serving as pastor of charges in Quebec, Ontario, Saskatchewan, and British Columbia, he was appointed in 1919 field secretary for the department of evangelism and social service in the Methodist Church. He continued in the same post with the United Church of Canada, after 1925; and retired only in 1937. He died at Toronto, Ontario, on February 19, 1940. He was the author of *Christian life in a changing world* (Toronto, 1937).

[*Can. who's who,* 1936-37.]

Thomas, Thomas (1766?-1828), surgeon and fur-trader, was born, probably in Wales, about 1766. He qualified as a surgeon, and in 1789 took service as a surgeon with the Hudson's Bay Company. He arrived at York Factory in the autumn of 1789, and was employed there for several years. From 1796 to 1810 he was master at Severn House; from 1810 to 1814 he was superintendent of the southern factories (Moose, Albany, and Eastmain); and from 1814 to 1815 he was governor of the northern department of Rupert's Land, pending the arrival of Robert Semple (q.v.). Later he retired from the Company's service, and settled at the Red River. He died at the Red River Settlement on November 24, 1828. He should not be confused with his son, Thomas Thomas, who became a councillor of Assiniboia; nor with another Thomas Thomas (known as the 2nd), who was also a surgeon, and entered the service of the Hudson's Bay Company in 1791, but deserted to the North West Company about 1804.

[E. E. Rich (ed.), *Colin Robertson's Correspondence book* (Toronto: The Champlain Society, 1939).]

Thomas, William (1800-1860), architect, was born in Stroud, Gloucestershire, England, in 1800. He became an architect, and practised his profession for some years in Leamington, England. He emigrated to Canada about 1842, and settled in Toronto. He was the architect of many of the public buildings built in Toronto in the fifties of last century, notably St. Michael's Cathedral, St. Lawrence Hall, the Toronto Gaol, and several churches. He died in Toronto on December 25, 1860.

[J. Ross Robertson, *Landmarks in Canada* (Toronto, 1917.]

Thompson, David (1770-1857), explorer and geographer, was born on April 30, 1770, in the parish of St. John the Evangelist, Westminster, England, the son of David Thompson. He was educated at the Grey Coat School, Westminster, and in 1784 he was apprenticed to the Hudson's Bay Company. He spent the years 1784-97 as a clerk in the service of the Hudson's Bay Company, either at the posts on Hudson Bay, or in the interior. In 1797 he transferred his services to the North West Company, in which he became a partner, and from this date until 1812 he was continuously engaged in fur-trading and exploring on the western plains and on the Pacific slope. He was the first white man to descend the Columbia River from its source to its mouth. Wherever he went he made traverses of his course and observed for longitude and latitude; and when he left the western country in 1812, he prepared a map of it which has been the basis of all subsequent maps. He settled at Terrebonne, Lower Canada, and later, at Williamstown, Upper Canada. From 1816 to 1826 he was employed in surveying the boundary line between Canada and the United States; and in later years he was employed on other surveys. He died, in circumstances of extreme poverty, at Longueuil, near Montreal, on February 10, 1857. In 1799, he married Charlotte Small, a half-breed; and by her he had sixteen children. His *Narrative of his explorations*, which remained for many years unpublished, has been edited, with introduction and notes, by J. B. Tyrrell (Toronto: The Champlain Society, 1916). His *Travels in western North America, 1784-1812* has been edited by V. G. Hopwood (Toronto, 1971).

[C. N. Cochrane, *David Thompson the explorer* (Toronto, 1924); E. Coues, *New light on the history of the greater North-West,* (2 vols., New York, 1897); J. B. Tyrrell, *David Thompson* (Geographical journal, 1911); W. S. Wallace, *By star and compass* (Toronto, 1922); F. Croft, *David Thompson's lonely crusade to open the west* (Maclean's magazine, Nov. 9, 1957); R. Glover, ed., *David Thompson's narrative, 1784-1812* (Toronto: The Champlain Society, 1962).

Thompson, David (1796?-1868), author, was born in Scotland about 1796. He enlisted in the Royal Scots, and after his discharge settled in Canada. He became a school-teacher in Niagara, Upper Canada; and in 1832 he published *A history of the late war between Great Britain and the United States of America* (Niagara, Upper Canada). Because of his inability to pay the cost of publication of this work, he was imprisoned. He died at Niagara, Ontario, in 1868.

[A. MacMurchy, *Handbook of Canadian literature* (Toronto, 1906).]

Thompson, David (1836-1886), politician, was born in Wainfleet, Welland county, Upper Canada, on December 7, 1836, the son of David Thompson, M.P.P. He represented Haldimand in the Legislative Assembly of Canada and in the Canadian House of Commons from 1863 to 1886, as a Liberal. He died at Ruthven Park, Indiana, Ontario, on April 18, 1886.

[*Dom. ann. reg.,* 1886; *Can. parl. comp.*]

Thompson, Dora Olive (d. 1934), writer of books for children, was the daughter of Henry L. Thompson, who was at the time of her death president of the Copp Clark Company, printers and publishers, Toronto, Ontario. She died at Toronto on September 29, 1934. She was the author of *Adèle in search of a home* (London, 1926), *A dealer in sunshine* (London, 1926), *Joy Meredith* (London, 1928), *Dimples* (London, 1929), *That girl Ginger* (London, 1931), *Nancy-Rose* (London, 1932), and *Kathleen and Peter* (London, 1934).

[Private information.]

Thompson, John (1834-1903), clergyman and author, was born at Norham, England, on December 31, 1834. He came to Canada with his parents when an infant, and was educated at the High School of Quebec and Knox College, Toronto (D.D., 1886). He was licensed as a minister of the Presbyterian Church in 1863; and from 1865 to his death he was minister of St. Andrew's Presbyterian Church, Sarnia, Ontario. In 1872 he married Mary, only daughter of the Hon. Alexander Mackenzie (q.v.), prime minister of Canada. He died at Sarnia, Ontario, on May 12, 1903. He was the author of *The lambs in the fold* (New York, 1893) and *Jesus, my Saviour* (New York, 1895).

[Morgan, *Can. men* (1898).]

Thompson, John Gawler (1787-1868), jurist, was born on January 7, 1787, and was educated at Quebec, Lower Canada. He was called to the bar of Lower Canada in 1814; and in 1827 he was appointed judge for the district of Gaspé. In 1859 he was appointed a judge of the Superior Court of the province for the same district; and he died on September 4, 1868.

[P. G. Roy, *Les juges de la province de Québec* (Quebec, 1933).]

Thompson, Sir John Sparrow David (1844-1894), prime minister of Canada (1892-94), was born in Halifax, Nova Scotia, on November 10, 1844, the son of John Sparrow Thompson, a civil servant, and Charlotte Pottinger. He was educated at the Free Church Academy in Halifax, and was called to the bar of Nova Scotia in 1865 (Q.C., 1879). In 1877 he was elected to the Legislative Assembly of Nova Scotia as a Liberal-Conservative for Antigonish; in 1878 he became attorney-general in the Holmes administration; and in 1882 he became prime minister. In the general elections of 1882, however, his ministry was defeated; and he himself, on his resignation, accepted appointment as a judge of the Supreme Court of Nova Scotia. After three years on the bench, he was offered by Sir John Macdonald (q.v.) in 1885 the post of minister of justice in the Dominion government; and was the same year elected to the House of Commons for Antigonish. "The great discovery of my life," said Macdonald later, "was my discovery of Thompson." As minister of justice, he handled with consummate skill the debate in 1886 on the execution of Louis Riel (q.v.), and that in 1889 on the Jesuits' Estates Act; and, on the death of Macdonald in 1891, he would undoubtedly have become prime minister, had he not been a convert to Roman Catholicism, and so not wholly acceptable to the Orange Order. Sir John Abbott (q.v.), the compromise candidate who became prime minister in 1891, resigned, however, in 1892; and Thompson then succeeded to the vacancy without opposition.

As prime minister, Thompson's tenure of office was too short to permit him to leave a deep impression on the history of Canada. Much of his time, moreover, was occupied with negotiations at the intercolonial conference in London over copyright and merchant shipping, and with his duties as the representative of Great Britain on the Behring Sea arbitration at Paris. But he established his reputation as a political leader of great ability and high character; and his sudden death at Windsor Castle, England, on December 12, 1894, was regarded everywhere as a profound tragedy.

In 1870 he married Annie, daughter of Captain Affleck of Halifax; and by her had two sons and three daughters. In 1888 he was created a K.C.M.G.; and just before his death in 1894 he was sworn of the Imperial Privy Council.

[J. Castell Hopkins, *Life and work of the Right Hon. Sir John Thompson* (Brantford, Ont., 1895); Senator Miller, *Incidents in the political career of the late Sir John Thompson* (pamphlet, Ottawa, 1895); Mr. Justice Russell, *The career of Sir John Thompson* (Dalhousie review, 1921); *Dict. nat. biog.*; Taché, *Men of the day*; Rose, *Cyc. Can. biog.* (1888); Le Jeune, *Dict. gén.*]

Thompson, Phillips. See **Thompson, Thomas Phillips.**

Thompson, Samuel (1810-1886), journalist, was born in London, England, in 1810, and came to Canada in 1833. He became a journalist, and established in 1838 the shortlived Toronto *Palladium*. He was later editor or publisher in Toronto of the *Herald*, the *Daily Colonist*, and *News of the Week*. In 1859, having obtained a contract for government printing, he removed to Quebec, and there he published in 1860 *Thompson's Mirror of Parliament*, a forerunner of Hansard. In his later years he retired from journalism, and was engaged in the insurance business. He died in Toronto on July 8, 1886. Shortly before his death he published his autobiography, under the title *Reminiscences of a Canadian pioneer* (Toronto, 1884).

[*Dom. ann. reg.*, 1886.]

Thompson, Thomas Phillips (1843-1933), journalist and author, was born at Newcastle-on-Tyne, England, in 1843, and came with his parents to Canada in 1857. He became a journalist, and he achieved a considerable reputation as a writer of humorous articles under the *nom de plume* of "Jimuel Briggs". He died at Oakville, Ontario, on May 22, 1933. He was the author of *The future government of Canada* (St. Catharines, C.W., 1864), *The politics of labour* (New York, 1887), and *The labour reform songster* (New York, 1892); and in 1902 he was the organizer in Ontario of the Socialist League.

[Morgan, *Can. men* (1912).]

Thompson, Walter Scott (1885-1966), public relations executive, was born at Newcastle-on-Tyne, England, October 22, 1885. As a young man he was on the editorial staffs of London newspapers. He came to Canada in 1911 after a tour of Australia, New Zealand, South Africa, and the South Sea Islands. He was telegraph editor and then city editor of the Montreal *Witness*. He became head of the press department of the Grand Trunk Railroad in 1914 and of the Canadian National Railways system in 1922. He was director of public relations for Trans-Canada Air Lines from 1941 to 1948. He handled the publicity for Canada's Diamond Jubilee in 1927, was made director of censorship in the Second World War, and in 1940 organized the department of public information for the Canadian government. He was awarded the C.B.E in 1946. He died at Montreal, Quebec, June 26, 1966.

[*Can. who's who*, 1964-66; Metropolitan Toronto Library Board, *Biographical scrapbooks*, vol. 26.]

Thomson, Andrew (1893-1974), meteorologist, was born in Owen Sound, Ontario, May 18, 1893. He was educated at the University of Toronto (M.A., 1916), Harvard University, and McGill University. He was associate physicist at the Carnegie Institute in Washington (1917-22), director of the Apia Observatory in Samoa (1922-29), aerologist for the Dominion of New Zealand (1929-30), and a member of the Meteorological Service of Canada from 1931 to 1959. He was director of the Canadian Meteorological Service from 1946 to 1959. He wrote *Upper winds over the South Pacific Ocean* (1927); *Upper winds over Samoa* (1930); *Upper winds, observations and results obtained on Cruise VII of the Carnegie* (1942). He was a fellow of the Royal Society of Canada (1935); received the Gold Medal of the Professional Institute of the Public Service of Canada (1952); and was awarded the O.B.E. in 1948. He died at Toronto, Ontario, October 18, 1974.

[*Can. who's who*, 1970-72.]

Thomson, Charles Poulette. See **Sydenham, Charles Poulett Thomson, Baron.**

Thomson, David Landsborough (1901-1964), biochemist, was born in Aberdeen, Scotland, November 14, 1901. His father was regius professor of natural history at the University of Aberdeen. David entered Aberdeen University, graduating with M.A. (1921) and B.Sc. (1924) degrees. He then went to Cambridge University, where he took the Ph.D. degree in 1928. He came to McGill as a lecturer in that year and spent his whole academic life at McGill University. He worked closely in publication with Collip, Browne, Selye, and others in the field of biochemistry, although he is best known for his *Life of the cell* (London, 1928), and his *Murder in the laboratory*, a "whodunit". During the Second World War he was a member of the advisory committee on nutrition, and for many years he was a member of the Fisheries Research Board of Canada, the National Research Council, and the Defence Research Board. He was chairman of the department of biochemistry at McGill University from 1941, in 1942 was made dean of the faculty of graduate studies and research, and in 1955, was made vice-principal in charge of research. He became a fellow of the Royal Society of Canada in 1936 and was awarded many honorary degrees. He died at Montreal, Quebec, October 2, 1964.

[*Proc. and Trans. Roy. Soc. Can.*, 1965.]

Thomson, Edward William (1849-1924), author and journalist, was born in Toronto township, Peel county, Upper Canada, on February 12, 1849, the son of William Thomson and Margaret Hamilton Foley. He was educated at Trinity College School, Weston. In 1864-65 he served in the Pennsylvania cavalry during the American Civil War; and in 1866 he served in the Queen's Own Rifles during the Fenian Raid in Canada. He was first a surveyor and civil engineer, and then he became a journalist. From 1879 to 1891 he was chief editorial writer on the Toronto *Globe*, and from 1891 to 1901 he was editor of the *Youth's Companion*. He then became Ottawa correspondent of the Boston *Transcript*, and devoted himself to independent journalism. He died at Boston, Massachusetts, on March 5, 1924. In 1873 he married Adelaide, daughter of Alexander St. Denis, of Port Fortune, Quebec. He was elected a fellow of the Royal Society of Canada in 1910; and he was the author of *Old man Savarin, and other stories* (Toronto, 1895; new ed., 1922), *Walter Gibbs, the young boss, and other stories* (Toronto, 1896), *Between earth and sky* (Toronto, 1897), *Smokey days* (Boston, 1901), *Peter Ottawa* (Toronto, 1905), *When Lincoln died, and other poems* (Boston and London, 1909), and *The many-mansioned house, and other poems* (Toronto, 1909).

[A. S. Bourinot, *Edward William Thomson* (Ottawa, 1955) and *The letters of Edward William Thomson to Archibald Lampman* (Ottawa, 1957); M. O. Hammond, *Edward William Thomson* (Queen's quarterly, 1931); *Dict. Am. biog.*; *Who was who in America*; Morgan, *Can. men* (1912).]

Thomson, Hugh Christopher (1791?-1834), printer and journalist, was born in Scotland about 1791. He came to Upper Canada after the War of 1812; and in 1819 he founded in Kingston the *Upper Canada Herald*, which he edited until his death. From 1824 to 1834 he represented Frontenac in the Legislative Assembly of Upper Canada. He died at Kingston on April 23, 1834. He was the author of a *Manual of parliamentary practice* (Kingston, U.C., 1828).

[W. S. Wallace, *The periodical literature of Upper Canada* (Can. hist. rev., 1931).]

Thomson, James Sutherland (1892-1972), theologian and university dean, was born in Stirling, Scotland, April 30, 1892. He was educated at the University of Glasgow (M.A. 1914); after service in the Cameron Highlanders and the Rifle Brigade in France and Flanders he enrolled in the divinity course at Trinity College, Glasgow (Hons. Dip., 1920). He was minister of Middle Church, Coatbridge, Scotland (1920-24); secretary for education, Church of Scotland (1924-30); professor at Pine Hill College, Halifax, Nova Scotia (1930-37); and president of the University of Saskatchewan (1937-49). He acted for one year as governor of the Canadian Broadcasting Corporation, and for two years (1956-58) was moderator of the United Church of Canada. His period of service at the University of Saskatchewan was very difficult, having begun in the depression and been carried out through five years of war. In 1949, he became dean of divinity at McGill University and returned to teaching philosophy and theology, retiring in 1957. He was a fellow of the Royal Society of Canada, and active in the United Church of Canada, the United Nations Society of Canada, and the National Conference of Canadian Universities.

His writings were mainly theological and religious: *Studies in the life of Jesus* (1927); *The way of Revelation* (1928); *The hope of the Gospel* (Toronto, 1955); *The divine mission* (Toronto, 1957); *The word of God* (Toronto, 1959); *God and His purpose* (Toronto, 1964); "Religion and theology" in *Literary history of Canada* (1965).

He died at Montreal, Quebec, November 18, 1972.

[*Can. who's who.*, 1967-69; *Proc. and Trans. Roy. Soc. Can.*, 1973.]

Thomson, John (d. 1828), fur-trader, was of Scottish origin. Possibly he was a son of John Thomson, the first postmaster of Montreal. He entered the service of the North West Company before 1789, for from that year to 1791 he was in charge of a post "near the lower part of Grass River in the Port Nelson track" In 1798 he was on the Peace River; in 1799 on Lake Athabaska; and in 1800 he built "Old Rocky Mountain House" on the Mackenzie River. He was stationed in the Athabaska department from 1806 to 1810, and in the English River department from 1811 to 1821. In 1804 he became a partner of the North West Company; and at the union of 1821 he became a chief factor of the Hudson's Bay Company. He retired from the service, however, on June 1, 1821; and he died on January 8, 1828, probably in the parish of Ste. Madeleine de Rigaud, Lower Canada, where he lived after his retirement. He married Françoise Boucher, and he had by her seven children.

[E. E. Rich (ed.), *Journal of occurrences in the Athabasca department, by George Simpson* (Toronto: The Champlain Society, 1938).]

Thomson, John Stuart (1869-1950), poet, was born in Montreal, Quebec, in 1869, and died at Glen Rock, New Jersey, on April 12, 1950. He was the author of *Estabelle and other verse* (Toronto, 1897) and *A day's song* (Toronto, 1900).

[R. E. Watters, *A check-list of Canadian literature* (Toronto, 1959).]

Thomson, Lesslie Rielle (1886-1958), engineer and author, was born in Toronto, Ontario, in 1886, and died at Montreal, Quebec, on April 27, 1958. He was educated at Upper Canada College and the University of Toronto (B.A.Sc., 1906), and became a consulting engineer. He was the author of *The Canadian railway problem* (Toronto, 1938). In 1946 he was created an O.B.E.

[*Can. who's who*, 1955-57]

Thomson, Thomas John (Tom) (1877-1917), painter, was born at Claremont, Ontario, on August 4, 1877. He was educated in the public schools of Owen Sound; and taught himself painting. He supported himself by serving as a bush-ranger in Algonquin Park, Ontario, during the greater part of the year; and here he obtained the inspiration for the pictures he painted in Toronto during the winter. These pictures are essentially Canadian, and betray a native-born genius. From them the group of Canadian painters known as "The Group of Seven" largely drew their ideas and style. Thomson, who was unmarried, was drowned in Algonquin Park on July 8, 1917.

[J. M. MacCallum, *Tom Thomson* (Can. mag., 1918); Blodwen Davies, *A study of Tom Thomson* (Toronto, 1935); A. H. Robson, *Tom Thomson* (Toronto, 1937); R. H. Hibbard, *Tom Thomson* (Toronto, 1962); B. Davies, *Tom Thomson: The story of a man who looked for beauty and for truth in the wilderness*. Foreword by A. Y. Jackson (Vancouver, 1967); O. Addison and E. Harwood, *Tom Thomson: The Algonquin years* (Toronto, 1969); N. MacTavish, *The fine arts in Canada* (Toronto, 1925); *Can. who was who*, vol. 1.]

Thomson, William J. (1857-1927), engraver, was born at Guelph, Ontario, in 1857. He was apprenticed to an engraving firm in Toronto about 1872; and he studied art under John A. Fraser (q.v.) at the Toronto Art School. He was one of the organizers of the Art Students League in 1886; and was its president in 1890-91. From 1916 to 1919 he was also the first president of the Society of Canadian Painter-Etchers. He became a master of etched work; and some of his etchings are in the National Gallery at Ottawa and the Art Gallery at Toronto. He died in Toronto on May 25, 1927.

[*William J. Thomson, Canada engraver— 1857-1927* (pamphlets, Toronto, 1930).]

Thorburn, Sir Robert (1836-1906), prime minister of Newfoundland (1885-89), was born on March 28, 1836, at Juniper Bank, Peebleshire, Scotland, and died at St. John's, Newfoundland, on April 12, 1906. He came to Newfoundland in 1852, and entered on a successful mercantile career. He was appointed a member of the Legislative Council in 1870. He resigned from the Council in 1885 to assume the leadership of the opposition in the Legislative Assembly, and was elected to represent Trinity in the Assembly. In the election of 1885 he led his party to victory, and was prime minister from 1885 to 1889. In 1887 he was created a K.C.M.G. In 1894 he was re-appointed a member of the Legislative Assembly.

[J. R. Smallwood (ed.), *The book of Newfoundland* (St. John's , 1937); D. W. Prowse, *History of Newfoundland* (London, 1895); *Who was who*, 1897-1916; *Encyc. Can.*]

Thorburn, William (*fl.* 1789-1805), furtrader, was a native of Scotland who entered the employ of the North West Company prior to 1789, when he was left in charge of "Finlay's old fort" on the Saskatchewan. He had become a partner of the North West Company by 1795, but had ceased to be a wintering partner by 1799. He relinquished his shares in the Company in 1805.

[W. S. Wallace (ed.), *Documents relating to the North West Company* (Toronto: The Champlain Society, 1934).]

Thornton, Sir Henry Worth (1871-1933), president of the Canadian National Railways (1922-32), was born at Logansport, Indiana, in the United States, on November 6, 1871. He was educated at the University of Pennsylvania, and entered the engineering department of the Pennsylvania Railroad in 1894. In 1911 he was appointed general superintendent of the Long Island Railroad; and in 1914 he went to England as general manager of the Great Eastern Railway. In 1917 his services were commandeered by the British government, and he became assistant director-general of movements and railways in France, with the temporary rank of colonel. In 1919 he was appointed inspector-general of transportation, with the rank of major-general; and he retained this position until 1922, when he was appointed president of the Canadian National Railways. He resigned from this position, because of adverse criticism, in 1932; and he died at New York on March 14, 1933. He was created a K.B.E. in 1919.

[D'Arcy Marsh, *The tragedy of Henry Thornton* (Toronto, 1935); *Who was who*, 1929-40; *Who was who in America*; *Americana annual*, 1934.]

Thorpe, Thomas (*fl.* 1781-1820), jurist, was a native of Ireland, and was called to the Irish bar in 1781. He became a protégé of Lord Castlereagh, and as a reward for some unknown services, probably in connection with the union of Great Britain and Ireland in 1801, was appointed in 1802 chief justice of Prince Edward Island. In 1805 he was appointed a puisne judge of the Court of King's Bench in Upper Canada, and he arrived in York (Toronto), in September, 1805. He assumed an attitude of hostility to the executive authorities in Upper Canada; and in 1806 he was elected to represent Durham, Simcoe, and the east riding of York in the Legislative Assembly. He headed in the Assembly the opposition to the government, and in 1807 he was suspended by Francis Gore (q.v.) from his position as judge. On his return to England, he was appointed chief justice of Sierra Leone; but he remained in this colony for only two years. The rest of his life he spent in poverty and obscurity; and he last appears in connection with a suit for criminal libel against Francis Gore in 1820. He was the author of *A letter to William Wilberforce* (London, 1815), *Reply to the special report of the directors of the African institution* (London, 1815), and *View of the present increase of the slave trade* (London, 1818).

[W. R. Riddell, *Mr. Justice Thorpe* (Can. law times, 1920); D. B. Read, *Lives of the judges of Upper Canada* (Toronto, 1888); Morgan, *Cel. Can.*]

Thorvaldson, Thorbergur (1883-1965), chemist and university dean, was born in Iceland, August 24, 1883, and emigrated to Canada with his parents, who settled near Gimli, Manitoba. He graduated from the University of Manitoba in honours chemistry in 1906 and received his doctorate from Harvard University in 1911. He studied in England and Europe from 1911 until his appointment to the department of chemistry at the University of Saskatchewan in 1914. From that time until his retirement as head of the department and dean of graduate studies in 1949 he remained at the University of Saskatchewan.

Dr. Thorvaldson was led into the study of the chemical properties of cement by the problems encountered when builders used the high sulphate ground waters of the prairies in making concrete. His work led to some fundamental research on the properties of cement, but he was always aware of the interrrelation of basic and applied science and he has been praised for his contribution to concrete construction methods.

He served on the National Research Council of Canada and on the Saskatchewan Research Council. He was active in organizing the Canadian Institute of Chemistry and the Chemical Institute of Canada and was awarded its first medal in 1951. He was a fellow of the Royal Society of Canada and recipient of the Tory Medal in 1951. He was made a member of the Icelandic Order of the Falcon. He died at Saskatoon, Saskatchewan, October 4, 1965.

[*Proc. Roy. Soc. Can.*, 1967; *Can. who's who*, 1955-57.]

Tiffany, Gideon (1774-1854), printer, was born in 1774. In 1794 he became the printer of the *Upper Canada Gazette* at Newark (Niagara), Upper Canada; and he published it until 1797. In 1799, with his brother Silvester (q.v.), he founded at Niagara the *Canada Constellation*, and he published this journal until toward the end of 1800. He then deserted printing and journalism for farming; and he died on his farm in Middlesex county, Ontario, in 1854.

[W. S. Wallace, *The periodical literature of Upper Canada* (Can. hist. rev., 1931); *The first journalists in Upper Canada* (Can. hist. rev., 1945).]

Tiffany, Silvester (1758-1811), printer, was born in Massachusetts, on August 9, 1758, the older brother of Gideon Tiffany (q.v.). He attended Dartmouth College from 1775 to 1777; but did not graduate. In 1799 he joined his brother Gideon in publishing the *Canada Constellation* at Newark (Niagara), Upper Canada; and when this journal ceased publication at the end of 1800, he became the editor and printer of the *Niagara Herald*, which he continued to publish until August 28, 1802. He then appears to have returned to the United States, and to have become the editor of a newspaper at Canandaigua, New York. He died at Canandaigua, New York, on March 24, 1811.

[W. S. Wallace, *The periodical literature of Upper Canada* (Can. hist. rev., 1931); *Michigan biographies*, vol. 1 (Lansing, Mich., 1924), under "Alexander F. Tiffany"; *The first journalists in Upper Canada* (Can. hist., rev., 1945).]

Tilley, Leonard Percy de Wolfe (1870-1947), prime minister of New Brunswick (1933-35), was born at Ottawa, Ontario, on May 21, 1870, the son of Sir Samuel Leonard Tilley (q.v.), and died at Saint John, New Brunswick, on December 28, 1947. He was educated at the University of New Brunswick and Dalhousie Law School, and was called to the New Brunswick bar in 1894 (K.C., 1914). In 1912 he was elected to represent Saint John as a Conservative in the New Brunswick legislature; and he became successively a minister without portfolio (1925-31), minister of lands and mines (1931-33), and prime minister (1933-35). He was defeated in the election of 1935, and retired from political life. He was then appointed to the bench as a judge of the Exchequer Court.

[*Can. parl. comp.*, 1935; *Can. who's who*, 1938-39; *Encyc. Can.*]

Tilley, Sir Samuel Leonard (1818-1896), statesman, was born at Gagetown, New Brunswick, on May 8, 1818, the son of Thomas

Morgan Tilley and Susan Ann Peters. He was educated at the Gagetown grammar school, and in 1831 began to earn his own livelihood as a clerk in an apothecary's office in Saint John, New Brunswick. In 1838 he went into business for himself, as a partner in the firm of Peters and Tilley. He was a member of the Legislative Assembly of New Brunswick from 1850 to 1851, from 1854 to 1856, and from 1857 to 1865. In 1854 he became provincial secretary in the Fisher administration, and from 1861 to 1865 was leader of the government. In 1864 he was a delegate to the conferences at Charlottetown and Quebec to discuss Confederation; and in 1866 he was a delegate to the London Conference, at which the British North America Act was drafted. The ministry of which he was a member was defeated in 1865 on the issue of Confederation, but was returned to power in 1866. In 1867 Tilley resigned from the New Brunswick cabinet, and became minister of customs in the first cabinet of the Dominion of Canada. This portfolio he retained until 1873, when he became minister of finance in the Macdonald government. On the fall of the government a few months later, he was appointed lieutenant-governor of New Brunswick; and his tenure of this office coincided with the period of office of the Mackenzie government. In 1878, therefore, he was free to become minister of finance in the second Macdonald goverment, and it fell to him to inaugurate the National Policy. Failing health compelled him to resign his portfolio in 1885, and he was then appointed lieutenant-governor of New Brunswick for a second term. This second term of office lasted until 1893; and on June 25, 1896, he died at Saint John, New Brunswick.

He was twice married, (1) to Julia Anna, daughter of James T. Hanford, of Saint John, and (2) in 1867 to Alice, daughter of Z. Chipman, of St. Stephen. He was created a C.B. (civil) in 1867, and a K.C.M.G. in 1879.

[J. Hannay, *The life and times of Sir Leonard Tilley* (Saint John, N.B., 1896), and *Sir Leonard Tilley* (Toronto, 1907); *Dict. nat. biog.*; *Cyc. Am. biog.*; Taylor, *Brit. Am.*, vol. 1; Dent, *Can. port.*, vol. 1; Taché, *Men of the day*; Rose, *Cyc. Can. biog.* (1888); *Can. parl. comp.*; *Can. who was who*, vol.2.]

Tilley, William Norman (1868-1942), lawyer, was born at Bowmanville, Ontario, on March 11, 1868. He was educated at the Osgoode Hall Law School, Toronto, was called to the bar in 1894 (K.C.,1916), and practised law in Toronto. He became an outstanding constitutional lawyer, and appeared frequently before the Judicial Committee of the Privy Council at Westminster. He died at Toronto on June 10, 1942.

[*Can. who's who*, 1936-37.]

Timmins, Noah Anthony (1867-1936), mining operator, was born at Mattawa,

Ontario, on March 31, 1867. He was educated at St. Mary's College, Montreal, and became interested in mining. In 1903 he and his brother Henry (d. 1930) acquired the LaRose mine at Cobalt, and in 1909 he, with his associates, developed the Hollinger mine in the Porcupine country. He was president of the Hollinger mine from its inception; and became a man of great wealth. He died at Palm Beach, Florida, on January 23, 1936. The town of Timmins is named after him.

[*New York Times*, Jan. 24, 1936.]

Timmins, Noah Anthony, Jr., (1898-1973), industrialist, was born at Mattawa, Ontario, April 30, 1898, the son of N. A. Timmins (q.v.). He was educated at Loyola College and McGill University (B.Sc.). He was associated with the mining interests of his family and became chairman of Timmins Investments and N. A. Timmins Limited; vice-president and director of Hollinger Mines Limited and St. Lawrence Corporation; and president of Timmins Mining Enterprises, South America, Tourlac Investments, South America, Quebec North Shore and Labrador Railway, Limited, Bank of Montreal, Labrador Mining and Exploration, and the Bank of London and Montreal (Nassau). He died at Nassau, December 16, 1973.

[*Can. who's who*, 1967-69.]

Tingle, John Bishop (1867?-1918), chemist, was born in Sheffield, England, about 1867; and was educated at Owens College, Manchester, and at the University of Munich (Ph.D., 1889). He came to America in 1896, occupied academic positions at the Lewis Institute, Chicago, at the Illinois College, Jacksonville, and at Johns Hopkins University, and was for a time assistant editor of the *American Chemical Journal*. In 1907 he was appointed professor of chemistry at McMaster University, Toronto; and he occupied this position until his death at Toronto, Ontario, on August 5, 1918. He was elected a fellow of the Royal Society of Canada shortly before his death; and he was joint author, with H. Meyer, of *Determination of radicals in carbon compounds* (New York, 1908).

[*Trans. Roy. Soc. Can.*, 1919; Morgan, *Can. men* (1912).]

Tisdale, David (1835-1911), minister of militia for Canada (1896), was born in Charlotteville, Norfolk county, Upper Canada, on September 8, 1835, the son of Ephraim Tisdale. He was educated at Simcoe grammar school, and was called to the bar of Upper Canada in 1858 (Q.C., 1872). In 1887 he was elected to represent South Norfolk in the Canadian House of Commons, and he held this seat continuously until his retirement from public life in 1908. On May 1, 1896, he became minister of militia in the Tupper administration, but he retired from office with his colleagues the following July. He died at Simcoe, Ontario, on March 31, 1911. In 1858 he married Sarah Araminta, daughter of James Walker; and by her he had two sons and two daughters.

[Morgan, *Can. men* (1912); *Can. who's who*, 1910; *Can. parl. comp.*]

Tocque, Philip (1814-1899), clergyman and author, was born at Carbonear, Newfoundland, in 1814. He became a schoolteacher in Newfoundland, and later clerk of the peace for southern Newfoundland; but in 1851 he embarked on the study of theology at the Berkeley Divinity School, Middletown, Connecticut; and he was ordained a priest of the Church of England in 1864. He occupied various charges in the Maritime provinces and in Ontario; and he died at Toronto, Ontario, on October 22, 1899. He was the author of *Wandering thoughts* (London, 1840), *A peep at Uncle Sam's farm, workshop, fisheries, &c.* (Boston, 1851), *Newfoundland, as it was and as it is* (London, 1878), and *Kaleidoscope echoes* (Toronto, 1895).

[Morgan, *Can. men* (1898).]

Tod, John (1791-1882), fur-trader, was born at Lochleven, Dumbartonshire, Scotland, in 1791. He entered the service of the Hudson's Bay Company and was for many years in charge of the Thompson River district in British Columbia. He retired from the company in 1849, and he was a member of the first council of Vancouver Island. He died at Victoria, British Columbia, on August 31, 1882.

[*Dom. ann. reg.*, 1882; F. H. Johnson, *John Tod* (Beaver, June, 1941).]

Todd, Alfred (1819-1874), civil servant and author, was born in England, on March 15, 1819. He came to Canada with his brother Alpheus Todd (q.v.) in 1833; and became chief clerk of the private bills office of the Legislative Assembly of Canada. He died at Ottawa, Ontario, on June 6, 1874. He was the author of *A treatise on the proceedings to be adopted in conducting or opposing private bills in the parliament of Canada* (Montreal, 1862).

[Morgan, *Bib. can.*; Cyc. Am. biog.]

Todd, Alpheus (1821-1884), librarian, was born in London, England, on July 30, 1821, the son of Henry Cooke Todd (q.v.). He came to Canada with his family in 1832, and in 1836 was employed as an assistant in the Library of the House of Assembly of Upper Canada. In 1841 he was appointed assistant librarian to the Legislative Assembly of Canada, and in 1854 librarian. In 1870 he was placed in charge of the Parliamentary Library at Ottawa; and he occupied this position until his death at Ottawa on January 22, 1884. In 1881 he was created a C.M.G., and he was given the degree of LL.D. by both Queen's University and McGill University. Though self-educated, he became the leading authority of his day on the law and custom of the Canadian constitution. He was the author of *The practice and privileges of the two houses of parliament* (Toronto, 1839); *Brief suggestions in regard to the formation of local governments for Upper and Lower Canada, in connection with a federal union of the British North American provinces* (Ottawa, 1866); *On parliamentary government in England* (2 vols., London, 1867); *A constitutional governor* (Ottawa, 1878); and *Parliamentary government in the British Colonies* (Boston, 1880).

[E. R. Cameron, *Alpheus Todd* (Canadian bar review, 1925); *Dom. ann. reg.*, 1884; Rose, *Cyc. Can. biog.* (1886); *Cyc. Am. biog.*; Morgan, *Bib. can.*; W. Kingsford, *The early bibliography of Ontario* (Toronto, 1892).]

Todd, Henry Cooke (d. 1862), author, was born in England, and was educated at Oxford University. He came to Canada with his family in 1832, and he died in 1862. He published, under the pen-name of "A Traveller", *Notes upon Canada and the United States, from 1832 to 1840, much in a small space, or a great deal in a little book* (Toronto, 1840); and under the pen-name of "One in Retirement", *Items (in the life of an usher) on travel, anecdote, and popular errors* (Quebec, 1855).

[W. Kingsford, *The early bibliography of Ontario* (Toronto, 1892).]

Todd, William Freeman (1854-1935), lieutenant-governor of New Brunswick (1923-28); was born at St. Stephen, New Brunswick, on May 2, 1854. He became a merchant in St. Stephen; and he represented Charlotte county in the Legislative Assembly of New Brunswick from 1899 to 1903 and in the Canadian House of Commons from 1908 to 1911. He was appointed lieutenant-governor of the province in 1923, and he retired from office in 1928. He died at St. Stephen, New Brunswick, on March 16, 1935.

[*Can. parl. comp.*]

Tolmie, Simon Fraser (1867-1937), prime minister of British Columbia (1928-33), was born at Victoria, British Columbia, on January 25, 1867, the son of William Fraser Tolmie (q.v.) and Jane Work. He was educated at the Ontario Veterinary College, Toronto; and became a farmer and breeder of pure-bred cattle on Vancouver Island. From 1917 to 1928 he represented Victoria in the Canadian House of Commons as a Conservative; and he was minister of agriculture in the Borden and Meighen cabinets from 1919 to 1921, and again in the second Meighen cabinet in 1926. In 1928 he resigned his seat in the House of Commons, was elected to represent Victoria in the legislature of British Columbia, and became prime minister of British Columbia and minister of railways. He continued in office until defeated at the polls in 1933. He was re-elected to represent Victoria in the

Canadian House of Commons in 1936; but he died at Victoria, British Columbia, on October 13, 1937. He was an honorary LL.D. of the University of British Columbia.

[*Can. who's who*, 1936-37; *Can. parl. comp.*]

Tolmie, William Fraser (1812-1886), chief factor of the Hudson's Bay Company, was born at Inverness, Scotland, on February 3, 1812. He studied medicine at the University of Glasgow (M.D., 1832), and entered the service of the Hudson's Bay Company as a surgeon. He arrived at Fort Vancouver, British Columbia, in 1833; and from that date until his retirement in 1870 occupied various posts in the service of the company on the Pacific slope. In 1843 he became chief factor of the company's posts on Puget Sound; in 1855 he was chief factor at Fort Nisqually; and in 1859 a member of the Hudson's Bay Company board of management at Victoria. From 1861 to 1866 he was a member of the Legislative Assembly of Vancouver Island; and from 1874 to 1878 he represented the district of Victoria in the Legislative Assembly of British Columbia. In 1870 he took up farming, and he was the first to introduce thoroughbred stock into British Columbia. He died at Victoria, Vancouver Island, on December 8, 1886. In 1850 he married Jane, eldest daughter of John Work (q.v.); and by her he had seven sons and five daughters. One son, Simon Fraser Tolmie (q.v.), became prime minister of British Columbia. He was much interested in the ethnology and linguistics of the Pacific coast Indians; and, with George M. Dawson (q.v.), he published *Comparative vocabularies of the Indian tribes of British Columbia* (Montreal, 1884). Part of his diary for 1833 has been published by E. S. Meany (Washington historical quarterly, 1932).

[S. F. Tolmie, *My father* (British Columbia historical quarterly, 1937); *Dom. ann. reg.*, 1886; *Can. parl. comp.*, 1876; J. B. Kerr, *Biographical dictionary of well-known British Columbians* (Vancouver, B.C., 1890); W. J. Rattray, *The Scot in British North America* (4 vols., Toronto, 1880); J. T. Walbran, *British Columbia coast names* (Ottawa, 1909).]

Tomison, William (*fl.* 1739-1811), fur-trader, was born in South Ronaldsay, an island of the Orkney group, in 1739, and was apprenticed to the Hudson's Bay Company in 1760. In 1767 he was sent inland to Lake Winnipeg to counteract the influence on the Indians of the "Canada pedlars", and for over a third of a century he was foremost among the Hudson's Bay Company's servants in combating the encroachments of the traders from Canada. In 1777 he was placed in charge of Cumberland House; and in 1786 he was appointed "inland chief" from York Factory. He returned to England in 1811, and would appear to have died not long afterwards.

[R. H. G. Leveson Gower, *William Tomison* (Beaver, 1934); J. B. Tyrrell (ed.), *Journals of Samuel Hearne and Philip Turnor* (Toronto: The Champlain Society, 1934).]

Tompkins, James J. (1870-1953), priest and educationist, was born in Margaree, Nova Scotia, on September 7, 1870, and died at Antigonish, Nova Scotia, on May 5, 1953. He was educated at St. Francis Xavier University, and was a member of the faculty of this university from 1902 to 1922. He became a leader in the co-operative movement in Nova Scotia, and in his later years carried his ideas into practice as the parish priest, first at Canso, and then at Reserve Mines.

[G. Boyle, *Father Tompkins of Nova Scotia* (New York, 1943); *Can. who's who*, 1948; *Encyc. Can.*]

Tonty, or Tonti, Henri de (1650?-1704), explorer, was born about 1650, the son of Lorenzo de Tonty, an Italian banker who invented the "tontine". He entered the French army in 1668. In 1677 he lost his right hand in an action in Sicily, whence came his nickname of "Main-de-Fer". In 1678 he was recommended to La Salle (q.v.) as a lieutenant in his explorations, and he served under La Salle until the death of the latter in 1687. He remained in the Illinois country until the year 1700, and then he placed himself in the service of Iberville (q.v.) in Louisiana. He died at Mobile, Louisiana, in September, 1704.

[E. R. Murphy, *Henry de Tonty* (Baltimore, 1941); B. Sulte, *Les Tonty* (Trans. Roy. Soc. Can., 1893); Henry E. Legler, *Chevalier Henry de Tonty* (Parkman Club Publications, No. 3, Milwaukee, 1896); P. Margry, *Relations et mémoires inédites* (Paris, 1865); *Cyc. Am. biog.*; Le Jeune, *Dict. gén.*; *Dict. Can. biog.*, vol. 2.]

Torrance, David (1805-1876), president of the Bank of Montreal (1873-76), was born in New York, N.Y., in 1805. He came to Canada with his father, James Torrance, when a boy, and settled first in Kingston, Upper Canada, and then in Montreal, Lower Canada. In Montreal he became in 1821 a clerk in the business of his uncle, John Torrance; and in 1833 he was admitted to partnership in the firm. When his uncle retired, the firm was reorganized as David Torrance and Co., and became one of the leading mercantile firms in Montreal, with a fleet of steamships and with connections in the West Indies and China. In 1873 David Torrance was elected president of the Bank of Montreal, in succession to E. A. King (q.v.); and he retained this position until his death at Montreal, Quebec, on January 29, 1876.

[Rose, *Cyc. Can. biog.* (1888); *Dict. Can. biog.*, vol. 10.]

Torrance, Frederick William (1823-1887), jurist, was born in Montreal, Lower Canada, on July 16, 1823, the son of John Torrance, and the nephew of David Torrance (q.v.). He was educated at Edinburgh University (M.A., 1844), studied law in Montreal, and was in 1848 called to the bar of Lower Canada. He practised law in Montreal; and from 1854 to 1870 was professor of Roman law in McGill University. In 1868 he was appointed a judge of the Superior Court of Quebec; and he remained on the bench until his death at Montreal, Quebec, on January 2, 1887.

[P. G. Roy, *Les juges de la province de Québec* (Quebec, 1933); R. Campbell, *A history of the Scotch Presbyterian church, St. Gabriel Street, Montreal* (Montreal, 1887); Rose, *Cyc. Can. biog.* (1888).]

Torrance, John (1839-1881), clergyman and educationist, was born at Kilmarnock, Scotland, on December 6, 1839. He came to Canada with his parents in 1849, and became a school-teacher. He later attended the Woodstock Literary Institute, and graduated from the University of Toronto (B.A., 1873). He was ordained a Baptist minister in 1864; and he occupied pastorates at Mount Elgin, Cheltenham, and Yorkville, Ontario. In 1876 he was appointed professor of Greek exegesis and apologetics at the Woodstock Institute; in 1879 he was appointed principal of the Theological Department of the Institute; and in 1881, professor of New Testament interpretation in the new Baptist College in Toronto. He died shortly afterwards, on August 3, 1881, at Bobcaygeon, Ontario.

[*Dom. ann. reg.,* 1881.]

Torrance, Robert (1825-1908), clergyman, was born at Markethill, county Armagh, Ireland, on May 23, 1825. He was educated at the Royal Academical Institution, Belfast; and he studied divinity in the halls of the United Secession Church in Glasgow and in Edinburgh, Scotland. He was licensed to preach in 1845, and was sent to Upper Canada as a probationer. In 1846 he was ordained a minister of the United Presbyterian Church, and became pastor of the congregation in Guelph. He remained pastor of this church until 1882; and after this date he had no stated charge. He was elected moderator of the Presbyterian Church in Canada in 1898; and in 1885 Knox College, Toronto, conferred on him the degree of D.D. He died in Guelph, Ontario, on January 31, 1908.

[Rose, *Cyc. Can. biog.* (1888).]

Torrington, Frederic Herbert (1837-1917), musician, was born at Dudley, Worcestershire, England, on October 20, 1837. He came to Canada in 1857, and settled in Montreal. From 1869 to 1873 he was organist of King's Chapel, Boston, Massachusetts; but in 1873 he returned to Canada as organist and choirmaster of the Metropolitan Church, Toronto. In 1886 he organized the first musical festival in Toronto; and in 1888 he founded the Toronto College of Music. He died in Toronto on November 19, 1917. In 1902 he was honoured by the University of Toronto with the degree of Mus. Doc.

[Morgan, *Can. men* (1912); *Can. who was who,* vol. 1.]

Tory, Henry Marshall (1864-1947), educationist, was born in Guysborough county, Nova Scotia, on January 11, 1864, and died at Ottawa, Ontario, on February 6, 1947. He was educated at McGill University (B.A., 1890; M.A, 1896; D.Sc., 1903), and Wesleyan College, Montreal (B.D., 1892). He was ordained a minister of the Methodist Church; but turned to academic work. In 1893 he was appointed a lecturer in mathematics at McGill University; in 1906 he became the first principal of McGill College in Vancouver; and in 1908 he became the first president of the University of Alberta. He resigned from this post in 1928, and until 1935 was the president of the National Research Council in Ottawa. From 1942 to his death he was president and chairman of the board of governors of Carleton College (now Carleton University). He was elected a fellow of the Royal Society of Canada in 1909, and was its president in 1939-40. He edited *A history of science in Canada* (Toronto, 1939).

[E. A. Corbett, *Henry Marshall Tory* (Toronto, 1954); *Proc. Roy. Soc. Can.,* 1947; *Can. who's who* 1938-39; *Who was who,* 1941-1950; *Encyc. Can.*]

Tory, James Cranswick (1862-1944), lieutenant-governor of Nova Scotia, was born at Port Shoreham, Guysborough county, Nova Scotia, on October 24, 1862. He was educated at McGill University, and for many years was an officer of the Sun Life Assurance Company of Canada. From 1911 to 1925 he represented Guysborough county in the Legislative Assembly of Nova Scotia; and from 1921 to 1925 he was a minister without portfolio in the administration of the Hon. George H. Murray (q.v.). In 1925 he was appointed lieutenant-governor of Nova Scotia; and he continued in office until 1931. He died at Halifax, Nova Scotia, on June 26, 1944.

[*Can. parl. comp.*; *Can. who's who,* 1936-37.]

Tory, John Stewart Donald (1903-1965), lawyer and financier, was born in Detroit, Michigan, July 19, 1903. He was educated at the University of Toronto (B.A. Hons., 1924), Osgoode Hall (1927), and Harvard University (D.C.L., 1929). He was a member of various law firms until forming his own company, J.S.D. Tory and Associates in 1941. He played a leading role in the merger of the Massey-Harris Company with the Ferguson Tractor interests in Britain, and of the Simpson Company of Toronto with Sears Roebuck of Chicago; and in the acquisition of the Algoma Steel shares of Sir James Dunn's estate for Canadian interests. He was a member of the board of governors of the University of Toronto, the Toronto General Hospital, and other public bodies. He was chairman of the board of McIntyre Porcupine Mines, and a director of Sun Life Assurance, Royal Bank, Argus Corporation, Algoma Steel, Montreal Trust, Moore Corporation, and others. He died at Toronto, Ontario, August 27, 1965.

[*Can. who's who*, 1955-57; Metropolitan Toronto Library Board, *Biographical scrapbooks*, vol. 23.]

Toussaint, François Xavier (1821-1895), educationist, was born at St. Jean, Island of Orleans, Lower Canada, on March 1, 1821. He became a school-teacher in the Normal School of Laval University; and he died at Quebec City on December 2, 1895. He was the author of *Traité d'arithmétique* (Quebec, 1865), *Géographie moderne* (Quebec, 1868), and *Abrégé d'histoire du Canada* (Quebec, 1874).

[*Bull. rech. hist.*, 1929.]

Townley, Adam (1808-1887), clergyman and author, was born in England on February 11, 1808, became a Methodist minister in Lower Canada in 1833, and in 1840 became a clergyman of the Church of England in Canada. In his later years he was rector at Paris, Ontario; and here he died on February 11, 1887. He was the author of *Ten letters addressed to the Hon. W. H. Draper, M.P.P., on the Church and church establishments*, by an Anglo-Canadian (Toronto, 1839), *Denominational schools* (Toronto, 1853), *Seven letters on the non-religious common school system of Canada and the United States* (Toronto, 1853), *The sacerdotal tithe* (New York, 1856), *A report on ministerial incomes* (London, Canada West, 1859), *A letter to the lord bishop of Huron in personal vindication* (Brantford, 1862), and *Plain explanations* (Toronto, 1862 and 1865).

[Morgan, *Bib. can.*]

Townshend, Sir Charles James (1844-1924), chief justice of Nova Scotia (1907-15), was born at Amherst, Nova Scotia, on March 22, 1844, the son of the Rev. Canon Townshend and Elizabeth Stewart. He was educated at King's College, Windsor, Nova Scotia (B.A., 1863; B.C.L., 1872; D.C.L., 1908), and was called to the bar of Nova Scotia in 1866 (Q.C., 1881). He practised law at Amherst; and he represented Cumberland in the Legislative Assembly of Nova Scotia from 1878 to 1884, and in the Canadian House of Commons from 1884 to 1887. From 1878 to 1882 he was also a minister without portfolio in the provincial government. In 1887 he was appointed a puisne judge of the Supreme Court of Nova Scotia; and in 1907 he became chief justice of

this court. He retired from the bench in 1915, and he died at Wolfville, Nova Scotia, on June 16, 1924. He was twice married, (1) in 1877 to Laura (d. 1884), daughter of J. D. Kinnear, and (2) in 1887 to Margaret, daughter of John Macfarlane. He was created a knight bachelor in 1911. He contributed a number of historical papers to the *Collections* of the Nova Scotia Historical Society.

[*Who was who*, 1916-28; *Can. who was who*, vol. 2; Morgan, *Can. men* (1912); *Can. who's who*, 1910; *Can. parl. comp.*]

Townshend, George, Marquess (1724-1807), soldier, was born on February 28, 1724, the eldest son of the third Viscount Townshend. He entered the British army at an early age, and he saw active service at the battles of Dettingen, Fontenoy, and Culloden. When the expedition under Wolfe (q.v.) was sent to Canada in 1758, he was appointed one of Wolfe's brigadiers; and after the death of Wolfe on the Plains of Abraham in 1759, the command of the British forces in Canada devolved upon him. He returned to England, however, in the autumn of 1759, leaving General Murray (q.v.) in command. He rose to the rank of field marshal in the army, and master-general of ordnance. In 1767 he succeeded his father as fourth Viscount Townshend; and in 1787 he was created a marquess. He died on September 14, 1807. He was twice married, (1) in 1751 to Lady Charlotte Compton (d. 1770), daughter of the Earl of Northampton, and (2) in 1773 to Anne, daughter of Sir William Montgomery, Bart., by whom he had a large family.

[Sir C. V. F. Townshend, *The military life of Field-Marshal George, first Marquess Townshend* (London, 1901); *Dict. nat. biog.*; Le Jeune, *Dict. gén.*]

Townsley, Benjamin Franklin (1890-1939), mining engineer and author, was born in 1890, became a mining engineer in Toronto, Ontario, and died in Toronto on May 7, 1939. He was the author of *Mine-finders* (Toronto, 1935).

[Private information.]

Tracey, Daniel (1795-1832), physician and journalist, was born in Roscrea, Tipperary county, Ireland, in May, 1795, the son of Michael Tracey, a merchant. He was educated at Trinity College, Dublin, and after graduation studied medicine at the Royal College of Surgeons, Dublin. He practised medicine in Dublin for several years; but in 1825 he emigrated to Canada, and began the practice of medicine in Montreal. In 1828 he established the *Vindicator*, a Reform newspaper, and became its editor; and in May, 1832, he was elected to represent the west ward of Montreal in the Legislative Assembly of Lower Canada. He died of cholera in Montreal on July 18, 1832.

[E. J. Mullally, *Mr. Daniel Tracey* (Montreal, 1935); *Bull. rech. hist.*, 1927.]

Tracy, Alexandre de Prouville, Sieur de (1603-1670), lieutenant-general of the French territories in America (1663-67), was born in France in 1603, and became an officer in the French army. In 1663 he was appointed lieutenant-general of the French territories in North and South America; and he arrived in Canada in 1665, with military reinforcements to be employed against the Iroquois. In 1666 he made a successful expedition against the Iroquois, and thoroughly cowed them. He returned to France in 1667; and he then became, first, commandant at Dunkirk, and later governor of Château Trompette, the stronghold of Bordeaux. Here he died on April 28, 1670.

[*Bull. rech. hist.,* 1897, 1904, and 1905; *Cyc. Am. biog.*; Bibaud, *Panth. can.*; Le Jeune, *Dict. gén.*; A. Fauteux, *La carrière pré-canadienne de M. de Tracy* (Cahiers des dix, 1936) *Dict. Can. biog.,* vol. 1.]

Traill, Mrs. Catherine Parr, née **Strickland** (1802-1899), author, was born in London, England, on January 9, 1802, the daughter of Thomas Strickland, of Reydon Hall, Suffolk. In 1832, she married Lieut. Thomas Traill, 21st Fusiliers, and with him emigrated to Canada, and settled near Rice Lake, Ontario. Her first book was *The backwoods of Canada* (London, 1835; new ed., 1846); and this was followed by *Lady Mary and her nurse* (London, 1850), *The Canadian Crusoes* (London, 1852), afterwards published under the title *Lost in the backwoods, The female emigrant guide* (Toronto, 1855), *Rambles in the Canadian forest* (London, 1859), *Pearls and pebbles, or The notes of an old naturalist* (Toronto, 1894), *Cot and cradle stories* (Toronto, 1895), and *Studies in plant life in Canada, or Gleanings from forest, lake, and plain* (Ottawa, 1885). She died at Lakefield, Ontario, on August 29, 1899.

[S. Eaton, *Lady of the backwoods: A biography of C. P. Traill* (Toronto, 1969); Morgan, *Can. men and women* (1898) and *Bib. can.*; A. MacMurchy, *Handbook of Canadian literature* (Toronto, 1906); R. P. Baker, *A history of English-Canadian literature to the Confederation* (Cambridge, Mass., 1920); G. H. Needler, *Otonabee pioneers* (Toronto, 1953).]

Trant, William (1844-1924), journalist and civil servant, was born in Leeds, England, on March 13, 1844. He became a journalist, first in London, and then in India; and in 1889 he came to Canada, and settled in the north-west. In his later years he was police magistrate of Regina, Saskatchewan, and afterwards archivist of the province of Saskatchewan. He died at Victoria, British Columbia, on September 4, 1924. He was the author of *Trade unions, their origin and objects, influence and efficacy* (London, 1884).

[Morgan, *Can. men* (1912).]

Trapp, Ethlyn (1891-1972), medical specialist, was born in New Westminster, British Columbia, in 1891. She was educated at McGill University (M.D., 1927) and in postgraduate studies at Berlin and Vienna. She began practice as a pediatrician in New Westminster and after a time she returned to Europe to study radiotherapy. Returning to Canada she opened an office which became a private centre for cancer treatment. In partnership with Dr. Olive Sadler and Dr. Margaret Hardie she launched a clinical research project on cancer of the breast which was continued after her retirement by the Cancer Institute. She was president of the British Columbia Medical Association, and of the National Cancer Institute, and she received the Order of Canada. She died in Vancouver, British Columbia, July 31, 1972.

[Vancouver *Sun*, Aug. 6, 1972.]

Trémaudan, Auguste Henri de (1874-1929), author, was born at Châteauguay, Quebec, on July 14, 1874, the son of Auguste de Trémaudan and Jeanne-Marie Huet, both natives of France. He became a journalist, and lived during most of his life in Manitoba. He died at Los Angeles, California, whither he had gone in search of health, on October 29, 1929. He was the author of *The Hudson Bay road* (London, 1915), *Pourquoi nous parlons français* (Winnipeg, 1916), *Les précurseurs* (Winnipeg, 1917), *Le sang français* (Winnipeg, 1918), and two three-act plays, *De fil en aiguille* (Los Angeles, 1925) and *Quand même* (Montreal, 1928).

[*Bull. rech. hist.,* 1930.]

Tremblay, Jules (1879-1927), author, was born in Montreal, Quebec, in 1879. He became first a journalist, and then a translator on the staff of the House of Commons at Ottawa. He died at Ottawa on November 28, 1927. He was the author of *Des mots, des vers* (Montreal, 1911), *Du crépuscule aux aubes* (Ottawa, 1917), *Les ferments* (Ottawa, 1917), *Aromes du terroir* (Ottawa, 1918), *Les ailes qui montent* (Ottawa, 1918), *La vente de la poule noire* (Ottawa, 1920), *Trouées dans les novales* (Ottawa, 1921), *Nos lettres* (Ottawa, 1921), *Sainte-Anne d'Ottawa: Un résumé d'histoire* (Ottawa, 1925), and several other books and pamphlets.

[*Can. who was who,* vol. 1; Le Jeune, *Dict. gén.*; *Bull. rech. hist.,* 1928.]

Tremblay, Rémi (1847-1926), author, was born on April 2, 1847, at St. Barnabé, county of St. Hyacinthe, Quebec. When still in his teens, he fought in the American Civil War, and later he served in the Canadian militia during the Fenian Raid. He became a journalist, and was the editor of newspapers at Quebec, at Montreal, and at Fall River and Worcester in the United States. In 1897 he entered the Canadian civil service, and was employed successively in the library of parliament and on the staff of Hansard. He retired in 1923, and he died on the island of Guadeloupe, whither he had gone in search of health, on January 31, 1926. He was the author of *Caprices poétiques et chansons satiriques* (Montreal, 1883), *Un revenant* (Montreal, 1884), *Poésies diverses: Coups d'ailes et coups de bec* (Montreal, 1888), *Boutades et rêveries* (Fall River, 1893), *Vers l'idéal* (Ottawa, 1912), *Pierre qui roule* (Montreal, 1923), and *Mon dernier voyage à travers l'Europe* (Montreal, 1925).

[*Bull. rech. hist.*, 1926; Le Jeune, *Dict. gén.*]

Tremeear, William James (1864-1927), lawyer, was born at Bowmanville, Canada West, on May 5, 1864. He was educated at the Osgoode Hall Law School, Toronto, and was called to the bar in Ontario in 1886. He practised law in Toronto from 1891 to 1918; and in 1898 he began the publication of *Canadian criminal cases*. He died at Pasadena, California, on September 26, 1927. He was the author of *A treatise on the Canadian law of conditional sales of chattels, and chattel liens* (Toronto, 1899), *The criminal code and the law of criminal evidence in Canada* (Toronto, 1902), *The liquor laws of Canada* (Toronto, 1904), and *Tremeear's Canada statute citations* (Toronto, 1929).

[Morgan, *Can. men* (1912).]

Trenholme, Norman William (1837-1919), jurist, was born at Kingsey, Drummond county, Lower Canada, on August 18, 1837. He was educated at McGill University (B.A., 1863; B.C.L., 1865; M.A., 1878; D.C.L., 1887), and was called to the bar of Lower Canada in 1865 (Q.C., 1889). He practised law in Montreal, and in 1888 he was elected *bâtonnier* of the Montreal bar. From 1868 to 1888 he was a professor of law at McGill University; and from 1888 to 1895 he was dean of the faculty of law in McGill University. In 1901 he was appointed a judge of the Superior Court of Quebec for the district of Montreal; in 1904 he was transferred to the Court of King's Bench; and in 1909 he was for a time acting chief justice of the province. He died at Westmount, Quebec, on June 26, 1919.

[P. G. Roy, *Les juges de la province de Québec* (Quebec, 1933); Morgan, *Can. men* (1912).]

Trethewey, William Griffith (1867-1926), capitalist, was born in Muskoka, Ontario, in 1867. He discovered and developed the Trethewey mine in Cobalt, New Ontario; and acquired from it a large fortune. In 1913 he removed to England, and purchased an estate in Sussex; but in 1924 he returned to Canada, and interested himself in farming near Weston, Ontario. He died at Sarasota, Florida, on March 6, 1926. His brother, John L. Trethewey, with whom he was associated, died at Toronto, Ontario, on January 19, 1930, aged 68 years.

[Private information.]

Trotter, Bernard Freeman (1890-1917), poet, was born in Toronto, Ontario, on June 16, 1890, the son of the Rev. Professor Thomas Trotter (q.v.). He was educated at McMaster University, Toronto (B.A., 1914). In 1916 he received a commission in the British army; and he was killed in France on May 7, 1917. His poems were published after his death, with an introduction by W. S. W. McLay, under the title *A Canadian twilight; and other poems of war and peace* (Toronto, 1917).

[*McMaster University monthly*, 1917.]

Trotter, Reginald George (1888-1951), historian, was born at Woodstock, Ontario, on July 14, 1888, and died at Kingston, Ontario, on April 17, 1951. He was educated at Yale University (B.A., 1911) and Harvard University (M.A., 1915; Ph.D., 1921); and after teaching for a time in Leland Stanford University, he was appointed Douglas professor of Canadian and colonial history in Queen's University, Kingston, in 1924. This chair he held for the rest of his life. In 1938 Acadia University conferred on him the honorary degree of D.C.L.; and in 1940 he was elected a fellow of the Royal Society of Canada. He was the author of *Canadian federation* (Toronto, 1924) and of *Canadian history: A syllabus and guide to reading* (Toronto, 1926; new ed., 1934); and he was joint author, with Chester New (q.v.), of *Modern history* (Toronto, 1946; new ed., 1954); and, with C. C. Lingard, of *Canadian world affairs, 1941-44* (Toronto, 1952).

[*Proc. Roy. Soc. Can.*, 1951; *Can. who's who*, 1948; *Who was who*, 1951-60.]

Trotter, Thomas (1781?-1855), clergyman and author, was born in Berwickshire, Scotland, about 1781. He was educated at Edinburgh University, and was ordained a minister of the Presbyterian Church. He emigrated to Nova Scotia in 1818, and became the Presbyterian pastor in Antigonish. He died at Antigonish, Nova Scotia, in 1855. He was the author of *A treatise on geology, in which the discoveries of that science are reconciled with the Scriptures* (Pictou, N.S., 1845) and *Letters on the meaning of Baptized in the New Testament* (Pictou, N.S., 1848).

[Morgan, *Bib. can.*]

Trotter, Thomas (1853-1918), clergyman and educationist, was born at Thurlaston, Leicestershire, England, on August 11, 1853. He came to Canada with his parents in 1870, and was educated at the University of Toronto (B.A., 1882) and McMaster University (B.Th., 1892; D.D. 1897). After holding pastoral charges in Woodstock and Toronto, he was appointed in 1890 professor of homiletics and pastoral theology in McMaster University, and in 1896 president of Acadia University. He retired from the presidency of Acadia University in 1906, and in 1909 he was reappointed professor of homiletics in McMaster University. He died in Toronto, Ontario, on June 7, 1918. He received the honorary degree of D.D. from Queen's University in 1903, and that of LL.D. from Dalhousie University in 1906, and from Acadia University in 1907.

[Morgan, *Can. men* (1912); *McMaster University monthly*, 1918.]

Trout, John Malcolm (1837?-1876), journalist, was born about 1837, and with his brother Edward founded in Toronto, Ontario, in 1867 the *Monetary Times*. Of this journal he became the business manager. He died in Toronto on October 11, 1876. With his brother, he was joint author of *The railways of Canada for 1870-1* (Toronto, 1871).

[Private information.]

Trow, James (1825-1892), politician, was born at Newtown, Montgomeryshire, North Wales, on December 16, 1825. He came to Canada in 1841, and settled in the county of Perth, Canada West. He was warden of the county of Perth for over twenty years; from 1867 to 1871 he represented South Perth in the first legislature of Ontario; and from 1872 to his death he represented the same constituency in the Canadian House of Commons. For many years he was whip of the Liberal party in the House of Commons. He died in 1892. He was the author of *A trip to Manitoba* (Quebec, 1875) and *Manitoba and North West Territories* (Ottawa, 1878).

[Rose, *Cyc. Can. biog.* (1886); *Can. parl. comp.*]

Troyes, Pierre, Chevalier de (d. 1688), soldier, came to Canada in the summer of 1685. On his arrival, he was given command of one hundred men and sent to retake the forts on Hudson Bay. The party set out from Montreal on March 20, 1686, and after three months of travel, reached their destination, where they surprised and captured Forts Monsipi, Rupert, and Albany. Troyes returned to Montreal in October, 1686; and he was one of the commanders of the regular troops in Denonville's expedition of 1687. On the return march, he was left in command at Fort Niagara, and there he died of some malignant disease, on May 8, 1688.

[Abbé I. Caron, *Journal de l'expédition du Chevalier de Troyes à la Baie d'Hudson en 1686* (Beauceville, Que., 1918); P. G. Roy, *Le chevalier de Troye* (Bull. rech. hist., 1908); Le Jeune, *Dict. gén.*; *Dict. Can. biog.*, vol. 1.]

Trudel, François Xavier Anselme (1838-1890), senator of Canada, was born at Ste. Anne de la Pérade, Lower Canada, on April 29, 1838. He was called to the bar in 1861, but devoted himself mainly to journalism and politics. He was the editor of the Montreal *Etendard*; and from 1871 to 1873 he represented Champlain in the Canadian House of Commons. In 1873 he was called to the Senate; and he sat in the Senate until his death, at Montreal, on January 17, 1890. He was the author of *La tempérance au point de vue social* (Montreal, 1879) and *Nos chambres hautes: Sénat et Conseil législatif* (Montreal, 1880).

[*Bull. rech. hist.*, 1928; *Can. parl. comp.*]

Trudelle, Charles (1822-1904), priest and author, was born at Charlesbourg, Lower Canada, on January 28, 1822, the son of Jean Trudelle. He was ordained a priest of the Roman Catholic Church in 1845; and occupied many charges in the province of Quebec. He died at Quebec on July 14, 1904. He was the author of *Notes sur la famille Trudelle* (Quebec, 1875), *Trois souvenirs* (Quebec, 1878), *Paroisse de Charlesbourg* (Quebec, 1887), and *Le Frère Louis* (Quebec, 1898).

[Allaire, *Dict. biog.*; *Bull. rech. hist.*, 1932.]

Trudelle, Joseph (d. 1921), local historian, was assistant librarian in the Legislative Library of the province of Quebec; and died at Quebec City on July 2, 1921. He was the author of *Charlesbourg: Mélanges historiographiques* (Quebec, 1896) and *Les jubilés et les églises et chapelles de la ville et banlieue de Québec* (2 vols., Quebec, 1901-04).

[*Bull. rech. hist.*, index vol.]

Trueman, Howard Thompson (1837-1908), historian, was born at Pointe de Bute, Westmorland county, New Brunswick, on March 1, 1837; and he died at the same place on March 22, 1908. He was the author of *The Chignecto isthmus and its first settlers* (Toronto, 1902) and *Early agriculture in the Atlantic provinces* (Moncton, N.B., 1907).

[Private information.]

Trutch, Sir Joseph William (1826-1904), lieutenant-governor of British Columbia (1871-76), was born at Ashcott, Somerset, England, in 1826, the son of William Trutch, afterwards clerk of the peace of St. Thomas, Jamaica. He was educated at Exeter, England, and became a civil engineer. In 1849 he went to California; and until 1856 he practised his profession there and in the Oregon country. He was then employed on construction work in Illinois, but in 1859 he removed to British Columbia, and settled in Victoria. He built the road from Yale to Cariboo, and the Alexandria suspension bridge over the Fraser River. In 1864 he was appointed commissioner of lands and works, and subsequently surveyor-general for British Columbia, and a member of the Executive Council. In 1870 he was one of the delegates chosen to go to Ottawa to arrange the terms of union between British Columbia and Canada; and in 1871 he was appointed lieutenant-governor of the province. He occupied this office until 1876, and then retired to private life. He died in Taunton, Somerset, England, on March 4, 1904. In 1855 he married Julia Elizabeth, daughter of Louis Hyde, of New York. In 1889 he was created a K.C.M.G.

[J. B. Kerr, *Biographical dictionary of well-known British Columbians* (Vancouver, B.C., 1890); Morgan; *Can. men* (1898); *Can. parl. comp.*; F. W. Howay and E. O. S. Scholefield, *British Columbia* (4 vols., Vancouver, B.C., 1914).]

Tuck, William Henry (1831-1913), jurist, was born at Saint John, New Brunswick, on February 27, 1831. He was educated at Mount Allison University (D.C.L., 1874), and was called to the bar in 1855 (Q.C., 1867). He practised law in Saint John, and in 1885 was appointed a judge of the Supreme Court of New Brunswick. From 1896 to 1908 he was chief justice of the province; and he died at Saint John, New Brunswick, on April 8, 1913.

[Morgan, *Can. men* (1912).]

Tucker, Gilbert Norman (1896-1955), historian, was born in Vancouver, British Columbia, on November 11, 1896, and died there on May 21, 1955. He was educated at the University of Toronto and the University of Western Ontario (B.A., 1921; M.A., 1922); but his university career was interrupted by service in the First World War, in which he was seriously wounded. Later he pursued post-graduate work at Christ's College, Cambridge (Ph.D., 1930). From 1932 to 1940 he was an assistant professor of history at Yale University; from 1941 to 1947 he was the official naval historian at Ottawa; and from 1948 to his death he was professor of Canadian history at the University of British Columbia. He was the author of *The Canadian commercial revolution, 1845-1851* (New Haven, 1936) and *The naval service of Canada* (2 vols., Ottawa, 1952).

[W. N. Sage, *Gilbert Norman Tucker* (Can. hist. rev., Sept., 1955; *New York Times*, May 25, 1955.]

Tucker, James Alexander (1872-1903), poet and journalist, was born in Owen Sound, Ontario, on December 22, 1872; and he died at Toronto, Ontario, on December 19, 1903. He was educated at the University of Toronto, but did not graduate, having been expelled from the University in 1895 as the ringleader in the undergraduate "strike" of that year. He completed his academic course at Leland Stanford University in California (B.A., 1896); and then returned to Canada, where he entered journalism. After his death, his friends published a volume of his *Poems* (Toronto, 1904), with a prefatory memoir by Arthur Stringer.

[*Can. who was who*, vol. 2.]

Tucker, William Bowman (1859-1934), clergyman and author, was born in London, England, on February 27, 1859. He came to Canada in 1871, and for some years worked on a farm in Ontario. He became a school-teacher, and later in 1885, was ordained a minister of the Methodist Church. In 1910 he resigned from the Church to become the founder and superintendent of the Montreal City Mission for "New Canadians". This position he retained until his death in Bristol, England, on August 11, 1934. He was the author of *The Camden colony* (Montreal, 1908), republished as *The romance of the Palatine Millers* (Montreal, 1929); *Songs of the wayside* (Montreal, 1918); and *Laurentian tales* (Montreal, 1922).

[Montreal *Gazette*, Aug. 12, 1934.]

Tufts, John Freeman (1843-1921), educationist, was born at New Albany, Nova Scotia, on March 25, 1843. He was educated at Acadia College (B.A., 1868; D.C.L., 1900) and at Harvard University (B.A., 1872; M.A., 1874); and in 1874 he was appointed principal of Horton Academy, Wolfville, Nova Scotia. From 1881 to 1883 and from 1891 to 1920 he was professor of history at Acadia University; and during two periods he was acting president of the University. He died at Wolfville, Nova Scotia, on February 7, 1921.

[*Records of the graduates of Acadia University* (Wolfville, N.S., 1926); *Harvard College class of 1872: Eleventh report of the secretary* (Cambridge, Mass., 1924); Morgan, *Can. men* (1912).]

Tully, Kivas (1820-1905), architect, was born in Queen's county, Ireland, in 1820, the son of Commander John P. Tully, R.N. He studied architecture and civil engineering in Limerick, and in 1844 he came to Canada. For many years he practised as an architect in Toronto; and in 1867 he was appointed architect and engineer to the department of public works in Ontario. A large number of public buildings in this province were designed by him. He died at Toronto on April 24, 1905. He was twice married, (1) in 1844 to Elizabeth Drew (d. 1847), of Drewsboro', county Clare, Ireland; and (2) in 1852 to Maria (d. 1883), daughter of Lieut.-Col. Samuel Strickland (q.v.).

[Morgan, *Can. men* (1898).]

Tully, Sydney Strickland (1860-1911), painter, was born in Toronto, Canada, in 1860, the eldest daughter of Kivas Tully (q.v.), and Maria Strickland. She was educated in Toronto, and studied art in London, Paris, and New York. In 1889 she was elected an associate of the Royal Canadian Academy; and she exhibited at the Paris Salon, the Royal Academy, the World's Fair, Chicago, and other expositions. Her most notable work was as a portrait painter. She died in Toronto on July 18, 1911.

[Morgan, *Can. men and women* (1912); N. MacTavish, *The fine arts in Canada* (Toronto, 1925).]

Tumpane, Michael F. (1877-1961), editor and trade-union leader, was born in Toronto in 1877. He was apprenticed as a printer and became a printing pressman in 1906. He was active in trade-union organization and led a group which broke away from the United States union affiliations. In 1927 he founded the *Trade Unionist*, a paper which he edited until 1956. He was president of the Canadian Federation of Labour in 1920 and 1921. He died at Toronto, Ontario, May, 10, 1961.

[Metropolitan Toronto Library Board, *Biographical scrapbooks*, vol. 18.]

Tupper, Charles (1794-1881), clergyman, was born at Cornwallis, Nova Scotia, on August 6, 1794, the son of Eliakim Tupper, who came to Nova Scotia from Connecticut in 1763. He entered the Baptist ministry in 1817, and during the sixty-three years of his ministry was the pastor of a number of churches in the Maritime provinces. He died at Aylesford, Nova Scotia, on January 19, 1881. In 1818 he married Miriam, daughter of James Lockhart, and widow of John Lowe; and by her he had three sons. From 1832 to 1836 he was editor of the *Baptist Magazine;* and he was the author of *Scriptural baptism* (Halifax, Nova Scotia, 1850), as well as other theological works. Acadia College conferred on him the degree of D.D.

[*Cyc. Am. biog.*; E. M. Saunders, *Life and letters of the Rt. Hon. Sir Charles Tupper, Bart.* (London, 1916); W. G. MacFarlane, *New Brunswick bibliography* (Saint John, N.B., 1895).]

Tupper, Sir Charles, Bart. (1821-1915), prime minister of Canada (1896), was born in Amherst, Nova Scotia, on July 2, 1821, the son of the Rev. Charles Tupper (q.v.) and Miriam Lockhart. He was educated at Horton Academy, Wolfville, Nova Scotia, and he studied medicine at Edinburgh University (M.D., 1843). He obtained the diploma of the Royal College of Surgeons in 1843; and on his return to Nova Scotia, he practised medicine in his native town. From 1855 to 1867 he represented Cumberland in the Legislative Assembly of Nova Scotia; from 1856 to 1860 he was provincial secretary in the Johnson government; and from 1864 to 1867 he was prime minister of Nova Scotia. He took a leading part in the Confederation movement, was a delegate to the Charlottetown, Quebec, and London conferences, and replied to the anti-confederation campaign of Joseph Howe (q.v.) in his *Letter to the Earl of Carnarvon* (London, 1866). It was mainly through his efforts that Nova Scotia was brought into the union of 1867.

From 1867 to 1884 he represented Cumberland in the Canadian House of Commons. But in the first government of the Dominion he was not included, having stood aside, with T. D'Arcy McGee (q.v.), in order to make way for Edward Kenny (q.v.), a Roman Catholic from Nova Scotia. In 1868 he was instrumental in defeating the attempts of the anti-confederationists in Nova Scotia to obtain repeal of the union, and in persuading Joseph Howe (q.v.) to enter the government. In 1870 he himself entered the cabinet as president of the council; and in 1872 and 1873 he held the portfolios of minister of inland revenue and minister of customs. From 1873 to 1878 he was the right-hand man of Sir John Macdonald (q.v.), while in opposition; and when the Conservatives were returned to power in 1878, he became minister of public works. From 1879 to 1884 he was minister of railways and canals, and as such had supervision of the arrangements for the building of the Canadian Pacific Railway. In 1883 he was appointed high commissioner for Canada in London; and apart from a period of sixteen months in 1887-88, during which he held the portfolio of minister of finance in the Macdonald government, he retained the high-commissionership until 1896. He was then recalled to Canada, and assumed the leadership of the Conservative party, shortly before the general elections of that year. Not even his dauntless energy, however, sufficed to revive the fallen fortunes of the party, and he was defeated at the polls after only six months' tenure of office. From 1896 to 1900 he led the Conservative opposition in the Canadian House of Commons; but in the general elections of 1900 he was defeated in Cape Breton, and he thereupon retired to private life.

He died at Bexley Heath, Kent, England, on October 30, 1915, the last of the "Fathers of Confederation" to pass away. In 1846 he married Frances Amelia (d. 1912), daughter of Silas Hibbert Morse, of Amherst, Nova Scotia; and by her he had three sons and three daughters. He was created a C.B. in 1867, a K.C.M.G. in 1879, a G.C.M.G. in 1886, and a baronet of the United Kingdom in 1888. He was also an LL.D. of Acadia College, of Cambridge University, and of Edinburgh University. Just before his death he published his *Recollections of sixty years* (London, 1914).

[E. M. Saunders, *The life and letters of the Rt. Hon. Sir Charles Tupper, Bart.* (2 vols., London, 1916; supplement ed. by Sir C. H. Tupper, Toronto, 1926); W. A. Harkin (ed.), *Political reminiscences of the Rt. Hon. Sir Charles Tupper, Bart.* (London, 1914); J. W. Longley, *Sir Charles Tupper* (Toronto, 1917); C. Thibault, *Biography of Sir Charles Tupper* (Montreal, 1883); D. H. Tait, *Dr. Charles Tupper: A father of confederation,* (Coll. Nova Scotia Hist. Soc., XXXVI, 1968); Morgan, *Can. men* (1912) and *Bib. can.*; Taché, *Men of the day*; Rose, *Cyc. Can. biog.* (1886); *Can. parl. comp.*]

Tupper, Sir Charles Hibbert (1855-1927), lawyer and statesman, was born at Amherst, Nova Scotia, on August 3, 1855, the second son of Sir Charles Tupper, Bart. (q.v.). He was educated at McGill University and Harvard University (LL.B., 1876), and was called to the bar of Nova Scotia in 1878 (Q.C., 1890). From 1882 to 1904 he represented Pictou in the Canadian House of Commons. From 1888 to 1894 he was minister of marine and fisheries in the Macdonald, Abbott, and Thompson governments; and from 1894 to 1896 he was minister of justice in the Bowell government. He was one of the "bolters" of January 4, 1896; but resumed office as solicitor-general in the Tupper government. In 1892 he was agent for Great Britain in the Behring Sea arbitration; and he was created, for his services in this arbitration, a K.C.M.G. in 1893. In 1904 he retired from politics, and devoted himself to the practice of law in Vancouver, British Columbia. He died at Vancouver on March 30, 1927. In 1879 he married Janet, daughter of the Hon. James McDonald (q.v.); and by her he had four sons and three daughters. He edited a *Supplement* (Toronto, 1926) to the *Life and letters* of his father, by the Rev. E. M. Saunders.

[R. A. Shields, *Sir Charles Tupper and the Franco-Canadian treaty of 1895: A study in imperial relations* (Can. hist. rev., 1968); *Can. who was who*, vol. 1; *Who was who*, 1916-28; Morgan, *Can. men* (1912); *Can. parl. comp.*]

Tupper, William Johnston (1862-1947), lieutenant-governor of Manitoba (1934-40), was born in Halifax, Nova Scotia, on June 29, 1862, the third son of Sir Charles Tupper, Bart. (q.v.), and died at Winnipeg, Manitoba, on December 17, 1947. He was educated at Upper Canada College and the Harvard Law School; and was called to the bar in Nova Scotia in 1885, and in Manitoba in 1886 (K.C., 1912). He served as a private in the North West Rebellion in 1885; and thereafter practised law in Winnipeg. He represented Winnipeg in the Legislative Assembly of Manitoba from 1920 to 1922; and from 1934 to 1940 he was lieutenant-governor of the province.

[*Who was who*, 1941-50; *Can. who's who*, 1938-39; *Can. parl. comp.*, 1940; *Encyc. Can.*]

Turcotte, Joseph Edouard (1808-1864), solicitor-general for Lower Canada (1847-48), was born at Gentilly, Lower Canada, in 1808. He was admitted to the bar in 1834 (Q.C., 1847); and he sat in the Legislative Assembly of Canada for St. Maurice from 1841 to 1844, and from 1851 to 1854; for Maskinongé from 1854 to 1857; for Champlain from 1858 to 1861; and for Three Rivers from 1861 to 1864. In 1847-48 he was solicitor-general for Lower Canada in the Draper administration; and from 1862 to 1863 he was speaker of the

Assembly. He died at Three Rivers, Lower Canada, on December 20, 1864.

[*Cyc. Am. biog.*; *Can. parl. comp.*, 1864.]

Turcotte, Louis Philippe (1842-1878), historian, was born at St. John, Island of Orleans, Lower Canada, on July 11, 1842, and was educated at the Quebec Seminary. In 1859 he became, as the result of falling through the ice of the St. Lawrence, an invalid for the rest of his life; and he devoted himself thenceforth to historical studies. He published first an *Historie de l'Ile d'Orléans* (Quebec, 1867); then he brought out his best-known and most important work, *Canada sous l'union* (2 vols., Quebec, 1871-72; new ed., 1882); and after this, successively, biographies of *L'hon. R. E. Caron* (pamphlet, Quebec, 1873) and of *L'hon. Sir G. E. Cartier* (pamphlet, Quebec, 1873), *L'invasion du Canada, 1775-6* (Quebec, 1876), and *La société littéraire et historique de Québec* (Quebec, 1879). He died at Quebec, on April 3, 1878. His work, while conscientious, did not attain a high level.

[Faucher de St. Maurice, *L. P. Turcotte* (Trans. Roy. Soc. Can., 1883); Henri d'Arles, *Nos historiens* (Montreal, 1921); J. P. Tardivel, *Notice biographique sur L. P. Turcotte* (Annales de l'Institut Canadien de Québec, 1878); *Dom. ann. reg.*, 1878; Morgan, *Bib. can.*; Le Jeune, *Dict. gén.*; *Dict. Can. biog.*, vol. 10.]

Turgeon, Onésiphore (1849-1944), senator of Canada, was born at Lévis, Canada East, on September 6, 1849. He was educated at Laval University (B.A., 1869), and became a journalist. He represented Gloucester in the Canadian House of Commons from 1900 to 1923; and he was a member of the Senate from 1923 to his death, at Bathurst, New Brunswick, on November 18, 1944. He was the author of *Un tribut à la race acadienne: Mémoires, 1871-1921* (Montreal, 1928).

[*Can. who's who*, 1936-37; *Can. parl. comp.*]

Turgeon, Pierre Flavien (1787-1867), Roman Catholic archbishop of Quebec (1850-67), was born at Quebec on November 12, 1787, the son of Louis Turgeon and Louise Dumont. He was educated at the Quebec Seminary, and was ordained to the priesthood in 1810. From 1808 to 1820 he was secretary to Bishop Plessis (q.v.); in 1833 he was elected coadjutor to the archbishop of Quebec; and in 1834 he was consecrated titular bishop of Sidyme. He succeeded to the archbishopric of Quebec in 1850; but owing to ill-health he ceased to administer the affairs of the See after 1855, and he died at Quebec on August 25, 1867. He was conspicuously loyal to the British Crown during the rebellion of 1837-38, and he was of assistance to the government during the union period. In 1852 he was instrumental in getting a charter for Laval University; and it was he who opened it officially in 1854.

[C. Legaré, *Souvenir consacré à la mémoire vénérée de Mgr P. F. Turgeon* (Quebec, 1867); *Dict. nat. biog.*; Allaire, *Dict. biog.*; Le Jeune, *Dict. gén.*; Bibaud, *Panth. can.*; Morgan, *Cel. Can.*; H. Têtu, *Les évêques de Québec* (Quebec, 1889).]

Turgeon, William Ferdinand Alphonse (1877-1969), ambassador and judge, was born near Bathurst, New Brunswick, June 3, 1877, and educated at Lévis College, Quebec, and Laval University. He was called to the bar in New Brunswick in 1902 and in the North West Territories in 1903, where he set up practice in Prince Albert. He became attorney-general of the new province of Saskatchewan in 1907 on his election to the Legislative Assembly. As attorney-general (1907-21) and provincial secretary (1912-18) he was responsible for much of the legal system of Saskatchewan. He was appointed to the Saskatchewan Court of Appeal in 1921 and became chief in 1938. In 1941 he resigned to become the first Canadian minister appointed to Argentina and Chile (1941-44). He then became Canada's first ambassador to Mexico (1944); Canadian ambassador to Belgium (1944); High Commissioner to Ireland (1947-50), and ambassador (1950-55); and in 1955 became Canada's first ambassador to Portugal. He retired in 1956. He headed the Saskatchewan Royal Commission on grain marketing (1923) and on the coal industry (1934); the federal Royal Commission on the transfer of Manitoba's natural resources from the federal government to the province (1928-29), on the textile industry (1936), on the grain trade (1936), and on transportation (1948). He died at Prince Albert, Saskatchewan, January 11, 1969.

[*Can. who's who,* 1967-69; *Encyc. Can.* (1972).]

Turner, Guy Roderick (1889-1963), soldier, was born in Four Falls, New Brunswick, in 1889. He taught school and was a railway engineer in New Brunswick before the First World War. He had joined the militia in 1906 and went on active service in 1914. He was awarded the Distinguished Conduct medal and was commissioned in 1915. He was later awarded the Military Cross and Bar. He served at the School of Military Engineering in England (1920-22) and at the Staff College in Quetta, India (1925-26). He became deputy adjutant and quartermaster-general of the First Canadian Army in 1942 and in 1945 was appointed Inspector-General of Western Canada. He retired in 1946. He was made a Commander of the Bath in 1943. During the early planning stages of the Allied invasion of Europe he was General A.G.L. McNaughton's personal representative on the Chiefs of Staff of the Allied Supreme Command. He died at Ottawa, Ontario, February 22, 1963.

[Metropolitan Toronto Library Board, *Biographical scrapbooks,* vol. 21.]

Turner, John Herbert (1834-1923), prime minister of British Columbia (1895-98), was born at Claydon, near Ipswich, England, on May 7, 1834, the son of John and Martha Turner. He emigrated to Canada in 1856, and after spending several years in Prince Edward Island, he removed in 1862 to Victoria, British Columbia. From 1879 to 1881 he was mayor of Victoria; and from 1887 to 1901 he represented Victoria in the Legislative Assembly of British Columbia. He was minister of finance and agriculture in the provincial government from 1887 to 1898, and again from 1899 to 1901; and from 1895 to 1898 he was prime minister. In 1901 he was appointed agent-general for British Columbia in Great Britain; and this post he held until his death at London, England, on December 9, 1923. In 1860 he married Elizabeth Eilbeck, of Whitehaven, England.

[Morgan, *Can. men* (1912); *Can. parl. comp.*; J. B. Kerr, *Biographical dictionary of well-known British Columbians* (Vancouver, B.C., 1890).]

Turner, John Peter (1881?-1948), historian, was born about 1881, and died at Ottawa, Ontario, on June 28, 1948. In his later years he was conservation editor of the periodical *Rod and gun;* and he was commissioned by the Royal Canadian Mounted Police to write the early history of the force. This was published after his death under the title *The North West Mounted Police, 1873-1893* (2 vols., Ottawa, 1950).

[*New York Times,* June 30, 1948.]

Turner, Thomas Andrew (1775?-1834), merchant and banker, was born in Aberdeenshire, Scotland, about 1775. He emigrated to Canada, and became a partner in the mercantile house of Allison, Turner, and Co. in Montreal. He was one of the founders of the Bank of Montreal, and in 1820 he was elected president of the Bank of Canada. For a number of years he was the proprietor of the Montreal *Gazette.* He died at Montreal on July 21, 1834. He was the author of a paper on *Annexation of Canada to the United States* (Dublin University magazine, vol. xxxv).

[Morgan, *Bib. can.*; R. Campbell, *History of the Scotch Presbyterian Church, St. Gabriel Street, Montreal* (Montreal, 1887).]

Turnor, Philip (1752?-1800), surveyor, was a native of Laleham, Middlesex, England, and was born about 1752. In 1778 he was articled to the Hudson's Bay Company as a surveyor; and he served as surveyor in the Hudson's Bay Company's territories in North America until 1792. The map of North America published by Arrowsmith in London in 1795 embodied the results of his surveys; and it is noteworthy that it was from Turnor that David Thompson (q.v.) received his instruction in surveying. He died near London, England, in the early part of 1800. He was the author of a pamphlet entitled

Result of astronomical observations made in the interior parts of North America (London, 1794).

[J. B. Tyrrell (ed.), *Journals of Samuel Hearne and Philip Turnor* (Toronto: The Champlain Society, 1934).]

Tuttle, Charles Richard (b. 1848), journalist and author, was born at Wallace, Cumberland county, Nova Scotia, on March 14, 1848. He was mainly self-educated, and became first a school-teacher in Nova Scotia, and then a journalist in Boston, Massachusetts. In 1879 he went to Winnipeg, Manitoba, and founded there the *Daily Times*. He was census commissioner for Manitoba in 1881; and in 1884 he accompanied the expedition to Hudson Bay commanded by Lieut. Gordon. Shortly afterwards he went to Chicago, and entered journalism there. He appears to have lived in Chicago for the rest of his life; but the date of his death has not been ascertained. A most voluminous writer, he was the author of *General history of the state of Michigan* (Detroit, Mich., 1873), *History of the border wars of two centuries* (Chicago, 1874), *An illustrated history of the state of Wisconsin* (Boston, 1875), *History of Indiana* (Des Moines, Ind., 1875), *A new centennial history of the state of Texas* (Madison, Wis., 1876), *Family and school history of America* (Madison, Wis., 1876), *Tuttle's popular history of the Dominion of Canada* (Montreal, 1877), *Short history of the Dominion of Canada* (Boston, 1878), *That young man* (Boston, 1878), *The boss devil of America* (Boston, 1878), *Royalty in Canada* (Montreal, 1879), *Our north land* (Toronto, 1885), *Democratic gospel* (Chicago, 1895), *The new democracy and Bryan, its prophet* (Chicago, 1896), *How to govern Chicago* (Chicago, 1896), *The golden North* (Chicago, 1897), *Yang, all-in-all-ism* (Seattle, Wash., 1904), *Creation by thinking* (Cleveland, Ohio, 1906), *The life primer* (Cleveland, Ohio, 1906), *The new idea* (Seattle, Wash., 1908), *Alaska* (Seattle, Wash., 1914), *The great world conflict and its lessons* (Chicago, 1916), and *New coöperative order* (Chicago, 1918); and he was joint author, with D. S. Durrie, of *An illustrated history of the state of Iowa* (Chicago, 1876), and, with A. C. Pennock, of *The centennial Northwest* (Madison, Wis., 1876). He was also the editor of a book entitled *World's cooperative food supply association;* and of this association he described himself as founder.

[J. P. Robertson, *A political manual of the province of Manitoba* (Winnipeg, 1887); O. F. Adams, *A dictionary of American authors* (Boston, 1904).]

Tweedie, Lemuel John (1849-1917), prime minister of New Brunswick (1900-07) and lieutenant-governor (1907-12), was born at Chatham, New Brunswick, on November 30, 1849. He was educated at Chatham, and in 1871 was called to the bar of New Brunswick (Q.C., 1892). From 1874 to 1878, and from 1886 to 1907, he represented Northumberland in the Legislative Assembly of New Brunswick; and he was successively surveyor-general in the Blair administration, provincial secretary in the Emmerson administration, and from 1900 to 1907 prime minister. From 1907 to 1912 he was lieutenant-governor of New Brunswick; and he died at Chatham, New Brunswick, on July 15, 1917. In 1876 he married Agnes, daughter of Alexander Loudoun, of Chatham, New Brunswick.

[Morgan, *Can. men* (1912); *Can. parl. comp.*]

Tweedie, Thomas Mitchell March (1872-1944), jurist, was born at River John, Nova Scotia, on March 4, 1872. He was educated at Mount Allison University (B.A., 1902; D.C.L., 1933) and Harvard University (LL.B., 1905); and was called to the bar of Nova Scotia in 1905, and to that of Alberta in 1907. He practised law in Calgary, Alberta; and he represented Calgary in the Alberta legislature from 1911 to 1917, and in the Canadian House of Commons from 1917 to 1921. He was appointed a judge of the Supreme Court of Alberta in 1921; and in September, 1944, he was appointed chief justice of the province. He died at Lethbridge, Alberta, only a few days later, on October 4, 1944.

[*Can. who's who*, 1936-37.]

Tweedsmuir, John Buchan, first Baron (1875-1940), historian, novelist, and governor-general of Canada (1935-40), was born in Scotland on August 26, 1875, the son of the Rev. John Buchan. He was educated at Glasgow University and at Brasenose College, Oxford (B.A., 1899; D.C.L., 1934). He was called to the bar in 1901 from the Inner Temple; and from 1901 to 1903 he was secretary to Lord Milner, high commissioner for South Africa. For many years he was vice-president of Thomas Nelson and Sons, publishers. From 1927 to 1935 he was a member of the House of Commons for the Scottish Universities; and in 1935 he was appointed governor-general of Canada. In 1932 he was created a Companion of Honour, and in 1935 a G.C.M.G. and Baron Tweedsmuir. He was the author of a number of biographies and historical works, notable among which were *Sir Walter Raleigh* (London, 1911), *A history of the great war* (London, 1921-22), *Lord Minto* (London, 1924), *Montrose* (1928), *Sir Walter Scott* (London, 1932), *Julius Caesar* (London, 1932), *The massacre of Glencoe* (London, 1933), *Oliver Cromwell* (1934), *The King's grace* (London, 1935), and *Augustus* (London, 1937); and he wrote a long series of novels and romances, notable among which were *Salute to adventures* (London, 1915), *The thirty-nine steps* (London, 1915), *Greenmantle* (London, 1916), *Huntingtower* (London, 1922), *The three hostages* (London, 1924), *John Mac-*

nab (London, 1925), *The dancing floor* (London, 1926), *Witch Wood* (London, 1927), *The Runagates' club* (London, 1928), *The courts of the morning* (London, 1929), *Castle Gay* (London, 1930), *The gap in the curtain* (London, 1932), *The magic walking-stick* (London, 1932), *A prince of the captivity* (London, 1933), *The free fishers* (London, 1934), *The house of the four winds* (London, 1935), *The island of sheep* (London, 1936) and *Sick Heart river* (London, 1941). One of his last books was his autobiography, *Memory Hold-the-door* (London, 1940). He died in Montreal on February 11, 1940.

[*Who was who,* 1929-40; *Can. who's who,* 1938-39; *Queen's quarterly,* 1940; *Saturday night,* 1940; Anna Buchan, *Unforgettable, unforgotten* (London, 1945); *John Buchan, by his wife and friends* (London, 1947); J. A. Smith, *John Buchan: A biography* (Toronto, 1965).]

Twining, Sir Philip Geoffrey (1862-1920), soldier, was born, in Halifax, Nova Scotia, on September 7, 1862, the son of Edmund Twining and Elizabeth Whitman. He was educated at the Royal Military College, Kingston, Ontario; and in 1885 he obtained a commission in the Royal Engineers. From 1887 to 1893 he served in India and Africa; from 1893 to 1899 he was professor of military engineering at the Royal Military College, Kingston; and in 1899 he returned to the Indian army. In 1914 he went to France as C.R.E. of the Seventh Division of the Indian Expeditionary Force; and he served in France continuously until 1918, rising to the position of adjutant- and quartermaster-general of the First British Army. Invalided to England in 1918, he was appointed there director of fortification and works, and as such official head of the Royal Engineers. He died at London, England, on January 15, 1920. He married Louise Daly, of Kingston. In 1919 he was created a K.C.M.G.

[Mary C. Ritchie, *Major-general Sir Geoffrey Twining* (Montreal, 1922); *Can. who was who,* vol. 1.]

Tyrer, Alfred Henry (1870-1942), clergyman, was born near Liverpool, England, in 1870; and emigrated to Canada in 1887. He was ordained a priest of the Church of England in 1904; and he died at Toronto, Ontario, on April 28, 1942. He was the author of *Sex, marriage, and birth-control* (Toronto, 1936) and an autobiography entitled *And a new earth* (Toronto, 1941).

[Toronto *Globe and Mail,* April 29, 1942.]

Tyrrell, James Williams (1863-1945), civil engineer, explorer, and author, was born in Weston, Canada West, on May 10, 1863, the son of William Tyrrell (q.v.). He was educated at the School of Practical Science, Toronto (C.E., 1889); and in 1893 he accompanied his brother, J. B. Tyrell, on an expedition from Lake Athabaska through the barren lands of Chesterfield Inlet. He published an account of this expedition in a book entitled *Across the sub-arctics of Canada* (Toronto, 1897). He later made many surveys and explorations from Labrador to Great Slave Lake; and he was one of the first to undertake gold-mining in the Red Lake district of northern Ontario. He was president of the Tyrrell Red Lake Mines. He died at Bartonville, near Hamilton, Ontario, on January 16, 1945.

[*Can. who's who,* 1936-37; Morgan, *Can. men* (1910).]

Tyrrell, Joseph Burr (1858-1957), geologist and historian, was born at Weston, Canada West, on November 1, 1858, the son of William Tyrrell (q.v.), and died at Toronto, Ontario, on August 26, 1957. He was educated at the University of Toronto (B.A.,1880; M.A., 1889) and Victoria University (B.Sc., 1889). He joined the staff of the Geological Survey of Canada in 1881, and between that date and his resignation from the Survey in 1898 he carried out explorations in many parts of the North West Territories. From 1898 to 1906 he was a consulting geologist and engineer in Toronto. In 1924 he became president of the Kirkland Lake Gold Mining Co. From his early years he had taken an interest in the history of Western and North Western Canada, and after settling in Toronto he began the publication of some very important volumes in this field. He first edited Samuel Hearne's *Journey from Prince of Wales' Fort in Hudson Bay to the Northern Ocean* (Toronto: The Champlain Society, 1911); and he followed this with *David Thompson's narrative of his explorations in western America* (Toronto: The Champlain Society, 1916), and *The journals of Samuel Hearne and Philip Turnor* (Toronto: The Champlain Society, 1934). He was elected a fellow of the Royal Society of Canada in 1910; and from 1927 to 1932 he was president of the Champlain Society. The University of Toronto conferred on him the honorary degree of LL.D. in 1930, and Queen's University in 1940. He left his valuable library and his papers to the University of Toronto Library.

[W. J. Loudon, *A Canadian geologist* (Toronto, 1930); *Proc. Roy. Soc. Can.,* 1958; D. M. Le Bourdais, *Tyrrell of Canada* (Beaver, Dec., 1952); *Can. who's who,* 1952-54.]

Tyrrell, William (1816-1904), pioneer, was born at Grange Castle, Kildare county, Ireland, in 1816. He came to Canada in 1836, and became a pioneer of settlement and building on the Humber River, near Toronto. He came to be known as "the Squire of Weston", and was warden of York county in 1864. He died at Weston, Ontario, on November 8, 1904. In 1845 he married Elizabeth Burr; and by her he had nine children, of whom two, Joseph Burr and James Williams (q.v.), became well-known explorers of Canada's barren lands.

[Edith L. Morrison and J. E. Middleton, *William Tyrrell of Weston* (Toronto, 1937).]

Tyrwhitt-Drake, Montague William (1830-1908), politician and jurist, was born at King's Walden, Hertfordshire, England, on January 20, 1830. He was educated at Charterhouse, and was admitted a solicitor in England in 1851. In 1859 he emigrated to British Columbia, and became a solicitor there in 1860, and a barrister in 1873 (Q.C., 1883).

From 1868 to 1870 he was a member of the Legislative Council for Victoria; from 1883 to 1886 he represented Victoria in the Legislative Assembly; and from 1883 to 1884 he was president of the Executive Council of British Columbia. He was appointed a judge of the Supreme Court of the province in 1889, and retired in 1904. He died at Victoria, British Columbia, on April 19, 1908.

[*Can. parl. comp.*; E. O. S. Scholefield and R. E. Gosnell, *A history of British Columbia* (Vancouver, B.C., 1913).]

$\mathcal{U}$

Umfreville, Edward (*fl.* 1771-1790), fur-trader, was a writer in the service of the Hudson's Bay Company from 1771 to 1782. He was captured by the French under La Pérouse in 1782, and on his release in 1783 went to Canada, where he entered the service of the North West Company as a clerk. In 1784 he was employed to discover a new route from Lake Superior to Lake Winnipeg; and his journal of this exploration has been edited by R. Douglas, under the title *Nipigon to Winnipeg* (Ottawa, 1929). He spent the years 1784-88 on the north branch of the Saskatchewan, but left the North West Company's service in 1788, and returned to England by way of New York. It appears from the records of the Hudson's Bay Company that he applied to be taken back into the service of this company in 1789, but failed to obtain satisfactory terms. He then published a book, entitled *The present state of Hudson Bay* (London, 1790; new ed., Toronto, 1954), which was in part an attack on the Hudson's Bay Company. After this, he disappears from view.

[Morgan, *Bib. can.*; R. Douglas (ed.), *Nipigon to Winnipeg* (Ottawa, 1929).]

Underhill, Frank Hawkins (1889-1971), historian, was born in Stouffville, Ontario, November 26, 1889. He attended the University of Toronto (B.A., 1911), and Balliol College, Oxford (B.A., 1913). He served as a lieutenant in the First World War, and at the war's end contributed the articles on the Canadian forces to volume 2 of *The Empire at War*, edited by Sir Charles Lucas. He was appointed professor of history at the University of Saskatchewan in 1913 and was also Saskatchewan's first professor of political science. In 1927 he went to the University of Toronto, where he taught history until his retirement in 1955. On retirement he became curator of Laurier House, Ottawa, until 1958. He began writing for the *Canadian Forum* in 1929 and was for some years chairman of its editorial board. His commentary on the Canadian scene appearing under the caption "O Canada" was an incisive appraisal of Canadian government and society. A founder of the League for Social Reconstruction in the early thirties, he contributed many germinal ideas to the fledgling

Co-operative Commonwealth Federation and was responsible for the first draft of what came to be known as the *Regina Manifesto*. He contributed to *Social planning for Canada* (1935), and edited the *Dufferin-Carnarvon Correspondence, 1874-1878* for the Champlain Society (1955); and a series of his lectures were published as *The British Commonwealth* by Duke University Press, 1950. He also wrote *In search of Canadian Liberalism* (Toronto, 1960); *The image of Confederation* (Toronto, 1964); *Canadian political parties* (C.H.A. booklet, No. 8, 1960); and *Upper Canadian politics in the 1850's.* (Toronto, 1967). A stimulating teacher, a writer with a deep understanding of the nature of Canadian political life, and a lively commentator on the Canadian scene, Frank Underhill contributed to Canadians' understanding of themselves in the world of politics as the Group of Seven did in the world of art. He died at Ottawa, Ontario, on September 16, 1971. Frank Underhill was a fellow of the Royal Society of Canada (1949) and received the Canada Medal (1967).

[C. Berger, *The writing of Canadian history* (Toronto, 1976); *Can. who's who*, 1955-57; *Encyc. Can.*; *Canadian Forum*, November, 1971.]

Unger, Heinz (1895-1965), musician and conductor, was born in Berlin, Germany, December 14, 1895. He was educated at the University of Berlin, the University of Munich, and the Conservatory in Berlin. He lived in Berlin from 1919 to 1933 and was conductor of the Berlin Symphony. He left Germany in 1933 and spent fifteen years working with orchestras in Britain, Spain, and Latin America. He came to Canada in 1948 and in 1952 became conductor of the York Concert Society, which he built from a chamber group into a symphony orchestra. He was an outstanding exponent of the works of Gustav Mahler and said Mahler was for him a way of life. He was recognized by the West German government with the Commander's Cross of the Order of Merit in 1965. He was author of *Hammer, sickle and baton* (London, 1939). Heinz Unger died at Toronto, Ontario, February 22, 1965.

[*Can. who's who*, 1955-57; Metropolitan

Toronto Library Board, *Biographical scrapbooks*, vol. 23; Toronto *Saturday Night* (April 3, 1954).]

Uniacke, James Boyle (d. 1858), politician, was the fourth son of Richard John Uniacke (q.v.). He studied law at the Inner Temple, London, England, was called to the bar, and practised law in Nova Scotia. He was elected to the Legislative Assembly of Nova Scotia to represent Cape Breton, and became the Tory leader in the Assembly. In 1837 he was appointed a member of the Council of Twelve; but in 1840 he resigned from the council, and became an advocate of responsible government. Later in 1840 he re-entered the Executive Council, with Joseph Howe (q.v.); but in 1844 he and Howe resigned in protest against the action of Lord Falkland (q.v.) in appointing M. B. Almon (q.v.) to the Council. In 1848 he was invited to form a government; and from 1848 to 1854 he was nominal head of the administration, with the portfolio of attorney-general. He retired from public life in 1854, and accepted the non-political office of commissioner of crown lands. He died in March, 1858.

[J. A. Chisholme (ed.), *The speeches and letters of Joseph Howe* (Halifax, N.S., 1909); E. M. Saunders, *Three premiers of Nova Scotia* (Toronto, 1909); D. Campbell, *History of Nova Scotia* (Montreal, 1873); *The two Uniackes* (Nova Scotia journal of education, 1937).]

Uniacke, Norman Fitzgerald (1777?-1846), attorney-general of Lower Canada (1809-25), was born in Nova Scotia about 1777, the eldest son of Richard John Uniacke (q.v.). He studied law at the Inner Temple in England, and was called to the English bar. In 1809 he was appointed attorney-general of Lower Canada. He was suspended from office in 1810, but was reinstated, and continued as attorney-general until 1825. In 1824 he was also elected to represent the borough of William Henry in the Legislative Assembly of Lower Canada; but in 1825 he resigned the attorney-generalship and his seat in the House, to accept appointment as a judge of the Court of King's Bench in Montreal. He sat on the bench until about 1836; and he died in Halifax, Nova Scotia, on December 11, 1846. In 1818 he suffered the loss of a leg through amputation; and in 1819 he married Sophie Delesdernier.

[P. G. Roy, *Les juges de la province de Québec* (Lévis, Que., 1933); *New Brunswick magazine*, 1898, p. 385; P. Gagnon, *Essai de bibliographie canadienne* (2 vols., Quebec and Montreal, 1895-1913).]

Uniacke, Richard John (1753-1830), attorney-general of Nova Scotia (1797-1830), was born at Castletown, Cork county, Ireland, on November 22, 1753, the fourth son of Nor-

man Fitzgerald Uniacke and Alicia, daughter of Bartholomew Purdon. In 1769 he entered upon the study of law in Dublin; but in 1773 he emigrated to America. In 1774 he settled in Nova Scotia, and in 1781 he was admitted to practice as a barrister and attorney in that province. From 1783 to 1793 he sat in the House of Assembly of Nova Scotia; and from 1789 to 1793 he was its speaker. In 1782 he had been appointed solicitor-general, and in 1797 he was chosen attorney-general of the province, a position he occupied for the rest of his life. In 1798 he was again elected to the House of Assembly, and in 1799 he was a second time chosen speaker of the House. In 1806 he retired finally from the legislature, and in 1808 he was appointed a member of the Executive Council. He died at Mount Uniacke, Nova Scotia, on October 11, 1830. In 1775 he married Martha Maria Delesdernier (d. 1803), by whom he had six sons and six daughters; and in 1808 Eliza Newton, by whom he had one daughter. He published *Statutes passed in the General Assemblies held in Nova Scotia from 1758 to 1804 inclusive* (Halifax, 1805).

[L. G. Power, *Richard John Uniacke, a sketch* (Coll. of the Nova Scotia Hist. Soc., 1895); R. G. Trotter, *An early proposal for the federation of British North America* (Can. hist. rev., 1925); Morgan, *Bib. can.*; R. G. Riddell (ed.), *Canadian portraits* (Toronto, 1940); *The two Uniackes* (Nova Scotia journal of education, 1937).]

Upham, Joshua (1741-1808), loyalist, was born at Brookfield, Massachusetts, in 1741, the son of Dr. Jabez Upham. He was educated at Harvard College (B.A., 1763), and was called to the bar in Massachusetts. During the Revolutionary War he served as an officer in the King's American Dragoons; and at the close of the war he settled in New Brunswick. In 1784 he was appointed a member of the Executive and Legislative councils of New Brunswick, and a puisne judge of the Court of King's Bench. In 1807 he went on a mission to England, in connection with the salaries granted to judges in New Brunswick; and he died in England on November 1, 1808. He married (1) a daughter of the Hon. John Murray, of Rutland, Massachusetts, and (2) a daughter of the Hon. Joshua Chandler, a Connecticut loyalist. By his first marriage he had one daughter, and by his second one son and three daughters.

[J. W. Lawrence, *The judges of New Brunswick* (Saint John, N.B., 1907); *Cyc. Am. biog.*]

Ure, George P. (d. 1860), journalist, was a native of Scotland. He came to Canada, and became a journalist on the staff of the *North American*, and subsequently of the Toronto *Globe*. In 1859 he founded in Montreal the *Family Herald*, a weekly journal; and he died at Montreal on August 22, 1860. With A.

Farewell he published *The Maine law illustrated* (Toronto, 1855), an early contribution to temperance literature; and under the *nom de plume* of "A member of the press", he was the author of *The handbook of Toronto* (Toronto, 1858).

[Morgan, *Bib. can.*]

Urquhart, Hugh MacIntyre (1880-1950), soldier and author, was born in 1880, and died in 1950. In the First World War, he rose to command the 16th Battalion, Canadian Expeditionary Force, and was awarded the M.C. and D.S.O. He was the author of *The history of the 16th Battalion* (Toronto, 1932) and of *Arthur Currie: The biography of a great Canadian* (Toronto, 1950), which was published posthumously.

[Private information.]

Urquhart, Norman C. (1893-1966), financier, was born in Toronto, Ontario, October 7, 1893, and educated at Jarvis Collegiate Institute. He opened his own brokerage firm in 1921 and was one of the first large holders of Noranda Mines stock. He was president of the Standard Stock and Mining Exchange (1928-29), and played a prominent role in its merger with the Toronto Stock Exchange in 1938-39. He retired in 1941 to devote his time to the welfare of prisoners of war through the Canadian Red Cross and later served as chairman of the National Executive of the Red Cross. In 1945 he headed the building fund for the Hospital for Sick Children, Toronto. He was a member of the Board of Governors of the University of Toronto; president of Mining Corporation of Canada (1950-64); vice-president and director of the Royal Bank; vice-president of Noranda Mines; vice-president of Simpson's Limited; and a director of seven companies. He was made a C.B.E., a commander of the Order of St. John of Jerusalem, and an officer of the French Legion of Honour for his wartime activities. He died at Toronto, Ontario, September 3, 1966.

[Metropolitan Toronto Library Board, *Biographical scrapbooks*, vol. 23.]

Urwick, Edward Johns (1867-1945), educationist, was born in Cheshire, England, in 1867, the son of the Reverend William Urwick. He was educated at Oxford University (B.A., 1890; M.A., 1892), and became interested in social service. From 1899 to 1902 he was subwarden of Toynbee Hall in London; from 1902 to 1910 he was director of the London School of Sociology; and from 1912 to 1922 he was professor of social philosophy in the University of London. He came to Canada in 1924, and in 1925 he was appointed a special lecturer in the department of political economy in the University of Toronto. In 1927 he was appointed head of this department; and he continued in this chair until his retirement in 1937. He died at Vancouver, British Columbia, on February 18, 1945. He was the author of *Studies of boy life in great cities* (London, 1903), *Luxury and waste of life* (London, 1908), *A philosophy of social progress* (London, 1912), *The message of Plato* (London, 1920), and *The social good* (London, 1927).

[H. A. Innis (ed.), *Essays in political economy in honour of E. J. Urwick* (Toronto, 1938); *Can. who's who*, 1936-37.]

Uttley, William Velores (1865-1944), local historian, was born in 1865, and died at Elmira, Ontario, on May 25, 1944. He was the publisher of the Kitchener *Record*, and later of the Elmira *Signet*; and after his retirement from journalism he wrote *A history of Kitchener, Ontario* (Kitchener, 1937).

[Toronto *Globe and Mail*, May 27, 1944.]

Vachon, Alexandre (1885-1953), Roman Catholic archbishop, was born at St. Raymond, Quebec, on August 16, 1885, and died at Dallas, Texas, on March 30, 1953. He was educated at Laval University (B.A., 1906; Ph.M., 1907; Th.M., 1909; S.T.D., 1910; M.A., 1911); and in 1937 became dean of the faculty of science at Laval University. From 1940 until his death he was archbishop of Ottawa. He was the author of text-books on chemistry and geology. The University of Montreal conferred on him the degree of D.Sc. in 1935, McGill University and Queen's University that of LL.D. in 1939, and Laval that of LL.D. in 1940; and he was elected a fellow of the Royal Society of Canada in 1934.

[*Proc. Roy. Soc. Can.*, 1953; *Can. who's who*, 1948.]

Vail, Edwin Arnold (1817-1885), speaker of the Legislative Assembly of New Brunswick (1865-67 and 1871-74), was born at Sussex Vale, New Brunswick, on August 19, 1817, the son of the Hon. John Cougle Vail and Charlotte, daughter of the Rev. Oliver Arnold. He was educated at Edinburgh University and at the University of Glasgow (M.D., 1837), and thereafter practised medicine at Sussex, New Brunswick. From 1857 to 1867 he represented Kings county as a Liberal in the Legislative Assembly of New Brunswick, and from 1865 to 1867 he was its speaker. He was a strong opponent of Confederation, and in 1867 he resigned from the legislature in protest against it; but he was again elected to the Legislative Assembly of New Brunswick for Kings county in 1870, and, except for the years 1874-78, he continued to represent this constituency until his death. From 1871 to 1874 he was again speaker of the Assembly; and in 1883 he was appointed a member of the Executive Council of New Brunswick without portfolio. He died at Sussex, New Brunswick, in August, 1885.

[*Dom. ann. reg.*, 1885; *Can. parl. comp.*; *Canadian biographical dictionary*, Quebec and Maritime provinces vol. (Chicago, 1881).]

Vail, William Berrian (1823-1904), minister of militia and defence for Canada (1874-78), was born at Sussex Vale, New Brunswick, on December 19, 1823, the son of the Hon. John Cougle Vail and Charlotte, daughter of the Rev. Oliver Arnold. From 1846 to 1867 he carried on with his brother, J. O. Vail, a shipping business at Digby, Nova Scotia. He was, like another brother, Dr. E. A. Vail (q.v.), an opponent of Confederation; and in 1867 he was elected, as an anti-Confederation Liberal, to the Legislative Assembly of Nova Scotia for Digby. He continued to represent this constituency until 1874, and during the whole of this period he was provincial and financial secretary in the Annand administration. During the latter half of it he was also government leader in the lower house; and the acceptance of Confederation by Nova Scotia, on the granting of "better terms", was in part due to his influence. From 1874 to 1878, and again from 1882 to 1887, he represented Digby as a Liberal in the Canadian House of Commons; and from 1874 to 1878 he was minister of militia and defence in the Mackenzie government. His administration of this office was mainly notable for the establishment in 1876 of the Royal Military College at Kingston, Ontario. He died at Dover, England, on April 10, 1904. In 1850 he married Charlotte, daughter of Charles Jones, of Weymouth, Nova Scotia; and by her he had two daughters.

[Morgan, *Can. men* (1898); *Can. parl. comp.*; *Canadian biographical dictionary*, Quebec and Maritime provinces vol. (Chicago, 1881); Toronto *Globe*, Oct. 26, 1876.]

Vaillancourt, Joseph-Jacques-Janvier Emile (1889-1968), diplomat and author, was born in Montreal, Quebec, March 23, 1889. He was educated at the Montreal Jesuit College (Ste. Marie) and the University of Caen, France (Litt. D.). He was in the public service of the province of Quebec in the department of tourism and was manager of the Montreal Tourist and Convention Bureau (1936-40). He was first Canadian minister to Cuba (1945-48) and to Yugoslavia (1948-50), and was ambassador to Peru (1950-55). He was an advocate both of Canadian unity and of the recognition by Quebec of her French heritage. He received many honours for his public service on both sides of the Atlantic. His writings include *Une maîtrise d'art en Canada* (1920); *La conquête du Canada par les Normands* (1930); *Adresse à l'Université de Caen* (1932); *Unity of origin — unity of sentiment* (1934); *History vs. finance* (1934); *Broad side* (1936); *Guillaume d'Orange* (1938); *Knifed and thrown away like a dead cat* (1938); *Contributions unlimited* (1938); *Knots* (1939). He died at Montreal, Quebec, January 15, 1968.

[*Can. who's who*, 1955-57.]

Vallée, Arthur (1882-1939), physician and author, was born at Quebec City on November 5, 1882, the son of Dr. Arthur Vallée and Honorine, daughter of the Hon. P. J. O. Chauveau (q.v.). He was educated at the Quebec Seminary and at Laval University (M.D., 1904). After two years of study abroad, he began the practice of medicine in Quebec; and in 1907 he was appointed secretary of the faculty of medicine in Laval University, and a professor of pathological anatomy. In 1929 he was elected a fellow of the Royal Society of Canada. He died at Quebec City on January 8, 1939. He was the author of *Un biologiste canadien: Michel Sarrazin* (Quebec, 1927).

[*Proc. Roy. Soc. Can.*, 1939.]

Vallière de Saint-Réal, Joseph Rémi (1787-1847), jurist, was born at Carleton, on the Bay of Chaleur, on October 1, 1787, the son of Jean Baptiste Vallière de Saint-Réal and Marguerite Corneillier dit Grandchamp. He came with his father, who was a blacksmith, to the French royalist settlement in Markham county, Upper Canada, in 1799; but at his father's death he went to Quebec, and became a protégé of Bishop Plessis (q.v.). He was called to the bar of Lower Canada in 1812; and in 1814 he was elected to the Legislative Assembly of the province for St. Maurice. He failed of re-election in 1817; but in 1820 he was elected for the upper town of Quebec, and he represented this constituency continuously until 1829. In 1823, during the absence of L. J. Papineau (q.v.), he was speaker of the House. In 1829 he was appointed a judge for the district of Three Rivers; and in 1842 chief justice at Montreal. In 1838 he was suspended from the bench by Sir John Colborne (q.v.), in consequence of his having granted a writ of *habeas corpus* to the prisoners arrested during the rebellion of 1837-38; but was restored to office by Poulett Thomson (q.v.) in 1840. He died on February 17, 1847. In 1812 he married Louise Pezard de Champlain, in 1831 Ester Elora Hart, of Three Rivers, and in 1836 Jane (Kierman) Bird.

[F. J. Audet, *Les juges en chef de la province de Québec* (Quebec, 1927); P. G. Roy, *Les juges de la province de Québec* (Quebec, 1933); Morgan, *Cel. Can.*; Bibaud, *Panth. can.*; Le Jeune, *Dict. gén.*; *Bull. rech. hist.*, 1923.]

Van Alstine, Peter (1747-1811), loyalist, was born at Kinderhook, New York, in 1747, and became a blacksmith. In the American Revolutionary War he took the Loyalist side, and served first as a captain of batteau men, and later as a major in Cuyler's Corps. He was the leader of a group of Loyalists who left New York by ship in 1783, spent the winter of 1783-84 in tents at Sorel, Quebec, and were settled in 1784 about Cataraqui (later Kingston). He represented Lennox and Prince Edward counties in the first Legislative Assembly of Upper Canada, after the refusal of the first elected member, Philip Dorland, to take the oath of allegiance. He died on his farm near Adolphustown, Upper Canada, in 1811.

[H. H. Van Wart, *The Loyalist settlement of Adolphustown: A short history of Peter Van Alstine and his company* (Loyalist Gazette, Aug., 1932); W. Canniff, *History of the settlement of Upper Canada* (Toronto, 1869).]

Van Cortlandt, Edward (1805-1875), physician and author, was born in Newfoundland in 1805, and was educated at Dr. Wilkie's school in Quebec. He studied medicine in England, and passed the examination of the Royal College of Surgeons in London in 1827. He returned to Canada in 1832, and settled in Bytown, Upper Canada (now Ottawa), where he practised medicine for the rest of his life. He died in Ottawa on March 25, 1875. He was interested in geology, mineralogy, and botany; and, in addition to papers contributed to the *Canadian Journal* and other periodicals, he was the author of several pamphlets, *Lecture on Ottawa productions* (Bytown, 1853), *Observations on the building stone of the Ottawa country* (Ottawa, n.d.), *An essay on entozoa* (Ottawa, 1865), and *An essay on the native compounds and metallurgy of iron, especially in connection with the Ottawa valley* (Ottawa, 1867). His wife, Gertrude Van Cortlandt, was author of *Records of the rise and progress of Ottawa* (Ottawa, 1858).

[W. Canniff, *The medical profession in Upper Canada* (Toronto, 1894); *Dict. Can. biog.*, vol. 10.]

Vancouver, George (1757-1798), navigator, was born on June 22, 1757, and entered the navy in 1771 as an able seaman on the *Resolution*, under Capt. James Cook (q.v.). He became a midshipman on the *Discovery*, on Capt. Cook's third voyage; and in 1780 he passed his examination as a lieutenant. In 1790 he attained the rank of commander, and in 1791 he was sent in the *Discovery* to take over from the Spaniards in the Nootka Sound territory. He explored the Pacific coast of North America; and on his return to England in 1795 he devoted himself to preparing his journals for publication. He died, when the task was virtually completed, on May 10,

1798, at Petersham, England; and a few months later his brother John published his *Voyage of discovery to the North Pacific Ocean and round the world in the years 1790-1795* (3 vols., with atlas of plates, London, 1798).

[G. H. Anderson, *Vancouver and his great voyage* (King's Lynn, 1923); G. Godwin, *Vancouver: A life* (New York, 1931); B. Anderson, *Surveyor of the sea: The life and voyages of Captain George Vancouver* (Toronto, 1960); *Dict. nat. biog.*; *Cyc. Am. biog.*]

VanderSmissen, William Henry (1844-1929), scholar, was born in Toronto on August 18, 1844, and was educated at the University of Toronto (B.A., 1864; M.A., 1866). In 1866 he was appointed lecturer in German at the University of Toronto, and in 1892 professor of German. From 1873 to 1891 he was also librarian. He retired from his professor's chair in 1913; and he died at Toronto on January 3, 1929. With W. H. Fraser (q.v.), he was author of *The high school German grammar* (Toronto, 1894); and he translated into English verse, with commentary and notes, *Goethe's Faust* (London, 1926).

[*Can. who was who*, vol. 1; Morgan, *Can. men* (1912).]

Van Dusen, Conrad (1801-1878), clergyman and author, was born December 14, 1801, in Adolphustown, Upper Canada. He became in 1829 a minister of the Methodist Episcopal Church; and in 1833 a minister of the Wesleyan Methodist Church. From 1849 to 1851 he was treasurer of Victoria College, Cobourg. He died at Whitby, Ontario, on August 18, 1878. Under the pseudonym of "Enemikeese", he was the author of *The Indian chief* (London, 1867), and *The successful young evangelist* (Toronto, 1870).

[*Dom. ann. reg.*, 1878; G. H. Cornish, *Cyclopaedia of Methodism in Canada* (Toronto, 1881); *Dict. Can. biog.*, vol. 10.]

Van Egmond, Anthony (1771-1838), soldier, was born in Holland in 1771. He served as an officer in the Dutch army during the French invasion of the Netherlands in 1793-94; and later he joined the Dutch contingent under Napoleon. He served under Napoleon until after the retreat from Moscow, in which he took part; then he joined the allied armies, with the rank of colonel, and he was with Blücher at Waterloo. Soon after the close of the Napoleonic wars, he emigrated to America; and for eight years he lived in Indiana county, Pennsylvania. He then removed to Upper Canada; and he settled first in Waterloo county, and later in the Huron Tract. He took part in the rebellion of 1837, and was in command of the rebels at the engagement of Montgomery's Farm. He was captured by the loyalists, succumbed to the rigours of imprisonment in the

Toronto jail, and died in hospital on January 5, 1838.

[E. C. Guillet, *The lives and times of the patriots* (Toronto, 1938); J. C. Dent, *The Upper Canadian rebellion* (2 vols., Toronto, 1885); G. H. Needler, *Colonel Anthony Van Egmond* (Toronto, 1956).]

Vanfelson, George (1784-1856), jurist, was born at Quebec, Canada, on April 23, 1784; and was admitted to the bar of Lower Canada in 1805 (Q.C., 1843). He represented the upper town of Quebec in the Legislative Assembly of Lower Canada from 1815 to 1820, and the lower town from 1832 to 1837; and he was attorney-general of the province for two periods of office, from 1819 to 1820 and from 1830 to 1832. He was appointed a judge of the Superior Court of Lower Canada in 1849; and he sat on the bench until his death, at Montreal, Canada East, on February 16, 1856.

[P. G. Roy, *Les juges de la province de Québec* (Quebec, 1933) and *Fils de Québec*, vol. 3 (Lévis, Que., 1933).]

Van Horne, Sir William Cornelius (1843-1915), president and chairman of the board of directors of the Canadian Pacific Railway (1888-1910), was born in Illinois, United States, on February 3, 1843, the son of Cornelius Covenhoven Van Horne. He became a telegraph operator on the Illinois Central Railway in 1857, and served in various capacities on American railways until 1882. He was then appointed general manager of the Canadian Pacific Railway; and it was under him that the work of construction was pushed to completion. In 1884 he was elected vice-president of the company, and in 1888 its president. In 1899 he exchanged this position for that of president of the board of directors. He retired from active connection with the company in 1910, and he died at Montreal on September 11, 1915. In 1867 he married Lucy Adeline, daughter of Erastus Hurd, Galesburg, Illinois. He was created a K.C.M.G. in 1894.

[W. Vaughan, *The life and work of Sir William Van Horne* (New York and Toronto, 1920); *Who was who*, 1897-1916; Morgan, *Can. men* (1912); Taché, *Men of the day*; H. A. Innis, *History of the Canadian Pacific Railway* (London, 1923).]

Vanier, Georges Philias (1888-1967), soldier and diplomat, governor general of Canada, was born in Montreal, Quebec, April 23, 1888. He was educated at Loyola College and at Laval University (B.A., 1906; LL.B., 1911). He was called to the bar of Quebec in 1911. He served in the First World War as a major in the 22e Bataillon canadien français, where he won the M.C. and bar and the D.S.O.. He was seriously wounded. He was A.D.C. to the Governor General of Canada (1921-23 and 1926-28). From 1925 to 1928 he commanded the Royal

22nd Regiment at Quebec. In 1930 he represented Canada at the London Naval Conference and at the General Assembly of the League of Nations. From 1931 to 1938 he was secretary in the office of the Canadian High Commissioner in London and in 1939 was made Canadian minister to France. On the fall of France he returned to Canada as secretary of the Joint Permanent Board for the Defense of Canada and the United States (1940-42). In 1943 he returned to London as Canadian minister to the allied governments in exile. He became ambassador to France in 1944 and remained until his retirement in 1953. He became Governor General of Canada in 1959 and remained in office until his death on March 5, 1967. He became a chevalier of the Legion of Honour in 1917 and an associate member of the French academy of moral and political science in 1951. Georges Vanier was a heroic soldier, a courtly diplomat, a gracious governor general, and a tireless worker for Canadian unity.

[*Can. who's who*, 1964-66; Metropolitan Toronto Library Board, *Biographical scrapbooks*, vol. 38.]

Vankoughnet, Philip (1790-1873), legislative councillor of Upper Canada, was born in Cornwall, Upper Canada, on April 2, 1790, the son of Michael Vankoughnet, a United Empire Loyalist. He fought in the War of 1812; and in the rebellion of 1837 he commanded the 5th Battalion of Incorporated Militia. From 1820 to 1828 he represented Stormont and Dundas in the Legislative Assembly of Upper Canada; and in 1836 he was appointed a member of the Legislative Council of the province. He died on May 7, 1873. In 1819 he married Harriet Sophia, daughter of Matthew Scott, of Carrick-on-Suir, Tipperary county, Ireland.

[E. M. Chadwick, *Ontarian families* (2 vols., Toronto, 1894-98); *Cyc. Am. biog.*; *Dict. Can. biog.*, vol. 10.]

Vankoughnet, Philip Michael Matthew Scott (1823-1869), chancellor of Upper Canada (1862-67) and of Ontario (1867-69), was born at Cornwall, Upper Canada, on January 21, 1823, the eldest son of Philip Vankoughnet (q.v.) and Harriet Sophia, daughter of Matthew Scott, of Tipperary county, Ireland. He was educated at Dr. Urquhart's school in Cornwall, Upper Canada, and was called to the bar of Upper Canada in 1844 (Q.C., 1850). In 1849 he was one of the chief organizers of the British American League, formed to oppose the annexation movement; but he did not enter parliament until 1856, when he was returned for the Rideau division of Upper Canada to the Legislative Council, being the first elected member of the Council to take his seat. Before his election he had already replaced Sir Allan MacNab (q.v.) as president of the Executive Council and minister of agriculture in the Taché-Macdonald administration, and he im-

mediately became the government leader in the Upper House. He resigned from office with his colleagues in 1858; but, after the collapse of the short-lived Brown-Dorion administration, he resumed office as chief commissioner of Crown lands, and this portfolio he retained until 1862. He was then appointed chancellor of the Upper Canada Court of Chancery; and after 1867 he became chancellor of Ontario. He died at Toronto on November 7, 1869. In 1845 he married Elizabeth, daughter of Col. Barker Turner; and by her he had two sons.

[D. B. Read, *Lives of the judges* (Toronto, 1888); *Dict. nat. biog.*; *Cyc. Am. biog.*; Morgan, *Cel. Can.*; Dent, *Can. port.*, vol. 4; J. C. Dent, *The last forty years* (2 vols., Toronto, 1881).]

Van Rensselaer, Rensselaer (1801-1850), "patriot general", was born in 1801, the son of General Solomon Rensselaer, of Albany, New York. He became the proprietor of the Albany *Daily Advertiser*; and in December, 1837, was prevailed upon to accept the post of commander-in-chief of the "patriot" forces gathered by William Lyon Mackenzie (q.v.) and others at Navy Island. After the evacuation of Navy Island, he was in command of the "patriot" force that made an unsuccessful attempt to capture Kingston. Shortly after this, he resigned his command, was tried and convicted on a charge of breaking the neutrality laws of the United States, and was sentenced to a year in prison and a fine of $250. He died in Syracuse, New York, on January 1, 1850.

[E. C. Guillet, *The lives and times of the patriots* (Toronto, 1938); Mrs. C. V. R. Bonney (comp.), *A legacy of historical gleanings*, vol. 2 (Albany, N.Y., 1875).]

Vansittart, Henry (1779-1844), naval officer, was born in Bisham Abbey, Berkshire, England, in 1779. He entered the British navy as a midshipman in 1791, and served throughout the Revolutionary and Napoleonic wars. In 1830 he was promoted rear-admiral, and in 1841 vice-admiral. In 1834 he bought an estate near Woodstock, Upper Canada, on which he settled; and he died here in 1844.

[*Dict. nat. biog.*; *Cyc. Am. biog.*; Morgan, *Cel. Can.*]

Varennes, Pierre Gaultier de. See La Vérendrye, Pierre Gaultier de Varennes, Sieur de.

Vaudreuil, Philippe de Rigaud, Marquis de (1643-1725), governor of New France (1705-25), was born in France in 1643. He came to New France in 1687, as commander of the French troops in the colony, and served as chief of staff in Denonville's expedition against the Iroquois. In 1690 he was charged with guarding the north shore of the St. Lawrence against the English, at the siege of

Quebec by Phips (q.v.). He was appointed governor of Montreal in 1698, and in 1703, on the death of Callière (q.v.), he was appointed lieutenant-general and governor of New France. He administered the government of the colony until his death, at Quebec, on October 10, 1725. In 1690 he married Louise-Elisabeth, daughter of the Chevalier Joybert de Soulanges; and by her he had six sons.

[F. H. Hammang, *The Marquis de Vaudreuil: New France at the beginning of the eighteenth century* (Bruges, 1938); *Dict. Can. biog.*, vol. 2.]

Vaudreuil-Cavagnal, Pierre de Rigaud, Marquis de (1698-1778), last governor of New France (1755-60), was born at Quebec in 1698, the son of Philippe de Rigaud de Vaudreuil (q.v.) and Louise-Elisabeth Joybert de Soulanges. He became a captain in the *troupes de la marine*, and in 1733 was appointed governor of Three Rivers. From 1742 to 1755 he was governor of Louisiana. In 1755 he was appointed governor of New France, and he arrived at Quebec on June 23 of that year. He found Canada on the brink of war with Great Britain. He opened hostilities by sending, in March, 1756, a force to capture the forts on the road to Oswego, and in March of the following year, he sent a force against Fort William Henry, on Lake George. He became the tool of Bigot (q.v.) in his plundering of the colony; and throughout the war with Great Britain, he continually thwarted Montcalm (q.v.) and greatly hampered the conduct of the war by his vacillating policy. He was in command at Quebec during the battle of the Plains of Abraham, and on receiving the news of Montcalm's defeat, deserted the lines below the city, made a hurried retreat towards Jacques Cartier, and authorized the surrender of the city. Later in 1760, when the British were before Montreal, he himself surrendered all Canada. After the conquest, he went to France, and with Bigot, he was tried for maladministration, but was acquitted. He died in Paris on August 4, 1778. He married Charlotte Fleury de la Gorgendière, widow of François Le Verrier de Rousson, and had no children. His letters to the Chevalier de Lévis have been published by the Abbé H. R. Casgrain in his *Collection des manuscrits du Maréchal de Lévis*, vol. viii (Quebec, 1895).

[W. Wood, *The fight for Canada* (Westminster, 1904); A. G. Doughty, *The siege of Quebec* (Quebec, 1901); F. Parkman, *Montcalm and Wolfe* (Boston, 1892); T. Chapais, *Le Marquis de Montcalm* (Quebec, 1911); P. G. Roy, *Les familles de nos gouverneurs français* (Bull. rech. hist., 1920); Le Jeune, *Dict. gén.*; G. Frégault, *Le grand Marquis* (Montreal, 1952).]

Vaughan, Robert Charles (1883-1966), railway president, was born in Toronto, Ontario, December 1, 1883, and educated in Toronto schools. He joined the Grand Trunk Railway in 1898 as a messenger; he moved to the Canadian Northern Railway in 1902, and in 1903 became secretary and chief clerk to the vice-president and general manager. He became assistant to the vice-president in 1910 and had responsibility for the Royal Line of steamers from Montreal to the United Kingdom. With the formation of the Canadian National Railways system he became vice-president in charge of purchases, stores, and steamships. He was appointed chairman of the Defence Purchasing Board at Ottawa on the outbreak of the Second World War until it became the ministry of supply. From 1941 until his retirement in 1950 he was president of the Canadian National Railways. After retirement Mr. Vaughan became president of Commonwealth International Corporation and Commonwealth International Leverage Fund Limited. He was also a director of National Steel Car, Sherwin-Williams Company, Canadian International Growth Fund, Belding-Corticelli, Institutional Shares Limited (New York), Institutional Growth Fund (New York), and Provincial Transport. In 1946 he received the C.M.G. He died in Montreal, January 5, 1966.

[*Can. who's who*, 1955-57; Metropolitan Toronto Library Board, *Biographical scrapbooks*, vols. 11 & 26.]

Vaughan, Walter (1865-1922), biographer, was born in Monmouthshire, Wales, on May 8, 1865, and was privately educated. He was called to the English bar; but never practised. He came to Canada in 1890, and entered the legal department of the Canadian Pacific Railway in Montreal. Here he remained for seven years, and during this time he saw much of Sir William Van Horne (q.v.), whose biographer he became. From 1907 to 1918 he was bursar of McGill University; his remaining years were spent between England and California; and finally he returned to Montreal to die in June, 1922. He was the author of one book, *The life and work of Sir William Van Horne* (New York, 1920).

[Private information; *McGill News*, Sept., 1922.]

Vauquelin, Jean (1728-1772), sailor, was born at Dieppe, France, in February, 1728, the son of Jean Charles Vauquelin, captain of a merchant vessel. He entered the merchant marine, and by 1750 commanded his own ship. When the Seven Years' War broke out, he was entrusted with the command of the frigate *Aréthuse*; and he greatly distinguished himself at the siege of Louisbourg in 1758. He and his vessel finally escaped from the harbour, by running the British blockade; and in 1759 he was appointed commander-in-chief of the French flotilla in the St. Lawrence. He kept his flotilla intact until May 16, 1760, when he was defeated in an engagement with some British ships immediately above Quebec, and was taken prisoner. He was returned to France; and after serving for twelve more years in the French navy, he died at Rochefort on November 10, 1772. The statement has been made that he committed suicide; but there is doubt about this.

[A. Fauteux, *Jean Vauquelin* (Trans. Roy. Soc. Can., 1930); G. Gravier, *Notice sur Jean Vauquelin* (Rouen, 1885); Le Jeune, *Dict. gén.*]

Veniot, Peter John (1863-1936), prime minister of New Brunswick (1923-25) and postmaster-general of Canada (1926-30), was born at Richibuctou, New Brunswick, on October 4, 1863, the son of Stephen Veniot and Mary Morell. He was educated at Pictou Academy. From 1894 to 1900 he represented Gloucester in the Legislative Assembly of New Brunswick; but he resigned in 1900 to become collector of customs at Bathurst, and later secretary of the school board. In 1917, however, he was re-elected to the Legislative Assembly; and he continued to sit in it until defeated in 1925. In 1917 he became minister of public works in the Foster government; and in 1923 he succeeded W. E. Foster (q.v.) as prime minister of New Brunswick. Defeated at the polls in 1925, he was elected to represent Gloucester in the House of Commons in 1926; and later in 1926 he was sworn of the Privy Council and appointed postmaster-general in the Mackenzie government. He resigned office with the rest of the cabinet after the general election of 1930, though he retained his seat in the House until his death at Bathurst, on July 6, 1936. In 1885 he married Catherine Melanson; and by her he had six sons. He was an LL.D. of the University of New Brunswick (1923) and of Laval University (1924).

[H. Charlesworth, *A cyclopaedia of Canadian biography* (Toronto, 1919); *Can. parl. comp.*]

Vennor, Henry George (1841-1884), geologist, ornithologist, and meteorologist, was born in Montreal, in 1841, the son of a hardware merchant. He was educated at the Montreal High School and at McGill University. From 1865 to 1880 he was on the staff of the Geological Survey of Canada; and his reports contained much of practical value. In 1877 he published the first of his *Vennor almanacs*, in which he ventured, with surprising success, to predict the weather. As an ornithologist, his chief work was *Our birds of prey* (Montreal, 1876). He died in Montreal on June 8, 1884.

[*Dom. ann. reg.*, 1884; *Cyc. Am. biog.*; Morgan, *Bib. can.*]

Ventadour, Henri de Lévis, Duc de (1596-1651), viceroy of Canada (1625-31), was born in the castle of Moustier Ventadour, near Tulle, Corrèze, France, in 1596. After serving in the army, he took holy orders; and in 1625 he bought from his uncle, Henri, Duc de Montmorency, the vice-royalty of Canada, with the object of furthering the Canadian missions. It was through him that the Jesuits came to Canada. Shortly after the Company of New France was organized in 1627, the Duc de Ventadour was compelled to relinquish his office of viceroy; but he continued throughout his life to interest himself in the Jesuit missions in Canada. He died in Paris, France, in 1651. Pointe Lévis, or Lévy, opposite Quebec, was named after him.

[Le Jeune, *Dict. gén.*]

Verchères, Marie-Madeleine Jarret de (1678-1747), heroine, was born on her father's seigniory on the St. Lawrence River, twenty miles below Montreal, on March 3, 1678, the daughter of François Jarret and Marie Perrot. In October, 1692, when her parents were absent, a band of marauding Iroquois appeared at the fort. Madeleine at once took command, and, with the assistance of her two young brothers, two soldiers, and an old man of eighty, defended the fort for a week, when relief came from Montreal. In September, 1706, she married Pierre-Thomas de la Pérade. In her later years she was chiefly distinguished on account of the large number of law-suits in which she engaged. She died on August 8, 1747.

[P. G. Roy, *Madeleine de Verchères, plaideuse* (Trans. Roy. Soc. Can., 1921); A. G. Doughty, *A daughter of New France* (Ottawa, 1916); F. Parkman, *Count Frontenac and New France under Louis XIV* (Boston, 1892); Le Jeune, *Dict. gén.*; *Dict. Can. biog.*, vol. 3.]

Vergor, Louis Du Pont Duchambon, Sieur de (1713-1775?), soldier, was born on September 20, 1713, at Sérignac, Saintonge, France, the son of Louis Du Pont Duchambon. He obtained a commission in the French army, and in 1751 was sent to Canada, with the rank of captain. In 1754 he was placed in command at Fort Beauséjour, and he surrendered this fort to Monckton (q.v.) on June 16, 1755, without attempting a defence. He was tried by courtmartial at Quebec in 1757, but was acquitted of the charges brought against him, and returned to duty in the army. It was his misfortune that he was in command of the post at the Anse-au-Foulon (Wolfe's Cove) when the British made their landing here before the battle of the Plains. After the conclusion of peace, Vergor returned to France; but nothing appears to be known of his subsequent career. In 1752 he married Marie-Josephte Riverin; and by her he had four children, the youngest of whom was born in 1763. He died in France shortly after 1775.

[Le Jeune, *Dict. gén.*]

Verigin, Peter (d. 1924), leader of the Doukhobors, was born in Russia. He became the pseudo-divine leader of the Doukhobors, a sect of Russian Quakers, and on three occasions was exiled to Siberia by the Russian government. He came to Canada in 1903 to assume control of the Doukhobor settlements which had been established in Saskatchewan shortly before; and he remained in Canada during the rest of his life. A man of great ability, he guided the destinies of the Doukhobor settlements, first in Saskatchewan, and then in British Columbia, with great success. He was killed, on November 28, 1924, by the explosion of a time bomb in a railway carriage in which he was travelling, near Grand Forks, British Columbia.

[E. H. Oliver, *Peter Verigin* (Trans. Roy. Soc. Can., 1932); Morgan, *Can. men* (1912); A. Maude, *A peculiar people* (New York, 1904); J. F. C. Wright, *Slava Bohu* (New York, 1940).]

Verner, Frederick A. (1836-1928), painter, was born at Trafalgar, near Oakville, Upper Canada, in February, 1836. He was the nephew of Sir William Verner, Bart., and in 1856 went to England. He joined the British Legion, and served under Garibaldi in Italy in 1860. In 1862 he returned to Canada, and visited the North West. He became notable for his paintings of prairie life; and in 1880 he was elected an associate of the Royal Canadian Academy. During the latter half of his life he lived in England; and he died in London, England, on May 6, 1928.

[Morgan, *Can. men* (1912); N. MacTavish, *The fine arts in Canada* (Toronto, 1925); H. G. Jones and E. Dyonnet, *History of the Royal Canadian Academy of Arts* (Montreal, 1934); W. Colgate, *Canadian Art, 1820-1940* (Toronto, 1943).]

Vernon, Charles William (1871-1934), clergyman and author, was born in London, England, in 1871. He came to Canada in 1889, and studied at King's College, Windsor (B.A., 1896; M.A., 1901). He was ordained a priest of the Church of England in 1896, and in 1919 was appointed general secretary of the Social Service Council of the Church of England in Canada. He died at Toronto, Ontario, on January 30, 1934. He was the author of *Cape Breton at the beginning of the twentieth century* (Toronto, 1903), *Bicentenary sketches and early days of the Church in Nova Scotia* (Halifax, 1910), and *The old Church in the new Dominion* (London, 1929).

[*Who's who in Canada*, 1930-31; Morgan, *Can. men* (1912).]

Verrazzano, Giovanni da (1485?-1528), explorer, was born at Florence, Italy, about 1485, and about 1505 entered the maritime service of France. In 1524 he sailed from the Azores on a voyage of exploration to North America. He made his landfall on the coast of Florida, and explored the coast northward as far as the Gulf of St. Lawrence. A map or planisphere of his discoveries was drawn in 1529 by his brother Gerolamo, who accompanied him; and on this map appears for the first time the name "Gallia Nova" (New France). In 1528 Verrazzano set out on a second voyage to America, but was killed and eaten by cannibals, on an island which appears to have been one of the Lesser Antilles.

[J. C. Brevoort, *Verrazano the navigator* (privately printed, 1874); H. C. Murphy, *The voyage of Verrazzano* (New York, 1875); B. F. De Costa, *Verrazano the explorer* (New York, 1880); S. E. Dawson, *The St. Lawrence basin* (London, 1905), *New light on the Verrazzano brothers* (Geographical journal, 1910), and *More new light on the Verrazzano brothers* (Geographical journal, 1926); C. Newcomb, *Explorer with a heart: The story of Giovanni da Verrazzano* (New York, 1969); *Dict. Can. biog.*, vol. 1; *Cyc. Am. biog.*; Le Jeune, *Dict. gén.*]

Verreau, Hospice Anthelme Jean Baptiste (1828-1901), priest and historian, was born at L'Islet, Lower Canada, on September 6, 1828, the son of Germain Alexandre Verreau and Marie Ursule Fournier. He was educated at the Quebec Seminary, and was ordained a priest of the Roman Catholic Church in 1851. From 1851 to 1857 he was principal of the College of Ste. Thérèse, and in 1857 he became principal of the Jacques Cartier Normal School — a position he occupied for the rest of his life. In 1887 he was appointed also professor of Canadian history at Laval University. In 1873 the government of Quebec commissioned him to report on materials relating to Canadian history in the archives of Europe; and the results of his inquiry were published in the report of the minister of agriculture for 1875. Though a profound scholar, he published comparatively little. A number of his papers are printed in the *Transactions* of the Royal Society of Canada, of which he was a charter member, in the *Journal de l'Instruction Publique*, and in the *Mémoires* of the Société Historique de Montréal. He edited also a collection of documents entitled *Invasion du Canada: Collection des Mémoires* (2 vols., Montreal, 1870-73); and he published a play, *Saint Stanislas* (Montreal, 1879). He died in Montreal on May 15, 1901. In 1878 he was made an LL.D. of Laval University.

[Armand Yon, *L'abbé Verreau* (Montreal, 1946); Morgan, *Can. men* (1898); Le Jeune, *Dict. gén.*; Rose, *Cyc. Can. biog.* (1886); *Proc. Roy. Soc. Can.*, 1894 and 1901; *Bull. rech. hist.*, 1917.]

Vetch, Samuel (1668-1732), governor of Nova Scotia (1710-17), was born in Scotland on

December 9, 1668, the son of the Rev. William Vetch (or Veitch), a Covenanting minister who was compelled to flee in 1671 to England, and later to Holland. He was educated at the College of Utrecht, and returned to England in the army of William of Orange in 1688. He became an officer in the 26th or Cameronian Regiment, and served on the continent until 1697. In 1698 he took part in the unsuccessful attempt to found the Darien Colony; and in 1700 he went to New York. In 1705 he was sent on a diplomatic mission to Quebec; and in 1710 he was adjutant-general of the expedition sent to conquer Acadia. On the capture of Annapolis Royal, he was appointed the first English governor of Nova Scotia; and he administered the affairs of the province until relieved of his appointment in 1717. His later years are obscure; but he died in London, England, on April 30, 1732, in a debtors' prison. In 1700 he married Margaret, daughter of Robert Livingstone, of New York.

[G. Patterson, *Hon. Samuel Vetch* (Coll. Nova Scotia Hist. Soc., 1885); J. C. Webster, *Samuel Vetch* (Shediac, N.B., 1929); B. Murdoch, *History of Nova Scotia* (3 vols., Halifax, N.S., 1865); *Dict. Can. biog.*, vol. 2.]

Veyssière, Léger Jean Baptiste Noël (d. 1800), clergyman, was a Recollet priest who, in 1769, abjured the Roman Catholic faith, and became Protestant minister at Three Rivers, Quebec. He remained in this charge until his death, at Three Rivers, on May 26, 1800.

[J. E. Roy, *Les premiers pasteurs protestants au Canada* (Bull. rech. hist., 1897).]

Vézina, François (1818-1882), banker, was born in Quebec on August 30, 1818. In 1849 he founded the Caisse d'Economie de Notre Dame de Québec, of which he became secretary-treasurer; and in 1859 he was appointed cashier of the Banque Nationale on its foundation. This position he occupied until his death at Quebec on January 25, 1882. He published an *Etude historique de la progression financière de la Caisse d'Economie de N.D. de Québec* (3 vols., Quebec, 1878).

[J. C. Langelier, *Biographie de François Vézina* (Quebec, 1876); *Dom. ann. reg.*, 1882.]

Vidal, Alexander (1819-1906), senator of Canada, was born at Bracknell, Berkshire, England, on August 4, 1819, the son of Capt. Richard Emeric Vidal, R.N., and Charlotte Penrose Mitton. He was educated at the Royal Mathematical School, Christ's Hospital, London, England. In 1834 he came with his parents to Canada, and in 1835 he settled at Sarnia, Upper Canada. In 1843 he became a provincial land surveyor; but in 1853 he became the agent of the Bank of Upper Canada in Sarnia, and in 1866 the agent of the Bank of Montreal. From 1863 to 1867 he was an elected member for the St. Clair division in the Legis-

lative Council of Canada; and he was defeated as a Conservative candidate for the Canadian House of Commons in 1867. In 1873 he was called to the Senate of Canada, and he remained a senator until his death on November 18, 1906. In 1847 he married Catherine Louisa, daughter of Capt. William Elliott Wright, R.N.; and by her he had five sons and two daughters. He was an ardent temperance and social reformer; and in 1875 he was chairman of the Dominion Prohibitory Convention at Montreal.

[Morgan, *Can. men* (1898); *Can. parl. comp.*; Rose, *Cyc. Can. biog.* (1886); *Canadian biographical dictionary*, Ontario vol. (Toronto, 1881).]

Vieth, Frederick Harris D. (d. 1910), soldier and author, was born and educated in Halifax, Nova Scotia. In 1855, while on a visit to the British Isles, he obtained a commission as an ensign in the 63rd or West Suffolk (later the Manchester) Regiment; and he served with this regiment throughout the later stages of the Crimean War. After the war, he remained with the regiment for several years, when it was stationed in the Maritime provinces; and after he left the army he served as captain and adjutant of the 11th Halifax Regiment of the Nova Scotia militia. In his later years he was a clerk in the department of railways and canals at Ottawa; and he died in Ottawa in 1910. He was the author of *Recollections of the Crimean campaign and the expedition to Kinburn in 1855, including also sporting and dramatic incidents in connection with garrison life in the Canadian lower provinces* (Montreal, 1907).

[Private information.]

Vieux-Rouge (pseud.). See **Voyer, Pierre Arthur Joseph.**

Viger, Bonaventure (1804-1877), rebel, was born at Boucherville, Lower Canada, on May 14, 1804, son of Bonaventure Viger and Louise Carmel-Levasseur. On November 22, 1837, he commanded the group of rebels who rescued two prisoners from a detachment of British troops on the Chambly road, and thus gave the signal for the outbreak of rebellion. He was present at the engagement at St. Charles, a few days later, and was captured by the loyalists. In 1838 he was banished by Lord Durham (q.v.) to the Bermudas; but was released later in the year, and returned to Canada after the amnesty was granted. He settled down in Boucherville, married a sister of the Abbé Trudel, and became a Conservative. He died at Beloeil, Quebec, on December 15, 1877.

[L. O. David, *Les patriotes de 1837-38* (Montreal, 1884); *Dict. Can. biog.*, vol. 10.]

Viger, Denis Benjamin (1774-1861), president of the Executive Council of Canada (1844-46), was born at Montreal on August 19,

1774. He was educated at the College of St. Raphael, and was called to the bar of Lower Canada. He sat in the Legislative Assembly of Lower Canada for the west ward of Montreal from 1808 to 1810, for the county of Leinster from 1810 to 1816, and for the county of Kent from 1816 to 1830. In 1830 he was appointed a member of the Legislative Council of the province. He was an ardent coadjutor of his cousin, L. J. Papineau (q.v.), and in 1828 accompanied him on a mission to England to press the views of the Assembly on the Colonial Office. In 1834 he was a second time deputed to visit England as an agent of the French Canadians. In 1838 he was arrested on a charge of complicity in the rebellion of 1837, but was released without trial. From 1841 to 1845 he represented Richelieu in the Legislative Assembly of United Canada, and from 1845 to 1848 Three Rivers. He was not included in the first Baldwin-Lafontaine administration; and in 1844 he accepted office under Metcalfe (q.v.) as Lower Canadian leader of the government, with the portfolio of president of the council. He failed, however, to carry his compatriots with him, and he resigned from the government in 1846. In 1848 he was appointed to the Legislative Council, and he sat in the Council until 1858. He died at Montreal on February 13, 1861. He was the author of *Considérations sur les effets qu'ont produits en Canada la conservation des établissements du pays, les moeurs, l'éducation de ses habitants, et les conséquences qu'entraînerait leur décadence* (Montreal, 1809), *Analyse d'un entretien sur la conservation des établissements du Bas-Canada* (Montreal, 1826), *Considérations relatives à la dernière révolution de la Belgique* (Montreal, 1831), and *La crise ministérielle* (Kingston, 1844). Some poetry by him was published in *Le Spectateur* (Montreal, 1813-29). He was the first president of the Société de St. Jean Baptiste; and in 1855 he was made an LL.D. by St. John's College, New York.

[J. Royal and C. S. Cherrier, *Biographie de l'Hon. D. B. Viger* (Montreal, n.d.); *Mémoires relatifs à l'emprisonnement de l'Hon. D.B. Viger* (Montreal, 1840); *Dict. nat. biog.*; *Cyc. Am. biog.*; Bibaud, *Panth. can.*; Le Jeune, *Dict. gén.*; Morgan, *Cel. Can.* and *Bib. can.*]

Viger, Jacques (1787-1858), antiquarian, was a cousin of the Hon. D. B. Viger (q.v.), and was born at Montreal on May 7, 1787, the son of Jacques Viger and Amaranthe Prévost. He was educated at the College of St. Raphael, became a surveyor, and in 1813 was appointed an inspector of roads and bridges at Montreal. He fought in the War of 1812 as an officer of the Voltigeurs, and was present at the capture of Sackett's Harbour. In 1832 he was elected the first mayor of Montreal. He devoted his life to the collection of materials relating to Canadian history. Of these he left twenty-nine

manuscript volumes, which he called his "Sabredache", and an "Album" of original illustrations. Apart from some official reports, he was the author of only two pamphlets, *Archéologie religieuse du diocèse de Montréal* (Montreal, 1850) and *Souvenirs historiques sur la seigneurie de La Prairie* (Montreal, 1857). He died at Montreal on December 12, 1858. In 1808 he married Marie Marguerite, daughter of Lacorne de St. Luc (q.v.), and widow of Major the Hon. John Lennox. Some of his letters to his wife were published in the *Revue Canadienne*, 1914.

[E. Z. Massicotte, *Jacques Viger et sa famille* (Bull. rech. hist., 1915); *Dict. nat. biog.*; *Cyc. Am. biog.*; Morgan, *Cel. Can.*; C. Roy, *Nouveaux essais sur la littérature canadienne* (Quebec, 1914); Bibaud, *Panth. can.*; Le Jeune, *Dict. gén.*]

Viger, Louis Labrèche (1824-1872), journalist and politician, was born at Terrebonne, Lower Canada, and was educated at the College of Montreal. He was adopted by the Hon. Denis Benjamin Viger (q.v.), and on the death of Viger added the name of Viger to his own patronymic of Labrèche. He was successively a priest, a journalist, a lawyer, a merchant, a politician, and a company promoter. From 1861 to 1867 he represented Terrebonne in the Legislative Assembly of Canada; but he took almost no part in the debates. He died at Montreal on April 27, 1872.

[L. O. David, *Les gerbes canadiennes* (Montreal, 1921); *Can. parl. comp.*, 1864; *Dict. Can. biog.*, vol. 10.]

Viger, Louis Michel (1785-1855), receiver-general of Canada (1848-49), was born at Montreal on September 28, 1785, the son of Louis Viger, a blacksmith, and Marie Agnes Papineau. He was called to the bar of Lower Canada; from 1830 to 1838 he represented Chambly in the Legislative Assembly of Lower Canada; and in 1837 he was implicated in the rebellion, though not actually under arms. In the Legislative Assembly of united Canada he represented Nicolet from 1842 to 1844, Terrebonne from 1848 to 1851, and Leinster from 1851 to 1854. He was one of the founders of the *Parti rouge*, and in 1848 he became receiver-general in the second Baldwin-Lafontaine administration; but in 1849 he resigned over the question of the removal of the seat of government to Toronto. He died in 1855. He was known as "le beau Viger", and for many years he was president of the Banque du Peuple.

[F. J. Audet, *L'hon. Louis-Michel Viger* (Bull. rech. hist., 1927); L. O. David, *Les gerbes canadiennes* (Montreal, 1921); Le Jeune, *Dict. gén.*]

Villebon, Joseph Robinau de (1655-1700), governor of Acadia (1690-1700), was born in Quebec, Canada, on August 22, 1655, the second son of René Robinau de Bécancour, surveyor-general of New France. He was educated in France, and joined the army. He served with a dragoon regiment for about ten years, and then returned to Canada with the rank of captain. He was sent by Frontenac (q.v.) to Port Royal in Acadia; and in 1690 he was appointed governor of Acadia, in succession to Menneval (q.v.). He was exceptionally successful in defending the province against the aggressions of the English; and he retained office until his death at Fort St. John on July 5, 1700.

[J. C. Webster, *Acadia at the end of the seventeenth century: Letters, journals, and memoirs of Joseph Robineau de Villebon* (Saint John, N.B., 1934); Le Jeune, *Dict. gén.; Dict. Can. biog.*, vol. 1.]

Villeneuve, Alphonse (1843-1898), priest, was born at Laprairie, Canada East, in 1843, and was ordained a priest of the Roman Catholic Church in 1873. He spent a large part of his life as a priest in the United States; but he died at Montreal, Quebec, on March 23, 1898. He was the author of *La comédie infernale; ou, Conjuration libérale aux enfers* (Montreal, 1871).

[Allaire, *Dict. biog.*]

Villeneuve, Jean Marie Rodrique (1883-1947), cardinal of the Roman Catholic Church, was born in Montreal, Quebec, on November 2, 1883, and died in Los Angeles, California, on January 17, 1947. He was educated at the University of Ottawa, and in 1902 he entered the Oblate order. He was ordained a priest in 1907, and from 1907 to 1919 he taught in the University of Ottawa. He became dean of theology in this University in 1930, and was then appointed the first bishop of Gravelbourg in Saskatchewan. In 1931 he became Archbishop of Quebec, and in 1933 he was created a cardinal, the fourth Canadian to receive this honour. He was the author of *Quelques pierres de doctrine* (Montreal, 1938) and a number of pamphlets on religious questions.

[U. Villeneuve, *Vie illustrée du Prince de l'Eglise* (n.p., 1947); *Can. who's who*, 1938-39; *Encyc. Can.*]

Villeray, Louis Rouer de (1629-1700), first councillor of the Sovereign Council of New France (1663-1700), was born in Amboise, near Tours, France, in 1629, the son of Jacques Rouer de Villeray and Marie Perthuis. He came to Canada about 1650 as secretary to Lauzon (q.v.), and became a notary at Quebec. On September 18, 1663, he was chosen as the first councillor of the new Sovereign Council, and although he was expelled in 1664 by Mézy (q.v.), in 1670 by Courcelles (q.v.), and in 1679 by Frontenac (q.v.), he was in each case replaced; and he remained the first councillor until his death on December 6, 1700. He married, first, on February 16, 1658, Catherine,

daughter of Charles Sevestre (d. 1670), by whom he had three children, and second, in 1675, Marie-Anne Du Saussay de Bémont.

[P. G. Roy, *Louis Rouer de Villeray* (Trans. Roy. Soc. Can., 1919) and *La famille Rouer de Villeray* (Bull. rech. hist., 1910); C. P. Beaubien, *Louis Rouer de Villeray* (Bull. rech. hist., 1899); Le Jeune, *Dict. gén.; Dict. Can. biog.*, vol. 1.]

Villers, Paul de (1823-1883), priest and author, was born at Lotbinière, Lower Canada, on April 5, 1823; and was ordained a priest of the Roman Catholic Church in 1847. For nearly forty years he was parish priest at Ste. Gertrude, Quebec; and he died at Ste. Gertrude on January 30, 1883. He was the author of *Quelques leçons sur l'art épistolaire et la politesse* (Montreal, 1865).

[Allaire, *Dict. biog.*]

Vimont, Barthélemy (1594-1667), Jesuit priest, was born in France on January 17, 1594, and entered the Society of Jesus in 1613. He was ordained a priest about 1626, and from 1629 to 1630 was a missionary in Cape Breton. He came to America a second time in 1639, as third superior of the Jesuits in Canada, and as curé of Notre Dame in Montreal. He returned to France in 1659, and he died in 1667.

[Allaire, *Dict. biog.; Dict. Can. biog.*, vol. 1.]

Vincennes, François Marie Bissot, Sieur de (1700-1736), soldier, was born in Montreal, Canada, on June 17, 1700, the son of Jean Baptiste Bissot de Vincennes, an army officer, and Marguerite Forestier. In 1718 he joined his father as a cadet among the Miami Indians, south of Lake Erie; and in 1733, having been promoted in 1730 to the rank of lieutenant, he was made commandant in the Wabash country. He re-established Fort Vincennes, which was named after him, and he has been described as "the founder of Indiana". He was burnt at the stake by the Chicacha Indians in the Wabash country on March 25, 1736.

[P. G. Roy, *Le Sieur de Vincennes, fondateur de l'Indiana, et sa famille* (Quebec, 1919); Le Jeune, *Dict. gén.; Dict. Can. biog.*, vol. 2.]

Vincent, Irving Orrin (1885-1920), educationist, was born at St. Armand, near Frelighsburg, Quebec, in 1885; and was educated at McGill University (B.A., 1907; M.A., 1908). He became a school-teacher, first at Sherbrooke, Quebec, then at Cookshire, Quebec; and in 1912 he was appointed first principal at the King Edward VII school in Montreal. He died in Montreal on February 23, 1920. He was the author of *The right track: Compulsory education in the province of Quebec* (Toronto, 1920).

[J. A. Dale, "Introduction" to I. O. Vincent, *The right track* (Toronto, 1920).]

Vincent, John (1765-1848), soldier, was born in England in 1765. He entered the British army as an ensign in 1781, and in 1810 reached the rank of colonel. He served in Canada during the War of 1812, and was in command at Fort George, in the Niagara peninsula, when it was evacuated in 1813. He was created a major-general in 1813, a lieutenant-general in 1825, and a general in 1841. He died in London, England, on June 21, 1848.

[*Cyc. Am. biog.*; L. H. Irving, *Officers of the British forces in Canada during the war of 1812-15* (Welland, Ont., 1908).]

Vincent, Thomas (1776?-1832), fur-trader, was born in England about 1776, and entered the service of the Hudson's Bay Company as a writer at Albany in 1790. In 1814 he was governor of Moose Factory and the Southern Department; and in 1821 he was made a chief factor. He retired from the service of the Hudson's Bay Company, and returned to England in 1826; and he died on March 30, 1832.

[E. E. Rich (ed.), *Colin Robertson's correspondence book* (Toronto: The Champlain Society, 1939).]

Vogt, Augustus Stephen (1861-1926), musician, was born at Washington, Ontario, on August 14, 1861, of German-Swiss parentage. He studied music in the United States and in Germany. After his return to Canada, he founded in 1894 the Mendelssohn Choir, and he directed it until 1917. In 1913 he became principal of the Toronto Conservatory of Music, and in 1919 dean of the faculty of music in the University of Toronto. He died in Toronto on September 17, 1926. He was the author of *The standard anthem book* (Toronto, 1894) and *Modern pianoforte technique* (Toronto, 1900), of which several editions have been published.

[*Can. who was who*, vol. 1; Morgan, *Can. men* (1912).]

Volkoff, Boris (Boris Baskaroff) (1902-1974), dancer and choreographer, was born in Tula, Russia, May 15, 1902, and educated in Russia. He studied with Jan-Janowiz, Domaratski-Novakowski, and the Moscow State Ballet as well as with Gorski, Chaliapina, and Nekrosova at the Bolshoi Ballet. He began his dancing career in Baku, Russia in 1916, and danced in Moscow and with the touring Ballet Russe. He left Russia for the United States in 1928 and came to Canada in 1929 to dance at Loew's Uptown Theatre in Toronto. He remained to form a ballet school and a ballet company which preceded the National Ballet by some twenty years. Although he was not associated with the National Ballet, Volkoff continued to live and teach in Toronto and was responsible for a number of ballets on ice and the choreo-

graphing of Canadian legends for the Volkoff Ballet Company. He was a founder of the Canadian Ballet Festival, 1948. He received the Order of Canada in 1973. He died at Toronto, Ontario, March 12, 1974.

[*Can. who's who*, 1970-72; *Creative Canada* (Vol. 1).]

Vondenvelden, William (d. 1809), surveyor, was assistant surveyor-general of the province of Lower Canada, and collaborated with Louis Charland (q.v.) in the first authoritative map of the province published in 1813. He died in the parish of St. Henri, Lower Canada, on June 20, 1809, from an accident when riding his horse. He was, with Louis Charland (q.v.), compiler of *Extraits des titres des anciennes concessions de terre en fief et seigneurie...dans la partie actuellement appelée le Bas-Canada* (Quebec, 1803).

[Morgan, *Bib. can.*]

Von Iffland, Anthony (1799-1876), physician, was born in Quebec, Lower Canada, in 1799, of German and French parentage. He was educated at the High School in Quebec, and studied medicine in London, Edinburgh, and Paris. On his return to Canada, he founded in 1820 at Quebec the first anatomical school in Canada; but was compelled to give up his practice in Quebec because of the rousing of public feeling against his anatomical studies. He occupied various medical positions in the public service of Quebec; but he retired from practice in 1867, and became commissary of the Marine Hospital in Quebec. He died at Quebec on December 7, 1876. He was a voluminous writer; and a bibliography of his papers and articles is to be found in H. J. Morgan, *Bibliotheca canadensis* (Ottawa, 1867).

[P. G. Roy, *Fils de Québec*, vol. 3 (Lévis, Que., 1933).]

Von Shoultz, Nils Szolteosky (d. 1838), filibusterer, was a native of Poland who took refuge in the United States. His sympathies were engaged by the filibusterers in the United States who were planning to free Canada from the British yoke; and, being an experienced soldier, he was placed in command of a force which landed near Prescott, Upper Canada, on November 12, 1838. He took up his headquarters in a stone windmill, where he held out for three or four days; but on November 16, after what was known as the battle of the Windmill, he and his companions were compelled to surrender unconditionally. He was tried before a court-martial at Kingston, and though defended by John A. Macdonald (q.v.), then a rising young lawyer, he was sentenced to death, and was hanged at Kingston on December 8, 1838.

[I. E. Struthers, *The trial of Miles von Schoultz* (Can. mag., 1917); E. C. Guillet, *The lives and times of the patriots* (Toronto,

1938); J. C. Dent, *The Upper Canadian rebellion* (2 vols., Toronto, 1885).]

Voorhis, Ernest (1859-1933), clergyman and author, was born in New York, N.Y., in 1859; and was educated at private schools and at Princeton University. He was ordained a priest of the Episcopal Church in the diocese of New York in 1886; and from 1900 to 1912 he was canon precentor of the Cathedral of St. John the Divine in New York. In 1912 he removed to Canada and became a Canadian citizen. From 1919 to his retirement in 1931 he was employed on the staff of the department of the interior at Ottawa; and he died at Toronto, Ontario, in 1933. He was the author of *Historic forts and trading posts of the French régime and of the English fur trading companies* (Ottawa, 1930). In 1890 he married Isabelle Lampman, eldest sister of the poet Archibald Lampman (q.v.).
[Private information.]

Voyer, Ludger Napoléon (1842-1876), soldier and author, was born at Quebec, Canada East, on April 20, 1842. In 1858 he obtained a commission in the 100th Regiment (Royal Canadians), and he resigned his commission in 1865. In 1870 he was appointed superintendent of the provincial police of the province of Quebec; and he died at Quebec, on February 22, 1876, from the apparently accidental discharge of a pistol. He was the author of *Les qualités morales du bon militaire* (Quebec, 1865).
[P. G. Roy, *Fils de Québec*, vol. 4 (Lévis, Que., 1933); *Dict. Can. biog.* vol. 10.]

Voyer, Pierre Arthur Joseph (1861-1918), journalist and biographer, was born in 1861, and became a journalist. He was the author of a pamphlet of *Biographies* (Three Rivers, 1883); and, under the pen-name of "Vieux-Rouge", he published *Les contemporains* (2 vols., Montreal, 1898-99). He died in 1918.
[F. J. Audet and G. Malchelosse, *Pseudonymes canadiens* (Montreal, 1936).]

Voyer, Pierre de. See **Argenson, Vicomte d'.**

Vroom, Fenwick Williams (1856-1944), clergyman and educationist, was born at St. Stephen, New Brunswick, of Dutch Loyalist descent. He was educated at King's College, Windsor, Nova Scotia (B.A., 1880; M.A., 1883; B.D., 1890; D.D., 1901); and he was ordained a priest of the Church of England in 1881. After serving as rector in Richmond and Shediac, New Brunswick, he was appointed in 1888 a professor of divinity in King's College, Nova Scotia; and from 1927 to 1936 he was dean of the faculty of divinity. In 1919 he was appointed archdeacon of Nova Scotia; and from 1927 to 1930 he was president of the Nova Scotia Historical Society. He died at Halifax, Nova Scotia, on January 8, 1944. He was the author of *The first six centuries* (New York, 1923), *An introduction to the Prayer book* (New York, 1930), and *King's College: A chronicle* (Halifax, N.S., 1941).
[*Can. who's who*, 1936-37; Morgan, *Can. men* (1912).]

Wadden, Jean Etienne. See **Wadin, Jean Etienne.**

Waddilove, William James Darley (1785?-1859), clergyman and author, was born about 1785, the son of the Very Rev. Robert Darley Waddilove, dean of Ripon. He took holy orders, and was for several years a missionary in Canada, with the Right Rev. the Hon. Charles James Stewart (q.v.), bishop of Quebec. He returned to England before 1837; and he died near Hexham, Northumberland-shire, on October 28, 1859. He was the author of *The Stewart missions* (London, 1838), *Canadian church robbery* (pamphlet, New-castle-on-Tyne, 1840), and *The lamp in the wilderness* (Hexham, 1847).
    [Morgan, *Bib. can.*]

Waddington, Alfred (1801-1872), author and pioneer, was born at Crescent House, Brompton, London, England, on October 2, 1801. He went to British Columbia at the time of the "gold rush" of 1858, and became a merchant in Victoria. He wrote the first book published in Vancouver Island, *The Fraser mines vindicated, or the history of four months* (Victoria, 1858); and he became the leading advocate in British Columbia of the construction of a transcontinental railway. He died at Ottawa, whither he had gone to forward his plans for a railway, on February 26, 1872.
    [R. L. Reid, *Alfred Waddington* (Trans. Roy. Soc. Can., 1932); F. W. Howay and E. O. S. Scholefield, *British Columbia* (4 vols., Vancouver, B.C., 1914); *Dict. Can. biog.*, vol. 10.]

Waddington, Geoffrey (1904-1966), musician and conductor, was born in Leicester, England, in 1904 and came to Canada at the age of three. He studied at the Toronto Conservatory of Music and toured as a concert violinist before being appointed music director of the Canadian Radio Broadcasting Commission in 1933. He left this position in 1937 and was an independent conductor. During this period he was director of the Army Show. In 1952 he rejoined the C.B.C., where he was director of music and conductor of the C.B.C. Symphony Orchestra until it amalgamated with the Toronto Symphony Orchestra in 1963. He was first violinist with the Toronto Symphony and a member of the faculty of the Toronto Conservatory of Music. Under Waddington's direction the C.B.C. Symphony introduced many Canadian works and was able to commission some for special presentations. He died at Toronto, Ontario, in June, 1966.
    [Metropolitan Toronto Library Board, *Biographical scrapbooks*, vols. 26 & 61.]

Wade, Frederick Coate (1860-1924), lawyer, was born at Bowmanville, Ontario, on February 26, 1860, the son of William Wade. He was educated at the University of Toronto (B.A., 1882), and was called to the bar of Manitoba in 1886 (K.C., 1902). From 1897 to 1901 he was legal adviser to the Yukon Council; and in 1903 he served as one of the British counsel on the Alaska Boundary Commission. In 1918 he was appointed agent-general for British Columbia in London, England; and he died in London on November 9, 1924. In 1886 he married Edith Mabel, daughter of D. B. Read (q.v.), Toronto. He was the author of *The Manitoba school question* (Winnipeg, 1895), and a number of other pamphlets.
    [Morgan, *Can. men* (1912).]

Wade, Mark Sweeten (1858-1929), physician and historian, was born in Sunderland, England, in 1858. He came to America early in life, and was educated at the University of Toronto, at the University of California, and at the Medical College, Fort Wayne, Indiana. He became an assistant surgeon on the staff of the Canadian Pacific Railway; and in his later years he was police magistrate of Kamloops, British Columbia. He died at Vancouver, British Columbia, on April 19, 1929. He was the author of *The Thompson country* (Kamloops, B.C., 1907), *Mackenzie of Canada* (Edinburgh, 1927), and *The overlanders of '62* (Victoria, B.C., 1931).
    [*Who's who among North American authors*, vol. 3 (1927-28).]

Waden, Jean Etienne. See **Wadin, Jean Etienne.**

Wadin (Waden, Wadden, or Waddens), Jean Etienne (*fl.* 1761-1781) was a Swiss Protestant, the son of Adam Samuel Waddens (or Vuadin) and Bernardine Ermon, of La Tour-de-Paise, in the canton of Berne. His father is said to have been a professor at the University of Geneva; but no proof of this has been found. The son would appear to have come to Canada with the British army, and to have settled in Canada as a merchant and trader. On November 23, 1761, he married at St. Laurent, near Montreal, Marie-Joseph Deguire (b. 1739); and there is, in the register of Christ Church, Montreal, the record of the christening of a number of Wadin children after this date. On January 27, 1768, "Capt. Woden" appears in a list of signatories in the "Minutes of a general meeting of the proprietors of Canada bills", held in London, England; and in 1772 his name first appears in the fur-trade licences as trading to Grand Portage. About 1779 he formed a partnership with Venant St. Germain (q.v.); and he was one of the partners in the original sixteen-share North West Company in that year. In the winter of 1780-81, while at Lac la Ronge, he was killed in an altercation with Peter Pond (q.v.).

[W. S. Wallace (ed.), *Documents relating to the North West Company* (Toronto: The Champlain Society, 1934).]

Wainwright, William (1840-1914), railway executive, was born in Manchester, England, on April 30, 1840. He entered the service of the Manchester, Sheffield, and Lincolnshire Railway as a clerk in the accountant's office; and in 1862 he came to Canada, at the invitation of Sir E. W. Watkin (q.v.), as chief clerk in the accountant's office of the Grand Trunk Railway. In the service of the Grand Trunk he rose until he became in 1911 senior vice-president of this railway, and second vice-president of the Grand Trunk Pacific Railway. He died, after 52 years' service with the Grand Trunk Railway, at Atlantic City, U.S.A., on May 14, 1914.

[Morgan, *Can. men* (1912).]

Wait, Benjamin (1813-1895), rebel, was born in Markham township, Upper Canada, on September 7, 1813. He took part in the rebellion of 1837-38; and was captured on June 24, 1838, after the Short Hills raid. He was tried on a charge of high treason and was sentenced to death by hanging on August 25, 1838. His sentence was, however, later commuted to transportation for life to Van Diemen's Land. In 1842, as the result of the efforts of his wife, he received a pardon; but before this pardon reached him, he had escaped from Van Diemen's Land to the United States. He lived in the United States for the rest of his life, and he died at Grand Rapids, Michigan, on November 9, 1895. He was the author of *Letters from Van Dieman's Land* (Buffalo, N.Y., 1843).

[E. C. Guillet, *The lives and times of the patriots* (Toronto, 1938); *Cyc. Am. biog.*]

Wakefield, Edward Gibbon (1796-1862), colonial reformer, was born in London, England, on March 20, 1796. He was educated at Westminster and at Edinburgh, and entered the British diplomatic service. In 1826 he was involved in the abduction of an heiress of sixteen years of age, though he was already himself a widower; and he spent as a result three years in Newgate prison. His years in prison led to a sincere study of society, and particularly of the problems of the British Empire. He became an authority on colonization; and when Lord Durham (q.v.) was appointed high commissioner in Canada, he brought Wakefield with him, though in an unofficial capacity. Parts of Lord Durham's famous *Report on the affairs of British North America* (London, 1839) were undoubtedly his handiwork. He left Canada in 1839, but returned in 1841; and from 1842 to 1844 he represented Beauharnois in the legislature of united Canada. Under the pseudonym of "A member of the provincial parliament", he published *A view of Sir Charles Metcalfe's government of Canada* (London, 1844). After this episode, however, he transferred his activities to New Zealand; and he died in Wellington, New Zealand, on May 16, 1862.

[R. Garnett, *Edward Gibbon Wakefield* (London, 1898); Ursilla M. Macdonnell, *Gibbon Wakefield and Canada subsequent to the Durham mission* (Queen's quarterly, 1924-25); A. J. Harrop, *The amazing career of Edward Gibbon Wakefield* (London, 1928); Irma O'Connor, *Edward Gibbon Wakefield* (London, 1929); P. Bloomfield, *Edward Gibbon Wakefield: Builder of the British Commonwealth* (Toronto, 1961); H. T. Manning, *E. G. Wakefield and the Beauharnois canal* (Can. hist. rev., 1967); *Dict. nat. biog.*]

Walbran, John T. (1848-1913), sailor and author, was born on March 23, 1848, in Ripon, Yorkshire, England, and was educated at the grammar school in Ripon, Yorkshire. He became a sailor, and in 1881 obtained his certificate as master mariner. He joined the marine and fisheries service of Canada in 1891; and from this date to 1908 he commanded the government steamer *Quadra* in the lighthouse, buoy, and fishery service on the coast of British Columbia. He died at Victoria, British Columbia, on March 31, 1913. He was the author of *British Columbia coast names* (Ottawa, 1909).

[Private information.]

Wales, William (1734?-1798), astronomer, was born about 1734, and in 1769 was sent by the British government to Hudson Bay to observe the transit of Venus in that year. He afterwards accompanied Captain Cook on his second and third voyages; and on his return to England he was appointed mathematical master at Christ's Hospital. He died in London, England, in 1798. Among other works he published *General observations made at Hudson's Bay* (London, 1772).

[*Dict. nat. biog.*; *Cyc. Am. biog.*]

Walkem, George Anthony (1834-1908), prime minister of British Columbia (1874-76 and 1878), was born at Newry, Ireland, on November 15, 1834, the eldest son of Charles Walkem and Mary Ann Boomer. His father came to Canada in 1847 as a surveyor on the staff of the Royal Engineers, and was employed in fixing the boundary between Canada and the United States. He was educated at McGill University; and he was called to the bar of Lower Canada in 1858. In 1862 he went to Victoria, British Columbia, and he became a Q.C. in 1873. From 1864 to 1870 he was a member of the Legislative Council of British Columbia; and in 1871 he was elected a member of the Legislative Assembly of the province of Cariboo. In 1872 he was appointed chief commissioner of lands and works in the Executive Council of the province, and in 1873 attorney-general. From 1874 to 1876 he was prime minister, and again in 1878. In 1882 he was appointed a puisne judge of the Supreme Court of British Columbia; and he continued to occupy this post until his death at Victoria on January 13, 1908. In 1879 he married Sophie Edith, daughter of the Hon. Henry Rhodes, of Victoria and Hawaii; and by her he had one daughter.

[*Cyc. Am. biog.*; *Can. parl. comp.*; Morgan, *Can. men* (1898); Dent, *Can. port.*, vol. 2; J. B. Kerr, *Biographical dictionary of well-known British Columbians* (Vancouver, B.C., 1890).]

Walkem, William Wymond (1850-1919), author, was born at Montreal, Canada East, on June 25, 1850, the younger brother of George Anthony Walkem (q.v.). He was educated at McGill University (M.D., 1873), and in 1875 he went to British Columbia to become private secretary to his brother, who was then prime minister of the province. He was elected a member of the Legislative Assembly of British Columbia for Nanaimo South in 1894; but was defeated in the general election of 1898. He died at Vancouver, British Columbia, on September 29, 1919. He was the author of *Stories of early days in British Columbia* (Vancouver, 1914).

[*Can. parl. comp.*; private information.]

Walker, Alexander (*fl.* 1848-1867), poet, was a non-commissioned officer in the British army who came to Canada prior to 1848, when he contributed verse to the *Literary Garland* (Montreal). From 1857 to 1861 he was assistant editor of the *Quebec Gazette*; and later he was employed in the military stores

department at Quebec. But after 1867 he passes from view. He was the author of *The knapsack: A collection of fugitive poems* (Kingston, 1853) and *Hours off and on sentry; or, Personal recollections of military adventure in Great Britain, Portugal, and Canada* (Montreal, 1859).

[Morgan, *Bib. can.*]

Walker, Anna Louisa (1836-1907), poet and hymn-writer, was born in England in 1836, and came to Canada in early life, with her parents. She lived first at Point Levy, Canada East, and after 1858 at Sarnia, Canada West. At Sarnia she and her sisters conducted for some time a private school for young ladies. She later married a man named Harry Coghill; and she died in England, on July 7, 1907. She was the author of *Leaves from the Canadian backwoods* (Montreal, 1861), in which first appeared the words of the well-known hymn "Work, for the night is coming".

[A. Wylie Mahon, *Canadian hymns and hymn-writers* (St. Andrews-by-the-Sea, N.B., 1908).]

Walker, Sir Byron Edmund (1848-1924), president of the Canadian Bank of Commerce (1907-24), was born in Seneca township, Haldimand county, Upper Canada, on October 14, 1848, the son of Alfred E. Walker. He entered the service of the Canadian Bank of Commerce in 1868; in 1886 he became general manager of the bank; and in 1907 its president. He wrote a *History of Canadian banking* (Toronto, 1896); he published a large number of pamphlets and addresses on banking and kindred subjects; and he was regarded as an outstanding authority on financial questions. He had, however, a wide range of other interests. He was a well-known art connoisseur, and had much to do with establishing the National Art Gallery in Ottawa, of the board of which he became chairman; he was one of the founders of the Champlain Society, and its first president; for many years he was honorary president of the Mendelssohn Choir, of Toronto; and in 1898 he was elected president of the Canadian Institute. From 1910 to 1923 he was chairman of the board of governors of the University of Toronto; and in 1923 he was elected its chancellor. He died, at Toronto, on March 27, 1924. In 1874 he married Mary (d. 1923), daughter of Alexander Alexander, of Hamilton, Ontario; and by her he had four sons and three daughters. In 1908 he was created a C.V.O., and in 1910 a knight bachelor. In 1911 he was elected a fellow of the Royal Society of Canada.

[G. P. de T. Glazebrook, *Sir Edmund Walker* (Oxford, 1933); *Proc. Roy. Soc. Can.*, 1925; *Can. who was who*, vol. 1; *Who was who*, 1916-28; Morgan, *Can. men* (1912); V. Ross, *History of the Canadian Bank of Commerce* (2 vols., Toronto, 1920).]

Walker, Edmund Murton (1877-1969), entomologist, was born in Windsor, Ontario, October 5, 1877; he died at Toronto, Ontario, February 14, 1969. Professor Walker was educated at the University of Toronto (B.A., 1900; M.B., 1903), and at the University of Berlin. He interned at the Toronto General Hospital (1903-04), and became assistant in the department of biology of the University of Toronto in 1904, rising to be head of the department of zoology in 1934, a position which he held to retirement in 1948. Professor Walker was honorary curator of entomology at the Royal Ontario Museum, and a fellow of the Royal Society of Canada and of the Royal Entomological Society. He discovered many new insect species, including the so-called Canadian ice-bug, part cricket, part cockroach, which was found at the foot of an Alberta glacier in 1913. A complete list of his publications is given in G.B. Wiggins, ed., *Centennial of Entomology in Canada – 1863-1963* (Contribution 69, Life Sciences, Royal Ontario Museum, 1966).

[*Can. who's who*, 1955-57; *Proc. and Trans. Roy. Soc. Can.*, 1970; Toronto *Globe and Mail*, Feb. 16, 1969.]

Walker, Hiram (1816-1899), distiller, was born in East Douglass, Massachusetts, on July 4, 1816. He emigrated to Canada in 1858, and settled on the eastern side of the Detroit River. He opened here a distillery; and about this distillery the town of Walkerville, named after him, grew up. He was joined by his three sons, and the firm was known as Hiram Walker and Sons until 1890; it was then incorporated as Hiram Walker and Sons, Ltd. He died on January 12, 1899.

[R. G. Hoskins, *Hiram Walker and the origins and development of Walkerville, Ontario* (Ont. hist., 1972); Morgan, *Can. men* (1898).]

Walker, Sir Hovenden (d. 1728), rear-admiral, is said to have been born in Ireland about 1656, but was probably born later than this. He entered the service of the Royal Navy. On March 15, 1710-11, he was promoted to be rear-admiral of the white squadron; and about the same time he was knighted. In 1711 he was appointed to command an expedition against Quebec, consisting of ten ships of the line, a number of smaller vessels, and about thirty transports, with 5,000 troops on board. On August 11, 1711, part of this fleet was wrecked in the St. Lawrence as a result of fogs and gales; and Walker, after a council of war, decided that the only course open to him was to return, with the remnant of the fleet, to England. In 1715, after the accession of George I, he was dismissed from the service, ostensibly because of his conduct of the Quebec expedition, but more probably because he was suspected of Jacobite sympathies. He went to South Carolina, and became a planter; but after a few years he returned to England, and he died in Dublin, Ireland, in 1728. He was the author of *A journal or full account of the late expedition to Canada* (London, 1720). A new edition of this, with an introduction by Gerald S. Graham, has been published by the Champlain Society (Toronto, 1953).

[*Dict. nat. biog.*; *Cyc. Am. biog.*; Le Jeune, *Dict. gén.*; *Dict. Can. biog.*, vol. 2.]

Walker, James (1756-1800), jurist, was born in England in 1756. He came to Canada about 1770; and in 1777 was called to the bar of the province of Quebec. He represented the county of Montreal in the first Legislative Assembly of Lower Canada from 1792 to 1796. In 1794 he was appointed a judge of the Court of Common Pleas; and later in the same year he was promoted to the Court of King's Bench for the district of Montreal. He died at Montreal, Lower Canada, on January 31, 1800.

[P. G. Roy, *Les juges de la province de Québec* (Quebec, 1933).]

Walker, John Henry (1831?-1899), illustrator, was born about 1830, and set up in business in Montreal as an engraver in 1852. He enjoyed a long period of popularity as an illustrator; and he died at Montreal in June, 1899.

[E. Z. Massicotte, *L'artiste Walker* (Bull. rech. hist., 1943).]

Walker, Norma Ford (1893-1968), geneticist, was born at St. Thomas, Ontario, September 3, 1893. She entered the University of Toronto in 1914 as a science student. Her first interest was entomology and she received her Ph.D. in 1923. She became an instructor at the University of Toronto in that year and remained with the university for her whole academic life, becoming professor of human genetics and director of the department of genetics at the Hospital for Sick Children, Toronto. Dr. Walker was a pioneer in the study of dermatoglyphics, and of mental retardation and other inherited traits, and, with Oliver Smithers, described the mode of inheritance of the haptoglobin variants. She was a charter member of the Genetics Society of Canada, and of the American Society of Human Genetics. She was a trustee of the Queen Elizabeth II Fund for Research in Children's Diseases. She was elected a fellow of the Royal Society of Canada in 1958. The research fields she pioneered have yielded a rich harvest to her successors. She died at Toronto, August 9, 1968.

[*Proc. Roy. Soc. Can.*, 1969; *Can. who's who*, 1955-57.]

Walker, Thomas (*fl.* 1752-1785), merchant, was born in England, possibly in 1718. He emigrated to Boston, Massachusetts, in 1752, and settled in Montreal in 1763. Here he engaged in the fur-trade. In 1764 he was

866

appointed a justice of the peace, and shortly afterwards was the victim of an assault by the military, in which one of his ears was cut off. The incident greatly embittered feeling in the colony, and Walker became the centre of a violent agitation. In 1774, when the Americans invaded Quebec, Walker went over to them, and he left the province with them in 1776. In 1785 Pierre Du Calvet (q.v.) met him in London, England; but after that he passes from view.

[L. W. Sicotte, *The affair Walker* (Canadian antiquarian and numismatic journal, 1915); A. L. Burt, *The mystery of Walker's ear* (Can. hist. rev., 1922); W. S. Wallace (ed.), *The Maseres letters* (Toronto, 1920); Le Jeune, *Dict. gén.*]

Walker, Thomas Leonard (1867-1942), mineralogist, was born near Brampton, Ontario, on December 31, 1867, and was educated at Queen's University, Kingston (M.A., 1890) and at Leipzig University (Ph.D., 1896). From 1897 to 1901 he was assistant superintendent of the Geological Survey of India; and from 1901 to 1937 he was professor of mineralogy in the University of Toronto. In 1913 he was appointed also director of the Royal Ontario Museum of Mineralogy and Petrography in Toronto. He was elected a fellow of the Royal Society of Canada in 1919; and in 1941 he was awarded the Society's Flavelle medal for his contributions to scientific research. He received the honorary degree of D.Sc. from the University of Toronto in 1938. He died at Toronto, Ontario, on August 6, 1942. In 1906 he married Mary Augusta, daughter of Sir James Woods (q.v.); and by her he had two sons and one daughter. He was the author of *Crystallography* (New York, 1914); and he started the series of *Contributions to Canadian mineralogy*, published annually in the geological series of the *University of Toronto Studies* since 1921.

[*Proc. Roy. Soc. Can.*, 1943; *Can. who's who*, 1936-37; Morgan, *Can. men* (1912).]

Walker, William (1793-1863), legislative councillor of Canada, was born in Scotland in 1793. He emigrated to Canada in 1815; and he became a partner in the famous mercantile house of Forsyth, Richardson, and Co., of Montreal, which later became Forsyth, Walker, and Co., of Quebec. He was part owner of the *Royal William*, the first steamship that crossed the Atlantic. In 1838 he was appointed a member of the Special Council of Lower Canada; and in 1842 he was called to the Legislative Council of Canada. He retired from business in 1848, and he died at Quebec, on May 18, 1863. He was the first chancellor of Bishop's College, Lennoxville; and he received from this college the degree of D.C.L.

[*Cyc. Am. biog.*]

Walker, William (1797-1844), lawyer and journalist, was born at Three Rivers, Lower Canada, in 1797, and was called to the bar of Lower Canada in 1819. He became a successful lawyer; and in 1835 he was sent to England, with John Neilson (q.v.), to present the views of the British constitutional party in Lower Canada to the British government. During the Sydenham administration, he was the editor of the Montreal *Times*; and he represented Rouville in the Legislative Assembly of united Canada from 1842 to 1843. He died in Montreal on April 10, 1844.

[A. W. P. Buchanan, *The bench and bar of Lower Canada* (Montreal, 1925).]

Walker, William Wesley (1858-1945), clergyman and author, was born in York county, Canada West, in 1858, and died at Toronto, Ontario, on September 30, 1945. He was educated at the Wesleyan Theological College in Montreal, and was ordained a minister of the Methodist Church. He served first as a missionary in the Parry Sound district, and later was pastor of several churches in southern Ontario. He was the author of *By northern lakes* (Toronto, 1896), *Sabre-thrusts at free-thought* (Toronto, 1898), *Occident and Orient: A tale* (Toronto, 1905), and *Alter ego: A tale* (Toronto, 1907).

[Toronto, *Globe and Mail*, Oct. 1, 1945; Morgan, *Can. men* (1912).]

Walking Buffalo (1870-1967), Indian chief, was born March 20, 1870, in southern Alberta. Orphaned early in life, he was adopted by the Rev. John Maclean (q.v.), a Methodist missionary, in 1881 and given the name George Maclean. He attended a mission school and although he was admitted to a school of medicine in Eastern Canada he did not leave the West because he was the only one in his tribe who could speak English. He was elected chief of the Stony Indians in 1920 and relinquished the position in 1935; after that time he was consulted as an elder statesman of Canada's Indians. He became a believer in Moral Re-armament and travelled around the world urging men to become reconciled to nature and to one another. He died at Banff, Alberta, December 27, 1967.

[Metropolitan Toronto Library Board, *Biographical scrapbooks*, vols. 33 & 58.]

Wallace, Archer (1884-1958), clergyman and author, was born at Blyth, England, on May 10, 1884, and died at Newmarket, Ontario, on July 30, 1958. He was educated at Victoria College, University of Toronto, and at the University of Western Ontario, and was ordained a minister of the Methodist Church. He became associate editor of the United Church of Canada Sunday School publications. He was the author of numerous books for young people, of which the following are typical: *Stories of grit* (Toronto, 1925), *Blazing new trails* (Toronto, 1928), *I believe in people* (New York, 1936), *The silver lining* (New York,

1937), *Stars in the sky* (Toronto, 1944), and *The field of honor* (Toronto, 1949).

[*Can. who's who*, 1952-54.]

Wallace, Edward Wilson (1880-1941), educationist, was born at Metuchen, New Jersey, on November 2, 1880, the son of the Rev. Francis Huston Wallace (q.v.). He was educated at Victoria College, University of Toronto (B.A., 1904; B.D., 1906; D.D., 1921) and at Columbia University (M.A., 1921). He was sent to China in 1906 as an educational missionary of the Methodist Church, and from 1912 to 1923 he was a professor in the West China Union University. In 1923 he became general secretary of the China Christian Educational Association; and in 1930 he was appointed chancellor and president of Victoria College and University in the University of Toronto. He died at Toronto, Ontario, on June 20, 1941. He was the author of *The heart of Szchuan* (Toronto, 1904) and *The new life in China* (London, 1914).

[*Can. who's who*, 1936-37; *Who's who among North American authors.*]

Wallace, Francis Huston (1851-1930), theologian, was born at Ingersoll, Ontario, in 1851, the son of the Rev. Robert Wallace. He was educated at the University of Toronto (B.A., 1873; M.A., 1874), at Knox College, Toronto, and at the Drew Theological Seminary, New Jersey (B.D., 1876). He was ordained a minister of the Methodist Church in 1878, and he held several pastoral charges until 1887, when he was appointed professor of New Testament literature in Victoria University. In 1900 he became dean of the faculty of theology in Victoria University; and he held this post for many years. He died at Toronto on June 2, 1930. In 1895 he was made a D.D. of Victoria University; and he was the author of *Witnesses of truth* (Toronto, 1885) and *The interpretation of the Apocalypse* (Toronto, 1903).

[*Can. who was who*, vol. 1; Morgan, *Can. men* (1912).]

Wallace, Frederick William (1886-1958), journalist and author, was born in Glasgow, Scotland, on December 11, 1886, and died at Montreal, Quebec, on July 15, 1958. He came to Canada in 1904, and served an apprenticeship on several shipping lines. He turned to writing in 1908, and in 1913 founded the *Canadian fisherman*, a magazine of which he was editor for many years. Then he published his first novel, *Blue water* (Toronto, 1913), and this was followed by *The Viking blood* (Toronto, 1920) and *Captain Salvation* (Toronto, 1925), as well as by several collections of short stories, *The shack locker* (Toronto, 1916), *Salt seas and sailormen* (Toronto, 1922), and *Tea from China* (Toronto, 1926). He also published some historical works dealing with the days of sail: *Wooden ships*

and iron men (Toronto, 1924), *In the wake of the windships* (Toronto, 1926), *The record of Canadian shipping* (Toronto, 1929), and *Under sail in the last of the clippers* (Glasgow, 1936). Shortly before his death he published his autobiography under the title *Roving fisherman* (Gardenvale, Que., 1955).

[*Can. who's who*, 1955-57; *Who's who in Can.*, 1951-52; *Encyc. Can.*; V. B. Rhodenizer, *Handbook of Canadian literature* (Ottawa, 1930).]

Wallace, Isaiah (1826-1907), clergyman, was born at Coverdale, New Brunswick, on January 17, 1826. He was educated at the Fredericton Seminary and at Acadia University (B.A., 1855; M.A., 1859; D.D., 1905), and became a Baptist minister. He had charges at various places in New Brunswick and Nova Scotia; but his chief work was as an evangelist under the Baptist Home Mission Board. He died at Aylesford, Nova Scotia, on December 24, 1907. He was the author of *Revival reminiscences: An autobiography* (Wolfville, N.S., 1903).

[*Records of the graduates of Acadia University* (Wolfville, N.S., 1926).]

Wallace, Sir James (1731-1803), governor of Newfoundland (1794-97), was born in 1731, and died in London, England, on January 6, 1803. He entered the Royal Navy, was commissioned a lieutenant in 1755, and saw service during the American Revolution. He was knighted in 1777; and in 1794 he was promoted to the rank of rear-admiral, and was appointed governor of Newfoundland. In 1796 he was unfortunate in being unable to prevent a powerful French squadron from landing at Bay Bulls, Newfoundland, and burning the village, but otherwise he seems to have been a successful governor. He retired as governor in 1797, and was promoted to the rank of admiral in 1801.

[*Dict. nat. biog.*; *Encyc. Can.*]

Wallace, James Nevin (d. 1941), surveyor and historian, was a graduate of Trinity College, Dublin, who came to Canada, and had a long experience as a surveyor in the Canadian West. He became interested in the early history of the West, was the author of *The wintering partners on Peace River* (Ottawa, 1929), and was joint editor, with R. Douglas, of *Twenty years of York Factory* (Ottawa, 1926). He died at Spring Banks, Alberta, on January 12, 1941.

[*Can. hist. rev.*, 1941.]

Wallace, Malcolm William (1873-1960), educationist and author, was born in Essex county, Ontario, on May 1, 1873, and died at Toronto, Ontario, on April 8, 1960. He was educated at the University of Toronto (B.A., 1896) and the University of Chicago (Ph.D., 1899). He was professor of English in Beloit

College, Wisconsin, from 1899 to 1904; and from 1904 to 1944 he was a member of the staff of the English department in University College, Toronto. He became head of the department in 1926, and principal of the College in 1928. He was the author of *The life of Sir Philip Sidney* (Cambridge, 1915) and *English character and the English literary tradition* (Toronto, 1952); and he edited two early English plays.

[*Can. who's who*, 1948; Toronto *Globe and Mail*, April 9, 1960.]

Wallace, Michael (1747-1831), loyalist, was born in Scotland in 1747, and emigrated to America, where he established himself at Norfolk, Virginia. He lost his property during the American Revolution, and removed to Halifax, Nova Scotia. He became treasurer of the province for many years, and in his later days was several times administrator of the province. He died in 1831.

[B. Murdoch, *History of Nova Scotia* (3 vols., Halifax, 1867); Le Jeune, *Dict. gén.*]

Wallace, Nathaniel Clarke (1844-1901), controller of customs for Canada (1892-95), was born at Woodbridge, Upper Canada, on May 21, 1844, the third son of Capt. Nathaniel Wallace, of Sligo, Ireland. He was educated at the Weston grammar school, and for some years was a school-teacher. In 1867 he established a milling business at Woodbridge; and in 1874 he was elected a member of the county council of York. In 1878 he became warden of York county, and was elected to represent West York in the Canadian House of Commons — a constituency he continued to represent until his death. From 1887 to his death he was grand master of the Orange Association of British North America; and in 1888 he was one of the "Noble 13" who voted for the disallowance of the Jesuits' Estates Act. In 1892 he was appointed controller of customs in the Thompson government; but he retired from the government in 1895 because of his opposition to its policy in regard to the Manitoba separate school question. He died at Woodbridge, Ontario, on October 18, 1901. In 1877 he married Belinda, daughter of James Gilmour, of Ottawa.

[C. E. Perry, *Hon. N. Clarke Wallace* (Mimico, Ont., 1897); *Can. who was who*, vol. 1; Morgan, *Can. men* (1898); *Can. parl. comp.*]

Wallace, Robert Charles (1881-1955), educationist, was born in the Orkney Islands, on June 15, 1881, and died at Kingston, Ontario, on January 29, 1955. He was educated at Edinburgh University (M.A., 1901; B.Sc., 1906; D.Sc., 1912) and the University of Göttingen (Ph.D., 1909); and he came to Canada in 1910 as a lecturer in geology and mineralogy in the University of Manitoba. In 1928 he was appointed president of the Uni-

versity of Alberta, and in 1936, principal of Queen's University, a position from which he retired in 1951. He was elected a fellow of the Royal Society of Canada in 1921, and was its president in 1941-42. He was created a C.M.G. in 1944; and he received honorary degrees from twenty universities in Canada, the United States, and the British Isles. He was the author of *A liberal education in a modern world* (Toronto, 1932) and *Religion, science, and the modern world* (Toronto, 1952); he edited *Some great men of Queen's* (Toronto, 1941); and he published many papers and reports. Just before his death he published an interesting autobiographical sketch entitled *As I look back* (Queen's Quarterly, 1954).

[*Proc. Roy. Soc. Can.*, 1955; *Can. who's who*, 1952-54; *Who was who*, 1951-60; *Encyc. Can.*]

Wallace, William Bernard (1861-1928), jurist, was born at Port Mulgrave, Nova Scotia, on February 26, 1861. He was educated at Dalhousie University (LL.B., 1885), and was called to the bar of Nova Scotia in 1884. He practised law in Halifax; and he represented Halifax in the Legislative Assembly of Nova Scotia from 1896 to 1900. In 1901 he was appointed judge of the county court of Halifax; and he occupied this seat on the bench until his death at Halifax, Nova Scotia, on March 31, 1928. In 1925 he was appointed a member of the Dominion royal commission on maritime rights. He was the author of *The law of mechanics' liens in Canada* (Toronto, 1905) and *Decisions of the Supreme Court of Nova Scotia hitherto unreported* (Halifax, N.S., 1907).

[Morgan, *Can. men* (1912).]

Wallace, William Stewart (1884-1970), historian and librarian, was born at Georgetown, Ontario, June 23, 1884. He was educated at the University of Toronto (B.A., 1906), and Oxford University (B.A., 1909; M.A., 1912). He began his teaching career at the University of Western Ontario in 1906, joined the faculty of McMaster University in 1909, and taught also at the University of Toronto as lecturer in history from 1910. In 1920 he joined the staff of the University of Toronto, becoming assistant librarian in 1922 and librarian from 1923 to 1954. He served in the Canadian army in the First World War. He was president of the Champlain Society, Toronto (1943-47), and president of the Canadian Library Association (1951-52). He died at Toronto, March 11, 1970. He wrote *The United Empire Loyalists* (Toronto, 1914), *The family compact* (Toronto, 1915), *The Maseres letters* (ed., Toronto, 1920), *By star and compass* (Toronto, 1922), *Sir John Macdonald* (Toronto, 1924), *A new history of Great Britain and Canada* (Toronto, 1925), *A dictionary of Canadian biography* (Toronto, 1926), *A history of the University of Toronto* (Toronto,

1927), and *The growth of Canadian national feeling* (Toronto, 1927).

[*Can. hist. rev.*, vol. LI, 1970.]

Wallberg, Emil Andrew (1867?-1929), civil engineer, was born in Sweden about 1867, and came to America with his parents in 1875. He was educated at Clinton, Iowa, and at Augustana College, Rock Island, Illinois, from which he graduated in engineering. He later came to Canada, where he became in 1907 a naturalized British subject, and he was the designer and constructor of many industrial plants in Ontario and Quebec. He was the president of the Canada Wire and Cable Company and the Lake St. John Power and Paper Company; and he amassed a considerable fortune. He died at Battle Creek, Michigan, on March 30, 1929. He was not married; and on the death of his sister in 1933, the bulk of his estate was bequeathed to the University of Toronto.

[Private information.]

Wallbridge, Lewis (1816-1887), chief justice of Manitoba (1882-87), was born in Belleville, Upper Canada, on November 27, 1816. He was called to the bar of Upper Canada in 1839 (Q.C., 1856), and in 1857 he was elected to represent Hastings in the Legislative Assembly of Canada. In 1863 he became solicitor-general in the Macdonald-Dorion administration, and the same year he was elected speaker of the Assembly. In 1867 he retired from political life; and in 1882 he was appointed chief justice of Manitoba. He died at Winnipeg, Manitoba, on October 20, 1887.

[*Cyc. Am. biog.*; *Can. parl. comp.*; Rose, *Cyc. Can. biog.* (1888); J. P. Robertson, *A political manual of the province of Manitoba* (Winnipeg, 1887).]

Waller, Charles Cameron (1869-1944), clergyman and educationist, was born in London, England, on February 6, 1869. He was educated at St. John's College, Cambridge (B.A., 1890; M.A., 1902), came to Canada in 1890, and was ordained a priest of the Church of England in 1893. He went back to England in 1897; but in 1902 he returned to Canada as principal of Huron College, London, Ontario; and he retired from this position only in 1941. He died at London, Ontario, on December 11, 1944. The University of Western Ontario conferred on him the honorary degree of D.D.

[*Can. who's who*, 1936-37; Morgan, *Can. men* (1912).]

Waller, Jocelyn (d. 1828), journalist, was the son of Sir Robert Waller, Bart., of county Tipperary, Ireland. He came to Canada in 1820, and in 1823 he founded at Montreal the *Canadian Spectator* (1823-28), a Reform journal printed in the English language. He was persecuted in the courts by the government; and he died in prison at Montreal on December 2, 1828. His eldest son, Edmund, became in 1830 fourth baronet.

[A. Fauteux, *Jocelyn Waller* (Bull. rech. hist., 1920); Morgan, *Cel. Can.* and *Bib. can.*]

Wallis, Katherine Elizabeth (1861-1957), sculptress, was born at Peterborough, Canada West, in 1861, and died at Santa Cruz, California, on December 14, 1957. She studied art at the Royal College of Art in South Kensington, England, became a sculptress, and for many years had a studio in Paris. She first exhibited in Canada in 1920. Several of her pieces of sculpture are in the National Gallery in Ottawa. She was the author of *Chips from the block: Poems* (New York, 1955).

[A. R. Collins, *A biographical sketch of Katherine E. Wallis, Canadian artist* (Fort Erie, Ont., 1948).]

Walsh, Sir Albert Joseph (1900-1958), chief justice of the Supreme Court of Newfoundland (1949-58), was born at Conception Bay, Newfoundland, on April 30, 1900, and died at St. John's, Newfoundland, on December 18, 1958. He was educated at Dalhousie University (LL.B., 1925); and was called to the bar in Nova Scotia and in Newfoundland in 1928 (K.C., 1932). In 1928 he was elected a member of the Newfoundland House of Assembly for Harbour Main, and became speaker of the House. In 1932 he became secretary of state in the Squires cabinet, but was defeated in the subsequent election. After 1934, when Newfoundland came under a commission form of government, he occupied several administrative posts; and he was chairman of the Newfoundland delegation that negotiated the terms of the union with Canada in 1949. He became the first lieutenant-governor of the new province, but resigned after a few months to accept the post of chief justice of the Supreme Court. He was created a knight bachelor in 1949.

[*Can. who's who*, 1955-57; *Encyc. Can.*]

Walsh, Henry Horace (1899-1969), university professor and historian, was born in Ellerslie, Prince Edward Island, September 17, 1899. He was educated at King's College, Halifax (B.A., 1921; M.A., 1923); at Oxford (1923-24); at the General Theological Seminary, New York (S.T.M., 1930); and at Columbia University (Ph.D., 1933). He was rector of Christ Church, Dartmouth, Nova Scotia (1936-45), and was made associate professor and then professor of church history at McGill University in 1948, a position he held until retirement in 1968. He was president of the Canadian Church History Association in 1959 and editor of the *Anglican Outlook*. He wrote *The concordat of 1801* (1933); *The Christian church in Canada* (1956); and *The church in the French era from colonization to the British conquest* (1966).

[*Can. who's who*, 1967-69.]

Walsh, James Morrow (1843-1905), first commissioner of the Yukon district, was born at Prescott, Upper Canada, in 1843, the son of Lewis Walsh and Elizabeth, daughter of John Morrow. He joined the militia, and saw service in the Fenian Raid of 1866. In 1873 he was appointed an inspector in the North-West Mounted Police; and he served with this force until 1883, having established his reputation as an officer of great courage and firmness by his handling of the Sioux chief, Sitting Bull. In 1883 he resigned from the Police, and established the Dominion Coke, Coal, and Transportation Company; but in 1897 the discovery of gold in the Yukon brought him back to the North-West Mounted Police. He was appointed a superintendent of the Police, and the chief executive officer of Canada in the Yukon, with the title of commissioner of the Yukon district. He held this post until 1898, when he retired; and he died at Brockville, Ontario, on July 25, 1905. In 1870 he married Mary, daughter of John Mowat, of Prescott.

[I. Allan, *White Sioux; Major Walsh of the Mounted Police* (1969); *Can. who was who*, vol. 2; Morgan, *Can. men* (1898); A. L. Haydon, *The riders of the plains* (London, 1910).]

Walsh, John (1830-1898), Roman Catholic archbishop of Toronto (1889-98), was born in the parish of Mooncoin, Kilkenny county, Ireland, on May 23, 1830, the son of James Walsh and Ellen Macdonald. He was educated at St. John's College, Waterford, and at the Seminary of St. Sulpice, Montreal, Canada. He was ordained a priest of the Roman Catholic Church in 1854. In 1867 he was consecrated bishop of Sandwich, a title changed in 1868 to bishop of London; and in 1889 he was installed as archbishop of Toronto. He died in Toronto on July 31, 1898. In 1867 he received the degree of D.D. from the Vatican.

[*Can. who was who*, vol. 2; Morgan, *Can. men* (1898); *Cyc. Am. biog.*; Le Jeune, *Dict. gén.*]

Walsh, William (1804-1858), Roman Catholic Archbishop of Halifax (1852-58), was born in Waterford, Ireland, in November, 1804. He was educated at St. John's College, Waterford, and was ordained a priest of the Roman Catholic Church in 1828. In 1834 he was appointed coadjutor vicar apostolic of Nova Scotia; in 1845 he became bishop of Halifax; and in 1852 archbishop. He died in Halifax, Nova Scotia, on August 10, 1858. He published a number of pastoral letters, and some translations of devotional books.

[*Cyc. Am. biog.*; Morgan, *Bib. can.*; Le Jeune, *Dict. gén.*]

Walsh, William Legh (1857-1938), lieutenant-governor of Alberta (1931-36), was born at Simcoe, Canada West, on January 28, 1857. He was educated at the University of Toronto and Osgoode Hall, Toronto, and was called to the Ontario bar in 1880, to that of the Yukon in 1900, and that of the North West Territories in 1904 (K.C., 1903). He practised law in Orangeville, Ontario, from 1880 to 1900, and later in the Yukon, and in Calgary, Alberta. From 1912 to 1931 he was a judge of the Supreme Court of Alberta; and from 1931 to 1936 he was lieutenant-governor of the province of Alberta. He died at Victoria, British Columbia, on January 13, 1938.

[*Can. who's who*, 1936-37; *Can. parl. comp.*]

Walter, Arnold Maria (1902-1973), musician and conductor, was born at Hannsdorf, Moravia, August 30, 1902, and educated in Prague and Berlin. He studied musicology with Hermann Abert, Johannes Wolf, and Curt Sachs, composition with Bruno Weigl, and piano with R. M. Breithaupt and Frederic Lamond. He was well known as a lecturer and writer on musical subjects in Berlin papers until 1933. After studying folk music in Spain and England he came to Canada in 1937 and taught at Upper Canada College and the Royal Conservatory of Music. He became director of the Faculty of Music at the University of Toronto (1952-68) and was chairman of the editorial board of the *Canadian Music Journal* (1956). He was president of the International Society of Music Education (1953-55); and a member of the board of the National Arts Centre (1966-68). His compositions include two symphonies, a cantata, and works for voice, piano, and various instrumental combinations. He died at Toronto, Ontario, October 5, 1973.

[*Can. who's who*, 1967-69; *Encyc. Can.* (1972).]

Walter, Hermann (1863-1952), educationist, was born at Basle, Switzerland, in 1863, and died at Montreal, Quebec, on February 18, 1952. He was educated at the universities of Neuchatel, Edinburgh, and Tübingen, and came to Canada in 1900 as a lecturer in modern languages at McGill University. Later he became head of the department, and acting dean of arts. He retired from McGill in 1936. He was the author of *Heinrich Heine* (London, 1930) and *Moses Mendelssohn, critic and philosopher* (New York, 1930).

[*Montreal Gazette*, Feb. 19, 1952.]

Walters, Angus (1882-1968), *Bluenose* skipper, was born in Lunenburg, Nova Scotia, in 1882. He began his seagoing life at thirteen on his father's fishing schooner. He built his own ship in 1908 and after a chartered voyage to the Mediterranean he used her as a fishing schooner for the next eight years. After the First World War he sailed the *Gilbert B. Walters*, one of the largest salt-bankers ever built in Nova Scotia. She brought in the largest single catch of fish ever landed in the province—790,400 pounds. From 1921, when she was built, until she was sold in 1942 he was managing owner of the *Bluenose*, in which he won five international races. He sailed her to the Chicago World's Fair of 1933 and to the silver Jubilee celebrations of George V in London in 1935. Captain Walters retired from the sea after the Second World War and went into the dairy business. He died at Lunenburg, August 12, 1968.

[*Encyc. Can.* (1972); G. J. Gillespie, *Bluenose Skipper* (1955).]

Walwyn, Sir Humphrey Thomas (1879-1957), governor of Newfoundland (1936-46), was born on January 25, 1879, and died at Maiden Newton, England, on December 29, 1957. He joined the Royal Navy, and rose to the rank of vice-admiral. He was appointed governor of Newfoundland in 1936, and remained in office during most of the period when the colony was under commission government. He was created a K.C.S.I. in 1933, and a K.C.M.G. in 1939.

[*Who was who*, 1951-60: *Encyc. Can.*; *Newfoundland supp.*]

Wanlock, Rob (pseud.). See **Reid, Robert.**

Warburton, Alexander Bannerman (1852-1929), prime minister of Prince Edward Island (1897-98), was born at Charlottetown, Prince Edward Island, on April 5, 1852, the son of the Hon. James Warburton. He was educated at King's College, Windsor (B.A., 1874; B.C.L., 1876; D.C.L., 1897), and at Edinburgh University. He was called to the bar in 1879 (Q.C., 1897), and practised law in Charlottetown. He represented Queen's in the Legislative Assembly of Prince Edward Island from 1891 to 1898; and from 1897 to 1898 he was prime minister of the province. From 1898 to 1904 he was judge of the County Court in Queen's county, but resigned to re-enter politics. From 1908 to 1911 he represented Queen's in the Canadian House of Commons. In 1920 he was appointed surrogate and judge of probate for Prince Edward Island; and he died at Charlottetown on January 14, 1929. He was the author of *A history of Prince Edward Island* (Saint John, N.B., 1923).

[*Can. parl. comp.*]

Warburton, George Augustus (1859-1929), social service worker and author, was born in Sandford, England, on October 4, 1859. He came to America in 1880; and for 29 years he was a secretary of the Young Men's Christian Association in the United States. In 1909 he became general secretary of the Y.M.C.A. in Toronto, Ontario; and he remained in this position until his death at Toronto, on February 21, 1929. He was the author of *A typical general secretary: The life of Edwin F. See* (New York, 1908).

[Morgan, *Can. men* (1912).]

Ward, James Edward (1883-1958), clergyman and author, was born in Barrie, Ontario, on October 1, 1883, and died at Toronto, Ontario, on April 13, 1958. He was educated at the University of Toronto and Oxford University (B.A., 1913), and was ordained a clergyman of the Church of England. He served as a chaplain with the British army in the First World War, and was wounded. He returned to Canada in 1925 and for thirty-one years was rector of St. Stephen's Church in Toronto. He was the author of *The wayfarer* (Toronto, 1922), *Indian summer and other poems* (Toronto, 1933), *This England* (Toronto, 1941), *The Master on the mount* (Toronto, 1943), and *God's plenty* (Toronto, 1945).

[*Can. who's who*, 1955-57; *Encyc. Can.*; Toronto *Globe and Mail*, April 14, 1958.]

Warden, Robert H. (1841-1905), clergyman and financier, was born in Dundee, Scotland on January 4, 1841, the son of Alexander J. Warden, F.S.A. He was educated at Madras College, St. Andrews, Scotland; and in 1866 he was ordained a minister of the Presbyterian Church. The same year he came to Canada; and from 1866 to 1874 he was minister at Bothwell, Ontario. In 1875 he became agent at Montreal of the Presbyterian Church in Canada; and in 1895 he became general agent of the church, a position he occupied until his death. In 1902 he was elected moderator of the Presbyterian Church in Canada; and in 1903 he became president of the Metropolitan Bank. He died at Toronto on November 26, 1905. He married Jemima, daughter of William McCaskill, of the island of Skye, Scotland; and by her he had several children. In 1888 he was made a D.D. of the Montreal Presbyterian College.

[Morgan, *Can. men*(1898); J. T. McNeill, *The Presbyterian Church in Canada* (Toronto, 1925).]

Wardrope, Thomas (1819-1914), clergyman, was born at Ladykirk, Berwickshire, Scotland, in 1819. He came to Canada in 1834, and was educated at Queen's University, Kingston (D.D., 1878) and at Edinburgh. He was first a grammar-school teacher at Bytown (Ottawa), and then he was ordained a minister of the Presbyterian Church. He was first pastor of Knox Church, Ottawa, and then of Chalmers Church, Guelph. He was superannuated in 1892; and he died at Guelph, Ontario, on June 17, 1914. In 1891 he was elected moderator of the Presbyterian Church in Canada.

[Morgan, *Can. men* (1912).]

Wark, David (1804-1905), senator of Canada, was born near Londonderry, Ireland, on February 19, 1804. He came to New Brunswick in 1825, and went into business as a general merchant. He represented Kent in the

Legislative Assembly of New Brunswick from 1843 to 1851; from 1851 to 1867 he was a member of the Legislative Council of New Brunswick; and from 1867 to 1905 he was a member of the Canadian Senate. He had thus sixty-two years of continuous service in the legislatures of British North America; and he was, at the time of his death, probably the oldest parliamentarian in the world. The only period in which he held executive office was from 1858 to 1862, when he was a minister without portfolio in the Executive Council of New Brunswick. He died at Fredericton, New Brunswick, on August 20, 1905. Shortly after his arrival in New Brunswick he married Annie Elizabeth, daughter of Isaac Burpee (q.v.), of Sunbury; and one daughter survived him.

[*Can. who was who*, vol. 1; Morgan, *Can. men* (1898); *Can. parl. comp.*]

Warman, Cy (1855-1914), author, was born at Greenup, Illinois, on June 22, 1855. He was successively a farmer, a wheat broker, a locomotive engineer, an editor, an author, and a promoter. He settled in London, Ontario, in 1898; and he lived here during most of the rest of his life. He died in Chicago, Illinois, on April 7, 1914. He was the author of *Mountain melodies* (Denver, 1892), *Tales of an engineer* (New York, 1895), *The express messenger and other tales of the rail* (New York, 1897), *The story of the railroad* (New York, 1898), *Frontier stories* (New York, 1898), *The white mail* (New York, 1899), *Snow on the headlight* (New York, 1899), *Short rails* (New York, 1900), *The last spike, and other railroad stories* (New York, 1906), *Weiga of Temagami, and other Indian tales* (New York, 1908), and *Songs of Cy Warman* (Boston, 1911).

[*Dict. Am. biog.*; *Who was who in America*; Morgan, *Can. men* (1912).]

Warre, Sir Henry James (1819-1898), soldier, was born at the Cape of Good Hope on January 12, 1819, was educated at Sandhurst, and entered the British army in 1837. In 1845-46 he was employed on the staff in Canada; and he made, with Captain Vavasour, a reconnaissance of the Oregon territory to ascertain what military action should be taken in the case of war with the United States. During the trip he made many drawings; and most of these were published by him under the title, *Sketches in North America and the Oregon territory* (London, 1848). He later served with distinction in the Crimea, in New Zealand, and in India; and was promoted to the rank of general; and was awarded in 1886 the K.C.B. He died in London, England, on April 3, 1898.

[*Who was who*, 1897-1916.]

Warren, William Robertson (1879-1927), prime minister of Newfoundland (1923-24), was born in St. John's, Newfoundland, on

October 9, 1879, and died there on December 31, 1927. He was educated in Newfoundland and in England, and was called to the bar in Newfoundland in 1901 (K.C., 1910). He was elected a member of the Newfoundland House of Assembly, and sat successively for Trinity, Port de Grave, and Fortune Bay. He became minister of justice in the Squires administration in 1919, and in 1923 succeeded Sir Richard Squires (q.v.) as prime minister. He was forced to resign, however, in 1924; and in 1926 he was appointed a judge of the Supreme Court of Newfoundland.

[*Who was who*, 1921-30: *Encyc. Can.*; *Newfoundland supp.*]

Watkin, Sir Edward William, Bart. (1819-1901), president of the Grand Trunk Railway Company (1861-63), was born in Salford, England, on September 26, 1819, the son of Absalom Watkin. In 1845 he went into railway enterprise, and in 1853 became general manager of the Manchester, Sheffield, and Lincolnshire Railway Company. In 1861 he was commissioned by the Colonial Office to visit Canada to investigate the possibility of federating the provinces of British North America; and the same year he became president of the Grand Trunk Railway Company of Canada. He retired from this position in 1863, and the rest of his life was devoted to railway work in England. He died at Rose Hill, Northenden, Cheshire, on April 13, 1901. He was created a knight bachelor in 1868, and a baronet of the United Kingdom in 1880. Among other works, he was the author of *A trip to the United States and Canada* (London, 1851) and *Canada and the States: Recollections, 1851 to 1886* (London, 1887).

[E. A. Mitchell, *Edward Watkin and the buying-out of the Hudson's Bay Company* (Can. hist. rev., 1953); *Dict. nat. biog.*, supp. II; Morgan, *Bib. can.*]

Watson, Albert Durrant (1859-1926), physician and author, was born at Dixie, Canada West, on January 8, 1859, the youngest son of William Youle Watson and Mary Aldred. He studied medicine at Victoria University, Cobourg (M.D., C.M., 1883), and at Edinburgh University; and he was made in 1883 a fellow of the Royal College of Physicians, Edinburgh. He practised medicine successfully in Toronto for many years; but he found time also for the writing of both poetry and prose, and in his later years he became interested in psychical research. He died at Toronto on May 3, 1926. Among his published works were the following: *The sovereignty of ideals* (Toronto, 1904), *The sovereignty of character* (Toronto, 1906), *The wing of the wild bird, and other poems* (Toronto, 1908), *Love and the universe* (Toronto, 1913), *Heart of the hills* (Toronto, 1917), *Three comrades of Jesus* (Toronto, 1919), *A dream of God* (Toronto, 1922), *Robert Norwood* (Toronto, 1923), and

The twentieth plane (Toronto, 1925). In 1924 there was published a collected edition of his *Poetical works* (Toronto).

[L. A. Pierce, *Albert Durrant Watson, an appraisal* (Toronto, 1923); Morgan, *Can. men* (1912).]

Watson, Sir Brook, Bart. (1735-1807), merchant and official, was born at Plymouth, England, on February 7, 1735. He went to sea, and at the age of fourteen lost one of his legs to a shark at Havana. He served as a commissary with Monckton (q.v.) at Beauséjour in 1755, and with Wolfe (q.v.) at Louisbourg in 1758; and from 1782 to 1783 he was commissary-general of the army in Canada. From 1784 to 1793 he was a member of parliament for the city of London; and he was the first agent in London of the province of New Brunswick, after its creation in 1783. He died at East Sheen, Surrey, England, on October 2, 1807. In 1803 he was created a baronet of the United Kingdom.

[J. C. Webster, *Sir Brook Watson* (reprint from the *Argosy*, Shediac, N.B., Nov., 1924); *Dict. nat. biog.*; *Cyc. Am. biog.*]

Watson, Sir David (1871-1922), soldier and journalist, was born at Quebec on February 7, 1871, the son of William Watson and Jean Grant. He was educated in the public schools of Quebec, and became a journalist. In 1901 he became managing director of the Quebec *Chronicle*. In 1900 he was gazetted a lieutenant in the 8th Royal Rifles of Quebec, and in 1911 he became its commanding officer, with the rank of lieutenant-colonel. In 1914 he was given command of the 2nd Battalion of the Canadian Expeditionary Force; and he served throughout the First World War from 1914 to 1919. In 1915 he was promoted to be brigadier-general in command of the 5th Brigade of the Canadian Corps, and in 1916 he was given command of the 4th Canadian Division, with the rank of major-general. At the end of the war he was the senior divisional commander of the Canadian Corps. He died in Quebec on February 19, 1922. In 1893 he married Mary Browning, of Quebec; and by her he had three daughters. In 1918 he was created, in recognition of his war services, a K.C.B.

[H. Charlesworth (ed.), *A cyclopaedia of Canadian biography* (Toronto, 1919); *Who's who in Canada*, 1921; *Can. ann. review*, 1914-22.]

Watson, Homer Ransford (1855-1936), landscape painter, was born in Doon, Canada West, in 1855. He studied landscape painting in England and in the United States, but his first work was done without formal tuition. He became *par excellence* the painter of pioneer life in Ontario. In 1882 he was elected a fellow of the Royal Canadian Academy of Art; and from 1918 to 1922 he was its president. He was also the first president of the Canadian Art

Club in 1907. Some of his landscapes are in Windsor Castle; others are in the National Gallery in Ottawa; and many are in private collections. He died at Doon, Ontario, where he had lived virtually the whole of his life, on May 30, 1936.

[F. E. Page, *Homer Watson* (Kitchener, Ont., 1939); Muriel Miller, *Homer Watson* (Toronto, 1938); Morgan, *Can. men* (1912); N. MacTavish, *The fine arts in Canada* (Toronto, 1925); A. H. Robson, *Canadian landscape painters* (Toronto, 1932).]

Watson, John (1847-1939), philosopher, was born at Glasgow, Scotland, on February 25, 1847. He was educated at Glasgow University (M.A., 1872; LL.D., 1880), and in 1872 was appointed professor of logic, metaphysics, and ethics in Queen's University, Kingston, Ontario. Later he became professor of moral philosophy; and in 1901 he was appointed also vice-principal of the university. He retired on pension, with the status of professor emeritus, in 1924; and he died at Kingston, Ontario, on January 27, 1939. He was a charter member of the Royal Society of Canada; and he received the honorary degree of LL.D. from the University of Toronto, that of Litt. D. from the University of Michigan, and that of D.D. from Knox College, Toronto. He was one of the outstanding philosophers of his day; and he was the author of a number of books of high merit: *Kant and his English critics* (Glasgow, 1881), *Schelling's transcendental idealism* (Chicago, 1882), *The philosophy of Kant* (Glasgow, 1888), *Comte, Mill, and Spencer* (Glasgow, 1888), *Hedonistic theories from Aristippus to Spencer* (Glasgow, 1895), *Christianity and idealism* (New York, 1897), *An outline of philosophy* (New York, 1898), *The philosophical basis of religion* (Glasgow, 1907), *The philosophy of Kant explained* (Glasgow, 1908), *The interpretation of religious experience* (2 vols., Glasgow, 1912), and *The state in peace and war* (Glasgow, 1919).

[*Trans. Roy. Soc. Can.*, 1939; *Can. who's who*, 1936-37; Morgan, *Can. men* (1912); R. C. Wallace (ed.), *Some great men of Queen's* (Toronto, 1941).]

Watson, Robert (1882-1948), author, was born at Glasgow, Scotland, in 1882, and died at Laguna Beach, California, on January 15, 1948. He came to Canada in 1908, and was in business in Vancouver until 1932, when he went to live in California. He was the author of the following works of fiction: *My brave and gallant gentleman* (Toronto, 1918), *The girl of O.K. Valley* (Toronto, 1919), *Stronger than his sea* (Toronto, 1920), *The spoilers of the valley* (New York, 1921), *Gordon of the lost lagoon* (Toronto, 1924), *Me and Peter* (Toronto, 1926), *High hazard* (Montreal, 1929), *A boy of the great north-west* (Ottawa, 1930), and *When Christmas came to Fort Garry* (Toronto, 1935). He also wrote three volumes of verse: *The mad* minstrel (Toronto, 1923), *Canada's fur-bearers* (Ottawa, 1925), and *Dreams of Fort Garry* (Winnipeg, 1931).

[*Can. who's who*, 1938-39; *Who's who among North American authors.*]

Watson, Samuel James (1837-1881), author, was born in Armagh, Ireland, in 1837, and was educated at the Belfast Academy. He came to Canada in 1857, and became a newspaper reporter. In 1871 he was appointed librarian of the Legislative Library of Ontario. He died at Toronto on October 31, 1881. He was the author of a *Constitutional history of Canada*, vol. i (all published, Toronto, 1874), *The powers of Canadian parliaments* (Toronto, 1879), an historical romance entitled *The peace-killer; or, the massacre of Lachine* (published in the *Canadian Illustrated News*, Toronto, 1870), and a volume of poetry entitled *The legend of the roses; and Ravlan, a drama* (Toronto, 1876).

[*Dom. ann. reg.*, 1880-81; *Bull. rech. hist.*, 1918; A. MacMurchy, *Handbook of Canadian literature* (Toronto, 1906).]

Waudby, John (d. 1861), journalist, was born in England, and came to Canada prior to 1840. He became editor, and later proprietor, of the Kingston *Herald*; and in 1841 he founded, under the patronage of Lord Sydenham (q.v.), the *Monthly Review*. Later, he was appointed clerk of the peace for the counties of Frontenac, Lennox, and Addington. He died at Kingston, Canada West, on August 28, 1861.

[Morgan, *Bib. can.*]

Waugh, William Templeton (1884-1932), historian, was born at Manchester, England, on March 18, 1884. He was educated at Manchester University (B.A., 1903; B.D., 1906), and he became assistant lecturer in history at Manchester University in 1910, and reader in history in 1919. In 1922 he was appointed associate professor of history in McGill University, Montreal, and in 1925 professor of history and chairman of the department. He died at Montreal on October 17, 1932. He was the author of *The monarchy and the people* (London, 1913), *Germany* (London, 1915), *James Wolfe, man and soldier* (Montreal, 1928), and *A history of Europe from 1378 to 1494* (London, 1932).

[*Who was who*, 1929-40; *Who's who in Canada*, 1930-31; A. E. Prince, *Professor W. T. Waugh* (Can. hist. rev., 1932).]

Way, Charles Jones (1835-1919), painter, was born in Dartmouth, England, in 1835. He studied art in the South Kensington Art School, and came to Canada in 1858. He settled in Montreal; and he was elected president of the old Society of Canadian Artists in 1870. He became a charter member of the Royal Canadian Academy in 1880; but he spent the later years of his life in Switzerland. Here he died in 1919.

[N. MacTavish, *The fine arts in Canada* (Toronto, 1925); Morgan, *Can. men* (1912).]

Weatherbe Sir Robert Linton (1836-1915), chief justice of Nova Scotia (1905-07), was born at Bedeque, Prince Edward Island, on April 7, 1836, the son of Jonathan Weatherbe and Mary Baker. He was educated at Prince of Wales College, Charlottetown, and at Acadia University (B.A., 1858; M.A., 1861; D.C.L., 1883); and was called to the bar of Nova Scotia in 1863 (Q.C., 1876). From 1867 to 1878 he was law clerk of the Legislative Assembly of Nova Scotia; and in 1877 he represented the Dominion as counsel before the Halifax Fisheries Commission. In 1878 he was appointed a judge of the Supreme Court of Nova Scotia; and in 1905 he became chief justice of Nova Scotia. He retired from the bench in 1907; and he died at Halifax on April 27, 1915. He was created a knight bachelor in 1906.

[*Can. who was who*, vol. 1; Morgan, *Can. men* (1912).]

Weaver, Emily Poynton (1865-1943), novelist and historian, was born near Manchester, England, in 1865. She came to Canada with her parents in 1880; and for most of her life she lived in Toronto, Ontario. She died in Toronto on March 11, 1943. She was the author of *My Lady Nell* (Boston, 1889), *The rabbi's sons* (Boston, 1891), *Soldiers of liberty* (Toronto, 1892), *Prince Rupert's namesake* (Boston, 1893), *The rain-proof invention* (Boston, 1896), *A Canadian history for boys and girls* (Toronto, 1905), *Old Quebec* (Toronto, 1907), *The trouble man* (Toronto, 1911), *The story of the counties of Ontario* (Toronto, 1913), *Canada and the British immigrant* (London, 1914), *The only girl* (Toronto, 1925), and *The book of Canada* (Garden City, N.Y., 1928).

[Morgan, *Can. men and women* (1912); A. MacMurchy, *Handbook of Canadian literature* (Toronto, 1906).]

Webster, John Clarence (1863-1950), physician and historian, was born at Shediac, New Brunswick, on October 21, 1863, and died there on March 16, 1950. He was educated at Mount Allison University (B.A., 1882) and Edinburgh University (M.B., C.M., 1888; M.D., 1891); and he became an outstanding authority on obstetrics and gynaecology. He held teaching positions at Edinburgh University, McGill University, and the Rush Medical College in Chicago. From 1899 to 1920 he was the chief obstetrician and gynaecologist at the Chicago Presbyterian Hospital. On his retirement he returned to Shediac, and devoted himself to the study of the early history of the Maritime provinces. He was the author of *The forts of Chignecto* (Shediac, N.B., 1930), *Acadia at the end of the seventeenth century* (Saint John, N.B., 1934), *Thomas Pichon, "the spy of Beauséjour"* (Sackville, N.B., 1937), and a large number of pamphlets and papers. He was elected a fellow of the Royal Society of Canada in 1924; he was made a C.M.G. in 1935; and five universities conferred on him honorary degrees. He left his rich collection of Canadiana to the New Brunswick Museum.

[J. C. Webster, *Those crowded years* (Shediac, N.B., 1944); *Proc. Roy. Soc. Can.*, 1950; *Can. who's who*, 1948; *Encyc. Can.*]

Webster, Lorne Campbell (1871-1941), senator of Canada, was born in Quebec City on September 30, 1871. He was educated at the Quebec High School and Montmagny College, and entered the coal business in Quebec city. He extended his business to include Montreal and other distributing centres in Canada, and became a leading Canadian financier. In 1920 he was summoned to the Senate of Canada for the Stadacona division; and he remained an influential figure in the Senate until his death at Montreal, Quebec, on September 27, 1941.

[A. Phillips, *The unknown man who bought the* Globe and Mail (Maclean's magazine, April 30, 1955); *Can. parl. comp.*; *Can. who's who*, 1936-37; Morgan, *Can. men* (1912).]

Webster, Thomas (1809-1901), clergyman and author, was born at Glen Dhu, Loch Wicklow, Ireland, on October 29, 1809. He emigrated to Canada, and in 1838 became a minister of the Methodist Episcopal Church of Canada. He died at Newbury, Ontario, on May 2, 1901. He was the author of *The union considered, and the Methodist Episcopal Church in Canada defended* (Belleville, C.W., 1842; 2nd ed., enlarged, Hamilton, C.W., 1858), *History of the Methodist Episcopal Church in Canada* (Hamilton, Ont., 1870), *An essay on Methodist church polity* (Hamilton, Ont., 1871), and *The life of the Rev. James Richardson* (Toronto, 1876).

[G. H. Cornish, *A cyclopaedia of Methodism in Canada* (2 vols., Toronto, 1881-1903).]

Webster, William (1865-1934), anaesthetist and author, was born in Manchester, England, in 1865, and died at Winnipeg, Manitoba, on October 23, 1934. He was educated at the University of Manitoba (M.D., C.M.), and became professor of anaesthesiology in the University of Manitoba medical school and chief anaesthetist at the Winnipeg General Hospital. During the First World War he served as a colonel in the Canadian Army Medical Corps, and was awarded the D.S.O. He was the author of *The science and art of anesthesia* (St. Louis, 1924).

[*Who's who among North American authors*, vol. IV (1929-30); *Canadian Medical Association Journal*, Dec., 1934.]

Wedderburn, Alexander (1796?-1843), author, was born in Aberdeen, Scotland, about 1796, and for many years was British emigration officer in New Brunswick, as well as secretary of the Agricultural and Emigration Society of Saint John. He died at Saint John, New Brunswick, about June 19, 1843. He was the author of *Statistical and practical observations relative to the province of New Brunswick* (Saint John, N.B., 1836). He was not, as is stated in H.J. Morgan, *Bibliotheca canadensis* (Ottawa, 1867), and in W. G. MacFarlane, *New Brunswick bibliography* (Saint John, N.B., 1895), the author of *Notitia of New Brunswick* (Saint John, N.B., 1838). This was written by Peter Fisher (q.v.).

[Morgan, *Bib. can.*; W. G. MacFarlane, *New Brunswick bibliography* (Saint John, N.B., 1895).]

Weekes, William (d. 1806), politician, was a native of Ireland. He emigrated to the United States, and is said to have studied law in the law office of Aaron Burr. In 1798 he came to Upper Canada, and was admitted to the provincial bar. Almost immediately he plunged into politics, and in 1800 he was the chief agent in securing the election of Mr. Justice Allcock (q.v.) to the Legislative Assembly. In 1804 he was himself elected to represent Durham, Simcoe and East York in the Legislative Assembly; and he took a leading part in the House in attacking the administration of the province. He was, in fact, a pioneer of the Reform Party in Upper Canada. In the autumn of 1806 he came into conflict with William Dickson (q.v.), while arguing a case before Mr. Justice Thorpe (q.v.) at the assizes in Niagara; and in the duel which ensued he fell, mortally wounded, on October 10, 1806.

[W. R. Riddell, *The duel in early Upper Canada* (Journal of the American institute of criminal law and criminology, July, 1915); W. S. Wallace, *The family compact* (Toronto, 1915).]

Weir, Arthur (1864-1902), poet, was born in Montreal, Quebec, on June 17, 1864. He was educated at McGill University (B.A. Sc., 1886), and became a journalist. He was on the editorial staff of the Montreal *Star*, and later on that of the *Journal of Commerce*. He died in 1902. He was the author of three volumes of verse, *Fleur-de-lys and other poems* (Montreal, 1887), *The romance of Sir Richard: Sonnets, and other poems* (Montreal, 1890), and *The snow-flake, and other poems* (Montreal, 1897), as well as a prose volume, *A Canuck down south* (Montreal, 1898).

[Morgan, *Can. men* (1898); *Bull. rech. hist.*, 1933; C. C. James, *A bibliography of Canadian poetry* (Toronto, 1899).]

Weir, Frank (b. 1860), lawyer and author, was born in Montreal, Canada East, on December 9, 1860, the son of William Weir (q.v.). He was educated at McGill University (B.C.L., 1882), and was called to the bar in the province of Quebec. He practised law in Montreal; and while still a young man he published *The law and practice of banking corporations* (Montreal, 1888). The date of his death has not been ascertained.

[Private information.]

Weir, George Moir (1885-1949), educationist, was born at Miami, Manitoba, on May 10, 1885, and died at Vancouver, British Columbia, on December 4, 1949. He was educated at McGill University (B.A., 1911), the University of Saskatchewan (M.A., 1914), the University of Chicago, and Queen's University (D. Paed., 1918). After teaching school in Saskatchewan, he became inspector of schools in the province. Later, he was appointed head of the department of education in the University of British Columbia. He entered provincial politics in 1933, when he was elected to represent Vancouver-Point Grey in the legislature; and he served as provincial secretary and minister of education in the Pattullo government from 1933 to 1941. Re-elected in 1945, he was minister of education in the Johnson government until ill-health forced him to retire in 1947. He was the author of *A survey of nursing education in Canada* (Toronto, 1932) and of *The separate school question in Canada* (Toronto, 1934).

[*Can. who's who*, 1948; *Encyc. Can.*]

Weir, Logan (pseud.). See **Perry, James Black.**

Weir, Robert (1809?-1843), journalist, was born about 1809; and in 1833 he purchased the Montreal *Herald*, of which he became the editor. He was one of the most vigorous upholders of the loyalist cause during the rebellion of 1837. He died at Montreal, on May 16, 1843.

[Morgan, *Bib. can.*]

Weir, Robert (1882-1939), minister of agriculture for Canada (1930-35), was born at Wingham, Ontario, on December 5, 1882. He was educated at the University of Toronto (B.A., 1911), and became a school-teacher and later inspector of schools in Saskatchewan. From 1916 to 1918 he served in the Canadian Expeditionary Force, was promoted to the rank of major in the 78th Battalion, and was wounded at Passchendaele. In 1922 he became a farmer, specializing in horses, cattle, and hogs, near Weldon, Saskatchewan, and later at Pincher Creek, Alberta. In 1930, he was elected to represent Melfort in the Canadian House of Commons; and he was minister of agriculture in the Bennett government from 1930 to 1935. He died near Weldon, Saskatchewan, on March 7, 1939.

[*Can. who's who*, 1936-37; *Can. parl. comp.*]

Weir, Robert Stanley (1856-1926), jurist and author, was born at Hamilton, Ontario, on November 15, 1856, the son of William Park

Weir and Helen Smith. He was educated at McGill University (B.C.L., 1880; D.C.L., 1897), and was called to the Quebec bar in 1881. He practised law in Montreal; in 1899 he was appointed one of the two joint recorders of Montreal; and in 1926 he was named a judge of the Exchequer Court of Canada. Besides a number of legal works, he wrote some poetry; and his version of the song *O Canada* is the basis of that commonly used. In 1923 he was elected a fellow of the Royal Society of Canada. He died at his summer home, on Lake Memphramagog, Quebec, on August 20, 1926. His legal and historical publications were *An insolvency manual* (Montreal, 1890), *Administration of the old régime in Canada* (Montreal, 1897), *The Education Act of the province of Quebec* (Montreal, 1899), *The civil code of Lower Canada and the Bills of Exchange Act* (Montreal, 1899), and *Municipal institutions in the province of Quebec* (Toronto, 1907); and he published two volumes of poetry, *After Ypres, and other verses* (Toronto, 1917) and *Poems, early and late* (Toronto, 1923).

[P. G. Roy, *Les juges de la province de Québec* (Quebec, 1933); *Proc. Roy. Soc. Can.*, 1927; Morgan, *Can. men* (1912); *Bull. rech. hist.*, 1933.]

Weir, William (1823-1905), banker, was born at Greenden, near Brechin, Scotland, on October 28, 1823. He came to Canada in 1842, and became an exchange broker in Montreal. From 1856 to 1859 he lived in Toronto; and during this period he was the publisher of the *Canadian Merchants' Magazine*. In 1882 he became president of La Banque Ville Marie. He died in Westmount, Quebec, on March 25, 1905. He was the author of *Sixty years in Canada* (Montreal, 1903).

[Morgan, *Can. men* (1912); Rose, *Cyc. Can. biog.* (1888).]

Weir, William Alexander (1858-1929), jurist, was born in Montreal on October 15, 1858, the younger brother of Robert Stanley Weir (q.v.). He was educated at McGill University, Montreal (B.C.L., 1881), and he was called to the bar of Quebec in 1881 (Q.C., 1899). He represented Argenteuil in the Legislative Assembly of Quebec from 1897 to 1910; and he was a member without portfolio of the Parent and Gouin administrations (1903-05), speaker of the Assembly (1905-06), minister of public works (1906-07) and provincial treasurer (1907-10). In 1910 he was appointed a puisne judge of the Supreme Court of Quebec. He died at London, England, on October 21, 1929. He was the author of legal treatises on *The municipal code of the province of Quebec* (Montreal, 1889) and *The civil code of the province of Quebec* (Montreal, 1890).

[P. G. Roy, *Les juges de la province de Québec* (Quebec, 1933); *Bull. rech. hist.*, 1933; Morgan, *Can. men* (1912); *Can. parl. comp.*]

Welch, Edward Ashurst (1860-1932), provost of Trinity University (1895-99), was born at Orpington, Kent, England, on August 22, 1860. He was educated at Cambridge University (B.A., 1882; M.A., 1885); and in 1885 he was ordained a priest of the Church of England. In 1895 he was appointed provost of the University of Trinity College, Toronto; and he held this post until his appointment as rector of St. James Cathedral, Toronto, in 1899. In 1909, on becoming vicar of Wakefield, England, he left Canada; and he died in London, England, on August 6, 1932.

[F. C. Macdonald, *Edward Ashurst Welch* (Cambridge, 1936); Morgan, *Can. men* (1912).]

Weldon, Richard Chapman (1849-1925), lawyer and educationist, was born in Sussex, New Brunswick, on January 19, 1849. He was educated at Mount Allison University (B.A., 1866; M.A., 1870; D.C.L., 1893) and at Yale University (Ph.D., 1872). From 1875 to 1883 he was professor of mathematics at Mount Allison University; and in 1884 he was called to the bar of Nova Scotia (Q.C., 1890). In 1884 he was appointed dean of the law faculty of Dalhousie University; and he held this post for over thirty years. From 1887 to 1896 he represented the constituency of Albert, New Brunswick, in the Dominion parliament. He died at Dartmouth, Nova Scotia, on November 26, 1925.

[Morgan, *Can. men* (1912); *Can. parl. comp.*]

Weller, John Laing (1862-1932), civil engineer, was born at Cobourg, Canada West, on February 13, 1862. He was educated at the Royal Military College, Kingston; and entered the government service in the department of railways and canals. He was first engaged in the construction of the Trent and Murray canals, then on the enlargement of the Ontario-St. Lawrence canals, and finally as superintending engineer of the Welland Canal. In 1912, when the government decided to build the new Welland Ship Canal, he was placed in charge of the surveys, design, and construction of the canal, and continued in this position until the suspension of the work in 1917. In 1919 he was appointed consulting engineer for the Welland Canal development; and he died at Hamilton, Ontario, on May 24, 1932, only three months before the construction of the canal was completed. Port Weller, at the mouth of the canal, was named after him.

[*Engineering journal*, June, 1932; *Can. who was who*, vol. 1.]

Wells, George Anderson (1877-1964), bishop, was born in Newfoundland, December 18, 1877. At the age of twelve he went to sea on his father's schooner and he became a mate at seventeen. He saw service in the South African War as a trooper, in the First World War as a chaplain, and in the Second World War as chaplain of the Fleet.

He was educated at St. John's College, Winnipeg, ordained deacon in 1910, and served in various western parishes until he became warden at St. John's College in 1921. He retired in 1934 to become Bishop of the Cariboo diocese until returning to military service in 1939. From 1946 until 1951 he was assistant bishop to the Bishop of Toronto. He was a companion of the Order of St. Michael and St. George. He died at Toronto, Ontario, April 10, 1964.

[*Can. who's who*, 1961-63; Metropolitan Toronto Library Board, *Biographical scrapbooks*, vol. 22.]

Wells, James Edward (1836-1898), educationist and journalist, was born at Harvey, New Brunswick, on May 3, 1836. He was educated at Acadia University (B.A., 1860; M.A., 1863); and from 1868 to 1880 was principal of the Woodstock Collegiate Institute. He then became a journalist, and from 1889 to 1898 was editor of the *Canadian Baptist*. In 1897 McMaster University conferred on him the honorary degree of LL.D. He died at Toronto, Ontario, on September 18, 1898. He was the author of *Life and labors of Robert Alex. Fyfe* (Toronto, n.d.).

[*Records of the graduates of Acadia University* (Wolfville, N.S., 1926).]

Wells, Joseph (1773?-1853), executive councillor of Upper Canada, was a veteran of the Peninsular War who was born about 1773. He entered the British army in 1798, and by 1814 had attained the rank of lieutenant-colonel. In 1815 he came to Canada as an inspecting field officer, and was soon afterwards placed on half-pay. He settled at Davenport, near York (Toronto); and in 1820 he was appointed a member of the Legislative Council of Upper Canada, and in 1829 a member of the Executive Council. In 1836 he resigned from the Executive Council with his colleagues, as a protest against the policy of Sir F. Bond Head (q.v.). He died at Davenport, near Toronto, on February 4, 1853. In 1813 he married Harriet, daughter of George King; and by her he had eight sons and two daughters. From 1827 to 1839 he was bursar of King's College (University of Toronto).

[Morgan, *Cel. Can.*; E. M. Chadwick, *Ontarian families* (2 vols., Toronto, 1894-98).]

Wells, Rupert Mearse (1835-1902), speaker of the Legislative Assembly of Ontario (1873-80), was born near Prescott, Upper Canada, on November 28, 1835, the son of Sheriff Wells, of Prescott and Russell. He was educated at the University of Toronto (B.A., 1854), and was called to the bar in 1857

(Q.C., 1876). From 1872 to 1882 he represented South Bruce in the Legislative Assembly of Ontario; and from 1873 to 1880 he was the speaker of the Assembly. In 1882 he was elected to represent East Bruce in the Canadian House of Commons; but was defeated in 1887, and thereupon retired from politics. He practised law in Toronto, first as a partner of the Hon. Edward Blake (q.v.), and later as the solicitor in Toronto for the Canadian Pacific Railway; and he died on May 11, 1902. He was not married.

[Morgan, *Can. men* (1898); *Can. parl. comp.*; C. Clarke, *Sixty years in Upper Canada* (Toronto, 1908).]

Wells, William Benjamin (1809-1881), jurist and author, was born in Augusta, Upper Canada, on October 3, 1809, the son of Loyalist parents. He was educated at the Augusta grammar school, and in 1833 was called to the bar of Upper Canada. In 1834 he established at Prescott the *Vanguard*, a Reform newspaper; and from 1834 to 1837 he represented Grenville in the Legislative Assembly of Upper Canada. In 1836 he went to England, with Robert Baldwin (q.v.) and Dr. Charles Duncombe (q.v.), to make representations to the Colonial Office regarding the administration of Sir F. Bond Head (q.v.). While in England he published *Canadiana: containing sketches of Upper Canada and the crisis in its political affairs* (London, 1837). In 1837 he was expelled from the Assembly, and fled to the United States; but he returned under the amnesty, and in 1850 he was appointed judge of the united county of Kent and Lambton, and later of the county of Kent. He retired from the bench in 1878, and he died at Toronto on April 8, 1881.

[*Dom. ann. reg.*, 1880-81; Morgan, *Bib. can.*; W. Kingsford, *Early bibliography of Upper Canada* (Toronto, 1892).]

Wentworth, Sir John, Bart. (1737-1820), lieutenant-governor of Nova Scotia (1792-1808), was born in 1737, the son of Mark Hunking Wentworth, a merchant of Portsmouth, New Hampshire. He was educated at Harvard College (B.A., 1755; M.A., 1758); and in 1766 he was appointed governor of New Hampshire. He took refuge in Boston, Massachusetts, in 1775; in 1776 he went to Halifax, Nova Scotia, and in 1778 to England. He was appointed surveyor-general of the king's woods in North America in 1783; and in 1792 he became lieutenant-governor of Nova Scotia. Though personally popular, he was accused of filling the Council with his own relatives; and he had some difficulties with the House of Assembly. He was succeeded by Sir George Prevost in 1808; and he died at Halifax on April 8, 1820. In 1795 he was created a baronet of the United Kingdom; and he received the degree of D.C.L. from Oxford University (1766), from Dartmouth College

(1773), and from the University of Aberdeen (1773).

[L. S. Mayo, *John Wentworth* (Cambridge, Massachusetts, 1921); Sir A. Archibald, *Life of Sir John Wentworth* (Coll. Nova Scotia Hist. Soc., 1922); *Dict. nat. biog.*; D. Campbell, *Nova Scotia* (Montreal, 1873); B. Murdoch, *History of Nova Scotia* (3 vols., Halifax, N.S., 1867).]

Wentzel, Willard Ferdinand (d. 1832), fur-trader, was probably the son of Adam Wentzel, a Norwegian merchant in Montreal, and Endimia Grout, who were married in Montreal in 1779. He entered the service of the North West Company in 1799; and for many years he was a clerk in the Athabaska country. He was taken over as a clerk by the Hudson's Bay Company at the time of the union of 1821; but he retired to Canada in 1825. He re-entered the Hudson's Bay Company's service in 1827, and for two years was a clerk at Mingan, on the lower St. Lawrence, but in 1829 he retired a second time, and he fell a victim to the cholera epidemic of 1832.

[W. S. Wallace (ed.), *Documents relating to the North West Company* (Toronto: The Champlain Society, 1934).]

Wesbrook, Frank Fairchild (1868-1918), president of the University of British Columbia (1913-18), was born in Brant county, Ontario, on July 12, 1868, the son of H. S. Wesbrook, later mayor of Winnipeg, Manitoba, and Helen Marr Fairchild. He was educated at the University of Manitoba (B.A., 1887; M.D., C.M., 1890), and pursued postgraduate studies in pathology and bacteriology at McGill University, Cambridge University, King's College, London, and the Hygienic and Pathological Institute, Marburg, Germany. In 1896 he was appointed professor of pathology and bacteriology at the University of Minnesota, and in 1906 he became dean of the College of Medicine in this university. In 1913 he was offered and accepted the post of president of the new University of British Columbia, and this position he held until his death on October 20, 1918. In 1896 he married Annie, daughter of Sir Thomas Taylor (q.v.). In 1918 he was elected a fellow of the Royal Society of Canada.

[*Can. who was who*, vol. 1; *Proc. Roy. Soc. Can.*, 1919; Morgan, *Can. men* (1912).]

West, John (1775?-1845), missionary, was born in Farnham, Sussex, England, about 1775. He was ordained a priest of the Church of England; and in 1820 he was appointed chaplain to the Hudson's Bay Company, and sent out to the Red River settlement in northwest America. He remained at Red River until 1823; he then was employed in making a tour of inspection of the Indian settlements in Upper Canada and the Maritime provinces; and after this task was accomplished, he returned to England. In 1834 the living of Farnham was conferred on him; and he died here at the end of 1845. He was the author of *The substance of a journal during a residence at the Red River colony* (London, 1824), a second edition of which was published, with the addition of *A journal of a mission to the Indians of New Brunswick and Nova Scotia, and the Mohawks on the Ouse or Grand River, Upper Canada* (London, 1827).

[B. Heeney, *John West and his Red River mission* (Toronto, 1920); Morgan, *Bib. can.*]

Weston, Thomas Chesmer (1832-1911), geologist, was born in Birmingham, England, in October, 1832. He came to Canada in 1859, as an employee of the Canadian Geological Survey; and he continued in the service of the Survey until his retirement on pension in 1894. He died at Quebec, Que., on July 31, 1911. He was the author of an autobiography entitled *Reminiscences among the rocks* (Toronto, 1899).

[Private information.]

Weston, William Percy (1879-1967), artist, was born in London, England, November 30, 1879. He was educated in London at the Teacher Training College and at Putney Art School. He taught in London (1900-09) before emigrating to Vancouver. He was art supervisor in the Vancouver schools from 1910 to 1914 and taught in the Provincial Normal School from 1914 to 1946. He wrote the *Teacher's Manual of Drawing* (1934) and is represented in the National Gallery; Hart House, Toronto; and the Vancouver Art Gallery. He was a member of the Canadian Group of Painters, the British Columbia Society of Fine Arts, and the Western Group of Painters. He was an associate of the Royal Canadian Academy of Art. He died at Vancouver, British Columbia, December 21, 1967.

[*Can. who's who*, 1955-57.]

Wetherald, Agnes Ethelwyn (1857-1940), poet, was born at Rockwood, Canada West, on April 26, 1857; and was educated at the Friends' Boarding School, Union Springs, New York, and at Pickering College, Pickering, Ontario. She was for a time a journalist on the staff of the Toronto *Globe*; but for most of her life she was a free-lance writer, contributing verse to various periodicals. She died at Fenwick, Ontario, on March 9, 1940. She was the author of five volumes of verse: *The house of the trees, and other poems* (Boston, 1896), *Tangled in stars* (Boston, 1902), *The radiant road* (Boston, 1904), *The last robin* (Boston, 1907), and *Tree-top mornings* (Boston, 1921); and a complete edition of her *Lyrics and sonnets* (Toronto, 1931) was published, with an introduction by J. W. Garvin (q.v.). She was also joint author, with G. Mercer Adam (q.v.), of *An Algonquin maiden* (Montreal, 1887).

[*Can. who's who*, 1936-37; Morgan, *Can.*

men and women (1912); A. MacMurchy, *Handbook of Canadian literature* (Toronto, 1906); *Saturday night*, April 13, 1940.]

Wetherall, Sir George Augustus (1788-1868), soldier, was born at Penton, Hampshire, England, in 1788, the son of General Sir Frederick Wetherall. He entered the British army in 1803; and he served in Canada, with the rank of colonel, during the Rebellion of 1837. He was in command of the column that defeated the rebels in Lower Canada at St. Charles; and for his services was gazetted a C.B. From 1843 to 1850 he was deputy adjutant-general in Canada. He was knighted in 1856, created a lieutenant-general in 1857, and a G.C.B. in 1865. He died at Sandhurst, England, on April 8, 1868.

[*Dict. nat. biog.*; *Cyc. Am. biog.*]

Wetherell, James Elgin (1851-1940), educationist and author, was born at Port Dalhousie, Canada West, on September 20, 1851. He was educated at the University of Toronto (B.A., 1877), and became a secondary-school teacher. In 1906 he was appointed an inspector of high schools for Ontario, and in 1917 general editor of text-books in the department of education. He retired from this position in 1924; and he died at Toronto, Ontario, on October 20, 1940. He was the author of *Over the sea* (Strathroy, Ont., 1892), *Fields of fame in England and Scotland* (Toronto, 1915), *Aesop in verse* (Toronto, 1926), *Strange corners of the world* (New York, 1927), *The land of Troy and Tarsus* (London, 1931), *Tales of ancient Rome* (Toronto, 1932), and *Three centuries of Canadian story* (Toronto, 1937); and he was the editor of *Later Canadian poems* (Toronto, 1893), *Later American poets* (Toronto, 1896), and *Poems of the love of country* (Toronto, 1905).

[Toronto *Globe and Mail*, Oct. 21, 1940; Morgan, *Can. men* (1912).]

Wetherell, Mrs. Margaret Hubner, *née* **Smith** (d. 1933), local historian, was the anonymous author of the *Jubilee history of Thorold township and town from the time of the red man to the present* (Thorold, Ont., 1898). This was re-issued in 1933, under the author's name, with a supplement by John H. Thompson, covering the period from 1897 to 1932.

[*Can. hist. rev.*, 1935.]

Wetmore, Andrew Rainsford (1820-1892), prime minister of New Brunswick (1867-70), was born in Fredericton, New Brunswick, on August 16, 1820, the son of George Ludlow Wetmore. He was called to the bar of Nova Scotia in 1843 (Q.C., 1863). In 1865 he was elected to represent Saint John in the House of Assembly of New Brunswick as an anti-Confederation candidate; but he almost immediately seceded from the ranks of the opponents of Confederation, and in 1866 he was elected for Saint John as a confederationist. In 1867 he was entrusted with the formation of the first government of New Brunswick under Confederation, and he remained prime minister until 1870. He was then appointed a judge of the Supreme Court of New Brunswick; and he sat on the bench until his death, at Fredericton, on March 7, 1892. He married Louisa, daughter of Thomas Lansdowne, sheriff of Kent county, Nova Scotia.

[*Can. parl. comp.*; *The premiers of New Brunswick since Confederation* (Can. mag., 1897); J. Hannay, *Wilmot and Tilley* (Toronto, 1907).]

Wetmore, Edward Ludlow (1841-1922), chief justice of Saskatchewan (1907-22), was born at Fredericton, New Brunswick, on March 24, 1841, the son of Charles P. Wetmore and Sarah Ketchum. He was educated at the University of New Brunswick (B.A., 1859; LL.D., 1908), and was called to the bar of New Brunswick in 1864 (Q.C., 1881). From 1874 to 1876 he was mayor of Fredericton; and from 1883 to 1886 he represented York in the provincial House of Assembly. In 1887 he was appointed a judge of the Supreme Court of the North West Territories; and in 1907 he became chief justice of Saskatchewan. He retired from the bench in 1912, and he died at Victoria, British Columbia, on January 19, 1922. In 1872 he married Eliza, daughter of Charles Dickson. In 1907 he was elected chancellor of the University of Saskatchewan.

[*Can. parl. comp.*; Morgan, *Can. men* (1912); Le Jeune, *Dict. gén.*]

Wetmore, Frank Ellsworth Waring (1910-1963), chemist and university administrator, was born in Saint John, New Brunswick, March 19, 1910. He was educated at the University of New Brunswick (B.Sc., 1933), and at the University of Toronto (M.A., 1934; Ph.D., 1937). He lectured at the University of Toronto from 1937. In 1957 he became assistant dean of the faculty of arts and science. When New College was opened in 1962 he became its first principal. His research and teaching were in the field of electrochemistry. He was elected a fellow of the Royal Society of Canada in 1955 and was a member of the Comité International de Thermodynamique et de Cinétique Electrochimiques. He was frequently consulted by both government and industry and was long associated with the electro-chemical laboratories of the Defence Research Board. He wrote, with D. J. LeRoy, *Principles of phase equilibria* (1951). He died at Toronto, Ontario, January 20, 1963.

[*Can. who's who* 1955-57; *Proc. Roy Soc. Can.*, 1963.]

Wetmore, Thomas (1766?-1828), attorney-general of New Brunswick (1809-28), was born in New York about 1766, the son of Timothy Wetmore, one of the first graduates of King's College, New York. He accompanied his parents to New Brunswick in 1783, and studied law in Saint John. He was called to the bar of New Brunswick in 1788, and entered into partnership with his father. In 1809 he was elected to represent Saint John in the Legislative Assembly of New Brunswick, and in the same year he was appointed attorney-general of the province. This office he held until his death at Kingswood, York county, New Brunswick, on March 22, 1828.

[J. W. Lawrence, *The judges of New Brunswick* (Saint John, N.B., 1907); B. Murdoch, *History of Nova Scotia* (3 vols., Halifax, N.S., 1865-67).]

Whale, Robert R. (1805-1887), painter, was born at Alternun, Cornwall, England, on March 13, 1805. He studied art at the National Gallery, in London, and became a successful painter of portraits and landscapes. In 1848 he was elected an A.R.A. He came to Canada, and settled at Brantford, Ontario, in 1864; and here he pursued the occupation of portrait-painter and landscape-painter until his death on July 8, 1887. His son, John Claude Whale (1853-1905), was also a successful painter.

[N. MacTavish, *The fine arts in Canada* (Toronto, 1925); A. H. Robson, *Canadian landscape painters* (Toronto, 1938).]

Wheeler, Arthur Oliver (1860-1945), land-surveyor and mountaineer, was born in Kilkenny, Ireland, on May 1, 1860, and died at Banff, Alberta, on March 20, 1945. He came to Canada in 1876, and in 1881 qualified as a land-surveyor. He served in the North West Rebellion in 1885, and was wounded at Batoche. He devoted many years to making topographical surveys of the Rocky Mountains; and from 1913 to 1925 he was one of the commissioners on the Alberta-British Columbia boundary. He founded the Alpine Club of Canada in 1906, and was its first president; and for many years he was the editor of the *Canadian Alpine Journal*. He was the author of *The Selkirk range* (2 vols., Ottawa, 1905) and joint author, with Elizabeth Parker, of *The Selkirk mountains* (Winnipeg, 1912).

[*Can. alpine journal*, 1945; *Encyc. Can.*]

Whelan, Edward (1824-1867), author, was born in county Mayo, Ireland, in 1824. At an early age, he emigrated to Nova Scotia, and entered the employ of Joseph Howe (q.v.) as a printer's devil. In 1842 he went to Prince Edward Island, and he became editor and proprietor of the Charlottetown *Examiner*. In 1858 he was appointed a member of the Legislative Council of the island; and he died at Charlottetown on December 10, 1867. He published *The union of the British provinces* (Charlottetown, 1865; new ed., Gardenvale,

1927), an account of the Charlottetown and Quebec conferences.

[P. McCourt, *Biographical sketch of the Hon. Edward Whelan* (Charlottetown, 1880); D. C. Harvey, *The centenary of Edward Whelan* (Charlottetown, 1926); E. J. Mullaly, *Edward Whelan* (Canadian Catholic Historical Association report, 1938-39); Morgan, *Bib. can.*; N. F. Davin, *The Irishman in Canada* (Toronto, 1877).]

Whidden, David Graham (1857-1941), local historian, was born at Antigonish, Nova Scotia, on September 22, 1857, and died at Wolfville, Nova Scotia, on July 10, 1941. He was the author of *The history of the town of Antigonish* (Wolfville, N.S., 1934).

[Private information.]

Whitaker, George (1810?-1882), clergyman and educationist, was born in England about 1810. He was educated at Queen's College, Cambridge (B.A., 1833); and in 1834 was elected a fellow of the College. He was ordained a priest of the Church of England in 1838, and was appointed vicar of Oakington, Cambridgeshire. In 1851 he was appointed first provost of Trinity University, Toronto; and he resigned this post only in 1881. He then returned to England, and he died there on August 28, 1882. He was the author of *Two letters to the lord bishop of Toronto* (Toronto, 1860); and a volume of his *Sermons* was published posthumously (London, 1882).

[*Dom. ann. reg.*, 1882.]

Whitbourne, Sir Richard (*fl.* 1579-1628), writer on Newfoundland, was born at Exmouth, Devonshire, England, at some date not ascertained, and died at some date after 1628. He became "a traveller and adventurer in foreign countries" at an early age, and made his first voyage to Newfoundland in 1579. He visited the island frequently after that date, and in 1620 he published in London his *Discourse and discovery of New-found-land*, in which he advocated the establishment of a "plantation" in Newfoundland. It was after the publication of this book that he was knighted. Some parts of the *Discourse* were reprinted by T. Whitburn in 1870, under the title *Westward Hoe for Avalon*.

[*Dict. nat. biog.*; *Encyc. Can.*; *Dict. Can. biog.*, vol. 1.]

White, Albert Scott (1855-1931), politician and jurist, was born at Sussex, New Brunswick, on April 12, 1855. He was educated at Mount Allison University (B.A., 1873; M.A., 1892; D.C.L., 1900) and Harvard University (LL.B., 1877), and was called to the bar of New Brunswick in 1879 (Q.C., 1894). He practised law in Sussex, New Brunswick; and he represented Kings in the Legislative Assembly of New Brunswick from 1886 to 1900. He was elected speaker of the Assembly

in 1900; and he was solicitor-general, attorney-general, and commissioner of public works in successive provincial administrations. In 1908 he was appointed a judge of the Supreme Court of New Brunswick; and he sat on the bench until his death, at Saint John, New Brunswick, on March 17, 1931.

[Morgan, *Can. men* (1912); *Can. parl. comp.*]

White, Edwin Theodore (1869-1929), educationist, was born in 1869, and was educated at the University of Toronto (B.A., 1899). He became a school-teacher, and in his later years was on the staff of the Normal School in London, Ontario. He died at London, Ontario, on April 6, 1929. He was the author of *Public school text-books in Ontario* (London, Ont., 1922).

[Private information.]

White, George Robert (1854-1910), clergyman, was born at St. Martin's, New Brunswick, on September 1, 1854. He was educated at Acadia University (B.A., 1887), and was ordained in 1887 a Baptist minister. He was the pastor of churches in several places in the Maritime provinces; and he died at Charlottetown, Prince Edward Island, on June 7, 1910. He was the author of *Sparks of the tinder* (Montreal, 1893).

[*Records of the graduates of Acadia University* (Wolfville, N.S., 1926).]

White, Harlow (1817-1888), painter, was born in London, England, in 1817. He came to Canada in 1871, and in 1880 he was elected a member of the Royal Canadian Academy of Arts. Shortly afterwards, he returned to England; and he died at the Charterhouse, in London, in 1888.

[N. MacTavish, *The fine arts in Canada* (Toronto, 1925).]

White, Henry (d. 1879), author, was a provincial land surveyor in Ontario, who died at Beaverton, Ontario, on January 3, 1879. He was the author of *Geology, oil fields, and minerals of Canada West* (Toronto, 1865) and *Gold regions of Canada* (Toronto, 1867).

[*Dom. ann. reg.*, 1879; Morgan, *Bib. can.*]

White, James (1863-1928), geographer, was born in Ingersoll, Ontario, on February 3, 1863, the son of David White and Christina Hendry. He was educated in the public schools and at the Royal Military College, Kingston; and in 1884 he joined the Geological Survey of Canada. In 1894 he was appointed geographer of the Geological Survey, and in 1899 chief geographer of the department of the interior. In this capacity he published *The atlas of Canada* (1906; rev. ed., 1915), which was his chief contribution to Canadian geography. From 1909 to 1913 he was secretary of the Conservation Commission, and from 1913 to its abolition in 1921 its deputy head. From 1921 to his death he was technical adviser to the minister of justice; and in this capacity he played an important part in the litigation over the Labrador boundary between Canada and Newfoundland before the Judicial Committee of the Privy Council in 1926. In 1927 he was elected chairman of the Geographic Board of Canada, of which he had been a member since 1898. He died at Ottawa on February 26, 1928. He was the author of *Altitudes in Canada* (Ottawa, 1901), *Dictionary of altitudes in Canada* (Ottawa, 1903), *Place-names in Quebec* (Ottawa, 1910), *Place-names of northern Canada* (Ottawa, 1910), *Place-names of the Thousand Islands* (Ottawa, 1910), and *Boundaries and treaties* (Ottawa, 1913). He was a fellow of the Royal Geographical Society and of the Royal Society of Canada. In 1888 he married Rachel, daughter of Thomas Waddell, and by her he had two daughters.

[H. S. Spence, *James White: A biographical sketch* (Ont. Hist. Soc., papers and records, 1931); *Can. who was who*, vol. 2; *Proc. Roy. Soc. Can.*, 1928; Morgan, *Can. men* (1912).]

White, Peter (1838-1906), speaker of the Canadian House of Commons (1891-96), was born at Pembroke, Upper Canada, on August 30, 1838, the son of Lieut.-Col. Peter White, founder of the town of Pembroke. He was educated at the local schools; and, after a business training in Ottawa, founded a lumber business at Pembroke. In 1874 he was elected to represent North Renfrew in the Canadian House of Commons, as a Conservative; but was unseated. He was, however, again returned in 1876; and he sat for North Renfrew continuously until 1896. From 1891 to 1896 he was speaker of the House. He was defeated at the polls in 1896 and in 1900; but was again elected for North Renfrew in 1904. He died at Pembroke, Ontario, on May 3, 1906.

[*Can. parl. comp.*, 1905; Morgan, *Can. men* (1898).]

White, Richard (1834-1910), newspaper publisher, was born in Montreal, Lower Canada, on May 14, 1834. He was educated at the Montreal high school, and was for some years engaged in the lumber business; but in 1855 he joined his brother, Thomas White (q.v.), in the management of the *Peterborough Review*. In 1864 he and his brother purchased the Hamilton *Spectator*; and in 1870 they acquired control of the Montreal *Gazette*. When Thomas White entered the Canadian House of Commons in 1878, Richard White became president and managing director of the Gazette Printing Company; and he continued in this position until his death at Montreal, Quebec, on June 21, 1910.

[*Can. who's who*, 1910; Morgan, *Can. men* (1898).]

White, Robert Smeaton (1856-1944), journalist and politician, was born in Peterborough, Canada West, on May 15, 1856, the son of the Hon. Thomas White (q.v.). He was educated at McGill University, and became a member of the staff of the Montreal *Gazette*. In 1885 he succeeded his father as editor-in-chief of this paper. From 1888 to 1895 he represented Cardwell in the Canadian House of Commons; from 1895 to 1917 he was collector of customs at Montreal; and from 1925 to 1940 he represented the St. Antoine division of Montreal in the Canadian House of Commons, being during this period the "dean of the House". He died at Westmount, Quebec, on December 5, 1944.

[*Can. who's who*, 1936-37; *Can. parl. comp.*]

White, Thomas (1830-1888), minister of the interior for Canada (1885-88), was born in Montreal, Lower Canada, on August 7, 1830, the son of Thomas White, a leather merchant. He was educated at the Montreal high school, and became a journalist. In 1853 he founded, at Peterborough, Ontario, the *Peterborough Review*, and he conducted this paper until 1860. In 1864, after studying law for several years, he founded, with his brother, the Hamilton *Spectator*; in 1869 he was sent to England as an emigration agent of the Canadian government; and in 1870 he assumed control of the Montreal *Gazette*. After several unsuccessful attempts to enter parliament, he was in 1878 elected to represent Cardwell in the Canadian House of Commons as a Conservative; and he sat for this constituency for the rest of his life. In 1885 he became minister of the interior in the Macdonald government; and on him devolved the reorganization of the government of the North West Territories after the second Riel rebellion. He died at Ottawa on April 21, 1888.

[*Dict. nat. biog.*; *Cyc. Am. biog.*; Rose, *Cyc. Can. biog.* (1888); Morgan, *Bib. can.*]

White, Sir Thomas (1866-1955), war-time minister of finance, was born at Bronte, Canada West, on November 13, 1866, and died at Toronto, Ontario, on February 11, 1955. He was educated at the University of Toronto (B.A., 1895) and Osgoode Hall, and was called to the bar in Ontario in 1899, but never practised law. He became general manager of the National Trust Company, and in 1911 was one of the group of business men in Toronto who opposed the Liberal proposal of reciprocity with the United States. When the Borden government was formed, he was appointed minister of finance, and he continued in this position until the end of the First World War. The measures he adopted for financing the war were of crucial importance. He was acting prime minister during the absence of Sir Robert Borden (q.v.), and was expected to succeed him as prime minister, but he resigned his seat in the House of Commons in 1921, and retired from politics. He was created a K.C.M.G. in 1916 and a G.C.M.G. in 1935, and was sworn of the Imperial Privy Council in 1920. He was the author of *The story of Canada's war finance* (Montreal, 1921) and two volumes of verse, *The battle of Britain, and other poems* (Montreal, 1945) and *Essays of Francis Bacon ... paraphrased in blank verse* (Montreal, 1945).

[*Who was who*, 1951-60; *Can. who's who*, 1952-54; *Encyc. Can.*]

White, William (1830-1912), civil servant and author, was born in London, England, on January 6, 1830. He came to Canada in 1854, and entered the Post Office department of the Canadian government. He became secretary, and then deputy-minister, of the department; and he retired on pension in 1897. He joined the Canadian militia at an early date, served in the Fenian Raid of 1866, and rose to the rank of lieutenant-colonel. In 1897 he was awarded the C.M.G. He died at Ottawa, Ontario, on October 3, 1912. He was the author of *The annals of Canada* (2 parts, Toronto, 1875-78).

[Morgan, *Can. men* (1912).]

White, William Charles (1873-1960), bishop and archaeologist, was born in Devonshire, England, in 1873, and died at Toronto, Ontario, on January 24, 1960. He came to Canada when a child with his parents, and was educated at country schools and at Wycliffe College, Toronto. He was ordained a priest of the Church of England, and in 1897 went to China as a missionary. In 1909 he was consecrated as the first bishop of Honan. In 1934 he returned to Toronto, and became keeper of the East Asiatic Collection in the Royal Ontario Museum and professor of Chinese archaeology in the University of Toronto. He retired in 1948. He was the author of *Tombs of old Lo-yang* (Shanghai, 1934), *An album of Chinese bamboos* (Toronto, 1939), *Tomb tile pictures of ancient China* (Toronto, 1939), *Chinese temple frescoes* (Toronto, 1940), *Chinese Jews* (3 vols., Toronto, 1912), *Bone culture of ancient China* (Toronto, 1945), and *Bronze culture of ancient China* (Toronto, 1956), as well as of a biography of *Canon Cody of St. Paul's Church* (Toronto, 1953).

[*Who was who*, 1951-60; *Can. who's who*, 1952-54; Toronto *Globe and Mail*, Jan. 25, 1960.]

White, William John (1861-1934), lawyer, was born in Peterborough, Ontario, on January 29, 1861, the son of Richard White. He was educated at McGill University (B.A., 1881; B.C.L., 1882; M.A., 1885; D.C.L., 1902), and was called to the bar in 1883 (Q.C., 1899). He became *bâtonnier* of the Montreal bar in 1901. He took an interest in Canadian history and folk-lore; and from 1889 to 1891 he published a

monthly periodical, *Canadiana*. He died at Montreal, on January 22, 1934. He was the author of *A treatise of Canadian company law* (Montreal, 1901).

[Morgan, *Can. men* (1912).]

White, William Thomas (1836-1925), jurist, was born at Quebec, Lower Canada, on May 28, 1836; and was educated at the Quebec high school and at Bishop's College, Lennoxville. He was called to the bar of Quebec in 1868 (Q.C., 1883), and practised law in Sherbrooke, Quebec. He became an outstanding corporation lawyer; and in 1895 he was raised to the bench as a judge of the Superior Court of the province of Quebec for the district of St. François. His health compelled his retirement in 1904; and he died at Sherbrooke, Quebec, on April 4, 1925.

[P. G. Roy, *Les juges de la province de Québec* (Quebec, 1933); Morgan, *Can. men* (1912).]

Whiteaves, Joseph Frederick (1835-1909), palaeontologist, was born in Oxford, England, in 1835. He emigrated to Canada in 1862, and settled in Montreal. For twelve years he was curator of the museum of the Montreal Natural History Society; and then, in 1876, he was appointed to the staff of the Geological Survey of Canada as palaeontologist, in succession to Elkanah Billings (q.v.). He died on August 8, 1909. He was one of the original fellows of the Royal Society of Canada; and in 1900 McGill University conferred on him the degree of LL.D. A bibliography of his scientific papers includes nearly 150 titles; his most important publications were his *Contributions to Canadian palaeontology* (3 vols., Montreal, 1885-91) and his *Mesozoic fossils* (3 vols., Montreal, 1876-84).

[*Trans. Roy. Soc. Can.*, 1910; Morgan, *Can. men* (1898).]

Whitebone, James Alexander (1894-1970), labour executive, was born in Saint John, New Brunswick, May 31, 1894, and was educated at Saint John High School. He became a member of the International Alliance of Theatrical Stage Employees and Moving Picture Machine Operators in 1917, becoming business agent and secretary of local 440. He represented the Trades and Labor Congress of Canada at the World Trade Union Congress in London in 1945, and became Labour representative at the International Labour Organization in Geneva in 1951. He was a member of the Saint John city council for sixteen years and mayor in 1960. He was author of *Labour in New Brunswick* (Saint John, 1927). He died at Saint John, New Brunswick, February 17, 1970.

[*Can. who's who*, 1967-69.]

Whitelaw, John (1774-1853), physician and school-teacher, was born at Bothwell,

Scotland, in 1774. He studied medicine at Edinburgh; and for a time practised medicine in Quebec, Lower Canada. About 1807 he removed to Upper Canada, and here he became a school-teacher. For a number of years he was headmaster of the Kingston grammar school; but in 1830 he became headmaster of the grammar school at Niagara. He was one of the most notable teachers during the early days of Upper Canada. He retired from teaching in 1851; and he died at Niagara, Canada West, on January 25, 1853.

[J. Carnochan, *History of Niagara* (Toronto, 1914).]

Whitelaw, William Menzies (1890-1974), historian, was born at Valcartier, Quebec, May 13, 1890. He graduated from the University of Toronto (B.A., 1910) and Union Theological College, New York (M. Th., 1914). He arrived in Germany with a Schoales Travelling Fellowship just before the outbreak of the First World War, and, escaping internment, he made his way to Great Britain, where he became a student at Edinburgh University. From 1915 until the end of the war he served in Egypt, Mesopotamia, and East Africa. After the war he resumed his studies at Columbia University, New York (M.A., 1920; Ph. D., 1934). He was an instructor in history at Columbia (1925-26), assistant professor at Rutgers (1926-32), assistant professor of history at McGill, Montreal (1933-34), Secretary of the Public Archives of Canada (1937-40), associate professor of history, University of Saskatchewan (1940-45), professor of history, United College, Winnipeg (1945-46), and visiting professor, American International College, Springfield, Massachussetts, becoming professor and head of the department of history in 1950. He retired in 1955 and died February 4, 1974, in Carmel, New York. Menzies Whitelaw was an exacting scholar, an academic adventurer, and an individualist who left his imprint on his students rather than in his published works, although his book *The Maritimes and Canada before Confederation* (Toronto, 1934; reprinted, 1966) is still the standard work on the subject. He also wrote *American Influences on British Federal Systems or the Constitution Reconsidered* (New York, 1938), as well as a number of articles and reviews.

[*Directory of American Scholars*, 1963; *Can. hist. rev.*, vol. LVI, 1975; private information.]

Whiteway, Sir William Vallance (1828-1908), prime minister of Newfoundland (1878-85, 1889-94, and 1895-97), was born in Devonshire, England, on April 1, 1828, and died at St. John's, Newfoundland, on June 24, 1908. He came to Newfoundland in 1843, and was called to the Newfoundland bar in 1852 (Q.C., 1867). In 1859 he was elected to the House of Assembly, and he was speaker of the

House from 1865 to 1869. He was defeated at the polls in 1869, but was re-elected in 1873; and from 1873 to 1878 he was solicitor-general in the Carter administration. From 1878 to 1885 he was prime minister and attorney-general; from 1885 to 1889 he was out of politics; but in 1889 he led his party to victory at the polls, and was prime minister again until 1897, except for a short interval in 1894-95. In 1897 he was again defeated, and retired from public life. He was created a K.C.M.G. in 1880, and Oxford University conferred on him the degree of D.C.L.

[*Dict. nat. biog.*, 2nd supp., vol. III; *Who was who*, 1897-1916; *Encyc. Can.*]

Whitney, Sir James Pliny (1843-1914), prime minister of Ontario (1905-14), was born at Williamsburg, Upper Canada, on October 2, 1843, the son of Richard Leet Whitney and Clarissa Jane Fairman. He was educated at the Cornwall grammar school, and was called to the Ontario bar in 1876 (Q.C., 1890). From 1888 to his death he represented Dundas in the Legislative Assembly of Ontario; from 1896 to 1905 he was leader of the Conservative opposition; and from 1905 to his death he was prime minister of Ontario, with the portfolio of president of the council. During his period of office he captured the confidence of the electors by his downright, straightforward methods and by his bluff honesty; and his name became a talisman of success among his followers. His régime was perhaps most notable for the advance made during it in the direction of government ownership of public utilities, and especially for the success of the Hydro-Electric Power Commission in supplying the province with power from Niagara Falls. Whitney died at Toronto on September 25, 1914. He married in 1877 Alice, third daughter of William Park, Cornwall; and by her he had one son and two daughters. He was a D.C.L. of Trinity University, Toronto (1902), and an LL.D. of the University of Toronto (1902) and of Queen's University, Kingston (1903). In 1908 he was created a K.C.M.G.

[*Who was who*, 1897-1916; Morgan, *Can. men* (1912); *Can. parl. comp.*; *Can. ann. rev.*, 1901-14.]

Whitton, Charlotte Elizabeth (1896-1975), social worker, was born in Renfrew, Ontario, March 8, 1896. She was educated at Renfrew and at Queen's University, where she was a university medallist in English and history, and where she played on the championship basketball and hockey teams. She obtained her M.A. in 1917 and graduated in education in 1918 with the Governor-General's Medal. On graduation she became assistant secretary of the Social Service Council of Canada (1918-22), and then secretary to the minister of trade and commerce (1922-25). She was director of the Canadian Welfare Council and delegate to the League of Nations

Committee on Social Questions (1926-41). She was the first woman elected controller in the Ottawa city council (1950) and was mayor of the city (1951-56 and 1961-64). Much of her work was in publicizing social questions. She was editor of *Social Welfare* (1918-22), and founder-editor of *Canadian Welfare* (1926-41). Among her books are *The dawn of ampler life* (1943). She received honorary degrees from six universities and was made a C.B.E. (1934), and a member of the Order of Canada (1968). She died at Ottawa, Ontario, January 25, 1975.

[*Can. who's who*, 1970-72.]

Whyte, Sir William (1843-1914), railwayman, was born in Dunfermline, Fifeshire, Scotland, on September 15, 1843, the son of William Whyte and Christina Methven. He came to Canada in 1863, and entered the employ of the Grand Trunk Railway. In 1884 he entered the service of the Canadian Pacific Railway, as superintendent of the Ontario division. In 1901 he became assistant to the president of the Canadian Pacific Railway; and in 1904 second vice-president of the company. He retired from active business in 1911; and he died at Los Angeles, California, on April 14, 1914. In 1872 he married Jane, daughter of Adam Scott, Toronto; and by her he had two sons and three daughters. He was created a knight bachelor in 1911.

[R. G. MacBeth, *Sir William Whyte, a builder of the West* (Can. mag., 1914); *Can. who was who*, vol. 2; Morgan, *Can. men* (1912); Rose, *Cyc. Can. biog.* (1886).]

Whyte-Edgar, Mrs. C. M. (1869-1948), anthologist, was born in 1869, and died at Lancaster, Ontario, on December 19, 1948. She compiled an anthology entitled *A wreath of Canadian song* (Toronto, 1910).

[Private information.]

Wickett, Samuel Morley (1872-1915), political economist, was born at Brooklin, Ontario, on October 17, 1872. He was educated at the University of Toronto (B.A., 1894) and at the University of Leipzig (Ph.D., 1897); and from 1897 to 1899 he was Mackenzie fellow in political science at the University of Toronto. In 1898 he was appointed lecturer in political economy in this university, and he retained this position until 1905, when he went into business. He died, suddenly, at Toronto, Ontario, on December 7, 1915. He was the author of *Canadians in the United States* (Boston, 1906) and of a series of studies of municipal government in Canada, published in the *University of Toronto Studies*. He also translated into English Karl Bücher's *Industrial evolution* (New York, 1912).

[Morgan, *Can. men* (1912); *University of Toronto monthly*, 1916.]

Wickson, Paul Giovanni (1860-1922), painter, was born in Toronto, Canada, in 1860,

the son of the Rev. Arthur Wickson, classical tutor in the University of Toronto, and Mary Anne Thomas. He was educated at the Toronto grammar school, and studied art at the South Kensington School of Arts. He specialized in the painting of animal subjects; and he exhibited at the Royal Academy, London, and other galleries. He died in Paris, Ontario, on September 2, 1922. In 1884 he married Elizabeth, daughter of Norman Hamilton, of Paris, Ontario.

[T. G. Marquis, *The art of Paul Wickson* (Can. mag., May, 1904); N. MacTavish, *The fine arts in Canada* (Toronto, 1925); *Can. who was who*, vol. 1; Morgan, *Can. men* (1912).]

Wicksteed, Gustavus William (1799-1898), civil servant and poet, was born in Liverpool, England, on December 21, 1799, the son of Richard Wicksteed and Eliza Tatlock. He came to Canada in 1821, and was called to the bar of Lower Canada (Q.C., 1854). In 1828 he was appointed assistant law clerk to the Legislative Assembly of Lower Canada; and in 1838 law clerk to the Special Council of the province. In 1841 he became law clerk of the Legislative Assembly of united Canada; and in 1867 law clerk to the Canadian House of Commons. He was superannuated in 1887; and he died at Ottawa on August 18, 1898. He married (1) the daughter of John Gray, president of the Bank of Montreal, and (2) Anna, daughter of Capt. John Fletcher, of the 72nd Regiment. He published several indexes to the statutes of Canada; and he was the author of *Waifs in verse* (Montreal, 1878).

[*Can. who was who*, vol. 2; Morgan, *Can. men* (1898) and *Bib. can.*; Rose, *Cyc. Can. biog.* (1886); *Cyc. Am. biog.*; C. C. James, *A bibliography of Canadian poetry* (Toronto, 1899).]

Widdifield, Charles Howard (1859-1937), jurist and author, was born at Uxbridge, Canada West, on January 21, 1859; and was educated at Upper Canada College, Toronto. He was called to the bar of Ontario in 1881, and for many years practised law in Picton, Ontario. In 1905 he was appointed a judge of the court of Grey county, Ontario; and in 1918 of the court of York county, Ontario. He retired from the bench in 1933, and he died at Toronto, Ontario, on June 10, 1937. He was the author of *The law of costs in Canada* (Toronto, 1892), *Words and terms judicially defined* (Toronto, 1914), *The law and practice relating to the passing of executor's accounts* (Toronto, 1916), *Surrogate court practice and procedure* (Toronto, 1917), and *The Motor vehicle act and the Highway travel act* (Toronto, 1920).

[*Can. who's who*, 1936-37; Morgan, *Can. men* (1912).]

Widmer, Christopher (1780-1858), legislative councillor of Canada, was born in England in 1780. He served in the Peninsular War as surgeon of the 14th Light Dragoons; and during the War of 1812 he emigrated to Canada, and settled in Toronto. Here he was one of the early practitioners of medicine. In 1843 he was appointed a member of the Legislative Council of Canada; and in 1853 he was for a few weeks chancellor of the University of Toronto. He died in Toronto on May 2, 1858.

[W. Canniff, *The medical profession in Upper Canada* (Toronto, 1894); *Cyc. Am. biog.*]

Wiggins, Ezekiel Stone (1839-1910), civil servant and author, was born in Queens county, New Brunswick, on December 4, 1839. He was educated at Albert College, Belleville, Ontario (B.A., 1870; M.A., 1872), and afterwards he studied medicine in Philadelphia, but never practised. In 1879 he was appointed to a position in the civil service at Ottawa, after having unsuccessfully contested Queens county, New Brunswick, in the Dominion general elections of 1878; and he remained a civil servant until his death at Ottawa on August 14, 1910. He was the author of *The architecture of the heavens* (Montreal, 1864) and *Universalism unfounded* (Napanee, Ont., 1867); and he gained a wide reputation as a prophet of the weather. In 1862 he married his cousin, Susie Anna Wiggins; and she later published *The Gunhilda letters* (Ottawa, 1881).

[Rose, *Cyc. Can. biog.* (1886); Morgan, *Can. men* (1898).]

Wightman, Frederick Arnold (1860-1939), clergyman, was born at Bayswater, New Brunswick, on September 19, 1860, and died at Fredericton, New Brunswick, on August 2, 1939. He was the author of *Our Canadian heritage* (Toronto, 1905).

[Private information.]

Wigle, Hamilton (1858-1934), clergyman and poet, was born in Essex county, Canada West, in 1858. He was educated at Victoria University (B.A., 1889), and for many years was a Methodist minister in Saskatchewan and Manitoba. In 1910 he went to the Maritime provinces, and he remained there until his superannuation in 1932. He died at Sault Ste. Marie, Ontario, on January 7, 1934. He was the author of *The veteran, and other poems* (Toronto, 1910) and *Poems for pulpit and platform* (Toronto, 1911), and he collaborated in preparing the *History of the Wigle family* (Kingsville, Ont., 1931).

[Morgan, *Can. men* (1912).]

Wigmore, Rupert Wilson (1875-1939), minister of customs and inland revenue for Canada (1920-21), was born in Saint John, N.B., May 10, 1875. He became the manager of a milk company in Saint John, and later a partner in a firm of ship brokers. In 1917 he was elected to represent Saint John city in the

Canadian House of Commons; and in 1920 he was sworn in as minister of customs and inland revenue in the first Meighen administration. He retired from the cabinet in 1921, and retired to private life. He died at Saint John, New Brunswick, on April 3, 1939.

[*Can. who's who*, 1936-37; *Can. parl. comp.*]

Wilcocke, Samuel Hull (1766?-1833), author, was born about 1766 at Reigate, Surrey, England, the son of the Rev. Samuel Wilcocke. Before coming to Canada he published *Britannia: A poem* (London, 1797), *A new and complete dictionary of the English and Dutch languages* (London, 1798), and a *History of the vice-royalty of Buenos-Aires* (London, 1807; 2nd ed., 1820), as well as translations of books in Dutch, German, and French. He seems to have come to Canada about 1817 as a hack-writer in the service of the North West Company during the Selkirk controversy. He was the author of *A narrative of occurrences in the Indian countries of North America* (London, 1817; 2nd ed., Montreal, 1818), *Report of the trials of Charles de Reinhard and Archibald M'Lellan* (Montreal, 1818), *Report of the proceedings connected with the disputes between the Earl of Selkirk and the North West Company* (Montreal, 1819), and *Report of the proceedings at a court of oyer and terminer appointed for the investigation of cases from the Indian territories* (Montreal, 1819). In 1820 he fell out with the North West Company, was arrested on a charge of forgery, and spent nearly two years in the Montreal jail. From 1821 to 1827, first at Montreal, and then at Burlington, Vermont, Rouse's Point, New York, and Plattsburg, New York, he published the *Scribbler*, a scurrilous journal in which he lampooned, under thin disguises, many of the leading people in Montreal. About 1828 he returned to Canada, and became a reporter of the debates in the Lower Canada legislature. In 1828 he published a *History of the session of the first parliament of Lower Canada, for 1828-9*, which is the first approach in Canada to Hansard. He died at Quebec on July 3, 1833.

[A. H. U. Colquhoun, *A victim of Scottish Canadians* (Dalhousie review, 1924); W. S. Wallace (ed.), *Documents relating to the North West Company* (Toronto: The Champlain Society, 1934); *The literature relating to the Selkirk controversy* (Can. hist. rev., March, 1932).]

Wild, Joseph (1834-1908), clergyman and author, was born at Summit, Littleborough, Lancashire, England, on November 16, 1834, the youngest son of Joseph Wild. He came to America in 1855; and, after a course of study at the Boston Theological College, became a minister of the Protestant Episcopal Church in Canada. From 1864 to 1872 he was stationed at Belleville, Ontario; from 1872 to 1880, at Brooklyn, New York; and from 1880 to 1893 he was pastor of the Bond Street Congregational Church, Toronto. He died at Brooklyn, New York, on August 18, 1908. He was the author of *The lost ten tribes* (New York, 1878; London, 1880), *How and when the world will end* (New York, 1880), *Talks for the times* (Toronto, 1886), *The future of Israel and Judah* (London, 1886), *Songs of the sanctuary* (London, 1886), *The Bond Street pulpit* (Toronto, 1888), *Canada and the Jesuits* (Toronto, 1889), and *The origin and secrets of freemasonry* (Toronto, 1889).

[Rose, *Cyc. Can. biog.* (1888).]

Wilgress, Leolyn Dana (1892-1969), diplomat, was born in Vancouver, British Columbia, October 20, 1892. He was educated in Victoria, in Yokohama, Japan, where his father was a steamship agent, and at McGill University in Montreal (B.A., 1914). He entered the Canadian Trade Commission service in 1914 and was posted to Omsk, Siberia, arriving at his destination in 1916. Wilgress was in Russia during the revolutionary period and left in October, 1919, for Romania. From there he was posted to London and then to Hamburg. During the period of his service from 1930 until his retirement from government service in 1966 he was involved in the Commonwealth and world economic conferences in London, and the preparatory conferences for the United Nations. He was chairman of the General Agreement on Tariffs and Trade (1948-51 and 1951-56), and was permanent representative at the NATO Council and the Organization for European Economic Cooperation (OEEC, 1953-58). He was the first Canadian minister to the U.S.S.R. (1942), becoming ambassador (1944), and was minister to Switzerland (1947-49) and Canadian High Commissioner to the United Kingdom (1949-52). He was Under-Secretary of State for External Affairs (1952-53). Wilgress had an intimate knowledge of European, including Russian, affairs and was able to assist Canada in fulfilling her growing obligations in the complex world of the Second World War and its aftermath. He was a Companion of the Order of Canada (1967). He died at Ottawa, July 21, 1969. He wrote *The impact of European integration on Canada* (Montreal, 1962); and *Canada's approach to trade negotiations* (Montreal, 1963).

[D. Wilgress, *Memoirs* (Toronto, 1967); *Can. who's who*, 1967-69.]

Wilkes, Henry (1805-1886), Congregationalist minister, was born in Birmingham, England, on June 21, 1805. He came to Canada with his parents in 1820, and went into business in Montreal. In 1828 he entered Glasgow University (B.A., 1832), and in 1834 he was ordained a minister of the Congregationalist Church. In 1836 he became the first pastor of the First Congregationalist Church in Montreal, and he was the pastor of this church until

1870. He then became principal of the Congregational College in Montreal. In a large degree, he was the father of Congregationalism in Canada. He died in Montreal on November 17, 1886. He was the author of a large number of sermons and addresses.

[Rev. J. Wood, *Memoir of Henry Wilkes* (Montreal and London, 1887); *Dom. ann. reg.*, 1886; Morgan, *Bib. can.*]

Wilkie, Daniel (1777-1851), clergyman and educationist, was born at Tollcross, Scotland, in 1777. He was educated at the University of Glasgow (M.A., 1803; LL.D., 1837), was ordained a minister of the Church of Scotland, and came to Canada in 1803. For over forty years he conducted a famous grammar school at Quebec, Lower Canada; and he died here on May 10, 1851. Besides a number of papers contributed to the *Transactions* of the Literary and Historical Society of Quebec, he was the author of a *Letter to the Roman Catholic clergy and the seigniors of Lower Canada, recommending the establishment of schools* (Quebec, 1810).

[Morgan, *Cel. Can.* and *Bib. can.*; Rose, *Cyc. Can. biog.* (1886).]

Wilkie, Daniel Robert (1846-1914), president of the Imperial Bank of Canada (1906-14), was born at Quebec, Lower Canada, on December 14, 1846, the son of Daniel Wilkie, and the grandson of the Rev. Daniel Wilkie (q.v.). He was educated at the High School and at Morrin College, Quebec; and in 1862 he entered the service of the Quebec Bank. In 1875 he became the general manager of the Imperial Bank, on its foundation; and in 1906 its president. He died at Toronto on November 19, 1914. In 1870 he married Sarah Caroline (d. 1887), daughter of the Hon. J. R. Benson, of St. Catharines, Ontario. He was the author of a treatise on *The theory and practice of banking in Canada* (Toronto, 1908).

[Morgan, *Can. men* (1912); *Can. who's who*, 1910; Rose, *Cyc. Can. biog.* (1886).]

Wilkins, Harriet Annie (1829-1888), poetess, was born in England in 1829, the daughter of the Rev. John Wilkins, a Congregationalist minister. She emigrated to Canada with her family and settled in Hamilton, Upper Canada. Here she conducted for many years a "Ladies' Seminary". In her later years she was a music teacher. She died in Hamilton on January 7, 1888. She was the author of *The holly branch* (Hamilton, Ont., 1851), *The Acacia* (Hamilton, Ont., 1860; 2nd ed., 1863), *Autumn leaves* (Hamilton, Ont., 1869), *Wayside flowers* (Toronto, 1876), and *Victor Roy: A Masonic poem* (Hamilton, Ont., 1882).

[C. C. James, *A bibliography of Canadian poetry* (Toronto, 1899).]

Wilkins, Lewis Morris (1801-1885), politician and jurist, was born at Halifax, Nova

Scotia, on May 24, 1801, the son of the Hon. Lewis Morris Wilkins, a judge of the Supreme Court of Nova Scotia, and Sarah Creighton. He was educated at King's College, Windsor, Nova Scotia (B.A., 1819), was called to the Nova Scotia bar in 1823, and practised law at Windsor, Nova Scotia, until 1856. He represented Windsor in the Legislative Assembly of the province from 1834 to 1837; he was a member of the Legislative Council from 1837 to 1844; and he again represented Windsor in the Assembly from 1853 to 1856. From 1854 to 1856 he was provincial secretary and clerk of the Executive Council in the Young administration; and in 1856 he was appointed a puisne judge of the Supreme Court of Nova Scotia. He retired from the bench in 1878, and he died at Windsor, Nova Scotia, on March 15, 1885. He was a D.C.L. of King's College, Windsor; and he was the author of a pamphlet, *The Lord's Supper* (Halifax, 1881).

[*Dom. ann. reg.*, 1885; *Cyc. Am. biog.*; *Canadian biographical dictionary*, Quebec and Maritime provinces vol. (Chicago, 1881); Sir J. Bourinot, *Builders of Nova Scotia* (Trans. Roy. Soc. Can., 1899).]

Wilkins, Robert Charles (1782-1866), legislative councillor of Upper Canada, was born in 1782, and settled in the Bay of Quinte district, with his parents, who were loyalists, about 1792. Here he later engaged in timber and importing businesses. He was appointed a member of the Legislative Council of Upper Canada in 1839; but he was not reappointed to the Legislative Council of Canada after the union of 1841. He died at Belleville, Ontario, in March, 1866.

[*A brief biographical sketch of the Hon. Robert Charles Wilkins* (Belleville, C.W., 1866); A. Ewart and J. Jarvis, *The personnel of the family compact* (Can. hist. rev., 1926).]

Wilkinson, John R. (d. 1908), militia officer and poet, was a native of Leamington, Ontario, who raised and organized the 21st Battalion in Essex county at the time of the North-West Rebellion of 1885. He did not see active service, since the battalion was disbanded before being sent to the North-West; but he retained his rank as lieutenant-colonel in the militia. He died at Leamington, Ontario, on July 11, 1908. He was the author of *Canadian battlefields, and other poems* (Toronto, 1899).

[Private information.]

Willan, Healey (1880-1968), organist and composer, was born in London, England, October 12, 1880. He was educated at St. Saviour's Choir School, Eastbourne, and received his Mus.D. at the University of Toronto (1921). He came to Canada to head the theory department of the Royal Conservatory of Music (Toronto) in 1913 and was vice-principal of the Conservatory from 1920 to 1936. He was professor of music at the University of Toronto from 1937 to 1950. Dr. Willan began his career as a church organist before leaving England; he was elected a fellow of the Royal College of Organists in 1899, and played in St. Albans and in London. He became organist and choirmaster of St. Paul's Anglican Church, Toronto, in 1913 and of St. Mary Magdalene Church, Toronto, in 1921, where he remained as organist until his retirement. He was the University of Toronto organist from 1932 to 1952. He was well known both as conductor and composer, and his choir, which excelled in liturgical music, was famous throughout Canada.

His three hundred musical compositions include the *Introduction Passacaglia and Fugue* for organ (1916); *Dierdre of the Sorrows* (1944), an opera; the *Royce Hall Suite* for symphonic band; two symphonies; a piano concerto; and chamber music and choral music. His best-known choral work, *Apostrophe to the Heavenly Hosts*, was performed in London in 1952. He had many honorary degrees conferred upon him; was awarded the Canada Council Medal in 1961; and was created a Companion of the Order of Canada in 1967. He died at Toronto, Ontario, February 16, 1968.

[*Encyc. Can.* (1972); *Can. who's who*, 1955-57; G. Ridout, *Healey Willan* (Canadian Music Journal, Spring, 1959); *Grove's dictionary of music and musicians* (London, 1954).]

Willcocks, Joseph (d. 1814), journalist and agitator, was a native of Ireland. He was implicated in the Irish rebellion of 1798, and fled from Ireland to Upper Canada. Here he obtained the patronage of Mr. Justice Allcock (q.v.), and in 1803 he was appointed sheriff of the Home district. His *Diary* for 1799-1803 has been printed as an appendix to J.E. Middleton and F. Landon (eds.), *The province of Ontario*, vol. 2 (Toronto, 1927). He was dismissed from office by Francis Gore (q.v.) in 1806 for political opposition to the government; and in 1807 he founded the *Upper Canadian Guardian, or Freeman's Journal*, the first party newspaper in Upper Canada. From 1808 to 1812 he represented Lincoln, Haldimand, and West York in the Legislative Assembly of the province; and during the session of 1808 he was imprisoned by warrant of the speaker of the Assembly for making "false, slanderous, and highly derogatory" statements about the members of the Assembly. During the War of 1812, he went over to the Americans, and he was killed at the siege of Fort Erie, on October 4, 1814, while serving as a colonel in the American army.

[A. H. U. Colquhoun, *The career of Joseph Willcocks* (Can. hist. rev., 1926); W. R. Riddell, *Joseph Willcocks* (Ont. Hist. Soc., papers and records, 1927).]

Willey, Arthur (1867-1942), zoölogist, was born at Scarborough, England, in 1867. He was educated at University College, London (D.Sc., 1894); and after carrying on zoölogical research in Italy, in the United States, in the South Sea Islands, and in Ceylon, he was appointed in 1910 head of the department of zoölogy in McGill University. He retired from this post in 1932; and he died at Montreal, Quebec, on December 26, 1942. He was elected a fellow of the Royal Society in 1899, and a fellow of the Royal Society of Canada in 1912. He was the author of *Amphioxus and the ancestry of vertebrates* (New York, 1894), *Zoölogical results, based on material obtained from New Britain, New Guinea, Loyalty islands, and elsewhere* (6 vols., London, 1898-1902), *Convergence in evolution* (New York, 1911), and *Lectures on Darwinism* (Boston, 1930).

[*Proc. Roy. Soc. Can.*, 1943.]

Williams, Arthur Trefusis Heneage (1837-1885), soldier, was born at Port Hope, Upper Canada, in 1837, the son of Commander Tucker Williams, R.N., who sat in the Legislative Assembly of united Canada from 1840 to 1848. He was educated at Upper Canada College, Toronto, and at Edinburgh University. He returned to Canada, and became a gentleman farmer. He represented East Durham in the Legislative Assembly of Ontario from 1867 to 1875 and in the Canadian House of Commons from 1878 to 1885. As lieutenant-colonel commanding the 46th battalion of the volunteer militia, he served in the North West Rebellion of 1885; and he died near Fort Pitt, in the North West Territories, on July 4, 1885.

[*Dom. ann. reg.*, 1885; Rose, *Cyc. Can. biog.* (1886).]

Williams, Charles R. (d. 1859?), author, was a resident of Cobourg, Canada West, when he published *The rival families; or, Virtue and vice;* and *The stolen jewels; or, The matchmaking mamma* (Cobourg, C.W., 1858). He died about 1859.

[Morgan, *Bib. can.*]

Williams, David (1859-1931), Anglican archbishop of Huron, was born near Lampeter, Cardiganshire, Wales, on March 14, 1859. He was educated at St. David's College, Lampeter, and at Oxford University; and he was ordained a priest of the Church of England in 1886. He came to Canada in 1887; and from 1887 to 1892 he was a professor in Huron College, London, Ontario. In 1905 he was elected bishop of Huron, and in 1926 he became archbishop of this diocese and metropolitan of the ecclesiastical province of Ontario. He died at London, Ontario, on October 7, 1931. He was a D.D. of the Western University (1905) and an LL.D. of the University of Toronto (1907).

[B. Heeney, *Leaders of the Canadian church: Third series* (Toronto, 1943); Morgan, *Can. men* (1912).]

Williams, David (1869-1944), journalist, was born at Carlingford, Perth county, Ontario, in 1869. He was educated in Collingwood, Ontario; and in 1886 he became editor of the Collingwood *Bulletin*, a weekly newspaper that in 1932 became the *Enterprise-Bulletin*. He continued to edit this newspaper until his death, at Collingwood, Ontario, on October 20, 1944. A man of wide interests, he was president of the Canadian Press Association, the Ontario Historical Society, the Ontario Library Association, and the Ontario Hospital Association; he was one of the founders, and for many years the secretary, of the Huron Institute; and in 1941 he received from the University of Toronto the honorary degree of LL.D. He was the author of *The origin of the names of the post-offices in the county of Simcoe* (Toronto, 1906).

[*Can. who's who*, 1936-37; Morgan, *Can. men* (1912).]

Williams, James William (1825-1892), Anglican bishop of Quebec (1863-92), was born in Overton, Hampshire, England, on September 15, 1825, the son of the Rev. David Williams, rector of Banghurst. He was educated at Pembroke College, Oxford (B.A., 1851), and in 1856 was ordained a priest of the Church of England. In 1857 he came to Canada to take charge of a school in connection with Bishop's College, Lennoxville; and soon afterwards he became professor of classics in Bishop's College. In 1863 he was chosen bishop of Quebec, and he continued to administer this see until his death at Quebec on April 20, 1892. He published a lecture on *Self-education* (Quebec, 1865) and several papers in the *Transactions* of the Quebec Literary and Historical Society.

[*Cyc. Am. biog.*; Morgan, *Bib. can.*; Rose, *Cyc. Can. biog.* (1888); C. H. Mockridge, *The bishops of the Church of England in Canada* (Toronto, 1896).]

Williams, Jenkin (d. 1819), jurist, was a Welsh lawyer who came to Canada soon after the British conquest. His commission as barrister and attorney-at-law is dated October 16, 1767. From 1776 to 1791 he was clerk of the Legislative Council; and in 1782 he was appointed also solicitor-general for the province. In 1792 he was created a judge of the Court of Common Pleas in Lower Canada; and in 1794 a judge of the Court of King's Bench. In 1801 he was appointed an honorary member of the Executive Council, and in 1802 a member of the Legislative Council of the province. He retired from the bench, on account of old age, in 1812; and he died on October 30, 1819.

[P. G. Roy, *Les juges de la province de Québec* (Quebec, 1933).]

Williams, John Aethuruld (1817-1889), clergyman, was born at Caermarthen, Wales, on December 19, 1817. He emigrated to Canada in 1834; and in 1846 he entered the Methodist ministry. He became the pastor successively of many of the largest Methodist churches in Ontario; and at the general conference of the united Methodist churches in Canada in 1883 he was elected president. In 1885 he was appointed general superintendent of the Methodist Church in Canada; and he remained in this post until his death on December 17, 1889. In 1878 Victoria University conferred on him the honorary degree of D.D.

[Rose, *Cyc. Can. biog.* (1888); G. A. Cornish, *Cyclopædia of Canadian Methodism* (2 vols., Toronto, 1881-1903).]

Williams, Sir Ralph Champneys (1848-1927), governor of Newfoundland (1909-13), was born in England on March 9, 1848, and died at London, England, on June 22, 1927. He was educated at Rossal School in Lancashire. After a series of explorations in Patagonia, Central Africa, and Bechuanaland, he entered the British colonial service, and held posts in Gibraltar, Barbados, Bechuanaland, and the Windward Islands. He was governor of Newfoundland from 1909 to 1913, when he was transferred to British East Africa. Here his health broke down, and in 1915 he was invalided home. He was created a C.M.G. in 1901, and a K.C.M.G. in 1907. He was the author of *How I became a governor* (London, 1913).

[*Who was who*, 1916-28; *Encyc. Can.*]

Williams, William (d. 1837), fur-trader, was appointed resident governor of the Hudson's Bay Company's territories, with headquarters at York Factory, at the height of the Selkirk troubles in 1818. In 1819, in consequence of the aggressions of the North West Company, he took an expedition to the Grand Rapids at the mouth of the Saskatchewan, and arrested a number of partners and clerks of the North West Company, some of whom were sent to England for trial and one of whom, Benjamin Frobisher (q.v.), died while trying to escape. A warrant was issued for the arrest of Williams; and George Simpson (q.v.) was sent out to hold his position in case he was removed from the territories over which he was governor. At the union of 1821, he was appointed joint governor with Simpson; and in 1822 he was placed in charge of the Southern Department. He returned to England in 1826; and he died in 1837.

[E. E. Rich (ed.), *Journal of occurrences in the Athabasca department, by George Simpson* (Toronto: The Champlain Society, 1938).]

Williams, Sir William Fenwick, Bart. (1800-1883), lieutenant-governor of Nova Scotia (1865-70), was born at Annapolis, Nova Scotia, on December 4, 1800, the son of Commissary-general Thomas Williams,

Barrack-master at Halifax, and Maria Walker. He was educated at the Royal Military Academy at Woolwich, and in 1825 he received a commission in the Royal Artillery. He rose in the army to the rank of general, which he attained in 1868. In 1841 he was sent to Turkey, for employment in the arsenal at Constantinople; and in 1854 he was appointed British commissioner with the Turkish army in Anatolia. He became practically commander-in-chief of the Turkish forces; and in the Russo-Turkish War he greatly distinguished himself by his gallant, though unsuccessful, defence of Kars. From 1856 to 1859 he was general-commandant of the Woolwich garrison; from 1859 to 1865 he was commander-in-chief of the British forces in Canada; and in 1865 he was appointed lieutenant-governor of Nova Scotia. In this capacity he assisted greatly in bringing about the successful issue of the negotiations for the inclusion of Nova Scotia in the Canadian Confederation. He left Nova Scotia in 1870; and from 1870 to 1876 he was governor of Gibraltar. In 1881 he was appointed constable of the Tower of London; and he died at London, England, on July 26, 1883. In 1852 he was created a C.B. (civil), in 1856 a K.C.B., and in 1871 a G.C.B. For his services in the Russo-Turkish war he was made a baronet, "of Kars". He was not married.

[*Dict. nat. biog.*; *Dom. ann. reg.*, 1883; Dent, *Can. port.*, vol. 4; Taylor, *Brit. Am.*, vol. 1; Le Jeune, *Dict. gén.*]

Williamson, Albert Curtis (1867-1944), portrait-painter, was born at Brampton, Ontario, in 1867. He studied art in Toronto, Canada, and Paris, France; and for some years he lived in France and Holland. Eventually, however, he returned to Canada; and during the latter part of his life he had a studio in Toronto. He painted the portraits of a number of people prominent in the public life of Canada; and examples of his work are to be found in the National Gallery at Ottawa, in the Art Gallery at Toronto, in the Parliament Buildings at Toronto, and in various colleges and universities. In 1907 he was elected an academician of the Royal Canadian Academy of Arts. He died, unmarried, in Toronto, Ontario, on April 18, 1944.

[*Can. who's who*, 1936-37; Morgan, *Can. men* (1912); N. MacTavish, *The fine arts in Canada* (Toronto, 1925).]

Williamson, Alexander Johnston (1796?-1870), poet, was born about 1796. He became a physician, but does not appear to have practised medicine. He became a journalist in Upper Canada; and in 1831 was editor of the *Anglo-Canadian*, a short-lived journal in Belleville, Upper Canada. In his later years he was a clerk in the Education Office at Toronto; and he died at Toronto, Ontario, on October 13, 1870. He was the author of *Origi-*

nal poems on various subjects (Toronto, 1836), *There is a God, with other poems* (Toronto, 1839), and *Devotional poems* (Toronto, 1840).

[C. C. James, *A bibliography of Canadian poetry* (Toronto, 1899).]

Williamson, James (1806-1895), astronomer, was born in Edinburgh, Scotland, on October 19, 1806. He was educated at Edinburgh University, and was licensed as a minister of the Presbyterian Church. In 1842 he was appointed professor of mathematics and natural philosophy at Queen's College, Kingston, Canada; and he was later professor of astronomy, director of the Kingston observatory, and vice-principal of Queen's. He died at Kingston, Ontario, on September 26, 1895. He married a sister of Sir John Macdonald (q.v.). He was given the degree of LL.D. by Glasgow University in 1855; and he was the author of *The inland seas of North America* (Kingston, 1854).

[R. Vashon Rogers, *Professor James Williamson* (Queen's quarterly, 1896); *Cyc. Am. biog.*]

Williamson, John (d. 1840), veteran, was a former private soldier in the 78th Regiment of the British army, who came to Canada and served as a sergeant in the battalion of Montreal volunteers formed at the time of the rebellion of 1837-38. He died at Edinburgh, Scotland, in 1840. While in Canada he published his autobiography, under the title *The narrative of a commuted pensioner* (Montreal, 1838).

[Morgan, *Bib. can.*]

Williams-Taylor, Sir Frederick (1863-1945), banker, was born at Moncton, New Brunswick, on October 23, 1863. He was educated privately, and in 1878 he entered the service of the Bank of Montreal. He became general manager of this bank in 1913, and continued in this capacity until his retirement in 1929. He died in Montreal, Quebec, on August 2, 1945. He was created a knight bachelor in 1913; and in 1915 he received the honorary degree of LL.D. from the University of New Brunswick.

[*Who's who*, 1945; *Who's who in Canada*, 1943-44; *Can. who's who*, 1938-39.]

Willing, Thomas Nathaniel (1858-1920), naturalist, was born in Toronto, Canada West, in 1858. He went to the North West Territories as a surveyor in his youth, and settled near Calgary in 1881. In 1899 he became chief game guardian in the North West Territories; and in 1910 he was appointed a lecturer in the College of Agriculture in the University of Saskatchewan. He became professor of natural history in this university; and he died at Saskatoon, Saskatchewan, on November 30, 1920.

[Morgan, *Can. men* (1912).]

Willingdon, Freeman Freeman-Thomas, first Earl of (1866-1941), governor-general of Canada (1926-31), was born on September 12, 1866. He was educated at Eton College and Trinity College, Cambridge; and was captain of both the Eton and Cambridge cricket elevens. He sat in the British House of Commons as a member, first for Hastings, and then for the Bodmin division of Cornwall, from 1900 to 1910; and in 1905 he was appointed a junior lord of the Treasury. From 1913 to 1919 he was governor of Bombay, and from 1919 to 1924 of Madras; and in 1926 he was appointed governor-general of Canada. He remained in this position until 1931, when he was appointed to the post of viceroy and governor-general of India, a post which he retained until 1936. He was created first Baron of Ratton in 1910, a G.C.I.E. in 1913, a G.B.E. in 1917, a G.C.S.I. in 1918, first Viscount of Ratendane of Willingdon in 1924, a G.C.M.G. in 1926, and first Earl of Willingdon in 1931. He died in London, England, on August 12, 1941. In 1892 he married the Hon. Marie Adelaide, daughter of the first Earl of Brassey; and by her he had one son, who succeeded to the earldom.

[*Who's who*, 1941; *Can. who's who*, 1936-37; *Burke's Peerage*; Saturday night, August 23, 1941; J. B. Cowan, *Canada's governors-general* (Toronto, 1952).]

Willis, Errick French (1896-1967), politician and premier, was born in Boissevain, Manitoba, March 21, 1896. He was educated at the University of Toronto (B.A.); the University of Alberta (M.A.); and the University of Manitoba (LL.B., LL.D.). He first ran for a seat in the House of Commons in the 1926 general election but was defeated. He was elected in 1930, and defeated in 1935. In 1936 he became leader of the Manitoba Conservative party and remained leader until 1954. He was elected to the Manitoba Legislature in 1936; was minister of public works from 1940 to 1950; and was minister of agriculture from 1958 to 1960. He was the first native-born lieutenant-governor of Manitoba (1960-65). He died at Winnipeg, Manitoba, January 9, 1967.

[*Can. who's who*, 1964-66.]

Willis, John Walpole (1792-1877), jurist, was born in England in 1792, the son of Dr. Willis, one of the physicians to George III. He was educated at the Charterhouse School and at Trinity Hall, Cambridge; and was called to the English bar. He became an equity lawyer, and published a treatise on *Equity pleading* (London, 1820). In 1827 he was appointed by royal warrant a judge of the Court of King's Bench in Upper Canada; but in 1828 he came into conflict with the attorney-general of Upper Canada, John Beverley Robinson (q.v.), as well as his brother judge, Mr. Justice Sherwood (q.v.), and was summarily dismissed from office by the lieutenant-governor, Sir Peregrine Maitland (q.v.). The Privy Council held that the removal had been too summary; but the British government did not send Willis back to Canada. He was appointed a judge in Demerara, British Guiana. Later he received an appointment as district judge in New South Wales; but in 1843 he was dismissed from this post. In 1852 he succeeded to the Wick Episcopi estates in Worcestershire; and he lived there until his death in September, 1877. In 1823 he married Lady Mary Isabella Bowes-Lyon, daughter of the Earl of Strathmore. He was the author of a pamphlet, *On the government of the British colonies* (London, 1850), in which he advocated colonial representation in the British parliament.

[D. B. Read, *Lives of the judges of Upper Canada* (Toronto, 1888); Morgan, *Cel. Can. and Bib. can.*; *Annual register*, 1877; J.C. Dent, *The Upper Canadian rebellion* (2 vols., Toronto, 1885).]

Willis, Michael (1798-1879), principal of Knox College, Toronto, was born in Greenock, Scotland, in 1798, the son of the Rev. William Willis, of Greenock. He became a minister of the Presbyterian Church (Old Light Burghers); and in 1847 he came to Canada as professor of systematic theology in Knox College. Of this institution he became principal; and he continued as such until 1870, when he returned to Scotland. He died at Aberlour, Banffshire, on August 19, 1879. While in Canada he published *Collectanea, Graeca et Latina; or, Selections from the Greek and Latin fathers* (Toronto, 1865).

[*Dom. ann. reg.*, 1879; *Cyc. Am. biog.*; Morgan, *Bib. can.*; W. Gregg, *History of the Presbyterian church in Canada* (Toronto, 1885); *Dict. Can. biog.*, vol. 10.]

Willis-O'Connor, Henry (1886-1957), aide-de-camp and author, was born at Ottawa, Ontario, on April 1, 1886, and died there on April 26, 1957. He joined the Governor-General's Foot Guards in Ottawa in 1906, and served throughout the First World War with the Canadians. From 1915 to 1920 he was A.D.C. to Sir Arthur Currie (q.v.). In 1919 he transferred to the Canadian Permanent Force, and rose to the rank of colonel. He was A.D.C. successively to five governors-general, prior to his retirement in 1946. In collaboration with Madge MacBeth, he was the author of an autobiography, entitled *Inside Government House* (Toronto, 1954).

[*Can. who's who*, 1948.]

Willison, Sir John Stephen (1856-1927), journalist and author, was born at Hills Green, Huron county, Ontario, on November 9, 1856, the son of Stephen Willison. He was educated in the public schools, and in 1882 became a journalist. From 1890 to 1902 he was editor-in-chief of the Toronto *Globe*; from 1902 to 1910 he was editor of the Toronto *News*; and in 1910 he became Canadian correspondent of

The Times. Though a Liberal up to 1902, he became after that date more and more an exponent of the Conservative point of view in politics; and in 1913 he was made a knight bachelor on the recommendation of the Borden government. In 1906 he was made an LL.D. of Queen's University, Kingston. He died at Toronto on May 27, 1927. He was twice married, first, in 1885 to Rachel Wood (d. 1925), daughter of Mrs. Margaret Turner, of Tiverton, Ontario; and secondly, in 1926, to Marjory MacMurchy (q.v.). His most notable work was *Sir Wilfrid Laurier and the Liberal party: A political history* (2 vols., Toronto, 1903; new and revised ed., Toronto, 1926); but he was also the author of *The railway question in Canada* (Toronto, 1897), *Anglo-Saxon amity* (Toronto, 1906), *The United States and Canada* (New York, 1908), *The new Canada* (London, 1912), *Reminiscences* (Toronto, 1919), *Agriculture and industry* (Toronto, 1920), *Partners in peace* (Toronto, 1923), and *Sir George Parkin, a biography* (London, 1929). He also founded and edited *Willison's Monthly* (1925-29).

[A. H. U. Colquhoun (ed.), *Press, politics, and people: The life and letters of Sir John Willison* (Toronto, 1935); *Who was who*, 1916-28; Morgan, *Can. men* (1912).]

Willison, Marjory, Lady, *née* **MacMurchy** (d. 1938), journalist and author, was born at Toronto, Ontario, the daughter of Archibald MacMurchy (q.v.). In 1926 she married Sir John Willison (q.v.); and she died at Toronto on December 15, 1938. She was the author of *The woman—bless her* (Toronto, 1916), *The Canadian girl at work* (Toronto, 1919), *The child's house* (London, 1923), *Golden treasury of famous books* (Toronto, 1929), and *The longest way round* (Toronto, 1937).

[*Can. who's who*, 1936-37; *Saturday night*, Dec., 1938.]

Willmott, Arthur Brown (1867-1914), geologist, was born at Nanticoke, Ontario, on March 11, 1867. He was educated at the University of Toronto (B.A., 1887; B.Sc., 1887) and at Harvard University (M.A., 1891). From 1892 to 1900 he was professor of natural science at McMaster University, Toronto; and in 1900 he became geologist, and in 1903 mines manager, for the Lake Superior Corporation at Sault Ste. Marie. He died at Toronto, Ontario, on May 8, 1914. He was the author of *The mineral wealth of Canada* (Toronto, 1897).

[Morgan, *Can. men* (1912).]

Wills, John (d. 1814?), fur-trader, became a partner of the XY Company shortly after 1798, and was one of the six wintering partners of the XY Company who became parters of the North West Company in 1804. Soon after 1804 he built Fort Gibraltar at the junction of the Red and Assiniboine rivers; and he remained in charge of the Red River district until 1806, when he was transferred to Rat River. He returned to the Red River, however, in 1809; and he remained in charge of this department until he was relieved, because of ill-health, by J. D. Cameron (q.v.) in the summer of 1814. He died at Fort Gibraltar, either in the latter part of 1814, or in the beginning of 1815. He was elected a member of the Beaver Club of Montreal in 1807.

[W. S. Wallace (ed.), *Documents relating to the North West Company* (Toronto: The Champlain Society, 1934).]

Willson, David (1778-1866), religious enthusiast, was born in Dutchess county, New York, June 7, 1778, the son of John Willson, formerly of Carrickfergus, Antrim, Ireland. In 1801 he came to Canada, and in 1802 he settled in the township of East Gwillimbury, Upper Canada. About 1812 he organized there a religious sect known as "the Children of Peace"; and at the village of Sharon he built, between 1825 and 1831, the Temple of Sharon, which is still standing. For over fifty years he guided the destinies of the sect he had founded; and he died at Sharon on January 19, 1866. About 1801 he married Phoebe Titus; and by her he had two, or possibly three, sons. Though a man of little education, he published *The rights of Christ* (Philadelphia, 1815), *The impressions of the mind* (Toronto, 1835), *Letters to the Jews* (Toronto, 1835), *Hymns and prayers* (2 vols., Toronto, 1846-49), *Sacred impressions of the mind in praise and prayer* (Toronto, 1853), and *The practical life of the author* (Toronto, 1860).

[J. Squair, *The temple of peace* (Women's Canadian Historical Society of Toronto, Transaction No. 20, 1919-20); J. L. Hughes, *Sketches of the Sharon temple and its founder* (Toronto, 1918).]

Willson, Henry Beckles (1869-1942), journalist and author, was born at Montreal, Quebec, on August 26, 1869. He was educated at Kingston, Ontario, and became a journalist. After serving an apprenticeship on the staff of some American newspapers, he went to England in 1892, and joined the staff of the London *Daily Mail*. Later he became a freelance writer and a prolific author of books, many of which related to Canada. He died at Beaulieu-sur-Mer, unoccupied France, on September 18, 1942. He was the author of *The tenth island* (London, 1897), *The great company* (Toronto, 1899), *Lost England* (London, 1902), *Lord Strathcona* (London, 1902), *The new America* (London, 1903), *Ledger and sword* (2 vols., London, 1903), *The story of rapid transit* (New York, 1903), *The romance of Canada* (London, 1907), *George III* (London, 1907), *Occultism and common-sense* (London, 1908), *The life and letters of James Wolfe* (London, 1909), *Nova Scotia* (London, 1911), *Quebec* (London, 1913), *The life of Lord Strathcona and Mount Royal* (London, 1915), *In the Ypres salient* (London, 1916), *Ypres*

(Bruges, 1920), *England* (London, 1922), *Redemption: A novel* (1924), *The Paris embassy* (London, 1927), *America's ambassadors to England* (London, 1928), *America's ambassadors to France* (London, 1928), *From Quebec to Piccadilly and other places* (London, 1929), *If I had fifty millions!* (London, 1931), *John Slidell and the Confederates in Paris* (New York, 1932), *Friendly relations* (Boston, 1934), *Heartache in Canaan, and other poems* (Oxford, 1938), and *Youth be dammed!* (London, 1938).

[*Who's who*, 1941; Morgan, *Can. men* (1912); *New York Times*, Sept. 22, 1942.]

Willson, Hugh Bowlby (1813-1880), publicist, was born at Winona, Upper Canada, September 15, 1813, the son of the Hon. John Willson (q.v.). He was educated at the Gore District Grammar School, and in 1841 he was called to the bar of Upper Canada. In 1849 he was one of the founders of the *Independent*, a newspaper established in Toronto to advocate the annexation of Canada to the United States; and later he assisted in founding the Hamilton *Spectator*. He died at New York, on April 29, 1880. He published a number of pamphlets on a variety of subjects: *Great Western Railway of Canada* (Hamilton, 1860), *The military defences of Canada* (Quebec, 1862), *The science of ship-building considered* (London, 1863), *High speed steamers* (Albany, 1866), *The science of money considered* (Washington, 1869), *A plea for Uncle Sam's money* (New York, 1870), *The money question considered* (London, 1874), *Industrial crises* (Washington, 1879), and *Currency* (New York, 1882).

[*Dom. ann. reg.*, 1880; Morgan, *Bib. can.*; *Dict. Can. biog.*, vol. 10.]

Willson, John (1776-1860), speaker of the Legislative Assembly of Upper Canada, was born in New Jersey, on August 5, 1776. He settled in Upper Canada in 1790, and in 1810 he was elected a member of the Legislative Assembly of Upper Canada for the West riding of York. He sat in the Assembly from 1810 to 1834; and he was the author of the Common School Act of the province. From 1824 to 1828 he was the speaker of the Assembly. In 1839 he was appointed to the Legislative Council of the province; but he was not included in the Legislative Council of united Canada in 1841. He died at his home in Ontario (now Winona), on May 26, 1860. His portrait hangs in the Toronto Public Library.

[Pearl Wilson, *Irish John Willson, and family, loyalists* (Ontario Historical Society, papers and records, 1936); J. Ross Robertson, *Landmarks of Canada* (Toronto, 1917).]

Wilmot, Lemuel Allan (1809-1878), politician, jurist, and lieutenant-governor of New Brunswick, was born in the county of Sunbury, New Brunswick, on January 31, 1809, the son of William Wilmot and Hannah, daughter of the Hon. William Bliss. He was educated at the College of New Brunswick, Fredericton; and in 1832 he was called to the bar of New Brunswick. In 1836 he was elected to represent York county as a Reformer in the House of Assembly of New Brunswick; and he sat in the House continuously until 1851. In 1843 he was appointed a member of the Executive Council of the province; but he resigned in 1845, with his colleagues, in protest against the action of Sir William Colebrooke (q.v.) in making appointments without reference to the Council. In 1847, however, he became attorney-general in the first "responsible government" established in New Brunswick, and he was the virtual head of the administration. He held office until 1851; and then he resigned to accept an appointment as puisne judge of the Supreme Court of New Brunswick. He sat on the bench until 1868, when he was appointed lieutenant-governor of New Brunswick. His period of office terminated in 1873; and he died at Fredericton, on May 20, 1878. He was twice married, (1) in 1832 to Jane (d. 1833), daughter of James Balloch, of Saint John, New Brunswick, and (2) in 1834 to Elizabeth, daughter of the Hon. William Black (q.v.).

[J. Hannay, *Lemuel Allan Wilmot* (Toronto, 1907); Rev. J. Lathern, *The Hon. Judge Wilmot, a biographical sketch* (Toronto, 1881); *Dict. nat. biog.*; *Cyc. Am. biog.*; *Dom. ann. reg.*, 1878; Dent, *Can. port.*, vol. 3; *Dict. Can. biog.*, vol.10.]

Wilmot, Montagu (d. 1766), governor of Nova Scotia (1764-66), was a British army officer who came to Nova Scotia about 1754. In 1755 he was appointed a member of the Executive Council of Nova Scotia; in 1763, lieutenant-governor of the province; and in 1764, governor. He died on May 23, 1766.

[B. Murdoch, *History of Nova Scotia* (3 vols., Halifax, N.S., 1865); T. B. Akins (ed.), *Selections from the public documents of Nova Scotia* (Halifax, N.S., 1869); *Dict. Can. biog.*, vol. 3.]

Wilmot, Robert Duncan (1809-1891), lieutenant-governor of New Brunswick (1880-85), was born in Fredericton, New Brunswick, on October 16, 1809, the son of John M. Wilmot, and a cousin of the Hon. Lemuel Allan Wilmot (q.v.). He was educated at Saint John, New Brunswick, and entered the shipping and milling business. For a number of years he lived in Liverpool, England; but in 1840 he returned to New Brunswick, and in 1846 he was elected a member of the Legislative Assembly of the province for Saint John. He continued to sit in the legislature for this constituency until 1861; and from 1851 to 1854 he was a member of the Executive Council with the portfolio of surveyor-general, and from 1856 to 1857 with the portfolio of provincial secretary. He opposed Confederation; and in 1865 he became

a member of the anti-confederationist government formed by Albert J. Smith (q.v.), and was elected to the Assembly for St. John county. In 1866, however, he deserted the anti-confederationists, was elected as a confederationist, and became a minister without portfolio in the Mitchell administration. He was a delegate to the London conference of 1866; and in 1867 he was called to the Senate of Canada. In 1878 he became a minister without portfolio in the government of Sir John Macdonald (q.v.), and was appointed speaker of the Senate. In 1880 he resigned from the Senate to accept appointment as lieutenant-governor of New Brunswick; and this post he occupied until 1885. He died at Oromocto, New Brunswick, on February 11, 1891.

[*Cyc. Am. biog.*; Dent, *Can. port.*, vol. 4; *Can. parl. comp.*; J. Hannay, *History of New Brunswick* (2 vols., Saint John, N.B., 1909).]

Wilmot, Samuel (1822-1899), pisciculturist, was born at Belmont farm, Clarke township, West Durham, Upper Canada, on August 22, 1822, the youngest son of Major Samuel Street Wilmot. He was educated at Upper Canada College, and devoted his life to agriculture and pisciculture. He was a pioneer in the artificial propagation of fish: at the beginning of his operations he had in his pond only three grilse and eight grown salmon. From these he took 20,000 eggs, and in the following year he turned out 15,000 young salmon. He became superintendent of fish culture for Canada under the Dominion government; and he supervised the establishment of fish-breeding establishments from the Atlantic to the Pacific. He died on May 17, 1899. In 1872 he married Helen Matilda, daughter of Charles Clark, of Cobourg, Ontario; and by her he had four sons and three daughters.

[*Cyc. Am. biog.*; Rose, *Cyc. Can. biog.* (1886); J. Squair, *The townships of Darlington and Clarke* (Toronto, 1927).]

Wilson, Sir Adam (1814-1891), jurist, was born in Edinburgh, Scotland, on September 22, 1814. He came to Canada in 1830, and for a few years was in business in Halton county, Upper Canada. In 1834, however, he entered the law office of Robert Baldwin (q.v.), and in 1839 he was called to the bar of Upper Canada (Q.C., 1850). From 1840 to 1849 he was in partnership with Robert Baldwin. In 1859 he was elected mayor of Toronto, being the first mayor elected by direct popular vote; and the same year he became the representative of North York in the Legislative Assembly. From 1862 to 1863 he was solicitor-general in the S. Macdonald-Sicotte administration; but in 1863 he was raised to the bench as a judge of the Court of Queen's Bench for Upper Canada. In 1878 he became chief justice of the Court of Common Pleas, and in 1884 of the Court of King's Bench, in Ontario. He retired from the bench in 1887, and he died at Toronto on

December 28, 1891. He married a daughter of Thomas Dalton (q.v.), proprietor of the *Patriot*, Toronto; and he was created a knight bachelor in 1887. He was the author of *A sketch of the office of constable* (Toronto, 1859).

[*Cyc. Am. biog.*; Dent, *Can. port.*, vol. 3; Rose, *Cyc. Can. biog.* (1886); Morgan, *Bib. can.*; J. C. Dent, *The last forty years* (2 vols., Toronto, 1880); W. J. Rattray, *The Scot in British North America* (4 vols., Toronto, 1880).]

Wilson, Alice Elizabeth (1897-1934), poet, was born in 1897, and died at Sherbrooke, Quebec, in 1934. Her verses were published posthumously in a volume entitled *My sanctuary garden* (Toronto, 1937).

[*Canadian bookman*, 1937.]

Wilson, Alice Evelyn (1881-1964), geologist and first woman to be admitted to the Fellowship of the Royal Society of Canada, was born in Ontario in 1881. Because of ill-health her university life was interrupted several times, and although she entered the University of Toronto in 1901, she did not receive her B.A. until 1911 while she was employed by the Geological Survey of Canada. In 1925 she was awarded a Canadian Federation of University Women's Clubs Scholarship and continued her studies at the University of Chicago, receiving her Ph.D. degree in 1929.

Dr. Wilson was associated with the Geological Survey of Canada for fifty-four years, beginning as a cataloguer of the fossil collection, which had been accumulating since 1840, and going on to do an intensive study of the geology of the Ottawa Valley while continuing her duties as assistant palaeontologist. Eventually she completed a detailed geological map of the 5,500 square miles east of the Rideau Lakes, a descriptive memoir, and a series of studies and reports several of which were published by the Royal Society of Canada. On her retirement from the Canadian government service in 1946, Dr. Wilson became a lecturer in Carleton University, where she remained for ten years.

Dr. Wilson continued her Ottawa Valley studies until 1963 and was the author of *The earth beneath our feet*, a child's guide to geology. She died at Ottawa, April 15, 1964.

[*Proc. Roy. Soc. Can.,* 1966; *Can. who's who*, 1948.]

Wilson, Cairine Reay (1885-1962), senator, was born in Montreal, Quebec, February 4, 1885. She was educated at Misses Symmers and Smith's school and the Trafalgar Institute. She was president of the League of Nations Society for Canada and the National Federation of Liberal Women of Canada, chairman of the Canadian National Committee on Refugees, and the first Canadian woman delegate to the fourth session of the United Nations General Assembly (1948). She was a Dame of Grace of the Order of St. John of Jerusalem and held the Cross of the Chevalier, Legion of Honour (France). In 1930 she was the first woman summoned to the Senate of Canada. She died on March 3, 1962, at Ottawa, Ontario.

[*Can. who's who*, 1955-57; *Saturday Night*, vol. 70 (June, 1955).]

Wilson, Charles (1808-1877), senator of Canada, was born at Coteau du Lac, Lower Canada, in April, 1808, the son of Alexander Wilson. He was for many years head of a hardware firm in Montreal, and was mayor of Montreal by acclamation from 1851 to 1853. In 1852 he was appointed a member of the Legislative Council of united Canada; and in 1867 he was called to the Senate of Canada by royal proclamation. He died in Montreal, May 4, 1877.

[*Can. parl. comp.*; *Dict. Can. biog.*, vol. 10.]

Wilson, Sir Daniel (1816-1892), president of University College, Toronto (1880-92), was born in Edinburgh, Scotland, on January 5, 1816, the second son of Archibald Wilson. He was educated at the Edinburgh High School and at Edinburgh University (B.A., 1837). He became interested in Scottish archaeology, and published *Memorials of Edinburgh* (2 vols., Edinburgh, 1848) and *The archaeology and prehistoric annals of Scotland* (2 vols., Edinburgh, 1851). In 1853 he received the appointment of professor of history and English literature in University College, Toronto, and this chair he occupied until his death. In 1880 he was appointed president of University College, and, on its reorganization in 1887, president of the University of Toronto. He died at Toronto on August 6, 1892. He was created a knight bachelor in 1888; and in 1885 he was elected president of the Royal Society of Canada, of which he was a charter member. After coming to Canada he published, in addition to many papers in learned journals, *Prehistoric man* (Cambridge, 1862), *Chatterton* (London, 1869), *Caliban* (London, 1872), *Spring wild flowers: A collection of poems* (London, 1875), *Reminiscences of old Edinburgh* (2 vols., Edinburgh, 1878), *William Nelson, a memoir* (Edinburgh, 1889), *The right hand: Left-handedness* (London, 1891), and *The lost Atlantis and other ethnographic studies* (Edinburgh, 1892).

[H. H. Langton, *Sir Daniel Wilson* (Toronto, 1929); W. Kingsford, *In memoriam — Sir D. Wilson* (Trans. Roy. Soc. Can., 1893); *Dict. nat. biog.*; Rose, *Cyc. Can. biog.* (1888); Dent, *Can. port.*, vol. 4; *Review of historical publications relating to Canada*, vol. v (Toronto, 1901), with bibliography.]

Wilson, Erastus William (1860-1922), insurance manager and soldier, was born in Belleville, Canada West, on July 1, 1860. He was educated in Belleville and Oshawa, and entered the insurance business. He became manager of the Manufacturers Life Insurance Company in Montreal. In 1882 he entered the Victoria Rifles in Montreal as a private; and he rose to command the regiment from 1903 to 1907. In 1909 he was appointed officer commanding the 18th Infantry Brigade; and from 1914 to 1919 he was district officer commanding M.D. No. 4 at Montreal. In 1917 he was awarded the C.M.G., and in 1918 he was promoted to the rank of major-general. He died at Montreal, Quebec, on May 15, 1922.

[*Who was who*, 1916-28; Morgan, *Can. men* (1912).]

Wilson, Harold Sowerby (1904-1959), educationist and author, was born in Campbellton, New Brunswick, on June 14, 1904, and died at Toronto, Ontario, on May 14, 1959. He was educated at Dalhousie University (B.A., 1927) and Harvard University (A.M., 1929; Ph.D., 1939); and after holding teaching appointments on the staff of several universities in the United States, was appointed associate professor of English in University College, Toronto, in 1946. He was the author of *On the design of Shakespearian tragedy* (Toronto, 1957).

[*Can. who's who*, 1955-57.]

Wilson, Isaiah Woodworth (1848-1928), local historian, was born at Hill Grove, Nova Scotia, on March 8, 1848; and died at Smith's Cove, Nova Scotia, in October, 1928. He was the author of *A geography and history of the county of Digby, Nova Scotia* (Halifax, N.S., 1900).

[R. J. Long, *Nova Scotia authors* (East Orange, N.J., 1918).]

Wilson, Jean (1910-1933), skater, was born in 1910, and was the undefeated holder of the title of champion of the North American speed-skating contests at five distances, when she died at Toronto, Ontario, on September 3, 1933.

[Toronto *Globe*, Sept. 4, 1933.]

Wilson, John (1809-1869), jurist, was born at Paisley, Scotland, in November, 1809, the eldest son of Ebenezer Wilson. He came to Upper Canada with his parents about 1823, and in 1835 was called to the bar of Upper Canada (Q.C., 1856). He practised law in London, Upper Canada; and in 1847, and again in 1854, he was elected to represent London in the Legislative Assembly. In 1863 he was elected for the St. Clair division to the Legislative Council; but he did not take his seat, as he was shortly afterwards appointed a judge of the Court of Common Pleas for Upper Canada. He died, in office, on June 3, 1869. He married a sister of Judge Hughes of St. Thomas, Upper Canada.

[D. B. Read, *Lives of the judges* (Toronto, 1888).]

Wilson, John Henry (1833-1912), senator of Canada, was born near Bytown (Ottawa), Upper Canada, on February 14, 1833. He was educated at the New York Medical College and at Victoria University, Cobourg (M.D., 1858). He practised medicine in St. Thomas, Ontario; and he represented East Elgin in the Ontario legislature from 1871 to 1879, and in the Canadian House of Commons from 1882 to 1891. He was called to the Senate of Canada in 1904; and he sat in the Senate until his death, at St. Thomas, Ontario, on July 3, 1912.

[*Can. who's who*, 1910; *Can. parl. comp.*; Morgan, *Can. men* (1898).]

Wilson, Lawrence Alexander (1864?-1934), senator of Canada, was born in Montreal, Canada East, about 1864, the son of a Scottish-Canadian father and a French-Canadian mother. He was educated at St. Mary's College, Montreal; and went into the wholesale wine and spirits business. He became wealthy, and was noted for his philanthropies and benefactions. From 1925 to 1930 he represented Vaudreuil-Soulanges in the Canadian House of Commons; and in 1930 he was called to the Senate of Canada. He died at Montreal, Quebec, on March 2, 1934. In 1933 he was created by the Pope a knight commander of the order of St. Gregory the Great.

[*Can. parl. comp.*; *Who's who in Canada*, 1932-33; Morgan, *Can. men* (1912).]

Wilson, Morley Evans (1881-1965), geologist, was born at Bright, Ontario, February 8, 1881. He graduated in arts from the University of Toronto in 1907, and studied at the University of Wisconsin, at the University of Chicago, and at Yale, which awarded him a Ph.D. in 1912. He spent his working life with the Geological Survey of Canada, specializing in Precambrian geology and ore deposits. He was involved in the mapping of the Abitibi district of Quebec and the Temiskaming area of Ontario. His detailed study of the Noranda area and its mineral resources, *Memoir 229, Noranda District Quebec—1941*, is considered a classic, and in 1959 he published *Memoir 315, Geological Survey Rouyn-Beauchastel map areas, Quebec*, which lies immediately south of the Noranda district. Mines in this area have produced over $25,000,000 in gold and silver as well as other minerals. Dr. Wilson was a fellow of the Royal Society of Canada and of the Geological Society of America, as well as of many other mining and geological societies. He was awarded the Selwyn G. Blaylock Medal of the Institute of Mining and Metallurgy in 1950 and the Willet G. Miller Medal of the Royal Society of Canada. He was interested in the formation of Carleton College and lectured there from 1947 to 1953, helping also to build a collection of mineral specimens and a geological library. He died at Ottawa, October 27, 1965.

[*Proc. Roy. Soc. Can.*, 1966; *Can. who's who*, 1955-57.]

Wilson, Norman Richard (1879-1944), educationist, was born at Cobourg, Ontario, on March 23, 1879. He was educated at the University of Toronto (B.A., 1899; M.A., 1901) and at the University of Chicago (Ph.D., 1908). He became a professor of mathematics at the University of Manitoba, and ultimately head of the department of mathematics. He was elected a fellow of the Royal Society of Canada in 1930. He died at Winnipeg, Manitoba, on December 27, 1944. With L. A. H. Warren, he was joint author of *College algebra* (New York, 1928).

[*Proc. Roy. Soc. Can.*, 1945; *Can. who's who*, 1936-37.]

Wilson, Richard Albert (1874-1949), educationist and author, was born at Renfrew, Ontario, on March 18, 1874, and died at Vancouver, British Columbia, on January 2, 1949. He was educated at Queen's University (B.A., 1901; M.A., 1902; Ph.D., 1906), and became a school-teacher in Ontario, and later in Saskatchewan. In 1915 he became professor of English language and literature in the University of Saskatchewan; he retired from this post in 1940. He was the author of *The birth of language* (London, 1937), a popular edition of which was issued later, with a preface by George Bernard Shaw, under the title *The miraculous birth of language* (London, 1946).

[*Can. who's who*, 1948.]

Wilson, Robert (1833-1912), clergyman and author, was born at Fort George, Scotland, on February 18, 1833. He was educated at Prince of Wales College, Charlottetown, Prince Edward Island, and at the University of Chicago (Ph.D., 1887). He was ordained a minister of the Methodist Church in 1854; and after serving in many pastorates in the Maritime provinces, he retired from the pastorate in 1905. He died at Saint John, New Brunswick, on June 24, 1912. He wrote under the *nom de plume* of "Mark Mapleton"; and he was the author of *Methodism in the Maritime provinces* (Halifax, 1893), as well as of two novels, *Tried but true* (Saint John, N.B., 1874) and *Never give up* (Saint John, N.B., 1878).

[Morgan, *Can. men* (1912); W. G. MacFarlane, *New Brunswick bibliography* (Saint John, N.B., 1895).]

Wilson, William (1798-1869), clergyman, was born in Lincolnshire, England, in 1798, and became a Wesleyan minister. After serving for fourteen years as a missionary in Newfoundland, he settled in Nova Scotia, and preached at Yarmouth and other places. He died at Point de Bute, Nova Scotia, in 1869. He was the author of *The modern crusade; or, The present Russian war* (Boston, 1854) and *Newfoundland and its missionaries* (Cambridge, Mass., 1866).

[R. J. Long, *Nova Scotia authors* (East Orange, N.J., 1918).]

Wiman, Erastus (1834-1904), author and capitalist, was born at Churchville, Peel county, Upper Canada, on April 21, 1834. He was educated in Toronto, and became in 1854 a journalist on the staff of the Toronto *Globe*. In 1860 he joined the staff of R. G. Dunn and Co.'s mercantile agency; in 1866 he was transferred to the head office of the company in New York; and later he became its general manager. In 1881 he was elected president of the Great North Western Telegraph Company of Canada; and in 1885 he became the first president of the Canadian Club in New York. He acquired a wide notoriety as the advocate of commercial union between Canada and the United States, and may be regarded as the father of the "unrestricted reciprocity" movement of the eighties. In 1897 he became a citizen of the United States; and he died at New York on February 9, 1904. Besides a number of pamphlets on commercial union, he wrote *Chances of success: Episodes and observations in the life of a busy man* (New York, 1893).

[E. Myers, *A Canadian in New York* (Can. mag., 1893); *Who was who in North America*; *Dict. Am. biog.*; *Cyc. Am. biog.*; Morgan, *Can. men* (1898); Rose, *Cyc. Can. biog.* (1888).]

Windle, Sir Bertram Coghill Alan (1858-1929), anthropologist, was born at Mayfield, Staffordshire, England, on May 8, 1858. He was educated at Trinity College, Dublin (M.A., 1878; M.D., 1883); and after serving on the staff of University College, Cork, and of Birmingham University, he was appointed in 1905 president of Queen's College, Cork. He retired from this position in 1919; and became professor of anthropology in St. Michael's College, Toronto. Later he was appointed special lecturer in ethnology in the University of Toronto. He died in Toronto on February 14, 1929. He was created a knight bachelor in 1912. He was the author of a large number of books and papers on anatomy, anthropology, archaeology, and religious history. Some of his lectures at the University of Toronto were published under the title *The Romans in Britain* (London, 1923).

[Monica Taylor, *Sir Bertram Windle: A memoir* (London, 1932); *Who was who*, 1929-40; *Can. who was who*, vol. 1.]

Wingfield, Alexander Hamilton (1828-1896), poet, was born in Blantyre, Lanarkshire, Scotland, on August 1, 1828. He emigrated to the United States about 1847, and about 1850 settled in Hamilton, Ontario. For many years he was a mechanic in the shops of the Great Western Railway; and in his later years he was a landing waiter in the Customs department. He died in Hamilton in 1896. He published *Poems and songs, in Scotch and English* (Hamilton, Ont., 1873).

[C. C. James, *A bibliography of Canadian poetry* (Toronto, 1899).]

Winslow, Edward (1746?-1815), loyalist, was born in Massachusetts about 1746, the son of Edward Winslow, and a great-great-grandson of that Edward Winslow who was governor of Plymouth Colony (1633-44). He was educated at Harvard College (B.A., 1765). During the American Revolution he was muster-master-general of the British forces in North America; and in 1783 he accompanied the loyalist refugees to Halifax, Nova Scotia. For two years he was secretary to the commander-in-chief in North America; and in 1784 he was appointed a member of the Executive Council of New Brunswick, with the office of surrogate general. In 1806 he was appointed a judge of the Supreme Court of New Brunswick. In 1808, as senior member of the Council, he became president and commander-in-chief of New Brunswick for a few months. He died in Fredericton, New Brunswick, on May 13, 1815.

[C. W. Rife, *Edward Winslow* (Canadian Historical Association Report, 1928); W. O. Raymond, *The Winslow papers* (Saint John, N.B., 1901); J. W. Lawrence, *The judges of New Brunswick* (Saint John, N.B., 1907); *Cyc. Am. biog.*]

Winslow, Joshua (1727-1801), loyalist, was born in Boston, Massachusetts, on January 23, 1727, the son of John Winslow. He served with distinction at the capture of Louisbourg in 1745, and he was commissary-general with the expedition to Nova Scotia in 1755. At the beginning of the American Revolution he removed to Halifax, and became paymaster-general of the British forces in North America. After the Revolution he settled in Quebec; and here he died in 1801. In 1759 he married his cousin, Anna Green (d. 1816), and by her he had one daughter.

[Alice M. Earle (ed.), *Diary of Anna Green Winslow* (Boston and New York, 1894); *Cyc. Am. biog.*]

Wintemberg, William John (1876-1941), archaeologist, was born at New Dundee, Ontario, on May 18, 1876. He was largely self-educated, but about 1903 came under the influence of David Boyle (q.v.), and became a leading authority on the archaeology of Canada. In 1912 he was attached to the Geological Survey of Canada; and in 1925 he was appointed assistant archaeologist, and in 1937 associate archaeologist, on the staff of the National Museum of Canada in Ottawa. In 1934 he was elected a fellow of the Royal Society of Canada; and he contributed a large number of valuable papers to the annual reports of the Ontario Provincial Museum, to the publications of the National Museum, and to the *Transactions* of the Royal Society of Canada. He died in Ottawa, Ontario, on April 25, 1941.

[*Proc. Roy. Soc. Can.*, 1941; *Can. who's who*, 1936-37.]

Winter, Charles Francis (1863-1946), soldier and author, was born at Montreal, Canada East, in 1863, and died at Ottawa, Ontario, on October 20, 1946. He was a veteran of the Nile campaign of 1882, of the Riel rebellion of 1885, and of the South African War; and during the First World War he served on the staff at military headquarters in Ottawa. From the rank of private he rose to that of brigadier. He was the author of *Lieutenant-General the Hon. Sir Sam Hughes, Canada's war minister* (Toronto, 1931).

[Toronto *Globe and Mail*, Oct. 21, 1946.]

Winter, Sir James Spearman (1845-1911), prime minister of Newfoundland (1897-1900), was born at Lamaline, Newfoundland, on January 1, 1845, and died at Toronto, Ontario, on October 6, 1911. He was called to the Newfoundland bar in 1867 (Q.C., 1880), became an outstanding lawyer, and was first elected to the House of Assembly for Burin in 1872. He was speaker of the House from 1877 to 1879, solicitor-general in the Whiteway administration from 1882 to 1885, and attorney-general in the Thorburn administration from 1885 to 1889. In 1893 he was appointed a judge of the Supreme Court of Newfoundland; but he resigned from the bench in 1896 to become leader of the Conservative party, and in 1897 he became prime minister and attorney-general. He was defeated in the House in 1900, and soon afterwards retired from politics. He was created a K.C.M.G. in 1888.

[*Dict. nat. biog.*, 2nd supp.; *Who was who*, 1897-1916; *Encyc. Can.*]

Winters, Robert Henry (1910-1969), industrialist, was born at Lunenburg, Nova Scotia, August 18, 1910. He was educated at Mount Allison University (B.A., 1931), and the Massachusetts Institute of Technology (B.S., M.S., 1934). He joined the staff of the Northern Electric Company of Montreal in 1934. From 1939 to 1946 he served with the R.C.E.M.E. in the Canadian army in Canada and Europe as a lieutenant-colonel. In the 1945 general election he contested the Queens-Lunenburg riding and was elected to the House of Commons at Ottawa. He was re-elected until 1957, when he lost his seat in the Diefenbaker sweep. He was minister of reconstruction and supply (1948-50), minister of resources and development (1950-3), and minister of public works (1953-7). He became president of Rio Tinto in 1957 and during the ensuing eight years became director of some twenty companies. Much of his energy was devoted to the Churchill Falls hydro-electric project which was undertaken by the British Newfoundland Corporation, of which he was chairman and chief executive officer.

Mr. Winters re-entered politics in 1965, at the urging of Prime Minister Pearson, and became minister of trade and commerce. In

1968 he resigned to contest the leadership of the Liberal party and had the support of its more conservative members. At the leadership convention he lost out to Pierre Elliott Trudeau on the fourth ballot. He did not re-enter politics but became, instead, president of Canada's largest foreign-investment company, Brazilian Light and Power Company (Brascan). He was vice-president of the Canadian Imperial Bank of Commerce, and was director of Canadair, Royal Insurance, International Business Machines, and Alcan Aluminum. He was first chairman of the Board of Governors of York University, Toronto, and took an interest in the development of Toronto's second university. He died at Monterey, California, October 10, 1969.

[*Can. who's who*, 1967-69; Toronto *Globe and Mail*, Oct. 13, 1969.]

Wintle, Ernest Douglas (1852-1917), ornithologist, was born at Gloucester, England, on June 29, 1852; and died at Montreal, Quebec, on July 19, 1917. He was the author of *The birds of Montreal* (Montreal, 1896).

[*Ottawa naturalist*, 1918.]

Wishart, William Thomas (d. 1853), clergyman and author, was a native of Scotland, and was ordained a minister of the Church of Scotland. He came to Canada, and was stationed first at Shelburne, Nova Scotia, and then at Saint John, New Brunswick. He died at Saint John in 1853. He was the author of *The decalogue the best system of ethics* (Halifax, N.S., 1842), *Extracts of lectures on political economy* (Saint John, N.B., 1845), *A series of outlines or theological essays on various subjects connected with Christian doctrine and practice* (Saint John, N.B., 1847), and *Six disquisitions on doctrinal and practical theology* (Saint John, N.B., 1853).

[W. G. MacFarlane, *New Brunswick bibliography* (Saint John, N.B., 1895); Morgan, *Bib. can.*]

Withrow, Oswald Charles Joseph (1878-1946), physician and author, was born in Oxford county, Ontario, in 1878, and died at Toronto, Ontario, on February 5, 1946. He was educated at the University of Toronto (M.B., 1902), and he practised medicine, first in Fort William and then in Toronto. In 1927 he was convicted of performing an illegal operation (though he maintained his innocence), and was sentenced to seven years in the penitentiary. On his release, he published an attack on the penal system in Ontario, under the title *Shackling the transgressor* (Toronto, 1933). He also wrote *Talks on sex education* (Toronto, 1919), *The romance of the Canadian National Exhibition* (Toronto, 1936), and *Poems from prison* (Toronto, 1937).

[Toronto *Globe and Mail*, Feb. 6, 1946.]

Withrow, William Henry (1839-1908), clergyman, author, and journalist, was born in Toronto, Upper Canada, on August 6, 1839, the son of James Withrow and Ellen Sanderson. He was educated at the Toronto Academy, at Victoria College, Cobourg, and at the University of Toronto (B.A., 1863; M.A., 1864). In 1866 he was admitted to the ministry of the Methodist Church, and in 1874 he was appointed editor of the *Canadian Methodist Magazine*, a position which he continued to occupy for more than a quarter of a century. He was a voluminous writer, and published many books of an historical or religious nature. His most important work was *The catacombs of Rome* (New York, 1874). In 1880 he was made a D.D. of Victoria University; and in 1884 he was elected a fellow of the Royal Society of Canada. He died in Toronto on November 12, 1908.

[*Proc. Roy. Soc. Can.*, 1909; *Cyc. Am. biog.*; Morgan, *Can. men* (1898); Rose, *Cyc. Can. biog.* (1886); L. E. Horning and L. J. Burpee, *A bibliography of Canadian fiction* (Toronto, 1904); A. MacMurchy, *Handbook of Canadian literature* (Toronto, 1906).]

Wix, Edward (1802-1866), clergyman and author, was born in England, in 1802, and died there on November 24, 1866. He was educated at Trinity College, Oxford (B.A., 1820; M.A., 1828), and was ordained a clergyman of the Church of England. He served as an archdeacon in Newfoundland from 1830 to 1839; and he was the author of *Six months of a Newfoundland missionary's journal* (London, 1836; 2nd ed., 1836).

[J. A. Venn, *Alumni Cantabrigienses*, Part II, vol. VI; *Encyc. Can.*; *Newfoundland supp.*]

Wodson, Henry Milner (1874-1952), journalist and author, was born at Newcastle-on-Tyne, England, in 1874, and died at Toronto, Ontario, on March 8, 1952. He came to Canada after 1900, and for over thirty years was a reporter on the Toronto *Evening Telegram*. Under the pseudonym of "Henry Milner", he published a novel entitled *The lad Felix* (Toronto, 1912); and he was the author also of *Private Warwick: The musings of a Canuck in khaki* (Toronto, 1915), *The Whirlpool: Scenes from Toronto police court* (Toronto, 1917), and *The justice shop* (Toronto, 1931).

[Toronto *Globe and Mail*, March 9, 1952.]

Wolfe, James (1727-1759), soldier, was born at Westerham, Kent, England, on January 2, 1727, the son of Colonel Edward Wolfe. He was educated at Westerham and at Greenwich; and in 1741 he obtained a commission as second lieutenant in his father's regiment of Marines. In 1742 he was transferred to the 12th Foot; and during the next fifteen years he saw service in the Netherlands, in Germany, and in Scotland. He was present at Dettingen in 1743, and at Culloden in 1745. Promoted to be lieutenant-colonel in 1750, and colonel in 1757, he was appointed in 1758 a brigadier-general in the expedition against Louisbourg; and the capture of Louisbourg was mainly due to his dash and resourcefulness. William Pitt, disregarding the claims of senior officers, then appointed him to command the expedition against Quebec in 1759, with the rank of major-general, at the age of thirty-two years. He invested the citadel of Quebec during the summer of 1759, and on the night of September 12-13 he succeeded in placing his army on the Plains of Abraham, to the west of Quebec. The battle which followed, on the morning of September 13, resulted in the defeat of the French and the capture of Quebec. But during the battle Wolfe fell, mortally wounded, and died a few minutes later. He was not married.

[W. T. Waugh, *James Wolfe* (Montreal, 1928); B. Willson, *The life and letters of James Wolfe* (London, 1909); R. Wright, *The life of Major-general James Wolfe* (London, 1864); E. Salmon, *General Wolfe* (London, 1909); F. Parkman, *Montcalm and Wolfe* (2 vols., Boston, 1884); *Dict. nat. biog.*; F. E. Whitton, *Wolfe and North America* (New York, 1971); H. R. Casgrain, *Wolfe and Montcalm* (Toronto, 1964); O. Warner, *With Wolfe to Quebec* (Toronto, 1972); *Dict. Can. biog.*, vol. 3.]

Wolfenden, Richard (1836-1911), soldier and civil servant, was born in England on March 20, 1836. He entered the British army as an officer in the Royal Engineers, and was sent to British Columbia. Here he served as an engineer officer for five years; and then, after his retirement from the army, he became an officer in the Canadian militia, in which he rose to the rank of lieutenant-colonel. In 1863 he was appointed king's printer in British Columbia; and he retained this position until his death, at Victoria, British Columbia, on October 5, 1911. In 1903 he was awarded the Imperial Service Order.

[*Can. who's who*, 1910; J. B. Kerr, *Biographical dictionary of well-known British Columbians* (Vancouver, B.C., 1890).]

Wolseley, Garnet Joseph Wolseley, first Viscount (1833-1913), soldier, was born at Golden Bridge House, county Dublin, Ireland, on June 4, 1833, the son of Major Garnet Joseph Wolseley, of the 25th Borderers. He entered the army as a second lieutenant in 1852, and saw service successively in India, in the Crimea, and in China. In 1861 he was sent to Canada as assistant quartermaster-general, and in 1865 became deputy quartermaster-general, with the rank of colonel. In 1870 he was chosen to command the force sent west to the Red River to quell the Riel insurrection; and for his services in this expedition he received the C.B. and the K.C.M.G. Later he commanded the Ashanti expedition of

1873-74, the Egyptian expedition of 1882, and the Nile expedition of 1885; and for his services in the last two expeditions he was created first a baron and then a viscount. In 1895 he succeeded the Duke of Cambridge as commander-in-chief of the British army, with the rank of field marshal; but he retired in 1899, and he died at Menton, France, on March 25, 1913. He was the author of *The story of a soldier's life* (2 vols., London, 1903).

[Sir F. Maurice and Sir George Arthur, *The life of Lord Wolseley* (London, 1924); Sir George Arthur (ed.), *The letters of Lord and Lady Wolseley* (London, 1922); *Dict. nat. biog.*, 1912-21; *Who was who*, 1897-1916.]

Wood, Andrew Trew (1826-1903), senator of Canada, was born at Mount Norris, Armagh, Ireland, the son of David Wood and Frances Bigham Trew. He was educated in Ireland, but came to Canada while still in his teens, and in 1848 entered the hardware business in Hamilton, Upper Canada. He acquired wealth, and in 1881 was a member of the Howland syndicate that offered to construct the Canadian Pacific Railway. He represented Hamilton in the Canadian House of Commons from 1874 to 1878, and again from 1896 to 1900. In 1901 he was appointed to the Canadian Senate; and he died at Hamilton on January 21, 1903. He was twice married, (1) in 1851 to Mary, daughter of William Freeman, and (2) in 1863 to Jennie, daughter of George H. White, Yorkville, Upper Canada.

[Morgan, *Can. men* (1898); *Can. parl. comp.*; *Can. who was who*, vol. 2.]

Wood, Edmund Burke (1820-1882), chief justice of Manitoba (1874-82), was born near Fort Erie, Upper Canada, on February 13, 1820. He was educated at Overton College, Ohio (B.A., 1848), and was called to the bar of Upper Canada in 1848 (Q.C., 1872). From 1863 to 1867 he represented West Brant in the Legislative Assembly of Canada, and from 1867 to 1872 he represented the same constituency in both the Canadian House of Commons and the Legislative Assembly of Ontario. From 1867 to 1871 he was provincial treasurer of Ontario, in Sandfield Macdonald's "Patent Combination", and he incurred much obloquy on account of his desertion of Sandfield Macdonald (q.v.) in the crisis which led to the defeat of the government in 1871. In 1873 he re-entered the House of Commons as member for West Durham; but in 1874 he was appointed chief justice of Manitoba, and he held this post until his death at Winnipeg, on October 7, 1882. In parliament he was known by the *sobriquet* of "Big Thunder".

[*Dom. ann. reg.*, 1882; *Cyc. Am. biog.*; Dent, *Can. port.*; C. R. W. Biggar, *Sir Oliver Mowat* (2 vols., Toronto, 1905); J. P. Robertson, *A political manual of Manitoba* (Winnipeg, 1887).]

Wood, Elizabeth Wyn (1903-1966), sculptor, was born at Orillia, Ontario, October 8, 1903. She was educated in Toronto and studied with Emmanuel Hahn, Arthur Lismer, J. E. H. MacDonald, C. M. Manly, and others at the Ontario College of Art (1921-26) and with Edward McCarter and Robert Laurent at the Art Students League in New York (1926-27). She married Emmanuel Hahn in 1926. She was active in the Canadian Arts Council as its organizing secretary (1944-45); and was chairman of the International Relations Committee (1945-48) and vice-president (1948-49). She also lectured, in Canada and the United States, on Canadian art. She was a member of the Royal Canadian Academy. She is probably best known for her powerful Stephen Leacock (q.v.) memorial in Orillia, but she has done many sculptures, including a bust of Leslie Frost (q.v.), four fountains and a monument to King George VI at Niagara Falls, and a fountain at the Canadian National Institute for the Blind in Toronto. Her work may be seen in the National Gallery of Canada, the Winnipeg Art Gallery, the Vancouver Art Gallery, the Art Gallery of Ontario, and thirty other public collections. She died at Toronto, Ontario, January 27, 1966.

[*Can. who's who*, 1961-63; *Encyc. Can.* (1972); *Creative Canada*, vol. I. (1971).]

Wood, Enoch (1804-1888), clergyman, was born in Lincolnshire, England, in 1804. He entered the service of the Wesleyan Missionary Society in 1825; and from 1826 to 1846 he was stationed in various charges in New Brunswick. In 1847 he was appointed superintendent of missions in the Wesleyan Methodist Church in Canada, with headquarters in Toronto; and from 1851 to 1857, and again in 1862, he was president of the Wesleyan Methodist Conference. He was superannuated in 1881; and he died at Davenport, near Toronto, Ontario, on January 31, 1888. Victoria University conferred on him the honorary degree of D.D. in 1860.

[Rose, *Cyc. Can. biog.* (1888); G. H. Cornish, *A cyclopaedia of Methodism in Canada* (2 vols., Toronto, 1881-1903).]

Wood, Henry Wise (1860-1941), agriculturist, was born near Monroe City, Missouri, on May 31, 1860. He was educated at the Christian University, Canton, Missouri; and he became a farmer. He farmed in Missouri until 1905; then he settled in Alberta, and in 1911 became a naturalized British subject. He was elected president of the United Farmers of Alberta in 1916; and he exerted a profound influence on agrarian policies in Canada, especially in regard to the formation of wheat pools. He died at Calgary, Alberta, on June 10, 1941. He was awarded the C.M.G. in 1935 "for service to agriculture in western Canada".

[W. K. Rolph, *Henry Wise Wood of Alberta* (Toronto, 1950); *Can. who's who*, 1938-39.]

Wood, Herbert Fairlie (1914-1967), soldier and author, was born in Toronto, Ontario, July 25, 1914; he attended Upper Canada College, Canadian Army Staff College (1943), and Staff College, Camberley, England (1947). He served with the 4th Armoured Division in north-west Europe during the Second World War, becoming major in 1944. He was chief instructor of the Canadian Infantry School in 1949 and commanded the 3rd Battalion of the Princess Patricia's Canadian Light Infantry in Korea (1952-53). From 1956 to 1959 he was secretary of the Army Council. He was appointed army historian in 1959 and retired in 1965. *Strange battleground* (1966) is the official history of the Canadian participation in the Korean War. He also wrote *Forgotten Canadians* (1963), a series of biographies of interesting but neglected nineteenth-century Canadians; a humorous novel, *The Private War of Jacket Coates* (1966); *The Silent Witness* (1967); and *Vimy* (1967). His work is strongly nationalist and carefully researched. He died in London, England, May 13, 1967, and was buried in Surrey, England.

[*Saturday Night* (Toronto, June, July, 1963); *Can. who's who*, 1964-66; Metropolitan Toronto Library Board, *Biographical scrapbooks*, vol. 33.]

Wood, Joanna E. (d. 1919), novelist, was born in Lanarkshire, Scotland, and came to Canada with her parents in early life. For many years she lived at Queenston Heights, Ontario; and she died in Detroit, Michigan, in 1919. She was the author of *The untempered wind* (Toronto, 1898), *Judith Moore* (Toronto, 1898), *A daughter of witches* (Toronto, 1900), and *Farden Ha'* (London, 1902).

[L. E. Horning and L. J. Burpee, *A bibliography of Canadian fiction* (Toronto, 1904); Morgan, *Can. men and women* (1912).]

Wood, John Fisher (1852-1899), controller of inland revenue and customs for Canada (1892-96), was born in Elizabethtown, Canada West, on October 12, 1852, the son of John Wood. He was called to the bar of Ontario in 1876 (Q.C., 1890), and practised law in Brockville. He represented Brockville in the Canadian House of Commons from 1882 to his death; in 1890-91 he was deputy speaker of the house; and from 1892 to 1896 he was a member of the government, first as controller of inland revenue, and then as controller of customs. In 1896 he was one of the "nest of traitors", so called, who deserted Sir Mackenzie Bowell (q.v.). He died on March 14, 1899. He was not married.

[*Can. parl. comp.*; *Can. men* (1898); J. C. Hopkins, *Life and work of the Rt. Hon. Sir John Thompson* (Brantford, Ont., 1895).]

Wood, Josiah (1843-1927), lieutenant-governor of New Brunswick (1912-17), was born at Sackville, New Brunswick, on April

18, 1843, the son of Mariner Wood. He was educated at Mount Allison University (B.A., 1863; M.A., 1866; D.C.L., 1891), and was called to the bar in 1866. Later, he abandoned law, and entered his father's ship-building business, to the control of which he succeeded on his father's death. From 1882 to 1895 he represented Westmorland in the Canadian House of Commons; and in 1895 he was appointed a member of the Canadian Senate. In 1912 he was appointed lieutenant-governor of New Brunswick, and he retired from office in 1917. In 1912 he was made an LL.D. of the University of New Brunswick. He was for a number of years treasurer of Mount Allison University; and in 1925 he founded in connection with this university the Josiah Wood Lectures. He died at Sackville, New Brunswick, on May 13, 1927.

[*Can. who was who*, vol. 1; *Can. parl. comp.*; Morgan, *Can. men* (1912).]

Wood, Louis Aubrey (1883-1955), educationist and author, was born in London, Ontario, on August 19, 1883, and died at Eugene, Oregon, on February 5, 1955. He was educated at the University of Toronto (B.A., 1905), the Montreal Presbyterian College (B.D., 1908), and the University of Heidelberg (Ph.D., 1911); and from 1914 to 1923 he was on the staff of the University of Western Ontario. He was appointed assistant professor of economics in the University of Oregon in 1924, associate professor in 1930, professor in 1935, and emeritus professor in 1949. He was the author of *The war chief of the Six Nations* (Toronto, 1914), *The Red River colony* (Toronto, 1915), *A history of farmers' movements in Canada* (Toronto, 1924), and *Union-management co-operation on the railroads* (New Haven, 1931).

[*Can. who's who*, 1953-54.]

Wood, Samuel Casey (1830-1913), provincial secretary, commissioner of agriculture, and provincial treasurer of Ontario (1873-85), was born at Bath, Upper Canada, in 1830, the son of Thomas Smith Wood. From 1871 to 1883 he represented South Victoria in the Ontario legislature; and from 1875 to 1883 he was a member of the Mowat government. In 1883 he retired from politics, and devoted himself to business. He died at Toronto on April 11, 1913. He married in 1854 Charlotte Maria Parkinson, of Mariposa, Upper Canada; and by her had several children.

[Morgan, *Can. men* (1912); *Can. parl. comp.*; Rose, *Cyc. Can. biog.* (1886); *Cyc. Am. biog.*]

Wood, Samuel Thomas (1860-1917), journalist, was born in Wollaston township, Hastings county, Canada West, on January 16, 1860, and he was educated in Belleville, Ontario. He joined the staff of the Toronto *Globe* in 1891, and became an editorial writer.

A number of his nature studies, originally published as editorials, were published under the title *Rambles of a Canadian naturalist* (Toronto, 1915), and he was also the author of *A primer of political economy* (Toronto, 1901) and *How we pay each other* (Toronto, 1917). He died at Toronto on November 6, 1917.

[Sir J. Willison and others, *A tribute to S. T. Wood* (Toronto, 1917); *Can. who was who*, vol. 1; Morgan, *Can. men* (1912).]

Wood, Stuart Zachary Taylor (1889-1966), R.C.M.P. Commissioner, was born at Napanee, Ontario, October 17, 1889, the son of Zachary Taylor Wood (q.v.). He was educated at the Royal Military College and entered the Royal North West Mounted Police in 1912. He served in the First World War with the R.C.M.P. cavalry unit. On his return to Canada he served in many parts of the country, including five years on Herschel Island. He was in charge of the Regina detachment during the Regina Riots of 1935. In 1936 he went to Ottawa to head the Criminal Investigation Branch. He became commissioner in 1938, and retired in 1951. He died at Ottawa, Ontario, June 3, 1966.

[Metropolitan Toronto Library Board, *Biographical scrapbooks*, vol. 9; *Can. who's who*, 1961-63.]

Wood, William Charles Henry (1864-1947), historian, was born at Quebec, Canada East, on June 7, 1864, and died at Quebec on September 2, 1947. He was educated at Wellington School in England and at an English army tutor's in Germany. On his return to Canada in 1887, he was commissioned in the 8th Royal Rifles of Quebec; he was promoted lieutenant-colonel in command of the regiment in 1907, and colonel on retirement in 1910. He became an outstanding authority on Canadian military history. He was the author of *The fight for Canada* (London, 1904), and of eight volumes dealing with military and naval history in the *Chronicles of Canada* and the *Chronicles of America* series; and he edited for the Champlain Society *The logs of the conquest of Canada* (Toronto, 1909) and *Select British documents of the Canadian War of 1812* (3 vols., Toronto, 1920-28). He also wrote *In the heart of old Canada* (Toronto, 1913), and edited *The storied province of Quebec* (5 vols., Toronto, 1931-32). With A. G. Doughty (q.v.), he was joint author of *The King's book of Quebec* (2 vols., Quebec, 1911). He was elected a fellow of the Royal Society of Canada in 1905, and was president of Section II in 1908-09.

[*Proc. Roy. Soc. Can.*, 1948; *Can. who's who*, 1938-39; Morgan, *Can. men* (1912).]

Wood, Zachary Taylor (1860-1915), assistant commissioner of the Royal North West Mounted Police, was born in Nova Scotia on November 27, 1860, and was educated at the Royal Military College, Kingston. He served as adjutant of the Winnipeg battalion during the North West Rebellion, and was present at the battle of Batoche in 1885. After the rebellion he was appointed an inspector of the Royal North West Mounted Police; and he was in command of the detachment of the Police sent to the Yukon in 1897. He was promoted to the rank of assistant commissioner in 1902; and on several occasions he acted as administrator of the Yukon Territory. He died at Asheville, North Carolina, on January 15, 1915. He was a great-grandson of Zachary Taylor, twelfth president of the United States of America.

[Morgan, *Can. men* (1912).]

Woodhouse, Arthur Sutherland Pigott (1895-1964), scholar, was born at Port Hope, Ontario, September 27, 1895. He spent his childhood in England but received his high school education at Barrie, Ontario, and spent his undergraduate years at University College, University of Toronto, before entering Harvard University Graduate School (A.M., 1923). He became assistant professor of English at the University of Manitoba in 1923, remaining there until he joined the English department at Toronto in 1929. He became head of the department in University College in 1945 and of the school of graduate studies in 1948. He was not only a fine and stimulating teacher but a scholar of great distinction in Canada. Almost one hundred of his students became teachers of English in universities throughout the world. He served for thirteen years as editor of the *University of Toronto Quarterly* and was founder and long-time editor of the annual survey *Letters in Canada*. He lectured in universities in North America and Britain and his influence on the development of the humanities in Canada was not only that of an academic (with Watson Kirkconnell he produced a historic survey *The humanities in Canada (1947)*), but that of one who was able to influence the direction of grants and scholarships to enable Canadian scholars to undertake more extensive research and publication in this field. He was an authority on John Milton and the era of the Puritan Revolution, but this was but an outstanding evidence of his knowledge and understanding of the development of human relationships. His most outstanding work was *Puritanism and liberty* (Toronto, 1938). Other works were *Collins and the creative imagination* (Toronto, 1931), *Comus once more* (Toronto, 1950), and *The heavenly muse: A preface to Milton* (Toronto, 1972). He died at Toronto, October 31, 1964. He was a fellow of the Royal Society of Canada, and a founding member of the Humanities Research Council of Canada.

[*Trans. Roy. Soc. Can.*, 1965; *Can. who's who*, 1955-57; *Encyc. Can.*]

Woodley, Edward Carruthers (1878-1955), educationist and author, was born in Montreal, Quebec, on August 2, 1878, and died there on February 13, 1955. He was educated at McGill University (B.A., 1900; M.A., 1902), and during his earlier years was engaged in educational work in India and the Near East. He returned to Canada in 1920, taught school in Westmount, and from 1930 to his retirement in 1945 was a special officer of the department of education for the province of Quebec. In 1944 he was elected a fellow of the Royal Historical Society. He was the author of *Legends of French Canada* (Toronto, 1931), *Canada's romantic heritage* (Toronto, 1940), *Our Canadian government* (Toronto, 1944), *Old Quebec trails and homes* (1947), *Untold tales of old Quebec* (Toronto, 1949), and *The Bible in Canada* (Toronto, 1953).

[*Can. who's who*, 1952-54.]

Woodrow, Mrs. Constance, *née* **Davies** (1899-1937), poet, was born in 1899, lived in Toronto, Ontario, and died at Whitby, Ontario, on August 1, 1937. She was the author of *The Celtic heart* (Toronto, 1929).

[Private information.]

Woods, James Hossack (1867-1941), journalist, was born at Quebec City, July 12, 1867, and was educated at McGill University and the University of Manitoba. He became a journalist, and in 1907 was appointed editor and managing director of the Calgary *Daily Herald*. He was twice president of the Canadian Press Association; from 1929 to 1931 he was president of the Canadian Chamber of Commerce; and in 1935 he was head of the Canadian delegation to the League of Nations Assembly in Geneva. He was awarded in 1935 the C.M.G. He died at Calgary, Alberta, on May 21, 1941.

[*Can. who's who*, 1936-37; Morgan, *Can. men* (1912).]

Woods, Sir James William (1855-1941), merchant, was born in Woodstock, Canada West, in 1855. In 1874 he entered the employ of Gordon Mackay and Co., wholesale drygoods merchants, in Toronto; and he became the president of this company. During the First World War he was director of purchases on the British War Mission to the United States; and in 1919 he was created a K.B.E. He died in Toronto, Ontario, on April 25, 1941.

[*Can. who's who*, 1936-37; *Who's who*, 1940.]

Woods, Robert Stuart (1819-1906), jurist and historian, was born at Sandwich, Upper Canada, in 1819. He served as a volunteer during the rebellion of 1837, and was present at the cutting-out of the *Caroline* at Niagara Falls. In 1842 he was called to the bar of Upper Canada (Q.C., 1872), and in 1885 he was appointed a judge of the county of Kent. This position he retained until his death at

Chatham, Ontario, on November 20, 1906. He was the author of *The burning of the Caroline and other reminiscences of 1837-8* (pamphlet, Chatham, Ont., 1896) and *Harrison Hall and its associations* (Chatham, Ont., 1896).

[*Can. who was who*, vol. 1; Morgan, *Can. men* (1898); Rose, *Cyc. Can. biog.* (1886).]

Woods, William Carson (1860-1902), author, was born in 1860, the son of Alexander Woods, a merchant in Quebec. He was educated at the Quebec High School and at Stanstead College; and he entered his father's business. He lived successively in Winnipeg, Toronto, and Quebec; and he died in July, 1902. He was the author of *The isle of the massacre* (Toronto, 1901).

[L. E. Horning and L. J. Burpee, *A bibliography of Canadian fiction* (Toronto, 1904).]

Woodsworth, James (d. 1917), clergyman and author, was born in Toronto, the son of Richard Woodsworth, a local preacher in the Methodist Church. He was ordained a minister of the Methodist Church in 1864, and in 1882 he was sent to the Portage la Prairie circuit in the West. He remained in the West for the rest of his life, and for many years he was superintendent of north-west missions for the Methodist Church. He retired from this post in 1915; and he died in Winnipeg, Manitoba, on January 26, 1917. He was the author of *Thirty years in the Canadian north-west* (Toronto, 1917).

[Morgan, *Can. men* (1912).]

Woodsworth, James Shaver (1874-1942), clergyman, politician, and author, was born in Etobicoke township, near Toronto, Ontario, on July 29, 1874, the son of the Rev. James Woodsworth (q.v.). He was educated at the University of Manitoba (B.A., 1896) and at Victoria University, Toronto (B.D., 1900), and was ordained a minister of the Methodist Church in 1896. After several years of pastoral work, he became interested in social welfare work; and in 1919 he became implicated in the Winnipeg strike, when he was arrested on a charge of sedition—a charge later withdrawn. In 1921 he was elected to represent North Winnipeg in the Canadian House of Commons; and he continued to represent this constituency until his death. In 1932 he was elected chairman of the national council of the Co-operative Commonwealth Federation; and became the parliamentary leader of the C.C.F. party. He died at Vancouver, British Columbia, on March 21, 1942. He was the author of *The strangers within our gates* (Toronto, 1908), *My neighbor* (Toronto, 1910), and *Studies in rural citizenship* (Winnipeg, 1915).

[Olive O. Ziegler, *Woodsworth, social pioneer* (Toronto, 1935); *Can. who's who*, 1936-37; Morgan, *Can. men* (1912); Grace MacInnis, *J. S. Woodsworth* (Toronto, 1953).]

Woodward, William Culham (1885-1957), lieutenant-governor of British Columbia (1941-46), was born on Manitoulin Island, Ontario, on April 24, 1885, and died in Hawaii on February 24, 1957. He was educated in the public schools of Vancouver, and in 1901 entered the service of the Royal Bank of Canada; but in 1908 he joined the staff of the family business, the Woodward Stores, Ltd., and in 1937 he became its president. From 1941 to 1946 he was lieutenant-governor of British Columbia.

[*Can. who's who*, 1952-54; *Can. parl. guide*, 1946; *Encyc. Can.*]

Woolverton, Linus (1846-1914), horticulturist, was born at Grimsby, Canada West, in 1846. He was educated at the University of Toronto (B.A., 1869; M.A., 1870), and became a fruit-grower. From 1886 to 1901 he was secretary of the Ontario Fruit Growers' Association; and from 1886 to 1903, editor of the *Canadian Horticulturist*. He died at Grimsby, Ontario, on May 7, 1914. He was the author of *The Canadian apple-grower's guide* (Toronto, 1910).

[Morgan, *Can. men* (1912).]

Work, John (1792?-1861), fur-trader, was born in the north of Ireland about 1792. He entered the service of the Hudson's Bay Company in 1814; and for eight years he served at York Factory and other posts on Hudson Bay. In 1823 he was sent to the Pacific slope; and he spent the rest of his life in this region. In 1846 he was promoted to the rank of chief factor, and from 1857 to his death he was a member of the Executive and Legislative councils of Vancouver Island. He died at Victoria, British Columbia, on December 23, 1861. He married Susette Legace, a Spokane half-breed; and by her he had five daughters and one son. Work's papers are in the Provincial Library, Victoria, British Columbia.

[W. S. Lewis and P.C. Phillips (eds.) *The journal of John Work* (Cleveland, Ohio, 1923); H. D. Dee, *An Irishman in the fur-trade* (British Columbia historical quarterly, 1943).]

Workman, George Coulson (1848-1936), clergyman and author, was born at Grafton, Canada West, on September 28, 1848. He was educated at Victoria University, Cobourg (B.A., 1875; M.A., 1878) and at Leipzig University (Ph.D., 1889). He was ordained a minister of the Methodist Church in 1878; and in 1882 he was appointed associate professor of Hebrew in Victoria University. He was subsequently professor of Old Testament exegesis and professor of oriental languages; but he retired from the staff of Victoria in 1891. From 1904 to 1908 he was professor of Old Testament exegesis in the Montreal Wesleyan Theological College; but after this he devoted himself to private studies. He died at Toronto,

Ontario, on April 22, 1936. He was the author of *The text of Jeremiah* (Edinburgh, 1889), *The Old Testament vindicated* (Toronto, 1897), *The Messianic prophecy vindicated* (Toronto, 1899), *How to study the Bible* (Toronto, 1902), *The servant of Jehovah* (London, 1907), *Atonement; or, Reconciliation with God* (New York, 1911), *Armageddon; or, The world movement* (Toronto, 1917), *Divine healing* (Toronto, 1924), *Jesus the man and Christ the spirit* (New York, 1928), and *Immortal life* (Toronto, 1934).

[Morgan, *Can. men* (1912); *University of Toronto monthly*, 1936.]

Workman, Joseph (1805-1894), physician, was born near Lisburn, county Antrim, Ireland, on May 26, 1805. He emigrated to Canada with his parents in 1829, and obtained his diploma as doctor of medicine from McGill College in 1835. For a number of years he abandoned the practice of medicine, and engaged in business in Toronto, Ontario, but he resumed the practice of medicine in Toronto in 1846, and for several years he was on the staff of Dr. Rolph's Toronto School of Medicine. In 1849-50 he was a member of the royal commission appointed to inquire into the affairs of King's College; and the report of the commission was largely his work. In 1854 he was appointed superintendent of the Insane Asylum in Toronto; and he retained this position until 1875. He died at Toronto on April 15, 1894. His unpublished diary, covering the years 1867 to 1894, is in the University of Toronto Library.

[Rose, *Cyc. Can. biog.* (1888); W. Canniff, *The medical profession in Upper Canada* (Toronto, 1894).]

Worrell, Clarendon Lamb (1854-1934), primate of the Church of England in Canada (1931-34), was born at Smiths Falls, Canada West, on July 20, 1854. He was educated at Trinity University (B.A., 1873; M.A., 1884; D.C.L., 1902); and was ordained a priest of the Church of England in 1884. From 1891 to 1904 he was professor of English literature at the Royal Military College, Kingston; and in 1904 he was elected bishop of Nova Scotia. In 1915 he became archbishop of Nova Scotia and metropolitan of Canada, and in 1931 primate of all Canada. He died at Halifax, Nova Scotia, on August 10, 1934.

[*Can. who was who*, vol. 2; B. Heeney, *Leaders of the Canadian church: Third series* (Toronto, 1943).]

Worthington, Frederic Franklin (1889-1967), soldier, was born at Peterhead, Scotland, on September 17, 1889. Orphaned at an early age, he accompanied his half-brother to Mexico at age twelve. As a young man he was involved in service in Latin American revolutions in Guatemala, Nicaragua, and Mexico, and during the First World War he served with

the Canadian Expeditionary Force. He was wounded in France, won the Military Medal, and was given an Officer Training Course in England. He returned to France with the Canadian Machine Gun Corps and was awarded the Military Cross and Bar. He joined the permanent Canadian army and specialized in armoured warfare. In 1940 he was commander of the First Canadian Armoured Brigade. He served in England as commander of the First Canadian Army Tank Brigade (1941), and as commander of the 4th Canadian Armoured Division (1942-44), as major-general. He was appointed general officer commanding Pacific Command (1945). In 1948 he retired from the army and became co-ordinator of civil defence for Canada (1948-57). He was known as Canada's expert on armoured warfare. He died at Ottawa, Ontario, December 8, 1967, and was buried at Camp Borden.

[*Encyc. Can.* (1972); *Can. who's who*, 1955-57; L. Worthington, *Worthy* (Toronto, 1961).]

Wotherspoon, Ivan (d. 1908), lawyer and author, was called to the bar of Lower Canada in 1866, and practised law, first in Quebec, and then in Montreal. He was compelled to give up practice in 1884; and he died at Montreal on May 13, 1908. He was the author of *A manual of the practice and jurisdiction in the several courts having civil jurisdiction in the province of Quebec* (Montreal, 1870; 2nd ed., 1880) and *The Insolvent Act of 1875* (Montreal, 1875).

[P. G. Roy, *Les avocats de la région de Québec* (Lévis, Que., 1936).]

Wright, Adam Henry (1846-1930), professor of obstetrics, was born at Brampton, Ontario, on April 6, 1846. He was educated at the University of Toronto (B.A., 1866; M.B., 1873). From 1887 to 1914 he was professor of obstetrics in the University of Toronto; and in 1909 he was elected president of the Canadian Medical Association. He died at Toronto on August 20, 1930. He was a M.R.C.S., Eng. (1877); and he was the author of *Lectures on obstetrics* (Toronto, 1905).

[Morgan, *Can. men* (1912); *University of Toronto monthly*, 1930.]

Wright, Alonzo (1825-1894), capitalist and politician, was born at Hull, Lower Canada, on February 26, 1825, the son of Lieut.-Col. Tiberius Wright and the grandson of Philemon Wright (q.v.). He was educated at the Potsdam Academy, New York, and engaged in lumbering on the Ottawa River. He represented Ottawa county in the Legislative Assembly of Canada from 1862 to 1867, and in the Canadian House of Commons from 1867 to 1891. He died on January 7, 1894. In 1850 he married Mary, daughter of Nicholas Sparks. He was nicknamed "the King of the Gatineau".

[*Cyc. Am. biog.*; *Can. parl. comp.*; C. W.

Cochrane, *Men of Canada*, vol. 4 (Brantford, Ont., 1894).]

Wright, Arthur Walker (1855-1944), journalist and historian, was born in Nichol township, near Cumnock, Canada West, on February 12, 1855. He was educated at the University of Toronto (B.A., 1883), and for many years he was a school-teacher. In 1902 he became the proprietor and editor of the *Mount Forest Confederate*; and he continued to edit this newspaper until his death at Mount Forest, Ontario, on July 25, 1944. He was the author of *Pioneer days in Nichol* (Mount Forest, Ont., 1924).

[M. N. Ask (ed.), *Who's who in journalism* (New York, 1928).]

Wright, Philemon (1760-1839), pioneer, was born September 3, 1760, in Woburn, Massachusetts, and emigrated to Canada in 1800. He settled on the site of what is now Hull, Quebec, and was known as "the father of the Ottawa". He died at Hull on June 2, 1839. He published *An account of the first settlement of the township of Hull, on the Ottawa River, L.C.* (Canadian magazine, 1824).

[J. Tassé, *Philémon Wright, ou Colonisation et commerce de bois* (Montreal, 1871); B. Harris, *The white chief of the Ottawa* (Toronto, 1903); Rose, *Cyc. Can. biog.* (1888); Morgan, *Cel. Can.* and *Bib. can.*]

Wright, Robert Ramsay (1852-1933), biologist, was born in Alloa, Scotland, in 1852, and was educated at Edinburgh University (M.A., 1871; B.Sc., 1873). He came to Canada in 1874 as professor of natural science (later, of biology) in the University of Toronto; and in 1901 he became vice-president of the University. He retired in 1912, and went to live in England. There he died, at Droitwich, Worcestershire, on September 6, 1933. He was a fellow of the Royal Society of Canada, and was in 1910 its president. In addition to numerous scientific papers, he was the author of an *Introduction to zoology for high schools* (Toronto, 1889) and a report on *The fish and fisheries of Ontario* (Toronto, 1892).

[*Proc. Roy. Soc. Can.*, 1934; *Who was who*, 1929-40; Morgan, *Can. men* (1912).]

Wright, William Henry (1876-1951), mining magnate and newspaper publisher, was born in Lincolnshire, England, April 21, 1876, and died at Barrie, Ontario, on September 20, 1951. He served in the British army throughout the South African War, and he came to Canada in 1907. He became a prospector, and in 1911 made a rich gold discovery on Kirkland Lake. He became one of the richest mining men in Canada. It was he who enabled C. George McCullagh (q.v.) to buy the Toronto *Globe* and the Toronto *Mail and Empire*, and to combine them in 1936 as the *Globe and Mail*.

[*Can. who's who*, 1948; *Encyc. Can.*]

Wrong, Edward Murray (1889-1928), historian, was born in Toronto, Ontario, on April 14, 1889, the eldest son of Professor George M. Wrong (q.v.) and Sophia Hume, daughter of the Hon. Edward Blake (q.v.). He was educated at the University of Toronto (B.A., 1911) and at Balliol College, Oxford (B.A., 1913; M.A., 1916). In 1914 he was elected a fellow of Magdalen College, Oxford; from 1916 to 1919 he was vice-principal of the College of Technology, Manchester; in 1919 he was appointed fellow and tutor of Magdalen College, Oxford; and from 1919 to 1924 he was also Beit Lecturer in Colonial History at Oxford. He died in Oxford on February 16, 1928. In 1915 he married Rosalind, daughter of A. L. Smith, the Master of Balliol; and by her he had six children. He was the author of *Charles Buller and responsible government* (Oxford, 1926) and a *History of England, 1688 to 1815* (London, 1927); and he edited *Crime and detection* (Oxford, 1926).

[*Can. who was who*, vol. 1; *Who was who*, 1916-28; *Encyc. Can.*]

Wrong, George MacKinnon (1860-1948), historian, was born in Elgin county, Canada West, on June 25, 1860, and died at Toronto, Ontario, on June 29, 1948. He was educated at Wycliffe College and University College, in the University of Toronto (B.A., 1883; M.A., 1896), and was ordained a priest of the Church of England in 1883. From 1883 to 1892 he was lecturer in history and apologetics at Wycliffe College, from 1892 to 1894 he was lecturer in history at the University of Toronto, and from 1894 until his retirement in 1927 he was professor of history and head of the department. He was one of the founders of the Champlain Society, and was its editorial secretary from 1905 to 1922, and its president from 1924 to 1928. He also founded, in 1897, the *Review of historical publications relating to Canada*, which became, in 1920, the *Canadian historical review*. Besides several text-books on British and Canadian history, he was the author of *The Crusade of 1383* (London, 1892), *The Earl of Elgin* (Toronto, 1906), *A Canadian manor and its seigneurs* (Toronto, 1908; new ed., 1926), *The fall of Canada* (Oxford, 1914), *Washington and his comrades in arms* (New Haven, 1921), *The rise and fall of New France* (2 vols., Toronto, 1928), *Canada and the American Revolution* (Toronto, 1935), and *The Canadians* (Toronto, 1938). He edited for the Champlain Society Sagard's *Long journey to the country of the Hurons* (Toronto, 1939); and he was co-editor, with H. H. Langton (q.v.), of *The Chronicles of Canada* (32 vols., Toronto, 1914-16). He was elected a fellow of the Royal Society of Canada in 1908; and he received the honorary degree of LL.D. from McGill University in 1919, and from the University of Toronto in 1941.

[W. S. Wallace, *The life and work of George M. Wrong* (Can. hist. rev., 1948);

Proc. Roy. Soc. Can., 1949; *Who was who*, 1941-50; *Can. who's who*, 1948.]

Wrong, Humphrey Hume (1894-1954), diplomat, was born in Toronto, Ontario, on September 10, 1894, the youngest son of George M. Wrong (q.v.), and died at Ottawa, Ontario, on January 21, 1954. He was educated at Upper Canada College, Ridley College, the University of Toronto (B.A., 1915), and Balliol College, Oxford (B. Litt., 1921). He served in the British army during the First World War; and from 1921 to 1926 he was on the staff of the department of history in the University of Toronto. He then joined the staff of the department of external affairs at Ottawa. After holding various appointments, he became Canadian ambassador at Washington in 1946. In 1953 he was recalled to Ottawa to become under-secretary of state for foreign affairs; but he died soon afterwards. He was the author of *The government of the West Indies* (Oxford, 1923) and *Sir Alexander Mackenzie, explorer and fur-trader* (Toronto, 1927).

[*Who was who*, 1951-60; *Can. who's who*, 1952-54; *Encyc. Can.*]

Würtele, Jonathan Saxton Campbell (1828-1904), jurist, was born at Quebec, Lower Canada, on January 27, 1828, the son of Jonathan Würtele, seignior of River David, and Louisa Sophia Campbell. He was educated at the High School in Quebec; and was called to the bar of Lower Canada in 1850 (Q.C., 1873). From 1873 to 1886 he represented Yamaska in the Legislative Assembly of Quebec; from 1882 to 1884 he was provincial treasurer in the Quebec government, and from 1884 to 1886 he was speaker of the Assembly. In 1886 he was appointed a judge of the Superior Court of Quebec, and in 1892 a judge of the Court of Queen's Bench. He died on April 24, 1904.

[P. G. Roy, *Les juges de la province de Québec* (Quebec, 1933); Morgan, *Can. men* (1898).]

Wyle, Florence (1881-1968), sculptor, was born in Trenton, Illinois, November 24, 1881. She was educated at the University of Illinois and the Art Institute of Chicago. She became an associate of Frances Loring (q.v.) in New York and joined her in Toronto in 1913, where they shared a studio and an artistic life for over fifty years. Miss Wyle taught at Central Technical School, Toronto, and was an active promoter of Canadian art movements. She worked for Canadian War Memorials (1918-19) and among others designed the Edith Cavell Memorial. She is represented by bronze, stone, and wood sculptures in the Art Gallery of Ontario (Toronto) and in Winnipeg and Chicago, as well as in the National Gallery of Canada. She died at Newmarket, Ontario, on January 14, 1968. She was a member of the Royal Canadian Academy and a founder-member of the Sculptors' Society of Canada.

[*Can. who's who*, 1961-63; *Encyc. Can.*; R. Sisler, *The girls* (Toronto, 1972).]

Wylie, David (1811-1891), journalist and poet, was born in Johnstone, Renfrewshire, Scotland, on March 23, 1811. In 1825, he was apprenticed to the printing business in Paisley; and he became a journalist. In 1845 he emigrated to Canada, and from 1849 to 1878 he was editor and proprietor of the Brockville *Recorder*. In his later days he was known as "the father of the Canadian press". He died at Brockville on December 21, 1891. He contributed in his early days in Canada to the *Literary garland* (1838-51); and he was the author of *Recollections of a convict, and miscellaneous pieces in prose and verse* (Montreal, 1847) and *Metrical waifs from the Thousand Islands* (Brockville, Ont., 1869).

[Rose, *Cyc. Can. biog.* (1886); Morgan, *Bib. can.*; C. C. James, *A bibliography of Canadian poetry* (Toronto, 1899).]

Yale, James Murray (1798?-1871), fur-trader, was born at Lachine, Lower Canada, about 1798. He entered the service of the North West Company about 1815, and was taken over as a clerk by the Hudson's Bay Company in 1821. He was sent to New Caledonia in 1821; and he remained on the Pacific slope for the rest of his life. He was promoted to the rank of chief trader in 1844. He died at Saanich, British Columbia, on May 7, 1871. Fort Yale was named after him.

[E. E. Rich (ed.), *Journal of occurrences in the Athabaska department, by George Simpson* (Toronto: The Champlain Society, 1938); *Dict. Can. biog.*, vol. 10.]

Yeigh, Frank (1861-1935), author, was born at Burford, Canada West, on July 21, 1861, and was educated in the local schools. He entered the civil service of Ontario, and from 1880 to 1896 was the private secretary of the Hon. A. S. Hardy (q.v.). He left the civil service in 1908, and devoted himself to lecturing, journalism, and social service. He died at Toronto on October 26, 1935. In 1892 he married Kate Westlake (q.v.), and on her death he married secondly Annie Louise, daughter of the Rev. Robert Laird. He was the author of *Ontario's parliament buildings, or A century of legislation* (Toronto, 1893) and *The heart of Canada* (Toronto, 1910); and for over 25 years he published an annual volume entitled *Five thousand facts about Canada*.

[Morgan, *Can. men* (1912).]

Yeigh, Mrs. Kate, *née* Westlake (1856-1906), novelist, was born in London, Ontario, in 1856, and became a journalist. She married Frank Yeigh (q.v.), of Toronto, in 1892; and she died at Toronto on March 4, 1906. She was the author of a novel entitled *A specimen spinster* (Toronto, 1905).

[Toronto *Globe*, March 5, 1906.]

Yeo, Sir James Lucas (1782-1818), sailor, was born in Southampton, England, on October 7, 1782, the son of James Yeo, formerly agent-victualler at Minorca. He entered the British navy at an early age, and served throughout the Napoleonic Wars. His ability won him rapid promotion; and in 1813 he was sent to Canada, with the rank of commodore, to command the British naval forces on the Great Lakes during the later stages of the War of 1812. He engaged in a duel with the American commodore, Isaac Chauncey; and by the end of 1814 he had captured Oswego and bottled up Chauncey's fleet in Sackett's Harbour. On the conclusion of peace, he returned to England; and he was then ordered to duty off the west coast of Africa. He died on the voyage home from Africa, on August 21, 1818, aged only 35 years. He was created a knight bachelor in 1810. He was not married.

[*Dict. nat. biog.*; *Cyc. Am. biog.*; Sir C. P. Lucas, *The Canadian War of 1812* (Oxford, 1906).]

Yeo, John (1837-1924), senator of Canada, was born at Port Hill, Prince Edward Island, on June 29, 1837. He sat in the Legislative Assembly of Prince Edward Island from 1858 to 1891, and in the Canadian House of Commons from 1891 to 1898. On three occasions he was a member of the Executive Council of Prince Edward Island. In 1898 he was appointed to the Senate of Canada; and he sat in the Senate until his death, at Charlottetown, Prince Edward Island, on December 14, 1924.

[*Can. who was who*, vol. 1; *Can. parl. comp.*; Morgan, *Can. men* (1912).]

Yeoman, Eric McKay (1885-1909), poet, was born at Newcastle, New Brunswick, on October 9, 1885, and was educated at Dalhousie University, Halifax. He became a journalist, and contributed verses to various periodicals. He died in February, 1909. After his death a small volume of his *Poems* was published privately in Halifax, Nova Scotia.

[Mrs. C. M. Whyte-Edgar, *A wreath of Canadian song* (Toronto, 1910).]

Youmans, Mrs. Letitia, *née* Creighton (1827-1896), temperance reformer, was born at Cobourg, Upper Canada, on January 3, 1827, and was educated at the Cobourg Ladies' Academy and at the Burlington Academy, Hamilton, Canada West. In 1850 she married Arthur Youmans (d. 1882); and soon afterwards she became known as a lecturer on temperance reform. In 1878 she was elected president of the Ontario Women's Christian Temperance Union, and in 1883 of the Dominion temperance organization. She died in Toronto on July 18, 1896. She was the author of an autobiography, *Campaign echoes* (Toronto, 1893).

[*Can. who was who*, vol. 2; Rose, *Cyc. Can. biog.* (1886).]

Young, Archibald Hope (1863-1935), historian, was born at Sarnia, Ontario, on February 6, 1863. He was educated at Upper Canada College and at the University of Toronto (B.A., 1887); and from 1887 to 1892 he was a master of Upper Canada College. In 1892 he was appointed lecturer in modern languages at Trinity University, Toronto, and in 1900 professor. He retired on pension in 1931; and he died at Toronto on April 6, 1935. In his later years he took a great interest in the history of the Church of England in Canada; and he was the author of *The Revd. John Stuart, D.D., U.E.L., of Kingston, Upper Canada, and his family* (Kingston, 1920), as well as of numerous historical papers contributed to the *Papers and Records* of the Ontario Historical Society, the *Canadian Churchman*, the *Canadian Historical Review*, and other periodicals. He edited *The roll of pupils of Upper Canada College, Toronto* (Kingston, 1917), and *The parish register of Kingston, Upper Canada* (Kingston, 1921). At the time of his death he was engaged on a life of Bishop Strachan (q.v.), which has not been published.

[*Can. hist. rev.*, 1935; *Ontario Historical Society, papers and records*, 1936; *University of Toronto monthly*, 1935; Morgan, *Can. men* (1912).]

Young, Sir Aretas William (1778-1835), lieutenant-governor of Prince Edward Island (1831-35), was born about 1778, and entered the British army as an ensign in 1795. He served throughout the Revolutionary and Napoleonic wars in Ireland, in Egypt, and in the Peninsula. In 1813 he was sent to Trinidad; and in 1820 and in 1821-23 he administered the government of Trinidad during the absence of the governor. In 1826 he was appointed protector of the slaves in Trinidad; and in 1831 he was gazetted lieutenant-governor of Prince Edward Island. This post he occupied until his death at Charlottetown, Prince Edward Island, on December 1, 1835. He married Sarah Cox, of Coolcliffe, Wexford, England; and by her he had several children, one of whom was Sir Henry Edward Fox Young, governor of South Australia (1848-55) and of Tasmania (1855-61).

[*Dict. nat. biog.*; *Cyc. Am. biog.*; D. Campbell, *History of Prince Edward Island* (Charlottetown, P.E.I., 1875).]

Young, Egerton Ryerson (1840-1909), missionary and author, was born at Crosby,

Upper Canada, on April 7, 1840, the son of the Rev. William Young and Amanda Waldron. He was educated at the Provincial Normal School, Toronto; and for several years he was a school-teacher. In 1867 he was ordained a minister of the Methodist Church; and in 1868 he was sent to the North West as a missionary. He remained in the North West until 1876; from 1876 to 1888 he served in various charges in Ontario; and in 1888 he retired from active parochial work to devote himself to writing and lecturing. He died at Bradford, Ontario, on October 5, 1909. In 1867 he married Elizabeth Bingham, of Bradford, Ontario. He wrote a number of books based on his western experiences: *By canoe and dog-train among the Cree and Salteaux Indians* (London, 1890), *Stories from Indian wigwams and northern camp-fires* (London, 1893), *Oowikapun, or How the gospel reached the Nelson River Indians* (London, 1894), *On the Indian trail* (London, 1897), *The apostle of the north* (London, 1899), *Indian life in the great north west* (London, 1900), *My dogs in the northland* (Toronto, 1902), and *Algonquin Indian tales* (Toronto, 1903). He was also the author of a number of stories for boys: *Three boys in the wild north land* (London, 1896), *Winter adventures* (London, 1899), *The children of the forest* (Toronto, 1904), *The battle of the bears* (Toronto, 1907), and others.

[*Can. who was who*, vol. 1; Morgan, *Can. men* (1898); Rose, *Cyc. Can. biog.* (1886).]

Young, George (1821-1910), clergyman and author, was born in Prince Edward county, Upper Canada, on December 31, 1821, of United Empire Loyalist descent. He became in 1842 an itinerant preacher in the Methodist Church, and for many years he served in various parts of eastern Canada. In 1868 he went to Winnipeg, as superintendent of Methodist missions in the West; and he was the first president of the Manitoba and North West Conference. He was in Winnipeg throughout the North West rebellion of 1869-70, and attended Thomas Scott (q.v.) at his execution by the rebels. He was superannuated in 1884, and returned to Toronto, Ontario. Here he died on August 1, 1910. He was the author of *Manitoba memories, being leaves from my life in the prairie province* (Toronto, 1897).

[Morgan, *Can. men* (1898).]

Young, George Paxton (1819-1889), professor of logic, metaphysics, and ethics in University College, Toronto (1871-89), was born in Berwick-on-Tweed, England, in 1819, the son of a Scottish clergyman. He was educated at Edinburgh High School and University, and was trained for the ministry of the Presbyterian Church. In 1847 he came to Canada, and in 1850 he became minister of Knox Church, Hamilton, Canada West. From 1853 to 1864 he was a professor in Knox College, Toronto; and from 1864 to 1871 he was inspector of the grammar schools of Upper

Canada. He was then appointed professor of logic, metaphysics, and ethics in University College, Toronto; and in this position he acquired a remarkable reputation as a teacher. He died at Toronto on February 26, 1889. He was the author of *Miscellaneous discourses and expositions of scripture* (Edinburgh, 1854); and some of his lectures were published long after his death by J. G. Hume, under the title *The ethics of freedom* (Toronto, 1911).

[J. King, *McCaul: Croft: Forneri* (Toronto, 1914); *Cyc. Am. biog.*; Dent, *Can. port.*, vol. 3; Morgan, *Bib. can.*; W. S. Wallace, *A history of the University of Toronto* (Toronto, 1927).]

Young, George Renny (1802-1853), journalist and author, was born at Falkirk, Scotland, on July 4, 1802, the second son of John Young (q.v.), author of the *Letters of Agricola* (Halifax, 1822). He came to Nova Scotia with his father in 1815, and in 1824 he founded in Halifax the *Nova Scotian*, a weekly newspaper which he edited, until it was purchased by Joseph Howe (q.v.) in 1828. He then became a member of the legal profession, in partnership with his brother William Young (q.v.); and he was for many years a prominent member of the Liberal opposition in the Legislative Assembly of Nova Scotia. In 1848 he became a member of the Uniacke administration, which marked the transition to responsible government in Nova Scotia; but he resigned in 1851 as the result of a difference with one of his colleagues. He died at Halifax, Nova Scotia, on June 30, 1853. An active writer, he published *The British North American colonies: Letters to E. G. S. Stanley, M.P.* (London, 1834), *The history, principles, and prospects of the Bank of British North America and of the Colonial Bank* (London, 1838), *The Canadian question* (London, 1839), and *Articles on the great colonial project of connecting Halifax and Quebec with a railroad* (London, 1847); but his chief work was an essay *On colonial literature, science, and education,* of which only vol. i (London, 1842) appeared.

[*Dict. nat. biog.*; R. J. Long, *Nova Scotia authors* (East Orange, N.J., 1918); Morgan, *Bib. can.*]

Young, James (1835-1913), politician and author, was born at Galt, Upper Canada, on May 24, 1835, the eldest son of John Young and Janet Bell. He was educated at Galt, and from 1853 to 1863 was editor of the *Dumfries Reformer.* From 1867 to 1878 he represented South Waterloo in the Canadian House of Commons; and from 1879 to 1886 he sat for North Brant in the Legislative Assembly of Ontario. For a few months in 1883 he was provincial treasurer in the Mowat administration. In 1878 and in 1893 he was chairman of the Liberal conventions held in Toronto; and for a time he was president of the Ontario Reform Association. He died at Galt, Ontario, on January 29, 1913. In 1858 he married Margaret, daughter of John McNaught, of Brantford, Ontario. Besides a number of pamphlets and addresses on political subjects, he wrote *Reminiscences of the early history of Galt and the settlement of Dumfries* (Toronto, 1880) and *Public men and public life in Canada* (Toronto, 1902; new and enlarged ed., 2 vols., Toronto, 1912.)

[Morgan, *Can. men* (1912) and *Bib. can.*; *Can. parl. comp.*; Dent, *Can. port.*, vol. 3; Rose, *Cyc. Can. biog.* (1888).]

Young, John (d. 1819), executive councillor of Lower Canada, was a prominent merchant of the city of Quebec, who represented the lower town of Quebec in the Legislative Assembly of Lower Canada from 1792 to 1808. In 1794 he was appointed an honorary member of the Executive Council of the province, and in 1808 a regular member. He was selected by Sir Robert Milnes (q.v.) in 1799 as chairman of a commission for the regulation of pilots, and was instrumental in securing the incorporation of Trinity House at Quebec, of which he became in 1805 the first master. He was absent from the province from 1814 to 1817; but on his return he resumed his duties as a member of the Executive Council. He died on September 14, 1819.

[A. G. Doughty and D. A. McArthur (eds.), *Documents relating to the constitutional history of Canada, 1791-1818* (Ottawa, 1914).]

Young, John (1773-1837), agricultural writer, was born near Falkirk, Scotland, in September, 1773, and was educated at Glasgow University. He emigrated to Nova Scotia, with his wife and children, in 1815; and in 1818 he published in the Halifax *Recorder* a series of papers drawing attention to the backward state of agriculture in the province. These letters, which were published in book form, under the title *Letters of Agricola* (Halifax, 1822), secured the creation of a board of agriculture in Nova Scotia; and of this board Young became secretary. In 1825 he was elected a member of the Legislative Assembly of Nova Scotia; and he retained his seat until his death at Halifax on October 26, 1837. He married Agnes, daughter of George Renny, of Falkirk, Scotland; and by her he had three sons.

[R. Cumming, *The Junius of Nova Scotia* (Dalhousie review, 1933); *Dict. nat. biog.*; *Cyc. Am. biog.*; Morgan, *Bib. can.*; R. J. Long, *Nova Scotia authors* (East Orange, N.J., 1918).]

Young, John (1811-1878), commissioner of public works for Canada (1851-52), was born in Ayr, Scotland, on March 11, 1811. He was educated at the Ayr parish school; and in 1826 he emigrated to Canada. He went into business in Montreal, and ultimately became chairman of the board of harbour commissioners for the port of Montreal. From 1851 to 1857 he represented Montreal in the Legislative Assembly of Canada; and from 1851 to 1852 he was commissioner of public works in the Hincks-Morin administration. From 1872 to 1874 he represented Montreal also in the Canadian House of Commons. He died at Montreal on April 12, 1878. He published numerous pamphlets on Canadian trade and commerce; and he was the founder in 1846 of a Free Trade Association which published the *Canadian Economist* (Montreal, 1846-47).

[*Dom. ann. reg.*, 1878; Rose, *Cyc. Can. biog.* (1886); Dent, *Can. port.*, vol. 3; Taylor, *Brit. Am.*, vol. 2; Morgan, *Bib. can.*; *Dict. Can. biog.*, vol. 10.]

Young, Sir John, Bart. See **Lisgar, Sir John Young, Bart., first Baron.**

Young, Richard (1843-1905), Anglican bishop of Athabaska (1884-1903), was born at South Park, Lincolnshire, England, on September 7, 1843. He was educated at Clare College, Cambridge (B.A., 1868), and was ordained a priest of the Church of England in 1869. In 1875 he was sent to Canada by the Church Missionary Society, and took charge of the parish of St. Andrew's in Manitoba. On the erection of the diocese of Athabaska in 1884, he was appointed bishop of Athabaska; and he presided over this diocese until his retirement in 1903. He died at London, England, on July 14, 1905. In 1884 he received the honorary degree of D.D. from the University of Manitoba, and in 1893 that of D.C.L. from Trinity University, Toronto.

[*Who was who*, 1897-1916; Morgan, *Can. men* (1898).]

Young, Robert Evans (1861-1911), surveyor and civil servant, was born at Georgetown, Canada West, on March 17, 1861. He became a land surveyor; and from 1882 to 1902 he was employed in numerous surveys in Manitoba and British Columbia. In 1902 he was appointed superintendent of railway lands in the department of the interior, Ottawa; and in 1910 he became chief geographer of the department. He died at Ottawa, Ontario, on October 24, 1911. He was the author of *Canada's fertile northland* (Ottawa, 1909).

[Morgan, *Can. men* (1912).]

Young, Thomas (d. 1860), architect, was born in England, and came to Canada in 1836. In 1840 he was appointed the first city engineer of Toronto. He became a leading architect; and King's College, Toronto (the first home of what is now the University of Toronto), was built by him. He died at Toronto, Canada West, on October 3, 1860.

[J. Ross Robertson, *Landmarks of Canada* (Toronto, 1917).]

Young, Thomas Frederick (d. 1940), poet, was educated at the Collegiate Institute in Goderich, Ontario, and became a schoolteacher at Port Albert, a village near Goderich. He died at the Huron County Home in Goderich on May 25, 1940. When a young man, he wrote and published *Canada and other poems* (Toronto, 1885).

[Private information.]

Young, Sir William (1799-1887), prime minister and later chief justice of Nova Scotia, was born at Falkirk, Scotland, on September 8, 1799, the eldest son of John Young (q.v.), the author of the *Letters of Agricola*, and Agnes Renny. He was educated at Glasgow University (matriculation, 1813); and he emigrated with his father to Nova Scotia in 1815. In 1826 he was called to the bar of Nova Scotia; and he was a member of the Legislative Assembly of Nova Scotia from 1832 to 1860, representing Cape Breton from 1832 to 1837, Inverness from 1837 to 1859, and Cumberland from 1859 to 1860. He was a prominent supporter of Joseph Howe (q.v.). From 1843 to 1854 he was speaker of the Assembly; in 1854 he was appointed attorney-general of the province; and in 1859 he became prime minister. In 1860 he retired from political life, and was appointed chief justice of Nova Scotia, a position which he retained for twenty-one years. He died at Halifax on May 8, 1887. In 1869 he was created a knight bachelor, and in 1881 he was made an LL.D. of Dalhousie College, Halifax.

[*Dict. nat. biog.*; W. Innes Addison, *The matriculation albums of the University of Glasgow* (Glasgow, 1913).]

Youville, Marie Marguerite Dufrost de La Jemmerais, Mère d' (1701-1771), founder of the Grey Nuns of Montreal, was born in Varennes, Canada, on October 15, 1701. In 1722 she married M. d'Youville; but her husband died in 1730, leaving her with two children. She then began to devote herself to charity; and in 1747 she was placed in charge of the Hôpital-Général in Montreal. Here she founded the order of Grey Nuns, or Sisters of Charity; and was thus a pioneer in organized charity in Canada. She died in Montreal, on December 23, 1771.

[Lady Jetté, *Vie de la vénérable mère d'Youville* (Montreal, 1900); Mgr D. S. Ramsay, *Life of the vénérable M.-M. Dufrost de Lajemmerais, Mde d'Youville* (Montreal, 1896); Abbé Faillon, *Vie de Mme d'Youville* (Ville-Marie, 1852); *L'Hôpital Général de Montréal (Soeurs grises), 1692-1821*, vol. i (Montreal, 1916); Mary G. Duffin, *A heroine of charity* (New York, 1938); E. Mitchell, *Marguerite d'Youville, foundress of the Grey Nuns*; tr. from the French by Helena Nantais (Montreal, 1965); Le Jeune, *Dict. gén.*]

Yule, Mrs. Pamela S., *née* **Vining** (d. 1897), author, was born in the state of New York, and was educated at Albion College,

Michigan. When the Canadian Literary Institute was founded at Woodstock, Ontario, in 1860, she was appointed instructor in English art and literature. Later, she married Professor James Cotton Yule (d. 1876), of the Canadian Literary Institute. She died at Ingersoll, Ontario, on March 6, 1897. She was the author of *Poems of the heart and home* (Toronto, 1881), *Sowing and Reaping; or, Records of the Ellisson family* (Toronto, 1899), and *Up hill; or, Paul Sutherland's progress* (Philadelphia, n.d.); and she edited *Records of a vanished life: Lectures, addresses, etc., of James Cotton Yule* (Toronto, 1876).

[C. C. James, *A bibliography of Canadian poetry* (Toronto, 1899); A. MacMurchy, *Handbook of Canadian literature* (Toronto, 1906).]

Z

Zavitz, Charles Ambrose (1863-1942), educationist, was born at Coldstream, Canada West, in 1863; and was educated at the Guelph Agricultural College (B.S.A., 1888). For forty years he was professor of field husbandry at the Ontario Agricultural College, Guelph; and he played an important role in introducing scientific agriculture into Canada. He retired in 1927, and he died at Poplar Hill, near London, Ontario, on March 17, 1942. The University of Western Ontario conferred on him the honorary degree of LL.D. He was the author of *Spiritual life: Personal thoughts* (London, Ont., 1932).

[Morgan, *Can. men* (1912); private information.]

Zeisberger, David (1721-1808), missionary, was born in Zauchtenthal, Moravia, on April 11, 1721. He emigrated to America in 1740, and became a Moravian missionary among the Delaware Indians. In 1791 he led his band of Delaware Indians into Canada, and established them on the banks of the Thames River, in Upper Canada. In 1797, the colony having been well established, he returned to minister to the Indian converts remaining in Ohio. His *Diary of a Moravian missionary among the Indians of Ohio* was translated from the German manuscript and edited by Eugene F. Bliss (Grosse Pointe, Mich., 1972). He died at Goshen, Ohio, on November 17, 1808.

[Rev. J. Morrison, *David Zeisberger and his Delaware Indians* (Ontario Hist. Soc., papers and records, 1914); E. de Schweinitz, *The life and times of David Zeisberger* (Philadelphia, 1871); E. E. Gray, *Wilderness Christians: The Moravian mission to the Delaware Indians* (Toronto, 1956); *Cyc. Am. biog.*]

Zimmerman, Samuel (1815-1857), contractor, was born in Huntingdon county, Pennsylvania, in 1815. He came to Canada in 1842, and settled at Thorold, Canada West. His first undertaking was the construction of a part of the Welland Canal; and subsequently he built part of the Great Western, the Cobourg and Peterborough, the Port Hope and Lindsay, and the Erie and Ontario railways, and the suspension and railway bridges across the Niagara River. He rapidly acquired great wealth, and was perhaps the richest man in Canada at that time. He was killed in the Desjardins Canal accident on the Great Western Railway at Hamilton on March 12, 1857. He was twice married, first to the daughter (d. 1854) of William Woodruff, of St. David's, Upper Canada, and second to a Miss Dunn, of Three Rivers, Lower Canada.

[R. W. Geary, *Samuel Zimmerman* (Welland County Hist. Soc., papers and records, vol. iii); Morgan, *Cel. Can.*]